MW00565538

Mark Satern's
ILLUSTRATED GUIDE TO
Video's
Best
1996
MASTER EDITION

Video's Best

Authored By: Mark A. Satern

ISBN # 0-9643171-1-7

Printed in the United States of America. Published simultaneously in Canada.

Video Availability: Along with the other information we have provided for each video title, we have indicated who the last known manufacturer was, what the jacket art looked like for his product and what his related serial number was. However, videos may have or have had several manufacturers, there may be no manufacturer currently producing the video or supplies through distributors and wholesalers may be limited or non-existent. Therefore, the picture of the video jacket, the manufacturer and serial number shown may not represent the only version available on video, may not represent the most current manufacturer or the video may not be readily available to your video merchant.

Printed, bound and distributed by:

The Publishing Group

1200 North Seventh Street

Minneapolis, MN 55411

(612) 522-1200

A WORD FROM THE AUTHOR

"As a movie-lover, I had become frustrated and tired of continually bringing home bad videos. And...it was obvious that I was not alone. Everyone else seemed also to be blindly wandering the aisles at the local video store in these same long and fruitless searches. There had to be a better and more efficient way for me and everyone else to find a good video quickly - every time we went to the store. Then it hit me: Some independent third party needed to extensively research all the videos available, weed out the many bad ones and then, in a totally unbiased manner, ***present only important decision-making information*** on those remaining "best videos." Also key, was that the resulting material had to be presented in a way that made it fast, easy and even fun for people to use. I had been an accomplished researcher and report-writer for many years and quickly decided that someone should be me.

My years of research to compile the data shown here included conducting an extensive review of numerous professional critic's opinions, collecting information from other independent sources, soliciting movie studios and video distributors and, wherever possible, discovering the response of the general public itself. The information generated on each video was then evaluated to conclude upon one standardized numerical rating. ***The rating is designed to reflect the likely attitude of the video's most-likely audience.*** The remaining information was then organized into highly-visual "Standard Information Blocks." The Standard Information Blocks are designed so ***the rating is be used in the context of the narratives, pictures and icons***. In this way, the reader can quickly determine if the rating will apply to him, i.e. ***YOU decide if the video is <u>right for you</u>.*** The information blocks were themselves then organized in a common-sense manner that makes it easy to sort through all the many "good" video choices available.

Most importantly, and not coincidentally, the fundamental difference between this book and the others available is that I have made a conscious and concerted effort to create a book that always remains true to its two most fundamental principles: ***report only key decision-making information and <u>keep personal opinions to a minimum</u>."***

Mark A. Satern
Author

Should you have suggestions as to how Video's Best might be improved or should you discover an error, please feel free to write us at:

Video's Best Suggestions
c/o The Publishing Group
1200 North Seventh Street
Minneapolis, MN 55411

Table of Contents

Notices Acknowledgements and Credits

Video's Best would like to express its sincere appreciation to all those individuals and companies who have aided us in our efforts to compile the best possible consumer guide book. Should we have inadvertently failed to acknowledge any individual or group, either in the body of the work or in the notices which follow, or if we have made any factual errors either here or within the body of the book, we assure you that that is purely accidental. Please make us aware of our mistake and we will be pleased and grateful to make any necessary additions or corrections.

Standard Information Block

Video's Best

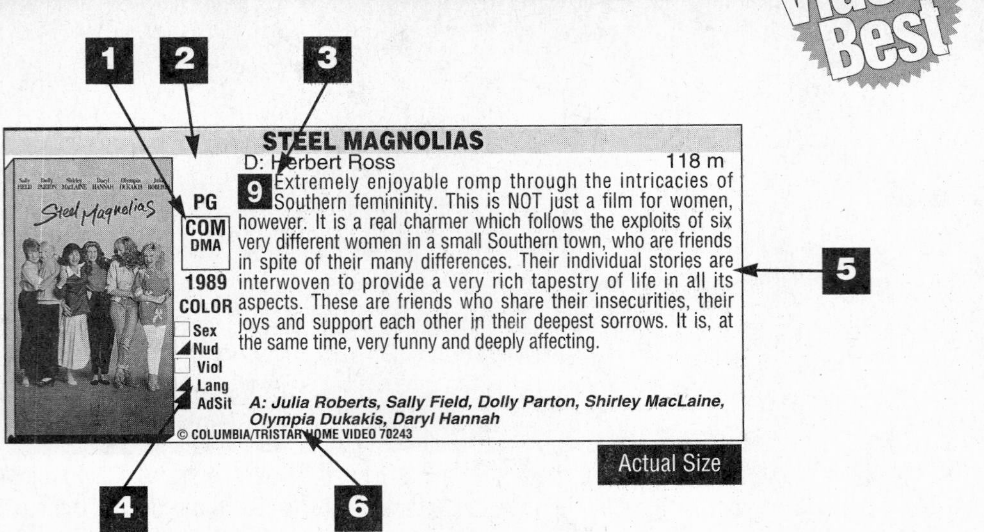

1 **MULTIPLE CATEGORIES: Video's Best** uses categories very differently than does any other book. Each video is first evaluated to determine what its characteristics or "personalities" are. Up to three of the possible personalities are then displayed within the box as shown above. The dominant personality is listed first and is bolder. The video will then appear within each personality section applicable to it. Not only does listing multiple personalities provide added information to better predict what to expect, but the reader now also has more than one opportunity to find a particular video which may appeal to him. The 15 personality categories this book uses are:

ACT	Action/Adventure	FAN	Fantasy	ROM	Romance
COM	Comedy	FOR	Foreign	SF	Science Fiction
CRM	Crime	HOR	Horror	SUS	Suspense
DOC	Documentary	MUS	Music	WAR	War
DMA	Drama	MYS	Mystery	WST	Western

In addition to the above "personality" categories, the video may also appear in FAMILY and/or CHILDREN sections. (The children's section is further divided - Feature Films, Animated Features, Cartoons and Informational). In total, **Video's Best** may have placed each information block in up to four different places in the book. That means you may have up to four different opportunities to find the video that will satisfy your needs.

Exceptions: Videos of movies which were released prior to 1956 will have all their personalities listed but these videos will not appear within the 15 major personality sections. Instead, they will appear in the OLDIES section, and there be listed only under their dominant personality. However, they may also yet appear again in the Children or Family sections if it applies.

2 **APPROPRIATE AUDIENCE:** This quick reference icon is special and unique to **Video's Best**. It is meant to indicate who the appropriate audience for this video is. It likely has nothing to do with levels of sex, violence, nudity, etc.- you should see the Motion Picture Arts Association Rating and **Video's Best's** Warning Blocks (Item 4 below) to discover what those concerns may be. This icon is meant solely to indicate the age group or level of maturity which will be most satisfied in viewing this video. The following definitions of **Video's Best** appropriate audience icons will help:

True family entertainment—something for everyone including the littlest children.

Largely designed for a family audience but will probably have little or no interest for the very youngest viewers. In some instances, the subject matter will likely interest older children (6-12) but it may have some items that parents should evaluate for their children.

This video is essentially designed for older audiences (usually minimum teenage level). It will likely require somewhat more mature levels of experience to fully understand, appreciate and enjoy. It may or may not also contain objectionable material.

This video is designed to be adult entertainment—this is either through the mature level of understanding it requires or because of particular adult elements intrinsic to its production (such as sexual references). Parents should evaluate its suitability for their teens.

3 **STANDARDIZED EVALUATIONS:** Each video has been evaluated on a standardized scale of 1-10. Only those videos which received a rating of 6 or above have been included. Each numerical rating is carefully defined to meet the standardized criteria which follow:

6 Above average TV quality. However, it may have a limited or narrow audience.

7 Good—This video's first-time audience will enjoy and be satisfied watching it once. However, they would likely not watch it again soon.

8 Very Good—Its first-time audience will enjoy this video and they would likely be interested in seeing it again relatively soon, particularly if it appeared on TV. They would recommend it to their friends.

9 Excellent—First-time viewers will be very pleased. They would definitely take the time to watch it again on TV and would even likely rent it again sometime in the near future. They will definitely recommend it highly to their friends.

10 Unforgettable masterpiece—This movie is so good that many people would spend money to see it again right away and will eagerly tell their friends to see it. It will be a popular rental for years to come.

Our ratings were carefully awarded after an extensive review of numerous professional critics, separate independent sources and the public's popular opinion, as reflected by the actual market acceptance of the movie. Ultimately, the final rating we awarded was the editor's subjective evaluation of *how the video will likely satisfy the viewing requirements of the video's intended or most likely audience*. We have endeavored to provide additional clues within the text of the narratives to better describe who that audience may be. (See also item 6 below.) You must evaluate ALL the information to specifically determine how *you should interpret our rating*.

4 **WARNING BLOCKS:** Each video is subjectively evaluated for the quantity or intensity of five items of particular interest to parents: Sex, Nudity, Violence, Language and Adult Situations. The levels are then graphically represented as follows:

☐ None of any consequence ◢ Some ■ Considerable Amount

5 **USEFUL NARRATIVES: Video's Best** narratives are especially designed to provide the information necessary for you to evaluate the video's suitability for you. Each video's narrative is designed to do three things: 1) to give a clear indication of the video's general plot, 2) to describe the general "feel" or personality of the video, 3) to warn of elements that may have a material impact on determining if this is a video for you. We endeavor to provide a maximum of information and a minimum of opinion.

6 **VIDEO AVAILABILITY:** Along with the other information we have provided for each video title, we have indicated who the last known manufacturer was, what the jacket art looked like for his product and what his related serial number was. However, videos may have or have had several manufacturers, there may be no manufacturer currently producing the video or supplies through distributors and wholesalers may be limited or non-existent. Therefore, the picture of the jacket sleeve, the manufacturer and serial number shown may not represent the only version available on video, may not represent the most current manufacturer or the video may not be readily available to your video merchant.

INDEXES: There are five separate indexes to help users in their quest to find a good video. Standard indexes list videos alphabetically by Titles, by Directors and by Actors. However, there is also a special index called "Heroes, Sequels, Subjects and Authors" which lists videos under various descriptions or items of interest. Plus, there is the "Best of the Best" index which prioritizes each primary category, listing the highest rated videos first.

Action

1956 and After

3:10 TO YUMA

D: Delmer Daves 92 m

NR | WST SUS ACT | 1957 | B&W

9 Top drawer Western, one of the best of the 1950s. Glenn Ford is a notorious gunman and powerful leader of a gang who holds up a stagecoach but gets caught when he stays behind to dally with a lonely barmaid. The wealthy owner of the stage company has offered Van Heflin, a poverty-struck farmer, $200 to guard Ford in a hotel room until lawmen arrive on the 3:10 train to take him into custody. Desperate for the money, Van Heflin agrees and becomes caught up in a psychological battle of wills with Ford, whose men begin to gather outside getting ready to break him out. Powerful stuff.

Sex, Nud, Viol, Lang, AdSit

A: Van Heflin, Glenn Ford, Felicia Farr, Richard Jaeckel, Henry Jones, Leora Dana

© COLUMBIA TRISTAR HOME VIDEO 60444

48 HOURS

D: Walter Hill 97 m

R | ACT COM CRM | 1983 | COLOR

9 A very popular blockbuster hit with good reason. It has plenty of realistic action, comedy, good acting, and is a good cop story, too. Nick Nolte is a veteran toughguy/boozehound cop but he needs help from a wiseguy/con man/convict (Eddie Murphy) in order to track down two extremely vicious cop killers. So, Nolte gets Murphy sprung from jail, but just for two days. Murphy turns out to be a good partner for the crazy cop. He is smart, cool under pressure, tough and funny, too (like when he terrorizes a redneck bar). Great entertainment on many levels all at once. Highly recommended.

Sex, Nud, Viol, Lang, AdSit

A: Eddie Murphy, Nick Nolte, Annette O'Toole, Frank McRae, James Remar, David Patrick Kelly

© PARAMOUNT HOME VIDEO 1139

52 PICKUP

D: John Frankenheimer 111 m

R | ACT SUS | 1986 | COLOR

7 A hard-edged and self-made man (Scheider) has a fling with a beautiful girl (Preston), where he is photographed by a group of pornographers, and becomes trapped in first blackmail and then murder. Scheider decides to fight back on his own, both to gain back his freedom but also to get revenge against the super-sleazy bad guys. This is a fast-paced thriller with a good story line, but it contains a very graphic and lurid depiction of underground sleaze and is a little too long.

Sex, Nud, Viol, Lang, AdSit

A: Roy Scheider, Ann-Margret, Vanity, John Glover, Clarence Williams, III, Kelly Preston

© VIDEO TREASURES SV9163

55 DAYS AT PEKING

D: Nicholas Ray 150 m

NR | DMA ACT | 1963 | COLOR

6 Semi-historical account of the Boxer Rebellion in China about 1900. Diplomatic staffs of eleven nations are trapped inside a walled-in compound with supplies running low. Stubborn English diplomat David Niven refuses to give in, even at the risk of his own family, and they are able to hold out for 55 days. Big sets and high production values combine with an excellent cast and good action sequences to offset the so-so story line that is built largely around not-too-attractive and now-dated stereotypical colonialist cliches.

Sex, Nud, Viol, Lang, AdSit

A: Charlton Heston, Ava Gardner, David Niven, Flora Robson, John Ireland, Paul Lukas

© BEST FILM & VIDEO CORP. 217

84 CHARLIE MOPIC

D: Patrick Duncan 95 m

R | WAR DMA ACT | 1989 | COLOR

8 Compelling and unique Vietnam war movie. The terrors and hardships of a dangerous jungle reconnaissance mission are told solely through the eye of a camera that is hand-held by an Army combat cameraman. He has been sent along with a six-man patrol into the highlands in 1969 to capture the experience of war for a training film. This filming technique is at times bothersome, but on whole it also adds a strong sense of reality in depicting the personal life-and-death quality of what it was actually like to be in the ground war in Vietnam on a daily basis.

Sex, Nud, Viol, Lang, AdSit

A: Jonathan Emerson, Nicholas Cascone, Richard Brooks, Jasons Tomlins, Christopher Burgard, Glenn Marshower

© COLUMBIA TRISTAR HOME VIDEO 09943

8 MILLION WAYS TO DIE

D: Hal Ashby 115 m

R | ACT SUS CRM | 1986 | COLOR

7 Brutal and cynical film in which Bridges, as an alcoholic ex-cop, is hired by a high-priced call girl (Arquette) to help her escape from her drug-dealing boyfriend and pimp (Garcia). Bridges gets drawn deep into a world of drugs, alcohol and sex and with his history, he may not make it back out. But - having Arquette there waiting for him at the end makes it worth the effort. This is a very violent and cynical cop film, punctuated with Bridges's character's personal crisis. However, it is also populated mostly with unsympathetic characters and that makes it a difficult film to get close to.

Sex, Nud, Viol, Lang, AdSit

A: Jeff Bridges, Rosanna Arquette, Alexandra Paul, Randy Brooks, Andy Garcia, Lisa Sloan

© CBS/FOX VIDEO 6118

ABOVE THE LAW

D: Andrew Davis 99 m

R | ACT | 1988 | COLOR

7 Plenty of action. Seagal, in his screen debut, plays a Chicago cop. When big-time drug suspects are allowed to walk free, Seagal starts to ask too many questions and soon he is forced to turn in his badge. That isn't going to stop him, he takes the law into his own hands. And, after he discovers corrupt government employees have sponsored a drug smuggling operation, he even takes on the CIA. But when his family is attacked, it's now no-holds barred, and he uses his martial arts training to dispense his own personal style of justice. Loads of action.

Sex, Nud, Viol, Lang, AdSit

A: Steven Seagal, Pam Grier, Sharon Stone, Daniel Faraldo, Henry Silva, Ron Dean

© WARNER HOME VIDEO 11786

ABYSS, THE

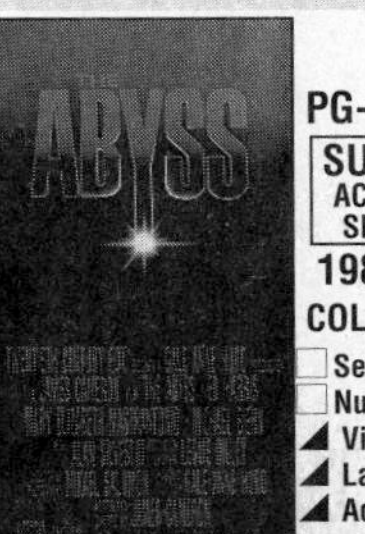

D: James Cameron 140 m

PG-13 | SUS ACT SF | 1989 | COLOR

7 Spectacular underwater adventure story about oil-platform workers and a Navy SEAL diving team who are paired in an attempt to find a mysteriously sunken nuclear submarine in extremely deep water. However, they encounter a wondrous deep water mystery on their trip into the deep. Absolutely riveting suspense, with intense action thrown in and a good plot twist. Although the fantasy element is a little weak, the thrills and the intense suspense more than compensate. Special effects are remarkable and were used again in TERMINATOR II.

Sex, Nud, Viol, Lang, AdSit

A: Ed Harris, Mary Elizabeth Mastrantonio, Michael Biehn, Leo Burmester, Todd Graff, John Bedford Lloyd

© FOXVIDEO 1561

ACROSS 110TH STREET

D: Barry Shear — 144 m

R | ACT CRM | 1972 | COLOR

Sex | Nud | Viol | Lang | AdSit

8 Unjustly overlooked film about N.Y.C. cops who are caught in the middle of a gang war. They are racing against the mob to catch the three black thieves who disguised themselves as cops so that they could steal $300,000 from a Mafia-controlled numbers bank. The mob wants their money back and they want revenge. Exciting, action-packed, but extremely violent. This is a highly suspenseful sleeper that should not be missed by action fans.

A: Anthony Quinn, Yaphet Kotto, Anthony Franciosa, Paul Benjamin, Richard Wind

Distributed By MGM/UA Home Video M203068

ACTION JACKSON

D: Craig R. Baxley — 96 m

R | ACT CRM | 1987 | COLOR

Sex | Nud | Viol | Lang | AdSit

6 Action hit. Weathers is a tough Detroit cop and Harvard graduate who, framed for murder, is being hunted down by his fellow cops. He has a serious run-in with a ruthless auto dealer (Nelson) after becoming involved with the man's wife and mistress. Not a lot of high drama and the very thin plot is also confusing, but there is plenty of non-stop action, in addition to the ample charms of both sultry rock star Vanity and Sharon Stone.

A: Carl Weathers, Craig T. Nelson, Vanity, Sharon Stone, Sonny Landham, Thomas F. Wilson

© WARNER HOME VIDEO 816

AGAINST ALL ODDS

D: Taylor Hackford — 122 m

R | MYS ACT | 1984 | COLOR

Sex | Nud | Viol | Lang | AdSit

6 Steamy thriller. A wealthy hood (Woods) hires an out-of-work ex-football star (Bridges) to find his girlfriend (Ward). Woods tells Bridges that she tried to kill him and also stole $50,000 that he wants back. Bridges chases her down to a beautiful island in Mexico but, instead, falls in love with the sensuous beauty. When Bridges doesn't return, Woods sends a henchman down to bring them both back. Then begins a series of plot twists brought on by jealousy, corruption and murder. Remake of OUT OF THE PAST.

A: Jeff Bridges, Rachel Ward, Alex Karras, James Woods, Richard Widmark, Jane Greer

© GOODTIMES 4621

ALAMO, THE

D: John Wayne — 162 m

NR | WST ACT | 1960 | COLOR

Sex | Nud | Viol | Lang | AdSit

8 John Wayne's action epic. It was Wayne's personal dream to see that this movie was made. He produced, directed and starred in this epic re-creation of the 1836 siege at San Antonio, Texas mission called the Alamo. The Duke gives a tough performance as Davy Crocket, but Widmark, Boone and Harvey also turn in excellent performances. Movie is a bit long, but when the action starts, Duke fans get their reward. Received seven Oscar nominations, including Best Picture. Also includes a 40-minute documentary about the filming of the movie.

A: John Wayne, Richard Widmark, Frankie Avalon, Richard Boone, Chill Wills, Laurence Harvey

Distributed By MGM/UA Home Video M302581

AL CAPONE

D: Richard Wilson — 104 m

NR | CRM ACT DMA | 1959 | B&W

Sex | Nud | Viol | Lang | AdSit

8 Excellent action movie. Solid telling of the life story of the infamous Chicago gangster who rises from being a hitman for Johnny Torrio (Persoff) to become the king of the Prohibition Era. After a bitter battle with the Feds, he is arrested and imprisoned for tax evasion. No other gangster so captured the imagination and the headlines of the country. Steiger is riveting in his portrayal of Capone, and the rest of the cast is perfect, too. For more of Capone see THE UNTOUCHABLES (1987) and SCARFACE (1932).

A: Rod Steiger, Fay Spain, Martin Balsam, Nehemiah Persoff

© CBS/FOX VIDEO 7750

ALIEN

D: Ridley Scott — 116 m

R | SUS ACT SF | 1979 | COLOR

Sex | Nud | Viol | Lang | AdSit

9 Heart-stopping terror and action galore. A spaceship crew finds that it has unwittingly taken on board an alien life form that uses human flesh to incubate its young, lives on human flesh and has the disconcerting ability to constantly change its form. Weaver is determined, tough and the only crewmember smart enough to stop it, and... she is determined to stop it. Gut-wrenching, non-stop suspense. Not for the faint-hearted. Followed by the equally good ALIENS and ALIEN 3, also with Weaver.

A: Tom Skerritt, Sigourney Weaver, John Hurt, Ian Holm, Harry Dean Stanton, Yaphet Kotto

© FOXVIDEO 1090

ALIEN 3

D: David Fincher — 115 m

R | SUS ACT SF | 1992 | COLOR

Sex | Nud | Viol | Lang | AdSit

8 Third entry in the chilling series. Sigourney Weaver is back. This time she crash-lands on a flea-infested maximum security prison planet which is occupied by some of the most violent criminals in the universe. However, the inmates there have found a sort of peace through religion and celibacy. In fact, Weaver poses a greater threat to them than they do to her because she has brought with her the Alien creature that lays its eggs inside humans. And, there are no weapons here to fight the deadly creatures. This one is more cerebral and less intense than the others, but it's no picnic either.

A: Sigourney Weaver, Charles Dutton, Charles Dance, Paul McGann, Brian Glover, Ralph Brown

© FOXVIDEO 5593

ALIEN NATION

D: Graham Baker — 90 m

R | CRM SF ACT | 1988 | COLOR

Sex | Nud | Viol | Lang | AdSit

8 Interesting and very entertaining slant on the buddy-cop theme. Earth has accepted, but not necessarily graciously, the refugees and former slaves of of another world. When cop James Caan's partner is killed in a shootout with a gang of the refugees, Caan is forced to unwillingly accept an alien "newcomer" as a replacement partner even though he is extremely prejudiced. Together, he and his new partner follow a trail of mysterious murders that leads them to discover what could become the worst drug epidemic the world has ever seen. Good action and humor, plus some very interesting human insights too. Great performances by Caan and Patinkin.

A: James Caan, Mandy Patinkin, Terence Stamp, Kevin Major Howard, Leslie Bevins

© FOXVIDEO 1585

ALIENS

D: James Cameron — 138 m

R | SUS ACT SF | 1986 | COLOR

Sex | Nud | Viol | Lang | AdSit

10 Wow! After 57 years of suspended animation, Weaver reawakens to find that the Alien's home planet has been colonized by humans, but now all contact with them has been lost. Weaver is determined to end her nightmares and to rid the universe of the Aliens. So, along with a Marine squad, she returns to the planet intent on saving the colonists. When they arrive, only a small girl is still living and they soon find themselves in an intense battle for their own lives. Every bit as intense as the original ALIEN and in some ways maybe better. Very heavy-duty action. Special effects won an Oscar.

A: Sigourney Weaver, Carrie Henn, Michael Biehn, Paul Reiser, Lance Henriksen, Bill Paxton

© FOXVIDEO 1504

ALIVE

D: Frank Marshall — 126 m

DMA ACT | 1992 | COLOR

Sex | Nud | Viol | Lang | AdSit

7 Gripping drama based upon the real-life 1972 plane crash in the snow-covered Andes Mountains. A team of rugby players managed to survive tremendous hardship and isolation for over 70 days at 11,500 feet, but only after having made the most difficult decisions. When the search for them was abandoned and they were left without hope, they survived by eating the dead bodies of their teammates. This is not a story about cannibalism. It is the story of survival in the face of devastating and debilitating odds. One of the most realistic films ever concerning a plane crash. Entertaining? No. Very interesting? Yes.

A: Ethan Hawke, Vincent Spano, Josh Hamilton, Bruce Ramsay, John Haymes Newton, David Kriegel

© TOUCHSTONE HOME VIDEO 1596

ALVAREZ KELLY

D: Edward Dmytryk — 110 m

NR | WST ACT | 1966 | COLOR

Sex | Nud | Viol | Lang | AdSit

7 A good Western. Richard Widmark has greatly complicated William Holden's life. Holden is a cowboy who has just sold a bunch of his cattle to the North during the Civil War. Politics are unimportant to him. Now Widmark, who is a Confederate colonel, captures Holden and wants him to help to steal the 2,500 head back for the starving South. Colorful if somewhat offbeat Western. Lots of two-fisted action and it is based upon an actual incident from the Civil War.

A: William Holden, Richard Widmark, Janice Rule, Victoria Shaw, Patrick O'Neal

© GOODTIMES 4210

AND THEN YOU DIE

D: Francis Mankiewicz — 115 m

R | ACT CRM | 1987 | COLOR

Sex | Nud | Viol | Lang | AdSit

8 Interesting and quite different. This is a unique film that captures your attention early and holds it throughout. It is the Canadian version of THE LONG GOOD FRIDAY. In it, a drug kingpin makes a fortune but then he gets caught between the police, a motor cycle gang, his own gang and other forces outside his organization - all of them are trying to get him and suddenly things are coming apart all around him. Thrill-a-minute. Excellent. Keeps you guessing right up to the last possible moment.

A: Kenneth Welsh, R.H. Thompson, Wayne Robson, Tom Harvey, George Bloomfield, Graeme Campbell

© VIDMARK ENTERTAINMENT M4708

ANGEL HEART

D: Alan Parker — 112 m

R | MYS SUS ACT | 1987 | COLOR

Sex / Nud / Viol / Lang / AdSit

8 Fascinatingly bizarre. In 1955 a cheesy private eye (Rourke) is hired by a mysterious stranger (De Niro) to track down a missing man. The trail leads from Harlem to New Orleans and to the home of a voodoo princess (Bonet). As his investigation proceeds, Rourke discovers more and more things that are very unusual indeed. The film is full of hallucinatory, sensual and frightening images. It is intriguing and fascinating, although not terribly appealing at times. As a film, it presents an interesting transformation from being a standard mystery at first into becoming a supernatural occult chiller at the end.

A: Mickey Rourke, Robert De Niro, Lisa Bonet, Charlotte Rampling

© LIVE HOME VIDEO 60459

ANOTHER 48 HOURS

D: Walter Hill — 98 m

R | ACT COM CRM | 1990 | COLOR

Sex / Nud / Viol / Lang / AdSit

7 That comic, wisecracking, crime-busting duo are back again for the second time around. This time, the boys make a huge mess of San Francisco as they try to bring down a very bad dude named Iceman. Nolte's got himself in a jam, so he turns to old friend/enemy Murphy - fresh out of prison himself - to save his career and clear his name by nailing Iceman to the wall in just 48 hours. Expect the usual bar brawls, tough talk, smart talk, humor and lots of violence and broken glass! Fun still, but not as good as the first time around in 48 HOURS.

A: Eddie Murphy, Nick Nolte, Brion James, Kevin Tighe, Ed O'Ross, David Anthony Marshall

© PARAMOUNT HOME VIDEO 32386

ANY WHICH WAY YOU CAN

D: Buddy Van Horn — 116 m

PG | COM ACT | 1980 | COLOR

Sex / Nud / Viol / Lang / AdSit

8 Sequel to EVERY WHICH WAY BUT LOOSE. Same cast of characters, same enjoyable formula. Eastwood is a beer drinkin' mechanic/streetfighter who is set to meet the King of the Streetfighters in an all-out fight in Jackson Hole, Wyoming. However, Clint falls in love and doesn't want to go. So a group of hoods kidnap his love to encourage him to show up. Clyde, the raunchy orangutan, is back, too. Certainly not highbrow entertainment, but it is a lot of fun and was very popular.

A: Clint Eastwood, Sondra Locke, Geoffrey Lewis, William Smith, Harry Guardino, Ruth Gordon

© WARNER HOME VIDEO 11077

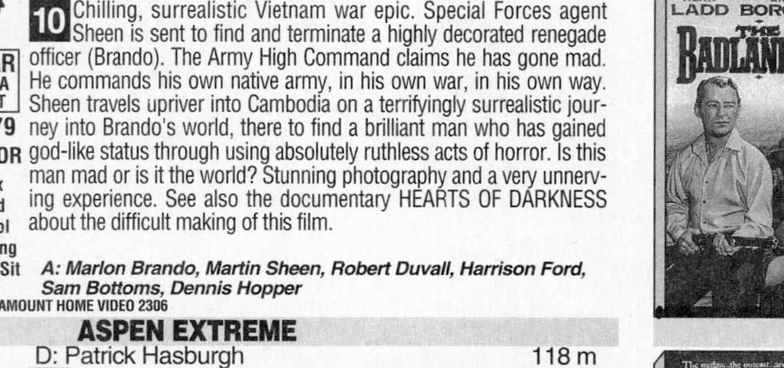

APOCALYPSE NOW

D: Francis Ford Coppola — 153 m

R | WAR DMA ACT | 1979 | COLOR

Sex / Nud / Viol / Lang / AdSit

10 Chilling, surrealistic Vietnam war epic. Special Forces agent Sheen is sent to find and terminate a highly decorated renegade officer (Brando). The Army High Command claims he has gone mad. He commands his own native army, in his own war, in his own way. Sheen travels upriver into Cambodia on a terrifyingly surrealistic journey into Brando's world, there to find a brilliant man who has gained god-like status through using absolutely ruthless acts of horror. Is this man mad or is it the world? Stunning photography and a very unnerving experience. See also the documentary HEARTS OF DARKNESS about the difficult making of this film.

A: Marlon Brando, Martin Sheen, Robert Duvall, Harrison Ford, Sam Bottoms, Dennis Hopper

© PARAMOUNT HOME VIDEO 2306

ASPEN EXTREME

D: Patrick Hasburgh — 118 m

PG-13 | ACT | 1992 | COLOR

Sex / Nud / Viol / Lang / AdSit

7 Two young best-friends and skiing buddies leave their blue-collar Detroit world behind to discover a luxurious new world when they arrive in Aspen, playground of the rich. Their goal is to become ski instructors and experience the excitement of extreme skiing - wild, unadventurous and dangerous skiing in virgin snow. However, they are also surrounded by temptation and are eventually seduced by the rich lifestyle. Their values and their friendship both have become challenged. What could easily have been a simple soap opera on snow was given reasonably good treatment. The characters are believable and likable, and there is some pretty good skiing action too.

A: Paul Gross, Peter Berg, Finola Hughes, Teri Polo

© HOLLYWOOD PICTURES HOME VIDEO 1776

ASSAULT ON PRECINCT 13

D: John Carpenter — 91 m

R | SUS CRM ACT | 1976 | COLOR

Sex / Nud / Viol / Lang / AdSit

8 Riveting thriller, taut suspense and lots of hard-hitting action. A nearly deserted LA police station is in the process of being closed down. There are only two deathrow prisoners, one cop and two secretaries waiting inside for the moving vans. Through the door runs a man who is being pursued by a gang of street kids. In a state of shock, he cannot tell the cop what is happening before the phone lines and the power are cut. They are all now trapped inside and the gang attacks. Widely recognized as an updated version of the Howard Hawks classic Western RIO BRAVO. Quite good.

A: Austin Stoker, Darwin Joston, Laurie Zimmer, Tony Burton, Nancy Loomis, Kim Richards

© UNITED AMERICAN VIDEO CORP. 5260

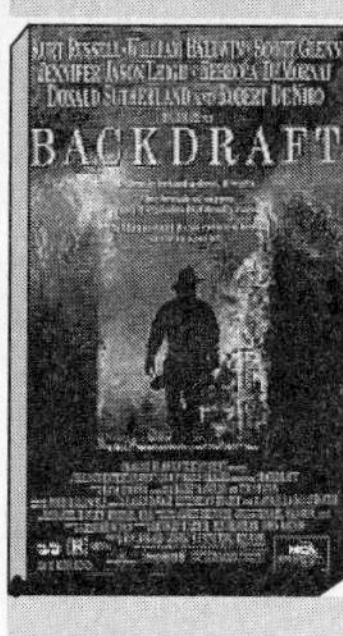

BACKDRAFT

D: Ron Howard — 135 m

R | ACT SUS MYS | 1991 | COLOR

Sex / Nud / Viol / Lang / AdSit

7 This is an involving film but the real star is the exciting high-tech special effects. Russell and Baldwin are two feuding brothers who must confront their personal differences and emotional scars after they are assigned to the same fire unit. Their personal drama unfolds against a backdrop in which an arsonist is lighting up the Windy City. The quest to stop him pits brother against brother in a battle of wills, fueled by their determination to live up to their heroic father's reputation. Spectacular special effects alone will keep you riveted, but it's a suspenseful mystery, too.

A: Kurt Russell, William Baldwin, Scott Glenn, Jennifer Jason Leigh, Rebecca De Mornay, Donald Sutherland

© MCA/UNIVERSAL HOME VIDEO, INC. 81078

BACKTRACK

D: Dennis Hopper — 102 m

R | CRM ACT | 1991 | COLOR

Sex / Nud / Viol / Lang / AdSit

6 Jodie Foster is an electronic artist who stumbles upon a mob hit. When she discovers that the police can't protect her from the mob, she decides to hide out on her own. The police however, need her as witness, so now she has both the police and the mob on her trail. To find her and kill her, the bad guys contract with top notch hit-man Dennis Hopper. He studies every aspect of her, discovers that she is in many ways like him, falls in love with her, and, after he catches up with her, he gives her the option of dying on the spot or leaving with him. Now they are both on the run together. Very unusual film. Not particularly outstanding, but curiously interesting.

A: Jodie Foster, Dennis Hopper, Dean Stockwell, Joe Pesci, John Turturro, Fred Ward

© LIVE HOME VIDEO 9952

BAD COMPANY

D: Damian Harris — 118 m

R | ACT | 1995 | COLOR

Sex / Nud / Viol / Lang / AdSit

6 Fishburne is a cool and calculating ex-CIA operative who has just been hired by a highly lucrative and privately owned, clandestine operation called The Toolshed, which specializes in wealthy corporate clients. The Toolshed is run by Langella and his right-hand woman, Barkin. After Fishburne's first major assignment goes off well, Barkin plots with him to murder Langella and take over the company. However, Barkin does not know that Fishburne is still under the thumb of the CIA, and the CIA wants The Toolshed too. Somewhat slow in the beginning and the characters are very cold and hard to care about. However, it is also an interesting plot and contains a neat twist.

A: Laurence Fishburne, Ellen Barkin, Frank Langella, Michael Beach, Gia Carides, David Ogden Stiers

© TOUCHSTONE HOME VIDEO 2757

BADLANDERS, THE

D: Delmer Daves — 84 m

NR | WST ACT | 1958 | COLOR

Sex / Nud / Viol / Lang / AdSit

7 Good Western action. It is the turn-of-the-century in Arizona. Alan Ladd and Ernest Borgnine have just been released from prison but they are eager to get even with the guy who sent them there in the first place and stole their gold mine in the process. To do it, they enlist a dynamite expert (Persoff) in their plot to steal $200,000 of their own gold back, right from under his nose. This is widely recognized as being a Western version of the gangster classic THE ASPHALT JUNGLE.

A: Alan Ladd, Ernest Borgnine, Katy Jurado, Claire Kelly

Distributed By MGM/UA Home Video M202710

BARBAROSA

D: Fred Schepisi — 90 m

PG | WST ACT | 1981 | COLOR

Sex / Nud / Viol / Lang / AdSit

8 Action packed and critically acclaimed Western. Willie Nelson puts in a fine performance as Barbarosa - a legendary, free-spirited outlaw who is joined by a ragged farmer/protege (Busey), on the run from an accidental killing. Barbarosa is running both from bounty hunters and his wife's family, who keeps sending their sons out to find and kill him. Together the two survive, while Busey gains a new trade and a growing respect for the strange loner Nelson. Majestic scenery, good period detail, realistic action and a sometimes funny script give it plenty of flavor. Solid Western.

A: Willie Nelson, Gary Busey, Isela Vega, Gilbert Roland, Danny De La Paz, George Voskovec

© J2 COMMUNICATIONS 0035

BAT 21

D: Peter Markle — 106 m

R | WAR ACT | 1988 | COLOR

Sex / Nud / Viol / Lang / AdSit

8 Excellent. Gene Hackman is a middle-aged career military officer in Vietnam who has safely fought his war from behind a desk or at 30,000 feet. But he is parachuted into the real war when he is shot down and lands inside enemy territory. Glover is a rescue pilot who doggedly tries to get him out as Hackman struggles to survive on the ground in a hostile territory and in a real down-to-earth shooting war. This film was based upon a real-life occurrence. This is a suspenseful and very well-acted story that keeps you on the edge of your seat. See the index for other Hackman movies.

A: Gene Hackman, Danny Glover, Jerry Reed, David Marshal Grant, Clayton Rohner, Erich Anderson

© VIDEO TREASURES MO12021

BATMAN

D: Tim Burton 126 m

PG-13 · ACT FAN · 1989 · COLOR · Sex · Nud · Viol · Lang · AdSit

8 A gloomy and foreboding Gotham City is out of control and run by hoods. In one of the opening sequences, one of them (Jack Nicholson) is dropped into a tub of acid by a newly-arrived powerful and sinister black hooded figure. Batman (Keaton) has come. Still, this acid bath has not killed Jack but it has contorted his face into a perpetual macabre smile and made him even more spiteful. He has now become Joker and seizes control of the underworld, immediately beginning a psychotic campaign of terror. This is not a comic book tale for the kiddies. It is an adult fantasy. The Joker is menacing and maniacal, and the violence is realistic (mostly). Exciting, definitely different.

A: Jack Nicholson, Michael Keaton, Kim Basinger, Pat Hingle, Billy Dee Williams, Jack Palance

© WARNER HOME VIDEO 12000

BATMAN: MASK OF THE PHANTASM

D: Eric Radomski, Bruce Timm 77 m

PG · ACT CLD · 1994 · COLOR · Sex · Nud · Viol · Lang · AdSit

8 After two super-budget feature films and a campy TV series, the Batman of the comic series returned in animated form this time. This version stays true to the style, and even the time (late 1930's) of the original. Andrea, Bruce Wayne's only true love, has come back to Gotham City but Batman (Bruce Wayne in disguise) is now suspected by the police in the murders of several major crime figures. One crime lord is so terrified of him that he has hired The Joker to protect him. However, the murderer is not Batman but yet another masked avenger. So, if Batman is to regain his good name, he must find out the truth. Exciting and well done but realistic and very violent, so this is not for very young. Many adults will like it too.

A:

© WARNER HOME VIDEO 15500

BATMAN RETURNS

D: Tim Burton 126 m

PG-13 · ACT FAN · 1992 · COLOR · Sex · Nud · Viol · Lang · AdSit

7 Awesome special effects and big budget production. Again, as in the first big-budget film, these characters are not just cartoon figures taken from the comic strip. They are presented as near-real psychotic characters. Catwoman, the Penguin and Batman all are given reasons for having become such social and psychological oddities. The three engage in a battle with each other and against a corrupt politician. Of course, you can expect the anticipated battle of good vs. evil, but this sequel is decidedly different than the comic strip. Gotham at Christmas is a truly freakish place. Outrageous and spectacular.

A: Michael Keaton, Michelle Pfeiffer, Danny DeVito, Christopher Walken, Michael Gough, Michael Murphy

© WARNER HOME VIDEO 15000

BEASTMASTER, THE

D: Don Coscarelli 119 m

PG · FAN ACT · 1982 · COLOR · Sex · Nud · Viol · Lang · AdSit

8 In a magical feudal world, a demented high priest enslaves a people and demands that they sacrifice their young children. A young warrior (Singer) is the only survivor of a tribal massacre, and he uses his ability to communicate telepathically with animals to aid him in his quest to defeat the evil sorcerer (Rip Torn) and to save the beautiful virgin (Tanya Roberts). Good special effects, and plenty of animals and action for kids of all ages.

A: Marc Singer, Tanya Roberts, Rip Torn, John Amos

Distributed By MGM/UA Home Video M800226

BEN HUR

D: William Wyler 211 m

G · ACT DMA · 1959 · COLOR · Sex · Nud · Viol · Lang · AdSit

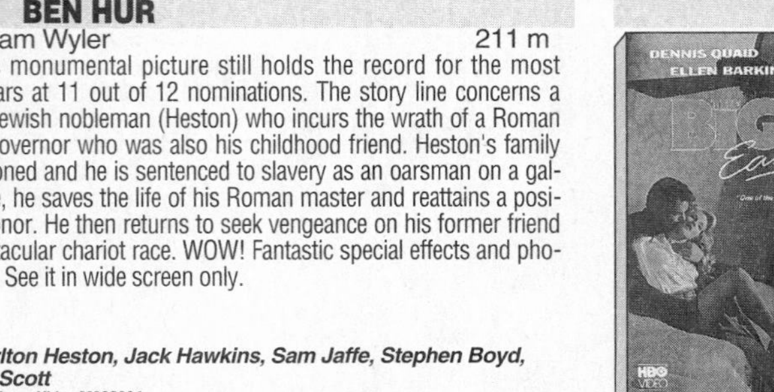

10 This monumental picture still holds the record for the most Oscars at 11 out of 12 nominations. The story line concerns a wealthy Jewish nobleman (Heston) who incurs the wrath of a Roman military governor who was also his childhood friend. Heston's family is imprisoned and he is sentenced to slavery as an oarsman on a galley. There, he saves the life of his Roman master and reattains a position of honor. He then returns to seek vengeance on his former friend in a spectacular chariot race. WOW! Fantastic special effects and photography. See it in wide screen only.

A: Charlton Heston, Jack Hawkins, Sam Jaffe, Stephen Boyd, Martha Scott

Distributed By MGM/UA Home Video M900004

BEST SELLER

D: John Flynn 95 m

R · ACT SUS · 1987 · COLOR · Sex · Nud · Viol · Lang · AdSit

8 Exciting and taut thriller. James Woods is a professional hitman and he wants revenge against a big-time industrialist - a man who he has worked for and trusted for years, but who has fired him. So, he enlists the aid of Brian Dennehy, a cop and successful crime-story writer, to help him tell his life's story. He will tell everything: about the extortion, murders and political corruption. The cop will get his story, but he's also going to have to keep his source alive. Even that is complicated, because neither of these two can completely trust the other. Tense, quick moving and exciting.

A: James Woods, Brian Dennehy, Victoria Tennant, Allison Balson, Paul Shenar, George Coe

© LIVE HOME VIDEO 6026

BEVERLY HILLS COP

D: Martin Brest 105 m

R · COM ACT CRM · 1984 · COLOR · Sex · Nud · Viol · Lang · AdSit

10 A huge box-office sensation, a perfect vehicle for the wise-cracking Eddie Murphy and a very funny and action-packed movie. A street-smart, smart aleck Detroit cop (Murphy) goes to L.A. intent upon tracking down a friend's killer. He ignores the by-the-book local cops and their warnings to stay away and instead blusters his way into high society, irritating everybody possible in the process. Following his killer's trail leads him to a major smuggling and drug ring. Cleverly woven fabric of comedy, characters and action. Excellent cast provides major support. Excellent score.

A: Eddie Murphy, Judge Reinhold, John Aston, Lisa Eibacher, Steven Berkoff, James Russo

© PARAMOUNT HOME VIDEO 1134

BEVERLY HILLS COP II

D: Tony Scott 103 m

R · COM ACT CRM · 1987 · COLOR · Sex · Nud · Viol · Lang · AdSit

7 Sequel to the megahit BEVERLY HILLS COP. It lacks the originality and major laughs of the first movie, but still has plenty of action and wise cracks. Murphy comes back to L.A. to investigate the shooting of his friend, police captain Cox, and runs up against hit woman Brigitte Nielsen. Murphy is again the likable smart-mouthed cop who runs over everyone to get the bad guys. Pretty good, but not close to the original. Don't miss Murphy's other megahit: 48 HOURS.

A: Eddie Murphy, Judge Reinhold, Jurgen Prochnow, Ronny Cox, John Aston, Brigitte Nielsen

© PARAMOUNT HOME VIDEO 1860

BIG BAD MAMA

D: Steve Carver 87 m

R · ACT COM · 1974 · COLOR · Sex · Nud · Viol · Lang · AdSit

7 Angie Dickinson stars in this light-hearted clone to BONNIE AND CLYDE. It is a pretty good action film about a depression-era mother who is tired of being poor and so, along with her teenage daughters, takes up robbing banks and other places for a living. Along the way to California, she and her girls take in accomplices, and boy-toys Tom Skerritt and William Shatner. While this film has a fair amount of action, it was most notable for its nude scenes, particularly Angie's, which has help to keep it a perennial favorite. Its success spawned a later and lessor clone.

A: Angie Dickinson, Tom Skerritt, William Shatner, Susan Sennett, Joan Prather, Robbie Lee

© WARNER HOME VIDEO 4013

BIG COUNTRY, THE

D: William Wyler 166 m

NR · WST ACT · 1958 · COLOR · Sex · Nud · Viol · Lang · AdSit

9 Big Western. Peck is a former sea captain who has abandoned the sea. He met Baker when she was in school, they're engaged and he has now come west to her father's (Bickford) ranch. Upon his arrival, he finds that he has stumbled into the middle of a vicious long-standing feud between Bickford and his neighbor Burl Ives (won Oscar) over water rights. However, the water is on land now owned by Jean Simmons who was willed it when her father died. Peck doesn't want to fight and is accused of being a coward, but he's going to have to. This is a big budget Western and is quite good too. Theme song is a classic.

A: Gregory Peck, Jean Simmons, Charlton Heston, Carroll Baker, Burl Ives, Charles Bickford

Distributed By MGM/UA Home Video M900917

BIG EASY, THE

D: Jim McBride 100 m

R · ACT MYS ROM · 1987 · COLOR · Sex · Nud · Viol · Lang · AdSit

9 Classy, sexy, exciting and refreshingly different. Quaid is a charming and dedicated homicide detective in New Orleans. Barkin is a by-the-book Assistant D.A. investigating corruption in the police ranks. She and her people catch him taking a small pay off (everybody does it) and goes after him. While they are on opposite sides on this case, she finds that she is still strongly attracted to him. She also discovers that he is truly a dedicated cop. When he uncovers a major scandal in the department and follows it out to the end - even though he is very close to the people involved. Excellent, intricate and well-crafted murder mystery - erotic, too.

A: Dennis Quaid, Ellen Barkin, Ned Beatty, John Goodman, Lisa Jane Persky, Charles Ludlum

© HBO VIDEO 0052

BIG JAKE

D: George Sherman 110 m

G · WST ACT · 1971 · COLOR · Sex · Nud · Viol · Lang · AdSit

6 It's 1909 and someone has kidnapped John Wayne's grandson (his real-life son John Ethan). They shouldn't have done that. His estranged wife of 18 years (Maureen O'Hara) has asked him to take one million dollars in ransom money to bad guy Richard Boone. Instead, Jake tries a double-cross that just about backfires. This movie also tried for some laughs... but shouldn't have. It works best as a shoot-'em-up Western for John Wayne fans. It's good at that.

A: John Wayne, Richard Boone, Maureen O'Hara, Patrick Wayne, Chris Mitchum, Bobby Vinton

© FOXVIDEO 7149

BIG RED ONE, THE

D: Samuel Fuller 114 m

PG
WAR DMA ACT
1980 COLOR
Sex Nud Viol Lang AdSit

9 A tough, gritty, realistic and brilliant war saga. Director Fuller spent 35 years trying to get this autobiographical movie of his first-hand memories of WWII made. The focus is upon the daily lives of the soldiers of the famous American First Infantry Division, called the Big Red One. Individual soldiers of the division are followed from their landing in North Africa all through Europe. Lee Marvin is a war-weary special infantry sergeant who is just trying to keep his young troops, most of them fresh out of high school, alive. The veterans survive but most replacements never live long enough to learn how to. Rich, moving and realistic. A terrific film.

A: Lee Marvin, Mark Hamill, Robert Carradine, Bobby DiCicco, Kelly Ward, Siegfried Rauch

© WARNER HOME VIDEO 939

BIG TROUBLE IN LITTLE CHINA

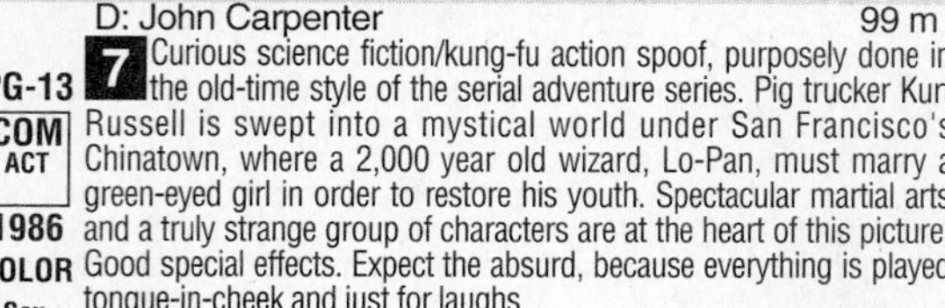

D: John Carpenter 99 m

PG-13
COM ACT
1986 COLOR
Sex Nud Viol Lang AdSit

7 Curious science fiction/kung-fu action spoof, purposely done in the old-time style of the serial adventure series. Pig trucker Kurt Russell is swept into a mystical world under San Francisco's Chinatown, where a 2,000 year old wizard, Lo-Pan, must marry a green-eyed girl in order to restore his youth. Spectacular martial arts and a truly strange group of characters are at the heart of this picture. Good special effects. Expect the absurd, because everything is played tongue-in-cheek and just for laughs.

A: Kurt Russell, Kim Cattrall, Victor Wong, Dennis Dun, Kate Burton, James Hong

© FOXVIDEO 1502

BILLY BATHGATE

D: Robert Benton 107 m

R
CRM ACT
1991 COLOR
Sex Nud Viol Lang AdSit

8 Absorbing and well-crafted gangster movie that was underappreciated on its release. Told through the eyes Billy (Loren Dean), a streetwise young kid trying to break out of the ghetto and into the rackets, this is the story of the final days of the infamous Dutch Schultz (Dustin Hoffman). More importantly, it is an involving depiction of the characters and lifestyle of that colorful era. Willis is Dutch's right-hand man who betrays him and earns a trip to the ocean floor in concrete boots. Kidman is the slumming socialite who enjoys living on the edge. Well done.

A: Dustin Hoffman, Nicole Kidman, Bruce Willis, Loren Dean, Steven Hill

© TOUCHSTONE HOME VIDEO 1337

BILLY JACK

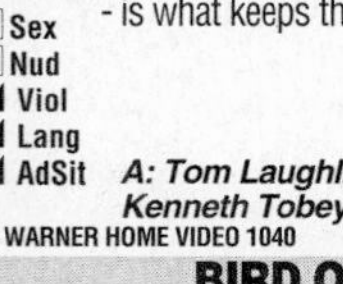

D: T.C. Frank 114 m

PG
ACT DMA
1971 COLOR
Sex Nud Viol Lang AdSit

7 A powerful, youth-oriented favorite. A huge film at the time of its release, it developed a cult following for its support of freedom, justice and anything anti-establishment. It made bold statements against bigotry, education and the government. Billy Jack (Laughlin) is a young half-breed Indian and a former Green Beret who is dedicated to single-handedly saving a "freedom school" for troubled children from reactionary townsfolk. His weapon - his finely honed karate skills - is what keeps their intrusions at bay.

A: Tom Laughlin, Deloris Taylor, Clark Howat, Bert Freed, Kenneth Tobey, Julie Webb

© WARNER HOME VIDEO 1040

BIRD ON A WIRE

D: John Badham 110 m

PG-13
COM ACT
1990 COLOR
Sex Nud Viol Lang AdSit

6 Cliched and predictable, but a good time if you'll check your brain at the door. Hawn is a successful BMW-driving yuppie lawyer who, while stopped for gas, thinks she recognizes Gibson as a long-dead lover with an appropriately aged face. It is! Gibson had snitched on an international ring of drug smugglers and is now protected by the FBI, but... on this very day, the killers are released from prison and have caught up with him. Hawn now rescues Gibson when the bullets start to fly, and the pair rekindle their romance on the lam, running from some very bad guys. Formula, but fun.

A: Mel Gibson, Goldie Hawn, David Carradine, Bill Duke, Joan Severance, Stephen Tobolowsky

© MCA/UNIVERSAL HOME VIDEO, INC. 80959

BITE THE BULLET

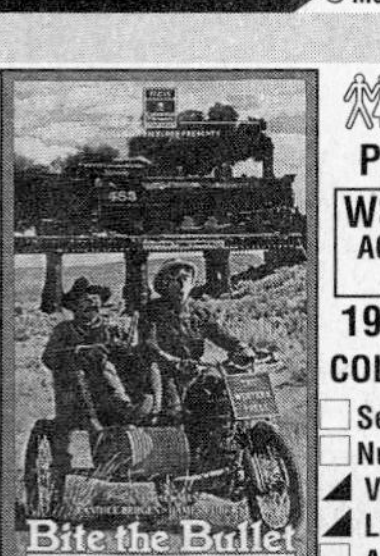

D: Richard Brooks 131 m

PG
WST ACT
1975 COLOR
Sex Nud Viol Lang AdSit

8 Excellent but unconventional Western that is a large-scale epic about a 700-mile endurance horserace (which were actually quite common in the West at the turn of the 20th century). This is a sleeper of a movie that was hardly noticed upon its release, but undeservedly so. The story revolves around the different types of people who compete in the rough-and-tumble race and the gradual respect that all the finalists gain for each other. There are many top stars in it - Hackman and Coburn in particular are excellent. Beautiful photography.

A: Gene Hackman, James Coburn, Candice Bergen, Ben Johnson, Jan-Michael Vincent, Dabney Coleman

© COLUMBIA TRISTAR HOME VIDEO VH10022

BLACK MARBLE, THE

D: Harold Becker 110 m

PG
CRM COM ACT
1980 COLOR
Sex Nud Viol Lang AdSit

7 An insightful, charming and sometimes funny look at a hard-drinking cop who is slowly killing himself with alcohol to dull the realities of his job. He is assigned a sexy new female detective who thinks he is crazy and obsolete. She wants to have as little as possible to do with him. When they are assigned the case of retrieving a kidnapped prize dog from a sleazy dog breeder, she changes her mind about him and falls in love with him. (There is a wonderful seduction scene in his apartment.) This movie slides from comedy into drama into action. It is good but also slightly uneven.

A: Paula Prentiss, Robert Foxworth, Harry Dean Stanton, Barbara Babcock, John Hancock, Judy Landers

© NEW LINE HOME VIDEO 1617

BLACK MOON RISING

D: Harley Cokliss 100 m

R
ACT
1986 COLOR
Sex Nud Viol Lang AdSit

6 A high-tech race car named The Black Moon is stolen by a ring of sophisticated car thieves who are led by industrialist Robert Vaughn. However, these guys are unaware that a highly secret government computer disk is hidden inside it. Tommy Lee Jones and Linda Hamilton team up to steal the car back. The plot has some interesting twists and turns, but the best reason to watch is some good special effects and high-speed action.

A: Tommy Lee Jones, Robert Vaughn, Linda Hamilton, Richard Jaeckel, Lee Ving, Bubba Smith

© R&G VIDEO, LP 90024

BLACK RAIN

D: Ridley Scott 125 m

R
ACT CRM
1989 COLOR
Sex Nud Viol Lang AdSit

9 Superior, high-intensity action thriller. Two New York police detectives take a vicious killer back to Japan where they are tricked into releasing him to the wrong people. The two now vow to get him back. However, their help is not welcomed by the Japanese police who have their own way of doing business. The Westerners soon find that their pursuit has entangled them with very powerful figures from the Japanese underworld, who are also engaged in an internal war. Loaded with non-stop action. Another very interesting Japanese-Mafia movie, but with a less-hyper air, is THE YAKUZA.

A: Michael Douglas, Andy Garcia, Ken Takakura, Kate Capshaw, Yusaku Matsuda, Tomisaburo Wakayama

© PARAMOUNT HOME VIDEO 32220

BLACK SUNDAY

D: John Frankenheimer 143 m

R
SUS ACT CRM
1977 COLOR
Sex Nud Viol Lang AdSit

9 Gripping thriller. An Arab guerrilla terrorist organization called Black September plans to attack America in the most painful way possible: they plan to blow up the Superbowl with the President in attendance. The terrorist leader gets shell-shocked Vietnam vet Bruce Dern to pilot the Goodyear Blimp into position, where they then plan to blow it up. Shaw is an Israeli agent who struggles against time to foil their plot. Terrific action sequences combine with genuine terror at the climax to create true excitement. Excellent.

A: Robert Shaw, Bruce Dern, Marthe Keller, Fritz Weaver, Steven Keats, William Daniels

© PARAMOUNT HOME VIDEO 8855

BLADE RUNNER

D: Ridley Scott 117 m

R
SF ACT
1982 COLOR
Sex Nud Viol Lang AdSit

8 A thought-provoking and visually impressive sci-fi movie. Ford is a bladerunner, a bountyhunter sent to chase down and "kill" four androids who have escaped from space and made their way to Earth. Ford is led on a chase through 21st-century Los Angeles where he falls in love with a woman who may be one of the androids. Ironically, his search leads him to discover that the androids have more soul than many humans. Intriguing blend of good science fiction and mystery. Rereleased later as Director's Cut with some previously excluded scenes put back and a different, darker ending added.

A: Harrison Ford, Rutger Hauer, Sean Young, Edward James Olmos, Joanna Cassidy, Daryl Hannah

© WARNER HOME VIDEO 12682

BLIND FURY

D: Phillip Noyce 86 m

R
ACT COM
1990 COLOR
Sex Nud Viol Lang AdSit

7 Odd action film with a premise that is sometimes unexpectedly funny while at the same time very violent. Rutger Hauer is a Vietnam vet who was blinded in a battle but has become a martial arts expert. So, when his best buddy (O'Quinn) is kidnapped by gangsters and forced into the drug business, Hauer sets off with O'Quinn's son to Las Vegas to bring down the bad guys. And, he makes mince meat out of them with his finely honed blind-man swordplay. The tongue-in-cheek humor will surprise you as they chop their way through one wild adventure after another. Very curious and interesting.

A: Rutger Hauer, Terry O'Quinn, Brandon Call, Lisa Blount, Randall Cobb, Meg Foster

© COLUMBIA TRISTAR HOME VIDEO 70253

BLOODSPORT

D: Newt Arnold — 92 m

R | ACT | 1987 | COLOR | Sex | Nud | Viol | Lang | AdSit

7 Kickboxing action to the absolute max! Martial arts guru Jean-Claude Van Damme arrives in Hong Kong to compete in the match of all matches, the Kumite - one of the most violent competitions around and one that is outlawed in Hong Kong. This is full-contact kickboxing. The rest of the plotline is immaterial. The purpose of the film is to show the fight sequences which contain lots of blood and the sharp crack of bones breaking into a zillion little pieces. However, it is based on the true story of the first Western man to win the brutal battle.

A: Jean-Claude Van Damme, Donald Gibb, Leah Ayres, Roy Chiao, Bolo Yeung, Norman Burton

© WARNER HOME VIDEO 37062

BLOWN AWAY

D: Stephen Hopkins — 121 m

R | ACT | 1994 | COLOR | Sex | Nud | Viol | Lang | AdSit

6 In spite of having an extremely powerful cast, this one turned out to be a fairly standard action picture. Its primary distinction is the huge number of explosions (103) it contained. Jeff Bridges is an Irish-American cop, working in Boston's bomb squad. He has just met the woman (Amis) he wants to marry and now he can no longer take the strain of his job. He has to quit. Then his town gets a visit from some-one from his past. Tommy Lee Jones plays an IRA bomber who has come to America to ply his wicked trade in Boston, and taunts Bridges with threats to his new family. So, Bridges must stay on the force to destroy the mad bomber.

A: Jeff Bridges, Tommy Lee Jones, Lloyd Bridges, Forest Whitaker, Suzy Amis, John Finn

Distributed By MGM/UA Home Video M904807

BLUE STEEL

D: Kathryn Bigelow — 103 m

R | ACT CRM | 1990 | COLOR | Sex | Nud | Viol | Lang | AdSit

6 A female rookie cop (Curtis), on her first day, is forced to shoot and kill an armed robber. She fired because she saw he had a weapon, but the pistol can't be found and she is suspended. However, an unseen witness was also there on that day and he picked up the gun. He has his own plans for it and for her. He is obsessed with Curtis. He is a smooth-talking handsome commodities broker (Silver) and he wins her over. But, unbeknownst to her or anyone else, he is also a serial killer who is using the missing gun to slam slugs into bodies. Plot is not particularly credible or even believable, but it does have a lot of gory action.

A: Jamie Lee Curtis, Ron Silver, Clancy Brown, Elizabeth Pena, Philip Bosco, Louise Fletcher

Distributed By MGM/UA Home Video M901885

BLUE THUNDER

D: John Badham — 108 m

R | ACT | 1983 | COLOR | Sex | Nud | Viol | Lang | AdSit

6 Intense flying action, but not a lot of sense. Roy Scheider is a Vietnam vet who is now an L.A. cop flying helicopters on a police surveillance squad. He is specially chosen to test pilot a new experimental attack helicopter. The craft is truly amazing in its capacities. But when he uncovers what the government plans to use it for, he and his partners decide to defeat the military master-minds and their plot. So they steal the chopper, and that sets up an exciting series of air duels above the streets of Los Angeles. Pretty unbelievable, but the action is hot and heavy.

A: Roy Scheider, Candy Clark, Malcolm McDowell, Warren Oates, Daniel Stern

© GOODTIMES 4619

BODYGUARD, THE

D: Mick Jackson — 130 m

R | ROM ACT SUS | 1993 | COLOR | Sex | Nud | Viol | Lang | AdSit

8 Frank Farmer (Kostner) is an ex-secret service agent who has now become a private bodyguard for hire. Whitney Houston is a pop-music star who has been receiving threatening messages. She reluctantly agrees to let her manager hire him, but she largely ignores his advice. That is, until Frank has to jump in to save her bacon after one particularly close call. Suddenly, she not only relies upon him but also begins to find her heart softening to him. Frank finds that he too is falling for her, but that is dangerous because feelings like those threaten his edge - and he needs his edge because the killer is still out there. Yes it's predictable, but hey - it's fun too.

A: Kevin Costner, Whitney Houston, Michele Lamar Richards, DeVaughn Nixon, Gary Kemp, Ralph Waite

© WARNER HOME VIDEO 12591

BOILING POINT

D: James B. Harris — 93 m

R | ACT CRM | 1993 | COLOR | Sex | Nud | Viol | Lang | AdSit

6 Tepid cop drama. Snipes is a Treasury Agent whose partner has been gunned down with a shotgun blast at a phony drug buy. Snipes is upset. He is now being transfered and will have to start over in another town, and his ex-wife has a new man. So, all he has is a friendly hooker (Davidovich), his anger and his job. However, he has talked his boss into one more week so he can find his partner's killer. The killer is a simpleton with a hair-trigger and no conscience. But, he is taking direction from a slick-talking conman (Dennis Hopper), just out of prison, who sets up various phony scams where the two steal the money and kill the other party.

A: Wesley Snipes, Dennis Hopper, Lolita Davidovich, Dan Hedaya, Valerie Perrine, Tony Lo Bianco

© WARNER HOME VIDEO 12976

BONNIE AND CLYDE

D: Arthur Penn — 112 m

NR | CRM ACT | 1967 | COLOR | Sex | Nud | Viol | Lang | AdSit

10 Blockbuster hit. Real-life depression-era folk heros Bonnie Parker (Dunaway) and Clyde Barro (Beatty) who proudly announced, "We rob banks," were immortalized by this landmark film which also transformed the whole action movie genre. The story follows the pair from when they first meet, through a series of highly publicized bank robberies, until their fateful and murderous end in a hail of many, many bullets. This is an exciting film which carefully weaves humor, human insight, social commentary and tenderness with graphic scenes of violence. 5 nominations and 2 Oscars.

A: Warren Beatty, Faye Dunaway, Michael J. Pollard, Gene Hackman, Estelle Parsons, Denver Pyle

© WARNER HOME VIDEO 1026

BORDER, THE

D: Tony Richardson — 107 m

R | ACT DMA | 1981 | COLOR | Sex | Nud | Viol | Lang | AdSit

7 Powerful performance by Nicholson as a border patrolman who is tempted into taking modest bribes in order to satisfy his demanding wife (Perrine). However, he is now being blackmailed by his neighbor and friend. A decent man, he eventually rebels against both the corruption and his corrupt fellow officers. He helps a desperate young Mexican mother, who was degraded into becoming a go-go dancer, recover her baby from an adoption ring. There are interesting moral aspects explored by Nicholson's character, but ultimately this is still an action movie, pitting Nicholson against other officers.

A: Jack Nicholson, Valerie Perrine, Harvey Keitel, Warren Oates, Elpidia Carrillo

© MCA/UNIVERSAL HOME VIDEO, INC. 71007

BOUNTY, THE

D: Roger Donaldson — 130 m

PG | DMA ACT | 1984 | COLOR | Sex | Nud | Viol | Lang | AdSit

8 This sweeping epic is the fourth screen retelling, and one of the best, of history's most famous mutiny. This screenplay concentrates on the personalities of the two principal characters and, as such, depicts the events somewhat more accurately. This Bligh (Hopkins) is just extremely stubborn - not crazy, and Christian (Gibson) is a shallow character. Beautiful scenery to watch and a fascinating story will hold your attention throughout. Also see the classic: MUTINY ON THE BOUNTY.

A: Mel Gibson, Anthony Hopkins, Laurence Olivier, Edward Fox, Daniel Day-Lewis, Bernard Hill

© UNITED AMERICAN VIDEO CORP. 5966

BOYS IN COMPANY C, THE

D: Sidney J. Furie — 125 m

R | WAR ACT | 1977 | COLOR | Sex | Nud | Viol | Lang | AdSit

7 Hard-hitting actioner about five young Marines who are sent to Vietnam together after having become friends in basic training. This was the first major studio war film about Vietnam after the war ended. Because of that, it is somewhat reminiscent of the standard war films following WWII and Korea and less like the more critical films which followed. Plenty of salty humor and comradery. The action scenes are gritty and very realistic.

A: Stan Shaw, Andrew Stevens, James Channing, Michael Lembeck, Craig Wasson

© COLUMBIA TRISTAR HOME VIDEO 60144

BRADDOCK: MISSING IN ACTION III

D: Aaron Norris — 104 m

R | ACT | 1988 | COLOR | Sex | Nud | Viol | Lang | AdSit

6 Rousing mindless actioner. US Army Colonel James Braddock returns to Vietnam in search of his Asian wife and Amerasian son, but he takes with him a whole assortment of high-tech weaponry. Norris fights his way in, grabs his family and a bunch of other Amerasian kids and battles his way out, hotly pursued by a sadistic Vietnamese officer. The film is typical Norris in that he applies liberal use of his considerable martial arts skills to destroy the opposition. Lots of action, little else.

A: Chuck Norris, Roland Harrah, III, Aki Aleong, Miki Kim, Yehuda Efroni

© VIDEO TREASURES M942

BRAVADOS, THE

D: Henry King — 99 m

NR | WST ACT DMA | 1958 | COLOR | Sex | Nud | Viol | Lang | AdSit

8 This is a powerful drama of fierce frontier justice and revenge gone wild. Peck plays a rancher whose wife is raped and then murdered by four men. He, however, is an expert tracker and pursues them to a Mexican border town where they are about to be hung for robbing a bank and killing a teller. Instead of hanging, they escape and take a beautiful young woman hostage. Now, taking charge of the posse, Peck tracks them down one by one, exacting his own vicious vengeance as he finds them. This is a stark and brooding Western where Peck becomes as bad as the killers he pursues. Thought provoking.

A: Gregory Peck, Joan Collins, Stephen Boyd, Albert Salmi, Henry Silva, Kathleen Gallant

© FOXVIDEO 1494

BREAKHEART PASS

PG | WST ACT MYS | 1976 | COLOR

Sex · Nud · Viol · Lang · AdSit

D: Tom Gries 96 m

7 Slam-bang action-filled Western starring Charles Bronson. He is an accused thief and an arsonist aboard a special government train that is heading through the snow-draped Rocky Mountains on a rescue mission to an Army outpost and is accompanied by a US Marshall. Also aboard are a governor, his secret mistress and a government engineer. When one of the passengers is murdered, it becomes apparent that all of them have something to hide and are not what they appear to be. Plenty of stunts and fights complement some interesting plot twists in a search for the answer to a

A: Charles Bronson, Ben Johnson, Ed Lauter, Richard Crenna, Charles Durning, Jill Ireland

Distributed By MGM/UA Home Video M201559

BRIDGE AT REMAGEN, THE

NR | WAR ACT | 1969 | COLOR

Sex · Nud · Viol · Lang · AdSit

D: John Guillermin 116 m

7 High intensity war flick recounting the real-life battle for a strategic WWII bridge. Near the end of WWII, Allied soldiers try to capture the last bridge into Germany intact so that it can be used in the Allied invasion efforts. The Germans desperately want the bridge destroyed for the same reason, but they are holding off to the last moment so that their retreating troops can get home. The war is coming to an end... this is the last hope for the Germans. There are very good action sequences, but fans of this genre should be sure to also see the similar but superior A BRIDGE TOO FAR.

A: George Segal, Ben Gazzara, Robert Vaughn, E.G. Marshall, Bradford Dillman, Peter Van Eyck

Distributed By MGM/UA Home Video M201533

BRIDGE ON THE RIVER KWAI, THE

NR | WAR DMA ACT | 1957 | COLOR

Sex · Nud · Viol · Lang · AdSit

D: David Lean 161 m

10 Powerful war drama which won 7 Academy Awards, including every major category. Much more than a standard war or action movie, this is the powerfully dramatic story of men under extreme stress. British soldiers in a Japanese prisoner-of-war camp are forced to construct a strategic bridge in Burma. For Guinness, the English commander, it is a source of pride for himself and his men, but Holden returns after escaping to blow it up as being a dangerous strategic target. Psychological battles of wills and major action sequences combine in a famous climax.

A: William Holden, Alec Guinness, Jack Hawkins, Sessue Hayakawa, James Donald, Geoffrey Horne

© COLUMBIA TRISTAR HOME VIDEO 60160

BRIDGE TOO FAR, A

PG | WAR ACT | 1977 | COLOR

Sex · Nud · Viol · Lang · AdSit

D: Richard Attenborough 178 m

9 Spectacular epic movie containing fictionalized personal accounts of the real-life, famous - but disastrous - Allied airborne assault during WWII to get major troop deployments behind the German lines. The objective was to drop 35,000 airborne troops into Eastern Holland to capture six major bridges over the Rhine river from Holland into Germany. This was history's largest airborne assault and before it was over more men had died than in the D-Day invasion. Yet, the people of Holland would have to wait another six months for liberation. Huge all-star cast. Action-packed battle scenes and charged dramatic moments. Beautiful photography of Dutch locations. Exciting.

A: Dirk Bogarde, James Caan, Michael Caine, Sean Connery, Laurence Olivier, Robert Redford

Distributed By MGM/UA Home Video M301838

BROTHERHOOD, THE

NR | CRM ACT | 1968 | COLOR

Sex · Nud · Viol · Lang · AdSit

D: Martin Ritt 96 m

7 A real sleeper. Two brothers are caught up in Mafia lifestyle and in a power struggle after their father dies leaving them the "business." Douglas believes in old-world traditions and is loyal to the Syndicate, but his brother Cord is different. Still, when Douglas kills Cord's father-in-law, Cord agrees to accept the contract to kill his own brother and Douglas must run away to hide in Sicily. This movie was made several years before THE GODFATHER, but contains many of the same elements that made GODFATHER such a big hit. Excellent story and a quality production.

A: Kirk Douglas, Alex Cord, Irene Papas, Luther Adler, Susan Strasberg, Eduardo Ciannelli

© PARAMOUNT HOME VIDEO 6815

BRUBAKER

R | CRM ACT | 1980 | COLOR

Sex · Nud · Viol · Lang · AdSit

D: Stuart Rosenberg 131 m

8 Redford plays Henry Brubaker, a reform-minded prison warden who arrives at his new assignment, a troubled prison, under cover as a new prisoner. He discovers that there is a conspiracy to murder prisoners by corrupt prison officials and then to cover it up. Based on the real-life experiences of Thomas O. Murlan, who was later dismissed as the Superintendent of the Arkansas State Penitentiary. Script was Oscar-nominated.

A: Robert Redford, Yaphet Kotto, Jane Alexander, Murray Hamilton, David Keith, Morgan Freeman

© FOXVIDEO 1098

BULLITT

PG | ACT CRM | 1968 | COLOR

Sex · Nud · Viol · Lang · AdSit

D: Peter Yates 114 m

9 This is the picture which set the standard in police action dramas for a long time, and it still stands up extremely well today. McQueen, in one of his best performances, plays a tough police detective assigned to guard a criminal witness for 48 hours and to then deliver him to testify. But his witness was shot and now he is chasing down the killer. Lots of plot twists make this a movie to be watched... but the car chase scenes make it a movie to watch over and over. Filmed at actual speeds in excess of 100 mph, they're excitement-plus, and some of the best ever done like it.

A: Steve McQueen, Robert Vaughn, Jacqueline Bisset, Norman Fell, Don Gordon, Robert Duvall

© WARNER HOME VIDEO 1029

BURN!

PG | DMA ACT | 1970 | COLOR

Sex · Nud · Viol · Lang · AdSit

D: Gillo Pontecorvo 113 m

7 Fascinating political intrigue set in the colonial Caribbean of 1845. Three hundred years earlier, the Portuguese had burned the entire island to put down an uprising and destroyed the entire native population. Black slaves were imported from Africa to replace them. Now the British send in an agent, egomaniacal Sir William Walker (Brando), to investigate a black uprising. Portraying himself as their savior, he incites the slaves to riot. But when the slaves throw the Portuguese out, he betrays their revolution and he simply replaces the Portuguese with the British.

A: Marlon Brando, Evaristo Marquez, Renato Salvatori, Tom Lyons, Norman Hill

Distributed By MGM/UA Home Video M202327

BUSTING

R | CRM COM ACT | 1973 | COLOR

Sex · Nud · Viol · Lang · AdSit

D: Peter Hyams 89 m

6 Gould and Blake are unconventional Los Angeles vice cops who are restricted to arresting small-time druggies and hookers because the big ones are getting protection from the higher-ups in the department. A fairly realistic, sometimes funny, depiction of police life. Gould and Blake are glib and have a good chemistry which makes this a reasonably entertaining buddy-cop movie.

A: Elliott Gould, Robert Blake, Allen Garfield, Antonio Fargas, Michael Lerner, Sid Haig

Distributed By MGM/UA Home Video M801407

CALL OF THE WILD

PG | ACT DMA | 1972 | COLOR

Sex · Nud · Viol · Lang · AdSit

D: Ken Annakin 104 m

7 Jack London's classic story remade. This time it has Charlton Heston in the lead role of an Alaskan gold prospector whose dog is stolen and forced into sad and sadistic service for others. This is good viewing, but there were three other productions of this story. Virtually all of them are better, but none are available on video except for the excellent 1991 variation by Disney called WHITE FANG.

A: Charlton Heston, Michele Mercier, Marla Rohm, Rik Battagila

© GOODTIMES 8385

CARLITO'S WAY

R | CRM ACT DMA | 1993 | COLOR

Sex · Nud · Viol · Lang · AdSit

D: Brian De Palma 145 m

8 Carlito (Pachino) was a big time drug dealer and a hood. He is tough and has stayed alive by doing what he has to do to survive. He was sent up for 30 years but his shyster lawyer (Penn) has gotten him out after only five. Still, that was enough time for Carlito. All he wants now is to go straight, stay out of trouble and he's got a plan to do it, too. He needs $75,000 to buy into a legit car rental business in the Bahamas and take his old flame (Miller) there with him. He is going to raise the money honestly by running a nightclub. The plan is working too. Then he gets a call from his lawyer buddy who is in trouble. Carlito feels honor-bound to help him, even though he risks everything.

A: Al Pacino, Sean Penn, Penelope Ann Miller, Luis Guzman, James Rebhorn, Viggo Mortensen

© MCA/UNIVERSAL HOME VIDEO, INC. 81630

CASUALTIES OF WAR

R | WAR DMA ACT | 1989 | COLOR

Sex · Nud · Viol · Lang · AdSit

D: Brian De Palma 120 m

8 This is a startling film that retells a real-life horror story from the Vietnam War. It occurred in 1966 and was first revealed in a magazine article. The story revolves around one incident when an out-of-control squad of American soldiers kidnaps, rapes and later murders a young Vietnamese girl after they are through with her. Fox is a new raw recruit, an innocent private, who watches as his crazed sergeant goes over the edge and leads his troops on this rampage. Fox is the only soldier who object. He tries to help the girl escape and later reports the incident, but he stands alone against his squad.

A: Michael J. Fox, Sean Penn, Thuy Thu Le, Don Harvey, John Leguizamo

© COLUMBIA TRISTAR HOME VIDEO 50183

CHARLEY VARRICK

D: Don Siegel 111 m

PG · SUS ACT · 1973 · COLOR

8 Very good and intelligent thriller. Walter Matthau plays a crop duster and small-time bank robber who only robs little back-country banks for little payrolls. But he gets much more than he bargained for when he and his partner rob a small rural bank of $750,000 that turns out to have been mob money. Now, they're in big trouble. The mob wants their money back and they send a sadistic and ruthless hit man, Joe Don Baker, to get it. Matthau must find a way to outfox both the mob and their hitman before it's too late. Fast-paced, thrilling action with lots of intriguing plot twists.

Sex · Nud · Viol · Lang · AdSit

A: Walter Matthau, Joe Don Baker, Felicia Farr, Andy Robinson, John Vernon, Sheree North

© MCA/UNIVERSAL HOME VIDEO, INC. 55062

CHINA GATE

D: Samuel Fuller 95 m

NR · ACT · 1957 · B&W

7 Prior to the major United States involvement in Indochina (Vietnam), it was a French colony. This film presents a very early view of Vietnam and France's troubles there. It is primarily an action story that concerns a group of Foreign Legion soldiers led by Sergeant Brock (Barry) who must go deep into the jungle to blow up a communist ammunition dump. They are led there by Lucky Legs, a beautiful Eurasian girl (Dickenson), and she and Brock are not strangers. They had a love affair which resulted in a child that Brock refuses to acknowledge.

Sex · Nud · Viol · Lang · AdSit

A: Gene Barry, Angie Dickinson, Nat King Cole, Paul Dubov, Lee Van Cleef, George Givot

© REPUBLIC PICTURES HOME VIDEO 0648

CHINA GIRL

D: Abel Ferrara 90 m

R · ACT ROM · 1987 · COLOR

7 This is a very slick low-budget movie that gives a tired old plot a present-day realness with a strong dose of believability. Set in lower Manhattan, an Italian boy working in a pizza parlor falls in love with a beautiful Chinese girl, but their forbidden romance leads to gang warfare between the neighborhood's Italian and Chinese gangs. This is a war that is carried out with a gritty realism in the back alleyways and dance floors of the neighborhood. A lot of energy and some attractive characters.

Sex · Nud · Viol · Lang · AdSit

A: James Russo, Sari Chang, Richard Panebianco, David Caruso

© LIVE HOME VIDEO 5238

CHINESE CONNECTION, THE

D: Lo Wei 107 m

R · ACT · 1973 · COLOR

7 Famed martial arts master Bruce Lee is at his best in this Kung Fu feast. In turn-of-the-century Shanghai, Bruce Lee searches for the killers of his revered Kung Fu teacher and mentor. His code of honor morally binds him to revenge the killing and he is pitted against some of his most formidable of foes - Japanese fighters who claim they are superior to Chinese fighters. Very violent.

Sex · Nud · Viol · Lang · AdSit

A: Bruce Lee, Miao Ker Hsio, James Tien, Robert Baker

© GOODTIMES 8471

CHISUM

D: Andrew V. McLaglen 111 m

G · WST ACT · 1970 · COLOR

8 This is a quite good Western. The Duke plays John Chisum, a land baron and a real-life character from the famous 1878 New Mexico Lincoln County War. Chisum is struggling against a wealthy land swindler (Forrest Tucker) who is cheating smaller ranchers and farmers out of their land. Excellent meaty characters add grit to the familiar story line: Corbett as Pat Garrett, Deuel as Billy the Kid, George as a bounty hunter and Ben Johnson as Wayne's foreman. Merle Haggard sings.

Sex · Nud · Viol · Lang · AdSit

A: John Wayne, Forrest Tucker, Christopher George, Ben Johnson, Glenn Corbett, Geoffrey Deuel

© WARNER HOME VIDEO 11089

CHOIRBOYS, THE

D: Robert Aldrich 120 m

R · CRM ACT DMA · 1977 · COLOR

6 Written by ex-detective Joseph Wambaugh, this is a story of the flip-side of some of the men in police work. Some L.A. cops meet periodically to let off some steam at frequent "choir practice" sessions, which are really wild booze and sex parties held in MacArthur Park. The story follows the lives of ten different cops. Most viewers will think that the depiction of their "choir practice" escapades are far too heavy-handed and foul. The film had a mixed reception at the box office upon its release, mostly because critics hated it.

Sex · Nud · Viol · Lang · AdSit

A: Charles Durning, Louis Gossett, Jr., Perry King, Clyde Kasatsu, Stephen Macht, Tim McIntire

© MCA/UNIVERSAL HOME VIDEO, INC. 55097

CLEAR AND PRESENT DANGER

D: Phillip Noyce 141 m

PG-13 · SUS ACT · 1994 · COLOR

9 Excellent. Jack Clancy's hero spy, Jack Ryan (Harrison Ford) is back. This time he has been promoted to Deputy Director of Intelligence for the CIA. When one of the President's friends and his family is killed by a Colombian drug dealer, the President authorizes a secret attack with US troops, led by field operative Willem Defoe. The druglord decides to fight back, however, but he is being manipulated and deceived by his own intelligence man, who has secret plans of his own. As Ryan, who knew nothing of the President's illegal war, begins to slowly unravel the pieces, he finds that he is being set up to take the fall. More an intelligent and intricate suspense film than an all-out action film.

Sex · Nud · Viol · Lang · AdSit

A: Harrison Ford, Willem Dafoe, Anne Archer, James Earl Jones, Joaquim De Almeida, Henry Czerny

© PARAMOUNT HOME VIDEO 32463

CLIFFHANGER

D: Renny Harlin 115 m

R · ACT · 1992 · COLOR

7 Action fans will enjoy this stunt-filled festival but the plot line is very slim, so others may not be so impressed. Still, the stunts are pretty terrific and the rugged mountain scenery is stunning. Stallone is a troubled park ranger who, along with his pretty park ranger girlfriend (Janine Turner), has gone on a mountain rescue mission to save the passengers from a wrecked plane. The trouble is that the rescuees are gang of thieves trying to escape with $100 million and they have taken his pretty girlfriend hostage to make sure they get away. Straight-forward film with some spectacular stunts.

Sex · Nud · Viol · Lang · AdSit

A: Sylvester Stallone, John Lithgow, Michael Rooker, Janine Turner, Paul Winfield, Ralph Waite

© COLUMBIA TRISTAR HOME VIDEO 52233

CODE OF SILENCE

D: Andrew Davis 100 m

R · ACT · 1985 · COLOR

8 This likely is Chuck Norris's best action film. When one gang breaks in on a drug deal of another gang to steal the drugs and money and kill everyone, there is big trouble and a vendetta. The family of the offending gang leader is killed, except for his daughter who is kidnapped. And, when a young cop refuses to break the policeman's "code of silence" to defend Chuck against false charges, Chuck is deserted by his fellow cops and left alone to retrieve the innocent girl from the vicious gang who has also vowed to kill him. Good solid action fare that you expect, but not as contrived as many of his others.

Sex · Nud · Viol · Lang · AdSit

A: Chuck Norris, Henry Silva, Bert Remsen, Dennis Farina, Mike Genovese, Ralph Foody

© GOODTIMES 045045

COLORS

D: Dennis Hopper 127 m

R · CRM ACT · 1988 · COLOR

8 Extremely intense police saga. However, the plot is rather tired: a well-seasoned and married cop (Duvall) with one year to go is unwillingly saddled with an over-eager green cop (Penn) who thinks he has all the answers. They are both assigned to a detail specializing in the extremely brutal streetgangs of East Los Angeles. Duvall and Penn play their roles with extreme intensity and the street life is presented with stark realism. That and the fact that many real-life gang members were cast to play themselves make this a very realistic and also very violent movie. Excellent, but definitely not for the squeamish.

Sex · Nud · Viol · Lang · AdSit

A: Sean Penn, Robert Duvall, Maria Conchita Alonso, Randy Brooks, Brand Bush, Don Cheadle

© ORION PICTURES CORPORATION 8711

COMANCHEROS, THE

D: Michael Curtiz 107 m

NR · WST ACT · 1961 · COLOR

8 Solid action Western. Wayne plays a Texas Ranger who has just captured a Mississippi riverboat dandy and gambler (Whitman) on charges of murder, for having killed a man in a duel. But, when Wayne comes up short of manpower, he drafts Whitman to help him chase down a band of outlaws called Comancheros who are supplying the dreaded Commanche Indians with rifles, ammunition and liquor. Typical Wayne, pretty good stuff. This is not his best movie - not his worst. There is plenty of action, some pathos, a little comedy and a great Elmer Bernstein score.

Sex · Nud · Viol · Lang · AdSit

A: John Wayne, Stuart Whitman, Lee Marvin, Ina Balin, Bruce Cabot, Nehemiah Persoff

© FOXVIDEO 1177

COMMANDO

D: Mark L. Lester 90 m

R · ACT COM · 1985 · COLOR

7 Arnold is the ultimate commando who eats Green Berets for breakfast. He is retired from a CIA special commando force but is forced out of retirement when an old enemy kidnaps his daughter in an effort to force him into helping them to dispose of a South American dictator. Arnold, however, has plans of his own and he is a one-man army. Chong is a stewardess who comes along with him for the ride, and what a ride! Plenty of action - guns everywhere, all the time. The intention was to make the movie campy, but most of the humor gets lost in the violence.

Sex · Nud · Viol · Lang · AdSit

A: Arnold Schwarzenegger, Rae Dawn Chong, Dan Hedaya, James Olson, Alyssa Milano, Vernon Wells

© FOXVIDEO 1484

CONAGHER

NR | WST ACT | 1991 | COLOR

D: Reynaldo Villalobos — 117 m

7 Very good made-for-cable Western, adapted from a novel by Louis L'Amour. Katharine Ross, her new husband and his children settle in the Western wilderness to start a cattle ranch. But, he never returns from a buying trip and they are left to survive alone. Elliot is a drifting cowpoke who meets her. They are attracted, but neither can or does do anything about it. He winters with an old rancher whose cattle are being stolen and, while tracking down the thieves, the two meet again. Very realistic and evocative for those times, but could have been improved with some editing. Slow.

Sex / Nud / Viol / Lang / AdSit

A: Sam Elliott, Katharine Ross, Barry Corbin, Billy Green Bush, Ken Curtis, Paul Koslo

© TURNER HOME ENTERTAINMENT 6081

CONAN THE BARBARIAN

R | ACT FAN | 1982 | COLOR

D: John Milius — 128 m

7 Schwarzenegger plays the mythical sword-swinging warrior who is seeking revenge on the snake cult leader (Jones) who massacred his village, including his parents, and then had him enslaved from the time he was just a small a boy. After fifteen years at the Wheel of Pain, grinding grain, he had developed a powerful body. Then he was trained as a gladiator and eventually freed. Now, he and his companions seek revenge and to learn the answer to "the riddle of steel" which his father had told him would give him the power to destroy his enemies. This intriguing movie is full of blood, gore, violence, big biceps and beautiful women. CONAN THE DESTROYER followed but was considerably tamer.

Sex / Nud / Viol / Lang / AdSit

A: Arnold Schwarzenegger, Sandahl Bergman, James Earl Jones, Mako, Ben Davidson, Max von Sydow

© MCA/UNIVERSAL HOME VIDEO, INC. 77010

CONAN THE DESTROYER

PG | ACT FAN | 1984 | COLOR

D: Richard Fleischer — 101 m

6 Far less violent than its predecessor CONAN THE BARBARIAN. Conan is recruited to accompany a beautiful princess (d'Abo) to a castle on a search for a magical gemstone. He and an assortment of accomplices he has picked up along the way, battle and defeat beasts and baddies as they proceed along. Played more for laughs this time. Still plenty of action, but certainly more suitable for the family.

Sex / Nud / Viol / Lang / AdSit

A: Arnold Schwarzenegger, Grace Jones, Wilt Chamberlain, Sarah Douglas, Olivia D'Abo, Mako

© MCA/UNIVERSAL HOME VIDEO, INC. 80079

COOGAN'S BLUFF

R | ACT CRM | 1968 | COLOR

D: Don Siegel — 93 m

8 This was the first break out of the cowboy mold by Clint Eastwood, although he didn't make it quite all the way. The character he creates here is the precursor to Dirty Harry Calahan. Clint plays an Arizona sheriff sent to NYC to bring back an extradited criminal (Don Stroud), but Stroud escapes. Clint becomes frustrated by the big city bureaucracy and employs his own down-home police tactics to get him back, much to the chagrin of the New York cops, and Lee J. Cobb in particular. An effective actioner with lots of action, including a big brawl. It inspired the TV series "McCloud."

Sex / Nud / Viol / Lang / AdSit

A: Clint Eastwood, Lee J. Cobb, Susan Clark, Don Stroud, Tisha Sterling, Betty Field

© MCA/UNIVERSAL HOME VIDEO, INC. 66042

COOL HAND LUKE

PG | DMA ACT | 1967 | COLOR

D: Stuart Rosenberg — 126 m

9 Hugely popular, very entertaining and a fascinating story of a fiercely independent loner (Newman) who wakes up in a Southern jail after a drunken night cutting the heads off parking meters. Newman refuses to give in to authority or the demands of his chain gang guards. He remains defiantly independent which gains him the admiration of his fellow prisoners, particularly their tough leader George Kennedy (who won an Oscar). He becomes their hero. Sometimes funny, sometimes poignant. Strother Martin went down in film history with his famed proclamation, "What we have here is a failure to communicate."

Sex / Nud / Viol / Lang / AdSit

A: Paul Newman, George Kennedy, Jo Van Fleet, J.D. Cannon, Strother Martin, Anthony Zerbe

© WARNER HOME VIDEO 11037

COP

R | CRM ACT | 1988 | COLOR

D: James Harris — 110 m

6 Chilling and visceral. James Woods plays a maverick cop who is barely hanging on to reality. He becomes obsessed with capturing a serial killer who has committed fifteen murders over the last ten years. Woods is so intense that the rest of the force wants no part of him and his wife leaves him. Several plot twists keeps your interest level high, but the logic does get strained at times. Very gritty and seamy. While much of this ground has been covered many times before, Woods's strong performance makes this believable and worth a watch.

Sex / Nud / Viol / Lang / AdSit

A: James Woods, Lesley Ann Warren, Charles Durning, Charles Haid, Randy Brooks

© UNITED AMERICAN VIDEO CORP. 5702

COTTON CLUB, THE

R | DMA ACT MUS | 1984 | COLOR

D: Francis Ford Coppola — 128 m

8 Very large budget movie that was fraught with scandal and controversy during production. It went way over budget and lacked a focus, so director Coppola was called in to "fix" it. Even so, the plot still tends to drift. However, this is also an opulent and evocative film depicting the excitement of the Jazz Age. Set against a background of great music and gangster violence, it is the story of a trumpeter (Gere) who falls in love with the mistress (Lane) of mobster Dutch Schultz; and, a dancer (Hines) who's in love with a black chorus girl, who is trying to pass for white. Even though flawed, this is still quite interesting, entertaining and worth spending time on.

Sex / Nud / Viol / Lang / AdSit

A: Richard Gere, Gregory Hines, Diane Lane, Lonette McKee, Bob Hoskins, Nicolas Cage

© NEW LINE HOME VIDEO 1714

COWBOYS

PG | WST ACT | 1972 | COLOR

D: Mark Rydell — 128 m

8 Good Western. John Wayne is Wil Andersen, a rancher whose hired-help desert him to prospect for gold just when he needs them to help to drive his herd 400 miles to market. Having no alternative, he reluctantly hires eleven local schoolboys to drive his cattle. On the trail, the boys face the normal hazards of nature, but also a wagon full of floozies, an outlaw band and their own fears... the boys become men. Bruce Dern is the menacing leader of the outlaw band and John is a gruff but believable father-figure. An unnecessarily cruel revenge mars the ending to otherwise good film.

Sex / Nud / Viol / Lang / AdSit

A: John Wayne, Roscoe Lee Browne, Bruce Dern, Colleen Dewhurst, Slim Pickens, Lonny Chapman

© WARNER HOME VIDEO 11213

CRIME STORY

NR | CRM ACT | 1985 | COLOR

D: Abel Ferrara — 96 m

8 This is the pilot for the TV series of the same name. It is a very atmospheric cops-and-robbers film depicting 1960s Chicago. There is lots of vintage rock 'n roll, cars with fins and some fascinating tough guys. Police Lt. Mike Torello heads the Major Crime Unit. He has set his sights on nailing a tough up-and-coming hood named Ray Lucca because Lucca killed two of Torello's friends. A very stylish film. Very strong character portrayals make this an excellent film for its genre. Many of the series's episodes are also available.

Sex / Nud / Viol / Lang / AdSit

A: Dennis Farina, Stephen Lang, Anthony Denison, Darlanne Fluegel, John Santucci, Bill Smitrovich

© R&G VIDEO, LP 90027

CROCODILE DUNDEE

PG-13 | COM ROM ACT | 1986 | COLOR

D: Peter Faiman — 98 m

9 Huge, world-wide box office phenomenon. A sexy rich-girl reporter (Kozlowski) goes to the Outback of Australia to interview a strange character, Mick "Crocodile" Dundee (Paul Hogan), when she hears tales of him having crawled for miles after having his leg bitten by a crocodile. Mick is a hero of giant proportions. He drinks. He fights. He wrestles crocs, and he obliges her by taking her with him on excursion out into his world. Then she reciprocates by bringing him into her jungle - Manhattan. Hilarious!! Followed by a pretty good CROCODILE DUNDEE II.

Sex / Nud / Viol / Lang / AdSit

A: Paul Hogan, Linda Kozlowski, John Meillon, David Gulpilil, Mark Blum, Michael Lombard

© PARAMOUNT HOME VIDEO 32029

CROCODILE DUNDEE II

PG | COM ACT | 1988 | COLOR

D: John Cornell — 110 m

7 Pleasant enough follow-up to the original. However, more action is added to the successful formula this time. Mick and Sue are now living in NYC, but things get too exciting for them when her ex-husband takes some pictures of some Columbian drug lords that he wasn't supposed to take and sends them to her for safekeeping. The Columbians want those pictures back and they are very nasty about it. Mick decides to even the odds by leading the bad guys onto his turf - the Outback of Australia. There, he is more than a match for the bad guys. Fun time.

Sex / Nud / Viol / Lang / AdSit

A: Paul Hogan, Linda Kozlowski, John Mellion, Charles Dutton, Hector Ubarry, Juan Fernandez

© PARAMOUNT HOME VIDEO 32147

CROSS OF IRON

R | WAR DMA ACT | 1977 | COLOR

D: Sam Peckinpah — 132 m

8 In the style of the famed German film THE BOAT (DAS BOOT), this is a solid American-made WWII adventure that also tells its story entirely from the German viewpoint. It is also a very realistic and action-packed look at war. Schell plays a German officer who is intent upon winning a hero's medal, while Coburn plays a capable war-weary sergeant who is comptemptuous of both the military and of war. Coburn is just trying to keep his troops from being ground up by the advancing Russian army in 1943. Great action scenes, particularly the tank scenes near the end.

Sex / Nud / Viol / Lang / AdSit

A: James Coburn, Maximilian Schell, James Mason, David Warner, Senta Berger

© MEDIA HOME ENTERTAINMENT, INC. M765

CROW, THE

D: Alex Proyas 117 m

R | ACT | 1994 | COLOR

Sex | Nud | Viol | Lang | AdSit

7 Mystical, dark, gloomy, extremely violent and profane. One year after his death on Halloween eve, a young rock musician arises from his grave to avenge his murder and the rape and murder of his fiancee. Guided and assisted by an ominous crow, he is both invincible and immortal. The city he has returned to is an evil, very bleak and cruel place, and its underlife is controlled by the murderous gang that violated him one year ago. The police have been unable to break the hold of the gangs because of the fear of the people. However, he has no fear because he is already dead. Lots of gratuitous violence and gloom that will appeal mostly to young people.

A: Brandon Lee, Ernie Hudson, Michael Wincott, David Patrick Kelly, Angel David, Rochelle Davis

© MIRAMAX HOME ENTERTAINMENT 3034

CRUSOE

D: Caleb Deschanel 95 m

PG-13 | ACT DMA | 1989 | COLOR

Sex | Nud | Viol | Lang | AdSit

8 The classic Defoe tale is updated into the nineteenth century. Crusoe, who is well played here by Aidan Quinn, is a ruthless Virginia slave trader who has become shipwrecked, washed up alone and naked on a desert island. On this island the merciless hunter must deal with basic survival, loneliness and something else, too. On this island there are cannibals. He, the hunter, has become the hunted... by those same people he would have enslaved and sold. In this production, there is no faithful man Friday but an independent and strong black warrior (Sapara)

A: Aidan Quinn, Ade Sapara, Warren Clark, Hebburn Graham, Jimmy Nail, Timothy Spall

© MCEG/STERLING 70064

CUBA

D: Richard Lester 121 m

R | ACT ROM | 1979 | COLOR

Sex | Nud | Viol | Lang | AdSit

7 Sean Connery plays a security advisor from England who is hired by Cuban dictator Batista to come to Cuba in 1959 to help put down the rebel insurgency. There, he meets his former lover Brooke Adams, who is now married to a shiftless playboy, and their passions reignite. He tries to convince her that Batista will fall and that she should leave Cuba with him. When the regime does fall, it is a mad scramble. This is a handsome film with strong cast and good period detail which was virtually and unduly ignored upon its release. Some say it was an attempt to remake CASABLANCA.

A: Brooke Adams, Sean Connery, Jack Weston, Hector Elizondo, Denholm Elliott, Chris Sarandon

Distributed By MGM/UA Home Video M201507

CULPEPPER CATTLE COMPANY, THE

D: Dick Richards 92 m

PG | WST ACT | 1972 | COLOR

Sex | Nud | Viol | Lang | AdSit

7 Ben Mockridge (Grimes) is an innocent 16-year-old farm boy in post-Civil War America. He yearns above all else to become a cowboy, so he persuades a trail boss to hire him even though he is young. He signs on as a cook's helper on a huge cattle drive where he is exposed to the harsh and unforgiving nature of the open trail and the sorry truth that 'Cowboyin' is somethin' you do when you can't do nothin' else." Very authentic in its details. Will please Western fans, but is pretty violent in places.

A: Gary Grimes, Billy Green Bush, Luke Sakew, Bo Hopkins, Geoffrey Lewis

© FOXVIDEO 1189

DAMN THE DEFIANT!

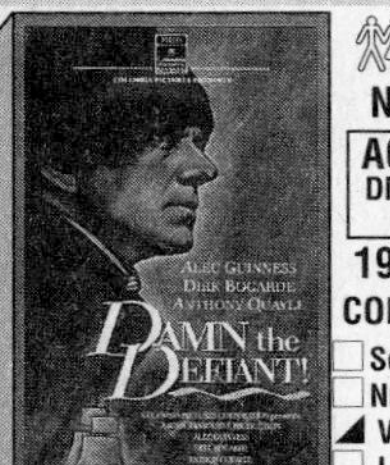

D: Lewis Gilbert 101 m

NR | ACT DMA | 1962 | COLOR

Sex | Nud | Viol | Lang | AdSit

8 Dramatic tale of an eighteenth-century British warship and its crew which is at war with both the French and with itself. Great attention to historic detail and a fine performances from its cast gives this production a first-rate quality. Guinness is the captain of the British warship H.M.S Defiant, but he is opposed by Bogarde, his cruel first officer, whose iron-fisted rule has the crew ready to mutiny. When Guinness is wounded and Bogarde takes command, the crew does mutiny - just as they are about to enter a major battle. Guinness must win them back.

A: Alec Guinness, Dirk Bogarde, Maurice Denham, Anthony Quayle, Peter Gill, Nigel Stock

© COLUMBIA TRISTAR HOME VIDEO 60825

DANCES WITH WOLVES

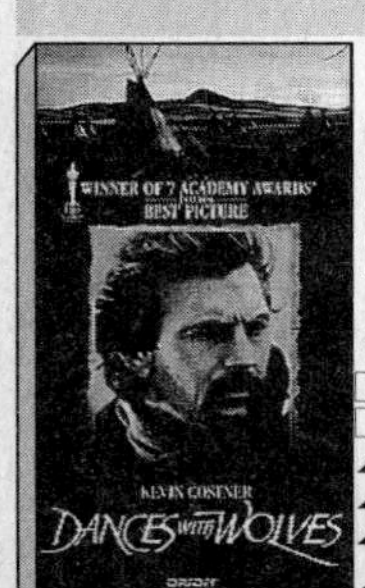

D: Kevin Costner 180 m

PG-13 | WST DMA ACT | 1990 | COLOR

Sex | Nud | Viol | Lang | AdSit

10 Wonderful, beautiful, grand and elegant. First-time director (and also the film's star) Costner scored a major win with this film. It won seven Oscars, including Best Picture and it struck a resilient chord in many viewers. It is the story of a disillusioned Civil War veteran who is stationed to a remote Army outpost in the Dakota territory. Finding it abandoned, he makes friends with a band of Lakota Sioux and is drawn into their extended family, their way of life and finds new meaning for his life. This is an exciting, thoroughly involving and sensitive telling of a time and a way of life long underappreciated. A must see!

A: Kevin Costner, Mary McDonnell, Graham Greene, Rodney A. Grant, Floyd Red Crow Westerman, Tantoo Cardinal

© ORION PICTURES CORPORATION 8768

DAY OF THE JACKAL, THE

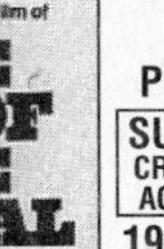

D: Fred Zinnemann 143 m

PG | SUS CRM ACT | 1973 | COLOR

Sex | Nud | Viol | Lang | AdSit

9 Mesmerizing tension. It is based upon the best selling novel of the same name and which, in turn, was based upon a real-life character. A terrorist organization hires the world's best professional hitman to assassinate French President Charles de Gaulle. The killer is a faceless man who is known only as the Jackal. French police learn of the plot, but the Jackal constantly changes disguises to stay just ahead of them. The scenes of the massive police manhunt are juxtaposed with the Jackal's compulsively meticulous preparations and the result is a buildup of an incredible tension. First-rate cast and absolutely compelling viewing.

A: Edward Fox, Alan Badel, Tony Britton, Cyril Cusack, Eric Porter, Michael Lonsdale

© MCA/UNIVERSAL HOME VIDEO, INC. 66040

DAYS OF THUNDER

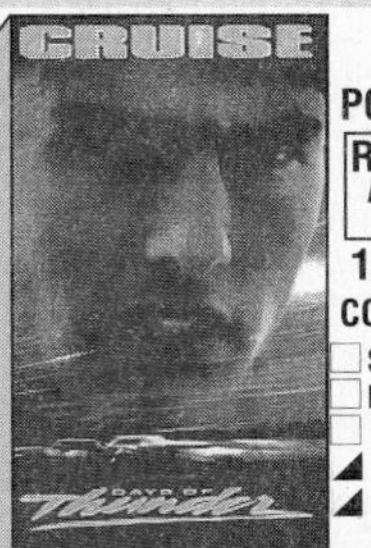

D: Tony Scott 107 m

PG-13 | ROM ACT | 1990 | COLOR

Sex | Nud | Viol | Lang | AdSit

6 This is a formula film but it is action-packed and of course - it has Tom Cruise. Cruise is intent on entering the adrenaline-pumping NASCAR car circuit and joins the racing team of veteran racer Duvall. However, his career is short-lived when he is badly injured in a crash. Lovely doctor Kidman patches him back together but discourages him from re-entering the circuit. Ignoring her fears, Cruise goes back to racing anyway. But now, he must deal with his own fears and the realization that he is mortal. The Kidman/Cruise on-screen romance was continued off-screen when they became husband and wife.

A: Tom Cruise, Robert Duvall, Randy Quaid, Nicole Kidman, Cary Elwes, Michael Rooker

© PARAMOUNT HOME VIDEO 32123

DEAD-BANG

D: John Frankenheimer 102 m

R | ACT CRM | 1989 | COLOR

Sex | Nud | Viol | Lang | AdSit

6 Don Johnson stars in this effective, but still more or less standard, cop flick - even though it is based upon a real character. He is an L.A. cop who has just been kicked out by his wife. He lives in a seedy apartment, drinks too much and the only thing he has left is his work. His investigation into the death of another cop leads him on a cross-country chase of a group of white supremacist killers that results in a major shootout in an underground bunker. Pretty good for what it is. Action fans might even want to add another point.

A: Don Johnson, Penelope Ann Miller, William Forsythe, Bob Balaban, Frank Military, Tate Donovan

© WARNER HOME VIDEO 658

DEAD CALM

D: Phillip Noyce 96 m

R | SUS ACT | 1989 | COLOR

Sex | Nud | Viol | Lang | AdSit

8 Extremely tense and effective thriller in which a married couple (Neil and Kidman), who have just lost a child, decide to spend some time together alone on a yacht 1200 miles off the coast of Australia. There they pick up a stranger (Zane) who is the sole survivor of a sinking ship. When Neil goes alone to check out the abandoned vessel, terror reigns at home. Zane is a psychotic killer who has killed all on board the ship he has just left. Now he commandeers Neil's boat and his wife, leaving Neil behind. She struggles alone in a cat-and-mouse survival game. Very impressive, intelligently made.

A: Sam Neill, Nicole Kidman, Billy Zane

© WARNER HOME VIDEO 11870

DEADLY COMPANIONS, THE

D: Sam Peckinpah 90 m

NR | WST ACT | 1961 | COLOR

Sex | Nud | Viol | Lang | AdSit

6 An ex-army sergeant (Brian Keith) accidentally kills a dancehall hostess's (O'Hara) son. To try to make amends, he escorts her and the body through deadly Apache territory. Along with them on their unhappy journey come two others, a half-crazed Confederate deserter (Wills) and a gun-happy young punk (Cochran). Three men and a beautiful woman become uneasy companions, alone in a hostile land. O'Hara must fight back both the unwanted advances of Cochran and her awakening feelings for the man she should hate (Keith). Most notable because this was Peckinpah's first picture.

A: Maureen O'Hara, Brian Keith, Steve Cochran, Chill Wills

© STARMAKER ENTERTAINMENT INC. 80045

DEADLY HERO

D: Ivan Nagy 102 m

PG | SUS ACT | 1975 | COLOR

Sex | Nud | Viol | Lang | AdSit

7 Engaging thriller. Murray is a cop who rescues a woman (Williams) from a vicious assault, killing her attacker in the process. At first she is grateful, but later she begins to suspect his actions, motives and continued attentions. Terrified, when she goes to his superiors to express her concerns, he begins to fear that he will lose his upcoming pension and decides that he must stop her. Gritty, bad-cop movie.

A: Don Murray, Diahn Williams, James Earl Jones, Lilia Skala, Treat Williams, Danny DeVito

© NEW LINE HOME VIDEO 2042

DEAD POOL, THE

D: Buddy Van Horn 91 m

R
ACT CRM
1988
COLOR
Sex Nud Viol Lang AdSit

7 Dirty Harry Callahan is back for a fifth time. Harry investigates a series of celebrity murders. The one common thread is that all the victims had their names included on a betting pool list, and Harry's name is on the list, too. The story's pretty straightforward. The characters, particularly Harry, are the real interest. There is plenty of action. A particularly interesting bit is a recreation of the famous car chase scene from the action classic BULLITT, except that here the chase involves a radio-controlled Corvette model car loaded with dynamite. Good action fun!

A: Clint Eastwood, Patricia Clarkson, Liam Neeson, David Hunt, Michael Curne, Evan C. Kim

© WARNER HOME VIDEO 11810

DEATH HUNT

D: Peter H. Hunt 97 m

R
ACT WST
1981
COLOR
Sex Nud Viol Lang AdSit

8 Thrilling actioner filmed in northern Canada. Lee Marvin is a tough Mountie nearing retirement who reluctantly agrees to leave Angie Dickinson to hunt down a fiercely independent trapper (Bronson) who has been framed for a murder he did not commit. These two skilled woodsman become engaged in a cat-and-mouse chase through icy wilderness, each pitting their skills against the other, each gaining respect for the other. This film based loosely on a real-life case from the 1930s.

A: Charles Bronson, Lee Marvin, Andrew Stevens, Angie Dickinson, Carl Weathers, Ed Lauter

© FOXVIDEO 1125

DEATH WISH

D: Michael Winner 93 m

R
ACT CRM
1974
COLOR
Sex Nud Viol Lang AdSit

9 This was an extremely popular film about a mild-mannered, liberal New Yorker who becomes radicalized after his wife and daughter are savagely raped and his wife dies. The system cannot or will not help him, so Bronson turns into a revenge-seeking vigilante out to destroy the street punks of New York. These he stalks by baiting traps to spring upon bad guys just when the unsuspecting vultures are about attack someone who they believe will be a victim. The vigilante becomes a hero to the people, but the cops must hunt him down. This hugely popular movie spawned many lessor sequels and imitators.

A: Charles Bronson, Hope Lange, Vincent Gardenia, Jeff Goldblum, Stuart Margolin, Olympia Dukakis

© PARAMOUNT HOME VIDEO 8774

DEEP, THE

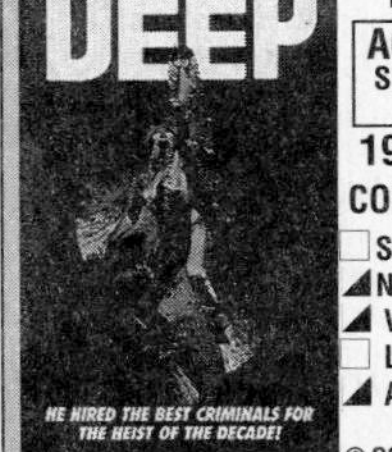

D: Peter Yates 120 m

R
ACT SUS
1977
COLOR
Sex Nud Viol Lang AdSit

6 Americans Nolte and Bisset are skin diving off the coast of Bermuda when they discover a sunken World War II ship containing a fortune in morphine. Lou Gossett is a voodoo wielding drug dealer on the island who has considerable interest in the treasure. His interest puts Nolte and Bisset in considerable danger. The two get help from a bitter recluse Shaw. Wonderful underwater scenery is the primary attraction and Bisset's eye-catching T-shirt adds to the excitement. Plot is so-so.

A: Robert Shaw, Jacqueline Bisset, Nick Nolte, Louis Gossett, Jr., Eli Wallach

© GOODTIMES 74205

DEEP COVER

D: Bill Duke 107 m

R
CRM ACT
1992
COLOR
Sex Nud Viol Lang AdSit

9 Far above average cop movie. Well written, excellently constructed, good action with solid believable acting. Fishburne is a cool-headed loner, but he is also a very motivated young cop who is recruited by the Feds to go undercover. He begins his new life on the street at as a low level hustler but quickly associates himself with a drug dealing, quirky and eccentric lawyer (Goldblum) who is hungry for money and thrills. As partners-in-crime, these two begin an assault on the drug hierarchy and eventually to arrive at the top. But once there, things take a drastic turn when the rules suddenly change for the undercover cop. Excellent.

A: Larry Fishburne, Jeff Goldblum, Victoria Dillard, Charles Martin Smith, Clarence Williams, III, Sidney Lassick

© TURNER HOME ENTERTAINMENT N4084

DEER HUNTER, THE

D: Michael Cimino 183 m

R
DMA WAR ACT
1978
COLOR
Sex Nud Viol Lang AdSit

10 Extraordinarily powerful winner of five Oscars, including Best Picture (nominated for nine). Young friends from a blue collar working class background in 1968 Pennsylvania leave their familiar land of hot blast furnaces and cool forests, from which they hunted deer, to go to Vietnam's steaming jungle to hunt men. This epic (long) movie is essentially shown in three parts: the hometown, the horrors of war and then back home again, now scarred both physically and emotionally. This powerful film packs a big wallop, but is not without controversy. Top-flight cast.

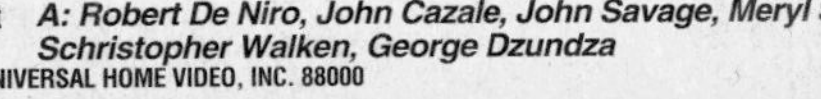

A: Robert De Niro, John Cazale, John Savage, Meryl Streep, Schristopher Walken, George Dzundza

© MCA/UNIVERSAL HOME VIDEO, INC. 88000

DEFIANT ONES, THE

D: Stanley Kramer 97 m

NR
DMA ACT
1958
B&W
Sex Nud Viol Lang AdSit

9 A major ground-breaking movie and great entertainment, too. It was nominated for seven Oscars and won three. Two prisoners who are chained together escape from a chain gang in the deep South. One is black and the other is white. Poitier and Curtis hate each other, but they are forced to work together and depend upon each other if they are first to escape and then to survive. This is a very well made and exciting movie that still packs a big punch today, while never sinking into platitudes and cliches. Powerful performances garnered four of the Oscar nominations.

A: Tony Curtis, Sidney Poitier, Theodore Bikel, Charles McGraw, Lon Chaney, Jr., Cara Williams

Distributed By MGM/UA Home Video M201557

DELIVERANCE

D: John Boorman 109 m

R
SUS DMA ACT
1972
COLOR
Sex Nud Viol Lang AdSit

10 Riveting account of four ordinary businessmen who decide to take a weekend whitewater canoe trip down a wild river before it is dammed up forever. What begins as a man-against-nature excursion becomes an exercise in gripping suspense, terror and survival. Four men become profoundly changed as they are forced to confront their fears alone when they are pursued by two demented hillbillies, intent upon murder and homosexual rape. The movie's theme song "Dueling Banjos" became a major pop hit. Excellent performances. Nominated for Best Picture. Totally involving.

A: Jon Voight, Burt Reynolds, Ned Beatty, Ronny Cox, Bill McKinney, James Dickey

© WARNER HOME VIDEO 1004

DELTA FORCE, THE

D: Menahem Golan 125 m

R
ACT
1986
COLOR
Sex Nud Viol Lang AdSit

7 Palestinian terrorists hijack an American airliner and take it to Beirut. America's crack anti-terrorist team, Delta Force, led by Lee Marvin, is called in to save the passengers and crew, and ex-team member Chuck Norris rejoins his old group to help them do it. Plenty of action to keep your adrenaline pumping. Never mind the abundant implausibilites, this isn't supposed to be a documentary. Very loosely based upon the actual 1985 hijacking, but this time the Yanks, with a lot of help from Hollywood, get to win.

A: Chuck Norris, Lee Marvin, Martin Balsam, Shelley Winters, Joey Bishop, George Kennedy

© VIDEO TREASURES SV9170

DIAMONDS ARE FOREVER

D: Guy Hamilton 121 m

PG
ACT
1971
COLOR
Sex Nud Viol Lang AdSit

7 James Bond's eighth outing (sixth for Connery and his second-to-last) - this time in the American Southwest. Bad guy (Charles Gray) uses the Las Vegas base of operations of a kidnapped millionaire recluse (Jimmy Dean) and a huge diamond-smuggling enterprise to finance his attempt to harness the sun's power. He intends to use a satellite-based light collector and laser beam to control the world. Not the best Bond effort, but pretty good - with plenty of action, gadgets and girls.

A: Sean Connery, Jill St. John, Charles Gray, Lana Wood, Jimmy Dean, Bruce Cabot

Distributed By MGM/UA Home Video M201406

DICK TRACY

D: Warren Beatty 105 m

PG
ACT CRM FAN
1990
COLOR
Sex Nud Viol Lang AdSit

7 Cartoon-like megabuck production that is a parody of the famous long-running comic-strip hero. There is a terrific line-up of major actors, however some are almost unrecognizable under makeup. (Al Pacino is despicable as the main villain who plans to unite all the bad guys. Madonna is marvelously vampy as Breathless Mahoney. Glenne Headly is lovely as Tracy's (Beatty) love interest.) Tracy rises to challenge the bad guys, but has trouble with his personal life. Plenty of shoot-'em-up action, against an unreal cartoon-like backdrop. Pretty good fun, not wonderful.

A: Warren Beatty, Madonna, Al Pacino, Dustin Hoffman, Mandy Patinkin, Paul Sorvino

© TOUCHSTONE HOME VIDEO 1066

DIE HARD

D: John McTiernan 132 m

R
ACT
1988
COLOR
Sex Nud Viol Lang AdSit

9 A rousing action flick that was a megahit in the theaters. Bruce Willis plays a New York cop who stumbles into an attempt by a group of terrorists to make hostages of the employees at a Christmas party in a Los Angeles high-rise building. The terrorists want to crack the computer code which controls a fortune in bonds. Willis is the only one who is in a position to help them escape. This is a powerhouse action yarn with great stunts, special effects and relentless, pounding action - punctuated with Willis's never-ending wisecracks. Dynamite stuff that spawned the sequel DIE HARD 2 and later DIE HARD WITH A VENGENCE.

A: Bruce Willis, Alan Rickman, Bonnie Bedelia, Alexander Godunov, Paul Gleason, William Atherton

© FOXVIDEO 1666

DIE HARD 2

D: Renny Harlin — 124 m

R | ACT | 1990 | COLOR

7 High intensity follow-up to the hugely successful original. Police detective McClane (Willis) is waiting at Washington's Dulles Airport for his wife to arrive on a Christmas Eve flight when the airport is seized by a renegade band of military commandos in a well-organized effort to free a drug lord from the government. The wise-cracking detective is again required to battle not only the bad guys, but incompetent good guys in order to free his wife and save the world. Full of action, some of it not too plausible, but all of it exciting.

Sex / Nud / Viol / Lang / AdSit

A: Bruce Willis, Dennis Franz, John Amos, Bonnie Bedelia, William Atherton, Reginald VelJohnson

© FOXVIDEO 1850

DIGGSTOWN

D: Michael Ritchie — 98 m

R | SUS ACT | 1992 | COLOR

7 James Woods, a sharp talking con-man just out of jail, is on his way to Diggstown, Georgia, where he has set up a crooked fight promoter (Dern) for a major tumble. Woods has primed Dern to fall for a bet that Woods's fighter (Gossett) can knock out any ten men in the county on the same day. What follows is a series of double-crosses and tricks by two major con men, each trying to outmaneuver and trick the other. Even though you're never quite sure who's out-conning whom until the last, this is not up to the standards of the great con movies like THE STING. Still, it is pretty entertaining.

Sex / Nud / Viol / Lang / AdSit

A: James Woods, Bruce Dern, Louis Gossett, Jr., Heather Graham, Randall "Tex" Cob, Thomas Wilson Brown

Distributed By MGM/UA Home Video 902692

DILLINGER

D: John Milius — 106 m

R | CRM ACT | 1973 | COLOR

8 A rip-roaring gangster movie with extremely violent but fascinating gun battles. Warren Oats was perfect for this part as Public Enemy Number One. The plot plays somewhat fast and loose with the facts, but great action sequences make up for that. The story follows Dillinger from midway in his bank-robbing career through until his death outside the Biograph Theater in Chicago at the hands of the G-men led by Melvin Purvis. You may also want to see LADY IN RED.

Sex / Nud / Viol / Lang / AdSit

A: Warren Oates, Ben Johnson, Michelle Phillips, Cloris Leachman, Harry Dean Stanton, Geoffrey Lewis

© ORION PICTURES CORPORATION SV9196

DIRTY DOZEN, THE

D: Robert Aldrich — 150 m

NR | WAR ACT | 1967 | COLOR

9 Major box office hit. Tough Army Major Lee Marvin recruits a bunch of violent convicts to go on a near-suicide commando raid behind German lines. Their reward, if they survive, is to have their records cleared and, if they don't, the opportunity of dying an honorable death. Marvin and his misfit team are to infiltrate a lush German retreat inside France where the German General Staff goes for its R&R. A great cast is well directed in this slick and highly entertaining war adventure which combines action, suspense and humor. Terrific entertainment and exciting, too.

Sex / Nud / Viol / Lang / AdSit

A: Lee Marvin, Ernest Borgnine, Charles Bronson, Jim Brown, John Cassavetes, Donald Sutherland

Distributed By MGM/UA Home Video M700008

DIRTY HARRY

D: Don Siegel — 102 m

R | ACT CRM | 1971 | COLOR

10 Excellent thriller. Clint Eastwood carved his name in American movie fame with this maverick San Francisco detective character, Harry Callahan. The city is desperate when it chooses Harry to be the one to track down a rooftop killer who has now captured a girl, buried her alive and will let her die if they don't pay a ransom. Harry tracks down this psychotic kidnapper/killer only to watch him get free on a legal technicality. Undeterred, Harry pursues the guy relentlessly, breaking all the rules along the way. Brilliant action and suspense. See Dirty Harry in the Heroes, Sequels, Subjects and Authors index for more in the series.

Sex / Nud / Viol / Lang / AdSit

A: Clint Eastwood, Reni Santoni, Harry Guardino, Andy Robinson, John Vernon, John Larch

© WARNER HOME VIDEO 1019

DISAPPEARANCE, THE

D: Stuart Cooper — 80 m

R | ACT SUS | 1977 | COLOR

7 Gripping intrigue draws you in early and holds you throughout. Donald Sutherland is a coolly competent professional hit man, but he is becoming morose and dissatisfied with his life. He loses himself to and becomes totally captivated with his wife, the only one he ever cared about or who has ever really cared about him. So one day when she disappears, he loses any ability to concentrate on his work. Oddly though, the next job offer he receives is to kill Plummer, his wife's lover and the man he believes to be responsible for her disappearance. Compelling performance by Sutherland.

Sex / Nud / Viol / Lang / AdSit

A: Donald Sutherland, Francine Racette, David Hemmings, John Hurt, Christopher Plummer, Virginia McKenna

© RHINO HOME VIDEO/RECORDS 2147

DIVA

D: Jean-Jacques Beineix — 119 m

R | FOR SUS ACT | 1981 | COLOR

8 Interesting French film which has become a cult favorite because it is so stylishly photographed. It also has a pretty good story. There are two separate plots interwoven. A mail messenger has a strong attraction to a black American opera singer (Fernandez). She has never allowed her voice to be recorded, so he secretly tapes a performance. He is seen. The next day a strange woman secretly drops another unrelated tape into his pocket, which incriminates a top cop, just before she dies. Soon the messenger is being chased all over Paris by two separate groups, both of whom are after his tapes. Some fans might even rate it higher. Subtitles.

Sex / Nud / Viol / Lang / AdSit

A: Frederic Andrei, Wilhemina Wiggins, Richard Bohringer, Thuy An Luu, Jacques Fabbri, Chantal Deruaz

Distributed By MGM/UA Home Video M800183

DOBERMAN GANG, THE

D: Byron Ross Chudnow — 85 m

G | ACT CRM | 1972 | COLOR

7 A con man who doesn't trust human partners, kidnaps six vicious Doberman Pinschers and a dog trainer, and then uses them to rob a particularly difficult bank. Six vicious-looking dogs rush into a bank with studded collars and saddlebags. One dog delivers a note to the tellers and the others stand guard. The real thieves are outside, but no one knows who they are. Ingenious low-budget flick that really works quite well. The dogs steal the show. Good family fare. Led to two sequels.

Sex / Nud / Viol / Lang / AdSit

A: Byron Mabe, Hal Reed, Julie Parrish, Simmy Bow, Jojo D'Amore, Juhn Tull

© CBS/FOX VIDEO 7793

DOLLARS ($)

D: Richard Brooks — 119 m

R | SUS ACT COM | 1972 | COLOR

9 Top notch heist film. Beatty is an American security technician who masterminds a plot to steal the ill-gotten gains from the security deposit boxes of crooks at a German bank. He enlists the aid of a dippy hooker (Hawn) to obtain copies of the keys that he needs for the three critical boxes. However, the film doesn't end after the robbery is over - because the owners of boxes, not nice guys at all, want everything back, and an elaborate chase across a frozen lake begins. Unexpected twists abound. Really good stuff.

Sex / Nud / Viol / Lang / AdSit

A: Warren Beatty, Goldie Hawn, Gert Frobe, Robert Webber, Scott Brady

© COLUMBIA TRISTAR HOME VIDEO 60450

DRAGON: THE BRUCE LEE STORY

D: Rob Cohen — 120 m

PG-13 | ACT DMA | 1993 | COLOR

8 High energy, action packed biography of one of the silver screen's action legends. Bruce Lee was a Chinese-American raised in Hong Kong, but who returned to the United States. Here he had to struggle against hostilities from both whites and Chinese to get a college education and to keep his Kung Fu school open. While the film does document Lee's inner turmoil, his love for his white wife and his rise in films, it focuses primarily upon the bigotry against which he rebelled and constantly fought (quite literally) against. He died at 32, before his biggest film ENTER THE DRAGON was released. Quite interesting and very involving.

Sex / Nud / Viol / Lang / AdSit

A: Jason Scott Lee, Lauren Holly, Michael Learned, Nancy Kwan, Robert Wagner

© MCA/UNIVERSAL HOME VIDEO, INC. 81480

DRAGONSLAYER

D: Matthew Robbins — 110 m

PG | ACT FAN | 1981 | COLOR

6 Enjoyable fantasy adventure. A horrible fire-breathing dragon is terrorizing the British countryside and an aging sorcerer is the only one who can stop it, but he is killed. So the job falls to his apprentice, who quickly finds himself in over his head, but only after he has already agreed to slay the dragon to save both a damsel in distress and the kingdom. Rich in special effects and period flavor. Set in 6th-century England and filmed on location in England, Scotland and Wales. Pretty scary and gruesome for real young ones and a little too corny for oldsters, but just right for those in between.

Sex / Nud / Viol / Lang / AdSit

A: Peter MacNicol, Caitlin Clarke, Ralph Richardson, John Hallam, Peter Eyre, Albert Salmi

© PARAMOUNT HOME VIDEO 1367

DRIVER, THE

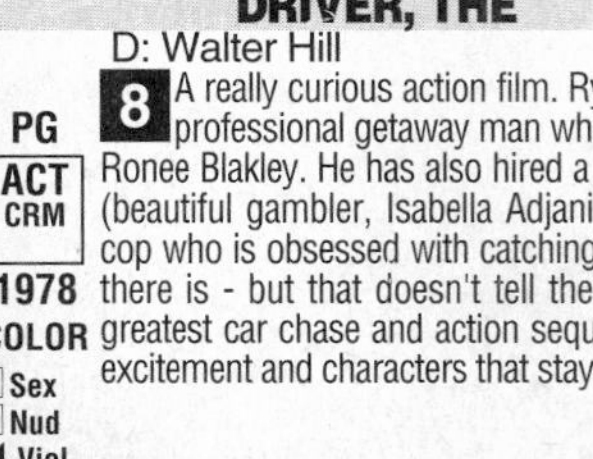

D: Walter Hill — 131 m

PG | ACT CRM | 1978 | COLOR

8 A really curious action film. Ryan O'Neal is a master driver and a professional getaway man who gets his jobs through middleman Ronee Blakley. He has also hired a woman to be his professional alibi (beautiful gambler, Isabella Adjani). Bruce Dern is an unscrupulous cop who is obsessed with catching him. That is just about all the plot there is - but that doesn't tell the story. This film has some of the greatest car chase and action sequences ever put on film. It is full of excitement and characters that stay with you after the film is over.

Sex / Nud / Viol / Lang / AdSit

A: Ryan O'Neal, Bruce Dern, Isabelle Adjani, Ronee Blakley, Matt Clark

© FOXVIDEO 1423

DR. NO

D: Terence Young — 112 m

PG | 9 | ACT | 1963 | COLOR

A James Bond winner. This is the film that launched the Bond juggernaut and made Sean Connery a superstar. It is less gimmicky than later ones, but the Bond elements are all there: nonstop action, witty dialogue, sexy women and humor. British Special Agent 007 is sent to Jamaica to investigate another agent's death. He is soon on his way to the mysterious island retreat of the evil Dr. No. where, with the help of CIA Agent Lord and beautiful Andress, he uncovers a sinister plot by Dr. No to take over the world. But, James defeats it just in the nick of time. Great fun!

Sex · Nud · Viol · Lang · AdSit

A: Sean Connery, Ursula Andress, Joseph Wiseman, Jack Lord, Bernard Lee, Lois Maxwell

Distributed By MGM/UA Home Video M201401

DROWNING POOL, THE

D: Stuart Rosenberg — 109 m

PG | 8 | MYS CRM ACT | 1975 | COLOR

Pretty good follow-up to a far-superior HARPER. Newman is back as the cynical private eye Lou Harper. This time he is hired by his former lover (Woodward) to find out who's blackmailing her. This is a seemingly simple case, but the further into it he gets, the more trouble he gets into. Newman's search takes him through some colorful Louisiana settings, gets him involved with all sorts of unsavory types, has him pursued by Woodward's sexy daughter (Melanie Griffith) and he winds up quite literally in water over his head. Slick and intelligent.

Sex · Nud · Viol · Lang · AdSit

A: Paul Newman, Joanne Woodward, Anthony Franciosa, Murray Hamilton, Gail Strickland, Melanie Griffith

© WARNER HOME VIDEO 11371

DUEL

D: Steven Spielberg — 91 m

NR | 8 | SUS ACT | 1971 | COLOR

Startling, effective thriller that was initially made for TV but was later released in theaters, too. This is also the film that made Steven Spielberg's reputation and gave him his big start in this film describing mindless terror. A salesman in a rented car, taking a leisurely drive down a remote stretch of road, finds himself relentlessly pursued by a maniacal driver at the wheel of a ten-ton tanker truck. He can't see this guy's face and he doesn't understand why, but one thing is for certain... this guy wants to kill him.. Superb suspense film with excellent pacing.

Sex · Nud · Viol · Lang · AdSit

A: Dennis Weaver, Tim Herbert, Charles Peel, Eddie Firestone, Gene Dynarksi, Alexander Lockwood

© MCA/UNIVERSAL HOME VIDEO, INC. 55096

DUEL AT DIABLO

D: Ralph Nelson — 130 m

NR | 8 | WST ACT | 1966 | COLOR

Garner is an embittered Army scout who is seeking revenge for his wife's murder while he is also guiding an Army ammunition train through hostile Indian territory. Also accompanying the train are Poitier, as an ex-sergeant who was forced to go along to break some horses that he wants to sell to the Army; and, an extremely bitter merchant (Weaver) and his wife (Anderson), who he despises because she was just recaptured from having lived with the Apaches and now has a half-breed son. This is an involving, solid, old-fashioned Western of the old school, with lots of action.

Sex · Nud · Viol · Lang · AdSit

A: James Garner, Sidney Poitier, Bibi Andersson, Dennis Weaver, Bill Travers, William Redfield

Distributed By MGM/UA Home Video M202957

DUELLISTS, THE

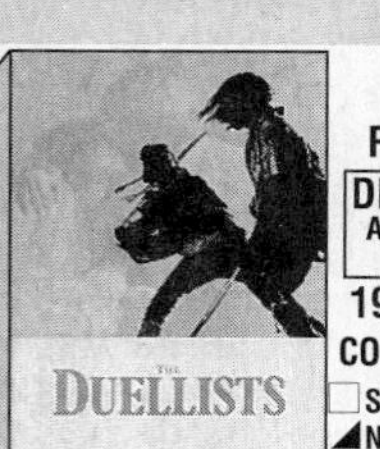

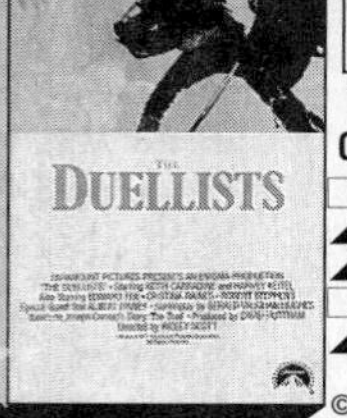

D: Ridley Scott — 101 m

PG | 8 | DMA ACT | 1978 | COLOR

Fascinating but unusual film dealing with obsession and honor. It is set between 1800 and 1815, in Napoleonic France. Calvary officer Carradine is sent by his superiors to confront Keitel over a duel he had had with someone else. Incensed at this affront to his dignity, the brutish Keitel challenges Carradine to a sword duel. Losing his challenge but surviving the duel, Keitel is now consumed by revenge and forces numerous other duels upon Carradine over succeeding years. The duels become more important to them both than all else in their lives.

Sex · Nud · Viol · Lang · AdSit

A: Keith Carradine, Harvey Keitel, Albert Finney, John McEnery

© PARAMOUNT HOME VIDEO 8975

EAGLE HAS LANDED, THE

D: John Sturges — 131 m

PG | 8 | ACT WAR | 1977 | COLOR

Fast moving and well-crafted high-adventure yarn set during World War II. Caine and Sutherland play 2 of 19 Nazi agents who are disguised as Polish soldiers and parachuted into England with the intent of kidnapping Winston Churchill and taking him back to Hitler. Their plans go awry when they are discovered early and must make a desperate attempt to complete the objective anyway. This is especially interesting because it is told from the German viewpoint. The agents aren't terrible, repulsive bad guys, just soldiers. Lots of twists, plenty of action and a surprise ending. Great acting.

Sex · Nud · Viol · Lang · AdSit

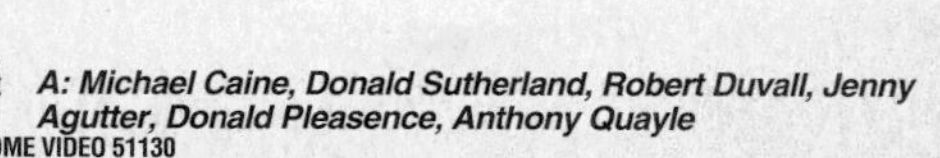

A: Michael Caine, Donald Sutherland, Robert Duvall, Jenny Agutter, Donald Pleasence, Anthony Quayle

© LIVE HOME VIDEO 51130

EARTHQUAKE

D: Mark Robson — 123 m

PG | 6 | ACT SUS | 1974 | COLOR

This was a monumental disaster film, one of the biggest ever done, in which California is destroyed by "the big one" - buildings collapse, streets buckle and chaos abounds. Theater audiences were also bombarded with "Sensurround" shock waves in addition to the terrific special effects upon the screen. It is packed with action, most of which will translate to the small screen, but the story line is minimal. As is typical in this genre, there are actually several stories running at the same time concerning the different effects of the quake on different people. Huge all-star cast.

Sex · Nud · Viol · Lang · AdSit

A: Charlton Heston, Ava Gardner, Lorne Greene, George Kennedy, Victoria Principal, Walter Matthau

© MCA/UNIVERSAL HOME VIDEO, INC. 55034

EDDIE MACON'S RUN

D: Jeff Kanew — 95 m

PG | 6 | ACT | 1983 | COLOR

OK car chase movie in which Schneider is wrongly convicted on trumped-up charges and sentenced to life. He has to get back with his wife and baby, so he escapes from jail and then runs across Texas toward Old Mexico. Kirk Douglas plays an aging cop who relentlessly pursues him. Douglas has his own agenda - he has to catch Sneider so he can prove that he is still valuable. Overall, it's pretty predictable but it does have a good assortment of stunts.

Sex · Nud · Viol · Lang · AdSit

A: Kirk Douglas, John Schneider, Lee Purcell, Leah Ayres, Lisa Dunsheath

© MCA/UNIVERSAL HOME VIDEO, INC. 77016

EIGER SANCTION, THE

D: Clint Eastwood — 130 m

R | 8 | ACT SUS | 1975 | COLOR

Clint Eastwood is a retired professional assassin who has taken up a much quieter occupation as an art collector, but he is called out of retirement to hunt down a double agent for the Agency. It is to be a sanctioned hit. His target will be one member of a group of mountain climbers that is seeking to climb the Alps, but he doesn't yet know which man it is. Some of the plot elements take a lot to swallow whole, but the action sequences of climbing the mountain make the movie worth while. Eastwood reportedly did his own climbing.

Sex · Nud · Viol · Lang · AdSit

A: Clint Eastwood, George Kennedy, Vonetta McGee, Jack Cassidy, Thayer David

© MCA/UNIVERSAL HOME VIDEO, INC. 66043

EL CID

D: Anthony Mann — 172 m

NR | 8 | ACT ROM DMA | 1961 | COLOR

Huge spectacle film containing some of the best old-world battle sequences ever filmed. There are miles of men in chain mail, knights on horseback and corpses everywhere. The action and spectacle are the real stars. It is the story of the eleventh-century Spanish warrior/hero El Cid (Heston), who battled Moorish invaders from the south, and the great love of his life (Loren). Magnificent settings and costumes. Much of the love story is overshadowed by the battles. Some of the splendor will be lost on the small screen.

Sex · Nud · Viol · Lang · AdSit

A: Charlton Heston, Sophia Loren, Raf Vallone, Hurd Hatfield, Genevieve Page

© BEST FILM & VIDEO CORP. 215

EL DORADO

D: Howard Hawks — 126 m

NR | 9 | WST ACT COM | 1967 | COLOR

Western fans line up. This is a big raucous John Wayne Western. Hawks revamped his big 1959 hit RIO BRAVO and this time has John Wayne being an aging gunfighter who helps his drunken friend, the sheriff (Mitchum), stop a range war. Great characters: Caan as a likable but odd-ball character who can't shoot; Arthur Hunnicut as a gnarled old Indian fighter and deputy; and Christopher George as a gunfighter on the other side but who has a sense of honor. Plenty of action and lots of humor, too. It was so successful it this time that it was redone one more time in 1970 as RIO LOBO.

Sex · Nud · Viol · Lang · AdSit

A: John Wayne, Robert Mitchum, James Caan, Arthur Hunnicutt, Edward Asner, Michelle Carey

© PARAMOUNT HOME VIDEO 6625

ELECTRA GLIDE IN BLUE

D: James William Guercio — 114 m

PG | 7 | CRM ACT DMA | 1973 | COLOR

Very violent crime melodrama about one cop's disillusionment. Blake is a smart, but undersized and over-macho, Arizona motorcycle cop who wants to become a detective in the worst way. He gets his chance when he finds an apparent suicide in a shack, exposes it as a murder and gets his promotion. However, his attitude gets him in trouble and he's soon busted back. Then he runs a foul of a group of hippies, who, ironically, are in many ways like him. Very fast and violent. Full of twists and turns. Blake is excellent, but the film has been criticized as being too arty (sort of MTV-like). Terrific motorcycle chase sequence.

Sex · Nud · Viol · Lang · AdSit

A: Robert Blake, Billy Green Bush, Mitchell Ryan, Jeannine Riley, Elisha Cook, Jr.

Distributed By MGM/UA Home Video M300871

EL MARIACHI

D: Robert Rodriguez 80 m

R | FOR ACT COM | 1992 | COLOR

Sex Nud Viol Lang AdSit

7 Most famous for being a film shot for only $7000 in 14 days and still being purchased for national release by a major studio (which then also gave its 24-year-old producer/director/co-writer/star a contract). The film is a quite choppy (what do you expect) spoof of spaghetti Westerns, even though it is set in modern times. It tells the unlikely story of an innocent guitar player dressed in black who wanders into a small Mexican town just after a hit man, who is also dressed in black and carries a guitar case full of weapons, has shot up the town. The poor hero is forced to defend himself over and over again. Subtitles.

A: Carlos Gallardo, Consuelo Gomez, Peter Marquardt, Jamie de Hoyos, Reinol Martinez

© COLUMBIA TRISTAR HOME VIDEO 53613

EMERALD FOREST, THE

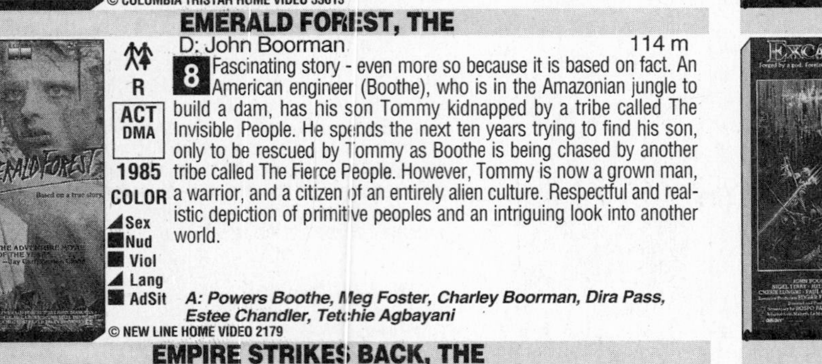

D: John Boorman 114 m

R | ACT DMA | 1985 | COLOR

Sex Nud Viol Lang AdSit

8 Fascinating story - even more so because it is based on fact. An American engineer (Boothe), who is in the Amazonian jungle to build a dam, has his son Tommy kidnapped by a tribe called The Invisible People. He spends the next ten years trying to find his son, only to be rescued by Tommy as Boothe is being chased by another tribe called The Fierce People. However, Tommy is now a grown man, a warrior, and a citizen of an entirely alien culture. Respectful and realistic depiction of primitive peoples and an intriguing look into another world.

A: Powers Boothe, Meg Foster, Charley Boorman, Dira Pass, Estee Chandler, Tetchie Agbayani

© NEW LINE HOME VIDEO 2179

EMPIRE STRIKES BACK, THE

D: Irvin Kershner 128 m

PG | SF ACT SUS | 1980 | COLOR

Sex Nud Viol Lang AdSit

10 A real winner! High intensity middle picture in the Star Wars trilogy. First came STAR WARS and after comes RETURN OF THE JEDI, but here, Luke Skywalker travels to the Jedi master Yoda to learn to the mystical and powerful ways of "The Source," Han Solo and Princess Leia get into deep trouble and develop "a thing" together, Billy Dee Williams joins the battle against the Empire, and Luke finds that Darth Vader not only wants to destroy the rebels, but wants Luke to join him in the "dark side" of the force. Excitement plus. WOW special effects.

A: Billy Dee Williams, Harrison Ford, Carrie Fisher, Mark Hamill, Anthony Daniels, Dave Prowse

© FOXVIDEO 1425

ENEMY BELOW, THE

D: Dick Powell 98 m

NR | WAR SUS ACT | 1957 | COLOR

Sex Nud Viol Lang AdSit

9 Gripping and extremely tense cat-and-mouse game between a German U-boat commanded by Curt Jurgens and an American destroyer escort captained by Robert Mitchum. The North Atlantic is the setting for this spellbinding study of bravery and tenacity, as two seasoned warriors engage in a chess game - a battle of experiences to see who will be the victor when hunter pursues hunter. Excellent photography. The special effects won an Oscar. An accurate portrayal of military tactics. Neither side is vilified nor is it glorified. This is highly watchable.

A: Robert Mitchum, Curt Jurgens, Theodore Bikel, Doug McClure, Russell Collins, David Hedison

© FOXVIDEO 1133

ENFORCER, THE

D: James Fargo 97 m

R | ACT SUS CRM | 1976 | COLOR

Sex Nud Viol Lang AdSit

9 Top-notch follow-up to MAGNUM FORCE in the DIRTY HARRY series. Harry gets in trouble again when he stops a holdup at a liquor store in his own way, but he doesn't stay in the doghouse long. He is needed. He is reluctantly teamed with a female cop (Tyne Daly) to track down a group of terrorists who have robbed a munitions warehouse and launched a terror spree, including kidnapping San Francisco's mayor. Daly seeks not only help to solve the case and take down the bad guys, but to gain Harry's approval. Solid action, good humor and a good plot make this a lot of fun - but very violent.

A: Clint Eastwood, Harry Guardino, Tyne Daly, Bradford Dillman, John Mitchum

© WARNER HOME VIDEO 11082

ENTER THE DRAGON

D: Robert Clouse 99 m

R | ACT | 1973 | COLOR

Sex Nud Viol Lang AdSit

9 mBruce Lee leapt upon the American scene with this big-budget Kung Fu action picture. In it, he and ex-Army buddies Saxon and Kelly join forces to infiltrate the secret society of an island fortress owned by a druglord to avenge his sister's death. There is only a minimal story line, but plenty of kung fu, karate, judo, tai kwan do, tai chi chuan and hapkido action - all choreographed by Lee. Enjoyable because it doesn't take itself too seriously. Lee died abruptly only two years later.

A: Bruce Lee, John Saxon, Jim Kelly, Ahna Capri, Shih Kien, Yang Tse

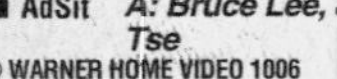

© WARNER HOME VIDEO 1006

EVERY WHICH WAY BUT LOOSE

D: James Fargo 114 m

PG | COM ACT | 1978 | COLOR

Sex Nud Viol Lang AdSit

8 Very popular and a big box office hit with wide public appeal. Eastwood plays a brawling boozy truck driver who chases a barroom country singer across the whole Southwest, while getting into fights with a motorcycle gang and a legendary barroom brawler named Tank Murdock. Far and away, the most appealing feature of the film is Eastwood's raunchy 165-pound Orangutan side-kick Clyde. A light-hearted good time. Great country-western songs, too. A lot of fun, but don't be expecting subtlety. This is all out low-brow stuff.

A: Clint Eastwood, Sondra Locke, Geoffrey Lewis, Beverly D'Angelo, Ruth Gordon

© WARNER HOME VIDEO 1028

EXCALIBUR

D: John Boorman 141 m

R | ACT FAN | 1981 | COLOR

Sex Nud Viol Lang AdSit

9 This is a gritty and extremely realistic telling of the classic Arthurian legend of the pursuit of truth, honor and pureness in mythical old England. So well done, it is as though you can smell and feel the time and the place. It is a magnificent production, filmed in beautiful Irish locations. It presents the entire 1500-year-old tale from the placing of the sword in the stone, the rise of King Arthur, the uniting of the land and the formation of the Round Table, to the forbidden love affair between Guinevere and Sir Lancelot, the fall of Camelot and the quest of the knights for the Holy Grail to restore it. Spellbinding storytelling with flashing swords, magic and forlorn love.

A: Nicol Williamson, Nigel Terry, Helen Mirren, Nicholas Clay, Cherie Lunghi, Corin Redgrave

© WARNER HOME VIDEO 22018

EXODUS

D: Otto Preminger 213 m

NR | DMA ACT | 1960 | COLOR

Sex Nud Viol Lang AdSit

7 Major box office hit which tells the story of the birth of the Jewish state, beginning with the resettlement of Palestine after World War II. The primary story line follows Paul Newman as a major political and military leader who guides European refugees after the war into British controlled Palestine. He later leads fighters in the resistance movement to win independence from Britain and separation from the Arabs, to form a separate Jewish state. The lives of several other characters are followed, including Sal Mineo as a young Auschwitz survivor who joins a terrorist group.

A: Paul Newman, Eva Marie Saint, Lee J. Cobb, Sal Mineo, Ralph Richardson

Distributed By MGM/UA Home Video M301455

EXPERIMENT IN TERROR

D: Blake Edwards 123 m

NR | SUS CRM ACT | 1962 | B&W

Sex Nud Viol Lang AdSit

8 Excellent, high-tension gripper about a sadistic psycho killer (Martin) who kidnaps a bank teller's (Remick) teenage sister (Powers). If she doesn't deliver $100,000 to him, her sister will be killed. Desperate, she contacts the FBI and an extensive surveillance is set up, but it doesn't work. The only way to draw him out is to use Remick as bait. Glenn Ford is the FBI agent who fights against the clock to save the girl and prevent tragedy. Suspense builds slowly and steadily throughout the entire picture. Excellent acting. Martin is particularly menacing.

A: Glenn Ford, Lee Remick, Stefanie Powers, Ross Martin, Ned Glass

© GOODTIMES 4443

EXTREME PREJUDICE

D: Walter Hill 104 m

R | ACT CRM | 1987 | COLOR

Sex Nud Viol Lang AdSit

7 Texas Ranger Nolte struggles each day to stop the drug traffic at the border, while his boyhood friend (Boothe) prospers as a major drug lord just across the border. The only thing they have left in common is Nolte's wife (Alonso), who was Booth's former lover. Now Booth's extravagant lifestyle is enticing her back to him. Into town comes a group of undercover agents whose mission it is to steal millions of drug dollars that Booth has stashed at the bank and also to take Boothe out with "extreme prejudice." Extremely violent.

A: Nick Nolte, Powers Boothe, Maria Conchita Alonso, Michael Ironside, Rip Torn, Clancy Brown

© LIVE HOME VIDEO 62178

EYE OF THE NEEDLE

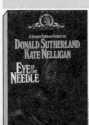

D: Richard Marquand 112 m

R | SUS ACT DMA | 1981 | COLOR

Sex Nud Viol Lang AdSit

8 Very taut espionage thriller. Sutherland plays a ruthless Nazi agent known as The Needle because of his penchant for killing with a switchblade knife. Operating in England, he learns of the plans for D-Day and makes a mad dash for the coast where he is to meet a U-boat. But a storm throws him up on the rocks of a desolate Scottish island inhabited only by a lonely and sexually frustrated woman, her crippled husband and young son. She allows Sutherland to seduce her and to win her trust - then she discovers what he is. She must stop him. High-tension. Very Good.

A: Donald Sutherland, Ian Bannen, Kate Nelligan, Christopher Cazenove, Philip Martin Brown

Distributed By MGM/UA Home Video M301303

FALLING DOWN

D: Joel Schumacher — 113 m

R | ACT DMA | 1993 | COLOR | Sex | Nud | Viol | Lang | AdSit

8 A striking portrait of a man who thought that he played by the rules but he never won the game, and now he has lost control. Michael Douglas plays D-FENS (a character known only by his personal license plate). D-FENS is an ordinary guy except that: he has lost his job, his wife, his child, his home - and his mind has cracked. Stuck in stalled freeway traffic, D-FENS abandons his car to begin a cross-city walk in a single-minded attempt to get "home." But, at each injustice or slight he encounters along the way, he lashes out, sometimes with vicious vengeance. Robert Duvall is a cop on his last day, who tracks D-FENS home.

A: Michael Douglas, Robert Duvall, Barbara Hershey, Rachel Ticotin, Frederic Forrest, Tuesday Weld

© WARNER HOME VIDEO 12648

FALL OF THE ROMAN EMPIRE, THE

D: Anthony Mann — 182 m

NR | DMA ACT | 1964 | COLOR | Sex | Nud | Viol | Lang | AdSit

8 Epic production with thrilling and spectacular action scenes, combined with intelligent scripting, depict the moral and political decay inside Imperial Rome. Emperor Commodus's actions bring about the fall of Rome, in spite of efforts by reformers to change it. Strong cast of beautiful people, beautiful sets and major budget, combined with intelligence, spectacle and action, create fascinating watching.

A: Sophia Loren, Stephen Boyd, James Mason, Alec Guinness, Christopher Plummer, Anthony Quayle

© BEST FILM & VIDEO CORP. 214

FANTASTIC VOYAGE

D: Richard Fleischer — 100 m

NR | SF ACT | 1966 | COLOR | Sex | Nud | Viol | Lang | AdSit

7 Set sometime in the near future, a scientist from a communist country defects to the West with a miniaturization process that will change the world - but he is nearly killed in an assassination attempt. A team of scientists and their submarine-like craft are shrunk to microscopic size and injected into the bloodstream of a his body in an attempt to save his life. They must get in and out within 60 minutes, but there is a saboteur on board and the ship is also being attacked by the body's natural defenses. Pretty good stuff, even today. Special Effects Oscar.

A: Stephen Boyd, Raquel Welch, Edmond O'Brien, Donald Pleasence, Arthur O'Connell, William Redfield

© FOXVIDEO 1002

FAR OFF PLACE, A

D: Mikael Solomon — 107 m

PG | ACT | 1993 | COLOR | Sex | Nud | Viol | Lang | AdSit

7 This is not at all a typical Walt Disney kid's adventure movie. It is more a video for teenagers (probably not for kids under 10 at all), because of graphic scenes of killing. It is the story of a 14-year-old girl named Nonnie, Xhabbo (a young bushman and her best friend) and Harry, a teenager from New York. Nonnie and her parents lived on the edge of Africa's Kalahari Desert and were fighting a battle against poachers who had been killing elephants for their ivory. However, now the poachers have killed Nonnie's parents and the three teenagers are forced to flee across 700 miles of open desert, with the poachers hot on their trial. Quite good.

A: Reese Witherspoon, Ethan Randall, Jack Thompson, Sarel Bok, Maximilian Schell, Robert Burke

© WALT DISNEY HOME VIDEO 1795

FATAL ATTRACTION

D: Adrian Lyne — 120 m

R | SUS ACT | 1987 | COLOR | Sex | Nud | Viol | Lang | AdSit

9 Terrific adult nail-biter. Douglas plays a happily married man who allows himself to be seduced one weekend when his wife is out of town. It was a fun weekend and it's over, right? Wrong! She is psychotically obsessed with him and she will not leave him alone. She calls him and his family constantly... and worse. This film holds your attention all the way from its super-sexy beginning to its nerve-jolting conclusion. Excellent cast, very exciting movie and major box office hit. Also check out similar PLAY MISTY FOR ME with Clint Eastwood.

A: Michael Douglas, Glenn Close, Anne Archer, Ellen Hamilton Latzen, Stuart Pankin

© PARAMOUNT HOME VIDEO 1762

FAT CITY

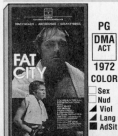

D: John Huston — 93 m

PG | DMA ACT | 1972 | COLOR | Sex | Nud | Viol | Lang | AdSit

8 Gritty realistic look at the hopeful, desperate and sleazy people of the fight game, and the least-savory aspects of a popular sport. It is probably one of the best films made about boxing, but it is also a portrayal of the lonesome life that goes with it. Very rich in atmosphere and characters. Stacy Keach plays a boozing has-been who goes back to the ring rather than to work at menial labor. Bridges is a hopeful young fighter, just beginning. Neither will give up his dreams. Excellent acting. Nomination for Best Supporting Actress.

A: Stacy Keach, Jeff Bridges, Susan Tyrrell, Nicholas Colasanto, Candy Clark

© COLUMBIA TRISTAR HOME VIDEO 60876

FEAR CITY

D: Abel Ferrara — 93 m

NR | CRM ACT | 1984 | COLOR | Sex | Nud | Viol | Lang | AdSit

6 A fairly standard thriller plot but with a very strong cast and very well executed. Set in the sleazy Times Square sex district of NYC, a psychopath is killing off strippers. Jack Scalia and Tom Berenger run a talent agency for strippers, but someone is killing off all their clients. Billy Dee Williams is a cop who is trying to get to the bottom of it. Berenger is also an ex-boxer who is out doing some detective work on his own because he's trying get things started back up his his old love (Griffith) and she is a stripper who is high on the psycho's list.

A: Jack Scalia, Tom Berenger, Melanie Griffith, Billy Dee Williams, Rossano Brazzi, Rae Dawn Chong

© HBO VIDEO TVA3000

FFOLKES

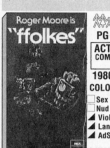

D: Andrew V. McLaglen — 99 m

PG | ACT COM | 1980 | COLOR | Sex | Nud | Viol | Lang | AdSit

7 Tongue-in-cheek characterization by Roger Moore in which he plays a character who acts exactly counter to his former role as James Bond. This guy hates women, but loves cats. He is a underwater sabotage expert who is called in by the British government to stop an impending attempt by a psychotic madman (Perkins) who is determined to blow up the largest oil rig in the North Sea unless the government pays him a ransom. This is no classic, but is an enjoyable diversion that is told with a touch of humor. The plot is actually more plausible than most of the James Bond plots.

A: Roger Moore, Anthony Perkins, James Mason, Michael Parks, David Hedison

© MCA/UNIVERSAL HOME VIDEO, INC. 80183

FINAL COUNTDOWN, THE

D: Don Taylor — 92 m

PG | SF ACT | 1980 | COLOR | Sex | Nud | Viol | Lang | AdSit

8 A very interesting but highly improbable concept for a movie. Suppose a nuclear aircraft carrier, equipped with 1980's weapons technology, slips into 1941 just before the Japanese are about to attack Pearl Harbor, by going into a time warp. Kirk Douglas, as the ship's captain, must decide whether to utilize his ship's overwhelming firepower to stop the impending attack and thus change the course of history. Pretty good yarn, if you can get past the premise.

A: Kirk Douglas, Martin Sheen, Katharine Ross, James Farentino, Ron O'Neal, Charles Durning

© LIVE HOME VIDEO VA4047

FIREFOX

D: Clint Eastwood — 136 m

PG | ACT | 1982 | COLOR | Sex | Nud | Viol | Lang | AdSit

7 The Russians have created a super fighter that can fly at Mach 6 and everything in it is controlled by the pilot's thoughts. American super-pilot Clint Eastwood is assigned the job of sneaking into a Russian air base and stealing their newest secret weapon, Firefox. Once he gets it off the ground, he still has to get it through the Russian's lethal air defense system. A little slow in the beginning, but then it takes off and gives you a good ride. Good special effects during the flight sequences.

A: Clint Eastwood, Freddie Jones, David Huffman, Warren Clarke, Ronald Lacey, Ken Colley

© WARNER HOME VIDEO 11219

FIREPOWER

D: Michael Winner — 107 m

R | ACT | 1979 | COLOR | Sex | Nud | Viol | Lang | AdSit

6 Sophia Loren is determined to avenge the letter-bomb death of her husband - a chemist who was about to prove that a drug company, controlled by the world's third-richest man, distributed the contaminated drugs that caused cancer and killed many people. She enlists the aid of an ex-lover (Coburn), who is now a government agent, to go with her to the Caribbean to flush out this Howard Hughes-like character - even though no one even knows what he looks like. Full of beautiful people, beautiful locations and lots of explosions. Passable action yarn.

A: Sophia Loren, James Coburn, O.J. Simpson, Eli Wallach, Anthony Franciosa, Vincent Gardenia

© LIVE HOME VIDEO 51111

FIRM, THE

D: Sydney Pollack — m

R | SUS ACT DMA | 1993 | COLOR | Sex | Nud | Viol | Lang | AdSit

8 Quite good thriller based on a blockbuster novel. Tom Cruise is a poor boy who has managed to graduate at the top of his Harvard law class and is recruited into a mysterious Memphis law firm with a huge salary. Only after he is in does he discover that he can't get out. The firm is a money-laundering machine for the Chicago mob. The FBI, on the other hand, sees him as their big opportunity to break the back of the mafia and is forcing him into becoming their snitch. If he doesn't help them, he'll go to jail. If he does, he will have to hide out forever. He is caught between two powerful forces who can crush him. Top-flight cast. Good, but book was better.

A: Tom Cruise, Jeanne Triplehorn, Gene Hackman, Holly Hunter, Ed Harris, Wilford Brimley

© PARAMOUNT HOME VIDEO 32523

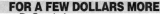

FIRST BLOOD (RAMBO)

D: Ted Kotcheff — 96 m

R | ACT | 1982 | COLOR

10 Red-hot, gritty and graphic! When ex-Green Beret Rambo (Stallone) happens upon Sheriff Dennehy's quiet small town, he ends up wrongfully arrested and thrown in the slammer, which for him reignites horrifying memories of Vietnam. He escapes into the Oregon woods, but has a bunch of vicious cops and the National Guard following him - and, all are intent on tracking him down. With a commando's guile and near superhuman strength, Rambo battles not only his pursuers but also the entire establishment that supports them. A colossal hit, full of explosive force and brutal violence. Two sequels.

Sex / Nud / Viol / Lang / AdSit

A: Sylvester Stallone, Richard Crenna, Brian Dennehy, David Caruso, Jack Starrett

© LIVE HOME VIDEO 65923

FIRST DEADLY SIN, THE

D: Brian G. Hutton — 112 m

R | CRM ACT | 1980 | COLOR

6 Gritty cop film about a weary detective (Sinatra) tracking down a psycho through the streets of New York at the same time that he is trying to cope with the fact that his wife (Dunaway) is slowly dying of a failed kidney operation. Normally a by-the-book guy, he sees a pattern in the killings that his superiors don't. If he is going to get this guy, he must bait a trap. Sinatra is convincing and the film is involving and believable, but it is also somber and slow moving.

Sex / Nud / Viol / Lang / AdSit

A: Frank Sinatra, Faye Dunaway, David Dukes, Brenda Vaccaro, Martin Gabel, James Whitmore

© WARNER HOME VIDEO 11368

FISTFUL OF DOLLARS, A

D: Sergio Leone — 102 m

NR | WST ACT | 1964 | COLOR

8 This was a watershed picture for Clint Eastwood, from it he became a giant star. In it, he played the "Man With No Name" - a strange gunslinger who single-handedly saves a small Mexican town being torn apart by two warring families. Interestingly, this film is actually based upon an excellent and funny samurai film, YOJIMBO. This was the first of several famed, action-packed spaghetti-Westerns (meaning Italian-made with dubbed-in English for some actors). It was followed by the successful sequel FOR A FEW DOLLARS MORE, and also inspired THE GOOD, THE BAD AND THE UGLY. Innovative and haunting score.

Sex / Nud / Viol / Lang / AdSit

A: Clint Eastwood, Gian Maria Volonte, Marianne Koch, Wolfgang Lukschy, Mario Brega, Carol Brown

Distributed By MGM/UA Home Video M201272

FLASHBACK

D: Franco Amurri — 108 m

R | COM ACT | 1990 | COLOR

6 Well cast and a pretty good time. Hopper is a radical hippie who never recovered from the '60s. Sutherland is a straightlaced yuppie FBI agent who never recovered from the '80s. Sutherland is charged with escorting the flipped-out Hopper from San Francisco to Spokane. But along the way they run afoul of corrupt cop and politician De Young. These two opposites are now running together for their lives; and, it is new experience and a surprise for Mr. F.B.I. to discover that he likes the hippie. Plays a little too fast and loose with believability, but still the characters are likable and fun.

Sex / Nud / Viol / Lang / AdSit

A: Dennis Hopper, Kiefer Sutherland, Carol Kane, Cliff De Young, Paul Dooley, Michael McKean

© PARAMOUNT HOME VIDEO 32110

FLASHPOINT

D: William Tannen — 95 m

R | ACT | 1984 | COLOR

7 Taut adventure story about two Texas border patrolmen who discover a long-abandoned jeep with a skeleton, a rifle, $800,000 cash and two phone numbers on board. One of the numbers belonged to the Dallas police department, when President Kennedy had been shot, twenty years ago and the other is in Washington DC. They have uncovered a major conspiracy; they are being pursued by an unknown quarry; and, they are up to their Stetsons in trouble. Someone wants them, and the twenty-year-old secret, dead. Action-filled thriller.

Sex / Nud / Viol / Lang / AdSit

A: Kris Kristofferson, Treat Williams, Rip Torn, Kevin Conway, Mark Slade, Tess Harper

© HBO VIDEO TVA2880

FLIGHT OF THE PHOENIX

D: Robert Aldrich — 143 m

NR | SUS DMA ACT | 1966 | COLOR

9 This is a gripping adventure story about a small planeful of men who are forced to crash in the North African desert. They are all trapped in a very hostile environment with only one way out. They must rebuild the plane and fly it out. Tension steadily builds as the men struggle both to endure the extreme rigors of desert survival and to rebuild the plane. An excellent international cast provides credibility and realism to an excellent script. Plus, there is a really unique twist as the climax builds. Very highly recommended viewing.

Sex / Nud / Viol / Lang / AdSit

A: James Stewart, Richard Attenborough, Peter Finch, Hardy Kruger, Ernest Borgnine, George Kennedy

© FOXVIDEO 1221

FOR A FEW DOLLARS MORE

D: Sergio Leone — 130 m

R | WST ACT | 1965 | COLOR

7 Action-packed sequel to A FISTFUL OF DOLLARS. The Man-with-no-name (Clint Eastwood) joins forces with another bounty hunter/gunslinger (Van Cleef) to track down a Mexican bandit and his cutthroat band. Both of them have their own reason for wanting this guy but to get him they have to form an uneasy partnership. This spaghetti-Western holds few surprises, but has plenty of what Westerns are most famous for, guns and action. Plus, it also has a truly outstanding score from Ennio Morricone. See also THE GOOD, THE BAD AND THE UGLY.

Sex / Nud / Viol / Lang / AdSit

A: Clint Eastwood, Lee Van Cleef, Gian Maria Volonte, Klaus Kinski, Rosemarie Dexter, Mario Brega

Distributed By MGM/UA Home Video M201577

FORCE 10 FROM NAVARONE

D: Guy Hamilton — 118 m

PG | WAR ACT | 1978 | COLOR

6 Almost a sequel to the far-superior THE GUNS OF NAVARONE. Members of American and British commando units join forces, under Harrison Ford's leadership, to sabotage a major bridge in the Balkans. The bridge is a vital link between the Germans and the Italians during World War II. Solid cast, with well-staged action sequences, but nothing distinguished in the plot or the execution.

Sex / Nud / Viol / Lang / AdSit

A: Robert Shaw, Harrison Ford, Edward Fox, Franco Nero, Barbara Bach

© WARNER HOME VIDEO 26018

FORT APACHE, THE BRONX

D: Daniel Petrie — 120 m

R | CRM ACT | 1981 | COLOR

8 Very tough cop story about the worst and most dangerous police district in New York - the South Bronx. Its precinct house is dubbed "Fort Apache" because it is encircled with barbed wire. Newman and Ken Wahl face a non-stop daily battle against the worst possible elements. Still, the idealistic veteran Newman keeps the faith. Then he witnesses two cops commit a brutal crime and he is forced to make a choice between loyalty and what's right. Tense and very realistic cop film about an urban nightmare. Excellent performances, especially by Newman and Ticotin.

Sex / Nud / Viol / Lang / AdSit

A: Paul Newman, Ken Wahl, Edward Asner, Kathleen Beller, Rachel Ticotin, Danny Aiello

© HBO VIDEO 90610

FOR YOUR EYES ONLY

D: John Glen — 129 m

PG | ACT | 1981 | COLOR

8 James Bond is back. After many frivolous outings, this fifth appearance of Roger Moore marks a return to a more serious attempt at the original James Bond "feel." Still, there are the beautiful women and action sequences, but its plot is less of a cartoon and more a spy adventure. Bond must gain the return of a top secret device from a sunken submarine with the aid of a Greek beauty - before the Russians get it.

Sex / Nud / Viol / Lang / AdSit

A: Roger Moore, Carole Bouquet, Chaim Topol, Lynn-Holly Johnson, Julian Glover, Jill Bennett

Distributed By MGM/UA Home Video M200180

FOUR MUSKETEERS, THE

D: Richard Lester — 107 m

PG | COM ACT | 1975 | COLOR

8 Highly entertaining, high-spirited comedy/adventure and sequel to THE THREE MUSKETEERS (although they were actually filmed at the same time). It is a tongue-in-cheek irreverent retelling of the Dumas classic of honor and comradeship between three valiant swordsmen. Full of swashbuckling sword play, slap stick humor and good story telling. It actually has a quite engrossing plot too, and Raquel Welch was never better. The final sword duel is a real piece of work.

Sex / Nud / Viol / Lang / AdSit

A: Oliver Reed, Raquel Welch, Richard Chamberlain, Frank Finlay, Michael York, Christopher Lee

© LIVE HOME VIDEO 215-280

FOURTH PROTOCOL, THE

D: John Mackenzie — 100 m

R | SUS ACT | 1987 | COLOR

8 Thrilling and excellent Cold War relic. Michael Caine is a British agent who suspects that something strange is up. He knows something is being smuggled into the country, but he doesn't know what it is at first. Then, he discovers that a Russian agent is smuggling an atom bomb into England and will detonate it next to an American airbase. The Americans will be blamed and a major spit will occur in the Western alliance. Non-stop pacing keeps suspense levels very high throughout. Very good.

Sex / Nud / Viol / Lang / AdSit

A: Michael Caine, Pierce Brosnan, Joanna Cassidy, Ned Beatty, Betsy Brantley, Peter Cartwright

© WARNER HOME VIDEO 320

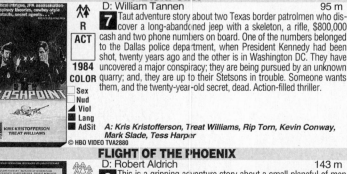

FOURTH WAR, THE

R | ACT | 1990 | COLOR

D: John Frankenheimer 90 m

6 The Cold War is dying right before their eyes, but two Cold War warriors are still facing each other down across the Czechoslovak-West German border. Then, when the Russian (Prochnow) orders a defector shot, the American (Scheider) strikes back and the two start their own private war. This is a thriller that doesn't really cover any new ground, but it does what it does quite well. Mildly involving. Fans of this kind of action in particular will be very entertained.

Sex / Nud / Viol / Lang / AdSit

A: Roy Scheider, Jurgen Prochnow, Tim Reid, Lara Harris, Harry Dean Stanton

© HBO VIDEO 90519

FREEBIE AND THE BEAN

R | ACT COM CRM | 1974 | COLOR

D: Richard Rush 113 m

8 Wild cop comedy. This is probably the first, and certainly one of the best, buddy-cop movies. It is the story of two odd-ball San Francisco cops: Freebie (Caan), who is a cheapskate, and Bean (Arkin), who is a very vocal Mexican-American. These two cops are trying to shut down a big numbers racket, but they rip up half of San Francisco in the process. Includes four car chases, and one super stunt ends up with their car crashing into the bedroom of a highrise apartment building. Caan and Arkin are great together. A lot of fun.

Sex / Nud / Viol / Lang / AdSit

A: Alan Arkin, James Caan, Loretta Swit, Valerie Harper, Jack Kruschen, Alex Rocco

© WARNER HOME VIDEO 11237

FRENCH CONNECTION, THE

R | ACT CRM SUS | 1971 | COLOR

D: William Friedkin 104 m

10 An exciting, landmark film that was a winner of five Oscars, including Best Picture. This is a realistic cop action yarn that trails a maverick, nearly amoral, New York cop and his wary partner as they obsessively and relentlessly investigate a huge heroin shipment from France. It is a thrilling and action-packed depiction of tough street-life. It is loaded with blood-pounding suspense and contains one of the most thrilling chase scenes ever recorded on film. Equally important, it also features an excellent plot, good character development, superb acting and was based upon real life.

Sex / Nud / Viol / Lang / AdSit

A: Gene Hackman, Fernando Rey, Roy Scheider, Eddie Egan, Sonny Grosso, Tony Lo Bianco

© FOXVIDEO 1009

FRESH

R | DMA ACT | 1994 | COLOR

D: Boaz Yakin 124 m

9 Fresh is his name. He has a job running heroin for one hood in the morning and another job in the afternoon selling crack for another hood. In his free time, he goes to the park to play speed chess with his derelict, chess-genius father. Everyone says that he is smart and someday he is going to be the man. Fresh is a 12 years old. He lives with his aunt with eleven of his cousins, jammed into a small apartment. His one goal has been to make enough money to escape. However, when he witnesses his young girlfriend being shot, he wants revenge but he needs to survive. He has only his street smarts and his chess skills to rely upon. Brilliant, riveting, realistic and sad.

Sex / Nud / Viol / Lang / AdSit

A: Sean Nelson, Giancarlo Esposito, Samuel L. Jackson, N'Bushe Wright, Ron Brice, Jean LaMarre

© MIRAMAX HOME ENTERTAINMENT 3041

FROM RUSSIA WITH LOVE

PG | ACT | 1964 | COLOR

D: Terence Young 119 m

9 This is thrilling and definitive Bond. Along with GOLDFINGER, it is one of the best of the James Bond superspy entries. It is a suspenseful adventure in which James becomes involved in a sinister plot which is baited with a beautiful Russian agent. He is pursued and almost done in on the Orient Express by a memorable and truly sinister bad guy (Robert Shaw). And, he is nearly toe-stabbed by a creepy Russian spy-master (Lotte Lenya) just as he thinks his job is complete. More realistic and believable than virtually all the other Bond flicks.

Sex / Nud / Viol / Lang / AdSit

A: Sean Connery, Daniela Bianchi, Lotte Lenya, Pedro Amendariz, Robert Shaw

Distributed By MGM/UA Home Video M201402

FUGITIVE, THE

PG-13 | SUS MYS ACT | 1994 | COLOR

D: Andrew Davis 131 m

9 A huge box office hit. Harrison Ford is Dr. Richard Kimble, who came home to find his wife dying after having been attacked. Kimble scuffled with the intruder and knows that the man has only one arm. However, all the physical evidence points to Kimble. No one believes his story and he is sentenced to die for the murder. But, while on the way to prison, the bus wrecks and he escapes. Tommy Lee Jones is a U.S. Marshall who has been assigned to recapture Kimble. He is good and he is dedicated. Kimble knows his only chance to regain his life is to find that one-armed man himself. Very suspenseful, good action, good mystery and excellent acting. 6 Oscar nominations, including Best Picture.

Sex / Nud / Viol / Lang / AdSit

A: Harrison Ford, Tommy Lee Jones, Sela Ward, Andreas Katsulas, Joe Pantoliano, Jereon Krabbe

© WARNER HOME VIDEO 21000

FULL METAL JACKET

R | WAR DMA ACT | 1987 | COLOR

D: Stanley Kubrick 117 m

8 A highly acclaimed, straightforward movie which follows a group of Marine recruits through basic training, where they are turned into killing machines, and on to Vietnam, where they do what they are trained to do. The picture is essentially divided into two halves. The beginning portion is dominated by the amazingly foul-mouthed verbal assaults of a real-life drill sergeant, molding the young recruits. The latter half relates the efforts of these Marines to do their job and to survive the 1968 Tet Offensive of Vietnam. It is a compelling depiction of the numbing dehumanization of war.

Sex / Nud / Viol / Lang / AdSit

A: Matthew Modine, Adam Baldwin, Vincent D'Onofrio, R. Lee Ermey, Dorian Harewood, Arliss Howard

© WARNER HOME VIDEO 11760

FUTUREWORLD

PG | SF ACT | 1976 | COLOR

D: Richard T. Heffron 107 m

7 Entertaining sequel to WEST WORLD. In a fantastic amusement park of the future, lifelike robots act out a customer's fantasies. But investigative reporters Fonda and Danner find out there is also a plan by one of the scientists to replace all the world's leaders with these robots and to control the world. (Similar plot to the cult classic INVASION OF THE BODY SNATCHERS). Yul Brynner is back in his WEST WORLD role. Pretty good escapism.

Sex / Nud / Viol / Lang / AdSit

A: Peter Fonda, Blythe Danner, Arthur Hill, Yul Brynner, Stuart Margolin, John P. Ryan

© GOODTIMES 04060

FX

R | ACT SUS | 1986 | COLOR

D: Robert Mandel 109 m

8 Fast-paced thriller. A special effects wizard is hired by the US Justice Department to stage what he thinks is a ploy to hide a protected witness from the mob. Instead, it is actually a plot by some corrupt Feds to kill off a dangerous witness who will incriminate them, too. When the high-tech wizard finds out the truth and discovers that he is also to be a victim, he has to use his tricks to vanish. But first he has to win a high-speed race through the streets of NYC. Lots of action, twists, and some good special effects.

Sex / Nud / Viol / Lang / AdSit

A: Bryan Brown, Brian Dennehy, Diane Verona, Cliff De Young, Mason Adams, Jerry Orbach

© HBO VIDEO TVA3769

GALLIPOLI

PG | WAR ACT | 1981 | COLOR

D: Peter Weir 111 m

9 Outstanding picture from Australia. Beautiful and powerful. Two adventurous young Australian idealists (Gibson and Lee) get caught up in a patriotic fever during World War I, join the army and are sent to Turkey. They are sent to Gallipoli, the site of a devastating WWI battle in which the Australian forces suffered tremendous casualties. A totally engrossing human drama and one of the best films ever of life on the battlefield. Striking period details, excellent production values and brilliant acting.

Sex / Nud / Viol / Lang / AdSit

A: Mel Gibson, Mark Lee, Bill Kerr, Robert Grubb, David Argue, Tim McKensie

© PARAMOUNT HOME VIDEO 1504

GATE OF HELL

NR | FOR ROM ACT | 1956 | COLOR

D: Tienosuk Kinugasa 86 m

9 Winner of Best Foreign Film Oscar, New York Film Critics and Cannes. Exquisitely beautiful, haunting and heart-wrenching Japanese tale of love. Set in the 12th-century, a warrior remains faithful to his Emperor in spite of overwhelming odds. When offered anything he wants for his reward, he asks for a beautiful lady he had met briefly but fell passionately in love with. However, she is happily married and refuses him. Yet, he is obsessed with her and refuses to leave her alone. Rebuffed on all fronts and desperate, he threatens to kill both her and her aunt, unless she agrees to let him kill her husband and then marry him. Instead, she kills herself. Beautiful photography. Subtitles.

Sex / Nud / Viol / Lang / AdSit

A: Machiko Kyo, Kazuo Hasegawa, Isao Yamagata

© HOME VISION GAT 020

GATOR

PG | ACT | 1976 | COLOR

D: Burt Reynolds 116 m

6 Gator McKlusky (Reynolds) is back in this sequel to the very popular WHITE LIGHTNING. Now on probation from moonshining charges, good ol' boy Gator is approached by an undercover Department of Justice agent (Weston) and blackmailed into finking on his backwoods buddy and local crime czar Jerry Reed. It seems the corrupt governor (Mike Douglas) needs a big bust to get reelected. But, Gator decides to get revenge on Douglas and his corrupt cronies too. Mildly entertaining, particularly for Reynolds fans.

Sex / Nud / Viol / Lang / AdSit

A: Burt Reynolds, Jack Weston, Lauren Hutton, Jerry Reed, Alice Ghostly, Dub Taylor

Distributed By MGM/UA Home Video M301623

GAUNTLET, THE

D: Clint Eastwood 109 m

R | ACT | 1977 | COLOR | Sex | Nud | Viol | Lang | AdSit

7 Stylish action flick in which Eastwood plays a hard-bitten disillusioned Phoenix cop trying to bring a hooker (Locke) back from Las Vegas to testify in a mob trial about a murder she witnessed. Eastwood must protect the girl against the mob, who wants her silenced. That's bad enough, but they soon find they are also the targets of corrupt politicians afraid of being exposed. The two of them are set up and the police are sent as yet another weapon to kill them both. Sometimes exciting, with plenty of violence, but ultimately not believable. Good action though.

A: Sondra Locke, Pat Hingle, William Prince, Bill McKinney, Mara Corday

© WARNER HOME VIDEO 11083

GERONIMO: AN AMERICAN LEGEND

D: Walter Hill 115 m

PG-13 | WST ACT | 1994 | COLOR | Sex | Nud | Viol | Lang | AdSit

7 A sincere, well acted and evocatively photographed attempt to present fairly both sides of the last of the Indian wars. The primary focus is on Geronimo and his band of renegade Apache raiders but is a reasonably accurate telling of the character and politics of the time. It is the end of an old way of life and the birth of a nation, but Geronimo and his group will live free or die free. General Crook (Hackman) is a fair and honest man who sends a young officer that Geronimo respects (Patric) to get him to surrender. Geronimo does, but is frustrated and breaks free, only to be hunted by a new and ruthless General. Well done, but tends to be slow in places.

A: Jason Patric, Gene Hackman, Robert Duvall, Wes Studi, Matt Damon, Rodney A. Grant

© COLUMBIA TRISTAR HOME VIDEO 58703

GETAWAY, THE

D: Sam Peckinpah 123 m

PG | ACT | 1972 | COLOR | Sex | Nud | Viol | Lang | AdSit

8 Exciting, very violent thriller. McQueen is a bankrobber who gets out of prison after his wife (MacGraw) goes to bed with the parole board chairman (Johnson). Johnson has also set up a bank robbery for them in which McQueen and two others are to rob a bank and MacGraw is to drive getaway. McQueen is furious with his wife for what she has done, but the robbery goes off as planned. McQueen and MacGraw then discover that it is also a setup and they are to be killed. Instead, the two take the money for themselves and set about killing Johnson before he can get them. Violent and fast-paced, with a great chase sequence. This film became a cult favorite and spawned a remake in 1994.

A: Steve McQueen, Ali MacGraw, Ben Johnson, Sally Struthers, Al Lettieri, Slim Pickens

© WARNER HOME VIDEO 11122

GETAWAY, THE

D: Roger Donaldson 116 m

NR | ACT CRM | 1994 | COLOR | Sex | Nud | Viol | Lang | AdSit

8 This is a high-energy remake of the 1972 action classic and cult film of the same name. Alec Baldwin and Kim Basinger star as a husband and wife robbery team. When Baldwin is caught and sent to a Mexican prison, he sends Basinger to talk a top gangster into getting him out in exchange for his special services. Woods does get him out, but only in part because he needs Baldwin's skills to rob a racetrack. The other reason was that Basinger slept with him. The heist goes down, but team turns on itself. Woods thinks Basinger will continue to betray Baldwin, but he is fooled. She and Baldwin keep the money and make a break, with the cops and the hoods in close pursuit.

A: Alec Baldwin, Kim Basinger, Michael Madsen, Jennifer Tilly, Richard Farnsworth, James Woods

© MCA/UNIVERSAL HOME VIDEO, INC. 82019

GETTYSBURG

D: Ronald Maxwell 254 m

PG | WAR DMA ACT | 1993 | COLOR | Sex | Nud | Viol | Lang | AdSit

9 On July 2, 1863, in the second year of the Civil War, the Union and Confederate Armies found each other outside a small Pennsylvania town and there fought the largest battle of the war. By the end of the third day of that battle 53,000 men lay dead - roughly the same number of men killed in the Vietnam War over twelve years. This is an epic film in both its scope and its intent. The battle sequences are extremely realistic and effectively convey the grandeur and the horror of that war like no other film before it. For history films it is a must see. Others, however, may find it to be slow, deliberate and long. Still, be patient. Also see terrific epic documentary THE CIVIL WAR.

A: Tom Berenger, Martin Sheen, Jeff Daniels, Sam Elliott, Richard Jordan

© TURNER HOME ENTERTAINMENT 6139

GLASS HOUSE, THE

D: Tom Gries 90 m

NR | DMA CRM ACT | 1972 | COLOR | Sex | Nud | Viol | Lang | AdSit

9 A gripping and hard-hitting realistic made-for-TV drama based on a story by Truman Capote, about what it is really like to be a convict behind bars. Three separate stories are merged to tell the larger story. A young kid is up on drug charges. Clu Gulager is an idealistic new prison guard. Alan Alda is a college professor up on manslaughter charges. Vic Morrow is a brutally powerful inmate boss who dominates his world and everyone in it. Savage and shocking depiction of life behind bars, where the guards look the other way while Morrow runs the "glass house." Filmed at Utah State Prison.

A: Vic Morrow, Clu Gulager, Billy Dee Williams, Dean Jagger, Alan Alda

© GOODTIMES 9252

GLORIA

D: John Cassavetes 121 m

PG | ACT CRM | 1980 | COLOR | Sex | Nud | Viol | Lang | AdSit

7 Surprisingly good story of an aging show girl and mob moll who saves her neighbor's eight-year-old boy from a mob hit. Gena Rowlands won an Oscar nomination for her hard-boiled gun-toting character portrayal. Just before both of the boy's parents are killed by mob hitmen, the father entrusts Rowlands with the boy's life and the mob's books. She and the boy are both now on the run and the mob's hot on their trail, but this is no ordinary woman - she knows how the mob works, what has to be done and she does it. Very good.

A: Gena Rowlands, Buck Henry, John Adames, Julie Carmen, Lupe Guarnica

© COLUMBIA TRISTAR HOME VIDEO 60196

GLORY

D: Edward Zwick 122 m

R | DMA ACT WAR | 1989 | COLOR | Sex | Nud | Viol | Lang | AdSit

9 Excellent story, based on fact, about the Civil War's first fighting regiment of black soldiers. The Civil War was fought largely because of the plight of black people, but blacks were not allowed to actually fight in it until near the end of the war. Broderick plays the black regiment's white officer who fights to get better treatment and pay for his men, and to gain for them the two things they want most - the opportunity go into battle and the dignity of being men. Extremely high production values, particularly in very realistic battle sequences. Winner of three Oscars, including Best Actor (Washington).

A: Matthew Broderick, Denzel Washington, Morgan Freeman, Cliff De Young, Cary Elwes

© COLUMBIA TRISTAR HOME VIDEO 11543

GODFATHER, THE

D: Francis Ford Coppola 171 m

R | DMA CRM ACT | 1972 | COLOR | Sex | Nud | Viol | Lang | AdSit

10 Inspired filmmaking. Absolutely everything, including production values, writing, casting, direction, acting and story-telling are all done to perfection. It was the winner of Best Picture, Actor and Screenplay. It is a riveting portrayal of a fictional immigrant family who have become ruthless leaders of a powerful Mafia clan. Story focuses primarily upon the father (Brando) and his youngest son, Michael (Pacino). The don has planned that Michael is to escape a life in the family business, but he is instead drawn into it and must lead the family when the father is shot. Masterpiece.

A: Marlon Brando, Al Pacino, James Caan, Robert Duvall, Talia Shire, Sterling Hayden

© PARAMOUNT HOME VIDEO 8049

GODFATHER EPIC, THE

D: Francis Ford Coppola 386 m

NR | DMA ACT CRM | 1977 | COLOR | Sex | Nud | Viol | Lang | AdSit

10 1+1=3. The original two GODFATHER movies are here edited together, with the sequences shown now in chronological order and other scenes added. As good as the first two films were, they pale alongside this compiled version. The surface story is that of an Italian immigrant who arrives in America and excels at surviving in a vicious turn-of-the-century ghetto. He and his family evolve into the underground masters of their vicious world. However, it is also the story of raw power, the corruption of power and the politics of power. This is genuine masterpiece and is an absolute must see.

A: Marlon Brando, Al Pacino, Robert De Niro, Robert Duvall, James Caan, Diane Keaton

© PARAMOUNT HOME VIDEO 8480

GODFATHER PART 2, THE

D: Francis Ford Coppola 200 m

R | DMA CRM ACT | 1974 | COLOR | Sex | Nud | Viol | Lang | AdSit

9 Fascinating follow-up to the powerhouse original. This one won 6 Oscars, including Best Picture. In it, Michael expands the family business to Las Vegas even though it destroys his marriage. It also explains how Michael's father came to leave Sicily for America in the first place. And, how he came to become involved in crime in the ghettos of Little Italy at the turn of the century. Robert De Niro here plays the younger don. (Marlon Brando played the older don in Part I.) Parts I & II were combined into a combined feature called GODFATHER, THE EPIC. As good as I & II are, the combination was better because it related events more sequentially for a better understanding.

A: Al Pacino, Robert De Niro, Robert Duvall, Talia Shire, Diane Keaton, Lee Strasberg

© PARAMOUNT HOME VIDEO 8459

GODFATHER PART 3, THE

D: Francis Ford Coppola 170 m

R | DMA CRM ACT | 1990 | COLOR | Sex | Nud | Viol | Lang | AdSit

8 A brilliant film, full of passion, and a rich conclusion to Coppola's trilogy of the lives and trials of a prominent mob family. At center stage again is Michael Corleone (Pacino). He has tired of the life and is taking the final step of making his family businesses legitimate and international. He has engineered a huge corporate takeover with the help of the Vatican, but finds that the organized grip of the mob is stronger than he is, and it destroys him. Exceptional performances, plus all of the drama, power and intrigue that we would expect to end this epic saga.

A: Al Pacino, Diane Keaton, Talia Shire, Andy Garcia, Eli Wallach, Joe Mantegna

© PARAMOUNT HOME VIDEO 32318

GODZILLA, KING OF THE MONSTERS

D: Terry Morse 80 m

NR | SF ACT CLD | 1956 | B&W

6 Campy original (American) version of the long-running Japanese classic horror film. Godzilla is a long dormant, huge, fire-breathing reptilian monster that is awakened by an atomic bomb blast, after which he goes on a reign of terror, destroying everything in his path. This original is far superior to the many clones which came later. It is most notable for the high quality of its special effects. (This version is not actually the original version. The original Japanese version was twenty minutes longer and did not have the subplot of the American scientist.)

Sex / Nud / Viol / Lang / AdSit

A: Inoshiro Honda, Raymond Burr, Takashi Shimura, Akihiko Hirata

© PARAMOUNT HOME VIDEO 12864

GOLDFINGER

D: Guy Hamilton 113 m

PG | ACT | 1964 | COLOR

10 Quintessential classic Bond! Third in the series and perhaps the best, although FROM RUSSIA WITH LOVE is right up there. James must rescue Fort Knox from the infamous Goldfinger's plot to contaminate its entire gold supply with radioactivity, thus making his own horde even more valuable. All the suave charm, excitement and thrills you expect are there, along with beautiful women. While the plot has its share of gadgets, it somehow never loses believability. Great entertainment and a memorable score, as well.

Sex / Nud / Viol / Lang / AdSit

A: Sean Connery, Gert Frobe, Honor Blackman, Shirley Eaton, Harold Sakata

Distributed By MGM/UA Home Video M201403

GOOD, THE BAD, AND THE UGLY, THE

Clint EASTWOOD
THE GOOD THE BAD THE UGLY

D: Sergio Leone 162 m

R | WST ACT | 1967 | COLOR

9 Third, last and best of a famous series of Westerns by Italian director Sergio Leone that were nicknamed spaghetti-Westerns and starred Clint Eastwood. In this one, Eastwood plays a bounty hunter and supposedly "The Good" part of a trio of gunslingers, which also consisted of Lee Van Cleef as an Army sergeant - "The Bad," and Eli Wallach as a thief - "The Ugly." Each man has one piece of a puzzle that will lead to $200,000 in buried Confederate gold. Very gritty and violent. See also A FISTFUL OF DOLLARS and A FEW DOLLARS MORE.

Sex / Nud / Viol / Lang / AdSit

A: Clint Eastwood, Lee Van Cleef, Eli Wallach, Rada Rassimov, Mario Brega, Chelo Alono

Distributed By MGM/UA Home Video M301465

GOODFELLAS

D: Martin Scorsese 146 m

R | CRM DMA ACT | 1990 | COLOR

9 This film is both masterful and perversely fascinating. It is based on the best selling novel GOODFELLAS and paints a fascinating picture of 30 years of the life and lifestyle of a real gangster. Henry Hill was fascinated as a boy with the money and the respect that the gangsters in his neighborhood had, so he became one. The "life" is one of decadent excesses of money, drinking, dining out, leisure time and women - counter-pointed by equal excesses of violence. The ruthlessness of these characters is absolute. Violence is business. There is no room for sympathy and emotion. Utterly intriguing.

Sex / Nud / Viol / Lang / AdSit

A: Robert De Niro, Ray Liotta, Lorraine Bracco, Joe Pesci, Paul Sorvino, Frank Sivero

© WARNER HOME VIDEO 12039

GORKY PARK

D: Michael Apted 127 m

R | MYS CRM ACT | 1983 | COLOR

8 An absorbing murder mystery set in Soviet Moscow. When three bodies, all with their faces and fingerprints destroyed, are discovered in Moscow's Gorky Park, a Russian police inspector (Hurt) begins an investigation. The trail leads him to a very wealthy and well-connected American fur trader (Marvin), a beautiful dissident (Pacula), the KGB and a New York cop (Dennehy). Lots of plot twists keep both Hurt and the viewer confused and guessing. A very involved but involving, and also somewhat uneven murder mystery. It has plenty of intrigue, plus an interesting window into life in a communist state.

Sex / Nud / Viol / Lang / AdSit

A: William Hurt, Lee Marvin, Joanna Pacula, Ian Bannen, Brian Dennehy

© GOODTIMES 04048

GO TELL THE SPARTANS

D: Ted Post 114 m

R | WAR DMA ACT | 1978 | COLOR

9 Superior and intelligent Vietnam war movie that was unjustly overlooked at the time of its release because of several other more highly-publicized pictures out at the same time. Set in 1964, before major US involvement in Vietnam, Lancaster is the commanding officer of an advisory group near Dienbienphu. The nature of the war is becoming apparent and he is already beginning to have doubts about the wisdom of being there, but still does his best to train his troops how to stay alive in jungle warfare. Excellent performances. Very realistic. True sleeper of a film.

Sex / Nud / Viol / Lang / AdSit

A: Burt Lancaster, Craig Wasson, Jonathan Goldsmith, Marc Singer, Joe Unger

© HBO VIDEO 90615

GREAT ESCAPE, THE

D: John Sturges 173 m

NR | ACT WAR DMA | 1963 | COLOR

10 Exciting blockbuster hit filled with major name international stars. An escape-prone group of cocky WWII Allied POWs are all gathered into one high security camp by the Germans, who wanted to put all their bad eggs into one high security basket. Instead, they get a massive POW escape attempt. This rousing adventure story is told as a series of character portraits which are then all linked together. It has a huge cast of top talent and a good script, plus pacing, humor and excitement aplenty. Watch for McQueen's thrilling motorcycle ride. Much copied - never equaled. Based upon an actual event. In the real event, 76 men broke out but only 3 found freedom.

Sex / Nud / Viol / Lang / AdSit

A: Steve McQueen, James Garner, Richard Attenborough, Charles Bronson, James Coburn, David McCallum

Distributed By MGM/UA Home Video M201257

GREAT LOCOMOTIVE CHASE, THE

D: Francis D. Lyon 85 m

NR | ACT | 1956 | COLOR

7 Colorful Disney production which depicts the true-life adventure story of a group of Union soldiers known as Andrews Raiders who launch a daring raid behind Confederate lines to steal a Confederate train and bring it home, blowing up the bridges behind it. However, their efforts are hampered by one rebel who will not stop trying to get his train back. Good family fun. This is a straightforward telling of the story with Disney emphasis on action and suspense. But there was another telling of the story - a great silent comedy classic by Buster Keaton in 1927 called THE GENERAL. See it, too.

Sex / Nud / Viol / Lang / AdSit

A: Fess Parker, Jeffrey Hunter, Jeff York, John Lupton, Eddie Firestone, Kenneth Tobey

© WALT DISNEY HOME VIDEO

GREAT NORTHFIELD MINNESOTA RAID, THE

D: Philip Kaufman 91 m

PG | WST ACT | 1972 | COLOR

7 Offbeat, but fact-based, Western about the famous raid on the "biggest bank west of the Mississippi" and the raid that ended the bankrobbing careers of the James-Younger gang. Contains vivid portraits of Cole Younger by Robertson and of Jesse James by Duvall. This is an attempt at a more realistic portrait of these bizarre and larger-than-life characters from the Old West, told from the other side - the seamy side - of the mirror. They are simple farmers, misfits who don't understand their times and become ruthless killers. Excellent characterizations but very different sort of Western.

Sex / Nud / Viol / Lang / AdSit

A: Cliff Robertson, Robert Duvall, Luke Askew, R.G. Armstrong, Dana Elcar, Donald Moffat

© MCA/UNIVERSAL HOME VIDEO, INC. 55106

GREAT TRAIN ROBBERY, THE

D: Michael Crichton 111 m

PG | ACT SUS | 1979 | COLOR

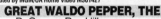

9 Stylish thriller about the very first robbery of a moving train - based upon a true incident in 1855 England. Sean Connery plays a dapper rogue of a thief who masterminds a daring plan to hijack gold bullion from a moving train. Beautiful production, with wonderful characters and a captivating plot. Lesley-Anne Down is Connery's beautiful mistress and also a disguise expert. Donald Sutherland is a braggart of a pickpocket. This is great entertainment that has you rooting for the bad guys.

Sex / Nud / Viol / Lang / AdSit

A: Sean Connery, Donald Sutherland, Lesley-Anne Down, Alan Webb, Malcolm Terris, Robert Lang

Distributed By MGM/UA Home Video M301427

GREAT WALDO PEPPER, THE

D: George Roy Hill 109 m

PG | DMA ACT | 1975 | COLOR

7 Appealing light adventure story. Redford is Waldo Pepper, a hot-shot, barnstorming pilot in the post-WWI 1920s who never had a chance to pit his skills against the German aces of the war and has always regretted it. However, when he gets the opportunity to fly a plane as a movie stuntman, he gets his chance. The other pilot is the WWI German fighter ace Ernst Kessler. Brilliant aerial footage and aerial acrobatics. Fun, even though the script is a little talky and uncertain.

Sex / Nud / Viol / Lang / AdSit

A: Robert Redford, Bo Svenson, Bo Brundin, Susan Sarandon, Geoffrey Lewis, Margot Kidder

© MCA/UNIVERSAL HOME VIDEO, INC. 55054

GREYSTOKE: THE LEGEND OF TARZAN, LORD OF THE APES

D: Hugh Hudson 130 m

PG | DMA ACT | 1983 | COLOR

7 This is a serious retelling of the classic Edgar Rice Burroughs character, and is told with style. An infant son of a dead ship-wrecked couple is discovered by apes and is raised as one of their own. Later discovered by a Belgian explorer, he is returned to civilization and is found to be the seventh Earl of Greystoke of Scotland. He is then taken to his doting grandfather (Richardson) and Tarzan attempts to become a civilized man. Wonderful ape-makeup. Even though it becomes slow and plodding near the end, it otherwise remains fun and very effective.

Sex / Nud / Viol / Lang / AdSit

A: Ralph Richardson, Christopher Lambert, Ian Holm, Andie MacDowell, Nigel Davenport, James Fox

© WARNER HOME VIDEO 11375

GUNFIGHT AT THE O.K. CORRAL

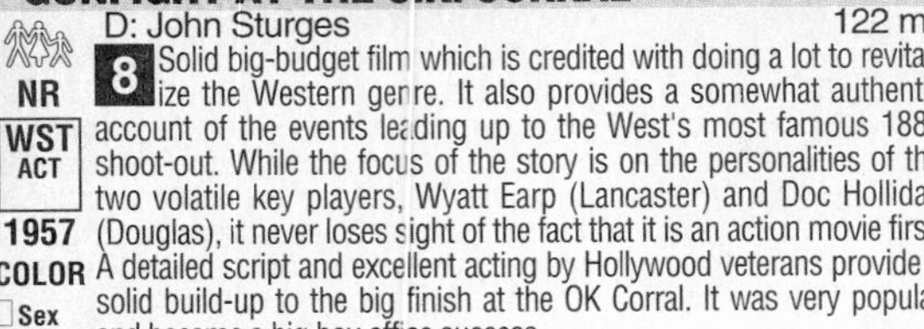

D: John Sturges — 122 m

NR | WST ACT | 1957 | COLOR

Sex / Nud / Viol ◢ / Lang / AdSit ◢

8 Solid big-budget film which is credited with doing a lot to revitalize the Western genre. It also provides a somewhat authentic account of the events leading up to the West's most famous 1881 shoot-out. While the focus of the story is on the personalities of the two volatile key players, Wyatt Earp (Lancaster) and Doc Holliday (Douglas), it never loses sight of the fact that it is an action movie first. A detailed script and excellent acting by Hollywood veterans provide a solid build-up to the big finish at the OK Corral. It was very popular and became a big box office success.

A: Burt Lancaster, Kirk Douglas, Rhonda Fleming, Jo Van Fleet, John Ireland, Lee Van Cleef

© PARAMOUNT HOME VIDEO 6218

GUNS OF NAVARONE, THE

D: J. Lee Thompson — 145 m

NR | WAR ACT | 1961 | COLOR

Sex / Nud / Viol ◢ / Lang / AdSit ◢

9 Action-packed WWII story about a multi-national Allied commando team sent onto a heavily guarded small Greek island in the Aegean Sea to destroy two radar-controlled batteries of huge German guns that threaten Allied troop ships. Excellent acting, first-rate production, high-intensity suspense and action. Nominated for seven Oscars, won Special Effects. Regarded among the best WWII flicks, along with THE GREAT ESCAPE, GUADALCANAL DIARY and SANDS OF IWO JIMA.

A: Gregory Peck, David Niven, Anthony Quinn, Stanley Baker, Anthony Quayle, James Darren

© COLUMBIA TRISTAR HOME VIDEO 60004

HAMBURGER HILL

D: John Irvin — 94 m

R | WAR ACT | 1987 | COLOR

Sex / Nud ◢ / Viol ■ / Lang ■ / AdSit ■

7 Very graphic grunt's-eye-view depiction of a 101st Airborne attack on a hill held by the North Vietnamese in 1969. It is a 10-day attack in which 14 men battle to take a muddy hill and receive 70% casualties. This is a straight-forward depiction of the horror and confusion of fighting, with battle scenes entirely from the soldier's viewpoint. The savage fighting is so graphic that it is sometimes hard to watch, but it is also not easily forgettable.

A: Michael Patrick Boatman, Tegan West, Dylan McDermott, Courtney Vance, Tommy Swerdlow, Steven Weber

© LIVE HOME VIDEO 6015

HAMMETT

D: Wim Wenders — 97 m

PG | MYS CRM ACT | 1982 | COLOR

Sex / Nud ◢ / Viol ◢ / Lang ◢ / AdSit ◢

7 Moody fictionalized screen portrait of the early years of famous mystery writer Dashiell Hammett (THE MALTESE FALCOLN and THE THIN MAN). In real life Hammett actually was a Pinkerton detective and this story has him personally becoming involved with a very baffling case about a missing Chinese woman. It is an authentic recreation of the 1930s film noir look and is a beautifully photographed film, but the very involved plot also requires the viewer's diligent attention in order to be appreciated.

A: Frederic Forrest, Peter Boyle, Marilu Henner, Roy Kinnear, Elisha Cook, Jr., Lydia Lei

© WARNER HOME VIDEO 22026

HANG 'EM HIGH

D: Ted Post — 114 m

NR | WST ACT | 1968 | COLOR

Sex / Nud / Viol ■ / Lang ◢ / AdSit ■

8 An action-packed American production that was done in the spaghetti-Western vein. In it, Eastwood plays an innocent rancher who is lynched by nine over-eager vigilantes who had mistaken him for a murderer. However, to their regret, he survived. Now hateful and sworn to vengeance, he sets about to get revenge. His first step is to get himself named as a marshall by a hanging judge who is bent on cleaning up the territory. The star gives him a "hunting license" and, one-by-one, Eastwood hunts down his victims. Excellently executed by a veteran staff of quality actors, this a solid but very violent, Western.

A: Clint Eastwood, Ed Begley, Pat Hingle, Arlene Golonka, Ben Johnson, Inger Stevens

Distributed By MGM/UA Home Video M201399

HARDER THEY FALL, THE

D: Mark Robson — 105 m

NR | DMA ACT | 1956 | B&W

Sex / Nud / Viol ■ / Lang / AdSit ■

9 Excellent. A moving and powerful sports drama that was also Bogie's last film. He plays an out-of-work sports writer who is reduced to writing PR releases for a boxing promoter (Steiger), and Steiger uses Bogart's help to build an upcoming boxer's image as a gentle giant. However, for the first time Bogart also comes to realize how corrupt the sport is because he discovers that Steiger has secretly been fixing fights. He just build the big guy up make a bundle when he loses the big championship match. Fast-paced, with excellent acting. A brutal indictment of boxing as a corrupt killer sport.

A: Humphrey Bogart, Rod Steiger, Jan Sterling, Mike Lane, Max Baer, Edward Andrews

© COLUMBIA TRISTAR HOME VIDEO 60010

HARD TIMES

D: Walter Hill — 97 m

PG | ACT DMA | 1975 | COLOR

Sex / Nud / Viol ■ / Lang ◢ / AdSit ◢

9 This is one of Charles Bronson's best roles. He plays a tough bare-knuckle boxer who is making a living by hustling street fights in Depression-era New Orleans. He and his sly manager (Coburn) stage a series of street bouts with the intention of setting up a "sting" of some local punks. Excellent recreation of period atmosphere and well-choreographed, violent and exciting fight sequences. Bronson was 54 when he made this film.

A: Charles Bronson, James Coburn, Jill Ireland, Strother Martin, Maggie Blye, Michael McGuire

© COLUMBIA TRISTAR HOME VIDEO 60008

HARD TO KILL

D: Bruce Malmuth — 96 m

R | ACT | 1990 | COLOR

Sex / Nud ◢ / Viol ■ / Lang ■ / AdSit ◢

6 Trademark martial arts action from this master of the genre. Seagal and his family are shot after he films a deal go down between a corrupt politician and the mob. He emerges after a seven-year coma to find that his family is dead. He wants revenge and enlists the help of the coma ward nurse (his then off-screen wife LeBrock) and his now-retired ex-partner to go after and nail the corrupt politician and his friends. Those guys think he's dead but they have a surprise in store.

A: Steven Seagal, Kelly LeBrock, Frederick Coffin, Bill Sadler

© WARNER HOME VIDEO 11914

HARD WAY, THE

D: John Badham — 115 m

R | COM ACT | 1991 | COLOR

Sex / Nud / Viol ■ / Lang ■ / AdSit ◢

6 Michael Fox is a spoiled Hollywood actor who is tired of playing the same old roles and wants desperately to have an exciting role in an upcoming cop movie which is supposed to go to Mel Gibson. Determined to "get into" the role, he wangles his way into two weeks of tagging along with a tough, nearly-out-of-control, cop (Woods) he saw on TV and who is currently trying to track down a particularly nasty killer. But - Woods doesn't want Fox along and does everything he can to discourage him. After this plot premise is laid out (in the first 20 minutes), things get predictable fast and pretty formula-driven. Still, the characters are fun to watch.

A: James Woods, Michael J. Fox, Stephen Lang, Annabella Sciorra, Penny Marshall

© MCA/UNIVERSAL HOME VIDEO, INC. 81079

HATARI!

D: Howard Hawks — 158 m

NR | ACT COM | 1961 | COLOR

Sex / Nud / Viol / Lang / AdSit

8 High energy and light-hearted fun. A great cast has a ball with a fun adventure story about a bunch of wild-animal trappers who capture African animals for zoos. This is good fun for adults and kids alike. John Wayne is at his macho best as the leader of the group. The simple story is amply spiced with doses of comedy, action, some excellent animal and scenic photography, and a little romance, too. Filmed on location in Tanganyika. Terrific Mancini score.

A: John Wayne, Elsa Martinelli, Red Buttons, Hardy Kruger, Gerard Blain

© PARAMOUNT HOME VIDEO 6629

HEARTBREAK RIDGE

D: Clint Eastwood — 130 m

R | WAR ACT | 1986 | COLOR

Sex / Nud ◢ / Viol ■ / Lang ■ / AdSit ■

6 This is an Eastwood vehicle pure and simple. He displays his starpower playing a tough, battle-scared, foul-mouthed gunnery sergeant with no wars to fight. He is serving his last tour as a boot-camp DI and gets a squad of misfits to train. While he loses the domestic battles with his ex-wife Marsha Mason, he turns his troops into a gung-ho fighting unit. He gets the job done just in time to take them to Grenada and kick communist butts. The whole thing is totally predictable, but just because we know where we're going doesn't mean we won't enjoy the trip.

A: Clint Eastwood, Marsha Mason, Everett McGill, Moses Gunn, Eileen Heckart, Bo Svenson

© WARNER HOME VIDEO 11701

HEART LIKE A WHEEL

D: Jonathan Kaplan — 113 m

PG | DMA ACT | 1983 | COLOR

Sex / Nud / Viol / Lang ◢ / AdSit ◢

7 Well-made sports biography about the pioneering female drag racer, Shirley "Cha-Cha" Muldowney. Bedelia gives a stellar performance as a hard-pressed woman who struggles to balance a career as a racer with being a wife. She also struggles to fight the sexist attitudes of a male-dominated sport into which she is the first woman to dare to enter. While the film does concern racing, it is really a human story of dedication and courage. It wins on both levels. Surprisingly good.

A: Bonnie Bedelia, Beau Bridges, Leo Rossi, Hoyt Axton, Bill McKinney, Dick Miller

© FOXVIDEO 1300

HELL IS FOR HEROS

D: Don Siegel — 90 m

NR | WAR DMA ACT | 1962 | COLOR

8 Quite good war drama in which character development is carefully interwoven into and necessary to the action sequences. The action scenes themselves are calculated realism, not empty-headed glory charges. A star-studded cast highlights this realistic war saga about a beleaguered Army squad which has survived Africa, France and Belgium, and is now assigned the job of plugging a hole in the front lines near the end of WWII. Steve McQueen is excellent as a tormented man who now requires battle as a drug to survive living.

Sex / Nud / Viol / Lang / AdSit

A: Steve McQueen, Bobby Darin, Fess Parker, Harry Guardino, James Coburn, Bob Newhart

© PARAMOUNT HOME VIDEO 6116

HELL TO ETERNITY

D: Phil Karlson — 132 m

NR | WAR DMA ACT | 1960 | B&W

8 Fascinating true story from World War II. Jeffery Hunter plays the real-life figure of Guy Gabaldon who was a Hispanic man raised by Japanese-Americans. Gabaldon could speak Japanese and became a hero of the South Pacific when he chose to fight his war on Saipan by going behind enemy lines each night to convince defeated Japanese soldiers to surrender, eventually winning a Silver Star for bringing in over 2,000 prisoners. Action aplenty, too, with very realistic battle scenes.

Sex / Nud / Viol / Lang / AdSit

A: Jeffrey Hunter, Vic Damone, David Janssen, Sessue Hayakawa

© CBS/FOX VIDEO 7351

HIDDEN, THE

D: Jack Sholder — 98 m

R | SF ACT CRM | 1987 | COLOR

8 Unique and exciting science fiction thriller. A Los Angeles cop is joined by a strange FBI agent (he chews Alka-Selzer tablets), in his attempt to get to the bottom of a rash of robberies and murders. The two are searching to find out how normal ordinary law-abiding citizens are being turned into such extremely violent killers. Then, the FBI agent informs the local cop that there is an alien creature who is invading these human bodies. He has a preference for heavy metal music, Ferraris and bloody violence. Full of high-intensity excitement, with good action sequences. Well made and very unpredictable.

Sex / Nud / Viol / Lang / AdSit

A: Michael Nouri, Kyle MacLachlan, Ed O'Ross, Clu Gulager, Claudia Christian, Clarence Felder

© MEDIA HOME ENTERTAINMENT, INC. M940

HIDDEN FORTRESS, THE

D: Akira Kurosawa — 139 m

NR | FOR ACT COM | 1958 | B&W

9 George Lucas acknowledges that this film, from the Japanese master filmmaker Akira Kurosawa, was the inspiration for his mega-smash hit STAR WARS. In it, a haughty young princess, a fortune in gold, a fugitive general and two bumbling and comic mercenary soldiers make a treacherous journey through enemy territory to get her back to her homeland. This one is so much fun you may even forget that its a foreign film. Subtitles.

Sex / Nud / Viol / Lang / AdSit

A: Toshiro Mifune, Misa Uehara, Minoru Chiaki, Kimatare Fugiwara, Susumu Fujita, Takashi Shimura

© HOME VISION HID 030

HIDING OUT

D: Bob Giraldi — 99 m

PG-13 | COM ACT | 1987 | COLOR

6 A 27-year-old commodities trader becomes a fugitive after he testifies against the mob and the mob kills the FBI agent sent to protect him. So he dyes his hair and registers as a senior at a high school in Delaware, where he becomes popular with the kids and dates the prettiest girl in school, but then the mob finds him. OK comedy. Teenagers will like it best.

Sex / Nud / Viol / Lang / AdSit

A: Jon Cryer, Keith Coogan, Annabeth Gish, Gretchen Cryer, Oliver Cotton

© HBO VIDEO 0042

HIGHLANDER

D: Russell Mulcahy — 110 m

R | ACT FAN | 1986 | COLOR

8 Flashy and intriguing fantasy in the romance tradition. It is the action-packed story of two immortal warriors who battle mightily in both 16th-century Scotland and 20th-century Manhatten to gain the "prize." Lambert receives tutelage in magic and warrior skills from his mentor Connery in 1536 - just in time to prepare himself for battle with the evil Kurgen (Brown) at that time and also again 400 years later. Spectacular swordplay and special effects mark this unusual tale which leaves some unaffected and others enthralled. An unworthy sequel followed and one only slightly better after that.

Sex / Nud / Viol / Lang / AdSit

A: Sean Connery, Christopher Lambert, Roxanne Hart, Clancy Brown

© HBO VIDEO TVA3761

HIGHLANDER: THE FINAL DIMENSION

D: Andy Morahan — 99 m

R | ACT FAN | 1994 | COLOR

6 Once again, the undying Highlander must do battle with another evil warrior. This time warriors from sixteenth-century Japan have freed themselves from being sealed inside a cavern after their underground prison is opened by unsuspecting archeologist team led by sexy Deborah Unger. The three become two, and then two become one, and that one will then do mortal combat with the Highlander to determine who will remain -- because ultimately there can only be one. For die-hard action fans only.

Sex / Nud / Viol / Lang / AdSit

A: Christopher Lambert, Mario Van Peebles, Deborah Unger, Mako, Raoul Trujillo, Martin Neufeld

© MIRAMAX HOME ENTERTAINMENT 3619

HIGH PLAINS DRIFTER

D: Clint Eastwood — 106 m

R | WST ACT | 1973 | COLOR

8 A very different sort of moral play. It is an immoral Western with a moral. The sleazy citizens of a corrupt mining town stand by while three outlaws brutally kill their Sheriff. Then, when gunslinger Eastwood comes to town, they hire him to replace the sheriff and protect them from the return of the bad guys. Instead, Eastwood takes charge of the town in a way they had not intended, and he begins a house-cleaning of his own. Very atmospheric, gritty, and violent, but told with a sense of ironic humor.

Sex / Nud / Viol / Lang / AdSit

A: Clint Eastwood, Verna Bloom, Marinna Hill, Mitchell Ryan, Jack Ging, Geoffrey Lewis

© MCA/UNIVERSAL HOME VIDEO, INC. 66038

HITMAN, THE

D: Aaron Norris — 94 m

R | ACT | 1991 | COLOR

6 This is a typical Chuck Norris vehicle - very violent, but his fans will be pleased. He plays a cop who is shot and left for dead by his partner (Parks) who had gone "dirty." Norris has recovered but has been pronounced dead so he can safely go under cover to infiltrate the Mafia, and also bring down his ex-partner who has become a kingpin. It is full of graphic and gory violence. For action and Norris fans only.

Sex / Nud / Viol / Lang / AdSit

A: Chuck Norris, Michael Parks, Alberta Watson, Al Waxman, Salim Grant

© CANNON VIDEO 32045

HOMBRE

D: Martin Ritt — 111 m

NR | WST ACT DMA | 1967 | COLOR

9 This is an intriguing and intelligent Western with powerhouse performances. Newman is a quiet loner, a white man who was raised by Apaches. He is onboard a 1880's stagecoach, along with a naive young married couple, a woman of the world, a corrupt Indian Agent with stolen money and his haughty wife and Richard Boone. Because Newman is so different he is shunned. However, he is the one they all later must rely upon to save them when their coach is robbed by Boone's killer gang and they are all left stranded to die. A captivating storyline, believable action and moving drama. Excellent.

Sex / Nud / Viol / Lang / AdSit

A: Paul Newman, Fredric March, Richard Boone, Diane Cliento, Cameron Mitchell, Barbara Rush

© FOXVIDEO 1012

HOMICIDE

D: David Mamet — 100 m

R | CRM DMA ACT | 1991 | COLOR

7 Intriguing police drama that is both a fascinating character portrait and a revealing view into the nature of a policeman's extended family. Joe Mantegna is a good and dedicated cop. He is a respected negotiator whose skills involve him in a major case with a real nasty killer. But, he is sidetracked when he stumbles onto the unrelated killing of an old Jewish woman. At first he wants no part of her case but quickly becomes fascinated with it because she was a hero in Israel's independence movement. She inspires a pride in the Jewish heritage he has long denied and he suddenly has a yearning to belong again. But, a man cannot have two families.

Sex / Nud / Viol / Lang / AdSit

A: Joe Mantegna, William H. Macy, Natalija Nogulich, Ving Rhames, Rebecca Pidgeon, Vincent Guastaferro

© COLUMBIA TRISTAR HOME VIDEO 91443

HOOPER

D: Hal Needham — 100 m

PG | ACT COM | 1978 | COLOR

8 Entertaining and light-hearted romp with fun-loving good-old-boys from Hollywood. Burt Reynolds and Sally Field recaptured much of the charm that they developed in SMOKEY AND THE BANDIT, but this time Burt plays an aging professional stuntman who is being challenged by an arrogant up-and-comer (Vincent) into doing the biggest stunt of his career. You should expect lots of thrilling stunts in cars and other places, but the real fun here is in the wise-cracking characters they create. Lots of fun.

Sex / Nud / Viol / Lang / AdSit

A: Burt Reynolds, Jan-Michael Vincent, Sally Field, Brian Keith, John Marley, Robert Klein

© WARNER HOME VIDEO 1008

HORSE SOLDIERS, THE

D: John Ford — 115 m

NR | WST ACT | 1959 | COLOR

7 Stirring John Ford adventure story - his only set during the Civil War. This "Western" is based upon an actual account of a Union raiding party sent into Rebel territory to cut supply lines into Vicksburg. Interestingly, the film takes no sides in the war. John Wayne plays the determined Union officer leading the raid, but he is accompanied by William Holden as a pacifistic Army doctor. Good action scenes, coupled with a romance between Wayne and a Southern girl (Towers) he must take captive on the way. Better than average as Westerns go, but suffers from preachy dialogue.

Sex · Nud · Viol · Lang · AdSit

A: John Wayne, William Holden, Constance Towers, Hoot Gibson, Althea Gibson, Ken Curtis

Distributed By MGM/UA Home Video M201772

HOUR OF THE GUN

D: John Sturges — 100 m

NR | WST ACT | 1967 | COLOR

7 Interesting twist to THE GUNFIGHT AT THE OK CORRAL -- the truth. James Garner plays a Wyatt Earp who is out for revenge and is ruthless in tracking down his brother's killers. There is lots of action, but this also presents a more complete and much darker picture of the situation surrounding the famous gunfight. Interestingly, it also presents a character, in Wyatt Earp, who is much less heroic and more spiteful. Well done. However, because the truth ran counter to the legend, this one had some difficulty at the box office. Still, this is one all Western fans should watch.

Sex · Nud · Viol · Lang · AdSit

A: James Garner, Jason Robards, Jr., Robert Ryan, Albert Salmi, Charles Aidman, Steve Ihnat

Distributed By MGM/UA Home Video M203118

HUNTER, THE

D: Buzz Kulik — 97 m

PG | ACT | 1980 | COLOR

6 Steve McQueen's last picture. He plays an aging modern-day bounty hunter hunting down bail jumpers and bringing them back to the law. His character, Papa Thorson, is based upon a real individual. Several excellent chase scenes keep the intensity level high, in spite of the fact that McQueen was dying of cancer as he made this picture.

Sex · Nud · Viol · Lang · AdSit

A: Steve McQueen, Eli Wallach, Kathryn Harrold, LeVar Burton, Ben Johnson

© PARAMOUNT HOME VIDEO 1192

HUNT FOR RED OCTOBER, THE

D: John McTiernan — 135 m

PG | SUS ACT | 1990 | COLOR

8 This is one of the last of the Cold War thrillers. It is based upon the best-selling Tom Clancy suspense novel set in 1984 - seven years prior to the actual downfall of the communist Soviet state. Connery plays a disenchanted commander of a new top-secret high-tech submarine code-named Red October and he plans to defect to the West with the secret sub. The Soviets race against time to sink him before he can deliver the sub and the Americans struggle to help him - both without starting a nuclear war. Very exciting and well done. However, purists will like the book better.

Sex · Nud · Viol · Lang · AdSit

A: Sean Connery, Alec Baldwin, Scott Glenn, Sam Neill, James Earl Jones

© PARAMOUNT HOME VIDEO 32020

HUSTLE

D: Robert Aldrich — 120 m

R | CRM MYS ACT | 1975 | COLOR

7 Effective but cynical detective thriller. Burt Reynolds is a bitter L.A. detective called in to investigate the murder of a young woman found dead on the beach, supposedly a suicide. Reynolds is an old fashioned kind of guy who believes in right and wrong, but each day he faces life's worst. So he spends his evenings with his girlfriend (Deneuve), a high-class hooker. Both dream of escaping their dreary lives, but neither does. Reynolds's investigations lead him to a lawyer (Albert) with mob connections. The girl was a hooker and a porn star. Pretty cynical stuff, but it is effective.

Sex · Nud · Viol · Lang · AdSit

A: Burt Reynolds, Catherine Deneuve, Ben Johnson, Paul Winfield, Eileen Brennan, Eddie Albert

© PARAMOUNT HOME VIDEO 8785

ICE STATION ZEBRA

D: John Sturges — 150 m

G | ACT SUS | 1968 | COLOR

6 This is a Cold War espionage flick in which Rock Hudson commands a submarine that is sent to the North Pole regions to retrieve Soviet spy satelite data from a weather station before the Russians get it. It is a large-scale picture with beautiful arctic photography, action and some suspense. Borgnine is a Russian defector. He is only one of several who are suspected of being the Russian spy which is known to be on board and which is being pursued by British agent Patrick McGoohan. This is a pretty typical Cold War movie. Still, it was supposedly the favorite of billionaire Howard Hughes.

Sex · Nud · Viol · Lang · AdSit

A: Rock Hudson, Ernest Borgnine, Patrick McGoohan, Jim Brown, Tony Bill, Lloyd Nolan

Distributed By MGM/UA Home Video M600160

I, THE JURY

D: Richard T. Heffron — 111 m

R | ACT MYS CRM | 1982 | COLOR

7 Mickey Spillane's gritty Mike Hammer character was born in the 1940s in his novel "I, the Jury." In this movie, the hard-boiled detective is updated into the 1980s as he investigates the murder of his Army buddy from Vietnam. His search takes him to Barbara Carrera's sex clinic. The seedy flavor of this film matches that of the novels. It is fast paced, has lots of action, a seedy atmosphere, plus lots of naked women and violence - all of which are befitting the character of Spillane's pulp novels and which also help to cover up some big plot holes.

Sex · Nud · Viol · Lang · AdSit

A: Armand Assante, Barbara Carrera, Alan King, Laurene Landon, Geoffrey Lewis, Paul Sorvino

© FOXVIDEO 1186

I'M GONNA GIT YOU SUCKA

D: Keenen Ivory Wayans — 89 m

R | COM ACT | 1988 | COLOR

8 Really funny spoof of the black exploitation movies of the early 1970s. Wayans comes home after a ten-year tour in the Army to find that his brother has died from an overdose of gold chains. Worse, he has left his family shackled with a big debt owed to the neighborhood's head punk. When the police don't help, Wayans rounds up a crew of over-the-hill heroes (Brown, Hayes, Casey and Fargas) to save the day. Major spoof, with laugh-out-loud gags.

Sex · Nud · Viol · Lang · AdSit

A: Keenan Ivory Wayans, Bernie Casey, Antonio Fargas, Steve James, Isaac Hayes, Jim Brown

Distributed By MGM/UA Home Video M901641

IMPOSSIBLE SPY, THE

D: Jim Goddard — 96 m

NR | SUS ACT | 1987 | COLOR

7 Intriguing espionage thriller - more so because it is based upon the real-life exploits of an Egyptain-born Israeli, Elie Cohen. Cohen is a mild mannered businessman who is recruited by Israeli intelligence (the Massad) in 1959 and sent to Argentina to infiltrate a group planning the overthrow of the Syran government. That experience provides him the means to become a spy inside Damascus itself, where he infiltrated the Syran government. The information he provided was, in large measure, responsible for the success of the Israelis in the Six-Day War... but the price is high.

Sex · Nud · Viol · Lang · AdSit

A: John Shea, Eli Wallach, Rami Danon, Michal Bat-Adam

© HBO VIDEO 0035

IMPULSE

D: Sondra Locke — 109 m

R | ACT CRM | 1990 | COLOR

8 Lottie Mason (Russell) is a beautiful female cop who likes taking risks. When a witness, who is to testify against a big-time narcotics dealer, steals $1 million and heads for cover, the D.A. (Fahey) has to get him back. He needs someone to go inside on a drug buy to trap his wayward witness and Lottie is just the one for the job, even though the D.A. has fallen in love with her. With her nerves on edge after the deal goes bad, Lottie stops at a bar and unknowingly meets the missing witness. Lottie follows an impulse and is where she isn't supposed to be when he is killed. Now she has the $1 million.

Sex · Nud · Viol · Lang · AdSit

A: Theresa Russell, Jeff Fahey, George Dzundza, Anal Rosenberg, Nicholas Mele

© WARNER HOME VIDEO 11887

INDIANA JONES AND THE LAST CRUSADE

D: Steven Spielberg — 126 m

PG-13 | ACT COM | 1989 | COLOR

8 Entertaining family flick in the Saturday matinee serial-action tradition. This is the last in the series of adventurous exploits of the famous Indiana Jones. Here, Indie (Ford) launches himself on a quest to find his father (Connery) who has disappeared while in search of the Holy Grail. Connery and Ford work well together as they endeavor to find the Grail and then to protect it from the evil Nazis, who are out to steal it. Thrills and style will delight viewers of all ages.

Sex · Nud · Viol · Lang · AdSit

A: Harrison Ford, Sean Connery, Denholm Elliott, Alison Doody, River Phoenix, Julian Glover

© PARAMOUNT HOME VIDEO 31859

INDIANA JONES AND THE TEMPLE OF DOOM

D: Steven Spielberg — 118 m

PG | ACT COM | 1984 | COLOR

8 Exciting follow-up (and first of two sequels) to super hit RAIDERS OF THE LOST ARK. This one is set at a place in time before the original and has Indie (Ford), a nightclub singer (Capshaw) and a resourceful Korean kid (Quan) embark on an adventure in India to retrieve a magic jewel and a village's children from a Maharaja's fortress where they have been forced to work his mines. Filled with action-packed sequences as the original was, but less effective now. May be too intense for very young viewers.

Sex · Nud · Viol · Lang · AdSit

A: Harrison Ford, Kate Capshaw, Ke Huy Quan, Amrish Puri, Philip Stone, Dan Aykroyd

© PARAMOUNT HOME VIDEO 1643

IN HARM'S WAY

D: Otto Preminger — 165 m

WAR / ACT — 1965 — B&W

8 This is an epic motion picture that uses the aftermath of the attack on Pearl Harbor and the beginning of WWII as the backdrop to explore its effects upon the lives and loves of several principal players. The most notable of these are John Wayne and Kirk Douglas. John begins a love affair with nurse Patricia Neal and leads the counterattack against the Japanese. While, Douglas disgraces himself by molesting a nurse and attempts to redeem himself with battle heroics. The credible personal subplots and some really good action sequences make for enjoyable entertainment. However, it was criticized as being too long.

Sex □ Nud □ Viol ◢ Lang □ AdSit ◢

A: John Wayne, Kirk Douglas, Patricia Neal, Tom Tryon, Paula Prentiss, Henry Fonda

© PARAMOUNT HOME VIDEO 6418

IN-LAWS, THE

D: Arthur Hiller — 103 m

PG — COM / ACT — 1979 — COLOR

8 Hysterically wacky and unpredictable. A normal neighborhood dentist (Arkin) agrees to do a small favor for his daughter's future father-in-law (Falk), supposedly a CIA agent. But it soon becomes obvious that Falk is more than a little crazy when the two rob an armored car of engraving plates from the U.S. Treasury and also find themselves in front of a firing squad in a South American country. Falk and Arkin are great together in this far-out comedy.

Sex □ Nud □ Viol □ Lang ◢ AdSit ◢

A: Peter Falk, Alan Arkin, Richard Libertini, Nancy Dussault, Penny Peyser, Michael Lembeck

© WARNER HOME VIDEO 1009

INNOCENT MAN, AN

D: Peter Yates — 113 m

R — CRM / ACT — 1989 — COLOR

7 Selleck is a happily married airline mechanic who is gets caught in a cop screw up. Two over-zealous cops mistake him for a drug dealer but, rather than admit a mistake and risk their necks, they frame him. When he is in prison, Selleck must fight for his life. In order to survive, he must become a very different man than he was when he went in and do things he never thought he would do. When he gets out, he, his wife and a con who helped him while he was in prison plot to get revenge on the two cops. Fast paced.

Sex ◢ Nud ◢ Viol ■ Lang ■ AdSit ■

A: Tom Selleck, F. Murray Abraham, Laila Robins, David Rasche, Richard Young, Badja Djola

© TOUCHSTONE HOME VIDEO 910

INTERNAL AFFAIRS

D: Mike Figgis — 114 m

R — SUS / ACT / CRM — 1990 — COLOR

8 A gripping police thriller. Andy Garcia is an internal affairs investigator, struggling to gain evidence against a respected veteran police officer (Gere) who he knows is using his position as a cop to manipulate and twist other cops into doing his bidding. Gere is deep into money laundering, robbery, drug running schemes and even murder. He is a control freak, but now he is up against someone he can't control... but he tries. He will protect himself no matter what it takes. Very tense believable plot.

Sex ◢ Nud ◢ Viol ■ Lang ■ AdSit ■

A: Richard Gere, Andy Garcia, Laurie Metcalf, Nancy Travis, William Baldwin

© PARAMOUNT HOME VIDEO 32245

IN THE LINE OF FIRE

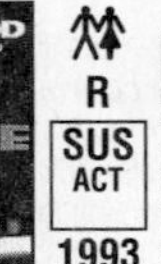

D: Wolfgang Petersen — 127 m

R — SUS / ACT — 1993 — COLOR

9 An exciting, very popular and gripping suspense film in which two government agents, both highly-trained and seasoned professionals, pit their skills against each other. Malcovich is extremely intelligent, totally ruthless and was assassin for the CIA. But, now he feels betrayed by his government and for him there is nothing left but the game. Clint Eastwood is an aging Secret Service agent who is haunted by his failure to protect President Kennedy. For Malcovich, the goal of this game of skills and retribution is his assassination of the President. His game is spiced by his highly-prized battle of wits against Eastwood, an adversary who he feels is his equal.

Sex □ Nud □ Viol ■ Lang ◢ AdSit ◢

A: Clint Eastwood, John Malkovich, Rene Russo, Dylan McDermott, Gary Cole, Fred Dalton Thompson

© COLUMBIA TRISTAR HOME VIDEO 52313

INTO THE NIGHT

D: John Landis — 115 m

R — ACT / ROM / COM — 1985 — COLOR

7 Jeff Goldblum is hopelessly boring and bored, plus his wife is having an affair with another man. While out on a midnight ramble, he stumbles into a beautiful woman (Pfeiffer) who is being pursued by a bunch of bad guys and accidentally gets involved with her, helping her to escape. Their adventure continues with repeated encounters with the killers and a quest to find some stolen emeralds. Criticized justly as being unnecessarily convoluted and difficult to follow, it is also, most times, a fun mix of romance, comedy and exciting action. Contains cameos from many leading directors.

Sex □ Nud ◢ Viol ■ Lang ■ AdSit ■

A: Jeff Goldblum, Michelle Pfeiffer, David Bowie, Richard Farnsworth, Vera Miles, Dan Aykroyd

© MCA/UNIVERSAL HOME VIDEO, INC. 80170

IPCRESS FILE, THE

D: Sidney J. Furie — 107 m

NR — SUS / MYS / ACT — 1965 — COLOR

9 This is a quite good and intelligent espionage thriller. Michael Caine is marvelous as a low-key Cockney crook turned secret agent. He is called in by London's top intelligence officials to investigate a series of kidnappings of top scientists, who are then brainwashed and taken behind the Iron Curtain. This is the best of three separate films based on three books from Len Deighton. It is taut and suspenseful, with numerous twists keeping interest levels high throughout. It was a very popular film and it made Caine into a star.

Sex □ Nud □ Viol ◢ Lang □ AdSit ◢

A: Michael Caine, Nigel Green, Sue Lloyd, Guy Coleman, Gordon Jackson

© MCA/UNIVERSAL HOME VIDEO, INC. 80518

IRON EAGLE

D: Sidney J. Furie — 117 m

PG-13 — ACT — 1986 — COLOR

6 Action fantasy fans only. The plot premise is totally without merit. Action is the thing here. An 18-year-old joins forces with a retired combat pilot to break into a top secret Air Force computer, steal a couple of jet fighters, launch an air raid into an Arab country and shoot down some MIG fighters in order to rescue the boy's father. Come on... but there is a lot of exciting aerial combat footage. Followed by IRON EAGLE II.

Sex □ Nud □ Viol ■ Lang ■ AdSit □

A: Louis Gossett, Jr., Jason Gedrick, David Suchet, Tim Thomerson

© CBS/FOX VIDEO 6160

IRON EAGLE II

D: Sidney J. Furie — 102 m

PG — ACT — 1988 — COLOR

6 The first mindless shoot-'em-up sold, so they built another one. This is the sequel to IRON EAGLE. This time Gossett is a general who recruits a team of fighter pilots from East and West to attack the Mid-East. Action fans will enjoy the thrills, but check your brains at the door.

Sex □ Nud □ Viol ◢ Lang ◢ AdSit ◢

A: Louis Gossett, Jr., Mark Humphrey, Stuart Margolin, Alan Scarfe, Sharon H. Brandon, Maury Chaykin

© LIVE HOME VIDEO 63258

IRON WILL

D: Charles Haid — 109 m

PG — ACT / DMA — 1994 — COLOR

8 It's 1917. Will Stoneman is a 17-year old South Dakota farm boy whose father raises sled dogs. When his father is killed, it looks like his mother may lose the farm and he'll never get to go to college. So, Will decides to enter a treacherous 522-mile dog-sled race through "the meanest stretch of land that God ever put together." For seven days, in mind-numbing 30-below cold, he will race against the best dog-sled racers in the world for the $10,000 prize, which he plans to win by running harder and sleeping less. This is a fictionalized account of an actual event. Predictable, but that doesn't stop it from being solid, rousing entertainment for the whole family.

Sex □ Nud □ Viol ◢ Lang □ AdSit ◢

A: Mackenzie Astin, Kevin Spacey, David Ogden Stiers, August Schellenberg, Brian Cox, George Gerdes

© WALT DISNEY HOME VIDEO 2545

JACKSON COUNTY JAIL

D: Michael Miller — 84 m

R — ACT — 1976 — COLOR

7 Pretty good action flick that has generated a fair cult following. Yvette Mimieux is a business woman who picks up a couple hitch-hiking while driving from California to New York. They rob her of everything she has, including her identification. When she goes for help, her story is doubted so she is held overnight until it is checked out. But that night, in her cell, she is brutally raped by a deputy. Another prisoner (Jones), in the next cell and up on charges of murder, helps her to escape. Together, they run away into a violent world she has never known.

Sex ■ Nud ◢ Viol ◢ Lang ◢ AdSit ■

A: Yvette Mimieux, Tommy Lee Jones, Robert Caradine, Severn Darden, Mary Woronov, Howard Hesseman

© WARNER HOME VIDEO 24001

JASON AND THE ARGONAUTS

D: Don Chaffey — 104 m

G — ACT / CLD — 1963 — COLOR

9 Exciting and very well done adventure story from Greek mythology. Jason, the son of a murdered Thessalian king, is cheated out of his birthright. So he gathers a crew for his ship and sets sail in search of the mythical Golden Fleece in order to reclaim his throne. This is an exciting adventure story which is made more so by stunning special effects (including a now classic scene with swordfighting skeletons). An interesting feature of this film for parents is that Jason and his crew are not portrayed as superheros, just mortal men performing great deeds. Great for kids.

Sex □ Nud □ Viol ◢ Lang □ AdSit □

A: Todd Armstrong, Gary Raymond, Honor Blackman, Nancy Kovack, Laurence Naismith, Niall MacGinnis

© COLUMBIA TRISTAR HOME VIDEO 60025

JAWS

D: Steven Spielberg 124 m

PG | **10** | SUS ACT DMA | 1975 | COLOR

A blockbuster hit that is both highly entertaining and technically masterful. An otherwise simplistic story line becomes a totally gripping adventure and leaves its audience terror-struck. A small town cop in a New England oceanside tourist town suspects that a great white shark is cruising the shoreline looking for lunch. Stubborn officials ignore his concerns until there is a major attack. The cop, a tenacious shark fisherman and a scientist set out to hunt down the shark, but... the gigantic creature turns to stalk them instead. Beware, this is a truly adrenaline pumping experience.

Sex Nud Viol Lang AdSit

A: Roy Scheider, Robert Shaw, Richard Dreyfuss, Larraine Gary, Murray Hamilton, Jeffrey Kramer

© MCA/UNIVERSAL HOME VIDEO, INC. 66001

JEREMIAH JOHNSON

D: Sydney Pollack 116 m

PG | **10** | WST ACT DMA | 1972 | COLOR

Hugely popular adventure story set in the mid-19th century Rocky Mountains. Jeremiah Johnson is a man who has lost all taste for civilization and so escapes into the unknown wilds of the Rockies. This grandly photographed spectacle follows the loner's early stumbling efforts at survival through to his mastery of the elements. However, his idyllic life is destroyed when his new family is murdered by raiding Indians. He launches himself into a murderous mission of revenge and his success at it leads him to become a feared and legendary figure among the Indians. An extraordinary adventure.

Sex Nud Viol Lang AdSit

A: Robert Redford, Will Geer, Charles Tyner, Stefan Glerasch, Allyn Ann McLerie

© WARNER HOME VIDEO 11061

JEWEL OF THE NILE, THE

D: Lewis Teague 106 m

PG | **7** | ACT ROM | 1985 | COLOR

This is an enjoyable follow-up to ROMANCING THE STONE, however it can't quite match the vitality of the earlier film. All the characters have here returned six months later to chase down yet another stone - this time in the Sahara Desert, in the middle of an Arab revolution. It seems Turner has writer's block and Douglas is tired of living in her shadow. The answer for them is an adventure to seek out he priceless Jewel of the Nile. Lots of money was spent on technical aspects and explosions. There are lots of good action sequences and some laughs too. Enjoyable.

Sex Nud Viol Lang AdSit

A: Michael Douglas, Kathleen Turner, Danny DeVito, Avner Eisenberg, Spiros Focas

© FOXVIDEO 1491

JIGSAW MAN, THE

D: Freddie Francis 90 m

PG | **7** | MYS ACT | 1984 | COLOR

Double agents and double-crosses will keep you guessing the whole way. Michael Caine is a former top British spy who has deserted to the Soviets. But he is really still an English agent, now only in the guise of a traitor? Before he left England, he had hidden a list of Soviet spies who were operating in England. Now, many years later, and after having his physical identity altered through plastic surgery, he is back in England to get his list... but for which side? An interesting caper, but not on a par with the lead's earlier pairing in SLEUTH.

Sex Nud Viol Lang AdSit

A: Laurence Olivier, Michael Caine, Susan George, Robert Powell, Eric Severeid

© HBO VIDEO TVA3219

JOE KIDD

D: John Sturges 88 m

PG | **6** | WST ACT | 1972 | COLOR

Eastwood and Duvall in top form cannot redeem the somewhat muddled quality of this movie. Nevertheless, it does contain some real bang-up action scenes. The time is the turn of the 20th century. The place is New Mexico. Robert Duvall is a land baron who has enticed Eastwood into helping him fight a group of Mexican-Americans who feel their land has been stolen from them and are now waging a guerrilla war against him. However, Eastwood soon discovers that they are right - he is on the wrong side and quickly joins the other side.

Sex Nud Viol Lang AdSit

A: Clint Eastwood, Robert Duvall, John Saxon, Don Stroud, Stella Garcia, James Wainwright

© MCA/UNIVERSAL HOME VIDEO, INC. 66050

JOHNNY HANDSOME

D: Walter Hill 96 m

R | **7** | ACT | 1989 | COLOR

Modern film noir with a twist. Mickey Rourke is Johnny Handsome and is called that because he has a severe facial disfigurement. His only friend is killed in a coin collector robbery gone bad, and Johnny was double-crossed and deserted by the other two partners (Ellen Barkin and Lance Henrickson). It seems that they had set him and his friend up, and then left him to take the rap. While in prison and in the mistaken belief that he will reform himself, he becomes the beneficiary of a new government program in which his deformed face is totally rebuilt. Instead, he uses his new face and identity to seek revenge on the two who betrayed him.

Sex Nud Viol Lang AdSit

A: Mickey Rourke, Ellen Barkin, Forest Whitaker, Elizabeth McGovern, Lance Henriksen, Morgan Freeman

© LIVE HOME VIDEO 68902

JOURNEY OF NATTY GANN, THE

D: Jeremy Paul Kagan 101 m

PG | **9** | DMA ACT CLD | 1985 | COLOR

This is a wonderfully endearing story that has the rare quality of being a family movie that has a genuine appeal both to young and to old. Natty Gann is a young girl in Depression-era Chicago, whose desperate father has to leave her, on short notice and without saying goodbye, with a very unpleasant old woman so he can take a good job in Seattle. Natty refuses to believe her father has deserted her and embarks on a cross-country trip by rail to go to him. She is all alone, except for a protective wolf and a hardened drifter she meets along the way. Very appealing, highly entertaining and very worthwhile.

Sex Nud Viol Lang AdSit

A: Meredith Salenger, John Cusack, Ray Wise, Lainie Kazan, Barry Miller, Scatman Crothers

© WALT DISNEY HOME VIDEO 400

JUBAL

D: Delmer Daves 101 m

NR | **8** | WST ACT | 1956 | COLOR

Interesting Western which is sometimes compared to OTHELLO. Glenn Ford is Jubal Troop, a drifter in Wyoming, who signs on as a hired hand at Ernest Borgnine's ranch. Borgnine is a likable oaf but he is having trouble with his sexy wife and he confides in Ford about it. Rod Steiger is one of his ranch hands and wants the woman, but she has rejected him. Steiger is also jealous of Ford's growing influence on Borgnine, so he plants suspicions in Borgnine's mind about Ford's intentions for the wife, which begins a series of events that leads to big trouble. An adult Western, well-acted and generally well done.

Sex Nud Viol Lang AdSit

A: Glenn Ford, Ernest Borgnine, Valerie French, Rod Steiger, Felicia Farr, Noah Beery, Jr.

© GOODTIMES 4510

JUDGMENT NIGHT

D: Stephen Hopkings 110 m

R | **7** | SUS ACT | 1993 | COLOR

A bunch of ordinary guys head out together in a motor home for a night out on the town, at a boxing match. When they become bogged down in a traffic jam, they head off to find a way around it on a detour through a bad neighborhood. Instead, they find themselves becoming witnesses to a murder and spend the rest of the film being chased from building to building by a gang of hoods who are trying to eliminate the witnesses. This is no DELIVERENCE but it is fast-paced and the characters are frequently believable.

Sex Nud Viol Lang AdSit

A: Emilio Estevez, Cuba Gooding, Jr., Denis Leary, Stephen Dorff, Jeremy Pevin, Erik Schrody

© MCA/UNIVERSAL HOME VIDEO, INC. 81563

JUGGERNAUT

D: Richard Lester 109 m

PG | **7** | SUS ACT | 1974 | COLOR

Very effective suspense thriller. A blackmailer has planted several bombs on board a luxury liner and is holding it for ransom while it sails on the high seas. Harris and a band of experts helicopter on board and must race against time to find all the bombs and defuse them. And, all the while they are looking, the blackmailer stays on the phone to taunt them with meager and cryptic clues as to where the bombs are. This could have been rather commonplace disaster movie, but instead it is raised, by excellent acting and direction, into an intense and realistic thriller.

Sex Nud Viol Lang AdSit

A: Richard Harris, Omar Sharif, David Hemmings, Anthony Hopkins, Shirley Knight, Ian Holm

Distributed By MGM/UA Home Video M203070

JUNGLE BOOK, THE

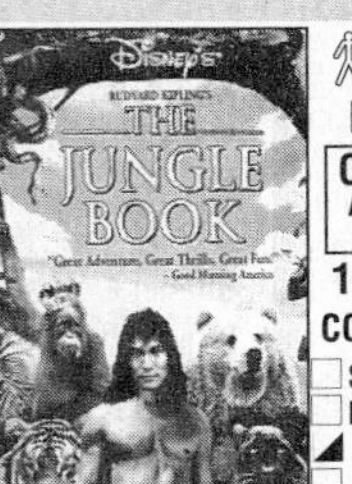

D: Steven Sommers 111 m

PG | **6** | CLD ACT | 1994 | COLOR

This is Rudyard Kipling's classic tale of Mowgli, a young boy from India who was lost in the jungle and raised to manhood by a pack of wolves. One day he chances upon a long-lost village containing great treasures of gold and jewels. But Mowgli has no use for these and takes only a jewel-encrusted dagger. Later still, Mowgli finds a beautiful girl in the jungle and follows her back to her village. Now for the first time, he discovers man and they discover his treasure. Don't expect to see a live-action version of Disney's cute animated classic. This attempts to follow more closely the original story, but it also takes considerable license. Very simply told. Too violent for very young however.

Sex Nud Viol Lang AdSit

A: Jason Scott Lee, Cary Elwes, Lena Hheadley, Sam Neill, John Cleese, Jason Fleming

© WALT DISNEY HOME VIDEO 4604

JURASSIC PARK

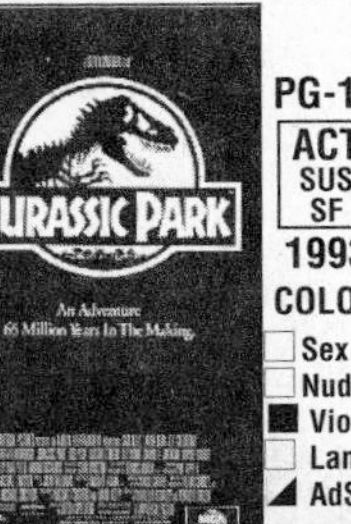

D: Steven Spielberg 126 m

PG-13 | **10** | ACT SUS SF | 1993 | COLOR

Masterful movie making is combined with wondrous special effects to create grippingly real terror. A wealthy industrialist has purchased in island off the coast of Costa Rica and plans to convert it into a fantastic tourist attraction. The featured attraction is live dinosaurs which have been miraculously reconstituted from "pickled" DNA fragments, taken from mosquitoes that have been entombed in amber for 100 million years. Two paleontologists (Neill and Dern) are called in to assure the investors that the park is safe. Instead, they are set upon and hunted by the carnivorous beasts who have been set free by sabotage and a massive power failure.

Sex Nud Viol Lang AdSit

A: Sam Neill, Laura Dern, Jeff Goldblum, Richard Attenborough

© MCA/UNIVERSAL HOME VIDEO, INC.

K2

D: Franc Roddam 104 m

R | ACT DMA | 1992 | COLOR | Sex | Nud | Viol | Lang | AdSit

7 Stunningly beautiful photography and dramatic mountain climbing sequences are the primary attractions to this film. Two best friends, one an aggressive, womanizing lawyer and the other a very married physics professor, talk their way into a group that will attempt to climb the second tallest mountain in the world, the 29,064 foot peak of K2 in the Himalayas. This pretty good man-verses-the-elements story is augmented with the lessor, but significant, parallel story of the personal realization by the lawyer of his self-imposed personal isolation. However, the thrill of the adventure is what most will remember.

A: Michael Biehn, Matt Craven, Raymond J. Barry, Hiroshi Fujioka, Patricia Charbonneau, Luca Bercovici

© PARAMOUNT HOME VIDEO 32828

KARATE KID, THE

D: John G. Avildsen 126 m

PG | ACT DMA | 1984 | COLOR | Sex | Nud | Viol | Lang | AdSit

9 A real audience pleaser. A fatherless kid (Macchio) arrives in Southern California from New Jersey. Out of place and constantly hassled by some street toughs, he finds an unlikely friend and mentor in the apartment complex's Japanese gardner (Morita). Morita gains the boy's confidence and decides to train the boy in karate to give him the confidence he needs. But, in so doing, he also instructs him in a personal code of honor. This is an old fashioned sort of feel-good movie that doesn't hide its attempts to play with your emotions, and you won't care. You'll be cheering.

A: Ralph Macchio, Noriyuki "Pat" Morita, Elisabeth Shue, Martin Kove, William Zabka

© COLUMBIA TRISTAR HOME VIDEO 60406

KARATE KID PART II, THE

D: John G. Avildsen 113 m

PG | ACT DMA | 1986 | COLOR | Sex | Nud | Viol | Lang | AdSit

7 This sequel begins immediately after the original ends. Morita receives notice that his father in Japan is dying. When he and "the kid" (Macchio) arrive in Okinawa, Morita is immediately and forcefully reminded of an old feud with an old rival. Morita sets about resolving that situation and also revives an old love. Macchio also finds love with a village girl and a new enemy in the nephew of Morita's old foe. This film is most notable for its repeat appearance of a cast of likable characters, and the feel-good finish. Enjoyable, but predictable.

A: Ralph Macchio, Noriyuki "Pat" Morita, Nobu McCarthy, Martin Kove, William Zabka

© COLUMBIA TRISTAR HOME VIDEO 60717

KELLY'S HEROES

D: Brian G. Hutton 146 m

PG | WAR ACT COM | 1970 | COLOR | Sex | Nud | Viol | Lang | AdSit

8 Entertaining tongue-in-cheek reverse-spin on the popular film DIRTY DOZEN. Clint Eastwood gathers up a group of misfits and thieves to form his own private army within the Army. His goal is to capture a small village behind German lines. Is he a patriot? No. He and his people launch a very effective and inspirational offensive spearhead against the enemy because there is Nazi gold stored in the town, and they're going to steal it. Sprawling and entertaining, with a large cast of odd-ball characters. Light spirits and some good action sequences keep it moving.

A: Clint Eastwood, Telly Savalas, Don Rickles, Donald Sutherland, Carroll O'Connor, Gavin MacLeod

Distributed By MGM/UA Home Video M700168

KHARTOUM

D: Basil Dearden 136 m

NR | ACT DMA | 1966 | COLOR | Sex | Nud | Viol | Lang | AdSit

8 Sweeping quasi-historical spectacle which tells the saga of Britain's battle for control over the Sudan, and of the rivalry between a British general (Heston) and a Moslem holy man (Olivier) named "The Mahdi" by his followers. In spite of their respect for each other, these two could not compromise and in 1883 The Mahdi led his followers in a long and arduous siege of the Sudanese city of Khartoum. The siege was eventually successful and led to the downfall of the British. Grand spectacle, well-mounted large battle sequences and some notable acting make this an entertaining diversion.

A: Charlton Heston, Laurence Olivier, Richard Johnson, Ralph Richardson, Alexander Knox, Johnny Sekka

Distributed By MGM/UA Home Video M202009

KID GALAHAD

D: Phil Karlson 95 m

NR | MUS ACT | 1962 | COLOR | Sex | Nud | Viol | Lang | AdSit

6 Elvis plays a young guy just back from the service. He's looking for a job and takes one as a sparring partner at a boxing camp, but instead he knocks out the camp's top boxer. So, the owner decides to make him into a champ, but this is a boxer that would rather be a mechanic and sing. Still, the promoter (Gig Young) can't let him get away because the kid is his one big chance to get out of debt to some hoods. Elvis agrees to fight for him, but that only gets him and his incorruptible trainer (Charles Bronson) in a whole lot of trouble. Pretty good, if you don't expect too much.

A: Elvis Presley, Gig Young, Charles Bronson, Lola Albright

Distributed By MGM/UA Home Video M701055

KIDNAPPED

D: Robert Stevenson 95 m

G | ACT CLD | 1960 | COLOR | Sex | Nud | Viol | Lang | AdSit

7 Great fun for kids of all ages from Disney. This is Disney's production of Robert Lewis Stevenson's swashbuckler classic. A young orphaned Scotsman is kidnapped by his cruel uncle just as he is about to inherit his family's estate. The boy is pressed into service as a cabin boy on a ship bound for the New World where, unknown to him, he is to be sold into slavery. But in their crossing they run over a small boat, killing all who were on board but a fellow Scotsman. The survivor and the boy become fast friends and escape the clutches of the foul ship they are captive to. Lots of high seas adventures.

A: Peter Finch, James MacArthur, Bernard Lee, Niall MacGinnis, Finlay Currie, Peter O'Toole

© WALT DISNEY HOME VIDEO 111

KILLER ELITE, THE

D: Sam Peckinpah 124 m

PG | ACT | 1975 | COLOR | Sex | Nud | Viol | Lang | AdSit

6 Secret Service agent James Caan is double-crossed by his partner (Duvall). Duvall has become a mercenary assassin and has seriously wounded Caan in an attack to get at a witness who he was guarding. Slowly recovering, Caan begins a relentless pursuit of his ex-partner, determined to get revenge. The plot becomes muddy and cynical with all the double-crosses and deceit, but the action and chase scenes are very intense. This is what you would expect from director Peckinpah.

A: James Caan, Robert Duvall, Arthur Hill, Gig Young, Mako, Bo Hopkins

Distributed By MGM/UA Home Video M301304

KILLER INSIDE ME, THE

D: Burt Kennedy 99 m

R | CRM ACT | 1976 | COLOR | Sex | Nud | Viol | Lang | AdSit

7 Taut thriller and a violent psychological study, with an exceptional acting job from Stacy Keach. He is a nice-guy deputy sheriff in a small midwestern town who goes off the deep end in a psychopathic spree of killing, while battling some redneck hoodlums. His suppressed violent personality is explained in a series of flashbacks exploring some deep childhood traumas. Excellent supporting cast, especially Susan Tyrell as a tough prostitute.

A: Stacy Keach, Susan Tyrrell, Keenan Wynn, Don Stroud, John Carradine, Charles McGraw

© WARNER HOME VIDEO 11708

KILLERS, THE

D: Don Siegel 95 m

NR | CRM ACT | 1964 | COLOR | Sex | Nud | Viol | Lang | AdSit

7 Terrific crime thriller that was Ronald Reagan's last picture, the only one where he played a bad guy and one where he got some of his best reviews. In it he hires two killers (Marvin and Gulager) to "hit" Cassavetes, but his hitmen start to wonder why he paid so much for the job, and why the intended victim refuses to run. When they investigate, they discover that Cassavetes was having an affair with Reagan's mistress (Dickenson) and that all three were involved in the robbery of an armored car where $1 million was taken. Very violent.

A: Lee Marvin, John Cassavetes, Angie Dickinson, Ronald Reagan, Clu Gulager, Norman Fell

© MCA/UNIVERSAL HOME VIDEO, INC. 55014

KILL ME AGAIN

D: John Dahl 95 m

R | SUS ACT | 1990 | COLOR | Sex | Nud | Viol | Lang | AdSit

6 Modern-day film noir in which a sexy femme fatal (Whalley-Kilmer) and her boyfriend steal some big-time money from the mob. She knocks her boyfriend in the head and takes off with the money. Then she seduces and tricks a private eye (Kilmer) into helping to fake her death so she can get both the boyfriend and the mob off her trail. But when she dumps Kilmer too, he goes after her and gets caught up in a chase which now includes the law, the ex-boyfriend and the mob. Other than lots of double-crosses, nothing much is new here, but what there is, is well done.

A: Joanne Whalley-Kilmer, Val Kilmer, Michael Madsen, Pat Mulligan, Bibi Besch

Distributed By MGM/UA Home Video M901835

KINDERGARTEN COP

D: Ivan Reitman 111 m

PG-13 | ACT COM CRM | 1990 | COLOR | Sex | Nud | Viol | Lang | AdSit

8 A nice little surprise film that has a little of everything. It has action, comedy, cuteness and romance! Tough police detective Kimble (Schwarzenegger) gets much more than he bargained for when he pretends to be a kindergarten teacher, while trying to track down the wife and son of a vicious drug lord who are in hiding. For the tough cop, the toughest part is dealing with a bunch of tiny kids. He fails miserably at it until he turns the classroom into boot camp. Don't be fooled though, all is not cuteness here. This is fundamentally an action flick with enough violence to get it a PG-13 rating.

A: Arnold Schwarzenegger, Penelope Ann Miller, Linda Hunt, Richard Tyson, Carroll Baker, Pamela Reed

© MCA/UNIVERSAL HOME VIDEO, INC. 81051

Action

KING KONG

D: John Guillermin — 135 m

PG | ACT FAN | 1976 | COLOR | Sex Nud Viol Lang AdSit

6 This was a big budget remake of the 1933 original black and white classic. The production values are much higher, the special effects have been updated, but it is most notable because it is also the first screen appearance of Jessica Lange. It is interesting, but in spite of color, better technology and a bigger budget, it is not in the same league as the original. It does not cast a spell over the audience as the original did and still does. There is no empathy for Kong. The romantic nature of the original is supplanted here by a cynicism and coarseness that dampen the viewer's enthusiasm.

A: Jeff Bridges, Jessica Lange, Charles Grodin, Ed Lauter

© PARAMOUNT HOME VIDEO 8872

KING OF NEW YORK

D: Abel Ferrara — 106 m

R | CRM ACT | 1990 | COLOR | Sex Nud Viol Lang AdSit

7 Extremely dark vision of a New York which becomes a battleground for the city's $1 billion drug trade. Christopher Walken is a ruthless criminal, just released from prison. He boldly announces that he and his henchmen will control the town's drug traffic, and will kill anyone and everyone who gets in their way. Very bloody and very violent. He and his army regularly kill Italian, Chinese and Columbian competitors, but the blood really flows when he puts out a contract on the cops. Fast-paced and action packed, but bloody.

A: Christopher Walken, Larry Fishburne, David Caruso, Victor Argo, Wesley Snipes, Giancarlo Esposito

© LIVE HOME VIDEO 68937

KRAYS, THE

D: Peter Medak — 119 m

R | CRM ACT | 1990 | COLOR | Sex Nud Viol Lang AdSit

8 Stylish and chilling portrayal of two of England's most vicious criminals. During the late '50s and early '60s, London's underworld was taken over by the sheer ruthlessness of twin brothers, Reggie and Ronnie Kray. Driven by ambition and bloodlust, and trained by their mother in the power of fear, these two rose quickly to power, and then, just as rapidly, crumbled as their psychosis caused them to lose control of the empire they had built. Both brothers were convicted of murder and are now serving 30-year sentences. Begins slow, but that changes.

A: Gary Kemp, Martin Kemp, Billie Whitelaw, Kate Hardie, Susan Fleetwood

© COLUMBIA TRISTAR HOME VIDEO 90973

LADYHAWKE

D: Richard Donner — 121 m

PG-13 | FAN ACT ROM | 1985 | COLOR | Sex Nud Viol Lang AdSit

8 Exciting and original medieval romantic adventure fantasy, set in the 13th century and beautifully photographed. A young pickpocket (Broderick) meets and becomes an ally to a dark knight whose constant companion is a hawk. The knight and his lady are the victims of an evil curse, where she is cursed into becoming a hawk by day and he into a wolf by night. Together all three embark on a quest to destroy the curse that tortures them by destroying the one who cast it. Very strong period flavor. Very well done and entertaining.

A: Matthew Broderick, Rutger Hauer, Michelle Pfeiffer, Leo McKern, John Wood, Ken Hutchison

© WARNER HOME VIDEO 11464

LADY IN RED

D: Lewis Teague — 90 m

R | CRM ACT | 1979 | COLOR | Sex Nud Viol Lang AdSit

7 Pamela Sue Martin puts in a very effective performance as a naive farm girl who escapes child abuse to enter into prostitution in Chicago during the 1920s. After a run-in with the law and jail time, she enters into service at a fancy bordello and there becomes the mistress of famous gangster John Dillinger. The FBI and her madame set her up to betray Dillinger and he is killed in a famous shoot-out at the Biograph Theater. Thereafter, she turns to a life of crime herself. Very fast-paced, with lots of blood, shoot-outs, sex and car chases. Effective and well done. Also see DILLINGER.

A: Pamela Sue Martin, Robert Conrad, Louise Fletcher, Robert Hogan, Laurie Heineman, Glenn Withrow

© LIVE HOME VIDEO VA4046

LA FEMME NIKITA

D: Luc Parriland — 117 m

R | FOR ACT SUS | 1990 | COLOR | Sex Nud Viol Lang AdSit

9 Action-filled, exotic, intelligent and thoroughly fascinating psychological character study of a supremely unique nature. Nikita is a profoundly lost young woman who is convicted of committing an extremely ruthless murder. But, after receiving a life sentence, the government fakes her suicide and enters her into an ultra-secret training program for assassins. There, her life gains a perverse meaning and focus, but she also gains an appreciation for the life she doesn't have. Haunting. Dubbed or subtitles. Beginning is very odd. Released in an Americanized version as POINT OF NO RETURN.

A: Anne Parriland, Jeanne Moreau, Tcheky Karyo, Jean Hugues Anglade

© VIDMARK ENTERTAINMENT 5471

LAGUNA HEAT

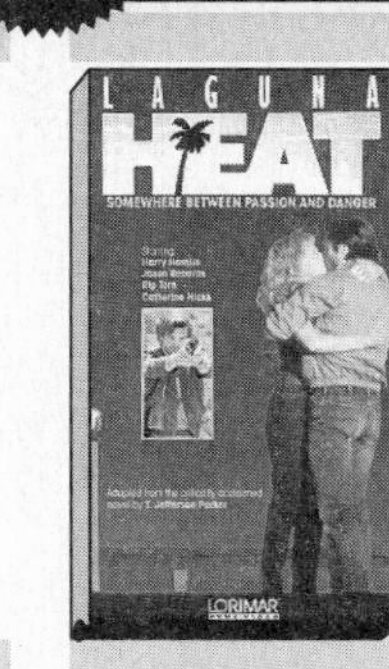

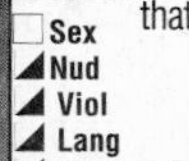
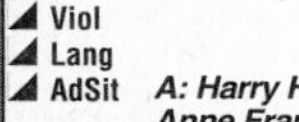
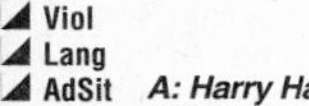
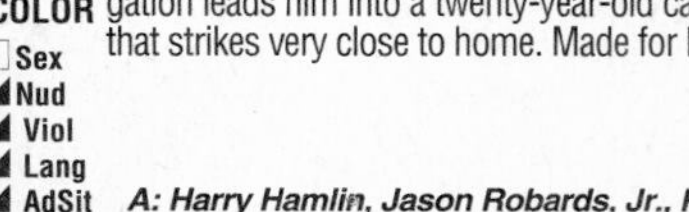

D: Simon Langton — 110 m

NR | MYS CRM ACT | 1987 | COLOR | Sex Nud Viol Lang AdSit

6 Witty mystery with a fair dose of action. Harry Hamlin, an L.A. detective who leaves his job after his divorce and the murder of his partner, has moved in with his father in a small coastal town. The town's peaceful facade is destroyed by two brutal murders tied to friends of his father's. Hamlin is drawn into the investigation when he gets involved with the daughter of one of the victims. Hamlin's investigation leads him into a twenty-year-old case of murder and corruption that strikes very close to home. Made for HBO cable TV.

A: Harry Hamlin, Jason Robards, Jr., Rip Torn, Catherine Hicks, Anne Francis

© WARNER HOME VIDEO 822

LAST AMERICAN HERO, THE

D: Lamont Johnson — 95 m

PG | ACT COM | 1973 | COLOR | Sex Nud Viol Lang AdSit

7 Underrated and interesting sports action film based on the life of real-life stock car racer, Junior Jackson, played by Jeff Bridges. He plays a guy who switches from running moonshine and racing Feds in North Carolina, to racing stock cars on the professional circuit so that he can raise enough money to hire a lawyer to help his moonshiner father. The hard-living driver rises through the pro ranks fast despite his unwillingness to do what the establishment wants him to do. Realistic racing sequences and three dimensional, believable characters make this an enjoyable experience.

A: Jeff Bridges, Valerie Perrine, Geraldine Fitzgerald, Art Lund, Gary Busey, Ned Beatty

© FOXVIDEO 1227

LAST MAN STANDING

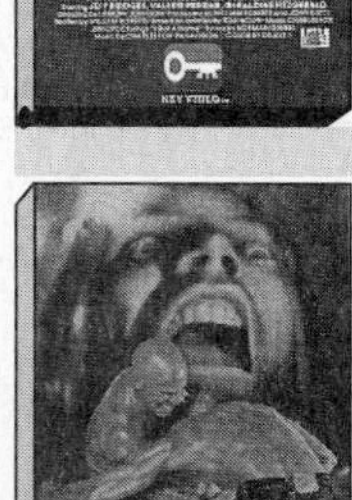

D: Damian Lee — 92 m

R | ACT | 1987 | COLOR | Sex Nud Viol Lang AdSit

6 Surprisingly good and underrated boxing film about a down-and-out fighter who tries to make it outside the ring but is unsuccessful and who then attempts a comeback in the brutal world of bare-knuckle boxing. Stars Vernon Wells, the villain from ROAD WARRIOR.

A: Vernon Wells, William Sanderson, Franco Columbu

© ACADEMY ENTERTAINMENT 1105

LAST OF THE MOHICANS, THE

D: Michael Mann — 114 m

R | WST ROM ACT | 1992 | COLOR | Sex Nud Viol Lang AdSit

10 Gorgeously photographed version of James Fenimore Cooper's classic story, set in northern New York during the mid-1700s, at the time of the French and Indian War. Hawkeye and his adoptive Indian father and brother agree to lead an English girl and her sister to their father commanding a remote fort besieged by French and Indian troops. He and the girl fall in love but they are overwhelmed by the war that threatens to consume them. Impeccable period details and intense and realistic violence make believable the desperate plight of these young lovers struggling to survive. This film contains none of Hollywood's typical gloss but rather a gripping realism that is rare to film. Wow!

A: Daniel Day-Lewis, Madeleine Stowe, Russell Means, Eric Schweig, Jodhi May, Wes Studi

© FOXVIDEO 1986

LAST TRAIN FROM GUN HILL

D: John Sturges — 94 m

NR | WST ACT | 1959 | COLOR | Sex Nud Viol Lang AdSit

7 Exciting Western. Douglas is a sheriff who has tracked down his wife's murderer to a small town that is under the almost total domination of Antony Quinn, the one-time best friend of Douglas. The murderer is discovered to have been Quinn's only son (Holliman). Quinn does not want his son to go back with Douglas, but neither does he want to hurt his old friend. Still, Douglas is determined to get Holliman out of town and back home to stand trial and hang - no matter what the cost. Confrontation is inevitable. Intelligently done. Above average.

A: Kirk Douglas, Anthony Quinn, Carolyn Jones, Earl Holliman, Ziva Rodann, Brad Dexter

© STARMAKER ENTERTAINMENT INC. 1058

LAWNMOWER MAN, THE

D: Bret Leonard — 108 m

R | SF ACT | 1992 | COLOR | Sex Nud Viol Lang AdSit

7 Dazzling, glitzy, high-tech computer wizardry is both the theme and the substance of this film. Well-meaning scientist Pierce Brosnan has created the means to accelerate the power of the mind through a combination of chemicals and "virtual" reality - a form of reality created within a computer and projected into a mind. He uses a retarded landscaper, the Lawnmower Man, as a new subject after a chimp he had used for nasty government experiments had become violent. The Lawnmower Man is transformed from being a meek moron into a malevolent maniac. Super special effects.

A: Jeff Fahey, Pierce Brosnan, Jenny Wright, Mark Bringleson, Geoffrey Lewis, Jeremy Slate

© TURNER HOME ENTERTAINMENT N4092

LAWRENCE OF ARABIA

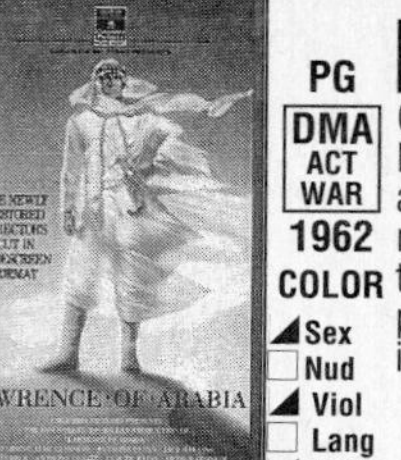

D: David Lean — 216 m

PG | DMA ACT WAR | 1962 | COLOR

10 A monumental accomplishment that fills the screen with majestic photography and gigantic spectacle. It was a winner of seven Oscars, including Best Picture, Director and Cinematography. Long before there was Operation Desert Storm (the 1991 Persian Gulf War), an enigmatic Englishman went into the deserts of Arabia and organized the scattered Arab tribes into an effective fighting force against the Ottoman Turks and the Germans during World War I. In the process, he created a new order in the Middle East and made himself into a legend. This one has everything: action, adventure and drama.

Sex / Nud / Viol / Lang / AdSit

A: Peter O'Toole, Alec Guinness, Anthony Quinn, Jack Hawkins, Claude Rains, Anthony Quayle

© COLUMBIA TRISTAR HOME VIDEO 50133

LEFT-HANDED GUN, THE

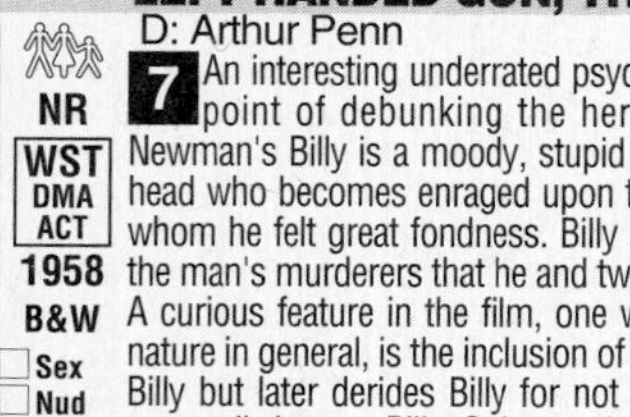

D: Arthur Penn — 1958 m

NR | WST DMA ACT | 1958 | B&W

7 An interesting underrated psychological Western which makes a point of debunking the hero-myth status of Billy the Kid. Newman's Billy is a moody, stupid and ruthless killer -- a lonely hothead who becomes enraged upon the murder of his boss, a man for whom he felt great fondness. Billy becomes so obsessed with killing the man's murderers that he and two others go on a wild killing spree. A curious feature in the film, one which comments upon on human nature in general, is the inclusion of a pulp writer who at first worships Billy but later derides Billy for not being the hero of his stories and eventually betrays Billy. Quite good.

Sex / Nud / Viol / Lang / AdSit

A: Paul Newman, Lita Milan, John Dehner, Hurd Hatfield, James Congdon, James Best

© WARNER HOME VIDEO 11067

LE MANS

D: Lee H. Katzin — 106 m

G | ACT | 1971 | COLOR

6 Exciting sports story about the famous 24-hour Grand Prix endurance auto race at Le Mans, France. Terrific photography intensifies the high-voltage racing atmosphere. Steve McQueen plays an American determined to rise above past calamities to capture the first place trophy. (McQueen raced in real life and did his own driving for the filming.)

Sex / Nud / Viol / Lang / AdSit

A: Steve McQueen, Siegfried Rauch, Elga Andersen

© CBS/FOX VIDEO 7156

LETHAL WEAPON

D: Richard Donner — 110 m

R | ACT CRM COM | 1987 | COLOR

10 Hugely popular high-voltage thriller which is fast, violent and funny. It owes its huge success to the unlikely chemistry of its two lead characters. One is an older, conservative family man and by-the-book cop (Glover). The other is a half-crazed lunatic cop (Gibson). When these guys discover that an apparent suicide is really a cover-up for a particularly raunchy drug ring, they set about destroying it with a vengeance. Very fast paced, with terrific action sequences and funny, with great chemistry between its two stars. It was followed by two very popular sequels.

Sex / Nud / Viol / Lang / AdSit

A: Mel Gibson, Danny Glover, Gary Busey, Mitchell Ryan, Tom Atkins, Darlene Love

© WARNER HOME VIDEO 11709

LETHAL WEAPON 2

D: Richard Donner — 114 m

R | ACT CRM COM | 1989 | COLOR

9 Action fans take note - they're back. Danny Glover and Mel Gibson reprised their roles as police partners - one normal, one a reckless lunatic. This time they are out to get some bad guy drug smugglers from South Africa, who are hiding behind diplomatic immunity, before the bad guys get mob accountant Joe Pesci. Wild and outlandish adventures ensue, loaded with lead-filled action, a little sex and a fair dose of laughs. Entertaining, but not at all believable. Still, this is fun. See also LETHAL WEAPON and LETHAL WEAPON 3.

Sex / Nud / Viol / Lang / AdSit

A: Mel Gibson, Danny Glover, Joe Pesci, Joss Ackland, Derrick O'Conner, Patsy Kensit

© WARNER HOME VIDEO 11876

LETHAL WEAPON 3

D: Richard Donner — 118 m

R | ACT CRM COM | 1992 | COLOR

7 True escapism - more from the hit cop combo of Gibson and Glover. Glover is straight-arrow family-man cop about to retire from the force but he is drawn back in to aid Gibson. They are tracking a cop gone bad who is now a major-league gun runner selling confiscated weapons to L.A. street gangs. The Hollywood folks pull out all the stops again. There is more of the fun glib comradery between the two, but there is also much more of the extravagant violence. The pairing is still good but it's getting a little old now.

Sex / Nud / Viol / Lang / AdSit

A: Mel Gibson, Danny Glover, Joe Pesci, Rene Russo, Stuart Wilson

© WARNER HOME VIDEO 12475

LICENCE TO KILL

D: John Glen — 133 m

PG-13 | ACT | 1989 | COLOR

8 One of the more serious of the James Bond flicks. This is the second outing with Timothy Dalton as Bond, and one of the best episodes since Sean Connery left the role. James defies his superiors when he takes revenge upon a Columbian drug lord, after the guy maims James's C.I.A. friend Felix Leiter and kills his bride. This is a tough Bond flick with lots of action, spectacular stunts and, of course, a sexy girl for Bond.

Sex / Nud / Viol / Lang / AdSit

A: Timothy Dalton, Carey Lowell, Robert Davi, Talsa Soto, Anthony Zerbe, Wayne Newton

© CBS/FOX VIDEO 4755

LIFE AND TIMES OF JUDGE ROY BEAN, THE

D: John Huston — 124 m

PG | WST COM ACT | 1972 | COLOR

8 Definitely strange but a fun Western with some really funny moments. Paul Newman creates a movie-variation on the real-life character Judge Roy Bean, who was famed as being a hanging judge. Newman's Bean rules over a two-bit Texas town like a lord, having run-ins (sometimes comical) with various odd-ball characters who stumble into his path. Stacy Keach is outstanding among these as the ferocious albino bad guy, Bad Bob. Filled with cameos by some of Hollywood's best. Very enjoyable even though sometimes it slows down too much.

Sex / Nud / Viol / Lang / AdSit

A: Paul Newman, Stacy Keach, Victoria Principal, Jacqueline Bisset, Ava Gardner, Anthony Perkins

© WARNER HOME VIDEO 11174

LIGHTHORSEMEN, THE

D: Simon Wincer — 116 m

PG | WAR ACT DMA | 1988 | COLOR

7 Stirring true story. Sweeping and episodic adventure which explores the lives of four Australian friends as they prepare for a decisive battle in WWI. The thrilling climax is a march through the desert by 800 Australian calvarymen who then mount a surprise calvary attack upon thousands of German and Turkish soldiers in a desert fortress. An impossible mission, but one which changed the course of history. A rousing and exciting calvary charge at the end makes up for its other slower and contemplative moments.

Sex / Nud / Viol / Lang / AdSit

A: Jon Blake, Peter Phelps, Tony Bonner, Bill Kerr, John Walton, Sigrid Thornton

© WARNER HOME VIDEO 762

LION OF THE DESERT

D: Moustapha Akkad — 164 m

PG | WAR ACT | 1979 | COLOR

8 An epic-scale film, based on the true story of a Bedouin teacher, Omar Mukhtar, who, at age 51, rose up to lead his people against the colonizing Italian armies of Mussolini (Steiger), led by a vicious general (Reed). Mukhtar (Quinn) led Bedouins on foot and on horseback in a guerrilla war against the mechanized Italian armies for twenty years until the Italians finally caught him and hung him. This is an impressive large-scale movie with high production values and well-staged battle scenes, but it is quite long.

Sex / Nud / Viol / Lang / AdSit

A: Anthony Quinn, Oliver Reed, Raf Vallone, Rod Steiger, John Gielgud

© LIVE HOME VIDEO 64104

LITTLE DRUMMER GIRL, THE

D: George Roy Hill — 130 m

R | ACT SUS | 1984 | COLOR

7 Intricate espionage thriller. Keaton is an outspoken actress and a Palestinian advocate. However, Israeli intelligence convinces her to become their double agent, involving her in plots of blackmail and terrorism. In actuality, she is being used as bait to catch a Palestinian terrorist. John Le Carre's brilliant and very complex novel is jam-packed into just over two hours. There is a lot to follow, and by trying to leave as much of the plot in as possible, much of the character development and involvement is lost - still, it holds your interest throughout.

Sex / Nud / Viol / Lang / AdSit

A: Diane Keaton, Yorgo Voyagis, Klaus Kinski, Sami Frey, Michael Cristofer

© WARNER HOME VIDEO 11416

LIVE AND LET DIE

D: Guy Hamilton — 123 m

PG | ACT | 1973 | COLOR

7 This is the first James Bond episode with Roger Moore as Bond. It is an interesting and fun excursion, but has a cartoonish plot. Bond is after a Caribbean diplomat Dr. Kanaga (Kotto), who is actually a drug kingpin intent upon giving away tons of heroin free, with the ultimate goal of creating a huge supply of junkies that he can then supply. Bond chases him in Harlem, his Caribbean island and through the swamps of Louisiana in a spectacular very high speed boat chase - "helped" by a good-ol'-boy sheriff. Seymore is Bond's love interest and Kotto's fortune-teller.

Sex / Nud / Viol / Lang / AdSit

A: Roger Moore, Yaphet Kotto, Jane Seymour, Clifton James, Geoffrey Holder

Distributed By MGM/UA Home Video M201418

LIVING DAYLIGHTS, THE

D: John Glen 131 m

PG | ACT | 1987 | COLOR

8 One of the best of the later James Bond films. It is the sixteenth in the series and Dalton is the fourth James Bond. This Bond is more mature in his attitudes and the plot is much less comic book in tone than many of the other recent entries. Bond is sent to help a KGB general (who turns out to be a double agent) and a pretty cellist escape over the Iron Curtain. Bond then gets involved with a crazy American gunrunner and a plot to smuggle tons of opium out of Afghanistan. Good and credible adventure.

Sex | Nud | Viol | Lang | AdSit

A: Timothy Dalton, Maryann d'Abo, Jeroen Krabbe, Joe Don Baker, John Rhys-Davies, Art Malik

Distributed By MGM/UA Home Video M202529

LOGAN'S RUN

D: Michael Anderson 119 m

PG | SF ACT | 1976 | COLOR

6 An intelligent adventure set in a strange futuristic society. Logan (York) is a policeman living and working in a carefree hedonistic domed city. His particular job is chasing down "runners" - individuals who run away rather than comply with a law requiring that they be "renewed" at age 30. This is an elaborate ceremony, after which the participants are never seen again. Facing his own renewal, York and and a girl escape outside the dome to discover another world that no one knew even existed. And it includes an old man (Ustinov) - something neither has ever seen or known to be possible. Entertaining.

Sex | Nud | Viol | Lang | AdSit

A: Michael York, Richard Jordan, Jenny Agutter, Farrah Fawcett, Peter Ustinov, Roscoe Lee Browne

Distributed By MGM/UA Home Video M600012

LONELY ARE THE BRAVE

D: David Miller 107 m

NR | WST DMA ACT | 1962 | B&W

8 A superb and penetrating character study. An easy-going 20th-century cowboy (Kirk Douglas) wants to help his friend break out of jail, so he gets into a bar fight and punches a cop. Now that he's in jail, his friend doesn't want to leave. Faced with the possibility of a year in prison, Douglas escapes from jail and heads into the hills on horseback. But the modern-day cops, headed up by Matthau, chase him down with help from trucks, helicopters and walkie-talkies. As the chase develops, Matthau gains respect for and begins to like his quarry. Good flick. Well done. One of Douglas's personal favorites.

Sex | Nud | Viol | Lang | AdSit

A: Kirk Douglas, Gena Rowlands, Walter Matthau, Michael Kane, Carroll O'Connor, George Kennedy

© MCA/UNIVERSAL HOME VIDEO, INC. 80143

LONESOME DOVE

D: Simon Wincer 372 m

NR | WST DMA ACT | 1990 | COLOR

10 Absolutely brilliant and totally engrossing made-for-TV miniseries adapted from Larry McMurtry's Pulitzer Prize-winning novel. This is an entirely believable, sweeping saga of two Texas Rangers who have out-lived their pioneering era in Texas. So, they strike out for Montana with a herd of cattle, intent upon establishing the first ranch in that virgin land. Striking performances by the entire cast paint a rich tapestry of colorful characters, adventure and romance in a realistically depicted Old West. A wonderful, totally involving, not-to-be-missed adventure.

Sex | Nud | Viol | Lang | AdSit

A: Robert Duvall, Tommy Lee Jones, Robert Urich, Danny Glover, Diane Lane, Ricky Schroder

© CABIN FEVER ENTERTAINMENT CF8371

LONE WOLF MCQUADE

D: Steve Carver 107 m

PG | ACT | 1983 | COLOR

8 Kung Fu verses karate. Chuck Norris is a maverick Texas Ranger who ignores the rules and so gets assigned to a new partner in the hopes that it will tame him down. Together they uncover a gun-running ring, led by bad guy David Carradine, which steals weapons from the Army and sells them to Central American terrorists. You'll see just about every kind of vicious weapon there is. The film is topped off by the climactic event of Norris and Carradine in a martial arts battle to the death. An action fan's delight.

Sex | Nud | Viol | Lang | AdSit

A: Chuck Norris, David Carradine, Barbara Carrera, Leon Isaac Kennedy, Robert Beltran

© GOODTIMES 5-74067

LONGEST DAY, THE

D: Ken Annakin, Andrew Marton 175 m

G | WAR ACT DMA | 1962 | B&W

9 Monumental epic war film documenting the massive invasion of Europe in WWII. 43 of Hollywood's biggest stars fill roles, big and small, to portray in detail the many events of D-Day. The story is essentially told in three parts: the planning; the behind-the-lines activities of the resistance forces and the initial paratrooper assault; and, the massive landings on the beaches of Normandy, France. The big story is evoked through a series of smaller stories from the many people involved. Spectacular!

Sex | Nud | Viol | Lang | AdSit

A: John Wayne, Robert Mitchum, Henry Fonda, Richard Burton, Rod Steiger, Sean Connery

© FOXVIDEO 1021

LONGEST YARD, THE

D: Robert Aldrich 121 m

R | COM ACT | 1974 | COLOR

9 Rousing and engaging comedy that is one of Reynolds's best efforts. He plays an ex-pro football quarterback sent to prison for stealing his girlfriend's car. Eddie Albert is a currupt prison warden who has created a semi-pro football team out of his prison guards. He is very proud of them and wants Reynolds to set up a prisoner-based team to play his guards and lose. What follows instead is a series of bone-crushing laughs as the prisoners get even with the guards. A great audience pleaser, in which we all root for the prisoners in a brutal football game that takes up 47 minutes of screen time.

Sex | Nud | Viol | Lang | AdSit

A: Burt Reynolds, Eddie Albert, Ed Lauter, Michael Conrad, James Hampton, Bernadette Peters

© PARAMOUNT HOME VIDEO 8708

LONG GOODBYE, THE

D: Robert Altman 113 m

R | MYS SUS ACT | 1973 | COLOR

7 Entertaining and stylish detective yarn based on the classic 1940s PI- character, Philip Marlowe, but updated to the 1970s with many interesting and off-beat twists added. Gould's Marlowe is a New York Jew out of step in hip, me-oriented California. It is frequently funny, but also remains an intense, action oriented mystery of the old school. Marlowe attempts to get an old friend released from a charge that he murdered his wife. A really off-the-wall ending.

Sex | Nud | Viol | Lang | AdSit

A: Elliott Gould, Sterling Hayden, Mark Rydell, Henry Gibson, Jim Bouton, Nina Van Pallandt

Distributed By MGM/UA Home Video M201409

LONG RIDERS, THE

D: Walter Hill 100 m

R | WST ACT | 1980 | COLOR

8 Excellent and intriguing Western about the famed James/Younger outlaw gang of the late 1800s that is historically fairly accurate. The film is long on action, short on plot, has an obscure moral and it is quite violent. However, it also contains the very interesting and very effective gimmick of having real-life brothers play the brothers of the gang. The Carradines are the Youngers, the Keaches are Frank and Jessie James and the Quaids are the Ford brothers. See also THE GREAT NORTHFIELD MINNESOTA RAID.

Sex | Nud | Viol | Lang | AdSit

A: David Carradine, Keith Carradine, Robert Carradine, Stacy Keach, James Keach, Dennis Quaid

Distributed By MGM/UA Home Video M600454

LORD JIM

D: Richard Brooks 154 m

NR | DMA ACT | 1965 | COLOR

8 Intriguing adaptation of a complex novel by Joseph Conrad. Many of the story's elements have been reduced or eliminated for the screen, but what remains is still rewarding. O'Toole is fascinating as a former British navel officer who forever clouds his record with one act of cowardice. Then, he receives a second chance to redeem his honor after being adopted by the native villagers on a small South Sea island. However, he is about to be put to the test by an invading group of Europeans.

Sex | Nud | Viol | Lang | AdSit

A: Peter O'Toole, James Mason, Curt Jurgens, Eli Wallach, Jack Hawkins, Paul Lukas

© COLUMBIA TRISTAR HOME VIDEO 60042

LOST COMMAND, THE

D: Mark Robson 129 m

NR | ACT WAR | 1966 | COLOR

7 Taut war actioner, with a good international cast. A group of French soldiers escape in defeat from French Indochina (Vietnam) after WWII. The group's disgraced leader (Quinn) has been relieved of all command. However, he gets one more chance to redeem himself when he is sent to fight against the guerrilla warfare breaking out in North African Algeria. He is determined to redeem himself at any cost and launches a bloody attack against the rebel forces led by Arab terrorist leader Segal. Some top notch action scenes

Sex | Nud | Viol | Lang | AdSit

A: Anthony Quinn, Alain Delon, George Segal, Michele Morgan, Claudia Cardinale

© COLUMBIA TRISTAR HOME VIDEO 60948

MADIGAN

D: Don Siegel 101 m

NR | CRM ACT | 1968 | COLOR

8 Realistic, hard-hitting action! Madigan (Widmark), is a tough cop, but he's in double trouble. In an attempt to capture a killer, he and his partner break in on a psychopathic killer, but they're momentarily distracted by a naked girl and the killer gets away. Hardball Commissioner Russell (Fonda) is outraged and gives Madigan only 72 hours to catch the guy. Madigan is hard-pressed but his socialite wife also is pressuring him to quit the police work he loves. Critically acclaimed for its revealing look into the workings of New York City detectives - its popularity launched the TV series.

Sex | Nud | Viol | Lang | AdSit

A: Richard Widmark, Henry Fonda, Inger Stevens, Harry Guardino, James Whitmore

© MCA/UNIVERSAL HOME VIDEO, INC. 80040

MAD MAX

D: George Miller — 90 m

R | ACT FAN | 1980 | COLOR

9 Excitement plus! This film began a trend and set the precedent for many action films (and sequels) to follow. Gibson stars as Max, a tough cop in post-nuclear Australia. The frustrated cop resigns his post, but when his wife and child are brutally murdered by a vagrant motorcycle gang, Max explodes back onto the scene with a vengeance. Weird surrealistic atmosphere and characters, plus extreme violence, made this one of the most successful Australian films of all time. Unbelievable stunt work and unusual atmosphere will keep you glued!

Sex Nud Viol Lang AdSit

A: Mel Gibson, Joanne Samuel, Tim Burns, Steve Bisley, Hugh Keays-Byrne, Roger Ward

© GOODTIMES 5-04051

MAD MAX BEYOND THUNDERDOME

D: George Miller, George Ogilvie — 107 m

PG-13 | ACT FAN | 1985 | COLOR

7 Superhero Max is back! Max enters ruthless Bartertown, run by Aunty Entity (Turner), where everything is traded - including lives. Aunty Entity sends Max to a battle in the Thunderdome with Blaster. When Max refuses, he is banished to the cruel desert to die. However, he is saved by a small band of orphans who believe him to be the messiah they have been waiting for. The big highlight is the thrilling fight scene when Max and Blaster finally do meet in the Thunderdome. Director Miller does a superb job of transforming Max into a mythological savior in this post-apocalypse adventure.

Sex Nud Viol Lang AdSit

A: Mel Gibson, Tina Turner, Bruce Spence, Helen Buday, Rod Zuanic, Angelo Rossitto

© WARNER HOME VIDEO 11519

MAGNIFICENT SEVEN, THE

D: John Sturges — 129 m

NR | WST ACT | 1960 | COLOR

9 Classic shoot-'em-up!!! Recurring raids from a small army of bandits inspire a delegation from a small Mexican town to seek out help from gunfighter Yul Brynner. Brynner rounds up six other misfits like himself, and together they redeem themselves by helping the people to banish the terrorizing banditos and to reestablish pride in the town. A direct American remake of the Japanese classic THE SEVEN SAMAURI, this immensely popular Western spawned three sequels. Except for Brynner, the other six hombres were unknowns at the time, and went on to become sought-after stars.

Sex Nud Viol Lang AdSit

A: Yul Brynner, Eli Wallach, Steve McQueen, Horst Buchholz, James Coburn, Charles Bronson

Distributed By MGM/UA Home Video M201268

MAGNUM FORCE

D: Ted Post — 122 m

R | ACT CRM | 1973 | COLOR

8 Very popular gritty action! Dirty Harry Callahan has a dirty police department. Someone is slowly killing off all the crime leaders in the City by the Bay. Harry discovers that the killers are none other than San Francisco's finest, taking short-cuts. Tired of the endless delays and red tape that go along with bringing the bad guys in the legal way, these guys just execute the bad guys on the spot. Holbrook is the head cop of the vigilante ring. He is also Harry's superior - and he hates Harry. Lots of fast macho action, with a good bit of humor thrown in, too.

Sex Nud Viol Lang AdSit

A: Clint Eastwood, Hal Holbrook, David Soul, Robert Urich, Mitchell Ryan, Felton Perry

© WARNER HOME VIDEO 1039

MAJOR DUNDEE

D: Sam Peckinpah — 124 m

NR | WST ACT | 1965 | COLOR

7 Lavishly produced Western in which Charlton Heston plays the title character, who is the warden of a Union Army prison that has been attacked by Apaches. He organizes his regulars and some prisoner volunteers (including a Confederate group whose leader, Richard Harris, is under a sentence of death) to chase the raiding party into Mexico. Complicated characters unduly confuse the plot, but the star power and the action is such that you will enjoy it anyway. The confusion resulted from director Peckinpah being removed. See also THE WILD BUNCH for many similarities.

Sex Nud Viol Lang AdSit

A: Charlton Heston, Richard Harris, Jim Hutton, James Coburn, Michael Anderson, Jr., Senta Berger

© COLUMBIA TRISTAR HOME VIDEO VH10370

MAN CALLED HORSE, A

D: Elliot Silverstein — 115 m

PG | WST DMA ACT | 1970 | COLOR

10 Powerful and thoroughly engrossing story of a haughty British aristocrat (Harris) who is captured by Sioux Indians while hunting in 1830s Dakotas. He is made into a slave by them, humiliated and then just ignored. He rebels, proving his manhood by undergoing a brutal tribal ritual called a sun dance (graphically shown). With his haughty noble exterior gone, his inner strength is unearthed, and he earns his way as a powerful and respected leader of the group. A gripping and realistic depiction of American Indian communal life. See also RETURN OF A MAN CALLED HORSE and DANCES WITH WOLVES.

Sex Nud Viol Lang AdSit

A: Richard Harris, Judith Anderson, Manu Tupou, Jean Gascon, Corinna Tsopei, Dub Taylor

© FOXVIDEO 7148

MAN FROM SNOWY RIVER, THE

D: George Miller — 104 m

G | WST ACT ROM | 1982 | COLOR

8 A rousing cinematic treat for the whole family! This is a beautiful and rousing adventure story that is based on a well-known Australian poem. An independent young man is hired by a wealthy cattle rancher in Australia's wilderness of the 1880s. He falls in love with the cattleman's daughter, but is not accepted by her father (Douglas - in a dual role, also as the father's maverick brother). The film culminates in a wild chase through mountainous terrain to capture a herd of wild horses, led by a magnificent stallion. Thrilling. Stunning scenery. Pretty good sequel in RETURN TO SNOWY RIVER.

Sex Nud Viol Lang AdSit

A: Kirk Douglas, Tom Burlinson, Terence Donovan, Sigrid Thornton, Jack Thompson, Lorraine Bayly

© FOXVIDEO 1233

MANHUNTER

D: Michael Mann — 120 m

R | CRM SUS ACT | 1986 | COLOR

9 Excellent! An ex-FBI agent (Peterson) is recalled to track a ruthless serial killer who is murdering entire families in the southeast. The psychopathic madman (Noonan) gets the name "The Tooth Fairy" for sadistically appropriate reasons. Clever and ever elusive, the only way Peterson can catch this crazed psycho is to actually think like the killer would - to get inside his head. This is the same method used in the later SILENCE OF THE LAMBS and in real life by the FBI. Very contemporary in style, with hard pounding music, this crime drama will take hold of you and won't let go.

Sex Nud Viol Lang AdSit

A: William L. Petersen, Kim Greist, Brian Cox, Dennis Farina, Stephen Lang, Tom Noonan

© WARNER HOME VIDEO 411

MAN IN THE IRON MASK, THE

D: Mike Newell — 108 m

NR | ACT DMA | 1977 | COLOR

8 Excellent and quite opulent made-for-TV movie of the classic and timeless tale from Alexander Dumas. Phillipe is one of two royal twin brothers. He is the rightful heir to the throne but is confined at birth to a remote island, and is there forced to wear an iron mask so no one will ever know his true identity. His foppish brother Louis is made king, but the real power rests with Finance Minister Fouget. France is corrupt. Captain D'Artagnan and another minister conspire to free Phillipe from prison so that he may publicly challenge Louis. Grand entertainment for the whole family.

Sex Nud Viol Lang AdSit

A: Richard Chamberlain, Patrick McGoohan, Louis Jourdan, Jenny Agutter, Vivien Merchant, Ian Holm

© LIVE HOME VIDEO 69940

MAN WHO SHOT LIBERTY VALANCE, THE

D: John Ford — 123 m

NR | WST ACT | 1962 | B&W

9 Excellent adult Western. Stewart stars as an idealistic Eastern-minded lawyer who wants to end the reign of terror of a ruthless killer, Liberty Valance (Marvin) in the lawless West. But the only tool he has is his lawbooks. Lawbooks aren't going to stop Liberty Valance. Stewart and tough rancher John Wayne compete for the love of pretty Vera Miles. Because Miles loves Stewart, and because Wayne knows that civilization must come and men like Stewart will make it happen, Wayne helps Stewart to defeat Valance, turning him into a hero. John Ford's last black and white Western packs a punch!

Sex Nud Viol Lang AdSit

A: James Stewart, John Wayne, Lee Marvin, Vera Miles, Edmond O'Brien, Andy Devine

© PARAMOUNT HOME VIDEO 6114

MAN WHO WOULD BE KING, THE

D: John Huston — 128 m

PG | ACT DMA | 1975 | COLOR

9 Excellent, rousing Rudyard Kipling adventure like they used to make! Two British ex-soldiers (Connery and Caine), in the fading days of colonial England, head to Kafiristan to plunder it and become rich. Connery is struck by an arrow in the chest but it hits a medal he wears and, when he just pulls the arrow out, the people declare him a god. The two soldiers enjoy their good fortune. Soon Caine wishes to leave but Connery likes being King. However, their deception is soon uncovered and they are ruined. Garnered four Oscar nominations. Caine and Connery are magic.

Sex Nud Viol Lang AdSit

A: Sean Connery, Michael Caine, Christopher Plummer, Saeed Jaffrey, Shakira Caine

© FOXVIDEO 7435

MAN WITH THE GOLDEN GUN, THE

D: Guy Hamilton — 127 m

PG | ACT | 1974 | COLOR

7 Golden action! Ninth in the series, Fleming's adaptation places 007 (Moore) in a desperate fight to retrieve the world's only solar harnessing device, the "Solex." The bad guy Scaramanga (Christopher Lee) has the device installed on his remote island retreat. The clue that leads Bond to the assassin's hideaway is the trail of an assassin's exotic weapon. This one is not as gadget-crazy as some of the others, but there are pandemonious chase scenes and car stunts, as well as beautiful scenery. A Pink Panther animated short adds to the amusement.

Sex Nud Viol Lang AdSit

A: Roger Moore, Christopher Lee, Britt Ekland, Maud Adams, Herve Villechaize, Clifton James

Distributed By MGM/UA Home Video M201419

MARATHON MAN

D: John Schlesinger 125 m

R | ACT SUS | 1976 | COLOR | Sex | Nud | ■ Viol | ◢ Lang | ■ AdSit

8 So tense your teeth will hurt. Hoffman stars a student who runs marathons. But he gets caught in the middle of a Nazi crime ring when his brother (Scheider) helps to sneak into the country an old Nazi, Christian Szell (Olivier), whose brother is guarding a horde of jewels that were taken from Jewish prisoners. But, when Olivier's brother dies, he kills Hoffman's brother and begins to torture Hoffman (in a famous scene with a dentist's drill) for information that he thinks he has, but doesn't. Then Hoffman escapes and the hunted becomes the hunter. Excellent. Olivier was Oscar-nominated.

A: Dustin Hoffman, Laurence Olivier, Marthe Keller, Roy Scheider, William Devane, Fritz Weaver

© PARAMOUNT HOME VIDEO 8789

MARLOWE

D: Paul Bogart 96 m

PG | MYS ACT | 1969 | COLOR | Sex | Nud | Viol | ◢ Lang | ◢ AdSit

8 Entertaining and intriguing mystery. The infamous Marlowe (Garner) is a hard-boiled detective who is hired by a girl (Farrell) to find her missing brother. Garner quickly finds that he has gotten more than he bargained for when kung fu king Bruce Lee (in his film debut) offers him a bribe to drop the case and then turns his office into a pile of broken sticks as a warning. There is blackmail, ice pick murders and a stripper (Moreno) who ultimately helps to solve the case. A good mystery is combined with clever dialogue to make this a real fun time. Based on the Chandler novel "The Little Sister."

A: James Garner, Gayle Hunnicutt, Carroll O'Connor, Rita Moreno, Sharon Farrell, Bruce Lee

Distributed By MGM/UA Home Video M200283

MASADA

D: Boris Sagal 131 m

NR | DMA ACT | 1984 | COLOR | Sex | Nud | Viol | Lang | ◢ AdSit

9 Excellent and moving epic drama of bravery and strength in this film dramatic depiction of a true event. In 70 A.D., a Roman general (O'Toole) is ordered to crush the Jewish uprising in Israel, and he does... Jerusalem is destroyed. However, a rebel zealot leader (Strauss) leads of a group of 980 zealots in an escape to Herod the Great's fortress palace high on Mt. Masada. There they hold out valiantly against 10,000 Roman soldiers in a prolonged 3-year Roman siege. Based on Ernest K. Gann's novel, this dramatic story was made into a very popular TV miniseries. O'Toole and Strauss deliver fine performances.

A: Peter O'Toole, Peter Strauss, Barbara Carrera

© MCA/UNIVERSAL HOME VIDEO, INC. 66125

MCCABE AND MRS. MILLER

D: Robert Altman 121 m

R | WST ACT | 1971 | COLOR | ◢ Sex | ◢ Nud | ■ Viol | ■ Lang | ■ AdSit

8 It is the turn of the century in the Pacific Northwest. McCabe (Beatty) is a small-time gambler and braggart with big ambitions who rides into a remote pioneer town. There he meets Mrs. Miller (Christie), a pretty madam who is motivated by money and who also has an entourage of expensive whores. She and McCabe become partners in a bordello, but its remarkable success attracts some big-time hoods, who intend to either buy it or steal it. Beautifully photographed, this story is a very realistic Western which takes much of the glamour from the time and out of its subject matter. Interesting.

A: Warren Beatty, Julie Christie, Rene Auberjonois, Keith Carradine, John Schuck, Bert Remsen

© WARNER HOME VIDEO 11055

MCQ

D: John Sturges 111 m

PG | ACT CRM | 1974 | COLOR | Sex | Nud | ■ Viol | ◢ Lang | ◢ AdSit

7 Wayne trades in his Old West six-shooters for a police badge in this fast-paced and suspenseful cop-action flick. A tough police lieutenant, Wayne goes after two drug dealers who killed his best friend on the force. His investigation leads him to a lonely barmaid (Dewhurst) and a villainous drug dealer, but he also uncovers a lot more when it turns out that many of his old friends on the force, including his ex-partner, are up to their eyes in dirty deeds, too. His new knowledge has put him in a very undesirable position. No shortage of action here. Good DIRTY HARRY-style shoot-'em-up.

A: John Wayne, Eddie Albert, Diana Muldaur, Colleen Dewhurst, Clu Gulager, David Huddleston

© WARNER HOME VIDEO 11140

MECHANIC, THE

D: Michael Winner 101 m

PG | ACT CRM | 1972 | COLOR | Sex | Nud | ◢ Viol | ◢ Lang | ◢ AdSit

8 Bronson is the ultimate professional assassin. There is no job or individual that he can't execute. He is a mafia favorite and they are his regular customer. Vincent is young, cold-blooded and interested in learning the business, so he went to the best. Bronson is wary and not keen on letting anyone into his private world, yet he is lonely and there is something about Vincent that draws him in. Vincent does become his protege, going along on a series of hits, and learns well -- maybe too well. Good action, good script and a good twist.

A: Charles Bronson, Jan-Michael Vincent, Keenan Wynn, Jill Ireland, Linda Ridgeway

Distributed By MGM/UA Home Video M201259

MEDICINE MAN

D: John McTiernan 105 m

PG-13 | DMA ACT | 1992 | COLOR | Sex | Nud | ◢ Viol | ◢ Lang | ◢ AdSit

6 Connery is a brilliant scientist who has found the cure for cancer in the Brazilian rain forest. He has created the serum once, but he can't duplicate it so he sends for a noted research assistant to come. Instead he gets Bracco, a tough-talking female scientist from the Bronx. Sparks fly between them as they try to find the missing element in the serum, but their attentions quickly turn instead to the rapidly burning rain forest which is threatening to destroy all of their work, plus the cure. The muddled script is saved only by Connery's presence.

A: Sean Connery, Lorraine Bracco, Jose Wilker

© HOLLYWOOD PICTURES HOME VIDEO 1358

MEMPHIS BELLE

D: Michael Caton-Jones 107 m

PG-13 | DMA WAR ACT | 1990 | COLOR | Sex | Nud | ◢ Viol | ◢ Lang | ◢ AdSit

8 Flying a bombing raid over Germany was about the most dangerous thing a man could do in WWII. The B-17 Memphis Belle had already flown 24 missions beating the odds. This next one would be its last and its last flight was being immortalized by a documentary for a bond drive, but its crew, all young men just barely out of their teens, don't care. They just want to get that last mission behind them and go home. Involving and entertaining. The film builds slowly, letting us get to know the characters. Then the last mission comes. Terrific air action. Also see TWELVE O'CLOCK HIGH.

A: Matthew Modine, Eric Stoltz, Billy Zane, Tate Donovan, Harry Connick, Jr., D.B. Sweeney

© WARNER HOME VIDEO 12040

MIAMI BLUES

D: George Armitage 97 m

R | CRM ACT | 1990 | COLOR | ◢ Sex | ◢ Nud | ■ Viol | ■ Lang | ■ AdSit

6 Intense drama with a dark comedic edge. Junior (Baldwin), is a psychopath, fresh out of prison. He moves to Miami and immediately kills a Hare Krishna at the airport. At a local hotel, he orders up a hooker and gets a not-too-bright girl named Pepper (Leigh), but the two like each other and attempt to settle down. A tough detective (Ward) is assigned the job of finding the airport murderer and quickly tracks down Junior, but Junior beats him up, steals his badge, gun and false teeth. Excessively violent and uneven, but also a very curious film with very unusual characters.

A: Alec Baldwin, Fred Ward, Jennifer Jason Leigh, Nora Dunn, Charles Napier, Obba Babatunde

© ORION PICTURES CORPORATION 8746

MIAMI VICE

D: Thomas Carter 99 m

NR | CRM ACT | 1984 | COLOR | Sex | Nud | ◢ Viol | Lang | ◢ AdSit

8 A lot of glamor, style and slam-bang action came with this pilot for the extremely popular and long-running TV series which followed during the late '80s. Tubbs (Thomas), is a New York cop who is after the drug kingpin who killed his brother. The trail of the killer leads him to Miami, where he runs headlong into Sonny Crockett (Johnson), a Miami cop hot on the trail of the same killer. The hard-driving contemporary music and rapid editing, along with the great screen personas of the two principle characters, set a new style for youth-oriented action films to come.

A: Don Johnson, Philip Michael Thomas, Saundra Santiago

© MCA/UNIVERSAL HOME VIDEO, INC. 80133

MIDNIGHT RUN

D: Martin Brest 125 m

R | COM ACT | 1988 | COLOR | Sex | Nud | ◢ Viol | ■ Lang | ◢ AdSit

8 Ex-cop and now bounty hunter Robert De Niro accepts a deceptively easy assignment. All he has to do is deliver a bail jumper from New York to L.A. on time and he'll get $100,000 for his troubles. Boy, has he got troubles! The bail jumper is a mild mannered ex-mob accountant (Grodin) who has embezzled $15 million from the mob and given it to charity. The mob wants him dead, and the FBI wants him before the mob gets to him. If that isn't enough trouble, Grodin never shuts up. The charismatic personalities of De Niro and Grodin blend to a make this a wonderful mix of fun.

A: Robert De Niro, Charles Grodin, John Ashton, Dennis Farina, Yaphet Kotto, Joe Pantoliano

© MCA/UNIVERSAL HOME VIDEO, INC. 80810

MIDWAY

D: Jack Smight 132 m

PG | WAR ACT | 1976 | COLOR | Sex | Nud | ◢ Viol | ◢ Lang | ◢ AdSit

7 Compelling war drama. Only six-months after the Japanese successful attack at Pearl Harbor, American naval and air forces delivered a crushing defeat to the overconfident Japanese Navy in the Battle of Midway, from which they never recovered. This film documents that battle and the events that lead up to it. Fonda shines as Commander Chester W. Nimitz. There is a needless romantic subplot where Heston helps his son deal with a romantic relationship with a Japanese/American. Factually correct, the studio used a mixture of real and created footage in depicting this epic battle.

A: Charlton Heston, Henry Fonda, Glenn Ford, Robert Mitchum, Edward Albert, Hal Holbrook

© MCA/UNIVERSAL HOME VIDEO, INC. 55030

MILLER'S CROSSING

D: Joel Coen, Ethan Coen 115 m

R | CRM ACT | 1990 | COLOR | Sex Nud Viol Lang AdSit

9 Excellent. Highly entertaining and stylish gangster film that spends more time on developing its characters and their society than most of the gangster films of the past, or the present. Set in an unnamed eastern city, an Irish gangster (Finney) and his right-hand man (Byrne) have a falling out over the same woman. Then when a rival Italian hood (Polito) sets his sights on Irish turf, Byrne apparently switches sides. Very violent at times, rich in character images and full of plot intrigue. This is also a film that you will think about for days after.

A: Albert Finney, Gabriel Byrne, Jon Polito, J.E. Freeman, Marcia Gay Harden, John Turturro

© FOXVIDEO 1852

MISSING IN ACTION

D: Joseph Zito 112 m

R | ACT | 1984 | COLOR | Sex Nud Viol Lang AdSit

7 Intense action! Chuck Norris plays Special Forces Colonel James Braddock, a former North Vietnamese prisoner. He escapes to the US and then returns to the jungles of Vietnam to finish some business and rescue POWs who he knows are still in captivity. Black market sidekick (Walsh), an old army buddy, helps him out, but most of the heavy combat is still up to Norris. Typical revisionist macho fantasy is more than a little unrealistic, but Norris makes it fun to watch. Sequel is MISSING IN ACTION 2.

A: Chuck Norris, M. Emmet Walsh, David Tress, James Hong

Distributed By MGM/UA Home Video M800557

MISSING IN ACTION 2 - THE BEGINNING

D: Joseph Zito 91 m

R | ACT | 1984 | COLOR | Sex Nud Viol Lang AdSit

6 Gritty and violent action! Technically the "prequel," this version tells the story of how Colonel Braddock escaped after ten years of Vietnamese captivity and sadistic torture. His capture begins when his helicopter crashes during an attempt to rescue other soldiers. His captors are incredibly cruel. It is plain to him that he must either escape or die trying. Norris fans will get all of the intense action they have come to expect.

A: Chuck Norris, M. Emmet Walsh, David Tress, James Hong

Distributed By MGM/UA Home Video M800658

MISSION, THE

D: Roland Joffe 125 m

PG | DMA ACT | 1986 | COLOR | Sex Nud Viol Lang AdSit

8 Sweeping drama set in the mid-18th century. Irons stars as a dedicated Jesuit priest who braves the jungles of South America and opens a mission there. De Niro is a slavetrader who is guilt-ridden for having murdered his own brother in a fit of rage. So he returns with Irons into the jungle, in an act of penance, to help convert the same people that in the past he would have made into slaves. Then when the small colony is sold to Portugal and slave trade is legalized, the two must fight the Portuguese and the church itself to save these native people from slavery. 7 nominations, including Best Picture.

A: Robert De Niro, Jeremy Irons, Liam Neeson, Ray McAnally, Aidan Quinn

© WARNER HOME VIDEO 11639

MOBSTERS

D: Michael Karbelnikoff 104 m

R | CRM ACT | 1991 | COLOR | Sex Nud Viol Lang AdSit

6 Sort of YOUNG GUNS in suits with tommy-guns. Some up-and-coming young stars of the early 90's were dressed up in a big money production. It is the supposed story of four young hoods who grew up together in the slums of New York and rose to transform the "mob" into a corporate-like business. The four are Lucky Luciano (Slater), Meyer Lanski (Dempsey), Ben "Bugsy" Segal (Grieco) and Frank Costello (Mandylor). In spite of a great deal of effort, the plot only generates slight momentum. However, there is a lot of starpower invested and plenty of violence and gore.

A: Christian Slater, Patrick Dempsey, Richard Grieco, Costas Mandylor, Anthony Quinn, Michael Gambon

© MCA/UNIVERSAL HOME VIDEO, INC. 81129

MOBY DICK

D: John Huston 116 m

NR | DMA ACT | 1956 | COLOR | Sex Nud Viol Lang AdSit

7 Based on Melville's classic, this gripping saga of revenge and the sea is first-rate! Against the warnings of a God-fearing preacher (Welles), seaman Richard Basehart joins ominous Quiquig and disfigured Captain Ahab (Peck) to set sail on a whaling ship in 1840. Ahab is quick to let his crew know that they are on a quest to kill the great white whale that made lunch of his leg. Ahab will let nothing stand in his way - not torturous seas, a mutiny or even the lives of his crew in his obsessive hunt to kill the great whale. Although a little heavy at times, this is excellent adventure.

A: Gregory Peck, Richard Basehart, Orson Welles, Leo Genn, Harry Andrews, Fredrich Ledebur

Distributed By MGM/UA Home Video M201643

MONA LISA

D: Neil Jordan 106 m

R | SUS ACT | 1986 | COLOR | Sex Nud Viol Lang AdSit

7 Absorbing British thriller. Hoskins plays a good-hearted small-time hood whose antics land him in prison. When he gets out, he goes to his former boss (Caine) who gives him a job chauffeuring a high-priced hooker (Tyson) around town. Hoskins falls in love with her and will do anything for her. She wants him to find her lost friend and that may get him killed. Critically acclaimed, the film capitalizes well on the chemistry between Hoskins and Tyson. Hoskins earned an Academy Award nomination for his stylish performance.

A: Bob Hoskins, Cathy Tyson, Michael Caine, Robbie Coltrane, Clark Peters, Kate Hardie

© HBO VIDEO 9955

MOONRAKER

D: Lewis Gilbert 128 m

PG | ACT | 1979 | COLOR | Sex Nud Viol Lang AdSit

6 Intergalactic adventure! Bond matches wits with evil industrialist Hugo Drax (Lonsdale). Drax is building a space station and plans to annihilate the planet with nerve gas dispensed from his fleet of space shuttles. After this is done he can then replace the earth's population with his own perfect super race. Bond's planet-saving efforts are full of cool spy stuff, exotic locations and witty dialogue. The freefall scene where 007 battles mega-villain Jaws for a single parachute is one of the film's best moments.

A: Roger Moore, Lois Chiles, Richard Kiel, Michael Lonsdale

Distributed By MGM/UA Home Video M201422

MOSQUITO COAST, THE

D: Peter Weir 119 m

PG | DMA ACT | 1986 | COLOR | Sex Nud Viol Lang AdSit

7 Gripping drama and action. An idealistic inventor and near lunatic (Ford) is fed up with life in America. So he uproots his entire family and moves them to Central America, hoping to create his own utopia there. He is a can-do kind of guy and manages to achieve some success. He begins to think of himself as a sort of god until three gun-toting terrorists arrive. Based on the best-seller by Paul Theroux, Ford's performance is stellar, although the character is an unsympathetic one. A serious and thought-provoking drama about one man's relentless search for perfection.

A: Harrison Ford, Helen Mirren, River Phoenix, Conrad Roberts, Butterfly McQueen, Martha Plimpton

© WARNER HOME VIDEO 11711

MOUNTAIN MEN, THE

D: Richard Lang 100 m

R | WST ACT | 1980 | COLOR | Sex Nud Viol Lang AdSit

7 A Western that really draws blood. Heston's son, Fraser-Clarke, wrote this extremely graphic depiction of white guys vs. Indians in hand-to-hand battle on the range and in the mountains. Set in the West during the 1830s, the wild lifestyle of two fur trappers (Heston and Keith) is coming to an end. That same way of life is also being threatened for the Indians and these two groups are now in perpetual conflict. The situation is further aggravated by the fact that the trappers have the runaway wife (Racimo) of a mean-spirited Indian Chief and he wants her back.

A: Charlton Heston, Brian Keith, Victoria Racimo, John Glover, Stephen Macht, Seymour Cassel

© GOODTIMES 4505

MOUNTAINS OF THE MOON

D: Bob Rafelson 140 m

R | DMA ACT | 1990 | COLOR | Sex Nud Viol Lang AdSit

8 Robust adventure! Two of history's most remarkable explorers from the Victorian era, undertake the last great challenge for mid-19th-century men of adventure - the search across totally uncharted and hostile lands for the source of the Nile. Sir Richard Burton and John Hanning Speke (Bergin and Glen) risked attacks by men, beasts and insects and bore unspeakable hardships to form strong personal bonds during their quest across Africa. This sweeping saga maintains historical integrity and sacrifices nothing to maintain gripping excitement. It doesn't have to. Gritty and realistically photographed at beautiful locations.

A: Patrick Bergin, Iain Glen, Richard E. Grant, Fiona Shaw, Bernard Hill, Paul Onsongo

© LIVE HOME VIDEO 68915

MS. 45

D: Abel Ferrara 82 m

R | ACT SUS | 1981 | COLOR | Sex Nud Viol Lang AdSit

7 Violent vengeance. When a beautiful young mute woman is brutally raped and beaten on her way home from work - and then is raped again by a robber waiting in her apartment when she gets home, she loses control. She kills her second attacker and uses his 45 to wreak revenge. The woman with a death wish shows no mercy as she seeks out men in this exploitative shocker - sort of a DEATH WISH from the other side. This violent movie has attained cult status, and the powerful ending is really a shocker.

A: Zoe Tamerlis, Steve Singer, Jack Thibeau, Peter Yellen

© LIVE HOME VIDEO 215147

MURPHY'S WAR

D: Peter Yates 106 m

PG | DMA ACT | 1971 | COLOR | Sex | Nud | Viol | Lang | AdSit

7 Near the end of WWII, an English ship is torpedoed and its crew gunned down by a German U-boat that prowls nearby waters. Irish merchantman (O'Toole) is the only survivor of the massacre. He is rescued by a French oil engineer and nursed back to health at a nearby village hospital. Now healthy, he hears of a wrecked old sea plane and decides to seek his own revenge by patching it up to conduct his own private war on the marauding U-boat's crew. O'Toole packs a powerful performance into this wartime story.

A: Peter O'Toole, Sian Phillips, Philippe Noiret, Horst Janson, John Hallam, Ingo Morgendorf

© PARAMOUNT HOME VIDEO 8047

MYSTERIOUS ISLAND

D: Cy Endfield 101 m

NR | ACT FAN CLD | 1961 | COLOR | Sex | Nud | Viol | Lang | AdSit

7 High-flying adventure from Jules Verne. Union soldiers escape from a Confederate prison in an observation balloon and are blown out to sea. They crash at sea and are spit up on the shores of the uncharted island of Captain Nemo (Lom). The island contains a volcano, pirates, incredibly large creatures (that mad-scientist Captain Nemo created to help with the world's food supply), two British girls who were also washed up on the island and Captain Nemo himself with his inoperative sub. Captain Nemo comes to their aid with all their other problems, but will he be able to save them when the volcano erupts?

A: Michael Craig, Joan Greenwood, Herbert Lom, Michael Callan, Gary Merrill

© COLUMBIA TRISTAR HOME VIDEO 60067

NAKED PREY, THE

D: Cornel Wilde 96 m

NR | ACT SUS | 1965 | COLOR | Sex | Nud | Viol | Lang | AdSit

9 An enthralling story of survival. Set in the 1860s, a white expedition in search of ivory offends a group of natives and is subsequently ambushed. All the members except Wilde are tortured to death. Impressed with his bravery, he is given a chance to survive. He is stripped naked, turned free, and then pursued by relentless native hunters. No matter how he struggles, he can keep no more than a few seconds in front of them. Alternately filmed from a distance and then close-up, this is a fascinating and intimate portrait of survival at its most basic level. Virtually no dialogue.

A: Cornel Wilde, Ken Gampu, Gert Van Den Bergh

© PARAMOUNT HOME VIDEO 6525

NARROW MARGIN, THE

D: Peter Hyams 99 m

R | SUS ACT | 1990 | COLOR | Sex | Nud | Viol | Lang | AdSit

8 Top rate action! Archer reluctantly agrees to a blind date, and then watches from behind a partially closed door as he is shot and killed. She flees to a hideaway in the mountains, but Hackman, the D.A., tracks her down and tries to persuade her to return to L.A. to testify against the killer. She refuses, but soon the hitmen have found her, too. She and Hackman escape and are on a speeding train back to L.A., but the hitmen are following close behind again. Archer fears for her life and Hackman tries to protect his frightened witness in this excellent remake of the 1952 original.

A: Gene Hackman, Anne Archer, James Sikking, J.T. Walsh, M. Emmet Walsh, Susan Hogan

© LIVE HOME VIDEO 68924

NAVY SEALS

D: Lewis Teague 113 m

R | ACT | 1990 | COLOR | Sex | Nud | Viol | Lang | AdSit

7 Heavy duty action but not much else! The Navy has underplayed the activities of their special SEAL (SEa, Air and Land) unit for decades, but the screenplay for this action-packed film was written by a real-live ex-SEAL. In it, an elite SEAL's unit, led by commander Biehn, travels to Beirut to stop dangerous terrorists who have gotten hold of American Stinger missiles. Lots of ground level action, authentic and sophisticated weapons and technology, and well-choreographed battle scenes will delight fans of this genre.

A: Charlie Sheen, Michael Biehn, Joanne Whalley-Kilmer, Rick Rossovich, Cybil O'Reilly, Bill Paxton

© ORION PICTURES CORPORATION 8729

NEVADA SMITH

D: Henry Hathaway 135 m

NR | WST ACT | 1966 | COLOR | Sex | Nud | Viol | Lang | AdSit

9 Solid hard-hitting Western. Steve McQueen comes home to find his Indian mother and white father have been tortured and killed by a outlaw band. He is now steeled by hate and, vowing vengeance, he sets off in pursuit of the killers. But he is just an inept hate-fueled farmboy until he stumbles onto a traveling gun merchant (Keith), who teaches him how to shoot and how to survive. Now, he has the tools he needs and he methodically pursues each man down and kills him, becoming nearly as bad as his quarry. Very good movie. The character came from the book THE CARPETBAGGERS, which was also made into a movie.

A: Steve McQueen, Karl Malden, Brian Keith, Suzanne Pleshette, Arthur Kennedy, Pat Hingle

© PARAMOUNT HOME VIDEO 6532

NEVER SAY NEVER AGAIN

D: Irvin Kershner 134 m

PG | ACT | 1983 | COLOR | Sex | Nud | Viol | Lang | AdSit

8 Sean Connery is back as James Bond after having been absent for 12 years. James is in pursuit of arch-villain Brandauer who is threatening the world with stolen missiles. Barbara Carrera is memorable as a sexy assassin Fatima Blush, out to get James - but she makes an explosive departure before she can get the job done. Sexy Kim Basinger plays Brandauer's naive girlfriend and ultimately James's love. Solid entry that is basically a remake of THUNDERBALL. Action-packed and witty.

A: Sean Connery, Klaus Maria Brandauer, Max von Sydow, Barbara Carrera, Kim Basinger, Bernie Casey

© WARNER HOME VIDEO 11337

NEW CENTURIONS, THE

D: Richard Fleischer 103 m

R | CRM DMA ACT | 1972 | COLOR | Sex | Nud | Viol | Lang | AdSit

8 An involving screen adaptation of Joseph Wambaugh's novel about the nature of street cops. Scott is a grizzled old veteran on the way out, teaching the new and enthusiastic rookie (Stacy Keach) the ropes. Keach loves it. He is hooked on the excitement, and he puts it before everything else even though it is destroying his marriage. Scott will soon retire but finds that he, too, is hooked, however he can't go back. This is a fascinating character study, but it is also ultimately pretty downbeat in nature. Great performances and a fascinating story.

A: George C. Scott, Stacy Keach, Jane Alexander, Rosalind Cash, Scott Wilson

© COLUMBIA TRISTAR HOME VIDEO 60070

NEW JACK CITY

D: Mario Van Peebles 101 m

R | CRM ACT | 1991 | COLOR | Sex | Nud | Viol | Lang | AdSit

6 Very gritty, hard-edged inner-city action flick. Two undercover cops lay everything on the line to bring down a ruthless Harlem drug lord (Snipes). Loads of action for the action crowd, but the hard, no-nonsense, repulsive realities about drugs and drug life also deliver a strong anti-drug message. The story line is essentially nothing new, however. The whole package is wrapped in a score heavily dosed with the rap music of Ice T, Christopher Williams and 2 Live Crew.

A: Wesley Snipes, Ice T, Mario Van Peebles, Alan Payne, Chris Rock, Vanessa Williams

© WARNER HOME VIDEO 12073

NEXT OF KIN

D: John Irvin 109 m

R | ACT | 1989 | COLOR | Sex | Nud | Viol | Lang | AdSit

7 Action-packed revenge flick in a similar vein to DEATH WISH. Patrick Swayze was a Kentucky hills boy, but now is a cop in Chicago. When his brother gets killed by a mob enforcer, Swayze is torn between his obligation to the law and his need for revenge as it would be in the hills. But his older brother arrives in town and there is no longer any doubt in his mind - he wants revenge, backwoods style. Largely predictable throughout, but it's still fun to watch the back-country boys whip the bad dudes from the big city.

A: Patrick Swayze, Liam Neeson, Adam Baldwin, Helen Hunt, Bill Paxton, Andreas Katsulas

© WARNER HOME VIDEO 670

NIGHTHAWKS

D: Bruce Malmuth 99 m

R | ACT SUS | 1981 | COLOR | Sex | Nud | Viol | Lang | AdSit

9 Supercharged action film and Stallone's best performance outside the ROCKY series. He and Williams, two New York street cops, get reassigned to a special unit that is charged with tracking down an especially ruthless and cunning international terrorist (Rutger Hauer), who is out to make a name for himself in America in a big way. Fast paced and very high intensity throughout, but especially tense when Hauer hijacks a tramway. Exciting and very well made.

A: Sylvester Stallone, Billy Dee Williams, Rutger Hauer, Nigel Davenport, Lindsay Wagner

© MCA/UNIVERSAL HOME VIDEO, INC. 71000

NO ESCAPE

D: Martin Campbell 118 m

R | ACT | 1994 | COLOR | Sex | Nud | Viol | Lang | AdSit

7 In the year 2022, prisons have become a business - a business that the politicians don't want to deal with. The worst of the murderers are sent to a remote and isolated island, hidden there and left to die. The prisoners have divided into two camps. The Outsiders are a ruthless group of the most cruel and merciless who have formed a warrior society. The Insiders have tried to maintain civility, but they are outnumbered 6 to 1 and if they are to survive, they have to let the world know what's happening. John Robbins (Liotta) is a Special Forces Marine Captain that was sent to the island to hide a mistake made by the Army. He is their only chance and they are his.

A: Ray Liotta, Michael Lerner, Stuart Wilson, Lanco Henricksen, Kevin Dillon, Kevin J. O'Connor

© HBO VIDEO 90982

NO MERCY

D: Richard Pearce 108 m

R

ACT SUS

1986 COLOR

Sex Nud Viol Lang AdSit

7 Richard Gere is an undercover cop whose partner is brutally and sadistically murdered. Swearing vengeance, he tracks the killers to Louisiana. There he uncovers a huge drug conspiracy involving the killers he is pursuing. The stakes go up. He kidnaps the druglord's beautiful woman (Basinger), the only witness, to flush out his quarry. He and Basinger make their escape into the Bayous, but ultimately he winds up protecting her from her former lover, who is now out to kill them both. Tense action in a traditional plot, but well done.

A: Richard Gere, Kim Basinger, Jeroen Krabbe, George Dzundza, Gary Basaraba, Ray Sharkey

© COLUMBIA TRISTAR HOME VIDEO 60791

NONE BUT THE BRAVE

D: Frank Sinatra 106 m

NR

ACT WAR

1965 COLOR

Sex Nud Viol Lang AdSit

6 Tense war drama about a plane full of Allied Marines that crash-lands on a Pacific island populated by small band of Japanese. Both groups have been cut off from the rest of the war. So, they conduct their own war with both sides plotting against the other and skirmishing. But when the Japanese commander offers water in exchange for help from the American's medic (Sinatra), who then amputates a man's leg and saves his life, a truce is worked out. An interesting, and a respectable entry, but it is most notable for being Sinatra's directorial debut.

A: Frank Sinatra, Clint Walker, Tommy Sands, Brad Dexter, Tony Bill, Sammy Jackson

© WARNER HOME VIDEO 11712

NORTH TO ALASKA

D: Henry Hathaway 117 m

NR

WST ACT COM

1960 COLOR

Sex Nud Viol Lang AdSit

9 Terrific good time in this light-hearted John Wayne Western. Wayne and Granger play turn-of-the-century Alaskan gold miners who strike it rich. Fabian is Granger's wet-behind-the-ears brother. Wayne goes to Seattle to pick up supplies and Granger's brand new mail-order bride. But when she is not there, Wayne "buys" saucy Capucine from a saloon and takes her back. Soon Granger and Wayne are both vying for her affections, as is young Fabian. Even while they're fighting each other, they're also fending off claim-jumpers lead by Kovacs. Great, fast-moving, tongue-in-cheek, fun.

A: John Wayne, Stewart Granger, Ernie Kovacs, Fabian, Capucine, Mickey Shaughnessy

© FOXVIDEO 1212

NO WAY OUT

D: Roger Donaldson 114 m

R

SUS MYS ACT

1987 COLOR

Sex Nud Viol Lang AdSit

9 Outstanding and totally engrossing remake of THE BIG CLOCK (1948). This intriguing and sexy suspense thriller will keep you guessing right up to the end. Costner plays a straight arrow from the Navy who is assigned as a CIA liaison to the Secretary of Defense (Hackman). Costner has a passionate affair with a super-sexy lady (Young). When she is murdered, he is assigned to investigate the murder, only to discover that all the clues are pointing to him and he is being framed for the girl's murder. He is being trapped by some very powerful people.

A: Kevin Costner, Gene Hackman, Sean Young, Will Patton, Howard Duff, George Dzundza

© HBO VIDEO 0051

OCTOPUSSY

D: John Glen 131 m

PG

ACT

1983 COLOR

Sex Nud Viol Lang AdSit

8 James Bond Number 13. Roger Moore is in pursuit of the killer of 009. He discovers a plot by a hard-line Soviet general, assisted by Octopussy (Maude Adams), to cripple the West's nuclear threat with public pressure. They will deliberately create a nuclear accident at a US base in Germany which will kill hundreds of thousands of people and force the removal of the nucs. Bond is launched on a fast-paced excursion through many countries and many women to prevent that from happening. Clever and humorous, but also one of the more believable adventures.

A: Roger Moore, Maud Adams, Louis Jourdan, Kristina Wayborn

Distributed By MGM/UA Home Video M200294

ODESSA FILE, THE

D: Ronald Neame 128 m

PG

SUS MYS ACT

1974 COLOR

Sex Nud Viol Lang AdSit

8 Gripping! John Voight is a German reporter who discovers, through reading the diary of a former death camp survivor, of the existence of Odessa, a secret German society that protects former SS officers who are now safely in positions of power within 1960s German centers of commerce and government. He also learns of the vicious and monstrously cruel Commandant (Maximilian Schell) of a Latvian camp. Voight goes undercover to infiltrate Odessa in search of Schell, but Odessa members are everywhere and he is in constant risk. Intricate plot can be confusing but is well worth the effort.

A: Jon Voight, Maximilian Schell, Derek Jacobi, Maria Schell, Mary Tamm, Klaus Lowitsch

© COLUMBIA TRISTAR HOME VIDEO 60317

OLD GRINGO

D: Luis Puenzo 120 m

R

WST ROM ACT

1989 COLOR

Sex Nud Viol Lang AdSit

7 A noble effort to dramatize Carlos Fuentes's novel revolving around the real-life character, and American journalist of the period, Ambrose Bierce. Jane Fonda plays an American spinster seeking adventure, who takes job as a teacher in old Mexico. Instead, she gets caught up in Pancho Villa's revolution and love. She becomes a realized woman, but is torn between her love for an old ex-patriot American journalist (Peck) and her passion for a young Mexican general (Smits), who is also the American's bastard son.

A: Jane Fonda, Jimmy Smits, Gregory Peck, Patricio Contreras, Jessica Tandy

© COLUMBIA TRISTAR HOME VIDEO 50203

OMEGA MAN, THE

D: Boris Sagal 98 m

PG

SF SUS ACT

1971 COLOR

Sex Nud Viol Lang AdSit

7 Well done and literate science fiction story about the breakdown of society after the world is largely destroyed in a biological war. Heston stars as a medical researcher who is strangely immune to the effects of all the germs. But a militant group of mutant survivors is now bent on destroying all technologies and has particularly targeted him to be killed. Heston discovers a few children who are also immune and being protected by Cash. The mutants want to kill them, too, but they are the future of the species and Heston must study them if there is to be a cure. Gripping suspense.

A: Charlton Heston, Anthony Zerbe, Rosalind Cash, Paul Koslo, Lincoln Kilpatrick, Eric Laneuville

© WARNER HOME VIDEO 11210

ONCE UPON A TIME IN AMERICA (LONG VERSION)

D: Sergio Leone 226 m

R

CRM ACT

1984 COLOR

Sex Nud Viol Lang AdSit

8 Very long and sometimes confusing, yet involving film depicting the relationship between two Jewish gangsters - from their beginnings as boys in the ghetto through their development into major hoods. Maxie (Woods) is too wild, so his friend Noodles (De Niro) tips off the police to an upcoming robbery so Maxie will get arrested and put safely behind bars before he gets killed. Instead, Maxie is apparently killed in a shoot out. Noodles leaves town. Now it's 1968, 35 years later, and Noodles mysteriously gets called back home to meet with his old friends.

A: Robert De Niro, James Woods, Elizabeth McGovern, Joe Pesci, Jennifer Connelly, Tuesday Weld

© WARNER HOME VIDEO 20019

ONCE UPON A TIME IN THE WEST

D: Sergio Leone 165 m

PG

WST ACT

1969 COLOR

Sex Nud Viol Lang AdSit

9 Masterful epic allegory for the ultimate taming of the West. Bronson has come to town to kill Fonda for having killed his brother years before. Fonda is a ruthless gunslinger who has also recently cold-bloodedly murdered a man and his children just to get the man's land to sell for a railroad station, and then he framed another outlaw (Robards) for those murders. However, Fonda's now in big trouble because both Robards and Bronson are out to kill him. Plus, a former prostitute (Cardinale), who, unknown to anyone, had married the murdered man, claims that the land is hers. Violent.

A: Henry Fonda, Jason Robards, Jr., Charles Bronson, Claudia Cardinale, Gabriele Ferzetti, Jack Elam

© PARAMOUNT HOME VIDEO 6830

ONE FALSE MOVE

D: Carl Franklin 106 m

R

CRM ACT

1992 COLOR

Sex Nud Viol Lang AdSit

6 Very gritty, low-budget crime story. It is not for everyone, but those intrigued by low-life characters and their psychology will find more than enough to hold their attention. Two bad guys and one bad girl kill off a house full of people for a load of drugs and slowly head east, back to her small hometown in Arkansas. Two cops from L.A. know where they are heading and solicit the help of the local hayseed sheriff, but he is more determined to prove himself the equal of big city cops. A major part of what makes this story interesting is the complex and seedy characters it explores.

A: Bill Paxton, Cynda Williams, Billy Bob Thornton, Michael Beach, Jim Metzler, Earl Billings

© COLUMBIA TRISTAR HOME VIDEO 91173

ONE GOOD COP

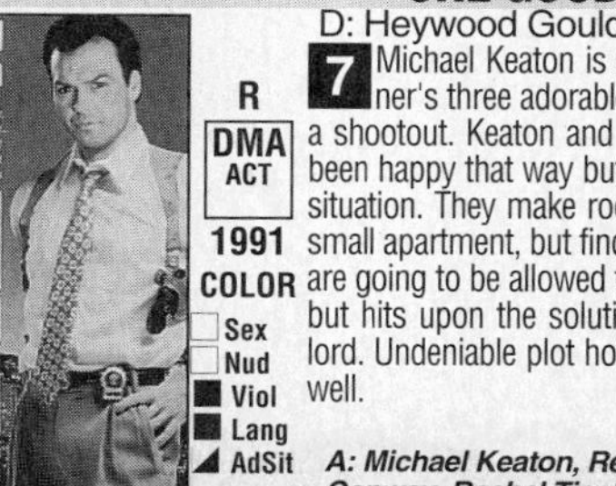

D: Heywood Gould 105 m

R

DMA ACT

1991 COLOR

Sex Nud Viol Lang AdSit

7 Michael Keaton is a dedicated N.Y.C. cop who inherits his partner's three adorable young daughters after the partner is killed in a shootout. Keaton and his wife have no kids of their own and have been happy that way but now they must come to grips with their new situation. They make room for the kids on a temporary basis in their small apartment, but find that they must get a bigger apartment if they are going to be allowed to keep them. Keaton doesn't have the money but hits upon the solution of "borrowing" some money from a drug lord. Undeniable plot holes and sentimentality, but it still works pretty well.

A: Michael Keaton, Rene Russo, Anthony Lapaglia, Kevin Conway, Rachel Ticotin, Tony Plana

© HOLLYWOOD PICTURES HOME VIDEO 1212

ON HER MAJESTY'S SECRET SERVICE

D: Peter H. Hunt 143 m

PG | ACT | 1969 | COLOR

Sex / Nud / Viol / Lang / AdSit

8 Fascinating James Bond entry. This was the first Bond film without Connery, but it was remarkably good - and gets better with age. This Bond is more vulnerable than Connery. He has tried and failed for two years to track down archvillian Blofeld (Savalas). He meets his match in beautiful and enchanting Dianna Rigg, and marries her. Through her gangster father, he gains entry into Blofeld's mountain stronghold to foil Blofeld's attempt to poison the world's food supply, but he does it at great cost. Less gimmicky, with great action.

A: George Lazenby, Diana Rigg, Telly Savalas, Gabriele Ferzetti, Bernard Lee, Lois Maxwell

Distributed By MGM/UA Home Video M201420

OPERATION CROSSBOW

D: Michael Anderson 116 m

NR | WAR ACT | 1965 | COLOR

Sex / Nud / Viol / Lang / AdSit

8 Rousing actioner set in WWII. A trio of British agents (Peppard, Courtenay and Kemp) are sent on a near-impossible mission to destroy a heavily guarded secret underground Nazi munitions installation, where German scientists are developing long range rockets. They impersonate German scientists to gain access to information which they are to send back. High intensity throughout, but it has a particularly sensational ending.

A: George Peppard, Sophia Loren, Trevor Howard, Tom Courtenay, Anthony Quayle, John Mills

Distributed By MGM/UA Home Video 202611

ORGANIZATION, THE

D: Don Medford 107 m

PG | CRM ACT | 1971 | COLOR

Sex / Nud / Viol / Lang / AdSit

6 The third and final appearance of Mr. Tibbs, the tough big city police detective Poitier created in IN THE HEAT OF THE NIGHT and followed up with in THEY CALL ME MR. TIBBS. This time in San Francisco, Poitier comes to the aid of a student vigilante group who raids a furniture factory that is really a front trafficking in heroin. When the manager is murdered, the group admits to Tibbs that they stole $5 million in dope to keep it off the streets but they didn't kill anyone. He rises to their defense but is suspended from the force. Good action flick with a realistic plot and believable climax.

A: Sidney Poitier, Barbara Mc Nair, Raul Julia, Sheree North, Ron O'Neal, Daniel J. Travanti

Distributed By MGM/UA Home Video M203136

OUR MAN FLINT

D: Daniel Mann 107 m

NR | ACT COM | 1966 | COLOR

Sex / Nud / Viol / Lang / AdSit

6 Outlandish James Bond spoof. Coburn is superagent Derek Flint from Z.O.W.I.E. who is sent to protect the world from a plot by the evil organization GALAXY and its top agent, the super seductive Gila Golan. GALAXY and its scientists are plotting to overtake and control the world's weather. It is up to superstud Flint to defeat them... but he does have the use of his special lighter that has 83 different uses, including: a blow torch, a derringer, a dart gun and a 2-way radio. Spectacular tongue-in-cheek spoof.

A: James Coburn, Lee J. Cobb, Gila Golan, Edward Mulhare, Benson Fong, Shelby Grant

© FOXVIDEO 1131

OUTLAND

D: Peter Hyams 111 m

R | SF ACT CRM | 1981 | COLOR

Sex / Nud / Viol / Lang / AdSit

8 Rousing space Western. Sean Connery is the new marshall assigned to police a dehumanized, rough-and-tumble mining colony on one of the moons of Jupiter. His search to identify the reasons behind a series of mysterious deaths leads him to the discovery of a pervasive corruption based upon the distribution of mind-altering drugs. Great special effects lend an air of realism and believability to this bleak other-world environment. The exciting action scenes could have occurred just as easily at the OK corral or on the streets of L.A. Exciting.

A: Sean Connery, Peter Boyle, Frances Sternhagen, James Sikking, Kika Markham

© WARNER HOME VIDEO 20002

OUTLAW JOSEY WALES, THE

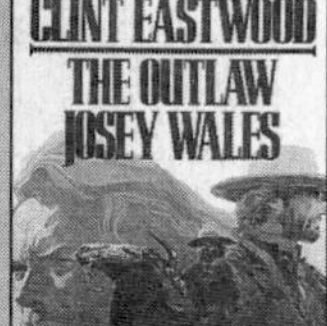

D: Clint Eastwood 136 m

PG | WST ACT | 1976 | COLOR

Sex / Nud / Viol / Lang / AdSit

9 Intriguing Civil War Western, highly acclaimed as one of Eastwood's best efforts both behind and in front of the camera. Josey Wales is a farmer whose family is brutalized and killed by renegade Union soldiers. Wales joins the Rebs seeking revenge and becomes one of their most effective weapons. At war's end, he refuses to surrender to corrupt Union troops he does not trust and so becomes a renegade. He seeks to escape into the West - but he is now being hunted as an outlaw. Rich characters and images. Exciting and believable.

A: Clint Eastwood, Chief Dan George, Sondra Locke, Bill Mc Kinney, John Vernon, Sam Bottoms

© WARNER HOME VIDEO 11125

PACIFIC HEIGHTS

D: John Schlesinger 103 m

R | SUS ACT | 1990 | COLOR

Sex / Nud / Viol / Lang / AdSit

8 A landlord's ultimate nightmare! Drake and Patty (Modine and Griffith) have him living right downstairs - in their new house! When the attractive, young couple spy the Victorian house of their dreams in Pacific Heights, they just know they have to have it. They pool their resources and decide that, if they rent out the bottom units, they can just make the mortgage. But their happiness is short lived when mysterious Keaton moves in and turns their lives into a living hell. He is a psychotic that even the legal system can't touch. A gripping, intelligent and believable psychothriller!

A: Melanie Griffith, Matthew Modine, Michael Keaton, Mako, Nobu McCarthy, Laurie Metcalf

© FOXVIDEO 1900

PACKAGE, THE

D: Andrew Davis 108 m

R | ACT SUS | 1989 | COLOR

Sex / Nud / Viol / Lang / AdSit

8 Nifty espionage thriller. Army sergeant Gene Hackman is assigned to escort another sergeant back to the U.S. from Germany and to his court-martial, but along the way the prisoner escapes. Hackman discovers that his prisoner was actually an imposter and that he is now neck deep in a cold war assassination plot to be carried out at an international disarmament conference. He and his officer ex-wife are left to figure out what's going on, how to clear his name and how to stop the plot from being carried out. Lots of surprises and twists add to the excitement.

A: Gene Hackman, Joanna Cassidy, Tommy Lee Jones, John Heard, Dennis Franz, Reni Santoni

© ORION PICTURES CORPORATION 8747

PALE RIDER

D: Clint Eastwood 116 m

R | WST ACT | 1985 | COLOR

Sex / Nud / Viol / Lang / AdSit

8 Nifty, quasi-mystical Western that many compare in its basic plot to the classic SHANE, but it also has elements of the 1973 HIGH PLAINS DRIFTER. Here Eastwood is Preacher, a very odd and mysterious stranger who rides into the middle of a battle between a group of independent miners and a powerful land baron who is trying to force them off their claims. But, Preacher is a strong character, an inordinately powerful and mystical superhero who gives the miners self-confidence and around whom they rally. It is never made clear, but it is hinted, that Preacher is the spirit of a gunslinger who seeks redemption so that his spirit may rest. Quite good with lots of Western action.

A: Clint Eastwood, Michael Moriarty, Carrie Snodgress, Christopher Penn, Richard Dysart, Sydney Penny

© WARNER HOME VIDEO 11475

PAPILLON

D: Franklin J. Schaffner 150 m

PG | DMA ACT SUS | 1973 | COLOR

Sex / Nud / Viol / Lang / AdSit

9 Exuberant testament to the triumph of the human spirit, based upon the real-life exploits of Henri Charriere, also called Papillon (meaning "the butterfly"). McQueen plays the Frenchman who is unjustly sentenced to the escape-proof hell of the infamous Devil's Island penal colony. In spite of overwhelming odds, he and his friend, a convicted forger (brilliantly played by Hoffman), make continued escape attempts - once succeeding for a short time and living in an idyllic Indian village. Each time they are captured, they again seek a new way to escape. There spirit is indomitable. Long but engrossing throughout.

A: Steve McQueen, Dustin Hoffman, Victor Jory, Anthony Zerbe, Don Gordon, Robert Deman

© WARNER HOME VIDEO 832

PARALLAX VIEW, THE

D: Alan J. Pakula 102 m

R | MYS SUS ACT | 1974 | COLOR

Sex / Nud / Viol / Lang / AdSit

9 Absolutely gripping, but strangely neglected, political thriller. Warren Beatty plays an alcoholic small-time reporter who witnesses the assassination of a Presidential candidate. As other witnesses mysteriously turn up dead, he begins his own investigations into their deaths. Each new piece of evidence he uncovers leads him to suspect that there is an elaborate coverup underway. An oppressive suspense builds steadily as the more he learns, the more likely it becomes that he will be eliminated, too.

A: Warren Beatty, Paula Prentiss, Hume Cronyn, William Daniels, Walter McGinn, Kelly Thordsen

© PARAMOUNT HOME VIDEO 8670

PASSENGER 57

D: Kevin Hooks 84 m

R | ACT | 1992 | COLOR

Sex / Nud / Viol / Lang / AdSit

6 Entertaining only to pure action fans. Snipes is the world's leading airline-security expert, who just happens to be aboard the same plane as Payne. Payne is a major-league hijacker who is being taken by the FBI back to L.A. However, also on board are a bunch of Payne's terrorist friends who want to set him free. They hijack the plane mid-flight and begin killing people. Sure was a lucky thing Snipes happened to be there and he comes to the rescue. Not much brainpower involved here but OK action.

A: Wesley Snipes, Bruce Payne, Tom Sizemore, Alex Datcher, Michael Horse

© WARNER HOME VIDEO 12569

PATRIOT GAMES

D: Phillip Noyce 117 m

R | ACT SUS | 1992 | COLOR

Sex / Nud / Viol / Lang / AdSit

7 Tom Clancy's CIA character Jack Ryan, first introduced in HUNT FOR RED OCTOBER, is back but this time he is played by Harrison Ford. Retired from the CIA and now a college professor in London with his wife (Archer) and daughter, Jack stumbles onto a plot by a splinter group of the IRA to assassinate English royalty. He breaks up the hit, killing one of the assassins in the process. The angry IRA tracks Jack back to America where he is forced to rejoin the CIA to protect his family and fight off the vengeful IRA. Not up to the standards of its predecessor, but still exciting and interesting if you're not too critical of some plot holes.

A: Harrison Ford, Anne Archer, James Earl Jones, Patrick Bergin, Thora Birch, Richard Harris

© PARAMOUNT HOME VIDEO 32530

PATTON

D: Franklin J. Schaffner 171 m

PG | DMA WAR ACT | 1970 | COLOR

Sex / Nud / Viol / Lang / AdSit

10 Brilliant portrait of an extremely colorful and unique historical figure - George S. "Blood-and-Guts" Patton. Winner of 8 Oscars, including Best Picture, Director, Screenplay and Actor. Patton, the man, was a brilliant battlefield tactician whose single-mindedness in and out of battle helped to win the North African campaign and to launch the initial assault into Europe at the beginning of WWII. It garnered him both the respect and the animosity of nearly everyone. Scott did a brilliant job with the role. Both fascinating and extremely enjoyable.

A: George C. Scott, Karl Malden, Stephen Young, Michael Strong, Tim Considine, Frank Latimore

© FOXVIDEO 1005

PINK CADILLAC

D: Buddy Van Horn 121 m

PG-13 | COM ACT | 1989 | COLOR

Sex / Nud / Viol / Lang / AdSit

6 Light-hearted Eastwood outing where he gets to pull out a bunch of his old characters and use them as he needs them. He plays skip-tracer Tommy Nowak who specializes in tracing down bail jumpers. But Tommy gets more than he bargained for when he chases down Bernadette Peters. She has skipped in a stolen pink Caddy, with a trunk full of counterfeit bills, and her eight-month-old baby. She is on the run from her husband's white supremist friends who want her, the Caddy and the money. Clint uses all sorts of disguises to con their way out of the mess.

A: Clint Eastwood, Bernadette Peters, Timothy Carhart, Tiffany Gale Robinson, John Dennis Johnston, Geoffrey Lewis

© WARNER HOME VIDEO 11877

PLATOON

D: Oliver Stone 120 m

R | WAR DMA ACT | 1986 | COLOR

Sex / Nud / Viol / Lang / AdSit

10 Profound statement on the harrowing experience of war - the utter terror of hand-to-hand combat and its lasting effects on ordinary people. A naive and idealistic replacement arrives at a battle-worn platoon in Vietnam. His innocence is soon lost to the realities of jungle warfare - where the slightest sound could warn of instant death. As bad as that is, he is also in the midst of an intercompany war where two sergeants (one decent and one ruthless) vie for control of the men. War's insanity was never made more personal, more real or more terrifying. 4 Oscars, including Picture and Director.

A: Charlie Sheen, Willem Dafoe, Tom Berenger, Francesco Quinn, Kevin Dillon, Forest Whitaker

© LIVE HOME VIDEO 6012

POINT BLANK

D: John Boorman 89 m

NR | CRM ACT SUS | 1967 | COLOR

Sex / Nud / Viol / Lang / AdSit

9 Violent and tense revenge flick that was largely ignored upon its release but is highly regarded now both for it's potency and its technical merits. Marvin is riveting as a vicious gangster who is shot and left for dead by his partner during a holdup, so he could run off with Marvin's wife and pay off a mob debt with the money they stole. Marvin recovers, and with help from sexy Angie Dickinson and a crooked accountant, he gains access inside the mob. He will get revenge, get his money back and kill off anyone who gets in his way. Very violent.

A: Lee Marvin, Angie Dickinson, Carroll O'Connor, Keenan Wynn, John Vernon, Lloyd Bochner

Distributed By MGM/UA Home Video M800278

POINT BREAK

D: Kathryn Bigelow 117 m

R | ACT | 1991 | COLOR

Sex / Nud / Viol / Lang / AdSit

6 High octane actioner that is most notable for its surfing scenes and two big chase scenes - one on foot and one while skydiving. Young maverick Reeves and old pro Busey are two FBI agents out to catch a Southern California group that has been pulling off a series of near-perfect bank robberies. The prime suspects are a bunch of adrenaline junkies led by hot-shot surfer Swayze. Reeves goes under cover into the surfing community so he can infiltrate the group. Terrific action but a pretty thin plot.

A: Patrick Swayze, Keanu Reeves, Gary Busey, Lori Petty, John C. McGinley

© FOXVIDEO 1870

POINT OF NO RETURN

D: John Badham 109 m

R | ACT SUS | 1992 | COLOR

Sex / Nud / Viol / Lang / AdSit

7 This is the Americanized (Hollywoodized) version of the very stylish French film LA FEMME NIKITA. It is the story of a beautiful but totally alienated young woman who had become a mindless killer and was sentenced to die. But, a government agency secretly arranged for her faked death so that it could secretly train her into a merciless assassin for them. However, their plans are fowled after her release into society, when she becomes humanized by the love of a gentle man. This version is virtually identical to the French version, except for being in English. However, because the actors are more familiar and the government is ours, it doesn't work as well.

A: Bridget Fonda, Anne Bancroft, Harvey Keitel, Gabriel Byrne, Miguel Ferrer, Olivia D'Abo

© WARNER HOME VIDEO 12819

POPE OF GREENWICH VILLAGE, THE

D: Stuart Rosenberg 121 m

R | CRM ACT | 1984 | COLOR

Sex / Nud / Viol / Lang / AdSit

7 Interesting character study, with insightful observations, of two small-time losers with big dreams who are constantly foiled by their own ineptitude. After getting fired from their restaurant jobs, and deeply in debt, Charlie (Rourke) and his cousin Paulie (Roberts) rob a safe containing Mafia money and accidentally kill an undercover cop. Now both the cops and the mob want them. Worse, while the two struggle just to stay alive in New York's Little Italy, Charlie's girlfriend (Hannah), who is tired of putting up with him, runs off with all their money.

A: Eric Roberts, Mickey Rourke, Daryl Hannah, Geraldine Page, Burt Young, Kenneth McMillan

Distributed By MGM/UA Home Video M800490

PORK CHOP HILL

D: Lewis Milestone 98 m

NR | WAR ACT | 1959 | B&W

Sex / Nud / Viol / Lang / AdSit

7 Realistic, believable and a grim portrait of one of the many insanities of war. During the Korean War, a beleaguered platoon of men lead by Peck are ordered to take a strategically useless hill. Despite punishing casualties, they manage to take that mound of earth. Then, without replacements or reinforcements, they are ordered to hold the hill - even in the face of a massive attack by an overwhelming force and just as cease-fire talks begin. Good solid performances. Based upon fact.

A: Gregory Peck, Harry Guardino, Rip Torn, George Peppard, Bob Steele, Robert Blake

Distributed By MGM/UA Home Video M301298

POSEIDON ADVENTURE, THE

D: Ronald Neame 117 m

PG | ACT DMA | 1972 | COLOR

Sex / Nud / Viol / Lang / AdSit

9 One of the best of many disaster films from the 1970s. An ocean-going luxury liner is overwhelmed by a massive tidal wave and left capsized, bobbing upside down on the open ocean. A few survivors, trapped below deck, must work their way into the deepest bowels of the ship, which is now the only part exposed to the air, in the hope that someone will find them and cut through the hull to save them. Their arduous trip provides numerous opportunities for an exploration of their motivations and individual life stories. Oscars for Special Effects and Theme Song: "The Morning After."

A: Gene Hackman, Ernest Borgnine, Carol Lynley, Red Buttons, Shelley Winters, Jack Albertson

© CBS/FOX VIDEO 1058

POSSE

D: Kirk Douglas 94 m

PG | WST DMA ACT | 1975 | COLOR

Sex / Nud / Viol / Lang / AdSit

8 Solid and interesting Western, with an odd edge. Kirk Douglas is both a cynical lawman and an ambitious politician, seeking to become a Senator from Texas. He sees an opportunity to capture the public's attention when he and his ruthless crew of deputies track down and try to capture an escaped robber, Bruce Dern. But Dern is a wily opponent who recognizes Douglas's self-serving agenda and uses it to gain the sympathy of the townspeople, turn the deputies against Douglas and then enlist them in his own cause.

A: Kirk Douglas, Bruce Dern, Bo Hopkins, James Stacy, Luke Askew, David Canary

© PARAMOUNT HOME VIDEO 8316

POSSE

D: Mario Van Peebles 113 m

R | WST ACT | 1993 | COLOR

Sex / Nud / Viol / Lang / AdSit

6 A very bloody and politically-correct Western. Five black soldiers and one white one, in Cuba during the Spanish-American War, rebel against a corrupt racist white colonel who has done his best to get them killed. They escape into the West with a cache of Cuban gold they have appropriated. Their sharp-shooting leader (Van Peebles) has unfinished business to take care of but the colonel is hot on their trial and has labeled them outlaws. Their arrival finds that the town is in the path of the on-coming railroad and that has made it the target of a bigoted white sheriff. A showdown is at hand.

A: Mario Van Peebles, Stephen Baldwin, Billy Zane, Charles Lane, Tiny Lister, Jr., Blair Underwood

© POLYGRAM VIDEO

PREDATOR

D: John McTiernan 107 m

R | ACT SUS SF | 1987 | COLOR | Sex Nud Viol Lang AdSit

9 Heart-pounding suspense. Schwarzenegger and his crew of trained mercenaries are hired by the CIA to go into a Latin American jungle to rescue a group South American officials kidnapped by terrorists. Just as they are about to complete their mission, they are surprised to discover that they are themselves being stalked by a fear-some other-world killer - a large, ugly, ferocious alien man/monster with truly awesome powers who enjoys hunting and killing. It has come to earth to hunt the hunters - humans. Fast-paced, intense suspense as team members are picked off one by one. Action-packed.

A: Arnold Schwarzenegger, Jesse Ventura, Bill Duke, Sonny Landham, Carl Weathers, Richard Chaves

© FOXVIDEO 1515

PRESIDIO, THE

D: Peter Hyams 97 m

R | CRM ACT | 1988 | COLOR | Sex Nud Viol Lang AdSit

8 An old-fashioned murder mystery with a couple of new twists. A female soldier is murdered while on patrol inside a military compound in San Francisco. The police detective (Mark Harmon) assigned to the case is distressed to learn that the base is being commanded by his old nemesis, Sean Connery. The state of their personal animosities is worsened when he also falls for Connery's daughter (Ryan). The two fight over jurisdiction on the case but a comradery grows when they combine their efforts and close in on the killer. Good action and chase sequences.

A: Sean Connery, Mark Harmon, Meg Ryan, Jack Warden, Mark Blum

© PARAMOUNT HOME VIDEO 31978

PRINCE OF THE CITY

D: Sidney Lumet 167 m

R | CRM DMA ACT | 1981 | COLOR | Sex Nud Viol Lang AdSit

8 A powerfully gripping and emotionally draining film, based on the true 1971 story of a member of an elite corp of New York drug cops who reveals a pervasive corruption on the force. It is his personal story of how he was moved to violate the policeman's code of silence. And, it is a story of the ability of power, drugs and money to corrupt even the best. Our cop is determined to expose the corruption, but do it without destroying his friends - after all, they are just victims of the process - but he can't. So, he becomes the biggest victim, when he cannot protect, and must betray and destroy, his best friends.

A: Treat Williams, Jerry Orbach, Richard Foronjy, Lindsay Crouse, Don Billett, Kenny Marino

© WARNER HOME VIDEO 22021

PROFESSIONAL, THE

D: Luc Besson 109 m

R | ACT DMA | 1995 | COLOR | Sex Nud Viol Lang AdSit

8 Very stylish, unique, involving and very curious film by the director of LA FEMME NIKITA. Leon is known as "the cleaner." He is an extremely competent assassin who can be counted upon to get any job done. He is also an extremely lonely and isolated man whose only purpose in life is his job. But that simple world is turned up-side-down, when he is befriended by an abused 12-year-old girl living next door. And, when her drug-dealing father and her family is brutally murdered by a corrupt DEA agent, she comes to her new friend for sanctuary...and to have him teach her his trade. This is a very realistic film. The characters are believable. The emotions are real but so is the bloody violence. Very interesting.

A: Jean Reno, Gary Oldman, Natalie Portman, Danny Aiello, Peter Appel, Michael Badalucco

© COLUMBIA TRISTAR HOME VIDEO 74743

PROFESSIONALS, THE

D: Richard Brooks 117 m

PG | WST ACT SUS | 1966 | COLOR | Sex Nud Viol Lang AdSit

9 Thrilling action-packed Western manned with some of the genre's best talent. A team of four mercenaries (an explosives expert, a horse trainer, an archer and a sharpshooter) are hired by a wealthy aging Texan to track down his beautiful young wife who has been kidnapped by a Mexican bandit. Heavily out-manned and out-gunned, their raid upon the stronghold yields up the woman, but they are hotly pursued on the way back and are surprised to find that the woman is not at all eager to go with them. Intense actioner with a high excitement quotient, top-flight performances and quality production values.

A: Burt Lancaster, Lee Marvin, Claudia Cardinale, Jack Palance, Woody Strode, Ralph Bellamy

© GOODTIMES 4501

PROGRAM, THE

D: David Ward 112 m

R | DMA ACT | 1993 | COLOR | Sex Nud Viol Lang AdSit

8 It is not necessary to be a fan of football to appreciate this video. Most of the action occurs off the field. The excitement of the game is there and there are plenty of football scenes, but the emphasis is on the people and pressures that make up the reality of big-time college football. This is not an indictment of the game but rather an attempt to reveal the real-life, behind the scenes truths: The coach who is pressured to win, so his school can reap the millions of dollars it brings in. The kid who wants to play the game so bad that he will risk his life with steroids. The quarterback who is a drunk. And, the poor kids looking for respect and a way out.

A: James Caan, Omar Epps, Crag Sheffer, Halle Berry, Kristy Swanson, Abraham Benrubi

© TOUCHSTONE HOME VIDEO 2312

Q&A

D: Sidney Lumet 132 m

R | CRM ACT | 1990 | COLOR | Sex Nud Viol Lang AdSit

8 Gritty hard-edged crime drama. Weather-beaten maverick cop Nolte kills a drug dealer in self defense. The seemingly open and shut case is routinely investigated by rookie district attorney Hutton, who discovers that Nolte has a dark side. He is a hard man, used to working alone in a cruel world. His methods are unorthodox and the characters of his world are weird and gruesome. Hutton wants to respect Nolte, but the more he investigates, the more his witnesses turn up dead. Nolte is a powerhouse the entire way. Exciting, but quite involved and saddled with a muddled ending.

A: Nick Nolte, Timothy Hutton, Armand Assante, Patrick O'Neal, Lee Richardson, Luis Guzman

© HBO VIDEO 0381

QUEST FOR FIRE

D: Jean-Jacques Annaud 100 m

R | DMA ACT | 1982 | COLOR | Sex Nud Viol Lang AdSit

8 Remarkable fictional epic that takes you back to the very dawn on mankind! When a primitive tribe loses the only source of fire they know, they send McGill, Perlman and El Kadi to find the elusive flame somewhere else. On their quest, the three encounter a tribe of cannibals, woolly mammoths and a woman (Chong). She teaches McGill about love and tenderness, and how to make real fire. Touching, warm, compelling. This is a serious and realistic odyssey with special custom-made languages and body movements that were all conceived by zoologist Desmond Morris. The costumes were an Oscar winner.

A: Everett McGill, Rae Dawn Chong, Ron Perlman, Nameer El Kadi

© FOXVIDEO 1148

QUICK AND THE DEAD, THE

D: Robert Day 91 m

NR | WST ACT | 1987 | COLOR | Sex Nud Viol Lang AdSit

8 Very good made-for-cable movie about a young family, uprooted by the Civil War, who attempt to make a home for themselves in the untamed West. When the family comes under attack, the father (Conti) accepts the advice and aid of a wanderer (Elliott) to help protect them. The green Conti and his family come to rely very heavily on Elliot's survival skills. Soon Conti's wife (Capshaw) and his boy begin to doubt him and become very enamored of their new protector. Based on the Louis L'Amour story, the flavor and feel of the lawless Old West is beautifully captured. A classy Western.

A: Sam Elliott, Tom Conti, Kate Capshaw, Kenny Morrison, Matt Clark, Lean Louis

© WARNER HOME VIDEO 818

QUIGLEY DOWN UNDER

D: Simon Wincer 121 m

PG-13 | WST ACT | 1990 | COLOR | Sex Nud Viol Lang AdSit

7 Entertaining "Western" with a decidedly different twist. Selleck plays Quigley, an American sharpshooter who has been hired by an Australian sheep rancher and land baron. He arrives in the Outback of the 1860s and is hauled across hundreds of miles to meet his employer. The two take an immediate dislike to each other, especially when Quigley finds that he has been hired to hunt down Aborigines. Quigley is beaten, tied to a crazy woman, the two are taken out into the wilderness and left to die, but they don't cooperate. Quigley is now in a war to the death with the vicious land baron.

A: Tom Selleck, Laura San Giacomo, Alan Rickman, Chris Haywood

Distributed By MGM/UA Home Video M902173

QUILLER MEMORANDUM, THE

D: Michael Anderson 103 m

NR | SUS ACT | 1966 | COLOR | Sex Nud Viol Lang AdSit

8 No gadgets or gimmicks in this intelligent espionage thriller! An American agent (Segal) in Berlin is recruited by head-Brit Guinness to help uncover a neo-Nazi group that is gaining momentum in Berlin. The two agents who were previously assigned to the project have been killed. Segal soon learns that even the guys on his side aren't trustworthy. He can trust no one - not Guinness, not sensuous teacher Senta Berger, and not Von Sydow, the scheming German aristocrat. He is alone. One mistake and he is dead, too.

A: George Segal, Senta Berger, Alec Guinness, Max von Sydow, George Sanders, Robert Helpmann

© FOXVIDEO 1403

RAGING BULL

D: Martin Scorsese 130 m

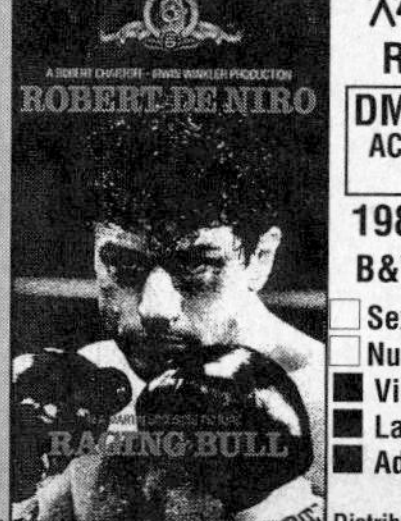

R | DMA ACT | 1980 | B&W | Sex Nud Viol Lang AdSit

9 Brutally compelling film! In and out of the ring, the only real opponent middleweight prize-fighter Jake LaMotta (De Niro) ever had was himself. In a remarkable effect, De Niro ages from an aggressive lean boxer in his twenties to a bloated overweight hack comic in mid-life. The story of his career is told in flashbacks. The rise to fame and his fall from it are all told with intelligence. Powerful and intense. The violent boxing scenes are graphically realistic. De Niro won an Academy Award - the film received eight nominations overall. This is one of the greats.

A: Robert De Niro, Joe Pesci, Cathy Moriarty, Frank Vincent, Nicholas Colasanto, Theresa Saldana

Distributed By MGM/UA Home Video M201322

RAIDERS OF THE LOST ARK

D: Steven Spielberg 115 m

PG | ACT SUS | 1981 | COLOR

Sex Nud Viol Lang AdSit

10 Rip-roaring, rousing, riotous adventure that never stops! Indiana Jones (Ford) is an archaeologist who embarks on a quest in 1936 to find the Lost Ark of the Covenant, a religious relic that possesses supernatural powers. Along the way, he battles Nazis, swordsmen, runaway boulders, venomous snakes and a whole vat of death and danger. Powerful, courageous, gritty - Ford is a huge screen hero. Spielberg's tribute to the Saturday matinees of old is better than any revival. The action just keeps coming at you in this thrilling roller-coaster ride! Followed by two sequels.

A: Harrison Ford, Karen Allen, Paul Freeman, Ronald Lacey, John Rhys-Davies, Denholm Elliott

© PARAMOUNT HOME VIDEO 1376

RAID ON ENTEBBE

D: Irvin Kershner 113 m

NR | ACT SUS | 1976 | COLOR

Sex Nud Viol Lang AdSit

7 A well-made dramatization of a real-life dramatic rescue! When terrorists hijacked an Israeli plane in 1976 and took 103 Israeli hostages to Uganda's Entebbe airport, the Israelies struck back. Israeli leader Finch orders a daring military rescue mission into a foreign country to get their people back. Bronson and Bucholz are to be at the helm of the mission. Made for TV, Finch received an Emmy nomination for this compelling drama. Although the impact was greater at the time it was released, it is still a good action film with strong suspenseful elements.

A: Charles Bronson, Peter Finch, Horst Buchholz, Martin Balsam, Jack Warden, Yaphet Kotto

© HBO VIDEO TVB2455

RAMBO: FIRST BLOOD II

D: George P. Cosmatos 95 m

R | ACT | 1985 | COLOR

Sex Nud Viol Lang AdSit

8 Rambo, the larger-than-life commando introduced in the film FIRST BLOOD, returns for more peril and risk in this action-packed war movie! Released from prison by his former Green Beret commander (Crenna), Rambo's mission is to rescue American MIA's detained and tortured for more than a decade inside Cambodia. Thick into the danger, his own government deserts him, but he goes on - undaunted. He enlists the aid of a beautiful gun-toting Vietnamese woman (Nickson) and vows vengeance on those who deserted him. A huge film. Lots of violence. A lean, mean, tough money machine!

A: Sylvester Stallone, Richard Crenna, Julia Nickson, Charles Napier, Steven Berkoff, Martin Kove

© LIVE HOME VIDEO 65924

RAMBO III

D: Peter MacDonald 102 m

R | ACT | 1988 | COLOR

Sex Nud Viol Lang AdSit

7 John Rambo is hammering at it again in this very gritty actioner! His friend and mentor, Crenna, is captured while on a top-secret mission in Afghanistan. Courageous Rambo disrupts his now serene life and, with the aid of Afghan rebels, sets out on a dangerous journey to rescue Crenna and wipe out the Soviets. The third film in the series features masterful explosions and graphic violence as the former and famous Vietnam vet does what he does best. Fans will love the hero as he risks life and limb to destroy evil.

A: Sylvester Stallone, Richard Crenna, Marc De Jonge, Kurtwood Smith, Spiros Focas, Sasson Gabai

© LIVE HOME VIDEO 65922

RAN

D: Akira Kurosawa 160 m

R | FOR DMA ACT | 1985 | COLOR

Sex Nud Viol Lang AdSit

8 This is an epic and masterful saga about a battle for a kingdom in Japan that was adapted from Shakespeare's King Lear by master film-maker Kurosawa. In the 16th century, Japanese King Hidetora (Nakadai) leaves his kingdom to his eldest son hoping to avoid bloodshed, but does not realize the implications of his decision because his evil daughter-in-law is plotting against him. His two younger sons are also in strong opposition to his decision. Soon they all plot against each other. This lavish Oscar-winning production was very highly acclaimed. A story of heartbreak, greed and war. Subtitles.

A: Tatsuya Nakadai, Jinpachi Nezu, Akira Terao, Daisuku Ryu, Mieko Harada, Yoshiko Miyazaki

© CBS/FOX VIDEO 3732

RAPID FIRE

D: Dwight H. Little 95 m

R | ACT | 1992 | COLOR

Sex Nud Viol Lang AdSit

8 Jake Lo is an art major at a California college. His father had been a CIA operative in communist China and but died at Tiananmen Square during the democracy demonstrations. Now Jake wants nothing to do with politics or causes of any kind. But, when he accidentally witnesses a murder by a Mafia kingpin, he becomes an unwilling big target and a key chess piece in a big game. Then, when his federal protectors turn out to also be secret Mafia hitmen, Jake has to take things into his own hands if he is to survive. His hands are lethal weapons. Slick action entertainment. Lots of fight scenes, as you would expect, but not cliched. Well done.

A: Brandon Lee, Powers Boothe, Nick Mancuso, Raymond J. Barry, Kate Hodge

© FOXVIDEO 1978

RAW DEAL

D: John Irvin 97 m

R | ACT | 1986 | COLOR

Sex Nud Viol Lang AdSit

6 Campy Schwarzenegger action flick. Former FBI agent (Schwarzenegger) falls from grace because he always does things his own way. So they throw him out. However, he is given one chance to come back. He has to infiltrate and destroy the head of the Chicago mob scene and his whole organization. The only catch is, the entire assignment is illegal. Striving to redeem himself, Schwarzenegger pulverizes everything in his path as he goes after the bad guys. The predictable plot and results are saved by some wry humor in this comic-book adventure. Arnold and action fans only.

A: Arnold Schwarzenegger, Ed Lauter, Sam Wanamaker, Darren McGavin, Kathryn Harrold, Paul Shenar

© HBO VIDEO TVA9982

RED HEAT

D: Walter Hill 106 m

R | ACT COM | 1988 | COLOR

Sex Nud Viol Lang AdSit

6 Unrelenting modern-day shoot-'em-up! Schwarzenegger is a tough and highly disciplined Russian detective who is sent to the United States to nab a Russian drug kingpin (O'Ross). When the druglord escapes Schwarzenegger's tight grip, Arnold pairs up with an obnoxious, lackadaisical Chicago cop (Belushi). Completely different in style, attitude and method, Schwarzenegger and Belushi clash in the biggest way, but eventually have a meeting of the minds and track down O'Ross through the tough streets of Chicago. Rough and sometimes funny!

A: Arnold Schwarzenegger, James Belushi, Peter Boyle, Ed O'Ross, Larry Fishburne, Gina Gershon

© LIVE HOME VIDEO 66057

RED TENT, THE

D: Mickail K. Kalatozov 121 m

G | DMA ACT | 1969 | COLOR

Sex Nud Viol Lang AdSit

7 Rugged adventure and a gripping saga about attempts to rescue a downed Italian dirigible crew. In 1928 the Italian dirigible "Italia" crashed in the Arctic while exploring the North Pole. For days the crew huddled inside the makeshift red tent sending out S.O.S. radio messages. Ronald Amundsen (Connery) leads a daring ground rescue attempt but dies trying to find the crew. Told in flashback form, this lavishly produced film is even more compelling because it is based upon a true story. Emotional and extremely well-acted. Beautiful photography.

A: Sean Connery, Peter Finch, Hardy Kruger, Claudia Cardinale

© PARAMOUNT HOME VIDEO 8041

REPO MAN

D: Alex Cox 93 m

R | COM ACT | 1983 | COLOR

Sex Nud Viol Lang AdSit

6 Quirky and peculiar comedy. An L.A. punkrocker (Estevez) takes a seedy job repossessing cars from owners who fall delinquent on their payments. His slimy mentor (Stanton) is an expert at the art of repo and takes the young punk under his wing, teaching him the ropes. However things get zany when they take back a vintage Chevy Malibu worth $20,000 and they find that the trunk is also stuffed full of radioactive aliens! An offbeat and often weird movie that is not for every taste, but if you're searching for something different - this is definitely it.

A: Harry Dean Stanton, Emilio Estevez, Vonetta McGee, Olivia Barash, Sy Richardson, Tracey Walter

© MCA/UNIVERSAL HOME VIDEO, INC. 80071

REPORT TO THE COMMISSIONER

D: Milton Katselas 113 m

PG | CRM ACT | 1974 | COLOR

Sex Nud Viol Lang AdSit

7 A tough and gritty crime drama. A naive and idealistic rookie cop (Moriarty) on the New York City beat accidentally kills an undercover agent. The beautiful female cop (Blakely) was posing as an accomplice and live-in lover to a big-time drug dealer (King). When Moriatry pulls that trigger, he also gets pulled into an elaborate cover-up by his corrupt superiors and he becomes their scapegoat.

A: Michael Moriarty, Yaphet Kotto, Susan Blakely, Hector Elizondo, Tony King

Distributed By MGM/UA Home Video M301297

RESERVOIR DOGS

D: Quentin Tarantino 99 m

R | CRM ACT | 1992 | COLOR

Sex Nud Viol Lang AdSit

7 Extremely violent crime film that uses extremes of violence and profanity to shock its audience into revulsion. However, it is also a very intriguing film that is reasonably well told, using a technique first used in the classic film THE ASPHALT JUNGLE. Most of the film takes place in an empty warehouse where a group of vicious thugs have gathered to figure out how the jewelry robbery they had tried to pull off could have gone so bad. Then, most of the story, in its many convolutions, unwinds as a series of flashbacks. This is a very hard-edged film. Don't watch it if you are easily offended.

A: Harvey Keitel, Tim Roth, Michael Madsen, Chris Penn, Steve Buscemi, Lawrence Tierney

© LIVE HOME VIDEO 48998

RETURN OF THE DRAGON

D: Bruce Lee — 90 m

R | ACT | 1973 | COLOR

7 Martial arts master Bruce Lee appears in this, his third and last, Kung Fu film (but it was actually filmed before ENTER THE DRAGON). He plays a distant cousin visiting relatives in Rome. Threatened by the Italian mob, the family is unconvinced when this shy quiet country boy insists on trying to help them, but they change their minds when he unleashes his lethal arsenal of punches, leaps and kicks. The Italian mob is forced to bring in their own heavy artillery in the form of seven-time US and World Karate Champion Chuck Norris (his film debut). Low-budget mindless fun.

Sex ☐ Nud ☐ Viol ■ Lang ☐ AdSit ◢

A: Bruce Lee, Chuck Norris, Nora Miao

© CBS/FOX VIDEO 6123

RETURN OF THE JEDI

D: Richard Marquand — 134 m

PG | SF ACT SUS | 1983 | COLOR

9 Thrilling finale to the hugely popular, exciting and imaginative STAR WARS trilogy from George Lucas. In this episode, Luke Skywalker has further mastered his skills as a Jedi Master of the "Force." He first rescues Princess Leia and Hans Solo from the vile and decadent Jabba-the-Hut, then aids in the destruction of the monstrously powerful Death Star by infiltrating the evil forces of the Empire, seeking out its all-powerful leader Darth Vader - to destroy him. Great characters. Great special effects. Great fun!

Sex ☐ Nud ☐ Viol ◢ Lang ☐ AdSit ☐

A: Mark Hamill, Carrie Fisher, Harrison Ford, Billy Dee Williams, Dave Prowse, Peter Mayhew

© FOXVIDEO 1478

RETURN TO LONESOME DOVE

D: Mike Robe — 330 m

NR | WST DMA ACT | 1993 | COLOR

8 Good follow-up to the fantastic original. Woodrow has taken his friend back to Texas to bury him. But, before going back, he stops off to ask another former Texas ranger to lead a group in capturing a herd of mustangs and driving them back to Montana. While they are doing that, he will stop off in Nebraska to buy blooded stock. He will breed the two to create a new hardier stock. Newt is to meet him in Nebraska, but instead gets in a gun fight and thrown into jail. He is paroled to a wealthy cattle baron with a pretty young wife. Much of the fire is gone from the original, but it is still well worth a watch.

Sex ☐ Nud ☐ Viol ◢ Lang ☐ AdSit ◢

A: John Voight, Barbara Hershey, Rick Schroder, Louis Gossett, Jr., William Petersen, Oliver Reed

© CABIN FEVER ENTERTAINMENT 9536

RIDE THE HIGH COUNTRY

D: Sam Peckinpah — 93 m

NR | WST ACT | 1962 | COLOR

9 Considered Peckinpah's finest film and one so good that two of Hollywood's biggest Western stars retired rather than try to top it. Two grizzled old friends and old-time gunfighters join forces to escort a large gold shipment. Along the way they reminisce, and even work together to aid a young bride (Hartley's debut) escape from her barbarian in-laws. While McCrea wants only to do a good and respectable job, Scott secretly wants to steal the gold they are supposed to be guarding. Beautiful photography, wonderful performances and an interesting story.

Sex ☐ Nud ☐ Viol ◢ Lang ☐ AdSit ☐

A: Randolph Scott, Joel McCrea, Mariette Hartley, Edgar Buchanan, Ronald Starr, Warren Oates

Distributed By MGM/UA Home Video M600850

RIGHT STUFF, THE

D: Philip Kaufman — 193 m

PG | DMA ACT | 1983 | COLOR

9 Fascinating and invigorating film that, even though quite long, is never boring. Seven pilots are chosen to be the first Americans in space under the NASA program, Project Mercury. This film tells their stories. Although the pivotal character is Chuck Yeager, all seven receive considerable attention, as does the entire training process that launched America's space program. An epic story, with plenty of exhilarating moments, that does not disappoint. Watch for the real Chuck Yeager in a cameo. Winner of four Oscars, including Score.

Sex ☐ Nud ☐ Viol ☐ Lang ◢ AdSit ◢

A: Charles Frank, Scott Glenn, Ed Harris, Sam Shepard, Fred Ward, Barbara Hershey

© WARNER HOME VIDEO 20014

RIO BRAVO

D: Howard Hawks — 141 m

NR | WST ACT COM | 1959 | COLOR

10 Exuberant Western with Wayne as the classic tough-guy sheriff who has arrested the brother of a wealthy rancher. The rancher wants his brother free. John wants him tried, but the rancher has a whole herd of cowboys and gunslingers ready to help him. John has a drunken deputy (Martin), a toothless, grizzled old man (Brennan) and a young untried gunhand (Nelson). Great fun. Lots of shootin' but good laughs too from a talented cast. Redone by Hawks, again with Wayne, in 1967 as EL DORADO - also was the model for ASSAULT ON PRECINCT 13 and RIO LOBO.

Sex ☐ Nud ☐ Viol ◢ Lang ☐ AdSit ☐

A: John Wayne, Dean Martin, Angie Dickinson, Walter Brennan, Ricky Nelson, Ward Bond

© WARNER HOME VIDEO 11050

RIO CONCHOS

D: Gordon Douglas — 107 m

NR | WST ACT | 1964 | COLOR

8 A rootin' shootin' good time! An ex-Confederate soldier (O'Brien) is still fighting the Civil War by running guns to the Apaches to get vengeance on the North. Four men, led by a US calvary captain (Whitman), are hunting for 2,000 stolen Spencer repeating rifles. They know O'Brien has them, so they are on their way into Mexico with a wagonload of gun powder to use as bait to draw him out. Boone, an Apache-hating ex-rebel; Franciosa, a charming killer avoiding the noose; and Brown, an Army sergeant, join Whitman in his quest. Some of the best in traditional action-packed Old West adventure.

Sex ☐ Nud ☐ Viol ◢ Lang ☐ AdSit ◢

A: Richard Boone, Stuart Whitman, Edmond O'Brien, Anthony Franciosa, Jim Brown

© FOXVIDEO 1224

RIO LOBO

D: Howard Hawks — 103 m

G | WST ACT | 1970 | COLOR

6 Second remake of the original giant 1959 hit RIO BRAVO and its 1967 follow-up EL DORADO. This time Wayne plays an ex-Union colonel who tracks down some Civil War traitors, who are also gold thieves. In the process, he winds up helping out a small town held hostage by a corrupt sheriff. An old story that gets a considerable boost from the talents of Wayne and Jack Elam, as a crazy old codger with a shotgun. This was also the last screen appearance of Sherry Lansing, who became a major studio exec.

Sex ☐ Nud ☐ Viol ◢ Lang ☐ AdSit ☐

A: John Wayne, Jennifer O'Neill, Jorge Rivero, Jack Elam, Sherry Lansing, Chris Mitchum

© FOXVIDEO 7016

RISING SUN

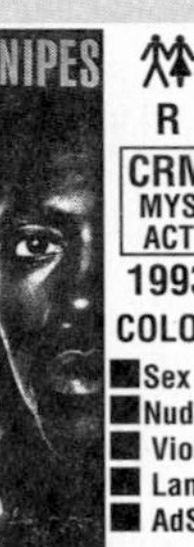

D: Philip Kaufman — 129 m

R | CRM MYS ACT | 1993 | COLOR

9 Very complicated, very sexy and enthralling. Snipes is an L.A. cop called in to investigate the death of a beautiful girl found dead on the boardroom table of very important Japanese company that is negotiating to purchase a sensitive American company. He is instructed to pick up Connery, a veteran officer experienced in the culture of the Japanese. Their investigation leads them through an intricate high-tech coverup concealing the business war between two Japanese companies. It is a battle between important and dangerous people and a complicated jigsaw puzzle of culture, intrigue and fast action. Excellent.

Sex ■ Nud ■ Viol ■ Lang ■ AdSit ■

A: Sean Connery, Wesley Snipes, Harvey Keitel, Cary-Hiroyuki Tagawa, Tia Carrere, Mako

© FOXVIDEO 8520

RIVER WILD, THE

D: Curtis Hanson — 112 m

PG-13 | ACT | 1994 | COLOR

6 Meryl Streep and her architect husband have just about had it. She had been a river guide when she was younger and they have planned to take a river rafting trip together with their son, to see if things can be put back together. However, their trip turns into a nightmare when they stumble on to two armed robbers who have planned their own trip down the river. But, their guide just died of bullet wounds he got in the hold up. So, they have decided to invite themselves along with Streep and her family on a wild ride down a rugged river. Some pretty exciting scenes running the rapids, but much is predictable and some of it doesn't hold water.

Sex ☐ Nud ☐ Viol ◢ Lang ■ AdSit ◢

A: Meryl Streep, Kevin Bacon, David Strathairn, Joseph Mazzello, John C. Reilly, Benjamin Bratt

© MCA/UNIVERSAL HOME VIDEO, INC. 82008

ROAD GAMES

D: Richard Franklin — 100 m

PG | SUS ACT | 1981 | COLOR

7 Intrigue and gore keep this offbeat thriller moving along. Oddball trucker Stacy Keach makes up stories about the people he meets to occupy his time on a long haul. This time, along the way, he picks up a female hitchhiker (Curtis), a rich girl looking for a change in her mundane life, and she joins him in his mind games. They spy one particular green van and become suspicious that there really may be something afoul with it and decide to investigate further. Director Franklin does a superb job of maintaining a high level of suspense. The audience is never really sure who it can trust and who it can't.

Sex ☐ Nud ☐ Viol ■ Lang ◢ AdSit ■

A: Stacy Keach, Jamie Lee Curtis, Marion Edward, Grant Page, Bill Stacey

© NEW LINE HOME VIDEO 90138

ROAD WARRIOR, THE - MAD MAX 2

D: George Miller — 96 m

R | SF ACT | 1982 | COLOR

8 Intense and very stylish action in this follow-up to MAD MAX. Gibson is roving the post-nuclear desolation in the Australian Outback when he is drawn into a frantic attempt to save one small band of survivors from a group of evil marauders and new wave warriors that is trying to take over the fuel depot belonging to the survivors. In the powerful climax, Max desperately leads the survivors in a headlong dash to safety through the Outback, driving a supertanker flat out across the desert while also conducting a running battle with the pursuing villains.

Sex ◢ Nud ◢ Viol ■ Lang ■ AdSit ◢

A: Mel Gibson, Bruce Spence, Vernon Wells, Virginia Hey, Mike Preston, Emil Minty

© WARNER HOME VIDEO 11181

ROBIN AND MARIAN

D: Richard Lester 107 m

PG

ROM ACT

1976

COLOR

Sex Nud Viol Lang AdSit

7 Robin Hood (Connery) returns to Sherwood Forest after 20 years of battling in the Crusades, along with Little John and King Richard (Harris). When King Richard is accidentally slain, his wicked brother John takes the throne and Robin heads for the woods. Robin's arch nemesis, the Sheriff of Nottingham (Shaw), is ordered to remove the clergy. Robin seeks out his love, Maid Marian (Hepburn), but finds that she has become a nun - the Mother Superior to be exact. The pair rekindle their love for each other and Robin prepares to confront his enemy. What a cast!

A: Sean Connery, Audrey Hepburn, Robert Shaw, Richard Harris, Nicol Williamson, Denholm Elliott

© COLUMBIA TRISTAR HOME VIDEO 60097

ROBIN HOOD: PRINCE OF THIEVES

D: Kevin Reynolds 144 m

PG-13

ACT ROM

1991

COLOR

Sex Nud Viol Lang AdSit

8 Good entertainment in a spectacular and lush swashbuckler! This 1990s version of the classic tale is a little more rugged, has a lot more gritty realism and less of the idealistic charm of past efforts. It is also lavishly produced, with great attention to detail. Costner's medieval Robin Hood is benevolent, tough, charming and gritty (but he doesn't have an English accent). Alan Rickman is deliciously sinister as the twisted Sheriff of Nottingham, and Mastrantonio holds her own as the captivating and feisty Maid Marian who captures Robin's heart. Action, suspense, romance - there's a little bit of everything all wrapped up in this delightful adventure!

A: Kevin Costner, Morgan Freeman, Mary Elizabeth Mastrantonio, Christian Slater, Alan Rickman, Geraldine Rickman

© WARNER HOME VIDEO 14000

ROBOCOP

D: Paul Verhoeven 103 m

R

ACT SF

1987

COLOR

Sex Nud Viol Lang AdSit

9 White-hot action! Detroit, in the not so far distant future, is a lawless city. A policeman (Weller) is killed on duty and the corporation that runs the police department uses what's left of him to create a bold new policeman. He is a fusion between man and machine. The dead cop is turned into the ultimate crime fighter - Robocop. However, Robocop still has residual memories that remind him of what he has lost and also information that will enable him to track down his own killers to exact a fierce revenge. A huge hit with unbelievable special effects. Tightly wound and powerfully violent.

A: Peter Weller, Nancy Allen, Ronny Cox, Kurtwood Smith, Miguel Ferrer, Robert Doqui

© ORION PICTURES CORPORATION 8610

ROBOCOP 2

D: Irvin Kershner 117 m

R

ACT SF

1990

COLOR

Sex Nud Viol Lang AdSit

7 Wildly violent action! There is big trouble in Detroit. A wicked drug kingpin (Noonan) wants to completely permeate the city with his own powerful new drug called "Nuke." Meanwhile, the company that created Robocop has made a newer version of the machine. However, this time the superhero's look-alike is a thoroughly evil cyborg. Robocop (Weller) must rid the city of both menaces - not an easy task. A very grim prediction for the future and a film that is full of fierce, ultra-violent, non-stop action.

A: Peter Weller, Nancy Allen, Dan O'Herlihy, Belinda Bauer, Tom Noonan, Gabriel Damon

© ORION PICTURES CORPORATION 8764

ROB ROY

D: Michael Caton-Jones 139 m

R

DMA ACT

1995

COLOR

Sex Nud Viol Lang AdSit

8 1717 Scotland was a feudal state in the process of breaking down. Poverty was widespread and many of its people were emigrating to "The Americas." The aristocrats controlled the land and the money. Robert Roy MacGregor was a real man and a legendary hero. He was the leader of his clan, a man of fiercely-defended honor and a dedicated husband. When he was cheated by a corrupt bureaucrat, his cattle killed, his home burned and his wife violated, he fought back against long odds to reclaim his defiled honor and became a national hero. Richly filmed against beautiful scenery, this film captures both the physical sense of the times and the feel of the everyday society. Beautiful, but somewhat ponderous.

A: Liam Neeson, Jessica Lange, John Hurt, Tim Roth, Eric Stoltz, Brian Cox

Distributed By MGM/UA Home Video M905228

ROCKETEER, THE

D: Joe Johnston 109 m

PG

ACT ROM

1991

COLOR

Sex Nud Viol Lang AdSit

7 Cliff Secord (Campbell) is an adventurous 1930s daredevil pilot who has discovered a secret government jet pack and takes to the skies with it on a wild joy ride. He's an adventurous sort and is just having fun, but the government wants it back. Unfortunately, so do some local hoods who are trying to deliver it to a secret buyer for a big payday. What they don't know is that their buyer, a famous Hollywood hero, is also a Nazi agent. Campbell's beautiful girlfriend (Connelly) gets unwillingly pulled into the fiasco too when she is romanced by the Hollywood hunk. Great period feel. Pretty good excitement, too, in spite of being overly long.

A: Bill Campbell, Alan Arkin, Jennifer Connelly, Paul Sorvino, Timothy Dalton, Terry O'Quinn

© WALT DISNEY HOME VIDEO 1239

ROCKY

D: John G. Avildsen 125 m

PG

DMA ACT

1976

COLOR

Sex Nud Viol Lang AdSit

10 Triple Academy Award-winning feel-good powerhouse! An unknown, small-time loser, a thumb-breaker from the streets of Philadelphia (Stallone), gets one miraculous shot at the boxing championship when champion Apollo Creed (Weathers) offers to fight him as a publicity stunt. For Appolo Creed, this is a joke - but for Rocky, it is everything. Rocky is relentlessly trained by a gnarled old has-been trainer (Meridith) and inspired by his shy girlfriend (Shire). This endearing film really went the distance with audiences and spawned numerous sequels. It is a rousing charmer that never gets old!

A: Sylvester Stallone, Talia Shire, Burt Young, Burgess Meredith, Carl Weathers, Thayer David

Distributed By MGM/UA Home Video M200249

ROCKY II

D: Sylvester Stallone 119 m

PG

DMA ACT

1979

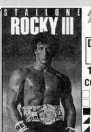

COLOR

Sex Nud Viol Lang AdSit

8 Rocky (Stallone) went from being a nobody to a national sensation in the first picture. Now he has become disenchanted with his new-found fame and is even unable to find work. After being taunted by his rival, Apollo Creed (Weathers), he accepts an offer for a rematch, in spite of the objections of his now-pregnant wife (Shire). Rocky rigorously trains under the keen eye of his personal trainer (Meredith), while also fighting with Shire at home. He is nearly destroyed when she, his tower of strength and inspiration, lapses into a coma after childbirth. Sentimental, powerful and uplifting!

A: Sylvester Stallone, Talia Shire, Carl Weathers, Burgess Meredith, Burt Young

Distributed By MGM/UA Home Video M200250

ROCKY III

D: Sylvester Stallone 103 m

PG

DMA ACT

1982

COLOR

Sex Nud Viol Lang AdSit

7 Stallone pounds out another rousing success! Rocky, now a man of wealth and leisure, is challenged into a new fight by the bullish Clubber Lang (Mr T.). However, Rocky is now soft and loses big, so he must reach deep within himself to find the inner strength needed to win a rematch - "the eye of the tiger." This time around, Rocky has to deal with a new challenger - fear. His longtime and trusted manager (Meredith) has died, but his new manager, Apollo Creed, teaches him some fancy footwork and quick moves in preparation for the big battle ahead.

A: Sylvester Stallone, Talia Shire, Hulk Hogan, Mr. T, Burt Young, Burgess Meredith

Distributed By MGM/UA Home Video M202086

ROCKY IV

D: Sylvester Stallone 93 m

PG

DMA ACT

1985

COLOR

Sex Nud Viol Lang AdSit

6 Rocky faces his biggest challenge. He is to represent America and avenge the death of his friend and teacher, Apollo Creed. This time Rocky prepares to do battle with Drago (Lundgren), a hulking superhuman Russian boxer with a death wish. Drago trains with stardust and sophisticated computer equipment, while Rocky has to train in a cold and rugged Siberia using old-fashioned primitive equipment. His wife (Shire) stands by him once again as he battles not only against the ominous powerhouse, but also for the good ol' USA. Intense and fierce, but much of the charm is gone.

A: Sylvester Stallone, Dolph Lundgren, Talia Shire, Carl Weathers, Burt Young, Brigitte Nielsen

Distributed By MGM/UA Home Video M202084

ROLLERBALL

D: Norman Jewison 118 m

R

ACT SF

1975

COLOR

Sex Nud Viol Lang AdSit

7 In the year 2018, corporations rule the world. All violence has been prohibited. There are no wars and no crime. Instead, the corporations have created the game of Rollerball, an extremely violent combination of football, basketball, hockey and roller derby. The game's best and most popular player is James Caan. He is so popular that he has become dangerous. The heads of the corporations want him to retire, but he refuses. They take away the woman he loves and still he refuses. Now they have changed the rules of the game. Now it is a game to the death.

A: James Caan, John Houseman, Maud Adams, John Beck, Moses Gunn, Ralph Richardson

Distributed By MGM/UA Home Video M300262

ROLLING THUNDER

D: John Flynn 99 m

R

ACT CRM

1977

COLOR

Sex Nud Viol Lang AdSit

8 Graphic action! A P.O.W. (Devane) returns to his small Texan home and family after eight miserable and brutal years in Vietnam. He is honored with 2000 silver dollars (symbolizing one for each day held captive) by the grateful town, but thieves quickly move in for the money. They torture him and murder his wife and child. Enraged, he enlists the aid of an ex-P.O.W. pal Jones. The two then methodically and systematically seek cold and emotionless revenge on the murderers. Very well done with well drawn characters. Bloody but engrossing.

A: William Devane, Tommy Lee Jones, James Best, Dabney Coleman, Linda Haynes, Lisa Richards

© GOODTIMES 74066

ROMANCING THE STONE

D: Michael Douglas 106 m

PG · ACT ROM COM · 1984 · COLOR

Sex Nud Viol Lang AdSit

8 Wildly fun! A shy romance novelist (Turner) receives a mysterious package from her dead brother-in-law which she must then take to the jungles of Columbia to rescue her kidnapped sister. Not knowing that she is carrying a treasure map, she finds herself embroiled in danger from the minute she steps off the plane. To her rescue comes wild and woolly Douglas, a gun-toting soldier of the jungle. Of course they fall in love, but the action never stops, nor does the humor, as Turner's drab existence is forever transformed. Followed by JEWEL OF THE NILE.

A: Michael Douglas, Kathleen Turner, Danny DeVito, Alfonso Arau, Zack Norman

© FOXVIDEO 1358

ROOKIE, THE

D: Clint Eastwood 121 m

R · ACT CRM · 1990 · COLOR

Sex Nud Viol Lang AdSit

6 Slam-bang action, more than enough to keep action fans happy, but not much else. Clint is a veteran cop saddled with an eager young by-the-book cop. Together they seek to hunt down a ruthless and murderous gang of auto thieves, led by Germans Raul Julia and a sadistic Sonia Braga. The film is loaded with the expected fights, shootings and chase scenes, plus a curious scene where Clint is raped by Sonia while he is tied to a chair.

A: Clint Eastwood, Charlie Sheen, Raul Julia, Sonia Braga, Lara Flynn Boyle

© WARNER HOME VIDEO 12061

ROOSTER COGBURN

D: Stuart Millar 108 m

PG · WST COM ACT · 1975 · COLOR

Sex Nud Viol Lang AdSit

8 TRUE GRIT meets THE AFRICAN QUEEN. John Wayne reprises his very popular and Oscar-winning title character from TRUE GRIT. Rooster is in pursuit of bad men who have lifted an Army wagonload of nitroglycerine. His search introduces him to a bible-thumping old-maid missionary played by Katharine Hepburn, whose father was also murdered by the bad guys. The fun starts when she insists on joining Wayne's expedition. An OK story line, but it is aided greatly by the presence of two screen legends who are just plain fun to watch, as well as a terrific supporting cast.

A: John Wayne, Katharine Hepburn, Anthony Zerbe, Strother Martin, John McIntire

© MCA/UNIVERSAL HOME VIDEO, INC. 55042

RUNAWAY

D: Michael Crichton 99 m

PG-13 · SF ACT · 1984 · COLOR

Sex Nud Viol Lang AdSit

6 Comic book-like Sci-Fi thriller. Someone is making minor modifications which are turning ordinary domestic robots into death machines. Tough-guy cop Selleck and his beautiful assistant (Rhodes) are assigned the job of bringing in the killer-robots and taking down their evil controller Luther (Simmons from the rock group KISS). However, when Luther catches on to Selleck's game, he kidnaps Selleck's child and holds him hostage on the roof of a building that is under construction. Great special effects help spice up the lukewarm plot and make this an interesting sci-fi flick.

A: Tom Selleck, Cynthia Rhodes, Gene Simmons, Kirstie Alley, Stan Shaw, Joey Cramer

© COLUMBIA TRISTAR HOME VIDEO 60469

RUNNING MAN, THE

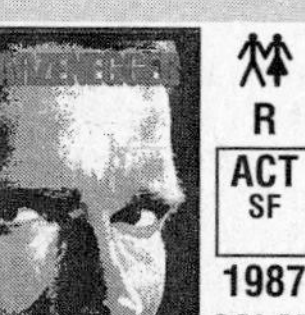

D: Paul Michael Glaser 101 m

R · ACT SF · 1987 · COLOR

Sex Nud Viol Lang AdSit

6 Horrifying peek into the future. Richard Dawson hosts a game show of death. In the year 2017, in the ravaged city of L.A., people have become very violent. For entertainment, they like to watch a gladiator game show where convicted felons literally run for their lives. If they win the game, they're pardoned, but most lose. Schwarzenegger is framed for murder and so becomes a reluctant contestant. Dawson runs him through his paces as fierce professional killers one after the other stalk him, but Schwarzenegger promises "I'll be back." Fast-paced, very violent action. Based on a novel by Stephen King.

A: Arnold Schwarzenegger, Richard Dawson, Maria Conchita Alonso, Yaphet Kotto, Jim Brown, Jesse Ventura

© LIVE HOME VIDEO 6021

RUNNING SCARED

D: Peter Hyams 108 m

R · ACT COM · 1986 · COLOR

Sex Nud Viol Lang AdSit

7 Witty and rousing adventure! Two tough Chicago street cops are tired of trying to control the influx of drugs into the city. So, after one particularly nasty day, they ponder retirement in the Florida Keys but decide that they must bring an aspiring godfather (Smits) - the source of much of their grief - down first. The wisecracking pair are magic on the screen with never-ending banter that is effortlessly funny. Some thrilling chase scenes and shootouts just add to the disarming fun of this bad guys vs. good guys actioner!

A: Gregory Hines, Billy Crystal, Steven Bauer, Darlanne Fluegel, Joe Pantoliano, Dan Hedaya

Distributed By MGM/UA Home Video M801008

RUN SILENT, RUN DEEP

D: Robert Wise 94 m

NR · WAR DMA ACT · 1958 · B&W

Sex Nud Viol Lang AdSit

8 Gripping WWII war drama. Burt Lancaster was to have become Captain of his own submarine, but instead is named first officer at the last minute when Clark Gable is given command. Gable is the only survivor of a Japanese attack on his old sub. In spite of being hampered by the suspicions and deep distrust of the entire crew and his first officer, and in the face of long odds, Gable is determined to sink a Japanese cruiser. Very tense drama, capturing the feeling of tight quarters and uncertainty. One of the best submarine movies ever.

A: Clark Gable, Burt Lancaster, Brad Dexter, Jack Warden, Nick Cravat, Don Rickles

Distributed By MGM/UA Home Video M202133

SACKETTS, THE

D: Robert Totten 198 m

NR · WST ACT · 1979 · COLOR

Sex Nud Viol Lang AdSit

7 Powerhouse cast of some of the biggest names in filmdom shine in this made-for-TV epic Western. Two Louis L'Amour novels ("The Daybreakers" and "The Sacketts") were combined to create this story. Three brothers choose to travel into the wild west to start new lives at the close of the Civil War rather than to return to a family feud in Tennessee. This is the saga of their trip west and their fortunes after getting there. Each plans to make it on his own there, but each knows he can rely on his brother. Rousing action flick with some truly sparkling performances.

A: Tom Selleck, Sam Elliott, Glenn Ford, Ben Johnson, Slim Pickens, Ruth Roman

© WARNER HOME VIDEO 957

SALVADOR

D: Oliver Stone 122 m

R · ACT DMA · 1985 · COLOR

Sex Nud Viol Lang AdSit

8 Intense and explosive film revealing the human tragedies of El Salvador in 1980! Based on a photojournalist's real-life experiences at the time, but did not become public until years later. Richard Boyle (Woods) is an American photojournalist sent to the embattled country to capture the nature of that war on film. He views first hand, and through the lenses of his camera, the murderous inhumanities and corruption that are a part of daily living there and raises questions about the motivations of the US-backed military. Woods's gripping performance was Oscar nominated. Intense and realistic.

A: James Woods, James Belushi, John Savage, Cynthia Gibb, Elpidia Carrillo, Michael Murphy

© LIVE HOME VIDEO VA5167

SAMURAI TRILOGY, THE

D: Hiroshi Inagaki 312 m

NR · FOR ACT · 1956 · COLOR

Sex Nud Viol Lang AdSit

9 Brilliant epic telling of the most famed of all Japanese swordsman, Musashi Miyomoto. This is actually three separate films: MUSASHI MIYAMOTO, DUEL AT ICHIJOJI TEMPLE and DUEL AT GANRYU ISLAND. Together, they are the most popular Japanese martial arts films ever. As a young man in 17th-century Japan, he seeks glory fighting in a civil war but finds defeat and returns as an outlaw. The love a girl and a Buddhist priest redeem him. Next he learns that death-blows are a small part of what makes a warrior, and he learns that mercy and kindness are powerful weapons too. But, at last he must fight his duel with his archrival Kojiro Sasaki. Japanese Western, compared to SHANE. Subtitles.

A: Toshiro Mifune, Koji Tsuruta, Kaoru Yachigusa, Rentaro Mikuni, Mariko Okada, Sachio Sakai

© HOME VISION SAM 040

SAND PEBBLES, THE

D: Robert Wise 180 m

NR · SUS DMA ACT · 1966 · COLOR

Sex Nud Viol Lang AdSit

8 Sprawling, intelligent and compelling epic film which garnered a nomination for Best Picture and numerous other technical Oscar nominations. An exceptionally strong performance from McQueen drives this film about a cynical, normally reclusive sailor assigned to the engine room of an American gunboat patrolling the Yangtze river of China about 1926... just as civil war begins. Commander Crenna must be diplomatic. He represents the United States. But McQueen will not watch passively as his best friend is tortured. And he also moves aggressively to protect a missionary's daughter.

A: Steve McQueen, Richard Crenna, Candice Bergen, Richard Attenborough, Mako, Gavin MacLeod

© FOXVIDEO 1029

SCALPHUNTERS, THE

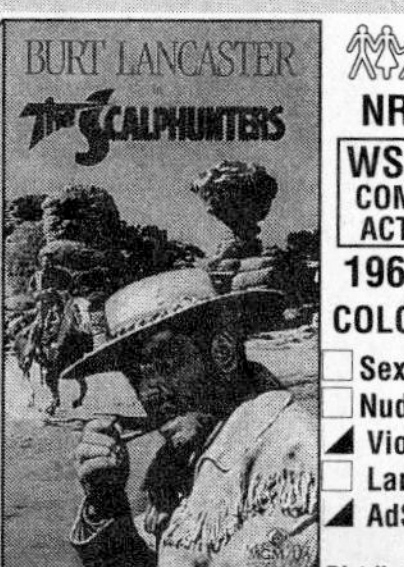

D: Sydney Pollack 100 m

NR · WST COM ACT · 1968 · COLOR

Sex Nud Viol Lang AdSit

8 Fun-filled and funny Western with truly interesting characters. A very determined fur trapper (Burt Lancaster) is forced by a group of Indians to swap his skins for a highly educated and uppity former slave (also a recent member of the Kiowa nation), Ossie Davis. He's not thrilled with the forced swap, so he sets out to get his furs back. But, by the time he catches them, an outlaw band of scalphunters headed by Savalas, has stolen the furs from the Indians and captured Davis, too. Undeterred, Burt hounds the scalphunters with guerrilla raids, getting occasional inside help from his uneasy ally, Davis. A real good time.

A: Burt Lancaster, Shelley Winters, Ossie Davis, Telly Savalas, Armando Silvestre, Nick Cravat

Distributed By MGM/UA Home Video M202033

SCARFACE

D: Brian De Palma — 170 m

R | CRM ACT | 1983 | COLOR | Sex | Nud | Viol | Lang | AdSit

8 One of the most gruesome, brutal and forceful gangster flicks ever made! A Cuban refugee, Tony Montana (Pacino), lands in the drug center of Miami. His ruthlessness causes him to quickly rise from a simple task man to drug kingpin, importing and selling cocaine. Along the way, Tony steals the crime lord's (Loggia) girlfriend (Pfeiffer), kills his kid sister's lover (Bauer), and spins himself into a web of tragedy with his cocaine abuses. This extremely violent remake of the 1932 classic is graphic and shocking from start to finish, and will not be easily forgotten. Too long, though.

A: Al Pacino, Steven Bauer, Michelle Pfeiffer, Mary Elizabeth Mastrantonio, Robert Loggia, Miriam Colon

© MCA/UNIVERSAL HOME VIDEO, INC. 80047

SCARLET AND THE BLACK, THE

D: Jerry London — 145 m

NR | SUS ACT | 1983 | COLOR | Sex | Nud | Viol | Lang | AdSit

7 Very good made-for-TV film relating the real-life exploits of a brave Irish priest, Monsignor Hugh O'Flaherty, during WWII. Operating from the Vatican, under the cloak of diplomatic immunity, O'Flaherty organizes a vast network of safe houses inside Nazi-occupied Rome and is responsible for the concealment and escape of hundreds of POWs and refugees. When Gestapo chief (Plummer) orders him killed or captured if he is spotted outside the Vatican, O'Flaherty assumes numerous disguises and plays cat-and-mouse games to keep operating.

A: Gregory Peck, Christopher Plummer, John Gielgud, Raf Vallone

© LIVE HOME VIDEO 69918

SEARCHERS, THE

D: John Ford — 144 m

NR | WST ACT | 1956 | COLOR | Sex | Nud | Viol | Lang | AdSit

10 Spectacular Western masterpiece from the two kings of the genre: John Ford and John Wayne. Beautiful scenery, fascinating characters and a thrilling story, rich in both psychological undercurrent and adventure. Wayne is a bitter ex-Confederate soldier who hates Indians. He and his brother's adopted son (who is half-Indian) come home to find that the brother and sister-in-law have been savagely murdered by Comanches and his niece is kidnapped. He and the boy form an uneasy partnership and set off to find her. This begins an epic 7-year odyssey in which Wayne rediscovers his humanity.

A: John Wayne, Jeffrey Hunter, Vera Miles, Ward Bond, Natalie Wood

© WARNER HOME VIDEO 1012

SEA WOLVES, THE

D: Andrew V. McLaglen — 120 m

PG | ACT WAR | 1980 | COLOR | Sex | Nud | Viol | Lang | AdSit

7 A riveting war adventure based on a true story! During WWII, aging British agents (Peck and Moore) recruit some retired members of a British calvary unit who are now members of an honorary drinking club in India for an espionage mission against the Germans. The team is after a clandestine radio transmitter on board a German ship that's anchored in a neutral Indian port. While Peck leads his over-the-hill recruits in their training sessions, Moore romances with a beautiful double agent (Kellerman). High flying adventure and a stellar cast.

A: Gregory Peck, Roger Moore, David Niven, Trevor Howard, Barbara Kellerman, Patrick Macnee

© WARNER HOME VIDEO 709

SERPICO

D: Sidney Lumet — 130 m

R | CRM ACT DMA | 1973 | COLOR | Sex | Nud | Viol | Lang | AdSit

10 Extremely tough and compelling police drama, based upon the true-life story of Frank Serpico, a cop whose public testimony in the early 70s about corruption and bribery, ripped open the NYC police department. Pacino's characterization is amazing. Serpico is an oddball, idealistic and obsessive cop who doesn't fit in as a regular cop, but his non-conformism is an asset as an undercover cop. It is as an undercover cop that he is exposed to the corrupt underbelly of the police force itself. When some corrupt cops find him to be incorruptible, he is determined to be too great a risk and he is set up to be killed. Instead of dying, he survived to testify against them.

A: Al Pacino, John Randolph, Jack Kehoe, Biff McGuire, Barbara Eda-Young, Tony Roberts

© PARAMOUNT HOME VIDEO 8689

SEVEN-UPS, THE

D: Philip D'Antoni — 109 m

PG | ACT CRM | 1973 | COLOR | Sex | Nud | Viol | Lang | AdSit

6 Made by the same producer as BULLITT and THE FRENCH CONNECTION, this film is first, foremost and almost solely an action picture - with a particularly great car chase. The action revolves around Scheider as the head of a special New York police unit that is charged with nailing major hoods for prison terms of seven or more years. His team utilizes stoolies to nail their quarry, but when one of his officers is killed by a stoolie who has turned the tables on them, the intense pursuit and the action begins. Good action picture.

A: Roy Scheider, Tony Lo Bianco, Bill Hickman, Richard Lynch, Larry Haines, Victor Arnold

© FOXVIDEO 1193

SHADOW OF THE WOLF

D: Jacques Dorfman — 108 m

PG-13 | DMA ACT | 1993 | COLOR | Sex | Nud | Viol | Lang | AdSit

7 Carefully drawn realistic portrait of the lifestyle of the Inuit of northern Canada. Set during the 1930s, this is the story of a young Inuit who rebels against the corruption brought to his people by the invasion of the whites. His people have forgotten the old ways and can no longer live without the white man's tools. His resentment leads him into a violent conflict with his father, who is the leader of the group. He leaves, but not before killing a corrupt white trader and taking a young woman away from his father. He struggles to survive, to find himself and to evade the white policeman who has come to find him.

A: Lou Diamond Phillips, Jennifer Tilly, Tosiroer Mifune, Donald Sutherland, Bernard-Pierre Donnadieu

© COLUMBIA TRISTAR HOME VIDEO 59893

SHAFT

D: Gordon Parks — 98 m

R | ACT CRM | 1971 | COLOR | Sex | Nud | Viol | Lang | AdSit

7 Heavy-duty brutal action. When the Mafia kidnaps a Harlem crimelord's daughter, he (Gunn) hires the toughest guy he can find, detective Shaft (Roundtree), to get his daughter back. This was one of the first and best crime dramas to feature a black hero in a leading role. Director Parks expertly mixes together threats of racial violence and mob wars as the story unfolds in this actioner with an impact that has not been dated by time. The score by Isaac Hayes was an Oscar winner.

A: Richard Roundtree, Moses Gunn, Charles Cioffi, Antonio Fargas, Christopher St. John, Drew Bundini Brown

Distributed By MGM/UA Home Video M700191

SHAKEDOWN

D: James Glickenhaus — 96 m

R | ACT CRM | 1988 | COLOR | Sex | Nud | Viol | Lang | AdSit

6 Two tough, streetwise guys, one a renegade cop and the other a burned-out legal aid attorney, team up to get rid of the corruption they suspect is running rampant in the New York Police Department. A drug dealer is charged with killing an undercover cop and Weller is the lawyer defending him. Elliott is an undercover cop who suspects that the police force is stealing money taken from drug dealers and has set the guy up. Together, the unlikely allies, the cop and the lawyer, struggle to get to the bottom of it all. This fast-paced action flick sports some incredible stunts, but is not too credible.

A: Peter Weller, Sam Elliott, Patricia Charbonneau, Antonio Fargas, Blanche Baker, Richard Brooks

© MCA/UNIVERSAL HOME VIDEO, INC. 80820

SHAMUS

D: Buzz Kulik — 106 m

PG | ACT COM | 1973 | COLOR | Sex | Nud | Viol | Lang | AdSit

6 Gimmicky and not particularly innovative, but still a fun private eye movie. Burt Reynolds is a quirky, wisecracking private eye who is hired to recover some stolen diamonds. In the process of his investigations, he runs across a a much bigger operation, including a warehouse full of stolen weapons and ammunition. Poor old Burt gets beat up at every other turn, but he does get some help from beautiful socialite Dyan Cannon. Fast moving, with lots of action and glib dialogue. Pretty good.

A: Burt Reynolds, Dyan Cannon, John P. Ryan, Giorgio Tozzi, Joe Santos, Ron Weyand

© COLUMBIA TRISTAR HOME VIDEO 60205

SHARKY'S MACHINE

D: Burt Reynolds — 123 m

R | CRM ACT SUS | 1981 | COLOR | Sex | Nud | Viol | Lang | AdSit

10 Top-drawer cop film - one of the best. Sharkey (Reynolds) is a hardened Atlanta narcotics cop demoted to working in vice after a shootout-gone-bad. He is bored, but when a high-priced hooker turns out to have connections with some very bad and very powerful people who were involved in his earlier narcotics case, Sharky becomes very interested. He sets up a round-the-clock observation of the girl's apartment and becomes totally enraptured by her as he voyeristically watches her every move... but a ruthless assassin is on the prowl and she is his target. Intelligent, realistic, very high intensity action.

A: Burt Reynolds, Vittorio Gassman, Brian Keith, Charles Durning, Rachel Ward, Vittorio Gassman

© WARNER HOME VIDEO 22024

SHENANDOAH

D: Andrew V. McLaglen — 106 m

NR | WST DMA ACT | 1965 | COLOR | Sex | Nud | Viol | Lang | AdSit

9 Emotional Western that captures well the heartbreak of the Civil War. Jimmy Stewart is a widowed father and farmer in Virginia, which was a major crossroads for both armies of the Civil War. Stewart wants no part of this war and vows to stay out of it. But when his young son is arrested after being mistaken for a rebel because he wore the wrong hat, Stewart gathers up the rest of his boys for a search to get their brother back. However, while on their long trip, the war arrives at his farm. This is a large scale picture that is very moving, emotionally charged and haunting. Katharine Ross's debut.

A: James Stewart, Doug McClure, Glenn Corbett, Patrick Wayne, Katharine Ross, George Kennedy

© MCA/UNIVERSAL HOME VIDEO, INC. 55033

SHINING THROUGH

D: David Seltzer 127 m

R | ROM ACT | 1992 | COLOR | Sex | Nud | Viol | Lang | AdSit

7 Griffith takes a job to Douglas's secretary just before WWII breaks out, only to soon discover that he is really an American spymaster. Her brains and guts soon win her a much more challenging job when his key operative in Berlin is killed. She is half-Irish and half German Jew, and she yearns to do something useful to the war effort. Because she is fluent in German, Douglas agrees to let her travel to Germany to gather top secret information for him, even though her only experience in the spy trade is what she has learned watching the movies. Griffith is disarmingly effective in this light weight but enjoyable little film.

A: Michael Douglas, Melanie Griffith, Liam Neeson, Joely Richardson, John Gielgud, Francis Guinan

© FOXVIDEO 5661

SHIPWRECKED

D: Nils Gaup 93 m

PG | ACT CLD | 1991 | COLOR | Sex | Nud | Viol | Lang | AdSit

8 A young boy joins the crew of a sailing ship as cabin boy to earn money to help save his parent's farm. They set sail for the South Seas, but on board is a pirate posing as a British naval officer. It is his plan to wait until the ship gets to the right location and then take control. However, just as he does, the ship is caught up in a terrible storm and is capsized. The lad makes it to a tropical island, but soon discovers that this is the island the pirate was seeking and it contains his buried treasure. Shipwrecked on a pirate island, the boy finds that he is not alone, and he must struggle to survive. Rousing Disney adventure film for young and old alike.

A: Stian Smestad, Gabriel Byrne, Louisa Haigh, Trond Munch, Bjorn Sundquist, Eva Von Honna

© WALT DISNEY HOME VIDEO 1168

SHOGUN

D: Jerry London 550 m

NR | DMA ROM ACT | 1980 | COLOR | Sex | Nud | Viol | Lang | AdSit

10 This is a landmark made-for-television mini-series based upon James Clavell's novel. It is the spellbinding epic story of a 17th-century English navigator, Blackthorne (Chamberlain), who is shipwrecked in Japan. Japan is a feudal society in which the nobility, the Samurai, have total and utter control over their lands and the people who go with them. Their master is the Shogun, the military leader of all Japan. Blackthorne is in an alien world, but he gains their respect, masters their language, their society and their many-layered plots of intrigue - and he discovers love. Wonderful stuff.

A: Richard Chamberlain, Toshiro Mifune, Yoko Shimada, Frankie Sakai, Alan Badel, Michael Hordern

© PARAMOUNT HOME VIDEO 80102

SHOOTING, THE

D: Monte Hellman 82 m

G | WST DMA ACT | 1967 | COLOR | Sex | Nud | Viol | Lang | AdSit

7 An unusual existential Western, similar to, but yet far from, the traditional shoot-'em-up. A strange woman (Perkins) hires bounty hunters Oates and Hutchins to escort her across the desert after her son is accidentally killed. A sadistic gunslinger (Nicholson) follows the trio and a bitter dispute develops between Nicholson and Hutchins over the woman and Nicholson kills him. The trio continue on through the relentless desert. Their water is running low and their horses are dying. This is not a typical Western, so don't expect a typical simple traditional resolution and ending.

A: Jack Nicholson, Will Hutchins, Warren Oates, Millie Perkins

© UNITED AMERICAN VIDEO CORP. 17193

SHOOTIST, THE

D: Don Siegel 100 m

PG | WST DMA ACT | 1976 | COLOR | Sex | Nud | Viol | Lang | AdSit

9 An intelligent triumph for John Wayne. As Wayne himself was dying of cancer (his last film), so is his character - an old gunfighter named J.B. Books. The time is 1901. Books has spent his life as a gunman, but both he and his era are dying. All he wants now is to be left alone, but wherever he goes his reputation precedes him. His enemies and even total strangers seek him out. Everybody wants to kill him or to make a profit from him. He has no real friends - only the woman who owns the boarding house where he is staying and her hero-worshipping son. Very believable and moving. A fitting last film for Wayne.

A: John Wayne, Lauren Bacall, Ron Howard, James Stewart, Scatman Crothers, Richard Boone

© PARAMOUNT HOME VIDEO 8904

SHOOT TO KILL

D: Roger Spottiswoode 109 m

R | SUS CRM ACT | 1988 | COLOR | Sex | Nud | Viol | Lang | AdSit

8 Thrilling game of cat and mouse! A ruthless killer joins a group of campers so that he can avoid the police. The group is hiking through the picturesque Pacific Northwest and is being led by Kirstie Alley. When things don't go his way, he begins killing off members of the group. FBI agent Poitier is coming after him, but the FBI man is way out of his element in the wilds and must rely on Alley's rugged boyfriend (Berenger) for help to track them down. This pair mix like oil and water, but they begin to work together when the pressure rises after Alley is taken hostage. Good job by Poitier.

A: Sidney Poitier, Tom Berenger, Kirstie Alley, Clancy Brown, Richard Masur, Andrew Robinson

© TOUCHSTONE HOME VIDEO 697

SILENCE OF THE LAMBS, THE

D: Jonathan Demme 118 m

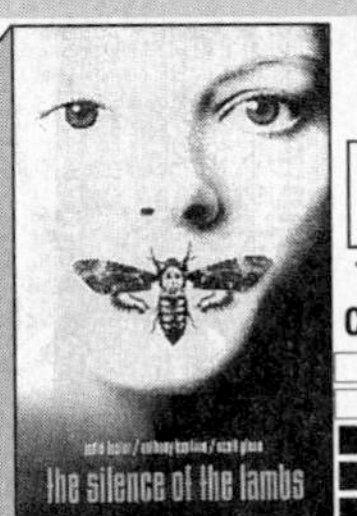

R | SUS CRM ACT | 1991 | COLOR | Sex | Nud | Viol | Lang | AdSit

9 Outstanding and deeply disturbing Oscar winner. Rookie FBI agent Starling (Foster) has been assigned the daunting task of helping to stop Buffalo Bill, a psycho serial killer who harvests his victim's skin. The key to finding Bill lies within the twisted mind of another brilliant serial killer, Hannibal the Cannibal, now serving time in a high security cell. Dr. Hannibal Lector (Hopkins) is also a brilliant psychiatrist and a master of manipulation. Hannibal knows Bill, but is fascinated with Starling and messes with her mind while she tries to get inside his. A magnificent, terrifying thriller. See MANHUNTER.

A: Jodie Foster, Anthony Hopkins, Scott Glenn, Ted Levine, Anthony Heald, Brooke Smith

© ORION PICTURES CORPORATION 8767

SILENCE OF THE NORTH

D: Allan Winton King 94 m

PG | WST DMA ACT | 1981 | COLOR | Sex | Nud | Viol | Lang | AdSit

7 Picturesque and inspirational. This is a story about a strong-willed woman (Burstyn) who falls in love with a rugged trapper (Skerritt) and follows him to live in the wilds of northern Canada. The story, based upon the actual autobiography of Olive Fredrickson, tells of her daily struggles, from being a young mother just after the turn of the 20th-century to later being a widow with three children. The wilderness can be cruel, and she and her family are left to brave nature's forces, survive cold winters and deal with tragedy on their own. Excellent.

A: Ellen Burstyn, Tom Skerritt, Gordon Pinsent, Jennifer McKinney, Colin Fox

© MCA/UNIVERSAL HOME VIDEO, INC. 71004

SILVERADO

D: Lawrence Kasdan 132 m

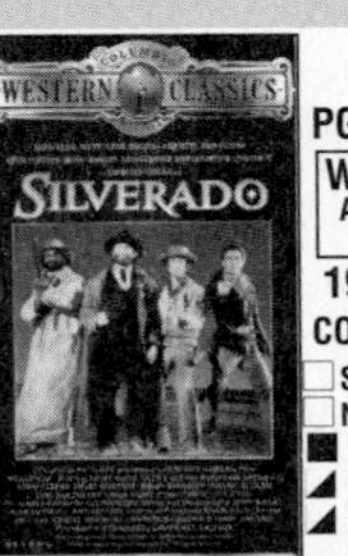

PG-13 | WST ACT | 1985 | COLOR | Sex | Nud | Viol | Lang | AdSit

9 Ripsnorter. A star-packed Western with action aplenty. Scott Glenn, on his way home from prison to his hot-headed brother (Costner), has to protect himself from three men who are trying to kill him. Then he stumbles onto another drifter (Kline) who has been stripped of everything he owns and left to die. The two of them team up to help a black man (Glover) out of a tough spot. Those three then team up with crazy brother Costner and all four help rid a small town of a corrupt sheriff. Relentless pacing provides a really good time, but it is very violent and don't think too long about the details.

A: Kevin Kline, Scott Glenn, Kevin Costner, Danny Glover, Linda Hunt, Rosanna Arquette

© COLUMBIA TRISTAR HOME VIDEO 60567

SILVER STREAK

D: Arthur Hiller 114 m

PG | COM ACT MYS | 1976 | COLOR | Sex | Nud | Viol | Lang | AdSit

9 Zany thriller. Wilder, a mild-mannered editor, is taking what he hopes to be a restful ride aboard a cross-country train. It seems to be even better when he seduces the girl in the next compartment (sexy Clayburgh). But she is an art scholar with information which will discredit both millionaire McGoohan and his Rembrandt letters as being fakes. Now, Wilder's leisurely trip turns overly exciting, when he spots a dead body being thrown from the train, and then hilarious, when small-time thief Pryor enters into the picture. Highly entertaining blend of romance, comedy and action.

A: Gene Wilder, Jill Clayburgh, Richard Pryor, Ned Beatty, Patrick McGoohan, Scatman Crothers

© FOXVIDEO 1080

SINK THE BISMARCK!

D: Lewis Gilbert 97 m

NR | WAR ACT | 1960 | B&W | Sex | Nud | Viol | Lang | AdSit

9 Powerful and involving first-class WWII actioner! The Bismarck was the biggest and most powerful battle ship ever built. It was supposed to be unsinkable and it was German. Upon the first reports of it leaving safe harbor, the best ship in the English navy was sent after the Bismarck - and was immediately sunk. The British admiralty then concocted a masterful campaign to find, attack and destroy the Nazi ship. It simply had to be done; the fate of the entire navy depended upon it. Historically, the film is reasonably accurate but it is also very exciting with a lot of actual war footage.

A: Kenneth More, Dana Wynter, Carl Mohner, Laurence Naismith, Geoffrey Keen, Karel Stepanek

© FOXVIDEO 1812

SMOKEY AND THE BANDIT

D: Hal Needham 96 m

PG | COM ACT | 1977 | COLOR | Sex | Nud | Viol | Lang | AdSit

9 Box office smash comedy. Good ol' boy Bandit (Burt Reynolds) gets hired to haul four hundred cases of Coors beer from Texarkana, Texas to Atlanta, Georgia. Since Coors is legal in Texas and not in Atlanta, there is a little bit of a situation - but if he can do it in 28 hours, he gets $80,000. So Burt runs interference, in a fast Camero, all across the South for the illegal load which is being driven in an 18-wheeler by Jerry Reed. Burt's job is keeping a herd of bumbling cops, led by local sheriff Jackie Gleason, occupied for his good buddy Reed. Loads of car stunts and gags. A rollicking good time.

A: Burt Reynolds, Sally Field, Jackie Gleason, Jerry Reed, Mike Henry, Paul Williams

© MCA/UNIVERSAL HOME VIDEO, INC. 66003

SMOKEY AND THE BANDIT II

D: Hal Needham — 101 m

PG | COM ACT | 1980 | COLOR | Sex Nud Viol Lang AdSit

7 Pretty good sequel to the original. This time the Bandit (Reynolds) and his buddy are hired to get a pregnant elephant to the Republican convention. But to do it, they have to go through the stomping grounds of their old arch-enemy sheriff Buford T. Justice (Gleeson). Dom DeLuis plays a gynecologist who gets to come along and treat the elephant. Contains a full assortment of the same sort of stunts that were the hallmark of the original, plus lots of clever dialogue, too. It doesn't have the same spark as the original did. Still, it's a good time.

A: Burt Reynolds, Sally Field, Jackie Gleason, Dom DeLuise, Jerry Reed, Paul Williams

© MCA/UNIVERSAL HOME VIDEO, INC. 66020

SNEAKERS

D: Phil Alden Robinson — 125 m

PG-13 | SUS COM ACT | 1992 | COLOR | Sex Nud Viol Lang AdSit

7 Entertaining caper. Redford and his group are very good thieves. They are hired by businesses to test for weaknesses in security systems by actually breaking in without getting caught. Then Redford is blackmailed by two CIA-types into having his team of misfits steal a black box from a brilliant inventor which contains the technology to decode any computer code in the world - a box many people would gladly kill for. Redford's team is made up of Poitier as an ex-CIA man and Aykroyd as an electronics specialist who sees conspiracies everywhere. Sometimes exciting, with several amusing moments.

A: Robert Redford, Sidney Poitier, Dan Aykroyd, River Phoenix, David Strathairn, Mary McDonnell

© MCA/UNIVERSAL HOME VIDEO, INC. 81282

SNIPER

D: Luis Llosa — 99 m

R | ACT | 1993 | COLOR | Sex Nud Viol Lang AdSit

6 This is a nearly straight-forward action flick, but it does have a slightly different bent. Berenger is a tough marine sniper/assassin with 74 kills to his credit, who has just received a new assignment and a new partner. The assignment is to take out a rebel general and the drug lord who is financing him. His new partner is a young staffer from the National Security Council who has a reputation as a sharpshooter but he has never killed anyone. The two mix like oil and water and they have to travel through miles of jungle to get into position to accomplish their mission. Not always successful but is never-the-less entertaining overall.

A: Tom Berenger, Billy Zane, J.T. Walsh, Aden Young, Ken Radley, Dale Dye

© COLUMBIA TRISTAR HOME VIDEO 70753

SOLDIER BLUE

D: Ralph Nelson — 105 m

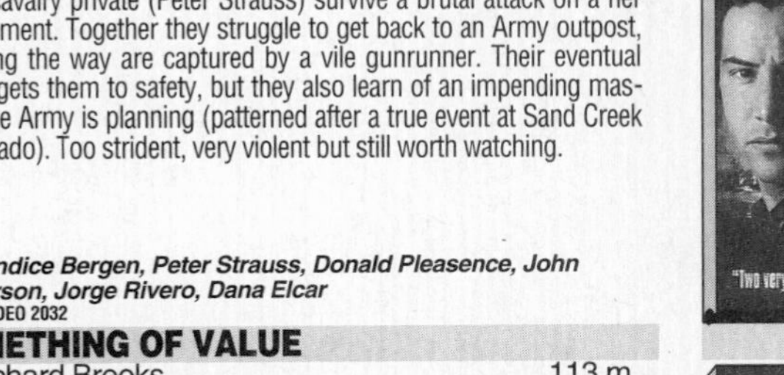

PG | WST ACT | 1974 | COLOR | Sex Nud Viol Lang AdSit

8 Controversial and violent Western. Bergen plays a white woman who had been captured by Indians two years before. She and a young cavalry private (Peter Strauss) survive a brutal attack on a her encampment. Together they struggle to get back to an Army outpost, but along the way are captured by a vile gunrunner. Their eventual escape gets them to safety, but they also learn of an impending massacre the Army is planning (patterned after a true event at Sand Creek in Colorado). Too strident, very violent but still worth watching.

A: Candice Bergen, Peter Strauss, Donald Pleasence, John Anderson, Jorge Rivero, Dana Elcar

© NEW LINE HOME VIDEO 2032

SOMETHING OF VALUE

D: Richard Brooks — 113 m

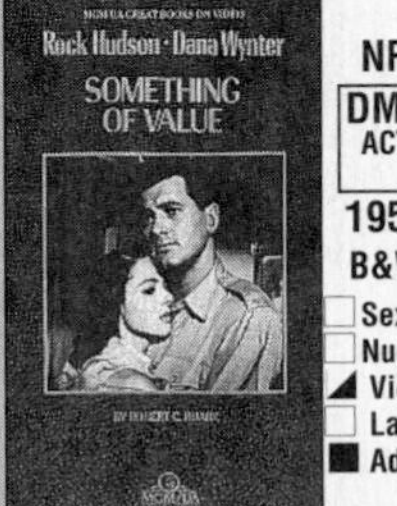

NR | DMA ACT | 1957 | B&W | Sex Nud Viol Lang AdSit

8 Powerful drama. White Hudson and black Poitier have been best friends ever since childhood. They have spent their days working side by side on Hudson's father's Kenyan plantation. But when Poitier is driven away by violent racists, he feels compelled to join the Mau Mau, a group of radical terrorists who are determined to end racial oppression in Kenya by driving all Englishmen out. Hudson's relationship with Poitier becomes very strained as the uprisings become increasingly violent. Exciting, builds steadily from a slow start. Prologue by Winston Churchill.

A: Rock Hudson, Sidney Poitier, Wendy Hiller, Dana Wynter, Frederick O'Neil

Distributed By MGM/UA Home Video M300840

SONS OF KATIE ELDER, THE

D: Henry Hathaway — 122 m

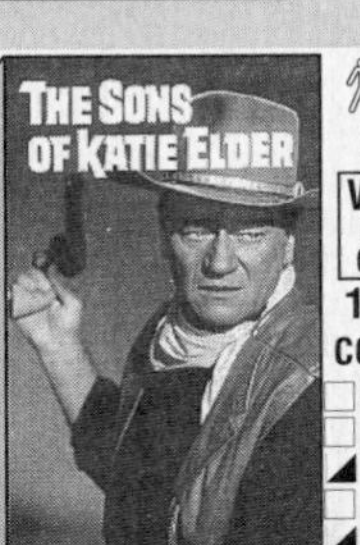

NR | WST ACT COM | 1965 | COLOR | Sex Nud Viol Lang AdSit

9 Fast-paced Wayne Western with action, good times and a heart! Katie was a loving mother who had four rough and rowdy sons. When she dies, the four come home to pay their respects and decide that the youngest should honor their mother and go to college. But first they make a pact to get back the land that was taken from Katie and to learn the truth about their father's murder six months earlier. The gunman (Wayne), the gambler (Martin), the quiet guy (Holliman) and the kid (Michael Anderson, Jr.) all put aside their differences to learn the truth and to protect each other's back. Rousing good time.

A: John Wayne, Dean Martin, Martha Hyer, Earl Holliman, Jeremy Slate, James Gregory

© PARAMOUNT HOME VIDEO 6729

SOUTHERN COMFORT

D: Walter Hill — 105 m

R | ACT SUS | 1981 | COLOR | Sex Nud Viol Lang AdSit

6 Pretty good action flick. When nine National Guardsmen converge on the Louisiana swamps for a weekend of practice maneuvers, they make the fatal mistake of stealing some canoes that belong to the local Cajun boys and then making fun of them. They shouldn't have ought to have done that. Because when war breaks out, the Guardsmen are armed only with rifles loaded with blanks. Slowly but surely the Cajuns kill the Guardsmen one by one until only Carradine and Boothe are left to fight for their lives in the intense climax. Unnerving and intense.

A: Keith Carradine, Powers Boothe, T.K. Carter, Fred Ward, Franklyn Seals, Lewis Smith

© UNITED AMERICAN VIDEO CORP. 5300

SPACECAMP

D: Harry Winer — 115 m

PG | ACT CLD | 1986 | COLOR | Sex Nud Viol Lang AdSit

6 An exciting adventure for anyone who ever dreamed of being an astronaut. Five awe-struck teenagers are chosen to spend the summer at a NASA space camp and learn all about the wonders of the space shuttle with the help of astronaut Capshaw. The summer program is sailing along until a robot, with a mind of its own, decides to launch the novice crew into space. When Capshaw gets injured, the teenage astronauts must figure out a way to get their hides back to earth in one piece. A fun trip.

A: Kate Capshaw, Lea Thompson, Tom Skerritt, Kelly Preston, Larry B. Scott, Tate Donovan

© LIVE HOME VIDEO VA5174

SPARTACUS

D: Stanley Kubrick — 196 m

PG-13 | ACT DMA | 1960 | COLOR | Sex Nud Viol Lang AdSit

10 Rousing and rewarding, intelligent and thrilling. A huge, epic human drama based solidly in historical fact. In 73 B.C. in republican Rome, a large and bloody slave revolt did, in fact, for a short time, challenge the Empire. Kirk Douglas plays Spartacus, a slave/gladiator who rose up first against the barbarism of his own master and later came to lead the entire slave revolt against all Rome. Brilliantly photographed - huge spectacle, with an involving script, exciting performances and thrilling battle sequences. Winner of four Oscars. Must see.

A: Kirk Douglas, Laurence Olivier, Jean Simmons, Charles Laughton, Peter Ustinov, Tony Curtis

© MCA/UNIVERSAL HOME VIDEO, INC. 81133

SPEED

D: Jan De Bont — 115 m

R | ACT SUS CRM | 1994 | COLOR | Sex Nud Viol Lang AdSit

9 Extremely high-octane film that was a huge summer hit and won two Oscars for Sound. Jack Traven is a member of the LA police SWAT team. When he and his partner break up the well-laid plans of a psychotic ex-cop named Howard Payne to extract money from the city, Howard decides to try again. And, this time he makes a personal challenge to Jack to beat him. This time he has placed a bomb on a city bus that becomes armed at 50 mph and will blow if the bus goes below 50. Jack makes it to the bus, but the bomb is armed and he is being helped by pretty passenger who is now driving. Electric and tense. Very well made. In spite of its implausibilites, you almost never doubt it. Great fun.

A: Keanu Reeves, Dennis Hopper, Sandra Bullock, Joe Morton, Jeff Daniels

© FOXVIDEO 8638

SPY WHO LOVED ME, THE

D: Lewis Gilbert — 128 m

PG | ACT | 1977 | COLOR | Sex Nud Viol Lang AdSit

8 Explosive Bond adventure! After US and Russian submarines are stolen by a shipping tycoon, Bond (Moore) must team up with a beautiful Soviet spy (Bach) in order to squash the evil Stromberg's (Jurgens) maniacal plans to destroy the world. Seems Stromberg wants to be the ruler of an undersea world which he will create after his provoked nuclear war destroys life as we know it on the surface. The major obstacle thrown in Bond's path is a hugely menacing seven foot hulk with a steel jaw - appropriately named "Jaws." Number 10 in the series is a boatload of fun.

A: Roger Moore, Barbara Bach, Curt Jurgens, Richard Kiel, Caroline Munro, Bernard Lee

Distributed By MGM/UA Home Video M201421

SQUANTO: A WARRIOR'S TALE

D: Xavier Koller — 112 m

PG | CLD ACT | 1994 | COLOR | Sex Nud Viol Lang AdSit

7 Squanto was an actual character from American history, whose story is here told by the people at Disney. Set in the early 1600s, Squanto was a young Indian warrior who was captured and returned to England as a prized slave. There, he escaped his captors and from a group of monks, learned both how to speak English and that not all Englishmen were bad. The monks eventually also helped him to return home, on a ship loaded with Pilgrims. However, when they arrive, the locals are prepared to fight this time. Even though his own tribe had been murdered, Squanto convinces these Indians that war brings only pain and successfully brokers a long-lived peace. The story is very simply told. Most suitable for children and teens.

A: Adam Beach, Eric Schweig, Mandy Patinkin, Michael Gambon, Nathaniel Parker, Alex Norton

© WALT DISNEY HOME VIDEO 2552

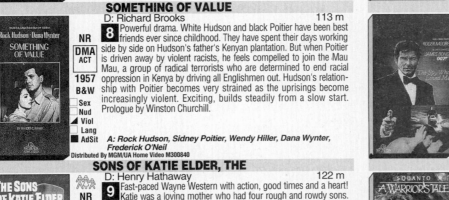

STAND ALONE

D: Alan Beattie — 94 m

R | ACT CRM | 1985 | COLOR

Sex □ Nud □ Viol ■ Lang ■ AdSit ◢

6 A dangerous showdown! An aging decorated war hero (Durning) decides to stand up against crime when he witnesses a murder committed by drug dealers in his neighborhood. He's had enough. Against the warnings of neighbors and friends, he teams up with police detective Keach to hunt the bad guys down. A lawyer counsels Durning not to risk his neck by testifying against the drug dealers - they can be ruthless and vindictive - but Durning decides that he's fed up with drugs in his neighborhood and decides to do whatever it takes to put 'em away.

A: Charles Durning, Pam Grier, James Keach, Bert Remsen, Barbara Sammeth, Lu Leonard

© R&G VIDEO, LP 80177

STAR CHAMBER, THE

D: Peter Hyams — 109 m

R | CRM ACT | 1982 | COLOR

Sex □ Nud □ Viol ■ Lang ■ AdSit ■

8 The justice system is unraveling and criminals are going free! Frustrated by a system that allows criminals to ply their trade with impunity, in the knowledge that a smart lawyer can always get them off, and frustrated by having to be part of that system, an idealistic Superior Court Judge (Douglas) and some others decide to do something about it. They decide to pass out their own justice, with their own law. However, when two innocent men are knowingly marked by them for death, Douglas is forced to reevaluate. Intelligent and provocative drama that stings. Not an exploitive rip-off.

A: Michael Douglas, Hal Holbrook, Sharon Gless, Yaphet Kotto, James Sikking, Joe Regalbuto

© CBS/FOX VIDEO 1295

STARGATE

D: Roland Emmerich — 119 m

PG-13 | SF ACT | 1994 | COLOR

Sex □ Nud □ Viol ◢ Lang ◢ AdSit ◢

7 James Spader is a brilliant linguistic professor whose unconventional ideas have gotten him in trouble, when he receives an invitation to work on a highly secret government project. His job is to decipher ancient symbols on a large round ring first discovered in 1928 at an Egyptian archeological dig, but never reported. His success leads to the discovery that the ring is in fact a portal through space that leads to another world. Now, he and a military team led by Kurt Russell have gone to that other world. It is very similar to earth, however its society has never changed. They remain slaves to the alien being who departed earth 10,000 years before. Some big plot holes diminish its effectiveness.

A: Kurt Russell, James Spader, Viveca Lindfors, Alexis Cruz, Mili Avital, Jaye Davidson

© LIVE HOME VIDEO 60222

STAR TREK: THE MOTION PICTURE

D: Robert Wise — 143 m

G | SF ACT | 1980 | COLOR

Sex □ Nud □ Viol □ Lang □ AdSit □

6 This is the first full-length motion picture spawned from the extremely popular TV series of 15 years prior, featuring the same cast. Driven by the huge popularity of that series, the picture generated terrific box office attention and spawned many sequels. This episode concerns an incoming ominous cloud that devours everything in its path. The Enterprise crew discovers that the cloud is really an intelligent machine. When one of it's crew has her body taken over by that intelligence, Kirk and company use her as a key to pursue the mystery of the machine and to venture inside it.

A: William Shatner, Leonard Nimoy, Persis Khambatta, Stephen Collins, DeForest Kelley, James Doohan

© PARAMOUNT HOME VIDEO 8858

STAR TREK GENERATIONS

D: David Carson — 117 m

PG | SF ACT | 1994 | COLOR

Sex □ Nud □ Viol ◢ Lang ◢ AdSit ◢

7 As this film was being made, STAR TREK: THE NEXT GENERATION was ceasing TV production. This film also marked the death of Captain Kirk and so set the stage for the succeeding sequels to revolve around the crew of the "NEXT GENERATION." Here Kirk is aboard the maiden flight of the Enterprise B, when he is apparently sucked into space by a hull breach after the ship confronts an energy field. Time advances 75 years. The crew of the Enterprise C again confronts the energy field. Guinan informs Captain Picard that it is the Nexus, a time-space phenomenon which is paradise-like inside. Mad-scientist, Dr. Soran, is willing to destroy a solar system to get there. Kirk and Picard, both inside the Nexus, must unite to defeat him.

A: Patrick Stewart, Jonathan Frakes, Brent Spinner, Levar Burton, Michael Dorn, William Shatner

© PARAMOUNT HOME VIDEO 32988

STAR TREK II: THE WRATH OF KHAN

D: Nicholas Meyer — 113 m

PG | SF ACT | 1982 | COLOR

Sex □ Nud □ Viol ◢ Lang □ AdSit □

8 Solid entry in the Star Trek series based upon one of the original 1960s TV plots. In that TV episode, the Enterprise crew had exiled several very aggressive genetic supermen on a lonely planet. They had been genetically engineered to be superior to ordinary humans but had become determined to dominate all society. They are led by Khan (Montalban). Now they have escaped. They have commandeered a war ship and are seeking possession of the new Genesis technology, which can create whole planets - but can also destroy them. And Khan seeks also to destroy his old nemesis, Kirk.

A: William Shatner, Leonard Nimoy, Ricardo Montalban, DeForest Kelley, James Doohan

© PARAMOUNT HOME VIDEO 1180

STAR TREK III: THE SEARCH FOR SPOCK

D: Leonard Nimoy — 105 m

PG | SF ACT | 1984 | COLOR

Sex □ Nud □ Viol ◢ Lang □ AdSit □

8 Spock is dead - or is he? In STAR TREK II, Spock had sacrificed himself in order to save the rest of the crew. His body was "buried" on the Genesis planet. Now there is evidence that Spock's intellect was not lost and his body is regenerating itself. Kirk and the crew steal their now-mothballed ship and return to rescue a young boy who may be Spock. However, they also find there a Klingon warship that is determined to capture the Genesis technology. Less emphasis on special effects and more on characters and plot.

A: William Shatner, DeForest Kelley, James Doohan, George Takei, Walter Koenig, Nichelle Nichols

© PARAMOUNT HOME VIDEO 1621

STAR TREK IV: THE VOYAGE HOME

D: William Shatner — 119 m

PG | SF ACT | 1989 | COLOR

Sex □ Nud □ Viol □ Lang ◢ AdSit □

7 Light-hearted and fun. Kirk and the crew of the Enterprise return home to earth in their commandeered Klingon ship (from STAR TREK III) to discover that earth's atmosphere is being bombarded by a message from an alien probe that cannot be returned. The probe is broadcasting in a language only understood by humpback whales, a species that is extinct in the 23rd century. The crew travels back in time to the 20th century to capture two whales to take forward in time and receive the messages. Very entertaining and somewhat comic in tone. A good time.

A: William Shatner, Leonard Nimoy, DeForest Kelley, James Doohan, Walter Koenig, Nichelle Nichols

© PARAMOUNT HOME VIDEO 1797

STAR TREK V: THE FINAL FRONTIER

D: William Shatner — 107 m

PG | SF ACT | 1989 | COLOR

Sex □ Nud □ Viol □ Lang ◢ AdSit □

6 Kirk and McCoy are trying to teach Spock some campfire songs when the Enterprise receives an emergency call to go to a distant planet which has apparently been taken over by a madman. However, it has all been a ruse. It was only a gambit to attract a starship, the Enterprise, which is then hijacked. The madman needs a vessel to take him to the Great Barrier - the edge of the Universe. He wants to talk to God. Kirk is uncertain why he would need to go to such lengths, but Spock is more receptive - the madman is his half-brother.

A: William Shatner, Leonard Nimoy, DeForest Kelley, James Doohan, Walter Koenig, Nichelle Nichols

© PARAMOUNT HOME VIDEO 32044

STAR TREK VI: THE UNDISCOVERED COUNTRY

D: Nicholas Meyer, William Shatner — 110 m

PG | SF ACT | 1991 | COLOR

Sex □ Nud □ Viol ◢ Lang □ AdSit □

7 The Klingon Empire is ready to make peace. One of their moons has exploded, the ozone on their home world is being destroyed, they do not have the resources to combat it themselves and they need the Federation. Even though Kirk loathes Klingons because they killed his son, the Enterprise is called upon to meet with the Klingons to prepare for peace talks -- but one of the Klingons is poisoned, Kirk and Dr. McCoy are accused of murder and are sentenced to a prison at a frozen Klingon outpost. Meanwhile, Spock has been able to prove that it was all a plot to destroy the talks. He must retrieve Kirk and McCoy and uncover the real plotters to salvage the peace.

A: William Shatner, Leonard Nimoy, DeForest Kelley, James Doonan, Walter Koenig, Nichelle Nicholes

© PARAMOUNT HOME VIDEO 32301

STAR WARS

D: George Lucas — 124 m

PG | SF ACT SUS | 1977 | COLOR

Sex □ Nud □ Viol ◢ Lang □ AdSit □

10 HUGE megahit and first of a trio of hits. Old-time Saturday matinee cliff-hanger intensity, Western shoot-`em-up action, mysticism, comedy, loveable characters and high tech wizardry - all set in a place long, long ago and far, far away. An ordinary boy, living with his adoptive parents on a remote farming colony, comes home to find them murdered by Imperial Stormtroopers. He soon also finds that he is not so ordinary and is launched into a mission to save the Universe. Won seven Oscars. Immensely entertaining. Followed by THE EMPIRE STRIKES BACK.

A: Carrie Fisher, Mark Hamill, Harrison Ford, Alec Guinness, Anthony Daniels, Peter Cushing

© FOXVIDEO 1130

STORMY MONDAY

D: Mike Figgis — 95 m

R | CRM ACT | 1987 | COLOR

Sex □ Nud ◢ Viol ■ Lang ◢ AdSit ■

7 A slick British thriller! Sting owns a fashionable nightclub in economically depressed Newcastle, England. Ruthless American businessman Jones wants that property along with all the others so that he can demolish them, redevelop the neighborhood into a stylish area and make a killing. But when Jones doesn't get what he wants easily, he decides to use violence to get things done. Sean Bean, who works for Sting, and his girlfriend Melanie Griffith help Sting to retaliate in kind. A well acted, slightly offbeat, atmospheric, suspense-filled modern-day (late '80s) film noir.

A: Melanie Griffith, Tommy Lee Jones, Sting, Sean Bean, James Cosmo, Mark Long

© GOODTIMES 4031

STRANGER AMONG US, A

D: Sidney Lumet 109 m

PG-13 | SUS ACT | 1992 | COLOR

6 Melanie Griffith puts in a credible performance as a tough New York policewoman. Because she believes the murder and robbery of a jewelry dealer was an inside job, she goes undercover. For this to work, she first must shed her toughcop persona in order to blend into Brooklyn's ultra-religious Hasidic Jews. This one begins with an intriguing premise and contains some good action scenes but is the plot is ultimately a pretty big reach.

Sex / Nud / Viol / Lang / AdSit

A: Melanie Griffith, Eric Thal, John Pankow, Tracy Pollan, Lee Richardson, Mia Sara

© HOLLYWOOD PICTURES HOME VIDEO 1480

STRIKING DISTANCE

D: Rowdy Herrington 102 m

R | ACT MYS CRM | 1993 | COLOR

6 Bruce Willis is a former homicide detective who now patrols the rivers of Pittsburgh on a speedboat because he said something he shouldn't have. What he said was that a serial murderer was a cop or a former cop and not the meek little man that was convicted. Cops don't badmouth cops, even if you are a fifth generation cop in a family of cops. What he didn't say is that he also knew each of the victims. He has just been assigned a woman as a new partner. She is the first one to learn of his secret - just as more dead women beginning to show up. Even though there are some interesting plot twists, there are also a whole lot of plot holes. Still, it works OK overall.

Sex / Nud / Viol / Lang / AdSit

A: Bruce Willis, Sarah Jessica Parker, Dennis Farina, Tom Sizemore, Brian James, Robert Pastorelli

© COLUMBIA TRISTAR HOME VIDEO 53683

STUNTMAN, THE

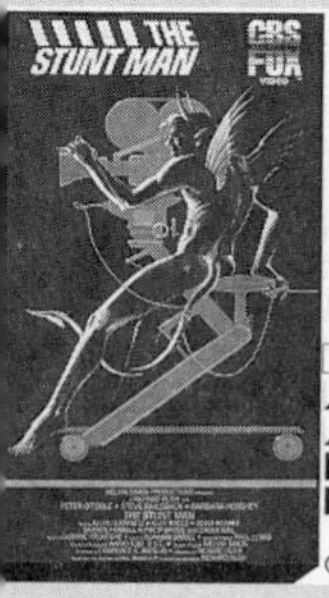

D: Richard Rush 130 m

R | SUS COM ACT | 1980 | COLOR

9 An uncommon black comedy with spirit! When Vietnam vet Railsback ventures onto a movie set and inadvertently causes the death of the top stuntman, Director O'Toole agrees to hide him from police. But Railsback must replace the dead stuntman. Railsback trains rigorously under O'Toole, who turns out to be a slightly sadistic coach. Then he uncovers the fact that O'Toole is planning to stage a stunt that will kill him. Slightly offbeat and frequently funny, the movie covers a lot of ground and has several twists. But if you stay with it, you will be rewarded.

Sex / Nud / Viol / Lang / AdSit

A: Peter O'Toole, Steve Railsback, Barbara Hershey, Alex Rocco, Chuck Bail, Alan Goorwitz

© FOXVIDEO 1110

ST. VALENTINE'S DAY MASSACRE

D: Roger Corman 100 m

NR | CRM ACT | 1967 | COLOR

7 A vividly graphic and explosively violent recreation of the gangland massacre that occurred in Chicago in 1929. Al Capone (Robards) and Bugsy Moran (Meeker) are rivals who start a gang war over control of the Windy City, a war that ends in Capone's favor. Capone and his men are thought to have staged the famous garage massacre to wipe out their opposition, but Capone, amazingly enough, gets off scott-free and is never proven to be the man behind the bloodbath. Told in semi-documentary format, the film is accurate, brutal and intense.

Sex / Nud / Viol / Lang / AdSit

A: Jason Robards, Jr., George Segal, Ralph Meeker, Jean Hale, Clint Ritchie, Frank Silvera

© FOXVIDEO 1153

SUDDEN IMPACT

D: Clint Eastwood 117 m

R | ACT CRM | 1983 | COLOR

8 Fourth entry in the DIRTY HARRY formula and the movie which gave the expression "Go ahead, make my day" new meaning. Harry is assigned to investigate a series of murders in which low-lifes have each been methodically shot in the forehead and in the the genitals. The maverick cop discovers a lead taking him to artist Sondra Locke who, along with her sister, was gang raped years before. Now she's is reaping revenge. How will Harry handle this "villian" whose tactics aren't that different from his own? Hard-hitting action flick with glimpses of humor.

Sex / Nud / Viol / Lang / AdSit

A: Clint Eastwood, Sondra Locke, Pat Hingle, Bradford Dillman, Paul Duke, Jack Thibeau

© WARNER HOME VIDEO 11341

SUPERMAN II

D: Richard Lester 127 m

PG | ACT COM FAN | 1979 | COLOR

8 Superman (Reeve) has his hands really full when three evil villains from his home planet Krypton come to earth and are intent on ruling it. They all possess the same powers that Superman has, and so the challenging battle to save the world begins. Meanwhile, Superman falls deeper in love with Lois Lane (Kidder), and arch rival Lex Luthor (Hackman) keeps persistently nipping at his heels. Much more brash and wild that the first film, this super adventure keeps the adrenaline pumping and the laughs coming at a very steady pace.

Sex / Nud / Viol / Lang / AdSit

A: Christopher Reeve, Margot Kidder, Gene Hackman, Ned Beatty, Valerie Perrine, Jackie Cooper

© WARNER HOME VIDEO 11120

SUPERMAN, THE MOVIE

D: Richard Donner 143 m

PG | ACT COM FAN | 1978 | COLOR

9 A super movie! Reeve is the man of steel from the planet Krypton who is sent to earth as a child and is raised in a small midwestern town. When he is grown he moves to the big city and uses his super powers to keep crime at bay. Clark Kent, the unassuming newspaper man, becomes Superman when duty calls. He fights for truth, justice and the American way while battling the evil Lex Luthor (Hackman). Superman also falls for the captivating Lois Lane (Kidder) in this infectious film that spawned three sequels. Plenty of humor, adventure and romance. Oscar winner for special effects!

Sex / Nud / Viol / Lang / AdSit

A: Christopher Reeve, Margot Kidder, Marlon Brando, Gene Hackman, Ned Beatty, Jackie Cooper

© WARNER HOME VIDEO 1013

SWISS FAMILY ROBINSON, THE

D: Ken Annakin 126 m

G | ACT CLD | 1960 | COLOR

9 Rousing fanciful adventure story that should be on every kid's - certainly every boy's - to-watch list, but is also entertaining for the entire family. Patented Disney adventure. Set in the early 19th-century, a family has set sail to escape the despotic rule of Napoleon but, under pursuit by pirates, they become shipwrecked on a tropical island paradise. The inventive father and his two older sons build a wonderland for the family out of native materials and an array of inventive weapons to ward off the impending assault of pirates led by Hayakawa. Top drawer entertainment.

Sex / Nud / Viol / Lang / AdSit

A: John Mills, Dorothy McGuire, James MacArthur, Janet Munro, Tommy Kirk, Sessue Hayakawa

© WALT DISNEY HOME VIDEO 053

SWORD OF LANCELOT

D: Cornel Wilde 115 m

NR | ACT ROM | 1963 | COLOR

7 Before CAMELOT, there was the story of King Arthur and his court - a rousing adventure based on Thomas Mallory's "Morte d'Arthur." This is the love story of forbidden passion between the dashing Sir Lancelot (Wilde) and the captivating Queen Guinevere. When the betrayed King Arthur finds out about their love affair, a vastly destructive war breaks out. Great performances of Lancelot and Guinevere are given by real-life husband and wife team Cornel Wilde and Jean Wallace. Loads of intricate swordplay add to the fun.

Sex / Nud / Viol / Lang / AdSit

A: Cornel Wilde, Jean Wallace, Brian Aherne, George Baker

© MCA/UNIVERSAL HOME VIDEO, INC. 80077

SWORD OF THE VALIANT

D: Stephen Weeks 102 m

PG | ACT | 1984 | COLOR

7 Nice mix of chivalry and adventure. Sean Connery is the supernatural Green Knight in the court of Camelot. When Sir Gawain (O'Keffe), a knight in King Arthur's court, cuts the Green Knight's head off, the magical Connery puts himself back together and makes Sir Gawain a bargain. O'Keffe must solve a riddle within one year or death is his consequence. Excellent period detail and production values, exciting swordplay and witty humor.

Sex / Nud / Viol / Lang / AdSit

A: Cyrielle Claire, Miles O'Keefe, Leigh Lawson, Sean Connery, Trevor Howard, Peter Cushing

Distributed By MGM/UA Home Video M700593

TAKING OF PELHAM ONE TWO THREE, THE

D: Joseph Sargent 115 m

R | SUS CRM ACT | 1974 | COLOR

8 Outstanding action thriller. Four ruthless terrorists, led by a thoroughly convincing Robert Shaw, hijack a loaded commuter train in the Bronx subway system. They demand to receive $1 million within one hour or they will start killing passengers one-by-one. Matthau is terrific as the gum-chewing transit chief of security who has to deal with them, the police and a vast government bureaucracy. Very fast-paced, interspersed with intense, high-speed action and cynical comedy relief. First-rate performances, accented by a pulse-pounding score. Excellent.

Sex / Nud / Viol / Lang / AdSit

A: Walter Matthau, Robert Shaw, Martin Balsam, Hector Elizondo, Tony Roberts, Jerry Stiller

Distributed By MGM/UA Home Video M301524

TANGO & CASH

D: Andrei Konchalovsky 104 m

R | ACT CRM | 1989 | COLOR

6 Wisecracking rivalry! Two Los Angeles cops each are convinced that they're the best there is. They are constant rivals even though they work together. That is until they are framed for a crime and sent to prison, then they join forces to become a powerful team. Jack Palance is the center of their troubles. He's the irritated drug kingpin that put them in the slammer because both were getting too close to his lucrative drug business. Stallone is a cop works strictly by the book but Russell flies by the seat of his pants - a volatile combination. Very predictable but OK.

Sex / Nud / Viol / Lang / AdSit

A: Sylvester Stallone, Kurt Russell, Jack Palance, Brion James, James Hong, Michael J. Pollard

© WARNER HOME VIDEO 11951

Action

TAPS

D: Harold Becker — 118 m

PG | ACT DMA | 1981 | COLOR

7 Unusual sort of action fare. Scott is the head of a financially strapped military academy. He is the role model and hero to all the cadets, but particularly to cadet major Hutton. Hutton and the rest of the cadets transform their sense of honor, duty, and love for their school and the military into an armed insurrection when the school's trustees decide to sell the grounds to a real estate developer for condominiums. Well-crafted and believable, with solid acting. (Note the early appearances of Tom Cruise and Sean Penn).

Sex · Nud · Viol · Lang · AdSit

A: George C. Scott, Timothy Hutton, Tom Cruise, Ronny Cox, Sean Penn

© FOXVIDEO 1128

TARGET

D: Arthur Penn — 117 m

R | ACT SUS | 1985 | COLOR

8 Good action adventure flick that overcomes some minor plot faults to deliver up an exciting experience. Dallas lumberyard owner Gene Hackman doesn't want to go to Europe for a vacation. So his wife (Hunnicutt) goes alone, hoping that he and their son (Dillon) will learn to get along in her absence. Then word comes that she has been kidnapped in Paris. He and the son fly to Paris, where assassins immediately attempt to kill him. For the first time, he reveals to his dumb-struck son that this boring, conservative old man is an ex-CIA agent, an expert in killing and surviving.

Sex · Nud · Viol · Lang · AdSit

A: Gene Hackman, Matt Dillon, Gayle Hunnicutt, Victoria Fyodorova, Josef Sommer, Guy Boyd

© CBS/FOX VIDEO 7097

TAXI DRIVER

D: Martin Scorsese — 114 m

R | DMA ACT | 1976 | COLOR

9 Intense, fascinating portrait of alienation made disturbingly real. De Niro is mesmerizing as ex-Marine Travis Bickle: quiet, a dutiful son, polite, well-meaning, but also socially inept, a loner and alone. As a night shift taxi driver, he witnesses a world of both seedy sex and beautiful women he does not know how to win. Frustratingly rejected by beautiful Shepherd, he snaps. The well-intentioned Bickle's torment focuses upon rescuing a 12-year-old whore (Foster). All his emotions boil over violently in a killing rampage directed against pimp Keitel and everything else corrupt.

Sex · Nud · Viol · Lang · AdSit

A: Robert De Niro, Cybill Shepherd, Peter Boyle, Jodie Foster, Harvey Keitel, Albert Brooks

© GOODTIMES 4226

TELEFON

D: Don Siegel — 102 m

PG | ACT SUS | 1977 | COLOR

8 Engrossing (even though improbable) and thrilling action adventure in which a crack KGB agent (Bronson) is sent to the USA to stop a Stalinist renegade agent from activating a series of previously planted KGB operatives. These operatives have been hypnotized and preprogrammed to begin a campaign of sabotage against American military bases. Bronson's job is to stop them before they start and so prevent the outbreak of WWIII. Assigned to help him is local KGB contact Lee Remick who is actually a CIA double agent. Very well-done espionage thriller.

Sex · Nud · Viol · Lang · AdSit

A: Charles Bronson, Lee Remick, Donald Pleasence, Tyne Daly, Patrick Magee, Sheree North

Distributed By MGM/UA Home Video M700127

TEQUILA SUNRISE

D: Robert Towne — 116 m

R | ACT ROM CRM | 1988 | COLOR

8 Good, spicy action flick, with some major Hollywood star power. The lives of two best friends from high school have gone in drastically different directions and are now seemingly headed headlong into conflict. Kurt Russell is an up-and-coming narcotics cop. Mel Gibson is basically a good guy but he has also become a major-league drug dealer and is now trying to get out of a nasty business. Russell is doing his best to try to catch Gibson. Between these two, in an involved plot, is sultry Michelle Pfeiffer, a beautiful restaurant owner whom they both love. Good action and well-paced with appealing stars.

Sex · Nud · Viol · Lang · AdSit

A: Mel Gibson, Michelle Pfeiffer, Kurt Russell, Raul Julia, Arliss Howard

© WARNER HOME VIDEO 11821

TERMINAL MAN, THE

D: Mike Hodges — 107 m

R | SF ACT | 1974 | COLOR

6 Engrossing science fiction thriller. George Segal plays a computer scientist who suffered some brain damage from an accident which causes him to erupt in violent outbursts. In desperation he agrees to have a microchip implanted within his brain which supposedly will control his violent urges, but there is a problem. The chip malfunctions and instead it turns him into a violent killer. Well acted, but pretty grim stuff.

Sex · Nud · Viol · Lang · AdSit

A: George Segal, Joan Hackett, Jill Clayburgh, Richard Dysart

© WARNER HOME VIDEO 11212

TERMINAL VELOCITY

D: Deran Sarafian — 132 m

PG-13 | ACT | 1994 | COLOR

6 Straight-forward action epic. Charlie Sheen is an ex-Olympic gymnast who is now a sky-jumping instructor outside Phoenix, Arizona. Kinski is a former KGB agent who is caught up in an attempt by the Russian mafia to steal a 747 planeload of Russian gold and hide it in Arizona. Right! Oh well, it's fine if you are just looking for some very light action entertainment.

Sex · Nud · Viol · Lang · AdSit

A: Charlie Sheen, Nastassja Kinski, James Gandolfini, Christopher McDonald, Suli McCullough, Hans R. Howes

© HOLLYWOOD PICTURES HOME VIDEO 3461

TERMINATOR, THE

D: James Cameron — 108 m

R | ACT SUS SF | 1984 | COLOR

10 A huge blockbuster hit that gained notoriety because of its extremely high intensity. Schwarzenneger, a cyborg (a lifelike robot), is sent back from the future to kill the mother (Hamilton) of a boy who is not yet born but who will later become a rebel leader. Arnold is an incredibly relentless and nearly indestructible killing machine from whom there is no escape. However, also arriving from the future is a resistance fighter (Biehn) who is0 here to help Hamilton defeat the Terminator. Terrific non-stop action flick, great special effects, believable and sympathetic characters and incredible pacing.

Sex · Nud · Viol · Lang · AdSit

A: Arnold Schwarzenegger, Michael Biehn, Linda Hamilton, Paul Winfield, Lance Henriksen, Rick Rossovich

© HBO VIDEO 2535

TERMINATOR 2: JUDGMENT DAY

D: James Cameron — 139 m

R | ACT SF | 1991 | COLOR

9 The action doesn't get much better than this! Hamilton and Schwarzenegger are powerhouses, poised to face their toughest challenges - and they do. The Terminator is back, but this time he is the good guy and the protector of Hamilton's son (Furlong), who is destined to eventually become a world leader in the eventual fight of men against the machines. When a new high tech Terminator that has been programmed to destroy the boy is dispatched from the future, Hamilton and Schwarzenegger find themselves involved in the ultimate battle with the ultimate killing machine. Will superior technology win over shear determination and the human spirit?

Sex · Nud · Viol · Lang · AdSit

A: Arnold Schwarzenegger, Linda Hamilton, Robert Patrick, Edward Furlong, Earl Boen, Joe Morton

© LIVE HOME VIDEO 68952

THELMA & LOUISE

D: Ridley Scott — 130 m

R | DMA ACT | 1991 | COLOR

9 This is the ultimate fugitive buddy road movie - only this time it's women, not men, who are living life on the lam! However, that is not to say that men won't enjoy it. Fed up with their oppressed and ordinary daily lives, two friends (Sarandon and Davis) just escape to the highway and decide to let their hair down. They experience more excitement than either of them expected and get into more trouble than they ever dreamed possible, but they decide that they will live life on their own terms. This is a heck of a film. It's very well done, well-acted and a lot of fun. It became a landmark film .

Sex · Nud · Viol · Lang · AdSit

A: Susan Sarandon, Geena Davis, Harvey Keitel, Michael Madsen, Christopher McDonald, Brad Pitt

Distributed By MGM/UA Home Video M902355

THERE WAS A CROOKED MAN

D: Joseph L. Mankiewicz — 123 m

R | WST ACT COM | 1970 | COLOR

8 Quirky and clever Western. Crooked man Kirk Douglas steals a small fortune. He is caught when he is spotted by his victim (who is looking through a voyeur's peep hole at a whorehouse) as he is celebrating his new fortune. He is sent to an Arizona prison which is wardened by revision-minded Henry Fonda. But, Douglas uses the opportunities created by Fonda's revisions to institute a riot and escape and immediately sets off to recover the buried booty. But, a very angry and exasperated Fonda has personally set out after him. Entertaining Western, with a clever and funny plot, and a powerhouse cast.

Sex · Nud · Viol · Lang · AdSit

A: Kirk Douglas, Henry Fonda, Warren Oates, Burgess Meredith, Hume Cronyn, Arthur O'Connell

© WARNER HOME VIDEO 11270

THIEF

D: Michael Mann — 124 m

R | CRM ACT | 1981 | COLOR

8 Interesting character study of an interesting character. After 11 years in prison, master thief James Caan is determined to create a normal life for himself. He is basically a decent sort of guy with normal dreams. So he gets married, buys a house and has kids, but they are all expensive and he is concerned that he may lose them. His reputation as a master thief has caught the attention of mob boss Prosky, who is pressuring Caan to work with him. Caan sees an opportunity for one last big job that will cement his life. Gripping, detailed and well-crafted.

Sex · Nud · Viol · Lang · AdSit

A: James Caan, Willie Nelson, Tuesday Weld, Tom Signorelli, Robert Prosky, James Belushi

Distributed By MGM/UA Home Video M201305

THOMAS CROWN AFFAIR, THE

D: Norman Jewison — 102 m

R | SUS ROM ACT | 1968 | COLOR

8 Stylish combination of a heist movie and a sophisticated romancer. Faye Dunaway is an unscrupulous insurance investigator hot on the trail of a bored millionaire (McQueen) who enjoys staging elaborate burglaries just for the thrill of it. Even as they play coy cat and mouse games and engage in clever and cryptic dialogue, he is plotting a daring bank heist that is to be carried off right under her nose. The emotional and mental games they play with each other inevitably lead to romance. Oscar for best song: "Windmills of Your Mind." Good entertainment.

Sex / Nud / Viol / Lang / AdSit

A: Steve McQueen, Faye Dunaway, Paul Burke, Yaphet Kotto, Jack Weston, Biff McGuire

Distributed By MGM/UA Home Video M201260

THREE DAYS OF THE CONDOR

D: Sydney Pollack — 118 m

R | SUS MYS ACT | 1975 | COLOR

9 Riveting spy suspensor. Very well done. Redford is an insignificant CIA researcher (he reads foreign novels to get espionage ideas) at a storefront office in NYC. One day, however, he happens to run an errand and comes back to the office to find that everyone in it has been slaughtered and he is a hunted man. He doesn't know who, he doesn't know why, and he can trust no one until he finds out. Having nowhere to hide, he forces his way into a lonely stranger's (Dunaway) apartment. At first she is terrified, but she begins to believe in him and an uneasy love affair blossoms. Thoroughly engrossing.

Sex / Nud / Viol / Lang / AdSit

A: Robert Redford, Faye Dunaway, Cliff Robertson, Max von Sydow, John Houseman

© PARAMOUNT HOME VIDEO 8803

THREE MUSKETEERS, THE

D: Richard Lester — 105 m

PG | ACT COM ROM | 1974 | COLOR

9 Great, well-rounded entertainment that has a little bit of everything. Dumas's classic tale has been filmed numerous times, but never this well. Michael York is determined to become one of the King's elite guards, the Musketeers, so he befriends three of them but, they are only interested in fighting, drinking and chasing women. However, they do become roused to action when York charms Welch, the Queen's lady-in-waiting, and she uncovers a plot to overcome the King. This news sends the Musketeers into rip roaring action. Rousing swashbuckling and hilarious slapstick. Top talent.

Sex / Nud / Viol / Lang / AdSit

A: Oliver Reed, Raquel Welch, Richard Chamberlain, Michael York, Frank Finlay, Geraldine Chaplin

© LIVE HOME VIDEO 67776

THREE MUSKETEERS, THE

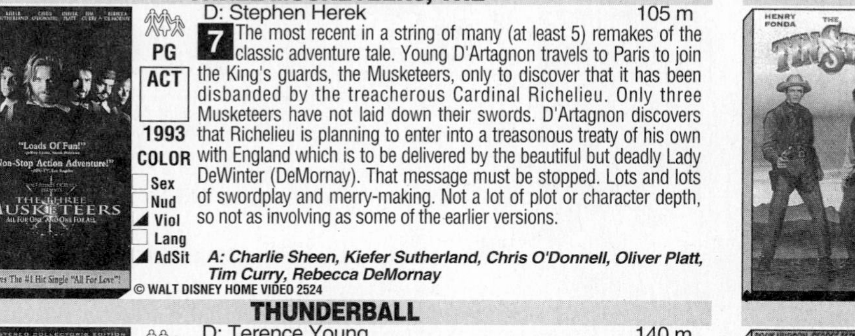

D: Stephen Herek — 105 m

PG | ACT | 1993 | COLOR

7 The most recent in a string of many (at least 5) remakes of the classic adventure tale. Young D'Artagnon travels to Paris to join the King's guards, the Musketeers, only to discover that it has been disbanded by the treacherous Cardinal Richelieu. Only three Musketeers have not laid down their swords. D'Artagnon discovers that Richelieu is planning to enter into a treasonous treaty of his own with England which is to be delivered by the beautiful but deadly Lady DeWinter (DeMornay). That message must be stopped. Lots and lots of swordplay and merry-making. Not a lot of plot or character depth, so not as involving as some of the earlier versions.

Sex / Nud / Viol / Lang / AdSit

A: Charlie Sheen, Kiefer Sutherland, Chris O'Donnell, Oliver Platt, Tim Curry, Rebecca DeMornay

© WALT DISNEY HOME VIDEO 2524

THUNDERBALL

D: Terence Young — 140 m

PG | ACT | 1965 | COLOR

8 James Bond is in pursuit of Spectre's number two man, Largo, and two stolen atom bombs - with which Largo intends to blackmail Miami. Along the way, James encounters Largo's mistress, Claudine Auger (the former Miss France), and seduces her into battling for truth and justice. 007 is as suave, as tough as ever and is loaded down with gadgets and pretty bikini-clad girls, too, but he is also all wet. Much of the filming was underwater, which makes it somewhat difficult to follow. Remade 14 years later as NEVER SAY NEVER AGAIN.

Sex / Nud / Viol / Lang / AdSit

A: Sean Connery, Claudine Auger, Adolfo Celi, Luciana Paluzzi, Rick Van Nutter

Distributed By MGM/UA Home Video M202729

THUNDERBOLT AND LIGHTFOOT

D: Michael Cimino — 117 m

R | ACT COM | 1974 | COLOR

8 Quirky action flick that Eastwood fans didn't quite know how to handle when it was released, but time has proven it to be a solid piece of action entertainment. Eastwood is a thief who is being hunted by his former partners (Kennedy and Lewis) who think that he set them up and then stole all their money from an earlier bank heist. When they do catch him, Eastwood and another young drifter (Bridges was Oscar-nominated) agree to join up with them and hit the same bank again in the same way as before. Colorful film, with great characters and an oddly interesting buddy element.

Sex / Nud / Viol / Lang / AdSit

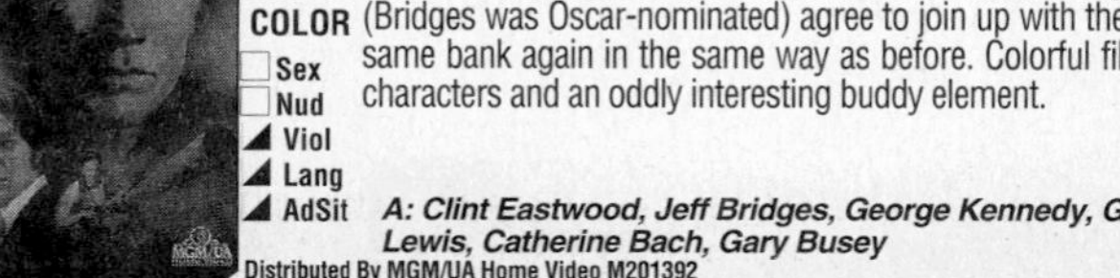

A: Clint Eastwood, Jeff Bridges, George Kennedy, Geoffrey Lewis, Catherine Bach, Gary Busey

Distributed By MGM/UA Home Video M201392

THUNDER ROAD

D: Arthur Ripley — 94 m

PG | ACT | 1958 | B&W

7 A pretty good action flick that was Mitchum's all the way. Mitchum co-wrote, produced and starred in this story of a Tennessee hill boy, just back from Korea and just out of prison, who goes back into the only business he knows - moonshining. Mitchum shines as a man whose own future is sealed but who cautions his younger brother to go into a real career. All the while he struggles against mobsters who want to take over his operation and the feds who want to shut him down. Mitchum even got a popular hit song from the film's theme - which he also wrote and sang.

Sex / Nud / Viol / Lang / AdSit

A: Robert Mitchum, Gene Barry, Keely Smith, James Mitchum, Jacques Auburchon, Trevor Bardette

Distributed By MGM/UA Home Video M601453

TIGHTROPE

D: Richard Tuggle — 118 m

R | CRM ACT DMA | 1984 | COLOR

9 Fascinating thriller which also has a compelling underlying story. Eastwood is a burned-out homicide detective. He has been deserted by his wife and is taking care of his two daughters. He has also taken to having kinky sex with the prostitutes on his beat, handcuffing them. When these same girls start to turn up dead, Eastwood realizes that he is being followed and that he and his daughters are in big danger. It is an intelligent script which allows Eastwood to analyze the dichotomy within his character, but it never forgets to be an action flick and refrains from exploitation.

Sex / Nud / Viol / Lang / AdSit

A: Clint Eastwood, Genevieve Bujold, Dan Hedaya, Alison Eastwood, Jennifer Beck

© WARNER HOME VIDEO 11400

TIMECOP

D: Peter Hyams — 99 m

R | SF ACT | 1994 | COLOR

8 This is Jean-Claude Van Damme's most interesting and intelligent flick to date. Blood-and-guts action fans certainly will not be disappointed - there is still plenty of both. However, this one actually has a pretty good premise and is well executed. Van Damme is a special officer assigned to a highly secret government agency in 2004. Their job is to go back into time to remove modern time travelers before they can alter history. The travelers he seeks have been sent by a corrupt politician who is using his access to the technology to generate money for a Presidential election campaign, no matter what the cost. Some plot holes, but over-all it is quite well done and fun.

Sex / Nud / Viol / Lang / AdSit

A: Jean-Claude Van Damme, Ron Silver, Mia Sara, Gloria Reuben, Bruce McGill, Scott Lawrence

© MCA/UNIVERSAL HOME VIDEO, INC. 82169

TIN STAR, THE

D: Anthony Mann — 93 m

NR | WST ACT | 1957 | B&W

9 Solid and well acted - a quality Western. Henry Fonda is a bounty hunter. He used to be a sheriff and had a family, but they died when he couldn't raise the money for doctor bills. Now, hard and bitter, he comes to a small town to await the arrival of a reward check. Anthony Perkins is the young sheriff in the town and is in way over his head with a local thug. Fonda, seeing a piece of his former self in the sheriff, helps Perkins learn what to do and, in the process, rediscovers a life for himself. An intelligent and affecting character study.

Sex / Nud / Viol / Lang / AdSit

A: Henry Fonda, Anthony Perkins, Betsy Palmer, Neville Brand, John McIntire, Lee Van Cleef

© PARAMOUNT HOME VIDEO 5708

TOBRUK

D: Arthur Hiller — 110 m

NR | ACT WAR | 1966 | COLOR

6 Thrilling World War II action movie in which a group of German Jews, disguised as Axis troops, together with some American and English commandos, undertake a daring mission across miles of desert wasteland to destroy the fuel supplies of Field Marshall Rommel's tanks in North Africa at Tobruk. Pretty good. There are some pretty big action scenes with tank battles, and some intrigue, too, when they suspect a traitor in their midst.

Sex / Nud / Viol / Lang / AdSit

A: Rock Hudson, George Peppard, Guy Stockwell, Nigel Green, Jack Watson, Norman Rossington

© MCA/UNIVERSAL HOME VIDEO, INC. 45014

TO LIVE AND DIE IN L.A.

D: William Friedkin — 114 m

R | ACT SUS CRM | 1985 | COLOR

8 High intensity action fare that is both riveting and disturbing. Secret Service Agent Petersen becomes obsessed with getting master counterfeiter Willem Dafoe, who had caused the death of his partner. A very cynical and violent film in which the good guys are only just a little better than the bad guys. The characters are complex and the story is loaded with a lot of twists and exciting action sequences. The problem that arises is that it becomes very difficult to determine which side to sympathize with or to even care about anyone at all.

Sex / Nud / Viol / Lang / AdSit

A: William L. Petersen, Willem Dafoe, John Pankow, Dean Stockwell, John Turturro

© LIVE HOME VIDEO VA5123

TOMBSTONE

R | WST ACT | 1994 | COLOR

D: George P. Cosmatos — 130 m

8 Critics dismissed this as just another remake, except more violent. In a literal sense, they were right. However, there is more to it than that. There is a genuine excitement. And, while all the characters and elements have been embellished by Hollywood, most of them, not all, are also generally true. Wyatt and his brothers did use their fearlessness and reputations to worm their way into much of the larcenous business of Tombstone, which put them on a collision course with a gang of hooligans called "The Cowboys". The blood war between these two factions began at the corral, killed Morgan, crippled Virgil, divided the town and destroyed The Cowboys.

Sex / Nud / Viol / Lang / AdSit

A: Kurt Russell, Val Kilmer, Michael Biehn, Powers Boothe, Dana Delany, Sam Elliott

© HOLLYWOOD PICTURES HOME VIDEO 2544

TOM HORN

R | WST ACT | 1980 | COLOR

D: William Wiard — 98 m

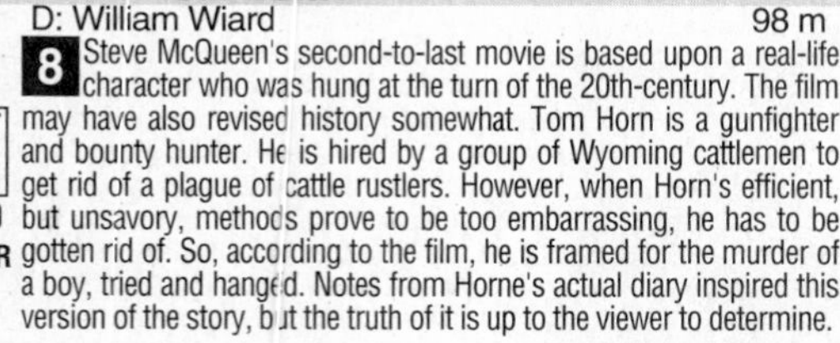

8 Steve McQueen's second-to-last movie is based upon a real-life character who was hung at the turn of the 20th-century. The film may have also revised history somewhat. Tom Horn is a gunfighter and bounty hunter. He is hired by a group of Wyoming cattlemen to get rid of a plague of cattle rustlers. However, when Horn's efficient, but unsavory, methods prove to be too embarrassing, he has to be gotten rid of. So, according to the film, he is framed for the murder of a boy, tried and hanged. Notes from Horne's actual diary inspired this version of the story, but the truth of it is up to the viewer to determine.

Sex / Nud / Viol / Lang / AdSit

A: Steve McQueen, Richard Farnsworth, Slim Pickens, Elisha Cook, Jr.

© WARNER HOME VIDEO 1042

TONY ROME

NR | MYS ACT | 1967 | COLOR

D: Gordon Douglas — 110 m

6 Sinatra stars in the title role as a private eye who is hired by his ex-partner to escort home the beautiful daughter of a wealthy industrialist when she is found drunk in a seedy Miami motel. After the girl's expensive diamond pin turns up missing, his place gets torn up, his ex-partner dies suspiciously and he finds that he is involved with blackmailers and junkies. Mildly diverting detective movie, somewhat reminiscent of the '40s film noir type. Sinatra's character is stylish and glib, but not altogether believable. Some good action helps a confusing plot become entertaining.

Sex / Nud / Viol / Lang / AdSit

A: Frank Sinatra, Jill St. John, Gena Rowlands, Richard Conte, Sue Lyon, Gena Rowlands

© FOXVIDEO 1338

TOO LATE THE HERO

PG | ACT WAR SUS | 1969 | COLOR

D: Robert Aldrich — 132 m

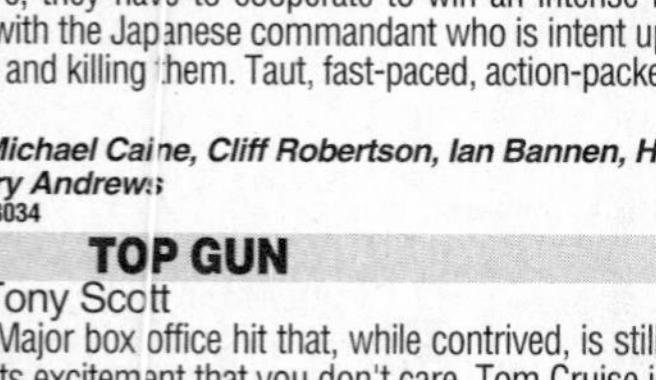

8 Good WWII action flick. A reluctant American is assigned to a unit of reluctant British commandos, who are to destroy the Japanese radio installation on the other end of their island in preparation for a major naval action. On their return, they discover a clandestine airfield and must get word of it back. Over the course of their mission, all but two are killed: the American (Robertson) and one Brit (Caine) - and they don't like each other. However, if they are going to survive, they have to cooperate to win an intense battle of wits and wills with the Japanese commandant who is intent upon hunting them down and killing them. Taut, fast-paced, action-packed thriller.

Sex / Nud / Viol / Lang / AdSit

A: Michael Caine, Cliff Robertson, Ian Bannen, Henry Fonda, Harry Andrews

© CBS/FOX VIDEO 8034

TOP GUN

PG | ACT ROM | 1986 | COLOR

D: Tony Scott — 109 m

10 Major box office hit that, while contrived, is still so captivating in its excitement that you don't care. Tom Cruise is a top Navy F-14 fighter pilot sent for additional "Top Gun" training at Miramar Naval Base in San Diego. This is a school which is reserved for only the best of the best. His cocky attitude gets him in trouble with nearly everyone there but he falls in love with his luscious physics instructor Kelly McGillis. Heartpoundingly thrilling flight sequences are at the heart of this film's big success for the men. Tom's smile wins over the women.

Sex / Nud / Viol / Lang / AdSit

A: Tom Cruise, Kelly McGillis, Anthony Edwards, Val Kilmer, Tim Robbins, Meg Ryan

© PARAMOUNT HOME VIDEO 1692

TORA! TORA! TORA!

G | WAR ACT | 1970 | COLOR

D: Richard Fleischer, Toshio Masuda — 144 m

8 Extravagant and historically accurate recreation of the events leading up to, and the actual bombing of, Pearl Harbor in 1941. Prepared by both Japanese and American production crews, two versions were prepared: one was released in America and was largely ignored by the public, the other was released in Japan becoming a major box office hit. Extraordinary effort was made to be both accurate and realistic. Much of the fact-based drama surrounding the events leading to the attack was thought to have been too slow for most Americans. Too bad. Very impressive action sequences.

Sex / Nud / Viol / Lang / AdSit

A: Martin Balsam, E.G. Marshall, James Whitmore, Jason Robards, Jr., Tatsuya Mihashi, Joseph Cotten

© FOXVIDEO 1017

TOTAL RECALL

R | SF ACT | 1990 | COLOR

D: Paul Verhoeven — 113 m

9 Spectacular special effects mark this high intensity actioner, set in the year 2084. Arnold Schwarzenegger is a construction worker who decides to take a fantasy trip to Mars from a machine that plants new memories in your mind. Instead, the machine brings back mysterious haunting old memories that have been taken from him. Why has someone wiped out his memories? Who is he really? He is driven to go to Mars to find out. He finds that he was a secret agent, and now they're trying to kill him. But, why? Very violent. Big, big budget was spent for special effects and scenery, and it shows.

Sex / Nud / Viol / Lang / AdSit

A: Arnold Schwarzenegger, Rachel Ticotin, Sharon Stone, Michael Ironside, Ronny Cox

© LIVE HOME VIDEO 68901

TOUCH OF EVIL

NR | CRM SUS ACT | 1958 | B&W

D: Orson Welles — 108 m

9 A seriously underrated film from Orson Welles - who wrote, directed and starred in it - that is essentially a fascinating character study. When a powerful American and his mistress are blown up at a Mexican border town, Welles, a corrupt American sheriff, blames the murder on a young Mexican and plants evidence on him to insure conviction. An honest Mexican cop (Heston) disputes the claim, so Welles frames Heston's American wife (Leigh) with murder and drugs and terrorizes her. Very famous three-minute continuous shot at beginning.

Sex / Nud / Viol / Lang / AdSit

A: Charlton Heston, Janet Leigh, Orson Welles, Joseph Calleia, Akim Tamiroff, Marlene Dietrich

© MCA/UNIVERSAL HOME VIDEO, INC. 55078

TOWERING INFERNO

PG | SUS ACT | 1974 | COLOR

D: Irwin Allen, John Guillermin — 165 m

8 First there was a crippled airliner (AIRPORT), then a capsized ship (THE POSEIDON ADVENTURE) and here there is a 150-story high-rise on fire. This was one of the biggest of the disaster flicks that were popular during the early 1970s. During the dedication ceremony of a new San Francisco hotel and office skyscraper that the developer had cut corners on, a fire breaks out, trapping people on the upper floors. Huge cast of blockbuster stars helps to carry this OK drama that is considerably spiced up with spectacular pyrotechnic special effects. 7 nominations, 2 Oscars.

Sex / Nud / Viol / Lang / AdSit

A: Steve McQueen, Paul Newman, William Holden, Faye Dunaway, Fred Astaire, Richard Chamberlain

© FOXVIDEO 1071

TOY SOLDIERS

R | ACT | 1991 | COLOR

D: Daniel Petrie, Jr. — 104 m

6 Silly and mindless action flick that still manages to be fun due largely to the strength of the acting power in its young cast and their likable characters. A group of Columbian terrorists takes over a military school that houses a bunch of rich-kid misfits, intending to hold them for ransom to gain the release of a powerful druglord. Poor terrorists, they don't know what they are getting into.

Sex / Nud / Viol / Lang / AdSit

A: Sean Astin, Louis Gossett, Jr., Andrew Divoff, Wil Wheaton, Keith Coogan

© COLUMBIA TRISTAR HOME VIDEO 70623

TRAIN, THE

NR | ACT SUS WAR | 1965 | B&W

D: John Frankenheimer — 133 m

9 Top-notch gripping action film set in France just as WWII is starting to turn for the Allies. Burt Lancaster is the head of the French railway system and is also in the underground movement. Paul Scofield is a driven German officer in charge of getting a train load of French art treasures, stolen from French museums, back to Germany. Lancaster is reluctant to risk lives for art until an old man he loves is killed by the Nazis as he trys to stop the train. Excellent, solid suspense. Fast moving, with a clever plot and good special effects. Based on a true story.

Sex / Nud / Viol / Lang / AdSit

A: Burt Lancaster, Paul Scofield, Michel Simon, Albert Remy, Wolfgang Preiss

Distributed By MGM/UA Home Video 202511

TRESPASS

R | ACT | 1992 | COLOR

D: Walter Hill — 101 m

7 High octane action thriller. Two white firemen from Arkansas stumble onto a treasure map drawn by a crazy man. 50 years before, the man had stolen a fortune in gold artifacts from a church and hidden them inside the East St. Louis factory where he had worked. The firemen chase their fortune to what is now an abandoned factory in a rundown, drug-infested area. Their treasure hunt turns into a nightmare, when they get caught accidentally witnessing a murder at a drug deal gone bad. Now they have become targets for execution in a fierce urban war. Very well done. Violent, tense and believable.

Sex / Nud / Viol / Lang / AdSit

A: Bill Paxton, Ice T, Ice Cube, William Sadler, Art Evans, De'Voreaux White

© MCA/UNIVERSAL HOME VIDEO, INC. 81281

TRIUMPH OF THE SPIRIT

D: Robert M. Young — 120 m

R | DMA ACT | 1989 | COLOR

6 Pretty good but a very sad drama based upon actual events. A young Greek Jewish boxer and street tough (Dafoe) is captured by the Nazis in 1943 and sent to Auschwitz, along with his family. There, the SS officers delight in watching boxing matches between the prisoners, where the contestants are like gladiators. They literally fight for their lives. The losers and their families are sent to the gas chambers. Blunt and grim.

Sex / Nud / Viol / Lang / AdSit

A: Willem Dafoe, Wendy Gazelle, Robert Loggia, Edward James Olmos, Kelly Wolf, Costas Mandylor

© COLUMBIA TRISTAR HOME VIDEO 59063

TRON

D: Steven Lisberger — 95 m

PG | SF ACT | 1982 | COLOR

6 Enjoyable Disney escapist adventure, geared to more than just kids. Set in the future, nearly everything is controlled by the Master Computer. Jeff Bridges is a computer whiz who sets out to prove that Warner, an unscrupulous executive, has stolen some of his programs. But before he gets very far, he is sucked inside the Master Computer's circuits where he, Boxleitner and Hughes must do battle against Warner and the Master Computer in a deadly video game. Exciting special effects. Plot is a little confusing, though.

Sex / Nud / Viol / Lang / AdSit

A: Jeff Bridges, Bruce Boxleitner, David Warner, Cindy Morgan, Barnard Hughes, Dan Shor

© WALT DISNEY HOME VIDEO 122

TRUE GRIT

D: Henry Hathaway — 128 m

G | WST ACT COM | 1969 | COLOR

9 Extremely popular Western for which Wayne finally won an Oscar, after 40 years in film. He is Rooster Cogburn, a crude old derelict of a marshall who helps out a young girl who wants him to track down her father's killer. They head off into Indian country, where they are joined by a young Texas ranger (Campbell). This is a very enjoyable movie that takes time for solid character development and creating interesting relationships between the principals. There is a rousing finish that is topped off with a near-classic shootout. Great entertainment.

Sex / Nud / Viol / Lang / AdSit

A: John Wayne, Glen Campbell, Kim Darby, Robert Duvall, Jeremy Slate, Strother Martin

© PARAMOUNT HOME VIDEO 6833

TRUE LIES

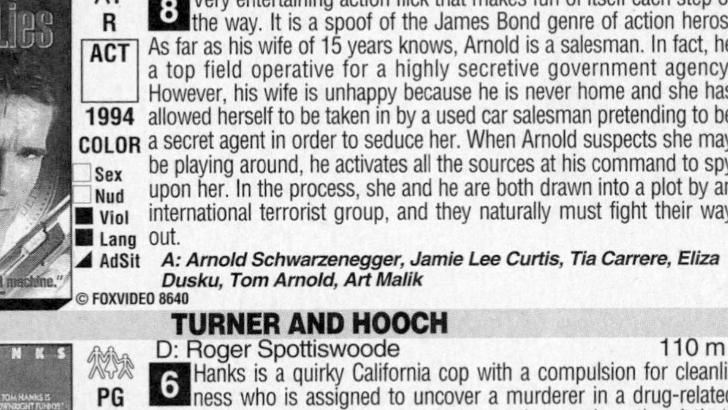

D: James Cameron — 141 m

R | ACT | 1994 | COLOR

8 Very entertaining action flick that makes fun of itself each step of the way. It is a spoof of the James Bond genre of action heros. As far as his wife of 15 years knows, Arnold is a salesman. In fact, he a top field operative for a highly secretive government agency. However, his wife is unhappy because he is never home and she has allowed herself to be taken in by a used car salesman pretending to be a secret agent in order to seduce her. When Arnold suspects she may be playing around, he activates all the sources at his command to spy upon her. In the process, she and he are both drawn into a plot by an international terrorist group, and they naturally must fight their way out.

Sex / Nud / Viol / Lang / AdSit

A: Arnold Schwarzenegger, Jamie Lee Curtis, Tia Carrere, Eliza Dusku, Tom Arnold, Art Malik

© FOXVIDEO 8640

TURNER AND HOOCH

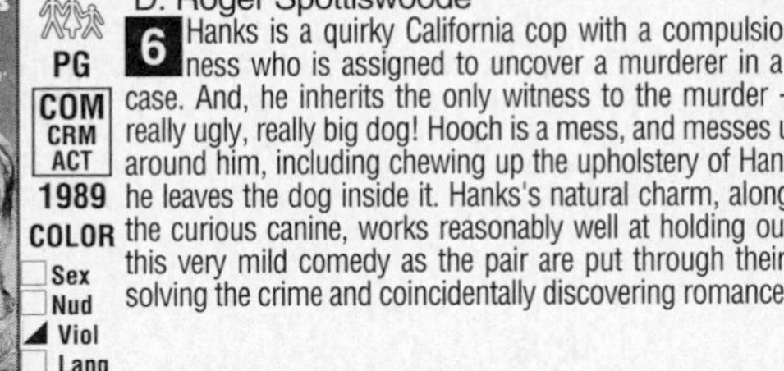

D: Roger Spottiswoode — 110 m

PG | COM CRM ACT | 1989 | COLOR

6 Hanks is a quirky California cop with a compulsion for cleanliness who is assigned to uncover a murderer in a drug-related case. And, he inherits the only witness to the murder - the victim's really ugly, really big dog! Hooch is a mess, and messes up everything around him, including chewing up the upholstery of Hanks's car after he leaves the dog inside it. Hanks's natural charm, along with that of the curious canine, works reasonably well at holding our attention in this very mild comedy as the pair are put through their paces while solving the crime and coincidentally discovering romance too.

Sex / Nud / Viol / Lang / AdSit

A: Tom Hanks, Mare Winningham, Craig T. Nelson, Reginald VelJohnson, Scott Paulin, J.C. Quinn

© TOUCHSTONE HOME VIDEO 911

TWO MULES FOR SISTER SARA

D: Don Siegel — 105 m

PG | WST ACT COM | 1969 | COLOR

8 Intriguing Western that lures you in, entertains you throughout and then hits you with a surprise curve. Clint is a drifter in Mexico during the revolution. He rescues a nun (MacLaine) from being raped but he is now burdened with her. He finds her to be both strangely unpious and fascinatingly appealing - all of which is very unsettling to him. She entices him into risking his neck by helping her to aid the rebel cause and eventually into helping her attack a French garrison. Light-hearted and action-packed fun - with a surprise inside.

Sex / Nud / Viol / Lang / AdSit

A: Shirley MacLaine, Clint Eastwood, Manolo Fabregas, Alberto Morin, Armando Silvestre, John Kelly

© MCA/UNIVERSAL HOME VIDEO, INC. 66046

TWO RODE TOGETHER

D: John Ford — 109 m

NR | WST DMA ACT | 1961 | COLOR

8 A worthy Western with Stewart in a somewhat uncharacteristically harsh role. He plays a hard-bitten and cynical marshall who has been hired by a naive calvary officer (Widmark) and a group of settlers to retrieve kidnapped white children from the Commanches. While Widmark and the settlers are optimistic, Stewart knows that what he will bring back is not what they expect. He also knows that the children will not be accepted. Interesting and somber take on the theme first explored in THE SEARCHERS, which is also highly recommended.

Sex / Nud / Viol / Lang / AdSit

A: James Stewart, Richard Widmark, Shirley Jones, Andy Devine, Woody Strode, Linda Cristal

© COLUMBIA TRISTAR HOME VIDEO 60762

ULZANA'S RAID

D: Robert Aldrich — 103 m

R | WST ACT | 1972 | COLOR

8 A tense and quite unusual Western that was viewed at the time by many critics as being an allegory for the fighting in Vietnam and so it received an unduly poor reception. That unfortunate aspect aside, this is quite an involving story. A seasoned old Army scout is sent along with a green officer in pursuit of a notoriously vicious Apache raiding party led by the cunning Ulzana. The inexperienced young lieutenant is tentative and uncertain, but Lancaster is as calculating as his cruel quarry, Ulzana. Very violent, an absorbing chess game of a pursuit and a thought provoking insight into the thin veil of civilization over us all. Great job by Lancaster. Based on fact.

Sex / Nud / Viol / Lang / AdSit

A: Burt Lancaster, Bruce Davison, Richard Jaeckel, Jorge Luke

© MCA/UNIVERSAL HOME VIDEO, INC. 80155

UNCOMMON VALOR

D: Ted Kotcheff — 105 m

R | ACT | 1983 | COLOR

7 Colonel Jason Rhodes (Hackman) is still pretty torn up about the apparent death of his son as a result of the Vietnam War. Ten years later, refusing to really believe that his son is gone, he learns that he may actually be alive but held prisoner in a Vietnamese camp. With the help of a powerful financial backer, Hackman assembles a crew of his son's Vietnam buddies and prepares to blast into Laos to free his son. A go-for-the-gusto adventure that holds nothing back.

Sex / Nud / Viol / Lang / AdSit

A: Gene Hackman, Fred Ward, Reb Brown, Robert Stack, Randall Cobb, Patrick Swayze

© PARAMOUNT HOME VIDEO 1657

UNDER SIEGE

D: Andrew Davis — 103 m

R | ACT | 1992 | COLOR

8 Solid action flick. Seagal is a highly-decorated Navy SEAL who was disgraced by a failed mission in Panama. So, he is given the chance to fill out his remaining 20-year tour as ship's cook on the battleship Missouri which is returning to port to be retired. However, psycho Executive Officer Busey has joined forces with a rogue CIA agent Jones and a crew of hired mercenaries who board the ship and capture it in a surprise raid. Their plan is to sell the ship's nuclear-tipped cruise missiles to various terrorist groups who will pay dearly. The only crew member who is capable of stopping them is the cook. Surprisingly well done and believable. Great action, but very violent.

Sex / Nud / Viol / Lang / AdSit

A: Steven Seagal, Tommy Lee Jones, Gary Busey, Erica Eleniak, Colm Meaney, Damian Chapa

© WARNER HOME VIDEO 12420

UNDERWORLD U.S.A.

D: Samuel Fuller — 99 m

NR | CRM ACT | 1960 | B&W

6 A young boy (Robertson) witnesses the brutal murder of his father by four up-and-coming mobsters. From that moment on, he decides to dedicate his life to taking revenge on the four and becomes a gangster himself to gain access into their world, even when it means going to prison. He infiltrates the mob, rises to the top and then locates the three hoods who are still alive. Then federal agents come to him looking for cooperation and he sees the perfect opportunity to gain his revenge by using the government to get what he wants most. All that is fine, except first he has to survive.

Sex / Nud / Viol / Lang / AdSit

A: Cliff Robertson, Dolores Dorn, Beatrice Coll, Larry Gates, Paul Dubov

© COLUMBIA TRISTAR HOME VIDEO 60918

UNFORGIVEN

D: Clint Eastwood — m

R | WST DMA ACT | 1992 | COLOR

10 Hugely successful and popular but very atypical Western that won Best Picture Oscar plus 3 more. Eastwood is an ex-gunslinger and outlaw who has been struggling to eke out a living as a farmer, but he and his family are starving. So, he and his ex-partner set off to collect a bounty by killing a couple of cowboys who have cut up a prostitute. Their mission, however, places them in direct conflict with another gunslinger (Hackman) who has become comfortable as the ruthless sheriff of the town. This is a no-nonsense, grittily realistic and unglamorous story of men pitted against each other, who are able to survive a brutal game by killing brutally without a thought.

Sex / Nud / Viol / Lang / AdSit

A: Clint Eastwood, Gene Hackman, Morgan Freeman, Richard Harris, Jaimz Woolvett

© WARNER HOME VIDEO 12531

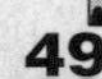

UNLAWFUL ENTRY

D: Jonathan Kaplan — 110 m

8 R — CRM ACT — 1992 — COLOR

■ Sex ■ Nud ■ Viol ■ Lang ■ AdSit

What happens when a psychotic bad cop uses all the power of the system against you? Kurt Russell and Madeleine Stowe are happily married and about to enter into a lucrative new business when their plush house is broken into. Ray Liotta is one of the cops who responds to the call. He is very helpful, and at first they think he is a friend, but he is in fact totally obsessed with Stowe. He is determined to win her away from Russell by showing her how weak Russell is compared to him. He uses his police access to their records to systematically terrorize and destroy their relationship. Very well acted and convincingly done, but also explicit and very violent.

A: Kurt Russell, Madeleine Stowe, Ray Liotta, Roger E. Mosley, Ken Lerner, Deborah Offner

© FOXVIDEO 1977

UNTOUCHABLES, THE

D: Brian De Palma — 119 m

10 R — CRM ACT SUS — 1987 — COLOR

□ Sex □ Nud ■ Viol ■ Lang ◢ AdSit

Outstanding! Some great talent combines forces to create a captivating high-energy excitement adventure set in prohibition-era Chicago. Costner is Elliot Ness, a very intense straight-arrow federal agent who arrives in a corrupt town, intent upon "getting" Al Capone (De Niro). He quickly sets about finding a few good men for his private force - beginning with a tough street cop (Connery - Oscar winner). Also included is an idealistic rookie (Garcia) and a bookish agent (Smith). A well-woven, realistic tapestry of drama, intrigue, suspense and high-intensity action. Highly recommended.

A: Kevin Costner, Sean Connery, Robert De Niro, Charles Martin Smith, Andy Garcia, Billy Drago

© PARAMOUNT HOME VIDEO 1886

UP PERISCOPE

D: Gordon Douglas — 111 m

6 NR — WAR ACT — 1959 — COLOR

□ Sex □ Nud ◢ Viol □ Lang ◢ AdSit

Good WWII actioner. James Garner is young and a brand new navy lieutenant. He is also a skindiver and a demolitions expert who is being sent to sabotage a Japanese radio transmitter on a South Pacific island. He travels to his location on board a submarine captained by Edmond O'Brien, who is under orders to take Garner in as close to shore as possible. Garner then is to leave the submarine while it is submerged and is to return to it when the job is complete. However, if he doesn't return by a predetermined time, he will be presumed dead. Well done. Still pretty effective today.

A: James Garner, Edmond O'Brien, Andra Martin, Alan Hale, Carleton Carpenter, Frank Gifford

© WARNER HOME VIDEO 12042

UTU

D: Geoff Murphy — 104 m

8 R — ACT DMA WST — 1983 — COLOR

□ Sex ◢ Nud ■ Viol □ Lang ◢ AdSit

Excellent (but very exotic) New Zealand import. It is set there, in the 1870s, but has definite overtones of the American Southwest. When a aboriginal tribesman, who is fighting for the British colonial army, comes home to find that his village has been massacred by the same white army he has been fighting for, he swears vengeance on all whites. He becomes a vicious raider of white settlements, hotly pursued by the army and even despised by many of his own people because of his ruthlessness. Lots of action, but also a moving moral play that is reminiscent of the American campaign against Geronimo.

A: Anzac Wallace, Kelly Johnson, Tim Elliot, Bruno Lawrence

© CBS/FOX VIDEO 6119

V

D: Kenneth Johnson — 197 m

9 NR — SF ACT — 1983 — COLOR

□ Sex □ Nud ◢ Viol □ Lang ◢ AdSit

This excellent made-for-TV miniseries held the fascination of the country. In it, fifty huge space ships appear in the skies over all the world's major cities. The human-like visitors relate that they are on a mission of peace, but soon they are moving to focus the fears of the masses. Blaming scientist's for all the ills of the mankind, they make their move to establish a world-wide fascist state, while also destroying the only force that can stop them. TV cameraman Mark Singer discovers the awful real truth and forms a rebel army to battle them. Very effective special effects create believability. Success brought another miniseries, then a TV series.

A: Mark Singer, Faye Grant, Michael Durrell, Peter Nelson, Jane Badler, Neva Patterson

© WARNER HOME VIDEO 11439

VALDEZ IS COMING

D: Edwin Sherin — 90 m

7 PG — WST ACT — 1971 — COLOR

□ Sex □ Nud ◢ Viol □ Lang □ AdSit

Pretty good Western. Burt Lancaster is Valdez, a Mexican/American sheriff who struggles to regain his dignity after having suffered years of racial degradation. After Valdez is forced to shoot a Mexican suspect, he tries to provide for the man's widow. His efforts trigger the hostilities of a ruthless cattle baron and gun-runner, who humiliates and then threatens Valdez. So Valdez captures the man's wife and the chase to kill Valdez is on - but Valdez is not a man to be taken lightly. Solid actioner, with some thought thrown in for good measure.

A: Burt Lancaster, Susan Clark, Frank Silvera, Richard Jordan, Jon Cypher, Barton Heyman

Distributed By MGM/UA Home Video M202961

VIEW TO A KILL, A

D: John Glen — 126 m

7 PG — ACT — 1985 — COLOR

□ Sex □ Nud ◢ Viol ◢ Lang ◢ AdSit

James's fellow agent has been killed in the Alps and when James goes to investigate, he barely escapes Soviet assassins. The trail leads him to a Russian spy in the Silicon Valley of California. Walken plans to induce a devastating earthquake there and take over the lucrative microchip market. The menacing Grace Jones is Walken's assistant, as is the captivating Roberts, but Roberts becomes Bond's ally and romantic interest. Edge-of-your seat adventure with spectacular stunts and action at every corner. This was Roger Moore's last outing as Bond.

A: Roger Moore, Christopher Walken, Grace Jones, Tanya Roberts, Patrick Macnee, Patrick Bauchau

Distributed By MGM/UA Home Video M202739

VIKINGS, THE

D: Richard Fleischer — 117 m

7 NR — ACT — 1958 — COLOR

□ Sex □ Nud ◢ Viol □ Lang ◢ AdSit

Well-done and rousing, an authentic-looking Viking action epic with a big-name cast. Tony Curtis is a slave of the Vikings. He is also Douglas's half-brother, although neither knows it. Curtis's mother was an English queen who was raped by Douglas's father, the Viking king (Borgnine). Douglas is a boisterous and rowdy carbon copy of his father. Both Douglas and Curtis are in love with the beautiful captured Welsh princess, Janet Leigh. However, Curtis and she escape, but Curtis and Douglas meet again and eventually unite to fight the English when their father is killed.

A: Kirk Douglas, Ernest Borgnine, Janet Leigh, Tony Curtis, James Donald

Distributed By MGM/UA Home Video M700579

VON RYAN'S EXPRESS

D: Mark Robson — 117 m

8 NR — ACT WAR — 1965 — COLOR

□ Sex □ Nud ◢ Viol □ Lang ◢ AdSit

Top-drawer WWII actioner. Sinatra is an American colonel shot down and placed in a POW camp. He is the ranking officer, but is not held in high regard by his fellow prisoners until he engineers the capture of the train in which 600 of them are being transported across Italy to Germany. The POWs want to divert their captured train toward Switzerland and freedom, but the Germans are not about to let that happen without a fight. Hard-hitting action, suspense, solid acting and well-paced directing make this a thrilling adventure story.

A: Frank Sinatra, Trevor Howard, Luther Adler, James Brolin, Brad Dexter, Edward Mulhare

© FOXVIDEO 1003

WAIT UNTIL DARK

D: Terence Young — 108 m

9 NR — SUS ACT — 1967 — COLOR

□ Sex □ Nud ◢ Viol □ Lang ◢ AdSit

Tense nail-biter for which Hepburn earned an Academy nomination. Her husband (Zimbalist) is tricked into bringing home a doll which he gives to his recently blinded wife. However, both are unaware that the doll contains heroin. Zimbalist is then lured away from the apartment so that psychotic Arkin and his two henchman Crenna and Weston can get the drugs back. But the trio get more than they bargained for when blind Hepburn turns out the lights... they are on equal footing in the dark. Still, Arkin is a ruthless killer. Riveting and gripping suspense made this into a very popular film.

A: Audrey Hepburn, Alan Arkin, Efrem Zimbalist, Jr., Jack Weston, Richard Crenna, Samantha Jones

© WARNER HOME VIDEO 11080

WALKING TALL

D: Phil Karlson — 126 m

7 R — ACT CRM — 1973 — COLOR

□ Sex □ Nud ■ Viol ■ Lang ◢ AdSit

Very popular but very violent revenge film in which a Tennessee man gets elected sheriff (Baker) by vowing to take back his town from corrupt politicians. He sets out to wage his war by ruthlessly swinging a baseball bat. This film was based upon a real-life character who ironically was later voted out of office because of his tough tactics, a fact the movie chooses to ignore. Spawned two lesser sequels and a TV series.

A: Joe Don Baker, Elizabeth Hartman, Noah Beery, Jr., Gene Evans, Brenda Benet, John Brascia

© LIVE HOME VIDEO LA9500

WAR AND PEACE

D: Sergei Bondarchuk — 360 m

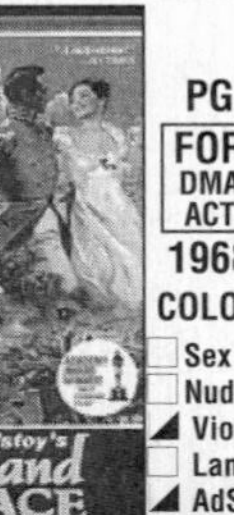

9 PG — FOR DMA ACT — 1968 — COLOR

□ Sex □ Nud ◢ Viol □ Lang ◢ AdSit

A dazzling masterpiece of a film and winner of Best Foreign Film. However, its extreme length and poor dubbing from Russian make this a difficult film for the average viewer to watch. Still, serious viewers should not miss it. Other attempts have been made to reduce the epic book to a scale suitable for the screen (most notably in 1956), however the story is just too big and too much was lost. This Russian version took over five years to make and cost a staggering $100 million. Outstanding production values.

A: Ludmila Savelyeva, Vyacheslav Tihonov, Sergei Bondarchuk, Victor Stanitsyn, Kira Golovko, Oleg Tabakov

© KULTUR VIDEO 1248

WARLOCK

D: Edward Dmytryk 122 m

NR | WST ACT | 1959 | COLOR

8 Intelligent and unusually complex psychological Western. The citizens of a small mining town find that they are being terrorized by a gang of outlaws. So they hire a gunslinger (Fonda) and his crippled gambler partner (Quinn) to stop the gang. Fonda and Quinn do what they were hired to do, but the town is distressed to learn that they have just exchanged one tyrant for another. Now the deputy (Widmark), himself a reformed bandit, must step in to stop a raging Quinn before he destroys the town.

Sex · Nud · Viol ✓ · Lang · AdSit ✓

A: Henry Fonda, Anthony Quinn, Richard Widmark, Dorothy Malone, Delores Michaels, Wallace Ford

© FOXVIDEO 1238

WARRIORS, THE

D: Walter Hill 94 m

R | ACT SF | 1979 | COLOR

7 Very stylized, surrealistic and almost cartoon-like vision of street-gang violence in New York City. Somewhat similar in "feel" to CLOCKWORK ORANGE. Two hundred street gangs (called tribes) hold a rally in downtown NYC. A small, little-known tribe calling itself "The Warriors" travels in with the rest. When the grand leader of all the tribes is killed, the unarmed Warriors are falsely blamed. Their leader is killed and the eight remaining members must get struggle to get back home. Their return trip is played out like a game where the subways are "safe" zones.

Sex · Nud · Viol ✓ · Lang ✓ · AdSit ✓

A: Michael Beck, James Remar, Deborah Van Valkenburgh, Thomas Waites, Dorsey Wright, Brian Tyler

© PARAMOUNT HOME VIDEO 1122

WAR WAGON, THE

D: Burt Kennedy 101 m

NR | WST ACT COM | 1967 | COLOR

7 Entertaining tongue-in-cheek John Wayne Western. John has had his fortune stolen, been framed by an unscrupulous cattle baron and mine owner (Cabot) and sent to prison. So, when John gets out, Cabot sends Kirk Douglas to kill him. Instead, John enlists Douglas in his plan to inflict sweet revenge and also gathers together several others in a gang to carry it out. He and his cronies are going to rob a big shipment of gold dust that Cabot transports in a special, heavily armed coach called the War Wagon. Good, mindless action adventure, amply spiced with humor. Hard to beat the combination of Wayne and Douglas.

Sex · Nud · Viol ✓ · Lang · AdSit

A: John Wayne, Kirk Douglas, Howard Keel, Robert Walker, Jr., Keenan Wynn

© MCA/UNIVERSAL HOME VIDEO, INC. 80016

WE OF THE NEVER NEVER

D: Igor Auzins 135 m

G | DMA WST ACT | 1982 | COLOR

8 Touching and captivating import from Australia, and winner of six Australian Academy Award nominations. It is a true story, taken from the diary of Jeannie Gunn, first published in 1908. She was the first white woman to travel deep into the Australian wilderness, called the Outback or the Never Never, to a cattle station with her husband. A stunning piece of camerawork depicts her story of survival in a rugged world dominated by men, their confrontation with the mystical world of the aborigines and their acceptance of her. However, her happiness is soon shattered with the death of her husband.

Sex · Nud · Viol ✓ · Lang ✓ · AdSit ✓

A: Angela Punch-McGregor, Tommy Lewis, Arthur Dignam, Tony Barry

© COLUMBIA TRISTAR HOME VIDEO 60256

WESTWORLD

D: Michael Crichton 90 m

PG | SF WST ACT | 1973 | COLOR

7 Very entertaining and inventive yarn about a high tech adult resort of the future, where wealthy patrons may live out their Wild West fantasies with amazingly lifelike robots. By day, the robots are shot up by the patrons. At night they are repaired. Everything is harmless and quite safe until one errant gunfighter robot (Brynner is terrific) refuses to play the game as it was written. He goes berserk and starts stalking the guests for real. Richard Benjamin and James Brolin are two tourists who are unfortunate enough to catch his attention. Well-done sequel is FUTUREWORLD.

Sex · Nud · Viol ✓ · Lang · AdSit

A: Yul Brynner, James Brolin, Richard Benjamin, Alan Oppenheimer, Victoria Shaw, Martin Jared

Distributed By MGM/UA Home Video M600097

WHERE EAGLES DARE

D: Brian G. Hutton 158 m

PG | WAR ACT | 1968 | COLOR

8 High intensity action film in which a small group of commandos, lead by Burton and Eastwood, attack a supposedly impregnable German-held castle high in the Bavarian Alps to rescue an American general being held captive there. They must get him out before the Nazis get critical secret information out of him, but their plans to do it are jeopardized by an unknown double-agent in their midst. Now, no one can be trusted. Lots of high-risk stunts, shootouts and thrilling adventure. A real hair-raiser.

Sex · Nud · Viol ✓ · Lang ✓ · AdSit ✓

A: Richard Burton, Clint Eastwood, Mary Ure, Michael Hordern, Patrick Wymark, Robert Beatty

Distributed By MGM/UA Home Video M700137

WHITE FANG

D: Randal Kleiser 109 m

PG | WST ACT CLD | 1991 | COLOR

9 Wonderful whole-family entertainment in the true sense of the phrase. This is an exciting adventure film that has something to satisfy everyone. It is a beautiful picture that evokes the actual feel of the Alaskan goldrush days. A young man follows his father's dying wishes to settle his gold claim deep in the wilds of a virgin Yukon wilderness. The film focuses upon the young man's journey there and upon his friendship with an orphaned wolf cub, White Fang. Spectacularly photographed, this is a tale of men in the wilderness and one man's love for his four-footed kindred spirit.

Sex · Nud · Viol ✓ · Lang · AdSit

A: Ethan Hawke, Klaus Maria Brandauer, James Remar, Seymour Cassel, Susan Hogan

© WALT DISNEY HOME VIDEO 1151

WHITE HUNTER, BLACK HEART

D: Clint Eastwood 112 m

PG | DMA ACT | 1990 | COLOR

7 An unusual departure from his typical fare, actor/director Eastwood presents a thinly veiled portrait of famed director John Houston and the filming of THE AFRICAN QUEEN. Eastwood's character takes the director's job only because it will pay off large personal debts and allow him to be able to go to Africa to shoot an elephant. The picture is only incidental to him. His obsession with the elephant hunt in fact jeopardizes the filming. Not a true action movie, this is an involving drama deriving its interest from the obsessive nature of the man and how that relates to the creative process.

Sex · Nud · Viol ✓ · Lang ✓ · AdSit ✓

A: Clint Eastwood, Jeff Fahey, Marisa Berenson, George Dzundza, Alun Armstrong

© WARNER HOME VIDEO 11916

WHITE LIGHTNING

D: Joseph Sargent 101 m

PG | ACT | 1973 | COLOR

8 Exciting action flick in which Burt Reynolds, as Gator McKlusky - a good ol' boy and moonshine runner - has been in prison. The Feds come to him with a proposition that they will free him if he helps them to trap a gang of moonshiners involving corrupt cop Beatty. Reynolds, however, has his own agenda. He wants to get Beatty, because Beatty killed his brother. Rousing adventure with top-notch acting and good driving stunts help raise this film above typical mindless action fare. This proved to be a popular film and Reynolds reprised his role later for the sequel GATOR.

Sex · Nud · Viol ✓ · Lang ✓ · AdSit ✓

A: Burt Reynolds, Ned Beatty, Jennifer Billingsley, Bo Hopkins, Matt Clark, Louise Latham

Distributed By MGM/UA Home Video M301431

WHITE LINE FEVER

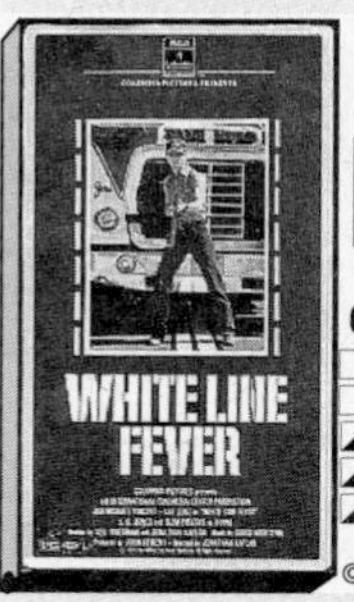

D: Jonathan Kaplan 92 m

PG | ACT | 1975 | COLOR

7 This was somewhat of a surprise hit. It is an entertaining morality-based actioner about a young returning Vietnam War veteran who gets married, buys a big rig and sets out to become an independent long haul trucker. He gets work through an old friend but balks when asked to carry an illegal load by a group of hoods. After his friend is killed, his wife is beaten (killing their unborn baby) and their house burned, he fights back. Solid direction, good acting, a plausible script and some really good action sequences have made this into a cult favorite.

Sex · Nud · Viol ✓ · Lang ✓ · AdSit ✓

A: Jan-Michael Vincent, Kay Lenz, Slim Pickens, L.Q. Jones, Don Porter, Sam Laws

© COLUMBIA TRISTAR HOME VIDEO VH10563

WHITE NIGHTS

D: Taylor Hackford 135 m

PG-13 | SUS ACT | 1985 | COLOR

8 Quite good. A famous Russian ballet dancer (Baryshnikov) who defected to America, finds himself captured again when the airplane on which he is traveling must make an emergency landing in the USSR. Hines is a privately remorseful American Army deserter and dancer who is charged by the KGB with keeping Baryshnikov from returning again to the West. The love for dance and the desire for freedom they share bonds them in friendship and, together, they concoct an elaborate plan for escape. Gripping drama, good action and exciting dance sequences.

Sex · Nud · Viol ✓ · Lang ✓ · AdSit ✓

A: Mikhail Baryshnikov, Gregory Hines, Isabella Rossellini, Jerzy Skolimowski, Helen Mirren, Geraldine Page

© COLUMBIA TRISTAR HOME VIDEO 60611

WHO'LL STOP THE RAIN

D: Karel Reisz 126 m

R | ACT SUS | 1978 | COLOR

8 Gripping and intense. A Vietnam veteran (Nolte) agrees to smuggle home some heroin for his buddy (Moriarity) who has a buyer for the stuff; but it's a set-up. A corrupt narcotics agent (Zerbe) and his partners are going to steal the dope and kill them all. Nolte shows up with the dope but heads out with Moriarity's addicted wife (Weld) when things go wrong. Moriarity is caught and tortured to reveal their whereabouts. They have fled through L.A. and to the mountains of New Mexico. Very intense and violent. There are no out-and-out good guys. Still an excellent and thoroughly spell-binding film.

Sex · Nud ✓ · Viol ✓ · Lang ✓ · AdSit ✓

A: Nick Nolte, Tuesday Weld, Michael Moriarty, Anthony Zerbe, Richard Masur, Ray Sharkey

Distributed By MGM/UA Home Video M201306

Action

WILBY CONSPIRACY, THE

D: Ralph Nelson — 113 m

PG — 8 — ACT DMA — 1974 — COLOR

Sex / Nud / Viol / Lang / AdSit

Set in South Africa but filmed in Kenya, Sidney Poitier is a militant African political activist. His attorney is Michael Caine's girlfriend. Poitier and Caine are chained together and then are allowed to escape by a vicious and bigoted policeman who is intent upon following Poitier to his underground leader. Poitier's and Caine's plight bring back reminders of THE DEFIANT ONES. It's the charm of Poitier and Caine that keep this film moving as an action film, while never losing the dramatic impact from the underlying causes.

A: Sidney Poitier, Michael Caine, Rutger Hauer, Nicol Williamson, Prunella Gee, Persis Khambatta

Distributed By MGM/UA Home Video M301294

WILD BUNCH, THE

D: Sam Peckinpah — 144 m

R — 9 — WST ACT — 1969 — COLOR

Sex / Nud / Viol / Lang / AdSit

Highly acclaimed Western, primarily because it ushered in a new era of graphic violence in film. However, it is also excellent entertainment. A veteran cast of prominent actors populate this action-packed story about a band of aging outlaws caught at the end of an era in 1913. Lead by Holden, the bunch decides to pull off one last big job. They hijack an ammunition train to take across the border to sell to a renegade Mexican General. They are pursued the whole way there by the Army, lead by a former member (Ryan), who is trying to earn his freedom. Non-stop very violent action.

A: William Holden, Robert Ryan, Ernest Borgnine, Edmond O'Brien, Ben Johnson, Warren Oates

© WARNER HOME VIDEO 1014

WILD ROVERS, THE

D: Blake Edwards — 138 m

PG — 8 — WST ACT COM — 1971 — COLOR

Sex / Nud / Viol / Lang / AdSit

An unheralded little gem. William Holden and Ryan O'Neal are two cowpoke buddies, one old and one young, who become disillusioned with their careers on the range when one of their friends is accidentally killed. On a whim, this not-too-bright pair decide to rob a bank and head out for Mexico. On a dead run with a posse hot on their heels, it occurs to them that this was not a wise career move. The pleasure in the movie comes from the relationship between these guys. A great buddy movie. Solid performances, particularly by Holden.

A: William Holden, Ryan O'Neal, Karl Malden, Lynn Carlin, Tom Skerritt, Joe Don Baker

Distributed By MGM/UA Home Video M600305

WILLOW

D: Ron Howard — 130 m

PG — 7 — ACT FAN CLD — 1988 — COLOR

Sex / Nud / Viol / Lang / AdSit

A kooky fantasy - sort of Star Wars meets the Wizard of Oz. Davis is Willow, 0an elf who is the protector of a small baby who will grow up, end the reign of the evil Queen Bavmorda (Marsh) and bring peace to the world. Warrior Kilmer offers his help to the little guy and along the way they encounter many wacky characters, some dangerous and some funny. This is a fanciful adventure that provides an eyeful of special effects. Although aimed at children, some of the violence might be too intense for the youngest ones.

A: Val Kilmer, Joanne Whalley-Kilmer, Warwick Davis, Jean Marsh, Patricia Hayes, Billy Barty

© COLUMBIA TRISTAR HOME VIDEO 60936

WILL PENNY

D: Tom Gries — 109 m

NR — 9 — WST ROM ACT — 1968 — COLOR

Sex / Nud / Viol / Lang / AdSit

Outstanding film that requires a Western setting to tell its perceptive and moving story, but this is not just a Western. Will Penny has spent his whole life as a cowboy and a loner. He has never thought of living any other way. However, after a run-in with a cruel rawhider and his boys who leave him to die, he is rescued by a pretty woman and her son who are traveling to Oregon to reunite with her settler-husband. For the first time, Will feels the tug of a home life and love. Heartwarming and evocative. Moving, understated performances make these characters human and very real. Excellent.

A: Charlton Heston, Joan Hackett, Donald Pleasence, Lee Majors, Bruce Dern

© PARAMOUNT HOME VIDEO 6723

WIND

D: Carroll Ballard — 140 m

PG-13 — 6 — ACT — 1992 — COLOR

Sex / Nud / Viol / Lang / AdSit

America's yacht has lost the America's Cup, and Matthew Modine has lost his love because he chose yachting over her so he could be in the race. Now, six months later, he rejoins her and her new master-designer boyfriend in a new high-tech race to build a new boat which will recover the lost grand prize for America. A great deal of money was spent on the production of this film and it shows because it is beautifully photographed. The plentiful racing scenes are exciting, however the stuff in the middle gets to be a bit of a stretch. Sailing fans will quite likely get their money's worth, others will be questionable.

A: Matthew Modine, Jennifer Grey, Cliff Robertson, Stellan Skarsgard, Rebecca Miller, Ned Vaughn

© COLUMBIA TRISTAR HOME VIDEO 70733

WIND AND THE LION, THE

D: John Milius — 120 m

PG — 8 — ACT ROM — 1975 — COLOR

Sex / Nud / Viol / Lang / AdSit

A rousing adventure story, very loosely based upon an actual event. In 1904 a beautiful American woman and her son are kidnapped in Morocco by a dashing rebel Berber chiefton (Connery). American President Teddy Roosevelt (Keith) threatens to send in American troops to retrieve her. This, however, sparks an international incident when the Germans fearing competition on their turf, send in troops to protect their own power play for North Africa. This is an action-packed adventure story, but it is also one of romance and political intrigue. Connery and Bergen shine. Very good.

A: Sean Connery, Candice Bergen, Brian Keith, John Huston, Geoffrey Lewis, Steve Kanaly

Distributed By MGM/UA Home Video M600662

WINDWALKER

D: Keith Merrill — 108 m

PG — 8 — WST DMA ACT — 1980 — COLOR

Sex / Nud / Viol / Lang / AdSit

Unusually well-rounded family entertainment in the form of the telling of a Cheyenne legend. As an old Cheyenne warrior lies dying, he tells his grandsons the story of how his wife was murdered and his son (their uncle) was kidnapped years before by a neighboring band of Crow Indians. The old man dies but comes back to life to protect his tribe from a Crow attack that is led by his lost son. A very unusual story of war, survival and love. The entire movie is spoken in the Cheyenne and Crow languages with English subtitles.

A: Trevor Howard, Nick Ramus, James Remar, Serene Hedin, Dusty Iron Wing McCrea, Silvana Gatlardo

© CBS/FOX VIDEO 6345

WINNING

D: James Goldstone — 123 m

PG — 6 — DMA ACT — 1969 — COLOR

Sex / Nud / Viol / Lang / AdSit

This a movie about racing, but it is more than that. Paul Newman is a race driver who marries a divorcee (Woodward) and adopts her son, but he is so dedicated to winning that he spends most of the season away from them. Even when they do reunite for the Indianapolis 500, he spends all his time with the car. Left alone, she finds herself attracted to another driver who pays attention to her. Very strong performance by both Newman and Woodward in a good story, with spectacular racing sequences. (Newman is a professional driver in real life.)

A: Paul Newman, Joanne Woodward, Robert Wagner, Richard Thomas, David Sheiner, Clu Gulager

© MCA/UNIVERSAL HOME VIDEO, INC. 45016

WITNESS

D: Peter Weir — 112 m

R — 10 — CRM ROM ACT — 1985 — COLOR

Sex / Nud / Viol / Lang / AdSit

Terrific. A young Amish widow (McGillis) and her son (Hass) travel to the city, but while they are waiting at the train station, the boy is a witness to a murder. John Book (Ford) is a jaded big city cop who wins over their confidence. However, they all get in big trouble when the boy identifies the murderer as being a narcotics cop (Glover). Ford is then shot and takes them back to their rustic home where he stays on to recover and hide with them. But, he is out of place as a hard-edged city boy dressed in simple Amish clothes, he is falling for McGillis, and the corrupt cops are coming to get them all. Romantic, thrilling and funny. This is a real winner.

A: Harrison Ford, Kelly McGillis, Josef Sommer, Lukas Haas, Jan Rubes, Alexander Godunov

© PARAMOUNT HOME VIDEO 1736

WYATT EARP

D: Lawrence Kasdan — 191 m

PG-13 — 9 — WST DMA ACT — 1994 — COLOR

Sex / Nud / Viol / Lang / AdSit

Excellent epic Western, telling the whole story of Wyatt Earp. It begins in Missouri and tells of his father's influence on all the boys. Follows Wyatt from the death of his first wife, becoming a buffalo hunter and then the man who tamed Dodge City. Only in the last half of a quite long movie does the story of the fight with the Clantons come along. A real attempt at telling history and the makeup of a complicated man was made. Wyatt is not painted as being a true hero in the classic Hollywood sense, but that actually makes the story much more interesting. It starts a little slow and is very deliberate in the telling, but it also tells a powerful and fascinating story. Hang in there.

A: Kevin Costner, Dennis Quaid, Gene Hackman, Michael Masden, Linden Ashby, Catherine O'Hara

© WARNER HOME VIDEO 13177

YAKUZA, THE

D: Sydney Pollack — 112 m

R — 9 — ACT SUS — 1975 — COLOR

Sex / Nud / Viol / Lang / AdSit

Excellent, high intensity blending of bone-jarring action with a fascinating cultural exploration into the Yakuza, Japan's Mafia-like underworld which has deep roots in the ancient Samurai ways. When Brian Keith's daughter is kidnapped and held for ransom by the Yakuza, he realizes the only chance he has to get her back is Harry Kilmer (Mitchum). Kilmer is a good friend and an ex-GI who is familiar with Yakuza ways, and Kilmer enlists the help of an old Japanese enemy who owes him a big debt. Absolutely gripping, intriguing and solid excitement. Excellent. See also 1989's BLACK RAIN.

A: Robert Mitchum, Takakura Ken, Brian Keith, Herb Edelman, Richard Jordan, Kishi Keiko

© WARNER HOME VIDEO 11397

YOJIMBO

D: Akira Kurosawa 110 m

NR
FOR ACT COM
1962
B&W
Sex
Nud
Viol
Lang
AdSit

9 Very funny, action packed and beautifully photographed Japanese "Western" - which became the model for A FISTFUL OF DOLLARS and many others. A samurai (Mifune), freed from his code of honor, roams from town to town selling his sword. In one small town, the sake dealer and the silk merchant are both trying to capture control of gambling, but both are cowards and so hire others to do their dirty work. Clever Mifune hires himself out to both sides and turns them against each other. In the end, they kill each other off and he gets the money, saying: "Now we'll have a little quiet in this town."

A: Toshiro Mifune, Eijiro Tono, Isuzu Yamada, Hiroshi Tachikawa, Kyu Sazanka

© NEW LINE HOME VIDEO 6144

YOUNG GUNS

D: Christopher Cain 102 m

R
WST ACT
1988
COLOR
Sex
Nud
Viol
Lang
AdSit

6 Hollywood retells the legend of Billy the Kid, done this time with the current group of young Hollywood hunks and bolstered by an MTV-type sound track and 20th-century political correctness. Old-timers will have a harder time cottonin' up to this version, but the younger generation turned out in big numbers. The story is that of a group of young toughs who are hired by a cultured Englishman to protect his New Mexico ranch. When he is killed, they turn into a marauding wild bunch led by Billy (Estevez) and are hunted down in a major man hunt. Watchable.

A: Emilio Estevez, Kiefer Sutherland, Lou Diamond Phillips, Charlie Sheen, Dermot Mulroney, Casey Siemaszko

© LIVE HOME VIDEO 5267

YOUNG GUNS 2

D: Geoff Murphy 105 m

PG-13
WST ACT
1990
COLOR
Sex
Nud
Viol
Lang
AdSit

6 This marked the return of the remaining half of the bunch from YOUNG GUNS. Same formula as before: lots of action supported by a heavy rock score and filled with Hollywood hunks. This time they have gathered up some new recruits and are heading off to Mexico. But they are being pursued by a band of government men led by Billy's one-time friend Pat Garrett.

A: Emilio Estevez, Kiefer Sutherland, Lou Diamond Phillips, Christian Slater, Balthazar Getty, Alan Ruck

© FOXVIDEO 1902

YOUNG LIONS, THE

D: Edward Dmytryk 167 m

NR
DMA WAR ACT
1958
B&W
Sex
Nud
Viol
Lang
AdSit

9 Excellent, gripping human drama that uses WWII as a backdrop to explore the war's effects on three very different men. Brando is a handsome and idealistic ski instructor who adopts Nazism as the answer to Germany's problems, until he discovers its realities. Montgomery Clift is an American Jew, a smallish man drafted into the Army, who must deal with anti-Semitic taunts both at home and in the service. Dean Martin is a popular playboy entertainer who must learn to face his own cowardice. The three separate stories are interwoven as the men are drawn together by the war. Very moving.

A: Marlon Brando, Montgomery Clift, Dean Martin, Hope Lange, Barbara Rush, Maximilian Schell

© FOXVIDEO 1057

YOU ONLY LIVE TWICE

D: Lewis Gilbert 118 m

PG
ACT
1967
COLOR
Sex
Nud
Viol
Lang
AdSit

8 Fifth in the Bond series and perhaps the most gadget-infested of them all. Set in Japan, James seeks out SPECTRE head man Biofeld (Pleasance) inside a volcano. Biofeld is engaged in an elaborate enterprise to steal both Russian and American spaceships. Each side is blaming the other. It appears that SPECTRE's plan to provoke World War III, so that it can emerge as the world's dominant force, is working. Some pretty nifty gadgets, pretty girls, of course, and a quick pace. Nancy Sinatra sings the title song.

A: Sean Connery, Akiko Wakabayashi, Tetsuro Tamba, Donald Pleasence, Karin Dor, Bernard Lee

Distributed By MGM/UA Home Video M201405

ZEPPELIN

D: Etienne Perrier 102 m

G
ACT WAR
1971
COLOR
Sex
Nud
Viol
Lang
AdSit

6 The time is WWI. The English military fears the German's newest weapon, the Zepplin, so they entice a German-born Scottish lieutenant (York) to "defect" to the Germans to collect information on the fearsome weapon. Now, as a German officer, he is almost unbelievably invited aboard the ship for a trial run. However, when it is airborne, he finds there is a reason he is there. The Germans plan to launch a daring raid into England and they need his knowledge of the countryside to carry it off. Entertaining and atmospheric with good special effects.

A: Michael York, Elke Sommer, Marius Goring, Anton Diffring, Rupert Davies, Peter Carsten

© WARNER HOME VIDEO 11562

ZERO TOLERANCE

D: Joseph Merhi 92 m

R
ACT
1994
COLOR
Sex
Nud
Viol
Lang
AdSit

6 Brutal drug lords have murdered FBI agent Robert Patrick's wife and children. They thought they killed him too. But, they didn't and now he is wreaking bloody revenge on them all. One-by-one he seeks each one out and then administers his own form of justice. Lots of bullets and blood.

A: Robert Patrick, Titus Welliver, Kristen Meadows, Mick Fleetwood, Barbara Patrick, Miles O'Keeffe

© LIVE HOME VIDEO 49206

ZULU

D: Cy Endfield 138 m

NR
ACT SUS
1964
COLOR
Sex
Nud
Viol
Lang
AdSit

8 Rousing adventure epic. This is the dramatization of an actual event which occurred on January 22, 1879. A small British garrison of 105 men, stationed at a remote outpost, learns that it is being approached by over 4000 Zulu warriors and that the only source of reinforcement, a force of 1200 men, has been totally wiped out. They are left alone, outnumbered 40-1, to withstand the onslaught. Refusing to abandon their post, they rally to victory. Well crafted, with massive and spectacular battle sequences. Excellent performances, including Caine in his first big role.

A: Jack Hawkins, Stanley Baker, Michael Caine, James Booth, Ulla Jacobsson

© NEW LINE HOME VIDEO 90002

Comedy

Video's Best

1956 and After

10

D: Blake Edwards 123 m

R

COM DMA

1979 COLOR

Sex ■ Nud ■ Viol □ Lang ◢ AdSit ■

9 A slick sophisticated comedy that became a huge blockbuster hit. Just after turning 40, songwriter Dudley Moore spies the fantasy woman of his dreams (Bo Derek). Even though it is her wedding day, he follows her into the church and then, totally smitten, leaves everything (including wife Andrews) to chase his mid-life crisis fantasy on her Acapulco honeymoon. Against all odds, she becomes fascinated with him and the sexually liberated beauty takes him into her bed. But Moore now becomes confused, suddenly aware that the realization of his dream is not what he had expected. Funny and very entertaining.

A: Bo Derek, Julie Andrews, Dudley Moore, Robert Webber, Dee Wallace

© WARNER HOME VIDEO 2002

29TH STREET

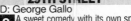

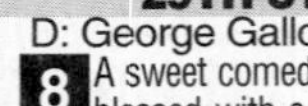

D: George Gallo 101 m

R

COM

1991 COLOR

Sex □ Nud □ Viol ◢ Lang ■ AdSit ◢

8 A sweet comedy with its own special kind of magic. Frank Jr. is blessed with a close-knit Italian family and uncommonly good luck. He's so lucky that when he was once stabbed, the doctors found a tumor and the incident actually saved his life. On the other hand, Frank Sr. never had anything but bad luck. His big dream is just to own his own house and to grow the best grass in the neighborhood. Instead, he has to spend his time ducking the neighborhood loan shark, to whom he owes $10,000. In his life, Sr. has bought boxes of lottery tickets and always lost, but now Jr. has bought one and he's a finalist for $6.2 million. Warm and funny.

A: Danny Aiello, Anthony Lapaglia, Lainie Kazan, Frank Pesce, Donna Maghani, Rick Aiello

© FOXVIDEO 1874

3 MEN AND A CRADLE

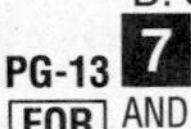

D: Coline Serreau 100 m

PG-13

FOR COM

1986 COLOR

Sex □ Nud ◢ Viol □ Lang ◢ AdSit ◢

7 This is the winning predecessor to and the inspiration for the later very successful Americanized version called THREE MEN AND A BABY. Three Parisian bachelors suddenly become fathers when they are presented with a little girl that one of them has fathered. The totally unprepared threesome suddenly have to learn to deal with diapers and crying, but also become hopelessly in love with her. It was also one of France's biggest films of all times. Subtitles or dubbed.

A: Roland Giraud, Michel Boujenah, Andre Dussollier, Phillippine Beaulieu, Dominique Lavanat

© LIVE HOME VIDEO 5192

48 HOURS

D: Walter Hill 97 m

R

ACT COM CRM

1983 COLOR

Sex ◢ Nud ◢ Viol ■ Lang ■ AdSit ◢

9 A very popular blockbuster hit with good reason. It has plenty of realistic action, comedy, good acting, and is a good cop story, too. Nick Nolte is a veteran toughguy/boozehound cop but he needs help from a wiseguy/con man/convict (Eddie Murphy) in order to track down two extremely vicious cop killers. So, Nolte gets Murphy sprung from jail, but just for two days. Murphy turns out to be a good partner for the crazy cop. He is smart, cool under pressure, tough and funny, too (like when he terrorizes a redneck bar). Great entertainment on many levels all at once. Highly recommended.

A: Eddie Murphy, Nick Nolte, Annette O'Toole, Frank McRae, James Remar, David Patrick Kelly

© PARAMOUNT HOME VIDEO 1139

5 CORNERS

D: Tony Bill 94 m

R

SUS COM

1987 COLOR

Sex □ Nud □ Viol ◢ Lang ■ AdSit ◢

7 This is a strange blending of melodrama and comedy, set in a 1960s Bronx atmosphere. Jodie Foster plays a pretty pet store worker who helped to convict a violent and unstable admirer, and her would-be rapist. Now he is out and is looking for her. Fearful, she seeks help from a friend and former neighborhood tough guy to help protect her from her obsessed fan. However, after a protracted bout of conscience, her toughguy-protector has become a pacifist and civil rights activist. Hard, reality-based suspense is offset by some offbeat comedy and interesting and curious characters.

A: Jodie Foster, Tim Robbins, John Turturro, Elizabeth Berridge, Todd Graff, Rose Gregorio

Distributed By MGM/UA Home Video M202773

9 TO 5

D: Colin Higgins 110 m

PG

COM

1980 COLOR

Sex □ Nud □ Viol □ Lang ◢ AdSit ◢

9 Great fun for nearly everybody from this very popular comedy. Three secretaries fantasize gleefully on how they will one day get even with their chauvinistic heal of a boss (Dabney Coleman). Then one day, circumstances suddenly do arise that give them a chance to act their fantasies out. The three women have a terrific time by becoming his torturers. Filled with outrageous slapstick sequences and lots of comedic one-liners. This was Dolly Parton's film debut and she also wrote and sang the theme song. Both were very big hits. Very enjoyable and funny.

A: Jane Fonda, Lily Tomlin, Dolly Parton, Dabney Coleman

© FOXVIDEO 1099

ABOUT LAST NIGHT

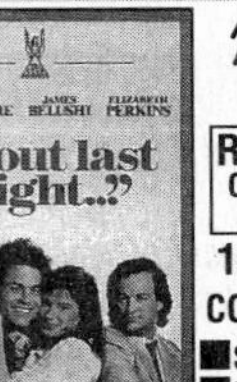

D: Edward Zwick 113 m

R

ROM COM

1986 COLOR

Sex ■ Nud ■ Viol □ Lang ■ AdSit ■

8 Witty, believable and touching romance comedy about an '80s kind of couple (Rob Lowe and Demi Moore). They are young singles committed only to having a good time, who meet at a ball game and again later at a bar. They share a great one-night stand that unexpectedly grows into a housekeeping arrangement. However, their relationship falls on hard times when, despite all their time together, he has a tough time making a total commitment to her and because their best friends are each doing their level best to break them apart. Interesting and funny reflection of yuppie love in the '80s.

A: Rob Lowe, Demi Moore, James Belushi, Elizabeth Perkins, George DiCenzo, Michael Alldredge

© COLUMBIA TRISTAR HOME VIDEO 60735

ABSENT-MINDED PROFESSOR, THE

D: Robert Stevenson 96 m

G

COM CLD

1961 B&W

Sex □ Nud □ Viol □ Lang □ AdSit □

8 A nerdy genius college professor (Fred MacMurry) accidentally discovers a gravity-defying glop he calls flubber. However, no one believes him except a nasty industrialist (Keenan Wynn), who tries to steal it. So, Fred uses the bouncy stuff on the shoes of school's losing basketball team, to make them into winners; and, in his old jalopy, to make it fly. Still great stuff for young kids, parents and maybe even a few teenagers.

A: Fred MacMurray, Nancy Olson, Keenan Wynn, Tommy Kirk, Leon Ames, Ed Wynn

© WALT DISNEY HOME VIDEO 028

ACCIDENTAL TOURIST, THE

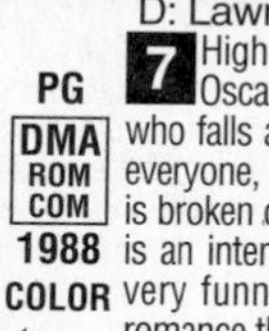

D: Lawrence Kasdan 121 m

PG

DMA ROM COM

1988

COLOR

Sex Nud Viol Lang AdSit

7 Highly acclaimed by critics and nominated for a Best Picture Oscar. William Hurt gives a strong performance as a travel writer who falls apart upon the death of his son. He distances himself from everyone, including Kathleen Turner, his estranged wife. His isolation is broken only when he is around kooky dog trainer Geena Davis. This is an intensely emotional film. While it is quirky and contains some very funny moments, this is primarily an intelligent drama and romance that takes its time to bring out the story. May be too slow for some.

A: William Hurt, Kathleen Turner, Geena Davis, Bill Pullman, Amy Wright, David Ogden Stiers

© WARNER HOME VIDEO 11825

ACE VENTURA: PET DETECTIVE

D: Tom Shadyac 87 m

PG-13

COM

1994

COLOR

Sex Nud Viol Lang AdSit

6 This is a video either for very dedicated fans of rubber-faced comic Jim Carrey, or really silly - make that stupid - and often crude slapstick. Carrey is extreme, absurdly silly and often vulgar, but he is also a very inventive comic. Here he plays Ace Ventura, a wacky super sleuth, specializing in retrieving pets. Ace has been hired by the Miami Dolphins to recover their stolen dolphin mascot, and he is assisted in his investigation by gorgeous Courtney Cox, who works for the Dolphins. However, the poor girl has also fallen in love with him - see, we said it was stupid. Ace is hindered in his efforts by spiteful beautiful police lieutenant Sean Young.

A: Jim Carrey, Sean Young, Courtney Cox, Tone Loc, Dan Marino, Noble Willingham

© WARNER HOME VIDEO 23000

ADDAMS FAMILY, THE

D: Barry Sonnenfeld 102 m

PG-13

COM

1991

COLOR

Sex Nud Viol Lang AdSit

8 A campy winner that's pure joy! Unorthodox and strange - sure. Kooky and spooky - you bet. That's the fun of it. The loveable, yet slightly sadistic, Addams Family lights up the screen in this comic tribute to creator cartoonist Charles Addams. A fake Uncle Fester comes to the mansion planning to steal the family fortune but is foiled by the sheer strangeness of the family's antics. Morticia (Huston) and Gomez (Julia) toss romantic sparks all over the place, and their daughter (Ricci) almost steals the show as she delivers ghoulish lines in deadpan fashion. Wonderful!

A: Anjelica Huston, Raul Julia, Christopher Lloyd, Christina Ricci, Jimmy Workman, Judith Malina

© PARAMOUNT HOME VIDEO 32689

ADDAMS FAMILY VALUES

D: Barry Sonnenfeld 94 m

PG-13

COM

1993

COLOR

Sex Nud Viol Lang AdSit

7 The morbid and very black humor from the New Yorker cartoon strip is back for a second run after the first big-screen outing in THE ADDAMS FAMILY proved to be a popular success. This time Morticia gives birth to a mustachioed miniature of Gomez. However, poor little Wednesday and Pugsley are homicidally jealous. So, Mom and Dad hire Debbie, a new nanny for the baby who promptly advises that the kids should be sent to a summer camp for overprivileged kids. That will leave Debbie more time to concentrate on Uncle Fester, who falls lustfully in love with the pulchritudinous Debbie. Debbie, however, is a black-widow murderess who marries for money and then kills.

A: Anjelica Huston, Raul Julia, Christopher Lloyd, Joan Cusack, Christina Ricci, Carol Kane

© PARAMOUNT HOME VIDEO 32806

ADVENTURES IN BABYSITTING

D: Chris Columbus 102 m

PG-13

COM

1987

COLOR

Sex Nud Viol Lang AdSit

7 Funny little comedy. Shue is stood up by her dream date so she agrees to be a baby sitter for the rest of the evening. However, she gets a call from a friend in the city who needs her help right away, so Shue gathers up her two babysitting charges and takes them along into downtown Chicago with her. There they embark on a riotous adventure where they are chased by street gangs, thieves, and mobsters. Fast-paced misadventure that snowballs into calamity. Its humor will be most entertaining to teenage and young adult viewers.

A: Elisabeth Shue, Maia Brewton, Keith Coogan, Anthony Rapp, Calvin Levels

© TOUCHSTONE HOME VIDEO 595

ADVENTURES OF BARON MUNCHAUSEN, THE

D: Terry Gilliam 122 m

PG

FAN COM CLD

1989

COLOR

Sex Nud Viol Lang AdSit

7 Inside the walls of a city under siege by the armies of the Ottoman Empire, a small troupe of actors puts on a play about the infamous German Baron Munchausen, who had claimed to have had many wildly extravagant exploits. Their presentation is interrupted by an old soldier who claims that he is, in fact, the real Baron. Vowing that he will rescue the town, the old soldier departs in a rag-tag home-made hot air balloon, off to enlist the aid of his superhuman partners of old: the strongest man on earth, the man who can blow stronger than a hurricane, and the fastest man alive. Silly, light-hearted fantasy.

A: John Neville, Robin Williams, Eric Idle, Oliver Reed, Sarah Polley, Uma Thurman

© COLUMBIA TRISTAR HOME VIDEO 50153

ADVENTURES OF BUCKAROO BANZAI ACROSS THE 8TH DIMEN

D: W.D. Richter 103 m

PG

SF COM

1984

B&W

Sex Nud Viol Lang AdSit

7 If you like really weird stuff, this farce is definitely for you. Peter Weller is a neurosurgeon/rock star/astro physicist who accidently frees some evil aliens from the 8th dimension. He and his companions must set things back the way they were. Film's tongue-in-cheek style and frantic pace are not for everyone, but it has become a cult favorite.

A: Peter Weller, John Lithgow, Ellen Barkin, Jeff Goldblum, Christopher Lloyd

© LIVE HOME VIDEO VA5056

ADVENTURES OF PRISCILLA, QUEEN OF THE DESERT, THE

D: Stephen Elliot 102 m

R

COM DMA

1994

COLOR

Sex Nud Viol Lang AdSit

8 Not at all your typical evening's entertainment. This curious and outrageous import from Australia won an Oscar for Best Costume Design. It is often funny and touching, but it also has a storyline you aren't likely encounter often. It is the story of the adventure of three drag queens, who make their living lip-syncing to 70's disco songs while dressed in fantastic flowing stage costumes. They have agreed to a performance in front of rugged crowds of rugged men in the rugged Outback, and they have set out on their adventure in a mechanically-uncertain bus which they have named Priscilla. Their trip is certainly not uneventful, but for drag queens that is normal. It is also certainly educational for most of us.

A: Terence Stamp, Hugo Weaving, Guy Pearce, Bill Hunter

© POLYGRAM VIDEO 33713-3

AFTER HOURS

D: Martin Scorsese 97 m

R

COM SUS

1985

COLOR

Sex Nud Viol Lang AdSit

6 Very bizarre and sophisticated black comedy. Be prepared for the unusual. Griffin Dunn is an uptight, word-processing trainer who is caught up in a nightmarish comedy of errors. He sets off to meet a sexy blind date (Arquette) at an artist's studio in Soho, but on the way there all his cash is blown out the window of his taxi. He goes to meet her anyway, but decides she is too strange and wants to leave but he doesn't have the subway fare home. So, he has become trapped, along with all the other weirdos, in Soho and that is when his troubles really begin.

A: Griffin Dunne, Rosanna Arquette, Teri Garr, John Heard, Linda Fiorentino, Richard"Cheech" Martin

© WARNER HOME VIDEO 11528

AIRPLANE

D: Jim Abrahams 88 m

PG

COM

1980

COLOR

Sex Nud Viol Lang AdSit

9 This is a wildly absurd spoof of the megahit AIRPORT and all the other disaster movies. It is filled with nonstop gags, bad puns and stupid jokes - most of which work. Hays is a washed-up anxiety-ridden pilot, flying onboard a plane where all the other people are stricken with food poisoning. That means everyone - including the pilot. So, he and his wacked-out ex-girlfriend stewardess are the only ones left who have a chance of landing the plane. This exercise in absolute silliness was a runaway hit in the theater. See also AIRPLANE II: THE SEQUEL; also THE NAKED GUN and NAKED GUN 2 1/2.

A: Robert Hayes, Julie Hagerty, Robert Stack, Lloyd Bridges, Peter Graves, Leslie Nielsen

© PARAMOUNT HOME VIDEO 1305

AIRPLANE 2 - THE SEQUEL

D: Ken Finkleman 84 m

PG

COM

1982

COLOR

Sex Nud Viol Lang AdSit

7 Hysterical sequel, with the same sort of silly, stupid jokes as were in the original AIRPLANE! And, there's a lot of them, too. This time, terrified pilot Hays must save the space shuttle from destruction. You also will want to see the original AIRPLANE! and the similar films of the NAKED GUN series.

A: Robert Hayes, Julie Hagerty, Lloyd Bridges, William Shatner, Raymond Burr, Chad Everett

© PARAMOUNT HOME VIDEO 1489

AIR UP THERE, THE

D: Paul M. Glaser 107 m

PG

COM

1994

COLOR

Sex Nud Viol Lang AdSit

6 Kevin Bacon is a former college basketball great who blew his knee out and so missed playing with the pros. Now he is, and has been for some time, the assistant coach at his alma-mater, St. Josephs. His ego has just gotten him in trouble again and it looks like he will never become coach. That's when he spots the 6'8"-answer to his prayers on a videotape that was shot at one of the school's missions in the middle of Africa. So, he's off to Africa to recruit the next NBA Hall-of-Famer. This is predictable all the way and is filled to the top with Hollywood cliches, but it still manages to kill time rather painlessly. Younger viewers will like it better than old cynics.

A: Kevin Bacon, Charles Gitonga Maina, Yolanda Vasquez, Winston Ntshona, Mabutho "Kid" Sithole, Sean McCann

© HOLLYWOOD PICTURES HOME VIDEO 2546

C
O
M

ALADDIN

D: John Musker, Ron Clements — 90 m

CLD COM — 1992 — COLOR

Sex / Nud / Viol / Lang / AdSit

10 Disney did it again. Hugely popular and an instant classic. The classic tale from the Arabian Nights was adapted to feature the manic, over-the-top energy and talent of Robin Williams as the genie. Aladdin is a poor street-smart peasant struggling to survive in the market of Agrabah, when he stumbles upon the beautiful Princess Jasmine who longs to be free. Aladdin is chosen to retrieve the magic lantern by the Sultan's evil counselor Jafar. Instead, Aladdin discovers for himself the magic of the genie in the lamp. Truly a for everyone. Charming, very funny, clever and extremely entertaining. 2 Oscars. Followed by RETURN OF JAFAR.

A:

© WALT DISNEY HOME VIDEO 1662

A LA MODE

D: Remy Duchemin — 99 m

R — FOR COM ROM — 1994 — COLOR

Sex / Nud / Viol / Lang / AdSit

8 Very entertaining piece of French fluff. Young Fausto has become an orphan and has been apprenticed to Mietek, a small-time tailor. Mietek is a bachelor with his own slant on life, but he takes a particular interest in Fausto. Fausto at first is interested in sewing clothes because he wants to meet pretty young women. He is particularly enamored of the very pretty daughter of the local mechanic. However, he soon discovers that he has a genuine flair for tailoring and a wild, imaginatively extravagant talent for promotion. A gentle story of no particular merit and a little bizarre, but it has very endearing characters. Quite good fun. Subtitles.

A: Jean Yanne, Florence Darel, Ken Higelin, Francois Hautesserre, Maurice Benichow, Maite Nahyr

© MIRAMAX HOME ENTERTAINMENT 3608

ALFIE

D: Lewis Gilbert — 113 m

NR — DMA COM — 1966 — COLOR

Sex / Nud / Viol / Lang / AdSit

8 Delightful but serious drama/comedy that was nominated for five Oscars, including Best Picture. This is also the movie that propelled Michael Caine into international stardom. Playboy Michael Caine finds women irresistable, and they can't resist him. He has a brief romance with Fields and she gets pregnant but, though he cares for her, he won't commitment to her. He continues to sleep with one woman after another, a sexual opportunist deriving little satisfaction from his activities. Only in the end does he begin to comprehend the harm that he has caused. Ribald comedy, but with a serious undercurrent.

A: Michael Caine, Shelley Winters, Millicent Martin, Julia Foster, Shirley Anne Field, Vivien Merchant

© PARAMOUNT HOME VIDEO 6604

ALICE

D: Woody Allen — 106 m

PG-13 — COM DMA — 1990 — COLOR

Sex / Nud / Viol / Lang / AdSit

7 A fine, whimsical adult fantasy from Woody Allen. Alice (Farrow) is a pampered shopaholic who lives in a Manhattan apartment with her very wealthy husband (Hurt), her two kids and her servants. She falls for a jazz saxophonist she meets while picking her kids up one day, and she begins to challenge her whole life. She goes to an Asian herbologist who gives her potions with magical powers that take her on an exotic journey into self-discovery and fulfillment. This is a dryly funny film which ventures out of Allen's traditional comfort zones and brings us some fresh life crises to be resolved.

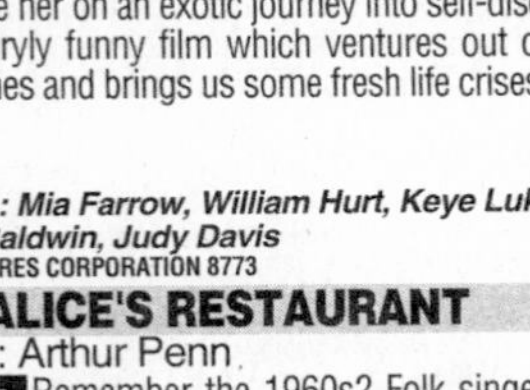

A: Mia Farrow, William Hurt, Keye Luke, Blythe Danner, Alec Baldwin, Judy Davis

© ORION PICTURES CORPORATION 8773

ALICE'S RESTAURANT

D: Arthur Penn — 111 m

PG — COM — 1969 — COLOR

Sex / Nud / Viol / Lang / AdSit

7 Remember the 1960s? Folk singer Arlo Guthrie had a big hit song which was given life within this film. Both the film and the song provide some revealing insights into the "hippie" counterculture of that era. The unusual and comic story chronicles Guthrie's ability to evade mandatory military service - the draft - after being deemed undesirable for having been arrested for littering. This is generally a fun blend of melodrama and whimsey.

A: Arlo Guthrie, Pat Quinn, James Broderick, Michael McClanathan, Geoff Outlaw, Tina Chen

Distributed By MGM/UA Home Video M201370

ALL OF ME

D: Carl Reiner — 93 m

PG — COM — 1984 — COLOR

Sex / Nud / Viol / Lang / AdSit

8 Wild slapstick. The spirit of a very eccentric and recently deceased heiress (Lily Tomlin) is accidentally injected into a lawyer's body (Steve Martin) after a guru's attempt to put her spirit into another woman's body fails. Since Martin is unwilling to give up possession, hilarity ensues. This is a great showcase for the comedic talents of the two stars as their two different-sex, totally mismatched personalities battle for possession of one body. It starts out sort of slow but gets better as it goes along. Martin's physical clowning steals the show.

A: Steve Martin, Lily Tomlin, Victoria Tennant, Jason Bernard, Madolyn Smith, Selma Diamond

© HBO VIDEO 2715

ALL THE MARBLES

D: Robert Aldrich — 113 m

R — COM — 1981 — COLOR

Sex / Nud / Viol / Lang / AdSit

7 Light-weight and fun little comedy about the trials and travails of a small-time hustler and promoter and his two gorgeous lady wrestlers, who are working the small-time Midwest circuit, hoping to get just one shot at the big time. With such a plot, the movie should not be as good as it is. Very entertaining, even without social redeeming qualities.

A: Peter Falk, Vicki Frederick, Laurene Landon, Burt Young, Tracy Reed, Susan Mechsner

Distributed By MGM/UA Home Video M800112

ALMOST PERFECT AFFAIR, AN

D: Michael Ritchie — 92 m

PG — ROM COM — 1979 — COLOR

Sex / Nud / Viol / Lang / AdSit

7 Carradine is a naive young director who has devoted the last two years to creating his film. Now he takes what little money he has left to finance a trip to take it to the Cannes Film Festival in France, where he hopes to sell it. But his film is held up at customs and is released only through the help of a famous producer's wife (Monica Vitti). He, the innocent, falls for and has an affair with her, the worldly. Starts slow but is entertaining and leaves you feeling good. Will appeal most to film fans.

A: Keith Carradine, Monica Vitti, Raf Vallone, Dick Anthony Williams

© PARAMOUNT HOME VIDEO 1221

ALWAYS

D: Henry Jaglom — 105 m

R — DMA ROM COM — 1985 — COLOR

Sex / Nud / Viol / Lang / AdSit

7 A very original film, largely a biography of director/actor Jaglom's real-life breakup with his wife Townsend. Three couples spend the Fourth of July together at a barbecue. One couple is getting married, one is solidly married, and David and Judy have been separated for two years and are on the verge of divorce. Judy stops by just to visit her almost ex-husband and ends up spending the weekend with him and the two other couples. They discuss love, romance, and each other. Some really funny dialogue, some interesting characters and some powerful human insights. Chocolate can be a powerful thing.

A: Henry Jaglom, Patrice Townsend, Melissa Leo, Joanna Frank, Alan Rachins, Michael Emil

© LIVE HOME VIDEO VA5161

ALWAYS

D: Steven Spielberg — 123 m

PG — ROM COM FAN — 1989 — COLOR

Sex / Nud / Viol / Lang / AdSit

7 Very pleasing remake of THE STORY OF JOE. Dreyfuss plays a bush pilot who is killed in a crash but is brought back by his guardian angel (Hepburn). He is to be the guardian angel of an awkward young flyer (Johnson). At first Dreyfuss likes his new job, but that all changes when he also has to help his girlfriend (Hunter) to move on with her life and does it by lining her up with Johnson. This is a light little movie with no major statements to make but it is still a lot of fun. However, you should see the original, too. It is one of director Spielberg's favorites, which was the reason why he redid it here.

A: Richard Dreyfuss, Holly Hunter, Brad Johnson, John Goodman, Audrey Hepburn, Keith David

© MCA/UNIVERSAL HOME VIDEO, INC. 80967

AMADEUS

D: Milos Forman — 158 m

PG — DMA COM MUS — 1984 — COLOR

Sex / Nud / Viol / Lang / AdSit

7 A witty production that won eight Oscars (including Best Picture, Actor and Director) with its literate, sophisticated script and superb performances. Salieri (Abraham) is a successful but mediocre composer. Still, he has great influence in the courts of Venice. Along comes Mozart, a brash young composer who effortlessly produces works of dazzling brilliance. Salieri is intensely jealous of Mozart's talent but is also disgusted with this boy-genius composer who is also a womanizer and a boor. So, he does all that he can to sabotage and destroy Mozart, but instead destroys himself. Slightly overlong.

A: Tom Hulce, F. Murray Abraham, Elizabeth Beridge, Simon Callow, Roy Dotrice, Christine Ebersole

© HBO VIDEO 2997

AMERICAN GRAFFITI

D: George Lucas — 112 m

PG — DMA COM — 1973 — COLOR

Sex / Nud / Viol / Lang / AdSit

10 A monster hit and a treasure trove of nostalgia. Also brilliant and unpretentious filmmaking that is just plain fun. It follows a group of high school students who are about to transition into another world. They nearing graduation from high school in 1962, in a small Northern California town. Lucas weaves their individual lives together into a vastly interesting, poignant, sensitive, frequently funny and always fascinating mosaic. An insightful and very entertaining package, wrapped up in terrific rock `n roll score. You really get to care about all these people. Highly recommended.

A: Richard Dreyfuss, Ron Howard, Paul LeMat, Cindy Williams, Candy Clark, Mackenzie Phillips

© MCA/UNIVERSAL HOME VIDEO, INC. 66010

AMERICANIZATION OF EMILY, THE

D: Arthur Hiller — 117 m

NR | COM DMA ROM | 1964 | B&W

◢ Sex □ Nud □ Viol □ Lang ◢ AdSit

8 Entertaining and daring comedy. Garner is a Navy officer whose main job is keeping his superiors comfortable and supplied with "everything." This suits Garner's larcenous and cowardly nature just fine. Andrews is his British war-widow chauffeur. She despises his avowed cowardice but falls for him anyway. However, things drastically change for them both when the admirals decide they want the first American naval casualty of the D-Day invasion filmed for publicity, and they order Garner to do it. Garner is afraid that the casualty is likely to be him. Compelling satire, with a hard edge.

A: James Garner, Julie Andrews, Melvyn Douglas, James Coburn, Joyce Grenfell, Keenan Wynn

Distributed By MGM/UA Home Video M200518

AMERICAN WEREWOLF IN LONDON, AN

D: John Landis — 97 m

R | HOR COM | 1981 | COLOR

□ Sex ◢ Nud ■ Viol ◢ Lang ■ AdSit

7 This is a literal depiction of the classic horror werewolf premise that had special effects so chilling that it won an Oscar. Two American students, backpacking through Europe, are attacked by a wolf on the English moors. Dunne is killed (although he keeps returning from the dead throughout the picture) and Naughton becomes a werewolf. There is also an interesting twist in the presentation because ample doses of humor are also interwoven into the genuine horror story, though this is not a spoof. There is genuine terror here. Great, sometimes gruesome, special effects.

A: David Naughton, Jenny Agutter, Griffin Dunne, John Woodvine, Brian Glover

© LIVE HOME VIDEO A5101

...AND GOD SPOKE

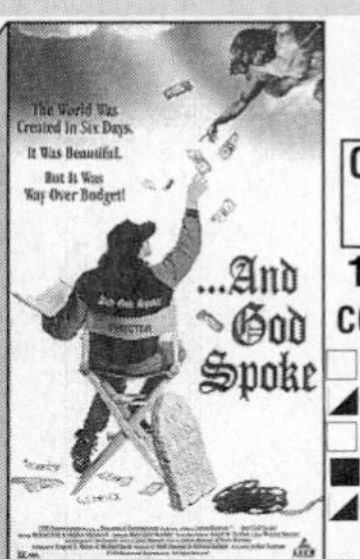

D: Arthur Borman — 82 m

R | COM | 1994 | COLOR

□ Sex ◢ Nud □ Viol ■ Lang ◢ AdSit

6 Low budget pseudo-documentary that makes light of the film-making business. Two self-absorbed nerdish producers have enticed a large studio into bankrolling their epic film based upon the Bible. A movie with a potential audience of 4 billion people can't go wrong, right? Wrong. Everything goes wrong. The film is terrible. As the documentary of the film-making itself progress, cast and crew are interviewed. Virtually all of them are as inept and as untalented as are the producers. Good natured and occasionally funny. True film fanatics will enjoy the inside jokes, and will certainly rate it higher - as did most critics. Everyone else will likely be much less enthused about it.

A: Michael Riley, Stephen Rappaport, Soupy Sales, Eve Plumb, Lou Ferrigno

© LIVE HOME VIDEO 60189

AND NOW FOR SOMETHING COMPLETELY DIFFERENT

D: Ian Mc Naughton — 88 m

PG | COM | 1972 | COLOR

□ Sex □ Nud □ Viol □ Lang ■ AdSit

8 Hilarious collection of sketches taken from TV's "Monty Python's Flying Circus," the British series. Typically bizarre selections, such as John Cleese as a Hungarian tourist using an "inappropriate phrase book," and the classic Lumberjack Song containing the memorable lyrics: "I cut down trees, I wear high heels, suspenders and a bra...." Really off-the-wall stuff. Lots of laughs for those with either a perverse or an English sense of humor.

A: John Cleese, Eric Idle, Terry Jones, Michael Palin, Graham Chapman, Terry Gilliam

© COLUMBIA TRISTAR HOME VIDEO 60123

AND NOW MY LOVE

D: Claude Lelouch — 121 m

PG | FOR ROM COM | 1975 | COLOR

□ Sex □ Nud □ Viol □ Lang ◢ AdSit

8 An entertaining bit of lighthearted romantic fluff about fate and love at first sight. How can it be that two people fall instantly and passionately in love with each other? The individual lives and three generations of family histories of two people are explored in parallel fashion to explain why they should fall instantly in love at their first meeting. A romantic and lyrical salute to life and love in the 20th century. However, it is a little involved and so requires patience. Dubbed or subtitles.

A: Marthe Keller, Andre Dussollier, Charles Denner

© NEW LINE HOME VIDEO 1505

ANGELS IN THE OUTFIELD

D: William Dear — 103 m

PG | COM | 1994 | COLOR

□ Sex □ Nud □ Viol □ Lang □ AdSit

7 Young Roger lives with his best friend in a foster home next to the ball park. When his father arrives for a last visit, Roger asks him when they can be together and Pop says, "When the Angels win the pennant." Even though the Angels are perennial losers, Roger prays that night that the Angels will win. Someone is listening, because soon a real angel (Christopher Lloyd) arrives to give the team some much-needed assistance. No one can see him, except that is for Roger, but everyone knows something is up. Coach Danny Glover hears of the boy's story and refuses to believe, but before long no one can deny that the Angels are winning. Charming, if simple and predictable, Disney family film.

A: Danny Glover, Tony Danza, Brenda Fricker, Ben Johnson, Christopher Lloyd, Joseph Gordon-Levitt

© WALT DISNEY HOME VIDEO 2753

ANNIE HALL

D: Woody Allen — 99 m

PG | ROM COM DMA | 1977 | COLOR

◢ Sex □ Nud □ Viol ◢ Lang ■ AdSit

9 Wonderful bittersweet movie, that nearly everybody (even most non-Allen fans) liked. Woody Allen's humor is very much alive here, but this is also a poignant and sophisticated look into '70s relationships. It is a four-Oscar movie, including Best Picture. It follows the relationship between neurotic New Yorkers, Allen and Keaton as first love grows, then it stutters, then it restarts and then it dies. Both outgrow each other to become different people than they were. Very funny but poignant and sad, too, because it rings so true with many who view it. It'll touch your heart.

A: Woody Allen, Diane Keaton, Tony Roberts, Paul Simon, Shelley Duvall, Carol Kane

Distributed By MGM/UA Home Video M200251

ANOTHER 48 HOURS

D: Walter Hill — 98 m

R | ACT COM CRM | 1990 | COLOR

□ Sex □ Nud ◢ Viol ■ Lang ■ AdSit

7 That comic, wisecracking, crime-busting duo are back again for the second time around. This time, the boys make a huge mess of San Francisco as they try to bring down a very bad dude named Iceman. Nolte's got himself in a jam, so he turns to old friend/enemy Murphy - fresh out of prison himself - to save his career and clear his name by nailing Iceman to the wall in just 48 hours. Expect the usual bar brawls, tough talk, smart talk, humor and lots of violence and broken glass! Fun still, but not as good as the first time around in 48 HOURS.

A: Eddie Murphy, Nick Nolte, Brion James, Kevin Tighe, Ed O'Ross, David Anthony Marshall

© PARAMOUNT HOME VIDEO 32386

ANOTHER STAKEOUT

D: John Badham — 109 m

PG-13 | COM | 1993 | COLOR

□ Sex □ Nud ◢ Viol ■ Lang ◢ AdSit

6 Richard Dreyfus and Emilio Estevez recreate their roles as two bickering cops. This time they go undercover with assistant D.A. Rosie O'Donnell, taking on the cover of man, his second wife and his live-at-home older son. Their job is to stake out a summer home, hoping to recapture a runaway witness against the mob. The threesome do not make a very loving, or convincing, family and that is where the comedy comes from... or it's supposed to. This is a pretty thin plot line, but the veterans manage to make passable entertainment out of the little they are given to work with.

A: Richard Dreyfus, Emilio Estevez, Rosie O'Donnell, Cathy Moriarty, Dennis Farina, Marcia Strassman

© TOUCHSTONE HOME VIDEO 2171

ANY WEDNESDAY

D: Robert Ellis Miller — 109 m

NR | COM ROM | 1966 | COLOR

◢ Sex □ Nud □ Viol □ Lang ■ AdSit

7 Every Wednesday Jason Robards cheats on his wife. Jane Fonda is the object of his weekly affections. Everything has been just great for them both. However, Jane is starting to feel a little put upon. Then something happens to change everything. Robards has been claiming her apartment as a business deduction, so his secretary accidentally gives out-of-town salesman Dean Jones the key. Jones finds out what's going on and wants to use the information to his advantage in a business deal with Robards, except he and Fonda have fallen for each other. Big hit on Broadway too. Funny, a good time.

A: Jane Fonda, Jason Robards, Jr., Dean Jones, Rosemary Murphy, Ann Prentis

© WARNER HOME VIDEO 11349

ANY WHICH WAY YOU CAN

D: Buddy Van Horn — 116 m

PG | COM ACT | 1980 | COLOR

◢ Sex □ Nud ◢ Viol ◢ Lang ◢ AdSit

8 Sequel to EVERY WHICH WAY BUT LOOSE. Same cast of characters, same enjoyable formula. Eastwood is a beer drinkin' mechanic/streetfighter who is set to meet the King of the Streetfighters in an all-out fight in Jackson Hole, Wyoming. However, Clint falls in love and doesn't want to go. So a group of hoods kidnap his love to encourage him to show up. Clyde, the raunchy orangutan, is back, too. Certainly not highbrow entertainment, but it is a lot of fun and was very popular.

A: Clint Eastwood, Sondra Locke, Geoffrey Lewis, William Smith, Harry Guardino, Ruth Gordon

© WARNER HOME VIDEO 11077

APARTMENT, THE

D: Billy Wilder — 126 m

NR | DMA COM ROM | 1960 | B&W

◢ Sex □ Nud □ Viol □ Lang ■ AdSit

10 Comedy and drama have rarely been so well woven together. In order to win favor with his boss (MacMurry) and other execs, Jack Lemmon agrees to lend his apartment to them so that they can carry on after-hours affairs. His stock rises and he quickly moves up to the 19th floor. He gets a key to the executive washroom, but he has to change his plans when he comes home to find his boss's latest girlfriend (MacLaine) has attempted suicide. He nurses her back to health and falls for her himself. Witty adult entertainment. Lemmon and MacLaine are great. Won the 1960 Best Picture Oscar.

A: Jack Lemmon, Shirley MacLaine, Fred MacMurray, Ray Walston, Jack Kuschen, Edie Adams

Distributed By MGM/UA Home Video M201307

APPRENTICESHIP OF DUDDY KRAVITZ, THE

D: Ted Kotcheff — 121 m

PG | COM DMA | 1974 | COLOR

7 Biting satire that was also Dreyfuss's first leading role. He plays a Jewish teenage hustler in 1940 Montreal who is determined to "do good," no matter what. He ruthlessly schemes to get money, women and power, no matter what the cost. This movie is exuberant and manic, as well as biting and sad, and is more than a little uneven too. However, it is also frequently hilarious. Dreyfuss displays his particular talent for sarcasm well and often, a trait that endures today. A wicked sophisticated comedy.

Sex | Nud | Viol | Lang | AdSit

A: Richard Dreyfuss, Randy Quaid, Jack Warden, Denholm Elliott

© PARAMOUNT HOME VIDEO 8791

APRIL FOOLS, THE

D: Stuart Rosenberg — 95 m

PG | COM ROM | 1969 | COLOR

6 Jack Lemmon is trapped in a bad marriage to lifeless Sally Kellerman. His boss gives him a big promotion and invites him to a big and glamorous, but boring, cocktail party. However, there he meets the very beautiful, but bored, Catherine Deneuve and the two of them leave together. They have a great time and fall in love. The problem is that they are both married -- she to the boss. This is an old-fashioned romantic comedy in many ways, except that the two of them do the unthinkable (in the 1960s) - they leave their spouses and the country to be together. Pleasant diversion.

Sex | Nud | Viol | Lang | AdSit

A: Jack Lemmon, Catherine Deneuve, Peter Lawford, Sally Kellerman

© CBS/FOX VIDEO 7129

ARACHNOPHOBIA

D: Frank Marshall — 110 m

PG-13 | SUS HOR COM | 1990 | COLOR

8 Killer spiders incite chaos in this very scary big bug movie! When a deadly spider is accidentally imported to the US, it breeds with local creepy crawlies and produces a herd of poisonous, mutant offspring that take special joy in eating humans. Daniels is the quiet family man who wanted to get his family away from the hustle and bustle of the city, but now faces a huge battle getting rid of the creatures that have invaded his new country home. Goodman provides comic relief as the exterminator on a mission. More fun than you can handle!

Sex | Nud | Viol | Lang | AdSit

A: Jeff Daniels, John Goodman, Julian Sands, Harley Jane Kozak, Stuart Pankin, Brian McNamera

© HOLLYWOOD PICTURES HOME VIDEO 1080

AROUND THE WORLD IN 80 DAYS

D: Michael Anderson — 179 m

G | COM | 1956 | COLOR

7 This successful extravaganza won five Oscars, including Best Picture, upon its release. It is a little dated now, but still offers up plenty of entertainment. It is the Jules Verne story of Phileous Fogg and his valet who are out to win a 19th-century bet that they can circle the world in 80 days. They encounter one adventure after another during their trip, each one populated with its own major star. Over 40 major stars appear in cameo roles. Very expensive - 68,894 people are photographed on 252 locations in 13 countries.

Sex | Nud | Viol | Lang | AdSit

A: David Niven, Cantinflas, Shirley MacLaine, Robert Newton, Marlene Dietrich, John Gielgud

© WARNER HOME VIDEO 11321

ARTHUR

D: Steve Gordon — 97 m

PG | COM ROM | 1981 | COLOR

10 Heartwarming and funny. Dudley Moore is Arthur. Arthur is a spoiled, rich and generally happy, alcoholic bachelor. But he is being forced to marry an up-tight heiress (Eikenberry) who he doesn't even like. Worse still, he has fallen for a lowly waitress and shoplifter (Minnelli). His family gives him an ultimatum: it's either a proper wife, continued money, power and elegance; or, love and total poverty. Moore is perfect and loveable as the drunken spoiled rich kid, but it's Gielgud as his sarcastic valet and surrogate father who steals the show and provides the belly laughs. Laugh-out-loud funny.

Sex | Nud | Viol | Lang | AdSit

A: Dudley Moore, Liza Minnelli, Stephen Elliott, John Gielgud, Jill Eikenberry

© WARNER HOME VIDEO 22020

ASK ANY GIRL

D: Charles Walters — 101 m

NR | COM ROM | 1959 | COLOR

7 Shirley MacLaine is a wide-eyed innocent girl who comes to the big city to find a husband, only to discover that most men are just lecherous skirthounds. She goes to work at an advertising agency and sets her sights on capturing one of the bosses (Gig Young), and she enlists the advertising techniques of his older brother (David Niven) to get her man. But things never work out as planned. Fun, light-hearted little fluff, carried off by a top-flight cast.

Sex | Nud | Viol | Lang | AdSit

A: David Niven, Shirley MacLaine, Gig Young, Rod Taylor, Jim Backus, Elisabeth Fraser

Distributed By MGM/UA Home Video 201128

AUNTIE MAME

D: Morton DaCosta — 144 m

NR | COM MUS | 1958 | COLOR

9 Funny and very entertaining. Russell is a tour-de-force in the title role as a colorful 1920's free-thinking eccentric aunt of an orphaned boy she adopts. She thinks "life is a banquet, and most poor suckers are starving to death." The boy, a sensible and down-to-earth type, has to learn to adapt to his lively live-for-today aunt. The story was first a hit Broadway play and the same cast was then transported into this film production. Hugely successful, it was nominated for six Academy Awards and was the top grossing film of 1959. A lot of fun.

Sex | Nud | Viol | Lang | AdSit

A: Rosalind Russell, Forrest Tucker, Coral Browne, Fred Clark, Peggy Cass, Roger Smith

© WARNER HOME VIDEO 11152

AUTHOR! AUTHOR!

D: Arthur Hiller — 110 m

PG | COM ROM | 1982 | COLOR

7 Al Pacino is a neurotic playwright who is just about to open a new play on Broadway, after a long dry spell. Just then, his flaky philandering wife (Weld) walks out on him for a new man, leaving him with her five kids - only one of which is his. Dyan Cannon is an actress with whom he falls in love and who helps him through his trials. Small but diverting little comedy with a happy ending and really cute kids. Good performances by everyone.

Sex | Nud | Viol | Lang | AdSit

A: Al Pacino, Tuesday Weld, Dyan Cannon, Alan King, Bob Elliott, Ray Gould

© FOXVIDEO 1181

AVANTI !

D: Billy Wilder — 144 m

R | COM ROM | 1972 | COLOR

8 Excellent but largely overlooked movie. Jack Lemmon is a wealthy American businessman who goes to Italy to recover the body of his tycoon father, only to discover that the old man died in the company of his long-time mistress. (The two went over a cliff together in his car.) However, his seemingly simple job is greatly complicated when he falls in love with the daughter of the other woman. The two of them struggle to get the bodies released from the stifling Italian bureaucracy. All of which gives them the time to discover more about their parents and themselves. Underrated Billy Wilder comedy. Entertaining.

Sex | Nud | Viol | Lang | AdSit

A: Jack Lemmon, Juliet Mills, Clive Revill, Edward Andrews, Gianfranco Barra, Franco Agrisano

Distributed By MGM/UA Home Video M203093

BABETTE'S FEAST

D: Gabriel Axel — 102 m

G | FOR DMA COM | 1987 | COLOR

8 Winner of Best Foreign Film Oscar. After her husband and son are killed, French exile (Audran) is taken in by two elderly sisters who live spartan and austere lives as religious leaders. After 14 years with them, Audran wins money in a lottery and prepares a sumptuous banquet in celebration of the women's father's 100th birthday. They and the stoic townspeople are at first hesitant but then join in. Soon long dormant earthly passions are resurrected in everyone. This is not for everyone because it is subtle, deliberate and slow, but it is funny, too, and a reward for the patient viewer. Dubbed.

Sex | Nud | Viol | Lang | AdSit

A: Stephane Audran, Birgitte Federspiel, Bodil Kjer, Vibeke Hastrup, Hanne Stensgard, Jarl Kulle

© ORION PICTURES CORPORATION 5040

BABY BOOM

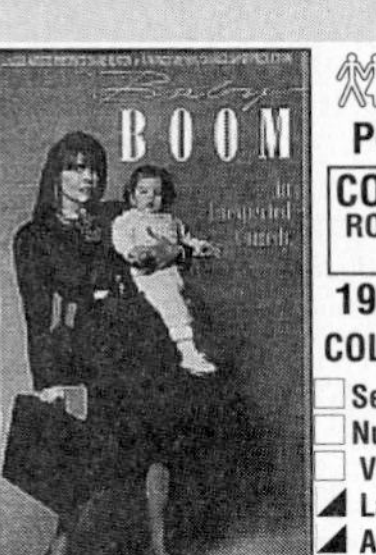

D: Charles Shyer — 110 m

PG | COM ROM | 1987 | COLOR

8 Funny light-weight little story about a high-powered yuppie Manhatten career-woman (Keaton) whose life abruptly changes when a distant cousin dies and she becomes an instant mom. Both her boss and live-in boyfriend recoil from the changes in her, so she moves to a simpler life in the country. She's not very well equipped for the simple life, though, and luckily she gets help from a friendly veterinarian (Shepard). Consistent and entertaining, but the story line is predictable. You might also want to see a similar story from the 1940s, BACHELOR MOTHER.

Sex | Nud | Viol | Lang | AdSit

A: Diane Keaton, Harold Ramis, Sam Wanamaker, Pat Hingle, Sam Shepard, Britt Leach

Distributed By MGM/UA Home Video M202520

BABY IT'S YOU

D: John Sayles — 105 m

R | ROM COM | 1983 | COLOR

7 Two high school kids in 1966 are total opposites, but they are in love. He is a working-class Catholic high school drop-out who dreams of becoming another Frank Sinatra in spite of rock-n-roll and calls himself the Sheik. She is an over-achieving college-bound Jewish girl who is determined to be a Broadway star. She goes off to college and he goes off to Miami to wait tables and await his big break. True, this slice-of-life story is predictable but it is also quite enjoyable, and has many worthwhile and insightful moments, too.

Sex | Nud | Viol | Lang | AdSit

A: Rosanna Arquette, Vincent Spano, Joanna Merlin, Jack Davidson, Nick Ferrari, Dolores Messina

© PARAMOUNT HOME VIDEO 1538

BACK TO SCHOOL

D: Alan Metter 96 m

PG-13 | COM | 1986 | COLOR

7 Rodney Dangerfield plays the uncouth but very rich owner of a chain of "Tall and Fat" stores. When his son wants to drop out of college because he is unpopular and depressed, Rodney decides to enter college himself to prove its value to his son. Trouble is, he never graduated from high school - but he is rich so he buys his way in. The slovenly Rodney takes the campus by storm, becomes BMOC and falls for pretty English teacher Kellerman. She changes his crude ways - somewhat. Full of some pretty funny one-liners. This is better than just a crude movie geared to teenagers. It has a heart.

Sex Nud Viol Lang AdSit

A: Rodney Dangerfield, Sally Kellerman, Burt Young, Keith Gordon, Robert Downey, Jr., Ned Beatty

© HBO VIDEO 2988

BACK TO THE FUTURE

D: Robert Zemeckis 116 m

PG | COM SF | 1985 | COLOR

9 Monster hit and great fun for everyone. Marty McFly (Fox) is an '80s teenager who gets zapped back to the '50s by crazed scientist Lloyd's souped-up Delorean, which was modified for time travel. There, he meets his future parents... but Mom has a crush on him (her own son-to-be) and Dad is a sniveling coward. Marty has to turn things around if he is ever to even be born. Mom must be convinced to give up on Marty so she can fall for Dad, but first Dad must be transformed from a wimpy nerd. The intricate and funny plot comes together for a satisfying ending. A great time.

Sex Nud Viol Lang AdSit

A: Michael J. Fox, Christopher Lloyd, Lea Thompson, Crispin Glover, Thomas F. Wilson, Wendie Jo Sperber

© MCA/UNIVERSAL HOME VIDEO, INC. 80196

BACK TO THE FUTURE, PART II

D: Robert Zemeckis 108 m

PG | COM SF | 1989 | COLOR

6 Michael J. Fox gets a second time-travel workout in this comic adventure when he tries to make things "right" that have gone wrong with the McFly family in the future. So, he and the Doc take to the time machine - the souped-up DeLorean - to 2015 to fix it. But when they return home to Hill Valley, they discover that home is not at all the way it should be. In order to fix their new problems in the present, they must again travel back into the past, 1955 to be exact. Be prepared, the ending leaves things unfinished to clear a wide path for the next sequel.

Sex Nud Viol Lang AdSit

A: Michael J. Fox, Christopher Lloyd, Lea Thompson, Thomas F. Wilson, Charles Fleischer, Joe Flaherty

© MCA/UNIVERSAL HOME VIDEO, INC. 80914

BACK TO THE FUTURE, PART III

D: Robert Zemeckis 118 m

PG | COM SF | 1990 | COLOR

7 A imaginative and thoroughly enjoyable adventure in time! The final entry in the trilogy has Marty (Fox) time traveling back to the old West, 1885. He must retrieve Doc (Lloyd - who was sent there by an ill-timed blast of lightning in Part II) and eventually even save himself from being killed by evil villain, Mad Dog Tannen (Wilson). But Doc has fallen hopelessly in love with a lovely school marm (Steenburgen) and isn't sure he wants to go. Now... with the DeLorean out of gas (gas hasn't even been invented in 1885) and Doc smitten with the love bug, how in the heck is Marty going to get back to the future?

Sex Nud Viol Lang AdSit

A: Michael J. Fox, Christopher Lloyd, Mary Steenburgen, Thomas F. Wilson, Lea Thompson, Elisabeth Shue

© MCA/UNIVERSAL HOME VIDEO, INC. 80976

BAD COMPANY

D: Robert Benton 94 m

PG | WST COM | 1972 | COLOR

7 Interesting and quite different kind of buddy-Western. It is part realistic adventure, part comedy. Two draft-dodgers each decide to head west rather than get caught up in the Civil War. Along the way, they meet some other young draft-dodgers and they form a small-time gang so they can rob and cheat to pay for their way west. However, when the group arrives in the West, it falls apart as they all turn on each other. An entertaining and clever combination of a fun buddy movie, raunchy humor and action. Brown and Bridges somehow manage to make their otherwise grungy characters appealing in spite of their unsavory natures.

Sex Nud Viol Lang AdSit

A: Jeff Bridges, Barry Brown, Jim Davis, David Huddleston, John Savage, Jerry Houser

© PARAMOUNT HOME VIDEO 8476

BAD NEWS BEARS, THE

D: Michael Ritchie 102 m

PG | COM | 1976 | COLOR

9 One of 1976's top grossing films, a terrific and funny comedy. Beer drinking ex-minor league pitcher Walter Matthau gets roped into coaching to a hopeless Little League baseball team, whose only talent seems to be spouting four-letter words and getting into fights. Enduring endless torment, he somehow turns a bunch of misfit boys into a team and then brings in an ace spitball pitcher - a girl (Tatum O'Neal) - to save the day. Riotous good fun. The movie's tremendous success spawned two sequels, only one of which is worth watching: BAD NEWS BEARS IN BREAKING TRAINING.

Sex Nud Viol Lang AdSit

A: Walter Matthau, Tatum O'Neal, Vic Morrow, Alfred Lutter, Jackie Earle Haley

© PARAMOUNT HOME VIDEO 8863

BAD NEWS BEARS IN BREAKING TRAINING, THE

D: Michael Ritchie 105 m

PG | COM | 1976 | COLOR

6 The Little Leaguers from THE BAD NEWS BEARS are back, but Walter Mathau isn't - so it isn't as good. Still, much of the charm is intact. Eager for a chance to play the Houston Toros so that they can get a shot at beating the Japanese champs, they first have to get a new coach. They find one guy, then dump him in favor of one kid's estranged father (Devane) who hopefully can teach their pitcher to get his fastball over the plate. Warm and sentimental, plus much of the language has been cleaned up from the first time, but it's not as much fun. Forget the next sequel.

Sex Nud Viol Lang AdSit

A: William Devane, Clifton James, Jackie Earle Haley, Jimmy Baio, Chris Barnes

© PARAMOUNT HOME VIDEO 8965

BAGDAD CAFE

D: Percy Adlon 91 m

PG | COM DMA | 1988 | COLOR

6 Looking for something really different? A really offbeat comedy. An overweight compulsive German tourist (Sagebrecht) leaves her husband after a fight in the middle of the Mojave desert. She seeks shelter at a seedy out-of-the-way motel/cafe whose owner is both constantly angry and totally disorganized. The regular clientele is a group of very strange and kooky eccentrics, like Jack Palance - who is obsessed with painting the chubby Sagebrect. The presence of this compulsive neatnic changes everyone at the cafe. She gives it order and turns it into a popular oasis. For seekers of the unusual only.

Sex Nud Viol Lang AdSit

A: Marianne Sagebrecht, Jack Palance, CCH Pounder, Christine Kaufmann, Monica Calhoun, George Aguilar

© MCEG/STERLING 70157

BAJA OKLAHOMA

D: Bobby Roth 100 m

NR | COM ROM | 1988 | COLOR

7 This is a bittersweet story of a small-town Texas barmaid who has the unfortunate tendency to always attract the wrong men. In fact, her life is totally occupied by strange characters and her passion to become a country song writer. When one of her many past lovers returns, she writes a song about him, but she is reluctant to give him a second chance. So, he sets about helping her to achieve her dream by working overtime to get her song made into a hit. Willie Nelson and Emmylou Harris make cameo appearances. Lots of colorful people and a good deal of fun, too.

Sex Nud Viol Lang AdSit

A: Lesley Ann Warren, Peter Coyote, Swoosie Kurtz, Billy Vera

© WARNER HOME VIDEO 827

BALLAD OF CABLE HOGUE, THE

D: Sam Peckinpah 122 m

R | WST COM | 1970 | COLOR

8 Truly enjoyable winner. It's 1908. Jason Robards is a prospector, abandoned by his partners in the desert and left to die. However, instead of dying, he discovers water in a land where there is little water, and that turns him into the wealthy owner of a stagecoach stopover. Still, he awaits the day when he will have the chance to get even with his partners. Stevens sparkles as a cowtown whore who loves him but leaves him for San Francisco anyway, only to come back later. Not much traditional action, but the characters are wonderful. Widely praised by the public and by critics, too.

Sex Nud Viol Lang AdSit

A: Jason Robards, Jr., Stella Stevens, Strother Martin, L.Q. Jones, David Warner, Slim Pickens

© WARNER HOME VIDEO 11298

BALTIMORE BULLET, THE

D: Robert Ellis Miller 103 m

PG | COM | 1980 | COLOR

7 Pleasant light-hearted little sports story about a couple of pool hustlers, a fast-talking veteran (Coburn) and a newcomer partner (Boxleitner) who con their way cross-country in an effort to raise some really big money, so they can play a high-stakes game with a suave gambler known as "The Deacon" (Sharif). Some remarkable pool shots, along with cameos by some of the sport's best, give the film the proper sense of atmosphere. See also THE HUSTLER and COLOR OF MONEY.

Sex Nud Viol Lang AdSit

A: James Coburn, Omar Sharif, Bruce Boxleitner, Ronee Blakley, Jack O'Halloran, Michael Lerner

© NEW LINE HOME VIDEO 90007

BANANAS

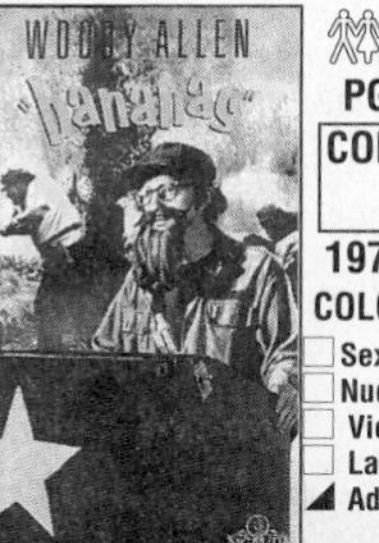

D: Woody Allen 83 m

PG | COM | 1971 | COLOR

9 Pure vintage Allen zaniness. Either you like him or you don't. It contains a wide variety of good and bad jokes in a bizarre story of a sex-starved gadget-tester who is jilted by his girlfriend, a political activist (Lassiter). Lovestruck, he follows her to the banana republic of San Marcos. There, after a set of Allen-like typically weird events, he inadvertently becomes president. A wacky movie with a funny score. Absurdity reigns.

Sex Nud Viol Lang AdSit

A: Woody Allen, Louise Lasser, Carlos Montalban, Howard Cosell, Rene Enriquez, Charlotte Rae

Distributed By MGM/UA Home Video M201764

BAREFOOT IN THE PARK

D: Gene Saks — 106 m

9 G | COM ROM | 1967 | COLOR

Neil Simon's consistently funny story of newlyweds adjusting to married life. A conservative young lawyer and his free-spirited, fun-loving young wife move into a rundown apartment building, where they are beset by a host of newlywed doubts and problems - including an intrusive mother-in-law, who is eventually wooed into retreat by their charming upstair's neighbor (Boyer). Things really boil, however, when Fonda becomes convinced that they are not meant for each other because Redford is too reserved and stuffy - all because he won't go barefoot in the park. A truly good time!

☐ Sex ☐ Nud ☐ Viol ☐ Lang ■ AdSit

A: Robert Redford, Jane Fonda, Charles Boyer, Mildred Natwick, Herb Edelman

© PARAMOUNT HOME VIDEO 8027

BARFLY

D: Barbet Schroeder — 100 m

8 R | COM DMA | 1987 | COLOR

Surprisingly enjoyable, literate, bittersweet comedy - but it is not for everybody. Exceptional performances by Rourke and Dunaway, and a dynamite jazz and R&B score highlight this guided tour through the gutters of Los Angeles. Rourke is a slovenly but eloquent poet and writer who prefers the bars and drinking over work. Dunaway is a fading beauty and his alcoholic soul and bedmate. But his work is ardently admired by pretty publisher Alice Krige, who is in competition with Dunaway for him. Very unusual, with characters that are hard for most people to identify with or care about.

◢ Sex ◢ Nud ◢ Viol ■ Lang ■ AdSit

A: Mickey Rourke, Faye Dunaway, Alice Krige, J.C. Quinn, Frank Stalone, Jack Nance

© WARNER HOME VIDEO 37212

BARTON FINK

D: John Turturro — 116 m

7 R | COM DMA | 1991 | COLOR

Surreal and quirky. It's a brilliant collage of colorful characterizations and black comedy, all packaged up as a spoof on 1930's Hollywoodishness. Fink (Turturro) is a Broadway playwright who, against his better judgment, takes a lucrative Hollywood writing job. However, the studio head wants him to write a movie screenplay about wrestling. Fink's brain locks up with writer's block and he begins to hallucinate. He can write nothing. His life is out of control, and he keeps getting interrupted by an insurance salesman (Goodman) who lives next door. Bizarre and sarcastic comedy.

☐ Sex ☐ Nud ☐ Viol ■ Lang ■ AdSit

A: John Goodman, John Turturro, John Mahoney, Judy Davis, Jon Polito, Michael Lerner

© FOXVIDEO 1905

BATTLE BEYOND THE STARS

D: Jimmy T. Murakami — 102 m

7 PG | SF COM | 1980 | COLOR

The planet Akir is a peaceful planet facing destruction by powerful forces, and it is beyond their own capacity to defend themselves. Richard Thomas becomes an emissary from Akir to Earth and other planets, seeking to recruit mercenaries to help save his world. He has recruited a lizard-like alien and some of his friends, a female Amazon warrior from the planet Valkyrie, and from earth - a cowboy and a computer specialist. Sort of a MAGNIFICENT SEVEN-in-outer-space. Genuinely enjoyable fantasy-comedy that never takes itself too seriously. Something for everyone.

☐ Sex ☐ Nud ◢ Viol ☐ Lang ☐ AdSit

A: Richard Thomas, John Saxon, Robert Vaughn, George Peppard, Sybil Danning, Darlanne Fluegel

© LIVE HOME VIDEO VA4044

BEETHOVEN'S 2ND

D: Rod Daniel — 89 m

8 PG | CLD COM | 1993 | COLOR

One of those rare sequels that is better than the original, at least most adults will think so. Beethoven is back, but the doggie drool quotient is way down. The dependence upon silliness and gross jokes has been replaced with interesting characters and situations. Much of the story is told from Beethoven's point of view. While on a stroll in the park one day, Beethoven spied his true love and four of the cutest puppies ever born. But, when the snarling owner of the new bride threatens to drown the furballs, Charles Grodin's kids decide to hide them in the basement, without telling Dad. This video is one the parents will enjoy right along with their kids.

☐ Sex ☐ Nud ☐ Viol ☐ Lang ☐ AdSit

A: Charles Grodin, Bonnie Hunt, Nicholle Tom, Christopher Castile, Sarah Rose Karr, Debi Mazar

© MCA/UNIVERSAL HOME VIDEO, INC. 81608

BEETLEJUICE

D: Tim Burton — 92 m

PG | COM | 1988 | COLOR

A loving, young couple sets up a perfect life for themselves in a pretty little farmhouse in Connecticut, but their perfect life is cut short when they drown accidentally. Being very new ghosts, and being inexperienced at such things, they continue to "live" in their farmhouse. But, a bizarre family has moved into their house and is intent upon destroying everything the couple had built. Because they are not yet good at haunting, they decide to call in professional help in the form of free-lance evil spirit Beetlejuice (Keaton). Good natured in spirit and good fun. Fun special effects.

☐ Sex ☐ Nud ◢ Viol ◢ Lang ☐ AdSit

A: Alec Baldwin, Geena Davis, Jeffrey Jones, Catherine O'Hara, Winona Ryder, Robert Goulet

© WARNER HOME VIDEO 11785

BEGINNER'S LUCK

D: Frank Mouris — 85 m

6 R | COM | 1984 | COLOR

A different little sex comedy. A lusty couple that is living together upstairs becomes friendly with an uptight virginal law student who is about to be married and is living downstairs. He talks the couple into living out their sex fantasies by running a personal ad for like-minded couples and when couples start to respond to the ads, things get strange. But things get complicated for our law student, when a comic menage a trois scene between the three of them develops, just as his intended shows up for a visit. There is no real sex and it is a little too silly at times, but it is also often funny.

☐ Sex ■ Nud ☐ Viol ■ Lang ■ AdSit

A: Sam Rush, Riley Steiner, Charles Humet, Kate Talbot, Mickey Coburn

© R&G VIDEO, LP 8601

BEING THERE

D: Hal Ashby — 130 m

8 PG | COM | 1979 | COLOR

This biting social satire has become a cult favorite. Sellers is brilliant as Chance, a simpleton gardner who has remained cloistered his whole life behind the walls of a mansion until his master dies. His only knowledge of the real world has come from watching the television, which is constantly on. When finally he does leave, his empty-headed chatter is misinterpreted by the rich and powerful as profound wisdom. He becomes an advisor to a giant of industry and is pursued by the man's sex-starved wife. Soon the powerful in politics seek his council and he is considered as a candidate for President. Curious black comedy. Sellers fans might rate it even higher.

☐ Sex ☐ Nud ☐ Viol ◢ Lang ■ AdSit

A: Peter Sellers, Shirley MacLaine, Melvyn Douglas, Jack Warden, Richard Dysart

© WARNER HOME VIDEO 938

BELL, BOOK AND CANDLE

D: Richard Quine — 103 m

7 NR | COM ROM | 1958 | COLOR

Kim Novak is a beautiful 1950s witch and a member of a family of witches which also includes her brother Nicky (Lemmon) and aunt Queeny (Lanchester). Lovely Kim falls in love with James Stewart on the eve of his wedding to someone else and so casts a spell over him to capture his heart. When Jimmy finds out why what has happened, happened... he wants out. So her warlock brother takes both Stewart and his partner (Kovacs) to another wacky witch (Hermione Gingold) to break the spell. Pleasant little comedy, expertly played by a talented cast.

☐ Sex ☐ Nud ☐ Viol ☐ Lang ◢ AdSit

A: James Stewart, Kim Novak, Jack Lemmon, Ernie Kovacs, Hermione Gingold, Elsa Lanchester

© COLUMBIA TRISTAR HOME VIDEO 60132

BELLBOY, THE

D: Jerry Lewis — 72 m

6 NR | COM CLD | 1960 | COLOR

Jerry Lewis at his silliest. Jerry is a ridiculous bellboy who fouls up everything at a ritzy Miami Beach hotel. What other bellboy in the world, when told to bring everything from the trunk of a Volkswagen, would remove the engine and take it up to their room. The film is a non-stop series of sight gags and slapstick. Young kids and Jerry Lewis fans will enjoy themselves.

☐ Sex ☐ Nud ☐ Viol ☐ Lang ☐ AdSit

A: Jerry Lewis, Alex Gerry, Bob Clayton, Sonnie Sands, Bill Richman

© VIDEO TREASURES 9740

BELLS ARE RINGING

D: Vincente Minnelli — 126 m

8 NR | COM MUS ROM | 1960 | COLOR

Upbeat musical that was brought to the big screen from Broadway. Judy Holliday plays a shy telephone answering service operator who uses her knowledge of her clients's problems to help them all out. She also has fallen secretly in love with playboy playwright Dean Martin, even though they have never met. He just thinks she is just a nice little old lady passing out advice and so thinks of her only as "Mom." A delightful MGM musical. 14 musical numbers. Songs include "Just in Time." See the Director's index under Vincente Minnelli for other classic musicals. He did a lot of them.

☐ Sex ☐ Nud ☐ Viol ☐ Lang ◢ AdSit

A: Judy Holliday, Dean Martin, Fred Clark, Eddie Foy, Jr., Jean Stapleton, Frank Gorshin

Distributed By MGM/UA Home Video M700063

BENNY & JOON

D: Jeremiah Chechik — 98 m

7 PG | ROM COM | 1993 | COLOR

Pleasing and odd little love story. Joon (Masterson) is Benny's mentally disturbed sister who lives at home with Benny. He has dedicated his life to her and her quirky eccentricities, to the point where he has no private life of his own. He is being counselled to place Joon in a group home but he rebels at the idea. Then Joon "wins" Sam (Depp) in a poker game. Sam is a friend's definitely quirky cousin who has taken on the persona of Buster Keaton. Sam's job is to take care of Joon while Benny's at work and the two misfits fall in love. Very enjoyable and fun time with some interesting characters.

☐ Sex ☐ Nud ☐ Viol ◢ Lang ◢ AdSit

A: Aidan Quinn, Johnny Depp, Mary Stuart Masterson

Distributed By MGM/UA Home Video 903007

BEST LITTLE WHOREHOUSE IN TEXAS, THE

D: Colin Higgins — 115 m

R | MUS COM | 1982 | COLOR

6 Light-hearted film version of the successful Broadway musical about one of the most famous real-life whorehouses of all time. Burt plays the unfortunate sheriff of a small Texas town who is getting severe pressure to put the town's most popular and revered institution (and his madam girlfriend Dolly Parton) out of business. That unpopular popular institution is the famous whorehouse called the Chicken Ranch. This film version is not as lively as the stage version and is somewhat slow in spots, but it still has enough going for it to recommend it as a good time.

Sex ◢ | Nud ◢ | Viol ☐ | Lang ■ | AdSit ■

A: Dolly Parton, Burt Reynolds, Lois Nettleton, Dom DeLuise, Charles Durning, Jim Nabors

© MCA/UNIVERSAL HOME VIDEO, INC. 77014

BEST OF CHEVY CHASE, THE

D: Lorne Michaels — 60 m

NR | COM | 1987 | COLOR

7 Goofy, comic fun! Pulled from various episodes of Saturday Night Live. Chase is joined by many of the hilarious comic geniuses he worked with on the series. Skits include the Weekend Update segments, the scene with Gerald Ford in the Oval Office and the land shark in Jaws. Classic SNL satire.

Sex ☐ | Nud ☐ | Viol ☐ | Lang ☐ | AdSit ◢

A: Chevy Chase, Dan Aykroyd, John Belushi, Jane Curtin, Garrett Morris, Bill Murray

© WARNER HOME VIDEO 805

BEST OF DAN AYKROYD, THE

D: Lorne Michaels — 56 m

NR | COM | 1986 | COLOR

7 Dan Aykroyd, in his peak comic form, hosts this hilarious compilation of classic Saturday Night Live skits taken from his tenure there from 1975-1979, including: "The Bass-O-Matic Salesman," "Fred Garvin: Male Prostitute," "Julie Child" and "The Final Days of the Nixon Presidency." A good time for SNL fans.

Sex ☐ | Nud ☐ | Viol ☐ | Lang ☐ | AdSit ◢

A: Dan Aykroyd, John Belushi, Chevy Chase, Jane Curtin, Garrett Morris, Bill Murray

© WARNER HOME VIDEO 35012

BEST OF EDDIE MURPHY, THE - SATURDAY NIGHT LIVE

D: — 78 m

NR | COM | 1989 | COLOR

8 Hilarious bunch of sketches taken from his years on Saturday Night Live. This is some of his best stuff. His skits include his riotous characterizations of Little Richard Simmons, Bill Cosby, James Brown, Buckwheat, Stevie Wonder and Mr. Robinson, the kiddie show host.

Sex ☐ | Nud ☐ | Viol ☐ | Lang ☐ | AdSit ◢

A: Eddie Murphy

© PARAMOUNT HOME VIDEO 12741

BEST OF GILDA RADNER, THE

D: Dave Wilson — 58 m

NR | COM | 1989 | COLOR

7 The much loved and very funny lady, Gilda Radner, packs a comic punch in this series of skits collected from her performances on Saturday Night Live. Some treasures are rock singer Candy Slice, consumer correspondent Roseanne Roseannadanna, and her characterization of TV news reporter and interviewer Barbara Walters - Baba Wawa. A wonderful tribute to her comic talent.

Sex ☐ | Nud ☐ | Viol ☐ | Lang ☐ | AdSit ◢

A: Gilda Radner, Dan Aykroyd, John Belushi, Steve Martin, Candice Bergen, Bill Murray

© WARNER HOME VIDEO 35148

BEST OF JOHN BELUSHI, THE

D: Lorne Michaels — 60 m

NR | COM | 1985 | COLOR

7 Belushi extracts the best of his comic form in sixteen skits from various Saturday Night Live performances between 1975 and 1979. The fun includes "Samurai Delicatessen" and his hysterical impression of Joe Cocker.

Sex ☐ | Nud ☐ | Viol ☐ | Lang ☐ | AdSit ◢

A: John Belushi, Dan Aykroyd, Chevy Chase, Jane Curtin, Garrett Morris, Bill Murray

© WARNER HOME VIDEO 34078

BEST OF NOT NECESSARILY THE NEWS, THE

D: Hoite C. Caston, John Moffitt — 57 m

NR | COM | 1988 | COLOR

7 Collection of some of the funniest moments from the HBO series that shows you the news as it was when it happened and how it might have been.

Sex ☐ | Nud ☐ | Viol ☐ | Lang ☐ | AdSit ◢

A: Anne Bloom, Danny Bren, Rich Hall, Mitchell Laurance, Stuart Pankin, Lucy Webb

© HBO VIDEO 0175

BEST OF TIMES, THE

D: Roger Spottiswoode — 104 m

PG-13 | DMA COM | 1986 | COLOR

7 Quite good and unduly underrated little "dramedy" about mid-life crisis. Robin Williams is vice president at the bank but he has never forgotten, or been able to live down, the biggest tragedy of his life - the night he dropped the football in the big high school game against their archrivals. So he and his best friend (Russell), the quarterback on that fateful night, decide to organize a rematch - 20 years later - and spice up life in their little town. Nice little story that leaves you satisfied when it's over.

Sex ◢ | Nud ☐ | Viol ◢ | Lang ◢ | AdSit ◢

A: Robin Williams, Kurt Russell, Pamela Reed, Holly Palance, Donovan Scott, Donald Moffat

© NEW LINE HOME VIDEO 1307

BETSY'S WEDDING

D: Alan Alda — 94 m

R | COM | 1990 | COLOR

7 The wedding of director Alda's own daughter gave him plenty of first-hand experience from which to create this wonderful wedding comedy. When Ringwald announces her marriage plans, father Alda enters into a seedy business arrangement with his mob brother-in-law (Pesci) so he can give his daughter away in grand style. Unfortunately, his dealings take on a slightly illegal bent and he almost ends up in the slammer instead of walking down the aisle. Funny lines from concerned relatives, plenty of bickering and last minute jitters. A charmer!

Sex ☐ | Nud ◢ | Viol ☐ | Lang ■ | AdSit ◢

A: Alan Alda, Molly Ringwald, Ally Sheedy, Madeline Kahn, Joe Pesci

© TOUCHSTONE HOME VIDEO 1067

BETTE MIDLER'S MONDO BEYONDO

D: — 60 m

NR | COM | 1988 | COLOR

6 Bette Midler plays an Italian sexpot hostess of an outlandish cable variety show, on which she introduces a series of film or tape clips from leading avant-garde performers. They are a wide assortment of oddball characters who engage in an even wider array of songs and skits - some very bizarre. Helps a lot if you are a Bette Midler fan.

Sex ☐ | Nud ☐ | Viol ☐ | Lang ◢ | AdSit ◢

A: Bette Midler

© HBO VIDEO 0154

BETWEEN THE LINES

D: Joan Micklin Silver — 101 m

R | COM | 1977 | COLOR

7 Funny little comedy about the staff of a youth-oriented counter-culture newspaper who must learn to deal with the paper's pending purchase by a large corporate conglomerate. Its an enjoyable gentle little sleeper of a comedy, dealing with people having to face a major change in lifestyle. Talented cast who were then all unknowns.

Sex ☐ | Nud ◢ | Viol ☐ | Lang ◢ | AdSit ■

A: John Heard, Lindsay Crouse, Jeff Goldblum, Jill Eikenberry, Gwen Welles, Stephen Collins

© LIVE HOME VIDEO VA5002

BEVERLY HILLBILLIES, THE

D: Penelope Spheeris — 93 m

PG | COM | 1994 | COLOR

7 Well, they're back... and just as silly as they were the first time 'round. But hey, that ain't all bad. The faces of the characters have changed but the characters haven't. Jed and his clan of hillbillies move themselves and their backwoods ways into the world of the super-rich. His neighbor is the greedy banker who only cares about keeping Jed's money in the bank. The banker's number one lackey, Miss Jane, is set upon winning the heart (and body) of Jed's nephew, the super-dumb Jethro (Diedrich Bader). Meanwhile, the banker's number two lackey (Rob Schneider) has set his girlfriend out to capture Jed's heart (and money). Fun blend of stupid humor and slapstick.

Sex | Nud | Viol | Lang | AdSit

A: Jim Varney, Cloris Leachman, Lilly Tomlin, Dabney Coleman, Erika Eleniak, Lea Thompson

© FOXVIDEO 8561

BEVERLY HILLS COP

D: Martin Brest 105 m

R | COM ACT CRM | 1984 | COLOR | Sex Nud Viol Lang AdSit

10 A huge box-office sensation, a perfect vehicle for the wise-cracking Eddie Murphy and a very funny and action-packed movie. A street-smart, smart aleck Detroit cop (Murphy) goes to L.A. intent upon tracking down a friend's killer. He ignores the by-the-book local cops and their warnings to stay away and instead blusters his way into high society, irritating everybody possible in the process. Following his killer's trail leads him to a major smuggling and drug ring. Cleverly woven fabric of comedy, characters and action. Excellent cast provides major support. Excellent score.

A: Eddie Murphy, Judge Reinhold, John Aston, Lisa Eibacher, Steven Berkoff, James Russo

© PARAMOUNT HOME VIDEO 1134

BEVERLY HILLS COP II

D: Tony Scott 103 m

R | COM ACT CRM | 1987 | COLOR | Sex Nud Viol Lang AdSit

7 Sequel to the megahit BEVERLY HILLS COP. It lacks the originality and major laughs of the first movie, but still has plenty of action and wise cracks. Murphy comes back to L.A. to investigate the shooting of his friend, police captain Cox, and runs up against hit woman Brigitte Nielsen. Murphy is again the likable smart-mouthed cop who runs over everyone to get the bad guys. Pretty good, but not close to the original. Don't miss Murphy's other megahit: 48 HOURS.

A: Eddie Murphy, Judge Reinhold, Jurgen Prochnow, Ronny Cox, John Aston, Brigitte Nielsen

© PARAMOUNT HOME VIDEO 1860

BEYOND THE VALLEY OF THE DOLLS

D: Russ Meyer 109 m

NC-17 | DMA COM | 1970 | COLOR | Sex Nud Viol Lang AdSit

6 Campy and sexy. This is an in-name-only sequel to VALLEY OF THE DOLLS, which was a movie soap opera of the same period. This would-be parody of a soap opera was co-written by film critic Roger Ebert and soft-porn director Russ Meyer. It is about a female rock group's attempts to do whatever it takes to make it in Hollywood. They encounter corruption, sex and a killing spree. Some viewers, who didn't take it too seriously, liked it - but the film got a decidedly mixed review. Originally rated X.

A: Dolly Read, Cynthia Meyers, Marcia McBroom, John LaZar, Michael Blodgett, Edy Williams

© FOX 1101

BIG

D: Penny Marshall 104 m

PG | COM DMA | 1988 | COLOR | Sex Nud Viol Lang AdSit

9 Sparkling, heartwarming blockbuster. When a 12-year-old boy is rejected by a fifteen-year-old girl, he makes a wish at a carnival's mechanical fortune teller to become big. The next morning he is - but he still has the mind and heart of a 12-year-old. Excellent vehicle for Hanks - it won him an Oscar nomination. This is much more a story about childhood innocence than a story for children. A major commercial success, it inspired other movies to use instant-grownup characters (although FREAKY FRIDAY was actually the first).

A: Tom Hanks, Elizabeth Perkins, Robert Loggia, John Heard, Jared Ruston, David Moscow

© FOXVIDEO 1658

BIG BAD MAMA

D: Steve Carver 87 m

R | ACT COM | 1974 | COLOR | Sex Nud Viol Lang AdSit

7 Angie Dickinson stars in this light-hearted clone to BONNIE AND CLYDE. It is a pretty good action film about a depression-era mother who is tired of being poor and so, along with her teenage daughters, takes up robbing banks and other places for a living. Along the way to California, she and her girls take in accomplices, and boy-toys Tom Skerritt and William Shatner. While this film has a fair amount of action, it was most notable for its nude scenes, particularly Angie's, which has help to keep it a perennial favorite. Its success spawned a later and lessor clone.

A: Angie Dickinson, Tom Skerritt, William Shatner, Susan Sennett, Joan Prather, Robbie Lee

© WARNER HOME VIDEO 4013

BIG BUS, THE

D: James Frawley 88 m

PG | COM | 1976 | COLOR | Sex Nud Viol Lang AdSit

6 Silly spoof of disaster films that predates AIRPLANE's spoof of AIRPORT by four years, but is not nearly as good. Still, it may be of interest to fans of the genre. It is the story of a super-luxurious, 75-ton, nuclear-powered bus with 32 wheels that is making its maiden run from New York to Denver. The bus carries a wide assortment of odd-ball characters, including a co-pilot who is prone to sudden black-outs.

A: Joseph Bologna, Stockard Channing, John Beck, Lynn Redgrave, Jose Ferrer, Ruth Gordon

© PARAMOUNT HOME VIDEO 8823

BIG BUSINESS

D: Jim Abrahams 98 m

PG | COM | 1988 | COLOR | Sex Nud Viol Lang AdSit

7 Clever. Two sets of identical twins, one born rich (the Midlers) and one born poor (the Tomlins) are mixed together at birth in the tiny town of Jupiter Hollow, which is owned by Midler's parents. One mismatched pair of Midler/Tomlins stays in town, poor. The other pair leaves rich - neither knowing of the colossal mix-up. Years later the wealthy New York twins, dominated by Midler, decide to sell the family interest in the town to a strip miner. Upset at that prospect, the poor country pair come to New York to fight for their town, only to discover their true long-lost twin. Fairly well-done and genuinely funny in several places.

A: Bette Midler, Lily Tomlin, Fred Ward, Edward Herrmann, Michele Placido, Daniel Gerroll

© TOUCHSTONE HOME VIDEO 605

BIG HAND FOR THE LITTLE LADY, A

D: Fielder Cook 95 m

WST COM SUS | 1966 | COLOR | Sex Nud Viol Lang AdSit

8 Great little comedy with lots of twists. It's a clever story about a farmer (Fonda) and his wife (Woodward) who arrive in town just in time for the annual big stakes poker game. He's a former gambler and has sworn off but, he has to get into that game. Against his wife's wishes, he does and then gets dealt the hand of his life. He bets until he runs out of cash, so he bets the farm (much to the wife's distress) and then has a heart attack. She now has everything in the world she owns at stake and bet on the unfinished game, so the little lady steps up to the table and says, "How do you play this game?"

A: Henry Fonda, Joanne Woodward, Jason Robards, Jr., Charles Bickford, Burgess Meredith, Paul Ford

© WARNER HOME VIDEO 11469

BIG PICTURE, THE

D: Christopher Guest 100 m

PG-13 | COM | 1988 | COLOR | Sex Nud Viol Lang AdSit

6 OK satire of Hollywood by Hollywood. Several of the same people involved with the successful satire THIS IS SPINAL TAP were involved here, but this one doesn't work quite so well. Still, for the theatrical set and Hollywood initiated, it's pretty good. They will want to add a point or two to the rating. A student movie maker (Bacon) wins an award for a small movie and gains attention from a major Hollywood agent. Bacon thinks he has arrived, but quickly learns that, in Hollywood, all ain't what it appears to be. Many of the inside jokes are lost on outsiders. Lots of major star cameos.

A: Kevin Bacon, Emily Longstreth, J.T. Walsh, Jennifer Jason Leigh, Michael McKean

© COLUMBIA TRISTAR HOME VIDEO 50263

BIG TOP PEE-WEE

D: Randal Kleiser 86 m

PG | CLD COM | 1988 | COLOR | Sex Nud Viol Lang AdSit

6 Farmer Pee-wee comes out of his cellar to find a circus has pitched its tent in his backyard. He decides to join up - but first he has to develop his own act. He also falls for the pretty trapeze artist Golino, much to the dismay of his girlfriend Miller. It's a simple story and there are some weak spots, but the kids will like it - even if it isn't up to the much better PEE-WEE'S BIG ADVENTURE.

A: Pee-wee Herman, Kris Kristofferson, Valeria Golino, Penelope Ann Miller, Susan Tyrrell, Albert Henderson

© PARAMOUNT HOME VIDEO 32076

BIG TROUBLE IN LITTLE CHINA

D: John Carpenter 99 m

PG-13 | COM ACT | 1986 | COLOR | Sex Nud Viol Lang AdSit

7 Curious science fiction/kung-fu action spoof, purposely done in the old-time style of the serial adventure series. Pig trucker Kurt Russell is swept into a mystical world under San Francisco's Chinatown, where a 2,000 year old wizard, Lo-Pan, must marry a green-eyed girl in order to restore his youth. Spectacular martial arts and a truly strange group of characters are at the heart of this picture. Good special effects. Expect the absurd, because everything is played tongue-in-cheek and just for laughs.

A: Kurt Russell, Kim Cattrall, Victor Wong, Dennis Dun, Kate Burton, James Hong

© FOXVIDEO 1502

BILL & TED'S BOGUS JOURNEY

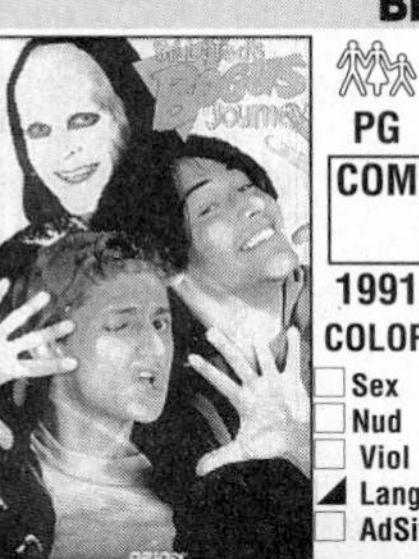

D: Peter Hewitt 98 m

PG | COM | 1991 | COLOR | Sex Nud Viol Lang AdSit

6 After skating through history class with the personal help of some of history's most prominent historical figures, cool dudes Reeves and Winter are desperately hoping that some twist of fate will bring them back to reality - any reality - in this funny sequel to BILL & TED'S EXCELLENT ADVENTURE. Once again, they travel through time in a phone booth, but this time their journey is literally to hell and back. After futuristic clones Evil Bill and Evil Ted are sent from above to end their "most excellent" lives, the pair will need much more than charm as they come face to face with the Grim Reaper. Radical, dude!

A: Keanu Reeves, Alex Winter, George Carlin, William Sadler, Joss Ackland

© ORION PICTURES CORPORATION 8765

BILL & TED'S EXCELLENT ADVENTURE

D: Stephen Herek — 90 m

PG | COM | 1989 | COLOR

7 A charmer and surprise hit! Two very hip but very stupid California high school radical dudes (Reeves and Winter) are failing history in grand fashion. To their rescue appears George Carlin, a futuristic guardian angel who possesses a magical phone booth that allows time travel. The pair climb aboard and experience history first hand, meeting the likes of Joan of Arc, Caesar, Napoleon, Beethoven and Socrates, all of whom make for an excellent history presentation. Loaded with laughs. Very cool, dude!

□ Sex □ Nud □ Viol ◢ Lang □ AdSit

A: Keanu Reeves, Alex Winter, George Carlin, Bernie Casey, Amy Stock-Poynton, Tony Camilieri

© NEW LINE HOME VIDEO 8741

BILL COSBY - HIMSELF

D: Bill Cosby, Jr. — 104 m

PG | COM | 1981 | COLOR

8 Concert footage filmed at Toronto's Hamilton Place Performing Arts Center of Bill Cosby imparting his wit and wisdom on such subjects as natural childbirth, raising children, going to the dentist and drinking.

□ Sex □ Nud □ Viol □ Lang ◢ AdSit

A: Bill Cosby

© CBS/FOX VIDEO 1350

BILLY CRYSTAL, A COMIC'S LINE

D: Bruce Gowers — 59 m

NR | COM | 1984 | COLOR

8 This was an HBO special that was later released on tape. Very funny and innovative performance. Billy presents a whole assortment of his patented characters.

□ Sex □ Nud □ Viol ◢ Lang ◢ AdSit

A: Billy Crystal

© PARAMOUNT HOME VIDEO 2329

BILLY CRYSTAL - DON'T GET ME STARTED

D: Paul Flaherty, Billy Crystal — 61 m

NR | COM | 1986 | COLOR

6 This is a two-part video. In the first part, Rob Reiner interviews Billy Crystal as he impersonates Sammy Davis Jr., Whoopi Goldberg and himself, about the behind-the-scenes happenings before showtime. The second part is Crystal live on stage at Hofstra University.

□ Sex □ Nud □ Viol ◢ Lang ◢ AdSit

A: Billy Crystal

© LIVE HOME VIDEO 3140

BILOXI BLUES

D: Mike Nichols — 105 m

PG-13 | COM DMA | 1988 | COLOR

7 Interesting and funny. The second Neil Simon story about his autobiographical character, Eugene Jerome, who was first introduced in BRIGHTON BEACH MEMOIRS. WWII is winding down now but Eugene still goes to Army basic training in Mississippi for ten weeks, where he is harassed by his sadistic drill sergeant and an equally hostile platoon. He has only two goals: to get through this ordeal and to lose his virginity. His only weapon in these battles is his sense of humor. Broderick narrates over the storyline, making interesting observations on his buddies and life in general.

◢ Sex □ Nud □ Viol ■ Lang ◢ AdSit

A: Matthew Broderick, Christopher Walken, Matt Mulhern, Casey Siemaszko, Penelope Ann Miller, Corey Parker

© MCA/UNIVERSAL HOME VIDEO, INC. 80799

BINGO LONG TRAVELING ALL-STARS, THE

D: John Badham — 111 m

PG | COM | 1976 | COLOR

8 Lively and funny comedy set in 1939, in the days of the old Negro Leagues, when blacks were barred from playing in the majors. Williams plays a baseball player who battles the Negro League's management by starting his own razzle dazzle team. His team of lively characters barnstorms its way through rural America, where they must also resort to conning, clowning and stealing just to survive. A great cast captures the feel of the period and has a whole lot of fun with the time and the subject. So do we... a real good time.

□ Sex □ Nud □ Viol ◢ Lang ◢ AdSit

A: Billy Dee Williams, James Earl Jones, Richard Pryor, Ted Ross

© MCA/UNIVERSAL HOME VIDEO, INC. 66056

BIRD ON A WIRE

D: John Badham — 110 m

PG-13 | COM ACT | 1990 | COLOR

6 Cliched and predictable, but a good time if you'll check your brain at the door. Hawn is a successful BMW-driving yuppie lawyer who, while stopped for gas, thinks she recognizes Gibson as a long-dead lover with an appropriately aged face. It is! Gibson had snitched on an international ring of drug smugglers and is now protected by the FBI, but... on this very day, the killers are released from prison and have caught up with him. Hawn now rescues Gibson when the bullets start to fly, and the pair rekindle their romance on the lam, running from some very bad guys. Formula, but fun.

□ Sex ◢ Nud ◢ Viol ◢ Lang ◢ AdSit

A: Mel Gibson, Goldie Hawn, David Carradine, Bill Duke, Joan Severance, Stephen Tobolowsky

© MCA/UNIVERSAL HOME VIDEO, INC. 80959

BLACK AND WHITE IN COLOR

D: Jean-Jacques Annaud — 90 m

PG | FOR COM | 1976 | COLOR

8 This is a very funny film and was the surprise winner in 1976 of the Oscar for Best Foreign Film over the more highly-touted COUSINE, COUSINE and SEVEN BEAUTIES. It is the whimsical story of two remote European settlements in Africa, one German and one French, which have been existing peacefully side-by-side for years. But with the outset of WWI, the French decide it is their duty to attack the Germans. So one of them recruits a bunch of surrounding natives and equips them with shoes, bayonets and French names for a battle which falters pitifully. Biting satire. Subtitles.

□ Sex ◢ Nud ◢ Viol ◢ Lang □ AdSit

A: Jean Carmet, Jacques Spiesser, Catherine Rouvel

© WARNER HOME VIDEO 803

BLACK MARBLE, THE

D: Harold Becker — 110 m

PG | CRM COM ACT | 1980 | COLOR

7 An insightful, charming and sometimes funny look at a hard-drinking cop who is slowly killing himself with alcohol to dull the realities of his job. He is assigned a sexy new female detective who thinks he is crazy and obsolete. She wants to have as little as possible to do with him. When they are assigned the case of retrieving a kidnapped prize dog from a sleazy dog breeder, she changes her mind about him and falls in love with him. (There is a wonderful seduction scene in his apartment.) This movie slides from comedy into drama into action. It is good but also slightly uneven.

□ Sex □ Nud ◢ Viol ◢ Lang ◢ AdSit

A: Paula Prentiss, Robert Foxworth, Harry Dean Stanton, Barbara Babcock, John Hancock, Judy Landers

© NEW LINE HOME VIDEO 1617

BLAZE

D: Ron Shelton — 117 m

R | DMA COM ROM | 1989 | COLOR

7 Hollywood's romantic-comedy version of the outlandish life and love of real-life Louisiana Governor Earl K. Long, who did have a scandalous affair with the flamboyant showgirl and stripper, Blaze Starr. Newman is energetic and full of ornery charm as the crusty Earl Long, and Lolita Davidovich puts in a "outstanding" and sexy performance as the famous Blaze Starr. The feisty Long struggles to survive repeated attacks on himself and his governorship, all the while it is he who is giving them some of their best ammunition. Look for the real Blaze Starr in a cameo role.

◢ Sex ■ Nud □ Viol ■ Lang ■ AdSit

A: Paul Newman, Lolita Davidovich, Robert Wuhl, Jeffrey DeMunn

© TOUCHSTONE HOME VIDEO 915

BLAZING SADDLES

D: Mel Brooks — 93 m

R | COM WST | 1974 | COLOR

9 Hilarious! This is a savage spoof of Westerns (DODGE CITY in particular). It is uproariously funny but also unflinchingly crude. The jokes are rapid fire and constant. The story revolves around Cleavon Little as the unlikely black sheriff being challenged by Harvey Korman's bad guy character. Madelin Kahn does a riotous Dietrich parody, Alex Karras knocks out a horse, and don't forget the beans around the campfire scene. Belly-laugh city. Also don't forget to see the unrelated but equally hilarious Western spoofs SUPPORT YOUR LOCAL SHERIFF and CAT BALLOU!

□ Sex □ Nud ◢ Viol ■ Lang ■ AdSit

A: Cleavon Little, Gene Wilder, Harvey Korman, Madeline Kahn, Mel Brooks, Slim Pickens

© WARNER HOME VIDEO 1001

BLIND FURY

D: Phillip Noyce — 86 m

R | ACT COM | 1990 | COLOR

7 Odd action film with a premise that is sometimes unexpectedly funny while at the same time very violent. Rutger Hauer is a Vietnam vet who was blinded in a battle but has become a martial arts expert. So, when his best buddy (O'Quinn) is kidnapped by gangsters and forced into the drug business, Hauer sets off with O'Quinn's son to Las Vegas to bring down the bad guys. And, he makes mince meat out of them with his finely honed blind-man swordplay. The tongue-in-cheek humor will surprise you as they chop their way through one wild adventure after another. Very curious and interesting.

□ Sex □ Nud ■ Viol ■ Lang ◢ AdSit

A: Rutger Hauer, Terry O'Quinn, Brandon Call, Lisa Blount, Randall Cobb, Meg Foster

© COLUMBIA TRISTAR HOME VIDEO 70253

BLISS

D: Ray Lawrence 112 m

R | DMA COM FAN | 1985 | COLOR

7 A very original, unusual and extremely black comedy, and the 1985 Australian Best Picture winner. A successful and seemingly happy advertising executive dies for four minutes and comes back into an apparently different world, which has many of the same players in it but they are all drastically changed. His wife is openly carrying on an affair with his partner, his son deals dope and wants to join the mob, his daughter is a doper and will do anything to get it and an elephant sits on his car. A very odd, nightmarish vision of modern life.

Sex, Nud, Viol, Lang, AdSit

A: Barry Otto, Lynette Curran, Helen Jones, Miles Buchanan

© R&G VIDEO, LP 80024

BORN YESTERDAY

D: Luis Mandoki 100 m

PG | COM ROM | 1993 | COLOR

7 Pleasant, but not sparkling, remake of the 1950 Judy Holliday classic. Billie (Melanie Griffith) is a sexy but dim-witted former showgirl who is mistress to a loutish real estate developer (John Goodman). They have come to Washington DC so that he can lobby some senators into keeping a military base open and get even richer. However, her ignorant comments have embarrassed him so much that he has hired a bookish reporter (Don Johnson) to tutor her. Instead, the seemingly dim-witted Billie learns too well. She learns that she doesn't have to accept being treated so badly and that she is also falling for the mild-mannered reporter.

Sex, Nud, Viol, Lang, AdSit

A: Melanie Griffith, John Goodman, Don Johnson, Edward Herrmann, Max Perlich, Fred Dalton Thomas

© HOLLYWOOD PICTURES HOME VIDEO 1740

BLISS OF MRS. BLOSSOM, THE

D: Joseph McGrath 93 m

PG | COM | 1968 | COLOR

7 An original oddball farcical comedy. Shirley MacLaine is a delight as the bored and unhappy wife of a successful bra manufacturer who she loves. One day her sewing machine breaks down, so she asks her husband to send someone to come fix it. He sends a little bumbler who fixes her machine, but she is so taken with him that she seduces him. He then refuses to leave and takes up permanent residence in her attic. She now has, for her, the perfect arrangement: a daytime lover in the attic and her husband at home each night. A truly strange premise, except that it is based upon fact.

Sex, Nud, Viol, Lang, AdSit

A: Shirley MacLaine, Richard Attenborough, James Booth, Freddie Jones, Bob Monkhouse, John Cleese

© PARAMOUNT HOME VIDEO 6810

BOY FRIEND, THE

D: Ken Russell 137 m

G | MUS COM | 1971 | COLOR

6 When the leading lady (Jackson) breaks her ankle, she is quickly replaced by the assistant stage manager (Twiggy). This is an interesting musical that works actually in two different ways. First, as a 1920s musical production of "The Boy Friend," which is being put on at a tacky matinee; and also as a vehicle for the much more elaborate Busby Berkeley production numbers which occur within the day-dreams of the matinee's participants. It will be most entertaining to fans of the '30s musicals genre. Fourteen songs in all. Glenda Jackson has a cameo as the lead hoofer.

Sex, Nud, Viol, Lang, AdSit

A: Twiggy, Christopher Gable, Moyra Fraser, Max Adrian, Vladek Sheybal, Glenda Jackson

Distributed By MGM/UA Home Video M200306

BLUES BROTHERS, THE

D: John Landis 133 m

R | COM MUS | 1980 | COLOR

8 Funny movie and some great music, too. It is a farcical adventure in which two losers (Aykroyd and Belushi) find that the orphanage they grew up in has fallen on hard times, so they decide to resurrect their old blues band to raise some money to save it. Riotous misadventures ensue as they gather everyone up, get a gig in a redneck bar and very nearly destroy Chicago with several car chases on their way to a benefit concert. Many major stars like Aretha Franklin, James Brown and Ray Charles cameo. A lot of slapstick and some dynamite music, too.

Sex, Nud, Viol, Lang, AdSit

A: John Belushi, Dan Aykroyd, John Candy, Carrie Fisher, Cab Calloway, Ray Charles

© MCA/UNIVERSAL HOME VIDEO, INC. 77000

BOYS NIGHT OUT

D: Michael Gordon 115 m

NR | COM | 1962 | COLOR

8 Entertaining comedy about a trio of married men from the suburbs, and one bachelor (Garner), who decide they need some extracurricular excitement and so lease an apartment in NYC for their activities. Gorgeous Kim Novak is a college student and is the object of their attentions. However, unknown to them, she is just doing research into sex, but her experiment has gotten out of hand. This is an early 60s screwball comedy in which innuendos are used liberally but there is no substance to back them up. The plot gains considerable comic support from these would-be playboy's wives.

Sex, Nud, Viol, Lang, AdSit

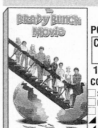

A: Kim Novak, James Garner, Tony Randall, Howard Duff, Janet Blair, Patti Page

Distributed By MGM/UA Home Video M204546

BLUME IN LOVE

D: Paul Mazursky 115 m

R | COM DMA | 1973 | COLOR

7 Enjoyable comedy/drama. George Segal is a philandering, successful divorce attorney who gets caught cheating by his wife. When she dumps him, he can't believe that it's over and that she doesn't love him anymore... he loves her. He still doesn't believe it, even after she moves in with hippie Kristofferson. He still loves her, pathetically pursuing her. In fact, he never knew how much he loved her until she divorced him. Funny, but too much truth in it to laugh too hard.

Sex, Nud, Viol, Lang, AdSit

A: George Segal, Susan Anspach, Kris Kristofferson, Marsha Mason, Shelley Winters

© WARNER HOME VIDEO 11085

BRADY BUNCH MOVIE, THE

D: Betty Thomas 90 m

PG-13 | COM | 1995 | COLOR

7 The 1970's TV series was a tremendous hit, particularly in reruns - although not usually because it was so true-to-life, but rather because it wasn't. Its audience loved to laugh at the overly-simplistic and moralizing plots; and the perpetually happy and too-nice characters. This film is a parody of that earlier unintentional parody, and it is so successful at it that you don't need to be a fan to laugh at the jokes. The plot is almost inconsequential. What is important is the premise. The Bradys are again a too-nice 70's family, happily dressed in polyester and walking on green shag carpet, however now they live in the rough-and-tumble 90s but are still happily ignorant of all the problems that surrounds them.

Sex, Nud, Viol, Lang, AdSit

A: Shelley Long, Gary Cole, Christine Taylor, Christopher Barnes, Jennifer Elise Cox, Michael McKean

© PARAMOUNT HOME VIDEO 32952

BOB & CAROL & TED & ALICE

D: Paul Mazursky 104 m

R | COM DMA | 1969 | COLOR

6 Satirical look at the changing and confused sexual mores in the 1960s. Robert Culp, a successful, sophisticated filmmaker, and his wife (Natalie Wood) go to a sensitivity-encounter institute just to observe, but get so involved that they decide to test their relationship with an affair with someone else. Who better to test their new freedom with than their best friends (Elliot Gould and Diane Cannon), who are confused by all this, especially when they wind up four to a bed. Lots of funny and some insightful moments.

Sex, Nud, Viol, Lang, AdSit

A: Natalie Wood, Robert Kulp, Elliott Gould, Dyan Cannon

© GOODTIMES 4204

BREAKFAST AT TIFFANY'S

D: Blake Edwards 114 m

NR | ROM DMA COM | 1961 | COLOR

9 Totally captivating. Audrey Hepburn plays young, beautiful and fanciful Holly Golightly. She is an innocent at play in an imagined world of elegance and fun and captures the imagination and the affections of a struggling writer, George Peppard. This is a tender love story of a small-town girl who caught up in the pursuit of the trappings of glamour and big-city life. Hepburn is absolutely captivating as this little girl lost. A charming and tender love story, perfectly complemented by Mancini's Oscar-winning score.

Sex, Nud, Viol, Lang, AdSit

A: Audrey Hepburn, George Peppard, Patricia Neal, Buddy Ebsen, Mickey Rooney, Martin Balsam

© PARAMOUNT HOME VIDEO 6505

BOB ROBERTS

D: Tim Robbins 102 m

R | DMA COM | 1992 | COLOR

8 Satire and parody of American politics. Tim Robbins plays Bob Roberts, an ultra-conservative child of liberal parents in the 60s. Bob, however, has risen from and abandoned his childhood roots in a commune, to become an unscrupulous multi-millionaire stocktrader and a born-again conservative. He released several "folk" albums and music videos which became popular, has promoted himself into a national sensation and is a populist candidate for a US Senate against a righteous and virtuous incumbent liberal (Gore Vidal). Very well received by the critics. However, its political theme and left-bias will limit its general audience appeal.

Sex, Nud, Viol, Lang, AdSit

A: Tim Robbins, Giancarlo Esposito, Alan Rickman, Gore Vidal, Brian Murray, Ray Wise

© LIVE HOME VIDEO 69898

BREAKFAST CLUB, THE

D: John Hughes 92 m

R | DMA COM | 1985 | COLOR

8 Quite good, perceptive, non-exploitive teen movie. A group of five totally different high school kids spend eight hours of detention together on a Saturday. At its start they have nothing in common, but during this day-long stretch of forced togetherness, the nerd, the jock, the delinquent, the prom queen and the kooky introvert all get to know each other, find that they have more in common than they ever thought and even become friends. Very funny at times, and interesting throughout.

Sex, Nud, Viol, Lang, AdSit

A: Molly Ringwald, Ally Sheedy, Emilio Estevez, Anthony Michael Hall, Judd Nelson

© MCA/UNIVERSAL HOME VIDEO, INC. 80167

BREAKING AWAY

D: Peter Yates — 100 m

PG | COM DMA | 1979 | COLOR

9 Wonderful sleeper and Best Picture Oscar nominee. It is a touching story of love, growing up and class differences. Four working-class teenagers just out of high school are scorned by the college kids in town. One becomes fixated on becoming a bicycle racing champion and tries to win a college girl over by pretending he's an Italian racer. When his cover is blown and the college boys further scorn his efforts, he and his friends decide to prove themselves as equals by winning the college bike race. This appealing, unpretentious film is funny, tender, insightful and entirely enjoyable.

□ Sex □ Nud □ Viol ◢ Lang ◢ AdSit

A: Dennis Christopher, Dennis Quaid, Robyn Douglas, Daniel Stern, Jackie Earle Haley, Barbara Barrie

© FOXVIDEO 1081

BREAKING IN

D: Bill Forsyth — 95 m

R | COM | 1989 | COLOR

7 Quirky and fun. Reynolds is in top form as an aging burglar who meets another younger burglar (Siemaszko) while each is breaking into the very same house. Reynolds seizes the opportunity and decides that Siemaszko would make a great partner. Reynolds takes him under his wing, teaching him some tricks of the trade, and together the pair commit one hilarious caper after another, trying very hard not to get caught. However, Siemaszko falls for a beautiful woman and starts spending too much money, which arouses police suspicion in no time. Spiffy and effervescent.

□ Sex □ Nud □ Viol ■ Lang ◢ AdSit

A: Burt Reynolds, Casey Siemaszko, Sheila Kelley, Lorraine Toussaint, Albert Salmi, Harry Carey, Jr.

© HBO VIDEO 0380

BREWSTER MC CLOUD

D: Robert Altman — 101 m

R | COM DMA | 1970 | COLOR

7 Definitely different. If you liked M*A*S*H or HAROLD AND MAUDE, or if your funny bone is off center, this black comedy may appeal to you. This is the story about a boy who grows up inside the Astrodome, in a bombshelter. He is protected by Sally Kellerman and taught by her to believe in dreams - even that he will be able to fly on his giant homemade wings. However, when some of Houston's richest citizens are murdered and are found covered in bird droppings, he becomes a prime suspect. A lot of quirky humor. Definitely original.

◢ Sex ◢ Nud ◢ Viol ◢ Lang ◢ AdSit

A: Bud Cort, Sally Kellerman, Michael Murphy, William Windom, Shelley Duvall, Stacy Keach

Distributed By MGM/UA Home Video M700466

BRIGHTON BEACH MEMOIRS

D: Gene Saks — 110 m

PG-13 | COM DMA | 1986 | COLOR

7 Neil Simon's semi-autobiographical comedy about a 15-year-old adolescent boy growing up in an overcrowded house in 1930s Brooklyn. It is the story of the whole family and their problems as seen from his viewpoint, while he is himself trying to deal with his own growing-up problems. Nostalgic and funny. If you like this, you may also be interested in seeing the next installment, BELOXI BLUES.

◢ Sex □ Nud □ Viol ◢ Lang ◢ AdSit

A: Jonathan Silverman, Blythe Danner, Bob Dishy, Brian Brillinger, Stacey Glick, Judith Ivey

© MCA/UNIVERSAL HOME VIDEO, INC. 80476

BRINK'S JOB, THE

D: William Friedkin — 103 m

PG | COM CRM | 1978 | COLOR

8 Highly entertaining and funny account of the famous 1950 Boston Brink's vault robbery, told with a light touch. Peter Falk stars as the head of a gang of klutzes that somehow pulls off the crime of the century - almost. They get $2.7 million, lead the government on a very long, very expensive chase and then get caught just one week before the statute of limitations runs out. Lots of fun.

□ Sex □ Nud ◢ Viol ◢ Lang □ AdSit

A: Peter Falk, Peter Boyle, Allen Garfield, Warren Oates, Paul Sorvino, Gena Rowlands

© MCA/UNIVERSAL HOME VIDEO, INC. 80062

BROADCAST NEWS

D: James L. Brooks — 132 m

R | COM DMA | 1987 | COLOR

9 Intelligent, extremely clever and entertaining take-no-prisoners look at TV news in general, and an odd love triangle in particular. Wonderful performances. Hurt is a popular, well-meaning and extremely photogenic anchorman, but he doesn't really understand the news he's reading. Hunter is a very bright and extremely driven producer who is attracted to him in spite of the fact that he represents everything she despises about TV news. She, is loved in turn by Brooks, who is a supercompetent reporter but becomes extremely nervous and sweats profusely when on camera. Five Oscar nominations. Great stuff.

□ Sex ◢ Nud □ Viol ■ Lang ■ AdSit

A: William Hurt, Albert Brooks, Holly Hunter, Robert Prosky, Lois Chiles, Jack Nicholson

© FOXVIDEO 1654

BROADWAY DANNY ROSE

D: Woody Allen — 85 m

PG | COM | 1984 | COLOR

7 Woody Allen wrote, directed and starred as talent agent Broadway Danny Rose. Danny Rose is a small-time manager who has no talent for selecting talent and has too soft of a heart to boot. His best chance to succeed and his principal client is an alcoholic over-the-hill crooner named Lou Canova, who is married but carrying on an affair with a gangster's tough-talking girlfriend, Mia Farrow. When Canova gets a chance to move up, Allen has to pretend to be Farrow's boyfriend, which is not a healthy thing to be. Entertaining little comic fable.

□ Sex □ Nud □ Viol ◢ Lang ◢ AdSit

A: Woody Allen, Mia Farrow, Milton Berle, Sandy Baron, Corbett Monica, Jackie Gayle

© LIVE HOME VIDEO 5041

BRONCO BILLY

D: Clint Eastwood — 117 m

PG | COM ROM | 1980 | COLOR

7 Engaging, lighthearted story of a troop of oddball characters working for a flea-bag wild west show. Eastwood is the idealistic owner, ace sharpshooter and self-styled star of his nearly-broke traveling Wild West Show. He and his troop of dedicated performers just want to entertain. Sondra Locke is a spoiled little rich girl who is abandoned by her husband on her honeymoon and finds a home when she becomes part of the show as Eastwood's assistant. Eastwood acts, directs and even sings with Merle Haggard. This simple little story has been unduly underrated by many critics. It's just fun.

□ Sex □ Nud □ Viol ◢ Lang ◢ AdSit

A: Clint Eastwood, Sondra Locke, Geoffrey Lewis, Scatman Crothers, Bill McKinney, Dan Vadis

© WARNER HOME VIDEO 11104

BRONX TALE, A

D: Robert De Niro — 122 m

R | DMA COM | 1993 | COLOR

9 Excellent. Colagero, C for short, is the son of Lorenzo, a hard working honest bus driver. The family lives two doors down from the neighborhood bar where Sonny, a gangster, holds court. C has two heros, his father and Sonny. Sonny spent ten years in prison and he spent his time reading. He is smart, he is tough and he loves C. Even though his father has forbidden it, C is infatuated with Sonny and Sonny watches out for him. From his father, C learns integrity and from Sonny he learns hard lessens about people and life. Brilliant first-time directing effort from De Niro, who flawlessly blends humor, drama and violence into a highly watchable tale of morality.

□ Sex □ Nud ■ Viol ■ Lang ◢ AdSit

A: Robert De Niro, Chazz Palminteri, Luillo Brancato, Francis Capra, Taral Hicks

© HBO VIDEO 90954

BUCK AND THE PREACHER

D: Sidney Poitier — 102 m

PG | WST COM | 1972 | COLOR

6 Pretty good and different sort of Western, but with a relatively thin plot. Buck (Poitier) is a black ex-Union Army Cavalry sergeant who agrees to act as scout for a wagon train of freed slaves heading to Colorado. Belafonte is a black con man and phony preacher who comes along. The preacher and Buck are forced to team up to defeat a group of white bounty hunters, led by the chief bad guy, Cameron Mitchell, who wants to kidnap them all and take them to Louisiana. Clever and light-hearted in spots. Warm with good characterizations.

□ Sex □ Nud □ Viol ◢ Lang □ AdSit

A: Sidney Poitier, Harry Belafonte, Cameron Mitchell, Ruby Dee

© COLUMBIA TRISTAR HOME VIDEO 60148

BUDDY SYSTEM, THE

D: Glenn Jordan — 110 m

PG | ROM COM | 1983 | COLOR

7 Nice little charmer. Wil Wheaton and his struggling, insecure, single Mom, make friends with a security guard, who is also a part-time novelist and a part-time inventor (Richard Dreyfuss), and is also struggling in a relationship with his ditzy, unfaithful girlfriend. Wil wants a father, but Mom and Dreyfuss are sure they are just friends. However, in spite of all their concerns and precautions, love triumphs. Dreyfuss learns to give up his unfaithful fantasy girl and Sarandon learns to trust again. This is a pleasing, enjoyable story, even if much of it is predictable. It is both funny and heartwarming.

□ Sex □ Nud □ Viol ◢ Lang ◢ AdSit

A: Richard Dreyfuss, Susan Sarandon, Jean Stapleton, Nancy Allen, Wil Wheaton

© FOXVIDEO 1316

BUFFY THE VAMPIRE SLAYER

D: Fran Rubel Kuzui — 86 m

PG-13 | COM HOR | 1992 | COLOR

7 Buffy is a spoiled and very popular "valley girl" totally into herself, her girl friends, her boy friend and cheerleading. Until, that is, she is visited by a mysterious old dude (Sutherland) who explains that the weird dreams she's been having are memories from her past lives. Buffy, you see, is the chosen one. Only she has the power to destroy the vampire plagues when they erupt, and one has now erupted in Southern California. Buffy must rise out of her innocent high school world to become the protector of the "real" world. This is a fun, wacky teen film that does a good job at making fun of itself and everything else.

□ Sex □ Nud ◢ Viol ◢ Lang ■ AdSit

A: Kristy Swanson, Luke Perry, Donald Sutherland, Rutger Hauer, Paul Reubens

© FOXVIDEO 1972

BULL DURHAM

D: Ron Shelton 108 m

R | COM ROM | 1988 | COLOR | Rating: 8

A truly charming and fun romantic comedy about the odd lifestyle surrounding a North Carolina minor league baseball team. Kevin Costner is an veteran catcher past his prime but who has been charged by management with helping to develop an immature young pitcher who has a powerful arm, a terrific fast ball and no brains. Susan Sarandon is a smart but quirky baseball groupie who each year chooses one player to give the benefit of her experience and her affections. This year she chooses the dumb pitcher, but Costner changes her mind. This is a quite intelligent little winner. You may also want to see LONG GONE.

Sex / Nud / Viol / Lang / AdSit

A: Kevin Costner, Susan Sarandon, Tim Robbins, Trey Wilson, Robert Wuhl, Jenny Robertson

© ORION PICTURES CORPORATION 8722

BULLETS OVER BROADWAY

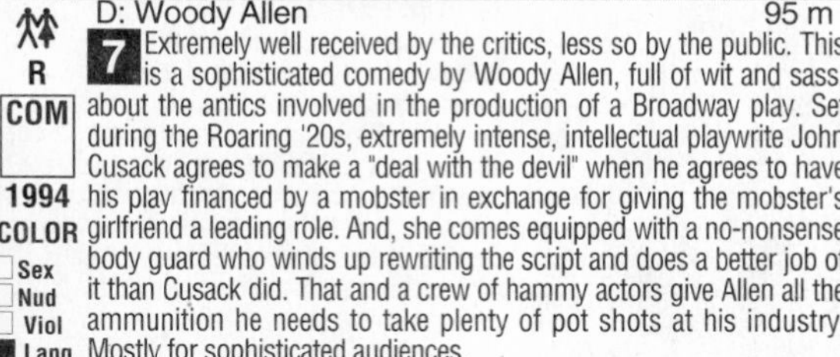

D: Woody Allen 95 m

R | COM | 1994 | COLOR | Rating: 7

Extremely well received by the critics, less so by the public. This is a sophisticated comedy by Woody Allen, full of wit and sass, about the antics involved in the production of a Broadway play. Set during the Roaring '20s, extremely intense, intellectual playwrite John Cusack agrees to make a "deal with the devil" when he agrees to have his play financed by a mobster in exchange for giving the mobster's girlfriend a leading role. And, she comes equipped with a no-nonsense body guard who winds up rewriting the script and does a better job of it than Cusack did. That and a crew of hammy actors give Allen all the ammunition he needs to take plenty of pot shots at his industry. Mostly for sophisticated audiences.

Sex / Nud / Viol / Lang / AdSit

A: John Cusack, Chazz Palminteri, Diane Weist, Jennifer Tilly, Tracey Ullman, Jim Broadbent

© MIRAMAX HOME ENTERTAINMENT 4368

BUONA SERA, MRS. CAMPBELL

D: Melvin Frank 111 m

NR | COM ROM | 1968 | COLOR | Rating: 7

Interesting premise for a comedy that works well due to an excellent cast. The beautiful Italian mother (Gina Lollogrigida) of a pretty 20-year-old daughter has been accepting support checks for years from three different American men who each think he fathered the girl during WWII. Now, all three men are coming back for a twentieth anniversary Army reunion, and they're bringing their wives along. Another further complication in Gina's life is that her daughter wants to meet her father. Gina is understandably in a panic. Good fun.

Sex / Nud / Viol / Lang / AdSit

A: Gina Lollobrigida, Peter Lawford, Shelley Winters, Phil Silvers, Telly Savalas, Lee Grant

Distributed By MGM/UA Home Video 203045

BURIED ALIVE

D: Frank Darabont 93 m

PG-13 | SUS COM | 1990 | COLOR | Rating: 7

A film that delights in bad taste and grotesque humor. A love-starved housewife who's terribly bored with her husband goes out and gets herself a new lover. She convinces her new boyfriend doctor that everything would be just wonderful if he would only kill her husband, and so he does. All is well for a short while but then all hell breaks loose when her presumed dead husband literally crawls back from the grave! Black comedy abounds, darkness surrounds, but all in a very slick way that will keep you glued to your seat and unwilling to turn away.

Sex / Nud / Viol / Lang / AdSit

A: Tim Matheson, Jennifer Jason Leigh, William Atherton, Hoyt Axton, Jay Gerber

© MCA/UNIVERSAL HOME VIDEO, INC. 80939

BUSTING

D: Peter Hyams 89 m

R | CRM COM ACT | 1973 | COLOR | Rating: 6

Gould and Blake are unconventional Los Angeles vice cops who are restricted to arresting small-time druggies and hookers because the big ones are getting protection from the higher-ups in the department. A fairly realistic, sometimes funny, depiction of police life. Gould and Blake are glib and have a good chemistry which makes this a reasonably entertaining buddy-cop movie.

Sex / Nud / Viol / Lang / AdSit

A: Elliott Gould, Robert Blake, Allen Garfield, Antonio Fargas, Michael Lerner, Sid Haig

Distributed By MGM/UA Home Video M801407

BUSTIN' LOOSE

D: Oz Scott 94 m

R | COM | 1981 | COLOR | Rating: 8

This is a warm and positive picture in spite of some pretty heavy-duty language that could just as well have been left out. Pryor plays a parolee who chooses to drive a busload of emotionally and physically handicapped youngsters across country to Washington State rather than go back to jail. However, his trip isn't a pleasant one. Along the way he must deal with the rebellious kids, their antagonistic teacher (Cicely Tyson), constant mechanical breakdowns and a confrontation with the KKK. There are some really funny moments here.

Sex / Nud / Viol / Lang / AdSit

A: Richard Pryor, Cicely Tyson, Alphonso Alexander, Robert Christian, George Coe, Janet Wong

© MCA/UNIVERSAL HOME VIDEO, INC. 77002

BUTCH AND SUNDANCE: THE EARLY DAYS

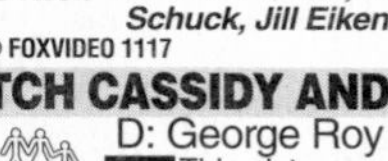

D: Richard Lester 111 m

PG | WST COM | 1979 | COLOR | Rating: 7

This prequel to the Redford/Newman pairing from the original blockbuster, imagines the same characters as they were when they were still just learning their trade. This easy-to-take follow up traces their adventures from the time of their first meeting, just after Butch is released from prison, and takes them through their early, not-too-good holdup attempts. The leads in this picture (Katt and Beringer), like Newman and Redford, are likable. The film is interesting in its own right, but is far overshadowed by its more illustrious predecessor.

Sex / Nud / Viol / Lang / AdSit

A: William Katt, Tom Berenger, Jeff Corey, John Corey, John Schuck, Jill Eikenberry

© FOXVIDEO 1117

BUTCH CASSIDY AND THE SUNDANCE KID

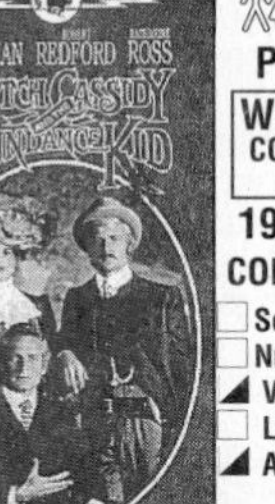

D: George Roy Hill 110 m

PG | WST COM | 1969 | COLOR | Rating: 10

This picture was a spectacular box office hit and deservedly so. It also won 4 Oscars. Newman and Redford are extremely likable as two fun-loving bank and train robbers who are relentlessly pursued by an unshakable Sheriff's posse... "Who is that guy anyway?" So they escape to Bolivia with Sundance's girlfriend (Ross) but they can't even rob the banks there properly because they can't speak the language. Great dialogue and chemistry between the players makes this an utter joy to watch. Extremely entertaining. Do not miss this one.

Sex / Nud / Viol / Lang / AdSit

A: Paul Newman, Robert Redford, Katharine Ross, Strother Martin, Cloris Leachman, Henry James

© FOXVIDEO 1061

BUTCHER'S WIFE, THE

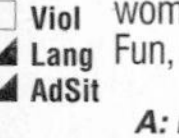
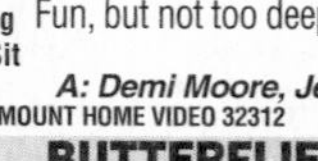

D: Terry Hughes 107 m

PG-13 | FAN COM ROM | 1991 | COLOR | Rating: 6

Curious and terribly fanciful! As a little girl, Marina (Moore) dreams that her true love will just simply find her. So one day when Dzunda washes up on shore, apparently right on cue, she believes that her psychic powers have drawn them together and they can't be denied. Without a second thought, she marries him and runs off to his Greenwich Village butcher shop with him. There, she promptly becomes a neighborhood sensation, when her uncannily perceptive advice consistently works and her predictions come true. Psychiatrist Daniels becomes especially entranced with this strange woman, but then love blooms between them and confuses everyone. Fun, but not too deep.

Sex / Nud / Viol / Lang / AdSit

A: Demi Moore, Jeff Daniels, George Dzundza, Mary Steenburgen

© PARAMOUNT HOME VIDEO 32312

BUTTERFLIES ARE FREE

D: Milton Katselas 149 m

PG | COM ROM DMA | 1972 | COLOR | Rating: 9

Genuine pleasure of a serio-comedy. Edward Albert is a blind young man struggling to become self-sufficient. He wants break free of his over-protective (but loving) mother and also to romance his kookie next-door neighbor (Hawn). Goldie is an eccentric, aspiring actress who has fallen for this guy but has to learn how to deal with things, too. Their relationship, and all the other complications, leads to a fast-paced comedy. Nominated for three Oscars, Heckart won Best Supporting Actress. A really good time and a great feel-good movie.

Sex / Nud / Viol / Lang / AdSit

A: Goldie Hawn, Edward Albert, Jr., Eileen Heckart, Mike Warren

© COLUMBIA TRISTAR HOME VIDEO 60149

BYE BYE BIRDIE

D: George Sidney 112 m

NR | MUS COM | 1963 | COLOR | Rating: 7

Lots of fun in this film adaptation of a big Broadway hit. An Elvis-like rock 'n roll sensation is being drafted into the Army. His manager, who is facing unemployment, launches a nationwide contest to find one lucky girl to give him a last goodbye kiss on the Ed Sullivan Show. When it turns out to be Ann-Margret, her home town, particularly her father (Paul Lynde), is thrown into a tizzy. Songs include "Kids" and "Put on a Happy Face." Really entertaining little piece of musical fluff. This was also Ann-Margret's film debut.

Sex / Nud / Viol / Lang / AdSit

A: Janet Leigh, Dick Van Dyke, Bobby Rydell, Maureen Stapleton, Paul Lynde, Ann-Margret

© COLUMBIA TRISTAR HOME VIDEO 60150

CABARET

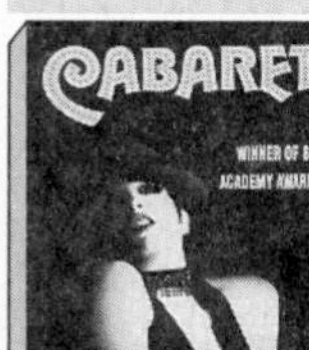

D: Bob Fosse 124 m

PG | MUS DMA COM | 1972 | COLOR | Rating: 9

A brilliant piece of work which won eight Oscars and is undoubtedly one of the best movie musicals ever. It is the story of Germany in 1931 and a young American girl caught up in its bawdy decadence. Hitler's Nazis had not yet captured full power and life was carefree, decadent and even sleazy; but doom is looming. Liza is a naive cabaret showgirl caught up in the carefree mood of the time and torn between two lovers. Wonderful songs steal the show; most notable are: "The Money Song" with Grey and Minnelli and the chorus line doing "Mein Heir."

Sex / Nud / Viol / Lang / AdSit

A: Liza Minnelli, Michael York, Helmut Griem, Joel Grey, Fritz Wepper, Marisa Berenson

© WARNER HOME VIDEO 785

CACTUS FLOWER

D: Gene Saks — 103 m

PG | COM ROM | 1969 | COLOR

8 Zany Broadway smash comedy brought to the screen. Matthau is a bachelor dentist having an affair with, and stringing along, pretty-young-thing Goldie Hawn, by telling her that he is married. When she attempts suicide, he says that he will marry her, but she refuses until she meets his wife. Having none, Matthau asks his straight-laced dowdy assistant (Bergman) to sit in as his wife. Both Matthau and Bergman are surprised to find that she is in love with him and he with her. Goldie falls for another guy - the nice guy next door. Hawn won an Oscar in her first big part. Great fun.

Sex / Nud / Viol / Lang / AdSit

A: Walter Matthau, Ingrid Bergman, Goldie Hawn, Jack Weston, Rick Lenz, Vito Scotti

© GOODTIMES 4229

CADDYSHACK

D: Harold Ramis — 98 m

R | COM | 1980 | COLOR

8 This is extraordinarily silly but it was also a major box office hit. The story is of the many tribulations occurring at and around a ritzy W.A.S.P.ish country club. A young caddy (O'Keefe) is trying to win a college scholarship. Bill Murray is a scream as a demented greenskeeper who is conducting a running battle with some particularly malicious gophers. Rodney Dangerfield is also genuinely funny as an obnoxious and crass real estate developer. It is sort of an imitation ANIMAL HOUSE but set on grass. Sophomoric and frequently crude humor.

Sex / Nud / Viol / Lang / AdSit

A: Chevy Chase, Rodney Dangerfield, Ted Knight, Michael O'Keefe, Bill Murray, Cindy Morgan

© WARNER HOME VIDEO 2005

CADILLAC MAN

D: Roger Donaldson — 97 m

R | COM DMA | 1990 | COLOR

6 Who has been sleeping with Tim Robbins's girlfriend? That's what gun-toting Robbins wants to know when he barges into a auto showroom full of customers demanding an answer. The sleezeball turns out to be salesman Robin Williams. In fact, he has been sleeping with a number of women, cheating on his wife, juggling a loan shark and trying to get his boss off his tail. Now, in this one perilous moment, Williams just may lose it all, and so he does verbal gymnastics trying to convince the crazed gunman to put that gun away. An inventive tale, hilarious in spots but uneven, too.

Sex / Nud / Viol / Lang / AdSit

A: Robin Williams, Tim Robbins, Pamela Reed, Annabella Sciorra, Fran Drescher, Zack Norman

© ORION PICTURES CORPORATION 8756

CALIFORNIA SUITE

D: Herbert Ross — 103 m

PG | COM | 1978 | COLOR

8 Neil Simon's story of one hotel room at the Beverly Hills Hotel and four separate couples who occupy it at different times. Therefore, there are four stories interwoven into this one package. The best one is that of Caine and Smith as a bickering and mismatched English couple in town for the Oscar ceremonies. Matthau trys to keep his wife from finding a hooker in his bed. Divorced Alda and Fonda fight over their daughter and his new California lifestyle. And, Bill Cosby and Richard Pryor have their friendship challenged when one thinks the other is getting snooty. Funny.

Sex / Nud / Viol / Lang / AdSit

A: Michael Caine, Maggie Smith, Jane Fonda, Alan Alda, Walter Matthau, Elaine May

© GOODTIMES 4225

CANNERY ROW

D: David S. Ward — 120 m

PG | ROM COM | 1982 | COLOR

7 Enjoyable people-story. Nick Nolte plays an ex-baseball player who has become a dedicated marine biologist. He is now conducting research in a rundown section of a California waterfront fishing village during the Depression and is also living there. Debra Winger plays an independent and likable prostitute who falls for him. She and a congregation of weird oddballs who live on Cannery Row with him give his life zest and add not-a-little confusion, but never boredom. In spite of some minor shortcomings, it's very hard not to like these characters, the story and the movie.

Sex / Nud / Viol / Lang / AdSit

A: Nick Nolte, Debra Winger, Audra Lindley, Frank McRae, M. Emmet Walsh, Sunshine Parker

Distributed By MGM/UA Home Video M800143

CAPTAIN NEWMAN, M.D.

D: David Miller — 126 m

NR | DMA COM | 1963 | COLOR

8 Affecting combination of drama and comedy. Peck is the hard-working head of psychiatry at an Army hospital at the close of WWII. He is trying to help his patients recover from serious war traumas, while also fighting off the military brass. Bobby Darin received an Oscar nomination for his performance as a war hero who has become afraid of being a coward. Tony Curtis provides laughs as a slick corporal who can be counted upon to get things done. A strong cast of supporting characters makes this realistic look inside a military mental hospital both largely-believable and enjoyable.

Sex / Nud / Viol / Lang / AdSit

A: Gregory Peck, Tony Curtis, Bobby Darin, Eddie Albert, Angie Dickinson, Jane Withers

© MCA/UNIVERSAL HOME VIDEO, INC. 80403

CARBON COPY

D: Michael Schultz — 91 m

PG | COM | 1981 | COLOR

7 This is a pleasant lightweight comedy starring George Segal as a corporate executive who is married to the boss's daughter and fully enjoying his life, when there comes a knock on the door. Standing there is the black son from a dalliance he had many years past, seeking out his father. Unfortunately for Segal, his wife and father-in-law do not take the news at all well. Sometimes silly, sometimes clever mix of social commentary and comedy.

Sex / Nud / Viol / Lang / AdSit

A: George Segal, Susan Saint James, Denzel Washington, Jack Warden, Dick Martin

© NEW LINE HOME VIDEO 1609

CARLIN AT CARNEGIE

D: Steven Santos — 596 m

NR | COM | 1983 | COLOR

6 Filmed live at Carnegie Hall. George discusses the fact that it is not always possible to "have a nice day." In fact, being told to have a nice day can be downright irritating. He also performs many of his famous routines, including the infamous "Seven Words You Can Never Say On TV." These are "big-time" words that are definitely for adults only.

Sex / Nud / Viol / Lang / AdSit

A: George Carlin

© LIVE HOME VIDEO 2017

CARLIN ON CAMPUS

D: Steven Santos — 59 m

NR | COM | 1985 | COLOR

7 One of America's funniest men is recorded live on the UCLA campus for HBO. Bits include "A Place for My Stuff." Carlin can be outrageously funny, but he is definitely outrageous and crude.

Sex / Nud / Viol / Lang / AdSit

A: George Carlin

© LIVE HOME VIDEO VA3061

CAR WASH

D: Michael Schultz — 97 m

PG | COM | 1976 | COLOR

8 Clever, fast-paced series of sketches and comedy bits revolving around the happenings at an inner-city car wash and it is all tied together with a solid rock/soul musical score. There is a whole cast of oddball characters who either work at, by or come through the car-wash, and they give this film its lighthearted flavor. Everybody gets a chance to strut their stuff, but Richard Pryor is outstanding as Daddy Rich, an evangelist with a gold limo. Plenty of slapstick, lots of laughs, some poignant moments, even a moral, but it also has its share of racial humor and vulgarity.

Sex / Nud / Viol / Lang / AdSit

A: Richard Pryor, Franklyn Ajaye, Sully Bayer, George Carlin, Irwin Corey, Melanie Mayron

© MCA/UNIVERSAL HOME VIDEO, INC. 66031

CASEY'S SHADOW

D: Martin Ritt — 117 m

PG | COM DMA CLD | 1977 | COLOR

7 Enjoyable old-time family fare. Walter Matthau is a ne'er-do-well and impoverished Cajun horse trainer whose wife has left him to raise their three sons by himself. Matthau is a simple man whose modest dream is to train a winning racehorse, but it is a dream he wants more than almost anything. He and his boys are grooming a quarter horse that the boys love, named Casey's Shadow for a million dollar race -- even though the wealthy owner Alexis Smith only wants to sell him. When the horse's leg is hurt just before the big race and even though the vet and his boys don't want the horse to race, Matthau enters the horse. Matthau almost single-handedly carries this movie.

Sex / Nud / Viol / Lang / AdSit

A: Walter Matthau, Andrew Rubin, Stephen Burns, Alexis Smith, Robert Webber, Murray Hamilton

© COLUMBIA TRISTAR HOME VIDEO 60153

CASUAL SEX ?

D: Genevieve Robert — 87 m

R | COM ROM | 1988 | COLOR

6 Two young women, Thompson and Jackson, are both looking for men but they also want a deep and meaningful relationship. So they decide to get into shape by taking a vacation at a health resort and use the opportunity to also scout out the men there. Both do their best to attract certain men that they have targeted, so that love can bloom. Unfortunately, all the men want is casual sex. Thompson does her best to fend off an obnoxious pig played by Andrew Dice Clay. Not uproariously funny, but it is amusing and a real try at talking frankly about safe sex.

Sex / Nud / Viol / Lang / AdSit

A: Lea Thompson, Victoria Jackson, Stephen Shellen, Mary Grass, Andrew Dice Clay, Jerry Levine

© MCA/UNIVERSAL HOME VIDEO, INC. 80788

CAT BALLOU

NR | COM WST | 1965 | COLOR

D: Elliot Silverstein — 96 m

10 Wonderfully funny spoof of Westerns. Jane Fonda plays a naive and innocent school teacher who turns to a life of crime after her father is killed by a crooked land baron seeking to gain control of her father's ranch. In response, she forms a rag tag gang, manned by a drunken ex-gunfighter and two cowards, to rob trains and avenge her father's murder. Lee Marvin is hysterical as both the drunken gunfighter (on a drunken horse) and his evil look-alike with a metal nose. Stubby Kaye and Nat King Cole, as traveling minstrels, punctuate the action and narrate the happenings with song. A great time.

Sex / Nud / Viol / Lang / AdSit

A: Jane Fonda, Lee Marvin, Michael Callan, Jay C. Flippen, Duane Hickman, John Marley

© COLUMBIA TRISTAR HOME VIDEO 60154

CATCH-22

R | COM WAR | 1970 | COLOR

D: Mike Nichols — 121 m

6 Captain Yossarian (Arkin) is a war-weary airman who, like most of his compatriots, wants to escape the insanity of combat. He, however, plans to do something about it and has decided to plead insanity. But according to Catch 22, if you are aware enough to say you are crazy, you can't be crazy... so you are qualified to be a soldier. Sarcastic, anti-war black comedy comes close, but sometimes misses the mark, too.

Sex / Nud / Viol / Lang / AdSit

A: Alan Arkin, Martin Balsam, Richard Benjamin, Anthony Perkins, Art Garfunkel, Bob Newhart

© PARAMOUNT HOME VIDEO 6924

CAVEMAN

PG | COM | 1981 | COLOR

D: Carl Gottlieb — 92 m

6 Silly, comic farce that is set in a prehistoric time. Ringo Starr makes the mistake of making eyes at the chief's voluptuous woman and is kicked out of the tribe for his indiscretion. So he forms his own tribe that is made up of other outcasts. Together they discover fire and create "rock" music. Slapstick aplenty and cute dinosaurs, but it's too bad that it's a too risque for kids because much of the silly humor is really better suited for them.

Sex / Nud / Viol / Lang / AdSit

A: Ringo Starr, Barbara Bach, Dennis Quaid, Shelley Long, Jack Gilford, John Matuszak

© FOXVIDEO 4543

CHANCES ARE

PG | ROM COM | 1989 | COLOR

D: Emile Ardolino — 108 m

7 Pretty good light-hearted comedy. Cybill Shepherd has remained true to her husband's memory for 23 years after his death, in spite of the persistent attentions of his best friend (Ryan O'Neal) who is also in love with her. Robert Downey Jr. is a college student who pursues Shepherd's grown daughter home from school. However, he soon uncomfortably discovers that he is the reincarnated spirit of her former husband, after being around Shepherd brings back all the feelings and memories from his former life. So he now sets out to help her to get her life back in motion and become happy again. Very well done. Sweet-natured and appealing.

Sex / Nud / Viol / Lang / AdSit

A: Cybill Shepherd, Robert Downey, Jr., Ryan O'Neal, Mary Stuart Masterson, Christopher McDonald, Josef Sommer

© COLUMBIA TRISTAR HOME VIDEO 70153

CHAPLIN REVUE, THE

NR | COM | 1958 | B&W

D: Charles Chaplin — 126 m

8 Three of Chaplin's best short features: "A Dog's Life," "Shoulder Arms," and "The Pilgrim." The pieces are woven together by music composed by Chaplin and his own narration and also includes some behind the scenes footage.

Sex / Nud / Viol / Lang / AdSit

A: Charlie Chaplin, Edna Purviance, Sydney Chaplin, Mack Swain

© CBS/FOX VIDEO 3001

CHAPTER TWO

PG | COM ROM | 1979 | COLOR

D: Robert Moore — 127 m

8 Neil Simon's autobiographical Broadway hit recounting many of his own painful personal experiences after the death of his first wife. James Caan plays a newly widowed writer (Caan) who meets a young actress (Marsha Mason, Neil Simon's real-life second wife) who is on the rebound after a failed marriage. They fall head-over-heels in love and ten days later they are married. It is only then he has a huge guilt attack over what he has just done. This makes him afraid for their futures and causes them both to analyze who and what they are. Very entertaining comedy which also will strike a resilient chord with many people.

Sex / Nud / Viol / Lang / AdSit

A: Marsha Mason, James Caan, Valerie Harper, Joseph Bologna

© GOODTIMES 4606

CHEAP DETECTIVE, THE

PG | COM MYS | 1978 | COLOR

D: Robert Moore — 92 m

7 Neil Simon has created a wacky parody of CASABLANCA, THE MALTESE FALCON and THE BIG SLEEP and it is filled with puns, sight gags and a huge bag of star players. Peter Falk plays a Bogart-like character who is in a search for a dozen diamond eggs and also becomes involved in a Casablanca-like love triangle. Very funny most of the time, particularly if you understand the references to these classic movies.

Sex / Nud / Viol / Lang / AdSit

A: Peter Falk, Ann-Margret, Eileen Brennan, Sid Caesar, Madeline Kahn, Marsha Mason

© COLUMBIA TRISTAR HOME VIDEO 90393

CHEECH AND CHONG'S NEXT MOVIE

R | COM | 1980 | COLOR

D: Thomas Chong — 95 m

6 This typical blend of the duo's patented drug humor and other irreverences is a small step above their usual silliness. Here, Cheech's cousin comes to visit. They smoke a lot of dope and wind up in a massage parlor. You either like this kind of stuff or you hate it. It is the follow up to UP IN SMOKE.

Sex / Nud / Viol / Lang / AdSit

A: Cheech Marin, Thomas Chong, Evelyn Guerrero, Betty Kennedy, Sy Kramer, Rikki Marin

© MCA/UNIVERSAL HOME VIDEO, INC. 66016

CHEYENNE SOCIAL CLUB, THE

PG | WST COM | 1970 | COLOR

D: Gene Kelly — 102 m

9 Light-hearted Western with plenty of action, too. Jimmy Stewart's brother Big John dies, leaving his "social club" to his brother. But Jimmy doesn't discover until he gets there that the club, which is Cheyenne's most popular business establishment, is also the local whorehouse. Jimmy and his scruffy long-time saddle partner (Henry Fonda) briefly enjoy their new-found career and its many benefits but then Jimmy has the misfortune to shoot an unruly customer. Now they are faced with the guy's very upset kinfolk, who are out for revenge. Great characters, all played just for fun... and fun it is. A great time.

Sex / Nud / Viol / Lang / AdSit

A: James Stewart, Henry Fonda, Shirley Jones, Sue Anne Langdon, Elaine Devry

© WARNER HOME VIDEO 11343

CHILLY SCENES OF WINTER

PG | ROM COM DMA | 1982 | COLOR

D: Joan Micklin Silver — 96 m

8 A Salt Lake City civil servant (Heard) falls very hard for pretty Hurt, who has just left her husband because he loved her too little. But now Heard loves her so intensely that she becomes scared by it all and cannot understand why she is now worthy of so much attention. Soon Heard's constant attentions and jealousy drive her back to her husband and the daughter she misses very much, but Heard still tries to win her back. Funny, but painful, too. Wonderful acting.

Sex / Nud / Viol / Lang / AdSit

A: John Heard, Mary Beth Hurt, Peter Riegert, Kenneth McMillan, Gloria Grahame

Distributed By MGM/UA Home Video M600726

CHOCOLATE WAR, THE

R | DMA COM | 1988 | COLOR

D: Keith Gordon — 103 m

7 Screen version of a very popular book set in a Catholic boys school. An idealistic freshman (Mitchell-Smith) is caught between an ambitious and ruthless teacher (Glover) and his own sense of honor. Glover wants to become headmaster through attaining the most-ever sales in the annual chocolate sale. He uses a group of bully-boys to pressure all the students into selling more than ever before, but new kid Mitchell-Smith refuses to cave in to Glover's demands and stands defiantly against him. Excellent performances and an interesting story that is best suited for teenagers.

Sex / Nud / Viol / Lang / AdSit

A: John Glover, Ilan Mitchell-Smith, Wally Ward, Bud Cort, Adam Baldwin, Jenny Wright

© VIDEO TREASURES SV9698

CHOOSE ME

R | COM DMA | 1984 | COLOR

D: Alan Rudolph — 106 m

8 Inventive and definitely different story concerning the love affairs of three loners. It is a sophisticated look at the truths and lies of love and sex in the 1980s in which the characters are actually more important than the storyline. Bujold is a radio talk show sex therapist who is actually hopelessly mixed up herself. Warren is a supposedly self-assured bar owner, but is actually constantly afraid and calls Bujold's radio show all the time for help. Carradine is the charming escaped mental case who seduces them both. This is a companion piece to WELCOME TO L.A. and REMEMBER MY NAME. Fine acting and a story that works on many levels at once.

Sex / Nud / Viol / Lang / AdSit

A: Genevieve Bujold, Keith Carradine, Lesley Ann Warren, Rae Dawn Chong, Patrick Bauchau, John Larroquette

© MEDIA HOME ENTERTAINMENT, INC. M787

CHRISTMAS STORY, A

D: Bob Clark — 95 m

PG | COM CLD | 1983 | COLOR

Sex · Nud · Viol · Lang · AdSit

9 Absolutely delightful story about growing up. Humorist Jean Sheperd relates a warmly comic story from his childhood in the 1940s, about his single-minded driving obsession with getting a Genuine Red Ryder Carbine Action Two Hundred Shot Lightning Loader BB rifle for Christmas - in spite of his mother's desperate concerns that he might put someone's eye out. Sheperd narrates the whimsical storyline himself and he is played wonderfully by Billingsley. An absolute and total delight for both young and old.

A: Peter Billingsley, Darren McGavin, Melinda Dillon, Ian Petrella, Scott Schwartz, Tedde Moore

Distributed By MGM/UA Home Video M800446

CIAO PROFESSORE!

D: Lina Wertmuller — 91 m

R | FOR COM DMA | 1994 | COLOR

Sex · Nud · Viol · ■ Lang · ■ AdSit

7 A dedicated and gentle teacher from the north of Italy is mistakenly assigned to teach a motley group of third graders at a seedy and poor town near Naples. It is a town almost without hope, as are its people. So, he is not prepared when he finds that his kids are charming. But, they are also irreverent, rebellious and extremely crude. They survive by being hard, but they want more and so they slowly begin to respond to his much softer ways. They learn from him, but he also learns from them. Consistently charming and quite funny in places, but you will have to be very tolerant of a never-ending string of vulgarities coming from the mouths of 10-year-olds. Subtitles.

A: Paolo Villaggia, Tsai Danieli, Gigio Morra, Sergio Lolli, Ester Carloni, Mario Bianco

© BUENA VISTA HOME VIDEO 3036

CINDERFELLA

D: Jerry Lewis — 88 m

NR | COM CLD | 1960 | COLOR

Sex · Nud · Viol · Lang · AdSit

6 Silly Jerry Lewis farce. The well-known children's fairy tale is rewritten to have wacky Ed Wynn become Jerry Lewis's godfather and save Jerry from his wicked stepmother and stepbrothers. Pretty weak over all, but children and Jerry Lewis fans will likely be entertained.

A: Jerry Lewis, Ed Wynn, Anna Maria Alberghetti

© VIDEO TREASURES SV9741

CITY SLICKERS

D: Ron Underwood — 114 m

PG-13 | COM DMA | 1991 | COLOR

Sex · Nud · Viol · ◢ Lang · ◢ AdSit

9 Hilarious! One heck of a good time! A real treasure. New Yorker Crystal and his friends (Stern and Kirby) are each trying to delay mid-life crises and Billy needs to find his smile again too. So, they decide that the best therapy would be to travel to the Wild West to herd cattle with a bunch of other dudes. However, they are in for a tough, soul-finding ride when the tough trail boss (Palance) dies and the real cow hands desert them, leaving the three city boys responsible for their own safety and for delivering the herd at the other end. Very believable and it will leave you smiling from ear to ear.

A: Billy Crystal, Daniel Stern, Bruno Kirby, Patricia Wettig, Helen Slater, Jack Palance

© NEW LINE HOME VIDEO 75263

CITY SLICKERS II

D: Paul Weiland — 115 m

PG-13 | COM | 1994 | COLOR

◢ Sex · Nud · ◢ Viol · ◢ Lang · ◢ AdSit

7 Like the original, this is funny, but not as. This time Mitch (Crystal) finds a map inside the brim of Curly's hat. It's a map to $20 million in gold bars that Curly's father robbed from a train in 1908. So, Mitch, his dead-beat good-for-nothing brother (Lovitz) and his pitiful best friend (Stern) head west to Nevada for treasure and adventure. They rent some horses and a buckboard, set off on a trip for lost gold and are immediately mugged by some bad guys, only to be saved by Curly's long-lost twin (also Palance). Their adventure is interspersed with episodes of self-discovery and is punctuated with several of Crystal's stand-up routines. Choppy. Fun, but not as much as the original.

A: Billy Crystal, Daniel Stern, Jon Lovitz, Jack Palance, Patricia Wettig, Noble Willingham

© COLUMBIA TRISTAR HOME VIDEO 71193

CLARA'S HEART

D: Robert Mulligan — 108 m

PG-13 | DMA COM | 1988 | COLOR

Sex · Nud · Viol · ■ Lang · ◢ AdSit

7 Whoopi Goldberg puts in an excellent performance as a Jamaican housekeeper in a torn household. The parents have just lost a baby and are on the brink of divorce. Their wise-guy son is caught up in his parent's anguish but feels neglected. He resents Goldberg's presence and takes great pleasure in giving her grief. But when the parents separate, it is she who gives him the love he craves and sets his life straight again. A winning, sentimental melodrama that is a showcase for Goldberg.

A: Whoopi Goldberg, Michael Ontkean, Kathleen Quinlan, Neil Patrick Harris, Spalding Gray, Beverly Todd

© WARNER HOME VIDEO 11823

CLASS

D: Lewis John Carlino — 98 m

R | DMA COM | 1983 | COLOR

◢ Sex · ■ Nud · Viol · ■ Lang · ■ AdSit

6 This is supposedly a comedy about a naive prep-school student (McCarthy) who falls into a wild weekend affair with a beautiful older woman (Bisset) in Chicago, only later to learn that she is also the alcoholic mother of his roommate (Lowe). As a comedy, it's only mildly entertaining and nothing special. But Bisset's troubled character gives this so-so comedy a serious overtone. The result is that some pretty good scenes get lost here amidst a lot of junk.

A: Rob Lowe, Jacqueline Bisset, Andrew McCarthy, Stuart Margolin, Cliff Robertson, John Cusack

© LIVE HOME VIDEO VA5026

CLERKS

D: Kevin Smith — m

R | COM | 1994 | B&W

Sex · Nud · Viol · ■ Lang · ■ AdSit

7 Very unusual low-budget comedy that definitely isn't for everyone. CLERKS is set largely inside a convenience store called Quick Stop Groceries. It is, in fact, written about the goings on inside and outside a convenience market and was written and directed by a 23-year-old who worked in the actual market that was featured. Dante, the principal character, is an aimless 23-year-old clerk who spends his days and nights dealing with the odd-ball characters who come in to shop, and talking with his buddy, who clerks at the video store next door and takes particular pleasure in antagonizing his customers. Amply laced with lots of vivid sex talk, but also very inventive and frequently very funny.

A: Brian O'Halloran, Jeff Anderson, Marilyn Ghigliotti, Lisa Spoonauer, Jason Mewes

© MIRAMAX HOME ENTERTAINMENT 3618

CLOSELY WATCHED TRAINS

D: Jiri Menzel — m

NR | FOR COM DMA | 1966 | B&W

◢ Sex · ◢ Nud · Viol · Lang · ■ AdSit

7 Touching Chech film about a young man who is trying to learn how to grow up in a Czechoslovakia that is under Nazi occupation. He is just a naive train dispatcher/trainee and inexperienced in virtually everything. Although he attempts to lose his virginity, he fails badly. So, his psychiatrist urges him to find an experienced woman to teach him. But his desperate search for love instead gets him involved in a plot to blow up a Nazi train. Sometimes funny and sometimes poignant. Subtitles.

A: Vaclav Neckar, Jitka Bendova

© COLUMBIA TRISTAR HOME VIDEO VH91058

COCA-COLA KID, THE

D: Dusan Makavejev — 949 m

R | COM ROM | 1985 | COLOR

◢ Sex · ■ Nud · Viol · ◢ Lang · ■ AdSit

6 Strange, light-hearted satire in which an intense young American executive arrives in Australia determined to spread Coca-Cola throughout the land. He discovers that one area is totally devoid of Coke and totally dominated by one old man's independent soft drink. With his savage intensity totally lost upon the laid-back Australians, and besieged by a kooky sexy secretary (Sacchi) who is bent on seducing him, he nevertheless endeavors to attract the stubborn old man into the Coca-Cola fold. Strange but humorous.

A: Eric Roberts, Greta Scacchi, Bill Kerr, Max Gillies, Chris Haywood, Kris McQuade

© LIVE HOME VIDEO VA5099

COCKTAIL

D: Roger Donaldson — 103 m

R | ROM COM | 1988 | COLOR

◢ Sex · ◢ Nud · ◢ Viol · ■ Lang · ◢ AdSit

6 A cocky young man (Cruise) breezes into New York determined to make it big. Instead, he becomes a hotshot bartender after veteran barkeep Brown takes him under his wing. Life is good, but when Cruise falls for charming and wealthy Shue, she gets pregnant while they frolic in Jamaica. From there on, the relationship gets badly bruised as Cruise tries to deal with this new twist of fate and Shue's father tries to keep Cruise away. Pretty basic. Critics didn't like it, but the colorful bar crowds and stylish atmosphere make this an enjoyable and attractive romance for young people.

A: Tom Cruise, Bryan Brown, Elisabeth Shue, Lisa Banes, Laurence Luckinbill, Kelly Lynch

© TOUCHSTONE HOME VIDEO 606

COCOON

D: Ron Howard — 117 m

PG-13 | SF COM DMA | 1985 | COLOR

◢ Sex · ◢ Nud · Viol · ◢ Lang · ◢ AdSit

9 Great stuff. Solid, good-time entertainment. A group of retired people in Florida discover a magical fountain of youth, secreted away in a seemingly abandoned swimming pool. After a few stolen swims in the pond, the old folks find that their dwindling energies have been mysteriously revitalized. The pool turns out to be a repository for friendly alien beings from another world and the old-timers are soon facing an unexpected dilemma. The aliens give them a chance to live forever but they must leave earth. Excellent cast (Ameche won an Oscar) and an endearing story line make this a real treat.

A: Don Ameche, Wilford Brimley, Hume Cronyn, Brian Dennehy, Jack Gilford, Steve Guttenberg

© FOXVIDEO 1476

COCOON: THE RETURN

D: Daniel Petrie — 116 m

PG | SF COM DMA | 1988 | COLOR

Sex / Nud / Viol / Lang / AdSit

7 Follow-up to the megahit COCOON. The oldsters return to earth five years later to help their alien friends rescue some cocoons which have become endangered by an earthquake. Now accustomed to a life free of pain and suffering, they have to readjust to life as it is on earth. This time around less attention is given to plot and more to character development. While this film has an excellent cast and is generally enjoyable, too, it lacks the energy and warmth of the earlier film.

A: Don Ameche, Wilford Brimley, Courtney Cox, Hume Cronyn, Brian Dennehy, Jack Gilford

© FOXVIDEO 1710

COLD TURKEY

D: Norman Lear — 99 m

PG | COM | 1971 | COLOR

Sex / Nud / Viol / Lang / AdSit

7 Clever little satire from Norman Lear about the small town of Eagle Rock, Iowa which accepts a challenge from a tobacco company to win $25 million. Madison Avenue PR guy Merwin Wren (Newhart) has convinced the tobacco company that no town could possibly win, but they didn't count on an ambitious minister (Dick Van Dyke) who leads the townsfolk in the crusade to quit smoking. Silly madness. Bob and Ray are hilarious.

A: Dick Van Dyke, Pippa Scott, Tom Poston, Bob Newhart, Vincent Gardenia, Edward Everett Horton

Distributed By MGM/UA Home Video M201581

COME BLOW YOUR HORN

D: Bud Yorkin — 115 m

NR | COM | 1963 | COLOR

Sex / Nud / Viol / Lang / AdSit

7 Fun, light-hearted early effort from Neil Simon (this was his first big stage hit) with a screen play written by Norman Lear. Frank Sinatra plays a free-living swinging bachelor with girls everywhere, who also has an admiring younger brother and a nagging father. Frank teaches his younger brother the ropes, only to have him steal own his girl away and to learn that playing the field can sometimes be a fool's game. Sinatra sings the title song.

A: Frank Sinatra, Lee J. Cobb, Molly Picon, Barbara Rush, Jill St. John, Tony Bill

© PARAMOUNT HOME VIDEO 6535

COMFORT AND JOY

D: Bill Forsyth — 93 m

PG | COM | 1984 | COLOR

Sex / Nud / Viol / Lang / AdSit

7 Quirky, fun little comedy. When a mild-mannered Scottish disk jockey's girl moves out on him, his world begins to fall apart. Even the birds begin to find more pleasure in decorating his BMW. He decides to find more meaning in his life by throwing himself into a noble struggle to reconcile two Mafia groups who are battling over territorial rights for their ice cream trucks. Full of dry wit and subtle humor. Sophisticated viewers are more likely to find this good fun. It takes a little patience. Amusing.

A: Bill Paterson, Eleanor David, C.P. Grogan, Alex Norton, Patrick Malahide, Rikki Fulton

© MCA/UNIVERSAL HOME VIDEO, INC. 80146

COMING TO AMERICA

D: John Landis — 116 m

R | COM | 1988 | COLOR

Sex / Nud / Viol / Lang / AdSit

8 Eddie Murphy plays a pampered African prince who rebels against his father's arranged marriage plans for him. He decides to go to America to find his own wife. Where does he go: to Queens, of course. This was a big box office hit, even though it is sometimes a little slow. It is nonetheless packed with more than enough laughs to keep you interested nearly all the way through it and, in the end, well entertained. Look for Murphy and Hall to each keep showing up (under heavy makeup) in other roles.

A: Eddie Murphy, Arsenio Hall, James Earl Jones, John Amos, Madge Sinclair, Shari Headley

© PARAMOUNT HOME VIDEO 32157

COMMANDO

D: Mark L. Lester — 90 m

R | ACT COM | 1985 | COLOR

Sex / Nud / Viol / Lang / AdSit

7 Arnold is the ultimate commando who eats Green Berets for breakfast. He is retired from a CIA special commando force but is forced out of retirement when an old enemy kidnaps his daughter in an effort to force him into helping them to dispose of a South American dictator. Arnold, however, has plans of his own and he is a one-man army. Chong is a stewardess who comes along with him for the ride, and what a ride! Plenty of action - guns everywhere, all the time. The intention was to make the movie campy, but most of the humor gets lost in the violence.

A: Arnold Schwarzenegger, Rae Dawn Chong, Dan Hedaya, James Olson, Alyssa Milano, Vernon Wells

© FOXVIDEO 1484

COMMITMENTS, THE

D: Alan Parker — 118 m

R | MUS COM | 1991 | COLOR

Sex / Nud / Viol / Lang / AdSit

8 Unusual, fun and infectiously upbeat. Set in the slums of North Dublin, a local hustler, Jimmy, is asked by two friends to transform their very bad wedding band into a successful one. Jimmy decides that they should recreate themselves into a soul band and recruits a Joe Cocker-like singer, three girl backup singers, and Joey (a middle-aged trumpeter who claims to have played with Otis Redding, Elvis Presley and others). They do it. They're a hit. They become The Commitments - even though some of them didn't even know what soul music was. This is very worthwhile viewing but it is "hampered" by intense Irish dialects and British humor.

A: Michael Aherne, Angeline Hall, Maria Doyle, Dave Finnegan, Bronagh Gallagher, Felim Gormley

© FOXVIDEO 1906

COMPROMISING POSITIONS

D: Frank Perry — 99 m

R | COM MYS | 1985 | COLOR

Sex / Nud / Viol / Lang / AdSit

7 A former investigative reporter, but now a bored housewife (Sarandon), decides to investigate the mysterious death of a Long Island dentist. The dentist, it turns out, was an incredible womanizer. So virtually every woman in town turns out to be a suspect. That element and the suburbia aspects set up a potential for a very clever and funny plot and the first part of the movie is very funny. However, the later part becomes pretty much a standard mystery. Still, a very worthwhile watch.

A: Susan Sarandon, Edward Herrmann, Raul Julia, Judith Ivey, Mary Beth Hurt, Anne DeSalvo

© PARAMOUNT HOME VIDEO 1928

CONTEMPT

D: Jean-Luc Godard — 102 m

NR | FOR COM DMA | 1964 | COLOR

Sex / Nud / Viol / Lang / AdSit

7 A satirical insider's look at European movie making. The plot revolves around an Italian filming of the classic Greek "The Odyssey." Piccoli is the script writer who would rather write for the stage. He reluctantly takes the movie job to appease what he feels are his wife's ambitions and greed. However, she is now disappointed in him for his lack of conviction. Sexy, sultry Bardot is his wife and she now begins what appears to him to be an affair with the vulgar producer (Palance) just to spite her husband. Everyone apparently is in contempt of everyone else. Film fans and film students are best audience.

A: Brigitte Bardot, Jack Palance, Fritz Lang, Michel Piccoli, Georgia Moll

© NEW LINE HOME VIDEO 2094

CONTINENTAL DIVIDE

D: Michael Apted — 103 m

PG | ROM COM | 1981 | COLOR

Sex / Nud / Viol / Lang / AdSit

7 A lightweight romantic comedy in which Belushi is a hard-edged Chicago political reporter who gets beat up by thugs because of a story. So, he is sent to hide out in the Rockies for a while by doing a story on a reclusive ornithologist (Brown) who is researching eagles. These two are total opposites. She is a country girl. He is a big city boy. Still, they fall in love and then they have to work out a solution to their totally different lifestyles - a modern twist on the old Tracy/Hepburn formula. A nice little comedy. Brown is attractive, Belushi mellowed out.

A: John Belushi, Blair Brown, Allen Garfield, Carlin Glynn

© MCA/UNIVERSAL HOME VIDEO, INC. 71001

COOKIE

D: Susan Seidelman — 93 m

R | COM | 1989 | COLOR

Sex / Nud / Viol / Lang / AdSit

6 Very light comedy. Falk is a Mafia don who is released on parole after thirteen years in the slammer. He returns to his loving wife (Vaccaro), his mistress (Wiest) and their smart-mouthed daughter (Lloyd). Falk must deal with rivalrous hoods, get even with a treacherous former partner and stay out of the clutches of a crooked D.A. He gets unexpected help from his gum-popping daughter who has been given the task of driving his limo. No side-splitting jokes or gags here, but still a pleasant evening's diversion.

A: Peter Falk, Emily Lloyd, Dianne Wiest, Brenda Vaccaro, Adrian Pasdar

© WARNER HOME VIDEO 660

COOLEY HIGH

D: Michael Schultz — 107 m

PG | COM | 1975 | COLOR

Sex / Nud / Viol / Lang / AdSit

6 Amusing little comedy. An inner-city version of AMERICAN GRAFFITI, set in 1964 Chicago. It is a series of incidents about inner-city high school life revolving around high school kids Turman and Jacobs. Their principal concerns are girl problems in the form of Cynthia Davis, but they also have to contend with teachers and a couple of street toughs. Instead of cruising Main Street in cars, they swipe rides on buses and trains. Sometimes funny, sometimes serious. It's generally OK, with warmth and good humor. It later became "What's Happening!" on TV.

A: Glynn Turman, Lawrence Hilton-Jacobs, Garrett Morris, Cynthia Davis, Corin Rogers, Maurice Leon Havis

© ORION PICTURES CORPORATION 7506

COOL RUNNINGS

D: Jon Turteltaub — 98 m

PG | COM | 1993 | COLOR

7 During the 1988 Winter Olympics, the small, very warm, Caribbean island of Jamaica placed an unlikely entry into the very cold bobsledding event. That actual event provoked Hollywood into creating its own version of the story. When a determined Jamaican sprinter's injury prevents him from entering into his preferred event, he gathers together some of his friends and together they enter the bobsledding event - even though none of them have ever even seen snow before. And, to give themselves a fighting chance, they entice a former bobsledder (John Candy) into coaching them. Silly, full of slap stick and predictable the whole way, but that doesn't prevent if from being a good time.

Sex | Nud | Viol | Lang | AdSit

A: Leon, Doug E. Doug, Rawle D. Lewis, Malik Yoba, John Candy

© WALT DISNEY HOME VIDEO 2325

CORRINA, CORRINA

D: Jessie Nelson — 115 m

PG | DMA COM | 1994 | COLOR

7 Sweet little 7-year-old Molly has just lost her mother and refuses to talk. Her father Manny (Ray Liotta) is heart-broken too, but he has to go on. After a couple of mistreats, he hires Corrina (Whoopi Goldberg) as his housekeeper. She is an highly-educated black woman who can't get other work using it, because this is the 1950s. Little Molly has never run into anyone quite like Whoopi. Her sense of fun breaks down the wall that sad little Molly has built up. But this creates another set of problems, because Molly starts to think of Corrina as her mother. What's more, Manny and Corrina become good friends and now their families are concerned. Not quite believable but fun anyway.

Sex | Nud | Viol | Lang | AdSit

A: Whoopie Goldberg, Ray Liotta, Tina Majorino, Wendy Crewson, Larry Miller, Don Ameche

© TURNER HOME ENTERTAINMENT N4013

COUPE DE VILLE

D: Joe Roth — 98 m

PG-13 | COM DMA | 1990 | COLOR

6 Interesting coming-of-age flick that rises above this oft-covered subject by having both a good cast and a slightly different twist on the subject. It is set in 1963, a time in American history before Vietnam, the civil rights movement and free love. Three feuding brothers are charged by their father with driving a powder blue 1954 Cadillac Coupe de Ville from Detroit to Miami for delivery to their mother for her 50th birthday. The fun comes from the conflict between three separate sibling personalities that somehow come to terms with each other by trip's end.

Sex | Nud | ◢ Viol | ◢ Lang | ◢ AdSit

A: Alan Arkin, Daniel Stern, Patrick Dempsey, Annabeth Gish, Rita Taggart, Joseph Bologna

© MCA/UNIVERSAL HOME VIDEO, INC. 80932

COURT JESTER, THE

D: Melvin Frank, Norman Panama — 101 m

NR | COM | 1956 | COLOR

9 One of the best comedies ever, certainly Kaye's best. He plays a lowly valet who rises to become a leader of a peasant revolt after he gets mixed up with some forest outlaws who are scheming to restore the rightful heir to the throne of England. For the love of a girl Kaye impersonates the Court Jester so he can gain access to the castle and then gets caught up in more swashbuckling than he wants. Delightfully complicated and very funny comic situations follow. Best gag: "The pellet with the poison's in the vessel with the pestle."

Sex | Nud | Viol | Lang | AdSit

A: Danny Kaye, Glynis Johns, Basil Rathbone, Angela Lansbury, Mildred Natwick, Cecil Parker

© PARAMOUNT HOME VIDEO 5512

COURTSHIP OF EDDIE'S FATHER, THE

D: Vincente Minnelli — 117 m

NR | COM ROM | 1962 | COLOR

8 Charming and highly entertaining comedy concerning a motherless 9-year-old boy (Ronny Howard) and his father (Glenn Ford). Life is hard for Ford, who is still trying to recover from the loss of his wife. So his son does his best to find himself a mother and his father a wife by trying to line Dad up with Shirley Jones, Dina Merrill and Stella Stevens. Heartwarming and funny. Very popular. It later it became a hit TV series starring Bill Bixby.

Sex | Nud | Viol | Lang | AdSit

A: Glenn Ford, Shirley Jones, Stella Stevens, Ron Howard, Dina Merrill, Jerry Van Dyke

Distributed By MGM/UA Home Video M200797

COUSINS

D: Joel Schumacher — 110 m

PG-13 | ROM COM | 1989 | COLOR

9 Charming love story that will leave your face smiling and your heart warmed. William Peterson and Sean Young meet at a big wedding and immediately fall into lust. The trouble is that they are both married to others. Their spouses, Ted Danson and Isabella Rossellini, discover what has happened and they become good friends. They decide to get even by faking their own affair, but surprise... their phony-affair turns into true love. Excellent, wonderful, winning and charming feel-good film. It is also the upbeat Americanized version of the 1976 French hit COUSIN, COUSINE.

◢ Sex | ◢ Nud | Viol | Lang | ■ AdSit

A: Ted Danson, Isabella Rossellini, Sean Young, William L. Petersen, Lloyd Bridges, Norma Aleandro

© PARAMOUNT HOME VIDEO 32181

CRAZY PEOPLE

D: Tony Bill — 91 m

R | COM | 1990 | COLOR

6 Creative fun tale about truth-in-advertising, and the lack of it! When a burned-out, stressed-out advertising executive (Moore) decides he's had enough of the corporate game, where hype is more important than truth. He decides instead to create some very truthful ads that are brutally frank. As a result, Moore's partner commits him to a mental hospital. However, when these ads become a surprising huge success and set the advertising world on its ear, Moore goes even farther with that idea when he makes use of the fertile minds of his fellow mental patients. Extra fun when he falls for wacked-out patient Hannah. Offbeat and funny.

Sex | Nud | Viol | ■ Lang | ■ AdSit

A: Dudley Moore, Daryl Hannah, Paul Reiser, Mercedes Ruehl, J.T. Walsh, Bill Smitrovich

© PARAMOUNT HOME VIDEO 32299

CRIMES AND MISDEMEANORS

D: Woody Allen — 104 m

PG-13 | DMA COM | 1990 | COLOR

8 Woody Allen creatively interweaves two separate stories. Landau, a distinguished doctor has an affair, but his mistress threatens to expose it and the fact that he is an embezzler. So, he arranges to have her killed, but then is tormented by what he did. Allen, in a more light-hearted vein, is a documentary film maker who is obsessed with besting his brother-in-law (Alda). These two quite different characters, and what they have in common, come together only at the film's end. Extremely strong cast explores virtually every issue of human importance, including family, friendship, love, murder and morality.

Sex | Nud | Viol | ◢ Lang | ■ AdSit

A: Martin Landau, Woody Allen, Mia Farrow, Anjelica Huston, Claire Bloom, Alan Alda

© ORION PICTURES CORPORATION 8755

CRIMES OF THE HEART

D: Bruce Beresford — 105 m

PG-13 | COM DMA | 1986 | COLOR

8 Very entertaining and provocative adaptation of a Pulitzer Prize-winning play. Three off-beat sisters reunite in their small Southern hometown on the occasion of their grandfather's failing health. Keaton is distraught because she is turning thirty, Spacek has shot her husband - just because she didn't like the way he looked, and Lange is giving up an unpromising singing career to work in a dog food factory. Now, after a long time apart, they are all back together under the same roof with the opportunity to recall their past and assess their futures. Zany and heartwarming, with biting humor.

Sex | Nud | Viol | ◢ Lang | ■ AdSit

A: Diane Keaton, Jessica Lange, Sissy Spacek, Sam Shepard, Tess Harper, Hurd Hatfield

© WARNER HOME VIDEO 421

CRITTERS

D: Shephen Herek — 86 m

PG-13 | HOR COM SF | 1986 | COLOR

7 Strange sort of mix between horror and comedy that proved to be quite popular and spawned three much-lessor sequels. Eight razor-toothed alien furballs have escaped from a prison in space and have landed near a farm family in Kansas. While Mom stays home to do battle the hungry little fellers who want to dine on humans, son Grimes goes to town to fetch help. On the way, he meets two intergalactic dead-pan bounty hunters who have come to kill off the bloodthirsty little monsters. Some very funny moments are mixed in with some really gory ones.

Sex | Nud | ■ Viol | ◢ Lang | ◢ AdSit

A: Dee Wallace, M. Emmet Walsh, Billy Green Bush, Scott Grimes, Nadine Van Der Velde, Don Opper

© TURNER HOME ENTERTAINMENT N4115

CROCODILE DUNDEE

D: Peter Faiman — 98 m

PG-13 | COM ROM ACT | 1986 | COLOR

9 Huge, world-wide box office phenomenon. A sexy rich-girl reporter (Kozlowski) goes to the Outback of Australia to interview a strange character, Mick "Crocodile" Dundee (Paul Hogan), when she hears tales of him having crawled for miles after having his leg bitten by a crocodile. Mick is a hero of giant proportions. He drinks. He fights. He wrestles crocs, and he obliges her by taking her with him on excursion out into his world. Then she reciprocates by bringing him into her jungle - Manhattan. Hilarious!! Followed by a pretty good CROCODILE DUNDEE II.

Sex | ◢ Nud | ◢ Viol | ◢ Lang | ◢ AdSit

A: Paul Hogan, Linda Kozlowski, John Meillon, David Gulpilil, Mark Blum, Michael Lombard

© PARAMOUNT HOME VIDEO 32029

CROCODILE DUNDEE II

D: John Cornell — 110 m

PG | COM ACT | 1988 | COLOR

7 Pleasant enough follow-up to the original. However, more action is added to the successful formula this time. Mick and Sue are now living in NYC, but things get too exciting for them when her ex-husband takes some pictures of some Columbian drug lords that he wasn't supposed to take and sends them to her for safekeeping. The Columbians want those pictures back and they are very nasty about it. Mick decides to even the odds by leading the bad guys onto his turf - the Outback of Australia. There, he is more than a match for the bad guys. Fun time.

Sex | Nud | ◢ Viol | ◢ Lang | ◢ AdSit

A: Paul Hogan, Linda Kozlowski, John Mellion, Charles Dutton, Hector Ubarry, Juan Fernandez

© PARAMOUNT HOME VIDEO 32147

CROOKLYN

PG-13 | DMA COM | 1994 | COLOR | Sex | Nud | Viol | Lang | AdSit

D: Spike Lee 114 m

7 This is a different sort of movie for Spike Lee. It is the story of a black family trying to survive hard times in Brooklyn during the 1970s. Alfre Woodard is the drill sergeant-like mother who is trying to raise her kids right, while the family struggles to get by on her teacher's salary. Her husband loves his family and is devoted to them, but is a musician trying to get recognised for playing his music, not other peoples. The story centers around the activities of their 10-year-old daughter as she trys to survive her four raucous older brothers. Highly praised by the critics. Funny at times, but more serious than billed. Will have some interest for everyone, but especially blacks.

A: Alfre Woodard, Delroy Lindo, David Patrick Kelly, Zelda Harris, Carlton Williams, Sharif Rashed

© MCA/UNIVERSAL HOME VIDEO, INC. 82069

DAD

PG | DMA COM | 1989 | COLOR | Sex | Nud | Viol | Lang | AdSit

D: Gary David Goldberg 117 m

8 Very touching dose of reality. A busy Wall Street yuppie (Ted Danson) must stop his life midstream to move in with his aged parents when his father becomes very ill. His previously distant and superficial relationship with his parents becomes radically altered as he faces the new reality of their mortality. For the first time, he also begins to understand them as adult individuals instead of parents. Lots of highs and lows, maybe too many, but definitely moving. It may also evoke painful feelings in old people and those who are dealing with old age in others. Lemmon is wonderful.

A: Jack Lemmon, Ted Danson, Olympia Dukakis, Kathy Baker, Kevin Spacey, Ethan Hawke

© MCA/UNIVERSAL HOME VIDEO, INC. 80933

DADDY'S DYIN' ... WHO'S GOT THE WILL?

PG-13 | COM | 1990 | COLOR | Sex | Nud | Viol | Lang | AdSit

D: Jack Fisk 97 m

6 Light-hearted little film in which a group of odd-ball characters, all brothers and sisters who can't stand each other, converge on their small Texas hometown to gather around, and to feud and fight upon their father's deathbed. Their one common thread is that they all hope to become wealthy... that is, if only they could find his will. Daddy can't remember where he put it. A terrific cast propels this film along, past some jokes that fall flat into some that are truly funny and through a back-biting honesty that makes it all work reasonably well.

A: Beau Bridges, Beverly D'Angelo, Tess Harper, Judge Reinhold, Amy Wright, Molly McClure

Distributed By MGM/UA Home Video M902089

DAMN YANKEES

NR | MUS COM | 1958 | COLOR | Sex | Nud | Viol | Lang | AdSit

D: George Abbott, Stanley Donen 111 m

8 Huge Broadway hit is brought to the screen in wonderful fashion. Joe Boyd is a middle-aged baseball fan that so wants to help his beloved Washington Senators whip the Yankees and win the pennant that he makes a deal with the devil (Walston) and his beautiful vamp Lola (Verdon) to become rejuvenated into a young player. Wonderful songs and dances. Oscar nominated score has "Whatever Lola Wants," "Heart" and "Two Lost Souls." Verdon is sexy and Walston is marvelously devilish.

A: Tab Hunter, Gwen Verdon, Ray Walston, Russ Brown, Shannon Bolin, Nathaniel Frey

© WARNER HOME VIDEO 35109

DARBY O'GILL AND THE LITTLE PEOPLE

G | COM CLD FAN | 1959 | COLOR | Sex | Nud | Viol | Lang | AdSit

D: Robert Stevenson 90 m

9 Wonderful fantasy about an an old caretaker at a wealthy Irish estate, Darby O'Gill, who falls into a well and discovers the leprechaun king. Darby tricks the king into granting him three wishes, but he soon wishes he hadn't. Poor old Darby has such a reputation for blarney that no one believes his preposterous tale, and the larcenous king has tricked him into wasting two wishes. Then comes a young Sean Connery, who has come to the estate to replace him, so he and his daughter are also about to lose their home. It is a magical tale with neat special effects. Among Disney's very best.

A: Albert Sharpe, Janet Munro, Sean Connery, Jimmy O'Dea, Kieron Moore, Estelle Winwood

© WALT DISNEY HOME VIDEO 038

DAVE

PG-13 | COM ROM | 1993 | COLOR | Sex | Nud | Viol | Lang | AdSit

D: Ivan Reitman 110 m

7 Dave owns a semi-successful temp agency but he also has an uncanny likeness for the President. So when the hard-hearted, stuffy and arrogant President needs a look-alike to stand in for him, Dave gets hired. However, when the Prez has a massive stroke while in the arms of a pretty blonde who is not his wife, Dave is drafted into the big leagues. But, Dave takes his role to heart when he is called upon to close a bunch of day care centers in the name of the budget, and he refuses. This precipitates a power struggle between him and the dead President's people who had hired him. There is some intrigue and romance, too. Very enjoyable, even though very predictable.

A: Kevin Kline, Sigourney Weaver, Ben Kingsley, Frank Langella

© WARNER HOME VIDEO 12962

DAY FOR NIGHT

PG | FOR DMA COM | 1971 | COLOR | Sex | Nud | Viol | Lang | AdSit

D: Francois Truffaut 116 m

9 French director Francois Truffaut's reverent satire of the movie-making business. The story reflects the pandemonium, activities, love lives and anxieties of the principal participants (the actors, director, producer and crew) in and during the making of a romance movie called "Meeting Pamela." This satirical film largely debunks the glamour of movie-making and is a favorite among film insiders. It has humor, but is not a true comedy. Oscar for Best Foreign Film. Dubbed. Sophisticated viewers and film fans only.

A: Jacqueline Bisset, Jean-Pierre Leaud, Valentina Cortese, Jean-Pierre Aumont

© WARNER HOME VIDEO 11134

DAYS OF THRILLS AND LAUGHTER

NR | COM | 1961 | B&W | Sex | Nud | Viol | Lang | AdSit

D: Robert Youngson 93 m

8 This is the third compilation of old movie clips prepared by Robert Youngson. It is a compilation of action and comedy scenes from the silent picture classics of Charlie Chaplin, Laurel and Hardy, the Keystone Cops, Fatty Arbuckle, Douglas Fairbanks, Pearl White and more. Quite good.

A:

© MPI HOME VIDEO MP1329

DAZED AND CONFUSED

R | COM DMA | 1993 | COLOR | Sex | Nud | Viol | Lang | AdSit

D: Richard Linklater 103 m

8 This is the kind of film that teens want to go see but makes parents cringe. It depicts one day and night at the end of the school year in 1976 at a small Texas town. Next year's seniors are hazing next year's freshman. They are all either cool or trying to be cool, and they are all having fun. They're too late for the 60's but that doesn't stop them from being rebellious - smoking pot and drinking beer. Anarchy rules. The plot generally follows about two dozen kids, but focuses more on the quarterback who doesn't want to sign a pledge to avoid smoking pot; and, a junior high kid trying to avoid being paddled by seniors. Best for teenagers and those who wish they still were.

A: Jason London, Rory Cochrane, Adam Goldberg, Anthony Rapp, Shasha Rapp, Wiley Wiggens

© MCA/UNIVERSAL HOME VIDEO, INC. 81495

DEAD HEAT

R | COM CRM | 1988 | COLOR | Sex | Nud | Viol | Lang | AdSit

D: Mark Goldblatt 86 m

6 An interesting idea for an off-beat crime spoof. A couple of LA cops discover that a series of jewelry heists is being carried out by dead criminals who have been turned into zombies. When one of the detectives is killed in the bad guy's laboratory, he is brought back as a good-guy zombie to help get the bad-guy zombies. Pretty gory in places and the comedy does not always connect, but still not too bad.

A: Treat Williams, Joe Piscopo, Lindsay Frost, Darren McGavin, Vincent Price

© R&G VIDEO, LP 90035

DEAD HEAT ON A MERRY-GO-ROUND

NR | CRM COM | 1966 | COLOR | Sex | Nud | Viol | Lang | AdSit

D: Bernard Girard 107 m

7 One of the greatest con artists of all times (Coburn) manages to win a parole from prison by seducing the lady shrink. Outside, he sets up an ingenious plan to rob the airport bank at the same time that airport security is occupied with the arrival of the Soviet Premier. The intelligent, sometimes witty script has a lot of complex twists in an intricate plot that will keep and hold your attention. Very entertaining. Perhaps Coburn's best performance. Watch for the surprise ending and keep an eye out for Harrison Ford in his first role.

A: James Coburn, Camilla Sparv, Aldo Ray, Ross Martin, Severn Darden, Robert Webber

© COLUMBIA TRISTAR HOME VIDEO 60963

DEAD MEN DON'T WEAR PLAID

PG | COM | 1982 | B&W | Sex | Nud | Viol | Lang | AdSit

D: Carl Reiner 89 m

7 Entertaining film noir parody. It is pretty good farce with an interesting twist. Steve Martin plays a private eye hired by beautiful Rachel Ward to solve the murder of her father, a famous cheese maker. Martin's search involves apparent conversations with famous movie people such as Humphrey Bogart, Cary Grant, Ingrid Bergman, Barbara Stanwyck, Fred MacMurray and Veronica Lake. (Film clips from old films are cleverly intermixed with Martin's live action and dialogue). The dead-pan humor is funny and sometimes even hilarious, but the one-note joke does wear thin after awhile.

A: Steve Martin, Rachel Ward, Reni Santoni, Carl Reiner, George Ganynes, Frank McCarthy

© MCA/UNIVERSAL HOME VIDEO, INC. 77011

DEATH BECOMES HER

D: Robert Zemeckis 103 m

PG-13 COM 1992 COLOR Sex Nud Viol Lang AdSit

6 A wicked farce that attacks America's obsession with beauty. Goldie Hawn and Meryl Streep grew up together. Streep rose to stardom on the stage but now both her beauty and her star are fading. So when Hawn brings her new plastic surgeon boyfriend (Willis) backstage for a visit, the vain Streep immediately charms him away and marries him. But, after seven years, even he is not enough to stave off the ravages of time. So, she buys an immortality potion from witch Rossellini. However, so has Hawn and she has come back to get her revenge. War erupts. The warriors are immortal but not unbreakable. Somewhat narrow and mean spirited but has a few moments.

A: Meryl Streep, Goldie Hawn, Bruce Willis, Isabella Rossellini

© MCA/UNIVERSAL HOME VIDEO, INC. 81279

DECLINE OF THE AMERICAN EMPIRE, THE

D: Denys Arcand 102 m

R FOR COM DMA 1986 COLOR Sex Nud Viol Lang AdSit

8 Enjoyable, but very sophisticated, look at sexual politics. A group of university teachers and students get together. Four men prepare a gourmet dinner while they swap stories about women and sex. The four women do the same while they exercise in a health club. Then they all meet for dinner and it becomes known that intimate secrets have been revealed. That inspires a very open sexual discussion which leads both to more revelations and experimentation. Intellectual, incisive and witty. However the subject matter, and the frank approach to it, makes this a video that is definitely not for everyone. Subtitles.

A: Dominique Michel, Dorothee Berryman, Louis Patal, Genevieve Rioux, Pierre Curzi, Remy Girard

© MCA/UNIVERSAL HOME VIDEO, INC. 80586

DEFENDING YOUR LIFE

D: Albert Brooks 112 m

PG COM ROM 1991 COLOR Sex Nud Viol Lang AdSit

7 Funny, offbeat Albert Brooks entry. Brooks is a self-involved advertising executive who, while in his brand new BMW, crashes headfirst into an oncoming bus. Dead, he is sent to Judgement City, a stop-over that allows the deceased to be "processed." There the newly-dead must defend their lives on earth. If they pass, they are sent to heaven. If they don't, they are sent back to earth to start all over again. Streep is perfect and she is heaven-bound. Brooks is taken with her and she is his new motivation to make it into heaven. Peculiar - yes, outrageous - no. Intelligent - yes, clever and witty - yes. Good - yes, great - no.

A: Albert Brooks, Meryl Streep, Rip Torn, Lee Grant, Buck Henry, George D. Wallace

© WARNER HOME VIDEO 12049

DELICATE DELINQUENT, THE

D: Don McGuire 101 m

NR COM CLD 1957 B&W Sex Nud Viol Lang AdSit

7 Jerry Lewis plays a bumbling janitor who pals around with juvenile delinquents. He joins the police force, with the help of Darren McGavin, but he is such a goofball that he has a hard time proving himself. This was Jerry's first effort after he split from Dean Martin, and it is one of his best efforts. It is also sentimental and contains the requisite assortment of Lewis slapstick and silliness.

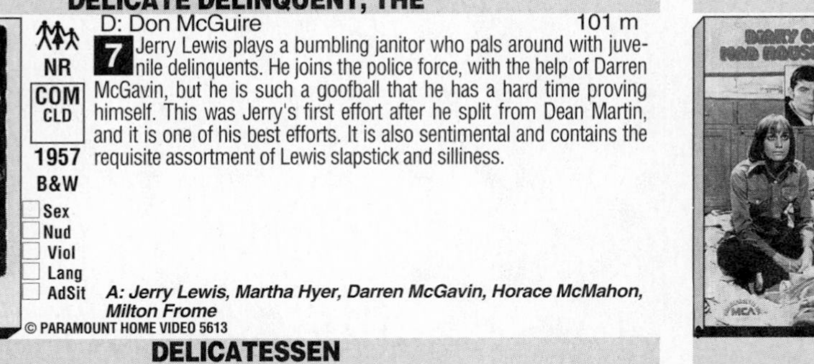

A: Jerry Lewis, Martha Hyer, Darren McGavin, Horace McMahon, Milton Frome

© PARAMOUNT HOME VIDEO 5613

DELICATESSEN

D: Marc Caro 95 m

R FOR COM 1992 COLOR Sex Nud Viol Lang AdSit

8 This French import is beyond bizarre. It's well into the really bizarre. It is not for the average viewer, but it is also strangely, perversely interesting and even hilarious at times. The time and location are never made clear, but the economic circumstances are definitely hard. The place is a rundown apartment building with a butcher shop on the first floor and upon which all the tenants rely for meat. But, there is never any meat until some unsuspecting person answers an advertisement for a handyman. Then there is meat. This time it is an out-of-work clown who comes knocking, but the butcher's daughter has fallen in love with him before he can become diner. Subtitles.

A: Dominique Pinon, Marie-Laure Dougnac, Jean-Claude Dreyfus, Karin Viard, Rufus, Ticky Holgado

© PARAMOUNT HOME VIDEO 15148

DELIRIOUS

D: Tom Mankiewicz 96 m

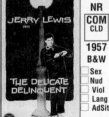

PG COM ROM 1991 COLOR Sex Nud Viol Lang AdSit

6 Slight but pleasant, goofy little comedy. John Candy is a writer for a TV soap opera. He gets conked on the head and wakes up to find himself living inside the story line of his soap and its small town of Ashford Falls. Furthermore, he finds that he can now control everything that happens to him and everyone in the soap, by simply typing the script the way way he wants it. Armed now with his new power, he sets out to capture the heart of beautiful-but-bitchy Emma Samms who he lusts after. However, his plans are constantly being foiled by good girl Mariel Hemingway.

A: John Candy, Raymond Burr, Mariel Hemingway, Emma Samms, Dylan Baker, Charles Rocket

Distributed By MGM/UA Home Video M902243

DESIGNING WOMAN

D: Vincente Minnelli 118 m

NR COM ROM 1957 COLOR Sex Nud Viol Lang AdSit

7 Oscars for Best Story and Screenplay. Good natured farce about a rough-natured sports writer (Peck) who meets and, after a whirl-wind courtship, marries a high fashion designer (Bacall). But then they discover that they have almost nothing in common. The fun begins to develop as each attempts to adapt to the other's odd habits and friends, and really it takes off when their old loves show up. Romantic and quite amusing.

A: Gregory Peck, Lauren Bacall, Dolores Gray, Sam Levene, Mickey Shaughnessy, Chuck Connors

Distributed By MGM/UA Home Video M201069

DESK SET

D: Walter Lang 103 m

NR ROM COM 1957 COLOR Sex Nud Viol Lang AdSit

7 Classic Hepburn/Tracy pairing. Tracy plays an efficiency expert hired to automate Katherine Hepburn's research department at a TV network with his computers. It is almost foreordained that these two will clash over the man (or woman) verses machine issue. That theme, as presented, seems quite simplistic now, but computers then represented a formidable threat and were a vital concern to much of America. Eventually love wins out and there is a place for both human and machine. The real reason to watch the movie is the sparks and repartee that flies between the two fiery leads.

A: Spencer Tracy, Katharine Hepburn, Gig Young, Joan Blondell, Dina Merrill, Neva Patterson

© FOXVIDEO 1244

DESPERATELY SEEKING SUSAN

D: Susan Seidelman 104 m

PG-13 COM 1985 COLOR Sex Nud Viol Lang AdSit

7 Interesting and sometimes funny, character study of a bored suburban housewife (Arquette) who gets vicarious thrills from reading the personal ads in the paper. She becomes fascinated with one in particular - a rock musician who is desperately seeking his girlfriend, the adventurous and exotic Susan (Madonna). Curiosity gets the better of Arquette and she decides to spy on the wonderfully mysterious Susan. When Susan sells her leather jacket, Arquette buys it and immediately becomes involved in a true adventure of her own when she discovers that the pockets contain diamond earrings which Susan had taken off a dead mobster. More amusing than laugh-out-loud.

A: Rosanna Arquette, Madonna, Aidan Quinn, Mark Blum, Robert Joy, Laurie Metcalf

© HBO VIDEO TVA2991

DIARY OF A MAD HOUSEWIFE

D: Frank Perry 100 m

R DMA COM 1970 COLOR Sex Nud Viol Lang AdSit

7 A bored New York housewife, who is burdened with a demeaning and abusive husband, tells her story. (His monumental abuses of her and his ruthless attempts at social climbing seem almost farcical - until you remember she is telling the story from her perspective.) She seeks relief from him with an affair with a dashing but selfish writer, and finds that he is no better than her husband. So, she seeks help in group therapy - which doesn't work either. This is a feminist satire from the feminist revolution which still works. Benjaman is so despicable, even his mother would hate him. Snodgress is marvelous.

A: Richard Benjamin, Carrie Snodgress, Frank Langella

© MCA/UNIVERSAL HOME VIDEO, INC. 66048

DINER

D: Barry Levinson 110 m

R COM DMA 1982 COLOR Sex Nud Viol Lang AdSit

8 A real sleeper that was much acclaimed by critics. It is a nostalgic, but not idealized, story of four young men growing up in 1959 Baltimore. They hang out at one particular diner, trying to learn how to deal with life and romance after leaving high school. One is married, one is engaged, one is trying to become engaged and one is playing the field. This is an insightful story of four flawed, inexperienced guys who meet over french fries to discuss life, music, and the best way to get women. Carefully and lovingly made.

A: Steve Guttenberg, Daniel Stern, Mickey Rourke, Kevin Bacon, Ellen Barkin, Paul Reiser

Distributed By MGM/UA Home Video M800164

DIRTY ROTTEN SCOUNDRELS

D: Frank Oz 110 m

PG COM 1988 COLOR Sex Nud Viol Lang AdSit

7 Funny and enjoyable tale of two con artists with very conflicting styles who are trampling on each other's toes. Michael Caine very successfully operates his scam with great style and panache in the south of France, bilking wealthy females. So when crude American interloper Steve Martin crashes into the territory, the town is quickly not big enough for the both of them. They decide to settle the issue through a competition to conquer the heart and wallet of pretty Glenne Headly, a wide-eyed American heiress. Top-notch comic antics from the two leads and some sharp plot twists.

A: Steve Martin, Michael Caine, Glenne Headly, Barbara Harris, Anton Rodgers, Ian McDiarmid

© ORION PICTURES CORPORATION 8725

DISCREET CHARM OF THE BOURGEOISIE, THE

D: Luis Bunuel 100 m

PG | FOR COM | 1972 | COLOR

9 A brilliant and caustic French work that pokes fun at the rich, the church, the police, and politics. Any attempt to describe the plot is nearly useless, because it is so convoluted. In essence, it all revolves around the frustrating attempts of three couples, diplomats from a South American country, to get dinner in Paris. It won the Oscar for Best Foreign Film. Full of delights and surprises. Hilarious. Subtitles or dubbed.

Sex / Nud / Viol / Lang / AdSit

A: Delphine Seyrig, Fernando Rey, Stephane Audran, Jean-Pierre Cassel

© XENON HOME VIDEO 8000

DISORDERLY ORDERLY

D: Frank Tashlin 90 m

NR | COM CLD | 1964 | COLOR

7 One of Jerry Lewis's best solo vehicles. Jerry is trying to earn money for medical school by working as a clumsy orderly in a hospital. Full of clever slapstick routines and sight gags. Jerry has one particular problem that is certainly going to be a major hindrance in learning to become a doctor: when people describe their pains, he begins to feel them, too. Silly, but this one is not just for Lewis fans - pretty good.

Sex / Nud / Viol / Lang / AdSit

A: Jerry Lewis, Glenda Farrell, Susan Oliver, Everett Sloane, Jack E. Leonard, Kathleen Freeman

© PARAMOUNT HOME VIDEO 6406

DIVINE MADNESS

D: 87 m

R | MUS COM | 1980 | COLOR

7 Bette Midler is sassy, bawdy, full of energy and unpredictable. She is also a talent which requires a particular "bent" to be fully appreciated and this concert film will either appeal to you or not based upon that. She sings 18 songs in all, punctuated by jokes and one-liners - some pretty risque. Songs include "Boogie Woogie Bugle Boy," "Do You Wanna Dance?" and "Leader of the Pack."

Sex / Nud / Viol / Lang / AdSit

A: Bette Midler

© WARNER HOME VIDEO 20001

DIVORCE - ITALIAN STYLE

D: Pietro Germi 104 m

NR | FOR COM | 1962 | B&W

8 Hilarious Italian comedy. A decadent Sicilian nobleman wants to get rid of his wife so that he can marry his young mistress, but the law forbids divorce. However, he can legally kill her if he catches her in the act with another man. So he sets about finding her one. This very funny satire on Italian mores won an Oscar for its story and screenplay. An ironic twist provides the perfect ending. Subtitles or dubbed.

Sex / Nud / Viol / Lang / AdSit

A: Marcello Mastroianni, Daniela Rocca, Leopoldo Trieste

© HEN'S TOOTH VIDEO 1020

DOC HOLLYWOOD

D: Michael Clayton-Jones 104 m

PG-13 | COM ROM | 1991 | COLOR

7 Upwardly mobile Michael J. Fox is looking forward to a very lucrative new career as a plastic surgeon in Beverly Hills. But then he has the misfortune to crash his little Porsche into a South Carolina fence. The powers that be in the small town of Grady sentence him to pay for the damages by doing some temporary medical services. This "fine" is designed to give the townsfolk time to seduce him into staying on in their little town. Even though he is melting, he is determined to leave. However, when he becomes interested in pretty local girl Julie Warner and she becomes interested back, things change. A cute film with both a healthy dose of humor and charm.

Sex / Nud / Viol / Lang / AdSit

A: Michael J. Fox, Julie Warner, Bridget Fonda, Woody Harrelson, Barnard Hughes, David Ogden Stiers

© WARNER HOME VIDEO 12222

DOGPOUND SHUFFLE

D: Jeffrey Bloom 98 m

PG | CLD COM | 1974 | COLOR

7 Fun light-weight little story about a homeless ex-vaudevillian tap dancer (Moody) whose dog, his only real friend, is impounded. In order to get the dog back, he must raise $30. Another drifter, a young harmonica-player (Soul), talks him into forming a street team to raise the money. Funny and sensitive performances, particularly by master character actor Ron Moody.

Sex / Nud / Viol / Lang / AdSit

A: Ron Moody, David Soul, Pamela McMyler, Ray Strucklyn, Raymond Sutton

© FOXVIDEO 9058

DOLLARS ($)

D: Richard Brooks 119 m

R | SUS ACT COM | 1972 | COLOR

9 Top notch heist film. Beatty is an American security technician who masterminds a plot to steal the ill-gotten gains from the security deposit boxes of crooks at a German bank. He enlists the aid of a dippy hooker (Hawn) to obtain copies of the keys that he needs for the three critical boxes. However, the film doesn't end after the robbery is over - because the owners of boxes, not nice guys at all, want everything back, and an elaborate chase across a frozen lake begins. Unexpected twists abound. Really good stuff.

Sex / Nud / Viol / Lang / AdSit

A: Warren Beatty, Goldie Hawn, Gert Frobe, Robert Webber, Scott Brady

© COLUMBIA TRISTAR HOME VIDEO 60450

DONA FLOR AND HER TWO HUSBANDS

D: Bruno Barreto 110 m

R | FOR COM | 1977 | COLOR

8 Very sexy, exotic and erotic comedy imported from Brazil. Sonia Braga is the sultry widow of a very exciting but totally irresponsible womanizer. After he dies in the middle of a tryst during Festival, she marries a dull but dependable pharmacist. However, she is a passionate woman and she longs for her first lover, and when her first husband starts showing up as a nude ghost at the very most inopportune times, she must decide between them. It was later remade for American audiences with Sally Fields as KISS ME GOODBYE, but was considerably toned down. Subtitles.

Sex / Nud / Viol / Lang / AdSit

A: Sonia Braga, Jose Wilker, Mauro Mendanca, Dinora Brillanti

© WARNER HOME VIDEO 34002

DONOVAN'S REEF

D: John Ford 109 m

NR | COM | 1963 | COLOR

7 Fun, light-hearted John Wayne comedy about three carefree pals on a Pacific island after WWII whose lives are up-ended by the unexpected arrival of a beautiful girl. Wayne and Marvin are co-owners of a raucous bar. Their buddy Warden, the island's doctor, has a Polynesian wife and several mixed-race children. The beautiful girl is Warden's stateside, fully-grown daughter, who's mother is a Boston blueblood and she doesn't know about her father's new family. Because Warden's not home, and fearing an embarrassing confrontation, Wayne and Lee hide his new family's identity from her. Seems quite patronizing now, but is also good-natured fun.

Sex / Nud / Viol / Lang / AdSit

A: John Wayne, Lee Marvin, Elizabeth Allen, Jack Warden, Cesar Romero, Dorothy Lamour

© PARAMOUNT HOME VIDEO 6220

DON'T DRINK THE WATER

D: Howard Morris 100 m

G | COM | 1969 | COLOR

6 Wacky little comedy, based on a Woody Allen play. Jackie Gleason is a caterer. He, his wife (Estelle Parsons) and daughter are on a European vacation when the plane taking them to Greece is hijacked and they are taken to a communist country instead. Stranded, they occupy themselves with taking pictures, but that is not a healthy thing to do in a paranoid country. They are immediately accused of being spies. They seek and find asylum in the US embassy, where they quickly become the focus of an international incident.

Sex / Nud / Viol / Lang / AdSit

A: Jackie Gleason, Estelle Parsons, Ted Bessell, Michael Constantine, Joan Delaney, Richard Libertini

© NEW LINE HOME VIDEO 00107

DOWN AND OUT IN BEVERLY HILLS

D: Paul Mazursky 103 m

R | COM DMA | 1986 | COLOR

9 Fun time. Nolte is a bum who is so despondent when his dog leaves him for a better home that he tries to drown himself in the swimming pool of a wealthy coat-hanger magnate (Dreyfuss). However, Dreyfuss spies him and saves him from drowning. The despondent Nolte then moves in with their largely disfunctional family. Oddly, his presence and unique perspective on things brings a strange calming effect to the household's peculiar occupants and everyone is changed for the better. While the film is somewhat uneven, the result is still very funny overall. Great performances especially by Mike the dog.

Sex / Nud / Viol / Lang / AdSit

A: Nick Nolte, Bette Midler, Richard Dreyfuss, Little Richard, Tracy Nelson, Elizabeth Pena

© TOUCHSTONE HOME VIDEO 473

DREAM TEAM, THE

D: Howard Zieff 113 m

PG-13 | COM | 1989 | COLOR

8 Clever comedy. A psychiatrist takes four mental patients on a field trip to watch a ball game in Yankee Stadium. But when the shrink gets separated from them, the loose loonies have to learn to deal with a truly insane environment on their own - New York City. Four crazies: Keaton is a liar with a violent streak, Lloyd is a clean freak, Boyle is a former advertising exec who thinks he's God, and Furst is a near-catatonic, all of whom must pool their talents to get their shrink back from two corrupt cops. Great individual performances of some looney characters make this an enjoyable diversion.

Sex / Nud / Viol / Lang / AdSit

A: Michael Keaton, Christopher Lloyd, Peter Boyle, Stephen Furst, Milo O'Shea

© MCA/UNIVERSAL HOME VIDEO, INC. 80882

DRIVING MISS DAISY

D: Bruce Beresford 99 m

PG | DMA COM | 1989 | COLOR | Sex | Nud | Viol | Lang | AdSit

8 A great feel-good film. In 1948 a wealthy Jewish merchant (Ackroyd) hires an elderly black man (Freeman) to drive and otherwise aid his crotchety old, widowed mother (Tandy - Oscar winner). At first reluctant, she accepts Morgan as an employee. Then, as she grows older and her friends die, she becomes more and more dependent on Morgan. These two are so different - yet an abiding best-friends sort of loving friendship develops. Great performances all around and very enjoyable, but perhaps oversold in the press. It is also rather slow. Oscars also for Best Picture and Screen Adaptation.

A: Jessica Tandy, Morgan Freeman, Dan Aykroyd, Esther Rolle, Patti Lupone

© WARNER HOME VIDEO 11931

DROWNING BY NUMBERS

D: Peter Greenaway 121 m

R | COM | 1991 | COLOR | Sex | Nud | Viol | Lang | AdSit

7 English Director Peter Greenaway has won a reputation as a creator of quite different and sometimes bizarre films. Here, three women, all with the same name -- Cissie, have systematically drown their sadistic husbands and each has won the cooperation of the local coroner through granting sexual favors. However, when a steadily growing crowd of witnesses begin to pressure him, the game-playing coroner decides to resolve the issue with a tug-of-war. As this story unfolds, the director literally labels the film on screen as it progresses from 1-100. No mere summary of the plot can satisfactorily impart the multitude of messages and subtleties. This is no simple who-dun-it, nor is it a simple anything.

A: Bernard Hill, Joan Plowright, Juliet Stevenson, Joely Richardson, Jason Edwards

© LIVE HOME VIDEO 69001

DR. STRANGELOVE OR: HOW I LEARNED TO STOP WORRYING

D: Stanley Kubrick 93 m

PG | COM DMA | 1964 | B&W | Sex | Nud | Viol | Lang | AdSit

10 Very funny black comedy and spoof of the nuclear confrontation between the East and West. Movies like this helped us get through the terror of living with "the bomb" by laughing at it. A renegade Air Force general takes it upon himself to save the world from the Russian menace by launching an unauthorized nuclear first strike. Sellars is hilarious in triple roles as the US President dealing with the Russians and unable to stop the bombers, as a British captain and as the crazy inventor of the bomb, Dr. Strangelove. Film also won four Oscar nominations, including Best Actor and Best Picture.

A: Peter Sellers, George C. Scott, Sterling Hayden, Slim Pickens, Keenan Wynn, James Earl Jones

© COLUMBIA TRISTAR HOME VIDEO 60172

DUMB & DUMBER

D: Peter Farrelly 110 m

PG-13 | COM | 1995 | COLOR | Sex | Nud | Viol | Lang | AdSit

6 Well, he's back. Fans of rubber-faced Jim Carrey will not be denied, nor will they be particularly surprised. He's just as ridiculous as always and just as crude - only this time he has a partner: Jeff Daniels plays Carrey's even dumber friend. After a beautiful woman leaves a briefcase behind, love-struck chauffeur Carrey becomes determined to return it to her, even though he must travel cross country to Aspen to do it. Recently fired Daniels joins his good buddy in the trip, unaware that the briefcase contains lots and lots of money, and some very bad people are now after them to get it back. Nothing interesting in the premise. The only reason to watch it is Carrey.

A: Jim Carrey, Jeff Daniels, Lauren Holly, Karen Duffy, Victoria Rowell, Teri Garr

© TURNER HOME ENTERTAINMENT N4036

EARTH GIRLS ARE EASY

D: Julien Temple 99 m

PG | COM MUS SF | 1989 | COLOR | Sex | Nud | Viol | Lang | AdSit

7 A wacky sci-fi spoof/musical about an alien space craft, occupied by some very hairy aliens, that crash-lands in the backyard swimming pool of Valley Girl Geena Davis. She and her ditsy girlfriend shave the hairy aliens and find that, underneath all their fur, they are hunks. Inspired, the girls take them on a fun-filled excursion into and through the live-for-today Southern California lifestyle. Lots of silly goofiness (plenty of sex jokes) and some good musical numbers, too. A pretty good time, but no masterpiece.

A: Geena Davis, Jeff Goldblum, Julie Brown, Jim Carrey, Damon Wayans, Michael McKean

© LIVE HOME VIDEO 5303

EATING

D: Henry Jaglom 110 m

R | COM | 1990 | COLOR | Sex | Nud | Viol | Lang | AdSit

8 Highly unusual but very entertaining film about a subject both near to the heart of and dreaded by many women. A group of trendy Southern California women have convened at a birthday party where the subject of the day becomes eating. It is explored in all its many manifestations, from its ultimate physical and sensual pleasures, to its darker psychological aspects. "I have sex before I eat, because if I have sex after I eat, I feel fat." Thirty women lounging along side the pool talking about themselves. Very different, but very interesting and worthwhile.

A: Nelly Allard, Frances Bergen, Mary Crosby, Lisa Richards, Gwen Welles, Dapha Kastner

© PARAMOUNT HOME VIDEO 83101

EATING RAOUL

D: Paul Bartel 87 m

R | COM | 1982 | COLOR | Sex | Nud | Viol | Lang | AdSit

8 Very black and sometimes hysterical comedy. Paul and Mary Bland, a non-descript average (but very prim) couple, want to open a gourmet restaurant but they are unable to finance it. Their salvation comes when Paul conks a would-be rapist over the head with a skillet, killing him. Paul gets rid of the body but keeps his money, and a new business is born. Mary runs an ad in a sex paper as a domitrix. Then, when the perverts show up, they get conked and the Blands keep their money.

A: Paul Bartel, Mary Woronov, Robert Beltran, Susan Salger, Buck Henry, Ed Begley, Jr.

© FOXVIDEO 1291

EDUCATING RITA

D: Lewis Gilbert 110 m

PG | COM DMA | 1983 | COLOR | Sex | Nud | Viol | Lang | AdSit

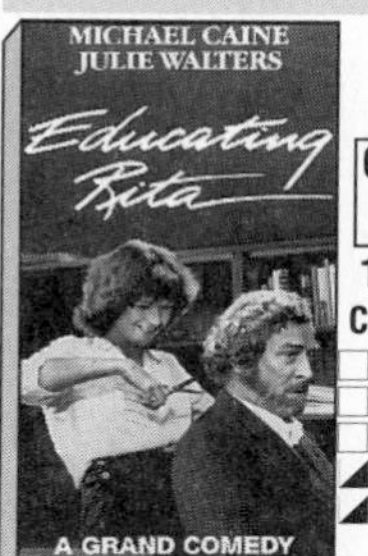

8 A likable movie and a big box office hit. It is the story of an uneducated English hairdresser who decides to better herself by going back to school. She has, as one of her teachers, a disaffected alcoholic English professor (Caine) who admires her zest for learning and life, and he becomes her mentor. Infected with her enthusiasm, his long-lost love of life and literature begins to return. But, as he watches her transform herself, he is also deeply unsettled to watch some of what he admired most in her slowly be changed. Three Oscar nominations for acting.

A: Michael Caine, Julie Walters, Michael Williams, Maureen Lipman, Jeananne Crowley, Malcolm Douglas

© GOODTIMES 7230

EDWARD SCISSORHANDS

D: Tim Burton 100 m

PG-13 | COM ROM FAN | 1990 | COLOR | Sex | Nud | Viol | Lang | AdSit

8 Heartwarming, heartbreaking and fanciful. Once upon a time, high on a hill, an inventor created a young man out of spare parts but died before he could give him hands and long scissors served as their awkward replacement. Thereafter, Edward Scissorhands (Depp) lived a lonely existence in the mansion until, one day, the Avon Lady (Wiest) came and took him to live with her family in the suburbs. But when Edward and her daughter (Ryder) fall in love, chaos breaks loose in the close-knit community and poor Edward is caught completely off guard. A very unusual semi-adult fantasy that can be very entertaining if you let it.

A: Johnny Depp, Winona Ryder, Dianne Wiest, Vincent Price, Alan Arkin, Anthony Michael Hall

© FOXVIDEO 0620

ED WOOD

D: Tim Burton 127 m

R | COM DMA | 1994 | B&W | Sex | Nud | Viol | Lang | AdSit

7 During the early 50s, an overly-enthusiastic Hollywood "go-for" named Ed Wood disregarded the fact that he had neither talent nor money and proceeded to produce, direct and star in some of the worst movies ever made, either before or since. His movies had virtually no plot, terrible production values and were notoriously overacted. He endured the pressures of his productions by dressing in women's clothes, showing a particular fondness for angora sweaters. No amount of failure or derision could dissuade him from his chosen profession. Johnny Depp plays Wood in this playful biography that won an Oscar for Best Makeup, and Landau won for Best Supporting Actor. Very Odd.

A: Johnny Depp, Sarah Jessica Parker, Martin Landau, Patricia Arquett, Bill Murray, Jeffrey Jones

© TOUCHSTONE HOME VIDEO 2758

EL DIABLO

D: Peter Markle 108 m

PG-13 | WST COM | 1990 | COLOR | Sex | Nud | Viol | Lang | AdSit

7 Tongue-in-cheek made-for-cable Western. Billy, a small town Texas schoolteacher loves to read novels of gunfighters and daydreams of being one. However, when a legendary outlaw named El Diablo actually rides into town, robs a bank and kidnaps one of his students, his daydreams come face to face with reality. While he sets off in pursuit, he is hopelessly outmatched in his quest, until he meets gunman Thomas Van Leek (Louis Gossett, Jr.). He and his cohorts make a new man out of Billy, even as they continue to chase down El Diablo. Full of gags and fun.

A: Anthony Edwards, Louis Gossett, Jr., John Glover, M.C. Gainey, Miguel Sandoval, Sarah Trigger

© HBO VIDEO 90435

EL DORADO

D: Howard Hawks 126 m

NR | WST ACT COM | 1967 | COLOR | Sex | Nud | Viol | Lang | AdSit

9 Western fans line up. This is a big raucous John Wayne Western. Hawks revamped his big 1959 hit RIO BRAVO and this time has John Wayne being an aging gunfighter who helps his drunken friend, the sheriff (Mitchum), stop a range war. Great characters: Caan as a likable but odd-ball character who can't shoot; Arthur Hunnicut as a gnarled old Indian fighter and deputy; and Christopher George as a gunfighter on the other side but who has a sense of honor. Plenty of action and lots of humor, too. It was so successful it this time that it was redone one more time in 1970 as RIO LOBO.

A: John Wayne, Robert Mitchum, James Caan, Arthur Hunnicutt, Edward Asner, Michelle Carey

© PARAMOUNT HOME VIDEO 6625

EL MARIACHI

D: Robert Rodriguez — 80 m

R | FOR ACT COM | 1992 | COLOR

□ Sex □ Nud ■ Viol □ Lang ◢ AdSit

7 Most famous for being a film shot for only $7000 in 14 days and still being purchased for national release by a major studio (which then also gave its 24-year-old producer/director/co-writer/star a contract). The film is a quite choppy (what do you expect) spoof of spaghetti Westerns, even though it is set in modern times. It tells the unlikely story of an innocent guitar player dressed in black who wonders into a small Mexican town just after a hit man, who is also dressed in black and carries a guitar case full of weapons, has shot up the town. The poor hero is forced to defend himself over and over again. Subtitles.

A: Carlos Gallardo, Consuelo Gomez, Peter Marquardt, Jamie de Hoyos, Reinol Martinez

© COLUMBIA TRISTAR HOME VIDEO 53613

EMO PHILIPS LIVE

D: Cynthia L. Sears — 60 m

NR | COM | 1988 | COLOR

□ Sex □ Nud □ Viol □ Lang ■ AdSit

8 Emo Philips has a totally off-center perspective on the world. Some would call it twisted. Almost everybody would call it very funny. See it before they lock him up.

A: Emo Phillips

© HBO VIDEO 0046

ENCHANTED APRIL

D: Mike Newell — 93 m

PG | COM ROM | 1992 | COLOR

□ Sex □ Nud □ Viol □ Lang ◢ AdSit

9 An enchanting and witty piece of delightful entertainment. Two middle class English women of the 1920s seek to escape the drizzly rains of home and the misery of their married lives, by renting a luxury villa on the sunny Italian Riviera for a month to sort through their problems. However, in order to afford it they accept two strangers in to share expenses. One is a cranky old woman and the other is jaded young beauty. The four women quickly relax, unwind their former lives and begin again with new understandings born of their interactions and new circumstances. Intelligent, romantic and charming.

A: Miranda Richardson, Josie Lawrence, Polly Walker, Joan Plowright, Alfred Molina, Michael Kitchen

© PARAMOUNT HOME VIDEO 15114

END, THE

D: Burt Reynolds — 100 m

R | COM DMA | 1978 | COLOR

□ Sex □ Nud ◢ Viol ■ Lang ■ AdSit

8 This is an outrageous black comedy and it is absolutely hysterical in places, but it is also slow in others. Burt Reynolds is a user-type of a guy who is stunned to discover that he is going to die from a rare disease. He can hardly believe his misfortune, but worse - nobody seems to care. So, he decides to commit suicide to get it all over. But when his attempt fails, he is sent to a mental institution. Now he is really desperate. There, he meets and befriends a crazy killer (loveably weird Dom DeLuise) who agrees, as a special favor, to kill him. This is a really left-handed comedy, but it definitely has some hysterical moments.

A: Burt Reynolds, Sally Field, Dom DeLuise, Joanne Woodward, David Steinberg, Pat O'Brien

Distributed By MGM/UA Home Video M203102

ENDLESS SUMMER, THE

D: Bruce Brown — 90 m

NR | DOC COM | 1964 | COLOR

□ Sex □ Nud □ Viol □ Lang □ AdSit

8 This is a perennial favorite and has not diminished with time. It is an extraordinarily fun documentary that captures the exhilaration and danger of surfing through beautiful photography of people in beautiful locations. It is a quasi-travelogue loosely patterned around the quest of two young surfers to find the perfect wave by exploring all the world's most famous beaches. Whimsically narrated by director Bruce Brown. In 1994, 30 years later, Brown retraced the steps in this documentary in ENDLESS SUMMER II.

A:

© TURNER HOME ENTERTAINMENT N4028

ENDLESS SUMMER II

D: Bruce Brown — 110 m

PG | DOC COM | 1994 | COLOR

□ Sex ◢ Nud □ Viol □ Lang □ AdSit

9 In 1964 director Bruce Brown created a now classic documentary in which two young surfers decided to follow the summer and the waves to all the places around the world where they could surf. Now, thirty years later, Brown goes back on the road again to retrace those footsteps, and it's even more fun than before. This is a very entertaining travelogue in which Brown narrates their trip with clever and funny dialogue. The photography is absolutely outstanding. He photographs surfing on big waves, on small waves, on almost no waves and on HUGE waves. He photographs it from in front of the waves, from behind the waves, on top of the wave, inside the wave and under the wave. Radical dude.

A: Robert"Wingnut" Weaver, Patrick O'Connell

© TURNER HOME ENTERTAINMENT N4052

ENEMIES, A LOVE STORY

D: Paul Mazursky — 121 m

R | DMA COM ROM | 1989 | COLOR

□ Sex ◢ Nud □ Viol ■ Lang ■ AdSit

8 Highly regarded and much talked about film of a Jewish refugee (Silver) and Holocaust survivor who is living in America after WWII. He is in the unfortunate position of juggling the three separate women that he loves, each in different ways. He is alive because a Polish family hid him and, largely out of gratitude, he married their daughter - a simple domestic woman who is totally dedicated to homemaking. He is involved in a passionate affair with a fiery married woman. And he has learned that his first wife, who he thought was dead, isn't. Intelligent and sophisticated but slow.

A: Ron Silver, Anjelica Huston, Lena Olin, Margaret Sophie Stein, Alan King, Judith Malina

© VIDEO TREASURES M012613

ENTER LAUGHING

D: Carl Reiner — 112 m

NR | COM | 1967 | COLOR

□ Sex □ Nud □ Viol □ Lang ◢ AdSit

6 Carl Reiner's semi-autobiographical account of a young man who gives up an unpromising career as a mechanic, and his mother's dreams of him becoming a pharmacist, to become a comedian instead. His stage debut is a total disaster and unorthodox, to say the least. This was a funny vehicle for Alan Arkin on Broadway and it made him into a star. There are also some good scenes with Jack Gilford and Elaine May. Generally funny - with some really funny bits.

A: Shelley Winters, Elaine May, Jose Ferrer, Jack Gilford, Reni Santoni, Don Rickles

© COLUMBIA TRISTAR HOME VIDEO 60624

ERRAND BOY, THE

D: Jerry Lewis — 93 m

NR | COM CLD | 1961 | B&W

□ Sex □ Nud □ Viol □ Lang □ AdSit

6 Jerry Lewis is given an under-cover job as an errand boy in a Hollywood movie studio, but his real job is supposed to be to uncover waste. However, inept and bumbling Jerry proceeds to destroy everything he touches. A lot of major-name character actors and Jerry's shtick make this an enjoyable diversion. Pretty good.

A: Jerry Lewis, Brian Donlevy, Sig Ruman, Howard McNear, Firtz Feld, Doodles Weaver

© LIVE HOME VIDEO 215-486

EVENING WITH BOBCAT GOLDTHWAIT: SHARE THE WARMTH

D: Anthony Eaton — 54 m

NR | COM | 1987 | COLOR

□ Sex □ Nud □ Viol ■ Lang ◢ AdSit

8 As a comedian, Bob Goldthwait is, at the very least, very different. His comedy is caustic and very funny. He attacks everybody: Ronald and Nancy Reagan, Bob Hope, Lucille Ball, Dr. Seuss, Rolling Stone Magazine and Bruce Willis. They're gonna lock him up. If you like the bizare and irreverent, see him soon. Heavy-duty profanity.

A: Bobcat Goldthwait

© LIVE HOME VIDEO 3159

EVENING WITH ROBIN WILLIAMS, AN

D: Don Mischer — 92 m

NR | COM | 1982 | COLOR

□ Sex □ Nud □ Viol ■ Lang ■ AdSit

8 Robin Williams is mania in motion. His energy is non-stop and unpredictable. His stand-up act at San Francisco's Great American Music Hall was filmed live.

A: Robin Williams

© PARAMOUNT HOME VIDEO 2319

EVERYTHING YOU ALWAYS WANTED TO KNOW ABOUT SEX

D: Woody Allen — 89 m

R | COM | 1972 | COLOR

◢ Sex ◢ Nud □ Viol ◢ Lang ■ AdSit

8 This is perhaps Woody Allen's most bizarre entry. It is not one that everyone will appreciate, but those who like Allen's absurd take on things will have a great time. Using Dr. David Reuben's sex manual of the same name as a premise, Allen creates a series of episodes, with each episode supposedly providing a response to a question. Topics in discussion include chastity belts, transvestites, breasts, sheep "lovers" and reluctant sperm. Uneven and sometimes tasteless; however, usually funny and sometimes hysterical.

A: Woody Allen, John Carradine, Lou Jacobi, Louise Lasser, Anthony Quayle, Lynn Redgrave

Distributed By MGM/UA Home Video M202106

EVERY WHICH WAY BUT LOOSE

D: James Fargo — 114 m

PG | 8 | COM ACT | 1978 | COLOR

Very popular and a big box office hit with wide public appeal. Eastwood plays a brawling boozy truck driver who chases a barroom country singer across the whole Southwest, while getting into fights with a motorcycle gang and a legendary barroom brawler named Tank Murdock. Far and away, the most appealing feature of the film is Eastwood's raunchy 165-pound Orangutan side-kick Clyde. A light-hearted good time. Great country-western songs, too. A lot of fun, but don't be expecting subtlety. This is all out low-brow stuff.

□ Sex ◢ Nud ◢ Viol ◢ Lang ◢ AdSit

A: Clint Eastwood, Sondra Locke, Geoffrey Lewis, Beverly D'Angelo, Ruth Gordon

© WARNER HOME VIDEO 1028

FABULOUS BAKER BOYS, THE

D: Steve Kloves — 116 m

R | 8 | ROM COM DMA | 1989 | COLOR

Excellent and curious character study of two piano playing brothers barely surviving by playing small clubs. Business has been even worse lately - that is, until they hire a sultry ex-hooker (Pfeiffer) as their vocalist. Suddenly they're in demand. Beau is excellent as the stalwart older brother who wants to hold the act together and play like they always have. But younger brother Jeff yearns to play solo jazz. Things come to an explosive head when Jeff and sexy Pfeiffer can't keep their hands off each other. Things will never be the same.

◢ Sex ◢ Nud □ Viol ■ Lang ◢ AdSit

A: Jeff Bridges, Michelle Pfeiffer, Beau Bridges, Ellie Raab, Jennifer Tilly

© LIVE HOME VIDEO 68910

FAMILY PLOT

D: Alfred Hitchcock — 121 m

PG | 8 | MYS COM | 1976 | COLOR

This is a winning, light-hearted, convoluted thriller/comedy from Mr. Hitchcock. A seedy pseudo-psychic (Harris) and her loser boyfriend (Dern) team up to track down a lost heir (Devane) and get a $10,000 reward. The target of all this attention is a man supposedly dead, not really dead, but who would much prefer to be thought of as dead. That is because he turns out to be a not-too-nice guy who, along with Karen Black, is in the process of launching a big kidnapping/extortion plot. A fun time, full of plot twists and black humor.

□ Sex □ Nud □ Viol □ Lang ◢ AdSit

A: Karen Black, Bruce Dern, Barbara Harris, William Devane, Ed Lauter, Cathleen Nesbitt

© MCA/UNIVERSAL HOME VIDEO, INC. 66054

FAST BREAK

D: Jack Smight — 107 m

PG | 6 | COM | 1979 | COLOR

A pretty good little comedy in which Gabe Kaplan, of TV's "Welcome Back Kotter," gives up his promising career as a cashier at a New York deli for a chance to coach an obscure Nevada college's pitiful basketball team. He is to get $50 for every game he wins and, if he beats their major rival, he gets to keep the job. He sets about recruiting his team by bringing in five street kids from New York to be on his team - and one of them is a girl.

□ Sex □ Nud □ Viol ◢ Lang □ AdSit

A: Gabe Kaplan, Harold Sylvester, Mike Warren, Bernard King, Reb Brown

© UNITED AMERICAN VIDEO CORP. 5970

FAST TIMES AT RIDGEMONT HIGH

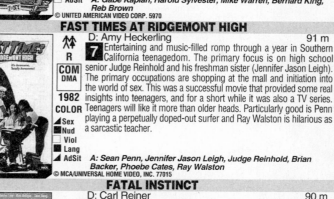

D: Amy Heckerling — 91 m

R | 7 | COM DMA | 1982 | COLOR

Entertaining and music-filled romp through a year in Southern California teenagedom. The primary focus is on high school senior Judge Reinhold and his freshman sister (Jennifer Jason Leigh). The primary occupations are shopping at the mall and initiation into the world of sex. This was a successful movie that provided some real insights into teenagers, and for a short while it was also a TV series. Teenagers will like it more than older heads. Particularly good is Penn playing a perpetually doped-out surfer and Ray Walston is hilarious as a sarcastic teacher.

◢ Sex ■ Nud □ Viol ■ Lang ◢ AdSit

A: Sean Penn, Jennifer Jason Leigh, Judge Reinhold, Brian Backer, Phoebe Cates, Ray Walston

© MCA/UNIVERSAL HOME VIDEO, INC. 77015

FATAL INSTINCT

D: Carl Reiner — 90 m

PG-13 | 6 | COM | 1994 | COLOR

One more in a string of wild spoofs of blockbuster movies. Like the name would imply, BASIC INSTINCT and FATAL ATTRACTION are in for major ribbing with this one, but they also take a serious shot at THE POSTMAN ALWAYS RINGS TWICE. Assante is an attorney/cop, who is oblivious to the longings his lovely and dutiful secretary has for him. And all that while, his wife and her lover try to kill him, even as he is also hotly pursued by the amorous Lola, who wants him in her lust-filled bed. Wild and silly slapstick competes with loads of puns to capture your groans. How well you like this one depends upon how you feel about silly spoofs, as well as how many of them you've already seen.

◢ Sex □ Nud □ Viol ◢ Lang AdSit

A: Armand Assante, Sherilyn Fenn, Kate Nelligan, Sean Young, Tony Randall, Christopher McDonald

Distributed By MGM/UA Home Video 03944

FATHER GOOSE

D: Ralph Nelson — 116 m

NR | 6 | COM ROM | 1964 | COLOR

Light-hearted romantic comedy. Grant is a carefree drunken bum living a carefree life in the islands of the South Pacific just before WWII breaks out and the Japanese begin their campaign of conquest. Wanting only to be left alone, he is tricked by Howard into becoming a coastwatcher for the Australian navy. If that predicament isn't bad enough, he is forced to rescue a prissy school teacher (Leslie Caron) and her young female charges, and winds up playing unwilling nursemaid to them. Enjoyable, even if undistinguished, romantic adventure that won an Oscar for Screenplay.

□ Sex □ Nud □ Viol □ Lang ◢ AdSit

A: Cary Grant, Leslie Caron, Trevor Howard, Jack Good, Nicole Felsette

© REPUBLIC PICTURES HOME VIDEO 5403

COM

FATHER OF THE BRIDE

D: Charles Shyer — 105 m

PG | 7 | COM | 1992 | COLOR

Steve Martin's little girl is getting married. This is not an easy thing for a father to deal with. She's just a baby. True, she is over 21 and she is marrying a computer whiz from a wealthy family, but still... Finally, after coming to grips with the idea of it all, he still has to face the reality of it. Particularly, he has to face wedding planner Martin Short and the bills. Pleasant, but undistinguished, remake of the 1950 classic with Spencer Tracy and Elizabeth Taylor. A little too silly in places, but Steve Martin fans will expect that.

□ Sex □ Nud □ Viol ◢ Lang ◢ AdSit

A: Steve Martin, Diane Keaton, Kimberly Williams, Martin Short, Kieran Culkin, George Newbern

© TOUCHSTONE HOME VIDEO 1335

FAVOR, THE

D: Donald Petrie — 97 m

R | 6 | COM | 1994 | COLOR

Kathy (Kozak) is happily married to a nice-guy and has two kids. However, she also has a dreadful problem. Ever since she received the invitation to her 15-year class reunion, she has been having romantic dreams about the hunk from highschool that she didn't sleep with all during the two years they went together. So, when she learns that her single best friend Emily (McGovern) will be going to Denver, she begs Emily to look him up, see what she has missed and report back. The reluctant Emily does what her friend requested, spending one glorious night in the sack with the dreamboat. But, now the happily married Kathy is jealous. Very slight comedy, covering no new ground.

□ Sex □ Nud □ Viol ■ Lang ■ AdSit

A: Harley Jane Kozak, Bill Pullman, Elizabeth McGovern, Brad Pitt, Ken Wahl

© ORION PICTURES CORPORATION 8775

FEARLESS VAMPIRE KILLERS, THE

D: Roman Polanski — 111 m

NR | 7 | COM HOR | 1967 | COLOR

Weird, odd-ball mixture of horror and humor that has achieved a significant cult following. Professor Abronsius (MacGowran) and his bumbling assistant (Polanski) travel to Transylvania to attempt to destroy a family of Slovokian vampires. While stopping at an inn, they spy the beautiful virginal innkeeper's daughter, Sarah (Sharon Tate). Later she is kidnapped by the vampires while she is taking a bath and the two attempt to infiltrate the vampire's annual ball to retrieve her - but will they get out again without becoming immortal themselves?

□ Sex ◢ Nud ◢ Viol □ Lang ◢ AdSit

A: Jack MacGowran, Roman Polanski, Alfie Bass, Jessie Robins, Sharon Tate, Ferdy Mayne

Distributed By MGM/UA Home Video M200138

FEAR OF A BLACK HAT

D: Anthony Drazan — 85 m

R | 8 | COM | 1994 | COLOR

Farcical pseudo-documentary that takes a wicked slap at gangsta-rap music and the people involved with it. It supposedly follows a group calling itself NWH (Niggaz With Hats) whose three members are Tone Def, Tasty-Taste and Ice Cold. This is a wildly outrageous satire that uses the vulgarity of the music-form to attack it. If a viewer can accept the premise and the constantly and purposely foul street language, there is much to enjoy. However, the unfortunate Catch 22 is, that those same people who will enjoy the satirical barbs thrown, must also endure the very music that is being spoofed. Fans of rap music may want to watch this, enjoy its humor and appreciate its sarcasm.

□ Sex ◢ Nud □ Viol ■ Lang ■ AdSit

A: Rusty Cundieff, Larry B. Scott, Mark Christophe Lawrence, Kasi Lemmons, Howie Gold, Barry Heins

© FOXVIDEO 5853

FERRIS BUELLER'S DAY OFF

D: John Hughes — 103 m

PG-13 | 7 | COM | 1986 | COLOR

On a pretty spring day, popular high school hero Ferris Bueller decides that he deserves a day off. So he tricks his parents into believing that he is sick and sets up an elaborate scheme to convince his high school principal of the same thing. Then he, his girlfriend and his best friend begin a wild adventure into downtown Chicago in his friend's Dad's vintage 1961 red Ferrari GT convertible which they "borrow." Their credo for the day: Don't take life too seriously. Despite some pretty universally funny moments, this is most attractive for teenagers.

□ Sex □ Nud □ Viol ◢ Lang ◢ AdSit

A: Matthew Broderick, Alan Ruck, Mia Sara, Jeffrey Jones, Jennifer Grey, Charlie Sheen

© PARAMOUNT HOME VIDEO 1890

FFOLKES

D: Andrew V. McLaglen 99 m

PG
ACT COM
1980
COLOR
Sex
Nud
Viol
Lang
AdSit

7 Tongue-in-cheek characterization by Roger Moore in which he plays a character who acts exactly counter to his former role as James Bond. This guy hates women, but loves cats. He is a underwater sabotage expert who is called in by the British government to stop an impending attempt by a psychotic madman (Perkins) who is determined to blow up the largest oil rig in the North Sea unless the government pays him a ransom. This is no classic, but is an enjoyable diversion that is told with a touch of humor. The plot is actually more plausible than most of the James Bond plots.

A: Roger Moore, Anthony Perkins, James Mason, Michael Parks, David Hedison

© MCA/UNIVERSAL HOME VIDEO, INC. 80183

FINDERS KEEPERS

D: Richard Lester 96 m

R
COM
1984
COLOR
Sex
Nud
Viol
Lang
AdSit

6 A moderately successful slapstick comedy in which circumstances build upon themselves to create mayhem. A couple has just stolen $5 million dollars from her father's safe and have it hidden inside a casket. A roller derby team manager escapes from disgruntled fans dressed in an army uniform and, by draping a flag over the coffin, pretends to escort the body home on a cross-country train trip. The characters and bizarre circumstances build from there. It is an OK farce with a crew of wacky characters. Standouts are Beverly D'Angelo and David Wayne, as the world's oldest conductor.

A: David Wayne, Beverly D'Angelo, Pamela Stephenson, Ed Lauter, Louis Gossett, Jr.

© CBS/FOX VIDEO 7079

FINE MADNESS, A

D: Irvin Kershner 104 m

NR
COM
1966
COLOR
Sex
Nud
Viol
Lang
AdSit

7 Black comedy and satire about an egotistical radical poet (Connery in a rare comedic role). He is Samson Shillitoe, a self-declared genius and part-time carpet cleaner. He lives in New York with his second wife (Woodward) and is being chased by a process server for the back alimony payments he owes his first wife. He can't keep his mouth shut, he can't get along with the women in his life, he can't deal with most forms of authority and he also has massive writer's block. So, he goes to a psychiatrist... and sleeps with the guy's wife. Sometimes uneven, but often very funny.

A: Sean Connery, Joanne Woodward, Jean Seberg, Patrick O'Neal, Colleen Dewhurst, Renee Taylor

© WARNER HOME VIDEO 11344

FINIAN'S RAINBOW

D: Francis Ford Coppola 142 m

G
MUS COM ROM
1968
COLOR
Sex
Nud
Viol
Lang
AdSit

7 This was a ground-breaking musical in the 1940s when it opened on Broadway, but is now dated in the way it deals with its theme of racial prejudice. Nevertheless, it still has some very fine moments and Tommy Steele is wonderful in the role of an effervescent leprechaun whose gold is stolen by Irishman Astaire. Astair has transplanted himself into the American South and Steele has followed him. Petula Clarke is Astaire's daughter and gets three wishes - one of which she uses to turn bigoted Southern Senator Wynn into a black man. Tuneful score includes, "How Are Things is Glocca Mora?"

A: Fred Astaire, Petula Clark, Tommy Steele, Keenan Wynn, Barbara Hanock, Don Francks

© WARNER HOME VIDEO 11208

FINNEGAN BEGIN AGAIN

D: Joan Micklin Silver 112 m

NR
ROM COM
1985
COLOR
Sex
Nud
Viol
Lang
AdSit

8 Touching and entertaining light comedy about the unlikely relationship that develops between a mismatched pair. He (Preston) is an aging and grouchy, once-good newspaper writer, who now is reduced to writing an advice column and taking care of his nearly-senile wife. She (Moore) is a middle-aged, widowed school teacher trapped in an affair with a married funeral director (Waterston). The platonic friendship between these two gradually drifts into romance. Winning performances, particularly by Preston, make this charming made-for-cable movie a very pleasant viewing experience.

A: Robert Preston, Mary Tyler Moore, Sylvia Sidney, Sam Waterston, David Huddleston

© HBO VIDEO TVF3243

FISH CALLED WANDA, A

D: Charles Crichton 108 m

R
COM CRM
1988
COLOR
Sex
Nud
Viol
Lang
AdSit

7 A bizarre farcical comedy with something to offend everyone. John Cleese, the Monty Python veteran, stars in this hilarious and/or ridiculous robbery caper - depending upon your tastes. Two Brits and two Americans team up to steal diamonds. When the one who has hidden the diamonds is caught, the others, particularly sexy Curtis, set about seducing and tricking his attorney (Cleese) into telling them where the take is hidden. Kline won Oscar.

A: John Cleese, Jamie Lee Curtis, Kevin Kline, Michael Palin, Maria Aitken, Tom Georgeson

© FOXVIDEO 4752

FISHER KING, THE

D: Terry Gilliam 138 m

R
FAN DMA COM
1991
COLOR
Sex
Nud
Viol
Lang
AdSit

7 Complex, surreal and painful. One of those movies you won't know if you should love or hate, but it is poignant and it cuts right to the bone. When it was released, it created a lot of controversy for its portrayal of homelessness and mental illness (which were handled lightly at times and very heavy at others). Williams was a history teacher but now is an upbeat, but deranged, street person. Bridges is a New York radio shock jock who goes too far, is fired, is forced on the street and finds a strange savior in wacked-out Williams. Shocking, emotional, mystical and sometimes funny.

A: Robin Williams, Jeff Bridges, Mercedes Ruehl, Michael Jeter, Harry Shearer, John de Lancie

© COLUMBIA TRISTAR HOME VIDEO 70613

FIVE HEARTBEATS, THE

D: Robert Townsend 120 m

R
MUS DMA COM
1991
COLOR
Sex
Nud
Viol
Lang
AdSit

8 Exuberant and fun (even if it's a little bit corny) ode to the heyday of Motown. This is the story of the rise of one fictional group to fame and is based loosely on the experiences of the R&B group, The Dells. It follows their rise from singing at amateur nights, to major success and then to personal failures. The film is not as cliched as it sounds. Although this is much-covered territory and is predictable, the characters are very likable and the music is fun and memory jogging. This is a good time, more so if you like this flavor of music or this was your era.

A: Robert Townsend, Michael Wright, Harry J. Lennix, Tico Wells, Diahann Carroll, Harold Nicholas

© FOXVIDEO 0630

FLAMINGO KID, THE

D: Garry Marshall 98 m

PG-13
DMA COM
1984
COLOR
Sex
Nud
Viol
Lang
AdSit

8 A real charmer. Very enjoyable and a credible coming-of-age story that is set in 1963 but could almost have been at any time. Dillon is a Brooklyn high-school grad, from a blue collar background, who lands a job as cabana boy at a private beach club on Long Island. He is immediately overwhelmed by the affluence of everything around him, particularly by Richard Crenna, the club's wealthy resident card-sharp. He determines that this is the life for him - he doesn't need college. However, this summer proves to be the biggest education of his life. It is the summer he grows up.

A: Matt Dillon, Richard Crenna, Jessica Walter, Janet Jones, Hector Elizondo, Fisher Stevens

© LIVE HOME VIDEO VA5072

FLASHBACK

D: Franco Amurri 108 m

R
COM ACT
1990
COLOR
Sex
Nud
Viol
Lang
AdSit

6 Well cast and a pretty good time. Hopper is a radical hippie who never recovered from the '60s. Sutherland is a straightlaced yuppie FBI agent who never recovered from the '80s. Sutherland is charged with escorting the flipped-out Hopper from San Francisco to Spokane. But along the way they run afoul of corrupt cop and politician De Young. These two opposites are now running together for their lives; and, it is new experience and a surprise for Mr. F.B.I. to discover that he likes the hippie. Plays a little too fast and loose with believability, but still the characters are likable and fun.

A: Dennis Hopper, Kiefer Sutherland, Carol Kane, Cliff De Young, Paul Dooley, Michael McKean

© PARAMOUNT HOME VIDEO 32110

FLETCH

D: Michael Ritchie 98 m

PG
COM
1985
COLOR
Sex
Nud
Viol
Lang
AdSit

7 Chevy Chase fans line up, everybody else - well, this IS one of his better efforts. He plays a wisecracking reporter who is always changing his identity. While investigating a drug case, Fletch is approached by a dying man who wants Fletch to murder him so his wife can get more insurance money, but Fletch smells more. He investigates and uncovers a drug smuggling ring including corrupt cop. Full of one-liners and non-sequiturs, generating laughs even if you're not a big fan. Plenty of action, too.

A: Chevy Chase, Dana Wheeler-Nicholson, Tim Matheson, Joe Don Baker, Richard Libertini, Geena Davis

© MCA/UNIVERSAL HOME VIDEO, INC. 80190

FLETCH LIVES

D: Michael Ritchie 95 m

PG
COM
1989
COLOR
Sex
Nud
Viol
Lang
AdSit

6 Wise-cracking Fletch inherits an 80-acre mansion and plantation in Louisiana. He quits his job at the newspaper and goes south to claim it. Trouble begins immediately when his beautiful neighbor turns up dead and he becomes a murder suspect. A beautiful real estate lady then shows up with an offer too good to be true and he has to deal with a never-ending string of stereotypical Southern buffoons. Silly sequel to FLETCH. Full of Chase's brand of humor. If you enjoy Chase and/or the original, you'll enjoy it. Others, be careful.

A: Chevy Chase, Hal Holbrook, Julianne Phillips, Cleavon Little, R. Lee Ermey, George Wyner

© MCA/UNIVERSAL HOME VIDEO, INC. 80881

FLIM-FLAM MAN, THE

D: Irvin Kershner 104 m

NR · COM · 1967 · COLOR · Rating: 7

Very entertaining comedy in which Scott is an old-time bunko artist who makes a living by charming the rural yokels of the South at the same time that he fleeces them. Along comes an AWOL soldier (Sarrazin) who Scott takes under his wing and teaches all the tricks of the trade. But Sarrazin, the ungrateful wretch, is essentially an honest man who tries to reform Scott instead. That is a gambit doomed to failure. Clever film with likable characters in which Scott really shines.

Sex / Nud / Viol / Lang / AdSit

A: George C. Scott, Sue Lyon, Michael Sarrazin, Harry Morgan, Jack Albertson, Slim Pickens

© FOXVIDEO 1210

FLINTSTONES, THE

D: Brian Levant 91 m

PG · COM CLD · 1994 · COLOR · Rating: 7

Anyone who compares this movie to the long-running TV cartoon series will be both disillusioned and satisfied. In spite of a $40 million budget that built fantastic sets plus some right-on casting, this film just does not have the same feel as the cartoon series did. However, that is not to say that it isn't fun. It is, if you are either a kid, or willing to accept the silly humor that appeals to a kid - like, say, those people who like The Three Stooges. In it, lovable, but not-too-bright Fred gets a big head when he is promoted by boss Rock Quarry. However, he was only promoted so he can take the fall for all the money Rock has embezzled. Also, poor Barney loses his job and has to move in with Fred and Wilma.

Sex / Nud / Viol / Lang / AdSit

A: John Goodman, Rick Moranis, Elizabeth Perkins, Rosie O'Donnell, Kyle MacLachlan, Halle Berry

© MCA/UNIVERSAL HOME VIDEO, INC. 81744

FOR KEEPS

D: John G. Avildsen 98 m

PG-13 · COM DMA · 1988 · COLOR · Rating: 7

Bittersweet coming-of-age film where growing up happens REAL fast. Ringwold and Batinkoff are two very popular high school kids with everything going for them: they are in love, have good grades, friends and college prospects. Then, she becomes pregnant. Their parents come unglued, so the kids leave to be on their own and are married. But it is soon very plain that things are now drastically different and they are never going to be the same again. This is an entertaining and light-hearted comedy, but it has a very serious undercurrent and contains documentary footage of a live birth.

Sex / Nud / Viol / Lang / AdSit

A: Molly Ringwald, Randall Batinkoff, Miriam Flynn, Kenneth Mars, Conchata Ferrell

© COLUMBIA TRISTAR HOME VIDEO 67005

FOR LOVE OR MONEY

D: Barry Sonneneld 96 m

PG · COM ROM · 1993 · COLOR · Rating: 6

Michael J. Fox is back in his element as a fast talking concierge at a posh hotel. He can get anything for anyone and can solve any problem - except his own. For years he has been saving all his tips and living in a ramshackle apartment so he can fulfill his life's ambition to create and own the plushest hotel in New York. He has just put all his money into an option to buy an island in the river and is close to making a deal with a major wheeler-dealer who can give him the rest of the money. The problem? The wheeler dealer is married, has a pretty young mistress he's leading along and the girl is also the girl of Michael's dreams. Which dream will it be? Fun, but not special.

Sex / Nud / Viol / Lang / AdSit

A: Michael J. Fox, Gabrielle Anwar, Anthony Higgins, Bob Balaban, Michael Tucker

© MCA/UNIVERSAL HOME VIDEO, INC. 81511

FORREST GUMP

D: Robert Zemeckis 142 m

PG-13 · DMA COM · 1994 · COLOR · Rating: 10

This was a monster hit. Both critics and general audiences loved it. It won 6 Oscars out of 13 nominations, including Best Picture, Actor and Director. It is the totally captivating story of a simple-minded man with a strange destiny. Forrest has an IQ of only 75, yet he has a heart that is unfailingly true. His strong legs earned him a football scholarship and a college degree. His single-minded determination caused him to repeatedly go back into a Vietnam battle to retrieve his friends and so he won the Congressional Medal of Honor. Forrest cannot understand much of what happens to him and around him. He focuses upon the simple truths...and so reminds us of them also. Wonderful.

Sex / Nud / Viol / Lang / AdSit

A: Tom Hanks, Robin Wright, Salley Field, Gary Sinise, Mykelti Williamson

© PARAMOUNT HOME VIDEO 32583

FOR THE BOYS

D: Mark Rydell 145 m

R · DMA COM · 1991 · COLOR · Rating: 8

Bittersweet entertainment. Midler and Caan are a long-time USO act. They cut it up on stage and have a ball entertaining troops - with Caan being a stuffy straightman and Milder's spicy tongue constantly dishing out surprises. With 50 years and three wars between them, each has helped the other through a myriad of lifetime troubles and triumphs, but when Midler's son is killed in the Vietnam War and Cann speaks of the honor of dying in battle, their long-time partnership comes to a rapid end. What will it take to reunite the pair that America so loves? Sentimental and rich with emotion.

Sex / Nud / Viol / Lang / AdSit

A: Bette Midler, James Caan, George Segal, Patrick O'Neal, Christopher Rydell, Arye Gross

© FOXVIDEO 5595

FOR THE LOVE OF BENJI

D: Joe Camp 85 m

G · COM CLD · 1977 · COLOR · Rating: 8

One of the most loveable characters in moviedom returns to charm his way into your heart. The whole family will enjoy his adventure through the streets of Athens, with Benji being chased by secret agents in search of the secret information tattooed on his paw. An interesting aspect of this film is that the movie is shot from Benji's point of view. Lovable. Preceeded by BENJI and followed by OH, HEAVENLY DOG!

Sex / Nud / Viol / Lang / AdSit

A: Benji, Patsy Garrett, Cynthia Smith, Allen Fiuzat, Ed Nelson, Bridget Armstrong

© BEST FILM & VIDEO CORP. 123

FORTUNE COOKIE, THE

D: Billy Wilder 126 m

NR · COM · 1966 · COLOR · Rating: 9

Hilarious Walter Matthau and Jack Lemmon comic pairing. When sports cameraman Lemmon gets knocked over while filming a football game, his shyster-lawyer brother-in-law, Whiplash Willie (Matthau), sees dollar signs. At first Jack plays along with the plan to collect $1 million, but soon his conscience gets the better of him and Willie has a struggle to keep Jack in the game. Matthau won an Oscar for his performance in Billy Wilder's laugh-out-loud comic masterpiece.

Sex / Nud / Viol / Lang / AdSit

A: Jack Lemmon, Walter Matthau, Ron Rich, Cliff Osmond, Judi West

Distributed By MGM/UA Home Video M202115

FOUL PLAY

D: Colin Higgins 116 m

PG · COM MYS CRM · 1978 · COLOR · Rating: 8

Very funny murder/mystery. A librarian (Hawn) picks up an undercover agent who gives her information that there will be an assassination attempt upon the Pope when he attends a performance of The Mikado. Quickly, there are several attempts made upon her life. Even though she tells all this to the police, they don't believe her. However, stumbling police detective Chevy Chases eventually comes to believe her and becomes both her protector and lover. A wide assortment of looneys and odd-balls add to the fun. The fine supporting cast includes Dudley Moore in his first American role.

Sex / Nud / Viol / Lang / AdSit

A: Goldie Hawn, Chevy Chase, Burgess Meredith, Rachel Roberts, Dudley Moore, Billy Barty

© PARAMOUNT HOME VIDEO 1116

FOUR MUSKETEERS, THE

D: Richard Lester 107 m

PG · COM ACT · 1975 · COLOR · Rating: 8

Highly entertaining, high-spirited comedy/adventure and sequel to THE THREE MUSKETEERS (although they were actually filmed at the same time). It is a tongue-in-cheek irreverent retelling of the Dumas classic of honor and comradeship between three valiant swordsmen. Full of swashbuckling sword play, slap stick humor and good story telling. It actually has a quite engrossing plot too, and Raquel Welch was never better. The final sword duel is a real piece of work.

Sex / Nud / Viol / Lang / AdSit

A: Oliver Reed, Raquel Welch, Richard Chamberlain, Frank Finlay, Michael York, Christopher Lee

© LIVE HOME VIDEO 215-280

FOUR SEASONS, THE

D: Alan Alda 109 m

PG · COM DMA · 1981 · COLOR · Rating: 7

A bittersweet, warm comedy about three middle-class couples who have always been very close friends and who vacation together once during each season of the year. They joke together and share each other's pain and joys - that is, until one couple divorces. Now the whole group relationship has to be reevaluated. This is generally endearing and entertaining and has some genuinely funny moments, but it's also a little too talky sometimes. Alda was Oscar-nominated for both acting and directing.

Sex / Nud / Viol / Lang / AdSit

A: Alan Alda, Carol Burnett, Len Carlou, Sandy Dennis, Rita Moreno, Jack Weston

© MCA/UNIVERSAL HOME VIDEO, INC. 77003

FOURTH STORY

D: Ivan Passer 91 m

PG-13 · MYS COM ROM · 1990 · COLOR · Rating: 7

Interesting and quirky made-for-cable-TV psychothriller. Mark Harmon plays a likable but average sort of PI who is hired by Mimi Rogers to find her husband after he just disappeared one morning after breakfast. The police don't believe that he's really in trouble and she needs him. Harmon search through the web of clues leads him to believe that there is indeed something afoot, but it is also linked to his own sordid past. What is more, the more they are together, the harder it is to deny that they are powerfully drawn to each other. Very enjoyable characters. However, the ending is a little messy.

Sex / Nud / Viol / Lang / AdSit

A: Mark Harmon, Mimi Rogers, Cliff De Young, Paul Gleason, M. Emmet Walsh

© VIDEO TREASURES M012778

FOUR WEDDINGS AND A FUNERAL

D: Mike Newell — 117 m

R | COM ROM | 1994 | COLOR | Sex, Nud, Viol, Lang, AdSit

8 Englishman Hugh Grant spends his Saturday's attending his friend's weddings. While all those around him seem to be falling into matrimonial bliss, his own love life is met with one misfire after another. Then, at one of these weddings, he chances to meet a gorgeous American (Andie MacDowell) and his heart feels a solid tug. But, after one blissful night together, she returns to America and he to his dull love life. Months later, at the next wedding, she returns. Again, they spend a blissful evening of lust, however this time she breaks the news that the next wedding he will go to is hers. Witty, and for most, quite amusing, but some will rate it higher, some lower.

A: Hugh Grant, Andie MacDowell, Kristin Scott Thomas, Simon Callow, Rowan Atkinson, James Fleet

© POLYGRAM VIDEO 6317693

FRANKIE & JOHNNY

D: Garry Marshall — 117 m

R | ROM DMA COM | 1991 | COLOR | Sex, Nud, Viol, Lang, AdSit

8 A captivating and unique love story. Pfeiffer and Pacino are very appealing in this endearing but decidedly unglamorous look at a last-chance love affair. Pacino is an ex-con who gets a job as a short order cook at a neighborhood diner. Pfeiffer is a waitress working there who has been burned one too many times and is not interested in a relationship of any kind. But Pacino falls hard for her. He will not retreat and continues to pursue her heart. He finally does charm her into bed, but still Pfeiffer retreats like a fragile bird, afraid of her ghosts. Enjoyable, realistic, believable, upbeat and very moving.

A: Al Pacino, Michelle Pfeiffer, Hector Elizondo, Kate Nelligan, Nathan Lane, Jane Morris

© PARAMOUNT HOME VIDEO 32222

FREAKY FRIDAY

D: Gary Nelson — 98 m

G | COM CLD | 1977 | COLOR | Sex, Nud, Viol, Lang, AdSit

8 Charming breezy comedy that is a truly fun time for the whole family - from Disney. Teenager Jodie Foster gets her wish when she and her mother (Barbara Harris) magically exchange personalities for a day and both of them find out that neither has such an easy time of things. Probably one of Disney's best-ever comedies. Lightweight fun from Mary Rogers's adaptation of her own book. This is the same premise as in the 1948 movie VICE VERSA, and it became very popular later with such other movies as BIG - but it was seldom used better than it was here.

A: Jodie Foster, Barbara Harris, John Astin, Ruth Buzzi, Kay Ballard, Patsy Kelly

© WALT DISNEY HOME VIDEO 056

FREEBIE AND THE BEAN

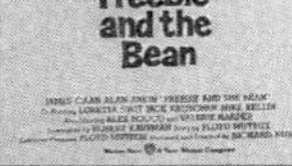

D: Richard Rush — 113 m

R | ACT COM CRM | 1974 | COLOR | Sex, Nud, Viol, Lang, AdSit

8 Wild cop comedy. This is probably the first, and certainly one of the best, buddy-cop movies. It is the story of two odd-ball San Francisco cops: Freebie (Caan), who is a cheapskate, and Bean (Arkin), who is a very vocal Mexican-American. These two cops are trying to shut down a big numbers racket, but they rip up half of San Francisco in the process. Includes four car chases, and one super stunt ends up with their car crashing into the bedroom of a highrise apartment building. Caan and Arkin are great together. A lot of fun.

A: Alan Arkin, James Caan, Loretta Swit, Valerie Harper, Jack Kruschen, Alex Rocco

© WARNER HOME VIDEO 11237

FRESHMAN, THE

D: Andrew Bergman — 102 m

PG | COM CRM | 1990 | COLOR | Sex, Nud, Viol, Lang, AdSit

7 A lighthearted charmer! Broderick is a naive freshman film student who, minutes after arriving in New York, has all his bags and belongings stolen. Broderick tracks the thief (Kirby) down, who surprisingly makes him an offer that he can't refuse. He now finds himself working for an irresistibly charismatic mob boss (Brando, in a spoof on his role in THE GODFATHER) running strange errands, while also being hotly pursued by the boss's sexy daughter. Among his odd duties is picking up a giant lizard from the airport and delivering that strange cargo unharmed to New Jersey.

A: Matthew Broderick, Marlon Brando, Bruno Kirby, Maximilian Schell, Penelope Ann Miller, Frank Whaley

© COLUMBIA TRISTAR HOME VIDEO 70293

FRIGHT NIGHT

D: Tom Holland — 105 m

R | COM HOR | 1985 | COLOR | Sex, Nud, Viol, Lang, AdSit

8 Wonderful little horror spoof. A reasonably sane and normal 17-year-old becomes convinced that his suave new neighbor (Sarandon) is a vampire, but no one believes him - not his mother, not his best friend and not even his devoted girlfriend. After the police ignore his pleas, he seeks the advice of a has-been movie actor (McDowall) who was known on TV as "The Great Vampire Killer" and who was also just fired as the host of the local TV's horror movie show. At first, McDowall just humors the kid but it soon turns out the guy really is a vampire. Ingenious blending of horror and humor.

A: Chris Sarandon, William Ragsdale, Roddy McDowall, Amanda Bearse, Stephen Geoffreys

© COLUMBIA TRISTAR HOME VIDEO 60562

FRISCO KID, THE

D: Robert Aldrich — 119 m

PG | WST COM | 1979 | COLOR | Sex, Nud, Viol, Lang, AdSit

8 Funny Western. Gene Wilder is a Polish rabbi who is on his way from Philadelphia, across the Wild West, to San Francisco and his new congregation. Except, he has no idea of how to get there and, while on his way, he is besieged by one misfortune after another. However, he meets a kindhearted cowpoke and part-time bankrobber (Ford) who takes pity upon this inept fish-out-of-water. Ford agrees to accompany him across country to San Francisco and together they manage to stay in one scrape or another the entire way. Good family fun.

A: Gene Wilder, Harrison Ford, Ramon Bieri, Val Bisoglio, Leo Fuchs

© WARNER HOME VIDEO 11095

FRONT, THE

D: Martin Ritt — 94 m

PG | DMA COM | 1976 | COLOR | Sex, Nud, Viol, Lang, AdSit

7 Witty comedy with a serious undercurrent. In the early 1950s, Senator Joseph McCarthy engaged in a national campaign to destroy all communist elements in the US. In the process, his witch hunt destroyed thousands of careers, particularly in the entertainment industry. Here Woody Allen plays a regular working stiff who is hired by a group of talented, but blacklisted, writers to represent their work as being his own so they can earn a living. However, he becomes a major success and finds himself also investigated. Some very funny scenes are mixed in with some poignant moments.

A: Woody Allen, Zero Mostel, Andrea Marcovicci, Joshua Shelley, Georgann Johnson

© GOODTIMES 4612

FUNNY THING HAPPENED ON THE WAY TO THE FORUM, A

D: Richard Lester — 100 m

NR | COM MUS | 1966 | COLOR | Sex, Nud, Viol, Lang, AdSit

8 Riotousness, bawdiness and absurdity abound in this fast-paced musical comedy. Zero Mostel excels as a scheming slave of ancient Rome whose sole goal is to earn his freedom. An outrageous slapstick comedy with a hopelessly convoluted plot that only adds to the insanity. It also combines the talents of veterans Buster Keaton, Jack Gilford and Phil Silvers with a then very young and very funny Michael Crawford ("Phantom of the Opera"). Wonderful Stephen Sondheim score. Expect the absurd and you won't be disappointed.

A: Zero Mostel, Phil Silvers, Jack Gilford, Buster Keaton, Michael Crawford

Distributed By MGM/UA Home Video M202258

FUN WITH DICK AND JANE

D: Ted Kotcheff — 95 m

PG | COM CRM | 1977 | COLOR | Sex, Nud, Viol, Lang, AdSit

8 Zany, polished fun-filled comedy. What do you do when you enjoy, and in fact are addicted to, the luxurious upper-middle-class lifestyle that your job as a highly-paid aerospace executive gives you, and you are suddenly fired? At first Dick and Jane tighten their belts and Jane gets a job. But Jane doesn't like her job and they don't like their belts tight. So, quite naturally, they decide to do the next best thing to earn a good living, they will rob and steal. See Dick and Jane steal. See Dick and Jane run. Really funny stuff.

A: George Segal, Jane Fonda, Ed McMahon, Dick Gautier, Allan Miller

© GOODTIMES 4431

GALLAGHER - MELON CRAZY

D: Joe Hostettler — 58 m

NR | COM | 1984 | COLOR | Sex, Nud, Viol, Lang, AdSit

8 The one-and-only madman Gallagher contemplates the mighty melon in all its many possibilities. There is no one like him or his Super-Sledge-o-Matic. Funny, funny man.

A: Gallagher

© PARAMOUNT HOME VIDEO 2339

GALLAGHER - OVER YOUR HEAD

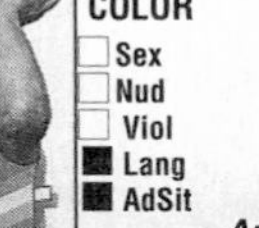

D: Joe Hostettler — 58 m

NR | COM | 1984 | COLOR | Sex, Nud, Viol, Lang, AdSit

8 Gallagher goes to Texas in a 20-gallon hat and with a six-shooter with a loooooong barrel. He discusses gun control and politics and whatever else pops into his mind. Crazy blend of stand-up and slapstick comedy like you will see from no one else.

A: Gallagher

© PARAMOUNT HOME VIDEO 2340

HAIRSPRAY

D: John Waters — 92 m

PG | COM | 1988 | COLOR

6 Goofball spoof of the early sixties. The story is intentionally bizarre and concerns a chubby adolescent girl who is consumed by a passion to dance on a Baltimore teen-TV dance show in 1963. She has the tallest tower of hair and the coolest dance moves, but before she can be on the show she has to de-thrône the reigning bouffant queen. Entertaining, if you are a fan of extravagant satire or of '60s music - of which there is a wide and very rich selection.

Sex Nud Viol Lang AdSit

A: Sonny Bono, Divine, Colleen Fitzpatrick, Deborah Harry, Jerry Stiller, Pia Zadora

© NEW LINE HOME VIDEO 62822

HANGIN' WITH THE HOMEBOYS

D: Joseph B. Vasquez — 90 m

R | DMA COM | 1991 | COLOR

7 Interesting bittersweet excursion, in which we go along with four young guys from the inner-city on a crucial Friday night of self discovery. Good friends, two black and two Puerto Rican buddies, are going nowhere with their lives and get together to hang out every Friday night. On this night, they cruise first their own neighborhood in the South Bronx and then enter over into whiteman's land, Manhatten. But, along the way, each has the veneer of who he thinks he is, scraped and chipped away. This is a non-romanticized, non-villainizing look at how most all of us just allow our lives to happen without ever taking charge ourselves. Most interesting to young people.

Sex Nud Viol Lang AdSit

A: Doug E. Doug, Mario Joyner, Nestor Serrano, John Leguizamo

© TURNER HOME ENTERTAINMENT N4113

HANNAH AND HER SISTERS

D: Woody Allen — 103 m

PG-13 | COM DMA | 1986 | COLOR

9 A heart-warming serious comedy from Woody Allen. This is one of his best (although ANNIE HALL is right up there). This is a two-year study of the lives of one of Woody's neurotic New York families that revolves around three sisters. Mia Farrow is the functional centerpin of the family. She plays peacemaker for all the other elements. However, her current husband is having an affair with one sister, and her ex-husband, hypochondriac Allen, is married to her other sister. In all, a dozen different characters are brought into the family. Three Oscars, nominated for seven.

Sex Nud Viol Lang AdSit

A: Woody Allen, Michael Caine, Mia Farrow, Carrie Fisher, Barbara Hershey, Maureen O'Sullivan

© HBO VIDEO 3897

HARD DAY'S NIGHT, A

D: Richard Lester — 90 m

G | MUS COM | 1964 | B&W

9 This is an exuberant and fun-filled musical romp with the Beatles - even for non-Beatles fans. The fab four had just reached the pinnacle of their popularity at the time of the release of this film and it does contain a full compliment of Lennon-McCartney songs, including: "Can't Buy Me Love," "And I Love Her" and "I Should Have Known Better"; but it is also a fast-paced and funny kaleidoscope of a rock group's frantic day by utilizing clever cinematic techniques. Good fun, even today, because it captures the charm and exuberant personalities that was a large part of how the group achieved the success it did.

Sex Nud Viol Lang AdSit

A: The Beatles, Wilfred Brambell, Victor Spinetti, Anna Quayle

© MPI HOME VIDEO MP1064

HARD WAY, THE

D: John Badham — 115 m

R | COM ACT | 1991 | COLOR

6 Michael Fox is a spoiled Hollywood actor who is tired of playing the same old roles and wants desperately to have an exciting role in an upcoming cop movie which is supposed to go to Mel Gibson. Determined to "get into" the role, he wangles his way into two weeks of tagging along with a tough, nearly-out-of-control, cop (Woods) he saw on TV and who is currently trying to track down a particularly nasty killer. But - Woods doesn't want Fox along and does everything he can to discourage him. After this plot premise is laid out (in the first 20 minutes), things get predictable fast and pretty formula-driven. Still, the characters are fun to watch.

Sex Nud Viol Lang AdSit

A: James Woods, Michael J. Fox, Stephen Lang, Annabella Sciorra, Penny Marshall

© MCA/UNIVERSAL HOME VIDEO, INC. 81079

HAROLD AND MAUDE

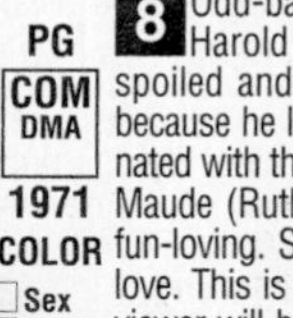

D: Hal Ashby — 91 m

PG | COM DMA | 1971 | COLOR

8 Odd-ball black comedy that has become a big cult favorite. Harold (Bud Cort) is a very strange young man. He is rich, spoiled and very confused. He repeatedly attempts suicide both because he likes to upset his snooty mother and because he is fascinated with the concept of death. And, that is what at first draws him to Maude (Ruth Gordon). Maude is old, but she is also eccentric and fun-loving. She is a laugh-riot. The two meet at a funeral and fall in love. This is not at all a typical comedy, but the patient open-minded viewer will be greatly rewarded with some laughs and some insights into human nature.

Sex Nud Viol Lang AdSit

A: Bud Cort, Ruth Gordon, Vivian Pickles, Cyril Cusack, Charles Tyner, Ellen Geer

© PARAMOUNT HOME VIDEO 8042

HARRY AND THE HENDERSONS

D: William Dear — 111 m

PG | COM CLD | 1987 | COLOR

7 Entertaining and pretty good family fun. Your typical suburban family is out on a trip in the wilds when father Lithgow runs over Harry, a real live man/ape - the fabled "Bigfoot". At first they think he's dead, but he's not. They bring him home to nurse him, but the big guy wreaks total havoc in their house. Still, he is a loveable sort and the family is growing more and more attached to him. Even so, they need to get him back to the woods where he belongs. That's a lot harder than it sounds... Harry doesn't want to go. But, he has to go because now everybody is after him. Good family entertainment.

Sex Nud Viol Lang AdSit

A: John Lithgow, Melinda Dillon, Don Ameche, Joshua Ruday, Margaret Langrick, Kevin Peter Hall

© MCA/UNIVERSAL HOME VIDEO, INC. 80677

HARRY AND TONTO

D: Paul Mazursky — 110 m

R | COM DMA | 1974 | COLOR

8 Touching story about an old man who is tired of being passed from one relative to the next and tired of letting life pass him by. So, he and his cat set out on a cross-country adventure in which they run across a varied, entertaining and interesting cast of odd-ball characters. By the time Harry finally arrives in LA, where he is was to move in with his son, Harry has discovered that he likes the adventure of the road. Carney won an Oscar for his portrayal of this dignified elderly adventure seeker. A truly entertaining journey of self discovery. Carney is a master. It doesn't deserve an R rating.

Sex Nud Viol Lang AdSit

A: Art Carney, Ellen Burstyn, Chief Dan George, Geraldine Fitzgerald, Larry Hagman, Melanie Mayron

© FOXVIDEO 1355

HATARI!

D: Howard Hawks — 158 m

NR | ACT COM | 1961 | COLOR

8 High energy and light-hearted fun. A great cast has a ball with a fun adventure story about a bunch of wild-animal trappers who capture African animals for zoos. This is good fun for adults and kids alike. John Wayne is at his macho best as the leader of the group. The simple story is amply spiced with doses of comedy, action, some excellent animal and scenic photography, and a little romance, too. Filmed on location in Tanganyika. Terrific Mancini score.

Sex Nud Viol Lang AdSit

A: John Wayne, Elsa Martinelli, Red Buttons, Hardy Kruger, Gerard Blain

© PARAMOUNT HOME VIDEO 6629

HEAR MY SONG

D: Peter Chelsom — 104 m

R | COM MUS | 1991 | COLOR

7 A likable comedy from Britain. Mickey (Dunbar) runs a Liverpool nightclub that caters to the local Irish community, and he loves Nancy (Fitsgerald). Mickey's club barely struggles along until he mistakenly hires a phony tenor who claims to be Joseph Locke (a famed real-life Irish tenor). However, the phony is found out and the mistake causes Mickey to lose his club. More importantly, he loses Nancy, whose mother knew the real Locke and was in love with him. So, the desperate Mickey sets off to Ireland to recover the real tenor (Beatty), who is in hiding there for tax evasion. Mickey must bring him back to his fans and to Nancy's mom. Charming and witty, but slow.

Sex Nud Viol Lang AdSit

A: Ned Beatty, Adrian Dunbar, Shirley Anne Field, Tara Fitsgerald, David McCallum, William Hootkins

© PARAMOUNT HOME VIDEO 15110

HEARTACHES

D: Donald Shebib — 93 m

R | COM DMA | 1982 | COLOR

7 Touching offbeat comedy about two women friends surviving in Toronto. Bonnie (Potts) is small-town girl who has left her hard-drinking husband (Carradine) rather than to tell him that he is not the father of her baby. On the bus, she runs into and befriends Rita, a kooky streetwise blond (Kidder) who has man-problems of her own. Even though these two are total opposites, they wind up becoming best friends. Rita protects Bonnie from Carradine, while she keeps getting into more man-problems herself. This is a fun lightweight comedy and a good female buddy movie.

Sex Nud Viol Lang AdSit

A: Annie Potts, Winston Rekert, Robert Carradine, Margot Kidder

© LIVE HOME VIDEO VA4024

HEARTBREAK HOTEL

D: Chris Columbus — 101 m

PG-13 | COM DMA | 1988 | COLOR

7 A far-out premise gets a respectable treatment by an excellent cast. It's 1972 and Tuesday Weld is depressed. Her husband has left her and her boyfriend beats her. Then she gets into a car accident, too. Her teenage guitarist son decides that he will get her the ultimate get well present. So, he kidnaps her idol, Elvis Presley. (Fabulous impersonation of Presley by David Keith.) However, Presley gains from the experience too, because he is guided back to his rock `n roll roots through the aspiring young musician and also gets to teach the boy's little sister to not be afraid of the dark.

Sex Nud Viol Lang AdSit

A: David Keith, Tuesday Weld, Charlie Schlatter, Angela Goethais, Jacque Lynn Colton, Chris Mulkey

© TOUCHSTONE HOME VIDEO 609

HEARTBREAK KID, THE

D: Elaine May 106 m

PG | COM DMA | 1972 | COLOR | Rating: 7

Neil Simon comedy about a young Jewish boy (Grodin) who meets a girl in a Manhattan singles bar and, shortly afterward, proposes to her. However, he already begins to grow tired of his new whining wife even as they drive to Florida for their honeymoon. When he meets a beautiful WASP girl (Shepherd) on the beach it's all over. Grodin woos and, after overcoming many obstacles, wins Shepherd, but this victory proves to be hollow. This is a subtle satiric look at love and marriage, not Simon's typical string of one liners. How funny it will be for you depends on how it hits you.

Sex | Nud | Viol | Lang | AdSit

A: Charles Grodin, Cybill Shepherd, Jeannie Berlin, Eddie Albert, Audra Lindley

© VIDEO TREASURES SV9088

HEARTBURN

D: Mike Nichols 109 m

R | DMA COM | 1986 | COLOR | Rating: 6

Starpower is the hallmark of this picture. Meryl Streep and Jack Nickolson play a New York writer who marries a Washington columnist. These are sophisticated people whose marriage seems fine until Nicholson steps out on her while she's pregnant. Some witty dialogue and some funny moments, but the glory is in the acting because the story itself is ultimately not very satisfying.

Sex | Nud | Viol | Lang | AdSit

A: Meryl Streep, Jack Nicholson, Maureen Stapleton, Jeff Daniels, Stockard Channing, Richard Masur

© PARAMOUNT HOME VIDEO 1688

HEART CONDITION

D: James D. Parriott 96 m

R | COM | 1990 | COLOR | Rating: 6

A mild comedy that is carried by the sheer force of its starpower. Hoskins is a bigot with a bad ticker. After he has a heart attack and wakes up with a transplanted new heart, he is very distressed to learn that it used to belong to a slick black lawyer who he had always despised. Then he also gets a visit from the ghost of the dead guy, who wants him to track down his murderers and also rescue the hooker that they both love. Not a laugh riot, but it does contain enough good times to make for a good evening's diversion.

Sex | Nud | Viol | Lang | AdSit

A: Denzel Washington, Bob Hoskins, Chloe Webb, Ray Baker, Jeffrey Meek, Kieran Mulroney

© TURNER HOME ENTERTAINMENT N4106

HEARTS OF THE WEST

D: Howard Zieff 103 m

PG | COM WST | 1975 | COLOR | Rating: 7

Pleasant light-hearted story about a starry-eyed young Iowa farm boy with a wild imagination (Bridges) who goes west to Hollywood in the 1920s, intent upon becoming a writer of Western movies. Along the way he stops into his Nevada correspondence school and discovers that it is just a post office box. However, he accidentally takes the crooks cash stash and escapes into the desert, where he is rescued by a movie crew in full Western costume. He becomes pals, gets a job as a B-movie actor, finds love with a script girl and meets a publisher for his novel. A fun and charming little film.

Sex | Nud | Viol | Lang | AdSit

A: Jeff Bridges, Alan Arkin, Blythe Danner, Andy Griffith, Donald Pleasence

Distributed By MGM/UA Home Video M600388

HEATHERS

D: Michael Lehmann 105 m

R | COM DMA | 1989 | COLOR | Rating: 7

If you love very black comedy in the form of quirky, offbeat drama, this flick is for you - and you don't have to be a teenager to get a kick out of it. The film is centered at Westerburg High, a place where the quest for popularity is the most important thing of all. The Heathers, a small group of gorgeous girls led by Doherty, are the ruling class. But when one of them (Ryder) breaks off from the others, her new outlaw boyfriend (Slater) decides that it is time to end the reign of the Heathers completely, and will stop at nothing to accomplish his goal. Darkly funny.

Sex | Nud | Viol | Lang | AdSit

A: Winona Ryder, Christian Slater, Shannen Doherty, Kim Walker, Lisanne Falk, Penelope Milford

© R&G VIDEO, LP 14014

HEAVEN CAN WAIT

D: Buck Henry 100 m

PG | COM FAN | 1978 | COLOR | Rating: 9

Highly entertaining and well-done remake of the charming 1941 smash hit HERE COMES MR. JORDAN. Warren Beatty plays Joe Pendleton, a good-natured football hero, whose soul has been accidentally removed too soon from his body by an over-eager angel. Then before they can get him back into it, his body is cremated. Bummer. So, the head angel (Mason) gets him another body to use until his time is really up. However, that presents a problem too. The new body belongs to a millionaire whose wife wants to kill him. Nine Oscar nominations.

Sex | Nud | Viol | Lang | AdSit

A: Warren Beatty, Julie Christie, Jack Warden, Dyan Cannon, Charles Grodin, James Mason

© PARAMOUNT HOME VIDEO 1109

HEAVY PETTING

D: Obie Benz 75 m

R | DOC COM | 1989 | COLOR | Rating: 7

Very funny but slightly sleazy documentary about the sexual and dating rituals of the '60s. Numerous clips from vintage sex education films and Hollywood's sexy scenes from the pre-sexual revolution of the '50s and '60s are interspersed with the frank confessions of several celebrities talking about their "first time." Ah, memories.

Sex | Nud | Viol | Lang | AdSit

A: Laurie Anderson, David Byrne, Sandra Bernhard, Allen Ginsberg, Abbie Hoffman, Spalding Gray

© ACADEMY ENTERTAINMENT 1197

HELLO, DOLLY

D: Gene Kelly 146 m

G | MUS COM | 1969 | COLOR | Rating: 6

This is a very lavish screen production of Broadway's smash hit about a turn-of-the-century matchmaker (played by Streisand) who hopes to snag one of her clients for herself. Extravagant film production and excellent musical productions cannot entirely make up for the fact that Barbara was much too young for that role. Even so, listen to the fantastic music: "Before the Parade Passes By" and, of course, "Hello Dolly" with Streisand in duet with Louis Armstrong. Based on the play and later movie THE MATCHMAKER.

Sex | Nud | Viol | Lang | AdSit

A: Barbra Streisand, Walter Matthau, Louis Armstrong, Michael Crawford, Tommy Tune, E.J. Peaker

© FOXVIDEO 1001

HELP!

D: Richard Lester 90 m

G | MUS COM | 1965 | COLOR | Rating: 8

Wild gags and lots of music populate this minor silly story about a group of religious zealots who want Ringo's (the Beatles drummer) ring for a sacrifice. Songs include: "Ticket to Ride," "Another Girl," "You've Got to Hide Your Love Away," and "Help!" If you are not a fan of either The Beatles or abject silliness, you might downgrade this to a 6, or perhaps even skip it. However, eccentrics, fans of the group or fans of silliness will have a good time. And, if you are a true Beatles fan, you MUST also see the excellent documentary, THE COMPLEAT BEATLES.

Sex | Nud | Viol | Lang | AdSit

A: The Beatles, Leo McKern, Eleanor Bran, Victor Spinetti

© MPI HOME VIDEO MP1342

HERO AT LARGE

D: Martin Davidson 99 m

PG | COM | 1980 | COLOR | Rating: 6

An out-of-work actor (Ritter), who is in a Captain Avenger costume while promoting a movie, foils a holdup attempt at a deli and the city begins to think that they are being protected by the real thing. The mayor, who is running for reelection, and his agents attempt to exploit the actor for their benefit. More than a little silly, but still enjoyable family fun.

Sex | Nud | Viol | Lang | AdSit

A: John Ritter, Anne Archer, Bert Convy, Devin McCarthy, Harry Bellaver, Anita Dangler

Distributed By MGM/UA Home Video M600316

HESTER STREET

D: Joan Micklin Silver 89 m

PG | DMA COM | 1975 | B&W | Rating: 7

Interesting reflection on a real problem from the days of mass immigrations to America at the turn of the 20th century. A Jewish immigrant (Steven Keats) arrives in New York first so that he can raise the money necessary to bring his wife (Kane) and child over from the old country. However, when she does arrive, she is disturbed to find that he is turning his back on the old world ways, and he is embarrassed by her cloddishness. They divorce and marry others. Great period detail and a simple and charming story. Fine performances. Kane received an Oscar nomination.

Sex | Nud | Viol | Lang | AdSit

A: Carol Kane, Steven Keats, Mel Howard, Dorrie Davanaugh

© LIVE HOME VIDEO A3068

HEY ABBOTT !

D: Jim Gates 76 m

NR | COM | 1978 | COLOR | Rating: 8

This is a collection of a series of hilarious skits by Abbott and Costello. This pair of vaudeville greats graduated from the vaudeville stage to film and then to TV. Vaudeville was slapstick comedy, sometimes with a heavy emphasis on word play. These guys were among the best at both. These skits (essentially all vaudeville) were taken from their 1950s TV series and the tape is hosted by comedic legend Milton Berle. Skits included: "Who's on First," "Oyster Stew," "Floogie Street" and "The Birthday Party."

Sex | Nud | Viol | Lang | AdSit

A: Bud Abbott, Lou Costello, Joe Besser, Phil Silvers, Steve Allen

© UNITED AMERICAN VIDEO CORP. 8152

HIDDEN FORTRESS, THE

D: Akira Kurosawa 139 m

NR | FOR ACT COM | 1958 | B&W

9 George Lucas acknowledges that this film, from the Japanese master filmmaker Akira Kurosawa, was the inspiration for his mega-smash hit STAR WARS. In it, a haughty young princess, a fortune in gold, a fugitive general and two bumbling and comic mercenary soldiers make a treacherous journey through enemy territory to get her back to her homeland. This one is so much fun you may even forget that its a foreign film. Subtitles.

Sex Nud Viol Lang AdSit

A: Toshiro Mifune, Misa Uehara, Minoru Chiaki, Kimatare Fugiwara, Susumu Fujita, Takashi Shimura

© HOME VISION HID 030

HIDING OUT

D: Bob Giraldi 99 m

PG-13 | COM ACT | 1987 | COLOR

6 A 27-year-old commodities trader becomes a fugitive after he testifies against the mob and the mob kills the FBI agent sent to protect him. So he dyes his hair and registers as a senior at a high school in Delaware, where he becomes popular with the kids and dates the prettiest girl in school, but then the mob finds him. OK comedy. Teenagers will like it best.

Sex Nud Viol Lang AdSit

A: Jon Cryer, Keith Coogan, Annabeth Gish, Gretchen Cryer, Oliver Cotton

© HBO VIDEO 0042

HIGH ANXIETY

D: Mel Brooks 94 m

PG | COM | 1977 | COLOR

6 Mel Brooks is at it again with his low-brow brand of slap-stick and shtick. This time he pokes fun at Hitchcock-type suspense movies as he plays the head of the Psycho-Neurotic Institute for the Very, Very Nervous. Cloris Leachman is his sadistic head nurse, Nurse Diesel, and he has a wide assortment of other looneys, too. Acceptable entertainment if you are a fan, but even non-fans will enjoy Brooks's classic BLAZING SADDLES and maybe even YOUNG FRANKENSTEIN.

Sex Nud Viol Lang AdSit

A: Mel Brooks, Madeline Kahn, Cloris Leachman, Harvey Korman, Ron Carey

© FOXVIDEO 1107

HIGH TIDE

D: Gillian Armstrong 102 m

PG-13 | DMA COM | 1987 | COLOR

7 Moving, emotional story set in Australia. Judy Davis plays a no-talent backup singer for a bad Elvis impersonator and she winds up being stranded in a small bleak coastal town. While staying in a trailer park, she chances upon a tomboyish teenage girl who she slowly recognises as being the daughter she had abandoned years before after her husband died. She begins to form a friendship with the girl that she thought she would never see again and gradually reveals who she is. Well acted and convincingly told even if the story's premise is a longshot.

Sex Nud Viol Lang AdSit

A: Judy Davis, Jan Adele, Claudia Karvan, Colin Friels

© NEW LINE HOME VIDEO 7722

HIT, THE

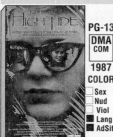

D: Stephen Frears 97 m

R | SUS COM | 1985 | COLOR

7 Offbeat and deceptively funny film. A stool pigeon (Stamp) has been in hiding in Spain for ten years but now has been found. Hurt and Roth are the two hit men who have been hired by the mob to bring him back to Paris where he is to be executed. However, when confronted by the two, Stamp is strangely compliant but begins to play mind games with them, making both them and the viewers, wonder what's going on. Then things get even more complicated for the two after they find that the car they hijacked to escape the police has a beautiful Spanish girl in it. Suspenseful, very funny in places and definitely unpredictable.

Sex Nud Viol Lang AdSit

A: Terence Stamp, John Hurt, Tim Roth, Laura Del Sol, Bill Hunter, Fernando Rey

© NEW LINE HOME VIDEO 7599

HOCUS POCUS

D: Kenny Ortega 96 m

PG | COM | 1993 | COLOR

6 One Halloween night, a teen-age boy playing with a spell, releases three witches who had been hung 300 years before. The three know that this time, if they are to survive, they must suck all the life's force from the town's children by daybreak. They crash a costume party where they escape detection by appearing to be just some more adults in costume. However, much to their dismay, the kid, his young sister, a pretty teenage girl and a talking 17th-century cat have set out determined to stop them. Starts slow and then picks up some steam, generally enjoyable but it never reaches its potential.

Sex Nud Viol Lang AdSit

A: Bette Midler, Sarah Jessica Parker, Kathy Najimy, Omri Katz, Thora Birch, Vinessa Shaw

© WALT DISNEY HOME VIDEO 2144

HOLLYWOOD HARRY

D: Robert Forster 99 m

PG-13 | COM MYS | 1986 | COLOR

7 A likable spoof of 40s-style PI mystery. A bored, down-and-out, not-too-bright private detective (Robert Forster) is jolted out of his lethargy by the mysterious case of the rich hog-farmer whose daughter is making porn movies. Daddy wants her back, so he hires our hero. But, the down-and-out Forster is joined in his search through the gutter by his own run-away niece, who adores him. However, neither one of them has a clue about what to do.

Sex Nud Viol Lang AdSit

A: Robert Forster, Joe Spinell, Shannon Wilcox, Kathrine Forster, Marji Martin, Mallie Jackson

© CANNON VIDEO M907

HOME ALONE

D: Chris Columbus 105 m

PG | CLD COM | 1990 | COLOR

9 This was a huge smash hit that kids loved because one of their own gets to cream the bad guys. 8-year-old Macaulay Culkin just wishes his parents would go away - and then they do! He wakes up one December morning to find that his family has left for their Christmas vacation to Paris and accidentally left him behind. Two thieves have targeted their supposedly vacant house to be ripped off, however they never counted on the little guy being there to stop them. Macaulay's war against the bad guys is the highlight of this entertaining film full of slap stick shenanigans. Parents won't like it as much as kids.

Sex Nud Viol Lang AdSit

A: Macaulay Culkin, Joe Pesci, Daniel Stern, John Heard, Catherine O'Hara, Kristin Minter

© FOXVIDEO 1866

HOME ALONE 2

D: Chris Columbus 120 m

PG | CLD COM | 1992 | COLOR

8 This is a cookie-cutter remake of the original. This time Macaulay gets separated from his parents by wandering onto the wrong plane in the Chicago airport and winds up in New York City. Because he has his father's credit cards, he checks into the Plaza Hotel and has a great time, until he runs into his old enemies Joe Pesci and Daniel Stem who have escaped from jail and are out for revenge. Macaulay, however sets up a new trap for them in a brownstone that is under renovation. The last 15 minutes are again filled with a slapstick war where the bad guys get their due.

Sex Nud Viol Lang AdSit

A: Macaulay Culkin, Joe Pesci, Daniel Stem, John Heard, Catherine O'Hara, Daniel Stern

© FOXVIDEO 1989

HOMEWARD BOUND: THE INCREDIBLE JOURNEY

D: Duwayne Dunham 84 m

G | COM CLD | 1993 | COLOR

8 Rock solid family entertainment and a lot of fun. Here, Disney has remade their 1963 hit THE INCREDIBLE JOURNEY, but this time they gave the cute animals real personalities and the voices of Michael J. Fox, Don Ameche and Sally Field. This is the extremely enjoyable and sometimes comic story of two dogs and a cat who are left temporarily several hundred miles away from home. However, they become worried that their masters are in trouble and so the three buddies begin a cross-country journey through the beautiful Sierra Mountains to get home. Very clever and highly entertaining story of their many encounters along the way. Truly a lot of fun. Some might even rate it higher.

Sex Nud Viol Lang AdSit

A:

© WALT DISNEY HOME VIDEO 1801

HONEY, I BLEW UP THE KID

D: Randal Kleiser 89 m

PG | COM CLD FAN | 1992 | COLOR

8 Sequel to HONEY, I SHRUNK THE KIDS. Moranis is now working for a corporation trying to develop a ray that, this time, will enlarge things. He is accidentally successful but accidentally blows up his two-year-old to the size of a ten-story building. There is something here for everyone to laugh at. Moranis is hysterical as he runs around Las Vegas trying to blast his kid with a ray gun to shrink him back down to size. Great special effects again. Overall, this is nearly as good as the original - only slightly less funny because some of the novelty is gone.

Sex Nud Viol Lang AdSit

A: Rick Moranis, Lloyd Bridges, Marcia Strassman, Robert Oliveri, Amy O'Neill

© WALT DISNEY HOME VIDEO 1371

HONEY, I SHRUNK THE KIDS

D: Joe Johnston 101 m

PG | COM CLD FAN | 1989 | COLOR

9 Big box office hit and great family fun-filled fantasy - in the old fashioned Disney tradition. Rick Moranis plays a klutzy scientist who is inventing an experimental ray gun in the attic. One day his kids and the neighbor's kids are playing with it and zap... they are all shrunk down to the size of ants. They become lost in the backyard, which, because of their size, has now been transformed into a forbidding jungle filled with terrible monsters. Really good special effects and fun gags that will satisfy all age groups. Good family entertainment.

Sex Nud Viol Lang AdSit

A: Rick Moranis, Matt Frewer, Marcia Strassman, Kristine Sutherland, Thomas Brown, Jared Rushton

© WALT DISNEY HOME VIDEO 909

HONEYMOON IN VEGAS

D: Andrew Bergman 95 m

PG-13 | ROM COM | 1992 | COLOR | ◢ Sex ☐ Nud ☐ Viol ◢ Lang ◢ AdSit

6 Mildly entertaining. Nicolas Cage is deathly afraid of getting married but at last gives in. He and his girl (Parker) fly off to Vegas to do the deed. However, in one last bout of cowardice, he delays the wedding for one quick game of poker. James Caan is a big time gambler who had earlier spotted Cage's girlfriend in the lobby. She happens to be a dead-ringer for his deceased wife. So he has arranged for the game and Cage loses $65,000 that he doesn't have. No problem says Caan, just loan me your girl for the weekend and we're even. There are a few funny moments and it is well acted, but there just isn't much meat to it.

A: James Caan, Sarah Jessica Parker, Nicolas Cage, Noriyuki "Pat" Morita, John Capodice, Robert Costanzo

© NEW LINE HOME VIDEO 75863

HONEYMOON MACHINE, THE

D: Richard Thorpe 87 m

NR | COM | 1961 | COLOR | ☐ Sex ☐ Nud ☐ Viol ☐ Lang ☐ AdSit

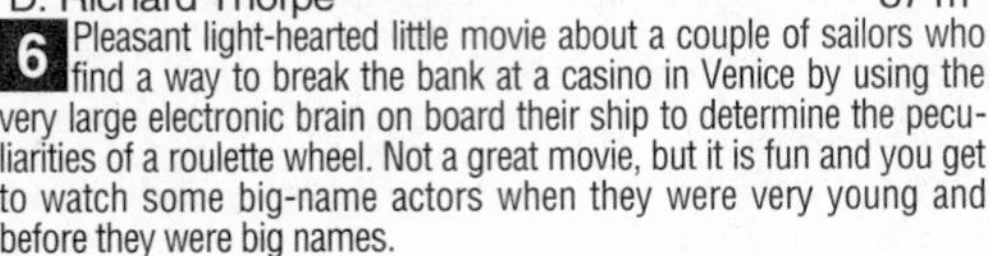

6 Pleasant light-hearted little movie about a couple of sailors who find a way to break the bank at a casino in Venice by using the very large electronic brain on board their ship to determine the peculiarities of a roulette wheel. Not a great movie, but it is fun and you get to watch some big-name actors when they were very young and before they were big names.

A: Steve McQueen, Brigid Brazlen, Jim Hutton, Paula Prentiss, Dean Jagger, Jack Weston

Distributed By MGM/UA Home Video 200795

HOOPER

D: Hal Needham 100 m

PG | ACT COM | 1978 | COLOR | ☐ Sex ☐ Nud ☐ Viol ◢ Lang ◢ AdSit

8 Entertaining and light-hearted romp with fun-loving good-old-boys from Hollywood. Burt Reynolds and Sally Field recaptured much of the charm that they developed in SMOKEY AND THE BANDIT, but this time Burt plays an aging professional stuntman who is being challenged by an arrogant up-and-comer (Vincent) into doing the biggest stunt of his career. You should expect lots of thrilling stunts in cars and other places, but the real fun here is in the wise-cracking characters they create. Lots of fun.

A: Burt Reynolds, Jan-Michael Vincent, Sally Field, Brian Keith, John Marley, Robert Klein

© WARNER HOME VIDEO 1008

HOPSCOTCH

D: Ronald Neame 107 m

R | COM SUS | 1980 | COLOR | ☐ Sex ☐ Nud ☐ Viol ■ Lang ◢ AdSit

8 Highly entertaining entry from two polished pros, even if the plot is contrived. Matthau plays a CIA agent put out to pasture by his pompous and idiotic boss (Beatty) - so Matthau decides to get even. He and his girl friend (Jackson) decide to publish his memoirs, detailing agency misdeeds and dirty tricks. Beatty doesn't take kindly to their revelations and a marvelously entertaining chase between professional chase-ors and chase-ees ensues. Not entirely believable, but Matthau and Jackson are an utter joy together. See them in HOUSE CALLS, too.

A: Walter Matthau, Glenda Jackson, Ned Beatty, Sam Waterston, Herbert Lom

© NEW LINE HOME VIDEO 00104

HORSE'S MOUTH, THE

D: Ronald Neame 96 m

NR | COM | 1958 | B&W | ☐ Sex ☐ Nud ☐ Viol ☐ Lang ◢ AdSit

8 Fans of wry English humor and Alec Guinness take note. Guinness both starred in and wrote this screenplay about an eccentric and driven painter who creates brilliant but bizarre art, and is always broke. He learns that a wealthy collector is interested in him, but the collector is out of town. So Guinness moves into the man's large flat and hangs his masterpieces. His artist friends, who are currently modeling their feet for him, also move in, cut a huge hole in the floor and drop in a huge block of granite. In short order, they have destroyed the building. Very funny satirical English comedy.

A: Alec Guinness, Kay Walsh, Renee Houston, Michael Gough

© HOME VISION HOR 130

HOSPITAL, THE

D: Arthur Hiller 102 m

PG | COM DMA | 1971 | COLOR | ◢ Sex ☐ Nud ☐ Viol ◢ Lang ◢ AdSit

8 An influential film and a bitingly funny black comedy about a chaotic modern hospital and its embittered chief surgeon (Scott) who is struggling against a system out of control. Scott battles a system in which patients come in relatively healthy but leave sicker or dead. His personal life is little better off until he has a brief encounter with a free spirit (Rigg) and her scheming father. The Paddy Chayefsky script won an Oscar and Scott was nominated. Funny in spite of the many uncomfortable truths it exposes - the film is based upon fact.

A: George C. Scott, Diana Rigg, Barnard Hughes, Nancy Marchand, Richard Dysart, Stephen Elliott

Distributed By MGM/UA Home Video M202361

HOTEL PARADISO

D: Peter Glenville 96 m

NR | COM | 1966 | COLOR | ☐ Sex ☐ Nud ☐ Viol ☐ Lang ■ AdSit

6 Alec Guiness is a 40ish married man who has developed a serious itch for his luscious next-door neighbor, Gina Lollabrigida. She feels neglected by her husband Robert Morley and so agrees to meet Guiness for a clandestine rendezvous at a flea-bag Parisian hotel. However, the consummation their carnal pleasures is constantly being frustrated by a series of unlikely coincidences and mistaken identities. This is a silly and mildly entertaining bedroom farce that succeeds only due to the talent of its stars.

A: Alec Guinness, Gina Lollobrigida, Robert Morley, Akim Tamiroff

Distributed By MGM/UA Home Video M200955

HOT MILLIONS

D: Eric Till 105 m

G | COM | 1968 | COLOR | ☐ Sex ☐ Nud ☐ Viol ☐ Lang ◢ AdSit

8 Highly entertaining laugh-getter, one of the surprise hits of the year and nominated for Best Original Screenplay. Peter Ustinov plays a roguish embezzler who is caught because of a computer. So, he decides to get his revenge by becoming an expert on computers himself in jail. When released, he conspires to get computer genius Robert Morley out of the country, and then, using his identity, he wheedles his way into Karl Malden's company, where he embezzles millions of dollars, marries his secretary and moves to Rio. But then, Malden sends Bob Newhart after him. Frequently hilarious.

A: Peter Ustinov, Maggie Smith, Karl Malden, Bob Newhart, Robert Morley, Cesar Romero

Distributed By MGM/UA Home Video M204550

HOT SHOTS

D: Jim Abrahams 83 m

PG-13 | COM | 1991 | COLOR | ☐ Sex ☐ Nud ☐ Viol ◢ Lang ◢ AdSit

8 Outlandish, occasionally hilarious, and usually - but not always - funny. A ridiculous spoof (in the tradition of NAKED GUN and AIRPLANE) of the megahit Tom Cruise movie TOP GUN. Charlie Sheen is a hotshot navy pilot who must live down the disastrous reputation his father has left him. It's full of wild puns and sight gags - most of which work, but some of which don't. Look for outrageous spoofs of other famous movie scenes from GONE WITH THE WIND, DANCES WITH WOLVES, THE FABULOUS BAKER BOYS and 9 1/2 WEEKS. Sheen is remarkably funny. So is Lloyd Bridges.

A: Charlie Sheen, Lloyd Bridges, Jon Cryer, Cary Elwes, Efrem Zimbalist, Jr., Valeria Golino

© FOXVIDEO 1930

HOT SHOTS! PART DEUX

D: Jim Abrahams 89 m

PG-13 | COM | 1993 | COLOR | ◢ Sex ◢ Nud ◢ Viol ◢ Lang ◢ AdSit

7 This is another one of those purposefully dumb, absolutely silly, slapstick gagfests. Sheen reprises a role from HOT SHOTS, this time spoofing Rambo. Also back are Valeria Golino and Lloyd Bridges. And, this time Richard Crenna plays Sheen's commanding officer (he played Sylvester Stalone's in the original RAMBO) directing Sheen on a mission into Iraq to rescue hostages. The film does murderous parodies of BASIC INSTINCT, APOCALYPSE NOW, LADY AND THE TRAMP and CASABLANCA. If you are a fan of this brand of zaniness or if you have never seen one, this will be fun. Even if you don't like them, it will make you laugh at times but it can also be tedious.

A: Charlie Sheen, Valeria Golino, Lloyd Bridges, Brenda Bakke, Richard Crenna

© FOXVIDEO 8507

HOUSEBOAT

D: Melville Shavelson 110 m

NR | ROM COM | 1958 | COLOR | ☐ Sex ☐ Nud ☐ Viol ☐ Lang ☐ AdSit

8 Predictable but highly enjoyable '50s-style romantic comedy about a Washington D.C. widowed attorney with three unruly kids living on a houseboat on the Potomac River. He hires a curvaceous music conductor's daughter, with no previous experience, as governess to take them in hand. Despite their relationships with others and numerous intervening catastrophies, they are... surprise... irresistibly drawn to each other. The star power of these two makes this a delight.

A: Cary Grant, Sophia Loren, Martha Hyer, Harry Guardino, Eduardo Ciannelli, Murray Hamilton

© PARAMOUNT HOME VIDEO 5806

HOUSE CALLS

D: Howard Zieff 98 m

PG | ROM COM | 1978 | COLOR | ◢ Sex ☐ Nud ☐ Viol ◢ Lang ◢ AdSit

9 This is a laugh-out-loud comedy about a recently widowed doctor, enjoying his sudden desirability and popularity with the ladies. But, he is distressed to find that he is irresistibly attracted to an outspoken divorcee (Jackson) who, if he isn't careful, will mess up everything. He doesn't want to give up his freedom, and she doesn't want to become a just another notch on his bedpost. Matthau and Jackson are wonderful together. Delightful comedy about two equally matched lovers, locked in a matrimonial battle of wits. Both Jackson and Matthau reappeared together in HOPSCOTCH.

A: Walter Matthau, Glenda Jackson, Art Carney, Richard Benjamin, Candice Azzara, Dick O'Neill

© MCA/UNIVERSAL HOME VIDEO, INC. 66045

HOUSEGUEST

D: Randall Miller 119 m

PG | COM | 1995 | COLOR

6 Silly family comedy. Sinbad is a former orphan who has never grown up. He is now a 35-year-old wannabe millionaire, chasing one get-rich scheme after another, but his luck has just ran out. He owes a loan-shark the $5,000 he borrowed, plus $45,000 in interest. His first bit of good luck is that the two goofy goons sent to collect from him are so stupid he is able to escape. The second is that he stumbles upon an uptight, middle-aged, upper-class white guy (Harrington) at the airport, who is waited for a black guy that he hasn't seen in years...and Sinbad is able to convince him that he is that guy. Then, silly Sinbad goes home with Harrington and teaches him and his family how to loosen-up.

Sex | Nud | Viol | Lang | AdSit

A: Sinbad, Phil Hartman, Jeffrey Jones, Kim Greist, Stan Shaw, Tony Longo

© HOLLYWOOD PICTURES HOME VIDEO 3631

HOUSE PARTY

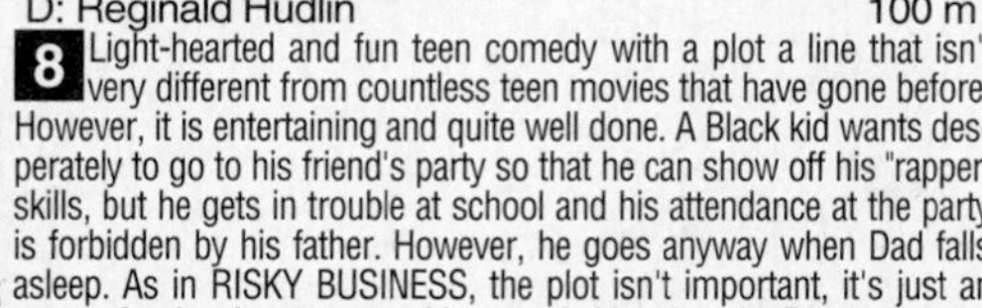

D: Reginald Hudlin 100 m

R | COM | 1990 | COLOR

8 Light-hearted and fun teen comedy with a plot a line that isn't very different from countless teen movies that have gone before. However, it is entertaining and quite well done. A Black kid wants desperately to go to his friend's party so that he can show off his "rapper" skills, but he gets in trouble at school and his attendance at the party is forbidden by his father. However, he goes anyway when Dad falls asleep. As in RISKY BUSINESS, the plot isn't important, it's just an excuse for the characters to shine... and shine they do. Funny, perceptive and a good time. Don't waste your time on the sequel.

Sex | Nud | Viol | Lang | AdSit

A: Christopher Reid, Christopher Martin, Robin Harris, Tisha Campbell, A.J. Johnson, Martin Lawrence

© TURNER HOME ENTERTAINMENT N4090

HOUSESITTER

D: Frank Oz 102 m

COM ROM | 1992 | COLOR

6 Mildly entertaining farce. Martin is a love-struck architect who hocks everything to build his dream house in his hometown to surprise his true love - except she says no. Heartbroken, he goes back to the city, leaving his dream house behind. There, he has a one night stand with pretty con-artist (Hawn), and when she discovers that there is a new house in a pretty little town with nobody in it - she decides to move in. Soon, she has put out the word that she is Martin's new wife, all of which is a surprise to Martin's parents, his girlfriend and most of all, to Martin. Basically ridiculous and silly, but OK if you are willing to accept it.

Sex | Nud | Viol | Lang | AdSit

A: Steve Martin, Goldie Hawn, Dana Delany, Julie Harris, Donald Moffat, Peter MacNicol

© MCA/UNIVERSAL HOME VIDEO, INC. 81280

HOWIE MANDEL'S NORTH AMERICAN WATUSI TOUR

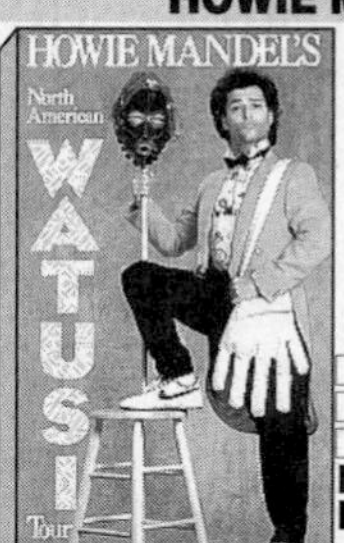

D: Jerry Kramer 52 m

COM | 1986 | COLOR

8 Howie Mandel's concert was filmed in Chicago. His sight gags and famous humor is here, but it is his off-the-wall improvisations with the audience that gets them and keeps them going.

Sex | Nud | Viol | Lang | AdSit

A: Howie Mandel

© PARAMOUNT HOME VIDEO 12546

HOW I WON THE WAR

D: Richard Lester 111 m

NR | COM WAR | 1967 | COLOR

6 Very British satire of one man's story of his military career. Michael Crawford plays an eccentric British officer who makes ridiculous demands of his troops and manages to stay alive when all those around him don't. Savage satire of war that may be lost on many because of very heavy British accents and very dry black humor. Others will find it hilarious.

Sex | Nud | Viol | Lang | AdSit

A: Michael Crawford, John Lennon, Roy Kinnear, Lee Montague, Jack MacGowran

Distributed By MGM/UA Home Video M600455

HOW TO MURDER YOUR WIFE

D: Richard Quine 120 m

NR | COM | 1965 | COLOR

6 Engaging comedy in which a cavalier, care-free bachelor (Lemmon) wakes up after a wild party to find that he has married the beautiful blond (Lisi) who came out of the cake, and she can't even speak English. A cartoonist and confirmed bachelor, he spends the rest of the film fantasizing ways to get out of his predicament, including an elaborate murder scheme. All of which leads to interesting, and sometimes funny, complications.

Sex | Nud | Viol | Lang | AdSit

A: Jack Lemmon, Verna Lisi, Terry-Thomas, Eddie Mayehoff, Claire Trevor, Jack Albertson

Distributed By MGM/UA Home Video M201466

HOW TO SUCCEED IN BUSINESS WITHOUT REALLY TRYING

D: David Swift 172 m

NR | MUS COM | 1967 | COLOR

8 Robert Morse brings his Broadway triumph successfully to the big screen in this musical satire about an ambitious and charming window washer who reads a book on success and immediately puts it to work. On his first day in the building, he charms pretty secretary Michele Lee into helping him to meet the chief of personnel. Soon he has everybody, including the President of the company, (Vallee) charmed - and, all with the help of the book. Entertaining with lots of good music including: "I Believe in You" and "Brotherhood of Man."

Sex | Nud | Viol | Lang | AdSit

A: Robert Morse, Michele Lee, Rudy Vallee, Anthony Teague, Maureen Arthur, Sammy Smith

Distributed By MGM/UA Home Video M200663

HUDSUCKER PROXY, THE

D: Joel Coen 111 m

PG | COM | 1994 | COLOR

7 This film received largely rave reviews from the critics. It is staffed with some of Hollywood's finest actors and is blessed with very rich production values. On its surface, it is a satire of how a group of executives in 1958, led by Paul Newman, connive to drive down the value of their company's stock so they can buy up controlling interest for themselves. To do this, they try to scare Wallstreet by putting a young and supposedly dim-witted guy in the executive's chair. However, he spoils their plan by instead driving up the stock prices by inventing the hula hoop and making millions. However, this film is also a rather slow-moving Hollywood inside-parody of itself, so it is for a select audience.

Sex | Nud | Viol | Lang | AdSit

A: Tim Robbins, Jennifer Jason Leigh, Paul Newman, Charles Durning, Jim True, John Mahoney

© WARNER HOME VIDEO 13166

ICE PIRATES

D: Stewart Raffill 95 m

PG | SF COM | 1984 | COLOR

6 Fun farce set in the future. Robert Urich plays a pirate leader in this tongue-in-cheek adventure story. He and his band of buccaneers come to the aid of beautiful princess (Crosby) in her battle against an evil force. Both she and the buccaneers are in pursuit of what is now the Universe's most precious commodity - water. The film is not always successful in its attempts at humor and excitement, but sometimes it is. The special effects aren't great, but they aren't bad, either. All this adds up to a passable evening's diversion for the family.

Sex | Nud | Viol | Lang | AdSit

A: Robert Urich, Mary Crosby, John Matuszak, Anjelica Huston, John Carradine

Distributed By MGM/UA Home Video M800427

ICICLE THIEF, THE

D: Maurizio Nichetti 84 m

NR | FOR COM | 1990 | COLOR

7 Very unusual and quite funny Italian satire. Its director has been called the Italian Woody Allen. This film is his lampoon of both classic Italian cinema and modern television advertising. In it, the film jumps back and forth between a black and white post-war Italy and a color contemporary Italy, and between poor households and middle-class ones. It is essentially a movie-within-a-series-of-movies. Featuring such things as a beautiful blond model diving into an ultramarine pool and emerging in a black and white river. Clearly for serious film fans only. Subtitles.

Sex | Nud | Viol | Lang | AdSit

A: Maurizio Nichetti, Caterina Sylos Labini, Claudio G. Fava, Heidi Komarek

© FOX/LORBER HOME VIDEO 1030

IF YOU COULD SEE WHAT I HEAR

D: Eric Till 100 m

PG | DMA COM | 1981 | COLOR

6 Interesting screen biography of real-life blind singer/composer Tom Sullivan. The story deals directly with his blindness and how he handles things. It begins with his college years, telling his story over time until he settles down after having several flings. The story stresses the more humorous elements of his situation and has, therefore, been criticized as being too simplistic, sugary-sweet and insubstantial. Others call it optimistic, life-affirming and uplifting. You'll get out of it whatever you look for.

Sex | Nud | Viol | Lang | AdSit

A: Marc Singer, R.H. Thomson, Sarah Torgov, Shari Belafonte Harper

© LIVE HOME VIDEO VA5014

I'LL DO ANYTHING

D: James L. Brooks 116 m

PG-13 | DMA COM | 1994 | COLOR

6 Nick Nolte plays Matt, a good but down-on-his-luck actor. Even after an Oscar nomination, he can't find steady work. And, now struggling, divorced and living in a rundown apartment, his spoiled 6-year-old daughter is moving in with him, and he has no idea what to do with her. His fortunes seem to have changed when an old friend gets him an audition but all that results is a job driving a second-rate movie director around. Then adding injury, his daughter lands a part. Originally planned to be a musical, but the preview audience responded badly, so the singing was pulled. Too slow for most, but fans of acting and Hollywood insiderisms may rate it even higher.

Sex | Nud | Viol | Lang | AdSit

A: Nick Nolte, Albert Brooks, Julie Kavner, Joely Richardson, Tracey Ulman, Whittni Wright

© COLUMBIA TRISTAR HOME VIDEO 52623

I LOVE YOU, ALICE B. TOKLAS

D: Hy Averback — 94 m

NR · COM · 1968 · COLOR

7 Peter Sellers is a scream as a conservative Los Angeles lawyer in the 1960s who, after he has an encounter with sexy young hippie Leigh Taylor-Young and some super-charged marijuana brownies, chucks everything to live in his car and let his hair grow. Sellers is wonderful as he discovers that the free-living lifestyle can be just as constraining as the old one. Even though many of the situations are obviously dated now, this is still a whole lot of fun.

Sex · ◢ Nud · Viol · ◢ Lang · ◢ AdSit

A: Peter Sellers, Leigh Taylor-Young, Jo Van Fleet, David Arkin, Joyce Van Patten

© WARNER HOME VIDEO 11127

I LOVE YOU TO DEATH

D: Lawrence Kasdan — 97 m

R · COM · 1990 · COLOR

7 Black, black comedy with, almost unbelievably, a happy ending. Tracey Ullman plays a woman who discovers that her husband (Kline) has been cheating on her - over and over again. So she enlists the aid of a young friend, her mother and a couple of dim-witted accomplices in her attempts to kill him. However, repeated attempts result in repeated failures, even though he is considerably worse for their efforts. Ultimately, her wayward husband is worn down, sees the light, changes his ways and she forgives him. Sound funny? It is. What's even funnier - it's based upon a true account.

◢ Sex · ◢ Nud · Viol · Lang · ◢ AdSit

A: Kevin Kline, Tracey Ullman, River Phoenix, Joan Plowright, William Hurt, Victoria Jackson

© COLUMBIA TRISTAR HOME VIDEO 70303

I'M ALL RIGHT, JACK

D: John Boulting — 101 m

NR · COM · 1960 · B&W

9 Wickedly funny satire which has some of England's finest funny men in top form for this spoof of the labor movement. A naive young man, a college man who works his way up from blue collar laborer, commits the unpardonable sin of improving his plant's efficiency. Sellers is hilarious as the outraged pompous labor leader who protests by calling a union strike, which closes down the plant. This causes other plants to close and soon strikes spread to cripple the entire country. Labor and management negotiations have rarely been this funny. Side-splitting at times.

Sex · Nud · Viol · Lang · ◢ AdSit

A: Ian Carmichael, Peter Sellers, Terry-Thomas, Richard Attenborough, Irene Handl, Margaret Rutherford

© HBO VIDEO TVC1113

I'M GONNA GIT YOU SUCKA

D: Keenen Ivory Wayans — 89 m

R · COM ACT · 1988 · COLOR

8 Really funny spoof of the black exploitation movies of the early 1970s. Wayans comes home after a ten-year tour in the Army to find that his brother has died from an overdose of gold chains. Worse, he has left his family shackled with a big debt owed to the neighborhood's head punk. When the police don't help, Wayans rounds up a crew of over-the-hill heroes (Brown, Hayes, Casey and Fargas) to save the day. Major spoof, with laugh-out-loud gags.

Sex · ◢ Nud · ◢ Viol · ■ Lang · ◢ AdSit

A: Keenan Ivory Wayans, Bernie Casey, Antonio Fargas, Steve James, Isaac Hayes, Jim Brown

Distributed By MGM/UA Home Video M901641

IMMEDIATE FAMILY

D: Jonathan Kaplan — 99 m

PG-13 · DMA COM · 1989 · COLOR

6 Glenn Close and James Woods are wealthy yuppies who have everything except what they want most - a baby. They have tried everything else and now, in desperation, they try a process called open adoption, where the adoptive parents meet the mother before the baby is born. The mother is Mary Stuart Masterson, a gritty blue collar unwed mother who isn't yet totally committed to giving up her baby. This is a relatively simple story that covers ground covered before, but it exceeds the more typical fare because of the excellent acting from Masterson.

Sex · Nud · Viol · ◢ Lang · ■ AdSit

A: Glenn Close, James Woods, Kevin Dillon, Mary Stuart Masterson, Linda Darlow

© COLUMBIA TRISTAR HOME VIDEO 50193

IMPROMPTU

D: James Lapine — 108 m

PG-13 · ROM COM · 1990 · COLOR

7 Witty, intellectual and romantic dramedy with a historical twist. Real-life 19th-century French novelist George Sand (played here by Judy Davis) was in fact not a man at all, but a free-spirited woman who enjoyed smoking cigars and cross-dressing. She also enjoyed scandalizing Paris by collecting a long list of lovers. This amusing film is about the strong-willed woman's pursuit of the delicate Polish composer, Frederic Chopin. He was in everything her opposite and was also not entirely open to her advances. Nor was her current lover eager to see her leave him. For sophisticated tastes.

Sex · ◢ Nud · Viol · ◢ Lang · ◢ AdSit

A: Judy Davis, Hugh Grant, Mandy Patinkin, Bernadette Peters, Julian Sands

© HEMDALE HOME VIDEO, INC. 7007

INDIANA JONES AND THE LAST CRUSADE

D: Steven Spielberg — 126 m

PG-13 · ACT COM · 1989 · COLOR

8 Entertaining family flick in the Saturday matinee serial-action tradition. This is the last in the series of adventurous exploits of the famous Indiana Jones. Here, Indie (Ford) launches himself on a quest to find his father (Connery) who has disappeared while in search of the Holy Grail. Connery and Ford work well together as they endeavor to find the Grail and then to protect it from the evil Nazis, who are out to steal it. Thrills and style will delight viewers of all ages.

Sex · Nud · ◢ Viol · ◢ Lang · ◢ AdSit

A: Harrison Ford, Sean Connery, Denholm Elliott, Alison Doody, River Phoenix, Julian Glover

© PARAMOUNT HOME VIDEO 31859

INDIANA JONES AND THE TEMPLE OF DOOM

D: Steven Spielberg — 118 m

PG · ACT COM · 1984 · COLOR

8 Exciting follow-up (and first of two sequels) to super hit RAIDERS OF THE LOST ARK. This one is set at a place in time before the original and has Indie (Ford), a nightclub singer (Capshaw) and a resourceful Korean kid (Quan) embark on an adventure in India to retrieve a magic jewel and a village's children from a Maharaja's fortress where they have been forced to work his mines. Filled with action-packed sequences as the original was, but less effective now. May be too intense for very young viewers.

Sex · Nud · ◢ Viol · ◢ Lang · ◢ AdSit

A: Harrison Ford, Kate Capshaw, Ke Huy Quan, Amrish Puri, Philip Stone, Dan Aykroyd

© PARAMOUNT HOME VIDEO 1643

INDIAN SUMMER

D: Mike Binder — 98 m

PG-13 · COM DMA · 1993 · COLOR

8 Seven thirty-something friends are invited back for a twenty-year reunion to a summer camp in Ontario. The camp's director (Alan Arkin) has selected them as his favorite residents from years past and he wants them to share one last week with him there before he closes the camp forever. The seven stay in the lakeside cabins and partake in all the activities that they did in their youths, but this time everything is punctuated with contemplations and discussions of their current lives. It is sort of like THE BIG CHILL but is set on a lake and is much more light-hearted. It is also a clever, warm and nostalgic feel-good film.

◢ Sex · Nud · Viol · ◢ Lang · ■ AdSit

A: Alan Arkin, Elizabeth Perkins, Vincent Spano, Diane Lane, Bill Paxton, Kevin Pollak

© TOUCHSTONE HOME VIDEO 1936

INDISCREET

D: Stanley Donen — 100 m

ROM COM · 1958 · COLOR

7 Delightful sophisticated comedy in which Cary Grant plays an American playboy diplomat who romances women and then tells them he is married to avoid being trapped into marriage. Then he romances a famous European film star (Bergman). He finds himself drawn to her but still he pretends to be married to escape commitment. However, she eventually discovers his lie and sets her own plans in motion to get even. Stylish and endearing performances from both. Charming.

Sex · Nud · Viol · Lang · ◢ AdSit

A: Cary Grant, Ingrid Bergman, Cecil Parker, Phylis Calvert, Megs Jenkins, David Kossoff

© REPUBLIC PICTURES HOME VIDEO 5404

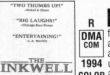

INKWELL, THE

D: Matty Rich — 122 m

R · DMA COM · 1994 · COLOR

6 Well-meaning story of an introverted black teenager who learns a lot about life and himself on one summer vacation. He and his family have been invited to stay for a couple of weeks with his wealthy aunt and uncle in their summer home at an affluent beach area known as The Inkwell. His father, who is an ex-black panther activist and his uncle, who is a black Republican, fight from the very first. His mother and his aunt fight too, but the shy youngster is having his own problems -- girls. He means well, but he is just not socially equipped for success. However, a couple of older women provide him with the means to gain confidence in himself and discover the new man buried deep inside.

Sex · Nud · Viol · ■ Lang · ◢ AdSit

A: Larenz Tate, Joe Morton, Suzzanne Douglas, Glynn Turman, Venessa Bell Calloway, Adrienne-Joi Johnson

© TOUCHSTONE HOME VIDEO 2749

IN-LAWS, THE

D: Arthur Hiller — 103 m

PG · COM ACT · 1979 · COLOR

8 Hysterically wacky and unpredictable. A normal neighborhood dentist (Arkin) agrees to do a small favor for his daughter's future father-in-law (Falk), supposedly a CIA agent. But it soon becomes obvious that Falk is more than a little crazy when the two rob an armored car of engraving plates from the U.S. Treasury and also find themselves in front of a firing squad in a South American country. Falk and Arkin are great together in this far-out comedy.

Sex · Nud · Viol · ◢ Lang · ◢ AdSit

A: Peter Falk, Alan Arkin, Richard Libertini, Nancy Dussault, Penny Peyser, Michael Lembeck

© WARNER HOME VIDEO 1009

INNERSPACE

D: Joe Dante 120 m

PG
COM SF
1987
COLOR
Sex
Nud
Viol
Lang
AdSit

7 Funny takeoff on FANTASTIC VOYAGE. Dennis Quaid is an astronaut who agrees to be miniaturized down to the size of a virus and then be injected into a rabbit. However, instead he accidentally gets shot into a hypochondriacal store clerk, Martin Short. What's worse, Short is now being chased by spies who want them both. Funny, off-the-wall stuff, with special effects that won an Oscar for Visual Effects. Short is perfect.

A: Dennis Quaid, Martin Short, Fiona Lewis, Vernon Wells, Meg Ryan, Kevin McCarthy

© WARNER HOME VIDEO 11754

INSIGNIFICANCE

D: Nicolas Roeg 110 m

R
DMA COM
1985
COLOR
Sex
Nud
Viol
Lang
AdSit

7 Intellectual and somewhat bizarre theatrical exercise. Four prominent public figures from the early '50s convene a very unusual impromptu meeting in a hotel room the evening before there is to be a congressional investigation into un-American activities. The characters, obviously Marilyn Monroe, Joe DiMaggio, Joseph McCarthy and Albert Einstein, engage in a sometimes humorous, sometimes serious discussion of sex, relativity and the nature of things. Clearly not for everyone's taste, but for the more esoteric viewer, an interesting and sometimes entertaining exercise.

A: Theresa Russell, Michael Emil, Gary Busey, Tony Curtis

© WARNER HOME VIDEO 014

IN THE MOOD

D: Phil Alden Robinson 98 m

PG-13
COM ROM
1987
COLOR
Sex
Nud
Viol
Lang
AdSit

7 Fascinating, more so because it was true. Sonny Wisecarver is a teenager in 1944 who has the strange propensity for falling in love with older women and then getting them to fall for him. He runs off with a married mother of two, only to have that relationship annulled. Whereupon, he marries another older woman, only to get in trouble again. Sweetly funny film, based upon a real live character from the '40s who the press labeled "The Woo Woo Kid." The real Sonny Wiscarver has a cameo as a mailman in a newsreel sequence.

A: Patrick Dempsey, Beverly D'Angelo, Talia Balsam, Michael Constantine, Betty Jinett

© WARNER HOME VIDEO 475

INTO THE NIGHT

D: John Landis 115 m

R
ACT ROM COM
1985
COLOR
Sex
Nud
Viol
Lang
AdSit

7 Jeff Goldblum is hopelessly boring and bored, plus his wife is having an affair with another man. While out on a midnight ramble, he stumbles into a beautiful woman (Pfeiffer) who is being pursued by a bunch of bad guys and accidentally gets involved with her, helping her to escape. Their adventure continues with repeated encounters with the killers and a quest to find some stolen emeralds. Criticized justly as being unnecessarily convoluted and difficult to follow, it is also, most times, a fun mix of romance, comedy and exciting action. Contains cameos from many leading directors.

A: Jeff Goldblum, Michelle Pfeiffer, David Bowie, Richard Farnsworth, Vera Miles, Dan Aykroyd

© MCA/UNIVERSAL HOME VIDEO, INC. 80170

I OUGHT TO BE IN PICTURES

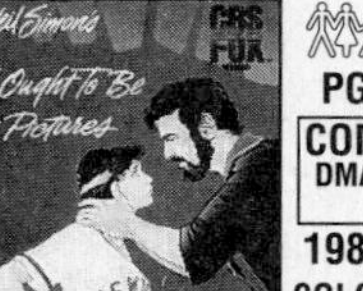

D: Herbert Ross 107 m

PG
COM DMA
1982
COLOR
Sex
Nud
Viol
Lang
AdSit

8 Heartwarming Neil Simon story about a 19-year-old girl who travels to Los Angeles to become a movie star and to look up her long lost father. Matthau plays a burned out screenwriter who spends more time drinking and at the race track than he does writing, and who abandoned his family back in Brooklyn many years ago. Ann-Margret plays his girlfriend, who mediates between the two to eventually brings them back together, and gets Matthau's paternal genes to kick in. Very funny and affecting.

A: Walter Matthau, Ann-Margret, Dinah Manoff, Lance Guest, Lewis Smith, Martin Ferrero

© FOXVIDEO 1150

I.Q.

D: Fred Schepisi 95 m

PG
COM ROM
1994
COLOR
Sex
Nud
Viol
Lang
AdSit

6 Lowly mechanic Tim Robbins is awe-struck by the arrival at his garage of Meg Ryan. She is very pretty; she is a brilliant mathematician; and, when Tim trys to return a watch she left, he discovers that she is also the niece of Albert Einstein (Walter Matthau). Oddly enough, Albert takes quite a liking to the boy. He and his three cronies decide that she would in fact be much happier with the mechanic than with the stuffy psychologist she is about to marry. The trouble is that she doesn't think Tim is smart enough. So, Albert and his buddies conspire to make Tim appear to be a latent genius - all of which leads to complications. Preposterous and implausible premise, but works because of star power.

A: Meg Ryan, Tim Robbins, Walter Mathau, Charles Durning, Shephen Fry, Lou Jacobi

© PARAMOUNT HOME VIDEO 32678

IRMA LA DOUCE

D: Billy Wilder 144 m

NR
COM
1963
COLOR
Sex
Nud
Viol
Lang
AdSit

7 Jack Lemmon plays a Parisian cop who has the misfortune of raiding the red light district while his boss is visiting. When he is fired, he takes up a new career as a pimp for streetwalker Shirley MacLaine, but has the added misfortune of falling in love with her. Now insanely jealous, he plots to keep customers away from her. Enjoyable comedy that attempted to rekindle the chemistry these two created in THE APARTMENT. Good, but it doesn't work quite as well. Andre Previn score won an Oscar.

A: Shirley MacLaine, Jack Lemmon, Lou Jacobi, Herschel Bernardi, Joan Shawlee, Hope Holiday

Distributed By MGM/UA Home Video M201582

IRRECONCILABLE DIFFERENCES

D: Charles Shyer 112 m

PG
COM DMA
1984
COLOR
Sex
Nud
Viol
Lang
AdSit

6 An unusual premise gives this picture a good opportunity to do something different and it almost does: a 10-year-old girl sues her parents for a divorce. A young couple have a good relationship until they each start to have some successes with their careers. Then they both become totally self-centered, devoted first to career and then to themselves. They exclude themselves from each other and even from their daughter. So she divorces them. A good premise, some funny moments and some poignant moments redeem this otherwise mediocre flick.

A: Drew Barrymore, Ryan O'Neal, Shelley Long, Sharon Stone, Sam Wanamaker

© LIVE HOME VIDEO VA5057

IT COULD HAPPEN TO YOU

D: Andrew Bergman 101 m

PG
ROM COM
1994
COLOR
Sex
Nud
Viol
Lang
AdSit

7 Lightweight and breezy entertainment. Nicolas Cage is a New York street cop and he loves it. His wife, Rosie Perez, is a hairdresser -- but she doesn't like it. She also doesn't like him being a cop and she doesn't even like him very much. Mostly, she doesn't like not being rich, so she is always having him buy lottery tickets. One day, when short on cash, Cage offered a down-on-her-luck, very sweet and very pretty waitress (Bridget Fonda) half his lottery ticket instead. But the idea backfired when the ticket turned out to be a winner and he had given away $2 million. Rosie really didn't like that and their marriage is in big trouble. Very predictable with absolutely no surprises, but fun.

A: Nicolas Cage, Bridget Fonda, Rosie Perez, Wendell Pierce, Isaac Hayes, Seymour Cassel

© COLUMBIA TRISTAR HOME VIDEO 72813

IT'S A MAD, MAD, MAD, MAD WORLD

D: Stanley Kramer 188 m

G
COM
1963
COLOR
Sex
Nud
Viol
Lang
AdSit

8 Three hours of zaniness from a virtual "Who's Who" of American comedy of the 1960s. An accident victim reveals the location of a buried "treasure" to a whole group of people who have surrounded him as he lays dying. Invigorated at their good fortune, they all charge off in a mad scramble to get their piece of the pie. But, it's stolen money and Spencer Tracy is a police detective who wants it back. However, he chooses to just sit back to watch this group of crazies do their level best to beat each other to $350,000 in stolen money and do his job for him. Sight-gags galore. Big cast and a good time.

A: Spencer Tracy, Edie Adams, Milton Berle, Sid Caesar, Ethel Merman, Jonathan Winters

Distributed By MGM/UA Home Video M302193

IT'S MY TURN

D: Claudia Weill 91 m

R
ROM COM
1980
COLOR
Sex
Nud
Viol
Lang
AdSit

7 Enjoyable sophisticated comedy about a modern-day woman's dilemma. She is successful - a brilliant mathematics professor, seemingly with everything. But she is also a klutz who can't seem to handle anything, including her life, very well. Her live-in lover is an aloof architect. Then, at her father's wedding, she meets her new step-mother's son (Douglas). He is a brash ex-baseball player with a beard. He is everything she shouldn't like, but she does. However, is this incest? Surprising little film that is consistently funny in a low-key witty sort of way.

A: Jill Clayburgh, Michael Douglas, Charles Grodin, Beverly Garland, Daniel Stern, Jennifer Salt

© COLUMBIA TRISTAR HOME VIDEO 60023

IT STARTED IN NAPLES

D: Melville Shavelson 100 m

NR
ROM COM
1960
COLOR
Sex
Nud
Viol
Lang
AdSit

6 Light-hearted fun. Clark Gable is a an American attorney who goes to Italy to settle the estate of his dead brother, only to find that there is a 10-year-old boy from a common-law marriage. His attempts to bring the boy back to the States are blocked by the boy's sexy Italian aunt (Sophia Loren). Guess what happens next. Lots of beautiful Italian scenery, including Sophia.

A: Clark Gable, Sophia Loren, Vittorio De Sica, Marietto, Paolo Carlini, Claudio Ermelli

© PARAMOUNT HOME VIDEO 6790

I WANNA HOLD YOUR HAND

D: Robert Zemeckis 99 m

PG | COM MUS | 1978 | COLOR

6 Delightful comedy produced by Steven Spielberg about six New Jersey teenagers in the early '60s who try to break into the Ed Sullivan Show the night that The Beatles are set to appear. Fast-paced, with a fine sense for the time period and the hysteria that surrounded the Fab Four's trip to America. Contains 17 Beatles songs.

Sex, Nud, Viol, Lang, AdSit

A: Nancy Allen, Bobby DiCicco, Mark McClure, Theresa Saldana, Eddie Deezen

© WARNER HOME VIDEO 35066

JERK, THE

D: Carl Reiner 94 m

R | COM | 1979 | COLOR

6 Ridiculous farce that will please Steve Martin fans (maybe Jerry Lewis's too), but will likely leave most others scratching their heads. Martin plays a happy, if none-too-bright, white "son" of black sharecropper parents. When he discovers that he is not really their son, he leaves home. He rises to fame and fortune as an inventor, only to fall again. But along the way, he marries the girl of his dreams, a coronet playing cosmetologist (Peters). Funny moments, but very uneven.

Sex, Nud, Viol, Lang, AdSit

A: Steve Martin, Bernadette Peters, Catlin Adams, Mabel King, Richard Ward, Bill Macey

© MCA/UNIVERSAL HOME VIDEO, INC. 66005

JESUS OF MONTREAL

D: Denys Arcand 119 m

R | FOR DMA COM | 1989 | COLOR

8 Nominated for Best Foreign Film. A group of unemployed actors get together some backers and form their own company for the presentation of the Passion Play on a hill overlooking Montreal. The play is in every way devout, but it does not follow traditional lines because it also attacks religious hypocrisy and commercialism. While it is well received by the community, the local clergy objects to it and so do its financial backers. The dilemma for the actors is whether to hold true to their ideals or to bow to pressure. Wickedly funny in places. Subtitles.

Sex, Nud, Viol, Lang, AdSit

A: Lothaire Bluteau, Catherine Wilkening, Johanne-Marie Tremblay, Remy Tirard, Robert Lepage, Gilles Pelletier

© ORION PICTURES CORPORATION 5057

JOHNNY STECCHINO

D: Roberto Benigni 122 m

R | FOR COM | 1991 | COLOR

7 This silly film is one of Italy's most popular hits. In it, Dante (Benigni) is a timid bus driver who is the spitting image of Johnny Stecchino, a notorious mob boss in hiding because other gangsters want to kill him. One night, Dante is seduced by beautiful Maria (Nicoletta Brashi) and is invited to return to Sicily with her. Believing that they are in love, he accepts her offer. However, her only plan is to trick the other gangsters into killing him instead of his look-alike, her husband. So, Dante is quite confused when he is constantly being shot at when all he has done is to have stolen a banana. Subtitles.

Sex, Nud, Viol, Lang, AdSit

A: Roberto Benigni, Nicoletta Brashi, Paolo Bonacelli, Ignazio Pappalardo, Franco Volpi

© TURNER HOME ENTERTAINMENT N4066

JOHNNY SUEDE

D: Tom DiCillo 92 m

R | COM | 1992 | COLOR

7 Playful, very quirky comedy. Johnny Suede is determined to become someone. He will become a teenage idol, but he will create something new. He will become a "retro-rocker" - a 50s sort of guy, but in the 90s. He's got the clothes. He's got a hollow-body electric guitar (although no talent). He's got really big, big hair, stacked into a super popadour (like his hero Ricky Nelson). What he doesn't got is black suede shoes - but then, one day while walking down the streets of his seedy neighborhood, his shoes literally hit him on the head. Now, he is ready to take on the world. Really unusual offbeat comedy.

Sex, Nud, Viol, Lang, AdSit

A: Brad Pitt, Catherine Keener, Calvin Levels, Alison Moir, Nick Cave, Tina Louise

© PARAMOUNT HOME VIDEO 15115

JO JO DANCER, YOUR LIFE IS CALLING

D: Richard Pryor 97 m

R | DMA COM | 1986 | COLOR

6 Alternately involving and boring, bitterly sad and riotously funny, this is the thinly veiled semi-autobiographical account of Richard Prior. Entertainer JoJo Dancer's spirit rises from his half-dead body to contemplate everything which got him to that point. The film chronicles his life's story from its earliest painful beginnings through to his peak as a popular entertainer, with an almost brutal honesty. Richard Prior fans will find it enlightening, others may not enjoy it.

Sex, Nud, Viol, Lang, AdSit

A: Richard Pryor, Debbie Allen, Carmen McRae, Diahnne Abbott, Barbara Williams

© GOODTIMES 4506

JOSHUA THEN AND NOW

D: Ted Kotcheff 102 m

R | COM DMA | 1985 | COLOR

7 Little-known Canadian gem that is the semi-autobiography of screenwriter Mordecai Richler (THE APPRENTICESHIP OF DUDDY KRAVITZ). James Woods plays a writer whose life is in shambles. He has just been falsely accused in the press of being homosexual and his wife has had a breakdown. His mind drifts and his life is shown in flashback. His father is a small-time gangster (Arkin is hysterical), who spent most of his time in prison, and his mother wanted to be a movie star, but was a stripper. No wonder his normal wife, the daughter of a rich senator, is crazy. Entertaining.

Sex, Nud, Viol, Lang, AdSit

A: James Woods, Gabrielle Lazure, Alan Arkin, Michael Sarrazin, Linda Sorenson, Alan Scarfe

© FOXVIDEO 1488

JUNIOR

D: Dilvan Reitman 110 m

PG-13 | COM | 1994 | COLOR

6 No one can ever accuse Arnold Schwarzenegger of failing to take chances. This time he plays a stuffy stoic Austrian scientist doing research in human fertility. When he and gynecologist DeVito lose both their grant and their university lab space to Emma Thompson, they decide to go all out. Arnold will take their new drug and DeVito will inject a fertilized human egg into his abdominal cavity. It works! But, more than that, as his "pregnency" develops, his feminine side makes a pronounced arrival. Not only does he suffer from morning sickness, but also bouts of over-sensitivity and crying, eventually even going to a spa for pregnant women. Sweet little comedy that stretches one joke to the max.

Sex, Nud, Viol, Lang, AdSit

A: Arnold Schwarzenegger, Danny DeVito, Emma Thompson, Frank Langella, Pamela Reed, Judy Collins

© MCA/UNIVERSAL HOME VIDEO, INC. 82213

JUNIOR BONNER

D: Sam Peckinpah 101 m

PG | DMA COM WST | 1972 | COLOR

8 Steve McQueen is an aging rodeo has-been who comes back to his hometown for one last ride and to try to make peace with his family in this modern-day Western. Everything and everybody there has changed. His mother and father are separated and his brother sells real estate. This is an interesting comedy/drama that explores life's changes for all the major characters involved but particularly McQueen. Preston is great as his hard-drinking dad but so is McQueen as the soft-spoken cowboy stumbling through life.

Sex, Nud, Viol, Lang, AdSit

A: Steve McQueen, Robert Preston, Ida Lupino, Ben Johnson, Joe Don Baker, Barbara Leigh

© CBS/FOX VIDEO 8019

JUST BETWEEN FRIENDS

D: Allan Burns 110 m

PG-13 | DMA COM | 1986 | COLOR

8 A likable different sort of tearjerker. Christine Lahti is a successful single newswoman who meets Mary Tyler Moore (married to Ted Danson) at an aerobics class, and they become fast friends because they have so much in common. Christine tells her friend that she is having an affair with a man who she knows is married. Yes, you guessed it - it's the same guy, but neither woman knows that. That is until the next twist comes when Christine finds that she is pregnant, at the same time that Danson is killed in a plane wreck. Good mixture of laughs and tears as these two try to sort out how they feel.

Sex, Nud, Viol, Lang, AdSit

A: Mary Tyler Moore, Christine Lahti, Sam Waterston, Ted Danson, Mark Blum, Jane Geer

© HBO VIDEO TVA3919

JUST ONE OF THE GUYS

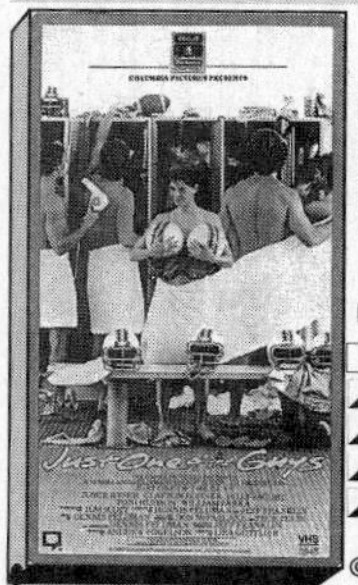

D: Lisa Gottlieb 100 m

PG-13 | COM | 1985 | COLOR

7 A pretty high school journalism student doesn't get the respect she thinks she would get if she were a boy, because her journalism teacher refuses to enter her paper into a newspaper contest. So she changes schools - but when she enrolls at a rival school, she enrolls as a boy; this time her paper, an expose on how boys are given preference, will get entered. She tangles with a bully, has to ward off the attacks of a passionate would-be girlfriend, and then falls for a loner - but he doesn't believe her story. Sort of TOOTSIE backwards. Fast-paced and well done.

Sex, Nud, Viol, Lang, AdSit

A: Joyce Hyser, Clayton Rohner, Billy Jacoby, Toni Hudson, William Zabka, Leigh McCloskey

© COLUMBIA TRISTAR HOME VIDEO 60493

JUST TELL ME WHAT YOU WANT

D: Sidney Lumet 114 m

R | COM ROM | 1979 | COLOR

6 Alan King puts in a flamboyant performance as a powerful mogul who is both happily married and also has a mistress, one of his top TV producers (Ali MacGraw). What does he do when his mistress finds true love with someone else? He sells the production company, rather than to let her run it. Fed up, she breaks free of him to be with her new man. But King outmaneuvers her to win her back. This is a sophisticated and cynical comedy whose charm may be lost on those who like their romances simple. Still, it has its moments.

Sex, Nud, Viol, Lang, AdSit

A: Ali MacGraw, Alan King, Peter Weller, Myrna Loy, Dina Merrill, Tony Roberts

© WARNER HOME VIDEO 11087

KELLY'S HEROES

D: Brian G. Hutton 146 m

PG | WAR ACT COM | 1970 | COLOR | Sex | Nud | Viol | Lang | AdSit

8 Entertaining tongue-in-cheek reverse-spin on the popular film DIRTY DOZEN. Clint Eastwood gathers up a group of misfits and thieves to form his own private army within the Army. His goal is to capture a small village behind German lines. Is he a patriot? No. He and his people launch a very effective and inspirational offensive spearhead against the enemy because there is Nazi gold stored in the town, and they're going to steal it. Sprawling and entertaining, with a large cast of odd-ball characters. Light spirits and some good action sequences keep it moving.

A: Clint Eastwood, Telly Savalas, Don Rickles, Donald Sutherland, Carroll O'Connor, Gavin MacLeod

Distributed By MGM/UA Home Video M700168

KENTUCKY FRIED MOVIE

D: John Landis 85 m

R | COM | 1977 | COLOR | Sex | Nud | Viol | Lang | AdSit

7 Frequently crude, lewd and definitely skewed, but also frequently hysterical. This is a series of short skits that satirize TV shows, commercials, and both Kung-fu and soft-porno movies. They are all strung together by the people who would later bring you AIRPLANE. Some of these jokes are really bad, but some are really good.

A: Evan C. Kim, Bill Bixby, Henry Gibson, Beorge Laxenby, Master Bang Soo Han, Donald Sutherland

© MEDIA HOME ENTERTAINMENT, INC. M233

KIDCO

D: Ronald F. Maxwell 104 m

PG | CLD COM | 1983 | COLOR | Sex | Nud | Viol | Lang | AdSit

7 Enjoyable story about a group of kids, between the ages of 9 and 16, who go into the fertilizer and pest control business for themselves. Much to everyone's surprise, their business takes off and they thrive. Soon it is the largest one of its type in all San Diego County. The kids are confronted with serious and unfair competition from unscrupulous adults and they are even under the scrutiny of the I.R.S, but they're not going to be beat. Very enjoyable excursion into American junior enterprise. The funniest part is that the story is based upon a real case.

A: Scott Schwartz, Cinnamopn Idles, Tristine Kkyler, Elizabeth Gorcey, Maggie Blye

© FOXVIDEO 1359

KIKA

D: Pedro Almodovar m

NR | FOR COM | 1994 | COLOR | Sex | Nud | Viol | Lang | AdSit

7 Kika is a make-up artist. She is sexy and she likes to have fun. She lives with Ramone, a kinky younger photographer of women's lingerie; but, she also has occasional interludes with his stepfather, who is also messing around with Kika's best friend. Her maid is a lesbian who wants to make love to her, to be a prison guard at a women's prison and is protecting her perverted brother, who is also an ex-porno star and escaped prisoner. Not nearly lastly, is Andrea Scarface, who was a former psychologist to Ramone, but is now host of a tabloid TV show. This film has enough sex and general weirdness to offend most people and is quite disjointed, but it is also strangely fascinating. Subtitles.

A: Veronica Forque, Peter Coyote, Victoria Abril, Alex Casanovas, Ross De Palma, Santiago LaJusticia

© VIDMARK ENTERTAINMENT VM 6103

KINDERGARTEN COP

D: Ivan Reitman 111 m

PG-13 | ACT COM CRM | 1990 | COLOR | Sex | Nud | Viol | Lang | AdSit

8 A nice little surprise film that has a little of everything. It has action, comedy, cuteness and romance! Tough police detective Kimble (Schwarzenegger) gets much more than he bargained for when he pretends to be a kindergarten teacher, while trying to track down the wife and son of a vicious drug lord who are in hiding. For the tough cop, the toughest part is dealing with a bunch of tiny kids. He fails miserably at it until he turns the classroom into boot camp. Don't be fooled though, all is not cuteness here. This is fundamentally an action flick with enough violence to get it a PG-13 rating.

A: Arnold Schwarzenegger, Penelope Ann Miller, Linda Hunt, Richard Tyson, Carroll Baker, Pamela Reed

© MCA/UNIVERSAL HOME VIDEO, INC. 81051

KING AND I, THE

D: Walter Lang 133 m

G | MUS ROM COM | 1956 | COLOR | Sex | Nud | Viol | Lang | AdSit

9 This is a sumptuous feast for the eyes and ears. Superb production values showcase a winning story. A spirited English widow (Kerr) is hired by the pompous King of Siam (Yul Brynner) in the 1860s to be governess for his many children. The clash of both cultures and personalities make for some interesting situations, but conflict gradually gives way to respect and to an unspoken and forbidden love. Wonderful music includes their duet "Shall We Dance." Winner of five Oscars and nominee for Best Picture.

A: Deborah Kerr, Yul Brynner, Rita Moreno, Martin Benson, Terry Sounders

© FOXVIDEO 1004

KING OF COMEDY, THE

D: Martin Scorsese 108 m

PG | DMA COM | 1982 | COLOR | Sex | Nud | Viol | Lang | AdSit

6 A strange black comedy with a daring performance by Robert De Niro. He plays a bizarre loser who is obsessed with becoming a comedian. His only audience has been a tape recorder, yet he believes he could become a famous if only he could get a big break on a popular late evening talk show, hosted by Jerry Lewis. So he creates an elaborate scheme to get on the program by kidnapping Lewis and holding him hostage until he can appear. The film does present a stark view of a cold-hearted and very unfair business, but the main character is also very unsympathetic.

A: Robert De Niro, Jerry Lewis, Sandra Bernhard, Shelley Hack, Tony Randall, Ed Herlihy

© COLUMBIA TRISTAR HOME VIDEO 60027

KING OF HEARTS

D: Phillippe De Broca 101 m

NR | FOR COM | 1967 | COLOR | Sex | Nud | Viol | Lang | AdSit

7 Large underground hit from the late 1960s and early '70s. It has diminished some with time but nonetheless maintains a big cult status with its fans. In it, Alan Bates is a WWI Scottish demolitions expert who is sent into a supposedly abandoned French village to dismantle explosive charges left by the retreating Germans. Instead, he finds that the loveable inmates of the local insane asylum have taken over the whole town and want to name him King of Hearts. Overly simplistic and idealistic statement about war that is, nonetheless, enjoyable to watch. Subtitles.

A: Pierre Brasseur, Genevieve Bujold, Alan Bates, Jean-Claude Brialy

Distributed By MGM/UA Home Video M201562

KISS ME GOODBYE

D: Robert Mulligan 101 m

PG | COM ROM | 1982 | COLOR | Sex | Nud | Viol | Lang | AdSit

6 Enjoyable, but very-much sanitized, version of the spicer (and funnier) Brazilian entry, DONA FLOR AND HER TWO HUSBANDS. A widow (Field) is about to marry stuffy Dr. Rupert Baines (Bridges) when she is confronted with the ghost of her dead husband (Caan), which only she can see and hear. Everything is quite predictable and most of the sexy humor has been altered to insignificance, but there is a comedic chemistry to the relationship between Fields and Bridges that is quite a lot of fun to watch.

A: Sally Field, James Caan, Jeff Bridges, Claire Trevor, Paul Dooley

© FOXVIDEO 1217

KOTCH

D: Jack Lemmon 114 m

PG | COM DMA | 1971 | COLOR | Sex | Nud | Viol | Lang | AdSit

9 Totally charming comedy about an old coot who keeps getting in the way living at his son's house, so they put him in an old age home. However he can't stand it there so he runs away and rents a small house to live in by himself. He befriends the pregnant young girl who used to babysit for his grandson and who has run away from home after being deserted by both her family and the baby's father. So, Kotch takes her into his little house and they take care of each other. This is a truly winning and heart-warming story, with a terrific performance by Matthau for which he received an Oscar nomination. The film got three other nominations, too. Excellent.

A: Walter Matthau, Deborah Winters, Felicia Farr, Ellen Geer, Charles Aidman, Lucy Saroyan

© MAGNETIC VIDEO 8008

LA CAGE AUX FOLLES

D: Edouard Molinaro 99 m

R | FOR COM | 1979 | COLOR | Sex | Nud | Viol | Lang | AdSit

7 Unique and frequently funny. One of the most successful foreign films ever shown in American theaters. The lives of a gay nightclub owner and his star impersonator/lover are thrown into turmoil when the son of one announces that he in going to be married. The girl's parents are prudish and would not understand his father's unique situation, so the two male lovers who have both helped to raise the boy decide to impersonate being man and wife. There are some genuinely hysterical scenes for those willing to accept the premise. Subtitles.

A: Ugo Totnazzi, Michel Serrault, Michel Balabru, Claire Maurier, Remy Laurent, Benny Luke

Distributed By MGM/UA Home Video M301580

LA NUIT DE VARENNES

D: Ettore Scola 128 m

R | FOR COM | 1982 | COLOR | Sex | Nud | Viol | Lang | AdSit

8 Imaginative but very talky French fiction. The night is June 22, 1791. Louis XVI and Marie Antoinette flee Paris and the Revolution. This fictitious flight provides an opportunity for the unlikely meeting of the fleeing pair with Casanova, American Thomas Paine and the Queen's own Lady-in-Waiting. The contradicting philosophies of the captive companions provide the basis for the witty dialogue which is the essence of this film. For discriminating and patient viewers.

A: Marcello Mastroianni, Harvey Keitel, Hanna Schygulla, Jean-Louis Barrault

© COLUMBIA TRISTAR HOME VIDEO 60033

LAST AMERICAN HERO, THE

D: Lamont Johnson 95 m

PG | ACT COM | 1973 | COLOR

7 Underrated and interesting sports action film based on the life of real-life stock car racer, Junior Jackson, played by Jeff Bridges. He plays a guy who switches from running moonshine and racing Feds in North Carolina, to racing stock cars on the professional circuit so that he can raise enough money to hire a lawyer to help his moonshiner father. The hard-living driver rises through the pro ranks fast despite his unwillingness to do what the establishment wants him to do. Realistic racing sequences and three dimensional, believable characters make this an enjoyable experience.

Sex, Nud, Viol, Lang, AdSit

A: Jeff Bridges, Valerie Perrine, Geraldine Fitzgerald, Art Lund, Gary Busey, Ned Beatty

© FOXVIDEO 1227

LAST DETAIL, THE

D: Hal Ashby 105 m

R | DMA COM | 1974 | COLOR

8 This was a superb and highly entertaining comedy/drama and it garnered Oscar nominations for both Jack Nicholson and Randy Quaid. Two long-time Navy men (Nicholson and Young) are assigned the task of bringing a naive AWOL young sailor (Quaid) back to serve a long jail sentence. These two old salts take pity on the kid and take it upon themselves to show the innocent young sailor what he will be missing while he is away. Alternately funny and sadly moving, it is also filled with some of the foulest language recorded up to that time.

Sex, Nud, Viol, Lang, AdSit

A: Jack Nicholson, Otis Young, Randy Quaid, Carol Kane, Michael Moriarty

© COLUMBIA TRISTAR HOME VIDEO 60034

L.A. STORY

D: Mick Jackson 98 m

PG-13 | COM ROM | 1991 | COLOR

7 A sometimes hilarious, sweet spoof about life in L.A. that has a ring of truth to it. TV weatherman Harris K. Telemacher (Martin) is hopelessly bored with the forever sunny/smoggy weather. He's bored with his girlfriend (Henner) and his younger diversion (Parker) is just a sexy airhead who fills his time. It's not until a quirky import from London (Tennant, his real-life wife) arrives that Martin's funky L.A. life gets some meaning and purpose. From freeway signs that communicate to snooty restaurants, this delightful farce is lightly seasoned with comic reality.

Sex, Nud, Viol, Lang, AdSit

A: Steve Martin, Victoria Tennant, Richard E. Grant, Marilu Henner, Sarah Jessica Parker

© LIVE HOME VIDEO 68964

LAST SEDUCTION, THE

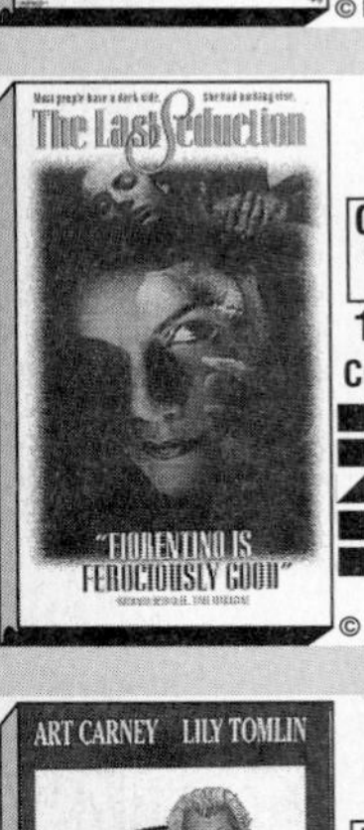

D: John Dahl 110 m

R | CRM COM | 1994 | COLOR

8 She loves breaking the rules. She is very, very clever. She has no heart. She uses sex as a substitute for love. She is ruthlessly scheming. She is totally self-serving. She loves money. She is Linda Fiorentino. And, she is perversely entertaining. This is one bad girl. She has stolen $700,000 that her student-doctor husband had made from selling drugs and she has run to a small town to hide for a while. There she meets a man who badly wants to get out and sees her as his ticket...only he doesn't know what he's let himself in for. Sophisticated black humor marks this quirky, tightly woven, slick tale of intrigue in the war of the sexes.

Sex, Nud, Viol, Lang, AdSit

A: Linda Fiorentino, Peter Berg, J.T. Walsh, Bill Nunn, Bill Pullman

© POLYGRAM VIDEO 34461-3

LATE SHOW, THE

D: Robert Benton 93 m

PG | MYS CRM COM | 1976 | COLOR

9 This is a highly entertaining mystery that works well on many levels at once. In it, a crusty old retired private eye (played to perfection by Art Carney) becomes drawn into a complex murder mystery. It begins simply enough being only a search to find a missing cat, but that quickly changes when he finds his ex-partner murdered. He sets off to find the murderer with the unwelcome assistance of a flaky flower child played to perfection by a goofy Lily Tomlin. New twists and clues are perfectly timed to keep the mystery interesting, but it is the relationship between its two principal players that is what is most appealing. Well done little gem. Very enjoyable.

Sex, Nud, Viol, Lang, AdSit

A: Art Carney, Lily Tomlin, Bill Macy, Eugene Roche, Joanna Cassidy, John Considine

© WARNER HOME VIDEO 11163

LEAGUE OF GENTLEMEN, THE

D: Basil Dearden 115 m

NR | COM CRM | 1960 | B&W

7 Witty and stylish caper flick. A group of shady ex-servicemen are blackmailed by their forcibly-retired army sergeant into becoming organized into an outlaw gang. He needs them so that they can pull off a complicated but very big bank robbery. Highly enjoyable lighthearted and witty English comedy, where the enjoyment comes from watching the characters succeed - almost.

Sex, Nud, Viol, Lang, AdSit

A: Jack Hawkins, Richard Attenborough, Nigel Patrick, Roger Livesey, Brian Forbes

© HOME VISION LEA 01

LEAGUE OF THEIR OWN, A

D: Penny Marshall m

PG | COM | 1992 | COLOR

8 Entertaining, light-hearted and winning portrait of Women's League baseball during WWII when most men were off fighting. The story follows the Peaches on their trip to the World Series and is based upon the real-life players Marge Maxwell and her sister Helen St. Aubin. Geena Davis plays the big sister and a big hitter, catcher and natural ballplayer who has a running battle of wills with her little sister (Petty), the pitcher. Hanks is a former-great-turned-drunk, who now has sunk to coaching a woman's team...but he is learning to like it. This is a pretty consistent good time, but it also has a couple of really hysterical moments.

Sex, Nud, Viol, Lang, AdSit

A: Tom Hanks, Geena Davis, Madonna, Lori Petty, Jon Lovitz, David Strathairn

© COLUMBIA TRISTAR HOME VIDEO 51223

LEAP OF FAITH

D: Richard Pearce 110 m

PG-13 | DMA COM | 1992 | COLOR

8 Steve Martin is a fraud. He is Rev. Jonas Nightengale, a revivalist minister who travels the country bilking the suckers and making them feel good while he does it. When one of his trucks breaks down in a small Kansas town, he sets up his tents and gets ready to put on a show while he waits for a part. Jonas spies a pretty waitress (Davidovich) and sets his sights on seducing her, but she will have no part of preachers who give her crippled little brother false hope. So, Jonas continues to fleece the flock but is eventually forced to confront of the human aspects of his trade, especially when a true miracle happens in front of his eyes.

Sex, Nud, Viol, Lang, AdSit

A: Steve Martin, Debra Winger, Lolita Davidovich, Liam Neeson, Lukas Haas

© PARAMOUNT HOME VIDEO 32792

LENNY BRUCE PERFORMANCE FILM, THE

D: John Magnuson 67 m

NR | COM DOC | 1968 | B&W

6 Controversial and irreverent stand-up comic Lenny Bruce was filmed in front of a live San Francisco audience. The photography is bad, but the film does give the viewer an opportunity to at least see the man who cleared the decks for the aggressive humor of later comedians. At the time of this filming, Bruce had been through many years of court battles on obscenity charges. This performance is mostly a tirade against the system that persecuted him. Funnier is a short animated feature that accompanies it: "Thank You Masked Man."

Sex, Nud, Viol, Lang, AdSit

A: Lenny Bruce

© RHINO HOME VIDEO/RECORDS 2014

LES GIRLS

D: George Cukor 155 m

NR | MUS COM | 1957 | COLOR

9 Winning musical from MGM. Lush musical with big production numbers, wonderful Cole Porter music and terrific performances by the entire cast. The story revolves around the turmoil created by a sensational book written by a former dancer (Kay Kendall) which concerned her days with a dance troop. One of the other members has sued her for libel and during the course of the trial, three separate showgirls reveal their romances with dancer Gene Kelley in a series of flashbacks. None of their memories match and they are all funny. Witty and stylish.

Sex, Nud, Viol, Lang, AdSit

A: Gene Kelly, Kay Kendall, Taina Elg, Mitzi Gaynor, Jacques Bergerac

Distributed By MGM/UA Home Video M300308

LETHAL WEAPON

D: Richard Donner 110 m

R | ACT CRM COM | 1987 | COLOR

10 Hugely popular high-voltage thriller which is fast, violent and funny. It owes its huge success to the unlikely chemistry of its two lead characters. One is an older, conservative family man and by-the-book cop (Glover). The other is a half-crazed lunatic cop (Gibson). When these guys discover that an apparent suicide is really a cover-up for a particularly raunchy drug ring, they set about destroying it with a vengeance. Very fast paced, with terrific action sequences and funny, with great chemistry between its two stars. It was followed by two very popular sequels.

Sex, Nud, Viol, Lang, AdSit

A: Mel Gibson, Danny Glover, Gary Busey, Mitchell Ryan, Tom Atkins, Darlene Love

© WARNER HOME VIDEO 11709

LETHAL WEAPON 2

D: Richard Donner 114 m

R | ACT CRM COM | 1989 | COLOR

9 Action fans take note - they're back. Danny Glover and Mel Gibson reprised their roles as police partners - one normal, one a reckless lunatic. This time they are out to get some bad guy drug smugglers from South Africa, who are hiding behind diplomatic immunity, before the bad guys get mob accountant Joe Pesci. Wild and outlandish adventures ensue, loaded with lead-filled action, a little sex and a fair dose of laughs. Entertaining, but not at all believable. Still, this is fun. See also LETHAL WEAPON and LETHAL WEAPON 3.

Sex, Nud, Viol, Lang, AdSit

A: Mel Gibson, Danny Glover, Joe Pesci, Joss Ackland, Derrick O'Conner, Patsy Kensit

© WARNER HOME VIDEO 11876

LETHAL WEAPON 3

D: Richard Donner — 118 m

R | ACT CRM COM | 1992 | COLOR

Sex ☐ Nud ☐ Viol ■ Lang ■ AdSit ■

7 True escapism - more from the hit cop combo of Gibson and Glover. Glover is straight-arrow family-man cop about to retire from the force but he is drawn back in to aid Gibson. They are tracking a cop gone bad who is now a major-league gun runner selling confiscated weapons to L.A. street gangs. The Hollywood folks pull out all the stops again. There is more of the fun glib comradery between the two, but there is also much more of the extravagant violence. The pairing is still good but it's getting a little old now.

A: Mel Gibson, Danny Glover, Joe Pesci, Rene Russo, Stuart Wilson

© WARNER HOME VIDEO 12475

LET'S DO IT AGAIN

D: Sidney Poitier — 113 m

PG | COM | 1975 | COLOR

Sex ☐ Nud ☐ Viol ☐ Lang ◢ AdSit ◢

8 Highly entertaining follow-up to UPTOWN SATURDAY NIGHT. Cosby and Poitier proved to be so popular as the larcenous lodge brothers that they decided to bring them back. This time they raise some money for their lodge by hypnotizing skinny Jimmy Walker and convincing him that he is a prize fighter. When he wins, the mob gets interested. A little silly, but a lot of fun, too.

A: Sidney Poitier, Bill Cosby, Calvin Lockhart, John Amos, Jimmie C. Walker, Ossie Davis

© WARNER HOME VIDEO 11137

LIFE AND TIMES OF JUDGE ROY BEAN, THE

D: John Huston — 124 m

PG | WST COM ACT | 1972 | COLOR

Sex ☐ Nud ☐ Viol ◢ Lang ☐ AdSit ◢

8 Definitely strange but a fun Western with some really funny moments. Paul Newman creates a movie-variation on the real-life character Judge Roy Bean, who was famed as being a hanging judge. Newman's Bean rules over a two-bit Texas town like a lord, having run-ins (sometimes comical) with various odd-ball characters who stumble into his path. Stacy Keach is outstanding among these as the ferocious albino bad guy, Bad Bob. Filled with cameos by some of Hollywood's best. Very enjoyable even though sometimes it slows down too much.

A: Paul Newman, Stacy Keach, Victoria Principal, Jacqueline Bisset, Ava Gardner, Anthony Perkins

© WARNER HOME VIDEO 11174

LIFE OF BRIAN

D: Terry Jones — 94 m

R | COM | 1979 | COLOR

Sex ☐ Nud ◢ Viol ☐ Lang ◢ AdSit ■

8 Religious people will likely be offended by the British comedy group Monty Python's outrageous spoof. The principal character, Brian, was unfortunate enough to be born in a stable just down the street from the Christ child. Now everyone keeps confusing him with Christ - especially the Romans. Being wanted by the Romans is not a pleasant predicament to be in. This is probably Python's most sustained comedy adventure off TV. However, unless you are a fan of their bizarre form of comedy, you'd better stay away. But others will enjoy it.

A: Terry Jones, John Cleese, Eric Idle, Michael Palin, Terry Tilliam, Graham Chapman

© WARNER HOME VIDEO 2003

LILIES OF THE FIELD

D: Ralph Nelson — 95 m

NR | DMA COM | 1963 | B&W

Sex ☐ Nud ☐ Viol ☐ Lang ☐ AdSit ☐

8 Extremely popular and heart-warming story of an itinerant handyman who happens upon a group of nuns recently escaped from East Germany. They are attempting to build a church but have no skills, no money for building materials and are barely able to communicate. Yet they charm and coerce him into helping them in their mission. This was a low-budget movie, but it had a winning story line and great characterizations that combined to make it a big hit with the public. Poitier won an Oscar and the movie received two other nominations, including Best Picture.

A: Sidney Poitier, Lilia Skala, Lisa Mann, Isa Crino, Stanley Adams

Distributed By MGM/UA Home Video M301762

LITTLE BIG LEAGUE

D: Andrew Scheinman — 120 m

PG | COM | 1994 | COLOR

Sex ☐ Nud ☐ Viol ☐ Lang ☐ AdSit ◢

8 Very well made family entertainment and you don't even need to like baseball to enjoy it - but if you do, you'll enjoy it even more. 12-year-old Billy is a baseball prodigy. He can't play any better than any other kid, but he knows everything there is to know about strategy. His grandpa owns the Minnesota Twins and when he dies, he leaves them to Billy. The Twins manager is sarcastic and derisive, and the team is losing. So, Billy fires the manager and hires himself. He revives many of the old plays from past days and teaches the team that having fun makes winners, but he is also soon overpowered by his place in a grownup world. Seems preposterous, but it really works.

A: Luke Edwards, Ashley Crow, Timothy Busfield, Jason Robards, Jr., John Ashton, Kevin Dunn

© COLUMBIA TRISTAR HOME VIDEO 72833

LITTLE BIG MAN

D: Arthur Penn — 147 m

PG | WST COM DMA | 1970 | COLOR

Sex ☐ Nud ◢ Viol ◢ Lang ☐ AdSit ◢

10 This is an outstanding and thoroughly enjoyable fable of the Old West. Dustin Hoffman plays Jack Crabb, a 121-year-old man living in a nursing home, who tells his colorful and not all-too-believable life's story to a doubtful young reporter through a series of flashbacks. His incredible stories begin when he was an orphaned pioneer boy adopted and raised by Cheyenne Indians. After he had returned to the white world, he became a terrible businessman and miserable husband, a dead-eyed gunfighter, a drunk and eventually a guide to Custer at his last stand. Wonderful characters, very clever, frequently funny, sometimes poignant, always extremely entertaining. Great fun.

A: Dustin Hoffman, Chief Dan George, Faye Dunaway, Martin Balsam, Jeff Corey, Richard Mulligan

© CBS/FOX VIDEO 7130

LITTLE GIANTS

D: Duwayne Dunham — 106 m

PG | COM CLD | 1994 | COLOR

Sex ☐ Nud ☐ Viol ☐ Lang ☐ AdSit ☐

6 Silly sort of sports film, mostly for kids. It's in the same vein as MIGHTY DUCKS and BAD NEWS BEARS, but not as as good. Two brothers living in the small town of Urbania, Ohio couldn't be more different. O'Neill is a former All-American and Heisman Trophy winner who now runs an auto dealership, and Moranis is just an ordinary sort who has always felt overrun by his hero brother. So, when O'Neill excludes a bunch of young geeky kids from his pee-wee football team, Moranis forms them all (including his daughter) into another team and challenges his brother to a game -- with the winner to represent the town. Captures well the way kids act, but too many body-function jokes.

A: Rick Moranis, Ed O'Neill, Brian Haley, Mary Ellen Trainor, Susanna Thompson, John Madden

© WARNER HOME VIDEO 16220

LITTLE MISS MARKER

D: Walter Bernstein — 103 m

PG | COM | 1980 | COLOR

Sex ☐ Nud ☐ Viol ☐ Lang ☐ AdSit ☐

8 Cute and winning Damon Runyon story set in the Depression. A charming little six-year-old girl was left with a crotchety bookie, named Sorrowful Jones (Walter Matthau), as security for payment on a bet. But when her father loses his bet and commits suicide, Sorrowful has a marker that he doesn't quite know how to handle. He doesn't know what to do with this kid and she is slowly melting his heart. So he asks his lady friend, a beautiful widow and socialite (Julie Andrews), for help. It gets a little slow-moving at times and is definitely very sentimental, but it is also great family entertainment.

A: Walter Matthau, Julie Andrews, Bob Newhart, Lee Grant, Sara Stimson

© MCA/UNIVERSAL HOME VIDEO, INC. 55082

LITTLE ROMANCE, A

D: George Roy Hill — 110 m

PG | ROM COM | 1979 | COLOR

Sex ☐ Nud ☐ Viol ☐ Lang ◢ AdSit ☐

7 Enchanting and delightful film which will appeal to all members of the family. It is a film about first love and the relationship that develops between two precocious kids, an American girl and a French boy, and an elderly ex-con man. The old man tells the young couple of an ages-old legend: if they kiss under the Bridge of Sighs in Venice at sunset, their love will last forever. This convinces the two, they are now determined to get there and he agrees to help them. This is a sweet movie that is full of surprises, laughs and will leave everyone feeling good. It is a sensitive and attractive treatment of adolescence.

A: Thelonlous Bernard, Diane Lane, Laurence Olivier, Sally Kellerman, Broderick Crawford, David Dukes

© WARNER HOME VIDEO 2001

LITTLE SHOP OF HORRORS, THE

D: Roger Corman — 72 m

NR | COM HOR | 1960 | COLOR

Sex ☐ Nud ☐ Viol ◢ Lang ☐ AdSit ◢

8 Hilarious and outrageous, very black comedy on a very low-budget. This is alternately known as "the film shot in two days" and plays like an extended vaudeville skit. In it, a very odd young florist's assistant is ignored by everyone until he develops a new exotic plant. Then he becomes very popular. However, unknown to nearly everyone, is how exotic that plant really is. It only prospers when it is fed human flesh, which our assistant provides. And, as the plant gets larger, it also begins to talk - demanding ever more and more. Later made into a successful Broadway play, this was then redone again on film in 1986, but this version is still best. Look for a very young Jack Nicholson as a masochist.

A: Jonathan Haze, Mel Welles, Jackie Joseph, Jack Nicholson, Dick Miller

© UNITED AMERICAN VIDEO CORP. 4043

LITTLE SHOP OF HORRORS

D: Frank Oz — 96 m

PG-13 | COM MUS HOR | 1986 | COLOR

Sex ☐ Nud ☐ Viol ◢ Lang ◢ AdSit ◢

6 Rick Moranis and an excellent cast - supported by a big budget, great special effects and some pretty neat musical production numbers - provide an entertaining and funny musical for the first 2/3 of the film. However, the black comedy plot - which concerns a very large, singing, man-eating plant - turns a little too macabre to be that funny in the last 1/3. Still - fans of the unusual should take note. This is actually a remake of a famous low-budget hit from 1960 done by Roger Corman which also included a very young Jack Nicholson.

A: Rick Moranis, Ellen Greene, Vincent Gardenia, Steve Martin, James Belushi, John Candy

© WARNER HOME VIDEO 11702

LOCAL HERO

D: Bill Forsyth 112 m

PG | COM | 1983 | COLOR

7 Off-beat comedy that pursues quirkiness instead of belly laughs. Careful observers will be rewarded, but the film does not contain the obvious comedy that mainstream audiences are used to seeing. A Huston oil executive and ace deal-maker is sent to a small town in Scotland in order to buy up the town and surrounding land so it can be developed into a refinery site. Most of the town is eager to sell out, but the more he gets exposed to the place and its people, he becomes reluctant himself to do the deal which will destroy the place. This story is most interesting for the rich assortment of oddball characters it presents.

Sex, Nud, Viol, Lang, AdSit

A: Peter Riegert, Burt Lancaster, Fulton MacKay, Denis Lawson, Norman Chancer, Peter Capaldi

© WARNER HOME VIDEO 11307

LOLITA

D: Stanley Kubrick 152 m

NR | COM | 1962 | B&W

6 A satire, black comedy and very controversial film at the time of its release, but quite tame by today's standards. The intention is to explore the sexual obsession and hypocrisy of James Mason, a sophisticated middle-aged man who is so obsessed with a precocious child/woman (Sue Lyon) that he marries her obnoxious sex-starved mother (Winters) just to be around the girl and, hopefully, to carry on an affair with her. Solid acting, particularly by Sellers as another obsessed pursuer.

Sex, Nud, Viol, Lang, AdSit

A: James Mason, Sue Lyon, Shelley Winters, Peter Sellers, Marianne Stone, Diana Decker

Distributed By MGM/UA Home Video M600068

LONELY GUY, THE

D: Arthur Hiller 91 m

R | COM | 1984 | COLOR

6 This is a movie for Steve Martin fans, mostly. There are some other redeeming factors, but the laughs are spread pretty thin. Steve is a greeting card writer whose girlfriend dumps him, thereby launching him into the world of lonely people and the not-so-swinging single set. He and buddy Grodin throw a party that bombs. Eventually Martin meets up with a woman who will have him, but he keeps losing her number. Sometimes poignant and occasionally funny.

Sex, Nud, Viol, Lang, AdSit

A: Steve Martin, Charles Grodin, Judith Ivey, Robyn Douglas, Steve Lawrence, Dr. Joyce Brothers

© MCA/UNIVERSAL HOME VIDEO, INC. 80014

LONELY HEARTS

D: Paul Cox 95 m

R | ROM COM | 1983 | COLOR

6 A touching and warm, but quirky, love story from Australia. A 50ish momma's boy piano tuner discovers a 30ish dowdy, extremely shy and sexually repressed bank clerk through a dating service after Momma dies. This is a warm story of these two, who have been too long burdened to and by others, who stumble and fumble their way into romance. It is a prize-winning, sometimes funny, sometimes heartwarming, but odd, look at another side of the human condition.

Sex, Nud, Viol, Lang, AdSit

A: Wendy Hughes, Norman Kaye, Jon Finlayson, Julia Blake, Jonathan Hardy

© NEW LINE HOME VIDEO 3023

LONGEST YARD, THE

D: Robert Aldrich 121 m

R | COM ACT | 1974 | COLOR

9 Rousing and engaging comedy that is one of Reynolds's best efforts. He plays an ex-pro football quarterback sent to prison for stealing his girlfriend's car. Eddie Albert is a currupt prison warden who has created a semi-pro football team out of his prison guards. He is very proud of them and wants Reynolds to set up a prisoner-based team to play his guards and lose. What follows instead is a series of bone-crushing laughs as the prisoners get even with the guards. A great audience pleaser, in which we all root for the prisoners in a brutal football game that takes up 47 minutes of screen time.

Sex, Nud, Viol, Lang, AdSit

A: Burt Reynolds, Eddie Albert, Ed Lauter, Michael Conrad, James Hampton, Bernadette Peters

© PARAMOUNT HOME VIDEO 8708

LONG GONE

D: Martin Davidson 113 m

NR | DMA COM | 1987 | COLOR

8 Loving and engaging look into America's favorite pastime. Stud Cantrell is a minor league baseball manager who has always managed to allude success until one fateful Florida summer in the early 1950s. That summer he is blessed with a winning team and a small town beauty queen who wants him to set up housekeeping. Now, with only one game left to win the pennant, the opposing team's owner offers him the chance of a life time, if only he'll throw the game. Enjoyable. Also see BULL DURHAM.

Sex, Nud, Viol, Lang, AdSit

A: William L. Petersen, Virginia Madsen, Dermot Mulroney, Henry Gibson

© WARNER HOME VIDEO 828

LOOK WHO'S TALKING

D: Amy Heckerling 96 m

PG-13 | COM | 1989 | COLOR

8 A simple-minded crowd pleaser that was quite popular. Kirstie Alley is an unwed accountant who is having an affair with a married man... that is, until she gets pregnant. Dumped, she has the baby on her own, except for the help of a cabbie friend (John Travolta), who later serves as her babysitter and a part-time surrogate father for the baby. However, the main charm and focus of the film are the baby's wisecrack "thoughts" and observations as voiced by Bruce Willis and written by Joan Rivers. Skip the sequels.

Sex, Nud, Viol, Lang, AdSit

A: John Travolta, Kirstie Alley, Olympia Dukakis, George Segal, Abe Vigoda, Bruce Willis

© COLUMBIA TRISTAR HOME VIDEO 70183

LORDS OF FLATBUSH, THE

D: Martin Davidson, Stephen Verona 88 m

PG | COM DMA | 1974 | COLOR

6 Interesting primarily because this film was the launching pad for four significant future stars. The film itself isn't too bad, but it isn't notable either... and it is very low budget. It is the story of the Flatbush gang - a group of male adolescents dipped in Brylcreem and wrapped in leather jackets, trying to proclaim themselves as men in 1957. Perry King falls for Susan Blakely. A pudgy Sly Stallone is dragged into marriage. Henry Winkler looks like the Fonz character he would later make famous on TV's "Happy Days".

Sex, Nud, Viol, Lang, AdSit

A: Martin Davidson, Perry King, Sylvester Stallone, Henry Winkler, Paul Mace, Susan Blakely

© COLUMBIA TRISTAR HOME VIDEO 60479

LOST IN AMERICA

D: Albert Brooks 91 m

R | COM | 1985 | COLOR

8 A sometimes hysterical look at yuppiedom in America. Super-achiever Brooks and his wife are about to move into their new $450,000 house when the promotion he is expecting falls through. Opting for a simpler life, the two sell everything and head across the country in a new Winnebago... their version of EASY RIDER. That dream suddenly evaporates too, when the wife looses everything in Las Vegas. Funny. However Brooks is also cocky and an acquired taste. Some like him, some don't.

Sex, Nud, Viol, Lang, AdSit

A: Albert Brooks, Julie Hagerty, Garry Marshall, Art Frankel, Michael Greene, Maggie Roswell

© WARNER HOME VIDEO 11460

LOST IN YONKERS

D: Martha Coolidge 114 m

PG | COM ROM DMA | 1993 | COLOR

8 Funny, touching and a real charmer from Neil Simon. Its 1942. Eddie is deep in debt from his dead wife's hospital expenses. His only chance is to leave his two boys behind in Yonkers with his stern mother and child-like sister, while he goes on the road for a year. Momma is a cold hard woman, but Aunt Bella is bubbly and full of life - even if her elevator doesn't quite make it to the top floor. Uncle Louie is a small-time hood who also comes to stay with Momma to hide out for a while. The two boys, Aunt Bella and Uncle Louie struggle to survive Momma's iron rule. Lots of clever dialogue from wonderfully drawn characters. Excellent.

Sex, Nud, Viol, Lang, AdSit

A: Richard Dreyfuss, Mercedes Ruehl, Irene Worth, David Strathairn, Brad Stoll, Mike Damus

© COLUMBIA TRISTAR HOME VIDEO 52663

LOVE AMONG THE RUINS

D: George Cukor 100 m

NR | ROM COM | 1975 | COLOR

8 Pleasant comedy which brings together two of the screen's biggest stars and one of its greatest directors. Set in 1911 London, Hepburn is being sued by a young gigolo for breach of promise when she fails to marry him. She seeks out the assistance of a long-ago lover (Olivier) who is now a famous barrister. He takes her case and though it all, their love is reborn. Made-for-TV, this piece rises far above the typical TV fare. Both Hepburn and Olivier won Emmys for their performances. Rich dialogue and performances. Entertaining.

Sex, Nud, Viol, Lang, AdSit

A: Katharine Hepburn, Laurence Olivier, Colin Blakely, Joan Sims, Richard Pearson, Leigh Lawson

© CBS/FOX VIDEO 8038

LOVE AND DEATH

D: Woody Allen 82 m

PG | COM | 1975 | COLOR

7 Woody Allen's mostly-funny spoof of "War and Peace." He plays a Slav in 1812 who is so in lust with his distant cousin (Keaton) that he agrees to help her assassinate Napoleon. Being a cowardly assistant though, he instead winds up in prison awaiting his execution. He has two hours with which to review his life - during which time he reflects upon Keaton, religion, philosophy, war, love and death. Pretty funny, but as always with Woody Allen's stuff... it helps to be a fan.

Sex, Nud, Viol, Lang, AdSit

A: Woody Allen, Diane Keaton, Harold Gould, Alfred Lutter, Olga Georges-Picot, Zvee Scooler

Distributed By MGM/UA Home Video M201765

LOVE AT FIRST BITE

D: Stan Dragoti 96 m

PG | COM | 1979 | COLOR

Sex Nud Viol Lang AdSit

8 A really good time. Funny, and more than a little silly, slapstick takeoff on the Dracula legend. Hamilton, as Dracula, finds himself evicted from his Transylvanian castle by the communists who want to make it into a gymnasium. So, he jets off to New York in search of his long lost love, now reborn as a fashion model who he saw on the front page of a magazine. Poor Drac, he is out of his element in New York. He even gets drunk on the blood of a wino. Even though her psychiatrist boyfriend tries to warn her, Drac's love still falls for the Count. So, the shrink becomes determined to save her. This is pretty heavy-handed slapstick humor but, hey, it's effective, and a lot of fun.

A: George Hamilton, Susan St. James, Richard Benjamin, Dick Shawn, Arte Johnson, Sherman Hemsley

© WARNER HOME VIDEO 26009

LOVE BUG, THE

D: Robert Stevenson 108 m

G | COM CLD | 1969 | COLOR

Sex Nud Viol Lang AdSit

9 Delightful Disney and cute comedy that is not just for kids. When a second-rate race driver (Dean Jones) defends a little VW from its abusive owner's kicks, interesting things begin to happen. The bug, Herbie by name, takes a shine to him. So later, when he gets teamed up with Herbie, he starts to win races. He thinks he's doing it on his own, but he's wrong. You see, Herbie has a mind of its own - some other pretty special other talents too - and, he is using them all to help them both win races. Lots of slapstick, stunts and warm-hearted fun. This film's success led to three sequels, but the original is the best.

A: Dean Jones, Michele Lee, Buddy Hackett, David Tomlinson, Joe Flynn

© WALT DISNEY HOME VIDEO 012

LOVED ONE, THE

D: Tony Richardson 122 m

NR | COM | 1965 | COLOR

Sex Nud Viol Lang AdSit

7 Very black comedy and an irreverent look at the funeral business. Sometimes hilarious but sometimes just gross. It was correctly advertised as the picture with something to offend everyone. British poet Robert Morse comes to Hollywood to visit his actor uncle and stays on to supervise his funeral after the uncle commits suicide. The funeral business, he discovers, is filled with very strange people. He even falls for a cosmetologist who was just promoted to embalmer. Winters plays twin morticians, both are cold-hearted - one buries people, the other pets.

A: Robert Morse, Jonathan Winters, Anjanette Comer, Rod Steiger, Dana Andrews, Milton Berle

Distributed By MGM/UA Home Video M200842

LOVE IN THE AFTERNOON

D: Billy Wilder 126 m

NR | COM ROM | 1957 | B&W

Sex Nud Viol Lang AdSit

7 An enchanting romantic comedy set in Paris. Gary Cooper is a rich American playboy businessman who is having an affair with another man's wife. Maurice Chevalier is a Parisian detective who specializes in spying upon adulterous wives. Audrey Hepburn, Chevalier's wistful and beautiful daughter, learns from her father that an angry husband is bent upon killing Cooper. So she warns Coop, saving him from the impending murder. She, however, begins to have her own rendezvous with him - but only in the afternoons and never telling him her name. Light-hearted and witty romantic comedy.

A: Gary Cooper, Audrey Hepburn, Maurice Chevalier, John McGiver

© CBS/FOX VIDEO 7428

LOVE POTION #9

D: Dale Launer 97 m

PG-13 | COM ROM | 1992 | COLOR

Sex Nud Viol Lang AdSit

6 Two biochemists are so nerdy that they don't even appeal to each other. Then a palm reader gives him love potion #8. At first he is a non-believer, but his newly-amorous cat changes his mind. So, the two chemists decide to experiment on themselves, but they take precautions to prevent "infecting" each other. Hey, the stuff works! They immediately become the objects of chemically-induced adoration from the other sex. However, the transformed twosome are also becoming genuinely attracted to each other. That is until she is stolen away by a hunk who has a love potion of his own. Our guy fights back, rallying with the antidote, love potion #9. No big laughs but entertaining.

A: Tate Donovan, Sandra Bullock, Dale Midkiff, Mary Mara, Anne Bancroft, Dylan Baker

© FOXVIDEO 1873

LOVES OF A BLONDE, THE

D: Milos Forman 88 m

NR | FOR COM ROM | 1965 | B&W

Sex Nud Viol Lang AdSit

9 Very likable and frequently hilarious portrait of a shy romantic young girl, coming of age in a small Czechoslovakia factory town where the women outnumber the men ten to one. This sort of an imbalance can cause a girl to wonder about love. Then a group of Army reservists visits town. Suddenly her girlish fantasies of love take flight. She meets Milda, becomes entranced with him and spends the night, but soon he is gone. A unique blending of pathos, sorrow and desire produces an engrossing and endearing comedy. A gem. A nominee for Best Foreign Film. Subtitles.

A: Hana Brejchova, Vladimir Pucholt

© HOME VISION LOV 100

LOVE WITH THE PROPER STRANGER

D: Robert Mulligan 102 m

NR | ROM COM | 1964 | B&W

Sex Nud Viol Lang AdSit

7 Wood and McQueen throw off sparks in this neat little romancer. McQueen is an independent sort, a musician. Natalie Wood is sweet and charming, a "good Italian girl." The two meet at a summer resort and share a moment of passion. She becomes pregnant and comes to him for help. McQueen trys to raise the money for an abortion, but it's then that he also begins to get to know her for the first time. So, when she breaks down while at a backroom abortionist, he pulls her out. It is then that they awkwardly begin afresh to discover each other. Touching, and frequently funny.

A: Natalie Wood, Steve McQueen, Edie Adams, Herschel Bernardi, Tom Bosley

© PARAMOUNT HOME VIDEO 6312

LUCAS

D: David Seltzer 100 m

PG-13 | ROM COM | 1986 | COLOR

Sex Nud Viol Lang AdSit

7 A brainy, but wimpy, 14-year-old has been accelerated into high-school. He is usually interested only in bugs and science, but over summer vacation, he falls in love with the pretty and friendly new girl in town. When fall comes though, she starts hanging out with the cool kids at school and she falls for the captain of the football team (Charlie Sheen). So, the love-smitten nerd decides to join the team, too. This is not a silly, condescending or trite film. It is a perceptive endearing story, that portrays the trials of puppy love. It is sweet, intelligent and enjoyable.

A: Corey Haim, Kerri Green, Charlie Sheen, Courtney Thorne-Smith, Winona Ryder

© FOXVIDEO 1495

M*A*S*H

D: Robert Altman 116 m

R | COM WAR DMA | 1970 | COLOR

Sex Nud Viol Lang AdSit

10 Hilarious irreverence! A Korean war Mobile Army Surgical Hospital is the setting for this dark and brash comedy. An unruly crew of oddball doctors and nurses survives the trauma of an endless war by concocting outlandish practical jokes to play upon each other - like selling tickets to an "unveiling" of a naked Hot Lips Houlihan in the shower. The result is big belly laughs all around. Winner of Oscar for Best Screenplay. Also nominated for Best Picture, Director and Supporting Actress. Inspired, but also very different from, the long-running TV series which became an attack on the Vietnam War.

A: Elliott Gould, Donald Sutherland, Sally Kellerman, Tom Skerritt, Robert Duvall, JoAnn Pflug

© FOXVIDEO 1038

MACARONI

D: Ettore Scola 104 m

PG | COM | 1985 | COLOR

Sex Nud Viol Lang AdSit

6 Jack Lemmon and Marcello Mastroianni star in this light-hearted comedy. Lemmon is a stuffy American business executive who returns to Italy after 40 years to visit Mastroianni. The pair were buddies during the war and Lemmon had fallen for Mastroianni's sister. Now, when Lemmon returns to Italy, he finds that for 40 years Mastroianni has been sending his sister amorous letters and signing Jack's name! Originally it was to help to ease her pain from his departure, but then he got carried away. Now Jack's got a big problem. Sparkling performances from both stars.

A: Jack Lemmon, Marcello Mastroianni, Isa Danieli, Daria Nicolodi, Maria Luisa Saniella

© PARAMOUNT HOME VIDEO 1937

MAGIC CHRISTIAN, THE

D: Joseph McGrath 101 m

PG | COM | 1969 | COLOR

Sex Nud Viol Lang AdSit

6 Man is motivated by greed - people will do anything for money. So says Sir Guy Grand, the richest man in the world (Peter Sellers). Sir Guy happens upon a young drifter (Ringo Starr) in the park and decides to adopt him. Then he concocts elaborate scenarios to prove to his new son this sad truth of life. The film was very politically correct for the 60s. The humor is also many times crude and may not appeal to many. Nevertheless, it is true - money does motivate and many of the results he is able to fabricate are amusing. The numerous star cameo appearances are part of the fun, too.

A: Peter Sellers, Ringo Starr, Raquel Welch, John Cleese, Christopher Lee, Richard Attenborough

© REPUBLIC PICTURES HOME VIDEO 2548

MAID, THE

D: Ian Toynton 91 m

PG | COM ROM | 1991 | COLOR

Sex Nud Viol Lang AdSit

6 Mildly enjoyable and entertaining, even though it's an entirely unbelievable little comedy. Martin Sheen is a high-powered Wall Street investment banker who has been transfered to Paris to take a position at a bank. There, he spies and becomes totally infatuated with a beautiful woman (Bisset). He decides to pursue her, to the point that he even takes a position as her new maid for the one month he has left before he is to start his new position at the bank, which it turns out, is her her old position. Fun little no-brainer.

A: Martin Sheen, Jacqueline Bisset, Jean-Pierre Cassel, Victoria Shalet, James Faulkner

© VIDEO TREASURES M012777

COM

MAID TO ORDER

D: Amy Jones 92 m

PG | COM | 1987 | COLOR

6 Slight but enjoyable little picture in which a spoiled little rich girl (Sheedy) gets a reverse-Cinderella treatment. Her chain-smoking fairy godmother takes away all her toys, her credit cards, even her identity and makes her penniless. She then is forced to take a position as a maid for spoiled rich people Valerie Perrine and Dick Shawn. Sheedy learns her lesson, meets her prince charming and gains some humility along the way.

Sex Nud Viol Lang AdSit

A: Ally Sheedy, Beverly D'Angelo, Dick Shawn, Michael Ontkean, Valerie Perrine, Tom Skerritt

© LIVE HOME VIDEO 64311

MAJOR LEAGUE

D: David S. Ward 107 m

R | COM | 1989 | COLOR

8 Wacky sports farce. A group of inept screw-ups are purposely recruited to play ball for the Cleveland Indians. You see, the team has a new owner - an ex-showgirl - and she wants to move to more stylish Miami, but the only way she can leave is to put together such a losing team that she can break the contract with the league. When the crew discovers her true intentions, the humiliated and frustrated team unites in a riotous effort to recover their pride, win the pennant and to defeat her plans. A genuine good time. Ex-con Sheen is especially entertaining as the pitcher, "Wild Thing." Uecker adds to the fun, too.

Sex Nud Viol Lang AdSit

A: Tom Berenger, Charlie Sheen, Corbin Bernsen, Margaret Whitton, Rene Russo, Bob Uecker

© PARAMOUNT HOME VIDEO 32270

MALCOLM

D: Nadia Tass 86 m

PG-13 | COM | 1986 | COLOR

7 Quirky award-winning Australian comedy with wit and whimsey. Malcolm is spacey and a little inept, but he is a genius when it comes to creating strange mechanical devices. After he is fired for tinkering on the job, he has to take as roommates an ex-con and his beautiful girlfriend to conserve on finances. The fun begins when the three of them scheme to pull off a bank robbery using one of Malcolm's wacky mechanical creations. Director Tass made this solid debut, basing Malcolm's character on her real-life brother. So successful, it was followed by RIKKI AND PETE.

Sex Nud Viol Lang AdSit

A: Colin Friels, John Hargreaves, Lindy Davies, Chris Haywood, Charles Tingwell, Beverly Phillips

© LIVE HOME VIDEO 5183

MAMA, THERE'S A MAN IN YOUR BED

D: Coline Serreau 107 m

PG-13 | FOR COM ROM | 1990 | COLOR

6 Quite unlikely, but still funny, comedy from the writer of THREE MEN AND A BABY. A successful executive of a Paris yogurt factory gets sabotaged by board members planning a takeover - but he finds an unlikely ally in the black cleaning lady. On her nightly rounds, she discovers what is going on and tells him. Together they plot to take back his company. But first he has to hide from the cops, so he stays at her three-room apartment where they sleep four to a bed and she has five kids, each by different husbands. Naturally, they fall in love.

Sex Nud Viol Lang AdSit

A: Daniel Arteuil, Firmine Richard, Pierre Vernier, Maxime Leroux

© HBO VIDEO 90560

MANHATTAN

D: Woody Allen 96 m

R | COM ROM | 1979 | B&W

9 Another brilliant and sophisticated slice-of-life look by Woody Allen at New York City neurotics - perhaps his best. A successful, but unfulfilled, TV writer (Allen) is running out of luck. His wife (Streep) has left him for another woman, and he has become involved in a string of love affairs that just aren't working out. This is an insightful Woody Allen-style comic look at life and the complications of adult love. The unforgettable Gershwin score successfully mixes with the black and white photography in this endearing adult comedy. See also ANNIE HALL.

Sex Nud Viol Lang AdSit

A: Woody Allen, Diane Keaton, Mariel Hemingway, Meryl Streep, Michael Murphy, Anne Byrne

Distributed By MGM/UA Home Video M800469

MANHATTAN MURDER MYSTERY

D: Woody Allen 108 m

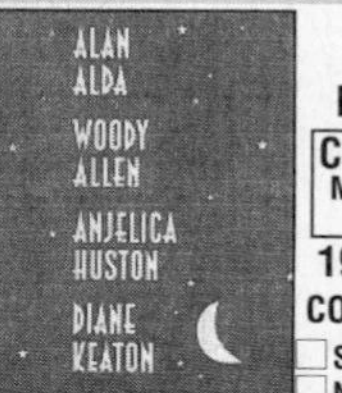

PG | COM MYS | 1993 | COLOR

8 The old Woody Allen is back. Gone are the angst-ridden self-examinations of much of his later work. This is a tightly scripted mystery, peppered with babbling conversations and Allen's one-liners. Back also is Diane Keaton. She plays Woody's bored wife who has become fascinated by the slightly odd activities of their neighbor after his wife dies of a heart attack. Woody thinks she's over-reacting saying, "There's nothing wrong with you that couldn't be cured with a little Prozac and a polo mallet." So, she enlists the help of their friend Alan Alda. The more they find out, the more it look's like she's right. Starts very slow, but then builds to a rapid fire conclusion.

Sex Nud Viol Lang AdSit

A: Diane Keaton, Woody Allen, Alan Alda, Anjelica Huston, Jerry Adler, Ron Rifkin

© COLUMBIA TRISTAR HOME VIDEO 71393

MANNEQUIN

D: Michael Gottlieb 90 m

PG | COM FAN | 1987 | COLOR

6 Comedy with a fantasy twist. A struggling artist (McCarthy) gets by, by sculpting mannequins and dressing store windows. However, one of his creations is special - into it he has designed all his fantasy elements. Then something mystical happens. An Egyptian spirit (Cattrall) comes and takes over the plaster body, but only he can see her. If anyone else comes around, it's back to plaster. Still, he is now an instant success. Taylor is amusing as his effeminate partner. This is a simple-minded, check-your-brain-at-the-door kind of comedy. Take it for what it is.

Sex Nud Viol Lang AdSit

A: Andrew McCarthy, Kim Cattrall, Estelle Getty, James Spader, Meshach Taylor, Carole Davis

© VIDEO TREASURES M920

MAN OF FLOWERS

D: Paul Cox 91 m

NR | DMA COM | 1984 | COLOR

7 Very odd and provocative drama, with a dark comedic edge. An eccentric old man (Kaye) is a collector of all things beautiful. Each week, he pays a lovely artist's model (Best), who he calls his "Little Flower," to strip for him while he plays classical music. However before she can finish, he runs to a church across the street to immediately vent his frustrations on the organ. The model he adores is torn between her relationship with her lesbian lover and her abusive boyfriend. But, when the boyfriend oversteps his bounds, the old man finds a beautiful way to protect his little flower.

Sex Nud Viol Lang AdSit

A: Norman Kaye, Alyson Best, Chris Haywood, Sarah Walker, Julia Blake, Bob Ellis

© LIVE HOME VIDEO VA4370

MAN WHO LOVED WOMEN, THE

D: Francois Truffaut 119 m

NR | FOR COM ROM | 1977 | COLOR

8 Wonderfully charming and sophisticated French comedy with serious undertones. The opening scene contains leg after beautiful female leg, filing slowly past the grave of Bertrand Morane. Bertrand, you see, is a man who loved women. He is a connoisseur of women. He loves all aspects of femaleness. And, women love him...even though he can be faithful to no one woman. He never abuses a woman, he just can't help himself from chasing the next one. This is his story and he tells it in flashback, as an autobiography. Spawned a much lesser American version with Burt Reynolds.

Sex Nud Viol Lang AdSit

A: Charles Denner, Brigitte Fossey, Nelly Borgeaud, Genevieve Fontanel, Nathalie Baye, Jean Daste

Distributed By MGM/UA Home Video M202962

MAN WITH TWO BRAINS, THE

D: Carl Reiner 90 m

R | COM SF | 1983 | COLOR

6 Mad-scientist farce. A brilliant brain surgeon's marriage to an ice queen (Turner) is falling apart. She is super-sexy but refuses him any satisfaction. Hoping to rekindle their romance, Dr. Hfuhruhur (Martin) takes her to Vienna but there he finds his true love. She is a disembodied brain in a jar that can communicate telepathically. So Martin schemes to find a way to "keep" the brain with him. In true Steve Martin form, this wacky comedy can be charming. Some of the scenes will have you in stitches while others leave you cold. Listen for Sissy Spacek as the voice of the brain.

Sex Nud Viol Lang AdSit

A: Steve Martin, Kathleen Turner, David Warner, Paul Benedict, Richard Brestoff, James Cromwell

© WARNER HOME VIDEO 11319

MARRIED TO THE MOB

D: Jonathan Demme 104 m

R | COM ROM | 1988 | COLOR

9 A delightful and winning comedy of errors. Angela (Pfeiffer) is a beautiful but unhappy housewife who is married to an unfaithful gangster husband. When he gets knocked off, she takes the opportunity to escape mob life altogether and flees to New York, sells all her worldly goods and rents a seedy apartment all on her own. She just might have a chance to be happy too - if it weren't for the head hood, who has the hots for her; his scheming wife, who thinks Angela is his seductress; and the FBI agents, who follow her everywhere. Funny and very likable, Pfeiffer turns out a sparkling performance.

Sex Nud Viol Lang AdSit

A: Michelle Pfeiffer, Matthew Modine, Dean Stockwell, Mercedes Ruehl, Alec Baldwin, Joan Cusack

© ORION PICTURES CORPORATION 8726

MASK, THE

D: Charles Russell 101 m

PG-13 | COM | 1994 | COLOR

7 Manic comedian Jim Carrey is the focus of this film. The plotline only provides a means for him to unleash his particular brand of craziness. Carry plays a milque-toastish bank clerk who discovers a strange and magical mask in the river, and when he wears it he is transformed into a green-faced, 1930's-like hipster who is also tornado of a superhero. All Carry's outlandish expressions and movements are further exaggerated by truly fantastic Looney-Toon-like special effects. Carry's character pursues romance with a beautiful sultry blonde bombshell, while battling a nasty gangster who is trying to take over the city. Utter silliness.

Sex Nud Viol Lang AdSit

A: Jim Carrey, Cameron Diaz, Peter Reigert, Peter Greene, Amy Yasbeck, Richard Jeni

© TURNER HOME ENTERTAINMENT N4011

MASS APPEAL

D: Glenn Jordan — 99 m

PG | DMA COM | 1984 | COLOR

Sex / Nud / Viol / ◢ Lang / ◢ AdSit

8 A young seminary student (Ivanek) wreaks holy havoc when he challenges a situation he finds at Father Tim Farley's (Lemmon) wealthy parish. Father Tim is laid-back. He cracks jokes from the pulpit and is much-loved by his parishioners. He even drives a Mercedes. Idealistic newcomer Ivaek questions Lemmon's methods and the two are launched on a collision course. Ivanek's confrontational path also gets him sideways of the inflexible Monsignor (Durning) and almost tossed out. But Lemmon protects his new charge and eventually they teach other about faith.

A: Jack Lemmon, Zeljko Ivanek, Charles Durning, Louise Latham, Lois de Banzie, James Ray

© MCA/UNIVERSAL HOME VIDEO, INC. 80168

MATCHMAKER, THE

D: Joseph Anthony — 110 m

NR | COM ROM | 1958 | B&W

Sex / Nud / Viol / Lang / ◢ AdSit

7 An endearing comedy. Shirley Booth stars as a crafty New York City matchmaker in the late 1800s. A wealthy widower and merchant (Ford) decides it is time to remarry, so he travels to New York to consult with a matchmaker for that purpose. There, he spies Shirley MacLaine and becomes intent on proposing his love to her. However, Shirley Booth has designs on him for herself and schemes to implement her plans. Any of this sound familiar? This is what later became the smash Broadway musical HELLO DOLLY.

A: Shirley Booth, Anthony Perkins, Shirley MacLaine, Paul Ford, Robert Morse, Wallace Ford

© PARAMOUNT HOME VIDEO 5736

MATINEE

D: Joe Dante — 99 m

PG | COM | 1993 | COLOR

Sex / Nud / Viol / ◢ Lang / AdSit

7 Sweet-natured and pleasant light entertainment that is meant to call up memories of another time. It is 1962 and master-promoter Lawrence Woolsey (Goodman) is about to personally launch his latest horror/monster movie. The movie is "Mant" (half man, half ant - all terror). The place is Key West, Florida just as the US Navy is heading out to enforce a blockade on Russian ships bound for Cuba. The world is terrorized by being on the brink of nuclear war; the patrons of the local theater are about to be terrorized by Mant; and, Gene (a 15-year-old horror movie fan) and his new girlfriend are locked together inside a bomb shelter in the theater's basement. Light-hearted.

A: John Goodman, Cathy Moriarty, Simon Fenton, Omri Katz, Kellie Martin, Lisa Jakub

© MCA/UNIVERSAL HOME VIDEO, INC. 81481

MATING GAME, THE

D: George Marshall — 96 m

NR | COM ROM | 1959 | COLOR

Sex / Nud / Viol / Lang / ◢ AdSit

8 Fast moving and fun sex romp. Tony Randall is a straight-laced IRS agent who descends upon an ornery farmer (Douglas) to see why he hasn't filed a tax return - ever. Tony does his best to pursue government business but the farmer's daughter (Reynolds) is doing her best to pursue him - and he's losing. Reynolds and Randall are both captivating in these fun roles from early in their careers.

A: Debbie Reynolds, Tony Randall, Paul Douglas, Fred Clark, Una Merkel, Philip Ober

Distributed By MGM/UA Home Video 203048

MATTER OF PRINCIPLE, A

D: Gwen Arner — 60 m

NR | COM DMA | 1984 | COLOR

Sex / Nud / Viol / Lang / ◢ AdSit

7 A lighthearted Scrooge-like Christmas story for everybody. The selfish and cantankerous father (Arkin) of a very large brood, ruins the family's Christmas when he decides he can't afford the expense. His wife (Dana) is fed up with his tyrannical behavior. She decides to take no more of it and leaves him, taking the kids. When he comes to realize that he might just have cost himself his family, he has a change of heart and comes to understand the true meaning of Christmas. Well done, a fun and entertaining holiday story.

A: Alan Arkin, Barbara Dana, Tony Arkin

© ACADEMY ENTERTAINMENT 1065

MAVERICK

D: Richard Donner — 127 m

PG | WST COM | 1994 | COLOR

Sex / Nud / ◢ Viol / ◢ Lang / AdSit

7 "Maverick" was one of TV's consistently best series, starred Garner and aired from 1957-1962. Maverick is a suave gambler who had a knack for getting into and out of trouble with a con, style and a grin. Gibson's 1994 Maverick is not Garner's, but he is still a fun-loving clever con-man. And, Garner is back too, but this time as a retired sheriff. Maverick needs to raise the last of the $25,000 stake he needs to get into a big game in St. Louis, but he has a struggle to get there -- with a sexy con-lady (Foster) who picks his pocket and various bad guys out for revenge. The plot is almost inconsequential. The focus is on the personalities. Enjoyable but not a laugh-riot.

A: Mel Gibson, Jodie Foster, James Garner, Graham Greene, Alfred Molina, James Coburn

© WARNER HOME VIDEO 13374

MAX DUGAN RETURNS

D: Herbert Ross — 98 m

PG | COM | 1983 | COLOR

Sex / Nud / Viol / ◢ Lang / ◢ AdSit

9 A warm and winning little comedy from Neil Simon that will warm your heart and tickle your funnybone. An ex-con and gambler (Robards) decides to try to regain the love of his daughter (Mason) after having been gone 26 years. Mason is a widowed school teacher, barely surviving with her son (Broderick), and she isn't very excited about seeing him again. Still, Robards is determined and he has a suitcase of money - even if it isn't his - to buy her love. So, he buries her and his grandson in presents. Imagine the difficult time she has explaining this to her new policeman boyfriend (Sutherland).

A: Jason Robards, Jr., Marsha Mason, Donald Sutherland, Matthew Broderick, Dody Goodman, Sal Viscuso

© FOXVIDEO 1236

MEATBALLS

D: Ivan Reitman — 94 m

PG | COM | 1980 | COLOR

Sex / ◢ Nud / Viol / ◢ Lang / ◢ AdSit

7 Irreverent, very lightweight, summertime fun! Murray stars as the lunatic summer counselor who leads his troops against their rivals in the camp olympics, while he also pays special attention to building their egos and helping one especially quiet kid. But, he also takes time for romance with pretty Kate Lynch. His wacky behavior is surprisingly easy to take, despite his sometimes tacky antics. Over all, it is touching and even irresistible at times, if you're ready for major silliness.

A: Bill Murray, Harvey Atkin, Kate Lynch, Russ Banham, Kristine DeBell, Sarah Torgov

© PARAMOUNT HOME VIDEO 1324

MEDITERRANEO

D: Gabriele Salvatores — 93 m

R | FOR COM | 1991 | COLOR

◢ Sex / ■ Nud / Viol / ■ Lang / ◢ AdSit

6 1991 winner of the Academy Award for Best Foreign film. However, it must have been a very slow year. This is a mildly entertaining story about a group of misfits from the Italian army who become stranded on a beautiful Greek island for nearly the entirety of WWII. There are no other men on the island, only women and children. One of the women is a pretty whore who sells them all her services but another woman lovingly shares herself for free with two brothers. There doesn't seem to be any real direction to this film. It is for serious and curious movie fans only. Subtitles.

A: Diego Abatantuono, Claudio Bigagli, Giuseppe Cederna, Claudio Bisio, Vanna Barba

© TOUCHSTONE HOME VIDEO 1593

MELVIN AND HOWARD

D: Jonathan Demme — 95 m

R | COM DMA | 1980 | COLOR

Sex / ■ Nud / Viol / ◢ Lang / ◢ AdSit

7 Unusual bittersweet comedy. Hollywood fabricated this story about the real-life character Melvin Dummar (LeMat), a down-on-his-luck gas station attendant in Utah who claimed to have once given Howard Hughes a ride, and claimed that Hughes later scrawled him a note which named him heir to $156 million. This odd-ball slice-of-life comedy works pretty well, if haltingly. It pokes fun both at society at large and at common-man Dummar's continual but ill-advised grabs for the American Dream. Academy Awards included Best Supporting Actress and Original Screenplay. Not a traditional comedy.

A: Paul LeMat, Jason Robards, Jr., Mary Steenburgen, Jack Kehoe, Pamela Reed, Dabney Coleman

© MCA/UNIVERSAL HOME VIDEO, INC. 66026

MEMOIRS OF AN INVISIBLE MAN

D: John Carpenter — 99 m

PG-13 | SF COM | 1992 | COLOR

◢ Sex / ◢ Nud / ◢ Viol / ◢ Lang / ◢ AdSit

6 Very light diversion. Chevy Chase is a securities analyst who decides to skip the lecture he's supposed to listen to at a government research facility and instead take a nap in a vacant room. Just then, there is an accident and everyone is evacuated from the building except for Chevy. When it is over, Chevy has become invisible. Sam Neill is a rogue CIA agent who is driven to make Chevy a key government asset, but Chevy is not eager to be partners with the CIA, so he makes a break and the chase is on. Chevy seeks out his new girlfriend, Daryl Hannah, for help. Clever. Although its not that funny, it is still reasonably enjoyable.

A: Chevy Chase, Daryl Hannah, Sam Neill, Michael McKean, Stephen Tobolowsky, Jim Norton

© WARNER HOME VIDEO 12310

MEMORIES OF ME

D: Henry Winkler — 103 m

PG-13 | COM DMA | 1988 | COLOR

Sex / Nud / Viol / ◢ Lang / ■ AdSit

7 The two of them couldn't be more different. Billy Crystal is a New York heart surgeon and his father (Alan King) is a California actor who has spent his whole career as an extra. When Crystal survives a mild heart attack, he decides to get his priorities in order. So his girl (Williams) encourages him to mend fences with his father. These two are so far apart that that isn't easy, and it does set up some pretty funny situations. However, when Billy finds that his father is terminally ill, they begin an adventure making up for lost time. Obviously contrived, but still an entertaining mixture of laughter and emotion.

A: Billy Crystal, Alan King, JoBeth Williams, Janet Carroll, David Ackroyd, Sean Connery

Distributed By MGM/UA Home Video M201514

MEN DON'T LEAVE

D: Paul Brickman 115 m

PG-13 | DMA COM | 1990 | COLOR

8 Moving and believable. Another victory for the director of RISKY BUSINESS! Jesseca Lange is a recently widowed mother of two left penniless, without hope and lonely when her husband is killed. She realizes that she must move to an apartment in the city and sell her big house to survive, but her young boys have a harder time understanding why things have changed so much. As she struggles with her own shattered dreams, loneliness, a new job and a likable but eccentric composer who's chasing her, she also must somehow give her teenage sons the means to survive in their own new worlds. Heartbreaking and heartwarming. Insightful comedy and moving drama. Excellent.

Sex, Nud, Viol, Lang, AdSit

A: Jessica Lange, Joan Cusack, Arliss Howard, Kathy Bates, Chris O'Connell, Charlie Korsmo

© WARNER HOME VIDEO 11897

MERMAIDS

D: Richard Benjamin 101 m

PG-13 | COM DMA | 1991 | COLOR

8 Offbeat and very different, but also a very entertaining comedy. Set in the '60s, Cher is the sexy mother of two girls. She's a looker. She loves men and can't keep her hands off them, but she's also so afraid of a permanent relationship that she's always running away from them. She just packs everybody up and leaves town. Her oldest daughter (Ryder) is just 15, trying to find her place in the world and trying to deal with her own hormones, but she's not getting much help from Mom. The youngest daughter's only concern is her dream to swim the English Channel. The three of them argue, laugh, and learn about family, life and love together.

Sex, Nud, Viol, Lang, AdSit

A: Cher, Bob Hoskins, Winona Ryder, Christina Ricci, Michael Schoeffling, Caroline McWilliams

© ORION PICTURES CORPORATION 8759

METEOR MAN

D: Robert Townsend 99 m

PG | FAN COM | 1994 | COLOR

6 Silly and farcical. Robert Townsend is a mild-mannered school teacher in a gang-terrorized neighborhood of Washington DC. His father wants to stand up to the gang but Townsend (and nearly everyone else) just wants to hide. That is until Townsend is struck by a magic green meteor which transforms him into Meteor Man, giving him the power to deflect lots and lots of bullets or catch them in his teeth, fly (even though he's afraid of heights), beat up bad guys and understand his dog speak to him. Even though the film lacks a sharp focus, it is so good natured that most will have fun, particularly black kids. Lots of painless-type violence.

Sex, Nud, Viol, Lang, AdSit

A: Robert Townsend, Marla Gibbs, Eddie Griffin, Robert Guillaume, James Earl Jones, Roy Fegan

Distributed By MGM/UA Home Video M903022

METROPOLITAN

D: Wilt Stillman 98 m

PG-13 | COM DMA | 1990 | COLOR

8 Refreshing, witty, intellectual comedy documenting the "trials" of a group of privileged NYC preppies. The story line itself is of little consequence because it only opens a window for us to see into their world. What is interesting, even fascinating at times, and almost always funny, is the amount of privileged ignorance these young people possess. This is a fact to which they themselves begin to gain some knowledge when a lack of escorts requires them to let into their privileged midst a middle-class outsider. For all that, this movie does not demean these people - it exposes their underlying humanity. If you liked this, also try BARCELONA.

Sex, Nud, Viol, Lang, AdSit

A: Edward Clements, Christopher Eigeman, Carolyn Farina, Isabel Gillies, Will Kempe, Taylor Nichols

© NEW LINE HOME VIDEO 75153

MICKI & MAUDE

D: Blake Edwards 118 m

PG-13 | COM ROM | 1984 | COLOR

7 A TV reporter (Dudley Moore) desperately wants to be a father, but his wife Micki (Ann Reinking) is a hard-driving career woman who doesn't want to take the time for a baby and barely for him. So, he has a fling with a pretty cellist named Maude (Irving), who shortly tells him that she is pregnant. Just as she does, his wife gives him the same news - and that's only part of his problems. He loves both women and can't pick between them. So, he marries Maude too, leads a secret double life and that works for a while - until, that is, the two women wind up in adjacent rooms at the hospital. Surprisingly winning and enjoyable.

Sex, Nud, Viol, Lang, AdSit

A: Dudley Moore, Amy Irving, Ann Reinking, Richard Mulligan, George Gaynes, Wallace Shawn

© COLUMBIA TRISTAR HOME VIDEO 60456

MIDNIGHT RUN

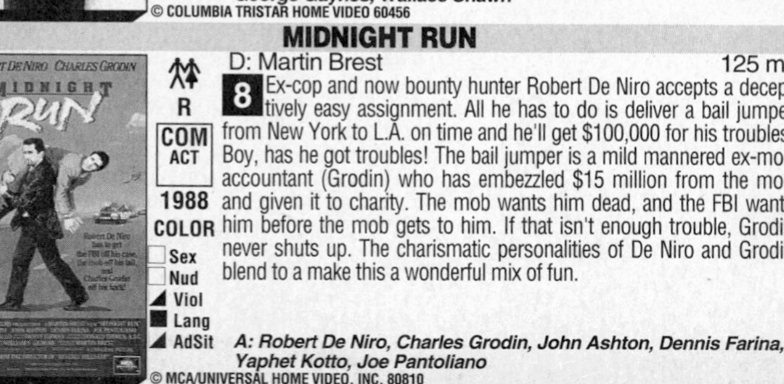

D: Martin Brest 125 m

R | COM ACT | 1988 | COLOR

8 Ex-cop and now bounty hunter Robert De Niro accepts a deceptively easy assignment. All he has to do is deliver a bail jumper from New York to L.A. on time and he'll get $100,000 for his troubles. Boy, has he got troubles! The bail jumper is a mild mannered ex-mob accountant (Grodin) who has embezzled $15 million from the mob and given it to charity. The mob wants him dead, and the FBI wants him before the mob gets to him. If that isn't enough trouble, Grodin never shuts up. The charismatic personalities of De Niro and Grodin blend to a make this a wonderful mix of fun.

Sex, Nud, Viol, Lang, AdSit

A: Robert De Niro, Charles Grodin, John Ashton, Dennis Farina, Yaphet Kotto, Joe Pantoliano

© MCA/UNIVERSAL HOME VIDEO, INC. 80810

MIDSUMMER NIGHT'S SEX COMEDY, A

D: Woody Allen 88 m

PG | COM ROM | 1982 | COLOR

7 This one is mostly for Woody Allen fans. It is set at the turn of the century and centers around three couples who decide to spend the weekend together at a beautiful estate in the country. Woody is there with his cold wife (Steenburgen). Ferrer is there with a promiscuous Mia Farrow. And Tony Roberts is there with his latest lover (Haggerty). Mischief-making soon ensues and it seems that everyone ends up falling in love with the wrong person. Quirky, but entertaining.

Sex, Nud, Viol, Lang, AdSit

A: Woody Allen, Mia Farrow, Jose Ferrer, Mary Steenburgen, Tony Roberts, Julie Hagerty

© WARNER HOME VIDEO 22025

MIGHTY DUCKS, THE

D: Stephen Herek 103 m

PG | COM CLD | 1992 | COLOR

8 Clever family fun. Estevez is a hotshot attorney who delights in humiliating his opponents - even the judges. So, when he is caught speeding once too often, they throw the book at him. However, he will be able to escape a jail sentence if he will perform community service. That is how he gets the job of coaching a kids's hockey team made up of inner-city misfits, called the Ducks. His anger and frustration at the situation soon give way to excitement over his successes with the team. The experience changes his attitude, helps the kids learn to play as a team and he also learns about love. Predictable, but a lot of fun anyway.

Sex, Nud, Viol, Lang, AdSit

A: Emilio Estevez, Lane Smith, Joss Ackland, Heidi Kling

© WALT DISNEY HOME VIDEO 1585

MILAGRO BEANFIELD WAR, THE

D: Robert Redford 118 m

R | DMA COM | 1988 | COLOR

8 Positively infectious good time. Based on Nicholas and David Ward's novel, this touching tale is set in a poor New Mexican town of Milagro. Bullying land developers plan to take over some farm land. So, handyman Vennera leads a rebellion against the big money interests by using their water to irrigate his dusty beanfield. His one act of defiance inspires all the others to gain courage, and to rise up and join him. An endearing story that, even with its simple plot, is sure to lift you up. The whimsical score won an Oscar.

Sex, Nud, Viol, Lang, AdSit

A: Sonia Braga, Chick Vennera, Ruben Blades, Christopher Walken, Daniel Stern, John Heard

© MCA/UNIVERSAL HOME VIDEO, INC. 80796

MISS FIRECRACKER

D: Thomas Schlamme 102 m

PG | COM DMA | 1988 | COLOR

6 Quirky and colorful comedy. Carnelle (Holly Hunter) is an insecure smalltown young girl who has grown up in the shadow of her lovely cousin (Steenburgen), a former Miss Firecracker. Carnelle dreams of gaining respectability, of changing her flirtatious image and wants to finally "be somebody," so she focuses all of her efforts upon entering and winning the local beauty contest. She will become Miss Firecracker, just as her cousin had done. This feel-good movie is peppered with all sorts of oddball characters and has its moments, but it is different.

Sex, Nud, Viol, Lang, AdSit

A: Holly Hunter, Mary Steenburgen, Tim Robbins, Scott Glenn, Alfre Woodard, Scott Glenn

© HBO VIDEO 0330

MODERN ROMANCE

D: Albert Brooks 940 m

R | COM | 1981 | COLOR

6 A comedy of neurosis and romantic errors! Albert Brooks stars an an obsessively compulsive Hollywood film editor who can't get the love thing right. He has absolutely no idea just how insensitive and rude he is. Kathryn Harrold, his girlfriend, is the best thing he's ever had but he breaks up with her because they can't communicate. Maybe there is someone else out there. But he almost immediately doubts that decision, too. As with many of Brooks's movies, his neurotic character is best appreciated by his fans.

Sex, Nud, Viol, Lang, AdSit

A: Albert Brooks, Kathryn Harrold, Bruno Kirby, James L. Brooks, Jane Hallaren, George Kennedy

© COLUMBIA TRISTAR HOME VIDEO 51083

MO' MONEY

D: Peter MacDonald 91 m

R | DMA COM | 1992 | COLOR

7 Damon Wayans and his brother Marlon star in this ethnic piece about two inner-city scam artists. Damon is the older brother who becomes infatuated with a beautiful and classy girl working in a credit card company. He knows he has no chance to win her over unless he straightens himself out. So he applies for a job there too, and gets it. However, the economic requirements of romance prove to be too much for his larcenous soul and he gives into the temptation to steal, which draws him into major trouble. Clever bits here and there, but will be most appealing to a younger audience.

Sex, Nud, Viol, Lang, AdSit

A: Damon Wayans, Marlon Wayans, Joe Santos, John Diehl, Stacey Dash, Harry J. Lennix

© COLUMBIA TRISTAR HOME VIDEO 51313

MONEY PIT, THE

D: Richard Benjamin 91 m

PG | COM | 1986 | COLOR

Sex | Nud | Viol | Lang | AdSit

6 A yuppie couple faces yuppie ruin in this innocuous misadventure. An up-and-coming rock and roll lawyer (Hanks) falls in love with a musician (Long). Just to "cement" their relationship, they decide to buy a mansion and fix it up. What they get is a house that just keeps sucking up money. Everything breaks, falls, collapses, deteriorates or blows up. Silly Spielberg creation begins to lose contact with reality as the house continues to ruin their lives. Can be fun if you're in the right state of unconsciousness.

A: Tom Hanks, Shelley Long, Alexander Godunov, Maureen Stapleton, Joe Mantegna, Philip Bosco

© MCA/UNIVERSAL HOME VIDEO, INC. 80387

MONKEY TROUBLE

D: Franco Amurri 93 m

PG | CLD COM | 1994 | COLOR

Sex | Nud | Viol | Lang | AdSit

6 Eva is a 9-year-old girl, who lives with her mother, step-father, half-brother and a new baby. She feels left out, even though everyone trys very hard to include her, and she really wants to have a dog. But, her step-father is allergic and besides she doesn't take care of things. Then one day, a tiny runaway monkey runs into her arms. Eva is in love, names him Dodger and hides him away in her room. However, Dodger has runaway from a crooked street performer who has trained him to be a thief, and who now wants Dodger back very badly. Very cute monkey. Mostly for younger kids.

A: Thora Birch, Mimi Rogers, Christopher McDonald, Harvey Keitel, Victor Argo, Robert Miranda

© TURNER HOME ENTERTAINMENT N4047

MON ONCLE

D: Jacques Tati 110 m

NR | FOR COM | 1958 | COLOR

Sex | Nud | Viol | Lang | AdSit

7 Outrageous foreign comedy farce that pokes fun at all things "modern." Mr. Hulot's brother-in-law's (Zola) home is a riotous mix of gadgets and mechanization. On the other hand, the quiet and unassuming Hulot (Tati) has a simple home. Hulot's adoring nephew (Bercort) prefers the simpler life, and it is from his perspective that the story is told. Included in his father's house is a grotesque fish fountain and some of the ugliest, most twisted furniture you've ever seen anywhere. The film is an ongoing series of sight gags with almost no dialogue. Best Foreign Picture Oscar. Subtitles.

A: Jacques Tati, Jean-Pierre Zola, Adrienne Servantie, Alain Bercourt

© HOME VISION ONC 020

MONSTER IN A BOX

D: Nick Broomfield 90 m

PG-13 | COM | 1992 | COLOR

Sex | Nud | Viol | Lang | AdSit

7 Very funny and quite curious filmed version of monologist Spalding Gray's stage play, consisting entirely of his lecture to the audience about himself. The "monster in a box" the title refers to is his 1900-page autobiography. His discussions constantly concern himself. However, since he is a great storyteller and most of the stories are at his own expense, they are almost always quite entertaining and sometimes very enlightening "pearls of wisdom". Such as: "Don't fly on an airline whose pilots believe in reincarnation."

A: Spalding Gray

© TURNER HOME ENTERTAINMENT N4134

MONSTER IN THE CLOSET

D: Bob Dahlin 90 m

PG | HOR COM | 1987 | COLOR

Sex | Nud | Viol | Lang | AdSit

6 Good natured humor and horror mix is this '50s-style spoof. A very Clark Kent-like obituary reporter (Grant) from the newspaper and a biology teacher (DuBarry) are sent to investigate a series of strange murders occurring in the closets of San Francisco. What they find is a music-loving mutant that commits brutal (and comic) murders but only in closets. A not-too-serious black comedy/horror movie in the same vein as LITTLE SHOP OF HORRORS. A very off-beat sort of movie.

A: Donald Grant, Denise DuBarry, Claude Akins, Howard Duff, John Carradine, Henry Gibson

© WARNER HOME VIDEO 783

MONTY PYTHON AND THE HOLY GRAIL

D: Terry Gilliam 90 m

PG | COM | 1974 | COLOR

Sex | Nud | Viol | Lang | AdSit

6 British lunacy abounds in this medieval farce. The Python gang goes after the legend of King Arthur and his knights in this comic assault on kings, communists and cowards, and the Knights of the Round Table embark on a perilous quest for the Holy Grail. This is wild and woolly stuff. Terribly uneven - sometimes terrible, sometime brilliant. One scene has a knight in a sword fight who has every limb cut off but is still so arrogant he won't admit he is losing. For Python fans, a most entertaining journey. Others beware.

A: Terry Jones, Graham Chapman, John Cleese, Terry Gilliam, Eric Idle, Michael Palin

© COLUMBIA TRISTAR HOME VIDEO 92253

MONTY PYTHON LIVE AT THE HOLLYWOOD BOWL

D: Terry Hughes 78 m

R | COM | 1982 | COLOR

Sex | Nud | Viol | Lang | AdSit

7 Madness! Those comic crazies from Britain are back, only this time they are live at the Hollywood Bowl in Los Angeles. The irreverent Python group presents a series of their favorite comic sketches, both old and new, to a crowd in the City of Angels. If you savor the flavor of Python humor, this madcap performance will definitely satisfy you.

A: Graham Chapman, John Cleese, Terry Gilliam, Eric Idle, Terry Jones, Michael Palin

© PARAMOUNT HOME VIDEO 12872

MONTY PYTHON'S THE MEANING OF LIFE

D: Terry Jones 103 m

R | COM | 1983 | COLOR

Sex | Nud | Viol | Lang | AdSit

6 Wicked humor, satire and irreverence mix in this set of comic sketches from the bawdy Python clan. From birth to death and everything in between, the Python crew leaves nothing sacred. They poke fun at all the important facets of life - religion, philosophy, history, medicine, birth control, death, the afterlife and - halibut! Look for the world's fattest man, and watch out - better have a strong stomach. Fans or eccentrics only.

A: Graham Chapman, John Cleese, Terry Gilliam, Eric Idle, Terry Jones, Michael Palin

© MCA/UNIVERSAL HOME VIDEO, INC. 71016

MOON OVER PARADOR

D: Paul Mazursky 103 m

PG-13 | COM | 1988 | COLOR

Sex | Nud | Viol | Lang | AdSit

6 Breezy and amusing tale of a hammy, out-of-work, off-Broadway actor (Dreyfuss) who gets shanghaied by the chief of the secret police (Julia) from a small Caribbean country. The figurehead leader of the country is dead from over-indulging in his excesses and Julia, the real power behind the throne, doesn't want to give up that power yet. So he needs Dreyfuss to impersonate the dead ruler until Julia can take over. However, Dreyfuss becomes a threat when he begins to enjoy his role and takes it too seriously. That threatens many political insiders but pleases beautiful Sonia Braga.

A: Richard Dreyfuss, Sonia Braga, Raul Julia, Jonathan Winters

© MCA/UNIVERSAL HOME VIDEO, INC. 80802

MOONSTRUCK

D: Norman Jewison 103 m

PG | COM ROM | 1987 | COLOR

Sex | Nud | Viol | Lang | AdSit

8 Absolutely delightful! Cher stars as an Italian-American widow living at home with her aging parents and engaged to marry an older man (Aiello), even though the romance is passionless. In spite of herself, she finds herself helplessly drawn to, and in love with, his younger brother (Cage). A whole bunch of romantic complications ensue. Jewison does a fantastic job of capturing the essence of Italian-American sensibilities - the warmth, humor and dialogue. Oscars for Cher, Dukakis and Patrick Stanley's script. That's amore!

A: Cher, Nicolas Cage, Olympia Dukakis, Vincent Gardenia, Danny Aiello, Julie Bovasso

Distributed By MGM/UA Home Video M901135

MOSCOW ON THE HUDSON

D: Paul Mazursky 107 m

R | COM DMA ROM | 1984 | COLOR

Sex | Nud | Viol | Lang | AdSit

8 The film is both comic and bittersweet and Robin Williams is an absolute charmer. While touring the United States, Williams, a musician for the Moscow Circus, is blown away by the wonders of Bloomingdales and defects to America right then. His adjustment to American life is difficult, often comedic and sad. He lives in fear that the KGB will capture him, until he gets his American citizenship. But he also has new friends in a black security guard, a sexy Italian lover and a cagey lawyer. America becomes home, but it doesn't happen all at once and it's a lot fun watching it happen.

A: Robin Williams, Maria Conchita Alonso, Cleavant Derricks, Alejandro Rey, Savely Kramarov, Elya Baskin

© COLUMBIA TRISTAR HOME VIDEO 60309

MOTHER, JUGS & SPEED

D: Peter Yates 98 m

PG | COM | 1976 | COLOR

Sex | Nud | Viol | Lang | AdSit

6 This is black comedy (in a sort of MASH vein) that is better that its title would indicate. The three primary characters are Cosby, Welch and Keitel. They are all drivers for a run-down ambulance company that is more concerned with the number of patients they see each day than the patient's health. Keitel is an ex-cop with a mixed past. Cosby is a free-wheeling driver and Welch is a dispatcher, studying nights to become a driver. Hagman is a show stopper as a driver with sex forever on his mind. They respond to call after call. Many are funny but some aren't. Not bad overall.

A: Bill Cosby, Raquel Welch, Larry Hagman, Harvey Keitel, Allen Garfield

© FOXVIDEO 1698

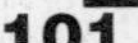

MOUSE THAT ROARED, THE

D: Jack Arnold — 83 m

NR | COM | 1959 | COLOR

8 Hilarious Sellers comedic satire. Grand Fenwick, a very, very small country - the smallest on earth - declares war on the United States because they hope to be defeated so they may collect foreign aid to rebuild their treasury. But when Sellers invades New York and captures an inventor of "the bomb" along with a sample bomb, they win and the US surrenders. Peter Sellers is masterful in this extravagant farce. He plays three separate roles to the hilt, each one severely lacking in brain power.

Sex / Nud / Viol / Lang / AdSit

A: Peter Sellers, Jean Seberg, David Kossoff, William Hartnell, Monty Landis, Leo McKern

© COLUMBIA TRISTAR HOME VIDEO 60062

MR. BASEBALL

D: Fred Schepisi — m

PG-13 | COM ROM | 1992 | COLOR

6 Intelligent and mildly entertaining serio-comedy about an American big league baseball former-great who is now on the downhill slide. His playing may be slipping, but his ego isn't. His agent gets him a job in Japan, playing for the Chunichi Dragons where his fierce independence and huge ego quickly get him into big trouble with the samurai-like coach (Takakura). He is definitely not a team player and he can't get used to the Japanese style of playing the game. However, Selleck and Takakura are eventually brought together by Selleck's romance with Takanashi, Takakura's daughter. Not hilarious but not too serious, either.

Sex / Nud / Viol / Lang / AdSit

A: Tom Selleck, Dennis Haysbert, Ken Takakura, Aya Takanashi

© MCA/UNIVERSAL HOME VIDEO, INC. 81231

MR. MOM

D: Stan Dragoti — 90 m

PG | COM | 1983 | COLOR

8 Hilarious flip-flop on the traditional American way of life. When a Detroit engineer (Keaton) loses his job and his wife (Garr) gets a high paying job with an advertising agency, they do the obvious thing: she goes to work and he stays home. This role reversal forces Keaton into some unfamiliar territory in dealing with the perils of running a household: the housework, the kids and a neighbor who wants to seduce him. How does he cope? He turns to alcohol and soap operas. Some really very funny moments happen when a traditional man gets out of his element.

Sex / Nud / Viol / Lang / AdSit

A: Michael Keaton, Teri Garr, Martin Mull, Ann Jillian, Christopher Lloyd, Frederick Koehler

© LIVE HOME VIDEO 5025

MR. NORTH

D: Danny Huston — 90 m

PG | COM FAN | 1988 | COLOR

6 Whimsical fantasy. A bright young Yale graduate (Edwards) arrives amid the upper-class society of Newport, R.I. of the 1920s. He is, it seems, endowed with magical healing powers. His body has an unusual amount of electricity and he can heal merely by touching. He begins to make a name for himself curing the wealthy sick and charming them, too, until the local medical community takes him to court. Based on Thornton Wilder's "Theophilus North," directed by John Huston's son with help from Dad before he died. Feel-good theme, but its very fanciful style might not be for all.

Sex / Nud / Viol / Lang / AdSit

A: Anthony Edwards, Robert Mitchum, Harry Dean Stanton, Anjelica Huston, Mary Stuart Masterson, Virginia Madsen

© MCEG/STERLING 70075

MR. SATURDAY NIGHT

D: Billy Crystal — 119 m

R | DMA COM | 1992 | COLOR

6 Billy Crystal stars, produces and directs this fictionalized biography of one of his stage characters, Buddy Young Jr. Buddy is a caustic old comedian who has short-circuited his own career his whole life by attacking everyone, including those who love him most: his brother, his wife, his friends and the people he works with. Now, he is an old man addicted to the applause of an audience, but there no longer is an audience who wants to hear him. The combination of good jokes that are nullified by a depressing pathetic character ultimately makes for a believable but unattractive character study.

Sex / Nud / Viol / Lang / AdSit

A: Billy Crystal, David Paymer, Julie Warner, Helen Hunt, Jerry Orbach, Ron Silver

© TURNER HOME ENTERTAINMENT N4064

MR. WONDERFUL

D: Anthony Menhella — 99 m

PG-13 | ROM COM | 1993 | COLOR

7 Matt Dillon is an electrician who has three problems. He wants very badly to invest with his friends in the rehabilitation of an old bowling alley. He can't because he is paying his ex-wife (Annabella Sciorra) so much money in alimony, so he needs to find her a new husband, a Mr. Wonderful, as quickly as possible. However, his last problem is the biggest -- he still loves her. And, while it was her that had walked out on him, intent upon getting an education that would lead her away from the blue-collar neighborhood that they both grew up in, she still loves him too. Pleasant romantic comedy, worthy of an hour and a half.

Sex / Nud / Viol / Lang / AdSit

A: Matt Dillon, Annabella Sciorra, Mary Louise Parker, William Hurt, Vincent D'Onofrio, David Barry Gray

© WARNER HOME VIDEO 12988

MUCH ADO ABOUT NOTHING

D: Kenneth Branagh — 110 m

PG-13 | COM ROM | 1993 | COLOR

8 This is one of the better screen productions of Shakespeare, but it is still Shakespeare. That means that educated and patient audiences will enjoy it, and others will wonder what all the fuss is about. Kenneth Branagh and his real-life wife Emma Thompson give the honey-tongued bard's words both sparkle and bite as the lovers Benedick and Beatrice, who spar with their wits as though they were swords. The story was filmed on location in sunny Tuscany, Italy. Prince Don Pedro and his men have just returned from war to skirmish amid the conflict and rivalries of love between men and women. Many critics would have rated it higher.

Sex / Nud / Viol / Lang / AdSit

A: Kenneth Branagh, Richard Briers, Michael Keaton, Keanu Reeves, Emma Thompson, Denzel Washington

© COLUMBIA TRISTAR HOME VIDEO 71753

MUPPET MOVIE, THE

D: James Frawley — 96 m

G | COM CLD MUS | 1979 | COLOR

8 Effervescent silliness, and some really baaaad puns, make this a delight for everyone. Kids like it because it is light-hearted and silly. Adults get their own special treats - such as when Dom DeLuise interrupts Kermit who's catching flys in the swamp. Dom tells Kermit that he is lost and in a big hurry because he has to "catch a plane." Kermit responds with "Not with a tongue like yours." Irresistable zaniness as the Muppets travel to Hollywood so that they can become movie stars. 15 cameo appearances from some big stars. See also THE MUPPETS TAKE MANHATTEN.

Sex / Nud / Viol / Lang / AdSit

A: Muppets, Milton Berle, Mel Brooks, Steve Martin, Bob Hope, Edgar Bergen

© CBS/FOX VIDEO 9001

MUPPETS TAKE MANHATTAN, THE

D: Frank Oz — 94 m

G | COM CLD | 1984 | COLOR

8 The Muppets return. After Kermit and his friends create a hit college show, they decide that they are ready for the big time... Broadway. Off they head for the Big Apple where they get taken in by a shyster lawyer. They're so broke they live in lockers at the bus station, Kermit gets amnesia on his way to his wedding to Miss Piggy. Muppet madness, and a wide selection of cameo appearances from some of the industry's biggest names, is again at the heart of this extravaganza in silliness.

Sex / Nud / Viol / Lang / AdSit

A: Art Carney, James Coco, Dabney Coleman, Elliott Gould, Joan Rivers, Linda Lavin

© CBS/FOX VIDEO 6731

MURDER BY DEATH

D: Robert Moore — 95 m

PG | MYS COM | 1976 | COLOR

8 Murder is on the dinner menu in this comic mystery! Eccentric millionaire Lionel Twain (Truman Capote) invites top detectives to his home for dinner and offers one million dollars to anyone who can solve the murder of the evening - someone at this table will be stabbed twelve times before midnight. Some of the dinner guests include prominent film detectives such as Sam Spade, Miss Marple and Charlie Chan. Written by Neil Simon, this hilarious film is really a spoof on the great super sleuths of film and features a fantastic all-star cast.

Sex / Nud / Viol / Lang / AdSit

A: Peter Sellers, Peter Falk, David Niven, Maggie Smith, James Coco, Alec Guinness

© COLUMBIA TRISTAR HOME VIDEO 60065

MURPHY'S ROMANCE

D: Martin Ritt — 107 m

PG-13 | ROM COM | 1985 | COLOR

7 Effortless romance in this charmer! A recently divorced young woman (Field) and her twelve-year-old son decide to make a fresh start in a small Arizona town and raise horses for a living. Almost immediately, she runs into crusty old druggist Murphy (Garner) and takes a liking to him, and he to her. But Field's old husband (Kerwin) throws a wrench in things when he shows up again. She doesn't know what to feel. Field and Garner are naturals together in this wonderful little slice of rural Americana that really works. Delightful!

Sex / Nud / Viol / Lang / AdSit

A: Sally Field, James Garner, Brian Kerwin, Corey Haim, Dennis Burkley, Georgann Johnson

© COLUMBIA TRISTAR HOME VIDEO 60649

MUSIC MAN, THE

D: Morton DaCosta — 151 m

G | MUS COM ROM | 1962 | COLOR

10 Golden Americana and a rousing good time too! A charming con artist and music "professor" (Preston) convinces a small turn-of-the-century Iowa town that he can teach the boys there to play musical instruments by using his Think Method. Then he convinces all the townsfolk that they should form a marching band - buying the costumes, instruments and all from him. Some of the Oscar-winning songs featured in this delightful musical include "76 Trombones," "'Til There Was You" and "Trouble." This wonderful slice of American apple pie was nominated for 6 Oscars, including Best Picture. Wonderful!!

Sex / Nud / Viol / Lang / AdSit

A: Robert Preston, Buddy Hackett, Hermione Gingold, Paul Ford, Pert Kelton, Shirley Jones

© WARNER HOME VIDEO 11473

MY BEAUTIFUL LAUNDRETTE

D: Stephen Frears 94 m

R | COM DMA | 1986 | COLOR | Sex Nud Viol Lang AdSit

8 Quirky and odd-ball art film that is very entertaining for the adventurous. Omar (Warnecke), a young Pakistani boy living in a rundown section of London, is given a beat-up launderette by his uncle. He teams up with Johnny (Day-Lewis), his punk boyfriend, and together they renovate the launderette into a neon dream. Everything goes great until a group of racist thugs decide to close down the operation. Although highly acclaimed for its poignant look at cultural differences, sexuality and economic problems, the plot may be a little remote for some. There also may be a problem for some because of the thick accents.

A: Daniel Day-Lewis, Saeed Jaffrey, Roshan Seth, Gordon Warnecke, Derrick Branche, Shirley Anne Field

© WARNER HOME VIDEO 784

MY BLUE HEAVEN

D: John Bailey 96 m

PG-13 | COM | 1990 | COLOR | Sex Nud Viol Lang AdSit

6 Mildly funny story about a minor NYC hip hood and mob informant (Martin) who gets dropped into a strange new world - Southern California suburbia - when he is placed into a FBI witness protection program. Add to that Rick Moranis as a boring straight-arrow G-man assigned to watch over him and you should have a formula for a laugh riot. What you get instead is a pretty good time, mostly carried along by Martin's Saturday Night Live-type characterizations.

A: Steve Martin, Rick Moranis, Joan Cusack, Carol Kane, Melanie Mayron, William Hickey

© WARNER HOME VIDEO 12003

MY BODYGUARD

D: Tony Bill 96 m

PG | COM DMA | 1980 | COLOR | Sex Nud Viol Lang AdSit

8 This is a winning and very likable charmer that will give everyone smiles. Clifford Peache (Makepeace) is a boy who has attended an exclusive private school for nine years, but now he is enrolled in a Chicago public high school, and that's a whole different world. The school is run by a gang of teenage thugs, lead by Dillon, who extort money from their classmates. But Clifford finds a unique solution. He hires Baldwin, a menacing older student, to protect him. However, their strictly-business relationship turns into a warm friendship with some surprises. A very funny and heartwarming movie.

A: Matt Dillon, Chris Makepeace, Adam Baldwin, Ruth Gordon, Matt Dillon, John Houseman

© FOXVIDEO 1111

MY BOYFRIEND'S BACK

D: Bob Balaban 85 m

PG-13 | ROM COM | 1993 | COLOR | Sex Nud Viol Lang AdSit

6 Silly little film about a love-struck teenager who dies after having been struck by a bullet that was meant for his beautiful but unattainable love. But before dying, he asks her to the prom and she, thinking it's a safe bet, agrees to go. However, so motivated is he that he arises from the grave to make his date on time. Being dead does have certain disadvantages though, such as having body parts that fall off and people just don't treat you the same either. The absurdity of it all gets carried away sometimes and it's also a long time to hear different variations on the same joke over and over, but it is sort of cute. Teenagers in particular might be its best audience.

A: Andrew Lowery, Traci Lind, Danny Zorn, Bob Dishy, Paul Dooley, Edward Herrmann

© TOUCHSTONE HOME VIDEO 2225

MY COUSIN VINNY

D: Jonathan Lynn 120 m

R | COM | 1992 | COLOR | Sex Nud Viol Lang AdSit

7 Predictable but likable. Two young guys driving through rural Alabama are blamed for the shooting of a store clerk. Macchio calls home for help and his mother sends his cousin Vinney (Pesci) to defend them. The trouble is that Vinney is a mechanic who just got his degree in night school. It took him six tries to pass the bar and he has spent the six weeks since then chasing ambulances. Soon, leather-clad and silver-chained, Vinney and his wisecracking girlfriend (Tomei won an Oscar) arrive in rural Alabama from Brooklyn. They blend right in...right! Fun characters, even if they're not very believable. But, the constant swearing is distracting and unnecessary.

A: Joe Pesci, Ralph Macchio, Marisa Tomei, Mitchell Whitfield, Fred Gwynne

© FOXVIDEO 1876

MY FAIR LADY

D: George Cukor 170 m

G | MUS ROM COM | 1964 | COLOR | Sex Nud Viol Lang AdSit

10 Outstanding winner of eight Oscars - including Best Picture! Shaw's enduring play (and film) PYGMALION is masterfully transformed into a magical musical by Lerner and Lowe. It is an exuberant story of the effort by a snooty Englishman to transform, on a bet, a guttersnipe flower peddler (Hepburn) into being able to pass for a respectable lady. In the process, he falls in love with her and she changes him forever. Just a few of the winning and memorable songs include "The Rain in Spain," "On the Street Where You Live" and "Get Me to the Church on Time." Wonderful.

A: Audrey Hepburn, Rex Harrison, Wilfrid Hyde-White, Stanley Holloway, Jeremy Brett, Theodore Bikel

© FOXVIDEO 7038

MY FATHER, THE HERO

D: Steve Miner 90 m

PG | COM | 1994 | COLOR | Sex Nud Viol Lang AdSit

6 Gerard Depardieu is a divorced over-achiever who hasn't had time to spend with his daughter for so long that he decides to take her on a dream vacation with him. However, she is now 15, resentful of his absence, embarrassed by being seen with her father and she's not a little girl anymore... but, she isn't grown up either - even though she looks like it. The boys all want to spend time with her and she doesn't want to be seen as a kid hanging with her father, but she somehow has to explain that old man who is always with her. So, she tells everyone that she is really his mistress, thinking that it will make her al-the-more mysterious. It does, but it also makes her father a child molester... and he has no idea what's going on. Not a hit, but a near miss.

A: Gerard Depardieu, Katherine Heigl, Dalton James, Lauren Hutton, Faith Prince, Stephen Tobolowsky

© TOUCHSTONE HOME VIDEO 2699

MY FAVORITE YEAR

D: Richard Benjamin 92 m

PG | COM | 1982 | COLOR | Sex Nud Viol Lang AdSit

7 This is an entertaining tribute to the Golden Age of television - when it was live. O'Toole stars as a Douglas Fairbanks-kind of hero who is going to make his television debut on a popular variety show as the guest star for the week. However, the bottle is O'Toole's method of dealing with the pressures of live performances, so the show's worried director assigns a young writer (Lynn-Baker) the impossible task of keeping O'Toole out of trouble, and sober. He, of course, does neither, and that opens the door for some riotous moments. O'Toole is perfect in the part.

A: Peter O'Toole, Mark Linn-Baker, Jessica Harper, Joseph Bologna, Bill Macy, Lainie Kazan

Distributed By MGM/UA Home Video M800188

MY LIFE AS A DOG

D: Lasse Hallstrom 101 m

NR | FOR COM DMA | 1987 | COLOR | Sex Nud Viol Lang AdSit

7 Offbeat and loveable. A young boy (Glanzelius) gets bundled up and shipped off to a country town in Sweden when his mother becomes seriously ill. This town is populated by offbeat characters and he feels deserted and alone. He comes to compare himself to the Russian dog Laika who was abandoned and left to die in space. But instead he learns to deal with his new surroundings, to understand loss, and even falls in love with a cute little tomboy. This is more than just a film about the pitfalls of growing up, this story is filled to the brim with humor and warmth. A Swedish surprise. Dubbed or subtitles.

A: Anton Glanzelius, Anki Liden, Tomas Von Bromssen, Melinda Kinnaman, Kicki Rundgren, Ing-mari Carlsson

© PARAMOUNT HOME VIDEO 12651

MY NEW GUN

D: Stacy Cochran 99 m

R | COM | 1992 | COLOR | Sex Nud Viol Lang AdSit

6 Quirky comedy with very dry humor. It concerns the mishappenings that occur when an overbearing doctor insists upon giving his pretty but vacuous wife a .38 special handgun for home self-defense. Things get very complicated when their wacky next-door neighbor borrows it. This is a strange little movie that may appeal to those who like their humor deadpan and whose funny bone is a little left of center, but others more conservative will be left scratching their head.

A: Diane Lane, James LeGros, Stephen Collins, Tess Harper, Bill Raymond, Bruce Altman

© COLUMBIA TRISTAR HOME VIDEO 93433

MYSTERY TRAIN

D: Jim Jarmusch 110 m

R | COM DMA | 1989 | COLOR | Sex Nud Viol Lang AdSit

6 Quirky and odd, but intriguing continuation of director Jarmusch's fascination with weird slices of America. This film contains three short stories woven together. An offbeat hotel in Memphis (the land of Elvis) attracts three groups of unique characters. Two Japanese teenage tourists who are ardent Elvis fans, an Italian widow here to take her husband's body home and Bracco, plus two others, who get involved in a robbery and a shooting. This clever study of characters can be slow in spots and is sometimes difficult to fathom, but has some sincerely funny moments, too. Be prepared.

A: Elizabeth Bracco, Nicolette Braschi, Youki Kudoh, Masatoshi Nagase, Joe Strummer, Steve Buscemi

© ORION PICTURES CORPORATION 5051

MYSTIC PIZZA

D: Donald Petrie 104 m

R | COM ROM | 1988 | COLOR | Sex Nud Viol Lang AdSit

7 Tasty coming-of-age comedy and the amorous misadventures of three young women. Working this summer at a pizza parlor in the town of Mystic, Connecticut, three young waitresses attempt a grab for their futures. One is set to marry her high school sweetheart, but faints at the alter. One is set to go to college on an astronomy scholarship, but instead falls in love with a married man. Her sister has looks, knows how to use them and is only out for a good time, but instead falls in love with a rich law student. Loveable characters. Good for everyone, but best audience is young women.

A: Annabeth Gish, Julia Roberts, Lili Taylor, Vincent D'Onofrio, William R. Moses, Adam Storke

© MCEG/STERLING 70054

COM

NADINE

PG | COM ROM | 1987 | COLOR | Sex | Nud | Viol | Lang | AdSit

D: Robert Benton 83 m

6 Nadine (Basinger) is a hairdresser in 1954 Texas. She is pregnant and about to be divorced from her looser bar-owner husband (Bridges). She has another problem, too. She was trying to get some "art" photographs back from a photographer when he was murdered and, in an hurry, she mistakenly picked up some other photos which he had taken of a map showing where a new road is to go. That is a secret that means money, and trouble... somebody wants the photos back. She's in big trouble. She seeks help from her reluctant ex and through it all, they fall in love all over again. Well-cast, light-hearted light-weight evening's diversion.

A: Jeff Bridges, Kim Basinger, Rip Torn, Gwen Verdon, Glenne Headly, Jerry Stiller

© CBS/FOX VIDEO 3841

NAKED GUN, THE

PG-13 | COM | 1988 | COLOR | Sex | Nud | Viol | Lang | AdSit

D: David Zucker 85 m

8 Zany, silly and filled with some of the stupidest jokes and puns of all time - but genuinely funny. Lt. Frank Derbin (Nielsen) is the dumbest cop to ever put on a badge. Nielsen and Presley begin a farcical affair and he discovers that tycoon Montalban has a plot to kill the Queen of England through mind control. Outfielder Reggie Jackson appears in the most hilarious Los Angeles Angels baseball game ever. If you enjoy outrageous silliness like this, you also should check out AIRPLANE. Followed by NAKED GUN 2 1/2.

A: Leslie Nielsen, Priscilla Presley, Ricardo Montalban, O.J. Simpson, George Kennedy

© PARAMOUNT HOME VIDEO 32100

NAKED GUN 2 1/2

PG-13 | COM | 1991 | COLOR | Sex | Nud | Viol | Lang | AdSit

D: David Zucker 85 m

7 Wacked-out, brain-dead police Lt. Frank Durbin (Nielsen) is back. He was the bumbling cop who somehow managed to save the Queen of England in the police parody, NAKED GUN. This time he is out to stop oil, gas, coal and nuclear interests from their attempts to sabotage a new environmental policy from being instituted in America. Just as many bad puns, gags and pratfalls as in the original, a few are hysterical and most of them are pretty funny. Still, that type of silliness gets a little thin and predictable, so some of the sparkle is gone.

A: Leslie Nielsen, Priscilla Presley, George Kennedy, O.J. Simpson, Robert Goulet, Richard Griffiths

© PARAMOUNT HOME VIDEO 32365

NAKED GUN 33 1/3: THE FINAL INSULT

PG-13 | COM | 1994 | COLOR | Sex | Nud | Viol | Lang | AdSit

D: Peter Segal 83 m

6 Detective Frank Drebin, master of the absurd, is back. This time the incredible bumbling detective, comes out of retirement to save the Oscars from a mad bomber. There are a host of unbilled cameos by many of Hollywood's biggest stars, plenty of sexual innuendos and a few big laughs scattered through it, but this song has been sung too many times now. True fans of the ridiculous would likely rate it higher.

A: Leslie Nielsen, Priscilla Presley, George Kennedy, O.J. Simpson, Fred Ward, Kathleen Freeman

© PARAMOUNT HOME VIDEO 32785

NASHVILLE

R | COM DMA | 1975 | COLOR | Sex | Nud | Viol | Lang | AdSit

D: Robert Altman 159 m

8 This picture was widely acclaimed by the critics and nominated for five Oscars, including Best Picture (won Best Song: Keith Carradine's "I'm Easy"). However, its somewhat elitist and condescending nature leaves others cold. It is a cynical character study of American culture, where 24 different characters, whose lives all revolve around the music business or someone in it, are followed for one solid weekend in and around Nashville. The one common thread tieing them all together is a political campaign by a populist candidate. Both comic and poignant, if you're receptive.

A: Henry Gibson, Lily Tomlin, Ronee Blakley, Keith Carradine, Geraldine Chaplin, Barbara Harris

© PARAMOUNT HOME VIDEO 8821

NASTY GIRL, THE

PG-13 | FOR COM DMA | 1990 | COLOR | Sex | Nud | Viol | Lang | AdSit

D: Michael Verhoeven 94 m

9 Delicious biting black comedy that sadly enough is based upon a true story. A German school girl, living in a picturesque Bavarian village, wants to write an essay to be entitled, "My Town During the Third Reich." Suddenly she is ostracized and threatened by the seemingly friendly people she has known all her life. This is a subject they don't want reopened and she is barred from the town archives. This story could easily enough have been turned into a very serious drama. Instead, it is presented as a biting satire, ripping apart hypocrisy. And, it does so in a way so that we see that her town is like all towns everywhere. Subtitles.

A: Lena Stolze, Monika Baumgartner, Michael Gahr, Elisabeth Bertram, Fred Stillkrauth, Robert Gioggenbach

© HBO VIDEO 90621

NATIONAL LAMPOON'S ANIMAL HOUSE

R | COM | 1978 | COLOR | Sex | Nud | Viol | Lang | AdSit

D: John Landis 109 m

9 Hilarious! Often tasteless and gross, nonetheless it is also outrageously funny. College fraternity life in 1962 at the Delta house is constantly rowdy, and they are the bane of the Dean's existence. He wants to close down Delta house in the worst way. The brothers are only too pleased to continue to make his life miserable. There is nothing too crude or outrageous for Bluto and the boys to do. This is a movie which was copied, but never equalled. You'll groan with disgust, but you're going to be laughing out loud, too.

A: John Belushi, Tim Matheson, John Vernon, Verna Bloom, Tom Hulce, Karen Allen

© MCA/UNIVERSAL HOME VIDEO, INC. 66000

NATIONAL LAMPOON'S CHRISTMAS VACATION

PG-13 | COM | 1989 | COLOR | Sex | Nud | Viol | Lang | AdSit

D: Jeremiah S. Chechik 97 m

7 Crazy, wacky, zany, and also the source for some very big laughs for fans of Chevy Chase's brand of crazy, wacky, zany slapstick. Clark Griswold (Chase) is a hapless family man who decides to spend the holiday vacation at home and have the relatives come to visit him. What a mess! Relatives bicker, create chaos and generally drive everyone nuts. Randy Quaid is one of those relatives who is in for the holidays and he is the quintessential slob. Predictable and not at all high-brow humor, but still a amusing good time.

A: Chevy Chase, Beverly D'Angelo, Randy Quaid, John Randolph, Diane Ladd, E.G. Marshall

© WARNER HOME VIDEO 11889

NATIONAL LAMPOON'S LOADED WEAPON 1

PG-13 | COM | 1993 | COLOR | Sex | Nud | Viol | Lang | AdSit

D: Gene Quintano 83 m

7 Parody run amok. This film is one more in the genre of wildly absurd takeoffs on popular films. This one takes aim at LOADED WEAPON, THE SILENCE OF THE LAMBS and BASIC INSTINCT. Its lead characters are a manic maniac white cop and a straight-arrow family man black cop. They are in hot pursuit of General Morters, who is smuggling cocaine inside packages of Wilderness Girl cookies. Assisting them are a likable slimeball and a lusty leather-loving sex kitten. Outlandish stunts and puns come in rapid fire machine gun fashion. If you're not tired of this kind of silliness, you might rate it as an 8.

A: Emilio Estevez, Samuel L. Jackson, Jon Lovitz, Tim Curry, Kathy Ireland, William Shatner

© NEW LINE HOME VIDEO 52363

NETWORK

R | COM DMA | 1976 | COLOR | Sex | Nud | Viol | Lang | AdSit

D: Sidney Lumet 122 m

10 Brilliant and not-too-kind satire of television and television news. This was a very popular and very biting black comedy in which a ruthless network executive (Duvall) is willing to do anything to get ratings and get his fourth-rate network out of the ratings basement. Even if it means allowing an off-his-rocker news anchorman (Finch) to become a hugely popular spectacle as the "mad prophet of the air-waves" by inciting his audience with ranting: "I'm mad as hell and I'm not going to take it anymore." Outstanding cast. Oscars: Actor, Actress, Supporting Actress and Screenplay.

A: Faye Dunaway, William Holden, Peter Finch, Robert Duvall, Wesley Addy, Ned Beatty

Distributed By MGM/UA Home Video M600012

NEVER ON SUNDAY

NR | COM | 1960 | B&W | Sex | Nud | Viol | Lang | AdSit

D: Jules Dassin 94 m

8 Delightful. Melina Mercouri is a simple woman who simply has fun with her life. She is a beautiful and whimsical creature with whom nearly every man in town is in love. For six days a week she's a whore, but on the seventh day she rests. Then, along comes an educated American. When he discovers that she loves the Greek Tragedies but has filled in the blank spots in her knowledge the way she wants to and that they all now end happily, he decides to educate her. His plan backfires when he discovers that the more she learns, the more she loses her zestful happiness. But, her education doesn't last long and his has just begun. Four Oscar nominations, won for Best Song.

A: Melina Mercouri, Jules Dassin, Tito Vandis, George Foundas

Distributed By MGM/UA Home Video M600659

NEW LEAF, A

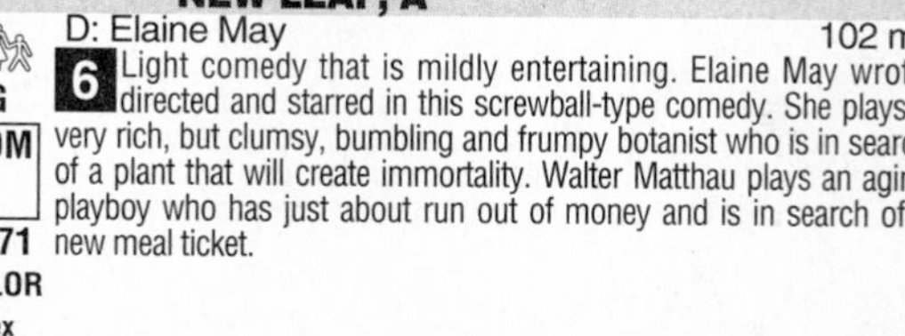

G | COM | 1971 | COLOR | Sex | Nud | Viol | Lang | AdSit

D: Elaine May 102 m

6 Light comedy that is mildly entertaining. Elaine May wrote, directed and starred in this screwball-type comedy. She plays a very rich, but clumsy, bumbling and frumpy botanist who is in search of a plant that will create immortality. Walter Matthau plays an aging playboy who has just about run out of money and is in search of a new meal ticket.

A: Walter Matthau, Elaine May, Jack Weston, James Coco, George Rose, William Redfield

© PARAMOUNT HOME VIDEO 8007

NEW LIFE, A

D: Alan Alda — 104 m

PG-13 | COM ROM | 1988 | COLOR | Sex | Nud | Viol | Lang | AdSit

6 Appealing little story about love in modern relationships. Alan Alda is an obnoxious stock broker and Ann-Margret is, or was, his wife. They divorce after twenty years of marriage. Each sets out to seek a new mate in the singles bars of New York. That turns out to be an unexpectedly painful process of bumps and bruises. Ultimately however, it is also a process that teaches to them both to become open and more understanding with each other and other people. They apply that lesson in their new relationships and also in their old ones. Pleasant and entertaining, but not profound.

A: Alan Alda, Ann-Margret, Hal Linden, Veronica Hamel, Mary Kay Place, John Shea

© PARAMOUNT HOME VIDEO 32160

NEW YORK STORIES

D: Woody Allen, Francis Ford Coppola — 126 m

PG | COM DMA | 1989 | COLOR | Sex | Nud | Viol | Lang | AdSit

6 Three entirely different short stories about New York people, from three of America's most prominent directors - Martin Scorsese, Francis Ford Coppola and Woody Allen. First is Scorsese's adult story about an obsessive artist (Nolte) trying to hang on to a student/lover (Arquette). Coppola's is a cute little story more for kids about a rich 12-year-old who lives alone in a hotel while her parents globe-trot. Allen's is the best and funniest, with the widest appeal, as he plays a middle-aged lawyer who is plagued by his nagging mother and is blessed when a magician "loses" her. Not for most people, but film students and film fans especially will enjoy themselves.

A: Nick Nolte, Rosanna Arquette, Talia Shire, Giancarlo Giannini, Mae Questal, Woody Allen

© TOUCHSTONE HOME VIDEO 952

NIGHT OF THE COMET

D: Thom Eberhardt — 95 m

PG-13 | SF COM HOR | 1984 | COLOR | Sex | Nud | Viol | Lang | AdSit

6 Quirky science fiction spoof. A couple of California "valley girls" are among the few humans left alive and unchanged on earth after a brilliant comet, that last passed earth when the dinosaurs died, again passes overhead. Most people are killed instantly, but some unfortunate others are turned into flesh-eating zombies. The girls, however, spend their time shopping in the deserted stores, looking for guys and dodging zombies. They eventually join a band of other survivors to do battle with the zombies. Sound silly? It is, but is still more than passable entertainment.

A: Robert Beltran, Catherine Mary Stewart, Kelli Maroney, Sharon Farrell

© GOODTIMES 4017

NIGHT ON EARTH

D: Jim Jarmusch — 128 m

R | COM | 1992 | COLOR | Sex | Nud | Viol | Lang | AdSit

6 Very quirky and strange. It is not one story line but rather five unrelated short stories, each set in a different place in the world, each about different things, but each is a little slice of life revolving around cab drivers and their fares. Incidents occur in Los Angeles, New York, Rome, Paris and Helsinki. Never a laugh riot but occasionally causes a chuckle. Interesting in the sort of way that watching people at the airport can sometimes be fun. Subtitles. Strange, best appreciated by film fans.

A: Gena Rowlands, Winona Ryder, Rosie Perez, Roberto Benigni, Giancarlo Esposito, Armin Mueller-Stahl

© TURNER HOME ENTERTAINMENT N4196

NIGHT SHIFT

D: Ron Howard — 106 m

R | COM ROM | 1982 | COLOR | Sex | Nud | Viol | Lang | AdSit

8 Clever and engaging comedy from Ron Howard. A shy and subdued nerd (Winkler) takes a night job at the city morgue for the peace and quiet he expects to find there. But his crazy co-worker (Keaton) and a sweet next door neighbor, who is also a hooker (Long), talk him into making a little extra money by running an escort service out of the morgue. This is a situation that is ripe with opportunities for laughs, and they all get used. Winkler and Long were good, but Keaton was so successful in his first screen lead that it launched him into major stardom. Fun.

A: Henry Winkler, Michael Keaton, Shelley Long, Kevin Costner, Bobby DiCicco, Nita Talbot

© WARNER HOME VIDEO 20006

NIGHT THEY RAIDED MINSKY'S, THE

D: William Friedkin — 990 m

PG | COM | 1968 | COLOR | Sex | Nud | Viol | Lang | AdSit

7 Cute and flavorful depiction of the story of striptease in burlesque. Britt Ekland is a naive Amish girl who has come to the big city to dance on Broadway. Instead, she ends up stripping and falling in love with a vaudeville comic (Robards) - much to the embarrassment and disdain of her very proper father. Some funny situations, but mostly the film provides an interesting look at what vaudeville and burlesque were actually like (it wasn't just strippers), and contains a lot of the racy humor that they were known for. There are several intact burlesque comedy skits.

A: Jason Robards, Jr., Britt Ekland, Norman Wisdom, Forrest Tucker, Harry Andrews, Joseph Wiseman

Distributed By MGM/UA Home Video M202363

NORTH DALLAS FORTY

D: Ted Kotcheff — 119 m

R | COM DMA | 1979 | COLOR | Sex | Nud | Viol | Lang | AdSit

9 Outstanding sports-oriented comedy with serious underpinnings - not the typical sports story. Nolte is a nearly over-the-hill pro football player. He loves the game, the good times and feelings of comradery he shares with his teammates. But his seven years in the pros have also taught him that he is just another piece of equipment - to be used up until there is nothing left. Still, he is hooked on the excitement and the way of life. Funny. Great football action. It makes no difference whether you are a fan - you'll have a good time.

A: Nick Nolte, Charles Durning, Bo Svenson, Mac Davis, John Matuszak, Dabney Coleman

© PARAMOUNT HOME VIDEO 8773

NORTH TO ALASKA

D: Henry Hathaway — 117 m

NR | WST ACT COM | 1960 | COLOR | Sex | Nud | Viol | Lang | AdSit

9 Terrific good time in this light-hearted John Wayne Western. Wayne and Granger play turn-of-the-century Alaskan gold miners who strike it rich. Fabian is Granger's wet-behind-the-ears brother. Wayne goes to Seattle to pick up supplies and Granger's brand new mail-order bride. But when she is not there, Wayne "buys" saucy Capucine from a saloon and takes her back. Soon Granger and Wayne are both vying for her affections, as is young Fabian. Even while they're fighting each other, they're also fending off claim-jumpers lead by Kovacs. Great, fast-moving, tongue-in-cheek, fun.

A: John Wayne, Stewart Granger, Ernie Kovacs, Fabian, Capucine, Mickey Shaughnessy

© FOXVIDEO 1212

NOTHING IN COMMON

D: Garry Marshall — 119 m

PG | COM DMA | 1986 | COLOR | Sex | Nud | Viol | Lang | AdSit

8 Touching, funny and entertaining. Tom Hanks is a fun-loving and totally irresponsible advertising hotshot who is forced to grow up suddenly when his parents separate after 34 years of marriage. Now the tables are switched and both have become dependent upon HIM for emotional support - this, when he never before had to be responsible for anything or to anybody. He reluctantly becomes his mother's closest confidant and also must provide encouragement to his aging, terrified father before a major operation, all while trying to help to mend their long-strained relationship.

A: Tom Hanks, Jackie Gleason, Eva Marie Saint, Bess Armstrong, Hector Elizondo, Barry Corbin

© HBO VIDEO TVR9960

NO TIME FOR SERGEANTS

D: Mervyn LeRoy — 119 m

NR | COM | 1958 | B&W | Sex | Nud | Viol | Lang | AdSit

9 Hilarious. Just basic goofball stuff, but very well done. This film marked Andy Griffith's first film role and launched his career. Will Stockdale (Griffith) is a simple mountain boy drafted into the Air Force and his simple ways are confused by his hard-pressed sergeant for dull-wittedness. Poor old good-natured Will can't seem to do anything right, but he keeps trying and his screw-ups drive everyone nuts. Very funny still. Don't expect any deep message, just a reeeal good time.

A: Andy Griffith, Myron McCormick, Nick Adams, Murray Hamilton, Don Knotts, Ed Begley

© WARNER HOME VIDEO 11195

NO WAY TO TREAT A LADY

D: Jack Smight — 108 m

NR | MYS SUS COM | 1968 | COLOR | Sex | Nud | Viol | Lang | AdSit

9 Terrific thriller that oddly also has a touch of comedy thrown in. Steiger puts in a dynamite performance as a demented and flamboyant killer. He is a transvestite who disguises himself as different people and then kills - but only dowdy older women, strangling them and leaving a gaudy red kiss on each victim. George Segal is an overly-mothered NY cop determined to find the killer. Segal's chief witness is Lee Remick, and he falls for her. Steiger keeps close tabs on the investigation and enjoys teasing Segal with clues. He also repeatedly taunts Segal with phone calls indicating that Remick may be next. Very well done.

A: Rod Steiger, Lee Remick, George Segal, Eileen Heckart, Murray Hamilton, Michael Dunn

© PARAMOUNT HOME VIDEO 6724

NUNS ON THE RUN

D: Jonathan Lynn — 94 m

PG-13 | COM | 1990 | COLOR | Sex | Nud | Viol | Lang | AdSit

7 A marvelously funny comic performance from Coltrane, who elevates this unimaginative premise above its apparent promise. He and Idle are a pair of lower echelon punks who decide to steal the proceeds of a bank heist from their partners and escape to South America. But their plans go awry and they are forced to take cover inside a convent, "concealing" their true identities under nun's habits. Lots of unexpected problems, like a priest who tries to grope one of them, and a drunken nun who likes to bet big. Lots of good-natured laughs.

A: Eric Idle, Robbie Coltrane, Tom Hickey, Doris Hare, Robert Patterson, Lila Kaye

© FOXVIDEO 1830

NUTTY PROFESSOR, THE

D: Jerry Lewis — 107 m

NR | COM | 1963 | COLOR

8 Jerry Lewis's most popular film. He directs himself in dual roles as the Jekyll and Hyde personalities hidden inside a super-shy, goofy-looking nerd of a college professor. Yearning for the love of beautiful student Stella Stevens, the professor creates a secret formula in his college lab which transforms the nerd into a suave but callous lady-killer (strangely similar in a cynical way, to his ex-partner, Dean Martin). Problems develop when the formula wears off at inopportune times.

Sex · Nud · Viol · Lang · AdSit

A: Jerry Lewis, Stella Stevens, Henry Gibson, Del Moore, Kathleen Freeman, Ned Flory

© PARAMOUNT HOME VIDEO 6712

OBJECT OF BEAUTY, THE

D: Michael Lindsay-Hogg — 105 m

R | COM ROM | 1991 | COLOR

8 A dark little love story - offbeat and intriguing. Malcovich and MacDowell, a once affluent couple, are now living way beyond their means. They get stuck in a posh hotel in London with a long-overdue hotel bill. Every day they are sinking deeper in debt, but they keep spending money they don't have and dodging hotel personnel. Malcovich finally suggests that they sell a rare and valuable sculpture that belongs to MacDowell, who refuses. So, when the little object turns up missing, each immediately suspects the other. An amusing test of love.

Sex · Nud · Viol · Lang · AdSit

A: John Malkovich, Andie MacDowell, Lolita Davidovich, Rudi Davies, Joss Ackland, Bill Paterson

© LIVE HOME VIDEO 68948

ODD COUPLE, THE

D: Gene Saks — 106 m

G | COM | 1968 | COLOR

10 Hugely popular, hilarious film that was taken from a Neil Simon comedy. Its success also launched a long-lived and very successful TV series of the same name. Felix and Oscar are poker buddies. Oscar is a divorced sportswriter and a slob of epic proportions. Felix is thrown out of his house and his marriage by his wife because of his obsessive neatness and quirky personality. Taking pity on Felix, Oscar lets him move in - creating a situation ripe with hilarious possibilities, none of which are missed. High quality everything. A scream!

Sex · Nud · Viol · Lang · AdSit

A: Jack Lemmon, Walter Matthau, John Fiedler, Herb Edelman, Monica Evans, Carole Shelley

© PARAMOUNT HOME VIDEO 8026

OH, GOD!

D: Carl Reiner — 98 m

PG | COM FAN | 1977 | COLOR

10 Wonderfully charming - and almost believable - story in which God creates a modern-day Moses in the form of a mild-mannered supermarket manager. George Burns is nearly perfect as God - or, at least, his version of God is one that is very appealing. John Denver is the manager, incredulous at his misfortune for having been chosen for such an unenviable job. However, everyone just thinks he is crazy and no one believes him.If God ever did come - this is exactly what you could expect the reaction to be. Inspired casting all around. Great entertainment!

Sex · Nud · Viol · Lang · AdSit

A: George Burns, John Denver, Teri Garr, Paul Sorvino, Ralph Bellamy, George Furth

© WARNER HOME VIDEO 1010

ON A CLEAR DAY YOU CAN SEE FOREVER

D: Vincente Minnelli — 129 m

G | MUS COM ROM | 1970 | COLOR

7 Entertaining and underrated. Barbra is a neurotic chain smoker who crashes a college class in hypnosis looking for a cure. Psychiatrist Yves Montand agrees to hypnotize her and is fascinated to discover that he has instead regressed her back into a former life - in 19th-century England. Intrigued by the woman he has found, he continues to hypnotize modern Barbra and soon falls in love with the intriguing woman from the past. However, modern Barbara thinks he is treating her smoking problem and she has fallen in love with him. Solid music and lush production.

Sex · Nud · Viol · Lang · AdSit

A: Barbra Streisand, Yves Montand, Bob Newhart, Larry Blyden, Simon Oakland, Jack Nicholson

© PARAMOUNT HOME VIDEO 6927

ONCE AROUND

D: Lasse Hallstrom — 114 m

R | ROM DMA COM | 1991 | COLOR

7 This movie is like getting wrapped up in a warm blanket on a freezing cold night. Dreyfuss is a super-salesman who sweeps a repressed Holly Hunter off her fee. He is annoying - but he is supposed to be. Hunter is strong emotionally - and she is not supposed to be. They are perfect for each other - but their family doesn't think so. Hunter is so tangled in family disapproval and so in love that she is extremely torn. The beauty of this one is that it is totally unpredictable, and charming, and irresistible, and very, very well acted.

Sex · Nud · Viol · Lang · AdSit

A: Richard Dreyfuss, Holly Hunter, Laura San Giacomo, Danny Aiello, Gena Rowlands, Roxanne Hart

© MCA/UNIVERSAL HOME VIDEO, INC. 81041

ONE FLEW OVER THE CUCKOO'S NEST

D: Milos Forman — 129 m

R | DMA COM | 1975 | COLOR

10 The first picture in 40 years to sweep all five top Academy Awards: Picture, Director, Actor, Actress and Screenplay. It is also a very entertaining and deeply moving film about a likable but unconventional and rebellious prisoner (Nicholson) who is transferred to a mental hospital. While there, much to the dismay of the establishment (in in the principal form of over-disciplined head nurse Rachet), this otherwise sane misfit rekindles a spirit of life in the other patients who have been beaten down by the system. A deeply moving story about the value of individual freedoms and diverse personalities. Must see.

Sex · Nud · Viol · Lang · AdSit

A: Jack Nicholson, Louise Fletcher, William Redfield, Danny DeVito, Christopher Lloyd, Scatman Crothers

© HBO VIDEO 1048

ONE, TWO, THREE

D: Billy Wilder — 110 m

NR | COM | 1961 | B&W

8 Winning fast-paced comedy that was James Cagney's last screen performance (until RAGTIME in 1981). He plays the manager of the Coca-Cola plant in West Berlin. He is in the middle of a promotional campaign when a state-side exec sends his empty-headed daughter to visit Germany and asks Cagney to look after her. All hell breaks loose when she slips over into East Germany and falls in love with a card-carrying, ardent Communist. And now there is a brand new little Commie on the way. Very funny.

Sex · Nud · Viol · Lang · AdSit

A: James Cagney, Horst Buchholz, Arlene Francis, Pamela Tiffin, Hans Lothar, Lilo Pulver

Distributed By MGM/UA Home Video M600882

ON GOLDEN POND

D: Mark Rydell — 105 m

PG | DMA COM | 1981 | COLOR

10 Big unexpected hit. Thoughtful, heartwarming and moving story of growing old and the reconciliation between a crotchety father and his alienated daughter. Winner of three Oscars: Actor (Fonda), Actress (Hepburn) and Screenplay. The daughter leaves her fiance's snotty son with her aging parents for the summer. The old man and the kid develop a relationship which teaches the kid to lighten up and the old man how to enjoy living again, to express love and to show his daughter the love she has long craved. Wonderful and uplifting. A real feel-good flick.

Sex · Nud · Viol · Lang · AdSit

A: Katharine Hepburn, Henry Fonda, Jane Fonda, Dabney Coleman, Doug McKeon, William Lanteau

© LIVE HOME VIDEO 27456

ONLY THE LONELY

D: Chris Columbus — 105 m

PG-13 | ROM COM | 1991 | COLOR

7 Sweet and sentimental little movie. John Candy is a 38-year-old Chicago cop who still lives with his widowed mother (Maureen O'Hara). She is a real piece of work who has opinions about everybody and everything and doesn't hesitate the share them. Ally Sheedy is a plain and painfully shy girl who graduated from beauty school but couldn't get a job, so she does the makeup on cadavers for her mortician father. John and Ally meet and fall in love, but Mom does her best to break them up. John loves this girl but is afraid of hurting Mom. This is sort of an update of 1955 Oscar winner MARTY. There are no Oscars here however, but it's nice.

Sex · Nud · Viol · Lang · AdSit

A: John Candy, Maureen O'Hara, Ally Sheedy, Anthony Quinn, James Belushi, Kevin Dunn

© FOXVIDEO 1877

ONLY TWO CAN PLAY

D: Sidney Gilliat — 106 m

NR | COM | 1962 | B&W

7 Would-be Lothario and low-level librarian Peter Sellers is bored and discouraged at living with an equally dispirited wife and two ornery kids in a run-down apartment. Looking for adventure and a major promotion, he responds to the amorous overtures from the sexy wife of a library board member. His repeated attempts to lustfully consummate their affair meet with constant comedic obstacles. Then the tables are totally turned on him when he discovers that his own wife is being pursued by a poet. Funny, but it helps to appreciate English humor.

Sex · Nud · Viol · Lang · AdSit

A: Peter Sellers, Virginia Maskell, Mai Zetterling, Richard Attenborough

© COLUMBIA TRISTAR HOME VIDEO 60725

ONLY WHEN I LAUGH

D: Glenn Jordan — 121 m

R | DMA COM | 1980 | COLOR

8 Bittersweet screenplay from Neil Simon. Marsha Mason is a has-been Broadway actress who has only just been released from a rehab clinic after three months treatment for alcoholism, when her 17-year-old daughter moves in with her after six years of living with her father. Mason must learn how to be a mother and friend all over again, even as she struggles to stay sober, get her career back on line and deal with a new love interest. Sometimes funny, sometimes sad, but always moving. Wonderful performances by everyone (three Oscar nominations). Heartwarming and entertaining, too.

Sex · Nud · Viol · Lang · AdSit

A: Marsha Mason, Kristy Mc Nichol, James Coco, Joan Hackett, David Dukes

© COLUMBIA TRISTAR HOME VIDEO 60079

OPERATION PETTICOAT

NR
COM ROM
1959
COLOR
Sex
Nud
Viol
Lang
AdSit

D: Blake Edwards 120 m

9 Hilarious and very popular comedy. Cary Grant is the captain of an unfortunate submarine which is beset by a never-ending series of embarrassing and very funny misfortunes in the South Pacific during World War II. The problems only begin when the sub must go to sea with the boat's paint job incomplete, leaving it pink. The problems are further compounded when first officer Curtis, a smooth-talking con man, squeezes five beautiful nurses into the sub. The stage is now set for some of Hollywood's biggest talents to work their comedic magic, and they do. Really funny. A great time.

A: Cary Grant, Tony Curtis, Gene Evans, Dina Merrill, Arthur O'Connell, Gavin MacLeod

© REPUBLIC PICTURES HOME VIDEO 5405

OPPOSITE SEX, THE

NR
MUS COM
1956
COLOR
Sex
Nud
Viol
Lang
AdSit

D: David Miller 117 m

7 This is the musical remake of the 1939 witty comedy THE WOMEN written by Clare Booth Luce. It is the story of a bunch of spoiled Park Avenue women discussing the basic licentious nature of men, while plotting to help one of their number (Allyson) to regain her husband from a floozy by teaching her the fine arts of backstabbing and gossip. Fun musical excursion, but also be sure to see the very funny 1939 original. Songs include: "A Perfect Love," "Jungle Red" and "Young Man with a Horn."

A: June Allyson, Joan Collins, Joan Blondell, Ann Miller, Agnes Moorehead

Distributed By MGM/UA Home Video M202134

OTHER PEOPLE'S MONEY

R
ROM COM
1992
COLOR
Sex
Nud
Viol
Lang
AdSit

D: Norman Jewison 101 m

7 This video is hard to classify. It is not a ha-ha comedy, a oh-ah romance, nor is it a drama. It is the sophisticated story of a nearly-despicable, cute and clever corporate raider Larry the Liquidator (DeVito), who's only lover is his computer, Carmen. Carmen has discovered a cash-rich cable and wire company. Because its industry is dying, its stock value is way below its salvage value. The old-line owner Gregory Peck refuses to liquidate, so Larry begins a hostile takeover. Peck counters by sending in a pretty but hard-as-nails corporate lawyer in as his attack dog. Larry has met his match. He is in love, but even love will not pull him off the scent of blood.

A: Danny DeVito, Gregory Peck, Penelope Ann Miller, Piper Laurie, Dean Jones, Tom Aldredge

© WARNER HOME VIDEO 12223

OUR MAN FLINT

NR
ACT COM
1966
COLOR
Sex
Nud
Viol
Lang
AdSit

D: Daniel Mann 107 m

6 Outlandish James Bond spoof. Coburn is superagent Derek Flint from Z.O.W.I.E. who is sent to protect the world from a plot by the evil organization GALAXY and its top agent, the super seductive Gila Golan. GALAXY and its scientists are plotting to overtake and control the world's weather. It is up to superstud Flint to defeat them... but he does have the use of his special lighter that has 83 different uses, including: a blow torch, a derringer, a dart gun and a 2-way radio. Spectacular tongue-in-cheek spoof.

A: James Coburn, Lee J. Cobb, Gila Golan, Edward Mulhare, Benson Fong, Shelby Grant

© FOXVIDEO 1131

OUTLAW BLUES

PG
COM
1977
COLOR
Sex
Nud
Viol
Lang
AdSit

D: Richard T. Heffron 101 m

7 Light-weight little comedy about a struggling country music song writer and ex-con (Fonda) who becomes a national folk hero. Years earlier he had one of his songs stolen from him. It then became a big hit and it made the thief (Callahan) famous. Now, in a confrontation with Callahan, Fonda accidentally shoots him and becomes the focus of statewide manhunt. His backup singer (Susan St. James) helps him hide out on the run, while she promotes his new song into a big hit for him. Pleasant and appealing no-brainer.

A: Peter Fonda, Susan St. James, James Callahan, John Crawford

© WARNER HOME VIDEO 11146

OUT-OF-TOWNERS, THE

G
COM
1970
COLOR
Sex
Nud
Viol
Lang
AdSit

D: Arthur Hiller 98 m

6 Successful adaptation of a Neil Simon screenplay about a Midwestern couple (Lemmon and Dennis) who come to the Big Apple for a job interview for Lemmon. They decide to also make it a romantic vacation, but their luggage gets lost, their hotel room reservations have been canceled, and they are mugged and hijacked. Just about everything that can go wrong does. Fast-paced with plenty of laughs, but uncomfortable and exasperating, too.

A: Jack Lemmon, Sandy Dennis, Anne Meara, Sandy Baron, Ron Carey, Billy Dee Williams

© PARAMOUNT HOME VIDEO 6914

OUTRAGEOUS FORTUNE

R
COM
1987
COLOR
Sex
Nud
Viol
Lang
AdSit

D: Arthur Hiller 99 m

8 Entertaining female-buddy flick, with two very unlikely buddies. Midler is brassy, rude and earthy. Long is a Yale grad, interested in refined beauty and art. Both are struggling actresses and are shocked to discover that they both have, or had, the same lover - and that he was a secret agent. Neither believes their Romeo is actually dead from an explosion, so they join forces and launch themselves into a hilarious cross-country search to find him, with both the KGB and the CIA in their wake.

A: Bette Midler, Shelley Long, George Carlin, Peter Coyote, Robert Prosky, John Schuck

© TOUCHSTONE HOME VIDEO 569

OVERBOARD

PG
COM ROM
1987
COLOR
Sex
Nud
Viol
Lang
AdSit

D: Garry Marshall 112 m

8 Clever, light-weight entertainment. Goldie Hawn is a spoiled and arrogant heiress who refuses to pay a carpenter (Russell) for a job. When he sees on the evening news that she has been found suffering from total amnesia, floating in the ocean (she fell from her yacht) - he sees a way both to get even with her and find a much-needed mother for his untamed kids. So he claims her from the authorities as his wife, and she - confused and not knowing any better - sets about taking up her new chores as mother. Good-natured and fun.

A: Goldie Hawn, Kurt Russell, Katherine Helmond, Edward Herrmann, Roddy McDowall, Michael Haggerty

Distributed By MGM/UA Home Video M201197

OWL AND THE PUSSYCAT, THE

PG
COM ROM
1970
COLOR
Sex
Nud
Viol
Lang
AdSit

D: Herbert Ross 95 m

8 Highly entertaining adaptation of a hit broadway comedy. In her first non-singing role, Streisand plays a kooky part-time model and sometime hooker living next door to a snooty book clerk, would-be writer and full-time snob (Segal). These two just cannot get along - barbs and insults fly back and forth, but love's sparks also fly between them. When he complains to the building's management about her late-night antics, she is expelled but manages to con her way into becoming his roommate. Zany, funny and sometimes hilarious.

A: Barbra Streisand, George Segal, Robert Klein, Allen Garfield, Roz Kelly

© COLUMBIA TRISTAR HOME VIDEO 60081

PAINT YOUR WAGON

PG
MUS COM WST
1970
COLOR
Sex
Nud
Viol
Lang
AdSit

D: Joshua Logan 164 m

9 A rousing good time with this fun-filled, Lerner and Loewe musical/Western/comedy set in the fictional gold-rich/women-poor California mining boom town of No-Name City in the mid-1800s. Two partners in a gold "mine" (Eastwood and Marvin mine the gold that falls through the floors at the saloons) purchase one of a Mormon traveler's extra wives (Seberg), and... they share her - all of her - 50/50. Clever and funny. Plus, some truly great music ("They Call the Wind Maria") that is only slightly diminished by Marvin's and Eastwood's singing.

A: Clint Eastwood, Lee Marvin, Jean Seberg, Harve Presnell, John Mitchum, Ray Walston

© PARAMOUNT HOME VIDEO 6933

PAJAMA GAME, THE

NR
MUS COM ROM
1957
COLOR
Sex
Nud
Viol
Lang
AdSit

D: George Abbott 102 m

8 Exuberant and enjoyable Hollywood conversion (largely intact) of the very successful Broadway play. Doris Day plays the head of the union's grievance committee at a pajama factory. She is heading up the charge to demand a 7 1/2 cent per hour pay raise. She must negotiate with the plant's foreman (Raitt) to get it, but love gets in the way. Light-hearted fun. Great songs and inventive Bob Fosse choreography. Songs include: "Hernando's Hideaway," "Hey There" and the big hit "Steam Heat."

A: Doris Day, John Raitt, Carol Haney, Eddie Foy, Jr., Reta Shaw

© WARNER HOME VIDEO 35085

PAL JOEY

NR
MUS COM
1957
COLOR
Sex
Nud
Viol
Lang
AdSit

D: George Sidney 109 m

8 Fun-filled and very entertaining, with a wonderful Rodgers and Hart score including 14 wonderful songs - many now classics themselves. The story is a pretty good one, too, about a brash heel of a singer (Sinatra) who wants to open a fancy nightclub. Rita Hayworth is a sexy, wealthy socialite who could be his ticket but she wants him to give up his love for Kim Novak. Songs include: "My Funny Valentine," "Bewitched Bothered and Bewildered" and "The Lady is a Tramp." Enjoyable.

A: Frank Sinatra, Rita Hayworth, Kim Novak, Bobby Sherwood, Elizabeth Patterson, Barbara Nichols

© COLUMBIA TRISTAR HOME VIDEO 60798

PAPA'S DELICATE CONDITION

D: George Marshall 98 m

NR | COM DMA | 1963 | COLOR

7 Pleasant light-hearted drama set in turn-of-the-century Texas. The setting evokes nostalgic feelings for a time past and the mood is light-hearted, but the subject has a serious overtone. Papa (Jackie Gleason) is a fun-loving railroader and the apple of his daughter's eye, but he is also a drunk and an embarrassment to his wife (Glynnis Johns). One day she packs up the kids and walks out. Gleason is quite charming in this enjoyable little story that also won an Oscar for Best Song: "Call Me Irresponsible."

Sex / Nud / Viol / Lang / AdSit

A: Jackie Gleason, Glynis Johns, Charlie Ruggles, Laurel Goodwin, Charles Lane, Elisha Cook, Jr.

© PARAMOUNT HOME VIDEO 6212

PAPER, THE

D: Ron Howard 112 m

R | DMA COM | 1994 | COLOR

7 A frenetic day in the life of a newspaper, in this case a New York scandal sheet called "The Sun." Michael Keaton is the metro editor and he loves his job. But: His wife is very pregnant and feeling left out of the newspaper world she had to leave behind. He has been made another offer by another paper and has to decide today. He missed out on the big story yesterday, but he thinks he has an even better one for today. He and paranoid columnist Randy Quaid are struggling to get that story by deadline, but he is in a battle with Glenn Close, an administrator who used to be a reporter but is now a bean counter, and she is fighting him on the deadline for his story. Fun, but a little overdone in places.

Sex / Nud / Viol / Lang / AdSit

A: Michael Keaton, Glenn Close, Marisa Tomei, Randy Quaid, Robert Duvall, Jason Alexander

© MCA/UNIVERSAL HOME VIDEO, INC. 82005

PAPER CHASE, THE

D: James Bridges 111 m

PG | DMA COM | 1973 | COLOR

9 Highly acclaimed and engrossing character study that spawned a TV series and a lot of other attention, too. Timothy Bottoms stars as a brilliant law student in his first year of law at Harvard. He is apparently in constant conflict with his extremely demanding and contentious law professor (Houseman). Houseman seems determined to make his life miserable. However, life becomes even more intense when Bottoms discovers that his new girl friend is also Houseman's daughter. Brilliant acting all around. Houseman won an Oscar and became a star.

Sex / Nud / Viol / Lang / AdSit

A: Timothy Bottoms, Lindsay Wagner, John Houseman, Graham Beckel, Craig Richard Nelson, Edward Herrmann

© FOXVIDEO 1046

PAPER MOON

D: Peter Bogdanovich 102 m

PG | COM | 1973 | B&W

9 Heart-warming and totally captivating story of a 1930s con-man (O'Neal) who agrees to drive the precocious, charming and worldly-wise 9-year-old daughter (his real-life daughter Tatum) of a dead former "girlfriend" to her aunt in Missouri. Along the way, he poses as a door-to-door Bible salesman and he is pleased to find that his cigarette-smoking young charge is very adept at helping him to charm widows out of their money. She's a natural. They are a happy family until they are joined by a wacky carny stripper (Kahn). A very colorful and funny film that is great fun, with loveable characters.

Sex / Nud / Viol / Lang / AdSit

A: Ryan O'Neal, Tatum O'Neal, Madeline Kahn, John Hillerman, P.J. Johnson, Randy Quaid

© PARAMOUNT HOME VIDEO 8465

PARENTHOOD

D: Ron Howard 124 m

PG-13 | COM DMA | 1989 | COLOR

8 Very popular and funny comedy about the joys and pitfalls of modern-day child rearing. At the center of all the mayhem is Steve Martin, a middle-aged father, who is trying to save his career while also coping with his neurotic eight-year old. His ex-hippie sister has got two problem teenagers and his neighbors are trying to raise their three-year-old to be a super-genius. Meanwhile, Martin's Dad is struggling with his own feelings of failure at raising another son who's an irresponsible gambler, deep in financial trouble. A bundle of laughs that rings true to life. A treat!

Sex / Nud / Viol / Lang / AdSit

A: Steve Martin, Jason Robards, Jr., Mary Steenburgen, Rick Moranis, Tom Hulce, Dianne Wiest

© MCA/UNIVERSAL HOME VIDEO, INC. 80921

PARENT TRAP, THE

D: David Swift 129 m

NR | COM CLD | 1961 | COLOR

9 Hugely popular Disney hit for the whole family. A prissy teenage girl from Boston runs into her spitting image in the form of a tomboy from California, at summer camp. The two mix like oil and water, at first. However, when they begin to compare notes, they discover that they are identical twins separated when their parents had divorced years before. Mom went east and Dad went west. The two decide to switch places at summer's end so each can meet the other parent and to begin a conspiracy designed to bring their still single parents back together again. Good fun for everyone. Hayley Mills is delightful.

Sex / Nud / Viol / Lang / AdSit

A: Hayley Mills, Maureen O'Hara, Brian Keith, Charlie Ruggles, Leo G. Carroll, Joanna Barnes

© WALT DISNEY HOME VIDEO 107

PARTY, THE

D: Blake Edwards 99 m

NR | COM | 1968 | COLOR

7 Hysterical sight gags frequent one of Peter Sellers's best (some think his best) and funniest work. You do, however, need to be a fan of absolute silliness. He plays a bumbling, dense actor who accidentally destroys an entire movie set, and he is fired for it. However, he is also mistakenly invited to a lavish party that evening at the director's extravagant house, and he wanders through the party inadvertently creating havoc wherever he goes. The movie begins to fall apart during the last third, but still great fun.

Sex / Nud / Viol / Lang / AdSit

A: Peter Sellers, Claudine Longet, Marge Champion, Denny Miller, Gavin MacLeod

Distributed By MGM/UA Home Video M201584

PASSED AWAY

D: Charlie Peters 97 m

PG-13 | COM DMA | 1992 | COLOR

6 Mildly likable and semi-interesting black comedy that explores the revelations of a colorful and contentious Irish family, reunited at the funeral of the family's patriarch (Warden). Dad had a heart attack and died when his nit-wit pretty-boy son literally scared him to death with a surprise welcome-back party after a stay in the hospital. In the family there is: an older tree-surgeon brother (Hoskins), who is dealing with his mid-life crisis; a sister, who is an activist nun hiding an illegal alien from the feds; a rebellious dancer sister (Reed); and, a mysterious strange other woman friend of Dad's. Interesting premise, with a good cast.

Sex / Nud / Viol / Lang / AdSit

A: Bob Hoskins, Blair Brown, Tim Curry, Frances McDormand, William L. Petersen, Pamela Reed

© HOLLYWOOD PICTURES HOME VIDEO 1453

PATERNITY

D: David Steinberg 94 m

PG | COM ROM | 1981 | COLOR

6 Pleasant and diverting light comedy about a generally happy and successful 44-year-old bachelor (Reynolds) who decides that he wants a baby, but he doesn't want a wife. So he strikes a bargain with a struggling musician and waitress (D'Angelo) to bear his child - no strings attached. Sure! Things start to get interesting when she starts to fall for him. Not a lot of big laughs, but it is a good time - particularly if you are a Reynolds fan.

Sex / Nud / Viol / Lang / AdSit

A: Burt Reynolds, Beverly D'Angelo, Norman Fell, Elizabeth Ashley

© PARAMOUNT HOME VIDEO 1401

PEGGY SUE GOT MARRIED

D: Francis Ford Coppola 103 m

PG-13 | COM ROM FAN | 1986 | COLOR

9 Provocative and thoroughly enjoyable adult fairy tale. Turner is a 43-year-old woman with two kids, who is separated and nearing divorce from her pitchman husband and high-school sweetheart. Then, when she is crowned queen at her 25th class reunion, she suddenly faints and is magically transported back to being 18 years old all over again. She has all the same experiences and opportunities as she did then, but this time she has the benefit of having 25 more years experience to make her decisions. Will she do again what she did then? Inventive and well acted.

Sex / Nud / Viol / Lang / AdSit

A: Kathleen Turner, Nicolas Cage, Barry Miller, Catherine Hicks, Maureen O'Sullivan, John Carradine

© CBS/FOX VIDEO 3800

PERSONAL SERVICES

D: Terry Jones 104 m

R | COM | 1987 | COLOR

8 Naughty English comedy, based upon the life of a real person. Cynthia Paine was a waitress who also managed apartments occupied by prostitutes. On one occasion when she is short her own rent, she takes a lesson from her tenants and trades sexual favors for her rent... and a new career is born. First she becomes a call girl, but eventually madam to one of Britain's kinkiest brothels. When it is discovered that her clientele includes some of England's biggest leaders and even some clergy members, she becomes a national sensation. Very blunt and forthright, scandalous and very funny.

Sex / Nud / Viol / Lang / AdSit

A: Terry Jones, Julie Walters, Alec McCowen, Danny Schiller, Shirley Stelfox

© LIVE HOME VIDEO 5221

PETER'S FRIENDS

D: Kenneth Branagh 102 m

NR | COM DMA | 1993 | COLOR

6 Sort of an English version of THE BIG CHILL. Peter has just inherited his father's estates and he has decided to call a ten-year reunion of college friends. They all arrive at Christmas time, but each has brought with him his own set of personal problems. Almost from the start, things go very badly. As time progresses, things get progressively worse. Just when all seems to be lost, Peter announces that the reason he has called them together is that he has HIV. In light of that overwhelmingly bad news, all the other problems begin to diminish in importance and the group can again recover old friendships. Slow.

Sex / Nud / Viol / Lang / AdSit

A: Emma Thompson, Kenneth Branagh, Stephen Fry, Rita Rudner, Alphonsia Emmanuel, Tony Slattery

© HBO VIDEO 90832

PETE 'N' TILLIE

D: Martin Ritt 100 m

PG

DMA COM

1972 COLOR

Sex / Nud / Viol / Lang / AdSit

6 Diverting little serio-comedy that works most of the time. Matthau plays a middle-aged wise-cracking market researcher. Burnett is a woman fast approaching spinsterhood. Lonely and tired of being alone, they have an affair, marry and have a child. But their world is turned upside down when the child is found to be dying. Matthau loses his hold on their relationship, has a series of affairs and their marriage is in deep trouble. Interesting in many ways and usually entertaining - but the mixed signals hurt it some.

A: Walter Matthau, Carol Burnett, Geraldine Page, Rene Auberjonois

© MCA/UNIVERSAL HOME VIDEO, INC. 80404

PETULIA

D: Richard Lester 105 m

R

DMA COM

1968 COLOR

Sex / Nud / Viol / Lang / AdSit

8 Highly regarded by the critics and serious movie fans as being one of the social hallmark films of the 1960s. This is the story of a prominent middle-aged doctor (Scott) who is getting divorced after many years of marriage. He finds himself tossed into a tumultuous relationship with a screwed-up, beautiful, kookie and frustrated young socialite (Christie) who has been married for only 6 months. Their bittersweet romance is designed to be an analogy for the turmoil and confusion of the late '60s. Superb cast. Dated now and a little too vague for most casual observers.

A: Julie Christie, George C. Scott, Richard Chamberlain, Arthur Hill, Shirley Knight, Joseph Cotten

© WARNER HOME VIDEO 11092

PILLOW TALK

D: Michael Gordon 103 m

NR

COM ROM

1959 COLOR

Sex / Nud / Viol / Lang / AdSit

9 Highly entertaining comedy that marked the first pairing of Rock Hudson and Doris Day. A huge box office hit that received five Oscar nominations - winning for Screenplay. Doris is an interior designer who shares a telephone line with Rock, a romeo playboy who is forever on the prowl for a new notch on his bedpost. She despises him for his insincere plotting and tells him so. But, she has never seen him so, when they finally meet, he pretends to be a gentlemanly Texan to charm and then seduce her. Instead, he falls in love with her - only to be scorned when he is discovered. Great supporting cast. A real winner.

A: Rock Hudson, Doris Day, Tony Randall, Thelma Ritter, Nick Adams, Julia Meade

© MCA/UNIVERSAL HOME VIDEO, INC. 55122

PINK CADILLAC

D: Buddy Van Horn 121 m

PG-13

COM ACT

1989 COLOR

Sex / Nud / Viol / Lang / AdSit

6 Light-hearted Eastwood outing where he gets to pull out a bunch of his old characters and use them as he needs them. He plays skip-tracer Tommy Nowak who specializes in tracing down bail jumpers. But Tommy gets more than he bargained for when he chases down Bernadette Peters. She has skipped in a stolen pink Caddy, with a trunk full of counterfeit bills, and her eight-month-old baby. She is on the run from her husband's white supremist friends who want her, the Caddy and the money. Clint uses all sorts of disguises to con their way out of the mess.

A: Clint Eastwood, Bernadette Peters, Timothy Carhart, Tiffany Gale Robinson, John Dennis Johnston, Geoffrey Lewis

© WARNER HOME VIDEO 11877

PINK PANTHER, THE

D: Blake Edwards 121 m

NR

COM

1964 COLOR

Sex / Nud / Viol / Lang / AdSit

9 Hysterical debut of the riotously inept French police inspector Jacques Clouseau (Sellers). The bumbling inspector has set his sights on capturing the dapper and notorious jewel thief "The Phantom." So intent is he that he fails to notice that the Phantom is also his wife's lover. Loaded with slapstick. It also marked the introduction of the animated cartoon character of the same name. Spawned six more sequels, followed immediately by A SHOT IN THE DARK, which many credit as being even funnier than the original.

A: Peter Sellers, David Niven, Capucine, Robert Wagner, Claudia Cardinale, Brenda de Banzie

Distributed By MGM/UA Home Video M203849

PINK PANTHER STRIKES AGAIN, THE

D: Blake Edwards 104 m

PG

COM

1976 COLOR

Sex / Nud / Viol / Lang / AdSit

8 Riotous fifth adventure of the bumbling French police inspector Clouseau. This time Clouseau's now insane supervisor (Lom) escapes from the asylum to which he has been confined. He commandeers a ray gun and threatens the city with total destruction if Clouseau is not destroyed. He has also hired a team of international killers to hunt Clouseau down. One of them, Lesley-Anne Down falls in love with the bumbler. Filled with the lots of slapstick and pain oriented jokes. Followed by REVENGE OF THE PINK PANTHER.

A: Peter Sellers, Herbert Lom, Colin Blakely, Leonard Rossiter, Lesley-Anne Down, Burt Kwouk

Distributed By MGM/UA Home Video M200252

PIRATES OF PENZANCE, THE

D: Wilford Leach 112 m

G

MUS COM

1983 COLOR

Sex / Nud / Viol / Lang / AdSit

7 Gilbert and Sullivan's perennial favorite comic-musical for the stage is given a good go on the screen (with most of the Broadway cast intact), but the use of very stylized sets and staged camera spectacles, reminiscent of Busby Berkely, will put off many reality-based filmgoers. Yet the story of an honest young man trapped into being a pirate and in love with the daughter of a Major General is still funny. The lyrics and score are simply wonderful. An impressive effort, but Ronstadt sings better than she acts.

A: Kevin Kline, Angela Lansbury, Linda Ronstadt, George Rose, Rex Smith, Tony Azito

© MCA/UNIVERSAL HOME VIDEO, INC. 71012

PLANES, TRAINS AND AUTOMOBILES

D: John Hughes 93 m

R

COM

1987 COLOR

Sex / Nud / Viol / Lang / AdSit

7 This amiable farce pits an uptight New York advertising executive (Martin) against a boisterously oafish, but good-natured, shower curtain salesman (Candy). Both are in a desperate race to get home to Chicago for Thanksgiving, but with their airplane flights indefinitely delayed, they opt to join forces and find alternate transportation - any kind of transportation. And so begins a series of preposterous disasters, one right after another. Through it all, the mismatched pair find a common bond at the finish line. Good fun for fans of these two comics.

A: Steve Martin, John Candy, Kevin Bacon, Michael McKean, William Windom, Dylan Baker

© PARAMOUNT HOME VIDEO 32036

PLAY IT AGAIN, SAM

D: Herbert Ross 85 m

PG

COM ROM

1972 COLOR

Sex / Nud / Viol / Lang / AdSit

8 Entertaining and different Woody Allen comedy that is more conventional than most of his films. Here he plays an insecure film critic, lost in his world of movies and suffering from recurring visits from the ghost of Humphrey Bogart - who is constantly giving him advice. When his bored wife divorces him to seek some adventure, Woody repeatedly fumbles in his attempts to meet new women. Even the assistance of his best friend (Roberts) fails. He simply can't say the right things... except, that is, to Diane, his best friend's wife. A funny movie that is also for non-Allen fans.

A: Woody Allen, Diane Keaton, Susan Anspach, Tony Roberts, Jerry Lacy, Jennifer Salt

© PARAMOUNT HOME VIDEO 8112

PLAZA SUITE

D: Arthur Hiller 114 m

PG

COM

1971 COLOR

Sex / Nud / Viol / Lang / AdSit

7 Pleasing Niel Simon collection of three comic vignettes, all of which occur in the same suite at New York City's exclusive Plaza Hotel and with comic veteran Walter Matthau playing all the male roles. 1) Stapleton and Matthau rent a room while the paint dries at home. Matthau is having an affair with his secretary. 2) Matthau is in town for a short time and calls up an old girlfriend who is married, bored and feeling guilty, and he tries to seduce her. 3) Matthau's young bride-to-be daughter locks herself in the bathroom and won't come out.

A: Walter Matthau, Maureen Stapleton, Barbara Harris, Lee Grant, Louise Sorel, Jenny Sullivan

© PARAMOUNT HOME VIDEO 8046

PLEASE DON'T EAT THE DAISIES

D: Charles Walters 112 m

NR

COM

1960 COLOR

Sex / Nud / Viol / Lang / AdSit

8 Bright and amiable family fare. David Niven and Doris Day have four kids. They leave their big city apartment to set up housekeeping in a big old house in the country when he begins a new job as a drama critic. And so begins not one storyline but a series of entertaining escapades: The big-city family learns to adjust to the country life. Doris struggles to renovate their house and deal with the P.T.A. David attempts to deal with an irate actress who he has panned in a review and a persistent cabbie who has a new script that he wants David to look at. Light-hearted farce.

A: David Niven, Doris Day, Janis Paige, Spring Byington, Richard Haydn, Jack Weston

Distributed By MGM/UA Home Video M201301

PLOT AGAINST HARRY, THE

D: Michael Roemer 81 m

NR

COM

1969 B&W

Sex / Nud / Viol / Lang / AdSit

7 This gem was made and then not released until 20 years later. Poor Harry. He's a small-time Jewish numbers banker in NYC who was sent up the river. Now he's out but the whole world has changed. He and his not-too-bright sidekick try to get his business back from an ex-employee who stole it. But in the process, they literally run into his tiger of an ex-wife, who also has their daughters in tow. He even tries to go straight at the urging of his relatives, but that doesn't work either. He just doesn't fit anywhere. A very funny previously unseen time capsule from the '60s. It was not released then because no one thought it would sell. They were wrong.

A: Martin Priest, Ben Lang, Maxine Woods, Henry Nemo

© NEW YORKER FILMS NYV00291

POCKETFUL OF MIRACLES

D: Frank Capra 137 m

NR | COM DMA | 1961 | COLOR

7 Sentimental favorite from Frank Capra. Bette Davis is delightful as Apple Annie, an old woman living in poverty, selling apples to support herself and her daughter who's away in boarding school. She spends everything on her daughter, who thinks her mother is wealthy and now is coming to visit. Annie is scared. Glenn Ford plays a soft-hearted crook who lines up a bunch of his toughguy friends to help Apple Annie convince her visiting daughter, and her rich fiance, that Annie is really a lady. This is Capra's own remake of his 1933 hit LADY FOR A DAY. Pleasing supersweet diversion. Ann-Margret's film debut.

Sex Nud Viol Lang AdSit

A: Bette Davis, Glenn Ford, Hope Lange, Arthur O'Connell, Peter Falk, Jack Elam

Distributed By MGM/UA Home Video M203855

POLICE ACADEMY

D: Hugh Wilson 96 m

R | COM | 1984 | COLOR

8 A surprise trash smash! The mayor of a large city waives the entrance requirements into the police academy and all sorts of social misfits join the ranks hoping for some really good partying. Officer Bailey does his best to make their lives miserable, but the misfits decide that they really do want to become officers in blue. Comic lunacy abounds in this sometimes funny, often tasteless and definitely outrageous popular comedy that was followed by five equally tasteless and outrageous sequels.

Sex Nud Viol Lang AdSit

A: Steve Guttenberg, Kim Cattrall, G.W. Bailey, Bubba Smith, Michael Winslow, Andrew Rubin

© WARNER HOME VIDEO 20016

POPEYE

D: Robert Altman 114 m

PG | COM CLD MUS | 1980 | COLOR

6 Curious live-action version of the famous cartoon character. Not a wonderful musical, but not too bad, either. It is an imaginative staging and production with some really wonderful characterizations from Duvall and especially Williams. All the famous characters are here. Popeye (Williams) rows into port looking for his pappy (Walston). He falls in love with skinny Olive (Duvall), even though she is engaged to Bluto (Smith). Interesting and clever. It was unfairly ignored at the box office by an audience that didn't know quite what how to take it. A good family movie.

Sex Nud Viol Lang AdSit

A: Robin Williams, Shelley Duvall, Ray Walston, Linda Hunt, Paul L. Smith, Paul Dooley

© PARAMOUNT HOME VIDEO 1171

PORKY'S

D: Bob Clark 99 m

R | COM | 1981 | COLOR

8 Monumental box office hit that is really little more than one long dirty joke. The story is of a bunch of 1950s Florida high school guys who sneak peaks at the girls in the showers at school and struggle mightily to lose their virginity. Their quest leads them to Porky's, a sleazy bar across the county line that is infamous for its loose women. Their arrival is met by abuse from the local bad-boy sheriff (Alex Karras), who is also Porky's brother. They are ripped off and thrown out, but the boys get their revenge. Loads of sex jokes and off-color humor.

Sex Nud Viol Lang AdSit

A: Dan Monahan, Wyatt Knight, Mark Herrier, Roger Wilson, Kim Cattrall, Alex Karras

© CBS/FOX VIDEO 1149

POSTCARDS FROM THE EDGE

D: Mike Nichols 101 m

R | COM DMA | 1990 | COLOR

8 Savvy, sophisticated, slick and brazenly funny. Streep is the drugged-out actress whose drug habit lands her in the detox center. Plagued with the feeling that she will forever be in her mother's shadow, she has turned to alternate evils for security. But her trouble starts afresh when the only way she can now get a job in Hollywood is to live in the "protective" care of that same overly-competitive mother. Her mother (MacLaine) was once a Hollywood glamour queen but has now become a domineering, alcoholic meddler. The conflict between these two is great entertainment. Based on Carrie Fisher's autobiographical novel.

Sex Nud Viol Lang AdSit

A: Meryl Streep, Shirley MacLaine, Dennis Quaid, Rob Reiner, Gene Hackman, Richard Dreyfuss

© COLUMBIA TRISTAR HOME VIDEO 50553

POWWOW HIGHWAY

D: Jonathan Wacks 91 m

R | COM | 1988 | COLOR

6 Satisfying buddy movie and a curious character study of a couple of unusual characters, two Northern Cheyenne Indians. The younger is a very intense Indian activist whose sister has been arrested in New Mexico. So he and his very large, amiable and slower moving friend set out in a beat-up Buick named Protector to free her. But the big man takes them there his way - by way of the Dakotas, because he is on a "Medicine trip." The trip is an adventure and a learning experience for both of them. They learn a lot about each other and we learn something, too. Clever and insightful, but unusual.

Sex Nud Viol Lang AdSit

A: A. Martinez, Gary Farmer, Amanda Wyss, Joanelle Romero, Sam Vlaos, Wayne Waterman

© CANNON VIDEO 31068

PRESIDENT'S ANALYST, THE

D: Theodore J. Flicker 100 m

NR | COM | 1967 | COLOR

7 Wild satire about a psychiatrist who is the President's secret shrink, but who gets fed up with the pressures of the job and just quits. However, he quickly discovers that is not an easy thing to do, because he immediately becomes the subject of an intense amount of interest by a horde of foreign spies, and the subject of a paranoia-induced frenzy in half the government's self-serving agencies. Totally wacky satire that attempts to skewer every sacred cow in its path.

Sex Nud Viol Lang AdSit

A: James Coburn, Godfrey Cambridge, Severn Darden, Pat Harrington, William Daniels, Will Geer

© PARAMOUNT HOME VIDEO 6716

PRETTY IN PINK

D: Howard Deutch 96 m

PG-13 | ROM COM | 1986 | COLOR

8 Effervescent, witty and disarmingly rich teenage comedy. A very bright but poor girl (Ringwald), from the wrong side of the tracks, and a rich boy (McCarthy) fall for each other. He asks her to the Senior Prom and their teen-age society erupts with the scandal. Can their romance survive all of the peer pressure? Their friends are doing everything to keep them apart, including Ringwald's pal Cryer (who is also in love with her). Some touching, funny and very tender moments fuse beautifully in this sparkling coming-of-age film. Good score, too.

Sex Nud Viol Lang AdSit

A: Molly Ringwald, Andrew McCarthy, Harry Dean Stanton, Jon Cryer, James Spader, Annie Potts

© PARAMOUNT HOME VIDEO 1858

PRETTY WOMAN

D: Garry Marshall 119 m

R | ROM COM | 1990 | COLOR

9 Endearing romantic Cinderella charmer. Gere is a hard-hearted corporate raider with no time for a meaningful relationship. Abandoned by his girlfriend, he meets pretty woman and street walker Julia Roberts - who charms him into buying an evening's entertainment. So charmed is he with her impishness that he also hires her to spend the entire week. Slowly his heart is melted by the hooker-with-a-heart, and her week with him opens up a whole new world for her... but what happens then? Extremely entertaining, sentimental favorite that was a massive popular hit.

Sex Nud Viol Lang AdSit

A: Julia Roberts, Richard Gere, Jason Alexander, Ralph Bellamy, Laura San Giacomo, Hector Elizondo

© TOUCHSTONE HOME VIDEO 1027

PRINCESS BRIDE, THE

D: Rob Reiner 98 m

PG | COM ROM FAN | 1987 | COLOR

7 Heroic fairy tale fantasy, designed for both young and old! A sick boy's grandfather (Falk) comes to read to him, promising him a story of monsters, fights, beasts, and, yes, a dose of romance, too. In the extravagant and adventurous story which comes to life on screen, a beautiful princess and a stableboy fall in love but are soon separated, and the evil king has her kidnapped so he can force her to marry him. Suddenly, a strange man in a mask appears poised to do battle for her. This brilliant adaptation of the whimsical cult novel comes alive at the hands of Rob Reiner.

Sex Nud Viol Lang AdSit

A: Peter Falk, Mandy Patinkin, Carol Kane, Billy Crystal, Chris Sarandon, Cary Elwes

© NEW LINE HOME VIDEO 7709

PRISONER OF SECOND AVENUE, THE

D: Melvin Frank 98 m

PG | DMA COM | 1975 | COLOR

8 A bittersweet reality-based quasi-comedy from Neil Simon. Jack Lemmon is hassled 48-year-old New Yorker who has received the unwelcome news that his position at a faltering ad agency has been eliminated. He is destroyed and reacts with a nervous breakdown. His loving, rock-solid and supportive wife Anne Bancroft has found work to support them while he has blackly comic bouts with obnoxious neighbors, intrusive relatives and shrink who really doesn't care. This is an odd blending of tragedy, melancholy and comedy that only Simon can carry off so well. Billed as a comedy but the neurosis is too real to laugh for long.

Sex Nud Viol Lang AdSit

A: Jack Lemmon, Anne Bancroft, M. Emmet Walsh, Gene Saks, Elizabeth Wilson, Florence Stanley

© WARNER HOME VIDEO 1035

PRISONER OF ZENDA, THE

D: Richard Quine 108 m

PG | COM | 1979 | COLOR

6 Comedic take off on the famous 1937 swashbuckling action movie of the same name. However, here Peter Sellers plays a Cockney cab driver who has been enlisted into being a look-alike stand-in for the endangered prince of the mythical nation of Ruritainia, after he is threatened with assassination by his evil half-brother. Things get further confused when the cabby falls for the prince's fiancee. This is a funny movie that didn't get much critical acclaim. It will be most enjoyed by fans of the zany, mix-up type comedies and by Peter Sellers fans.

Sex Nud Viol Lang AdSit

A: Peter Sellers, Lynne Frederick, Lionel Jeffries, Elke Sommer, Gregory Sierra, Jeremy Kemp

© MCA/UNIVERSAL HOME VIDEO, INC. 66057

PRIVATE BENJAMIN

D: Howard Zieff 110 m

R | COM | 1980 | COLOR

9 A clever and bubbly comedy, hilarious in spots, that was a big, big box office hit and also received three Oscar nominations. Spoiled little rich girl Goldie Hawn is severely depressed when her brand new, second husband croaks on their wedding night. A scheming army recruiter convinces her that a stint in the army is just what she needs... it'll be just like a vacation... it isn't. Great fun when the spoiled rich kid has to discover how to deal with things on her own, without a safety net and for the first time in her life. Really entertaining.

Sex / Nud / Viol / Lang / AdSit

A: Goldie Hawn, Eileen Brennan, Albert Brooks, Armand Assante, Robert Webber, Sam Wanamaker

© WARNER HOME VIDEO 11075

PRIVATE FUNCTION, A

D: Malcolm Mowbray 96 m

R | COM | 1985 | COLOR

7 Very British satiric comedy. Set in post-war England, amidst the severe rationing of the period, and upon the occasion of the wedding of Princess Elizabeth to Prince Phillip. The gentry of a small community wishes to celebrate the marriage and so they have raised a contraband pig to be roasted at their private banquet. Palin is a wimpy and henpecked podiatrist who has a social-climber for a wife. So intent is she upon throwing their own party, that she coerces him into pignapping the main course. Caution: very droll, very British.

Sex / Nud / Viol / Lang / AdSit

A: Maggie Smith, Michael Palin, Denholm Elliott, Liz Smith, Richard Griffiths, Tony Haygarth

© PARAMOUNT HOME VIDEO 12998

PRIZZI'S HONOR

D: John Huston 130 m

R | COM CRM SUS | 1985 | COLOR

9 Devilishly delicious black comedy. Nicholson is a Mafia hit man for the Prizzi family. He becomes fascinated with a sexy mystery woman (Turner), who turns out to be a free-lance hitter, too. But things become greatly complicated for them when it turns out she has stolen some of the family's money and he gets an order to kill her. Nicholson's loyalties are severely tested: should he hit her, or marry her. Now that he is no longer trustworthy, the family hires her to hit him. Terrific performances, witty dialogue, fascinating plotting. Eight Oscar nominations.

Sex / Nud / Viol / Lang / AdSit

A: Jack Nicholson, Kathleen Turner, Anjelica Huston, John Randolph, William Hickey, Robert Loggia

© LIVE HOME VIDEO 5106

PRODUCERS, THE

D: Mel Brooks 90 m

NR | COM MUS | 1968 | COLOR

9 Hysterical farce from Mel Brooks. This, his first film, won him an Oscar for Best Screenplay and he also directed. It is about a shyster promoter (Mostel) who cons a meek accountant (Wilder) into helping him with a terrific get-rich-quick scheme. They will sell interests in a new (and very bad) Broadway play ("Springtime for Hitler") which they will produce... but they will sell 25 times more shares than are available. Then when the thing flops, they will take all the extra money to Rio with them. But when it becomes a big hit instead, they are in big-time trouble.

Sex / Nud / Viol / Lang / AdSit

A: Zero Mostel, Gene Wilder, Dick Shawn, Kenneth Mars, Lee Meredith, Christopher Hewett

© NEW LINE HOME VIDEO 2051

PROTOCOL

D: Herbert Ross 96 m

PG | COM | 1984 | COLOR

7 Pleasant, but highly contrived, movie in which a bubble-headed waitress (Goldie Hawn) inadvertently foils an assassination plot against an Arab Potentate. She becomes an overnight hero and is awarded a job in the State Protocol Department, but quickly becomes a pawn in games of state. Simple Goldie rises to the challenge and transforms herself into a meaningful person. Light-hearted, frivolous entertainment that was made for Goldie and is more than a little like her character in PRIVATE BENJAMIN. Likable.

Sex / Nud / Viol / Lang / AdSit

A: Goldie Hawn, Chris Sarandon, Gail Strickland, Cliff De Young, Richard Romanus, Ed Begley, Jr.

© WARNER HOME VIDEO 11434

PULP

D: Mike Hodges 95 m

PG | SUS COM | 1972 | COLOR

6 Pretty good spoof thriller. Michael Caine is a hack writer from Hollywood who is hired by a retired film star (Rooney), to ghost write his autobiography. Rooney made his name playing gangsters and now lives in Italy. Caine travels to Italy and begins his interviews of Rooney, but they are cut short when Rooney is murdered. Now someone is apparently after Caine, too. Maybe Rooney was so good at playing gangsters because he wasn't acting after all.

Sex / Nud / Viol / Lang / AdSit

A: Michael Caine, Mickey Rooney, Lionel Stander, Lizabeth Scott, Nadia Cassini, Al Lettieri

© WOOD KNAPP VIDEO 1025

PUNCHLINE

D: David Seltzer 123 m

R | DMA COM | 1988 | COLOR

6 Interesting curiosity of a movie about comedians struggling to master their craft in the face of real-life worries. Tom Hanks plays a medical student who is caustic and a failure in his life, but a natural comedian and a hit in the clubs. Sally Field is a wife and mother who desperately wants to be a comedienne. She struggles daily to balance home responsibilities with the pleasure/pain of performing with only mild success. Hanks and Field are friends drawn together by their pain. She helps him to hold together and he helps to punch up her act. Well acted.

Sex / Nud / Viol / Lang / AdSit

A: Tom Hanks, Sally Field, John Goodman, Mark Rydell, Pam Matteson, Kim Greist

© COLUMBIA TRISTAR HOME VIDEO 65010

PURPLE ROSE OF CAIRO, THE

D: Woody Allen 84 m

PG | COM FAN | 1985 | COLOR

8 Inventive bittersweet fantasy treat for Woody Allen fans and most others, too. Mia Farrow has a gloomy existence. She is a Depression-era waitress married to an unemployed bully. Her only escape and joy is the movies. One day, upon her fifth viewing of her favorite soaper, the handsome lead steps down off the screen and into her life. But the character's sudden absence from the film causes chaos on the screen. Seeking to find out what happened, the actor who plays the character, visits her and also falls in love with her.

Sex / Nud / Viol / Lang / AdSit

A: Mia Farrow, Jeff Daniels, Danny Aiello, Edward Herrmann, John Wood, Dianne Weist

© LIVE HOME VIDEO VA5068

Q

D: Larry Cohen 92 m

R | HOR COM | 1982 | COLOR

6 Campy, gory, creature feature with a sense of humor. Manhattan is being terrorized by a giant winged lizard-beast that is swooping down from the huge skyscrapers and brutally killing New Yorkers. Window washers go up, but come down without their heads. When crazy Moriarty uncovers the location of the gruesome creature's nest - the Chrysler Building - the small-time crook decides to cash in and holds the city for ransom. Tongue-in-cheek humor and cheesy acting adds to the fun of this giant monster horror movie.

Sex / Nud / Viol / Lang / AdSit

A: David Carradine, Richard Roundtree, Michael Moriarty, Candy Clark, Malachy McCourt

© MCA/UNIVERSAL HOME VIDEO, INC. 71017

QUEEN OF HEARTS

D: Jon Amiel 112 m

PG | COM ROM | 1989 | COLOR

8 Warm and endearing jewel. Rosa and Danilo are young Italian lovers who elope after WWII to London because Rosa has been promised to marry the wealthy butcher, Barbariccia. After twenty happy years of marriage, four children and making a good life with their restaurant, Barbariccia arrives in London to spoil it. He has become the owner of several gambling houses and has won everything Danilo has in a card game. However, the family has arranged a "sting" to get all their money back and get rid of Barbariccia in the process. Witty and funny. Mostly in English, some subtitles.

Sex / Nud / Viol / Lang / AdSit

A: Anita Zagaria, Joseph Long, Eileen Way, Vittorio Duse, Vittorio Amandola, Tat Whalley

© MCEG/STERLING 70188

QUEEN'S LOGIC

D: Steve Rash 116 m

R | DMA COM | 1991 | COLOR

7 Offbeat and slow to develop, but some interesting moments that make this worthwhile for the thoughtful viewer. Five buddies who grew up together in the Queens borough of NYC get together when one of them is about to be married... or will he? His imminent wedding has become a time for a reevaluation of everything by everyone. Olin's not sure that he should get married. Mantegna is on the outs with his wife. Kevin Bacon is a failed Hollywood musician. Malkovich is a homosexual who doesn't like homosexuals. Eventually interesting, but it takes a while to get the characters straight and to understand them.

Sex / Nud / Viol / Lang / AdSit

A: Kevin Bacon, Linda Fiorentino, John Malkovich, Joe Mantegna, Ken Olin, Tony Spiridakis

© LIVE HOME VIDEO 68923

QUICK CHANGE

D: Bill Murray, Howard Franklin 89 m

R | COM CRM | 1990 | COLOR

7 After staging what could have been the perfect bank robbery, three New Yorkers attempt to get out of the city and hop a plane headed for the South Pacific. Unfortunately, almost everything that can go wrong does, and Murray, Davis and Quaid barely manage to stay one step ahead of the police on their calamity-filled trek to the airport. This is a film that could be cliched and predictable, but it is not. It is surprisingly funny and sports some outstanding slapstick and sight gags.

Sex / Nud / Viol / Lang / AdSit

A: Bill Murray, Geena Davis, Randy Quaid, Jason Robards, Jr., Bob Elliott, Philip Bosco

© WARNER HOME VIDEO 12004

COM

RACING WITH THE MOON

D: Richard Benjamin 108 m

PG | ROM COM | 1984 | COLOR | Sex ◢ | Nud ◢ | Viol ☐ | Lang ◢ | AdSit ◢

7 Touching, entertaining and nostalgic look back. Two young men (Penn and Cage) are about to be sent off to the Marines during WWII and decide to make the most of their last few weeks together in 1942. Penn is a young man from common roots who falls for who he thinks is a rich girl. Emboldened by his imminent departure, he chases her, not knowing that she is a maid's daughter. Meanwhile, his buddy has gotten a girl pregnant, so Penn enlists his new girl's help in raising the necessary $150. Touching and sweet film. Highly likable, a reminder of lost innocence.

A: Sean Penn, Nicolas Cage, Elizabeth McGovern, John Karlen, Rutanya Alda, Carol Kane

© PARAMOUNT HOME VIDEO 1668

RADIO DAYS

D: Woody Allen 96 m

PG | COM DMA | 1986 | COLOR | Sex ☐ | Nud ◢ | Viol ☐ | Lang ◢ | AdSit ◢

7 Witty and sentimental tribute to the pre-television era. Radio then was filled with much more than just music and talk. In the 1940s, it was also theater and entertainment, and people tuned in regularly to intently follow the radio legends. In the Queens, a young boy and his eccentric extended family listen with rapt attention to this other world. It is the world they all aspire to; however, their dream world is not what they have envisioned. The Masked Avenger is really short and bald and the charming talk show host is just a playboy. Critically acclaimed as one of Allen's best films.

A: Mia Farrow, Seth Green, Julie Kavner, Josh Mostel, Michael Tucker, Diane Keaton

© HBO VIDEO 0014

RADIOLAND MURDERS

D: Mel Smith 108 m

PG | COM | 1994 | COLOR | Sex ☐ | Nud ☐ | Viol ☐ | Lang ☐ | AdSit ◢

6 Frenetic slap-stick comedy not that far removed from what you would expect from the Three Stooges. Loaded with a cast of prominent stars in cameo roles, this is the story of the antics going on behind the scenes of a live radio broadcast for a new network in 1939. Behind the scenes everything is going wrong. The sponsors have demanded that the entire script be rewritten at the last minute. The writers haven't been paid in weeks. The director is romancing the manager's wife. The head writer is trying to win back his wife, the show's assistant manager. And both he and she are trying to solve some very real murders that started about as soon as the show did. Very goofy and not for everyone.

A: Brian Benben, Ned Beatty, George Burns, Brion James, Michael Lerner

© MCA/UNIVERSAL HOME VIDEO, INC. 82206

RAIN MAN

D: Barry Levinson 134 m

R | DMA COM | 1988 | COLOR | Sex ☐ | Nud ☐ | Viol ☐ | Lang ■ | AdSit ■

9 An exceptional lesson in humanity! Cocky super-salesman Cruise goes home to his father's funeral hoping the expected inheritance will save his fledgling car business. Instead he discovers that he has an autistic savant brother (Hoffman) - kept a secret from him his whole life - who's inherited most of Dad's estate. Cruise nabs Hoffman and takes him on a cross-country odyssey, hoping to get a bigger share. Except, quite unexpectedly, the brothers forge a deep bond. Hoffman's outstanding performance was an Oscar-winner, and the film won for Best Picture, Director and Screenplay.

A: Dustin Hoffman, Tom Cruise, Valeria Golino, Jerry Molden, Jack Murdock, Michael Roberts

Distributed By MGM/UA Home Video M901648

RAISING ARIZONA

D: Joel Coen 94 m

PG-13 | COM | 1987 | COLOR | Sex ☐ | Nud ☐ | Viol ◢ | Lang ◢ | AdSit ■

6 Very different, almost bizarre, film. Cage is a petty crook with a compulsion to hold up convenience stores. He is arrested so many times that he and the police photographer (Hunter) fall in love and get married. They discover that she can't have kids and, because of his record, they can't adopt - so they decide to steal one of the quintuplets born to a wealthy dealer in unfinished furniture. Thereafter begins a series of disasters and car chases. Very offbeat and fast-paced. If you like your comedies bizarre, add 1 to rating.

A: Nicolas Cage, Holly Hunter, John Goodman, William Forsythe, Trey Wilson

© FOXVIDEO 5191

RAMBLING ROSE

D: Martha Coolidge 115 m

R | DMA COM | 1991 | COLOR | Sex ■ | Nud ◢ | Viol ☐ | Lang ◢ | AdSit ■

8 Delightful and quite different. Set in a small Southern town during the depression years, Robert Duvall and his family take in an orphan girl as a domestic, but she quickly becomes much more. Rose is very likable, full of life and energy, totally without guile and highly-sexed. She quickly adopts this family as her own - almost too literally. She looks upon the children as peers, the mother as a kindred spirit and upon Duvall with a very undaughterly kind of love. Rose, in fact, is a pathetic creature in desperate need of love and she sets out to find it with other men. Sensitive portrait, very well done.

A: Laura Dern, Diane Ladd, Robert Duvall, Lukas Haas

© LIVE HOME VIDEO 69000

RANCHO DELUXE

D: Frank Perry 93 m

R | COM WST | 1975 | COLOR | Sex ◢ | Nud ◢ | Viol ☐ | Lang ■ | AdSit ■

8 Quirky modern-day Western. Two listless, fun-lovin', ne'r-do-well, part-time cowboys and cattle rustlers decide to have fun by pestering a bored but rich cattleman who bought his huge ranch with the profits from a chain of beauty parlors. These two are so lazy that their modus operandi is to cut up the dead animals with a chain saw. Their coup de grace comes when they kidnap his prize bull and hold it for ransom, keeping it inside a motel room. A lot of fun and always good-natured, but underlying it all is a sense of pity for the cast of listless characters, because all of them are really only wasting their time in life.

A: Jeff Bridges, Sam Waterston, Elizabeth Ashley, Charlene Dallas, Clifton James, Slim Pickens

Distributed By MGM/UA Home Video 202643

READY TO WEAR

D: Robert Altman 133 m

R | COM | 1995 | COLOR | Sex ◢ | Nud ■ | Viol ◢ | Lang ■ | AdSit ■

6 Director Robert Altman again gathered together a mammoth collection of Hollywood stars to populate this supposed satirical send-up of the fashion industry. All the beautiful people are converging upon Paris for the season when all the pretentious fashion designers are about to tell all the world's women how they are to look. The film weaves together dozens of stories over the course of one week...stories of petty jealousies, private passions, neurotic egotistical people and skinny models, and it is all held together by the thread of Kim Basinger as a pseudo-important reporter who interviews them all. Got very mixed to poor reaction from viewers. Recommended for sophisticated and pseudo-sophisticated viewers only.

A: Sophia Loren, Marcello Mastroianni, Kim Basinger, Forest Whitaker, Tim Robbins, Julia Roberts

© MIRAMAX HOME ENTERTAINMENT 4438

REAL GENIUS

D: Martha Coolidge 106 m

PG | COM | 1985 | COLOR | Sex ☐ | Nud ☐ | Viol ☐ | Lang ◢ | AdSit ◢

7 Fast-paced and involving teen-comedy! A young genius (Jarret) enrolls at Pacific Tech and is recruited to join the school's think tank whose brilliant members are working on a laser project. They are led by unethical professor Atherton, who is really building a secret death weapon for the US Government. The guys live a carefree life and party hearty, but when Jarret and his fellow team members learn of the truth, they formulate an elaborate scheme to thwart the plan of their corrupt professor. Full of college highjinks and sex jokes.

A: Val Kilmer, Gabe Jarret, Michelle Meyrink, William Atherton, Jonathan Gries, Patti D'Arbanville

© COLUMBIA TRISTAR HOME VIDEO 60568

REALITY BITES

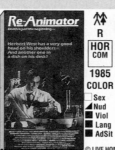

D: Ben Stiller 99 m

PG-13 | DMA COM | 1994 | COLOR | Sex ☐ | Nud ☐ | Viol ☐ | Lang ◢ | AdSit ■

6 This is an attempt to define the characteristics of Generation X, or the children of the children of the '60s. However, since this group does not have any singular philosophically defining characteristics or direction, neither does this movie. Winona Ryder and her friends have just graduated from college and are caught up in a sort of listless drift and a lot of TV trivia. Winona spends her time videotaping her friends while working as a flunky at a TV station, her roommate has been promoted to store manager and her neo-beatnik almost-boyfriend (Ethan Hawk) leads a grunge band. But, she is also seeing a young executive. What will become of her?

A: Winona Ryder, Ethan Hawk, Ben Stiller, Janeane Garolalo, Steve Zahn, Swoosie Kurtz

© MCA/UNIVERSAL HOME VIDEO, INC. 81929

RE-ANIMATOR

D: Stuart Gordon 86 m

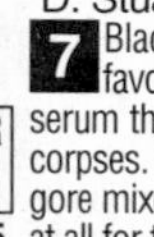

R | HOR COM | 1985 | COLOR | Sex ☐ | Nud ◢ | Viol ■ | Lang ■ | AdSit ■

7 Black humor in a chilling horror film that has become a cult favorite! When a medical student (Combs) discovers a magical serum that can bring the dead back to life, he uses it. He re-animates corpses. But when they come alive, they are extremely violent. Classic gore mixes with modern special effects to produce results that are not at all for the faint at heart. The video cassette version contains violence removed from the screen version that was so grizzly that it had caused the R rating to be revoked. Very, very dark.

A: Jeffrey Combs, Bruce Abbott, Barbara Crampton, David Gale, Robert Sampson

© LIVE HOME VIDEO VA5136

RED HEAT

D: Walter Hill 106 m

R | ACT COM | 1988 | COLOR | Sex ☐ | Nud ◢ | Viol ■ | Lang ■ | AdSit ◢

6 Unrelenting modern-day shoot-'em-up! Schwarzenegger is a tough and highly disciplined Russian detective who is sent to the United States to nab a Russian drug kingpin (O'Ross). When the druglord escapes Schwarzenegger's tight grip, Arnold pairs up with an obnoxious, lackadaisical Chicago cop (Belushi). Completely different in style, attitude and method, Schwarzenegger and Belushi clash in the biggest way, but eventually have a meeting of the minds and track down O'Ross through the tough streets of Chicago. Rough and sometimes funny!

A: Arnold Schwarzenegger, James Belushi, Peter Boyle, Ed O'Ross, Larry Fishburne, Gina Gershon

© LIVE HOME VIDEO 66057

REIVERS, THE

NR | DMA COM | 1969 | COLOR | Sex Nud Viol Lang AdSit

D: Mark Rydell — 107 m

9 Absolutely wonderful and delightful tale taken from William Faulkner. It is the story of the innocent 12-year-old son of a wealthy Mississippian who begins to grow up during the summer of 1905. While his family is away, he is charmed by two fun-loving, but scurrilous, rogues (McQueen and Crosse) into "borrowing" his granddaddy's brand new automobile for a grandly adventurous trip to far away Memphis. There, he will spend the night in a bordello, while McQueen visits his girlfriend and as Crosse schemes to trade the new automobile for a race horse, which he then plans to race to win the car back. This is a sentimental charmer, a real winner and a lot of fun.

A: Steve McQueen, Sharon Farrell, Will Geer, Michael Constantine, Rupert Crosse, Mitch Vogel

© CBS/FOX VIDEO 7153

REUBEN, REUBEN

R | COM ROM | 1983 | COLOR | Sex Nud Viol Lang AdSit

D: Robert Ellis Miller — 100 m

7 Offbeat sophisticated and witty comedy. Conti is wonderful as a British poet with terminal writer's block. He is also a charming freeloader, who lives by the bottle and makes a game of seducing women. When the Brit is transplanted to Connecticut, he lectures on the college circuit to make ends meet, but there he falls for a beautiful young farm girl student (McGillis) and he struggles mightily turn himself around in hopes of winning her over. Witty and sophisticated, this comedy was adapted from the novel by Peter DeVires. Two Oscar nominations. Certainly not typical movie fair and perhaps not for all tastes.

A: Tom Conti, Kelly McGillis, Cynthia Harris, Joel Fabiani, Roberts Blossom, E. Katherine Kerr

© CBS/FOX VIDEO 1435

RELUCTANT DEBUTANTE, THE

NR | COM | 1958 | COLOR | Sex Nud Viol Lang AdSit

D: Vincente Minnelli — 97 m

6 Lively and refreshing comedy. The on- (and off) screen husband and wife team (Harrison and Kendall) are making elaborate preparations to present their daughter (Sandra Dee) to society. It's the social season in London, where promising seventeen-year-olds take part in lavish balls specially designed for the momentous occasion. Unfortunately, Harrison's Americanized daughter (by another marriage) is quickly bored by English etiquette and tradition and instead takes up with a bad boy American drummer (Saxon). Sprightly and fun.

A: Rex Harrison, Kay Kendall, John Saxon, Sandra Dee, Angela Lansbury

Distributed By MGM/UA Home Video M202364

REVENGE OF THE NERDS

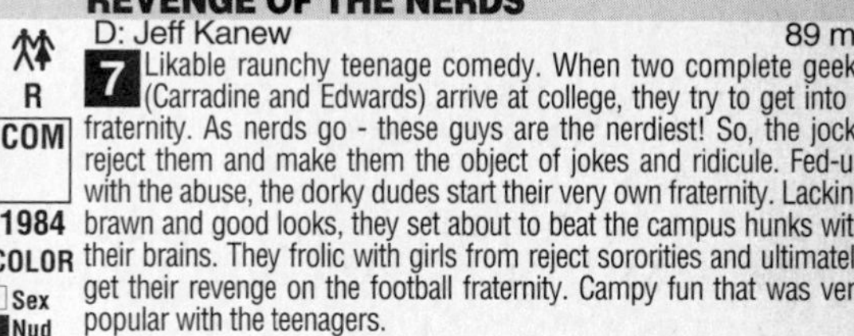

R | COM | 1984 | COLOR | Sex Nud Viol Lang AdSit

D: Jeff Kanew — 89 m

7 Likable raunchy teenage comedy. When two complete geeks (Carradine and Edwards) arrive at college, they try to get into a fraternity. As nerds go - these guys are the nerdiest! So, the jocks reject them and make them the object of jokes and ridicule. Fed-up with the abuse, the dorky dudes start their very own fraternity. Lacking brawn and good looks, they set about to beat the campus hunks with their brains. They frolic with girls from reject sororities and ultimately get their revenge on the football fraternity. Campy fun that was very popular with the teenagers.

A: Robert Carradine, Anthony Edwards, Julie Montgomery, Curtis Armstrong, Ted McGinley, Michelle Meyrink

© FOXVIDEO 1439

RENAISSANCE MAN

PG-13 | COM DMA | 1994 | COLOR | Sex Nud Viol Lang AdSit

D: Penny Marshall — 138 m

6 Danny DeVito is a former top-flight ad-writer, but now he's all washed up. Just fired from his last job and in desperate need of money, he agrees to take a civilian teaching position at an Army base. His job - teach the dumbest of the dumb. Reluctant Danny was not thrilled about teaching anyway, but this is way more than he bargained for. But, these troops have nowhere else to go and he is determined to reach them. In order to do it, he has to first get his student's attention, and he has to fight his non-Army ways - which place him in constant conflict with devoted drill sergeant Gregory Hines. Well-meaning time-killer, upbeat and occasionally has some funny stuff.

A: Danny DeVito, Gregory Hines, James Remar, Ed Begley, Jr., Lillo Brancato, Jr., Stacey Dash

© TOUCHSTONE HOME VIDEO 2754

REVENGE OF THE PINK PANTHER, THE

PG | COM | 1972 | COLOR | Sex Nud Viol Lang AdSit

D: Blake Edwards — 100 m

7 The bumbling Inspector Clouseau is at it again. When the French Inspector (Sellers) is tipped off that he is to be killed, he foils the assassination attempt, but pretends to be dead. Ditzy but resourceful, he hopes to be able to find his would-be killer if he can remain incognito. This means that he appears in a never-ending series of disguises. His search leads him to Hong Kong, where he attempts to break up the heroin ring of his would-be assassin. As in the others of the series, this also contains a series of pratfalls and slapstick jokes. The last in the series by Sellers.

A: Peter Sellers, Herbert Lom, Dyan Cannon, Robert Webber, Burt Kwouk, Robert Loggia

Distributed By MGM/UA Home Video M201448

REPO MAN

R | COM ACT | 1983 | COLOR | Sex Nud Viol Lang AdSit

D: Alex Cox — 93 m

6 Quirky and peculiar comedy. An L.A. punkrocker (Estevez) takes a seedy job repossessing cars from owners who fall delinquent on their payments. His slimy mentor (Stanton) is an expert at the art of repo and takes the young punk under his wing, teaching him the ropes. However things get zany when they take back a vintage Chevy Malibu worth $20,000 and they find that the trunk is also stuffed full of radioactive aliens! An offbeat and often weird movie that is not for every taste, but if you're searching for something different - this is definitely it.

A: Harry Dean Stanton, Emilio Estevez, Vonetta McGee, Olivia Barash, Sy Richardson, Tracey Walter

© MCA/UNIVERSAL HOME VIDEO, INC. 80071

RICHARD PRYOR HERE AND NOW

R | COM | 1983 | COLOR | Sex Nud Viol Lang AdSit

D: Richard Pryor — 83 m

6 Filmed live on Bourbon Street in New Orleans, this is Pryor's fourth and probably worst live concert. Still, Pryor's outlandish comedy is very much in evidence; however, only his most devoted fans will wait through the rest to find it. Included here for his fans only.

A: Richard Pryor

© COLUMBIA TRISTAR HOME VIDEO VH10468

RETURN OF THE LIVING DEAD, THE

R | HOR COM | 1985 | COLOR | Sex Nud Viol Lang AdSit

D: Dan O'Bannon — 86 m

7 A terrifying horror flick that you can laugh at too! Part fright, part funny. It takes up where NIGHT OF THE LIVING DEAD left off. When medical supply workers (James Karen and Thom Mathews) unwittingly release some poisonous gas from sealed drums, the vapors enliven several corpses in a small New Orleans town. Dead for years, these bodies wake up starving - hungry for human brains. The plentiful humor does not diminish the nail-biting gore splattered throughout. Acting is well-done with special effects that are outrageously sick. Not for those with sensitive stomachs.

A: Clu Gulager, James Karen, Don Calfa, Thom Mathews, Linnea Quigley

© HBO VIDEO TVA3395

RICHARD PRYOR - LIVE AND SMOKIN'

NR | COM | 1971 | COLOR | Sex Nud Viol Lang AdSit

D: Michael Blum — 45 m

6 Richard Pryor fans only. He performs live at New York City's Improvisation. There are some very, very funny moments, but Pryor is extremely vulgar. Included is his famous skit, "Wino and the Junkie."

A: Richard Pryor

© LIVE HOME VIDEO 3075

RETURN OF THE PINK PANTHER

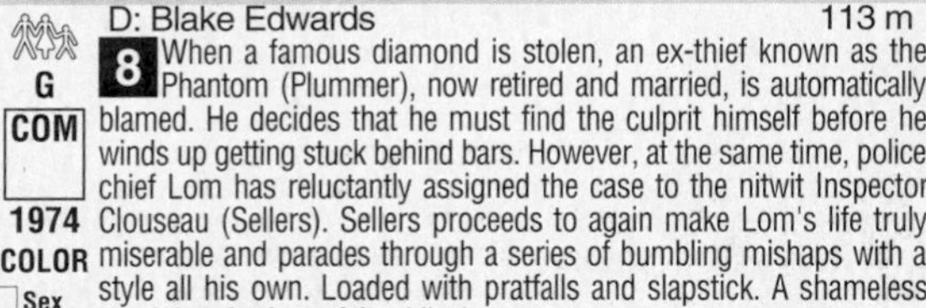

G | COM | 1974 | COLOR | Sex Nud Viol Lang AdSit

D: Blake Edwards — 113 m

8 When a famous diamond is stolen, an ex-thief known as the Phantom (Plummer), now retired and married, is automatically blamed. He decides that he must find the culprit himself before he winds up getting stuck behind bars. However, at the same time, police chief Lom has reluctantly assigned the case to the nitwit Inspector Clouseau (Sellers). Sellers proceeds to again make Lom's life truly miserable and parades through a series of bumbling mishaps with a style all his own. Loaded with pratfalls and slapstick. A shameless good time for fans of the ridiculous.

A: Peter Sellers, Christopher Plummer, Catherine Schell, Herbert Lom, Burt Kwouk, Peter Arne

© LIVE HOME VIDEO 27480

RICHARD PRYOR - LIVE IN CONCERT

NR | COM | 1979 | COLOR | Sex Nud Viol Lang AdSit

D: Jeff Margolis — 78 m

8 This is the first, and widely recognized as the best, of his recorded concert films. Filmed live in Long Beach, California. Uncensored, this is pretty blue material, but it is also hilarious. He speaks of being arrested for shooting his car, of his heart attack and of when his grandmother caught him with cocaine.

A: Richard Pryor

© LIVE HOME VIDEO 4000

RICHARD PRYOR LIVE ON SUNSET STRIP

D: Joe Layton 82 m

R | COM | 1982 | COLOR

7 Pryor's hilarious comments on Africa, lawyers, sex and the time when he set himself on fire while freebasing cocaine are all spliced together from two separate concerts at the Hollywood Palladium. Prior's comedy is caustic, hilarious, oddly moving and always very blue - both profane and vulgar.

Sex / Nud / Viol / Lang / AdSit

A: Richard Pryor

© GOODTIMES 4237

RIKKY AND PETE

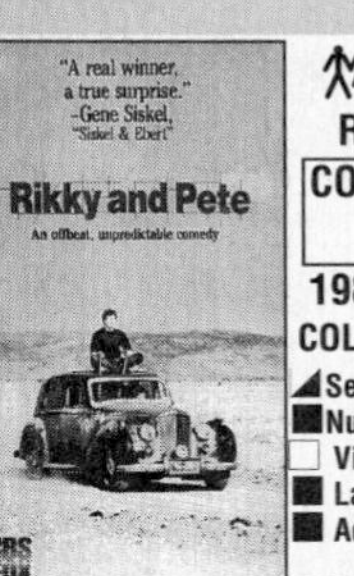

D: Nadia Tass 103 m

R | COM | 1988 | COLOR

6 Delightful but quirky import from Australia, a sequel to MALCOLM. Rikki and Pete are an oddball brother and sister couple. Rikki is a geologist and part-time folk singer. Pete is a weird mechanical genius who invents Rube Goldberg-type devices. Trying to duck a policeman who is out to get Pete for a stunt he pulled, the two head out into the Australian Outback. They wind up in a small mining town full of all kinds of other oddball characters. Somewhat disorganized and hard to follow, but also fun and chock full of "gross-out" slapstick jokes.

Sex / Nud / Viol / Lang / AdSit

A: Nina Landis, Stephen Kearney, Tetchie Agbayani, Bill Hunter

© CBS/FOX VIDEO 4750

RIO BRAVO

D: Howard Hawks 141 m

NR | WST ACT COM | 1959 | COLOR

10 Exuberant Western with Wayne as the classic tough-guy sheriff who has arrested the brother of a wealthy rancher. The rancher wants his brother free. John wants him tried, but the rancher has a whole herd of cowboys and gunslingers ready to help him. John has a drunken deputy (Martin), a toothless, grizzled old man (Brennan) and a young untried gunhand (Nelson). Great fun. Lots of shootin' but good laughs too from a talented cast. Redone by Hawks, again with Wayne, in 1967 as EL DORADO - also was the model for ASSAULT ON PRECINCT 13 and RIO LOBO.

Sex / Nud / Viol / Lang / AdSit

A: John Wayne, Dean Martin, Angie Dickinson, Walter Brennan, Ricky Nelson, Ward Bond

© WARNER HOME VIDEO 11050

RISKY BUSINESS

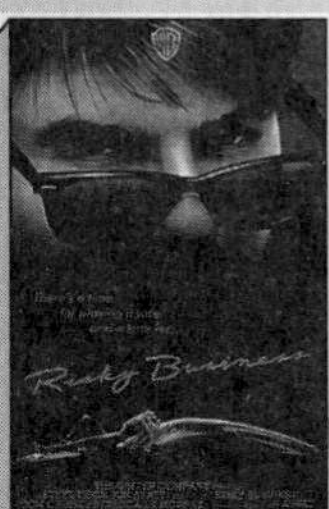

D: Paul Brickman 99 m

R | COM ROM | 1983 | COLOR

9 Disarming, sexy, stylish and a whole lotta fun! High schooler Tom Cruise is every mother's dream, so when his parents went on vacation, they left him with the house and the Porsche. Then one of his friends orders a call girl for him and his life (and his parent's house) is turned inside out. After the Porsche winds up in the lake, the desperate Cruise allows himself to be charmed by sexy call girl (De Mornay), who is also deeply in debt to her pimp, into turning the affluent home into a bordello for one night. But it all backfires when Cruise falls for her and her pimp steals a whole house full of his parent's furniture. Charming, funny and a huge boost for Tom Cruise.

Sex / Nud / Viol / Lang / AdSit

A: Tom Cruise, Rebecca De Mornay, Curtis Armstrong, Bronson Pinchot, Raphael Sbarge, Joe Pantoliano

© WARNER HOME VIDEO 11323

RITA, SUE AND BOB TOO

D: Alan Clarke 94 m

R | COM | 1987 | COLOR

6 Spicy British sex-comedy. Costigan and his wife (Sharp) are having marriage problems, which originate in the bedroom. Two slightly overweight teenage babysitters (Finneran and Homes) regularly watch their children and are eager to grow up. So, when he flippantly makes a suggestive remark concerning the two of them, they take him up on it. They make a happy love trio, too, until his wife finally finds out. Things become even more complicated when Finneran gets pregnant and Holmes gets a new boyfriend. A fun and outrageous British frolic. For open-minded viewers only.

Sex / Nud / Viol / Lang / AdSit

A: George Costigan, Siobhan Finneran, Michelle Homes, Lesley Sharp

© WARNER HOME VIDEO 445

RITZ, THE

D: Richard Lester 91 m

R | COM | 1976 | COLOR

7 Witty sophisticated farce with a fast pace! When Jack Weston's father dies, his ruthless mobster brother-in-law (Stiller) puts out a contract on him to keep Weston from getting a piece of the family's garbage business. Weston flees to New York City and holes up into an all-male hotel called the Ritz, notorious as a gay hangout. There he meets a ditzy torch singer who can't hold a tune (Moreno) but is still waiting for her big break. Unfortunately, Stiller owns the Ritz and Weston is tracked down by Stiller's resourceful wife. Sophisticated fun.

Sex / Nud / Viol / Lang / AdSit

A: Jack Weston, Jerry Stiller, Rita Moreno, Treat Williams, Kay Ballard, F. Murray Abraham

© WARNER HOME VIDEO 11356

ROAD TO HONG KONG, THE

D: Norman Panama 92 m

NR | MUS COM | 1962 | B&W

6 Lively formula comedy. Two ex-vaudeville performers turned con men end up in a plot filled with international intrigue. A secret formula has been submerged inside one of their minds. Somewhere along the line, Hope loses his memory and that unfortunate incident leads them to involvement with a spy (Collins) and a nutty gang of baddies. Sellers makes an exuberant performance in his cameo as the doctor who examines Hope. Inside jokes between Hope and Crosby add some zest to the last film in the series.

Sex / Nud / Viol / Lang / AdSit

A: Bob Hope, Bing Crosby, Joan Collins, Dorothy Lamour, Robert Morley, Walter Gotell

Distributed By MGM/UA Home Video M202078

ROBIN AND THE SEVEN HOODS

D: Gordon Douglas 123 m

NR | MUS COM | 1964 | COLOR

6 A jazzy musical spoof, both of gangsters and of the classic English adventure tale. Set in 1928 Chicago, gangster Sinatra strikes upon a brilliant move. He will set up various charity groups and then take his cut right off the top. However, all the good will he generates also turns out to be very good for the business at his speakeasies. His chief rival in town (Falk) is more than a little upset because he's losing so much business and he decides to do something about it. A frothy light-hearted musical comedy, featuring the Oscar-nominated songs "My Kind of Town" and "All for One."

Sex / Nud / Viol / Lang / AdSit

A: Frank Sinatra, Dean Martin, Bing Crosby, Sammy Davis, Jr., Peter Falk, Barbara Rush

© WARNER HOME VIDEO 11369

ROBIN HOOD: MEN IN TIGHTS

D: Mel Brooks 105 m

PG-13 | COM | 1993 | COLOR

6 Mel Brooks fans only. Silly satirical farce by Brooks, wherein he puts his own spin on the events of Sherwood Forest and even puts in a small appearance as Rabbi Tuckman (in place of Friar Tuck). In spite of a few good bits, much of it is slow going. Still, for Brooks' die-hards it may be worth the time spent.

Sex / Nud / Viol / Lang / AdSit

A: Cary Elwes, Richard Lewis, Amy Yasbeck, Roger Rees, Dave Chappelle, Mark Blankfield

© FOXVIDEO 8522

ROBIN WILLIAMS LIVE

D: Bruce Gowers 65 m

NR | COM | 1986 | COLOR

8 Witty, wacky, wonderfully funny and woefully blue. True to his comic form, Robin Williams offers up a hilarious performance, filmed at the Metropolitan Opera House in San Francisco. His extraordinary ability to mimic personalities and improvise on cue are brilliantly showcased here. Often blue and sometimes vulgar, topics include sex and politics. Adults will certainly enjoy this, but it's not for kids.

Sex / Nud / Viol / Lang / AdSit

A: Robin Williams

© LIVE HOME VIDEO 3147

ROCKET GIBRALTAR

D: Daniel Petrie 100 m

PG | COM DMA | 1988 | COLOR

7 Bittersweet drama about love and family. A much-loved patriarch, Levi Rockwell (Lancaster), has called his family together to celebrate his 77th birthday. His large family, children and grandchildren, all gather on his beautiful estate on Long Island. Although his children love him, it's his grandchildren that make a heartfelt connection with him and carry out his most cherished last wish. Sentimental, touching and emotional. Have a box of tissue ready for the last few scenes.

Sex / Nud / Viol / Lang / AdSit

A: Burt Lancaster, Suzy Amis, John Glover, Bill Pullman, Patricia Clarkson, Frances Conroy

© COLUMBIA TRISTAR HOME VIDEO 65009

ROCKY HORROR PICTURE SHOW, THE

D: Jim Sharman 106 m

R | MUS COM SF | 1975 | COLOR

9 Wacky, purposely goofy, full of rock `n roll energy and lots of fun! On one dark and stormy night, a stuffy young couple (Bostwick and Sarandon) get a flat tire and come knocking on the door of extra-terrestrial transvestite Dr. Frank N. Furter's mysterious castle looking for a phone. They find that they have arrived on a very special night. It's a party! The castle is full of kinky guests and the bisexual doctor teaches the up-tight pair to loosen up by seducing them both. That's not all - he's an alien. This film inspired a huge unprecedented cult following. Very very different. Be open minded.

Sex / Nud / Viol / Lang / AdSit

A: Barry Bostwick, Susan Sarandon, Tim Curry, Charles Gray, Richard O'Brien, Patricia Quinn

© FOXVIDEO 1424

ROCK 'N' ROLL HIGH SCHOOL

D: Allan Arkush — 93 m

PG | MUS COM | 1979 | COLOR

6 Rowdy teenage rebels are seeking reform in this fast-paced teenage musical comedy! A new principal (Woronov) comes to Vince Lombardi High School and tries to cramp the kid's style, but one rebellious teenager, a die-hard "Ramones" fan, blasts their music out into the halls, and even succeeds at bringing her favorite group to the school. A confrontation is now at hand. The students go nuts and conduct a huge revolt against the suppressive and stifling establishment. A cult favorite for teens, with some genuine humor and outstanding rock 'n' roll.

Sex | Nud | Viol | Lang | AdSit

A: P.J. Soles, Vincent Van Patten, Clint Howard, Dey Young, The Ramones, Mary Woronov

© WARNER HOME VIDEO 24054

ROMANCING THE STONE

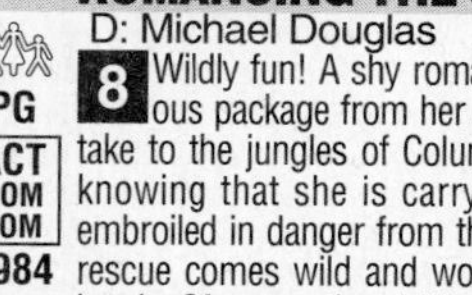

D: Michael Douglas — 106 m

PG | ACT ROM COM | 1984 | COLOR

8 Wildly fun! A shy romance novelist (Turner) receives a mysterious package from her dead brother-in-law which she must then take to the jungles of Columbia to rescue her kidnapped sister. Not knowing that she is carrying a treasure map, she finds herself embroiled in danger from the minute she steps off the plane. To her rescue comes wild and woolly Douglas, a gun-toting soldier of the jungle. Of course they fall in love, but the action never stops, nor does the humor, as Turner's drab existence is forever transformed. Followed by JEWEL OF THE NILE.

Sex | Nud | Viol | Lang | AdSit

A: Michael Douglas, Kathleen Turner, Danny DeVito, Alfonso Arau, Zack Norman

© FOXVIDEO 1358

ROOKIE OF THE YEAR

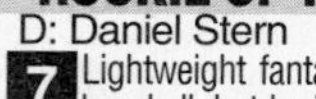

D: Daniel Stern — 103 m

PG | CLD COM | 1993 | COLOR

7 Lightweight fantasy adventure for kids. Nicholas is crazy about baseball, but he is so clumsy that he's always the last kid on the bench to get played. Then a miracle happens... he breaks his arm. It's a miracle because when it heals on its own, he discovers that the tendons have been stretched too tight, so his arm now is like a catapult. Those shortened tendons have given him a 100 mph fastball. Now the kid who could never play, has just signed a contract to pitch for the Chicago Cubs. He's got the power but he needs help to put it to use. Gary Busy is a nearly over-the-hill pitcher that shows him how to get the job done. Pleasant enough pastime for kids.

Sex | Nud | Viol | Lang | AdSit

A: Thomas Ian Nicholas, Gary Busy, Albert Hall, Amy Morton, Dan Hedaya, Bruce Altman

© FOX 8521

ROOSTER COGBURN

D: Stuart Millar — 108 m

PG | WST COM ACT | 1975 | COLOR

8 TRUE GRIT meets THE AFRICAN QUEEN. John Wayne reprises his very popular and Oscar-winning title character from TRUE GRIT. Rooster is in pursuit of bad men who have lifted an Army wagonload of nitroglycerine. His search introduces him to a bible-thumping old-maid missionary played by Katharine Hepburn, whose father was also murdered by the bad guys. The fun starts when she insists on joining Wayne's expedition. An OK story line, but it is aided greatly by the presence of two screen legends who are just plain fun to watch, as well as a terrific supporting cast.

Sex | Nud | Viol | Lang | AdSit

A: John Wayne, Katharine Hepburn, Anthony Zerbe, Strother Martin, John McIntire

© MCA/UNIVERSAL HOME VIDEO, INC. 55042

ROSALIE GOES SHOPPING

D: Percy Adlon — 96 m

PG | COM | 1990 | COLOR

6 A German woman has moved to America with her American husband - to a little town in Arkansas. Rosalie (Sagebrecht) is a warm-hearted mother, just searching for her American Dream. She goes on a credit card rampage and buys everything in sight. Soon, she has to become a wizard at creative finance as she alters checks, lies daily to credit collectors and runs up $1 million in debts. She has become a genius at creative finance. She just wants her family to have a piece of the American Pie. A quirky look at American consumerism and consumption.

Sex | Nud | Viol | Lang | AdSit

A: Marianne Sagebrecht, Brad Davis, Judge Reinhold, Alex Winter, John Hawkes, David Denney

© VIDMARK ENTERTAINMENT VM5275

ROSEANNE BARR SHOW, THE

D: Rocco Urbishi — 60 m

NR | COM | 1987 | COLOR

7 Hysterics from the "Domestic Goddess"! Before Roseanne Barr was Roseanne Arnold, before she had created the biggest television comedy show, and before she had become a household name, she was a standup comic. In 1987 she did a hilarious standup special about her own household for HBO. This special splices parts of the star's routine in with her family's humble life at the mobile home. Much of this material certainly became the inspiration for her hit TV show "Roseanne." Very funny, and easy to relate to.

Sex | Nud | Viol | Lang | AdSit

A: Roseanne Barr

© HBO VIDEO 0056

ROUNDERS, THE

D: Burt Kennedy — 85 m

NR | WST COM | 1964 | COLOR

7 Likable little comedy about the adventures of two nearly over-the-hill modern-day cowboy buddies working for a stingy rancher (Chill Wills). Ben and Howdy spend nearly the entire movie trying to best an ornery roan named "Ol' Fooler" nearly destroying a small town in the process. Their adventures with the horse becomes the central gag, tieing together a pleasant time-killer of a film which became a minor sleeper hit the year it was released.

Sex | Nud | Viol | Lang | AdSit

A: Glenn Ford, Henry Fonda, Sue Ann Langdon, Hope Holiday, Chill Wills, Edgar Buchanan

Distributed By MGM/UA Home Video M200975

ROXANNE

D: Fred Schepisi — 107 m

PG | COM ROM | 1987 | COLOR

8 Clever and winning comedy that is one of Steve Martin's most pleasing efforts. He is C.D., the chief of a small town's fire department, with a super-sized snoz and a rapier wit. Arriving one summer are Roxanne, a beautiful astronomy student (Hannah); and a handsome, but shy and shallow, hunk of a fireman (Rossovich). The shy hunk asks C.D. to contribute eloquent words to help him to woo Roxanne. It works, but poor C.D. has also fallen for Roxanne. She likes C.D., but she has fallen for the hunky man with wit and words - unaware that the words and wit come from C.D. Funny remake of CYRANO DE BERGERAC.

Sex | Nud | Viol | Lang | AdSit

A: Steve Martin, Daryl Hannah, Rick Rossovich, Shelley Duvall

© COLUMBIA TRISTAR HOME VIDEO 60853

RUDE AWAKENING

D: Aaron Russo — 100 m

R | COM | 1989 | COLOR

6 In 1969 two free-wheeling, flower-loving hippies seek to avoid the draft and dodge the FBI, so they take flight to Central America where they form an isolated commune. Twenty years later, they discover that there is a CIA plot to invade their new homeland, so they decide to return to New York to expose the plot to the world. Only the world they return to is nothing like the one they left. New York and their old friends have all changed. The yuppies have arrived, among other things! Good-humored silly satire.

Sex | Nud | Viol | Lang | AdSit

A: Cheech Marin, Eric Roberts, Julie Hagerty, Robert Carradine, Buck Henry, Louise Lasser

© HBO VIDEO 0352

RULING CLASS, THE

D: Peter Medak — 154 m

PG | COM DMA | 1972 | COLOR

9 Thoroughly irreverent British comedy - a classic with a cult following. The totally mad heir to a British lordship (O'Toole) thinks that he is Jesus Christ. At first, his family goes along with his bizarre belief so that they can live off of his money, but when it gets out of hand, they all plot against him. Dark and surrealistic, the film comes complete with chaos and spontaneous song and dance. Fans of British irreverence will love it, but it is not for every taste. Based on the play by Peter Medak, it takes a big bite out of the British upper-crust.

Sex | Nud | Viol | Lang | AdSit

A: Peter O'Toole, Alastair Sim, Coral Browne, Arthur Lowe, Harry Andrews, Michael Bryant

© NEW LINE HOME VIDEO 2085

RUNNING SCARED

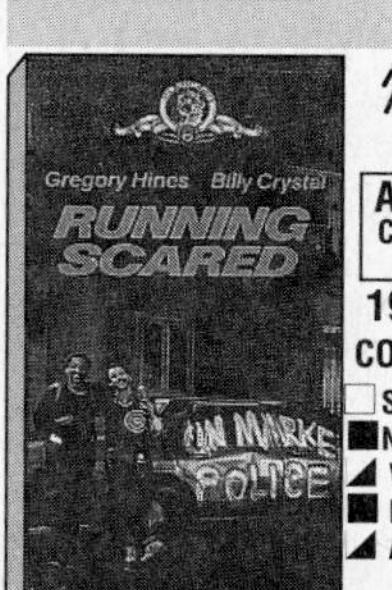

D: Peter Hyams — 108 m

R | ACT COM | 1986 | COLOR

7 Witty and rousing adventure! Two tough Chicago street cops are tired of trying to control the influx of drugs into the city. So, after one particularly nasty day, they ponder retirement in the Florida Keys but decide that they must bring an aspiring godfather (Smits) - the source of much of their grief - down first. The wisecracking pair are magic on the screen with never-ending banter that is effortlessly funny. Some thrilling chase scenes and shootouts just add to the disarming fun of this bad guys vs. good guys actioner!

Sex | Nud | Viol | Lang | AdSit

A: Gregory Hines, Billy Crystal, Steven Bauer, Darlanne Fluegel, Joe Pantoliano, Dan Hedaya

Distributed By MGM/UA Home Video M801008

RUSSIANS ARE COMING, THE RUSSIANS ARE COMING, THE

D: Norman Jewison — 127 m

NR | COM | 1966 | COLOR

8 Zany comedy that was a surprise big hit. Set at the height of the Cold War, imagine the hysterics that would ensue if a Russian submarine, intent only upon getting a close look at a typically picturesque small Maine fishing village, runs aground upon a sandbar. And then an inept crewman (Alan Arkin) is sent ashore to capture a civilian boat large enough to tow the submarine free. Instead, Arkin nearly starts a war when he is confronted by the local make-shift militia, led by an inept old soldier (Paul Ford) and a bungling deputy sheriff (Jonathan Winters). Solid light-hearted comedy with good gags.

Sex | Nud | Viol | Lang | AdSit

A: Carl Reiner, Eva Marie Saint, Alan Arkin, Brian Keith, Jonathan Winters, Paul Ford

Distributed By MGM/UA Home Video M201490

RUSSKIES

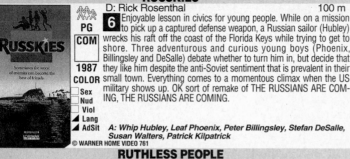

D: Rick Rosenthal — 100 m

PG · COM · 1987 · COLOR

6 Enjoyable lesson in civics for young people. While on a mission to pick up a captured defense weapon, a Russian sailor (Hubley) wrecks his raft off the coast of the Florida Keys while trying to get to shore. Three adventurous and curious young boys (Phoenix, Billingsley and DeSalle) debate whether to turn him in, but decide that they like him despite the anti-Soviet sentiment that is prevalent in their small town. Everything comes to a momentous climax when the US military shows up. OK sort of remake of THE RUSSIANS ARE COMING, THE RUSSIANS ARE COMING.

Sex · Nud · Viol · Lang · AdSit

A: Whip Hubley, Leaf Phoenix, Peter Billingsley, Stefan DeSalle, Susan Walters, Patrick Kilpatrick

© WARNER HOME VIDEO 761

RUTHLESS PEOPLE

D: Jim Abrahams — 93 m

R · COM · 1986 · COLOR

8 Zany comedy in which Danny DeVito is a scheming millionaire who is tired of his acerbic, overweight wife (Bette Midler). He's planning to have her killed so he can run off with his mistress. But before he can do it, she is kidnapped by a gentle down-on-their-luck couple. (He's so gentle that he won't even step on a spider.) These two are just looking for a piece of the good life, but DeVito's dream has just came true and he won't pay. When Midler learns that sorry news, she also realizes who her friends are - her kidnappers. So they all plot together to separate poor old Danny from his money.

Sex · Nud · Viol · Lang · AdSit

A: Danny DeVito, Judge Reinhold, Helen Slater, Bette Midler, Anita Morris, Bill Pullman

© TOUCHSTONE HOME VIDEO 485

SAMANTHA

D: Stephen La Rocque — 101 m

PG · COM ROM · 1992 · COLOR

6 Samantha is a wildly eccentric (some might say goofy) girl. On her 21st birthday, her mother and father tell her that she was actually left on their doorstep 21 years before in a wicker basket. Samantha, is overcome by the news, locks herself in her room and sits in front of her almost-father's ancient blunderbuss. She has jury-rigged it to the door to await her imminent demise, but her ill-considered attempt is thwarted. So, she decides to move in with her life-long best friend Henry while she begins her quest to discover her real parents, and screws up his love life in the bargain - for a while. Sometimes wacky and funny, sometimes just strange and sometimes entertaining.

Sex · Nud · Viol · Lang · AdSit

A: Martha Plimpton, Dermot Mulroney, Hector Elizondo, Mary Kay Place, Ione Skye

© ACADEMY ENTERTAINMENT 1480

SAME TIME, NEXT YEAR

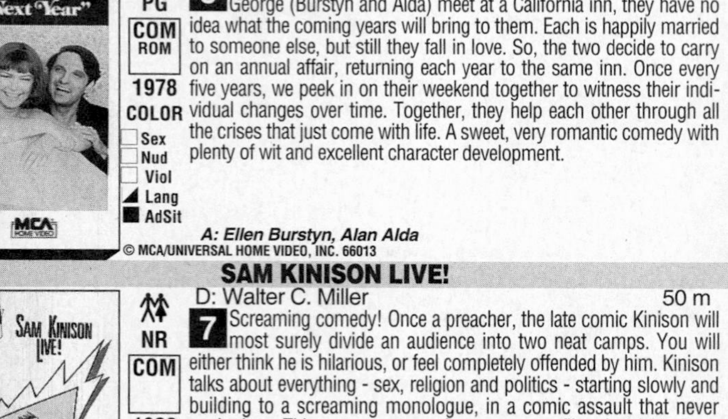

D: Robert Mulligan — 119 m

PG · COM ROM · 1978 · COLOR

8 A warm, human and truly romantic comedy! When Doris and George (Burstyn and Alda) meet at a California inn, they have no idea what the coming years will bring to them. Each is happily married to someone else, but still they fall in love. So, the two decide to carry on an annual affair, returning each year to the same inn. Once every five years, we peek in on their weekend together to witness their individual changes over time. Together, they help each other through all the crises that just come with life. A sweet, very romantic comedy with plenty of wit and excellent character development.

Sex · Nud · Viol · Lang · AdSit

A: Ellen Burstyn, Alan Alda

© MCA/UNIVERSAL HOME VIDEO, INC. 66013

SAM KINISON LIVE!

D: Walter C. Miller — 50 m

NR · COM · 1988 · COLOR

7 Screaming comedy! Once a preacher, the late comic Kinison will most surely divide an audience into two neat camps. You will either think he is hilarious, or feel completely offended by him. Kinison talks about everything - sex, religion and politics - starting slowly and building to a screaming monologue, in a comic assault that never apologizes. This outrageous performance was filmed at LA's Roxy Theatre. Kinison's comic style fires at everything, from point-blank range.

Sex · Nud · Viol · Lang · AdSit

A: Sam Kinison

© HBO VIDEO 0047

SAMMY AND ROSIE GET LAID

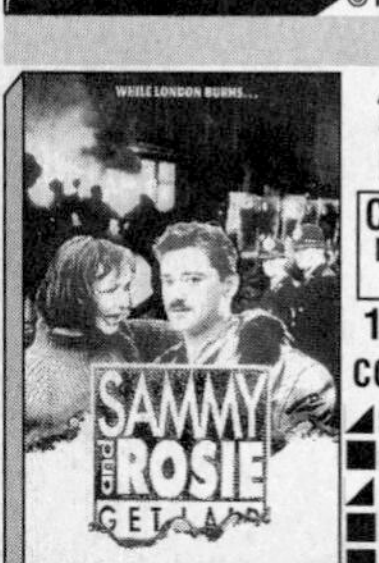

D: Stephen Frears — 97 m

NR · COM DMA · 1987 · COLOR

7 A very direct little British sex comedy that wastes no time getting right to the heart of matter. A radical young married couple (Din and Barber) live in London and share a very sexually liberated and open marriage. When Kapoor, Din's very traditional but wealthy Pakistani father, comes for a visit, his whole world is shaken by their behavior. Whatever happened to the England he used to know? The sexual exploits and political views of the 80's, particularly of Rosie, go completely unchecked. But, if Sammy and Rosie want some of daddy's money they are going to have to produce an heir. Darkly funny - not for all tastes.

Sex · Nud · Viol · Lang · AdSit

A: Claire Bloom, Roland Gift, Shashi Kapoor, Frances Barber, Ayub Khan Din, Wendy Gazelle

© WARNER HOME VIDEO 763

SAVANNAH SMILES

D: Pierre DeMoro — 105 m

PG · COM CLD · 1982 · COLOR

8 A real charmer. Savannah (Anderson) is a six-year old who runs away from her snooty, rich parents and she winds up in the back seat of a car belonging to two soft-hearted escaped convicts. Her father has offered a huge reward for her return, but who's going to believe the story of two convicts. So, they try valiantly to get her back without blowing their cover. Meanwhile, the three hide out in an abandoned house where they all become a loving "family," experiencing feelings none of them has ever known before. Chock-full of tender moments, sincere laughs and an ending that packs an emotional punch. A gem!

Sex · Nud · Viol · Lang · AdSit

A: Mark Miller, Donovan Scott, Bridgette Andersen, Peter Graves, Michael Parks, Noriyuki "Pat" Morita

© NEW LINE HOME VIDEO 2058

SAVING GRACE

D: Robert M. Young — 112 m

PG · COM · 1986 · COLOR

7 Sweet-natured and sentimental little comedy about a young Pope. He is a man-of-the-people and is very frustrated at becoming bogged down with the bureaucracy and bureaucrats of the Vatican... so he just leaves. He just wanders away to a small remote village that has no priest and is desperately poor. There, he gets a chance to help people again. Several cute moments, including watching three Cardinals try to cover up the fact that the Pope is missing. Not very believable, but well-intentioned and fun... as long as you don't think too hard about it.

Sex · Nud · Viol · Lang · AdSit

A: Tom Conti, Fernando Rey, Erland Josephson, Giancarlo Giannini, Donald Hewlett, Edward James Olmos

© NEW LINE HOME VIDEO 2180

SCALPHUNTERS, THE

D: Sydney Pollack — 100 m

NR · WST COM ACT · 1968 · COLOR

8 Fun-filled and funny Western with truly interesting characters. A very determined fur trapper (Burt Lancaster) is forced by a group of Indians to swap his skins for a highly educated and uppity former slave (also a recent member of the Kiowa nation), Ossie Davis. He's not thrilled with the forced swap, so he sets out to get his furs back. But, by the time he catches them, an outlaw band of scalphunters headed by Savalas, has stolen the furs from the Indians and captured Davis, too. Undeterred, Burt hounds the scalphunters with guerrilla raids, getting occasional inside help from his uneasy ally, Davis. A real good time.

Sex · Nud · Viol · Lang · AdSit

A: Burt Lancaster, Shelley Winters, Ossie Davis, Telly Savalas, Armando Silvestre, Nick Cravat

Distributed By MGM/UA Home Video M202033

SCAVENGER HUNT

D: Michael Schultz — 116 m

PG · COM · 1979 · COLOR

6 Silly, campy fun. When game manufacturer Vincent Price dies, he leaves a huge amount of money to his friends and relatives, but only the winning team of an insane scavenger hunt will get to claim the grand prize - the entire two hundred million dollar estate of the dearly-departed. Included in the odd assortment of required collectibles are commodes, ostriches, fat people, beehives and all sorts of other very strange items. Nutty.

Sex · Nud · Viol · Lang · AdSit

A: Richard Benjamin, James Coco, Scatman Crothers, Ruth Gordon, Cloris Leachman, Cleavon Little

© CBS/FOX VIDEO 6224

SCENES FROM A MALL

D: Paul Mazursky — 87 m

R · COM DMA · 1991 · COLOR

6 Fans of Woody Allen and Bette Midler should get a kick out of this film - others may have a tougher time with it. Trendy California couple Midler and Allen are shopping at an upscale mall for gifts and apparel for their 16th anniversary party the following night, when Allen's conscience gets the best of him and he confesses that he has had an affair. They fight and make up. And then Midler turns around and confesses the very same sin to him. Will they even make it through to tomorrow? Dramatic tension and mildly funny moments ensue in this comedy/drama.

Sex · Nud · Viol · Lang · AdSit

A: Bette Midler, Woody Allen, Bill Irwin, Daren Firestone, Rebecca Nickels, Paul Mazursky

© TOUCHSTONE HOME VIDEO 1163

SCENES FROM THE CLASS STRUGGLE IN BEVERLY HILLS

D: Paul Bartel — 103 m

R · COM · 1989 · COLOR

6 Outrageously naughty, but silly and fun. When two socially pretentious and affluent Beverly Hills families are forced to share one smallish mansion for a weekend, all sorts of wild sexual antics erupt. Divorcee Wornov's house is being fumigated, so she and her son take refuge next door at neighbor Bisset's house. Bisset is an ex-TV star trying to make a comeback. Her husband has just died, but his ghost keeps popping up. Just to complicate things even more, the families's two gardeners plot to see who can seduce their employer first. Don't expect great satire, just silliness.

Sex · Nud · Viol · Lang · AdSit

A: Jacqueline Bisset, Ed Begley, Jr., Ray Sharkey, Mary Woronov, Robert Beltran, Wallace Shawn

© VIDEO TREASURES SV9689 1

SCHOOL DAZE

D: Spike Lee 114 m

R | COM MUS | 1987 | COLOR | Sex | Nud | Viol | Lang | AdSit

7 Insightful and honest comedy. During homecoming weekend at a black college, two factions of the school, the Wanabee fraternity and the Jigaboo fraternity, clash in every way. The Wanabees work to lose or disguise their racial identity, while the Jigaboos are comfortable and secure with their's, and the two groups torment each other. From all this energized ruckus, director Spike Lee skillfully extracts a lesson in social values and explores subjects not often talked about in film, or elsewhere. Spirited dance numbers intermix with the outrageous goings-on during the celebratory weekend. Criticized as being unstructured.

A: Larry Fishburne, Giancarlo Esposito, Joe Seneca, Tisha Campbell, Kyme, Ossie Davis

© COLUMBIA TRISTAR HOME VIDEO 65006

SCROOGED

D: Richard Donner 101 m

PG-13 | COM | 1989 | COLOR | Sex | Nud | Viol | Lang | AdSit

7 Heartwarming holiday comedy with spirit! Frank (Murray) is a cold-hearted network TV executive who doesn't have time for anybody but himself. Frank's holiday attitude needs an adjustment. When three ghosts, the ghosts of Christmas past (a maniacal New York cabbie), present (a zany Carol Kane) and a ghoul from the future, come to visit, they manage to put a little love in back into his heart and ignite his holiday spirit, too. Murray's trademark style of humor adds a zany quality to this film and it surprises you with its unexpected emotional ending.

A: Bill Murray, John Forsythe, Carol Kane, David Johansen, Karen Allen, Bobcat Goldthwait

© PARAMOUNT HOME VIDEO 32054

SEEMS LIKE OLD TIMES

D: Jay Sandrich 103 m

PG | COM | 1980 | COLOR | Sex | Nud | Viol | Lang | AdSit

8 Romantically zany Neil Simon comedy. A beautiful attorney (Hawn), with a soft heart, finds herself torn between her ex-husband (Chase), who needs her help, and her new husband (Grodin), on a career fast-track. When Chase is accused of bank robbery, he goes to Hawn for help. But Chase's predicament could harm Grodin's chances of becoming the next Attorney General. Clever and funny situations occur as Hawn helps Chase, but also struggles to maintain proper appearances for her husband. A well-cast 1930s-style screwball comedy-like farce, overflowing with wit and charm.

A: Chevy Chase, Goldie Hawn, Charles Grodin, Robert Guillaume, Harold Gould, George Grizzard

© COLUMBIA TRISTAR HOME VIDEO 60200

SEE NO EVIL, HEAR NO EVIL

D: Arthur Hiller 103 m

R | COM | 1989 | COLOR | Sex | Nud | Viol | Lang | AdSit

6 A blind man and a deaf man (Pryor and Wilder) both witness a murder. A customer is shot at Wilder's Manhattan newsstand but all he catches is a peek at her sexy legs while Pryor gets a whiff of her perfume. The cops show up and arrest the inept pair because they are the only two potential suspects they can find. Never mind that they aren't even capable of such an elaborate scheme. Together, the pair sets out to prove their innocence and, along the way, deftly extract a mild amount of humor from their unfortunate situations. Recommended for Wilder or Pryor fans only.

A: Richard Pryor, Gene Wilder, Joan Severance, Kevin Spacey

© COLUMBIA TRISTAR HOME VIDEO 70223

SEMI-TOUGH

D: Michael Ritchie 108 m

R | COM ROM | 1977 | COLOR | Sex | Nud | Viol | Lang | AdSit

8 Fun comic showcase for Reynolds' easy-going charm. Two professional football players - star running back Reynolds and his best buddy, roommate and wide receiver, Kristofferson - share the same girlfriend/buddy, Jill Clayburgh. The lucky girl is also the owner's carefree daughter. They make a happy threesome until Kristofferson joins a self-awareness group, talks her into joining too and then asks her to marry him. Now third man out, Reynolds seeks to debunk the group and win her back for himself. Light-hearted fun that is frequently hilarious.

A: Burt Reynolds, Kris Kristofferson, Jill Clayburgh, Robert Preston, Bert Convy, Lotte Lenya

Distributed By MGM/UA Home Video M201219

SEND ME NO FLOWERS

D: Norman Jewison 100 m

NR | COM | 1964 | COLOR | Sex | Nud | Viol | Lang | AdSit

7 Classic Hudson/Day fun! Rock Hudson, a hopeless hypochondriac, overhears a bleak prognosis at a hospital one day and becomes convinced that it's his own. Wanting to make sure that his family and wife (Day) are provided for when he is gone, he enlists the aid of best friend Randall to find a new husband for Day. The laughs break loose when Day convinces herself that his strange behavior is a cover-up for an affair he is having and he's just feeling guilty. This buoyant and funny film was the last of the Hudson/Day pairings.

A: Rock Hudson, Doris Day, Tony Randall, Clint Walker, Paul Lynde, Hal March

© MCA/UNIVERSAL HOME VIDEO, INC. 80405

SEPTEMBER GUN

D: Don Taylor 94 m

NR | WST COM | 1983 | COLOR | Sex | Nud | Viol | Lang | AdSit

6 This unconventional Western/comedy starts out a bit slowly but builds into an action-packed adventure. A crusty old gunslinger (Preston) is coerced into helping a stubborn nun (Duke) and a group of orphaned children reach a remote mission school located in Colorado, some three hundred miles away. However, when they get there, the mission school that Sister Dulcina expects to find has been taken over by an outlaw. It is now a bar, and worse. She wants it back for her school and Preston gets the unwelcome job of helping her do it. Made for TV.

A: Robert Preston, Patty Duke, Geoffrey Lewis, Sally Kellerman, Christopher Lewis

© GOODTIMES 9153

SERIAL

D: Bill Persky 90 m

R | COM | 1980 | COLOR | Sex | Nud | Viol | Lang | AdSit

7 Comic satire of the '70s-style ardent pursuit of deep inner-meanings found in the antics of affluent Marin County, California. These pursuits include hot tubs, religious cults, sex and drugs...and, the Holroyd family is about to go through some changes. Mom (Weld) is having an affair with the poodle's groomer, and daughter McAlister has run off to join a religious cult. But Dad's (Mull) problems are just beginning. From Moonies to free love and funky fads, this funny parody is right on the mark, although some of '70s foolishness may seem even more foolish and dated now. It is entertaining, nonetheless.

A: Martin Mull, Tuesday Weld, Sally Kellerman, Tom Smothers, Bill Macy, Christopher Lee

© PARAMOUNT HOME VIDEO 1191

SERIAL MOM

D: John Waters 93 m

R | COM | 1994 | COLOR | Sex | Nud | Viol | Lang | AdSit

6 On the outside, Kathleen Turner is the perfect suburban housewife. In public, she always has a smile and a helpful hand. However, behind closed doors, she ardently reads about mass-murderers and even corresponds with mass-murderer Richard Speck. She also makes filthy phone calls to torment the widow next door. All of life's little annoyances are becoming too much for her and she snaps. Her first victim is her son's math teacher, the next is the boy who slighted her daughter and then comes the old woman who defiantly refused to rewind the video tapes she rented. This is a very black comedy. Lovers of macabre humor (which is overplayed for effect) will enjoy themselves. Others, will be left wanting.

A: Kathleen Turner, Sam Waterston, Ricki Lake, Matthew Lillard, Scott Wesley Morgan, Walt MacPherson

© HBO VIDEO 90980

SEVEN BEAUTIES

D: Lina Wertmuller 116 m

R | FOR DMA COM | 1976 | COLOR | Sex | Nud | Viol | Lang | AdSit

8 Award-winning, powerful and near-surrealist story of a man willing to sacrifice anything to survive. A small-time hood in WWII Italy trys to commit a murder but fails miserably and is caught. He pleads insanity rather than go to prison. Finding that intolerable, he accepts the opportunity to join the army, but deserts when sent to the Russian front - for which he is sent to a concentration camp where he encounters more intensely grotesque horrors. He seduces an obese, sadistic prison warden to get out. The raw ugliness his situations depicted will test your sensibilities. Ardent film fans only.

A: Giancarlo Giannini, Fernando Rey, Shirley Stoler, Elena Fiore, Enzo Vitale

© COLUMBIA TRISTAR HOME VIDEO 60203

SHAG: THE MOVIE

D: Zelda Barron 96 m

PG | DMA COM | 1989 | COLOR | Sex | Nud | Viol | Lang | AdSit

7 Surprisingly pleasing female coming-of-age-type movie, set in the South in the summer of 1963. Four best friends from high school decide to spend one last fling together before one gets married, one leaves town and two go off to college. They go to Myrtle Beach for their last weekend of fun at a Shag contest (briefly-popular type of '60s dance). The movie does not open any new ground here, but the four leads are very appealing. Sort of a throwback to the BEACH PARTY movies, with a bit of DIRTY DANCING thrown in. Great '60s sound track and good period details.

A: Phoebe Cates, Annabeth Gish, Bridget Fonda, Tyrone Power, Jr., Robert Rusler, Page Hannah

© HBO VIDEO 0214

SHAGGY DOG, THE

D: Charles Barton 101 m

G | CLD COM | 1959 | B&W | Sex | Nud | Viol | Lang | AdSit

8 A winning classic Disney fantasy! A young Wilby Daniels (Tommy Kirk) has found an ancient ring and mutters the magic words inscribed inside. He suddenly discovers that he has now cast a magical spell which transforms him into a sheepdog - and does it at the worst possible random moments. His predicament is made even worse because his dad (Fred MacMurray) is allergic to dogs. The only way he can break the spell and be turned back into a boy permanently is by an act of heroism. Disney's first attempt at a live action film is chock full of fun gags and charm. A good time!

A: Fred MacMurray, Jean Hagen, Tommy Kirk, Annette Funicello, Tim Considine, Kevin Corcoran

© WALT DISNEY HOME VIDEO 43

SHAMPOO

D: Hal Ashby 112 m

R | COM DMA | 1975 | COLOR

Sex Nud Viol Lang AdSit

7 A provocative sex comedy set in liberated 1968 Southern California. Warren Beatty is sexy and a top-notch hairdresser in Beverly Hills, but not too bright. He wants to open his own shop and needs to borrow the money from investment counselor, Jack Warden. However, he is sleeping with Warden's wife, his mistress and his daughter; plus he's also trying to keep up his relationship with his girlfriend Goldie Hawn. This is an interesting comedic study, exploring the morals of the time and the level of satisfaction or dissatisfaction that so much sex brings. Funny, but not uproarious. Lee Grant won an Oscar.

A: Warren Beatty, Lee Grant, Jack Warden, Julie Christie, Goldie Hawn, Carrie Fisher

© GOODTIMES 4223

SHAMUS

D: Buzz Kulik 106 m

PG | ACT COM | 1973 | COLOR

Sex Nud Viol Lang AdSit

6 Gimmicky and not particularly innovative, but still a fun private eye movie. Burt Reynolds is a quirky, wisecracking private eye who is hired to recover some stolen diamonds. In the process of his investigations, he runs across a a much bigger operation, including a warehouse full of stolen weapons and ammunition. Poor old Burt gets beat up at every other turn, but he does get some help from beautiful socialite Dyan Cannon. Fast moving, with lots of action and glib dialogue. Pretty good.

A: Burt Reynolds, Dyan Cannon, John P. Ryan, Giorgio Tozzi, Joe Santos, Ron Weyand

© COLUMBIA TRISTAR HOME VIDEO 60205

SHE'S GOTTA HAVE IT

D: Spike Lee 84 m

R | COM | 1986 | B&W

Sex Nud Viol Lang AdSit

7 Inventive comedy with a very different look - this time from the woman's side of sex and love! The beautiful and sexy Nora Darling (Johns) is struggling to juggle the amorous attentions of three different suitors. Spike Lee wrote, directed and starred in this sexually uninhibited comedy that is fresh, witty and frank. It is simply the story, set in Brooklyn, of the adventures of the free-spirited Nora who dallies with three men, each very different. She takes exactly what she wants from each one of them, while committing herself to none of them.

A: Spike Lee, Tommy Redmond Hicks, Tracy Camila Johns, Raye Dowell, John Canada Terrell, Bill Lee

© CBS/FOX VIDEO 3860

SHIRLEY VALENTINE

D: Lewis Gilbert 108 m

R | COM ROM DMA | 1989 | COLOR

Sex Nud Viol Lang AdSit

8 Frolicsome fun little comedy in which a frumpy middle-aged London housewife looks out upon her comfortable but routine existence and decides that life is passing her by. She loves her husband, but she is bored. So, when she gets a chance to go to Greece, she takes it; and when her husband won't go with her, she goes alone. In beautiful Greece she discovers a freedom that she hasn't known and becomes reborn by a brief romantic interlude with a local lothario. She has fun, recaptures the life that was slipping away and when her husband comes after her, he does too. Involving and fun.

A: Pauline Collins, Tom Conti, Julia McKenzie, Alison Steadman, Joanna Lumley, Bernard Hill

© PARAMOUNT HOME VIDEO 32248

SHOCK TO THE SYSTEM, A

D: Jan Egleson 88 m

R | SUS COM | 1990 | COLOR

Sex Nud Viol Lang AdSit

7 Slick little black comedy. Caine's a New York advertising executive who has backed himself into a corner. He has an impossible wife and some major debts, but the worst thing is that a young wippersnapper has just snatched up the promotion he's had his eye on. In a rage of fury, he decides that murder is the answer. He smiles secretly to himself when two of his esteemed colleagues end up on the missing-persons list, and he gets his advancement. But a curious detective may make his new hard-won position in life short-lived. Wickedly sophisticated.

A: Michael Caine, Elizabeth McGovern, Swoosie Kurtz, Peter Riegert, Will Patton, John McMartin

© HBO VIDEO 0378

SHORT CIRCUIT

D: John Badham 98 m

PG | COM SF | 1986 | COLOR

Sex Nud Viol Lang AdSit

8 Sparkling comedic farce for the family! No. 5 is a military robot that was developed to be a weapon by the government, but it was zapped with a bolt of lightning and now the little guy seems nearly human. No. 5 has also taken off to see the world on his own. He finds a friend in animal lover Ally Sheedy and learns American culture by watching TV. Sheedy and the newly educated No. 5 develop an affection for each other, but the military is steadfastly after his adorable little tail, with his creator Guttenberg leading the chase. Naturally, she hides him from them. Charming entertainment.

A: Ally Sheedy, Steve Guttenberg, Fisher Stevens, Austin Pendleton, G.W. Bailey, David Oliver

© FOXVIDEO 3724

SHORT CIRCUIT 2

D: Kenneth Johnson 110 m

PG | COM SF | 1988 | COLOR

Sex Nud Viol Lang AdSit

7 Johnny Five (formerly No. 5) is the cute military robot that was struck by lightning in the original film and then became almost human. In this sequel, Johnny comes to the big city to help out one of his inventors who has now gone into the toy business. Johnny hits the streets looking for some "urban input" but attracts some unsavory friends. Some street punks want to trick the naive robot into helping them to pull off a jewel robbery. Cute, but mostly for the younger set this time.

A: Fisher Stevens, Michael McKean, Cynthia Gibb, Jack Weston

© COLUMBIA TRISTAR HOME VIDEO 67008

SHOT IN THE DARK, A

D: Blake Edwards 103 m

PG | COM | 1964 | COLOR

Sex Nud Viol Lang AdSit

9 Hilarious follow up to THE PINK PANTHER. The bumbling and incredibly inept Parisian Inspector Clouseau is assigned to investigate a murder where all the clues point to very sexy maid Elke Sommer as being the murderer. In spite of overwhelming evidence to the contrary, Clouseau sets out to prove that she is innocent. Slapstick and hilarity abound. Wherever he goes, he leaves an ever-increasing pile of dead bodies. Very fast-paced. The success of this picture assured that a long, and successful, string of sequels would follow - and they did.

A: Peter Sellers, Elke Sommer, George Sanders, Herbert Lom, Burt Kwouk, Tracy Reed

Distributed By MGM/UA Home Video M201446

SILENT MOVIE

D: Mel Brooks 87 m

PG | COM | 1976 | COLOR

Sex Nud Viol Lang AdSit

6 A washed-up movie director (Brooks) gets a wild idea that just might revive his career: revive the silent movie. He realizes that silent films were often the funniest kind, so he and a few of his friends (Feldman and DeLuise) hire a crew of big name stars (Burt Reynolds, Paul Newman, James Caan, Liza Minnelli and Anne Bancroft) and convince an influential movie producer to back their film. There are some really funny scenes and sight gags, although a few attempts at humor fall flat. Amusing nonetheless. It includes music and sound effects but only one line of spoken dialogue.

A: Mel Brooks, Marty Feldman, Sid Caesar, Dom DeLuise, Bernadette Peters, Harold Gould

© FOXVIDEO 1437

SILVER STREAK

D: Arthur Hiller 114 m

PG | COM ACT MYS | 1976 | COLOR

Sex Nud Viol Lang AdSit

9 Zany thriller. Wilder, a mild-mannered editor, is taking what he hopes to be a restful ride aboard a cross-country train. It seems to be even better when he seduces the girl in the next compartment (sexy Clayburgh). But she is an art scholar with information which will discredit both millionaire McGoohan and his Rembrandt letters as being fakes. Now, Wilder's leisurely trip turns overly exciting, when he spots a dead body being thrown from the train, and then hilarious, when small-time thief Pryor enters into the picture. Highly entertaining blend of romance, comedy and action.

A: Gene Wilder, Jill Clayburgh, Richard Pryor, Ned Beatty, Patrick McGoohan, Scatman Crothers

© FOXVIDEO 1080

SISTER ACT

D: Emile Ardolino 100 m

PG | COM | 1992 | COLOR

Sex Nud Viol Lang AdSit

8 Very popular comedy. Whoopi is a singer in a Vegas nightclub act and the girlfriend of the club's mobster owner. But, when she has the misfortune of catching him in the act of murdering someone, she knows she's in big trouble and heads underground. The cops offer her protection if she will testify. She agrees but, much to her surprise and dismay, the place they choose to hide her is a convent. This is not a lifestyle which comes easy to a Vegas lounge singer. What's even worse, their choir is terrible. So, Whoopi transforms this boring bunch of off-key nuns into a rock-'n-roll sensation. But being on network news is not a good thing for a nun on the run. Lot of fun.

A: Whoopi Goldberg, Maggie Smith, Harvey Keitel, Mary Wickes

© TOUCHSTONE HOME VIDEO 1452

SISTER ACT 2

D: Bill Duke 107 m

PG | COM | 1994 | COLOR

Sex Nud Viol Lang AdSit

6 Sister Whoopi is back. This time the nuns are in trouble and they need her help. Bad guy, James Coburn is trying to shut down their inner-city San Francisco high school. These kids really need their school and only Whoopi can help them. How? By what else? Let's put on a show! There is not a lot of plot here, nor is there much suspense or even much involvement with the characters. What there is, is some fun choral efforts by a bunch of talented kids. Predictable but genuinely wholesome, even if it isn't very funny or exciting.

A: Whoopi Goldberg, Maggie Smith, Kathy Najimy, Bernard Hughes, Mary Wickes, James Coburn

© TOUCHSTONE HOME VIDEO 2525

SIX DEGREES OF SEPARATION

D: Fred Schepisi m

R | COM | 1994 | COLOR | Sex | Nud | Viol | Lang | AdSit

6 Ouisa and Flan (Channing and Sutherland) are pretentious, urbanely witty, pampered and rich liberal snobs who's luxurious Fifth Avenue Apartment is invaded by a cultured, intelligent and well-spoken young black man. The guy claims to know their children from Harvard and charms them with his extravagant stories, indicating that he is the son of Sidney Poitier. The star-struck pair are bowled over by his charm and offer him their home and money, too. Then they discover that he is a fraud and has pulled this very same stunt on others. Still, they have a hard time getting him out of their lives. While it does poke fun and holes in pretense, it also suffers from that same malady.

A: Stockard Channing, Will Smith, Donald Sutherland, Mary Beth Hurt, Bruce Davidson, Heather Graham

Distributed By MGM/UA Home Video M904745

SIXTEEN CANDLES

D: John Hughes 93 m

PG | COM | 1984 | COLOR | Sex | Nud | Viol | Lang | AdSit

8 Hilarious snapshot of teenage life, pain and love, but you don't have to be sixteen to love it. Every girl awaits her sixteenth birthday with dreamy anticipation. Unfortunately for Ringwald, her family is busy with her sister's wedding and they all forget her big day. Just to make matters worse, she has a huge crush on a boy (Schoeffling) who doesn't even know she exists. Everything else in her life is all wrong, too. Things look up when Schoeffling, the man of her dreams, takes notice, and she discovers that a "geek" who likes her isn't so much of a geek after all. Vivid, lively and endearing.

A: Molly Ringwald, Paul Dooley, Justin Henry, Michael Schoeffling, Anthony Michael Hall, John Cusack

© MCA/UNIVERSAL HOME VIDEO, INC. 80076

SKIN DEEP

D: Blake Edwards 102 m

R | COM | 1989 | COLOR | Sex | Nud | Viol | Lang | AdSit

6 Some guys will do anything for true love. So will this guy - as long as he doesn't have to give up women, get a job or stop drinking. Ritter is the man with all the bad habits, habits he developed to cure his chronic case of writer's block. His worst habit is that he is painfully in love with his ex-wife, but he just can't rid himself of his other vices, even though they are the ones that caused the breakup of his marriage in the first place. Not always funny, but it has a few spots, especially his search for "safe sex."

A: John Ritter, Vincent Gardenia, Alyson Reed, Julianne Phillips, Chelsea Field

© VIDEO TREASURES M012336

SKIN GAME

D: Paul Bogart 102 m

PG | WST COM | 1971 | COLOR | Sex | Nud | Viol | Lang | AdSit

9 First-class comedy! Two men of the Old West really have a good con game going in this top-notch comedy with a social conscience. Set just before the Civil War, Garner and Gossett pose as master and slave. Their scam is that Garner sells Gossett for a high price, Gossett escapes and they split the dough. Then they can do it all over again in the next town. Everything is going great, too, until Susan Clark steals their money and Garner's heart; and a slave trader (Asner) takes Gossett and his girlfriend South into real slavery. Always entertaining. Has some really funny moments.

A: James Garner, Louis Gossett, Jr., Susan Clark, Edward Asner, Andrew Duggan

© WARNER HOME VIDEO 11406

SLAP SHOT

D: George Roy Hill 123 m

R | COM | 1977 | COLOR | Sex | Nud | Viol | Lang | AdSit

8 Outrageous and irreverent fun! Newman is the coach of a losing hockey team that plays the game like a bunch of delicate ballerinas. Hoping to turn things around for his bumbling minor-league team, Newman instructs his men to get out there and act like animals. They do and they start winning, but the crowd is more interested in the team's violent ice antics than the fact that they're winning. We're not just talking bad sportsmanship here, but out and out fistfights and martial arts, etc. The results are extremely funny, although the film was criticized for its heavy use of profanity.

A: Paul Newman, Strother Martin, Jennifer Warren, Michael Ontkean, Lindsay Crouse, Melinda Dillon

© MCA/UNIVERSAL HOME VIDEO, INC. 66012

SLEEPER

D: Woody Allen 88 m

PG | COM | 1973 | COLOR | Sex | Nud | Viol | Lang | AdSit

8 Woody Allen silliness supreme. Ridiculous farce in which Woody is a mild-mannered owner of a health food store who goes in to have an ulcer operation only to wake up - or rather, be defrosted - 200 years later, after having been wrapped in aluminum foil and frozen. This world is a vastly changed place from the one he left. He is almost immediately sought out to be recruited into an underground movement that is trying to overthrow the dictator, but Woody hides out instead, pretending to be a robot. Wacky silliness, slapstick gags aplenty and one liners flying everywhere.

A: Woody Allen, Diane Keaton, Mary Gregory, John Beck, Don Keefer, Don McLiam

Distributed By MGM/UA Home Video M201463

SLEEPLESS IN SEATTLE

D: Nora Ephron 105 m

PG | ROM COM | 1993 | COLOR | Sex | Nud | Viol | Lang | AdSit

9 Wonderfully endearing feel-good movie. The love of Tom Hanks' life has just died, leaving him and his young son heartbroken and lonely. He has left Chicago to get away from the memories but still he is always sad. So, his son contacts a radio show shrink to get help. In Baltimore, Meg Ryan is about to get married. She does her best to convince herself that she is doing the right thing in marrying this guy, but she is also powerfully drawn to the voice of a lonely, sleepless man a continent away she heard on the radio. As silly as it sounds, this is a charming and funny video that draws you to its attractive characters who you badly want to see get together and be happy.

A: Tom Hanks, Meg Ryan, Bill Pullman, Rosie O'Donnell, Rita Wilson, Rob Reiner

© COLUMBIA TRISTAR HOME VIDEO 52413

SLEUTH

D: Joseph L. Mankiewicz 139 m

PG | SUS MYS COM | 1968 | COLOR | Sex | Nud | Viol | Lang | AdSit

9 A delicious and winning film that is made even better by some really superb talent! Caine and Olivier play a masterful cat-and-mouse game, each trying to outsmart and outdo the other. Caine has had an affair with Olivier's wife. So, Olivier devises a clever plot to get even by trying to trick Caine into getting caught committing a crime. However, Caine figures out Olivier's plan and turns the table on Olivier, enacting his own kind of revenge. This totally unpredictable and inventive plot takes some terrific sharp turns that will leave you guessing! Both Olivier and Caine were Oscar-nominated.

A: Laurence Olivier, Michael Caine, Alec Cawthorne, Margo Channing, John Mathews, Teddy Martin

© VIDEO TREASURES SV9069

SLITHER

D: Howard Zieff 92 m

PG | COM | 1973 | COLOR | Sex | Nud | Viol | Lang | AdSit

7 Zany comic farce. James Caan and his cellmate Harry, were just released from prison but they are immediately attacked. Harry is killed but, with his dying breath, gives Caan a clue to $300,000 in stolen loot. This launches a wacky adventure in which a group of odd-ball characters - Caan, his amphetamine-addicted girlfriend (Kellerman), Harry's ex-partner Barry and Harry's wife (Lasser) - chase all over Southern California countryside in Barry's RV in search of the fortune. However there are two ominous black vans always in pursuit and everyone takes frequent comedic stops along the way.

A: James Caan, Peter Boyle, Sally Kellerman, Louise Lasser, Allen Garfield, Richard B. Shull

Distributed By MGM/UA Home Video M200171

SMILE

D: Michael Ritchie 113 m

PG | COM | 1975 | COLOR | Sex | Nud | Viol | Lang | AdSit

7 A sarcastic, comic poke at beauty pageants. The chief judge is a mobile home salesman (Dern), whose son snaps pictures of the contestants naked and tries to sell the pictures to his friends, but gets caught. The choreographer (Kidd) is trying to revive his flagging career. The head of the proceedings (Feldon) is a prude. Since there are a multitude of story lines going on at the same time, we are not allowed to get involved with any one character. That, along with its unflattering portrait of pageants, caused the public to stay away. This is unfortunate because the film is also frequently hilarious.

A: Bruce Dern, Barbara Feldon, Melanie Griffith, Michael Kidd, Geoffrey Lewis, Nicholas Pryor

Distributed By MGM/UA Home Video M201288

SMOKEY AND THE BANDIT

D: Hal Needham 96 m

PG | COM ACT | 1977 | COLOR | Sex | Nud | Viol | Lang | AdSit

9 Box office smash comedy. Good ol' boy Bandit (Burt Reynolds) gets hired to haul four hundred cases of Coors beer from Texarkana, Texas to Atlanta, Georgia. Since Coors is legal in Texas and not in Atlanta, there is a little bit of a situation - but if he can do it in 28 hours, he gets $80,000. So Burt runs interference, in a fast Camero, all across the South for the illegal load which is being driven in an 18-wheeler by Jerry Reed. Burt's job is keeping a herd of bumbling cops, led by local sheriff Jackie Gleeson, occupied for his good buddy Reed. Loads of car stunts and gags. A rollicking good time.

A: Burt Reynolds, Sally Field, Jackie Gleason, Jerry Reed, Mike Henry, Paul Williams

© MCA/UNIVERSAL HOME VIDEO, INC. 66003

SMOKEY AND THE BANDIT II

D: Hal Needham 101 m

PG | COM ACT | 1980 | COLOR | Sex | Nud | Viol | Lang | AdSit

7 Pretty good sequel to the original. This time the Bandit (Reynolds) and his buddy are hired to get a pregnant elephant to the Republican convention. But to do it, they have to go through the stomping grounds of their old arch-enemy sheriff Buford T. Justice (Gleeson). Dom DeLuis plays a gynecologist who gets to come along and treat the elephant. Contains a full assortment of the same sort of stunts that were the hallmark of the original, plus lots of clever dialogue, too. It doesn't have the same spark as the original did. Still, it's a good time.

A: Burt Reynolds, Sally Field, Jackie Gleason, Dom DeLuise, Jerry Reed, Paul Williams

© MCA/UNIVERSAL HOME VIDEO, INC. 66020

SNAPPER, THE

D: Stephen Frears 95 m

R | COM | 1993 | COLOR

7 A working class Irish family is thrown into turmoil when their eldest, a 20-year old unmarried daughter, announces that she is pregnant. The embarrassing situation is made nearly unbearable for mom and dad when she steadfastly refuses to name the father, because the unspoken truth is even more embarrassing. Rumors of who the father is begin to fly in the neighborhood causing an even bigger scandal. Poor old dad wants to do the right thing, but he just doesn't know what that is. Heavy Irish accents make this one difficult to catch much of the humor. Occasional gems pop through.

Sex / Nud / Viol / Lang / AdSit

A: Colm Meaney, Tina Kellegher, Ruth McCabe, Colm O'Byrne, Eanna Macliam, Ciara Duffy

© MIRAMAX HOME ENTERTAINMENT 2523

SNEAKERS

D: Phil Alden Robinson 125 m

PG-13 | SUS COM ACT | 1992 | COLOR

7 Entertaining caper. Redford and his group are very good thieves. They are hired by businesses to test for weaknesses in security systems by actually breaking in without getting caught. Then Redford is blackmailed by two CIA-types into having his team of misfits steal a black box from a brilliant inventor which contains the technology to decode any computer code in the world - a box many people would gladly kill for. Redford's team is made up of Poitier as an ex-CIA man and Aykroyd as an electronics specialist who sees conspiracies everywhere. Sometimes exciting, with several amusing moments.

Sex / Nud / Viol / Lang / AdSit

A: Robert Redford, Sidney Poitier, Dan Aykroyd, River Phoenix, David Strathairn, Mary McDonnell

© MCA/UNIVERSAL HOME VIDEO, INC. 81282

SOAPDISH

D: Michael Hoffman 97 m

PG-13 | COM | 1991 | COLOR

6 A comic farce that pokes fun at the characters, producers and actors involved in soap opera land. Field is a neurotic soap opera queen who fears she is past her prime. She's having big troubles on-screen, backstage and personally, too. The scandals on-screen can't compare to the scandals off-screen. Kline is a has-been actor and her ex-lover, brought back to the show; and Downey is her callous producer, who only thinks about the ratings game. Plot lines and implausible scripts are also wreaking havoc on the set, and everybody is working only for their own advantage. Silly screwball farce.

Sex / Nud / Viol / Lang / AdSit

A: Sally Field, Kevin Kline, Robert Downey, Jr., Cathy Moriarty, Whoopi Goldberg, Elisabeth Shue

© PARAMOUNT HOME VIDEO 32445

S.O.B.

D: Blake Edwards 121 m

R | COM | 1981 | COLOR

6 Hollywood takes a direct hit in this comic attack. When a crazed producer's (Mulligan) "G" rated musical turns out to be a disaster, he has a nervous breakdown. Overnight, he is about to be all washed up. Then he decides to spice his flop up. Maybe some smut will turn things around and he can save himself. So he tries to convince his wife (Andrews) to bare her chest for some scenes so he can radically recut the film into a softporn production. Edwards's film pokes fun at the games Hollywood plays, and he achieves a small revenge for Hollywood's rough treatment of him during the '70s.

Sex / Nud / Viol / Lang / AdSit

A: William Holden, Robert Preston, Julie Andrews, Richard Mulligan, Robert Vaughn, Loretta Swit

© WARNER HOME VIDEO 699

SO FINE

D: Andrew Bergman 91 m

R | COM | 1981 | COLOR

6 Wacky, silly comedy. When his father's (Warden) dress-making company gets in debt trouble with the mob, pop calls in his tightly wound English professor son (O'Neal) to help. He does help but he also quickly winds up in bed with a gangster's wife (Melato) just as her husband shows up. O'Neal makes for a fast-break escape, grabbing her jeans by mistake on the way out, they split right down the middle when he tries to put them on and, voila, a new fashion craze is ignited. In spite of his rousing success in the fashion biz, he tries to go back to teaching game but she is still following him, and her husband is right behind.

Sex / Nud / Viol / Lang / AdSit

A: Ryan O'Neal, Jack Warden, Mariangela Melato, Richard Kiel, David Rounds

© WARNER HOME VIDEO 11143

SO I MARRIED AN AXE MURDERER

D: Thomas Schlamme 93 m

PG-13 | COM ROM | 1993 | COLOR

7 Charlie Mackenzie has trouble committing to a woman. He always finds a problem with them. Sherri was a kleptomaniac, Jill was in the mafia and Pam smelled like soup. Now Charlie has discovered the girl of his dreams at the butcher shop. She is smart and a real babe too. However, on a trip to visit his parents, his mother shows him an article from her tabloid magazine that describes a woman who has murdered her three previous husbands before moving on to a new town to begin again. Slowly, the paranoid Charlie begins to discover clues that point to his new love. Light-hearted and fun overall, but somewhat uneven. In an earlier time, it could have starred Bob Hope.

Sex / Nud / Viol / Lang / AdSit

A: Mike Meyers, Nancy Travis, Anthony LaPaglia, Amanda Plummer, Brenda Fricker, Alan Arkin

© COLUMBIA TRISTAR HOME VIDEO 52423

SOLDIER IN THE RAIN

D: Blake Edwards 88 m

NR | COM DMA | 1963 | B&W

7 A wonderful mix of comedy, sincere drama and some loveable wacky characters. Two Army sergeants share a very different sort of relationship. Gleason is a high-living wheeler-dealer who loves the service and is planning to stay for good. McQueen is sort of a boob who worships the ground Gleason walks on but is about to get back to civilian life and hopes Gleason will join him. Their relationship becomes strained when McQueen introduces Gleason to a very beautiful but ditzy young woman (Weld). The comic banter ranges from slapstick to sentimental.

Sex / Nud / Viol / Lang / AdSit

A: Steve McQueen, Jackie Gleason, Tuesday Weld, Tony Bill, Tom Poston, Ed Nelson

© CBS/FOX VIDEO 7737

SOME KIND OF WONDERFUL

D: Howard Deutch 93 m

PG-13 | ROM COM | 1987 | COLOR

8 Uniquely wonderful. This is a lovely story of a lovelorn teenager's romantic pursuits. Stoltz is a poor boy from the wrong side of the tracks who has fallen so head-over-heels in love with beautiful and classy Thompson that he is blind to the fact that his best pal, tomboy Masterson, is seriously in love with him. Wonderful exploration of the trials of teenage love that will leave you feeling wonderful. Funny and warm.

Sex / Nud / Viol / Lang / AdSit

A: Eric Stoltz, Lea Thompson, Mary Stuart Masterson, Craig Sheffer, John Ashton, Elias Koteas

© PARAMOUNT HOME VIDEO 31979

SOME LIKE IT HOT

D: Billy Wilder 120 m

NR | COM | 1959 | B&W

10 Wildly funny and now a legendary comedy. Two second-rate musicians witness the infamous St. Valentine's Day massacre in Chicago. That's a very unhealthy situation to be in. So with the mob in hot pursuit, the two disguise themselves as women and take up with an all-girl band that is leaving by train to a gig in Miami. Marilyn was rarely, if ever, more casually sensual than here; Curtis and Lemmon are a delight; and Joe E. Brown is a scream as a rich playboy with the hots for Jack Lemmon (in drag). Dazzling performances in a truly funny comedy.

Sex / Nud / Viol / Lang / AdSit

A: Marilyn Monroe, Tony Curtis, Jack Lemmon, George Raft, Pat O'Brien, Joe E. Brown

Distributed By MGM/UA Home Video M203848

SOMEONE TO LOVE

D: Henry Jaglom 110 m

R | COM | 1988 | COLOR

6 Film director Jaglom plays himself in this insightful mock-documentary that takes place over dinner. He plays a filmmaker who is frustrated with his relationship with a beautiful but noncommittal girlfriend (Marcovicci). So he gathers a bunch of his single friends together for a Valentine's Day dinner. Once seated, he begins to systematically ask all of his friends to answer into the camera the question, "Why are you alone?" Orson Welles (in his last film role) sits in the balcony, commenting Greek tragedy-like on the activities below him. A witty and intelligent look into human nature.

Sex / Nud / Viol / Lang / AdSit

A: Orson Welles, Andrea Marcovicci, Sally Kellerman, Oja Kodar, Michael Emil, Ronee Blakley

© PARAMOUNT HOME VIDEO 12673

SOMETHING FOR EVERYONE

D: Harold Prince 112 m

R | COM SUS | 1970 | COLOR

6 Angela Lansbury is the head of a previously wealthy German family just after WWII. The answer to her prayers appears to be a dynamic young man (York) who wants her to hire him as their footman. It seems he can do anything. But almost immediately, he begins an affair with her homosexual son and at the same time marries a beautiful young woman. York will go to any lengths to further his social standing. He has no morality or social conscience. This is a very well done and interesting black comedy with a twist ending, but the unattractive characters will leave some cold.

Sex / Nud / Viol / Lang / AdSit

A: Angela Lansbury, Michael York, John Gill, Anthony Corlan

© CBS/FOX VIDEO 7174

SOMETHING WILD

D: Jonathan Demme 113 m

R | COM SUS | 1986 | COLOR

7 An offbeat roller coaster ride full of comedy, fun, thrills and violence. A burned-out '80s accountant (Daniels) is looking for something to spice up his life and he finds it in Lulu (Griffith). She is a sexy flirt who invites him into her life and bed. She leads him on a wild ride back to her home town to meet her mother and then to her high school reunion where they run headlong into her psychotic ex-con ex-husband (Liotta) who terrorizes them. What starts out very funny and sexy becomes an intense story full of twists and turns. The soundtrack is outstanding, the acting is solid, and the plot compelling.

Sex / Nud / Viol / Lang / AdSit

A: Jeff Daniels, Melanie Griffith, Ray Liotta, Margaret Colin, Tracey Walter, Dana Preu

© HBO VIDEO 0001

SONGWRITER

D: Alan Rudolph 94 m

R · MUS COM · 1984 · COLOR · Sex Nud Viol Lang AdSit

6 Kristofferson and Nelson play fictional forms of themselves who, together, take the music industry by storm. Early in their career the country-western sensations split up to pursue their own interests. Nelson goes on to become a superstar of country song while Kristofferson remains the country rebel with a huge heart. When Nelson's wife throws him out and he gets into a sticky situation with a manager who wants to steal his material, he calls on his old pal to help him. An enjoyable story that takes you along at an even clip, and features a lot of country music.

A: Kris Kristofferson, Willie Nelson, Melinda Dillon, Rip Torn, Lesley Ann Warren, Mickey Raphael

© COLUMBIA TRISTAR HOME VIDEO 60437

SON-IN-LAW

D: Steve Rash 96 m

PG-13 · COM · 1993 · COLOR · Sex Nud Viol Lang AdSit

7 A pretty South Dakota farm girl leaves wholesome home to go to school in weird California. A short time on campus and she knows that this isn't the life for her, but then a wacked-out former geek (Pauly Shore) convinces her to loosen up a little and see what there is to see. It works, but when Thanksgiving time comes and the geek has no place to go, she decides to take him, along with her new clothes and orange hair, back to the farm with her. The folks don't know quite what to do with the long haired wild man, but soon they start to see that under that flashy shirt beats a heart of gold. Really silly. Maybe dumb would be a better word. But, it is also surprisingly fun.

A: Pauly Shore, Carla Gugino, Lane Smith, Cindy Pickett, Mason Adams, Patrick Renna

© HOLLYWOOD PICTURES HOME VIDEO 1998

SONS OF KATIE ELDER, THE

D: Henry Hathaway 122 m

NR · WST ACT COM · 1965 · COLOR · Sex Nud Viol Lang AdSit

9 Fast-paced Wayne Western with action, good times and a heart! Katie was a loving mother who had four rough and rowdy sons. When she dies, the four come home to pay their respects and decide that the youngest should honor their mother and go to college. But first they make a pact to get back the land that was taken from Katie and to learn the truth about their father's murder six months earlier. The gunman (Wayne), the gambler (Martin), the quiet guy (Holliman) and the kid (Michael Anderson, Jr.) all put aside their differences to learn the truth and to protect each other's back. Rousing good time.

A: John Wayne, Dean Martin, Martha Hyer, Earl Holliman, Jeremy Slate, James Gregory

© PARAMOUNT HOME VIDEO 6729

SPIES LIKE US

D: John Landis 102 m

PG · COM · 1985 · COLOR · Sex Nud Viol Lang AdSit

6 A very kooky and silly comedy. Aykroyd and Chase are two nitwit government employees recruited by a US intelligence organization for a perilous Russian spy mission. The pair couldn't fight their way out of a wet paper bag but, once deployed, manage to avoid all sorts of sticky situations anyway. However, they eventually come to realize that they've been had. They are really just a pair of decoys who have been sent out to get the Soviets off the tail of the real spies. A fun screwball comedy that ends up getting quite dangerous. Fans of wacky humor will enjoy!

A: Chevy Chase, Dan Aykroyd, Steve Forrest, Donna Dixon, Bruce Davison, William Prince

© WARNER HOME VIDEO 11533

SPLASH

D: Ron Howard 109 m

PG · COM ROM FAN · 1984 · COLOR · Sex Nud Viol Lang AdSit

9 An unbelievable plot is made both believable and captivating, thanks to outstanding acting by Hanks and Hannah and deft direction by Howard. Hanks is a wealthy businessman who has everything but love. When he nearly drowns off the coast of Cape Cod, it is a beautiful mermaid (Hannah) who rescues him. She is infatuated with him and grows legs to search the big city for him. She charms him with her incredible innocence and they fall madly in love, but Hanks still has a hard time learning to deal with her nautical nature. Fantastic movie-making and a wonderful blending of fantasy and romance.

A: Tom Hanks, Daryl Hannah, Eugene Levy, John Candy, Dody Goodman, Richard B. Shull

© TOUCHSTONE HOME VIDEO 213

SPLITTING HEIRS

D: Robert Young 87 m

PG-13 · COM · 1993 · COLOR · Sex Nud Viol Lang AdSit

6 Silly English farce that was written by Monty Python alumnus Eric Idle. In it, Idle plays the rightful sixteenth duke of Bournemouth who was switched at birth by his hippie American mother (Hershey), so he has been raised by Pakistani foster parents in London. Rick Moranis is the grown-up son of an English cook who has been raised thinking that he is the duke-to-be. Moranis and Idle become friends and that is how Idle discovers his lost true heritage. He then seeks help from wacky lawyer John Cleese to regain his title, who instructs him that the only way he will do it is if Moranis is "accidentally" killed. Fans of goofy humor only.

A: Rick Moranis, Eric Idle, Barbara Hershey, Catherine Zeta Jones, John Cleese, Sadie Frost

© MCA/UNIVERSAL HOME VIDEO, INC. 81494

STAKEOUT

D: John Badham 115 m

R · COM CRM · 1987 · COLOR · Sex Nud Viol Lang AdSit

8 A funny cop flick. Dreyfuss and Estevez are two undercover cops who derive great joy out of one-upping the other guy. They are given an "easy" assignment - simply to watch the girlfriend of a guy who has escaped from jail. The pair park their buns across the street and stakeout the subject, but she turns out to be beautiful. Dreyfuss falls in love with her and decides to pursue her! For Estevez, this this is the last straw. The charismatic pair works wonders on the screen in this hilarious buddy cop film.

A: Emilio Estevez, Richard Dreyfuss, Madeleine Stowe, Aidan Quinn, Dan Lauria, Forest Whitaker

© TOUCHSTONE HOME VIDEO 596

STAND BY ME

D: Rob Reiner 87 m

R · DMA COM · 1986 · COLOR · Sex Nud Viol Lang AdSit

9 Wonderful, endearing, funny and highly entertaining story of the turning point in the lives of four 12-year-old buddies who enjoy one last summer together as children in 1959. One is an imaginative storyteller, one an overweight wimp, one a foolhardy daredevil and another a troubled and lonely toughguy. Richard Dreyfuss narrates this story, as a now-grown writer remembering an adventurous two-day camping trip with his three friends as they set out to find the dead body of a boy hit by a train. This is not a morbid outing but rather a grand adventure. Deeply affecting. Very special.

A: Wil Wheaton, River Phoenix, Corey Feldman, Jerry O'Connell, Richard Dreyfuss, Kiefer Sutherland

© COLUMBIA TRISTAR HOME VIDEO 60736

STARDUST MEMORIES

D: Woody Allen 89 m

PG · DMA COM · 1980 · B&W · Sex Nud Viol Lang AdSit

6 Allen is unabashedly playing himself in this unique but mean-spirited film. Sandy Bates (Allen) is a filmmaker whose earlier stuff can't compare (according to his fans) to his later stuff. He is a lonely genius who nobody understands. When a director cuts up his first serious film, he seeks solace by attending a seminar, but is immediately stampeded by fans, favor-seekers and film critics. Allen shows a side of himself that fans may not like, and takes a poke at those who have been critical of his work. Still, very interesting.

A: Woody Allen, Charlotte Rampling, Jessica Harper, Marie-Christine Barrault, Tony Roberts, Daniel Stern

Distributed By MGM/UA Home Video M203033

STARTING OVER

D: Alan J. Pakula 106 m

R · ROM COM · 1979 · COLOR · Sex Nud Viol Lang AdSit

8 Hilarious, and also good therapy for everyone who is recovering from divorce. Poor Burt Reynolds really needs to get on with his life, but he can't shake off his feelings for his ex (Bergen). Lonely and insecure, he joins a self-help group and relies upon his his brother (Durning) for support. His life is a mess until Durning introduces him to a schoolteacher (Clayburgh). Together, they are magic and become lovers, but when Bergen comes back, Burt is confused all over again. Very perceptive, charming and very funny. A warm and witty winner!

A: Burt Reynolds, Jill Clayburgh, Candice Bergen, Charles Durning, Frances Sternhagen, Austin Pendleton

© PARAMOUNT HOME VIDEO 1239

START THE REVOLUTION WITHOUT ME

D: Bud Yorkin 91 m

PG · COM · 1970 · COLOR · Sex Nud Viol Lang AdSit

7 Hilarious confusion! Set in 17th-century France, a peasant lady and an aristocrat each have twins, which are inadvertently mixed up. One Wilder/Sutherland combo grows up as aristocrats and the other as poor peasants. Years later, the mis-matched brothers first meet when both sets are sent to the the King's palace to prepare for the impending revolution. With the mixed-up pairs having one member each on opposite sides of the warring fence, absolute chaos erupts as they try to figure out which one is to be where and who is who. This madcap film developed a cult following.

A: Gene Wilder, Donald Sutherland, Billie Whitelaw, Hugh Griffith, Jack MacGowran, Victor Spinetti

© WARNER HOME VIDEO 11296

STEEL MAGNOLIAS

D: Herbert Ross 118 m

PG · COM DMA · 1989 · COLOR · Sex Nud Viol Lang AdSit

9 Extremely enjoyable romp through the intricacies of Southern femininity. This is NOT just a film for women, however. It is a real charmer which follows the exploits of six very different women in a small Southern town, who are friends in spite of their many differences. Their individual stories are interwoven to provide a very rich tapestry of life in all its aspects. These are friends who share their insecurities, their joys and support each other in their deepest sorrows. It is, at the same time, very funny and deeply affecting.

A: Julia Roberts, Sally Field, Dolly Parton, Shirley MacLaine, Olympia Dukakis, Daryl Hannah

© COLUMBIA TRISTAR HOME VIDEO 70243

ST. ELMO'S FIRE

D: Joel Schumacher 110 m

R | DMA COM | 1985 | COLOR | Sex, Nud, Viol, Lang, AdSit

8 Outstanding reality check! A group of Georgetown graduates are finding that the real world is a little hard to take and, as the pressures of real life mount, their friendships are tested. A cocaine addict sleeps with her boss, a guy pines away for a sophisticated lady, a virgin has the hots for an irresponsible hunk, a yuppie cheats on his live-in and his best friend wants a piece of the action. These messed-up friends really need each other! A unique slice of life story that neatly puts together a colorful puzzle all about growing up.

A: Emilio Estevez, Rob Lowe, Judd Nelson, Andrew McCarthy, Demi Moore, Ally Sheedy

© COLUMBIA TRISTAR HOME VIDEO 60559

STEVE MARTIN LIVE

D: Carl Gottlieb, Gary Wels 60 m

NR | COM | 1986 | COLOR | Sex, Nud, Viol, Lang, AdSit

7 The wild and crazy guy is up to his comic antics again in his first concert that was made available on video. Comic highlights in this performance filmed live in 1979 include "King Tut," "Wild and Crazy Guy," "Fun Balloon Animals" and the hilarious comic short "The Absent Minded Waiter," which was nominated for an Academy award. Martin fans will have a very good time sampling Martin's early humor.

A: Steve Martin, David Letterman, Henny Youngman, Paul Simon, Buck Henry, Teri Garr

© LIVE HOME VIDEO VA3134

STING, THE

D: George Roy Hill 129 m

PG | SUS COM | 1973 | COLOR | Sex, Nud, Viol, Lang, AdSit

10 Very popular and hugely entertaining reteaming of the winning duo from BUTCH CASSIDY AND THE SUNDANCE KID, and the winner of 7 Oscars - including Best Picture. After his partner and friend is killed by a NYC hood (Shaw), a small-time con man Redford enlists Newman's help in a big-time scheme to take the guy down, hard. Very talented cast. A clever and intricate plot keeps moving and keeps you guessing and second-guessing. You know there's a con being worked, but you don't ever really know how or who. A very lively Scott Joplin ragtime score from Marvin Hamlisch adds to the fun.

A: Paul Newman, Robert Redford, Robert Shaw, Eileen Brennan, Charles Durning, Ray Walston

© MCA/UNIVERSAL HOME VIDEO, INC. 66009

STIR CRAZY

D: Sidney Poitier 111 m

R | COM | 1980 | COLOR | Sex, Nud, Viol, Lang, AdSit

8 Pryor and Wilder really deliver the laughs as two average Joes blow off the big city and head for the wonderful West hoping for a change of luck. The wacky pair manage to run out of money in Arizona and take a job that requires them to wear ridiculous woodpecker costumes for a bank promotion. When two bank robbers steal their costumes, Wilder and Pryor are arrested for the robbery and sentenced to 120 years in the slammer. Now there's a sadistic warden, a huge mass-murderer and scheming guards to survive. This effortless silly slice-of-prison life comedy had audiences rolling in the aisles.

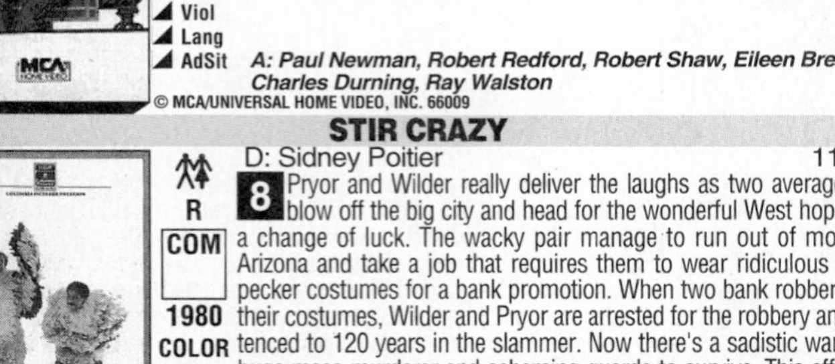

A: Gene Wilder, Richard Pryor, JoBeth Williams, Georg Stanford Brown, Craig T. Nelson, Barry Corbin

© COLUMBIA TRISTAR HOME VIDEO 60216

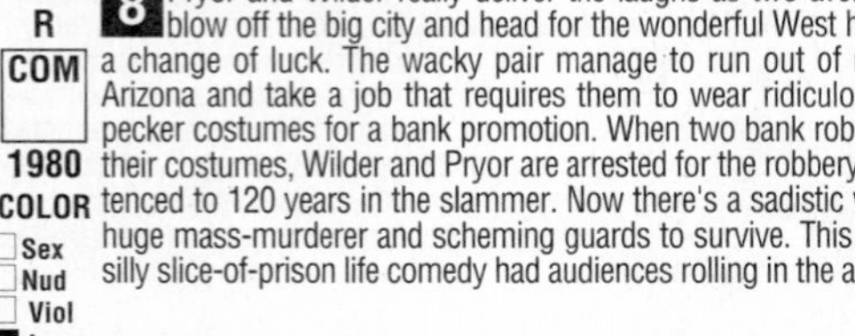

STRANGERS IN GOOD COMPANY

D: Cynthia Scott 101 m

PG | COM DMA | 1991 | COLOR | Sex, Nud, Viol, Lang, AdSit

9 Absolutely delightful. A small group of old ladies, all from widely different backgrounds, is on a field trip on a back road when their bus breaks down. They are stranded twenty miles from help, so they take refuge in an old house, scrounge for food from nature and talk. Who would have expected listening to these women talk to be such a good time. True, it is slow at times, but never for too long... and then something will happen that makes the wait entirely worth while. It is like a fine wine which must be slipped slowly. Worthwhile for everyone but, like fine wine, is likely better appreciated by more experienced consumers.

A: Alice Diablo, Constance Garneau, Winifred Holden, Cissy Meddings, Mary Meigs, Catherine Roche

© TOUCHSTONE HOME VIDEO 1354

STRICTLY BALLROOM

D: Baz Luhrmann 94 m

PG | ROM COM | 1993 | COLOR | Sex, Nud, Viol, Lang, AdSit

8 A very different sort of comedy from Australia. Paul Mercurio has been in training, under the tutelage of his very driven mother, since he was six years old to win the Pan-Pacific Grand Prix Dance Championship. She desperately wants the championship for her son, that was denied to her and his father. The son, however, is frustrated by the rigid confines of tradition and wants to dance his own steps. His mother is furious with him, but he is determined. He will dance his way and he selects as his dance partner lowly Fran, a mousey-looking beginner, because she believes in him. Critics and regular folks loved this quirky charmer that is sort of a combination of ROCKY and FLASHDANCE.

A: Paul Mercurio, Tara Morice, Bill Hunter, Shirley Hastings, Liz Holt, Les Kendall

© TOUCHSTONE HOME VIDEO 1701

STRIPES

D: Ivan Reitman 106 m

R | COM | 1981 | COLOR | Sex, Nud, Viol, Lang, AdSit

8 This riotous farce was a well-designed vehicle for Murray's casual and caustic wit. When he loses his girlfriend, his job and his apartment, Murray and his best friend (Ramis) decide to join the Army. These two screwups make life a misery for their platoon sergeant Warren Oates, until the very last days of their training when Murray decides to shape up his platoon in his own hilarious fashion. From basic training, these clowns head to Europe where they borrow a nuclear weapons carrier disguised as an RV. Ridiculous, silly and very funny.

A: Bill Murray, Harold Ramis, Warren Oates, P.J. Soles, John Candy, John Larroquette

© COLUMBIA TRISTAR HOME VIDEO 60221

STUNTMAN, THE

D: Richard Rush 130 m

R | SUS COM ACT | 1980 | COLOR | Sex, Nud, Viol, Lang, AdSit

9 An uncommon black comedy with spirit! When Vietnam vet Railsback ventures onto a movie set and inadvertently causes the death of the top stuntman, Director O'Toole agrees to hide him from police. But Railsback must replace the dead stuntman. Railsback trains rigorously under O'Toole, who turns out to be a slightly sadistic coach. Then he uncovers the fact that O'Toole is planning to stage a stunt that will kill him. Slightly offbeat and frequently funny, the movie covers a lot of ground and has several twists. But if you stay with it, you will be rewarded.

A: Peter O'Toole, Steve Railsback, Barbara Hershey, Alex Rocco, Chuck Bail, Alan Goorwitz

© FOXVIDEO 1110

SUBURBAN COMMANDO

D: Burt Kennedy 88 m

PG | CLD COM | 1991 | COLOR | Sex, Nud, Viol, Lang, AdSit

7 Wrestling's superstar Hulk Hogan is surprisingly likable and effective as Shep Ramsey, an alien warrior who has battled General Ball and defeated his plan to take over the Universe. He has come to earth to get a little well-deserved rest but instead becomes involved with the troubled lives of a down-on-their-luck urban family. Father Christopher Lloyd is too mild-mannered and is being over-run by his boss, so Shep gives him some lessons and helps to revive their luck. Mostly for kids.

A: Hulk Hogan, Christopher Lloyd, Shelley Duvall, Larry Miller, William Ball, JoAnn Dearing

© TURNER HOME ENTERTAINMENT N4098

SUGARLAND EXPRESS, THE

D: Steven Spielberg 109 m

PG | DMA COM | 1974 | COLOR | Sex, Nud, Viol, Lang, AdSit

8 Oddly fascinating film that was Steven Spielberg's first feature film. A simple-minded girl, just released from jail after having served a short sentence for a minor theft, learns that her baby is being adopted by a family in Sugarland, Texas. In a fit of desperation, she breaks her husband out of prison, kidnapping a cop along the way. They all set off to Sugarland in a stolen cop car to get her baby back. Pursued by an armada of police cars, she gets major publicity and becomes a folk hero. Based upon an actual 1969 event.

A: Goldie Hawn, Ben Johnson, William Atherton, Michael Sacks

© MCA/UNIVERSAL HOME VIDEO, INC. 55052

SUMMER SCHOOL

D: Carl Reiner 98 m

PG-13 | COM | 1987 | COLOR | Sex, Nud, Viol, Lang, AdSit

8 Excellent summer fun - at school! Harmon is a laid-back high school coach and teacher whose mellow teaching style gets him in hot water. His students aren't doing very well, and so the administration forces Harmon to stay home from a Hawaiian vacation to prepare some kids for a big remedial English test. If they don't pass, he loses his job! Summer love ignites when Harmon falls for Alley. She isn't interested in him in the beginning, but soon comes around and even helps out. Reiner's deft direction makes this a blast for teenagers and middle-agers alike.

A: Mark Harmon, Kirstie Alley, Robin Thomas, Dean Cameron, Patrick Labyorteaux, Courtney Thorne-Smith

© PARAMOUNT HOME VIDEO 1518

SUNDOWNERS, THE

D: Fred Zinnemann 133 m

NR | WST DMA COM | 1960 | COLOR | Sex, Nud, Viol, Lang, AdSit

9 Wonderfully winning film that was a Best Picture nominee and received four other nominations. One of the best-ever of many Mitchum/Kerr pairings. It is the loving character study of a headstrong rover who insists upon taking his wife and family with him from job to job, herding and shearing sheep in Australia's outback during the 1920s. He loves his family and he loves the life, but she thinks its time to settle down. Shot on location in Australia. Numerous winning vignettes and a crew of fascinating characters populate this endearing story. Highly recommended and rewarding viewing for all ages.

A: Deborah Kerr, Robert Mitchum, Peter Ustinov, Michael Anderson, Jr., Glynis Johns, Dina Merrill

© WARNER HOME VIDEO 11215

SUNSHINE BOYS, THE

D: Herbert Ross 102 m

PG | COM | 1975 | COLOR | Sex | Nud | Viol | Lang | AdSit

8 Very popular and appealing Neil Simon Broadway comedy brought to the screen. Richard Benjamin is a talent agent who schemes to entice his retired old uncle and former partner to revive their one-time top vaudeville act for a TV special. The problem is that, while the two were great together on stage, they hated each other's guts offstage and have been feuding for years. This is the first screen appearance of George Burns since 1939 and he received a Best Supporting Actor Oscar for his efforts. With Burns and Matthau this film can't miss and it doesn't.

A: George Burns, Walter Matthau, Richard Benjamin, Lee Meredith, Carol Arthur, Howard Hesseman

Distributed By MGM/UA Home Video M600014

SUPERMAN II

D: Richard Lester 127 m

PG | ACT COM FAN | 1979 | COLOR | Sex | Nud | Viol | Lang | AdSit

8 Superman (Reeve) has his hands really full when three evil villains from his home planet Krypton come to earth and are intent on ruling it. They all possess the same powers that Superman has, and so the challenging battle to save the world begins. Meanwhile, Superman falls deeper in love with Lois Lane (Kidder), and arch rival Lex Luthor (Hackman) keeps persistently nipping at his heels. Much more brash and wild that the first film, this super adventure keeps the adrenaline pumping and the laughs coming at a very steady pace.

A: Christopher Reeve, Margot Kidder, Gene Hackman, Ned Beatty, Valerie Perrine, Jackie Cooper

© WARNER HOME VIDEO 11120

SUPERMAN, THE MOVIE

D: Richard Donner 143 m

PG | ACT COM FAN | 1978 | COLOR | Sex | Nud | Viol | Lang | AdSit

9 A super movie! Reeve is the man of steel from the planet Krypton who is sent to earth as a child and is raised in a small midwestern town. When he is grown he moves to the big city and uses his super powers to keep crime at bay. Clark Kent, the unassuming newspaper man, becomes Superman when duty calls. He fights for truth, justice and the American way while battling the evil Lex Luthor (Hackman). Superman also falls for the captivating Lois Lane (Kidder) in this infectious film that spawned three sequels. Plenty of humor, adventure and romance. Oscar winner for special effects!

A: Christopher Reeve, Margot Kidder, Marlon Brando, Gene Hackman, Ned Beatty, Jackie Cooper

© WARNER HOME VIDEO 1013

SUPPORT YOUR LOCAL GUNFIGHTER

D: Burt Kennedy 92 m

PG | COM WST | 1971 | COLOR | Sex | Nud | Viol | Lang | AdSit

8 The uproariously funny SUPPORT YOUR LOCAL SHERIFF! was so successful that they decided to do another one. Technically, this is not a sequel, because the characters are different (although the actors aren't). This time around Garner is a con artist who has spied an opportunity to make a fortune in a mining dispute. But, in order to do it he has to convince everyone that the bumbling Jack Elam is really a notorious gunfighter and killer. While this one doesn't have the sparkle and punch of the first one, it is still a darn good time and well worth the time spent.

A: James Garner, Suzanne Pleshette, Jack Elam, Harry Morgan, John Dehner, Joan Blondell

Distributed By MGM/UA Home Video M201122

SUPPORT YOUR LOCAL SHERIFF

D: Burt Kennedy 92 m

G | COM WST | 1969 | COLOR | Sex | Nud | Viol | Lang | AdSit

10 A very, very funny picture - that shoots holes in just about every cliche ever packed into a Western. James Garner is a drifter, passing through a gold-mining boomtown. He's got the fastest wit in the West but at heart he is just a peace lover and it is only his economics which force him into becoming the town sheriff. He is quick to point out that he is really just on his way to Australia. The only one in town actively on his side is the one-eyed town drunk (Eliam). Against him is a cantankerous old man, his snide gunslinger son and the mayor's spoiled suffragette daughter. Absolutely hilarious! Also, see BLAZING SADDLES.

A: James Garner, Joan Hackett, Walter Brennan, Harry Morgan, Jack Elam, Bruce Dern

Distributed By MGM/UA Home Video M202031

SURE THING, THE

D: Rob Reiner 94 m

PG-13 | COM ROM | 1985 | COLOR | Sex | Nud | Viol | Lang | AdSit

7 Sure entertainment! College freshman and party hound John Cusack, and prudish Daphne Zuniga accidentally wind up sharing a ride to California over Christmas break. Cusack, who is actually a strike-out with women, is traveling to see surfer girl Nicollette Sheridan who is supposed to be a "sure thing". Zunigan is supposed to reunite with her equally uptight boyfriend. But, Cusack and Zunigan fight so much that their ride deserts them and to their mutual surprise, they find themselves falling in love with each other on this comic road trip wrought with misadventure.

A: John Cusack, Daphne Zuniga, Anthony Edwards, Viveca Lindfors, Nicollette Sheridan, Tim Robbins

© NEW LINE HOME VIDEO 2178

SWAN, THE

D: Charles Vidor 109 m

NR | ROM COM | 1956 | COLOR | Sex | Nud | Viol | Lang | AdSit

6 The beautiful princess (Kelly) is supposed to marry the prince (Guinness) and save her family's declining fortunes, however she would rather spend her time with her handsome tutor, a common man (Jourdan). Still, when she spies the prince, she is immediately taken by him. However the prince is cool to the arranged wedding, so her mother sets about plotting to make him jealous. It is ironic that this was Grace Kelly's last film before her marriage to Prince Rainier. Slow in spots, and the humor is subtle but the story is captivating and heartwarming. As always, Grace is delightful.

A: Grace Kelly, Alec Guinness, Louis Jourdan, Agnes Moorehead, Jessie Royce Landis, Brian Aherne

Distributed By MGM/UA Home Video M201068

SWEET HEARTS DANCE

D: Robert Greenwald 101 m

R | ROM COM | 1988 | COLOR | Sex | Nud | Viol | Lang | AdSit

6 Nice little change-of-pace film for tough guy Don Johnson. It is the parallel love stories of two high school buddies. Johnson has married his high school sweetheart (Sarandon), is a carpenter, has three kids and is going through a mid-life crisis about his relationship with her. However, his buddy (Daniels) is single, has played around for years, is a school principal, but has fallen in love with a teacher (Perkins) and is about to begin his first real relationship. Entertaining story of the changing natures of both life and love. A little slow-moving in places.

A: Don Johnson, Susan Sarandon, Jeff Daniels, Elizabeth Perkins

© COLUMBIA TRISTAR HOME VIDEO 67012

SWEETIE

D: Jane Campion m

R | COM DMA | 1990 | COLOR | Sex | Nud | Viol | Lang | AdSit

7 A very unique comedy drama from Australia. In the tradition of BLUE VELVET and ERASERHEAD, the strange photography and shady characters give this film a very offbeat, surrealistic feeling. Story centers around two sisters: one a very quiet, depressed wallflower (Lemon), and Sweetie (Colson), the obese nutcase who turns her and her family's lives completely inside out. A very strange but intriguing study of human nature, relationships and sibling rivalry that is not for all tastes.

A: Genevieve Lemon, Karen Colston, Tom Lycos, Dorothy Barry, Jon Darling, Michael Lake

© LIVE HOME VIDEO 68929

SWEET LORRAINE

D: Steve Gomer 91 m

PG-13 | COM DMA | 1987 | COLOR | Sex | Nud | Viol | Lang | AdSit

7 Sentimental sleeper that packs a big punch in a small package! Once a grand hotel in the Catskills, the Lorraine is now 80-years-old and is badly in need of extensive repairs, but the money for the renovation just isn't there. Owner Stapleton is very fond of the hotel and staff, but she faces bankruptcy. Alvarado is her granddaughter who helps wherever she can and finds herself drawn into a love for the old place, too. Developers anxious to get ahold of the prime land offer a tempting price. Could this be the last summer for the memorable hotel? An atmospheric and sentimental journey.

A: Maureen Stapleton, Trini Alvarado, Lee Richardson, John Bedford Lloyd, Giancarlo Esposito, Edie Falco

© PARAMOUNT HOME VIDEO 12606

SWEPT AWAY...

D: Lina Wertmuller 116 m

R | FOR COM ROM | 1975 | COLOR | Sex | Nud | Viol | Lang | AdSit

8 Provocative, saucy Italian comedy with a rough edge. Melato is a spoiled, rich, arrogant woman who continually humiliates the staff aboard her yacht and degrades her servant (Giannini). However, when they end up stranded together on a deserted island, the wars erupt. They can agree upon nothing. She is a rich capitalist. He is a deckhand and a communist. But the sex is great and their roles are quickly reversed. Giannini becomes the dominator, completely controlling Melato's every thought and stripping her of all dignity and vanity. A delightful mixed bag of morality and humor. Dubbed.

A: Giancarlo Giannini, Mariangela Melato

© COLUMBIA TRISTAR HOME VIDEO 60224

SWIMMING TO CAMBODIA

D: Jonathan Demme 85 m

NR | COM | 1987 | COLOR | Sex | Nud | Viol | Lang | AdSit

7 A very unique, disarming film. The entire film is a shot showing performing artist Gray sitting on a stage, behind his desk and delivering a wry and often hilarious monologue about his experiences in Thailand during the filming of THE KILLING FIELDS. Gray's often humorous, often tragic account of his experiences also sports an occasional movie clip or bar of music to supplement the monologue that expertly evokes vivid pictures. Don't write this one off, it is very different, but it is completely absorbing and compellingly interesting. You may also want to see his MONSTER IN A BOX.

A: Spalding Gray

© WARNER HOME VIDEO 760

SWING SHIFT

D: Jonathan Demme 100 m

PG | DMA COM | 1984 | COLOR

6 A WWII period piece, with fine attention to detail. It attempts to capture, through a fictionalized account, the feel of the first time that women joined the work force as their husbands were sent off to war. However, the film takes an unfortunate turn when it concentrates on romance instead. When Hawn's husband (Harris) is shipped off to fight, she takes a job as a riveter in a munitions plant to make ends meet. While there, she catches the eye of the macho Russell and the pair have an affair. Things get messy when Hawn's husband finds out about it. Lahti was Oscar-nominated.

Sex / Nud / Viol / Lang / AdSit

A: Goldie Hawn, Kurt Russell, Christine Lahti, Ed Harris

SWITCH

D: Blake Edwards 104 m

R | COM | 1990 | COLOR

7 A funny farce. Steve (King) is a womanizing slimeball who faces his personal judgment day when three discarded ex-lovers murder him. God makes a deal with the devil to send Steve back and give him one more chance - but he must find just one woman who truly likes him or he will go straight to hell. Satan agrees but adds his own twist by insisting that he return as a female. Thus, sexist Steve wakes up in sexy Barkin's body. Barkin is terrific as he/she tries to meet the sex change challenge, including coping with high heals, and deciding whether to date a man or woman. Lighthearted fun.

Sex / Nud / Viol / Lang / AdSit

A: Ellen Barkin, Jimmy Smits, JoBeth Williams, Lorraine Bracco, Tony Roberts, Perry King

TAKE DOWN

D: Keith Merrill 96 m

PG | COM DMA | 1978 | COLOR

7 Light-hearted sports serio-comedy. The high school in a little Utah town has a perpetually losing football team. Still they are determined to win at something. So they start a wrestling team, even though the only coach they have is a stuffy English teacher and Shakespeare scholar (Herrmann) who has no understanding at all of sports - and he isn't very excited by the prospect of coaching either. However, urged on by his wife, Herrmann learns to loosen up. Surprise, he develops a winning team but has to he struggle to keep his rebellious star athlete from dropping out of school. Rousing finish.

Sex / Nud / Viol / Lang / AdSit

A: Edward Herrmann, Kathleen Lloyd, Lorenzo Lamas, Maureen McCormick, Stephen Furst, Kevin Hooks

TAKE THE MONEY AND RUN

D: Woody Allen 86 m

PG | COM | 1969 | COLOR

7 Woody Allen's directorial debut. He plays a loser who tries to support his wife through an ill-advised career as a bank robber. In a great scene, he tries to stick up a bank with a demand note that is so poorly written that the teller can't even read it. ("Does this say gun or gub?") Bumbling Woody is caught and sent to prison but he escapes while working on an all-black chain gang. Still, when the group is approached by searchers, they all, including Woody, try to pose as a "very close family." Nonstop Woody Allen-type jokes, some of which are hysterical.

Sex / Nud / Viol / Lang / AdSit

A: Woody Allen, Janet Margolin, Marcel Hillaire, Jacquelyn Hyde, Lonny Chapman, Jackson Beck

TAKING CARE OF BUSINESS

D: Arthur Hiller 108 m

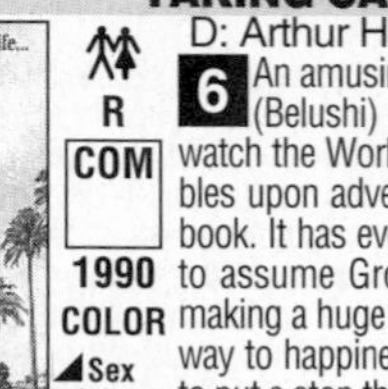

R | COM | 1990 | COLOR

6 An amusingly offbeat, somewhat campy, buddy movie. A convict (Belushi) engineers a daring escape from prison just so he can watch the World Series in person. However, while he is out, he stumbles upon advertising executive Grodin's coveted organizer and datebook. It has everything in it he needs. He seizes upon the opportunity to assume Grodin's identity and is now running around generally making a huge mess of Grodin's once perfect life. Belushi hot-tubs his way to happiness in Grodin's mansion, while Grodin tries desperately to put a stop the madness. Enjoyable light-hearted farce.

Sex / Nud / Viol / Lang / AdSit

A: James Belushi, Charles Grodin, Anne DeSalvo, Loryn Locklin, Stephen Elliott, Hector Elizondo

TALL GUY, THE

D: Mel Smith 92 m

R | COM | 1990 | COLOR

7 Wacky, quirky British comedy about a failed American actor (Goldblum) in England, scratching out an existence as the straight man to a loud and egotistical comedian. He is getting nowhere fast until he gets sick and winds up under the care of a sexy, take-charge nurse (Thompson). He pursues her persistently, inventing weekly illnesses, enduring weekly shots, until he wins her over. Just then he gets fired - but his acting career is resurrected when he gains the lead role in the musical version of THE ELEPHANT MAN. Somewhat spotty but also riotously hilarious in places.

Sex / Nud / Viol / Lang / AdSit

A: Jeff Goldblum, Rowan Atkinson, Emma Thompson, Geraldine James, Emil Wolk

TALL STORY

D: Joshua Logan 90 m

NR | COM | 1960 | B&W

7 Enjoyable little piece of froth about a man-hungry college co-ed who has fallen for the college basketball star Anthony Perkins. She is trying to get both her degree and her man. He, however, has unwittingly been bribed to throw the big basketball game between the American and the Soviet teams and is trying to get out of it. Light-hearted farcical fun. This was also Jane Fonda's film debut.

Sex / Nud / Viol / Lang / AdSit

A: Anthony Perkins, Jane Fonda, Ray Walston, Marc Connelly, Anne Jackson, Murray Hamilton

TAMING OF THE SHREW, THE

D: Franco Zeffirelli 122 m

NR | COM | 1967 | COLOR

9 Shakespeare for the masses, or at least as close as it gets. Director Zeffirelli has filmed this comedy more as a movie and less as a stage play. Richard Burton is a chauvinistic, poverty-stricken 16th-century Italian nobleman who seeks a wealthy wife. Rich merchant Hordern fears he will never find a man for his sharp-tongued, independent and free-thinking daughter. It seems like a perfect match, except for Taylor's protestations. Sparks fly from the then-married actor-couple as Burton attempts to woo Taylor. Lots of slapstick comedy. Highly entertaining.

Sex / Nud / Viol / Lang / AdSit

A: Elizabeth Taylor, Richard Burton, Vernon Dobtcheff, Michael Hordern, Natasha Pyne, Michael York

TAMMY AND THE BACHELOR

D: Joseph Pevney 89 m

NR | ROM COM | 1957 | COLOR

7 Simple and charming little romancer. It's a little corny but fun, and it made Debbie Reynolds into a national star. (It also gave her a very popular song: "Tammy.") When rich boy Nielson's private plane crashlands near poor Bayou-country girl Debbie's houseboat, she and her rascal grandfather (Brennan) rescue him, nurse him back to health and a romance is born. But cultures clash, too, when she is invited to stay with his wealthy family. Never fear, all ends well. Sweet, charming and so successful that it led to two sequels and a TV series.

Sex / Nud / Viol / Lang / AdSit

A: Debbie Reynolds, Leslie Nielsen, Walter Brennan, Mala Powers, Fay Wray, Mildred Natwick

TATIE DANIELLE

D: Etienne Chatliez 114 m

PG-13 | FOR COM | 1991 | COLOR

7 Very unusual and very black French satire. Auntie Danielle is 83. She lost her husband 50 years ago in the Great War and has been talking to his picture ever since. She is bitter, cantankerous, demanding and manipulative. She purposely strives to make everyone around her unhappy, it is her only real joy. Then, her well-meaning great-nephew asks her to move in with them, little knowing what he and his family are in for. Auntie makes their life miserable, so they leave on vacation with her in the care of a young woman they have hired. In her, Auntie has met her match. This is a very dark comedy that will not appeal to everyone. Subtitles.

Sex / Nud / Viol / Lang / AdSit

A: Tsilla Chelton, Catherine Jacob, Isabelle Nanty, Neige Dolsky, Eric Prat, Laurence Fevrier

TAXING WOMAN, A

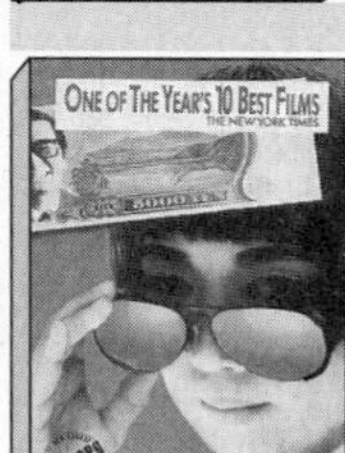

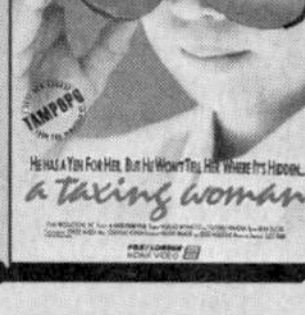

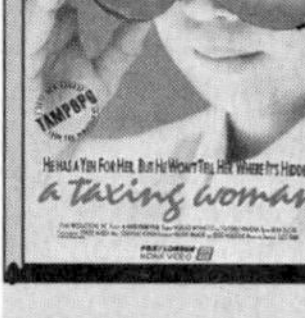

D: Juzo Itami 127 m

NR | FOR COM | 1987 | COLOR

8 Subtle and disarming Japanese black satire that was a winner of 9 Japanese Academy Awards, including Best Picture. Ryoko is innocent-looking and pretty, but she is also one of Tokyo's most single-mindedly determined tax collectors. She is so dedicated that she will sit outside a restaurant to compare the number of customers leaving to the receipts reported. Then, she sets her sights on one of Tokyo's best tax dodges, their famous love hotels. She is persistent in her efforts to catch its owner cheating, but he is just as persistent in his efforts to duck her - while they both fight their growing mutual attraction. Subtitles.

Sex / Nud / Viol / Lang / AdSit

A: Nobuko Miyamoto, Tsutomu Yamazaki

TEACHERS

D: Arthur Hiller 106 m

R | DMA COM | 1984 | COLOR

6 Well intentioned and mildly entertaining statement about the state of public schools of the time. John F. Kennedy High School is sued by a former student who graduated, even though he couldn't even read. JoBeth Williams is his attorney who does battle with the conservative school system and also carries on a romance with burned-out good teacher Nick Nolte. Nolte is caught between both warring factions, while also trying to deal with rebellious student Macchio. Some good comedic moments, good acting, over-all enjoyable but a little heavy-handed at times.

Sex / Nud / Viol / Lang / AdSit

A: Nick Nolte, JoBeth Williams, Lee Grant, Judd Hirsch, Richard Mulligan, Ralph Macchio

TEACHER'S PET

D: George Seaton 120 m

NR | COM ROM | 1958 | B&W

6 Enjoyable little farce. When hard-boiled city editor Clark Gable is roundly criticized by a night school journalism instructor, he is intent upon getting even. So he joins her class, unbeknownst to her. Instead of getting even, he becomes her star pupil, falls in love with her and seeks to win her heart away from her intellectual boyfriend Gig Young. Light, witty, bright and breezy. Gig Young is hilarious. Gable is winning, even though he was really too old for the role.

Sex Nud Viol Lang AdSit

A: Doris Day, Clark Gable, Gig Young, Mamie Van Doren, Nick Adams, Charles Lane

© PARAMOUNT HOME VIDEO 5716

TEAHOUSE OF THE AUGUST MOON, THE

D: Daniel Mann 124 m

NR | COM | 1956 | COLOR

9 Warm and winning. The US Army assigns a young officer (Glenn Ford) the task of teaching the tiny Okinawan village of Tobiki the benefits of democracy and free enterprise in the wake of World War II. Marlon Brando plays the overly large (he's supposed to be Japanese), shrewd and roguish peasant interpreter who helps Ford with his daunting task. Charming and witty compendium of the tribulations occurring when widely different cultures collide. Rarely has it been so much fun, however. Interesting characters, funny, with clever dialogue. Successful transition from Broadway play.

Sex Nud Viol Lang AdSit

A: Marlon Brando, Glenn Ford, Machiko Kyo, Eddie Albert, Paul Ford

Distributed By MGM/UA Home Video M200665

TERMS OF ENDEARMENT

D: James L. Brooks 132 m

PG | DMA ROM COM | 1983 | COLOR

10 Mesmerizing and totally heartwarming drama that captured five major Oscars, including Picture, Screenplay, Director, Actress and Supporting Actress. It is an intimate and winning character study of the relationship between a mother and daughter as it evolves over a period of years. MacLaine is wonderful as a neurotic, domineering mother and Winger is equally good as her independent-minded daughter who marries a cheating English teacher against her mother's wishes and later is to die of cancer. Totally captivating performances and story that surely will warm your heart and wet your eyes.

Sex Nud Viol Lang AdSit

A: Shirley MacLaine, Debra Winger, Jack Nicholson, John Lithgow, Danny DeVito, Jeff Daniels

© PARAMOUNT HOME VIDEO 1407

THAT DARN CAT!

D: Robert Stevenson 115 m

G | CLD COM | 1965 | COLOR

8 Lively Disney comedy about a Siamese cat named DC (Darned Cat), belonging to Hayley Mills, who comes home one night after its regular excursion with the wristwatch of a kidnapped bank teller around its neck. Hayley calls the FBI and agent Dean Jones (who is allergic to cats) trails DC through one slapstick adventure after another in his search to find the kidnapped woman. Bright and lively comedy with plenty of interesting characters, much like you would expect from the Disney fun factory.

Sex Nud Viol Lang AdSit

A: Hayley Mills, Dean Jones, Dorothy Provine, Roddy McDowall, Neville Brand, Elsa Lanchester

© WALT DISNEY HOME VIDEO 4125

THAT'S LIFE!

D: Blake Edwards 102 m

PG-13 | DMA COM | 1986 | COLOR

6 Harvey is wealthy and his wife is throwing him a big birthday party with all his friends and family in attendance. But Harvey is miserable and is making everybody else miserable. Harvey is turning 60, and he doesn't like it. His wife (Andrews) is having her own personal crisis. She will not know until after the party whether the biopsy for cancer, which she told no one about, was positive. Harvey is Jack Lemmon (or is it director Blake Edwards). This film has been criticized for unfolding just as though it was a home movie. Believable, funny in spots and moving.

Sex Nud Viol Lang AdSit

A: Julie Andrews, Jack Lemmon, Sally Kellerman, Robert Loggia, Emma Walton, Felicia Farr

© LIVE HOME VIDEO 5203

THAT TOUCH OF MINK

D: Delbert Mann 99 m

NR | COM ROM | 1962 | COLOR

7 Amusing romantic comedy. Ever-virginal Doris Day is naive and unemployed, walking through the canyons of New York when she is splashed by hot shot executive Cary Grant's limo. Smitten with the charms of Miss Day, Cary attempts to woo her with his charm and his money. That's it, that's all there really is - but it is a proven formula, has winning stars, sparkling dialogue and good support from a talented cast, particularly Gig Young. Enjoy.

Sex Nud Viol Lang AdSit

A: Cary Grant, Doris Day, Audrey Meadows, Gig Young, John Astin, Dick Sargent

© REPUBLIC PICTURES HOME VIDEO 5407

THEATER OF BLOOD

D: Douglas Hickox 105 m

R | HOR COM | 1973 | COLOR

6 Flamboyant film in which Price plays a Shakespearean actor who fakes his own death so that he can get revenge upon nine critics who have been less than kind to him throughout his career and have denied him the Best Actor of the Year Award. With the aid of his equally demented daughter (delicious Diana Rigg), he recreates particularly appropriate Shakespearean scenarios within which to extract his ghoulish punishments. Somewhat gory, but funny, too. A combination that has gained it a cult following.

Sex Nud Viol Lang AdSit

A: Vincent Price, Diana Rigg, Ian Hendry, Robert Morley, Jack Hawkins, Harry Andrews

Distributed By MGM/UA Home Video M600902

THERE'S A GIRL IN MY SOUP

D: Roy Boulting 97 m

R | COM | 1970 | COLOR

6 Light-hearted sex romp. Set in England, Peter Sellers is a TV gourmet who also has a taste for women. When his free-loving next door neighbor, Goldie Hawn in her patented "Laugh-In" ditzy blonde image, has a falling out with her live-in lover, Sellers falls in lust with her. Complications complicate when lust turns to love. Not terrific, but not terrible, either.

Sex Nud Viol Lang AdSit

A: Peter Sellers, Goldie Hawn, Diana Dors, Tony Britton

© GOODTIMES 4213

THERE WAS A CROOKED MAN

D: Joseph L. Mankiewicz 123 m

R | WST ACT COM | 1970 | COLOR

8 Quirky and clever Western. Crooked man Kirk Douglas steals a small fortune. He is caught when he is spotted by his victim (who is looking through a voyeur's peep hole at a whorehouse) as he is celebrating his new fortune. He is sent to an Arizona prison which is wardened by revision-minded Henry Fonda. But, Douglas uses the opportunities created by Fonda's revisions to institute a riot and escape and immediately sets off to recover the buried booty. But, a very angry and exasperated Fonda has personally set out after him. Entertaining Western, with a clever and funny plot, and a powerhouse cast.

Sex Nud Viol Lang AdSit

A: Kirk Douglas, Henry Fonda, Warren Oates, Burgess Meredith, Hume Cronyn, Arthur O'Connell

© WARNER HOME VIDEO 11270

THEY CALL ME TRINITY

D: E.B. Clucher 109 m

G | WST COM | 1971 | COLOR

6 A wild spoof of the very popular "speghetti Westerns" of the time, which became a surprise international hit on its own. Terence Hill is an amoral sheriff helped out by his dim-witted half-brother, but the two unexpectedly become the saviors of a group of Morman settlers who are being harassed by a group of marauding Mexican bandits. Mostly good fun and spiced with ample doses of slapstick humor and comic action.

Sex Nud Viol Lang AdSit

A: Terence Hill, Bud Spencer, Farley Granger, Gisela Hahn, Stephen Zacharias, Dan Sturkie

© UNITED AMERICAN VIDEO CORP. 5464

THEY MIGHT BE GIANTS

D: Anthony Harvey 98 m

G | COM ROM | 1971 | COLOR

6 Curious, interesting and quirky little comedy. When a retired judge (Scott) begins to believe that he is the great Sherlock Holmes, his brother sees an easy opportunity to grab his money. So the brother hires a female psychiatrist, coincidentally named Dr. Watson (Woodward), to investigate Scott. This she does, following Scott, fully dressed as Holmes, all around New York, while he is in search of the illusive Moriarity. Oddly, she soon begins to believe that he could actually be Holmes. More important than his true identity, she believes in him and two lonely people find and enjoy each other.

Sex Nud Viol Lang AdSit

A: George C. Scott, Joanne Woodward, Jack Gilford, Lester Rawlins, Rue McClanahan, Ron Weyand

© MCA/UNIVERSAL HOME VIDEO, INC. 80408

THINGS CHANGE

D: David Mamet 105 m

PG | COM | 1988 | COLOR

6 Don Ameche is great as an old shoeshine man who bears a striking resemblance to a Mafia don. The don makes a deal with the old man: if Ameche agrees to go to jail for him, he will set the old man up for retirement with a fishing boat in Sicily. A soft-hearted and soft-headed, low-level hood is assigned to watch the old guy during his last weekend of freedom, but decides to treat him to a wild weekend at Lake Tahoe instead. Things take a surprising turn when these two arrive in Reno. Everyone thinks the old man is a real Mafia king and they are given the royal treatment. Subtle and witty comedy.

Sex Nud Viol Lang AdSit

A: Don Ameche, Joe Mantegna, J.J. Johnson, Robert Prosky, Ricky Jay, Mike Nussbaum

© COLUMBIA TRISTAR HOME VIDEO 65011

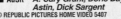

THIS IS MY LIFE

D: Nora Ephron 94 m

PG-13 | COM | 1992 | COLOR

6 Engaging little comedy. While there are no big laughs and it's a little too slow, this video will also generally keep a grin on your face. It is the story of a single mother with two daughters who struggles against long odds to make it as a performing stand-up comedienne. (Oddly, the funniest parts of the movie are when she is off-stage, not on.) Suddenly, almost overnight, she's a big hit, but now she has to deal with the kids's resentment and her own guilt for leaving them alone too much. Moderately interesting characters.

Sex / Nud / Viol / Lang / AdSit

A: Julie Kavner, Dan Aykroyd, Carrie Fisher, Samantha Mathis, Gaby Hoffman, Danny Zorn

© FOXVIDEO 1953

THIS IS SPINAL TAP

D: Rob Reiner 88 m

R | COM | 1984 | COLOR

6 A purposely absurd pseudo-documentary in which Rob Reiner, playing documentary producer Marty DeBregi, follows the decline of a fictitious British heavy-metal rock group which is sliding into obscurity on a disastrous American tour to promote their new album "Smell the Glove." Extremely satirical, with lots of insider jokes and some hysterical moments, but also a lot of misfires. This is not a movie for everyone, but those who appreciate this type of thing will have a good time.

Sex / Nud / Viol / Lang / AdSit

A: Rob Reiner, Michael McKean, Christopher Guest, Harry Shearer, R.J. Parnell, David Kaff

© NEW LINE HOME VIDEO 2081

THOROUGHLY MODERN MILLIE

D: George Roy Hill 138 m

G | MUS COM | 1967 | COLOR

6 Cute musical fluff that received 7 Oscar nominations and won Best Original Score. Julie Andrews arrives in the big city and quickly transforms herself into a 1920s modern woman - a flapper. She is also determined to realize her life's ambition: to become a stenographer and marry her boss. But, she becomes so caught up in her fantasy that she doesn't see that she really doesn't want her boss because she really is in love with someone else. All the while, her equally innocent new-found friend (Moore) has become the object of a white slaver's interest. Light-hearted light-weight campy farce.

Sex / Nud / Viol / Lang / AdSit

A: Julie Andrews, Mary Tyler Moore, Carol Channing, John Gavin, Beatrice Lillie, James Fox

© MCA/UNIVERSAL HOME VIDEO, INC. 55028

THOUSAND CLOWNS, A

D: Fred Coe 114 m

NR | COM | 1965 | B&W

8 Hilarious comedy about a non-conformist writer (Robards) who drops out of society. He lives with his precocious 12-year-old nephew and aspires to teach the boy his peculiar ways. All this makes him unpopular with the welfare department and he is being pressured by a social worker (Gordon) to go out and get a "regular job" - or they'll take the boy away. Filmed in NYC and taken from a big Broadway play. Witty, poignant, heart-warming and very funny. It is still very worthwhile, even though it is dated slightly because non-conformist Robards does have to sell out and get a job in the end.

Sex / Nud / Viol / Lang / AdSit

A: Jason Robards, Jr., Barbara Harris, Martin Balsam, Barry Gordon, Gene Saks, William Daniels

Distributed By MGM/UA Home Video M202365

THREE FUGITIVES

D: Francis Veber 96 m

PG-13 | COM | 1989 | COLOR

7 Cute little comedy with a sentimental twist. Nick Nolte is just out of jail and determined to go straight but, while he is at the bank trying to open up a new account, a bumbling would-be stick-up man (Martin Short) takes him as a hostage. No one will believe that Nolte was not in on it from the beginning. He and they are now wanted. So, having no choice, he, Short and Short's 6-year-old daughter make a mad dash for the border. Plenty of enthusiasm and lots of slapstick, but there are some sweet moments, too, between Nolte and the girl.

Sex / Nud / Viol / Lang / AdSit

A: Nick Nolte, Martin Short, James Earl Jones, Sarah Rowland Doroff, Kenneth McMillan, Alan Ruck

© TOUCHSTONE HOME VIDEO 950

THREE MEN AND A BABY

D: Leonard Nimoy 102 m

PG | COM | 1988 | COLOR

9 Lively, warm and very enjoyable (also extremely popular) comedy. Three carefree bachelors suddenly have unwanted responsibility thrust upon them. A destitute and distraught former girlfriend of bachelor Danson leaves a baby, his baby, on the doorstep of the trio's swinging, impeccably furnished and maintained bachelor digs. This is bubbly, brainless fun when the three party animals become instant, bumbling, overly-protective "fathers." Winning performances all around. It is an American remake of the French THREE MEN AND A CRADLE and was followed by THREE MEN AND A LITTLE LADY.

Sex / Nud / Viol / Lang / AdSit

A: Tom Selleck, Steve Guttenberg, Ted Danson, Nancy Travis, Margaret Colin, Philip Bosco

© TOUCHSTONE HOME VIDEO 658

THREE MEN AND A LITTLE LADY

D: Emile Ardolino 103 m

PG | COM ROM | 1990 | COLOR

8 Some liked this follow-up even better than the original! The men have all matured, baby Mary has now grown into an adorable 5-year-old, and Mom Travis has become an engaging romantic interest. All five live together in a happy home and all three men are dedicated fathers. But when Travis decides to move to England for the love of another man (Cazenove), Selleck's love for her is awakened and the men set out to prove Cazenove's true intentions and that he doesn't care a bit about little Mary. A genuine treasure with plenty love and laughter to go around.

Sex / Nud / Viol / Lang / AdSit

A: Tom Selleck, Steve Guttenberg, Ted Danson, Nancy Travis, Robin Weisman, Christopher Cazenove

© TOUCHSTONE HOME VIDEO 1139

THREE MUSKETEERS, THE

D: Richard Lester 105 m

PG | ACT COM ROM | 1974 | COLOR

9 Great, well-rounded entertainment that has a little bit of everything. Dumas's classic tale has been filmed numerous times, but never this well. Michael York is determined to become one of the King's elite guards, the Musketeers, so he befriends three of them but, they are only interested in fighting, drinking and chasing women. However, they do become roused to action when York charms Welch, the Queen's lady-in-waiting, and she uncovers a plot to overcome the King. This news sends the Musketeers into rip roaring action. Rousing swashbuckling and hilarious slapstick. Top talent.

Sex / Nud / Viol / Lang / AdSit

A: Oliver Reed, Raquel Welch, Richard Chamberlain, Michael York, Frank Finlay, Geraldine Chaplin

© LIVE HOME VIDEO 67776

THRILL OF IT ALL, THE

D: Norman Jewison 108 m

NR | COM | 1963 | COLOR

7 Cute little '60s spoof of the TV industry and commercials, in particular. Doris Day and her doctor hubby James Garner are happily married, but that is all drastically changed when a bored Day accepts a high-paying job as a spokesperson in TV commercials. She becomes an overnight sensation and their domestic bliss is transformed into a nightmare for Garner. All he wants is to have his old life back and he schemes to get it. Written by Carl Reiner. Fast and funny.

Sex / Nud / Viol / Lang / AdSit

A: Doris Day, James Garner, Arlene Francis, Edward Andrews, Elliott Reid, Carl Reiner

© MCA/UNIVERSAL HOME VIDEO, INC. 80320

THROW MOMMA FROM THE TRAIN

D: Danny DeVito 88 m

PG-13 | COM | 1987 | COLOR

6 DeVito is a hack would-be mystery writer taking a college class from almost-writer Crystal. Crystal is currently driven to distraction by his ex-wife who has stolen his unpublished book and gotten rich after selling it as her own. DeVito is tormented by a brutally domineering mother. When DeVito suffers from writer's block and Crystal suggests that he see Hitchcock's STRANGERS ON A TRAIN (in which two strangers agree to kill the other's "problem"), DeVito thinks it is an offer to swap similar services and takes him up on it. Very black comedy. A few big hit gags, but a lot of misses, too.

Sex / Nud / Viol / Lang / AdSit

A: Danny DeVito, Billy Crystal, Anne Ramsey, Kim Griest, Rob Reiner, Kate Mulgrew

© ORION PICTURES CORPORATION 8719

THUNDERBOLT AND LIGHTFOOT

D: Michael Cimino 117 m

R | ACT COM | 1974 | COLOR

8 Quirky action flick that Eastwood fans didn't quite know how to handle when it was released, but time has proven it to be a solid piece of action entertainment. Eastwood is a thief who is being hunted by his former partners (Kennedy and Lewis) who think that he set them up and then stole all their money from an earlier bank heist. When they do catch him, Eastwood and another young drifter (Bridges was Oscar-nominated) agree to join up with them and hit the same bank again in the same way as before. Colorful film, with great characters and an oddly interesting buddy element.

Sex / Nud / Viol / Lang / AdSit

A: Clint Eastwood, Jeff Bridges, George Kennedy, Geoffrey Lewis, Catherine Bach, Gary Busey

Distributed By MGM/UA Home Video M201392

TIE ME UP! TIE ME DOWN!

D: Pedro Almodovar 105 m

NC-17 | FOR COM | 1990 | COLOR

6 Controversial import from Spain. An orphan and mental patient (Banderas) is released from the hospital. He has nowhere to go, no skills (except in bed) and no one who cares for him. But he becomes fascinated with a porno star and convinces himself that she will grow to love him if she just has the time. So he barges into her apartment and ties her up until she can come to her senses. Oddly, she slowly does begin to develop a strange affection for this pathetic guy, which grows into love. Fresh and original, but somewhat slow and definitely odd.

Sex / Nud / Viol / Lang / AdSit

A: Antonio Banderas, Victoria Abril, Loles Leon, Francisco Rabal

© COLUMBIA TRISTAR HOME VIDEO 90903

TIME BANDITS

D: Terry Gilliam 116 m

PG | SF COM | 1981 | COLOR

6 A near-hit from Monty Python alumni Michael Palin and Terry Gilliam. It's witty and clever, with very high production values, but somehow doesn't connect big-time. A bored English schoolboy is escorted through time and space by six dwarves who have stolen a map of time holes from the Supreme Being. They are out to steal treasures from one time and escape into another time. Along the way they have encounters with Robin Hood, Agamemnon, Napoleon and the Titanic. Doesn't work real well as a comedy, but passes fairly well as an adventure.

Sex / Nud / ■ Viol / Lang / ■ AdSit

A: John Cleese, Sean Connery, Ian Holm, Shelley Duvall, Katherine Helmond, Michael Palin

© PARAMOUNT HOME VIDEO 2310

TIN MEN

D: Barry Levinson 112 m

R | COM | 1987 | COLOR

7 Clever comedy with both funny and telling moments, revealing human nature. Set in 1963, a couple of glorified con men - with big macho egos and even bigger cars - make a barely-legal living by tricking gullible homeowners into buying unneeded aluminum siding for their houses. When DeVito crunches the fender of Dreyfuss's brand new Cadillac, a war with escalating levels of revenge culminates when Dreyfuss sets out to seduce DeVito's wife (Hershey). But Devito hates her anyway. Hershey however, is transformed and she and Dreyfuss fall in love. Great dialogue and supporting cast.

Sex / Nud / ■ Viol / ■ Lang / ■ AdSit

A: Danny DeVito, Richard Dreyfuss, Barbara Hershey, John Mahoney, Jackie Gayle, J.T. Walsh

© TOUCHSTONE HOME VIDEO 571

TOM JONES

D: Tony Richardson 127 m

NR | COM | 1963 | COLOR

9 Sexy, extremely popular and funny. This is a spirited and flavorful story of an orphaned rascal and rake who lustily pursues his fortune, and all the women he meets, in an 18th-century England that is faithfully-reproduced for the screen. Hugely popular, it was the winner of four major Oscars: Best Picture, Director, Score and Screenplay. Also nominated in all four major acting categories. Ribald Tom Jones makes his way in the world by loving life, and women, to the fullest. That is a formula that makes him both envied and hated. Sometimes hilarious, often bawdy, frequently witty, and always sumptuous. A real treat.

■ Sex / Nud / ■ Viol / Lang / ■ AdSit

A: Albert Finney, Susannah York, Hugh Griffith, Edith Evans, Joan Greenwood, David Warner

© HBO VIDEO 90664

TOOTSIE

D: Sydney Pollack 116 m

PG | COM ROM | 1982 | COLOR

10 Wonderfully delightful picture and a huge blockbuster hit. Dustin Hoffman is an out-of-work actor who can't get a job, so he dresses up as a woman to win a part on a daytime soap opera. Quite by accident, he becomes a huge hit and is trapped into playing the role of a woman both onscreen and off. This is particularly distressing to him because he is falling in love with the leading lady (Jessica Lange) who thinks of him/her as a girlfriend. Worse, on a short trip home with Lange, her father makes a pass at him/her. Interesting insights on differences in sexes. 10 Oscar nominations. Funny!!

Sex / Nud / Viol / ■ Lang / ■ AdSit

A: Dustin Hoffman, Jessica Lange, Charles Durning, Bill Murray, Teri Garr, Dabney Coleman

© COLUMBIA TRISTAR HOME VIDEO 60246

TOTO THE HERO

D: Jaco van Dormael 94 m

PG-13 | FOR COM | 1992 | COLOR

8 Thomas is a cranky old man who is convinced that he was switched at birth with the rich kid next door who has now become a powerful industrialist. He has become obsessed with winning back the life that he is convinced was stolen from him. Ever since he was young, Thomas has had a fantasy that he is Toto the Hero, a secret agent. The movie's clever plot line concerns his plan to reclaim the heritage that is rightfully his, and the various flash backs and flash forwards used explain how he came to have such a skewed view of circumstances. Clever, original and fun. Subtitles.

Sex / ■ Nud / ■ Viol / Lang / ■ AdSit

A: Michel Bouquet, Mireille Perrier, Jo de Backer, Gisela Uhlen, Peter Bohlke, Thomas Godet

© PARAMOUNT HOME VIDEO 83088

TOUGH GUYS

D: Jeff Kanew 103 m

PG | COM | 1986 | COLOR

6 This picture was custom-made for Lancaster and Douglas, two screen legends. It was also their seventh time together on screen. In it, they play the last two successful train robbers in America, who are just now being released after a thirty-year stretch in prison. They are woefully out of place in the world of the 1980's and are given no respect because they are old. Lancaster winds up in a nursing home and Douglas can only find work doing menial labor. Demoralized, they decide to go back into the business that they know best, for one last big heist. Not hilarious, but still fun.

Sex / Nud / Viol / Lang / ■ AdSit

A: Burt Lancaster, Kirk Douglas, Charles Durning, Eli Wallach, Alexis Smith, Dana Carvey

© TOUCHSTONE HOME VIDEO 511

TOY, THE

D: Richard Donner 102 m

PG | COM | 1982 | COLOR

6 A very successful, but out of touch, businessman (Gleason) takes his spoiled kid (Schwartz) shopping for Christmas and tells him that he can have absolutely anything he wants in the store. The kid decides that he wants the janitor (Pryor), a down-and-out journalist who will gladly take the money. High comedy unleashes itself as janitor Pryor teaches Gleason and the kid a few things about love, life and happiness and helping to change their lives. Pretty simple and predictable but entertaining.

Sex / Nud / Viol / ■ Lang / AdSit

A: Richard Pryor, Jackie Gleason, Scott Schwartz, Wilfrid Hyde-White, Ned Beatty

© GOODTIMES 4499

TRADING PLACES

D: John Landis 118 m

R | COM | 1983 | COLOR

9 Wild and fun, silly comedy. Two wealthy brothers (Bellamy and Ameche) are at odds about whether environment or heredity has more to do with success. So, to settle the score, they make a bet using a fellow commodities broker (Aykroyd) and a homeless street hustler (Murphy) as unsuspecting guinea pigs. Suddenly, streetwise Eddie Murphy finds himself thrust into the lap of luxury and haughty broker Aykroyd must learn how to survive on the streets. Tough-talking hooker Curtis keeps Aykroyd from going off the deep end, while Murphy rapidly excels in his new job. Powerfully funny!

Sex / ■ Nud / Viol / ■ Lang / ■ AdSit

A: Dan Aykroyd, Eddie Murphy, Ralph Bellamy, Don Ameche, Jamie Lee Curtis, Paul Gleason

© PARAMOUNT HOME VIDEO 1551

TREMORS

D: Ron Underwood 95 m

PG-13 | HOR COM | 1989 | COLOR

7 A genuinely exciting and yet funny monster movie that is a direct throw-back to the 50s. Two comic handymen (Bacon and Ward), whose prime ambition is just to leave the dead-end town of Perfection, Nevada, have their departure interrupted and they get a little more excitement than usual when the town is attacked by hungry giant worm-like creatures capable of swallowing a car. The two join forces with a pretty female seismology student (Carter) and a heavily-armed survivalist couple (Gross and McEntire) in a battle to defeat the scheming treacherous worms. Genuinely fun. Fast-paced with good special effects.

Sex / Nud / ■ Viol / ■ Lang / ■ AdSit

A: Kevin Bacon, Fred Ward, Finn Carter, Michael Gross, Reba McEntire

© MCA/UNIVERSAL HOME VIDEO, INC. 80957

TRIBES

D: Joseph Sargent 90 m

G | DMA COM | 1970 | COLOR

8 Excellent made-for-TV movie. It was made during the time of the Vietnam war and revolves around many of the issues that concerned everyone then. It has become a little dated but it is also still both insightful and funny. Imagine a hippie, in a robe, with long hair and sandals, getting drafted into the Marines. Darin McGavin is the tough DI given the responsibility of turning this flower into a lean, mean, fighting machine. The trouble is, he is already lean and tough, but he's a dedicated peacenik. Worse yet, he's also a natural leader and everyone in the platoon is following him, not the tough DI. Really quite good.

Sex / Nud / Viol / Lang / ■ AdSit

A: Jan-Michael Vincent, Darren McGavin, Earl Holliman, John Gruber, Danny Goldman, Richard Yniguez

© FOXVIDEO 1669

TROUBLE WITH ANGELS, THE

D: Ida Lupino 110 m

NR | COM CLD | 1966 | COLOR

7 Charming light-weight fare in which two rambunctious young girls (Hayley Mills and June Harding) are constantly playing pranks and raising Cain at a Catholic convent school. They are driving the normally sane and saintly Mother Superior (Rosalind Russell) nuts. Warm and genial comedy suitable for the whole family.

Sex / Nud / Viol / Lang / AdSit

A: Hayley Mills, June Harding, Rosalind Russell, Binnie Barnes, Mary Wickes, Gypsy Rose Lee

© COLUMBIA TRISTAR HOME VIDEO 60250

TRUE GRIT

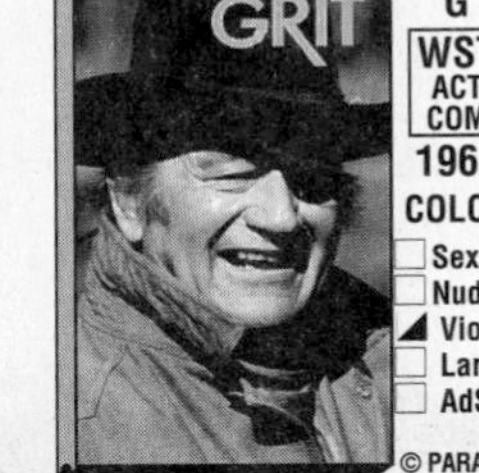

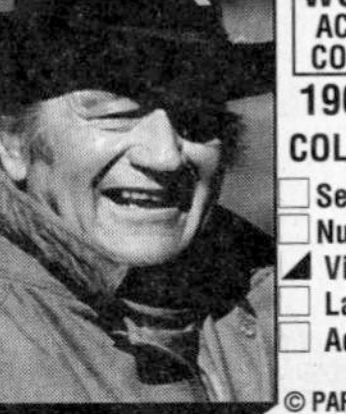

D: Henry Hathaway 128 m

G | WST ACT COM | 1969 | COLOR

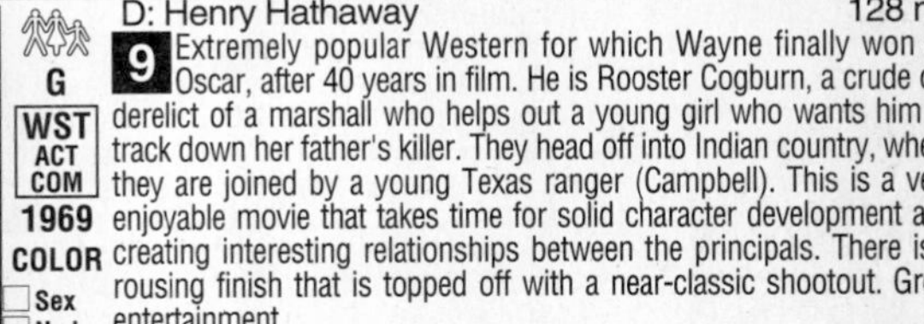

9 Extremely popular Western for which Wayne finally won an Oscar, after 40 years in film. He is Rooster Cogburn, a crude old derelict of a marshall who helps out a young girl who wants him to track down her father's killer. They head off into Indian country, where they are joined by a young Texas ranger (Campbell). This is a very enjoyable movie that takes time for solid character development and creating interesting relationships between the principals. There is a rousing finish that is topped off with a near-classic shootout. Great entertainment.

Sex / Nud / ■ Viol / Lang / AdSit

A: John Wayne, Glen Campbell, Kim Darby, Robert Duvall, Jeremy Slate, Strother Martin

© PARAMOUNT HOME VIDEO 6833

COM

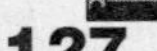

TRUE LOVE

D: Nancy Savoca — 101 m

R | COM DMA | 1989 | COLOR

6 A young Bronx working couple is getting married, even though they are just now discovering that they hardly know each other. The ball is rolling and they aren't going to let that stop one of the most extravagant, garish and tacky weddings ever (the mashed potatoes are dyed blue to match the dresses) from happening. Even though he proves to be an irresponsible sort, in their world men and women do what is expected of them and she's going to get him to the alter no matter what it takes. The film has some riotously funny scenes, but its characters are obnoxious at times and difficult to sympathize with.

Sex / Nud / Viol / Lang / AdSit

A: Annabella Sciorra, Ron Eldard, Roger Rignack, Aida Turturro, Star Jasper, Michael J. Wolfe

Distributed By MGM/UA Home Video M901763

TRUST

D: Hal Hartley — 107 m

R | DMA COM | 1991 | COLOR

8 Quirky, almost surreal black comedy. A pretty 16-year-old finds that she is pregnant. She tells her father. He insults her. She slaps him. He falls dead. She leaves home and meets up with a 17-year-old electronics whiz-kid who also left home because he can't get along with his dad. He can't hold a job because he refuses to stoop to work on TVs and he carries around his father's Korean War vintage hand grenade, just in case he wants to commit suicide. Deadpan dialogue. Stylish photography and plenty of off-beat moments. Can these two misfits find happiness? Likely will become a cult favorite.

Sex / Nud / Viol / Lang / AdSit

A: Adrienne Shelly, Martin Donovan, Merritt Nelson, Edie Falco, John Mc Kay

© REPUBLIC PICTURES HOME VIDEO 4205

TUNE IN TOMORROW

D: Jon Amiel — 90 m

PG-13 | COM | 1990 | COLOR

6 Oddball but amiable comedy. Reeves is a 21-year-old writer at a struggling New Orleans radio station in 1951. Along comes a flamboyant oddball writer (Falk) that the station has hired to write an original soap opera and boost their ratings. Falk becomes the younger's mentor and uses that relationship to develop a scandalous hit radio program that is based upon the love affair that has developed between Reeves and his 36-year-old aunt by marriage. Wacky Falk manipulates both of them and their relationship to get his soap opera material. Occasionally hilarious but also confusing at times.

Sex / Nud / Viol / Lang / AdSit

A: Barbara Hershey, Keanu Reeves, Peter Falk, Bill McCutcheon, Patricia Clarkson, Jerome Dempsey

© HBO VIDEO 90526

TUNNEL OF LOVE, THE

D: Gene Kelly — 98 m

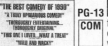

NR | COM ROM | 1958 | B&W

8 Richard Widmark and Doris Day desperately want a child but they can't seem to connect. But, their best friends and neighbors, Gig Young and Elisabeth Fraser, are a virtual baby factory. Doris and Richard decide to adopt. Gig, however has system which he imparts to Richard: Gig stays virile by playing around. Widmark is reminded of this when, nine months after he awakens in a motel room after a night on the town with a pretty investigator for the adoption agency, that same agency delivers Richard and Doris a new baby. Hit Broadway play that made it intact to the screen.

Sex / Nud / Viol / Lang / AdSit

A: Doris Day, Richard Widmark, Gig Young, Gia Scala, Elisabeth Fraser, Elizabeth Wilson

Distributed By MGM/UA Home Video 203047

TURNER AND HOOCH

D: Roger Spottiswoode — 110 m

PG | COM CRM ACT | 1989 | COLOR

6 Hanks is a quirky California cop with a compulsion for cleanliness who is assigned to uncover a murderer in a drug-related case. And, he inherits the only witness to the murder - the victim's really ugly, really big dog! Hooch is a mess, and messes up everything around him, including chewing up the upholstery of Hanks's car after he leaves the dog inside it. Hanks's natural charm, along with that of the curious canine, works reasonably well at holding our attention in this very mild comedy as the pair are put through their paces while solving the crime and coincidentally discovering romance too.

Sex / Nud / Viol / Lang / AdSit

A: Tom Hanks, Mare Winningham, Craig T. Nelson, Reginald VelJohnson, Scott Paulin, J.C. Quinn

© TOUCHSTONE HOME VIDEO 911

TURTLE DIARY

D: John Irvin — 96 m

PG | ROM COM | 1986 | COLOR

7 Different, offbeat romantic comedy from Britain. Two lonely, repressed Londoners are brought together and discover love under odd circumstances. She is an author of children's books. He is a clerk at a bookstore. However, both have become obsessed with the plight of three sea turtles at the London Zoo and plot together, along with the help of the zoo keeper, to free them into the open ocean. Fresh and low-key. Intelligent and quite touching.

Sex / Nud / Viol / Lang / AdSit

A: Ben Kingsley, Glenda Jackson, Michael Gambon, Richard Johnson, Rosemary Leach, Eleanor Bron

© LIVE HOME VIDEO VA5173

TWINS

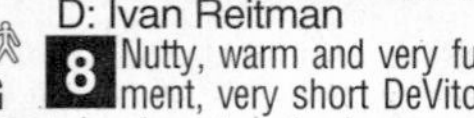

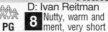

D: Ivan Reitman — 107 m

PG | COM | 1989 | COLOR

8 Nutty, warm and very funny. As the result of a genetic experiment, very short DeVito and mega-man Schwarzenegger are twins (yes, twins) who were separated at birth and have now been reunited in their adult life. When the pair figure out that it is actually true, they embark on a comic road trip to find their natural mother. Although this is a very unlikely plot, this hilarious film that has somehow been made to be believable and is highly satisfying. That is do in large measure to help from the natural wit and humor of the stars. A lot of fun!

Sex / Nud / Viol / Lang / AdSit

A: Arnold Schwarzenegger, Danny DeVito, Kelly Preston, Chloe Webb, Bonnie Bartlett, Marshall Bell

© MCA/UNIVERSAL HOME VIDEO, INC. 80873

TWO MULES FOR SISTER SARA

D: Don Siegel — 105 m

PG | WST ACT COM | 1969 | COLOR

8 Intriguing Western that lures you in, entertains you throughout and then hits you with a surprise curve. Clint is a drifter in Mexico during the revolution. He rescues a nun (MacLaine) from being raped but he is now burdened with her. He finds her to be both strangely unpious and fascinatingly appealing - all of which is very unsettling to him. She entices him into risking his neck by helping her to aid the rebel cause and eventually into helping her attack a French garrison. Light-hearted and action-packed fun - with a surprise inside.

Sex / Nud / Viol / Lang / AdSit

A: Shirley MacLaine, Clint Eastwood, Manolo Fabregas, Alberto Morin, Armando Silvestre, John Kelly

© MCA/UNIVERSAL HOME VIDEO, INC. 66046

UFORIA

D: John Binder — 92 m

PG | SF COM | 1981 | COLOR

7 Eccentric personalities mix with funky science fiction and make a thoroughly enjoyable film. Quirky supermarket checkout clerk Williams is a born again Christian with some wild ideas. She believes she is the chosen one, that salvation will come in the form of UFOs and that she will lead humanity to safety. Wanderer Ward falls in love with her, and preacher/huckster Stanton decides that this is a great opportunity to make some serious money, if he can just milk it from the right angle. But... what happens if she's right? Good natured fun, offbeat and more than a little zany.

Sex / Nud / Viol / Lang / AdSit

A: Cindy Williams, Harry Dean Stanton, Fred Ward, Harry Carey, Jr., Darrell Larson

© MCA/UNIVERSAL HOME VIDEO, INC. 80042

UNCLE BUCK

D: John Hughes — 100 m

PG | COM CLD | 1989 | COLOR

7 Lightweight but enjoyable farce that is mostly for the younger set. When the family is hit by a crisis and Mom and Dad have to leave for a while, they bring in big, oafish, clumsy, bachelor Uncle Buck to look after his nephew and nieces. In spite of his faltering attempts at surrogate parenthood, the kids, particularly teenage daughter Kelly, come to realize that old Buck isn't so bad after all. Contrary to how it might appear, there is some intelligence behind the slapstick. It'll leave your heart a little warmer, too.

Sex / Nud / Viol / Lang / AdSit

A: John Candy, Amy Madigan, Jean Kelly, Macaulay Culkin, Gaby Hoffman

© MCA/UNIVERSAL HOME VIDEO, INC. 80900

UNMARRIED WOMAN, AN

D: Paul Mazursky — 124 m

R | DMA COM ROM | 1978 | COLOR

9 An unforgettable look at life, love and relationships. Jill Clayburgh appears to have everything. Then suddenly her husband of 17 years tearfully confesses he's in love with a younger woman. Destroyed, she is forced to start over. She ventures tentatively out into the singles scene. It is an uncomfortable experience but, after one false start, she meets an oddball artist who restores her spirit and confidence. Insightful, witty and believable. This was a Best Picture nominee. Also nominated was Clayburgh for Best Actress and Mazursky for Best Screenplay. Excellent.

Sex / Nud / Viol / Lang / AdSit

A: Jill Clayburgh, Alan Bates, Michael Murphy, Cliff Gorman, Pat Quinn, Kelly Bishop

© FOXVIDEO 1088

UNSINKABLE MOLLY BROWN, THE

D: Charles Walters — 128 m

NR | MUS COM | 1964 | COLOR

6 Big-budget screen version of the successful Broadway musical. Debbie Reynolds puts in an enthusiastic and rambunctious performance in the title role. Her character is based upon a real-life character from the Colorado gold rush days. She is an unsophisticated, but energetic, backwoods girl who marries a miner just before he strikes it rich. She is determined, but unsuccessful, at making it into Denver society, even though she is the richest woman in town - that is until she gains notoriety as a being survivor of the sinking Titanic. Bouncy, but mostly for musical fans.

Sex / Nud / Viol / Lang / AdSit

A: Debbie Reynolds, Ed Begley, Harve Presnell, Hermione Baddeley, Jack Kruschen, Harvey Lembeck

Distributed By MGM/UA Home Video M600578

UP THE SANDBOX

D: Irvin Kershner 98 m

R | COM DMA | 1972 | COLOR

Sex Nud ◢ Viol ■ Lang ■ AdSit

6 Streisand is a neglected New York housewife and mother of two who is feeling like life has passed her by. She fears even more the effect that the impending birth of her third child will have on her and her family. Her professor husband Selby barely notices her anxiety and unhappiness, he's all wrapped up in his work. So she seeks solace in fantasy. Streisand's performance helps to save this weird, somewhat uneven, but still touching, funny and warm feminist statement.

A: Barbra Streisand, David Selby, Jane Hoffman, John C. Becher

© WARNER HOME VIDEO 11325

UPTOWN SATURDAY NIGHT

D: Sidney Poitier 104 m

PG | COM | 1974 | COLOR

Sex Nud ◢ Viol ◢ Lang ◢ AdSit

7 Good time entertainment. Cosby and Poitier sneak out of their houses for a night together of gambling at an illicit gambling parlor. But things go drastically awry when the game is raided by a band of hoods and everyone there is robbed. However, things get really desperate for them, when they learn that one of them had a winning lottery ticket tucked away in his wallet. Now they are determined to get that wallet back. Hilarity reigns when these two ordinary Joes go up against the mob. Very popular comedy that was followed by LET'S DO IT AGAIN.

A: Bill Cosby, Sidney Poitier, Flip Wilson, Harry Belafonte, Richard Pryor, Rosalind Cash

© WARNER HOME VIDEO 11101

USED CARS

D: Robert Zemeckis 111 m

R | COM | 1980 | COLOR

Sex ◢ Nud Viol ■ Lang ◢ AdSit

7 Brash, often tasteless, but undeniably funny! Russell is outstanding as the irreverent and unscrupulous used car salesman with a mission. He is determined to outdo all the other rival car salesmen and he will spare no effort to crush the competition. When the car salesman across the street kills Russell's boss (Warden), hoping to kill the competition too, Russell and his cohort (Graham) pretend Warden is still alive so Warden's corrupt brother won't take over the dealership. Inventive with some absolutely hilarious moments!

A: Kurt Russell, Jack Warden, Gerrit Graham, Frank McRae, Deborah Harmon, Joe Flaherty

© GOODTIMES 4603

VALLEY GIRL

D: Martha Coolidge 95 m

R | COM ROM | 1983 | COLOR

Sex ◢ Nud Viol ◢ Lang ◢ AdSit

7 A cut above the typical teen fare. This is an appealing story of a cute teenage girl's dilemma. Should she, like, dump this gnarly blond hunk for this really wierded-out punk? The punk (Cage) makes her laugh and she likes him. The hunk is boring and he steals her french fries. Her friends think she's crazy, so she caves in and goes to the prom with the hunk. But the goofy dude doesn't quit. This is a cute film because it's an intelligent depiction of teen problems and it treats everyone, both teens and parents, with both a degree of respect and disrespect.

A: Nicolas Cage, Deborah Foreman, Frederic Forrest, Lee Purcell, Colleen Camp, Elizabeth Daily

© GOODTIMES 4038

VANYA ON 42ND STREET

D: Louis Malle 119 m

PG | DMA COM | 1994 | COLOR

Sex Nud Viol Lang ■ AdSit

8 Intelligent update (but not by much) of famed Russian Anton Chekhov's literary masterpiece UNCLE VANYA. The three collaborators of MY DINNER WITH ANDRE, Wallace Shawn, Andre Gregory and director Louis Malled have once again combined their talents for this production. This play dramatizes people trapped between the harsh realities of their lives and the longings of their hearts. It is a timeless drama of faith, hope and the redemptive power of love. It is also very very obviously a play. Incessant conversation and soliloquies, not action, relate the intent of the author. This is a video primarily for patient, intelligent and literarily-informed audiences - not the general public.

A: Julianne Moore, Brooke Smith, George Gaynes, Wallace Shawn, Andre Gregory

© COLUMBIA TRISTAR HOME VIDEO 74983

VICE VERSA

D: Brian Gilbert 97 m

PG | COM | 1988 | COLOR

Sex Nud Viol ◢ Lang ◢ AdSit

6 Father and son trade places! Marshall Seymour (Reinhold) is a workaholic department store executive who never has time for his son. His son (Savage) thinks that his Dad is completely out of touch. But the pair learn what it is like to be in the other's shoes when the powers of a magical skull enable their bodies to trade places while their minds stay put. Even though the plot has been recycled, the chemistry between Savage and Reinhold make this a real winner. If you like this one, see also FREAKY FRIDAY or BIG.

A: Judge Reinhold, Fred Savage, Swoosie Kurtz, David Proval, Corinne Bohrer, Jane Kaczmarek

© COLUMBIA TRISTAR HOME VIDEO 65007

VICTOR/VICTORIA

D: Blake Edwards 134 m

PG-13 | COM ROM | 1982 | COLOR

Sex Nud Viol ◢ Lang ■ AdSit

8 Riotous good time. Julie Andrews is an unemployed torch singer in 1930's Paris. Starving, she runs into an equally unemployed gay entertainer (Preston). They strike upon a brilliant idea and form an act which quickly makes them the toast of Paris: offstage she poses as a man who impersonates being a woman onstage. The ruse works until an American (Garner) becomes convinced that Andrews is a woman, falls in love with her/him and sets out to prove his point. But Garner's jilted girlfriend (Warren) is spreading rumors that he's in love with a man. Hilarious comedy of errors.

A: Julie Andrews, Robert Preston, Lesley Ann Warren, John Rhys-Davies, James Garner, Alex Karras

Distributed By MGM/UA Home Video M800151

VIRGIN SOLDIERS, THE

D: John Dexter 96 m

R | COM ROM | 1969 | COLOR

◢ Sex ◢ Nud ◢ Viol ◢ Lang ■ AdSit

7 A group of young soldiers are as inexperienced on the battlefield as they are in bed. Stationed in Singapore, the subject of all the young men's speculation is the beautiful virginal Army brat Lynn Redgrave. Poor Private Brigg makes a pass at her at a dance but is so drunk he can't follow up on it. Instead, he takes beginner's lessons from a pretty local prostitute. Meanwhile, Redgrave has taken solace in the arms of older man Davenport. However, in the midst of a guerrilla raid, while taking refuge together in the jungle, the two inexperienced lovers discover passion in the bushes.

A: Lynn Redgrave, Nigel Davenport, Hywel Bennett, Nigel Patrick, Rachel Kempson, Tsai Chin

© COLUMBIA TRISTAR HOME VIDEO 60737

VOYAGE ROUND MY FATHER, A

D: Alvin Rakoff 85 m

NR | DMA COM | 1983 | COLOR

Sex Nud Viol Lang ◢ AdSit

8 A powerful emotional journey that also has a strong comedic undercurrent. When an eccentric but successful older lawyer (Olivier) loses his sight, he decides to continue his battles in the courtroom anyway, and turns to his family and son for help. As his son (Bates) helps his difficult father through this trying time, he begins to remember all of the good times and the bitterly bad times that he and his father have shared in their troubled relationship. And, he learns to stop trying to understand his father and to just love him. Beautifully filmed and acted. A good lesson for most fathers and sons.

A: Laurence Olivier, Alan Bates, Elizabeth Sellars, Jane Asher

© HBO VIDEO 0329

WACKIEST SHIP IN THE ARMY, THE

D: Richard Murphy 99 m

NR | COM WAR | 1961 | COLOR

Sex Nud ◢ Viol Lang AdSit

6 Pleasing light-weight entertainment. Jack Lemmon is a young Navy lieutenant who, because he has some sailing experience, is conned into commanding a run-down old sailing ship through the waters of the South Pacific during WWII. He and his motley crew of inexperienced Army soldier/sailors are charged with getting a man onto an island behind Japanese lines to spy on Japanese movements. This is a light-hearted comedy that also plays serious for a while with the dangerous aspects of war. Most of the time it is fun and funny, but it has its serious moments, too.

A: Jack Lemmon, Ricky Nelson, Chips Rafferty, John Lund, Tom Tully, Warren Berlinger

© COLUMBIA TRISTAR HOME VIDEO 60596

WALK, DON'T RUN

D: Charles Walters 114 m

NR | COM ROM | 1966 | COLOR

Sex Nud Viol Lang AdSit

7 Very entertaining romantic comedy starring Cary Grant in his last film. He is a dapper English industrialist who arrives in Tokyo just before the Olympics. Tokyo is faced with a severe housing shortage, he is two days too early to get the room he has reserved and he is homeless. Seeing a notice at the embassy, he rents a room from very beautiful but very proper Samantha Eggar. She is engaged to stuffy John Standing, who Grant can't stand. So Grant sublets his half of the apartment to American race walker Jim Hutton, of whom he does approve, and proceeds to play cupid for the two.

A: Cary Grant, Samantha Eggar, Jim Hutton, John Standing, Miiko Taka, Ted Hartley

© COLUMBIA TRISTAR HOME VIDEO 60875

WALTZ OF THE TOREADORS

D: John Guillermin 100 m

NR | COM | 1962 | COLOR

Sex Nud Viol Lang ◢ AdSit

7 Zany Sellers is a lecherous retired general just before WWI who has been locked into a loveless marriage with a shrew for a wife. They have two vacuous daughters. For years he has loved a French woman but has never been in a position to be able to consummate the relationship. He has now retreated to his castle to figure out what he will do and to chase his maids around, when his sexy French friend turns up, determined to change things. The wife and an amorous doctor have their own plans. Slapstick farce with a heart. Fans of Sellers will be delighted, but others will also have a good time, too.

A: Peter Sellers, Margaret Leighton, John Fraser, Dany Robin

© UNITED AMERICAN VIDEO CORP. 7034

COM

WANDERERS

D: Philip Kaufman — 117 m

R | DMA COM | 1979 | COLOR | Viol, Lang, AdSit

8 Entertaining film which follows the exploits of a gang of high school kids from the Italian section of the Bronx in 1963. It has a good mix of comedy, excitement and '60s music (Dion, The Shirelles, The Four Seasons and many others). Their gang, The Wanderers, spends most of its time in the streets in frequent encounters (usually non-violent) with other gangs from other neighborhoods and ethnic groups. Their biggest concerns are school and chasing girls. Eventful but somewhat uneven. Nevertheless, its infectiousness and some good performances have made it a cult favorite.

A: Ken Wahl, John Friedrich, Karen Allen, Olympia Dukakis, Tony Ganlos, Toni Kalem

© WARNER HOME VIDEO 22009

WAR OF THE ROSES, THE

D: Danny DeVito — 116 m

R | COM DMA | 1989 | COLOR | Viol, Lang, AdSit

7 Very black comedy which is, at the same time, very funny and very painful - painful because it is based upon some bitter truths about human relationships. Two perfectly matched young lovers fall in love, marry, have kids, build a text book life and collect a houseful of beautiful things. He becomes a very successful attorney and she a successful caterer. Then their love dies and gives birth to one of the bitterest divorces ever. Each would rather destroy the other than to give ground. Sometimes hysterically funny, but at others just hysterical.

A: Michael Douglas, Kathleen Turner, Danny DeVito, Heather Fairfield, Sean Astin

© FOXVIDEO 1800

WAR WAGON, THE

D: Burt Kennedy — 101 m

NR | WST ACT COM | 1967 | COLOR | Viol

7 Entertaining tongue-in-cheek John Wayne Western. John has had his fortune stolen, been framed by an unscrupulous cattle baron and mine owner (Cabot) and sent to prison. So, when John gets out, Cabot sends Kirk Douglas to kill him. Instead, John enlists Douglas in his plan to inflict sweet revenge and also gathers together several others in a gang to carry it out. He and his cronies are going to rob a big shipment of gold dust that Cabot transports in a special, heavily armed coach called the War Wagon. Good, mindless action adventure, amply spiced with humor. Hard to beat the combination of Wayne and Douglas.

A: John Wayne, Kirk Douglas, Howard Keel, Robert Walker, Jr., Keenan Wynn

© MCA/UNIVERSAL HOME VIDEO, INC. 80016

WATCH IT

D: Tom Flynn — 102 m

COM ROM | 1993 | COLOR | Sex, Nud, Lang, AdSit

6 Sometimes funny, sometimes genuine, sometimes aggravating, sometimes implausible. John comes back to Chicago to visit his estranged cousin Michael and moves as a fourth roommate with Michael's other friends. The boys are engaged in a never-ending game of competing practical jokes they call "Watch It". All four act like college freshman, however John does have an ounce of maturity. When Michael's girl friend discovers him in the act of cheating on her, John walks her home. They fall for each other but John can't commit. Then Michael charms her back to him and conflict is born. It has some good moments.

A: Peter Gallagher, Suzy Amis, John C. McGinley, Lili Taylor, Tom Sizemore, Jon Tenney

© PARAMOUNT HOME VIDEO 83126

WATERHOLE NO. 3

D: William Graham — 100 m

NR | WST COM | 1967 | COLOR | Viol, AdSit

7 Amusing, somewhat racy, Western farce. Three confederates have stolen a Union Army gold shipment and have hidden it in a desert waterhole. James Coburn is a gambler and lady's man, hot in pursuit of the gold. He has sampled the sheriff's amorous daughter's charms. Now the girl is chasing after him and so is the sheriff, but mostly because Coburn stole the sheriff's prize horse, and they're all converging on the waterhole with the gold. Slapstick comedy, combined with some clever and bawdy dialogue. Good time.

A: James Coburn, Carroll O'Connor, Joan Blondell, Claude Akins, Bruce Dern, Margaret Blye

© PARAMOUNT HOME VIDEO 6707

WAYNE'S WORLD 2

D: Stephen Surjik — 94 m

PG-13 | COM | 1993 | COLOR | Viol, Lang, AdSit

6 Young fans of WAYNES WORLD will enjoy the return of their dweebish duo, but the rest of the world will likely heave a collective yawn. The two high school pseudo-cool dudes that created their own public-access cable TV show have left home and set up their own pad. They have also talked Wayne's "babe" girlfriend into singing in their Waynestock music festival. Garth is being seduced by Honey Hornee (Kim Basinger) who really just wants him to kill off her pesky husband, while Wayne's jealousy has driven the babe into marrying someone else unless he can get to the church on time. Lots of tired gags and sophomoric suggestive humor.

A: Mike Meyers, Dana Carvey, Tia Carrere, Christopher Walken, Kim Basinger, Ralph Brown

© PARAMOUNT HOME VIDEO 32845

WAYNE'S WORLD

D: Penelope Spheeris — 95 m

PG-13 | COM | 1992 | COLOR | Sex, Nud, Lang, AdSit

8 Campy fun at its most ridiculous - a huge surprise hit. Wayne and Garth (Myers and Carvey), of TV's Saturday Night Live fame, take to the movies in this very funny film about a not-so-smart teenage duo who are trying to take their homemade cable-access show to the networks. The film is really a bunch of comic skits stitched together in a way that affords an opportunity for the two main characters to do their funny stuff. Teenagers and Saturdaynight Live fans, however, will most likely be the audience that will get the most enjoyment out of this wacked-out film! A sweet little story - NOT!!!

A: Mike Myers, Dana Carvey, Rob Lowe, Tia Carrere, Brian Doyle-Murray, Lara Flynn Boyle

© PARAMOUNT HOME VIDEO 32706

WEEKEND AT BERNIE'S

D: Ted Kotcheff — 101 m

PG-13 | COM | 1989 | COLOR | Viol, Lang, AdSit

6 Silly, raucous farce. Two low-level employees win a weekend at their boss's exclusive beach house after they uncover an embezzlement scheme at work. When the two arrive, they find that their boss (Kiser) is dead - killed by a professional hit man. Fearing for their own safety but not wanting to lose the opportunity for a wild weekend, they prop the dead man up, pretend that he is alive and proceed to have a good time. Very silly, lots of sight gags. Kiser is terrific as the dead man.

A: Andrew McCarthy, Jonathan Silverman, Catherine Mary Stewart, Terry Kiser, Don Calfa

© LIVE HOME VIDEO 68904

WHAT ABOUT BOB?

D: Frank Oz — 99 m

PG | COM | 1991 | COLOR

8 Zany good time. Wacked-out, phobic and totally dependent neurotic (Bill Murray) pursues his pompous shrink (Dreyfuss) on his summer vacation. Murray just doesn't want to be left alone. Wherever Dreyfuss turns, there's Murray. Worse still, Murray has endeared himself to Dreyfuss's family. Dreyfuss wants to lose Murray but his family likes him, so there is no respite for Dreyfuss anywhere. The head-doctor is himself driven to madness. Hilarious in places, just plain silly in others, but almost always enjoyable. Even non-fans of the wise-cracking Bill Murray will have a good time with him in this one.

A: Richard Dreyfuss, Bill Murray, Julie Hagerty, Charlie Korsmo, Kathryn Bowen, Tom Aldredge

© TOUCHSTONE HOME VIDEO 1224

WHAT'S NEW PUSSYCAT?

D: Clive Donner — 110 m

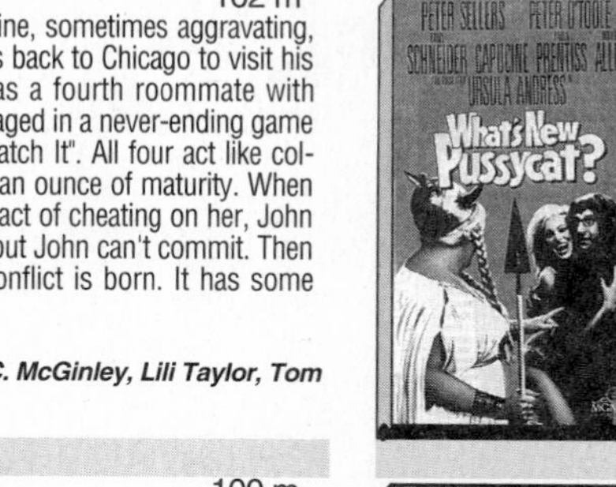

NR | COM | 1965 | COLOR | AdSit

6 Once very daring, now only a slightly sexy, silly farce - but it still has its funny moments. Written by Woody Allen (who has a small part as a frustrated stripper's assistant), it is the story of a fashion editor who seeks help from an analyst because he keeps becoming romantically involved with his models, who all chase him. But he has turned in his desperation, to a psychiatrist (Sellers) who has more problems than the patient. Much of the humor is dated but there are moments that are worth waiting for - including the scenes of the gorgeous Ursula Andress. Tom Jones had a major pop hit with the theme song.

A: Peter Sellers, Peter O'Toole, Ursula Andress, Paula Prentiss, Woody Allen, Capucine

Distributed By MGM/UA Home Video M202079

WHAT'S UP, DOC?

D: Peter Bogdanovich — 94 m

PG | COM ROM | 1972 | COLOR

8 Zany '70s remake of 1938s BRINGING UP BABY. A fast-paced comedy in which a stuffy musicologist (O'Neal) and his fiancee (Kahn) become involved with an outlandish college student (Streisand) after they all get thrown in together in a wild adventure to get back four identical flight bags which have gotten mixed up. One bag contains Streisand's clothes, and one O'Neal's music - but one of the others contains a wealth of stolen jewels and there are top secrets in the other. Non-stop running gags produce some real big belly laughs and a riotous final chase scene.

A: Barbra Streisand, Ryan O'Neal, Kenneth Mars, Austin Pendleton, Madeline Kahn, Sorrell Booke

© WARNER HOME VIDEO 1041

WHAT'S UP TIGER LILY

D: Woody Allen — 80 m

PG | COM | 1966 | COLOR | Viol, Lang

6 At the height of the James Bond craze, Woody Allen came up with this one-joke spy farce that works quite well through most of its length. He's taken a fourth-rate Japanese rip-off of the spy genre, over-dubbed all the Japanese dialogue with English and substituted his own wacky plot. Under Woody's revised plot, there is a devious plan afoot to steal the world's best egg salad recipe. Silliness reigns. Music is provided by The Lovin' Spoonful.

A: Woody Allen, Tatsuya Mihashi, Hana Miya, Tadao Nakamura

© GOODTIMES 9148

WHEN COMEDY WAS KING

D: 81 m

NR | COM | 1959 | B&W

Sex / Nud / Viol / Lang / AdSit

9 This is a compilation of some of the best clips from the comedies of the silent era. Included are clips from Charlie Chaplin, Buster Keaton, Laurel and Hardy, Ben Turpin, Fatty Arbuckle, Wallace Beery, Gloria Swanson, The Keystone Kops and more. Comedy like this doesn't diminish with time.

A: Charlie Chaplin, Harry Langdon, Buster Keaton, Fatty Arbuckle, Mabel Normand, Snub Pollard

© UNITED AMERICAN VIDEO CORP. 7124

WHEN HARRY MET SALLY ...

D: Rob Reiner 96 m

R | COM ROM | 1989 | COLOR

Sex / Nud / Viol / Lang / AdSit

10 This huge comic hit took the viewing public by storm! Ryan and Crystal are at first two college students who agree to travel across the country together to save on costs. Crystal hypothesizes that men and women can't be just friends because the sex thing always gets in the way. In New York they part ways, mildly annoyed with each other. Years later, now bruised and wiser, they meet again by chance. Their friendship blooms but they are determined to keep it platonic. However, that is soon put to the test. A heart-warming, touching comic masterpiece - a real gem, because it's humor is so firmly based in reality!

A: Billy Crystal, Meg Ryan, Carrie Fisher, Bruno Kirby, Steven Ford, Lisa Jane Persky

© NEW LINE HOME VIDEO 7732

WHERE'S POPPA?

D: Carl Reiner 85 m

R | COM | 1970 | COLOR

Sex / Nud / Viol / Lang / AdSit

9 Bizarre black comedy. If you are not a fan of the off-beat, leave this one on the shelf. But if you have a warped funny bone, this is for you. George Segal is a young attorney who is taking care of his 87-year-old mother rather than to have her committed to a nursing home. He keeps bringing home pretty nurses to take care of her; nurses with whom he keeps falling in love and who his mother keeps driving off with her bawdy and wacky antics. When she drives off Van Devere too, he vows to get rid of Mom by causing a her to have a heart attack. Nothing is sacred here. Totally irreverent comedy.

A: George Segal, Ruth Gordon, Trish Van Devere, Ron Leibman, Rob Reiner, Vincent Gardenia

Distributed By MGM/UA Home Video M201583

WHICH WAY IS UP?

D: Michael Schultz 94 m

R | COM | 1977 | COLOR

Sex / Nud / Viol / Lang / AdSit

6 This is mostly a film for Richard Prior fans. It is the story of a desperately poor citrus picker from Central California who becomes a labor union hero by accident. He leaves his wife and sells out for the high life in the big city and pretty McKee. Prior has three different roles: he is the picker, a minister and a dirty old man. The story itself seems to always come up short, but Prior is a riot. Lots of adult humor.

A: Richard Pryor, Lonette McKee, Margaret Avery, Dolph Sweet, Morgan Woodward, Marilyn Coleman

© MCA/UNIVERSAL HOME VIDEO, INC. 66014

WHITE MEN CAN'T JUMP

D: Ron Shelton 115 m

R | COM | 1992 | COLOR

Sex / Nud / Viol / Lang / AdSit

7 A brash, vulgar, sometimes hilarious comedy about playground basketball (the game, the hustlers and their quest to earn a decent, but dishonest living). Together, Woody and Wesley hustle their way across L.A.'s neighborhood courts. Woody wants to make enough money to pay off a big debt he owes to a bunch of bad guys, and his corrupt partner's wife wants to move to a bigger house. The snappy, but relentlessly vulgar dialogue between the two is a highlight. However, Woody's inability to control his compulsiveness gets to be frustrating - you really want him to make it and learn to grow up, but he just isn't going to. Raunchy.

A: Woody Harrelson, Wesley Snipes, Rosie Perez, Tyra Ferrell, Cylk Cozart, Kadeem Hardison

© FOXVIDEO 1959

WHO FRAMED ROGER RABBIT

D: Robert Zemeckis 106 m

PG | COM | 1988 | COLOR

Sex / Nud / Viol / Lang / AdSit

8 Fun blending of real and fantasy worlds in this technically very difficult combination of live-action and animation. The plot is set in Hollywood in 1947. Cartoon character Roger Rabbit is framed for murder and seeks the help of hard-boiled real-world detective Eddie Valiant (Hoskins), but must first pull him out of his self-induced retirement. Hoskins's investigation leads him into the animated world of Toon Town, a place that is inhabited by famous cartoon characters, and a place where anything can happen and usually does. Funny, fast-paced and very entertaining.

A: Bob Hoskins, Christopher Lloyd, Joanna Cassidy, Stubby Kaye, Alan Tilvern

© TOUCHSTONE HOME VIDEO 940

WHOSE LIFE IS IT ANYWAY?

D: John Badham 119 m

R | DMA COM | 1981 | COLOR

Sex / Nud / Viol / Lang / AdSit

9 Richard Dreyfuss puts in another sterling performance as a rising young sculptor who becomes paralyzed from the neck down in an auto accident. While he remains an impressive intellectual force, he becomes so depressed that he hires an attorney to pursue his right to die. Doctors Cassavetes and Lahti try desperately to convince him to live. Extremely potent performances keep this from being just another tragedy movie. And, it is ultimately, and unexpectedly, an upbeat movie. Excellent.

A: Richard Dreyfuss, John Cassavetes, Christine Lahti, Bob Balaban, Kenneth McMillan, Kaki Hunter

Distributed By MGM/UA Home Video M800140

WHO'S MINDING THE MINT?

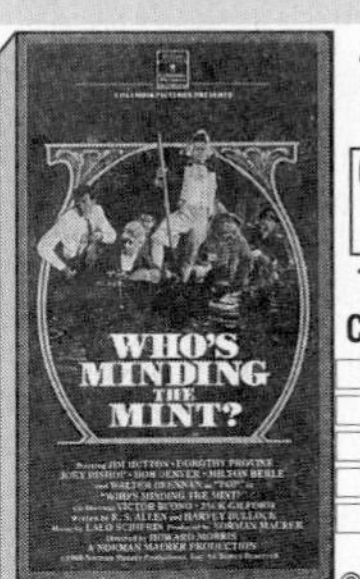

D: Howard Morris 97 m

NR | COM | 1967 | COLOR

Sex / Nud / Viol / Lang / AdSit

8 Hilarious farce in the same vein as IT'S A MAD, MAD, MAD, MAD WORLD. A really top-flight cast of talented people makes this zaniness work, and work well it does. Jim Hutton is a worker at the US Mint who accidentally destroys $50,000 in new bills. He enlists the help of an odd assortment of friendly thieves to help him reprint the missing money. Things get really wacky, though, when he has to hurriedly move the plan up one night and it turns into an outrageous come-as-you-are fest. Plus, they have printed up not $50,000 but $7,000,000. Truly entertaining - a riotous good time.

A: Jim Hutton, Walter Brennan, Jack Gilford, Milton Berle, Joey Bishop, Victor Buono

© COLUMBIA TRISTAR HOME VIDEO 60439

WILD AT HEART

D: David Lynch 125 m

R | DMA ROM COM | 1990 | COLOR

Sex / Nud / Viol / Lang / AdSit

8 Maverick director Lynch has created an oddly fascinating series of images, characters and events - if taken individually. But if taken as a whole, it is a confusing experience. The principal focus is upon Lula (Dern) and Sailor (Cage). She is a 20-year-old gum-popping, sex-crazed daughter of witch of a woman. Cage is a rebellious 23-year-old who spurned mama's advances and killed the thug she sent to beat him. Just out of prison, Sailor and Lula head across the country, meeting more strange characters and avoiding the killers her Mom has sent after them.

A: Laura Dern, Willem Dafoe, Crispin Glover, Diane Ladd, Isabella Rossellini, Harry Dean Stanton

© VIDEO TREASURES M012765

WILDCATS

D: Michael Ritchie 106 m

R | COM | 1986 | COLOR

Sex / Nud / Viol / Lang / AdSit

7 Goldie Hawn is charming as a football-crazy divorcee who just happens to be the daughter of a famous football coach. She has two wishes: coach a boys football team and win the custody of her children from her ex-husband. Wish number one comes true when she accepts a coaching position at a tough inner-city high school, but she must fight to earn the brash students's approval and respect. Wish number two is a little harder because achieving wish one gets in the way, but she tackles it with the same wit, humor and determination that made her a star coach. A lot of fun!

A: Goldie Hawn, Swoosie Kurtz, Robyn Lively, Brandy Gold, James Keach, Jan Hooks

© WARNER HOME VIDEO 11583

WILD ROVERS, THE

D: Blake Edwards 138 m

PG | WST ACT COM | 1971 | COLOR

Sex / Nud / Viol / Lang / AdSit

8 An unheralded little gem. William Holden and Ryan O'Neal are two cowpoke buddies, one old and one young, who become disillusioned with their careers on the range when one of their friends is accidentally killed. On a whim, this not-too-bright pair decide to rob a bank and head out for Mexico. On a dead run with a posse hot on their heels, it occurs to them that this was not a wise career move. The pleasure in the movie comes from the relationship between these guys. A great buddy movie. Solid performances, particularly by Holden.

A: William Holden, Ryan O'Neal, Karl Malden, Lynn Carlin, Tom Skerritt, Joe Don Baker

Distributed By MGM/UA Home Video M600305

WILLIE AND PHIL

D: Paul Mazursky 116 m

R | ROM COM | 1980 | COLOR

Sex / Nud / Viol / Lang / AdSit

7 Odd but interesting love story. Two guys meet and become fast friends at a screening of JULES AND JIM, a French film by Francois Truffaut about two friends who strike up a relationship with an amoral woman in a three-way love affair. They soon meet and become friends and lovers of free-spirited Margot Kidder. The film follows their relationships through nine years of the sexual revolution, which gives it the opportunity to track the changes that occur in society as witnessed by these players.

A: Michael Ontkean, Margot Kidder, Ray Sharkey, Natalie Wood, Jan Miner, Tom Brennan

© FOXVIDEO 1132

WINGS OF EAGLES, THE

D: John Ford 107 m

NR · DMA COM · 1957 · COLOR

6 Fairly interesting biography of the remarkable real-life character - Frank "Spig" Wead. He was a daring Navy pilot in WWI. However, he was severely paralyzed after breaking his neck in an accident. Forced out of the service, he became a Hollywood screenwriter. He even went on to serve again in WWII. John Wayne plays the part with two-fisted gusto and Maureen O'Hara is his wife. This is a somewhat confusing film to watch if you're not clued in, because the first half plays like a slapstick comedy and the last is much more sedate. This is also one of Wayne's better acting jobs.

Sex · Nud · Viol · Lang · AdSit

A: John Wayne, Dan Dailey, Maureen O'Hara, Ward Bond, Ken Curtis, Edmund Lowe

Distributed By MGM/UA Home Video M200513

WINTER KILLS

D: William Richert 97 m

R · DMA COM · 1979 · COLOR

8 A peculiar combination of political intrigue and black comedy. This is a farfetched and paranoid tongue-in-cheek vision of power in America. Bridges is the younger brother of a President who was slain in 1960. He was never satisfied with the official story so now, 19 years later, he launches his own investigation into a new conspiracy theory. A circuitous trip through oddball characters, places and people brings him back to his own father as a prime suspect. Its eccentric flavor and characters have made this a cult favorite. Not for the casual viewer.

Sex · Nud · Viol · Lang · AdSit

A: Jeff Bridges, John Huston, Anthony Perkins, Belinda Bauer, Eli Wallach, Sterling Hayden

© NEW LINE HOME VIDEO 2056

WISE GUYS

D: Brian De Palma 100 m

R · COM · 1986 · COLOR

6 Silly black comedy in which two very low-level hoods (Piscopo and DeVito), who are tired of running menial errands, risk some of the boss's (Hedaya) money at a race track and lose it. Hedaya gets even by telling each one separately that, in order to redeem himself, he has to kill the other. Instead, the two flee to Atlantic City hoping to win back the missing money, but now there is a hit man after them both. DeVito's energy is what carries this one.

Sex · Nud · Viol · Lang · AdSit

A: Danny DeVito, Joe Piscopo, Dan Hedaya, Harvey Keitel, Patti Lupone, Ray Sharkey

Distributed By MGM/UA Home Video M201031

WISH YOU WERE HERE

D: David Leland 92 m

R · DMA COM · 1987 · COLOR

8 Bittersweet British production. It is the portrait of a 16-year-old girl growing up in the very straight-laced culture of the late '40s and '50s. Her mother is dead and her father is a drunk. She has no direction. Worse, she refuses to recognize her "place." She is also a spirited girl who enjoys the power her new sensuousness gives her, and she refuses to be repressed. She's just trying to have fun and find love, but she gets much more than that. This film is very funny and shocking to some, but is also a very sensitive and touching story. Strong performances.

Sex · Nud · Viol · Lang · AdSit

A: Emily Lloyd, Tom Bell, Jesse Birdsall, Geoffrey Durham, Claire Clifford, Barbara Durkin

© FRIES HOME VIDEO 99400

WITCHES OF EASTWICK, THE

D: George Miller 118 m

R · COM DMA · 1987 · COLOR

8 Wicked little comedy. Three women, bored with small town life and the lack of eligible bachelors, fantasize one night about the perfect man. They don't know that they possess supernatural powers and that they have just summoned up their dreamboat from Hell. When the rich charmer (Nicholson) moves to town, he seduces all three of them, but none of them realizes until it is almost too late that he is truly evil, he is in fact the Devil. Loosely based on John Updike's novel. Very funny in places, but a very dark comedy... not for everyone.

Sex · Nud · Viol · Lang · AdSit

A: Jack Nicholson, Cher, Susan Sarandon, Michelle Pfeiffer, Veronica Cartwright, Richard Jenkins

© WARNER HOME VIDEO 11741

WITH HONORS

D: Alex Keshishian 101 m

PG-13 · DMA COM · 1994 · COLOR

6 Harvard senior Brendan Fraser has just experienced the ultimate college horror - his hard drive just crashed and with it, his entire thesis. He has one copy printed however, but while going to get a copy made, he slips on the ice and the paper winds up in the hands of a philosophical bum (Pesci) living in the furnace room at the library. To get it back - one page at a time - Fraser must commit certain kindnesses and listen to the bum's words of wisdom. At first this price is a gross injustice, then a mild imposition, but then a labor of love. Pesci's life has been one of mistakes, Fraser had no father and so the relationship grows. Quite funny in places but also obvious and grating at times.

Sex · Nud · Viol · Lang · AdSit

A: Joe Pesci, Brendan Fraser, Moria Kelly, Patrick Dempsey, Josh hamilton, Gore Vidal

© WARNER HOME VIDEO 13079

WITHOUT A CLUE

D: Thom Eberhardt 107 m

PG · COM MYS · 1988 · COLOR

8 Funny high-spirited farce that takes an entirely different slant to the oft-used mystery/detective movie vehicle of Sherlock Holmes and Dr. Watson - suppose Sherlock Holmes was just a drunken bumbling actor and Watson was the real deductive genius. Kingsley plays Watson, a doctor who enjoys investigating crimes and then writing about them. He uses the mythical figure of Sherlock Holmes as the detective, but one day is called upon to present him. So he hires Caine to be Holmes and forever after has to keep him out of trouble. Inventive and funny.

Sex · Nud · Viol · Lang · AdSit

A: Michael Caine, Ben Kingsley, Jeffrey Jones, Lysette Anthony, Paul Freeman

© ORION PICTURES CORPORATION 8733

WOMAN IN RED, THE

D: Gene Wilder 87 m

PG-13 · COM ROM · 1984 · COLOR

6 Wilder is a successful advertising executive who is happily married. One day, however, he spies the fantastically gorgeous LeBrock in a parking garage and falls head-over-heels in love with her. It just doesn't stop there, however. Wilder pursues her with wild abandon, while Gilda Radner, who he has spurned, seeks revenge. All of which yields some pretty good laughs and unleashes wild chaos. Oscar-winning score includes the smash hit from Stevie Wonder "I Just Called to Say I Love You." Americanized version of the French PARDON MON AFFAIRE.

Sex · Nud · Viol · Lang · AdSit

A: Gene Wilder, Gilda Radner, Kelly LeBrock, Charles Grodin, Joseph Bologna, Judith Ivey

© LIVE HOME VIDEO VA5055

WORKING GIRL

D: Mike Nichols 115 m

R · COM ROM · 1988 · COLOR

8 Tough, funny and sophisticated comedy! A smart but struggling working girl (Griffith) is trying to climb the corporate ladder. When her slimy boss (Weaver) steals an idea from her, she realizes that she is going to have to employ other tactics in order to get to the top. With her boss on vacation, secretary Griffith sneakily takes her boss's place and puts together a handsome financial deal with unsuspecting help of a high powered wheeler-dealer (Ford), but Weaver gets wind of the plan and proceeds to make life hell for Griffith. Very entertaining, a real charmer with wit and grit.

Sex · Nud · Viol · Lang · AdSit

A: Sigourney Weaver, Melanie Griffith, Harrison Ford, Alec Baldwin, Joan Cusack, Philip Bosco

© FOXVIDEO 1709

WORLD ACCORDING TO GARP, THE

D: George Roy Hill 136 m

R · COM DMA · 1982 · COLOR

7 A very unusual movie, taken from a book by John Irving. However, it is not one which the casual observer can easily understand. That is not to say that this isn't an enjoyable movie - but you do have to work to understand the meaning and value in it. It is the story of a man who is the offspring of a very eccentric and independent-minded feminist who surrounds herself with odd people. Garp is a somewhat ordinary kind of guy, but his world is a strange one occupied by strange people. It is also a sad one where bizarre happenings are commonplace. Big cast, great acting.

Sex · Nud · Viol · Lang · AdSit

A: Robin Williams, Mary Beth Hurt, John Lithgow, Glenn Close, Amanda Plummer, Jessica Tandy

© WARNER HOME VIDEO 11261

WORLD OF HENRY ORIENT, THE

D: George Roy Hill 106 m

NR · COM · 1964 · COLOR

7 Clever, quirky but sensitive comedy with a sugar-coated message. Sellers is Henry Orient, an egocentric, eccentric pianist who manages to make a living in New York City, but he is much better at chasing women. Henry finds himself being idolized and obsessively chased around town by two rich teenage girl, who are following Henry because of a lack of love in their own lives. This is a point which gains importance when lecherous Henry hits on one of the girl's mothers. The two teenagers nearly steal the show away from a talented cast of veterans.

Sex · Nud · Viol · Lang · AdSit

A: Peter Sellers, Paula Prentiss, Tom Bosley, Angela Lansbury, Phyllis Thaxter

Distributed By MGM/UA Home Video M202876

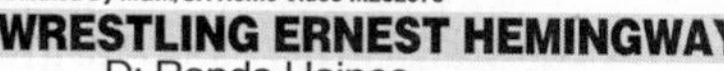

WRESTLING ERNEST HEMINGWAY

D: Randa Haines 123 m

PG-13 · DMA COM · 1993 · COLOR

8 Extremely engaging and likable story of two very unlikely friends. Richard Harris is a 75-year old, slovenly, retired sea captain who's been married four times. Robert Duvall is a very neat and very proper, retired Cuban barber who has never been married. Both live alone in Florida, trying to make the days pass, and it is there they meet one day in the park by the sea. Two more unlikely friends are possible, but their loneliness draws them together. Their similarities melt away their differences and make their friendship fascinating and fun. Funny, sometimes very funny, but this also deliberate and thought-provoking. Fascinating, very real characters.

Sex · Nud · Viol · Lang · AdSit

A: Richard Harris, Robert Duvall, Shirley MacLaine, Piper Laurie, Sandra Bullock

© WARNER HOME VIDEO 12993

WRONG ARM OF THE LAW, THE

D: Cliff Owen — 94 m

NR | COM CRM | 1962 | B&W

Sex / Nud / Viol / Lang / AdSit

7 Silly farce of the variety that made Sellers famous. He plays Pearly Gates, the leader of a Cockney band of thieves that is so prosperous that it has set up a welfare-like system to take care of its members. All that is threatened now because each time they carry off a heist, they are confronted by a group of cops that confiscates everything. The problem is that these guys are not really cops. So Pearly calls a conference between the real cops and the other hoods, and they all agree to call a truce and cooperate long enough to get these cop/thieves put in jail. Wacky and zany, wild fun.

A: Peter Sellers, Lionel Jeffries, Bernard Cribbins, Nanette Newman, Davey Kaye

© MONTEREY HOME VIDEO 34860

WRONG BOX, THE

D: Bryan Forbes — 105 m

NR | COM | 1966 | COLOR

Sex / Nud / Viol / Lang / AdSit

7 Wildly irreverent and typically British black comedy. The survivor of two elderly Victorian brothers will inherit a very large trust fund. When neither of the old timers appears to be willing to cooperate any time soon, two of the younger cousins and eventual beneficiaries conspire to assist Mother Nature. One of the brothers is supposedly killed, but really isn't... but, if he's not dead, who is in the box? Fans of British humor will especially find this interesting, and they should also check out KIND HEARTS AND CORONETS.

A: Michael Caine, Peter Cook, Dudley Moore, Peter Sellers, John Mills, Ralph Richardson

© COLUMBIA TRISTAR HOME VIDEO 60416

YESTERDAY, TODAY AND TOMORROW

D: Vittorio De Sica — 119 m

NR | FOR COM | 1964 | COLOR

Sex / Nud / Viol / Lang / AdSit

9 Three saucy, sexy, comic tales that won the Best Foreign Film Oscar. Three beautiful Italian women (all Sophia Loren, at her sexiest) use sex to get what they want from their men. In one story, she uses it to stay out of jail by staying pregnant year after year. In another, she is a flirt who seduces men and then drops them. In the last, she is a prostitute who tempts the seminary student who wants to "save" her. It is during this story when she performs a super-sexy strip that can still make blood pressures rise, and is one of the most famous scenes of her career. Funny, too. Subtitles.

A: Sophia Loren, Marcello Mastroianni, Tina Pica, Giovanni Ridolfi

© UNITED AMERICAN VIDEO CORP. 5197

YOJIMBO

D: Akira Kurosawa — 110 m

NR | FOR ACT COM | 1962 | B&W

Sex / Nud / Viol / Lang / AdSit

9 Very funny, action packed and beautifully photographed Japanese "Western" - which became the model for A FISTFUL OF DOLLARS and many others. A samurai (Mifune), freed from his code of honor, roams from town to town selling his sword. In one small town, the sake dealer and the silk merchant are both trying to capture control of gambling, but both are cowards and so hire others to do their dirty work. Clever Mifune hires himself out to both sides and turns them against each other. In the end, they kill each other off and he gets the money, saying: "Now we'll have a little quiet in this town."

A: Toshiro Mifune, Eijiro Tono, Isuzu Yamada, Hiroshi Tachikawa, Kyu Sazanka

© NEW LINE HOME VIDEO 6144

YOUNG DOCTORS IN LOVE

D: Garry Marshall — 97 m

R | COM | 1982 | COLOR

Sex / Nud / Viol / Lang / AdSit

6 Outlandish takeoff on TV soap operas that is very entertaining for those who are open-minded and prepared for the offbeat. It does to soap operas what AIRPLANE did to disaster movies. Chaotic comedy filled with gags - some work and some don't, but still enjoyable overall. The story is populated with characters who have everything else in mind except the best interests of their patients. Coleman is a wacked-out surgeon. Nurse Pamela Reed is a prude. Sean Young definitely isn't. Elizondo is a hood who likes to dress in drag, and Doctor McKean can't stand blood. Raunchy.

A: Michael McKean, Sean Young, Harry Dean Stanton, Patrick Macnee, Hector Elizondo, Dabney Coleman

© VIDEO TREASURES SV9152

YOUNG FRANKENSTEIN

D: Mel Brooks — 106 m

PG | COM HOR | 1974 | B&W

Sex / Nud / Viol / Lang / AdSit

9 This ranks right up there with BLAZING SADDLES, the other masterpiece from Mel Brooks - master of zany spoofs. This one rips into Frankenstein movies. Gene Wilder is a modern-day college professor who disdains his family's jaded history and goes back to Transylvania to get it right this time. Gags are nonstop. Hysterical scenes with Boyle as his monster and Marty Feldman as his hunchback assistant. Music, sets and props, which are reminiscent of the '30s, all add to the fun. Hilarious the whole way through.

A: Gene Wilder, Peter Boyle, Marty Feldman, Madeline Kahn, Cloris Leachman, Teri Garr

© FOXVIDEO 1103

YOU'RE A BIG BOY NOW

D: Francis Ford Coppola — 98 m

NR | COM | 1966 | COLOR

Sex / Nud / Viol / Lang / AdSit

8 Offbeat comedy that may not appeal to everybody, but those whose funnybone is a little crooked will enjoy Francis Ford Coppola's UCLA master's thesis. Bernard Chanticleer is a nice boy, a stock boy at the library, a dreamer and an over-protected mama's boy. His father has kicked him out of the house for his own good, so he can grow up. Bernard gets an 8th-floor walk-up apartment in Greenich Village. He becomes infatuated with and learns of life from a man-hating go-go dancer (Hartman) before he meets up with shy and pretty librarian Karen Black. Fun score from Lovin' Spoonful.

A: Elizabeth Hartman, Peter Kastner, Geraldine Page, Julie Harris, Michael Dunn, Tony Bill

© WARNER HOME VIDEO 11312

ZELIG

D: Woody Allen — 79 m

PG | COM | 1983 | B&W

Sex / Nud / Viol / Lang / AdSit

7 Clever bit of film making from Woody Allen. Allen plays Zelig, The Human Chameleon. Zelig is so eager to be accepted that he repeatedly changes his appearance and takes on the demeanor of whatever group he is with in order to become part of it. Zelig becomes a celebrity in the '20s, when he is seen to appear with such diverse people as F. Scott Fitgerald, Jack Dempsey, Babe Ruth, Herbert Hoover and Adolph Hitler. Excellently photographed, mimicking a documentary style reminiscent of the period. Clever, but a one-joke film; best for fans of Woody Allen and movie making.

A: Woody Allen, Mia Farrow, Saul Bellow, Susan Sontag, Garrett Brown, Stephanie Farrow

© WARNER HOME VIDEO 22027

ZORBA THE GREEK

D: Michael Cacoyannis — 142 m

NR | DMA COM | 1964 | B&W

Sex / Nud / Viol / Lang / AdSit

9 Invigorating and captivating Best Picture nominee about a totally uncomplicated man with a zest for life - Zorba - is played to perfection by Anthony Quinn. When an uptight young English intellectual (Bates) comes to Zorba's small village on the Greek isle of Crete to reopen a small mine he has inherited, Zorba appoints himself as the man's tutor. He will teach the Englishman how to live life. This is a highly emotional and at times highly exuberant exploration of all that life has to offer. Highly recommended. Won three other Oscars, including Best Supporting Actress.

A: Anthony Quinn, Alan Bates, Irene Papas, Lila Kedrova, George Foundas

© FOXVIDEO 1106

C R M

Crime

1956 and After

10 RILLINGTON PLACE

PG | CRM DMA | 1971 | COLOR | Sex | Nud | Viol | Lang | AdSit

D: Richard Fleischer 111 m

7 Fascinating true story which so upset the English public that it brought about the end to the death penalty there. John Hurt is utterly believable and pitiable as a simple man who is wrongly sent to his death for the hideous murders of his wife and child. In actuality, his landlord had offered to abort the unwanted baby, but had instead raped the woman and then killed both her and another child. The landlord then lied at the trial, helping to convict the husband. The truth was not discovered until years after the execution, when the landlord was brought up on other murder charges.

A: John Hurt, Judy Geeson, Richard Attenborough, Andre Morell

© COLUMBIA TRISTAR HOME VIDEO 60593

12 ANGRY MEN

NR | CRM DMA | 1957 | B&W | Sex | Nud | Viol | Lang | AdSit

D: Sidney Lumet 93 m

9 Compelling courtroom drama. Twelve jurors, all men, convene to decide the fate of a boy accused of murdering his father. The case is seemingly cut-and-dried and all vote guilty - except one, Fonda. For him, the situation is not so clear cut. Against considerable pressure from the other eleven, he slowly builds a case for acquittal out of his concerns for the boy's innocence and gradually wins over the others - all except Cobb who holds out. Tense, engrossing and impressive, it received Oscar nominations for Best Picture, Director and Screenplay.

A: Henry Fonda, Lee J. Cobb, Martin Balsam, Jack Klugman, Jack Warden, E.G. Marshall

Distributed By MGM/UA Home Video M301270

48 HOURS

R | ACT COM CRM | 1983 | COLOR | Sex | Nud | Viol | Lang | AdSit

D: Walter Hill 97 m

9 A very popular blockbuster hit with good reason. It has plenty of realistic action, comedy, good acting, and is a good cop story, too. Nick Nolte is a veteran toughguy/boozehound cop but he needs help from a wiseguy/con man/convict (Eddie Murphy) in order to track down two extremely vicious cop killers. So, Nolte gets Murphy sprung from jail, but just for two days. Murphy turns out to be a good partner for the crazy cop. He is smart, cool under pressure, tough and funny, too (like when he terrorizes a redneck bar). Great entertainment on many levels all at once. Highly recommended.

A: Eddie Murphy, Nick Nolte, Annette O'Toole, Frank McRae, James Remar, David Patrick Kelly

© PARAMOUNT HOME VIDEO 1139

8 MILLION WAYS TO DIE

R | ACT SUS CRM | 1986 | COLOR | Sex | Nud | Viol | Lang | AdSit

D: Hal Ashby 115 m

7 Brutal and cynical film in which Bridges, as an alcoholic ex-cop, is hired by a high-priced call girl (Arquette) to help her escape from her drug-dealing boyfriend and pimp (Garcia). Bridges gets drawn deep into a world of drugs, alcohol and sex and with his history, he may not make it back out. But - having Arquette there waiting for him at the end makes it worth the effort. This is a very violent and cynical cop film, punctuated with Bridges's character's personal crisis. However, it is also populated mostly with unsympathetic characters and that makes it a difficult film to get close to.

A: Jeff Bridges, Rosanna Arquette, Alexandra Paul, Randy Brooks, Andy Garcia, Lisa Sloan

© CBS/FOX VIDEO 6118

AARON LOVES ANGELA

R | ROM CRM | 1975 | B&W | Sex | Nud | Viol | Lang | AdSit

D: Gordon Parks 99 m

6 Star-crossed "Romeo and Juliet" story, Harlem style. A black boy (Hooks) falls for a sweet and pretty Puerto Rican girl (Cara) in a drug infested neighborhood of Harlem. They are in love but love, in their world, is dangerous. They struggle against the nature of their circumstances, a Puerto Rican gang and his bitter father, to meet in secret in a condemned building. Unknown to them, this is also a place where there is going to be a big drug buy. Jose Feliciano music. Also see the original ROMEO AND JULIET or WEST SIDE STORY.

A: Kevin Hooks, Irene Cara, Moses Gunn, Robert Hooks, Ernestine Jackson, Jose Feliciano

© COLUMBIA TRISTAR HOME VIDEO 60480

ACCUSED, THE

R | DMA CRM | 1988 | COLOR | Sex | Nud | Viol | Lang | AdSit

D: Jonathan Kaplan 110 m

9 Powerful, intense drama with an important moral question to ask. Foster won an Oscar for her riveting performance as a somewhat sleazy and deliberately provocative woman who is gang raped at a neighborhood bar. Female public prosecutor McGillis is intent upon dealing with the rape in a typically bureaucratic manner, but the incensed victim demands a public trial. An unexpectedly compelling, non-exploitive drama about a sleazy, foul-mouthed, but yet amazingly naive young woman who gets her day in court. Excellent drama and a powerhouse film.

A: Jodie Foster, Kelly McGillis, Bernie Coulsen, Leo Rossi, Ann Hearn, Carmen Argenziano

© PARAMOUNT HOME VIDEO 1760

ACROSS 110TH STREET

R | ACT CRM | 1972 | COLOR | Sex | Nud | Viol | Lang | AdSit

D: Barry Shear 144 m

8 Unjustly overlooked film about N.Y.C. cops who are caught in the middle of a gang war. They are racing against the mob to catch the three black thieves who disguised themselves as cops so that they could steal $300,000 from a Mafia-controlled numbers bank. The mob wants their money back and they want revenge. Exciting, action-packed, but extremely violent. This is a highly suspenseful sleeper that should not be missed by action fans.

A: Anthony Quinn, Yaphet Kotto, Anthony Franciosa, Paul Benjamin, Richard Wind

Distributed By MGM/UA Home Video M203068

ACTION JACKSON

R | ACT CRM | 1987 | COLOR | Sex | Nud | Viol | Lang | AdSit

D: Craig R. Baxley 96 m

6 Action hit. Weathers is a tough Detroit cop and Harvard graduate who, framed for murder, is being hunted down by his fellow cops. He has a serious run-in with a ruthless auto dealer (Nelson) after becoming involved with the man's wife and mistress. Not a lot of high drama and the very thin plot is also confusing, but there is plenty of non-stop action, in addition to the ample charms of both sultry rock star Vanity and Sharon Stone.

A: Carl Weathers, Craig T. Nelson, Vanity, Sharon Stone, Sonny Landham, Thomas F. Wilson

© WARNER HOME VIDEO 816

AFTER DARK MY SWEET

D: James Foley — 114 m

R | SUS CRM | 1990 | COLOR | Sex Nud Viol Lang AdSit

8 Sexy modern-day film noir. A seemingly punch-drunk ex-boxer drifter (Patric), recently escaped from a mental institution, finds himself irresistibly attracted to a seductive widow (Ward). She and a disgraced ex-cop, now a sleazy con man (Dern), draw him into an ill-conceived kidnap and ransom plot. When Patric discovers that he has been duped and is just a pawn in their plan, things get deadly. They picked on the wrong guy. Lots of plot twists in this steamy thriller that is also rife with cynicism and paranoia. Patric puts in a superb performance.

A: Jason Patric, Rachel Ward, Bruce Dern, George Dickerson, James Cotton, Rocky Giordani

© LIVE HOME VIDEO 68943

AL CAPONE

D: Richard Wilson — 104 m

NR | CRM ACT DMA | 1959 | B&W | Sex Nud Viol Lang AdSit

8 Excellent action movie. Solid telling of the life story of the infamous Chicago gangster who rises from being a hitman for Johnny Torrio (Persoff) to become the king of the Prohibition Era. After a bitter battle with the Feds, he is arrested and imprisoned for tax evasion. No other gangster so captured the imagination and the headlines of the country. Steiger is riveting in his portrayal of Capone, and the rest of the cast is perfect, too. For more of Capone see THE UNTOUCHABLES (1987) and SCARFACE (1932).

A: Rod Steiger, Fay Spain, Martin Balsam, Nehemiah Persoff

© CBS/FOX VIDEO 7750

ALIEN NATION

D: Graham Baker — 90 m

R | CRM SF ACT | 1988 | COLOR | Sex Nud Viol Lang AdSit

8 Interesting and very entertaining slant on the buddy-cop theme. Earth has accepted, but not necessarily graciously, the refugees and former slaves of of another world. When cop James Caan's partner is killed in a shootout with a gang of the refugees, Caan is forced to unwillingly accept an alien "newcomer" as a replacement partner even though he is extremely prejudiced. Together, he and his new partner follow a trail of mysterious murders that leads them to discover what could become the worst drug epidemic the world has ever seen. Good action and humor, plus some very interesting human insights too. Great performances by Caan and Patinkin.

A: James Caan, Mandy Patinkin, Terence Stamp, Kevin Major Howard, Leslie Bevins

© FOXVIDEO 1585

AMERICAN ME

D: Edward James Olmos — 125 m

R | CRM DMA | 1992 | COLOR | Sex Nud Viol Lang AdSit

7 Powerful, violent and brutal film about brutality, violence, power and respect. Olmos also stars in this his directing debut. This film graphically illustrates the patterns of behavior that seduce some into a cycle of gang violence. Olmos plays a man who has spent most of his life in prison but has gained self-worth and respect as a ruthless crime lord. However, when he learns the personal price he has paid, it has become too late for him to benefit. This is not a pleasant film to watch because what it reflects is uncompromising, graphic and real. Ultimately it makes a powerful anti-gang and anti-violence statement.

A: Edward James Olmos, William Forsythe, Pepe Serna, Danny De La Paz, Evelina Fernandez, Sal Lopez

© MCA/UNIVERSAL HOME VIDEO, INC. 81265

ANATOMY OF A MURDER

D: Otto Preminger — 161 m

NR | SUS MYS CRM | 1959 | B&W | Sex Nud Viol Lang AdSit

9 Extremely strong movie. Fascinating courtroom drama with a strong sense of realism. A gripping story that was nominated for seven Oscars, including Best Picture. Jimmy Stewart defends an Army lieutenant (Gazzara) who is on trial for having murdered his sexy wife's (Remick) rapist. Excellent legal drama, considered to be among the best of all time, with some absolutely riveting scenes. Stuart is a witty, cagey defense lawyer. Scott is a stuffy big-city prosecuting attorney. First-rate stuff that was also considered very daring for its time.

A: James Stewart, Arthur O'Connell, Lee Remick, Ben Gazzara, Eve Arden, George C. Scott

© COLUMBIA TRISTAR HOME VIDEO 60701

ANDERSON TAPES, THE

D: Sidney Lumet — 98 m

PG | SUS CRM | 1971 | COLOR | Sex Nud Viol Lang AdSit

7 Really neat thriller. Connery is a master crook who has just been released from prison. He plans the holdup of the entire Fifth Avenue apartment building where his girlfriend lives in New York City and the plan is bankrolled by a big underworld boss. The best specialists there are have been hired to work with him. Disguised as moving men, the team systematically loots each apartment, but things start to unravel. Tight editing and excellent performances keep the viewer totally involved and on edge. Climax is particularly good.

A: Sean Connery, Dyan Cannon, Martin Balsam, Ralph Meeker, Alan King, Margaret Hamilton

© COLUMBIA TRISTAR HOME VIDEO 60124

AND HOPE TO DIE

D: Rene Clement — 95 m

R | CRM | 1972 | COLOR | Sex Nud Viol Lang AdSit

7 French criminal (Trintignant) is on the run and being pursued by a band of gypsies. He reaches Montreal where Ryan, an aging gangster and father-figure for a gang of thugs, takes him in. Ryan gets him involved in a kidnap plan where they are hired to kidnap a gangster's moll and hold her for ransom for $1 million. They are betrayed and their plan goes bad, but they go through with the kidnapping plan anyway - even though the victim is dead. Above-average caper with weird touches.

A: Robert Ryan, Jean-Louis Trintignant, Aldo Ray, Lea Massari, Tisa Farrow

© MONTEREY HOME VIDEO B762

AND THEN YOU DIE

D: Francis Mankiewicz — 115 m

R | ACT CRM | 1987 | COLOR | Sex Nud Viol Lang AdSit

8 Interesting and quite different. This is a unique film that captures your attention early and holds it throughout. It is the Canadian version of THE LONG GOOD FRIDAY. In it, a drug kingpin makes a fortune but then he gets caught between the police, a motor cycle gang, his own gang and other forces outside his organization - all of them are trying to get him and suddenly things are coming apart all around him. Thrill-a-minute. Excellent. Keeps you guessing right up to the last possible moment.

A: Kenneth Welsh, R.H. Thompson, Wayne Robson, Tom Harvey, George Bloomfield, Graeme Campbell

© VIDMARK ENTERTAINMENT M4708

ANOTHER 48 HOURS

D: Walter Hill — 98 m

R | ACT COM CRM | 1990 | COLOR | Sex Nud Viol Lang AdSit

7 That comic, wisecracking, crime-busting duo are back again for the second time around. This time, the boys make a huge mess of San Francisco as they try to bring down a very bad dude named Iceman. Nolte's got himself in a jam, so he turns to old friend/enemy Murphy - fresh out of prison himself - to save his career and clear his name by nailing Iceman to the wall in just 48 hours. Expect the usual bar brawls, tough talk, smart talk, humor and lots of violence and broken glass! Fun still, but not as good as the first time around in 48 HOURS.

A: Eddie Murphy, Nick Nolte, Brion James, Kevin Tighe, Ed O'Ross, David Anthony Marshall

© PARAMOUNT HOME VIDEO 32386

APOLOGY

D: Robert Bierman — 98 m

NR | SUS CRM | 1986 | COLOR | Sex Nud Viol Lang AdSit

8 An intriguingly different story. An artist (Warren) has what she thinks is a brilliant idea. She starts an anonymous phone service, as an artistic experiment. People are to call in to leave their confessions anonymously to free their consciences. But the plan takes a macabre twist when a psychopath begins a killing spree, just so that he has something to confess to her. Soon he begins to pursue her, too. Weller is the cop who trys to help her by catching him first. Stylish suspense thriller. Made for cable TV.

A: Lesley Ann Warren, Peter Weller, John Glover, Jimmie Ray Weeks, George Loros, Harvey Fierstein

© HBO VIDEO 9975

ASSAULT ON PRECINCT 13

D: John Carpenter — 91 m

R | SUS CRM ACT | 1976 | COLOR | Sex Nud Viol Lang AdSit

8 Riveting thriller, taut suspense and lots of hard-hitting action. A nearly deserted LA police station is in the process of being closed down. There are only two deathrow prisoners, one cop and two secretaries waiting inside for the moving vans. Through the door runs a man who is being pursued by a gang of street kids. In a state of shock, he cannot tell the cop what is happening before the phone lines and the power are cut. They are all now trapped inside and the gang attacks. Widely recognized as an updated version of the Howard Hawks classic Western RIO BRAVO. Quite good.

A: Austin Stoker, Darwin Joston, Laurie Zimmer, Tony Burton, Nancy Loomis, Kim Richards

© UNITED AMERICAN VIDEO CORP. 5260

AT CLOSE RANGE

D: James Foley — 115 m

R | SUS CRM | 1986 | COLOR | Sex Nud Viol Lang AdSit

8 A powerful thriller. A rural Pennsylvania hood returns home to the family he abandoned years before. His two listless and admiring sons long to prove themselves to their father to be worthy of joining his gang, but the two have no idea of how ruthless their father can be. When the cops begin to close in on him, he becomes fearful his own sons know too much and decides that they must be eliminated to remove any threat. Vivid and shocking in its ruthless violence - particularly since it is based upon a real-life situation. Excellent and forceful acting.

A: Sean Penn, Christopher Walken, Mary Stuart Masterson, Christopher Penn, Millie Perkins, Candy Clark

© LIVE HOME VIDEO VA5170

BACK TRACK

D: Dennis Hopper — 102 m

R | CRM ACT | 1991 | COLOR

Sex / Nud / Viol / Lang / AdSit

6 Jodie Foster is an electronic artist who stumbles upon a mob hit. When she discovers that the police can't protect her from the mob, she decides to hide out on her own. The police however, need her as witness, so now she has both the police and the mob on her trail. To find her and kill her, the bad guys contract with top notch hitman Dennis Hopper. He studies every aspect of her, discovers that she is in many ways like him, falls in love with her, and, after he catches up with her, he gives her the option of dying on the spot or leaving with him. Now they are both on the run together. Very unusual film. Not particularly outstanding, but curiously interesting.

A: Jodie Foster, Dennis Hopper, Dean Stockwell, Joe Pesci, John Turturro, Fred Ward

© LIVE HOME VIDEO 9952

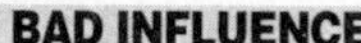

BAD INFLUENCE

D: Curtis Hanson — 99 m

R | SUS CRM | 1990 | COLOR

Sex / Nud / Viol / Lang / AdSit

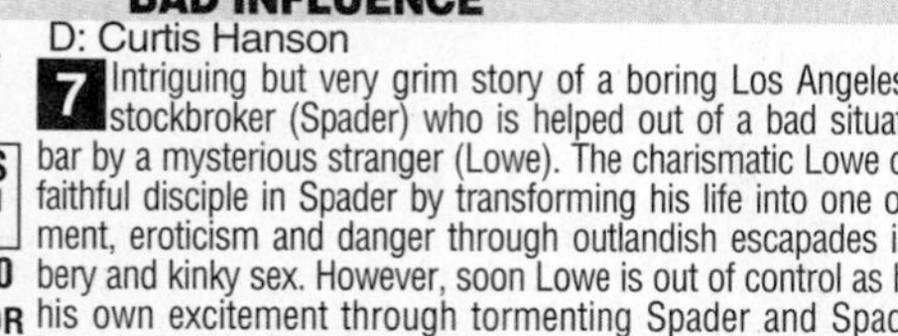

7 Intriguing but very grim story of a boring Los Angeles yuppie stockbroker (Spader) who is helped out of a bad situation in a bar by a mysterious stranger (Lowe). The charismatic Lowe creates a faithful disciple in Spader by transforming his life into one of excitement, eroticism and danger through outlandish escapades into robbery and kinky sex. However, soon Lowe is out of control as he seeks his own excitement through tormenting Spader and Spader's life becomes a surrealistic nightmare. Nothing is too much for Lowe, including murder. Vivid and sometimes lurid.

A: Rob Lowe, James Spader, Lisa Zane, Christian Clemenson, Kathleen Wilhoite, Tony Maggio

© COLUMBIA TRISTAR HOME VIDEO 59233

BADLANDS

D: Terrence Malick — 94 m

PG | CRM DMA | 1973 | COLOR

Sex / Nud / Viol / Lang / AdSit

9 Chilling true story. In 1958 Charles Starkweather began an extended cross-country killing spree. By the time he and his teenage girlfriend were apprehended, ten people were dead. This real-life event is grippingly captured in this very disturbing drama that you won't soon forget. Excellent acting, fine craftsmanship and striking photography bring this uncomfortable story of cool, almost casual, killing to life. See also IN COLD BLOOD.

A: Martin Sheen, Sissy Spacek, Warren Oates, Ramon Bieri, Alan Vint

© WARNER HOME VIDEO 11135

BASIC INSTINCT

D: Paul Verhoeven — 123 m

R | SUS CRM | 1992 | COLOR

Sex / Nud / Viol / Lang / AdSit

7 A taut and intense psychosexual thriller! Set in San Francisco, a tough cop (Douglas) investigates a brutal ice pick murder and finds himself uncontrollably attracted to an overtly sexual novelist (Stone), who is the prime suspect in the case. Despite her ominous and provocative warnings that he's in way over his head, Douglas pursues the unabashedly sexual Stone, never really knowing for sure if he'll be the next to die by the pierce of the pick. Fast paced with graphic sex scenes. But its intense presentation also hides some major plot flaws which don't stand up on later reflection.

A: Michael Douglas, Sharon Stone, George Dzundza, Jeanne Tripplehorn, Denis Arndt, Leilani Sarelle

© LIVE HOME VIDEO 48961

BETRAYED

D: Constantine Costa-Gavras — 128 m

R | CRM DMA | 1988 | COLOR

Sex / Nud / Viol / Lang / AdSit

7 FBI agent Debra Winger is sent undercover in a rural community when a left-wing talk show host is murdered by right-wing extremists. The chief suspect is a warm-hearted, single-parent farmer that she falls in love with. The longer she is around him, the more she discovers that he is also a very paranoid bigot who is deeply involved with a heavily armed extremist group. Winger gives a strong performance as a woman torn by the profound moral dilemma of despising and having to arrest the man she also loves. However, the potential impact is diminished by some holes in plot.

A: Debra Winger, Tom Berenger, John Heard, Betsy Blair, Ted Levine, John Mahoney

Distributed By MGM/UA Home Video M901553

BEVERLY HILLS COP

D: Martin Brest — 105 m

R | COM ACT CRM | 1984 | COLOR

Sex / Nud / Viol / Lang / AdSit

10 A huge box-office sensation, a perfect vehicle for the wise-cracking Eddie Murphy and a very funny and action-packed movie. A street-smart, smart aleck Detroit cop (Murphy) goes to L.A. intent upon tracking down a friend's killer. He ignores the by-the-book local cops and their warnings to stay away and instead blusters his way into high society, irritating everybody possible in the process. Following his killer's trail leads him to a major smuggling and drug ring. Cleverly woven fabric of comedy, characters and action. Excellent cast provides major support. Excellent score.

A: Eddie Murphy, Judge Reinhold, John Aston, Lisa Eibacher, Steven Berkoff, James Russo

© PARAMOUNT HOME VIDEO 1134

BEVERLY HILLS COP II

D: Tony Scott — 103 m

R | COM ACT CRM | 1987 | COLOR

Sex / Nud / Viol / Lang / AdSit

7 Sequel to the megahit BEVERLY HILLS COP. It lacks the originality and major laughs of the first movie, but still has plenty of action and wise cracks. Murphy comes back to L.A. to investigate the shooting of his friend, police captain Cox, and runs up against hit woman Brigitte Nielsen. Murphy is again the likable smart-mouthed cop who runs over everyone to get the bad guys. Pretty good, but not close to the original. Don't miss Murphy's other megahit: 48 HOURS.

A: Eddie Murphy, Judge Reinhold, Jurgen Prochnow, Ronny Cox, John Aston, Brigitte Nielsen

© PARAMOUNT HOME VIDEO 1860

BILLY BATHGATE

D: Robert Benton — 107 m

R | CRM ACT | 1991 | COLOR

Sex / Nud / Viol / Lang / AdSit

8 Absorbing and well-crafted gangster movie that was underappreciated on its release. Told through the eyes Billy (Loren Dean), a streetwise young kid trying to break out of the ghetto and into the rackets, this is the story of the final days of the infamous Dutch Schultz (Dustin Hoffman). More importantly, it is an involving depiction of the characters and lifestyle of that colorful era. Willis is Dutch's right-hand man who betrays him and earns a trip to the ocean floor in concrete boots. Kidman is the slumming socialite who enjoys living on the edge. Well done.

A: Dustin Hoffman, Nicole Kidman, Bruce Willis, Loren Dean, Steven Hill

© TOUCHSTONE HOME VIDEO 1337

BLACK MARBLE, THE

D: Harold Becker — 110 m

PG | CRM COM ACT | 1980 | COLOR

Sex / Nud / Viol / Lang / AdSit

7 An insightful, charming and sometimes funny look at a hard-drinking cop who is slowly killing himself with alcohol to dull the realities of his job. He is assigned a sexy new female detective who thinks he is crazy and obsolete. She wants to have as little as possible to do with him. When they are assigned the case of retrieving a kidnapped prize dog from a sleazy dog breeder, she changes her mind about him and falls in love with him. (There is a wonderful seduction scene in his apartment.) This movie slides from comedy into drama into action. It is good but also slightly uneven.

A: Paula Prentiss, Robert Foxworth, Harry Dean Stanton, Barbara Babcock, John Hancock, Judy Landers

© NEW LINE HOME VIDEO 1617

BLACK RAIN

D: Ridley Scott — 125 m

R | ACT CRM | 1989 | COLOR

Sex / Nud / Viol / Lang / AdSit

9 Superior, high-intensity action thriller. Two New York police detectives take a vicious killer back to Japan where they are tricked into releasing him to the wrong people. The two now vow to get him back. However, their help is not welcomed by the Japanese police who have their own way of doing business. The Westerners soon find that their pursuit has entangled them with very powerful figures from the Japanese underworld, who are also engaged in an internal war. Loaded with non-stop action. Another very interesting Japanese-Mafia movie, but with a less-hyper air, is THE YAKUZA.

A: Michael Douglas, Andy Garcia, Ken Takakura, Kate Capshaw, Yusaku Matsuda, Tomisaburo Wakayama

© PARAMOUNT HOME VIDEO 32220

BLACK SUNDAY

D: John Frankenheimer — 143 m

R | SUS ACT CRM | 1977 | COLOR

Sex / Nud / Viol / Lang / AdSit

9 Gripping thriller. An Arab guerrilla terrorist organization called Black September plans to attack America in the most painful way possible: they plan to blow up the Superbowl with the President in attendance. The terrorist leader gets shell-shocked Vietnam vet Bruce Dern to pilot the Goodyear Blimp into position, where they then plan to blow it up. Shaw is an Israeli agent who struggles against time to foil their plot. Terrific action sequences combine with genuine terror at the climax to create true excitement. Excellent.

A: Robert Shaw, Bruce Dern, Marthe Keller, Fritz Weaver, Steven Keats, William Daniels

© PARAMOUNT HOME VIDEO 8855

BLACK WIDOW

D: Bob Rafelson — 101 m

R | SUS CRM | 1987 | COLOR

Sex / Nud / Viol / Lang / AdSit

8 Absorbing sexy thriller. Debra Winger is a Justice Department investigator who becomes intently suspicious of Theresa Russell because Russell is constantly being widowed only a very short time after having married wealthy men. Intensity builds as Winger's obsession with convicting Russell of murder becomes as strong as Russell's own compulsion to continue to get away with murder. Winger becomes so fixated that she quits her job just so she can continue to follow Russell. Solid plotting and the leads are both beautiful - and very believable. Good stuff.

A: Debra Winger, Theresa Russell, Sami Frey, Dennis Hopper, Nicol Williamson, Terry O'Quinn

© FOXVIDEO 5033

BLOOD IN, BLOOD OUT

D: Taylor Hackford 180 m

R | CRM DMA | 1993 | COLOR | Sex | Nud | Viol | Lang | AdSit

7 The lives of three young Latinos, two half-brothers and a cousin, from the barrios of East Los Angeles are followed from their days together in a street gang in 1973 to their very different lives in 1984. Epic in length, there are several episodes of very involving drama, but they are bracketed by long episodes of violence. One of the friends is an artist whose back is broken and becomes a drug addict; one becomes a police detective and the other, who is tortured by being half-white, becomes the leader of a Latino gang in San Quentin prison. This is not a casual film. It takes effort to watch this much violence and pain, but it also provides an effective window into that culture.

A: Jesse Borrego, Benjamine Bratt, Enrique Castillo, Damian Chapa, Delroy Lindo, Tom Wilson

© HOLLYWOOD PICTURES HOME VIDEO 2015

BLOW OUT

D: Brian De Palma 108 m

R | SUS CRM | 1981 | COLOR | Sex | Nud | Viol | Lang | AdSit

7 Travolta is a motion picture sound effects man who inadvertently records the sounds of a car accident which killed a potential Presidential candidate. He also saves the life of a young prostitute who is in that car. Now, listening over and over to his tapes, he becomes certain that something is just not right, that was no accident. He holds the key evidence in a major political conspiracy, but the only one who believes him is the girl. Their knowledge puts both their lives in danger, and they are both targets for murder. Good suspense.

A: John Travolta, Nancy Allen, John Lithgow, Dennis Franz, Peter Boyden

© GOODTIMES 74063

BLOWUP

D: Michelangelo Antonioni 102 m

NR | SUS CRM | 1966 | COLOR | Sex | Nud | Viol | Lang | AdSit

8 Solid thriller. A brilliant London photographer travels about London capturing the sights and sounds of the city, particularly beautiful fashion models. One day he photographs a couple embracing in the park, but the girl runs after him, demanding the film back. He refuses and when he develops the film, he thinks he sees a gun trained on her partner. He goes back to the park to investigate and finds a body, but the next morning it's gone. This film is rich in many-layered meanings but remains, at its essence, an elegant murder mystery. Very influential film. Sexy. Would be considered R-rated today.

A: Vanessa Redgrave, David Hemmings, Sarah Miles, Jill Kennington, Verushka, The Yardbirds

Distributed By MGM/UA Home Video M600015

BLUE STEEL

D: Kathryn Bigelow 103 m

R | ACT CRM | 1990 | COLOR | Sex | Nud | Viol | Lang | AdSit

6 A female rookie cop (Curtis), on her first day, is forced to shoot and kill an armed robber. She fired because she saw he had a weapon, but the pistol can't be found and she is suspended. However, an unseen witness was also there on that day and he picked up the gun. He has his own plans for it and for her. He is obsessed with Curtis. He is a smooth-talking handsome commodities broker (Silver) and he wins her over. But, unbeknownst to her or anyone else, he is also a serial killer who is using the missing gun to slam slugs into bodies. Plot is not particularly credible or even believable, but it does have a lot of gory action.

A: Jamie Lee Curtis, Ron Silver, Clancy Brown, Elizabeth Pena, Philip Bosco, Louise Fletcher

Distributed By MGM/UA Home Video M901885

BODY DOUBLE

D: Brian De Palma 114 m

R | MYS SUS CRM | 1984 | COLOR | Sex | Nud | Viol | Lang | AdSit

8 Slick, clever, suspenseful and sexy. De Palma borrows from Hitchcock (VERTIGO and REAR WINDOW) and even himself (OBSESSION, DRESSED TO KILL and BLOW OUT) to create a fascinating and controversial piece of work. Wasson is an out-of-work actor who is set up to be a witness for a murder. He is asked to house-sit at an expensive home where a telescope is trained upon a sexy neighbor who does a nightly dance naked in front of her window. Melanie Griffith is sexy and hilarious as a porno star who holds a key to the mystery of a grisly murder.

A: Craig Wasson, Deborah Shelton, Dennis Franz, Melanie Griffith, Gregg Henry, Guy Boyd

© GOODTIMES 4239

BODY HEAT

D: Lawrence Kasdan 113 m

R | SUS MYS CRM | 1981 | COLOR | Sex | Nud | Viol | Lang | AdSit

10 Gripping erotic thriller. Hurt is a second-rate lawyer who is sucked into a torrid affair with a sizzlingly lustful Turner. Their chemistry sets the screen ablaze. Turner is beautiful, sexy and rich, but she is married to a rich man (Crenna). She entices Hurt into a torrid affair and then into plot to kill Crenna, but has some devious twists and turns she has kept to herself. Very steamy and sexy, but that never gets in the way of the suspense and the surprises which hold your attention until the very last minute.

A: William Hurt, Kathleen Turner, Richard Crenna, Ted Danson, Mickey Rourke, J.A. Preston

© WARNER HOME VIDEO 20005

BOILING POINT

D: James B. Harris 93 m

R | ACT CRM | 1993 | COLOR | Sex | Nud | Viol | Lang | AdSit

6 Tepid cop drama. Snipes is a Treasury Agent whose partner has been gunned down with a shotgun blast at a phony drug buy. Snipes is upset. He is now being transfered and will have to start over in another town, and his ex-wife has a new man. So, all he has is a friendly hooker (Davidovich), his anger and his job. However, he has talked his boss into one more week so he can find his partner's killer. The killer is a simpleton with a hair-trigger and no conscience. But, he is taking direction from a slick-talking conman (Dennis Hopper), just out of prison, who sets up various phony scams where the two steal the money and kill the other party.

A: Wesley Snipes, Dennis Hopper, Lolita Davidovich, Dan Hedaya, Valerie Perrine, Tony Lo Bianco

© WARNER HOME VIDEO 12976

BONNIE AND CLYDE

D: Arthur Penn 112 m

NR | CRM ACT | 1967 | COLOR | Sex | Nud | Viol | Lang | AdSit

10 Blockbuster hit. Real-life depression-era folk heros Bonnie Parker (Dunaway) and Clyde Barro (Beatty) who proudly announced, "We rob banks," were immortalized by this landmark film which also transformed the whole action movie genre. The story follows the pair from when they first meet, through a series of highly publicized bank robberies, until their fateful and murderous end in a hail of many, many bullets. This is an exciting film which carefully weaves humor, human insight, social commentary and tenderness with graphic scenes of violence. 5 nominations and 2 Oscars.

A: Warren Beatty, Faye Dunaway, Michael J. Pollard, Gene Hackman, Estelle Parsons, Denver Pyle

© WARNER HOME VIDEO 1026

BOSTON STRANGLER, THE

D: Richard Fleischer 116 m

NR | CRM SUS | 1968 | COLOR | Sex | Nud | Viol | Lang | AdSit

8 Startling true story. Albert DeSalvo was a seemingly ordinary plumber and family man, but it was he who was the infamous Boston Strangler who terrorized Boston during the 1960s, killing only women - each murder more gruesome than the last. This is a non-sensationalized account of the search for, the capture of and the prosecution of DeSalvo. The documentary style of presentation creates a heightened sense of realism. Fonda plays the criminologist who found him, and Curtis is remarkably believable in a powerful performance as DeSalvo.

A: Tony Curtis, Henry Fonda, George Kennedy, Mike Kellin, Murray Hamilton, Sally Kellerman

© FOXVIDEO 1015

BOYZ N THE HOOD

D: John Singleton 112 m

R | CRM DMA | 1991 | COLOR | Sex | Nud | Viol | Lang | AdSit

9 An emotionally charged portrait of young men growing up in the very violent society of the inner-city. Brash and painfully insightful, this film looks at the way of life in the inner-city of Los Angeles, and the poverty, crime and gang wars that come with it. The story centers around one father and his desperate attempt to keep his son (Cuba Gooding, Jr.) out of trouble and to instill some sense of values in him. At 23, director John Singleton has done some incredible work and was honored by the New York Film Circle for this project.

A: Ice Cube, Cuba Gooding, Jr., Morris Chestnut, Larry Fishburne, Tyra Ferrell, Angela Bassett

© COLUMBIA TRISTAR HOME VIDEO 50813

BRINK'S JOB, THE

D: William Friedkin 103 m

PG | COM CRM | 1978 | COLOR | Sex | Nud | Viol | Lang | AdSit

8 Highly entertaining and funny account of the famous 1950 Boston Brink's vault robbery, told with a light touch. Peter Falk stars as the head of a gang of klutzes that somehow pulls off the crime of the century - almost. They get $2.7 million, lead the government on a very long, very expensive chase and then get caught just one week before the statute of limitations runs out. Lots of fun.

A: Peter Falk, Peter Boyle, Allen Garfield, Warren Oates, Paul Sorvino, Gena Rowlands

© MCA/UNIVERSAL HOME VIDEO, INC. 80062

BROTHERHOOD, THE

D: Martin Ritt 96 m

NR | CRM ACT | 1968 | COLOR | Sex | Nud | Viol | Lang | AdSit

7 A real sleeper. Two brothers are caught up in Mafia lifestyle and in a power struggle after their father dies leaving them the "business." Douglas believes in old-world traditions and is loyal to the Syndicate, but his brother Cord is different. Still, when Douglas kills Cord's father-in-law, Cord agrees to accept the contract to kill his own brother and Douglas must run away to hide in Sicily. This movie was made several years before THE GODFATHER, but contains many of the same elements that made GODFATHER such a big hit. Excellent story and a quality production.

A: Kirk Douglas, Alex Cord, Irene Papas, Luther Adler, Susan Strasberg, Eduardo Ciannelli

© PARAMOUNT HOME VIDEO 6815

BRUBAKER

D: Stuart Rosenberg — 131 m

R · **8** · CRM ACT · 1980 · COLOR

Redford plays Henry Brubaker, a reform-minded prison warden who arrives at his new assignment, a troubled prison, under cover as a new prisoner. He discovers that there is a conspiracy to murder prisoners by corrupt prison officials and then to cover it up. Based on the real-life experiences of Thomas O. Murlan, who was later dismissed as the Superintendent of the Arkansas State Penitentiary. Script was Oscar-nominated.

Sex · Nud · Viol · Lang · AdSit

A: Robert Redford, Yaphet Kotto, Jane Alexander, Murray Hamilton, David Keith, Morgan Freeman

© FOXVIDEO 1098

BUGSY

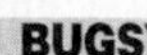

D: Barry Levinson — 135 m

R · **8** · DMA CRM · 1991 · COLOR

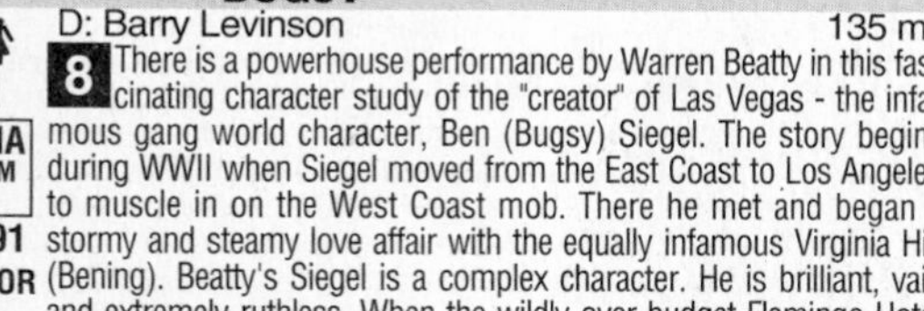

There is a powerhouse performance by Warren Beatty in this fascinating character study of the "creator" of Las Vegas - the infamous gang world character, Ben (Bugsy) Siegel. The story begins during WWII when Siegel moved from the East Coast to Los Angeles to muscle in on the West Coast mob. There he met and began a stormy and steamy love affair with the equally infamous Virginia Hill (Bening). Beatty's Siegel is a complex character. He is brilliant, vain and extremely ruthless. When the wildly over-budget Flamingo Hotel flops, Bugsy meets with swift mob justice.

Sex · Nud · Viol · Lang · AdSit

A: Warren Beatty, Ben Kingsley, Annette Bening, Lewis Van Bergen, Harvey Keitel, Richard Sarafian

© COLUMBIA TRISTAR HOME VIDEO 70673

BULLITT

D: Peter Yates — 114 m

PG · **9** · ACT CRM · 1968 · COLOR

This is the picture which set the standard in police action dramas for a long time, and it still stands up extremely well today. McQueen, in one of his best performances, plays a tough police detective assigned to guard a criminal witness for 48 hours and to then deliver him to testify. But his witness was shot and now he is chasing down the killer. Lots of plot twists make this a movie to be watched... but the car chase scenes make it a movie to watch over and over. Filmed at actual speeds in excess of 100 mph, they're excitement-plus, and some of the best ever done like it.

Sex · Nud · Viol · Lang · AdSit

A: Steve McQueen, Robert Vaughn, Jacqueline Bisset, Norman Fell, Don Gordon, Robert Duvall

© WARNER HOME VIDEO 1029

BUSTING

D: Peter Hyams — 89 m

R · **6** · CRM COM ACT · 1973 · COLOR

Gould and Blake are unconventional Los Angeles vice cops who are restricted to arresting small-time druggies and hookers because the big ones are getting protection from the higher-ups in the department. A fairly realistic, sometimes funny, depiction of police life. Gould and Blake are glib and have a good chemistry which makes this a reasonably entertaining buddy-cop movie.

Sex · Nud · Viol · Lang · AdSit

A: Elliott Gould, Robert Blake, Allen Garfield, Antonio Fargas, Michael Lerner, Sid Haig

Distributed By MGM/UA Home Video M801407

CAPE FEAR

D: J. Lee Thompson — 106 m

NR · **8** · SUS CRM · 1961 · B&W

Riveting tale of revenge and terror. Robert Mitchum is truly fearsome as a convicted sadistic rapist who is newly released from prison and who now has come back to terrorize Peck and his family. Peck was the attorney who sent him up. Mitchum stalks Peck's wife and his pretty teenage daughter but, though his actions are despicable, nothing that he does is illegal. The police can do nothing to protect them so, if Peck is going to save his family, he has to set a trap and bait it with those he loves most. Excruciatingly tense drama. Brilliant study of psycopathic sadism. Remade in 1992.

Sex · Nud · Viol · Lang · AdSit

A: Gregory Peck, Polly Bergen, Robert Mitchum, Lori Martin, Martin Balsam, Telly Savalas

© MCA/UNIVERSAL HOME VIDEO, INC. 80514

CAPE FEAR

D: Martin Scorsese — 128 m

R · **8** · SUS CRM · 1992 · COLOR

Excellent remake of 1961 classic. When wacked-out, self-educated De Niro gets out of jail after 14 long years, he decides to go after the lawyer who let him down and didn't get him off. De Niro methodically torments and terrorizes Nolte's family, paying special attention to his young daughter, but always staying just inside the law. He becomes their ultimate nightmare because the cops can do nothing. Even when Nolte decides he has had enough and takes his family away to hide out, De Niro secretly goes along for the ride. Criticized as being overblown, this is still a nail-biting, teeth-grinding, psychological thriller that really bites, but see the 1961 original too.

Sex · Nud · Viol · Lang · AdSit

A: Robert De Niro, Nick Nolte, Jessica Lange, Juliette Lewis, Joe Don Baker, Robert Mitchum

© MCA/UNIVERSAL HOME VIDEO, INC. 81105

CARLITO'S WAY

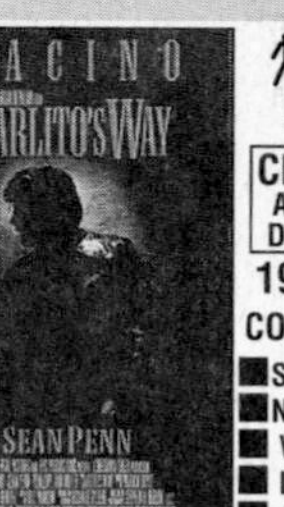

D: Brian De Palma — 145 m

R · **8** · CRM ACT DMA · 1993 · COLOR

Carlito (Pachino) was a big time drug dealer and a hood. He is tough and has stayed alive by doing what he has to do to survive. He was sent up for 30 years but his shyster lawyer (Penn) has gotten him out after only five. Still, that was enough time for Carlito. All he wants now is to go straight, stay out of trouble and he's got a plan to do it, too. He needs $75,000 to buy into a legit car rental business in the Bahamas and take his old flame (Miller) there with him. He is going to raise the money honestly by running a nightclub. The plan is working too. Then he gets a call from his lawyer buddy who is in trouble. Carlito feels honor-bound to help him, even though he risks everything.

Sex · Nud · Viol · Lang · AdSit

A: Al Pacino, Sean Penn, Penelope Ann Miller, Luis Guzman, James Rebhorrn, Viggo Mortensen

© MCA/UNIVERSAL HOME VIDEO, INC. 81630

CHINATOWN

D: Roman Polanski — 131 m

R · **10** · MYS SUS CRM · 1974 · COLOR

Landmark film and one of the greatest detective stories of all times. It won eleven Oscar nominations. Jack Nicholson plays Jake Gittes, a small-time 1930's California private detective who is hired by a beautiful socialite (Dunaway) to investigate her husband's affair. But Gittes gets much more than he bargained for when he stumbles into a major case involving double dealing, land swindles, water rights, murder, incest and major political figures. It is a bizarre story which leads us on a complex and fascinating journey. Sequel: THE TWO JAKES.

Sex · Nud · Viol · Lang · AdSit

A: Jack Nicholson, Faye Dunaway, John Huston, Perry Lopez, John Hillerman, Diane Ladd

© PARAMOUNT HOME VIDEO 8674

CHOIRBOYS, THE

D: Robert Aldrich — 120 m

R · **6** · CRM ACT DMA · 1977 · COLOR

Written by ex-detective Joseph Wambaugh, this is a story of the flip-side of some of the men in police work. Some L.A. cops meet periodically to let off some steam at frequent "choir practice" sessions, which are really wild booze and sex parties held in MacArthur Park. The story follows the lives of ten different cops. Most viewers will think that the depiction of their "choir practice" escapades are far too heavy-handed and foul. The film had a mixed reception at the box office upon its release, mostly because critics hated it.

Sex · Nud · Viol · Lang · AdSit

A: Charles Durning, Louis Gossett, Jr., Perry King, Clyde Kasatsu, Stephen Macht, Tim McIntire

© MCA/UNIVERSAL HOME VIDEO, INC. 55097

CLIENT, THE

D: Joel Schumacher — 121 m

PG-13 · **8** · CRM SUS · 1994 · COLOR

Quite good thriller that was translated from John Grisham's best-seller. A mafia lawyer confesses the whereabouts of dead Senator to an 11-year-old just before committing suicide. The smart kid has watched enough TV to know that he is in trouble if he talks. But, a glory-grabbing federal prosecutor (Jones) knows he knows, so he's in trouble even if he doesn't. He and his single Mom have no money, but he needs a lawyer. He gets the help he needs from an ex-alcoholic ex-mother, Susan Sarandon. Smart and now with a second chance, she is going to protect this kid no matter what. Fascinating battle of wills and maneuvers between the lawyers - and a war to stay alive between the kid and the hoods.

Sex · Nud · Viol · Lang · AdSit

A: Susan Sarandon, Tommy Lee Jones, Mary-Louise Parker, Anthony LaPaglia, Brad Renfro, Ossie Davis

© WARNER HOME VIDEO 13233

COLORS

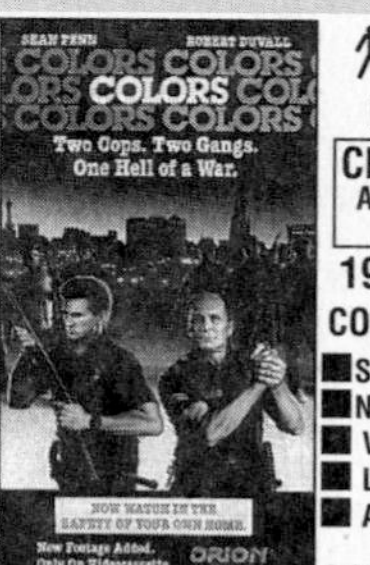

D: Dennis Hopper — 127 m

R · **8** · CRM ACT · 1988 · COLOR

Extremely intense police saga. However, the plot is rather tired: a well-seasoned and married cop (Duvall) with one year to go is unwillingly saddled with an over-eager green cop (Penn) who thinks he has all the answers. They are both assigned to a detail specializing in the extremely brutal streetgangs of East Los Angeles. Duvall and Penn play their roles with extreme intensity and the street life is presented with stark realism. That and the fact that many real-life gang members were cast to play themselves make this a very realistic and also very violent movie. Excellent, but definitely not for the squeamish.

Sex · Nud · Viol · Lang · AdSit

A: Sean Penn, Robert Duvall, Maria Conchita Alonso, Randy Brooks, Brand Bush, Don Cheadle

© ORION PICTURES CORPORATION 8711

CONSENTING ADULTS

D: Alan J. Pakula — 99 m

R · **6** · SUS CRM · 1992 · COLOR

Kline and Mastrantonio are happily married professionals living next door to Spacey and Miller. Kline and Mastrantonio become more and more impressed with the apparent ease with which Spacey can generate income. Then Spacey provides them with some helpful assistance and draws them further into his confidence. They are friends. However, one day he proposes a strange bargain to Kline, that they trade places in the middle of the night... their wives won't even know. They do, but the next morning Spacey's wife is dead, and the police are holding an astounded Kline for the murder. Contrived, but it still it holds your attention.

Sex · Nud · Viol · Lang · AdSit

A: Kevin Kline, Kevin Spacey, Mary Elizabeth Mastrantonio, Rebecca Miller, Forest Whitaker

© HOLLYWOOD PICTURES HOME VIDEO HPH1523

COOGAN'S BLUFF

D: Don Siegel — 93 m

R | ACT CRM | 1968 | COLOR

8 This was the first break out of the cowboy mold by Clint Eastwood, although he didn't make it quite all the way. The character he creates here is the precursor to Dirty Harry Calahan. Clint plays an Arizona sheriff sent to NYC to bring back an extradited criminal (Don Stroud), but Stroud escapes. Clint becomes frustrated by the big city bureaucracy and employs his own down-home police tactics to get him back, much to the chagrin of the New York cops, and Lee J. Cobb in particular. An effective actioner with lots of action, including a big brawl. It inspired the TV series "McCloud."

Sex / Nud / Viol / Lang / AdSit

A: Clint Eastwood, Lee J. Cobb, Susan Clark, Don Stroud, Tisha Sterling, Betty Field

© MCA/UNIVERSAL HOME VIDEO, INC. 66042

COP

D: James Harris — 110 m

R | CRM ACT | 1988 | COLOR

6 Chilling and visceral. James Woods plays a maverick cop who is barely hanging on to reality. He becomes obsessed with capturing a serial killer who has committed fifteen murders over the last ten years. Woods is so intense that the rest of the force wants no part of him and his wife leaves him. Several plot twists keeps your interest level high, but the logic does get strained at times. Very gritty and seamy. While much of this ground has been covered many times before, Woods's strong performance makes this believable and worth a watch.

Sex / Nud / Viol / Lang / AdSit

A: James Woods, Lesley Ann Warren, Charles Durning, Charles Haid, Randy Brooks

© UNITED AMERICAN VIDEO CORP. 5702

CRIMES OF PASSION

D: Ken Russell — 107 m

R | CRM DMA | 1985 | COLOR

6 At night, China Blue (Kathleen Turner) is the sexiest and best of the $50 whores in the red light district, but in the daytime she is a compulsive fashion designer. She loves to play power games with her customers. Laughlin is an unhappy suburban husband who gets involved with her. Turner is being stalked. Perhaps it is by Anthony Perkins. He plays a street corner preacher who is obsessed with her. She haunts his fantasies. Not a particularly distinctive movie, but it is interesting and Turner does put in a powerful and sexy performance.

Sex / Nud / Viol / Lang / AdSit

A: Kathleen Turner, Anthony Perkins, John Laughlin, Annie Potts, Bruce Davison

© R&G VIDEO, LP 14005

CRIME STORY

D: Abel Ferrara — 96 m

NR | CRM ACT | 1985 | COLOR

8 This is the pilot for the TV series of the same name. It is a very atmospheric cops-and-robbers film depicting 1960s Chicago. There is lots of vintage rock `n roll, cars with fins and some fascinating tough guys. Police Lt. Mike Torello heads the Major Crime Unit. He has set his sights on nailing a tough up-and-coming hood named Ray Lucca because Lucca killed two of Torello's friends. A very stylish film. Very strong character portrayals make this an excellent film for its genre. Many of the series's episodes are also available.

Sex / Nud / Viol / Lang / AdSit

A: Dennis Farina, Stephen Lang, Anthony Denison, Darlanne Fluegel, John Santucci, Bill Smitrovich

© R&G VIDEO, LP 90027

CUTTER'S WAY

D: Ivan Passer — 110 m

R | CRM SUS | 1981 | COLOR

7 A small-time hustler and gigolo (Bridges) witnesses a wealthy murderer dumping a young girl's body in an alley. When he is charged with the murder, his best friend (John Heard), an embittered and crippled Vietnam veteran, is determined to help. Heard is extremely bitter toward anyone of privilege - those who sent others off to do their dirty work, like in Vietnam. He now becomes obsessed with exposing the wealthy killer so that he can validate his own tarnished sense of morality. The three leads are all very good, but the gloomy atmosphere may not appeal to all.

Sex / Nud / Viol / Lang / AdSit

A: Jeff Bridges, John Heard, Lisa Eichhorn, Ann Dusenberry, Stephen Elliott, Nina Van Pallandt

Distributed By MGM/UA Home Video M700154

DAY OF THE JACKAL, THE

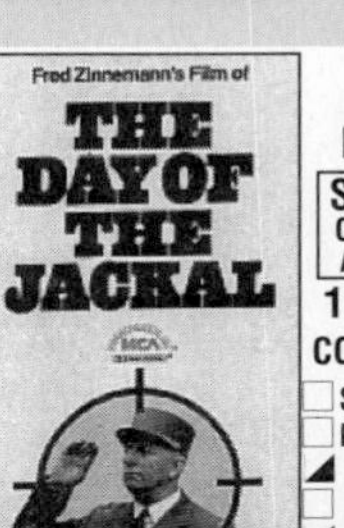

D: Fred Zinnemann — 143 m

PG | SUS CRM ACT | 1973 | COLOR

9 Mesmerizing tension. It is based upon the best selling novel of the same name and which, in turn, was based upon a real-life character. A terrorist organization hires the world's best professional hitman to assassinate French President Charles de Gaulle. The killer is a faceless man who is known only as the Jackal. French police learn of the plot, but the Jackal constantly changes disguises to stay just ahead of them. The scenes of the massive police manhunt are juxtaposed with the Jackal's compulsively meticulous preparations and the result is a buildup of an incredible tension. First-rate cast and absolutely compelling viewing.

Sex / Nud / Viol / Lang / AdSit

A: Edward Fox, Alan Badel, Tony Britton, Cyril Cusack, Eric Porter, Michael Lonsdale

© MCA/UNIVERSAL HOME VIDEO, INC. 66040

DEAD-BANG

D: John Frankenheimer — 102 m

R | ACT CRM | 1989 | COLOR

6 Don Johnson stars in this effective, but still more or less standard, cop flick - even though it is based upon a real character. He is an L.A. cop who has just been kicked out by his wife. He lives in a seedy apartment, drinks too much and the only thing he has left is his work. His investigation into the death of another cop leads him on a cross-country chase of a group of white supremacist killers that results in a major shootout in an underground bunker. Pretty good for what it is. Action fans might even want to add another point.

Sex / Nud / Viol / Lang / AdSit

A: Don Johnson, Penelope Ann Miller, William Forsythe, Bob Balaban, Frank Military, Tate Donovan

© WARNER HOME VIDEO 658

DEAD HEAT

D: Mark Goldblatt — 86 m

R | COM CRM | 1988 | COLOR

6 An interesting idea for an off-beat crime spoof. A couple of LA cops discover that a series of jewelry heists is being carried out by dead criminals who have been turned into zombies. When one of the detectives is killed in the bad guy's laboratory, he is brought back as a good-guy zombie to help get the bad-guy zombies. Pretty gory in places and the comedy does not always connect, but still not too bad.

Sex / Nud / Viol / Lang / AdSit

A: Treat Williams, Joe Piscopo, Lindsay Frost, Darren McGavin, Vincent Price

© R&G VIDEO, LP 90035

DEAD HEAT ON A MERRY-GO-ROUND

D: Bernard Girard — 107 m

NR | CRM COM | 1966 | COLOR

7 One of the greatest con artists of all times (Coburn) manages to win a parole from prison by seducing the lady shrink. Outside, he sets up an ingenious plan to rob the airport bank at the same time that airport security is occupied with the arrival of the Soviet Premier. The intelligent, sometimes witty script has a lot of complex twists in an intricate plot that will keep and hold your attention. Very entertaining. Perhaps Coburn's best performance. Watch for the surprise ending and keep an eye out for Harrison Ford in his first role.

Sex / Nud / Viol / Lang / AdSit

A: James Coburn, Camilla Sparv, Aldo Ray, Ross Martin, Severn Darden, Robert Webber

© COLUMBIA TRISTAR HOME VIDEO 60963

DEAD POOL, THE

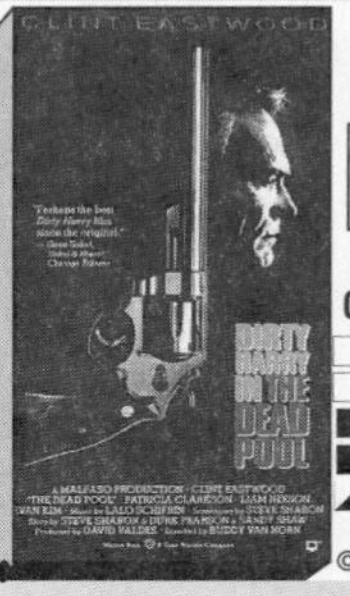

D: Buddy Van Horn — 91 m

R | ACT CRM | 1988 | COLOR

7 Dirty Harry Callahan is back for a fifth time. Harry investigates a series of celebrity murders. The one common thread is that all the victims had their names included on a betting pool list, and Harry's name is on the list, too. The story's pretty straightforward. The characters, particularly Harry, are the real interest. There is plenty of action. A particularly interesting bit is a recreation of the famous car chase scene from the action classic BULLITT, except that here the chase involves a radio-controlled Corvette model car loaded with dynamite. Good action fun!

Sex / Nud / Viol / Lang / AdSit

A: Clint Eastwood, Patricia Clarkson, Liam Neeson, David Hunt, Michael Curne, Evan C. Kim

© WARNER HOME VIDEO 11810

DEATH WISH

D: Michael Winner — 93 m

R | ACT CRM | 1974 | COLOR

9 This was an extremely popular film about a mild-mannered, liberal New Yorker who becomes radicalized after his wife and daughter are savagely raped and his wife dies. The system cannot or will not help him, so Bronson turns into a revenge-seeking vigilante out to destroy the street punks of New York. These he stalks by baiting traps to spring upon bad guys just when the unsuspecting vultures are about attack someone who they believe will be a victim. The vigilante becomes a hero to the people, but the cops must hunt him down. This hugely popular movie spawned many lessor sequels and imitators.

Sex / Nud / Viol / Lang / AdSit

A: Charles Bronson, Hope Lange, Vincent Gardenia, Jeff Goldblum, Stuart Margolin, Olympia Dukakis

© PARAMOUNT HOME VIDEO 8774

DEEP COVER

D: Bill Duke — 107 m

R | CRM ACT | 1992 | COLOR

9 Far above average cop movie. Well written, excellently constructed, good action with solid believable acting. Fishburne is a coolheaded loner, but he is also a very motivated young cop who is recruited by the Feds to go undercover. He begins his new life on the street at as a low level hustler but quickly associates himself with a drug dealing, quirky and eccentric lawyer (Goldblum) who is hungry for money and thrills. As partners-in-crime, these two begin an assault on the drug hierarchy and eventually to arrive at the top. But once there, things take a drastic turn when the rules suddenly change for the undercover cop. Excellent.

Sex / Nud / Viol / Lang / AdSit

A: Larry Fishburne, Jeff Goldblum, Victoria Dillard, Charles Martin Smith, Clarence Williams, III, Sidney Lassick

© TURNER HOME ENTERTAINMENT N4084

DEFENSELESS

D: Martin Campbell 106 m

R | SUS CRM | 1991 | COLOR | Sex | Nud | Viol | Lang | AdSit

7 Slick psychological thriller. Barbara Hershey is an attorney who is unfortunate enough to find her client (and lover) dead. However, she has also been framed for his murder and she may also be the killer's next victim. Her client was a real estate tycoon who she had been defending against charges of child pornography and, who it turns out, had also been married to an old friend of hers. Perhaps he was killed by the irate father of one of his young victims, or maybe there is another motive - but she must depend on an enigmatic police detective (Sam Shepard) to find out who the real murderer is, and do it in time to save her.

A: Barbara Hershey, Sam Shepard, J.T. Walsh, John Kapelos, Mary Beth Hurt

© LIVE HOME VIDEO 61704

DICK TRACY

D: Warren Beatty 105 m

PG | ACT CRM FAN | 1990 | COLOR | Sex | Nud | Viol | Lang | AdSit

7 Cartoon-like megabuck production that is a parody of the famous long-running comic-strip hero. There is a terrific line-up of major actors, however some are almost unrecognizable under makeup. (Al Pacino is despicable as the main villain who plans to unite all the bad guys. Madonna is marvelously vampy as Breathless Mahoney. Glenne Headly is lovely as Tracy's (Beatty) love interest.) Tracy rises to challenge the bad guys, but has trouble with his personal life. Plenty of shoot-'em-up action, against an unreal cartoon-like backdrop. Pretty good fun, not wonderful.

A: Warren Beatty, Madonna, Al Pacino, Dustin Hoffman, Mandy Patinkin, Paul Sorvino

© TOUCHSTONE HOME VIDEO 1066

DILLINGER

D: John Milius 106 m

R | CRM ACT | 1973 | COLOR | Sex | Nud | Viol | Lang | AdSit

8 A rip-roaring gangster movie with extremely violent but fascinating gun battles. Warren Oats was perfect for this part as Public Enemy Number One. The plot plays somewhat fast and loose with the facts, but great action sequences make up for that. The story follows Dillinger from midway in his bank-robbing career through until his death outside the Biograph Theater in Chicago at the hands of the G-men led by Melvin Purvis. You may also want to see LADY IN RED.

A: Warren Oates, Ben Johnson, Michelle Phillips, Cloris Leachman, Harry Dean Stanton, Geoffrey Lewis

© ORION PICTURES CORPORATION SV9196

DIRTY HARRY

D: Don Siegel 102 m

R | ACT CRM | 1971 | COLOR | Sex | Nud | Viol | Lang | AdSit

10 Excellent thriller. Clint Eastwood carved his name in American movie fame with this maverick San Francisco detective character, Harry Callahan. The city is desperate when it chooses Harry to be the one to track down a rooftop killer who has now captured a girl, buried her alive and will let her die if they don't pay a ransom. Harry tracks down this psychotic kidnapper/killer only to watch him get free on a legal technicality. Undeterred, Harry pursues the guy relentlessly, breaking all the rules along the way. Brilliant action and suspense. See Dirty Harry in the Heroes, Sequels, Subjects and Authors index for more in the series.

A: Clint Eastwood, Reni Santoni, Harry Guardino, Andy Robinson, John Vernon, John Larch

© WARNER HOME VIDEO 1019

DOBERMAN GANG, THE

D: Byron Ross Chudnow 85 m

G | ACT CRM | 1972 | COLOR | Sex | Nud | Viol | Lang | AdSit

7 A con man who doesn't trust human partners, kidnaps six vicious Doberman Pinschers and a dog trainer, and then uses them to rob a particularly difficult bank. Six vicious-looking dogs rush into a bank with studded collars and saddlebags. One dog delivers a note to the tellers and the others stand guard. The real thieves are outside, but no one knows who they are. Ingenious low-budget flick that really works quite well. The dogs steal the show. Good family fare. Led to two sequels.

A: Byron Mabe, Hal Reed, Julie Parrish, Simmy Bow, Jojo D'Amore, Juhn Tull

© CBS/FOX VIDEO 7793

DRESSED TO KILL

D: Brian De Palma 105 m

R | SUS CRM | 1980 | COLOR | Sex | Nud | Viol | Lang | AdSit

8 High-tension drama as a psychopath stalks two women. Angie Dickinson is a sexually frustrated housewife caught up in her sexual fantasies and is talking with her psychiatrist about her problem. However, she is brutally slashed after she has an affair with a total stranger. A hooker (Nancy Allen) who saw the killer leave, is soon being pursued by the psychopathic killer. So she teams up with Dickenson's young son in an effort to trap the murderer - a tall blonde named Bobbi. Michael Caine plays Angie's psychiatrist and he may hold the key, but beware... all things aren't as they appear to be. Unexpected ending.

A: Michael Caine, Angie Dickinson, Nancy Allen, Keith Gordon, Dennis Franz, David Margulies

© WARNER HOME VIDEO 26008

DRIVER, THE

D: Walter Hill 131 m

PG | ACT CRM | 1978 | COLOR | Sex | Nud | Viol | Lang | AdSit

8 A really curious action film. Ryan O'Neal is a master driver and a professional getaway man who gets his jobs through middleman Ronee Blakley. He has also hired a woman to be his professional alibi (beautiful gambler, Isabella Adjani). Bruce Dern is an unscrupulous cop who is obsessed with catching him. That is just about all the plot there is - but that doesn't tell the story. This film has some of the greatest car chase and action sequences ever put on film. It is full of excitement and characters that stay with you after the film is over.

A: Ryan O'Neal, Bruce Dern, Isabelle Adjani, Ronee Blakley, Matt Clark

© FOXVIDEO 1423

DROWNING POOL, THE

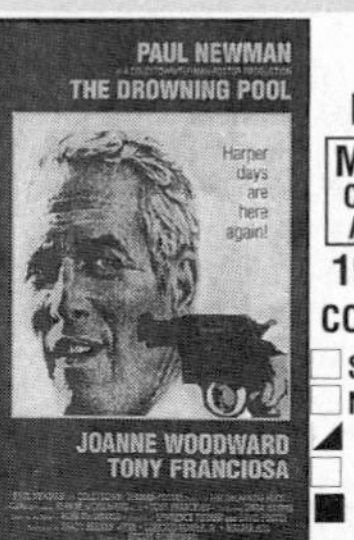

D: Stuart Rosenberg 109 m

PG | MYS CRM ACT | 1975 | COLOR | Sex | Nud | Viol | Lang | AdSit

8 Pretty good follow-up to a far-superior HARPER. Newman is back as the cynical private eye Lou Harper. This time he is hired by his former lover (Woodward) to find out who's blackmailing her. This is a seemingly simple case, but the further into it he gets, the more trouble he gets into. Newman's search takes him through some colorful Louisiana settings, gets him involved with all sorts of unsavory types, has him pursued by Woodward's sexy daughter (Melanie Griffith) and he winds up quite literally in water over his head. Slick and intelligent.

A: Paul Newman, Joanne Woodward, Anthony Franciosa, Murray Hamilton, Gail Strickland, Melanie Griffith

© WARNER HOME VIDEO 11371

ELECTRA GLIDE IN BLUE

D: James William Guercio 114 m

PG | CRM ACT DMA | 1973 | COLOR | Sex | Nud | Viol | Lang | AdSit

7 Very violent crime melodrama about one cop's disillusionment. Blake is a smart, but undersized and over-macho, Arizona motorcycle cop who wants to become a detective in the worst way. He gets his chance when he finds an apparent suicide in a shack, exposes it as a murder and gets his promotion. However, his attitude gets him in trouble and he's soon busted back. Then he runs a foul of a group of hippies, who, ironically, are in many ways like him. Very fast and violent. Full of twists and turns. Blake is excellent, but the film has been criticized as being too arty (sort of MTV-like). Terrific motorcycle chase sequence.

A: Robert Blake, Billy Green Bush, Mitchell Ryan, Jeannine Riley, Elisha Cook, Jr.

Distributed By MGM/UA Home Video M300871

ENFORCER, THE

D: James Fargo 97 m

R | ACT SUS CRM | 1976 | COLOR | Sex | Nud | Viol | Lang | AdSit

9 Top-notch follow-up to MAGNUM FORCE in the DIRTY HARRY series. Harry gets in trouble again when he stops a holdup at a liquor store in his own way, but he doesn't stay in the doghouse long. He is needed. He is reluctantly teamed with a female cop (Tyne Daly) to track down a group of terrorists who have robbed a munitions warehouse and launched a terror spree, including kidnapping San Francisco's mayor. Daly seeks not only help to solve the case and take down the bad guys, but to gain Harry's approval. Solid action, good humor and a good plot make this a lot of fun - but very violent.

A: Clint Eastwood, Harry Guardino, Tyne Daly, Bradford Dillman, John Mitchum

© WARNER HOME VIDEO 11082

ESCAPE FROM ALCATRAZ

D: Don Siegel 112 m

PG | SUS CRM | 1979 | COLOR | Sex | Nud | Viol | Lang | AdSit

7 Very intriguing and involving "true" story. It is the straightforward telling of the "facts" (although somewhat romanticized by Hollywood) surrounding the actual 1962 breakout of three prisoners from the supposedly escape-proof Alcatraz prison. The prisoners did get off the island but were never heard of again. The movie would have you believe that they survived. Eastwood plays Frank Morris who masterminded the escape for himself and two others. McGoohan plays a cold-hearted tough warden. It maintains your interest throughout and is largely credible.

A: Clint Eastwood, Patrick McGoohan, Roberts Blossom, Jack Thibeau, Fred Ward, Paul Benjamin

© PARAMOUNT HOME VIDEO 1256

EXECUTIONER'S SONG, THE

D: Lawrence Schiller 136 m

NR | DMA CRM | 1982 | COLOR | Sex | Nud | Viol | Lang | AdSit

9 Riveting true tale of condemned killer Gary Gilmore's struggle to get Utah authorities to execute him. Norman Mailer adapted his book to create this excellent made-for-TV movie about a socially maladjusted killer who responds to his isolation by striking out like a vicious and utterly cruel animal. The story is also about his doomed love affair with a desperate young woman. Convicted for the senseless murder of two people, Gilmore sought to die with dignity. On January 17, 1977 he got his wish. Brilliant efforts by both Jones and Arquette. Scenes have been added to the TV version.

A: Tommy Lee Jones, Rosanna Arquette, Christine Lahti, Eli Wallach, Steven Keats, Jordon Clarke

© LIVE HOME VIDEO 215-507

EXPERIMENT IN TERROR

D: Blake Edwards 123 m

NR | SUS CRM ACT | 1962 | B&W

Sex · Nud · Viol · Lang · AdSit

8 Excellent, high-tension gripper about a sadistic psycho killer (Martin) who kidnaps a bank teller's (Remick) teenage sister (Powers). If she doesn't deliver $100,000 to him, her sister will be killed. Desperate, she contacts the FBI and an extensive surveillance is set up, but it doesn't work. The only way to draw him out is to use Remick as bait. Glenn Ford is the FBI agent who fights against the clock to save the girl and prevent tragedy. Suspense builds slowly and steadily throughout the entire picture. Excellent acting. Martin is particularly menacing.

A: Glenn Ford, Lee Remick, Stefanie Powers, Ross Martin, Ned Glass

© GOODTIMES 4443

EXTREME PREJUDICE

D: Walter Hill 104 m

R | ACT CRM | 1987 | COLOR

Sex · Nud · Viol · Lang · AdSit

7 Texas Ranger Nolte struggles each day to stop the drug traffic at the border, while his boyhood friend (Boothe) prospers as a major drug lord just across the border. The only thing they have left in common is Nolte's wife (Alonso), who was Booth's former lover. Now Booth's extravagant lifestyle is enticing her back to him. Into town comes a group of undercover agents whose mission it is to steal millions of drug dollars that Booth has stashed at the bank and also to take Boothe out with "extreme prejudice." Extremely violent.

A: Nick Nolte, Powers Boothe, Maria Conchita Alonso, Michael Ironside, Rip Torn, Clancy Brown

© LIVE HOME VIDEO 62178

EYEWITNESS

D: Peter Yates 103 m

R | SUS CRM | 1981 | COLOR

Sex · Nud · Viol · Lang · AdSit

7 William Hurt is a janitor in a New York building who discovers a dead man's murdered body. Hurt has long been infatuated with a beautiful television news reporter, so he uses his limited knowledge of the case to get close to her. Then, in order to prolong their relationship, he claims that he actually witnessed the murder. His lies put them both in the middle of international intrigue and in serious danger. A quirky love story and interesting characters just add to a pretty good suspense flick.

A: William Hurt, Sigourney Weaver, Christopher Plummer, James Woods

© CBS/FOX VIDEO 1116

FAMILY BUSINESS

D: Sidney Lumet 113 m

R | DMA CRM | 1989 | COLOR

Sex · Nud · Viol · Lang · AdSit

6 Three superb leads make this a watchable and enjoyable film. A bright MIT scholar (Broderick) conjures up the perfect crime and enlists the aid of a veteran thief, his Granddad (Connery), to carry it off. His Dad (Hoffman) violently disapproves of the caper, but decides that the only way to protect his son is to go along with the plan. Everything goes well until Broderick gets caught. The Dad and Granddad, who have never liked each other, find themselves in the moral dilemma of their lives, they can free the boy if they turn themselves in.

A: Sean Connery, Dustin Hoffman, Matthew Broderick, Rosana DeSoto, Janet Carroll, Victoria Jackson

© COLUMBIA TRISTAR HOME VIDEO 70233

FATAL VISION

D: David Greene 192 m

NR | CRM MYS | 1984 | COLOR

Sex · Nud · Viol · Lang · AdSit

9 Excellent made-for-TV miniseries about a real event that stunned the American public when it happened and had a recurring place in headlines for years after. In 1970, Dr. Jeffrey MacDonald - a former Green Beret - was accused of brutally murdering his pregnant wife and two daughters. MacDonald claimed the murders were done by drug-crazed hippies, but his father-in-law soon came to believe MacDonald had killed his own family. After a military hearing dropped charges due to inconclusive evidence, the father pursued the case and, ten years later, MacDonald was convicted. Compelling drama.

A: Karl Malden, Gary Cole, Eva Marie Saint, Gary Grubbs, Mitchell Ryan, Andy Griffith

© COLUMBIA TRISTAR HOME VIDEO 60770

FEAR CITY

D: Abel Ferrara 93 m

NR | CRM ACT | 1984 | COLOR

Sex · Nud · Viol · Lang · AdSit

6 A fairly standard thriller plot but with a very strong cast and very well executed. Set in the sleazy Times Square sex district of NYC, a psychopath is killing off strippers. Jack Scalia and Tom Berenger run a talent agency for strippers, but someone is killing off all their clients. Billy Dee Williams is a cop who is trying to get to the bottom of it. Berenger is also an ex-boxer who is out doing some detective work on his own because he's trying get things started back up his his old love (Griffith) and she is a stripper who is high on the psycho's list.

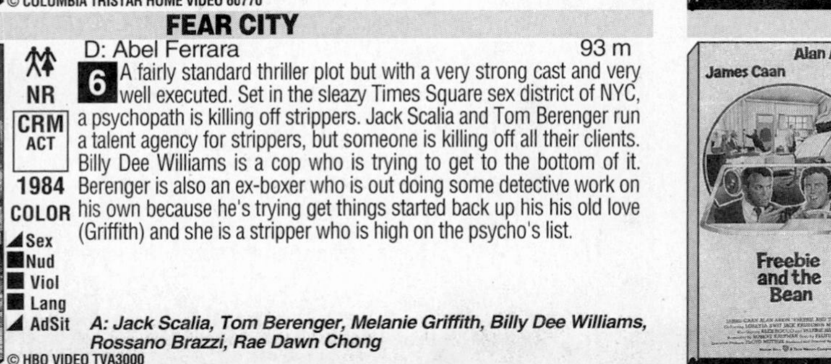

A: Jack Scalia, Tom Berenger, Melanie Griffith, Billy Dee Williams, Rossano Brazzi, Rae Dawn Chong

© HBO VIDEO TVA3000

FIRST DEADLY SIN, THE

D: Brian G. Hutton 112 m

R | CRM ACT | 1980 | COLOR

Sex · Nud · Viol · Lang · AdSit

6 Gritty cop film about a weary detective (Sinatra) tracking down a psycho through the streets of New York at the same time that he is trying to cope with the fact that his wife (Dunaway) is slowly dying of a failed kidney operation. Normally a by-the-book guy, he sees a pattern in the killings that his superiors don't. If he is going to get this guy, he must bait a trap. Sinatra is convincing and the film is involving and believable, but it is also somber and slow moving.

A: Frank Sinatra, Faye Dunaway, David Dukes, Brenda Vaccaro, Martin Gabel, James Whitmore

© WARNER HOME VIDEO 11368

FISH CALLED WANDA, A

D: Charles Crichton 108 m

R | COM CRM | 1988 | COLOR

Sex · Nud · Viol · Lang · AdSit

7 A bizarre farcical comedy with something to offend everyone. John Cleese, the Monty Python veteran, stars in this hilarious and/or ridiculous robbery caper - depending upon your tastes. Two Brits and two Americans team up to steal diamonds. When the one who has hidden the diamonds is caught, the others, particularly sexy Curtis, set about seducing and tricking his attorney (Cleese) into telling them where the take is hidden. Kline won Oscar.

A: John Cleese, Jamie Lee Curtis, Kevin Kline, Michael Palin, Maria Aitken, Tom Georgeson

© FOXVIDEO 4752

FLESH AND BONE

D: Steve Kloves 127 m

R | DMA CRM | 1993 | COLOR

Sex · Nud · Viol · Lang · AdSit

7 Very unusual but yet compelling viewing. Dennis Quaid is Arlis, a 40ish loner, who spends his time driving from town to town, stocking his string of vending machines, sleeping with other men's wives and avoiding relationships. That is, until he runs across Kay (Meg Ryan), a hard-drinking woman escaping from a bad marriage. Arlis has good reason for being the way he is. His father (James Cann) is about as cold and mean as a man can be. 30 years ago, he had Arlis let him into a farmer's house and then shotgunned the man, his wife and son. The only one left live was a baby. Kay is an orphan and she carries with her a picture of that same farmhouse.

A: Dennis Quaid, Meg Ryan, James Caan, Gweneth Paltrow, Scott Wilson, Christopher Rydell

© PARAMOUNT HOME VIDEO 32899

FORT APACHE, THE BRONX

D: Daniel Petrie 120 m

R | CRM ACT | 1981 | COLOR

Sex · Nud · Viol · Lang · AdSit

8 Very tough cop story about the worst and most dangerous police district in New York - the South Bronx. Its precinct house is dubbed "Fort Apache" because it is encircled with barbed wire. Newman and Ken Wahl face a non-stop daily battle against the worst possible elements. Still, the idealistic veteran Newman keeps the faith. Then he witnesses two cops commit a brutal crime and he is forced to make a choice between loyalty and what's right. Tense and very realistic cop film about an urban nightmare. Excellent performances, especially by Newman and Ticotin.

A: Paul Newman, Ken Wahl, Edward Asner, Kathleen Beller, Rachel Ticotin, Danny Aiello

© HBO VIDEO 90610

FOUL PLAY

D: Colin Higgins 116 m

PG | COM MYS CRM | 1978 | COLOR

Sex · Nud · Viol · Lang · AdSit

8 Very funny murder/mystery. A librarian (Hawn) picks up an undercover agent who gives her information that there will be an assassination attempt upon the Pope when he attends a performance of The Mikado. Quickly, there are several attempts made upon her life. Even though she tells all this to the police, they don't believe her. However, stumbling police detective Chevy Chases eventually comes to believe her and becomes both her protector and lover. A wide assortment of looneys and odd-balls add to the fun. The fine supporting cast includes Dudley Moore in his first American role.

A: Goldie Hawn, Chevy Chase, Burgess Meredith, Rachel Roberts, Dudley Moore, Billy Barty

© PARAMOUNT HOME VIDEO 1116

FREEBIE AND THE BEAN

D: Richard Rush 113 m

R | ACT COM CRM | 1974 | COLOR

Sex · Nud · Viol · Lang · AdSit

8 Wild cop comedy. This is probably the first, and certainly one of the best, buddy-cop movies. It is the story of two odd-ball San Francisco cops: Freebie (Caan), who is a cheapskate, and Bean (Arkin), who is a very vocal Mexican-American. These two cops are trying to shut down a big numbers racket, but they rip up half of San Francisco in the process. Includes four car chases, and one super stunt ends up with their car crashing into the bedroom of a highrise apartment building. Caan and Arkin are great together. A lot of fun.

A: Alan Arkin, James Caan, Loretta Swit, Valerie Harper, Jack Kruschen, Alex Rocco

© WARNER HOME VIDEO 11237

FRENCH CONNECTION, THE

D: William Friedkin 104 m

R | ACT CRM SUS | 1971 | COLOR | Sex Nud Viol Lang AdSit

10 An exciting, landmark film that was a winner of five Oscars, including Best Picture. This is a realistic cop action yarn that trails a maverick, nearly amoral, New York cop and his wary partner as they obsessively and relentlessly investigate a huge heroin shipment from France. It is a thrilling and action-packed depiction of tough street-life. It is loaded with blood-pounding suspense and contains one of the most thrilling chase scenes ever recorded on film. Equally important, it also features an excellent plot, good character development, superb acting and was based upon real life.

A: Gene Hackman, Fernando Rey, Roy Scheider, Eddie Egan, Sonny Grosso, Tony Lo Bianco

© FOXVIDEO 1009

FRENZY

D: Alfred Hitchcock 116 m

R | SUS CRM MYS | 1972 | COLOR | Sex Nud Viol Lang AdSit

8 Hitchcock, the master filmmaker, returned to England after 30 years in America to create this, his second-to-last film. It is the story of a "necktie sex-murderer" who is raping and killing women in London. Hitchcock also returns to his favorite theme of an innocent man trapped under the weight of circumstantial evidence. In this case, our man suffers while the suave real killer evades suspicion. Very suspenseful and contains all of the masterful camera tricks, pacing and black humor that are Hitchcock's trademarks.

A: Jon Finch, Barry Foster, Barbara Leigh-Hunt, Anna Massey, Alec McCowen

© MCA/UNIVERSAL HOME VIDEO, INC. 55011

FRESHMAN, THE

D: Andrew Bergman 102 m

PG | COM CRM | 1990 | COLOR | Sex Nud Viol Lang AdSit

7 A lighthearted charmer! Broderick is a naive freshman film student who, minutes after arriving in New York, has all his bags and belongings stolen. Broderick tracks the thief (Kirby) down, who surprisingly makes him an offer that he can't refuse. He now finds himself working for an irresistibly charismatic mob boss (Brando, in a spoof on his role in THE GODFATHER) running strange errands, while also being hotly pursued by the boss's sexy daughter. Among his odd duties is picking up a giant lizard from the airport and delivering that strange cargo unharmed to New Jersey.

A: Matthew Broderick, Marlon Brando, Bruno Kirby, Maximilian Schell, Penelope Ann Miller, Frank Whaley

© COLUMBIA TRISTAR HOME VIDEO 70293

FUN WITH DICK AND JANE

D: Ted Kotcheff 95 m

PG | COM CRM | 1977 | COLOR | Sex Nud Viol Lang AdSit

8 Zany, polished fun-filled comedy. What do you do when you enjoy, and in fact are addicted to, the luxurious upper-middle-class lifestyle that your job as a highly-paid aerospace executive gives you, and you are suddenly fired? At first Dick and Jane tighten their belts and Jane gets a job. But Jane doesn't like her job and they don't like their belts tight. So, quite naturally, they decide to do the next best thing to earn a good living, they will rob and steal. See Dick and Jane steal. See Dick and Jane run. Really funny stuff.

A: George Segal, Jane Fonda, Ed McMahon, Dick Gautier, Allan Miller

© GOODTIMES 4431

GETAWAY, THE

D: Roger Donaldson 116 m

NR | ACT CRM | 1994 | COLOR | Sex Nud Viol Lang AdSit

8 This is a high-energy remake of the 1972 action classic and cult film of the same name. Alec Baldwin and Kim Basinger star as a husband and wife robbery team. When Baldwin is caught and sent to a Mexican prison, he sends Basinger to talk a top gangster into getting him out in exchange for his special services. Woods does get him out, but only in part because he needs Baldwin's skills to rob a racetrack. The other reason was that Basinger slept with him. The heist goes down, but team turns on itself. Woods thinks Basinger will continue to betray Baldwin, but he is fooled. She and Baldwin keep the money and make a break, with the cops and the hoods in close pursuit.

A: Alec Baldwin, Kim Basinger, Michael Madsen, Jennifer Tilly, Richard Farnsworth, James Woods

© MCA/UNIVERSAL HOME VIDEO, INC. 82019

GLASS HOUSE, THE

D: Tom Gries 90 m

NR | DMA CRM ACT | 1972 | COLOR | Sex Nud Viol Lang AdSit

9 A gripping and hard-hitting realistic made-for-TV drama based on a story by Truman Capote, about what it is really like to be a convict behind bars. Three separate stories are merged to tell the larger story. A young kid is up on drug charges. Clu Gulager is an idealistic new prison guard. Alan Alda is a college professor up on manslaughter charges. Vic Morrow is a brutally powerful inmate boss who dominates his world and everyone in it. Savage and shocking depiction of life behind bars, where the guards look the other way while Morrow runs the "glass house." Filmed at Utah State Prison.

A: Vic Morrow, Clu Gulager, Billy Dee Williams, Dean Jagger, Alan Alda

© GOODTIMES 9252

GLORIA

D: John Cassavetes 121 m

PG | ACT CRM | 1980 | COLOR | Sex Nud Viol Lang AdSit

7 Surprisingly good story of an aging show girl and mob moll who saves her neighbor's eight-year-old boy from a mob hit. Gena Rowlands won an Oscar nomination for her hard-boiled gun-toting character portrayal. Just before both of the boy's parents are killed by mob hitmen, the father entrusts Rowlands with the boy's life and the mob's books. She and the boy are both now on the run and the mob's hot on their trail, but this is no ordinary woman - she knows how the mob works, what has to be done and she does it. Very good.

A: Gena Rowlands, Buck Henry, John Adames, Julie Carmen, Lupe Guarnica

© COLUMBIA TRISTAR HOME VIDEO 60196

GODFATHER, THE

D: Francis Ford Coppola 171 m

R | DMA CRM ACT | 1972 | COLOR | Sex Nud Viol Lang AdSit

10 Inspired filmmaking. Absolutely everything, including production values, writing, casting, direction, acting and story-telling are all done to perfection. It was the winner of Best Picture, Actor and Screenplay. It is a riveting portrayal of a fictional immigrant family who have become ruthless leaders of a powerful Mafia clan. Story focuses primarily upon the father (Brando) and his youngest son, Michael (Pacino). The don has planned that Michael is to escape a life in the family business, but he is instead drawn into it and must lead the family when the father is shot. Masterpiece.

A: Marlon Brando, Al Pacino, James Caan, Robert Duvall, Talia Shire, Sterling Hayden

© PARAMOUNT HOME VIDEO 8049

GODFATHER TRILOGY, THE

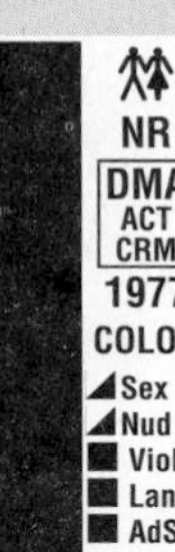

D: Francis Ford Coppola 386 m

NR | DMA ACT CRM | 1977 | COLOR | Sex Nud Viol Lang AdSit

10 1+1=3. The original two GODFATHER movies are here edited together, with the sequences shown now in chronological order and other scenes added. As good as the first two films were, they pale alongside this compiled version. The surface story is that of an Italian immigrant who arrives in America and excels at surviving in a vicious turn-of-the-century ghetto. He and his family evolve into the underground masters of their vicious world. However, it is also the story of raw power, the corruption of power and the politics of power. This is genuine masterpiece and is an absolute must see.

A: Marlon Brando, Al Pacino, Robert De Niro, Robert Duvall, James Caan, Diane Keaton

© PARAMOUNT HOME VIDEO 8480

GODFATHER PART 2, THE

D: Francis Ford Coppola 200 m

R | DMA CRM ACT | 1974 | COLOR | Sex Nud Viol Lang AdSit

9 Fascinating follow-up to the powerhouse original. This one won 6 Oscars, including Best Picture. In it, Michael expands the family business to Las Vegas even though it destroys his marriage. It also explains how Michael's father came to leave Sicily for America in the first place. And, how he came to become involved in crime in the ghettos of Little Italy at the turn of the century. Robert De Niro here plays the younger don. (Marlon Brando played the older don in Part I.) Parts I & II were combined into a combined feature called GODFATHER, THE EPIC. As good as I & II are, the combination was better because it related events more sequentially for a better understanding.

A: Al Pacino, Robert De Niro, Robert Duvall, Talia Shire, Diane Keaton, Lee Strasberg

© PARAMOUNT HOME VIDEO 8459

GODFATHER PART 3, THE

D: Francis Ford Coppola 170 m

R | DMA CRM ACT | 1990 | COLOR | Sex Nud Viol Lang AdSit

8 A brilliant film, full of passion, and a rich conclusion to Coppola's trilogy of the lives and trials of a prominent mob family. At center stage again is Michael Corleone (Pacino). He has tired of the life and is taking the final step of making his family businesses legitimate and international. He has engineered a huge corporate takeover with the help of the Vatican, but finds that the organized grip of the mob is stronger than he is, and it destroys him. Exceptional performances, plus all of the drama, power and intrigue that we would expect to end this epic saga.

A: Al Pacino, Diane Keaton, Talia Shire, Andy Garcia, Eli Wallach, Joe Mantegna

© PARAMOUNT HOME VIDEO 32318

GOODFELLAS

D: Martin Scorsese 146 m

R | CRM DMA ACT | 1990 | COLOR | Sex Nud Viol Lang AdSit

9 This film is both masterful and perversely fascinating. It is based on the best selling novel GOODFELLAS and paints a fascinating picture of 30 years of the life and lifestyle of a real gangster. Henry Hill was fascinated as a boy with the money and the respect that the gangsters in his neighborhood had, so he became one. The "life" is one of decadent excesses of money, drinking, dining out, leisure time and women - counter-pointed by equal excesses of violence. The ruthlessness of these characters is absolute. Violence is business. There is no room for sympathy and emotion. Utterly intriguing.

A: Robert De Niro, Ray Liotta, Lorraine Bracco, Joe Pesci, Paul Sorvino, Frank Sivero

© WARNER HOME VIDEO 12039

GORKY PARK

D: Michael Apted 127 m

R | MYS CRM ACT | 1983 | COLOR

Sex Nud Viol Lang AdSit

8 An absorbing murder mystery set in Soviet Moscow. When three bodies, all with their faces and fingerprints destroyed, are discovered in Moscow's Gorky Park, a Russian police inspector (Hurt) begins an investigation. The trail leads him to a very wealthy and well-connected American fur trader (Marvin), a beautiful dissident (Pacula), the KGB and a New York cop (Dennehy). Lots of plot twists keep both Hurt and the viewer confused and guessing. A very involved but involving, and also somewhat uneven murder mystery. It has plenty of intrigue, plus an interesting window into life in a communist state.

A: William Hurt, Lee Marvin, Joanna Pacula, Ian Bannen, Brian Dennehy

© GOODTIMES 04048

GUARDIAN, THE

D: David Greene 102 m

NR | CRM DMA | 1984 | COLOR

Sex Nud Viol Lang AdSit

6 Provocative. A Manhattan apartment building hires a no-nonsense ex-military man (Gossett) as a security guard for their building, after they become concerned for their safety because of the direction their neighborhood is taking. While he does clean out the building of lawbreakers, a liberal tenant (Sheen) begins to question their savior's brutal methods and whether the safety of the building is worth that kind of cost. Interesting flick which was made for cable TV.

A: Louis Gossett, Jr., Martin Sheen, Arthur Hill, Tandy Cronyn, Arthur Hill, Kate Lynch

© ASTRAL VIDEO E104

HAMMETT

D: Wim Wenders 97 m

PG | MYS CRM ACT | 1982 | COLOR

Sex Nud Viol Lang AdSit

7 Moody fictionalized screen portrait of the early years of famous mystery writer Dashiell Hammett (THE MALTESE FALCOLN and THE THIN MAN). In real life Hammett actually was a Pinkerton detective and this story has him personally becoming involved with a very baffling case about a missing Chinese woman. It is an authentic recreation of the 1930s film noir look and is a beautifully photographed film, but the very involved plot also requires the viewer's diligent attention in order to be appreciated.

A: Frederic Forrest, Peter Boyle, Marilu Henner, Roy Kinnear, Elisha Cook, Jr., Lydia Lei

© WARNER HOME VIDEO 22026

HARPER

D: Jack Smight 121 m

NR | MYS SUS CRM | 1966 | COLOR

Sex Nud Viol Lang AdSit

9 Excellent, a rousing detective yarn that was the first of Newman's career and is credited with causing the resurrection of the private-eye genre. Harper (Newman) is a smooth private eye who is hired by a rich man's wife (Bacall) to find her husband when he doesn't come home. The investigative trail leads Harper through a curious cast of oddball characters, eventually to a smuggling ring and murder. Fast paced, rapid-fire dialogue and sophisticated plot twists. Followed by THE DROWNING POOL. Excellent.

A: Paul Newman, Lauren Bacall, Shelley Winters, Arthur Hill, Julie Harris, Janet Leigh

© WARNER HOME VIDEO 11175

HEAVENLY CREATURES

D: Peter Jackson 99 m

R | CRM DMA | 1994 | COLOR

Sex Nud Viol Lang AdSit

8 Based upon an actual incident, this is both the recreation of those events and a remarkable depiction of the nature of self-delusion. Pauline at 14, was reclusive and a loner. Juliet was the new girl, and was so over-bearing that she was equally ostracized. Left outside the mainstream, the two loners discovered each other. Both were intensely romantic in their notion of how things should be and created a perfect fanciful world that became very real to them, and into which both would frequently escape. However, when their new-found kinship was threatened with separation, both girls conspired to brutally murder their perceived enemy, Pauline's mother. Remarkable acting and special effects.

A: Kate Winslet, Melanie Lynskey, Sarah Peirse, Diana Kent, Clive Merrison, Simon O'Connor

© MIRAMAX HOME ENTERTAINMENT 4371

HELTER SKELTER

D: Tom Gries 119 m

NR | CRM DMA | 1976 | COLOR

Sex Nud Viol Lang AdSit

9 Superb made-for-TV production of the best-selling book which chronicles the people and events surrounding the grisly and infamous 1969 Tate/La Bianca murders, and the subsequent trials of the notorious Charles Manson and his "family." While it is a recreation of the events surrounding the murders, it is also a mesmerizing portrait of a psychotic killer who had his followers convinced that he was the messiah. The novel upon which the movie was based was written by the state's actual prosecutor, Vincent Bugliosi. Very intense, electrifying and disturbing film.

A: George DiCenzo, Steve Railsback, Nancy Wolfe, Marilyn Burns, Christina Hart, Cathey Paine

© CBS/FOX VIDEO 7713

HENRY - PORTRAIT OF A SERIAL KILLER

D: John Mc Naughton 90 m

NR | DMA CRM | 1990 | COLOR

Sex Nud Viol Lang AdSit

8 Brutal and extremely unpleasant but also utterly fascinating look into the mind of a serial murderer. Loosely based upon the self-confessed Texas serial murderer Henry Lee Lucas, this film is quasi-documentary. It is not exploitative, but it faithfully and graphically depicts scene after scene of rapes and murders, including one in which Henry and his roommate record the murder of a family on video tape so they can watch it over and over. This is both a very grisly and a very moving picture, but it is definitely not for everyone.

A: Michael Rooker, Tom Towles, Tracy Arnold

© MPI HOME VIDEO 3108

HIDDEN, THE

D: Jack Sholder 98 m

R | SF ACT CRM | 1987 | COLOR

Sex Nud Viol Lang AdSit

8 Unique and exciting science fiction thriller. A Los Angeles cop is joined by a strange FBI agent (he chews Alka-Selzer tablets), in his attempt to get to the bottom of a rash of robberies and murders. The two are searching to find out how normal ordinary law-abiding citizens are being turned into such extremely violent killers. Then, the FBI agent informs the local cop that there is an alien creature who is invading these human bodies. He has a preference for heavy metal music, Ferraris and bloody violence. Full of high-intensity excitement, with good action sequences. Well made and very unpredictable.

A: Michael Nouri, Kyle MacLachlan, Ed O'Ross, Clu Gulager, Claudia Christian, Clarence Felder

© MEDIA HOME ENTERTAINMENT, INC. M940

HIDDEN AGENDA

D: Ken Loach 108 m

R | MYS CRM | 1990 | COLOR

Sex Nud Viol Lang AdSit

8 Superb political conspiracy and intrigue, in the tradition of Z. An American civil rights investigator, documenting atrocities in Northern Ireland in the 1980s, is murdered in a police ambush. His girlfriend (McDormand) and a British police investigator come to unravel the mystery that surrounds his death and also uncover a military plot to cover up the systematic torture of IRA sympathizers and operatives, including the murder of McDormand's boyfriend. A little hard to follow the dialects at first, but ultimately engrossing and believable viewing.

A: Frances McDormand, Brad Dourif, Brian Cox, Mai Zetterling, Jim Norton, Maurice Roeves

© HBO VIDEO 90558

HOMICIDE

D: David Mamet 100 m

R | CRM DMA ACT | 1991 | COLOR

Sex Nud Viol Lang AdSit

7 Intriguing police drama that is both a fascinating character portrait and a revealing view into the nature of a policeman's extended family. Joe Mantegna is a good and dedicated cop. He is a respected negotiator whose skills involve him in a major case with a real nasty killer. But, he is sidetracked when he stumbles onto the unrelated killing of an old Jewish woman. At first he wants no part of her case but quickly becomes fascinated with it because she was a hero in Israel's independence movement. She inspires a pride in the Jewish heritage he has long denied and he suddenly has a yearning to belong again. But, a man cannot have two families.

A: Joe Mantegna, William H. Macy, Natalija Nogulich, Ving Rhames, Rebecca Pidgeon, Vincent Guastaferro

© COLUMBIA TRISTAR HOME VIDEO 91443

HUSTLE

D: Robert Aldrich 120 m

R | CRM MYS ACT | 1975 | COLOR

Sex Nud Viol Lang AdSit

7 Effective but cynical detective thriller. Burt Reynolds is a bitter L.A. detective called in to investigate the murder of a young woman found dead on the beach, supposedly a suicide. Reynolds is an old fashioned kind of guy who believes in right and wrong, but each day he faces life's worst. So he spends his evenings with his girlfriend (Deneuve), a high-class hooker. Both dream of escaping their dreary lives, but neither does. Reynolds's investigations lead him to a lawyer (Albert) with mob connections. The girl was a hooker and a porn star. Pretty cynical stuff, but it is effective.

A: Burt Reynolds, Catherine Deneuve, Ben Johnson, Paul Winfield, Eileen Brennan, Eddie Albert

© PARAMOUNT HOME VIDEO 8785

I, THE JURY

D: Richard T. Heffron 111 m

R | ACT MYS CRM | 1982 | COLOR

Sex Nud Viol Lang AdSit

7 Mickey Spillane's gritty Mike Hammer character was born in the 1940s in his novel "I, the Jury." In this movie, the hard-boiled detective is updated into the 1980s as he investigates the murder of his Army buddy from Vietnam. His search takes him to Barbara Carrera's sex clinic. The seedy flavor of this film matches that of the novels. It is fast paced, has lots of action, a seedy atmosphere, plus lots of naked women and violence - all of which are befitting the character of Spillane's pulp novels and which also help to cover up some big plot holes.

A: Armand Assante, Barbara Carrera, Alan King, Laurene Landon, Geoffrey Lewis, Paul Sorvino

© FOXVIDEO 1186

IMPULSE

D: Sondra Locke 109 m

R | ACT CRM | 1990 | COLOR | Sex Nud Viol Lang AdSit

8 Lottie Mason (Russell) is a beautiful female cop who likes taking risks. When a witness, who is to testify against a big-time narcotics dealer, steals $1 million and heads for cover, the D.A. (Fahey) has to get him back. He needs someone to go inside on a drug buy to trap his wayward witness and Lottie is just the one for the job, even though the D.A. has fallen in love with her. With her nerves on edge after the deal goes bad, Lottie stops at a bar and unknowingly meets the missing witness. Lottie follows an impulse and is where she isn't supposed to be when he is killed. Now she has the $1 million.

A: Theresa Russell, Jeff Fahey, George Dzundza, Anal Rosenberg, Nicholas Mele

© WARNER HOME VIDEO 11887

INCIDENT, THE

D: Larry Pierce 99 m

NR | SUS CRM | 1967 | B&W | Sex Nud Viol Lang AdSit

8 Brutal, disturbing story of urban violence witnessed first hand. Martin Sheen made his screen debut as one of two drunken street punks in the New York subway system. Bored, they begin to terrorize, one-by-one, the passengers of a subway car. Their panic-stricken victims become so afraid for themselves that they all but abandon concern for anyone else. Very unpleasant, but still a valid and timely drama with a top-notch cast. This was Donna Mills's first screen outing, as well.

A: Tony Musante, Martin Sheen, Beau Bridges, Jack Gilford, Thelma Ritter, Donna Mills

© FOXVIDEO 1290

IN COLD BLOOD

D: Richard Brooks 134 m

R | CRM SUS DMA | 1968 | B&W | Sex Nud Viol Lang AdSit

10 A chilling, very intense masterpiece relating the real world senseless murders of a Kansas farm family and the character of their psychotic murderers. It is taken from Truman Capote's best-selling book of the same name, which he based upon his extensive prison interviews of the two murderers. The events related are all the more chilling because of their matter-of-fact presentation. Blake and Wilson put in the performances of their lives as uncaring remorseless killers and the story related is their's from the time of the crime itself, through to their executions. Extremely powerful.

A: Robert Blake, Scott Wilson, John Forsythe, Jeff Corey, Will Geer, Paul Stewart

© COLUMBIA TRISTAR HOME VIDEO VH10342

INNOCENT MAN, AN

D: Peter Yates 113 m

R | CRM ACT | 1989 | COLOR | Sex Nud Viol Lang AdSit

7 Selleck is a happily married airline mechanic who is gets caught in a cop screw up. Two over-zealous cops mistake him for a drug dealer but, rather than admit a mistake and risk their necks, they frame him. When he is in prison, Selleck must fight for his life. In order to survive, he must become a very different man than he was when he went in and do things he never thought he would do. When he gets out, he, his wife and a con who helped him while he was in prison plot to get revenge on the two cops. Fast paced.

A: Tom Selleck, F. Murray Abraham, Laila Robins, David Rasche, Richard Young, Badja Djola

© TOUCHSTONE HOME VIDEO 910

INTERNAL AFFAIRS

D: Mike Figgis 114 m

R | SUS ACT CRM | 1990 | COLOR | Sex Nud Viol Lang AdSit

8 A gripping police thriller. Andy Garcia is an internal affairs investigator, struggling to gain evidence against a respected veteran police officer (Gere) who he knows is using his position as a cop to manipulate and twist other cops into doing his bidding. Gere is deep into money laundering, robbery, drug running schemes and even murder. He is a control freak, but now he is up against someone he can't control... but he tries. He will protect himself no matter what it takes. Very tense believable plot.

A: Richard Gere, Andy Garcia, Laurie Metcalf, Nancy Travis, William Baldwin

© PARAMOUNT HOME VIDEO 32245

IN THE HEAT OF THE NIGHT

D: Norman Jewison 110 m

NR | CRM MYS DMA | 1967 | COLOR | Sex Nud Viol Lang AdSit

9 Powerhouse film that won 5 Oscars, including Best Picture, Best Screenplay and Best Actor. A black Philadelphia homicide detective is arrested at a Mississippi train station after a very important white man is found dead nearby. The gruff redneck sheriff (Steiger) is forced by the facts to release him and then is forced to ask the big city cop for his help in solving the mystery. This a film that works on every level. It is a good mystery, great drama and has not lost any of its considerable punch with time. It is simply excellent.

A: Sidney Poitier, Rod Steiger, Warren Oates, Lee Grant, Scott Wilson, Quentin Dean

Distributed By MGM/UA Home Video M201265

INTO THIN AIR

D: Roger Young 97 m

NR | DMA CRM | 1985 | COLOR | Sex Nud Viol Lang AdSit

8 Chilling and poignant fact-based story about a Canadian mother (Burstyn) who is absolutely relentless in her pursuit of her missing son. While on a trip back to summer school in Colorado, after visiting home, he just vanishes. Burstyn doggedly seeks out the facts about what happened to him, with the help of a retired detective. This is an excellent made-for-TV movie, but it is depressing.

A: Ellen Burstyn, Robert Prosky, Sam Robards, Nicholas Pryor, Caroline McWilliams, John Dennis Johnston

© NEW STAR ENTERTAINMENT 1005

JENNIFER 8

D: Bruce Robinson 127 m

R | MYS CRM SUS | 1992 | COLOR | Sex Nud Viol Lang AdSit

8 Tightly wound thriller. LA homicide detective John Berlin (Garcia) has transfered to a northern California police department to escape big city burnout and to work with his best friend (Henricksen). He arrives just in time to be on-site when a woman's severed hand is found and begins to uncover clues that tie it to an unsolved murder, and that leads him to suspect that there is a serial murderer killing blind women. But, his suspicions are based on few facts and the other cops thinks he's a big city showboat. His fears are very real for him because he has uncovered a pretty blind witness (Thurman) who is now in serious danger because no one believes him.

A: Andy Garcia, Uma Thurman, Lance Henriksen, Kathy Baker, Kevin Conway, John Malkovich

© PARAMOUNT HOME VIDEO 32495

KALIFORNIA

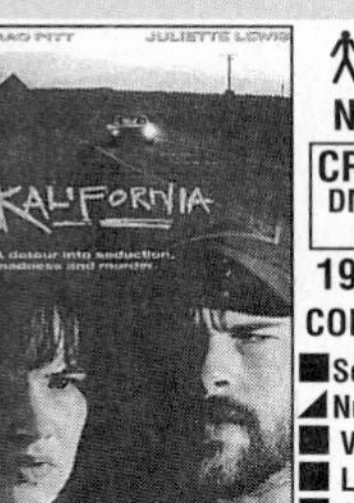

D: Dominic Sena 118 m

NR | CRM DMA | 1993 | COLOR | Sex Nud Viol Lang AdSit

7 Extremely intense portrait of a serial killer. Brian is a writer and his girlfriend Carrie is a photographer. They want a new start in California, so they plan a cross-country trip, visiting sites of serial murders along the way. He will write and she will take pictures. They place an advertisement on the bulletin board for someone to share their expenses. Their ad is answered by Early and Adele. Early is a crude live-in-the-moment kind, and Adele is a simple-minded waitress. Brian admires Early's attitude, but Carrie sees danger in him. She is right, Early is a remorseless killer and they will now witness murder first hand. Brilliant, brutal acting by Pitt. Not a pretty picture to watch.

A: Brad Pitt, Juliette Lewis, David Duchovny, Michelle Forbes

© POLYGRAM VIDEO 88933-3

KILLER INSIDE ME, THE

D: Burt Kennedy 99 m

R | CRM ACT | 1976 | COLOR | Sex Nud Viol Lang AdSit

7 Taut thriller and a violent psychological study, with an exceptional acting job from Stacy Keach. He is a nice-guy deputy sheriff in a small midwestern town who goes off the deep end in a psychopathic spree of killing, while battling some redneck hoodlums. His suppressed violent personality is explained in a series of flashbacks exploring some deep childhood traumas. Excellent supporting cast, especially Susan Tyrell as a tough prostitute.

A: Stacy Keach, Susan Tyrrell, Keenan Wynn, Don Stroud, John Carradine, Charles McGraw

© WARNER HOME VIDEO 11708

KILLERS, THE

D: Don Siegel 95 m

NR | CRM ACT | 1964 | COLOR | Sex Nud Viol Lang AdSit

7 Terrific crime thriller that was Ronald Reagan's last picture, the only one where he played a bad guy and one where he got some of his best reviews. In it he hires two killers (Marvin and Gulager) to "hit" Cassavetes, but his hitmen start to wonder why he paid so much for the job, and why the intended victim refuses to run. When they investigate, they discover that Cassavetes was having an affair with Reagan's mistress (Dickenson) and that all three were involved in the robbery of an armored car where $1 million was taken. Very violent.

A: Lee Marvin, John Cassavetes, Angie Dickinson, Ronald Reagan, Clu Gulager, Norman Fell

© MCA/UNIVERSAL HOME VIDEO, INC. 55014

KILLING, THE

D: Stanley Kubrick 85 m

NR | CRM SUS | 1956 | B&W | Sex Nud Viol Lang AdSit

9 Excellent film noir thriller that established Stanley Kubrick as a director. Sterling Hayden masterminds an intricate plot, requiring split-second timing, to rob a racetrack payroll of $2 million. This extremely well made picture investigates the personality and motivation behind each member of the group. Each story is told up until the same climactic moment in time, but then the next story is begun. When all of the stories have been told up to that same climactic moment, they proceed together to the conclusion. Intriguing idea, spell-binding plot.

A: Sterling Hayden, Coleen Gray, Jay C. Flippen, Marie Windsor, Timothy Carey, Vince Edwards

Distributed By MGM/UA Home Video 201704

KILLING TIME, THE

D: Rick King — 94 m

R | CRM SUS | 1987 | COLOR | Sex | Nud | Viol | Lang | AdSit

6 Very involved, twisting story line. A small-town sheriff (Baker) is about to retire and is to be replaced by his deputy (Bridges), whose ex-wife is being abused by her new and wealthy husband. She fears for her life, so Bridges helps her plan to murder him, but their plan is threatened by the new deputy (Sutherland). Except Sutherland turns out to be a serial killer who has stolen someone else's identity. Tense drama of suspicion, deception and murder with more twists than a bag of pretzels, but slow to develop.

A: Beau Bridges, Kiefer Sutherland, Wayne Rogers, Joe Don Baker, Camelia Kath, Janet Carroll

© R&G VIDEO, LP 80098

KINDERGARTEN COP

D: Ivan Reitman — 111 m

PG-13 | ACT COM CRM | 1990 | COLOR | Sex | Nud | Viol | Lang | AdSit

8 A nice little surprise film that has a little of everything. It has action, comedy, cuteness and romance! Tough police detective Kimble (Schwarzenegger) gets much more than he bargained for when he pretends to be a kindergarten teacher, while trying to track down the wife and son of a vicious drug lord who are in hiding. For the tough cop, the toughest part is dealing with a bunch of tiny kids. He fails miserably at it until he turns the classroom into boot camp. Don't be fooled though, all is not cuteness here. This is fundamentally an action flick with enough violence to get it a PG-13 rating.

A: Arnold Schwarzenegger, Penelope Ann Miller, Linda Hunt, Richard Tyson, Carroll Baker, Pamela Reed

© MCA/UNIVERSAL HOME VIDEO, INC. 81051

KING OF NEW YORK

D: Abel Ferrara — 106 m

R | CRM ACT | 1990 | COLOR | Sex | Nud | Viol | Lang | AdSit

7 Extremely dark vision of a New York which becomes a battleground for the city's $1 billion drug trade. Christopher Walken is a ruthless criminal, just released from prison. He boldly announces that he and his henchmen will control the town's drug traffic, and will kill anyone and everyone who gets in their way. Very bloody and very violent. He and his army regularly kill Italian, Chinese and Columbian competitors, but the blood really flows when he puts out a contract on the cops. Fast-paced and action packed, but bloody.

A: Christopher Walken, Larry Fishburne, David Caruso, Victor Argo, Wesley Snipes, Giancarlo Esposito

© LIVE HOME VIDEO 68937

KISS BEFORE DYING, A

D: James Dearden — 93 m

R | SUS CRM | 1991 | COLOR | Sex | Nud | Viol | Lang | AdSit

7 A tightly-wound thriller! Dillon is handsome, but poor and utterly ruthless. He decides that the best way out of poverty is to marry very well, so he chooses Sean Young's prominent family to marry into. He researches everything about them, then he makes his move. Young (in two roles) plays twin sisters both courted by Dillon. Dillon kills off the first one while he charms and marries the other sister. The tension mounts when Young slowly gets really curious about her twin's strange death. For the viewer, it doesn't matter that you know who the killer is - suspense hangs in the air and danger looms at every corner.

A: Matt Dillon, Sean Young, Max von Sydow, Diane Ladd, James Russo, Martha Gehman

© MCA/UNIVERSAL HOME VIDEO, INC. 81068

KLUTE

D: Alan J. Pakula — 114 m

R | SUS MYS CRM | 1971 | COLOR | Sex | Nud | Viol | Lang | AdSit

9 Compelling and provocative psychological thriller, with a mesmerizing (Oscar-winning) performance by Jane Fonda. Fonda plays a sultry high-class NYC hooker who gets in over her head. Small-town private detective Donald Sutherland is searching for a husband who is missing after a trip to NYC and who had visited Fonda. Neurotic Fonda only feels in control when she is manipulating a trick. But now she finds herself falling in love with Sutherland as she comes to rely more and more upon him - because she is being relentlessly pursued by the same sadistic killer. A real nail-biter finish.

A: Jane Fonda, Donald Sutherland, Charles Cioffi, Roy Scheider, Dorothy Tristan, Rita Gam

© WARNER HOME VIDEO 1027

KNIGHT MOVES

D: Carl Schenkel — 105 m

R | SUS MYS CRM | 1993 | COLOR | Sex | Nud | Viol | Lang | AdSit

7 Competent murder thriller. A chess champion (Christopher Lambert) has gone to the Pacific Northwest to participate in a chess championship and also finds himself incriminated in a series of serial murders. Several beautiful young women have been ritualistically murdered and drained of blood, with cryptic messages then scrawled in their blood. Top cop Tom Skerritt is not certain if Peter, who is receiving phone messages from the killer and supposedly using his game skills to help solve the murders, is the victim of the plot or really is the secret instigator of it. Psychologist Diane Lane too, is caught between love and fear. Not great, but not bad either.

A: Christopher Lambert, Diane Lane, Tom Skerritt, Daniel Baldwin, Charles Bailey-Gates, Ferdinand Mayne

© REPUBLIC PICTURES HOME VIDEO 2200

KRAYS, THE

D: Peter Medak — 119 m

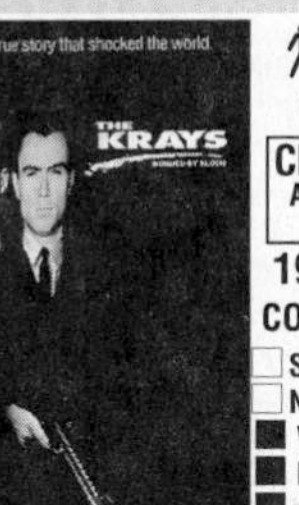

R | CRM ACT | 1990 | COLOR | Sex | Nud | Viol | Lang | AdSit

8 Stylish and chilling portrayal of two of England's most vicious criminals. During the late '50s and early '60s, London's underworld was taken over by the sheer ruthlessness of twin brothers, Reggie and Ronnie Kray. Driven by ambition and bloodlust, and trained by their mother in the power of fear, these two rose quickly to power, and then, just as rapidly, crumbled as their psychosis caused them to lose control of the empire they had built. Both brothers were convicted of murder and are now serving 30-year sentences. Begins slow, but that changes.

A: Gary Kemp, Martin Kemp, Billie Whitelaw, Kate Hardie, Susan Fleetwood

© COLUMBIA TRISTAR HOME VIDEO 90973

KUFFS

D: Bruce Evans — 102 m

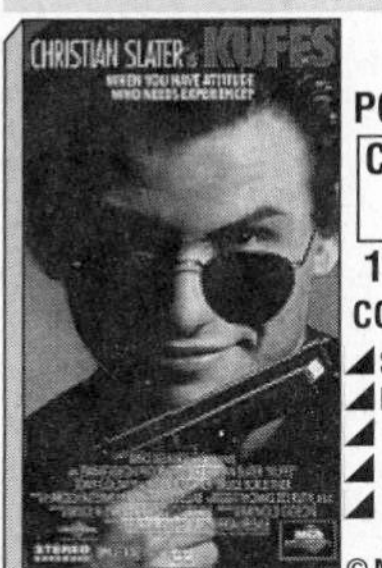

PG-13 | CRM | 1991 | COLOR | Sex | Nud | Viol | Lang | AdSit

7 Off-beat crime drama. Wise-guy drop out Slater is out of work and down on his luck, but he still balks at his brother Brad's (Boxleitner) offer to come to work for him at his security company. When Brad is killed in the line of duty, Slater inherits the company, Patrol Special Team. At first Slater hates it, but soon he becomes determined to find his brother's killer and, in the process, learns about responsibility and being a good cop. It has an interesting gimmick in that Slater speaks to the camera in between scenes, but it is way too flippant in spots and is more suited for younger people.

A: Christian Slater, Tony Goldwyn, Milla Jovovich, Bruce Boxleitner, George De La Pena, Troy Evans

© MCA/UNIVERSAL HOME VIDEO, INC. 81245

LADY IN RED

D: Lewis Teague — 90 m

R | CRM ACT | 1979 | COLOR | Sex | Nud | Viol | Lang | AdSit

7 Pamela Sue Martin puts in a very effective performance as a naive farm girl who escapes child abuse to enter into prostitution in Chicago during the 1920s. After a run-in with the law and jail time, she enters into service at a fancy bordello and there becomes the mistress of famous gangster John Dillinger. The FBI and her madame set her up to betray Dillinger and he is killed in a famous shoot-out at the Biograph Theater. Thereafter, she turns to a life of crime herself. Very fast-paced, with lots of blood, shoot-outs, sex and car chases. Effective and well done. Also see DILLINGER.

A: Pamela Sue Martin, Robert Conrad, Louise Fletcher, Robert Hogan, Laurie Heineman, Glenn Withrow

© LIVE HOME VIDEO VA4046

LAGUNA HEAT

D: Simon Langton — 110 m

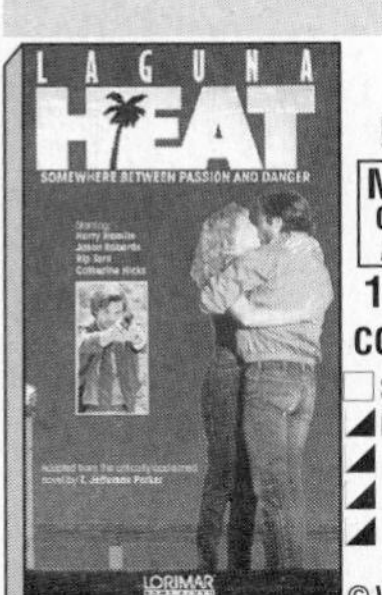

NR | MYS CRM ACT | 1987 | COLOR | Sex | Nud | Viol | Lang | AdSit

6 Witty mystery with a fair dose of action. Harry Hamlin, an L.A. detective who leaves his job after his divorce and the murder of his partner, has moved in with his father in a small coastal town. The town's peaceful facade is destroyed by two brutal murders tied to friends of his father's. Hamlin is drawn into the investigation when he gets involved with the daughter of one of the victims. Hamlin's investigation leads him into a twenty-year-old case of murder and corruption that strikes very close to home. Made for HBO cable TV.

A: Harry Hamlin, Jason Robards, Jr., Rip Torn, Catherine Hicks, Anne Francis

© WARNER HOME VIDEO 822

LASSITER

D: Roger Young — 100 m

R | CRM | 1983 | COLOR | Sex | Nud | Viol | Lang | AdSit

6 Pretty good actioner set in London just prior to the outbreak of WWII. Tom Selleck is a slick American cat burglar who is coerced by a gritty English cop (Hoskins) into stealing a fortune in diamonds from the German embassy and safely out of the hands of the Third Reich. Hopskins's plot includes Selleck's seduction of sexy Lauren Hutton, which does not, in the slightest, make Selleck's girlfriend Seymour happy.

A: Tom Selleck, Jane Seymour, Lauren Hutton, Bob Hoskins, Joe Regalbuto, Ed Lauter

© WARNER HOME VIDEO 11372

LAST SEDUCTION, THE

D: John Dahl — 110 m

R | CRM COM | 1994 | COLOR | Sex | Nud | Viol | Lang | AdSit

8 She loves breaking the rules. She is very, very clever. She has no heart. She uses sex as a substitute for love. She is ruthlessly scheming. She is totally self-serving. She loves money. She is Linda Fiorentino. And, she is perversely entertaining. This is one bad girl. She has stolen $700,000 that her student-doctor husband had made from selling drugs and she has run to a small town to hide for a while. There she meets a man who badly wants to get out and sees her as his ticket...only he doesn't know what he's let himself in for. Sophisticated black humor marks this quirky, tightly woven, slick tale of intrigue in the war of the sexes.

A: Linda Fiorentino, Peter Berg, J.T. Walsh, Bill Nunn, Bill Pullman

© POLYGRAM VIDEO 34461-3

LATE SHOW, THE

D: Robert Benton 93 m

PG
MYS CRM COM
1976
COLOR
Sex
Nud
Viol
Lang
AdSit

9 This is a highly entertaining mystery that works well on many levels at once. In it, a crusty old retired private eye (played to perfection by Art Carney) becomes drawn into a complex murder mystery. It begins simply enough being only a search to find a missing cat, but that quickly changes when he finds his ex-partner murdered. He sets off to find the murderer with the unwelcome assistance of a flaky flower child played to perfection by a goofy Lily Tomlin. New twists and clues are perfectly timed to keep the mystery interesting, but it is the relationship between its two principal players that is what is most appealing. Well done little gem. Very enjoyable.

A: Art Carney, Lily Tomlin, Bill Macy, Eugene Roche, Joanna Cassidy, John Considine

© WARNER HOME VIDEO 11163

LEAGUE OF GENTLEMEN, THE

D: Basil Dearden 115 m

NR
COM CRM
1960
B&W
Sex
Nud
Viol
Lang
AdSit

7 Witty and stylish caper flick. A group of shady ex-servicemen are blackmailed by their forcibly-retired army sergeant into becoming organized into an outlaw gang. He needs them so that they can pull off a complicated but very big bank robbery. Highly enjoyable lighthearted and witty English comedy, where the enjoyment comes from watching the characters succeed - almost.

A: Jack Hawkins, Richard Attenborough, Nigel Patrick, Roger Livesey, Brian Forbes

© HOME VISION LEA 01

LETHAL WEAPON

D: Richard Donner 110 m

R
ACT CRM COM
1987
COLOR
Sex
Nud
Viol
Lang
AdSit

10 Hugely popular high-voltage thriller which is fast, violent and funny. It owes its huge success to the unlikely chemistry of its two lead characters. One is an older, conservative family man and by-the-book cop (Glover). The other is a half-crazed lunatic cop (Gibson). When these guys discover that an apparent suicide is really a cover-up for a particularly raunchy drug ring, they set about destroying it with a vengeance. Very fast paced, with terrific action sequences and funny, with great chemistry between its two stars. It was followed by two very popular sequels.

A: Mel Gibson, Danny Glover, Gary Busey, Mitchell Ryan, Tom Atkins, Darlene Love

© WARNER HOME VIDEO 11709

LETHAL WEAPON 2

D: Richard Donner 114 m

R
ACT CRM COM
1989
COLOR
Sex
Nud
Viol
Lang
AdSit

9 Action fans take note - they're back. Danny Glover and Mel Gibson reprised their roles as police partners - one normal, one a reckless lunatic. This time they are out to get some bad guy drug smugglers from South Africa, who are hiding behind diplomatic immunity, before the bad guys get mob accountant Joe Pesci. Wild and outlandish adventures ensue, loaded with lead-filled action, a little sex and a fair dose of laughs. Entertaining, but not at all believable. Still, this is fun. See also LETHAL WEAPON and LETHAL WEAPON 3.

A: Mel Gibson, Danny Glover, Joe Pesci, Joss Ackland, Derrick O'Conner, Patsy Kensit

© WARNER HOME VIDEO 11876

LETHAL WEAPON 3

D: Richard Donner 118 m

R
ACT CRM COM
1992
COLOR
Sex
Nud
Viol
Lang
AdSit

7 True escapism - more from the hit cop combo of Gibson and Glover. Glover is straight-arrow family-man cop about to retire from the force but he is drawn back in to aid Gibson. They are tracking a cop gone bad who is now a major-league gun runner selling confiscated weapons to L.A. street gangs. The Hollywood folks pull out all the stops again. There is more of the fun glib comradery between the two, but there is also much more of the extravagant violence. The pairing is still good but it's getting a little old now.

A: Mel Gibson, Danny Glover, Joe Pesci, Rene Russo, Stuart Wilson

© WARNER HOME VIDEO 12475

LIST OF ADRIAN MESSENGER, THE

D: John Huston 98 m

NR
SUS MYS CRM
1963
B&W
Sex
Nud
Viol
Lang
AdSit

8 Entertaining witty mystery which has the interesting gimmick of having four of Hollywood's biggest names - Tony Curtis, Burt Lancaster, Frank Sinatra and Robert Mitchum - all buried under make-up for short cameo appearances. Someone is killing off all the potential heirs to the family fortune. Now, there is only one heir, a young grandson, left. The only clue to the murderer is a list of names from one of the murdered heirs, Adrian Messinger. Eleven down, one to go. George C. Scott is a retired British intelligence officer who is on the murderer's trail. Entertaining with lots of twists.

A: George C. Scott, Clive Brook, Dana Wynter, Herbert Marshall, Frank Sinatra, Robert Mitchum

© MCA/UNIVERSAL HOME VIDEO, INC. 80165

MADIGAN

D: Don Siegel 101 m

NR
CRM ACT
1968
COLOR
Sex
Nud
Viol
Lang
AdSit

8 Realistic, hard-hitting action! Madigan (Widmark), is a tough cop, but he's in double trouble. In an attempt to capture a killer, he and his partner break in on a psychopathic killer, but they're momentarily distracted by a naked girl and the killer gets away. Hardball Commissioner Russell (Fonda) is outraged and gives Madigan only 72 hours to catch the guy. Madigan is hard-pressed but his socialite wife also is pressuring him to quit the police work he loves. Critically acclaimed for its revealing look into the workings of New York City detectives - its popularity launched the TV series.

A: Richard Widmark, Henry Fonda, Inger Stevens, Harry Guardino, James Whitmore

© MCA/UNIVERSAL HOME VIDEO, INC. 80040

MAGNUM FORCE

D: Ted Post 122 m

R
ACT CRM
1973
COLOR
Sex
Nud
Viol
Lang
AdSit

8 Very popular gritty action! Dirty Harry Callahan has a dirty police department. Someone is slowly killing off all the crime leaders in the City by the Bay. Harry discovers that the killers are none other than San Francisco's finest, taking short-cuts. Tired of the endless delays and red tape that go along with bringing the bad guys in the legal way, these guys just execute the bad guys on the spot. Holbrook is the head cop of the vigilante ring. He is also Harry's superior - and he hates Harry. Lots of fast macho action, with a good bit of humor thrown in, too.

A: Clint Eastwood, Hal Holbrook, David Soul, Robert Urich, Mitchell Ryan, Felton Perry

© WARNER HOME VIDEO 1039

MANHUNTER

D: Michael Mann 120 m

R
CRM SUS ACT
1986
COLOR
Sex
Nud
Viol
Lang
AdSit

9 Excellent! An ex-FBI agent (Peterson) is recalled to track a ruthless serial killer who is murdering entire families in the southeast. The psychopathic madman (Noonan) gets the name "The Tooth Fairy" for sadistically appropriate reasons. Clever and ever elusive, the only way Peterson can catch this crazed psycho is to actually think like the killer would - to get inside his head. This is the same method used in the later SILENCE OF THE LAMBS and in real life by the FBI. Very contemporary in style, with hard pounding music, this crime drama will take hold of you and won't let go.

A: William L. Petersen, Kim Greist, Brian Cox, Dennis Farina, Stephen Lang, Tom Noonan

© WARNER HOME VIDEO 411

MCQ

D: John Sturges 111 m

PG
ACT CRM
1974
COLOR
Sex
Nud
Viol
Lang
AdSit

7 Wayne trades in his Old West six-shooters for a police badge in this fast-paced and suspenseful cop-action flick. A tough police lieutenant, Wayne goes after two drug dealers who killed his best friend on the force. His investigation leads him to a lonely barmaid (Dewhurst) and a villainous drug dealer, but he also uncovers a lot more when it turns out that many of his old friends on the force, including his ex-partner, are up to their eyes in dirty deeds, too. His new knowledge has put him in a very undesirable position. No shortage of action here. Good DIRTY HARRY-style shoot-'em-up.

A: John Wayne, Eddie Albert, Diana Muldaur, Colleen Dewhurst, Clu Gulager, David Huddleston

© WARNER HOME VIDEO 11140

MECHANIC, THE

D: Michael Winner 101 m

PG
ACT CRM
1972
COLOR
Sex
Nud
Viol
Lang
AdSit

8 Bronson is the ultimate professional assassin. There is no job or individual that he can't execute. He is a mafia favorite and they are his regular customer. Vincent is young, cold-blooded and interested in learning the business, so he went to the best. Bronson is wary and not keen on letting anyone into his private world, yet he is lonely and there is something about Vincent that draws him in. Vincent does become his protege, going along on a series of hits, and learns well -- maybe too well. Good action, good script and a good twist.

A: Charles Bronson, Jan-Michael Vincent, Keenan Wynn, Jill Ireland, Linda Ridgeway

Distributed By MGM/UA Home Video M201259

MENACE II SOCIETY

D: Allen Hughes, Albert Hughes 97 m

R
CRM DMA
1993
COLOR
Sex
Nud
Viol
Lang
AdSit

9 Highly praised portrait of the rough and ugly life that is everyday existence in the ghettos of Los Angeles. The praise is well deserved but this video is very difficult to watch. The characters are mean and remorseless killers who value nobody's life, many times including their own, and respect nothing. The story revolves around one young black man, whose father dealt drugs and died when he was ten. His mother gave him to his grandparents and then died herself of an overdose. His grandparents raised him as best they could, but his world is the streets and his family are the other tough kids who are just like him. A brutal film about a brutal life.

A: Tyrin Turner, Jada Pinkett, Larenz Tate, Arnold Johnson, M C Eiht , Marilyn Coleman

© TURNER HOME ENTERTAINMENT N4165

MIAMI BLUES

D: George Armitage — 97 m

R · CRM ACT · 1990 · COLOR

6 Intense drama with a dark comedic edge. Junior (Baldwin), is a psychopath, fresh out of prison. He moves to Miami and immediately kills a Hare Krishna at the airport. At a local hotel, he orders up a hooker and gets a not-too-bright girl named Pepper (Leigh), but the two like each other and attempt to settle down. A tough detective (Ward) is assigned the job of finding the airport murderer and quickly tracks down Junior, but Junior beats him up, steals his badge, gun and false teeth. Excessively violent and uneven, but also a very curious film with very unusual characters.

Sex · Nud · Viol · Lang · AdSit

A: Alec Baldwin, Fred Ward, Jennifer Jason Leigh, Nora Dunn, Charles Napier, Obba Babatunde

© ORION PICTURES CORPORATION 8746

MIAMI VICE

D: Thomas Carter — 99 m

NR · CRM ACT · 1984 · COLOR

8 A lot of glamor, style and slam-bang action came with this pilot for the extremely popular and long-running TV series which followed during the late '80s. Tubbs (Thomas), is a New York cop who is after the drug kingpin who killed his brother. The trail of the killer leads him to Miami, where he runs headlong into Sonny Crockett (Johnson), a Miami cop hot on the trail of the same killer. The hard-driving contemporary music and rapid editing, along with the great screen personas of the two principle characters, set a new style for youth-oriented action films to come.

Sex · Nud · Viol · Lang · AdSit

A: Don Johnson, Philip Michael Thomas, Saundra Santiago

© MCA/UNIVERSAL HOME VIDEO, INC. 80133

MIGHTY QUINN, THE

D: Carl Schenkel — 98 m

R · MYS CRM · 1989 · COLOR

6 There are flavorful and interesting characters set in a beautiful location and, taken as a whole, this is a worthwhile excursion. Denzel is a likable local figure whose intelligence and character have earned him the job of police chief. But his life gets messy when his friend since childhood (Townsend) appears to be the murderer of a rich white man at a local resort. And things get even messier when he finds that there is a lot of covert money that has been sent to his island by the US government, they want it back and have sent on of their agents to get it. Good, but the plot gets fairly involved and has a few too many diversions.

Sex · Nud · Viol · Lang · AdSit

A: Denzel Washington, Robert Townsend, James Fox, Mimi Rogers, M. Emmet Walsh

© CBS/FOX VIDEO 4761

MILLER'S CROSSING

D: Joel Coen, Ethan Coen — 115 m

R · CRM ACT · 1990 · COLOR

9 Excellent. Highly entertaining and stylish gangster film that spends more time on developing its characters and their society than most of the gangster films of the past, or the present. Set in an unnamed eastern city, an Irish gangster (Finney) and his right-hand man (Byrne) have a falling out over the same woman. Then when a rival Italian hood (Polito) sets his sights on Irish turf, Byrne apparently switches sides. Very violent at times, rich in character images and full of plot intrigue. This is also a film that you will think about for days after.

Sex · Nud · Viol · Lang · AdSit

A: Albert Finney, Gabriel Byrne, Jon Polito, J.E. Freeman, Marcia Gay Harden, John Turturro

© FOXVIDEO 1852

MISSISSIPPI BURNING

D: Alan Parker — 127 m

R · CRM SUS DMA · 1988 · COLOR

9 Hard-edged and mesmerizing drama that is based on fact. It's 1964 and change is coming to Mississippi. Three young civil rights workers are missing and the FBI is investigating. Willem Dafoe is a dedicated young agent sent in to run the investigation, but Gene Hackman is the local agent who understands these people. He and Dafoe are not friends but they are both dedicated to stopping the reign of terror of the KKK. Still, the FBI is not welcomed by any of the locals, black or white. And as Dafoe brings in hundreds of agents, the national press moves in and the fires start to burn. Nominated for seven Academy Awards. Excellent.

Sex · Nud · Viol · Lang · AdSit

A: Gene Hackman, Willem Dafoe, Frances McDormand, Brad Dourif, R. Lee Ermey, Gailard Sartain

© ORION PICTURES CORPORATION 8727

MOBSTERS

D: Michael Karbelnikoff — 104 m

R · CRM ACT · 1991 · COLOR

6 Sort of YOUNG GUNS in suits with tommy-guns. Some up-and-coming young stars of the early 90's were dressed up in a big money production. It is the supposed story of four young hoods who grew up together in the slums of New York and rose to transform the "mob" into a corporate-like business. The four are Lucky Luciano (Slater), Meyer Lanski (Dempsey), Ben "Bugsy" Segal (Grieco) and Frank Costello (Mandylor). In spite of a great deal of effort, the plot only generates slight momentum. However, there is a lot of starpower invested and plenty of violence and gore.

Sex · Nud · Viol · Lang · AdSit

A: Christian Slater, Patrick Dempsey, Richard Grieco, Costas Mandylor, Anthony Quinn, Michael Gambon

© MCA/UNIVERSAL HOME VIDEO, INC. 81129

MONEY FOR NOTHING

D: Ramon Menendez — 100 m

R · CRM · 1993 · COLOR

6 What would you do if you found $1.2 million? That was the real-life situation that Joey Coyle was faced with when he and a friend stumbled on money that had just fallen out of the back of an armored car. John Cusack plays Joey Coyle, an out of work laborer from South Philadelphia. Poor Joey decided to keep the money. Just as soon as the decision was made, his world started to fall apart. He did all the wrong things with the wrong people and his secret rapidly started to unwind, with him caught in the middle. Cusack's Joey is a well-meaning, generous, good guy. In real life, the real Joey was forever haunted by his notoriety and eventually committed suicide.

Sex · Nud · Viol · Lang · AdSit

A: John Cusack, Michael Madsen, Debi Mazor, Benicio Del Toro, Maury Chaykin, Michael Rapaport

© HOLLYWOOD PICTURES HOME VIDEO 2313

MONSIEUR HIRE

D: Patrice Leconte — 88 m

PG-13 · FOR SUS CRM · 1990 · COLOR

8 Brilliant and gripping suspense import from France. A balding reclusive tailor, Monsieur Hire, becomes obsessed with the beautiful young lady across his courtyard, peeping at her constantly from his darkened windows. One day a flash of lightning reveals his embarrassing activities to her and she confronts him. When another young woman is found dead nearby and she is terrified. It is natural that Monsieur Hire would becomes the police's natural suspect. However, the snoopy Monsieur Hire knows who the real killer is. Subtly erotic, but also extraordinary in its drama and its perceptiveness.

Sex · Nud · Viol · Lang · AdSit

A: Michel Blanc, Sandrine Bonnaire, Andre Wilms, Luc Thuiller

© ORION PICTURES CORPORATION 5053

MORNING AFTER, THE

D: Sidney Lumet — 103 m

R · CRM MYS ROM · 1986 · COLOR

8 Complex thriller! A beautiful washed-up actress (Fonda), now an alcoholic, is having a very bad morning. After a night of an excess of everything, she wakes up to find that the man in bed next to her is dead, with a dagger through his heart. She remembers nothing. Terrified, she erases all trace of her presence and evades the police. She lives in fear until she bumps into ex-cop and ex-alcoholic (Bridges) who becomes charmed by this girl with a problem and who unravels the mystery for her. Both Fonda's and Bridges's characters are complex, appealing and quite believable.

Sex · Nud · Viol · Lang · AdSit

A: Jane Fonda, Jeff Bridges, Raul Julia, Diane Salinger, Richard Foronjy, Geoffery Scott

© WARNER HOME VIDEO 419

MORTAL THOUGHTS

D: Alan Rudolph — 104 m

R · CRM MYS · 1991 · COLOR

6 Who killed Headly's abusive, drug-addicted and nasty husband (Bruce Willis)? Did she or did her best friend (Demi Moore)? It is a question that the movie never really answers... but the story and accompanying theories are compelling and involving. Filmed in flash-back, the story is told how Moore, Willis and a Headly go out one night to a carnival but Willis never makes it home. The two women decide to hide his death and bury him in a ditch. When an inspector comes calling, their friendship unravels as each is pressed hard to present her side of the story. Curious and downbeat.

Sex · Nud · Viol · Lang · AdSit

A: Demi Moore, Bruce Willis, Glenne Headly, John Pankow, Harvey Keitel, Billie Neal

© COLUMBIA TRISTAR HOME VIDEO 50743

MURDER IN THE FIRST

D: Marc Rocco — 123 m

R · DMA CRM · 1995 · COLOR

8 In 1930, a 17-year-old orphan stole $5 from a rural store to feed his hungry sister. The store doubled as a post office, so he was sent to federal prison and later was transfered to Alcatraz. After a failed escape attempt, and accused of being the ring-leader, a vengeful warden ordered him into solitary confinement - a cold, wet, pitilessly dark, pest-infested hole - where he was left and repeatedly beaten for three years. Within hours of his release, and now a totally demented wreck, he fatally stabbed the man who ratted on him. His supposed cut-and-dried case is assigned to a novice attorney, who instead won his case by attacking the cruel system which created him and then destroyed him. Based on true story.

Sex · Nud · Viol · Lang · AdSit

A: Christian Slater, Kevin Bacon, Gary Oldman, Embeth Davidtz, Brad Dourif, Lee Ermey

© WARNER HOME VIDEO 13895

MURDER, SHE SAID

D: George Pollock — 87 m

NR · MYS CRM · 1962 · B&W

8 The intrigue never stops in this wonderful whodunit! A dozing Miss Marple (Rutherford) awakens and witnesses a murder on a passing train. Naturally, the police think she is only dreaming. However, convinced of what she saw, she takes a job as a domestic at an estate, hoping to find all the clues she needs to put the case to bed. A very skillful adaptation of Agatha Christie's "4:50 to Paddington" that is great fun for mystery buffs.

Sex · Nud · Viol · Lang · AdSit

A: Margaret Rutherford, Arthur Kennedy, Muriel Pavlow, James Robertson Justice, Charles Tingwell, Thorley Walters

Distributed By MGM/UA Home Video M201994

MURPH THE SURF

PG | CRM | 1975 | COLOR

D: Marvin J. Chomsky — 102 m

6 The impossible heist. A story of how two Florida beach bums conspired to steal the 564-carat Star of India sapphire from New York's American Museum of Natural History. Believe it or not, they actually succeeded, and the story is based on the truth. The real crime was committed in 1964. It was the biggest jewel heist in history. There is some solid suspense in this film and a pretty good boat chase, too.

Sex | Nud | Viol | Lang | AdSit

A: Robert Conrad, Don Stroud, Donna Mills, Robyn Millan, Burt Young, Luther Adler

NEW CENTURIONS, THE

R | CRM DMA ACT | 1972 | COLOR

D: Richard Fleischer — 103 m

8 An involving screen adaptation of Joseph Wambaugh's novel about the nature of street cops. Scott is a grizzled old veteran on the way out, teaching the new and enthusiastic rookie (Stacy Keach) the ropes. Keach loves it. He is hooked on the excitement, and he puts it before everything else even though it is destroying his marriage. Scott will soon retire but finds that he, too, is hooked, however he can't go back. This is a fascinating character study, but it is also ultimately pretty downbeat in nature. Great performances and a fascinating story.

Sex | Nud | Viol | Lang | AdSit

A: George C. Scott, Stacy Keach, Jane Alexander, Rosalind Cash, Scott Wilson

NEW JACK CITY

R | CRM ACT | 1991 | COLOR

D: Mario Van Peebles — 101 m

6 Very gritty, hard-edged inner-city action flick. Two undercover cops lay everything on the line to bring down a ruthless Harlem drug lord (Snipes). Loads of action for the action crowd, but the hard, no-nonsense, repulsive realities about drugs and drug life also deliver a strong anti-drug message. The story line is essentially nothing new, however. The whole package is wrapped in a score heavily dosed with the rap music of Ice T, Christopher Williams and 2 Live Crew.

Sex | Nud | Viol | Lang | AdSit

A: Wesley Snipes, Ice T, Mario Van Peebles, Alan Payne, Chris Rock, Vanessa Williams

NIGHT VISITOR, THE

PG | CRM SUS | 1970 | COLOR

D: Laslo Benedek — 94 m

6 An interesting and clever chiller. Max Von Sydow is imprisoned inside a supposedly escape-proof prison for the criminally insane for having committed a grisly axe murder two years before. He has devised a devious plot to reap vengeance on those who he holds responsible for his conviction. He will escape from prison for one night only and steal across the frozen Scandinavian winterscape in only his underwear and shoes. He will kill his sister and a farm girl, and leave his brother-in-law to take blame. Then he will return to his cell. It's the perfect alibi. Trevor Howard is the detective who investigates the new murderers. Fine performances.

Sex | Nud | Viol | Lang | AdSit

A: Max von Sydow, Liv Ullmann, Trevor Howard, Per Oscarsson

NORTH BY NORTHWEST

NR | SUS CRM | 1959 | COLOR

D: Alfred Hitchcock — 136 m

10 All-time classic suspensor and quintessential Hitchcock. This highly entertaining thriller starred Cary Grant when he was at the height of his career and at his most charming. He plays a bewildered advertising executive who is being chased cross-country by both the police (who think he is a murderer) and by foreign spies (who think he is a double-agent). Then, he is unexpectedly charmed and aided by beautiful Eva Marie Saint, but soon has reason to question her motives, too. A masterpiece of intrigue. Several now-classic and often imitated scenes. See also NOTORIOUS.

Sex | Nud | Viol | Lang | AdSit

A: Cary Grant, Eva Marie Saint, James Mason, Leo G. Carroll, Jessie Royce Landis, Philip Ober

ONCE UPON A TIME IN AMERICA (LONG VERSION)

R | CRM ACT | 1984 | COLOR

D: Sergio Leone — 226 m

8 Very long and sometimes confusing, yet involving film depicting the relationship between two Jewish gangsters - from their beginnings as boys in the ghetto through their development into major hoods. Maxie (Woods) is too wild, so his friend Noodles (De Niro) tips off the police to an upcoming robbery so Maxie will get arrested and put safely behind bars before he gets killed. Instead, Maxie is apparently killed in a shoot out. Noodles leaves town. Now it's 1968, 35 years later, and Noodles mysteriously gets called back home to meet with his old friends.

Sex | Nud | Viol | Lang | AdSit

A: Robert De Niro, James Woods, Elizabeth McGovern, Joe Pesci, Jennifer Connelly, Tuesday Weld

ONE FALSE MOVE

R | CRM ACT | 1992 | COLOR

D: Carl Franklin — 106 m

6 Very gritty, low-budget crime story. It is not for everyone, but those intrigued by low-life characters and their psychology will find more than enough to hold their attention. Two bad guys and one bad girl kill off a house full of people for a load of drugs and slowly head east, back to her small hometown in Arkansas. Two cops from L.A. know where they are heading and solicit the help of the local hayseed sheriff, but he is more determined to prove himself the equal of big city cops. A major part of what makes this story interesting is the complex and seedy characters it explores.

Sex | Nud | Viol | Lang | AdSit

A: Bill Paxton, Cynda Williams, Billy Bob Thornton, Michael Beach, Jim Metzler, Earl Billings

ONION FIELD, THE

R | CRM DMA | 1979 | COLOR

D: Harold Becker — 126 m

10 Superb and fascinating crime drama adapted from real life by ex-cop and author Joseph Wambaugh. In 1963 two small-time criminals kidnap two cops. In the middle of an onion field, they kill one, but the other escapes. The killers are captured and convicted, but for years are able to frustrate justice by manipulating the legal system. In the interim, the surviving cop is slowly consumed with guilt for having lived while his partner died, and with the frustration of not being able to do anything to see justice done. An exceptional film

Sex | Nud | Viol | Lang | AdSit

A: John Savage, James Woods, Ronny Cox, Franklyn Seales, Ted Danson, Christopher Lloyd

ORGANIZATION, THE

PG | CRM ACT | 1971 | COLOR

D: Don Medford — 107 m

6 The third and final appearance of Mr. Tibbs, the tough big city police detective Poitier created in IN THE HEAT OF THE NIGHT and followed up with in THEY CALL ME MR. TIBBS. This time in San Francisco, Poitier comes to the aid of a student vigilante group who raids a furniture factory that is really a front trafficking in heroin. When the manager is murdered, the group admits to Tibbs that they stole $5 million in dope to keep it off the streets but they didn't kill anyone. He rises to their defense but is suspended from the force. Good action flick with a realistic plot and believable climax.

Sex | Nud | Viol | Lang | AdSit

A: Sidney Poitier, Barbara Mc Nair, Raul Julia, Sheree North, Ron O'Neal, Daniel J. Travanti

OUTLAND

R | SF ACT CRM | 1981 | COLOR

D: Peter Hyams — 111 m

8 Rousing space Western. Sean Connery is the new marshall assigned to police a dehumanized, rough-and-tumble mining colony on one of the moons of Jupiter. His search to identify the reasons behind a series of mysterious deaths leads him to the discovery of a pervasive corruption based upon the distribution of mind-altering drugs. Great special effects lend an air of realism and believability to this bleak other-world environment. The exciting action scenes could have occurred just as easily at the OK corral or on the streets of L.A. Exciting.

Sex | Nud | Viol | Lang | AdSit

A: Sean Connery, Peter Boyle, Frances Sternhagen, James Sikking, Kika Markham

OUT OF THE DARKNESS

R | CRM MYS SUS | 1985 | COLOR

D: Jud Taylor — 96 m

8 Fascinating story of the New York cop Ed Zigo, who tracked down the infamous "Son of Sam" killer in 1976-77. This was the vicious real-life murderer who shot young lovers in their cars with a large bore revolver, and then wrote taunting notes to reporters and the police to brag of his successes. This gripping story focuses on the cop and the chase, not the killer. A solid and interesting script with tight pacing and an excellent performance from Martin Sheen make this a gripping crime mystery.

Sex | Nud | Viol | Lang | AdSit

A: Martin Sheen, Hector Elizondo, Matt Clark, Jennifer Salt

OVER THE EDGE

PG | DMA CRM | 1980 | COLOR

D: Jonathan Kaplan — 95 m

7 Disturbing portrait of alienated rich kids. Quite good in its own right but most notable for being Mat Dillon's screen debut. It is a powerful and unsettling portrait of lost and disaffected rich kids who play with booze, drugs and guns, and who spend their idle time committing robbery and violence. A familiar story line, but one especially well done. Excellent sound track featuring music by "Cheap Trick," "The Cars" and "The Ramones." Not released until Dillon was a star, it was originally thought to be too provocative.

Sex | Nud | Viol | Lang | AdSit

A: Michael Kramer, Pamela Ludwig, Matt Dillon, Vincent Spano, Tom Fergus, Ellen Geer

PERFECT WORLD, A

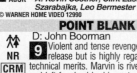

D: Clint Eastwood 138 m

PG-13 | CRM DMA | 1993 | COLOR

8 An unusual sort of drama that is both convincing and touching. Costner is Butch, a career criminal who has broken out of prison. He and another escapee take Phillip, a 7-year-old boy, hostage on their getaway flight. Clint Eastwood is a veteran Texas Ranger who leads up the team, including Laura Dern as a criminologist consultant, that is out to get him back. Young Phillip has no father and Butch never really had one either, so the two are drawn ever closer to each other as they combine forces to help Butch escape. Sometimes funny, but this is no comedy. Butch is an emotional cripple who wants to give Phillip what he craves for himself, but he must do it while on the run.

Sex | Nud | Viol | Lang | AdSit

A: Kevin Costner, Clint Eastwood, Laura Dern, T.J. Lowther, Keith Szarabajka, Leo Bermester

© WARNER HOME VIDEO 12990

POINT BLANK

D: John Boorman 89 m

NR | CRM ACT SUS | 1967 | COLOR

9 Violent and tense revenge flick that was largely ignored upon its release but is highly regarded now both for it's potency and its technical merits. Marvin is riveting as a vicious gangster who is shot and left for dead by his partner during a holdup, so he could run off with Marvin's wife and pay off a mob debt with the money they stole. Marvin recovers, and with help from sexy Angie Dickinson and a crooked accountant, he gains access inside the mob. He will get revenge, get his money back and kill off anyone who gets in his way. Very violent.

Sex | Nud | Viol | Lang | AdSit

A: Lee Marvin, Angie Dickinson, Carroll O'Connor, Keenan Wynn, John Vernon, Lloyd Bochner

Distributed By MGM/UA Home Video M800278

POPE OF GREENWICH VILLAGE, THE

D: Stuart Rosenberg 121 m

R | CRM ACT | 1984 | COLOR

7 Interesting character study, with insightful observations, of two small-time losers with big dreams who are constantly foiled by their own ineptitude. After getting fired from their restaurant jobs, and deeply in debt, Charlie (Rourke) and his cousin Paulie (Roberts) rob a safe containing Mafia money and accidentally kill an undercover cop. Now both the cops and the mob want them. Worse, while the two struggle just to stay alive in New York's Little Italy, Charlie's girlfriend (Hannah), who is tired of putting up with him, runs off with all their money.

Sex | Nud | Viol | Lang | AdSit

A: Eric Roberts, Mickey Rourke, Daryl Hannah, Geraldine Page, Burt Young, Kenneth McMillan

Distributed By MGM/UA Home Video M800490

POSTMAN ALWAYS RINGS TWICE, THE

D: Bob Rafelson 121 m

R | SUS CRM DMA | 1981 | COLOR

6 Super-sexy remake of the classic 1946 film about the passion between a cook at a roadside cafe and a handyman which led to their conspired murder of her husband. Unhampered by the censorship of 1946, this remake dives headlong into the passions only alluded to in the earlier version. After a strong beginning, things begin to wander some. Ultimately, this version is not as satisfying as the original because much of the empathy for the characters which was created in the original is lost here. Still... interesting.

Sex | Nud | Viol | Lang | AdSit

A: Jack Nicholson, Jessica Lange, Michael Lerner, John Colicos

© WARNER HOME VIDEO 673

PRESIDIO, THE

D: Peter Hyams 97 m

R | CRM ACT | 1988 | COLOR

8 An old-fashioned murder mystery with a couple of new twists. A female soldier is murdered while on patrol inside a military compound in San Francisco. The police detective (Mark Harmon) assigned to the case is distressed to learn that the base is being commanded by his old nemesis, Sean Connery. The state of their personal animosities is worsened when he also falls for Connery's daughter (Ryan). The two fight over jurisdiction on the case but a comradery grows when they combine their efforts and close in on the killer. Good action and chase sequences.

Sex | Nud | Viol | Lang | AdSit

A: Sean Connery, Mark Harmon, Meg Ryan, Jack Warden, Mark Blum

© PARAMOUNT HOME VIDEO 31978

PRESUMED INNOCENT

D: Alan J. Pakula 127 m

R | MYS SUS CRM | 1990 | COLOR

8 This is a sexy and thoroughly involving thriller (based on a best-selling novel) which was a big hit at the box office. Ford plays Rusty Sabich, a hard-working up-and-coming attorney at the county prosecutor's office. However, he has a brief affair with a stunningly sexy female attorney (Sacchi) that ends badly. His marriage is damaged but survives. Then the woman turns up raped and murdered. His finger prints and blood are found at the scene and the prosecutor's office that he was so committed to, is now doing its best to nail him. This is a fascinating mystery and courtroom drama that is full of red herrings and plot twists and is very well done.

Sex | Nud | Viol | Lang | AdSit

A: Harrison Ford, Brian Dennehy, Raul Julia, Bonnie Bedelia, Paul Winfield, Greta Scacchi

© WARNER HOME VIDEO 12034

PRINCE OF THE CITY

D: Sidney Lumet 167 m

R | CRM DMA ACT | 1981 | COLOR

8 A powerfully gripping and emotionally draining film, based on the true 1971 story of a member of an elite corp of New York drug cops who reveals a pervasive corruption on the force. It is his personal story of how he was moved to violate the policeman's code of silence. And, it is a story of the ability of power, drugs and money to corrupt even the best. Our cop is determined to expose the corruption, but do it without destroying his friends - after all, they are just victims of the process - but he can't. So, he becomes the biggest victim, when he cannot protect, and must betray and destroy, his best friends.

Sex | Nud | Viol | Lang | AdSit

A: Treat Williams, Jerry Orbach, Richard Foronjy, Lindsay Crouse, Don Billett, Kenny Marino

© WARNER HOME VIDEO 22021

PRIZZI'S HONOR

D: John Huston 130 m

R | COM CRM SUS | 1985 | COLOR

9 Devilishly delicious black comedy. Nicholson is a Mafia hit man for the Prizzi family. He becomes fascinated with a sexy mystery woman (Turner), who turns out to be a free-lance hitter, too. But things become greatly complicated for them when it turns out she has stolen some of the family's money and he gets an order to kill her. Nicholson's loyalties are severely tested: should he hit her, or marry her. Now that he is no longer trustworthy, the family hires her to hit him. Terrific performances, witty dialogue, fascinating plotting. Eight Oscar nominations.

Sex | Nud | Viol | Lang | AdSit

A: Jack Nicholson, Kathleen Turner, Anjelica Huston, John Randolph, William Hickey, Robert Loggia

© LIVE HOME VIDEO 5106

PUBLIC EYE, THE

D: Howard Franklin 99 m

R | CRM MYS | 1992 | COLOR

7 Before there were pictures on TV news, there were sensational pictures on the front pages of newspapers. Joe Pesci is perfect as the premier free-lance tabloid photographer in 1940's New York. He is a grubby little man in a squashed hat with a stubby cigar always stuck in his face. Always the first one on the scene of a shooting, he is friendly with cops and crooks alike. But, he is also a lonely loner with the soul of an artist. His infatuation for a beautiful night club owner (Hershey) involves him in a mob investigation that proves to be deadly. Interesting film noir mystery, but patience required.

Sex | Nud | Viol | Lang | AdSit

A: Joe Pesci, Barbara Hershey, Stanley Tucci, Jerry Alder, Jared Harris, Garry Becker

© MCA/UNIVERSAL HOME VIDEO, INC. 81284

Q&A

D: Sidney Lumet 132 m

R | CRM ACT | 1990 | COLOR

8 Gritty hard-edged crime drama. Weather-beaten maverick cop Nolte kills a drug dealer in self defense. The seemingly open and shut case is routinely investigated by rookie district attorney Hutton, who discovers that Nolte has a dark side. He is a hard man, used to working alone in a cruel world. His methods are unorthodox and the characters of his world are weird and gruesome. Hutton wants to respect Nolte, but the more he investigates, the more his witnesses turn up dead. Nolte is a powerhouse the entire way. Exciting, but quite involved and saddled with a muddled ending.

Sex | Nud | Viol | Lang | AdSit

A: Nick Nolte, Timothy Hutton, Armand Assante, Patrick O'Neal, Lee Richardson, Luis Guzman

© HBO VIDEO 0381

QUICK CHANGE

D: Bill Murray, Howard Franklin 89 m

R | COM CRM | 1990 | COLOR

7 After staging what could have been the perfect bank robbery, three New Yorkers attempt to get out of the city and hop a plane headed for the South Pacific. Unfortunately, almost everything that can go wrong does, and Murray, Davis and Quaid barely manage to stay one step ahead of the police on their calamity-filled trek to the airport. This is a film that could be cliched and predictable, but it is not. It is surprisingly funny and sports some outstanding slapstick and sight gags.

Sex | Nud | Viol | Lang | AdSit

A: Bill Murray, Geena Davis, Randy Quaid, Jason Robards, Jr., Bob Elliott, Philip Bosco

© WARNER HOME VIDEO 12004

RAGTIME

D: Milos Forman 156 m

PG | DMA CRM | 1981 | COLOR

8 A colorful portrait of life at the beginning of the 20th century, set amidst scandal and middle-class morals of the time. Too many subplots confuse the beginning of the film, but things pick up when the focus narrows. While on his way to his own wedding, a black man is accosted by a raucous group of firemen who harass him and then vandalize his car. After repeated attempts to receive justice within the system fail, he takes drastic measures on his own and holds the town hostage. Now, finally, the system takes notice but fights back with a vengeance. Excellent, lots of major stars and a big budget. Nominated for eight Oscars.

Sex | Nud | Viol | Lang | AdSit

A: James Cagney, Brad Dourif, Moses Gunn, Elizabeth McGovern, Kenneth McMillan, James Olson

© PARAMOUNT HOME VIDEO 1486

C R M

REAL MCCOY, THE

D: Russell Mulcahy 106 m

PG-13 | CRM | 1993 | COLOR

Sex | Nud | Viol | Lang | AdSit

6 This is a minor league caper flick. Kim Basinger is a master bankrobber whose specialty is stealth and brains. However, she got caught and has just been released from a long stretch in the pen. She is determined to go straight this time, but her sleazy parole officer is in cahoots with a major league bad guy who wants her to do one more big one for him. When she refuses, the bad guys kidnap her son and bounce her around to encourage her participation. Mildly interesting.

A: Kim Basinger, Val Kilmer, Gailard Sartain, Terance Stamp, Raynor Scheine, Nick Searcy

© MCA/UNIVERSAL HOME VIDEO, INC. 81604

REPORT TO THE COMMISSIONER

D: Milton Katselas 113 m

PG | CRM ACT | 1974 | COLOR

Sex | Nud | Viol | Lang | AdSit

7 A tough and gritty crime drama. A naive and idealistic rookie cop (Moriarty) on the New York City beat accidentally kills an undercover agent. The beautiful female cop (Blakely) was posing as an accomplice and live-in lover to a big-time drug dealer (King). When Moriatry pulls that trigger, he also gets pulled into an elaborate coverup by his corrupt superiors and he becomes their scapegoat.

A: Michael Moriarty, Yaphet Kotto, Susan Blakely, Hector Elizondo, Tony King

Distributed By MGM/UA Home Video M301297

RESERVOIR DOGS

D: Quentin Tarantino 99 m

R | CRM ACT | 1992 | COLOR

Sex | Nud | Viol | Lang | AdSit

7 Extremely violent crime film that uses extremes of violence and profanity to shock its audience into revulsion. However, it is also a very intriguing film that is reasonably well told, using a technique first used in the classic film THE ASPHALT JUNGLE. Most of the film takes place in an empty warehouse where a group of vicious thugs have gathered to figure out how the jewelry robbery they had tried to pull off could have gone so bad. Then, most of the story, in its many convolutions, unwinds as a series of flashbacks. This is a very hard-edged film. Don't watch it if you are easily offended.

A: Harvey Keitel, Tim Roth, Michael Madsen, Chris Penn, Steve Buscemi, Lawrence Tierney

© LIVE HOME VIDEO 48998

RIDER ON THE RAIN

D: Rene Clement 119 m

PG | SUS CRM | 1970 | COLOR

Sex | Nud | Viol | Lang | AdSit

8 This is a tightly-plotted and well-executed thriller that is loaded with suspense! A young French housewife (Jobert) is brutally raped by a stranger. She kills him in self defense and disposes of his body in the sea. When the body washes up on shore, she receives a visit from a mysterious stranger (Bronson). He tells her he suspects she killed the man. He had been a prison escapee and had a flight bag with $60,000 of US Army money. Bronson won't leave her alone until he gets the money back, and she doesn't know who he is. This is a fine film that has a chilling, polished and unpredictable script. It is also one of Bronson's finest performances.

A: Charles Bronson, Marlene Jobert, Jill Ireland, Annie Cordy

© MONTEREY HOME VIDEO 33708

RISING SUN

D: Philip Kaufman 129 m

R | CRM MYS ACT | 1993 | COLOR

Sex | Nud | Viol | Lang | AdSit

9 Very complicated, very sexy and enthralling. Snipes is an L.A. cop called in to investigate the death of a beautiful girl found dead on the boardroom table of very important Japanese company that is negotiating to purchase a sensitive American company. He is instructed to pick up Connery, a veteran officer experienced in the culture of the Japanese. Their investigation leads them through an intricate high-tech coverup concealing the business war between two Japanese companies. It is a battle between important and dangerous people and a complicated jigsaw puzzle of culture, intrigue and fast action. Excellent.

A: Sean Connery, Wesley Snipes, Harvey Keitel, Cary-Hiroyuki Tagawa, Tia Carrere, Mako

© FOXVIDEO 8520

ROLLING THUNDER

D: John Flynn 99 m

R | ACT CRM | 1977 | COLOR

Sex | Nud | Viol | Lang | AdSit

8 Graphic action! A P.O.W. (Devane) returns to his small Texan home and family after eight miserable and brutal years in Vietnam. He is honored with 2000 silver dollars (symbolizing one for each day held captive) by the grateful town, but thieves quickly move in for the money. They torture him and murder his wife and child. Enraged, he enlists the aid of an ex-P.O.W. pal Jones. The two then methodically and systematically seek cold and emotionless revenge on the murderers. Very well done with well drawn characters. Bloody but engrossing.

A: William Devane, Tommy Lee Jones, James Best, Dabney Coleman, Linda Haynes, Lisa Richards

© GOODTIMES 74066

ROMEO IS BLEEDING

D: Peter Medak 108 m

R | CRM | 1994 | COLOR

Sex | Nud | Viol | Lang | AdSit

7 The critics were not very kind to this one. It is a raw, somewhat bizarre and not entirely believable story, but it also has hard edge that is strangely fascinating. Oldman is a New York cop who is supplementing his take-home pay by providing inside tips to mob king Scheider. His tips are getting people killed but he likes the money. He also loves his wife, but that doesn't stop him from cheating on her with a mistress, and cheating on them both when tempted by a beautiful and totally ruthless professional killer (Lena Olin). His world crashes in on him when Scheider wants him to kill Olin but she offers him her body and more money not to.

A: Gary Oldman, Lena Olin, Annabella Sciorra, Juliette Lewis, Roy Scheider

© POLYGRAM VIDEO 30445-3

ROOKIE, THE

D: Clint Eastwood 121 m

R | ACT CRM | 1990 | COLOR

Sex | Nud | Viol | Lang | AdSit

6 Slam-bang action, more than enough to keep action fans happy, but not much else. Clint is a veteran cop saddled with an eager young by-the-book cop. Together they seek to hunt down a ruthless and murderous gang of auto thieves, led by Germans Raul Julia and a sadistic Sonia Braga. The film is loaded with the expected fights, shootings and chase scenes, plus a curious scene where Clint is raped by Sonia while he is tied to a chair.

A: Clint Eastwood, Charlie Sheen, Raul Julia, Sonia Braga, Lara Flynn Boyle

© WARNER HOME VIDEO 12061

RUSH

D: Lili Fini Zanuck 120 m

R | CRM DMA | 1992 | COLOR

Sex | Nud | Viol | Lang | AdSit

6 Unrelentingly grim portrait of a 1975 Texas undercover narcotics team. A young undercover cop (Patric) selects a female recruit to be his new partner to aid him in gathering evidence with which to convict a bunch of seedy local low-lifes of distributing drugs. But in order to gain the confidence of their quarry, they have to become like them, including taking drugs. This is a story of conflicting morals and of a life where the thrill of the hunt, and the fear it brings, is as big a high as are the drugs themselves. A realistic but ultimately unsatisfying experience.

A: Jason Patric, Jennifer Jason Leigh, Gregg Allman, Sam Elliott, Max Perlich

Distributed By MGM/UA Home Video 902527

SCARFACE

D: Brian De Palma 170 m

R | CRM ACT | 1983 | COLOR

Sex | Nud | Viol | Lang | AdSit

8 One of the most gruesome, brutal and forceful gangster flicks ever made! A Cuban refugee, Tony Montana (Pacino), lands in the drug center of Miami. His ruthlessness causes him to quickly rise from a simple task man to drug kingpin, importing and selling cocaine. Along the way, Tony steals the crime lord's (Loggia) girlfriend (Pfeiffer), kills his kid sister's lover (Bauer), and spins himself into a web of tragedy with his cocaine abuses. This extremely violent remake of the 1932 classic is graphic and shocking from start to finish, and will not be easily forgotten. Too long, though.

A: Al Pacino, Steven Bauer, Michelle Pfeiffer, Mary Elizabeth Mastrantonio, Robert Loggia, Miriam Colon

© MCA/UNIVERSAL HOME VIDEO, INC. 80047

SEA OF LOVE

D: Harold Becker 113 m

R | CRM SUS MYS | 1989 | COLOR

Sex | Nud | Viol | Lang | AdSit

9 Very steamy murder mystery. Al Pacino is a cynical and alcoholic cop who has no life outside his work, except the bottle. He is assigned, along with a cop from another precinct (Goodman), to the investigation of a series of murdered dead men, all of which have Ellen Barkin as a common thread. Pacino falls hard for the fiery Barkin and refuses to believe that she is the murderer, even though everyone else has made her their prime suspect. She has revived Pacino's life and he desperately wants to believe she's innocent. Tension builds as he begins a torrid relationship with her, never really knowing for sure if she is a murderer, even as his investigation continues.

A: Al Pacino, Ellen Barkin, John Goodman, Michael Rooker, William Hickey

© MCA/UNIVERSAL HOME VIDEO, INC. 80883

SERPICO

D: Sidney Lumet 130 m

R | CRM ACT DMA | 1973 | COLOR

Sex | Nud | Viol | Lang | AdSit

10 Extremely tough and compelling police drama, based upon the true-life story of Frank Serpico, a cop whose public testimony in the early 70s about corruption and bribery, ripped open the NYC police department. Pacino's characterization is amazing. Serpico is an oddball, idealistic and obsessive cop who doesn't fit in as a regular cop, but his non-conformism is an asset as an undercover cop. It is as an undercover cop that he is exposed to the corrupt underbelly of the police force itself. When some corrupt cops find him to be incorruptible, he is determined to be too great a risk and he is set up to be killed. Instead of dying, he survived to testify against them.

A: Al Pacino, John Randolph, Jack Kehoe, Biff McGuire, Barbara Eda-Young, Tony Roberts

© PARAMOUNT HOME VIDEO 8689

SEVEN-UPS, THE

D: Philip D'Antoni 109 m

PG | ACT CRM | 1973 | COLOR

6 Made by the same producer as BULLITT and THE FRENCH CONNECTION, this film is first, foremost and almost solely an action picture - with a particularly great car chase. The action revolves around Scheider as the head of a special New York police unit that is charged with nailing major hoods for prison terms of seven or more years. His team utilizes stoolies to nail their quarry, but when one of his officers is killed by a stoolie who has turned the tables on them, the intense pursuit and the action begins. Good action picture.

Sex Nud Viol Lang AdSit

A: Roy Scheider, Tony Lo Bianco, Bill Hickman, Richard Lynch, Larry Haines, Victor Arnold

© FOXVIDEO 1193

SHAFT

D: Gordon Parks 98 m

R | ACT CRM | 1971 | COLOR

7 Heavy-duty brutal action. When the Mafia kidnaps a Harlem crimelord's daughter, he (Gunn) hires the toughest guy he can find, detective Shaft (Roundtree), to get his daughter back. This was one of the first and best crime dramas to feature a black hero in a leading role. Director Parks expertly mixes together threats of racial violence and mob wars as the story unfolds in this actioner with an impact that has not been dated by time. The score by Isaac Hayes was an Oscar winner.

Sex Nud Viol Lang AdSit

A: Richard Roundtree, Moses Gunn, Charles Cioffi, Antonio Fargas, Christopher St. John, Drew Bundini Brown

Distributed By MGM/UA Home Video M700191

SHAKEDOWN

D: James Glickenhaus 96 m

R | ACT CRM | 1988 | COLOR

6 Two tough, streetwise guys, one a renegade cop and the other a burned-out legal aid attorney, team up to get rid of the corruption they suspect is running rampant in the New York Police Department. A drug dealer is charged with killing an undercover cop and Weller is the lawyer defending him. Elliott is an undercover cop who suspects that the police force is stealing money taken from drug dealers and has set the guy up. Together, the unlikely allies, the cop and the lawyer, struggle to get to the bottom of it all. This fast-paced action flick sports some incredible stunts, but is not too credible.

Sex Nud Viol Lang AdSit

A: Peter Weller, Sam Elliott, Patricia Charbonneau, Antonio Fargas, Blanche Baker, Richard Brooks

© MCA/UNIVERSAL HOME VIDEO, INC. 80820

SHARKY'S MACHINE

D: Burt Reynolds 123 m

R | CRM ACT SUS | 1981 | COLOR

10 Top-drawer cop film - one of the best. Sharkey (Reynolds) is a hardened Atlanta narcotics cop demoted to working in vice after a shootout-gone-bad. He is bored, but when a high-priced hooker turns out to have connections with some very bad and very powerful people who were involved in his earlier narcotics case, Sharky becomes very interested. He sets up a round-the-clock observation of the girl's apartment and becomes totally enraptured by her as he voyeristically watches her every move... but a ruthless assassin is on the prowl and she is his target. Intelligent, realistic, very high intensity action.

Sex Nud Viol Lang AdSit

A: Burt Reynolds, Vittorio Gassman, Brian Keith, Charles Durning, Rachel Ward, Vittorio Gassman

© WARNER HOME VIDEO 22024

SHOOT TO KILL

D: Roger Spottiswoode 109 m

R | SUS CRM ACT | 1988 | COLOR

8 Thrilling game of cat and mouse! A ruthless killer joins a group of campers so that he can avoid the police. The group is hiking through the picturesque Pacific Northwest and is being led by Kirstie Alley. When things don't go his way, he begins killing off members of the group. FBI agent Poitier is coming after him, but the FBI man is way out of his element in the wilds and must rely on Alley's rugged boyfriend (Berenger) for help to track them down. This pair mix like oil and water, but they begin to work together when the pressure rises after Alley is taken hostage. Good job by Poitier.

Sex Nud Viol Lang AdSit

A: Sidney Poitier, Tom Berenger, Kirstie Alley, Clancy Brown, Richard Masur, Andrew Robinson

© TOUCHSTONE HOME VIDEO 697

SILENCE OF THE LAMBS, THE

D: Jonathan Demme 118 m

R | SUS CRM ACT | 1991 | COLOR

9 Outstanding and deeply disturbing Oscar winner. Rookie FBI agent Starling (Foster) has been assigned the daunting task of helping to stop Buffalo Bill, a psycho serial killer who harvests his victim's skin. The key to finding Bill lies within the twisted mind of another brilliant serial killer, Hannibal the Cannibal, now serving time in a high security cell. Dr. Hannibal Lector (Hopkins) is also a brilliant psychiatrist and a master of manipulation. Hannibal knows Bill, but is fascinated with Starling and messes with her mind while she tries to get inside his. A magnificent, terrifying thriller. See MANHUNTER.

Sex Nud Viol Lang AdSit

A: Jodie Foster, Anthony Hopkins, Scott Glenn, Ted Levine, Anthony Heald, Brooke Smith

© ORION PICTURES CORPORATION 8767

SOLDIER'S STORY, A

D: Norman Jewison 102 m

PG | MYS CRM DMA | 1984 | COLOR

9 Powerful and riveting psychological drama and solid mystery. Set in the segregated Army of 1944, a proud black attorney from Washington is sent to a Louisiana military post to investigate the death of the master sergeant of an all-black unit. He could have been murdered by a white racist, but it could also have been any of the black men in his unit, all of whom hated him. This is a fascinating look into human nature and into the nature of those times. However, it is also a solid whodunit, with a wide assortment of characters, all with compelling reasons for wanting the man dead. Works well on many levels all at once. Sterling performances. Excellent.

Sex Nud Viol Lang AdSit

A: Howard E. Rollins, Jr., Adolph Caesar, Art Evans, Dennis Lipscomb, Denzel Washington, Patti LaBelle

© COLUMBIA TRISTAR HOME VIDEO 60408

SOMEONE TO WATCH OVER ME

D: Ridley Scott 106 m

R | SUS CRM ROM | 1987 | COLOR

8 Brightly polished thriller! An incredibly beautiful and rich member of the New York's social elite (Rogers) witnesses a gruesome murder that was committed by the mob. She escapes by the skin of her teeth, but is now being stalked by the ruthless killer (Katsulas). Berenger is a happily married cop who is assigned to protect her around the clock. In spite of themselves, the pair begin a passionate affair. When the killer is unsuccessful at nabbing Rogers directly, he kidnaps Berenger's wife and kids to hold hostage. Berenger is being forced to choose between them. A visually stunning, heart-stopping and atmospheric suspensor!

Sex Nud Viol Lang AdSit

A: Tom Berenger, Mimi Rogers, Lorraine Bracco, Jerry Orbach, John Rubinstein, Andreas Katsulas

© COLUMBIA TRISTAR HOME VIDEO 60877

SPEED

D: Jan De Bont 115 m

R | ACT SUS CRM | 1994 | COLOR

9 Extremely high-octane film that was a huge summer hit and won two Oscars for Sound. Jack Traven is a member of the LA police SWAT team. When he and his partner break up the well-laid plans of a psychotic ex-cop named Howard Payne to extract money from the city, Howard decides to try again. And, this time he makes a personal challenge to Jack to beat him. This time he has placed a bomb on a city bus that becomes armed at 50 mph and will blow if the bus goes below 50. Jack makes it to the bus, but the bomb is armed and he is being helped by pretty passenger who is now driving. Electric and tense. Very well made. In spite of its implausibilites, you almost never doubt it. Great fun.

Sex Nud Viol Lang AdSit

A: Keanu Reeves, Dennis Hopper, Sandra Bullock, Joe Morton, Jeff Daniels

© FOXVIDEO 8638

STAKEOUT

D: John Badham 115 m

R | COM CRM | 1987 | COLOR

8 A funny cop flick. Dreyfuss and Estevez are two undercover cops who derive great joy out of one-upping the other guy. They are given an "easy" assignment - simply to watch the girlfriend of a guy who has escaped from jail. The pair park their buns across the street and stakeout the subject, but she turns out to be beautiful. Dreyfuss falls in love with her and decides to pursue her! For Estevez, this this is the last straw. The charismatic pair works wonders on the screen in this hilarious buddy cop film.

Sex Nud Viol Lang AdSit

A: Emilio Estevez, Richard Dreyfuss, Madeleine Stowe, Aidan Quinn, Dan Lauria, Forest Whitaker

© TOUCHSTONE HOME VIDEO 596

STAND ALONE

D: Alan Beattie 94 m

R | ACT CRM | 1985 | COLOR

6 A dangerous showdown! An aging decorated war hero (Durning) decides to stand up against crime when he witnesses a murder committed by drug dealers in his neighborhood. He's had enough. Against the warnings of neighbors and friends, he teams up with police detective Keach to hunt the bad guys down. A lawyer counsels Durning not to risk his neck by testifying against the drug dealers - they can be ruthless and vindictive - but Durning decides that he's fed up with drugs in his neighborhood and decides to do whatever it takes to put 'em away.

Sex Nud Viol Lang AdSit

A: Charles Durning, Pam Grier, James Keach, Bert Remsen, Barbara Sammeth, Lu Leonard

© R&G VIDEO, LP 80177

STAR CHAMBER, THE

D: Peter Hyams 109 m

R | CRM ACT | 1982 | COLOR

8 The justice system is unraveling and criminals are going free! Frustrated by a system that allows criminals to ply their trade with impunity, in the knowledge that a smart lawyer can always get them off, and frustrated by having to be part of that system, an idealistic Superior Court Judge (Douglas) and some others decide to do something about it. They decide to pass out their own justice, with their own law. However, when two innocent men are knowingly marked by them for death, Douglas is forced to reevaluate. Intelligent and provocative drama that stings. Not an exploitive rip-off.

Sex Nud Viol Lang AdSit

A: Michael Douglas, Hal Holbrook, Sharon Gless, Yaphet Kotto, James Sikking, Joe Regalbuto

© CBS/FOX VIDEO 1295

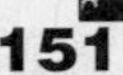

STATE OF GRACE

D: Phil Joanou 134 m

R | CRM DMA | 1990 | COLOR

Sex | Nud | Viol | Lang | AdSit

8 This is a grimly realistic portrait of the Irish gangsters and punks living in the tenements of Manhattan's Hell's Kitchen. Sean Penn is Terry Noonan, a graduate of the Kitchen, back home to reacquaint himself with old friends. Of particular interest to him are his former girlfriend (Robin Wright) and former best buddy Jackie Flannery (Gary Oldman). Terry asks Jackie if he can help him get a job with his brother Frankie, the local kingpin. Both brothers are psychopaths but Frankie is a cold-hearted manipulator while Jackie will literally do anything for his friends. Jackie gets Terry in, but Terry is an undercover cop. Extremely violent, but very believable.

A: Sean Penn, Ed Harris, Gary Oldman, Robin Wright, John C. Reilly, Burgess Meredith

© ORION PICTURES CORPORATION 8760

STORMY MONDAY

D: Mike Figgis 95 m

R | CRM ACT | 1987 | COLOR

Sex | Nud | Viol | Lang | AdSit

7 A slick British thriller! Sting owns a fashionable nightclub in economically depressed Newcastle, England. Ruthless American businessman Jones wants that property along with all the others so that he can demolish them, redevelop the neighborhood into a stylish area and make a killing. But when Jones doesn't get what he wants easily, he decides to use violence to get things done. Sean Bean, who works for Sting, and his girlfriend Melanie Griffith help Sting to retaliate in kind. A well acted, slightly offbeat, atmospheric, suspense-filled modern-day (late '80s) film noir.

A: Melanie Griffith, Tommy Lee Jones, Sting, Sean Bean, James Cosmo, Mark Long

© GOODTIMES 4031

STREET SMART

D: Jerry Schatzberg 97 m

R | CRM SUS | 1987 | COLOR

Sex | Nud | Viol | Lang | AdSit

6 Corruption, greed and murder meld together in this taut crime drama. Reeve is an unscrupulous magazine reporter in need of a sensational story. So he concocts a front-page story about a New York pimp living high on the hog. When a real-life pimp named Fast Black (Freeman), who resembles the man in the story, is implicated in a murder, Reeve's secure world is threatened. Freeman desperately needs an alibi and Reeve is it. Suddenly, he is embroiled in a murder case and in deep trouble, but he gets help from one of Fast Black's hookers (Baker).

A: Christopher Reeve, Morgan Freeman, Mimi Rogers, Kathy Baker, Jay Patterson, Andre Gregory

© CANNON VIDEO M930

STRIKING DISTANCE

D: Rowdy Herrington 102 m

R | ACT MYS CRM | 1993 | COLOR

Sex | Nud | Viol | Lang | AdSit

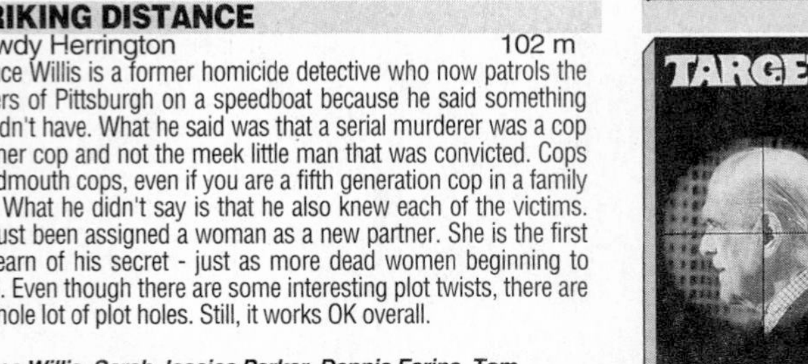

6 Bruce Willis is a former homicide detective who now patrols the rivers of Pittsburgh on a speedboat because he said something he shouldn't have. What he said was that a serial murderer was a cop or a former cop and not the meek little man that was convicted. Cops don't badmouth cops, even if you are a fifth generation cop in a family of cops. What he didn't say is that he also knew each of the victims. He has just been assigned a woman as a new partner. She is the first one to learn of his secret - just as more dead women beginning to show up. Even though there are some interesting plot twists, there are also a whole lot of plot holes. Still, it works OK overall.

A: Bruce Willis, Sarah Jessica Parker, Dennis Farina, Tom Sizemore, Brian James, Robert Pastorelli

© COLUMBIA TRISTAR HOME VIDEO 53683

ST. VALENTINE'S DAY MASSACRE

D: Roger Corman 100 m

NR | CRM ACT | 1967 | COLOR

Sex | Nud | Viol | Lang | AdSit

7 A vividly graphic and explosively violent recreation of the gangland massacre that occurred in Chicago in 1929. Al Capone (Robards) and Bugsy Moran (Meeker) are rivals who start a gang war over control of the Windy City, a war that ends in Capone's favor. Capone and his men are thought to have staged the famous garage massacre to wipe out their opposition, but Capone, amazingly enough, gets off scott-free and is never proven to be the man behind the bloodbath. Told in semi-documentary format, the film is accurate, brutal and intense.

A: Jason Robards, Jr., George Segal, Ralph Meeker, Jean Hale, Clint Ritchie, Frank Silvera

© FOXVIDEO 1153

SUDDEN IMPACT

D: Clint Eastwood 117 m

R | ACT CRM | 1983 | COLOR

Sex | Nud | Viol | Lang | AdSit

8 Fourth entry in the DIRTY HARRY formula and the movie which gave the expression "Go ahead, make my day" new meaning. Harry is assigned to investigate a series of murders in which low-lifes have each been methodically shot in the forehead and in the the genitals. The maverick cop discovers a lead taking him to artist Sondra Locke who, along with her sister, was gang raped years before. Now she's is reaping revenge. How will Harry handle this "villian" whose tactics aren't that different from his own? Hard-hitting action flick with glimpses of humor.

A: Clint Eastwood, Sondra Locke, Pat Hingle, Bradford Dillman, Paul Duke, Jack Thibeau

© WARNER HOME VIDEO 11341

SUSPECT

D: Peter Yates 101 m

R | SUS CRM | 1987 | COLOR

Sex | Nud | Viol | Lang | AdSit

8 Highly entertaining. Cher has a seemingly impossible task at hand. As a public defender, she has been assigned to prove a deaf and mute, homeless Vietnam vet (Neeson) is innocent of a grisly crime. She finds some unexpected help when one of the jurors (Quaid) contacts her directly. This is highly improper and puts her career in jeopardy, but he has evidence that is so compelling and dangerous that there is no choice but to work with him. Their job is made even more difficult by the stubborn judge, a corrupt senator and a prosecutor with an attitude. Stellar performances all around.

A: Dennis Quaid, Cher, Liam Neeson, John Mahoney, Joe Mantegna, Philip Bosco

© COLUMBIA TRISTAR HOME VIDEO 67002

TAKING OF PELHAM ONE TWO THREE, THE

D: Joseph Sargent 115 m

R | SUS CRM ACT | 1974 | COLOR

Sex | Nud | Viol | Lang | AdSit

8 Outstanding action thriller. Four ruthless terrorists, led by a thoroughly convincing Robert Shaw, hijack a loaded commuter train in the Bronx subway system. They demand to receive $1 million within one hour or they will start killing passengers one-by-one. Matthau is terrific as the gum-chewing transit chief of security who has to deal with them, the police and a vast government bureaucracy. Very fast-paced, interspersed with intense, high-speed action and cynical comedy relief. First-rate performances, accented by a pulse-pounding score. Excellent.

A: Walter Matthau, Robert Shaw, Martin Balsam, Hector Elizondo, Tony Roberts, Jerry Stiller

Distributed By MGM/UA Home Video M301524

TANGO & CASH

D: Andrei Konchalovsky 104 m

R | ACT CRM | 1989 | COLOR

Sex | Nud | Viol | Lang | AdSit

6 Wisecracking rivalry! Two Los Angeles cops each are convinced that they're the best there is. They are constant rivals even though they work together. That is until they are framed for a crime and sent to prison, then they join forces to become a powerful team. Jack Palance is the center of their troubles. He's the irritated drug kingpin that put them in the slammer because both were getting too close to his lucrative drug business. Stallone is a cop works strictly by the book but Russell flies by the seat of his pants - a volatile combination. Very predictable but OK.

A: Sylvester Stallone, Kurt Russell, Jack Palance, Brion James, James Hong, Michael J. Pollard

© WARNER HOME VIDEO 11951

TARGETS

D: Peter Bogdanovich 90 m

PG | SUS CRM | 1968 | COLOR

Sex | Nud | Viol | Lang | AdSit

8 Chilling debut for director Peter Bogdanovich. This film has a dual plotline which comes together only at the end. An aging actor in horror movies (Karloff) decides to retire rather than compete with the horrors occurring every day in the real world; and a seemingly normal Vietnam veteran (O'Kelly) loses control and murders his family. Later O'Kelly stations himself high in the screen of a drive-in movie theater and begins to take random shots at the patrons - one of whom is Karloff, there on a promotion stint. Intense suspense builds at the rousing conclusion.

A: Boris Karloff, Tim O'Kelly, Randy Quaid, Nancy Hsueh, James Brown, Arthur Peterson

© PARAMOUNT HOME VIDEO 6824

TEQUILA SUNRISE

D: Robert Towne 116 m

R | ACT ROM CRM | 1988 | COLOR

Sex | Nud | Viol | Lang | AdSit

8 Good, spicy action flick, with some major Hollywood star power. The lives of two best friends from high school have gone in drastically different directions and are now seemingly headed headlong into conflict. Kurt Russell is an up-and-coming narcotics cop. Mel Gibson is basically a good guy but he has also become a major-league drug dealer and is now trying to get out of a nasty business. Russell is doing his best to try to catch Gibson. Between these two, in an involved plot, is sultry Michelle Pfeiffer, a beautiful restaurant owner whom they both love. Good action and well-paced with appealing stars.

A: Mel Gibson, Michelle Pfeiffer, Kurt Russell, Raul Julia, Arliss Howard

© WARNER HOME VIDEO 11821

THIEF

D: Michael Mann 124 m

R | CRM ACT | 1981 | COLOR

Sex | Nud | Viol | Lang | AdSit

8 Interesting character study of an interesting character. After 11 years in prison, master thief James Caan is determined to create a normal life for himself. He is basically a decent sort of guy with normal dreams. So he gets married, buys a house and has kids, but they are all expensive and he is concerned that he may lose them. His reputation as a master thief has caught the attention of mob boss Prosky, who is pressuring Caan to work with him. Caan sees an opportunity for one last big job that will cement his life. Gripping, detailed and well-crafted.

A: James Caan, Willie Nelson, Tuesday Weld, Tom Signorelli, Robert Prosky, James Belushi

Distributed By MGM/UA Home Video M201305

THIN BLUE LINE, THE

D: Errol Morris 101 m

NR | DOC CRM | 1988 | COLOR | Sex Nud Viol Lang AdSit

8 Fascinating documentary investigation into the conviction of Randall Adams, a hitchhiker, for the 1976 murder of a Dallas policeman. He was sentenced to death based largely upon the testimony of runaway David Harris, who was later convicted of another murder. Director Errol Morris, who formerly was a private detective, became interested in the case. Through a series of interviews and recreations, which he presents in this documentary, he created so much doubt about the nature of the facts that convicted Adams that he was eventually released.

A:

© HBO VIDEO 0177

THUNDERHEART

D: Michael Apted 118 m

R | MYS CRM | 1992 | COLOR | Sex Nud Viol Lang AdSit

9 Compelling and totally engrossing mystery. Kilmer stars as a hotshot FBI agent who is chosen, because he is part Sioux, to accompany veteran agent Sam Shepard to the Pine Ridge Indian Reservation and investigate a murder. However, his Indian blood gives him no advantage in the investigation. The locals just mock him, calling him a Washington Redskin. However, his encounters with the local sheriff (Green) and religious leader (Thin Elk) teach him things about his own past and he begins to suspect that the government has framed an innocent man. See also the documentary by the same director: INCIDENT AT OGLALA.

A: Val Kilmer, Sam Shepard, Fred Ward, Graham Greene, John Trudell, Chief Ted Thin Elk

© COLUMBIA TRISTAR HOME VIDEO 70693

TIGHTROPE

D: Richard Tuggle 118 m

R | CRM ACT DMA | 1984 | COLOR | Sex Nud Viol Lang AdSit

9 Fascinating thriller which also has a compelling underlying story. Eastwood is a burned-out homicide detective. He has been deserted by his wife and is taking care of his two daughters. He has also taken to having kinky sex with the prostitutes on his beat, handcuffing them. When these same girls start to turn up dead, Eastwood realizes that he is being followed and that he and his daughters are in big danger. It is an intelligent script which allows Eastwood to analyze the dichotomy within his character, but it never forgets to be an action flick and refrains from exploitation.

A: Clint Eastwood, Genevieve Bujold, Dan Hedaya, Alison Eastwood, Jennifer Beck

© WARNER HOME VIDEO 11400

TIME AFTER TIME

D: Nicholas Meyer 112 m

PG | SF CRM | 1979 | COLOR | Sex Nud Viol Lang AdSit

8 Very imaginative and engaging story that is quite literate and very enjoyable in spite of its apparently bizarre premise. H.G. Welles (Malcolm McDowell) is compelled to chase Jack the Ripper (David Warner) into the future after the Ripper uses Welles's time machine to escape from Victorian England. The future he escapes to is San Francisco in 1979. Welles and the Ripper engage in a lively battle of wits in an environment that is totally alien to both of them. An amusing and engaging subplot is Welles's burgeoning romance with a modern-day bank teller (Mary Steenburgen).

A: David Warner, Mary Steenburgen, Malcolm McDowell, Charles Cioffi, Joseph Maher, Patti D'Arbanville

© WARNER HOME VIDEO 22017

TO LIVE AND DIE IN L.A.

D: William Friedkin 114 m

R | ACT SUS CRM | 1985 | COLOR | Sex Nud Viol Lang AdSit

8 High intensity action fare that is both riveting and disturbing. Secret Service Agent Petersen becomes obsessed with getting master counterfeiter Willem Dafoe, who had caused the death of his partner. A very cynical and violent film in which the good guys are only just a little better than the bad guys. The characters are complex and the story is loaded with a lot of twists and exciting action sequences. The problem that arises is that it becomes very difficult to determine which side to sympathize with or to even care about anyone at all.

A: William L. Petersen, Willem Dafoe, John Pankow, Dean Stockwell, John Turturro

© LIVE HOME VIDEO VA5123

TOUCH OF EVIL

D: Orson Welles 108 m

NR | CRM SUS ACT | 1958 | B&W | Sex Nud Viol Lang AdSit

9 A seriously underrated film from Orson Welles - who wrote, directed and starred in it - that is essentially a fascinating character study. When a powerful American and his mistress are blown up at a Mexican border town, Welles, a corrupt American sheriff, blames the murder on a young Mexican and plants evidence on him to insure conviction. An honest Mexican cop (Heston) disputes the claim, so Welles frames Heston's American wife (Leigh) with murder and drugs and terrorizes her. Very famous three-minute continuous shot at beginning.

A: Charlton Heston, Janet Leigh, Orson Welles, Joseph Calleia, Akim Tamiroff, Marlene Dietrich

© MCA/UNIVERSAL HOME VIDEO, INC. 55078

TRUE BELIEVER

D: Joseph Ruben 103 m

R | CRM SUS | 1989 | COLOR | Sex Nud Viol Lang AdSit

8 Taut and fierce - a fast ride! A powerful attorney (Woods), once a crusading idealist in the '60s, is now a wealthy but cynical defender of drug dealers. His assistant (Downey) worships him and, in an effort to revitalize him, convinces him to take on an almost impossible case - get a convicted killer who was framed out of prison. Reluctantly at first, Woods takes the case. He finds himself up to his neck in corrupt cops and politicians, but he also rediscovers a passion for his work once again. Highly entertaining build-up to a powerful conclusion that will take you by surprise.

A: James Woods, Robert Downey, Jr., Margaret Colin, Kurtwood Smith, Yuji Okumoto, Tom Bower

© COLUMBIA TRISTAR HOME VIDEO 65012

TRUE ROMANCE

D: Tony Scott 121 m

R | CRM DMA | 1993 | COLOR | Sex Nud Viol Lang AdSit

7 This is no WUTHERING HEIGHTS. The romance here is between a ditzy novice call girl named Alabama and an not-too-bright Elvis-admirer named Clarence, who was only her third-ever trick. When Clarence learns that her pimp has threatened her, Clarence goes to gain her freedom back. However, in the process, he kills the pimp and accidentally picks up the wrong suitcase - this one has a major shipment of cocaine in it. Clarence and Alabama head off to California with their treasure and with the mob and the cops on their trail. A very violent movie that has occasional stabs at black comedy thrown in. Not a pretty portrait of people, but one that is perversely believable.

A: Christian Slater, Patricia Arquette, Dennis Hopper, Val Kilmer, Gary Oldman, Brad Pitt

© WARNER HOME VIDEO 13158

TURNER AND HOOCH

D: Roger Spottiswoode 110 m

PG | COM CRM ACT | 1989 | COLOR | Sex Nud Viol Lang AdSit

6 Hanks is a quirky California cop with a compulsion for cleanliness who is assigned to uncover a murderer in a drug-related case. And, he inherits the only witness to the murder - the victim's really ugly, really big dog! Hooch is a mess, and messes up everything around him, including chewing up the upholstery of Hanks's car after he leaves the dog inside it. Hanks's natural charm, along with that of the curious canine, works reasonably well at holding our attention in this very mild comedy as the pair are put through their paces while solving the crime and coincidentally discovering romance too.

A: Tom Hanks, Mare Winningham, Craig T. Nelson, Reginald VelJohnson, Scott Paulin, J.C. Quinn

© TOUCHSTONE HOME VIDEO 911

TWO JAKES, THE

D: Jack Nicholson 137 m

R | CRM MYS | 1990 | COLOR | Sex Nud Viol Lang AdSit

6 Involved and convoluted follow-up to CHINATOWN. It's now ten years later. Jake (Nicholson) is a war hero. He owns a successful detective agency and is a member of the country club. Against his better judgment, he accepts a divorce job to spy on the wife (Tilly) of another Jake, who is a shady land developer (Keitel). Shortly into his investigation, Keitel's partner is murdered. It is pretty obvious Keitel did it and now our Jake's right in the middle. Very convoluted, but if you rent CHINATOWN first to provide a basis for what you will see here, you'll enjoy it - but pay attention.

A: Jack Nicholson, Harvey Keitel, Meg Tilly, Madeleine Stowe, Ruben Blades, Eli Wallach

© PARAMOUNT HOME VIDEO 1854

UNDER SUSPICION

D: Simon Moore 100 m

R | SUS CRM | 1992 | COLOR | Sex Nud Viol Lang AdSit

7 Well-made thriller from England. In 1959 England, divorces could only be obtained through proof of adultery. Neeson was a cop but now is a sleazy PI scraping up a living by setting up scenes of faked adultery to photograph for a fee - many times using his own wife. On one such escapade, he breaks into a room on que but finds his wife and her male companion have been shot dead. He becomes the chief suspect. With the help of an old friend, he struggles to prove himself innocent. But wait, the story's not that simple. Several neat twists keep you guessing. Even when you think it's over, it's not. Over-all, pretty good, but it does stretch credibility at times.

A: Liam Neeson, Laura San Giacomo, Kenneth Cranham, Alphonsia Emmanuel, Maggie O'Neill, Martin Grace

© COLUMBIA TRISTAR HOME VIDEO 51133

UNDERWORLD U.S.A.

D: Samuel Fuller 99 m

NR | CRM ACT | 1960 | B&W | Sex Nud Viol Lang AdSit

6 A young boy (Robertson) witnesses the brutal murder of his father by four up-and-coming mobsters. From that moment on, he decides to dedicate his life to taking revenge on the four and becomes a gangster himself to gain access into their world, even when it means going to prison. He infiltrates the mob, rises to the top and then locates the three hoods who are still alive. Then federal agents come to him looking for cooperation and he sees the perfect opportunity to gain his revenge by using the government to get what he wants most. All that is fine, except first he has to survive.

A: Cliff Robertson, Dolores Dorn, Beatrice Coll, Larry Gates, Paul Dubov

© COLUMBIA TRISTAR HOME VIDEO 60918

UNLAWFUL ENTRY

D: Jonathan Kaplan — 110 m

R | CRM ACT | 1992 | COLOR

8 What happens when a psychotic bad cop uses all the power of the system against you? Kurt Russell and Madeleine Stowe are happily married and about to enter into a lucrative new business when their plush house is broken into. Ray Liotta is one of the cops who responds to the call. He is very helpful, and at first they think he is a friend, but he is in fact totally obsessed with Stowe. He is determined to win her away from Russell by showing her how weak Russell is compared to him. He uses his police access to their records to systematically terrorize and destroy their relationship. Very well acted and convincingly done, but also explicit and very violent.

Sex · Nud · Viol · Lang · AdSit

A: Kurt Russell, Madeleine Stowe, Ray Liotta, Roger E. Mosley, Ken Lerner, Deborah Offner

© FOXVIDEO 1977

UNTOUCHABLES, THE

D: Brian De Palma — 119 m

R | CRM ACT SUS | 1987 | COLOR

10 Outstanding! Some great talent combines forces to create a captivating high-energy excitement adventure set in prohibition-era Chicago. Costner is Elliot Ness, a very intense straight-arrow federal agent who arrives in a corrupt town, intent upon "getting" Al Capone (De Niro). He quickly sets about finding a few good men for his private force - beginning with a tough street cop (Connery - Oscar winner). Also included is an idealistic rookie (Garcia) and a bookish agent (Smith). A well-woven, realistic tapestry of drama, intrigue, suspense and high-intensity action. Highly recommended.

Sex · Nud · Viol · Lang · AdSit

A: Kevin Costner, Sean Connery, Robert De Niro, Charles Martin Smith, Andy Garcia, Billy Drago

© PARAMOUNT HOME VIDEO 1886

WALKING TALL

D: Phil Karlson — 126 m

R | ACT CRM | 1973 | COLOR

7 Very popular but very violent revenge film in which a Tennessee man gets elected sheriff (Baker) by vowing to take back his town from corrupt politicians. He sets out to wage his war by ruthlessly swinging a baseball bat. This film was based upon a real-life character who ironically was later voted out of office because of his tough tactics, a fact the movie chooses to ignore. Spawned two lesser sequels and a TV series.

Sex · Nud · Viol · Lang · AdSit

A: Joe Don Baker, Elizabeth Hartman, Noah Beery, Jr., Gene Evans, Brenda Benet, John Brascia

© LIVE HOME VIDEO LA9500

WHISPERS IN THE DARK

D: Crowe Christopher — 103 m

R | SUS MYS CRM | 1992 | COLOR

7 Supersexy murder mystery. A beautiful patient (Unger) reports her vivid and provocative sexual encounters with bondage to her female psychiatrist (Sciorra). Sciorra is distressed to learn her own new boyfriend (Sheridan) knows Unger. Is he the man of her torrid stories? ...or is it another of her patients, one who was just released from prison for torturing women? That question becomes critical when Unger is found hanging bound, naked and very dead. Good plot twists and effective murder mystery despite some flaws, but the overt sexuality will diminish it for many.

Sex · Nud · Viol · Lang · AdSit

A: Annabella Sciorra, Jamey Sheridan, Deborah Unger, Alan Alda, Anthony Lapaglia, Jill Clayburgh

© PARAMOUNT HOME VIDEO 32756

WHITE MISCHIEF

D: Michael Radford — 108 m

R | DMA CRM | 1988 | COLOR

7 Elegantly filmed, sensuous, scandalous, bizarre-but-true story. It's 1940 and England is being bombed to pieces at the outset of WWII. An aging colonialist from Kenya, in need of a wife, has returned to England and married ravishing Gretta Sacchi. All she really wanted was the money and the title, but when she arrives back in Kenya's Happy Valley, she discovers a decadent lifestyle of elegant parties, drugs, drinking and wife-swapping. The world outside is ignored. She has a passionate affair with a handsome young man who is later found dead. Very naughty, voyeuristic and sexy.

Sex · Nud · Viol · Lang · AdSit

A: Greta Scacchi, Charles Dance, Sarah Miles, John Hurt, Trevor Howard, Hugh Grant

© NEW LINE HOME VIDEO 7724

WITNESS

D: Peter Weir — 112 m

R | CRM ROM ACT | 1985 | COLOR

10 Terrific. A young Amish widow (McGillis) and her son (Hass) travel to the city, but while they are waiting at the train station, the boy is a witness to a murder. John Book (Ford) is a jaded big city cop who wins over their confidence. However, they all get in big trouble when the boy identifies the murderer as being a narcotics cop (Glover). Ford is then shot and takes them back to their rustic home where he stays on to recover and hide with them. But, he is out of place as a hard-edged city boy dressed in simple Amish clothes, he is falling for McGillis, and the corrupt cops are coming to get them all. Romantic, thrilling and funny. This is a real winner.

Sex · Nud · Viol · Lang · AdSit

A: Harrison Ford, Kelly McGillis, Josef Sommer, Lukas Haas, Jan Rubes, Alexander Godunov

© PARAMOUNT HOME VIDEO 1736

WITNESS FOR THE PROSECUTION

D: Billy Wilder — 116 m

NR | MYS CRM | 1957 | B&W

10 Absolutely wonderful screen adaptation of one of Agatha Christie's best mysteries and one of the best courtroom dramas ever. An aging barrister (Laughton) is called from retirement to defend a married man (Power) who is accused of murdering a wealthy woman that he had been seeing. He claims he didn't do it, but the only witness he has is his icy wife (Dietrich), and she has testified that he is guilty. Wonderful performances (Dietrich's last), more plot twists than a bag of pretzels and a startling ending. Excellent - don't miss it! Four Academy Award nominations.

Sex · Nud · Viol · Lang · AdSit

A: Marlene Dietrich, Tyrone Power, Charles Laughton, Elsa Lanchester, John Williams, Henry Daniell

Distributed By MGM/UA Home Video M202517

WRONG ARM OF THE LAW, THE

D: Cliff Owen — 94 m

NR | COM CRM | 1962 | B&W

7 Silly farce of the variety that made Sellers famous. He plays Pearly Gates, the leader of a Cockney band of thieves that is so prosperous that it has set up a welfare-like system to take care of its members. All that is threatened now because each time they carry off a heist, they are confronted by a group of cops that confiscates everything. The problem is that these guys are not really cops. So Pearly calls a conference between the real cops and the other hoods, and they all agree to call a truce and cooperate long enough to get these cop/thieves put in jail. Wacky and zany, wild fun.

Sex · Nud · Viol · Lang · AdSit

A: Peter Sellers, Lionel Jeffries, Bernard Cribbins, Nanette Newman, Davey Kaye

© MONTEREY HOME VIDEO 34860

WRONG MAN, THE

D: Alfred Hitchcock — 105 m

NR | SUS MYS CRM | 1956 | B&W

7 A harrowing and ultimately terrifying Hitchcock movie - because it is so believable, because it is based upon a true event and because it could happen to you, too. Henry Fonda plays a New York jazz musician who is confronted at his home by police, arrested, fingerprinted, jailed and tried for a series of crimes he didn't commit because there were eye witnesses who swore he was the culprit. And, before the look-alike crook is found, even his wife comes to believe he is guilty. She has a nervous breakdown and is institutionalized. Compelling but unnerving to watch.

Sex · Nud · Viol · Lang · AdSit

A: Henry Fonda, Vera Miles, Anthony Quayle, Harold J. Stone, Nehemiah Persoff, Esther Minciotti

© WARNER HOME VIDEO 11155

Documentary

Video's Best

DOC

1956 and After

35 UP

D: Michael Apted — 127 m

NR · DOC · 1991 · COLOR

Sex · Nud · Viol · Lang · AdSit

9 In 1963, Director Michael Apted documented the lives and circumstances of fourteen selected English 7-year-olds and he has returned to review their individual situations every seven years since. Now 35 years old, this is a fascinating and revealing portrait of these same people as we witness their lives again seven more years later and as we watch them again change right before our eyes. This particular entry in the series, as were the others before it, was filmed for British TV and was preceeded by 28 UP, which is also available on video.

A:

© ACADEMY ENTERTAINMENT 1705

AMERICAN DREAM

D: Barbara Kopple — 98 m

PG-13 · DOC · 1991 · COLOR

Sex · Nud · Viol · Lang · AdSit

8 1991's winner of the Oscar for Best Documentary. It is a perceptive postmortem examination of a very divisive labor strike. In 1984 the Hormel Company declared a profit but still asked its workers at a Minnesota plant to accept a significant pay cut. This precipitated a long and bitter strike that pitted virtually everyone against everyone. The national union refused to support the local's call for a strike, and management called for outside workers to replace the union people - and had the National Guard protect them. Townspeople and families were set against each other in a very deep and very bitter battle.

A:

© HBO VIDEO 90811

ANIMALS ARE BEAUTIFUL PEOPLE

D: Jamie Uys — 92 m

G · DOC · CLD · 1974 · COLOR

Sex · Nud · Viol · Lang · AdSit

8 This fun documentary was made by the maker of THE GODS MUST BE CRAZY. It is a humorous and interesting review of the animals of the deserts and the jungles of Africa. It covers all the animals from the largest to the smallest using sharp portraits that remain interesting and do not become too cute. Examples include such things as the mother fish who hides her babies in her mouth, and the "good time" that some elephants and other animals have when they eat the well-fermented Marula tree berries.

A:

© WARNER HOME VIDEO 11105

BEACH BOYS, THE - AN AMERICAN BAND

D: — 103 m

PG-13 · MUS · DOC · 1985 · COLOR

Sex · Nud · Viol · Lang · AdSit

6 This is the "authorized," therefore somewhat sanitized, story of the rock 'n roll group with the happy California sun-filled beach sound who, along with the English invasion of groups like The Beatles in the early 60s, came to mark the beginning of a significant change in the direction of rock 'n roll music. The Beach Boys had been an American institution for 25 years by the time this film was made and it is primarily a celebration of their brand of music. It contains over 40 original songs and lots of behind-the-scenes footage. However, none of the band's troubles behind the glamour is discussed.

A: The Beach Boys

© LIVE HOME VIDEO VA5080

BEST BOY

D: Ira Wohl — 105 m

DOC · DMA · 1981 · COLOR

Sex · Nud · Viol · Lang · AdSit

8 This is the moving real-life story of Philly, a 52-year-old retarded man and it won an Oscar for Best Documentary. Philly has been living at home with his parents ever since he was born, but now his parents are very old. His cousin Ira has become concerned about what will happen to Philly. So he talks Philly's parents into letting him help Philly to learn how to become more independent. This is a film that documents his efforts to do just that. Contrary to being a depressing film, Philly's enthusiasm and joy at accomplishing even the littlest tasks is contagious. A heart-warming, uplifting film. Recommended.

A:

© TAPEWORM VIDEO 1020

BRIEF HISTORY OF TIME

D: Errol Morris — 84 m

G · DOC · 1992 · COLOR

Sex · Nud · Viol · Lang · AdSit

8 Stephen Hawking has one of the most brilliant minds the modern world has known. Yet, that fact wasn't fully appreciated until he was stricken with a devastatingly crippling disease, ALS. The disease has left that mind trapped in a useless shell of a body and confined to a wheelchair. However, it was only then that he began to truly become productive with his mind, and he now endlessly contemplates the subtleties and vastness of space and time from his wheelchair. This documentary combines an anecdotal biography of his life with a discussion of a major part of his life's work: What is the nature of time and is it infinite? Fascinating stuff. It requires your attention but not a PHD in physics.

A:

© PARAMOUNT HOME VIDEO 83100

BRING ON THE NIGHT

D: Michael Apted — 90 m

PG-13 · MUS · DOC · 1986 · COLOR

Sex · Nud · Viol · Lang · AdSit

7 This is an interesting behind the scenes look at Sting and his band for his fans. It allows you to meet each one individually and to watch them while they are creating, rehearsing, meeting the press, performing and dealing with their own private lives.

A: Sting

© WARNER HOME VIDEO 344

CHICKEN RANCH

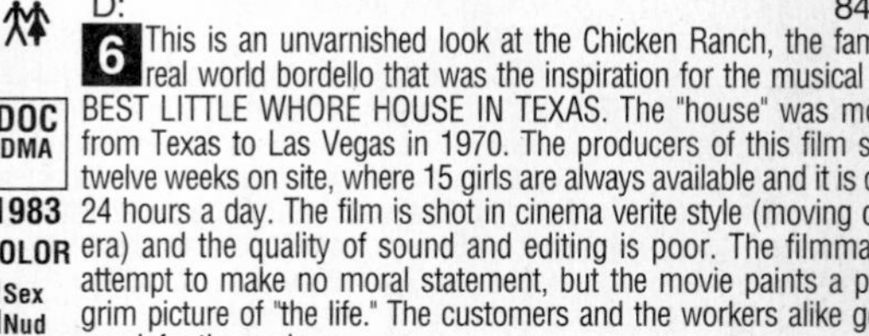

D: — 84 m

DOC · DMA · 1983 · COLOR

Sex · Nud · Viol · Lang · AdSit

6 This is an unvarnished look at the Chicken Ranch, the famous real world bordello that was the inspiration for the musical THE BEST LITTLE WHORE HOUSE IN TEXAS. The "house" was moved from Texas to Las Vegas in 1970. The producers of this film spent twelve weeks on site, where 15 girls are always available and it is open 24 hours a day. The film is shot in cinema verite style (moving camera) and the quality of sound and editing is poor. The filmmakers attempt to make no moral statement, but the movie paints a pretty grim picture of "the life." The customers and the workers alike get to speak for themselves.

A:

© LIVE HOME VIDEO VA3052

CHUCK BERRY HAIL HAIL! ROCK 'N' ROLL

D: Taylor Hackford — 121 m

PG | DOC MUS | 1987 | COLOR

10 If you like classic rock 'n roll, you've got to see this movie. Chuck Berry, the father of rock 'n roll, had his sixtieth birthday tribute concert in St. Louis at the Fox Theatre - and this is it. Singing back-up are some of the greatest singers and stylists of classic and '80s rock 'n roll. Berry sings all of his greatest songs including: "Maybellene," "Memphis," "Nadine" and "Roll Over Beethoven."

☐ Sex ☐ Nud ☐ Viol ☐ Lang ☐ AdSit

A: Chuck Berry, Keith Richards, Eric Clapton, Robert Cray, Etta James, Julian Lennon

© MCA/UNIVERSAL HOME VIDEO, INC. 80465

COMPLEAT BEATLES, THE

D: — 119 m

NR | DOC MUS | 1984 | B&W

9 A fascinating documentary, even to non-Beatle fans. It is an extensive and quite entertaining look at the evolution and promotion of an international phenomenon. It documents their very earliest beginnings, the changes they underwent and all the people involved in their creation and promotion; and, it is punctuated with a very liberal use of actual interviews, newsreel footage and concert excerpts - including their US tour. The primary focus is on their development - from the early days as "The Quarrymen", through their maturation to more complex music, to their breakup after the 1969 film LET IT BE.

☐ Sex ☐ Nud ☐ Viol ☐ Lang ☐ AdSit

A: The Beatles

Distributed By MGM/UA Home Video M700166

CONCERT FOR BANGLADESH, THE

D: Saul Swimmer — 90 m

G | MUS DOC | 1971 | COLOR

9 In August 1971 at Madison Square Garden, former Beatle George Harrison put on a benefit concert to raise money to help the starving people of Bangladesh. It was a huge rock concert that gained international recognition and support. This is a straight-forward recording of that concert. Lots of great rock music from many giants of the period, but you might want to fast-forward through a long stretch of Ravi Shankar's sitar music if you aren't a fan.

☐ Sex ☐ Nud ☐ Viol ☐ Lang ☐ AdSit

A: George Harrison, Bob Dylan, Eric Clapton, Ringo Starr, Leon Russell, Ravi Shankar

© PARAMOUNT HOME VIDEO 15167

DEAR AMERICA: LETTERS HOME FROM VIETNAM

D: Bill Couturie — 84 m

PG | DOC DMA WAR | 1988 | COLOR

9 An extremely moving and powerful documentary. This is a non-political, award-winning documentary which examines the Vietnam War from the soldier's perspective. Actual letters, written home at the time, are read by numerous prominent actors and are accompanied by '60s music, news footage, still photographs, and even home movies. This is a gut-wrenchingly presentation of the personal face of war. It is neither politicized nor glamorized, only human. Originally made-for-TV and later released to theaters.

☐ Sex ☐ Nud ☑ Viol ☑ Lang ☑ AdSit

A:

© HBO VIDEO 0207

ELVIS: THAT'S THE WAY IT IS

D: Dennis Sanders — 109 m

G | DOC MUS | 1970 | COLOR

8 Excellent documentary made in 1970 of Elvis's preparations for a run in the Las Vegas International Hotel. Well filmed, with numerous excerpts of Elvis offstage and rehearsing. Also interspersed are numerous interviews of various backstage people, fans and musicians. The film culminates with his opening night act which includes "All Shook Up," "Blue Suede Shoes" and "Bridge Over Troubled Waters." 27 songs in all.

☐ Sex ☐ Nud ☐ Viol ☐ Lang ☐ AdSit

A: Elvis Presley

Distributed By MGM/UA Home Video M700373

ENDLESS SUMMER, THE

D: Bruce Brown — 90 m

NR | DOC COM | 1964 | COLOR

8 This is a perennial favorite and has not diminished with time. It is an extraordinarily fun documentary that captures the exhilaration and danger of surfing through beautiful photography of people in beautiful locations. It is a quasi-travelogue loosely patterned around the quest of two young surfers to find the perfect wave by exploring all the world's most famous beaches. Whimsically narrated by director Bruce Brown. In 1994, 30 years later, Brown retraced the steps in this documentary in ENDLESS SUMMER II.

☐ Sex ☐ Nud ☐ Viol ☐ Lang ☐ AdSit

A:

© TURNER HOME ENTERTAINMENT N4028

ENDLESS SUMMER II

D: Bruce Brown — 110 m

PG | DOC COM | 1994 | COLOR

9 In 1964 director Bruce Brown created a now classic documentary in which two young surfers decided to follow the summer and the waves to all the places around the world where they could surf. Now, thirty years later, Brown goes back on the road again to retrace those footsteps, and it's even more fun than before. This is a very entertaining travelogue in which Brown narrates their trip with clever and funny dialogue. The photography is absolutely outstanding. He photographs surfing on big waves, on small waves, on almost no waves and on HUGE waves. He photographs it from in front of the waves, from behind the waves, on top of the wave, inside the wave and under the wave. Radical dude.

☐ Sex ☑ Nud ☐ Viol ☐ Lang ☐ AdSit

A: Robert "Wingnut" Weaver, Patrick O'Connell

© TURNER HOME ENTERTAINMENT N4052

GIMME SHELTER

D: — 91 m

PG | DOC MUS | 1970 | COLOR

7 Critically acclaimed, but disturbing, documentary of the 1969 Rolling Stone concert tour of America, with particular focus upon a free concert at Altamount Speedway that resulted in chaos and an off-camera knifing and murder. The Hells Angels were hired as security for the event. Stones perform some of their best songs including "Brown Sugar," but the film is more a disturbing display of the drug culture of the 1960s.

☐ Sex ☐ Nud ☑ Viol ☑ Lang ☑ AdSit

A: The Rolling Stones, Jefferson Airplane, Tina Turner

© ABKCO VIDEO 1001-3

GIZMO

D: — 76 m

G | DOC COM | 1980 | B&W

8 Funny documentary revealing America's passion for zany inventions. Footage was largely gleaned from newsreels dating back to the '30s. The inventions include a dimple making machine, wet diaper alarms and an anti-snore device.

☐ Sex ☐ Nud ☐ Viol ☐ Lang ☐ AdSit

A:

© WARNER HOME VIDEO 28002

GOLDEN AGE OF COMEDY, THE

D: Robert Youngson — 78 m

NR | DOC | 1957 | B&W

7 Fun compilation of some of the silent era's greatest comedy moments created by some of its then zaniest stars: Charlie Chaplin, Laurel and Hardy, the Keystone Kops, Will Rogers, Carole Lombard, Ben Turpin, Harry Langdon and others. This wide assortment of slapstick excerpts, from the heyday of silent film 1914-1929, presents the comedy that brought tears of laughter to the entertainment-deprived and relatively unsophisticated audiences of its day, however much of what was hysterical then provokes mostly yawns now.

☐ Sex ☐ Nud ☐ Viol ☐ Lang ☐ AdSit

A:

© UNITED AMERICAN VIDEO CORP. 216

GOSPEL

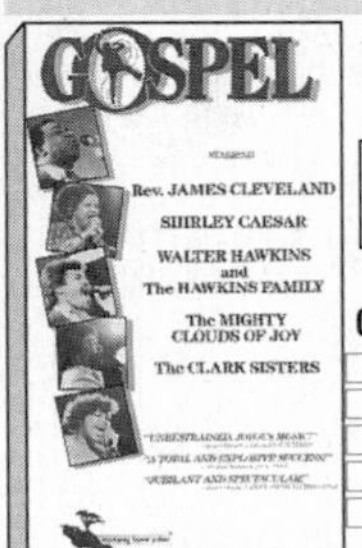

D: — 92 m

DOC MUS | 1982 | COLOR

9 A rousing and exuberant, high-energy concert including several top gospel performers of the '70s and '80s in very entertaining performances before a very enthusiastic crowd. There is no commentary, only music. The groups include: James Cleveland and the Southern California Community Choir, Walter Hawkins and the Hawkins Family, Mighty Clouds of Joy, Shirley Caesar, Twinkie Clark and the Clark Sisters. If you enjoyed this you should also see another documentary SAY AMEN, SOMEBODY.

☐ Sex ☐ Nud ☐ Viol ☐ Lang ☐ AdSit

A:

© MONTEREY HOME VIDEO 31944

HEARTS OF DARKNESS - A FILMMAKER'S APOCALYPSE

D: Fax Bahr, Eleanor Coppola — 96 m

R | DOC | 1991 | COLOR

8 Coppola invested everything - his reputation, his personal assets and his sanity - in the creation of his personal vision. APOCALYPSE NOW was a combination of America's experiences in Vietnam and a radio play from 1939 called "Hearts of Darkness," with Orson Welles. It was also a recipe for trouble. It was one of the most complex films, both technically and artistically, ever attempted. And it was complicated further by Martin Sheen's heart attack at age 36, a typhoon, threats of communist attacks and the lack of a real ending for a $13 million film that had already cost over $20 million.

☐ Sex ☐ Nud ☐ Viol ☑ Lang ☑ AdSit

A:

© PARAMOUNT HOME VIDEO 83081

HEAVY PETTING

D: Obie Benz — 75 m

R | DOC COM | 1989 | COLOR

Sex / Nud / Viol / Lang / AdSit

7 Very funny but slightly sleazy documentary about the sexual and dating rituals of the '60s. Numerous clips from vintage sex education films and Hollywood's sexy scenes from the pre-sexual revolution of the '50s and '60s are interspersed with the frank confessions of several celebrities talking about their "first time." Ah, memories.

A: Laurie Anderson, David Byrne, Sandra Bernhard, Allen Ginsberg, Abbie Hoffman, Spalding Gray

© ACADEMY ENTERTAINMENT 1197

HELL'S ANGELS FOREVER

D: Lee Madden — 93 m

R | DOC | 1983 | COLOR

Sex / Nud / Viol / Lang / AdSit

6 This is a rare insider's look at the famous motorcycle gang. Beginning after WWII with a bunch of daredevil bombers, its name has become synonymous with renegades and violence. Witness the life, the weddings, the funerals, the violence and the independence. Sometimes crude, but still a very interesting look into this strange fraternity of rebels.

A:

© VIDEO TREASURES M264

HOLLYWOOD - 13 VOLUMES

D: — 676 m

NR | DOC | 1989 | B&W

Sex / Nud / Viol / Lang / AdSit

8 This is a top-notch documentary that is narrated by James Mason and which examines the many aspects of Hollywood during the early years of the silent era. Shown in 13 separate volumes and filmed for British TV, it explores virtually every aspect of those times and contains numerous interviews with Hollywood insiders and stars, plus some rarely seen film footages. A must for serious film fans.

A: James Mason

© HBO VIDEO 0263

HOOP DREAMS

D: Steve James — 176 m

NR | DOC | 1994 | COLOR

Sex / Nud / Viol / Lang / AdSit

8 An amazing documentary follows four years in the lives of two very promising young basketball players - William Gates and Arthur Agee. These inner-city Chicago kids are both recruited out of grammer school to play for a private high school on a scholarship. However, very soon tuition prices were raised and one is forced to drop out. He returns to a neighborhood public school and plays there. Their lives are not lived in a basketball vacuum, nor do they live their dreams only for themselves. They represent hope where there is little. They have troubled homes and live in rough neighborhoods where failure is a way of life. Fascinating but very long. 250 hours of tape were pared to just 3, but should have been edited to 2.

A:

© TURNER HOME ENTERTAINMENT N4021

HUGH HEFNER: ONCE UPON A TIME

D: Robert Heath — m

R | DOC | 1992 | COLOR

Sex / Nud / Viol / Lang / AdSit

8 America before 1950 and Hugh Hefner was a very different place. World War II came along to break down the old complacent and self-assured Puritan values. Change burst forth to challenge all the old ideas. Changes like: rock `n roll music, the cold war, civil rights and "Playboy" magazine. "Playboy" and Hugh Hefner said that the girl next door was sexy, that it was OK to enjoy sex. That novel idea began what became a tidal wave of changes. The man who led the charge to the new morality was a 27-year-old from a repressed background. This documentary is obviously biased, however his story is truly a fascinating one and his influence has in fact been extremely substantial.

A:

© PLAYBOY HOME VIDEO 0733

IMAGINE: JOHN LENNON

D: — 104 m

R | DOC MUS | 1988 | COLOR

Sex / Nud / Viol / Lang / AdSit

8 This documentary is really quite good and contains rare live concert footage, home movies of John Lennon's private life, plus TV footage and much of Lennon's own music (36 songs in all). The film is punctuated with commentary from Lennon himself, that was excerpted from elsewhere. It is insightful, odd at times, funny, emotionally moving and lovingly done.

A: John Lennon, Yoko Ono, George Harrison

© WARNER HOME VIDEO 11819

INCIDENT AT OGLALA - THE LEONARD PELTIER STORY

D: Michael Apted — 90 m

PG | DOC | 1992 | COLOR

Sex / Nud / Viol / Lang / AdSit

8 During a politically turbulent time in 1975, two FBI agents and one Native American were killed in a shoot-out on the Pine Ridge Reservation in South Dakota. After an extensive search, three Native Americans were arrested. One, Leonard Peltier, was convicted and sentenced to two life terms. This incisive documentary reexamines the issues surrounding the case in detail, including interviews with people from both sides. It is not a tirade, but rather a step-by-step analysis which indicates that Peltier may have been framed. Also see the similar commercial release, but fictional, THUNDERHEART.

A: Robert Redford

© LIVE HOME VIDEO 69013

JAZZ ON A SUMMER'S DAY

D: Bert Stern — 84 m

NR | MUS DOC | 1959 | COLOR

Sex / Nud / Viol / Lang / AdSit

9 Jazz fans take note. On a summer's day in 1958 at Newport, Road Island, the Newport Jazz Festival was born. This is a candid and thoroughly enjoyable documentary of the musical event that preceeded Woodstock by more than ten years. Virtually all the legendary greats of jazz are in attendance including: Louis Armstrong, Dinah Washington, Mahalia Jackson, Thelonious Monk, Anita O'Day, Chuck Berry and George Shearing.

A: Louis Armstrong, Big Maybell, Chuck Berry, Dianah Washington, Gerry Mulligan, Thelonious Monk

© NEW YORKER FILMS NYV16590

KING: MONTGOMERY TO MEMPHIS

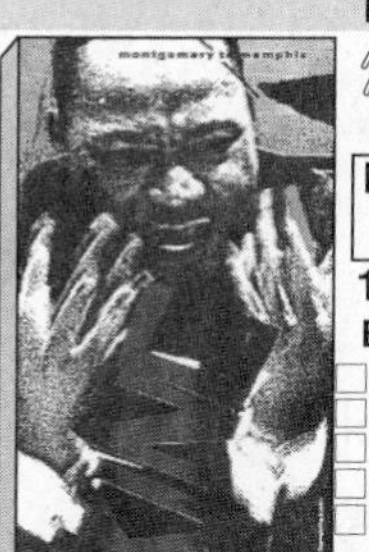

D: — 103 m

NR | DOC | 1970 | B&W

Sex / Nud / Viol / Lang / AdSit

9 A eloquent documentary of the life and accomplishments of the man and a dream. Numerous pieces of film are brilliantly edited together documenting the highlights of his career, beginning with the bus boycott in Montgomery, through his address at the Lincoln Memorial and the Nobel Peace Prize, to his murder in Memphis.

A:

© PACIFIC ARTS VIDEO 680

KOYAANISQATSI

D: Godfrey Reggio — 87 m

DOC | 1983 | COLOR

Sex / Nud / Viol / Lang / AdSit

8 Strangely compelling viewing. It is a fascinating kaleidoscopic view of the many majesties and not so majestic objects and activities to be found in both nature and within man's cities. It is a total flight of photographic fancy, where the only sound is a symbiotic score by Philip Glass. There is no narration, no dialogue. There is only a never-ending string of compelling images. Koyaanisqatsi is a word from the language of the Southwestern Hopi Indians. It means "life out of balance."

A:

© PACIFIC ARTS VIDEO PAVR539

LAST WALTZ, THE

D: Martin Scorsese — 117 m

PG | DOC MUS | 1976 | COLOR

Sex / Nud / Viol / Lang / AdSit

9 A major lineup of 1976 rock `n roll talent. This is the actual farewell concert for the rock group called "The Band," taped as it happened. Onstage production numbers are interspersed with back stage goings on and interviews. It is a must see for rock `n roll fans. Note the partial lineup, shown below, of the rock stars included and in attendance.

A: The Band, Bob Dylan, Neil Young, Joni Mitchell, Van Morrison, Eric Clapton

Distributed By MGM/UA Home Video M200482

LENNY BRUCE PERFORMANCE FILM, THE

D: John Magnuson — 67 m

NR | COM DOC | 1968 | B&W

Sex / Nud / Viol / Lang / AdSit

6 Controversial and irreverent stand-up comic Lenny Bruce was filmed in front of a live San Francisco audience. The photography is bad, but the film does give the viewer an opportunity to at least see the man who cleared the decks for the aggressive humor of later comedians. At the time of this filming, Bruce had been through many years of court battles on obscenity charges. This performance is mostly a tirade against the system that persecuted him. Funnier is a short animated feature that accompanies it: "Thank You Masked Man."

A: Lenny Bruce

© RHINO HOME VIDEO/RECORDS 2014

MAN WHO SAW TOMORROW, THE

D: Robert Guenette 88 m

PG · DOC · 1981 · COLOR

Sex · Nud · Viol · Lang · AdSit

8 An amazing 16th-century poet and mystic Nostradamus made extremely accurate and thought-provoking predictions that will confound and terrify you. Welles narrates this documentary detailing the predicted events that have occurred and the many still to come. Amazingly accurate, his prophecies included the rise and fall of Hitler and the assassinations of Presidents Lincoln and Kennedy. Nostradamus even gives names and dates in some cases. Haunting.

A: Orson Welles

© WARNER HOME VIDEO 11246

MONTEREY POP

D: James Desmond 88 m

NR · DOC MUS · 1967 · COLOR

Sex · Nud · Viol · Lang · AdSit

9 White Hot! This is the first major rock concert film and was shot at the Monterey Pop Festival in California in 1967. This landmark concert featured some of the biggest musical stars (15) of the time, in their brightest moments, and it kicked off the rock summer series (Summer of Love) that culminated in Woodstock. Performances include Janis Joplin's "Ball and Chain" and an intense rendition of "My Generation" by The Who. Brilliant historical time-piece and a must-see for anyone with more than a passing interest in music.

A: Jimi Hendrix, Otis Redding, The Who, Jefferson Airplane, Janis Joplin, The Animals

© COLUMBIA TRISTAR HOME VIDEO RO162VH

MY FRIEND LIBERTY

D: Jimmy Picker 30 m

DOC CLD · 1986 · COLOR

Sex · Nud · Viol · Lang · AdSit

7 Animated history lesson. The famous lady Liberty comes to life, steps down and educates a young man about the history of the statue and the meaning behind her name. Entertaining and educational, this program is done in clay animation by the Academy Award winner Jimmy Picker. Great for children and adults alike.

A:

© WARNER HOME VIDEO 130

PARIS IS BURNING

D: Jennie Livingston 78 m

R · DOC · 1991 · COLOR

Sex · Nud · Viol · Lang · AdSit

9 Utterly fascinating, non-condescending and revealing trip into what, for most, is a very bizarre world - NYC's gay scene. However, this film is not just for gays. This is a world where fantasy becomes reality - not sexual but acceptual. It is a world with its own culture. Where hispanic and black gay men seek to achieve a level of acceptance and pride that they are denied elsewhere. It is characterized by competitions, known as drag balls, where contestants "walk" or parade in front of their peers to win best of such categories as "most real" or "prettiest." Poignant and provocative.

A:

© ACADEMY ENTERTAINMENT 1495

PUMPING IRON

D: George Butler, Robert Flore 90 m

PG · DOC · 1977 · COLOR

Sex · Nud · Viol · Lang · AdSit

6 Fascinating look inside the world of male body building. The primary focus is upon six-time Mr. Olympia, Arnold Schwarzenegger, and his attempt to retain his title. (This film was the first major exposure of Schwarzenegger to the bulk of the American public.) Also included are many of the major body builders of the time, including Lou Ferrigno (The Incredible Hulk). Much of the behind-the-scenes filming concerns Arnold's efforts at psyching out Ferrigno. See also companion film PUMPING IRON II: THE WOMEN.

A: Arnold Schwarzenegger, Lou Ferrigno, Mike Katz, Franco Columbu

© COLUMBIA TRISTAR HOME VIDEO 60085

PUMPING IRON II: THE WOMEN

D: George Butler 107 m

NR · DOC · 1985 · COLOR

Sex · Nud · Viol · Lang · AdSit

6 Curious documentary covering the 1983 Women's World Cup held at Caesar's Palace in Las Vegas. It is a straightforward documentary whose primary focus is the contrasting physiques of massive Australian Bev Francis and the more curvy Rachel McLish. An interesting curiosity is that the winners are offered their prizes either in cash, by check or with poker chips. It was derived from the earlier documentary with Arnold Schwarzenegger and Lou Ferrigno, PUMPING IRON.

A: Rachel McLish, Lori Bowden, Carla Dunlap, Bev Francis, Kris Alexander, George Plimpton

© LIVE HOME VIDEO VA5093

ROGER & ME

D: Michael Moore 91 m

R · DOC · 1989 · COLOR

Sex · Nud · Viol · Lang · AdSit

7 This was a controversial, clever and humorous film that was released during an economic recession and became a testament to the plight of the unemployed. When GM closed several plants in Flint, Michigan, 35,000 of the 150,000 residents lost their jobs. This film's director, Michael Moore, embarked on a personal crusade to show to the indifferent chairman of GM, Roger Smith, the effect the plant closing had on the small town. He also narrates his own documentary, injecting a good dose of humor into some truly sad and disturbing scenes of the homelessness and poverty of the jobless residents. Sobering.

A:

© WARNER HOME VIDEO 11978

SAY AMEN, SOMEBODY

D: George T. Nierenberg 100 m

G · DOC MUS · 1983 · COLOR

Sex · Nud · Viol · Lang · AdSit

9 A riotous celebration of Gospel music! This documentary captures the energetic feeling and uplifting essence of the songs, the sound, the meanings, the joy and inspiration of music made for the senses and soul. Featured are two of Gospel's greats: Thomas A. Dorsey and Willie Mae Ford Smith. Their lives and their careers are explored and spliced with more than two dozen exuberant songs. A glistening, shining film that is wonderful for the whole family and will leave you feeling jubilant and refreshed. If you enjoy this, you should also see the documentary GOSPEL.

A: Willie Mae Ford Smith, Thomas A. Dorsey, Sallie Martin

© PACIFIC ARTS VIDEO 547

STATUE OF LIBERTY, THE

D: Ken Burns 60 m

DOC · 1986 · B&W

Sex · Nud · Viol · Lang · AdSit

8 A fascinating historic journey! The famous "Lady" that has welcomed countless immigrants to America is the feature of this Academy Award-nominated documentary. Researched to the last detail, New York Governor Mario Cuomo makes a guest appearance and interviews some of the most intriguing and famous immigrants. The legend, facts and history of Lady Liberty are explored from the very beginning up until her restoration in 1986. An outstanding tribute, narrated by David McCullough. Another documentary about the statue but aimed more for children is MY FRIEND LIBERTY.

A:

© LIVE HOME VIDEO VA1049

STREETWISE

D: Martin Bell 92 m

NR · DOC DMA · 1985 · COLOR

Sex · Nud · Viol · Lang · AdSit

8 This is not a pretty picture. This in an intense, real and horrifying look at the lives of a group of teenage runaways who make their home the streets of Seattle and the things that they endure to survive. Most of them are victims of a destructive homelife or parents who are out of touch. They eat out of trash bins, stick needles up their arms, drink, sell themselves and their souls. The only thing they really have is each other. It is that strong bond that keeps them going. Real teenagers, real life, and a real heartbreaking account of life far outside of what, for most of us, is normal.

A:

© R&G VIDEO, LP 9548

STRIPPER

D: Jerome Gary 90 m

R · DOC · 1985 · COLOR

Sex · Nud · Viol · Lang · AdSit

7 A compassionate, quirky, honest semi-documentary that takes a real-life look at the lives of five strippers who put bread on the table by taking off their clothes. It is much more than a strip story. The focus is on their individual lives, their challenges, and the reasoning behind their chosen profession. The story follows the women to the First Annual Stripper's Convention where they compete for the $25,000 prize.

A: Sara Costa, Kimberly Holcomb, Loree Menton, Lisa Suarez, Janet Boyd

© CBS/FOX VIDEO 6749

THAT'S ENTERTAINMENT!

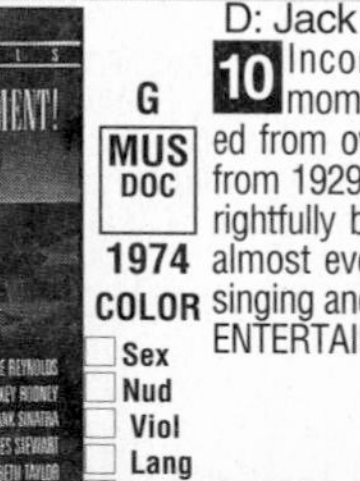

D: Jack Haley, Jr. 134 m

G · MUS DOC · 1974 · COLOR

Sex · Nud · Viol · Lang · AdSit

10 Incomparable compilation of some of the most magical moments from MGM's monumental mound of musicals, extracted from over 100 of its best films, and taken over a 29-year period from 1929 to 1958. This was the glory period at MGM when it could rightfully boast of "having more stars than there are in heaven" and almost every one of them gets at least one appearance. Non-stop singing and dancing. Something for nearly everyone. See also THAT'S ENTERTAINMENT, PART 2, which added comedies and dramas.

A: Fred Astaire, Bing Crosby, Gene Kelly, Peter Lawford, Liza Minnelli, Donald O'Connor

Distributed By MGM/UA Home Video M600007

THAT'S ENTERTAINMENT III

D: Bud Friedgen, Michael J. Sheridan 108 m

G | MUS DOC | 1994 | COLOR

9 Once again they dug back into the vaults at MGM's dream factory and resurrected some of the greatest musical sequences produced there. This one differs from the others in that it also includes many complete musical sequences which were pulled and were never shown in the final productions. We get to watch Fred Astaire do the same dance sequence on two different sets at the same time on a split screen. And, we get to watch a fabulous Eleanor Powell dance sequence on one screen at the same time we watch the buz of the stage hands and cameras as they film the same sequence, on another screen.

Sex / Nud / Viol / Lang / AdSit

A: June Allyson, Ctd Charisse, Lena Horne, Gene Kelly, Debbie Reynolds, Mickey Rooney

Distributed By MGM/UA Home Video

THAT'S ENTERTAINMENT, PART 2

D: Gene Kelly 129 m

G | MUS DOC | 1976 | COLOR

9 Inevitable sequel to the very popular THAT'S ENTERTAINMENT, that had been made two years earlier. This time comedy and drama, also taken from MGM's impressive vault of major movies, are included along with musicals. When you have that kind of selection to choose from, it is impossible to disappoint, and this film certainly doesn't. Still, the original is even better.

Sex / Nud / Viol / Lang / AdSit

A: John Barrymore, Clark Gable, Greta Garbo, Gene Kelly, Bing Crosby, Judy Holliday

Distributed By MGM/UA Home Video M700075

THAT WAS ROCK

D: Steve Binder, Larry Peerce 90 m

NR | MUS DOC | 1964 | B&W

9 One of the best collections of rock `n roll and R&B talent from the '60s. See Chuck Berry, James Brown, Ray Charles, Marvin Gaye, The Rolling Stones, The Supremes, Smokey Robinson and the Miracles, Gerry and the Pacemakers, The Ronettes and Tina Turner. Originally recorded on B&W videotape, the recording quality is not good - but the material is priceless. The clips were also originally released in two rock extravaganza-type films: "The T.A.M.I. Show" (1964) and "The Big T.N.T. Show" (1966).

Sex / Nud / Viol / Lang / AdSit

A: Chuck Berry, James Brown, Marvin Gaye, The Rolling Stones, The Supremes, Smokey Robinson

© MUSIC MEDIA M434

THIN BLUE LINE, THE

D: Errol Morris 101 m

NR | DOC CRM | 1988 | COLOR

8 Fascinating documentary investigation into the conviction of Randall Adams, a hitchhiker, for the 1976 murder of a Dallas policeman. He was sentenced to death based largely upon the testimony of runaway David Harris, who was later convicted of another murder. Director Errol Morris, who formerly was a private detective, became interested in the case. Through a series of interviews and recreations, which he presents in this documentary, he created so much doubt about the nature of the facts that convicted Adams that he was eventually released.

Sex / Nud / Viol / Lang / AdSit

A:

© HBO VIDEO 0177

THIS IS ELVIS

D: Andrew Solt, Malcolm Leo 144 m

PG | DOC MUS | 1981 | COLOR

8 An entertaining and controversial film which combines interviews, documentary footage, concert clips, home movies and dramatic recreations to portray many different aspects of Presley's life and career. The film begins with his death at age 42 and uses a series of flashbacks to illustrate his beginnings as a truck driver, his early career (including his appearance on The Ed Sullivan Show), his induction into the army, his comeback show with Frank Sinatra and his big TV special from 1968. Includes 38 songs.

Sex / Nud / Viol / Lang / AdSit

A: Elvis Presley

© WARNER HOME VIDEO 11173

TIMES OF HARVEY MILK, THE

D: Robert Epstein 90 m

NR | DOC | 1984 | COLOR

9 Winner of the 1984 Academy Award for Best Documentary. Harvey Milk was the first openly gay person ever to be elected to public office in California. In 1978 he and San Francisco Mayor George Moscone were shot and killed by clean-cut council member Dan White. This film covers not only the trial of White and his famous "twinkie defense," but also the influence Milk had on politics and his fight for the civil rights of everyone. This is a very moving experience, regardless of your sexual orientation.

Sex / Nud / Viol / Lang / AdSit

A:

© PACIFIC ARTS VIDEO 632

TRUTH OR DARE

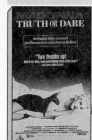

D: Alek Keshishian 131 m

R | DOC MUS | 1991 | COLOR

8 Controversial, revealing, manipulative and daring. Madonna bravely holds nothing back in this back stage documentary about the controversial performer's life. It's not all pretty; she can be bitchy - barking orders at her dancers and crew - but in the next frame she's vulnerable, mourning at her mother's grave. She has decided to let the audience see everything. You have to decide if it's calculated or just spontaneous. Simply put, if you like Madonna, you will really enjoy this, if not - you won't. You might also be interested to see Julie Brown's biting satire of it called MEDUSA: DARE TO BE TRUTHFUL.

Sex / Nud / Viol / Lang / AdSit

A: Madonna

© LIVE HOME VIDEO 69021

U2: RATTLE AND HUM

D: Phil Joanou 90 m

PG-13 | MUS DOC | 1988 | B&W

8 Much more than just a concert film! From Ireland to the States, this is an outstanding concert tour of one of the hottest rock bands of the '80s and beyond as they promote their phenomonenal "Joshua Tree" album. U2, the Grammy award-winning band, is one with a message and a conscience. The first half of film is filmed in black and white, the second in color - as four of the members discover not only their musical personality but also their individual inspirations and musical histories.

Sex / Nud / Viol / Lang / AdSit

A:

© PARAMOUNT HOME VIDEO 32228

VICTORY AT SEA - SERIES

D: 780 m

NR | DOC WAR | 1960 | B&W

10 This is a very popular and multi-award-winning documentary series that was created for TV during the early 1950s, in 26 30-minute segments (also available). It documents the Allied struggle during WWII over five continents. The entire series is now available in one six-volume tape set. It is an extremely well-written documentary, containing excellent photography (including some amazing archival footage), magnificently narrated by Alexander Scourby and accompanied by a rousing Richard Rodgers score.

Sex / Nud / Viol / Lang / AdSit

A:

© NEW LINE HOME VIDEO 7659

VIETNAM: A TELEVISION HISTORY

D: 780 m

NR | DOC | 1983 | COLOR

9 Winner of six Emmys from its original airing on PBS. This very highly acclaimed series sets out, over 13 hours and in seven volumes, the torturous history of Vietnam - beginning with a historical background for this tiny country which has been constantly invaded for centuries. In 1885, the French claimed it as a colony. The Japanese took it in WWII. There was a brief flirtation with independence after WWII when Ho Chi Minh approached the US, but instead the US supported the French. The US entered in the early '60s and did not get out again until it evacuated Hanoi in defeat 1975.

Sex / Nud / Viol / Lang / AdSit

A:

© COLUMBIA TRISTAR HOME VIDEO D0489VH

VISION SHARED: TRIBUTE TO W. GUTHRIE AND LEADBELLY

D: Jim Brown 70 m

DOC MUS | 1988 | COLOR

8 Fascinating! Two of the great musical pioneers are paid just tribute by 1988 musicians from many venues in this fantastic documentary. The stories of the lives of folksingers Woody Gutherie and Leadbelly are interspersed with their music which is played by themselves and also performed by many music greats of 1988. This salute to the pair includes songs like "Vigilante Man," "Jesus Christ," "This Land is Your Land" and "Do Re Me." A sparkling look to the recent past and the foundations of popular modern music.

Sex / Nud / Viol / Lang / AdSit

A: Bruce Springsteen, Pete Seeger, Bob Dylan, John Cougar Mellencamp, Willie Nelson, Arlo Guthrie

© CBS MUSIC VIDEO ENTERPRISES 19V-49006

WAR ROOM, THE

D: D. A. Pennebaker, Chris Hegedus 95 m

NR | DOC | 1993 | COLOR

6 This film was named for the computer filled-room in Littlerock, Arkansas from which the 1992 campaign of Bill Clinton for the Presidency was directed. Documentary cameras followed the myriad of events that surrounded both the race for the Democratic nomination and the Presidency itself. Primary focus is upon the team of James Carville and George Stephanopoulos, the political strategist and communications director respectively, as they struggle to promote their candidate against Republican George Bush and strong independent candidate Ross Perot. Entertaining, instructive and unbiased day-to-day coverage of a hard fought and close campaign. Still, Clinton supporters may rate it higher.

Sex / Nud / Viol / Lang / AdSit

A:

© VIDMARK ENTERTAINMENT 5894

WEAVERS: WASN'T THAT A TIME!

D: Jim Brown 78 m

DOC MUS

1980

COLOR

Sex
Nud
Viol
Lang
AdSit

10 Wonderfully joyous. For those who don't know - for much of the '40s and '50s The Weavers were the preeminent musical quartet in the country and had a string of top ten hits. The performers were: Lee Hayes, Ronnie Gilbert, Fred Hellerman and Pete Seeger. They and their music formed the basis for the folk phenomena of the late '50s and early '60s. They were magical. This film features archival footage and documents their 1980 reunion at Carnegie Hall. Songs: "Goodnight Irene," "Kisses Sweeter Than Wine," "If I Had a Hammer" (they wrote it) and much, much more.

A: The Weavers

WOODSTOCK

D: Michael Wadleigh 184 m

R

DOC MUS

1970

COLOR

Sex
Nud
Viol
Lang
AdSit

10 Brilliant film which won the 1970 Oscar for Best Documentary and totally captures the spirit of the weekend in 1969 when a farm in New York became the third largest city in the State of New York - with over 400,000 people. This was at the height of the hippie age and it was the Summer of Love. It was the granddaddy if all rock concerts and had virtually every major rock band of the era in attendance. This film is a behind-the-scenes look at both the performers and the people. It was a real "Happening," and this is a valuable time capsule. Great music. Fascinating people.

A: Joan Baez, Joe Cocker, The Who, Country Joe&The Fish, Crosby,Stills & Nash, Jimi Hendrix

Drama

1956 and After

10

D: Blake Edwards — 123 m

R | COM DMA | 1979 | COLOR | ■ Sex ■ Nud □ Viol ◢ Lang ■ AdSit

9 A slick sophisticated comedy that became a huge blockbuster hit. Just after turning 40, songwriter Dudley Moore spies the fantasy woman of his dreams (Bo Derek). Even though it is her wedding day, he follows her into the church and then, totally smitten, leaves everything (including wife Andrews) to chase his mid-life crisis fantasy on her Acapulco honeymoon. Against all odds, she becomes fascinated with him and the sexually liberated beauty takes him into her bed. But Moore now becomes confused, suddenly aware that the realization of his dream is not what he had expected. Funny and very entertaining.

A: Bo Derek, Julie Andrews, Dudley Moore, Robert Webber, Dee Wallace

© WARNER HOME VIDEO 2002

10 RILLINGTON PLACE

D: Richard Fleischer — 111 m

PG | CRM DMA | 1971 | COLOR | □ Sex □ Nud ◢ Viol ◢ Lang ◢ AdSit

7 Fascinating true story which so upset the English public that it brought about the end to the death penalty there. John Hurt is utterly believable and pitiable as a simple man who is wrongly sent to his death for the hideous murders of his wife and child. In actuality, his landlord had offered to abort the unwanted baby, but had instead raped the woman and then killed both her and another child. The landlord then lied at the trial, helping to convict the husband. The truth was not discovered until years after the execution, when the landlord was brought up on other murder charges.

A: John Hurt, Judy Geeson, Richard Attenborough, Andre Morell

© COLUMBIA TRISTAR HOME VIDEO 60593

12 ANGRY MEN

D: Sidney Lumet — 93 m

NR | CRM DMA | 1957 | B&W | □ Sex □ Nud □ Viol □ Lang ◢ AdSit

9 Compelling courtroom drama. Twelve jurors, all men, convene to decide the fate of a boy accused of murdering his father. The case is seemingly cut-and-dried and all vote guilty - except one, Fonda. For him, the situation is not so clear cut. Against considerable pressure from the other eleven, he slowly builds a case for acquittal out of his concerns for the boy's innocence and gradually wins over the others - all except Cobb who holds out. Tense, engrossing and impressive, it received Oscar nominations for Best Picture, Director and Screenplay.

A: Henry Fonda, Lee J. Cobb, Martin Balsam, Jack Klugman, Jack Warden, E.G. Marshall

Distributed By MGM/UA Home Video M301270

2001 - A SPACE ODYSSEY

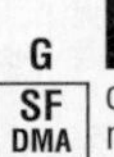

D: Stanley Kubrick — 139 m

G | SF DMA | 1968 | COLOR | □ Sex □ Nud □ Viol □ Lang ◢ AdSit

8 Highly acclaimed science fiction epic based on a book by Arthur C. Clarke. In the year 2001, men working on a moon base discover a mysterious monolith beneath the moon's surface, proving that mankind is not alone in the universe. The discovery of a second monolith on earth leads to an expedition to Jupiter, where there is to be a third. Along the way, the spaceship's all-powerful main computer (HAL) malfunctions, causing the pilots to try to shut it down. Oscar for special effects. Good, but doesn't merit its very lofty reputation and may be overly mystical for many.

A: Keir Dullea, William Sylvester, Gary Lockwood, Daniel Richter

Distributed By MGM/UA Home Video M202233

2010

D: Peter Hyams — 117 m

PG | SF DMA | 1984 | COLOR | □ Sex □ Nud □ Viol □ Lang ◢ AdSit

8 Sequel to 2001, A SPACE ODESSEY. In the year 2010, a team of astronauts leaves earth on a Russian spaceship, bound for Jupiter to discover what happened to the original spaceship which was lost. When the team finds the earlier ship, they reactivate the ship's computer, discover a survivor from the original mission and also discover the mystery behind the monoliths. More "down-to-earth" than the original and, therefore, easier to follow. (This satisfies some and disappoints others.) Good special effects again, too.

A: Roy Scheider, John Lithgow, Bob Balaban, Helen Mirren, Keir Dullea

Distributed By MGM/UA Home Video M800591

400 BLOWS, THE

D: Francois Truffaut — 99 m

NR | FOR DMA | 1959 | B&W | □ Sex □ Nud ◢ Viol □ Lang ◢ AdSit

8 A sensitive, powerful and sometimes very sad film. It was also a daring movie for its time because it dared to challenge the establishment. It is the story of a disaffected 12-year-old boy who is failed and virtually abandoned by his parents, his teachers and all the other institutions around him. Deeply embittered, he strikes out at them all by committing a series of petty crimes. If he is to survive, he will have to find strength within himself. Famed as being one of the most memorable French New Wave ultra-realist films of the period, it is also worthy and affecting on a personal, non-technical basis. Subtitles. The character is picked up in later life in LOVE ON THE RUN.

A: Jean-Pierre Leaud, Patrick Auffay, Claire Maurier, Albert Remy

© HOME VISION FOU040

55 DAYS AT PEKING

D: Nicholas Ray — 150 m

NR | DMA ACT | 1963 | COLOR | □ Sex □ Nud ◢ Viol □ Lang ◢ AdSit

6 Semi-historical account of the Boxer Rebellion in China about 1900. Diplomatic staffs of eleven nations are trapped inside a walled-in compound with supplies running low. Stubborn English diplomat David Niven refuses to give in, even at the risk of his own family, and they are able to hold out for 55 days. Big sets and high production values combine with an excellent cast and good action sequences to offset the so-so story line that is built largely around not-too-attractive and now-dated stereotypical colonialist cliches.

A: Charlton Heston, Ava Gardner, David Niven, Flora Robson, John Ireland, Paul Lukas

© BEST FILM & VIDEO CORP. 217

8 1/2

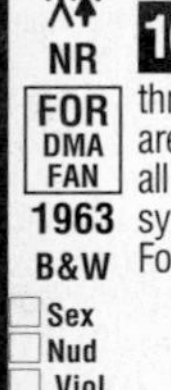

D: Federico Fellini — 138 m

NR | FOR DMA FAN | 1963 | B&W | □ Sex □ Nud □ Viol □ Lang ■ AdSit

10 For very sophisticated viewers only. This is a semiautobiographical film in which master Italian filmmaker Federico Fellini depicts, through a visual "diary," the director's difficulties in making the film we are watching. Viewers witness his memories, fantasies and problems, all through a storyline which ebbs and flows between reality and fantasy, eventually evolving to a world in between the two. Winner of Foreign Film Oscar. Subtitles.

A: Marcello Mastroianni, Claudia Cardinale, Anouk Aimee, Sandra Milo, Barbara Steele

© MPI HOME VIDEO 1398

84 CHARING CROSS ROAD

D: David Jones — 100 m

PG | ROM DMA | 1986 | COLOR

6 Sweet adult romance about two letter correspondents who never meet. True story of a struggling writer in New York, with an intense passion for books she can't really afford, who responds to an ad placed by a London-based used book store in a New York paper. A 20-year relationship ensues between the writer and the store's unhappily married owner which evolves from business to love - but they never meet. Their love exists only through the mail. A beautiful film that is virtually all talk. It is a lovely, literate story, but may be too slow for many.

□ Sex □ Nud □ Viol ◢ Lang ■ AdSit

A: Anne Bancroft, Anthony Hopkins, Judi Dench, Maurice Denham, Jean De Baer, Eleanor David

© COLUMBIA TRISTAR HOME VIDEO 60815

84 CHARLIE MOPIC

D: Patrick Duncan — 95 m

R | WAR DMA ACT | 1989 | COLOR

8 Compelling and unique Vietnam war movie. The terrors and hardships of a dangerous jungle reconnaissance mission are told solely through the eye of a camera that is hand-held by an Army combat cameraman. He has been sent along with a six-man patrol into the highlands in 1969 to capture the experience of war for a training film. This filming technique is at times bothersome, but on whole it also adds a strong sense of reality in depicting the personal life-and-death quality of what it was actually like to be in the ground war in Vietnam on a daily basis.

□ Sex □ Nud ■ Viol ■ Lang ■ AdSit

A: Jonathan Emerson, Nicholas Cascone, Richard Brooks, Jasons Tomlins, Christopher Burgard, Glenn Marshower

© COLUMBIA TRISTAR HOME VIDEO 09943

8 SECONDS

D: John G. Avildsen — 104 m

PG-13 | DMA | 1994 | COLOR

6 If you are a cowboy, or if your taste and background lean toward cowboyin', you may want to increase the rating one notch. However, most people will find this biography about rodeo great Lane Frost only mildly interesting at best. Lane Frost was the son of a former rodeo great and a genuinely nice guy - the kind of guy that cowboys aren't supposed to be. He didn't drink, didn't fight and always took time to talk to kids. Still, after he reached the top - after he became the world's best cowboy - even he, for a time, lost sight of where he was headed. A nice little movie with some effective acting with Luke Perry as Frost and Stephen Baldwin as his hard-living cowboy buddy.

□ Sex □ Nud □ Viol ◢ Lang ◢ AdSit

A: Luke Perry, Stephen Baldwin, Cynthia Geary, James Rebhorn, Carrie Snodgrass, Red Mitchell

© TURNER HOME ENTERTAINMENT N4023

ABOVE THE RIM

D: Jeff Pollack — m

R | DMA | 1994 | COLOR

6 To many inner-city black kids, basketball is an obsession. To a very few, it is a way out. Kyle (Martin) is cocky and selfish, but he is also a talented high school kid who has a chance to make it. He's waiting for his ticket to arrive in the form of a scholarship to Georgetown, but he also has a chance to play for a tough street team run by a drug dealer (Shakur). His mother is working overtime to insure that he goes to school with or without a scholarship, but his world is basketball. The school coach has arranged for a hard-luck former basketball All-American to get a job as a security guard, in hopes that he will take over teaching when he leaves. His first job will be Kyle.

□ Sex □ Nud ◢ Viol ■ Lang ◢ AdSit

A: Duane Martin, Leon, Tonya Pinkins, Tupac Shakur, Marlon Wayons, Bernie Mac

© TURNER HOME ENTERTAINMENT N4046

ABSENCE OF MALICE

D: Sydney Pollack — 116 m

PG | DMA ROM | 1981 | COLOR

9 Excellent, thought-provoking entertainment about an innocent man who is convicted by innuendo in the media. Sally Fields is a naive reporter, tricked into printing a story which falsely implicates innocent businessman Paul Newman. Newman fights to clear his name and to get revenge. Fields does what she can to help and in the process he and the conscience-stricken Fields unexpectedly fall for each other. However, it is not the romance that most effects you, it is the timely and probably timeless drama of the story you will remember. This is powerful, thoughtful drama about the potentially abusive power of the press. Received three Oscar nominations.

□ Sex □ Nud ◢ Viol ◢ Lang ◢ AdSit

A: Paul Newman, Sally Field, Bob Balaban, Melinda Dillon, Wilford Brimley, Luther Adler

© GOODTIMES 4222

ACCIDENTAL TOURIST, THE

D: Lawrence Kasdan — 121 m

PG | DMA ROM COM | 1988 | COLOR

7 Highly acclaimed by critics and nominated for a Best Picture Oscar. William Hurt gives a strong performance as a travel writer who falls apart upon the death of his son. He distances himself from everyone, including Kathleen Turner, his estranged wife. His isolation is broken only when he is around kooky dog trainer Geena Davis. This is an intensely emotional film. While it is quirky and contains some very funny moments, this is primarily an intelligent drama and romance that takes its time to bring out the story. May be too slow for some.

◢ Sex □ Nud □ Viol ◢ Lang ■ AdSit

A: William Hurt, Kathleen Turner, Geena Davis, Bill Pullman, Amy Wright, David Ogden Stiers

© WARNER HOME VIDEO 11825

ACCUSED, THE

D: Jonathan Kaplan — 110 m

R | DMA CRM | 1988 | COLOR

9 Powerful, intense drama with an important moral question to ask. Foster won an Oscar for her riveting performance as a somewhat sleazy and deliberately provocative woman who is gang raped at a neighborhood bar. Female public prosecutor McGillis is intent upon dealing with the rape in a typically bureaucratic manner, but the incensed victim demands a public trial. An unexpectedly compelling, non-exploitive drama about a sleazy, foul-mouthed, but yet amazingly naive young woman who gets her day in court. Excellent drama and a powerhouse film.

■ Sex ■ Nud ■ Viol ■ Lang ■ AdSit

A: Jodie Foster, Kelly McGillis, Bernie Coulsen, Leo Rossi, Ann Hearn, Carmen Argenziano

© PARAMOUNT HOME VIDEO 1760

ACROSS THE GREAT DIVIDE

D: Stewart Raffill — 102 m

G | DMA CLD | 1977 | COLOR

6 A very well done children's film about the adventures of two orphans. While on their way to Oregon in 1876, the two young children are orphaned when their grandfather dies, but they decide that they must continue on by themselves to claim their family's land in Oregon. Along the way they stumble into a loveable old con man and the threesome adopt each other and continue to pursue their dream traveling through the beautiful and threatening mountains. Fun for young people. See also THE ADVENTURES OF THE WILDERNESS FAMILY and THE WILDERNESS FAMILY, PART 2.

□ Sex □ Nud □ Viol □ Lang □ AdSit

A: Robert Logan, George "Buck" Flower, Heather Rattray, Mark Edward Hall

© VIDEO TREASURES M206

ACT OF VENGEANCE

D: John Mackenzie — 979 m

NR | DMA | 1986 | COLOR

7 An excellent drama based upon real events. Joseph Yablonski (Bronson) was an honest man who wanted to reform the corrupted United Mine Workers coal miner's union by running against the corrupt and ruthless Tony Boyle (Brimley). But in 1969, after a particularly bitter election fight, Yablonski and his family are found murdered. This film provides a three-pronged exploration of the murders: Yablonski's personal life, union politics and physical descriptions of his murderers. Boyle was later convicted of the murders. Bronson, Burstyn and Brimley all excel in their roles. First-rate drama.

□ Sex □ Nud ◢ Viol ◢ Lang ◢ AdSit

A: Charles Bronson, Ellen Burstyn, Wilford Brimley, Hoyt Axton, Ellen Barkin

© HBO VIDEO 0002

ADAM

D: Michael Tuchner — 96 m

NR | DMA | 1983 | COLOR

8 Heart rending real-life story of John and Reve William's search for their son Adam after he had mysteriously disappeared. This is compelling, wrenching drama, detailing the months of uncertainty and anguish. Eventually their lobby of Congress led to legislation which today permits parents to use the FBI's national crime computer to help locate missing children.

□ Sex □ Nud □ Viol □ Lang ◢ AdSit

A: Daniel J. Travanti, JoBeth Williams, Martha Scott, Richard Masur, Paul Regina, Mason Adams

© STAR CLASSICS L1761

ADAM AT 6 A.M.

D: Robert Scheerer — 100 m

PG | DMA | 1970 | COLOR

7 This is an underrated film with heart and is particularly good at capturing the restlessness of a pivotal period in American history. Set in the restlessness and uncertainty of the late 1960s, a hip California college professor (Douglas) begins to question his sheltered academic lifestyle. Hoping to experience the real world and to learn what it is all about, he takes off to spend a summer in Missouri working as a laborer with "regular people." There he falls in love and is happy, but doubts again surface about his life.

□ Sex □ Nud ◢ Viol □ Lang ■ AdSit

A: Michael Douglas, Joe Don Baker, Lee Purcell, Meg Foster, Grayson Hall

© CBS/FOX VIDEO 7166

ADVENTURES OF HUCK FINN, THE

D: Stephen Sommers — 108 m

PG | DMA CLD | 1993 | COLOR

9 Wonderful adaptation of Mark Twain's classic adventure story set in the pre-Civil War South. Huck Finn is a fun-loving boy that is as wild as the river, but he has been taken in by the widow Douglas who has vowed to civilize him. However, his thieving father has come and stolen him back, so Huck has faked his own murder and run away. In the uproar, the household slave, and Huck's friend Jim, also runs away. Now everyone thinks that Jim has murdered Huck. Instead, they have joined up on a grand adventure down the river, which turns into a run for their lives. Fast-moving and funny. Never misses a beat.

□ Sex □ Nud ◢ Viol ◢ Lang □ AdSit

A: Elijah Wood, Courtney B. Vance, Robbie Coltrane, Jason Robards, Jr., Ron Pearlman, Dana Ivey

© WALT DISNEY HOME VIDEO 1896

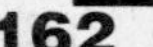

ADVENTURES OF HUCKLEBERRY FINN, THE

D: Michael Curtiz — 108 m

7 G · DMA CLD · 1960 · COLOR

Very good version of Twain's classic story with a very appealing cast. More true to Twain's original story than earlier films. An independent boy, Huckleberry Finn, and escaped slave, Jim, travel down the Mississippi River and get more adventure than they had counted on when they run into two con men who convince them that they are a king and duke. Eddie Hodges is appealing as Huck and famed boxer Archie Moore is a standout as Jim.

Sex · Nud · Viol · Lang · AdSit

A: Tony Randall, Eddie Hodges, Archie Moore, Patty McCormack, Neville Brand, Buster Keaton

Distributed By MGM/UA Home Video M201279

ADVENTURES OF PRISCILLA, QUEEN OF THE DESERT, THE

D: Stephen Elliot — 102 m

8 R · COM DMA · 1994 · COLOR

Not at all your typical evening's entertainment. This curious and outrageous import from Australia won an Oscar for Best Costume Design. It is often funny and touching, but it also has a storyline you aren't likely encounter often. It is the story of the adventure of three drag queens, who make their living lip-syncing to 70's disco songs while dressed in fantastic flowing stage costumes. They have agreed to a performance in front of rugged crowds of rugged men in the rugged Outback, and they have set out on their adventure in a mechanically-uncertain bus which they have named Priscilla. Their trip is certainly not uneventful, but for drag queens that is normal. It is also certainly educational for most of us.

Sex · Nud · Viol · Lang · AdSit

A: Terence Stamp, Hugo Weaving, Guy Pearce, Bill Hunter

© POLYGRAM VIDEO 33713-3

ADVENTURES OF THE WILDERNESS FAMILY, THE

D: Stewart Raffill — 100 m

8 G · DMA CLD · 1976 · COLOR

This is a very good, family-oriented human interest drama but is mostly geared for young people. An urban family escapes the city and pollution to the majestic wonders of nature for the sake of a sick daughter. There they build a cabin in the magnificent Rockies and brave the dangers of the wild. Lots of animals and scenery. See also WILDERNESS FAMILY, PART 2 and similar ACROSS THE GREAT DIVIDE.

Sex · Nud · Viol · Lang · AdSit

A: Robert Logan, Susan D. Shaw, Ham Larsen, Heather Rattray, George "Buck" Flower, William Cornford

© VIDEO TREASURES 9655

ADVISE AND CONSENT

D: Otto Preminger — 142 m

7 NR · DMA · 1962 · B&W

This is a long but engrossing tale of Washington political intrigue and backroom wheeling and dealing. Henry Fonda has been appointed as Secretary of State, but he is not a popular choice. There is extensive opposition to his appointment and the debate over his confirmation is intense. The vote will be very close, which prompts one ruthless politician to resort to attempt blackmail. Praised as being largely realistic in flavor and subdued in its characterizations. Charles Laughton, in his last movie, is a crusty old Senator from the South. Excellent performances all around by an all-star cast.

Sex · Nud · Viol · Lang · AdSit

A: Henry Fonda, Don Murray, Charles Laughton, Walter Pidgeon, Peter Lawford, Gene Tierney

© VIDEO TREASURES HR9613

ADVOCATE, THE

D: Leslie Megahey — 102 m

7 R · DMA MYS · 1994 · COLOR

15th-century France was rife with ignorance, superstition and corruption. Law is attempted for the protection of order, but it is also subject to the interpretation of both the church and the local aristocracy. One of its more bizarre aspects is that animals were held to the same laws as were man. This presents an interesting background for this film to present its story of an ardent lawyer who has escaped the corrupt politics of Paris, only to be trapped in even more corrupt and bizarre local politics, when he is forced to defend a pig accused of killing a Jewish boy. Quite unusual, yet also quite fascinating -- both from a historical aspect and philosophical one. Based upon fact.

Sex · Nud · Viol · Lang · AdSit

A: Colin Firth, Ian Holm, Donald Pleasence, Amina Annabi, Nicol Williamson, Michael Gough

© MIRAMAX HOME ENTERTAINMENT 2560

AGE OF INNOCENCE, THE

D: Martin Scorsese — 138 m

9 PG · ROM DMA · 1993 · COLOR

It is New York City in the 1870's. Newland (Daniel Day-Lewis), a wealthy attorney and the son of a prominent old family, is set to marry the beautiful but very proper May (Winona Ryder), the daughter of another fine old family. Then May's cousin Ellen (Michelle Pfeiffer) returns from Europe, seeking a divorce from her brutish husband. Worse, she wants to live alone and be her own person, which just isn't done. So, Newland is asked to help save the family's good name. Instead, his heart is set pounding with passion for the unconventional Ellen. Against a background of gossip and hypocrisy, they must decide whether they should follow their hearts or do the proper thing. 4 Oscar nominations.

Sex · Nud · Viol · Lang · AdSit

A: Daniel Day-Lewis, Michelle Pfeiffer, Winona Ryder

© COLUMBIA TRISTAR HOME VIDEO 52633

AGE OLD FRIENDS

D: Allan Kroeker — 89 m

7 NR · DMA · 1989 · COLOR

Heart-rending and heart-warming. John (Cronyn) is an aging man who gets an offer to move in with his daughter (Tandy Cronyn - real-life daughter) but he turns it down to instead move into a retirement home. There he meets Michael (Gardenia) who becomes his good friend. But Michael soon develops the beginning signs of senility and over time grows to rely heavily on John for support and day-to-day tasks. John's daughter again makes the offer to live with her and John is forced to chose between a better life with her or staying to help his old friend. A very moving story of friendship and life.

Sex · Nud · Viol · Lang · AdSit

A: Hume Cronyn, Vincent Gardenia, Esther Rolle, Tandy Cronyn, Michele Scarabelli

© HBO VIDEO 0427

AGNES OF GOD

D: Norman Jewison — 90 m

7 PG-13 · DMA MYS · 1985 · COLOR

Truly unusual film. An apparently unbalanced young nun (Tilly) is accused of killing her own newborn baby, which she claims is not even hers. A court-appointed psychiatrist (Fonda) is sent to investigate this strange situation, but finds no easy explanations. Is the girl devout and sane, with some greater mystery at play here? Soon Fonda and the Mother Superior (Bancroft) are sparring over the fate of the girl. Very strong acting - two Oscar nominations. At times fascinating, but also disturbing and not always satisfying. From a hit Broadway play.

Sex · Nud · Viol · Lang · AdSit

A: Jane Fonda, Anne Bancroft, Meg Tilly, Anne Pitoniak, Winston Rekert, Gratien Gelians

© COLUMBIA TRISTAR HOME VIDEO 60563

D M A

AGONY AND THE ECSTASY, THE

D: Carol Reed — 139 m

7 NR · DMA · 1965 · COLOR

This is the story of the four-year battle of wills between two of the most colorful figures from the Italian Renaissance period. The soldier/Pope Julius II asks Michaelangelo to paint the ceiling of the Sistine Chapel, but Michaelangelo refuses when they violently disagree on Michelangelo's vision of what it should be. Then, virtually forced to do the work, Michelangelo begins but soon destroys what he has done and leaves Rome. Later, he returns to finish the task. Very lush production values mark this historical drama of two powerful, willful individuals in conflict.

Sex · Nud · Viol · Lang · AdSit

A: Charlton Heston, Rex Harrison, Diane Cilento, Harry Andrews, Alberto Lupo, Adolfo Celi

© FOXVIDEO 1007

AIRPORT

D: George Seaton — 137 m

9 PG · SUS DMA · 1970 · COLOR

This was the first of the major disaster epics which were very popular for nearly a decade. Here, a crazed bomber blows a hole in an airliner while it is in flight. Badly crippled, the plane must land immediately at a snowbound airport whose runway is blocked by an another airliner stuck in the mud. This type of plot provides an opportunity for the film to explore the lives of several different people affected by the disaster. So, there are several stories going on all at the same time. Pretty good stuff. Helen Hayes won an Oscar. Taut and suspenseful. See also AIRPORT 1975, AIRPORT '77, THE POSIDEON ADVENTURE, EARTHQUAKE and TOWERING INFERNO.

Sex · Nud · Viol · Lang · AdSit

A: Burt Lancaster, Dean Martin, George Kennedy, Helen Hayes, Jean Seberg, Jacqueline Bisset

© MCA/UNIVERSAL HOME VIDEO, INC. 55031

AIRPORT 1975

D: Jack Smight — 107 m

7 PG · SUS DMA · 1974 · COLOR

AIRPORT disaster sequel. When the cockpit of a 747 is struck by a small plane in mid-air, the entire flight crew is killed. It is up to stewardess Karen Black to fly the plane by Heston's radioed instructions, that is until Heston himself can be "dropped" into the ripped-open cock-pit by a helicopter from overhead. Not terribly believable but it is very entertaining - in part because there were 22 major stars aboard that airplane. See also AIRPORT and AIRPORT '77.

Sex · Nud · Viol · Lang · AdSit

A: Charlton Heston, Karen Black, George Kennedy, Efrem Zimbalist, Jr., Susan Clark, Helen Reddy

© GOODTIMES 4107

AIRPORT '77

D: Jerry Jameson — 114 m

7 PG · SUS DMA · 1977 · COLOR

This is another AIRPORT disaster flick sequel. This time, millionaire Jimmy Stewart has a converted 747 jumbo jet transport a large group of VIP guests along with a fortune in his art treasures to the grand opening of a museum in Palm Beach. However, the plane is hijacked along the way and forced to crash land into the open ocean within the famed Bermuda Triangle. Then, in order to be rescued, the plane and passengers, who are alive inside, must be lifted whole from the ocean floor. See also AIRPORT and AIRPORT 1975.

Sex · Nud · Viol · Lang · AdSit

A: Jack Lemmon, Lee Grant, Brenda Vaccaro, Darren McGavin, Christopher Lee, James Stewart

© MCA/UNIVERSAL HOME VIDEO, INC. 66039

AKIRA KUROSAWA'S DREAMS

D: Akira Kurosawa 120 m

PG | FOR DMA | 1990 | COLOR | Sex | Nud | Viol | Lang | AdSit

9 Rich in imagery, famed Japanese director Akira Kurosawa has created a screen depiction of eight dreams which separately contemplate and explore the consequences of man's world and his effect upon differing aspects of it. Very personal and philosophical, some stories are much more effective than others, however all are eerie and not totally resolved, much like real dreams. Film fans will enjoy the master's cinematography, but casual observers may be left wanting. Subtitles.

A: Akira Terao, Mieko Harada, Chishu Ryu, Martin Scorsese

© WARNER HOME VIDEO 11911

ALAMO BAY

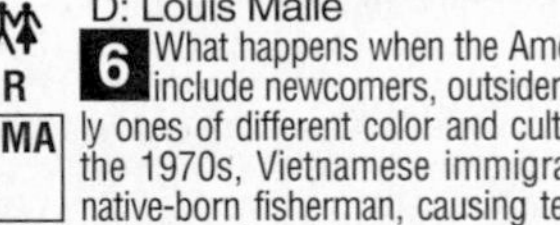

D: Louis Malle 99 m

R | DMA | 1985 | COLOR | Sex | Nud | Viol | Lang | AdSit

6 What happens when the American dream must be broadened to include newcomers, outsiders from a different country, especially ones of different color and culture? On the Gulf Coast of Texas in the 1970s, Vietnamese immigrants work very hard and outwork native-born fisherman, causing tension and deep-seated animosities to flair up. Amy Madigan supports Ho Nguyen's right to be there, but her boyfriend, Ed Harris, joins the KKK. Based on true events.

A: Ed Harris, Amy Madigan, Ho Nquyen, Donald Moffat, Truyer Tran, Rudy Young

© COLUMBIA TRISTAR HOME VIDEO 60561

AL CAPONE

D: Richard Wilson 104 m

NR | CRM ACT DMA | 1959 | B&W | Sex | Nud | Viol | Lang | AdSit

8 Excellent action movie. Solid telling of the life story of the infamous Chicago gangster who rises from being a hitman for Johnny Torrio (Persoff) to become the king of the Prohibition Era. After a bitter battle with the Feds, he is arrested and imprisoned for tax evasion. No other gangster so captured the imagination and the headlines of the country. Steiger is riveting in his portrayal of Capone, and the rest of the cast is perfect, too. For more of Capone see THE UNTOUCHABLES (1987) and SCARFACE (1932).

A: Rod Steiger, Fay Spain, Martin Balsam, Nehemiah Persoff

© CBS/FOX VIDEO 7750

ALFIE

D: Lewis Gilbert 113 m

NR | DMA COM | 1966 | COLOR | Sex | Nud | Viol | Lang | AdSit

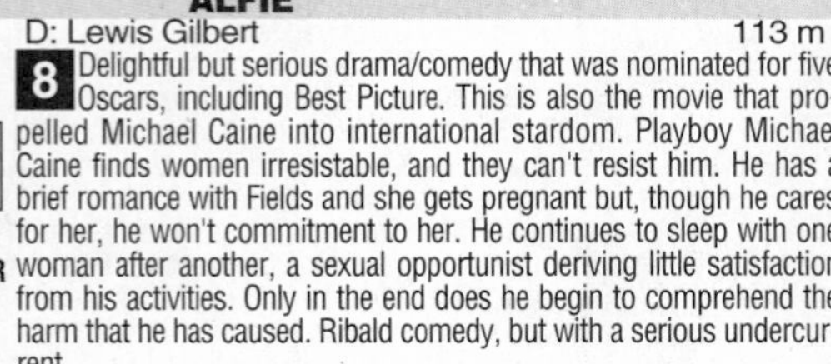

8 Delightful but serious drama/comedy that was nominated for five Oscars, including Best Picture. This is also the movie that propelled Michael Caine into international stardom. Playboy Michael Caine finds women irresistable, and they can't resist him. He has a brief romance with Fields and she gets pregnant but, though he cares for her, he won't commitment to her. He continues to sleep with one woman after another, a sexual opportunist deriving little satisfaction from his activities. Only in the end does he begin to comprehend the harm that he has caused. Ribald comedy, but with a serious undercurrent.

A: Michael Caine, Shelley Winters, Millicent Martin, Julia Foster, Shirley Anne Field, Vivien Merchant

© PARAMOUNT HOME VIDEO 6604

ALICE

D: Woody Allen 106 m

PG-13 | COM DMA | 1990 | COLOR | Sex | Nud | Viol | Lang | AdSit

7 A fine, whimsical adult fantasy from Woody Allen. Alice (Farrow) is a pampered shopaholic who lives in a Manhattan apartment with her very wealthy husband (Hurt), her two kids and her servants. She falls for a jazz saxophonist she meets while picking her kids up one day, and she begins to challenge her whole life. She goes to an Asian herbologist who gives her potions with magical powers that take her on an exotic journey into self-discovery and fulfillment. This is a dryly funny film which ventures out of Allen's traditional comfort zones and brings us some fresh life crises to be resolved.

A: Mia Farrow, William Hurt, Keye Luke, Blythe Danner, Alec Baldwin, Judy Davis

© ORION PICTURES CORPORATION 8773

ALICE DOESN'T LIVE HERE ANYMORE

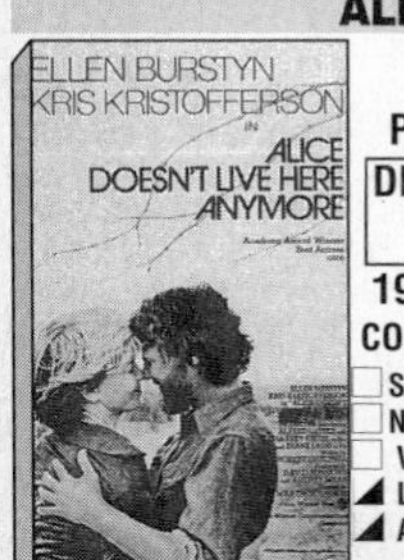

D: Martin Scorsese 112 m

PG | DMA | 1974 | COLOR | Sex | Nud | Viol | Lang | AdSit

9 This is a wonderful story of a woman who is determined to make it on her own after her husband is killed. Alice has dreams to fulfill and she also wants to change her life, but is broke and has a young son to support. She is 35 and has no skills but heads out anyway. She finds work both as a singer and as a waitress. As she rebuilds her life, she discovers a self she hadn't known was there. Burstyn richly deserved her Oscar for Best Actress. Also nominated for two other Oscars. Inspired a long-running TV series. Excellent.

A: Ellen Burstyn, Kris Kristofferson, Harvey Keitel, Billy Green Bush, Alfred Lutter, Jodie Foster

© WARNER HOME VIDEO 1034

ALIVE

D: Frank Marshall 126 m

DMA ACT | 1992 | COLOR | Sex | Nud | Viol | Lang | AdSit

7 Gripping drama based upon the real-life 1972 plane crash in the snow-covered Andes Mountains. A team of rugby players managed to survive tremendous hardship and isolation for over 70 days at 11,500 feet, but only after having made the most difficult decisions. When the search for them was abandoned and they were left without hope, they survived by eating the dead bodies of their teammates. This is not a story about cannibalism. It is the story of survival in the face of devastating and debilitating odds. One of the most realistic films ever concerning a plane crash. Entertaining? No. Very interesting? Yes.

A: Ethan Hawke, Vincent Spano, Josh Hamilton, Bruce Ramsay, John Haymes Newton, David Kriegel

© TOUCHSTONE HOME VIDEO 1596

ALL QUIET ON THE WESTERN FRONT

D: Delbert Mann 131 m

NR | WAR DMA | 1978 | COLOR | Sex | Nud | Viol | Lang | AdSit

9 Extremely strong made-for-TV remake of the 1930 classic. It is war in the mud as told from the German point of view. A young idealistic student-turned-soldier is caught up in the romance of the idea of war and dives excitedly in. But, at the front lines of WWI he discovers the dark realities of war really is. Ernest Borgnine is a seasoned veteran who teaches Richard Thomas how to stay alive. Borgnine, Neal and the movie each received Emmy nominations. Despite being an excellent, high quality production with top notch photography and effects, it still is not as good as the 1930 classic version.

A: Ernest Borgnine, Richard Thomas, Patricia Neal, Ian Holm

© LIVE HOME VIDEO 51115

ALL THAT JAZZ

D: Bob Fosse 123 m

R | DMA MUS | 1980 | COLOR | Sex | Nud | Viol | Lang | AdSit

7 Adult autobiographical musical from Bob Fosse. A driven, egotistical chainsmoker encounters the angel of death (in the lovely form of Jessica Lange) after suffering a heart attack resulting from the overwhelming pressures caused by working on a film, working on a Broadway musical, as well as trying to please his wife, his mistress, and his daughter. The musical numbers are quite extraordinary - stunning and sometimes shocking. Scheider's finest performance, with solid assistance from Ben Vereen and Cliff Gorman.

A: Roy Scheider, Ann Reinking, Jessica Lange, Leland Palmer, Cliff Gorman, Ben Vereen

© FOXVIDEO 1095

ALL THE PRESIDENT'S MEN

D: Alan J. Pakula 139 m

PG | DMA MYS | 1976 | COLOR | Sex | Nud | Viol | Lang | AdSit

10 Nominated for 8 Oscars, won 4, including Best Picture. On June 17, 1972, well-dressed burglars were caught inside the offices of national Democratic party headquarters. This film is a modern classic and is also a landmark film about events that lead to President Nixon's downfall and his eventual resignation. Even though the final result is known, the way in which the drama unfolds is still fascinating. The complex issues surrounding the Watergate break-in are explained in understandable terms by using the best elements of a mystery/thriller, presented in a documentary style. Great story telling.

A: Dustin Hoffman, Robert Redford, Jason Robards, Jr., Jane Alexander, Jack Warden, Martin Balsam

© WARNER HOME VIDEO 1018

ALL THE RIGHT MOVES

D: Michael Chapman 90 m

R | DMA | 1983 | COLOR | Sex | Nud | Viol | Lang | AdSit

7 Tom Cruise (in one of his earliest hits) wants to become an engineer after high school and is looking to escape from the dreary dying steel mill town in which he lives. His only chance is by winning a football scholarship. His football coach (Nelson) has his own chance to get out as a college coach of a big league school, and he puts tremendous pressure on his kids to perform. However, after they lose one particularly important game, he comes down hard on the team. Cruise objects and gets thrown off the team for it. His dream has just died. This is a very believable portrait and extremely well acted.

A: Tom Cruise, Craig T. Nelson, Lea Thompson, Charles Cioffi, Christopher Penn, Paul Carafotes

© CBS/FOX VIDEO 1299

ALPINE FIRE

D: Fredi M. Murer 115 m

R | FOR DMA | 1987 | COLOR | Sex | Nud | Viol | Lang | AdSit

6 A farm family living in a remote mountainous area of the Swiss Alps struggles to survive. The two children are extraordinarily close due to their physical isolation and the emotional remoteness of their parents. The boy is a deaf-mute who is struggling with his adolescence. His older sister protects him fiercely and loves him unconditionally, but she struggles with her own loneliness and their passions lead them into a tragic incestuous relationship. This is not an exploitation film. It is interesting and very different, but also ultimately not completely satisfying. Subtitles.

A: Thomas Nook, Johanna Lier, Dorothea Moritz, Rolf Illig

© LIVE HOME VIDEO 5235

ALWAYS

D: Henry Jaglom 105 m

R | DMA ROM COM | 1985 | COLOR

Sex Nud Viol Lang AdSit

7 A very original film, largely a biography of director/actor Jaglom's real-life breakup with his wife Townsend. Three couples spend the Fourth of July together at a barbecue. One couple is getting married, one is solidly married, and David and Judy have been separated for two years and are on the verge of divorce. Judy stops by just to visit her almost ex-husband and ends up spending the weekend with him and the two other couples. They discuss love, romance, and each other. Some really funny dialogue, some interesting characters and some powerful human insights. Chocolate can be a powerful thing.

A: Henry Jaglom, Patrice Townsend, Melissa Leo, Joanna Frank, Alan Rachins, Michael Emil

© LIVE HOME VIDEO VA5161

AMADEUS

D: Milos Forman 158 m

PG | DMA COM MUS | 1984 | COLOR

Sex Nud Viol Lang AdSit

7 A witty production that won eight Oscars (including Best Picture, Actor and Director) with its literate, sophisticated script and superb performances. Salieri (Abraham) is a successful but mediocre composer. Still, he has great influence in the courts of Venice. Along comes Mozart, a brash young composer who effortlessly produces works of dazzling brilliance. Salieri is intensely jealous of Mozart's talent but is also disgusted with this boy-genius composer who is also a womanizer and a boor. So, he does all that he can to sabotage and destroy Mozart, but instead destroys himself. Slightly overlong.

A: Tom Hulce, F. Murray Abraham, Elizabeth Beridge, Simon Callow, Roy Dotrice, Christine Ebersole

© HBO VIDEO 2997

AMBASSADOR, THE

D: J. Lee Thompson 97 m

R | SUS DMA | 1984 | COLOR

Sex Nud Viol Lang AdSit

7 Political intrigue set in the Middle East. Mitchum is a dedicated American ambassador to Israel who is working hard to find a solution to the Palestinian issue. He efforts make him the target of numerous terrorist attacks including being blackmailed with a film of his adulterous wife's illicit affair with a PLO powerbroker. Hudson is a security officer. This is an intelligent and entertaining thriller. This is also Rock Hudson's last major film. It is loosely based upon the book 52 PICKUP which was itself made into a good film and released two years later.

A: Robert Mitchum, Ellen Burstyn, Rock Hudson, Fabio Testi, Donald Pleasence

Distributed By MGM/UA Home Video M800765

AMERICAN FLYERS

D: John Badham 113 m

PG-13 | DMA | 1985 | COLOR

Sex Nud Viol Lang AdSit

7 This is a very likable story about two estranged brothers attempt to recover their relationship. One is an over-achieving sports doctor, dying of an incurable disease (Costner). The younger brother is drifting with no direction (Grant). Their strained relationship, and that with their mother, is further complicated because she had deserted their father as he was dying of the same disease that Costner suffers from. The one common thread linking the brothers is bicycle racing and a grueling three-day bicycle race through the mountains of Colorado. This is a highly enjoyable feel-good movie.

A: Kevin Costner, David Marshal Grant, Rae Dawn Chong, Alexandra Paul, Janice Rule, John Amos

© WARNER HOME VIDEO 11520

AMERICAN GRAFFITI

D: George Lucas 112 m

PG | DMA COM | 1973 | COLOR

Sex Nud Viol Lang AdSit

10 A monster hit and a treasure trove of nostalgia. Also brilliant and unpretentious filmmaking that is just plain fun. It follows a group of high school students who are about to transition into another world. They nearing graduation from high school in 1962, in a small Northern California town. Lucas weaves their individual lives together into a vastly interesting, poignant, sensitive, frequently funny and always fascinating mosaic. An insightful and very entertaining package, wrapped up in terrific rock `n roll score. You really get to care about all these people. Highly recommended.

A: Richard Dreyfuss, Ron Howard, Paul LeMat, Cindy Williams, Candy Clark, Mackenzie Phillips

© MCA/UNIVERSAL HOME VIDEO, INC. 66010

AMERICAN HEART

D: Martin Bell 114 m

R | DMA | 1993 | COLOR

Sex Nud Viol Lang AdSit

8 Sobering and very realistic portrait of an American family/non-family. Bridges is an ex-convict just out on parole, when he discovers that his young son has runaway to come to live with him. He has no job, no skills, no home, no money, no desire to take care of a kid or any idea how to be a father. Furlong is a very sad kid who has no mother. All he has is his father and that isn't much. But, Bridges is determined to go straight this time and also trys to become a father, agreeing to take the boy in saying: "You keep me straight and I'll keep you straight." To see this movie is, for most of us, to see a tough, very different, but very real world for too many others.

A: Jeff Bridges, Edward Furlong, Lucinda Jenney, Tracey Kapisky, Don Harvey, Maggie Welsh

© LIVE HOME VIDEO 69940

AMERICANIZATION OF EMILY, THE

D: Arthur Hiller 117 m

NR | COM DMA ROM | 1964 | B&W

Sex Nud Viol Lang AdSit

8 Entertaining and daring comedy. Garner is a Navy officer whose main job is keeping his superiors comfortable and supplied with "everything." This suits Garner's larcenous and cowardly nature just fine. Andrews is his British war-widow chauffeur. She despises his avowed cowardice but falls for him anyway. However, things drastically change for them both when the admirals decide they want the first American naval casualty of the D-Day invasion filmed for publicity, and they order Garner to do it. Garner is afraid that the casualty is likely to be him. Compelling satire, with a hard edge.

A: James Garner, Julie Andrews, Melvyn Douglas, James Coburn, Joyce Grenfell, Keenan Wynn

Distributed By MGM/UA Home Video M200518

AMERICAN ME

D: Edward James Olmos 125 m

R | CRM DMA | 1992 | COLOR

Sex Nud Viol Lang AdSit

7 Powerful, violent and brutal film about brutality, violence, power and respect. Olmos also stars in this his directing debut. This film graphically illustrates the patterns of behavior that seduce some into a cycle of gang violence. Olmos plays a man who has spent most of his life in prison but has gained self-worth and respect as a ruthless crime lord. However, when he learns the personal price he has paid, it has become too late for him to benefit. This is not a pleasant film to watch because what it reflects is uncompromising, graphic and real. Ultimately it makes a powerful anti-gang and anti-violence statement.

A: Edward James Olmos, William Forsythe, Pepe Serna, Danny De La Paz, Evelina Fernandez, Sal Lopez

© MCA/UNIVERSAL HOME VIDEO, INC. 81265

ANDERSONVILLE TRIAL, THE

D: George C. Scott 150 m

NR | DMA WST | 1970 | COLOR

Sex Nud Viol Lang AdSit

9 Riveting psychological and courtroom drama based upon solid historical fact. During the Civil War, the Confederate prison at Andersonville, Georgia housed over 50,000 prisoners under absolutely squalid conditions. This is the gripping account of the moral issues surrounding the post-war trial of the Prussian administrator of that camp, whose German military training required him to follow orders without question even though these orders lead to over 14,000 deaths. It is one of the most tragic stories to come out of the Civil War and is an issue that would be revisited in WWII. Thought-provoking and powerful stuff.

A: Martin Sheen, William Shatner, Buddy Ebsen, Richard Basehart, Cameron Mitchell, Jack Cassidy

© LIVE HOME VIDEO 51065

AND GOD CREATED WOMAN

D: Roger Vadim 90 m

PG | FOR DMA | 1957 | COLOR

Sex Nud Viol Lang AdSit

6 This is a famous ground-breaking French film that is the story of a voluptuous orphan woman/child (super-sexy Brigitte Bardot). She is a passionate girl who can't help being a manteaser. She embarrasses her adoptive parents who then threaten her with being forced to leave town. Instead, she agrees to marry the younger son of a straight-laced family who is enchanted with her. However, she has long lusted after not him, but his older brother... and when she gets a chance, she seduces him - only to regret her actions later. It is relatively tame today but it was a breakthrough at the time.

A: Brigitte Bardot, Curt Jurgens, Jean-Louis Trintignant, Christian Marquand, Georges Poujouly, Jean Tissier

© LIVE HOME VIDEO 3002

AND THE BAND PLAYED ON

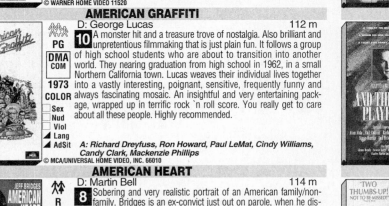

D: Roger Spottiswoode 140 m

PG | DMA | 1993 | COLOR

Sex Nud Viol Lang AdSit

8 Excellent made-for-cable TV movie that dramatizes the true-life story of AIDS. The individually devastating nature of the disease required the Center for Disease Control (CDC) to evaluate it, but when its highly communicable nature became known, they knew they also had a full-blown world-wide mass-killer. Matthew Modine is the central character in a cast that includes many of the biggest names in Hollywood. He plays the key CDC researcher who led the search to first discover what the absolutely devastating disease was and how it was transmitted, to the prolonged and politically unpopular fight with the government and public to respect the severity of the problem.

A: Matthew Modine, Alan Alda, Phil Collins, Richard Gere, Glenne Headley, Lily Tomlin

© HBO VIDEO 90962

ANGEL AT MY TABLE, AN

D: Jane Champion 157 m

R | FOR DMA | 1991 | COLOR

Sex Nud Viol Lang AdSit

6 A critically acclaimed film, this was originally made for New Zealand television. It is an adaptation of the autobiographies of Janet Frame, New Zealand's most famous poet and writer. Hers is the story of a sad and very shy childhood. Her shyness resulted in a such a total lack of social skills that it was misdiagnosed as being schizophrenia. She spent eight years in a mental institution before being released to begin anew acquiring the confidence and skills to live a somewhat normal life. Well-done and heartfelt, but very detailed, very deliberate and very slow. Very patient viewers only.

A: Kerry Fox, Kerry Fox, Aleia Keogh, Karen Fergusson, Iris Churn, K.J. Wilson

© TURNER HOME ENTERTAINMENT N4124

ANGELO MY LOVE

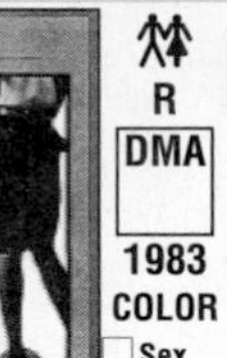

D: Robert Duvall 115 m

R | DMA | 1983 | COLOR

7 A fascinating journey into the real-life world of modern-day gypsies. The film itself follows a streetwise 11-year-old hustler in New York City on his search to recover a stolen $10,000 ring that is a family heirloom and destined to belong to his wife one day. However, the real focus is upon the nature of the gypsy lifestyle. It is a fascinating portrait of a life that few can imagine. Real gypsies, not actors were used in the roles. You may also want to see KING OF THE GYPSIES.

Sex / Nud / Viol / Lang / AdSit

A: Michael Evans, Ruthie Evans, Angelo Evans, Tony Evans, Steve Tsingonoff

© COLUMBIA TRISTAR HOME VIDEO 60125

ANGIE

D: Martha Coolidge 108 m

R | DMA | 1994 | COLOR

7 Angie (Geena Davis) has grown up in a working-class Italian neighborhood of Brooklyn. She has a dead-end job and has been going with a plumber named Vinnie and is now pregnant with his child. Vinnie is ecstatic and proposes immediately, everything seems on track for a normal life, but Angie wants more. When she was three, her mother deserted her and her father. Angie never really knew her mother and her father won't talk about it but Angie wonders if she hadn't felt trapped too. Unwilling to be locked into a future she is not sure of, Angie breaks free to search for the better life she knows is out there, but she is not prepared for what she discovers.

Sex / Nud / Viol / Lang / AdSit

A: Geena Davis, James Gandolfin, Aida Turturro, Philip Basco, Jenny O'Hara, Stephen Rea

© HOLLYWOOD PICTURES HOME VIDEO 2556

ANNE OF AVONLEA

D: Kevin Sullivan 224 m

NR | DMA ROM | 1988 | COLOR

9 Sparkling sequel to ANNE OF GREEN GABLES and a rare event where the sequel is as good as the original. Anne, the idealistic redheaded orphan who was adopted by a bachelor farmer and his old-maid sister, is now 18. She is an intelligent young woman and a budding writer who becomes a teacher at Avonlea. There she wins the hearts of everyone around her, including the stubborn headmistress who is determined to make her life miserable, and where she has her first brush with adult love. Absolutely charming story that will win over everyone of every age. Extremely well done.

Sex / Nud / Viol / Lang / AdSit

A: Megan Follows, Colleen Dewhurst, Wendy Hiller, Frank Converse, Schuyyler Grant, Jonathan Crombie

© WALT DISNEY HOME VIDEO 650

ANNE OF GREEN GABLES

D: Kevin Sullivan 199 m

NR | DMA | 1985 | COLOR

10 Wonderfully well-made. This endearing classic story is brought to life by an excellent cast and set in beautifully scenic Nova Scotia. A charming orphan girl with a wild imagination and flaming red hair is adopted by a bachelor farmer and his old-maid sister. They are kind hard-working people, but very plain and stoic; and, Anne is vibrant, full of wonder for life and bounding with enthusiasm. As much as they resist her, she brings profound changes into their quiet lives, and they love her in return. Heartwarming and thoroughly uplifting story. A true treat for everyone. See also ANNE OF AVONLEA.

Sex / Nud / Viol / Lang / AdSit

A: Megan Follows, Colleen Dewhurst, Patricia Hamilton, Marilyn Lightstone, Charmion King, Richard Farnsworth

© WALT DISNEY HOME VIDEO 642

ANNE OF THE THOUSAND DAYS

D: Charles Jarrott 145 m

PG | DMA | 1969 | COLOR

8 Engrossing generally true story of 16th-century England's King Henry VIII. Henry wants an heir and he wants Anne Boleyn (Bujold), so he decides to throw away his current childless wife, but the Pope will not let him divorce her. Further, the crafty Anne will not lay with the King unless any heir she bears him is declared legitimate. The battle between them rages on for six years. Eventually Henry forms his own church, the Church of England, and marries Anne - but she produces only a daughter. So, Henry takes still another wife and Anne's days are numbered. Great performances, fascinating. 9 Oscar nominations.

Sex / Nud / Viol / Lang / AdSit

A: Richard Burton, Genevieve Bujold, Anthony Quayle, Irene Papas, Peter Jeffrey

© MCA/UNIVERSAL HOME VIDEO, INC. 80163

ANNIE HALL

D: Woody Allen 99 m

PG | ROM COM DMA | 1977 | COLOR

9 Wonderful bittersweet movie, that nearly everybody (even most non-Allen fans) liked. Woody Allen's humor is very much alive here, but this is also a poignant and sophisticated look into '70s relationships. It is a four-Oscar movie, including Best Picture. It follows the relationship between neurotic New Yorkers, Allen and Keaton as first love grows, then it stutters, then it restarts and then it dies. Both outgrow each other to become different people than they were. Very funny but poignant and sad, too, because it rings so true with many who view it. It'll touch your heart.

Sex / Nud / Viol / Lang / AdSit

A: Woody Allen, Diane Keaton, Tony Roberts, Paul Simon, Shelley Duvall, Carol Kane

Distributed By MGM/UA Home Video M200251

ANOTHER WOMAN

D: Woody Allen 81 m

PG | DMA | 1988 | COLOR

8 Gena Rowlands is a 50ish New York philosophy professor who discovers her life is not as stable as she has assumed. Instead, she has only managed to shield herself from all emotions. She is forced to seriously reappraise herself when she accidentally overhears another woman's conversation in a session with a psychoanalyst next door. As the woman (Farrow) explains how she feels her marriage is beginning to crumble, Rowlands begins to look at her own life in a new way. This is a stark adult drama and is well-cast - but it is a serious-minded Woody Allen film without clear cut answers and not for everyone.

Sex / Nud / Viol / Lang / AdSit

A: Gena Rowlands, Mia Farrow, Ian Holm, Blythe Danner, Gene Hackman, Betty Buckley

© ORION PICTURES CORPORATION 8735

APARTMENT, THE

D: Billy Wilder 126 m

NR | DMA COM ROM | 1960 | B&W

10 Comedy and drama have rarely been so well woven together. In order to win favor with his boss (MacMurry) and other execs, Jack Lemmon agrees to lend his apartment to them so that they can carry on after-hours affairs. His stock rises and he quickly moves up to the 19th floor. He gets a key to the executive washroom, but he has to change his plans when he comes home to find his boss's latest girlfriend (MacLaine) has attempted suicide. He nurses her back to health and falls for her himself. Witty adult entertainment. Lemmon and MacLaine are great. Won the 1960 Best Picture Oscar.

Sex / Nud / Viol / Lang / AdSit

A: Jack Lemmon, Shirley MacLaine, Fred MacMurray, Ray Walston, Jack Kuschen, Edie Adams

Distributed By MGM/UA Home Video M201307

APOCALYPSE NOW

D: Francis Ford Coppola 153 m

R | WAR DMA ACT | 1979 | COLOR

10 Chilling, surrealistic Vietnam war epic. Special Forces agent Sheen is sent to find and terminate a highly decorated renegade officer (Brando). The Army High Command claims he has gone mad. He commands his own native army, in his own war, in his own way. Sheen travels upriver into Cambodia on a terrifyingly surrealistic journey into Brando's world, there to find a brilliant man who has gained god-like status through using absolutely ruthless acts of horror. Is this man mad or is it the world? Stunning photography and a very unnerving experience. See also the documentary HEARTS OF DARKNESS about the difficult making of this film.

Sex / Nud / Viol / Lang / AdSit

A: Marlon Brando, Martin Sheen, Robert Duvall, Harrison Ford, Sam Bottoms, Dennis Hopper

© PARAMOUNT HOME VIDEO 2306

APPRENTICESHIP OF DUDDY KRAVITZ, THE

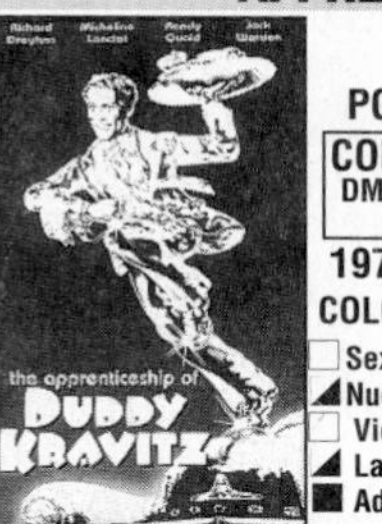

D: Ted Kotcheff 121 m

PG | COM DMA | 1974 | COLOR

7 Biting satire that was also Dreyfuss's first leading role. He plays a Jewish teenage hustler in 1940 Montreal who is determined to "do good," no matter what. He ruthlessly schemes to get money, women and power, no matter what the cost. This movie is exuberant and manic, as well as biting and sad, and is more than a little uneven too. However, it is also frequently hilarious. Dreyfuss displays his particular talent for sarcasm well and often, a trait that endures today. A wicked sophisticated comedy.

Sex / Nud / Viol / Lang / AdSit

A: Richard Dreyfuss, Randy Quaid, Jack Warden, Denholm Elliott

© PARAMOUNT HOME VIDEO 8791

ASHES AND DIAMONDS

D: Andrzej Wajda 105 m

NR | FOR DMA WAR | 1958 | B&W

9 An extremely powerful and influential Polish film. WWII has just ended and a new peace dominated by Russian communists is beginning. Three young Poles, former members of the resistance movement, have just killed three Polish workers, believing that the communist party chief is among them. One of the assassins realizes that their target was in fact not killed. Spending the night at a hotel, the war-hardened young man has an affair with a pretty and tender barmaid. For the first time, he feels the war is over and begins to doubt his continuing role as a bitter political fanatic and soldier. Made a star of Cybulski and is considered the last in a trilogy of war films from director Wajda. Subtitles.

Sex / Nud / Viol / Lang / AdSit

A: Zbigniew Cybulski, Eva Krzyzewska, Adam Pawlikowski, Waclaw Zastrzezynski

© HOME VISION ASH 020

AS SUMMERS DIE

D: Jean-Claude Tramont 88 m

NR | DMA | 1986 | COLOR

7 Excellent made-for-TV movie. Glenn Scott is a struggling small town Georgia lawyer in 1959, who takes on the town's wealthiest family. He defends an old black woman against a rich white family's attempt to take back some land the family patriarch had given her earlier, after oil is found on it. He gets some unexpected help from the old man's feisty old sister (Davis). He soon finds that he has to defend this old woman too when the rest of the family begins to question her sanity. And the more he becomes involved with their family, he is drawn to the old woman's niece (Curtis). Excellent acting bring sparkle to a pretty good drama.

Sex / Nud / Viol / Lang / AdSit

A: Scott Glenn, Bette Davis, Jamie Lee Curtis, Penny Fuller, Beah Richards, John McIntire

© HBO VIDEO 9977

ATLANTIC CITY

D: Louis Malle — 104 m

R — DMA — 1981 — COLOR

9 A superb picture. A little group of losers struggles to "make good" in a seedy Atlantic City that is itself trying to be reborn into an eastcoast gambling Mecca. Lancaster is wonderful playing an aging small-time hood just out of prison. He is imagines himself to be more than he is and is all style and no real substance. Susan Sarandon is a poor girl next door who is working as a clam-shucker in a restaurant, while going to school to learn to become a casino dealer. She and Lancaster gain one brief shot at glory when her drug-dealing husband dies. They sell off his inventory, and for a short time they're on top.

Sex, Nud, Viol, Lang, AdSit

A: Burt Lancaster, Susan Sarandon, Kate Reid, Michel Piccoli, Hollis McLaren, Robert Joy

© PARAMOUNT HOME VIDEO 1460

AT PLAY IN THE FIELDS OF THE LORD

D: Hector Babenco — 190 m

R — DMA — 1991 — COLOR

8 Beautiful photography and earnest performances capture the spirit of the novel's intent. Excellent drama, however things do bog down in places. Set in the '80s, three very different Americans, each with very different motivations, affect the lives of a remote tribe of Brazilian rainforest Indians with almost equal doses of harm. Lithgow is a sanctimonious Protestant missionary who is willing to destroy their way of life so he can accomplish his selfish ends. Quinn is an earnest missionary who unwittingly provides Lithgow the access to the Indians he couldn't get himself. Berenger is a lost and tortured soul who wants to become part of the forest tribe's innocence.

Sex, Nud, Viol, Lang, AdSit

A: Tom Berenger, John Lithgow, Daryl Hannah, Aidan Quinn, Tom Waits, Kathy Bates

© MCA/UNIVERSAL HOME VIDEO, INC. 81246

AU REVOIR LES ENFANTS

D: Louis Malle — 103 m

PG — FOR DMA WAR — 1987 — COLOR

8 Goodbye children. Powerful Oscar nominee for Best Foreign Film. During WWII, at a French Catholic boarding school, the headmaster and the monks shield several Jewish children from the occupying Nazis. This is the story of two boys, one Catholic and one Jewish, who develop a close relationship during that winter - a relationship that is cut short when the Nazis discover the Jewish children-in-hiding. Deeply felt and moving, though a little slow at times. A devastating ending. Dubbed.

Sex, Nud, Viol, Lang, AdSit

A: Gaspard Manesse, Raphael Fejto, Francine Racette, Stanislas de Malberg, Phillipe Morier-Genoud, Francois Berleand

© ORION PICTURES CORPORATION 5041

AUTOBIOGRAPHY OF MISS JANE PITMAN

D: John Korty — 106 m

NR — DMA — 1974 — COLOR

10 This terrific made-for-TV movie is a triumph, and it won nine Emmys. It is essentially the story of much of black-American history, and it is told as it was "witnessed" in the person of one woman, Jane Pitman. Upon the event of her 110th birthday, just as the civil rights movement of the 1960s has begun, she begins to tell her story. The story line follows her from age 19 when she was a slave girl during the Civil War South, through to womanhood, in the Jim Crow era, to being an old woman and witnessing the civil rights movement of the 1960s. Excellent stuff!

Sex, Nud, Viol, Lang, AdSit

A: Cicely Tyson, Richard Dysart, Odetta, Michael Murphy, Thalmus Rasulala, Barbara Chaney

© UNITED AMERICAN VIDEO CORP. 5917

AVALON

D: Barry Levinson — 126 m

PG — DMA — 1991 — COLOR

7 A warm telling of an immigrant's story, which is also the story of a growing nation. An immigrant family seeks the American dream in the town of Avalon, near Baltimore, just prior to WWII. It is the story of what fifty years of changes bring to this large and boisterous family. The father struggles to become an entrepreneur in discount merchandising and to keep his family from drifting apart. Grandmother and Grandfather are not sure that they like the changes that industrialization is bringing, and desperately try to recall the good times so long ago. Long, but lovingly created, and well worth the time invested.

Sex, Nud, Viol, Lang, AdSit

A: Aidan Quinn, Joan Plowright, Armin Mueller-Stahl, Elizabeth Perkins, Lou Jacobi, Leo Fuchs

© COLUMBIA TRISTAR HOME VIDEO 70543

AWAKENINGS

D: Penny Marshall — 120 m

PG-13 — DMA — 1990 — COLOR

8 A charmer, a heartbreaker and a tearjerker. Williams puts in a strong performance as a shy reclusive doctor who decides to risk everything to try to treat a ward of comatose patients. He believes that there is a person alive inside the apparently frozen shells, and they all may be recoverable. His research leads him to a new treatment which he tries first on patient De Niro, who has been "asleep" for 30 years. De Niro does respond. He comes to back to "life" one night, an eerily "normal" person, but the drugs diminish in effectiveness and he fades away. Based on fact and the experiences of Dr. Oliver Sacks.

Sex, Nud, Viol, Lang, AdSit

A: Robin Williams, Robert De Niro, Julie Kavner, Ruth Nelson, John Heard, Penelope Ann Miller

© COLUMBIA TRISTAR HOME VIDEO 50563

BABE, THE

D: Arthur Hiller — 115 m

PG — DMA — 1992 — COLOR

7 Baseball's larger-than-life hero is given good old-fashioned hero treatment in this entertaining, sentimental and pleasing Hollywood biography. All the well-known Babe Ruth trivia is included, including his famous called home run shot over the center field wall in the 1932 World Series, his love for children and also his many excesses. However, this is not a mindless tribute or exploitive trivialization. The man is given substance and dignity. Although his shortcomings are there too, we are never allowed to lose our love for the oversized hero. Goodman does a great job. Enjoyable.

Sex, Nud, Viol, Lang, AdSit

A: John Goodman, Kelly McGillis, Trini Alvarado, Bruce Boxleitner, Peter Donat, Richard Tyson

© MCA/UNIVERSAL HOME VIDEO, INC. 81286

BABETTE'S FEAST

D: Gabriel Axel — 102 m

G — FOR DMA COM — 1987 — COLOR

8 Winner of Best Foreign Film Oscar. After her husband and son are killed, French exile (Audran) is taken in by two elderly sisters who live spartan and austere lives as religious leaders. After 14 years with them, Audran wins money in a lottery and prepares a sumptuous banquet in celebration of the women's father's 100th birthday. They and the stoic townspeople are at first hesitant but then join in. Soon long dormant earthly passions are resurrected in everyone. This is not for everyone because it is subtle, deliberate and slow, but it is funny, too, and a reward for the patient viewer. Dubbed.

Sex, Nud, Viol, Lang, AdSit

A: Stephane Audran, Birgitte Federspiel, Bodil Kjer, Vibeke Hastrup, Hanne Stensgard, Jarl Kulle

© ORION PICTURES CORPORATION 5040

BABY DOLL

D: Elia Kazan — 115 m

R — DMA — 1956 — B&W

8 Tennessee Williams's sordid tale, set in a decaying South, of a child bride and her empty-headed middle-aged husband (Malden). Malden is allowed to marry Baby, but he may not consummate their marriage until she is 20 and he has proven that he can successfully provide for her. A new cotton gin has come to town and is causing Malden's cotton gin to go bankrupt. So he burns down the new competition. Its vengeful owner (Wallach) suspects Malden, and he seduces Baby to get her to incriminate Malden. Banned when released but is relatively tame now. Baby doll nighties became popular after this film.

Sex, Nud, Viol, Lang, AdSit

A: Carroll Baker, Eli Wallach, Karl Malden, Mildred Dunnock, Lonny Chapman, Rip Torn

© WARNER HOME VIDEO 34074

BABY, THE RAIN MUST FALL

D: Robert Mulligan — 100 m

NR — DMA — 1964 — B&W

6 An underrated movie about an irresponsible guitar playing would-be rockabilly singer who gets sent to jail for stabbing someone. McQueen is perfect in the role of this misfit who is now out on parole and trying to start a new life with his wife (Remick) and daughter. Murray is a local sheriff who tries to help him go straight, but the hot-headed McQueen can't change his ways. The title song became a major pop hit for singer Glen Yarlborough. Worth a look.

Sex, Nud, Viol, Lang, AdSit

A: Steve McQueen, Lee Remick, Don Murray, Paul Fix, Josephine Hutchinson, Ruth White

© GOODTIMES 4211

BACKBEAT

D: Ian Softley — 100 m

R — DMA MUS — 1994 — COLOR

8 Before there were The Beatles, John Lennon and Stuart Sutcliff were best friends. This film is set in 1960, before The Beatles were discovered and is not really a story of the group. It is more the story of the relationship between Lennon and Sutcliff. The group, then including Sutcliff, had gone to Germany to play in strip joints, hone their skills and have some fun. The band was Lennon's dream. Sutcliff was only a so-so musician, but he was a talented painter and in Germany he met a beautiful avant-guarde photographer Astrid Kirchherr. He fell in love and eventually left both Lennon and the group, but he died of a brain hemorrhage at only 21. An interesting look at backstage life.

Sex, Nud, Viol, Lang, AdSit

A: Sheryl Lee, Stephen Dorff, Ian Hart, Gary Bakewell, Chris O'Neill, Hellena Schmied

© POLYGRAM VIDEO 6317713

BADLANDS

D: Terrence Malick — 94 m

PG — CRM DMA — 1973 — COLOR

9 Chilling true story. In 1958 Charles Starkweather began an extended cross-country killing spree. By the time he and his teenage girlfriend were apprehended, ten people were dead. This real-life event is grippingly captured in this very disturbing drama that you won't soon forget. Excellent acting, fine craftsmanship and striking photography bring this uncomfortable story of cool, almost casual, killing to life. See also IN COLD BLOOD.

Sex, Nud, Viol, Lang, AdSit

A: Martin Sheen, Sissy Spacek, Warren Oates, Ramon Bieri, Alan Vint

© WARNER HOME VIDEO 11135

BAGDAD CAFE

D: Percy Adlon — 91 m

PG | COM DMA | 1988 | COLOR

6 Looking for something really different? A really offbeat comedy. An overweight compulsive German tourist (Sagebrecht) leaves her husband after a fight in the middle of the Mojave desert. She seeks shelter at a seedy out-of-the-way motel/cafe whose owner is both constantly angry and totally disorganized. The regular clientele is a group of very strange and kooky eccentrics, like Jack Palance - who is obsessed with painting the chubby Sagebrect. The presence of this compulsive neatnic changes everyone at the cafe. She gives it order and turns it into a popular oasis. For seekers of the unusual only.

Sex / Nud / Viol / Lang / AdSit

A: Marianne Sagebrecht, Jack Palance, CCH Pounder, Christine Kaufmann, Monica Calhoun, George Aguilar

© MCEG/STERLING 70157

BALLAD OF GREGORIO CORTEZ, THE

D: Robert M. Young — 105 m

PG | WST DMA | 1983 | COLOR

7 This is the true story, set in 1901 Texas, of a Mexican cowhand who was falsely accused of horse theft after a series of errors which stemmed from an otherwise innocent misunderstood word in Spanish. The incident explodes out of control and he kills the local sheriff who came to arrest him. For the next 11 days, he is pursued by 600 rangers for over 450 miles in one of Texas's biggest manhunts. A very different sort of Western that realistically captures the era and recreates the bordertowns. Olmos does an excellent job with the character of a man who is a fugitive for no good reason.

Sex / Nud / Viol / Lang / AdSit

A: Edward James Olmos, James Gammon, Tom Bower, Bruce McGill, Alan Vint, Timothy Scott

© NEW LINE HOME VIDEO 2062

BALLAD OF LITTLE JO, THE

D: Maggie Greenwald — 124 m

R | WST DMA | 1993 | COLOR

7 This is a very curious video. While it is a Western, it is a very different sort of Western. Suzy Amis plays the daughter of a wealthy easterner, who is thrown out by her father after she has an illegitimate child. She sets out in a westerly direction, not really knowing where to go. She does however soon discover that a woman alone on the road is a target. So, she cut off her hair and donned a man's clothes. She is safe from unwanted advances, but she also soon discovers that she is trapped in her secret. The video is very evocative of the period and presents a window onto not-so-flattering aspects that are usually glossed over. It is interesting, but it does tend to be a little slow.

Sex / Nud / Viol / Lang / AdSit

A: Suzy Amis, Bo Hopkins, Ian McKellen, David Chung, Anthony Heald, Heather Graham

© TURNER HOME ENTERTAINMENT N4156

BALLAD OF NARAYAMA, THE

D: Shohei Imamura — 129 m

NR | FOR DMA | 1983 | COLOR

9 Truly unusual Canne Film Festival winner, set in the late 19th century in a remote and very primitive Japanese mountain village. Here people live extremely close to nature and are not far above animals themselves. Life is very rudimentary and very fragile, because food is very short. So, the people have adopted a ruthless survival code. Some male babies are abandoned and left to die in rice paddies and old people, people reaching 70 years of age, are carried to a spot high on the mountain Narayama and left there to die. An old woman is still in good health, but she feels obligated to fulfill her obligation and welcomes death, even though her son fights to avoid her fate. Subtitles.

Sex / Nud / Viol / Lang / AdSit

A: Ken Ogata, Sumiko Sakamoto, Tonpei Hidari, Seiji Kurazaki, Junko Takada

© HOME VISION BAL 08

BANG THE DRUM SLOWLY

D: John Hancock — 98 m

PG | DMA | 1974 | COLOR

9 Moving and powerful story of two major league baseball players, who are best friends. While Moriarty is a good-looking hero and star pitcher, De Niro is a somewhat dim-witted farmboy and a work-horse-type catcher, who is just trying to complete the season. He also has a secret. He has Hodgkin's Disease and no one knows except Moriarty. Even though Moriarty is constantly teased by the rest of the team for standing by De Niro, on a team that is torn apart by bickering, this unlikely pair remain best friends. A sensitive, moving story with outstanding performances.

Sex / Nud / Viol / Lang / AdSit

A: Michael Moriarty, Robert De Niro, Vincent Gardenia, Danny Aiello, Ann Wedgeworth, Selma Diamond

© PARAMOUNT HOME VIDEO 8732

BARABBAS

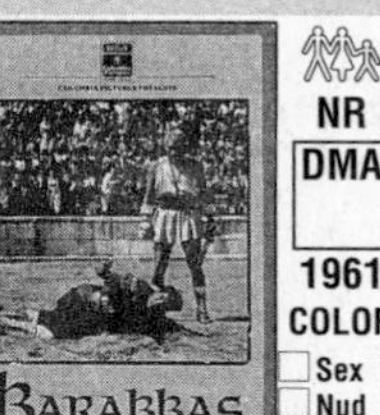

D: Richard Fleischer — 134 m

NR | DMA | 1961 | COLOR

8 Fictionalized Biblical epic of the life of Barabbas, the thief who was freed by Pontius Pilate when Jesus Christ was condemned to die. Barabbas is a non-believer, but spends the troubled years after his release first as a slave and later as a gladiator. He constantly mocks Christ, while all the time he is struggling to understand the meaning of it all. Only in the end does he discover faith. Plenty of spectacle and action. Quinn and a solid cast of veterans give credibility to this screen adaptation of a novel by Par Lagerkvist.

Sex / Nud / Viol / Lang / AdSit

A: Anthony Quinn, Silvana Mangano, Arthur Kennedy, Katy Jurado, Harry Andrews, Vittorio Gassman

© COLUMBIA TRISTAR HOME VIDEO 60129

BARBARIANS AT THE GATE

D: Glenn Jordan — 107 m

R | DMA | 1992 | COLOR

8 Wallstreet gone wild. Greed gone amuck. Tussles at the top. The politics of power. This entertaining film documents one of the biggest purchases of of the 1980s or any century - the $30.6 billion leveraged buyout of R.J.R. Nabisco. It is the blow by blow account of the battle between Nabisco's flamboyant CEO F. Ross Johnson who wanted to take the company private (and make a fortune for himself) and outsider Henry Kravis, a cold and steely master of the artform of the leveraged buyout. Very interesting, entertaining and informative.

Sex / Nud / Viol / Lang / AdSit

A: James Garner, Jonathan Pryce, Peter Riegert, Joanna Cassidy, Fred Dalton Thompson, Lielani Ferrer

© HBO VIDEO 90835

BARFLY

D: Barbet Schroeder — 100 m

R | COM DMA | 1987 | COLOR

8 Surprisingly enjoyable, literate, bittersweet comedy - but it is not for everybody. Exceptional performances by Rourke and Dunaway, and a dynamite jazz and R&B score highlight this guided tour through the gutters of Los Angeles. Rourke is a slovenly but eloquent poet and writer who prefers the bars and drinking over work. Dunaway is a fading beauty and his alcoholic soul and bedmate. But his work is ardently admired by pretty publisher Alice Krige, who is in competition with Dunaway for him. Very unusual, with characters that are hard for most people to identify with or care about.

Sex / Nud / Viol / Lang / AdSit

A: Mickey Rourke, Faye Dunaway, Alice Krige, J.C. Quinn, Frank Stalone, Jack Nance

© WARNER HOME VIDEO 37212

BARRY LYNDON

D: Stanley Kubrick — 185 m

PG | DMA | 1975 | COLOR

7 A sumptuous feast for the eyes and winner of four Oscars. Contains absolutely stunning photography and exquisite mid-18th century period detail. (The actors did not wear costumes but actual antique clothes.) The story is that of a personable but roguish Irishman of common birth and very flexible morals, who uses any means necessary to elevate his station in life. He eventually marries a wealthy and beautiful noblewoman but abuses her badly and loses it all. The film remains interesting throughout but the lead character is hard to respect and it is sometimes quite slow moving.

Sex / Nud / Viol / Lang / AdSit

A: Ryan O'Neal, Marisa Barenson, Patrick Magee, Hardy Druger, Steven Berkoff, Gay Hamilton

© WARNER HOME VIDEO 11178

BARTON FINK

D: John Turturro — 116 m

R | COM DMA | 1991 | COLOR

7 Surreal and quirky. It's a brilliant collage of colorful characterizations and black comedy, all packaged up as a spoof on 1930's Hollywoodishness. Fink (Turturro) is a Broadway playwright who, against his better judgment, takes a lucrative Hollywood writing job. However, the studio head wants him to write a movie screenplay about wrestling. Fink's brain locks up with writer's block and he begins to hallucinate. He can write nothing. His life is out of control, and he keeps getting interrupted by an insurance salesman (Goodman) who lives next door. Bizarre and sarcastic comedy.

Sex / Nud / Viol / Lang / AdSit

A: John Goodman, John Turturro, John Mahoney, Judy Davis, Jon Polito, Michael Lerner

© FOXVIDEO 1905

BEACHES

D: Garry Marshall — 123 m

PG-13 | DMA | 1988 | COLOR

8 A two hankie tearjerker! A charmer, a heartbreaker and an inspiration. Two young girls from very different backgrounds meet and, over the years, become very close. Their friendship endures numerous trials and tribulations - marriage, divorce, jealousy and career disasters - but they survive with each other's love. Midler is a struggling actress who finally makes it big. Hershey becomes a wealthy young lawyer who marries the man of her dreams and has a wonderful child. But in the end it is tragedy that brings them closest together, just before it tears them apart. Unforgettable!

Sex / Nud / Viol / Lang / AdSit

A: Bette Midler, Barbara Hershey, John Heard, Spalding Gray, Lainie Kazan, James Read

© TOUCHSTONE HOME VIDEO 797

BEAR, THE

D: Jean-Jacques Annaud — 92 m

PG | DMA CLD | 1989 | COLOR

9 Excellent family entertainment that was roundly praised by critics and loved by audiences. It is a big-budget movie that took several years to film and is the story, set in 1885 British Columbia, of a huge injured kodiak bear that adopts an orphaned cub. Fearing gunfire from approaching hunters, the two flee across a vast expanse of beautiful but foreboding wilderness. But in the end, the bears still must face the hunter. This is not a schmaltzy Disney knock-off. This is special. Adults will enjoy this as much as the kids.

Sex / Nud / Viol / Lang / AdSit

A: Tcheky Karyo, Jack Wallace

© COLUMBIA TRISTAR HOME VIDEO 70213

BECKET

D: Peter Glenville 150 m

NR | DMA | 1964 | COLOR

Sex, Nud, Viol, Lang, AdSit

10 Magnificent, stunning and powerful. This is a beautiful costume drama revolving around the stormy friendship of two of 12th-century England's most powerful people. Henry II (O'Toole) is ruler of Saxony, and Becket (Burton) is his closest friend and a brilliant man who Henry made Archbishop of Canterbury to turn the church into his ally. However, Becket is profoundly moved by a new devotion to God and church, and so becomes the King's enemy instead. Henry, rebuffed by his friend, becomes obsessed with destroying him. Wonderful pageantry. Twelve Oscar Nominations. Historically credible, too.

A: Richard Burton, Peter O'Toole, John Gielgud, Donald Wolfit, Martita Hunt, Pamela Brown

© MPI HOME VIDEO MP1053

BEDFORD INCIDENT, THE

D: James Harris 102 m

NR | DMA SUS | 1965 | B&W

Sex, Nud, Viol, Lang, AdSit

7 Tense nuclear-age Cold War thriller. Poitier is a cocky magazine reporter on board an American destroyer to record a typical day tracking subs off the coast of Greenland. This destroyer is skippered by an authoritarian near-maniacal Navy captain (Widmark), who keeps his near-exhausted but devoted crew on a razor's edge and is also especially fond of harassing one particular Russian sub. This ongoing battle of wits with the sub builds into a destructive pressure within the ship's crew that leads to a numbing climax. Well-acted, with a good script.

A: Richard Widmark, Sidney Poitier, James MacArthur, Martin Balsam, Wally Cox, Eric Portman

© COLUMBIA TRISTAR HOME VIDEO 60130

BEGUILED, THE

D: Don Siegel 109 m

R | WST DMA | 1970 | COLOR

Sex, Nud, Viol, Lang, AdSit

7 Offbeat story set in the South during the Civil War. It is an oddly compelling story of a wounded Union soldier who is taken in at a girl's boarding school. There, he becomes the cause of sexual tensions, leading to a flurry of jealousy and hatred as both students and teachers vie for his affections. He is held hostage by the women, each of whom holds his life in the balance with their vow of secrecy, however he is a schemer and a liar who will say and do anything to get what he wants. Rather slow-paced, but rewarding for the patient viewer, with a startling conclusion. Another interesting and somewhat similar theme was provocatively explored in BLACK NARCISSUS.

A: Clint Eastwood, Geraldine Page, Elizabeth Hartman, Jo Ann Harris, Darleen Carr, Mae Mercer

© MCA/UNIVERSAL HOME VIDEO, INC. 55059

BELIZAIRE THE CAJUN

D: Glen Pitre 113 m

PG | DMA WST | 1986 | COLOR

Sex, Nud, Viol, Lang, AdSit

6 Rich and faithful portrait of the Louisiana bayou country in the early 1800s. The rhythms of the place and the time provide a backdrop for this piece of Cajun folklore, and are also some of the film's most inviting qualities. Belizair is a self-assured traditional Cajun herbal healer who is in trouble because of his love for the Cajun wife of a rich Anglo, and because of his continued defense of his people against the prejudice of the other locals. Belizair is framed for murder after he helps a persecuted friend. Sincere effort that has worthy moments, but also some shortcomings.

A: Armand Assante, Gail Youngs, Michael Schoeffling, Stephen McHatti, Will Patton, Nancy Barrett

© CBS/FOX VIDEO 3740

BEN HUR

D: William Wyler 211 m

G | ACT DMA | 1959 | COLOR

Sex, Nud, Viol, Lang, AdSit

10 This monumental picture still holds the record for the most Oscars at 11 out of 12 nominations. The story line concerns a wealthy Jewish nobleman (Heston) who incurs the wrath of a Roman military governor who was also his childhood friend. Heston's family is imprisoned and he is sentenced to slavery as an oarsman on a galley. There, he saves the life of his Roman master and reattains a position of honor. He then returns to seek vengeance on his former friend in a spectacular chariot race. WOW! Fantastic special effects and photography. See it in wide screen only.

A: Charlton Heston, Jack Hawkins, Sam Jaffe, Stephen Boyd, Martha Scott

Distributed By MGM/UA Home Video M900004

BENIKER GANG, THE

D: Ken Kwapis 87 m

G | CLD DMA | 1984 | COLOR

Sex, Nud, Viol, Lang, AdSit

7 Heartwarming made-for-TV film about five orphans in an orphanage who have formed their own unorthodox family and are determined to stay together no matter what. The five even conspire to find ways to ward off potential parents. But when the family is finally threatened with breakup because of adoptions that can't be avoided, they all run off together and the oldest ghostwrites an advice column to support them all. This is actually quite well-done and not overly-sweet, as you might expect. A real sleeper.

A: Andrew McCarthy, Jennie Dundas, Danny Dintanro, Charles Fields, Jeff Alan-Lee

© WARNER HOME VIDEO 223

BERNICE BOBS HER HAIR

D: Joan Micklin Silver 49 m

NR | DMA | 1976 | COLOR

Sex, Nud, Viol, Lang, AdSit

8 This is F. Scott Fitzgerld's delightful and sensitive story of a shy young girl (Shelly Duvall) who is transformed by her cousin into a femme fatale on a summer's visit in 1919. She sacrifices her beautiful long hair so that she will be accepted by an in-group of pleasure-seeking would-be flappers from the jazz-age, and becomes a big success. But her success is also a source of unexpected problems when she captures all the boys's hearts. A fun but perceptive movie that explores our perceptions of self-worth and personal integrity. Introduction by Henry Fonda.

A: Shelley Duvall, Veronica Cartwright, Bud Cort, Dennis Christopher, Gary Springer, Land Binkley

© MONTEREY HOME VIDEO 30434

BEST BOY

D: Ira Wohl 105 m

DOC DMA | 1981 | COLOR

Sex, Nud, Viol, Lang, AdSit

8 This is the moving real-life story of Philly, a 52-year-old retarded man and it won an Oscar for Best Documentary. Philly has been living at home with his parents ever since he was born, but now his parents are very old. His cousin Ira has become concerned about what will happen to Philly. So he talks Philly's parents into letting him help Philly to learn how to become more independent. This is a film that documents his efforts to do just that. Contrary to being a depressing film, Philly's enthusiasm and joy at accomplishing even the littlest tasks is contagious. A heart-warming, uplifting film. Recommended.

A:

© TAPEWORM VIDEO 1020

BEST MAN, THE

D: Franklin J. Schaffner 103 m

NR | DMA | 1964 | B&W

Sex, Nud, Viol, Lang, AdSit

9 Excellent. This is one of America's most insightful movies ever about the true nature of politics. It concerns the backstage maneuvering and dirt-digging ruthlessness at a political convention. Two very different opponents for their party's Presidential nomination (Robertson and Fonda) battle for the endorsement of the retiring President (Tracy). One is a conscience-ridden intellectual and the other is an opportunist. Given the likelihood that nothing will ever really change in this regard, this is probably a particularly timeless story.

A: Cliff Robertson, Henry Fonda, Lee Tracy, Edie Adams, Shelley Berman, Ann Sothern

Distributed By MGM/UA Home Video M301775

BEST OF TIMES, THE

D: Roger Spottiswoode 104 m

PG-13 | DMA COM | 1986 | COLOR

Sex, Nud, Viol, Lang, AdSit

7 Quite good and unduly underrated little "dramedy" about mid-life crisis. Robin Williams is vice president at the bank but he has never forgotten, or been able to live down, the biggest tragedy of his life - the night he dropped the football in the big high school game against their archrivals. So he and his best friend (Russell), the quarterback on that fateful night, decide to organize a rematch - 20 years later - and spice up life in their little town. Nice little story that leaves you satisfied when it's over.

A: Robin Williams, Kurt Russell, Pamela Reed, Holly Palance, Donovan Scott, Donald Moffat

© NEW LINE HOME VIDEO 1307

BEST OF UPSTAIRS DOWNSTAIRS, THE

D: 700 m

NR | DMA | 1971 | COLOR

Sex, Nud, Viol, Lang, AdSit

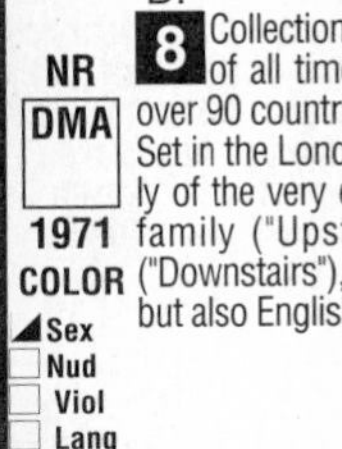

8 Collection of one of the best and most popular television series of all time. Produced in England for the BBC, it was shown in over 90 countries. It won seven Emmys, plus numerous other awards. Set in the London household of the wealthy upper-class Bellamy family of the very early 20th century, it follows both the members of the family ("Upstairs") and the lives of its many staff members ("Downstairs"), providing glimpses not only into their personal lives but also English society of that era. 14 separate volumes.

A:

© HBO VIDEO 2853

BETRAYAL

D: David Jones 95 m

R | DMA | 1983 | COLOR

Sex, Nud, Viol, Lang, AdSit

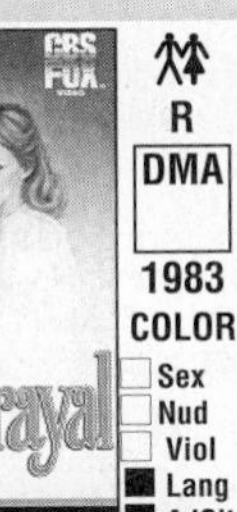

7 This was a high quality stage play that was brought to the screen with three distinguished actors who each give wonderful performances - but it is not for everyone. It is a somewhat talky story of the slow death of a marriage (Kingsley and Hodge) and a look into the long-term extramarital affair between Hodge and her husband's best friend, Irons. It uses the interesting gimmick of telling the story backwards - from the breakup of the affair to the beginning. High quality but arty.

A: Jeremy Irons, Ben Kingsley, Patricia Hodge

© FOXVIDEO 1296

BETRAYED

R | CRM DMA | 1988 | COLOR

D: Constantine Costa-Gavras 128 m

7 FBI agent Debra Winger is sent undercover in a rural community when a left-wing talk show host is murdered by right-wing extremists. The chief suspect is a warm-hearted, single-parent farmer that she falls in love with. The longer she is around him, the more she discovers that he is also a very paranoid bigot who is deeply involved with a heavily armed extremist group. Winger gives a strong performance as a woman torn by the profound moral dilemma of despising and having to arrest the man she also loves. However, the potential impact is diminished by some holes in plot.

Sex / Nud / Viol / Lang / AdSit

A: Debra Winger, Tom Berenger, John Heard, Betsy Blair, Ted Levine, John Mahoney

Distributed By MGM/UA Home Video M901553

BETSY, THE

R | DMA ROM | 1978 | COLOR

D: Daniel Petrie 132 m

6 Amusing diversion. A powerful cast throws itself into this soap opera adaptation of a best-seller-brought-to-the-screen, with major gusto. It is the lurid tale of members of an automobile dynasty family. We have here a selection of power brokering, conventional sex, incest and homosexuality. Plot moves pretty slow but it is nonetheless an interesting piece of trash.

Sex / Nud / Viol / Lang / AdSit

A: Laurence Olivier, Tommy Lee Jones, Robert Duvall, Katharine Ross, Lesley-Anne Down, Jane Alexander

© CBS/FOX VIDEO 7190

BETWEEN TWO WOMEN

NR | DMA | 1986 | COLOR

D: Jon Avnet 95 m

8 Excellent, very serious drama. Dewherst won an Emmy playing a strong-willed mother-in-law who was once a great singer and who lived her own life as she wanted, but now she has come to live with her son's family after having had a stroke. A proud woman and not at all eager to accept help, she must now come to depend upon her naive daughter-in-law's strength. Fawcett must learn to deal with this very difficult woman, while at the same time that she struggles to keep her faltering marriage together. The resulting conflict causes them both to grow in ways that neither expected possible. Powerful drama. Excellent performances.

Sex / Nud / Viol / Lang / AdSit

A: Farrah Fawcett, Colleen Dewhurst, Michael Nouri, Bridgette Andersen, Danny Corkill, Steven Hill

© WARNER HOME VIDEO 35018

BEYOND THE VALLEY OF THE DOLLS

NC-17 | DMA COM | 1970 | COLOR

D: Russ Meyer 109 m

6 Campy and sexy. This is an in-name-only sequel to VALLEY OF THE DOLLS, which was a movie soap opera of the same period. This would-be parody of a soap opera was co-written by film critic Roger Ebert and soft-porn director Russ Meyer. It is about a female rock group's attempts to do whatever it takes to make it in Hollywood. They encounter corruption, sex and a killing spree. Some viewers, who didn't take it too seriously, liked it - but the film got a decidedly mixed review. Originally rated X.

Sex / Nud / Viol / Lang / AdSit

A: Dolly Read, Cynthia Meyers, Marcia McBroom, John LaZar, Michael Blodgett, Edy Williams

© FOX 1101

BIBLE, THE

NR | DMA | 1966 | COLOR

D: John Huston 171 m

8 A major cinematic rendering of the ancient stories from the first twenty-two chapters of Genesis. They include: the creation, Adam and Eve, Cain and Able, Noah's Ark, the Tower of Babel, Sodom and Gomorrah, and the story of Abraham and Sarah. It is somewhat long on grandeur and short on intimacy with the characters, nevertheless it is also a spectacular vision of a film.

Sex / Nud / Viol / Lang / AdSit

A: George C. Scott, Peter O'Toole, Ava Gardner, Richard Harris, Franco Nero, Michael Parks

© FOXVIDEO 1020

BIG

PG | COM DMA | 1988 | COLOR

D: Penny Marshall 104 m

9 Sparkling, heartwarming blockbuster. When a 12-year-old boy is rejected by a fifteen-year-old girl, he makes a wish at a carnival's mechanical fortune teller to become big. The next morning he is - but he still has the mind and heart of a 12-year-old. Excellent vehicle for Hanks - it won him an Oscar nomination. This is much more a story about childhood innocence than a story for children. A major commercial success, it inspired other movies to use instant-grownup characters (although FREAKY FRIDAY was actually the first).

Sex / Nud / Viol / Lang / AdSit

A: Tom Hanks, Elizabeth Perkins, Robert Loggia, John Heard, Jared Ruston, David Moscow

© FOXVIDEO 1658

BIG CHILL, THE

R | DMA | 1983 | COLOR

D: Lawrence Kasdan 103 m

8 This was a major film that was very popular because it struck a resonant chord with many who watched it and served as a wake-up call for others. Seven college friends from the radical '60s get back together at the funeral of one of their former group after he has committed suicide. All of them had been rebels and non-conformists but now they are settled into being typical establishment types, more or less. The death of their friend forces each to reevaluate what they have done with themselves and where they are going with the rest of their lives. Very strong cast. Great '60s music.

Sex / Nud / Viol / Lang / AdSit

A: Tom Berenger, Glenn Close, Jeff Goldblum, William Hurt, Kevin Kline, Meg Tilly

© COLUMBIA TRISTAR HOME VIDEO 60112

BIG RED ONE, THE

PG | WAR DMA ACT | 1980 | COLOR

D: Samuel Fuller 114 m

9 A tough, gritty, realistic and brilliant war saga. Director Fuller spent 35 years trying to get this autobiographical movie of his first-hand memories of WWII made. The focus is upon the daily lives of the soldiers of the famous American First Infantry Division, called the Big Red One. Individual soldiers of the division are followed from their landing in North Africa all through Europe. Lee Marvin is a war-weary special infantry sergeant who is just trying to keep his young troops, most of them fresh out of high school, alive. The veterans survive but most replacements never live long enough to learn how to. Rich, moving and realistic. A terrific film.

Sex / Nud / Viol / Lang / AdSit

A: Lee Marvin, Mark Hamill, Robert Carradine, Bobby DiCicco, Kelly Ward, Siegfried Rauch

© WARNER HOME VIDEO 939

BILLY BUDD

NR | DMA | 1962 | B&W

D: Peter Ustinov 123 m

8 This is a powerful and provocative story taken from Herman Melville's novella and set in the 1797 British Navy that raises some unsettling and thought-provoking questions. Robert Ryan is an iron-handed, tyrannical and sadistic first mate of a British naval ship who torments an innocent and naive young sailor Billy Budd (Terrance Stamp) to distraction. When Stamp, in a fit of induced rage, accidentally kills Ryan, he is placed on trial for murder. What is justice? Where does blame lie? A terrific cast makes this a powerful film.

Sex / Nud / Viol / Lang / AdSit

A: Robert Ryan, Peter Ustinov, Melvyn Douglas, Terrence Stamp, Paul Rogers, David McCallum

© CBS/FOX VIDEO 7196

BILLY JACK

PG | ACT DMA | 1971 | COLOR

D: T.C. Frank 114 m

7 A powerful, youth-oriented favorite. A huge film at the time of its release, it developed a cult following for its support of freedom, justice and anything anti-establishment. It made bold statements against bigotry, education and the government. Billy Jack (Laughlin) is a young half-breed Indian and a former Green Beret who is dedicated to single-handedly saving a "freedom school" for troubled children from reactionary townsfolk. His weapon - his finely honed karate skills - is what keeps their intrusions at bay.

Sex / Nud / Viol / Lang / AdSit

A: Tom Laughlin, Deloris Taylor, Clark Howat, Bert Freed, Kenneth Tobey, Julie Webb

© WARNER HOME VIDEO 1040

BILOXI BLUES

PG-13 | COM DMA | 1988 | COLOR

D: Mike Nichols 105 m

7 Interesting and funny. The second Neil Simon story about his autobiographical character, Eugene Jerome, who was first introduced in BRIGHTON BEACH MEMOIRS. WWII is winding down now but Eugene still goes to Army basic training in Mississippi for ten weeks, where he is harassed by his sadistic drill sergeant and an equally hostile platoon. He has only two goals: to get through this ordeal and to lose his virginity. His only weapon in these battles is his sense of humor. Broderick narrates over the storyline, making interesting observations on his buddies and life in general.

Sex / Nud / Viol / Lang / AdSit

A: Matthew Broderick, Christopher Walken, Matt Mulhern, Casey Siemaszko, Penelope Ann Miller, Corey Parker

© MCA/UNIVERSAL HOME VIDEO, INC. 80799

BIRCH INTERVAL

PG | DMA | 1978 | COLOR

D: Delbert Mann 104 m

6 An uplifting family story of a 12-year-old girl who is sent to live with her Amish grandfather, Eddie Albert, in rural 1947 Pennsylvania. She eagerly anticipates her visit there, but she soon learns that things aren't as idyllic as she has imagined and also learns some of life's sadder truths through some painful experiences. An excellent cast and outstanding performances make this sensitive coming-of-age story a memorable experience for both young and old.

Sex / Nud / Viol / Lang / AdSit

A: Eddie Albert, Rip Torn, Ann Wedgeworth, Susan McClung, Anne Revere

© MEDIA HOME ENTERTAINMENT, INC. M867

BIRD

D: Clint Eastwood 161 m

R | DMA MUS | 1988 | COLOR

7 Heartfelt story about the sad life of a jazz giant. Legendary, brilliant saxophonist Charlie Parker revolutionized jazz in the 1940s, but Charlie Parker was also addicted to drugs and booze and died young. Eastwood's direction captures the spirit of the seedy hotel rooms and bars that made up Parker's life, and Whitaker is excellent as Bird Parker. The sax music you hear is actually Parker's, but it is accompanied by modern recordings by studio musicians.

Sex / Nud / Viol / Lang / AdSit

A: Forest Whitaker, Diane Venora, Samuel E. Wright, Keith David, Michael McGuire, James Handy

© WARNER HOME VIDEO 11820

BIRDMAN OF ALCATRAZ

D: John Frankenheimer 141 m

NR | DMA | 1962 | COLOR

8 Excellent, but romanticized, screenplay about a man who got along better with birds than he did with people. It is an intense character study of the real-life prisoner Robert Stroud who became a world renown expert on birdlife while serving 40 years in solitary confinement for murder, in some of the toughest prisons in the country. Stroud eventually spent 53 years in prisons, including Alcatraz - a prison which was reserved to house the worst of the worst. Lancaster puts in one of his best performances.

Sex / Nud / Viol / Lang / AdSit

A: Burt Lancaster, Karl Malden, Thelma Ritter, Betty Field, Neville Brand, Telly Savalas

Distributed By MGM/UA Home Video M202269

BIRDY

D: Alan Parker 120 m

R | DMA | 1984 | COLOR

8 Powerful statement on the traumatizing effects of war. Cage and Modine grow up together in South Philadelphia and both go to Vietnam. Birdy (Modine) has always wished he was a bird so he could escape from his troubles but, as a result of being in Vietnam, Birdy comes to believe he really is a bird. He exists now in a near-catatonic state in an Army hospital. His childhood friend (Cage) tries to bring him back to reality by recalling their youth. Great performances all the way around. Some really terrific film footage recreates Birdy's flight fantasies. Not for everyone, but a powerful movie.

Sex / Nud / Viol / Lang / AdSit

A: Matthew Modine, Nicolas Cage, John Harkins, Sandy Baron, Karen Young, Bruno Kirby

© COLUMBIA TRISTAR HOME VIDEO 60457

BITTER HARVEST

D: Roger Young 98 m

NR | DMA | 1981 | COLOR

8 Excellent drama. Everything goes wrong for young dairy farmer Ron Howard, whose cattle first take sick and then start to die. Howard is convincing as the scared and panicky farmer who has to battle an unfeeling government bureaucracy to discover that there is a fat-soluble chemical in his dairy feed that is killing his cows, and affecting over 8 million Americans, too. This was a made-for-TV movie that was based upon a true incident. Far above typical TV fare.

Sex / Nud / Viol / Lang / AdSit

A: Ron Howard, Art Carney, Richard Dysart

© FRIES HOME VIDEO 90700

BLACK BEAUTY

D: James Hill 105 m

G | DMA CLD | 1971 | B&W

7 This is the beloved classic children's story of a young boy's relentless quest in Victorian England to find his missing black colt as it passes from owner to owner, until once again it is back home with him. It will definitely hold a kid's attention throughout and will likely hold the attention of many adults, too. Plus, it quite probably will also bring a tear to everyone's eye.

Sex / Nud / Viol / Lang / AdSit

A: Mark Lester, Walter Slezak, Peter Lee Lawrence, Ursla Glas

© PARAMOUNT HOME VIDEO 8079

BLACK LIKE ME

D: Carl Lerner 107 m

NR | DMA | 1964 | B&W

6 Controversial and interesting film based upon the best-selling book of the same name. It is the true story of a white writer in the 1950s who wishes to learn what it is actually like to be a black man in the South. So he darkens his skin with chemicals and takes a trip through the pre-civil rights South to experience the bigotry rampant at the time for himself. Some production aspects are dated now, but many of the lessons still have value today.

Sex / Nud / Viol / Lang / AdSit

A: James Whitmore, Roscoe Lee Browne, Sorrell Booke, Will Geer, Dan Priest, Al Freeman, Jr.

© XENON HOME VIDEO 1506

BLACK ROBE

D: Bruce Beresford 101 m

R | DMA WST | 1991 | COLOR

8 Stunningly photographed quasi-historical portrait of very early North America (Quebec in 1634) and an idealistic young Jesuit's expedition into the virgin wilderness to bring Christianity to the Huron Indians. Leaving a small French outpost, he and a white companion travel with a band of Algonquins through land controlled by the ferocious Iroquois. The priest's concepts of God become unexpectedly challenged when confronted with the Iroquois and God, both in their own elements. Intelligent and intense. A fictional account, but scrupulously based on carefully researched fact.

Sex / Nud / Viol / Lang / AdSit

A: August Schellenberg, Lothaire Bluteau, Aden Young, Sandrine Holt, Tantoo Cardinal

© VIDMARK ENTERTAINMENT VM5543

BLACK STALLION, THE

D: Carroll Ballard 117 m

G | DMA CLD | 1979 | COLOR

9 The wonderful and moving story of a boy and his relationship with a beautiful black Arabian stallion. The two were stranded together on a desert island after a shipwreck. They have become best friends and, after they are rescued, the horse goes home with the boy. The primary thrust of the story is upon the training and racing of his horse, with the help of a wise old horse trainer (Mickey Rooney). One of the best children's films ever, and fun for adults, too. It proved to be so popular that it was followed with THE BLACK STALLION RETURNS.

Sex / Nud / Viol / Lang / AdSit

A: Kelly Reno, Mickey Rooney, Teri Garr, Clarence Huse, Hoyt Axton

Distributed By MGM/UA Home Video M201604

D
M
A

BLACK STALLION RETURNS, THE

D: Robert Dalva 105 m

PG | DMA CLD | 1983 | COLOR

8 Rousing sequel to THE BLACK STALLION. When the black stallion is stolen back by an Arab chieftain and taken to the Sahara, Kelly Reno, now a teenager, goes there to get him back. In his ordeal to get his friend back, he has to travel across miles of hot desert sands and deal with not always friendly local tribesmen. Pretty good action scenes, particularly the big race climax scene. This is not a cheap rip-off of the original. It is good in its own right. But still, it doesn't quite have the same magic as the original. Excellent family entertainment.

Sex / Nud / Viol / Lang / AdSit

A: Kelly Reno, Vincent Spano, Teri Garr, Allen Garfield, Woody Strode, Jodi Thelen

Distributed By MGM/UA Home Video M201864

BLAZE

D: Ron Shelton 117 m

R | DMA COM ROM | 1989 | COLOR

7 Hollywood's romantic-comedy version of the outlandish life and love of real-life Louisiana Governor Earl K. Long, who did have a scandalous affair with the flamboyant showgirl and stripper, Blaze Starr. Newman is energetic and full of ornery charm as the crusty Earl Long, and Lolita Davidovich puts in a "outstanding" and sexy performance as the famous Blaze Starr. The feisty Long struggles to survive repeated attacks on himself and his governorship, all the while it is he who is giving them some of their best ammunition. Look for the real Blaze Starr in a cameo role.

Sex / Nud / Viol / Lang / AdSit

A: Paul Newman, Lolita Davidovich, Robert Wuhl, Jeffrey DeMunn

© TOUCHSTONE HOME VIDEO 915

BLISS

D: Ray Lawrence 112 m

R | DMA COM FAN | 1985 | COLOR

7 A very original, unusual and extremely black comedy, and the 1985 Australian Best Picture winner. A successful and seemingly happy advertising executive dies for four minutes and comes back into an apparently different world, which has many of the same players in it but they are all drastically changed. His wife is openly carrying on an affair with his partner, his son deals dope and wants to join the mob, his daughter is a doper and will do anything to get it and an elephant sits on his car. A very odd, nightmarish vision of modern life.

Sex / Nud / Viol / Lang / AdSit

A: Barry Otto, Lynette Curran, Helen Jones, Miles Buchanan

© R&G VIDEO, LP 80024

BLOODBROTHERS

D: Robert Mulligan 117 m

R | DMA | 1978 | COLOR

7 Story of a 19-year-old's growing pains within a traditional Brooklyn Italian family. It is an interesting drama, even if it is a little over-blown, and is brought realistically to life by a high-quality stable of actors. Richard Gere's father (Lo Bianco) and his uncle (Sorvino) are macho big-city construction workers. Gere is a good-looking guy, with girls and a good-paying union job that his father and uncle got for him, but he thinks he wants to do something different with his life. That places him in conflict with those he loves most. He's at a crossroads. Many moving moments.

Sex / Nud / Viol / Lang / AdSit

A: Richard Gere, Paul Sorvino, Tony Lo Bianco, Marilu Henner, Lelia Goldoni, Danny Aiello

© WARNER HOME VIDEO 11088

BLOOD IN, BLOOD OUT

D: Taylor Hackford 180 m

R | CRM DMA | 1993 | COLOR | Sex | Nud | Viol | Lang | AdSit

7 The lives of three young Latinos, two half-brothers and a cousin, from the barrios of East Los Angeles are followed from their days together in a street gang in 1973 to their very different lives in 1984. Epic in length, there are several episodes of very involving drama, but they are bracketed by long episodes of violence. One of the friends is an artist whose back is broken and becomes a drug addict; one becomes a police detective and the other, who is tortured by being half-white, becomes the leader of a Latino gang in San Quentin prison. This is not a casual film. It takes effort to watch this much violence and pain, but it also provides an effective window into that culture.

A: Jesse Borrego, Benjamine Bratt, Enrique Castillo, Damian Chapa, Delroy Lindo, Tom Wilson

© HOLLYWOOD PICTURES HOME VIDEO 2015

BLUE

D: Krzysztof Kieslowski 98 m

R | FOR DMA | 1993 | COLOR | Sex | Nud | Viol | Lang | AdSit

7 Plodding but oddly interesting French film. Juliette Binoche is the wife of a world famous composer who, along with their young daughter, is killed in an auto wreck. Only she survives. Numbed by the enormity of her loss, she sells everything she has, leaving her memories behind, and vanishes to live in a small apartment in Paris to contemplate all that has happened. Sophisticated and patient viewers will find it to have literary merit. Subtitles.

A: Juliette Binoch, Benoit Regent, Florence Pernel, Charlotte Very, Helene Vincent, Philippe Volter

© TOUCHSTONE HOME VIDEO 2759

BLUE CHIPS

D: William Friedkin m

PG-13 | DMA | 1994 | COLOR | Sex | Nud | Viol | Lang | AdSit

8 Nick Nolte plays the hard-driving basketball coach of a school that has for years reigned as a college basketball power. However, last year, even though his kids gave him everything they had to give, they came up losers. The press belittles him, the alumni are upset and he wants to be a winner. The truth is that he simply does not have the horsepower it takes. He is losing the big players, the blue chips, to other schools. Desperate, even though he has always been scrupulous in avoiding payoffs, Nolte realizes that the only way he can win is to allow the alumni to buy him the best players. This is an effective vehicle that portrays the sad truth behind college sports.

A: Nick Nolte, Mary McDonell, J.T. Walsh, Ed O'Neill, Alfre Woodard, Shaquille O'Neal

© PARAMOUNT HOME VIDEO 32741

BLUE COLLAR

D: Paul Schrader 114 m

R | DMA | 1978 | COLOR | Sex | Nud | Viol | Lang | AdSit

8 Intensely realistic, but underrated drama about dead-ended people. Three very close friends, Detroit auto workers Prior, Keitel and Kotto, find their lives as assembly line workers pure drudgery. Their dispair becomes profound when they discover that it isn't only management that is their problem, the union is corrupt, too. Their friendship begins to fall apart. Then they plot to rob the union to set themselves free. The film focuses on the fears and repressed anger of men who have nowhere to turn. All three leads provide convincing performances and make this a very effective film.

A: Richard Pryor, Harvey Keitel, Yaphet Kotto, Ed Begley, Jr., Harry Bellaver, George Memmoli

© MCA/UNIVERSAL HOME VIDEO, INC. 66044

BLUE VELVET

D: David Lynch 121 m

R | SUS DMA | 1986 | COLOR | Sex | Nud | Viol | Lang | AdSit

8 Audacious, brilliant and disturbing. A young college student returns to his home town and becomes enraptured with a haunting nightclub singer. He soon discovers that there is a bizarre and hidden world of decadence and terror just under the surface of his little town that he and most others never knew was there. It is a perverted world that the surface calm belies. Hopper is fascinating as a sadistic kidnapper/drug dealer. Weird, surreal stuff. Undeniably gripping, but not easily enjoyable. Strong stuff. Keep an open mind.

A: Kyle MacLachlan, Isabella Rossellini, Dennis Hopper, Laura Dern, Dean Stockwell

© WARNER HOME VIDEO 692

BLUME IN LOVE

D: Paul Mazursky 115 m

R | COM DMA | 1973 | COLOR | Sex | Nud | Viol | Lang | AdSit

7 Enjoyable comedy/drama. George Segal is a philandering, successful divorce attorney who gets caught cheating by his wife. When she dumps him, he can't believe that it's over and that she doesn't love him anymore... he loves her. He still doesn't believe it, even after she moves in with hippie Kristofferson. He still loves her, pathetically pursuing her. In fact, he never knew how much he loved her until she divorced him. Funny, but too much truth in it to laugh too hard.

A: George Segal, Susan Anspach, Kris Kristofferson, Marsha Mason, Shelley Winters

© WARNER HOME VIDEO 11085

BOAT, THE (FORMERLY DAS BOOT)

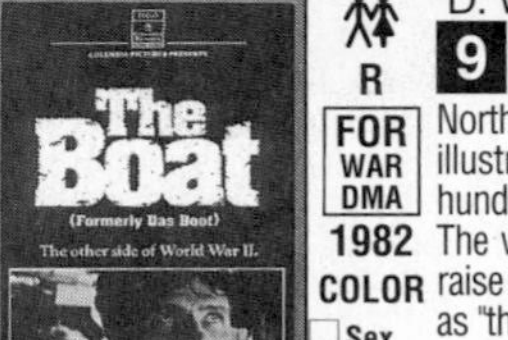

D: Wolfgang Petersen 150 m

R | FOR WAR DMA | 1982 | COLOR | Sex | Nud | Viol | Lang | AdSit

9 Extremely realistic depiction of the claustrophobic life aboard a German U-boat on the prowl, attacking and under attack in the North Atlantic of World War II. German-made, the film meticulously illustrates the crowding, grime and absolute terror of being several hundred feet below water while those overhead are trying to kill you. The war-weary captain guides his desperate crew as they attempt to raise the damaged ship from the ocean floor. Brilliant. Superb. Billed as "the most expensive and most successful motion picture in the history of German cinema." Dubbed/subtitles.

A: Jurgen Prochnow, Herbert Granemeyer, Klause Wenneman, Hubertus Bengsch, Martin Semmelrogge

© COLUMBIA TRISTAR HOME VIDEO 60139

BOB & CAROL & TED & ALICE

D: Paul Mazursky 104 m

R | COM DMA | 1969 | COLOR | Sex | Nud | Viol | Lang | AdSit

6 Satirical look at the changing and confused sexual mores in the 1960s. Robert Culp, a successful, sophisticated filmmaker, and his wife (Natalie Wood) go to a sensitivity-encounter institute just to observe, but get so involved that they decide to test their relationship with an affair with someone else. Who better to test their new freedom with than their best friends (Elliot Gould and Diane Cannon), who are confused by all this, especially when they wind up four to a bed. Lots of funny and some insightful moments.

A: Natalie Wood, Robert Kulp, Elliott Gould, Dyan Cannon

© GOODTIMES 4204

BOB ROBERTS

D: Tim Robbins 102 m

R | DMA COM | 1992 | COLOR | Sex | Nud | Viol | Lang | AdSit

8 Satire and parody of American politics. Tim Robbins plays Bob Roberts, an ultra-conservative child of liberal parents in the 60s. Bob, however, has risen from and abandoned his childhood roots in a commune, to become an unscrupulous multi-millionaire stocktrader and a born-again conservative. He released several "folk" albums and music videos which became popular, has promoted himself into a national sensation and is a populist candidate for a US Senate against a righteous and virtuous incumbent liberal (Gore Vidal). Very well received by the critics. However, its political theme and left-bias will limit its general audience appeal.

A: Tim Robbins, Giancarlo Esposito, Alan Rickman, Gore Vidal, Brian Murray, Ray Wise

© LIVE HOME VIDEO 69898

BORDER, THE

D: Tony Richardson 107 m

R | ACT DMA | 1981 | COLOR | Sex | Nud | Viol | Lang | AdSit

7 Powerful performance by Nicholson as a border patrolman who is tempted into taking modest bribes in order to satisfy his demanding wife (Perrine). However, he is now being blackmailed by his neighbor and friend. A decent man, he eventually rebels against both the corruption and his corrupt fellow officers. He helps a desperate young Mexican mother, who was degraded into becoming a go-go dancer, recover her baby from an adoption ring. There are interesting moral aspects explored by Nicholson's character, but ultimately this is still an action movie, pitting Nicholson against other officers.

A: Jack Nicholson, Valerie Perrine, Harvey Keitel, Warren Oates, Elpidia Carrillo

© MCA/UNIVERSAL HOME VIDEO, INC. 71007

BORN FREE

D: James Hill 95 m

NR | DMA CLD | 1966 | COLOR | Sex | Nud | Viol | Lang | AdSit

9 This is an exceptional film with universal appeal. It is also a true story. Elsa, a young lioness, is one of three lion cubs who are raised in captivity by two Kenyan game wardens after they are forced to kill the cub's parents. The wardens want Elsa to be free when she is grown. So, as Elsa matures, they have to teach her how to survive on her own in the wilderness. This is a true family film and not just for the young kids. Immensely popular upon its release, it has lost none of its charm over time. The title song won an Oscar and was also a significant pop hit.

A: Virginia McKenna, Bill Travers, Geoffrey Keen, Peter Lukoye

© COLUMBIA TRISTAR HOME VIDEO 60142

BORN ON THE FOURTH OF JULY

D: Oliver Stone 145 m

R | DMA WAR | 1989 | COLOR | Sex | Nud | Viol | Lang | AdSit

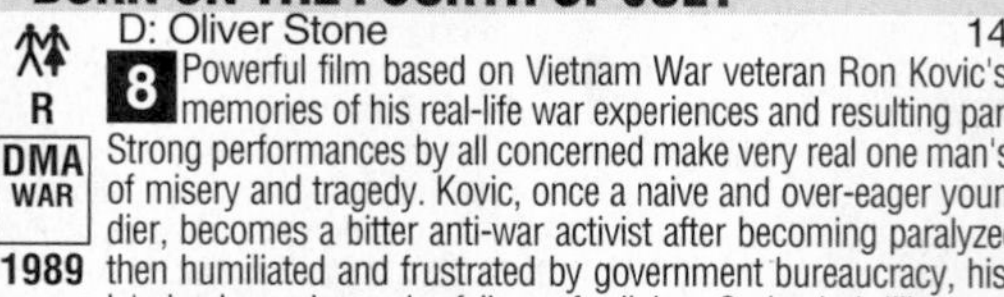

8 Powerful film based on Vietnam War veteran Ron Kovic's bitter memories of his real-life war experiences and resulting paralysis. Strong performances by all concerned make very real one man's story of misery and tragedy. Kovic, once a naive and over-eager young soldier, becomes a bitter anti-war activist after becoming paralyzed, and then humiliated and frustrated by government bureaucracy, his family's inadequacies and a failure of religion. Cruise is brilliant as a tortured man. This is a very moving film, but it is also very heavy-handed in making its point.

A: Tom Cruise, Raymond J. Barry, Caroline Kava, Willem Dafoe, Kyra Sedgwick, Tom Berenger

© MCA/UNIVERSAL HOME VIDEO, INC. 80901

BOUND FOR GLORY

D: Hal Ashby 149 m

PG | DMA MUS | 1976 | COLOR

Rating: 8

This moving biography is of Woodie Guthrie, a famous singer/composer of some of America's most favorite folk songs ("This Land is Your land"). It focuses primarily on the depression years when Guthrie traveled across America primarily by rail. The vignettes of that sad period of American history and those hit hardest by it, provide us with a window into the suffering that made up the soul of his songs. Carradine is superb as Gutherie. Won 2 Oscars: Photography and Score.

Sex | Nud | Viol | Lang | AdSit

A: David Carradine, Ronny Cox, Melinda Dillon, Gail Strickland, Randy Quaid, John Lehne

Distributed By MGM/UA Home Video M600878

BOUNTY, THE

D: Roger Donaldson 130 m

PG | DMA ACT | 1984 | COLOR

Rating: 8

This sweeping epic is the fourth screen retelling, and one of the best, of history's most famous mutiny. This screenplay concentrates on the personalities of the two principal characters and, as such, depicts the events somewhat more accurately. This Bligh (Hopkins) is just extremely stubborn - not crazy, and Christian (Gibson) is a shallow character. Beautiful scenery to watch and a fascinating story will hold your attention throughout. Also see the classic: MUTINY ON THE BOUNTY.

Sex | Nud | Viol | Lang | AdSit

A: Mel Gibson, Anthony Hopkins, Laurence Olivier, Edward Fox, Daniel Day-Lewis, Bernard Hill

© UNITED AMERICAN VIDEO CORP. 5966

BOYS FROM BRAZIL, THE

D: Franklin J. Schaffner 123 m

R | SUS DMA | 1978 | COLOR

Rating: 8

This is an entertaining thriller with an interesting premise. Suppose the infamous Nazi doctor who murdered thousands in "medical experiments," Dr. Josef Mengele, was still alive, living in Brazil and was attempting to clone ninety-four brand new boy-Hitlers from which to create a new Reich. Gregory Peck gets a rare opportunity to play a bad guy as Josef Mengele, and does quite well at it, too. But Olivier is brilliant as Nazi hunter Libermann who tries to stop Peck and his hideous cloning project.

Sex | Nud | Viol | Lang | AdSit

A: Gregory Peck, Laurence Olivier, James Mason, Lilli Palmer, Uta Hagen, Rosemary Harris

© LIVE HOME VIDEO 51117

BOYS IN THE BAND, THE

D: William Friedkin 119 m

R | DMA | 1970 | COLOR

Rating: 6

This was an interesting and widely acclaimed film which was also quite daring for Hollywood to do. It is the screen version of a successful off-Broadway play concerning the conversations at a gay man's birthday party, attended by nine men. Eight of the men are gay, one insists he is not. The party degenerates into a series of bitchy confrontations, which result in personal revelations of the loneliness and heartbreaks of being homosexual. Sometimes funny, sometimes sad, but almost always interesting.

Sex | Nud | Viol | Lang | AdSit

A: Kenneth Nelson, Peter White, Leonard Frey, Cliff Gorman, Frederick Coumbs, Laurence Luckinbill

© CBS/FOX VIDEO 7017

BOYS ON THE SIDE

D: Herbert Ross 117 m

R | DMA | 1995 | COLOR

Rating: 8

Quite involving girl-buddy-movie. Jane hasn't been successful in love (she's a lesbian) or in her singing career, so...she answers an ad, carpools with Robin (a middle-class real estate agent) and they both leave New York headed for Los Angeles. When they stop in Pittsburg to see Holly, Jane's ditsy nymphomaniac girlfriend, she and her drug-dealing live-in get in a fight and she conks him on the head with a bat. The three girls leave together only to later discover that he is dead. The three now race non-stop across country, but stop in Tucson when Robin gets sick and where Holly falls for a cop. Sometimes funny and sometimes very touching. Women will cheer, but most men will like it too.

Sex | Nud | Viol | Lang | AdSit

A: Whoopi Goldberg, Mary-Louise Parker, Drew Barrymore, Matthew McConaughey, James Remar, Estelle Parsons

© WARNER HOME VIDEO 13570

BOY WHO COULD FLY, THE

D: Nick Castle 114 m

PG | FAN DMA | 1986 | COLOR

Rating: 8

Highly enjoyable and uplifting film, excellent family entertainment. When her husband commits suicide after learning he has cancer, the hard-pressed Bonnie Bedelia and her two children move in next door to a troubled autistic boy who has lost his parents in a plane wreck and now just sits on the roof dreaming that he can fly. No one can reach him, but Bedelia's troubled daughter (Deakins) slowly draws him out of his private world and becomes the only true friend he has. Genuinely heartwarming picture about the value of love and of never giving up.

Sex | Nud | Viol | Lang | AdSit

A: Lucy Deakins, Jay Underwood, Bonnie Bedelia, Fred Savage, Colleen Dewhurst, Fred Gwynne

© WARNER HOME VIDEO 781

BOYZ N THE HOOD

D: John Singleton 112 m

R | CRM DMA | 1991 | COLOR

Rating: 9

An emotionally charged portrait of young men growing up in the very violent society of the inner-city. Brash and painfully insightful, this film looks at the way of life in the inner-city of Los Angeles, and the poverty, crime and gang wars that come with it. The story centers around one father and his desperate attempt to keep his son (Cuba Gooding, Jr.) out of trouble and to instill some sense of values in him. At 23, director John Singleton has done some incredible work and was honored by the New York Film Circle for this project.

Sex | Nud | Viol | Lang | AdSit

A: Ice Cube, Cuba Gooding, Jr., Morris Chestnut, Larry Fishburne, Tyra Ferrell, Angela Bassett

© COLUMBIA TRISTAR HOME VIDEO 50813

BRAVADOS, THE

D: Henry King 99 m

NR | WST ACT DMA | 1958 | COLOR

Rating: 8

This is a powerful drama of fierce frontier justice and revenge gone wild. Peck plays a rancher whose wife is raped and then murdered by four men. He, however, is an expert tracker and pursues them to a Mexican border town where they are about to be hung for robbing a bank and killing a teller. Instead of hanging, they escape and take a beautiful young woman hostage. Now, taking charge of the posse, Peck tracks them down one by one, exacting his own vicious vengeance as he finds them. This is a stark and brooding Western where Peck becomes as bad as the killers he pursues. Thought provoking.

Sex | Nud | Viol | Lang | AdSit

A: Gregory Peck, Joan Collins, Stephen Boyd, Albert Salmi, Henry Silva, Kathleen Gallant

© FOXVIDEO 1494

BREAKER MORANT

D: Bruce Beresford 103 m

PG | DMA SUS | 1980 | COLOR

Rating: 9

Very potent drama and a winner of 10 Australian awards. Set in 1901 during the Boer War in South Africa, three young Australian officers are made into scapegoats and forced to stand trial on trumped up charges of having killed civilian prisoners, one of which was a German. It is preordained that they must be convicted. If they aren't, the political plans of the British Empire will be stunted. Based upon an actual event, this is a gripping story that is beautifully crafted. Strong rich performances bring us close to these tragic characters. Captivating. This is a must see.

Sex | Nud | Viol | Lang | AdSit

A: Edward Woodward, Jack Thompson, John Waters, Charles Tingwell, Bryan Brown, Vincent Ball

© COLUMBIA TRISTAR HOME VIDEO 60145

BREAKFAST AT TIFFANY'S

D: Blake Edwards 114 m

NR | ROM DMA COM | 1961 | COLOR

Rating: 9

Totally captivating. Audrey Hepburn plays young, beautiful and fanciful Holly Golightly. She is an innocent at play in an imagined world of elegance and fun and captures the imagination and the affections of a struggling writer, George Peppard. This is a tender love story of a small-town girl who caught up in the pursuit of the trappings of glamour and big-city life. Hepburn is absolutely captivating as this little girl lost. A charming and tender love story, perfectly complemented by Mancini's Oscar-winning score.

Sex | Nud | Viol | Lang | AdSit

A: Audrey Hepburn, George Peppard, Patricia Neal, Buddy Ebsen, Mickey Rooney, Martin Balsam

© PARAMOUNT HOME VIDEO 6505

BREAKFAST CLUB, THE

D: John Hughes 92 m

R | DMA COM | 1985 | COLOR

Rating: 8

Quite good, perceptive, non-exploitive teen movie. A group of five totally different high school kids spend eight hours of detention together on a Saturday. At its start they have nothing in common, but during this day-long stretch of forced togetherness, the nerd, the jock, the delinquent, the prom queen and the kooky introvert all get to know each other, find that they have more in common than they ever thought and even become friends. Very funny at times, and interesting throughout.

Sex | Nud | Viol | Lang | AdSit

A: Molly Ringwald, Ally Sheedy, Emilio Estevez, Anthony Michael Hall, Judd Nelson

© MCA/UNIVERSAL HOME VIDEO, INC. 80167

BREAKING AWAY

D: Peter Yates 100 m

PG | COM DMA | 1979 | COLOR

Rating: 9

Wonderful sleeper and Best Picture Oscar nominee. It is a touching story of love, growing up and class differences. Four working-class teenagers just out of high school are scorned by the college kids in town. One becomes fixated on becoming a bicycle racing champion and tries to win a college girl over by pretending he's an Italian racer. When his cover is blown and the college boys further scorn his efforts, he and his friends decide to prove themselves as equals by winning the college bike race. This appealing, unpretentious film is funny, tender, insightful and entirely enjoyable.

Sex | Nud | Viol | Lang | AdSit

A: Dennis Christopher, Dennis Quaid, Robyn Douglas, Daniel Stern, Jackie Earle Haley, Barbara Barrie

© FOXVIDEO 1081

BREATHLESS

D: Jean-Luc Godard 90 m

NR | FOR DMA | 1959 | B&W

7 Belmondo became a huge star because of this film. In it he plays a playful small-time hood in Paris who steals a car. Jean Seberg is a beautiful free-spirited American who is seduced by his charm and follows him. When he accidentally shoots a cop who is chasing him, he hides out in Seberg's apartment. She remains captivated by his spirit but will not commit herself to him. Then, as the police close in on him, Seberg betrays him, but he refuses to run. This film appealed greatly to a "live for today" attitude prevalent after the War in France and became a big French cult favorite. Subtitles.

Sex, Nud, Viol, Lang, AdSit

A: Jean-Paul Belmondo, Daniel Boulanger, Jean Seberg

© CONNOISSEUR VIDEO COLLECTION 1021

BREWSTER MC CLOUD

D: Robert Altman 101 m

R | COM DMA | 1970 | COLOR

7 Definitely different. If you liked M*A*S*H or HAROLD AND MAUDE, or if your funny bone is off center, this black comedy may appeal to you. This is the story about a boy who grows up inside the Astrodome, in a bombshelter. He is protected by Sally Kellerman and taught by her to believe in dreams - even that he will be able to fly on his giant homemade wings. However, when some of Houston's richest citizens are murdered and are found covered in bird droppings, he becomes a prime suspect. A lot of quirky humor. Definitely original.

Sex, Nud, Viol, Lang, AdSit

A: Bud Cort, Sally Kellerman, Michael Murphy, William Windom, Shelley Duvall, Stacy Keach

Distributed By MGM/UA Home Video M700466

BRIAN'S SONG

D: Buzz Kulik 74 m

G | DMA | 1970 | COLOR

10 Truly exceptional made-for-TV movie recounting the real-life deep friendship between Chicago Bears players Brian Piccolo and Gale Sayers. It won five Emmy Awards. This odd-ball pair made news as the first interracial roommates in professional football, but their relationship only began on the playing field. They became best friends too. Brian Piccolo (Caan) is witty and free-spirited. Gale Sayers (Williams) is serious and all business. When Sayers gets badly hurt, Piccolo prods him into full recovery. Then it's Sayers turn when Piccolo is found to have cancer. Heartwarming. A milestone in TV movies.

Sex, Nud, Viol, Lang, AdSit

A: James Caan, Billy Dee Williams, Jack Warden, Judy Pace, Shelley Fabares

© COLUMBIA TRISTAR HOME VIDEO 60156

BRIDGE ON THE RIVER KWAI, THE

D: David Lean 161 m

NR | WAR DMA ACT | 1957 | COLOR

10 Powerful war drama which won 7 Academy Awards, including every major category. Much more than a standard war or action movie, this is the powerfully dramatic story of men under extreme stress. British soldiers in a Japanese prisoner-of-war camp are forced to construct a strategic bridge in Burma. For Guinness, the English commander, it is a source of pride for himself and his men, but Holden returns after escaping to blow it up as being a dangerous strategic target. Psychological battles of wills and major action sequences combine in a famous climax.

Sex, Nud, Viol, Lang, AdSit

A: William Holden, Alec Guinness, Jack Hawkins, Sessue Hayakawa, James Donald, Geoffrey Horne

© COLUMBIA TRISTAR HOME VIDEO 60160

BRIGHTON BEACH MEMOIRS

D: Gene Saks 110 m

PG-13 | COM DMA | 1986 | COLOR

7 Neil Simon's semi-autobiographical comedy about a 15-year-old adolescent boy growing up in an overcrowded house in 1930s Brooklyn. It is the story of the whole family and their problems as seen from his viewpoint, while he is himself trying to deal with his own growing-up problems. Nostalgic and funny. If you like this, you may also be interested in seeing the next installment, BELOXI BLUES.

Sex, Nud, Viol, Lang, AdSit

A: Jonathan Silverman, Blythe Danner, Bob Dishy, Brian Brillinger, Stacey Glick, Judith Ivey

© MCA/UNIVERSAL HOME VIDEO, INC. 80476

BROADCAST NEWS

D: James L. Brooks 132 m

R | COM DMA | 1987 | COLOR

9 Intelligent, extremely clever and entertaining take-no-prisoners look at TV news in general, and an odd love triangle in particular. Wonderful performances. Hurt is a popular, well-meaning and extremely photogenic anchorman, but he doesn't really understand the news he's reading. Hunter is a very bright and extremely driven producer who is attracted to him in spite of the fact that he represents everything she despises about TV news. She, is loved in turn by Brooks, who is a supercompetent reporter but becomes extremely nervous and sweats profusely when on camera. Five Oscar nominations. Great stuff.

Sex, Nud, Viol, Lang, AdSit

A: William Hurt, Albert Brooks, Holly Hunter, Robert Prosky, Lois Chiles, Jack Nicholson

© FOXVIDEO 1654

BRONX TALE, A

D: Robert De Niro 122 m

R | DMA COM | 1993 | COLOR

9 Excellent. Colagero, C for short, is the son of Lorenzo, a hard working honest bus driver. The family lives two doors down from the neighborhood bar where Sonny, a gangster, holds court. C has two heros, his father and Sonny. Sonny spent ten years in prison and he spent his time reading. He is smart, he is tough and he loves C. Even though his father has forbidden it, C is infatuated with Sonny and Sonny watches out for him. From his father, C learns integrity and from Sonny he learns hard lessens about people and life. Brilliant first-time directing effort from De Niro, who flawlessly blends humor, drama and violence into a highly watchable tale of morality.

Sex, Nud, Viol, Lang, AdSit

A: Robert De Niro, Chazz Palminteri, Luillo Brancato, Francis Capra, Taral Hicks

© HBO VIDEO 90954

BROTHERS KARAMAZOV, THE

D: Richard Brooks 147 m

NR | DMA | 1958 | COLOR

7 Dostoyevsky's classic Russian novel about a 19th-century domineering and lecherous father and his four sons. One son is an intellectual, one a religious zealot, one an illegitimate schemer and the oldest loves the same woman as does his father. Cobb was Oscar-nominated. An excellent cast works hard to bring life to the screenplay about the effect that the father's death, and the inheritance he leaves, has on his sons. Production is well-done but cannot live up to the full promise of the monumental novel.

Sex, Nud, Viol, Lang, AdSit

A: Yul Brynner, Claire Bloom, Lee J. Cobb, Maria Schell, Richard Basehart, William Shatner

Distributed By MGM/UA Home Video M300375

BUDDY HOLLY STORY, THE

D: Steve Rash 113 m

PG | DMA MUS | 1978 | COLOR

8 One of the best rock `n roll movies ever. Gary Busey was Oscar-nominated for his bravura performance as Buddy Holly - the legendary Texas boy who combined country music with rhythm and blues. This is not the typical glossed-over Hollywood version of a poor boy made good, but an accurate representation of the Texas rock legend up until his tragic death. Busey's energetic impersonation of Holly includes live performances of the classic "That'll Be the Day," "It's So Easy," "Peggy Sue" and others. See also LA BAMBA for Richie Valens's story.

Sex, Nud, Viol, Lang, AdSit

A: Gary Busey, Charles Martin Smith, Dick O'Neil, Maria Richwine, Conrad Janis, Amy Johnson

© COLUMBIA TRISTAR HOME VIDEO 60801

BUGSY

D: Barry Levinson 135 m

R | DMA CRM | 1991 | COLOR

8 There is a powerhouse performance by Warren Beatty in this fascinating character study of the "creator" of Las Vegas - the infamous gang world character, Ben (Bugsy) Siegel. The story begins during WWII when Siegel moved from the East Coast to Los Angeles to muscle in on the West Coast mob. There he met and began a stormy and steamy love affair with the equally infamous Virginia Hill (Bening). Beatty's Siegel is a complex character. He is brilliant, vain and extremely ruthless. When the wildly over-budget Flamingo Hotel flops, Bugsy meets with swift mob justice.

Sex, Nud, Viol, Lang, AdSit

A: Warren Beatty, Ben Kingsley, Annette Bening, Lewis Van Bergen, Harvey Keitel, Richard Sarafian

© COLUMBIA TRISTAR HOME VIDEO 70673

BURMESE HARP, THE

D: Kon Ichikawa 116 m

NR | FOR WAR DMA | 1956 | B&W

9 Powerful and moving anti-war film from Japan. Nearing the end of WWII, a harp-playing Japanese soldier's unit tries to steal away into neutral territory but he volunteers to stay behind and journey into the mountains to convince other renegade fighters that Japan has officially surrendered. But along the way, he is wounded and saved by a Buddhist priest. Now transformed and wearing the robes of the monk, he traverses endless plains of dead soldiers and begins to methodically bury and burn the bodies of his countrymen. And when other soldiers leave to retreat, he stays behind to finish his task. Subtitles. Also known as THE HARP OF BURMA.

Sex, Nud, Viol, Lang, AdSit

A: Shoji Yasui, Rentaro Mikuni, Tatsuya Mihashi, Tanie Kitabayashi, Yunosuke Ito

© HOME VISION BUR 110

BURN!

D: Gillo Pontecorvo 113 m

PG | DMA ACT | 1970 | COLOR

7 Fascinating political intrigue set in the colonial Caribbean of 1845. Three hundred years earlier, the Portuguese had burned the entire island to put down an uprising and destroyed the entire native population. Black slaves were imported from Africa to replace them. Now the British send in an agent, egomaniacal Sir William Walker (Brando), to investigate a black uprising. Portraying himself as their savior, he incites the slaves to riot. But when the slaves throw the Portuguese out, he betrays their revolution and he simply replaces the Portuguese with the British.

Sex, Nud, Viol, Lang, AdSit

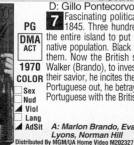

A: Marlon Brando, Evaristo Marquez, Renato Salvatori, Tom Lyons, Norman Hill

Distributed By MGM/UA Home Video M202327

BURNING BED, THE

D: Robert Greenwald 95 m

NR DMA 1984 COLOR

9 Farrah Fawcett received an Emmy nomination for her performance in this excellent made-for-TV movie, which was based on a true story. Farrah plays Francine Hughes, a battered Michigan housewife who became so desperate that on March 9, 1977 that she set fire to her ex-husband while he was asleep in their bed, rather than to allow herself to be beaten again. The husband's abusive nature later became the major issue at her murder trial which followed. Far superior to typical television fare. For another excellent Fawcett performance, see BETWEEN TWO WOMEN.

Sex Nud Viol Lang AdSit

A: Farrah Fawcett, Paul Masur, James Callahan, Richard Masur, Grace Zabriskie, Penelope Milford

© CBS/FOX VIDEO 6889

BURNING SEASON, THE

D: John Frankenheimer 123 m

NR DMA 1994 COLOR

8 Winner of 3 Golden Globe Awards, this is the true story of a hero in the battle for the preservation of the Brazilian rain forest. For generations, poor rubber-tappers had been cheated, beaten down and even killed by powerful men. But, they had the forest...it was the law. Then, in the 1980s, the burning came. Again, powerful people had corrupted the system and this time were stealing the land to make cattle ranches. But, this time the peasants fought back...not with guns, but with non-violent demonstrations led by Chico Mendes. When a documentary showed the world what was happening, Chico became a spokesman to the world. He won the battle for his forrest, but he paid for it with his life.

Sex Nud Viol Lang AdSit

A: Raul Julia, Carmen Argenziano, Sonia Braga, Kamala Dawson, Luis Guzman, Edward James Olmos

© WARNER HOME VIDEO 13883

BUSTER AND BILLIE

D: Daniel Petrie 100 m

R ROM DMA 1974 COLOR

6 A perceptive little story about teenage love between two mismatched Georgia high school students in 1948. A potential for cheap exploitation is averted and becomes instead an affecting young-love story. The most popular boy in school (Vincent) is surprised when he is attracted to a plain girl that he dates only because everyone tells him that she is a tramp. Instead, he sees a warm and sensitive girl who is crying out to be accepted. He finds something sweet and attractive in her, but their love is severely challenged when she is attacked by a group of tough guys.

Sex Nud Viol Lang AdSit

A: Jan-Michael Vincent, Joan Goodfellow, Pamela Sue Martin, Clifton James, Robert Englund

© COLUMBIA TRISTAR HOME VIDEO 60481

BUTTERFIELD 8

D: Daniel Mann 110 m

NR DMA ROM 1960 COLOR

6 Very daring for its day, Elizabeth Taylor won her first Oscar playing a model and high-class call girl who flutters from one man to another. She's very popular, just call Butterfield 8. She meets and falls in love with a very prominent man (Harvey). Their passions rage and he wants to leave his wife to be with her, but cannot come to grips with her past life and eventually refuses to leave his wealthy wife for her. Glossy soap opera.

Sex Nud Viol Lang AdSit

A: Elizabeth Taylor, Laurence Harvey, Mildred Dunnock, Dina Merrill, Betty Field, Eddie Fisher

Distributed By MGM/UA Home Video M300272

BUTTERFLIES ARE FREE

D: Milton Katselas 149 m

PG COM ROM DMA 1972 COLOR

9 Genuine pleasure of a serio-comedy. Edward Albert is a blind young man struggling to become self-sufficient. He wants break free of his over-protective (but loving) mother and also to romance his kookie next-door neighbor (Hawn). Goldie is an eccentric, aspiring actress who has fallen for this guy but has to learn how to deal with things, too. Their relationship, and all the other complications, leads to a fast-paced comedy. Nominated for three Oscars, Heckart won Best Supporting Actress. A really good time and a great feel-good movie.

Sex Nud Viol Lang AdSit

A: Goldie Hawn, Edward Albert, Jr., Eileen Heckart, Mike Warren

© COLUMBIA TRISTAR HOME VIDEO 60149

CABARET

D: Bob Fosse 124 m

PG MUS DMA COM 1972 COLOR

9 A brilliant piece of work which won eight Oscars and is undoubtedly one of the best movie musicals ever. It is the story of Germany in 1931 and a young American girl caught up in its bawdy decadence. Hitler's Nazis had not yet captured full power and life was carefree, decadent and even sleazy; but doom is looming. Liza is a naive cabaret showgirl caught up in the carefree mood of the time and torn between two lovers. Wonderful songs steal the show; most notable are: "The Money Song" with Grey and Minnelli and the chorus line doing "Mein Heir."

Sex Nud Viol Lang AdSit

A: Liza Minnelli, Michael York, Helmut Griem, Joel Grey, Fritz Wepper, Marisa Berenson

© WARNER HOME VIDEO 785

CADILLAC MAN

D: Roger Donaldson 97 m

R COM DMA 1990 COLOR

6 Who has been sleeping with Tim Robbins's girlfriend? That's what gun-toting Robbins wants to know when he barges into a auto showroom full of customers demanding an answer. The sleezeball turns out to be salesman Robin Williams. In fact, he has been sleeping with a number of women, cheating on his wife, juggling a loan shark and trying to get his boss off his tail. Now, in this one perilous moment, Williams just may lose it all, and so he does verbal gymnastics trying to convince the crazed gunman to put that gun away. An inventive tale, hilarious in spots but uneven, too.

Sex Nud Viol Lang AdSit

A: Robin Williams, Tim Robbins, Pamela Reed, Annabella Sciorra, Fran Drescher, Zack Norman

© ORION PICTURES CORPORATION 8756

CALL OF THE WILD

D: Ken Annakin 104 m

PG ACT DMA 1972 COLOR

7 Jack London's classic story remade. This time it has Charlton Heston in the lead role of an Alaskan gold prospector whose dog is stolen and forced into sad and sadistic service for others. This is good viewing, but there were three other productions of this story. Virtually all of them are better, but none are available on video except for the excellent 1991 variation by Disney called WHITE FANG.

Sex Nud Viol Lang AdSit

A: Charlton Heston, Michele Mercier, Marla Rohm, Rik Battagila

© GOODTIMES 8385

CAMILLE CLAUDEL

D: Bruno Nuytten 149 m

R FOR DMA 1989 COLOR

6 A bit long but involving look at the artistic genius of the famous French sculptress and her slide into insanity. A very independent woman, Camille (Adjani) is consumed with her art but finds conflict in the male-dominated art world. She studies under the noted sculptor August Rodin (Depardieu) and soon develops a romantic, but stormy, relationship with him. Sadly, she spends her last years in an asylum, suffering with an insanity brought on by the turbulence surrounding her work and her relationship with Rodin. Wonderful period detail but the film is likely leave you unsatisfied. Subtitles.

Sex Nud Viol Lang AdSit

A: Isabelle Adjani, Gerard Depardieu, Daniele Lebrun, Laurent Grevill, Katrine Boorman, Alain Cuny

© ORION PICTURES CORPORATION 5050

CANDIDATE, THE

D: Michael Ritchie 110 m

PG DMA 1972 COLOR

7 Redford plays an idealistic attorney who agrees to run for a US Senator's seat against long odds, but only if he can do it on his terms. He soon realizes that he is going to lose big and if he wants to win, he is going to have to give way to some powerful forces. Unless he wins, he can achieve nothing. This is an insider's view on how politicians are packaged and sold. Screenwriter and director were both active in '60s politics and have injected a lot of realism and believability into the story. Screenplay won an Oscar.

Sex Nud Viol Lang AdSit

A: Robert Redford, Melvyn Douglas, Peter Boule, Karen Carlson, Allen Garfield

© WARNER HOME VIDEO 1022

CAPTAIN NEWMAN, M.D.

D: David Miller 126 m

NR DMA COM 1963 COLOR

8 Affecting combination of drama and comedy. Peck is the hard-working head of psychiatry at an Army hospital at the close of WWII. He is trying to help his patients recover from serious war traumas, while also fighting off the military brass. Bobby Darin received an Oscar nomination for his performance as a war hero who has become afraid of being a coward. Tony Curtis provides laughs as a slick corporal who can be counted upon to get things done. A strong cast of supporting characters makes this realistic look inside a military mental hospital both largely-believable and enjoyable.

Sex Nud Viol Lang AdSit

A: Gregory Peck, Tony Curtis, Bobby Darin, Eddie Albert, Angie Dickinson, Jane Withers

© MCA/UNIVERSAL HOME VIDEO, INC. 80403

CARDINAL, THE

D: Otto Preminger 175 m

NR DMA 1963 COLOR

7 Tom Tryon plays a Roman Catholic priest, Stephen Fermoyle, who has come from a humble background and Irish parents, all the while doubting himself and his calling. This is a handsomely produced soap opera that follows his career from parish priest to the lofty level of Cardinal over a period of three decades. The story is long but nonetheless compelling due to Otto Preminger's deft touch. Beautiful pageantry and some good acting don't hurt, either.

Sex Nud Viol Lang AdSit

A: Tom Tryon, Carol Lynley, Romy Schneider, John Huston, Burgess Meredith

© VIDEO TREASURES SV9030

CAREFUL, HE MIGHT HEAR YOU

D: Carl Schultz 113 m

PG | DMA | 1984 | COLOR | Sex, Lang, AdSit

9 A heart-wrenching, emotional drama from Australia about a bitter custody battle between two sisters. One is rich and one not and they are fighting over their 7-year-old nephew who has been left alone after his mother dies and his dad deserts him. The story is particularly poignant because it is told entirely from the boy's perspective as he tries to understand the adult-world happenings around him. The movie is a credible depiction of a situation that is at times heartwarming and at other times bitterly sad. Winner of 8 Australian awards.

A: Robyn Nevin, Richolas Gledhill, Wendy Hughes, John Hargreaves

© FOXVIDEO 1436

CARLITO'S WAY

D: Brian De Palma 145 m

R | CRM ACT DMA | 1993 | COLOR | Sex, Nud, Viol, Lang, AdSit

8 Carlito (Pachino) was a big time drug dealer and a hood. He is tough and has stayed alive by doing what he has to do to survive. He was sent up for 30 years but his shyster lawyer (Penn) has gotten him out after only five. Still, that was enough time for Carlito. All he wants now is to go straight, stay out of trouble and he's got a plan to do it, too. He needs $75,000 to buy into a legit car rental business in the Bahamas and take his old flame (Miller) there with him. He is going to raise the money honestly by running a nightclub. The plan is working too. Then he gets a call from his lawyer buddy who is in trouble. Carlito feels honor-bound to help him, even though he risks everything.

A: Al Pacino, Sean Penn, Penelope Ann Miller, Luis Guzman, James Rebhorrn, Viggo Mortensen

© MCA/UNIVERSAL HOME VIDEO, INC. 81630

CARNAL KNOWLEDGE

D: Mike Nichols 98 m

R | DMA | 1971 | COLOR | Sex, Nud, Lang, AdSit

7 America's sexual mores and attitudes are followed through the experiences of two men, from their college days in the late '40s into their middle age, in the early '70s. Nicholson is an amoral user of people, incapable of any real intimacy. Garfunkel is his shy buddy. Nicholson and Garfunkel are college roommates who both lose their virginity to the same girl, but Garfunkel marries her. Nicholson carries on a relationship with a fading sex goddess Ann-Margret, but also requires visits to prostitute Moreno for satisfaction. Powerful, insightful and thought-provoking, but depressing.

A: Jack Nicholson, Candice Bergen, Art Garfunkel, Ann-Margret, Rita Moreno, Carol Kane

© NEW LINE HOME VIDEO 2030

CARNY

D: Robert Kaylor 106 m

R | DMA | 1980 | COLOR | Sex, Nud, Viol, Lang, AdSit

8 Very different but strangely fascinating and voyeuristic look inside the seedy world of carnival workers. The story is about the relationship that develops between a pair of carnival buddies, who make their living hustling the suckers - one in clown makeup hurls insults at people passing by and the other sells balls to them to throw at him. Foster is a teenage runaway who joins them both on the road. This is an atmospheric film that concentrates on the bond that develops between these odd characters, in a life where they have their own rules and it's OK to cheat, lie, and steal. Foster's first adult role.

A: Gary Busey, Jodie Foster, Robbie Robertson, Meg Foster, Bert Remsen, Craig Wasson

© WARNER HOME VIDEO 940

CASEY'S SHADOW

D: Martin Ritt 117 m

PG | COM DMA CLD | 1977 | COLOR

7 Enjoyable old-time family fare. Walter Matthau is a ne'er-do-well and impoverished Cajun horse trainer whose wife has left him to raise their three sons by himself. Matthau is a simple man whose modest dream is to train a winning racehorse, but it is a dream he wants more than almost anything. He and his boys are grooming a quarter horse that the boys love, named Casey's Shadow for a million dollar race -- even though the wealthy owner Alexis Smith only wants to sell him. When the horse's leg is hurt just before the big race and even though the vet and his boys don't want the horse to race, Matthau enters the horse. Matthau almost single-handedly carries this movie.

A: Walter Matthau, Andrew Rubin, Stephen Burns, Alexis Smith, Robert Webber, Murray Hamilton

© COLUMBIA TRISTAR HOME VIDEO 60153

CASUALTIES OF WAR

D: Brian De Palma 120 m

R | WAR DMA ACT | 1989 | COLOR | Sex, Nud, Viol, Lang, AdSit

8 This is a startling film that retells a real-life horror story from the Vietnam War. It occurred in 1966 and was first revealed in a magazine article. The story revolves around one incident when an out-of-control squad of American soldiers kidnaps, rapes and later murders a young Vietnamese girl after they are through with her. Fox is a new raw recruit, an innocent private, who watches as his crazed sergeant goes over the edge and leads his troops on this rampage. Fox is the only soldier who object. He tries to help the girl escape and later reports the incident, but he stands alone against his squad.

A: Michael J. Fox, Sean Penn, Thuy Thu Le, Don Harvey, John Leguizamo

© COLUMBIA TRISTAR HOME VIDEO 50183

CATERED AFFAIR, THE

D: Richard Brooks 95 m

NR | DMA | 1956 | B&W | AdSit

7 Bette Davis is cast exactly opposite her usual glamour role. Here she is Aggie, an Irish cabbie's shrew of a wife. When her daughter (Debbie Reynolds) announces that she will be married, Aggie is determined to give her daughter the ritzy wedding that she never had - even if it means that she spends all their savings and destroys her husband's (Borgnine) dream of buying his own cab business. Aggie can see nothing but her own dream in her compulsion to impress others.

A: Bette Davis, Ernest Borgnine, Debbie Reynolds, Barry Fitzgerald, Rod Taylor

Distributed By MGM/UA Home Video M201845

CATHOLICS

D: Jack Gold 86 m

NR | DMA | 1973 | COLOR | AdSit

8 A far above average made-for-TV movie, set somewhere in the future. An emissary from the Pope (Martin Sheen) comes to Ireland to convince the priests at an ancient monastery to change their old conservative ways and to conform to the new revised thinkings of the church. Trevor Howard plays a strong-willed abbot who is unwilling to change because truth cannot be altered to fit the temperature of the times. A thought-provoking drama with riveting performances.

A: Trevor Howard, Martin Sheen, Raf Vallone, Andrew Keir, Cyril Cusack, Michael Bambon

© LIVE HOME VIDEO 215-249

CAT ON A HOT TIN ROOF

D: Richard Brooks 108 m

NR | DMA | 1958 | COLOR | AdSit

9 Very potent human drama which won six Oscar nominations, including Best Picture. It is Tennessee Williams's explosive play about the crisis in a powerful Southern family, headed up by a domineering patriarch. Big Daddy (Burl Ives) is dying and he has called his family in. He wants an heir. Paul Newman is the favored son. However, he is also a faded former football hero who is unable to face responsibility and remains dominated by Daddy. He has become a drunk, married to sexy, greedy Maggie (Taylor), who no longer even shares his bed. They are all there to get some of Daddy's money.

A: Elizabeth Taylor, Paul Newman, Burl Ives, Jack Carson, Judith Anderson, Madeleine Sherwood

Distributed By MGM/UA Home Video M600060

CEASE FIRE

D: David Nutter 97 m

R | DMA WAR | 1985 | COLOR | Viol, Lang, AdSit

7 After fifteen years of trying to fit back into society, Johnson's Vietnam-induced flashbacks are ripping at his marriage. When he loses his job, the pain of his experiences overwhelm him. Then fellow vet Lyons convinces him to acknowledge that he has a problem and to seek help in group therapy sessions at a Veterans Center. This is an earnest and heartfelt drama that reflects the other side of RAMBO, which is too true for too many. Slowly, with the help of therapy and the love of his family, he starts to win his way back.

A: Don Johnson, Lisa Biount, Robert F. Lyons, Richard Chaves, Rick Richards, Chris Noel

© CONGRESS VIDEO GROUP 02780

CEMETERY CLUB, THE

D: Bill Duke 107 m

PG-13 | DMA ROM | 1992 | COLOR | Sex, Lang, AdSit

7 Three older women have been friends for a very long time - since before their husbands died. Now all three husbands are dead and the three are trying to decide what to do with the rest of their lives. One day their cemetery visit is disrupted by a loud argument taking place between a very mad Danny Aiello and the groundskeeper for not having taken care of his wife's grave. Later, Aiello meets Burstyn at her music store and again apologizes for the argument, but he also asks her out. Their budding relationship not only confuses the both of them, but it also disrupts the serenity of the Cemetery Club.

A: Danny Aiello, Olympia Dukakis, Ellen Burstyn, Diane Ladd

© TOUCHSTONE HOME VIDEO 1481

CHALK GARDEN, THE

D: Ronald Neame 106 m

NR | DMA | 1964 | COLOR | AdSit

8 When her father remarries, young Hayley Mills is sent to live with her grandmother. Grandmother spoils her shamefully and the girl has become a terror because she rightfully feels as though no one loves her. Both her mother and father have deserted her and her grandmother's prime concern is her garden. She has become an extremely disagreeable girl and she lashes out at everyone. Then a governess (Kerr), with a dark past, battles everyone to give the girl the love, support and direction she needs. A very high quality soap opera for discriminating audiences. Entertaining, too.

A: Deborah Kerr, Hayley Mills, Edith Evans, Felix Aylmer, Elizabeth Sellars, John Mills

© MCA/UNIVERSAL HOME VIDEO, INC. 80639

CHAMP, THE

D: Franco Zeffirelli 121 m

PG | DMA CLD | 1979 | COLOR | Sex | Nud | Viol | Lang | AdSit

7 Sentimental remake of the 1931 Wallace Beery/Jackie Cooper classic, this time set at a Florida racetrack. Billy Flynn is an alcoholic ex-prize fighter who keeps promising his young son that he will one day again become champ, but instead he drinks and is perpetually broke. After seven years, the boy's now-wealthy mother sees him again and challenges Billy for custody of the boy. Billy now desperately needs to attempt a real come back so he can keep his son, even though the doctor says it will kill him. Not up to the original but still jerks plenty of tears. Very young Schroder is outstanding.

A: Jon Voight, Faye Dunaway, Ricky Schroder, Jack Warden

Distributed By MGM/UA Home Video M600034

CHAMPIONS

D: John Irvin 113 m

PG | DMA | 1984 | COLOR | Sex | Nud | Viol | Lang | AdSit

7 Heartwarming true story from England of the triumph of the human spirit - in the tradition of CHARIOTS OF FIRE. It is the comeback story of two champions: a talented young jockey with his eye set upon winning the Grand National Steeplechase, but who is stricken with cancer at 31; and his horse Aldaniti, that is crippled in a horse race. Both overcame long odds to ride in the National during the rousing finish to an uplifting film. Well-made and affecting film.

A: John Hurt, Edward Woodward, Jan Francis, Ben Johnson

© NEW LINE HOME VIDEO 2086

CHAPLIN

D: Richard Attenborough 135 m

PG-13 | DMA | 1992 | COLOR | Sex | Nud | Viol | Lang | AdSit

7 Quite comprehensive but very sober biography of one of the greatest comedians ever in film. It follows Chaplin's entire life: beginning in the slums of London; his mother's insanity; his career on the stages of London, the American vaudeville stage, in silent films and talkies; his wives, women and children; his politics; and, his running battle with J. Edgar Hoover who eventually drove him from America. Excellent acting throughout, particularly by Downey, but it does tend to be quite slow moving - particularly in the last half. And, for a film about a comic, it isn't nearly as funny as it should be.

A: Robert Downey, Jr., Dan Aykroyd, Geraldine Chaplin, Anthony Hopkins, Milla Jovovich, Moira Kelly

© LIVE HOME VIDEO 69897

CHARIOTS OF FIRE

D: Hugh Hudson 124 m

PG | DMA | 1981 | COLOR | Sex | Nud | Viol | Lang | AdSit

8 A major box office hit and highly acclaimed by the critics. It is an unusual and absorbing drama about two Englishmen, one a devout Scottish Christian missionary and the other a Jewish student, who are both training to run in the 1924 Olympics. However, neither is running for personal glory or for the glory of England - one is running for the glory of God, the other just to gain acceptance. It is a thought-provoking drama that also beautifully captures both the spirit and the atmosphere of the times. It won Best Picture of 1981 and three other Oscars.

A: Ben Cross, Ian Charleson, Nigel Havers, Nicolas Farrell, Alice Krige, Cheryl Campbell

© WARNER HOME VIDEO 20004

CHARLY

D: Ralph Nelson 104 m

PG | DMA SF | 1968 | COLOR | Sex | Nud | Viol | Lang | AdSit

8 Endearing sentimental favorite with an interesting premise that also explores some fascinating philosophical territory. Cliff Robertson won an Oscar for his role as Charley, a gentle, retarded man with a powerful drive to learn. When Charley is asked to try a breakthrough surgical procedure that may help him get smarter, he readily agrees. He does quickly attain genius-level brain powers, but no one counted on the complex emotions that develop, too. Claire Bloom is a caseworker who works to help Charley adapt to the changes and find a brief period of happiness before, unexpectedly, the process reverses.

A: Cliff Robertson, Claire Bloom, Lilia Skala, Leon Janney, Dick Van Patten

© CBS/FOX VIDEO 8020

CHASE, THE

D: Arthur Penn 135 m

NR | DMA | 1966 | COLOR | Sex | Nud | Viol | Lang | AdSit

6 A small town in Texas is torn apart when a local boy (Robert Redford), imprisoned on false charges, breaks out of jail and returns home for his wife (Jane Fonda). E.G. Marshall is a local baron who wants Redford shot before it becomes known that his son was having an affair with Fonda. Brando, as the sheriff, is tracking Redford down both to capture a runaway and to protect him from a drunken posse with a reward on their minds. OK melodrama, but some problems during production severely hurt the quality. Should have been much better, but Redford shows an early glimpse of his starpower.

A: Marlon Brando, Jane Fonda, Robert Redford, E.G. Marshall, Angie Dickinson, Janice Rule

© COLUMBIA TRISTAR HOME VIDEO 60617

CHEYENNE AUTUMN

D: John Ford 155 m

NR | WST DMA | 1964 | COLOR | Sex | Nud | Viol | Lang | AdSit

8 Director John Ford came to be virtually synonymous with cowboy heros and the Western movie. This film was his last movie and here he strayed away from his typical glorification of the white man's West. This is the story of a group of starving and desperate Cheyenne Indians who leave their barren reservation in Oklahoma to struggle back home to Wyoming. It is a pitiful tale of privation and hardship. They must travel across 1500 miles of bleak winter landscape, all the while pursued by the US Calvary, who will only take them back where they started. Worthy viewing.

A: Richard Widmark, Carroll Baker, Karl Malden, Dolores Del Rio, Sal Mineo, Edward G. Robinson

© WARNER HOME VIDEO 11052

CHICKEN RANCH

D: 84 m

DOC DMA | 1983 | COLOR | Sex | Nud | Viol | Lang | AdSit

6 This is an unvarnished look at the Chicken Ranch, the famous real world bordello that was the inspiration for the musical THE BEST LITTLE WHORE HOUSE IN TEXAS. The "house" was moved from Texas to Las Vegas in 1970. The producers of this film spent twelve weeks on site, where 15 girls are always available and it is open 24 hours a day. The film is shot in cinema verite style (moving camera) and the quality of sound and editing is poor. The filmmakers attempt to make no moral statement, but the movie paints a pretty grim picture of "the life." The customers and the workers alike get to speak for themselves.

A:

© LIVE HOME VIDEO VA3052

CHILD IS WAITING, A

D: John Cassavetes 105 m

NR | DMA | 1963 | B&W | Sex | Nud | Viol | Lang | AdSit

8 A moving, poignant and provocative story of an overly-committed music teacher (Garland) and psychologist (Lancaster) at a school for the mentally retarded who desperately attempt to reach out to the children who will always remain children. One particular situation becomes the focus of the drama, but the story chosen could have been that of any one of the children because of the many similarities they all share. Actual retarded children were used in the filming, producing a poignant and gripping story. Not for overly sensitive people.

A: Burt Lancaster, Judy Garland, Steven Hill, Gena Rowlands

Distributed By MGM/UA Home Video M301824

CHILDREN OF A LESSER GOD

D: Randa Haines 119 m

R | ROM DMA | 1986 | COLOR | Sex | Nud | Viol | Lang | AdSit

9 An exceptional movie that both the critics and the public liked. William Hurt is a dedicated teacher at a school for the deaf who becomes fascinated with a very beautiful and obviously intelligent, but exceedingly bitter, young woman who continues to work at the school as a janitor after graduating. He seeks to uncover her secrets and to help her but instead falls in love with her. A very unusual and moving love story made more involving by impeccable performances. Matlin, deaf in real life, won an Oscar for her film debut.

A: William Hurt, Marlee Matlin, Piper Laurie, Philip Bosco

© PARAMOUNT HOME VIDEO 1839

CHILLY SCENES OF WINTER

D: Joan Micklin Silver 96 m

PG | ROM COM DMA | 1982 | COLOR | Sex | Nud | Viol | Lang | AdSit

8 A Salt Lake City civil servant (Heard) falls very hard for pretty Hurt, who has just left her husband because he loved her too little. But now Heard loves her so intensely that she becomes scared by it all and cannot understand why she is now worthy of so much attention. Soon Heard's constant attentions and jealousy drive her back to her husband and the daughter she misses very much, but Heard still tries to win her back. Funny, but painful, too. Wonderful acting.

A: John Heard, Mary Beth Hurt, Peter Riegert, Kenneth McMillan, Gloria Grahame

Distributed By MGM/UA Home Video M600726

CHINA SYNDROME, THE

D: James Bridges 123 m

PG | SUS DMA | 1979 | COLOR | Sex | Nud | Viol | Lang | AdSit

10 A huge box office hit because it was very intense and believable drama. A novice TV reporter (Fonda) and her cameraman are at a nuclear generating station when there is a near-meltdown situation. It is averted only by a quick-thinking engineer (Lemon), but the TV station refuses to televise their video tapes. When Lemmon releases X-rays revealing that it could happen again, another reporter is killed. There is no doubt now that there is a ruthless coverup underway by very powerful people. Feeling he has no alternative Lemmon seizes control of the plant and invites the media in. Excellent.

A: Jane Fonda, Jack Lemmon, Michael Douglas, Scott Brady, James Hampton, Peter Donat

© GOODTIMES 4200

D M A

CHOCOLATE WAR, THE

D: Keith Gordon 103 m

R | DMA COM | 1988 | COLOR

7 Screen version of a very popular book set in a Catholic boys school. An idealistic freshman (Mitchell-Smith) is caught between an ambitious and ruthless teacher (Glover) and his own sense of honor. Glover wants to become headmaster through attaining the most-ever sales in the annual chocolate sale. He uses a group of bully-boys to pressure all the students into selling more than ever before, but new kid Mitchell-Smith refuses to cave in to Glover's demands and stands defiantly against him. Excellent performances and an interesting story that is best suited for teenagers.

Sex / Nud / Viol / Lang / AdSit

A: John Glover, Ilan Mitchell-Smith, Wally Ward, Bud Cort, Adam Baldwin, Jenny Wright

© VIDEO TREASURES SV9698

CHOIRBOYS, THE

D: Robert Aldrich 120 m

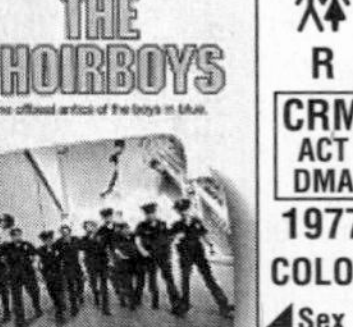

R | CRM ACT DMA | 1977 | COLOR

6 Written by ex-detective Joseph Wambaugh, this is a story of the flip-side of some of the men in police work. Some L.A. cops meet periodically to let off some steam at frequent "choir practice" sessions, which are really wild booze and sex parties held in MacArthur Park. The story follows the lives of ten different cops. Most viewers will think that the depiction of their "choir practice" escapades are far too heavy-handed and foul. The film had a mixed reception at the box office upon its release, mostly because critics hated it.

Sex / Nud / Viol / Lang / AdSit

A: Charles Durning, Louis Gossett, Jr., Perry King, Clyde Kasatsu, Stephen Macht, Tim McIntire

© MCA/UNIVERSAL HOME VIDEO, INC. 55097

CHOOSE ME

D: Alan Rudolph 106 m

R | COM DMA | 1984 | COLOR

8 Inventive and definitely different story concerning the love affairs of three loners. It is a sophisticated look at the truths and lies of love and sex in the 1980s in which the characters are actually more important than the storyline. Bujold is a radio talk show sex therapist who is actually hopelessly mixed up herself. Warren is a supposedly self-assured bar owner, but is actually constantly afraid and calls Bujold's radio show all the time for help. Carradine is the charming escaped mental case who seduces them both. This is a companion piece to WELCOME TO L.A. and REMEMBER MY NAME. Fine acting and a story that works on many levels at once.

Sex / Nud / Viol / Lang / AdSit

A: Genevieve Bujold, Keith Carradine, Lesley Ann Warren, Rae Dawn Chong, Patrick Bauchau, John Larroquette

© MEDIA HOME ENTERTAINMENT, INC. M787

CHORUS LINE, A

D: Richard Attenborough 117 m

PG-13 | MUS DMA | 1985 | COLOR

6 Broadway's longest running hit, winner of 9 Tony Awards and the Pulitzer Prize, is transferred to the silver screen with only mediocre success. The story concerns a succession of dancing hopefuls who audition in front of a tough director, played by Michael Douglas. In between big production numbers, they have intimate discussions between themselves, in which they bare their souls and relate their innermost dreams and secrets. This is still acceptable entertainment, but does not contain the same vitality, pacing and energy of, nor live up to the promise of, the stage play.

Sex / Nud / Viol / Lang / AdSit

A: Michael Douglas, Terrence Mann, Alyson Reed, Cameron English, Vicki Frederick, Audrey Landers

© NEW LINE HOME VIDEO 2183

CHOSEN, THE

D: Jeremy Paul Kagan 107 m

PG | DMA | 1982 | COLOR

8 A provocative and very moving story about two very different views of the world, plus the conflict that develops between the two people and the friendship that bridges it. Two Jewish-American boys in 1940s Brooklyn become fast friends, but that friendship also provokes a deep inner struggle. Miller is a the son of a devout Jew who is a liberal scholar (Schell). He has been raised to question everything. Benson is the son of a very strict Hasidic rabbi (Steiger), who has been taught to forsake the 20th century entirely and not to question either his faith or his heritage. Very good drama. The religion aspect is only incidental to the larger cultural one.

Sex / Nud / Viol / Lang / AdSit

A: Maximilian Schell, Rod Steiger, Robby Benson, Barry Miller, Hildy Brooks, Ron Rifkin

© FOXVIDEO 1297

CHRISTMAS WIFE, THE

D: David Jones 73 m

NR | ROM DMA | 1988 | COLOR

9 A lonely widower (Jason Robards), alone for the first time at Christmas, submits an ad to the newspaper in which he seeks to find someone to share the holiday season with. Iris (Julie Harris) answers the ad. Iris is shy and reserved, and asks only that he ask no questions, and he "hires" her to spend Christmas with him at his mountain cabin. Two of America's greatest actors give beautiful poignancy to this story of love in life's later years. Solid character study and a delight to watch.

Sex / Nud / Viol / Lang / AdSit

A: Jason Robards, Jr., Julie Harris, Don Francks, James Eckhouse, Patricia Hamilton, Deborah Glover

© HBO VIDEO 0323

CHRISTOPHER COLUMBUS - THE DISCOVERY

D: John Glen 121 m

PG-13 | DMA | 1992 | COLOR

6 Made for the occasion of the 500th anniversary of the discovery of the New World, this film and another: 1492: CONQUEST OF PARADISE met with very little box office attention. This was partly due to the condensed nature of its historical subject, and partly due to its attempt to make a historical figure of questionable heroics palatable and interesting. In a broad historical sense the film is accurate, however many of the details are questionable. Still, it does do a reasonably good job of capturing much of the character, feel and attitudes of the times. Quite luxuriant sets and costuming.

Sex / Nud / Viol / Lang / AdSit

A: George Corraface, Marlon Brando, Tom Selleck, Rachel Ward, Robert Davi, Benicio del Toro

© WARNER HOME VIDEO 12592

CIAO PROFESSORE!

D: Lina Wertmuller 91 m

R | FOR COM DMA | 1994 | COLOR

7 A dedicated and gentle teacher from the north of Italy is mistakenly assigned to teach a motley group of third graders at a seedy and poor town near Naples. It is a town almost without hope, as are its people. So, he is not prepared when he finds that his kids are charming. But, they are also irreverent, rebellious and extremely crude. They survive by being hard, but they want more and so they slowly begin to respond to his much softer ways. They learn from him, but he also learns from them. Consistently charming and quite funny in places, but you will have to be very tolerant of a never-ending string of vulgarities coming from the mouths of 10-year-olds. Subtitles.

Sex / Nud / Viol / Lang / AdSit

A: Paolo Villaggia, Tsai Danieli, Gigio Morra, Sergio Lolli, Ester Carloni, Mario Bianco

© BUENA VISTA HOME VIDEO 3036

CINCINNATI KID, THE

D: Norman Jewison 104 m

NR | DMA | 1965 | COLOR

8 Steve McQueen plays the "Cincinnati Kid," a roving young cardshark looking for the big time. Despite a couple of side trips for romance with Tuesday Weld and Ann-Margret, the true and sole object of this boy's attention is cards and his search for the big game. The big game is with "The Man" (Robinson) in New Orleans. That game will be a non-stop, winner-take-all five card stud poker battle. Their card game is the film's finale and the definite highlight of the movie. Blondell is wonderful as the dealer, "Ladyfingers."

Sex / Nud / Viol / Lang / AdSit

A: Steve McQueen, Ann-Margret, Edward G. Robinson, Karl Malden, Tuesday Weld, Joan Blondell

Distributed By MGM/UA Home Video 600135

CINDERELLA LIBERTY

D: Mark Rydell 117 m

R | ROM DMA | 1973 | COLOR

9 Not your typical kind of romance. This is a heartwarming story of a troubled Seattle hooker, her bastard half-black son and the sailor who learns to love them both. James Caan plays a good-hearted sailor-on-pass who falls for a very likable hooker (Mason), who is in deep trouble. She is determined never to fall in love again and he is determined to change her mind. Great performances by both of them - Mason won an Oscar nomination for her performance. It is a wonderfully warm, non-schmaltzy story where the characters win you over easily, and a strong dose of realism makes it all believable.

Sex / Nud / Viol / Lang / AdSit

A: James Caan, Marsha Mason, Eli Wallach, Burt Young, Dabney Coleman, Kirk Calloway

© FOXVIDEO 1738

CINEMA PARADISO

D: Giuseppe Tornatore 121 m

PG | FOR DMA | 1989 | COLOR

8 Bittersweet winner of the Oscar for Best Foreign Film. Salvatore is a young boy whose sole diversion in his small rural Italian town shortly after WWII is the magical world of movies. The crusty projectionist there becomes his friend and mentor, and the classic American, French and Italian movies he watches become his window to the world outside. They teach him how to court his first love and eventually how to escape his small town by making movies of his own. Then one day, thirty years later, he is called back for a beautiful secret. Captivating. Subtitles or dubbed.

Sex / Nud / Viol / Lang / AdSit

A: Philippe Noiret, Jaques Perrin, Salvatore Cascio, Agnese Nano

© HBO VIDEO 0376

CITIZEN COHN

D: Frank Pierson 112 m

R | DMA | 1992 | COLOR

9 Roy Cohn was the powerful legal mind behind one of the most infamous characters of the 1950s, Senator Joseph McCarthy. Cohn was a Jewish homosexual who was both an antiSemite and a homophobic. James Woods does an incredible job of portraying him, both as he lay in a hospital bed hallucinating and dying of AIDS in 1988, and as the story is revealed in a series of flashbacks. His is a powerful story of powerful people guiding the steamroller of the House Committee on Un-American Activities which left thousands of people and careers ruined in its wake. A fascinating story that was originally made for cable.

Sex / Nud / Viol / Lang / AdSit

A: James Woods, Joe Don Baker, Joseph Bologna, Ed Flanders, Frederic Forrest, Lee Grant

© HBO VIDEO 90826

CITY OF HOPE

D: John Sayles — 129 m

R — DMA — 1991 — COLOR

8 Wide-sweeping, excellently crafted and satisfying - a rich tapestry of everyday gritty real life in the inner-city. These are real people - not good, not bad - just people trying to survive. For them, corruption is everywhere - yet honest people continue to try. Five different stories are told, and all are successfully brought together in the end. Perhaps because of its bleekness (more probably because it did not get any major publicity), the word on this film did not get out. That's a real shame. It deserved better. This is a real sleeper.

Sex, Nud, Viol, Lang, AdSit

A: Tony Lo Bianco, Vincent Spano, Joe Morton, John Sayles, Angela Bassett, David Strathairn

© SVS/TRIUMPH 92053

CITY OF JOY

D: Roland Joffe — 135 m

PG-13 — DMA — 1992 — COLOR

6 An American doctor, Max Lowe (Patrick Swayze), loses direction for his life after a young patient dies on the operating table. That is, until he stumbles into a dedicated British nurse (Collins), working in the oppressing slums of Calcutta, running a free clinic. His sense of purpose is rekindled there. However, her clinic and the rickshaw pullers of her neighborhood are threatened by a brutal Mafia-like crime lord. Max rallies the locals against their own fears, giving them all a renewed sense of pride, and teaches them the strength that they gain from banding together.

Sex, Nud, Viol, Lang, AdSit

A: Patrick Swayze, Pauline Collins, Om Puri

© COLUMBIA TRISTAR HOME VIDEO 70683

CITY SLICKERS

D: Ron Underwood — 114 m

PG-13 — COM DMA — 1991 — COLOR

9 Hilarious! One heck of a good time! A real treasure. New Yorker Crystal and his friends (Stern and Kirby) are each trying to delay mid-life crises and Billy needs to find his smile again too. So, they decide that the best therapy would be to travel to the Wild West to herd cattle with a bunch of other dudes. However, they are in for a tough, soul-finding ride when the tough trail boss (Palance) dies and the real cow hands desert them, leaving the three city boys responsible for their own safety and for delivering the herd at the other end. Very believable and it will leave you smiling from ear to ear.

Sex, Nud, Viol, Lang, AdSit

A: Billy Crystal, Daniel Stern, Bruno Kirby, Patricia Wettig, Helen Slater, Jack Palance

© NEW LINE HOME VIDEO 75263

CIVIL WAR, THE

D: Burns Ken — 680 m

NR — DMA — 1990 — COLOR

10 Director Ken Burns captivated the American public with his nine part PBS TV-series, which made the magnitude and horror of the American Civil War become real. Never before has it been made so plain to so many what a truly cataclysmic event the War was, not only for Americans but for the whole world. It was the crowning event of all civilization from the advent of recorded history. It was a monumental conflict that defined warfare for the two World Wars to come, but it also decided the value of life and the practicality of a nation of laws for all the people. With this as a backdrop, Lincoln's two-minute Gettysburg Address garners real and profound meaning. Magnificent.

Sex, Nud, Viol, Lang, AdSit

A:

© TURNER HOME ENTERTAINMENT 1861

CLARA'S HEART

D: Robert Mulligan — 108 m

PG-13 — DMA COM — 1988 — COLOR

7 Whoopi Goldberg puts in an excellent performance as a Jamaican housekeeper in a torn household. Their parents have just lost a baby and are on the brink of divorce. Their wise-guy son is caught up in his parent's anguish but feels neglected. He resents Goldberg's presence and takes great pleasure in giving her grief. But when the parents separate, it is she who gives him the love he craves and sets his life straight again. A winning, sentimental melodrama that is a showcase for Goldberg.

Sex, Nud, Viol, Lang, AdSit

A: Whoopi Goldberg, Michael Ontkean, Kathleen Quinlan, Neil Patrick Harris, Spalding Gray, Beverly Todd

© WARNER HOME VIDEO 11823

CLASH OF THE TITANS

D: Desmond Davis — 118 m

PG — DMA FAN CLD — 1981 — COLOR

8 Ancient Greek mythology is given life by some pretty good special effects and a big-name cast. The hero Perseus (Hamlin), son of Zeus (Olivier), must battle magic, monsters and the gods to save beautiful Andromeda (Bowker) from danger and to win her hand. Special effects are the real stars, however, particularly the flying horse Pegasus and Medusa, the woman with hair of snakes who can turn you to stone if you look at her.

Sex, Nud, Viol, Lang, AdSit

A: Laurence Olivier, Harry Hamlin, Judi Bowker, Burgess Meredith, Maggie Smith

Distributed By MGM/UA Home Video M700074

CLASS

D: Lewis John Carlino — 98 m

R — DMA COM — 1983 — COLOR

6 This is supposedly a comedy about a naive prep-school student (McCarthy) who falls into a wild weekend affair with a beautiful older woman (Bisset) in Chicago, only later to learn that she is also the alcoholic mother of his roommate (Lowe). As a comedy, it's only mildly entertaining and nothing special. But Bisset's troubled character gives this so-so comedy a serious overtone. The result is that some pretty good scenes get lost here amidst a lot of junk.

Sex, Nud, Viol, Lang, AdSit

A: Rob Lowe, Jacqueline Bisset, Andrew McCarthy, Stuart Margolin, Cliff Robertson, John Cusack

© LIVE HOME VIDEO VA5026

CLASS ACTION

D: Michael Apted — 110 m

R — DMA — 1990 — COLOR

8 This excellent drama is really a story within a story. A noted lawyer, (Hackman), who became famous for fighting for liberal causes, takes a case against an auto manufacturer which made cars that blow up on impact. However, his bright lawyer/daughter (Mastrantonio) agrees to represent the other side. Not only do they fight battles in court, but their already stormy personal relationship takes a further beating as Mastrantonio endeavors to prove to her Dad that she is a good lawyer, and to pay him back for ignoring her as a child. Intelligent, suspenseful, engrossing and effective.

Sex, Nud, Viol, Lang, AdSit

A: Gene Hackman, Mary Elizabeth Mastrantonio, Colin Friels, Joanna Merlin, Larry Fishburne, Donald Moffat

© FOXVIDEO 1869

D M A

CLEAN AND SOBER

D: Glenn Gordon Caron — 124 m

R — DMA — 1988 — COLOR

8 Michael Keaton gives a brilliant performance as a hot shot real estate executive who decides to hide out in a 21-day drug and alcohol detox program after he gets himself into trouble. The police want to talk to him about $92,000 he has embezzled, and he discovers that the woman he picked up in a bar the night before is dead in his bed from a cocaine overdose. In spite of all this, he doesn't realize that his biggest problem is himself. However, that is about to change. Convincing and thought-provoking.

Sex, Nud, Viol, Lang, AdSit

A: Michael Keaton, Kathy Baker, Morgan Freeman, M. Emmet Walsh

© WARNER HOME VIDEO 11824

CLEOPATRA

D: Joseph L. Mankiewicz — 246 m

NR — DMA ROM — 1963 — COLOR

7 This film created a big commotion in 1963. It had spectacular pageantry, a hugely expensive production cost and was very highly publicized (in part because of an on-going love affair between its two stars, Burton and Taylor). Its story, of the lusty ambitious Egyptian queen (Taylor) who used her charms in hopes of conquering the world through marrying Julius Caesar Emperor of Rome (Harrison), and then also having an ill-fated romance with his general Mark Antony (Burton) after Caesar's death, is ripe with pagentry and spectacle. It won four Oscars and was nominated for more. Rex Harrison was brilliant.

Sex, Nud, Viol, Lang, AdSit

A: Elizabeth Taylor, Richard Burton, Rex Harrison, Roddy McDowall, Pamela Brown, Martin Landau

© FOXVIDEO 1143

CLOCKWORK ORANGE

D: Stanley Kubrick — 137 m

R — SF DMA — 1971 — COLOR

8 Surrealistic look at an ultra-violent future. Alex is human on the outside and machine-like and cold on the inside. Alex (McDowell) is a thrill-criminal. He and his gang spend their nights practicing "ultra-violence"; that is, raping, beating and terrorizing. He's captured by the authorities and is psychologically reconditioned to become physically nauseous when he witnesses violence. However, when he is again turned loose into his old world, he is like a cat with no claws and soon reverts to his former ways. Moral: You can't cure a thrill criminal. Weird but intriguing.

Sex, Nud, Viol, Lang, AdSit

A: Malcolm McDowell, Patrick Magee, Adrienne Corri, Aubrey Morris, James Marcus

© WARNER HOME VIDEO 1031

CLOSE ENCOUNTERS OF THE THIRD KIND

D: Steven Spielberg — 132 m

PG — SF DMA — 1977 — COLOR

9 Excellent science fiction. After a mysterious encounter with an alien craft, Richard Dreyfuss becomes consumed with trying to understand a mysterious and recurring dream. Before long, he discovers that he is not alone - there are many tormented others like him who are all converging on an isolated mesa in the West, which has become very heavily populated by scientists and cordoned off by the military. Soon the reason becomes known, the mesa is being visited by wondrous spacecrafts which contain child-like beings, wonderful visitors from another world seeking their first contact with earthlings.

Sex, Nud, Viol, Lang, AdSit

A: Richard Dreyfuss, Francois Truffaut, Teri Garr, Melinda Dillon

© COLUMBIA TRISTAR HOME VIDEO 60162

CLOSELY WATCHED TRAINS

D: Jiri Menzel m

NR | FOR COM DMA | 1966 | B&W

7 Touching Chech film about a young man who is trying to learn how to grow up in a Czechoslovakia that is under Nazi occupation. He is just a naive train dispatcher/trainee and inexperienced in virtually everything. Although he attempts to lose his virginity, he fails badly. So, his psychiatrist urges him to find an experienced woman to teach him. But his desperate search for love instead gets him involved in a plot to blow up a Nazi train. Sometimes funny and sometimes poignant. Subtitles.

Sex / Nud / Viol / Lang / AdSit

A: Vaclav Neckar, Jitka Bendova

© COLUMBIA TRISTAR HOME VIDEO VH91058

COAL MINER'S DAUGHTER

D: Michael Apted 124 m

PG | DMA MUS | 1980 | COLOR

9 This is the true-life rags-to-riches story of the "First Lady of County Music," Loretta Lynn - but it is more than that. It's a fascinating character study, independent of its central character's connection to country music. Sissy Spacek won a well-deserved Oscar for her portrayal of Lynn's rise from being an impoverished Appalachian child-bride (a mother of four at eighteen) to becoming an American icon, and all the unexpected problems that followed her rise to fame.

Sex / Nud / Viol / Lang / AdSit

A: Sissy Spacek, Tommy Lee Jones, Beverly D'Angelo, Levon Helm, Phyllis Boyens, Ernest Tubb

© MCA/UNIVERSAL HOME VIDEO, INC. 66015

D
M
A

COBB

D: Ron Shelton 129 m

R | DMA | 1994 | COLOR

8 Famed baseball hero Ty Cobb had a phenomenal lifetime batting average of .367. He batted over .300 in 23 seasons and over .400 in five. He also spiked twelve men into the hospital in just one year. Baseball for Ty Cobb wasn't a game, it was war - so was his entire life. While baseball was the focus of Cobb's life, the focus of this film is Cobb. It is the story of his life as revealed to Al Stump, a sports writer he hand-picked at the age of 70, on the verge of his death. Despite his impending death, Cobb had not moderated his lifestyle in any regard. He still made a point to antagonize anyone in his presence, including Stump who despised him and yet pitied the man who had fame and fortune, but not one friend.

Sex / Nud / Viol / Lang / AdSit

A: Tommy Lee Jones, Robert Wuhl, Lolita Davidovich, Lou Meyers, Bradley Witford, Stephen Mendillo

© WARNER HOME VIDEO 13365

COCOON

D: Ron Howard 117 m

PG-13 | SF COM DMA | 1985 | COLOR

9 Great stuff. Solid, good-time entertainment. A group of retired people in Florida discover a magical fountain of youth, secreted away in a seemingly abandoned swimming pool. After a few stolen swims in the pond, the old folks find that their dwindling energies have been mysteriously revitalized. The pool turns out to be a repository for friendly alien beings from another world and the old-timers are soon facing an unexpected dilemma. The aliens give them a chance to live forever but they must leave earth. Excellent cast (Ameche won an Oscar) and an endearing story line make this a real treat.

Sex / Nud / Viol / Lang / AdSit

A: Don Ameche, Wilford Brimley, Hume Cronyn, Brian Dennehy, Jack Gilford, Steve Guttenberg

© FOXVIDEO 1476

COCOON: THE RETURN

D: Daniel Petrie 116 m

PG | SF COM DMA | 1988 | COLOR

7 Follow-up to the megahit COCOON. The oldsters return to earth five years later to help their alien friends rescue some cocoons which have become endangered by an earthquake. Now accustomed to a life free of pain and suffering, they have to readjust to life as it is on earth. This time around less attention is given to plot and more to character development. While this film has an excellent cast and is generally enjoyable, too, it lacks the energy and warmth of the earlier film.

Sex / Nud / Viol / Lang / AdSit

A: Don Ameche, Wilford Brimley, Courtney Cox, Hume Cronyn, Brian Dennehy, Jack Gilford

© FOXVIDEO 1710

COLD SASSY TREE

D: Joan Tewkesbury 97 m

NR | DMA ROM | 1989 | COLOR

7 A superb made-for-TV drama that is told through the eyes of a 15-year-old boy. Grandpa Rucker Blakeslee (Widmark) is the supporting pillar of the small Southern town of Cold Sassy. Widmark is the prosperous owner of most of the town's major businesses and is also at the firm head of his family. But he shocks both the town and his family when he returns from a buying trip up North with a new, much younger and very independent bride (Dunaway), who has a dark secret in her past. Their's is a special relationship that each has entered into for separate reasons, but it sets the town buzzing.

Sex / Nud / Viol / Lang / AdSit

A: Faye Dunaway, Richard Widmark, Neil Patrick Harris, Frances Fisher, Lee Garlington, John Jackson

© TURNER HOME ENTERTAINMENT 6057

COLLECTOR, THE

D: William Wyler 116 m

NR | SUS DMA | 1965 | COLOR

8 Chilling, claustrophobic and fascinating character study by a master director. A pathetic young neurotic clerk has no friends and so, instead, he has become a collector. He collects things... all kinds of things. He is desperately lonely, so he kidnaps a beautiful art student and then holds her as his captive, trying to force her to love him. This is a very powerful suspense vehicle and a disturbing probe into the mind of a pathetic desperate man driven to extreme behavior.

Sex / Nud / Viol / Lang / AdSit

A: Terence Stamp, Samantha Eggar, Maurice Dallimore, Mona Washbourne

© COLUMBIA TRISTAR HOME VIDEO 60163

COLONEL CHABERT

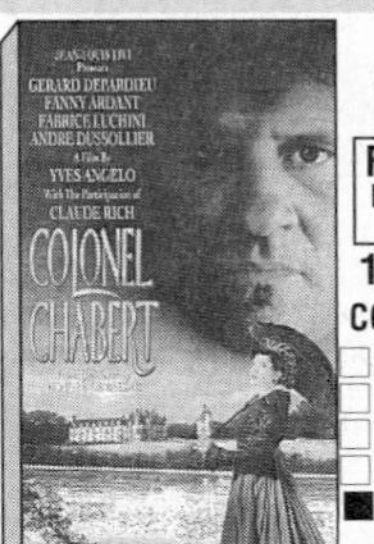

D: Jean-Louis Livi 111 m

NR | FOR DMA | 1995 | COLOR

8 Quite intriguing and lush French drama based upon the novel by Honore De Balzac. It is 1817, ten years after Colonel Chabert was reported killed in Russia. However, he was not dead. He was discovered alive and nursed back to health, but it has taken ten years to regain his strength and his memory. He has returned now to Paris to reclaim his name, his fortune and his wife. But, his beautiful wife has remarried and now refuses to acknowledge him. To do so would cost her her wealth, her husband and her position in society. Chabert has lived through death and no longer treasures life, but he will not be denied or betrayed - so he hires a brilliant attorney to fight for him. Subtitles.

Sex / Nud / Viol / Lang / AdSit

A: Gerard Depardieu, Fanny Ardant, Fabrice Luchinin, Andre Dussollier, Daniel Prevost, Romane Bohringer

© REPUBLIC PICTURES HOME VIDEO 6136

COLOR OF MONEY, THE

D: Martin Scorsese 119 m

R | DMA | 1986 | COLOR

9 Excellent. This is the 1986 sequel to the 1961 hit THE HUSTLER, which also starred Paul Newman. Newman has given up hustling to become a wealthy whiskey distributor. His passion for the hunt is rekindled when he spies a promising but cocky small-time hustler (Tom Cruise). Newman takes him under his wing to teach him that hustling is not just being able to shoot pool well. Cruise graduates from the small-time into the big leagues and Newman becomes determined to once again be good at the game he loves, leading to a shoot-off at the national championship. Great fun. Newman won an Oscar.

Sex / Nud / Viol / Lang / AdSit

A: Paul Newman, Tom Cruise, Mary Elizabeth Mastrantonio, Helen Shaver, John Turturro, Forest Whitaker

© TOUCHSTONE HOME VIDEO 513

COLOR PURPLE, THE

D: Steven Spielberg 154 m

PG-13 | DMA | 1985 | COLOR

9 This is simply masterful movie making by Steven Spielburg and it garnered eleven Oscar nominations. It is a story of the survival of the spirit, even in the face of overwhelming obstacles. It is the heart-rending, beautifully photographed story of one woman's struggle to survive severe loneliness in an absence of all love and in the presence of both physical and emotional abuse. After years of cruelty, it is the love, friendship, guidance and encouragement of another woman that gives her the courage to free herself and to realize her dreams. An uncommon and deeply moving experience.

Sex / Nud / Viol / Lang / AdSit

A: Whoopi Goldberg, Danny Glover, Adolph Caesar, Margaret Avery, Oprah Winfrey, Rae Dawn Chong

© WARNER HOME VIDEO 11534

COMES A HORSEMAN

D: Alan J. Pakula 118 m

PG | WST DMA | 1978 | COLOR

8 Modern-day Western, set in the 1940s just after the end of the War. Jane Fonda plays a spinster rancher who is being set upon by her powerful neighbor (Jason Robards). He is intent upon creating a vast empire in the style of the land barons of the old West. Helping her in her fight are her aging hired hand (Farnsworth) and a World War II veteran (Caan), who is trying to forget what he has seen. A simple story, this is nonetheless an engrossing film, beautifully photographed with majestic scenery, but it is a little slow-moving at times.

Sex / Nud / Viol / Lang / AdSit

A: Jane Fonda, James Caan, Jason Robards, Jr., George Grizzard, Richard Farnsworth, Mark Harmon

© FOXVIDEO 4552

COMIC, THE

D: Carl Reiner 96 m

PG | DMA | 1969 | COLOR

7 Dick Van Dyke plays a silent film star (who is a composite of several real-life people - Chaplin, Keaton, Langdon, Arbuckle and Lloyd). His on-screen character is much beloved by the public, but off-screen he is a self-destructive autocrat. His egotism and philandering, combined with alcoholism, drive those around him away. Then when talking movies come in and his old style of physical comedy becomes less popular, his career is gone. This is a powerful piece that is alternately both funny and sad - particularly the ending.

Sex / Nud / Viol / Lang / AdSit

A: Dick Van Dyke, Mickey Rooney, Michele Lee, Cornel Wilde, Nina Wayne, Pert Kelton

© COLUMBIA TRISTAR HOME VIDEO 60589

COMING HOME

D: Hal Ashby 130 m

R | DMA ROM WAR | 1978 | COLOR

9 Extremely powerful early attempt to explore the effects of the Vietnam war. A gung-ho career Marine officer's (Dern) naive wife (Fonda) finds real love with a bitter paraplegic (Voight) while volunteering at the hospital when her husband is away at war. Dern comes back from Vietnam very mixed up himself. He is having great difficulty adjusting to all the changes in himself and his wife because she is now independent, and deeply involved with Voight. Politics of Vietnam are downplayed, this is a very human drama. Oscars for Fonda, Voight and script. Best Picture nominee, too.

Sex Nud Viol Lang AdSit

A: Jane Fonda, Jon Voight, Bruce Dern, Robert Carradine, Robert Ginty, Penelope Milford

Distributed By MGM/UA Home Video M301428

CONFORMIST, THE

D: Bernardo Bertolucci 108 m

R | FOR DMA | 1970 | COLOR

8 A French character study and a portrait of the decadence of fascism prevalent during Mussolini's reign in Italy. In 1938, a weak-willed man wants to advance his career in radio so he joins the Italian fascist party. However, in a test of his fascist loyalties, he is ordered to go to Paris to kill his college professor who is now in exile. Instead, he becomes infatuated with the professor's lesbian wife, who unfortunately is more interested in his wife than in him. He then also has to repress his own childhood homosexual experiences with his chauffeur and he slowly begins to self-destruct. Powerful. Dubbed.

Sex Nud Viol Lang AdSit

A: Stefania Sandrelli, Dominique Sanda

© PARAMOUNT HOME VIDEO 8121

CONRACK

D: Martin Ritt 111 m

PG | DMA | 1974 | COLOR

8 Simple but involving true story of Pat Conroy, a white teacher who goes to a small, isolated island off the South Carolina coast to teach its culturally deprived black kids. It is a moving story about a dedicated teacher who will go to almost any lengths to reach his kids, even if it means some very unconventional teaching methods or placing himself in direct conflict with the school superintendent. A very affecting and effective movie, with a satisfying upbeat story to tell. Outstanding job by Jon Voight.

Sex Nud Viol Lang AdSit

A: Jon Voight, Hume Cronyn, Paul Winfield, Madge Sinclair, Tina Andrews, Antonio Fargas

© FOXVIDEO 1469

CONSPIRACY: THE TRIAL OF THE CHICAGO 8

D: Jeremy Paul Kagan 118 m

NR | DMA | 1987 | COLOR

8 This excellent courtroom drama was originality made for cable TV. It is the recreation of one of the pivotal events of the 1960s - the 1969 trial of eight anti-war activists who were charged with conspiracy to riot, from the 1968 riots at the Democratic National Convention. The dialogue for the movie was created from actual court transcripts, actual news footage and actual interviews with the principals as they were at the time of the filming.

Sex Nud Viol Lang AdSit

A: Peter Boyle, Robert Carradine, Elliott Gould, Robert Loggia, Michael Lembeck, David Opatoshu

© HBO VIDEO 0026

CONTEMPT

D: Jean-Luc Godard 102 m

NR | FOR COM DMA | 1964 | COLOR

7 A satirical insider's look at European movie making. The plot revolves around an Italian filming of the classic Greek "The Odyssey." Piccoli is the script writer who would rather write for the stage. He reluctantly takes the movie job to appease what he feels are his wife's ambitions and greed. However, she is now disappointed in him for his lack of conviction. Sexy, sultry Bardot is his wife and she now begins what appears to him to be an affair with the vulgar producer (Palance) just to spite her husband. Everyone apparently is in contempt of everyone else. Film fans and film students are best audience.

Sex Nud Viol Lang AdSit

A: Brigitte Bardot, Jack Palance, Fritz Lang, Michel Piccoli, Georgia Moll

© NEW LINE HOME VIDEO 2094

CONVERSATION, THE

D: Francis Ford Coppola 113 m

PG | DMA SUS | 1974 | COLOR

9 Best Picture nominee. Hackman is a top surveillance expert, for sale to the highest bidder, but he has become a loner, isolated and extremely weary. He is hired by a mysterious, powerful man to follow a woman and to record her conversations. When he records her with another man, he learns that she is the mystery man's wife, having an affair. She is in great danger. Hackman's work has hurt people in the past, so he becomes obsessed now with protecting her. However, as the movie evolves, it becomes more a fascinating character study. It is the story of moral man who is deteriorating at an immoral job. Excellent.

Sex Nud Viol Lang AdSit

A: Gene Hackman, John Cazale, Allen Garfield, Harrison Ford, Cindy Williams, Teri Garr

© PARAMOUNT HOME VIDEO 2307

CONVICTION, THE

D: Marco Bellocchio 92 m

NR | FOR DMA ROM | 1994 | COLOR

8 An unusual and strangely compelling Italian film that proposes insight into, the mystery of female sexuality: Why are many, if not most women, powerfully drawn to "dangerous" men? A woman is inadvertently locked into a museum for the night, only to discover that she is not alone. With her is a man, who totally captivates her and compellingly engages her in a wild night of mutually consuming passion. In the morning, she discovers that he had had the keys all the time, and files charges against him for rape. In court, he does not deny her claims that he overpowered her with his will, but insists that it was seduction not rape. Very unusual and very adult.

Sex Nud Viol Lang AdSit

A: Pietro Valsecchi, Nella Banfi, Vittorio Mezzogiorno, Andrzej Seweryn, Claire Nebout, Grazny Szapolowska

© ORION PICTURES CORPORATION FLV1151

COOL HAND LUKE

D: Stuart Rosenberg 126 m

PG | DMA ACT | 1967 | COLOR

9 Hugely popular, very entertaining and a fascinating story of a fiercely independent loner (Newman) who wakes up in a Southern jail after a drunken night cutting the heads off parking meters. Newman refuses to give in to authority or the demands of his chain gang guards. He remains defiantly independent which gains him the admiration of his fellow prisoners, particularly their tough leader George Kennedy (who won an Oscar). He becomes their hero. Sometimes funny, sometimes poignant. Strother Martin went down in film history with his famed proclamation, "What we have here is a failure to communicate."

Sex Nud Viol Lang AdSit

A: Paul Newman, George Kennedy, Jo Van Fleet, J.D. Cannon, Strother Martin, Anthony Zerbe

© WARNER HOME VIDEO 11037

CORRINA, CORRINA

D: Jessie Nelson 115 m

PG | DMA COM | 1994 | COLOR

7 Sweet little 7-year-old Molly has just lost her mother and refuses to talk. Her father Manny (Ray Liotta) is heart-broken too, but he has to go on. After a couple of mistreats, he hires Corrina (Whoopi Goldberg) as his housekeeper. She is an highly-educated black woman who can't get other work using it, because this is the 1950s. Little Molly has never run into anyone quite like Whoopi. Her sense of fun breaks down the wall that sad little Molly has built up. But this creates another set of problems, because Molly starts to think of Corrina as her mother. What's more, Manny and Corrina become good friends and now their families are concerned. Not quite believable but fun anyway.

Sex Nud Viol Lang AdSit

A: Whoopie Goldberg, Ray Liotta, Tina Majorino, Wendy Crewson, Larry Miller, Don Ameche

© TURNER HOME ENTERTAINMENT N4013

COTTON CLUB, THE

D: Francis Ford Coppola 128 m

R | DMA ACT MUS | 1984 | COLOR

8 Very large budget movie that was fraught with scandal and controversy during production. It went way over budget and lacked a focus, so director Coppola was called in to "fix" it. Even so, the plot still tends to drift. However, this is also an opulent and evocative film depicting the excitement of the Jazz Age. Set against a background of great music and gangster violence, it is the story of a trumpeter (Gere) who falls in love with the mistress (Lane) of mobster Dutch Schultz; and, a dancer (Hines) who's in love with a black chorus girl, who is trying to pass for white. Even though flawed, this is still quite interesting, entertaining and worth spending time on.

Sex Nud Viol Lang AdSit

A: Richard Gere, Gregory Hines, Diane Lane, Lonette McKee, Bob Hoskins, Nicolas Cage

© NEW LINE HOME VIDEO 1714

COUNTERFEIT TRAITOR, THE

D: George Seaton 140 m

NR | SUS DMA ROM | 1962 | COLOR

8 Tense WWII thriller, based upon a real-life character. Eric Ericson (Holden) has been raised in America but is technically a Swedish citizen. He is also an international businessman and so he travels freely between Allied Europe and Nazi Germany. Because he wants to remain neutral, British agents set him up and then blackmail him into becoming a spy. He is to be a double agent. The Germans are to think that he is one of theirs, but he is one of ours. He becomes a very effective agent for the Allies, working with the German underground, where he meets and falls in love (Lilli Palmer), but their love is doomed.

Sex Nud Viol Lang AdSit

A: William Holden, Lilli Palmer, Hugh Griffith, Erica Beer, Werner Peters

© PARAMOUNT HOME VIDEO 6113

COUNTRY

D: Richard Pearce 109 m

PG | DMA | 1984 | COLOR

7 Sympathetic story of a rural Iowa family's struggle to save their farm when the faceless government wants to foreclose on their loan. This is a believable look at the trauma and the drama that occurs within this torn farm family when farmer Shepard falls apart and escapes the relentless pressure by resorting to the bottle. His wife (Lange) is forced to become strong enough to hold her family together and to fight off the government. Excellent performances. Lange received an Oscar nomination.

Sex Nud Viol Lang AdSit

A: Jessica Lange, Sam Shepard, Matt Clark, Wilford Brimley

© TOUCHSTONE HOME VIDEO 241

D M A

COUPE DE VILLE

D: Joe Roth 98 m

PG-13 COM DMA 1990 COLOR

6 Interesting coming-of-age flick that rises above this oft-covered subject by having both a good cast and a slightly different twist on the subject. It is set in 1963, a time in American history before Vietnam, the civil rights movement and free love. Three feuding brothers are charged by their father with driving a powder blue 1954 Cadillac Coupe de Ville from Detroit to Miami for delivery to their mother for her 50th birthday. The fun comes from the conflict between three separate sibling personalities that somehow come to terms with each other by trip's end.

Sex Nud Viol Lang AdSit

A: Alan Arkin, Daniel Stern, Patrick Dempsey, Annabeth Gish, Rita Taggart, Joseph Bologna

© MCA/UNIVERSAL HOME VIDEO, INC. 80932

CRAZY FROM THE HEART

D: Thomas Schlamme 94 m

NR ROM DMA 1991 COLOR

8 Delightful and charming. Lahti is the principal at Tidewater Texas High School. She and the football coach have had an "understanding." For the past eight years he has gone to her house on Thursday nights, had dinner and watched her TV. However, he refuses to marry her. Ruben Blades is a small rancher who takes a janitor's job at her school to make ends meet. He immediately likes Lahti, asks her out and, in an act of rebellion, she goes out with the Mexican janitor. She has a ball. They dance, get very drunk and wind up on a Mexican beach, married. However, reality hits on Monday morning, she is married to a Mexican in a very small Texas town. Fun.

Sex Nud Viol Lang AdSit

A: Christine Lahti, Ruben Blades, William Russ, Mary Kay Place, Louise Latham, Tommy Mendez

© TURNER HOME ENTERTAINMENT 6171

CRIES AND WHISPERS

D: Ingmar Bergman 95 m

R FOR DMA 1972 COLOR

9 This is a very heavy adult drama that won Best Film at New York Film Critics, also four Oscar nominations, including Best Picture. It won Best Cinematography. A woman lies dying of cancer around 1900 and searches for peace. Her two sisters have come to stay with her but all three are haunted by unhappy pasts and are bitter. The peasant servant girl is the only positive force and is closer to the dying woman than are her sisters. Each of the women seek to reconnect through internal evaluations of their past in this barren landscape. Masterful use of light, shadow and sound, plus flawless acting imparts a sense of deep suffering and pain. Intense and slow moving. Subtitled.

Sex Nud Viol Lang AdSit

A: Liv Ullmann, Ingrid Thulin, Harriet Anderson, Kari Sylwan, Erland Josephson, Georg Arlin

© HOME VISION CRI 050

CRIMES AND MISDEMEANORS

D: Woody Allen 104 m

PG-13 DMA COM 1990 COLOR

8 Woody Allen creatively interweaves two separate stories. Landau, a distinguished doctor has an affair, but his mistress threatens to expose it and the fact that he is an embezzler. So, he arranges to have her killed, but then is tormented by what he did. Allen, in a more light-hearted vein, is a documentary film maker who is obsessed with besting his brother-in-law (Alda). These two quite different characters, and what they have in common, come together only at the film's end. Extremely strong cast explores virtually every issue of human importance, including family, friendship, love, murder and morality.

Sex Nud Viol Lang AdSit

A: Martin Landau, Woody Allen, Mia Farrow, Anjelica Huston, Claire Bloom, Alan Alda

© ORION PICTURES CORPORATION 8755

CRIMES OF PASSION

D: Ken Russell 107 m

R CRM DMA 1985 COLOR

6 At night, China Blue (Kathleen Turner) is the sexiest and best of the $50 whores in the red light district, but in the daytime she is a compulsive fashion designer. She loves to play power games with her customers. Laughlin is an unhappy suburban husband who gets involved with her. Turner is being stalked. Perhaps it is by Anthony Perkins. He plays a street corner preacher who is obsessed with her. She haunts his fantasies. Not a particularly distinctive movie, but it is interesting and Turner does put in a powerful and sexy performance.

Sex Nud Viol Lang AdSit

A: Kathleen Turner, Anthony Perkins, John Laughlin, Annie Potts, Bruce Davison

© R&G VIDEO, LP 14005

CRIMES OF THE HEART

D: Bruce Beresford 105 m

PG-13 COM DMA 1986 COLOR

8 Very entertaining and provocative adaptation of a Pulitzer Prize-winning play. Three off-beat sisters reunite in their small Southern hometown on the occasion of their grandfather's failing health. Keaton is distraught because she is turning thirty, Spacek has shot her husband - just because she didn't like the way he looked, and Lange is giving up an unpromising singing career to work in a dog food factory. Now, after a long time apart, they are all back together under the same roof with the opportunity to recall their past and assess their futures. Zany and heartwarming, with biting humor.

Sex Nud Viol Lang AdSit

A: Diane Keaton, Jessica Lange, Sissy Spacek, Sam Shepard, Tess Harper, Hurd Hatfield

© WARNER HOME VIDEO 421

CRISIS AT CENTRAL HIGH

D: Lamont Johnson 120 m

NR DMA 1981 COLOR

9 Compelling made-for-TV documentary-like recreation of the events surrounding the 1957 integration of Central High in Little Rock, Arkansas. The Supreme Court had ordered the all-white school to admit nine black students, creating a crisis situation. White crowds picketed the school, taunted and even beat up blacks. This film is a recreation of the actual events as they were recorded at the time in the journal of assistant principal Elizabeth Huckaby, who played a critical role in achieving a peaceful resolution. Woodward is stunning as Huckaby and received an Emmy nomination for her efforts.

Sex Nud Viol Lang AdSit

A: Joanne Woodward, Charles Durning, Henderson Forsythe, William Russ, Calvin Levels

© LIVE HOME VIDEO LA9509

CRISSCROSS

D: Chris Menges 101 m

R DMA 1992 COLOR

6 An adolescent boy is living with his mother in 1969 at the cheap Key West, Florida hotel where they also work. The boy's father was a Vietnam fighter pilot who has self-destructed and left them after he returned home a broken man. The daily struggle to survive slowly destroys the relationship between mother and son. So, in her earnest attempt to make more money, she becomes a topless dancer. While the boy understands why she did it, inside he is deeply hurt and humiliated. Their relationship is redeemed however, when he is caught selling drugs to make more money for them, forcing them both to recognize what they've lost. A good try, but also unsatisfying.

Sex Nud Viol Lang AdSit

A: Goldie Hawn, Arliss Howard, James Gammon, David Arnott, Keith Carradine, J.C. Quinn

Distributed By MGM/UA Home Video 902496

CROOKLYN

D: Spike Lee 114 m

PG-13 DMA COM 1994 COLOR

7 This is a different sort of movie for Spike Lee. It is the story of a black family trying to survive hard times in Brooklyn during the 1970s. Alfre Woodard is the drill sergeant-like mother who is trying to raise her kids right, while the family struggles to get by on her teacher's salary. Her husband loves his family and is devoted to them, but is a musician trying to get recognised for playing his music, not other peoples. The story centers around the activities of their 10-year-old daughter as she trys to survive her four raucous older brothers. Highly praised by the critics. Funny at times, but more serious than billed. Will have some interest for everyone, but especially blacks.

Sex Nud Viol Lang AdSit

A: Alfre Woodard, Delroy Lindo, David Patrick Kelly, Zelda Harris, Carlton Williams, Sharif Rashed

© MCA/UNIVERSAL HOME VIDEO, INC. 82069

CROSSING THE BRIDGE

D: Mike Binder 104 m

R DMA 1992 COLOR

6 The intelligent and reflective remembrances of a middle-aged writer, concerning the events leading up to the single most fateful night of his life, are the basis for this film. Two years out of high school, he and his two best friends, Tim and Danny, still do everything together just as they always did. They all still live at home, sleep in late after getting drunk the night before and ride around in an old car they call The War Wagon. However, they are forced to face the fact of their aimless lives, when they discover themselves on trip back from Canada with a spare tire full of heroin. Well done, but slow.

Sex Nud Viol Lang AdSit

A: Stephen Baldwin, Josh Charles, Jason Gedrick, Jeffery Tambor

© TOUCHSTONE HOME VIDEO 1584

CROSS OF IRON

D: Sam Peckinpah 132 m

R WAR DMA ACT 1977 COLOR

8 In the style of the famed German film THE BOAT (DAS BOOT), this is a solid American-made WWII adventure that also tells its story entirely from the German viewpoint. It is also a very realistic and action-packed look at war. Schell plays a German officer who is intent upon winning a hero's medal, while Coburn plays a capable war-weary sergeant who is comptemptuous of both the military and of war. Coburn is just trying to keep his troops from being ground up by the advancing Russian army in 1943. Great action scenes, particularly the tank scenes near the end.

Sex Nud Viol Lang AdSit

A: James Coburn, Maximilian Schell, James Mason, David Warner, Senta Berger

© MEDIA HOME ENTERTAINMENT, INC. M765

CRUSH

D: Alison Maclean 97 m

DMA 1993 COLOR

6 Oddly intriguing import from New Zealand. Lane and Christina are two female friends traveling together to interview a writer. On the way there, while Lane was driving, there is a violent accident which leaves Christina paralyzed in a coma in the hospital. The stunned Lane shows up at the door of the writer and begins a friendship with the man's lonely 15-year-old daughter Angela, but soon Lane is also sleeping with the father. Angela feels that her new best friend has deserted her. Jealous and hostile, Angela goes to visit Christina in the hospital, spending hours. As Christina begins to recover, Angela holds up tiny picture of Lane and says, "She is the one who did this to you."

Sex Nud Viol Lang AdSit

A: Marcia Gay Harden, Donough Rees, Caitlin Bossley, William Zappa

© ORION PICTURES CORPORATION FLV1128

CRUSOE

D: Caleb Deschanel 95 m

PG-13 | 8 | ACT DMA | 1989 | COLOR

The classic Defoe tale is updated into the nineteenth century. Crusoe, who is well played here by Aidan Quinn, is a ruthless Virginia slave trader who has become shipwrecked, washed up alone and naked on a desert island. On this island the merciless hunter must deal with basic survival, loneliness and something else, too. On this island there are cannibals. He, the hunter, has become the hunted... by those same people he would have enslaved and sold. In this production, there is no faithful man Friday but an independent and strong black warrior (Sapara).

Sex Nud Viol Lang AdSit

A: Aidan Quinn, Ade Sapara, Warren Clark, Hebburn Graham, Jimmy Nail, Timothy Spall

© MCEG/STERLING 70064

CRY FREEDOM

D: Richard Attenborough 157 m

PG | 9 | DMA | 1987 | COLOR

Sweeping film chronicles the true story of two men, one white and one black, in South Africa. In 1975 newspaperman Donald Woods (Kline) meets a crusading non-violent black leader Steve Biko (Washington) and they become friends. It is only through Biko, that Woods comes to understand the true horror of the system of which he is a part. Later, when Biko is murdered in prison, Woods courageously risks his own life to press the government for an inquest. That determined action causes his own persecution by the same system. He must escape, as he fights to get the real story told to the rest of the world. Excellent.

Sex Nud Viol Lang AdSit

A: Kevin Kline, Denzel Washington, Penelope Wilton, Kevin MacNally, John Thaw, Timothy West

© MCA/UNIVERSAL HOME VIDEO, INC. 80763

CRYING GAME, THE

D: Neil Jordan 112 m

R | 8 | DMA ROM | 1992 | COLOR

Intelligent and very unusual piece of filmmaking that is not for the casual observer. It starts you firmly in one direction and then suddenly jerks you in another, as it takes on two dramatic themes at one time. It begins in the ruthless politics of the Irish Republican Army when a team of volunteers kidnaps a British soldier (Whitaker) as a hostage. Fergus (Rea) is his guard but he allows himself to begin to like his charge and also begins to question his mission. When Whitaker is killed, Fergus goes to London to see the soldier's girlfriend and again is forced question his values when he falls for the girl too, only to discover that she is a he. Quite compelling.

Sex Nud Viol Lang AdSit

A: Stephen Rea, Miranda Richardson, Jaye Davidson, Forest Whitaker

© LIVE HOME VIDEO 69039

CRY IN THE DARK, A

D: Fred Schepisi 122 m

PG-13 | 9 | DMA | 1988 | COLOR

An astonishing and chilling true story about an Australian Seventh-Day Adventist minister (Neill) and his wife (Streep) who claimed that their child was carried off by a wild dog when they were on a camping trip in 1980. Vicious rumors soon surface that the baby was actually sacrificed in a ritual killing. Streep is then charged with murder, even though there is no body, no evidence and no motive. She is tried against a backdrop of media hype and innuendo. Streep's acting is truly amazing. Fascinating, but a little slow in places.

Sex Nud Viol Lang AdSit

A: Meryl Streep, Sam Neill, Bruce Myles, Charles Tingwell, Nick Tate, Neil Fitzpatrick

© WARNER HOME VIDEO 11868

DA

D: Matt Clark 102 m

PG | 8 | DMA | 1988 | COLOR

Martin Sheen plays a New York City playwright who returns to Ireland for his 83-year-old father's funeral. While in the house where he was raised, he is visited by the ghost of his father, conjured up by his own imagination. Possessed of a troubled childhood and a tortured love/hate relationship with his father, Sheen and the ghost of his father discuss their very troubled history. Sometimes sentimental but always uncompromising, it is both touching and affecting. Extremely powerful performances.

Sex Nud Viol Lang AdSit

A: Barnard Hughes, Martin Sheen, William Hickey, Doreen Hepburn, Karl Hayden

© MCEG/STERLING 70090

DAD

D: Gary David Goldberg 117 m

PG | 8 | DMA COM | 1989 | COLOR

Very touching dose of reality. A busy Wall Street yuppie (Ted Danson) must stop his life midstream to move in with his aged parents when his father becomes very ill. His previously distant and superficial relationship with his parents becomes radically altered as he faces the new reality of their mortality. For the first time, he also begins to understand them as adult individuals instead of parents. Lots of highs and lows, maybe too many, but definitely moving. It may also evoke painful feelings in old people and those who are dealing with old age in others. Lemmon is wonderful.

Sex Nud Viol Lang AdSit

A: Jack Lemmon, Ted Danson, Olympia Dukakis, Kathy Baker, Kevin Spacey, Ethan Hawke

© MCA/UNIVERSAL HOME VIDEO, INC. 80933

DAMAGE

D: Louis Malle 112 m

NR | 6 | DMA | 1992 | COLOR

An upper class Englishman (Irons) falls passionately and unreasoningly in love with his son's enigmatic lover (Binoche). She warns him that "damaged people are dangerous" but he cannot stop. She is a tragic figure who's brother committed suicide over his love for her. Ever since, she has tried to resolve her feelings of guilt and confused sexuality. She loves both the son and the father, will give up neither and that leads to more tragedy. Based upon popular book. It was very controversial upon its release for the overt sexuality. High production standards, excellent acting but slow. Some critics liked it, most didn't.

Sex Nud Viol Lang AdSit

A: Jeremy Irons, Miranda Richardson, Juliette Binoche, Leslie Caron, Rupert Graves

© TURNER HOME ENTERTAINMENT N4286

DAMN THE DEFIANT!

D: Lewis Gilbert 101 m

NR | 8 | ACT DMA | 1962 | COLOR

Dramatic tale of an eighteenth-century British warship and its crew which is at war with both the French and with itself. Great attention to historic detail and a fine performances from its cast gives this production a first-rate quality. Guinness is the captain of the British warship H.M.S Defiant, but he is opposed by Bogarde, his cruel first officer, whose iron-fisted rule has the crew ready to mutiny. When Guinness is wounded and Bogarde takes command, the crew does mutiny - just as they are about to enter a major battle. Guinness must win them back.

Sex Nud Viol Lang AdSit

A: Alec Guinness, Dirk Bogarde, Maurice Denham, Anthony Quayle, Peter Gill, Nigel Stock

© COLUMBIA TRISTAR HOME VIDEO 60825

DANCES WITH WOLVES

D: Kevin Costner 180 m

PG-13 | 10 | WST DMA ACT | 1990 | COLOR

Wonderful, beautiful, grand and elegant. First-time director (and also the film's star) Costner scored a major win with this film. It won seven Oscars, including Best Picture and it struck a resilient chord in many viewers. It is the story of a disillusioned Civil War veteran who is stationed to a remote Army outpost in the Dakota territory. Finding it abandoned, he makes friends with a band of Lakota Sioux and is drawn into their extended family, their way of life and finds new meaning for his life. This is an exciting, thoroughly involving and sensitive telling of a time and a way of life long underappreciated. A must see!

Sex Nud Viol Lang AdSit

A: Kevin Costner, Mary McDonnell, Graham Greene, Rodney A. Grant, Floyd Red Crow Westerman, Tantoo Cardinal

© ORION PICTURES CORPORATION 8768

DANCE WITH A STRANGER

D: Mike Newell 101 m

R | 8 | DMA | 1984 | COLOR

Fascinating true story of the last woman to be executed in England. Ruth Ellis was a platinum-blond hostess in a working class pub. She fell in love with, and became pregnant by, a sharp-dressing and handsome ne'er-do-well upper-class snob who drank too much and neglected her. In spite of the emotional and physical abuse he heaped upon her, she refused to leave him. Then when he threatened to leave her, she was overwhelmed by an intense jealousy and she shot him. She was hung for it July 13, 1955. Completely convincing and totally involving.

Sex Nud Viol Lang AdSit

A: Miranda Richardson, Rupert Everett, Ian Holm, Matthew Carroll, Tom Chadbon

© LIVE HOME VIDEO VA5137

DANGEROUS LIAISONS

D: Stephen Frears 120 m

R | 8 | DMA ROM | 1988 | COLOR

Nominated for 7 Oscars, including Best Picture, and won 3. It is a marvelous story of 18th-century gamesmanship among the bored, unscrupulous aristocracy of a decadent France. Ex-lovers Close and Malkovich are engaged in a contest. They manipulate the lives of those around them through calculated sexual liasons. They seek both their pleasures and revenge through games of seduction and betrayal, but are eventually destroyed by their own shallowness. Pfeiffer is the virtuous beauty that destroys them when Malkovich breaks the rules - he falls in love with her. Lush settings.

Sex Nud Viol Lang AdSit

A: Glenn Close, John Malkovich, Michelle Pfeiffer, Mildred Natwick, Swoosie Kurtz, Keanu Reeves

© WARNER HOME VIDEO 11872

DANGEROUS WOMAN, A

D: Stephen Gyllenhaal 93 m

R | 6 | DMA | 1993 | COLOR

Martha (Debra Winger) is slow-witted, has a child-like innocence and she lives with her wealthy aunt (Barbary Hershey) in the guest house on her estate. Her aunt is trapped in a relationship with a married man and although she loves Martha, she treats her like a child. David Straithairn is a drifting alcoholic loner who stays on to do odd jobs. He sees his opposite in simple Martha and, though he knows better, he gives over to his loneliness and allows himself one night of peace with her. All three are only trying to get by the best they can, but it is Martha who sees through all the lies they tell themselves. Well acted and intense, but also sometimes aimless and slow.

Sex Nud Viol Lang AdSit

A: Debra Winger, Barbara Hershey, Gabriel Byrne, David Straithairn, Chloe Webb, John Terry

© MCA/UNIVERSAL HOME VIDEO, INC. 81723

DANTON

D: Andrzej Wajda 136 m

PG | FOR DMA | 1983 | COLOR

8 Intriguing historical drama. In post-revolutionary France anarchy rages. A strong-willed fanatic, Robespierre, is using the revolution to further his own goals. He and his allies have set up a dictatorship which will lead to what will be called the "Reign of Terror." His former friend and ally Danton declares that the revolution has gone too far and seeks an end to the destruction. Robespierre is now threatened, he publicly denounces Danton and Danton is executed. Strong parallels to many of the occurances in late 20th-century Eastern Europe. A brilliant and absorbing film. Subtitles.

Sex, Nud, Viol, Lang, AdSit

A: Gerard Depardieu, Wojciech Pszoniak, Patrice Chereau, Angela Winkler

© COLUMBIA TRISTAR HOME VIDEO VH91053

DARLING

D: John Schlesinger 122 m

NR | DMA | 1965 | B&W

7 Interesting psychological profile of a beautiful girl from a commonplace background who decides to sleep her way to the top. She uses and discards men along the way until she finally marries a wealthy Italian nobleman. But, after "arriving" at the top, she discovers that the life she has sought for so long and hard is depressing, meaningless and lonely. This was a very trendy film in the '60s. It is slick and very cynical. Nominated for 5 Oscars - it won Screenplay and Costume Design. Julie Christie won Best Actress.

Sex, Nud, Viol, Lang, AdSit

A: Julie Christie, Dirk Bogarde, Laurence Harvey, Roland Curram, Jose Luis de Villalonga, Alex Scott

© NEW LINE HOME VIDEO 2011

DAUGHTERS OF THE DUST

D: Julie Dash 113 m

NR | DMA | 1991 | COLOR

7 A beautifully photographed, often quite interesting, sometimes fascinating but unfortunately also quite slow-moving portrait of an isolated group of former slaves, living on the islands off the coasts of South Carolina and Georgia. These are a people who have retained their West African culture into the modern era. The time is 1902 and the story focuses on one family that is leaving the island to find prosperity in the North and the ceremony that marks their departure.

Sex, Nud, Viol, Lang, AdSit

A: Cora Lee Day, Barbara-O, Cheryl Lynn Bruce, Tommy Hicks, Kaycee Moore, Alva Rogers

© KINO INTERNATIONAL VIDEO

DAVID AND LISA

D: Frank Perry 94 m

NR | DMA ROM | 1962 | B&W

8 Highly-watchable, sensitive and rewarding story of two mentally disturbed teenagers who meet while they are institutionalized. David is a 17-year-old who is absolutely terrified of being touched. 15-year-old Lisa is a schizophrenic who vacillates between being a 4-year-old and a voiceless adolescent. Their unlikely friendship and emotional attachment is nurtured by an understanding doctor (DaSilva). Slowly they begin to build faith, which in turn begins to help them overcome their disturbed natures. Based on fact, this low-budget sleeper won 2 Oscar nominations.

Sex, Nud, Viol, Lang, AdSit

A: Keir Dullea, Janet Margolin, Howard da Silva, Neva Patterson, Clifton James

© COLUMBIA TRISTAR HOME VIDEO 60761

DAY FOR NIGHT

D: Francois Truffaut 116 m

PG | FOR DMA COM | 1971 | COLOR

9 French director Francois Truffaut's reverent satire of the moviemaking business. The story reflects the pandemonium, activities, love lives and anxieties of the principal participants (the actors, director, producer and crew) in and during the making of a romance movie called "Meeting Pamela." This satirical film largely debunks the glamour of movie-making and is a favorite among film insiders. It has humor, but is not a true comedy. Oscar for Best Foreign Film. Dubbed. Sophisticated viewers and film fans only.

Sex, Nud, Viol, Lang, AdSit

A: Jacqueline Bisset, Jean-Pierre Leaud, Valentina Cortese, Jean-Pierre Aumont

© WARNER HOME VIDEO 11134

DAY OF THE LOCUST, THE

D: John Schlesinger 140 m

R | DMA | 1975 | COLOR

8 Spellbinding look into the depressing underbelly of 1930s Hollywood decadence. Atherton is a young Yale graduate screenwriter trying to survive in Hollywood, coping with its more unglamorous failings. His encounters with various unsuccessful wannabes become the movie's focus. Karen Black is a sexy, bad actress, making the rounds on the casting couches and living with her alcoholic father (Meredith) - a former vaudevillian, now a door-to-door salesman. When she becomes destitute enough, she moves in with an oafish accountant (Sutherland) who she ridicules. Very grim ending.

Sex, Nud, Viol, Lang, AdSit

A: Donald Sutherland, Karen Black, William Atherton, Burgess Meredith, Geraldine Page, Bo Hopkins

© PARAMOUNT HOME VIDEO 8679

DAYS OF HEAVEN

D: Terrence Malick 95 m

PG | DMA ROM | 1978 | COLOR

9 Hailed as a great cinematic achievement, the stunningly beautiful photography won an Oscar. Gere, his sister and his girlfriend (Adams) leave the poverty of Chicago in turn-of-the-century America. Traveling as a brother and his two sisters, they settle in Kansas on the farm of a wealthy, but dying, young farmer (Sheppard). Sheppard falls in love with Adams, unaware of her real relationship to Gere. Sensing an opportunity to get rich quick, Gere encourages her to marry Sheppard anyway. For a while, they all live in luxury, but when Adams falls for Sheppard, the deception is revealed.

Sex, Nud, Viol, Lang, AdSit

A: Richard Gere, Brooke Adams, Sam Shepard, Linda Manz, Robert Wilke, Stuart Margolin

© PARAMOUNT HOME VIDEO 8942

DAYS OF WINE AND ROSES

D: Blake Edwards 118 m

NR | DMA | 1962 | B&W

9 Hugely successful, very provocative drama of modern-day life - just as relevant now as when released in 1962. In powerful Oscar-nominated performances, Lemmon and Remick are an attractive newlywed couple who innocently stumble into alcoholism. Jack is a top notch PR guy who must "socialize," but he also seeks relief from the day's job pressures with a drink. He encourages Remick to join him. They live the good life, but then the life owns them. Lemmon faces up to his problem and finds help through Alcoholics Anonymous but not Remick. Powerful film - realistic, not patronizing.

Sex, Nud, Viol, Lang, AdSit

A: Jack Lemmon, Lee Remick, Charles Bickford, Jack Klugman, Alan Hewitt, Jack Albertson

© WARNER HOME VIDEO 11161

DAY THE EARTH CAUGHT FIRE, THE

D: Val Guest 95 m

NR | SF DMA | 1962 | B&W

8 One of the most intelligent science fiction entries out of Britain. Edward Judd is a cynical reporter who uncovers this incredible story: when the Americans and the Russians inadvertently conducted nuclear tests on the same day, the earth was sent off its orbit to spiral inward toward the sun. The earth is doomed. This is a realistic treatment of the subject of the last days of the earth, both scientifically and emotionally. The film creates a believable sense of doom and the insightful observations of human nature produce a tense, thought-provoking experience.

Sex, Nud, Viol, Lang, AdSit

A: Edward Judd, Janet Munro, Leo McKern, Michael Goodliffe, Bernard Braden

© CONGRESS VIDEO GROUP 03615

DAZED AND CONFUSED

D: Richard Linklater 103 m

R | COM DMA | 1993 | COLOR

8 This is the kind of film that teens want to go see but makes parents cringe. It depicts one day and night at the end of the school year in 1976 at a small Texas town. Next year's seniors are hazing next year's freshman. They are all either cool or trying to be cool, and they are all having fun. They're too late for the 60's but that doesn't stop them from being rebellious - smoking pot and drinking beer. Anarchy rules. The plot generally follows about two dozen kids, but focuses more on the quarterback who doesn't want to sign a pledge to avoid smoking pot; and, a junior high kid trying to avoid being paddled by seniors. Best for teenagers and those who wish they still were.

Sex, Nud, Viol, Lang, AdSit

A: Jason London, Rory Cochrane, Adam Goldberg, Anthony Rapp, Shasha Rapp, Wiley Wiggens

© MCA/UNIVERSAL HOME VIDEO, INC. 81495

DEAD, THE

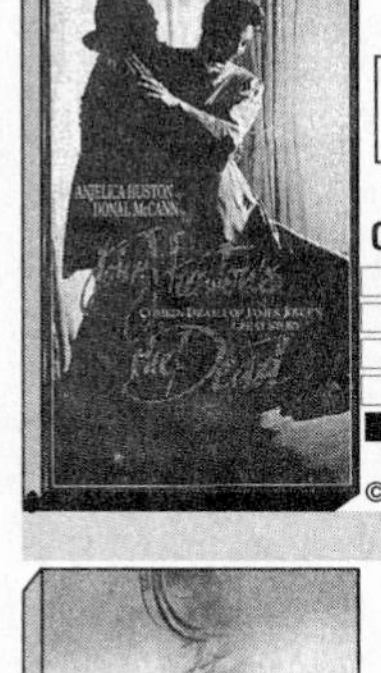

D: John Huston 82 m

PG | DMA | 1988 | COLOR

8 Elegant adaptation of the James Joyce short story of personal discovery set at a holiday dinner party in 1904. The party is thrown by a young couple who have invited all of their dearest friends. When conversation turns to discussions of the people who have influenced the people at the party and who are no longer alive, the wife remembers a past lover and the couple gradually comes to realize that there is no longer any love left between them. This was Huston's last directing effort. The screenplay was Oscar-nominated. It is touching and emotional film, but also somber and not for everyone.

Sex, Nud, Viol, Lang, AdSit

A: Anjelica Huston, Donal McCann, Rachael Dowling, Cathleen Kelany, Ingrid Cragie, Dan O'Herlihy

© LIVE HOME VIDEO 6019

DEAD AGAIN

D: Kenneth Branagh 107 m

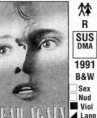

R | SUS DMA | 1991 | B&W

7 In a world of high-tech, big budget thrillers, along comes this little gem that did very well at the box office. Branagh is a modern-day private eye who takes in a lovely amnesiac (Thompson, his real life wife) and agrees to help her discover who she is. And when she is hypnotized, they find out that they have both lived a former life together in 1949. One was a noted pianist and the other was her conductor husband and the husband was later convicted of murdering his wife with a pair of scissors. Will the past recreate itself? An interesting suspense thriller with style, class and intelligence.

Sex, Nud, Viol, Lang, AdSit

A: Kenneth Branagh, Emma Thompson, Andy Garcia, Derek Jacobi, Hanna Schygulla

© PARAMOUNT HOME VIDEO 32057

DEAD MAN OUT

D: Richard Pierce 87 m

NR | SUS DMA | 1989 | COLOR

8 Intense made-for-TV prison drama. Ben (Blades) has brutally murdered four innocent people and is now awaiting execution, but the extreme pressures on Death Row have pushed him over the edge. The State has a problem. They legally can not execute an insane man, even though he was sane when he committed the murders. Glover is a psychiatrist hired by the state to cure Ben. But Glover becomes tortured by his task. Does he cure the man and thereby help to kill him. Or does he leave him to suffer in his torment, but stay alive. Powerful performance by Blades.

Sex Nud Viol Lang AdSit

A: Danny Glover, Ruben Blades, Tom Atkins, Larry Block, Samuel L. Jackson, Maria Ricossa

© HBO VIDEO 0221

DEAD POET'S SOCIETY

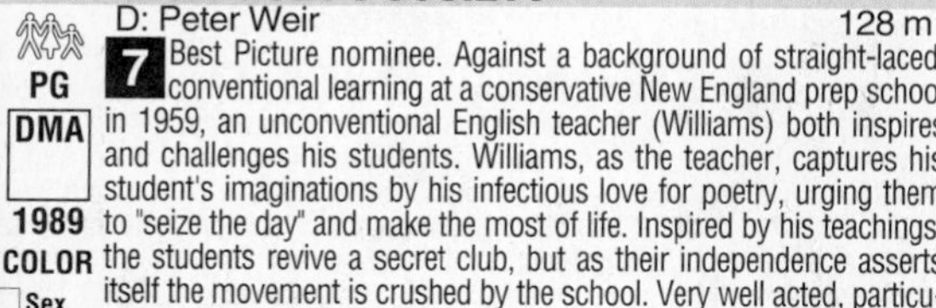

D: Peter Weir 128 m

PG | DMA | 1989 | COLOR

7 Best Picture nominee. Against a background of straight-laced, conventional learning at a conservative New England prep school in 1959, an unconventional English teacher (Williams) both inspires and challenges his students. Williams, as the teacher, captures his student's imaginations by his infectious love for poetry, urging them to "seize the day" and make the most of life. Inspired by his teachings, the students revive a secret club, but as their independence asserts itself the movement is crushed by the school. Very well acted, particularly Williams. Oscar for Screenplay.

Sex Nud Viol Lang AdSit

A: Robin Williams, Robert Sean Leonard, Ethan Hawke, Kurtwood Smith, Josh Charles, Gale Hansen

© TOUCHSTONE HOME VIDEO 947

DEAD RINGERS

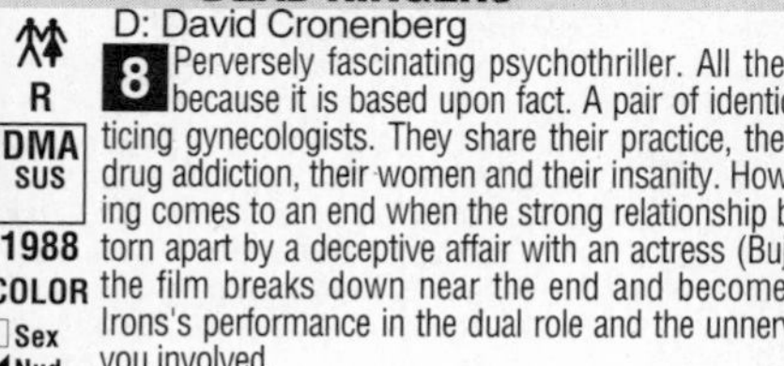

D: David Cronenberg 117 m

R | DMA SUS | 1988 | COLOR

8 Perversely fascinating psychothriller. All the more fascinating because it is based upon fact. A pair of identical twins are practicing gynecologists. They share their practice, their apartment, their drug addiction, their women and their insanity. However, all that sharing comes to an end when the strong relationship between the two is torn apart by a deceptive affair with an actress (Bujold). Even though the film breaks down near the end and becomes gory in places, Irons's performance in the dual role and the unnerving premise keep you involved.

Sex Nud Viol Lang AdSit

A: Jeremy Irons, Genevieve Bujold, Heidi Von Palleske, Barbara Gordon, Shirley Douglas, Stephen Lack

© VIDEO TREASURES M012168

DEAR AMERICA: LETTERS HOME FROM VIETNAM

D: Bill Couturie 84 m

PG | DOC DMA WAR | 1988 | COLOR

9 An extremely moving and powerful documentary. This is a non-political, award-winning documentary which examines the Vietnam War from the soldier's perspective. Actual letters, written home at the time, are read by numerous prominent actors and are accompanied by '60s music, news footage, still photographs, and even home movies. This is a gut-wrenchingly presentation of the personal face of war. It is neither politicized nor glamorized, only human. Originally made-for-TV and later released to theaters.

Sex Nud Viol Lang AdSit

A:

© HBO VIDEO 0207

DEATH AND THE MAIDEN

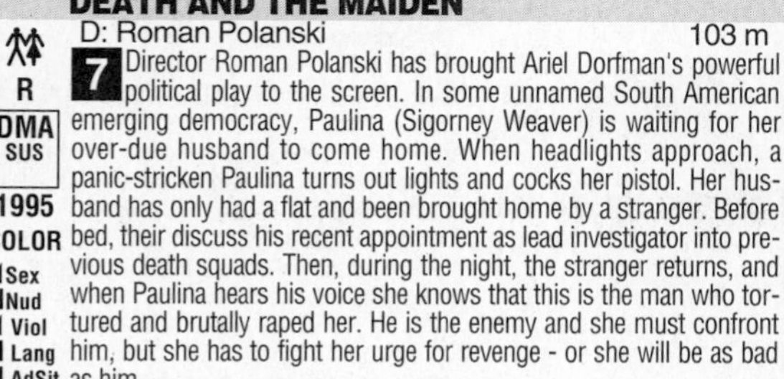

D: Roman Polanski 103 m

R | DMA SUS | 1995 | COLOR

7 Director Roman Polanski has brought Ariel Dorfman's powerful political play to the screen. In some unnamed South American emerging democracy, Paulina (Sigorney Weaver) is waiting for her over-due husband to come home. When headlights approach, a panic-stricken Paulina turns out lights and cocks her pistol. Her husband has only had a flat and been brought home by a stranger. Before bed, their discuss his recent appointment as lead investigator into previous death squads. Then, during the night, the stranger returns, and when Paulina hears his voice she knows that this is the man who tortured and brutally raped her. He is the enemy and she must confront him, but she has to fight her urge for revenge - or she will be as bad as him.

Sex Nud Viol Lang AdSit

A: Sigorney Weaver, Ben Kingsley, Stuart Wilson

© TURNER HOME ENTERTAINMENT N4119

DEATH IN VENICE

D: Luchino Visconti 124 m

PG | DMA | 1971 | COLOR

8 Widely critically acclaimed and controversial study of an aging, world famous composer (thinly veiled Gustav Mahler). This man has denied most emotion all his life and is now on the verge of a nervous breakdown while on vacation in Venice in the summer of 1911. Suddenly, however, he spies what he believes to be perfection and beauty in the person of a pretty young boy, traveling with his mother and sisters. He becomes obsessed with the boy and follows him everywhere, without ever making contact. Beautifully shot, with excellent use of music, but the homosexual theme is not for everybody.

Sex Nud Viol Lang AdSit

A: Dirk Bogarde, Bjorne Andresen, Silvana Mangano, Marisa Berenson

© WARNER HOME VIDEO 11060

DEATH OF A SALESMAN

D: Volker Schlondorff 135 m

NR | DMA | 1985 | COLOR

9 This is a very highly regarded made-for-TV production of the American theater classic. The Arthur Miller story concerns the disintegrating life of an aging traveling salesman who can't understand how and why his business and family life have all failed. For years he has pursued the American Dream and only now, in this shattering climax to his life, does he come to realize that all which he has chased, his whole life, is hollow. This production was filmed on a Broadway stage set, but numerous flashback sequences are interwoven into it on film. Brilliant acting.

Sex Nud Viol Lang AdSit

A: Dustin Hoffman, Kate Reid, John Malkovich, Stephen Lang, Charles Durning

© WARNER HOME VIDEO 380

DECLINE OF THE AMERICAN EMPIRE, THE

D: Denys Arcand 102 m

R | FOR COM DMA | 1986 | COLOR

8 Enjoyable, but very sophisticated, look at sexual politics. A group of university teachers and students get together. Four men prepare a gourmet dinner while they swap stories about women and sex. The four women do the same while they exercise in a health club. Then they all meet for dinner and it becomes known that intimate secrets have been revealed. That inspires a very open sexual discussion which leads both to more revelations and experimentation. Intellectual, incisive and witty. However the subject matter, and the frank approach to it, makes this a video that is definitely not for everyone. Subtitles.

Sex Nud Viol Lang AdSit

A: Dominique Michel, Dorothee Berryman, Louis Patal, Genevieve Rioux, Pierre Curzi, Remy Girard

© MCA/UNIVERSAL HOME VIDEO, INC. 80586

DEER HUNTER, THE

D: Michael Cimino 183 m

R | DMA WAR ACT | 1978 | COLOR

10 Extraordinarily powerful winner of five Oscars, including Best Picture (nominated for nine). Young friends from a blue collar working class background in 1968 Pennsylvania leave their familiar land of hot blast furnaces and cool forests, from which they hunted deer, to go to Vietnam's steaming jungle to hunt men. This epic (long) movie is essentially shown in three parts: the hometown, the horrors of war and then back home again, now scarred both physically and emotionally. This powerful film packs a big wallop, but is not without controversy. Top-flight cast.

Sex Nud Viol Lang AdSit

A: Robert De Niro, John Cazale, John Savage, Meryl Streep, Schristopher Walken, George Dzundza

© MCA/UNIVERSAL HOME VIDEO, INC. 88000

DEFIANT ONES, THE

D: Stanley Kramer 97 m

NR | DMA ACT | 1958 | B&W

9 A major ground-breaking movie and great entertainment, too. It was nominated for seven Oscars and won three. Two prisoners who are chained together escape from a chain gang in the deep South. One is black and the other is white. Poitier and Curtis hate each other, but they are forced to work together and depend upon each other if they are first to escape and then to survive. This is a very well made and exciting movie that still packs a big punch today, while never sinking into platitudes and cliches. Powerful performances garnered four of the Oscar nominations.

Sex Nud Viol Lang AdSit

A: Tony Curtis, Sidney Poitier, Theodore Bikel, Charles McGraw, Lon Chaney, Jr., Cara Williams

Distributed By MGM/UA Home Video M201557

DELIVERANCE

D: John Boorman 109 m

R | SUS DMA ACT | 1972 | COLOR

10 Riveting account of four ordinary businessmen who decide to take a weekend whitewater canoe trip down a wild river before it is dammed up forever. What begins as a man-against-nature excursion becomes an exercise in gripping suspense, terror and survival. Four men become profoundly changed as they are forced to confront their fears alone when they are pursued by two demented hillbillies, intent upon murder and homosexual rape. The movie's theme song "Dueling Banjos" became a major pop hit. Excellent performances. Nominated for Best Picture. Totally involving.

Sex Nud Viol Lang AdSit

A: Jon Voight, Burt Reynolds, Ned Beatty, Ronny Cox, Bill McKinney, James Dickey

© WARNER HOME VIDEO 1004

DESERT BLOOM

D: Eugene Corr 103 m

PG | DMA | 1986 | COLOR

7 Poignant study of a 13-year-old girl (Gish) struggling to grow up in 1951 Nevada. She lives at a gas station in the desert with her dreamer mother (Williams) and abusive stepfather (Voight), who was a war hero and is now an embittered alcoholic still struggling with his demons. Her young life is thrown into further turmoil when her sexy show-girl aunt (Barkin) moves in while waiting for her divorce to become final. Barkin's presence sparks a confrontation between the girl's mother and her stepfather. Study of a faltering family's struggle to survive under pressure.

Sex Nud Viol Lang AdSit

A: Jon Voight, JoBeth Williams, Ellen Barkin, Allen Garfield, Annabeth Gish, Jay Underwood

© GOODTIMES 4516

D M A

DEVILS, THE

D: Ken Russell 103 m

R | DMA SUS | 1971 | COLOR

8 Very controversial and bizarre, but true, story (documented in 1634 France) presented in a nearly hallucinogenic way. Reed plays a cynical and amoral priest (he has a very active sex life) who gets in trouble with his Cardinal for opposing his political plans. Soon a hysterical nun (Redgrave) steps forward, accusing Reed of having seduced her and the other nuns through witchcraft. A charismatic exorcist (Gothard) arrives in town to conduct a mass exorcism, after which Reed is burned at the stake. Some pretty grotesque scenes will surely offend devout believers, but this is fascinating stuff.

Sex Nud Viol Lang AdSit

A: Vanessa Redgrave, Oliver Reed, Murray Melvin, Max Adrian, Gemma Jones, Michael Gothard

© WARNER HOME VIDEO 11110

DIARY OF A MAD HOUSEWIFE

D: Frank Perry 100 m

R | DMA COM | 1970 | COLOR

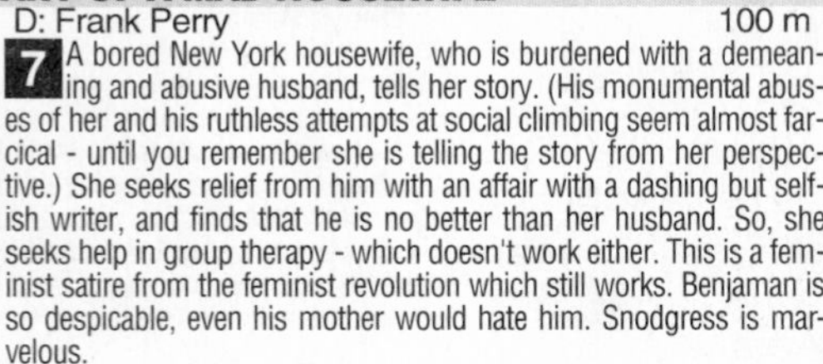

7 A bored New York housewife, who is burdened with a demeaning and abusive husband, tells her story. (His monumental abuses of her and his ruthless attempts at social climbing seem almost farcical - until you remember she is telling the story from her perspective.) She seeks relief from him with an affair with a dashing but selfish writer, and finds that he is no better than her husband. So, she seeks help in group therapy - which doesn't work either. This is a feminist satire from the feminist revolution which still works. Benjaman is so despicable, even his mother would hate him. Snodgress is marvelous.

Sex Nud Viol Lang AdSit

A: Richard Benjamin, Carrie Snodgress, Frank Langella

© MCA/UNIVERSAL HOME VIDEO, INC. 66048

D M A

DIARY OF ANNE FRANK, THE

D: George Stevens 151 m

NR | DMA SUS | 1959 | B&W

9 Very moving screen depiction of a real-life WWII tragedy. The story was written based upon an actual diary of a young Jewish girl while she was in hiding with her family inside Nazi-occupied Holland. In the diary, she tells of the daily lives of her family and a few friends who are forced to hide in secret rooms hidden behind the false walls of an Amsterdam factory building during the occupation. The threat of discovery is ever-present and they lived their lives under extreme pressure. Still, throughout harrowing daily routines and constant fear, Anne manages to keep hope alive. 3 Oscars.

Sex Nud Viol Lang AdSit

A: Millie Perkins, Joseph Schildkraut, Shelley Winters, Richard Beymer, Lou Jacobi, Ed Wynn

© FOXVIDEO 1074

DIFFERENT STORY, A

D: Paul Aaron 104 m

PG | ROM DMA | 1979 | COLOR

7 A decidedly different sort of love story. A male homosexual and a lesbian (King and Foster) are only just stumbling along in their relationships with other people. Then, they discover each other. He is handsome, charming and intelligent and she is quick-witted and pretty. At first, they form a close friendship -- just that -- but then one night, it turns into love. They marry and have a baby. Sounds like a strange one, but is remarkably good -- due largely to the excellent and convincing efforts of Meg Foster. A little uneven at times, but still a sensitive love story.

Sex Nud Viol Lang AdSit

A: Perry King, Meg Foster, Valerie Curtin, Peter Donat

© NEW LINE HOME VIDEO 2177

DINER

D: Barry Levinson 110 m

R | COM DMA | 1982 | COLOR

8 A real sleeper that was much acclaimed by critics. It is a nostalgic, but not idealized, story of four young men growing up in 1959 Baltimore. They hang out at one particular diner, trying to learn how to deal with life and romance after leaving high school. One is married, one is engaged, one is trying to become engaged and one is playing the field. This is an insightful story of four flawed, inexperienced guys who meet over french fries to discuss life, music, and the best way to get women. Carefully and lovingly made.

Sex Nud Viol Lang AdSit

A: Steve Guttenberg, Daniel Stern, Mickey Rourke, Kevin Bacon, Ellen Barkin, Paul Reiser

Distributed By MGM/UA Home Video M800164

DIRTY DANCING

D: Emile Ardolino 105 m

PG-13 | ROM DMA | 1987 | COLOR

9 A gigantic box office hit - primarily because of its sexy, sensual and energetic dance sequences. Jennifer Grey is a seventeen-year-old girl on vacation with her parents in the Catskills in the 1960s. There she falls for sexy dance instructor Patrick Swayze and becomes his prize pupil. She learns something about dancing and about life, too. This is a coming-of-age story that has little that's new, but tells it with a whole lot of energy and steamy sensuality. Appealing, exuberant and fun. Women especially loved it. Best Song Oscar.

Sex Nud Viol Lang AdSit

A: Jennifer Grey, Patrick Swayze, Cynthia Rhodes, Jerry Orbach, Jack Weston

© LIVE HOME VIDEO 6013

DISCLOSURE

D: Barry Levinson 129 m

R | SUS DMA | 1995 | COLOR

7 Michael Douglas has spent the last ten years heading the manufacturing division at a high-tech company. Now that company is about to become part of a multi-million dollar merger. Just as it looks as though he's going to make a lot of money and be promoted in the bargain, he learns that his old flame Demi Moore will get the promotion instead. He can live with that, but she has other plans. That evening she trys to seduce him and when he resists, she claims sexual harassment. He now stands to loose everything, including his family. The only option he has left is to sue her for sexual harassment. This kind of news in the press is very hard on mergers, so now everyone, is playing hardball. Quite involving and not sensationalized.

Sex Nud Viol Lang AdSit

A: Michael Douglas, Demi Moore, Donald Sutherland, Caroline Goodall, Dylan Baker, Roma Maffia

© WARNER HOME VIDEO 13575

DISTANT VOICES, STILL LIVES

D: Terence Davies 87 m

PG-13 | DMA | 1988 | COLOR

8 British. An interesting offbeat, highly stylized autobiographical sketch of the director's own family, which is a family plagued by the lasting effects created by an erratic father. It is told as a series of excerpts from each of the lives of the members of this working class English family in the years just after World War II. It doesn't contain a continuous stream of narrative, but rather relies upon an effective sound track and a series of family "snapshots" to effectively create the images of time and place, and tie them all together. Not for everyone.

Sex Nud Viol Lang AdSit

A: Freda Dowie, Peter Postlethwaite, Angela Walsh, Dean Williams, Lorraine Ashbourne

© LIVE HOME VIDEO 68907

DOCTOR, THE

D: Randa Haines 123 m

PG-13 | DMA | 1991 | COLOR

8 Elegant, enlightening and heart-wrenching. Hurt is a callous heart surgeon who pays little attention to his patients's concerns and dismisses their questions with flippant answers. But things change drastically for him when his nagging cough turns out to be throat cancer. Suddenly, he becomes the victim of hospital bureaucracy, foreboding darkness and uncertainty - and he gets to experience all of the same indignities he inflicted on his patients. An extremely well-acted true story based on Dr. Edward Rosembaum's "A Taste Of My Own Medicine."

Sex Nud Viol Lang AdSit

A: William Hurt, Elizabeth Perkins, Christine Lahti, Mandy Patinkin, Adam Arkin, Charlie Korsmo

© TOUCHSTONE HOME VIDEO 1257

DOCTOR ZHIVAGO

D: David Lean 200 m

PG | ROM DMA | 1965 | COLOR

9 A beautiful and painfully romantic love story. It is also a mammoth epic spectacle with stunning photography and a beautiful score. It won 5 Oscars. The story was taken from Boris Pasternak's Nobel Prize-winning novel. It is the tale of life in Russia before, during and after the 1917 Russian revolution for a doctor/poet, his wife and his lover. It also paints a vivid portrait of a whole society through a painful and trying time. The movie is long, but can be forgiven because of the gorgeous scenery, the spectacular photography, and the tragic love story it tells. A very watchable movie.

Sex Nud Viol Lang AdSit

A: Omar Sharif, Julie Christie, Geraldine Chaplin, Rod Steiger, Alec Guinness, Tom Courtenay

Distributed By MGM/UA Home Video M900003

DOG DAY AFTERNOON

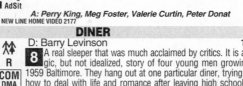

D: Sidney Lumet 125 m

R | SUS DMA | 1975 | COLOR

9 Gripping, bizarre but true story of a sweaty, loser of a man (Pacino) and his slow-witted partner who hold up a bank in Brooklyn to get money, mostly to finance Pacino's boyfriend's sex-change operation. This is an acting tour de force by Pacino as the small-time bank job is bungled and turned into a full blown hostage situation and media-circus, shown live on television news. Great pacing and suspense as Pacino negotiates the release of his prisoners. Nominated for six Oscars, including Best Picture. Highly recommended viewing.

Sex Nud Viol Lang AdSit

A: Al Pacino, John Cazale, Charles Durning, Carol Kane, James Broderick, Chris Sarandon

© WARNER HOME VIDEO 1024

DOGFIGHT

D: Nancy Savoca 94 m

R | ROM DMA | 1991 | COLOR

7 Four young buddies, Marines on their last night in the States before leaving for Vietnam in 1963, stage a dogfight. A dogfight is a contest where each gets a date with the ugliest girl he can find and brings her back to a party where the winner is chosen. However, Phoenix unexpectedly comes to like the girl he finds (Taylor). But when she learns of the cruel joke that has been played on her, she lashes back at him. Now wiser, he leaves his buddies behind to spend the evening with her. That one experience, and the war he goes to fight, marks the end of his arrogance and ignorance, and things are never so simple for him again.

Sex Nud Viol Lang AdSit

A: River Phoenix, Lili Taylor, Richard Panebianco, Anthony Clark, Mitchell Whitfield, E.G. Daily

© WARNER HOME VIDEO 12051

DOG OF FLANDERS, A

D: James B. Clark — 96 m

NR | CLD DMA | 1959 | COLOR | Rating: 9

This is a wonderful children's story, but it is also good viewing for the whole family. Set in turn-of-the-century Belgium, a young boy who is living with his grandfather, dreams of becoming a great painter, but they are very poor. He and his grandfather adopt a stray dog who pulls the old man's milk cart, and when the dog becomes sick, they have to struggle to save him. However, then the grandfather dies, and the boy and the dog are left alone. Get out your hankies - this is going to hit you just as hard as OLD YELLER. It is particularly good for kids.

Sex / Nud / Viol / Lang / AdSit

A: David Ladd, Donald Crisp, Theodore Bikel, Max Croiset, Monique Ahrens, Siohban Taylor

© PARAMOUNT HOME VIDEO 2325

DOLLMAKER, THE

D: Daniel Petrie — 140 m

NR | DMA | 1984 | COLOR | Rating: 8

Excellent made-for-TV movie. Nominated for a total of six Emmy awards. Jane Fonda won an Emmy for her portrayal of a simple Kentucky hills housewife and mother whose family is uprooted from their mountain home at the start of World War II when her husband takes a high-paying factory job in Detroit. Lonely, her only personal pleasure comes from carving wooden dolls. Later she must turn to her carvings to raise the money they need when tragedy strikes. This is a brilliant salute to the strength of the human spirit. Great period detail. Sensitive story, lovingly told. Excellent family viewing.

Sex / Nud / Viol / Lang / AdSit

A: Jane Fonda, Levon Helm, Susan Kingsley, Nikki Cresswell

© FOXVIDEO 5538

DOMINICK AND EUGENE

D: Robert M. Young — 111 m

PG-13 | DMA | 1988 | COLOR | Rating: 9

Very moving story of twin brothers. One (Liotta) is a bright medical college student devoted to his brother. The other (Hulce) is mildly retarded but is supporting them both by working as a garbage man. Liotta is hard-pressed to go to school, take care of his brother and have a relationship with Curtis, too. Then things get even more complicated when he gets an offer to serve his residency at the prestigious Stanford University hospital because that means leaving his brother behind for two years. Deeply touching story of love and responsibility. Terrific acting from everyone.

Sex / Nud / Viol / Lang / AdSit

A: Tom Hulce, Ray Liotta, Jamie Lee Curtis, Robert Levine, Todd Graff, Bill Cobbs

© ORION PICTURES CORPORATION 8716

DON'T CRY, IT'S ONLY THUNDER

D: Peter Werner — 108 m

PG | DMA | 1981 | COLOR | Rating: 8

Heartwarming little movie that never got big promotion when it was released. It is based upon a true incident from the Vietnam War. In 1968, a US Army medic (Christopher) has a profitable little business set up on the side dealing in black market items. But he gets caught, court-martialed and sent to work in a mortuary in Saigon. There, he is recruited by a group of nuns and a dedicated Army doctor who need his special talent to help supply their orphanage. Now, things take on a new meaning for him. A truly inspirational movie that never drifts into melodrama.

Sex / Nud / Viol / Lang / AdSit

A: Dennis Christopher, Susan Saint James, Roger Aaron Brown, Lisa Lu, James Whitmore, Jr., Thu Thuy

© COLUMBIA TRISTAR HOME VIDEO 60170

DON'T LOOK NOW

D: Nicolas Roeg — 110 m

R | SUS DMA | 1974 | COLOR | Rating: 8

Gripping, eerie psychic thriller. After their 10 year-old daughter drowns, Christie and Sutherland go to Venice where he is to help to restore a church. She befriends two strange sisters, one of whom is a blind psychic who tells them that their daughter is happy. He does not believe the psychic, but then sees a strange figure in a red raincoat who reminds him of his daughter. The psychic also warns Sutherland of great impending danger. Meanwhile, in another subplot, random murders are occurring about town. Really spooky occult stuff, a sexy scene and big climax.

Sex / Nud / Viol / Lang / AdSit

A: Julie Christie, Donald Sutherland, Hilary Mason, Cielia Matania, Massimo Serato, Renato Scarpa

© PARAMOUNT HOME VIDEO 8704

DOORS, THE

D: Oliver Stone — 135 m

R | DMA MUS | 1991 | COLOR | Rating: 7

Alternatingly powerful and boring, invigorating and demoralizing, impressive and pompous, this is director Oliver Stone's extravaganza recreating the ambience of an era and a state of mind. Unfortunately the mind in question (Doors singer Jim Morrison), though brilliant, was in serious disarray. He was a self-destructive genius/icon who, in many ways, personified the era and he self-destructed at 27. Very interesting to Morrison's fans but ultimately, the film cannot help but be a downer, man. The photography which made the film an impressive experience in theaters is diminished on video. Fans only.

Sex / Nud / Viol / Lang / AdSit

A: Val Kilmer, Meg Ryan, Kyle MacLachlan, Frank Whaley, Michael Madsen, Billy Idol

© LIVE HOME VIDEO 68956

DO THE RIGHT THING

D: Spike Lee — 120 m

R | DMA | 1989 | COLOR | Rating: 8

Intriguing, much talked about and controversial film by black director Spike Lee. Tensions build on a summer's day within an impoverished neighborhood of Brooklyn. It is populated entirely by black people, except for the white Italian owner (Aiello) of the pizza parlor which has been there for many years and is a major focal point in the neighborhood. The picture is a composite of several individual's lives and the events of a hot summer's day which culminate in a riot at the day's end. Insightful but troubling, and a not altogether pleasant reflection on modern-day life.

Sex / Nud / Viol / Lang / AdSit

A: Danny Aiello, Spike Lee, Ossie Davis, Ruby Dee, John Turturro, Richard Edson

© MCA/UNIVERSAL HOME VIDEO, INC. 80894

DOUBLE SUICIDE

D: Masahiro Shinoda — 105 m

NR | FOR DMA ROM | 1969 | B&W | Rating: 8

A Japanese traditional puppet play dating back to 1720 is the source of the story line and the stylized feel to this film. A newspaper vendor has a passionate love affair with a beautiful geisha and she loves him. He cannot control himself and vows to purchase her freedom although he is already very deep in debt. His business is bankrupted. His wife and two small children are suffering terribly. She is neglected, deprived and abused, yet she is bound to him by duty. It is hopeless for everyone. A romantic tragedy laden with symbolism and steeped in Japanese culture. Not for everyone. Subtitles.

Sex / Nud / Viol / Lang / AdSit

A: Shima Iwashita, Kichiemon Nakamura, Hosei Komatsu

© COLUMBIA TRISTAR HOME VIDEO K0677

DOWN AND OUT IN BEVERLY HILLS

D: Paul Mazursky — 103 m

R | COM DMA | 1986 | COLOR | Rating: 9

Fun time. Nolte is a bum who is so despondent when his dog leaves him for a better home that he tries to drown himself in the swimming pool of a wealthy coat-hanger magnate (Dreyfuss). However, Dreyfuss spies him and saves him from drowning. The despondent Nolte then moves in with their largely disfunctional family. Oddly, his presence and unique perspective on things brings a strange calming effect to the household's peculiar occupants and everyone is changed for the better. While the film is somewhat uneven, the result is still very funny overall. Great performances especially by Mike the dog.

Sex / Nud / Viol / Lang / AdSit

A: Nick Nolte, Bette Midler, Richard Dreyfuss, Little Richard, Tracy Nelson, Elizabeth Pena

© TOUCHSTONE HOME VIDEO 473

DOWNHILL RACER

D: Michael Ritchie — 102 m

PG | DMA | 1969 | COLOR | Rating: 7

Sports story about what it sometimes takes to be a winner. It was a very influential and well-done sports film that provides a not-often-seen look behind the glamour. It is also the character study of a loner's empty life. Redford plays an egotistical ski bum who wins a place on the US Olympic ski team when a racer gets hurt. His character is very unappealing, however. This makes him a source of trouble for the team, and a not very appealing hero for the film. The film works best for its exciting skiing sequences, which are dazzling. Redford did much of his own skiing and stunts.

Sex / Nud / Viol / Lang / AdSit

A: Robert Redford, Gene Hackman, Camilla Sparv, Kar Michael Vogler, Jim McMullan, Chiristian Dormer

© PARAMOUNT HOME VIDEO 6910

DRAGON: THE BRUCE LEE STORY

D: Rob Cohen — 120 m

PG-13 | ACT DMA | 1993 | COLOR | Rating: 8

High energy, action packed biography of one of the silver screen's action legends. Bruce Lee was a Chinese-American raised in Hong Kong, but who returned to the United States. Here he had to struggle against hostilities from both whites and Chinese to get a college education and to keep his Kung Fu school open. While the film does document Lee's inner turmoil, his love for his white wife and his rise in films, it focuses primarily upon the bigotry against which he rebelled and constantly fought (quite literally) against. He died at 32, before his biggest film ENTER THE DRAGON was released. Quite interesting and very involving.

Sex / Nud / Viol / Lang / AdSit

A: Jason Scott Lee, Lauren Holly, Michael Learned, Nancy Kwan, Robert Wagner

© MCA/UNIVERSAL HOME VIDEO, INC. 81480

DREAMCHILD

D: Gavin Millar — 90 m

PG | DMA | 1985 | COLOR | Rating: 7

In 1932 an eighty-year-old woman came to Columbia University to help everyone there celebrate the 100th birthday of Lewis Carroll (author of "Alice's Adventures in Wonderland"). She was present because, when she was just 10, she was the inspiration for Carroll to create the story - she was Alice. Those true facts led to the making of this film. Here, Alice recalls her relationship with Carroll in mid-19th century England. She recalls her idyllic childhood through a blend of reality and Jim Henson's muppets. Well done unusual treat, worth watching.

Sex / Nud / Viol / Lang / AdSit

A: Coral Browne, Peter Gallagher, Ian Holm, Jane Asher, Nicola Cowper, Amelia Shankley

Distributed By MGM/UA Home Video M202767

DREAM OF KINGS, A

D: Daniel Mann — 107 m

R | DMA | 1969 | COLOR | Sex | Nud | Viol | Lang | AdSit

8 Moving, emotional story about the robust and proud Greek father of a very sick son. Anthony Quinn is unforgettable as a proud man and a respected member of Chicago's vibrant Greek community, even though he makes his living as a gambler. He is desperately trying to raise enough money to take his son back to Greece. He will in fact do anything to get the money, including risk his reputation. Irene Papas is his wife and Inger Stevens is excellent as the lonely widow he teaches to learn how to live. An affecting character study of tragedy.

A: Anthony Quinn, Irene Papas, Inger Stevens, Val Avery, Sam Levene

© UNITED AMERICAN VIDEO CORP. 5297

DREAMSCAPE

D: Joseph Ruben — 99 m

PG-13 | SF SUS DMA | 1983 | COLOR | Sex | Nud | Viol | Lang | AdSit

7 A really imaginative and intriguing premise. Suppose psychics could be trained to enter into the dreams or nightmares of others and to then help calm their fears. Quaid and other psychics have been recruited into a huge government program to do just that. He is so successful that he is assigned the special job of helping the President deal with his recurring fears of a nuclear holocaust. However, Quaid also uncovers a plot involving one of his fellow psychics, who is supposed to use these same techniques to kill the President. Good special effects.

A: Dennis Quaid, Max von Sydow, Christopher Plummer, Eddie Albert, Kate Capshaw

© HBO VIDEO TVA2722

D
M
A

DRESSER, THE

D: Peter Yates — 118 m

PG | DMA | 1983 | COLOR | Sex | Nud | Viol | Lang | AdSit

9 Fascinating study of the symbiotic relationship between an aging actor and his dresser. Set in wartime England, an eccentric, crotchety old actor (Finney) has been the mainstay of his touring company for a long time and he is now beginning to crumble under the pressure. He depends upon his manservant to do virtually everything for him because his love of theater exceeds all other desires. The dresser, on the other hand, lives his entire life vicariously through the old man's performances. Witty writing and complex characters. Recommended viewing, even for non-thespians.

A: Albert Finney, Tom Cortenay, Edward Fox, Zena Walker, Eileen Atkins, Michael Gough

© COLUMBIA TRISTAR HOME VIDEO VH10184

DRIVING MISS DAISY

D: Bruce Beresford — 99 m

PG | DMA COM | 1989 | COLOR | Sex | Nud | Viol | Lang | AdSit

8 A great feel-good film. In 1948 a wealthy Jewish merchant (Ackroyd) hires an elderly black man (Freeman) to drive and otherwise aid his crotchety old, widowed mother (Tandy - Oscar winner). At first reluctant, she accepts Morgan as an employee. Then, as she grows older and her friends die, she becomes more and more dependent on Morgan. These two are so different - yet an abiding best-friends sort of loving friendship develops. Great performances all around and very enjoyable, but perhaps oversold in the press. It is also rather slow. Oscars also for Best Picture and Screen Adaptation.

A: Jessica Tandy, Morgan Freeman, Dan Aykroyd, Esther Rolle, Patti Lupone

© WARNER HOME VIDEO 11931

DR. STRANGELOVE OR: HOW I LEARNED TO STOP WORRYING

D: Stanley Kubrick — 93 m

PG | COM DMA | 1964 | B&W | Sex | Nud | Viol | Lang | AdSit

10 Very funny black comedy and spoof of the nuclear confrontation between the East and West. Movies like this helped us get through the terror of living with "the bomb" by laughing at it. A renegade Air Force general takes it upon himself to save the world from the Russian menace by launching an unauthorized nuclear first strike. Sellars is hilarious in triple roles as the US President dealing with the Russians and unable to stop the bombers, as a British captain and as the crazy inventor of the bomb, Dr. Strangelove. Film also won four Oscar nominations, including Best Actor and Best Picture.

A: Peter Sellers, George C. Scott, Sterling Hayden, Slim Pickens, Keenan Wynn, James Earl Jones

© COLUMBIA TRISTAR HOME VIDEO 60172

DRUGSTORE COWBOY

D: Gus Van Sant, Jr. — 104 m

R | DMA | 1989 | COLOR | Sex | Nud | Viol | Lang | AdSit

8 Very realistic, intense and uncompromising look at the lives of drug addicts. This is the story of two junkie couples who support their daily habits with a never-ending series of petty thefts. Uninviting though it is, the life still has its moments. Then, when it looks like luck is running out and death may be a blessing, Dillon decides that he has to get out - even if it means leaving his love behind. Excellently acted and well structured, this is a very affecting look into a world most of us never, thankfully, see.

A: Matt Dillon, Kelly Lynch, William Borroughs, James Remar, James Le Gros, Heather Graham

© LIVE HOME VIDEO 68911

DRY WHITE SEASON, A

D: Euzhan Palcy — 107 m

R | DMA | 1989 | COLOR | Sex | Nud | Viol | Lang | AdSit

7 Highly touted upon its release and worthwhile viewing. However, this film is still a promise not fully met. It is the story of a complaisant, comfortable and kindly South African prep school teacher who gradually comes to realize the true nature of the system of apartheid he has always lived under when his black gardener's son is victimized and terribly beaten by a perverse security chief. Brando received an Oscar nomination for his portrayal of a liberal attorney who fights a court battle he cannot win. The film's effectiveness is diminished by melodrama.

A: Donald Sutherland, Susan Sarandon, Marlon Brando, Janet Suzman, Zakes Mokae

© CBS/FOX VIDEO 4768

DUELLISTS, THE

D: Ridley Scott — 101 m

PG | DMA ACT | 1978 | COLOR | Sex | Nud | Viol | Lang | AdSit

8 Fascinating but unusual film dealing with obsession and honor. It is set between 1800 and 1815, in Napoleonic France. Calvary officer Carradine is sent by his superiors to confront Keitel over a duel he had had with someone else. Incensed at this affront to his dignity, the brutish Keitel challenges Carradine to a sword duel. Losing his challenge but surviving the duel, Keitel is now consumed by revenge and forces numerous other duels upon Carradine over succeeding years. The duels become more important to them both than all else in their lives.

A: Keith Carradine, Harvey Keitel, Albert Finney, John McEnery

© PARAMOUNT HOME VIDEO 8975

DYING YOUNG

D: Joel Schumacher — 111 m

R | ROM DMA | 1991 | COLOR | Sex | Nud | Viol | Lang | AdSit

7 A competent weeper. Poor, young and inexperienced, Roberts answers a newspaper ad to become a nurse for rich cancer patient (Scott). She is very uncertain that she can handle such a daunting task, but his need for her pulls her in. The two are immediately drawn to each other and, when Scott's cancer suddenly goes into remission, their romance blooms. But when he gets ill again and gives up the fight, it is Roberts who has now grown strong enough to give him the courage he needs to continue fighting. Strong performances from both elevate a simple story.

A: Julia Roberts, Campbell Scott, Vincent D'Onofrio, Colleen Dewhurst, David Selby, Ellen Burstyn

© FOXVIDEO 1914

EARLY FROST, AN

D: John Erman — 97 m

NR | DMA | 1985 | COLOR | Sex | Nud | Viol | Lang | AdSit

8 Highly acclaimed Emmy-winning made-for-TV movie that rises far above the typical TV fare. This is an emotion-packed story of an apparently successful and normal son who breaks the news to his parents at their thirtieth anniversary that, not only is he gay, but he is also dying of AIDS. Powerful and sensitively acted, emotion-packed but not sensationalized. Very high quality performances add to the film's effectiveness. One of the first films to deal openly with AIDS.

A: Aidan Quinn, Gena Rowlands, Ben Gazzara, Sylvia Sidney, John Glover, Sydney Walsh

© COLUMBIA TRISTAR HOME VIDEO 60760

EASY RIDER

D: Dennis Hopper — 94 m

R | DMA | 1969 | COLOR | Sex | Nud | Viol | Lang | AdSit

8 This was a landmark film and a watershed for the 1960s - but its strong counter-culture statement makes it seem pretty dated now. However, this low-budget little film turned into a big box office success and, therefore, it spawned many copycats. The film concerns two hippies who sell some drugs to finance a motorcycle excursion across the Southwest and then on into the South. Along the way they meet rednecks, hippies, dopers, hookers and Jack Nicholson (Oscar nomination). It also has some truly memorable and great rock music.

A: Peter Fonda, Dennis Hopper, Jack Nicholson, Luana Anders, Robert Walker, Jr., Karen Black

© COLUMBIA TRISTAR HOME VIDEO 60174

EDUCATING RITA

D: Lewis Gilbert — 110 m

PG | COM DMA | 1983 | COLOR | Sex | Nud | Viol | Lang | AdSit

8 A likable movie and a big box office hit. It is the story of an uneducated English hairdresser who decides to better herself by going back to school. She has, as one of her teachers, a disaffected alcoholic English professor (Caine) who admires her zest for learning and life, and he becomes her mentor. Infected with her enthusiasm, his long-lost love of life and literature begins to return. But, as he watches her transform herself, he is also deeply unsettled to watch some of what he admired most in her slowly be changed. Three Oscar nominations for acting.

A: Michael Caine, Julie Walters, Michael Williams, Maureen Lipman, Jeananne Crowley, Malcolm Douglas

© GOODTIMES 7230

ED WOOD

D: Tim Burton — 127 m

R | COM DMA | 1994 | B&W

7 During the early 50s, an overly-enthusiastic Hollywood "go-for" named Ed Wood disregarded the fact that he had neither talent nor money and proceeded to produce, direct and star in some of the worst movies ever made, either before or since. His movies had virtually no plot, terrible production values and were notoriously over-acted. He endured the pressures of his productions by dressing in women's clothes, showing a particular fondness for angora sweaters. No amount of failure or derision could dissuade him from his chosen profession. Johnny Depp plays Wood in this playful biography that won an Oscar for Best Makeup, and Landau won for Best Supporting Actor. Very Odd.

Sex · Nud · Viol · Lang · AdSit

A: *Johnny Depp, Sarah Jessica Parker, Martin Landau, Patricia Arquett, Bill Murray, Jeffrey Jones*

© TOUCHSTONE HOME VIDEO 2758

EIGHT MEN OUT

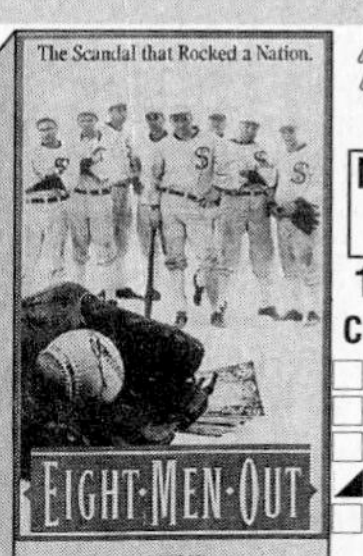

D: John Sayles — 120 m

PG | DMA | 1988 | COLOR

7 Intriguing sports drama about the 1919 World Series where the Chicago White Sox intentionally threw the Series. That actual event became known as the Black Sox scandal. A superb ensemble cast and excellent period detail illustrate the story of a team that felt so motivated by the stinginess of their team owner they felt justified in selling out a World Series game - the game they loved and their fans - for cash. They were all caught and everyone involved was banned from ever playing the game professionally again. The story is true.

Sex · Nud · Viol · Lang · AdSit

A: *Charlie Sheen, John Cusack, Christopher Lloyd, D.B. Sweeney, David Strathairn, Michael Lerner*

© ORION PICTURES CORPORATION 8723

EL CID

D: Anthony Mann — 172 m

NR | ACT ROM DMA | 1961 | COLOR

8 Huge spectacle film containing some of the best old-world battle sequences ever filmed. There are miles of men in chain mail, knights on horseback and corpses everywhere. The action and spectacle are the real stars. It is the story of the eleventh-century Spanish warrior/hero El Cid (Heston), who battled Moorish invaders from the south, and the great love of his life (Loren). Magnificent settings and costumes. Much of the love story is overshadowed by the battles. Some of the splendor will be lost on the small screen.

Sex · Nud · Viol · Lang · AdSit

A: *Charlton Heston, Sophia Loren, Raf Vallone, Hurd Hatfield, Genevieve Page*

© BEST FILM & VIDEO CORP. 215

ELECTRA GLIDE IN BLUE

D: James William Guercio — 114 m

PG | CRM ACT DMA | 1973 | COLOR

7 Very violent crime melodrama about one cop's disillusionment. Blake is a smart, but undersized and over-macho, Arizona motorcycle cop who wants to become a detective in the worst way. He gets his chance when he finds an apparent suicide in a shack, exposes it as a murder and gets his promotion. However, his attitude gets him in trouble and he's soon busted back. Then he runs a foul of a group of hippies, who, ironically, are in many ways like him. Very fast and violent. Full of twists and turns. Blake is excellent, but the film has been criticized as being too arty (sort of MTV-like). Terrific motorcycle chase sequence.

Sex · Nud · Viol · Lang · AdSit

A: *Robert Blake, Billy Green Bush, Mitchell Ryan, Jeannine Riley, Elisha Cook, Jr.*

Distributed By MGM/UA Home Video M300871

ELECTRIC HORSEMAN, THE

D: Sydney Pollack — 120 m

PG | DMA ROM WST | 1979 | COLOR

7 Entertaining modern-day Western about an ex-rodeo star who has become an alcoholic cowboy appearing on cereal boxes riding a horse and promoting the cereal by appearing live on a champion racehorse, in a suit studded with flashing lights. Fonda, a reporter out for a good story, gets one. Redford becomes so upset when the horse he rides is exploited, too, that he steals the horse and rides across Utah looking for a place to set it free. Fonda stays one step of ahead the cops and finds him, but at first doesn't believe him about what he is trying to do. Eventually she does and falls for him.

Sex · Nud · Viol · Lang · AdSit

A: *Robert Redford, Jane Fonda, Valerie Perrine, Willie Nelson, John Saxon, Wilford Brimley*

© MCA/UNIVERSAL HOME VIDEO, INC. 66006

ELEPHANT MAN, THE

D: David Lynch — 124 m

PG | DMA | 1980 | B&W

8 Moving story, remarkably based upon a real individual - John Merrick (beautifully played by John Hurt under masses of make-up). Merrick was massively deformed and was dubbed the Elephant Man by the freak show where he lived until being rescued by a Victorian doctor (Hopkins). Degraded, beaten and humiliated, Merrick is at last given a chance to gain some dignity and respect for himself. This is the story of a man's struggle to survive and achieve dignity against hopeless odds. Beautiful period details. Top performances. 8 Oscar nominations. Unforgettable.

Sex · Nud · Viol · Lang · AdSit

A: *Anthony Hopkins, John Hurt, Anne Bancroft, John Gielgud, Wendy Hiller, Freddie Jones*

© PARAMOUNT HOME VIDEO 1347

ELMER GANTRY

D: Richard Brooks — 147 m

NR | DMA | 1960 | COLOR

9 Provocative and juicy Sinclair Lewis drama about phony evangelism in the Bible belt during the 1920s. This story is just as valid today, and maybe more so, than when it was released. Lancaster plays a salesman who worms his way into a barnstorming evangelist's group and transforms it into a money machine. But everything is jeopardized when a prostitute and old girlfriend (Jones) shows up. Lancaster and Jones both won acting Oscars. Director Brooks won an Oscar, plus there were nominations for Best Picture and Score. This is a must see.

Sex · Nud · Viol · Lang · AdSit

A: *Burt Lancaster, Jean Simmons, Dean Jagger, Arthur Kennedy, Shirley Jones, Patti Page*

Distributed By MGM/UA Home Video M301601

ELVIS - THE MOVIE

D: John Carpenter — 117 m

NR | DMA MUS | 1979 | COLOR

9 Highly regarded and excellent depiction of Elvis's life, from rising from poverty as a truck driver to headlining in Las Vegas showrooms. Russell won universal acclaim for his right-on portrait of The King. His became the standard for the comparison of all other impersonators. This was a made-for-TV production, but is far better than that might indicate. It was one of the highest rated TV movies of all time. Excellent acting support came from Shelly Winters as Elvis's mother.

Sex · Nud · Viol · Lang · AdSit

A: *Kurt Russell, Shelley Winters, Season Hubley, Pat Hingle, Bing Russell*

© LIVE HOME VIDEO 4080

D M A

EMERALD FOREST, THE

D: John Boorman — 114 m

R | ACT DMA | 1985 | COLOR

8 Fascinating story - even more so because it is based on fact. An American engineer (Boothe), who is in the Amazonian jungle to build a dam, has his son Tommy kidnapped by a tribe called The Invisible People. He spends the next ten years trying to find his son, only to be rescued by Tommy as Boothe is being chased by another tribe called The Fierce People. However, Tommy is now a grown man, a warrior, and a citizen of an entirely alien culture. Respectful and realistic depiction of primitive peoples and an intriguing look into another world.

Sex · Nud · Viol · Lang · AdSit

A: *Powers Boothe, Meg Foster, Charley Boorman, Dira Pass, Estee Chandler, Tetchie Agbayani*

© NEW LINE HOME VIDEO 2179

EMPIRE OF THE SUN

D: Steven Spielberg — 154 m

PG | DMA | 1987 | COLOR

6 Epic in length, grand scale and beautifully photographed. An upper-class British family living in pre-WWII Shanghi experiences all the luxuries available in their colonial lifestyle. But when war breaks out, they flee in terror with the common masses. However, in the panic their young son (Bale) is left behind and becomes a Japanese POW. A privileged boy who is now growing up in a place of no privileges, Bale is "adopted" by an amoral American seaman and scavenger (Malkovich), but he learns to survive on his own. Long and slow. Bale is marvelous. Film purists will increase the rating.

Sex · Nud · Viol · Lang · AdSit

A: *Christian Bale, John Malkovich, Miranda Richardson, Nigel Havers*

© WARNER HOME VIDEO 11753

END, THE

D: Burt Reynolds — 100 m

R | COM DMA | 1978 | COLOR

8 This is an outrageous black comedy and it is absolutely hysterical in places, but it is also slow in others. Burt Reynolds is a user-type of a guy who is stunned to discover that he is going to die from a rare disease. He can hardly believe his misfortune, but worse - nobody seems to care. So, he decides to commit suicide to get it all over. But when his attempt fails, he is sent to a mental institution. Now he is really desperate. There, he meets and befriends a crazy killer (loveably weird Dom DeLuise) who agrees, as a special favor, to kill him. This is a really left-handed comedy, but it definitely has some hysterical moments.

Sex · Nud · Viol · Lang · AdSit

A: *Burt Reynolds, Sally Field, Dom DeLuise, Joanne Woodward, David Steinberg, Pat O'Brien*

Distributed By MGM/UA Home Video M203102

END OF THE ROAD

D: Avram Avakian — 110 m

X | DMA | 1970 | COLOR

6 Very peculiar but haunting story about an unstable and depressed college professor (Keach) who has just been released from a mental institution and who has an illicit affair with a fellow professor's wife. Jones plays a quack of a doctor who gives Keach bizarre shock treatments for his depression. Excellent performances by all, but the heavy use of symbolism makes for difficult and sometimes confused watching. Some critics rate this film quite highly, others despise it. The original X rating would be more of an R today. Obviously not for the casual observer.

Sex · Nud · Viol · Lang · AdSit

A: *Stacy Keach, Dorothy Tristan, Harris Yulin, James Earl Jones, Grayson Hall, James Coco*

© CBS/FOX VIDEO 7290

ENEMIES, A LOVE STORY

R | DMA COM ROM | 1989 | COLOR

D: Paul Mazursky 121 m

8 Highly regarded and much talked about film of a Jewish refugee (Silver) and Holocaust survivor who is living in America after WWII. He is in the unfortunate position of juggling the three separate women that he loves, each in different ways. He is alive because a Polish family hid him and, largely out of gratitude, he married their daughter - a simple domestic woman who is totally dedicated to homemaking. He is involved in a passionate affair with a fiery married woman. And he has learned that his first wife, who he thought was dead, isn't. Intelligent and sophisticated but slow.

Sex Nud Viol Lang AdSit

A: Ron Silver, Anjelica Huston, Lena Olin, Margaret Sophie Stein, Alan King, Judith Malina

© VIDEO TREASURES M012613

EUROPA EUROPA

R | FOR DMA | 1991 | COLOR

D: Agnieszka Holland 115 m

8 Utterly fascinating true story of survival from WWII. 13-year-old Jew, Simon Perel, and his family escape Germany to Poland in 1938 only to be overrun there by the Nazi blitzkrieg in 1939. Caught away from home, he is picked up by a Russian soldier and placed in an orphanage where he learns Russian. He first masquerades as a Communist, and later as a Hitler Youth until is drafted into the German army where he become an interpreter. For seven harrowing years he survives by adapting as needed - all the while desperate to hide the biggest symbol of his Jewishness. He is circumcised. Subtitles.

Sex Nud Viol Lang AdSit

A: Marco Hofschneider, Rene Hofschneider, Julie Delpy, Ashley Wanninger, Piotr Kozlowski

© ORION PICTURES CORPORATION 5064

ENTRE NOUS

PG | FOR DMA | 1983 | COLOR

D: Diane Kurys 110 m

9 Intelligent and poignant adult drama - a big hit in the art theaters and it received a nomination for Best Foreign Film. It is an autobiographical work depicting the director's own mother's story and begins in France during the German occupation. A Russian Jewish woman escapes prison by agreeing to marry a total stranger. Another woman sees her husband shot in front of her eyes. Later, in 1952, these two women are brought together by tragedy and meet again by chance. A relationship develops and both leave their husbands to start a new life together. The subject of the film is their deep friendship, but there is a subtle hint of lesbianism present as well. Subtitles.

Sex Nud Viol Lang AdSit

A: Isabelle Huppert, Miou-Miou, Guy Marchand, Jean-Pierre Bacri

Distributed By MGM/UA Home Video M800492

EVERYBODY'S ALL AMERICAN

R | DMA | 1988 | COLOR

D: Taylor Hackford 127 m

8 Eye-opening portrait of an aging sports hero. Quaid plays a 1950s college football hero who marries the homecoming queen and then enters a career in professional football. All is perfect, but their idyllic life is short-circuited when his career is suddenly over. He is no longer a hero. He becomes a caricature of his former self. His wife has always been in the background, but now she must be strong if they are to survive. Lange is sympathetic and entirely believable in her role as a woman torn between her love for her husband and her fear for what he has become.

Sex Nud Viol Lang AdSit

A: Jessica Lange, Dennis Quaid, Timothy Hutton, John Goodman, Carl Lumbly, Ray Barker

© WARNER HOME VIDEO 11827

EQUUS

R | DMA | 1977 | COLOR

D: Sidney Lumet 145 m

7 Interesting and absorbing adaptation of a major stage success (although not as good). Richard Burton is a psychiatrist who is given the task of examining a young stable boy's intense sexual and mystical fascination with horses - after he blinds six of them. This is a thought-provoking drama about a passion and insanity which stemmed from the boy's oddly-directed religious fervor. As Burton explores his patient more and more deeply, he also learns more and more about himself. Burton won a Best Actor nomination. This was also his last quality role before his death.

Sex Nud Viol Lang AdSit

A: Richard Burton, Peter Firth, Colin Blakely, Joan Plowright, Eileen Atkins, Jenny Agutter

Distributed By MGM/UA Home Video M700675

EXECUTIONER'S SONG, THE

NR | DMA CRM | 1982 | COLOR

D: Lawrence Schiller 136 m

9 Riveting true tale of condemned killer Gary Gilmore's struggle to get Utah authorities to execute him. Norman Mailer adapted his book to create this excellent made-for-TV movie about a socially maladjusted killer who responds to his isolation by striking out like a vicious and utterly cruel animal. The story is also about his doomed love affair with a desperate young woman. Convicted for the senseless murder of two people, Gilmore sought to die with dignity. On January 17, 1977 he got his wish. Brilliant efforts by both Jones and Arquette. Scenes have been added to the TV version.

Sex Nud Viol Lang AdSit

A: Tommy Lee Jones, Rosanna Arquette, Christine Lahti, Eli Wallach, Steven Keats, Jordon Clarke

© LIVE HOME VIDEO 215-507

ESCAPE FROM SOBIBOR

PG-13 | DMA SUS | 1987 | COLOR

D: Jack Gold 120 m

8 Exciting drama based upon the real-life 1943 breakout of prisoners from a Nazi concentration camp. An exceptional cast and script, plus top-notch production values, bring a vibrant sense of reality to this story of the largest-ever prisoner escape from a Nazi death camp. A captured Russian officer, a Polish Jew and a seamstress lead the camp against impossible odds in this last-ditch effort to survive. Alan Arkin in particular puts in a standout performance. Originally made for TV.

Sex Nud Viol Lang AdSit

A: Alan Arkin, Rutger Hauer, Joanna Pacula, Hartman Becker, Jack Shepherd

© LIVE HOME VIDEO 69004

EXECUTION OF PRIVATE SLOVIK, THE

NR | DMA WAR | 1974 | COLOR

D: Lamont Johnson 122 m

8 Riveting true-life account of the first American soldier to be executed for desertion since the Civil War. World War II soldier Eddie Slovik was at first disqualified from active military duty during the war because of a teenage criminal record. However, he was eventually called up and placed in a front line position. Then, under an enemy attack, Slovik froze, could not fire his rifle and deserted his position. This action led to his eventual court-martial and execution by firing squad. Sheen's performance as Slovik is masterful. Powerful drama.

Sex Nud Viol Lang AdSit

A: Martin Sheen, Mariclare Costello, Ned Beatty, Gary Busey, Matt Clark, Ben Hammer

© MCA/UNIVERSAL HOME VIDEO, INC. 80569

E.T. THE EXTRA-TERRESTRIAL

PG | SF DMA CLD | 1982 | COLOR

D: Steven Spielberg 115 m

10 Huge blockbuster hit and instant classic. Wonderful, warm story of a lovable little visitor from another world who is stranded on Earth and befriended by a 10-year-old boy. Elliott tries to keep little E.T. hidden, but soon the rest of his family knows the secret and then they are all helping to hide the little guy from the government people who are now out to capture him. But, all little E.T. wants is just to go home. No wonder this is the #1 box office hit of all time. It has captured the hearts and imaginations of all who have ever watched it - all over the world.

Sex Nud Viol Lang AdSit

A: Dee Wallace, Henry Thomas, Peter Coyote, Robert MacNaughton, Drew Barrymore, K.C. Martel

© MCA/UNIVERSAL HOME VIDEO, INC. 77012

EXODUS

NR | DMA ACT | 1960 | COLOR

D: Otto Preminger 213 m

7 Major box office hit which tells the story of the birth of the Jewish state, beginning with the resettlement of Palestine after World War II. The primary story line follows Paul Newman as a major political and military leader who guides European refugees after the war into British controlled Palestine. He later leads fighters in the resistance movement to win independence from Britain and separation from the Arabs, to form a separate Jewish state. The lives of several other characters are followed, including Sal Mineo as a young Auschwitz survivor who joins a terrorist group.

Sex Nud Viol Lang AdSit

A: Paul Newman, Eva Marie Saint, Lee J. Cobb, Sal Mineo, Ralph Richardson

Distributed By MGM/UA Home Video M301455

EUREKA

R | DMA | 1983 | COLOR

D: Nicolas Roeg 130 m

6 Hackman puts in another yeoman performance, this time as a prospector in Canada's northern wilderness who stumbles frozen into a cave and discovers a huge gold deposit. Twenty years later, he has bought his own island in the Caribbean, but - his wife is an alcoholic, his daughter is seduced away by a gigolo and some ruthless mobsters want his island for a casino. Hackman is so paranoid, he can't enjoy anything he has and his life is crumbling around him. Very odd, but morbidly fascinating drama.

Sex Nud Viol Lang AdSit

A: Gene Hackman, Theresa Russell, Rutger Hauer, Jane Lapotaire, Mickey Rourke, Joe Pesci

Distributed By MGM/UA Home Video M800683

EYE OF THE NEEDLE

R | SUS ACT DMA | 1981 | COLOR

D: Richard Marquand 112 m

8 Very taut espionage thriller. Sutherland plays a ruthless Nazi agent known as The Needle because of his penchant for killing with a switchblade knife. Operating in England, he learns of the plans for D-Day and makes a mad dash for the coast where he is to meet a U-boat. But a storm throws him up on the rocks of a desolate Scottish island inhabited only by a lonely and sexually frustrated woman, her crippled husband and young son. She allows Sutherland to seduce her and to win her trust - then she discovers what he is. She must stop him. High-tension. Very Good.

Sex Nud Viol Lang AdSit

A: Donald Sutherland, Ian Bannen, Kate Nelligan, Christopher Cazenove, Philip Martin Brown

Distributed By MGM/UA Home Video M301303

FABULOUS BAKER BOYS, THE

D: Steve Kloves — 116 m

R | ROM COM DMA | 1989 | COLOR

8 Excellent and curious character study of two piano playing brothers barely surviving by playing small clubs. Business has been even worse lately - that is, until they hire a sultry ex-hooker (Pfeiffer) as their vocalist. Suddenly they're in demand. Beau is excellent as the stalwart older brother who wants to hold the act together and play like they always have. But younger brother Jeff yearns to play solo jazz. Things come to an explosive head when Jeff and sexy Pfeiffer can't keep their hands off each other. Things will never be the same.

Sex · Nud · Viol · Lang · AdSit

A: Jeff Bridges, Michelle Pfeiffer, Beau Bridges, Ellie Raab, Jennifer Tilly

© LIVE HOME VIDEO 68910

FACE IN THE CROWD, A

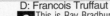

D: Elia Kazan — 126 m

NR | DMA | 1957 | B&W

8 Fascinating early look at the power of television. A big, likable, teddy bear of a man, who tells stories and picks his guitar, becomes a hit on TV. He is Lonesome Rhodes (Andy Griffith). Overnight he goes from being in the jailhouse to becoming a major TV star. Soon he is overpowered by sex, booze, corruption and power, saying: "I'm not just an entertainer. I'm a force, a power!" He's become monster. This film made Griffith into a star and also introduced Lee Remick. Neal plays the reporter who discovered him, made him into a star and eventually destroys him. Still relevant.

Sex · Nud · Viol · Lang · AdSit

A: Andy Griffith, Patricia Neal, Anthony Franciosa, Walter Matthau, Lee Remick, Kay Medford

© WARNER HOME VIDEO 34075

FAHRENHEIT 451

D: Francois Truffaut — 112 m

NR | SF DMA | 1966 | COLOR

6 This is Ray Bradbury's well-known story about a time in the future when society's forbidden books are burned, and readers are hunted down as criminals by a special corp of "firemen." One fireman (Werner) questions his job and his life when a young rebel (Christie) challenges him and changes his mind. He is now forced to choose between a safe life and intellectual freedom. Interesting and different subject matter, but slow-moving and has a reserved quality which prevents you from becoming deeply involved with the characters.

Sex · Nud · Viol · Lang · AdSit

A: Julie Christie, Oskar Werner, Cyril Cusack, Anton Diffring, Jeremy Spenser, Bee Duffell

© MCA/UNIVERSAL HOME VIDEO, INC. 80199

FAIL SAFE

D: Sidney Lumet — 111 m

NR | SUS DMA | 1964 | B&W

9 High-tension nail-biter about what might happen if the US had accidentally bombed Moscow. Through a series of errors, US bombers armed with nuclear weapons are sent to bomb Moscow. They are under strict orders that, once they are on the way, nothing - not even direct orders from the President - will turn them back. The tension becomes intense as time runs down, military leaders struggle to call the planes back and world leaders try to determine what to do to prevent total destruction. Very intelligent production.

Sex · Nud · Viol · Lang · AdSit

A: Henry Fonda, Walter Matthau, Fritz Weaver, Larry Hagman, Frank Overton, Sorrell Booke

© GOODTIMES 4228

FALCON AND THE SNOWMAN, THE

D: John Schlesinger — 131 m

R | DMA | 1985 | COLOR

8 How could two young friends, both from affluent California families, be convicted of treason. Boyce is an idealist who is disillusioned after discovering, through his top-secret job at TRW, that the CIA has meddled in the internal affairs of Australia. His friend Lee is a heroin addict and a thrill junkie. So the two just decide to sell secrets to the Russians, which they do - that is until they get caught in 1977. Very strong performances, particularly by Penn, paint a fascinating portrait of these two very strange characters.

Sex · Nud · Viol · Lang · AdSit

A: Timothy Hutton, Sean Penn, Pat Hingle, Lori Singer, Richard Dysart, Chris Makepeace

© LIVE HOME VIDEO VA5073

FALLING DOWN

D: Joel Schumacher — 113 m

R | ACT DMA | 1993 | COLOR

8 A striking portrait of a man who thought that he played by the rules but he never won the game, and now he has lost control. Michael Douglas plays D-FENS (a character known only by his personal license plate). D-FENS is an ordinary guy except that: he has lost his job, his wife, his child, his home - and his mind has cracked. Stuck in stalled freeway traffic, D-FENS abandons his car to begin a cross-city walk in a single-minded attempt to get "home." But, at each injustice or slight he encounters along the way, he lashes out, sometimes with vicious vengeance. Robert Duvall is a cop on his last day, who tracks D-FENS home.

Sex · Nud · Viol · Lang · AdSit

A: Michael Douglas, Robert Duvall, Barbara Hershey, Rachel Ticotin, Frederic Forrest, Tuesday Weld

© WARNER HOME VIDEO 12648

FALL OF THE ROMAN EMPIRE, THE

D: Anthony Mann — 182 m

NR | DMA ACT | 1964 | COLOR

8 Epic production with thrilling and spectacular action scenes, combined with intelligent scripting, depict the moral and political decay inside Imperial Rome. Emperor Commodus's actions bring about the fall of Rome, in spite of efforts by reformers to change it. Strong cast of beautiful people, beautiful sets and major budget, combined with intelligence, spectacle and action, create fascinating watching.

Sex · Nud · Viol · Lang · AdSit

A: Sophia Loren, Stephen Boyd, James Mason, Alec Guinness, Christopher Plummer, Anthony Quayle

© BEST FILM & VIDEO CORP. 214

FAMILY, THE

D: Ettore Scola — 128 m

PG | FOR DMA | 1987 | COLOR

7 Nominated in 1987 for the Best Foreign Film Oscar. This is a colorful bittersweet portrait of the people who have populated one man's long life. The story is set almost entirely in his living room. The patriarch of an Italian family (Grassman) is celebrating his 80th birthday. As his relatives arrive and he is getting ready, the story of his and his family's lives are told as a series of flashbacks. The past 80 years have brought a lot of changes to the family. They have endured war, love, hate, triumph and tragedy - all of the things that go along with living a rich existence. Dubbed.

Sex · Nud · Viol · Lang · AdSit

A: Vittorio Gassman, Fanny Ardant, Andrea Occhipinti, Stefania Sandrelli, Jo Ciampa, Philippe Noiret

© LIVE HOME VIDEO 5268

FAMILY BUSINESS

D: Sidney Lumet — 113 m

R | DMA CRM | 1989 | COLOR

6 Three superb leads make this a watchable and enjoyable film. A bright MIT scholar (Broderick) conjures up the perfect crime and enlists the aid of a veteran thief, his Granddad (Connery), to carry it off. His Dad (Hoffman) violently disapproves of the caper, but decides that the only way to protect his son is to go along with the plan. Everything goes well until Broderick gets caught. The Dad and Granddad, who have never liked each other, find themselves in the moral dilemma of their lives, they can free the boy if they turn themselves in.

Sex · Nud · Viol · Lang · AdSit

A: Sean Connery, Dustin Hoffman, Matthew Broderick, Rosana DeSoto, Janet Carroll, Victoria Jackson

© COLUMBIA TRISTAR HOME VIDEO 70233

FANNY

D: Joshua Logan — 128 m

NR | ROM DMA | 1961 | COLOR

8 Moving love story that received five Oscar nominations, including Best Picture. Leslie Caron is Fanny, a beautiful young girl who falls in love with Marius, a bartender's son. They live in the French seaport town of Marseilles. Marius has two loves, Fanny and the sea. The two lovers give in to their passions, but he leaves to go to sea, unknowingly leaving her pregnant. To protect her family, she enters into a marriage of convenience with a loving but much older man (Chevalier). When Marius returns, she finds that her love for him has not diminished and three lives are thrown into turmoil.

Sex · Nud · Viol · Lang · AdSit

A: Leslie Caron, Maurice Chevalier, Charles Boyer, Horst Buchholz, Baccaloni, Lionel Jeffries

© WARNER HOME VIDEO 11159

FANNY AND ALEXANDER

D: Ingmar Bergman — 188 m

R | FOR DMA | 1983 | COLOR

7 A rewarding experience for patient sophisticated viewers. Set in turn-of-the-century Sweden, two young children are raised within an affluent and warm theatrical family. Life is exciting and fun. However, when their father dies, their mother is consoled by and marries a strict minister. That marriage requires them all to make severe adjustments in their lives. This is a rich tapestry of life in 1907 Sweden and a powerful indictment of religious excess. The story is largely viewed through the eyes of Alexander and is richly orchestrated in lavish period details. Demanding viewing, but richly rewarding.

Sex · Nud · Viol · Lang · AdSit

A: Pernilla Allwin, Bertil Guve, Ewa Froling, Jan Malmsjo, Harriet Andersson, Erland Josephson

© NEW LINE HOME VIDEO 2067

FAR AND AWAY

D: Ron Howard — 140 m

PG-13 | DMA WST ROM | 1992 | COLOR

8 Enjoyable, sweeping near-epic. A poor Irish tenant farmer (Cruise) is upset with the absentee landlord whom he blames for his father's death. He narrowly escapes dying in a duel with the man and escapes to America in 1890, along with the man's spoiled daughter (Kidman) in tow. Their first stop is Boston where he finds work as a bare-knuckle boxer and she plucks chickens. However, quickly they make their way west to attempt to claim free land in the great Oklahoma Land Rush. True, the story line is a little thin but the characters (Cruise and Kidman were married in real life) are a lot of fun to watch and the photography is grand.

Sex · Nud · Viol · Lang · AdSit

A: Tom Cruise, Nicole Kidman, Thomas Gibson, Colm Meaney, Barbara Babcock, Robert Prosky

© MCA/UNIVERSAL HOME VIDEO, INC. 81415

FAR AWAY, SO CLOSE

D: Wim Wenders 146 m

PG-13 | FOR FAN DMA | 1994 | COLOR | Sex | Nud | Viol | Lang | AdSit

8 Intriguing concept first used in 1988's WINGS OF DESIRE. Angels flitter around listening into the lives and thoughts of ordinary people. And, as in the earlier film, one angel longs to see and feel what it is like to be human. However, he wants to do more. He wants to do good. His exposure to real world of humans leads him to discover how ill-prepared he is, particularly for the aloneness of each human soul. Still, he struggles to learn and even gains some mild assistance from another former angel and now immigrant, but he is also struggling against an evil angel sent by the other side to foil his efforts.

A: Otto Sander, Peter Falk, Horst Buchholz, Natassia Kinski, Heinz Ruhmann, Willem Dafoe

© COLUMBIA TRISTAR HOME VIDEO 79968

FAREWELL MY CONCUBINE

D: Chen Kaige 157 m

R | FOR DMA | 1993 | COLOR | Sex | Nud | Viol | Lang | AdSit

8 An beautifully filmed epic import from mainland China which follows 50 years in the careers of two actors. The two meet as young boys and students at an unbelievably cruel acting school. There they become friends while finely honing their skills at performing one particular classic opera. They will perform it throughout their lives. It is about an ancient king and his concubine who died for him. All actors in Chinese opera are men and the man in the female role gives himself totally to his character, even off stage. The two act as though they are married, except in one way, and when a woman comes between them their relationship falters. Very long and Chinese opera is very shrill. Subtitles.

A: Leslie Cheung, Zhang Fengyi, Gong Li, Lu Qi, Ying Da

© MIRAMAX HOME ENTERTAINMENT 2522

FAR FROM THE MADDING CROWD

D: John Schlesinger 165 m

PG | ROM DMA | 1967 | COLOR | Sex | Nud | Viol | Lang | AdSit

8 Lovely and intelligent adaptation of Thomas Hardy's romance novel, set in Victorian England of 1874. A beautiful farm girl (Julie Christie) inherits her father's farm. She longs to be free from society's constraints and also to better her station in life. She is a sensual creature who is loved by three men and has a devastating effect on their lives. They are a common herdsman (Bates), a gentleman farmer (Finch) and a dashing calvaryman (Stamp). Her situation unleashes a firestorm of passions and conflict, but eventually yields love, too. Superb production values and beautiful photography.

A: Julie Christie, Terence Stamp, Alan Bates, Peter Finch, Prunella Ransome

Distributed By MGM/UA Home Video M300514

FAR PAVILIONS, THE

D: Peter Duffell 108 m

NR | ROM DMA | 1984 | COLOR | Sex | Nud | Viol | Lang | AdSit

8 Hugely popular. A grand tale of romance, love, treachery and intrigue. This was originally made as a miniseries for cable TV and is edited down here into feature film length. Ben Cross is a 19th-century Indian-born Englishman who was raised as a Hindu until he was 11. He has now returned to India as an army officer and he falls in love with his former childhood playmate (Irving), who is now a beautiful princess promised to an elderly Rajah (Brazzi). He is torn between his love for her and his duty to the crown. Huge international cast. Beautiful scenery and sets.

A: Ben Cross, Amy Irving, Omar Sharif, John Gielgud, Christopher Lee, Rossano Brazzi

© HBO VIDEO TVC2717

FAST TIMES AT RIDGEMONT HIGH

D: Amy Heckerling 91 m

R | COM DMA | 1982 | COLOR | Sex | Nud | Viol | Lang | AdSit

7 Entertaining and music-filled romp through a year in Southern California teenagedom. The primary focus is on high school senior Judge Reinhold and his freshman sister (Jennifer Jason Leigh). The primary occupations are shopping at the mall and initiation into the world of sex. This was a successful movie that provided some real insights into teenagers, and for a short while it was also a TV series. Teenagers will like it more than older heads. Particularly good is Penn playing a perpetually doped-out surfer and Ray Walston is hilarious as a sarcastic teacher.

A: Sean Penn, Jennifer Jason Leigh, Judge Reinhold, Brian Backer, Phoebe Cates, Ray Walston

© MCA/UNIVERSAL HOME VIDEO, INC. 77015

FAT CITY

D: John Huston 93 m

PG | DMA ACT | 1972 | COLOR | Sex | Nud | Viol | Lang | AdSit

8 Gritty realistic look at the hopeful, desperate and sleazy people of the fight game, and the least-savory aspects of a popular sport. It is probably one of the best films made about boxing, but it is also a portrayal of the lonesome life that goes with it. Very rich in atmosphere and characters. Stacy Keach plays a boozing has-been who goes back to the ring rather than to work at menial labor. Bridges is a hopeful young fighter, just beginning. Neither will give up his dreams. Excellent acting. Nomination for Best Supporting Actress.

A: Stacy Keach, Jeff Bridges, Susan Tyrrell, Nicholas Colasanto, Candy Clark

© COLUMBIA TRISTAR HOME VIDEO 60876

FAT MAN AND LITTLE BOY

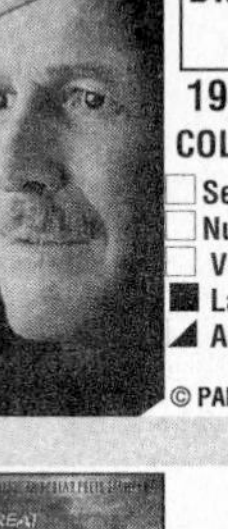
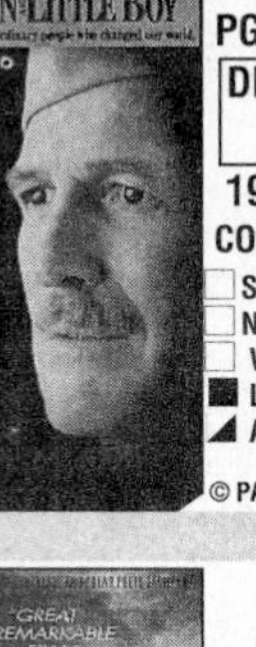

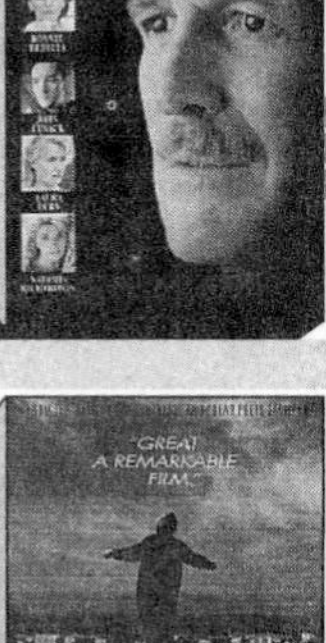

D: Roland Joffe 127 m

PG-13 | DMA | 1989 | COLOR | Sex | Nud | Viol | Lang | AdSit

6 Dramatization of the WWII story concerning the development of the atomic bomb. The primary focus of this film is upon two characters. Paul Newman is the hard-headed and driven General Leslie Groves - who will use any means necessary to ensure that the project proceeds on schedule. Dwight Schultz plays the brilliant physicist Robert Oppenheimer - who is both driven to complete his task and torn by the horror of what he is setting out to do. While this is neither a riveting drama nor an entirely accurate history lesson, it is still a realistic and involving depiction of the mood of the time.

A: Paul Newman, Dwight Schultz, John Cusack, Laura Dern, Natasha Richardson, Bonnie Bedelia

© PARAMOUNT HOME VIDEO 32252

FEARLESS

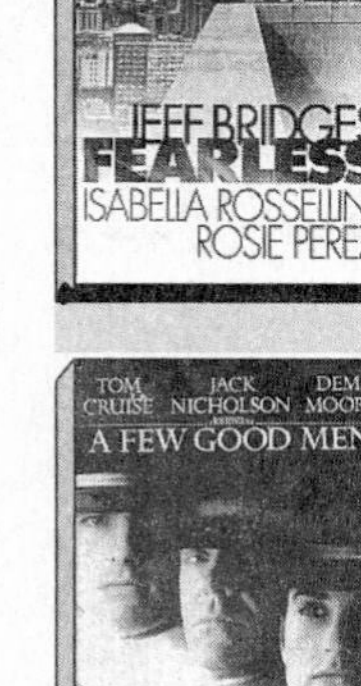

D: Peter Weir 122 m

R | DMA | 1993 | COLOR | Sex | Nud | Viol | Lang | AdSit

7 Very intense drama. Jeff Bridges is a man with a morbid fear of flying but who becomes transformed after he survives an air crash. The others who lived through the experience are all fearful, grieving and guilt-ridden, but he now feels invincible. However, while he is not dead, he is not alive either. Rosie Perez is a deeply religious young mother who has become totally withdrawn because she could not hold on to her baby son who was killed. So, these two emotional cripples are brought together by a psychiatrist hoping they can bring each other back to reality. Excellent acting, very high quality and it is interesting - but this is not entertainment. It is heavy and sometimes painful to watch.

A: Jeff Bridges, Isabella Rossellini, Tom Hulce, John Turturro, Benicio Del Toro

© WARNER HOME VIDEO 12986

FEW GOOD MEN, A

D: Rob Reiner 138 m

R | DMA SUS | 1992 | COLOR | Sex | Nud | Viol | Lang | AdSit

10 Terrific courtroom drama. Intelligent, classy and believable. A young Marine at Guantanamo base in Cuba, commanded by a gung-ho Colonel (Nicholson) dies an apparent victim of murder. Two Marines are arrested and charged, but Demi Moore is a military attorney who smells a coverup. She brings it to her superior's attention, who assigns a brilliant smart-aleck Harvard grad (Cruise) to the case instead of her. But, she wangles her way onto the team anyway. It is quickly learned that the death was an accident but that it resulted from an illegal order from commander Nicholson. How to prove it in court. Powerful personalities and performances. Dynamite!

A: Tom Cruise, Jack Nicholson, Demi Moore, Kevin Bacon, Kiefer Sutherland, Kevin Pollack

© COLUMBIA TRISTAR HOME VIDEO 27893

FIDDLER ON THE ROOF

D: Norman Jewison 180 m

G | MUS DMA | 1971 | COLOR | Sex | Nud | Viol | Lang | AdSit

8 Lavish production of the very entertaining and long-running Broadway hit musical. Anatevka is a small Russian Jewish village where milkman Tevye, his wife and their five daughters live. Poor Tevya tries to marry off his dowryless daughters to wealthy husbands, but his foolish daughters want to marry for love. All the while, the Jews of his town are being persecuted by the Czarist pograms. Rich in grand music, with memorable lyrics (some are now standards) and high production values. This production received five Oscar nominations - including Best Picture, Actor and Director.

A: Topol, Norman Crane, Leonard Frey, Molly Picon, Paul Mann, Rosalind Harris

Distributed By MGM/UA Home Video M201320

FIELD, THE

D: Jim Sheridan 113 m

PG-13 | DMA | 1990 | COLOR | Sex | Nud | Viol | Lang | AdSit

6 Beautifully photographed and wonderfully acted. The place is Ireland in the 1930s, in a very small poverty-ridden village. Bull McCabe (Harris), as his father did before him, has dedicated his life to transforming a three-acre rented piece of land into a fertile and lush field so that it can be passed down to his son. The woman who owns the field is now going to sell it at auction and a rich American wants it just so he can pave it over for his project. Bull can not accept this. This is a tale of unreasoning stubbornness and fierce community loyalties. Despite everything, this is a film one can only respect and admire, not truly enjoy.

A: Richard Harris, John Hurt, Sean Bean, Tom Berenger, Brenda Fricker, Frances Tomelty

© LIVE HOME VIDEO 68965

FIELD OF DREAMS

D: Phil Alden Robinson 106 m

PG | DMA FAN | 1989 | COLOR | Sex | Nud | Viol | Lang | AdSit

8 This was the feel-good movie of 1989 and a Best Picture nominee. Costner plays a dreamer, an Iowa farmer who hears a voice that says, "If you build it, he will come." After he convinces himself and his wife that he is not crazy, he sets out to build a baseball diamond in the middle of his corn field. Then, mystically and magically, Shoeless Joe Jackson of the Chicago White Sox of 1918, his father's hero, does come. Then Costner sets off to find a reclusive writer (Jones) who returns with Costner to witness the wonder. Soon a whole team of people, all with unfulfilled dreams, arrives at the magic corn field. Excellent acting but "corny".

A: Kevin Costner, Amy Madigan, Gaby Hoffman, Ray Liotta, Timothy Busfield, James Earl Jones

© MCA/UNIVERSAL HOME VIDEO, INC. 80884

FINGERS

R | DMA | 1978 | COLOR
■ Sex ■ Nud ■ Viol ■ Lang ■ AdSit

D: James Toback — 89 m

8 Fascinating but bizarre, and sometimes unappealing, story of a man torn between two extremely opposite worlds. Keitel is a man who can't be himself because he doesn't know who that is. He is trying to be a concert pianist for his mother and he is also a vicious debt collector for his loan-shark father. He does his best to please both parents, but can please neither. He is desperate for love and looks for it with women. But he gets into trouble there, too, when he falls for a black mobster's girlfriend. Extremely violent. Not for all tastes.

A: Harvey Keitel, Jim Brown, Tisa Farrow, Michael Gazzo, Tanya Roberts, Danny Aiello

© TURNER HOME ENTERTAINMENT 6299

FIRE DOWN BELOW

NR | DMA | 1957 | COLOR
☐ Sex ☐ Nud ☐ Viol ☐ Lang ◢ AdSit

D: Robert Parrish — 116 m

7 Sultry Rita Hayworth is a lady with a tainted past. She is a passenger on tramp steamer with Mitchum and Lemmon on a trip between islands in the Caribbean. Both men fall in love with her, compete against each other and deceive each other for her attentions. They become bitter rivals until an explosion below decks traps Lemmon. His friend Mitchum must now save him. While this is a well-worn story line, it is nonetheless very entertaining because of a top-flight cast which creates good characters and beautiful scenery - particularly sexy Hayworth.

A: Rita Hayworth, Robert Mitchum, Jack Lemmon, Anthony Newley, Herbert Lom

© COLUMBIA TRISTAR HOME VIDEO 60647

FIRM, THE

R | SUS ACT DMA | 1993 | COLOR
◢ Sex ☐ Nud ◢ Viol ■ Lang ■ AdSit

D: Sydney Pollack — m

8 Quite good thriller based on a blockbuster novel. Tom Cruise is a poor boy who has managed to graduate at the top of his Harvard law class and is recruited into a mysterious Memphis law firm with a huge salary. Only after he is in does he discover that he can't get out. The firm is a money-laundering machine for the Chicago mob. The FBI, on the other hand, sees him as their big opportunity to break the back of the mafia and is forcing him into becoming their snitch. If he doesn't help them, he'll go to jail. If he does, he will have to hide out forever. He is caught between two powerful forces who can crush him. Top-flight cast. Good, but book was better.

A: Tom Cruise, Jeanne Triplehorn, Gene Hackman, Holly Hunter, Ed Harris, Wilford Brimley

© PARAMOUNT HOME VIDEO 32523

FIRST BORN

PG-13 | DMA SUS | 1984 | COLOR
☐ Sex ☐ Nud ◢ Viol ◢ Lang ◢ AdSit

D: Michael Apted — 100 m

6 An intense and believable story of a struggling young divorced woman (Terry Garr), with two sons, who falls in love with tough guy Peter Weller. He moves in with them and later turns out to be an abusive cocaine dealer. His menacing presence becomes a real danger for all of them and it appears they are trapped. But help for the family comes from within when her oldest teenage son (Collett) stands up to Weller. Good performances make this a credible picture, in spite of its overly-violent conclusion.

A: Teri Garr, Peter Weller, Christopher Collet, Robert Downey, Jr., Corey Haim, Sarah Jessica Parker

© PARAMOUNT HOME VIDEO 1744

FISHER KING, THE

R | FAN DMA COM | 1991 | COLOR
◢ Sex ☐ Nud ■ Viol ■ Lang ■ AdSit

D: Terry Gilliam — 138 m

7 Complex, surreal and painful. One of those movies you won't know if you should love or hate, but it is poignant and it cuts right to the bone. When it was released, it created a lot of controversy for its portrayal of homelessness and mental illness (which were handled lightly at times and very heavy at others). Williams was a history teacher but now is an upbeat, but deranged, street person. Bridges is a New York radio shock jock who goes too far, is fired, is forced on the street and finds a strange savior in wacked-out Williams. Shocking, emotional, mystical and sometimes funny.

A: Robin Williams, Jeff Bridges, Mercedes Ruehl, Michael Jeter, Harry Shearer, John de Lancie

© COLUMBIA TRISTAR HOME VIDEO 70613

FISH HAWK

G | DMA CLD | 1979 | COLOR
☐ Sex ☐ Nud ☐ Viol ☐ Lang ◢ AdSit

D: Donald Shebib — 95 m

7 Fish Hawk is an old alcoholic Osage Indian living alone in the turn-of-the-century Ozarks. He is a lonely old man who is scorned by everyone. In his drunkenness one day, he kills his dog - one of the few friends he has. He vows to reform and to track down and kill a bear that has been terrorizing the town. In the woods, he meets a lonely young farm boy. They become friends and their friendship causes him to remember much of what he has forgotten. He vows to give up his old ways, but he also must leave his new friend to go back home to his people. A gentle story that is well done.

A: Will Sampson, Charles Fields, Geoffrey Bowes, Mary Pirie, Don Francks

© VIDEO TREASURES M297

F.I.S.T.

PG | DMA | 1978 | COLOR
☐ Sex ☐ Nud ◢ Viol ◢ Lang ◢ AdSit

D: Norman Jewison — 144 m

6 This is a well-produced film about the rise of a Hoffa-like character through the ranks of a trucker's union to eventually become its president. Stallone is an idealistic man who begins as a truck driver. He first becomes a union activist, then rises in the union. On his way up, he has accepted Mafia favors and he has learned some effective methods of his own. He has become as ruthless as the men he has replaced. Now, after a twenty-year rise to power, he runs headlong into Rod Steiger, a crusading US senator. Good production values and excellent performances, but it is predictable.

A: Sylvester Stallone, Rod Steiger, Peter Boyle, Melinda Dillon, David Huffman, Tony Lo Bianco

Distributed By MGM/UA Home Video M300337

FITZCARRALDO

PG | FOR DMA | 1982 | COLOR
☐ Sex ◢ Nud ◢ Viol ◢ Lang ◢ AdSit

D: Werner Herzog — 150 m

7 A fascinating portrait of a man obsessed. A crazy Irishman in turn-of-the-century Peru becomes obsessed with opening a shipping lane through the Amazonian rain forest to gain access to fourteen million rubber trees. His other burning goal is to open his own personal opera house in the middle of the Amazonian jungle. In order to do all this, he must drag a 320-ton steamboat over a mountain. An astonishing movie about one man's perseverance in the face of overwhelming odds. Involving, but slow moving.

A: Klaus Kinski, Claudia Cardinale, Paul Hittscher, Jose Lewgoy

© WARNER HOME VIDEO 24003

D M A

FIVE EASY PIECES

R | DMA | 1970 | COLOR
◢ Sex ◢ Nud ◢ Viol ■ Lang ■ AdSit

D: Bob Rafelson — 98 m

8 Best Picture nominee, plus a Best Actor nomination for Nicholson. This is also the film that made Nicholson a star. He is a drifter and a drunk going from job to job, and woman to woman. He is also a gifted classical pianist running from his wealthy, sophisticated and very stuffy family. While working as an oil rig laborer and living with a sexy but empty-headed waitress (Karen Black), he learns that his father, with whom he never got along, has been crippled by two strokes. He comes home to face his family and ultimately himself. A simple premise, excellent in its execution.

A: Jack Nicholson, Karen Black, Susan Anspach, Billy Green Bush, Sally Struthers, Ralph Waite

© COLUMBIA TRISTAR HOME VIDEO 60965

FIVE HEARTBEATS, THE

R | MUS DMA COM | 1991 | COLOR
☐ Sex ☐ Nud ◢ Viol ■ Lang ◢ AdSit

D: Robert Townsend — 120 m

8 Exuberant and fun (even if it's a little bit corny) ode to the heyday of Motown. This is the story of the rise of one fictional group to fame and is based loosely on the experiences of the R&B group, The Dells. It follows their rise from singing at amateur nights, to major success and then to personal failures. The film is not as cliched as it sounds. Although this is much-covered territory and is predictable, the characters are very likable and the music is fun and memory jogging. This is a good time, more so if you like this flavor of music or this was your era.

A: Robert Townsend, Michael Wright, Harry J. Lennix, Tico Wells, Diahann Carroll, Harold Nicholas

© FOXVIDEO 0630

FLAMINGO KID, THE

PG-13 | DMA COM | 1984 | COLOR
◢ Sex ☐ Nud ☐ Viol ◢ Lang ◢ AdSit

D: Garry Marshall — 98 m

8 A real charmer. Very enjoyable and a credible coming-of-age story that is set in 1963 but could almost have been at any time. Dillon is a Brooklyn high-school grad, from a blue collar background, who lands a job as cabana boy at a private beach club on Long Island. He is immediately overwhelmed by the affluence of everything around him, particularly by Richard Crenna, the club's wealthy resident card-sharp. He determines that this is the life for him - he doesn't need college. However, this summer proves to be the biggest education of his life. It is the summer he grows up.

A: Matt Dillon, Richard Crenna, Jessica Walter, Janet Jones, Hector Elizondo, Fisher Stevens

© LIVE HOME VIDEO VA5072

FLASHDANCE

R | DMA MUS | 1983 | COLOR
☐ Sex ◢ Nud ☐ Viol ◢ Lang ■ AdSit

D: Adrian Lyne — 95 m

8 Huge, huge hit. Jennifer Beals plays an 18-year-old welder during the day and an erotic dancer at a local bar at night - but, just until the time when she can enter formal dance school to become a ballerina. In the meantime, she enjoys being able to improvise dance sequences at the bar and the audiences love her. She is being courted by her rich and handsome boss but becomes incensed when he intervenes for her to get her admitted to school. Very slight story but high in energy and slightly sexy, with a pulsating soundtrack. It's been likened to an hour and a half of MTV.

A: Jennifer Beals, Michael Nouri, Lilia Skala, Cynthia Rhodes, Belinda Bauer, Phil Burns

© PARAMOUNT HOME VIDEO 1454

FLESH AND BONE

D: Steve Kloves 127 m

R | DMA CRM | 1993 | COLOR

7 Very unusual but yet compelling viewing. Dennis Quaid is Arlis, a 40ish loner, who spends his time driving from town to town, stocking his string of vending machines, sleeping with other men's wives and avoiding relationships. That is, until he runs across Kay (Meg Ryan), a hard-drinking woman escaping from a bad marriage. Arlis has good reason for being the way he is. His father (James Cann) is about as cold and mean as a man can be. 30 years ago, he had Arlis let him into a farmer's house and then shotgunned the man, his wife and son. The only one left live was a baby. Kay is an orphan and she carries with her a picture of that same farmhouse.

Sex / Nud / Viol / Lang / AdSit

A: Dennis Quaid, Meg Ryan, James Caan, Gweneth Paltrow, Scott Wilson, Christopher Rydell

© PARAMOUNT HOME VIDEO 32899

FLIGHT OF THE PHOENIX

D: Robert Aldrich 143 m

NR | SUS DMA ACT | 1966 | COLOR

9 This is a gripping adventure story about a small planeful of men who are forced to crash in the North African desert. They are all trapped in a very hostile environment with only one way out. They must rebuild the plane and fly it out. Tension steadily builds as the men struggle both to endure the extreme rigors of desert survival and to rebuild the plane. An excellent international cast provides credibility and realism to an excellent script. Plus, there is a really unique twist as the climax builds. Very highly recommended viewing.

Sex / Nud / Viol / Lang / AdSit

A: James Stewart, Richard Attenborough, Peter Finch, Hardy Kruger, Ernest Borgnine, George Kennedy

© FOXVIDEO 1221

FLOATING WEEDS

D: Yasurjiro Ozu 119 m

NR | DMA | 1959 | COLOR

10 Japanese director Ozu is famed for his careful use of visuals -- motion and camera -- and this film is highly regarded as one of his best. This is one of his last works and is a remake of his silent version from 1934. An aging actor returns, with his troup, to visit a remote island town. There he is reunited with a former lover and his illegitimate son who believes him to be his uncle. But, the actor's growing desire to reclaim his family makes his current mistress jealous and she viciously plots against him - including having a member of the troup seduce his son. Critically hailed, this one is for sophisticated audiences and students of film only. Subtitles.

Sex / Nud / Viol / Lang / AdSit

A: Ganjiro Kakamura, Haruko Sugimura, Hiroshi Kawaguchi, Machiko Kyo

© HOME VISION FLO 050

FLY, THE

D: Kurt Neumann 94 m

NR | SF DMA HOR | 1958 | B&W

9 This is a superior science fiction story. A scientist, experimenting with a machine that disintegrates matter in one place and reintegrates it again in another place, has a serious accident when his genes are mixed with those of a household fly. His head has become attached to the fly's body, and vice versa. He is now a gruesome freak struggling to return to normal. This film has become a cult favorite for very good reason. It was produced with care, high production values, good special effects and good acting. It was remade in 1986 in an equally good but much more grizzly manner.

Sex / Nud / Viol / Lang / AdSit

A: David Hedison, Patricia Owens, Vincent Price, Herbert Marshall, Kathleen Freeman

© FOXVIDEO 1190

FLY, THE

D: David Cronenberg 96 m

R | SF HOR DMA | 1986 | COLOR

8 Equally good (but much more graphic and intense) remake of the 1958 classic science fiction horror story. A brilliant scientist has built a matter transportation device which he decides to try out on himself. Unknown to him, a fly is in the chamber with him when the machine is activated and their genes are mixed together. He becomes horribly disfigured. Very interesting premise, combined with a credible love story. Excellent makeup won an Oscar.

Sex / Nud / Viol / Lang / AdSit

A: Jeff Goldblum, Geena Davis, John Getz, Joy Boushel, Les Carlson

© FOXVIDEO 1503

FOOL FOR LOVE

D: Robert Altman 108 m

R | DMA ROM | 1985 | COLOR

6 Arty play about a cowboy/stuntman drifter (Shepard) who continues to pursue a romance with an unsettled woman (Basinger) who has rejected him, but yet retains strong feelings for him. These two meet up at a seedy motel at the edge of nowhere to work out their problems. A series of flashbacks reveal that they both have a common kinship relationship with a mysterious character (Stanton). Very intense performances by two very competent actors, but it is hard to develop warm feelings for either of them. Will appeal most to fans of more adventurous types of drama.

Sex / Nud / Viol / Lang / AdSit

A: Sam Shepard, Kim Basinger, Harry Dean Stanton, Randy Quaid, Martha Crawford

Distributed By MGM/UA Home Video M800894

FOOL KILLER, THE

D: Servando Gonzalez 100 m

NR | DMA SUS | 1965 | B&W

7 Unusual adventure story in which George, a 12-year-old runaway orphan boy in the post-Civil War South, rides the rails. He strikes up a relationship with a crusty old-timer who intrigues him with stories of an eight-foot-tall axe-wielding murderer who is supposedly roaming the countryside. He calls him the "fool killer." Later, young George teams up with a tormented, very tall war veteran who has lost his memory. They travel together, but slowly George begins to fear that his new companion may, in fact, be the fool killer. Somewhat arty and offbeat, but it definitely has its moments.

Sex / Nud / Viol / Lang / AdSit

A: Anthony Perkins, Edward Albert, Dana Elcar, Henry Hull, Salome Jens, Arnold Moss

© REPUBLIC PICTURES HOME VIDEO 1352

FOOTLOOSE

D: Herbert Ross 107 m

PG | DMA | 1984 | COLOR

7 When big-city kid Bacon moves into a small town, he finds a few surprises in store for him. The biggest surprise is that dancing is outlawed. Bible belt minister Lithgow has taken it upon himself to institute the ban in their little town. However, when Bacon falls for the minister's daughter, the two team up to make a formidable opponent in the battle to bring back fun. The memorable score did very well on the charts, and Bacon's spirited determination makes this a "feel good" film that's especially well suited for younger teenagers.

Sex / Nud / Viol / Lang / AdSit

A: Kevin Bacon, Lori Singer, John Lithgow, Dianne Wiest, Christopher Penn, Sarah Jessica Parker

© PARAMOUNT HOME VIDEO 1589

FORBIDDEN CHOICES

D: Jennifer Warren 109 m

R | DMA | 1995 | COLOR

7 The Beans lived across the road from Earlene Pomerleau. They were dirt poor, crude, ill-mannered and extremely independent. Earlene watched them live their lives through her picture window. There were countless kids whose parentage wasn't always clear. Earlene's father despised them, but Earlene envied their free spirit and the way they stuck together. They lived life. They always had each other and they were never alone. This is the story of the Beans as told by Earlene. It also became her story as her resistance gave way to her curiosity, and to her feelings for the tortured Beale Bean. Curiously interesting. More than a soap opera. It did not get the attention it deserved.

Sex / Nud / Viol / Lang / AdSit

A: Martha Plimpton, Kelly Lynch, Rutger Hauer, Patrick McGaw, Richard Sanders, Michael MacRae

© LIVE HOME VIDEO 69981

FOR KEEPS

D: John G. Avildsen 98 m

PG-13 | COM DMA | 1988 | COLOR

7 Bittersweet coming-of-age film where growing up happens REAL fast. Ringwold and Batinkoff are two very popular high school kids with everything going for them: they are in love, have good grades, friends and college prospects. Then, she becomes pregnant. Their parents come unglued, so the kids leave to be on their own and are married. But it is soon very plain that things are now drastically different and they are never going to be the same again. This is an entertaining and light-hearted comedy, but it has a very serious undercurrent and contains documentary footage of a live birth.

Sex / Nud / Viol / Lang / AdSit

A: Molly Ringwald, Randall Batinkoff, Miriam Flynn, Kenneth Mars, Conchata Ferrell

© COLUMBIA TRISTAR HOME VIDEO 67005

FORREST GUMP

D: Robert Zemeckis 142 m

PG-13 | DMA COM | 1994 | COLOR

10 This was a monster hit. Both critics and general audiences loved it. It won 6 Oscars out of 13 nominations, including Best Picture, Actor and Director. It is the totally captivating story of a simple-minded man with a strange destiny. Forrest has an IQ of only 75, yet he has a heart that is unfailingly true. His strong legs earned him a football scholarship and a college degree. His single-minded determination caused him to repeatedly go back into a Vietnam battle to retrieve his friends and so he won the Congressional Medal of Honor. Forrest cannot understand much of what happens to him and around him. He focuses upon the simple truths...and so reminds us of them also. Wonderful.

Sex / Nud / Viol / Lang / AdSit

A: Tom Hanks, Robin Wright, Salley Field, Gary Sinise, Mykelti Williamson

© PARAMOUNT HOME VIDEO 32583

FOR THE BOYS

D: Mark Rydell 145 m

R | DMA COM | 1991 | COLOR

8 Bittersweet entertainment. Midler and Caan are a long-time USO act. They cut it up on stage and have a ball entertaining troops - with Caan being a stuffy straightman and Milder's spicy tongue constantly dishing out surprises. With 50 years and three wars between them, each has helped the other through a myriad of lifetime troubles and triumphs, but when Midler's son is killed in the Vietnam War and Cann speaks of the honor of dying in battle, their long-time partnership comes to a rapid end. What will it take to reunite the pair that America so loves? Sentimental and rich with emotion.

Sex / Nud / Viol / Lang / AdSit

A: Bette Midler, James Caan, George Segal, Patrick O'Neal, Christopher Rydell, Arye Gross

© FOXVIDEO 5595

D M A

FOUR HORSEMEN OF THE APOCALYPSE

D: Vincente Minnelli 154 m

NR | DMA | 1962 | COLOR

7 This is a large-scale drama set in a Paris that is on the brink of war. It is the story about a wealthy family whose member's politics become divided and the family's loyalty is torn. Brothers join opposing sides as the world gets set to tear itself apart. Brother will fight brother. Searing drama of love, honor and passion. The title refers to the biblical story of the end of the earth when it is visited by four horsemen: Conquest, War, Pestilence and Death. This is an entertaining remake of the superior 1921 classic silent movie with Valentino, but updated from WWI to WWII.

Sex / Nud / Viol / Lang / AdSit

A: Glenn Ford, Ingrid Thulin, Lee J. Cobb, Charles Boyer, Paul Henreid

Distributed By MGM/UA Home Video M300650

FOUR SEASONS, THE

D: Alan Alda 109 m

PG | COM DMA | 1981 | COLOR

7 A bittersweet, warm comedy about three middle-class couples who have always been very close friends and who vacation together once during each season of the year. They joke together and share each other's pain and joys - that is, until one couple divorces. Now the whole group relationship has to be reevaluated. This is generally endearing and entertaining and has some genuinely funny moments, but it's also a little too talky sometimes. Alda was Oscar-nominated for both acting and directing.

Sex / Nud / Viol / Lang / AdSit

A: Alan Alda, Carol Burnett, Len Carlou, Sandy Dennis, Rita Moreno, Jack Weston

© MCA/UNIVERSAL HOME VIDEO, INC. 77003

FOXES

D: Adrian Lyne 106 m

R | DMA | 1980 | COLOR

7 Touchingly realistic film about four teenage girls who share an apartment in suburban Los Angeles. These are girls who don't come from "Leave It To Beaver" families. Each girl has problems - but the story's primary focus is upon Foster's attempt to protect her sweet but irresponsible girlfriend, and her own personal struggle to maintain some sort of normal home life with her neurotic mother. Involving, memorable and meaningful. Unduly ignored by critics at the time of its release.

Sex / Nud / Viol / Lang / AdSit

A: Jodie Foster, Cherie Currie, Scott Baio, Sally Kellerman, Randy Quaid, Louis Smith

Distributed By MGM/UA Home Video M203087

FRANCES

D: Graeme Clifford 134 m

R | DMA | 1982 | COLOR

9 Poignant and chilling tale of a tormented woman whose only fault was being independent at a time when it wasn't allowed - and it destroyed her. Jessica Lange is absolutely brilliant in her depiction of the real-life character Francis Farmer. As teenager, her contest-winning essay launched her on a promising path that would let her taste the glories of stardom in Hollywood and Broadway. However, through time, her independent nature, plus too much booze and pills, set her in conflict with powerful forces. That led to personal torment, a mental institution and obscurity. Excellent. Unforgettable.

Sex / Nud / Viol / Lang / AdSit

A: Jessica Lange, Kim Stanley, Sam Shepard, Bart Burns, Jeffrey DeMunn, Jordan Charney

© HBO VIDEO TVB1621

FRANKIE & JOHNNY

D: Garry Marshall 117 m

R | ROM DMA COM | 1991 | COLOR

8 A captivating and unique love story. Pfeiffer and Pacino are very appealing in this endearing but decidedly unglamorous look at a last-chance love affair. Pacino is an ex-con who gets a job as a short order cook at a neighborhood diner. Pfeiffer is a waitress working there who has been burned one too many times and is not interested in a relationship of any kind. But Pacino falls hard for her. He will not retreat and continues to pursue her heart. He finally does charm her into bed, but still Pfeiffer retreats like a fragile bird, afraid of her ghosts. Enjoyable, realistic, believable, upbeat and very moving.

Sex / Nud / Viol / Lang / AdSit

A: Al Pacino, Michelle Pfeiffer, Hector Elizondo, Kate Nelligan, Nathan Lane, Jane Morris

© PARAMOUNT HOME VIDEO 32222

FREE WILLY

D: Simon Wincer 112 m

PG | CLD DMA | 1993 | COLOR

8 This is a very good movie for all kids, most parents and some adults. Jesse is a 12-year-old parentless kid who gets one more chance. He gets assigned kindly foster parents to take care of him while he is to wash off the paint that he and some of his homeless friends had sprayed on the walls of a second-rate seaquarium. While working at the park, he meets Willy. Willy is an orca, a killer whale who has been taken from his family. Willy is unhappy and no one can train him, but lonely Jesse and lonely Willy become fast friends when Willy is attracted to Jesse's harmonica. This film was a big hit.

Sex / Nud / Viol / Lang / AdSit

A: Jason James Richter, Lori Petty, Jayne Atkinson, August Schellenberg, Michael Madsen

© WARNER HOME VIDEO 18000

FRENCH LIEUTENANT'S WOMAN, THE

D: Karel Reisz 124 m

R | ROM DMA | 1982 | COLOR

6 Well-crafted telling of a multilayered story which was first related in a very popular novel. The movie version is a much simplified version of that story, yet it requires rapt attention to digest its subtlety and worth. It is an examination of the similarities and contrasts in the parallel stories, separated by time, of a modern-day love affair between two actors (who are creating a film about a love affair between a haunting Victorian woman and her lover) and the love affair of the Victorian people they portray. Intriguing with wonderful acting. Five Academy Award nominations.

Sex / Nud / Viol / Lang / AdSit

A: Meryl Streep, Jeremy Irons, Leo McKern, Hilton McRae, Emily Morgan

Distributed By MGM/UA Home Video M200181

FRESH

D: Boaz Yakin 124 m

R | DMA ACT | 1994 | COLOR

9 Fresh is his name. He has a job running heroin for one hood in the morning and another job in the afternoon selling crack for another hood. In his free time, he goes to the park to play speed chess with his derelict, chess-genius father. Everyone says that he is smart and someday he is going to be the man. Fresh is a 12 years old. He lives with his aunt with eleven of his cousins, jammed into a small apartment. His one goal has been to make enough money to escape. However, when he witnesses his young girlfriend being shot, he wants revenge but he needs to survive. He has only his street smarts and his chess skills to rely upon. Brilliant, riveting, realistic and sad.

Sex / Nud / Viol / Lang / AdSit

A: Sean Nelson, Giancarlo Esposito, Samuel L. Jackson, N'Bushe Wright, Ron Brice, Jean LaMarre

© MIRAMAX HOME ENTERTAINMENT 3041

FRIED GREEN TOMATOES

D: Jon Avnet 130 m

PG-13 | DMA | 1991 | COLOR

9 Absolutely wonderful! Two endearing and heartwarming stories for the price of one. An old woman in a nursing home (Tandy) captures the imagination of a frumpy and unhappy middle-aged housewife (Bates) with her stories of two girls from her childhood days, Izzy and Ruth. These two were no ordinary girls and their's was a extraordinary friendship, deep and true. Taking courage from the old woman's stories, Bates is given new confidence. She is transformed into a new woman, and she and Tandy become as close as Izzy and Ruth. Heartwarming and invigorating.

Sex / Nud / Viol / Lang / AdSit

A: Kathy Bates, Mary Stuart Masterson, Mary-Louise Parker, Cicely Tyson, Stan Shaw

© MCA/UNIVERSAL HOME VIDEO, INC. 81228

FRIENDLY FIRE

D: David Greene 146 m

NR | DMA | 1979 | COLOR

7 Superb made-for-TV and Emmy-winning drama. In 1970 an Iowa farm couple (Beatty and Burnett) receive a visit from an Army officer who tells them that their son was killed in Vietnam in an American artillery barrage - friendly fire. When their efforts to find out more about their son's death meet with government indifference, they become more and more aggressive in their search, disillusioned in their government and eventually become anti-war activists. This is a gripping and moving account of a real life occurrence. Both Burnett and Beatty put in strong performances.

Sex / Nud / Viol / Lang / AdSit

A: Carol Burnett, Ned Beatty, Sam Waterston, Timothy Hutton

© CBS/FOX VIDEO 9074

FRIENDLY PERSUASION

D: William Wyler 138 m

NR | WST DMA WAR | 1956 | COLOR

9 Wonderfully warm and charming film about the moral quandaries experienced by a Southern Indiana Quaker family during the heartbreak of the Civil War. Gary Cooper and Dorothy McGuire play the Quaker parents of Anthony Perkins (in an Oscar-nominated performance). Their tranquil life is violently challenged when their eldest son goes off to join in the battles to prove that he is no coward. It is a moving tale of love and honor. Cooper is also perfectly cast. Six Oscar nominations, including Best Picture and Best Director, plus a beautiful Dimitri Tiomkin score.

Sex / Nud / Viol / Lang / AdSit

A: Gary Cooper, Dorothy McGuire, Marjorie Main, Anthony Perkins, Robert Middleton, Richard Eyer

© CBS/FOX VIDEO 7318

FROM THE TERRACE

D: Mark Robson 144 m

NR | DMA ROM | 1960 | COLOR

8 Well-acted, involving and entertaining high-class soap opera. A young Paul Newman struggles to become successful and advance in society. He does all the right things. He marries the right woman (Joanne Woodward), a rich and spoiled socialite, and he works very long hours. He struggles to succeed in the corporate world while his marriage deteriorates and he has no personal life. Then he meets and falls in love with a woman who forces him to reevaluate everything he has become. Taken from a hugely popular novel about love, romance and power among the idle rich by John O'Hara.

Sex / Nud / Viol / Lang / AdSit

A: Paul Newman, Joanne Woodward, Myrna Loy, Ina Balin, Leon Ames

© FOXVIDEO 1036

FRONT, THE

D: Martin Ritt — 94 m

PG | DMA COM | 1976 | COLOR

7 Witty comedy with a serious undercurrent. In the early 1950s, Senator Joseph McCarthy engaged in a national campaign to destroy all communist elements in the US. In the process, his witch hunt destroyed thousands of careers, particularly in the entertainment industry. Here Woody Allen plays a regular working stiff who is hired by a group of talented, but blacklisted, writers to represent their work as being his own so they can earn a living. However, he becomes a major success and finds himself also investigated. Some very funny scenes are mixed in with some poignant moments.

Sex · Nud · Viol · Lang · AdSit

A: Woody Allen, Zero Mostel, Andrea Marcovicci, Joshua Shelley, Georgann Johnson

© GOODTIMES 4612

FULL METAL JACKET

D: Stanley Kubrick — 117 m

R | WAR DMA ACT | 1987 | COLOR

8 A highly acclaimed, straightforward movie which follows a group of Marine recruits through basic training, where they are turned into killing machines, and on to Vietnam, where they do what they are trained to do. The picture is essentially divided into two halves. The beginning portion is dominated by the amazingly foul-mouthed verbal assaults of a real-life drill sergeant, molding the young recruits. The latter half relates the efforts of these Marines to do their job and to survive the 1968 Tet Offensive of Vietnam. It is a compelling depiction of the numbing dehumanization of war.

Sex · Nud · Viol · Lang · AdSit

A: Matthew Modine, Adam Baldwin, Vincent D'Onofrio, R. Lee Ermey, Dorian Harewood, Arliss Howard

© WARNER HOME VIDEO 11760

FUNNY GIRL

D: William Wyler — 165 m

G | MUS DMA | 1968 | COLOR

9 Wonderful, Oscar-winning Barbara Streisand triumph in which she recreates her successful role in the hit Broadway musical. Fantastic music: "People," "Don't Rain on My Parade," "My Man" and much more. It is also the unhappy semi-biography of Fanny Brice, the singer-comedienne who rose from obscurity to the heights of stardom in the Ziegfield Follies. While her stage career was a success, her private life was a shambles. Heart-warming performance by Streisand. Followed by the sequel "FUNNY LADY."

Sex · Nud · Viol · Lang · AdSit

A: Barbra Streisand, Omar Sharif, Kay Medford, Anne Francis, Walter Pidgeon, Lee Allen

© COLUMBIA TRISTAR HOME VIDEO 60191

FUNNY LADY

D: Herbert Ross — 136 m

PG | MUS DMA | 1975 | COLOR

8 Successful, if less endearing, sequel to the megahit FUNNY GIRL. This one was nominated for five Oscars. Lavish production, top-notch talent and great music keep this sequel afloat, in spite of a cliche-ridden script. The story is a continuation of the troubled off-stage life of famous comedienne Fanny Brice. After leaving Nicky Arnstein (Sharif), she meets and marries Billy Rose (Caan), but with little success. In spite of some short-comings, it is still well worth a watch.

Sex · Nud · Viol · Lang · AdSit

A: Barbra Streisand, James Caan, Omar Sharif, Roddy McDowall, Ben Vereen, Heidi O'Rourke

© COLUMBIA TRISTAR HOME VIDEO 60685

GABY - A TRUE STORY

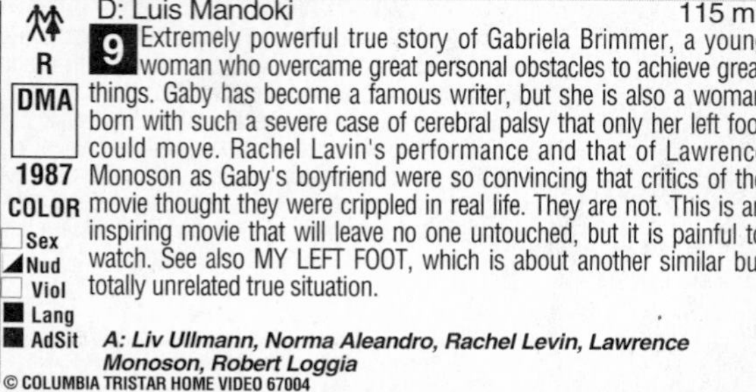

D: Luis Mandoki — 115 m

R | DMA | 1987 | COLOR

9 Extremely powerful true story of Gabriela Brimmer, a young woman who overcame great personal obstacles to achieve great things. Gaby has become a famous writer, but she is also a woman born with such a severe case of cerebral palsy that only her left foot could move. Rachel Lavin's performance and that of Lawrence Monoson as Gaby's boyfriend were so convincing that critics of the movie thought they were crippled in real life. They are not. This is an inspiring movie that will leave no one untouched, but it is painful to watch. See also MY LEFT FOOT, which is about another similar but totally unrelated true situation.

Sex · Nud · Viol · Lang · AdSit

A: Liv Ullmann, Norma Aleandro, Rachel Levin, Lawrence Monoson, Robert Loggia

© COLUMBIA TRISTAR HOME VIDEO 67004

GAL YOUNG'UN

D: Victor Nunez — 105 m

NR | DMA | 1979 | COLOR

8 Poignant and absorbing low-budget gem. A relatively-wealthy, middle-aged, backwoods woman during the Depression is charmed by a young dandy into marrying him. Then, after they are married, he uses her money to build a still. He turns her farmhouse into a moonshine operation and runs around with other women. The ultimate humiliation comes when he brings home another unfortunate young woman whom he has also conned. But - the two conspire to get sweet revenge. Based on a short story by Marjorie Rawlings.

Sex · Nud · Viol · Lang · AdSit

A: Dana Preu, David Peck, J. Smith, Gene Densmore, Jenny Stringfellow, Tim McCormick

© ACADEMY ENTERTAINMENT 1068

GAMBLER, THE

D: Karel Reisz — 111 m

R | DMA | 1974 | COLOR

7 Intelligent, gritty and grim story of a compulsive gambler driven by urges beyond his control. James Caan gives one of his best performances as a college professor, the son of a doctor and grandson of a prominent and forceful man. He is an educated man of some privilege who gambles. Caan's character is not just satisfied with gambling - his compulsion is much deeper. His is a compulsion for danger - he gambles to lose. Interesting, if grim, character study.

Sex · Nud · Viol · Lang · AdSit

A: James Caan, Paul Sorvino, Lauren Hutton

© PARAMOUNT HOME VIDEO 8678

GANDHI

D: Richard Attenborough — 188 m

PG | DMA | 1982 | COLOR

9 Epic and grand scale picture, with stunningly beautiful photography, about one of the most influential men of the 20th century. Mahatma Gandhi created the non-violent methods which have now become standard in instituting political change in societies all over the world. Gandhi's gentle personality and life story is sensitively portrayed, providing the viewer with the background necessary to understand the development of his revolutionary method of conducting a revolution: humiliate a tyrant on the world stage and give dignity to your cause. Winner of 9 Oscars, including Best Picture.

Sex · Nud · Viol · Lang · AdSit

A: Ben Kingsley, John Gielgud, Martin Sheen, Candice Bergen, Trevor Howard, John Mills

© COLUMBIA TRISTAR HOME VIDEO 50503

GARDEN OF DELIGHTS, THE

D: Carlos Saura — 101 m

NR | FOR DMA | 1970 | COLOR

7 Critically acclaimed, complex and surrealist black comedy from Spain. An extremely rich industrialist is crippled in a car crash. He is paralyzed and he has lost his memory. This is an economic disaster for his relatives. So, confined to a wheel chair, the poor man is forced to watch painful incidents from his past being reenacted by his supposed respected family, in an heartless attempt to resurrect his memory long enough to recover the number of his Swiss bank account. Subtitles.

Sex · Nud · Viol · Lang · AdSit

A: Jose Luis Lopez Vasques, Luchy Soto, Francisco Pierra, Charo Soriano, Lina Canalejas

© HOME VISION GAR 050

GARDENS OF STONE

D: Francis Ford Coppola — 112 m

R | DMA | 1987 | COLOR

7 Somber reflection on the divisive nature of the Vietnam war. James Caan plays a battle-toughened sergeant who has returned stateside from Vietnam to the elite Old Guard ceremonial unit at Arlington National Cemetery. He takes an eager young private (Siemaszko), who is the son of a former buddy from Korea, under his wing like he would his own son. His young charge wants desperately to see action. Caan is a dedicated and loyal soldier who feels the war is wrong and surrounding him daily is the fresh shipment home of dead bodies from Vietnam. He desperately wants to help prepare young soldiers to survive combat, but instead must remain in the Gardens of Stone.

Sex · Nud · Viol · Lang · AdSit

A: James Caan, Anjelica Huston, James Earl Jones, Rick Washburn, Casey Siemaszko, Mary Stuart Masterson

© CBS/FOX VIDEO 3731

GEORGY GIRL

D: Silvio Narizzano — 100 m

NR | COM DMA | 1966 | B&W

8 Excellent offbeat English moral comedy from the sixties, set in a very "mod" London. Redgrave won an Oscar nomination as Georgy, the chubby roommate who doesn't fit into the swinging scene, so she lives her life vicariously through a very promiscuous and bitchy Charlotte Rampling. Still, Redgrave yearns for a traditional life, with romance. When Rampling becomes pregnant, Georgy is thrilled and treats the child as her own. Mason puts in his usual fine characterization as a wealthy aging man who wants Georgy to be his mistress. Funny and moving. The theme song became a big pop hit.

Sex · Nud · Viol · Lang · AdSit

A: Lynn Redgrave, James Mason, Alan Bates, Charlotte Rampling, Rachel Kempson, Bill Owen

© COLUMBIA TRISTAR HOME VIDEO 60783

GERMINAL

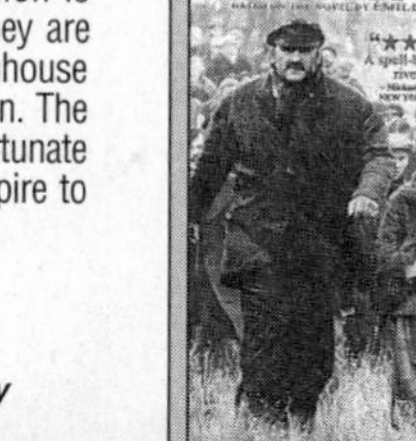

D: Claude Berri — 166 m

R | FOR DMA | 1993 | COLOR

8 Lushly made French epic from the novel by Emile Zola. It is said to be the most expensive French film made to date, at $30 million. Set in the coal mines of 19th-century France, this is the story of the pitiful lives of the poverty-struck miners, as they struggle to survive both in the dangerous, bleak and filthy holes from which they scrape a living; and, from the merciless owners of the mine, who also own their houses, the food they eat and ultimately their souls. After repeated abuses by their masters, the miners rise up in rebellion, holding out against impossible odds for change. Beautifully photographed, highly evocative and morbidly realistic, as well as being very, very long.

Sex · Nud · Viol · Lang · AdSit

A: Gerard Depardieu, Miou-Miou, Renaud, Jean Carmet, Judith Henry, Jean-Roger Milo

© COLUMBIA TRISTAR HOME VIDEO 72673

GETTING IT RIGHT

R | DMA COM | 1989 | COLOR

D: Randal Kleiser — 101 m

8 Wry English drama/comedy about a pleasant, soft-spoken 31-year old, who leads a quiet safe life, still living at home. Gavin Lamb is a hair dresser at Mr. Adrian's in London. He is very uncertain of himself outside the shop, so he does not ask girls out. Instead of blaming himself, however, he always finds some fatal flaw in each girl he meets. So, he is a 31-year old virgin. Then, he attends a trendy party and meets two women who will change his life. Slowly, he begins to understand himself and that he should not worry about being loved but rather learn to love instead. Starts out rather strange and slowly but improves as it progresses.

Sex, Nud, Viol, Lang, AdSit

A: Jesse Birdsall, Helena Bonham Carter, Peter Cook, Lynn Redgrave, Jane Heywood, Judy Parfitt

© MCEG/STERLING MV89003

GETTYSBURG

PG | WAR DMA ACT | 1993 | COLOR

D: Ronald Maxwell — 254 m

9 On July 2, 1863, in the second year of the Civil War, the Union and Confederate Armies found each other outside a small Pennsylvania town and there fought the largest battle of the war. By the end of the third day of that battle 53,000 men lay dead - roughly the same number of men killed in the Vietnam War over twelve years. This is an epic film in both its scope and its intent. The battle sequences are extremely realistic and effectively convey the grandeur and the horror of that war like no other film before it. For history films it is a must see. Others, however, may find it to be slow, deliberate and long. Still, be patient. Also see terrific epic documentary THE CIVIL WAR.

Sex, Nud, Viol, Lang, AdSit

A: Tom Berenger, Martin Sheen, Jeff Daniels, Sam Elliott, Richard Jordan

© TURNER HOME ENTERTAINMENT 6139

GIANT

G | DMA ROM | 1956 | COLOR

D: George Stevens — 202 m

9 This is a giant, sprawling soap opera saga that garnered ten Oscar nominations. It is Edna Ferber's three-generation story about the maturation of Texas from the days of cattle to oil. The story revolves around Rock Hudson, his Eastern-born wife Taylor and James Dean (in his last film role), as a young ranch hand who is totally captivated by Taylor. Dean grows rich with oil and disillusioned with life. Hudson and Taylor raise three kids on what is the biggest ranch in Texas. Weak in spots, but still quite impressive. Two weeks after filming was complete, Dean was killed in a car wreck.

Sex, Nud, Viol, Lang, AdSit

A: James Dean, Rock Hudson, Elizabeth Taylor, Carroll Baker, Dennis Hopper, Chill Wills

© WARNER HOME VIDEO 11414

GIG, THE

NR | COM DMA | 1985 | COLOR

D: Frank D. Gilroy — 92 m

6 Engaging buddy story about a group of middle-aged professional men who meet once a week to play Dixieland music. Then they get their dream opportunity, a chance to be professional musicians during a two-week stint in a resort in the Catskills of upper-New York. It is a touching comedy about dreams that meet reality. It has interesting characters, is frequently amusing and has a couple of really good laughs. Well worth a try.

Sex, Nud, Viol, Lang, AdSit

A: Wayne Rogers, Cleavon Little, Andrew Duncan, Jerry Matz, Daniel Nalbach, Joe Silver

© WARNER HOME VIDEO 381

GIRL FRIENDS

PG | DMA COM | 1978 | COLOR

D: Claudia Weill — 87 m

7 Highly acclaimed low-budget picture that was not considered commercial enough to get wide release. It is the affectionate growing-up story of two female friends and roommates. One is a likable but frumpy Jewish girl who leaves her friend to get married. The other is a Midwestern girl who is just out of college and trying to become an independent career girl as a photographer in Manhattan. But - she is paying her dues. Warm performances overcome the lack of a big budget.

Sex, Nud, Viol, Lang, AdSit

A: Melanie Mayron, Anita Skinner, Eli Wallach, Christopher Guest, Bob Balaban

© WARNER HOME VIDEO 11130

GIRL WHO SPELLED FREEDOM, THE

NR | DMA CLD | 1986 | COLOR

D: Simon Wincer — 90 m

8 Heartwarming true story of a young Cambodian girl who is determined to master English after her family flees war-torn Cambodia and settles in Tennessee. In spite of the difficulties she and her family have struggling to learn new ways and a new language, she becomes a spelling-bee champion within a just a few months. Good entertainment for all ages.

Sex, Nud, Viol, Lang, AdSit

A: Wayne Rogers, Mary Kay Place, Kieu Chinh, Kathleen Sisk, Jade Chinn, Margot Pinvidic

© WALT DISNEY HOME VIDEO 416V

GLASS HOUSE, THE

NR | DMA CRM ACT | 1972 | COLOR

D: Tom Gries — 90 m

9 A gripping and hard-hitting realistic made-for-TV drama based on a story by Truman Capote, about what it is really like to be a convict behind bars. Three separate stories are merged to tell the larger story. A young kid is up on drug charges. Clu Gulager is an idealistic new prison guard. Alan Alda is a college professor up on manslaughter charges. Vic Morrow is a brutally powerful inmate boss who dominates his world and everyone in it. Savage and shocking depiction of life behind bars, where the guards look the other way while Morrow runs the "glass house." Filmed at Utah State Prison.

Sex, Nud, Viol, Lang, AdSit

A: Vic Morrow, Clu Gulager, Billy Dee Williams, Dean Jagger, Alan Alda

© GOODTIMES 9252

GLASS MENAGERIE, THE

PG | DMA | 1987 | COLOR

D: Paul Newman — 134 m

8 Well made version of Tennessee Williams's classic masterpiece play about an overbearing former Southern belle whose strong opinions stifle her son and drive her crippled daughter ever more inward and repressed. Even though she is severely dominated by her mother, the girl still finds hope through her brother and a gentleman caller. Malkovich puts in a brilliant performance as the narrator-brother.

Sex, Nud, Viol, Lang, AdSit

A: Joanne Woodward, John Malkovich, Karen Allen, James Naughton

© MCA/UNIVERSAL HOME VIDEO, INC. 80787

D M A

GLENGARRY GLEN ROSS

R | DMA | 1992 | COLOR

D: James Foley — 100 m

8 Some of Hollywood's best actors deliver stellar performances in this highly-regarded film adapted from a Pulitzer Prize-winning play. While the performances are flawless and compelling, the subject matter is depressing and the people portrayed are unappealing. The title refers to a tract of land the four principal players are charged with selling. They are salesmen who are given an ultimatum: close deals or you're gone. These are ruthless people who generate self-worth and status among their peers thru their sales volumes, regardless of who they hurt. Revealing and powerful look at a seedy world.

Sex, Nud, Viol, Lang, AdSit

A: Jack Lemmon, Al Pacino, Ed Harris, Alan Arkin, Kevin Spacey, Alec Baldwin

© LIVE HOME VIDEO 69921

GLORY

R | DMA ACT WAR | 1989 | COLOR

D: Edward Zwick — 122 m

9 Excellent story, based on fact, about the Civil War's first fighting regiment of black soldiers. The Civil War was fought largely because of the plight of black people, but blacks were not allowed to actually fight in it until near the end of the war. Broderick plays the black regiment's white officer who fights to get better treatment and pay for his men, and to gain for them the two things they want most - the opportunity go into battle and the dignity of being men. Extremely high production values, particularly in very realistic battle sequences. Winner of three Oscars, including Best Actor (Washington).

Sex, Nud, Viol, Lang, AdSit

A: Matthew Broderick, Denzel Washington, Morgan Freeman, Cliff De Young, Cary Elwes

© COLUMBIA TRISTAR HOME VIDEO 11543

GODDESS, THE

NR | DMA | 1957 | B&W

D: John Cromwell — 105 m

8 Moving and haunting screenplay by Paddy Chayefsky about a Marilyn Monroe-type character. She is a lonely girl who possesses a great sensuality and craves attention. Her career is going nowhere until her marriage to ex-prize fighter Lloyd Bridges brings her to the attention of some powerful people. Then she sleeps her way to the top to become "a love goddess of the silver screen." But for all her success, she only discovers that hers is a lonely and empty life, full of phonies. Excellent, powerful performance by Kim Stanley.

Sex, Nud, Viol, Lang, AdSit

A: Kim Stanley, Lloyd Bridges, Steven Hill

© COLUMBIA TRISTAR HOME VIDEO 60728

GODFATHER, THE

R | DMA CRM ACT | 1972 | COLOR

D: Francis Ford Coppola — 171 m

10 Inspired filmmaking. Absolutely everything, including production values, writing, casting, direction, acting and story-telling are all done to perfection. It was the winner of Best Picture, Actor and Screenplay. It is a riveting portrayal of a fictional immigrant family who have become ruthless leaders of a powerful Mafia clan. Story focuses primarily upon the father (Brando) and his youngest son, Michael (Pacino). The don has planned that Michael is to escape a life in the family business, but he is instead drawn into it and must lead the family when the father is shot. Masterpiece.

Sex, Nud, Viol, Lang, AdSit

A: Marlon Brando, Al Pacino, James Caan, Robert Duvall, Talia Shire, Sterling Hayden

© PARAMOUNT HOME VIDEO 8049

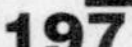

GODFATHER TRILOGY, THE

D: Francis Ford Coppola — 386 m

NR | DMA ACT CRM | 1977 | COLOR

10 1+1=3. The original two GODFATHER movies are here edited together, with the sequences shown now in chronological order and other scenes added. As good as the first two films were, they pale alongside this compiled version. The surface story is that of an Italian immigrant who arrives in America and excels at surviving in a vicious turn-of-the-century ghetto. He and his family evolve into the underground masters of their vicious world. However, it is also the story of raw power, the corruption of power and the politics of power. This is genuine masterpiece and is an absolute must see.

Sex / Nud / Viol / Lang / AdSit

A: Marlon Brando, Al Pacino, Robert De Niro, Robert Duvall, James Caan, Diane Keaton

© PARAMOUNT HOME VIDEO 8480

GODFATHER PART 2, THE

D: Francis Ford Coppola — 200 m

R | DMA CRM ACT | 1974 | COLOR

9 Fascinating follow-up to the powerhouse original. This one won 6 Oscars, including Best Picture. In it, Michael expands the family business to Las Vegas even though it destroys his marriage. It also explains how Michael's father came to leave Sicily for America in the first place. And, how he came to become involved in crime in the ghettos of Little Italy at the turn of the century. Robert De Niro here plays the younger don. (Marlon Brando played the older don in Part I.) Parts I & II were combined into a combined feature called GODFATHER, THE EPIC. As good as I & II are, the combination was better because it related events more sequentially for a better understanding.

Sex / Nud / Viol / Lang / AdSit

A: Al Pacino, Robert De Niro, Robert Duvall, Talia Shire, Diane Keaton, Lee Strasberg

© PARAMOUNT HOME VIDEO 8459

GODFATHER PART 3, THE

D: Francis Ford Coppola — 170 m

R | DMA CRM ACT | 1990 | COLOR

8 A brilliant film, full of passion, and a rich conclusion to Coppola's trilogy of the lives and trials of a prominent mob family. At center stage again is Michael Corleone (Pacino). He has tired of the life and is taking the final step of making his family businesses legitimate and international. He has engineered a huge corporate takeover with the help of the Vatican, but finds that the organized grip of the mob is stronger than he is, and it destroys him. Exceptional performances, plus all of the drama, power and intrigue that we would expect to end this epic saga.

Sex / Nud / Viol / Lang / AdSit

A: Al Pacino, Diane Keaton, Talia Shire, Andy Garcia, Eli Wallach, Joe Mantegna

© PARAMOUNT HOME VIDEO 32318

GOD'S LITTLE ACRE

D: Anthony Mann — 120 m

NR | DMA | 1958 | B&W

7 Erskine Caldwell's adult novel is set in rural Georgia. A poor farmer (Ryan) and his sons are convinced that there is gold buried on their land and have been compulsively digging for it for fifteen years. Tina Louis is the sexy daughter-in-law married to son Jack Lord. However, she and Aldo Ray (husband of Ryan's daughter) are also former lovers causing constant trouble. Ryan is a good-hearted man but he is a fool. He has dedicated himself to the gold, even though his family is collapsing around him. Convincing atmosphere, sensitive and intelligent. Sometimes bawdy and humorous. More or less faithful to the book.

Sex / Nud / Viol / Lang / AdSit

A: Robert Ryan, Tina Louise, Aldo Ray, Buddy Hackett, Jack Lord, Vic Morrow

© UNITED AMERICAN VIDEO CORP. 5031

GOING IN STYLE

D: Martin Brest — 91 m

PG | COM DMA | 1979 | COLOR

9 Absolutely delightful. Three old men share an apartment in Queens, a bench in the park and a boring existence. When one of their sons needs some help with his finances, Burns convinces the other two that they should help the boy out and spice up their lives a little, too. They should rob a bank. You would expect a film with this quality of talent and a good plot gimmick like that to be funny and it is, but it also proves to be a moving experience, too. Burns is a standout.

Sex / Nud / Viol / Lang / AdSit

A: George Burns, Art Carney, Lee Strasberg, Charles Hallahan, Pamela Payton-Wright

© WARNER HOME VIDEO 1030

GOING PLACES

D: Bertrand Blier — 122 m

R | FOR COM DMA | 1974 | COLOR

7 There are widely differing opinions on this one. It was very controversial but it launched the career of Gerard Depardieu. It is the story of two likable louts who cavort through the French countryside stealing cars, terrorizing people and having their way with numerous women. They are searching for the one woman who can understand them, and they find her in a beautiful ex-convict, Jeanne Moreau. It is provocative, funny, disturbing and outrageous. For the most open-minded viewers only.

Sex / Nud / Viol / Lang / AdSit

A: Gerard Depardieu, Miou-Miou, Jeanne Moreau, Patrick Dewaere, Brigitte Fossey

© INTERAMA VIDEO CLASSICS 0021

GOOD FATHER, THE

D: Mike Newell — 121 m

NR | DMA | 1987 | COLOR

7 Brilliant and absorbing drama, but a decidedly downbeat tale of bitterness. Hopkins is compelling as an embittered middle-aged executive who is losing influence over his son's life after having lost a custody battle in his divorce. When his friend's wife announces that she is seeking a divorce and will leave for Australia with her lesbian lover, Hopkins makes it his personal campaign to fight her. Very well acted. Imported from England.

Sex / Nud / Viol / Lang / AdSit

A: Anthony Hopkins, Jim Broadbent, Harriet Walter, Fanny Viner, Simon Callow, Joanne Whalley-Kilmer

© FOXVIDEO 3588

GOODFELLAS

D: Martin Scorsese — 146 m

R | CRM DMA ACT | 1990 | COLOR

9 This film is both masterful and perversely fascinating. It is based on the best selling novel GOODFELLAS and paints a fascinating picture of 30 years of the life and lifestyle of a real gangster. Henry Hill was fascinated as a boy with the money and the respect that the gangsters in his neighborhood had, so he became one. The "life" is one of decadent excesses of money, drinking, dining out, leisure time and women - counter-pointed by equal excesses of violence. The ruthlessness of these characters is absolute. Violence is business. There is no room for sympathy and emotion. Utterly intriguing.

Sex / Nud / Viol / Lang / AdSit

A: Robert De Niro, Ray Liotta, Lorraine Bracco, Joe Pesci, Paul Sorvino, Frank Sivero

© WARNER HOME VIDEO 12039

GOOD MORNING, VIETNAM

D: Barry Levinson — 121 m

R | COM DMA | 1988 | COLOR

8 Entertaining movie, due almost entirely to Williams's manic monologues and shtick. Williams plays a rogue disc jockey who revolutionizes Vietnam's Armed Services Radio airwaves and aggravates the big brass. The real Adrian Cronauer bore very little resemblance to the character created by Williams. Nor did the actual events surrounding him compare to those of the movie. Nonetheless, this is still an entertaining piece of work, with good performances by Williams and by others, too - most notably Forest Whitaker. Forget the attempts at drama, just enjoy the fun.

Sex / Nud / Viol / Lang / AdSit

A: Robin Williams, Forest Whitaker, Tung Thanh Tran, Chantara Sukapotana, Bruno Kirby, Robert Wuhl

© TOUCHSTONE HOME VIDEO 660

GORILLAS IN THE MIST

D: Michael Apted — 129 m

PG-13 | DMA | 1988 | COLOR

8 Absorbing drama about the real-life naturalist, Diane Fossey, who changed the world's perceptions of gorillas being kong-like killers, into being gentle giants. Beginning in 1967, she went to live in the remote wilds of Africa for The National Geographic Society, to monitor the habits of the nearly-extinct mountain gorilla. This film documents her early triumphs at being accepted by the wild gorillas, her developing attachment for them and her later obsessive attempts to protect them from poachers. Sigourney Weaver is very powerful - painting Fossey as a complex individual. Good entertainment, too.

Sex / Nud / Viol / Lang / AdSit

A: Sigourney Weaver, Bryan Brown, Julie Harris, John Omirah Miluwi

© MCA/UNIVERSAL HOME VIDEO, INC. 80851

GO TELL THE SPARTANS

D: Ted Post — 114 m

R | WAR DMA ACT | 1978 | COLOR

9 Superior and intelligent Vietnam war movie that was unjustly overlooked at the time of its release because of several other more highly-publicized pictures out at the same time. Set in 1964, before major US involvement in Vietnam, Lancaster is the commanding officer of an advisory group near Dienbienphu. The nature of the war is becoming apparent and he is already beginning to have doubts about the wisdom of being there, but still does his best to train his troops how to stay alive in jungle warfare. Excellent performances. Very realistic. True sleeper of a film.

Sex / Nud / Viol / Lang / AdSit

A: Burt Lancaster, Craig Wasson, Jonathan Goldsmith, Marc Singer, Joe Unger

© HBO VIDEO 90615

GRADUATE, THE

D: Mike Nichols — 106 m

PG | DMA COM ROM | 1967 | COLOR

9 A huge box office smash and a landmark film of the 1960s. 7 nominations, 1 Oscar. Hoffman, in his first major role, plays Benjamin, a very confused and naive college graduate, who returns to his affluent parents's home not knowing what to do with his life. Then Mrs. Robinson (Bancroft), the wife of his father's best friend, seduces him, adding to his confusion. Hoffman is both funny and poignant as he is seduced by this older woman, only to fall in madly love with her daughter. Now, for the first time, Benjamin knows what he wants. A brilliant score by Simon and Garfunkel: "Mrs. Robinson" and "Sounds of Silence" made them international music stars.

Sex / Nud / Viol / Lang / AdSit

A: Anne Bancroft, Dustin Hoffman, Katharine Ross, Murray Hamilton, Norman Fell, Alice Ghostly

© NEW LINE HOME VIDEO 2071

GRAND CANYON

D: Lawrence Kasdan 134 m

R | DMA | 1991 | COLOR

7 A thought-provoking and mildly engrossing drama about how chance encounters can affect the daily challenges people face. Kline and Glover are quite different but yet they meet quite by accident late one night in South-Central L.A. and become friends. One good turn is followed by another. A series of events occurs that changes both of their lives, and the lives of their families and friends. In an increasingly changing world, sometimes you need to put things into perspective by focusing on that which is extraordinary - like the Grand Canyon.

Sex Nud Viol Lang AdSit

A: Danny Glover, Kevin Kline, Steve Martin, Mary McDonnell, Mary-Louise Parker, Alfre Woodward

© FOXVIDEO 5596

GRASSHOPPER, THE

D: Jerry Paris 96 m

R | DMA | 1970 | COLOR

8 This is an undeservedly overlooked film about a beautiful 19-year-old girl from British Columbia who is bored at home and drawn into show business as a Las Vegas showgirl. She has no real talent or ambition, nor does she have any real understanding of life in general or this world she has entered. She is lost, so she gets married. When that doesn't work, she becomes a rich man's mistress. Eventually, she becomes hooked on drugs and then a full-time prostitute... all by age 22. Quite good performances, including that of football great Jim Brown as a good guy who helps her.

Sex Nud Viol Lang AdSit

A: Jacqueline Bisset, Jim Brown, Joseph Cotten, Corbett Monica, Ramon Bieri

© UNITED AMERICAN VIDEO CORP. 5199

GREAT BALLS OF FIRE

D: Jim McBride 108 m

PG-13 | DMA MUS | 1989 | COLOR

8 Jerry Lee Lewis was an icon of the early rock `n roll period and his life was as raucous as his music. Dennis Quaid captures the wild spirit of "The Killer" in his rise from obscurity to international fame, and his abrupt fall from grace after he married his 13-year-old second cousin, played by Winona Ryder. This biography is full of energy and style. Dennis Quaid throws in all the enthusiasm he can muster and has great support provided from a good cast.

Sex Nud Viol Lang AdSit

A: Dennis Quaid, Winona Ryder, Alec Baldwin, Trey Wilson, John Doe, Peter Cook

© ORION PICTURES CORPORATION 8743

GREAT ESCAPE, THE

D: John Sturges 173 m

NR | ACT WAR DMA | 1963 | COLOR

10 Exciting blockbuster hit filled with major name international stars. An escape-prone group of cocky WWII Allied POWs are all gathered into one high security camp by the Germans, who wanted to put all their bad eggs into one high security basket. Instead, they get a massive POW escape attempt. This rousing adventure story is told as a series of character portraits which are then all linked together. It has a huge cast of top talent and a good script, plus pacing, humor and excitement aplenty. Watch for McQueen's thrilling motorcycle ride. Much copied - never equaled. Based upon an actual event. In the real event, 76 men broke out but only 3 found freedom.

Sex Nud Viol Lang AdSit

A: Steve McQueen, James Garner, Richard Attenborough, Charles Bronson, James Coburn, David McCallum

Distributed By MGM/UA Home Video M201257

GREATEST STORY EVER TOLD, THE

D: George Stevens 199 m

G | DMA | 1965 | COLOR

9 Epic and grand-scale telling of the life of Christ, presenting all the traditional Biblical stories. It traces his life from birth through the crucifixion to the resurrection. It includes a huge star-studded cast. It earned five Oscar nominations and has become an enduring perennial favorite.

Sex Nud Viol Lang AdSit

A: Max von Sydow, Charlton Heston, Roddy McDowall, Robert Loggia, Jose Ferrer, Dorothy McGuire

Distributed By MGM/UA Home Video M301653

GREAT GATSBY, THE

D: Jack Clayton 146 m

PG | DMA ROM | 1974 | COLOR

7 F. Scott Fitzgerald's popular romantic tragedy about the flamboyant flapper era of the Roaring Twenties. Jay Gatsby (Redford) lost Daisy, the spoiled woman that he loved, years ago when she married a rich blueblood. He has now become wealthy himself, though through bootlegging. He throws mammoth parties at his Long Island mansion and invites the beautiful society people, hoping once again to get close to his lost love - Daisy Buchanan (Farrow). This is an enjoyable romancer, even though it is slightly flawed. An excellent re-creation of the period.

Sex Nud Viol Lang AdSit

A: Robert Redford, Mia Farrow, Sam Waterston, Bruce Dern, Karen Black, Lois Chiles

© PARAMOUNT HOME VIDEO 8469

GREAT SANTINI, THE

D: Lewis John Carlino 116 m

PG | DMA | 1980 | COLOR

8 Powerful drama of a family in total disarray. Robert Duvall won universal acclaim in his portrayal of Bull Meechum, a tough Marine fighterpilot who has no war to fight. Bull runs roughshod over his family, as he would a troop of recruits. He is a rowdy, hard-drinking military man, married to a demure Southern belle (Danner). His failure to reveal his inner feelings leads to heartbreaking conflicts with his teenage son (O'Keefe was Oscar nominated) and within himself.

Sex Nud Viol Lang AdSit

A: Robert Duvall, Blythe Danner, Michael O'Keefe, Lisa Jane Persky, Stan Shaw, Theresa Merritt

© WARNER HOME VIDEO 22010

GREAT WALDO PEPPER, THE

D: George Roy Hill 109 m

PG | DMA ACT | 1975 | COLOR

7 Appealing light adventure story. Redford is Waldo Pepper, a hotshot, barnstorming pilot in the post-WWI 1920s who never had a chance to pit his skills against the German aces of the war and has always regretted it. However, when he gets the opportunity to fly a plane as a movie stuntman, he gets his chance. The other pilot is the WWI German fighter ace Ernst Kessler. Brilliant aerial footage and aerial acrobatics. Fun, even though the script is a little talky and uncertain.

Sex Nud Viol Lang AdSit

A: Robert Redford, Bo Svenson, Bo Brundin, Susan Sarandon, Geoffrey Lewis, Margot Kidder

© MCA/UNIVERSAL HOME VIDEO, INC. 55054

D M A

GREAT WHITE HOPE, THE

D: Martin Ritt 103 m

PG | DMA | 1970 | COLOR

8 Passionate recreation of the successful original Broadway play which also starred James Earl Jones and Jane Alexander. This is a play about the famed black heavyweight boxing champion from the early 20th-century, Jack Johnson. It is an emotional portrait of a man who was endlessly harassed in spite of his many successes in the ring and because of them... and because he was black, he had a white mistress, he was outspoken and he didn't "know his place." He is a prideful man, who is eventually humiliated by being forced to lose to a white boxer. Rich period details. Jones was nominated for Best Actor Oscar.

Sex Nud Viol Lang AdSit

A: James Earl Jones, Jane Alexander, Lou Gilbert, Joel Fluellen, Hal Holbrook, R.G. Armstrong

© FOXVIDEO 1151

GREY FOX, THE

D: Phillip Borsos 92 m

PG | WST DMA | 1983 | COLOR

8 Elegant and warm-hearted story of a real life stagecoach bandit named Bill Miner, who was also nick-named the "Gentleman Bandit." After 33 years in prison for stagecoach robbery, he was released into the twentieth century on June 17, 1901 from San Quentin Prison. Farnsworth is excellent as a man who must adjust to an entirely new world and becomes inspired on how to "adapt" to these modern times after he watches THE GREAT TRAIN ROBBERY. Charming and thoughtful entertainment.

Sex Nud Viol Lang AdSit

A: Richard Farnsworth, Jackie Borroughs, Ken Pogue, Timothy Webber

© MEDIA HOME ENTERTAINMENT, INC. M258

GREYSTOKE: THE LEGEND OF TARZAN, LORD OF THE APES

D: Hugh Hudson 130 m

PG | DMA ACT | 1983 | COLOR

7 This is a serious retelling of the classic Edgar Rice Burroughs character, and is told with style. An infant son of a dead shipwrecked couple is discovered by apes and is raised as one of their own. Later discovered by a Belgian explorer, he is returned to civilization and is found to be the seventh Earl of Greystoke of Scotland. He is then taken to his doting grandfather (Richardson) and Tarzan attempts to become a civilized man. Wonderful ape-makeup. Even though it becomes slow and plodding near the end, it otherwise remains fun and very effective.

Sex Nud Viol Lang AdSit

A: Ralph Richardson, Christopher Lambert, Ian Holm, Andie MacDowell, Nigel Davenport, James Fox

© WARNER HOME VIDEO 11375

GRIFTERS, THE

D: Stephen Frears 114 m

R | DMA | 1990 | COLOR

8 Roy is a young grifter, a con man, making his living with small-time cons. Then into his life come two women. One is his mother, a veteran big-time grifter who has been out of her grown son's life for a long time and now is on the run from a big con gone bad. The other is Myra - a sexy con with eyes on a big prize, and she wants Roy to help her to get it. Ironically, there is very little difference between the two women and ultimately Roy doesn't want much to do with either of them, but still is sucked in. Strange journey to an underground world where seduction and deceit are the norm.

Sex Nud Viol Lang AdSit

A: Anjelica Huston, Annette Bening, John Cusack, Pat Hingle, Henry Jones, J.T. Walsh

© HBO VIDEO 90545

GROSS ANATOMY

D: Thom Eberhardt 109 m

PG-13 | COM DMA | 1989 | COLOR

6 This is an attempt at a medical version of THE PAPER CHASE. Modine plays a poor fisherman's son. He is a likable and very bright student at medical school, but he is going into medicine only for the money, so he doesn't study any harder than he has to and has no passion for it. He is smart and so is confident that he can bluff his way through med school, like he has nearly everything else, and still get to romance all the girls at the same time. However, then he meets someone who will unexpectedly change his life.

Sex Nud Viol Lang AdSit

A: Matthew Modine, Christine Lahti, Daphne Zuniga, Todd Field, John Scott Clough, Zakes Mokae

© TOUCHSTONE HOME VIDEO 961

GUARDIAN, THE

D: David Greene 102 m

NR | CRM DMA | 1984 | COLOR

6 Provocative. A Manhattan apartment building hires a no-nonsense ex-military man (Gossett) as a security guard for their building, after they become concerned for their safety because of the direction their neighborhood is taking. While he does clean out the building of lawbreakers, a liberal tenant (Sheen) begins to question their savior's brutal methods and whether the safety of the building is worth that kind of cost. Interesting flick which was made for cable TV.

Sex Nud Viol Lang AdSit

A: Louis Gossett, Jr., Martin Sheen, Arthur Hill, Tandy Cronyn, Arthur Hill, Kate Lynch

© ASTRAL VIDEO E104

GUARDING TESS

D: Hugh Wilson 99 m

PG-13 | DMA COM | 1994 | COLOR

8 While this film does have some very funny moments, it is not a straight-forward comedy. Nicolas Cage is a secret service agent, assigned against his will to guard Tess (MacLaine), an independent and cantankerous widow to an ex-President. And, Tess absolutely delights in tormenting him. During the first half of the film their tumultuous and sometimes funny relationship is set up, but it is the last part of the film where the film takes wing. Tess is here revealed to actually be a frustrated and vital woman who despises being relegated to the backroads of history. It is also here that their troubled relationship deepens, truly becoming interesting and here that the plot takes a surprising twist.

Sex Nud Viol Lang AdSit

A: Nicolas Cage, Shirley MacLaine, Austin Pendleton, Edward Albert, James Rebhorn, Richard Griffiths

© COLUMBIA TRISTAR HOME VIDEO 78703

GUESS WHO'S COMING TO DINNER

D: Stanley Kramer 108 m

NR | DMA | 1967 | COLOR

7 This film is best remembered as being the last screen pairing of Tracy and Hepburn (Tracy died only weeks after it was finished), although it did garner a couple of Oscars. It is the story about a high-class, politically liberal parents who have preached liberal attitudes but are suddenly faced with a real-world dilemma when their college senior daughter brings home a brilliant research physician who is black. His family isn't too excited about it either. Entertaining enough, but a little too strident and somewhat quaint now.

Sex Nud Viol Lang AdSit

A: Spencer Tracy, Katharine Hepburn, Sidney Poitier, Katharine Houghton, Cecil Kellaway, Beah Richards

© COLUMBIA TRISTAR HOME VIDEO 60541

GUILTY BY SUSPICION

D: Irwin Winkler 105 m

PG-13 | DMA | 1991 | COLOR

7 A poignant drama about the disastrous Communist witch hunts in the early '50s that put a lot of creative people in Hollywood out of work and turned Hollywood against itself. De Niro is a movie director who is pressured relentlessly to confirm the suspicions that his friends are Communists. If he does, his stalled career will get a boost. Bening is his ex-wife who lends a supportive shoulder. Wettig delivers a stellar performance as a victim of that process, and Wendt is a writer unable to save himself. De Niro's character refuses to buckle, even under great pressure.

Sex Nud Viol Lang AdSit

A: Robert De Niro, Annette Bening, Sam Wanamaker, Martin Scorsese, Patricia Wettig, George Wendt

© WARNER HOME VIDEO 12053

HAMBONE AND HILLIE

D: Roy Watts 97 m

PG | DMA CLD | 1984 | COLOR

7 Heartwarming story of devotion. An elderly woman returns to Los Angeles from a trip to New York to visit her grandson by plane. However, her dog, Hambone, who must travel as baggage, escapes from his travel case and gets loose in the big world, far way from home. But Hambone will not be separated from his mistress for long, and a cross-country 3,300 mile journey of many travails begins. Very good entertainment for the whole family, but especially the kids.

Sex Nud Viol Lang AdSit

A: Lillian Gish, O.J. Simpson, Timothy Bottoms, Candy Clark, Jack Carter

© R&G VIDEO, LP 80072

HAMLET

D: Franco Zeffirelli 135 m

PG | DMA | 1990 | COLOR

9 Excellent screen version of the 400-year-old Shakespeare masterpiece that was described by its director as "Hamlet for the '90s." What has, in fact, happened is that a little of the dialogue has been trimmed to make the play quicker moving and a little more accessible for modern-day audiences. Mel Gibson's Hamlet is a little less cerebral and more physical. Hamlet returns to Denmark from Germany to find his father, the King, dead and his mother married to his uncle. However, Hamlet's father's ghost tells Hamlet that he was truly murdered and demands that Hamlet reap revenge.

Sex Nud Viol Lang AdSit

A: Mel Gibson, Glenn Close, Alan Bates, Ian Holm, Paul Scofield, Helena Bonham-Carter

© WARNER HOME VIDEO 12200

HANDFUL OF DUST, A

D: Charles Sturridge 118 m

PG | ROM DMA | 1988 | COLOR

8 Very elegant English drama by Evelyn Waugh, the author of "Brideshead Revisited," which is done in a sort of Masterpiece Theatre style. A seemingly happily married upper-crust English couple of the 1930s have their lives torn apart when the husband invites a dashing but penniless socialite for a weekend. By comparison to their guest, the husband is revealed to be a stuffy and tradition-bound husband, and the dormant passions of a bored and selfish wife are ignited by the visitor.

Sex Nud Viol Lang AdSit

A: James Wilby, Rupert Graves, Kristin Scott Thomas, Anjelica Huston, Alec Guinness

© NEW LINE HOME VIDEO 62825

HANDMAID'S TALE, THE

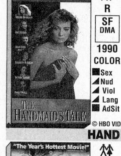

D: Volker Schlondorff 109 m

R | SF DMA | 1990 | COLOR

6 An interesting premise is given a little bit better than mediocre treatment, despite top-notch acting. Set in a bleak future-America, the few remaining fertile women are forced to become surrogate breeders for the ruling military elite. This story follows the fortunes of one such girl. Excellent performances fail to inspire a more than a moderately empathetic response. However, this is a very thought-provoking subject that deserves consideration by viewers interested in non-traditional and thought-provoking viewing.

Sex Nud Viol Lang AdSit

A: Natasha Richardson, Faye Dunaway, Aidan Quinn, Elizabeth McGovern, Victoria Tennant, Robert Duvall

© HBO VIDEO 0431

HAND THAT ROCKS THE CRADLE, THE

D: Curtis Hanson 110 m

R | SUS DMA | 1992 | COLOR

8 Disturbing thriller that will bristle the hair on the back of your neck! De Mornay is married to an obstetrician who kills himself when patient Sciorra accuses him of molesting her at the office. The trauma prompts De Mornay's miscarriage and she is told she can never have children again. Destroyed, she is determined to get revenge. She takes a job as nanny to Sciorra's two young children and slowly, she plots to take over Sciorra's life. She schemes to win over both the love of Sciorra's children and her husband. De Mornay's character is evil, diabolical and ruthless. Quite compelling and disturbing viewing.

Sex Nud Viol Lang AdSit

A: Rebecca De Mornay, Annabella Sciorra, Ernie Hudson, Matt McCoy, Ernie Hudson

© HOLLYWOOD PICTURES HOME VIDEO 1334

HANGING TREE, THE

D: Delmer Daves 108 m

NR | WST DMA | 1959 | COLOR

9 A solid, intelligent Western, that was unjustly overlooked upon its release. It is 1870s Montana in a gold camp called Skull Creek. The town is populated by fortune seekers of all types. There mountain men, saloons, prostitutes, bad people and good people too -- but they are all after gold. Dr. Joseph Frail (Cooper) is a quiet doctor, haunted by his past, who has come to town to hang out his shingle. But his life is thrown into violent turmoil when he comes to the aid of a pretty immigrant girl (Maria Schell) who has been blinded. It is a woman-poor town and the two of them are hounded by a fire-brand minister (George C. Scott) and a hot-headed jealous miner (Karl Malden.)

Sex Nud Viol Lang AdSit

A: Gary Cooper, Maria Schell, Karl Malden, George C. Scott, Ben Piazza, Virginia Gregg

© WARNER HOME VIDEO 11049

HANGIN' WITH THE HOMEBOYS

D: Joseph B. Vasquez 90 m

R | DMA COM | 1991 | COLOR

7 Interesting bittersweet excursion, in which we go along with four young guys from the inner-city on a crucial Friday night of self discovery. Good friends, two black and two Puerto Rican buddies, are going nowhere with their lives and get together to hang out every Friday night. On this night, they cruise first their own neighborhood in the South Bronx and then enter over into whiteman's land, Manhatten. But, along the way, each has the veneer of who he thinks he is, scraped and chipped away. This is a non-romanticized, non-villainizing look at how most all of us just allow our lives to happen without ever taking charge ourselves. Most interesting to young people.

Sex Nud Viol Lang AdSit

A: Doug E. Doug, Mario Joyner, Nestor Serrano, John Leguizamo

© TURNER HOME ENTERTAINMENT N4113

HANNAH AND HER SISTERS

D: Woody Allen 103 m

PG-13 | COM DMA | 1986 | COLOR

9 A heart-warming serious comedy from Woody Allen. This is one of his best (although ANNIE HALL is right up there). This is a two-year study of the lives of one of Woody's neurotic New York families that revolves around three sisters. Mia Farrow is the functional centerpin of the family. She plays peacemaker for all the other elements. However, her current husband is having an affair with one sister, and her ex-husband, hypochondriac Allen, is married to her other sister. In all, a dozen different characters are brought into the family. Three Oscars, nominated for seven.

Sex | Nud | Viol | Lang | AdSit

A: Woody Allen, Michael Caine, Mia Farrow, Carrie Fisher, Barbara Hershey, Maureen O'Sullivan

© HBO VIDEO 3897

HARDER THEY FALL, THE

D: Mark Robson 105 m

NR | DMA ACT | 1956 | B&W

9 Excellent. A moving and powerful sports drama that was also Bogie's last film. He plays an out-of-work sports writer who is reduced to writing PR releases for a boxing promoter (Steiger), and Steiger uses Bogart's help to build an upcoming boxer's image as a gentle giant. However, for the first time Bogart also comes to realize how corrupt the sport is because he discovers that Steiger has secretly been fixing fights. He just build the big guy up make a bundle when he loses the big championship match. Fast-paced, with excellent acting. A brutal indictment of boxing as a corrupt killer sport.

Sex | Nud | Viol | Lang | AdSit

A: Humphrey Bogart, Rod Steiger, Jan Sterling, Mike Lane, Max Baer, Edward Andrews

© COLUMBIA TRISTAR HOME VIDEO 60010

HARD TIMES

D: Walter Hill 97 m

PG | ACT DMA | 1975 | COLOR

9 This is one of Charles Bronson's best roles. He plays a tough bare-knuckle boxer who is making a living by hustling street fights in Depression-era New Orleans. He and his sly manager (Coburn) stage a series of street bouts with the intention of setting up a "sting" of some local punks. Excellent recreation of period atmosphere and well-choreographed, violent and exciting fight sequences. Bronson was 54 when he made this film.

Sex | Nud | Viol | Lang | AdSit

A: Charles Bronson, James Coburn, Jill Ireland, Strother Martin, Maggie Blye, Michael McGuire

© COLUMBIA TRISTAR HOME VIDEO 60008

HAROLD AND MAUDE

D: Hal Ashby 91 m

PG | COM DMA | 1971 | COLOR

8 Odd-ball black comedy that has become a big cult favorite. Harold (Bud Cort) is a very strange young man. He is rich, spoiled and very confused. He repeatedly attempts suicide both because he likes to upset his snooty mother and because he is fascinated with the concept of death. And, that is what at first draws him to Maude (Ruth Gordon). Maude is old, but she is also eccentric and fun-loving. She is a laugh-riot. The two meet at a funeral and fall in love. This is not at all a typical comedy, but the patient open-minded viewer will be greatly rewarded with some laughs and some insights into human nature.

Sex | Nud | Viol | Lang | AdSit

A: Bud Cort, Ruth Gordon, Vivian Pickles, Cyril Cusack, Charles Tyner, Ellen Geer

© PARAMOUNT HOME VIDEO 8042

HARRY AND TONTO

D: Paul Mazursky 110 m

R | COM DMA | 1974 | COLOR

8 Touching story about an old man who is tired of being passed from one relative to the next and tired of letting life pass him by. So, he and his cat set out on a cross-country adventure in which they run across a varied, entertaining and interesting cast of odd-ball characters. By the time Harry finally arrives in LA, where he is was to move in with his son, Harry has discovered that he likes the adventure of the road. Carney won an Oscar for his portrayal of this dignified elderly adventure seeker. A truly entertaining journey of self discovery. Carney is a master. It doesn't deserve an R rating.

Sex | Nud | Viol | Lang | AdSit

A: Art Carney, Ellen Burstyn, Chief Dan George, Geraldine Fitzgerald, Larry Hagman, Melanie Mayron

© FOXVIDEO 1355

HAVANA

D: Sydney Pollack 145 m

R | DMA ROM | 1990 | COLOR

7 A high-stakes romance set in 1958 amidst the tremors of a communist revolution in Havana. Redford is Jack Weil, a high-rolling gambler who is hoping to make it big in Cuba. En route he meets Olin, the beautiful wife of a revolutionary leader, who is in need of some help. Her husband has been reported killed and now she needs some protection. However, the attraction that propells Redford to her and their budding relationship will certainly hurt his chances at his big break, but Redford realizes that there other dreams worth chasing.

Sex | Nud | Viol | Lang | AdSit

A: Robert Redford, Lena Olin, Alan Arkin, Thomas Milian, Daniel Davis, Tony Plana

© MCA/UNIVERSAL HOME VIDEO, INC. 81049

HAWAII

D: George Roy Hill 190 m

NR | DMA | 1966 | COLOR

7 Sprawling Michener saga about the white settlement of Hawaii in the early 1800s. The missionaries came to bring God but instead nearly destroyed a people and a culture. Max von Sydow plays the stridently religious missionary who is sent to convert the natives. Julie Andrews plays his wife who struggles to stand by him, even though she is in love with dashing sea captain Richard Harris. Beautiful photography and scenery. Received six Oscar nominations. The second half of Michener's book was made into the sequel: THE HAWAIIANS.

Sex | Nud | Viol | Lang | AdSit

A: Julie Andrews, Max von Sydow, Richard Harris, Torin Thatcher, Gene Hackman, Carroll O'Connor

Distributed By MGM/UA Home Video M301464

HEARTACHES

D: Donald Shebib 93 m

R | COM DMA | 1982 | COLOR

7 Touching offbeat comedy about two women friends surviving in Toronto. Bonnie (Potts) is small-town girl who has left her hard-drinking husband (Carradine) rather than to tell him that he is not the father of her baby. On the bus, she runs into and befriends Rita, a kooky streetwise blond (Kidder) who has man-problems of her own. Even though these two are total opposites, they wind up becoming best friends. Rita protects Bonnie from Carradine, while she keeps getting into more man-problems herself. This is a fun lightweight comedy and a good female buddy movie.

Sex | Nud | Viol | Lang | AdSit

A: Annie Potts, Winston Rekert, Robert Carradine, Margot Kidder

© LIVE HOME VIDEO VA4024

HEARTBREAK HOTEL

D: Chris Columbus 101 m

PG-13 | COM DMA | 1988 | COLOR

7 A far-out premise gets a respectable treatment by an excellent cast. It's 1972 and Tuesday Weld is depressed. Her husband has left her and her boyfriend beats her. Then she gets into a car accident, too. Her teenage guitarist son decides that he will get her the ultimate get well present. So, he kidnaps her idol, Elvis Presley. (Fabulous impersonation of Presley by David Keith.) However, Presley gains from the experience too, because he is guided back to his rock 'n roll roots through the aspiring young musician and also gets to teach the boy's little sister to not be afraid of the dark.

Sex | Nud | Viol | Lang | AdSit

A: David Keith, Tuesday Weld, Charlie Schlatter, Angela Goethais, Jacque Lynn Colton, Chris Mulkey

© TOUCHSTONE HOME VIDEO 609

HEARTBREAK KID, THE

D: Elaine May 106 m

PG | COM DMA | 1972 | COLOR

7 Neil Simon comedy about a young Jewish boy (Grodin) who meets a girl in a Manhattan singles bar and, shortly afterward, proposes to her. However, he already begins to grow tired of his new whining wife even as they drive to Florida for their honeymoon. When he meets a beautiful WASP girl (Shepherd) on the beach it's all over. Grodin woos and, after overcoming many obstacles, wins Shepherd, but this victory proves to be hollow. This is a subtle satiric look at love and marriage, not Simon's typical string of one liners. How funny it will be for you depends on how it hits you.

Sex | Nud | Viol | Lang | AdSit

A: Charles Grodin, Cybill Shepherd, Jeannie Berlin, Eddie Albert, Audra Lindley

© VIDEO TREASURES SV9088

HEARTBURN

D: Mike Nichols 109 m

R | DMA COM | 1986 | COLOR

6 Starpower is the hallmark of this picture. Meryl Streep and Jack Nickolson play a New York writer who marries a Washington columnist. These are sophisticated people whose marriage seems fine until Nicholson steps out on her while she's pregnant. Some witty dialogue and some funny moments, but the glory is in the acting because the story itself is ultimately not very satisfying.

Sex | Nud | Viol | Lang | AdSit

A: Meryl Streep, Jack Nicholson, Maureen Stapleton, Jeff Daniels, Stockard Channing, Richard Masur

© PARAMOUNT HOME VIDEO 1688

HEART IS A LONELY HUNTER, THE

D: Robert Ellis Miller 124 m

G | DMA | 1968 | COLOR

8 A real tearjerker. Alan Arkin won an Oscar nomination for his stunning portrait of a lonely deaf-mute living in a small Southern town. He is a sensitive and compassionate man who struggles to help all those around him, particularly a spoiled teenager Sandra Locke (Oscar nominated). But, no one recognizes the depth of his personal despair. He is virtually friendless and pathetically, totally alone. A heart-rending story. This was the screen debut for both Locke and Keach.

Sex | Nud | Viol | Lang | AdSit

A: Alan Arkin, Sondra Locke, Laurinda Barrett, Stacy Keach, Chuck McCann, Cicely Tyson

© WARNER HOME VIDEO 11194

HEARTLAND

D: Richard Pearce — 95 m

PG | DMA WST | 1979 | COLOR

7 Moving realistic story about pioneer life in the far-flung virgin lands of Wyoming in 1910, based upon the actual diaries of a frontier woman. Ferrell plays a young widow who accepts a job as a housekeeper for a sour homesteader and eventually marries him. They become devoted to each other and their family. She and her daughter learn to deal with the hardships of isolation and having to confront nature on its own terms. Thoughtful with beautiful photography. Excellent acting. Moving, well-crafted and worthy story that was critically acclaimed but is also slow moving.

Sex / Nud / Viol / Lang / AdSit

A: Conchata Ferrell, Rip Torn, Lilia Skala, Megan Folson, Amy Wright

© HBO VIDEO 608

HEART LIKE A WHEEL

D: Jonathan Kaplan — 113 m

PG | DMA ACT | 1983 | COLOR

7 Well-made sports biography about the pioneering female drag racer, Shirley "Cha-Cha" Muldowney. Bedelia gives a stellar performance as a hard-pressed woman who struggles to balance a career as a racer with being a wife. She also struggles to fight the sexist attitudes of a male-dominated sport into which she is the first woman to dare to enter. While the film does concern racing, it is really a human story of dedication and courage. It wins on both levels. Surprisingly good.

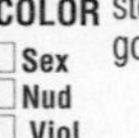
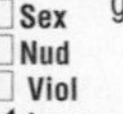

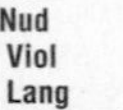
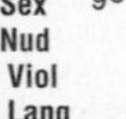
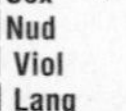

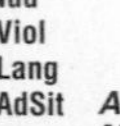

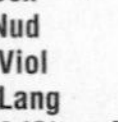

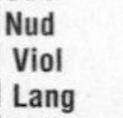
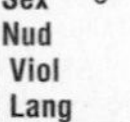
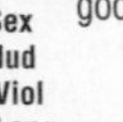

Sex / Nud / Viol / Lang / AdSit

A: Bonnie Bedelia, Beau Bridges, Leo Rossi, Hoyt Axton, Bill McKinney, Dick Miller

© FOXVIDEO 1300

D M A

HEATHERS

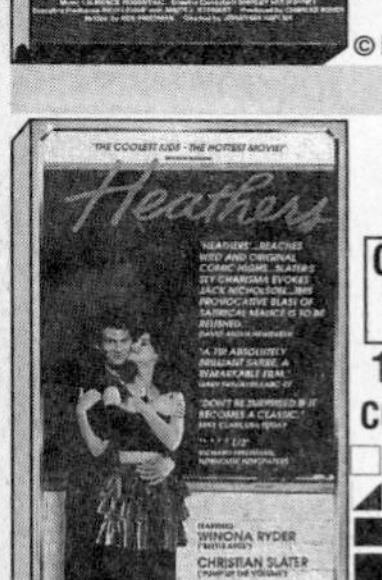

D: Michael Lehmann — 105 m

R | COM DMA | 1989 | COLOR

7 If you love very black comedy in the form of quirky, offbeat drama, this flick is for you - and you don't have to be a teenager to get a kick out of it. The film is centered at Westerburg High, a place where the quest for popularity is the most important thing of all. The Heathers, a small group of gorgeous girls led by Doherty, are the ruling class. But when one of them (Ryder) breaks off from the others, her new outlaw boyfriend (Slater) decides that it is time to end the reign of the Heathers completely, and will stop at nothing to accomplish his goal. Darkly funny.

Sex / Nud / Viol / Lang / AdSit

A: Winona Ryder, Christian Slater, Shannen Doherty, Kim Walker, Lisanne Falk, Penelope Milford

© R&G VIDEO, LP 14014

HEAVEN AND EARTH

D: Oliver Stone — 142 m

R | DMA WAR | 1993 | COLOR

6 This is the last in Oliver Stone's Vietnam trilogy following PLATOON and BORN ON THE FOURTH OF JULY. It is based upon the memoirs of Le Ly, a Vietnamese farm girl whose quiet life took a violent turn when her village became the center of a battleground. She is raped and escapes to Da Nang. There she becomes pregnant by a rich man who sends her to Saigon, where she turns to prostitution and she meets Tommy Lee Jones who takes her back to America. Stone uses the sorrowful experiences of one woman to represent all the tragedies of that small country and the American involvement in it. That is a gross simplification and a mistake. Beautifully filmed but slanted and flawed.

Sex / Nud / Viol / Lang / AdSit

A: Tommy Lee Jones, Hiep Thi Le, Joan Chen, Haing S. Ngor, Debbie Reynolds, Conchata Ferrell

© WARNER HOME VIDEO 12983

HEAVENLY CREATURES

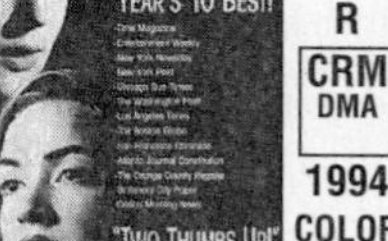

D: Peter Jackson — 99 m

R | CRM DMA | 1994 | COLOR

8 Based upon an actual incident, this is both the recreation of those events and a remarkable depiction of the nature of self-delusion. Pauline at 14, was reclusive and a loner. Juliet was the new girl, and was so over-bearing that she was equally ostracized. Left outside the mainstream, the two loners discovered each other. Both were intensely romantic in their notion of how things should be and created a perfect fanciful world that became very real to them, and into which both would frequently escape. However, when their new-found kinship was threatened with separation, both girls conspired to brutally murder their perceived enemy, Pauline's mother. Remarkable acting and special effects.

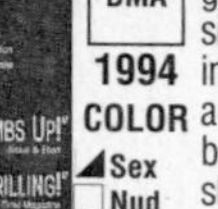
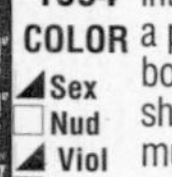
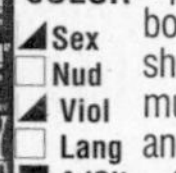

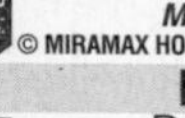

Sex / Nud / Viol / Lang / AdSit

A: Kate Winslet, Melanie Lynskey, Sarah Peirse, Diana Kent, Clive Merrison, Simon O'Connor

© MIRAMAX HOME ENTERTAINMENT 4371

HELL IN THE PACIFIC

D: John Boorman — 101 m

G | WAR DMA | 1968 | COLOR

6 An unusual twist to a World War II theme. An American pilot (Marvin) becomes stranded on an island that is already occupied by a lone Japanese officer. If this were any other time or place, they would have helped each other. But they are at war. At first they launch minor raids against each other, but then they realize that they stand a better chance of surviving by cooperating, so they strike an uneasy truce. They combine their energies to build a raft so they can both get off the island.

Sex / Nud / Viol / Lang / AdSit

A: Lee Marvin, Toshiro Mifune

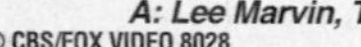

© CBS/FOX VIDEO 8028

HELL IS FOR HEROES

D: Don Siegel — 90 m

NR | WAR DMA ACT | 1962 | COLOR

8 Quite good war drama in which character development is carefully interwoven into and necessary to the action sequences. The action scenes themselves are calculated realism, not empty-headed glory charges. A star-studded cast highlights this realistic war saga about a beleaguered Army squad which has survived Africa, France and Belgium, and is now assigned the job of plugging a hole in the front lines near the end of WWII. Steve McQueen is excellent as a tormented man who now requires battle as a drug to survive living.

Sex / Nud / Viol / Lang / AdSit

A: Steve McQueen, Bobby Darin, Fess Parker, Harry Guardino, James Coburn, Bob Newhart

© PARAMOUNT HOME VIDEO 6116

HELL TO ETERNITY

D: Phil Karlson — 132 m

NR | WAR DMA ACT | 1960 | B&W

8 Fascinating true story from World War II. Jeffery Hunter plays the real-life figure of Guy Gabaldon who was a Hispanic man raised by Japanese-Americans. Gabaldon could speak Japanese and became a hero of the South Pacific when he chose to fight his war on Saipan by going behind enemy lines each night to convince defeated Japanese soldiers to surrender, eventually winning a Silver Star for bringing in over 2,000 prisoners. Action aplenty, too, with very realistic battle scenes.

Sex / Nud / Viol / Lang / AdSit

A: Jeffrey Hunter, Vic Damone, David Janssen, Sessue Hayakawa

© CBS/FOX VIDEO 7351

HELTER SKELTER

D: Tom Gries — 119 m

NR | CRM DMA | 1976 | COLOR

9 Superb made-for-TV production of the best-selling book which chronicles the people and events surrounding the grisly and infamous 1969 Tate/La Bianca murders, and the subsequent trials of the notorious Charles Manson and his "family." While it is a recreation of the events surrounding the murders, it is also a mesmerizing portrait of a psychotic killer who had his followers convinced that he was the messiah. The novel upon which the movie was based was written by the state's actual prosecutor, Vincent Bugliosi. Very intense, electrifying and disturbing film.

Sex / Nud / Viol / Lang / AdSit

A: George DiCenzo, Steve Railsback, Nancy Wolfe, Marilyn Burns, Christina Hart, Cathey Paine

© CBS/FOX VIDEO 7713

HENRY & JUNE

D: Philip Kaufman — 136 m

NC-17 | DMA | 1990 | COLOR

8 Stylish, intelligent and sensual adaptation, taken from the actual diaries of writer Anais Nin, of her passionate affair with expatriate American author Henry Miller and his sensuous wife June in Paris, 1931. Paris at that time was an extravagantly wild, anything goes mecca for the intellectual and creative people of Europe and America who were drawn to its Bohemian lifestyle. Although this film does contain very erotic and explicit sequences, this is not pornographic material. It was the first film to officially receive the MPAA rating of NC-17.

Sex / Nud / Viol / Lang / AdSit

A: Fred Ward, Maria de Medeiros, Uma Thurman, Richard E. Grant, Kevin Spacey

© MCA/UNIVERSAL HOME VIDEO, INC. 81050

HENRY - PORTRAIT OF A SERIAL KILLER

D: John Mc Naughton — 90 m

NR | DMA CRM | 1990 | COLOR

8 Brutal and extremely unpleasant but also utterly fascinating look into the mind of a serial murderer. Loosely based upon the self-confessed Texas serial murderer Henry Lee Lucas, this film is quasi-documentary. It is not exploitative, but it faithfully and graphically depicts scene after scene of rapes and murders, including one in which Henry and his roommate record the murder of a family on video tape so they can watch it over and over. This is both a very grisly and a very moving picture, but it is definitely not for everyone.

Sex / Nud / Viol / Lang / AdSit

A: Michael Rooker, Tom Towles, Tracy Arnold

© MPI HOME VIDEO 3108

HENRY V

D: Kenneth Branagh — 138 m

NR | DMA WAR | 1989 | COLOR

9 Extraordinarily well done version of the Shakespeare classic telling of King Henry V's war with the French. When a young Henry is thrust onto the throne of England and insulted by the French envoy, Henry is determined to be seen as a strong king. So he exercises his hereditary right to the French crown, gathers his army together and goes to France to claim it. Notable for the inclusion of a very realistic, but small in scale, presentation of medieval warfare. An Oscar nomination went to Kenneth Branagh for his stunning performance as Henry, and the film won the Oscar for Costume Design.

Sex / Nud / Viol / Lang / AdSit

A: Kenneth Branagh, Paul Scofield, Derek Jacobi, Ian Holm, Alec McGowen, Judi Dench

© CBS/FOX VIDEO 2575

HERO

D: Stephen Frears 116 m

PG-13 | DMA | 1992 | COLOR

6 Hoffman is a small-time crook and people-user who happens to be the first to arrive at an airliner crash site. Without really intending to, he becomes a hero leading passengers out of the burning wreckage, and then he just leaves. However, a local TV news reporter (Davis) was on board and, in a big publicity stunt, she gets her station to post a huge reward for the hero. Garcia is a gentle homeless Vietnam vet and recluse. After Hoffman doesn't show, Garcia decides to claim the reward and use the money for good. Hoffman discovers too late about the reward and now who'll believe him. This is a well-intentioned indictment of the press, but is also heavy-handed.

Sex | Nud | Viol | Lang | AdSit

A: Geena Davis, Dustin Hoffman, Andy Garcia, Joan Cusack, Tom Arnold

© COLUMBIA TRISTAR HOME VIDEO 51563

HESTER STREET

D: Joan Micklin Silver 89 m

PG | DMA COM | 1975 | B&W

7 Interesting reflection on a real problem from the days of mass immigrations to America at the turn of the 20th century. A Jewish immigrant (Steven Keats) arrives in New York first so that he can raise the money necessary to bring his wife (Kane) and child over from the old country. However, when she does arrive, she is disturbed to find that he is turning his back on the old world ways, and he is embarrassed by her cloddishness. They divorce and marry others. Great period detail and a simple and charming story. Fine performances. Kane received an Oscar nomination.

Sex | Nud | Viol | Lang | AdSit

A: Carol Kane, Steven Keats, Mel Howard, Dorrie Davanaugh

© LIVE HOME VIDEO A3068

HIDE IN PLAIN SIGHT

D: James Caan 96 m

PG | DMA | 1979 | COLOR

8 Very watchable dramatization of a true story about a divorced man (Caan) who becomes the victim of the government's Witness Relocation Program. His ex-wife marries a hood who later turns state's evidence. Then the guy and his new family, which includes Caan's kids, are given new identities. Caan's family disappears overnight and the government refuses to help him find his kids. He launches into an 18-month gut-wrenching search to find them.

Sex | Nud | Viol | Lang | AdSit

A: James Caan, Jill Eikenberry, Robert Viharo, Joe Grifasi, Barbara Rae, Danny Aiello

Distributed By MGM/UA Home Video M600047

HIGH HEELS

D: Pedro Almodovar 113 m

R | FOR DMA | 1992 | COLOR

6 Spanish import that is supposed to be a black comedy. If it is, it is so black that its comedy is virtually hidden. Still, it does work as a somewhat involving drama with a mystery element. Sexy Victoria Abril has been long separated from her celebrity mother (Paredes), whom she compulsively adores. Mother returns to Spain to find that daughter has married mother's former lover. Later, when the husband/lover is murdered in his bed, mother and daughter are both suspects of an investigator - who turns out to be a former lover of Abril - but is unknown to her because he was disguised at the time. Subtitles.

Sex | Nud | Viol | Lang | AdSit

A: Victoria Abril, Miguel Bose, Marisa Paredes, Ama Lizaran, Mairata O Wisiedo, Cristina Marcos

© PARAMOUNT HOME VIDEO 15121

HIGH TIDE

D: Gillian Armstrong 102 m

PG-13 | DMA COM | 1987 | COLOR

7 Moving, emotional story set in Australia. Judy Davis plays a no-talent backup singer for a bad Elvis impersonator and she winds up being stranded in a small bleak coastal town. While staying in a trailer park, she chances upon a tomboyish teenage girl who she slowly recognises as being the daughter she had abandoned years before after her husband died. She begins to form a friendship with the girl that she thought she would never see again and gradually reveals who she is. Well acted and convincingly told even if the story's premise is a longshot.

Sex | Nud | Viol | Lang | AdSit

A: Judy Davis, Jan Adele, Claudia Karvan, Colin Friels

© NEW LINE HOME VIDEO 7722

HOFFA

D: Danny DeVito 140 m

R | DMA | 1992 | COLOR

7 Jimmy Hoffa was one of labor's greatest champions. He was also utterly ruthless in his efforts to advance union's causes. Early on in his career, he made an alliance with organized crime wherein they would not get in his way and provide him with occasional services and he would help to make them rich. This film chronicles 40 years of Hoffa's career - from the beginning, through his corruption conviction by Robert Kennedy and on to his never-solved murder and disappearance. A great deal of money was spent on the film and it shows. It is generally interesting and informative but, it is also far and away too forgiving of a vicious bone-breaker and schemer.

Sex | Nud | Viol | Lang | AdSit

A: Jack Nicholson, Danny DeVito, Armand Assante, J.T. Walsh, Robert Prosky

© FOXVIDEO 1991

HOMBRE

D: Martin Ritt 111 m

NR | WST ACT DMA | 1967 | COLOR

9 This is an intriguing and intelligent Western with powerhouse performances. Newman is a quiet loner, a white man who was raised by Apaches. He is onboard a 1880's stagecoach, along with a naive young married couple, a woman of the world, a corrupt Indian Agent with stolen money and his haughty wife and Richard Boone. Because Newman is so different he is shunned. However, he is the one they all later must rely upon to save them when their coach is robbed by Boone's killer gang and they are all left stranded to die. A captivating storyline, believable action and moving drama. Excellent.

Sex | Nud | Viol | Lang | AdSit

A: Paul Newman, Fredric March, Richard Boone, Diane Cliento, Cameron Mitchell, Barbara Rush

© FOXVIDEO 1012

HOMECOMING, THE

D: Fielder Cook 98 m

NR | DMA | 1971 | COLOR

8 Award-winning and sentimental telling of rural life during the Great Depression. It is also the pilot for the extremely popular TV series, "The Waltons." It is Christmas Eve in 1933. The large Walton family is anxiously awaiting the return home of their father, who has gone to town in search of work. He is long over due. The beleaguered mother decides to send her oldest son off in search of news. Heartwarming.

Sex | Nud | Viol | Lang | AdSit

A: Patricia Neal, Richard Thomas, Edgar Bergen, Ellen Corby, William Windom, Cleavon Little

© FOXVIDEO 7134

HOME FROM THE HILL

D: Vincente Minnelli 151 m

NR | DMA | 1960 | COLOR

8 This was one of Robert Mitchum's juiciest roles. He plays a wealthy, domineering father and a philandering husband. That sets the stage for an absorbing melodrama about the conflicts which explode within his troubled Texas family. This carousing father constantly battles both with his wife and his two sons, one of whom is illegitimate. And, there's more hot water for the pot - the sons are both in love with the same girl. A little long, but it holds your attention the whole way. This was also the screen debuts of both George Peppard and George Hamilton.

Sex | Nud | Viol | Lang | AdSit

A: Robert Mitchum, Eleanor Parker, George Peppard, George Hamilton, Luana Patten, Everett Sloane

Distributed By MGM/UA Home Video M300802

HOME OF OUR OWN, A

D: Tony Bill 104 m

PG | DMA | 1993 | COLOR

6 Kathy Bates is a single mother in 1960 with six kids, no money and an ardent wish to finally have a home of their own. So, she packs her kids into their beat-up old Plymouth and just heads out, leaving Los Angeles in their past. Their future turns out to be in Hankston, Idaho. That's where she spies a half-finished house that has no electricity, no bathroom, no windows and no roof. She has no money but she sweet-talks its owner into selling. She takes a waitress job at the bowling alley and some of the other kids get jobs. They're the poorest people in town but they won't take charity, and they all begin to build a home of their own. Very predictable, yet it has charm.

Sex | Nud | Viol | Lang | AdSit

A: Kathy Bates, Edward Furlong, Soon-Teck Oh, Tony Campidi, Clarissa Lassig, Sarah Schaub

© POLYGRAM VIDEO 30447-3

HOMICIDE

D: David Mamet 100 m

R | CRM DMA ACT | 1991 | COLOR

7 Intriguing police drama that is both a fascinating character portrait and a revealing view into the nature of a policeman's extended family. Joe Mantegna is a good and dedicated cop. He is a respected negotiator whose skills involve him in a major case with a real nasty killer. But, he is sidetracked when he stumbles onto the unrelated killing of an old Jewish woman. At first he wants no part of her case but quickly becomes fascinated with it because she was a hero in Israel's independence movement. She inspires a pride in the Jewish heritage he has long denied and he suddenly has a yearning to belong again. But, a man cannot have two families.

Sex | Nud | Viol | Lang | AdSit

A: Joe Mantegna, William H. Macy, Natalija Nogulich, Ving Rhames, Rebecca Pidgeon, Vincent Guastaferro

© COLUMBIA TRISTAR HOME VIDEO 91443

HOOSIERS

D: David Anspaugh 114 m

PG | DMA | 1987 | COLOR

9 Thoroughly enjoyable slice of Americana. A very satisfying experience that the whole family will truly enjoy. Gene Hackman plays an unorthodox coach who gets one last chance at coaching in a small town high school in Indiana. His methods rankle everyone, on and off the team, until his team starts to win. He takes his underdogs to the championship. The town, the school, everybody is excited. The thrill is infectious even to the viewer. What is particularly gratifying is that this story was based upon a real-life incident in 1951 Indiana.

Sex | Nud | Viol | Lang | AdSit

A: Gene Hackman, Barbara Hershey, Dennis Hopper, Sheb Wooley, Fern Parsons, Brad Boyle

© LIVE HOME VIDEO 5191

HOPE AND GLORY

D: John Boorman 118 m

PG-13 · DMA WAR · 1987 · COLOR

9 This is an extremely well made English film that was highly praised by critics and was also a Best Picture nominee. It is the story of WWII and the London blitz as it was viewed from the eyes of a nine-year-old boy. Writer/director Boorman recaptures those experience as a time of great trauma and reappraisals for the adults, but just a grand adventure for him. His father is away, his mother is distracted and school is closed because of bombing raids. There is excitement, heroism, friendly soldiers and a live-for-today attitude everywhere. Alternately dramatic and funny, it is rich in characters and atmosphere.

Sex · Nud · Viol · Lang · AdSit

A: Sebastian Rice Edwards, Sarah Miles, David Hayman, Derrick O'Connor, Sammi Davis, Ian Bannen

© NEW LINE HOME VIDEO 7713

HOSPITAL, THE

D: Arthur Hiller 102 m

PG · COM DMA · 1971 · COLOR

8 An influential film and a bitingly funny black comedy about a chaotic modern hospital and its embittered chief surgeon (Scott) who is struggling against a system out of control. Scott battles a system in which patients come in relatively healthy but leave sicker or dead. His personal life is little better off until he has a brief encounter with a free spirit (Rigg) and her scheming father. The Paddy Chayefsky script won an Oscar and Scott was nominated. Funny in spite of the many uncomfortable truths it exposes - the film is based upon fact.

Sex · Nud · Viol · Lang · AdSit

A: George C. Scott, Diana Rigg, Barnard Hughes, Nancy Marchand, Richard Dysart, Stephen Elliott

Distributed By MGM/UA Home Video M202361

HOT SPOT, THE

D: Dennis Hopper 130 m

R · DMA · 1990 · COLOR

7 Sexy and sleazy modern-day film noir. Don Johnson is a scheming low-life, armed with a lack of morals and plenty of sex appeal, who drifts into a small Texas town where he gets a job selling cars to the yokels. In his off-hours, he romances both the boss's sultry wife and a sexy sweet young co-worker, while planning the robbery of the local bank. Instead, he gets sucked into a web of blackmail and murder. Trashy pulp spiced with some very interesting visuals from director Dennis Hopper. A little too long, and it comes up short in places - but you won't leave it.

Sex · Nud · Viol · Lang · AdSit

A: Don Johnson, Virginia Madsen, Jennifer Connelly, Jerry Hardin

© ORION PICTURES CORPORATION 8754

HOUSE OF THE SPIRITS

D: Bille August 109 m

R · ROM DMA · 1994 · COLOR

7 Meryl Streep and Jeremy Irons almost recapture the fire they created in THE FRENCH LIEUTENANT'S WOMAN. As a young man, Irons leaves to earn his fortune so that he may marry his love, but she dies before he can return. Distressed, he retreats to a remote ranch and becomes a despotic tyrant. Lonely, he returns to marry the gentle sister of his lost love. They develop a deep tender love, but still his oppressive ways hang like a pall over their house. Told over 50 years' time, this is the story of lost opportunity and the consequences of bitterness. Much of the complexity and motivations from the book are lost, but it still holds your attentions.

Sex · Nud · Viol · Lang · AdSit

A: Meryl Streep, Glenn Close, Jeremy Irons, Winona Ryder, Antonio Banderas, Teri Polo

© LIVE HOME VIDEO 49143

HOWARD'S END

D: James Ivory 143 m

PG · DMA · 1992 · COLOR

8 Beautifully executed film of E. M. Forster's English classic. Still, its very nature precludes it from being a film for general audiences. Set in very proper Edwardian England, it is the story of what happens when the very conservative, laisser-faire-wealthy Wilcoxes become entwined with the old-money, proto-feminist, Schlegel women. The Wilcoxes are staid, stuffy and stingy. The Schlegels are liberal, open and casual. Yet, their fates become intertwined when Ruth Wilcox (Redgrave) and Margaret Schlegel (Thompson) become friends and Ruth leaves Margaret her home called Howard's End. 9 Oscar nominations, won 3.

Sex · Nud · Viol · Lang · AdSit

A: Emma Thompson, Anthony Hopkins, Vanessa Redgrave, Helena Bonham-Carter, Samuel West

© COLUMBIA TRISTAR HOME VIDEO 26773

HUD

D: Martin Ritt m

DMA WST · 1963 · B&W

9 A very powerful adult drama and modern Western that contains one of the most memorable performances from Newman. Newman plays a selfish and irresponsible rake. He is the 30ish son of a Texas rancher (Douglas) who is now old and has fallen on hard times. Brandon de Wilde is the teenage son of Newman's dead brother. All three, and their salty housekeeper (Neal), live together on their dusty cattle ranch. The boy idolizes Newman, but the old man detests his son for his callous disregard for anyone but himself. Newman is tortured and bitter because his father rejects him. Their conflict has come to a head when their cattle become infected and must be destroyed. Winner of 3 Oscars.

Sex · Nud · Viol · Lang · AdSit

A: Paul Newman, Melvyn Douglas, Patricia Neal, Brandon de Wilde, John Ashley, Whit Bissell

© PARAMOUNT HOME VIDEO 6630

HUSTLER, THE

D: Robert Rossen 135 m

NR · DMA · 1962 · B&W

10 An outstanding and compelling drama of a cocky but self-destructive drifter who is striving for his place in the sun. Newman is outstanding as "Fast" Eddie Felson, a small-time pool hustler making a living in sleazy backstreet poolhalls. Eddie is so driven he feels compelled to play his game even after his hands are broken and when it means the destruction of relationship with the woman who loves him. His compulsive pursuit of the game leads him to the big leagues and a long-sought match with Minnesota Fats. Sequel 25 years later: THE COLOR OF MONEY.

Sex · Nud · Viol · Lang · AdSit

A: Paul Newman, Jackie Gleason, Piper Laurie, George C. Scott, Myron McCormick, Murray Hamilton

© CBS/FOX VIDEO 1006

ICE CASTLES

D: Donald Wrye 109 m

PG · DMA · 1979 · COLOR

7 An Iowa farm girl strives her whole life to become a world class figure skater. She even forsakes her boyfriend and her widowed father in her consuming pursuit of the Olympic gold in ice skating. But she is forced to change her plans when an accident leaves her blinded. However, with the help of her father and her boyfriend, she regains the courage needed to beat the odds and to skate again. Sentimental overload? Yes, but effectively done, bringing both laughter and tears. Enjoyable. Melissa Manchester sings Marvin Hamlisch's Oscar-nominated theme "Through the Eyes of Love."

Sex · Nud · Viol · Lang · AdSit

A: Robby Benson, Lynn-Holly Johnson, Colleen Dewhurst, Tom Skerritt, Jennifer Warren

© COLUMBIA TRISTAR HOME VIDEO 60018

ICEMAN

D: Fred Schepisi 101 m

PG · SF DMA · 1984 · COLOR

8 Fascinating and credible premise: An arctic exploration team finds a pre-historic Neanderthal man frozen in the ice. Incredibly, they are successful in restoring the man to life out of his frozen coma. Now the question becomes what to do with this incredible find. Some want even to dissect him, but anthropologist Hutton is interested in him as a human being and develops a strong rapport with the man. Very well done. The serious approach to the subject matter and excellent performances by the leads make this an intriguing adventure story.

Sex · Nud · Viol · Lang · AdSit

A: Timothy Hutton, Lindsay Crouse, John Lone, Josef Sommer, David Strathairn, Danny Glover

© MCA/UNIVERSAL HOME VIDEO, INC. 80074

IDOLMAKER, THE

D: Taylor Hackford 119 m

PG · DMA MUS · 1980 · COLOR

7 Slick filmmaking tells the story of a failed-songwriter turned promoter (played well by Sharkey) who stops at nothing to push, pull and shove two young Philadelphia boys into becoming national pop idols at the beginning of the rock `n roll revolution of the late '50s. Quite well done, even though some felt that it fell short at the end. Energetic performances and music recapture much of the feel of the period. Based upon the real-life rise of Frankie Avalon and Fabian.

Sex · Nud · Viol · Lang · AdSit

A: Ray Sharkey, Peter Gallagher, Paul Land, Maureen McCormick, Olympia Dukakis

Distributed By MGM/UA Home Video M600370

IF YOU COULD SEE WHAT I HEAR

D: Eric Till 100 m

PG · DMA COM · 1981 · COLOR

6 Interesting screen biography of real-life blind singer/composer Tom Sullivan. The story deals directly with his blindness and how he handles things. It begins with his college years, telling his story over time until he settles down after having several flings. The story stresses the more humorous elements of his situation and has, therefore, been criticized as being too simplistic, sugary-sweet and insubstantial. Others call it optimistic, life-affirming and uplifting. You'll get out of it whatever you look for.

Sex · Nud · Viol · Lang · AdSit

A: Marc Singer, R.H. Thomson, Sarah Torgov, Shari Belafonte Harper

© LIVE HOME VIDEO VA5014

I LIKE IT LIKE THAT

D: Darnell Martin 106 m

R · DMA · 1994 · COLOR

7 Lisette and Chino are the focus of a very loud but absorbing film about a disfunctional young Latino family. They live in the barrios of Bronx, crowded in and surrounded by poverty, drugs and joblessness. In spite of all that surrounds them, they love each other and their three children. Still, it is difficult and their fragile world begins to collapse when Chino gets thrown into jail for stealing a stereo for her. When Lisette is seen in a fancy car with another man, rumors begin. Chino believes them and cheats with another woman. Their relationship explodes. Very loud at first, but also very perceptive and it draws you in.

Sex · Nud · Viol · Lang · AdSit

A: Lauren Velez, Jon Seda, Rita Moreno, Jesse Borrego, Tomas Melly, Griffin Dunne

© COLUMBIA TRISTAR HOME VIDEO 73653

I'LL CRY TOMORROW

D: Daniel Mann 120 m

NR | DMA | 1956 | B&W | Sex | Nud | Viol | Lang | AdSit

8 Excellent and moving biography of actress and singer Lillian Roth. She was a very popular and highly envied celebrity from her youngest days as a child actress, but her personal life was one racked with doubt, failed marriages and alcoholism. Her inner turmoil led to total collapse into alcoholism. Then, on skid-row, she began to fight her way back. Susan Hayward received universal acclaim and an Oscar nomination for her masterful portrayal. She even did her own singing and did it very well. The real Lillian Roth eventually incorporated some of Hayward's singing style.

A: Susan Hayward, Eddie Albert, Richard Conte, Jo Van Fleet, Don Taylor, Ray Danton

Distributed By MGM/UA Home Video M301484

I'LL DO ANYTHING

D: James L. Brooks 116 m

PG-13 | DMA COM | 1994 | COLOR | Sex | Nud | Viol | Lang | AdSit

6 Nick Nolte plays Matt, a good but down-on-his-luck actor. Even after an Oscar nomination, he can't find steady work. And, now struggling, divorced and living in a rundown apartment, his spoiled 6-year-old daughter is moving in with him, and he has no idea what to do with her. His fortunes seem to have changed when an old friend gets him an audition but all that results is a job driving a second-rate movie director around. Then adding injury, his daughter lands a part. Originally planned to be a musical, but the preview audience responded badly, so the singing was pulled. Too slow for most, but fans of acting and Hollywood insiderisms may rate it even higher.

A: Nick Nolte, Albert Brooks, Julie Kavner, Joely Richardson, Tracey Ulman, Whittni Wright

© COLUMBIA TRISTAR HOME VIDEO 52623

IMAGE, THE

D: Peter Werner 91 m

NR | DMA | 1990 | COLOR | Sex | Nud | Viol | Lang | AdSit

8 Provocative and involving made-for-cable movie that was made in the same vein as NETWORK. A highly-rated television newsman, on a "60 Minutes"-type news show, is America's most-trusted man. However, he is so eager for good ratings that he cuts corners, resulting in the false accusation of a savings and loan vice president, who then commits suicide. This and a crumbling marriage cause him to suffer a serious moral crisis. Distressed, he reopens his investigation, revealing the truth to the public, even including his own mistake - much to the dismay of the network. Strong performance from Finney.

A: Albert Finney, Marsha Mason, Kathy Baker, Swoosie Kurtz

© HBO VIDEO 0384

IMAGINARY CRIMES

D: Anthony Drazan 106 m

PG | DMA | 1994 | COLOR | Sex | Nud | Viol | Lang | AdSit

7 A devastating portrait of the severely damaged lives caused by a man who has deluded himself and dragged his wife and his children along with him in an endless chase after a pot of gold that is perpetually only a "technicality away". His single-minded and careless determination to strike it rich, allows him to justify lying to and cheating people, all the while he destroys the love and respect of his family. His story is told from the perspective of his 17-year-old daughter. She eloquently describes the pain and embarrassment he unknowingly causes until eventually he runs out of new people to cheat and his lies have left him with no options. Somewhat slow, but very powerful.

A: Harvey keitel, Fairuza Balk, Kelly Lynch, Vincent Donofrio, Diane Baker, Chris Penn

© WARNER HOME VIDEO 13888

IMITATION OF LIFE

D: Douglas Sirk 124 m

NR | DMA | 1959 | COLOR | Sex | Nud | Viol | Lang | AdSit

7 Excellent soapbox drama. Lana Turner is a driven actress and Juanita Moore is her black housekeeper. Turner has been so dedicated to her career that she ignores the needs of her daughter (Dee), who then turns to Moore for the mothering she needs. But Moore is heart-broken because her own daughter is embarrassed about being black and tries to pass as white, which becomes the major focus of the movie. Fine performances by everyone make this a very effective and memorable tearjerker.

A: Lana Turner, John Gavin, Sandra Dee, Dan O'Herlihy, Susan Kohner, Juanita Moore

© MCA/UNIVERSAL HOME VIDEO, INC. 80152

IMMEDIATE FAMILY

D: Jonathan Kaplan 99 m

PG-13 | DMA COM | 1989 | COLOR | Sex | Nud | Viol | Lang | AdSit

6 Glenn Close and James Woods are wealthy yuppies who have everything except what they want most - a baby. They have tried everything else and now, in desperation, they try a process called open adoption, where the adoptive parents meet the mother before the baby is born. The mother is Mary Stuart Masterson, a gritty blue collar unwed mother who isn't yet totally committed to giving up her baby. This is a relatively simple story that covers ground covered before, but it exceeds the more typical fare because of the excellent acting from Masterson.

A: Glenn Close, James Woods, Kevin Dillon, Mary Stuart Masterson, Linda Darlow

© COLUMBIA TRISTAR HOME VIDEO 50193

IN COLD BLOOD

D: Richard Brooks 134 m

R | CRM SUS DMA | 1968 | B&W | Sex | Nud | Viol | Lang | AdSit

10 A chilling, very intense masterpiece relating the real world senseless murders of a Kansas farm family and the character of their psychotic murderers. It is taken from Truman Capote's best-selling book of the same name, which he based upon his extensive prison interviews of the two murderers. The events related are all the more chilling because of their matter-of-fact presentation. Blake and Wilson put in the performances of their lives as uncaring remorseless killers and the story related is their's from the time of the crime itself, through to their executions. Extremely powerful.

A: Robert Blake, Scott Wilson, John Forsythe, Jeff Corey, Will Geer, Paul Stewart

© COLUMBIA TRISTAR HOME VIDEO VH10342

IN COUNTRY

D: Norman Jewison 116 m

R | DMA | 1989 | COLOR | Sex | Nud | Viol | Lang | AdSit

7 Powerful story about a 17-year-old recent high school graduate (Emily Lloyd) who discovers some letters written by the father she never knew, who died in Vietnam. Searching to discover more about her father, she turns to her reclusive uncle (Bruce Willis). Willis puts in a solid performance as a veteran who has never come to grips with his own memories of the war and his feelings of guilt for having survived it. He has become a cynic and an alcoholic, but he pulls himself together to help her. Stirring and memorable final scene at the Vietnam Memorial.

A: Bruce Willis, Emily Lloyd, Joan Allen, Kevin Anderson, Richard Hamilton, Judith Ivey

© WARNER HOME VIDEO 11888

INCREDIBLE SHRINKING MAN, THE

D: Jack Arnold 81 m

NR | SF DMA | 1957 | B&W | Sex | Nud | Viol | Lang | AdSit

9 Thoughtful, well-made and intelligent science fiction classic that has not diminished with time. Grant Williams is an ordinary business man who, oddly, begins to shrink after walking through a strange mist. All science's efforts are unable to stop him from shrinking. As he shrinks, his status regarding all things around him alters. Eventually his trip ever smaller makes him invisible to the normal world. He is alone. Great special effects and action create excitement, but the lasting power of the film comes from the forced reevaluation of life as we know it. Excellent.

A: Grant Williams, Randy Stuart, Paul Lanton, April Kent, Raymond Bailey

© MCA/UNIVERSAL HOME VIDEO, INC. 80765

INDECENT PROPOSAL

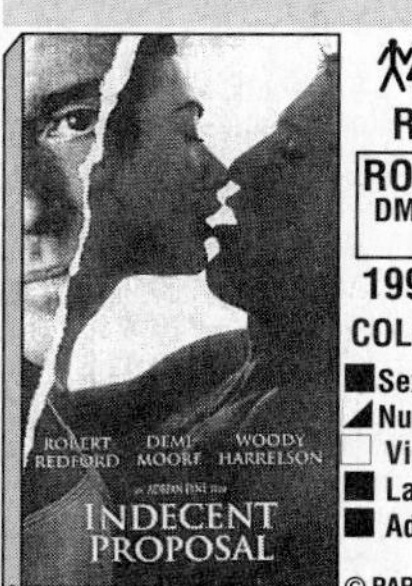

D: Adrian Lyne 119 m

R | ROM DMA | 1993 | COLOR | Sex | Nud | Viol | Lang | AdSit

7 Deeply-in-love newly-weds Demi Moore and Woody Harrelson had gotten themselves into a deep financial hole. They owed $50,000 on a loan that they couldn't repay. Then they thought they had found a way out. Billionaire Robert Redford offered them one million dollars if Woody will let Demi sleep with him for one night. They discussed it. They thought they could handle it. They agreed to do it. But, now the guilt and the doubt about having done it are tearing them both up inside. Its tearing the two of them apart, because all of a sudden, the money problem doesn't matter any more. Not great drama or even great soap opera, but it is interesting.

A: Robert Redford, Demi Moore, Woody Harrelson, Ikuver Platt, Seymour Cassel

© PARAMOUNT HOME VIDEO 32453

INDIAN SUMMER

D: Mike Binder 98 m

PG-13 | COM DMA | 1993 | COLOR | Sex | Nud | Viol | Lang | AdSit

8 Seven thirty-something friends are invited back for a twenty-year reunion to a summer camp in Ontario. The camp's director (Alan Arkin) has selected them as his favorite residents from years past and he wants them to share one last week with him there before he closes the camp forever. The seven stay in the lakeside cabins and partake in all the activities that they did in their youths, but this time everything is punctuated with contemplations and discussions of their current lives. It is sort of like THE BIG CHILL but is set on a lake and is much more light-hearted. It is also a clever, warm and nostalgic feel-good film.

A: Alan Arkin, Elizabeth Perkins, Vincent Spano, Diane Lane, Bill Paxton, Kevin Pollak

© TOUCHSTONE HOME VIDEO 1936

INDOCHINE

D: Regis Wargnier 156 m

PG-13 | FOR DMA | 1993 | COLOR | Sex | Nud | Viol | Lang | AdSit

7 Indochine is French for Indo-China or Vietnam. Catherine Deneuve is the middle-aged daughter of a French-colonialist rubber plantation owner. She has no permanent man but she has adopted the orphaned daughter of friends and the girl is her treasure. Deneuve has a brief, passionate affair with a French officer. So, when her daughter falls in love with the same man, Deneuve sees that he is sent to a remote post. But her daughter follows him there and is soon swallowed up in the communist rebellion that is beginning to swell up from the countryside. The film unwinds over 25 years of history and 2 1/2 hours on screen. It won Best Foreign Film Oscar, is beautifully filmed but is very long. Subtitles.

A: Catherine Deneuve, Vincent Perez, Linh Dan Pham, Jean Yanne, Dominique Blanc, Henri Marteau

© COLUMBIA TRISTAR HOME VIDEO 27233

I NEVER PROMISED YOU A ROSE GARDEN

D: Anthony Page — 92 m

R | DMA | 1977 | COLOR

8 This is a very intelligent and realistic depiction of a 16-year-old girl's (Quinlan) fight against schizophrenia. Her life is extremely frustrating for her with one day fading into the real world and the next slipping into a world of illusion and delusion. The only thing that gives her comfort is her relationship with her dedicated and caring psychiatrist (Anderson). Graphic and realistic, so it is also often unpleasant and unforgettable. Powerful performances.

Sex / Nud / Viol / Lang / AdSit

A: Bibi Andersson, Kathleen Quinlan, Reni Santoni, Susan Tyrrell, Signe Hasso, Diane Varsi

© WARNER HOME VIDEO 24033

I NEVER SANG FOR MY FATHER

D: Gilbert Cates — 90 m

PG | DMA | 1970 | COLOR

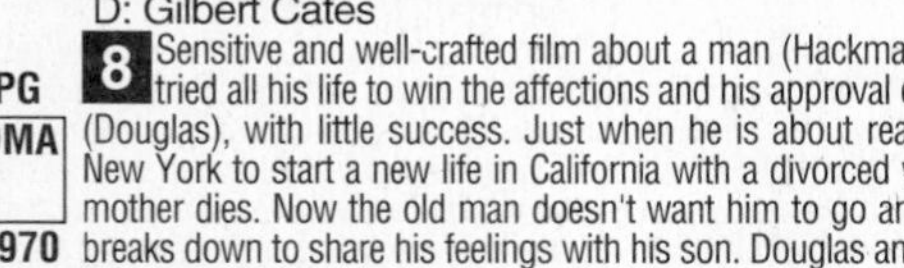

8 Sensitive and well-crafted film about a man (Hackman) who has tried all his life to win the affections and his approval of his father (Douglas), with little success. Just when he is about ready to leave New York to start a new life in California with a divorced woman, his mother dies. Now the old man doesn't want him to go and he finally breaks down to share his feelings with his son. Douglas and Hackman both received Oscar nominations for their powerful performances. Superb, but depressing.

Sex / Nud / Viol / Lang / AdSit

A: Melvyn Douglas, Gene Hackman, Dorothy Stickney, Estelle Parsons, Elizabeth Hubbard, Conrad Bain

© COLUMBIA TRISTAR HOME VIDEO 60847

INHERIT THE WIND

D: Stanley Kramer — 127 m

NR | DMA | 1960 | B&W

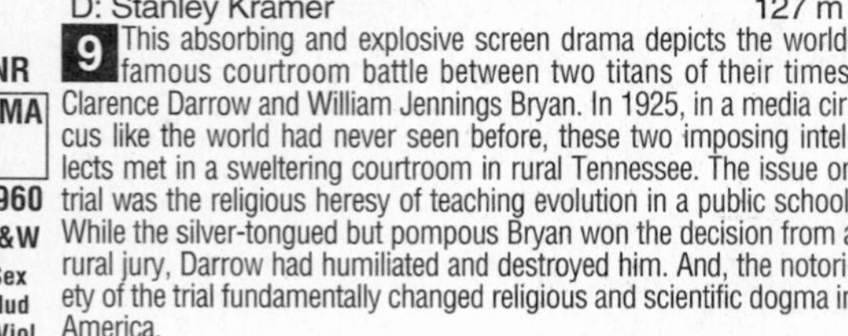

9 This absorbing and explosive screen drama depicts the world-famous courtroom battle between two titans of their times, Clarence Darrow and William Jennings Bryan. In 1925, in a media circus like the world had never seen before, these two imposing intellects met in a sweltering courtroom in rural Tennessee. The issue on trial was the religious heresy of teaching evolution in a public school. While the silver-tongued but pompous Bryan won the decision from a rural jury, Darrow had humiliated and destroyed him. And, the notoriety of the trial fundamentally changed religious and scientific dogma in America.

Sex / Nud / Viol / Lang / AdSit

A: Spencer Tracy, Fredric March, Gene Kelly, Dick York, Claude Akins, Harry Morgan

Distributed By MGM/UA Home Video M201649

INKWELL, THE

D: Matty Rich — 122 m

R | DMA COM | 1994 | COLOR

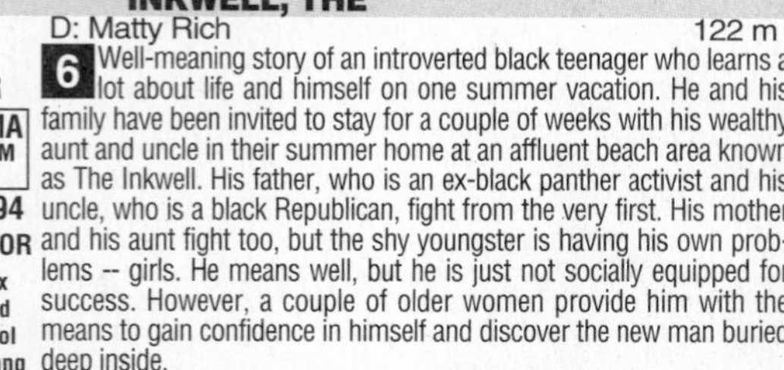

6 Well-meaning story of an introverted black teenager who learns a lot about life and himself on one summer vacation. He and his family have been invited to stay for a couple of weeks with his wealthy aunt and uncle in their summer home at an affluent beach area known as The Inkwell. His father, who is an ex-black panther activist and his uncle, who is a black Republican, fight from the very first. His mother and his aunt fight too, but the shy youngster is having his own problems -- girls. He means well, but he is just not socially equipped for success. However, a couple of older women provide him with the means to gain confidence in himself and discover the new man buried deep inside.

Sex / Nud / Viol / Lang / AdSit

A: Larenz Tate, Joe Morton, Suzzanne Douglas, Glynn Turman, Venessa Bell Calloway, Adrienne-Joi Johnson

© TOUCHSTONE HOME VIDEO 2749

INNER CIRCLE, THE

D: Andrei Konchalovsky — 122 m

PG-13 | DMA | 1992 | COLOR

6 Hulce is a young movie projectionist, newly married to Davidovich, living in pre-WWII Moscow. He, like many of the Russians of the time, is so enraptured with Stalin and the hope of communism that he blinds himself to the dehumanization it also brings. Dedicated to his job, he is made projectionist to Stalin himself and is so proud of his accomplishment that he naively becomes even more blinded - this time to the erosion of his wife's love for him and her brooding sadness. Slowly they are destroyed. Interesting, well photographed and sadly believable, but also grim, depressing and slow.

Sex / Nud / Viol / Lang / AdSit

A: Tom Hulce, Lolita Davidovich, Bob Hoskins, Alexandre Zbruev, Fedoor Chaliapin, Jr., Bess Beyer

© COLUMBIA TRISTAR HOME VIDEO 51073

INNOCENT, THE

D: Luchino Visconti — 125 m

R | FOR ROM DMA | 1979 | COLOR

9 Lush and beautifully photographed erotic tragedy of Italian decadence. A lustful nineteenth-century Italian nobleman (Giannini) ignores his beautiful wife (Antonelli) and pursues other women, particularly a beautiful widow (O'Neill). He not only fails to hide his escapades, but expects Antonelli to understand. She has an affair of her own with a young author. She has turned the tables on him. He is very surprised to learn that his lust for her has returned and he is now insanely jealous. Highly charged. Famed director Visconti's last film. Subtitles.

Sex / Nud / Viol / Lang / AdSit

A: Giancarlo Giannini, Laura Antonelli, Jennifer O'Neill, Rina Morelli, Massimo Girotti

© CONNOISSEUR VIDEO COLLECTION 1064

INN OF THE SIXTH HAPPINESS, THE

D: Mark Robson — 158 m

NR | DMA | 1958 | COLOR

8 Effective and heartwarming true story of English missionary Gladys Alward (Bergman) who determinedly opens a mission prior to the outbreak of World War II. She earns the respect and love of the locals and, in particular, the Mandarin (Donat), who agreed to convert to Christianity just for her. She falls in love with a Eurasian colonel (Jergens) but is forced to leave the country at the outbreak of the war. So she takes a group of war orphans on a dangerous cross country flight with her. Very involving. A simple, true story - well told.

Sex / Nud / Viol / Lang / AdSit

A: Ingrid Bergman, Curt Jurgens, Robert Donat, Ronald Squire

© FOXVIDEO 1170

INSIGNIFICANCE

D: Nicolas Roeg — 110 m

R | DMA COM | 1985 | COLOR

7 Intellectual and somewhat bizarre theatrical exercise. Four prominent public figures from the early '50s convene a very unusual impromptu meeting in a hotel room the evening before there is to be a congressional investigation into un-American activities. The characters, obviously Marilyn Monroe, Joe DiMaggio, Joseph McCarthy and Albert Einstein, engage in a sometimes humorous, sometimes serious discussion of sex, relativity and the nature of things. Clearly not for everyone's taste, but for the more esoteric viewer, an interesting and sometimes entertaining exercise.

Sex / Nud / Viol / Lang / AdSit

A: Theresa Russell, Michael Emil, Gary Busey, Tony Curtis

© WARNER HOME VIDEO 014

INTERIORS

D: Woody Allen — 92 m

PG | DMA | 1978 | COLOR

8 Extremely well-done but very downbeat serious work from Woody Allen. He examines the tortured lives of each member of an upper-class family that is tearing itself apart and who meet in a family gathering at a seaside retreat. Their troubled existences are exposed when the father announces that he is divorcing the cold mother to marry a spunky widow. Extremely serious stuff with no laughs here. Excellent performances provide insights into the causes of the frustrations that cause their heartbreaks. Moving, memorable and affecting, but not much fun.

Sex / Nud / Viol / Lang / AdSit

A: Diane Keaton, E.G. Marshall, Geraldine Page, Richard Jordan, Sam Waterston, Maureen Stapleton

Distributed By MGM/UA Home Video M800369

INTERNATIONAL VELVET

D: Bryan Forbes — 126 m

PG | DMA CLD | 1978 | COLOR

8 Entertaining sequel to the 1944 classic NATIONAL VELVET which starred a young Elizabeth Taylor. The English Steeplechase winner (Newman) is now forty years old. She has an orphaned American niece (O'Neal) who is determined to become an Olympic riding champion. A tough trainer (Hopkins) shows her the dedication it takes to become a winner. Excellent photography and fine acting help offset the fact that it is slightly overlong. Still, this is interesting human drama and enjoyable family entertainment.

Sex / Nud / Viol / Lang / AdSit

A: Tatum O'Neal, Christopher Plummer, Anthony Hopkins, Nanette Newman, Dinsdale Landen

Distributed By MGM/UA Home Video M600296

INTERVIEW WITH THE VAMPIRE

D: Neil Jordan — 123 m

R | DMA HOR | 1995 | COLOR

8 Brad Pitt plays Louis, a 200 year-old vampire, who has come to tell his melancholy story to reporter Christian Slater. In 1790's Louisiana, 24-year-old Louis had lost both his young wife in childbirth and his will to live, when he was "seduced" to the vampire-way by Lestat (Tom Cruise), an arrogant, consciousless, vampire killer. The guilt-ridden Louis refuses to kill humans and instead sucks the blood of rats, but yet looks upon Lestat as his mentor and teacher. When the tortured Louis takes pity upon a motherless girl, Lestat "converts" her for his friend Louis. But, Louis and the girl conspire to kill Lestat and then to travel the world to find more of their kind, to better understand their fate.

Sex / Nud / Viol / Lang / AdSit

A: Tom Cruise, Brad Pitt, Antonio Banderas, Stephen Rea, Christian Slater, Kirsten Dunst

© WARNER HOME VIDEO 13176

IN THE HEAT OF THE NIGHT

D: Norman Jewison — 110 m

NR | CRM MYS DMA | 1967 | COLOR

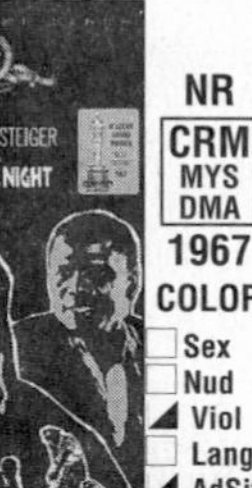

9 Powerhouse film that won 5 Oscars, including Best Picture, Best Screenplay and Best Actor. A black Philadelphia homicide detective is arrested at a Mississippi train station after a very important white man is found dead nearby. The gruff redneck sheriff (Steiger) is forced by the facts to release him and then is forced to ask the big city cop for his help in solving the mystery. This is a film that works on every level. It is a good mystery, great drama and has not lost any of its considerable punch with time. It is simply excellent.

Sex / Nud / Viol / Lang / AdSit

A: Sidney Poitier, Rod Steiger, Warren Oates, Lee Grant, Scott Wilson, Quentin Dean

Distributed By MGM/UA Home Video M201265

IN THE NAME OF THE FATHER

D: Jim Sheridan 133 m

R | DMA | 1994 | COLOR

8 7 Oscar nominations, including Best Picture. Based upon actual events, this is the story of Gerry Conlon, a petty Irish thief who finds himself caught between the IRA and the British Army. Gerry is sent to London by his father to start over but he remains a thief, but soon he is accused falsely by the police of masterminding a pub-bombing for the IRA. When his father comes to help, he too finds himself arrested as an accomplice. Both are then railroaded, convicted and sent to prison. Finally, after 15 years, a sympathetic lawyer has their case reheard and Gerry is released. He has finally matured, but his father is now dead. Stunning indictment of English law. Long and hindered by accents.

□ Sex ◢ Nud ◢ Viol ■ Lang ■ AdSit

A: Daniel Day-Lewis, Pete Postlethwaite, Emma Thompson, John Lynch, Corin Redgrave, Beatie Edney

© MCA/UNIVERSAL HOME VIDEO, INC. 81800

INTIMATE CONTACT

D: Waris Hussein 159 m

NR | DMA | 1987 | COLOR

8 Powerful human drama, originally made for British TV and shown on American cable in two parts. A successful businessman, his wife and their two children all have their comfortable lives turned upside down when he learns that he has contracted AIDS from a weekend encounter with a prostitute while away on a business trip. His wife decides to stand by him, even when they are both ostracized by friends and neighbors. She befriends other victims and comes to be a crusader for the rights of victims - while they both await his inevitable death. Moving and sympathetic. Very well done.

□ Sex □ Nud □ Viol ◢ Lang ■ AdSit

A: Claire Bloom, Daniel Massey, Abigail Cruttenden, Mark Kingston

© HBO VIDEO 0093

INTO THE WEST

D: Mike Newell 97 m

PG | CLD DMA | 1993 | COLOR

8 Excellent adventure story for kids over 10 and their parents. Set in modern-day Ireland, two young boys, 8 and 12 years old, are struggling to understand their place in the world. Their mother has died and their father has been drinking ever since. They are poor, nearly alone and they are gypsies, so they are despised by everyone. But, their grandfather has been followed home by a beautiful white horse which adopts the boys. The three are inseparable. The horse even stays with them in their 16th floor apartment until he is taken away by the authorities. So, the boys steal him back and begin a cross country odyssey, with the horse leading the way and their father and the police in pursuit.

□ Sex □ Nud ◢ Viol ◢ Lang ◢ AdSit

A: Gabriel Byrne, Ellen Barkin, Ruaidhri Conroy, Ciaran Fitzgerald, David Kelly, Johnny Murphy

© TOUCHSTONE HOME VIDEO 1594

INTO THIN AIR

D: Roger Young 97 m

NR | DMA CRM | 1985 | COLOR

8 Chilling and poignant fact-based story about a Canadian mother (Burstyn) who is absolutely relentless in her pursuit of her missing son. While on a trip back to summer school in Colorado, after visiting home, he just vanishes. Burstyn doggedly seeks out the facts about what happened to him, with the help of a retired detective. This is an excellent made-for-TV movie, but it is depressing.

□ Sex □ Nud ◢ Viol □ Lang ◢ AdSit

A: Ellen Burstyn, Robert Prosky, Sam Robards, Nicholas Pryor, Caroline McWilliams, John Dennis Johnston

© NEW STAR ENTERTAINMENT 1005

INVITATION TO A GUNFIGHTER

D: Richard Wilson 92 m

NR | WST DMA | 1964 | COLOR

7 A very different sort of Western. When a small town learns that a local outcast is returning home, they fear for the safety of their town, so they hire a tough gunslinger (Brynner) to kill him when he shows up. However, a major problem develops for the townsfolk when Brynner determines that the returning bad guy is a more worthwhile human being than anyone in the town he has been hired to protect. This may be too slow for some action fans, but it is interesting and definitely puts a different spin on things.

□ Sex □ Nud ◢ Viol □ Lang ◢ AdSit

A: Yul Brynner, George Segal, Janice Rule, Pat Hingle, Brad Dexter

Distributed By MGM/UA Home Video M202958

I OUGHT TO BE IN PICTURES

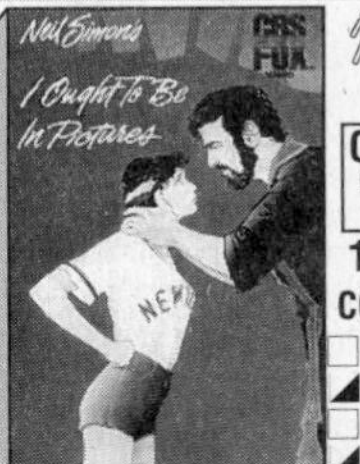

D: Herbert Ross 107 m

PG | COM DMA | 1982 | COLOR

8 Heartwarming Neil Simon story about a 19-year-old girl who travels to Los Angeles to become a movie star and to look up her long lost father. Matthau plays a burned out screenwriter who spends more time drinking and at the race track than he does writing, and who abandoned his family back in Brooklyn many years ago. Ann-Margret plays his girlfriend, who mediates between the two to eventually brings them back together, and gets Matthau's paternal genes to kick in. Very funny and affecting.

□ Sex ◢ Nud □ Viol ◢ Lang ◢ AdSit

A: Walter Matthau, Ann-Margret, Dinah Manoff, Lance Guest, Lewis Smith, Martin Ferrero

© FOXVIDEO 1150

IRONWEED

D: Hector Babenco 135 m

R | DMA | 1987 | COLOR

6 Oscar-nominated performances by the lead actors and a brilliant recreation of the Depression-era atmosphere only add to the sense of despair that this movie imparts. Nicholson and Streep both play homeless alcoholics living hand-to-mouth existences in 1938 Albany, New York. The story explores the histories and long-time relationship between these two miserable characters. It is unremittingly gloomy and bleak. But the movie's salvation lies in the brilliance of its two stars.

□ Sex ◢ Nud ◢ Viol ■ Lang ■ AdSit

A: Jack Nicholson, Meryl Streep, Carroll Baker, Michael O'Keefe, Diane Venora, Fred Gwynne

© LIVE HOME VIDEO 6022

IRON WILL

D: Charles Haid 109 m

PG | ACT DMA | 1994 | COLOR

8 It's 1917. Will Stoneman is a 17-year old South Dakota farm boy whose father raises sled dogs. When his father is killed, it looks like his mother may lose the farm and he'll never get to go to college. So, Will decides to enter a treacherous 522-mile dog-sled race through "the meanest stretch of land that God ever put together." For seven days, in mind-numbing 30-below cold, he will race against the best dog-sled racers in the world for the $10,000 prize, which he plans to win by running harder and sleeping less. This is a fictionalized account of an actual event. Predictable, but that doesn't stop it from being solid, rousing entertainment for the whole family.

□ Sex □ Nud ◢ Viol □ Lang ◢ AdSit

A: Mackenzie Astin, Kevin Spacey, David Ogden Stiers, August Schellenberg, Brian Cox, George Gerdes

© WALT DISNEY HOME VIDEO 2545

IRRECONCILABLE DIFFERENCES

D: Charles Shyer 112 m

PG | COM DMA | 1984 | COLOR

6 An unusual premise gives this picture a good opportunity to do something different and it almost does: a 10-year-old girl sues her parents for a divorce. A young couple have a good relationship until they each start to have some successes with their careers. Then they both become totally self-centered, devoted first to career and then to themselves. They exclude themselves from each other and even from their daughter. So she divorces them. A good premise, some funny moments and some poignant moments redeem this otherwise mediocre flick.

□ Sex ◢ Nud □ Viol ◢ Lang ◢ AdSit

A: Drew Barrymore, Ryan O'Neal, Shelley Long, Sharon Stone, Sam Wanamaker

© LIVE HOME VIDEO VA5057

ISADORA

D: Karel Reisz 153 m

NR | DMA MUS | 1968 | COLOR

6 Interesting, but very long, biography of a controversial and truly unique individual and a pivotal figure in creative dance. Isadora Duncan was a free-spirited artist who created scandal where ever she went. She was also one of the primary innovators of what became modern dance. Her animalistic and suggestive dancing style was considered very daring and her private life, having several relationships ongoing at the same time, was equally scandalous. The film explores it all, including the deaths of her children and her own bizarre death. Redgrave received an Oscar nomination for her efforts.

◢ Sex ◢ Nud □ Viol ◢ Lang ■ AdSit

A: Vanessa Redgrave, James Fox, Jason Robards, Jr., Ivan Tchenko, John Fraser, Bessie Love

© MCA/UNIVERSAL HOME VIDEO, INC. 80519

ISLANDS IN THE STREAM

D: Franklin J. Schaffner 110 m

PG | DMA | 1979 | COLOR

7 Ernest Hemingway's last and unfinished novel is here adapted for the screen. George C. Scott puts in one of the best performances of his life as a self-absorbed sculptor living an isolated and solitary life on a remote island at the outset of World War II. When he is visited by his three sons and ex-wife, his complacency is thrown into disarray and he is forced to reevaluate his life. However, he is shocked back into reality after one son is killed in the war, and he returns to humanity by helping to save a fleeing family. Emotion filled.

□ Sex □ Nud □ Viol ◢ Lang ■ AdSit

A: George C. Scott, David Hemmings, Claire Bloom, Susan Tyrrell, Gilbert Roland

© PARAMOUNT HOME VIDEO 8782

IS PARIS BURNING?

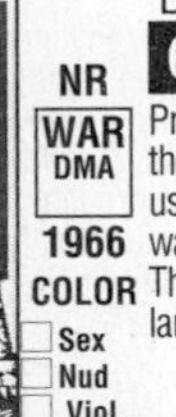

D: Rene Clement 173 m

NR | WAR DMA | 1966 | COLOR

6 This is a star-studded extravaganza, telling of the period in time from the Allied landing at Normandy to the recapture of Paris. Principally, the film concerns the Allied rush to reclaim Paris before the Nazis could destroy it. It is told in a semi-documentary style and uses many stories unfolding parallel to each other (much the same way as it was done in THE LONGEST DAY), to tell the over-all story. The numerous moderately involving stories are told with the help of a large international cast of actors.

□ Sex □ Nud □ Viol ◢ Lang ◢ AdSit

A: Jean-Paul Belmondo, Charles Boyer, Leslie Caron, Alain Delon, Kirk Douglas, Glenn Ford

© PARAMOUNT HOME VIDEO 6603

I WANT TO LIVE!

D: Robert Wise — 122 m

NR | DMA SUS | 1958 | B&W

8 Gripping movie that won Susan Hayward an Oscar for Best Actress and received five other nominations. It is based upon the true story of the 1955 execution of Barbara Graham, in California's San Quentin prison, for murder. Hayward is mesmerizing as she plays a girl who lived dangerously. She stole, was a drug addict and a prostitute but, according to the film, was framed for the robbery/murder of a widow. This is a bleak and downbeat story, but it is nonetheless gripping and compelling throughout.

Sex / Nud / Viol / Lang / AdSit

A: Susan Hayward, Simon Oakland, Virginia Vincent, Theodore Bikel

Distributed By MGM/UA Home Video M600760

I WILL FIGHT NO MORE FOREVER

D: Richard T. Heffron — 105 m

NR | WST DMA | 1975 | COLOR

8 Dramatic telling of the true story of the Nez Perce Indians and their leader Chief Joseph. In 1877 Chief Joseph attempted to lead his people north to Canada and to freedom in defiance of a government order to move them onto a reservation. The US government sent the Army to stop them and to bring them back. It was the last major calvary campaign for the plains Indians. The Nez Perce tied the Army up in a chase that lasted for five months, even though they had only 100 warriors. Excellent telling of a moving and affecting story.

Sex / Nud / Viol / Lang / AdSit

A: Ned Romero, James Whitmore, Sam Elliott, Linda Redfern

© GOODTIMES 8387

JACKNIFE

D: David Jones — 102 m

R | DMA ROM | 1989 | COLOR

8 This is powerful and captivating human drama that was created through the masterful performances of its stars. Ed Harris is a tormented Vietnam vet who lost his best friend in the war. He has become an alcoholic and now lives alone with his shy wallflower sister. Ten years after the war, he receives an unannounced visit from Robert De Niro, another friend from Vietnam and De Niro forces him to come to grips with the feelings that he has repressed for a long time. However, he also causes trouble in their complacent lives when De Niro begins courting Harris's sister. Moving drama.

Sex / Nud / Viol / Lang / AdSit

A: Robert De Niro, Ed Harris, Kathy Baker, Charles Dutton, Louden Wainwright, III

© HBO VIDEO 0213

JANE EYRE

D: Julian Amyes — 239 m

NR | ROM DMA | 1983 | COLOR

8 Classic tale of courage and romance from a 19th-century novel by Charlotte Bronte. A young girl is orphaned, mistreated and unloved. Now older, and possessing a strength born of that childhood, she is hired as governess for the household of the darkly moody and mysterious Mr. Rochester. Her willfulness brings her to his special attention and they fall in love. But their happiness is soon threatened by his dark secret. Exceptional presentation produced by the BBC.

Sex / Nud / Viol / Lang / AdSit

A: Timothy Dalton, Zelah Clarke

© FOXVIDEO 3760

JAWS

D: Steven Spielberg — 124 m

PG | SUS ACT DMA | 1975 | COLOR

10 A blockbuster hit that is both highly entertaining and technically masterful. An otherwise simplistic story line becomes a totally gripping adventure and leaves its audience terror-struck. A small town cop in a New England oceanside tourist town suspects that a great white shark is cruising the shoreline looking for lunch. Stubborn officials ignore his concerns until there is a major attack. The cop, a tenacious shark fisherman and a scientist set out to hunt down the shark, but... the gigantic creature turns to stalk them instead. Beware, this is a truly adrenaline pumping experience.

Sex / Nud / Viol / Lang / AdSit

A: Roy Scheider, Robert Shaw, Richard Dreyfuss, Larraine Gary, Murray Hamilton, Jeffrey Kramer

© MCA/UNIVERSAL HOME VIDEO, INC. 66001

JEAN DE FLORETTE

D: Claude Berri — 122 m

PG | FOR DMA | 1987 | COLOR

9 Emotionally powerful and beautifully filmed first half of the classic French tragedy of greed set in southeast France during the mid-1920s. A proud and greedy farmer (Yves Montand) plots with his simple-minded nephew to obtain much-needed water and to financially destroy their new neighbor during a drought. They do not tell him of a hidden spring on his land, which they want for themselves. Their new neighbor is a city-born hunchback (Depardieu) whose only dream is to be a farmer. Extremely moving performances evoke deep feelings. The second portion is MANON OF THE SPRING. Subtitles.

Sex / Nud / Viol / Lang / AdSit

A: Yves Montand, Daniel Auteuil, Gerard Depardieu, Elisabeth Depardieu

© ORION PICTURES CORPORATION 5033

JEREMIAH JOHNSON

D: Sydney Pollack — 116 m

PG | WST ACT DMA | 1972 | COLOR

10 Hugely popular adventure story set in the mid-19th century Rocky Mountains. Jeremiah Johnson is a man who has lost all taste for civilization and so escapes into the unknown wilds of the Rockies. This grandly photographed spectacle follows the loner's early stumbling efforts at survival through to his mastery of the elements. However, his idyllic life is destroyed when his new family is murdered by raiding Indians. He launches himself into a murderous mission of revenge and his success at it leads him to become a feared and legendary figure among the Indians. An extraordinary adventure.

Sex / Nud / Viol / Lang / AdSit

A: Robert Redford, Will Geer, Charles Tyner, Stefan Glerasch, Allyn Ann McLerie

© WARNER HOME VIDEO 11061

JESSE OWENS STORY, THE

D: Richard Irving — 174 m

NR | DMA | 1984 | COLOR

7 This is a made-for-TV docudrama that tells the story of famed American hero Jesse Owens. Owens was a black sharecropper's son who rose above his family's circumstances to go to college. At college, he broke track record after record and went on to the 1936 Olympics in Nazi Germany. There he won a fabulous, four gold medals and embarrassed Hitler and his prized supermen. For a brief while he was the pride of America, but he went home to face the same prejudices he had left, in the land that he loved and had called him a hero. For 30 years more he was both embarrassed and exploited, but he never faltered in his struggle for dignity.

Sex / Nud / Viol / Lang / AdSit

A: Dorian Harewood, Georg Stanford Brown, Debbi Morgan, Barry Corbin, Kai Wulff, George Kennedy

© PARAMOUNT HOME VIDEO 85040

JESUS

D: John Kirsh, Peter Sykes — 118 m

G | DMA | 1979 | COLOR

7 Unusually faithful reconstruction of the life of Christ as taken from the Gospel of Luke. Filmed in the Holyland with Israeli actors, this is a quite literal interpretation of Luke, backed by nine years of intensive research. All the props used in the filming and every aspect of the peoples lives depicted on screen are as authentic as was possible. Wherever possible authentic locations were used. This is a very sober "informational" film with no attempt to create any entertainment value. Narrated by Alexander Scourby.

Sex / Nud / Viol / Lang / AdSit

A: Brian Deacon, Rivka Noiman, Joseph Shiloah, Niko Nitai, Gadi Rol

© WARNER HOME VIDEO 11139

JESUS OF MONTREAL

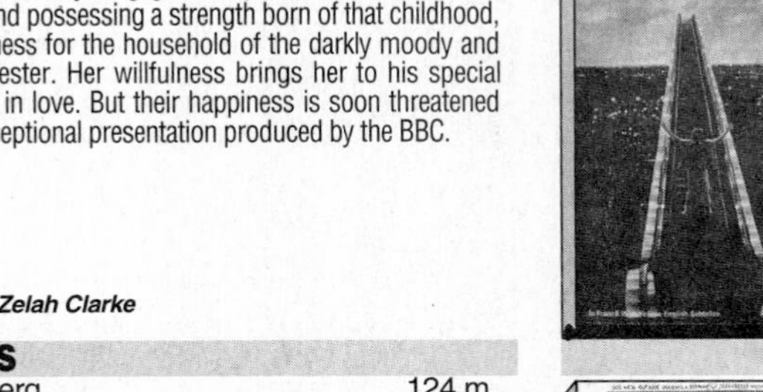

D: Denys Arcand — 119 m

R | FOR DMA COM | 1989 | COLOR

8 Nominated for Best Foreign Film. A group of unemployed actors get together some backers and form their own company for the presentation of the Passion Play on a hill overlooking Montreal. The play is in every way devout, but it does not follow traditional lines because it also attacks religious hypocrisy and commercialism. While it is well received by the community, the local clergy objects to it and so do its financial backers. The dilemma for the actors is whether to hold true to their ideals or to bow to pressure. Wickedly funny in places. Subtitles.

Sex / Nud / Viol / Lang / AdSit

A: Lothaire Bluteau, Catherine Wilkening, Johanne-Marie Tremblay, Remy Tirard, Robert Lepage, Gilles Pelletier

© ORION PICTURES CORPORATION 5057

JESUS OF NAZARETH

D: Franco Zeffirelli — 279 m

NR | DMA | 1976 | COLOR

9 Widely regarded as one of, if not the best, film telling of the story of Christ. Originally filmed for television, and populated by a huge big-name cast of Who's Whos, this is an extremely detailed and reverent recounting of the life of Christ as told by the four Gospels. It begins before his birth and goes through to the Crucifixion and Resurrection. Visually splendid and narratively involving, it was acclaimed by critics and religious leaders too. Very long, even though it has been edited down from the original TV length, but well worth the time spent.

Sex / Nud / Viol / Lang / AdSit

A: Robert Powell, Anne Bancroft, James Mason, Laurence Olivier, Rod Steiger, Ernest Borgnine

© LIVE HOME VIDEO 48988

JFK

D: Oliver Stone — 189 m

R | DMA MYS | 1991 | COLOR

9 Sensational and controversial, this is director Oliver Stone's alternative to the traditional and widely accepted (but not uncontested) Warren Commission version of the JFK assassination. Huge cast of talented big name actors and very high production standards combine with a long running time to cast the view that the assassination was inspired in the halls of government and involved both Cubans and New Orlean's homosexual community. Whether you accept Stone's allegations as fact or fiction, you will still find this to be compelling watching and a fascinatingly interwoven story.

Sex / Nud / Viol / Lang / AdSit

A: Kevin Costner, Tommy Lee Jones, Donald Sutherland, Jack Lemmon, Walter Matthau, Joe Pesci

© WARNER HOME VIDEO 12306

JOE

D: John G. Avildsen 107 m

R | DMA | 1970 | COLOR

Sex Nud Viol Lang AdSit

7 This is a controversial picture, both in content and style, and it reflected the broad divisions in America during the social turmoil of the late '60s. Bill, an affluent and liberal businessman, has killed his daughter's hippie/druggie boyfriend in a fit of rage. At a local bar, he lets the news slip to Joe, an ultra-conservative redneck. Both because Joe now knows his secret and because Joe is sympathetic to his reasons, he befriends Joe. He soon finds that he is more like the redneck than he thought possible, and he gets drawn ever deeper into Joe's world. Overly simplistic and not pleasant, but intriguing.

A: Peter Boyle, Susan Sarandon, Dennis Patrick, K. Callan, Audrey Caire, Patrick McDermick

Distributed By MGM/UA Home Video M203170

JO JO DANCER, YOUR LIFE IS CALLING

D: Richard Pryor 97 m

R | DMA COM | 1986 | COLOR

Sex Nud Viol Lang AdSit

6 Alternately involving and boring, bitterly sad and riotously funny, this is the thinly veiled semi-autobiographical account of Richard Prior. Entertainer JoJo Dancer's spirit rises from his half-dead body to contemplate everything which got him to that point. The film chronicles his life's story from its earliest painful beginnings through to his peak as a popular entertainer, with an almost brutal honesty. Richard Prior fans will find it enlightening, others may not enjoy it.

A: Richard Pryor, Debbie Allen, Carmen McRae, Diahnne Abbott, Barbara Williams

© GOODTIMES 4506

JOSEPHINE BAKER STORY, THE

D: Brian Gibson 129 m

R | DMA MUS | 1991 | COLOR

Sex Nud Viol Lang AdSit

8 One of the most outrageous, controversial and best loved entertainers of all time was Josephine Baker. This is her story. She was born at the turn of the 20th-century, desperately poor and black in St. Louis. Beginning on the vaudeville circuit in America, she parlayed her effervescent personality, unique singing and sizzling hot dancing into a trip to Paris. There, her nude dancing made her an international sensation and Paris became her home. She took life head on. She married royalty, was extravagant in every way possible. Interesting woman and entertaining film.

A: Lynn Whitfield, Ruben Blades, David Dukes, Louis Gossett, Jr., Craig T. Nelson

© HBO VIDEO 90571

JOSHUA THEN AND NOW

D: Ted Kotcheff 102 m

R | COM DMA | 1985 | COLOR

Sex Nud Viol Lang AdSit

7 Little-known Canadian gem that is the semi-autobiography of screenwriter Mordecai Richler (THE APPRENTICESHIP OF DUDDY KRAVITZ). James Woods plays a writer whose life is in shambles. He has just been falsely accused in the press of being homosexual and his wife has had a breakdown. His mind drifts and his life is shown in flashback. His father is a small-time gangster (Arkin is hysterical), who spent most of his time in prison, and his mother wanted to be a movie star, but was a stripper. No wonder his normal wife, the daughter of a rich senator, is crazy. Entertaining.

A: James Woods, Gabrielle Lazure, Alan Arkin, Michael Sarrazin, Linda Sorenson, Alan Scarfe

© FOXVIDEO 1488

JOURNEY OF HOPE

D: Xavier Koller 111 m

PG | FOR DMA | 1991 | COLOR

Sex Nud Viol Lang AdSit

9 Compelling winner of the 1990 Best Foreign Language Film Oscar. Haydar and his family are desperately poor and persecuted Kurds living in a small village in Turkey. Distraught and tired of his plight, he decides to emigrate to Switzerland - to Paradise - after receiving a post card from there. He sells everything he has, except for a few small possessions. Then, he and his wife take one son and leave the other six children behind to begin their clandestine journey of hope. However, before their journey is over, he will be lied to repeatedly, savagely abused and swindled out of all their money. Heartbreaking, but extremely powerful. Subtitles.

A: Necmettin Cobanoglu, Emin Sivas, Nur Surer

© HBO VIDEO 90675

JOURNEY OF NATTY GANN, THE

D: Jeremy Paul Kagan 101 m

PG | DMA ACT CLD | 1985 | COLOR

Sex Nud Viol Lang AdSit

9 This is a wonderfully endearing story that has the rare quality of being a family movie that has a genuine appeal both to young and to old. Natty Gann is a young girl in Depression-era Chicago, whose desperate father has to leave her, on short notice and without saying goodbye, with a very unpleasant old woman so he can take a good job in Seattle. Natty refuses to believe her father has deserted her and embarks on a cross-country trip by rail to go to him. She is all alone, except for a protective wolf and a hardened drifter she meets along the way. Very appealing, highly entertaining and very worthwhile.

A: Meredith Salenger, John Cusack, Ray Wise, Lainie Kazan, Barry Miller, Scatman Crothers

© WALT DISNEY HOME VIDEO 400

JOY LUCK CLUB, THE

D: Wayne Wong 139 m

R | DMA | 1993 | COLOR

Sex Nud Viol Lang AdSit

9 An extremely moving drama. Four women, each of whom has emigrated from China under tragic circumstances, has met each week for years to play mah-jongg and to compare their lives; and, each has a daughter. Now, one of the four mothers has died and the survivors have met. Through a series of flashbacks, each mother's story is told and a each daughter's life is explored. The hopes of the old-world mothers for their prosperous new-world daughters have caused much pain and a lack of understanding between the generations. It doesn't matter that these women are Chinese. This is a universal story of mothers and daughters, love, anger and self-doubt resolved. Beautiful and extremely popular.

A: France Nuyen, Rosalind Chao, Ming-Na Wen, Tsai Chin, Tamlyn Tomita, Lisa Lu

© HOLLYWOOD PICTURES HOME VIDEO 2291

JUDGEMENT AT NUREMBURG

D: Stanley Kramer 187 m

NR | DMA WAR | 1961 | B&W

Sex Nud Viol Lang AdSit

10 12 Oscar nominations. Galvanizing and masterful production of the post World War II war-crimes trials at Nuremberg, Germany. Tracy is an American judge who must decide the fate of four German judges charged with manipulating the law to help Nazis prosecute Jews in the Holocaust. In pursuit of that end, the film examines the lives of several people deeply affected by the tragedy. The ultimate question to be answered is, how responsible are people for following the orders of their superiors? An intelligent and thoughtful production with a large cast and excellent performances.

A: Spencer Tracy, Burt Lancaster, Maximilian Schell, Richard Widmark, Marlene Dietrich, Montgomery Clift

Distributed By MGM/UA Home Video M301536

JUDGMENT IN BERLIN

D: Leo Penn 92 m

PG | DMA SUS | 1988 | COLOR

Sex Nud Viol Lang AdSit

8 Interesting, intense and unusual courtroom drama based upon the actual 1978 hijacking of a Polish airliner to a US base in West Germany by an East German couple using a toy gun. The communists want the criminals returned. Trying to defuse an embarrassing and politically explosive situation, an American judge (Sheen) is brought in by the American government to decide if a hijacking to escape communism is justifiable. Excellent performances by Sheen and Penn (in a small role) make this a very involving and very watchable experience.

A: Martin Sheen, Sam Wanamaker, Max Gail, Heinz Hoenig, Carl Lumbly, Sean Penn

© NEW LINE HOME VIDEO 62774

JU DOU

D: Zhang Yimou 98 m

NR | FOR ROM DMA | 1991 | COLOR

Sex Nud Viol Lang AdSit

9 Magnificent and visually stunning picture from China that Chinese officials tried to hide. At the urging of major American directors, it received a much-deserved nomination for the Best Foreign Film. It is the story of a beautiful young woman purchased by a wealthy bitter old man in 1920 China. He is sterile but, because she is unable to bear him the son that he wants, he beats her and treats her as an animal. The man's near-slave adopted son consoles her. They meet in secret and become passionate lovers. But when she becomes pregnant, their lives become hell. Powerful. Subtitles.

A: Gong Li, Li Baotian, Li Wei, Zhang Yi, Zheng Jian

© LIVE HOME VIDEO 68983

JUICE

D: Ernest R. Dickerson 95 m

R | DMA | 1992 | COLOR

Sex Nud Viol Lang AdSit

6 Realistic and very downbeat story of four high school-aged black kids in Harlem skipping school and going nowhere fast. Epps is the only one of the four who has any ambition. He wants to become a DJ, but his friends only aspire to doing small-time scams and acting tough. Against his wishes, he accompanies them on a robbery of the local market, but things go drastically wrong when one of them shoots the clerk. This causes a split in their group and the shooter shoots two of his friends. Very unattractive characters and constant swearing diminish effectiveness.

A: Omar Epps, Jermaine Hopkins, Tupac Shakur, Khalil Kain, Cindy Herron, Vincent Laresca

© PARAMOUNT HOME VIDEO 32758

JULIA

D: Fred Zinnemann 118 m

PG | DMA SUS | 1977 | COLOR

Sex Nud Viol Lang AdSit

9 This is a captivating human thriller, written by the late author Lillian Hellman concerning her life-time friendship with her unusual friend Julia. Lillian (Fonda) and Julia (Redgrave) were childhood friends. Julia was born to wealth and has devoted her life to activist causes. It is now the 1930s and Julia is an activist fighting against the relentless onslaught of Nazism inside Germany. While traveling in Europe, Lillian is approached to smuggle money to her friend Julia inside Germany. This is a very involving production that was extremely well done and was very popular. Three Oscars.

A: Jane Fonda, Vanessa Redgrave, Jason Robards, Jr., Maximilian Schell, Meryl Streep, Hal Holbrook

© FOXVIDEO 1091

JULIET OF THE SPIRITS

D: Federico Fellini — 142 m

NR | FOR DMA FAN | 1964 | COLOR

8 A famous Fellini film. Juliet is an Italian housewife who is complacent in her dull life, thinking that the reason her husband largely ignores her is only because he works too much. However, one night, they hold a seance and she finds that she can actually talk to the spirits. They tell her that she deserves to enjoy life more. The film then becomes an attempt to illustrate the penetration the female psyche through a series of symbolic, surrealistic and gaudy images which fly by the viewer so fast that it is hard to keep track of them. Sort of a female 8 1/2. Largely for film fans. Subtitles.

Sex Nud Viol Lang AdSit

A: Giulietta Masina, Sandra Milo, Mario Pisu, Valentina Cortese, Lou Gilbert, Sylva Koscina

© CONNOISSEUR VIDEO COLLECTION 1017

JUNGLE FEVER

D: Spike Lee — 131 m

R | DMA ROM | 1991 | COLOR

7 Independent director Spike Lee once again raises some controversial questions when he explores racism from both sides of an interracial love affair. It is not a feel good film, nor a naively idealistic one - but one much more realistic, and one that takes a hard look at love, life and society. Snipes is a successful, upwardly mobile happily married black architect from Harlem who falls for his blue collar Italian secretary (Sciorra). Their affair ignites explosive intolerance from both of their families and their friends that is so fierce that they buckle under the pressure.

Sex Nud Viol Lang AdSit

A: Wesley Snipes, Annabella Sciorra, Spike Lee, Ossie Davis, Ruby Dee, Samuel L. Jackson

© MCA/UNIVERSAL HOME VIDEO, INC. 81093

JUNIOR BONNER

D: Sam Peckinpah — 101 m

PG | DMA COM WST | 1972 | COLOR

8 Steve McQueen is an aging rodeo has-been who comes back to his hometown for one last ride and to try to make peace with his family in this modern-day Western. Everything and everybody there has changed. His mother and father are separated and his brother sells real estate. This is an interesting comedy/drama that explores life's changes for all the major characters involved but particularly McQueen. Preston is great as his hard-drinking dad but so is McQueen as the soft-spoken cowboy stumbling through life.

Sex Nud Viol Lang AdSit

A: Steve McQueen, Robert Preston, Ida Lupino, Ben Johnson, Joe Don Baker, Barbara Leigh

© CBS/FOX VIDEO 8019

JUST BETWEEN FRIENDS

D: Allan Burns — 110 m

PG-13 | DMA COM | 1986 | COLOR

8 A likable different sort of tearjerker. Christine Lahti is a successful single newswoman who meets Mary Tyler Moore (married to Ted Danson) at an aerobics class, and they become fast friends because they have so much in common. Christine tells her friend that she is having an affair with a man who she knows is married. Yes, you guessed it - it's the same guy, but neither woman knows that. That is until the next twist comes when Christine finds that she is pregnant, at the same time that Danson is killed in a plane wreck. Good mixture of laughs and tears as these two try to sort out how they feel.

Sex Nud Viol Lang AdSit

A: Mary Tyler Moore, Christine Lahti, Sam Waterston, Ted Danson, Mark Blum, Jane Geer

© HBO VIDEO TVA3919

K2

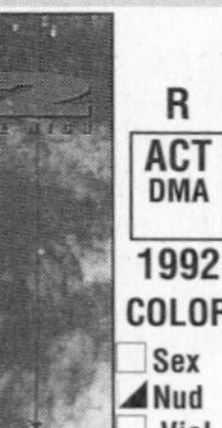

D: Franc Roddam — 104 m

R | ACT DMA | 1992 | COLOR

7 Stunningly beautiful photography and dramatic mountain climbing sequences are the primary attractions to this film. Two best friends, one an aggressive, womanizing lawyer and the other a very married physics professor, talk their way into a group that will attempt to climb the second tallest mountain in the world, the 29,064 foot peak of K2 in the Himalayas. This pretty good man-verses-the-elements story is augmented with the lessor, but significant, parallel story of the personal realization by the lawyer of his self-imposed personal isolation. However, the thrill of the adventure is what most will remember.

Sex Nud Viol Lang AdSit

A: Michael Biehn, Matt Craven, Raymond J. Barry, Hiroshi Fujioka, Patricia Charbonneau, Luca Bercovici

© PARAMOUNT HOME VIDEO 32828

KALIFORNIA

D: Dominic Sena — 118 m

NR | CRM DMA | 1993 | COLOR

7 Extremely intense portrait of a serial killer. Brian is a writer and his girlfriend Carrie is a photographer. They want a new start in California, so they plan a cross-country trip, visiting sites of serial murders along the way. He will write and she will take pictures. They place an advertisement on the bulletin board for someone to share their expenses. Their ad is answered by Early and Adele. Early is a crude live-in-the-moment kind, and Adele is a simple-minded waitress. Brian admires Early's attitude, but Carrie sees danger in him. She is right, Early is a remorseless killer and they will now witness murder first hand. Brilliant, brutal acting by Pitt. Not a pretty picture to watch.

Sex Nud Viol Lang AdSit

A: Brad Pitt, Juliette Lewis, David Duchovny, Michelle Forbes

© POLYGRAM VIDEO 88933-3

KANAL

D: Andrzej Wajda — 96 m

NR | FOR WAR DMA | 1956 | B&W

9 It is May of 1944 and Warsaw has been reduced to rubble by the Nazis. There is only one small chance for the defeated and demoralized Resistance fighters to escape. They are ordered to descend into the foul, dark and claustrophobic sewers. The terror and despair is palpable. The Germans will shoot at them if they emerge and throw grenades down manholes when they don't. Only one, a young woman, knows the way out, but her boyfriend is desperately wounded. They are trapped down below. One of three in a trilogy of Polish war films by Wajda. Others include: A GENERATION and ASHES AND DIAMONDS. Subtitles.

Sex Nud Viol Lang AdSit

A: Teresa Izewska, Tadeusz Janczar, Wienczyslaw Glinski, Tadeusz Gwiazdowski

© HOME VISION KAN 020

KARATE KID, THE

D: John G. Avildsen — 126 m

PG | ACT DMA | 1984 | COLOR

9 A real audience pleaser. A fatherless kid (Macchio) arrives in Southern California from New Jersey. Out of place and constantly hassled by some street toughs, he finds an unlikely friend and mentor in the apartment complex's Japanese gardner (Morita). Morita gains the boy's confidence and decides to train the boy in karate to give him the confidence he needs. But, in so doing, he also instructs him in a personal code of honor. This is an old fashioned sort of feel-good movie that doesn't hide its attempts to play with your emotions, and you won't care. You'll be cheering.

Sex Nud Viol Lang AdSit

A: Ralph Macchio, Noriyuki "Pat" Morita, Elisabeth Shue, Martin Kove, William Zabka

© COLUMBIA TRISTAR HOME VIDEO 60406

KARATE KID PART II, THE

D: John G. Avildsen — 113 m

PG | ACT DMA | 1986 | COLOR

7 This sequel begins immediately after the original ends. Morita receives notice that his father in Japan is dying. When he and "the kid" (Macchio) arrive in Okinawa, Morita is immediately and forcefully reminded of an old feud with an old rival. Morita sets about resolving that situation and also revives an old love. Macchio also finds love with a village girl and a new enemy in the nephew of Morita's old foe. This film is most notable for its repeat appearance of a cast of likable characters, and the feel-good finish. Enjoyable, but predictable.

Sex Nud Viol Lang AdSit

A: Ralph Macchio, Noriyuki "Pat" Morita, Nobu McCarthy, Martin Kove, William Zabka

© COLUMBIA TRISTAR HOME VIDEO 60717

KHARTOUM

D: Basil Dearden — 136 m

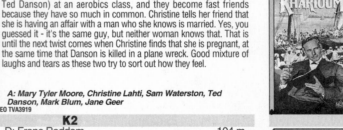

NR | ACT DMA | 1966 | COLOR

8 Sweeping quasi-historical spectacle which tells the saga of Britain's battle for control over the Sudan, and of the rivalry between a British general (Heston) and a Moslem holy man (Olivier) named "The Mahdi" by his followers. In spite of their respect for each other, these two could not compromise and in 1883 The Mahdi led his followers in a long and arduous siege of the Sudanese city of Khartoum. The siege was eventually successful and led to the downfall of the British. Grand spectacle, well-mounted large battle sequences and some notable acting make this an entertaining diversion.

Sex Nud Viol Lang AdSit

A: Charlton Heston, Laurence Olivier, Richard Johnson, Ralph Richardson, Alexander Knox, Johnny Sekka

Distributed By MGM/UA Home Video M202009

KILLING FIELDS, THE

D: Roland Joffe — 142 m

R | DMA WAR SUS | 1984 | COLOR

10 An absolutely unforgettable picture. A lacerating and highly charged emotional drama based upon the real events surrounding the fall of Cambodia and the American evacuation. New York Times correspondent Sidney Schanberg is aided in a last minute escape by his close friend and interpretor Dith Pran, but Pran can't get out. He is left to face the horrifying re-education camps of the Khmer Rouge and murder on a massive scale, but Schanberg never stops in his struggles to find and free him. Stunning portrait of a society gone mad! Three Oscars and three additional nominations.

Sex Nud Viol Lang AdSit

A: Sam Waterston, Haing S. Ngor, John Malkovich, Julian Sands, Craig T. Nelson

© WARNER HOME VIDEO 11419

KING CREOLE

D: Michael Curtiz — 116 m

NR | DMA MUS | 1958 | B&W

8 Presley surprised quite a few critics with this performance. He was an unexpected choice for this dramatization of "A Stone for Danny Fisher" after James Dean died, but Hal Wallis tailored it perfectly for him. He plays a young would-be singer, bordering on delinquency and working as a busboy in a mobster's (Matthau) nightclub. Carolyn Jones is Matthau's mistress. When she is publicly mistreated, Presley comes to her defense. So, to embarrass him, Matthau makes him stand up before the crowd and sing, but instead he is a hit. Over a dozen songs including "Hard Headed Woman" and "Trouble."

Sex Nud Viol Lang AdSit

A: Elvis Presley, Carolyn Jones, Dolores Hart, Dean Jagger, Liliane Montevecchi, Walter Matthau

© CBS/FOX VIDEO 2005

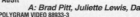

KING LEAR

D: 170 m

NR | DMA | 1984 | COLOR

9 A stellar production, by an all-star cast, headed by the brilliant Olivier (at age 75) playing the old king driven to madness by his scheming daughters. It is a story of greed, lust for power and an old man longing for past loyalties. It is tragedy on a grand scale, and a fitting climax to a triumphant career for one of the world's finest actors. Made for television, and winner of an Emmy.

Sex / Nud / Viol / Lang / AdSit

A: Laurence Olivier, Diana Rigg, John Hurt, Leo McKern, Colin Blakely

© KULTUR VIDEO 1223

KING OF COMEDY, THE

D: Martin Scorsese 108 m

PG | DMA COM | 1982 | COLOR

6 A strange black comedy with a daring performance by Robert De Niro. He plays a bizarre loser who is obsessed with becoming a comedian. His only audience has been a tape recorder, yet he believes he could become a famous if only he could get a big break on a popular late evening talk show, hosted by Jerry Lewis. So he creates an elaborate scheme to get on the program by kidnapping Lewis and holding him hostage until he can appear. The film does present a stark view of a cold-hearted and very unfair business, but the main character is also very unsympathetic.

Sex / Nud / Viol / Lang / AdSit

A: Robert De Niro, Jerry Lewis, Sandra Bernhard, Shelley Hack, Tony Randall, Ed Herlihy

© COLUMBIA TRISTAR HOME VIDEO 60027

KING OF KINGS

D: Nicholas Ray 170 m

NR | DMA | 1961 | COLOR

9 A reverent and very traditional telling of the life of Christ. It is a story simply yet intelligently told, and grandly filmed in CinemaScope. Christ's life is told from its beginning in the manger, through to his death on the cross, and including such important events as his wandering in the desert, The Sermon on the Mount and, of course, The Last Supper. A large-scale spectacular that had a cast of thousands. Narrated by Orson Welles.

Sex / Nud / Viol / Lang / AdSit

A: Jeffrey Hunter, Siobhan McKenna, Robert Ryan, Hurd Hatfield, Viveca Lindfors, Rita Gam

Distributed By MGM/UA Home Video M700326

KING OF MARVIN GARDENS

D: Bob Rafelson 104 m

R | DMA | 1972 | COLOR

8 This film came two years after Jack Nicholson's smash success in FIVE EASY PIECES, also directed by Rafelson. This time he plays the younger brother of a big-time dreamer and a small time schemer, Bruce Dern. Nicholson has dubbed his brother the king of Marvin Gardens and has come to visit him in Atlantic City. Dern has just been released on bail and introduces Nicholson to fading beauty queen Ellen Burstyn and her step-daughter. Dern has come up with a new scheme: he will create a beauty contest and use the proceeds to buy an island near Hawaii. Interesting characters and performances, sometimes depressing but also frequently haunting.

Sex / Nud / Viol / Lang / AdSit

A: Jack Nicholson, Bruce Dern, Ellen Burstyn, Julia Anne Robinson, Scatman Crothers

© COLUMBIA TRISTAR HOME VIDEO 52803

KING OF THE GYPSIES

D: Frank Pierson 112 m

R | DMA | 1978 | COLOR

6 Fascinating but unpleasant look into a culture foreign to virtually all others. It is one based upon dishonesty, deception, fortune tellers and all-night celebrations. Sterling Hayden is a dying Gypsy king who elects to skip over his son and leave the tribe's leadership to his grandson, who would rather escape his heritage but ultimately cannot. Hirsch, the son passed over, sets about on a quest to kill his own son. Based upon a non-fiction best-seller by Peter Maas. See also ANGELO MY LOVE.

Sex / Nud / Viol / Lang / AdSit

A: Sterling Hayden, Shelley Winters, Susan Sarandon, Judd Hirsch, Eric Roberts, Brooke Shields

© PARAMOUNT HOME VIDEO 8868

KING OF THE HILL

D: Steven Soderbergh 103 m

PG-13 | DMA | 1993 | COLOR

7 An intelligent and earnest film describing the effects of the Great Depression on one bright but innocent young boy, trying to grow up in St. Louis in 1933. He and his younger brother have lived with his tubercular mother and salesman father in middle-class harmony, until his father lost his job. The four of them have been forced to move into a cheep hotel, but he is embarrassed and doesn't want his friends to know what has happened. So, he has created a web of deception to try to maintain his middle class identity, even when his brother had to be sent away, his mother went into the hospital and his father had to take to the road, leaving him behind alone. Well done.

Sex / Nud / Viol / Lang / AdSit

A: Jerone Krabbe, Lisa Eichhorn, Karen Allen, Spalding Greey, Elizabeth McGovern, Jesse Bradford

© MCA/UNIVERSAL HOME VIDEO, INC. 81651

KING RAT

D: Bryan Forbes 135 m

NR | DMA WAR | 1965 | B&W

8 Excellent drama based on the daily life in a WWII Japanese POW camp in Singapore. This story, taken from a James Clavell (author of SHOGUN) novel, is that of a streetwise opportunistic American who rises above everyone else in his prison camp to become the unscrupulous and powerful head of the camp's black market. Known to his fellow prisoners as King Rat, even the officers assist him in his powerplays in exchange for food and money. This is an unvarnished story of survival on a basic level. Segal is convincingly despicable in a role that Newman and McQueen turned down.

Sex / Nud / Viol / Lang / AdSit

A: George Segal, Tom Cortenay, James Fox, Patrick O'Neal, Denholm Elliott, James Donald

© COLUMBIA TRISTAR HOME VIDEO 60028

KINGS GO FORTH

D: Delmer Daves 110 m

NR | DMA ROM | 1958 | COLOR

7 Extremely controversial upon its release, this film still has relevance today. Two American soldiers, a veteran sergeant (Sinatra) and a recent newcomer and playboy (Tony Curtis), fight together on the battlefield of WWII France. Off the battlefield, they compete for the heart of a beautiful French girl (Natalie Wood). However, both of their characters are severely tested when she reveals to them that she is half-white and half-black. A little soapy, but with this quality of talent, that is easy to overlook.

Sex / Nud / Viol / Lang / AdSit

A: Frank Sinatra, Tony Curtis, Natalie Wood, Leora Dana, Karl Swenson

Distributed By MGM/UA Home Video M301730

KISS OF THE SPIDER WOMAN

D: Hector Babenco 120 m

R | DMA | 1985 | COLOR

7 Compelling and unusual English-language film from Brazil that was a Best Picture nominee. Two vastly different men are confined together in a Brazilian prison. Raul Julia is a political activist and Hurt (who won an Oscar) is just a gay window dresser. At first the two have nothing in common, but gradually Julia lets Hurt help him pass the days and entertain him with his vibrant retellings of old movies. Gradually each man begins to understand the other and they become close friends. Daring and oddly compelling movie.

Sex / Nud / Viol / Lang / AdSit

A: William Hurt, Raul Julia, Sonia Braga, Jose Lewgoy

© NEW LINE HOME VIDEO 90001

KITCHEN TOTO, THE

D: Harry Hook 96 m

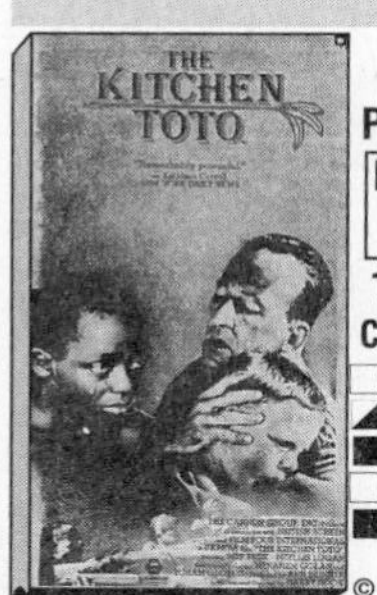

PG-13 | DMA | 1987 | COLOR

7 Critically acclaimed and powerful film about a ten-year-old orphaned black boy in 1950s British colonial Kenya. When his pacifist father is murdered, the boy is taken in by the white chief of police, as a kindness, to be a kitchen servant. When massive racial violence between East African tribesmen and the British break out in the famous Mau Mau uprising, the Mau Mau rebels, who had killed his father, demand that he kill his white masters or be killed himself. The film is slowly paced and demands your attention, but patient viewing will be rewarded.

Sex / Nud / Viol / Lang / AdSit

A: Edwin Mahinda, Bob Peck, Phyllis Logan, Kirsten Hughes, Robert Urouhart, Nicholas Chase

© WARNER HOME VIDEO 37069

KNIFE IN THE WATER

D: Roman Polanski 95 m

NR | FOR DMA | 1962 | B&W

9 Roman Polanski's first, and some think his best, picture. A minor official and his younger wife are off for a weekend of sailing. Along the way they pick up a young student hitchhiker. Polanski's masterful storytelling unveils that there are major problems underlying this marriage. The young rider proves to be a rival for the girl and sexual tensions steadily build. The husband attempts to prove himself to his wife, and to himself, by engaging the boy in petty games. He wins, but by so doing, only proves his own childishness. Powerful and fascinating. Subtitles.

Sex / Nud / Viol / Lang / AdSit

A: Leon Niemczyk, Jolanta Umecka, Zygmunt Malanowicz

© HOME VISION KN101

KOTCH

D: Jack Lemmon 114 m

PG | COM DMA | 1971 | COLOR

9 Totally charming comedy about an old coot who keeps getting in the way living at his son's house, so they put him in an old age home. However he can't stand it there so he runs away and rents a small house to live in by himself. He befriends the pregnant young girl who used to babysit for his grandson and who has run away from home after being deserted by both her family and the baby's father. So, Kotch takes her into his little house and they take care of each other. This is a truly winning and heart-warming story, with a terrific performance by Matthau for which he received an Oscar nomination. The film got three other nominations, too. Excellent.

Sex / Nud / Viol / Lang / AdSit

A: Walter Matthau, Deborah Winters, Felicia Farr, Ellen Geer, Charles Aidman, Lucy Saroyan

© MAGNETIC VIDEO 8008

KRAMER VS. KRAMER

D: Robert Benton 105 m

PG | DMA | 1979 | COLOR

Sex | ◢Nud | Viol | ◢Lang | ■AdSit

10 Enormously powerful and deeply moving picture that won 4 Oscars, including Best Picture. When an alienated mother and wife (Streep) walks out on her executive husband (Hoffman) and small son, Hoffman is destroyed. The out-of-touch father and husband is forced to learn to deal with life and his son on a new, much more intimate level. All his priorities must change. Just when he has come to understand and cope with the changes, the mother returns demanding custody of the child. This is a deeply affecting movie which causes you swing violently between tears and laughter. A must see.

A: Dustin Hoffman, Meryl Streep, Justin Henry, JoBeth Williams, Jane Alexander, Howard Duff

© COLUMBIA TRISTAR HOME VIDEO 60030

LA BAMBA

D: Luis Valdez 103 m

PG-13 | DMA MUS | 1987 | COLOR

Sex | ◢Nud | Viol | ■Lang | ■AdSit

8 Entertaining biography of the short life of one of rock `n roll's major early stars whose early death both affected the course of music and ended an era. Richie Valens's real-life rise from abject poverty to fame and riches, only to die young suddenly, is a blend of soap opera and excitement that makes it a natural for the movies. Viewers won't be disappointed. Fans of '50s music will enjoy it, yes - but so will everyone else. It's just a good story that has something for nearly everyone and is well presented.

A: Lou Diamond Phillips, Rosana De Soto, Esai Morales, Danielle von Zerneck, Elizabeth Pena

© COLUMBIA TRISTAR HOME VIDEO 60854

D
M
A

LA DOLCE VITA

D: Federico Fellini 174 m

NR | FOR DMA | 1961 | B&W

◢Sex | ◢Nud | Viol | Lang | ■AdSit

7 This is considered a landmark film and won an Oscar for Best Foreign Film, but it will have a select audience. Fellini's typical surrealism was tempered greatly, but not altogether. Mastroianni is a man with serious ambitions as an author, but he cannot give up the money he makes as a tabloid writer and the carefree life it buys him. So, he wonders aimlessly from party to party monitoring and participating in the shallow, decadent lives of the rich and famous that his readers envy. Long and rambling.

A: Marcello Mastroianni, Yvonne Furneaux, Anita Ekberg, Anouk Aimee, Magali Noel, Alain Cuny

© GOODTIMES 8298

LADY SINGS THE BLUES

D: Sidney J. Furie 144 m

R | DMA MUS | 1972 | COLOR

Sex | ◢Nud | ◢Viol | ■Lang | ■AdSit

7 Billy Holiday is an icon in African-American culture and a pillar in American jazz. This film is her fictionalized Hollywood biography. As a biography it has many shortcomings; but as a soap opera drama, it's not bad. It attracted five Oscar nominations, including one for Diana Ross in her powerful screen debut. The story supposedly chronicles Holiday's rise from singing in brothels through her destruction by drug addiction. Great songs include "Strange Fruit" and "God Bless the Child."

A: Diana Ross, Billy Dee Williams, Richard Pryor, James Callahan, Paul Hampton, Sid Melton

© PARAMOUNT HOME VIDEO 8374

LAST ANGRY MAN, THE

D: Daniel Mann 100 m

NR | DMA | 1959 | B&W

Sex | Nud | Viol | Lang | ◢AdSit

7 Paul Muni received his fifth Oscar nomination in this his last picture. Although a little overly-sentimental, this is still a very enjoyable story about a selfless doctor who has dedicated 45 years of service as a general practitioner in a poor Brooklyn neighborhood. Now a TV show wants to honor him with a depiction of his life's story, but the old man's principals are threatened by an overly-enthusiastic TV producer. Excellent performances raise this above a mere soap opera.

A: Paul Muni, David Wayne, Betsy Palmer, Luther Adler, Joby Baker, Joanna Moore

© COLUMBIA TRISTAR HOME VIDEO 60956

LAST DETAIL, THE

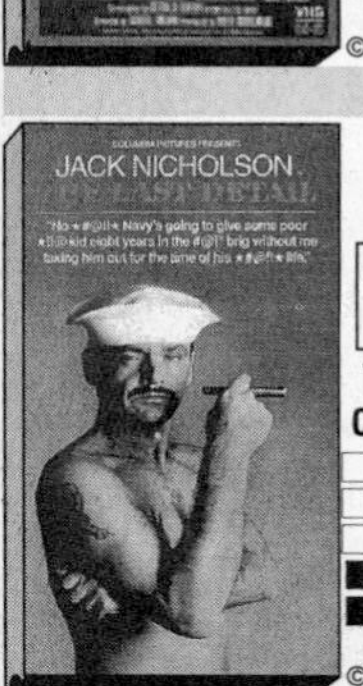

D: Hal Ashby 105 m

R | DMA COM | 1974 | COLOR

Sex | Nud | Viol | ■Lang | ■AdSit

8 This was a superb and highly entertaining comedy/drama and it garnered Oscar nominations for both Jack Nicholson and Randy Quaid. Two long-time Navy men (Nicholson and Young) are assigned the task of bringing a naive AWOL young sailor (Quaid) back to serve a long jail sentence. These two old salts take pity on the kid and take it upon themselves to show the innocent young sailor what he will be missing while he is away. Alternately funny and sadly moving, it is also filled with some of the foulest language recorded up to that time.

A: Jack Nicholson, Otis Young, Randy Quaid, Carol Kane, Michael Moriarty

© COLUMBIA TRISTAR HOME VIDEO 60034

LAST EMPEROR, THE

D: Bernardo Bertolucci 164 m

PG-13 | DMA | 1987 | COLOR

◢Sex | ◢Nud | ◢Viol | Lang | ◢AdSit

9 Beautiful, epic, true biography. Winner of nine Oscars, including Best Picture and Best Director. Pu Yi was taken from his home at age three, in 1908, to be crowned the Emperor of China. Whereupon he was compelled to live an opulent but entirely isolated life inside the fabled Forbidden City. But with the onset of the communist revolution, he is suddenly deposed and forced to live out his life as a common gardener. Massive picture with lush production, actually filmed inside the Forbidden City.

A: John Lone, Joan Chen, Peter O'Toole, Ying Ruocheng, Victor Wong, Dennis Dun

© NEW LINE HOME VIDEO 7715

LAST EXIT TO BROOKLYN

D: Uli Edel 103 m

R | DMA | 1990 | COLOR

■Sex | ■Nud | ◢Viol | ■Lang | ■AdSit

7 Powerful, but very disturbing drama reflecting the lives of three troubled people in a 1952 blue collar Brooklyn neighborhood. One story is of a homosexual union boss, another is the semi-comic love life and marriage of a factory worker's daughter to one of his young co-workers, but the last is the most troubling. Jennifer Jason Leigh is startling as a troubled, confused and ultimately tragic prostitute. This is a powerful and evocative drama, but is not an enjoyable or satisfying experience.

A: Jennifer Jason Leigh, Burt Young, Peter Dobson, Jerry Orbach, Ricki Lake, Alexis Arquette

© COLUMBIA TRISTAR HOME VIDEO 90633

LAST HURRAH, THE

D: John Ford 125 m

NR | DMA | 1958 | B&W

Sex | Nud | Viol | Lang | ◢AdSit

8 Top-notch cast of veteran character actors support Spencer Tracy in this sentimental political portrait of a big-city mayor and old-style political boss running for one last election. Tracy is a man running against a weak candidate, but who is backed by powerful forces. The ultimate tragedy is that of a man who fails to recognize the changes of time. The film is loosely based upon the story of Boston's Mayor Curley and was taken from a best-selling novel.

A: Spencer Tracy, Jeffrey Hunter, Dianne Foster, Pat O'Brien, Basil Rathbone, Donald Crisp

© COLUMBIA TRISTAR HOME VIDEO 60922

LAST PICTURE SHOW, THE

D: Peter Bogdanovich 118 m

R | DMA | 1971 | B&W

■Sex | ■Nud | ◢Viol | Lang | ■AdSit

10 Brilliant, moving portrait of small town people, struggling to be happy and survive in a dying Texas town of the early 1950s. Two young men attempt to grow up and navigate through life (and trouble caused by spoiled rich girl Shepherd), without a roadmap. Johnson is perfect as a grizzled old man who is the commonsense anchor for both of them and the whole town. Leachman is touching as a lonely, neglected wife of the football coach who seeks love. Very rich characters and brilliant performances (Oscars to Leachman and Johnson) make a sensitive story, all the more poignant. A must see!

A: Timothy Bottoms, Jeff Bridges, Ben Johnson, Cloris Leachman, Ellen Burstyn, Cybill Shepherd

© COLUMBIA TRISTAR HOME VIDEO 50423

LAST SUMMER

D: Frank Perry 97 m

R | DMA | 1969 | COLOR

◢Sex | ◢Nud | Viol | ■Lang | ■AdSit

7 Engrossing dramatic study of four unchaperoned teenagers who begin to discover themselves on the summer beaches of the resort area of New York's Fire Island. They get drunk, smoke pot, experiment with sex and enter into contests of power and gamesmanship. Excellent performances from some then up-and-comers in this powerful story which won wide critical acclaim.

A: Richard Thomas, Barbara Hershey, Bruce Davison, Cathy Burns, Ernesto Gonzalez, Peter Turgeon

© CBS/FOX VIDEO 7406

LAST TANGO IN PARIS

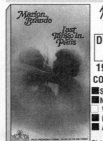

D: Bernardo Bertolucci 130 m

X | DMA | 1973 | COLOR

■Sex | ■Nud | Viol | ■Lang | ■AdSit

6 Very controversial film which was initially banned upon its release. Rated X, it is still explicit by today's standards. It is the story of an American in Paris who is tormented by his wife's suicide. While looking for an apartment, he has a passionate encounter with a total stranger and they enter into a torrid no-obligation sexual adventure. This is ultimately a psychological study of a guilt-ridden man, but it is also so entwined in sex that the one overshadows the other.

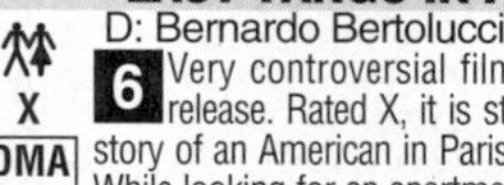

A: Marlon Brando, Maria Schneider, Jean-Pierre Leaud, Massimo Girotti, Darling Legitimus, Catherine Allegret

Distributed By MGM/UA Home Video M301733

LAST TEMPTATION OF CHRIST, THE

D: Martin Scorsese 163 m

R | DMA | 1988 | COLOR | Sex | Nud | Viol | Lang | AdSit

9 Much maligned but extremely thought-provoking film which, for some, commits the "blasphemy" of speculating (beyond the four Gospels) on an alternate vision of Christ's last minute thoughts (hallucinations) on the cross. The bulk of the picture is a faithful and very realistically depicted (including sex and nudity) restatement of the traditional Biblical stories. The key departure is the addition of having the tormented Christ hallucinate as to what his life might have been like as a normal man, only to discover that this too is another trick of the devil. Very moving and actually quite pious.

A: Willem Dafoe, Harvey Keitel, Barbara Hershey, Harry Dean Stanton, David Bowie, Verna Bloom

© MCA/UNIVERSAL HOME VIDEO, INC. 80842

LAST TYCOON, THE

D: Elia Kazan 123 m

PG | DMA | 1977 | COLOR | Sex | Nud | Viol | Lang | AdSit

6 This is a laudable effort to adapt F. Scott Fitzgerald's last and unfinished book - analyzing the character, general underbelly and power structure of the movie industry of the 1930s - for the big screen. It is the beneficiary of one of De Niro's best and most subtle performances and the presence of a lot of major stars. De Niro's character is one patterned after Irving Tahlberg. He is a manipulative power broker who is slowly working himself to death, fighting change in the movie industry.

A: Robert De Niro, Tony Curtis, Jeanne Moreau, Jack Nicholson, Donald Pleasence, Peter Strauss

© PARAMOUNT HOME VIDEO 8776

L'AVVENTURA

D: Michelangelo Antonioni 145 m

NR | FOR DMA | 1960 | B&W | Sex | Nud | Viol | Lang | AdSit

9 Both praised and booed, this is not a film for a casual observer. On the surface, it is the story of the search for a missing woman. A group of wealthy Italians visit a barren rock of an island near Crete. There a woman disappears after having an argument with her lover. The lover and the woman's best friend to scour the island for her, but after finding no trace, they leave the island and make inquiries at a near-by town. Soon, the two find themselves falling into a tempestuous relationship of their own. Below the surface story, this is an allegorical depiction of the decay of the idle rich. Demands attention but became a very influential film.

A: Monica Vitti, Gabriele Ferzetti, Lea Massari, Dominique Blanchar

© HOME VISION AVV 030

LAWMAN

D: Michael Winner 98 m

PG | WST DMA | 1971 | COLOR | Sex | Nud | Viol | Lang | AdSit

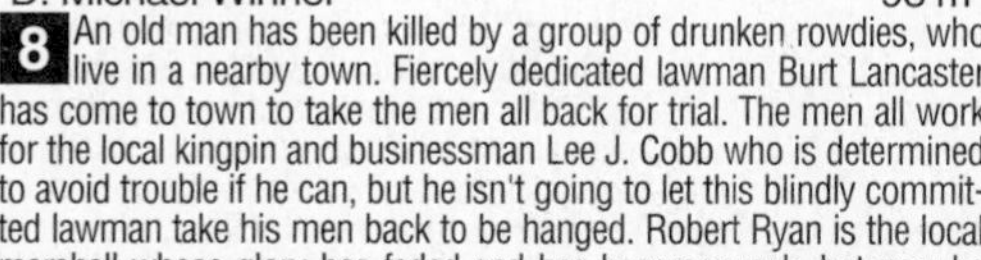

8 An old man has been killed by a group of drunken rowdies, who live in a nearby town. Fiercely dedicated lawman Burt Lancaster has come to town to take the men all back for trial. The men all work for the local kingpin and businessman Lee J. Cobb who is determined to avoid trouble if he can, but he isn't going to let this blindly committed lawman take his men back to be hanged. Robert Ryan is the local marshall whose glory has faded and has become weak, but now he must decide on which side he will team. Curious and quite different Western that explores whether the end justifies the means. Cobb is terrific.

A: Burt Lancaster, Robert Ryan, Lee J. Cobb, Sheree North, Joseph Wiseman, Robert Duvall

Distributed By MGM/UA Home Video M202960

LAWRENCE OF ARABIA

D: David Lean 216 m

PG | DMA ACT WAR | 1962 | COLOR | Sex | Nud | Viol | Lang | AdSit

10 A monumental accomplishment that fills the screen with majestic photography and gigantic spectacle. It was a winner of seven Oscars, including Best Picture, Director and Cinematography. Long before there was Operation Desert Storm (the 1991 Persian Gulf War), an enigmatic Englishman went into the deserts of Arabia and organized the scattered Arab tribes into an effective fighting force against the Ottoman Turks and the Germans during World War I. In the process, he created a new order in the Middle East and made himself into a legend. This one has everything: action, adventure and drama.

A: Peter O'Toole, Alec Guinness, Anthony Quinn, Jack Hawkins, Claude Rains, Anthony Quayle

© COLUMBIA TRISTAR HOME VIDEO 50133

LEAN ON ME

D: John G. Avildsen 109 m

PG-13 | DMA | 1989 | COLOR | Sex | Nud | Viol | Lang | AdSit

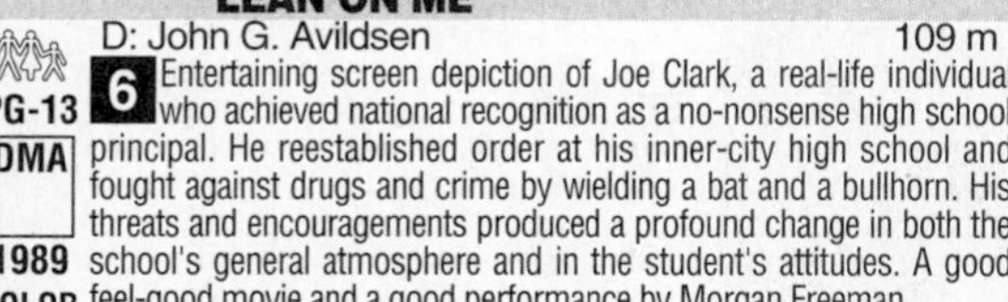

6 Entertaining screen depiction of Joe Clark, a real-life individual who achieved national recognition as a no-nonsense high school principal. He reestablished order at his inner-city high school and fought against drugs and crime by wielding a bat and a bullhorn. His threats and encouragements produced a profound change in both the school's general atmosphere and in the student's attitudes. A good feel-good movie and a good performance by Morgan Freeman.

A: Morgan Freeman, Robert Guillaume, Beverly Todd, Alan North, Lynne Thigpen, Robin Bartlett

© WARNER HOME VIDEO 11875

LEAP OF FAITH

D: Richard Pearce 110 m

PG-13 | DMA COM | 1992 | COLOR | Sex | Nud | Viol | Lang | AdSit

8 Steve Martin is a fraud. He is Rev. Jonas Nightengale, a revivalist minister who travels the country bilking the suckers and making them feel good while he does it. When one of his trucks breaks down in a small Kansas town, he sets up his tents and gets ready to put on a show while he waits for a part. Jonas spies a pretty waitress (Davidovich) and sets his sights on seducing her, but she will have no part of preachers who give her crippled little brother false hope. So, Jonas continues to fleece the flock but is eventually forced to confront of the human aspects of his trade, especially when a true miracle happens in front of his eyes.

A: Steve Martin, Debra Winger, Lolita Davidovich, Liam Neeson, Lukas Haas

© PARAMOUNT HOME VIDEO 32792

LEARNING TREE

D: Gordon Parks 107 m

PG | DMA | 1969 | COLOR | Sex | Nud | Viol | Lang | AdSit

7 Sensitive autobiographical story by famed Life magazine photographer Gordon Parks. It is the story of a young black man growing up in Kansas in the 1920s. That summer he learns of many things, but struggles with the moral dilemma of his life when, after he witnesses a murder, he must decide whether he should speak up. Revealing what he saw will free the white man falsely charged, convict the black man who did it and risk personal retribution that is sure to come from the black man's son. This is a beautifully photographed story of growing up black.

A: Kyle Johnson, Estelle Evans, Dana Elcar, Mita Waters, Alex Clarke

© WARNER HOME VIDEO 11591

LEAVE 'EM LAUGHING

D: Jackie Cooper 103 m

NR | DMA | 1981 | COLOR | Sex | Nud | Viol | Lang | AdSit

9 Outstanding, heartwarming, true-life story of Jack Thum. Jack Thum was a Chicago supermarket clown and real-life hero. He and his wife took in and cared for dozens of homeless, neglected and unwanted children. This is a real tearjerker but it is never manipulative. It is a moving testimony to an extraordinarily good man's life. Mickey Rooney is brilliant. He is totally believable as a simple man struggling both to help these desperate kids and to make ends meet. Then it tears your heart out when he learns that he will die of cancer and thinks he is a failure. Must-see family entertainment.

A: Mickey Rooney, Anne Jackson, Red Buttons, William Windom, Elisha Cook, Jr.

© FRIES HOME VIDEO 94950

LEAVING NORMAL

D: Edward Zwick 110 m

R | DMA | 1992 | COLOR | Sex | Nud | Viol | Lang | AdSit

6 Odd little female-buddy drama that also has some lighter moments. Two misfits - one (Tilly) a twice-married, abused mouse and the other (Lahti) a boisterous ex-bar maid - are strangers. Nevertheless, they head off together to Alaska to claim a small piece of land that Lahti owns. Neither one has roots and both are looking for a new start. It is a journey, filled with oddball characters and problems one after the other. The problems don't end when they get to Alaska, but the women do discover that they have each other. Well acted, but not everyone will identify with it or the characters.

A: Christine Lahti, Meg Tilly, Lenny Von Dohlen, Maury Chaykin, James Gammon, Patrika Darbo

© MCA/UNIVERSAL HOME VIDEO, INC. 81230

LEFT-HANDED GUN, THE

D: Arthur Penn 1958 m

NR | WST DMA ACT | 1958 | B&W | Sex | Nud | Viol | Lang | AdSit

7 An interesting underrated psychological Western which makes a point of debunking the hero-myth status of Billy the Kid. Newman's Billy is a moody, stupid and ruthless killer -- a lonely hothead who becomes enraged upon the murder of his boss, a man for whom he felt great fondness. Billy becomes so obsessed with killing the man's murderers that he and two others go on a wild killing spree. A curious feature in the film, one which comments upon on human nature in general, is the inclusion of a pulp writer who at first worships Billy but later derides Billy for not being the hero of his stories and eventually betrays Billy. Quite good.

A: Paul Newman, Lita Milan, John Dehner, Hurd Hatfield, James Congdon, James Best

© WARNER HOME VIDEO 11067

LEGENDS OF THE FALL

D: Edward Zwick 134 m

R | DMA ROM | 1995 | COLOR | Sex | Nud | Viol | Lang | AdSit

7 Beginning at the end of the 1800s, this film documents the tale of a prosperous Montana family that self-destructs. Hopkins has three sons. The oldest (Quinn) is the most practical. The middle son (Pitt) is a wild spirit and is his father's favorite. And, the youngest is a romantic who brings home a beautiful young woman to marry, but leaves with his brothers to fight in WWI. Only the two oldest return. Pitt is destroyed because he could not save his brother's life. However, he falls for his brother's fiance - only to leave her and home, destroying his father. She then marries the oldest brother. Years later Pitt returns to begin again but also rekindles old fires. Winner of an Oscar for Best Cinematography.

A: Brad Pitt, Anthony Hopkins, Aidan Quinn, Julia Ormand, Henry Thomas, Karina Lombard

© COLUMBIA TRISTAR HOME VIDEO 78723

D
M
A

LENNY

D: Bob Fosse — 112 m

R | DMA | 1974 | B&W

9 Brilliant character portrait of an extremely controversial and self-destructive comedian who was a brazen challenger of the status quo during the late '50s and early '60s. This fact earned him the ire of the social establishment, but also the adoration of a rebellious few. Hoffman's depiction of this tormented individual won him an Oscar nomination. Numerous other Oscar nominations included Best Picture, Director and Screenplay. But this is definitely not for everyone. See also THE LENNY BRUCE PERFORMANCE FILM.

Sex | Nud | Viol | Lang | AdSit

A: Dustin Hoffman, Valerie Perrine, Jan Miner, Stanley Beck, Gary Morton

Distributed By MGM/UA Home Video M801663

LES MISERABLES

D: Glenn Jordan — 123 m

NR | DMA | 1978 | COLOR

8 Involving and lavishly produced, made-for-TV version of the Victor Hugo classic, set in France in the grim days just prior to the French Revolution. Valjean (Jordan) is a wretched woodcutter who, caught trying to steal bread for his starving sister and her family, is sentenced to five years in prison. That sentence keeps getting extended each time he is caught trying to escape. Finally succeeding in escaping, he becomes respected, prosperous and even a mayor. But he is tormented for years by his former jailer (Perkins) who obsessively pursues him. Very well done.

Sex | Nud | Viol | Lang | AdSit

A: Richard Jordan, Anthony Perkins, John Gielgud, Cyril Cusack, Celia Robson

© LIVE HOME VIDEO 69925

LET HIM HAVE IT

D: Peter Medak — 115 m

R | DMA | 1992 | COLOR

7 Powerful drama. In 1952 London, everything was in short supply, except guns, and a group of bored school boys becomes carried away in their movie-based fantasies of rich gangland heros. This is the true story that outraged all England. A 19-year old child-like retarded epileptic, Dereck Bentley (with the mental age of 11) was caught up in that fantasy, too, and he wanted to be part of the group. So, when the younger boys decide to rob a warehouse, he went along. But, during the robbery, one particularly nasty boy killed a policeman. Still, Derek, who had nothing to do with the killing but was old enough, was executed for it. Absorbing, but heavy English accents.

Sex | Nud | Viol | Lang | AdSit

A: Christopher Eccleston, Paul Reynolds, Eileen Atkins, Tom Bell, Clare Holman, Michael Gough

© TURNER HOME ENTERTAINMENT N4093

LIAR'S MOON

D: David Fisher — 106 m

PG | ROM DMA | 1981 | COLOR

7 Interesting slightly soap opera-ish romance story about two young lovers in 1949 Texas. Both are young, one is rich and one is poor. They have fallen in love but their parents have forcefully forbidden them to see each other. However, she is pregnant, so they run off together. The two lovers have all the typical problems that you would expect... no money, incompatibility, etc. but they have another problem, too ... they may also be brother and sister. This is not nearly as tacky as it sounds. This is well done and has quite affecting performances, especially by Dillon.

Sex | Nud | Viol | Lang | AdSit

A: Matt Dillon, Cindy Fisher, Christopher Connelly, Hoyt Axton, Yvonne De Carlo, Broderick Crawford

© LIVE HOME VIDEO VA4020

LIES

D: Jim Wheat, Ben Wheat — 93 m

R | SUS DMA | 1983 | COLOR

6 Interesting psychological thriller about an out-of-work actress who is unwittingly drawn into a plan, by an unscrupulous psychiatrist and scheming film director, to trick an heiress out of her fortune. Set inside a secluded mental institution, she is to portray a murder witness who has committed suicide. However, she learns that there is no film - she is instead a key player in a dangerous scam. The plot is filled with double-crosses and twists (probably too many), but interest is maintained by excellent acting, particularly by Gail Strickland and Ann Dusenberry.

Sex | Nud | Viol | Lang | AdSit

A: Ann Dusenberry, Gail Strickland, Bruce Davison, Clu Gulager, Terence Knox, Bert Remsen

© CBS/FOX VIDEO 3842

LIFE AND NOTHING BUT

D: Bertrand Tavernier — 135 m

PG | FOR DMA WAR | 1989 | COLOR

8 Two years after the armistice, French Major Noiret is still sorting through the dead. He is trying to locate one certifiable unknown soldier for the Arc de Triomphe. His job is a seemingly endless one in that he has over 400,000 dead French soldiers to investigate. His strange occupation also places him into the paths of two women who come to represent all those looking for loved ones. One is a young aristocrat obsessively looking for her dead husband. The other is looking for her fiance. This is a story of tortured lives that are held in limbo by war. Brilliant photography. A major award winner. Well done. Subtitles.

Sex | Nud | Viol | Lang | AdSit

A: Philippe Noiret, Sabine Azema, Pascale Vidal, Maurice Barrier, Francois Perrot, Jean-Pol Dubois

© ORION PICTURES CORPORATION 5056

LIFEGUARD

D: Daniel Petrie — 96 m

PG | DMA | 1976 | COLOR

7 This is a likable and occasionally involving movie that was fairly well received by both audiences and critics. Sam Elliot is a carefree lifeguard on California's beaches. He is pushing 30 and begins to question both his lifestyle and his future after he goes to his 15-year high school reunion. Should he give up the women and the fun to seek out a stable income and a job with a future? Ann Archer is waiting there for him if he does. But there are pretty beach groupies if he doesn't. An attractive cast and pleasant scenery make this an enjoyable diversion - not an intense introspective.

Sex | Nud | Viol | Lang | AdSit

A: Sam Elliott, Anne Archer, Kathleen Quinlan, Stephen Young, Parker Stevenson

© PARAMOUNT HOME VIDEO 8813

LIGHTHORSEMEN, THE

D: Simon Wincer — 116 m

PG | WAR ACT DMA | 1988 | COLOR

7 Stirring true story. Sweeping and episodic adventure which explores the lives of four Australian friends as they prepare for a decisive battle in WWI. The thrilling climax is a march through the desert by 800 Australian calvarymen who then mount a surprise calvary attack upon thousands of German and Turkish soldiers in a desert fortress. An impossible mission, but one which changed the course of history. A rousing and exciting calvary charge at the end makes up for its other slower and contemplative moments.

Sex | Nud | Viol | Lang | AdSit

A: Jon Blake, Peter Phelps, Tony Bonner, Bill Kerr, John Walton, Sigrid Thornton

© WARNER HOME VIDEO 762

LIGHT SLEEPER

D: Paul Schrader — 103 m

R | DMA | 1992 | COLOR

7 Willem Dafoe is a 40-year-old man being forced to start his life over. He is basically a good and ethical man but he is a former drug addict who still makes his living delivering drugs to New York's high-end clientele for his long-time friend and pal, Ann (Sarandon). He knows no other life outside his job and now Ann is closing down her business to go straight. Making his life worse, the cops are after a killer and think he may be their key, so they are dogging him; his ex-girl friend, that he still loves, won't have anything to do with him; and, he is all alone facing a new and uncertain life. Realistic.

Sex | Nud | Viol | Lang | AdSit

A: Willem Dafoe, Susan Sarandon, Dana Delany, David Clennon, Mary Beth Hurt

© LIVE HOME VIDEO 69006

LILIES OF THE FIELD

D: Ralph Nelson — 95 m

NR | DMA COM | 1963 | B&W

8 Extremely popular and heart-warming story of an itinerant handyman who happens upon a group of nuns recently escaped from East Germany. They are attempting to build a church but have no skills, no money for building materials and are barely able to communicate. Yet they charm and coerce him into helping them in their mission. This was a low-budget movie, but it had a winning story line and great characterizations that combined to make it a big hit with the public. Poitier won an Oscar and the movie received two other nominations, including Best Picture.

Sex | Nud | Viol | Lang | AdSit

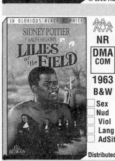

A: Sidney Poitier, Lilia Skala, Lisa Mann, Isa Crino, Stanley Adams

Distributed By MGM/UA Home Video M301762

LILITH

D: Robert Rossen — 114 m

NR | DMA ROM | 1964 | B&W

7 An intelligent and sensitive study in madness. The story is that of a dedicated young trainee (Beatty) in an exclusive mental institution who falls obsessively in love with a beautiful patient (Seberg). She is bewitching to all who see her, but she is also living in her own dream world. His growing love for this schizophrenic girl draws him ever deeper into her tortured world and eventually into his own madness. This tragic love story is slow to unwind and is ultimately unsatisfying. However, it is also very intriguing and involving. Patience in viewing is required.

Sex | Nud | Viol | Lang | AdSit

A: Warren Beatty, Jean Seberg, Peter Fonda, Kim Hunter, Gene Hackman

© COLUMBIA TRISTAR HOME VIDEO 60443

LION IN WINTER, THE

D: Anthony Harvey — 134 m

PG | DMA | 1968 | COLOR

9 Grand and elegant - but very heavy - historical drama which won 3 Oscars. It is a brilliant portrayal of the many squabbles, incessant plotting and constant turmoil occurring near the end of the reign of England's twelfth-century Henry II. Which of his three contentious sons (all of whom are fighting like dogs for a fresh bone) would succeed him to power? O'Toole is brilliant as the scheming Henry, but Katharine Hepburn took home her third Oscar as his imprisoned queen, Eleanor of Aquitaine. Fans of historical epics should also see O'Toole and Burton in BECKET.

Sex | Nud | Viol | Lang | AdSit

A: Peter O'Toole, Katharine Hepburn, Jane Merrow, Timothy Dalton, Anthony Hopkins, Nigel Terry

© NEW LINE HOME VIDEO 2057

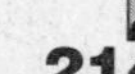

LITTLE BIG MAN

D: Arthur Penn 147 m

PG | WST COM DMA | 1970 | COLOR

10 This is an outstanding and thoroughly enjoyable fable of the Old West. Dustin Hoffman plays Jack Crabb, a 121-year-old man living in a nursing home, who tells his colorful and not all-too-believable life's story to a doubtful young reporter through a series of flashbacks. His incredible stories begin when he was an orphaned pioneer boy adopted and raised by Cheyenne Indians. After he had returned to the white world, he became a terrible businessman and miserable husband, a dead-eyed gunfighter, a drunk and eventually a guide to Custer at his last stand. Wonderful characters, very clever, frequently funny, sometimes poignant, always extremely entertaining. Great fun.

Sex | Nud | Viol | Lang | AdSit

A: Dustin Hoffman, Chief Dan George, Faye Dunaway, Martin Balsam, Jeff Corey, Richard Mulligan

© CBS/FOX VIDEO 7130

LITTLE BUDDHA

D: Bernardo Bertolucci 133 m

PG | DMA | 1994 | COLOR

7 Very unusual and yet oddly fascinating film that intertwines two tales. One is of a modern day Buddhist monk who has followed his dream to America to locate the reincarnated spirit of his former teacher. He believes the answer to his search lies in a precocious 8-year-old. The boy's parents are very skeptical but their fears are layed to rest by the kindly old man, who then tells the 2500 year-old story, beautifully photographed, of the Buddha (Reeves) who gave up his life of luxury to search out true contentment. The stories are well interwoven and strangely intriguing, resulting in a meaningful primer into Buddhism and a philosophical insight into the value of earthly things.

Sex | Nud | Viol | Lang | AdSit

A: Keanu Reeves, Ying Ruocheng, Chris Isaak, Alex Wiesendanger, Raju Lal, Bridget Fonda

© MIRAMAX HOME ENTERTAINMENT 2548

LITTLE MAN TATE

D: Jodie Foster 99 m

PG | DMA | 1991 | COLOR

8 Heartbreaking, heartwarming charmer. What's a poor waitress mom (Foster) to do when she realizes that her genius son needs to be raised in an environment that she can't provide ... love isn't enough, he needs stimulation. So, when he gets an opportunity to go to a special summer college session, though she resists at first, she sends him. He is to stay with the well-meaning director of the special school (Wiest), but her focus is always on his mind and she doesn't know how to give him the love he needs. He feels alone, unloved, misunderstood and rejected. Extremely well done. A real winner for Foster.

Sex | Nud | Viol | Lang | AdSit

A: Jodie Foster, Dianne Wiest, Adam Hann-Byrd, Harry Connick, Jr., David Pierce, P.J. Ochlan

© ORION PICTURES CORPORATION 8778

LITTLE THIEF, THE

D: Claude Miller 108 m

R | FOR DMA | 1989 | COLOR

7 Set in post-war 1950 France, this represents the turmoil of that time. It is the story of a pretty young girl who is abandoned to relatives by her mother. She feels deserted and strikes out at the world by stealing. She runs away from everyone and lives only for the day. She even hires on as a maid and seduces the man of the house just before she steals from them. Then she falls for Raoul who is another young thief, and they continue to steal from her employers until she is arrested. However, now she has become pregnant. This film was intended to be the female counterpart for Truffaut's classic in a similar vein: 400 BLOWS. Subtitles.

Sex | Nud | Viol | Lang | AdSit

A: Charlotte Gainsbourg, Didier Bezace, Simon de la Brosse, Raoul Billery

© HBO VIDEO 0377

LITTLE WOMEN

D: Gillian Armstrong 118 m

PG | DMA | 1994 | COLOR

9 This is the fourth version of Louisa May Alcott's classic book which has been brought to the American movie screen. The first was silent. There was also an English version, also silent, and a TV version. The 1933 version is still the reigning champion. That said, this version is widely regarded as being an excellent adaptation of Alcott's semi-autobiographical story of the March sisters, a book that has inspired generations of teenage girls to strive to reach beyond the limits others have set for them. Suddenly poverty struck by their father's absence because of the Civil War, the girls and their mother survive with grace, and the girls - particularly Jo (Ryder) - go on to achieve their dreams.

Sex | Nud | Viol | Lang | AdSit

A: Winona Ryder, Susan Sarandon, Gabriel Byrne, Trini Alvarado, Samantha Mathis, Kirsten Dunst

© COLUMBIA TRISTAR HOME VIDEO 01023

LONDON KILLS ME

D: Hanif Kureishi 107 m

R | DMA | 1992 | COLOR

6 Curious slice of life story concerning the bizarre lifestyle of some of London's street people. The central focus is upon a 20 year-old character (Chadwick) who is desperately tired of his life struggling to survive by scamming and selling drugs. Then, he finds hope in an offer of a job by a restaurant owner, if he only gets new shoes. He wants out so bad that he becomes obsessed with getting new shoes. However, he also wants to gain the attentions of the newest member of his street family (McCourt), but he is in competition with his best friend and the group's leader (Mackintosh). Strange story about strange people in a strange environment.

Sex | Nud | Viol | Lang | AdSit

A: Justin Chadwick, Steven Mackintosh, Emer Mc Court, Roshan Seth, Brad Dourif, Mona Shaw

© LIVE HOME VIDEO 69029

LONELINESS OF THE LONG DISTANCE RUNNER, THE

D: Tony Richardson 104 m

NR | DMA | 1962 | B&W

9 An engrossing exploration of an embittered and rebellious young man who is sent to a reformatory after robbing a bakery. There he encounters a strict but sympathetic warden who believes in rehabilitation. Using the boy's need for recognition, the warden prods him into joining the track team, where he is chosen to be on the team and represent the school. Excellent acting, and a very highly critically acclaimed film from England. However, it is slow-moving and bleak.

Sex | Nud | Viol | Lang | AdSit

A: Tom Courtenay, Michael Redgrave, Avis Bunnage, Peter Madden, Alec McCowen, James Fox

© WARNER HOME VIDEO 11755

LONELY ARE THE BRAVE

D: David Miller 107 m

NR | WST DMA ACT | 1962 | B&W

8 A superb and penetrating character study. An easy-going 20th-century cowboy (Kirk Douglas) wants to help his friend break out of jail, so he gets into a bar fight and punches a cop. Now that he's in jail, his friend doesn't want to leave. Faced with the possibility of a year in prison, Douglas escapes from jail and heads into the hills on horseback. But the modern-day cops, headed up by Matthau, chase him down with help from trucks, helicopters and walkie-talkies. As the chase develops, Matthau gains respect for and begins to like his quarry. Good flick. Well done. One of Douglas's personal favorites.

Sex | Nud | Viol | Lang | AdSit

A: Kirk Douglas, Gena Rowlands, Walter Matthau, Michael Kane, Carroll O'Connor, George Kennedy

© MCA/UNIVERSAL HOME VIDEO, INC. 80143

D
M
A

LONESOME DOVE

D: Simon Wincer 372 m

NR | WST DMA ACT | 1990 | COLOR

10 Absolutely brilliant and totally engrossing made-for-TV miniseries adapted from Larry McMurtry's Pulitzer Prize-winning novel. This is an entirely believable, sweeping saga of two Texas Rangers who have out-lived their pioneering era in Texas. So, they strike out for Montana with a herd of cattle, intent upon establishing the first ranch in that virgin land. Striking performances by the entire cast paint a rich tapestry of colorful characters, adventure and romance in a realistically depicted Old West. A wonderful, totally involving, not-to-be-missed adventure.

Sex | Nud | Viol | Lang | AdSit

A: Robert Duvall, Tommy Lee Jones, Robert Urich, Danny Glover, Diane Lane, Ricky Schroder

© CABIN FEVER ENTERTAINMENT CF8371

LONG DAY'S JOURNEY INTO NIGHT

D: Sidney Lumet 180 m

NR | DMA | 1962 | B&W

9 Stunning adaptation of the autobiographical play from Eugene O'Neill. An unforgettable dissection of a family in disarray and decline. Katharine Hepburn was Oscar-nominated for her portrayal of the drug-addicted mother slipping backward into her addiction. Richardson plays the successful, but pompous and extremely miserly, actor/father who cannot forget his poverty-stricken youth. One son is an alcoholic and the other is dying of TB. Extremely powerful, but depressing.

Sex | Nud | Viol | Lang | AdSit

A: Katharine Hepburn, Ralph Richardson, Jason Robards, Jr., Dean Stockwell, Jeanne Barr

© REPUBLIC PICTURES HOME VIDEO 5548

LONGEST DAY, THE

D: Ken Annakin, Andrew Marton 175 m

G | WAR ACT DMA | 1962 | B&W

9 Monumental epic war film documenting the massive invasion of Europe in WWII. 43 of Hollywood's biggest stars fill roles, big and small, to portray in detail the many events of D-Day. The story is essentially told in three parts: the planning; the behind-the-lines activities of the resistance forces and the initial paratrooper assault; and, the massive landings on the beaches of Normandy, France. The big story is evoked through a series of smaller stories from the many people involved. Spectacular!

Sex | Nud | Viol | Lang | AdSit

A: John Wayne, Robert Mitchum, Henry Fonda, Richard Burton, Rod Steiger, Sean Connery

© FOXVIDEO 1021

LONG GONE

D: Martin Davidson 113 m

NR | DMA COM | 1987 | COLOR

8 Loving and engaging look into America's favorite pastime. Stud Cantrell is a minor league baseball manager who has always managed to allude success until one fateful Florida summer in the early 1950s. That summer he is blessed with a winning team and a small town beauty queen who wants him to set up housekeeping. Now, with only one game left to win the pennant, the opposing team's owner offers him the chance of a life time, if only he'll throw the game. Enjoyable. Also see BULL DURHAM.

Sex | Nud | Viol | Lang | AdSit

A: William L. Petersen, Virginia Madsen, Dermot Mulroney, Henry Gibson

© WARNER HOME VIDEO 828

LONG, HOT SUMMER, THE

D: Martin Ritt 117 m

NR | DMA | 1958 | COLOR

8 Powerful blending of several William Faulkner short stories into one brooding drama. It's the film that made Newman a star. Newman is a handyman who drifts into a corrupt, small, backwater Mississippi town dominated by its rich patriarch (Welles). Spunky Newman becomes a sharecropper for Welles, battles with him and decides to pursue marrying Welles's spinster daughter (Woodward). Newman's arrival stirs up passions in the little town - changing it forever. Well acted!

Sex / Nud / Viol / Lang / AdSit

A: Paul Newman, Joanne Woodward, Anthony Franciosa, Orson Welles, Lee Remick, Angela Lansbury

© FOXVIDEO 1045

LONGTIME COMPANION

D: Norman Rene 100 m

R | DMA | 1990 | COLOR

8 Emotional, intelligent, sensitive and highly acclaimed examination of the effect that AIDS has and has had - in human and in personal terms. The primary focus of this film is upon a closely knit group of gay men in NYC. It follows them over a nine-year period, from the earliest days of the epidemic in the early '80s, when the risk was virtually unknown. We watch the steady effect the disease has upon them all as it evolves from being just another story in the newspaper, to one that affects each one of them personally in some profound way. This is not just a "gay movie" nor is it sensationalized. It is a people story and it is very affecting.

Sex / Nud / Viol / Lang / AdSit

A: Bruce Davison, Stephen Caffrey, Patrick Cassidy, John Dossett, Mark Lamos, Dermot Mulroney

© VIDMARK ENTERTAINMENT VM5357

LONG WALK HOME, THE

D: Richard Pearce 98 m

PG | DMA | 1991 | COLOR

7 Intriguing and non-sensationalized account of two very different people's personal confrontation with the widely accepted nature of things in the South during the late 1950s. Odessa (Goldberg) is a black housekeeper for Miriam (Spacek). Spacek is the wife of one of the white community's biggest pillars. When black leaders call upon all black people to boycott the segregated buses, Odessa is forced to walk nine miles to and from work. Miriam, however, is determined to give her maid a ride, even though her husband and her society object. She is therefore forced into a moral confrontation with her husband, her society and her heritage. Involving.

Sex / Nud / Viol / Lang / AdSit

A: Sissy Spacek, Whoopi Goldberg, Dwight Schultz, Ving Rhames, Dylan Baker, Mary Steenburgen

© LIVE HOME VIDEO 68913

LOOK BACK IN ANGER

D: Tony Richardson 99 m

NR | DMA | 1959 | B&W

8 Powerful and riveting drama from England, set in the late 1950s. England was a country in social turmoil at this time, and this is the story of a young man who reflected that turmoil. Burton is passionate as the disillusioned and frustrated Jimmy Porter, a college graduate who rejects his middle class prospects to open a candy shop. However, unsatisfied and frustrated with his life, he betrays his wife by having an affair with her best friend. High quality drama and impassioned performances by the three principal actors. Realistic with bristling dialogue.

Sex / Nud / Viol / Lang / AdSit

A: Richard Burton, Claire Bloom, Mary Ure, Edith Evans, Donald Pleasence, Gary Raymond

© UNITED AMERICAN VIDEO CORP. 5303

LOOKING FOR MR. GOODBAR

D: Richard Brooks 136 m

R | DMA | 1977 | COLOR

7 A controversial portrait of an emotionally crippled woman (brilliantly portrayed by Diane Keaton) who is struggling from being raised in a claustrophobic family atmosphere. She leads a tragic double life. By day she is a caring Catholic teacher of deaf-mute children, and by night she cruises singles bars picking up men. Somewhat heavy-handed psychological story of a woman possessed of a destructive childhood, who is now looking for sexual and emotional gratification in an empty, degrading and self-destructive manner. A violent and disturbing ending.

Sex / Nud / Viol / Lang / AdSit

A: Diane Keaton, Tuesday Weld, William Atherton, Richard Kiley, Richard Gere, Tom Berenger

© PARAMOUNT HOME VIDEO 8874

LORD JIM

D: Richard Brooks 154 m

NR | DMA ACT | 1965 | COLOR

8 Intriguing adaptation of a complex novel by Joseph Conrad. Many of the story's elements have been reduced or eliminated for the screen, but what remains is still rewarding. O'Toole is fascinating as a former British navel officer who forever clouds his record with one act of cowardice. Then, he receives a second chance to redeem his honor after being adopted by the native villagers on a small South Sea island. However, he is about to be put to the test by an invading group of Europeans.

Sex / Nud / Viol / Lang / AdSit

A: Peter O'Toole, James Mason, Curt Jurgens, Eli Wallach, Jack Hawkins, Paul Lukas

© COLUMBIA TRISTAR HOME VIDEO 60042

LORD OF THE FLIES

D: Harry Hook 90 m

R | DMA | 1990 | COLOR

6 This is an Americanization of (plus an attempt to update and contemporize) the story first depicted in a novel and later adapted to the screen in 1963. A planeful of boys is stranded on an island when their plane is forced to crash-land. At first the group organizes in a civilized fashion, but soon its members begin to depart to join a rebel segment. Gradually the thin veneer of civilization is chipped away and the society of the entire group reverts back into tribalism and barbarism. This is an effective presentation, but the earlier black and white British version is considered by most to be superior.

Sex / Nud / Viol / Lang / AdSit

A: Balthazar Getty, Christopher Furrh, Danuel Pipoly, Badgett Dale

© NEW LINE HOME VIDEO 7746

LORD OF THE RINGS, THE

D: Ralph Bakshi 133 m

PG | FAN DMA | 1978 | COLOR

8 J.R.R. Tolkein fans only. This brilliantly animated feature compiles 1 1/2 books of the 3-book "Lord of the Rings" series into one longish feature film. The animation is truly impressive, but if the viewer is unfamiliar with this story of hobbits, dwarves, magicians and the other characters from Middle Earth who search out the magic rings, he will be entirely lost. Read the books first, then watch this... but definitely read the books. What an adventure!

Sex / Nud / Viol / Lang / AdSit

A:

© HBO VIDEO TVE1049

LORDS OF FLATBUSH, THE

D: Martin Davidson, Stephen Verona 88 m

PG | COM DMA | 1974 | COLOR

6 Interesting primarily because this film was the launching pad for four significant future stars. The film itself isn't too bad, but it isn't notable either... and it is very low budget. It is the story of the Flatbush gang - a group of male adolescents dipped in Brylcreem and wrapped in leather jackets, trying to proclaim themselves as men in 1957. Perry King falls for Susan Blakely. A pudgy Sly Stallone is dragged into marriage. Henry Winkler looks like the Fonz character he would later make famous on TV's "Happy Days".

Sex / Nud / Viol / Lang / AdSit

A: Martin Davidson, Perry King, Sylvester Stallone, Henry Winkler, Paul Mace, Susan Blakely

© COLUMBIA TRISTAR HOME VIDEO 60479

LORENZO'S OIL

D: George Miller 136 m

PG-13 | DMA | 1993 | COLOR

7 Extremely powerful, emotionally draining and eventually satisfying film, but it is definitely not entertainment. It is the true story of two very intelligent and determined people who are given the devastating news that their vibrant 5-year-old boy has a disease which will destroy his mind inch-by-inch and then kill him within a very short period of time. However, these two extremely determined people refuse to accept the very slow and deliberate pace of the on-going research. They defy medical convention and authority to instead launch their own search for an answer, scouring libraries for previously unassociated research to find a therapy to save their son.

Sex / Nud / Viol / Lang / AdSit

A: Susan Sarandon, Nick Nolte, Peter Ustinov, Kathleen Wilhoite, Zack O'Malley Greenburg

© MCA/UNIVERSAL HOME VIDEO, INC. 81290

LOST IN YONKERS

D: Martha Coolidge 114 m

PG | COM ROM DMA | 1993 | COLOR

8 Funny, touching and a real charmer from Neil Simon. Its 1942. Eddie is deep in debt from his dead wife's hospital expenses. His only chance is to leave his two boys behind in Yonkers with his stern mother and child-like sister, while he goes on the road for a year. Momma is a cold hard woman, but Aunt Bella is bubbly and full of life - even if her elevator doesn't quite make it to the top floor. Uncle Louie is a small-time hood who also comes to stay with Momma to hide out for a while. The two boys, Aunt Bella and Uncle Louie struggle to survive Momma's iron rule. Lots of clever dialogue from wonderfully drawn characters. Excellent.

Sex / Nud / Viol / Lang / AdSit

A: Richard Dreyfuss, Mercedes Ruehl, Irene Worth, David Strathairn, Brad Stoll, Mike Damus

© COLUMBIA TRISTAR HOME VIDEO 52663

LOVE CHILD

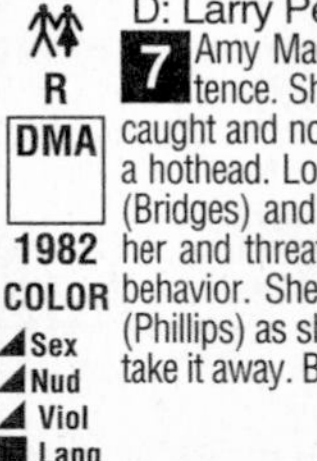

D: Larry Peerce 97 m

R | DMA | 1982 | COLOR

7 Amy Madigan is a 21-year-old girl serving a 7-year prison sentence. She and her wild cousin tried to steal at gunpoint, she got caught and now she is having a difficult time in prison because she is a hothead. Lonely, she has an affair with a sympathetic prison guard (Bridges) and gets pregnant. Now aware of the baby growing inside her and threatened with losing it, she begins to reform her extreme behavior. She receives help from a young but tough lesbian inmate (Phillips) as she fights to keep her baby from the system that wants to take it away. Based upon a true story and not as trite as it sounds.

Sex / Nud / Viol / Lang / AdSit

A: Amy Madigan, Beau Bridges, Mackenzie Phillips, Albert Salmi, Joanna Merlin, Rhea Perlman

© WARNER HOME VIDEO 20007

LOVE FIELD

D: Jonathan Kaplan 104 m

PG-13 | ROM DMA | 1992 | COLOR | Sex Nud Viol Lang AdSit

6 Michelle Pfeiffer is a naive Dallas housewife in 1963 who feels totally inadequate in her own life and idolizes Jacqueline Kennedy. When the President is killed she feels compelled to go to his funeral in spite of her husband forbidding her to do it. She heads north on a Greyhound bus upon which she meets a black man (Haysbert) and his little girl. He sees trouble coming and does his best to avoid her but can't. She simply does not know what kind of trouble she is making for him. She only wants to be friendly, but soon they are in trouble, and are forced to head north together in a stolen car with the FBI in pursuit.

A: Michelle Pfeiffer, Dennis Haysbert, Brian Kerwin, Stephanie McFadden

© ORION PICTURES CORPORATION 8789

LOVE LETTERS

D: Amy Jones 88 m

R | ROM DMA | 1983 | COLOR | Sex Nud Viol Lang AdSit

7 An intelligent, interesting and worthy exploration of human nature, that asks some uneasy questions. Jamie Lee Curtis plays a disc jockey who discovers some passionate love letters in the personal effects of her mother, who has died very young. The letters reveal that her mother had had a passionate and consuming, but adulterous, affair with a married man. Curtis longs for the same sort of all-consuming love that her mother had experienced. She gets her chance but the man she has found (Keach) is also married. This is an adult movie that asks adult questions.

A: Jamie Lee Curtis, James Keach, Amy Madigan, Bud Cort, Matt Clark, Sally Kirkland

© LIVE HOME VIDEO 5051

LOVE ON THE RUN

D: Francoit Truffaut 95 m

NR | FOR DMA | 1978 | COLOR | Sex Nud Viol Lang AdSit

8 The character of Antoine Doinel was first introduced at age 13 in Truffaut's famous film 400 BLOWS. It is actually the fifth is a series of films which depict other times in this character's lives. This film picks up his life in his mid-thirties. He is freshly divorced and has begun new love affairs with women from his past. (This film is amply injected with clips from the past films.) But the death of his mother reveals to him the deep emotional scars which have yet to heal and have left him an emotional cripple. If you have missed the earlier films this one will be largely wasted on you.

A: Jean-Pierre Leaud, Marie-France Pisier, Claude Jade, Dani, Dorthee

© HOME VISION LOV 070

LOVER, THE

D: Jean-Jacques Annaud 103 m

R | ROM DMA | 1992 | COLOR | Sex Nud Viol Lang AdSit

7 Explicit, seductive story of forbidden passion in 1920s Vietnam. Leung, a young, rich Chinese man, becomes obsessed with March, a poor ex-patriot French schoolgirl. Their banned relationship is one of uncontrollable desire. She keeps her emotions aloof and revels only in the excitement of the experience because she always dreamed of making love to faceless men. Although he declares that he will always love March, he marries a woman chosen by his parents. It is only as March returns to France that she realizes that she loves him, too. Nominated for its cinematography, but the plotting suffers because of its vagaries and an over-reliance upon sex.

A: Jane March, Tony Leung, Frederique Meininger, Arnaud Giovaninetti, Melvil Poupaud

Distributed By MGM/UA Home Video 903183

LUST FOR LIFE

D: Vincente Minnelli 123 m

NR | DMA | 1956 | COLOR | Sex Nud Viol Lang AdSit

9 Compelling drama about the life of the master-painter Vincent Van Gogh, as passionately portrayed by Kirk Douglas. Van Gogh was largely ignored as a painter in his lifetime and had to deal with constant heartbreak and poverty. His best friend and constant critic was Paul Gauguin and is here played by Anthony Quinn (who took home an Oscar for Best Supporting Actor). This is an exquisite production and some claim it to be the best movie ever made about an artist, but this is by no means just for art fans. Superb. See also VINCENT & THEO for a more subdued but equally intense portrait.

A: Kirk Douglas, Anthony Quinn, James Donald, Pamela Brown, Everett Sloane

Distributed By MGM/UA Home Video M200510

M*A*S*H

D: Robert Altman 116 m

R | COM WAR DMA | 1970 | COLOR | Sex Nud Viol Lang AdSit

10 Hilarious irreverence! A Korean war Mobile Army Surgical Hospital is the setting for this dark and brash comedy. An unruly crew of oddball doctors and nurses survives the trauma of an endless war by concocting outlandish practical jokes to play upon each other - like selling tickets to an "unveiling" of a naked Hot Lips Houlihan in the shower. The result is big belly laughs all around. Winner of Oscar for Best Screenplay. Also nominated for Best Picture, Director and Supporting Actress. Inspired, but also very different from, the long-running TV series which became an attack on the Vietnam War.

A: Elliott Gould, Donald Sutherland, Sally Kellerman, Tom Skerritt, Robert Duvall, JoAnn Pflug

© FOXVIDEO 1038

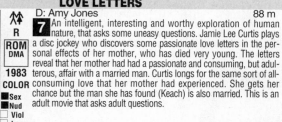

MAC

D: John Turturro 118 m

R | DMA | 1993 | COLOR | Sex Nud Viol Lang AdSit

8 Heartfelt tribute to the American work ethic and a vivid portrait of Italian/American family life. Mac is the oldest of three brothers whose father was a craftsman of the old school and who took great pride in his work. Mac feels the same way. The time is in the early 50s. The brothers had been working for a penny-pinching contractor who cut corners and cheated. Mac becomes so incensed that he forms a new construction company along with his brothers. Mac is compulsively driven to excellence and success, but his brothers have other more moderate goals. Sometimes funny, sometimes moving, most of the time very loud and always heartfelt. Not for everyone.

A: John Turturro, Michael Badalucco, Carl Capotoro, Katherine Borowitz, Ellen Barkin, John Amos

© COLUMBIA TRISTAR HOME VIDEO 93693

MACARTHUR

D: Joseph Sargent 131 m

PG | DMA WAR | 1979 | COLOR | Sex Nud Viol Lang AdSit

8 History buffs take note! This portrayal of one of history's most intriguing figures follows MacArthur's career from his controversial island-hopping campaign of WWII, through his governorship of Japan after the war, to the Korean War, when he was fired. The story is revealed between bits of his farewell address given before a group of West Point cadets. Necessarily, many of the details were sacrificed for the sake of time, but enough remains to make this an excellent production. Peck did an admirable job of retaining MacArthur's contentious and regal air.

A: Gregory Peck, Ed Flanders, Dan O'Herlihy, Sandy Kenyon, Dick O'Neill, Marj Dusay

© MCA/UNIVERSAL HOME VIDEO, INC. 55041

MACBETH

D: Roman Polanski 139 m

R | DMA | 1971 | COLOR | Sex Nud Viol Lang AdSit

8 Polanski's controversial rendition of Shakespeare's tragic play is both very violent and very powerful. A Scottish warrior's lust for power, plus the encouragements of a scheming wife and the prophesy of three evil witches, lead him ever deeper onto a path that will eventually lead to his destruction. The violence is extreme, gripping and not for the faint-at-heart. The finale features some magnificent sword-wielding battles. This is the first film Polanski made after the murder of his wife (see HELTER SKELTER) and was originally and undeservedly rated X for gore and nudity.

A: Jon Finch, Nicholas Selby, Francesca Annis, Martin Shaw, John Stride

© COLUMBIA TRISTAR HOME VIDEO 60622

MADAME SOUSATZKA

D: John Schlesinger 121 m

PG-13 | DMA | 1988 | COLOR | Sex Nud Viol Lang AdSit

6 Interesting and quirky character study of an eccentric piano teacher who takes a young prodigy under her wing. She is a failed near-great pianist who takes it upon herself to not only teach her students piano, but personal discipline of her own design. This student is still only a teenager and he has desires of his own. He rebels against her tutelage and, encouraged by his ambitious mother and a greedy talent agent, he begins a stage career before he is really ready. Not a great film, but an entertaining human drama. Excellent performances.

A: Shirley MacLaine, Peggy Ashcroft, Twiggy, Navin Chowdhry, Leigh Lawson, Shabana Azmi

© MCA/UNIVERSAL HOME VIDEO, INC. 80840

MADAME X

D: David Lowell Rich 100 m

NR | DMA | 1966 | COLOR | Sex Nud Viol Lang AdSit

8 Get your hankies out! Turner plays the wife of an inattentive and absent diplomat who was blackmailed by her mother-in-law into abandoning him and her young son. Now, 20 years later, she is destitute and up on charges of murder. In a perverse twist of fate, she is defended at her trial by her now-grown son - only he has no idea that he is defending his own mother. Turner's attempts at preventing her son from finding out the truth are truly heart-wrenching. Slow in spots, but Turner delivers a very moving performance. This is the sixth filming of this popular soap opera since 1909.

A: Lana Turner, John Forsythe, Ricardo Montalban, Burgess Meredith, Constance Bennett, Keir Dullea

© MCA/UNIVERSAL HOME VIDEO, INC. 80154

MAD DOG AND GLORY

D: John McNaughton 97 m

R | ROM DMA | 1993 | COLOR | Sex Nud Viol Lang AdSit

6 De Niro is a murder investigator for the Chicago police but he is also so shy that his friends have jokingly nicknamed him "Mad Dog." Then Mad Dog accidentally saves the life of a small-time hood, Bill Murray. In gratitude, Murray sends Glory (Uma Thurman) his virtual slave, to "entertain" him for a week. When the two fall in love, Mad Dog must dig down inside himself to find the courage to face up to this hood who wants to take his property back. This is not a comedy, nor is it a true drama or even a true romance. In spite of its uncertain nature, it's a mildly interesting story.

A: Robert De Niro, Uma Thurman, Bill Murray, Kathy Baker, David Caruso, Mike Starr

© MCA/UNIVERSAL HOME VIDEO, INC. 81278

MAHOGANY

D: Berry Gordy 109 m

PG | DMA ROM | 1975 | COLOR

6 Diana Ross goes from rags to riches in this likable soap opera. Perkins is a gay fashion photographer who discovers poor Chicago girl Ross working as a secretary and she is rocketed to international fame as a high-fashion model. However, she is soon dissatisfied and she goes out on a limb wearing one of her own designs at a fashion show. Now she has become a famous clothing designer, too! With all of this new-found fame, Ross leaves her wanna-be politician boyfriend Williams, but she discovers that her life is empty without him. This mildly popular soap opera has its moments.

Sex Nud Viol Lang AdSit

A: Diana Ross, Billy Dee Williams, Jean-Pierre Aumont, Anthony Perkins, Beah Richards, Nina Foch

© PARAMOUNT HOME VIDEO 8835

MALCOLM X

D: Spike Lee 201 m

DMA | 1992 | COLOR

8 Intelligent and genuinely interesting portrait of a complex man who became a pivotal figure in the beginning of America's transition under the civil rights movement. Malcolm X was a small-time thief and hustler who found religion, pride and purpose while serving time in prison. It was there tha he was converted into a radical Muslim sect. His energies were transferred into his new cause and he rose to become one of its national leaders teaching pride in being black. However, after he discovered the corruption in his group, he chose to denounce it and leave to seek a more peaceful He was then assassinated by his former colleagues. Over-long.

Sex Nud Viol Lang AdSit

A: Denzel Washington, Spike Lee, Angela Basset, Al Freeman, Jr., Delroy Lindo, Albert Hall

© WARNER HOME VIDEO 12596

MAMBO KINGS, THE

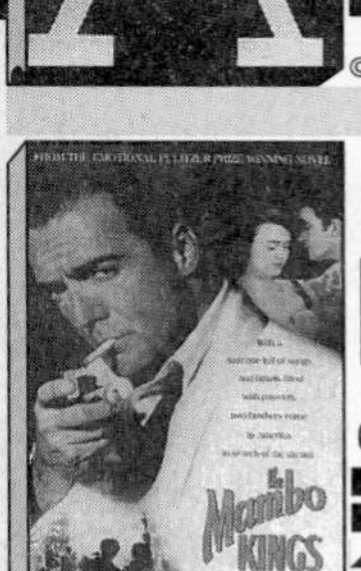

D: Arne Glimcher 104 m

R | DMA MUS | 1992 | COLOR

7 Colorful involving story of the trials of two musical brothers who flee Cuba in the early '50s, arriving in New York determined to break into its musical scene with their enthusiastic performances and lively Latin rhythms. In spite of the long odds, they do meet with quick success, but are stopped dead when they refuse to bow to the powerful leader of the local entertainment community. They are forced into becoming butchers to survive, until they get a big break on the "I Love Lucy Show" with Desi Arnaz. This is not a story of music however, it is an involving portrait of the deep love between two brothers through their struggle. The enthusiastic music is fun, too.

Sex Nud Viol Lang AdSit

A: Armand Assante, Antonio Banderas, Cathy Moriarty, Maruschka Detmers, Desi Arnaz, Jr., Celia Cruz

© WARNER HOME VIDEO 12308

MAN CALLED HORSE, A

D: Elliot Silverstein 115 m

PG | WST DMA ACT | 1970 | COLOR

10 Powerful and thoroughly engrossing story of a haughty British aristocrat (Harris) who is captured by Sioux Indians while hunting in 1830s Dakotas. He is made into a slave by them, humiliated and then just ignored. He rebels, proving his manhood by undergoing a brutal tribal ritual called a sun dance (graphically shown). With his haughty noble exterior gone, his inner strength is unearthed, and he earns his way as a powerful and respected leader of the group. A gripping and realistic depiction of American Indian communal life. See also RETURN OF A MAN CALLED HORSE and DANCES WITH WOLVES.

Sex Nud Viol Lang AdSit

A: Richard Harris, Judith Anderson, Manu Tupou, Jean Gascon, Corinna Tsopei, Dub Taylor

© FOXVIDEO 7148

MANCHURIAN CANDIDATE, THE

D: John Frankenheimer 127 m

PG-13 | SUS DMA | 1962 | B&W

9 Fully-loaded political thriller! When a highly decorated Korean war vet (Harvey) comes home, nobody suspects that he might actually be a fully-conditioned lethal killing machine. After their platoon is taken by Communists during the war, its members are either killed or brainwashed and then made to forget. However, one survivor (Sinatra) starts to have dreams that give him clues about his returning buddy's real mission. This is a scathing indictment of political extremism on both sides. Lansbury plays the meddling mother who has lofty Republican intentions. Poignant and suspenseful.

Sex Nud Viol Lang AdSit

A: Frank Sinatra, Laurence Harvey, Angela Lansbury, Janet Leigh, James Gregory, Henry Silva

Distributed By MGM/UA Home Video M801369

MAN FOR ALL SEASONS, A

D: Fred Zinnemann 120 m

G | DMA | 1966 | COLOR

10 Winner of six Academy Awards, including Best Picture! This is a magnificent portrayal of Sir Thomas More's (Scofield) battles with King Henry VIII (Shaw). Henry wants to divorce his wife who has not born him an heir. More refuses to support Henry's request of the Pope for a divorce so he can marry Anne Boleyn. Then Henry creates and declares himself to be the head of the Church of England and demands the clergy swear allegiance to him and not the Pope. More refuses. Cromwell frames More, who is eventually beheaded. Scofield's golden performance won him an Oscar for Best Actor.

Sex Nud Viol Lang AdSit

A: Wendy Hiller, Leo McKern, Robert Shaw, Orson Welles, Susannah York, Paul Scofield

© COLUMBIA TRISTAR HOME VIDEO 60047

MAN IN LOVE, A

D: Diane Kurys 110 m

R | ROM DMA | 1987 | COLOR

8 Steamy romance. An American actor (Coyote) is in Italy, making a film about the life of a notable Italian writer. But he becomes hopelessly infatuated with his sultry leading lady (Scacchi). Sparks begin to fly between them. The romance of the script leads them straight into a high-voltage affair, which jeopardizes everything for them both. He is married to Jamie Curtis, who wants him to come home. Director Kurys' first English language film is believable, sensual and interesting. As the characters develop, their everyday concerns about marriage and commitment are lost to passion.

Sex Nud Viol Lang AdSit

A: Peter Coyote, Jamie Lee Curtis, Greta Scacchi, Peter Riegert, Claudia Cardinale, John Berry

© NEW LINE HOME VIDEO 7711

MAN IN THE IRON MASK, THE

D: Mike Newell 108 m

NR | ACT DMA | 1977 | COLOR

8 Excellent and quite opulent made-for-TV movie of the classic and timeless tale from Alexander Dumas. Phillipe is one of two royal twin brothers. He is the rightful heir to the throne but is confined at birth to a remote island, and is there forced to wear an iron mask so no one will ever know his true identity. His foppish brother Louis is made king, but the real power rests with Finance Minister Fouget. France is corrupt. Captain D'Artagnan and another minister conspire to free Phillipe from prison so that he may publicly challenge Louis. Grand entertainment for the whole family.

Sex Nud Viol Lang AdSit

A: Richard Chamberlain, Patrick McGoohan, Louis Jourdan, Jenny Agutter, Vivien Merchant, Ian Holm

© LIVE HOME VIDEO 69940

MAN OF FLOWERS

D: Paul Cox 91 m

NR | DMA COM | 1984 | COLOR

7 Very odd and provocative drama, with a dark comedic edge. An eccentric old man (Kaye) is a collector of all things beautiful. Each week, he pays a lovely artist's model (Best), who he calls his "Little Flower," to strip for him while he plays classical music. However before she can finish, he runs to a church across the street to immediately vent his frustrations on the organ. The model he adores is torn between her relationship with her lesbian lover and her abusive boyfriend. But, when the boyfriend oversteps his bounds, the old man finds a beautiful way to protect his little flower.

Sex Nud Viol Lang AdSit

A: Norman Kaye, Alyson Best, Chris Haywood, Sarah Walker, Julia Blake, Bob Ellis

© LIVE HOME VIDEO VA4370

MANON OF THE SPRING

D: Claude Berri 113 m

PG-13 | FOR DMA | 1987 | COLOR

9 Visually stunning and profoundly moving conclusion to the dramatization of the classic French story first begun in JEAN DE FLORETTE. Manon is the beautiful grown daughter of the now-dead hunchback farmer who had been deceived and destroyed in the earlier story. She has learned the secret behind the death of her father - that is, who had blocked up the spring on her father's farm. That vicious and cruel act destroyed a simple man with a simple dream, only to become a farmer. So, now she plots her revenge. Please see both films together. English subtitles.

Sex Nud Viol Lang AdSit

A: Yves Montand, Emmanuelle Beart, Daniel Auteuil, Hippolyte Hiradot, Elisabeth Depardieu

© ORION PICTURES CORPORATION 5035

MAN WHO WOULD BE KING, THE

D: John Huston 128 m

PG | ACT DMA | 1975 | COLOR

9 Excellent, rousing Rudyard Kipling adventure like they used to make! Two British ex-soldiers (Connery and Caine), in the fading days of colonial England, head to Kafiristan to plunder it and become rich. Connery is struck by an arrow in the chest but it hits a medal he wears and, when he just pulls the arrow out, the people declare him a god. The two soldiers enjoy their good fortune. Soon Caine wishes to leave but Connery likes being King. However, their deception is soon uncovered and they are ruined. Garnered four Oscar nominations. Caine and Connery are magic.

Sex Nud Viol Lang AdSit

A: Sean Connery, Michael Caine, Christopher Plummer, Saeed Jaffrey, Shakira Caine

© FOXVIDEO 7435

MAN WITHOUT A COUNTRY, THE

D: Delbert Mann 78 m

NR | DMA | 1973 | COLOR

8 Stirring and thought-provoking adaptation of the classic Edward Everett Hale novel. It is a brilliant character study of a fictional early 1800 character named Philip Nolan. Nolan is an overly-zealous patriot who is eager to join in Aaron Burr's plan to bring Texas and Mexico into the United States. When he is caught, he boldly states that if his country stayed as it was, he wished that he did not have a country. At his court-martial, Nolan is granted his wish: he would be condemned to a ship and never be allowed to receive news of or even see American soil again.

Sex Nud Viol Lang AdSit

A: Cliff Robertson, Robert Ryan, Peter Strauss, Beau Bridges, Walter Abel, John Cullum

© WORLDVISION HOME VIDEO, INC. 4105

MAN WITHOUT A FACE

D: Mel Gibson 115 m

PG-13 | DMA | 1993 | COLOR

Sex | Nud | Viol | Lang | AdSit

7 It is the summer of 1968 in a small Maine village. Nick Stahl is an adolescent and one of three children of a wealthy and beautiful woman, however each was fathered by a different man. He is troubled and confused and his primary goal is to escape his family by being accepted at a military school. To do that, he needs help with mathematics and Latin. Mel Gibson is a former teacher who was horribly disfigured in a car accident that killed one of his students. He was unjustly accused of child abuse and served three years in jail. Now, he is alone and an outcast, but he is a good teacher. Fate has drawn the two together, but fate will also be harsh.

A: Mel Gibson, Nick Stahl, Margaret Whitton, Fay Masterson, Gaby Hoffman, Richard Masur

© WARNER HOME VIDEO 12987

MARJORIE MORNINGSTAR

D: Irving Rapper 125 m

NR | DMA ROM | 1958 | COLOR

Sex | Nud | Viol | Lang | AdSit

6 Natalie Wood is a beautiful 18-year-old girl from New York, with stars in her eyes, who leaves her family and sweetheart behind to venture off into the excitement of the theatre. She changes her name from Morgenstern to Morningstar and joins a summer stock group. There, she falls in love with an older performer (Kelly). He leaves the group to go to New York and the big time and she goes with him. She loves him even when he fails, but he does not treat her nearly so well. Adapted from Herman Wouk's novel, Wood and Kelly give touching performances.

A: Gene Kelly, Natalie Wood, Claire Trevor, Ed Wynn, Everett Sloane, Carolyn Jones

© REPUBLIC PICTURES HOME VIDEO 5552

MARNIE

D: Alfred Hitchcock 130 m

PG | DMA SUS | 1964 | COLOR

Sex | Nud | Viol | Lang | AdSit

6 A beautiful blond (Hedron) has the nasty habit of stealing money from her employers and leaving without a clue. When she is caught by her current boss (Connery) before she gets gone, he becomes determined to find out what's behind her kleptomaniac habits and blackmails her into marrying him while he struggles to understand her demons. Hitchcock uses varied innovative filming techniques to hint at the inner turmoil and the underlying psychosis of Hedren's past. Dismissed when it was originally released, the film has since won the respect it deserves.

A: Tippi Hedren, Sean Connery, Diane Baker, Louise Latham, Martin Gabel, Alan Napier

© MCA/UNIVERSAL HOME VIDEO, INC. 80156

MARRIAGE OF MARIA BRAUN, THE

D: Rainer Werner Fassbinder 120 m

R | FOR DMA WAR | 1979 | COLOR

Sex | Nud | Viol | Lang | AdSit

9 Challenging and intelligent look at German society in the wake of World War II. In the final days of the war, Maria marries a Wehrmacht officer, even as the bombs fall. They have one night together, he goes off to war and is presumed dead. However, he returns, finding her in bed with an American soldier. He is enraged, attacks the soldier and is sent to prison. The sensuous Maria emotionally isolates herself and does what it takes to get him out, including ruthlessly sleeping her way to the top of the corporate heap in a power-hungry charge, and he betrays his soul to let her do it. Brilliant performances.

A: Hanna Schygulla, Klaus Lowitsch, Ivan Desny

© COLUMBIA TRISTAR HOME VIDEO 60718

MARRIED TO IT

D: Arthur Hiller 112 m

R | DMA | 1993 | COLOR

Sex | Nud | Viol | Lang | AdSit

6 A mildly interesting drama which documents the married lives of three quite different couples who meet, become unlikely friends and help each other through some major potholes in life. Bridges and Channing are a struggling but mostly happy middle-aged couple with Woodstock roots in the 60s. Masterson and Leonard are newly married, fresh out of college, new to love, new to the world, and... he was just indicted for stock manipulations. Silver and Shepherd are wealthy urbanites caught up in a wild passion for each other but their relationship is complicated by misplaced values and a daughter from a previous marriage.

A: Beau Bridges, Stockard Channing, Robert Sean Leonard, Mary Stuart Masterson, Cybill Shepherd, Ron Silver

© ORION PICTURES CORPORATION 8790

MARY SHELLEY'S FRANKENSTEIN

D: Kenneth Branagh 123 m

R | DMA SF HOR | 1994 | COLOR

Sex | Nud | Viol | Lang | AdSit

7 This $45 million faithful adaptation of Mary Shelly's novel is set at the end of the eighteenth century. Devastated by the death of his wife, aristocrat Frankenstein (Branagh) studies to become a doctor. His interest lies not in healing the sick but by studying the mysteries of death. As a student, he builds upon the work of a brilliant teacher to actually recreate life by combining the stolen body parts of the dead. Stunned by the pitiful human result of his experiments, who escapes, he vows never to play with life again. However, the hideous and merciless creature he has created (De Niro) is constantly tormented by people. Terribly lonely, he now seeks out his "father" to force him to create a companion for him too.

A: Kenneth Branagh, Robert De Niro, Tom Hulce, Helena Bonham Carter, Aidan Quinn, Ian Holm

© COLUMBIA TRISTAR HOME VIDEO 78713

MASADA

D: Boris Sagal 131 m

NR | DMA ACT | 1984 | COLOR

Sex | Nud | Viol | Lang | AdSit

9 Excellent and moving epic drama of bravery and strength in this film dramatic depiction of a true event. In 70 A.D., a Roman general (O'Toole) is ordered to crush the Jewish uprising in Israel, and he does... Jerusalem is destroyed. However, a rebel zealot leader (Strauss) leads of a group of 980 zealots in an escape to Herod the Great's fortress palace high on Mt. Masada. There they hold out valiantly against 10,000 Roman soldiers in a prolonged 3-year Roman siege. Based on Ernest K. Gann's novel, this dramatic story was made into a very popular TV miniseries. O'Toole and Strauss deliver fine performances.

A: Peter O'Toole, Peter Strauss, Barbara Carrera

© MCA/UNIVERSAL HOME VIDEO, INC. 66025

MASK

D: Peter Bogdanovich 120 m

PG-13 | DMA | 1985 | COLOR

Sex | Nud | Viol | Lang | AdSit

9 Be prepared to shed some tears. This film is a dramatization of the real-life story of a severely disfigured boy (Stoltz) who suffering from Elephantitis. His rowdy, biker mother (Cher) is an inspiring tower of strength on the outside, but inside she can barely keep herself together. She loves her son unconditionally, teaching him the wonders of living in spite of the taunting of others and the pain of loneliness. She instills in him strength, a self-confidence and a zest for life that keep both of them going. Cher and Stoltz are outstanding in this most touching and moving drama.

A: Cher, Sam Elliott, Eric Stoltz, Laura Dern, Estelle Getty, Richard Dysart

© MCA/UNIVERSAL HOME VIDEO, INC. 80173

D M A

MASS APPEAL

D: Glenn Jordan 99 m

PG | DMA COM | 1984 | COLOR

Sex | Nud | Viol | Lang | AdSit

8 A young seminary student (Ivanek) wreaks holy havoc when he challenges a situation he finds at Father Tim Farley's (Lemmon) wealthy parish. Father Tim is laid-back. He cracks jokes from the pulpit and is much-loved by his parishioners. He even drives a Mercedes. Idealistic newcomer Ivaek questions Lemmon's methods and the two are launched on a collision course. Ivanek's confrontational path also gets him sideways of the inflexible Monsignor (Durning) and almost tossed out. But Lemmon protects his new charge and eventually they teach other about faith.

A: Jack Lemmon, Zeljko Ivanek, Charles Durning, Louise Latham, Lois de Banzie, James Ray

© MCA/UNIVERSAL HOME VIDEO, INC. 80168

MATEWAN

D: John Sayles 100 m

PG-13 | DMA | 1987 | COLOR

Sex | Nud | Viol | Lang | AdSit

9 Powerful and gripping dramatization of a true story. It's 1920 and the coal miners in West Virginia are working under terrible conditions. A young union organizer (Cooper) leads the frustrated miners in a strike. He is intent upon avoiding conflict, but the Italians continue to work in spite of the strike and the owners bring in black workers from Alabama. There is inevitable conflict, but eventually the three groups settle into an uneasy alliance. Then the owners fight back again, this time with violence. The result is a massacre that is now infamous in labor relations.

A: James Earl Jones, Mary McDonnell, William Oldham, Chris Cooper, Bob Gunton, Kevin Tighe

© WARNER HOME VIDEO 384

MATTER OF PRINCIPLE, A

D: Gwen Arner 60 m

NR | COM DMA | 1984 | COLOR

Sex | Nud | Viol | Lang | AdSit

7 A lighthearted Scrooge-like Christmas story for everybody. The selfish and cantankerous father (Arkin) of a very large brood, ruins the family's Christmas when he decides he can't afford the expense. His wife (Dana) is fed up with his tyrannical behavior. She decides to take no more of it and leaves him, taking the kids. When he comes to realize that he might just have cost himself his family, he has a change of heart and comes to understand the true meaning of Christmas. Well done, a fun and entertaining holiday story.

A: Alan Arkin, Barbara Dana, Tony Arkin

© ACADEMY ENTERTAINMENT 1065

MEAN STREETS

D: Martin Scorsese 112 m

R | DMA | 1973 | COLOR

Sex | Nud | Viol | Lang | AdSit

9 Gritty, ultra-realistic character study of seedy low-life characters in Little Italy. George (Keitel) aspires to move up in his Mafia circle, and must keep his friendship with reckless and psychotic Lennie (De Niro) a secret. Lennie seems to be forever in trouble and George is always bailing him out. When Lennie defaults on a payment to a loan shark, George must help him to get out of town. This film has no plot in a traditional sense, but it rather is a fascinating character study and a realistic depiction of small-time Mafia life. One of Scorsese's first directorial attempts, and a big critical success.

A: Robert De Niro, Harvey Keitel, David Proval, Amy Robinson, Richard Romanus, Cesare Danova

© WARNER HOME VIDEO 11081

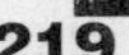

MEDICINE MAN

D: John McTiernan 105 m

PG-13 DMA ACT 1992 COLOR

Sex Nud Viol Lang AdSit

6 Connery is a brilliant scientist who has found the cure for cancer in the Brazilian rain forest. He has created the serum once, but he can't duplicate it so he sends for a noted research assistant to come. Instead he gets Bracco, a tough-talking female scientist from the Bronx. Sparks fly between them as they try to find the missing element in the serum, but their attentions quickly turn instead to the rapidly burning rain forest which is threatening to destroy all of their work, plus the cure. The muddled script is saved only by Connery's presence.

A: Sean Connery, Lorraine Bracco, Jose Wilker

© HOLLYWOOD PICTURES HOME VIDEO 1358

MELVIN AND HOWARD

D: Jonathan Demme 95 m

R COM DMA 1980 COLOR

Sex Nud Viol Lang AdSit

7 Unusual bittersweet comedy. Hollywood fabricated this story about the real-life character Melvin Dummar (LeMat), a down-on-his-luck gas station attendant in Utah who claimed to have once given Howard Hughes a ride, and claimed that Hughes later scrawled him a note which named him heir to $156 million. This odd-ball slice-of-life comedy works pretty well, if haltingly. It pokes fun both at society at large and at common-man Dummar's continual but ill-advised grabs for the American Dream. Academy Awards included Best Supporting Actress and Original Screenplay. Not a traditional comedy.

A: Paul LeMat, Jason Robards, Jr., Mary Steenburgen, Jack Kehoe, Pamela Reed, Dabney Coleman

© MCA/UNIVERSAL HOME VIDEO, INC. 66026

MEMORIES OF ME

D: Henry Winkler 103 m

PG-13 COM DMA 1988 COLOR

Sex Nud Viol Lang AdSit

7 The two of them couldn't be more different. Billy Crystal is a New York heart surgeon and his father (Alan King) is a California actor who has spent his whole career as an extra. When Crystal survives a mild heart attack, he decides to get his priorities in order. So his girl (Williams) encourages him to mend fences with his father. These two are so far apart that that isn't easy, and it does set up some pretty funny situations. However, when Billy finds that his father is terminally ill, they begin an adventure making up for lost time. Obviously contrived, but still an entertaining mixture of laughter and emotion.

A: Billy Crystal, Alan King, JoBeth Williams, Janet Carroll, David Ackroyd, Sean Connery

Distributed By MGM/UA Home Video M201514

MEMPHIS BELLE

D: Michael Caton-Jones 107 m

PG-13 DMA WAR ACT 1990 COLOR

Sex Nud Viol Lang AdSit

8 Flying a bombing raid over Germany was about the most dangerous thing a man could do in WWII. The B-17 Memphis Belle had already flown 24 missions beating the odds. This next one would be its last and its last flight was being immortalized by a documentary for a bond drive, but its crew, all young men just barely out of their teens, don't care. They just want to get that last mission behind them and go home. Involving and entertaining. The film builds slowly, letting us get to know the characters. Then the last mission comes. Terrific air action. Also see TWELVE O'CLOCK HIGH.

A: Matthew Modine, Eric Stoltz, Billy Zane, Tate Donovan, Harry Connick, Jr., D.B. Sweeney

© WARNER HOME VIDEO 12040

MENACE II SOCIETY

D: Allen Hughes, Albert Hughes 97 m

R CRM DMA 1993 COLOR

Sex Nud Viol Lang AdSit

9 Highly praised portrait of the rough and ugly life that is everyday existence in the ghettos of Los Angeles. The praise is well deserved but this video is very difficult to watch. The characters are mean and remorseless killers who value nobody's life, many times including their own, and respect nothing. The story revolves around one young black man, whose father dealt drugs and died when he was ten. His mother gave him to his grandparents and then died herself of an overdose. His grandparents raised him as best they could, but his world is the streets and his family are the other tough kids who are just like him. A brutal film about a brutal life.

A: Tyrin Turner, Jada Pinkett, Larenz Tate, Arnold Johnson, M C Eiht, Marilyn Coleman

© TURNER HOME ENTERTAINMENT N4165

MEN DON'T LEAVE

D: Paul Brickman 115 m

PG-13 DMA COM 1990 COLOR

Sex Nud Viol Lang AdSit

8 Moving and believable. Another victory for the director of RISKY BUSINESS! Jesseca Lange is a recently widowed mother of two left penniless, without hope and lonely when her husband is killed. She realizes that she must move to an apartment in the city and sell her big house to survive, but her young boys have a harder time understanding why things have changed so much. As she struggles with her own shattered dreams, loneliness, a new job and a likable but eccentric composer who's chasing her, she also must somehow give her teenage sons the means to survive in their own new worlds. Heartbreaking and heartwarming. Insightful comedy and moving drama. Excellent.

A: Jessica Lange, Joan Cusack, Arliss Howard, Kathy Bates, Chris O'Connell, Charlie Korsmo

© WARNER HOME VIDEO 11897

MEPHISTO

D: Istvan Szabo 150 m

NR FOR DMA 1981 COLOR

Sex Nud Viol Lang AdSit

8 A very stylish and controversial war drama best suited for sophisticated audiences. It was also the Academy Award winner for the Best Foreign Film of 1981. A talented but egotistical actor, living in Germany just before the War, is given a chance by a powerful Nazi to advance his career if he will just renounce his past politics. He does but only when it is too late does he realize that he has paid a very high price for what he has gained. Based on the book by Klaus Mann, who committed suicide due to the difficulties encountered in getting the book published - it was banned in Germany for forty years.

A: Klaus Maria Brandauer, Krystyna Janda, Ildiko Bansagi, Karen Boyd, Rolf Hope, Christina Harbot

© TVS INC.

MERMAIDS

D: Richard Benjamin 101 m

PG-13 COM DMA 1991 COLOR

Sex Nud Viol Lang AdSit

8 Offbeat and very different, but also a very entertaining comedy. Set in the '60s, Cher is the sexy mother of two girls. She's a looker. She loves men and can't keep her hands off them, but she's also so afraid of a permanent relationship that she's always running away from them. She just packs everybody up and leaves town. Her oldest daughter (Ryder) is just 15, trying to find her place in the world and trying to deal with her own hormones, but she's not getting much help from Mom. The youngest daughter's only concern is her dream to swim the English Channel. The three of them argue, laugh, and learn about family, life and love together.

A: Cher, Bob Hoskins, Winona Ryder, Christina Ricci, Michael Schoeffling, Caroline McWilliams

© ORION PICTURES CORPORATION 8759

METROPOLITAN

D: Wilt Stillman 98 m

PG-13 COM DMA 1990 COLOR

Sex Nud Viol Lang AdSit

8 Refreshing, witty, intellectual comedy documenting the "trials" of a group of privileged NYC preppies. The story line itself is of little consequence because it only opens a window for us to see into their world. What is interesting, even fascinating at times, and almost always funny, is the amount of privileged ignorance these young people possess. This is a fact to which they themselves begin to gain some knowledge when a lack of escorts requires them to let into their privileged midst a middle-class outsider. For all that, this movie does not demean these people - it exposes their underlying humanity. If you liked this, also try BARCELONA.

A: Edward Clements, Christopher Eigeman, Carolyn Farina, Isabel Gillies, Will Kempe, Taylor Nichols

© NEW LINE HOME VIDEO 75153

MIDNIGHT CLEAR, A

D: Keith Gordon 107 m

R DMA WAR 1992 COLOR

Sex Nud Viol Lang AdSit

6 A sad and emotional anti-war statement, very well received critically. It is Christmas 1944. The war is very near to an end. Six young soldiers are all who remain of a special squad of 16 whiz kids, stationed in a forward position to collect information about an expected desperate Nazi offensive. Scared, they are approached by a group of equally scared German soldiers who want to surrender before they get killed in the big upcoming battle. The two sides even celebrate Christmas together. However, because of a misunderstanding, the peace is broken and the two sides get into a big fire fight anyway. Draining, frustrating and unsatisfying.

A: Peter Berg, Kevin Dillon, Arye Gross, Ethan Hawke, Gary Sinise, Frank Whaley

© COLUMBIA TRISTAR HOME VIDEO 92833

MIDNIGHT COWBOY

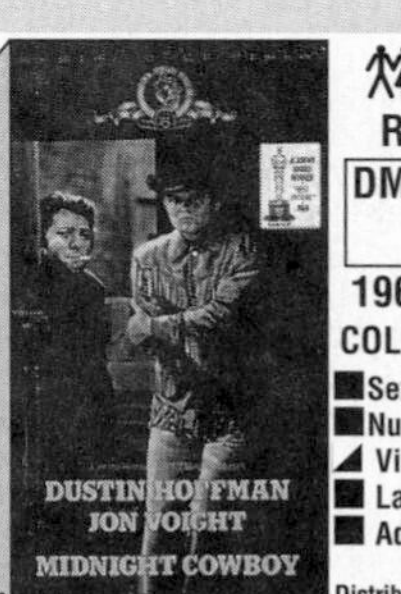

D: John Schlesinger 113 m

R DMA 1969 COLOR

Sex Nud Viol Lang AdSit

8 Shocking drama that holds the distinction of being the only movie ever to win Best Picture and be rated X (would only be an R today). Buck (Voight) is a handsome dim-witted dishwasher in Texas but imagines himself to be a natural source of satisfaction for rich New York women. So, he travels there to become rich. His first NY conquest, however, is so broke that he has to give her cab fare to get home. Then he meets Ratso Rizzo, a diminutive, sleazy con man who has tuberculosis and dreams as big as Buck's. Ratso offers to become Buck's manager and to also share the rundown building he calls home. Gloomy and depressing, slice of sleazy life.

A: Dustin Hoffman, Jon Voight, Sylvia Miles, Brenda Vaccaro, John McGiver, Barnard Hughes

Distributed By MGM/UA Home Video M700193

MIDNIGHT EXPRESS

D: Alan Parker 123 m

R DMA SUS 1978 COLOR

Sex Nud Viol Lang AdSit

9 Unrelenting reality-based terror! A forceful adaptation of the true story of Billy Hayes (Davis), a young man who was sentenced to 30 years in a sub-human Turkish prison after being caught with hashish strapped to his body. Inside prison, he is subjected to harrowing and violent torture by the Turkish government. This graphic depiction of his chilling experience will most likely stick with you for long while - the nightmarish helplessness and terror of it all goes right to the bone. Oliver Stone won an Oscar for Best Screenplay.

A: Brad Davis, Randy Quaid, John Hurt, Bo Hopkins, Ira Miracle, Mike Kellin

© GOODTIMES 4238

MILAGRO BEANFIELD WAR, THE

D: Robert Redford — 118 m

R — DMA COM — 1988 — COLOR — **8**

Positively infectious good time. Based on Nichols and David Ward's novel, this touching tale is set in a poor New Mexican town of Milagro. Bullying land developers plan to take over some farm land. So, handyman Vennera leads a rebellion against the big money interests by using their water to irrigate his dusty beanfield. His one act of defiance inspires all the others to gain courage, and to rise up and join him. An endearing story that, even with its simple plot, is sure to lift you up. The whimsical score won an Oscar.

Sex · Nud · Viol · Lang · AdSit

A: Sonia Braga, Chick Vennera, Ruben Blades, Christopher Walken, Daniel Stern, John Heard

© MCA/UNIVERSAL HOME VIDEO, INC. 80796

MIRACLE, THE

D: Neil Jordan — 100 m

NR — DMA — 1991 — COLOR — **7**

Curious and interesting English import. Jimmy and Rose are best friends. Jimmy's father is a saxophonist, a former swinger and now a drunk, working at an Irish seaside resort. He and Jimmy live together there alone. Each day Jimmy and Rose patrol the beachfront, watching the people to make up stories of their own to match what they think they see. Then one day a beautiful older woman catches their attention. Jimmy becomes strangely fascinated with her, his adolescent hormones boiling. However, the truth about this woman is more than Jimmy and Rose could ever have guessed.

Sex · Nud · Viol · Lang · AdSit

A: Donal McCann, Beverly D'Angelo, Niall Byrne, Lorraine Pilkington

© LIVE HOME VIDEO 68989

MIRACLE WORKER, THE

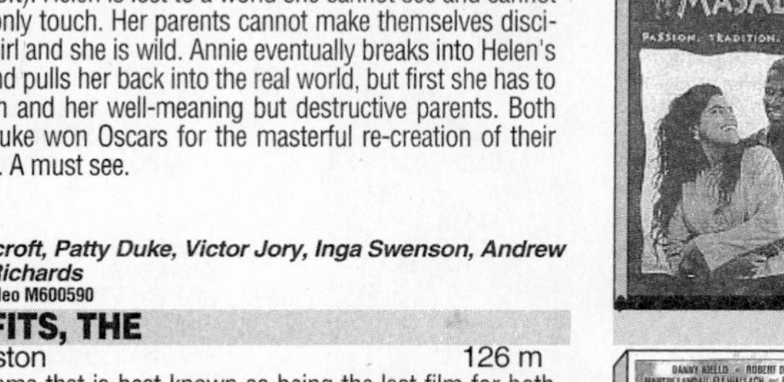

D: Arthur Penn — 107 m

NR — DMA — 1962 — B&W — **9**

Truly inspiring! A brilliant film depiction of the life of Helen Keller (Duke) and her unforgettable and determined teacher Annie Sullivan (Bancroft). Helen is lost to a world she cannot see and cannot hear. She can only touch. Her parents cannot make themselves discipline the poor girl and she is wild. Annie eventually breaks into Helen's private world and pulls her back into the real world, but first she has to fight both Helen and her well-meaning but destructive parents. Both Bancroft and Duke won Oscars for the masterful re-creation of their Broadway roles. A must see.

Sex · Nud · Viol · Lang · AdSit

A: Anne Bancroft, Patty Duke, Victor Jory, Inga Swenson, Andrew Prine, Beah Richards

Distributed By MGM/UA Home Video M600590

MISFITS, THE

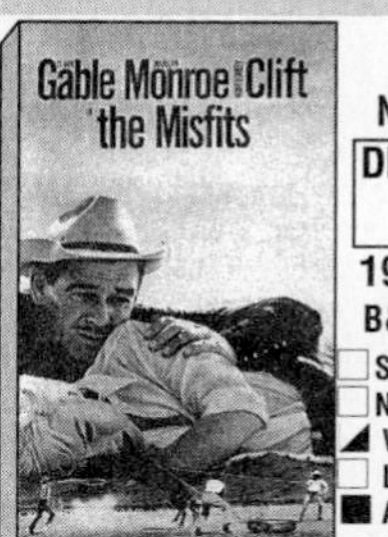

D: John Huston — 126 m

NR — DMA — 1961 — B&W — **6**

Moody drama that is best known as being the last film for both Gable and Monroe. He died 8 days before it finished - she halfway into her next picture. A beautiful idealist and one-time stripper (Monroe), unhappy with her marriage to a businessman, travels to Reno, Nevada to get a divorce. There she meets a rugged drifting cowboy (Gable), falls for him and leaves with him, and his pals Wallach and Clift to capture misfits, horses too small for anything but being made into dogmeat. When she discovers the purpose of their mission, she is very upset and battles Gable but Gable refuses to back down.

Sex · Nud · Viol · Lang · AdSit

A: Clark Gable, Marilyn Monroe, James Barton, Montgomery Clift, Eli Wallach, Thelma Ritter

Distributed By MGM/UA Home Video M201650

MISS FIRECRACKER

D: Thomas Schlamme — 102 m

PG — COM DMA — 1988 — COLOR — **6**

Quirky and colorful comedy. Carnelle (Holly Hunter) is an insecure smalltown young girl who has grown up in the shadow of her lovely cousin (Steenburgen), a former Miss Firecracker. Carnelle dreams of gaining respectability, of changing her flirtatious image and wants to finally "be somebody," so she focuses all of her efforts upon entering and winning the local beauty contest. She will become Miss Firecracker, just as her cousin had done. This feel-good movie is peppered with all sorts of oddball characters and has its moments, but it is different.

Sex · Nud · Viol · Lang · AdSit

A: Holly Hunter, Mary Steenburgen, Tim Robbins, Scott Glenn, Alfre Woodard, Scott Glenn

© HBO VIDEO 0330

MISSING

D: Constantine Costa-Gavras — 122 m

PG — DMA SUS — 1982 — COLOR — **8**

Solid political intrigue! At the height of a violent military coup in South America, a young American journalist (Shea) disappears. His wife (Spacek) and conservative businessman father (Lemmon) put past differences behind them to embark on a desperate search to find him there. When their inquiries meet with stonewalling at the American Embassy, the pair come to the uncomfortable conclusion that their own government may be in collusion with the local bureaucracy in preventing them from finding the truth. Best Screenplay, plus nominated for Actor, Actress and Best Picture.

Sex · Nud · Viol · Lang · AdSit

A: Jack Lemmon, Sissy Spacek, John Shea, Melanie Mayron, Charles Cioffi, David Clennon

© MCA/UNIVERSAL HOME VIDEO, INC. 71009

MISSION, THE

D: Roland Joffe — 125 m

PG — DMA ACT — 1986 — COLOR — **8**

Sweeping drama set in the mid-18th century. Irons stars as a dedicated Jesuit priest who braves the jungles of South America and opens a mission there. De Niro is a slavetrader who is guilt-ridden for having murdered his own brother in a fit of rage. So he returns with Irons into the jungle, in an act of penance, to help convert the same people that in the past he would have made into slaves. Then when the small colony is sold to Portugal and slave trade is legalized, the two must fight the Portuguese and the church itself to save these native people from slavery. 7 nominations, including Best Picture.

Sex · Nud · Viol · Lang · AdSit

A: Robert De Niro, Jeremy Irons, Liam Neeson, Ray McAnally, Aidan Quinn

© WARNER HOME VIDEO 11639

MISSISSIPPI BURNING

D: Alan Parker — 127 m

R — CRM SUS DMA — 1988 — COLOR — **9**

Hard-edged and mesmerizing drama that is based on fact. It's 1964 and change is coming to Mississippi. Three young civil rights workers are missing and the FBI is investigating. Willem Dafoe is a dedicated young agent sent in to run the investigation, but Gene Hackman is the local agent who understands these people. He and Dafoe are not friends but they are both dedicated to stopping the reign of terror of the KKK. Still, the FBI is not welcomed by any of the locals, black or white. And as Dafoe brings in hundreds of agents, the national press moves in and the fires start to burn. Nominated for seven Academy Awards. Excellent.

Sex · Nud · Viol · Lang · AdSit

A: Gene Hackman, Willem Dafoe, Frances McDormand, Brad Dourif, R. Lee Ermey, Gailard Sartain

© ORION PICTURES CORPORATION 8727

MISSISSIPPI MASALA

D: Mira Nair — 117 m

R — DMA ROM — 1992 — COLOR — **7**

An unusual and intelligent film. A wealthy Indian attorney, who was born in African Uganda, is forced to leave by dictator Idi Amin. He, his wife and daughter settle down and work for relatives at their motel in an Indian enclave of Mississippi, where they are neither white or black. His beautiful daughter meets and falls for a successful young black man (Washington). She has really never known discrimination but, when their relationship is discovered, they are both immediately chastised by Indians, blacks and whites. Involving, well-conceived and executed, but a little slow.

Sex · Nud · Viol · Lang · AdSit

A: Denzel Washington, Sarita Choudhury, Roshan Seth, Sharmila Tagore, Charles Dutton, Joe Seneca

© COLUMBIA TRISTAR HOME VIDEO 92693

MISTRESS

D: Barry Primus — 112 m

R — DMA — 1992 — COLOR — **6**

Where THE PLAYER dealt satirically with a Hollywood filled with beautiful people double-talking and cutting each other's throats, this film is populated with very unattractive people doing the same thing. While being much closer to the truth, the film is also too close to the truth to be funny, although it trys. It is the story of a once-promising filmmaker, who is being wooed by a has-been producer. The producer is trying to entice him into altering his script (about an artist who refuses to be corrupted) so that the investors can put their mistresses in the movies. Film insiders only.

Sex · Nud · Viol · Lang · AdSit

A: Danny Aiello, Robert De Niro, Martin Landau, Eli Wallach, Robert Wuhl

© LIVE HOME VIDEO 9864

MI VIDA LOCA (MY CRAZY LIFE)

D: Allison Anders — 100 m

R — DMA — 1994 — COLOR — **6**

Young Latino women who try to mix growing up with too-early motherhood, and who do it while substituting gang life for real family, is the subject of this film. Two Hispanic girls have grown up being best friends, but they have now became mortal enemies, after both have a child fathered by the same boy. They are children playing at being adults. They struggle to build a life for themselves but have no effective and successful model to guide them. Not particularly insightful, and this is ground well-covered before...but never from a female perspective.

Sex · Nud · Viol · Lang · AdSit

A: Angel Aviles, Seidy Lopez, Jacob Vargas, Panchito Gomex, Julian Reyes, Marlo Marron

© HBO VIDEO 91188

MOBY DICK

D: John Huston — 116 m

NR — DMA ACT — 1956 — COLOR — **7**

Based on Melville's classic, this gripping saga of revenge and the sea is first-rate! Against the warnings of a God-fearing preacher (Welles), seaman Richard Basehart joins ominous Quiquig and disfigured Captain Ahab (Peck) to set sail on a whaling ship in 1840. Ahab is quick to let his crew know that they are on a quest to kill the great white whale that made lunch of his leg. Ahab will let nothing stand in his way - not torturous seas, a mutiny or even the lives of his crew in his obsessive hunt to kill the great whale. Although a little heavy at times, this is excellent adventure.

Sex · Nud · Viol · Lang · AdSit

A: Gregory Peck, Richard Basehart, Orson Welles, Leo Genn, Harry Andrews, Fredrich Ledebur

Distributed By MGM/UA Home Video M201643

MODERNS, THE

D: Alan Rudolph — 126 m

R | DMA | 1988 | COLOR | Sex, Nud, Viol, Lang, AdSit

6 There was nothing more romantic or modern than an American living in Paris in the '20s. Nick (Carradine) is a struggling American artist living in Paris who stumbles upon his old love Rachael (Fiorentio) and seduces her, even though she is now married to a prominent businessman. Mildly humorous, this film takes a back seat to historical documentation but transforms the mild story into a cinematic treat for the senses, capturing the beautiful surroundings and the art of the times.

A: Keith Carradine, John Lone, Linda Fiorentino, Genevieve Bujold, Wallace Shawn

© NEW LINE HOME VIDEO 7712

MOLLY MAGUIRES, THE

D: Martin Ritt — 123 m

PG | DMA | 1970 | COLOR | Sex, Nud, Viol, Lang, AdSit

6 Powerful story of a battle for dignity. In 1870 the immigrant Irish coal miners in Pennsylvania worked under terrible conditions. The Molly Maguires were a group of rebels that violently battled against those inhuman conditions. Connery, the leader of the group, considers a new arrival in town (Harris) to be a friend. However he is really a Pinkerton detective whose mission is to betray the Mollies, even though it is a difficult task to deal with in his own conscience. This story evokes vivid images of the sad day-to-day drone of the miners' existence and is based on fact. Beautiful Mancini score.

A: Sean Connery, Richard Harris, Samantha Eggar, Frank Finlay, Art Lund, Anthony Costello

© PARAMOUNT HOME VIDEO 6905

MOMMIE DEAREST

D: Frank Perry — 129 m

PG | DMA | 1981 | COLOR | Sex, Nud, Viol, Lang, AdSit

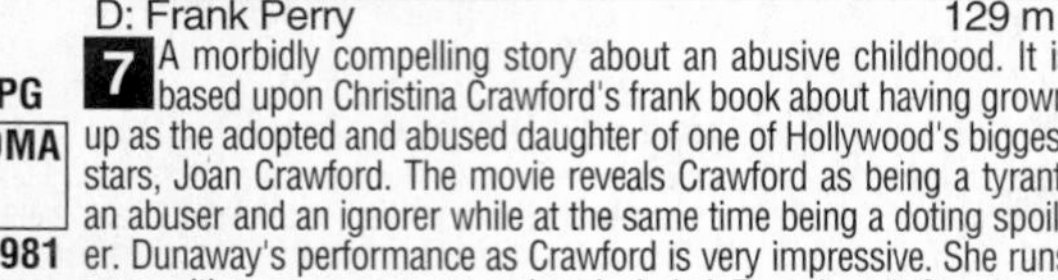

7 A morbidly compelling story about an abusive childhood. It is based upon Christina Crawford's frank book about having grown up as the adopted and abused daughter of one of Hollywood's biggest stars, Joan Crawford. The movie reveals Crawford as being a tyrant, an abuser and an ignorer while at the same time being a doting spoiler. Dunaway's performance as Crawford is very impressive. She runs away with every scene, cast and set included. Even though Crawford's actions are seemingly ludicrous at times, still you feel compelled to watch this film through.

A: Faye Dunaway, Diana Scarwid, Steve Forrest, Howard da Silva, Mara Hobel

© PARAMOUNT HOME VIDEO 1263

MO' MONEY

D: Peter MacDonald — 91 m

R | DMA COM | 1992 | COLOR | Sex, Nud, Viol, Lang, AdSit

7 Damon Wayans and his brother Marlon star in this ethnic piece about two inner-city scam artists. Damon is the older brother who becomes infatuated with a beautiful and classy girl working in a credit card company. He knows he has no chance to win her over unless he straightens himself out. So he applies for a job there too, and gets it. However, the economic requirements of romance prove to be too much for his larcenous soul and he gives into the temptation to steal, which draws him into major trouble. Clever bits here and there, but will be most appealing to a younger audience.

A: Damon Wayans, Marlon Wayans, Joe Santos, John Diehl, Stacey Dash, Harry J. Lennix

© COLUMBIA TRISTAR HOME VIDEO 51313

MOSCOW ON THE HUDSON

D: Paul Mazursky — 107 m

R | COM DMA ROM | 1984 | COLOR | Sex, Nud, Viol, Lang, AdSit

8 The film is both comic and bittersweet and Robin Williams is an absolute charmer. While touring the United States, Williams, a musician for the Moscow Circus, is blown away by the wonders of Bloomingdales and defects to America right then. His adjustment to American life is difficult, often comedic and sad. He lives in fear that the KGB will capture him, until he gets his American citizenship. But he also has new friends in a black security guard, a sexy Italian lover and a cagey lawyer. America becomes home, but it doesn't happen all at once and it's a lot fun watching it happen.

A: Robin Williams, Maria Conchita Alonso, Cleavant Derricks, Alejandro Rey, Savely Kramarov, Elya Baskin

© COLUMBIA TRISTAR HOME VIDEO 60309

MOSQUITO COAST, THE

D: Peter Weir — 119 m

PG | DMA ACT | 1986 | COLOR | Sex, Nud, Viol, Lang, AdSit

7 Gripping drama and action. An idealistic inventor and near lunatic (Ford) is fed up with life in America. So he uproots his entire family and moves them to Central America, hoping to create his own utopia there. He is a can-do kind of guy and manages to achieve some success. He begins to think of himself as a sort of god until three gun-toting terrorists arrive. Based on the best-seller by Paul Theroux, Ford's performance is stellar, although the character is an unsympathetic one. A serious and thought-provoking drama about one man's relentless search for perfection.

A: Harrison Ford, Helen Mirren, River Phoenix, Conrad Roberts, Butterfly McQueen, Martha Plimpton

© WARNER HOME VIDEO 11711

MOUNTAINS OF THE MOON

D: Bob Rafelson — 140 m

R | DMA ACT | 1990 | COLOR | Sex, Nud, Viol, Lang, AdSit

8 Robust adventure! Two of history's most remarkable explorers from the Victorian era, undertake the last great challenge for mid-19th-century men of adventure - the search across totally uncharted and hostile lands for the source of the Nile. Sir Richard Burton and John Hanning Speke (Bergin and Glen) risked attacks by men, beasts and insects and bore unspeakable hardships to form strong personal bonds during their quest across Africa. This sweeping saga maintains historical integrity and sacrifices nothing to maintain gripping excitement. It doesn't have to. Gritty and realistically photographed at beautiful locations.

A: Patrick Bergin, Iain Glen, Richard E. Grant, Fiona Shaw, Bernard Hill, Paul Onsongo

© LIVE HOME VIDEO 68915

MR. & MRS. BRIDGE

D: James Ivory — 127 m

PG-13 | DMA | 1990 | COLOR | Sex, Nud, Viol, Lang, AdSit

7 Critically acclaimed but slow moving drama of an all-American couple from the 1930s. He is a successful attorney in Kansas City, staid and in firm control of his family, with a sharply defined sense of what's right and what's wrong. She has been his devoted and self-sacrificing wife. Both are now challenged by a world that is rapidly changing around them, and by their own children who march to different drummers. Sharply defined characters, brilliant acting (Woodward was Oscar-nominated) and brief vignettes define this picture, rather than any specific plot. Slow.

A: Joanne Woodward, Paul Newman, Robert Sean Leonard, Kyra Sedgwick, Lyndon Ashby

© HBO VIDEO 90533

MR. SATURDAY NIGHT

D: Billy Crystal — 119 m

R | DMA COM | 1992 | COLOR | Sex, Nud, Viol, Lang, AdSit

6 Billy Crystal stars, produces and directs this fictionalized biography of one of his stage characters, Buddy Young Jr. Buddy is a caustic old comedian who has short-circuited his own career his whole life by attacking everyone, including those who love him most: his brother, his wife, his friends and the people he works with. Now, he is an old man addicted to the applause of an audience, but there no longer is an audience who wants to hear him. The combination of good jokes that are nullified by a depressing pathetic character ultimately makes for a believable but unattractive character study.

A: Billy Crystal, David Paymer, Julie Warner, Helen Hunt, Jerry Orbach, Ron Silver

© TURNER HOME ENTERTAINMENT N4064

MRS. PARKER AND THE VICIOUS CIRCLE

D: Alan Rudolph — 124 m

R | DMA | 1994 | COLOR | Sex, Nud, Viol, Lang, AdSit

8 Literate and well-read viewers will enjoy this film biography of famed writer Dorothy Parker. Mrs. Parker was known for her extremely biting wit and savage one-liners. During the 1920s, she and her like-minded fellow writers would gather at the Algonquin Hotel for long drinking sessions wherein they would entertain themselves with fiercely competitive verbal jousts, skewering themselves and anyone else they chose. Mrs. Parker's bitter wit descends over time, many lovers and many more alcoholic hazes, into a cynicism that led to deep depression and even suicide attempts. This is not an entertaining film for general audiences. It is for sophisticated viewers only, who may rate it even higher.

A: Jennifer Jason Leigh, Matthew Broderick, Campbell Scott, Peter Gallagher, Jennifer Beals, Andrew McCarthy

© TURNER HOME ENTERTAINMENT N4020

MRS. SOFFEL

D: Gillian Armstrong — 113 m

PG-13 | DMA ROM | 1985 | COLOR | Sex, Nud, Viol, Lang, AdSit

6 Curiously interesting but also a slow-moving and gloomy drama that was based upon a real incident. In 1901 Pittsburgh, a repressed warden's wife (Keaton) is permitted to distribute Bibles to prisoners on death row. She becomes infatuated with the charismatic older of two brothers (Gibson), who are up for a murder which they may not have committed. She not only falls in love him and then helps them to escape, but she leaves with them, too. She is transformed from being a devoutly religious woman to being the adulterous lover of a man on the run from the law.

A: Diane Keaton, Mel Gibson, Edward Herrmann, Matthew Modine, Trini Alvarado, Jennie Dundas

Distributed By MGM/UA Home Video M800600

MURDERERS AMONG US: THE SIMON WIESENTHAL STORY

D: Brian Gibson — 157 m

NR | DMA | 1989 | COLOR | Sex, Nud, Viol, Lang, AdSit

8 Powerful and moving true life account of an Austrian Jew who survives the terror of German Nazi war camps to reunite with his family, and then dedicates his life to a search for justice by hunting down Nazi war criminals. Among the men that Simon Wiesenthal is credited for bringing in are Adolf Eichmann and Franz Murer. Ben Kingsley is brilliant in the title role. This made-for-cable movie is not for the squeamish - the scenes in the war camps are very real.

A: Ben Kingsley, Craig T. Nelson, Renee Soutendijk, Louisa Haig, Paul Freeman, Anton Lesser

© HBO VIDEO 0321

MURDER IN THE FIRST

D: Marc Rocco 123 m

R | DMA CRM | 1995 | COLOR | Sex | Nud | Viol | Lang | AdSit

8 In 1930, a 17-year-old orphan stole $5 from a rural store to feed his hungry sister. The store doubled as a post office, so he was sent to federal prison and later was transfered to Alcatraz. After a failed escape attempt, and accused of being the ring-leader, a vengeful warden ordered him into solitary confinement - a cold, wet, pitilessly dark, pest-infested hole - where he was left and repeatedly beaten for three years. Within hours of his release, and now a totally demented wreck, he fatally stabbed the man who ratted on him. His supposed cut-and-dried case is assigned to a novice attorney, who instead won his case by attacking the cruel system which created him and then destroyed him. Based on true story.

A: Christian Slater, Kevin Bacon, Gary Oldman, Embeth Davidtz, Brad Dourif, Lee Ermey

© WARNER HOME VIDEO 13895

MURPHY'S WAR

D: Peter Yates 106 m

PG | DMA ACT | 1971 | COLOR | Sex | Nud | Viol | Lang | AdSit

7 Near the end of WWII, an English ship is torpedoed and its crew gunned down by a German U-boat that prowls nearby waters. Irish merchantman (O'Toole) is the only survivor of the massacre. He is rescued by a French oil engineer and nursed back to health at a nearby village hospital. Now healthy, he hears of a wrecked old sea plane and decides to seek his own revenge by patching it up to conduct his own private war on the marauding U-boat's crew. O'Toole packs a powerful performance into this wartime story.

A: Peter O'Toole, Sian Phillips, Philippe Noiret, Horst Janson, John Hallam, Ingo Morgendorf

© PARAMOUNT HOME VIDEO 8047

MUSIC BOX

D: Constantine Costa-Gavras 126 m

PG-13 | DMA SUS | 1989 | COLOR | Sex | Nud | Viol | Lang | AdSit

8 An unusual, passionate and gripping courtroom drama. A working class Hungarian immigrant is accused of having committed atrocious war crimes. He turns to his daughter, a lawyer (Lange), to defend him and prove his innocence. Lange agrees, never once doubting her father's innocence, but soon shocking developments require that she prove everything to herself, too. This is an intense and gripping drama and will have you guessing what the truth is the whole way. Lange received an Oscar nomination for her powerful and convincing performance.

A: Jessica Lange, Armin Mueller-Stahl, Frederic Forrest, Lukas Haas, Cheryl Lynn Bruce, Donald Moffat

© LIVE HOME VIDEO 68903

MY BEAUTIFUL LAUNDRETTE

D: Stephen Frears 94 m

R | COM DMA | 1986 | COLOR | Sex | Nud | Viol | Lang | AdSit

8 Quirky and odd-ball art film that is very entertaining for the adventurous. Omar (Warnecke), a young Pakistani boy living in a rundown section of London, is given a beat-up launderette by his uncle. He teams up with Johnny (Day-Lewis), his punk boyfriend, and together they renovate the launderette into a neon dream. Everything goes great until a group of racist thugs decide to close down the operation. Although highly acclaimed for its poignant look at cultural differences, sexuality and economic problems, the plot may be a little remote for some. There also may be a problem for some because of the thick accents.

A: Daniel Day-Lewis, Saeed Jaffrey, Roshan Seth, Gordon Warnecke, Derrick Branche, Shirley Anne Field

© WARNER HOME VIDEO 784

MY BODYGUARD

D: Tony Bill 96 m

PG | COM DMA | 1980 | COLOR | Sex | Nud | Viol | Lang | AdSit

8 This is a winning and very likable charmer that will give everyone smiles. Clifford Peache (Makepeace) is a boy who has attended an exclusive private school for nine years, but now he is enrolled in a Chicago public high school, and that's a whole different world. The school is run by a gang of teenage thugs, lead by Dillon, who extort money from their classmates. But Clifford finds a unique solution. He hires Baldwin, a menacing older student, to protect him. However, their strictly-business relationship turns into a warm friendship with some surprises. A very funny and heartwarming movie.

A: Matt Dillon, Chris Makepeace, Adam Baldwin, Ruth Gordon, Matt Dillon, John Houseman

© FOXVIDEO 1111

MY DINNER WITH ANDRE

D: Louis Malle 110 m

PG | DMA | 1981 | COLOR | Sex | Nud | Viol | Lang | AdSit

6 Curious twist on traditional film formats. In this strange film, two old friends just sit down to dinner and discuss everything that is going on in their lives. That's it! One is a playwright actor (Shawn), the other is a theatre director (Gregory) and they just discuss philosophy, the meaning of life, etc. It is a daring premise - the entire film is taken up just with their conversation only... they just talk. The thought-provoking movie was a surprise hit with the art crowd, but the nonstop talking will likely seem a bit much for the ordinary viewer. Art people will rate it much higher.

A: Andre Gregory, Wallace Shawn

© PACIFIC ARTS VIDEO 532

MY FATHER'S GLORY

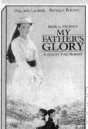

D: Yves Robert 110 m

G | FOR DMA | 1991 | COLOR | Sex | Nud | Viol | Lang | AdSit

9 Very highly acclaimed literary triumph. It is the richly painted portrait of the memories of author and filmmaker Marcel Pagnol's childhood in rural France at the turn of the 20th-century. It is primarily the story of a summer trip that he took, along with his parents, where even the most commonplace of situations become fascinating to a precocious boy totally involved in the rural lifestyle. This marvelous experience was followed by the equally fascinating MY MOTHER'S CASTLE. In French with subtitles.

A: Philippe Caubere, Nathalie Roussel, Julian Ciamaca, Therese Liotard, Didier Pain

© ORION PICTURES CORPORATION 5066

MY GIRL

D: Howard Zieff 102 m

PG | DMA ROM CLD | 1991 | COLOR | Sex | Nud | Viol | Lang | AdSit

8 Irresistable weeper. Eleven-year-old Chlumsky is the precocious daughter of a widowed mortician (Aydroyd) and because their house doubles for a mortuary, death is everywhere. Aykroyd doesn't have much time for his daughter, nor does he know how to reach out to her, not knowing that she feels responsible for her mother's death or that she's jealous when he falls for the new cosmetologist (Curtis) he has hired. But Macauly Culkin is her neighbor and that summer she and Culkin become best friends and experience the beginnings of young love. However, their summer together comes to a tragic end. Parents, share this one with your kids.

A: Anna Chlumsky, Macaulay Culkin, Dan Aykroyd, Jamie Lee Curtis, Richard Masur, Griffin Dunne

© COLUMBIA TRISTAR HOME VIDEO 50993

MY LEFT FOOT

D: Jim Sheridan 103 m

R | DMA | 1989 | COLOR | Sex | Nud | Viol | Lang | AdSit

9 Inspiring true story! Born with cerebral palsy and thought to be a vegetable, a young Irishman, Christy Brown (Daniel Day-Lewis), astounds his family by writing a message on the floor by using his foot. He's alive in there! His mother devoted herself to him, scrimping to save to get him the help he needed. With the support of her unselfish love, Christy goes on to become an accomplished painter and writer. He even types his memoirs using his left foot. He overcame great obstacles to have a life. Oscar for Day-Lewis, as Best Actor, and Fricker, for Supporting Actress. Astounding!

A: Daniel Day-Lewis, Brenda Fricker, Ray McAnally, Hugh O'Conor, Fiona Shaw, Cyril Cusack

© HBO VIDEO 0373

MY LIFE

D: Bruce Rubin 117 m

PG-13 | DMA | 1993 | COLOR | Sex | Nud | Viol | Lang | AdSit

8 Michael Keaton is young, successful and married to beautiful Nicole Kidman. She is pregnant with their first child when he discovers that he is going to die soon from an incurable cancer. Keaton is determined that his unborn child will know who he is. So, even as he struggles to find a way to stay alive, he also begins, on videotape, to pass on all the life's instructions that he can. He also wants to document his life, which causes him to uncover and then to heal old wounds. While dying is the subject of this video, it is more about the reevaluation of life that the contemplation of death brings. There is nothing here overly profound, but it is involving and sobering.

A: Michael Keaton, Nicole Kidman, Bradley Whitford, Queen Latifah, Michael Constantina, Hang S. Ngor

© COLUMBIA TRISTAR HOME VIDEO 71143

MY LIFE AS A DOG

D: Lasse Hallstrom 101 m

NR | FOR COM DMA | 1987 | COLOR | Sex | Nud | Viol | Lang | AdSit

7 Offbeat and loveable. A young boy (Glanzelius) gets bundled up and shipped off to a country town in Sweden when his mother becomes seriously ill. This town is populated by offbeat characters and he feels deserted and alone. He comes to compare himself to the Russian dog Laika who was abandoned and left to die in space. But instead he learns to deal with his new surroundings, to understand loss, and even falls in love with a cute little tomboy. This is more than just a film about the pitfalls of growing up, this story is filled to the brim with humor and warmth. A Swedish surprise. Dubbed or subtitles.

A: Anton Glanzelius, Anki Liden, Tomas Von Bromssen, Melinda Kinnaman, Kicki Rundgren, Ing-mari Carlsson

© PARAMOUNT HOME VIDEO 12651

MY NAME IS BILL W.

D: Daniel Petrie 100 m

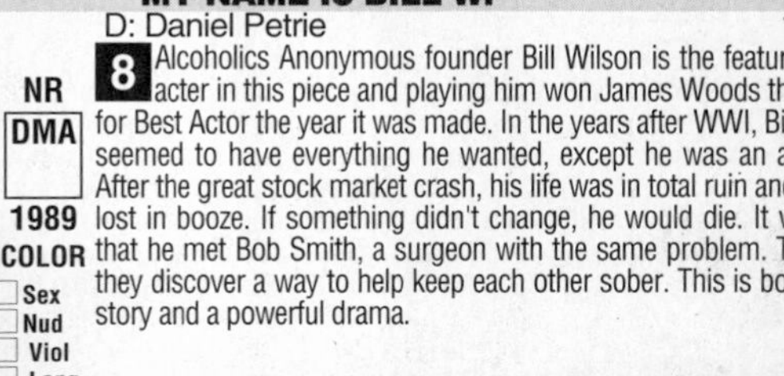

NR | DMA | 1989 | COLOR | Sex | Nud | Viol | Lang | AdSit

8 Alcoholics Anonymous founder Bill Wilson is the featured character in this piece and playing him won James Woods the Emmy for Best Actor the year it was made. In the years after WWI, Bill Wilson seemed to have everything he wanted, except he was an alcoholic. After the great stock market crash, his life was in total ruin and he was lost in booze. If something didn't change, he would die. It was then that he met Bob Smith, a surgeon with the same problem. Together, they discover a way to help keep each other sober. This is both a true story and a powerful drama.

A: James Woods, JoBeth Williams, James Garner, Fritz Weaver, Robert Harper, Gary Sinise

© WARNER HOME VIDEO 13371

D M A

MY OWN PRIVATE IDAHO

D: Gus Van Sant, Jr. 105 m

R | DMA | 1991 | COLOR | Sex ■ Nud ■ Viol ◢ Lang ■ AdSit ■

6 Extremely well made, acted and photographed, but its subject matter will limits its appeal. It is a depressing tale of a young male street prostitute (Phoenix), hampered by narcolepsy, and his best friend (Reeves). Phoenix is surviving day-to-day, lost and alone except for the band of misfits and hustlers he lives with, who are just like him. Reeves is the rebellious son of Portland's wealthy mayor, but living with the group. Phoenix's single overriding obsession is to find the loving mother of his childhood memories - the mother who deserted him. The film successfully evokes an unpleasant empathy for pitiable characters, but heavy going.

A: River Phoenix, Keanu Reeves, James Russo, William Richert, Rodney Harvey, Flea

© TURNER HOME ENTERTAINMENT N4095

MY SIDE OF THE MOUNTAIN

D: James B. Clark 100 m

G | DMA CLD | 1969 | COLOR | Sex ☐ Nud ☐ Viol ☐ Lang ☐ AdSit ☐

7 This is an entertaining back-to-nature tale in which a thirteen-year-old boy gives up all of his worldly possessions and the comforts of home, to test his survival skills by emulating his idol, Henry David Thoreau. He runs away intending to make the Canadian mountains his home for one year and takes nothing with him but his mind and his courage. Refreshing and charming, this is a film that the whole family will enjoy. It's not just for kids.

A: Ted Eccles, Theodore Bikel, Tudi Wiggins, Frank Perry, Prggi Loder

© PARAMOUNT HOME VIDEO 6813

MYSTERY TRAIN

D: Jim Jarmusch 110 m

R | COM DMA | 1989 | COLOR | Sex ☐ Nud ■ Viol ☐ Lang ■ AdSit ■

6 Quirky and odd, but intriguing continuation of director Jarmusch's fascination with weird slices of America. This film contains three short stories woven together. An offbeat hotel in Memphis (the land of Elvis) attracts three groups of unique characters. Two Japanese teenage tourists who are ardent Elvis fans, an Italian widow here to take her husband's body home and Bracco, plus two others, who get involved in a robbery and a shooting. This clever study of characters can be slow in spots and is sometimes difficult to fathom, but has some sincerely funny moments, too. Be prepared.

A: Elizabeth Bracco, Nicolette Braschi, Youki Kudoh, Masatoshi Nagase, Joe Strummer, Steve Buscemi

© ORION PICTURES CORPORATION 5051

MY SWEET CHARLIE

D: Lamont Johnson 97 m

NR | DMA | 1969 | COLOR | Sex ☐ Nud ☐ Viol ☐ Lang ☐ AdSit ◢

8 An intelligent made-for-television production that won three Emmys, including Best Actress. Two of society's outcasts are thrown together against their will. A bigoted young white girl (Duke) is disowned by her family because she is pregnant; and, a black New York lawyer (Freeman) is running from the law because he killed a white man in self-defense. These two very different people find themselves forced to hide in the same abandoned house on the Texas coast. Duke is faced with, for her, a terrible moral dilemma: He's black and he's wanted by the law, but she needs his help badly. The truth is they both need each other's help. Very well done.

A: Patty Duke, Al Freeman, Jr., William Hardy, Ford Rainey, Chris Wilson, Noble Willingham

© MCA/UNIVERSAL HOME VIDEO, INC. 80326

NAKED

D: Mike Leigh 131 m

R | DMA | 1994 | COLOR | Sex ■ Nud ■ Viol ◢ Lang ■ AdSit ■

8 Very, very dark, but yet perversely fascinating English film. Johnny is a dead-broke intellectual with an acidly sarcastic wit and a deep-seated cynicism. He has escaped to London, arriving at the apartment of a former girlfriend and her pitifully insecure roommate, who immediately becomes fascinated with him. But, Johnny only uses her, immediately discards her and decides to leave them both to move back to the streets. It is then that we begin to understand the workings of Johnny's tormented genius mind and soul. Much of NAKED is philosophical, while being bitterly funny. Accents are difficult. Mostly for a thinking audience with a strong stomach. Should have been shorter.

A: David Thewis, Lesley Sharp, Katrin Cartlidge, Greg Cruttwell, Peter Wight, Claire Skinner

© TURNER HOME ENTERTAINMENT N4311

NAKED KISS, THE

D: Samuel Fuller 90 m

NR | DMA | 1964 | B&W | Sex ☐ Nud ☐ Viol ◢ Lang ☐ AdSit ■

7 This is fascinating "B" movie, extremely provocative for its time. In the opening scene, a bald woman beats a man with a telephone. He was her pimp, had cheated her and shaved her head. She has gotten even but now she must run away. At first she plies her trade in small towns but she decides to go straight. She becomes a nurse's aid at a handicapped children's hospital where she becomes popular and marries a cultured, handsome millionaire, who knows of her past. But, she is startled to learn that he is a pervert and a child molester and she kills him. No one will believe her story, especially with her past...that is until they find a dead little girl.

A: Constance Towers, Anthony Eisley, Virginia Grey, Betty Bronson, Patsy Kelly, Michael Dante

© HOME VISION NAK 01

NASHVILLE

D: Robert Altman 159 m

R | COM DMA | 1975 | COLOR | Sex ☐ Nud ◢ Viol ◢ Lang ■ AdSit ■

8 This picture was widely acclaimed by the critics and nominated for five Oscars, including Best Picture (won Best Song: Keith Carradine's "I'm Easy"). However, its somewhat elitist and condescending nature leaves others cold. It is a cynical character study of American culture, where 24 different characters, whose lives all revolve around the music business or someone in it, are followed for one solid weekend in and around Nashville. The one common thread tieing them all together is a political campaign by a populist candidate. Both comic and poignant, if you're receptive.

A: Henry Gibson, Lily Tomlin, Ronee Blakley, Keith Carradine, Geraldine Chaplin, Barbara Harris

© PARAMOUNT HOME VIDEO 8821

NASTY GIRL, THE

D: Michael Verhoeven 94 m

PG-13 | FOR COM DMA | 1990 | COLOR | Sex ☐ Nud ◢ Viol ◢ Lang ◢ AdSit ■

9 Delicious biting black comedy that sadly enough is based upon a true story. A German school girl, living in a picturesque Bavarian village, wants to write an essay to be entitled, "My Town During the Third Reich." Suddenly she is ostracized and threatened by the seemingly friendly people she has known all her life. This is a subject they don't want reopened and she is barred from the town archives. This story could easily enough have been turned into a very serious drama. Instead, it is presented as a biting satire, ripping apart hypocrisy. And, it does so in a way so that we see that her town is like all towns everywhere. Subtitles.

A: Lena Stolze, Monika Baumgartner, Michael Gahr, Elisabeth Bertram, Fred Stillkrauth, Robert Gioggenbach

© HBO VIDEO 90621

NATURAL, THE

D: Barry Levinson 134 m

PG | DMA | 1984 | COLOR | Sex ☐ Nud ☐ Viol ◢ Lang ◢ AdSit ◢

8 Sentimental film favorite, extremely popular with the public. Roy Hobbs (Redford) is a natural baseball player, but his career is stopped dead by a bullet from a crazy woman (Hershey) while on his way up to the big leagues. Sidelined for 16 years, Hobbs makes a hard-fought comeback attempt. Inspired by his hometown sweetheart, his batting leads his team into the pennant. But the owner will take a financial loss if the team wins, so Kim Basinger is brought in to distract Redford for a while. Rewarding, old-fashioned fun.

A: Robert Redford, Robert Duvall, Glenn Close, Kim Basinger, Barbara Hershey

© COLUMBIA TRISTAR HOME VIDEO 60380

NELL

D: Michael Apted 113 m

PG-13 | DMA | 1994 | COLOR | Sex ☐ Nud ■ Viol ☐ Lang ■ AdSit ◢

7 Jodie Foster plays Nell, a young woman who has grown up in near-total isolation ever since her birth to a mother who could not talk, had been raped, lived as a hermit and hid her from the world too. But now her mother is dead, Nell has no knowledge of the world and can not even speak - except in a language that is all her own. Liam Neeson is a local doctor who discovers Nell and, along with psychologist Natasha Richardson, trys to protect her while Nell is slowly made aware of the much larger unknown world around her. A very interesting concept that is reasonably well executed, although it does tend to preach in places. As usual, Jodie Foster's performance is outstanding.

A: Jodie Foster, Liam Neeson, Natasha Richardson, Richard Libertini, Nick Searey, Jeremy Davies

© FOXVIDEO 8737

NETWORK

D: Sidney Lumet 122 m

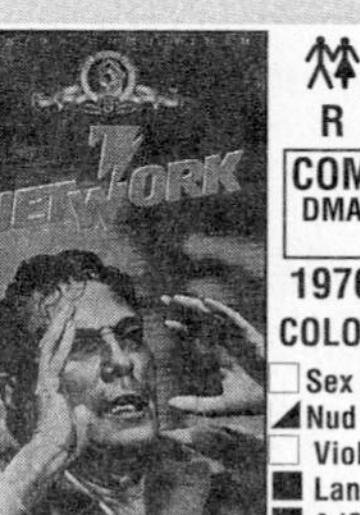

R | COM DMA | 1976 | COLOR | Sex ☐ Nud ◢ Viol ☐ Lang ■ AdSit ■

10 Brilliant and not-too-kind satire of television and television news. This was a very popular and very biting black comedy in which a ruthless network executive (Duvall) is willing to do anything to get ratings and get his fourth-rate network out of the ratings basement. Even if it means allowing an off-his-rocker news anchorman (Finch) to become a hugely popular spectacle as the "mad prophet of the airwaves" by inciting his audience with ranting: "I'm mad as hell and I'm not going to take it anymore." Outstanding cast. Oscars: Actor, Actress, Supporting Actress and Screenplay.

A: Faye Dunaway, William Holden, Peter Finch, Robert Duvall, Wesley Addy, Ned Beatty

Distributed By MGM/UA Home Video M600012

NEVER CRY WOLF

D: Carroll Ballard 105 m

PG | DMA | 1983 | COLOR | Sex ☐ Nud ◢ Viol ◢ Lang ◢ AdSit ◢

8 This "nature" film proved to be very popular across a broad spectrum of the viewing public. It is the story of a field biologist (Smith) who is sent into the barren wilds of the Arctic to study wolves. Absolutely alone in the vast wilderness, we watch Smith set up his observations of a pack of wolves and then watch the relationship that develops between the two. There is stunning scenery and beautiful photography, but this is also an absorbing, and sometimes humorous, adventure story worthy of viewing by everyone from the very youngest to the oldest. Taken from the best-selling memoirs of Farley Mowat. Done by Disney's studios.

A: Charles Martin Smith, Brian Dennehy, Samson Jorah

© WALT DISNEY HOME VIDEO 182

NEW AGE, THE

D: Michael Tolkin — 112 m

R | DMA | 1994 | COLOR | Sex ■ | Nud ■ | Viol □ | Lang ■ | AdSit ■

7 Very intense dissection of economic and social pretense, combined with spiritual emptiness. Peter Weller and Judy Davis are an apparently successful couple. However, he has lost interest in his advertising career and cannot refrain from engaging in affairs, even though his wife is his best friend. Her graphics business has fallen on to hard times and she feels betrayed by him. They agree to live separate lives, each with someone else, but remain inside the same expensive house, which they can't afford. They also start a new equally-pretentious business together -- only to fail at that too. Everything is falling down around them and they are lost. Very heavy and slow moving.

A: Peter Weller, Judy Davis, Patrick Bauchau, Corbin Bernen, John Diehl, Adam West

© WARNER HOME VIDEO 13030

NEW CENTURIONS, THE

D: Richard Fleischer — 103 m

R | CRM DMA ACT | 1972 | COLOR | Sex □ | Nud □ | Viol ■ | Lang ■ | AdSit ■

8 An involving screen adaptation of Joseph Wambaugh's novel about the nature of street cops. Scott is a grizzled old veteran on the way out, teaching the new and enthusiastic rookie (Stacy Keach) the ropes. Keach loves it. He is hooked on the excitement, and he puts it before everything else even though it is destroying his marriage. Scott will soon retire but finds that he, too, is hooked, however he can't go back. This is a fascinating character study, but it is also ultimately pretty downbeat in nature. Great performances and a fascinating story.

A: George C. Scott, Stacy Keach, Jane Alexander, Rosalind Cash, Scott Wilson

© COLUMBIA TRISTAR HOME VIDEO 60070

NEW YEAR'S DAY

D: Henry Jaglom — 90 m

R | DMA ROM | 1989 | COLOR | Sex □ | Nud ◢ | Viol □ | Lang ■ | AdSit ■

7 Interesting character studies are drawn from the opportunity presented when two groups of strangers are forced occupy the same apartment for one day. Three young women have been renting an apartment in New York. They are moving out but thought they had until the end of the day. In walks the owner, recently arrived from California and wanting to move in because he thought their lease was up at the beginning of the day. This film explores the personalities of those moving out and a depressed man in mid-life crisis moving in. That one day leaves a lasting impression on them all forever.

A: Maggie Jakobson, Gwen Welles, David Duchovny, Melanie Winter, Harvey Miller, Irene Moore

© PARAMOUNT HOME VIDEO 12780

NEW YORK STORIES

D: Woody Allen, Francis Ford Coppola — 126 m

PG | COM DMA | 1989 | COLOR | Sex □ | Nud □ | Viol □ | Lang ◢ | AdSit ◢

6 Three entirely different short stories about New York people, from three of America's most prominent directors - Martin Scorsese, Francis Ford Coppola and Woody Allen. First is Scorsese's adult story about an obsessive artist (Nolte) trying to hang on to a student/lover (Arquette). Coppola's is a cute little story more for kids about a rich 12-year-old who lives alone in a hotel while her parents globe-trot. Allen's is the best and funniest, with the widest appeal, as he plays a middle-aged lawyer who is plagued by his nagging mother and is blessed when a magician "loses" her. Not for most people, but film students and film fans especially will enjoy themselves.

A: Nick Nolte, Rosanna Arquette, Talia Shire, Giancarlo Giannini, Mae Questal, Woody Allen

© TOUCHSTONE HOME VIDEO 952

NICHOLAS AND ALEXANDRA

D: Franklin J. Schaffner — 172 m

PG | DMA | 1971 | COLOR | Sex □ | Nud □ | Viol □ | Lang □ | AdSit ◢

7 Done with a big budget and beautifully photographed, this film won 6 Oscar nominations. It is the insightful and detailed chronicling of the last years of the Russian aristocracy. Czar Nicholas and his domineering wife, Alexandra, govern over a declining empire while they are both desperately concerned for their hemophiliac son. They have lost contact with their people and Alexandra is more and more influenced by the mad monk Rasputin, because she believed that without his help her son would die. Excellent acting and historically accurate, yet sometimes slow-moving. Also see RASPUTIN AND THE EMPRESS.

A: Michael Jayston, Janet Suzman, Laurence Olivier, Jack Hawkins, Tom Baker, Alexander Knox

© COLUMBIA TRISTAR HOME VIDEO 60072

NIGHT AND THE CITY

D: Irwin Winkler — 104 m

R | DMA | 1992 | COLOR | Sex ◢ | Nud □ | Viol ◢ | Lang ■ | AdSit ◢

6 De Niro is Harry, a scuzzy ambulance-chasing New York lawyer. Harry hangs out at a midtown Manhattan bar who's owner hates him, even without the knowledge that Harry is having an affair with his wife (Lange). Harry schemes to become a boxing promoter and Lange is helping him, in the hopes of opening her own bar and leaving her husband. By lying and cheating, Harry manages to promote a fight in spite of the efforts of a big-time hood and promoter (King) to stop him. There are top notch people involved with this film but good acting cannot overcome the repulsive characters they play.

A: Robert De Niro, Jessica Lange, Alan King, Eli Wallach, Jack Warden, Cliff Gorman

© FOXVIDEO 1987

NIGHTBREAKER

D: Peter Markle — 99 m

NR | DMA | 1989 | COLOR | Sex □ | Nud □ | Viol □ | Lang □ | AdSit ◢

7 Moving and powerful fact-based drama that uses the interesting dramatic trick of having Martin Sheen's son (Estevez) play Martin as a young man. In the early 1950s, the US military had used 235,000 soldiers as unwitting guinea pigs in the nuclear testing in the Nevada desert. As a young psychologist, Estevez's job is to observe. Even though his wife is a researcher and warns him against it, he goes. Now, 30 years later, the older Sheen plays a research neurologist who must deal with the trauma of his own involvement in that program. Told through a series of flashbacks. Made-for-cable.

A: Martin Sheen, Emilio Estevez, Lea Thompson, Melinda Dillon

© TURNER HOME ENTERTAINMENT 6021

NIGHT OF THE IGUANA, THE

D: John Huston — 117 m

NR | DMA | 1964 | B&W | Sex □ | Nud □ | Viol □ | Lang □ | AdSit ■

6 Even powerful performances and John Huston's direction cannot make this Tennessee Williams play truly successful. It remains, however, a very engrossing picture. Burton plays a defrocked alcoholic minister eking out a living as a tour guide in Mexico, while struggling to maintain his sanity. He becomes entangled with three strikingly different women, who each try to rescue him from his spiral downward. First is an 18-year-old nymphette (Lyon). Kerr is a more mature woman who helps to stabilize him, but he is then confronted with sultry Gardner, an old flame. Dark and moody.

A: Richard Burton, Deborah Kerr, Ava Gardner, Sue Lyon, James Ward, Grayson Hall

Distributed By MGM/UA Home Video M600080

NIGHT TO REMEMBER, A

D: Roy Ward Baker — 119 m

NR | DMA | 1958 | B&W | Sex □ | Nud □ | Viol □ | Lang □ | AdSit ◢

9 Compelling, detailed and authentic documentary-like accounting of the events surrounding the sinking of the H.M.S. Titanic in April of 1912. That wreck cost 1302 lives (705 survived). The human story of that tragedy is told through a series of vignettes by using a huge cast. (There are over 200 speaking roles.) The stories told are the personal stories of heroism, self-sacrifice, grace under pressure and also the immense tragedy in the face of panic and terrible confusion. The "unsinkable" ship hit an iceberg and sank in 1 1/2 hours.

A: Kenneth More, David McCallum, Honor Blackman, Robert Ayers, Anthony Bushell

© PARAMOUNT HOME VIDEO 12580

NINTH CONFIGURATION, THE

D: William Peter Blatty — 115 m

R | SUS DMA | 1979 | COLOR | Sex □ | Nud ◢ | Viol ■ | Lang ■ | AdSit ■

8 A very intense and almost surrealist film that is hard to follow. Its characters are also very bizarre, so it is not for everyone. Stacy Keach plays a psychiatrist at a remote military mental institution which is charged with caring for deeply disturbed Vietnam War veterans. It soon becomes apparent that the doctor may be as nutty as the patients and he begins to have very strange effects on the patients. This film appears to swing violently from dark comedy to tragedy and almost loses viewers, but the obscure plot does come together in the end.

A: Stacy Keach, Scott Wilson, Jason Miller, Ed Flanders, Neville Brand, George DiCenzo

© R&G VIDEO, LP 90006

NORMA RAE

D: Martin Ritt — 117 m

PG | DMA | 1979 | COLOR | Sex □ | Nud □ | Viol ◢ | Lang ◢ | AdSit ◢

9 Powerfully moving, but also highly entertaining, this is a story taken from the pages of real life. It is the story of the organization of a labor union at small-town Southern textile mill during the Depression years. Sally Field won her much-deserved first Oscar as the impassioned poor Southern woman who is won over to the union cause by a NY organizer (Leibman) and then who wins over her co-workers. But... it is also a very human story of the relationships between regular people, depicting courage and personal growth of the individual. Superior.

A: Sally Field, Ron Leibman, Beau Bridges, Pat Hingle, Barbara Baxley, Gail Strickland

© FOXVIDEO 1082

NORTH DALLAS FORTY

D: Ted Kotcheff — 119 m

R | COM DMA | 1979 | COLOR | Sex □ | Nud ■ | Viol ■ | Lang ■ | AdSit ◢

9 Outstanding sports-oriented comedy with serious underpinnings - not the typical sports story. Nolte is a nearly over-the-hill pro football player. He loves the game, the good times and feelings of comradery he shares with his teammates. But his seven years in the pros have also taught him that he is just another piece of equipment - to be used up until there is nothing left. Still, he is hooked on the excitement and the way of life. Funny. Great football action. It makes no difference whether you are a fan - you'll have a good time.

A: Nick Nolte, Charles Durning, Bo Svenson, Mac Davis, John Matuszak, Dabney Coleman

© PARAMOUNT HOME VIDEO 8773

NORTHERN LIGHTS

D: John Hanson, Rob Nilsson 96 m

NR | DMA | 1979 | COLOR

8 Stark survival on the Northern prairie, taken from the diaries of real-life pioneer Ray Sorenson. Set in 1915 North Dakota, this is the story of fiercely determined Norwegian and Swedish settlers and their struggles to survive the harshness of a barren, virgin landscape, plus the powerful pressures from outside forces, both government and commercial, all of which endeavor to destroy them. Realistic and unforgettable story of human courage and determination in the face of overpowering obstacles.

Sex | Nud | Viol | Lang | AdSit

A: Joe Spano, Robert Behling, Susan Lynch, Henry Martinson

© R&G VIDEO, LP A86520

NOSTRADAMUS

D: Roger Christian 118 m

R | DMA | 1994 | COLOR

8 It is the early 1500s. France is laid waste by the horrors of the black plague and the Inquisition. Nostradamus is a physician whose radical scientific beliefs and medical treatments run counter to the teachings of the church. That conflict causes him to take refuge with an older doctor who has, along with a group of intellectuals, collected and hidden any ancient books of wisdom. When the older man learns of Nostradamus' prophetic dreams, he administers drugs to enhance their intensity. Nostradamus then must write down and publish a warning of the terrors he foresees. Whatever the historical accuracy, the film is also an intriguing portrait of a tortured soul.

Sex | Nud | Viol | Lang | AdSit

A: Tcheky Karyo, Amanda Plummer, Assumpta Serna, Julia Ormond, Rutger Hauer, F. Murray Abraham

© ORION PICTURES CORPORATION 8808

D
M
A

NOTHING IN COMMON

D: Garry Marshall 119 m

PG | COM DMA | 1986 | COLOR

8 Touching, funny and entertaining. Tom Hanks is a fun-loving and totally irresponsible advertising hotshot who is forced to grow up suddenly when his parents separate after 34 years of marriage. Now the tables are switched and both have become dependent upon HIM for emotional support - this, when he never before had to be responsible for anything or to anybody. He reluctantly becomes his mother's closest confidant and also must provide encouragement to his aging, terrified father before a major operation, all while trying to help to mend their long-strained relationship.

Sex | Nud | Viol | Lang | AdSit

A: Tom Hanks, Jackie Gleason, Eva Marie Saint, Bess Armstrong, Hector Elizondo, Barry Corbin

© HBO VIDEO TVR9960

NOT WITHOUT MY DAUGHTER

D: Brian Gilbert 107 m

PG-13 | DMA | 1991 | COLOR

6 An absorbing story based upon the real situation encountered by a Michigan housewife, Betty Mahmoody, who was married to an Iranian-born doctor. He took his wife and daughter on a visit home to Iran, but while there he was converted to Islam and decided to stay. Thereafter, he tells his wife that she may leave if she chooses, but their daughter will stay with him. In Iran, Betty is horrified to discover, a woman has no rights and the full power of a police-state government is now set against her. She has no power, no money and no friends, but still she is determined to take her daughter home.

Sex | Nud | Viol | Lang | AdSit

A: Sally Field, Alfred Molina, Shelia Rosenthal, Roshan Seth

Distributed By MGM/UA Home Video M902257

NUN'S STORY, THE

D: Fred Zinnemann 152 m

NR | DMA | 1959 | COLOR

8 An outstanding drama and a major box office success. Nominated six times, including Best Picture and Actress. Hepburn is a young woman who has constant, recurring doubts about her decision to be a nun. A brilliant nurse, she is assigned first to a psychiatric hospital and then to the Belgian Congo. She wrestles with her conscience constantly because of the conflicts between her pride and her desires to help people with her medical skills. She knows she is good and finds it very difficult to be humble and subservient so that she can be a good nun. She cannot find peace. Engrossing human drama.

Sex | Nud | Viol | Lang | AdSit

A: Audrey Hepburn, Peter Finch, Edith Evans, Peggy Ashcroft, Dean Jagger, Mildred Dunnock

© WARNER HOME VIDEO 11171

NUTS

D: Martin Ritt 116 m

R | DMA | 1987 | COLOR

8 Compelling psychological and courtroom drama derived from a prostitute's refusal to plead guilty. Streisand plays a strong-willed, high-class hooker up on murder charges for having killed a client. Her court-appointed lawyer (Dreyfuss) and her embarrassed parents want her to take the plea-bargained offer of manslaughter by reason of insanity. She refuses to admit to them or anyone else that she is insane, demanding instead a court trial. She will not be railroaded. Powerful character portrayals by high-class cast.

Sex | Nud | Viol | Lang | AdSit

A: Barbra Streisand, Richard Dreyfuss, Maureen Stapleton, Eli Wallach, Robert Webber, James Whitmore

© WARNER HOME VIDEO 11756

OFFICER AND A GENTLEMAN, AN

D: Taylor Hackford 126 m

R | ROM DMA | 1982 | COLOR

9 Immensely popular and sentimental soap opera with a hard edge. Richard Gere is a Navy brat, a loner and a social misfit. He sees his only chance for respectability in becoming a Navy pilot, but he first has to get past a tough drill instructor (Gossett) who is intent upon breaking down his selfish independence. Winger is a poor local girl, who sees her only chance at a way out to a good life in being married to a pilot. These two are cut from the same cloth and you can see things coming from a mile away, but this is still a very well done, compelling and heartwarming movie. A real feel good movie.

Sex | Nud | Viol | Lang | AdSit

A: Richard Gere, Debra Winger, David Keith, Louis Gossett, Jr., Harold Sylvester, Robert Loggia

© PARAMOUNT HOME VIDEO 1467

OFFICIAL STORY, THE

D: Luis Puenzo 112 m

NR | FOR DMA SUS | 1985 | COLOR

9 This is an extremely powerful Oscar winner for Best Foreign Film. It is a devastating story about a sheltered, middle-class Argentinian woman and wife of a politician, who gradually comes to the realization that her adopted daughter was forcefully torn away from her mother by the government. The mother had been a political activist, was tortured and then murdered. Worse than that news, she also learns that her otherwise-loving husband has always known about it. Her world, and all that she has naively believed in, is utterly destroyed. The scene where she views photos of someone, who is obviously her child's mother, with the child's grandmother is devastating. Subtitles.

Sex | Nud | Viol | Lang | AdSit

A: Norma Aleandro, Hector Alterio, Analia Castro

© PACIFIC ARTS VIDEO 630

OF HUMAN BONDAGE

D: Kenneth Hughes 100 m

NR | DMA ROM | 1964 | B&W

7 This is the third movie version made of Somerset Maugham's novel. The first, with Bette Davis, is generally considered to be the better, but the lesser quality early production values of it make this one a more popular version. The story concerns the sad obsession a sensitive club-footed medical student (Harvey) has for a promiscuous London barmaid (Novak) who constantly abuses his attraction for her. His attraction for the faithless girl nearly destroys his career and his life.

Sex | Nud | Viol | Lang | AdSit

A: Kim Novak, Laurence Harvey, Siobhan McKenna, Robert Morley, Roger Livesey, Nanette Newman

Distributed By MGM/UA Home Video M300745

OF MICE AND MEN

D: Reza Badiyi 150 m

NR | DMA | 1981 | COLOR

8 Excellent made-for-TV version of Steinbeck's classic morality play. George and Lenny are migrant workers in California during the Depression years. Lenny is a big and powerful man, but he is also mentally retarded. He looks constantly to George, like a brother, for guidance. George truly cares for Lenny and he does his best to keep Lenny out of trouble so they can just live peacefully on this new job. But, Lenny's size and childish ways invite trouble and the spoiled son of the ranch owner provides it. Sensitive and compelling.

Sex | Nud | Viol | Lang | AdSit

A: Robert Blake, Pat Hingle, Ted Neeley, Randy Quaid, Lew Ayres, Cassie Yates

© PRISM ENTERTAINMENT 1934

OF MICE AND MEN

D: Gary Sinise m

DMA | 1993 | COLOR

9 Beautifully crafted and thoroughly involving recreation of John Steinbeck's classic novel. Lenny and George are migratory field hands traveling together in California's Salinas Valley during the Depression years. George is Lenny's protector. Lenny is a large and powerful, but feeble-minded, man who has a great passion for soft things. All the two of them want is to live peaceably, but Lenny's simple innocence and lack of understanding, even of the simplest things, repeatedly gets them into trouble. Each time they settle, they are forced to move on again. Excellent!

Sex | Nud | Viol | Lang | AdSit

A: John Malkovich, Gary Sinise, Alexis Arquette, Sherilyn Fenn, Ray Walston, Joe Morton

Distributed By MGM/UA Home Video M902693

OLD YELLER

D: Robert Stevenson 84 m

G | DMA CLD | 1957 | COLOR

10 Wonderful, endearing Disney story that has been and will continue to be a perpetual family favorite for very good reason. Set in the Texas wilderness of 1859, a pioneer father leaves his family and homestead to join a cattle drive for a short while, leaving his young son "in charge" of the family. In the father's absence, the boy adopts a mongrel dog he names Old Yeller. Soon Old Yeller becomes his best friend and the family's protector. The two are inseparable. Then tragedy strikes and the boy must become a man. It is a powerful story for children but adults love it, too. See also THE YEARLING.

Sex | Nud | Viol | Lang | AdSit

A: Dorothy McGuire, Fess Parker, Tommy Kirk, Kevin Corcoran, Jeff York, Chuck Connors

© WALT DISNEY HOME VIDEO 037

OLIVER!

G · MUS DMA · 1968 · COLOR

D: Carol Reed — 145 m

10 An absolutely outstanding musical and winner of the Best Picture Oscar and six others. Great entertainment. Dickens was never this much fun. All the story's touching elements are here, but the tragedy of an eight-year-old orphan's utter aloneness and helpless, living in the streets during desperate times, is much less traumatic when it is set to music and dance. Plus, the colorful characters were wonderfully captured by a terrific cast. There are lavish production numbers and sets. The truly wonderful and memorable songs include: "Consider Yourself," "As Long as He Needs Me" and "Who Will Buy."

Sex · Nud · Viol · Lang · AdSit

A: Mark Lester, Jack Wild, Ron Moody, Oliver Reed, Shani Wallace

© COLUMBIA TRISTAR HOME VIDEO 60526

O LUCKY MAN!

R · DMA · 1973 · COLOR

D: Lindsay Anderson — 178 m

9 A big critical success and a favorite of serious film fans, but very heavy going for most everyone else. It is an epic-scale allegory, set in post-industrial England, which follows an enthusiastic young coffee salesman through a series of life's adventures and misadventures on his trek up and down the ladder of success - some of which are funny, some not, some very surreal. His adventures expose him to all manner of people, most of whom are very unpleasant. An altogether cynical depiction of capitalistic society, but the more arty viewer will be more than satisfied.

Sex · Nud · Viol · Lang · AdSit

A: Malcolm McDowell, Ralph Richardson, Arthur Lowe, Rachel Roberts

© WARNER HOME VIDEO 11249

ONCE AROUND

R · ROM DMA COM · 1991 · COLOR

D: Lasse Hallstrom — 114 m

7 This movie is like getting wrapped up in a warm blanket on a freezing cold night. Dreyfuss is a super-salesman who sweeps a repressed Holly Hunter off her fee. He is annoying - but he is supposed to be. Hunter is strong emotionally - and she is not supposed to be. They are perfect for each other - but their family doesn't think so. Hunter is so tangled in family disapproval and so in love that she is extremely torn. The beauty of this one is that it is totally unpredictable, and charming, and irresistible, and very, very well acted.

Sex · Nud · Viol · Lang · AdSit

A: Richard Dreyfuss, Holly Hunter, Laura San Giacomo, Danny Aiello, Gena Rowlands, Roxanne Hart

© MCA/UNIVERSAL HOME VIDEO, INC. 81041

ONE FLEW OVER THE CUCKOO'S NEST

R · DMA COM · 1975 · COLOR

D: Milos Forman — 129 m

10 The first picture in 40 years to sweep all five top Academy Awards: Picture, Director, Actor, Actress and Screenplay. It is also a very entertaining and deeply moving film about a likable but unconventional and rebellious prisoner (Nicholson) who is transferred to a mental hospital. While there, much to the dismay of the establishment (in in the principal form of over-disciplined head nurse Rachet), this otherwise sane misfit rekindles a spirit of life in the other patients who have been beaten down by the system. A deeply moving story about the value of individual freedoms and diverse personalities. Must see.

Sex · Nud · Viol · Lang · AdSit

A: Jack Nicholson, Louise Fletcher, William Redfield, Danny DeVito, Christopher Lloyd, Scatman Crothers

© HBO VIDEO 1048

ONE GOOD COP

R · DMA ACT · 1991 · COLOR

D: Heywood Gould — 105 m

7 Michael Keaton is a dedicated N.Y.C. cop who inherits his partner's three adorable young daughters after the partner is killed in a shootout. Keaton and his wife have no kids of their own and have been happy that way but now they must come to grips with their new situation. They make room for the kids on a temporary basis in their small apartment, but find that they must get a bigger apartment if they are going to be allowed to keep them. Keaton doesn't have the money but hits upon the solution of "borrowing" some money from a drug lord. Undeniable plot holes and sentimentality, but it still works pretty well.

Sex · Nud · Viol · Lang · AdSit

A: Michael Keaton, Rene Russo, Anthony Lapaglia, Kevin Conway, Rachel Ticotin, Tony Plana

© HOLLYWOOD PICTURES HOME VIDEO 1212

ONE ON ONE

PG · DMA · 1977 · COLOR

D: Lamont Johnson — 100 m

8 An upbeat "little" film in which Robby Benson is a small town boy who is awarded a basketball scholarship to a big West Coast university. There he runs head-on into the corruption of big-time college athletics and an extremely demanding coach. Naive Benson trys to buck both the system and his coach. He gains help for his studies and strength for his battles with his coach through the encouragement of his pretty tutor, Annette O'Toole. It is an inspiring story in which the little guy takes on the power and wins.

Sex · Nud · Viol · Lang · AdSit

A: Robby Benson, Annette O'Toole, G.D. Spradlin, Gail Strickland, Melanie Griffith

© WARNER HOME VIDEO 11141

ON GOLDEN POND

PG · DMA COM · 1981 · COLOR

D: Mark Rydell — 105 m

10 Big unexpected hit. Thoughtful, heartwarming and moving story of growing old and the reconciliation between a crotchety father and his alienated daughter. Winner of three Oscars: Actor (Fonda), Actress (Hepburn) and Screenplay. The daughter leaves her fiance's snotty son with her aging parents for the summer. The old man and the kid develop a relationship which teaches the kid to lighten up and the old man how to enjoy living again, to express love and to show his daughter the love she has long craved. Wonderful and uplifting. A real feel-good flick.

Sex · Nud · Viol · Lang · AdSit

A: Katharine Hepburn, Henry Fonda, Jane Fonda, Dabney Coleman, Doug McKeon, William Lanteau

© LIVE HOME VIDEO 27456

ONION FIELD, THE

R · CRM DMA · 1979 · COLOR

D: Harold Becker — 126 m

10 Superb and fascinating crime drama adapted from real life by ex-cop and author Joseph Wambaugh. In 1963 two small-time criminals kidnap two cops. In the middle of an onion field, they kill one, but the other escapes. The killers are captured and convicted, but for years are able to frustrate justice by manipulating the legal system. In the interim, the surviving cop is slowly consumed with guilt for having lived while his partner died, and with the frustration of not being able to do anything to see justice done. An exceptional film

Sex · Nud · Viol · Lang · AdSit

A: John Savage, James Woods, Ronny Cox, Franklyn Seales, Ted Danson, Christopher Lloyd

© NEW LINE HOME VIDEO 2034

ONLY WHEN I LAUGH

R · DMA COM · 1980 · COLOR

D: Glenn Jordan — 121 m

8 Bittersweet screenplay from Neil Simon. Marsha Mason is a has-been Broadway actress who has only just been released from a rehab clinic after three months treatment for alcoholism, when her 17-year-old daughter moves in with her after six years of living with her father. Mason must learn how to be a mother and friend all over again, even as she struggles to stay sober, get her career back on line and deal with a new love interest. Sometimes funny, sometimes sad, but always moving. Wonderful performances by everyone (three Oscar nominations). Heartwarming and entertaining, too.

Sex · Nud · Viol · Lang · AdSit

A: Marsha Mason, Kristy Mc Nichol, James Coco, Joan Hackett, David Dukes

© COLUMBIA TRISTAR HOME VIDEO 60079

ON THE BEACH

NR · DMA · 1959 · B&W

D: Stanley Kramer — 135 m

6 After a nuclear war strikes the Northern Hemisphere, the only survivors are a few people in Australia and those on board a submerged American submarine captained by Gregory Peck. As the ominous nuclear clouds gradually descend upon these people, too, Peck attempts to save this one small group of survivors, which includes a young couple (Perkins and Anderson), an alcoholic nuclear scientist (Astaire), and Peck and his adventurous love interest (Gardner). Very well done, but gloomy. It was a highly-celebrated anti-nuclear war film from the '50s.

Sex · Nud · Viol · Lang · AdSit

A: Gregory Peck, Ava Gardner, Fred Astaire, Anthony Perkins, Donna Anderson, John Tate

Distributed By MGM/UA Home Video M202267

ORDINARY PEOPLE

R · DMA · 1980 · COLOR

D: Robert Redford — 124 m

9 Powerhouse drama and winner of four Academy Awards, including Best Picture and Director. It is the heart-rending story about a typical family torn apart by a simple failure to communicate with each other. Lost in their own worlds - living alone together - each slowly grows away from the others. When one son dies tragically in a boating accident, the remaining distraught and isolated son attempts suicide and seeks outside help from a psychiatrist. The mother never recognizes her own isolation and alienates herself further from both her son and her husband. Stunning and provocative stuff.

Sex · Nud · Viol · Lang · AdSit

A: Mary Tyler Moore, Judd Hirsch, Donald Sutherland, Timothy Hutton, Elizabeth McGovern, Dinah Manoff

© PARAMOUNT HOME VIDEO 8964

ORPHANS

R · DMA · 1987 · COLOR

D: Alan J. Pakula — 116 m

6 Interesting drama with an odd twist and weird characters. Two orphaned brothers live in squalor and isolation. One brother is very naive and reclusive. The other is an angry punk who supports both of them by occasional excursions into New York to steal. On one occasion, he kidnaps an alcoholic gangster (Finney) to hold him hostage. But Finney was an orphan, too, and a strange and unlikely fatherly relationship develops between him and the boys. Great acting, but very unusual characters and situations.

Sex · Nud · Viol · Lang · AdSit

A: Albert Finney, Matthew Modine, Kevin Anderson, John Kelloggn, Anthony Heald

© WARNER HOME VIDEO 453

OTELLO

D: Franco Zeffirelli — 123 m

PG · MUS DMA · 1986 · COLOR · **8**

Opera fans will delight in this production of the classic Italian opera based upon Shakespeare's hero, Otello, starring tenor Placido Domingo. Otello, the jealous Moorish general, is driven into a murderous rage by the scheming Iago who has created lies about Otello's beautiful wife Desdemona. Filmed on locations throughout the Mediterranean. English subtitles.

Sex · Nud · Viol · Lang · ◢ AdSit

A: Placido Domingo, Justino Diaz, Katia Ricciarelli

© KULTUR VIDEO 1184

OTHER SIDE OF THE MOUNTAIN, THE

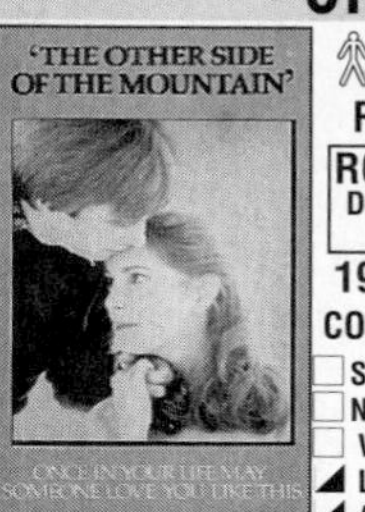

D: Larry Peerce — 102 m

PG · ROM DMA · 1975 · COLOR · **8**

Popular love story taken from the pages of real life. Jill Kinmont (Hassett) was a talented skier who seemed destined for the 1956 Olympic team. Instead she was left a paraplegic after a tragic skiing accident. Despondent over her circumstances, she is revitalized by the love of Beau Bridges, but then tragedy strikes again. Hers is truly a story of determination in the face of overwhelming adversity. Guaranteed to jerk more than a few tears.

Sex · Nud · Viol · ◢ Lang · ◢ AdSit

A: Marilyn Hassett, Beau Bridges, Dabney Coleman, Belinda J. Montgomery

© MCA/UNIVERSAL HOME VIDEO, INC. 55116

OTHER SIDE OF THE MOUNTAIN, PART II, THE

D: Larry Peerce — 99 m

PG · ROM DMA · 1978 · COLOR · **8**

In this sequel, also taken from real life, the paralyzed skier Jill Kinmont (Hassett) is now a teacher in L.A. after having lost her lover in a plane crash. On vacation to her hometown, she meets a divorced trucker (Bottoms) who pursues her. After having been so heartbroken before, she is very reluctant to allow yet another man into her life, but his persistence breaks down her resistance. This is a good love story. It is involving and credible. As in the first film, be prepared to get a few tears jerked.

Sex · Nud · Viol · Lang · ◢ AdSit

A: Marilyn Hassett, Timothy Bottoms, Belinda J. Montgomery, Nan Martin

© MCA/UNIVERSAL HOME VIDEO, INC. 55117

OUT OF AFRICA

D: Sydney Pollack — 161 m

PG · ROM DMA · 1985 · COLOR · **9**

Epic love story and winner of seven Oscars, including Best Picture. It is the romantic story of a strong-willed Danish woman (Streep) who married for convenience and then moved to Africa in 1913 with her philandering husband to run their coffee plantation. There, she develops a deep love for the land, its ways, its peoples, and also for an English adventurer (Redford) who loved what she loved. They are two rugged individualists who continually move in and out of each other's lives, torn between love for adventure and each other. Based upon the experiences of writer Isak Dinesen.

◢ Sex · Nud · Viol · Lang · ◢ AdSit

A: Robert Redford, Meryl Streep, Klaus Maria Brandauer, Michael Kitchen, Malick Bowens, Michael Gough

© MCA/UNIVERSAL HOME VIDEO, INC. 80350

OUTSIDERS, THE

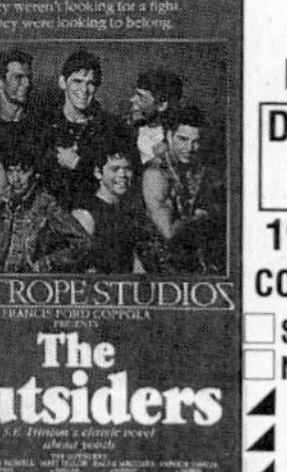

D: Francis Ford Coppola — 91 m

PG · DMA · 1983 · COLOR · **7**

Diverting soap opera about teenagers, faithfully taken from the very popular novel by S.E. Hinton. Set in 1966 Oklahoma, this film explores conflict in the lives of a group troubled, poor teenagers - outsiders who just want to belong. But the stakes are raised too high when Howell and Macchio have to go into hiding after Macchio accidentally kills a rich kid while rescuing his friend. Later, things get worse when Macchio is killed saving some young kids from a fire and a distraught Dillon attempts a robbery. Good period details and performances from a young cast who all became major stars.

Sex · Nud · ◢ Viol · ◢ Lang · ◢ AdSit

A: Matt Dillon, C. Thomas Howell, Ralph Macchio, Rob Lowe, Diane Lane, Emilio Estevez

© WARNER HOME VIDEO 11310

OVER THE EDGE

D: Jonathan Kaplan — 95 m

PG · DMA CRM · 1980 · COLOR · **7**

Disturbing portrait of alienated rich kids. Quite good in its own right but most notable for being Mat Dillon's screen debut. It is a powerful and unsettling portrait of lost and disaffected rich kids who play with booze, drugs and guns, and who spend their idle time committing robbery and violence. A familiar story line, but one especially well done. Excellent sound track featuring music by "Cheap Trick," "The Cars" and "The Ramones." Not released until Dillon was a star, it was originally thought to be too provocative.

Sex · Nud · ◢ Viol · ◢ Lang · ◢ AdSit

A: Michael Kramer, Pamela Ludwig, Matt Dillon, Vincent Spano, Tom Fergus, Ellen Geer

© WARNER HOME VIDEO 22008

PAPA'S DELICATE CONDITION

D: George Marshall — 98 m

NR · COM DMA · 1963 · COLOR · **7**

Pleasant light-hearted drama set in turn-of-the-century Texas. The setting evokes nostalgic feelings for a time past and the mood is light-hearted, but the subject has a serious overtone. Papa (Jackie Gleason) is a fun-loving railroader and the apple of his daughter's eye, but he is also a drunk and an embarrassment to his wife (Glynnis Johns). One day she packs up the kids and walks out. Gleason is quite charming in this enjoyable little story that also won an Oscar for Best Song: "Call Me Irresponsible."

Sex · Nud · Viol · Lang · ◢ AdSit

A: Jackie Gleason, Glynis Johns, Charlie Ruggles, Laurel Goodwin, Charles Lane, Elisha Cook, Jr.

© PARAMOUNT HOME VIDEO 6212

PAPER, THE

D: Ron Howard — 112 m

R · DMA COM · 1994 · COLOR · **7**

A frenetic day in the life of a newspaper, in this case a New York scandal sheet called "The Sun." Michael Keaton is the metro editor and he loves his job. But: His wife is very pregnant and feeling left out of the newspaper world she had to leave behind. He has been made another offer by another paper and has to decide today. He missed out on the big story yesterday, but he thinks he has an even better one for today. He and paranoid columnist Randy Quaid are struggling to get that story by deadline, but he is in a battle with Glenn Close, an administrator who used to be a reporter but is now a bean counter, and she is fighting him on the deadline for his story. Fun, but a little overdone in places.

Sex · Nud · ◢ Viol · ■ Lang · ◢ AdSit

A: Michael Keaton, Glenn Close, Marisa Tomei, Randy Quaid, Robert Duvall, Jason Alexander

© MCA/UNIVERSAL HOME VIDEO, INC. 82005

PAPER CHASE, THE

D: James Bridges — 111 m

PG · DMA COM · 1973 · COLOR · **9**

Highly acclaimed and engrossing character study that spawned a TV series and a lot of other attention, too. Timothy Bottoms stars as a brilliant law student in his first year of law at Harvard. He is apparently in constant conflict with his extremely demanding and contentious law professor (Houseman). Houseman seems determined to make his life miserable. However, life becomes even more intense when Bottoms discovers that his new girl friend is also Houseman's daughter. Brilliant acting all around. Houseman won an Oscar and became a star.

Sex · Nud · Viol · ◢ Lang · ◢ AdSit

A: Timothy Bottoms, Lindsay Wagner, John Houseman, Graham Beckel, Craig Richard Nelson, Edward Herrmann

© FOXVIDEO 1046

PAPILLON

D: Franklin J. Schaffner — 150 m

PG · DMA ACT SUS · 1973 · COLOR · **9**

Exuberant testament to the triumph of the human spirit, based upon the real-life exploits of Henri Charriere, also called Papillon (meaning "the butterfly"). McQueen plays the Frenchman who is unjustly sentenced to the escape-proof hell of the infamous Devil's Island penal colony. In spite of overwhelming odds, he and his friend, a convicted forger (brilliantly played by Hoffman), make continued escape attempts - once succeeding for a short time and living in an idyllic Indian village. Each time they are captured, they again seek a new way to escape. There spirit is indomitable. Long but engrossing throughout.

◢ Sex · ◢ Nud · ◢ Viol · ◢ Lang · ◢ AdSit

A: Steve McQueen, Dustin Hoffman, Victor Jory, Anthony Zerbe, Don Gordon, Robert Deman

© WARNER HOME VIDEO 832

PARADISE

D: Mary Agnes Donoghue — 111 m

PG-13 · DMA ROM · 1991 · COLOR · **7**

An old-fashioned summer film all about love, relationships and heartbreak. Ben and Lily (Johnson and Griffith) are married, but you wouldn't know it from the cold shoulder they give each other. When 10-year old Elijah Wood is sent to live with them for the summer, he becomes intrigued with discovering why their relationship is so strained and discovers that they are still suffering from the pain of losing their own three year-old son. Since that time, Lily and Ben have withdrawn from each other. However, the boy's presence resurrects the love the two once had felt for each other and they receive a second chance. Refreshing and heartwarming.

Sex · Nud · ◢ Viol · ◢ Lang · ◢ AdSit

A: Melanie Griffith, Don Johnson, Elijah Wood, Thora Birch, Sheila McCarthy, Eve Gordon

© TOUCHSTONE HOME VIDEO 1258

PARENTHOOD

D: Ron Howard — 124 m

PG-13 · COM DMA · 1989 · COLOR · **8**

Very popular and funny comedy about the joys and pitfalls of modern-day child rearing. At the center of all the mayhem is Steve Martin, a middle-aged father, who is trying to save his career while also coping with his neurotic eight-year old. His ex-hippie sister has got two problem teenagers and his neighbors are trying to raise their three-year-old to be a super-genius. Meanwhile, Martin's Dad is struggling with his own feelings of failure at raising another son who's an irresponsible gambler, deep in financial trouble. A bundle of laughs that rings true to life. A treat!

Sex · Nud · Viol · ■ Lang · ◢ AdSit

A: Steve Martin, Jason Robards, Jr., Mary Steenburgen, Rick Moranis, Tom Hulce, Dianne Wiest

© MCA/UNIVERSAL HOME VIDEO, INC. 80921

PARIS, TEXAS

R | DMA | 1984 | COLOR

D: Wim Wenders — 145 m

7 Critical success and winner of the Grand Prize at the Cannes Film Festival in 1984, but very heavy going, slow and overly long. It is a powerful screenplay from Sam Shepard, in his frequently repeated male/female theme. This concerns the return of a man after a four-year absence. When his wife abandoned the family, he fell apart and wandered, lonely and lost, having forgotten who he was. Now he returns to reclaim his son from his brother, to find his lost wife and to reclaim his lost life. Excellent drama, but only for the serious and patient viewer.

Sex / Nud / Viol / Lang / AdSit

A: Nastassia Kinski, Harry Dean Stanton, Dean Stockwell, Aurore Clement, Hunter Carson

© FOXVIDEO 1457

PARIS TROUT

R | DMA | 1991 | COLOR

D: Stephen Gyllenhaal — 98 m

6 Perversely interesting character study of the self-destruction of a locally powerful, and particularly venal, small-town shopkeeper. Set in 1949 Georgia, Paris Trout is a deeply disturbed and uncaring paranoid, married to Barbara Hershey. He delights in her sadistic humiliation. His cruelty eventually drives her into the arms Ed Harris, an attorney in the District Attorney's office who is prosecuting Trout for the senseless murder of a young black girl. Excellent acting, high quality production values, but unremittingly grim and depressing.

Sex / Nud / Viol / Lang / AdSit

A: Dennis Hopper, Barbara Hershey, Ed Harris

© VIDEO TREASURES M012814

PASSAGE TO INDIA, A

PG | DMA | 1984 | COLOR

D: David Lean — 163 m

8 Nominated for 11 Oscars - Winner of 2. This is a beautifully photographed and widely distributed British film exploring colonialism in India, the clashes of cultures and Victorian attitudes of morality. Set in 1924, two English women are dismayed to witness the widespread racism in the ruling upper-crust English toward Indians. However, after making friends with an Indian doctor, the two overstep the bounds of accepted decency when they agree to picnic at a cave with him and so the younger woman accuses him of rape. What did happen? Sumptuous, interesting and satisfying, but ambiguous.

Sex / Nud / Viol / Lang / AdSit

A: Judy Davis, Peggy Ashcroft, James Fox, Alec Guinness, Victor Banerjee, Nigel Havers

© COLUMBIA TRISTAR HOME VIDEO 60485

PASSED AWAY

PG-13 | COM DMA | 1992 | COLOR

D: Charlie Peters — 97 m

6 Mildly likable and semi-interesting black comedy that explores the revelations of a colorful and contentious Irish family, reunited at the funeral of the family's patriarch (Warden). Dad had a heart attack and died when his nit-wit pretty-boy son literally scared him to death with a surprise welcome-back party after a stay in the hospital. In the family there is: an older tree-surgeon brother (Hoskins), who is dealing with his mid-life crisis; a sister, who is an activist nun hiding an illegal alien from the feds; a rebellious dancer sister (Reed); and, a mysterious strange other woman friend of Dad's. Interesting premise, with a good cast.

Sex / Nud / Viol / Lang / AdSit

A: Bob Hoskins, Blair Brown, Tim Curry, Frances McDormand, William L. Petersen, Pamela Reed

© HOLLYWOOD PICTURES HOME VIDEO 1453

PASSION FISH

R | DMA | 1992 | COLOR

D: John Sayles — 135 m

7 McDonnell is a successful soap opera queen until her career is cut short by a New York taxi, which left her paralyzed from the waist down and extremely bitter. She retreats to the safety of her childhood home on the Louisiana bayous, there to drink away her misfortune and hide behind a TV remote control. Woodard is the umpteenth nurse who has been hired to take care of her. The others have all been driven away because McDonnell is so caustic. Woodard, however, can't leave because she is putting her own life back together after leaving a detox center for drug addiction. These two last chance people help each other to come back to life. 2 Oscar nominations.

Sex / Nud / Viol / Lang / AdSit

A: Mary McDonnell, Alfre Woodard, Nora Dunn, David Strathairn, Sheila Kelley, Angela Bassett

© COLUMBIA TRISTAR HOME VIDEO 53283

PASSION OF ANNA, THE

R | FOR DMA SUS | 1970 | COLOR

D: Ingmar Bergman — 101 m

8 Max von Sydow is an ex-convict living alone in a farmhouse on a small island and is visited one day by a crippled woman (Ulmann) requesting to use the telephone. When she leaves, she forgets her purse behind. He gets her name from it to return it to her but also learns from letters inside of her troubled marriage. They become friends and she moves into his farmhouse but their relationship becomes very strained, in part because of reports of an axe murderer being at large. She believes he may be the axe murderer and he believes she is trying to kill him as she probably killed her husband and child.

Sex / Nud / Viol / Lang / AdSit

A: Max von Sydow, Liv Ullmann, Bibi Andersson, Erland Josephson

Distributed By MGM/UA Home Video M202786

PATCH OF BLUE, A

NR | DMA ROM | 1965 | COLOR

D: Guy Green — 106 m

8 A sensitive and moving drama, which held the potential to be badly exploitive, but it isn't at all. This is a thoughtful drama about an 18-year-old blind white girl whose mother is a prostitute. She keeps the girl uneducated, confined to their apartment and uses her as a servant. One day, on a rare trip alone to the park, the girl meets a young man who helps her and encourages her to learn about life. She falls in love with him, the only one who ever helped her, not knowing that he is black. Good drama, well acted, not overly sentimental or sensationalized. 5 Oscar nominations.

Sex / Nud / Viol / Lang / AdSit

A: Sidney Poitier, Elizabeth Hartman, Shelley Winters, Wallace Ford, Ivan Dixon, John Qualen

Distributed By MGM/UA Home Video M202010

PATHS OF GLORY

NR | DMA WAR | 1957 | B&W

D: Stanley Kubrick — 89 m

9 Stunning and provocative statement about the excesses which can occur from vanity and abuses of power inside the insane framework of war. Set in WWI France, a vain and inconsistent general orders his troops into an ill-advised attack upon an impenetrable position. After many men are killed, the troops sanely hold back. However, rather than admit his failure, and incensed by their insubordination, the General orders that one man from each of three platoons be chosen to be court-martialed and then executed for cowardice. Powerful, believable and convincingly acted.

Sex / Nud / Viol / Lang / AdSit

A: Kirk Douglas, Ralph Meeker, Adolphe Menjou, George Macready, Timothy Carey, Wayne Morris

Distributed By MGM/UA Home Video M301735

PATTON

PG | DMA WAR ACT | 1970 | COLOR

D: Franklin J. Schaffner — 171 m

10 Brilliant portrait of an extremely colorful and unique historical figure - George S. "Blood-and-Guts" Patton. Winner of 8 Oscars, including Best Picture, Director, Screenplay and Actor. Patton, the man, was a brilliant battlefield tactician whose single-mindedness in and out of battle helped to win the North African campaign and to launch the initial assault into Europe at the beginning of WWII. It garnered him both the respect and the animosity of nearly everyone. Scott did a brilliant job with the role. Both fascinating and extremely enjoyable.

Sex / Nud / Viol / Lang / AdSit

A: George C. Scott, Karl Malden, Stephen Young, Michael Strong, Tim Considine, Frank Latimore

© FOXVIDEO 1005

PAWNBROKER, THE

NR | DMA | 1965 | B&W

D: Sidney Lumet — 120 m

9 Outstanding and fascinating portrait of a man totally lost to all feeling. Steiger's performance is stunning and it won him an Oscar nomination. He plays a Jewish survivor of Nazi torture and imprisonment. He is now an empty, totally isolated man and a pawnbroker in Harlem. His black landlord is a racketeer dealing in prostitution and slum misery - but Steiger doesn't care. His one employee (Sanchez) and a social worker try to get through to him to break down his icy wall, but he resolutely resists them until Sanchez is killed while protecting him in a robbery. Somber and very powerful.

Sex / Nud / Viol / Lang / AdSit

A: Rod Steiger, Geraldine Fitzgerald, Brock Peters, Jaime Sanchez

© REPUBLIC PICTURES HOME VIDEO 3162

PELLE THE CONQUEROR

PG-13 | FOR DMA | 1988 | COLOR

D: Bille August — 138 m

9 A wonderful exploration of the power of the human spirit and winner of Best Foreign Film, but its slow pace and earnestness will diminish its appeal to many. An impoverished peasant, Max Von Sydow (Oscar nominated), takes a desperate chance at a better life by leaving Sweden to become a farm laborer in Denmark. Because he is older and has a young son, he is the last chosen among the many laborers. He must accept a job with a wealthy tyrant. There, he must suffer many hardships to achieve only the most modest successes, but he has his son Pelle whom he dotes upon. Pelle will be what he was not and sets off on a quest to conquer the world. Subtitles.

Sex / Nud / Viol / Lang / AdSit

A: Max von Sydow, Pelle Hvenegaard, Erik Paaske

© HBO VIDEO 0210

PERFECT WORLD, A

PG-13 | CRM DMA | 1993 | COLOR

D: Clint Eastwood — 138 m

8 An unusual sort of drama that is both convincing and touching. Costner is Butch, a career criminal who has broken out of prison. He and another escapee take Phillip, a 7-year-old boy, hostage on their getaway flight. Clint Eastwood is a veteran Texas Ranger who leads up the team, including Laura Dern as a criminologist consultant, that is out to get him back. Young Phillip has no father and Butch never really had one either, so the two are drawn ever closer to each other as they combine forces to help Butch escape. Sometimes funny, but this is no comedy. Butch is an emotional cripple who wants to give Phillip what he craves for himself, but he must do it while on the run.

Sex / Nud / Viol / Lang / AdSit

A: Kevin Costner, Clint Eastwood, Laura Dern, T.J. Lowther, Keith Szarabajka, Leo Bermester

© WARNER HOME VIDEO 12990

D M A

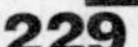

PERMANENT RECORD

D: Marisa Silver 92 m

PG-13 | DMA | 1988 | COLOR

8 Moving and sensitive drama exploring the subject of teenage suicide. This is not a simplistic melodrama but a serious study of a sad fact of life, and it packs a wallop. It is thought provoking and recommended viewing for all teenagers and parents. David is a very talented high school kid, seemingly with a solid future. He seems to have no real problems, yet he is profoundly unhappy. Then one night he kills himself - leaving all those around him trying to understand why, and having to deal with the results of David's decision.

Sex | Nud | Viol | Lang | AdSit

A: Alan Boyce, Keanu Reeves, Jennifer Rubin, Michelle Meyrink, Pamela Gidley, Michael Elgart

© PARAMOUNT HOME VIDEO 32039

PERSONAL BEST

D: Robert Towne 128 m

R | DMA ROM | 1982 | COLOR

7 Sensitive and honest story about the close personal relationship which develops between two female track-and-field athletes who are in training together for the 1980 Olympics. Truly excellent performances make this an interesting and worthy offering - both as a sports movie and as an honest, non-exploitive look into a loving lesbian relationship which develops between the two leads, a relationship that is destroyed under the pressure of competition.

Sex | Nud | Viol | Lang | AdSit

A: Mariel Hemingway, Scott Glenn, Patrice Donnelly, Kenny Moore

© WARNER HOME VIDEO 11242

PETER'S FRIENDS

D: Kenneth Branagh 102 m

NR | COM DMA | 1993 | COLOR

6 Sort of an English version of THE BIG CHILL. Peter has just inherited his father's estates and he has decided to call a ten-year reunion of college friends. They all arrive at Christmas time, but each has brought with him his own set of personal problems. Almost from the start, things go very badly. As time progresses, things get progressively worse. Just when all seems to be lost, Peter announces that the reason he has called them together is that he has HIV. In light of that overwhelmingly bad news, all the other problems begin to diminish in importance and the group can again recover old friendships. Slow.

Sex | Nud | Viol | Lang | AdSit

A: Emma Thompson, Kenneth Branagh, Stephen Fry, Rita Rudner, Alphonsia Emmanuel, Tony Slattery

© HBO VIDEO 90832

PETE 'N' TILLIE

D: Martin Ritt 100 m

PG | DMA COM | 1972 | COLOR

6 Diverting little serio-comedy that works most of the time. Matthau plays a middle-aged wise-cracking market researcher. Burnett is a woman fast approaching spinsterhood. Lonely and tired of being alone, they have an affair, marry and have a child. But their world is turned upside down when the child is found to be dying. Matthau loses his hold on their relationship, has a series of affairs and their marriage is in deep trouble. Interesting in many ways and usually entertaining - but the mixed signals hurt it some.

Sex | Nud | Viol | Lang | AdSit

A: Walter Matthau, Carol Burnett, Geraldine Page, Rene Auberjonois

© MCA/UNIVERSAL HOME VIDEO, INC. 80404

PETULIA

D: Richard Lester 105 m

R | DMA COM | 1968 | COLOR

8 Highly regarded by the critics and serious movie fans as being one of the social hallmark films of the 1960s. This is the story of a prominent middle-aged doctor (Scott) who is getting divorced after many years of marriage. He finds himself tossed into a tumultuous relationship with a screwed-up, beautiful, kookie and frustrated young socialite (Christie) who has been married for only 6 months. Their bittersweet romance is designed to be an analogy for the turmoil and confusion of the late '60s. Superb cast. Dated now and a little too vague for most casual observers.

Sex | Nud | Viol | Lang | AdSit

A: Julie Christie, George C. Scott, Richard Chamberlain, Arthur Hill, Shirley Knight, Joseph Cotten

© WARNER HOME VIDEO 11092

PEYTON PLACE

D: Mark Robson 157 m

NR | DMA ROM | 1957 | COLOR

8 In the 1950s Grace Matalious wrote a spicy book that ripped the cover off the hypocrisy of middle-class morality, depicting the sexual maneuvering and horseplay going on behind the closed doors of a fictitious small New England town of the early '50s. It, of course, was a monumental hit. This is a toned-down version of the book, but it still was a jolt to the prevailing sensibilities of the times. At its heart, it is essentially a melodramatic soap opera - but one that is very well done, with some of the best talent that was available. Still quite involving today. Nominated for 9 Oscars in 1957.

Sex | Nud | Viol | Lang | AdSit

A: Lana Turner, Hope Lange, Russ Tamblyn, Arthur Kennedy, Diane Varsi

© FOXVIDEO 1855

PHAR LAP

D: Simon Wincer 107 m

PG | DMA | 1984 | COLOR

9 Rousing family entertainment. This is the true account of the legendary Australian thoroughbred horse from the 1930s that became an national hero after overcoming huge odds to be a winner. Told in a series of flashbacks. Phar Lap was trained by a brutal trainer and was nearly ruined by him. But through the devotion of a shy stableboy and the dedication of his Jewish owner (who had to fight mindless prejudice just to get his horse entered), this horse became the winner of 33 races in just three years. You'll be cheering, too.

Sex | Nud | Viol | Lang | AdSit

A: Tom Burlinson, Ron Leibman, Judy Morris, Martin Vaughan, Celia De Burgh, Vincent Ball

© FOXVIDEO 1444

PHILADELPHIA

D: Jonathan Demme 125 m

PG-13 | DMA | 1994 | COLOR

9 Tom Hanks deserved and won an Oscar for Best Actor in his stunning portrait of a dedicated and brilliant young lawyer, fighting back against the prominent Philadelphia law firm that fired him for incompetence after they learned he had AIDS. This is a story of AIDS, but it is much more than that. It is the story of a young man struggling to gain internal acceptance of his own mortality. It is the story of a man's struggle to regain his dignity. It is a powerful courtroom drama that makes an eloquent case for justice. This film makes no statement about homosexuality itself, but about humanity. No matter what your prejudices, you cannot escape this film unmoved.

Sex | Nud | Viol | Lang | AdSit

A: Tom Hanks, Denzel Washington, Jason Robards, Jr., Mary Steenburgen, Antonio Banderas, Ron Vawter

© COLUMBIA TRISTAR HOME VIDEO 52613

PIANO, THE

D: Jane Campion 121 m

R | ROM DMA | 1993 | COLOR

9 This is a highly acclaimed romantic drama that received 7 Oscar nominations, including Best Picture. It is also the quite unusual love story of an extremely repressed Victorian woman (Hunter) who will no longer talk but only communicates in writing and expresses her emotions through her piano. She is a mail-order bride who has just arrived, quite literally, upon the shore of a very primitive New Zealand, along with her piano and young daughter. Her new husband (Neil) chooses to leave her beloved piano on the beach, but it is retrieved by their neighbor (Keitel) who then uses it to bribe her into sexual adventures. Soon their passions evolve into forbidden love.

Sex | Nud | Viol | Lang | AdSit

A: Holly Hunter, Harvey Keitel, Sam Neil, Anna Paquin, Kerry Walker, Genevieve Lemon

© LIVE HOME VIDEO 69974

PICNIC

D: Joshua Logan 113 m

NR | DMA ROM | 1956 | COLOR

8 William Holden is a drifter who arrives on a freight train in a small Kansas town on a Labor Day weekend to visit his friend from college, wealthy Cliff Robertson. Holden had been a big man with the women and a hero on the football team, but now goes from one deadend job to another. Robertson invites him along with his pretty girlfriend Kim Novak to the big town picnic. Holden's easy charm and overt sexuality ignites the passions of all the women, including Novak, who is powerfully drawn to this man who is in many ways just like her. Nominated for six Oscars, including Best Picture, won two. Some overly melodramatic moments diminish its effectiveness today.

Sex | Nud | Viol | Lang | AdSit

A: Kim Novak, William Holden, Susan Strasberg, Rosalind Russell, Cliff Robertson, Arthur O'Connell

© COLUMBIA TRISTAR HOME VIDEO 90613

PIXOTE

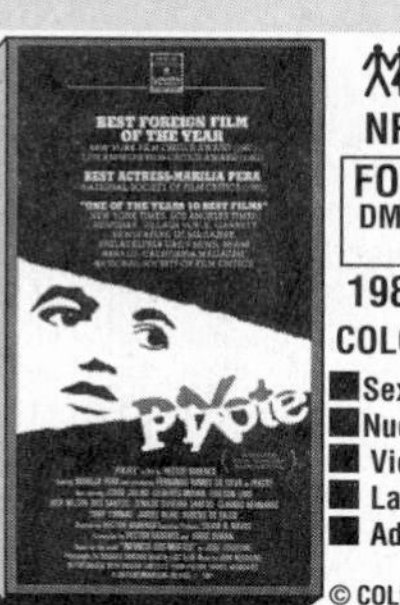

D: Hector Babenco 127 m

NR | FOR DMA | 1981 | COLOR

9 Overwhelmingly powerful, thoroughly engrossing and unrelentingly grim multi-award winning film from Brazil. Set in the slums of Sao Paulo, this is the true story of Pixote. He was abandoned by his parents and left to survive on his own. By age ten he is a pimp, a thief and a murderer. This could easily be too overwhelming for some because it holds back nothing - but neither does it exploit. The performance of the ten-year-old star is all the more haunting because in real life, five years after the completion of the film, he was killed in a shootout with police. Subtitles.

Sex | Nud | Viol | Lang | AdSit

A: Marilia Pera, Fernando Ramos da Silva, Jardel Filho, Rubens de Falco, Elke Maraviha, Tony Tornado

© COLUMBIA TRISTAR HOME VIDEO 60083

PLACES IN THE HEART

D: Robert Benton 113 m

PG | DMA | 1984 | COLOR

9 A wonderful, sensitive charmer for which Sally Field won an Oscar and which also was a big box office hit. In Depression-plagued Waxahachie, Texas, Sally Field's sheriff husband is accidentally killed. Widowed, with children and no money, she is suddenly faced with the possible loss of her farm. Desperate, she agrees to take in an alienated blind boarder (Malkovich) and also accepts an offer from a vagabond black fieldhand (Glover) to help her farm her cotton. A bond of love grows between this mismatched, makeshift family as they struggle to save their home against over-whelming odds. A definite must-see, watch it.

Sex | Nud | Viol | Lang | AdSit

A: Sally Field, John Malkovich, Danny Glover, Ed Harris, Amy Madigan, Lindsay Crouse

© CBS/FOX VIDEO 6836

PLATOON

R
WAR DMA ACT
1986
COLOR
Sex
Nud
Viol
Lang
AdSit

D: Oliver Stone 120 m

10 Profound statement on the harrowing experience of war - the utter terror of hand-to-hand combat and its lasting effects on ordinary people. A naive and idealistic replacement arrives at a battle-worn platoon in Vietnam. His innocence is soon lost to the realities of jungle warfare - where the slightest sound could warn of instant death. As bad as that is, he is also in the midst of an intercompany war where two sergeants (one decent and one ruthless) vie for control of the men. War's insanity was never made more personal, more real or more terrifying. 4 Oscars, including Picture and Director.

A: Charlie Sheen, Willem Dafoe, Tom Berenger, Francesco Quinn, Kevin Dillon, Forest Whitaker

© LIVE HOME VIDEO 6012

PLAYBOYS, THE

PG-13
ROM DMA
1992
COLOR
Sex
Nud
Viol
Lang
AdSit

D: Gillies Mackinnon 113 m

7 The place is an isolated little town in Ireland and it's 1957. An independent and sassy beauty (Wright) has a child out of wedlock. She will not tell who the father is, nor will she marry the town's middle-aged cop (Finney) as the village priest wants her to. The tongues of townspeople wag and they taunt her, but deep down they know that, without her fire, their town is nothing. Finney is perfect as an older man consumed by his love for the girl who will not have him and who is losing her to a handsome drifter/actor from a traveling troup called The Playboys. Gentle, sophisticated romance.

A: Aidan Quinn, Albert Finney, Robin Wright, Milo O'Shea, Alan Devlin

© HBO VIDEO 99710

PLAYER, THE

R
DMA
1992
COLOR
Sex
Nud
Viol
Lang
AdSit

D: Robert Altman 124 m

7 Critics loved this sophisticated and vicious satire of the shallowness of corporate Hollywood. However, commoners will be less kind. True, for those who are interested in such things, it is a right-on portrait, but it is also a story about unsavory people and there is no one to care about. Robbins is an exec who is trying to protect his job, which is mostly to say "No" to writers and to look good while doing it. However, he has antagonized one writer too many, and one is now sending him threatening notes. He accidentally kills the man in a fight, steals the guy's girl and then spends the rest of the film ducking the cops. 50 major stars cameo.

A: Tim Robbins, Greta Scacchi, Whoopi Goldberg, Fred Ward, Peter Gallagher

© TURNER HOME ENTERTAINMENT N4032

PLAYING FOR TIME

NR
DMA
1980
COLOR
Sex
Nud
Viol
Lang
AdSit

D: Daniel Mann 148 m

9 Outstanding and stunning true story of how a French cabaret singer, Fania Fenelon (Redgrave), and a few others, survived the Auschwitz concentration camp by performing in a bizarre orchestra - an orchestra which played for other inmates as they marched off to their deaths, as well as for Nazi officers. But each member of the orchestra lived in terror because they all knew that at any time they could be next. This first-rate made-for-TV movie won four Emmys, including Drama Special, Actress (Redgrave), Supporting Actress (Alexander) and Writing.

A: Vanessa Redgrave, Jane Alexander, Maud Adams, Viveca Lindfors, Shirley Knight, Melanie Mayron

© MCEG/STERLING 70034

POCKETFUL OF MIRACLES

NR
COM DMA
1961
COLOR
Sex
Nud
Viol
Lang
AdSit

D: Frank Capra 137 m

7 Sentimental favorite from Frank Capra. Bette Davis is delightful as Apple Annie, an old woman living in poverty, selling apples to support herself and her daughter who's away in boarding school. She spends everything on her daughter, who thinks her mother is wealthy and now is coming to visit. Annie is scared. Glenn Ford plays a soft-hearted crook who lines up a bunch of his toughguy friends to help Apple Annie convince her visiting daughter, and her rich fiance, that Annie is really a lady. This is Capra's own remake of his 1933 hit LADY FOR A DAY. Pleasing supersweet diversion. Ann-Margret's film debut.

A: Bette Davis, Glenn Ford, Hope Lange, Arthur O'Connell, Peter Falk, Jack Elam

Distributed By MGM/UA Home Video M203855

POSEIDON ADVENTURE, THE

PG
ACT DMA
1972
COLOR
Sex
Nud
Viol
Lang
AdSit

D: Ronald Neame 117 m

9 One of the best of many disaster films from the 1970s. An ocean-going luxury liner is overwhelmed by a massive tidal wave and left capsized, bobbing upside down on the open ocean. A few survivors, trapped below deck, must work their way into the deepest bowels of the ship, which is now the only part exposed to the air, in the hope that someone will find them and cut through the hull to save them. Their arduous trip provides numerous opportunities for an exploration of their motivations and individual life stories. Oscars for Special Effects and Theme Song: "The Morning After."

A: Gene Hackman, Ernest Borgnine, Carol Lynley, Red Buttons, Shelley Winters, Jack Albertson

© CBS/FOX VIDEO 1058

POSSE

PG
WST DMA ACT
1975
COLOR
Sex
Nud
Viol
Lang
AdSit

D: Kirk Douglas 94 m

8 Solid and interesting Western, with an odd edge. Kirk Douglas is both a cynical lawman and an ambitious politician, seeking to become a Senator from Texas. He sees an opportunity to capture the public's attention when he and his ruthless crew of deputies track down and try to capture an escaped robber, Bruce Dern. But Dern is a wily opponent who recognizes Douglas's self-serving agenda and uses it to gain the sympathy of the townspeople, turn the deputies against Douglas and then enlist them in his own cause.

A: Kirk Douglas, Bruce Dern, Bo Hopkins, James Stacy, Luke Askew, David Canary

© PARAMOUNT HOME VIDEO 8316

POSTCARDS FROM THE EDGE

R
COM DMA
1990
COLOR
Sex
Nud
Viol
Lang
AdSit

D: Mike Nichols 101 m

8 Savvy, sophisticated, slick and brazenly funny. Streep is the drugged-out actress whose drug habit lands her in the detox center. Plagued with the feeling that she will forever be in her mother's shadow, she has turned to alternate evils for security. But her trouble starts afresh when the only way she can now get a job in Hollywood is to live in the "protective" care of that same overly-competitive mother. Her mother (MacLaine) was once a Hollywood glamour queen but has now become a domineering, alcoholic meddler. The conflict between these two is great entertainment. Based on Carrie Fisher's autobiographical novel.

A: Meryl Streep, Shirley MacLaine, Dennis Quaid, Rob Reiner, Gene Hackman, Richard Dreyfuss

© COLUMBIA TRISTAR HOME VIDEO 50553

D
M
A

POSTMAN ALWAYS RINGS TWICE, THE

R
SUS CRM DMA
1981
COLOR
Sex
Nud
Viol
Lang
AdSit

D: Bob Rafelson 121 m

6 Super-sexy remake of the classic 1946 film about the passion between a cook at a roadside cafe and a handyman which led to their conspired murder of her husband. Unhampered by the censorship of 1946, this remake dives headlong into the passions only alluded to in the earlier version. After a strong beginning, things begin to wander some. Ultimately, this version is not as satisfying as the original because much of the empathy for the characters which was created in the original is lost here. Still... interesting.

A: Jack Nicholson, Jessica Lange, Michael Lerner, John Colicos

© WARNER HOME VIDEO 673

POWER OF ONE, THE

PG-13
DMA
1992
COLOR
Sex
Nud
Viol
Lang
AdSit

D: John G. Avildsen 127 m

7 An effective and mildly inspirational story about trying to make a difference when the odds are against you. The story is told essentially in two parts. In the first, a young boy of English parentage is orphaned in South Africa during the late '30s, where being white is of little value in a society that hates the English nearly as much as it does blacks. He takes as his mentors two prison inmates, one white and one black. They teach him how to box in the ring and how to survive life out of it. In the film's second half, when he is a grown man, he courageously defies the country's legal color line and agrees to box against blacks.

A: Steven Dorff, Armin Mueller-Stahl, Morgan Freeman, John Gielgud, Fay Masterson, Daniel Craig

© WARNER HOME VIDEO 12411

PRIME OF MISS JEAN BRODIE, THE

PG
DMA
1969
COLOR
Sex
Nud
Viol
Lang
AdSit

D: Ronald Neame 116 m

9 Captivating character study and a showcase for Smith's powerful Oscar-winning performance. She plays a hopelessly romantic and idealistic schoolteacher in a 1930s Scottish girls school who delights in her ability to hold the rapt attention of her impressionable charges with glossy tales of her dreamy philosophies. However, when her students begin to emulate her ideals, her influence proves to be very dangerous. One girl is dead and another's innocence is lost when she succeeds in seducing one of Miss Brodie's admirers. Miss Brodie is exposed and destroyed. Excellent and compelling.

A: Maggie Smith, Robert Stephens, Pamela Franklin, Gordon Jackson, Celia Johnson

© FOXVIDEO 1744

PRINCE OF THE CITY

R
CRM DMA ACT
1981
COLOR
Sex
Nud
Viol
Lang
AdSit

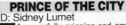

D: Sidney Lumet 167 m

8 A powerfully gripping and emotionally draining film, based on the true 1971 story of a member of an elite corp of New York drug cops who reveals a pervasive corruption on the force. It is his personal story of how he was moved to violate the policeman's code of silence. And, it is a story of the ability of power, drugs and money to corrupt even the best. Our cop is determined to expose the corruption, but do it without destroying his friends - after all, they are just victims of the process - but he can't. So, he becomes the biggest victim, when he cannot protect, and must betray and destroy, his best friends.

A: Treat Williams, Jerry Orbach, Richard Foronjy, Lindsay Crouse, Don Billett, Kenny Marino

© WARNER HOME VIDEO 22021

PRINCE OF TIDES

D: Barbra Streisand — 132 m

R | DMA ROM | 1991 | COLOR

7 Heartfelt, emotional telling of two lives which touch to "heal" each other. Nolte plays a sad man wearing a happy face and hiding a tortured soul. When his twin sister attempts suicide again, Nolte seeks to help her psychiatrist (Streisand) explore into his sister's continuing profound despair. As their long-repressed sordid family history is released from inside him, he learns to confront his own ghosts. Then Streisand's growing affections for this man, who can reach the son she cannot, reveals the extent of her own isolation and unhappiness. Powerful performances and a moving experience.

Sex / Nud / Viol / Lang / AdSit

A: Nick Nolte, Barbra Streisand, Kate Nelligan, Melinda Dillon, Jeroen Krabbe, Jason Gould

© COLUMBIA TRISTAR HOME VIDEO 50943

PRINCESS CARABOO

D: Michael Austin — 96 m

PG | DMA MYS | 1994 | COLOR

6 An unusual idea for a movie. It is 1787 and a young woman is discovered in the English countryside wearing a turban, speaking no English, dressed rather commonly, but also having an elegant (and some think a regal) bearing. Who is this very strange woman? She is taken into the home of a local aristocrat and as word of her spreads, people become more and more convinced that she is a princess from a foreign land, stranded in England. She becomes the focus of the country's interest and even a favorite in the royal court. All the while, a newspaperman is struck by her beauty and fascinated with her. He must learn who she is. Curious film, but also very contrived and full of holes.

Sex / Nud / Viol / Lang / AdSit

A: Phoebe Cates, Jim Broadbent, Wendy Hughes, Kevin Kline, John Lithgow, Stephen Rea

© COLUMBIA TRISTAR HOME VIDEO 73503

D
M
A

PRISONER OF HONOR

D: Ken Russell — 90 m

PG | DMA | 1991 | COLOR

8 Compelling made-for-TV telling of the famous Dreyfus affair - a scandal in the French military of the 1890s, which both helped to establish greater justice in France and contributed to the outbreak WWI. A minor military leak is wrongly blamed on an obscure officer only because the man is a Jew. In Watergate fashion, the problem starts very small and grows to eventually destroy an institution. One officer (Richard Dreyfuss) discovers that the man is innocent, but the pompous General staff refuses to admit publicly that they were ever wrong and attempt to cover it up, leaving the man in prison. Continual coverup destroy all the parties and eventually destroys France.

Sex / Nud / Viol / Lang / AdSit

A: Richard Dreyfuss, Oliver Reed, Peter Firth, Jeremy Kemp, Brian Blessed, Peter Vaughan

© HBO VIDEO 90685

PRISONER OF SECOND AVENUE, THE

D: Melvin Frank — 98 m

PG | DMA COM | 1975 | COLOR

8 A bittersweet reality-based quasi-comedy from Neil Simon. Jack Lemmon is hassled 48-year-old New Yorker who has received the unwelcome news that his position at a faltering ad agency has been eliminated. He is destroyed and reacts with a nervous breakdown. His loving, rock-solid and supportive wife Anne Bancroft has found work to support them while he has blackly comic bouts with obnoxious neighbors, intrusive relatives and shrink who really doesn't care. This is an odd blending of tragedy, melancholy and comedy that only Simon can carry off so well. Billed as a comedy but the neurosis is too real to laugh for long.

Sex / Nud / Viol / Lang / AdSit

A: Jack Lemmon, Anne Bancroft, M. Emmet Walsh, Gene Saks, Elizabeth Wilson, Florence Stanley

© WARNER HOME VIDEO 1035

PROFESSIONAL, THE

D: Luc Besson — 109 m

R | ACT DMA | 1995 | COLOR

8 Very stylish, unique, involving and very curious film by the director of LA FEMME NIKITA. Leon is known as "the cleaner." He is an extremely competent assassin who can be counted upon to get any job done. He is also an extremely lonely and isolated man whose only purpose in life is his job. But that simple world is turned up-side-down, when he is befriended by an abused 12-year-old girl living next door. And, when her drug-dealing father and her family is brutally murdered by a corrupt DEA agent, she comes to her new friend for sanctuary...and to have him teach her his trade. This is a very realistic film. The characters are believable. The emotions are real but so is the bloody violence. Very interesting.

Sex / Nud / Viol / Lang / AdSit

A: Jean Reno, Gary Oldman, Natalie Portman, Danny Aiello, Peter Appel, Michael Badalucco

© COLUMBIA TRISTAR HOME VIDEO 74743

PROGRAM, THE

D: David Ward — 112 m

R | DMA ACT | 1993 | COLOR

8 It is not necessary to be a fan of football to appreciate this video. Most of the action occurs off the field. The excitement of the game is there and there are plenty of football scenes, but the emphasis is on the people and pressures that make up the reality of big-time college football. This is not an indictment of the game but rather an attempt to reveal the real-life, behind the scenes truths: The coach who is pressured to win, so his school can reap the millions of dollars it brings in. The kid who wants to play the game so bad that he will risk his life with steroids. The quarterback who is a drunk. And, the poor kids looking for respect and a way out.

Sex / Nud / Viol / Lang / AdSit

A: James Caan, Omar Epps, Crag Sheffer, Halle Berry, Kristy Swanson, Abraham Benrubi

© TOUCHSTONE HOME VIDEO 2312

PROMISES IN THE DARK

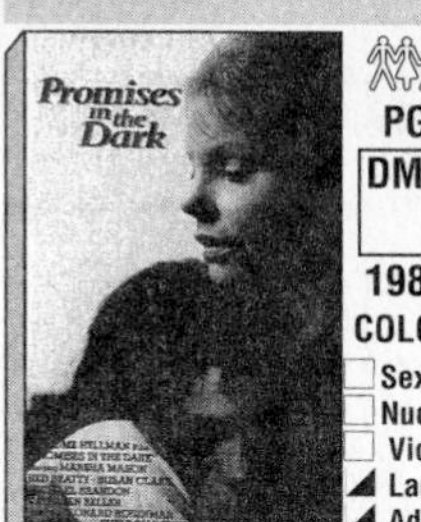

D: Jerome Hellman — 118 m

PG | DMA | 1980 | COLOR

8 Intense and very realistic tearjerker about the relationship that develops between a doctor (Mason) and her patient, a seventeen-year-old girl who is dying of cancer. Mason is tormented by the fact that there is nothing she can do for her charge. Now that the girl is getting worse each day, Mason must decide whether she will honor her promise to let the girl die with dignity or sustain her on life support systems. Top-notch acting and an unrelenting realism make this a sensitive, moving, compassionate experience, and a depressing one.

Sex / Nud / Viol / Lang / AdSit

A: Ned Beatty, Susan Clark, Marsha Mason, Michael Brandon, Kathleen Beller

© WARNER HOME VIDEO 22011

PROSPERO'S BOOKS

D: Peter Greenaway — 126 m

R | FAN DMA | 1991 | COLOR

9 Extremely complex, esoterically offbeat, exquisite, sumptuously photographed and very personalized version of Shakespeare's THE TEMPEST - which must be read first to appreciate the film. Even then, it may take several viewings to absorb what is happening on screen. Prospero and his daughter, set adrift in a small boat by his brother (who wants to steal his Dukedom), survive because a faithful servant has packed food and Prospero's most prized books on board. The film provides a vision of all the books's contents, which are magically depicted by fairies. For very sophisticated viewers only.

Sex / Nud / Viol / Lang / AdSit

A: John Gielgud, Isabelle Pasco, Michel Blanc, Erland Josephson, Tom Bell, Kenneth Cranham

© VIDEO TREASURES MO12883

PUMP UP THE VOLUME

D: Alan Moyle — 105 m

R | DMA | 1990 | COLOR

8 Not just another teenage movie - this one's loaded with integrity. By day, he is just a shy newcomer to an Arizona high school. By night, he is "Hard Harry," a progressive radio talk show host who runs his nightly pirated show out of his basement. He's the voice of the times and speaks to the feelings of anger and hopelessness felt by the student body. He encourages his young audience to act out their feelings and buck the establishment. But when one of his followers goes too far, the FCC comes in for the kill and leads a manhunt to shut him down.

Sex / Nud / Viol / Lang / AdSit

A: Christian Slater, Cheryl Pollack, Samantha Mathis, Ellen Greene, Annie Ross, Scott Paulin

© TURNER HOME ENTERTAINMENT N40974

PUNCHLINE

D: David Seltzer — 123 m

R | DMA COM | 1988 | COLOR

6 Interesting curiosity of a movie about comedians struggling to master their craft in the face of real-life worries. Tom Hanks plays a medical student who is caustic and a failure in his life, but a natural comedian and a hit in the clubs. Sally Field is a wife and mother who desperately wants to be a comedienne. She struggles daily to balance home responsibilities with the pleasure/pain of performing with only mild success. Hanks and Field are friends drawn together by their pain. She helps him to hold together and he helps to punch up her act. Well acted.

Sex / Nud / Viol / Lang / AdSit

A: Tom Hanks, Sally Field, John Goodman, Mark Rydell, Pam Matteson, Kim Greist

© COLUMBIA TRISTAR HOME VIDEO 65010

PURE COUNTRY

D: Christopher Cain — 113 m

PG | ROM DMA | 1992 | COLOR

7 If you like your country music pure, and if you like your story simple and sweet, this is for you. George is a country music star who has become very unhappy with the demands of his life on the road and the course his stage career (managed by Warren) has taken. So he leaves, right in the middle of a concert tour. He winds up on the ranch of a pretty cowgirl, her gnarly father and her two brothers. George's focus begins to return just as Warren hunts him down and takes him back for a big Las Vegas concert and a happy ending. There are ten different country songs scattered through the storyline.

Sex / Nud / Viol / Lang / AdSit

A: George Straight, Lesley Ann Warren, Isabel Glasser, Kyle Chandler, John Doe, Rory Calhoun

© WARNER HOME VIDEO 12593

PURPLE RAIN

D: Albert Magnoli — 113 m

R | MUS DMA | 1984 | COLOR

6 Prince's notorious screen debut is a semi-autobiographical story of a rock musician who can't get along with his parents, his band or his girlfriend. The film is most notable for its striking score, which won an Oscar. Rock `n' roll hits include the smash hits: "When Doves Cry," "Let's Go Crazy," "I Would Die 4 U," "Darling Nikki" and "Purple Rain."

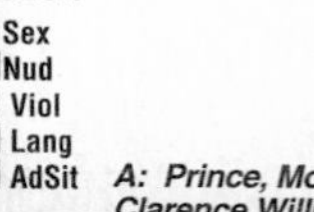

Sex / Nud / Viol / Lang / AdSit

A: Prince, Morris Day, Apollonia Kotero, Jill Jones, Olga Karlatos, Clarence Williams, III

© WARNER HOME VIDEO 11398

QUEEN MARGOT

D: Patrice Chereau 153 m

R | FOR DMA ROM | 1995 | COLOR | Sex | Nud | Viol | Lang | AdSit

9 Brilliant French epic historical drama. It is 1572, and religious wars are raging throughout Europe. Charles IX, the son of the shrewd and absolutely ruthless Catherine de Medicis, is King of France. Catholic Catherine has lost her influence over Charles to a Protestant advisor. She now plots to regain control, while also claiming credit for preventing war, by marrying her daughter Margot to the Protestant King of a French province. But when the marriage does not achieve her goals, she and her sons resort to assassination and murder, and Margot, at first a pawn, becomes a queen. Intelligent, exquisitely complex and intricate. Requires and inspires rapt attention. Wonderfully acted and filmed. Subtitles.

A: Isabelle Adjani, Daniel Auteuil, Jean-Hugues Anglade, Vincent Perez, Virna Lisi

© MIRAMAX HOME ENTERTAINMENT 4439

QUEEN'S LOGIC

D: Steve Rash 116 m

R | DMA COM | 1991 | COLOR | Sex | Nud | Viol | Lang | AdSit

7 Offbeat and slow to develop, but some interesting moments that make this worthwhile for the thoughtful viewer. Five buddies who grew up together in the Queens borough of NYC get together when one of them is about to be married... or will he? His imminent wedding has become a time for a reevaluation of everything by everyone. Olin's not sure that he should get married. Mantegna is on the outs with his wife. Kevin Bacon is a failed Hollywood musician. Malkovich is a homosexual who doesn't like homosexuals. Eventually interesting, but it takes a while to get the characters straight and to understand them.

A: Kevin Bacon, Linda Fiorentino, John Malkovich, Joe Mantegna, Ken Olin, Tony Spiridakis

© LIVE HOME VIDEO 68923

QUEST FOR FIRE

D: Jean-Jacques Annaud 100 m

R | DMA ACT | 1982 | COLOR | Sex | Nud | Viol | Lang | AdSit

8 Remarkable fictional epic that takes you back to the very dawn on mankind! When a primitive tribe loses the only source of fire they know, they send McGill, Perlman and El Kadi to find the elusive flame somewhere else. On their quest, the three encounter a tribe of cannibals, woolly mammoths and a woman (Chong). She teaches McGill about love and tenderness, and how to make real fire. Touching, warm, compelling. This is a serious and realistic odyssey with special custom-made languages and body movements that were all conceived by zoologist Desmond Morris. The costumes were an Oscar winner.

A: Everett McGill, Rae Dawn Chong, Ron Perlman, Nameer El Kadi

© FOXVIDEO 1148

QUIET EARTH, THE

D: Geoff Murphy 91 m

R | SF DMA | 1985 | COLOR | Sex | Nud | Viol | Lang | AdSit

6 An intelligent New Zealand Sci-Fi thriller. The earth has become very quiet one morning when a scientist wakes up to find that all human life on earth has been virtually wiped out. He concludes that one of the top secret government projects he has been working on may be the reason, the fabric of time/space may have been torn apart. He seeks to discover if there is other life left. He does find a young woman and a Maori tribesman and together, they realize that it is up to them to find the answer to restoring mankind. Serious food for thought and a technically astute production.

A: Bruno Lawrence, Alison Routledge, Peter Smith

© CBS/FOX VIDEO 3042

QUIZ SHOW

D: Robert Redford 143 m

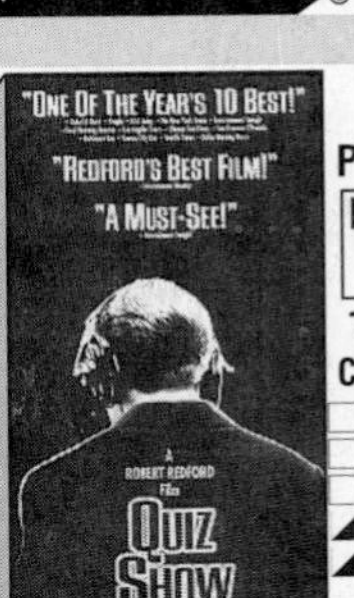

PG-13 | DMA | 1994 | COLOR | Sex | Nud | Viol | Lang | AdSit

9 Fascinating and entertaining tale of how early TV used fame and fortune to corrupt a few, deceive an entire country and sell a lot of Geritol. Selling and selling out is what this show is about. In only ten years, TV had captured America. The game shows, in which ordinary people could win huge sums of money, were the most seductive. However, the producers were giving the answers to the contestant could draw the biggest audience. On 21, that had been Herb Stemple, but when his ratings peaked it was time to crown a new king - clean cut college professor Charles Van Dorn - Herb fought back and spilled the beans to congressional attorney Rob Morrow. Terrific. Four Oscar nominations.

A: John Turturro, Rob Morrow, Ralph Fiennes, David Paymer, Christopher McDonald, Paul Scofield

© HOLLYWOOD PICTURES HOME VIDEO 2558

RACHEL, RACHEL

D: Paul Newman 102 m

R | DMA ROM | 1968 | COLOR | Sex | Nud | Viol | Lang | AdSit

6 Sensitive, grown-up coming out story. Woodward is a socially repressed schoolteacher during the day. At night she is her aging mother's servant. She prepares her mother's drinks and arranges her parties. Then an old classmate (Olson) appears on the scene and offers Woodward a chance at her first love relationship and she is determined to take it. This very sensitive story about a young woman trying to come out of her shell was nominated for four Oscars, including Best Picture and Director. Woodward gives a compelling performance in Newman's first directorial attempt. A little slow.

A: Joanne Woodward, Estelle Parsons, James Olson, Geraldine Fitzgerald, Kate Harrington, Donald Moffat

© WARNER HOME VIDEO 11333

RADIO DAYS

D: Woody Allen 96 m

PG | COM DMA | 1986 | COLOR | Sex | Nud | Viol | Lang | AdSit

7 Witty and sentimental tribute to the pre-television era. Radio then was filled with much more than just music and talk. In the 1940s, it was also theater and entertainment, and people tuned in regularly to intently follow the radio legends. In the Queens, a young boy and his eccentric extended family listen with rapt attention to this other world. It is the world they all aspire to; however, their dream world is not what they have envisioned. The Masked Avenger is really short and bald and the charming talk show host is just a playboy. Critically acclaimed as one of Allen's best films.

A: Mia Farrow, Seth Green, Julie Kavner, Josh Mostel, Michael Tucker, Diane Keaton

© HBO VIDEO 0014

RAGGEDY MAN

D: Jack Fisk 94 m

PG | DMA SUS | 1981 | COLOR | Sex | Nud | Viol | Lang | AdSit

8 Gripping character study. A young divorcee (Spacek) is trying to forge a life for herself and her two sons in a small Texas Gulf town. The two single men in town (except for the mysterious raggedy man) are convinced that, since she is divorced, she must be eager and they harass her. Instead, she has a loving affair with a sailor (Roberts) passing through and gains a new inner strength. Now she is determined to go somewhere new, but is again confronted by the two. In a needlessly horrifying ending, she receives help from the mysterious "raggedy man." Otherwise sensitive and unassuming.

A: Sissy Spacek, Eric Roberts, Sam Shepard, William Sanderson, Tracey Walter, Henry Thomas

© MCA/UNIVERSAL HOME VIDEO, INC. 71003

RAGING BULL

D: Martin Scorsese 130 m

R | DMA ACT | 1980 | B&W | Sex | Nud | Viol | Lang | AdSit

9 Brutally compelling film! In and out of the ring, the only real opponent middleweight prize-fighter Jake LaMotta (De Niro) ever had was himself. In a remarkable effect, De Niro ages from an aggressive lean boxer in his twenties to a bloated overweight hack comic in mid-life. The story of his career is told in flashbacks. The rise to fame and his fall from it are all told with intelligence. Powerful and intense. The violent boxing scenes are graphically realistic. De Niro won an Academy Award - the film received eight nominations overall. This is one of the greats.

A: Robert De Niro, Joe Pesci, Cathy Moriarty, Frank Vincent, Nicholas Colasanto, Theresa Saldana

Distributed By MGM/UA Home Video M201322

RAGTIME

D: Milos Forman 156 m

PG | DMA CRM | 1981 | COLOR | Sex | Nud | Viol | Lang | AdSit

8 A colorful portrait of life at the beginning of the 20th century, set amidst scandal and middle-class morals of the time. Too many subplots confuse the beginning of the film, but things pick up when the focus narrows. While on his way to his own wedding, a black man is accosted by a raucous group of firemen who harass him and then vandalize his car. After repeated attempts to receive justice within the system fail, he takes drastic measures on his own and holds the town hostage. Now, finally, the system takes notice but fights back with a vengeance. Excellent, lots of major stars and a big budget. Nominated for eight Oscars.

A: James Cagney, Brad Dourif, Moses Gunn, Elizabeth McGovern, Kenneth McMillan, James Olson

© PARAMOUNT HOME VIDEO 1486

RAINBOW, THE

D: Ken Russell 104 m

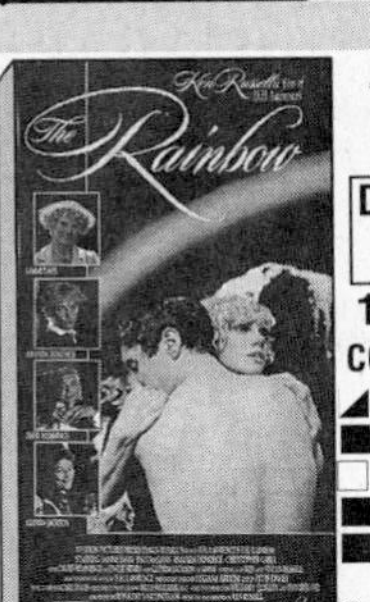

R | DMA | 1989 | COLOR | Sex | Nud | Viol | Lang | AdSit

7 Taken from D.H. Lawrence's novel of the same name, this is in essence a prequel to WOMEN IN LOVE. It is an intelligent telling of the dawning of a young woman's sexual awareness in a restrained Victorian England. A young English schoolteacher (Davis) searches for a more satisfying existence and, defying her parents, she embraces promiscuity to forge relationships first with a female teacher and then with a soldier. These experiences open her to a new spiritual and sensual self-discovery, resulting in a more open life.

A: Sammi Davis, Paul McGann, Amanda Donohoe, Christopher Gable, David Hemmings, Glenda Jackson

© LIVE HOME VIDEO 5336

RAINMAKER, THE

D: John Anthony 121 m

NR | ROM DMA | 1956 | COLOR | Sex | Nud | Viol | Lang | AdSit

7 More than just a romance, an invigorating film about faith in yourself. When a drought-stricken midwestern town is praying for rain, a charming and bombastic rainmaker (Lancaster) emerges, promising miracles. He successfully charms all the desperate farmers, but the lonely and insecure spinster Hepburn dismisses his promises of hope and deflects his romantic advances. He does not relent. His contagious enthusiasm soon inspires her to believe in herself, and in her beauty - both inside and out. When the moment of truth comes, Hepburn emerges triumphant - forever a changed woman.

A: Burt Lancaster, Katharine Hepburn, Wendell Corey, Lloyd Bridges, Earl Holliman, Cameron Prud'homme

© PARAMOUNT HOME VIDEO 5606

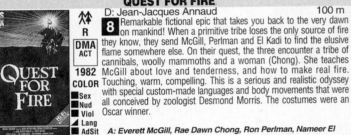

RAIN MAN

D: Barry Levinson 134 m

R · DMA COM · 1988 · COLOR

9 An exceptional lesson in humanity! Cocky super-salesman Cruise goes home to his father's funeral hoping the expected inheritance will save his fledgling car business. Instead he discovers that he has an autistic savant brother (Hoffman) - kept a secret from him his whole life - who's inherited most of Dad's estate. Cruise nabs Hoffman and takes him on a cross-country odyssey, hoping to get a bigger share. Except, quite unexpectedly, the brothers forge a deep bond. Hoffman's outstanding performance was an Oscar-winner, and the film won for Best Picture, Director and Screenplay.

Sex · Nud · Viol · Lang · AdSit

A: Dustin Hoffman, Tom Cruise, Valeria Golino, Jerry Molden, Jack Murdock, Michael Roberts

Distributed By MGM/UA Home Video M901648

RAIN PEOPLE, THE

D: Francis Ford Coppola 102 m

R · DMA · 1969 · COLOR

6 Early Coppola sleeper and a cult favorite! Bored and feeling trapped in her marriage, a pregnant Long Island housewife (Knight) takes off on a flight of discovery. She is overwhelmed and must get away to discover herself. Leaving her husband behind and looking for a lover, she picks up James Caan on the highway, but he is a brain-damaged football player who is child-like and instead she has to take care of him. Robert Duvall is a traffic cop who was also to be her lover, but this relationship also ends in tragedy. This is an intriguing character study whose feminist subject matter was way ahead of its time.

Sex · Nud · Viol · Lang · AdSit

A: James Caan, Shirley Knight, Robert Duvall, Tom Aldredge, Marya Zimmet, Lloyd Crews

© WARNER HOME VIDEO 11058

D M A

RAINTREE COUNTY

D: Edward Dmytryk 173 m

NR · ROM DMA · 1957 · COLOR

6 Epic soap opera. Set during the Civil War, high school sweethearts (Saint and Clift) are in love. But when beautiful but bratty Southern belle Taylor comes for a visit, she charms Clift into marriage. Only too late does Clift realize that Taylor possesses a streak of insanity. She becomes more and more obsessed with the idea that she is the illegitimate daughter of her father and a servant girl. She becomes more unhappy and tormented, making Clift more unhappy and tormented, too. This lavish production was intended to compare with GONE WITH THE WIND but didn't make it that far.

Sex · Nud · Viol · Lang · AdSit

A: Montgomery Clift, Elizabeth Taylor, Eva Marie Saint, Lee Marvin, Nigel Patrick, Rod Taylor

Distributed By MGM/UA Home Video M900401

RAISE THE RED LANTERN

D: Zhang Yimou 125 m

PG · FOR DMA · 1991 · COLOR

9 Exquisitely photographed import from mainland China. The subject is the feudal marriage of a beautiful girl who is forced to leave college at 19 because her father has died, to become the fourth wife of a wealthy landlord. Each evening each wife must stand in front of the door to her quarters as the master signals which wife he will sleep with by ordering the red lanterns lit in that house. The women's days are spent in gilded boredom and so pass their time by plotting against each other for advancement within the household. Elegant and very dramatic, but also staid and very slow. Subtitles.

Sex · Nud · Viol · Lang · AdSit

A: Gong Li, Ma Jingwu, Jin Shuyuan, Cao Cuifeng, He Caifei

© ORION PICTURES CORPORATION 5068

RAISIN IN THE SUN, A

D: Daniel Petrie 128 m

NR · DMA · 1961 · B&W

8 Penetrating drama of the life of a black family in 1950s Chicago. The mother, sister, brother and his wife all live in a small tenement apartment. But their life is thrown into turmoil by the impending receipt of a $10,000 insurance payment. For Mom it means an opportunity to escape the claustrophobic life they lead and move into the all-white suburbs. Poitier wants to realize the dream of owning his own business, and his sister wants to finish medical school. For us, it is an opportunity to witness the effect of dreams denied. Based on Lorraine Hansberry's Pulitzer Prize-winning play.

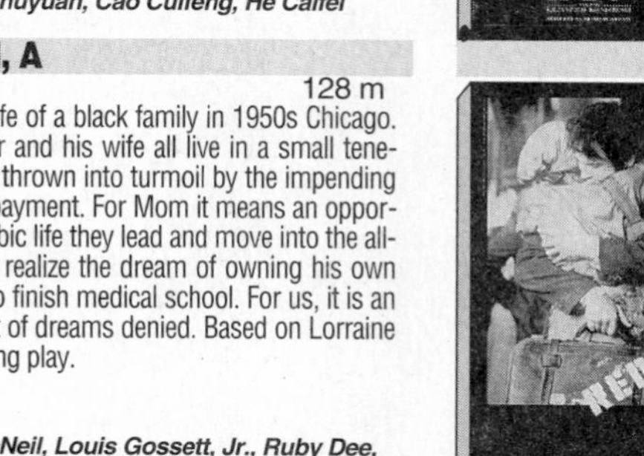

Sex · Nud · Viol · Lang · AdSit

A: Sidney Poitier, Claudia McNeil, Louis Gossett, Jr., Ruby Dee, Ivan Dixon, Diana Sands

© COLUMBIA TRISTAR HOME VIDEO 60091

RAMBLING ROSE

D: Martha Coolidge 115 m

R · DMA COM · 1991 · COLOR

8 Delightful and quite different. Set in a small Southern town during the depression years, Robert Duvall and his family take in an orphan girl as a domestic, but she quickly becomes much more. Rose is very likable, full of life and energy, totally without guile and highly-sexed. She quickly adopts this family as her own - almost too literally. She looks upon the children as peers, the mother as a kindred spirit and upon Duvall with a very undaughterly kind of love. Rose, in fact, is a pathetic creature in desperate need of love and she sets out to find it with other men. Sensitive portrait, very well done.

Sex · Nud · Viol · Lang · AdSit

A: Laura Dern, Diane Ladd, Robert Duvall, Lukas Haas

© LIVE HOME VIDEO 69000

RAN

D: Akira Kurosawa 160 m

R · FOR DMA ACT · 1985 · COLOR

8 This is an epic and masterful saga about a battle for a kingdom in Japan that was adapted from Shakespeare's King Lear by master film-maker Kurosawa. In the 16th century, Japanese King Hidetora (Nakadai) leaves his kingdom to his eldest son hoping to avoid bloodshed, but does not realize the implications of his decision because his evil daughter-in-law is plotting against him. His two younger sons are also in strong opposition to his decision. Soon they all plot against each other. This lavish Oscar-winning production was very highly acclaimed. A story of heartbreak, greed and war. Subtitles.

Sex · Nud · Viol · Lang · AdSit

A: Tatsuya Nakadai, Jinpachi Nezu, Akira Terao, Daisuku Ryu, Mieko Harada, Yoshiko Miyazaki

© CBS/FOX VIDEO 3732

RAPTURE, THE

D: Michael Tolkin 100 m

R · DMA · 1991 · COLOR

8 Stellar acting in a deliberately provocative plot. Mimi Rogers provides a forceful portrait of a beautiful woman, aimless and stuck in a monotonous dead-end job. Her major excitement has come from kinky group sex, but she is tired of the shallow meaninglessness of that existence. There has to be a better reason for living. She throws away her hedonistic lifestyle, gives herself over to a fundamentalist Christian sect and sits back to await the Second Coming which she believes is imminent. But when The Rapture appears to actually happen, she rejects it for what it has caused her to become. Intriguing, thought-provoking, but ultimately disturbing.

Sex · Nud · Viol · Lang · AdSit

A: Mimi Rogers, David Duchovny, Patrick Bauchau, Will Pappon, Kimberly Cullum, Terri Hanover

© TURNER HOME ENTERTAINMENT N4114

REALITY BITES

D: Ben Stiller 99 m

PG-13 · DMA COM · 1994 · COLOR

6 This is an attempt to define the characteristics of Generation X, or the children of the children of the '60s. However, since this group does not have any singular philosophically defining characteristics or direction, neither does this movie. Winona Ryder and her friends have just graduated from college and are caught up in a sort of listless drift and a lot of TV trivia. Winona spends her time videotaping her friends while working as a flunky at a TV station, her roommate has been promoted to store manager and her neo-beatnik almost-boyfriend (Ethan Hawk) leads a grunge band. But, she is also seeing a young executive. What will become of her?

Sex · Nud · Viol · Lang · AdSit

A: Winona Ryder, Ethan Hawk, Ben Stiller, Janeane Garolalo, Steve Zahn, Swoosie Kurtz

© MCA/UNIVERSAL HOME VIDEO, INC. 81929

RED

D: Krzysztof Kieslowski 109 m

R · FOR DMA · 1995 · COLOR

6 This is the third in the series of "color movies" from director Kieslowski. The other two were BLUE and WHITE. Luscious fashion model Valentine is in a dying relationship when she accidentally hits a dog with her car. She seeks out the owner, who is a world-worn former judge and now spends his time listening in on the phone calls of his neighbors. At first Valentine is upset by his activities, but then she becomes drawn into the pain to which the old man has become witness. An odd intellectual relationship develops between the two. The old man tells her of how the loss of his love dominated his life and he then sets about making certain the same does not happen to Valentine.

Sex · Nud · Viol · Lang · AdSit

A: Irene Jacob, Jean-Louis Trintignant

© MIRAMAX HOME ENTERTAINMENT 4373

REDS

D: Warren Beatty 195 m

PG · DMA ROM · 1981 · COLOR

7 Monumental and ambitious personal film by Director/actor Warren Beatty. It is the story of the American radical leftist journalist, John Reed (Beatty), and his love affair with feminist Louise Bryant (Keaton). Their love affair, marriage and eventual breakup is set against the backdrop of the tumultuous events surrounding the Russian Revolution of 1917. Beautifully photographed and a critical success, but also a ponderously long lesson in communist history. Winner of three Oscars, including Best Director, Supporting Actress and Cinematography.

Sex · Nud · Viol · Lang · AdSit

A: Warren Beatty, Diane Keaton, Maureen Stapleton, Edward Herrmann, Jerzy Kosinski, Jack Nicholson

© PARAMOUNT HOME VIDEO 1331

RED TENT, THE

D: Mickail K. Kalatozov 121 m

G · DMA ACT · 1969 · COLOR

7 Rugged adventure and a gripping saga about attempts to rescue a downed Italian dirigible crew. In 1928 the Italian dirigible "Italia" crashed in the Arctic while exploring the North Pole. For days the crew huddled inside the makeshift red tent sending out S.O.S. radio messages. Ronald Amundsen (Connery) leads a daring ground rescue attempt but dies trying to find the crew. Told in flashback form, this lavishly produced film is even more compelling because it is based upon a true story. Emotional and extremely well-acted. Beautiful photography.

Sex · Nud · Viol · Lang · AdSit

A: Sean Connery, Peter Finch, Hardy Kruger, Claudia Cardinale

© PARAMOUNT HOME VIDEO 8041

REGARDING HENRY

D: Mike Nichols 85 m

PG-13 DMA ROM 1991 COLOR

8 Unscrupulous, ruthless and callous - that is a telling description of attorney Henry Turner (Ford). Then he is shot in the head in a robbery attempt and everything changes. He has survived the bullet but he has lost his memory. His wife (Bening) helps nurse him back to health and she finds that she is falling in love again, but this time with a different, better man who is emerging. The recovering Ford discovers that they had been drifting apart. Both he and his wife had been having affairs, their marriage had been near breakup and that he was the principal cause. Emotional, yes, but not smarmy or manipulative. This is very believable and rewarding watching.

Sex Nud Viol Lang AdSit

A: Harrison Ford, Annette Bening, Mikki Allen, Bill Nunn, Donald Moffat, Nancy Marchand

© PARAMOUNT HOME VIDEO 32403

REIVERS, THE

D: Mark Rydell 107 m

NR DMA COM 1969 COLOR

9 Absolutely wonderful and delightful tale taken from William Faulkner. It is the story of the innocent 12-year-old son of a wealthy Mississippian who begins to grow up during the summer of 1905. While his family is away, he is charmed by two fun-loving, but scurrilous, rogues (McQueen and Crosse) into "borrowing" his granddaddy's brand new automobile for a grandly adventurous trip to far away Memphis. There, he will spend the night in a bordello, while McQueen visits his girlfriend and as Crosse schemes to trade the new automobile for a race horse, which he then plans to race to win the car back. This is a sentimental charmer, a real winner and a lot of fun.

Sex Nud Viol Lang AdSit

A: Steve McQueen, Sharon Farrell, Will Geer, Michael Constantine, Rupert Crosse, Mitch Vogel

© CBS/FOX VIDEO 7153

REMAINS OF THE DAY

D: James Ivory 134 m

DMA 1993

8 8 Oscar nominations, including Picture, Director, Actress and Actor. Beautifully acted and photographed, and highly literate screen adaptation of Kazuo Ishiguro's famed 1989 novel. Anthony Hopkins is a very proper English butler totally dedicated to his profession. He has no life of his own and denies himself all pleasures, even an admission of his love for Emma Thompson. She is an immensely competent housekeeper, who has no family other than the staff at the manor and no love other than that for Hopkins. Yet, neither will speak of it and so it remains unspoken and unfulfilled. The house and service is all that is important, even as their lives are being spent. Very slow.

Sex Nud Viol Lang AdSit

A: Anthony Hopkins, Emma Thompson, James Fox, Christopher Reeve, Peter Vaughn, Hugh Grant

© COLUMBIA TRISTAR HOME VIDEO 71093

RENAISSANCE MAN

D: Penny Marshall 138 m

PG-13 COM DMA 1994 COLOR

6 Danny DeVito is a former top-flight ad-writer, but now he's all washed up. Just fired from his last job and in desperate need of money, he agrees to take a civilian teaching position at an Army base. His job - teach the dumbest of the dumb. Reluctant Danny was not thrilled about teaching anyway, but this is way more than he bargained for. But, these troops have nowhere else to go and he is determined to reach them. In order to do it, he has to first get his student's attention, and he has to fight his non-Army ways - which place him in constant conflict with devoted drill sergeant Gregory Hines. Well-meaning time-killer, upbeat and occasionally has some funny stuff.

Sex Nud Viol Lang AdSit

A: Danny DeVito, Gregory Hines, James Remar, Ed Begley, Jr., Lillo Brancato, Jr., Stacey Dash

© TOUCHSTONE HOME VIDEO 2754

RESURRECTION

D: Daniel Petrie 102 m

PG DMA FAN 1980 COLOR

9 An underrated gem. Burstyn (Oscar nominated) creates a fascinating character - a simple, ordinary and pleasant woman who survives a traffic accident that killed her husband. She returns from near-death to discover that she has received a miraculous gift, the ability to heal both herself and others. This gentle, gracious woman then heals all those who come to her for help. However, the young farmer with whom she was falling in love, tries to force her to confess that she is Jesus reborn. Others accuse her of being a charlatan or resent her power. Everyone wants something. Her gift has now become a burden.

Sex Nud Viol Lang AdSit

A: Ellen Burstyn, Sam Shepard, Roberts Blossom, Eva LeGallienne, Richard Farnsworth, Clifford David

© MCA/UNIVERSAL HOME VIDEO, INC. 66047

RETURN TO LONESOME DOVE

D: Mike Robe 330 m

NR WST DMA ACT 1993 COLOR

8 Good follow-up to the fantastic original. Woodrow has taken his friend back to Texas to bury him. But, before going back, he stops off to ask another former Texas ranger to lead a group in capturing a herd of mustangs and driving them back to Montana. While they are doing that, he will stop off in Nebraska to buy blooded stock. He will breed the two to create a new hardier stock. Newt is to meet him in Nebraska, but instead gets in a gun fight and thrown into jail. He is paroled to a wealthy cattle baron with a pretty young wife. Much of the fire is gone from the original, but it is still well worth a watch.

Sex Nud Viol Lang AdSit

A: John Voight, Barbara Hershey, Rick Schroder, Louis Gossett, Jr., William Petersen, Oliver Reed

© CABIN FEVER ENTERTAINMENT 9586

REVERSAL OF FORTUNE

D: Barbet Schroeder 104 m

R DMA MYS 1990 COLOR

9 An absorbing docudrama that provides a fascinating look inside the mysterious and decadent world of the super rich. The film is based upon a real-life case from the early 1980s that had the entire nation's attention. It is the intriguing story of the second trial of Claus von Bulow - an icy European aristocrat who was accused of murdering his wife Sunny, a spoiled wealthy American heiress. He hired a Harvard law professor to appeal his conviction and then to fight for him in a new trial. The murder is explored from many different viewpoints, but the film itself never takes a position. It is a fascinating study in people and the legal system.

Sex Nud Viol Lang AdSit

A: Jeremy Irons, Glenn Close, Ron Silver, Uta Hagen, Annabella Sciorra, Fisher Stevens

© WARNER HOME VIDEO 11934

RHAPSODY IN AUGUST

D: Akira Kurosawa 98 m

PG FOR DMA 1991 COLOR

6 Famed Japanese filmmaker Akira Kurosawa's morality play that comments both upon the destructive nature of war, even years after it is over. An old woman, living outside of Nagasaki, has her grandchildren over for the summer while their parents are in Hawaii to visit the family of her wealthy brother who is now near death. The children discover for the first time that their grandfather was killed in the atomic bomb blast and at first resent their parents for going to America. The old woman chastises them for blaming Americans and instead blames war itself. Kurosawa's approach is very simplistic and seems more directed toward young people, but should not be lost.

Sex Nud Viol Lang AdSit

A: Sachiko Murase, Hidetaka Yoshioka, Tomoko Onatakara, mie Suzuki, Mitsunori Isaki, Richard Gere

© ORION PICTURES CORPORATION 5062

RICH AND FAMOUS

D: George Cukor 117 m

R DMA 1981 COLOR

6 Two Smith college graduates remain friends through 20 years of rivalry in love and in work. One achieves critical but not economic success writing serious novels. The other becomes rich and famous writing soap opera novels. Sensitive and energetic acting from two of Hollywood's best fails to raise this film above the 1943 version (OLD ACQUAINTANCE), also by Cukor (but not available on video). 20 years of emotional turmoil, is a lot of turmoil. Still, this is an interesting film, but likely more interesting to women than men.

Sex Nud Viol Lang AdSit

A: Jacqueline Bisset, Candice Bergen, David Selby, Hart Bochner, Meg Ryan, Steven Hill

Distributed By MGM/UA Home Video M800111

RICH IN LOVE

D: Bruce Beresford m

PG-13 DMA 1993 COLOR

6 Kathryn Erbe comes home from high school to find a note from her mother (Clayburgh) that was really meant for her father (Finney). The note says she feels trapped, has to leave them and start over again. Kathryn and her father spend the next year trying desperately to find the mother. In the interim, her unhappily pregnant sister and her new husband have moved in with them. Papa eventually discovers a new love with the local beautician (Laurie) and Kathryn attempts to find love for herself by staging the seduction of her high school boyfriend, but she only finds satisfaction with her sister's troubled husband. Pleasant enough, but slow moving.

Sex Nud Viol Lang AdSit

A: Kathryn Erbe, Albert Finney, Kyle MacLachlan, Suzy Amis, Piper Laurie, Jill Clayburgh

Distributed By MGM/UA Home Video M902691

RIGHT STUFF, THE

D: Philip Kaufman 193 m

PG DMA ACT 1983 COLOR

9 Fascinating and invigorating film that, even though quite long, is never boring. Seven pilots are chosen to be the first Americans in space under the NASA program, Project Mercury. This film tells their stories. Although the pivotal character is Chuck Yeager, all seven receive considerable attention, as does the entire training process that launched America's space program. An epic story, with plenty of exhilarating moments, that does not disappoint. Watch for the real Chuck Yeager in a cameo. Winner of four Oscars, including Score.

Sex Nud Viol Lang AdSit

A: Charles Frank, Scott Glenn, Ed Harris, Sam Shepard, Fred Ward, Barbara Hershey

© WARNER HOME VIDEO 20014

RIVER NIGER, THE

D: Krishna Shah 104 m

R DMA 1978 COLOR

7 Realistic, emotional and tough. Based on the Tony Award-winning play, a black family, living in an inner-city ghetto, struggles to come to terms with a violent revolution going on outside their door that is brought about by the grinding poverty they live in. James Earl Jones is a poet who dives deeply into his poetry to escape from that turmoil, but the ugly reality is that he remains trapped in his house with his wife (Cicely Tyson). They are supported, both emotionally and financially, by his friend Dr. Dudley (Lou Gossett Jr.).

Sex Nud Viol Lang AdSit

A: Louis Gossett, Jr., Cicely Tyson, James Earl Jones, Glynn Turman, Roger E. Mosley

© CONTINENTAL VIDEO 1017

DMA

RIVER RUNS THROUGH IT, A

D: Robert Redford — 124 m

PG | DMA | 1992 | COLOR

9 Norman and Paul are the sons of a strict Presbyterian minister in a small Montana town in the early 20th-century. The boys were always very different from each other and from their father. Norman was quiet and studious, but Paul was rebellious and rowdy. Norman grew up to study English literature at Dartmouth, but Paul became a newspaper reporter, a gambler, a heavy drinker and thrived on scandal. Through everything, the one thing that these very different boys and their strict father all shared was a deep love for fly fishing. This critically acclaimed autobiography of Norman Maclean was said to be unfilmable. However, this stunning film is a brilliant success.

Sex Nud Viol Lang AdSit

A: Robert Redford, Craig Sheffer, Brad Pitt, Tom Skerritt, Emily Lloyd, Brenda Blethyn

© COLUMBIA TRISTAR HOME VIDEO 51573

RIVER'S EDGE

D: Tim Hunter — 99 m

R | DMA | 1987 | COLOR

7 A riveting, powerful and extremely disturbing story of teenage alienation and murder - all the more so, because it is based on an actual event. A group of alienated teenagers have formed a into tight family-like group. So, when one of them murders his girlfriend, the others are ill-prepared to separate right and wrong from loyalty to each other. At first they choose loyalty, but Reeves eventually goes to the police, so he soon finds himself in conflict with their stoned leader Glover. Glover flees for protection to drug dealer Hopper, the only only adult friend he has. This is a hard look at troubled youth. Controversial, often bleak, but extremely thought provoking.

Sex Nud Viol Lang AdSit

A: Crispin Glover, Keanu Reeves, Ione Skye Leitch, Roxana Zal, Daniel Roebuck, Tom Bower

© NEW LINE HOME VIDEO 7690

ROB ROY

D: Michael Caton-Jones — 139 m

R | DMA ACT | 1995 | COLOR

8 1717 Scotland was a feudal state in the process of breaking down. Poverty was widespread and many of its people were emigrating to "The Americas." The aristocrats controlled the land and the money. Robert Roy MacGregor was a real man and a legendary hero. He was the leader of his clan, a man of fiercely-defended honor and a dedicated husband. When he was cheated by a corrupt bureaucrat, his cattle killed, his home burned and his wife violated, he fought back against long odds to reclaim his defiled honor and became a national hero. Richly filmed against beautiful scenery, this film captures both the physical sense of the times and the feel of the everyday society. Beautiful, but somewhat ponderous.

Sex Nud Viol Lang AdSit

A: Liam Neeson, Jessica Lange, John Hurt, Tim Roth, Eric Stoltz, Brian Cox

Distributed By MGM/UA Home Video M905228

ROCKET GIBRALTAR

D: Daniel Petrie — 100 m

PG | COM DMA | 1988 | COLOR

7 Bittersweet drama about love and family. A much-loved patriarch, Levi Rockwell (Lancaster), has called his family together to celebrate his 77th birthday. His large family, children and grandchildren, all gather on his beautiful estate on Long Island. Although his children love him, it's his grandchildren that make a heartfelt connection with him and carry out his most cherished last wish. Sentimental, touching and emotional. Have a box of tissue ready for the last few scenes.

Sex Nud Viol Lang AdSit

A: Burt Lancaster, Suzy Amis, John Glover, Bill Pullman, Patricia Clarkson, Frances Conroy

© COLUMBIA TRISTAR HOME VIDEO 65009

ROCKY

D: John G. Avildsen — 125 m

PG | DMA ACT | 1976 | COLOR

10 Triple Academy Award-winning feel-good powerhouse! An unknown, small-time loser, a thumb-breaker from the streets of Philadelphia (Stallone), gets one miraculous shot at the boxing championship when champion Apollo Creed (Weathers) offers to fight him as a publicity stunt. For Appolo Creed, this is a joke - but for Rocky, it is everything. Rocky is relentlessly trained by a gnarled old has-been trainer (Meridith) and inspired by his shy girlfriend (Shire). This endearing film really went the distance with audiences and spawned numerous sequels. It is a rousing charmer that never gets old!

Sex Nud Viol Lang AdSit

A: Sylvester Stallone, Talia Shire, Burt Young, Burgess Meredith, Carl Weathers, Thayer David

Distributed By MGM/UA Home Video M200249

ROCKY II

D: Sylvester Stallone — 119 m

PG | DMA ACT | 1979 | COLOR

8 Rocky (Stallone) went from being a nobody to a national sensation in the first picture. Now he has become disenchanted with his new-found fame and is even unable to find work. After being taunted by his rival, Apollo Creed (Weathers), he accepts an offer for a rematch, in spite of the objections of his now-pregnant wife (Shire). Rocky rigorously trains under the keen eye of his personal trainer (Meredith), while also fighting with Shire at home. He is nearly destroyed when she, his tower of strength and inspiration, lapses into a coma after childbirth. Sentimental, powerful and uplifting!

Sex Nud Viol Lang AdSit

A: Sylvester Stallone, Talia Shire, Carl Weathers, Burgess Meredith, Burt Young

Distributed By MGM/UA Home Video M200250

ROCKY III

D: Sylvester Stallone — 103 m

PG | DMA ACT | 1982 | COLOR

7 Stallone pounds out another rousing success! Rocky, now a man of wealth and leisure, is challenged into a new fight by the bullish Clubber Lang (Mr T.). However, Rocky is now soft and loses big, so he must reach deep within himself to find the inner strength needed to win a rematch - "the eye of the tiger." This time around, Rocky has to deal with a new challenger - fear. His longtime and trusted manager (Meredith) has died, but his new manager, Apollo Creed, teaches him some fancy footwork and quick moves in preparation for the big battle ahead.

Sex Nud Viol Lang AdSit

A: Sylvester Stallone, Talia Shire, Hulk Hogan, Mr. T, Burt Young, Burgess Meredith

Distributed By MGM/UA Home Video M202086

ROCKY IV

D: Sylvester Stallone — 93 m

PG | DMA ACT | 1985 | COLOR

6 Rocky faces his biggest challenge. He is to represent America and avenge the death of his friend and teacher, Apollo Creed. This time Rocky prepares to do battle with Drago (Lundgren), a hulking superhuman Russian boxer with a death wish. Drago trains with stardust and sophisticated computer equipment, while Rocky has to train in a cold and rugged Siberia using old-fashioned primitive equipment. His wife (Shire) stands by him once again as he battles not only against the ominous powerhouse, but also for the good ol' USA. Intense and fierce, but much of the charm is gone.

Sex Nud Viol Lang AdSit

A: Sylvester Stallone, Dolph Lundgren, Talia Shire, Carl Weathers, Burt Young, Brigitte Nielsen

Distributed By MGM/UA Home Video M202084

ROE VS. WADE

D: Gregory Hoblit — 92 m

NR | DMA | 1989 | COLOR

7 This is the powerful true story of Texan Ellen Campbell's precedent-setting court battle to gain the legal right to an abortion. It is also a balanced portrayal of this very emotional issue and her confrontation. In 1973, unmarried and trapped in an unwanted pregnancy, Campbell (Holly Hunter) discovered a young attorney (Amy Madigan) who was willing to pursue her case. Together they took it to the Supreme Court and established that the Texas law was unconstitutional, which opened the way for national change. Nominated for six Emmys - won two, including Holly Hunter as Best Actress.

Sex Nud Viol Lang AdSit

A: Holly Hunter, Amy Madigan, Kathy Bates, Terry O'Quinn, Stephen Tobolowsky, Dion Anderson

© PARAMOUNT HOME VIDEO 12771

ROLLOVER

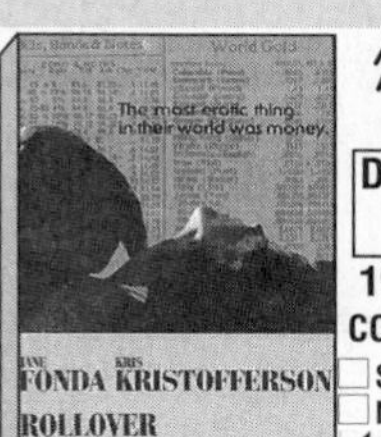

D: Alan J. Pakula — 117 m

R | DMA | 1981 | COLOR

6 High stakes suspense! When Fonda's husband, the owner of a huge petrochemical company, mysteriously dies, she calls in a high-powered troubleshooter (Kristoffersson) to help her save the sinking company. They develop a strategy which requires Arab venture capital. But, during a trip to Saudi Arabia, they stumble onto a conspiracy discovering that Arab oil money is not being "rolled over" into American banks - instead it is being withdrawn. This is an action which will have disastrous consequences to the world economy. This is a complex but intriguing look into the world of high finance. A polished production.

Sex Nud Viol Lang AdSit

A: Jane Fonda, Kris Kristofferson, Hume Cronyn, Josef Sommer

© WARNER HOME VIDEO 22022

ROMEO AND JULIET

D: Franco Zeffirelli — 138 m

PG | ROM DMA | 1968 | COLOR

9 The classic Shakespearean tragedy and ultimate love story is brilliantly retold here! Romeo (Whiting) and Juliet (Hussey) are two teenagers who fall deeply in love, but their families are warring. That ensures that their love will never bloom and tragedy soon strikes the forlorn lovers. Whiting and Hussey interpreted their complex roles excellently, despite their young age. The two were 17 and 15, respectively, when the movie was made. The photography and production values will take your breath away. Oscar winner for both Cinematography and Costume Design.

Sex Nud Viol Lang AdSit

A: Olivia Hussey, Leonard Whiting, Milo O'Shea, Michael York

© PARAMOUNT HOME VIDEO 6809

ROMERO

D: John Duigan — 105 m

PG-13 | DMA | 1989 | COLOR

7 Set against the background of a country that is torn apart by oppression and civil unrest, this is an affecting biography/drama of a mild mannered and tormented Salvadoran Catholic Archbishop who was transformed into becoming a political activist. He rose up and eventually took an eloquent social stand against the injustices which ran rampant in his country of El Salvador. However, his commitment to change also eventually led to his assassination in 1980. This is quite an involving film. It was financed by the United States Roman Catholic Church. Raul Julia did an outstanding job.

Sex Nud Viol Lang AdSit

A: Raul Julia, Richard Jordan, Ana Alicia, Eddie Velez, Tony Piana, Harold Gould

© VIDMARK ENTERTAINMENT 5228

ROOM WITH A VIEW, A

D: James Ivory 117 m

NR | ROM DMA | 1986 | COLOR | Sex, Nud, Viol, Lang, AdSit

8 Enchanting intelligent surprise! A young Englishwoman (Carter) travels on holliday to sensuous Florence, Italy, to view the world and broaden her horizons. There she finds a young man to whom she is very attracted (Sands). Her meddling chaperone, however, doesn't approve of him and she is torn between her love for this common man and her proper engagement back home to a stuffy and self-absorbed Englishman (Day-Lewis). Based on a novel by E.M. Forster, this film is an elegant, witty and evocative portrayal of the upper-crust manners and mores of the Edwardian English of 1907.

A: Helena Bonham Carter, Maggie Smith, Daniel Day-Lewis, Denholm Elliott, Julian Sands, Simon Callow

© CBS/FOX VIDEO 6915

ROOTS

D: Marvin J. Chomsky 562 m

NR | DMA SUS | 1977 | COLOR | Sex, Nud, Viol, Lang, AdSit

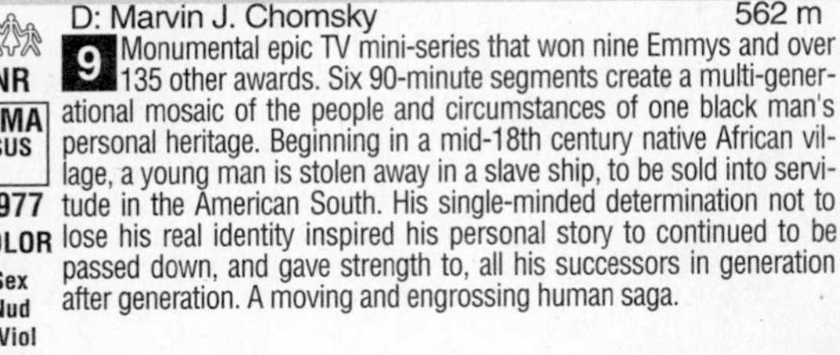

9 Monumental epic TV mini-series that won nine Emmys and over 135 other awards. Six 90-minute segments create a multi-generational mosaic of the people and circumstances of one black man's personal heritage. Beginning in a mid-18th century native African village, a young man is stolen away in a slave ship, to be sold into servitude in the American South. His single-minded determination not to lose his real identity inspired his personal story to continued to be passed down, and gave strength to, all his successors in generation after generation. A moving and engrossing human saga.

A: Edward Asner, Lloyd Bridges, Cicely Tyson, Lorne Greene, Ben Vereen, Levar Burton

© WARNER HOME VIDEO 11111

ROSE, THE

D: Mark Rydell 134 m

R | DMA MUS | 1979 | COLOR | Sex, Nud, Viol, Lang, AdSit

7 Midler, in her starring debut, brilliantly plays a brassy, extremely successful but lonely rock star who succumb to the perils of stardom and life on the road. She falls prey to alcohol and drug abuse, and gets involved in several destructive relationships, all as a vain attempt to seek solace for her loneliness. Midler's character was modeled after the ill-fated life of singer Janis Joplin. An insightful look into the not-always-glamorous life of rock and roll, with some of the best musical footage ever captured on film. "The Rose" is one of the outstanding songs from the film.

A: Bette Midler, Alan Bates, Frederic Forrest, Harry Dean Stanton, Barry Primus, David Keith

© FOXVIDEO 1092

RUBY

D: John Mackenzie 111 m

R | DMA | 1992 | COLOR | Sex, Nud, Viol, Lang, AdSit

6 Very well-acted but fictionalized account of the low-life Dallas strip-club owner who shot Lee Harvey Oswald (President Kennedy's assassin) on live TV. This is the dramatization of his supposed complicity in a CIA plot to cover up its involvement with the mob in the assassination of the President. Good characterizations combine with intense realism to provide more than passable entertainment... but the history is questionable. For another questionable view of the Kennedy assassination see JFK.

A: Danny Aiello, Sherilyn Fenn, Arliss Howarde, Tobin Bell, David Duchovny, Richard Sarafian

© COLUMBIA TRISTAR HOME VIDEO 92183

RUDY

D: David Anspaugh 112 m

PG | DMA | 1993 | COLOR | Sex, Nud, Viol, Lang, AdSit

7 Likable story about an unlikely but real-life sports hero, Daniel E. "Rudy" Ruettiger. Rudy wanted more than anything to play football for Notre Dame but he was too short, too light, too poor and didn't have good grades. So, for four years after highschool, he worked in the mills. But when his best friend was killed, Rudy knew he had to chase his dream, no matter how long the odds. When Notre Dame wouldn't admit him, he worked his way through Holy Cross until his grades were good enough. And, when he couldn't make the the 1st, 2nd or even 3rd teams, he became Notre Dame's tackling dummy. Too Hollywood to believe all of it, but you can't escape liking it either.

A: Sean Astin, Ned Beatty, Charles S. Dutton, Jason Miller, Lili Taylor, Robert Prosky

© COLUMBIA TRISTAR HOME VIDEO 53723

RULING CLASS, THE

D: Peter Medak 154 m

PG | COM DMA | 1972 | COLOR | Sex, Nud, Viol, Lang, AdSit

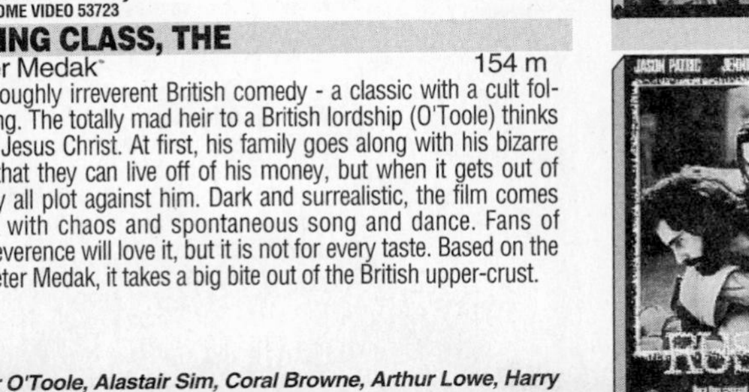

9 Thoroughly irreverent British comedy - a classic with a cult following. The totally mad heir to a British lordship (O'Toole) thinks that he is Jesus Christ. At first, his family goes along with his bizarre belief so that they can live off of his money, but when it gets out of hand, they all plot against him. Dark and surrealistic, the film comes complete with chaos and spontaneous song and dance. Fans of British irreverence will love it, but it is not for every taste. Based on the play by Peter Medak, it takes a big bite out of the British upper-crust.

A: Peter O'Toole, Alastair Sim, Coral Browne, Arthur Lowe, Harry Andrews, Michael Bryant

© NEW LINE HOME VIDEO 2085

RUMBLE FISH

D: Francis Ford Coppola 94 m

R | DMA | 1983 | B&W | Sex, Nud, Viol, Lang, AdSit

6 A bold teenage movie. A young punk (Dillon) is growing up on the wrong side of the tracks in Tulsa and is looking to escape his hellish life. He lives with an alcoholic father (Hopper) and worships his motorcycle riding brother (Rourke). So, Dillon readily goes along with his brother's scheme to free exotic fish from a pet store, but that only ends up with him getting into trouble with the cops. This adaptation of S.E. Hinton's novel is filmed in black and white except for some scenes with Siamese fighting fish. That's only part of the symbolism cram-packed into this film.

A: Matt Dillon, Mickey Rourke, Dennis Hopper, Diane Lane, Diana Scarwid, Vincent Spano

© MCA/UNIVERSAL HOME VIDEO, INC. 80056

RUMOR OF WAR, A

D: Richard T. Heffron 106 m

NR | DMA WAR | 1980 | COLOR | Sex, Nud, Viol, Lang, AdSit

9 Riveting made-for-television war drama based upon a real individual. Philip Caputo (Davis) was a young and idealistic college student who joined the Marines. He went off to fight the brutal war in Vietnam and watched his friends die. Then, while leading his men into combat at a small Vietnamese village, things went terribly awry and he found himself facing a court martial for murder and his once loyal attitude to the Corps changed. A gripping true story about one man's political transformation from an enthusiastic soldier to a bitter veteran. Adapted from the novel by John Sacret Young.

A: Brad Davis, Keith Carradine, Stacy Keach, Michael O'Keefe, Richard Bradford, Brian Dennehy

© FRIES HOME VIDEO 97700

RUNAWAY TRAIN

D: Andrei Konchalovsky 112 m

R | SUS DMA | 1985 | COLOR | Sex, Nud, Viol, Lang, AdSit

7 An intriguing combination of intense suspense, action and intellectual drama. Two desperate and hardened convicts break out of a maximum security prison in Alaska during the dead of winter. They hop a ride on a freight train only to discover that the engineer has died of a heart attack and now they are trapped on a high speed runaway. The authorities know they are onboard and are intent upon derailing the massive rolling deathtrap until they and the convicts both discover that there is another passenger on board. Voight and Roberts received Oscar nominations for their vivid portraits.

A: Jon Voight, Eric Roberts, Rebecca De Mornay, Kyle T. Heffner, John P. Ryan, Kenneth McMillan

Distributed By MGM/UA Home Video M800867

RUNNING ON EMPTY

D: Sidney Lumet 117 m

PG-13 | DMA | 1988 | COLOR | Sex, Nud, Viol, Lang, AdSit

8 A radical political pair (Lahti and Hirsch) blew up a napalm plant in the '60s. Now, 17 years later and parents, they have been raising their family while on the lam. They are constantly afraid the FBI will find them. So every time their past begins to catch up with them, they uproot and move, having to change their names, disrupt their children and through all their lives into turmoil. However, when their son (Phoenix) is accepted at the Julliard School of Music, the family is faced with a huge decision. Phoenix is emotionally powerful as a 17-year-old who must chose between a life of his own, on his own, or staying with his fugitive family. Engrossing drama.

A: Christine Lahti, Judd Hirsch, River Phoenix, Martha Plimpton, Jonas Arby, Ed Crowley

© WARNER HOME VIDEO 11843

RUN SILENT, RUN DEEP

D: Robert Wise 94 m

NR | WAR DMA ACT | 1958 | B&W | Sex, Nud, Viol, Lang, AdSit

8 Gripping WWII war drama. Burt Lancaster was to have become Captain of his own submarine, but instead is named first officer at the last minute when Clark Gable is given command. Gable is the only survivor of a Japanese attack on his old sub. In spite of being hampered by the suspicions and deep distrust of the entire crew and his first officer, and in the face of long odds, Gable is determined to sink a Japanese cruiser. Very tense drama, capturing the feeling of tight quarters and uncertainty. One of the best submarine movies ever.

A: Clark Gable, Burt Lancaster, Brad Dexter, Jack Warden, Nick Cravat, Don Rickles

Distributed By MGM/UA Home Video M202133

RUSH

D: Lili Fini Zanuck 120 m

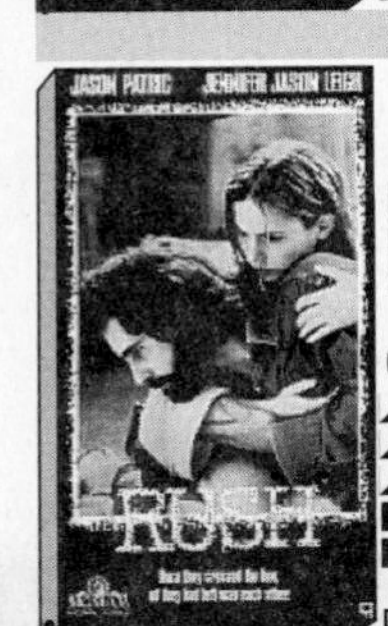

R | CRM DMA | 1992 | COLOR | Sex, Nud, Viol, Lang, AdSit

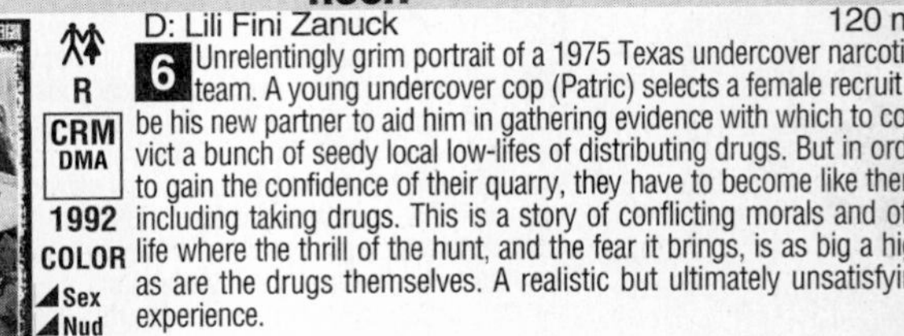

6 Unrelentingly grim portrait of a 1975 Texas undercover narcotics team. A young undercover cop (Patric) selects a female recruit to be his new partner to aid him in gathering evidence with which to convict a bunch of seedy local low-lifes of distributing drugs. But in order to gain the confidence of their quarry, they have to become like them, including taking drugs. This is a story of conflicting morals and of a life where the thrill of the hunt, and the fear it brings, is as big a high as are the drugs themselves. A realistic but ultimately unsatisfying experience.

A: Jason Patric, Jennifer Jason Leigh, Gregg Allman, Sam Elliott, Max Perlich

Distributed By MGM/UA Home Video 902527

RYAN'S DAUGHTER

D: David Lean — 194 m

PG | ROM DMA | 1970 | COLOR

8 Sweeping story of tragic love. It's 1916. Mitchum is a quiet, middle-aged school teacher who marries a pretty young local girl (Miles) in the small Northern Ireland village where he teaches. Their's is not a loveless union but it is uninspired. Then, tragically, she falls passionately in love with with a doubly forbidden lover. Her torrid affair is with a shell-shocked British officer who was sent to monitor the activities of the local IRA. When their forbidden affair is discovered, the passions in the little village boil over. Stunning photography. Two Oscars.

Sex ◢ Nud ◢ Viol ◢ Lang □ AdSit ◢

A: Sarah Miles, Robert Mitchum, Christopher Jones, John Mills, Trevor Howard, Leo McKern

Distributed By MGM/UA Home Video M700163

SAILOR WHO FELL FROM GRACE WITH THE SEA, THE

The sailor who fell from grace with the sea

D: Lewis John Carlino — 105 m

R | DMA ROM | 1976 | COLOR

7 Stirring and erotic romantic drama. A lonely British widow (Miles) meets an American merchant seaman (Kristofferson) and a passionate romance develops between them. Miles sees the sailor as a symbol of honor and trust. However, her troubled young son, who is at first pleased that his mother has someone, is soon convinced by his friends that the sailor won't be true to her and will revert back to sailor ways. Over time, the boy turns violent and a plot for murder develops. The film stays true to Yukio Mishima's novel. The ending is quite bizarre.

Sex ■ Nud ■ Viol ■ Lang ■ AdSit ■

A: Sarah Miles, Kris Kristofferson, Jonathan Kanh, Margo Cunningham, Earl Rhodes

© GOODTIMES 9181

SAINT JACK

D: Peter Bogdanovich — 112 m

R | DMA | 1979 | COLOR

6 A curious character profile. Jack Flowers (Gazzara) is an American businessman in Singapore. He is a simple, good-hearted man who doesn't make judgments on what people do. So, at night, he is also a pimp and hopes to get rich running the classiest whorehouse in town by specializing in the American servicemen on vacation from the Vietnam War. However, the Chinese competition decides he is infringing on their business and they destroy his operation, exposing him to a flood of political corruption. A vivid portrayal of a corrupt and sinful Singapore during the Vietnan war.

Sex □ Nud ◢ Viol □ Lang ■ AdSit ◢

A: Ben Gazzara, Denholm Elliott, James Villiers, David Lazenby

© LIVE HOME VIDEO VA4067

SAINT OF FORT WASHINGTON

D: Tim Hunter — 103 m

R | DMA | 1993 | COLOR

7 Danny Glover and Matt Dillon are homeless men who meet one cold night at an armory that provides temporary shelter. Glover instructs him to pin his shoes under the bedposts to keep them from being stolen and later also protects him from being beaten. Dillon is a meek schizophrenic who hears voices and fancies himself a photographer, even though his camera has no film. Glover is a veteran of the streets. He has a wife and two daughters that he hasn't seen in years and shrapnel in his leg from Vietnam. The two agree to take care of each other and share one simple dream: of getting their own apartment by selling fruit. This is a haunting portrait of life in the streets.

Sex □ Nud □ Viol ◢ Lang ■ AdSit ■

A: Danny Glover, Matt Dillon, Rick Aviles, Nina Slemaszko, Ving Rhames, Joe Seneca

© WARNER HOME VIDEO 12805

SALVADOR

D: Oliver Stone — 122 m

R | ACT DMA | 1985 | COLOR

8 Intense and explosive film revealing the human tragedies of El Salvador in 1980! Based on a photojournalist's real-life experiences at the time, but did not become public until years later. Richard Boyle (Woods) is an American photojournalist sent to the embattled country to capture the nature of that war on film. He views first hand, and through the lenses of his camera, the murderous inhumanities and corruption that are a part of daily living there and raises questions about the motivations of the US-backed military. Woods's gripping performance was Oscar nominated. Intense and realistic.

Sex ◢ Nud ◢ Viol ■ Lang ■ AdSit ■

A: James Woods, James Belushi, John Savage, Cynthia Gibb, Elpidia Carrillo, Michael Murphy

© LIVE HOME VIDEO VA5167

SAMMY AND ROSIE GET LAID

D: Stephen Frears — 97 m

NR | COM DMA | 1987 | COLOR

7 A very direct little British sex comedy that wastes no time getting right to the heart of matter. A radical young married couple (Din and Barber) live in London and share a very sexually liberated and open marriage. When Kapoor, Din's very traditional but wealthy Pakistani father, comes for a visit, his whole world is shaken by their behavior. Whatever happened to the England he used to know? The sexual exploits and political views of the 80's, particularly of Rosie, go completely unchecked. But, if Sammy and Rosie want some of daddy's money they are going to have to produce an heir. Darkly funny - not for all tastes.

Sex ◢ Nud ■ Viol ◢ Lang ◢ AdSit ■

A: Claire Bloom, Roland Gift, Shashi Kapoor, Frances Barber, Ayub Khan Din, Wendy Gazelle

© WARNER HOME VIDEO 763

SAND PEBBLES, THE

D: Robert Wise — 180 m

NR | SUS DMA ACT | 1966 | COLOR

8 Sprawling, intelligent and compelling epic film which garnered a nomination for Best Picture and numerous other technical Oscar nominations. An exceptionally strong performance from McQueen drives this film about a cynical, normally reclusive sailor assigned to the engine room of an American gunboat patrolling the Yangtze river of China about 1926... just as civil war begins. Commander Crenna must be diplomatic. He represents the United States. But McQueen will not watch passively as his best friend is tortured. And he also moves aggressively to protect a missionary's daughter.

Sex □ Nud □ Viol ◢ Lang □ AdSit ◢

A: Steve McQueen, Richard Crenna, Candice Bergen, Richard Attenborough, Mako, Gavin MacLeod

© FOXVIDEO 1029

SARAFINA!

D: Darrell James Roodt — 98 m

PG-13 | MUS DMA | 1992 | COLOR

6 This film version of the hit Broadway musical is a near miss for most of the typical public, but it will satisfy some. Sarafina is a black teenage girl living in the South African segregated township of Soweto. She dreams of becoming a movie star but idolizes Nelson Mandella and becomes politicized by the brutalities of the white soldiers who terrorize the people. She and the other students rally around a charismatic history teacher (Goldberg) who teaches them to be proud and reject apartheid. The energetic Afro-pop music and dancing invigorates the plot which is well intentioned but too heavy handed.

Sex □ Nud □ Viol ■ Lang ◢ AdSit ◢

A: Whoopi Goldberg, Miriam Makeba, Leleti Khumalo, John Kani, Mbongeni Ngema

© TOUCHSTONE HOME VIDEO 1595

SARAH, PLAIN AND TALL

D: Glenn Jordan — 98 m

G | ROM DMA | 1991 | COLOR

8 Endearing and wonderfully acted sentimental charmer, produced to very high standards for TV's "Hallmark Hall of Fame." In 1910, a lonely Kansas farmer and widower (Walken), with two motherless children, advertises back East for a wife. Glen Close is a spinsterly Maine schoolteacher who agrees to a one-month sexless trial "marriage." When she arrives, she finds two kids who quickly warm to her mothering. Her month is an eventful one - they are hit with a big storm and she helps a neighbor give birth, but Walken still grieves for his long-dead wife and it looks at first like her time was wasted.

Sex □ Nud □ Viol □ Lang □ AdSit □

A: Glenn Close, Christopher Walken, Lexi Randall, Margaret Sophie Stein, Jon De Vries, Christopher Bell

© REPUBLIC PICTURES HOME VIDEO 1821

SATURDAY NIGHT FEVER

D: John Badham — 118 m

R | DMA ROM MUS | 1977 | COLOR

8 Huge box office smash! Tony (Travolta) is just a paint salesman in Brooklyn but on Saturday night, the highlight of his week, he dances at the neighborhood disco where he's the star. He decides to take a shot at the big time with a new partner (Gorney) and enters a dance contest that he hopes will serve as a springboard to the place where dreams come true - Manhattan. Instead, he unexpectedly begins to question the shallowness of his existence. The pulse pounding soundtrack and beat of the Bee Gee's helped to define the dynamic dance mood of '70s disco and of an era. Electric!

Sex ◢ Nud ◢ Viol □ Lang ■ AdSit ■

A: John Travolta, Karen Lynn Gorney, Donna Pescow, Barry Miller, Joseph Cali, Paul Pape

© PARAMOUNT HOME VIDEO 1113

SAVE THE TIGER

D: John G. Avildsen — 100 m

R | DMA | 1973 | COLOR

6 Serious and involving, but depressing, exploration of the pressures created by the pursuit of the American Dream. Jack Lemon won an Oscar for his portrayal of a formerly successful businessman whose garment business is now on the ropes. Desperate, he wants to burn the place down for the insurance money, but he has to fight his partner Jack Gilford, who doesn't want him to do it. Lemon is at the end of his rope and just about to lose his mind. Sometimes slow moving, but also a very powerful statement.

Sex □ Nud □ Viol □ Lang ■ AdSit ■

A: Jack Lemmon, Jack Gilford, Patricia Smith, Laurie Heineman

© PARAMOUNT HOME VIDEO 8479

SAYONARA

D: Joshua Logan — 147 m

NR | ROM DMA | 1957 | COLOR

9 Thought provoking, highly regarded and deeply affecting film from James Michener. It is a story of romance and love, but also of the conflict love creates when cultures and human nature clashes. This Best Picture nominee is set just after WWII in occupied Japan. Brando is a racist American air ace who has his self-assured notions severely tested when the government's refusal to allow the interracial marriage of Red Buttons and Miyoshi Umeki precipitates their suicide pact. His notions are really challenged when he falls in love with a beautiful Japanese dancer himself. Winner of 4 Oscars.

Sex □ Nud □ Viol □ Lang ◢ AdSit ◢

A: Marlon Brando, James Garner, Ricardo Montalban, Red Buttons, Miyoshi Umeki, Miiko Taka

© CBS/FOX VIDEO 7146

SCANDAL

D: Michael Caton-Jones 106 m

R | DMA | 1989 | COLOR | Sex | Nud | Viol | Lang | AdSit

8 Spicy retelling of England's infamous Profumo sex-scandal of the mid-1960s. An impressionable and beautiful young showgirl named Christine Keeler gains the attention of one of London's socialite power-brokers. He initiates her into the glamorous, exciting and fun world of swinging fraternizations with the rich and powerful. She and her female friend (Fonda) reign over their social domain until she tells the press of her simultaneous relationships both with England's ruling conservative party Secretary of State and a suspected Soviet spy. True story.

A: John Hurt, Joanne Whalley-Kilmer, Ian McKellen, Bridget Fonda, Leslie Phillips, Britt Ekland

© HBO VIDEO 0212

SCARECROW

D: Jerry Schatzberg 112 m

R | DMA | 1973 | COLOR | Sex | Nud | Viol | Lang | AdSit

6 Hackman, an ex-con, dreams of opening a carwash business in Pittsburgh with the savings he has accumulated in prison. In California he meets Pacino, a seaman just back from a five year trip, after abandoning his pregnant wife in Detroit. The pair hit it off and team up for a cross-country journey in search of their dreams, staying with old friends along the way. However, the closer they get to the end of the journey, the more worried Pacino becomes. After calling his wife, he has a nervous breakdown and Hackman has to use his savings, his dream, to help his friend to survive.

A: Gene Hackman, Al Pacino, Dorothy Tristan, Eileen Brennan, Ann Wedgeworth, Richard Lynch

© WARNER HOME VIDEO 11098

SCARLETT

D: John Erman 360 m

NR | ROM DMA | 1994 | COLOR | Sex | Nud | Viol | Lang | AdSit

7 This expensive and much ballyhooed 6-hour epic is the made-for-TV mini-series which supposedly picks up where GONE WITH THE WIND left off. Spoiled Southern belle Scarlett O'Hara is now determined to win back the heart of the gambler cad Rhett Butler. She simply must have him back, and she pursues him everywhere at all cost. Essentially, this is a lushly produced soap opera which will more than maintain the rapt attention of the romantics, but it will not inspire them.

A: Joanne Whalley-Kilmer, Timothy Dalton, Ann-Margret, Paul Winfield, Annabeth Gish, John Gielgud

© CABIN FEVER ENTERTAINMENT 9506

SCENES FROM A MALL

D: Paul Mazursky 87 m

R | COM DMA | 1991 | COLOR | Sex | Nud | Viol | Lang | AdSit

6 Fans of Woody Allen and Bette Midler should get a kick out of this film - others may have a tougher time with it. Trendy California couple Midler and Allen are shopping at an upscale mall for gifts and apparel for their 16th anniversary party the following night, when Allen's conscience gets the best of him and he confesses that he has had an affair. They fight and make up. And then Midler turns around and confesses the very same sin to him. Will they even make it through to tomorrow? Dramatic tension and mildly funny moments ensue in this comedy/drama.

A: Bette Midler, Woody Allen, Bill Irwin, Daren Firestone, Rebecca Nickels, Paul Mazursky

© TOUCHSTONE HOME VIDEO 1163

SCENES FROM A MARRIAGE

D: Ingmar Bergman 168 m

PG | FOR DMA ROM | 1973 | COLOR | Sex | Nud | Viol | Lang | AdSit

9 Very highly acclaimed by the critics and winner of many awards. This is a challenging, very in-depth and sometimes very truthful, therefore quite painful, look at a relationship between two people over 20 years. Originally made as six 50-minute segments for a Swedish TV mini-series by famed director Ingmar Bergman, it is here edited down to 168 minutes. The two are married for ten years, when there is a painful breakup after he leaves her for a younger woman. They both marry others, only to later reconcile into a new and more mature relationship. Dubbed.

A: Liv Ullmann, Erland Josephson, Bibi Andersson, Jan Malmsjo, Anita Wall, Gunnel Lindblom

© COLUMBIA TRISTAR HOME VIDEO VCF3225

SCENT OF A WOMAN

D: Martin Brest 157 m

R | DMA | 1992 | COLOR | Sex | Nud | Viol | Lang | AdSit

8 Al Pacino won Best Actor Oscar as Lieutenant Colonel Frank Slade, a 26-year career Army man. A brilliant officer, he was destined for big things, but his wildness and his mouth always got in the way. Now, he is a bitter alcoholic living in a small apartment at his niece's house after being blinded when juggled hand grenades in a stunt. His niece is going way for the Thanksgiving weekend so she has hired a young prep student with troubles of his own to watch him. Instead, Colonel Slade has decided to take the boy to have one last glorious weekend in New York City before killing himself, but his plans get changed. Believable, very enjoyable and leaves you feeling good.

A: Al Pacino, Chris O'Donnell, Gabrielle Anwar, James Rebhorn, Richard Bradford, Bradley Whitford

© MCA/UNIVERSAL HOME VIDEO, INC. 81283

SCHINDLER'S LIST

D: Steven Spielberg 197 m

R | DMA WAR | 1994 | B&W | Sex | Nud | Viol | Lang | AdSit

10 Mind-boggling true story. Oscar Schindler was a promoter, a playboy and a Nazi in Krakow, Poland. In 1939, he seized the opportunity to make his fortune by arm-twisting several wealthy Jews from the ghetto into investing in a new factory that he would front. The company was to make pots for the German war machine with Jewish slave labor. He was a success and did make a fortune, but it also forced him daily to witness the mindless cruelty and absolute horror of the Nazis. His realization transformed him. Soon he was struggling to protect his workers, ultimately even purchasing 1100 Jews from the Nazis. Riveting and true. 10 Oscar nominations, won Best Picture.

A: Liam Neeson, Ralph Fiennes, Ben Kingsley, Caroline Goodall, Jonathan Sagalle, Embeth Davidtz

© MCA/UNIVERSAL HOME VIDEO, INC. 82153

SCHOOL TIES

D: Robert Mandel 110 m

PG-13 | DMA | 1992 | COLOR | Sex | Nud | Viol | Lang | AdSit

7 A 1950's working class kid with a good throwing arm gets a big break and a chance to go to Harvard when an upper-crust prep school needs a star quarterback to have a winning season. Brendan Fraser becomes the team hero and a popular man on campus in spite of being poor. However, the bubble bursts when it also becomes known that he is a Jew. Predictable and a little slow to get started, but well acted with convincing performances.

A: Brendan Fraser, Chris O'Donnell, Andrew Lowery, Matt Damon, Randall Batinkoff, Amy Locane

© PARAMOUNT HOME VIDEO 32290

SEANCE ON A WET AFTERNOON

D: Bryan Forbes 115 m

NR | SUS DMA | 1964 | B&W | Sex | Nud | Viol | Lang | AdSit

8 Excellent psychological drama! An eccentric psychic medium (Stanley), who is barely able to maintain her grip on sanity after the loss of her baby, invents a shady scheme to further her career. She decides to have her weak-willed husband (Attenborough) kidnap a wealthy young girl, collect the ransom and then she can reveal the girl's hiding place during a seance to become famous. The plot is full of unpredictable twists and turns, because her plan does not go off as planned. Stanley's outstanding performance of the off-balance psychic earned her an Oscar nomination.

A: Richard Attenborough, Kim Stanley, Patrick Magee, Nanette Newman, Judith Donner, Gerald Sim

© HOME VISION SEA 030

SEARCHING FOR BOBBY FISCHER

D: Steven Zaillian 111 m

PG | DMA | 1993 | COLOR | Sex | Nud | Viol | Lang | AdSit

8 Who would of thought that a movie about chess would be so interesting, fun and exciting too. For some chess is a game, for some it is war and for some it is an obsession. This is the story of 7-year old Josh who has a genius for chess. For him chess is fun and it is an artform, like it was for American and world champion Bobby Fischer. That makes Josh the focus of everyone's aspirations. In him, they see the next Fischer and they are determined to see that dream, their dream, come true. They are the chess hustler in the park, his chess master instructor and his own father. Josh doesn't want to disappoint anyone, he only wants to have fun. Based on truth.

A: Max Pomerane, Joe Montegna, Joan Allen, Ben Kingsley, Laurence Fishburne, Robert Stephens

© PARAMOUNT HOME VIDEO 32673

SECRET CEREMONY

D: Joseph Losey 109 m

R | DMA | 1968 | COLOR | Sex | Nud | Viol | Lang | AdSit

7 Intriguing, psychological tale of sex, murder and suicide. Farrow plays a psychotic nympho who has seduced her stepfather (Mitchum) and caused her mother's marriage to fail. When her mother dies, the guilt-ridden girl kidnaps an aging prostitute (Taylor) because she bears a striking resemblance to her. However, Taylor gradually eases into the role of Farrow's mother because Taylor also thinks that the girl looks a great deal like her own deceased daughter. It is then that Mitchum reappears and threatens their relationship, telling the truth of what Farrow has done. Quite good and very different.

A: Elizabeth Taylor, Mia Farrow, Robert Mitchum, Pamela Brown, Peggy Ashcroft

© MCA/UNIVERSAL HOME VIDEO, INC.

SECRET GARDEN, THE

D: Agnieszka Holland 103 m

PG | DMA CLD | 1993 | COLOR | Sex | Nud | Viol | Lang | AdSit

9 A sumptuously photographed screen adaptation of Frances Hodgson Burnett's classic 1911 novel. Ten-year-old Mary is a sad orphaned girl who has been returned to England from India after her parents were killed. She is to live with her cold uncle, who is still mourning his wife's death, and his bed-ridden ten-year-old son. Their huge mansion, on the cold and misty moors, is a lifeless loveless place. Mary begins to explore her new home and discovers a garden that has been locked away since her aunt's death. She begins to nurture the neglected garden and to draw out her sick cousin. Slowly life begins to return to them all. Excellent, but too intense and slow for young kids. 10 and up.

A: Kate Maberly, Heydon Prowse, Andrew Knott, John Lynch, Laura Crossley, Maggie Smith

© WARNER HOME VIDEO 19000

D M A

SEDUCTION OF JOE TYNAN, THE

D: Jerry Schatzberg 107 m

R | DMA | 1979 | COLOR | Sex Nud Viol Lang AdSit

8 A young liberal senator (Alda) from New York seems to have it all. He is suave, bright, rapidly rising to success and at ease with his constituents. To top it off, he has a lovely wife (Harris). But he is slowly corrupted by the world in which he lives. He quickly disregards his conscience to begin an affair with a beautiful labor attorney (Streep) while working on a project with her, and he also sells out an older colleague just to gain some publicity. Power, and the pursuit of it, corrupts. Alda wrote this sometimes good and sometimes funny screenplay, tailor-making the lead role for himself.

A: Alan Alda, Meryl Streep, Barbara Harris, Rip Torn, Melvyn Douglas

© MCA/UNIVERSAL HOME VIDEO, INC. 66008

SEIZE THE DAY

D: Fielder Cook 93 m

NR | DMA | 1986 | COLOR | Sex Nud Viol Lang AdSit

8 An excellent and insightful look at the steady disintegration of one man's life. A washed up salesman (Williams), out of luck and out of money, returns to his native New York hoping to get some help from his cold-hearted father (Wiseman). Turned down, Williams looks to his friends for comfort, but they also offer little solace. In desperation, he gambles the very last of his savings on a risky investment in the commodities market. Williams's first dramatic role was faithfully adapted from the novella by Saul Bellow. This is not light entertainment, this is the dramatic destruction of a desperate man.

A: Robin Williams, Joseph Wiseman, Jerry Stiller, Glenne Headly

© HBO VIDEO TVA9970

SEPARATE BUT EQUAL

D: George Stevens, Jr. 193 m

PG | DMA | 1991 | COLOR | Sex Nud Viol Lang AdSit

9 Subtly intelligent and totally absorbing made-for-cable-TV film. In one of his finest performances, Poitier is stunning as Thurgood Marshall, the brilliant NAACP lawyer who fought a four-year battle that resulted in the famous Supreme Court ruling of 1954: Brown vs. Board of Education. This momentous ruling declared that separate was inherently not equal. All performances, and the entire play itself, are doubly effective because none of the people in it, on either side, are not portrayed as simplistic caricatures, but as real people - neither all good, nor all bad. Gripping and powerful.

A: Sidney Poitier, Burt Lancaster, Richard Kiley, Cleavon Little, John McMartin

© REPUBLIC PICTURES HOME VIDEO 3617

SEPARATE TABLES

D: Delbert Mann 118 m

NR | DMA ROM | 1958 | B&W | Sex Nud Viol Lang AdSit

8 Winner of 7 Oscar nominations, including Best Picture. It is an emotional peek into troubled lives. Based on the play by Terence Rattigan, the guests at a small British seaside hotel develop cautious relationships with each other as they try to sort out their troubled lives. Lancaster and Hayworth are a divorced couple trying to mend their relationship, while Lancaster's lover (Hiller) looks on. The lonely daughter (Kerr) of an overbearing and domineering mother (Cooper) is attracted to a boastful war hero (Niven). Very well-acted, this pair of one-act plays won Niven and Hiller Oscars.

A: Rita Hayworth, Deborah Kerr, David Niven, Wendy Hiller, Burt Lancaster, Gladys Cooper

Distributed By MGM/UA Home Video M301759

SERGEANT RUTLEDGE

D: John Ford 112 m

WST DMA | 1960 | Sex Nud Viol Lang AdSit

8 In the aftermath of the Civil War, two U.S. Calvary units were created specifically for black soldiers. These units served with distinction in helping to open the developing West. The plains Indians came to call these men Buffalo soldiers. Famed Western director John Ford uses that actual situation to create a story of one black soldier who has been wrongly accused of rape and murder. Sergeant Rutledge (Woody Strode) is on trial and his story is told in a series of flashbacks. Lt. Cantrell (Jeffrey Hunter) defends Rutledge as witnesses come to the stand to tell their stories, which are then woven into his. Very unusual for the time. Very interesting material, well presented.

A: Jeffrey Hunter, Woody Strode, Constance Towers, Billie Burke, Carleton Young, Juano Hernandez

© WARNER HOME VIDEO 12272

SERGEANT RYKER

D: Buzz Kulik 85 m

NR | DMA WAR | 1968 | COLOR | Sex Nud Viol Lang AdSit

7 Sgt. Paul Ryker has been accused of defecting to Communist China during the Korean War. He claims that he was actually on a secret mission behind enemy lines, but his story doesn't agree with the evidence and he is convicted. The prosecuting attorney believes that Ryker's attorney was incompetent. He reviews the case and succeeds in getting the case reopened, but in the process he has fallen in love with Ryker's wife and is himself now being charged for criminal misconduct. Based upon a made-for-TV film.

A: Lee Marvin, Bradford Dillman, Vera Miles, Peter Graves, Lloyd Nolan, Murral Hamilton

© GOODTIMES 4115

SERPICO

D: Sidney Lumet 130 m

R | CRM ACT DMA | 1973 | COLOR | Sex Nud Viol Lang AdSit

10 Extremely tough and compelling police drama, based upon the true-life story of Frank Serpico, a cop whose public testimony in the early 70s about corruption and bribery, ripped open the NYC police department. Pacino's characterization is amazing. Serpico is an oddball, idealistic and obsessive cop who doesn't fit in as a regular cop, but his non-conformism is an asset as an undercover cop. It is as an undercover cop that he is exposed to the corrupt underbelly of the police force itself. When some corrupt cops find him to be incorruptible, he is determined to be too great a risk and he is set up to be killed. Instead of dying, he survived to testify against them.

A: Al Pacino, John Randolph, Jack Kehoe, Biff McGuire, Barbara Eda-Young, Tony Roberts

© PARAMOUNT HOME VIDEO 8689

SERVANT, THE

D: Joseph Losey 112 m

NR | DMA | 1963 | B&W | Sex Nud Viol Lang AdSit

8 A shocking and highly plausible psychological thriller from England. A decadent and lazy, wealthy London playboy (Fox) needs someone to help him run his mansion, so he hires low-life Bogarde to be his personal valet and caretaker. Bogarde slowly begins to take over the life of his employer by taking advantage of his many weaknesses, sexual being foremost, and, in a psychological battle of wits, reduces Fox to being his mere puppet. The servant has become the master. This brooding character study is fascinating and well acted. Although a little slow to develop, patience is rewarded.

A: Dirk Bogarde, James Fox, Sarah Miles, Wendy Craig, Catherine Lacey, Patrick Magee

© CONGRESS VIDEO GROUP 60880

SEVEN BEAUTIES

D: Lina Wertmuller 116 m

R | FOR DMA COM | 1976 | COLOR | Sex Nud Viol Lang AdSit

8 Award-winning, powerful and near-surrealist story of a man willing to sacrifice anything to survive. A small-time hood in WWII Italy trys to commit a murder but fails miserably and is caught. He pleads insanity rather than go to prison. Finding that intolerable, he accepts the opportunity to join the army, but deserts when sent to the Russian front - for which he is sent to a concentration camp where he encounters more intensely grotesque horrors. He seduces an obese, sadistic prison warden to get out. The raw ugliness his situations depicted will test your sensibilities. Ardent film fans only.

A: Giancarlo Giannini, Fernando Rey, Shirley Stoler, Elena Fiore, Enzo Vitale

© COLUMBIA TRISTAR HOME VIDEO 60203

SEVEN DAYS IN MAY

D: John Frankenheimer 118 m

NR | SUS DMA | 1964 | B&W | Sex Nud Viol Lang AdSit

8 A tense and entirely believable nail-biter of how it really might happen... the military's overthrow of the US government. An intelligent screenplay from Rod Serling builds tension slowly but unalterably as an Army colonel's (Douglas) suspicions about the intentions of a right-wing general (Lancaster) develop into the reality that there is an active plot within the Pentagon to overthrow the President (March). Powerful climax. Terrific performances by an all-star cast. See also THE MANCHURIAN CANDIDATE.

A: Burt Lancaster, Kirk Douglas, Fredric March, Ava Gardner, Edmond O'Brien, Martin Balsam

© WARNER HOME VIDEO 12776

SEVENTH SEAL, THE

D: Ingmar Bergman 96 m

NR | FOR DMA | 1956 | B&W | Sex Nud Viol Lang AdSit

10 Acclaimed as being one of the greatest works ever in cinema, and the best-known effort of famed director Ingmar Bergman. This is very serious and heavy material, but it also tackles some very profound philosophical questions that no other film has ever explored quite so deeply. Von Sydow plays a 14th-century knight finding his way back home from the Crusades, traveling though a countryside that is infested with plague and death. Meeting the figure of Death on the road, he bargains with Death, through a chess game, for more time to learn life's meanings. Subtitles or dubbed.

A: Gunnar Bjornstrand, Max von Sydow, Bibi Andersson, Nils Poppe, Maud Hansson, Bengt Ekerot

© HOME VISION SEV 090

SEX, LIES AND VIDEOTAPE

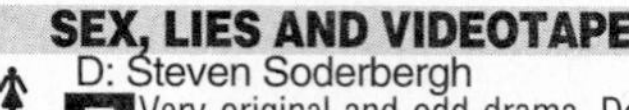

D: Steven Soderbergh 99 m

R | DMA | 1989 | COLOR | Sex Nud Viol Lang AdSit

7 Very original and odd drama. Double winner at Cannes and Oscar-nominated for Screenplay. Spader visits his old friend Gallagher who is now a successful attorney and married to MacDowell. Gallagher has become selfish and MacDowell has lost interest in him, so he begins a torrid affair with her sultry sister, San Giacomo. Spader, however, is impotent and receives his only gratification from interviewing women on videotape regarding their sex lives. When MacDowell learns of her husband's affair, she turns to Spader and wants to be on one of his tapes. Talky and slow, but quite interesting.

A: James Spader, Peter Gallagher, Andie MacDowell, Laura San Giacomo

© NEW LINE HOME VIDEO 90483

SHADOWLANDS

D: Richard Attenborough — 133 m

PG | ROM DMA | 1993 | COLOR

9 Wonderful, wrenching and true. English writer C.S. Lewis had won great fame from his children's classic "Chronicles of Narnia". In 1952, he was a middle-aged man, long a confirmed bachelor and a professor at Oxford. He was a master of his world of books. But that Christmas, he met an American writer. She was only in England for a short time with her son, who wanted to meet the author of his favorite book. Their relationship was very polite, but when she left, he felt her absence. Months later, she returned as a divorced woman and it was then that he began to feel love and also, for the first time, profoundly alive. Flawless in all aspects. Hopkins is brilliant.

Sex / Nud / Viol / Lang / AdSit

A: Anthony Hopkins, Debra Winger, Edward Hardwicke, John Wood, Michael Denison, Joseph Mazzello

© HBO VIDEO 90968

SHADOW OF THE WOLF

D: Jacques Dorfman — 108 m

PG-13 | DMA ACT | 1993 | COLOR

7 Carefully drawn realistic portrait of the lifestyle of the Inuit of northern Canada. Set during the 1930s, this is the story of a young Inuit who rebels against the corruption brought to his people by the invasion of the whites. His people have forgotten the old ways and can no longer live without the white man's tools. His resentment leads him into a violent conflict with his father, who is the leader of the group. He leaves, but not before killing a corrupt white trader and taking a young woman away from his father. He struggles to survive, to find himself and to evade the white policeman who has come to find him.

Sex / Nud / Viol / Lang / AdSit

A: Lou Diamond Phillips, Jennifer Tilly, Tosiroer Mifune, Donald Sutherland, Bernard-Pierre Donnadieu

© COLUMBIA TRISTAR HOME VIDEO 59893

SHAG: THE MOVIE

D: Zelda Barron — 96 m

PG | DMA COM | 1989 | COLOR

7 Surprisingly pleasing female coming-of-age-type movie, set in the South in the summer of 1963. Four best friends from high school decide to spend one last fling together before one gets married, one leaves town and two go off to college. They go to Myrtle Beach for their last weekend of fun at a Shag contest (briefly-popular type of '60s dance). The movie does not open any new ground here, but the four leads are very appealing. Sort of a throwback to the BEACH PARTY movies, with a bit of DIRTY DANCING thrown in. Great '60s sound track and good period details.

Sex / Nud / Viol / Lang / AdSit

A: Phoebe Cates, Annabeth Gish, Bridget Fonda, Tyrone Power, Jr., Robert Rusler, Page Hannah

© HBO VIDEO 0214

SHAMPOO

D: Hal Ashby — 112 m

R | COM DMA | 1975 | COLOR

7 A provocative sex comedy set in liberated 1968 Southern California. Warren Beatty is sexy and a top-notch hairdresser in Beverly Hills, but not too bright. He wants to open his own shop and needs to borrow the money from investment counselor, Jack Warden. However, he is sleeping with Warden's wife, his mistress and his daughter; plus he's also trying to keep up his relationship with his girlfriend Goldie Hawn. This is an interesting comedic study, exploring the morals of the time and the level of satisfaction or dissatisfaction that so much sex brings. Funny, but not uproarious. Lee Grant won an Oscar.

Sex / Nud / Viol / Lang / AdSit

A: Warren Beatty, Lee Grant, Jack Warden, Julie Christie, Goldie Hawn, Carrie Fisher

© GOODTIMES 4223

SHAWSHANK REDEMPTION

D: Frank Darabont — 142 m

R | DMA | 1994 | COLOR

8 This is a powerful but grim drama concerning the nature of lives of the people we place behind bars. Its primary focus is upon Tim Robbins as a banker who is sent to prison in 1947 for the murder of his wife and her lover; and, his long-term friendship with another con, Morgan Freeman. Over the course of their 20 years together, they develop a deep friendship and respect for one another as they both struggle to survive their days and the brutality of a system from which there is no escape. Yet, through persistence and shear force of will, they do manage fill their empty days and even achieve an ultimate victory. Excellent performances. Nominated for seven Oscars.

Sex / Nud / Viol / Lang / AdSit

A: Tim Robbins, Morgan Freeman, Bob Gunton, William Sadler, Clancy Brown, James Whitmore

© COLUMBIA TRISTAR HOME VIDEO 74593

SHELTERING SKY, THE

D: Bernardo Bertolucci — 139 m

R | DMA | 1990 | COLOR

6 Beautifully photographed and well acted, but long, with an enigmatic story line. Not for everyone. Much has been left out and it will be very difficult to understand unless you have read the book. An American couple, married for ten years but with a troubled relationship, have gone in search of adventure in North Africa immediately after WWII. They are on an intellectual search of discovery and they have taken along with them a socialite friend who becomes the third leg of a romantic triangle. The film's confusion in part stems from attempts to non-verbally depict the characters' intense feelings and emotions through the use of various odd camera angles and long shots.

Sex / Nud / Viol / Lang / AdSit

A: Debra Winger, John Malkovich, Campbell Scott, Jill Bennett, Timothy Spall, Eric Vu-an

© WARNER HOME VIDEO 12062

SHENANDOAH

D: Andrew V. McLaglen — 106 m

NR | WST DMA ACT | 1965 | COLOR

9 Emotional Western that captures well the heartbreak of the Civil War. Jimmy Stewart is a widowed father and farmer in Virginia, which was a major crossroads for both armies of the Civil War. Stewart wants no part of this war and vows to stay out of it. But when his young son is arrested after being mistaken for a rebel because he wore the wrong hat, Stewart gathers up the rest of his boys for a search to get their brother back. However, while on their long trip, the war arrives at his farm. This is a large scale picture that is very moving, emotionally charged and haunting. Katharine Ross's debut.

Sex / Nud / Viol / Lang / AdSit

A: James Stewart, Doug McClure, Glenn Corbett, Patrick Wayne, Katharine Ross, George Kennedy

© MCA/UNIVERSAL HOME VIDEO, INC. 55033

SHIP OF FOOLS

D: Stanley Kramer — 149 m

NR | DMA | 1965 | B&W

9 A powerhouse film that is part heavy drama and part soap opera. It is an engrossing dissection of the lives and the attitudes of the people aboard a German ship sailing from Mexico to Germany in 1933. The ship's atmosphere is saturated with the feelings of those times, born of the depression and the rise of Nazism. There is a neurotic divorcee, a baseball player, an anti-Semite and the ship's doctor, who is in love with a depressed drug addict. Huge all-star cast. Winner of Best Cinematography. Nominated for Best Picture and 7 other Oscars.

Sex / Nud / Viol / Lang / AdSit

A: Vivien Leigh, Simone Signoret, Oskar Werner, Heinz Ruehmann, Jose Ferrer, Lee Marvin

© COLUMBIA TRISTAR HOME VIDEO 60542

SHIRLEY VALENTINE

D: Lewis Gilbert — 108 m

R | COM ROM DMA | 1989 | COLOR

8 Frolicsome fun little comedy in which a frumpy middle-aged London housewife looks out upon her comfortable but routine existence and decides that life is passing her by. She loves her husband, but she is bored. So, when she gets a chance to go to Greece, she takes it; and when her husband won't go with her, she goes alone. In beautiful Greece she discovers a freedom that she hasn't known and becomes reborn by a brief romantic interlude with a local lothario. She has fun, recaptures the life that was slipping away and when her husband comes after her, he does too. Involving and fun.

Sex / Nud / Viol / Lang / AdSit

A: Pauline Collins, Tom Conti, Julia McKenzie, Alison Steadman, Joanna Lumley, Bernard Hill

© PARAMOUNT HOME VIDEO 32248

SHOCK CORRIDOR

D: Samuel Fuller — 101 m

NR | DMA MYS | 1963 | B&W

8 Condemned by many at the time of its release as being trash, this film has risen to become a cult favorite. An immature and self-serving young journalist decides that he will be committed to an insane asylum so that he can uncover a murderer that the police can't -- and he will win himself a Pulitzer Prize in the process. So, he forces his stripteaser girlfriend to claim that she is his sister and that he has been making advances to her. Once inside, he is confronted with the real pain of the other inmates and the delusions they use to escape. After being attacked by nymphomaniacs and convincing himself that his girlfriend is cheating, he too begins to lose his mind.

Sex / Nud / Viol / Lang / AdSit

A: Peter Breck, Constance Towers, James Best, Hari Rhodes, Gen Evans, Larry Tucker

© HOME VISION SHO 01

SHOGUN

D: Jerry London — 550 m

NR | DMA ROM ACT | 1980 | COLOR

10 This is a landmark made-for-television mini-series based upon James Clavell's novel. It is the spellbinding epic story of a 17th-century English navigator, Blackthorne (Chamberlain), who is shipwrecked in Japan. Japan is a feudal society in which the nobility, the Samurai, have total and utter control over their lands and the people who go with them. Their master is the Shogun, the military leader of all Japan. Blackthorne is in an alien world, but he gains their respect, masters their language, their society and their many-layered plots of intrigue - and he discovers love. Wonderful stuff.

Sex / Nud / Viol / Lang / AdSit

A: Richard Chamberlain, Toshiro Mifune, Yoko Shimada, Frankie Sakai, Alan Badel, Michael Hordern

© PARAMOUNT HOME VIDEO 80102

SHOOTING, THE

D: Monte Hellman — 82 m

G | WST DMA ACT | 1967 | COLOR

7 An unusual existential Western, similar to, but yet far from, the traditional shoot-'em-up. A strange woman (Perkins) hires bounty hunters Oates and Hutchins to escort her across the desert after her son is accidentally killed. A sadistic gunslinger (Nicholson) follows the trio and a bitter dispute develops between Nicholson and Hutchins over the woman and Nicholson kills him. The trio continue on through the relentless desert. Their water is running low and their horses are dying. This is not a typical Western, so don't expect a typical simple traditional resolution and ending.

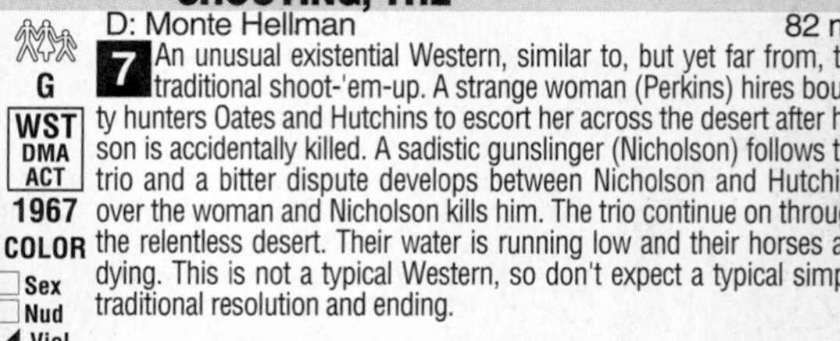

Sex / Nud / Viol / Lang / AdSit

A: Jack Nicholson, Will Hutchins, Warren Oates, Millie Perkins

© UNITED AMERICAN VIDEO CORP. 17193

DMA

SHOOTIST, THE

PG | WST DMA ACT | 1976 | COLOR | Sex | Nud | Viol | Lang | AdSit

D: Don Siegel — 100 m

9 An intelligent triumph for John Wayne. As Wayne himself was dying of cancer (his last film), so is his character - an old gunfighter named J.B. Books. The time is 1901. Books has spent his life as a gunman, but both he and his era are dying. All he wants now is to be left alone, but wherever he goes his reputation precedes him. His enemies and even total strangers seek him out. Everybody wants to kill him or to make a profit from him. He has no real friends - only the woman who owns the boarding house where he is staying and her hero-worshipping son. Very believable and moving. A fitting last film for Wayne.

A: John Wayne, Lauren Bacall, Ron Howard, James Stewart, Scatman Crothers, Richard Boone

© PARAMOUNT HOME VIDEO 8904

SHOOT THE MOON

R | DMA | 1981 | COLOR | Sex | Nud | Viol | Lang | AdSit

D: Alan Parker — 125 m

7 A very emotional look at the demolition of a marriage and the destruction of a family. A successful writer (Finney) wakes up one day convinced that he is no longer happy or satisfied in his current life, so he leaves his wife (Keaton) and his four children for the arms of a younger woman (Allen). Keaton now struggles to deal with the hurt of rejection, to come to terms with her anger and to calm the anxieties of her four confused daughters. As the film progresses, the irony becomes more evident that it is Finney who has lost the most because the problem always was his, and now his family is gone, too. Turbulent, convincing and raw.

A: Diane Keaton, Albert Finney, Peter Weller, Karen Allen, Dana Hill, Viveka Davis

Distributed By MGM/UA Home Video M800141

SHOOT THE PIANO PLAYER

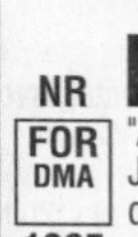

NR | FOR DMA | 1960 | B&W | Sex | Nud | Viol | Lang | AdSit

D: Francois Truffaut — 84 m

7 Film fans only, this is an interesting mixed bag of offbeat and colorful characters. A brilliant concert pianist (Aznavour) is haunted by his wife's suicide and begins a rapid spiral downward. Soon he finds himself playing to a sleazy crowd at a cheap Parisian cafe, where he is being pressured to get his life together by his new girlfriend, a waitress at the cafe. He gets into a fight with the bartender over her. And, his brother gets involved with the gangsters that frequent the place. This is an uncompromising New Wave film that takes the viewer across the emotional spectrum from dark comedy to tragedy. Subtitles.

A: Charles Aznavour, Marie Dubois, Nicole Berger, Michele Mercier

© HOME VISION SHO 100

SHOP ON MAIN STREET, THE

NR | FOR DMA | 1965 | B&W | Sex | Nud | Viol | Lang | AdSit

D: Jan Kadar, Elmar Klos — 128 m

9 Impassioned and bittersweet Best Foreign Film Oscar-winner. Tono, a man who cares nothing about politics, is appointed "Aryan Controller," by his Nazi brother. He is to oversee an elderly Jewish lady who owns a button shop in WWII Czechoslovakia. She doesn't understand and thinks he is her assistant. Gradually, the odd pair build a deep friendship, but when the Nazis mandate that all Jews are to be deported, Tono must make the decision of his life. The woman is deaf, poor, has no idea that there is even a war going on - and she trusts him completely. Sensitive and funny at times. Subtitles.

A: Josef Kroner, Hana Slivkova, Ida Kaminska, Frantisek Zvarik, Helena Zvarikov, Martin Holly

© HOME VISION SHO 110

SHORT CUTS

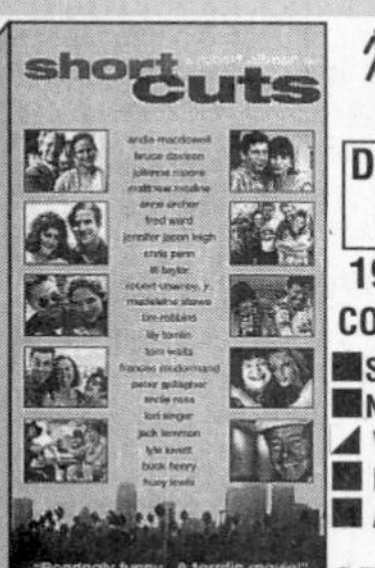

R | DMA | 1993 | COLOR | Sex | Nud | Viol | Lang | AdSit

D: Robert Altman — 189 m

9 Near unanimous accolades from virtually all the critics. Once again director Robert Altman takes his audience on an odyssey of the human condition. Intelligent viewers, with the patience to sit through over three hours of popping into and out of the lives of about two dozen various true-to-life people, will be richly rewarded. Each character has his own degree of desperation and his own way of dealing with it. However, it takes about an hour of watching before we even begin to understand the varying characters and how they are all inter-related. If you are interested in casual entertainment, this isn't it. If you enjoy trying to understand people this is a valuable tool.

A: Tim Robbins, Madeleine Stowe, Andie MacDowell, Jennifer Jason Lee, Anne Archer, Bruce Davidson

© TURNER HOME ENTERTAINMENT N4288

SILAS MARNER

NR | DMA | 1985 | COLOR | Sex | Nud | Viol | Lang | AdSit

D: Giles Foster — 92 m

8 Wonderful, touching BBC adaptation of George Eliot's classic tale. Set in 18th-century England, a crusty old linen weaver (Kingsley) has become a bitter man. His life has become dull and uninspired after he was wrongly accused of stealing. So, dejected and betrayed, he retreats into seclusion. However, a powerful twist of fate brings a young abandoned girl to his home and he is reborn. Suddenly, he has someone who needs him, and she brings a great deal of joy into his lonely existence and changes his life. However, everything is threatened when her real father returns. Enchanting.

A: Ben Kingsley, Jenny Agutter, Patrick Ryecart, Jonathan Coy, Freddie Jones, Frederick Treves

© CBS/FOX VIDEO 3711

SILENCE, THE

NR | FOR DMA | 1963 | B&W | Sex | Nud | Viol | Lang | AdSit

D: Ingmar Bergnam — 95 m

7 This is the third film of Bergman's religious trilogy (THROUGH A GLASS DARKLY and WINTER LIGHT) and here God is silent. Two sisters have been bound up in a love-hate incestuous relationship since childhood. The older is a lesbian but the younger is heterosexual and promiscuous. The two and the 10-year-old son of the younger are on a trip and stop in a hotel. There the younger sister picks up a waiter and inflames the older. Surreal and very dark. Subtitles.

A: Ingrid Thulin, Gunnel Lindblom, Jorgen Lindstrom, Hakan Jahnberg, Birger Malmsten

© HOME VISION SIL 100

SILENCE OF THE NORTH

PG | WST DMA ACT | 1981 | COLOR | Sex | Nud | Viol | Lang | AdSit

D: Allan Winton King — 94 m

7 Picturesque and inspirational. This is a story about a strong-willed woman (Burstyn) who falls in love with a rugged trapper (Skerritt) and follows him to live in the wilds of northern Canada. The story, based upon the actual autobiography of Olive Fredrickson, tells of her daily struggles, from being a young mother just after the turn of the 20th-century to later being a widow with three children. The wilderness can be cruel, and she and her family are left to brave nature's forces, survive cold winters and deal with tragedy on their own. Excellent.

A: Ellen Burstyn, Tom Skerritt, Gordon Pinsent, Jennifer McKinney, Colin Fox

© MCA/UNIVERSAL HOME VIDEO, INC. 71004

SILENT RUNNING

G | SF DMA | 1972 | COLOR | Sex | Nud | Viol | Lang | AdSit

D: Douglas Trumbull — 90 m

8 Dramatic family entertainment with a message. A spaceship floating about in space houses the only remaining vegetation left from an earth where a nuclear war has destroyed all plant life. Dern is a devoted botanist who has spent eight years tending this ark and now he has received an order from earth to destroy everything. The enormity of what is being asked of him is more than he can bare. Instead, he hijacks the vessel, kills off the other crewmen and takes his cargo into the safety of the rings of Saturn. His only companions now are the two robots with very human-like qualities that help him to tend his garden.

A: Bruce Dern, Cliff Potts, Ron Rifkin, Jesse Vint

© MCA/UNIVERSAL HOME VIDEO, INC. 55029

SILKWOOD

R | DMA | 1983 | COLOR | Sex | Nud | Viol | Lang | AdSit

D: Mike Nichols — 132 m

8 Riveting true story of a major corporate coverup and the personal hardship of the woman who tried to expose it. Karen Silkwood (Streep) is a worker at a nuclear plant and lives with her lover (Russell) and her gay roommate (Cher). When Silkwood realizes how unsafe working conditions are at her plant, she rebels becoming a union activist and begins to gather incriminating evidence. This is how she comes to discover that defective and potentially deadly materials are being produced. Just as she is about to blow the lid off the scandal, she is mysteriously killed in a car accident. Based on a true incident. Nominated for 5 Oscars.

A: Meryl Streep, Kurt Russell, Cher, Craig T. Nelson, Diana Scarwid, Fred Ward

© NEW LINE HOME VIDEO 1377

SIMPLE TWIST OF FATE, A

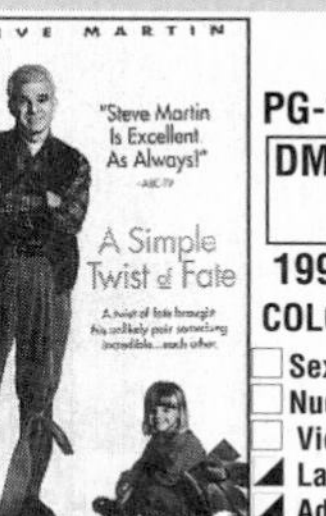

PG-13 | DMA | 1994 | COLOR | Sex | Nud | Viol | Lang | AdSit

D: Gilles MacKinnon — 116 m

7 This is quite a different sort of outing for Steve Martin. Not only did he star in this one, but he also wrote it. Based upon the classic SILAS MARNER, it is the story of a sad and lonely man who had become a miser and a drunk until a little girl walked into his life. Just as his life had hit bottom, this little joy came to him and gave him back his life. However, his life is dealt another blow when the child's wealthy father reveals himself and begins a court battle to reclaim the child he had abandoned. This has virtually no comedy, unlike you would expect, and it takes way to long to get rolling, but it is well-crafted and will leave you with warm fuzzies.

A: Steve Martin, Gabriel Byrne, Catherine O'Hara, Stephen Baldwin, Laura Linney, Alana Austin

© TOUCHSTONE HOME VIDEO 3081

SINGLES

PG-13 | DMA ROM | 1992 | COLOR | Sex | Nud | Viol | Lang | AdSit

D: Cameron Crowe — 100 m

7 An enjoyable exploration of the turmoils of love and dating for the young single residents of one particular apartment building in Seattle. Steve is a traffic engineer who is plotting to win the heart of his love, Linda - but Linda has been burned too many times. Janet is a student who is working in a coffee house. She is head over heels in love with Cliff - but Cliff is preoccupied with driving his mediocre rock band to greatness. How will each win what he or she wants, and will they still want it when they get it? No great revelations, but still enjoyable - particularly if you're young and single.

A: Bridget Fonda, Campbell Scott, Kyra Sedgwick, Matt Dillon, Sheila Kelley, Jim True

© WARNER HOME VIDEO 12410

SKEEZER

D: Peter H. Hunt 96 m

NR
DMA CLD
1981
COLOR
Sex Nud Viol Lang AdSit

8 A surprising true story that is sure to touch a soft spot in even the hardest of hearts. In this heartwarming, made-for-TV drama, a social worker discovers that letting troubled and lonely children play with Skeezer, a loveable sheepdog, produces wonderful results. After just a few hours with the dog, the children with emotional disorders in the home where she works, are much more calm and receptive to others. This true-life tale merely exposes the simple truth that we all need acceptance and love.

A: Karen Valentine, Dee Wallace, Justin Lord, Tom Atkins

© LIVE HOME VIDEO 66870

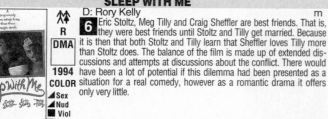

SLEEP WITH ME

D: Rory Kelly m

R
DMA
1994
COLOR
Sex Nud Viol Lang AdSit

6 Eric Stoltz, Meg Tilly and Craig Sheffler are best friends. That is, they were best friends until Stoltz and Tilly get married. Because it is then that both Stoltz and Tilly learn that Sheffler loves Tilly more than Stoltz does. The balance of the film is made up of extended discussions and attempts at discussions about the conflict. There would have been a lot of potential if this dilemma had been presented as a situation for a real comedy, however as a romantic drama it offers only very little.

A: Eric Stoltz, Craig Sheffler, Meg Tilly, Quentin Tarantino, June Lockhart

Distributed By MGM/UA Home Video M905306

SMOOTH TALK

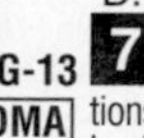

D: Joyce Chopra 92 m

PG-13
DMA
1985
COLOR
Sex Nud Viol Lang AdSit

7 Disturbing and provocative. Child/woman Laura Dern is poised on the brink of adulthood and through her, the trials and emotions associated with that often troubling time are explored. Her story begins with a close examination of the effect Dern's troubled parent's (Place and Helm) and their not-so-wonderful relationship has had on her. However, this psychological drama gets especially intense when the sultry young girl gets in over her head after catching the fancy of a seedy drifter (Williams). It is based on the short story by Joyce Carol Oats, "Where Are You Going? Where Have You Been?" Excellent job by young Dern.

A: Treat Williams, Laura Dern, Mary Kay Place, Levon Helm, Elizabeth Berridge

© LIVE HOME VIDEO VA5143

SOFT SKIN, THE

D: Francois Truffaut 118 m

NR
FOR DMA
1964
B&W
Sex Nud Viol Lang AdSit

7 While on a business trip, a happily married man meets a beautiful airline hostess. They have a passionate affair and as his love for her grows, his difficulties with his wife increase at home. Yet, he is unable to choose between his wife and his mistress. He has discovered his dream woman but now he is in a situation he cannot control and becomes more and more lost. Ultimately, his infidelity will spawn its own solution.

A: Jean Desailly, Francoise Dorleac, Nelly Benedetti, Daniel Ceccaldi

© HOME VISION SOF 020

SOLDIER IN THE RAIN

D: Blake Edwards 88 m

NR
COM DMA
1963
B&W
Sex Nud Viol Lang AdSit

7 A wonderful mix of comedy, sincere drama and some loveable wacky characters. Two Army sergeants share a very different sort of relationship. Gleason is a high-living wheeler-dealer who loves the service and is planning to stay for good. McQueen is sort of a boob who worships the ground Gleason walks on but is about to get back to civilian life and hopes Gleason will join him. Their relationship becomes strained when McQueen introduces Gleason to a very beautiful but ditzy young woman (Weld). The comic banter ranges from slapstick to sentimental.

A: Steve McQueen, Jackie Gleason, Tuesday Weld, Tony Bill, Tom Poston, Ed Nelson

© CBS/FOX VIDEO 7737

SOLDIER'S STORY, A

D: Norman Jewison 102 m

PG
MYS CRM DMA
1984
COLOR
Sex Nud Viol Lang AdSit

9 Powerful and riveting psychological drama and solid mystery. Set in the segregated Army of 1944, a proud black attorney from Washington is sent to a Louisiana military post to investigate the death of the master sergeant of an all-black unit. He could have been murdered by a white racist, but it could also have been any of the black men in his unit, all of whom hated him. This is a fascinating look into human nature and into the nature of those times. However, it is also a solid whodunit, with a wide assortment of characters, all with compelling reasons for wanting the man dead. Works well on many levels all at once. Sterling performances. Excellent.

A: Howard E. Rollins, Jr., Adolph Caesar, Art Evans, Dennis Lipscomb, Denzel Washington, Patti LaBelle

© COLUMBIA TRISTAR HOME VIDEO 60408

SOMEBODY HAS TO SHOOT THE PICTURE

D: Frank Pierson 104 m

R
SUS DMA
1990
COLOR
Sex Nud Viol Lang AdSit

8 Gripping made-for-cable TV movie. Scheider plays a burned-out, Pulitzer Prize-winning photojournalist who is hired by a small-time druglord (Howard) who was convicted of shooting a police officer seven years before. Now on death row and facing execution, Howard wants someone to film his last seconds. During one of the inevitable delays which frequent the capital punishment process, Scheider uncovers some evidence that may prove that his man is innocent. Then, he and the victim's own widow rush to prove the man's innocence in time to save him. Grabs you early and never lets go. Probably too intense for younger viewers.

A: Roy Scheider, Bonnie Bedelia, Arliss Howard, Robert Carradine, Andre Braugher

© MCA/UNIVERSAL HOME VIDEO, INC. 81038

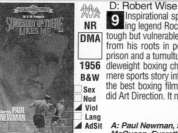

SOMEBODY UP THERE LIKES ME

D: Robert Wise 97 m

NR
DMA
1956
B&W
Sex Nud Viol Lang AdSit

9 Inspirational sports drama and the top-notch biography of boxing legend Rocky Graziano. Newman throws off sparks playing a tough but vulnerable Rocky. This is an inspiring story that follows him from his roots in poverty on the streets of NYC, through a stint in prison and a tumultuous army career, on to his rise to becoming middleweight boxing champion. This is a story that rises above being a mere sports story into being a true dramatic gem - but it is also one of the best boxing films ever made. Cinematography won an Oscar, as did Art Direction. It made Newman a star.

A: Paul Newman, Sal Mineo, Pier Angeli, Robert Loggia, Steve McQueen, Everett Sloane

Distributed By MGM/UA Home Video M300640

SOME CAME RUNNING

D: Vincente Minnelli 137 m

NR
DMA
1958
COLOR
Sex Nud Viol Lang AdSit

7 Great performances. Sinatra is a troubled writer who has come home to a small midwestern town just after the war, with a floozy (MacLaine) on his arm. Sinatra hangs out with his kindred spirit, Dean Martin, and is chastised by his brother (Kennedy) for his relationships with Martin and MacLaine in spite of the fact that Kennedy is himself carrying on an affair with his secretary. This is an intriguing character study of disappointment, disillusionment and of small-town hypocrisy, all powered by some great performances. Received 5 Oscar nominations, including one for MacLaine.

A: Frank Sinatra, Dean Martin, Shirley MacLaine, Martha Hyer, Arthur Kennedy, Nancy Gates

Distributed By MGM/UA Home Video M300964

SOMETHING OF VALUE

D: Richard Brooks 113 m

NR
DMA ACT
1957
B&W
Sex Nud Viol Lang AdSit

8 Powerful drama. White Hudson and black Poitier have been best friends ever since childhood. They have spent their days working side by side on Hudson's father's Kenyan plantation. But when Poitier is driven away by violent racists, he feels compelled to join the Mau Mau, a group of radical terrorists who are determined to end racial oppression in Kenya by driving all Englishmen out. Hudson's relationship with Poitier becomes very strained as the uprisings become increasingly violent. Exciting, builds steadily from a slow start. Prologue by Winston Churchill.

A: Rock Hudson, Sidney Poitier, Wendy Hiller, Dana Wynter, Frederick O'Neil

Distributed By MGM/UA Home Video M300840

SOMETIMES A GREAT NOTION

D: Paul Newman 115 m

PG
DMA
1971
COLOR
Sex Nud Viol Lang AdSit

7 Interesting drama that is sort of a mid-20th-century Western. Henry Fonda and his sons Newman and Sarrazin are stubborn independent loggers in Oregon. They constantly fight against each other and everybody else. Their motto is "Never give an inch." So, when the local industry declares a strike, they naturally defy it to deliver some logs so they can keep their small operation going. But they pay a severe price for their independence as they struggle to get their harvest to market. Good acting and beautiful scenery. Newman's directing debut.

A: Paul Newman, Henry Fonda, Lee Remick, Michael Sarrazin, Richard Jaeckel, Linda Lawson

© MCA/UNIVERSAL HOME VIDEO, INC. 55081

SOMMERSBY

D: Jon Amiel 114 m

PG-13
ROM WST DMA
1993
COLOR
Sex Nud Viol Lang AdSit

9 Very involving and highly romantic Civil War saga, but with a very different bent. Jack Sommersby (Gere) has been away from his Tennessee farm for six years, locked up in a Yankee prison. His wife Laurel and his son have given him up for dead, and yet one day he comes walking back into his war-torn town and onto their decimated farm. Jack has changed. He left as a disagreeable sort and came back as a thoughtful and caring man. Jack wins back Laurel and then even organizes a recovery plan for the town. But soon he is arrested for murder and is accused of being someone else. This one starts slow but comes to a powerful and unusual finish.

A: Richard Gere, Jodie Foster, James Earl Jones, Bill Pullman, William Windom, Brett Kelly

© WARNER HOME VIDEO 12649

SON OF THE MORNING STAR

D: Mike Robe 186 m

PG | WST DMA | 1991 | COLOR

7 Excellent and revealing made-for-TV miniseries covering the period from the time of the Civil War to the 1876 Battle at the Little Big Horn. It is the fact-based story of both the peoples and politics of the time, using George Custer as the pivotal figure. It is told from both the Anglo perspective of Custer's wife (Arquette) and a young Indian woman's (voice of Buffy St. Marie) perspective. What emerges is a comprehensive, insightful and personalized picture of a pivotal time in American history. If you are a history fan, it is worthy of at least an 8. However, it is slow-moving in places.

Sex Nud Viol Lang AdSit

A: Gary Cole, Rosanna Arquette, Dean Stockwell, Rodney A. Grant, Stanley Anderson, Ed Blatchford

© REPUBLIC PICTURES HOME VIDEO RN043810

SOPHIE'S CHOICE

D: Alan J. Pakula 155 m

R | DMA ROM | 1982 | COLOR

9 Stunning portrait by Meryl Streep that earned her a Best Actress Oscar. Sophie is a survivor of the Nazi concentration camps. Now safe in America just after the war and living with an explosive biologist (Kline), she is tormented by her own survival from the death camps when so many others did not survive. A young and naive writer (MacNicol) living downstairs from the mysterious pair is drawn to this odd couple. He becomes fascinated with her and an odd relationship develops between the two men and the tragic Sophie. Compelling story and an utterly fascinating performance by Streep. 4 other nominations.

Sex Nud Viol Lang AdSit

A: Meryl Streep, Kevin Kline, Peter MacNicol, Rita Karin, Stephen D. Newman, Josh Mostel

© CBS/FOX VIDEO 9076

D M A

SOUNDER

D: Martin Ritt 105 m

G | DMA | 1972 | COLOR

9 Moving, beautifully made, thought provoking, highly acclaimed and a truly excellent family movie. Nominated for Best Picture. Set in Louisiana during the Great Depression, a black sharecropper's family must survive very hard times alone after the father is caught trying to steal food for his family and is sent to prison for a year. His wife struggles to to keep them all whole until he can return. Utterly believable performances by the entire cast, but particularly Tyson, give this story a universal appeal that transcends any racial lines.

Sex Nud Viol Lang AdSit

A: Cicely Tyson, Paul Winfield, Carmen Mathews, Kevin Hooks, Taj Mahal, James Best

© PARAMOUNT HOME VIDEO 2324

SOUND OF MUSIC, THE

D: Robert Wise 175 m

G | MUS DMA | 1965 | COLOR

9 Immensely popular film adapted from an immensely popular Broadway musical and taken from the pages of real life. Winner of the Best Picture and four other Oscars. Andrews is Maria, a spunky girl who doesn't fit in at the convent, so she is sent to be the governess for the family of widower Baron Von Trapp (Plummer). She falls in love with him and the family, and they are married. But it is 1938, the Nazis are menacing Austria and have targeted their whole family. So the entire family is forced into making a daring escape over the mountains. Warm and wonderful with memorable songs. Sweet and timeless.

Sex Nud Viol Lang AdSit

A: Julie Andrews, Christopher Plummer, Peggy Wood, Angela Cartwright, Richard Haydn, Eleanor Parker

© FOXVIDEO 1051

SOUTH CENTRAL

D: Steve Anderson 99 m

R | DMA | 1992 | COLOR

8 A hard-edged portrait that lets you feel the mean life in the streets of South Los Angeles. It is a place where your only family is your gang. Bobby is a product of those streets, where it pays to be selfish and cruel... for a while. Bobby is a founding member of a gang called the Dueces, but his glory is short-lived. Just has he has become a father, he receives a 10-year sentence for murder. As his term ends, he learns that his son has been shot in a robbery. His vow of vengeance is stifled when a lifer and converted Muslim makes him understand that he is the reason his son was shot, and only he can prevent his son from reliving his doomed and empty life. See also BOYZ N THE HOOD.

Sex Nud Viol Lang AdSit

A: Glenn Plummer, Carl Lumbly, Christian Coleman, Byron Keith Minns, LaRita Shelby, Lexie D. Bingham

© WARNER HOME VIDEO 12594

SPARTACUS

D: Stanley Kubrick 196 m

PG-13 | ACT DMA | 1960 | COLOR

10 Rousing and rewarding, intelligent and thrilling. A huge, epic human drama based solidly in historical fact. In 73 B.C. in republican Rome, a large and bloody slave revolt did, in fact, for a short time, challenge the Empire. Kirk Douglas plays Spartacus, a slave/gladiator who rose up first against the barbarism of his own master and later came to lead the entire slave revolt against all Rome. Brilliantly photographed - huge spectacle, with an involving script, exciting performances and thrilling battle sequences. Winner of four Oscars. Must see.

Sex Nud Viol Lang AdSit

A: Kirk Douglas, Laurence Olivier, Jean Simmons, Charles Laughton, Peter Ustinov, Tony Curtis

© MCA/UNIVERSAL HOME VIDEO, INC. 81133

SPIRIT OF THE BEEHIVE, THE

D: Victor Erice 93 m

NR | FOR DMA | 1973 | COLOR

9 Haunting and poignant story of a lonely little girl. In the mountains of Spain just after the revolution, an 8-year-old girl lives with her 10-year-old sister and their parents. Their village has been spared the destruction of the revolution but despair abounds. The father tends bees and ponders existence, while the mother writes letters to an imagined lover. No one speaks and there is no love in the house. One day the girls watch Boris Karloff's FRANKENSTEIN in which the monster befriends a little girl, and the little girl is drawn to him. So lonely is she that she becomes obsessed with finding the monster. Reality fades from her world and she becomes lost to her imagination. Subtitles.

Sex Nud Viol Lang AdSit

A: Ana Torrent, Isabel Telleria, Fernando Fernan Gomez, Teresa Gimpera, Jose Villasante

© HOME VISION SPI 080

SPLENDOR IN THE GRASS

D: Elia Kazan 124 m

NR | ROM DMA | 1961 | COLOR

7 A tragic tale of an intense, forbidden young love. Beatty is a rich young man who falls deeply in love with his high school sweetheart, the not-so-wealthy Wood. The pair struggle with awakened intense sexual feelings, but do not give in to them. This is 1920 Kansas and Beatty's self-righteous father and Wood's shrewish mother forbid it. They stop seeing each other, Beatty dates an infamous bad girl and Wood has a breakdown. Beatty goes off to college. His father commits suicide when he goes broke and Beatty marries someone else. Nomination for Woods. Debut for Diller and Dennis.

Sex Nud Viol Lang AdSit

A: Natalie Wood, Warren Beatty, Audrey Christie, Sean Garrison, Sandy Dennis, Phyllis Diller

© WARNER HOME VIDEO 11164

SPLIT IMAGE

D: Ted Kotcheff 113 m

R | DMA | 1982 | COLOR

7 An intense thought-provoking drama. O'Keefe is a clean-cut college athlete. He is very bright and seems to have everything going for him. However, after he becomes involved with a sexy student (Allen) who persuades him to join a cult led by Peter Fonda, he becomes so embroiled in the cult that he rejects his family and everything that he has ever known. His disturbed mother and father send an expert to kidnap and deprogram him - to bring back the son they used to know. He begins to respond well to the deprogramming, but things soon begin unravel again when Fonda and Allen come to win him back to the fold. Gripping and topical.

Sex Nud Viol Lang AdSit

A: Michael O'Keefe, Karen Allen, Peter Fonda, James Woods, Elizabeth Ashley, Brian Dennehy

© NEW LINE HOME VIDEO 1322

SQUARE DANCE

D: Daniel Petrie 118 m

PG-13 | DMA | 1986 | COLOR

7 A winning coming-of-age drama. A young girl (Ryder) is about to begin to experience some of the uncomfortable complexities that life has to offer. At 13, Ryder is living a comfortable and relatively happy life on her grandfather's (Robards) ranch in Texas. Her trampy mother (Alexander) shows up for a visit and Ryder decides to follow her to the big city. There she learns the truth about her mother and the father she never knew. Feeling lost and alone, she develops a relationship with a retarded boy (Rob Lowe). Sensitive and tough with superb performances from all.

Sex Nud Viol Lang AdSit

A: Jason Robards, Jr., Jane Alexander, Rob Lowe, Winona Ryder, Deborah Richter, Gulch Koock

© PACIFIC ARTS VIDEO 673

STACKING

D: Martin Rosen 96 m

PG | DMA | 1987 | COLOR

6 The Morgan family is down on its luck in 1950s Montana. They are about to lose their farm because the husband and father has had a bad accident in the field and now spends most of his time drinking. Mother (Lahti) is fed up with her life, yearns to escape it and has become enamored with a handsome drifter (Coyote). So, fourteen-year-old Anna Mae (Follows) is the only one who is left to do what has to be done. She and their hard-drinking fieldhand (Forrest) struggle to make their stacking machine work so they can harvest the hay they need to save the farm.

Sex Nud Viol Lang AdSit

A: Christine Lahti, Frederic Forrest, Megan Follows, Peter Coyote, Jason Gedrick

© NEW LINE HOME VIDEO 90227

STAND AND DELIVER

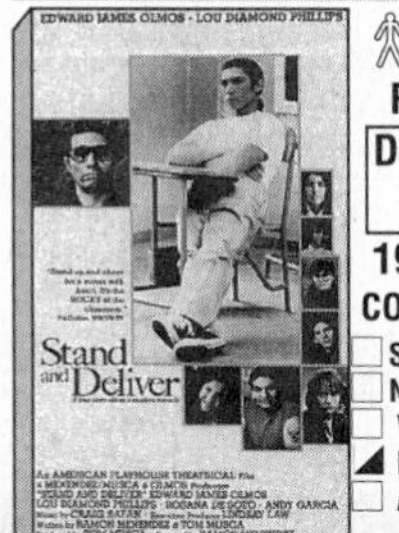

D: Ramon Menendez 103 m

PG | DMA | 1988 | COLOR

8 Inspiring true story. Jamie Escalante (Olmos) is a tough Los Angeles high school teacher who gives up a prestigious job to become an inner-city math teacher. He believes he can impact the lives of inner-city students who are on a fast track to nowhere. Armed with a forceful, unique and caring style, and a power to motivate even the most rebellious students, he challenges, pokes, prods and inspires his kids, kids who could barely do basic math, to become math masters and pass the state Advanced Placement Test in calculus - their ticket into college. Heartwarming, funny and true.

Sex Nud Viol Lang AdSit

A: Edward James Olmos, Andy Garcia, Lou Diamond Phillips, Rosana De Soto, Will Gotay, Ingrid Oliu

© WARNER HOME VIDEO 11805

STAND BY ME

D: Rob Reiner 87 m

R | DMA COM | 1986 | COLOR

9 Wonderful, endearing, funny and highly entertaining story of the turning point in the lives of four 12-year-old buddies who enjoy one last summer together as children in 1959. One is an imaginative storyteller, one an overweight wimp, one a foolhardy daredevil and another a troubled and lonely toughguy. Richard Dreyfuss narrates this story, as a now-grown writer remembering an adventurous two-day camping trip with his three friends as they set out to find the dead body of a boy hit by a train. This is not a morbid outing but rather a grand adventure. Deeply affecting. Very special.

Sex | Nud | Viol | Lang | AdSit

A: Wil Wheaton, River Phoenix, Corey Feldman, Jerry O'Connell, Richard Dreyfuss, Kiefer Sutherland

© COLUMBIA TRISTAR HOME VIDEO 60736

STANLEY & IRIS

D: Martin Ritt 105 m

PG-13 | ROM DMA | 1990 | COLOR

7 Iris is a middle-aged woman, newly widowed. She is adrift, struggling with her grief while trying to support her household. Stanley is a very bright middle-aged guy. He is a mechanical genius who is able to build almost anything, but he is working only as a cook. Then his employers fire him after they too find out his dark secret - he can't read. Stanley has met Iris at the factory where they both worked. After Stanley gets fired (as a safety risk), he can no longer support his old and sick father. He is so despondent that he goes to Iris to ask for her help in learning how to read. This is an affecting drama and a sweet romance story too.

Sex | Nud | Viol | Lang | AdSit

A: Jane Fonda, Robert De Niro, Swoosie Kurtz, Martha Plimpton, Harley Cross, Jamey Sheridan

Distributed By MGM/UA Home Video M901694

STARDUST MEMORIES

D: Woody Allen 89 m

PG | DMA COM | 1980 | B&W

6 Allen is unabashedly playing himself in this unique but mean-spirited film. Sandy Bates (Allen) is a filmmaker whose earlier stuff can't compare (according to his fans) to his later stuff. He is a lonely genius who nobody understands. When a director cuts up his first serious film, he seeks solace by attending a seminar, but is immediately stampeded by fans, favor-seekers and film critics. Allen shows a side of himself that fans may not like, and takes a poke at those who have been critical of his work. Still, very interesting.

Sex | Nud | Viol | Lang | AdSit

A: Woody Allen, Charlotte Rampling, Jessica Harper, Marie-Christine Barrault, Tony Roberts, Daniel Stern

Distributed By MGM/UA Home Video M203033

STATE OF GRACE

D: Phil Joanou 134 m

R | CRM DMA | 1990 | COLOR

8 This is a grimly realistic portrait of the Irish gangsters and punks living in the tenements of Manhattan's Hell's Kitchen. Sean Penn is Terry Noonan, a graduate of the Kitchen, back home to reacquaint himself with old friends. Of particular interest to him are his former girlfriend (Robin Wright) and former best buddy Jackie Flannery (Gary Oldman). Terry asks Jackie if he can help him get a job with his brother Frankie, the local kingpin. Both brothers are psychopaths but Frankie is a cold-hearted manipulator while Jackie will literally do anything for his friends. Jackie gets Terry in, but Terry is an undercover cop. Extremely violent, but very believable.

Sex | Nud | Viol | Lang | AdSit

A: Sean Penn, Ed Harris, Gary Oldman, Robin Wright, John C. Reilly, Burgess Meredith

© ORION PICTURES CORPORATION 8760

STEALING HOME

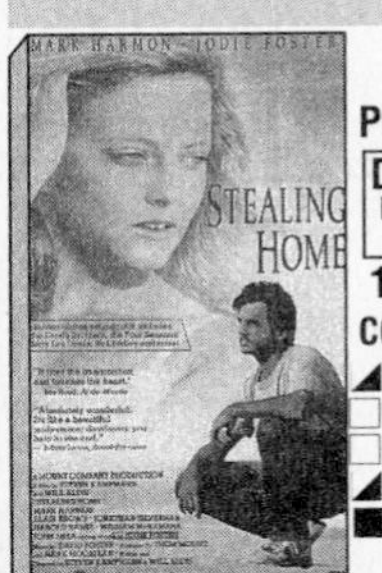

D: Steven Kampmann 98 m

PG-13 | DMA ROM | 1988 | COLOR

8 A bittersweet story that didn't get its proper due upon release. Harmon plays a nearly washed-up minor league baseball player who is just barely hanging on to his sanity. Then he gets a call to come home. His best friend has committed suicide and has willed him her ashes. She was a free-spirit and was his babysitter when he was young. As he grew up she became his mentor and lover. Their story is told through a series of flashbacks and flashforwards, and as it is explored over time his life slowly comes into focus for him. Somewhat corny and overstated, but also memorable. Foster is unforgettable.

Sex | Nud | Viol | Lang | AdSit

A: Mark Harmon, Jodie Foster, Blair Brown, Harold Ramis, Jonathan Silverman, William McNamara

© WARNER HOME VIDEO 11818

STEEL MAGNOLIAS

D: Herbert Ross 118 m

PG | COM DMA | 1989 | COLOR

9 Extremely enjoyable romp through the intricacies of Southern femininity. This is NOT just a film for women, however. It is a real charmer which follows the exploits of six very different women in a small Southern town, who are friends in spite of their many differences. Their individual stories are interwoven to provide a very rich tapestry of life in all its aspects. These are friends who share their insecurities, their joys and support each other in their deepest sorrows. It is, at the same time, very funny and deeply affecting.

Sex | Nud | Viol | Lang | AdSit

A: Julia Roberts, Sally Field, Dolly Parton, Shirley MacLaine, Olympia Dukakis, Daryl Hannah

© COLUMBIA TRISTAR HOME VIDEO 70243

ST. ELMO'S FIRE

D: Joel Schumacher 110 m

R | DMA COM | 1985 | COLOR

8 Outstanding reality check! A group of Georgetown graduates are finding that the real world is a little hard to take and, as the pressures of real life mount, their friendships are tested. A cocaine addict sleeps with her boss, a guy pines away for a sophisticated lady, a virgin has the hots for an irresponsible hunk, a yuppie cheats on his live-in and his best friend wants a piece of the action. These messed-up friends really need each other! A unique slice of life story that neatly puts together a colorful puzzle all about growing up.

Sex | Nud | Viol | Lang | AdSit

A: Emilio Estevez, Rob Lowe, Judd Nelson, Andrew McCarthy, Demi Moore, Ally Sheedy

© COLUMBIA TRISTAR HOME VIDEO 60559

STERILE CUCKOO, THE

D: Alan J. Pakula 107 m

R | DMA ROM | 1970 | COLOR

8 Liza Minnelli won a much-deserved Oscar nomination for her role as the wisecracking, insecure, vulnerable Pookie Adams. Her mother died in childbirth (Pookie says she was her first victim) and she has been a problem ever since. Her father doesn't know how to deal with her, so he keeps putting her in different boarding schools. On the bus to college, she meets shy Jerry (Burton) who is on his way to a neighboring school and immediately decides that they should be friends, instead she only embarrasses him. However, later she turns up to spend the weekend and they become friends and lovers. Poignant and bittersweet.

Sex | Nud | Viol | Lang | AdSit

A: Liza Minnelli, Wendell Burton, Tim McIntire, Elizabeth Harrower

© PARAMOUNT HOME VIDEO 6904

D M A

STONE BOY, THE

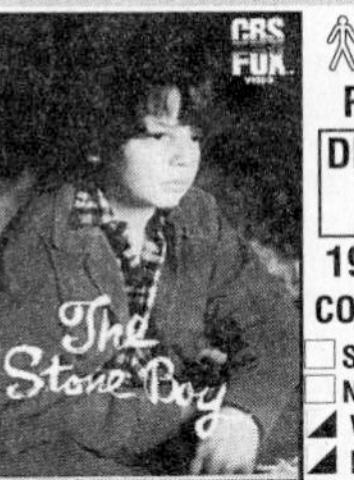

D: Christopher Cain 93 m

PG | DMA | 1984 | COLOR

9 Powerfully moving. On a hunting expedition, 12-year-old Presson accidentally kills his older brother. At first he doesn't know what to do, but eventually he does go home to tell his parents what happened. However, now wrought with guilt, he retreats behind a dark and quiet wall of seclusion. He doesn't even cry and his quietness is perceived as being a lack of caring. He receives an overwhelming dose of rejection and anger from his father (Duvall). While, his mother wants to reach out to him, she is restrained by the distraught father. This is an intensely sad but very realistic story of family that is nearly destroyed by a lack of communication.

Sex | Nud | Viol | Lang | AdSit

A: Robert Duvall, Glenn Close, Jason Presson, Frederic Forrest, Wilford Brimley, Gail Youngs

© FOXVIDEO 1445

STORY OF WOMEN, THE

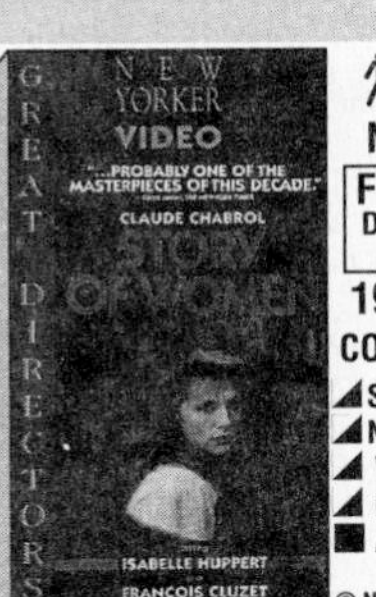

D: Claude Chabrol 110 m

NR | FOR DMA | 1988 | COLOR

8 A remarkable award-winning film. Isabelle Huppert received a Best Actress award for her portrayal of the real-life French woman who was the last woman to be guillotined. She was a cold and childlike woman who had struggled in abject poverty in Nazi-occupied France at the beginning of the war. Then when her neighbor became pregnant, she performed an amateur abortion for her. Soon she was in the business and had developed a grand lifestyle. However, her humiliated husband turned her in when she is so bold as to take a Nazi collaborator for her lover. It is then that she is condemned to die by the same townspeople who she had served. Subtitles.

Sex | Nud | Viol | Lang | AdSit

A: Isabelle Huppert, Francois Cluzet, Marie Trintignant, Louis Ducreux, Michel Beaune, Dominique Blanc

© NEW YORKER FILMS NYV59091

STRAIGHT TIME

D: Ulu Grosbard 114 m

R | DMA | 1978 | COLOR

7 This is a straight forward hard look at a man who is firmly trapped in a life of crime. Hoffman is a career criminal who has just served time for armed robbery and was released after six years. He has every intention of going straight this time and he does his best to make it. He finds a girlfriend and tries to find a job but, after a bad run-in with his menacing parole officer, he starts a rapid downward spiral again. He doesn't know how to make it straight. Crime and even prison is an easier life for him than being on the outside. There he knows the rules. Gritty, sober and realistic look at life behind bars and on the streets.

Sex | Nud | Viol | Lang | AdSit

A: Dustin Hoffman, Gary Busey, Theresa Russell, M. Emmet Walsh, Rita Taggart

© WARNER HOME VIDEO 11124

STRANGERS IN GOOD COMPANY

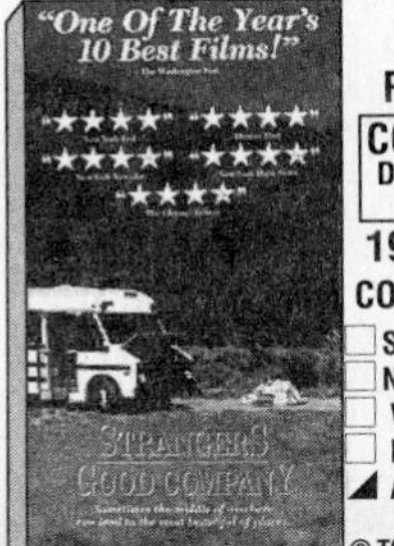

D: Cynthia Scott 101 m

PG | COM DMA | 1991 | COLOR

9 Absolutely delightful. A small group of old ladies, all from widely different backgrounds, is on a field trip on a back road when their bus breaks down. They are stranded twenty miles from help, so they take refuge in an old house, scrounge for food from nature and talk. Who would have expected listening to these women talk to be such a good time. True, it is slow at times, but never for too long... and then something will happen that makes the wait entirely worth while. It is like a fine wine which must be slipped slowly. Worthwhile for everyone but, like fine wine, is likely better appreciated by more experienced consumers.

Sex | Nud | Viol | Lang | AdSit

A: Alice Diablo, Constance Garneau, Winifred Holden, Cissy Meddings, Mary Meigs, Catherine Roche

© TOUCHSTONE HOME VIDEO 1354

STRANGERS WHEN WE MEET

D: Richard Quine 117 m

7 NR | ROM DMA | 1960 B&W | Sex Nud Viol Lang AdSit

Martial discontent runs rampant in this lush and enjoyable soap opera. A brilliant architect (Douglas) is frustrated with his money-obsessed wife (Rush). Just down the street, neighbor Novak feels worthless and taken for granted by her dull husband (Bryant). Douglas and Novak fall head over heels in love, igniting a heated affair, but their happiness is threatened when Douglas is offered the job of his life and must choose between his family, his career, and Novak. Matthau is wonderful as their mutual friend who knows of their affair and begins to make passes at Rush.

A: Kirk Douglas, Kim Novak, Ernie Kovacs, Barbara Rush, Walter Matthau, Virginia Bruce

© COLUMBIA TRISTAR HOME VIDEO 60944

STRAPLESS

D: David Hare 99 m

7 R | DMA ROM | 1990 COLOR | Sex Nud Viol Lang AdSit

Intelligent drama that has many aspects to it. A middle-aged American doctor, working in London under England's socialized medical system, has devoted her life to her work. However, after observing her carefree sister, she decides she has missed out on too much. She needs excitement too and takes a chance with a charming man while on a vacation in Portugal. She does have a good time, but she refuses invitations to his bed. Still he persists. Eventually she marries him and gives over to passion. Life now appears to be wonderful, that is until she finds that he has taken her money and is already is married. Passion is not always free.

A: Blair Brown, Bridget Fonda, Bruno Ganz, Hugh Laurie

© COLUMBIA TRISTAR HOME VIDEO 90893

STRAW DOGS

D: Sam Peckinpah 117 m

9 R | DMA | 1971 COLOR | Sex Nud Viol Lang AdSit

This is not especially easy to watch, but it is a powerful film. Hoffman is a quiet American math teacher who moves with his beautiful wife (George) to her native village in England. The village workmen leer at and taunt the sexy George and Hoffman's reluctance to fight with them causes a rift to develop when she thinks he is a coward. So, when she is raped by the men, she doesn't even tell him. However, when a young retarded man Hoffman is sheltering is beaten and the same mob attacks their house, it's too much for Hoffman and he fights back, killing several. George now learns what violence is and has to shoot a man herself. Forceful and brilliantly acted.

A: Dustin Hoffman, Susan George, Peter Vaughan, T.P. McKenna, Peter Arne, David Warner

© CBS/FOX VIDEO 8005

STREETWISE

D: Martin Bell 92 m

8 NR | DOC DMA | 1985 COLOR | Sex Nud Viol Lang AdSit

This is not a pretty picture. This in an intense, real and horrifying look at the lives of a group of teenage runaways who make their home the streets of Seattle and the things that they endure to survive. Most of them are victims of a destructive homelife or parents who are out of touch. They eat out of trash bins, stick needles up their arms, drink, sell themselves and their souls. The only thing they really have is each other. It is that strong bond that keeps them going. Real teenagers, real life, and a real heartbreaking account of life far outside of what, for most of us, is normal.

A:

© R&G VIDEO, LP 9548

SUDDENLY, LAST SUMMER

D: Joseph L. Mankiewicz 114 m

8 NR | DMA | 1959 B&W | Sex Nud Viol Lang AdSit

A compelling, riveting, sinister Tennessee Williams concoction. Taylor plays a woman who is hopelessly neurotic, largely due to the ever-present memory of her much loved, homosexual cousin's violent death. His wealthy mother (Hepburn) is willing to go to any lengths to put that memory to rest, including convincing neurosurgeon Clift that they are only hallucinations. If Clift will perform a lobotomy to stop them, Hepburn will make a huge donation to his hospital. However, under pentothal, Taylor reveals the real reasons for her urgency. Brilliantly acted - Hepburn and Taylor were Oscar nominated.

A: Katharine Hepburn, Elizabeth Taylor, Montgomery Clift, Albert Dekker

© COLUMBIA TRISTAR HOME VIDEO VH10518

SUGARLAND EXPRESS, THE

D: Steven Spielberg 109 m

8 PG | DMA COM | 1974 COLOR | Sex Nud Viol Lang AdSit

Oddly fascinating film that was Steven Spielberg's first feature film. A simple-minded girl, just released from jail after having served a short sentence for a minor theft, learns that her baby is being adopted by a family in Sugarland, Texas. In a fit of desperation, she breaks her husband out of prison, kidnapping a cop along the way. They all set off to Sugarland in a stolen cop car to get her baby back. Pursued by an armada of police cars, she gets major publicity and becomes a folk hero. Based upon an actual 1969 event.

A: Goldie Hawn, Ben Johnson, William Atherton, Michael Sacks

© MCA/UNIVERSAL HOME VIDEO, INC. 55052

SUMMER AND SMOKE

D: Peter Glenville 118 m

8 NR | DMA ROM | 1962 COLOR | Sex Nud Viol Lang AdSit

From the Tennessee Williams play comes this film full of despair, sadness and love unfulfilled. Yet, it is also extremely involving. Geraldine Page (in a repeat of her stage role) stars as a small town spinster with a set of overbearing parents. She is head over heels in love with the town's handsome young doctor (Harvey). But his disregard for her causes both of them a great deal of pain and agony, especially when he falls for a sexy dancehall girl. Dazzling performances throughout, Page gives an especially outstanding performance. Profound and moving, but also slow and depressing.

A: Geraldine Page, Laurence Harvey, Rita Moreno, Una Merkel, John McIntire, Pamela Tiffin

© PARAMOUNT HOME VIDEO 6107

SUMMER OF '42

D: Robert Mulligan 104 m

8 PG | ROM DMA | 1971 COLOR | Sex Nud Viol Lang AdSit

This is a lovely, tender and endearing coming-of-age movie, evocatively set in 1940s atmosphere at the beginning of WWII, on a summer resort island. Three adolescent boys are both fascinated and frustrated with sex. They pour over the marriage manual of one of their parents and even make faltering attempts at acquiring condoms from the local pharmacy. But, sex takes on a new meaning when Grimes falls in deeply in love with a 22-year-old war bride who has just sent her new husband off to war. A sweet and tender movie that garnered four Oscar nominations and was hugely popular.

A: Jennifer O'Neill, Gary Grimes, Jerry Houser, Oliver Conant, Christopher Norris, Lou Frizell

© WARNER HOME VIDEO 1033

SUMMER PLACE, A

D: Delmer Daves 130 m

7 NR | ROM DMA | 1959 COLOR | Sex Nud Viol Lang AdSit

Top-notch soaper! McGuire and Egan, once teenage lovers, find themselves together again after parental disapproval had catapulted them into 20 years of separation. Egan, now a successful businessman, returns to an island off the coast of Maine and finds that his old flame (McGuire) is stuck in a very unhappy marriage. Romance once again ignites. Each divorce their current spouses and marry each other. Then love strikes again and Egan's daughter (Dee) falls in love with McGuire's son (Donahue). The theme song by Max Steiner was a monumental hit.

A: Troy Donahue, Sandra Dee, Dorothy McGuire, Richard Egan, Arthur Kennedy, Constance Ford

© WARNER HOME VIDEO 11593

SUMMER STORY, A

D: Piers Haggard 97 m

7 PG-13 | ROM DMA | 1988 COLOR | Sex Nud Viol Lang AdSit

A romantic and picturesque story of love and life at the turn of the century in England. A beautiful young farmgirl (Stubbs) falls madly in love with an affluent but weak-willed British attorney (Wilby). He does love her, but the social consciousness of the time will not readily allow him in such an arrangement. So, he ultimately makes the decision that changes the course of their romance and breaks Stubbs's fragile heart. An endearing romance tale based on Galsworthy's novel "The Apple Tree."

A: Imogen Stubbs, James Wilby, Ken Colley, Sophie Ward, Susannah York, Jerome Flynn

© MEDIA HOME ENTERTAINMENT, INC. M012485

SUNDOWNERS, THE

D: Fred Zinnemann 133 m

9 NR | WST DMA COM | 1960 COLOR | Sex Nud Viol Lang AdSit

Wonderfully winning film that was a Best Picture nominee and received four other nominations. One of the best-ever of many Mitchum/Kerr pairings. It is the loving character study of a headstrong rover who insists upon taking his wife and family with him from job to job, herding and shearing sheep in Australia's outback during the 1920s. He loves his family and he loves the life, but she thinks its time to settle down. Shot on location in Australia. Numerous winning vignettes and a crew of fascinating characters populate this endearing story. Highly recommended and rewarding viewing for all ages.

A: Deborah Kerr, Robert Mitchum, Peter Ustinov, Michael Anderson, Jr., Glynis Johns, Dina Merrill

© WARNER HOME VIDEO 11215

SUNRISE AT CAMPOBELLO

D: Vincent J. Donehue 144 m

8 NR | DMA | 1960 COLOR | Sex Nud Viol Lang AdSit

Fascinating biography of President Franklin D. Roosevelt's courageous struggle to keep polio from taking over his life. Bellamy expertly plays the determined president who is stricken with the debilitating disease and paralyzed in the 1920s. His wife Eleanor (Garson) and trusted friend (Cronyn) inspire him to face the disease head-on and try to walk again. Outstanding and educational, the acting is first-rate and absolutely inspirational. Adapted from Schary's hit play. Four Oscar nominations.

A: Ralph Bellamy, Greer Garson, Hume Cronyn, Jean Hagen, Ann Shoemaker, Alan Bunce

© WARNER HOME VIDEO 11214

SWEET BIRD OF YOUTH

D: Richard Brooks 120 m

NR | DMA | 1962 | COLOR

9 Screen adaptation of Tennessee Williams's big Broadway hit! A gigolo (Newman) returns to his hometown and causes quite a ruckus when he brings back with him a sultry but aging movie queen (Page) who takes her pleasure in alcohol and sex. When Newman seeks to reawaken an old romance with Knight, the daughter of the town's political boss (Begley) who he had once made pregnant, her father doesn't like the idea at all. Begley and his son (Torn) plot a vicious revenge against Newman. This was considerably toned down to get it past the censors of the time. Still, it is a powerful drama.

Sex Nud Viol Lang AdSit

A: Paul Newman, Geraldine Page, Shirley Knight, Ed Begley, Rip Torn, Mildred Dunnock

Distributed By MGM/UA Home Video M200793

SWEET DREAMS

D: Karel Reisz 115 m

PG-13 | DMA MUS | 1985 | COLOR

8 Jessica Lange gives a nearly flawless performance in this brilliant biography of the late Patsy Cline, one of country music's largest icons. This film documents her rise to fame but dwells mostly on her turbulent marriage. When Cline met her husband (Ed Harris), she fell in love quickly. But with fame fast approaching, her husband turned abusive and resentful and their's was a troubled and turbulent marriage. A tragic plane crash silenced forever Cline's wonderful voice, but Lange brings it back to life with her Oscar-nominated portrayal, lip syncing the original songs with absolute precision. Outstanding supporting cast.

Sex Nud Viol Lang AdSit

A: Jessica Lange, Ed Harris, Ann Wedgeworth, David Clennon, Gary Basaraba

© HBO VIDEO TVA3666

SWEETIE

D: Jane Campion m

R | COM DMA | 1990 | COLOR

7 A very unique comedy drama from Australia. In the tradition of BLUE VELVET and ERASERHEAD, the strange photography and shady characters give this film a very offbeat, surrealistic feeling. Story centers around two sisters: one a very quiet, depressed wallflower (Lemon), and Sweetie (Colson), the obese nutcase who turns her and her family's lives completely inside out. A very strange but intriguing study of human nature, relationships and sibling rivalry that is not for all tastes.

Sex Nud Viol Lang AdSit

A: Genevieve Lemon, Karen Colston, Tom Lycos, Dorothy Barry, Jon Darling, Michael Lake

© LIVE HOME VIDEO 68929

SWEET LORRAINE

D: Steve Gomer 91 m

PG-13 | COM DMA | 1987 | COLOR

7 Sentimental sleeper that packs a big punch in a small package! Once a grand hotel in the Catskills, the Lorraine is now 80-years-old and is badly in need of extensive repairs, but the money for the renovation just isn't there. Owner Stapleton is very fond of the hotel and staff, but she faces bankruptcy. Alvarado is her granddaughter who helps wherever she can and finds herself drawn into a love for the old place, too. Developers anxious to get ahold of the prime land offer a tempting price. Could this be the last summer for the memorable hotel? An atmospheric and sentimental journey.

Sex Nud Viol Lang AdSit

A: Maureen Stapleton, Trini Alvarado, Lee Richardson, John Bedford Lloyd, Giancarlo Esposito, Edie Falco

© PARAMOUNT HOME VIDEO 12606

SWEET SMELL OF SUCCESS

D: Alexander Mackendrick 97 m

NR | DMA | 1957 | B&W

8 Lancaster stars as J.J. Hunsecker, an egomaniacal, all-powerful New York newspaper columnist. Curtis is a press agent whose livelihood depends upon getting his client's exposure. Because Lancaster's column provides the best exposure available, Curtis will do anything to get it. Lancaster is driven and has no interest in women, except for his sister who lives with him. When she takes up with a musician (Milner), Lancaster wants it stopped and offers Curtis whatever it takes if he'll do it. Though he feels guilty, Curtis is too drawn by the offer to refuse. Blistering look at power and the press.

Sex Nud Viol Lang AdSit

A: Burt Lancaster, Tony Curtis, Martin Milner, Sam Levene, Barbara Nichols, Susan Harrison

Distributed By MGM/UA Home Video M301434

SWIMMER, THE

D: Frank Perry 94 m

PG | DMA | 1968 | COLOR

7 A thoughtful sleeper! One sunny Sunday morning, middle-aged advertising exec (Lancaster) decides to commute home by "swimming," stopping at each friend, neighbor and ex-lover's pool in his upscale Connecticut neighborhood on the way. Each stop in his travels evokes powerful memories. Each memory recounted paints an ever clearer picture of a man whose life is in a shambles. He is compulsively self-deluded and shallow. Each stop is sobering, especially the last one - his own empty house. This clever film, overlooked when it was released, certainly deserves a second look.

Sex Nud Viol Lang AdSit

A: Burt Lancaster, Janet Landgard, Janice Rule, Tony Bickley, Marge Champion, Bill Fiore

© COLUMBIA TRISTAR HOME VIDEO 60543

SWING SHIFT

D: Jonathan Demme 100 m

PG | DMA COM | 1984 | COLOR

6 A WWII period piece, with fine attention to detail. It attempts to capture, through a fictionalized account, the feel of the first time that women joined the work force as their husbands were sent off to war. However, the film takes an unfortunate turn when it concentrates on romance instead. When Hawn's husband (Harris) is shipped off to fight, she takes a job as a riveter in a munitions plant to make ends meet. While there, she catches the eye of the macho Russell and the pair have an affair. Things get messy when Hawn's husband finds out about it. Lahti was Oscar-nominated.

Sex Nud Viol Lang AdSit

A: Goldie Hawn, Kurt Russell, Christine Lahti, Ed Harris

© WARNER HOME VIDEO 11376

SYBIL

D: Daniel Petrie 122 m

NR | DMA | 1977 | COLOR

8 Excellent made-for-TV drama in which Sally Field gives an outstanding performance as Sybil - a very disturbed young woman with 17 different personalities. Joanne Woodward plays her psychiatrist who slowly reveals each of the different characters, and the intense childhood trauma that caused Sybil to take the extreme measure of creating different personalities to escape her pain and deal with daily life. Fascinating drama based upon an actual case history. Sally Field deservedly won an Emmy for her performance.

Sex Nud Viol Lang AdSit

A: Sally Field, Joanne Woodward, Brad Davis, Martine Bartlett, Jane Hoffman, William Prince

© CBS/FOX VIDEO 00122

SYLVESTER

D: Tim Hunter 104 m

PG | DMA CLD | 1984 | COLOR

8 NATIONAL VELVET fans take note! Sylvester is an untamed jumping horse that catches the fancy of sixteen year-old tomboy Gilbert. She and her two brothers are orphaned and are under the care of a crusty old horse trainer (Farnsworth). Gilbert falls in love with the beautiful white horse and enlists the aid of Farnsworth to help train it, even though he doesn't think the horse has a chance. But with his help, she and Sylvester do train the horse for the event of her life held in Lexington, Kentucky. A charmer that lifts you up and leaves you feeling very good.

Sex Nud Viol Lang AdSit

A: Melissa Gilbert, Richard Farnsworth, Michael Schoeffling, Constance Towers

© COLUMBIA TRISTAR HOME VIDEO 60476

TABLE FOR FIVE

D: Robert Lieberman 120 m

PG | DMA | 1983 | COLOR

8 A very effective drama which reflects a situation many can identify with. Jon Voight is a divorced father who, after a long absence is now estranged from his children. He hopes to reestablish his relationship with them. So, he picks them from his ex-wife (Perkins) and her new husband (Crenna) to go on an extended ocean voyage. But, he finds that it is very difficult to regain his children's respect and affections. Then news arrives that their mother has been killed in a car accident and he has to battle stepfather Crenna for custody. Solid tear-jerker.

Sex Nud Viol Lang AdSit

A: Jon Voight, Millie Perkins, Richard Crenna, Kevin Costner, Roxana Zal, Marie-Christine Barrault

© CBS/FOX VIDEO 7043

TAKE DOWN

D: Keith Merrill 96 m

PG | COM DMA | 1978 | COLOR

7 Light-hearted sports serio-comedy. The high school in a little Utah town has a perpetually losing football team. Still they are determined to win at something. So they start a wrestling team, even though the only coach they have is a stuffy English teacher and Shakespeare scholar (Herrmann) who has no understanding at all of sports - and he isn't very excited by the prospect of coaching either. However, urged on by his wife, Herrmann learns to loosen up. Surprise, he develops a winning team but has to he struggle to keep his rebellious star athlete from dropping out of school. Rousing finish.

Sex Nud Viol Lang AdSit

A: Edward Herrmann, Kathleen Lloyd, Lorenzo Lamas, Maureen McCormick, Stephen Furst, Kevin Hooks

© UNICORN VIDEO, INC. 564

TALK RADIO

D: Oliver Stone 110 m

R | DMA | 1989 | COLOR

6 An obnoxious late-night Dallas radio talk show host, who has become very popular because of his abusive style. He will do virtually anything to antagonize and belittle his audience, so he can promote himself into national celebrity status. (Based upon the real-life character Alan Berg.) One particular weekend he discovers that he has a chance to get a national syndication, so he turns the heat up even higher under his audience of lonely and angry people. This story is strangely curious and is well-acted, but it also has very unappealing characters and is essentially very downbeat in tone. Not for everyone.

Sex Nud Viol Lang AdSit

A: Eric Bogosian, Alec Baldwin, Ellen Greene, Leslie Hope, John C. McGinley, John Pankow

© MCA/UNIVERSAL HOME VIDEO, INC. 80841

TAP

D: Nick Castle 110 m

PG-13 · MUS DMA · 1989 · COLOR · Sex · Nud · Viol · Lang · AdSit

7 Enjoyable old-style musical with a very talented cast. Hines stars as a recently released convict who has just served a stretch for a jewel robbery. He is an excellent tap dancer, but rock `n roll has destroyed his chances at making a living practicing his craft. Nevertheless, he trys to establish a dancing career for himself instead of returning to crime. His girl friend and her father (Davis), an old-time tap dancer, seek to help him. However, this story line, just as in the old time musical, is just a ruse to showcase some of the best tap dancing you'll ever see anywhere.

A: Gregory Hines, Sammy Davis, Jr., Suzanne Douglas, Savion Glover, Sandman Simms, Joe Morton

© COLUMBIA TRISTAR HOME VIDEO 70143

TAPS

D: Harold Becker 118 m

PG · ACT DMA · 1981 · COLOR · Sex · Nud · Viol · Lang · AdSit

7 Unusual sort of action fare. Scott is the head of a financially strapped military academy. He is the role model and hero to all the cadets, but particularly to cadet major Hutton. Hutton and the rest of the cadets transform their sense of honor, duty, and love for their school and the military into an armed insurrection when the school's trustees decide to sell the grounds to a real estate developer for condominiums. Well-crafted and believable, with solid acting. (Note the early appearances of Tom Cruise and Sean Penn).

A: George C. Scott, Timothy Hutton, Tom Cruise, Ronny Cox, Sean Penn

© FOXVIDEO 1128

TAXI BLUES

D: Pavel Lounguine 110 m

NR · FOR DMA · 1990 · COLOR · Sex · Nud · Viol · Lang · AdSit

8 Powerful import from post-perestroika Moscow. It is intended to be an allegory describing the whole of the Russian people's post-Soviet dilemma. That dilemma is personified by the two principal players. One is a burly, solidly working-class Russian taxi driver whose world is simple and tough. The other is a self-destructive Jewish jazz musician, an emaciated alcoholic whose wife has just thrown him out. When he can't pay his 70-ruble fare, the driver beats him up and confiscates his sax. But then he takes pity on the sorry guy and an odd relationship develops where each begins to learn about the other man's world.

A: Piotr Mamonov, Piotr Zaitchenko, Natalia Koliakanova, Vladimir Kachpour, Hal Singer, Elena Saphonova

© NEW YORKER FILMS NYV10092

TAXI DRIVER

D: Martin Scorsese 114 m

R · DMA ACT · 1976 · COLOR · Sex · Nud · Viol · Lang · AdSit

9 Intense, fascinating portrait of alienation made disturbingly real. De Niro is mesmerizing as ex-Marine Travis Bickle: quiet, a dutiful son, polite, well-meaning, but also socially inept, a loner and alone. As a night shift taxi driver, he witnesses a world of both seedy sex and beautiful women he does not know how to win. Frustratingly rejected by beautiful Shepherd, he snaps. The well-intentioned Bickle's torment focuses upon rescuing a 12-year-old whore (Foster). All his emotions boil over violently in a killing rampage directed against pimp Keitel and everything else corrupt.

A: Robert De Niro, Cybill Shepherd, Peter Boyle, Jodie Foster, Harvey Keitel, Albert Brooks

© GOODTIMES 4226

TEACHERS

D: Arthur Hiller 106 m

R · DMA COM · 1984 · COLOR · Sex · Nud · Viol · Lang · AdSit

6 Well intentioned and mildly entertaining statement about the state of public schools of the time. John F. Kennedy High School is sued by a former student who graduated, even though he couldn't even read. JoBeth Williams is his attorney who does battle with the conservative school system and also carries on a romance with burned-out good teacher Nick Nolte. Nolte is caught between both warring factions, while also trying to deal with rebellious student Macchio. Some good comedic moments, good acting, over-all enjoyable but a little heavy-handed at times.

A: Nick Nolte, JoBeth Williams, Lee Grant, Judd Hirsch, Richard Mulligan, Ralph Macchio

Distributed By MGM/UA Home Video M202814

TELL THEM WILLIE BOY IS HERE

D: Abraham Polonsky 98 m

PG · WST DMA · 1969 · COLOR · Sex · Nud · Viol · Lang · AdSit

6 Unusual modern Western that is based upon an actual 1909 incident. Robert Blake is a Paiute Indian who wants to wed white Katharine Ross, but her father (Angel) reacts violently to the news and Blake kills him in self-defense. He and Ross then flee together to avoid arrest. Sheriff Redford is reluctant to arrest Willie, but prissy Susan Clark and racist rancher Sullivan urge him on. President Grover Cleveland is also in the area, and the press corp with him promotes Willie's case nationally into the appearance of a major Indian uprising. Compelling viewing, even though heavy-handed.

A: Robert Redford, Katharine Ross, Robert Blake, Susan Clark, Barry Sullivan, Mikel Angel

© MCA/UNIVERSAL HOME VIDEO, INC. 55084

TEN COMMANDMENTS, THE

D: Cecil B. DeMille 219 m

G · DMA · 1956 · COLOR · Sex · Nud · Viol · Lang · AdSit

9 DeMille's second spectacular biblical epic. The Old Testament story of Moses is told with great detail (Oscar for Special Effects) and as much presence and conviction as Charlton Heston can muster. Moses's life is depicted from the time of his birth, his adoption into royalty, his banishment to the desert, his anointment by God, the many trials endured by the Egyptian king Ramses and the exodus of the Jews from Egypt. DeMille didn't miss anything. The parting of the Red Sea is still spectacular. Solid reverent family entertainment. See also equally grand BEN HUR, filmed three years later.

A: Charlton Heston, Yul Brynner, John Derek, Anne Baxter, Yvonne De Carlo, Edward G. Robinson

© PARAMOUNT HOME VIDEO 6524

TENDER MERCIES

D: Bruce Beresford 93 m

PG · DMA · 1983 · COLOR · Sex · Nud · Viol · Lang · AdSit

8 Bittersweet story of a once famous, but now down-and-out, alcoholic country singer who stumbles into a rundown Texas motel and a meaningful relationship with a kind-hearted widow and her son. Mac Sledge (Duvall) begins to patch his life back together and discovers that there is someone who loves him and for him to love, that he still has songs he needs to write and old problems he has yet to resolve. Interesting and believable characters are given real depth by top quality acting, particularly by Duvall, who won an Oscar. An interesting aside is that Duvall both wrote and sang all the songs himself.

A: Robert Duvall, Tess Harper, Betty Buckley, Allan Hubbard, Ellen Barkin, Wilford Brimley

© HBO VIDEO 1640

TENTH MAN, THE

D: Richard T. Heffron 99 m

NR · DMA · 1988 · COLOR · Sex · Nud · Viol · Lang · AdSit

8 A fascinating premise. Hopkins is a wealthy attorney who lives on an estate near a village just outside of WWII Paris and commutes in to work each day. However, one day he is picked up totally at random by a Nazi patrol and is thrown into prison. He and the other prisoners are told that they are to single out ten from their number, who will then be shot. They make the choice at random and he is one that is selected. Terrified, he makes a contract with a fellow prisoner who will die in his place and he will give everything he owns to the man's impoverished mother and sister. Years later, tormented and destitute he visits his house not telling them who he is. Excellent.

A: Anthony Hopkins, Kristin Scott Thomas, Derek Jacobi, Cyril Cusack

Distributed By MGM/UA Home Video 803941

TERMS OF ENDEARMENT

D: James L. Brooks 132 m

PG · DMA ROM COM · 1983 · COLOR · Sex · Nud · Viol · Lang · AdSit

10 Mesmerizing and totally heartwarming drama that captured five major Oscars, including Picture, Screenplay, Director, Actress and Supporting Actress. It is an intimate and winning character study of the relationship between a mother and daughter as it evolves over a period of years. MacLaine is wonderful as a neurotic, domineering mother and Winger is equally good as her independent-minded daughter who marries a cheating English teacher against her mother's wishes and later is to die of cancer. Totally captivating performances and story that surely will warm your heart and wet your eyes.

A: Shirley MacLaine, Debra Winger, Jack Nicholson, John Lithgow, Danny DeVito, Jeff Daniels

© PARAMOUNT HOME VIDEO 1407

TESS

D: Roman Polanski 136 m

PG · ROM DMA · 1980 · COLOR · Sex · Nud · Viol · Lang · AdSit

8 Extremely handsome production of "Tess of the D'Urbervilles," the tragic story of a beautiful but desperately poor girl in Victorian England. She is sent to live with distant relations when her parents learn that their family was once one of prominence, hoping that she will be able to better herself. Instead, she is seduced by her roguish cousin and abandoned when she becomes pregnant. The baby dies. She marries a minister's son but he, too, abandons her on the night of their wedding when he discovers her tainted past. Beautiful and haunting period piece. 6 nominations - 3 Oscars.

A: Nastassia Kinski, Peter Firth, Leigh Lawson, John Bett, Rosemary Martin, Sylvia Coleridge

© COLUMBIA TRISTAR HOME VIDEO 50633

THAT'S LIFE

D: Blake Edwards 102 m

PG-13 · DMA COM · 1986 · COLOR · Sex · Nud · Viol · Lang · AdSit

6 Harvey is wealthy and his wife is throwing him a big birthday party with all his friends and family in attendance. But Harvey is miserable and is making everybody else miserable. Harvey is turning 60, and he doesn't like it. His wife (Andrews) is having her own personal crisis. She will not know until after the party whether the biopsy for cancer, which she told no one about, was positive. Harvey is Jack Lemmon (or is it director Blake Edwards). This film has been criticized for unfolding just as though it was a home movie. Believable, funny in spots and moving.

A: Julie Andrews, Jack Lemmon, Sally Kellerman, Robert Loggia, Emma Walton, Felicia Farr

© LIVE HOME VIDEO 5203

THAT WAS THEN... THIS IS NOW

D: Christopher Cain 102 m

R | DMA | 1985 | COLOR

6 Worthy adaptation by Emilio Estevez of "The Outsiders; Rumble Fish" by S.E. Hinton. It is an unvarnished character portrait of two young men who grew up together as brothers in a rough neighborhood and are now entering into adulthood together. Estevez is an orphan raised by a working class widow (Babcock) along with her own son (Sheffer). The boys have been close but now Sheffer accepts responsibility and woos waitress Delaney, while Estevez deals drugs. One grows up, one doesn't. Strong performances, but depressing.

Sex / Nud / Viol / Lang / AdSit

A: Emilio Estevez, Craig Sheffer, Kim Delaney, Barbara Babcock, Jill Schoelen, Morgan Freeman

© PARAMOUNT HOME VIDEO 1954

THELMA & LOUISE

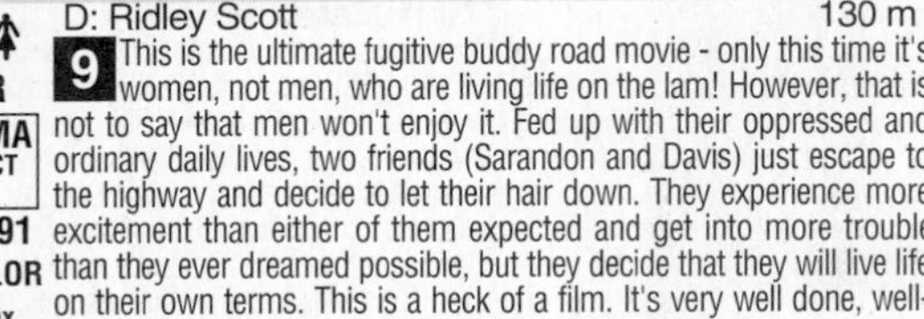

D: Ridley Scott 130 m

R | DMA ACT | 1991 | COLOR

9 This is the ultimate fugitive buddy road movie - only this time it's women, not men, who are living life on the lam! However, that is not to say that men won't enjoy it. Fed up with their oppressed and ordinary daily lives, two friends (Sarandon and Davis) just escape to the highway and decide to let their hair down. They experience more excitement than either of them expected and get into more trouble than they ever dreamed possible, but they decide that they will live life on their own terms. This is a heck of a film. It's very well done, well-acted and a lot of fun. It became a landmark film .

Sex / Nud / Viol / Lang / AdSit

A: Susan Sarandon, Geena Davis, Harvey Keitel, Michael Madsen, Christopher McDonald, Brad Pitt

Distributed By MGM/UA Home Video M902355

THIEF OF HEARTS

D: Douglas Day Stewart 101 m

R | ROM DMA | 1984 | COLOR

7 This is a fascinating premise gets pretty fair treatment. A cat burglar breaks into a house and steals the diaries of a beautiful young married woman. By reading them, he now possesses all her innermost secrets and desires and strikes upon a well-calculated plan. He spies upon her and then sets out to seduce her by fulfilling all her fantasies. He will become her perfect lover. At first she fails to recognize the ruse and becomes a willing participant in his plan, but then as she begins to suspect, things take a bad turn. Well-done and very erotic, with reedited scenes added for the video version.

Sex / Nud / Viol / Lang / AdSit

A: Barbara Williams, Steven Bauer, John Getz, David Caruso, George Wendt, Christine Ebersole

© PARAMOUNT HOME VIDEO 1660

THIS BOY'S LIFE

D: Michael Caton-Jones m

R | DMA | 1993 | COLOR

8 Child abuse is not always only physical. Jack's mother had a way of getting out of trouble - she always just ran. She ran from one bad relationship to another until she ran into Dwight. Dwight wasn't the man of her dreams but Jack needed a father and she was tired of running. So, she married Dwight and moved to tiny Concrete, Oregon. But, Dwight was a small-minded man and everyone else was more powerful than he was - except, that is, for Jack. So under the guise of straightening him out, Dwight constantly hounded and belittled Jack. Excellent performances and believable drama, but this is not light entertainment. It is also based on fact.

Sex / Nud / Viol / Lang / AdSit

A: Robert De Niro, Ellen Barkin, Leonardo DiCaprio, Jonah Blechman, Eliza Dushku, Chris Cooper

© WARNER HOME VIDEO 12650

THIS PROPERTY IS CONDEMNED

D: Sydney Pollack 109 m

NR | DMA | 1966 | COLOR

6 Film adaptation of a Tennessee Williams play. Like virtually all Williams's works, this is a gritty story of troubled lives. Set in the depression years, a handsome young man (Redford) comes into a small Southern town, taking up residence at the boarding house for railway workers run by Natalie Wood's mother. A stifled Wood quickly becomes infatuated with Redford and seizes upon him as a way out of this life, but cold-hearted Redford is just there to lay off railway workers. He becomes so hated that he is being driven out of town, and she gets caught in the fury of the townsfolk.

Sex / Nud / Viol / Lang / AdSit

A: Robert Redford, Natalie Wood, Charles Bronson, Kate Reid, Robert Blake, Dabney Coleman

© PARAMOUNT HOME VIDEO 6534

THREE OF HEARTS

D: Yurek Bogayevicz 101 m

R | ROM DMA | 1993 | COLOR

7 A very unusual premise produces a film that is difficult for many people to accept. Ignoring that, it is quite likable. Kelly Lynch and Sherilyn Fenn have been lesbian lovers. Now Fenn wants to call it quits, but Lynch is still very much in love with her and does not want to lose her. Meanwhile Lynch has become buddies with Baldwin, a likable gigolo she had hired to escort her to a family wedding. This unlikely pair strikes upon a plan to win Fenn back to Lynch. He will seduce her and then dump her, breaking her heart and causing her to return to Lynch. Baldwin, however, is disillusioned with his life and falls for Fenn instead and Lynch eventually decides to help him.

Sex / Nud / Viol / Lang / AdSit

A: William Baldwin, Kelly Lynch, Sherilyn Fenn, Joe Pantoliano, Gail Strickland, Cec Verrell

© TURNER HOME ENTERTAINMENT N4034

THRONE OF BLOOD

D: Akira Kurosawa 105 m

FOR DMA | 1957 | B&W

10 Grippingly powerful Japanese retelling of Shakespeare's "MacBeth." This is masterful filmmaking, but it is also very heavy going - be prepared. Japan's master director Kurosawa has taken the Shakespearean themes of overpowering pride and bloody treachery and set them within the framework of 16th-century feudal Japan's brutality. Mufune is a paranoid warlord who is hounded by his greedy wife Yamada and driven by his lust for power. Strikingly powerful images evoke Shakespeare's vision, but do so in such a way that the story is singularly valid in its own right. In Japanese, with subtitles.

Sex / Nud / Viol / Lang / AdSit

A: Toshiro Mifune, Isuzu Yamada, Minoru Chiaki, Takashi Shimura

© HOME VISION THR 090

THROUGH A GLASS DARKLY

D: Ingmar Bergman 90 m

NR | FOR DMA | 1961 | B&W

9 Mostly for serious film fans - this was the first in Bergman's "faith" trilogy. It is the dark psychological study of the events and relationships surrounding four persons - a schizophrenic woman just released from a mental institution, her husband, her younger brother and her psychologist father - who all spend the summer together on an isolated island. It is Bergman's philosophic probe of man's relationship to God. We watch this woman slowly descend back into the hell of her insanity. Best Foreign Film Oscar. Subtitles or dubbed.

Sex / Nud / Viol / Lang / AdSit

A: Harriet Andersson, Max von Sydow, Gunnar Bjornstrand, Lars Passgard

© HOME VISION THR 100

TIGHTROPE

D: Richard Tuggle 118 m

R | CRM ACT DMA | 1984 | COLOR

9 Fascinating thriller which also has a compelling underlying story. Eastwood is a burned-out homicide detective. He has been deserted by his wife and is taking care of his two daughters. He has also taken to having kinky sex with the prostitutes on his beat, handcuffing them. When these same girls start to turn up dead, Eastwood realizes that he is being followed and that he and his daughters are in big danger. It is an intelligent script which allows Eastwood to analyze the dichotomy within his character, but it never forgets to be an action flick and refrains from exploitation.

Sex / Nud / Viol / Lang / AdSit

A: Clint Eastwood, Genevieve Bujold, Dan Hedaya, Alison Eastwood, Jennifer Beck

© WARNER HOME VIDEO 11400

TIME MACHINE, THE

D: George Pal 103 m

PG | SF DMA | 1960 | COLOR

8 Lush adaptation of the H.G. Welles novel. A Victorian inventor (Taylor) develops a time machine and, full of hope, he travels ahead in time only to encounter numerous world wars and destruction. Disturbed, he leaps far ahead into the year 802,701. There he discovers a peaceful, carefree race living in an apparent Garden of Eden. But there are dangers here as well. These people are mutants, born of atomic wars, who are totally ignorant and apathetic to everything - to the point that they won't even defend themselves against a race of subsurface dwellers which preys upon them. Special Effects Oscar.

Sex / Nud / Viol / Lang / AdSit

A: Rod Taylor, Alan Young, Yvette Mimieux, Sebastian Cabot, Tom Helmore, Whit Bissell

Distributed By MGM/UA Home Video M600152

TIME TO LOVE AND A TIME TO DIE, A

D: Douglas Sirk 133 m

NR | DMA ROM WAR | 1958 | COLOR

8 Poignant, moving, believable and sad anti-war film. It is the story of an ordinary German soldier caught up in the chaos occurring during the closing days of World War II. He returns home on furlough from the Russian front to his hometown which has been almost totally destroyed by the Allied bombing raids and his parents are missing. All the townsfolk are as severely demoralized and fearful as is he, but there he meets a beautiful young woman. They fall in love and marry, all the while knowing that their time together will be brief because he must soon return to the front.

Sex / Nud / Viol / Lang / AdSit

A: John Gavin, Lilo Pulver, Jock Mahoney, Keenan Wynn, Jim Hutton, Klaus Kinski

© MCA/UNIVERSAL HOME VIDEO, INC.

TIN DRUM, THE

D: Volker Schlondorff 142 m

R | FOR FAN DMA | 1979 | COLOR

9 Very bizarre and "artsy" fantasy, or rather nightmare, taken from a world-renown novel by Gunter Grass. Visually stunning, it was the winner of the Best Foreign Film Oscar. The story is that of young boy in 1920s Germany who is so distraught by the Nazis and their bleak world that he decides to stop growing. Instead, he becomes obsessed with beating on his toy drum to drown out horror, and also develops a piercing scream. However, these strange talents only make him into a popular source of entertainment for the Nazis, and ultimately he survives when others others around him suffer. Subtitles.

Sex / Nud / Viol / Lang / AdSit

A: Mario Adorf, Angela Winkler, David Bennent, Daniel Olbrychski, Katharina Thalbach, Heinz Bennent

© WARNER HOME VIDEO 24053

TO DANCE WITH THE WHITE DOG

PG · ROM DMA · 1993 · COLOR
D: Glenn Jordan — 98 m

9 Beautiful made-for-TV movie that was done for the Hallmark Hall of Fame. Sam and Cora are an old couple that have lived together for all their lives and live surrounded by their family. Still deeply in love after 50 years of marriage, Cora is stricken and dies. Sam is struggling with his loneliness and is in poor health himself. Suddenly one day, a stray white dog shows up at his door. The two become fast friends, but the dog only comes around when he is alone and his children fear he is losing his mind. But the dog is real and it is there to protect and love him, just as Cora had done. Extremely well done and very moving. Reportedly based upon an actual incidence.

Sex · Nud · Viol · Lang ◢ · AdSit ◢

A: Hume Cronyn, Jessica Tandy, Christine Baranski, Terry Beaver, Harley Cross, Ester Rolle

© REPUBLIC PICTURES HOME VIDEO 0837

TO KILL A MOCKINGBIRD

NR · DMA · 1962 · B&W
D: Robert Mulligan — 131 m

9 Outstanding and flavorful film about a small-town 1930s Alabama lawyer who defends a black man who was falsely charged of raping a white woman. Peck is outstanding (Oscar) as the hard-pressed lawyer and widowed father who is trying to raise two impressionable young children against a background of hate and fear. He is ostracized by the whole town for standing up for what is right. An extremely powerful film that takes its time but never bogs down. Winner of three Oscars, including Peck's, plus two other nominations, including Best Picture.

Sex · Nud · Viol ◢ · Lang · AdSit ◢

A: Gregory Peck, Mary Badham, Philip Alford, Brock Peters, Robert Duvall, John Megna

© MCA/UNIVERSAL HOME VIDEO, INC. 55032

TOM & VIV

PG-13 · DMA · 1994 · COLOR
D: Brian Tilbert — 125 m

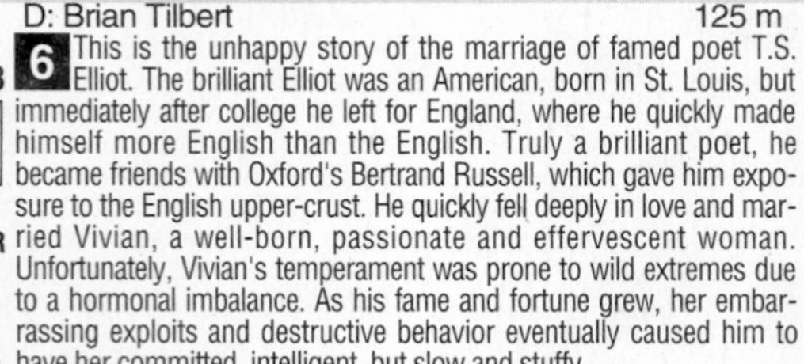

6 This is the unhappy story of the marriage of famed poet T.S. Elliot. The brilliant Elliot was an American, born in St. Louis, but immediately after college he left for England, where he quickly made himself more English than the English. Truly a brilliant poet, he became friends with Oxford's Bertrand Russell, which gave him exposure to the English upper-crust. He quickly fell deeply in love and married Vivian, a well-born, passionate and effervescent woman. Unfortunately, Vivian's temperament was prone to wild extremes due to a hormonal imbalance. As his fame and fortune grew, her embarrassing exploits and destructive behavior eventually caused him to have her committed. intelligent, but slow and stuffy.

Sex · Nud · Viol · Lang ◢ · AdSit ■

A: Willem Dafoe, Miranda Richardson, Rosemary Harris, Tim Dutton, Nickolas Grace

© MIRAMAX HOME ENTERTAINMENT 4441

TO SIR, WITH LOVE

NR · DMA · 1967 · COLOR
D: James Clavell — 105 m

8 Powerful and affecting melodrama that was very popular - and for good reason. Sidney Poitier is a new, untried teacher who is assigned a teaching position at a London slum school that is populated by alienated and abusive teenagers. His determined persistence and unorthodox teaching methods break through their walls of hostility and instill in them a renewed sense of hope. A heartfelt and believable film in which Poitier shines in one of his best performances. Similar to equally good BLACKBOARD JUNGLE from 10 years earlier.

Sex · Nud · Viol · Lang · AdSit ◢

A: Sidney Poitier, Judy Geeson, Christian Roberts, Suzy Kendall, Lulu, Faith Brook

© COLUMBIA TRISTAR HOME VIDEO 60247

TO SLEEP WITH ANGER

PG · DMA FAN · 1990 · COLOR
D: Charles Burnett — 102 m

8 Unusual and offbeat but enchanting film about the conflicts between old and new values, between one generation and the next, and between an old black culture and an emerging new one. Parents Gideon and Suzie cling to their old ways from the deep South, to the embarrassment and consternation of their youngest son and his wife. Into Gideon's home, on a tree-lined Los Angeles street, walks jovial Harry Mention (Glover), an old friend of Gideon. But Harry is much more. He is a charmer, a storyteller and an evil "trickster" who has come to charm their souls from them.

Sex · Nud · Viol · Lang ◢ · AdSit ◢

A: Danny Glover, Paul Butler, Mary Alice, Sheryl Lee Ralph, Carl Lumbly, Richard Brooks

© COLUMBIA TRISTAR HOME VIDEO F0734

TOUCHED BY LOVE

PG · DMA · 1980 · COLOR
D: Gus Trikonis — 95 m

7 Touching true story. A nursing trainee who works with kids afflicted with cerebral palsy has one particular girl who is totally incommunicative until she strikes upon the unconventional idea of talking the girl into writing to her idol, Elvis Presley. When Presley returns her letter and becomes the girl's pen pal, she begins a remarkable turnaround in attitude which results in a new life for her. Understated performances add significantly to this uplifting and sentimental (but not overly so) effective tearjerker.

Sex · Nud · Viol · Lang ◢ · AdSit

A: Deborah Raffin, Diane Lane, Michael Learned, Cristina Raines, Mary Wickes, Clu Gulager

© COLUMBIA TRISTAR HOME VIDEO 60307

TRIBES

G · DMA COM · 1970 · COLOR
D: Joseph Sargent — 90 m

8 Excellent made-for-TV movie. It was made during the time of the Vietnam war and revolves around many of the issues that concerned everyone then. It has become a little dated but it is also still both insightful and funny. Imagine a hippie, in a robe, with long hair and sandals, getting drafted into the Marines. Darin McGavin is the tough DI given the responsibility of turning this flower into a lean, mean, fighting machine. The trouble is, he is already lean and tough, but he's a dedicated peacenik. Worse yet, he's also a natural leader and everyone in the platoon is following him, not the tough DI. Really quite good.

Sex · Nud · Viol · Lang · AdSit ◢

A: Jan-Michael Vincent, Darren McGavin, Earl Holliman, John Gruber, Danny Goldman, Richard Yniguez

© FOXVIDEO 1669

TRIP TO BOUNTIFUL, THE

PG · DMA · 1985 · COLOR
D: Peter Masterson — 107 m

9 Poignant, moving and rich in texture. An old woman (Page) is living with her son and his discontented, demanding wife in a crowded apartment in 1947. Desperately unhappy and lonely, she longs for the happier days when she lived in Bountiful, Texas and hoping to recapture that happiness, she escapes on a bus to visit her hometown. On the bus to Bountiful, she meets a kindred spirit in a young woman (DeMornay), but upon her arrival her hopes are dashed when she discovers that all her old friends are dead and Bountiful is abandoned. Excellent, but sometimes slow. Best Actress Oscar for a brilliant job by Page.

Sex · Nud · Viol · Lang · AdSit ◢

A: Geraldine Page, John Heard, Carlin Glynn, Rebecca De Mornay, Richard Bradford

© NEW LINE HOME VIDEO 1341

TRIUMPH OF THE SPIRIT

R · DMA ACT · 1989 · COLOR
D: Robert M. Young — 120 m

6 Pretty good but a very sad drama based upon actual events. A young Greek Jewish boxer and street tough (Dafoe) is captured by the Nazis in 1943 and sent to Auschwitz, along with his family. There, the SS officers delight in watching boxing matches between the prisoners, where the contestants are like gladiators. They literally fight for their lives. The losers and their families are sent to the gas chambers. Blunt and grim.

Sex · Nud · Viol ■ · Lang ◢ · AdSit ■

A: Willem Dafoe, Wendy Gazelle, Robert Loggia, Edward James Olmos, Kelly Wolf, Costas Mandylor

© COLUMBIA TRISTAR HOME VIDEO 59063

TROPIC OF CANCER

NC-17 · DMA · 1970 · COLOR
D: Joseph Strick — 87 m

7 Henry Miller's underground classic book was banned for 27 years. It was a semi-autobiographical novel that purports to document the sexual exploits of of a free-spirited hedonistic American in the Paris of the 1920's. The film is an updated version of the book and is a series of earthy but good-natured vignettes. Ellen Burstyn has only a tiny role as Miller's upset wife.

Sex ■ · Nud ■ · Viol · Lang ■ · AdSit ■

A: Rip Torn, Ellen Burstyn, David Bauer, James Callahan, Laurence Ligneres, Phil Brown

© PARAMOUNT HOME VIDEO 6922

TRUE COLORS

R · DMA · 1991 · COLOR
D: Herbert Ross — 111 m

7 Interesting portrait in ambition, shown in the contrast of two characters. Two best friends from law school both enter into the political process. Rich kid Spader chooses to join the Justice Department. Poor boy Cusack enters directly into politics. Cusack has no personal passion for any political agenda; his only goal is the pursuit of power. He is not morally corrupt, but he is driven so hard to be somebody that he allows himself to betray his friend to satisfy a political patron. When Spader learns he was betrayed, he sets a trap for his old friend that will destroy his political career.

Sex ◢ · Nud · Viol ◢ · Lang ■ · AdSit ■

A: James Spader, John Cusack, Imogen Stubbs, Mandy Patinkin, Richard Widmark, Dina Merrill

© PARAMOUNT HOME VIDEO 32127

TRUE CONFESSIONS

R · DMA · 1981 · COLOR
D: Ulu Grosbard — 107 m

8 A thoughtful and powerful film. Two brothers in 1930s Los Angles are on very different tracks. One (Duvall) is a hard-edged, formerly corrupt cop and the other (De Niro) is an ambitious priest of a wealthy parish. These two come into conflict when the reformed Duvall traces the murder of a young prostitute to a heavy contributor to De Niro's church (Durning). Duvall wants his brother's help to nail a murderer, but De Niro balks. Solid character studies. A little slow, but a very powerful story of power politics.

Sex · Nud ◢ · Viol ◢ · Lang ■ · AdSit ◢

A: Robert De Niro, Robert Duvall, Charles Durning, Ed Flanders, Burgess Meredith, Rose Gregorio

Distributed By MGM/UA Home Video M800145

TRUE LOVE

D: Nancy Savoca — 101 m

R | COM DMA | 1989 | COLOR

6 A young Bronx working couple is getting married, even though they are just now discovering that they hardly know each other. The ball is rolling and they aren't going to let that stop one of the most extravagant, garish and tacky weddings ever (the mashed potatoes are dyed blue to match the dresses) from happening. Even though he proves to be an irresponsible sort, in their world men and women do what is expected of them and she's going to get him to the alter no matter what it takes. The film has some riotously funny scenes, but its characters are obnoxious at times and difficult to sympathize with.

Sex / Nud / Viol / Lang / AdSit

A: Annabella Sciorra, Ron Eldard, Roger Rignack, Aida Turturro, Star Jasper, Michael J. Wolfe

Distributed By MGM/UA Home Video M901763

TRUE ROMANCE

D: Tony Scott — 121 m

R | CRM DMA | 1993 | COLOR

7 This is no WUTHERING HEIGHTS. The romance here is between a ditzy novice call girl named Alabama and an not-too-bright Elvis-admirer named Clarence, who was only her third-ever trick. When Clarence learns that her pimp has threatened her, Clarence goes to gain her freedom back. However, in the process, he kills the pimp and accidentally picks up the wrong suitcase - this one has a major shipment of cocaine in it. Clarence and Alabama head off to California with their treasure and with the mob and the cops on their trail. A very violent movie that has occasional stabs at black comedy thrown in. Not a pretty portrait of people, but one that is perversely believable.

Sex / Nud / Viol / Lang / AdSit

A: Christian Slater, Patricia Arquette, Dennis Hopper, Val Kilmer, Gary Oldman, Brad Pitt

© WARNER HOME VIDEO 13158

TRULY, MADLY, DEEPLY

D: Anthony Minghella — 107 m

NR | ROM DMA FAN | 1992 | COLOR

7 Touching and comedic. British couple Stevenson and Rickman are deeply in love. So when Rickman dies, Stevenson can't seem to find the will to go on. In her grief, she simply exists, losing track of days and withdrawing into a dark shell of sadness. However, one day he mysteriously reappears to her as a ghost and helps her through her grief. It is then that she realizes that he can no longer give her the kind of relationship she really needs and she finds the strength to live again. The wonderful thing about this movie is that it just happens, no explanation is ever offered as to Rickman's reappearance, and ultimately it really isn't needed.

Sex / Nud / Viol / Lang / AdSit

A: Juliet Stevenson, Alan Rickman, Bill Paterson, Michael Maloney, Christopher Rozycki, Keith Bartlett

© TOUCHSTONE HOME VIDEO 1353

TRUST

D: Hal Hartley — 107 m

R | DMA COM | 1991 | COLOR

8 Quirky, almost surreal black comedy. A pretty 16-year-old finds that she is pregnant. She tells her father. He insults her. She slaps him. He falls dead. She leaves home and meets up with a 17-year-old electronics whiz-kid who also left home because he can't get along with his dad. He can't hold a job because he refuses to stoop to work on TVs and he carries around his father's Korean War vintage hand grenade, just in case he wants to commit suicide. Deadpan dialogue. Stylish photography and plenty of off-beat moments. Can these two misfits find happiness? Likely will become a cult favorite.

Sex / Nud / Viol / Lang / AdSit

A: Adrienne Shelly, Martin Donovan, Merritt Nelson, Edie Falco, John Mc Kay

© REPUBLIC PICTURES HOME VIDEO 4205

TUCKER: THE MAN AND HIS DREAM

D: Francis Ford Coppola — 111 m

PG | DMA | 1988 | COLOR

8 In 1948 the man before his time built the car before its time. This true story of Preston Tucker (Bridges) is told with spirit and verve and is brilliantly directed by longtime admirer Coppola. Tucker built a safer and more affordable car than anyone else after the war, but interests in Washington joined forces with the big three car manufacturers and launched a smear campaign against the car, destroying Tucker's dream. Undaunted, Tucker emerged with his character unshaken and his optimism intact. Inspiring!

Sex / Nud / Viol / Lang / AdSit

A: Jeff Bridges, Joan Allen, Martin Landau, Frederic Forrest, Ako, Dean Stockwell

© PARAMOUNT HOME VIDEO 32144

TUNES OF GLORY

D: Ronald Neame — 106 m

NR | DMA | 1960 | COLOR

8 Superb and gripping British character drama about a rivalry which develops between two soldiers. Alec Guiness, an older Scottish colonel from common roots, has been in temporary command of his regiment and is about to retire. He drinks too much and his discipline is lax, but the men like him. He is replaced by Mills, a much younger, high-born, by-the-book and very competent officer. Guiness resents Mills and loses no opportunity to belittle and torment him. It reaches the point where they are at war with each other and Guiness alienates himself from everyone. Solid Oscar-nominated screenplay.

Sex / Nud / Viol / Lang / AdSit

A: Alec Guinness, John Mills, Kay Walsh, Susannah York, Dennis Price, John Fraser

© NEW LINE HOME VIDEO 6020

TURNING POINT

D: Herbert Ross — 119 m

PG | DMA | 1979 | COLOR

8 Highly acclaimed, high quality drama. Two friends who were both promising dancers, take different paths at their turning points. Bancroft gives up a home and family for a life in ballet. MacLaine gives up dancing to become a wife and mother in Oklahoma. But her daughter is now a budding ballerina who is at her own turning point and the long-standing relationship between the two old friends is in jeopardy. Raw emotions are unleashed as their histories are revealed. Eleven Oscar nominations. Excellent acting and beautiful dance sequences featuring Mikhail Baryshnikov.

Sex / Nud / Viol / Lang / AdSit

A: Shirley MacLaine, Anne Bancroft, Leslie Browne, Mikhail Baryshnikov, Tom Skerritt, Martha Scott

© FOXVIDEO 1089

TWICE IN A LIFETIME

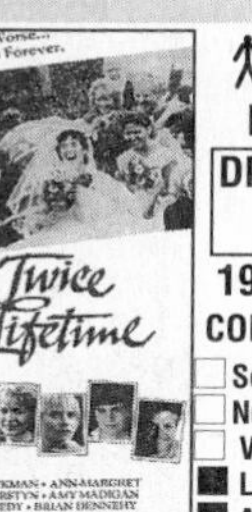

D: Bud Yorkin — 117 m

R | DMA | 1985 | COLOR

8 Powerful and realistic slice-of-life drama that will strike a responsive chord in many viewers. A middle-aged millworker (Gene Hackman) is stuck in a routine marriage to Ellen Burstyn, his wife of 30 years. His dissatisfaction is brought to a head when he falls for a local barmaid (Ann-Margret). He leaves Burstyn, but is tormented by the pain he has caused his wife and two daughters. One daughter (Madigan) is unable to forgive him, but the other (Sheedy) relents and invites him to her wedding - over Madigan's objections. Solid cast raises this far above a soap opera. Meaningful and evocative.

Sex / Nud / Viol / Lang / AdSit

A: Gene Hackman, Ellen Burstyn, Ann-Margret, Amy Madigan, Ally Sheedy, Brian Dennehy

© LIVE HOME VIDEO VA5119

TWILIGHT ZONE: THE MOVIE

D: Joe Dante, John Landis — 101 m

PG | SUS DMA FAN | 1983 | COLOR

7 Intriguing collection of four tales of the thought-provoking variety, made famous in the 1960s TV series of the same name. In fact, three of the episodes are remakes from that series. All are interesting and done with much higher production values, but oddly they lack the punch of the originals and overall are not as good - still worth a look, though. Example: "Nightmare at 20,000 Feet" - Lithgow is terrified because he is the only passenger on an airliner who can see the gremlin that is on the craft's wing working hard to rip it off.

Sex / Nud / Viol / Lang / AdSit

A: Dan Aykroyd, Albert Brooks, Scatman Crothers, John Lithgow, Vic Morrow, Kevin McCarthy

© WARNER HOME VIDEO 11314

TWO RODE TOGETHER

D: John Ford — 109 m

NR | WST DMA ACT | 1961 | COLOR

8 A worthy Western with Stewart in a somewhat uncharacteristically harsh role. He plays a hard-bitten and cynical marshall who has been hired by a naive calvary officer (Widmark) and a group of settlers to retrieve kidnapped white children from the Commanches. While Widmark and the settlers are optimistic, Stewart knows that what he will bring back is not what they expect. He also knows that the children will not be accepted. Interesting and somber take on the theme first explored in THE SEARCHERS, which is also highly recommended.

Sex / Nud / Viol / Lang / AdSit

A: James Stewart, Richard Widmark, Shirley Jones, Andy Devine, Woody Strode, Linda Cristal

© COLUMBIA TRISTAR HOME VIDEO 60762

TWO WOMEN

D: Vittorio De Sica — 99 m

NR | FOR DMA WAR | 1961 | B&W

9 Extremely intense and moving drama. Sophia Loren received an Oscar for her powerful performance. It is a story of survival under extraordinary circumstances. It is Italy during WWII, just as the Germans are retreating and the Allies are advancing. Sophia is the mother of a 13-year-old daughter and both are struggling just to survive. They are also just learning to deal with the girl's awakening womanhood, because both mother and daughter have both fallen in love with a farmer's son (Belmundo), when both are raped by advancing soldiers. Heart-wrenching. Subtitles or dubbed.

Sex / Nud / Viol / Lang / AdSit

A: Sophia Loren, Raf Vallone, Jean-Paul Belmondo, Eleanora Brown, Renato Salvatori

© GOODTIMES 4240

UNBEARABLE LIGHTNESS OF BEING

D: Philip Kaufman — 172 m

R | DMA ROM | 1988 | COLOR

9 Sensual, aesthetic and mesmerizing. The setting is Prague - 1966. A brilliant Czech doctor (Day Lewis) is a real lady killer and he believes very strongly that it is this free spirit that keeps him sane. He is married to Olin, who he truly does love, but he is also having a torrid affair with a beautiful waitress (Binoche). His wife also wants to experience this feeling, but for her it's a disaster. Then the Russian tanks move in and the trio flees to Geneva. There they further explore life, politics and their relationships, forming a sensuous love triangle. Provocative, emotionally appealing, physically sexy.

Sex / Nud / Viol / Lang / AdSit

A: Daniel Day-Lewis, Juliette Binoche, Lena Olin, Derek de Lint, Erland Josephson, Pavel Landovsky

© ORION PICTURES CORPORATION 8721

UNDER THE VOLCANO

D: John Huston 112 m

R · DMA · 1984 · COLOR

6 Somber. Set in Mexico, November 1939 on the Day of the Dead, a day set aside to celebrate death, a British diplomat (Finney) living in Mexico is drowning his sorrows with alcohol. A rash of recent crises and his wife's love affair have nearly driven him over the edge. His wife (Bisset) and half brother (Andrews) do everything they can to bring him out of his alcoholic state, but their efforts are to no avail; he seems to be inviting death on this black day. A critically acclaimed drama from the noted directorial hand of John Huston. However, much of the book's symbolism hasn't translated well.

Sex · Nud · Viol · Lang · AdSit

A: Albert Finney, Jacqueline Bisset, Anthony Andrews, Katy Jurado, Ignacio Lopez Tarso, James Villiers

© MCA/UNIVERSAL HOME VIDEO, INC. 80125

UNFORGIVEN, THE

D: John Huston 123 m

NR · WST DMA · 1960 · COLOR

7 In the Texas panhandle immediately after the Civil War, memories of the fierce battles with the Kiowa are still fresh in minds on both sides. So when a figure from the past claims that Hepburn is a full-blooded Kiowa who was adopted by white settlers as a baby, tensions erupt. The Kiowa want to reclaim her into the tribe and the local whites want her gone. Both she and her adopted family are torn by the conflict that threatens to consume them all. One "brother" clearly loves her in a non-brotherly way and another hates Indians so much he is willing to leave his family. Intense.

Sex · Nud · Viol · Lang · AdSit

A: Burt Lancaster, Audrey Hepburn, Lillian Gish, Audie Murphy, John Saxon, Charles Brickford

Distributed By MGM/UA Home Video M601123

UNFORGIVEN

D: Clint Eastwood m

R · WST DMA ACT · 1992 · COLOR

10 Hugely successful and popular but very atypical Western that won Best Picture Oscar plus 3 more. Eastwood is an ex-gunslinger and outlaw who has been struggling to eke out a living as a farmer, but he and his family are starving. So, he and his ex-partner set off to collect a bounty by killing a couple of cowboys who have cut up a prostitute. Their mission, however, places them in direct conflict with another gunslinger (Hackman) who has become comfortable as the ruthless sheriff of the town. This is a no-nonsense, grittily realistic and unglamorous story of men pitted against each other, who are able to survive a brutal game by killing brutally without a thought.

Sex · Nud · Viol · Lang · AdSit

A: Clint Eastwood, Gene Hackman, Morgan Freeman, Richard Harris, Jaimz Woolvett

© WARNER HOME VIDEO 12531

UNMARRIED WOMAN, AN

D: Paul Mazursky 124 m

R · DMA COM ROM · 1978 · COLOR

9 An unforgettable look at life, love and relationships. Jill Clayburgh appears to have everything. Then suddenly her husband of 17 years tearfully confesses he's in love with a younger woman. Destroyed, she is forced to start over. She ventures tentatively out into the singles scene. It is an uncomfortable experience but, after one false start, she meets an oddball artist who restores her spirit and confidence. Insightful, witty and believable. This was a Best Picture nominee. Also nominated was Clayburgh for Best Actress and Mazursky for Best Screenplay. Excellent.

Sex · Nud · Viol · Lang · AdSit

A: Jill Clayburgh, Alan Bates, Michael Murphy, Cliff Gorman, Pat Quinn, Kelly Bishop

© FOXVIDEO 1088

UP THE SANDBOX

D: Irvin Kershner 98 m

R · COM DMA · 1972 · COLOR

6 Streisand is a neglected New York housewife and mother of two who is feeling like life has passed her by. She fears even more the effect that the impending birth of her third child will have on her and her family. Her professor husband Selby barely notices her anxiety and unhappiness, he's all wrapped up in his work. So she seeks solace in fantasy. Streisand's performance helps to save this weird, somewhat uneven, but still touching, funny and warm feminist statement.

Sex · Nud · Viol · Lang · AdSit

A: Barbra Streisand, David Selby, Jane Hoffman, John C. Becher

© WARNER HOME VIDEO 11325

URBAN COWBOY

D: James Bridges 132 m

PG · ROM DMA · 1980 · COLOR

8 Sassy cowboy slice-of-life romance with plenty of twang! Newcomer Travolta breezes into a tough Texas town and hangs out at the very popular Gilley's bar. He picks up and soon marries local girl Winger, but strays to make his bed with rich girl Smith for a while. Winger retaliates and moves in with local bad boy Glenn, creating a spicy romantic mess. At the center of everything is the symbol of courage and bravery for all the cowboys in the bar - the mechanical bull - a device the men ride as a testament to their manhood. Very flavorful honky-tonk fare! Good star chemistry. Very popular movie.

Sex · Nud · Viol · Lang · AdSit

A: John Travolta, Debra Winger, Scott Glenn, Madolyn Smith, Barry Corbin, Brooke Alderson

© PARAMOUNT HOME VIDEO 1285

UTU

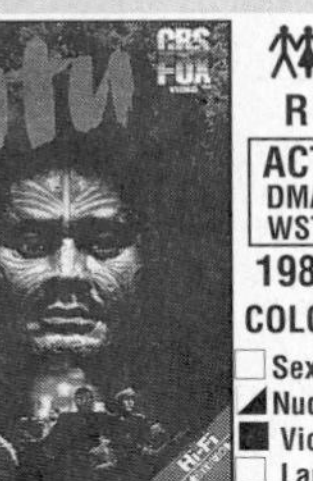

D: Geoff Murphy 104 m

R · ACT DMA WST · 1983 · COLOR

8 Excellent (but very exotic) New Zealand import. It is set there, in the 1870s, but has definite overtones of the American Southwest. When a aboriginal tribesman, who is fighting for the British colonial army, comes home to find that his village has been massacred by the same white army he has been fighting for, he swears vengeance on all whites. He becomes a vicious raider of white settlements, hotly pursued by the army and even despised by many of his own people because of his ruthlessness. Lots of action, but also a moving moral play that is reminiscent of the American campaign against Geronimo.

Sex · Nud · Viol · Lang · AdSit

A: Anzac Wallace, Kelly Johnson, Tim Elliot, Bruno Lawrence

© CBS/FOX VIDEO 6119

VALMONT

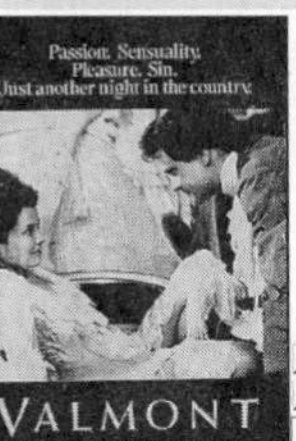

D: Milos Forman 137 m

R · DMA ROM · 1990 · COLOR

6 The cast is younger and the budget was bigger, but it came too close on the heels of the very successful DANGEROUS LIASONS to be a big box office hit. It is essentially the same story, although it has been softened a little. Two decadent 18th-century French aristocrats and former lovers make a callous bet. She (Benning) wants him (Firth) to cockold her unfaithful lover (Jones) by seducing his 15-year-old fiance (Balk). He counters that he can bed the timid and very married Meg Tilly. If he wins, Benning must be his bedmate.

Sex · Nud · Viol · Lang · AdSit

A: Colin Firth, Annette Bening, Meg Tilly, Henry Thomas, Fairuza Balk, Sian Phillips

© ORION PICTURES CORPORATION 8753

VANYA ON 42ND STREET

D: Louis Malle 119 m

PG · DMA COM · 1994 · COLOR

8 Intelligent update (but not by much) of famed Russian Anton Chekhov's literary masterpiece UNCLE VANYA. The three collaborators of MY DINNER WITH ANDRE, Wallace Shawn, Andre Gregory and director Louis Malled have once again combined their talents for this production. This play dramatizes people trapped between the harsh realities of their lives and the longings of their hearts. It is a timeless drama of faith, hope and the redemptive power of love. It is also very very obviously a play. Incessant conversation and soliloquies, not action, relate the intent of the author. This is a video primarily for patient, intelligent and literarily-informed audiences - not the general public.

Sex · Nud · Viol · Lang · AdSit

A: Julianne Moore, Brooke Smith, George Gaynes, Wallace Shawn, Andre Gregory

© COLUMBIA TRISTAR HOME VIDEO 74983

VERDICT, THE

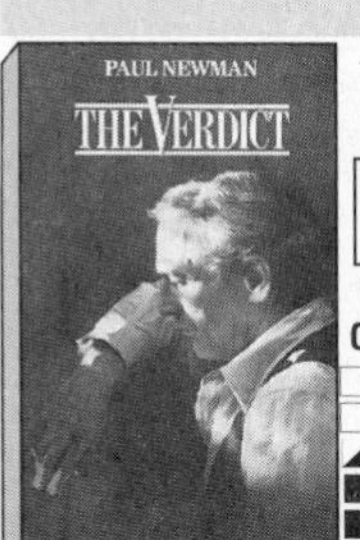

D: Sidney Lumet 129 m

R · DMA · 1982 · COLOR

9 Excellent, emotionally-charged courtroom drama in which Paul Newman really sparkles. He plays an alcoholic has-been Boston lawyer who has arrived at the bottom. He is given a simple straightforward malpractice case by a friend. All he needs to do is settle to collect his fee, but for him the case becomes a moral challenge. It is his last chance to redeem himself. He pursues his case, virtually alone, against the Archdiocese of Boston and one of Boston's biggest law firms, battling in a court where the judge despises him. It that isn't enough, the enemy has planted a spy in his camp. Compelling viewing on many levels.

Sex · Nud · Viol · Lang · AdSit

A: Paul Newman, Jack Warden, Charlotte Rampling, James Mason, Lindsay Crouse, James Handy

© FOXVIDEO 1188

VICTIM

D: Basil Dearden 100 m

NR · SUS DMA · 1961 · B&W

8 Exhilarating English drama. Bogarde is a successful young lawyer, but he has a secret. When his homosexual lover (McEnery) approaches Bogarde to defend him from phony robbery charges, Bogarde refuses fearing that he may become blackmailed. Then McEnery is found murdered, himself a victim of blackmail. But before he died, he had destroyed any evidence that might have implicated Bogarde with him. Now Bogard feels compelled to go after the murderers, even if it means risking his career, his marriage and his life. A stunning thriller that deftly deals with homosexuality.

Sex · Nud · Viol · Lang · AdSit

A: Dirk Bogarde, Sylvia Sims, Dennis Price, John Barrie, Peter McEnery, Donald Churchill

© NEW LINE HOME VIDEO 6134

VINCENT & THEO

D: Robert Altman 140 m

PG-13 · DMA · 1990 · COLOR

8 Beautifully photographed and compelling, but slow-going account of the intense and strangely symbiotic relationship that existed between artist Vincent van Gogh and his art-dealer brother Theo. Although barely able to support himself, Theo also supported his brother throughout his lifetime. He also endlessly endeavored to promote Vincent's artwork because Theo was uncomfortable in both business and love and had no artistic outlet of his own. Tortured Vincent struggled to impart his visions, caring about nothing else, but nobody listens, ironically, until he is dead. See also LUST FOR LIFE.

Sex · Nud · Viol · Lang · AdSit

A: Tim Roth, Johanna Ter Steege, Jip Wjingaarden, Jean-Francois Perrier, Vincent Vallier

© HEMDALE HOME VIDEO, INC. 7010

VOYAGE OF THE DAMNED

D: Stuart Rosenberg 134 m

PG | DMA | 1976 | COLOR

8 A heartbreaking drama based on the true story of the ship St. Louis in 1939. The ship, loaded with German Jews seeking refuge, sets sail from Nazi Germany for Cuba. The refugees are denied entry and the ship is forced to return to Germany, even though the passengers are all bound for certain death or imprisonment. The passengers are unaware that from the beginning, the whole expedition was a stunt by Nazi propaganda minister Goebbels who knew what would happen. Von Sydow is the non-German ship's captain and is the focal point around which the many stories of the passengers revolve and are revealed.

Sex | Nud | Viol | Lang | AdSit

A: Faye Dunaway, Oskar Werner, Max von Sydow, Orson Welles, Malcolm McDowell, Lynne Frederick

© LIVE HOME VIDEO 51135

VOYAGE ROUND MY FATHER, A

D: Alvin Rakoff 85 m

NR | DMA COM | 1983 | COLOR

8 A powerful emotional journey that also has a strong comedic undercurrent. When an eccentric but successful older lawyer (Olivier) loses his sight, he decides to continue his battles in the courtroom anyway, and turns to his family and son for help. As his son (Bates) helps his difficult father through this trying time, he begins to remember all of the good times and the bitterly bad times that he and his father have shared in their troubled relationship. And, he learns to stop trying to understand his father and to just love him. Beautifully filmed and acted. A good lesson for most fathers and sons.

Sex | Nud | Viol | Lang | AdSit

A: Laurence Olivier, Alan Bates, Elizabeth Sellars, Jane Asher

© HBO VIDEO 0329

WALK ON THE WILD SIDE

D: Edward Dmytryk 114 m

NR | DMA ROM | 1962 | B&W

8 Saucy and shocking (for the early '60s) soap opera set in the Great Depression years. A good-natured Texan (Harvey) searches for his lost love and finds her working in a New Orleans whorehouse, The Doll House, under the close supervision of lesbian madam Barbara Stanwyck. Distraught at her circumstances, he forgives her and vows to get her released. Stanwyck has her own plans and sets about to make his life miserable. Four solid female roles and performances, including then-newcomer Jane Fonda. Famous opening sequence.

Sex | Nud | Viol | Lang | AdSit

A: Jane Fonda, Laurence Harvey, Barbara Stanwyck, Capucine, Anne Baxter

© COLUMBIA TRISTAR HOME VIDEO 60923

WALL STREET

D: Oliver Stone 126 m

R | DMA | 1987 | COLOR

9 Spellbinding tale of a personal tragedy and the moral corruption brought on by the lust for money and power. Charlie Sheen is young and aggressive, but he doesn't get anywhere until he works his way into the confidence of Douglas, one of Wall Street's biggest wheeler-dealers. However, Douglas doesn't make his money by accident and he encourages Sheen to provide him with insider information. Even though he knows it's wrong, Sheen can't resist. Soon he is riding in limos, running with beautiful women, and living in a luxury apartment - but he has also sold out his father's trust to do it. Absorbing drama. Douglas won Oscar.

Sex | Nud | Viol | Lang | AdSit

A: Michael Douglas, Charlie Sheen, Martin Sheen, Daryl Hannah, Terence Stamp, James Spader

© FOXVIDEO 1653

WANDERERS

D: Philip Kaufman 117 m

R | DMA COM | 1979 | COLOR

8 Entertaining film which follows the exploits of a gang of high school kids from the Italian section of the Bronx in 1963. It has a good mix of comedy, excitement and '60s music (Dion, The Shirelles, The Four Seasons and many others). Their gang, The Wanderers, spends most of its time in the streets in frequent encounters (ususally non-violent) with other gangs from other neighborhoods and ethnic groups. Their biggest concerns are school and chasing girls. Eventful but somewhat uneven. Nevertheless, its infectiousness and some good performances have made it a cult favorite.

Sex | Nud | Viol | Lang | AdSit

A: Ken Wahl, John Friedrich, Karen Allen, Olympia Dukakis, Tony Ganlos, Toni Kalem

© WARNER HOME VIDEO 22009

WANNSEE CONFERENCE, THE

D: Heinz Schirk 85 m

NR | FOR DMA | 1987 | COLOR

9 Chilling historical film which recounts nearly verbatim the actual events of a meeting which took place on January 20, 1942. In this meeting, the hierarchy of the German government -- high ranking officials of the SS, the Nazi Party and other government bureaucrats -- discussed with casual coolness, the way in which they would exterminate eleven million people. Much of the dialogue was taken from actual minutes of the meeting and the drama is allowed to evolve in real-time over the course of a fine buffet lunch that included brandy and cigarettes. Their cold-blooded, matter-of-fact and almost casual conversational tones make this an even more chilling experience. Subtitles.

Sex | Nud | Viol | Lang | AdSit

A: Robert Artzhorn, Friedrich Beckhaus, Gerd Bockmann, Jochen Busse, Hans W. Bussinger

© HOME VISION WAN 020

WAR, THE

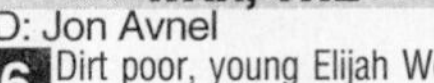

D: Jon Avnel 126 m

PG-13 | DMA | 1994 | COLOR

6 Dirt poor, young Elijah Wood, his sister and his hard-pressed mother struggle to survive in Mississippi in the early 1970's. Dad (Kevin Costner) can't hold a job and has just come back after being away for several months. The kids thought he was off looking for work, but he was in a veteran's hospital trying to ward off his recurring nightmares from Vietnam. However, his kids demons are more immediate - they are the children in the unruly and unkempt family that runs the neighborhood junk yard, who terrorize them just for fun. His kids want to fight back but Dad is convinced that violence only brings more violence and once started, it never stops. Ernest and slow, but worthwhile, especially for older kids.

Sex | Nud | Viol | Lang | AdSit

A: Elijah Wood, Kevin Costner, Mare Winningham, Lexi Randall, Christine Baranski, Gary Basaraba

© MCA/UNIVERSAL HOME VIDEO, INC. 82214

WAR AND PEACE

D: Sergei Bondarchuk 360 m

PG | FOR DMA ACT | 1968 | COLOR

9 A dazzling masterpiece of a film and winner of Best Foreign Film. However, its extreme length and poor dubbing from Russian make this a difficult film for the average viewer to watch. Still, serious viewers should not miss it. Other attempts have been made to reduce the epic book to a scale suitable for the screen (most notably in 1956), however the story is just too big and too much was lost. This Russian version took over five years to make and cost a staggering $100 million. Outstanding production values.

Sex | Nud | Viol | Lang | AdSit

A: Ludmila Savelyeva, Vyacheslav Tihonov, Sergei Bondarchuk, Victor Stanitsyn, Kira Golovko, Oleg Tabakov

© KULTUR VIDEO 1248

D M A

WARM NIGHTS ON A SLOW MOVING TRAIN

D: Bob Ellis 90 m

R | DMA ROM | 1989 | COLOR

7 Interesting Australian import. An art teacher from a Melborne Catholic school supplements her income to support her morphine-addicted brother. Every Sunday night she rides the train between Melborne and Sydney and entices men into her room for sex for a price. She successfully avoids any entanglements with any of her customers until she encounters one who has a proposition of his own and she is drawn to him. Her carefully isolated, detached self gives way to a new and overwhelming passion. Erotic - without any actual sex, but a little talky.

Sex | Nud | Viol | Lang | AdSit

A: Wendy Hughes, Colin Friels, Norman Kaye, John Clayton, Rod Zuanic, Peter Whitford

© PRISM ENTERTAINMENT 51352

WAR OF THE ROSES, THE

D: Danny DeVito 116 m

R | COM DMA | 1989 | COLOR

7 Very black comedy which is, at the same time, very funny and very painful - painful because it is based upon some bitter truths about human relationships. Two perfectly matched young lovers fall in love, marry, have kids, build a text book life and collect a houseful of beautiful things. He becomes a very successful attorney and she a successful caterer. Then their love dies and gives birth to one of the bitterest divorces ever. Each would rather destroy the other than to give ground. Sometimes hysterically funny, but at others just hysterical.

Sex | Nud | Viol | Lang | AdSit

A: Michael Douglas, Kathleen Turner, Danny DeVito, Heather Fairfield, Sean Astin

© FOXVIDEO 1800

WATERDANCE, THE

D: Neal Jimenez, Michael Steinberg 106 m

R | DMA ROM | 1992 | COLOR

8 A surprisingly revealing and frank story about Joel, a young writer who wakes up after a hiking accident, permanently paralyzed from the waist down. Joel is wheeled into a ward at a rehabilitation center with other patients paralyzed as he is. But they are not like him; they are each different. There is a racist white biker and a black lothario, whose family has left him. Still, while Joel is educated and has a pretty girlfriend who wants to stand by him, each of these three have more in common than they ever thought. If you think this dramatic ground that has all been covered before, you're wrong. This is a quite revealing and very involving movie.

Sex | Nud | Viol | Lang | AdSit

A: Wesley Snipes, Eric Stoltz, William Forsythe, Helen Hunt, Elizabeth Pena

© COLUMBIA TRISTAR HOME VIDEO 91243

WATERLAND

D: Stephen Gyllenhaal 95 m

R | DMA | 1993 | COLOR

9 Brilliant, provocative and compelling adult drama. Jeremy Irons is brilliant playing a high school history teacher who is struggling both with students who don't care, and a personal history that has driven him to the brink of mental collapse. So, he decides to tell his students (who are confused by his motives) very personal and revealing stories of himself, both to help to exorcise his demons and to lead his students to realize how history is made up of the personal stories of real people. Still, his particular stories are extraordinary. They soon draw the students and you in, and command your fascination. Unusual and quite extraordinary.

Sex | Nud | Viol | Lang | AdSit

A: Jeremy Irons, Ethan Hawke, Sinead Cusack, John Heard, Grant Warnock, Lena Headley

© TURNER HOME ENTERTAINMENT N4126

WATERSHIP DOWN

D: Martin Rosen 93 m

PG · DMA FAN · 1978 · COLOR · Sex · Nud · Viol · Lang · AdSit

8 Although this is an animated feature, it is not a cartoon for little kiddies. It is an allegorical story for adults and older kids. It involves the human-like story of the survival of a small group of rabbits who leave the apparent safety of their home because Hazel foresees impending doom. She leads a group of males in search of a new home, past the dangers of foxes, owls, dogs and men, to reach a hill called Watership Down. There, they make a new home and set about attracting females from neighboring, but hostile clans, of rabbits. Well-done, thoughtful entertainment.

A:

© WARNER HOME VIDEO 34003

WAY WE WERE, THE

D: Sydney Pollack 118 m

PG · ROM DMA · 1973 · COLOR · Sex · Nud · Viol · Lang · AdSit

9 Their romance begins in the late '30s. A scruffy college activist (Streisand) has a big crush on handsome athlete (Redford), but nothing happens. Seven years later she finds him again. He is now a writer, drunk in a bar and romance blooms. But she is a Jew - he is a WASP. She is a strident political liberal - politics are a nuisance to him. So they split and reunite, and split again. Beautiful story of how two people can love each other deeply but cannot live together. 5 Oscar nominations: Streisand, Score and Title Song won. One of the public's all-time romance favorites.

A: Barbra Streisand, Robert Redford, Bradford Dillman, Murray Hamilton, Patrick O'Neal, Viveca Lindfors

© COLUMBIA TRISTAR HOME VIDEO 60254

WEDDING BANQUET, THE

D: Ang Lee 108 m

R · DMA · 1993 · COLOR · Sex · Nud · Viol · Lang · AdSit

7 A very different sort of film. Not a comedy, but occasionally funny. An ambitious gay Chinese-American businessman has been living with his lover for five years in New York. However, his parents, who want grandchildren, are constantly pestering him to get married. So, at his lover's suggestion and to get his parents to leave him alone, he agrees to marry a Chinese girl who is about to be deported. However, trouble develops when the jubilant parents insist upon coming to America to be at the wedding, which they expect to be a huge traditional Chinese celebration. Rapidly, lies multiply and take on a life of their own. Approximately half of the film is in Chinese, with subtitles.

A: Ah-Leh Gua, Sihung Lung, May Chin, Winston Chao, Mitchell Lichtenstein

© FOXVIDEO 8170

WEDDING GIFT, THE

D: Richard Loncraine 87 m

PG-13 · DMA · 1994 · COLOR · Sex · Nud · Viol · Lang · AdSit

7 Diana is slowing being paralyzed and nobody knows why. Yet, she is a feisty woman, who struggles to maintain her good humor in the face of terrible uncertainty and great physical pain. Deric, her husband, strains to maintain his wife's spirits and keep his stumbling company afloat. The doctors can not explain what is happening to her, but Diana knows she is dying. She begins to squirrel sleeping pills away, but she is holding out for her son's wedding and she has taken on the job of finding her husband a new wife. Based upon a true story, this is not just another disease-of-the-week film. Made in England.

A: Julie Walters, Jim Broadbent, Thora Hird, Sian Thomas

© MIRAMAX HOME ENTERTAINMENT 3038

WEEDS

D: John Hancock 109 m

R · DMA · 1987 · COLOR · Sex · Nud · Viol · Lang · AdSit

6 Nick Nolte has been sentenced to life without parole in San Quentin. Helplessly distraught and faced with a hopeless future, he begins to read for the first time in his life. Inspired, he writes and then stages a prison play describing the inmates's life behind bars. The play is seen by a critic (Taggart) who lobbies for and eventually wins Nolte's release from prison. Outside, Nolte romances Taggart and forms his own acting troop that is made up of ex-cons, but when it falters he considers a robbery to support it. Based upon a true story. Earnest and well acted, but uneven.

A: Nick Nolte, Rita Taggart, Joe Mantegna, Ernie Hudson, John Toles-Bey, Lane Smith

© HBO VIDEO 0062

WE OF THE NEVER NEVER

D: Igor Auzins 135 m

G · DMA WST ACT · 1982 · COLOR · Sex · Nud · Viol · Lang · AdSit

8 Touching and captivating import from Australia, and winner of six Australian Academy Award nominations. It is a true story, taken from the diary of Jeannie Gunn, first published in 1908. She was the first white woman to travel deep into the Australian wilderness, called the Outback or the Never Never, to a cattle station with her husband. A stunning piece of camerawork depicts her story of survival in a rugged world dominated by men, their confrontation with the mystical world of the aborigines and their acceptance of her. However, her happiness is soon shattered with the death of her husband.

A: Angela Punch-McGregor, Tommy Lewis, Arthur Dignam, Tony Barry

© COLUMBIA TRISTAR HOME VIDEO 60256

WEST SIDE STORY

D: Robert Wise, Jerome Robbins 153 m

NR · MUS ROM DMA · 1961 · COLOR · Sex · Nud · Viol · Lang · AdSit

10 Great entertainment, a landmark film and winner of ten Oscars, including Best Picture. The huge Broadway musical smash hit (which transformed Romeo and Juliet into members of rival New York ethnic gangs) was transferred to the silver screen with absolutely nothing lost in the translation. Beautiful and memorable songs (most of which have become standards): "Maria," "Tonight," "I Feel Pretty," "America" and more. Dance sequences won a special Oscar. Very importantly, the beautiful and tragic love story itself is not lost in the beautiful music either. A must see!

A: Natalie Wood, Richard Beymer, Rita Moreno, Russ Tamblyn, George Chakiris

Distributed By MGM/UA Home Video M201266

WHALES OF AUGUST, THE

D: Lindsay Anderson 91 m

NR · DMA · 1987 · COLOR · Sex · Nud · Viol · Lang · AdSit

6 Two elderly sisters (Lillian Gish and Bette Davis) live together on the coast of Maine. Their lives consist primarily of reminiscences of days gone by. Davis is nearly blind and may also be going senile. Their life-long friend (Ann Sothern was Oscar nominated) trys to convince them that they should sell the house. Another neighbor (Vincent Price) is trying to charm them into staying because he is looking for a place to live after his landlady dies. Great acting all the way around by some of the screen's biggest names, but slow moving.

A: Lillian Gish, Bette Davis, Ann Sothern, Vincent Price, Harry Carey, Jr., Mary Steenburgen

© NEW LINE HOME VIDEO 7600

WHAT'S EATING GILBERT GRAPE?

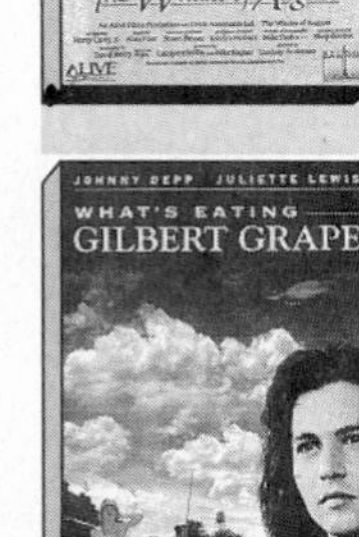

D: Lasse Hallstrom 118 m

PG-13 · DMA · 1993 · COLOR · Sex · Nud · Viol · Lang · AdSit

6 Gilbert Grape is stuck in a small town working at a small grocery story so he can help support his VERY big mother (who is so big, she hasn't left the house in seven years), his retarded brother (who he has to watch constantly) and his two sisters (one of which is a young teenager totally involved only with herself). No wonder Gilbert is depressed. He's trapped and there isn't any way out. His only excitement has been a new girl who is only in town for as long as it will take to ship in the part their car needs. There are no great revelations here, only some nice human vignettes and pretty good acting.

A: Johnny Depp, Juliette Lewis, Leonardo DiCaprio, Darlene Gates, Laura Harrington, Mary Steenburgen

© PARAMOUNT HOME VIDEO 32955

WHAT'S LOVE GOT TO DO WITH IT

D: Brian Gibson 118 m

R · DMA MUS · 1993 · COLOR · Sex · Nud · Viol · Lang · AdSit

9 Hard-hitting biography of R & B and Rock legend, Tina Turner. While the film traces her musical history, and is peppered with some great music, it is more the story of a survivor. She had been abandoned as a child by her mother and left in the care of her grandmother. As a teenager, she rejoined her mother in the big city, where she met Ike Turner. He was immediately struck by her raw talent and singing style. He quickly incorporated her into his band and set about making them into a national name. However, as her popularity rose so did his deep-seated insecurities. He beat her regularly, and it took years for her to break free. An excellent, but sobering, film.

A: Angela Bassett, Laurence Fishburne, Venessa Bell Calloway, Jenifer Lewis, Chi, Phylis Yvonne Stickney

© TOUCHSTONE HOME VIDEO 2011

WHEN A MAN LOVES A WOMAN

D: Luis Mandoki 136 m

R · DMA · 1994 · COLOR · Sex · Nud · Viol · Lang · AdSit

7 Meg Ryan is a school guidance counselor and Andy Garcia is an airline pilot. They are successful, apparently wildly in love and wonderously happy. They have two charming little girls that they both love but there is a secret that they both are reluctant to face. Meg is an alcoholic and he helps to cover it up. She has a constant nagging feeling of inadequacy that only goes away when she drinks. So, she drinks a lot. Finally, it can no longer be denied. She commits herself to a rehab center to dry out. When she returns, it is not the same. She has faced the dragon and is no longer willing to live in her husband's shadow. Even though she loves him, she has to do this on her own.

A: Andy Garcia, Meg Ryan, Lauren Tom, Phillip Seymor Hoffman, Tina Majorino, Ellen Burstyn

© TOUCHSTONE HOME VIDEO 2549

WHEN THE LEGENDS DIE

D: Stuart Millar 105 m

PG · DMA WST · 1972 · COLOR · Sex · Nud · Viol · Lang · AdSit

7 A perceptive and sensitive story about the relationship that develops between an aging, hard-drinking cowboy, who is having a hard time dealing with his declining rodeo skills, and a rebellious young Ute Indian, who has freshly arrived from the reservation after his parents have died. The old man exploits the youngster and his riding abilities for a meal ticket when he trains the boy to ride broncs in the rodeo. However, their relationship becomes severely strained when Widmark encourages him to lose so they can make money on the bets. One of Widmark's better performances.

A: Frederic Forrest, Richard Widmark, Luana Anders, Vito Scotti

© FOXVIDEO 1293

WHERE THE DAY TAKES YOU

D: Marc Rocco — 107 m

R | DMA | 1992 | COLOR | Sex | Nud | Viol | Lang | AdSit

6 What is life like on the streets of L.A. for runaways? This film tries to tell you. It is told in a semi-documentary style with social worker interviewing a young street person on videotape. King is 20 or 21, he really doesn't know, but he is the leader of the family. The "family" is a group of kids that hang out together for mutual support and friendship. Their day is spent hustling, watching their backs and trying to have some fun. (They are after all, just kids.) However, their's is a particularly nasty, dirty, treacherous world full of drugs, sex-for-sale and violence. This is an interesting premise and an OK film, but it is a little overstated.

A: Sean Astin, Lara Flynn Boyle, Peter Dobson, Balthazar Getty, Ricki Lake, James Le Gros

© COLUMBIA TRISTAR HOME VIDEO 92883

WHERE THE RIVER FLOWS NORTH

D: Jay Craven — 105 m

PG-13 | DMA | 1993 | COLOR | Sex | Nud | Viol | Lang | AdSit

6 It is Vermont in 1927. There has been a great deal of change over the years. Most of the big trees have been logged away. Old-time logger Rip Torn and the crusty Indian woman who lives with him, survive by eking out a living boiling leaves down for their oil. However, change is coming again. A huge dam is going to be built down stream and their valley will be flooded. In spite of numerous generous offers the old man refuses to sell. He has his own dreams and his own agenda. Even though, he is up against more than he possibly defeat, he persists in chasing his dreams. And, even though the old woman fears for their future, she cannot leave him. Thoughtfully executed with well-drawn characters.

A: Rip Torn, Tantoo Cardinal, Bill Raymond, Michael J. Fox, Mark Margolis, Treat Williams

© A-PIX ENTERTAINMENT 21041

WHISTLE DOWN THE WIND

D: Bryan Forbes — 99 m

NR | DMA | 1962 | B&W | Sex | Nud | Viol | Lang | AdSit

8 A fugitive murderer is found hiding in the barn by three innocent young children. When they ask who he is, he is so relieved they are just children that he says, "Jesus Christ!" - and they take him at his word. Word of him spreads through the children but none tells their parents. They keep his secret and hide him in the barn. Excellent performances by everyone, especially the children. This is a fascinating story about the nature of a child's trust and innocence. There is a memorable conclusion that makes it especially worthwhile viewing for the whole family.

A: Hayley Mills, Alan Bates, Bernard Lee, Norman Bird, Elsie Wagstaffe

© NEW LINE HOME VIDEO 6040

WHITE

D: Krzystof Kieslowski — 102 m

R | FOR DMA | 1994 | COLOR | Sex | Nud | Viol | Lang | AdSit

6 Poor little Karol has a right to be depressed. He is impotent and so his beautiful wife has just divorced him (even though they still love each other), taken all his money and left him humiliated, totally broke and broken on the streets of Paris. Yet, from somewhere he summons the strength to return home to Poland where he becomes determined to remake himself into a rich and powerful man. He will return to Paris and have his revenge. This is a curious storyline and strange characters that manages to hold your attention. Sub-titles.

A: Zbignew Zamachowski, Julie Delpy

© MIRAMAX HOME ENTERTAINMENT 3039

WHITE DAWN, THE

D: Philip Kaufman — 110 m

PG | DMA | 1975 | COLOR | Sex | Nud | Viol | Lang | AdSit

6 Slightly offbeat drama. Three whalers find themselves separated from the others, lost and alone in the Arctic of 1896. Nearly frozen, they are discovered and taken in by a group of Eskimos. Soon the civilized men are exploiting the innocents. They find a way to make alcohol. They steal, lie and take advantage of the women. This is not just a simplistic melodrama but is well done and thought provoking. Beautiful cinematography, too.

A: Warren Oates, Timothy Bottoms, Louis Gossett, Jr., Simonie Kopapik, Joanasie Salominie, Pilitak

© PARAMOUNT HOME VIDEO 8724

WHITE HUNTER, BLACK HEART

D: Clint Eastwood — 112 m

PG | DMA ACT | 1990 | COLOR | Sex | Nud | Viol | Lang | AdSit

7 An unusual departure from his typical fare, actor/director Eastwood presents a thinly veiled portrait of famed director John Houston and the filming of THE AFRICAN QUEEN. Eastwood's character takes the director's job only because it will pay off large personal debts and allow him to be able to go to Africa to shoot an elephant. The picture is only incidental to him. His obsession with the elephant hunt in fact jeopardizes the filming. Not a true action movie, this is an involving drama deriving its interest from the obsessive nature of the man and how that relates to the creative process.

A: Clint Eastwood, Jeff Fahey, Marisa Berenson, George Dzundza, Alun Armstrong

© WARNER HOME VIDEO 11916

WHITE MISCHIEF

D: Michael Radford — 108 m

R | DMA CRM | 1988 | COLOR | Sex | Nud | Viol | Lang | AdSit

7 Elegantly filmed, sensuous, scandalous, bizarre-but-true story. It's 1940 and England is being bombed to pieces at the outset of WWII. An aging colonialist from Kenya, in need of a wife, has returned to England and married ravishing Gretta Sacchi. All she really wanted was the money and the title, but when she arrives back in Kenya's Happy Valley, she discovers a decadent lifestyle of elegant parties, drugs, drinking and wife-swapping. The world outside is ignored. She has a passionate affair with a handsome young man who is later found dead. Very naughty, voyeuristic and sexy.

A: Greta Scacchi, Charles Dance, Sarah Miles, John Hurt, Trevor Howard, Hugh Grant

© NEW LINE HOME VIDEO 7724

WHITE PALACE

D: Luis Mandoki — 103 m

R | ROM DMA | 1990 | COLOR | Sex | Nud | Viol | Lang | AdSit

8 Likable Cinderella-story about two of the most unlikely of lovers, linked together by loss and lust. He (Spader) is a 27-year-old successful and wealthy yuppie from a wealthy family, mourning the death of his young wife. She (Sarandon) is a friendly but broke, over-40, down-to-earth waitress trying to drink away the death of her son. Oil and water, nonetheless these two escape together for one night of lust that is so good that a strange and powerful relationship develops which compels and captures them both. However, they must live in the real world and deal with their friends and family.

A: Susan Sarandon, James Spader, Eileen Brennan, Kathy Bates, Rachel Levin, Renee Taylor

© MCA/UNIVERSAL HOME VIDEO, INC. 81019

WHO'S AFRAID OF VIRGINIA WOOLF?

D: Mike Nichols — 131 m

NR | DMA | 1966 | B&W | Sex | Nud | Viol | Lang | AdSit

8 Searing, intensely powerful drama that was nominated for 13 Oscars and won 5. It is a very intense dissection of lives in turmoil. An English professor (Burton) and his bitchy wife (Taylor) invite a young faculty couple to their house for late-night drinks. The evening's discussions quickly erupt into bombastic and degrading tirades from an unfulfilled Taylor toward Burton. He is humiliated and becomes vengeful in response. Segal and Dennis are the young couple who receive more than they bargained for. Gut wrenching, loud and evocative, this is not light entertainment.

A: Richard Burton, Elizabeth Taylor, George Segal, Sandy Dennis

© WARNER HOME VIDEO 11056

WHOSE LIFE IS IT, ANYWAY?

D: John Badham — 119 m

R | DMA COM | 1981 | COLOR | Sex | Nud | Viol | Lang | AdSit

9 Richard Dreyfuss puts in another sterling performance as a rising young sculptor who becomes paralyzed from the neck down in an auto accident. While he remains an impressive intellectual force, he becomes so depressed that he hires an attorney to pursue his right to die. Doctors Cassavetes and Lahti try desperately to convince him to live. Extremely potent performances keep this from being just another tragedy movie. And, it is ultimately, and unexpectedly, an upbeat movie. Excellent.

A: Richard Dreyfuss, John Cassavetes, Christine Lahti, Bob Balaban, Kenneth McMillan, Kaki Hunter

Distributed By MGM/UA Home Video M800140

WHO'S THAT KNOCKING AT MY DOOR?

D: Martin Scorsese — 90 m

R | DMA | 1968 | B&W | Sex | Nud | Viol | Lang | AdSit

8 Film fans take note. This was the first film by Martin Scorsese. It is a reworking of a film he did while at a student NYU and is autobiographical. It is also the first feature film for Harvey Keitel. This is an unpleasant but fascinating study of a young Italian-American street punk trying to relate his feelings for a beautiful independent art student to his strict Catholic upbringing. His confusion is only amplified when he discovers that she was once raped. Very stylized and will likely not appeal to mainstream audiences.

A: Zina Bethune, Harvey Keitel, Anne Collette, Lennard Kuras, Michael Scala, Harry Northrup

© WARNER HOME VIDEO 11582

WIDE SARGASSO SEA

D: John Duigan — 100 m

NR | ROM DMA | 1993 | COLOR | Sex | Nud | Viol | Lang | AdSit

7 This is a literate romantic tale of love promised and then lost. It is an adaptation of a novel by Jean Rhys that presents a possible explanation as to where the crazy woman who lived in the attic in JANE EYRE came from. An Englishman has traveled to Jamaica in the 1840s to marry a woman he has never met. She is the wealthy, lonely daughter of a dead former slave owner. They marry and move to her mountain home. At first, they are deeply in love, then he begins to receive letters that cause him to doubt her. They are soon destroyed. The Sargasso Sea is a wide bed of floating sea weed in the Caribbean that traps sailors just as they are about to reach their goal. Very slow.

A: Karina Lombard, Nathaniel Parker, Claudia Robinson, Rowena King, Martine Beswicke, Huw Christie Williams

© TURNER HOME ENTERTAINMENT N4297

WILBY CONSPIRACY, THE

D: Ralph Nelson — 113 m

PG | ACT DMA | 1974 | COLOR

8 Set in South Africa but filmed in Kenya, Sidney Poitier is a militant African political activist. His attorney is Michael Caine's girlfriend. Poitier and Caine are chained together and then are allowed to escape by a vicious and bigoted policeman who is intent upon following Poitier to his underground leader. Poitier's and Caine's plight bring back reminders of THE DEFIANT ONES. It's the charm of Poitier and Caine that keep this film moving as an action film, while never losing the dramatic impact from the underlying causes.

Sex Nud Viol Lang AdSit

A: Sidney Poitier, Michael Caine, Rutger Hauer, Nicol Williamson, Prunella Gee, Persis Khambatta

Distributed By MGM/UA Home Video M301294

WILD AT HEART

D: David Lynch — 125 m

R | DMA ROM COM | 1990 | COLOR

8 Maverick director Lynch has created an oddly fascinating series of images, characters and events - if taken individually. But if taken as a whole, it is a confusing experience. The principal focus is upon Lula (Dern) and Sailor (Cage). She is a 20-year-old gum-popping, sex-crazed daughter of witch of a woman. Cage is a rebellious 23-year-old who spurned mama's advances and killed the thug she sent to beat him. Just out of prison, Sailor and Lula head across the country, meeting more strange characters and avoiding the killers her Mom has sent after them.

Sex Nud Viol Lang AdSit

A: Laura Dern, Willem Dafoe, Crispin Glover, Diane Ladd, Isabella Rossellini, Harry Dean Stanton

© VIDEO TREASURES M012765

WILD HEARTS CAN'T BE BROKEN

D: Steve Minor — 89 m

G | DMA | 1991 | COLOR

9 Truly wonderful family picture. A rebellious 17-year-old orphan girl flees her aunt's stifling home by answering a newspaper advertisement seeking a rider for a diving horse in a traveling show. But this is more than just a story about a girl who rides a horse through forty feet of empty space into a tank of water. It is the story of a girl who struggles for happiness and to succeed in a world where the chips are stacked against her. Not only does she succeed once, but twice. And she finds a family and love. Terrific feel for an era and absolutely charming. Based on truth.

Sex Nud Viol Lang AdSit

A: Gabrielle Anwar, Cliff Robertson, Michael Schoeffling

© WALT DISNEY HOME VIDEO 1223

WILD STRAWBERRIES

D: Ingmar Bergman — 90 m

NR | FOR DMA | 1959 | B&W

9 Less enigmatic than most of Bergman's works this is also one of his best works. This is a must for film buffs, but it is also accessible to many ordinary viewers too. An old man has had a fearsome nightmare the night before. In it he discovered his own corpse. On this day, he is in a carriage on the way to receive an honorary degree and on this day he also begins to feel his own mortality. Along the way, he offers a ride to three young hitchhikers who remind him of people in his past. Through a series of flashbacks he begins to review his life and also begins to realize that his life is almost over and he has never lived. Subtitles.

Sex Nud Viol Lang AdSit

A: Victor Sjostrom, Bibi Andersson, Ingrid Thulin, Gunnar Bjornstrand, Max Von Sydow

© HOME VISION WIL 140

WINDWALKER

D: Keith Merrill — 108 m

PG | WST DMA ACT | 1980 | COLOR

8 Unusually well-rounded family entertainment in the form of the telling of a Cheyenne legend. As an old Cheyenne warrior lies dying, he tells his grandsons the story of how his wife was murdered and his son (their uncle) was kidnapped years before by a neighboring band of Crow Indians. The old man dies but comes back to life to protect his tribe from a Crow attack that is led by his lost son. A very unusual story of war, survival and love. The entire movie is spoken in the Cheyenne and Crow languages with English subtitles.

Sex Nud Viol Lang AdSit

A: Trevor Howard, Nick Ramus, James Remar, Serene Hedin, Dusty Iron Wing McCrea, Silvana Gatlardo

© CBS/FOX VIDEO 6345

WINGS OF EAGLES, THE

D: John Ford — 107 m

NR | DMA COM | 1957 | COLOR

6 Fairly interesting biography of the remarkable real-life character - Frank "Spig" Wead. He was a daring Navy pilot in WWI. However, he was severely paralyzed after breaking his neck in an accident. Forced out of the service, he became a Hollywood screenwriter. He even went on to serve again in WWII. John Wayne plays the part with two-fisted gusto and Maureen O'Hara is his wife. This is a somewhat confusing film to watch if you're not clued in, because the first half plays like a slapstick comedy and the last is much more sedate. This is also one of Wayne's better acting jobs.

Sex Nud Viol Lang AdSit

A: John Wayne, Dan Dailey, Maureen O'Hara, Ward Bond, Ken Curtis, Edmund Lowe

Distributed By MGM/UA Home Video M200513

WINNING

D: James Goldstone — 123 m

PG | DMA ACT | 1969 | COLOR

6 This a movie about racing, but it is more than that. Paul Newman is a race driver who marries a divorcee (Woodward) and adopts her son, but he is so dedicated to winning that he spends most of the season away from them. Even when they do reunite for the Indianapolis 500, he spends all his time with the car. Left alone, she finds herself attracted to another driver who pays attention to her. Very strong performance by both Newman and Woodward in a good story, with spectacular racing sequences. (Newman is a professional driver in real life.)

Sex Nud Viol Lang AdSit

A: Paul Newman, Joanne Woodward, Robert Wagner, Richard Thomas, David Sheiner, Clu Gulager

© MCA/UNIVERSAL HOME VIDEO, INC. 45016

WINTER KILLS

D: William Richert — 97 m

R | DMA COM | 1979 | COLOR

8 A peculiar combination of political intrigue and black comedy. This is a farfetched and paranoid tongue-in-cheek vision of power in America. Bridges is the younger brother of a President who was slain in 1960. He was never satisfied with the official story so now, 19 years later, he launches his own investigation into a new conspiracy theory. A circuitous trip through oddball characters, places and people brings him back to his own father as a prime suspect. Its eccentric flavor and characters have made this a cult favorite. Not for the casual viewer.

Sex Nud Viol Lang AdSit

A: Jeff Bridges, John Huston, Anthony Perkins, Belinda Bauer, Eli Wallach, Sterling Hayden

© NEW LINE HOME VIDEO 2056

WINTER LIGHT

D: Ingmar Bergman — 80 m

NR | FOR DMA | 1962 | B&W

9 A penetrating look into a disillusioned Protestant minister who has lost his faith and watches his congregation crumble when he cannot give them the guidance he craves so desperately for himself. Great performances mark this central entry in Bergman's religious trilogy which also includes THROUGH A GLASS DARKLY and THE SILENCE. This will be a difficult film for non- Bergman fans to watch but it is a powerful film for those who are. Subtitles.

Sex Nud Viol Lang AdSit

A: Ingrid Thulin, Gunnar Bjornstrand, Max Von Sydow, Gunnel Lindblom

© HOME VISION WIN 140

WISH YOU WERE HERE

D: David Leland — 92 m

R | DMA COM | 1987 | COLOR

8 Bittersweet British production. It is the portrait of a 16-year-old girl growing up in the very straight-laced culture of the late '40s and '50s. Her mother is dead and her father is a drunk. She has no direction. Worse, she refuses to recognize her "place." She is also a spirited girl who enjoys the power her new sensuousness gives her, and she refuses to be repressed. She's just trying to have fun and find love, but she gets much more than that. This film is very funny and shocking to some, but is also a very sensitive and touching story. Strong performances.

Sex Nud Viol Lang AdSit

A: Emily Lloyd, Tom Bell, Jesse Birdsall, Geoffrey Durham, Claire Clifford, Barbara Durkin

© FRIES HOME VIDEO 99400

WITCHES OF EASTWICK, THE

D: George Miller — 118 m

R | COM DMA | 1987 | COLOR

8 Wicked little comedy. Three women, bored with small town life and the lack of eligible bachelors, fantasize one night about the perfect man. They don't know that they possess supernatural powers and that they have just summoned up their dreamboat from Hell. When the rich charmer (Nicholson) moves to town, he seduces all three of them, but none of them realizes until it is almost too late that he is truly evil, he is in fact the Devil. Loosely based on John Updike's novel. Very funny in places, but a very dark comedy... not for everyone.

Sex Nud Viol Lang AdSit

A: Jack Nicholson, Cher, Susan Sarandon, Michelle Pfeiffer, Veronica Cartwright, Richard Jenkins

© WARNER HOME VIDEO 11741

WITH HONORS

D: Alex Keshishian — 101 m

PG-13 | DMA COM | 1994 | COLOR

6 Harvard senior Brendan Fraser has just experienced the ultimate college horror - his hard drive just crashed and with it, his entire thesis. He has one copy printed however, but while going to get a copy made, he slips on the ice and the paper winds up in the hands of a philosophical bum (Pesci) living in the furnace room at the library. To get it back - one page at a time - Fraser must commit certain kindnesses and listen to the bum's words of wisdom. At first this price is a gross injustice, then a mild imposition, but then a labor of love. Pesci's life has been one of mistakes, Fraser had no father and so the relationship grows. Quite funny in places but also obvious and grating at times.

Sex Nud Viol Lang AdSit

A: Joe Pesci, Brendan Fraser, Moria Kelly, Patrick Dempsey, Josh hamilton, Gore Vidal

© WARNER HOME VIDEO 13079

WITHOUT A TRACE

D: Stanley R. Jaffee — 119 m

PG | DMA SUS | 1983 | COLOR | Sex Nud Viol Lang AdSit

8 An extremely well-done and reality-based depiction of the trauma caused by the disappearance of a child. A mother gets her child up, dressed, sends him off to school, goes to work and then waits for him to get home after school - but he never comes. The police begin an intensive search and she launches herself into a door-to-door campaign - all of which results in nothing for months on end. This story is based upon a real incident in New York. It is a highly suspenseful tear-jerker that presents no easy solutions. Thought provoking.

A: Kate Nelligan, Judd Hirsch, Stockard Channing, David Dukes, Danny Corkill

© FOXVIDEO 1235

WOMAN'S TALE, A

D: Paul Cox — 93 m

NR | DMA | 1992 | COLOR | Sex Nud Viol Lang AdSit

7 Martha is almost eighty years old. Even though she is feisty, loves life and is free-spirited, her body is betraying her. She has cancer. She lives alone in the apartment she has lived in for years with her things, her cat and her parakeet. Her son comes to visit her regularly. Her friends are the incapacitated old man next door, the neighborhood prostitute and a dedicated nurse who takes care of her and who she allows to use the apartment to meet her married boyfriend. Martha's story is in many ways typical of many old people. It is slow, largely predictable and depressing, but it is also very effective.

A: Sheila Florance, Gosia Dobrowolska, Norman Kaye, Chris Haywood, Myrtle Woods, Ernest Gray

© ORION PICTURES CORPORATION 5072

WOMAN UNDER THE INFLUENCE, A

D: John Cassavetes — 147 m

R | DMA | 1974 | COLOR | Sex Nud Viol Lang AdSit

7 Technically brilliant - Oscar nominations for Acting and Directing. However, the subject matter is not much fun. This is serious stuff. Gena Rowlands is a mother and a wife to hardhat husband Peter Falk who is doing her best to hold on, but she is walking the line between sanity and insanity. One moment she is child-like innocent and near normal in appearance, the next her desperation drives her to give way to her impulses. Peter Falk is doing his best to deal with her mood swings and to be understanding, but he is losing control to his frustration and is striking out. Brilliant acting. Emotionally powerful.

A: Peter Falk, Gena Rowlands, Katherine Cassavetes, Lady Rowlands, Fred Draper

© TOUCHSTONE HOME VIDEO 1344

WORKING GIRLS

D: Lizzie Borden — 93 m

NR | DMA | 1987 | COLOR | Sex Nud Viol Lang AdSit

8 Documentary-style depiction of a day in the life of a Manhatten brothel. This is an odd sort of movie that is both funny and thought provoking. There is a lot of nudity and sex, but this is all business. The result is definitely not erotic. For these women, it is just another day at the office. The women are of different types: one is a lesbian whose girlfriend doesn't know what she does, some are housewives, some are students working their way through school, but all are professionals. Sometimes forced and stagey, but also honest and fascinating. You may also want to see the documentary CHICKEN RANCH.

A: Louise Smith, Ellen McElduff, Amanda Goodwin, Marusia Zach, Janne Peters, Helen Nicholas

© NEW LINE HOME VIDEO 90204

WORLD ACCORDING TO GARP, THE

D: George Roy Hill — 136 m

R | COM DMA | 1982 | COLOR | Sex Nud Viol Lang AdSit

7 A very unusual movie, taken from a book by John Irving. However, it is not one which the casual observer can easily understand. That is not to say that this isn't an enjoyable movie - but you do have to work to understand the meaning and value in it. It is the story of a man who is the offspring of a very eccentric and independent-minded feminist who surrounds herself with odd people. Garp is a somewhat ordinary kind of guy, but his world is a strange one occupied by strange people. It is also a sad one where bizarre happenings are commonplace. Big cast, great acting.

A: Robin Williams, Mary Beth Hurt, John Lithgow, Glenn Close, Amanda Plummer, Jessica Tandy

© WARNER HOME VIDEO 11261

WORLD APART

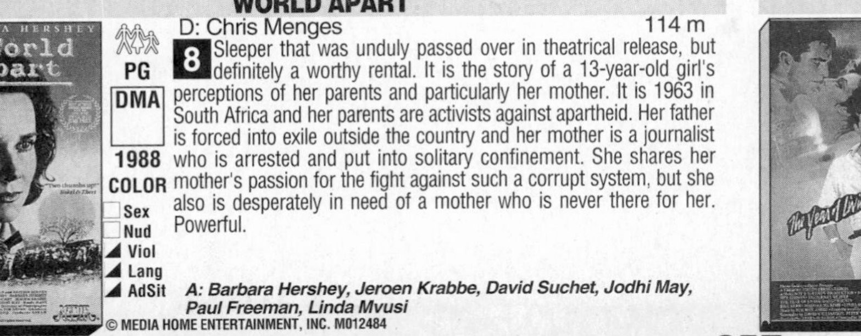

D: Chris Menges — 114 m

PG | DMA | 1988 | COLOR | Sex Nud Viol Lang AdSit

8 Sleeper that was unduly passed over in theatrical release, but definitely a worthy rental. It is the story of a 13-year-old girl's perceptions of her parents and particularly her mother. It is 1963 in South Africa and her parents are activists against apartheid. Her father is forced into exile outside the country and her mother is a journalist who is arrested and put into solitary confinement. She shares her mother's passion for the fight against such a corrupt system, but she also is desperately in need of a mother who is never there for her. Powerful.

A: Barbara Hershey, Jeroen Krabbe, David Suchet, Jodhi May, Paul Freeman, Linda Mvusi

© MEDIA HOME ENTERTAINMENT, INC. M012484

WRESTLING ERNEST HEMINGWAY

D: Randa Haines — 123 m

PG-13 | DMA COM | 1993 | COLOR | Sex Nud Viol Lang AdSit

8 Extremely engaging and likable story of two very unlikely friends. Richard Harris is a 75-year old, slovenly, retired sea captain who's been married four times. Robert Duvall is a very neat and very proper, retired Cuban barber who has never been married. Both live alone in Florida, trying to make the days pass, and it is there they meet one day in the park by the sea. Two more unlikely friends are possible, but their loneliness draws them together. Their similarities melt away their differences and make their friendship fascinating and fun. Funny, sometimes very funny, but this also deliberate and thought-provoking. Fascinating, very real characters.

A: Richard Harris, Robert Duvall, Shirley MacLaine, Piper Laurie, Sandra Bullock

© WARNER HOME VIDEO 12993

WRITTEN ON THE WIND

D: Douglas Sirk — 99 m

NR | DMA ROM | 1956 | COLOR | Sex Nud Viol Lang AdSit

8 Steamy potboiler from the '50s which has lost only a little of the steam. Robert Stack, the spoiled and alcoholic grandson of a Texas oil baron, marries beautiful Lauren Bacall. Dorothy Malone (Oscar winner) is his trampy sister who isn't at all happy to see him bring Bacall home, especially since she is love with his best friend (Hudson) and Hudson is also in love with Bacall. Things really get messy when Stack, who thinks he's sterile, goes for his gun when he finds that Bacall is pregnant. Very high quality soaper.

A: Rock Hudson, Lauren Bacall, Robert Stack, Dorothy Malone, Robert Keith, Grant Williams

© MCA/UNIVERSAL HOME VIDEO, INC. 80582

WYATT EARP

D: Lawrence Kasdan — 191 m

PG-13 | WST DMA ACT | 1994 | COLOR | Sex Nud Viol Lang AdSit

9 Excellent epic Western, telling the whole story of Wyatt Earp. It begins in Missouri and tells of his father's influence on all the boys. Follows Wyatt from the death of his first wife, becoming a buffalo hunter and then the man who tamed Dodge City. Only in the last half of a quite long movie does the story of the fight with the Clantons come along. A real attempt at telling history and the makeup of a complicated man was made. Wyatt is not painted as being a true hero in the classic Hollywood sense, but that actually makes the story much more interesting. It starts a little slow and is very deliberate in the telling, but it also tells a powerful and fascinating story. Hang in there.

A: Kevin Costner, Dennis Quaid, Gene Hackman, Michael Masden, Linden Ashby, Catherine O'Hara

© WARNER HOME VIDEO 13177

YANKS

D: John Schlesinger — 139 m

R | ROM DMA | 1979 | COLOR | Sex Nud Viol Lang AdSit

8 Lavishly produced film about the effects of WWII on a small English town which was inundated by the Americans who were stationed there just before D-Day. Three relationships between American men and English women and their families are featured. It is a passionate portrait of a troubled time and how different people came to deal with it. One of the women is married, one has a boy friend who is away and already in the fighting, and the third woman throws herself headlong into a romance without thought of tomorrow. Good period details.

A: Richard Gere, Vanessa Redgrave, William Devane, Lisa Eichhorn, Rachel Roberts, Chick Vennera

© MCA/UNIVERSAL HOME VIDEO, INC. 80123

YEAR MY VOICE BROKE, THE

D: John Duigan — 103 m

PG-13 | DMA ROM | 1988 | COLOR | Sex Nud Viol Lang AdSit

8 Sensitive story from Australia which won its equivalent of a Best Picture award. Excellent. A 14-year-old boy (Taylor) has a difficult time when he is confronted with the pangs of growing up. His major crisis comes when his long-time girlfriend (who is 15 and maturing much faster) falls for an older boy. The other guy is an athlete and also a bit of a troublemaker. Set in 1962, major trouble ensues when she gets pregnant and leaves town, even though Taylor tries to help her. This is a well-handled teen drama that is heartwarming, frank, honest and not sensationalized.

A: Noah Taylor, Loene Carmen, Ben Mendelsohn, Graeme Blundell, Lynette Curran, Malcolm Robertson

© LIVE HOME VIDEO 68865

YEAR OF LIVING DANGEROUSLY, THE

D: Peter Weir — 115 m

PG | DMA SUS ROM | 1983 | COLOR | Sex Nud Viol Lang AdSit

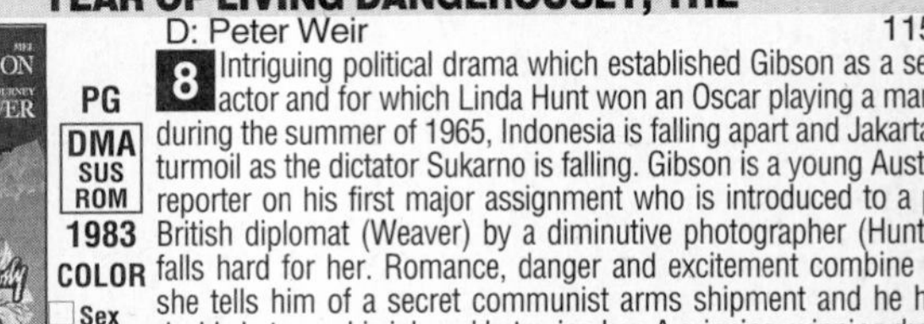

8 Intriguing political drama which established Gibson as a serious actor and for which Linda Hunt won an Oscar playing a man. Set during the summer of 1965, Indonesia is falling apart and Jakarta is in turmoil as the dictator Sukarno is falling. Gibson is a young Australian reporter on his first major assignment who is introduced to a pretty British diplomat (Weaver) by a diminutive photographer (Hunt) and falls hard for her. Romance, danger and excitement combine when she tells him of a secret communist arms shipment and he has to decide between his job and betraying her. A gripping, winning drama.

A: Mel Gibson, Sigourney Weaver, Linda Hunt, Michael Murphy

Distributed By MGM/UA Home Video M800243

D M A

YOUNG LIONS, THE

D: Edward Dmytryk 167 m

NR
DMA WAR ACT
1958
B&W
Sex
Nud
Viol
Lang
AdSit

9 Excellent, gripping human drama that uses WWII as a backdrop to explore the war's effects on three very different men. Brando is a handsome and idealistic ski instructor who adopts Nazism as the answer to Germany's problems, until he discovers its realities. Montgomery Clift is an American Jew, a smallish man drafted into the Army, who must deal with anti-Semitic taunts both at home and in the service. Dean Martin is a popular playboy entertainer who must learn to face his own cowardice. The three separate stories are interwoven as the men are drawn together by the war. Very moving.

A: Marlon Brando, Montgomery Clift, Dean Martin, Hope Lange, Barbara Rush, Maximilian Schell

© FOXVIDEO 1057

YOUNG PHILADELPHIANS, THE

D: Vincent Sherman 131 m

NR
DMA ROM
1959
B&W
Sex
Nud
Viol
Lang
AdSit

8 Superb, involving melodrama about a poor boy (Newman) who has dedicated himself to become a lawyer and advance his station. He is so intent upon rising the ladder that he throws away an opportunity for love with a beautiful society girl (Rush) because she doesn't fit into his plans at the moment. However, when he is called upon by his desperate old Army buddy (Vaughn), a blue-blooded outcast, to defend him in a murder trial, Newman finally must make a choice between his goals and his principals. He regains his perspective and also gets another chance to win back Rush's love.

A: Paul Newman, Barbara Rush, Brian Keith, Alexis Smith, Robert Vaughn, Adam West

© WARNER HOME VIDEO 11157

Z

D: Constantine Costa-Gavras 128 m

PG
FOR SUS DMA
1969
COLOR
Sex
Nud
Viol
Lang
AdSit

9 Spellbinding and highly influential political thriller that was banned in several right-wing countries and which won the Oscar for Best Foreign Film. A conservative investigator of the supposed accidental death of a popular left-wing political activist discovers that, not only was it a murder and that the conservative government is covering up, but that the government played an active role in the murder. His decision to pursue the case may result in the downfall of the government. Based on an actual case in Greece in 1963.

A: Yves Montand, Irene Papas, Jean-Louis Trintignant

© COLUMBIA TRISTAR HOME VIDEO 60266

ZENTROPA

D: Lars von Trier 112 m

B&W
FOR DMA
1992
COLOR
Sex
Nud
Viol
Lang
AdSit

8 Excellent, innovative and intriguing cinematography - but very challenging, enigmatic and surreal plotting. The storyline is set in Germany in the days immediately following the fall of Hitler, while under the occupation of the American army. A young American has come to take a job as a railroad conductor, but becomes involved with the daughter of the railroad's founder and gets caught up in post-war intrigue and murder. The story is presented as a sort of hypnotic hallucination and has many of the disjointed qualities of a dream. It is both very intriguing and very frustrating. A must see for film fans. Others, however, are cautioned.

A: Jean-Marc Barr, Barbara Sukowa, Lawrence Hartman, Udo Kier, Eddie Constantine

© TOUCHSTONE HOME VIDEO 1599

ZORBA THE GREEK

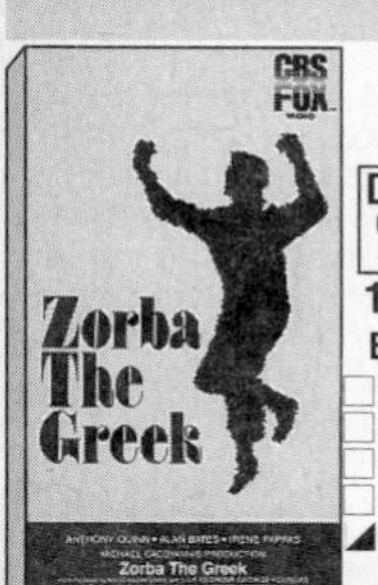

D: Michael Cacoyannis 142 m

NR
DMA COM
1964
B&W
Sex
Nud
Viol
Lang
AdSit

9 Invigorating and captivating Best Picture nominee about a totally uncomplicated man with a zest for life - Zorba - is played to perfection by Anthony Quinn. When an uptight young English intellectual (Bates) comes to Zorba's small village on the Greek isle of Crete to reopen a small mine he has inherited, Zorba appoints himself as the man's tutor. He will teach the Englishman how to live life. This is a highly emotional and at times highly exuberant exploration of all that life has to offer. Highly recommended. Won three other Oscars, including Best Supporting Actress.

A: Anthony Quinn, Alan Bates, Irene Papas, Lila Kedrova, George Foundas

© FOXVIDEO 1106

Fantasy

Video's Best

1956 and After

3 WORLDS OF GULLIVER, THE

D: Jack Sher — 100 m

NR | FAN CLD | 1960 | COLOR

7 This fanciful story, designed in the 18th century to be biting satire, is considerably toned down here. Now it is just good family entertainment. It is the story of Gulliver, who was swept overboard while at sea and washed ashore first on Lilliput, an island totally inhabited by very, very tiny people. Later Gulliver travels to another island, Brobdingnag, where the people are as much taller than Gulliver as he was than the Lilliputians. It's all done in live action through a trick photography process called dynavision. OK for everyone, but best for young children.

Sex / Nud / Viol / Lang / AdSit

A: Kerwin Mathews, Jo Morrow, June Thorburn, Lee Patterson, Gregoire Aslan, Basil Sydney

© COLUMBIA TRISTAR HOME VIDEO 60924

7 FACES OF DR. LAO

D: George Pal — 101 m

NR | FAN WST CLD | 1963 | COLOR

9 Absolutely delightful and heartwarming fantasy. A small Old West town newspaper editor (Ericson) is trying to win the hand of a pretty widow (Eden) and fighting a lonely battle against a villain (O'Connell), who is trying to grab up all the land around. A truly strange helpmate arrives in the form of a mysterious and wise old Chinese magician named Dr. Lao (Randall). Dr. Lao is the proprietor of a traveling circus containing a fantastic array of wondrous sideshow creatures. Fabulous makeup and special effects. Randall is truly outstanding, playing multiple roles. Great fun for all.

Sex / Nud / Viol / Lang / AdSit

A: Tony Randall, Barbara Eden, Arthur O'Connell, John Ericson, Lee Patrick, Noah Beery, Jr.

Distributed By MGM/UA Home Video M600667

7TH VOYAGE OF SINBAD, THE

D: Nathan Juran — 94 m

G | FAN CLD | 1958 | COLOR

8 Flavorful Arabian Nights tale of Sinbad the Sailor. An evil wizard has shrunk the beautiful Princess (and Sinbad's true love) to only six inches high. In order to restore her, Sinbad must battle a giant bird, a giant cyclops, a dragon and a sword-wielding living skeleton. Wonderful special effects and a thrilling, well-paced, fanciful adventure story that will please both young and old alike. The stop motion animation created for this picture is still very highly regarded, and for years was held as the standard for the industry.

Sex / Nud / Viol ◢ / Lang / AdSit

A: Kerwin Mathews, Kathryn Grant, Richard Eyer, Torin Thatcher

© COLUMBIA TRISTAR HOME VIDEO 60114

8 1/2

D: Federico Fellini — 138 m

NR | FOR DMA FAN | 1963 | B&W

10 For very sophisticated viewers only. This is a semiautobiographical film in which master Italian filmmaker Federico Fellini depicts, through a visual "diary," the director's difficulties in making the film we are watching. Viewers witness his memories, fantasies and problems, all through a storyline which ebbs and flows between reality and fantasy, eventually evolving to a world in between the two. Winner of Foreign Film Oscar. Subtitles.

Sex / Nud / Viol / Lang / AdSit ■

A: Marcello Mastroianni, Claudia Cardinale, Anouk Aimee, Sandra Milo, Barbara Steele

© MPI HOME VIDEO 1398

ADVENTURES OF BARON MUNCHAUSEN, THE

D: Terry Gilliam — 122 m

PG | FAN COM CLD | 1989 | COLOR

7 Inside the walls of a city under siege by the armies of the Ottoman Empire, a small troupe of actors puts on a play about the infamous German Baron Munchausen, who had claimed to have had many wildly extravagant exploits. Their presentation is interrupted by an old soldier who claims that he is, in fact, the real Baron. Vowing that he will rescue the town, the old soldier departs in a rag-tag homemade hot air balloon, off to enlist the aid of his superhuman partners of old: the strongest man on earth, the man who can blow stronger than a hurricane, and the fastest man alive. Silly, light-hearted fantasy.

Sex / Nud ◢ / Viol ◢ / Lang / AdSit

A: John Neville, Robin Williams, Eric Idle, Oliver Reed, Sarah Polley, Uma Thurman

© COLUMBIA TRISTAR HOME VIDEO 50153

ALWAYS

D: Steven Spielberg — 123 m

PG | ROM COM FAN | 1989 | COLOR

7 Very pleasing remake of THE STORY OF JOE. Dreyfuss plays a bush pilot who is killed in a crash but is brought back by his guardian angel (Hepburn). He is to be the guardian angel of an awkward young flyer (Johnson). At first Dreyfuss likes his new job, but that all changes when he also has to help his girlfriend (Hunter) to move on with her life and does it by lining her up with Johnson. This is a light little movie with no major statements to make but it is still a lot of fun. However, you should see the original, too. It is one of director Spielberg's favorites, which was the reason why he redid it here.

Sex / Nud / Viol / Lang ◢ / AdSit ◢

A: Richard Dreyfuss, Holly Hunter, Brad Johnson, John Goodman, Audrey Hepburn, Keith David

© MCA/UNIVERSAL HOME VIDEO, INC. 80967

ARMY OF DARKNESS

D: Sam Raimi — 81 m

R | FAN HOR | 1992 | COLOR

6 Silly, gory, pseudo-campy, sword-and-sorcery gore fest. Our hero is transported back in time from the modern-day housewares department of S-Mart into the Middle Ages along with his shotgun, chainsaw and a beat-up Oldsmobile. There he is first enslaved only to be transformed into the hero that he truly is, after he defeats the vile evil thing in the pit into which he was thrown. Thereafter, he is sent in search of the "Necronomicon", a magic book bound in human skin. He succeeds, but in the process also sets free an army of the dead (called the Deadites) which he then must also defeat. This is for a select and discriminating audience - that is hopefully not too big.

Sex / Nud / Viol ■ / Lang ■ / AdSit ◢

A: Bruce Campbell, Embeth Davidtz, Marcus Gilbert, Ian Abercrombie, Richard Grove, Timothy Patrick Quill

© MCA/UNIVERSAL HOME VIDEO, INC. 81288

BATMAN

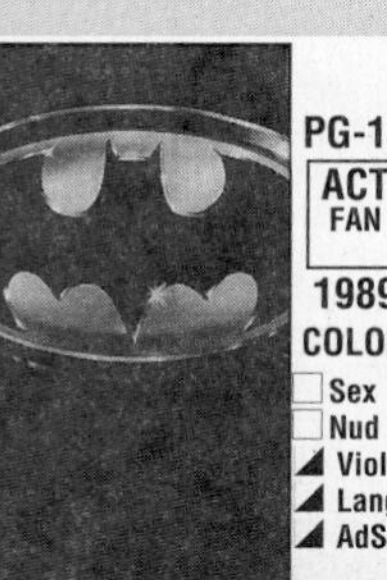

D: Tim Burton — 126 m

PG-13 | ACT FAN | 1989 | COLOR

8 A gloomy and foreboding Gotham City is out of control and run by hoods. In one of the opening sequences, one of them (Jack Nicholson) is dropped into a tub of acid by a newly-arrived powerful and sinister black hooded figure. Batman (Keaton) has come. Still, this acid bath has not killed Jack but it has contorted his face into a perpetual macabre smile and made him even more spiteful. He has now become Joker and seizes control of the underworld, immediately beginning a psychotic campaign of terror. This is not a comic book tale for the kiddies. It is an adult fantasy. The Joker is menacing and maniacal, and the violence is realistic (mostly). Exciting, definitely different.

Sex / Nud / Viol ◢ / Lang ◢ / AdSit ◢

A: Jack Nicholson, Michael Keaton, Kim Basinger, Pat Hingle, Billy Dee Williams, Jack Palance

© WARNER HOME VIDEO 12000

BATMAN RETURNS

D: Tim Burton 126 m

PG-13 | ACT FAN | 1992 | COLOR

7 Awesome special effects and big budget production. Again, as in the first big-budget film, these characters are not just cartoon figures taken from the comic strip. They are presented as near-real psychotic characters. Catwoman, the Penguin and Batman all are given reasons for having become such social and psychological oddities. The three engage in a battle with each other and against a corrupt politician. Of course, you can expect the anticipated battle of good vs. evil, but this sequel is decidedly different than the comic strip. Gotham at Christmas is a truly freakish place. Outrageous and spectacular.

Sex, Nud, Viol, Lang, AdSit

A: Michael Keaton, Michelle Pfeiffer, Danny DeVito, Christopher Walken, Michael Gough, Michael Murphy

© WARNER HOME VIDEO 15000

BEASTMASTER, THE

D: Don Coscarelli 119 m

PG | FAN ACT | 1982 | COLOR

8 In a magical feudal world, a demented high priest enslaves a people and demands that they sacrifice their young children. A young warrior (Singer) is the only survivor of a tribal massacre, and he uses his ability to communicate telepathically with animals to aid him in his quest to defeat the evil sorcerer (Rip Torn) and to save the beautiful virgin (Tanya Roberts). Good special effects, and plenty of animals and action for kids of all ages.

Sex, Nud, Viol, Lang, AdSit

A: Marc Singer, Tanya Roberts, Rip Torn, John Amos

Distributed By MGM/UA Home Video M800226

BLACK ORPHEUS

D: Marcel Camus 103 m

NR | FOR ROM FAN | 1958 | COLOR

8 This winner of the Oscar for the Best Foreign Film is a modernized version of an old Greek legend. The story is set in Rio de Janeiro during Carnival, Brazil's version of Marde Gras. A streetcar conductor (Mello) and a shy, beautiful country girl fall passionately in love. The lovers lose themselves in the frenzy of Carnival but she is followed through the streets of Rio by a stranger dressed as death and is killed. Mello attempts to resurrect her through magic but must eventually join her in the next world. Hauntingly beautiful score. Subtitles.

Sex, Nud, Viol, Lang, AdSit

A: Breno Mello, Marpessa Dawn, Lourdes de Oliveira, Lea Garcia, Adhemar da Silva, Alexandro Constantino

© HOME VISION BLA 170

BLACK RAINBOW

D: Mike Hodges 103 m

R | SUS FAN | 1991 | COLOR

7 Neat little mystical thriller. Rosanna Arquette and her drunken father (Jason Robards) make a dishonest living with a traveling stage act. She is a medium, relaying messages from the dead to the living. However, one day she really does see the future. She tells a woman about her dead husband and how he was murdered - before it happens. She not only accurately predicted the future, she also knows the name of the killer, which makes her and her father targets. But worse that that, she is now perpetually haunted by countless other secrets and impending deaths. Hulce is a young reporter hooked on the story and who follows them on the road.

Sex, Nud, Viol, Lang, AdSit

A: Rosanna Arquette, Jason Robards, Jr., Tom Hulce, Mark Joy, Ron Rosenthal, John Bennes

© VIDEO TREASURES M012820

BLISS

D: Ray Lawrence 112 m

R | DMA COM FAN | 1985 | COLOR

7 A very original, unusual and extremely black comedy, and the 1985 Australian Best Picture winner. A successful and seemingly happy advertising executive dies for four minutes and comes back into an apparently different world, which has many of the same players in it but they are all drastically changed. His wife is openly carrying on an affair with his partner, his son deals dope and wants to join the mob, his daughter is a doper and will do anything to get it and an elephant sits on his car. A very odd, nightmarish vision of modern life.

Sex, Nud, Viol, Lang, AdSit

A: Barry Otto, Lynette Curran, Helen Jones, Miles Buchanan

© R&G VIDEO, LP 80024

BOY WHO COULD FLY, THE

D: Nick Castle 114 m

PG | FAN DMA | 1986 | COLOR

8 Highly enjoyable and uplifting film, excellent family entertainment. When her husband commits suicide after learning he has cancer, the hard-pressed Bonnie Bedelia and her two children move in next door to a troubled autistic boy who has lost his parents in a plane wreck and now just sits on the roof dreaming that he can fly. No one can reach him, but Bedelia's troubled daughter (Deakins) slowly draws him out of his private world and becomes the only true friend he has. Genuinely heartwarming picture about the value of love and of never giving up.

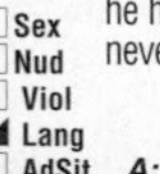
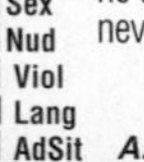

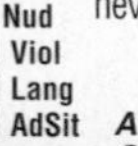

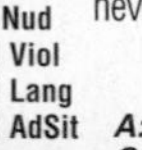

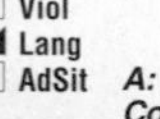

Sex, Nud, Viol, Lang, AdSit

A: Lucy Deakins, Jay Underwood, Bonnie Bedelia, Fred Savage, Colleen Dewhurst, Fred Gwynne

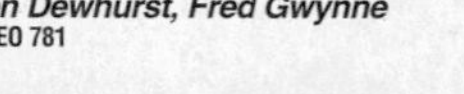

© WARNER HOME VIDEO 781

BUTCHER'S WIFE, THE

D: Terry Hughes 107 m

PG-13 | FAN COM ROM | 1991 | COLOR

6 Curious and terribly fanciful! As a little girl, Marina (Moore) dreams that her true love will just simply find her. So one day when Dzunda washes up on shore, apparently right on cue, she believes that her psychic powers have drawn them together and they can't be denied. Without a second thought, she marries him and runs off to his Greenwich Village butcher shop with him. There, she promptly becomes a neighborhood sensation, when her uncannily perceptive advice consistently works and her predictions come true. Psychiatrist Daniels becomes especially entranced with this strange woman, but then love blooms between them and confuses everyone. Fun, but not too deep.

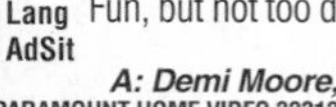

Sex, Nud, Viol, Lang, AdSit

A: Demi Moore, Jeff Daniels, George Dzundza, Mary Steenburgen

© PARAMOUNT HOME VIDEO 32312

CLASH OF THE TITANS

D: Desmond Davis 118 m

PG | DMA FAN CLD | 1981 | COLOR

8 Ancient Greek mythology is given life by some pretty good special effects and a big-name cast. The hero Perseus (Hamlin), son of Zeus (Olivier), must battle magic, monsters and the gods to save beautiful Andromeda (Bowker) from danger and to win her hand. Special effects are the real stars, however, particularly the flying horse Pegasus and Medusa, the woman with hair of snakes who can turn you to stone if you look at her.

Sex, Nud, Viol, Lang, AdSit

A: Laurence Olivier, Harry Hamlin, Judi Bowker, Burgess Meredith, Maggie Smith

Distributed By MGM/UA Home Video M700074

CONAN THE BARBARIAN

D: John Milius 128 m

R | ACT FAN | 1982 | COLOR

7 Schwarzenegger plays the mythical sword-swinging warrior who is seeking revenge on the snake cult leader (Jones) who massacred his village, including his parents, and then had him enslaved from the time he was just a small a boy. After fifteen years at the Wheel of Pain, grinding grain, he had developed a powerful body. Then he was trained as a gladiator and eventually freed. Now, he and his companions seek revenge and to learn the answer to "the riddle of steel" which his father had told him would give him the power to destroy his enemies. This intriguing movie is full of blood, gore, violence, big biceps and beautiful women. CONAN THE DESTROYER followed but was considerably tamer.

Sex, Nud, Viol, Lang, AdSit

A: Arnold Schwarzenegger, Sandahl Bergman, James Earl Jones, Mako, Ben Davidson, Max von Sydow

© MCA/UNIVERSAL HOME VIDEO, INC. 77010

CONAN THE DESTROYER

D: Richard Fleischer 101 m

PG | ACT FAN | 1984 | COLOR

6 Far less violent than its predecessor CONAN THE BARBARIAN. Conan is recruited to accompany a beautiful princess (d'Abo) to a castle on a search for a magical gemstone. He and an assortment of accomplices he has picked up along the way, battle and defeat beasts and baddies as they proceed along. Played more for laughs this time. Still plenty of action, but certainly more suitable for the family.

Sex, Nud, Viol, Lang, AdSit

A: Arnold Schwarzenegger, Grace Jones, Wilt Chamberlain, Sarah Douglas, Olivia D'Abo, Mako

© MCA/UNIVERSAL HOME VIDEO, INC. 80079

CROSSROADS

D: Walter Hill 100 m

R | FAN MUS | 1986 | COLOR

7 Enjoyable fantasy about a young classical guitar student (Macchio) who tracks down a legendary blues musician, Willie Brown (Seneca), in a Harlem hospital. He is obsessed with seeking the mysteries of the blues, so he breaks Willie out and together they travel to the heart of the Delta to "go down to the crossroads" (the lyrics of blues great - Robert Johnson). It is a trip in which Machio seeks fame, finds romance and together he and Willie seek to release Willie from an immortal deal he had made with the devil years before. An interesting character study with a great blues score.

Sex, Nud, Viol, Lang, AdSit

A: Ralph Macchio, Joe Seneca, Jami Gertz, Joe Morton, Robert Judd

© COLUMBIA TRISTAR HOME VIDEO 60665

DARBY O'GILL AND THE LITTLE PEOPLE

D: Robert Stevenson 90 m

G | COM CLD FAN | 1959 | COLOR

9 Wonderful fantasy about an an old caretaker at a wealthy Irish estate, Darby O'Gill, who falls into a well and discovers the leprechaun king. Darby tricks the king into granting him three wishes, but he soon wishes he hadn't. Poor old Darby has such a reputation for blarney that no one believes his preposterous tale, and the larcenous king has tricked him into wasting two wishes. Then comes a young Sean Connery, who has come to the estate to replace him, so he and his daughter are also about to lose their home. It is a magical tale with neat special effects. Among Disney's very best.

Sex, Nud, Viol, Lang, AdSit

A: Albert Sharpe, Janet Munro, Sean Connery, Jimmy O'Dea, Kieron Moore, Estelle Winwood

© WALT DISNEY HOME VIDEO 038

FAN

DARK CRYSTAL, THE

D: Jim Henson, Frank Oz — 93 m

PG | FAN | 1982 | COLOR | Sex | Nud | Viol | Lang | AdSit

6 The creators of the Muppets have created a full-length feature film that is totally populated by puppets. It is a fanciful tale depicting good versus evil. In it, a young Gelfling (elf-like creature) hero must find and replace a missing piece of the dark crystal in order to protect the world and restore it to light. If he is unsuccessful, the terribly evil Skeksis (vulture-like creatures) will defeat the benevolent Mystics and the world will decay. The Skeksis are such absolutely repugnant and evil characters that they are likely to be far too scary for small kids. Better for older kids and teenagers.

A:

© WALT DISNEY HOME VIDEO 2596

DARKMAN

D: Sam Raimi — 96 m

R | SF FAN | 1990 | COLOR | Sex | Nud | Viol | Lang | AdSit

7 This is a violent comic book-like fantasy thriller that pulls out all the stops! A brilliant scientist (Neeson), who is very close to discovering ways to regenerate body parts, is savagely attacked by a gang and his laboratory is set on fire. He is left to die and is burned beyond all recognition. Even though he recovers, using his special knowledge skin regeneration, he is now consumed by revenge and he uses his special knowledge to create the alternate identity of Darkman to fight crime. Spectacular big-budget special effects and the wildly improbable stunts and heroics more than make up for plot holes.

A: Liam Neeson, Frances McDormand, Colin Friels, Larry Drake, Jesse Lawrence Ferguson, Rafael H. Robledo

© MCA/UNIVERSAL HOME VIDEO, INC. 80978

D.A.R.Y.L

D: Simon Wincer — 100 m

PG | SF FAN CLD | 1985 | COLOR | Sex | Nud | Viol | Lang | AdSit

8 Charming story about a childless urban couple who adopt an apparently amnesiatic ten-year-old. He is a perfect child. He is a math whiz, works wonders with video games, is the hero of the baseball team and he changes their lives. But D.A.R.Y.L. is really an advanced robot... so advanced that he has developed human feelings. He has run away from the government program that created him and now the government wants him back. A delightful fantasy which will be entertaining for the whole family.

A: Barret Oliver, Mary Beth Hurt, Michael McKean, Josef Sommer, Kathryn Walker

© PARAMOUNT HOME VIDEO 1810

DICK TRACY

D: Warren Beatty — 105 m

PG | ACT CRM FAN | 1990 | COLOR | Sex | Nud | Viol | Lang | AdSit

7 Cartoon-like megabuck production that is a parody of the famous long-running comic-strip hero. There is a terrific line-up of major actors, however some are almost unrecognizable under makeup. (Al Pacino is despicable as the main villain who plans to unite all the bad guys. Madonna is marvelously vampy as Breathless Mahoney. Glenne Headly is lovely as Tracy's (Beatty) love interest.) Tracy rises to challenge the bad guys, but has trouble with his personal life. Plenty of shoot-'em-up action, against an unreal cartoon-like backdrop. Pretty good fun, not wonderful.

A: Warren Beatty, Madonna, Al Pacino, Dustin Hoffman, Mandy Patinkin, Paul Sorvino

© TOUCHSTONE HOME VIDEO 1066

DOUBLE LIFE OF VERONIQUE, THE

D: Krzysztof Kieslowski — 96 m

R | FOR FAN | 1991 | COLOR | Sex | Nud | Viol | Lang | AdSit

6 Exotic and haunting portrait of two young women born on the same day - one in Poland, one in France. They are identical in appearance, personality, talent and frail health. One says, "I know that I am not alone," although she does not know what it means. When the Polish girl is chosen to be a featured singer at a concert and dies on stage, the other feels grief and ends her own singing lessons. Later she finds the image of the dead girl on a photograph she took on a trip to Poland. A feeling of mysticism and an eerie mood are the only purpose for the film. Subtitles.

A: Irene Jacob, Philippe Volter, Sandrine Dumas, Aleksander Bardini, Louis Ducreux, Claude Duneton

© PARAMOUNT HOME VIDEO 15122

DRAGONSLAYER

D: Matthew Robbins — 110 m

PG | ACT FAN | 1981 | COLOR | Sex | Nud | Viol | Lang | AdSit

6 Enjoyable fantasy adventure. A horrible fire-breathing dragon is terrorizing the British countryside and an aging sorcerer is the only one who can stop it, but he is killed. So the job falls to his apprentice, who quickly finds himself in over his head, but only after he has already agreed to slay the dragon to save both a damsel in distress and the kingdom. Rich in special effects and period flavor. Set in 6th-century England and filmed on location in England, Scotland and Wales. Pretty scary and gruesome for real young ones and a little too corny for oldsters, but just right for those in between.

A: Peter MacNicol, Caitlin Clarke, Ralph Richardson, John Hallam, Peter Eyre, Albert Salmi

© PARAMOUNT HOME VIDEO 1367

EDWARD SCISSORHANDS

D: Tim Burton — 100 m

PG-13 | COM ROM FAN | 1990 | COLOR | Sex | Nud | Viol | Lang | AdSit

8 Heartwarming, heartbreaking and fanciful. Once upon a time, high on a hill, an inventor created a young man out of spare parts but died before he could give him hands and long scissors served as their awkward replacement. Thereafter, Edward Scissorhands (Depp) lived a lonely existence in the mansion until, one day, the Avon Lady (Wiest) came and took him to live with her family in the suburbs. But when Edward and her daughter (Ryder) fall in love, chaos breaks lose in the close-knit community and poor Edward is caught completely off guard. A very unusual semi-adult fantasy that can be very entertaining if you let it.

A: Johnny Depp, Winona Ryder, Dianne Wiest, Vincent Price, Alan Arkin, Anthony Michael Hall

© FOXVIDEO 0620

EXCALIBUR

D: John Boorman — 141 m

R | ACT FAN | 1981 | COLOR | Sex | Nud | Viol | Lang | AdSit

9 This is a gritty and extremely realistic telling of the classic Arthurian legend of the pursuit of truth, honor and pureness in mythical old England. So well done, it is as though you can smell and feel the time and the place. It is a magnificent production, filmed in beautiful Irish locations. It presents the entire 1500-year-old tale from the placing of the sword in the stone, the rise of King Arthur, the uniting of the land and the formation of the Round Table, to the forbidden love affair between Guinevere and Sir Lancelot, the fall of Camelot and the quest of the knights for the Holy Grail to restore it. Spellbinding storytelling with flashing swords, magic and forlorn love.

A: Nicol Williamson, Nigel Terry, Helen Mirren, Nicholas Clay, Cherie Lunghi, Corin Redgrave

© WARNER HOME VIDEO 22018

FAR AWAY, SO CLOSE

D: Wim Wenders — 146 m

PG-13 | FOR FAN DMA | 1994 | COLOR | Sex | Nud | Viol | Lang | AdSit

8 Intriguing concept first used in 1988's WINGS OF DESIRE. Angels flitter around listening into the lives and thoughts of ordinary people. And, as in the earlier film, one angel longs to see and feel what it is like to be human. However, he wants to do more. He wants to do good. His exposure to real world of humans leads him to discover how ill-prepared he is, particularly for the aloneness of each human soul. Still, he struggles to learn and even gains some mild assistance from another former angel and now immigrant, but he is also struggling against an evil angel sent by the other side to foil his efforts.

A: Otto Sander, Peter Falk, Horst Buchholz, Natassia Kinski, Heinz Ruhmann, Willem Dafoe

© COLUMBIA TRISTAR HOME VIDEO 79968

FIELD OF DREAMS

D: Phil Alden Robinson — 106 m

PG | DMA FAN | 1989 | COLOR | Sex | Nud | Viol | Lang | AdSit

8 This was the feel-good movie of 1989 and a Best Picture nominee. Costner plays a dreamer, an Iowa farmer who hears a voice that says, "If you build it, he will come." After he convinces himself and his wife that he is not crazy, he sets out to build a baseball diamond in the middle of his corn field. Then, mystically and magically, Shoeless Joe Jackson of the Chicago White Sox of 1918, his father's hero, does come. Then Costner sets off to find a reclusive writer (Jones) who returns with Costner to witness the wonder. Soon a whole team of people, all with unfulfilled dreams, arrives at the magic corn field. Excellent acting but "corny".

A: Kevin Costner, Amy Madigan, Gaby Hoffman, Ray Liotta, Timothy Busfield, James Earl Jones

© MCA/UNIVERSAL HOME VIDEO, INC. 80884

FIRST MEN IN THE MOON

D: Nathan Juran — 103 m

NR | SF FAN | 1964 | COLOR | Sex | Nud | Viol | Lang | AdSit

7 Entertaining adaptation of the fanciful H.G. Wells novel in which a crew from 1899 Victorian England sets out on an expedition to the moon. When they arrive there, they find that the moon is occupied by human-like ant forms that live in immense crystal caverns. It is told in a sort of tongue-in-cheek fashion and its special effects including the monsters, are fun. They are not too scary for the younger viewers but still manage to be exciting for everyone. Good family entertainment.

A: Edward Judd, Martha Hyer, Lionel Jefferies, Peter Finch, Erik Chitty, Betty McDowall

© COLUMBIA TRISTAR HOME VIDEO 60958

FISHER KING, THE

D: Terry Gilliam — 138 m

R | FAN DMA COM | 1991 | COLOR | Sex | Nud | Viol | Lang | AdSit

7 Complex, surreal and painful. One of those movies you won't know if you should love or hate, but it is poignant and it cuts right to the bone. When it was released, it created a lot of controversy for its portrayal of homelessness and mental illness (which were handled lightly at times and very heavy at others). Williams was a history teacher but now is an upbeat, but deranged, street person. Bridges is a New York radio shock jock who goes too far, is fired, is forced on the street and finds a strange savior in wacked-out Williams. Shocking, emotional, mystical and sometimes funny.

A: Robin Williams, Jeff Bridges, Mercedes Ruehl, Michael Jeter, Harry Shearer, John de Lancie

© COLUMBIA TRISTAR HOME VIDEO 70613

GHOST

D: Jerry Zucker 127 m

PG-13 | ROM FAN COM | 1990 | COLOR

Rating: 9

This romantic charmer was the big box office smash of 1990. Demi Moore and Patrick Swayze are deeply in love and are about to be married, but on the way home one night Swayze is mugged and shot. Now a ghost, Swayze learns that his murder was not accidental. It was actually a planned murder by his friend and former partner at the bank, who is laundering money, and that his love is still in grave danger. So, he seeks help from a very surprised phony medium (Goldberg), who, after some unexpected and very funny, supernatural communication with Swayze, realizes that she is the only one who can help save Moore. This is a wonderful film that rings true and has a little of everything for everybody.

Sex Nud Viol Lang AdSit

A: Patrick Swayze, Demi Moore, Whoopi Goldberg, Tony Goldwyn, Rick Aviles, Vincent Schiavelli

© PARAMOUNT HOME VIDEO 32004

GHOSTBUSTERS

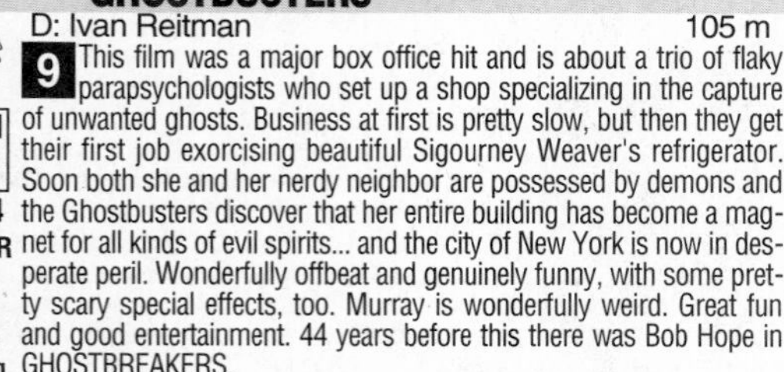

D: Ivan Reitman 105 m

PG | COM HOR FAN | 1984 | COLOR

Rating: 9

This film was a major box office hit and is about a trio of flaky parapsychologists who set up a shop specializing in the capture of unwanted ghosts. Business at first is pretty slow, but then they get their first job exorcising beautiful Sigourney Weaver's refrigerator. Soon both she and her nerdy neighbor are possessed by demons and the Ghostbusters discover that her entire building has become a magnet for all kinds of evil spirits... and the city of New York is now in desperate peril. Wonderfully offbeat and genuinely funny, with some pretty scary special effects, too. Murray is wonderfully weird. Great fun and good entertainment. 44 years before this there was Bob Hope in GHOSTBREAKERS.

Sex Nud Viol Lang AdSit

A: Bill Murray, Dan Aykroyd, Sigourney Weaver, Harold Ramis, Annie Potts, Rick Moranis

© COLUMBIA TRISTAR HOME VIDEO 60413

GHOSTBUSTERS II

D: Ivan Reitman 102 m

PG | COM HOR FAN | 1989 | COLOR

Rating: 7

Entertaining follow-up to the original blockbuster. This time the ghostbusting team sets about rescuing Sigourney Weaver, her infant son and all of NYC from a river of pink slime negative energy, which is flowing under the streets of the city. This one seems rather long and is not as captivating as the original, but is still a good time for fans. Teenagers are probably its best audience.

Sex Nud Viol Lang AdSit

A: Bill Murray, Dan Aykroyd, Sigourney Weaver, Harold Ramis, Rick Moranis, Ernie Hudson

© COLUMBIA TRISTAR HOME VIDEO 50163

GOLDEN VOYAGE OF SINBAD, THE

D: Gordon Hessler 105 m

G | FAN CLD | 1974 | COLOR

Rating: 8

Tales of Captain Sinbad have thrilled generations. Great special effects add to the mystical charm of this ancient hero in a film that still captures the fantasies of kids today. Sinbad sets sail for an uncharted island with a beautiful slave girl (Munro) and the Grand Vizier of the land on board his ship. An evil wizard is trying to gain control of the kingdom and is using evil spirits to do it. Great special effects include both a ship's figurehead and a sword wielding six-armed statue coming to life. Then throw in a one-eyed centaur and a griffin. Great entertainment for kids.

Sex Nud Viol Lang AdSit

A: John Phillip Law, Caroline Monro, Tom Baker, Douglas Wilmer, Gregoire Aslan, John Garfield, Jr.

© COLUMBIA TRISTAR HOME VIDEO 60199

GOONIES, THE

D: Richard Donner 114 m

PG | FAN CLD | 1985 | COLOR

Rating: 8

Rousing old-fashioned adventure yarn for kids. Spielberg produced this fantasy about a neighborhood group of kids who call themselves the Goonies. Their neighborhood is going to be razed by greedy developers so they all get together for one last time. Then, wonderfully, they discover a real-life treasure map that will provide more than enough money to save their neighborhood. They set off on a trek for the treasure, a trek which leads them into a subterranean world of caves, caverns, booby-traps, a real pirate ship and a monster. Plenty of action and thrills to keep the kids fascinated.

Sex Nud Viol Lang AdSit

A: Sean Astin, Josh Brolin, Corey Feldman, Martha Plimpton, Ke Huy Quan, John Matuszak

© WARNER HOME VIDEO 11474

GREMLINS

D: Joe Dante 106 m

PG | COM FAN HOR | 1984 | COLOR

Rating: 8

Entertaining and very different. Steven Spielberg put together this combination "horror"/comedy - so this is not your typical flick. The premise is that an inventor (Axton) goes on a Christmas shopping trip to Chinatown looking for the perfect gift for his son. He decides upon a strange but cute little creature called a "mowgli," but is given three warnings: Do not get it wet, keep it out of bright light and never to feed it after midnight. When these rules are ignored, hordes of mischievous gremlins result. Fascinating special effects. Really wacky.

Sex Nud Viol Lang AdSit

A: Zach Galligan, Phoebe Cates, Hoyt Axton, Frances Lee McCain, Polly Holliday, Glynn Turman

© WARNER HOME VIDEO 11388

GREMLINS 2: THE NEW BATCH

D: Joe Dante 107 m

PG-13 | COM FAN HOR | 1990 | COLOR

Rating: 8

Those weird little creatures are back to raise havoc in a New York office complex and with its tycoon owner. The film is filled with the same odd mixture of non-toxic horror and comedy as in the original. It is also filled with Hollywood insider-type jokes and plot spins. A little more violence than the first one earned it a PG-13. Some think it's not as good as the original. Others think it's better. Fun, no matter how it's sliced.

Sex Nud Viol Lang AdSit

A: Zach Galligan, Phoebe Cates, John Glover, Christopher Lee, Robert Prosky, Dick Miller

© WARNER HOME VIDEO 11886

HEAVEN CAN WAIT

D: Buck Henry 100 m

PG | COM FAN | 1978 | COLOR

Rating: 9

Highly entertaining and well-done remake of the charming 1941 smash hit HERE COMES MR. JORDAN. Warren Beatty plays Joe Pendleton, a good-natured football hero, whose soul has been accidentally removed too soon from his body by an over-eager angel. Then before they can get him back into it, his body is cremated. Bummer. So, the head angel (Mason) gets him another body to use until his time is really up. However, that presents a problem too. The new body belongs to a millionaire whose wife wants to kill him. Nine Oscar nominations.

Sex Nud Viol Lang AdSit

A: Warren Beatty, Julie Christie, Jack Warden, Dyan Cannon, Charles Grodin, James Mason

© PARAMOUNT HOME VIDEO 1109

HIGHLANDER

D: Russell Mulcahy 110 m

R | ACT FAN | 1986 | COLOR

Rating: 8

Flashy and intriguing fantasy in the romance tradition. It is the action-packed story of two immortal warriors who battle mightily in both 16th-century Scotland and 20th-century Manhatten to gain the "prize." Lambert receives tutelage in magic and warrior skills from his mentor Connery in 1536 - just in time to prepare himself for battle with the evil Kurgen (Brown) at that time and also again 400 years later. Spectacular swordplay and special effects mark this unusual tale which leaves some unaffected and others enthralled. An unworthy sequel followed and one only slightly better after that.

Sex Nud Viol Lang AdSit

A: Sean Connery, Christopher Lambert, Roxanne Hart, Clancy Brown

© HBO VIDEO TVA3761

HIGHLANDER: THE FINAL DIMENSION

D: Andy Morahan 99 m

R | ACT FAN | 1994 | COLOR

Rating: 6

Once again, the undying Highlander must do battle with another evil warrior. This time warriors from sixteenth-century Japan have freed themselves from being sealed inside a cavern after their underground prison is opened by unsuspecting archeologist team led by sexy Deborah Unger. The three become two, and then two become one, and that one will then do mortal combat with the Highlander to determine who will remain -- because ultimately there can only be one. For die-hard action fans only.

Sex Nud Viol Lang AdSit

A: Christopher Lambert, Mario Van Peebles, Deborah Unger, Mako, Raoul Trujillo, Martin Neufeld

© MIRAMAX HOME ENTERTAINMENT 3619

HOBBIT, THE

D: Arthur Rankin, Jr. 78 m

FAN | 1977 | COLOR

Rating: 6

J.R.R. Tolkien's classic fantasy is set in a time and place long ago. It is the story of a strange little man-like creature named Bilbo Baggins and his perilous adventures in the marvelously wondrous world of middle-earth, which is populated by wizards, dwarves, goblins, wargs and the terrible dragon Smaug. The book is magical but it is reduced here to little more than a children's fairy tale. Perhaps it is too much to expect that this fantasy masterpiece should translate well to the screen. Nevertheless, there is value for those familiar with the book, but please read the book. Sequel is RETURN OF THE KING.

Sex Nud Viol Lang AdSit

A:

© WARNER HOME VIDEO 716

HONEY, I BLEW UP THE KID

D: Randal Kleiser 89 m

PG | COM CLD FAN | 1992 | COLOR

Rating: 8

Sequel to HONEY, I SHRUNK THE KIDS. Moranis is now working for a corporation trying to develop a ray that, this time, will enlarge things. He is accidentally successful but accidentally blows up his two-year-old to the size of a ten-story building. There is something here for everyone to laugh at. Moranis is hysterical as he runs around Las Vegas trying to blast his kid with a ray gun to shrink him back down to size. Great special effects again. Overall, this is nearly as good as the original - only slightly less funny because some of the novelty is gone.

Sex Nud Viol Lang AdSit

A: Rick Moranis, Lloyd Bridges, Marcia Strassman, Robert Oliveri, Amy O'Neill

© WALT DISNEY HOME VIDEO 1371

HONEY, I SHRUNK THE KIDS

D: Joe Johnston — 101 m

9 PG | COM CLD FAN | 1989 | COLOR

☐ Sex ☐ Nud ☐ Viol ☐ Lang ☐ AdSit

Big box office hit and great family fun-filled fantasy - in the old fashioned Disney tradition. Rick Moranis plays a klutzy scientist who is inventing an experimental ray gun in the attic. One day his kids and the neighbor's kids are playing with it and zap... they are all shrunk down to the size of ants. They become lost in the backyard, which, because of their size, has now been transformed into a forbidding jungle filled with terrible monsters. Really good special effects and fun gags that will satisfy all age groups. Good family entertainment.

A: Rick Moranis, Matt Frewer, Marcia Strassman, Kristine Sutherland, Thomas Brown, Jared Rushton

© WALT DISNEY HOME VIDEO 909

HOOK

D: Steven Spielberg — 142 m

7 PG | FAN CLD | 1991 | COLOR

☐ Sex ☐ Nud ◢ Viol ☐ Lang ☐ AdSit

Peter Pan (Williams) is all grown up and has become a stressed-out exec who doesn't spend enough time with his children. However, while he is in London visiting Aunt Wendy, his old arch enemy Captain Hook (Hoffman) kidnaps his kids and Peter must return to Never Never Land to get them back. But Peter is so changed that he can't remember how to fly or how to fight. Fortunately, Tinkerbell (Roberts) comes to the rescue and helps him to remember and to get ready for the big showdown with Hook. Not wonderful, but pleasant. Enjoy this big-budget high tech Spielberg fantasy, but please also see the wonderful low-tech 1960 TV production of PETER PAN.

A: Robin Williams, Dustin Hoffman, Julia Roberts, Bob Hoskins, Maggie Smith, Caroline Goodall

© COLUMBIA TRISTAR HOME VIDEO 70603

IN SEARCH OF THE CASTAWAYS

D: Robert Stevenson — 98 m

8 G | CLD FAN | 1962 | COLOR

☐ Sex ☐ Nud ☐ Viol ☐ Lang ☐ AdSit

Fun-filled Disney adaptation of Jules Verne's adventure story. A young girl (Mills) launches an expedition into the South Pacific, headed by professor Chevalier, to find her missing sea captain father. Their fanciful journey requires them to overcome the perils of earthquakes and volcanos, and do battle with a giant condor and cannibals. Great special effects provide an involving fantasy to stimulate the adventurous spirit in young and old alike.

A: Maurice Chevalier, Hayley Mills, George Sanders, Wilfrid Hyde-White, Michael Anderson, Jr.

© WALT DISNEY HOME VIDEO 131

JOURNEY TO THE CENTER OF THE EARTH

D: Henry Levin — 129 m

7 G | FAN CLD | 1959 | COLOR

☐ Sex ☐ Nud ◢ Viol ☐ Lang ☐ AdSit

Jules Verne's fantasy adventure about a 19th-century expedition to the center of the earth is still imaginative and fun, but its sense of innocence, especially with today's sophisticated audiences, makes it most attractive to children and fanciful adults. A scientist and his small party descend into the earth's bowels. Along the way they encounter dangerous giant reptiles, a beautiful quartz cavern, the lost city of Atlantis, a treacherous and traitorous count and other adventures. High production values and good special effects.

A: James Mason, Pat Boone, Arlene Dahl, Diane Baker, Peter Ronsen, Thayer David

© FOXVIDEO 1248

JULIET OF THE SPIRITS

D: Federico Fellini — 142 m

8 NR | FOR DMA FAN | 1964 | COLOR

◢ Sex ☐ Nud ☐ Viol ☐ Lang ■ AdSit

A famous Fellini film. Juliet is an Italian housewife who is complacent in her dull life, thinking that the reason her husband largely ignores her is only because he works too much. However, one night, they hold a seance and she finds that she can actually talk to the spirits. They tell her that she deserves to enjoy life more. The film then becomes an attempt to illustrate the penetration the female psyche through a series of symbolic, surrealistic and gaudy images which fly by the viewer so fast that it is hard to keep track of them. Sort of a female 8 1/2. Largely for film fans. Subtitles.

A: Giulietta Masina, Sandra Milo, Mario Pisu, Valentina Cortese, Lou Gilbert, Sylva Koscina

© CONNOISSEUR VIDEO COLLECTION 1017

KING KONG

D: John Guillermin — 135 m

6 PG | ACT FAN | 1976 | COLOR

☐ Sex ◢ Nud ◢ Viol ◢ Lang ◢ AdSit

This was a big budget remake of the 1933 original black and white classic. The production values are much higher, the special effects have been updated, but it is most notable because it is also the first screen appearance of Jessica Lange. It is interesting, but in spite of color, better technology and a bigger budget, it is not in the same league as the original. It does not cast a spell over the audience as the original did and still does. There is no empathy for Kong. The romantic nature of the original is supplanted here by a cynicism and coarseness that dampen the viewer's enthusiasm.

A: Jeff Bridges, Jessica Lange, Charles Grodin, Ed Lauter

© PARAMOUNT HOME VIDEO 8872

LADYHAWKE

D: Richard Donner — 121 m

8 PG-13 | FAN ACT ROM | 1985 | COLOR

☐ Sex ☐ Nud ■ Viol ◢ Lang ☐ AdSit

Exciting and original medieval romantic adventure fantasy, set in the 13th century and beautifully photographed. A young pick-pocket (Broderick) meets and becomes an ally to a dark knight whose constant companion is a hawk. The knight and his lady are the victims of an evil curse, where she is cursed into becoming a hawk by day and he into a wolf by night. Together all three embark on a quest to destroy the curse that tortures them by destroying the one who cast it. Very strong period flavor. Very well done and entertaining.

A: Matthew Broderick, Rutger Hauer, Michelle Pfeiffer, Leo McKern, John Wood, Ken Hutchison

© WARNER HOME VIDEO 11464

LAND THAT TIME FORGOT

D: Kevin Connor — 90 m

6 PG | FAN | 1975 | COLOR

☐ Sex ☐ Nud ☐ Viol ☐ Lang ☐ AdSit

Lightweight production of Edgar Rice Burroughs's (Tarzan) adventure story set in 1918. A group of Germans from a WWI submarine and some American survivors of a sunk Allied ship, who had also been aboard the sub, discover a lost and secret prehistoric land in South America that is still dominated by dinosaurs. This is a pretty good adventure story for young people, but story line is pretty simple and the special effects are only mediocre at best.

A: Doug McClure, Susan Penhaligon, John McEnery

© LIVE HOME VIDEO VA3027

LIKE WATER FOR CHOCOLATE

D: Alphonso Arau — 105 m

8 R | FAN ROM | 1992 | COLOR

◢ Sex ■ Nud ◢ Viol ☐ Lang ■ AdSit

Sensuous fantasy import from Mexico. Set in the early 20th-century, this is the story of a young woman's enormously frustrated life which was twisted by her selfish shrew of a mother. The tradition of their family demanded that the youngest daughter would not marry but would remain home to take care of the mother until she died. However, the youngest daughter was deeply in love to a boy who married her sister. Her passion denied, the only pleasure she has in life is her cooking, and it is quite literally magical and mystical. Even when mama is dead, the poor girl is haunted by her past and her mother's ghost. Erotic and mystical, not for everyone. Subtitles.

A: Lumi Cavazos, Marco Leonardi, Regina Torne, Mario Ivan Martinez, Ada Carrasco

© TOUCHSTONE HOME VIDEO 2111

LITTLE PRINCE, THE

D: Stanley Donen — 88 m

6 G | MUS FAN | 1974 | COLOR

☐ Sex ☐ Nud ☐ Viol ☐ Lang ■ AdSit

This is a valiant effort and it was a major production effort, but is also very difficult to follow. Still, dedicated fans of musicals and/or students of Lerner and Loewe shouldn't miss it. It is a highly romanticized story in which a pilot (Kiley) is forced to land in the desert. He and his wrecked plane are chanced upon by an alien from outer space in the form of a little boy. However, this little boy has the mind of a very mature old soul. Together these two explore matters of life and love. Very curious, but not one of the great team's better efforts.

A: Richard Kiley, Steven Warner, Gene Wilder, Bob Fosse, Clive Revill, Donna McKechnie

© PARAMOUNT HOME VIDEO 8017

LORD OF THE RINGS, THE

D: Ralph Bakshi — 133 m

8 PG | FAN DMA | 1978 | COLOR

☐ Sex ☐ Nud ◢ Viol ☐ Lang ◢ AdSit

J.R.R. Tolkein fans only. This brilliantly animated feature compiles 1 1/2 books of the 3-book "Lord of the Rings" series into one longish feature film. The animation is truly impressive, but if the viewer is unfamiliar with this story of hobbits, dwarves, magicians and the other characters from Middle Earth who search out the magic rings, he will be entirely lost. Read the books first, then watch this... but definitely read the books. What an adventure!

A:

© HBO VIDEO TVE1049

MAD MAX

D: George Miller — 90 m

9 R | ACT FAN | 1980 | COLOR

☐ Sex ☐ Nud ■ Viol ■ Lang ■ AdSit

Excitement plus! This film began a trend and set the precedent for many action films (and sequels) to follow. Gibson stars as Max, a tough cop in post-nuclear Australia. The frustrated cop resigns his post, but when his wife and child are brutally murdered by a vagrant motorcycle gang, Max explodes back onto the scene with a vengeance. Weird surrealistic atmosphere and characters, plus extreme violence, made this one of the most successful Australian films of all time. Unbelievable stunt work and unusual atmosphere will keep you glued!

A: Mel Gibson, Joanne Samuel, Tim Burns, Steve Bisley, Hugh Keays-Byrne, Roger Ward

© GOODTIMES 5-04051

MAD MAX BEYOND THUNDERDOME

D: George Miller, George Ogilvie 107 m

PG-13 | ACT FAN | 1985 | COLOR | Sex | Nud | Viol | Lang | AdSit

7 Superhero Max is back! Max enters ruthless Bartertown, run by Aunty Entity (Turner), where everything is traded - including lives. Aunty Entity sends Max to a battle in the Thunderdome with Blaster. When Max refuses, he is banished to the cruel desert to die. However, he is saved by a small band of orphans who believe him to be the messiah they have been waiting for. The big highlight is the thrilling fight scene when Max and Blaster finally do meet in the Thunderdome. Director Miller does a superb job of transforming Max into a mythological savior in this post-apocalypse adventure.

A: Mel Gibson, Tina Turner, Bruce Spence, Helen Buday, Rod Zuanic, Angelo Rossitto

© WARNER HOME VIDEO 11519

MANNEQUIN

D: Michael Gottlieb 90 m

PG | COM FAN | 1987 | COLOR | Sex | Nud | Viol | Lang | AdSit

6 Comedy with a fantasy twist. A struggling artist (McCarthy) gets by, by sculpting mannequins and dressing store windows. However, one of his creations is special - into it he has designed all his fantasy elements. Then something mystical happens. An Egyptian spirit (Cattrall) comes and takes over the plaster body, but only he can see her. If anyone else comes around, it's back to plaster. Still, he is now an instant success. Taylor is amusing as his effeminate partner. This is a simple-minded, check-your-brain-at-the-door kind of comedy. Take it for what it is.

A: Andrew McCarthy, Kim Cattrall, Estelle Getty, James Spader, Meshach Taylor, Carole Davis

© VIDEO TREASURES M920

MARY POPPINS

D: Robert Stevenson 139 m

G | MUS CLD FAN | 1964 | COLOR | Sex | Nud | Viol | Lang | AdSit

10 Absolutely delightful! An enchanting magical nanny, Mary Poppins (Andrews), glides into a banker's home in 1910 London and brings happiness into everyone's lives. Who else can have a tea party on the ceiling? She and a chimney sweep (Van Dyke) sing the song "Chim-Chim-Cheree" and dance with magic feet on London rooftops. Van Dyke's animated scene where he frolics with little penguins is unforgettable. This top-shelf musical won five Academy Awards: Best Actress, Film Editing, Original Music, Song and Visual Effects. It was nominated for thirteen. You, as well as the kids, will find your smiles!

A: Julie Andrews, Dick Van Dyke, David Tomlinson, Glynis Johns, Ed Wynn, Hermione Baddeley

© WALT DISNEY HOME VIDEO 023

METEOR MAN

D: Robert Townsend 99 m

PG | FAN COM | 1994 | COLOR | Sex | Nud | Viol | Lang | AdSit

6 Silly and farcical. Robert Townsend is a mild-mannered school teacher in a gang-terrorized neighborhood of Washington DC. His father wants to stand up to the gang but Townsend (and nearly everyone else) just wants to hide. That is until Townsend is struck by a magic green meteor which transforms him into Meteor Man, giving him the power to deflect lots and lots of bullets or catch them in his teeth, fly (even though he's afraid of heights), beat up bad guys and understand his dog speak to him. Even though the film lacks a sharp focus, it is so good natured that most will have fun, particularly black kids. Lots of painless-type violence.

A: Robert Townsend, Marla Gibbs, Eddie Griffin, Robert Guillaume, James Earl Jones, Roy Fegan

Distributed By MGM/UA Home Video M903022

MR. NORTH

D: Danny Huston 90 m

PG | COM FAN | 1988 | COLOR | Sex | Nud | Viol | Lang | AdSit

6 Whimsical fantasy. A bright young Yale graduate (Edwards) arrives amid the upper-class society of Newport, R.I. of the 1920s. He is, it seems, endowed with magical healing powers. His body has an unusual amount of electricity and he can heal merely by touching. He begins to make a name for himself curing the wealthy sick and charming them, too, until the local medical community takes him to court. Based on Thornton Wilder's "Theophilus North," directed by John Huston's son with help from Dad before he died. Feel-good theme, but its very fanciful style might not be for all.

A: Anthony Edwards, Robert Mitchum, Harry Dean Stanton, Anjelica Huston, Mary Stuart Masterson, Virginia Madsen

© MCEG/STERLING 70075

MYSTERIOUS ISLAND

D: Cy Endfield 101 m

NR | ACT FAN CLD | 1961 | COLOR | Sex | Nud | Viol | Lang | AdSit

7 High-flying adventure from Jules Verne. Union soldiers escape from a Confederate prison in an observation balloon and are blown out to sea. They crash at sea and are spit up on the shores of the uncharted island of Captain Nemo (Lom). The island contains a volcano, pirates, incredibly large creatures (that mad-scientist Captain Nemo created to help with the world's food supply), two British girls who were also washed up on the island and Captain Nemo himself with his inoperative sub. Captain Nemo comes to their aid with all their other problems, but will he be able to save them when the volcano erupts?

A: Michael Craig, Joan Greenwood, Herbert Lom, Michael Callan, Gary Merrill

© COLUMBIA TRISTAR HOME VIDEO 60067

NAKED LUNCH

D: David Cronenberg 115 m

R | FAN | 1991 | COLOR | Sex | Nud | Viol | Lang | AdSit

6 An attempt to film the unfilmable results in film that is only for the most dedicated of film fans, or those who have already read Burroughs's 1959 novel. Weller plays a struggling New York writer who makes his living as an exterminator. His wife (Davis) is a junkie addicted to the bug powder he uses. Soon he is too and he becomes haunted by a hallucinogenic nightmare occurring in a surrealistic Casablanca-like setting, filled with odd characters - including his typewriter, which has been transformed into a cockroach-like monster. The reports he sends back home become the the book/movie we are watching.

A: Peter Weller, Judy Davis, Julian Sands, Roy Scheider, Ian Sands, Monique Mercure

© FOXVIDEO 5614

NIGHTMARE BEFORE CHRISTMAS, THE

D: Tim Burton 76 m

SEPT | FAN CLD | 1993 | COLOR | Sex | Nud | Viol | Lang | AdSit

8 Wonderfully bizarre. Welcome to a land where each holiday has its own town. Jack Skellington is the Pumpkin King of freakish Halloween Town. He is the master of all things in his domain, but has become bored with it. He longs for something more and thinks he has found it when he discovers Christmas Town. The answer for him is simple, he will kidnap Santa Claus and take his place. Even though his Frankenstein-like rag doll girlfriend Sally cautions against it, Jack proceeds with his plan to make Christmas his too. Don't expect a typical Christmas tale. Expect something very different. Wonderful stop-action puppet animation flows as smoothly as real life and was Oscar-nominated.

A:

© TOUCHSTONE HOME VIDEO 2236

OH, GOD!

D: Carl Reiner 98 m

PG | COM FAN | 1977 | COLOR | Sex | Nud | Viol | Lang | AdSit

10 Wonderfully charming - and almost believable - story in which God creates a modern-day Moses in the form of a mild-mannered supermarket manager. George Burns is nearly perfect as God - or, at least, his version of God is one that is very appealing. John Denver is the manager, incredulous at his misfortune for having been chosen for such an unenviable job. However, everyone just thinks he is crazy and no one believes him.If God ever did come - this is exactly what you could expect the reaction to be. Inspired casting all around. Great entertainment!

A: George Burns, John Denver, Teri Garr, Paul Sorvino, Ralph Bellamy, George Furth

© WARNER HOME VIDEO 1010

ORLANDO

D: Sally Potter 93 m

PG-13 | FAN | 1993 | COLOR | Sex | Nud | Viol | Lang | AdSit

8 This one is for a select audience. Virginia Woolf's novel has been interpreted with extravagantly opulent camerawork and rich period flavors. Orlando is a feminine spirit who slowly evolves over a-year period, learning from life experiences. Orlando begins as a young Englishman in the year 1600, where he/she is a favorite of old Queen Elizabeth I and who grants him a substantial estate on the condition that he/she never grows old. Orlando's first lesson is learned from a broken heart when a beautiful Russian princess refuses his love. Subsequent lessons are learned in later ages until Orlando finally finds fulfillment as a modern-day single mother and writer. Slow, very odd.

A: Tilda Swinton, Billy Zane, Lothaire Bluteau, John Wood, Charlotte Valandrey, Heathcote Williams

© COLUMBIA TRISTAR HOME VIDEO 71543

PAPERHOUSE

D: Bernard Rose 92 m

PG-13 | SUS HOR FAN | 1989 | COLOR | Sex | Nud | Viol | Lang | AdSit

7 Bizarre, original and strangely captivating fantasy and psychological thriller. At school, Anna (a 13-year-old girl who is prone to vivid dreams) draws a strange house and, in the upstairs window, a lonely boy who cannot move. Then, feeling ill, she heads home but falls into a culvert on the way and there she has a nightmare where she sees the house and meets the boy of her picture. Anna is found and taken home. Now, she alters her drawing to match her new dream. But when the dream returns again, it has evolved once again. It is then that she learns that her doctor has another patient, a paralyzed boy and he's the boy in the window. Her dream is alive.

A: Ben Cross, Glenne Headly, Charlotte Burke, Elliott Spiers, Gemma Jones

© LIVE HOME VIDEO 5283

PEGGY SUE GOT MARRIED

D: Francis Ford Coppola 103 m

PG-13 | COM ROM FAN | 1986 | COLOR | Sex | Nud | Viol | Lang | AdSit

9 Provocative and thoroughly enjoyable adult fairy tale. Turner is a 43-year-old woman with two kids, who is separated and nearing divorce from her pitchman husband and high-school sweetheart. Then, when she is crowned queen at her 25th class reunion, she suddenly faints and is magically transported back to being 18 years old all over again. She has all the same experiences and opportunities as she did then, but this time she has the benefit of having 25 more years experience to make her decisions. Will she do again what she did then? Inventive and well acted.

A: Kathleen Turner, Nicolas Cage, Barry Miller, Catherine Hicks, Maureen O'Sullivan, John Carradine

© CBS/FOX VIDEO 3800

PRINCESS BRIDE, THE

PG | COM ROM FAN | 1987 | COLOR

D: Rob Reiner 98 m

7 Heroic fairy tale fantasy, designed for both young and old! A sick boy's grandfather (Falk) comes to read to him, promising him a story of monsters, fights, beasts, and, yes, a dose of romance, too. In the extravagant and adventurous story which comes to life on screen, a beautiful princess and a stableboy fall in love but are soon separated, and the evil king has her kidnapped so he can force her to marry him. Suddenly, a strange man in a mask appears poised to do battle for her. This brilliant adaptation of the whimsical cult novel comes alive at the hands of Rob Reiner.

Sex Nud Viol Lang AdSit

A: Peter Falk, Mandy Patinkin, Carol Kane, Billy Crystal, Chris Sarandon, Cary Elwes

© NEW LINE HOME VIDEO 7709

PROSPERO'S BOOKS

R | FAN DMA | 1991 | COLOR

D: Peter Greenaway 126 m

9 Extremely complex, esoterically offbeat, exquisite, sumptuously photographed and very personalized version of Shakespeare's THE TEMPEST - which must be read first to appreciate the film. Even then, it may take several viewings to absorb what is happening on screen. Prospero and his daughter, set adrift in a small boat by his brother (who wants to steal his Dukedom), survive because a faithful servant has packed food and Prospero's most prized books on board. The film provides a vision of all the books's contents, which are magically depicted by fairies. For very sophisticated viewers only.

Sex Nud Viol Lang AdSit

A: John Gielgud, Isabelle Pasco, Michel Blanc, Erland Josephson, Tom Bell, Kenneth Cranham

© VIDEO TREASURES M012883

PURPLE ROSE OF CAIRO, THE

PG | COM FAN | 1985 | COLOR

D: Woody Allen 84 m

8 Inventive bittersweet fantasy treat for Woody Allen fans and most others, too. Mia Farrow has a gloomy existence. She is a Depression-era waitress married to an unemployed bully. Her only escape and joy is the movies. One day, upon her fifth viewing of her favorite soaper, the handsome lead steps down off the screen and into her life. But the character's sudden absence from the film causes chaos on the screen. Seeking to find out what happened, the actor who plays the character, visits her and also falls in love with her.

Sex Nud Viol Lang AdSit

A: Mia Farrow, Jeff Daniels, Danny Aiello, Edward Herrmann, John Wood, Dianne Weist

© LIVE HOME VIDEO VA5068

RED BALLOON, THE

FAN CLD FOR | 1956 | COLOR

D: Albert Lamorisse 34 m

10 A brilliant children's treasure! While there is no dialogue in this classic fantasy, it remains one of the most charming films of all time. In this engaging story, a young boy (Lamorisse) makes friends with a red balloon, and it follows him all around Paris. It goes to school with him. It even waits for him outside his window when he is in his room. The film is so visually flawless that the story is crystal clear - it needs no dialogue. A winner for both children and adults alike with a sparkling musical score. Winner of an Academy Award for Best Original Screenplay. Unequaled!

Sex Nud Viol Lang AdSit

A: Pascal Lamorisse, Georges Seliler

© NEW LINE HOME VIDEO 6001

RESURRECTION

PG | DMA FAN | 1980 | COLOR

D: Daniel Petrie 102 m

9 An underrated gem. Burstyn (Oscar nominated) creates a fascinating character - a simple, ordinary and pleasant woman who survives a traffic accident that killed her husband. She returns from near-death to discover that she has received a miraculous gift, the ability to heal both herself and others. This gentle, gracious woman then heals all those who come to her for help. However, the young farmer with whom she was falling in love, tries to force her to confess that she is Jesus reborn. Others accuse her of being a charlatan or resent her power. Everyone wants something. Her gift has now become a burden.

Sex Nud Viol Lang AdSit

A: Ellen Burstyn, Sam Shepard, Roberts Blossom, Eva LeGallienne, Richard Farnsworth, Clifford David

© MCA/UNIVERSAL HOME VIDEO, INC. 66047

RETURN OF THE KING, THE

NR | FAN | 1979 | COLOR

D: Jules Bass 98 m

6 J.R.R. Tolkein's ever-popular tale about an epic battle between good and evil is greatly diminished in scope and scale. For the uninitiated, this conclusion to the story begun in THE HOBBIT may be slightly confusing. For those already initiated to the grand story, much has been removed from it to get the story on film. Consequently, not many viewers will be totally satisfied. However, it is still worthy of watching. Both the initiated and in-initiated will find something that they will find to be of interest. For a grittier version check out LORD OF THE RINGS.

Sex Nud Viol Lang AdSit

A:

© WARNER HOME VIDEO 843

SOMEWHERE IN TIME

PG | ROM FAN | 1980 | COLOR

D: Jeannot Szwarc 104 m

8 Very entertaining and intensely romantic story of love found and lost! Reeve is a handsome playwrite (from the 1980s) who sees a picture of a beautiful actress (Seymour) that was taken in 1912. He immediately falls in love with her. He believes that they had been lovers in a past life and through self-hypnosis he manages to transports himself back in time to be with her. He finds her at the Grand Hotel on Michigan's Mackinac Island and they fall deeply in love, despite the objections of her manager (Plummer) who does everything he can to break them up. This is an entrancing, even though fanciful, love story with beautiful photography of picturesque settings.

Sex Nud Viol Lang AdSit

A: Christopher Reeve, Jane Seymour, Christopher Plummer, Teresa Wright, Bill Erwin, George Voskovec

© MCA/UNIVERSAL HOME VIDEO, INC. 66024

SPLASH

PG | COM ROM FAN | 1984 | COLOR

D: Ron Howard 109 m

9 An unbelievable plot is made both believable and captivating, thanks to outstanding acting by Hanks and Hannah and deft direction by Howard. Hanks is a wealthy businessman who has everything but love. When he nearly drowns off the coast of Cape Cod, it is a beautiful mermaid (Hannah) who rescues him. She is infatuated with him and grows legs to search the big city for him. She charms him with her incredible innocence and they fall madly in love, but Hanks still has a hard time learning to deal with her nautical nature. Fantastic movie-making and a wonderful blending of fantasy and romance.

Sex Nud Viol Lang AdSit

A: Tom Hanks, Daryl Hannah, Eugene Levy, John Candy, Dody Goodman, Richard B. Shull

© TOUCHSTONE HOME VIDEO 213

STARMAN

PG | ROM SF FAN | 1984 | COLOR

D: John Carpenter 115 m

8 An endearing charmer. An space ship is shot down and crashes in rural Wisconsin. The scared alien escapes from the crash site before the government gets to it and stumbles upon the cabin of a young woman (Allen) who is newly widowed and still grieving the loss of her husband. The alien will die if he doesn't make it to Arizona where he will be rescued in three days. So he, takes on the form of her dead husband and makes her drive him there. She is not pleased but along the way, while they are dodging the pursuing FBI, she discovers a sweetness about him. That, and because he looks like her dead husband, she falls in love with him. Very entertaining and uplifting.

Sex Nud Viol Lang AdSit

A: Jeff Bridges, Karen Allen, Charles Martin Smith, Richard Jaeckel

© COLUMBIA TRISTAR HOME VIDEO 60412

SUPERMAN II

PG | ACT COM FAN | 1979 | COLOR

D: Richard Lester 127 m

8 Superman (Reeve) has his hands really full when three evil villains from his home planet Krypton come to earth and are intent on ruling it. They all possess the same powers that Superman has, and so the challenging battle to save the world begins. Meanwhile, Superman falls deeper in love with Lois Lane (Kidder), and arch rival Lex Luthor (Hackman) keeps persistently nipping at his heels. Much more brash and wild that the first film, this super adventure keeps the adrenaline pumping and the laughs coming at a very steady pace.

Sex Nud Viol Lang AdSit

A: Christopher Reeve, Margot Kidder, Gene Hackman, Ned Beatty, Valerie Perrine, Jackie Cooper

© WARNER HOME VIDEO 11120

SUPERMAN, THE MOVIE

PG | ACT COM FAN | 1978 | COLOR

D: Richard Donner 143 m

9 A super movie! Reeve is the man of steel from the planet Krypton who is sent to earth as a child and is raised in a small midwestern town. When he is grown he moves to the big city and uses his super powers to keep crime at bay. Clark Kent, the unassuming newspaper man, becomes Superman when duty calls. He fights for truth, justice and the American way while battling the evil Lex Luthor (Hackman). Superman also falls for the captivating Lois Lane (Kidder) in this infectious film that spawned three sequels. Plenty of humor, adventure and romance. Oscar winner for special effects!

Sex Nud Viol Lang AdSit

A: Christopher Reeve, Margot Kidder, Marlon Brando, Gene Hackman, Ned Beatty, Jackie Cooper

© WARNER HOME VIDEO 1013

TIN DRUM, THE

R | FOR FAN DMA | 1979 | COLOR

D: Volker Schlondorff 142 m

9 Very bizarre and "artsy" fantasy, or rather nightmare, taken from a world-renown novel by Gunter Grass. Visually stunning, it was the winner of the Best Foreign Film Oscar. The story is that of young boy in 1920s Germany who is so distraught by the Nazis and their bleak world that he decides to stop growing. Instead, he becomes obsessed with beating on his toy drum to drown out horror, and also develops a piercing scream. However, these strange talents only make him into a popular source of entertainment for the Nazis, and ultimately he survives when others others around him suffer. Subtitles.

Sex Nud Viol Lang AdSit

A: Mario Adorf, Angela Winkler, David Bennent, Daniel Olbrychski, Katharina Thalbach, Heinz Bennent

© WARNER HOME VIDEO 24053

TO SLEEP WITH ANGER

D: Charles Burnett 102 m

PG · DMA FAN · 1990 · COLOR · Sex · Nud · Viol · Lang · AdSit

8 Unusual and offbeat but enchanting film about the conflicts between old and new values, between one generation and the next, and between an old black culture and an emerging new one. Parents Gideon and Suzie cling to their old ways from the deep South, to the embarrassment and consternation of their youngest son and his wife. Into Gideon's home, on a tree-lined Los Angeles street, walks jovial Harry Mention (Glover), an old friend of Gideon. But Harry is much more. He is a charmer, a storyteller and an evil "trickster" who has come to charm their souls from them.

A: Danny Glover, Paul Butler, Mary Alice, Sheryl Lee Ralph, Carl Lumbly, Richard Brooks

© COLUMBIA TRISTAR HOME VIDEO F0734

TRULY, MADLY, DEEPLY

D: Anthony Minghella 107 m

NR · ROM DMA FAN · 1992 · COLOR · Sex · Nud · Viol · Lang · AdSit

7 Touching and comedic. British couple Stevenson and Rickman are deeply in love. So when Rickman dies, Stevenson can't seem to find the will to go on. In her grief, she simply exists, losing track of days and withdrawing into a dark shell of sadness. However, one day he mysteriously reappears to her as a ghost and helps her through her grief. It is then that she realizes that he can no longer give her the kind of relationship she really needs and she finds the strength to live again. The wonderful thing about this movie is that it just happens, no explanation is ever offered as to Rickman's reappearance, and ultimately it really isn't needed.

A: Juliet Stevenson, Alan Rickman, Bill Paterson, Michael Maloney, Christopher Rozycki, Keith Bartlett

© TOUCHSTONE HOME VIDEO 1353

TUCK EVERLASTING

D: Frederick King Keller 90 m

NR · FAN CLD · 1981 · COLOR · Sex · Nud · Viol · Lang · AdSit

8 Enchanting, entertaining and intelligent fantasy that the whole family can enjoy. One day, while walking through the woods, Young Whynnie discovers the Tuck family. The Tucks feel no pain, never grow old and will never die. The Tucks come to like and eventually trust her enough to reveal to her their secret. This is a charming story that is not at all patronizing to kids and is a rewarding experience for the whole family. The film was adapted from Natalie Babbitt's novel of the same title.

A: Margaret Chamberlain, Paul Flessa, Fred A. Keller, James McGuire, Sonia Raimi, Bruce D'Auria

© LIVE HOME VIDEO VA4228

TWICE UPON A TIME

D: John Korty, Charles Swenson 75 m

PG · FAN CLD · 1983 · COLOR · Sex · Nud · Viol · Lang · AdSit

8 Imaginative and captivating cartoon fable that is only marginally for young kids. It is much too fast-paced, complex and filled with word-play for the average youngster and is more suited to older children, teenagers and fanciful adults. That is why this deserving video did not get wide theatrical release, even though it was produced by George Lucas. An almost indescribable bunch of characters sets out to save the world from the greedy owner of the Murkworks Nightmare Factory and to prevent him from blanketing the world with bad dreams. Funny and enjoyable.

A:

© WARNER HOME VIDEO 20012

TWILIGHT ZONE: THE MOVIE

D: Joe Dante, John Landis 101 m

PG · SUS DMA FAN · 1983 · COLOR · Sex · Nud · Viol · Lang · AdSit

7 Intriguing collection of four tales of the thought-provoking variety, made famous in the 1960s TV series of the same name. In fact, three of the episodes are remakes from that series. All are interesting and done with much higher production values, but oddly they lack the punch of the originals and overall are not as good - still worth a look, though. Example: "Nightmare at 20,000 Feet" - Lithgow is terrified because he is the only passenger on an airliner who can see the gremlin that is on the craft's wing working hard to rip it off.

A: Dan Aykroyd, Albert Brooks, Scatman Crothers, John Lithgow, Vic Morrow, Kevin McCarthy

© WARNER HOME VIDEO 11314

WARLOCK: THE ARMAGEDDON

D: Anthony Hickox 98 m

R · HOR FAN · 1993 · COLOR · Sex · Nud · Viol · Lang · AdSit

6 Once every millennium the devil trys to reappear upon and reclaim earth. In order to accomplish his complete return, his agent must possess the five magic rune stones. It is the God-given task of the Druids to prevent that from happening. Now is the time of this millennium for Satan to return. The Warlock has come to recover the stones to make way for his coming. He captures three of the stones and makes his way to California to recover the last two which are in the possession of a small group of Druids. The son and daughter of two of them are chosen to be warriors to battle the Warlock and prevent his recovering the last stones. Extremely gory and violent.

A: Julian Sands, Chris Young, Paula Marshall, Steve Kahan, Charles Hallahan, R.G. Armstrong

© VIDMARK ENTERTAINMENT 5518

WATERSHIP DOWN

D: Martin Rosen 93 m

PG · DMA FAN · 1978 · COLOR · Sex · Nud · Viol · Lang · AdSit

8 Although this is an animated feature, it is not a cartoon for little kiddies. It is an allegorical story for adults and older kids. It involves the human-like story of the survival of a small group of rabbits who leave the apparent safety of their home because Hazel foresees impending doom. She leads a group of males in search of a new home, past the dangers of foxes, owls, dogs and men, to reach a hill called Watership Down. There, they make a new home and set about attracting females from neighboring, but hostile clans, of rabbits. Well-done, thoughtful entertainment.

A:

© WARNER HOME VIDEO 34003

WILLOW

D: Ron Howard 130 m

PG · ACT FAN CLD · 1988 · COLOR · Sex · Nud · Viol · Lang · AdSit

7 A kooky fantasy - sort of Star Wars meets the Wizard of Oz. Davis is Willow, 0an elf who is the protector of a small baby who will grow up, end the reign of the evil Queen Bavmorda (Marsh) and bring peace to the world. Warrior Kilmer offers his help to the little guy and along the way they encounter many wacky characters, some dangerous and some funny. This is a fanciful adventure that provides an eyeful of special effects. Although aimed at children, some of the violence might be too intense for the youngest ones.

A: Val Kilmer, Joanne Whalley-Kilmer, Warwick Davis, Jean Marsh, Patricia Hayes, Billy Barty

© COLUMBIA TRISTAR HOME VIDEO 60936

WITCHES, THE

D: Nicolas Roeg 92 m

PG · FAN CLD · 1990 · COLOR · Sex · Nud · Viol · Lang · AdSit

9 Terrific spooky story for kids, but not under 8 or so. Luke is a 9-year-old boy whose loving grandmother tells him bedtime stories and always warns him of the dangers of witches (they like to kill little children). However, he and his grandmother happen to stay at a hotel where there is also a conference of witches and, it seems, the head witch (Huston) has created a magic potion that will turn all the children in England into mice. Then, she spots Luke. He escapes from her, but not before she turns him into a mouse. Now it is up to Luke to save himself and all the other children. That's not an easy job for a mouse.

A: Jasen Fisher, Mai Zetterling, Anjelica Huston, Rowan Atkinson, Bill Paterson, Brenda Blethyn

© WARNER HOME VIDEO 671

WONDERFUL WORLD OF THE BROTHERS GRIM, THE

D: Henry Levin, George Pal 128 m

NR · FAN CLD MUS · 1962 · COLOR · Sex · Nud · Viol · Lang · AdSit

6 Fanciful depiction of the lives of the famous story-telling brothers, which combines a telling of their life stories with three of their fairy tales: "The Dancing Princess," in which a princess finds her true love in a common woodsman; "The Cobbler and the Elves," in which an overworked shoemaker receives overnight assistance from some helpful elves (George Pal's famous Puppetoons); and, "The Singing Bone," where a pompous and cowardly knight relies upon his lowly servant to fight a fire-breathing dragon.

A: Laurence Harvey, Claire Bloom, Jim Backus, Yvette Mimieux, Buddy Hackett, Barbara Eden

Distributed By MGM/UA Home Video M200693

YELLOW SUBMARINE

D: George Dunning 87 m

G · MUS FAN · 1968 · COLOR · Sex · Nud · Viol · Lang · AdSit

8 Imaginative and clever animated feature with a score filled with fun Beatles music. Beatles fans will of course be particularly interested, but others should take note as well. The storyline has animated Beatles traveling by a yellow submarine to the fantasy land of Pepperland where their music and love will overcome the Blue Meanies, who have declared war on all that is good. Surrealistic pop art combines with lots of jokes and puns, plus these and more songs: "Lucy in the Sky With Diamonds," "When I'm 64," "All You Need is Love" and "Yellow Submarine."

A: The Beatles

Distributed By MGM/UA Home Video M301170

Foreign

Video's Best

1956 and After

3 MEN AND A CRADLE

D: Coline Serreau 100 m

PG-13 | FOR COM | 1986 | COLOR | Sex | Nud | Viol | Lang | AdSit

7 This is the winning predecessor to and the inspiration for the later very successful Americanized version called THREE MEN AND A BABY. Three Parisian bachelors suddenly become fathers when they are presented with a little girl that one of them has fathered. The totally unprepared threesome suddenly have to learn to deal with diapers and crying, but also become hopelessly in love with her. It was also one of France's biggest films of all times. Subtitles or dubbed.

A: Roland Giraud, Michel Boujenah, Andre Dussollier, Phillippine Beaulieu, Dominique Lavanat

© LIVE HOME VIDEO 5192

400 BLOWS, THE

D: Francois Truffaut 99 m

NR | FOR DMA | 1959 | B&W | Sex | Nud | Viol | Lang | AdSit

8 A sensitive, powerful and sometimes very sad film. It was also a daring movie for its time because it dared to challenge the establishment. It is the story of a disaffected 12-year-old boy who is failed and virtually abandoned by his parents, his teachers and all the other institutions around him. Deeply embittered, he strikes out at them all by committing a series of petty crimes. If he is to survive, he will have to find strength within himself. Famed as being one of the most memorable French New Wave ultra-realist films of the period, it is also worthy and affecting on a personal, non-technical basis. Subtitles. The character is picked up in later life in LOVE ON THE RUN.

A: Jean-Pierre Leaud, Patrick Auffay, Claire Maurier, Albert Remy

© HOME VISION FOU040

8 1/2

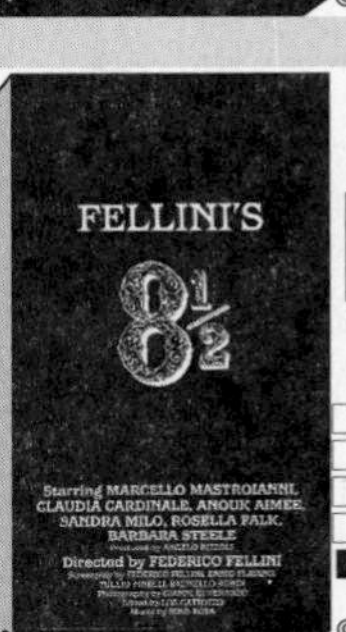

D: Federico Fellini 138 m

NR | FOR DMA FAN | 1963 | B&W | Sex | Nud | Viol | Lang | AdSit

10 For very sophisticated viewers only. This is a semiautobiographical film in which master Italian filmmaker Federico Fellini depicts, through a visual "diary," the director's difficulties in making the film we are watching. Viewers witness his memories, fantasies and problems, all through a storyline which ebbs and flows between reality and fantasy, eventually evolving to a world in between the two. Winner of Foreign Film Oscar. Subtitles.

A: Marcello Mastroianni, Claudia Cardinale, Anouk Aimee, Sandra Milo, Barbara Steele

© MPI HOME VIDEO 1398

AKIRA KUROSAWA'S DREAMS

D: Akira Kurosawa 120 m

PG | FOR DMA | 1990 | COLOR | Sex | Nud | Viol | Lang | AdSit

9 Rich in imagery, famed Japanese director Akira Kurosawa has created a screen depiction of eight dreams which separately contemplate and explore the consequences of man's world and his effect upon differing aspects of it. Very personal and philosophical, some stories are much more effective than others, however all are eerie and not totally resolved, much like real dreams. Film fans will enjoy the master's cinematography, but casual observers may be left wanting. Subtitles.

A: Akira Terao, Mieko Harada, Chishu Ryu, Martin Scorsese

© WARNER HOME VIDEO 11911

A LA MODE

D: Remy Duchemin 99 m

R | FOR COM ROM | 1994 | COLOR | Sex | Nud | Viol | Lang | AdSit

8 Very entertaining piece of French fluff. Young Fausto has become an orphan and has been apprenticed to Mietek, a small-time tailor. Mietek is a bachelor with his own slant on life, but he takes a particular interest in Fausto. Fausto at first is interested in sewing clothes because he wants to meet pretty young women. He is particularly enamored of the very pretty daughter of the local mechanic. However, he soon discovers that he has a genuine flair for tailoring and a wild, imaginatively extravagant talent for promotion. A gentle story of no particular merit and a little bizarre, but it has very endearing characters. Quite good fun. Subtitles.

A: Jean Yanne, Florence Darel, Ken Higelin, Francois Hautesserre, Maurice Benichow, Maite Nahyr

© MIRAMAX HOME ENTERTAINMENT 3608

ALL THE MORNINGS OF THE WORLD

D: Alain Marielle 110 m

NR | FOR MUS | 1993 | COLOR | Sex | Nud | Viol | Lang | AdSit

9 This is a wonderfully photographed French period piece, set in the 17th-century, that won 7 Cesar Awards, including Best Picture. While it is a favorite of the critics, it is also ponderous and very slow-moving. It is the story of a reclusive genius composer, who locks himself and his two beautiful daughters away from the world upon the death of his wife. The arrival of a flamboyant and talented young student draws the old man out enough to allow the younger one in for lessons. All of which is much to the approval of one of the daughters, but she is soon destroyed by her passions. The average viewer will be bored, but sophisticated romantic ones will be captivated. Subtitled.

A: Jean-Pierre Marielle, Gerard Depardieu, Anne Brochet, Guillaume Depardieu, Michel Bouquet, Jean-Claude Dreyfus

© TOUCHSTONE HOME VIDEO 2234

ALPINE FIRE

D: Fredi M. Murer 115 m

R | FOR DMA | 1987 | COLOR | Sex | Nud | Viol | Lang | AdSit

6 A farm family living in a remote mountainous area of the Swiss Alps struggles to survive. The two children are extraordinarily close due to their physical isolation and the emotional remoteness of their parents. The boy is a deaf-mute who is struggling with his adolescence. His older sister protects him fiercely and loves him unconditionally, but she struggles with her own loneliness and their passions lead them into a tragic incestuous relationship. This is not an exploitation film. It is interesting and very different, but also ultimately not completely satisfying. Subtitles.

A: Thomas Nook, Johanna Lier, Dorothea Moritz, Rolf Illig

© LIVE HOME VIDEO 5235

AND GOD CREATED WOMAN

D: Roger Vadim 90 m

PG | FOR DMA | 1957 | COLOR | Sex | Nud | Viol | Lang | AdSit

6 This is a famous ground-breaking French film that is the story of a voluptuous orphan woman/child (super-sexy Brigitte Bardot). She is a passionate girl who can't help being a manteaser. She embarrasses her adoptive parents who then threaten her with being forced to leave town. Instead, she agrees to marry the younger son of a straight-laced family who is enchanted with her. However, she has long lusted after not him, but his older brother... and when she gets a chance, she seduces him - only to regret her actions later. It is relatively tame today but it was a breakthrough at the time.

A: Brigitte Bardot, Curt Jurgens, Jean-Louis Trintignant, Christian Marquand, Georges Poujouly, Jean Tissier

© LIVE HOME VIDEO 3002

AND NOW MY LOVE

D: Claude Lelouch 121 m

8 An entertaining bit of lighthearted romantic fluff about fate and love at first sight. How can it be that two people fall instantly and passionately in love with each other? The individual lives and three generations of family histories of two people are explored in parallel fashion to explain why they should fall instantly in love at their first meeting. A romantic and lyrical salute to life and love in the 20th century. However, it is a little involved and so requires patience. Dubbed or subtitles.

PG | FOR ROM COM | 1975 | COLOR | Sex Nud Viol Lang AdSit

A: Marthe Keller, Andre Dussollier, Charles Denner

© NEW LINE HOME VIDEO 1505

ANGEL AT MY TABLE, AN

D: Jane Champion 157 m

6 A critically acclaimed film, this was originally made for New Zealand television. It is an adaptation of the autobiographies of Janet Frame, New Zealand's most famous poet and writer. Hers is the story of a sad and very shy childhood. Her shyness resulted in a such a total lack of social skills that it was misdiagnosed as being schizophrenia. She spent eight years in a mental institution before being released to begin anew acquiring the confidence and skills to live a somewhat normal life. Well-done and heartfelt, but very detailed, very deliberate and very slow. Very patient viewers only.

R | FOR DMA | 1991 | COLOR | Sex Nud Viol Lang AdSit

A: Kerry Fox, Kerry Fox, Aleia Keogh, Karen Fergusson, Iris Churn, K.J. Wilson

© TURNER HOME ENTERTAINMENT N4124

F O R

ASHES AND DIAMONDS

D: Andrzej Wajda 105 m

9 An extremely powerful and influential Polish film. WWII has just ended and a new peace dominated by Russian communists is beginning. Three young Poles, former members of the resistance movement, have just killed three Polish workers, believing that the communist party chief is among them. One of the assassins realizes that their target was in fact not killed. Spending the night at a hotel, the war-hardened young man has an affair with a pretty and tender barmaid. For the first time, he feels the war is over and begins to doubt his continuing role as a bitter political fanatic and soldier. Made a star of Cybulski and is considered the last in a trilogy of war films from director Wajda. Subtitles.

NR | FOR DMA WAR | 1958 | B&W | Sex Nud Viol Lang AdSit

A: Zbigniew Cybulski, Eva Krzyzewska, Adam Pawlikowski, Waclaw Zastrzezynski

© HOME VISION ASH 020

AU REVOIR LES ENFANTS

D: Louis Malle 103 m

8 Goodbye children. Powerful Oscar nominee for Best Foreign Film. During WWII, at a French Catholic boarding school, the headmaster and the monks shield several Jewish children from the occupying Nazis. This is the story of two boys, one Catholic and one Jewish, who develop a close relationship during that winter - a relationship that is cut short when the Nazis discover the Jewish children-in-hiding. Deeply felt and moving, though a little slow at times. A devastating ending. Dubbed.

PG | FOR DMA WAR | 1987 | COLOR | Sex Nud Viol Lang AdSit

A: Gaspard Manesse, Raphael Fejto, Francine Racette, Stanislas de Malberg, Phillipe Morier-Genoud, Francois Berleand

© ORION PICTURES CORPORATION 5041

BABETTE'S FEAST

D: Gabriel Axel 102 m

8 Winner of Best Foreign Film Oscar. After her husband and son are killed, French exile (Audran) is taken in by two elderly sisters who live spartan and austere lives as religious leaders. After 14 years with them, Audran wins money in a lottery and prepares a sumptuous banquet in celebration of the women's father's 100th birthday. They and the stoic townspeople are at first hesitant but then join in. Soon long dormant earthly passions are resurrected in everyone. This is not for everyone because it is subtle, deliberate and slow, but it is funny, too, and a reward for the patient viewer. Dubbed.

G | FOR DMA COM | 1987 | COLOR | Sex Nud Viol Lang AdSit

A: Stephane Audran, Birgitte Federspiel, Bodil Kjer, Vibeke Hastrup, Hanne Stensgard, Jarl Kulle

© ORION PICTURES CORPORATION 5040

BALLAD OF NARAYAMA

D: Shohei Imamura 129 m

9 Truly unusual Canne Film Festival winner, set in the late 19th century in a remote and very primitive Japanese mountain village. Here people live extremely close to nature and are not far above animals themselves. Life is very rudimentary and very fragile, because food is very short. So, the people have adopted a ruthless survival code. Some male babies are abandoned and left to die in rice paddies and old people, people reaching 70 years of age, are carried to a spot high on the mountain Narayama and left there to die. An old woman is still in good health, but she feels obligated to fulfill her obligation and welcomes death, even though her son fights to avoid her fate. Subtitles.

NR | FOR DMA | 1983 | COLOR | Sex Nud Viol Lang AdSit

A: Ken Ogata, Sumiko Sakamoto, Tonpei Hidari, Seiji Kurazaki, Junko Takada

© HOME VISION BAL 08

BELLE EPOQUE

D: Fernando Trueba 109 m

7 Delightfully saucy story from Spain. It is 1931, the country is in civil war and young Fernando has just deserted from the army. Arriving in a small town, he makes a friend in an old man who lets him stay with him. But when the man's daughters are to arrive, Fernando is asked to leave. He agrees, but then he sees Clara, Violeta, Rocia and young Luz, and he conveniently arranges to miss his train. Returning to the house, the old man allows him to stay. Four beautiful women - surely he can seduce one of them. However, young Fernando is surprised when one by one, they seduce him. Bawdy and sexy, but not crude. Actually quite charming. Best Foreign Film Oscar. Subtitles.

R | FOR ROM | 1994 | COLOR | Sex Nud Viol Lang AdSit

A: Jorge Sanz, Maribel Verdu, Ariadna Gil, Miriam Diaz-Aroca, Penelope Cruz, Fernando Fernan Gomez

© COLUMBIA TRISTAR HOME VIDEO 79373

BIZET'S CARMEN

D: 151 m

7 Opera is taken off the stage and into the streets when this opera favorite is filmed on location. Placido Domingo plays the aristocratic Spanish soldier who loses his heart and ruins his life when he frees a faithless, beautiful Spanish gypsy from prison in this classic opera. Actually filmed on location in the streets of Spain, this production has true dramatic force, as well as powerful music and beautiful singing.

PG | MUS FOR ROM | 1983 | COLOR | Sex Nud Viol Lang AdSit

A: Julia Migenes-Johnson, Placido Domingo, Ruggero Raimondi, Faith Esham, Jean-Philippe Lafont

© COLUMBIA TRISTAR HOME VIDEO 60487

BLACK AND WHITE IN COLOR

D: Jean-Jacques Annaud 90 m

8 This is a very funny film and was the surprise winner in 1976 of the Oscar for Best Foreign Film over the more highly-touted COUSINE, COUSINE and SEVEN BEAUTIES. It is the whimsical story of two remote European settlements in Africa, one German and one French, which have been existing peacefully side-by-side for years. But with the outset of WWI, the French decide it is their duty to attack the Germans. So one of them recruits a bunch of surrounding natives and equips them with shoes, bayonets and French names for a battle which falters pitifully. Biting satire. Subtitles.

PG | FOR COM | 1976 | COLOR | Sex Nud Viol Lang AdSit

A: Jean Carmet, Jacques Spiesser, Catherine Rouvel

© WARNER HOME VIDEO 803

BLACK ORPHEUS

D: Marcel Camus 103 m

8 This winner of the Oscar for the Best Foreign Film is a modernized version of an old Greek legend. The story is set in Rio de Janeiro during Carnival, Brazil's version of Marde Gras. A streetcar conductor (Mello) and a shy, beautiful country girl fall passionately in love. The lovers lose themselves in the frenzy of Carnival but she is followed through the streets of Rio by a stranger dressed as death and is killed. Mello attempts to resurrect her through magic but must eventually join her in the next world. Hauntingly beautiful score. Subtitles.

NR | FOR ROM FAN | 1958 | COLOR | Sex Nud Viol Lang AdSit

A: Breno Mello, Marpessa Dawn, Lourdes de Oliveira, Lea Garcia, Adhemar da Silva, Alexandro Constantino

© HOME VISION BLA 170

BLUE

D: Krzysztof Kieslowski 98 m

7 Plodding but oddly interesting French film. Juliette Binoche is the wife of a world famous composer who, along with their young daughter, is killed in an auto wreck. Only she survives. Numbed by the enormity of her loss, she sells everything she has, leaving her memories behind, and vanishes to live in a small apartment in Paris to contemplate all that has happened. Sophisticated and patient viewers will find it to have literary merit. Subtitles.

R | FOR DMA | 1993 | COLOR | Sex Nud Viol Lang AdSit

A: Juliette Binoch, Benoit Regent, Florence Pernel, Charlotte Very, Helene Vincent, Philippe Volter

© TOUCHSTONE HOME VIDEO 2759

BOAT, THE (FORMERLY DAS BOOT)

D: Wolfgang Petersen 150 m

9 Extremely realistic depiction of the claustrophobic life aboard a German U-boat on the prowl, attacking and under attack in the North Atlantic of World War II. German-made, the film meticulously illustrates the crowding, grime and absolute terror of being several hundred feet below water while those overhead are trying to kill you. The war-weary captain guides his desperate crew as they attempt to raise the damaged ship from the ocean floor. Brilliant. Superb. Billed as "the most expensive and most successful motion picture in the history of German cinema." Dubbed/subtitles.

R | FOR WAR DMA | 1982 | COLOR | Sex Nud Viol Lang AdSit

A: Jurgen Prochnow, Herbert Granemeyer, Klause Wenneman, Hubertus Bengsch, Martin Semmelrogge

© COLUMBIA TRISTAR HOME VIDEO 60139

BREATHLESS

D: Jean-Luc Godard 90 m

NR | FOR DMA | 1959 | B&W

7 Belmondo became a huge star because of this film. In it he plays a playful small-time hood in Paris who steals a car. Jean Seberg is a beautiful free-spirited American who is seduced by his charm and follows him. When he accidentally shoots a cop who is chasing him, he hides out in Seberg's apartment. She remains captivated by his spirit but will not commit herself to him. Then, as the police close in on him, Seberg betrays him, but he refuses to run. This film appealed greatly to a "live for today" attitude prevalent after the War in France and became a big French cult favorite. Subtitles.

Sex | Nud | Viol | Lang | AdSit

A: Jean-Paul Belmondo, Daniel Boulanger, Jean Seberg

© CONNOISSEUR VIDEO COLLECTION 1021

BURMESE HARP, THE

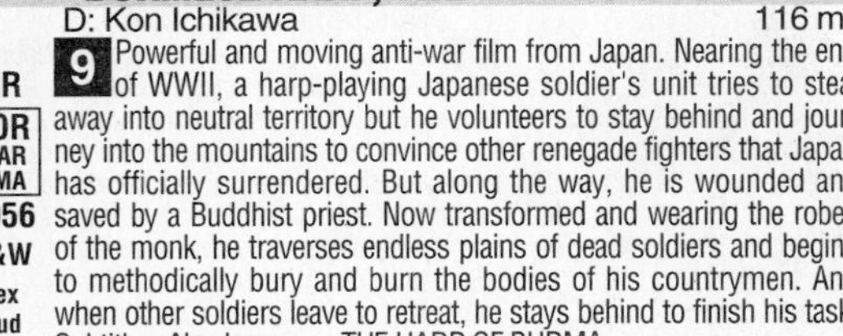

D: Kon Ichikawa 116 m

NR | FOR WAR DMA | 1956 | B&W

9 Powerful and moving anti-war film from Japan. Nearing the end of WWII, a harp-playing Japanese soldier's unit tries to steal away into neutral territory but he volunteers to stay behind and journey into the mountains to convince other renegade fighters that Japan has officially surrendered. But along the way, he is wounded and saved by a Buddhist priest. Now transformed and wearing the robes of the monk, he traverses endless plains of dead soldiers and begins to methodically bury and burn the bodies of his countrymen. And when other soldiers leave to retreat, he stays behind to finish his task. Subtitles. Also known as THE HARP OF BURMA.

Sex | Nud | Viol | Lang | AdSit

A: Shoji Yasui, Rentaro Mikuni, Tatsuya Mihashi, Tanie Kitabayashi, Yunosuke Ito

© HOME VISION BUR 110

CAMILLE CLAUDEL

D: Bruno Nuytten 149 m

R | FOR DMA | 1989 | COLOR

6 A bit long but involving look at the artistic genius of the famous French sculptress and her slide into insanity. A very independent woman, Camille (Adjani) is consumed with her art but finds conflict in the male-dominated art world. She studies under the noted sculptor August Rodin (Depardieu) and soon develops a romantic, but stormy, relationship with him. Sadly, she spends her last years in an asylum, suffering with an insanity brought on by the turbulence surrounding her work and her relationship with Rodin. Wonderful period detail but the film is likely leave you unsatisfied. Subtitles.

Sex | Nud | Viol | Lang | AdSit

A: Isabelle Adjani, Gerard Depardieu, Daniele Lebrun, Laurent Grevill, Katrine Boorman, Alain Cuny

© ORION PICTURES CORPORATION 5050

CIAO PROFESSORE!

D: Lina Wertmuller 91 m

R | FOR COM DMA | 1994 | COLOR

7 A dedicated and gentle teacher from the north of Italy is mistakenly assigned to teach a motley group of third graders at a seedy and poor town near Naples. It is a town almost without hope, as are its people. So, he is not prepared when he finds that his kids are charming. But, they are also irreverent, rebellious and extremely crude. They survive by being hard, but they want more and so they slowly begin to respond to his much softer ways. They learn from him, but he also learns from them. Consistently charming and quite funny in places, but you will have to be very tolerant of a never-ending string of vulgarities coming from the mouths of 10-year-olds. Subtitles.

Sex | Nud | Viol | Lang | AdSit

A: Paolo Villaggia, Tsai Danieli, Gigio Morra, Sergio Lolli, Ester Carloni, Mario Bianco

© BUENA VISTA HOME VIDEO 3036

CINEMA PARADISO

D: Giuseppe Tornatore 121 m

PG | FOR DMA | 1989 | COLOR

8 Bittersweet winner of the Oscar for Best Foreign Film. Salvatore is a young boy whose sole diversion in his small rural Italian town shortly after WWII is the magical world of movies. The crusty projectionist there becomes his friend and mentor, and the classic American, French and Italian movies he watches become his window to the world outside. They teach him how to court his first love and eventually how to escape his small town by making movies of his own. Then one day, thirty years later, he is called back for a beautiful secret. Captivating. Subtitles or dubbed.

Sex | Nud | Viol | Lang | AdSit

A: Philippe Noiret, Jaques Perrin, Salvatore Cascio, Agnese Nano

© HBO VIDEO 0376

CLOSELY WATCHED TRAINS

D: Jiri Menzel m

NR | FOR COM DMA | 1966 | B&W

7 Touching Chech film about a young man who is trying to learn how to grow up in a Czechoslovakia that is under Nazi occupation. He is just a naive train dispatcher/trainee and inexperienced in virtually everything. Although he attempts to lose his virginity, he fails badly. So, his psychiatrist urges him to find an experienced woman to teach him. But his desperate search for love instead gets him involved in a plot to blow up a Nazi train. Sometimes funny and sometimes poignant. Subtitles.

Sex | Nud | Viol | Lang | AdSit

A: Vaclav Neckar, Jitka Bendova

© COLUMBIA TRISTAR HOME VIDEO VH91058

COLONEL CHABERT

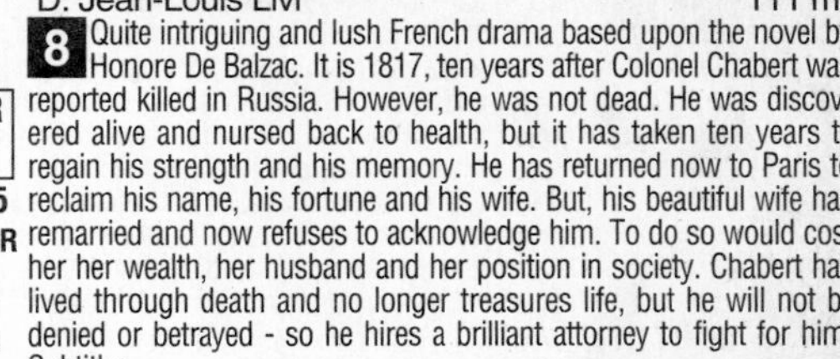

D: Jean-Louis Livi 111 m

NR | FOR DMA | 1995 | COLOR

8 Quite intriguing and lush French drama based upon the novel by Honore De Balzac. It is 1817, ten years after Colonel Chabert was reported killed in Russia. However, he was not dead. He was discovered alive and nursed back to health, but it has taken ten years to regain his strength and his memory. He has returned now to Paris to reclaim his name, his fortune and his wife. But, his beautiful wife has remarried and now refuses to acknowledge him. To do so would cost her her wealth, her husband and her position in society. Chabert has lived through death and no longer treasures life, but he will not be denied or betrayed - so he hires a brilliant attorney to fight for him. Subtitles.

Sex | Nud | Viol | Lang | AdSit

A: Gerard Depardieu, Fanny Ardant, Fabrice Luchinin, Andre Dussollier, Daniel Prevost, Romane Bohringer

© REPUBLIC PICTURES HOME VIDEO 6136

CONFIDENTIALLY YOURS

D: Francois Truffaut 110 m

NR | FOR SUS | 1983 | B&W

7 This was famed director Francois Truffaut's last film. It is light and entertaining, and is also a film very like his favorite director Alfred Hitchcock would have done. However, it is not very highly regarded. It is the story of a real estate agent who is accused of murdering his wife's lover. His secretary, who has been secretly in love with him, turns detective to uncover the mystery of who has framed him. Like Hitchcock's films, this one too has romance and humor thrown in with the thrills. Subtitled.

Sex | Nud | Viol | Lang | AdSit

A: Fanny Ardant, Jean-Louis Trintignat, Philippe Laudenbach, Caroline Sihol, Philippe Morier-Genoud

© HOME VISION CON 050

CONFORMIST, THE

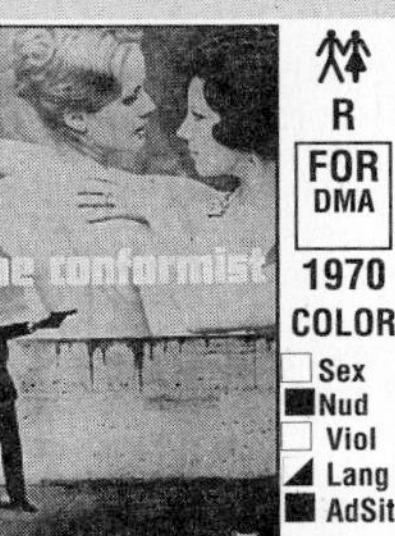

D: Bernardo Bertolucci 108 m

R | FOR DMA | 1970 | COLOR

8 A French character study and a portrait of the decadence of fascism prevalent during Mussolini's reign in Italy. In 1938, a weak-willed man wants to advance his career in radio so he joins the Italian fascist party. However, in a test of his fascist loyalties, he is ordered to go to Paris to kill his college professor who is now in exile. Instead, he becomes infatuated with the professor's lesbian wife, who unfortunately is more interested in his wife than in him. He then also has to repress his own childhood homosexual experiences with his chauffeur and he slowly begins to self-destruct. Powerful. Dubbed.

Sex | Nud | Viol | Lang | AdSit

A: Stefania Sandrelli, Dominique Sanda

© PARAMOUNT HOME VIDEO 8121

FOR

CONTEMPT

D: Jean-Luc Godard 102 m

NR | FOR COM DMA | 1964 | COLOR

7 A satirical insider's look at European movie making. The plot revolves around an Italian filming of the classic Greek "The Odyssey." Piccoli is the script writer who would rather write for the stage. He reluctantly takes the movie job to appease what he feels are his wife's ambitions and greed. However, she is now disappointed in him for his lack of conviction. Sexy, sultry Bardot is his wife and she now begins what appears to him to be an affair with the vulgar producer (Palance) just to spite her husband. Everyone apparently is in contempt of everyone else. Film fans and film students are best audience.

Sex | Nud | Viol | Lang | AdSit

A: Brigitte Bardot, Jack Palance, Fritz Lang, Michel Piccoli, Georgia Moll

© NEW LINE HOME VIDEO 2094

CONVICTION, THE

D: Marco Bellocchio 92 m

NR | FOR DMA ROM | 1994 | COLOR

8 An unusual and strangely compelling Italian film that proposes insight into, the mystery of female sexuality: Why are many, if not most women, powerfully drawn to "dangerous" men? A woman is inadvertently locked into a museum for the night, only to discover that she is not alone. With her is a man, who totally captivates her and compellingly engages her in a wild night of mutually consuming passion. In the morning, she discovers that he had had the keys all the time, and files charges against him for rape. In court, he does not deny her claims that he overpowered her with his will, but insists that it was seduction not rape. Very unusual and very adult.

Sex | Nud | Viol | Lang | AdSit

A: Pietro Valsecchi, Nella Banfi, Vittorio Mezzogiorno, Andrzej Seweryn, Claire Nebout, Grazny Szapolowska

© ORION PICTURES CORPORATION FLV1151

CRIES AND WHISPERS

D: Ingmar Bergman 95 m

R | FOR DMA | 1972 | COLOR

9 This is a very heavy adult drama that won Best Film at New York Film Critics, also four Oscar nominations, including Best Picture. It won Best Cinematography. A woman lies dying of cancer around 1900 and searches for peace. Her two sisters have come to stay with her but all three are haunted by unhappy pasts and are bitter. The peasant servant girl is the only positive force and is closer to the dying woman than are her sisters. Each of the women seek to reconnect through internal evaluations of their past in this barren landscape. Masterful use of light, shadow and sound, plus flawless acting imparts a sense of deep suffering and pain. Intense and slow moving. Subtitled.

Sex | Nud | Viol | Lang | AdSit

A: Liv Ullmann, Ingrid Thulin, Harriet Anderson, Kari Sylwan, Erland Josephson, Georg Arlin

© HOME VISION CRI 050

CYRANO DE BERGERAC

D: Jean-Paul Rappeneau 138 m

PG | FOR ROM | 1990 | COLOR

9 An inspired version of the classic tearjerker by Edmond Rostand. This is an extremely lavish French production (filmed in French and shown with subtitles) and may well be the definitive filmed version of the story. It is the story of an 17th-century eloquent swordsman with the romantic soul, who was so self-conscious of his looks that he held back telling his beloved Roxanne of his own deep feeling for her and helped his friend to win her heart for him. Acclaimed as France's greatest actor, Depardieu is charismatic in the role and received an Oscar nomination. Excellent. Subtitles.

Sex / Nud / Viol / Lang / AdSit

A: Gerard Depardieu, Anne Brochet, Vincent Perez, Jacques Weber, Roland Bertin

© ORION PICTURES CORPORATION 5058

DANTON

D: Andrzej Wajda 136 m

PG | FOR DMA | 1983 | COLOR

8 Intriguing historical drama. In post-revolutionary France anarchy rages. A strong-willed fanatic, Robespierre, is using the revolution to further his own goals. He and his allies have set up a dictatorship which will lead to what will be called the "Reign of Terror." His former friend and ally Danton declares that the revolution has gone too far and seeks an end to the destruction. Robespierre is now threatened, he publicly denounces Danton and Danton is executed. Strong parallels to many of the occurances in late 20th-century Eastern Europe. A brilliant and absorbing film. Subtitles.

Sex / Nud / Viol / Lang / AdSit

A: Gerard Depardieu, Wojciech Pszoniak, Patrice Chereau, Angela Winkler

© COLUMBIA TRISTAR HOME VIDEO VH91053

DANZON

D: Maria Novaro 103 m

PG-13 | FOR ROM | 1991 | COLOR

8 Highly regarded film from Mexico. Julia is a telephone operator who lives in Mexico City with her teenage daughter. Her life is boring, monotonous and uneventful - except for Wednesday nights. Wednesday night is when she goes ballroom dancing, performing a dance known as the Danzon. However, her life is upset when Carmelo, her long-time dance partner but about whom she know very little, suddenly disappears. Uncharacteristically following an impulse, she follows him to Veracruz. Suddenly the woman who has no excitement in her life and has seen little of the world, is deeply immersed in mystery and romance. Spanish with subtitles.

Sex / Nud / Viol / Lang / AdSit

A: Maria Rojo, Carmen Salinas, Blanca Guerra, Margarita Isabel, Tito Vasconcelos

© COLUMBIA TRISTAR HOME VIDEO 53463

DAY FOR NIGHT

D: Francois Truffaut 116 m

PG | FOR DMA COM | 1971 | COLOR

9 French director Francois Truffaut's reverent satire of the moviemaking business. The story reflects the pandemonium, activities, love lives and anxieties of the principal participants (the actors, director, producer and crew) in and during the making of a romance movie called "Meeting Pamela." This satirical film largely debunks the glamour of movie-making and is a favorite among film insiders. It has humor, but is not a true comedy. Oscar for Best Foreign Film. Dubbed. Sophisticated viewers and film fans only.

Sex / Nud / Viol / Lang / AdSit

A: Jacqueline Bisset, Jean-Pierre Leaud, Valentina Cortese, Jean-Pierre Aumont

© WARNER HOME VIDEO 11134

DECLINE OF THE AMERICAN EMPIRE, THE

D: Denys Arcand 102 m

R | FOR COM DMA | 1986 | COLOR

8 Enjoyable, but very sophisticated, look at sexual politics. A group of university teachers and students get together. Four men prepare a gourmet dinner while they swap stories about women and sex. The four women do the same while they exercise in a health club. Then they all meet for dinner and it becomes known that intimate secrets have been revealed. That inspires a very open sexual discussion which leads both to more revelations and experimentation. Intellectual, incisive and witty. However the subject matter, and the frank approach to it, makes this a video that is definitely not for everyone. Subtitles.

Sex / Nud / Viol / Lang / AdSit

A: Dominique Michel, Dorothee Berryman, Louis Patal, Genevieve Rioux, Pierre Curzi, Remy Girard

© MCA/UNIVERSAL HOME VIDEO, INC. 80586

DELICATESSEN

D: Marc Caro 95 m

R | FOR COM | 1992 | COLOR

8 This French import is beyond bizarre. It's well into the really bizarre. It is not for the average viewer, but it is also strangely, perversely interesting and even hilarious at times. The time and location are never made clear, but the economic circumstances are definitely hard. The place is a rundown apartment building with a butcher shop on the first floor and upon which all the tenants rely for meat. But, there is never any meat until some unsuspecting person answers an advertisement for a handyman. Then there is meat. This time it is an out-of-work clown who comes knocking, but the butcher's daughter has fallen in love with him before he can become diner. Subtitles.

Sex / Nud / Viol / Lang / AdSit

A: Dominique Pinon, Marie-Laure Dougnac, Jean-Claude Dreyfus, Karin Viard, Rufus, Ticky Holgado

© PARAMOUNT HOME VIDEO 15148

DISCREET CHARM OF THE BOURGEOISIE, THE

D: Luis Bunuel 100 m

PG | FOR COM | 1972 | COLOR

9 A brilliant and caustic French work that pokes fun at the rich, the church, the police, and politics. Any attempt to describe the plot is nearly useless, because it is so convoluted. In essence, it all revolves around the frustrating attempts of three couples, diplomats from a South American country, to get dinner in Paris. It won the Oscar for Best Foreign Film. Full of delights and surprises. Hilarious. Subtitles or dubbed.

Sex / Nud / Viol / Lang / AdSit

A: Delphine Seyrig, Fernando Rey, Stephane Audran, Jean-Pierre Cassel

© XENON HOME VIDEO 8000

DIVA

D: Jean-Jacques Beineix 119 m

R | FOR SUS ACT | 1981 | COLOR

8 Interesting French film which has become a cult favorite because it is so stylishly photographed. It also has a pretty good story. There are two separate plots interwoven. A mail messenger has a strong attraction to a black American opera singer (Fernandez). She has never allowed her voice to be recorded, so he secretly tapes a performance. He is seen. The next day a strange woman secretly drops another unrelated tape into his pocket, which incriminates a top cop, just before she dies. Soon the messenger is being chased all over Paris by two separate groups, both of whom are after his tapes. Some fans might even rate it higher. Subtitles.

Sex / Nud / Viol / Lang / AdSit

A: Frederic Andrei, Wilhemina Wiggins, Richard Bohringer, Thuy An Luu, Jacques Fabbri, Chantal Deruaz

Distributed By MGM/UA Home Video M800183

DIVORCE - ITALIAN STYLE

D: Pietro Germi 104 m

NR | FOR COM | 1962 | B&W

8 Hilarious Italian comedy. A decadent Sicilian nobleman wants to get rid of his wife so that he can marry his young mistress, but the law forbids divorce. However, he can legally kill her if he catches her in the act with another man. So he sets about finding her one. This very funny satire on Italian mores won an Oscar for its story and screenplay. An ironic twist provides the perfect ending. Subtitles or dubbed.

Sex / Nud / Viol / Lang / AdSit

A: Marcello Mastroianni, Daniela Rocca, Leopoldo Trieste

© HEN'S TOOTH VIDEO 1020

DONA FLOR AND HER TWO HUSBANDS

D: Bruno Barreto 110 m

R | FOR COM | 1977 | COLOR

8 Very sexy, exotic and erotic comedy imported from Brazil. Sonia Braga is the sultry widow of a very exciting but totally irresponsible womanizer. After he dies in the middle of a tryst during Festival, she marries a dull but dependable pharmacist. However, she is a passionate woman and she longs for her first lover, and when her first husband starts showing up as a nude ghost at the very most inopportune times, she must decide between them. It was later remade for American audiences with Sally Fields as KISS ME GOODBYE, but was considerably toned down. Subtitles.

Sex / Nud / Viol / Lang / AdSit

A: Sonia Braga, Jose Wilker, Mauro Mendanca, Dinora Brillanti

© WARNER HOME VIDEO 34002

DOUBLE LIFE OF VERONIQUE, THE

D: Krzysztof Kieslowski 96 m

R | FOR FAN | 1991 | COLOR

6 Exotic and haunting portrait of two young women born on the same day - one in Poland, one in France. They are identical in appearance, personality, talent and frail health. One says, "I know that I am not alone," although she does not know what it means. When the Polish girl is chosen to be a featured singer at a concert and dies on stage, the other feels grief and ends her own singing lessons. Later she finds the image of the dead girl on a photograph she took on a trip to Poland. A feeling of mysticism and an eerie mood are the only purpose for the film. Subtitles.

Sex / Nud / Viol / Lang / AdSit

A: Irene Jacob, Philippe Volter, Sandrine Dumas, Aleksander Bardini, Louis Ducreux, Claude Duneton

© PARAMOUNT HOME VIDEO 15122

DOUBLE SUICIDE

D: Masahiro Shinoda 105 m

NR | FOR DMA ROM | 1969 | B&W

8 A Japanese traditional puppet play dating back to 1720 is the source of the story line and the stylized feel to this film. A newspaper vendor has a passionate love affair with a beautiful geisha and she loves him. He cannot control himself and vows to purchase her freedom although he is already very deep in debt. His business is bankrupted. His wife and two small children are suffering terribly. She is neglected, deprived and abused, yet she is bound to him by duty. It is hopeless for everyone. A romantic tragedy laden with symbolism and steeped in Japanese culture. Not for everyone. Subtitles.

Sex / Nud / Viol / Lang / AdSit

A: Shima Iwashita, Kichiemon Nakamura, Hosei Komatsu

© COLUMBIA TRISTAR HOME VIDEO K0677

EL MARIACHI

D: Robert Rodriguez 80 m

R | FOR ACT COM | 1992 | COLOR | □ Sex □ Nud ■ Viol □ Lang ◢ AdSit

7 Most famous for being a film shot for only $7000 in 14 days and still being purchased for national release by a major studio (which then also gave its 24-year-old producer/director/co-writer/star a contract). The film is a quite choppy (what do you expect) spoof of spaghetti Westerns, even though it is set in modern times. It tells the unlikely story of an innocent guitar player dressed in black who wonders into a small Mexican town just after a hit man, who is also dressed in black and carries a guitar case full of weapons, has shot up the town. The poor hero is forced to defend himself over and over again. Subtitles.

A: Carlos Gallardo, Consuelo Gomez, Peter Marquardt, Jamie de Hoyos, Reinol Martinez

© COLUMBIA TRISTAR HOME VIDEO 53613

ELVIRA MADIGAN

D: Bo Widerberg 90 m

PG | FOR ROM | 1967 | COLOR | □ Sex □ Nud □ Viol □ Lang ■ AdSit

9 Acclaimed as one of the most romantic films of all times. It is based upon a true story about a Swedish Army officer and a famous circus tightrope walker who fall so desperately in love that they abandon all their obligations to run away together. Their pictures are appearing in the newspapers, so they must hide and keep moving. But soon they are out of money and are hungry. That leaves them only one way out. Loving but yet unsentimental. Beautiful images. Subtitles.

A: Pia Degermark, Thommy Berggren

© FOOTHILLS VIDEO

ENTRE NOUS

D: Diane Kurys 110 m

PG | FOR DMA | 1983 | COLOR | ◢ Sex ◢ Nud ◢ Viol □ Lang ◢ AdSit

9 Intelligent and poignant adult drama - a big hit in the art theaters and it received a nomination for Best Foreign Film. It is an autobiographical work depicting the director's own mother's story and begins in France during the German occupation. A Russian Jewish woman escapes prison by agreeing to marry a total stranger. Another woman sees her husband shot in front of her eyes. Later, in 1952, these two women are brought together by tragedy and meet again by chance. A relationship develops and both leave their husbands to start a new life together. The subject of the film is their deep friendship, but there is a subtle hint of lesbianism present as well. Subtitles.

A: Isabelle Huppert, Miou-Miou, Guy Marchand, Jean-Pierre Bacri

Distributed By MGM/UA Home Video M800492

EUROPA EUROPA

D: Agnieszka Holland 115 m

R | FOR DMA | 1991 | COLOR | □ Sex ◢ Nud ◢ Viol □ Lang ■ AdSit

8 Utterly fascinating true story of survival from WWII. 13-year-old Jew, Simon Perel, and his family escape Germany to Poland in 1938 only to be overrun there by the Nazi blitzkrieg in 1939. Caught away from home, he is picked up by a Russian soldier and placed in an orphanage where he learns Russian. He first masquerades as a Communist, and later as a Hitler Youth until is drafted into the German army where he become an interpreter. For seven harrowing years he survives by adapting as needed - all the while desperate to hide the biggest symbol of his Jewishness. He is circumcised. Subtitles.

A: Marco Hofschneider, Rene Hofschneider, Julie Delpy, Ashley Wanninger, Piotr Kozlowski

© ORION PICTURES CORPORATION 5064

FAMILY, THE

D: Ettore Scola 128 m

PG | FOR DMA | 1987 | COLOR | □ Sex □ Nud □ Viol ◢ Lang ◢ AdSit

7 Nominated in 1987 for the Best Foreign Film Oscar. This is a colorful bittersweet portrait of the people who have populated one man's long life. The story is set almost entirely in his living room. The patriarch of an Italian family (Grassman) is celebrating his 80th birthday. As his relatives arrive and he is getting ready, the story of his and his family's lives are told as a series of flashbacks. The past 80 years have brought a lot of changes to the family. They have endured war, love, hate, triumph and tragedy - all of the things that go along with living a rich existence. Dubbed.

A: Vittorio Gassman, Fanny Ardant, Andrea Occhipinti, Stefania Sandrelli, Jo Ciampa, Philippe Noiret

© LIVE HOME VIDEO 5268

FANNY AND ALEXANDER

D: Ingmar Bergman 188 m

R | FOR DMA | 1983 | COLOR | ◢ Sex ◢ Nud □ Viol ◢ Lang ◢ AdSit

7 A rewarding experience for patient sophisticated viewers. Set in turn-of-the-century Sweden, two young children are raised within an affluent and warm theatrical family. Life is exciting and fun. However, when their father dies, their mother is consoled by and marries a strict minister. That marriage requires them all to make severe adjustments in their lives. This is a rich tapestry of life in 1907 Sweden and a powerful indictment of religious excess. The story is largely viewed through the eyes of Alexander and is richly orchestrated in lavish period details. Demanding viewing, but richly rewarding.

A: Pernilla Allwin, Bertil Guve, Ewa Froling, Jan Malmsjo, Harriet Andersson, Erland Josephson

© NEW LINE HOME VIDEO 2067

FAR AWAY, SO CLOSE

D: Wim Wenders 146 m

PG-13 | FOR FAN DMA | 1994 | COLOR | □ Sex □ Nud ◢ Viol ■ Lang ■ AdSit

8 Intriguing concept first used in 1988's WINGS OF DESIRE. Angels flitter around listening into the lives and thoughts of ordinary people. And, as in the earlier film, one angel longs to see and feel what it is like to be human. However, he wants to do more. He wants to do good. His exposure to real world of humans leads him to discover how ill-prepared he is, particularly for the aloneness of each human soul. Still, he struggles to learn and even gains some mild assistance from another former angel and now immigrant, but he is also struggling against an evil angel sent by the other side to foil his efforts.

A: Otto Sander, Peter Falk, Horst Buchholz, Natassia Kinski, Heinz Ruhmann, Willem Dafoe

© COLUMBIA TRISTAR HOME VIDEO 79968

FAREWELL MY CONCUBINE

D: Chen Kaige 157 m

R | FOR DMA | 1993 | COLOR | □ Sex □ Nud ◢ Viol ■ Lang ■ AdSit

8 An beautifully filmed epic import from mainland China which follows 50 years in the careers of two actors. The two meet as young boys and students at an unbelievably cruel acting school. There they become friends while finely honing their skills at performing one particular classic opera. They will perform it throughout their lives. It is about an ancient king and his concubine who died for him. All actors in Chinese opera are men and the man in the female role gives himself totally to his character, even off stage. The two act as though they are married, except in one way, and when a woman comes between them their relationship falters. Very long and Chinese opera is very shrill. Subtitles.

A: Leslie Cheung, Zhang Fengyi, Gong Li, Lu Qi, Ying Da

© MIRAMAX HOME ENTERTAINMENT 2522

FITZCARRALDO

D: Werner Herzog 150 m

PG | FOR DMA | 1982 | COLOR | □ Sex ◢ Nud ◢ Viol ◢ Lang ◢ AdSit

7 A fascinating portrait of a man obsessed. A crazy Irishman in turn-of-the-century Peru becomes obsessed with opening a shipping lane through the Amazonian rain forest to gain access to fourteen million rubber trees. His other burning goal is to open his own personal opera house in the middle of the Amazonian jungle. In order to do all this, he must drag a 320-ton steamboat over a mountain. An astonishing movie about one man's perseverance in the face of overwhelming odds. Involving, but slow moving.

A: Klaus Kinski, Claudia Cardinale, Paul Hittscher, Jose Lewgoy

© WARNER HOME VIDEO 24003

GARDEN OF DELIGHTS, THE

D: Carlos Saura 101 m

NR | FOR DMA | 1970 | COLOR | □ Sex □ Nud □ Viol □ Lang ■ AdSit

7 Critically acclaimed, complex and surrealist black comedy from Spain. An extremely rich industrialist is crippled in a car crash. He is paralyzed and he has lost his memory. This is an economic disaster for his relatives. So, confined to a wheel chair, the poor man is forced to watch painful incidents from his past being reenacted by his supposed respected family, in an heartless attempt to resurrect his memory long enough to recover the number of his Swiss bank account. Subtitles.

A: Jose Luis Lopez Vasques, Luchy Soto, Francisco Pierra, Charo Soriano, Lina Canalejas

© HOME VISION GAR 050

GATE OF HELL

D: Tienosuk Kinugasa 86 m

NR | FOR ROM ACT | 1956 | COLOR | □ Sex □ Nud ■ Viol □ Lang ◢ AdSit

9 Winner of Best Foreign Film Oscar, New York Film Critics and Cannes. Exquisitely beautiful, haunting and heart-wrenching Japanese tale of love. Set in the 12th-century, a warrior remains faithful to his Emperor in spite of overwhelming odds. When offered anything he wants for his reward, he asks for a beautiful lady he had met briefly but fell passionately in love with. However, she is happily married and refuses him. Yet, he is obsessed with her and refuses to leave her alone. Rebuffed on all fronts and desperate, he threatens to kill both her and her aunt, unless she agrees to let him kill her husband and then marry him. Instead, she kills herself. Beautiful photography. Subtitles.

A: Machiko Kyo, Kazuo Hasegawa, Isao Yamagata

© HOME VISION GAT 020

GERMINAL

D: Claude Berri 166 m

R | FOR DMA | 1993 | COLOR | ■ Sex ■ Nud ◢ Viol ◢ Lang ■ AdSit

8 Lushly made French epic from the novel by Emile Zola. It is said to be the most expensive French film made to date, at $30 million. Set in the coal mines of 19th-century France, this is the story of the pitiful lives of the poverty-struck miners, as they struggle to survive both in the dangerous, bleak and filthy holes from which they scrape a living; and, from the merciless owners of the mine, who also own their houses, the food they eat and ultimately their souls. After repeated abuses by their masters, the miners rise up in rebellion, holding out against impossible odds for change. Beautifully photographed, highly evocative and morbidly realistic, as well as being very, very long.

A: Gerard Depardieu, Miou-Miou, Renaud, Jean Carmet, Judith Henry, Jean-Roger Milo

© COLUMBIA TRISTAR HOME VIDEO 72673

GET OUT YOUR HANDKERCHIEFS

D: Bertrand Blier 109 m

R | FOR COM | 1978 | COLOR | Sex | Nud | Viol | Lang | AdSit

7 Controversial quirky black comedy from France that won the Best Foreign Picture Oscar. It is a very unconventional film about a man whose wife is very unhappy. She won't smile or even talk. He doesn't know what is wrong but he loves her and will do almost anything to make her happy. Sensing that the thing she needs most is a lover, he sets out to find her one. Still, she just sits and knits and knits. Then she meets a remarkable 13-year-old boy. A funny and intelligent work of biting satire that is definitely adult in character. Subtitles.

A: Carole Laure, Gerard Depardieu, Patrick Dewaere, Ritan, Michel Serrault, Eleonore Hirt

© WARNER HOME VIDEO 28001

GOING PLACES

D: Bertrand Blier 122 m

R | FOR COM DMA | 1974 | COLOR | Sex | Nud | Viol | Lang | AdSit

7 There are widely differing opinions on this one. It was very controversial but it launched the career of Gerard Depardieu. It is the story of two likable louts who cavort through the French countryside stealing cars, terrorizing people and having their way with numerous women. They are searching for the one woman who can understand them, and they find her in a beautiful ex-convict, Jeanne Moreau. It is provocative, funny, disturbing and outrageous. For the most open-minded viewers only.

A: Gerard Depardieu, Miou-Miou, Jeanne Moreau, Patrick Dewaere, Brigitte Fossey

© INTERAMA VIDEO CLASSICS 0021

HIDDEN FORTRESS, THE

D: Akira Kurosawa 139 m

NR | FOR ACT COM | 1958 | B&W | Sex | Nud | Viol | Lang | AdSit

9 George Lucas acknowledges that this film, from the Japanese master filmmaker Akira Kurosawa, was the inspiration for his mega-smash hit STAR WARS. In it, a haughty young princess, a fortune in gold, a fugitive general and two bumbling and comic mercenary soldiers make a treacherous journey through enemy territory to get her back to her homeland. This one is so much fun you may even forget that its a foreign film. Subtitles.

A: Toshiro Mifune, Misa Uehara, Minoru Chiaki, Kimatare Fugiwara, Susumu Fujita, Takashi Shimura

© HOME VISION HID 030

HIGH HEELS

D: Pedro Almodovar 113 m

R | FOR DMA | 1992 | COLOR | Sex | Nud | Viol | Lang | AdSit

6 Spanish import that is supposed to be a black comedy. If it is, it is so black that its comedy is virtually hidden. Still, it does work as a somewhat involving drama with a mystery element. Sexy Victoria Abril has been long separated from her celebrity mother (Paredes), whom she compulsively adores. Mother returns to Spain to find that daughter has married mother's former lover. Later, when the husband/lover is murdered in his bed, mother and daughter are both suspects of an investigator - who turns out to be a former lover of Abril - but is unknown to her because he was disguised at the time. Subtitles.

A: Victoria Abril, Miguel Bose, Marisa Paredes, Ama Lizaran, Mairata O Wisiedo, Cristina Marcos

© PARAMOUNT HOME VIDEO 15121

HOUR OF THE WOLF

D: Ingmar Bergman 88 m

NR | FOR HOR | 1968 | B&W | Sex | Nud | Viol | Lang | AdSit

7 The very dark side of a brooding artist (Max Von Sydow) is revealed when he and his pregnant wife retreat to a deserted island. He is plagued with surrealistic dreams and each day they become more and more real to him. Soon his bizarre hallucinations become his realities. His wife does her best to save him from them, but she is nearly destroyed as well. This is supposed to be one of Ingmar Bergman's lesser efforts, but still is powerful stuff. Subtitles.

A: Max von Sydow, Liv Ullmann, Erland Josephson, Gertrud Fridh, Gudrun Brost

Distributed By MGM/UA Home Video M202934

ICICLE THIEF, THE

D: Maurizio Nichetti 84 m

NR | FOR COM | 1990 | COLOR | Sex | Nud | Viol | Lang | AdSit

7 Very unusual and quite funny Italian satire. Its director has been called the Italian Woody Allen. This film is his lampoon of both classic Italian cinema and modern television advertising. In it, the film jumps back and forth between a black and white post-war Italy and a color contemporary Italy, and between poor households and middle-class ones. It is essentially a movie-within-a-series-of-movies. Featuring such things as a beautiful blond model diving into an ultramarine pool and emerging in a black and white river. Clearly for serious film fans only. Subtitles.

A: Maurizio Nichetti, Caterina Sylos Labini, Claudio G. Fava, Heidi Komarek

© FOX/LORBER HOME VIDEO 1030

INDOCHINE

D: Regis Wargnier 156 m

PG-13 | FOR DMA | 1993 | COLOR | Sex | Nud | Viol | Lang | AdSit

7 Indochine is French for Indo-China or Vietnam. Catherine Deneuve is the middle-aged daughter of a French-colonialist rubber plantation owner. She has no permanent man but she has adopted the orphaned daughter of friends and the girl is her treasure. Deneuve has a brief, passionate affair with a French officer. So, when her daughter falls in love with the same man, Deneuve sees that he is sent to a remote post. But her daughter follows him there and is soon swallowed up in the communist rebellion that is beginning to swell up from the countryside. The film unwinds over 25 years of history and 2 1/2 hours on screen. It won Best Foreign Film Oscar, is beautifully filmed but is very long. Subtitles.

A: Catherine Deneuve, Vincent Perez, Linh Dan Pham, Jean Yanne, Dominique Blanc, Henri Marteau

© COLUMBIA TRISTAR HOME VIDEO 27233

INNOCENT, THE

D: Luchino Visconti 125 m

R | FOR ROM DMA | 1979 | COLOR | Sex | Nud | Viol | Lang | AdSit

9 Lush and beautifully photographed erotic tragedy of Italian decadence. A lustful nineteenth-century Italian nobleman (Giannini) ignores his beautiful wife (Antonelli) and pursues other women, particularly a beautiful widow (O'Neill). He not only fails to hide his escapades, but expects Antonelli to understand. She has an affair of her own with a young author. She has turned the tables on him. He is very surprised to learn that his lust for her has returned and he is now insanely jealous. Highly charged. Famed director Visconti's last film. Subtitles.

A: Giancarlo Giannini, Laura Antonelli, Jennifer O'Neill, Rina Morelli, Massimo Girotti

© CONNOISSEUR VIDEO COLLECTION 1064

JEAN DE FLORETTE

D: Claude Berri 122 m

PG | FOR DMA | 1987 | COLOR | Sex | Nud | Viol | Lang | AdSit

9 Emotionally powerful and beautifully filmed first half of the classic French tragedy of greed set in southeast France during the mid-1920s. A proud and greedy farmer (Yves Montand) plots with his simple-minded nephew to obtain much-needed water and to financially destroy their new neighbor during a drought. They do not tell him of a hidden spring on his land, which they want for themselves. Their new neighbor is a city-born hunchback (Depardieu) whose only dream is to be a farmer. Extremely moving performances evoke deep feelings. The second portion is MANON OF THE SPRING. Subtitles.

A: Yves Montand, Daniel Auteuil, Gerard Depardieu, Elisabeth Depardieu

© ORION PICTURES CORPORATION 5033

JESUS OF MONTREAL

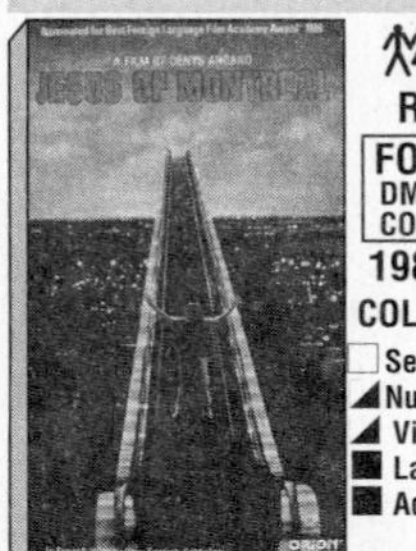

D: Denys Arcand 119 m

R | FOR DMA COM | 1989 | COLOR | Sex | Nud | Viol | Lang | AdSit

8 Nominated for Best Foreign Film. A group of unemployed actors get together some backers and form their own company for the presentation of the Passion Play on a hill overlooking Montreal. The play is in every way devout, but it does not follow traditional lines because it also attacks religious hypocrisy and commercialism. While it is well received by the community, the local clergy objects to it and so do its financial backers. The dilemma for the actors is whether to hold true to their ideals or to bow to pressure. Wickedly funny in places. Subtitles.

A: Lothaire Bluteau, Catherine Wilkening, Johanne-Marie Tremblay, Remy Tirard, Robert Lepage, Gilles Pelletier

© ORION PICTURES CORPORATION 5057

JOHNNY STECCHINO

D: Roberto Benigni 122 m

R | FOR COM | 1991 | COLOR | Sex | Nud | Viol | Lang | AdSit

7 This silly film is one of Italy's most popular hits. In it, Dante (Benigni) is a timid bus driver who is the spitting image of Johnny Stecchino, a notorious mob boss in hiding because other gangsters want to kill him. One night, Dante is seduced by beautiful Maria (Nicoletta Brashi) and is invited to return to Sicily with her. Believing that they are in love, he accepts her offer. However, her only plan is to trick the other gangsters into killing him instead of his look-alike, her husband. So, Dante is quite confused when he is constantly being shot at when all he has done is to have stolen a banana. Subtitles.

A: Roberto Benigni, Nicoletta Brashi, Paolo Bonacelli, Ignazio Pappalardo, Franco Volpi

© TURNER HOME ENTERTAINMENT N4066

JOURNEY OF HOPE

D: Xavier Koller 111 m

PG | FOR DMA | 1991 | COLOR | Sex | Nud | Viol | Lang | AdSit

9 Compelling winner of the 1990 Best Foreign Language Film Oscar. Haydar and his family are desperately poor and persecuted Kurds living in a small village in Turkey. Distraught and tired of his plight, he decides to emigrate to Switzerland - to Paradise - after receiving a post card from there. He sells everything he has, except for a few small possessions. Then, he and his wife take one son and leave the other six children behind to begin their clandestine journey of hope. However, before their journey is over, he will be lied to repeatedly, savagely abused and swindled out of all their money. Heartbreaking, but extremely powerful. Subtitles.

A: Necmettin Cobanoglu, Emin Sivas, Nur Surer

© HBO VIDEO 90675

FOR

JU DOU

D: Zhang Yimou 98 m

NR
FOR ROM DMA
1991
COLOR
Sex Nud Viol Lang AdSit

9 Magnificent and visually stunning picture from China that Chinese officials tried to hide. At the urging of major American directors, it received a much-deserved nomination for the Best Foreign Film. It is the story of a beautiful young woman purchased by a wealthy bitter old man in 1920 China. He is sterile but, because she is unable to bear him the son that he wants, he beats her and treats her as an animal. The man's near-slave adopted son consoles her. They meet in secret and become passionate lovers. But when she becomes pregnant, their lives become hell. Powerful. Subtitles.

A: Gong Li, Li Baotian, Li Wei, Zhang Yi, Zheng Jian

© LIVE HOME VIDEO 68983

JULES AND JIM

D: Francois Truffaut 105 m

NR
FOR ROM
1962
B&W
Sex Nud Viol Lang AdSit

10 Considered by many to be famed French director Truffaut's masterpiece. It is the story of two best friends and their love for the mystical Catherine. Jim and Jules are writers who meet in 1912 at an ancient stone carving of a beautiful woman. They find that they agree on nearly everything, then they meet the enchanting Catherine, who is the image of the carving. The three become great friends and both men adore her. She is a child-woman who embodies all that draws out the passions in a man, but Catherine can commitment to no one man. She marries Jules, but he must suffer through her infidelities. Then she wants Jim. So rather than for anyone to loose, they share each other. Subtitles.

A: Oskar Werner, Henri Serre, Jeanne Moreau, Marie Dubois, Vanna Urbino, Sabine Haudepin

© HOME VISION JUL 050

JULIET OF THE SPIRITS

D: Federico Fellini 142 m

NR
FOR DMA FAN
1964
COLOR
Sex Nud Viol Lang AdSit

8 A famous Fellini film. Juliet is an Italian housewife who is complacent in her dull life, thinking that the reason her husband largely ignores her is only because he works too much. However, one night, they hold a seance and she finds that she can actually talk to the spirits. They tell her that she deserves to enjoy life more. The film then becomes an attempt to illustrate the penetration the female psyche through a series of symbolic, surrealistic and gaudy images which fly by the viewer so fast that it is hard to keep track of them. Sort of a female 8 1/2. Largely for film fans. Subtitles.

A: Giulietta Masina, Sandra Milo, Mario Pisu, Valentina Cortese, Lou Gilbert, Sylva Koscina

© CONNOISSEUR VIDEO COLLECTION 1017

KANAL

D: Andrzej Wajda 96 m

NR
FOR WAR DMA
1956
B&W
Sex Nud Viol Lang AdSit

9 It is May of 1944 and Warsaw has been reduced to rubble by the Nazis. There is only one small chance for the defeated and demoralized Resistance fighters to escape. They are ordered to descend into the foul, dark and claustrophobic sewers. The terror and despair is palpable. The Germans will shoot at them if they emerge and throw grenades down manholes when they don't. Only one, a young woman, knows the way out, but her boyfriend is desperately wounded. They are trapped down below. One of three in a trilogy of Polish war films by Wajda. Others include: A GENERATION and ASHES AND DIAMONDS. Subtitles.

A: Teresa Izewska, Tadeusz Janczar, Wienczyslaw Glinski, Tadeusz Gwiazdowski

© HOME VISION KAN 020

KIKA

D: Pedro Almodovar m

NR
FOR COM
1994
COLOR
Sex Nud Viol Lang AdSit

7 Kika is a make-up artist. She is sexy and she likes to have fun. She lives with Ramone, a kinky younger photographer of women's lingerie; but, she also has occasional interludes with his stepfather, who is also messing around with Kika's best friend. Her maid is a lesbian who wants to make love to her, to be a prison guard at a women's prison and is protecting her perverted brother, who is also an ex-porno star and escaped prisoner. Not nearly lastly, is Andrea Scarface, who was a former psychologist to Ramone, but is now host of a tabloid TV show. This film has enough sex and general weirdness to offend most people and is quite disjointed, but it is also strangely fascinating. Subtitles.

A: Veronica Forque, Peter Coyote, Victoria Abril, Alex Casanovas, Ross De Palma, Santiago LaJusticia

© VIDMARK ENTERTAINMENT VM 6103

KING OF HEARTS

D: Phillippe De Broca 101 m

NR
FOR COM
1967
COLOR
Sex Nud Viol Lang AdSit

7 Large underground hit from the late 1960s and early '70s. It has diminished some with time but nonetheless maintains a big cult status with its fans. In it, Alan Bates is a WWI Scottish demolitions expert who is sent into a supposedly abandoned French village to dismantle explosive charges left by the retreating Germans. Instead, he finds that the loveable inmates of the local insane asylum have taken over the whole town and want to name him King of Hearts. Overly simplistic and idealistic statement about war that is, nonetheless, enjoyable to watch. Subtitles.

A: Pierre Brasseur, Genevieve Bujold, Alan Bates, Jean-Claude Brialy

Distributed By MGM/UA Home Video M201562

KNIFE IN THE WATER

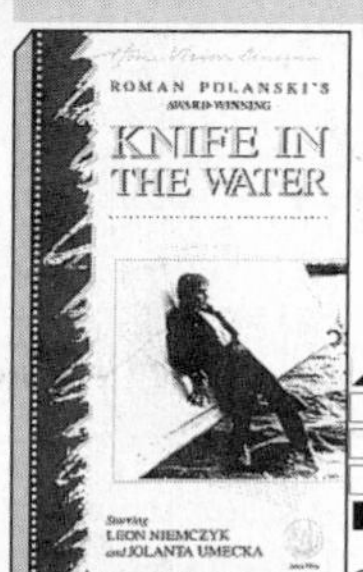
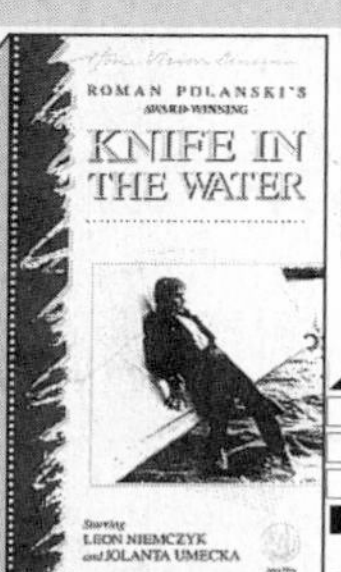

D: Roman Polanski 95 m

NR
FOR DMA
1962
B&W
Sex Nud Viol Lang AdSit

9 Roman Polanski's first, and some think his best, picture. A minor official and his younger wife are off for a weekend of sailing. Along the way they pick up a young student hitchhiker. Polanski's masterful storytelling unveils that there are major problems underlying this marriage. The young rider proves to be a rival for the girl and sexual tensions steadily build. The husband attempts to prove himself to his wife, and to himself, by engaging the boy in petty games. He wins, but by so doing, only proves his own childishness. Powerful and fascinating. Subtitles.

A: Leon Niemczyk, Jolanta Umecka, Zygmunt Malanowicz

© HOME VISION KN101

KWAIDAN

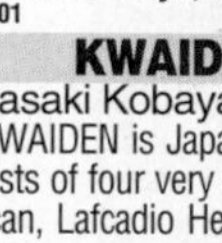
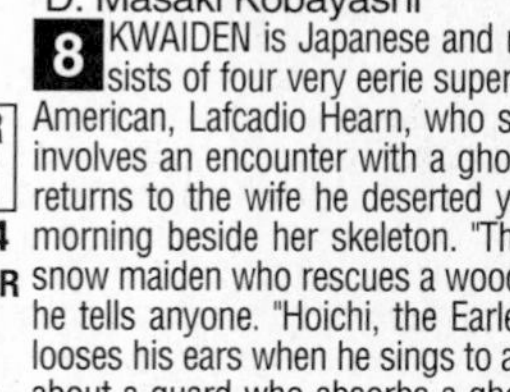
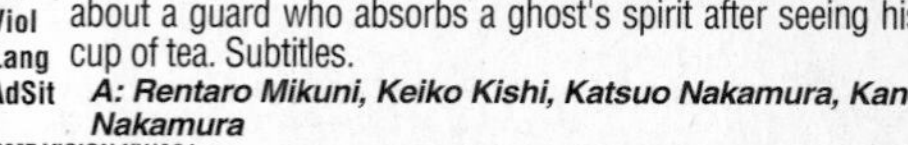

D: Masaki Kobayashi 164 m

NR
FOR HOR SUS
1964
COLOR
Sex Nud Viol Lang AdSit

8 KWAIDEN is Japanese and means "Ghost Story." This film consists of four very eerie supernatural tales that were written by an American, Lafcadio Hearn, who settled in Japan in 1890. Each story involves an encounter with a ghost. "Black Hair" is of a samurai who returns to the wife he deserted years before and wakes up the next morning beside her skeleton. "The Woman of the Snow" is about a snow maiden who rescues a woodcutter and then swears to kill him if he tells anyone. "Hoichi, the Earless" is about a blind musician who looses his ears when he sings to a Samurai ghost. "In A Cup of Tea" is about a guard who absorbs a ghost's spirit after seeing his face in a cup of tea. Subtitles.

A: Rentaro Mikuni, Keiko Kishi, Katsuo Nakamura, Kanemon Nakamura

© HOME VISION KWA01

LA CAGE AUX FOLLES

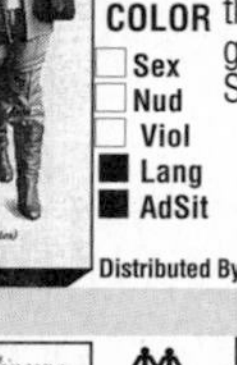

D: Edouard Molinaro 99 m

R
FOR COM
1979
COLOR
Sex Nud Viol Lang AdSit

7 Unique and frequently funny. One of the most successful foreign films ever shown in American theaters. The lives of a gay nightclub owner and his star impersonator/lover are thrown into turmoil when the son of one announces that he is going to be married. The girl's parents are prudish and would not understand his father's unique situation, so the two male lovers who have both helped to raise the boy decide to impersonate being man and wife. There are some genuinely hysterical scenes for those willing to accept the premise. Subtitles.

A: Ugo Totnazzi, Michel Serrault, Michel Balabru, Claire Maurier, Remy Laurent, Benny Luke

Distributed By MGM/UA Home Video M301580

LACEMAKER, THE

D: Claude Goretta 107 m

R
FOR ROM
1977
COLOR
Sex Nud Viol Lang AdSit

8 This was the break-through film for French star Isabelle Huppert. In it, she plays a simple and sweet 19-year old beautician. While on a trip to the beach with her friend, she meets a handsome student writer. She falls immediately and rapturously in love with him, and he is infatuated with her innocence and beauty. They return to Paris and immediately move in together. She is desperately in love with him and wants nothing else, but he becomes more and more aware of their differences. She shares none of his interests and wants more from her. Eventually asks her to move out. She is devastated and suffers a mental collapse.

A: Isabelle Huppert, Yves Beneyton, Florence Giorgietti, Anne-Marie Duringer, Jean Obe, Monique Chaumette

© HOME VISION LAC 01

LA DOLCE VITA

D: Federico Fellini 174 m

NR
FOR DMA
1961
B&W
Sex Nud Viol Lang AdSit

7 This is considered a landmark film and won an Oscar for Best Foreign Film, but it will have a select audience. Fellini's typical surrealism was tempered greatly, but not altogether. Mastroianni is a man with serious ambitions as an author, but he cannot give up the money he makes as a tabloid writer and the carefree life it buys him. So, he wonders aimlessly from party to party monitoring and participating in the shallow, decadent lives of the rich and famous that his readers envy. Long and rambling.

A: Marcello Mastroianni, Yvonne Furneaux, Anita Ekberg, Anouk Aimee, Magali Noel, Alain Cuny

© GOODTIMES 8298

LA FEMME NIKITA

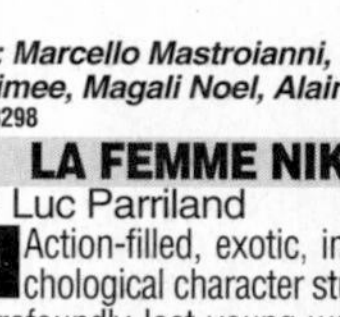

D: Luc Parriland 117 m

R
FOR ACT SUS
1990
COLOR
Sex Nud Viol Lang AdSit

9 Action-filled, exotic, intelligent and thoroughly fascinating psychological character study of a supremely unique nature. Nikita is a profoundly lost young woman who is convicted of committing an extremely ruthless murder. But, after receiving a life sentence, the government fakes her suicide and enters her into an ultra-secret training program for assassins. There, her life gains a perverse meaning and focus, but she also gains an appreciation for the life she doesn't have. Haunting. Dubbed or subtitles. Beginning is very odd. Released in an Americanized version as POINT OF NO RETURN.

A: Anne Parrilland, Jeanne Moreau, Tcheky Karyo, Jean Hugues Anglade

© VIDMARK ENTERTAINMENT 5471

LA NUIT DE VARENNES

D: Ettore Scola — 128 m

R | FOR COM | 1982 | COLOR

8 Imaginative but very talky French fiction. The night is June 22, 1791. Louis XVI and Marie Antoinette flee Paris and the Revolution. This fictitious flight provides an opportunity for the unlikely meeting of the fleeing pair with Casanova, American Thomas Paine and the Queen's own Lady-in-Waiting. The contradicting philosophies of the captive companions provide the basis for the witty dialogue which is the essence of this film. For discriminating and patient viewers.

Sex, Nud, Viol, Lang, AdSit

A: Marcello Mastroianni, Harvey Keitel, Hanna Schygulla, Jean-Louis Barrault

© COLUMBIA TRISTAR HOME VIDEO 60033

LAST METRO, THE

D: Francois Truffaut — 131 m

PG | FOR ROM | 1980 | COLOR

7 Nominated for Best Picture Oscar. It is 1942 Paris. The Nazis rule, so a brilliant Jewish theatrical director is forced to go into hiding in the basement of the theater. In his place, his beautiful and loving wife, Catherine Deneuve, must see that the troup stays together. She must deal with the very constrictive boundaries placed upon her by the occupiers, the barbs of a vicious pro-Nazi critic, while also fighting off her growing affections for her lead actor Gerard Depardieu. In spite of everything, the show must go on.

Sex, Nud, Viol, Lang, AdSit

A: Catherine Deneuve, Gerard Depardieu, Jean Poiret, Heinz Bennent, Andrea Ferreol, Jean-Louis Richard

© HOME VISION LAS 070

L'AVVENTURA

D: Michelangelo Antonioni — 145 m

NR | FOR DMA | 1960 | B&W

9 Both praised and booed, this is not a film for a casual observer. On the surface, it is the story of the search for a missing woman. A group of wealthy Italians visit a barren rock of an island near Crete. There a woman disappears after having an argument with her lover. The lover and the woman's best friend to scour the island for her, but after finding no trace, they leave the island and make inquiries at a near-by town. Soon, the two find themselves falling into a tempestuous relationship of their own. Below the surface story, this is an allegorical depiction of the decay of the idle rich. Demands attention but became a very influential film.

Sex, Nud, Viol, Lang, AdSit

A: Monica Vitti, Gabriele Ferzetti, Lea Massari, Dominique Blanchar

© HOME VISION AVV 030

LIFE AND NOTHING BUT

D: Bertrand Tavernier — 135 m

PG | FOR DMA WAR | 1989 | COLOR

8 Two years after the armistice, French Major Noiret is still sorting through the dead. He is trying to locate one certifiable unknown soldier for the Arc de Triomphe. His job is a seemingly endless one in that he has over 400,000 dead French soldiers to investigate. His strange occupation also places him into the paths of two women who come to represent all those looking for loved ones. One is a young aristocrat obsessively looking for her dead husband. The other is looking for her fiance. This is a story of tortured lives that are held in limbo by war. Brilliant photography. A major award winner. Well done. Subtitles.

Sex, Nud, Viol, Lang, AdSit

A: Philippe Noiret, Sabine Azema, Pascale Vidal, Maurice Barrier, Francois Perrot, Jean-Pol Dubois

© ORION PICTURES CORPORATION 5056

LITTLE THIEF, THE

D: Claude Miller — 108 m

R | FOR DMA | 1989 | COLOR

7 Set in post-war 1950 France, this represents the turmoil of that time. It is the story of a pretty young girl who is abandoned to relatives by her mother. She feels deserted and strikes out at the world by stealing. She runs away from everyone and lives only for the day. She even hires on as a maid and seduces the man of the house just before she steals from them. Then she falls for Raoul who is another young thief, and they continue to steal from her employers until she is arrested. However, now she has become pregnant. This film was intended to be the female counterpart for Truffaut's classic in a similar vein: 400 BLOWS. Subtitles.

Sex, Nud, Viol, Lang, AdSit

A: Charlotte Gainsbourg, Didier Bezace, Simon de la Brosse, Raoul Billery

© HBO VIDEO 0377

LOVE ON THE RUN

D: Francoit Truffaut — 95 m

NR | FOR DMA | 1978 | COLOR

8 The character of Antoine Doinel was first introduced at age 13 in Truffaut's famous film 400 BLOWS. It is actually the fifth is a series of films which depict other times in this character's lives. This film picks up his life in his mid-thirties. He is freshly divorced and has begun new love affairs with women from his past. (This film is amply injected with clips from the past films.) But the death of his mother reveals to him the deep emotional scars which have yet to heal and have left him an emotional cripple. If you have missed the earlier films this one will be largely wasted on you.

Sex, Nud, Viol, Lang, AdSit

A: Jean-Pierre Leaud, Marie-France Pisier, Claude Jade, Dani, Dorthee

© HOME VISION LOV 070

LOVES OF A BLONDE, THE

D: Milos Forman — 88 m

NR | FOR COM ROM | 1965 | B&W

9 Very likable and frequently hilarious portrait of a shy romantic young girl, coming of age in a small Czechoslovakia factory town where the women outnumber the men ten to one. This sort of an imbalance can cause a girl to wonder about love. Then a group of Army reservists visits town. Suddenly her girlish fantasies of love take flight. She meets Milda, becomes entranced with him and spends the night, but soon he is gone. A unique blending of pathos, sorrow and desire produces an engrossing and endearing comedy. A gem. A nominee for Best Foreign Film. Subtitles.

Sex, Nud, Viol, Lang, AdSit

A: Hana Brejchova, Vladimir Pucholt

© HOME VISION LOV 100

MAMA, THERE'S A MAN IN YOUR BED

D: Coline Serreau — 107 m

PG-13 | FOR COM ROM | 1990 | COLOR

6 Quite unlikely, but still funny, comedy from the writer of THREE MEN AND A BABY. A successful executive of a Paris yogurt factory gets sabotaged by board members planning a takeover - but he finds an unlikely ally in the black cleaning lady. On her nightly rounds, she discovers what is going on and tells him. Together they plot to take back his company. But first he has to hide from the cops, so he stays at her three-room apartment where they sleep four to a bed and she has five kids, each by different husbands. Naturally, they fall in love.

Sex, Nud, Viol, Lang, AdSit

A: Daniel Arteuil, Firmine Richard, Pierre Vernier, Maxime Leroux

© HBO VIDEO 90560

MAN AND A WOMAN, A

D: Claude Lelouch — 103 m

NR | FOR ROM | 1966 | COLOR

8 Passionate love story that became very popular. A widowed script girl and a race car driver whose wife had committed suicide, meet at their children's boarding school. They fall in love, but their romance is complicated because she is haunted by memories from her past. Set against the international auto racing circuit, the movie was one of America's most popular French films in the '60s. It was stylish and intensely romantic. It was the Oscar winner for Best Foreign Film and Screenplay. It was remade in '77 and was followed with a sequel in '86. The musical score is fantastic - the acting is potent. Dubbed.

Sex, Nud, Viol, Lang, AdSit

A: Anouk Aimee, Jean-Louis Trintignant, Pierre Barouh, Valerie Lagrange

© WARNER HOME VIDEO 11655

MANON OF THE SPRING

D: Claude Berri — 113 m

PG-13 | FOR DMA | 1987 | COLOR

9 Visually stunning and profoundly moving conclusion to the dramatization of the classic French story first begun in JEAN DE FLORETTE. Manon is the beautiful grown daughter of the now-dead hunchback farmer who had been deceived and destroyed in the earlier story. She has learned the secret behind the death of her father - that is, who had blocked up the spring on her father's farm. That vicious and cruel act destroyed a simple man with a simple dream, only to become a farmer. So, now she plots her revenge. Please see both films together. English subtitles.

Sex, Nud, Viol, Lang, AdSit

A: Yves Montand, Emmanuelle Beart, Daniel Auteuil, Hippolyte Hiradot, Elisabeth Depardieu

© ORION PICTURES CORPORATION 5035

MAN WHO LOVED WOMEN, THE

D: Francois Truffaut — 119 m

NR | FOR COM ROM | 1977 | COLOR

8 Wonderfully charming and sophisticated French comedy with serious undertones. The opening scene contains leg after beautiful female leg, filing slowly past the grave of Bertrand Morane. Bertrand, you see, is a man who loved women. He is a connoisseur of women. He loves all aspects of femaleness. And, women love him...even though he can be faithful to no one woman. He never abuses a woman, he just can't help himself from chasing the next one. This is his story and he tells it in flashback, as an autobiography. Spawned a much lesser American version with Burt Reynolds.

Sex, Nud, Viol, Lang, AdSit

A: Charles Denner, Brigitte Fossey, Nelly Borgeaud, Genevieve Fontanel, Nathalie Baye, Jean Daste

Distributed By MGM/UA Home Video M202962

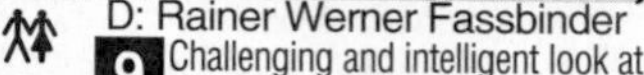

MARRIAGE OF MARIA BRAUN, THE

D: Rainer Werner Fassbinder — 120 m

R | FOR DMA WAR | 1979 | COLOR

9 Challenging and intelligent look at German society in the wake of World War II. In the final days of the war, Maria marries a Wehrmacht officer, even as the bombs fall. They have one night together, he goes off to war and is presumed dead. However, he returns, finding her in bed with an American soldier. He is enraged, attacks the soldier and is sent to prison. The sensuous Maria emotionally isolates herself and does what it takes to get him out, including ruthlessly sleeping her way to the top of the corporate heap in a power-hungry charge, and he betrays his soul to let her do it. Brilliant performances.

Sex, Nud, Viol, Lang, AdSit

A: Hanna Schygulla, Klaus Lowitsch, Ivan Desny

© COLUMBIA TRISTAR HOME VIDEO 60718

FOR

MEDITERRANEO

D: Gabriele Salvatores 93 m

R | FOR COM | 1991 | COLOR | 6

1991 winner of the Academy Award for Best Foreign film. However, it must have been a very slow year. This is a mildly entertaining story about a group of misfits from the Italian army who become stranded on a beautiful Greek island for nearly the entirety of WWII. There are no other men on the island, only women and children. One of the women is a pretty whore who sells them all her services but another woman lovingly shares herself for free with two brothers. There doesn't seem to be any real direction to this film. It is for serious and curious movie fans only. Subtitles.

Sex / Nud / Viol / Lang / AdSit

A: Diego Abatantuono, Claudio Bigagli, Giuseppe Cederna, Claudio Bisio, Vanna Barba

© TOUCHSTONE HOME VIDEO 1593

MEPHISTO

D: Istvan Szabo 150 m

NR | FOR DMA | 1981 | COLOR | 8

A very stylish and controversial war drama best suited for sophisticated audiences. It was also the Academy Award winner for the Best Foreign Film of 1981. A talented but egotistical actor, living in Germany just before the War, is given a chance by a powerful Nazi to advance his career if he will just renounce his past politics. He does but only when it is too late does he realize that he has paid a very high price for what he has gained. Based on the book by Klaus Mann, who committed suicide due to the difficulties encountered in getting the book published - it was banned in Germany for forty years.

Sex / Nud / Viol / Lang / AdSit

A: Klaus Maria Brandauer, Krystyna Janda, Ildiko Bansagi, Karen Boyd, Rolf Hope, Christina Harbot

© TVS INC.

MON ONCLE

D: Jacques Tati 110 m

NR | FOR COM | 1958 | COLOR | 7

Outrageous foreign comedy farce that pokes fun at all things "modern." Mr. Hulot's brother-in-law's (Zola) home is a riotous mix of gadgets and mechanization. On the other hand, the quiet and unassuming Hulot (Tati) has a simple home. Hulot's adoring nephew (Bercort) prefers the simpler life, and it is from his perspective that the story is told. Included in his father's house is a grotesque fish fountain and some of the ugliest, most twisted furniture you've ever seen anywhere. The film is an ongoing series of sight gags with almost no dialogue. Best Foreign Picture Oscar. Subtitles.

Sex / Nud / Viol / Lang / AdSit

A: Jacques Tati, Jean-Pierre Zola, Adrienne Servantie, Alain Bercourt

© HOME VISION ONC 020

MONSIEUR HIRE

D: Patrice Leconte 88 m

PG-13 | FOR SUS CRM | 1990 | COLOR | 8

Brilliant and gripping suspense import from France. A balding reclusive tailor, Monsieur Hire, becomes obsessed with the beautiful young lady across his courtyard, peeping at her constantly from his darkened windows. One day a flash of lightning reveals his embarrassing activities to her and she confronts him. When another young woman is found dead nearby and she is terrified. It is natural that Monsieur Hire would becomes the police's natural suspect. However, the snoopy Monsieur Hire knows who the real killer is. Subtly erotic, but also extraordinary in its drama and its perceptiveness.

Sex / Nud / Viol / Lang / AdSit

A: Michel Blanc, Sandrine Bonnaire, Andre Wilms, Luc Thuiller

© ORION PICTURES CORPORATION 5053

MY FATHER'S GLORY

D: Yves Robert 110 m

G | FOR DMA | 1991 | COLOR | 9

Very highly acclaimed literary triumph. It is the richly painted portrait of the memories of author and filmmaker Marcel Pagnol's childhood in rural France at the turn of the 20th-century. It is primarily the story of a summer trip that he took, along with his parents, where even the most commonplace of situations become fascinating to a precocious boy totally involved in the rural lifestyle. This marvelous experience was followed by the equally fascinating MY MOTHER'S CASTLE. In French with subtitles.

Sex / Nud / Viol / Lang / AdSit

A: Philippe Caubere, Nathalie Roussel, Julian Ciamaca, Therese Liotard, Didier Pain

© ORION PICTURES CORPORATION 5066

MY LIFE AS A DOG

D: Lasse Hallstrom 101 m

NR | FOR COM DMA | 1987 | COLOR | 7

Offbeat and loveable. A young boy (Glanzelius) gets bundled up and shipped off to a country town in Sweden when his mother becomes seriously ill. This town is populated by offbeat characters and he feels deserted and alone. He comes to compare himself to the Russian dog Laika who was abandoned and left to die in space. But instead he learns to deal with his new surroundings, to understand loss, and even falls in love with a cute little tomboy. This is more than just a film about the pitfalls of growing up, this story is filled to the brim with humor and warmth. A Swedish surprise. Dubbed or subtitles.

Sex / Nud / Viol / Lang / AdSit

A: Anton Glanzelius, Anki Liden, Tomas Von Bromssen, Melinda Kinnaman, Kicki Rundgren, Ing-mari Carlsson

© PARAMOUNT HOME VIDEO 12651

NASTY GIRL, THE

D: Michael Verhoeven 94 m

PG-13 | FOR COM DMA | 1990 | COLOR | 9

Delicious biting black comedy that sadly enough is based upon a true story. A German school girl, living in a picturesque Bavarian village, wants to write an essay to be entitled, "My Town During the Third Reich." Suddenly she is ostracized and threatened by the seemingly friendly people she has known all her life. This is a subject they don't want reopened and she is barred from the town archives. This story could easily enough have been turned into a very serious drama. Instead, it is presented as a biting satire, ripping apart hypocrisy. And, it does so in a way so that we see that her town is like all towns everywhere. Subtitles.

Sex / Nud / Viol / Lang / AdSit

A: Lena Stolze, Monika Baumgartner, Michael Gahr, Elisabeth Bertram, Fred Stillkrauth, Robert Gioggenbach

© HBO VIDEO 90621

OFFICIAL STORY, THE

D: Luis Puenzo 112 m

NR | FOR DMA SUS | 1985 | COLOR | 9

This is an extremely powerful Oscar winner for Best Foreign Film. It is a devastating story about a sheltered, middle-class Argentinian woman and wife of a politician, who gradually comes to the realization that her adopted daughter was forcefully torn away from her mother by the government. The mother had been a political activist, was tortured and then murdered. Worse than that news, she also learns that her otherwise-loving husband has always known about it. Her world, and all that she has naively believed in, is utterly destroyed. The scene where she views photos of someone, who is obviously her child's mother, with the child's grandmother is devastating. Subtitles.

Sex / Nud / Viol / Lang / AdSit

A: Norma Aleandro, Hector Alterio, Analia Castro

© PACIFIC ARTS VIDEO 630

PASSION OF ANNA, THE

D: Ingmar Bergman 101 m

R | FOR DMA SUS | 1970 | COLOR | 8

Max von Sydow is an ex-convict living alone in a farmhouse on a small island and is visited one day by a crippled woman (Ulmann) requesting to use the telephone. When she leaves, she forgets her purse behind. He gets her name from it to return it to her but also learns from letters inside of her troubled marriage. They become friends and she moves into his farmhouse but their relationship becomes very strained, in part because of reports of an axe murderer being at large. She believes he may be the axe murderer and he believes she is trying to kill him as she probably killed her husband and child.

Sex / Nud / Viol / Lang / AdSit

A: Max von Sydow, Liv Ullmann, Bibi Andersson, Erland Josephson

Distributed By MGM/UA Home Video M202786

PELLE THE CONQUEROR

D: Bille August 138 m

PG-13 | FOR DMA | 1988 | COLOR | 9

A wonderful exploration of the power of the human spirit and winner of Best Foreign Film, but its slow pace and earnestness will diminish its appeal to many. An impoverished peasant, Max Von Sydow (Oscar nominated), takes a desperate chance at a better life by leaving Sweden to become a farm laborer in Denmark. Because he is older and has a young son, he is the last chosen among the many laborers. He must accept a job with a wealthy tyrant. There, he must suffer many hardships to achieve only the most modest successes, but he has his son Pelle whom he dotes upon. Pelle will be what he was not and sets off on a quest to conquer the world. Subtitles.

Sex / Nud / Viol / Lang / AdSit

A: Max von Sydow, Pelle Hvenegaard, Erik Paaske

© HBO VIDEO 0210

PIXOTE

D: Hector Babenco 127 m

NR | FOR DMA | 1981 | COLOR | 9

Overwhelmingly powerful, thoroughly engrossing and unrelentingly grim multi-award winning film from Brazil. Set in the slums of Sao Paulo, this is the true story of Pixote. He was abandoned by his parents and left to survive on his own. By age ten he is a pimp, a thief and a murderer. This could easily be too overwhelming for some because it holds back nothing - but neither does it exploit. The performance of the ten-year-old star is all the more haunting because in real life, five years after the completion of the film, he was killed in a shootout with police. Subtitles.

Sex / Nud / Viol / Lang / AdSit

A: Marilia Pera, Fernando Ramos da Silva, Jardel Filho, Rubens de Falco, Elke Maraviha, Tony Tornado

© COLUMBIA TRISTAR HOME VIDEO 60083

QUEEN MARGOT

D: Patrice Chereau 153 m

R | FOR DMA ROM | 1995 | COLOR | 9

Brilliant French epic historical drama. It is 1572, and religious wars are raging throughout Europe. Charles IX, the son of the shrewd and absolutely ruthless Catherine de Medicis, is King of France. Catholic Catherine has lost her influence over Charles to a Protestant advisor. She now plots to regain control, while also claiming credit for preventing war, by marrying her daughter Margot to the Protestant King of a French province. But when the marriage does not achieve her goals, she and her sons resort to assassination and murder, and Margot, at first a pawn, becomes a queen. Intelligent, exquisitely complex and intricate. Requires and inspires rapt attention. Wonderfully acted and filmed. Subtitles.

Sex / Nud / Viol / Lang / AdSit

A: Isabelle Adjani, Daniel Auteuil, Jean-Hugues Anglade, Vincent Perez, Virna Lisi

© MIRAMAX HOME ENTERTAINMENT 4439

FOR

RAISE THE RED LANTERN

D: Zhang Yimou — 125 m

PG | FOR DMA | 1991 | COLOR | Rating: 9 | Sex

Exquisitely photographed import from mainland China. The subject is the feudal marriage of a beautiful girl who is forced to leave college at 19 because her father has died, to become the fourth wife of a wealthy landlord. Each evening each wife must stand in front of the door to her quarters as the master signals which wife he will sleep with by ordering the red lanterns lit in that house. The women's days are spent in gilded boredom and so pass their time by plotting against each other for advancement within the household. Elegant and very dramatic, but also staid and very slow. Subtitles.

A: Gong Li, Ma Jingwu, Jin Shuyuan, Cao Cuifeng, He Caifei

© ORION PICTURES CORPORATION 5068

RAN

D: Akira Kurosawa — 160 m

R | FOR DMA ACT | 1985 | COLOR | Rating: 8 | Viol

This is an epic and masterful saga about a battle for a kingdom in Japan that was adapted from Shakespeare's King Lear by master film-maker Kurosawa. In the 16th century, Japanese King Hidetora (Nakadai) leaves his kingdom to his eldest son hoping to avoid bloodshed, but does not realize the implications of his decision because his evil daughter-in-law is plotting against him. His two younger sons are also in strong opposition to his decision. Soon they all plot against each other. This lavish Oscar-winning production was very highly acclaimed. A story of heartbreak, greed and war. Subtitles.

A: Tatsuya Nakadai, Jinpachi Nezu, Akira Terao, Daisuku Ryu, Mieko Harada, Yoshiko Miyazaki

© CBS/FOX VIDEO 3732

RED

D: Krzysztof Kieslowski — 109 m

R | FOR DMA | 1995 | COLOR | Rating: 6 | Sex, Nud, AdSit

This is the third in the series of "color movies" from director Kieslowski. The other two were BLUE and WHITE. Luscious fashion model Valentine is in a dying relationship when she accidentally hits a dog with her car. She seeks out the owner, who is a world-worn former judge and now spends his time listening in on the phone calls of his neighbors. At first Valentine is upset by his activities, but then she becomes drawn into the pain to which the old man has become witness. An odd intellectual relationship develops between the two. The old man tells her of how the loss of his love dominated his life and he then sets about making certain the same does not happen to Valentine.

A: Irene Jacob, Jean-Louis Trintignant

© MIRAMAX HOME ENTERTAINMENT 4373

RED BALLOON, THE

D: Albert Lamorisse — 34 m

FAN CLD FOR | 1956 | COLOR | Rating: 10

A brilliant children's treasure! While there is no dialogue in this classic fantasy, it remains one of the most charming films of all time. In this engaging story, a young boy (Lamorisse) makes friends with a red balloon, and it follows him all around Paris. It goes to school with him. It even waits for him outside his window when he is in his room. The film is so visually flawless that the story is crystal clear - it needs no dialogue. A winner for both children and adults alike with a sparkling musical score. Winner of an Academy Award for Best Original Screenplay. Unequaled!

A: Pascal Lamorisse, Georges Seliler

© NEW LINE HOME VIDEO 6001

RHAPSODY IN AUGUST

D: Akira Kurosawa — 98 m

PG | FOR DMA | 1991 | COLOR | Rating: 6

Famed Japanese filmmaker Akira Kurosawa's morality play that comments both upon the destructive nature of war, even years after it is over. An old woman, living outside of Nagasaki, has her grandchildren over for the summer while their parents are in Hawaii to visit the family of her wealthy brother who is now near death. The children discover for the first time that their grandfather was killed in the atomic bomb blast and at first resent their parents for going to America. The old woman chastises them for blaming Americans and instead blames war itself. Kurosawa's approach is very simplistic and seems more directed toward young people, but should not be lost.

A: Sachiko Murase, Hidetaka Yoshioka, Tomoko Onatakara, mie Suzuki, Mitsunori Isaki, Richard Gere

© ORION PICTURES CORPORATION 5062

SAMURAI TRILOGY, THE

D: Hiroshi Inagaki — 312 m

NR | FOR ACT | 1956 | COLOR | Rating: 9 | Viol

Brilliant epic telling of the most famed of all Japanese swordsman, Musashi Miyomoto. This is actually three separate films: MUSASHI MIYAMOTO, DUEL AT ICHIJOJI TEMPLE and DUEL AT GANRYU ISLAND. Together, they are the most popular Japanese martial arts films ever. As a young man in 17th-century Japan, he seeks glory fighting in a civil war but finds defeat and returns as an outlaw. The love a girl and a Buddhist priest redeem him. Next he learns that death-blows are a small part of what makes a warrior, and he learns that mercy and kindness are powerful weapons too. But, at last he must fight his duel with his archrival Kojiro Sasaki. Japanese Western, compared to SHANE. Subtitles.

A: Toshiro Mifune, Koji Tsuruta, Kaoru Yachigusa, Rentaro Mikuni, Mariko Okada, Sachio Sakai

© HOME VISION SAM 040

SCENES FROM A MARRIAGE

D: Ingmar Bergman — 168 m

PG | FOR DMA ROM | 1973 | COLOR | Rating: 9 | Lang, AdSit

Very highly acclaimed by the critics and winner of many awards. This is a challenging, very in-depth and sometimes very truthful, therefore quite painful, look at a relationship between two people over 20 years. Originally made as six 50-minute segments for a Swedish TV mini-series by famed director Ingmar Bergman, it is here edited down to 168 minutes. The two are married for ten years, when there is a painful breakup after he leaves her for a younger woman. They both marry others, only to later reconcile into a new and more mature relationship. Dubbed.

A: Liv Ullmann, Erland Josephson, Bibi Andersson, Jan Malmsjo, Anita Wall, Gunnel Lindblon

© COLUMBIA TRISTAR HOME VIDEO VCF3225

SEVEN BEAUTIES

D: Lina Wertmuller — 116 m

R | FOR DMA COM | 1976 | COLOR | Rating: 8 | Nud, Viol, Lang, AdSit

Award-winning, powerful and near-surrealist story of a man willing to sacrifice anything to survive. A small-time hood in WWII Italy trys to commit a murder but fails miserably and is caught. He pleads insanity rather than go to prison. Finding that intolerable, he accepts the opportunity to join the army, but deserts when sent to the Russian front - for which he is sent to a concentration camp where he encounters more intensely grotesque horrors. He seduces an obese, sadistic prison warden to get out. The raw ugliness his situations depicted will test your sensibilities. Ardent film fans only.

A: Giancarlo Giannini, Fernando Rey, Shirley Stoler, Elena Fiore, Enzo Vitale

© COLUMBIA TRISTAR HOME VIDEO 60203

SEVENTH SEAL, THE

D: Ingmar Bergman — 96 m

NR | FOR DMA | 1956 | B&W | Rating: 10 | Viol, AdSit

Acclaimed as being one of the greatest works ever in cinema, and the best-known effort of famed director Ingmar Bergman. This is very serious and heavy material, but it also tackles some very profound philosophical questions that no other film has ever explored quite so deeply. Von Sydow plays a 14th-century knight finding his way back home from the Crusades, traveling though a countryside that is infested with plague and death. Meeting the figure of Death on the road, he bargains with Death, through a chess game, for more time to learn life's meanings. Subtitles or dubbed.

A: Gunnar Bjornstrand, Max von Sydow, Bibi Andersson, Nils Poppe, Maud Hansson, Bengt Ekerot

© HOME VISION SEV 090

SHOOT THE PIANO PLAYER

D: Francois Truffaut — 84 m

NR | FOR DMA | 1960 | B&W | Rating: 7 | Viol, AdSit

Film fans only, this is an interesting mixed bag of offbeat and colorful characters. A brilliant concert pianist (Aznavour) is haunted by his wife's suicide and begins a rapid spiral downward. Soon he finds himself playing to a sleazy crowd at a cheap Parisian cafe, where he is being pressured to get his life together by his new girlfriend, a waitress at the cafe. He gets into a fight with the bartender over her. And, his brother gets involved with the gangsters that frequent the place. This is an uncompromising New Wave film that takes the viewer across the emotional spectrum from dark comedy to tragedy. Subtitles.

A: Charles Aznavour, Marie Dubois, Nicole Berger, Michele Mercier

© HOME VISION SHO 100

SHOP ON MAIN STREET, THE

D: Jan Kadar, Elmar Klos — 128 m

NR | FOR DMA | 1965 | B&W | Rating: 9 | AdSit

Impassioned and bittersweet Best Foreign Film Oscar-winner. Tono, a man who cares nothing about politics, is appointed "Aryan Controller," by his Nazi brother. He is to oversee an elderly Jewish lady who owns a button shop in WWII Czechoslovakia. She doesn't understand and thinks he is her assistant. Gradually, the odd pair build a deep friendship, but when the Nazis mandate that all Jews are to be deported, Tono must make the decision of his life. The woman is deaf, poor, has no idea that there is even a war going on - and she trusts him completely. Sensitive and funny at times. Subtitles.

A: Josef Kroner, Hana Slivkova, Ida Kaminska, Frantisek Zvarik, Helena Zvarikov, Martin Holly

© HOME VISION SHO 110

SILENCE, THE

D: Ingmar Bergnam — 95 m

NR | FOR DMA | 1963 | B&W | Rating: 7 | Sex, Nud, AdSit

This is the third film of Bergman's religious trilogy (THROUGH A GLASS DARKLY and WINTER LIGHT) and here God is silent. Two sisters have been bound up in a love-hate incestuous relationship since childhood. The older is a lesbian but the younger is heterosexual and promiscuous. The two and the 10-year-old son of the younger are on a trip and stop in a hotel. There the younger sister picks up a waiter and inflames the older. Surreal and very dark. Subtitles.

A: Ingrid Thulin, Gunnel Lindblom, Jorgen Lindstrom, Hakan Jahnberg, Birger Malmsten

© HOME VISION SIL 100

SOFT SKIN, THE

D: Francois Truffaut 118 m

NR | FOR DMA | 1964 | B&W

Sex / Nud / Viol / Lang / AdSit

7 While on a business trip, a happily married man meets a beautiful airline hostess. They have a passionate affair and as his love for her grows, his difficulties with his wife increase at home. Yet, he is unable to choose between his wife and his mistress. He has discovered his dream woman but now he is in a situation he cannot control and becomes more and more lost. Ultimately, his infidelity will spawn its own solution.

A: Jean Desailly, Francoise Dorleac, Nelly Benedetti, Daniel Ceccaldi

© HOME VISION SOF 020

SPIRIT OF THE BEEHIVE, THE

D: Victor Erice 93 m

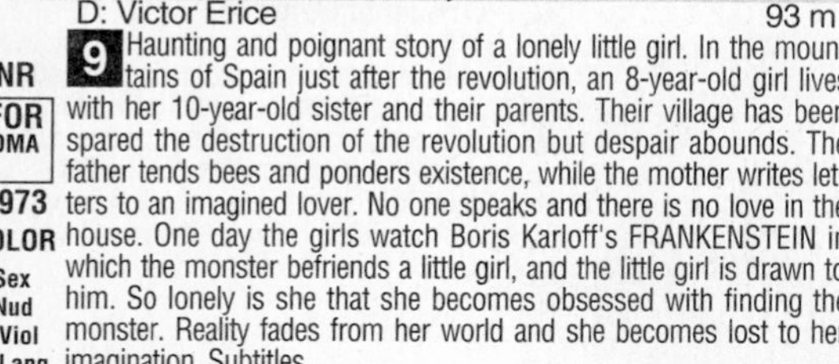

NR | FOR DMA | 1973 | COLOR

Sex / Nud / Viol / Lang / AdSit

9 Haunting and poignant story of a lonely little girl. In the mountains of Spain just after the revolution, an 8-year-old girl lives with her 10-year-old sister and their parents. Their village has been spared the destruction of the revolution but despair abounds. The father tends bees and ponders existence, while the mother writes letters to an imagined lover. No one speaks and there is no love in the house. One day the girls watch Boris Karloff's FRANKENSTEIN in which the monster befriends a little girl, and the little girl is drawn to him. So lonely is she that she becomes obsessed with finding the monster. Reality fades from her world and she becomes lost to her imagination. Subtitles.

A: Ana Torrent, Isabel Telleria, Fernando Fernan Gomez, Teresa Gimpera, Jose Villasante

© HOME VISION SPI 080

STORY OF WOMEN, THE

D: Claude Chabrol 110 m

NR | FOR DMA | 1988 | COLOR

Sex / Nud / Viol / Lang / AdSit

8 A remarkable award-winning film. Isabelle Huppert received a Best Actress award for her portrayal of the real-life French woman who was the last woman to be guillotined. She was a cold and childlike woman who had struggled in abject poverty in Nazi-occupied France at the beginning of the war. Then when her neighbor became pregnant, she performed an amateur abortion for her. Soon she was in the business and had developed a grand lifestyle. However, her humiliated husband turned her in when she is so bold as to take a Nazi collaborator for her lover. It is then that she is condemned to die by the same townspeople who she had served. Subtitles.

A: Isabelle Huppert, Francois Cluzet, Marie Trintignant, Louis Ducreux, Michel Beaune, Dominique Blanc

© NEW YORKER FILMS NYV59091

SWEPT AWAY...

D: Lina Wertmuller 116 m

R | FOR COM ROM | 1975 | COLOR

Sex / Nud / Viol / Lang / AdSit

8 Provocative, saucy Italian comedy with a rough edge. Melato is a spoiled, rich, arrogant woman who continually humiliates the staff aboard her yacht and degrades her servant (Giannini). However, when they end up stranded together on a deserted island, the wars erupt. They can agree upon nothing. She is a rich capitalist. He is a deckhand and a communist. But the sex is great and their roles are quickly reversed. Giannini becomes the dominator, completely controlling Melato's every thought and stripping her of all dignity and vanity. A delightful mixed bag of morality and humor. Dubbed.

A: Giancarlo Giannini, Mariangela Melato

© COLUMBIA TRISTAR HOME VIDEO 60224

TATIE DANIELLE

D: Etienne Chatliez 114 m

PG-13 | FOR COM | 1991 | COLOR

Sex / Nud / Viol / Lang / AdSit

7 Very unusual and very black French satire. Auntie Danielle is 83. She lost her husband 50 years ago in the Great War and has been talking to his picture ever since. She is bitter, cantankerous, demanding and manipulative. She purposely strives to make everyone around her unhappy, it is her only real joy. Then, her well-meaning great-nephew asks her to move in with them, little knowing what he and his family are in for. Auntie makes their life miserable, so they leave on vacation with her in the care of a young woman they have hired. In her, Auntie has met her match. This is a very dark comedy that will not appeal to everyone. Subtitles.

A: Tsilla Chelton, Catherine Jacob, Isabelle Nanty, Neige Dolsky, Eric Prat, Laurence Fevrier

© LIVE HOME VIDEO 69002

TAXI BLUES

D: Pavel Lounguine 110 m

NR | FOR DMA | 1990 | COLOR

Sex / Nud / Viol / Lang / AdSit

8 Powerful import from post-perestroika Moscow. It is intended to be an allegory describing the whole of the Russian people's post-Soviet dilemma. That dilemma is personified by the two principal players. One is a burly, solidly working-class Russian taxi driver whose world is simple and tough. The other is a self-destructive Jewish jazz musician, an emaciated alcoholic whose wife has just thrown him out. When he can't pay his 70-ruble fare, the driver beats him up and confiscates his sax. But then he takes pity on the sorry guy and an odd relationship develops where each begins to learn about the other man's world.

A: Piotr Mamonov, Piotr Zaitchenko, Natalia Koliakanova, Vladimir Kachpour, Hal Singer, Elena Saphonova

© NEW YORKER FILMS NYV10092

TAXING WOMAN, A

D: Juzo Itami 127 m

NR | FOR COM | 1987 | COLOR

Sex / Nud / Viol / Lang / AdSit

8 Subtle and disarming Japanese black satire that was a winner of 9 Japanese Academy Awards, including Best Picture. Ryoko is innocent-looking and pretty, but she is also one of Tokyo's most single-mindedly determined tax collectors. She is so dedicated that she will sit outside a restaurant to compare the number of customers leaving to the receipts reported. Then, she sets her sights on one of Tokyo's best tax dodges, their famous love hotels. She is persistent in her efforts to catch its owner cheating, but he is just as persistent in his efforts to duck her - while they both fight their growing mutual attraction. Subtitles.

A: Nobuko Miyamoto, Tsutomu Yamazaki

© FOX/LORBER HOME VIDEO 1001

THRONE OF BLOOD

D: Akira Kurosawa 105 m

FOR DMA | 1957 | B&W

Sex / Nud / Viol / Lang / AdSit

10 Grippingly powerful Japanese retelling of Shakespeare's "MacBeth." This is masterful filmmaking, but it is also very heavy going - be prepared. Japan's master director Kurosawa has taken the Shakespearean themes of overpowering pride and bloody treachery and set them within the framework of 16th-century feudal Japan's brutality. Mufune is a paranoid warlord who is hounded by his greedy wife Yamada and driven by his lust for power. Strikingly powerful images evoke Shakespeare's vision, but do so in such a way that the story is singularly valid in its own right. In Japanese, with subtitles.

A: Toshiro Mifune, Isuzu Yamada, Minoru Chiaki, Takashi Shimura

© HOME VISION THR 090

THROUGH A GLASS DARKLY

D: Ingmar Bergman 90 m

NR | FOR DMA | 1961 | B&W

Sex / Nud / Viol / Lang / AdSit

9 Mostly for serious film fans - this was the first in Bergman's "faith" trilogy. It is the dark psychological study of the events and relationships surrounding four persons - a schizophrenic woman just released from a mental institution, her husband, her younger brother and her psychologist father - who all spend the summer together on an isolated island. It is Bergman's philosophic probe of man's relationship to God. We watch this woman slowly descend back into the hell of her insanity. Best Foreign Film Oscar. Subtitles or dubbed.

A: Harriet Andersson, Max von Sydow, Gunnar Bjornstrand, Lars Passgard

© HOME VISION THR 100

TIE ME UP! TIE ME DOWN!

D: Pedro Almodovar 105 m

NC-17 | FOR COM | 1990 | COLOR

Sex / Nud / Viol / Lang / AdSit

6 Controversial import from Spain. An orphan and mental patient (Banderas) is released from the hospital. He has nowhere to go, no skills (except in bed) and no one who cares for him. But he becomes fascinated with a porno star and convinces himself that she will grow to love him if she just has the time. So he barges into her apartment and ties her up until she can come to her senses. Oddly, she slowly does begin to develop a strange affection for this pathetic guy, which grows into love. Fresh and original, but somewhat slow and definitely odd.

A: Antonio Banderas, Victoria Abril, Loles Leon, Francisco Rabal

© COLUMBIA TRISTAR HOME VIDEO 90903

TIN DRUM, THE

D: Volker Schlondorff 142 m

R | FOR FAN DMA | 1979 | COLOR

Sex / Nud / Viol / Lang / AdSit

9 Very bizarre and "artsy" fantasy, or rather nightmare, taken from a world-renown novel by Gunter Grass. Visually stunning, it was the winner of the Best Foreign Film Oscar. The story is that of young boy in 1920s Germany who is so distraught by the Nazis and their bleak world that he decides to stop growing. Instead, he becomes obsessed with beating on his toy drum to drown out horror, and also develops a piercing scream. However, these strange talents only make him into a popular source of entertainment for the Nazis, and ultimately he survives when others others around him suffer. Subtitles.

A: Mario Adorf, Angela Winkler, David Bennent, Daniel Olbrychski, Katharina Thalbach, Heinz Bennent

© WARNER HOME VIDEO 24053

TOTO LE HEROS

D: Jaco van Dormael 94 m

PG-13 | FOR COM | 1992 | COLOR

Sex / Nud / Viol / Lang / AdSit

8 Thomas is a cranky old man who is convinced that he was switched at birth with the rich kid next door who has now become a powerful industrialist. He has become obsessed with winning back the life that he is convinced was stolen from him. Ever since he was young, Thomas has had a fantasy that he is Toto the Hero, a secret agent. The movie's clever plot line concerns his plan to reclaim the heritage that is rightfully his, and the various flash backs and flash forwards used explain how he came to have such a skewed view of circumstances. Clever, original and fun. Subtitles.

A: Michel Bouquet, Mireille Perrier, Jo de Backer, Gisela Uhlen, Peter Bohlke, Thomas Godet

© PARAMOUNT HOME VIDEO 83088

TWO ENGLISH GIRLS

D: Francois Truffaut — 130 m

NR · FOR ROM · 1971 · COLOR

9 Often referred to as being the flip-side of Truffaut's film JULES AND JIM. This is a civilized and tender love story of a Frenchman who falls in love with two lovely but innocent sisters. Set just prior to WWI, the Frenchman is repressed by his inability to choose between the two, the demands of his over-powering mother and the girl's own repressed passions, so their relationship remains an jangled emotional triangle for over seven years before any can consummate their loves. In 1983 Truffaut managed to get 22 minutes restored which had to be expunged upon the original release in 1971. Subtitles.

Sex ✓ · Nud ✓ · Viol · Lang · AdSit ■

A: Jean-Pierre Leaud, Kika Markham, Stacey Tendeter, Sylvia Marriott, Marie Mansart, Philippe Leotard

© HOME VISION TWO 050

TWO WOMEN

D: Vittorio De Sica — 99 m

NR · FOR DMA WAR · 1961 · B&W

9 Extremely intense and moving drama. Sophia Loren received an Oscar for her powerful performance. It is a story of survival under extraordinary circumstances. It is Italy during WWII, just as the Germans are retreating and the Allies are advancing. Sophia is the mother of a 13-year-old daughter and both are struggling just to survive. They are also just learning to deal with the girl's awakening womanhood, because both mother and daughter have both fallen in love with a farmer's son (Belmundo), when both are raped by advancing soldiers. Heart-wrenching. Subtitles or dubbed.

Sex ✓ · Nud · Viol ✓ · Lang · AdSit ■

A: Sophia Loren, Raf Vallone, Jean-Paul Belmondo, Eleanora Brown, Renato Salvatori

© GOODTIMES 4240

VANISHING, THE

D: George Sluizer — 105 m

NR · FOR HOR SUS · 1991 · COLOR

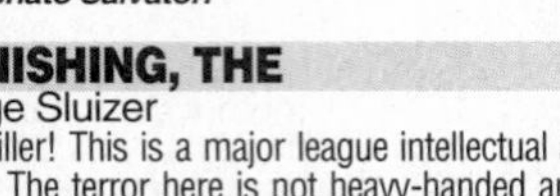

9 Icy thriller! This is a major league intellectual and psychological chiller. The terror here is not heavy-handed and obvious, but is more of the Hitchcock or the Edgar Allen Poe variety. Two young lovers are traveling when they run out of gas. He thoughtlessly leaves her behind, terrified and alone. She's furious but they make up and go to a rest area to play. She leaves to go to a store but she never returns. Haunted by her loss, he places posters all over requesting information. After three years, a seemingly genteel professor sends him a tantalizing note. Subtle, but deeply and profoundly shocking. Subtitles.

Sex · Nud · Viol ✓ · Lang · AdSit ■

A: Gene Bervoets, Johanna Ter Steege, Bernard-Pierre Donnadieu

© FOX/LORBER HOME VIDEO 1037

WANNSEE CONFERENCE, THE

D: Heinz Schirk — 85 m

NR · FOR DMA · 1987 · COLOR

9 Chilling historical film which recounts nearly verbatim the actual events of a meeting which took place on January 20, 1942. In this meeting, the hierarchy of the German government -- high ranking officials of the SS, the Nazi Party and other government bureaucrats -- discussed with casual coolness, the way in which they would exterminate eleven million people. Much of the dialogue was taken from actual minutes of the meeting and the drama is allowed to evolve in real-time over the course of a fine buffet lunch that included brandy and cigarettes. Their cold-blooded, matter-of-fact and almost casual conversational tones make this an even more chilling experience. Subtitles.

Sex · Nud · Viol · Lang · AdSit ✓

A: Robert Artzhorn, Friedrich Beckhaus, Gerd Bockmann, Jochen Busse, Hans W. Bussinger

© HOME VISION WAN 020

WAR AND PEACE

D: Sergei Bondarchuk — 360 m

PG · FOR DMA ACT · 1968 · COLOR

9 A dazzling masterpiece of a film and winner of Best Foreign Film. However, its extreme length and poor dubbing from Russian make this a difficult film for the average viewer to watch. Still, serious viewers should not miss it. Other attempts have been made to reduce the epic book to a scale suitable for the screen (most notably in 1956), however the story is just too big and too much was lost. This Russian version took over five years to make and cost a staggering $100 million. Outstanding production values.

Sex · Nud · Viol ✓ · Lang · AdSit ✓

A: Ludmila Savelyeva, Vyacheslav Tihonov, Sergei Bondarchuk, Victor Stanitsyn, Kira Golovko, Oleg Tabakov

© KULTUR VIDEO 1248

WHITE

D: Krzystof Kieslowski — 102 m

R · FOR DMA · 1994 · COLOR

6 Poor little Karol has a right to be depressed. He is impotent and so his beautiful wife has just divorced him (even though they still love each other), taken all his money and left him humiliated, totally broke and broken on the streets of Paris. Yet, from somewhere he summons the strength to return home to Poland where he becomes determined to remake himself into a rich and powerful man. He will return to Paris and have his revenge. This is a curious storyline and strange characters that manages to hold your attention. Sub-titles.

Sex ✓ · Nud · Viol ✓ · Lang ✓ · AdSit ■

A: Zbignew Zamachowski, Julie Delpy

© MIRAMAX HOME ENTERTAINMENT 3039

WILD STRAWBERRIES

D: Ingmar Bergman — 90 m

NR · FOR DMA · 1959 · B&W

9 Less enigmatic than most of Bergman's works this is also one of his best works. This is a must for film buffs, but it is also accessible to many ordinary viewers too. An old man has had a fearsome nightmare the night before. In it he discovered his own corpse. On this day, he is in a carriage on the way to receive an honorary degree and on this day he also begins to feel his own mortality. Along the way, he offers a ride to three young hitchhikers who remind him of people in his past. Through a series of flashbacks he begins to review his life and also begins to realize that his life is almost over and he has never lived. Subtitles.

Sex ✓ · Nud · Viol · Lang · AdSit ■

A: Victor Sjostrom, Bibi Andersson, Ingrid Thulin, Gunnar Bjornstrand, Max Von Sydow

© HOME VISION WIL 140

WINTER LIGHT

D: Ingmar Bergman — 80 m

NR · FOR DMA · 1962 · B&W

9 A penetrating look into a disillusioned Protestant minister who has lost his faith and watches his congregation crumble when he cannot give them the guidance he craves so desperately for himself. Great performances mark this central entry in Bergman's religious trilogy which also includes THROUGH A GLASS DARKLY and THE SILENCE. This will be a difficult film for non- Bergman fans to watch but it is a powerful film for those who are. Subtitles.

Sex · Nud · Viol · Lang · AdSit ■

A: Ingrid Thulin, Gunnar Bjornstrand, Max Von Sydow, Gunnel Lindblom

© HOME VISION WIN 140

YESTERDAY, TODAY AND TOMORROW

D: Vittorio De Sica — 119 m

NR · FOR COM · 1964 · COLOR

9 Three saucy, sexy, comic tales that won the Best Foreign Film Oscar. Three beautiful Italian women (all Sophia Loren, at her sexiest) use sex to get what they want from their men. In one story, she uses it to stay out of jail by staying pregnant year after year. In another, she is a flirt who seduces men and then drops them. In the last, she is a prostitute who tempts the seminary student who wants to "save" her. It is during this story when she performs a super-sexy strip that can still make blood pressures rise, and is one of the most famous scenes of her career. Funny, too. Subtitles.

Sex ✓ · Nud ✓ · Viol · Lang · AdSit ■

A: Sophia Loren, Marcello Mastroianni, Tina Pica, Giovanni Ridolfi

© UNITED AMERICAN VIDEO CORP. 5197

YOJIMBO

D: Akira Kurosawa — 110 m

NR · FOR ACT COM · 1962 · B&W

9 Very funny, action packed and beautifully photographed Japanese "Western" - which became the model for A FISTFUL OF DOLLARS and many others. A samurai (Mifune), freed from his code of honor, roams from town to town selling his sword. In one small town, the sake dealer and the silk merchant are both trying to capture control of gambling, but both are cowards and so hire others to do their dirty work. Clever Mifune hires himself out to both sides and turns them against each other. In the end, they kill each other off and he gets the money, saying: "Now we'll have a little quiet in this town."

Sex · Nud · Viol ■ · Lang · AdSit ✓

A: Toshiro Mifune, Eijiro Tono, Isuzu Yamada, Hiroshi Tachikawa, Kyu Sazanka

© NEW LINE HOME VIDEO 6144

Z

D: Constantine Costa-Gavras — 128 m

PG · FOR SUS DMA · 1969 · COLOR

9 Spellbinding and highly influential political thriller that was banned in several right-wing countries and which won the Oscar for Best Foreign Film. A conservative investigator of the supposed accidental death of a popular left-wing political activist discovers that, not only was it a murder and that the conservative government is covering up, but that the government played an active role in the murder. His decision to pursue the case may result in the downfall of the government. Based on an actual case in Greece in 1963.

Sex · Nud · Viol ✓ · Lang ✓ · AdSit ✓

A: Yves Montand, Irene Papas, Jean-Louis Trintignant

© COLUMBIA TRISTAR HOME VIDEO 60266

ZENTROPA

D: Lars von Trier — 112 m

B&W · FOR DMA · 1992 · COLOR

8 Excellent, innovative and intriguing cinematography - but very challenging, enigmatic and surreal plotting. The storyline is set in Germany in the days immediately following the fall of Hitler, while under the occupation of the American army. A young American has come to take a job as a railroad conductor, but becomes involved with the daughter of the railroad's founder and gets caught up in post-war intrigue and murder. The story is presented as a sort of hypnotic hallucination and has many of the disjointed qualities of a dream. It is both very intriguing and very frustrating. A must see for film fans. Others, however, are cautioned.

Sex ✓ · Nud · Viol ✓ · Lang ✓ · AdSit ✓

A: Jean-Marc Barr, Barbara Sukowa, Lawrence Hartman, Udo Kier, Eddie Constantine

© TOUCHSTONE HOME VIDEO 1599

Horror

Videos Best

1956 and After

13 GHOSTS

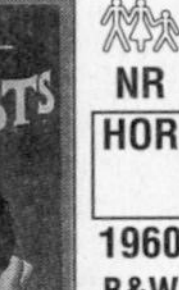

D: William Castle — 88 m

NR | HOR | 1960 | B&W

6 An enjoyable family spookfest. A normal ordinary family - a mom, a dad and two kids - inherits an old house which comes equipped with a spooky housekeeper (who may also be a witch), a secret fortune (hidden somewhere inside) and 13 ghosts. Viewers of the original theater version were issued special glasses which allowed them to see the ghosts in 3D. Light-hearted fun, with some laughs and some scares, too.

Sex | Nud | Viol | Lang | AdSit

A: Charles Herbert, Donald Woods, Martin Milner, Rosemary DeCamp, Jo Morrow, Margaret Hamilton

© COLUMBIA TRISTAR HOME VIDEO 60488

ABOMINABLE DR. PHIBES

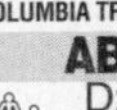

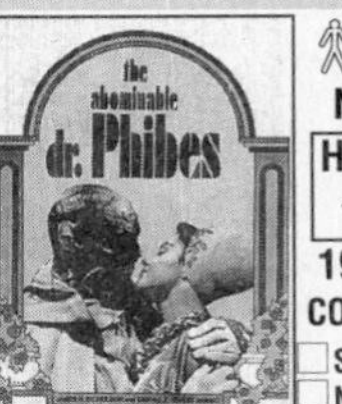

D: Robert Fuest — 90 m

NR | HOR | 1971 | COLOR

7 Dr. Phibes and his wife are in a terrible car accident about 1929. He has survived even though he is horribly disfigured. However, his wife has died during surgery. The crazed Dr. Phibes is incensed that the doctors let his wife die and has stalked and tormented them. Now, he has decided that he will to get even with them by inflicting upon his nine victims the same ten plagues from the Old Testament which God had visited upon the Egyptian Pharaoh Ramses. And, at the same time, he will search for a way to bring his beloved back to life. Filmed amid gothic backdrops, this is a stylish picture that is reminiscent of 1930s horror flicks. Price is at his campy best.

Sex | Nud | Viol | Lang | AdSit

A: Vincent Price, Joseph Cotten, Hugh Griffith, Terry-Thomas, Virginia North

© LIVE HOME VIDEO 3029

AMERICAN WEREWOLF IN LONDON, AN

D: John Landis — 97 m

R | HOR COM | 1981 | COLOR

7 This is a literal depiction of the classic horror werewolf premise that had special effects so chilling that it won an Oscar. Two American students, backpacking through Europe, are attacked by a wolf on the English moors. Dunne is killed (although he keeps returning from the dead throughout the picture) and Naughton becomes a werewolf. There is also an interesting twist in the presentation because ample doses of humor are also interwoven into the genuine horror story, though this is not a spoof. There is genuine terror here. Great, sometimes gruesome, special effects.

Sex | Nud | Viol | Lang | AdSit

A: David Naughton, Jenny Agutter, Griffin Dunne, John Woodvine, Brian Glover

© LIVE HOME VIDEO A5101

ANGUISH

D: Bigas Luna — 85 m

R | HOR SUS | 1988 | COLOR

7 A bizarre twist is at the heart of this movie. The principal character (Lerner) has lost his job as an orderly due to blindness brought on by diabetes. His mother telepathically talks him into murdering his enemies and then plucking out their eyes for revenge. Then we, the viewers, discover that what we just saw was an on-screen depiction of another movie. That film is being watched by still another audience, whose members are being killed off one-by-one. We are watching two movies for the price of one, one is within the other, and there is a killer in both of them. Scary and compelling.

Sex | Nud | Viol | Lang | AdSit

A: Michael Lerner, Zelda Rubinstein, Talia Paul, Clara Pastor, Angel Jove

© CBS/FOX VIDEO 5145

ARACHNOPHOBIA

D: Frank Marshall — 110 m

PG-13 | SUS HOR COM | 1990 | COLOR

8 Killer spiders incite chaos in this very scary big bug movie! When a deadly spider is accidentally imported to the US, it breeds with local creepy crawlies and produces a herd of poisonous, mutant offspring that take special joy in eating humans. Daniels is the quiet family man who wanted to get his family away from the hustle and bustle of the city, but now faces a huge battle getting rid of the creatures that have invaded his new country home. Goodman provides comic relief as the exterminator on a mission. More fun than you can handle!

Sex | Nud | Viol | Lang | AdSit

A: Jeff Daniels, John Goodman, Julian Sands, Harley Jane Kozak, Stuart Pankin, Brian McNamera

© HOLLYWOOD PICTURES HOME VIDEO 1080

ARMY OF DARKNESS

D: Sam Raimi — 81 m

R | FAN HOR | 1992 | COLOR

6 Silly, gory, pseudo-campy, sword-and-sorcery gore fest. Our hero is transported back in time from the modern-day housewares department of S-Mart into the Middle Ages along with his shotgun, chainsaw and a beat-up Oldsmobile. There he is first enslaved only to be transformed into the hero that he truly is, after he defeats the vile evil thing in the pit into which he was thrown. Thereafter, he is sent in search of the "Necronomicon", a magic book bound in human skin. He succeeds, but in the process also sets free an army of the dead (called the Deadites) which he then must also defeat. This is for a select and discriminating audience - that is hopefully not too big.

Sex | Nud | Viol | Lang | AdSit

A: Bruce Campbell, Embeth Davidtz, Marcus Gilbert, Ian Abercrombie, Richard Grove, Timothy Patrick Quill

© MCA/UNIVERSAL HOME VIDEO, INC. 81288

ASPHYX, THE

D: Peter Newbrook — 96 m

PG | SUS HOR | 1972 | COLOR

8 A Victorian scientist discovers the spirit of death which is possessed within all beings. Life only exists when the spirit is in the body and death can only occur when that spirit leaves the body. Trap it and life becomes eternal - but is eternal life really a good thing to pursue? Excellent thriller, told with conviction.

Sex | Nud | Viol | Lang | AdSit

A: Robert Powell, Robert Stephens, Jane Lapotaire, Ralph Arliss, Alex Scott

© MAGNUM ENTERTAINMENT, INC. M3117

ATTIC, THE

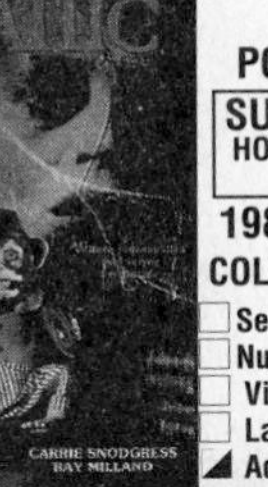

D: George Edwards — 92 m

PG | SUS HOR | 1981 | COLOR

6 Chilling little story of a domineering father (Milland), confined to a wheel chair, who stops at nothing to intimidate his mousey daughter (Snodgrass) into caring for him. All her dreams for herself are always ruined. Her fiance even disappears, strangely, just before they are to be married. But the tables are about to be turned on Daddy when Louise finds out what's in the attic. Interesting and eerie psychological character study.

Sex | Nud | Viol | Lang | AdSit

A: Carrie Snodgress, Ray Milland, Rosemary Murphy, Ruth Cox, Rancis Bay, Marjorie Eaton

© MONTEREY HOME VIDEO B763

AUDREY ROSE

D: Robert Wise 113 m

PG | HOR | 1977 | COLOR

Sex Nud Viol Lang AdSit

6 Ivy is an 11-year-old child and the daughter of an otherwise happily married couple (Mason and Beck). However, Ivy becomes repeatedly besieged by a frenzied behavior and terrible nightmares. Anthony Hopkins is mysterious stranger who is seen following Ivy around. Mason and Beck are startled to discover that he believes that Ivy is the reincarnated soul of his daughter, Audrey Rose, who was killed in a burning car - but they also quickly come to believe him because they have seen Ivy's behavior. Spooky, but the emphasis is on the relationships, not on cheap scares.

A: Marsha Mason, Anthony Hopkins, John Beck, Susan Swift

Distributed By MGM/UA Home Video M600418

BAD SEED, THE

D: Mervyn LeRoy 129 m

NR | SUS HOR | 1956 | B&W

Sex Nud Viol Lang AdSit

8 Creepy, chilling, spellbinding account of seemingly sweet, but truly evil, six-year old child who coldly and casually murders her classmate for a penmanship medal, and then lures even more people to their deaths. Only her mother begins to suspect who the killer is when she discovers her own dark secret. She carries a bad seed within her, a profound immorality that somehow missed being expressed in her but has come out in her daughter. Great little shocker, with quality production. An unnerving experience, based upon a stageplay. Four Oscar nominations, three for acting.

A: Nancy Kelly, Patty McCormack, Henry Jones, Eileen Heckart, Evelyn Varden, Jesse White

© WARNER HOME VIDEO 11342

BASKET CASE

D: Frank Henenlotter 89 m

R | HOR | 1982 | COLOR

Sex Nud Viol Lang AdSit

7 Gory low-budget film which has become quite a cult favorite. Siamese twins (one large and one very small) are surgically separated, but still remain emotionally attached and telepathically linked. So upset are they with being separated that they travel to New York, with Duane carrying his deformed little brother around in a wicker basket. Their mission is to kill the doctors responsible for separating them. Genuinely weird characters and lots of gore.

A: Kevin Van Hentryck, Terri Susan Smith, Beverly Bonner, Lloyd Pace, Robert Vogel

© VIDEO TREASURES SV9231

BELIEVERS, THE

D: John Schlesinger 114 m

R | HOR SUS | 1987 | COLOR

Sex Nud Viol Lang AdSit

8 Gripping and genuinely frightening story of a recently widowed psychiatrist (Sheen) who has moved from Minneapolis to NYC to work for the police department treating cases of stress. He begins treating a cop who is acting strangely and suffers from nightmares arising from the ritualistic child murders he is investigating. Sheen at first does not believe in the power of the voodoo cult, but is forced to change his mind when the cop commits suicide and Sheen discovers that his own son may be sacrificed by the cult. Suspenseful throughout, with a give-no-mercy climax.

A: Martin Sheen, Helen Shaver, Richard Masur, Harley Cross, Jimmy Smits, Robert Loggia

© HBO VIDEO 0034

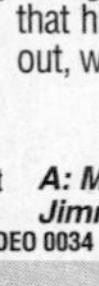

BIRDS, THE

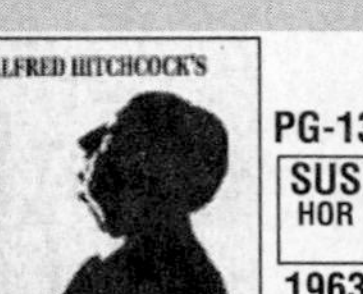

D: Alfred Hitchcock 119 m

PG-13 | SUS HOR | 1963 | COLOR

Sex Nud Viol Lang AdSit

8 Hitchcock classic. Tippy Hedren is a beautiful, wealthy, spoiled, young socialite (Hedron) who has her sites set on a handsome attorney (Taylor), much to the dismay of his schoolteacher girlfriend (Pleshette). However, that quickly takes a backseat when nature rebels in Northern California. Suddenly thousands of birds, for no apparent reason, attack the small coastal town of Bedoega Bay and all the townsfolk are pursued wherever they go. Alfred Hitchcock's technical mastery allows the viewer to suspend his suspicions, to believe and then fear that what he is seeing is real. Not for the fainthearted.

A: Rod Taylor, Tippi Hedren, Suzanne Pleshette, Jessica Tandy, Veronica Cartwright, Ethel Griffies

© MCA/UNIVERSAL HOME VIDEO, INC. 55010

BLACK SABBATH

D: Mario Bava 99 m

NR | HOR | 1964 | COLOR

Sex Nud Viol Lang AdSit

7 Spooky! An anthology of three horror tales, all hosted by Boris Karloff: 1. A nurse steals a diamond ring from a corpse. 2. A phone call from the beyond. But the best is saved for last. 3. A young man discovers a horse carrying the headless body of a man. He takes the body to a farmhouse where he discovers the horrible truth. The father of the house had gone off to kill a special variety of vampire called a wurdalak. This vampire only attacks the ones he loves. Instead, the father was killed, has himself become a wurdalak and is preying upon his own family. Wonderful spooky atmosphere.

A: Boris Karloff, Mark Damon, Suzy Anderson, Jacqueline Pierreux, Milli Monti, Michele Mercier

© HBO VIDEO 3354

BLOB, THE

D: Irvin Yeaworth, Jr. 82 m

NR | HOR SF | 1958 | COLOR

Sex Nud Viol Lang AdSit

6 This is a campy science fiction/horror "classic" from the '50s genre of cheap horror movies. It is mostly interesting for having been Steve McQueen's first starring role and because the theme song, "Beware the Blob, It Leaps, and Creeps, and Leaps," was written by Burt Bacharach and Hal David. The fairly silly plot has Steve as a teenager, fighting the disbelief of his folks and the townsfolk about a big glob of jello from outer space that oozes into, onto and eats everything - and continues to grow. Remade in 1988 with "real" special effects.

A: Steve McQueen, Aneta Corseaut, Olin Howlin, Earl Rowe

© GOODTIMES 8146

BLOB, THE

D: Chuck Russell 92 m

R | SF HOR | 1988 | COLOR

Sex Nud Viol Lang AdSit

7 This is a high-budget, high-tech remake of a low-budget cult favorite from the '50s that starred Steve McQueen. The special effects and production values are much better here, but the story is essentially the same: A meteor brings a pink glop from space to a small ski resort town. The ooze eats anything, everything and everybody. The more it eats, the more it grows and the bigger its appetite gets. Only two high school kids have what it takes to fight it. Good special effects make the suspense and thrills more intense this time around, though - and more violent.

A: Kevin Dillon, Shawnee Smith, Donovan Leitch, Jeffrey DeMunn, Candy Clark, Joe Seneca

© COLUMBIA TRISTAR HOME VIDEO 67010

BLOOD ON SATAN'S CLAW

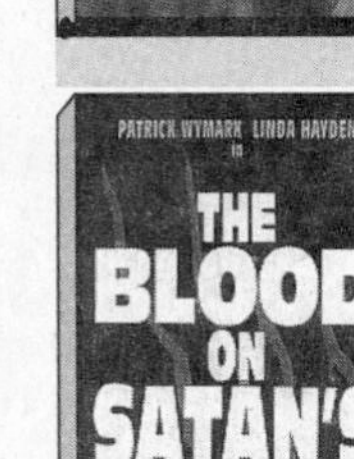

D: Piers Haggard 103 m

R | HOR | 1970 | COLOR

Sex Nud Viol Lang AdSit

8 Chilling and very atmospheric. In rural England of 1670, the deadly trials for witchcraft are everywhere and a gloomy atmosphere of suspense hangs over everything. A group of small children unearth strange skeletal remains which are believed to be those of a demon. They begin to worship it, and soon even sacrifice other children to him. The rich period atmosphere presented creates an air of believability. That, and a certain amount of gruesomeness, make this a film that is definitely not for the squeamish or for young children.

A: Patrick Wymark, Linda Hayden, Barry Andrews, Michele Dotrice, Tamara Ustinov, Simon Williams

Distributed By MGM/UA Home Video M204524

BLUE MONKEY

D: William Fruet 97 m

R | HOR | 1987 | COLOR

Sex Nud Viol Lang AdSit

6 A small city hospital is contaminated by a patient who is infected by a very peculiar insect. It is a bug that causes terminal gangrene when its eggs grow inside a body. Then one of these little guys mutates into a ten-foot monster and takes after doctors and patients. The film's low budget and none-too-original plot give it the impression of being a '50ish version of ALIENS (even though it was released in '87). Still, a decent cast, plus some charm and suspense, make it more than a little interesting.

A: Steve Railsback, Susan Anspach, Gwynyth Walsh, John Vernon, Joe Flaherty

© COLUMBIA TRISTAR HOME VIDEO 20874

BLUE SUNSHINE

D: Jeff Lieberman 94 m

R | SUS HOR | 1977 | COLOR

Sex Nud Viol Lang AdSit

8 Terrifying psychological shocker. When an innocent man is falsely accused of brutal murders, he evades police while he rushes to uncover who the real murderer is, and what the motive could be. His clues lead him to a discover a whole group of people who are all going bald. What else he discovers is terrifying: there is no rational motive for the murders. Students who took a particular brand of high-octane hallucinogenic LSD in the '60s that was called "Blue Sunshine" are now having violent after-effects - they are becoming crazed killers. This a truly terrifying film about losing control of your mind and a real shocker in spite of its low budget.

A: Zalman King, Mark Goddard, Robert Walden, Deborah Winters, Charles Siebert

© LIVE HOME VIDEO VA4124

BODY SNATCHERS

D: Abel Ferrara 87 m

R | HOR SF | 1994 | COLOR

Sex Nud Viol Lang AdSit

7 This is the third time that the 1954 novel has been filmed. While the first two, both named INVASION OF THE BODY SNATCHERS are better, this one too is involving and spooky. This time, a rebellious teenage girl moves with her family to an Army base where her chemist father is to check out spills for the EPA. However, something far more sinister is afoot. Slowly she notices that the people on the base all act quite wooden, soulless and altogether strange. The reason becomes all too clear when she discovers that alien creatures are able to extract your DNA while you sleep and then to replicate you. The real you is disposed of and emotionless drones replace you.

A: Gabrielle Anwar, Terry Kinney, Billy Wirth, Christine Elise, Forest Whitaker, Meg Tilly

© WARNER HOME VIDEO 13027

BRAIN DAMAGE

D: Frank Henenlotter — 89 m

R | HOR | 1988 | COLOR

Sex Nud Viol Lang AdSit

7 For lovers of the Bizarre. Brian (Rick Herbst) is a lonely boy looking for thrills and he finds some. He gets injected with a blue venom from a wisecracking eel-like monster called Elmer whose injections provide him some mind-blowing psychedelic highs and do a lot more besides. He becomes addicted to Elmer's potion. The serious trouble is that Elmer is a mutant parasite that lives on human brains and he relies on Brian to get them for him. From the writer/director of BASKET CASE.

A: Rick Herbst, Gordon MacDonald, Jennifer Lowery, Theo Barnes, Lucille Saint-Peter, Vicki Darnell

© PARAMOUNT HOME VIDEO 12671

BRAINSCAN

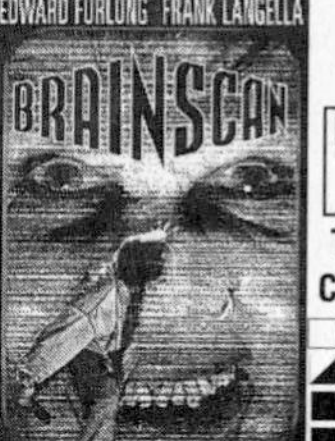

D: John Flynn — 96 m

R | HOR | 1994 | COLOR

Sex Nud Viol Lang AdSit

7 Michael Brower is a lonely teenager, his mother is dead and his father is always away. He has three interests: horror movies dealing with death, the girl next door and computer gadgetry. So when his buddy calls to tell him about a new state-of-the-art interactive video game about fear and death, Michael calls the makers. But as soon as he does, the powerful game and its ghoulish master, The Trickster, penetrate into his consciousness and toy with his darkest impulses. The Trickster has taken control of his life and has also made him into a murderer. Very ghoulish and grotesque in places. Too bad it didn't tone it down, because it's too gross for the younger set which is its best audience.

A: Edward Furlong, Frank Langella, Amy Hargraves, Jamie Marsh, Victor Ertmanis, T. Ryder Smith

© COLUMBIA TRISTAR HOME VIDEO 72773

BRAM STOKER'S DRACULA

D: Francis Ford Coppola — 130 m

R | HOR | 1992 | COLOR

Sex Nud Viol Lang AdSit

8 Opulent, stylish, ghoulish and sexy. Count Dracula has forsaken God because God allowed his beloved to think he had been killed in battle, whereupon she killed herself. So, in response, God has cursed Dracula to a ghoulish eternal life. But now, 400 years later, Dracula believes his love has been reborn and has come to Victorian London to pursue her. However, he is challenged there by a brilliant scientist who believes the curse of Dracula is real and seeks to destroy him. A great deal of money and time was spent to create marvelous special effects that inspire moments of genuine terror. However, the characters too are stylized, so unfortunately some of the impact is lost.

A: Gary Oldman, Winona Ryder, Anthony Hopkins, Keanu Reaves, Richard E. Grant, Cary Elwes

© COLUMBIA TRISTAR HOME VIDEO 51413

BUFFY THE VAMPIRE SLAYER

D: Fran Rubel Kuzui — 86 m

PG-13 | COM HOR | 1992 | COLOR

Sex Nud Viol Lang AdSit

7 Buffy is a spoiled and very popular "valley girl" totally into herself, her girl friends, her boy friend and cheerleading. Until, that is, she is visited by a mysterious old dude (Sutherland) who explains that the weird dreams she's been having are memories from her past lives. Buffy, you see, is the chosen one. Only she has the power to destroy the vampire plagues when they erupt, and one has now erupted in Southern California. Buffy must rise out of her innocent high school world to become the protector of the "real" world. This is a fun, wacky teen film that does a good job at making fun of itself and everything else.

A: Kristy Swanson, Luke Perry, Donald Sutherland, Rutger Hauer, Paul Reubens

© FOXVIDEO 1972

CANDYMAN

D: Bernard Rose — 98 m

R | HOR | 1992 | COLOR

Sex Nud Viol Lang AdSit

6 For fans of gore only. The story revolves around the quest of a beautiful grad student to uncover the mystery behind the legend of Candyman. He is the spirit of a former black slave who was killed for having loved a white woman. She gets her wish and soon is also pursued by the dead man with no hands, only a hook that he uses to split his victims wide open. Lots of gore, not much else.

A: Virginia Madsen, Tony Todd, Vanessa Williams, Xander Berkeley, Kasi Lemmons

© COLUMBIA TRISTAR HOME VIDEO 94633

CARNIVAL OF SOULS

D: Herk Harvey — 84 m

PG | HOR SUS | 1962 | B&W

Sex Nud Viol Lang AdSit

8 This is a cult favorite that was made for just $30,000 in Kansas. It is a really eerie little gem about an uninvolved, non-caring, emotionally detached young woman. The car in which she is riding crashes into a river and she survives - or does she - because it strangely takes her three hours to resurface. Afterward she is plagued by recurring black-outs and is haunted by a ghoulish, zombie-like character which only she can see. Leave the lights on for this one.

A: Candace Hillgoss, Sidney Berger, Frances Feist

© UNITED AMERICAN VIDEO CORP. 7227

CARRIE

D: Brian De Palma — 100 m

R | HOR SUS | 1976 | COLOR

Sex Nud Viol Lang AdSit

9 In spite of being tormented at home by her religiously fanatic mother and ridiculed at school as a weirdo, suddenly Sissy Spacek's dream appears to have come true when she is asked to the prom by the school hunk. When it turns out to be just a cruel practical joke, everyone pays when Sissy unleashes her secret. She has devastating telekinetic powers and she uses them now to torment her tormentors. This film is very well done. Spacek and Laurie both received Oscar nominations. This is also the film that gave Spacek her big break. High quality spookiness.

A: Sissy Spacek, Piper Laurie, William Katt, John Travolta, Amy Irving, Nancy Allen

Distributed By MGM/UA Home Video M200261

CAT PEOPLE

D: Paul Schrader — 119 m

R | HOR SUS | 1982 | COLOR

Sex Nud Viol Lang AdSit

7 Erotic remake of the 1942 original. Beautiful Kinski and her brother are cursed to turn into killer panthers when they become sexually aroused. Kinski investigates a series of killings, reportedly by a panther, which she fears may have been committed by her brother. Then she meets and falls passionately in love with the zookeeper (Hurt). What will she do? Plenty eerie and plenty sexy, too. Lots of atmosphere, but it becomes a little too surreal in places. Its gore and nudity will offend some.

A: Nastassia Kinski, Malcolm McDowell, Annette O'Toole, John Heard, Ruby Dee, Ed Begley, Jr.

© MCA/UNIVERSAL HOME VIDEO, INC. 77008

CAT'S EYE

D: Lewis Teague — 94 m

PG-13 | SUS HOR | 1985 | COLOR

Sex Nud Viol Lang AdSit

8 Some really scary bedtime stories. This is an anthology of three Stephen King tales: Alan King's clinic produces a shocking cure for James Woods's smoking, Tennis pro Hays accepts a challenge to walk around a building on its ledge, and little Drew Barrymore is protected from a deadly troll living in the wall by a stray cat. Some gruesome scenes, but mostly this is just plain scary stuff.

A: Drew Barrymore, James Woods, Robert Hayes, Alan King, Kenneth McMillan, Candy Clark

© CBS/FOX VIDEO 4731

CHANGELING, THE

D: Peter Medak — 113 m

R | SUS HOR | 1979 | COLOR

Sex Nud Viol Lang AdSit

8 Solid suspense thriller that is also a really scary ghost story. Music professor Scott loses his wife and daughter in a terrible traffic accident and when he moves into an old house, he finds that it is haunted by the spirit of a child who lived and died there 70 years before. Van Devere is the real estate agent who helps Scott to discover the secret of the house, even as Scott becomes the unwilling accomplice to the ghost's revenge. An excellent cast and an intense performance by Scott provide the essence of what every spook story needs, believability.

A: George C. Scott, Trish Van Devere, Melvyn Douglas, John Colicos, Jean Marsh, Madeleine Thornton-Sherwood

© HBO VIDEO 90630

CHILD'S PLAY

D: Tom Holland — 88 m

R | HOR SUS | 1988 | COLOR

Sex Nud Viol Lang AdSit

8 When 6-year-old Andy is asked how his babysitter was pushed out a window to a violent death, he simply says Chucky did it. A dead psycho murderer (Brad Dourif) has transfered his soul into a doll and Andy was given the doll on his birthday by his widowed Mom (Hicks). Now the doll "Chucky" seeks vengeance on those who killed him, but no one believes poor Andy. However, the real scare is that now Chucky wants to transfer his soul into a live body. A well-crafted horror thriller that builds slowly, leaving the best for last. Great special effects.

A: Catherine Hicks, Chris Sarandon, Alex Vincent, Brad Dourif, Dinah Manoff, Tommy Swerdlow

Distributed By MGM/UA Home Video M901593

COMPANY OF WOLVES

D: Neil Jordan — 95 m

R | HOR | 1984 | COLOR

Sex Nud Viol Lang AdSit

6 Decidedly adult retelling of "Little Red Riding Hood." This psychological retelling of the classic story has Lansbury as Grandma who shows up to visit. She turns the dreams which her adolescent 13-year-old granddaughter (Patterson) has into tales about men and wolves, fables full of sexual symbolism and mysterious happenings. Eccentric. Not for the casual viewer.

A: Angela Lansbury, David Warner, Sarah Patterson, Graham Crowden, Stephen Rea, Tusse Silberg

© LIVE HOME VIDEO VA5092

CREEPING FLESH, THE

D: Freddie Francis 94 m

PG
HOR
1972
COLOR

7 A scientist, trying to create a serum from the blood of evil men to counteract insanity, is injecting the serum into his daughter, whose mother had been insane. However, she has become insane, too, and is placed in her uncle's asylum. Her father continues his experiments, this time on an ancient skeleton that grows flesh when touched with water and he accidentally brings back to life a long dormant evil spirit. He is slowly goes insane himself, and as he does, the monster is turned loose on the world. This is an old-fashioned monster thriller, with a good cast, that will run a few icy chills up and down your spine.

Sex / Nud / Viol / Lang / AdSit

A: Peter Cushing, Christopher Lee, Lorna Hellbron, George Benson, Kenneth J. Warren

© COLUMBIA TRISTAR HOME VIDEO VH10147

CREEPSHOW

D: George A. Romero 120 m

R
HOR
1982
COLOR

7 Stephen King's anthology of five short stories is here presented in the same manner that the E.C. comic book series used years ago. (King was enamored with these when he was a child. It was also entitled "Creepshow.") King's own son, Joe, plays a young boy who is reading the stories and they provide the central focus for five separate vignettes that are played out on screen. The subjects of the stories range from the undead to angry cockroaches. Sometimes funny and sometimes really scary. It was successful enough to spawn a sequel: CREEPSHOW 2.

Sex / Nud / Viol / Lang / AdSit

A: Hal Holbrook, Adrienne Barbeau, Fritz Weaver, Leslie Nelson, Carrie Nye, Stephen King

© WARNER HOME VIDEO 11306

CREEPSHOW 2

D: George A. Romero 92 m

R
HOR
1987
COLOR

6 Three more short stories from Stephen King in a follow-up to the original CHREEPSHOW. These three gruesome tales are connected by animation. A wooden Indian comes to life, an oil slick devours teenagers and a hit-and-run driver is terrorized by the hitchhiker she hit. This is not as good as the original but still is OK, especially for fans.

Sex / Nud / Viol / Lang / AdSit

A: Lois Chiles, George Kennedy, Dorothy Lamour, Daniel Beer, Page Hannah

© R&G VIDEO, LP 90001

CRITTERS

D: Shephen Herek 86 m

PG-13
HOR COM SF
1986
COLOR

7 Strange sort of mix between horror and comedy that proved to be quite popular and spawned three much-lessor sequels. Eight razor-toothed alien furballs have escaped from a prison in space and have landed near a farm family in Kansas. While Mom stays home to do battle the hungry little fellers who want to dine on humans, son Grimes goes to town to fetch help. On the way, he meets two intergalactic dead-pan bounty hunters who have come to kill off the bloodthirsty little monsters. Some very funny moments are mixed in with some really gory ones.

Sex / Nud / Viol / Lang / AdSit

A: Dee Wallace, M. Emmet Walsh, Billy Green Bush, Scott Grimes, Nadine Van Der Velde, Don Opper

© TURNER HOME ENTERTAINMENT N4115

CUJO

D: Lewis Teague 93 m

R
HOR SUS
1983
COLOR

7 A genuinely frightening story from Stephen King. Dee Wallace is a young mother in a Maine village whose marriage is slowly disintegrating. She has had a brief affair, and she and her husband have had a fight. She has left the house with their young son in their car. Terror strikes when the car stalls and the two are attacked by a crazed and rabid Saint Bernard. This is a film where the plot builds slowly throughout and results in a solid, chilling climax. A skillfully crafted chiller that is definitely not for kids.

Sex / Nud / Viol / Lang / AdSit

A: Dee Wallace, Danny Pintauro, Daniel Hugh-Kelly, Christopher Stone, Ed Lauter, Mills Watson

© WARNER HOME VIDEO 11331

CURSE OF THE DEMON

D: Jacques Tourneur 81 m

NR
HOR SUS
1957
B&W

9 Exceptional. One of the best horror films ever. Dana Andrews plays a stuffy New York clinical psychologist who travels to London to help expose a group of devil worshipers as being a hoax. His colleague has been mysteriously and brutally murdered, but Andrews refuses to believe that a demon called up by the group did it. Unfortunately for Dana, they aren't a hoax, and their leader (MacGinnis) calls up a demon from Hell to deal with him, too. Very moody and atmospheric, with misty English locations. Gripping and chilling terror. True genre classic.

Sex / Nud / Viol / Lang / AdSit

A: Dana Andrews, Peggy Cummins, Niall MacGinnis, Maurice Denham

© GOODTIMES 4424

CURSE OF THE WEREWOLF, THE

D: Terence Fisher 93 m

NR
HOR
1961
COLOR

7 Very good chiller. A young mute girl is brutally raped by a mysterious street beggar. She gives birth to a son, whose violent heritage is withheld from him throughout his childhood. Now in adulthood, he began to undergo a very strange physical transformation after he was denied his girlfriend's love. Now, upon the arrival of each full moon, he strangely begins to develop an overpowering thirst for blood and with its appearance is physically transformed into a werewolf. This is a superior, well-crafted movie with more adult considerations than is typical for the genre.

Sex / Nud / Viol / Lang / AdSit

A: Oliver Reed, Clifford Evans, Yvonne Romain, Anthony Dawson

© MCA/UNIVERSAL HOME VIDEO, INC. 80543

DAMIEN: OMEN II

D: Don Taylor 107 m

R
HOR
1978
COLOR

7 Sequel to THE OMEN. In the original, Damien's father is killed by police as he attempts to kill his own son, who he believed to be the Antichrist - the son of the devil. Damien has now grown into an obnoxious teenager at a military school, as the ward of his very wealthy uncle (Holden). While there, Damien reads the Book of Revelations and discovers his true identity. Very soon he begins to kill off his second family and anyone else who gets in his way. Very grisly and gory.

Sex / Nud / Viol / Lang / AdSit

A: William Holden, Lee Grant, Lew Ayres, Sylvia Sidney, Johnathan Scott-Taylor

© FOXVIDEO 1087

DARK HALF, THE

D: George A. Romero 122 m

R
HOR SUS
1993
COLOR

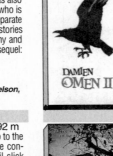

6 Hutton is college professor who has been trying to write legitimate works of literature, but so far his major successes, and a good living, have come from writing trash under a pseudonym. The recurring star of those novels is a ruthless antihero who will stop at nothing. When Hutton's secret life is threatened by a blackmailer, he decides to go public and to "kill off" his pseudonym, thereby also the book and its character. However, that character was created out of Hutton's own repressed self (his dark half). That half has gained a life of its own and is brutally killing all of those people who have a part in killing him off. Starts stronger than it finishes.

Sex / Nud / Viol / Lang / AdSit

A: Timothy Hutton, Amy Madigan, Julie Harris, Michael Rooker, Robert Joy, Kent Broadhurst

© ORION PICTURES CORPORATION 8787

DAWN OF THE DEAD

D: George A. Romero 126 m

NR
HOR
1979
COLOR

8 This was the long-awaited sequel to the horror masterpiece NIGHT OF THE LIVING DEAD. Opinions on this movie are widely divided, due mostly to extreme gore and graphic violence. A female TV reporter, her boyfriend (a helicopter pilot) and two members of a SWAT team escape marauding bands of flesh-eating Zombies in the chopper. They land on top of a shopping center that has everything they could need and barricade themselves inside. They are then set upon both by zombies and a motorcycle gang. Your evaluation of this movie will depend upon the strength of your stomach.

Sex / Nud / Viol / Lang / AdSit

A: David Emge, Ken Foree, Scott Reiniger, Gaylen Ross, Tom Savini

© HBO VIDEO TVB1977

DAY OF THE TRIFFIDS, THE

D: Steve Sekely 95 m

NR
SF HOR
1962
COLOR

7 Most of the people of Earth are blinded when the earth is bombarded by a meteor shower. The shower also contains strange other-world seeds, seeds which grow into walking, man-eating plants. Howard Keel leads a small group in a last stand against the marauding plants while scientist Moor and his wife struggle to find a scientific answer. Intelligent dialogue separates this from most of the other invasion/disaster films of the same period. Pretty good special effects. Enjoyable piece of science fiction.

Sex / Nud / Viol / Lang / AdSit

A: Howard Keel, Nicole Maurey, Janette Scott, Kieron Moore, Mervyn Johns

© GOODTIMES VGT5090

DEAD AND BURIED

D: Gary A. Sherman 95 m

R
HOR
1981
COLOR

6 The sheriff and coroner of a small sea-side fishing town have their hands full when grisly murders begin to occur. A man is beaten up, tied to a tree and then set ablaze. Things become even more bizarre when other bodies come back to life as zombies. And, their hearts have been removed and hidden by the voodoo master, so that he can keep them under his control. Very Gory. Really good makeup work. Campy and entertaining horror flick.

Sex / Nud / Viol / Lang / AdSit

A: James Farentino, Melody Anderson, Jack Albertson, Nancy Locke Hauser

© LIVE HOME VIDEO VA4060

DOCTOR PHIBES RISES AGAIN

PG | HOR | 1972 | COLOR

D: Robert Fuest — 89 m

7 This is a terror flick in the innocent '60s tradition. It brings back the Dr. Phibes character from THE ABOMINABLE DR. PHIBES. Mad Dr. Phibes (Price, at his campy best) goes off to an Egyptian tomb in search of a magic potion - the elixir of life - which will bring his dead wife back to life. But he is not alone. A wealthy man named Biederbeck wants it, too. So to gain possession of the stuff, and to assure it is he who wins, Phibes gradually kills off all the members of the other side except Biederbeck. Soon it is a personal battle and both men are determined to win. Entertaining.

Sex, Nud, Viol, Lang, AdSit

A: Vincent Price, Robert Quarry, Hugh Griffith, Valli Kemp, Peter Cushing, Terry-Thomas

© LIVE HOME VIDEO VA4349

DR. GIGGLES

R | HOR | 1992 | COLOR

D: Manny Coto — 96 m

6 Intentionally campy gore blood fest which will be of interest only to those who revel in such things. Drake is the grown son of a 50's heart surgeon who was killed by irate customers for having botched so many operations. 30 years later, Drake has escaped from an institution for the criminally insane and taken up residency at his father's old digs. His specialties are extracting the hearts from unwilling patients without sedation and cracking a series of very bad jokes at the same time: "Either you're dead or my watch has stopped" or, how about: "If you think this is bad, wait until you get my bill."

Sex, Nud, Viol, Lang, AdSit

A: Larry Drake, Holly Marie Combs, Glenn Quinn, Cliff DeYoung, Richard Bradford, Nancy Fish

© MCA/UNIVERSAL HOME VIDEO, INC. 81422

DR. TERROR'S HOUSE OF HORRORS

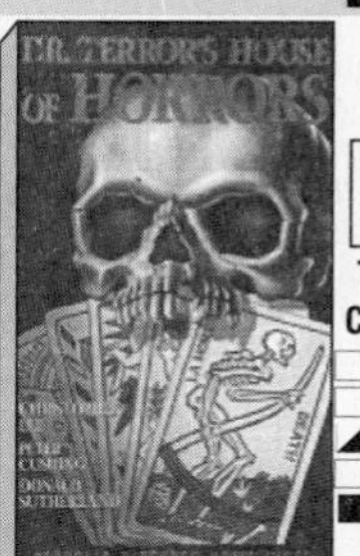

NR | SUS HOR | 1965 | COLOR

D: Freddie Francis — 98 m

7 Intelligent, very well done film. A mysterious doctor who calls himself Dr. Terror and who reads Tarot cards, enters into the private traveling compartment of five men on a train. He is really Death in disguise and he tells each man his fortune. For each man he predicts death - grotesque and macabre deaths. What follows is an anthology of the separate tales of each man, which are all then interwoven together. They are tales of the macabre and bizarre. Everything is very credibly done, with a top-flight cast. Gruesome, but fun.

Sex, Nud, Viol, Lang, AdSit

A: Peter Cushing, Christopher Lee, Donald Sutherland, Neil McCallum, Roy Castle, Max Adrian

© REPUBLIC PICTURES HOME VIDEO 1067

EVIL, THE

R | HOR SUS | 1978 | COLOR

D: Gus Trikonis — 80 m

8 Genuine hard-boiled chills come when psychiatrist Richard Crenna and his wife rent a gothic mansion in the country for his summer drug rehabilitation program. While he and some others are renovating the property, they discover a locked trap door. They should not have opened that door. Now the building has a tenant they don't want - the devil himself (Victor Buono) - who imprisons them all... and then, one by one, kills each one of them off. Genuinely scary stuff of the supernatural variety.

Sex, Nud, Viol, Lang, AdSit

A: Richard Crenna, Joanna Pettet, Victor Buono, Andrew Prine, Cassie Yates

© NEW LINE HOME VIDEO 4006

EXORCIST, THE

R | SUS HOR | 1973 | COLOR

D: William Friedkin — 122 m

10 Extraordinarily powerful, deeply evocative and very believable story of the satanic possession. It is so believable that it could literally SCARE the hell out of you. Nominated for 10 Oscars, including Best Picture. A 12-year-old girl (Blair) is possessed by an ancient demon and is transformed into a vile, hideous and truly repulsive creature. Her desperate mother (Burstyn) seeks out a troubled priest (Miller) to confront the demon, but the demon turns the priest's own failing faith and sense of guilt against him. So, Miller calls in a seasoned old priest (von Sydow) to help him exorcise the demon. You may never turn the lights out again.

Sex, Nud, Viol, Lang, AdSit

A: Ellen Burstyn, Max von Sydow, Linda Blair, Jason Miller, Lee J. Cobb

© WARNER HOME VIDEO 1007

EXORCIST II: THE HERETIC

R | SUS HOR | 1977 | COLOR

D: John Boorman — 118 m

6 This is a relatively undistinguished sequel to the devastatingly horrific original. Still, this one does contain some genuinely chilling moments. Four years after she was exorcised of the demon Pazuzu, Linda Blair is again suffering from recurring nightmares and is now under treatment by psychoanalyst Louise Fletcher. Under hypnosis, it is discovered she is still possessed. Burton is the Vatican's investigator Father Lamont. He knows that he needs help so he searches through Africa to find former possession survivor James Earl Jones to urge him to once again face the evil that he had barely escaped before.

Sex, Nud, Viol, Lang, AdSit

A: Richard Burton, Linda Blair, Louise Fletcher, Kitty Will, James Earl Jones, Ned Beatty

© WARNER HOME VIDEO 1023

FALL OF THE HOUSE OF USHER, THE

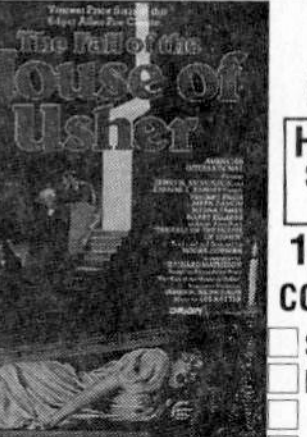

NR | HOR SUS | 1960 | COLOR

D: Roger Corman — 79 m

8 Classic Edgar Allan Poe horror tale about a family and its legacy of madness and doom. When her suitor (Mark Damon) arrives at an old, dreary, decaying mansion to take a beautiful girl (Myrna Fahey) away to be married, her older brother (Vincent Price) becomes desperate for his sister to stay and reveals to Damon the secret. All Ushers are condemned to eventual madness and to an early death. Undeterred, he yet attempts to get his intended to leave. It is then that the terror begins. This film captures the flavor of Poe as no other has yet done, even though it was filmed in only 15 days with virtually no budget.

Sex, Nud, Viol, Lang, AdSit

A: Vincent Price, Mark Damon, Myrna Fahey, Harry Ellerbe

© WARNER HOME VIDEO 26004

FEARLESS VAMPIRE KILLERS, THE

NR | COM HOR | 1967 | COLOR

D: Roman Polanski — 111 m

7 Weird, odd-ball mixture of horror and humor that has achieved a significant cult following. Professor Abronsius (MacGowran) and his bumbling assistant (Polanski) travel to Transylvania to attempt to destroy a family of Slovokian vampires. While stopping at an inn, they spy the beautiful virginal innkeeper's daughter, Sarah (Sharon Tate). Later she is kidnapped by the vampires while she is taking a bath and the two attempt to infiltrate the vampire's annual ball to retrieve her - but will they get out again without becoming immortal themselves?

Sex, Nud, Viol, Lang, AdSit

A: Jack MacGowran, Roman Polanski, Alfie Bass, Jessie Robins, Sharon Tate, Ferdy Mayne

Distributed By MGM/UA Home Video M200138

FIRESTARTER

R | SUS HOR | 1984 | COLOR

D: Mark L. Lester — 113 m

8 Excellent screen version of Stephen King's strange story of a little girl who has the telekinetic power to start fires by merely thinking of it. Some times she can control her thoughts, sometimes she can't - for which she feels guilty. Her nice-guy father (Sheen) does his best to comfort her and also to protect her from George C. Scott. Scott is an agent for the government. It wants to either use her as their secret weapon or to eliminate her. There is real suspense generated here and great special effects, too. Horror fans will be more than satisfied. Fast paced, with a top-flight cast.

Sex, Nud, Viol, Lang, AdSit

A: Drew Barrymore, David Keith, George C. Scott, Martin Sheen, Art Carney, Louise Fletcher

© MCA/UNIVERSAL HOME VIDEO, INC. 80075

FLY, THE

NR | SF DMA HOR | 1958 | B&W

D: Kurt Neumann — 94 m

9 This is a superior science fiction story. A scientist, experimenting with a machine that disintegrates matter in one place and reintegrates it again in another place, has a serious accident when his genes are mixed with those of a household fly. His head has become attached to the fly's body, and vice versa. He is now a gruesome freak struggling to return to normal. This film has become a cult favorite for very good reason. It was produced with care, high production values, good special effects and good acting. It was remade in 1986 in an equally good but much more grizzly manner.

Sex, Nud, Viol, Lang, AdSit

A: David Hedison, Patricia Owens, Vincent Price, Herbert Marshall, Kathleen Freeman

© FOXVIDEO 1190

FLY, THE

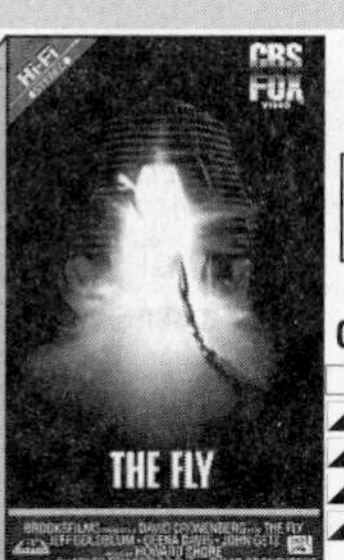

R | SF HOR DMA | 1986 | COLOR

D: David Cronenberg — 96 m

8 Equally good (but much more graphic and intense) remake of the 1958 classic science fiction horror story. A brilliant scientist has built a matter transportation device which he decides to try out on himself. Unknown to him, a fly is in the chamber with him when the machine is activated and their genes are mixed together. He becomes horribly disfigured. Very interesting premise, combined with a credible love story. Excellent makeup won an Oscar.

Sex, Nud, Viol, Lang, AdSit

A: Jeff Goldblum, Geena Davis, John Getz, Joy Boushel, Les Carlson

© FOXVIDEO 1503

FRIGHT NIGHT

R | COM HOR | 1985 | COLOR

D: Tom Holland — 105 m

8 Wonderful little horror spoof. A reasonably sane and normal 17-year-old becomes convinced that his suave new neighbor (Sarandon) is a vampire, but no one believes him - not his mother, not his best friend and not even his devoted girlfriend. After the police ignore his pleas, he seeks the advice of a has-been movie actor (McDowall) who was known on TV as "The Great Vampire Killer" and who was also just fired as the host of the local TV's horror movie show. At first, McDowall just humors the kid but it soon turns out the guy really is a vampire. Ingenious blending of horror and humor.

Sex, Nud, Viol, Lang, AdSit

A: Chris Sarandon, William Ragsdale, Roddy McDowall, Amanda Bearse, Stephen Geoffreys

© COLUMBIA TRISTAR HOME VIDEO 60562

FURY, THE

R | SUS HOR | 1978 | COLOR

D: Brian De Palma — 119 m

8 Chilling contemporary tale of an ordinary man (Kirk Douglas) who's son is kidnapped by a supersecret government agency. Its agents have kidnapped his son so that they can use his psychic powers for their own purposes or, if they can't, to kill him. Amy Irving may look as innocent as a school girl - but one look from her can literally kill. Douglas enlists her help and together they track down his missing son and confront the kidnappers. This is a very effective suspense flick, but it is also very intense, very bloody and violent in places... and it has an explosive ending.

Sex | Nud | Viol | Lang | AdSit

A: Kirk Douglas, Andrew Stevens, Amy Irving, Fiona Lewis, John Cassavetes, Charles Durning

© FOXVIDEO 1097

GHOSTBUSTERS

PG | COM HOR FAN | 1984 | COLOR

D: Ivan Reitman — 105 m

9 This film was a major box office hit and is about a trio of flaky parapsychologists who set up a shop specializing in the capture of unwanted ghosts. Business at first is pretty slow, but then they get their first job exorcising beautiful Sigourney Weaver's refrigerator. Soon both she and her nerdy neighbor are possessed by demons and the Ghostbusters discover that her entire building has become a magnet for all kinds of evil spirits... and the city of New York is now in desperate peril. Wonderfully offbeat and genuinely funny, with some pretty scary special effects, too. Murray is wonderfully weird. Great fun and good entertainment. 44 years before this there was Bob Hope in GHOSTBREAKERS.

Sex | Nud | Viol | Lang | AdSit

A: Bill Murray, Dan Aykroyd, Sigourney Weaver, Harold Ramis, Annie Potts, Rick Moranis

© COLUMBIA TRISTAR HOME VIDEO 60413

GHOSTBUSTERS II

PG | COM HOR FAN | 1989 | COLOR

D: Ivan Reitman — 102 m

7 Entertaining follow-up to the original blockbuster. This time the ghostbusting team sets about rescuing Sigourney Weaver, her infant son and all of NYC from a river of pink slime negative energy, which is flowing under the streets of the city. This one seems rather long and is not as captivating as the original, but is still a good time for fans. Teenagers are probably its best audience.

Sex | Nud | Viol | Lang | AdSit

A: Bill Murray, Dan Aykroyd, Sigourney Weaver, Harold Ramis, Rick Moranis, Ernie Hudson

© COLUMBIA TRISTAR HOME VIDEO 50163

GREMLINS

PG | COM FAN HOR | 1984 | COLOR

D: Joe Dante — 106 m

8 Entertaining and very different. Steven Spielberg put together this combination "horror"/comedy - so this is not your typical flick. The premise is that an inventor (Axton) goes on a Christmas shopping trip to Chinatown looking for the perfect gift for his son. He decides upon a strange but cute little creature called a "mowgli," but is given three warnings: Do not get it wet, keep it out of bright light and never to feed it after midnight. When these rules are ignored, hordes of mischievous gremlins result. Fascinating special effects. Really wacky.

Sex | Nud | Viol | Lang | AdSit

A: Zach Galligan, Phoebe Cates, Hoyt Axton, Frances Lee McCain, Polly Holliday, Glynn Turman

© WARNER HOME VIDEO 11388

GREMLINS 2: THE NEW BATCH

PG-13 | COM FAN HOR | 1990 | COLOR

D: Joe Dante — 107 m

8 Those weird little creatures are back to raise havoc in a New York office complex and with its tycoon owner. The film is filled with the same odd mixture of non-toxic horror and comedy as in the original. It is also filled with Hollywood insider-type jokes and plot spins. A little more violence than the first one earned it a PG-13. Some think it's not as good as the original. Others think it's better. Fun, no matter how it's sliced.

Sex | Nud | Viol | Lang | AdSit

A: Zach Galligan, Phoebe Cates, John Glover, Christopher Lee, Robert Prosky, Dick Miller

© WARNER HOME VIDEO 11886

HALLOWEEN

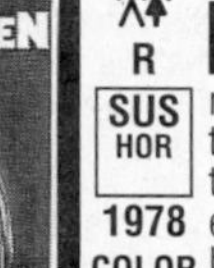

R | SUS HOR | 1978 | COLOR

D: John Carpenter — 92 m

9 This is the low-budget thriller which launched a seemingly endless series of much lessor sequels. A young boy was sent to a mental institution after he had killed his sister on Halloween. Now, fifteen years later he has escaped and he has returned to terrorize three teenage girls. This is one of the scariest films since PSYCHO. The emphasis is very much on suspense and terror in this well-crafted horror gem, because the killer enjoys mercilessly taunting his victims before he kills. But, there is gore, too. Several sequels of much lessor quality followed. This is also the film that made Jamie Lee Curtis into a star.

Sex | Nud | Viol | Lang | AdSit

A: Donald Pleasence, Jamie Lee Curtis, Nancy Loomis, P.J. Sales, Charles Cyphers, Kyle Richards

© MEDIA HOME ENTERTAINMENT, INC. M131

HAUNTING, THE

G | SUS HOR | 1963 | B&W

D: Robert Wise — 112 m

9 This is a masterful psychological horror movie that manipulates your mind rather than overloads your senses. A ninety-year-old New England house has long been rumored to be haunted. Over the years it has been the setting for a series of tragedies. Dr. Markway (Johnson) is determined to explore its secrets. So he, two female psychic researchers (Harris and Bloom) and the nephew (Tamblyn) of the old woman who has inherited it enter. It soon appears to the group that the house "wants" Julie Harris. But was what we/they just saw real, or was it just our/their imagination? Truly hair-raising.

Sex | Nud | Viol | Lang | AdSit

A: Julie Harris, Claire Bloom, Richard Johnson, Russ Tamblyn, Lois Maxwell, Fay Compton

Distributed By MGM/UA Home Video M600903

HITCHER, THE

R | HOR SUS | 1985 | COLOR

D: Robert Harmon — 98 m

7 A young California-bound motorist (Howell) picks up a hitchhiker (Hauer) somewhere in Texas. He shouldn't have. The thumber is actually a murderous psychotic who has killed his previous ride and now holds a knife to Howell's throat. In a happy piece of good luck, Hower pushes the hitcher out the door and leaves him behind. He has escaped from the hitcher - or has he. His terror is refreshed anew when a car goes by with the hitcher and his next victims inside - a family with children. Edge-of-your-seat suspense. Gobs of violence and gore.

Sex | Nud | Viol | Lang | AdSit

A: Rutger Hauer, C. Thomas Howell, Jennifer Jason Leigh, Jeffrey DeMunn, Henry Darrow

© HBO VIDEO TVA3756

HORROR OF DRACULA

NR | HOR SUS | 1958 | COLOR

D: Terence Fisher — 82 m

8 Genuinely scary film. Christopher Lee is marvelous as he creates a sinister portrait of the charismatic but vile and evil Count who prowls gothic London as a blood-thirsty vampire. This is a very stylish film that captures the feel of a Dracula whose blood sucking induces an orgasmic-like high in his willing female bloodbanks. Peter Cushing is also very good as Dracula's nemesis, Dr. Van Helsing. This is a very high quality version of the timeless story, equal to Lugosi's 1931 portrait in DRACULA. The success of this film spawned many lessor sequels.

Sex | Nud | Viol | Lang | AdSit

A: Christopher Lee, Peter Cushing, Michael Gough, Melissa Stribling, Carol Marsh, John Van Eyssen

© WARNER HOME VIDEO 11499

HOUR OF THE WOLF

NR | FOR HOR | 1968 | B&W

D: Ingmar Bergman — 88 m

7 The very dark side of a brooding artist (Max Von Sydow) is revealed when he and his pregnant wife retreat to a deserted island. He is plagued with surrealistic dreams and each day they become more and more real to him. Soon his bizarre hallucinations become his realities. His wife does her best to save him from them, but she is nearly destroyed as well. This is supposed to be one of Ingmar Bergman's lesser efforts, but still is powerful stuff. Subtitles.

Sex | Nud | Viol | Lang | AdSit

A: Max von Sydow, Liv Ullmann, Erland Josephson, Gertrud Fridh, Gudrun Brost

Distributed By MGM/UA Home Video M202934

HOWLING, THE

R | HOR | 1981 | COLOR

D: Joe Dante — 90 m

8 A well-made horror flick that has just about every kind of horror trick ever used in it. A beautiful TV reporter (Wallace) is attacked by a man she was to meet at a porno booth. While the police did kill him, his body later disappears from the morgue. Distraught over the experience, she and her husband are invited to stay at a secluded retreat for therapy, but there is no rest there. Outside she hears a piercing shriek. Finally, unable to stand it any longer, she goes outside to investigate the strange howling. There she finds she is in a den of werewolves. Gruesome, great special effects and very scary.

Sex | Nud | Viol | Lang | AdSit

A: Dee Wallace, Christopher Stone, Patrick Macnee, Dennis Dugan, Slim Pickens, John Carradine

© NEW LINE HOME VIDEO 1615

HUSH... HUSH, SWEET CHARLOTTE

NR | HOR SUS | 1964 | COLOR

D: Robert Aldrich — 133 m

8 Near-classic chiller. Bette Davis is astonishing as a reclusive, wealthy old woman notorious for having killed her lover years before and who now lives on the edge of reality. When the State wants to tear down her house to build a highway, she turns to her cousin Olivia de Havilland. But de Havilland and her boyfriend Joseph Cotten instead plot to drive her into total insanity. Winner of seven Oscar nominations, this is no ordinary horror movie. Highly suspenseful all the way until the tragic end. Reunites the two stars from WHAT EVER HAPPENED TO BABY JANE.

Sex | Nud | Viol | Lang | AdSit

A: Bette Davis, Olivia de Havilland, Joseph Cotten, Agnes Moorehead, Cecil Kellaway, Mary Astor

© FOXVIDEO 1245

INTERVIEW WITH THE VAMPIRE

D: Neil Jordan — 123 m

R | DMA HOR | 1995 | COLOR | Sex | Nud | Viol | Lang | AdSit

8 Brad Pitt plays Louis, a 200 year-old vampire, who has come to tell his melancholy story to reporter Christian Slater. In 1790's Louisiana, 24-year-old Louis had lost both his young wife in childbirth and his will to live, when he was "seduced" to the vampire-way by Lestat (Tom Cruise), an arrogant, consciousless, vampire killer. The guilt-ridden Louis refuses to kill humans and instead sucks the blood of rats, but yet looks upon Lestat as his mentor and teacher. When the tortured Louis takes pity upon a motherless girl, Lestat "converts" her for his friend Louis. But, Louis and the girl conspire to kill Lestat and then to travel the world to find more of their kind, to better understand their fate.

A: Tom Cruise, Brad Pitt, Antonio Banderas, Stephen Rea, Christian Slater, Kirsten Dunst

© WARNER HOME VIDEO 13176

INVASION OF THE BODY SNATCHERS

D: Don Siegel — 80 m

NR | SF SUS HOR | 1956 | B&W | Sex | Nud | Viol | Lang | AdSit

9 A chilling and frightening film that is every bit as powerful today as when released. Kevin McCarthy is a small town doctor who observes that all those around him - his patients, his friends and even his family - are slowly being transformed into emotionless, cold, inhuman beings. They look the same but they are different, very different. Slowly he uncovers the truth, that earth has been invaded by strange aliens who consume humans and then replace them with identical replicas that emerge from strange "pods." This has a subtle understated terror that found its intellectual inspiration in McCarthy-era politics.

A: Kevin McCarthy, Dana Wynter, Carolyn Jones, King Donovan, Larry Gates, Virginia Christine

© REPUBLIC PICTURES HOME VIDEO 2018

INVASION OF THE BODY SNATCHERS

D: Philip Kaufman — 117 m

PG | SF HOR | 1978 | COLOR | Sex | Nud | Viol | Lang | AdSit

8 Good remake of the 1956 classic, with slight alteration. Donald Sutherland is a city health official who discovers that there is an epidemic of mindless and soulless people loose on the streets of San Francisco. Further investigation leads to the startling discovery that the real people have been destroyed but not before they have been duplicated. The affected people had taken home the flowers which grew from an invasion of spores from space. Then, at home, as they sleep, the plants creep over their victims, stealing their form, their life and their soul. Good cast and quite well done, but purists will like the original better.

A: Donald Sutherland, Brooke Adams, Leonard Nimoy, Jeff Goldblum, Veronica Cartwright

Distributed By MGM/UA Home Video M600297

ISLAND OF DR. MOREAU, THE

D: Don Taylor — 104 m

PG | SF HOR | 1977 | COLOR | Sex | Nud | Viol | Lang | AdSit

6 Seventeen days adrift alone at sea in 1896, Michael York at last drifts up on the shores of an island, but he is not alone there. The island is populated by the half-animal/half-human creatures created by the experiments of a demented scientist. Dr. Moreau's (Lancaster) creations are the remnants of his experiments to transform animals into men. York meets Moreau and falls in love with his beautiful adopted daughter (Carrera), even as he also begins to discover the full extent of the horrors Moreau has committed.

A: Burt Lancaster, Michael York, Barbara Carrera, Nigel Davenport, Richard Basehart

© GOODTIMES 04062

I WAS A TEENAGE WEREWOLF

D: Gene Fowler, Jr. — 75 m

NR | HOR | 1957 | B&W | Sex | Nud | Viol | Lang | AdSit

6 So bad it's good. It is also most notable because it was Michael Landon's screen debut. In it, he plays Tony, a high-school kid with a tendency to explode into raving fits of violence. He is being "treated" by his doctor for his aggressive behavior but things are only getting worse. Finally Tony becomes fully transformed and the reason for his rampage becomes obvious. He is a werewolf. This film was very popular with teenagers of the day, particularly at drive-in movies. Now it is a big cult film.

A: Michael Landon, Yvonne Lime, Whit Bissell, Vladimir Sokoloff, Guy Williams

© COLUMBIA TRISTAR HOME VIDEO 60906

KWAIDAN

D: Masaki Kobayashi — 164 m

NR | FOR HOR SUS | 1964 | COLOR | Sex | Nud | Viol | Lang | AdSit

8 KWAIDEN is Japanese and means "Ghost Story." This film consists of four very eerie supernatural tales that were written by an American, Lafcadio Hearn, who settled in Japan in 1890. Each story involves an encounter with a ghost. "Black Hair" is of a samurai who returns to the wife he deserted years before and wakes up the next morning beside her skeleton. "The Woman of the Snow" is about a snow maiden who rescues a woodcutter and then swears to kill him if he tells anyone. "Hoichi, the Earless" is about a blind musician who looses his ears when he sings to a Samurai ghost. "In A Cup of Tea" is about a guard who absorbs a ghost's spirit after seeing his face in a cup of tea. Subtitles.

A: Rentaro Mikuni, Keiko Kishi, Katsuo Nakamura, Kanemon Nakamura

© HOME VISION KWA01

LADY IN WHITE

D: Frank Laloggia — 113 m

PG-13 | SUS HOR | 1988 | COLOR | Sex | Nud | Viol | Lang | AdSit

7 Eerily effective thriller. Unlike some films which rely on outlandish events to create a chilling effect, this film simply allows you to believe that what you see could be real. A very bright young boy is locked in the cloakroom at school as a prank. During the night he is visited by the ghost of one of several children who have been mysteriously killed in recent years. In his vision he can also, but not quite, make out the killer... or is all this occurring in his imagination? An absorbing thriller, well worth watching.

A: Lukas Haas, Len Carlou, Alex Rocco, Katherine Helmond, Jason Bresson, Lucy Lee Flippin

© VIDEO TREASURES SV9693

LAIR OF THE WHITE WORM

D: Ken Russell — 93 m

R | HOR | 1988 | COLOR | Sex | Nud | Viol | Lang | AdSit

6 Strange, outrageous and, some say, perverse tale set in the British countryside. An archaeologist unearths a strange-looking skull. He takes it and two young ladies to the festivities at a local castle, where the lady of the manor steals the skull and takes it to her dungeon. It turns out that the skull is the missing ingredient in her bizarre sect's quest to restore to life an ancient evil huge white worm. She then uses her wiley charms to lure in the last remaining ingredient... a virgin. Kinky and surrealistic, this is not for everyone but is definitely a different brand of horror.

A: Amanda Donohoe, Hugh Grant, Catherine Oxenberg, Sammi Davis, Peter Capaldi, Stratford Johns

© LIVE HOME VIDEO 5282

LEGEND OF HELL HOUSE, THE

D: John Hough — 94 m

PG | HOR SUS | 1973 | COLOR | Sex | Nud | Viol | Lang | AdSit

7 Thrilling tale of the occult. A wealthy man hires a team of four psychic researchers to occupy a haunted house which has already destroyed one team of investigators. This group is to stay for one week to determine why there have been so many mysterious deaths there. Roddy McDowall is the only survivor of the previous team and he is back again. In addition to him, this time there is a psychiatrist, his wife and a medium. Before their stay is done they will see madness and murder. This is very different from most other ghost movies. There are some real scares here. Top flight cast.

A: Pamela Franklin, Roddy McDowall, Clive Revill, Gayle Hunnicutt

© FOXVIDEO 1465

LITTLE SHOP OF HORRORS, THE

D: Roger Corman — 72 m

NR | COM HOR | 1960 | COLOR | Sex | Nud | Viol | Lang | AdSit

8 Hilarious and outrageous, very black comedy on a very low-budget. This is alternately known as "the film shot in two days" and plays like an extended vaudeville skit. In it, a very odd young florist's assistant is ignored by everyone until he develops a new exotic plant. Then he becomes very popular. However, unknown to nearly everyone, is how exotic that plant really is. It only prospers when it is fed human flesh, which our assistant provides. And, as the plant gets larger, it also begins to talk - demanding ever more and more. Later made into a successful Broadway play, this was then redone again on film in 1986, but this version is still best. Look for a very young Jack Nicholson as a masochist.

A: Jonathan Haze, Mel Welles, Jackie Joseph, Jack Nicholson, Dick Miller

© UNITED AMERICAN VIDEO CORP. 4043

LITTLE SHOP OF HORRORS

D: Frank Oz — 96 m

PG-13 | COM MUS HOR | 1986 | COLOR | Sex | Nud | Viol | Lang | AdSit

6 Rick Moranis and an excellent cast - supported by a big budget, great special effects and some pretty neat musical production numbers - provide an entertaining and funny musical for the first 2/3 of the film. However, the black comedy plot - which concerns a very large, singing, man-eating plant - turns a little too macabre to be that funny in the last 1/3. Still - fans of the unusual should take note. This is actually a remake of a famous low-budget hit from 1960 done by Roger Corman which also included a very young Jack Nicholson.

A: Rick Moranis, Ellen Greene, Vincent Gardenia, Steve Martin, James Belushi, John Candy

© WARNER HOME VIDEO 11702

MAGIC

D: Richard Attenborough — 106 m

R | SUS HOR | 1978 | COLOR | Sex | Nud | Viol | Lang | AdSit

7 Reality checks out and eerie insanity checks in. Hopkins plays a ventriloquist who lets his dummy, Fats, slowly take over his personality. His insecurities about the act propel him back to his hometown, where he finds his high school sweetheart (Ann-Margaret) involved in a nasty marriage to a loathsome country boy. The love triangle that develops spells disaster. He is slowly losing himself to the growing personality of his dummy (which is manifesting all his worst desires), and she is searching vainly for happiness lost in her past.

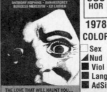

A: Anthony Hopkins, Ann-Margret, Burgess Meredith, Ed Lauter, Jerry Hauser, E.J. Andre

© UNITED AMERICAN VIDEO CORP. 5866

MARTIN

D: George A. Romero — 96 m

R | SUS HOR | 1978 | COLOR | Sex | Nud | Viol | Lang | AdSit

8 Terror and horror. Martin (Amplas) is just a little crazy. He thinks he is a vampire. Martin is a teenage boy who goes out at night committing all sorts of grizzly murders. First he drugs his victims with a hypodermic, then he opens their veins with a razorblade and then he drinks their blood! Poor Martin becomes even more confused when he is attracted to a depressed young married woman. What's he to do now? Then, Martin's grandfather makes his life even more difficult because he is determined to stop this family curse. This bit of true gore is in fact quite well done.

A: John Amplas, Lincoln Maazel, Christine Forrest, Elayne Nadeau, Tom Savini, Sarah Venable

© HBO VIDEO TVB1976

MARY SHELLEY'S FRANKENSTEIN

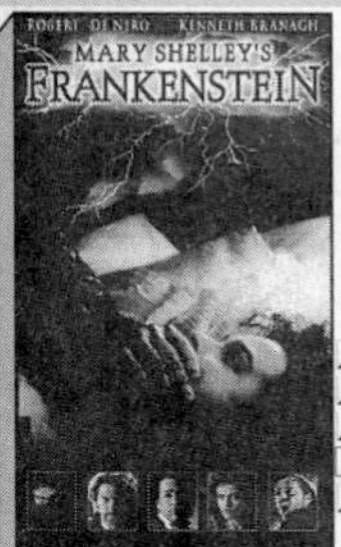

D: Kenneth Branagh — 123 m

R | DMA SF HOR | 1994 | COLOR | Sex | Nud | Viol | Lang | AdSit

7 This $45 million faithful adaptation of Mary Shelly's novel is set at the end of the eighteenth century. Devastated by the death of his wife, aristocrat Frankenstein (Branagh) studies to become a doctor. His interest lies not in healing the sick but by studying the mysteries of death. As a student, he builds upon the work of a brilliant teacher to actually recreate life by combining the stolen body parts of the dead. Stunned by the pitiful human result of his experiments, who escapes, he vows never to play with life again. However, the hideous and merciless creature he has created (De Niro) is constantly tormented by people. Terribly lonely, he now seeks out his "father" to force him to create a companion for him too.

A: Kenneth Branagh, Robert De Niro, Tom Hulce, Helena Bonham Carter, Aidan Quinn, Ian Holm

© COLUMBIA TRISTAR HOME VIDEO 78713

MEPHISTO WALTZ, THE

D: Paul Wendkos — 109 m

R | SUS HOR | 1971 | COLOR | Sex | Nud | Viol | Lang | AdSit

7 This is a demonic chiller that will possess you. The world's greatest pianist (Jurgens) is dying of leukemia and so he has become eager to find a new body in which to live. Journalist (Alda) is surprised to be granted a long sought-after interview with the famous pianist but soon, Alda's wife (Bisset) begins to notice a marked change in his personality. Jurgens and his daughter (Parkins), it turns out, are both devil worshipers and Alda body has been possessed by Jurgens. The spooky atmosphere may seem a little overdone at first, but the haunting ending will likely stay with you for awhile.

A: Alan Alda, Curt Jurgens, Jacqueline Bisset, Barbara Parkins

© FOXVIDEO 1200

MISERY

D: Rob Reiner — 107 m

R | SUS HOR | 1990 | COLOR | Sex | Nud | Viol | Lang | AdSit

8 Paul Sheldon (Caan) is a writer of successful series of "Misery Chastain" romance novels. His self-proclaimed number one fan is Annie Wilkes (Bates). So, after sliding off the road in a remote region of Colorado and breaking his legs, Paul is pleased that Annie, this rather plain and matronly nurse, has rescued him from the ditch and taken him to her house. However, after she reads his latest novel and discovers that he has killed off her heroine, Paul discovers the dark side of his deranged "angel." The obsessed Annie tortures him and refuses to let him leave until he resurrects Misery in a new novel.

A: Kathy Bates, James Caan, Richard Farnsworth, Frances Sternhagen, Lauren Bacall

© NEW LINE HOME VIDEO 77773

MONKEY SHINES

D: George A. Romero — 113 m

R | HOR SUS | 1988 | COLOR | Sex | Nud | Viol | Lang | AdSit

6 Hair raising! When a young law student (Beghe) is injured in an accident, he is rendered a quadraplegic. His best friend recruits an animal trainer to educate a lab monkey that will help Beghe to do everyday tasks. However, because the monkey's brain has been altered in the lab, the monkey also begins to carry out the subconscious evil aspirations of Beghe and embarks on a rampage of revenge and murder. The monkey delivers an amazing performance in this chilling flick under the direction of shockmaster George Romero.

A: Jason Beghe, John Pankow, Kate McNeil, Joyce Van Patten

© ORION PICTURES CORPORATION 8728

MONSTER IN THE CLOSET

D: Bob Dahlin — 90 m

PG | HOR COM | 1987 | COLOR | Sex | Nud | Viol | Lang | AdSit

6 Good natured humor and horror mix is this '50s-style spoof. A very Clark Kent-like obituary reporter (Grant) from the newspaper and a biology teacher (DuBarry) are sent to investigate a series of strange murders occurring in the closets of San Francisco. What they find is a music-loving mutant that commits brutal (and comic) murders but only in closets. A not-too-serious black comedy/horror movie in the same vein as LITTLE SHOP OF HORRORS. A very off-beat sort of movie.

A: Donald Grant, Denise DuBarry, Claude Akins, Howard Duff, John Carradine, Henry Gibson

© WARNER HOME VIDEO 783

NEEDFUL THINGS

D: Fraser C. Heston — 120 m

SUS HOR | 1993 | Sex | Nud | Viol | Lang | AdSit

7 A new business called Needful Things has opened in a small Maine town. It is run by a kindly man, who always knows just the right thing will be for anyone who comes into his store. And, he will sell it for a very reasonable price, asking only that you also do him a very small favor in return - just play a small trick on someone. However, all the tricks, when put together, are an unholy conspiracy that has turned everyone in town against each other. Hate has come to town, neighbor murders neighbor. There is riot in the streets. Max von Sydow is the kindly man who is also the devil come to earth. Ed Harris is a cop who just put all the pieces together. From Stephen King.

A: Ed Harris, Max von Sydow, Bonnie Bedelia, J.T. Walsh, Valri Bromfield, Amanda Plummer

© TURNER HOME ENTERTAINMENT N4167

NIGHTMARE ON ELM STREET, A

D: Wes Craven — 92 m

R | HOR | 1984 | COLOR | Sex | Nud | Viol | Lang | AdSit

7 For horror movie fans only - but they will be delighted. An imaginative premise with good special effects. The teenagers in the neighborhood discover that they are having very similar dreams of a horrific stalking figure. It seems that, many years ago, neighborhood vigilantes set fire to Freddie Kruger, accusing him of being a child murderer. Now Freddie haunts the dreams of the children of his tormentors. And these dreams are becoming their realities and many are turning up unexplainedly dead. Followed by a long string of exploitive and gory sequels.

A: John Saxon, Ronee Blakley, Heather Langenkamp, Robert Englund, Amanda Wyss, Nick Corri

© VIDEO TREASURES M790

NIGHT OF THE COMET

D: Thom Eberhardt — 95 m

PG-13 | SF COM HOR | 1984 | COLOR | Sex | Nud | Viol | Lang | AdSit

6 Quirky science fiction spoof. A couple of California "valley girls" are among the few humans left alive and unchanged on earth after a brilliant comet, that last passed earth when the dinosaurs died, again passes overhead. Most people are killed instantly, but some unfortunate others are turned into flesh-eating zombies. The girls, however, spend their time shopping in the deserted stores, looking for guys and dodging zombies. They eventually join a band of other survivors to do battle with the zombies. Sound silly? It is, but is still more than passable entertainment.

A: Robert Beltran, Catherine Mary Stewart, Kelli Maroney, Sharon Farrell

© GOODTIMES 4017

NIGHT OF THE DEMONS

D: Kevin S. Tenney — 87 m

R | HOR | 1988 | COLOR | Sex | Nud | Viol | Lang | AdSit

6 As a prank, a group of teenagers hold a party on Halloween night inside an old abandoned funeral parlor. In the spirit of the moment, they cast a spell to call up demons from the nether world... but the spell works, and their demon is hungry for souls. Mildly gory.

A: William Gallor, Hal Havins, Mimi Kinkade, Cathy Podewell, Linnea Quigley

© REPUBLIC PICTURES HOME VIDEO 3019

NIGHT OF THE LIVING DEAD

D: George A. Romero — 95 m

R | HOR | 1968 | B&W | Sex | Nud | Viol | Lang | AdSit

9 Gruesome granddaddy of all modern horror films. This low-budget chiller was panned by the critics because of its graphic violence, but the public loved it. Its cheap grainy quality only adds to the effectiveness of the tone of terror the picture sets. Seven people are forced to lock themselves inside a farmhouse to escape rampaging flesh-eating zombies which relentlessly besiege the house. There are several scenes where you will jump right out of your skin. Watch it with a friend.

A: Judith O'Dea, Russell Streiner, Duane Jones, Keith Wayne

© COLUMBIA TRISTAR HOME VIDEO 77173

NIGHT STALKER, THE

D: Don Weis — 98 m

NR | HOR SUS | 1971 | COLOR | Sex | Nud | Viol | Lang | AdSit

8 Quite good and involving thriller with personality that was originally made for TV. It proved to be so successful that it launched a short-lived series of the same name. Darin McGavin plays a persistent wise-cracking reporter on the crime beat in Las Vegas. The city has recently been plagued by a series of grisly Jack-the-Ripper-like murders. McGavin hounds the city's establishment and keeps turning up new clues in his pursuit of the ghoulish vampirish killer. Extremely tight script with a good blending of believability, mystery, comedy, suspense and horror.

A: Darren McGavin, Simon Oakland, Carol Lynley, Claude Akins, Ralph Meeker

© MCA/UNIVERSAL HOME VIDEO, INC. 80011

OMEN, THE

D: Richard Donner 111 m

R — HOR SUS — 1976 — COLOR — Viol, Lang, AdSit

8 Very well done, high tension horror flick with a top flight cast and a good storyline. American ambassador Gregory Peck is convinced by a priest to substitute another child for his own dead newborn baby, without telling his wife (Remick). Five years later, all Hell breaks loose when several people around Damien are all killed. Peck investigates further to find that his own baby had actually been murdered at birth and that the substitute baby, Damien, is the Anti-Christ. According to the New Testament, with the arrival of the Anti-Christ the final battle between good and evil has begun. Peck must kill Damien. Thoroughly frightening. Sequel is DAMIEN - OMEN II.

A: Gregory Peck, Lee Remick, David Warner, Billie Whitelaw, Harvey Stephens, Leo McKern

© FOXVIDEO 1079

OTHER, THE

D: Robert Mulligan 100 m

PG — SUS HOR — 1972 — COLOR — Viol, Lang, AdSit

7 An eerie tale of the unnatural. During the summer of 1935, near a small Connecticut farm, there occurs a series of tragic and bizarre murders. While this film begins at an apparently slow pace, it is only laying careful groundwork and clues for the chilling story which soon begins to unwind. Two 12-year-old boys are twins. They look alike, act alike and are very dedicated to each other. But, they are different - one is very evil. People die. Only their mother and their grandmother have any suspicions of what the truth may be. This is a real chiller from Tom Tryon.

A: Uta Hagen, Diana Muldaur, John Ritter, Chris Udvarnoky, Martin Udvarnoky, Victor French

© FOXVIDEO 1729

PAPERHOUSE

D: Bernard Rose 92 m

PG-13 — SUS HOR FAN — 1989 — COLOR — Viol, Lang, AdSit

7 Bizarre, original and strangely captivating fantasy and psychological thriller. At school, Anna (a 13-year-old girl who is prone to vivid dreams) draws a strange house and, in the upstairs window, a lonely boy who cannot move. Then, feeling ill, she heads home but falls into a culvert on the way and there she has a nightmare where she sees the house and meets the boy of her picture. Anna is found and taken home. Now, she alters her drawing to match her new dream. But when the dream returns again, it has evolved once again. It is then that she learns that her doctor has another patient, a paralyzed boy and he's the boy in the window. Her dream is alive.

A: Ben Cross, Glenne Headly, Charlotte Burke, Elliott Spiers, Gemma Jones

© LIVE HOME VIDEO 5283

PEEPING TOM

D: Michael Powell 101 m

NR — SUS HOR — 1960 — COLOR — Nud, Viol, AdSit

8 This film was widely panned (and even denounced) by the critics upon its release, but it is now regarded as a significant pioneering film in psychological explorations and has become a cult favorite. It is the story of a psychopathic woman-killer. As a young boy, his father studied fear and used him as a subject. Now he is grown and he photographs his victims as they are being stabbed with his tripod, just as they die, because he enjoys the look of fear on their faces. The filming technique forces us to become voyeurs to the victim's deaths, right along with him. Very different and highly suspenseful.

A: Carl Boehm, Moira Shearer, Anna Massey, Maxine Audley, Brenda Bruce, Martin Miller

© HOME VISION PEE 030

PET SEMATARY

D: Mary Lambert 103 m

R — HOR — 1989 — COLOR — Viol, Lang, AdSit

8 Popular chiller adapted from a Stephen King novel. The Creed family has moved into a typical rural home along side a highway in the Maine wilderness. When the family's cat is hit by a car their elderly neighbor tells them of an ancient Indian legend, that if they bury the cat in a nearby ancient Indian burial ground it will be brought back. They do and the cat is brought back to life. Later, when their son is killed on the same highway and the family begins to disintegrate, they try to bring the boy back the same way. To their regret, they succeed. He is not dead, but he isn't alive either.

A: Fred Gwynne, Dale Midkiff, Denise Crosby, Miko Hughes, Brad Greenquist, Michael Lombard

© PARAMOUNT HOME VIDEO 1949

PET SEMATARY II

D: Mary Lambert 102 m

R — HOR — 1992 — COLOR — Nud, Viol, Lang, AdSit

8 A LA veterinarian takes Jeff, his 13-year-old son, back to his wife's hometown of Ludlow, Maine to bury her after she is accidentally killed, and they stay on to live there. The son is devastated by his mother's death and is struggling to fit in in this new town. His best friend is a boy who lives in fear of his violent stepfather Gus. When Gus shoots the boy's dog, the boys decide to bury him in the legendary Indian cemetery, which is said to revive the dead. When the dog is resurrected, Jeff decides that he will do the same thing with Mom. Very gory and violent, and it manages to create some moments of genuine fear. This is not a picture for kids.

A: Edward Furlong, Anthony Edwards, Clancy Brown, Jared Rushton

© PARAMOUNT HOME VIDEO 32747

PHANTASM

D: Don Coscarelli 87 m

R — HOR SF — 1979 — COLOR — Sex, Nud, Viol, Lang, AdSit

6 Popular, but bizarre, mixture of horror and science fiction that definitely does have some jump-out-your-seat moments. A 13-year-old ignores the orders of his older brother not to go to the funeral of a friend who was killed (after having sex with a strange woman in the cemetery). From the bushes, he spies a villainous, very tall man steal the body away. The two brothers follow the sinister man back to a mausoleum and find there a very bizarre world which includes a very deadly flying silver sphere with protruding daggers.

A: Michael Baldwin, Bill Thornbury, Reggie Bannister, Angus Scrimm, Ken Jones, Kathy Lester

© NEW LINE HOME VIDEO 2005

PIT AND THE PENDULUM, THE

D: Roger Corman 80 m

NR — HOR SUS — 1961 — COLOR — Viol, AdSit

6 Edgar Allan Poe's short story inspired this low-budget thriller. Vincent Price is the son of the 16th-century Spanish Inquisition's most notorious torturer, who is tortured himself by his belief that he has buried his own wife alive. Price also now believes himself to actually be his father. When his wife's brother comes to investigate his sister's death, Price takes him to the pit and the pendulum - a room where a razor sharp pendulum moves ever lower and closer to its victim with each successive sweep. A little hokey in a few spots, still very well staged and acted. Guaranteed to put a chill up your spine.

A: Vincent Price, John Kerr, Barbara Steele, Luana Anders, Anthony Carbone

© GOODTIMES 5-74043

POLTERGEIST

D: Tobe Hooper 115 m

PG — HOR — 1982 — COLOR — Viol, Lang, AdSit

9 Terrrrrriffic and chilling ghost yarn. A young family moves into a new house which, unknown to them, has been built on top of a cemetery. The unsettled spirits ("poltergeists" in German) of the cemetery are not at all pleased. At first they only move their furniture around, but then they steal away the 5-year-old daughter. All that remains of her is her voice which emanates from another world on the other side of the closet door. The family calls in a diminutive spiritualist to get the girl back. Some really nifty special effects and fast-paced excitement. Fun spookfest and a big hit, but not for most kids.

A: JoBeth Williams, Craig T. Nelson, Dominique Dunne, Oliver Robbins, Heather O'Rourke

Distributed By MGM/UA Home Video M800165

POLTERGEIST II: THE OTHER SIDE

D: Brian Gibson 92 m

PG-13 — HOR — 1986 — COLOR — Viol, Lang, AdSit

6 The TV promo announced "They're back!," and they were, but it isn't quite as much fun this time. The family moves in with the grandmother, who is a psychic, but she dies and her house is invaded by a host of evil demons (great special effects again). This time the family gets help from an Indian mystic (Sampson). He crosses over into the netherworld to do battle with their enemies there, and is assisted by the grandmother's ghost. Pretty good ghost flick. Not as good as the original, but that was a tough act to follow. Not for little kids.

A: JoBeth Williams, Craig T. Nelson, Heather O'Rourke, Zelda Rubinstein, Oliver Robins, Will Sampson

Distributed By MGM/UA Home Video M800940

POSSESSION OF JOEL DELANEY, THE

D: Waris Hussein 105 m

R — HOR — 1972 — COLOR — Nud, Viol, AdSit

6 Offbeat horror flick. Joel Delaney (King) is bored and boring. He is Shirley MacLaine's brother and he has a Puerto Rican friend, a voodoo freak, who delights in ritualistically whacking off the heads of girls. When his odd friend dies, Joel suddenly decides to move into the dead guy's apartment and has also become prone to violent outbursts. It becomes clear to MacLaine that her brother is possessed by the spirit of his dead friend. She wants her brother back and seeks the help of a voodoo priest from Spanish Harlem. But his efforts at exorcising the possessing spirit doesn't work and Joel is now out to get her, too.

A: Shirley MacLaine, Perry King, Lisa Kohane, David Elliott, Michael Hordern, Miriam Colon

© PARAMOUNT HOME VIDEO 8111

PSYCHO

D: Alfred Hitchcock 109 m

NR — SUS HOR — 1960 — B&W — Nud, Viol, AdSit

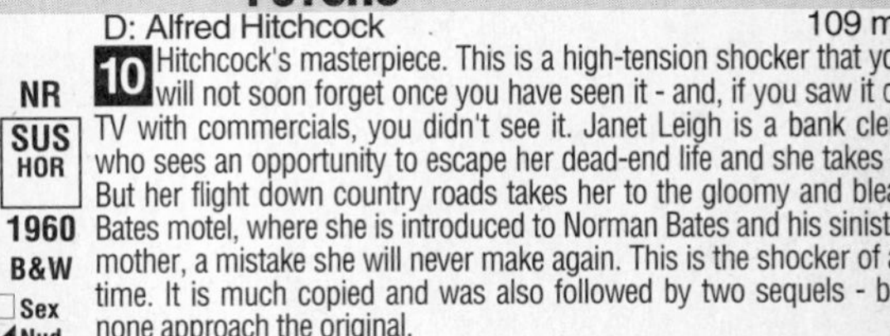

10 Hitchcock's masterpiece. This is a high-tension shocker that you will not soon forget once you have seen it - and, if you saw it on TV with commercials, you didn't see it. Janet Leigh is a bank clerk who sees an opportunity to escape her dead-end life and she takes it. But her flight down country roads takes her to the gloomy and bleak Bates motel, where she is introduced to Norman Bates and his sinister mother, a mistake she will never make again. This is the shocker of all time. It is much copied and was also followed by two sequels - but none approach the original.

A: Anthony Perkins, Janet Leigh, Martin Balsam, Vera Miles, John Gavin, John McIntire

© MCA/UNIVERSAL HOME VIDEO, INC. 55001

HOR

PSYCHO II

D: Richard Franklin 113 m

R — SUS HOR — 1983 — COLOR

7 Quite good remake of Hitchcock's masterpiece. 22 years after Norman was locked up - he's out, on the recommendation of his shrink and against the objections of Vera Miles, his previous victim's sister. Norman returns to his old neighborhood and tries to go straight. He gets a job at a local restaurant and strikes up a relationship with waitress Meg Tilly. However, it isn't long before he begins getting notes from a woman claiming to be his dead mother. Soon, the killings begin again. Respectful, and effective, remake.

Sex Nud Viol Lang AdSit

A: Anthony Perkins, Vera Miles, Meg Tilly, Robert Loggia, Dennis Franz, Hugh Gillin

© MCA/UNIVERSAL HOME VIDEO, INC. 80008

PULSE

D: Paul Golding 90 m

PG-13 — HOR SF — 1988 — COLOR

6 Well-crafted but mindless scare flick. David (Lawrence) is an 11-year-old who is visiting his father and step-mother for the summer. He is excited about being there but has become very suspicious that something is going on with the electricity. The appliances seem to have taken on a vengeful personality. The televisions and microwave seem determined to kill them. And then, the old man next door is electrocuted and his house destroyed. Now David and his stepmother are certain there is trouble, but his father refuses to believe. Tension builds slowly and believably until the exciting finish.

Sex Nud Viol Lang AdSit

A: Cliff De Young, Roxanne Hart, Joey Lawrence, Matthew Lawrence, Charles Tyner, Dennis Redfield

© COLUMBIA TRISTAR HOME VIDEO 65004

Q

D: Larry Cohen 92 m

R — HOR COM — 1982 — COLOR

6 Campy, gory, creature feature with a sense of humor. Manhattan is being terrorized by a giant winged lizard-beast that is swooping down from the huge skyscrapers and brutally killing New Yorkers. Window washers go up, but come down without their heads. When crazy Moriarty uncovers the location of the gruesome creature's nest - the Chrysler Building - the small-time crook decides to cash in and holds the city for ransom. Tongue-in-cheek humor and cheesy acting adds to the fun of this giant monster horror movie.

Sex Nud Viol Lang AdSit

A: David Carradine, Richard Roundtree, Michael Moriarty, Candy Clark, Malachy McCourt

© MCA/UNIVERSAL HOME VIDEO, INC. 71017

RE-ANIMATOR

D: Stuart Gordon 86 m

R — HOR COM — 1985 — COLOR

7 Black humor in a chilling horror film that has become a cult favorite! When a medical student (Combs) discovers a magical serum that can bring the dead back to life, he uses it. He re-animates corpses. But when they come alive, they are extremely violent. Classic gore mixes with modern special effects to produce results that are not at all for the faint at heart. The video cassette version contains violence removed from the screen version that was so grizzly that it had caused the R rating to be revoked. Very, very dark.

Sex Nud Viol Lang AdSit

A: Jeffrey Combs, Bruce Abbott, Barbara Crampton, David Gale, Robert Sampson

© LIVE HOME VIDEO VA5136

REPULSION

D: Roman Polanski 105 m

NR — HOR SUS — 1965 — B&W

9 Controversial and shocking! A beautiful but sexually repressed young woman (Deneuve) lives with her sister (Furneaux) in a London flat. She is both repulsed by sex and fascinated with it, and she can't escape it because of the affair her sister is having. When Furneaux goes on vacation for two weeks with her lover and leaves her sister alone in the apartment, Deneuve crumbles, a psychological nightmare ensues and she begins to suffer from compelling hallucinations which lead her into a murderous rampage. A thrilling psychological horror masterpiece that is sure to affect you.

Sex Nud Viol Lang AdSit

A: Catherine Deneuve, Ian Hendry, Yvonne Furneaux, John Fraser, Patrick Wymark, James Villiers

© VIDEO DIMENSIONS

RETURN OF THE LIVING DEAD, THE

D: Dan O'Bannon 86 m

R — HOR COM — 1985 — COLOR

7 A terrifying horror flick that you can laugh at too! Part fright, part funny. It takes up where NIGHT OF THE LIVING DEAD left off. When medical supply workers (James Karen and Thom Mathews) unwittingly release some poisonous gas from sealed drums, the vapors enliven several corpses in a small New Orleans town. Dead for years, these bodies wake up starving - hungry for human brains. The plentiful humor does not diminish the nail-biting gore splattered throughout. Acting is well-done with special effects that are outrageously sick. Not for those with sensitive stomachs.

Sex Nud Viol Lang AdSit

A: Clu Gulager, James Karen, Don Calfa, Thom Mathews, Linnea Quigley

© HBO VIDEO TVA3395

ROSEMARY'S BABY

D: Roman Polanski 134 m

R — HOR SUS — 1968 — COLOR

9 Stunning and compelling, stylish and chilling tale of witchcraft that is taken nearly verbatim from Ira Levin's best-selling novel. Cassavetes and Mia Farrow move into a stylish New York apartment building where, unknown to Farrow, husband Cassavetes becomes involved in a neighborhood witch's coven. Slowly she becomes aware that those seemingly friendly people around her all have ulterior motives. They want her unborn baby! Very well done, with a top-drawer cast. Terrifying because the presentation makes the story entirely believable. Ruth Gordon won Oscar for Best Supporting Actress.

Sex Nud Viol Lang AdSit

A: Mia Farrow, John Cassavetes, Ruth Gordon, Ralph Bellamy, Maurice Evans, Charles Grodin

© PARAMOUNT HOME VIDEO 6831

SALEM'S LOT

D: Tobe Hooper 111 m

NR — HOR SUS — 1979 — COLOR

7 Chilling Stephen King adaptation. A writer (David Soul) returns to the small New England town of Salem's Lot, where his aunt used to live. He hopes to derive some inspiration from her creepy old house, sitting high on a hilltop. He discovers that the house has been sold to a wicked antiques dealer (Mason) and that now the house has become a source of real evil. It is the home of a group of vampires that is determined to create an army of new followers. Soul and two friends set out to destroy them. Originally a two-part TV movie, the video contains more devilish violence. One of the best of King's film adaptations.

Sex Nud Viol Lang AdSit

A: David Soul, James Mason, Lance Kerwin, Bonnie Bedelia, Lew Ayres, Reggie Nalder

© WARNER HOME VIDEO 11336

SCANNERS

D: David Cronenberg 104 m

R — HOR SF — 1981 — COLOR

7 Shocking and gruesome, yet a perversely riveting horror tale. It is discovered too late, that a drug which was created to calm a shaky pregnancy causes the child's telekinetic powers to become dramatically increased. The child becomes a "scanner," able to probe into other people's minds. Two of the scanners (Ironside and Dane) have hatched a plot to control the world. However, the doctor who invented the drug (McGoohan) has recruited a good scanner (Lack) to block them. Beware, there is a truly mind-blowing conclusion. Intensely graphic special effects.

Sex Nud Viol Lang AdSit

A: Jennifer O'Neill, Stephen Lack, Patrick McGoohan, Lawrence Dane, Charles Shamata, Michael Ironside

© NEW LINE HOME VIDEO 2080

SCARECROWS

D: William Wesley 80 m

R — HOR SUS — 1988 — COLOR

8 Truly horrifying, hair-raising and chilling! Five ex-military men rob a bank and take off with over $3 million in cash. They hijack a cargo plane for their escape, but when one of the robbers parachutes out with all the cash, the others are forced to land the plane in an isolated cornfield that is filled with scarecrows - scarecrows which are possessed by some strange supernatural force and one by one, each man is hunted down. An excellent and well made horror flick that is finely acted and somehow made believable. Not for the faint-at-heart, there is graphic violence that die-hard horror fans will just eat up.

Sex Nud Viol Lang AdSit

A: Ted Vernon, Michael Simms, Richard Vidan

© FORUM HOME VIDEO FH79013

SENDER, THE

D: Roger Christian 92 m

R — HOR SUS — 1982 — COLOR

7 A very disturbed young man is so terrified by his nightmares that he becomes suicidal and is hospitalized. It is then discovered that he is also telepathic and can choose others to receive his projected thoughts. When his psychiatrist (Harrold) attempts to help him, she discovers that she has been chosen by him to share his tormented dreams and nightmares. Soon he loses control of his powers and the entire hospital becomes terrorized by his dreams. This is a low-key thriller in the Hitchcock vein. A good cast does a good job.

Sex Nud Viol Lang AdSit

A: Kathryn Harrold, Shirley Knight, Zeljko Ivanek, Paul Freeman, Sean Hewitt, Harry Ditson

© PARAMOUNT HOME VIDEO 1537

SENTINEL, THE

D: Michael Winner 92 m

R — HOR — 1977 — COLOR

7 A gripping and unrelenting thriller. A beautiful fashion model (Raines) moves into a Brooklyn Heights brownstone after the death of her father, but she is soon plagued by nightmares. She likes her new neighbors, so she is shocked when she is told that only she and an old priest live in the building. Her boyfriend thinks she is losing her mind. However, she soon discovers that the building is in fact occupied by demons. More disconcerting, the building is actually the gateway to Hell and she is to be the next gatekeeper. A truly unsettling film, with a really chilling climax. Based on the best-seller by Jeffrey Konvitz.

Sex Nud Viol Lang AdSit

A: Cristina Raines, Chris Sarandon, Martin Balsam, Jose Ferrer, John Carradine, Ava Gardner

© MCA/UNIVERSAL HOME VIDEO, INC. 45011

SEVENTH SIGN, THE

R | SUS HOR | 1988 | COLOR | Sex | Nud | Viol | Lang | AdSit

D: Carl Schultz 97 m

6 The seventh sign, as described in the book of Revelations, signals the end of the world. When six of the seven signs come to pass, pregnant Demi Moore begins having terrible nightmares. A strange-acting boarder (Prochnow) has taken up residence in her house. She discovers that he is carrying out the ancient prophecies from the Bible and through him she also learns that she has been chosen as an instrument of the Seventh Sign. It will come with the birth of her baby. She is having a hard time getting her husband or anyone else to believe her. Still, she is determined to stop it... but, can she.

A: Demi Moore, Michael Biehn, Jurgen Prochnow, Peter Friedman, Manny Jacobs, John Taylor

© COLUMBIA TRISTAR HOME VIDEO 67007

SHINING, THE

R | HOR SUS | 1980 | COLOR | Sex | Nud | Viol | Lang | AdSit

D: Stanley Kubrick 144 m

7 Jack Nicholson is a writer who takes a winter job as caretaker at a snowbound resort in the Rockies, where years before the caretaker had killed his family. Nicholson too becomes haunted by the isolation and the specters of the past consume him. He is possessed by the evil spirits of the place and launches a relentless assault on his own family. The horror and violence come at you with a driving force. Fans are sure to love the special effects and Nicholson's performance, although the pace can drag in spots. Stephen King's book provided the basis for this chiller.

A: Jack Nicholson, Shelley Duvall, Scatman Crothers, Danny Lloyd, Barry Nelson, Joel Turkel

© WARNER HOME VIDEO 11079

SHOUT, THE

R | SUS HOR | 1980 | COLOR | Sex | Nud | Viol | Lang | AdSit

D: Jerzy Skolimowski 90 m

7 Offbeat macabre thriller. Imagine someone who can kill just by screaming. Alan Bates is an inmate at an English asylum who claims that he can kill with a horrifying scream he learned while he lived in Australian outback with the Aborigines. Is he crazy? Ask composer John Hurt and his wife (Susannay York). He terrorized them both by demonstrating his power when he killed an innocent shepherd. Then, slowly, he began to take over their lives and seduced her. It was then that the husband discovered for himself the secret of the shout and that is how Bates came to be in the asylum. A very strange and twisted story that will hold your attention.

A: Alan Bates, Susannah York, John Hurt, Tim Curry, Robert Stephens

© UNITED AMERICAN VIDEO CORP. 17198

SILVER BULLET

R | HOR | 1985 | COLOR | Sex | Nud | Viol | Lang | AdSit

D: Daniel Attias 95 m

7 Gruesome and gory adaptation of the Stephen King novel. In a small town, someone, or something, is savagely murdering the townsfolk. Only one young boy, who has been confined to a wheelchair since birth, knows the answer and has the courage to face the monstrous killer. His problem is that he must convince his sister and alcoholic uncle (Busey) that a werewolf is the unknown murderer. The final confrontation between the werewolf and a silver bullet is a fast-paced, white knuckle ride.

A: Gary Busey, Everett McGill, Corey Haim, Megan Follows, Terry O'Quinn, Robin Groves

© PARAMOUNT HOME VIDEO 1827

SISTERS

R | SUS HOR | 1973 | COLOR | Sex | Nud | Viol | Lang | AdSit

D: Brian De Palma 92 m

7 A hair-raising psychological thriller in the Hitchcock tradition! A pair of identical Siamese twins (Margot Kidder) are surgically separated as teenagers. One twin makes it out of the operation with her sanity intact and is gentle and kind, but the other becomes a homicidal maniac. The trouble is, you see, you never really know which is which. Peering from a bedroom window, a newspaper reporter (Jennifer Salt) witnesses the brutal stabbing of a talk show host, but not the killer. The police don't believe her, so she hires a private detective (Durning). Together they seek to expose the killer and also uncover the nightmare of the sisters. Intense suspense.

A: Margot Kidder, Jennifer Salt, Charles Durning, Barnard Hughes, William Finley, Mary Davenport

© WARNER HOME VIDEO 26002

STEPFATHER, THE

R | SUS HOR | 1987 | COLOR | Sex | Nud | Viol | Lang | AdSit

D: Joseph Ruben 89 m

8 A chilling story about a charming man with a great smile and who seemingly has a perfect family. But, when they disappoint him - he kills them. And, when no one catches him, he just settles in a new town and gets a new family. The stepfather (O'Quinn) is obsessed with setting up the ideal family and this time it's with Shelly Hack and teenager Jill Schoelen. He's so friendly that no one suspects him, but something doesn't feel right to Schoelen. She has him checked out and begins to suspect the awful truth. Now she's become a risk to dad. Touches of humor are interjected throughout that provide an escape from the madness.

A: Terry O'Quinn, Jill Schoelen, Shelley Hack

© NEW LINE HOME VIDEO 7567

SWEENEY TODD

NR | MUS HOR | 1982 | COLOR | Sex | Nud | Viol | Lang | AdSit

D: Harold Prince 139 m

8 Truly spooky! A demented barber is the center of focus in this film that is really the Sondheim stage musical filmed in its entirety. The barber Todd (Hearn), falsely sent to prison by the Mayor, is released to find his wife gone mad and his daughter kidnapped by the Mayor. He loses his grip in seeking revenge against the system and begins slashing the throats of his customers. Their remains, given to the haunting Mrs. Lovett (Lansbury), are then baked in her meat pies. Filmed before a live audience at the Dorothy Chandler Pavilion in L.A. The play won 8 Tony Awards in 1979, including Best Musical and Best Actress.

A: Angela Lansbury, George Hearn, Sara Woods

© TURNER HOME ENTERTAINMENT 1002

TALES FROM THE DARKSIDE: THE MOVIE

R | HOR | 1990 | COLOR | Sex | Nud | Viol | Lang | AdSit

D: John Harrison 93 m

6 Three solid horror tales are connected by the narration of a boy who is telling the tales while trying to hold off the threat of a cannibalistic housewife and modern-day witch (Deborah Harry) who wants to put him in the oven. The stories are: a cat from hell that seeks revenge for the deaths of laboratory animals, a mummy that is loose in a college fraternity, and a gargoyle that comes to life to terrorize New York. This is not a masterpiece but it is at least a good step above TV fare. Gory.

A: Deborah Harry, Christian Slater, William Hickey, David Johansen, Rae Dawn Chong, James Remar

© PARAMOUNT HOME VIDEO 32360

TENANT, THE

R | SUS HOR | 1976 | COLOR | Sex | Nud | Viol | Lang | AdSit

D: Roman Polanski 126 m

8 Very unique and unusual film. Polanski cast himself as a timid Polish clerk who rents a flat in a seedy Parisian apartment building. The previous tenant, a young girl, committed suicide by leaping to her death. He has great difficulty interacting with his neighbors. Gradually, he begins to lose his grip on reality and begins to fear that the people in the building are also trying to drive him into suicide too. Bizarrely fascinating and darkly comic, but this is a film about burgeoning madness and is not at all a typical horror film, yet in many ways it is more creepy.

A: Isabelle Adjani, Melvin Douglas, Jo Van Fleet, Bernard Fresson, Shelley Winters

© PARAMOUNT HOME VIDEO 8676

THEATER OF BLOOD

R | HOR COM | 1973 | COLOR | Sex | Nud | Viol | Lang | AdSit

D: Douglas Hickox 105 m

6 Flamboyant film in which Price plays a Shakespearean actor who fakes his own death so that he can get revenge upon nine critics who have been less than kind to him throughout his career and have denied him the Best Actor of the Year Award. With the aid of his equally demented daughter (delicious Diana Rigg), he recreates particularly appropriate Shakespearean scenarios within which to extract his ghoulish punishments. Somewhat gory, but funny, too. A combination that has gained it a cult following.

A: Vincent Price, Diana Rigg, Ian Hendry, Robert Morley, Jack Hawkins, Harry Andrews

Distributed By MGM/UA Home Video M600902

THING, THE

R | HOR SF SUS | 1982 | COLOR | Sex | Nud | Viol | Lang | AdSit

D: John Carpenter 109 m

7 The 1951 classic has been remade. However, it would be more accurate to say that this is more of a sequel. This version, however, is not for the little kiddies - it is filled with gore. Where the original relied upon your imagination to create fear, this version gives you a series of state-of-the-art gory special effects. Kurt Russell and his people arrive at the remote arctic station just after an alien creature, which had been defrosted after having been frozen for years, has depleted the supply of live bodies. This new crew will soon be his new supply. This is scary and fun, but check out the original, too. It is, in many ways, better.

A: Kurt Russell, Wilford Brimley, Richard Dysart, Richard Masur, T.K. Carter, Richard Dysart

© MCA/UNIVERSAL HOME VIDEO, INC. 77009

TOMB OF LIGEIA

VINCENT PRICE stars in this Edgar Allan Poe classic
TOMB of LIGEIA

NR | HOR | 1964 | COLOR | Sex | Nud | Viol | Lang | AdSit

D: Roger Corman 82 m

7 Stylish and spooky film by Roger Corman. It is his last entry in a series of horror flicks that were inspired by the stories of Edgar Alan Poe. Vincent Price is obsessed with his dead wife and he marries a woman who looks like her. She, however, is understandably upset when she discovers that he sleeps in the crypt of his dead wife. The spirit of the dead woman returns first in the form of their cat and then in the new bride herself. This is a well-done spook film that was also shot on the sets left over from the filming of BECKET.

A: Vincent Price, Elizabeth Shepherd, John Westbrook, Richard Johnson, Derek Francis

© HBO VIDEO TVC3681

TREMORS

D: Ron Underwood 95 m

PG-13 | HOR COM | 1989 | COLOR | Sex | Nud | Viol | Lang | AdSit

7 A genuinely exciting and yet funny monster movie that is a direct throw-back to the 50s. Two comic handymen (Bacon and Ward), whose prime ambition is just to leave the dead-end town of Perfection, Nevada, have their departure interrupted and they get a little more excitement than usual when the town is attacked by hungry giant worm-like creatures capable of swallowing a car. The two join forces with a pretty female seismology student (Carter) and a heavily-armed survivalist couple (Gross and McEntire) in a battle to defeat the scheming treacherous worms. Genuinely fun. Fast-paced with good special effects.

A: Kevin Bacon, Fred Ward, Finn Carter, Michael Gross, Reba McEntire

TWICE-TOLD TALES

D: Sidney Salkow 120 m

NR | HOR | 1963 | COLOR | Sex | Nud | Viol | Lang | AdSit

6 Fright fans take notice. Vincent Price stars in three separate thrillers loosely based on stories from the famous 19th-century writer Nathaniel Hawthorne. The stories are: "Dr. Heidegger's Experiment" - a doctor brings his dead wife back to life and she then tells him a secret; "Rappaccini's Daughter" - who was raised on deadly herbs by her brilliant father and now just her touch is deadly; and "The House of the Seven Gables" - a man returns to the house to search for hidden treasure and is haunted by a vengeful spirit. Rich in atmosphere, with good characterizations from a talented cast.

A: Vincent Price, Sebastian Cabot, Brett Halsey, Joyce Taylor, Beverly Garland

VANISHING, THE

D: George Sluizer 105 m

NR | FOR HOR SUS | 1991 | COLOR | Sex | Nud | Viol | Lang | AdSit

9 Icy thriller! This is a major league intellectual and psychological chiller. The terror here is not heavy-handed and obvious, but is more of the Hitchcock or the Edgar Allen Poe variety. Two young lovers are traveling when they run out of gas. He thoughtlessly leaves her behind, terrified and alone. She's furious but they make up and go to a rest area to play. She leaves to go to a store but she never returns. Haunted by her loss, he places posters all over requesting information. After three years, a seemingly genteel professor sends him a tantalizing note. Subtle, but deeply and profoundly shocking. Subtitles.

A: Gene Bervoets, Johanna Ter Steege, Bernard-Pierre Donnadieu

HOR

VANISHING, THE

D: George Sluizer 110 m

R | SUS HOR | 1993 | COLOR | Sex | Nud | Viol | Lang | AdSit

8 One of the most diabolical plots ever put on the screen was first done in Holland. It proved to be so successful that Hollywood redid it here, using the same director. The story concerns a young man (Sutherland) and his girlfriend (Bullock) who leave together to go on a trip. Midway into the trip, she just disappears without a trace at a roadside stop. Sutherland is consumed with finding her, but after three years, he would be satisfied to only know what happened. Jeff Bridges is a quirky chemistry professor who knows the answer and offers to show him. Not as good as the original but still plenty of sheer terror.

A: Kiefer Sutherland, Jeff Bridges, Sandra Bullock, Nancy Travis, Park Overall, Maggie Linderman

VILLAGE OF THE DAMNED

D: Wolf Rilla 77 m

HOR SF | 1960 | B&W | Sex | Nud | Viol | Lang | AdSit

8 Eerie, suspenseful and frightening! All the women in a small English village mysteriously become pregnant at the same time and give birth to a strange group of emotionless, super-intelligent children. They all have blond hair, physically develop very rapidly, and also possess telekinetic powers. George Sanders is the father of the children's leader. He takes it upon himself to become their teacher and he learns even more about them. Then the children, with an eerie calmness, begin to terrorize the village. Even though they can read his every thought, Sanders decides that they must be destroyed.

A: George Sanders, Barbara Shelley, Michael Gwynne, Laurence Naismith, John Phillips, Richard Vernon

WARLOCK: THE ARMAGEDDON

D: Anthony Hickox 98 m

R | HOR FAN | 1993 | COLOR | Sex | Nud | Viol | Lang | AdSit

6 Once every millennium the devil trys to reappear upon and reclaim earth. In order to accomplish his complete return, his agent must possess the five magic rune stones. It is the God-given task of the Druids to prevent that from happening. Now is the time of this millennium for Satan to return. The Warlock has come to recover the stones to make way for his coming. He captures three of the stones and makes his way to California to recover the last two which are in the possession of a small group of Druids. The son and daughter of two of them are chosen to be warriors to battle the Warlock and prevent his recovering the last stones. Extremely gory and violent.

A: Julian Sands, Chris Young, Paula Marshall, Steve Kahan, Charles Hallahan, R.G. Armstrong

WES CRAVEN'S NEW NIGHTMARE

D: Wes Craven 111 m

R | HOR | 1994 | COLOR | Sex | Nud | Viol | Lang | AdSit

6 Yes, Freddy Krueger is back yet again. Unlike, most of the many sequels that followed the original NIGHTMARE ON ELMSTREET, this one has something that makes it slightly different, if no less gory and mindless. This time, the stars of the preceeding movies appear playing themselves. Heather Langenkamp is now grown, a mother of a little boy and married to a special effects man. Wes Craven, the director of the other films, has called her into his office to ask her to again reprise her role. However, she has been having real-life nightmares and been getting menacing phone calls. It seems that the spirit of Freddy has made the leap from movies to become her real-life nemesis.

A: Heather Langenkamp, Robert Englund, Miko Hughes, Wes Craven, John Saxon

WHAT EVER HAPPEND TO BABY JANE?

D: Robert Aldrich 134 m

NR | SUS HOR | 1962 | B&W | Sex | Nud | Viol | Lang | AdSit

8 A truly scary journey into strange minds. This is a character profile of two perverse and rivalrous personalities which are masterfully portrayed by two screen legends. Bette Davis is Baby Jane. She is a child star from the silent era who never made it in talking pictures. Joan Crawford is her sister who did, but she was mysteriously crippled in a car accident and has been an invalid for 30 years. For 30 years Davis has taken care of her sister and tormented her. When Crawford announces she is going to sell the house, Davis really goes off her rocker and reverts to her childhood. A masterpiece of terror. A big hit.

A: Bette Davis, Joan Crawford, Victor Buono, Anna Lee, Marjorie Bennett

WHEN A STRANGER CALLS

D: Fred Walton 97 m

R | SUS HOR | 1979 | COLOR | Sex | Nud | Viol | Lang | AdSit

8 A genuinely scary thriller. A teenage baby sitter (Carol Kane) is terrorized by a mysterious phone caller. Police detective Durning traces the calls and discovers that the man (Beckley) is already inside the house. He captures the invader but not before he has killed the children in the house. The murderous intruder is sent away, but seven years later he escapes and he has come back to torment Kane again. This time she has kids of her own and she is terrified. Kane again calls Durning who is now a private detective to help her again. This is a very high intensity suspense film for the first part, but it lets down some near the end. Still, it is a real shocker.

A: Charles Durning, Carol Kane, Colleen Dewhurst, Tony Beckley, Rachel Roberts, Ron O'Neal

WHITE OF THE EYE

D: Donald Cammell 111 m

R | SUS HOR | 1987 | COLOR | Sex | Nud | Viol | Lang | AdSit

6 Bizarre little thriller. A psycho is loose in a small Arizona town. If you are beautiful and rich you are more likely to see him. That is unwelcome because he is torturing and then dissecting his female victims. David Keith is an audio expert unfaithfully married to an immigrant from New York. She is understandably upset because she and her daughter are getting threatening messages - and her husband is the chief suspect of head cop Evans. The interesting photography and ample twists hold your attention and keep you guessing all the way to the end. And, the ending will leave many unsettled.

A: David Keith, Cathy Moriarty, Art Evans, Alberta Watson

WOLF

D: Mike Nichols 125 m

R | SUS HOR | 1994 | COLOR | Sex | Nud | Viol | Lang | AdSit

7 Senior book editor Jack Nicholson's car strikes a wolf on a lonely stretch of Vermont highway. As Jack attempts to move the animal out of the roadway he is bitten. Just days later, the area around the bite begins to grow hair and he also becomes aware that all his senses are now heightened. Formerly a non-aggressive type, he strikes back now with a vengeance when his job is given to his underhanded protege after their publishing house becomes the subject of a tycoon's takeover; and, Jack's passions become aroused by the man's beautiful but troubled daughter (Pfeiffer). Sophisticated storytelling where the werewolf's bite is only a key that unlocks its victim's true nature.

A: Jack Nicholson, Michelle Pfeiffer, James Spader

WOLFEN

D: Michael Wadleigh 114 m

R | HOR SUS | 1981 | COLOR | Sex | Nud | Viol | Lang | AdSit

8 Effective surrealistic chiller with some really terrifying moments. Albert Finney is a NYC detective who sets out to penetrate the mystery surrounding a series of particularly gory and grisly murders that appear at first to have nothing in common. Aided by a psychologist (Venora) and a wry coroner (Hines), his search leads him to the discovery of a group of American Indians who control a pack of ancient, truly evil supernatural superwolves. Superior special effects and innovative camera work combine with some excellent acting to overcome some other minor shortcomings to make this a chilling experience.

A: Albert Finney, Diane Venora, Edward James Olmos, Gregory Hines, Tom Noonan, Dick O'Neill

YOUNG FRANKENSTEIN

D: Mel Brooks 106 m

PG

COM HOR

1974

B&W

Sex
Nud
Viol
Lang
AdSit

9 This ranks right up there with BLAZING SADDLES, the other masterpiece from Mel Brooks - master of zany spoofs. This one rips into Frankenstein movies. Gene Wilder is a modern-day college professor who disdains his family's jaded history and goes back to Transylvania to get it right this time. Gags are nonstop. Hysterical scenes with Boyle as his monster and Marty Feldman as his hunch-back assistant. Music, sets and props, which are reminiscent of the '30s, all add to the fun. Hilarious the whole way through.

A: Gene Wilder, Peter Boyle, Marty Feldman, Madeline Kahn, Cloris Leachman, Teri Garr

© FOXVIDEO 1103

Musicals

1956 and After

1776

G | MUS | 1972 | COLOR

D: Peter H. Hunt — 148 m

8 This is a witty and spirited musical retelling of how the United States was founded. This Pulitzer Prize-winning film is a re-creation of the hit Broadway musical stage play by Peter Stone, and it includes nearly all of the original cast. The primary focus is the signing of the Declaration of Independence and it includes the discussions and debate over who should write it - John Adams (Daniels) or Tom Jefferson (Howard). Ben Franklin (da Silva), however, wonders if the document will even be passed in such a divided congress. Entertaining and fun!

Sex / Nud / Viol / Lang / AdSit

A: William Daniels, Howard da Silva, Ken Howard, Blythe Danner, Ronald Holgate, John Cullum

© COLUMBIA TRISTAR HOME VIDEO 60204

ABSOLUTE BEGINNERS

PG-13 | MUS ROM | 1986 | COLOR

D: Julien Temple — 107 m

6 Enthusiastic British musical production made especially for the screen by a director of music videos. Set in 1958 London, it is the somewhat typical story of love sought for, found, lost and found again. At times it reminds one of WEST SIDE STORY but, overall, falls short of that lofty goal. While the plot is weak, the music and dance scenes do redeem any shortcomings. (However, it also helps if the viewer is British.) Outstanding jazz score. See also WEST SIDE STORY, to see how a truly great teenage-love musical is done.

Sex / Nud / Viol / Lang / AdSit

A: Eddie O'Connell, Patsy Kensit, David Bowie, James Fox, Ray Davies, Ege Ferret

© HBO VIDEO TVA3900

ALL THAT JAZZ

R | DMA MUS | 1980 | COLOR

D: Bob Fosse — 123 m

7 Adult autobiographical musical from Bob Fosse. A driven, egotistical chainsmoker encounters the angel of death (in the lovely form of Jessica Lange) after suffering a heart attack resulting from the overwhelming pressures caused by working on a film, working on a Broadway musical, as well as trying to please his wife, his mistress, and his daughter. The musical numbers are quite extraordinary - stunning and sometimes shocking. Scheider's finest performance, with solid assistance from Ben Vereen and Cliff Gorman.

Sex / Nud / Viol / Lang / AdSit

A: Roy Scheider, Ann Reinking, Jessica Lange, Leland Palmer, Cliff Gorman, Ben Vereen

© FOXVIDEO 1095

ALL THE MORNINGS OF THE WORLD

NR | FOR MUS | 1993 | COLOR

D: Alain Marielle — 110 m

9 This is a wonderfully photographed French period piece, set in the 17th-century, that won 7 Cesar Awards, including Best Picture. While it is a favorite of the critics, it is also ponderous and very slow-moving. It is the story of a reclusive genius composer, who locks himself and his two beautiful daughters away from the world upon the death of his wife. The arrival of a flamboyant and talented young student draws the old man out enough to allow the younger one in for lessons. All of which is much to the approval of one of the daughters, but she is soon destroyed by her passions. The average viewer will be bored, but sophisticated romantic ones will be captivated. Subtitled.

Sex / Nud / Viol / Lang / AdSit

A: Jean-Pierre Marielle, Gerard Depardieu, Anne Brochet, Guillaume Depardieu, Michel Bouquet, Jean-Claude Dreyfus

© TOUCHSTONE HOME VIDEO 2234

AMADEUS

PG | DMA COM MUS | 1984 | COLOR

D: Milos Forman — 158 m

7 A witty production that won eight Oscars (including Best Picture, Actor and Director) with its literate, sophisticated script and superb performances. Salieri (Abraham) is a successful but mediocre composer. Still, he has great influence in the courts of Venice. Along comes Mozart, a brash young composer who effortlessly produces works of dazzling brilliance. Salieri is intensely jealous of Mozart's talent but is also disgusted with this boy-genius composer who is also a womanizer and a boor. So, he does all that he can to sabotage and destroy Mozart, but instead destroys himself. Slightly overlong.

Sex / Nud / Viol / Lang / AdSit

A: Tom Hulce, F. Murray Abraham, Elizabeth Beridge, Simon Callow, Roy Dotrice, Christine Ebersole

© HBO VIDEO 2997

ANNIE

PG | MUS CLD | 1982 | COLOR

D: John Huston — 128 m

8 The comic strip story of the little orphan girl with the perpetual optimism comes to life. Annie (Quinn) is a red-haired orphan girl who dreams of life outside the orphanage, but her plans to escape are constantly foiled by Miss Hannigan, the drunken head mistress (Burnett). One day Annie is chosen to go to live for a short time with hugely rich Daddy Warbucks (Finney). They hit it off and days become weeks. But Miss Hannigan continues to plot to get her back. Big, splashy and over-produced, but it's still all there and it's fine family entertainment.

Sex / Nud / Viol / Lang / AdSit

A: Albert Finney, Carol Burnett, Aileen Quinn, Bernadette Peters, Tim Curry, Geoffrey Holder

© COLUMBIA TRISTAR HOME VIDEO 60127

AUNTIE MAME

NR | COM MUS | 1958 | COLOR

D: Morton DaCosta — 144 m

9 Funny and very entertaining. Russell is a tour-de-force in the title role as a colorful 1920's free-thinking eccentric aunt of an orphaned boy she adopts. She thinks "life is a banquet, and most poor suckers are starving to death." The boy, a sensible and down-to-earth type, has to learn to adapt to his lively live-for-today aunt. The story was first a hit Broadway play and the same cast was then transported into this film production. Hugely successful, it was nominated for six Academy Awards and was the top grossing film of 1959. A lot of fun.

Sex / Nud / Viol / Lang / AdSit

A: Rosalind Russell, Forrest Tucker, Coral Browne, Fred Clark, Peggy Cass, Roger Smith

© WARNER HOME VIDEO 11152

BACKBEAT

R | DMA MUS | 1994 | COLOR

D: Ian Softley — 100 m

8 Before there were The Beatles, John Lennon and Stuart Sutcliff were best friends. This film is set in 1960, before The Beatles were discovered and is not really a story of the group. It is more the story of the relationship between Lennon and Sutcliff. The group, then including Sutcliff, had gone to Germany to play in strip joints, hone their skills and have some fun. The band was Lennon's dream. Sutcliff was only a so-so musician, but he was a talented painter and in Germany he met a beautiful avant-guarde photographer Astrid Kirchherr. He fell in love and eventually left both Lennon and the group, but he died of a brain hemorrhage at only 21. An interesting look at backstage life.

Sex / Nud / Viol / Lang / AdSit

A: Sheryl Lee, Stephen Dorff, Ian Hart, Gary Bakewell, Chris O'Neill, Hellena Schmied

© POLYGRAM VIDEO 6317713

BEACH BOYS, THE - AN AMERICAN BAND

PG-13 | MUS DOC | 1985 | COLOR

D: — 103 m

6 This is the "authorized," therefore somewhat sanitized, story of the rock `n roll group with the happy California sun-filled beach sound who, along with the English invasion of groups like The Beatles in the early 60s, came to mark the beginning of a significant change in the direction of rock `n roll music. The Beach Boys had been an American institution for 25 years by the time this film was made and it is primarily a celebration of their brand of music. It contains over 40 original songs and lots of behind-the-scenes footage. However, none of the band's troubles behind the glamour is discussed.

Sex / Nud / Viol / Lang / AdSit

A: The Beach Boys

© LIVE HOME VIDEO VA5080

BEAUTY AND THE BEAST

G | CLD MUS | 1991 | COLOR

D: Gary Trousdale, Kirk Wise — 90 m

10 Disney received the first-ever Best Picture nomination for an animated feature for this delightful instant classic. The story is that of the beautiful daughter of an eccentric father, who is made a prisoner in the isolated and desolate castle of a hideous beast that loves her. The essentials of the classic storyline are all there but everything is given a Disney twist and set to music in a score that took home an Oscar, as did its title tune. Except, this time around everything is more fanciful: All the household fixtures come to life and sing. Delightful. Children 6 & up are held spellbound, but it's a little slow for the very youngest ones.

Sex / Nud / Viol / Lang / AdSit

A:

© WALT DISNEY HOME VIDEO 1325

BELLS ARE RINGING

NR | COM MUS ROM | 1960 | COLOR

D: Vincente Minnelli — 126 m

8 Upbeat musical that was brought to the big screen from Broadway. Judy Holliday plays a shy telephone answering service operator who uses her knowledge of her clients's problems to help them all out. She also has fallen secretly in love with playboy playwright Dean Martin, even though they have never met. He just thinks she is just a nice little old lady passing out advice and so thinks of her only as "Mom." A delightful MGM musical. 14 musical numbers. Songs include "Just in Time." See the Director's index under Vincente Minnelli for other classic musicals. He did a lot of them.

Sex / Nud / Viol / Lang / AdSit

A: Judy Holliday, Dean Martin, Fred Clark, Eddie Foy, Jr., Jean Stapleton, Frank Gorshin

Distributed By MGM/UA Home Video M700063

BEST LITTLE WHOREHOUSE IN TEXAS, THE

R | MUS COM | 1982 | COLOR

D: Colin Higgins — 115 m

6 Light-hearted film version of the successful Broadway musical about one of the most famous real-life whorehouses of all time. Burt plays the unfortunate sheriff of a small Texas town who is getting severe pressure to put the town's most popular and revered institution (and his madam girlfriend Dolly Parton) out of business. That unpopular popular institution is the famous whorehouse called the Chicken Ranch. This film version is not as lively as the stage version and is somewhat slow in spots, but it still has enough going for it to recommend it as a good time.

Sex / Nud / Viol / Lang / AdSit

A: Dolly Parton, Burt Reynolds, Lois Nettleton, Dom DeLuise, Charles Durning, Jim Nabors

© MCA/UNIVERSAL HOME VIDEO, INC. 77014

BIRD

R | DMA MUS | 1988 | COLOR

D: Clint Eastwood — 161 m

7 Heartfelt story about the sad life of a jazz giant. Legendary, brilliant saxophonist Charlie Parker revolutionized jazz in the 1940s, but Charlie Parker was also addicted to drugs and booze and died young. Eastwood's direction captures the spirit of the seedy hotel rooms and bars that made up Parker's life, and Whitaker is excellent as Bird Parker. The sax music you hear is actually Parker's, but it is accompanied by modern recordings by studio musicians.

Sex / Nud / Viol / Lang / AdSit

A: Forest Whitaker, Diane Venora, Samuel E. Wright, Keith David, Michael McGuire, James Handy

© WARNER HOME VIDEO 11820

BIZET'S CARMEN

PG | MUS FOR ROM | 1983 | COLOR

D: — 151 m

7 Opera is taken off the stage and into the streets when this opera favorite is filmed on location. Placido Domingo plays the aristocratic Spanish soldier who loses his heart and ruins his life when he frees a faithless, beautiful Spanish gypsy from prison in this classic opera. Actually filmed on location in the streets of Spain, this production has true dramatic force, as well as powerful music and beautiful singing.

Sex / Nud / Viol / Lang / AdSit

A: Julia Migenes-Johnson, Placido Domingo, Ruggero Raimondi, Faith Esham, Jean-Philippe Lafont

© COLUMBIA TRISTAR HOME VIDEO 60487

BLUE HAWAII

NR | MUS ROM | 1961 | COLOR

D: Norman Taurog — 106 m

6 One of Elvis's most popular flicks. Elvis plays the son of a rich family who returns home to Hawaii after a stint in the service. The heir to a pineapple fortune, he upsets his parents by wanting to work in a tourist bureau instead. Great locations. Plenty of music, pretty girls and romance. Over a dozen songs, including one of his prettiest-ever hits: "Can't Help Falling in Love With You." The sound track was the fastest-selling album of 1961.

Sex / Nud / Viol / Lang / AdSit

A: Elvis Presley, Joan Blackman, Nancy Walters, Angela Lansbury, Roland Winters, Iris Adrian

© CBS/FOX VIDEO 2001

BLUES BROTHERS, THE

R | COM MUS | 1980 | COLOR

D: John Landis — 133 m

8 Funny movie and some great music, too. It is a farcical adventure in which two losers (Aykroyd and Belushi) find that the orphanage they grew up in has fallen on hard times, so they decide to resurrect their old blues band to raise some money to save it. Riotous misadventures ensue as they gather everyone up, get a gig in a redneck bar and very nearly destroy Chicago with several car chases on their way to a benefit concert. Many major stars like Aretha Franklin, James Brown and Ray Charles cameo. A lot of slapstick and some dynamite music, too.

Sex / Nud / Viol / Lang / AdSit

A: John Belushi, Dan Aykroyd, John Candy, Carrie Fisher, Cab Calloway, Ray Charles

© MCA/UNIVERSAL HOME VIDEO, INC. 77000

BOUND FOR GLORY

PG | DMA MUS | 1976 | COLOR

D: Hal Ashby — 149 m

8 This moving biography is of Woodie Guthrie, a famous singer/composer of some of America's most favorite folk songs ("This Land is Your land"). It focuses primarily on the depression years when Guthrie traveled across America primarily by rail. The vignettes of that sad period of American history and those hit hardest by it, provide us with a window into the suffering that made up the soul of his songs. Carradine is superb as Gutherie. Won 2 Oscars: Photography and Score.

Sex / Nud / Viol / Lang / AdSit

A: David Carradine, Ronny Cox, Melinda Dillon, Gail Strickland, Randy Quaid, John Lehne

Distributed By MGM/UA Home Video M600878

BOY FRIEND, THE

G | MUS COM | 1971 | COLOR

D: Ken Russell — 137 m

6 When the leading lady (Jackson) breaks her ankle, she is quickly replaced by the assistant stage manager (Twiggy). This is an interesting musical that works actually in two different ways. First, as a 1920s musical production of "The Boy Friend," which is being put on at a tacky matinee; and also as a vehicle for the much more elaborate Busby Berkeley production numbers which occur within the daydreams of the matinee's participants. It will be most entertaining to fans of the '30s musicals genre. Fourteen songs in all. Glenda Jackson has a cameo as the lead hoofer.

Sex / Nud / Viol / Lang / AdSit

A: Twiggy, Christopher Gable, Moyra Fraser, Max Adrian, Vladek Sheybal, Glenda Jackson

Distributed By MGM/UA Home Video M200306

BRING ON THE NIGHT

PG-13 | MUS DOC | 1986 | COLOR

D: Michael Apted — 90 m

7 This is an interesting behind the scenes look at Sting and his band for his fans. It allows you to meet each one individually and to watch them while they are creating, rehearsing, meeting the press, performing and dealing with their own private lives.

Sex / Nud / Viol / Lang / AdSit

A: Sting

© WARNER HOME VIDEO 344

BRUCE SPRINGSTEEN VIDEO ANTHOLOGY/1978-88

MUS | 1988 | COLOR

D: — 100 m

8 Concert footage of Springsteen. Contains eighteen of his songs.

Sex / Nud / Viol / Lang / AdSit

A: Bruce Springsteen

© CBS MUSIC VIDEO ENTERPRISES 24V-49010

BUDDY HOLLY STORY

D: Steve Rash — 113 m

PG · DMA MUS · 1978 · COLOR

8 One of the best rock `n roll movies ever. Gary Busey was Oscar-nominated for his bravura performance as Buddy Holly - the legendary Texas boy who combined country music with rhythm and blues. This is not the typical glossed-over Hollywood version of a poor boy made good, but an accurate representation of the Texas rock legend up until his tragic death. Busey's energetic impersonation of Holly includes live performances of the classic "That'll Be the Day," "It's So Easy," "Peggy Sue" and others. See also LA BAMBA for Richie Valens's story.

Sex · Nud · Viol · Lang · ◢ AdSit

A: Gary Busey, Charles Martin Smith, Dick O'Neil, Maria Richwine, Conrad Janis, Amy Johnson

© COLUMBIA TRISTAR HOME VIDEO 60801

BYE BYE BIRDIE

D: George Sidney — 112 m

NR · MUS COM · 1963 · COLOR

7 Lots of fun in this film adaptation of a big Broadway hit. An Elvis-like rock `n roll sensation is being drafted into the Army. His manager, who is facing unemployment, launches a nationwide contest to find one lucky girl to give him a last goodbye kiss on the Ed Sullivan Show. When it turns out to be Ann-Margret, her home town, particularly her father (Paul Lynde), is thrown into a tizzy. Songs include "Kids" and "Put on a Happy Face." Really entertaining little piece of musical fluff. This was also Ann-Margret's film debut.

Sex · Nud · Viol · Lang · AdSit

A: Janet Leigh, Dick Van Dyke, Bobby Rydell, Maureen Stapleton, Paul Lynde, Ann-Margret

© COLUMBIA TRISTAR HOME VIDEO 60150

CABARET

D: Bob Fosse — 124 m

PG · MUS DMA COM · 1972 · COLOR

9 A brilliant piece of work which won eight Oscars and is undoubtedly one of the best movie musicals ever. It is the story of Germany in 1931 and a young American girl caught up in its bawdy decadence. Hitler's Nazis had not yet captured full power and life was carefree, decadent and even sleazy; but doom is looming. Liza is a naive cabaret showgirl caught up in the carefree mood of the time and torn between two lovers. Wonderful songs steal the show; most notable are: "The Money Song" with Grey and Minnelli and the chorus line doing "Mein Heir."

Sex · Nud · Viol · ◢ Lang · ■ AdSit

A: Liza Minnelli, Michael York, Helmut Griem, Joel Grey, Fritz Wepper, Marisa Berenson

© WARNER HOME VIDEO 785

CAMELOT

D: Joshua Logan — 179 m

G · MUS ROM · 1967 · COLOR

8 The beautiful and fanciful romance legend of King Arthur and the Round Table was first brought to the Broadway stage by Lerner & Loewe. This is a thoroughly enjoyable big-budget film presentation of that same musical. It is the story of one man trying to balance his dream for justice in a better world and his great love for Guenevere, who loves someone else more than him. Beautiful sets, wonderful music and a tragic story, from the first meeting of Arthur and Guenevere, through the forbidden love affair with Guenevere and Lancelot, and finally to the downfall of Camelot. 3 Oscars.

Sex · Nud · Viol · Lang · ◢ AdSit

A: Richard Harris, Vanessa Redgrave, Franco Nero, David Hemmings, Lionel Jefferies

© WARNER HOME VIDEO 11084

CAN-CAN

D: Walter Lang — 131 m

NR · MUS · 1960 · COLOR

7 It's 1896 Paris and the Can-Can just has been banned. Shirley MacLaine performs the naughty dance in her Paris nightclub anyway because her attorney (Frank Sinatra) has a judge (Chevalier) in his pocket. But everything changes when a new judge (Jourdan) threatens to stop it. Cole Porter's music is outstanding and there is a lot of energy expended in the dances. It's the music and dancing that make this worth watching. Everything else is so-so.

Sex · Nud · Viol · Lang · ◢ AdSit

A: Frank Sinatra, Shirley MacLaine, Maurice Chevalier, Louis Jordan, Juliet Prowse, Marcel Dalio

© FOXVIDEO 1016

CAROUSEL

D: Henry King — 128 m

NR · MUS ROM · 1956 · COLOR

10 Rogers and Hammerstein's classic musical is memorably brought to life with lavish production numbers and the beautiful voices of Gordon MacRae and Shirley Jones. A handsome and charming carnival barker (MacRae) falls in love and marries a beautiful girl (Jones), but he panics when he realizes she is pregnant and he must support them. He feels he must get money fast so he attempts an ill-fated robbery, is killed and then he looks down on her from heaven. Memorable songs include "If I Loved You," "You'll Never Walk Alone" and "June is Bustin' Out All Over." Just wonderful. See OKLAHOMA, too.

Sex · Nud · Viol · Lang · ◢ AdSit

A: Gordon MacRae, Shirley Jones, Cameron Mitchell, Barbara Ruick, Claramae Turner, Gene Lockhart

© FOXVIDEO 1713

CHITTY CHITTY BANG BANG

D: Kenneth Hughes — 147 m

G · MUS CLD · 1968 · COLOR

7 This very lavish musical was based upon a book by Ian Fleming. Dick Van Dyke plays an inventor with two children who creates a magical flying automobile. On a trip to the beach, he, his girlfriend and the children are all kidnapped into a magical world. It is dominated by the evil Baron Bomburst and his child-hating wife, who has kidnapped the children. With the help of a toymaker (Benny Hill), Dick seeks to rescue the kids. This picture cost a huge amount of money for its time ($10,000,000) and was supposed to be more of a family picture, but really is most appealing to smaller children.

Sex · Nud · Viol · Lang · AdSit

A: Dick Van Dyke, Sally Ann Howes, Anna Quayle, Lionel Jeffries, Benny Hill

Distributed By MGM/UA Home Video M201647

CHORUS LINE, A

D: Richard Attenborough — 117 m

PG-13 · MUS DMA · 1985 · COLOR

6 Broadway's longest running hit, winner of 9 Tony Awards and the Pulitzer Prize, is transferred to the silver screen with only mediocre success. The story concerns a succession of dancing hopefuls who audition in front of a tough director, played by Michael Douglas. In between big production numbers, they have intimate discussions between themselves, in which they bare their souls and relate their innermost dreams and secrets. This is still acceptable entertainment, but does not contain the same vitality, pacing and energy of, nor live up to the promise of, the stage play.

Sex · Nud · Viol · ■ Lang · ■ AdSit

A: Michael Douglas, Terrence Mann, Alyson Reed, Cameron English, Vicki Frederick, Audrey Landers

© NEW LINE HOME VIDEO 2183

CHUCK BERRY HAIL HAIL! ROCK `N' ROLL

D: Taylor Hackford — 121 m

PG · DOC MUS · 1987 · COLOR

10 If you like classic rock `n roll, you've got to see this movie. Chuck Berry, the father of rock `n roll, had his sixtieth birthday tribute concert in St. Louis at the Fox Theatre - and this is it. Singing back-up are some of the greatest singers and stylists of classic and '80s rock `n roll. Berry sings all of his greatest songs including: "Maybellene," "Memphis," "Nadine" and "Roll Over Beethoven."

Sex · Nud · Viol · Lang · AdSit

A: Chuck Berry, Keith Richards, Eric Clapton, Robert Cray, Etta James, Julian Lennon

© MCA/UNIVERSAL HOME VIDEO, INC. 80465

COAL MINER'S DAUGHTER

D: Michael Apted — 124 m

PG · DMA MUS · 1980 · COLOR

9 This is the true-life rags-to-riches story of the "First Lady of County Music," Loretta Lynn - but it is more than that. It's a fascinating character study, independent of its central character's connection to country music. Sissy Spacek won a well-deserved Oscar for her portrayal of Lynn's rise from being an impoverished Appalachian child-bride (a mother of four at eighteen) to becoming an American icon, and all the unexpected problems that followed her rise to fame.

Sex · Nud · Viol · Lang · ◢ AdSit

A: Sissy Spacek, Tommy Lee Jones, Beverly D'Angelo, Levon Helm, Phyllis Boyens, Ernest Tubb

© MCA/UNIVERSAL HOME VIDEO, INC. 66015

COMMITMENTS, THE

D: Alan Parker — 118 m

R · MUS COM · 1991 · COLOR

8 Unusual, fun and infectiously upbeat. Set in the slums of North Dublin, a local hustler, Jimmy, is asked by two friends to transform their very bad wedding band into a successful one. Jimmy decides that they should recreate themselves into a soul band and recruits a Joe Cocker-like singer, three girl backup singers, and Joey (a middle-aged trumpeter who claims to have played with Otis Redding, Elvis Presley and others). They do it. They're a hit. They become The Commitments - even though some of them didn't even know what soul music was. This is very worthwhile viewing but it is "hampered" by intense Irish dialects and British humor.

◢ Sex · Nud · ◢ Viol · ■ Lang · ◢ AdSit

A: Michael Aherne, Angeline Hall, Maria Doyle, Dave Finnegan, Bronagh Gallagher, Felim Gormley

© FOXVIDEO 1906

COMPLEAT BEATLES, THE

D: — 119 m

NR · DOC MUS · 1984 · B&W

9 A fascinating documentary, even to non-Beatle fans. It is an extensive and quite entertaining look at the evolution and promotion of an international phenomenon. It documents their very earliest beginnings, the changes they underwent and all the people involved in their creation and promotion; and, it is punctuated with a very liberal use of actual interviews, newsreel footage and concert excerpts - including their US tour. The primary focus is on their development - from the early days as "The Quarrymen", through their maturation to more complex music, to their breakup after the 1969 film LET IT BE.

Sex · Nud · Viol · Lang · AdSit

A: The Beatles

Distributed By MGM/UA Home Video M700166

MUS

CONCERT FOR BANGLADESH, THE

D: Saul Swimmer 90 m

G | MUS DOC | 1971 | COLOR

9 In August 1971 at Madison Square Garden, former Beatle George Harrison put on a benefit concert to raise money to help the starving people of Bangladesh. It was a huge rock concert that gained international recognition and support. This is a straight-forward recording of that concert. Lots of great rock music from many giants of the period, but you might want to fast-forward through a long stretch of Ravi Shankar's sitar music if you aren't a fan.

Sex / Nud / Viol / Lang / AdSit

A: George Harrison, Bob Dylan, Eric Clapton, Ringo Starr, Leon Russell, Ravi Shankar

© PARAMOUNT HOME VIDEO 15167

COTTON CLUB, THE

D: Francis Ford Coppola 128 m

R | DMA ACT MUS | 1984 | COLOR

8 Very large budget movie that was fraught with scandal and controversy during production. It went way over budget and lacked a focus, so director Coppola was called in to "fix" it. Even so, the plot still tends to drift. However, this is also an opulent and evocative film depicting the excitement of the Jazz Age. Set against a background of great music and gangster violence, it is the story of a trumpeter (Gere) who falls in love with the mistress (Lane) of mobster Dutch Schultz; and, a dancer (Hines) who's in love with a black chorus girl, who is trying to pass for white. Even though flawed, this is still quite interesting, entertaining and worth spending time on.

Sex / Nud / Viol / Lang / AdSit

A: Richard Gere, Gregory Hines, Diane Lane, Lonette McKee, Bob Hoskins, Nicolas Cage

© NEW LINE HOME VIDEO 1714

CROSSROADS

D: Walter Hill 100 m

R | FAN MUS | 1986 | COLOR

7 Enjoyable fantasy about a young classical guitar student (Macchio) who tracks down a legendary blues musician, Willie Brown (Seneca), in a Harlem hospital. He is obsessed with seeking the mysteries of the blues, so he breaks Willie out and together they travel to the heart of the Delta to "go down to the crossroads" (the lyrics of blues great - Robert Johnson). It is a trip in which Machio seeks fame, finds romance and together he and Willie seek to release Willie from an immortal deal he had made with the devil years before. An interesting character study with a great blues score.

Sex / Nud / Viol / Lang / AdSit

A: Ralph Macchio, Joe Seneca, Jami Gertz, Joe Morton, Robert Judd

© COLUMBIA TRISTAR HOME VIDEO 60665

DAMN YANKEES

D: George Abbott, Stanley Donen 111 m

NR | MUS COM | 1958 | COLOR

8 Huge Broadway hit is brought to the screen in wonderful fashion. Joe Boyd is a middle-aged baseball fan that so wants to help his beloved Washington Senators whip the Yankees and win the pennant that he makes a deal with the devil (Walston) and his beautiful vamp Lola (Verdon) to become rejuvenated into a young player. Wonderful songs and dances. Oscar nominated score has "Whatever Lola Wants," "Heart" and "Two Lost Souls." Verdon is sexy and Walston is marvelously devilish.

Sex / Nud / Viol / Lang / AdSit

A: Tab Hunter, Gwen Verdon, Ray Walston, Russ Brown, Shannon Bolin, Nathaniel Frey

© WARNER HOME VIDEO 35109

DIVINE MADNESS

D: 87 m

R | MUS COM | 1980 | COLOR

7 Bette Midler is sassy, bawdy, full of energy and unpredictable. She is also a talent which requires a particular "bent" to be fully appreciated and this concert film will either appeal to you or not based upon that. She sings 18 songs in all, punctuated by jokes and one-liners - some pretty risque. Songs include "Boogie Woogie Bugle Boy," "Do You Wanna Dance?" and "Leader of the Pack."

Sex / Nud / Viol / Lang / AdSit

A: Bette Midler

© WARNER HOME VIDEO 20001

DOCTOR DOLITTLE

D: Richard Fleischer 145 m

G | MUS CLD | 1967 | COLOR

8 This is a musical adaptation of Hugh Lofting's children's classic about an eccentric doctor (Rex Harrison) who loves animals so much better than people that he speaks 498 animal languages. He goes off on an adventure, from his home at Puddleby-on-the-Marsh, in search of new ones and he and his fiancee (Samantha Eggar) discover some very strange ones indeed. Won an Oscar for Best Song: "Talk to the Animals." While it was a box office flop and most critics were unkind, it still manages to please little kids who aren't aware of any of that.

Sex / Nud / Viol / Lang / AdSit

A: Rex Harrison, Samantha Eggar, Anthony Newley, Richard Attenborough, Peter Bull, Geoffrey Holder

© FOXVIDEO 1025

DON GIOVANNI

D: 177 m

MUS | 1978 | COLOR

9 Opera fan's delight. Some of the best voices in the operatic world unite in Mozart's classic opera of a unsatisfiable rogue who seduces his way to hell. Filmed on location in Venice with lavish production values.

Sex / Nud / Viol / Lang / AdSit

A: Ruggero Raimondi, Kiri Te Kanawa, Edda Moser, Jose Van Dam, Kenneth Riegel, Teresa Berganza

© KULTUR VIDEO 1185

DOORS, THE

D: Oliver Stone 135 m

R | DMA MUS | 1991 | COLOR

7 Alternatingly powerful and boring, invigorating and demoralizing, impressive and pompous, this is director Oliver Stone's extravaganza recreating the ambience of an era and a state of mind. Unfortunately the mind in question (Doors singer Jim Morrison), though brilliant, was in serious disarray. He was a self-destructive genius/icon who, in many ways, personified the era and he self-destructed at 27. Very interesting to Morrison's fans but ultimately, the film cannot help but be a downer, man. The photography which made the film an impressive experience in theaters is diminished on video. Fans only.

Sex / Nud / Viol / Lang / AdSit

A: Val Kilmer, Meg Ryan, Kyle MacLachlan, Frank Whaley, Michael Madsen, Billy Idol

© LIVE HOME VIDEO 68956

EARTH GIRLS ARE EASY

D: Julien Temple 99 m

PG | COM MUS SF | 1989 | COLOR

7 A wacky sci-fi spoof/musical about an alien space craft, occupied by some very hairy aliens, that crash-lands in the backyard swimming pool of Valley Girl Geena Davis. She and her ditsy girlfriend shave the hairy aliens and find that, underneath all their fur, they are hunks. Inspired, the girls take them on a fun-filled excursion into and through the live-for-today Southern California lifestyle. Lots of silly goofiness (plenty of sex jokes) and some good musical numbers, too. A pretty good time, but no masterpiece.

Sex / Nud / Viol / Lang / AdSit

A: Geena Davis, Jeff Goldblum, Julie Brown, Jim Carrey, Damon Wayans, Michael McKean

© LIVE HOME VIDEO 5303

ELVIS: THAT'S THE WAY IT IS

D: Dennis Sanders 109 m

G | DOC MUS | 1970 | COLOR

8 Excellent documentary made in 1970 of Elvis's preparations for a run in the Las Vegas International Hotel. Well filmed, with numerous excerpts of Elvis offstage and rehearsing. Also interspersed are numerous interviews of various backstage people, fans and musicians. The film culminates with his opening night act which includes "All Shook Up," "Blue Suede Shoes" and "Bridge Over Troubled Waters." 27 songs in all.

Sex / Nud / Viol / Lang / AdSit

A: Elvis Presley

Distributed By MGM/UA Home Video M700373

ELVIS - THE MOVIE

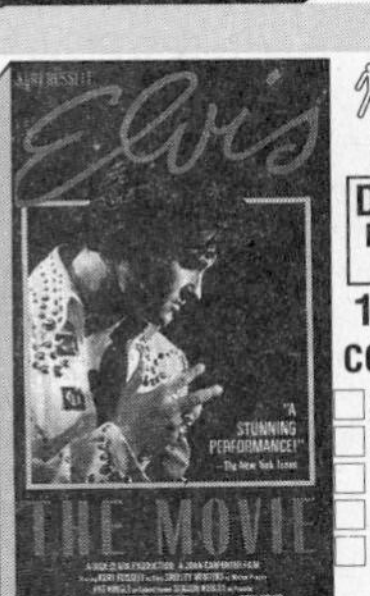

D: John Carpenter 117 m

NR | DMA MUS | 1979 | COLOR

9 Highly regarded and excellent depiction of Elvis's life, from rising from poverty as a truck driver to headlining in Las Vegas showrooms. Russell won universal acclaim for his right-on portrait of The King. His became the standard for the comparison of all other impersonators. This was a made-for-TV production, but is far better than that might indicate. It was one of the highest rated TV movies of all time. Excellent acting support came from Shelly Winters as Elvis's mother.

Sex / Nud / Viol / Lang / AdSit

A: Kurt Russell, Shelley Winters, Season Hubley, Pat Hingle, Bing Russell

© LIVE HOME VIDEO 4080

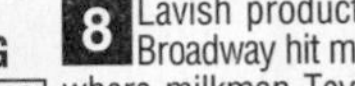

FIDDLER ON THE ROOF

D: Norman Jewison 180 m

G | MUS DMA | 1971 | COLOR

8 Lavish production of the very entertaining and long-running Broadway hit musical. Anatevka is a small Russian Jewish village where milkman Tevye, his wife and their five daughters live. Poor Tevya tries to marry off his dowryless daughters to wealthy husbands, but his foolish daughters want to marry for love. All the while, the Jews of his town are being persecuted by the Czarist pograms. Rich in grand music, with memorable lyrics (some are now standards) and high production values. This production received five Oscar nominations - including Best Picture, Actor and Director.

Sex / Nud / Viol / Lang / AdSit

A: Topol, Norman Crane, Leonard Frey, Molly Picon, Paul Mann, Rosalind Harris

Distributed By MGM/UA Home Video M201320

FINIAN'S RAINBOW

G · MUS COM ROM · 1968 · COLOR

D: Francis Ford Coppola 142 m

7 This was a ground-breaking musical in the 1940s when it opened on Broadway, but is now dated in the way it deals with its theme of racial prejudice. Nevertheless, it still has some very fine moments and Tommy Steele is wonderful in the role of an effervescent leprechaun whose gold is stolen by Irishman Astaire. Astaire has transplanted himself into the American South and Steele has followed him. Petula Clarke is Astaire's daughter and gets three wishes - one of which she uses to turn bigoted Southern Senator Wynn into a black man. Tuneful score includes, "How Are Things is Glocca Mora?"

Sex · Nud · Viol · Lang · AdSit

A: Fred Astaire, Petula Clark, Tommy Steele, Keenan Wynn, Barbara Hanock, Don Francks

© WARNER HOME VIDEO 11208

FIVE HEARTBEATS, THE

R · MUS DMA COM · 1991 · COLOR

D: Robert Townsend 120 m

8 Exuberant and fun (even if it's a little bit corny) ode to the heyday of Motown. This is the story of the rise of one fictional group to fame and is based loosely on the experiences of the R&B group, The Dells. It follows their rise from singing at amateur nights, to major success and then to personal failures. The film is not as cliched as it sounds. Although this is much-covered territory and is predictable, the characters are very likable and the music is fun and memory jogging. This is a good time, more so if you like this flavor of music or this was your era.

Sex · Nud · Viol · Lang · AdSit

A: Robert Townsend, Michael Wright, Harry J. Lennix, Tico Wells, Diahann Carroll, Harold Nicholas

© FOXVIDEO 0630

FIVE PENNIES, THE

NR · MUS · 1959 · COLOR

D: Melville Shavelson 117 m

6 This is a sentimental biography of jazz trumpeter Red Nichols. It is almost solely a musical entry, so it will be enjoyed most by jazz fans. It contains more that 20 tunes from many of the greats of the '30s and '40s. Of particular interest is Louis "Satchmo" Armstrong and a rousing duet version of "When The Saints Go Marching In." The musical solos were provided by Nichols himself.

Sex · Nud · Viol · Lang · AdSit

A: Danny Kaye, Barbara Bel Geddes, Tuesday Weld, Louis Armstrong, Bob Crosby, Bobby Troup

© PARAMOUNT HOME VIDEO 5823

FLASHDANCE

R · DMA MUS · 1983 · COLOR

D: Adrian Lyne 95 m

8 Huge, huge hit. Jennifer Beals plays an 18-year-old welder during the day and an erotic dancer at a local bar at night - but, just until the time when she can enter formal dance school to become a ballerina. In the meantime, she enjoys being able to improvise dance sequences at the bar and the audiences love her. She is being courted by her rich and handsome boss but becomes incensed when he intervenes for her to get her admitted to school. Very slight story but high in energy and slightly sexy, with a pulsating soundtrack. It's been likened to an hour and a half of MTV.

Sex · Nud · Viol · Lang · AdSit

A: Jennifer Beals, Michael Nouri, Lilia Skala, Cynthia Rhodes, Belinda Bauer, Phil Burns

© PARAMOUNT HOME VIDEO 1454

FLOWER DRUM SONG

NR · MUS ROM · 1961 · COLOR

D: Henry Koster 133 m

7 Pleasant adaptation of the Rodgers & Hammerstein Broadway musical. A picture-bride (Umeki) comes from China to San Francisco's Chinatown for an arranged marriage to a night-club owner (Soo). However, Soo is in love with a sultry singer (Kwan). But that's OK because Umeki falls in love with a handsome stranger (Shigeta). However, Kwan wants Shigeta. Some wonderful songs have become familiar standards: "I Enjoy Being a Girl" and "You Are Wonderful." The story line is not outstanding, but pleasing performances by some very talented people make this a very entertaining diversion.

Sex · Nud · Viol · Lang · AdSit

A: Jack Soo, Nancy Kwan, Benson Fong, Miyoshi Umeki, Juanita Hall, James Shigeta

© MCA/UNIVERSAL HOME VIDEO, INC. 80198

FUNNY FACE

NR · MUS ROM · 1957 · COLOR

D: Stanley Donen 103 m

9 Stylish and elegant fairy tale romance story that only happens in the movies. Fred Astair is a charming and sophisticated fashion photographer who discovers an impishly charming Audrey Hepburn working as a clerk in a bookstore. He transforms her into a high-fashion model sensation and falls in love with her. Wonderful Gershwin score: "How Long Has This Been Going On" and "S'Wonderful." One of Astair's best later efforts. Top-notch escapism.

Sex · Nud · Viol · Lang · AdSit

A: Fred Astaire, Audrey Hepburn, Kay Thompson, Michel Auclair, Ruta Lee, Suzy Parker

© PARAMOUNT HOME VIDEO 5608

FUNNY GIRL

G · MUS DMA · 1968 · COLOR

D: William Wyler 165 m

9 Wonderful, Oscar-winning Barbara Streisand triumph in which she recreates her successful role in the hit Broadway musical. Fantastic music: "People," "Don't Rain on My Parade," "My Man" and much more. It is also the unhappy semi-biography of Fanny Brice, the singer-comedienne who rose from obscurity to the heights of stardom in the Ziegfeld Follies. While her stage career was a success, her private life was a shambles. Heart-warming performance by Streisand. Followed by the sequel "FUNNY LADY."

Sex · Nud · Viol · Lang · AdSit

A: Barbra Streisand, Omar Sharif, Kay Medford, Anne Francis, Walter Pidgeon, Lee Allen

© COLUMBIA TRISTAR HOME VIDEO 60191

FUNNY LADY

PG · MUS DMA · 1975 · COLOR

D: Herbert Ross 136 m

8 Successful, if less endearing, sequel to the megahit FUNNY GIRL. This one was nominated for five Oscars. Lavish production, top-notch talent and great music keep this sequel afloat, in spite of a cliche-ridden script. The story is a continuation of the troubled off-stage life of famous comedienne Fanny Brice. After leaving Nicky Arnstein (Sharif), she meets and marries Billy Rose (Caan), but with little success. In spite of some short-comings, it is still well worth a watch.

Sex · Nud · Viol · Lang · AdSit

A: Barbra Streisand, James Caan, Omar Sharif, Roddy McDowall, Ben Vereen, Heidi O'Rourke

© COLUMBIA TRISTAR HOME VIDEO 60685

FUNNY THING HAPPENED ON THE WAY TO THE FORUM, A

NR · COM MUS · 1966 · COLOR

D: Richard Lester 100 m

8 Riotousness, bawdiness and absurdity abound in this fast-paced musical comedy. Zero Mostel excels as a scheming slave of ancient Rome whose sole goal is to earn his freedom. An outrageous slapstick comedy with a hopelessly convoluted plot that only adds to the insanity. It also combines the talents of veterans Buster Keaton, Jack Gilford and Phil Silvers with a then very young and very funny Michael Crawford ("Phantom of the Opera"). Wonderful Stephen Sondheim score. Expect the absurd and you won't be disappointed.

Sex · Nud · Viol · Lang · AdSit

A: Zero Mostel, Phil Silvers, Jack Gilford, Buster Keaton, Michael Crawford

Distributed By MGM/UA Home Video M202258

GIGI

G · MUS ROM COM · 1958 · COLOR

D: Vincente Minnelli 117 m

8 Huge hit. Nine Oscars. This is Lerner and Lowe's charming story about a French tomboy (Caron) who is being groomed by her grandmother and aunt to become a courtesan to wealthy playboy Jourdan - but Gigi wants true love. Jourdan too is bored with his decadent life and has long been charmed by Gigi's exuberance and innocence as a child, but he discovers that she is now a woman and that he has grown to love her. Exquisitely filmed by the musical master Vincente Minelli. Wonderful tunes: "Thank Heaven for Little Girls" and "I Remember It Well."

Sex · Nud · Viol · Lang · AdSit

A: Leslie Caron, Maurice Chevalier, Louis Jourdan, Hermione Gingold, Jacques Bergerac, Eva Gabor

Distributed By MGM/UA Home Video M700050

GIMME SHELTER

PG · DOC MUS · 1970 · COLOR

D: 91 m

7 Critically acclaimed, but disturbing, documentary of the 1969 Rolling Stone concert tour of America, with particular focus upon a free concert at Altamount Speedway that resulted in chaos and an off-camera knifing and murder. The Hells Angels were hired as security for the event. Stones perform some of their best songs including "Brown Sugar," but the film is more a disturbing display of the drug culture of the 1960s.

Sex · Nud · Viol · Lang · AdSit

A: The Rolling Stones, Jefferson Airplane, Tina Turner

© ABKCO VIDEO 1001-3

GOSPEL

DOC MUS · 1982 · COLOR

D: 92 m

9 A rousing and exuberant, high-energy concert including several top gospel performers of the '70s and '80s in very entertaining performances before a very enthusiastic crowd. There is no commentary, only music. The groups include: James Cleveland and the Southern California Community Choir, Walter Hawkins and the Hawkins Family, Mighty Clouds of Joy, Shirley Caesar, Twinkie Clark and the Clark Sisters. If you enjoyed this you should also see another documentary SAY AMEN, SOMEBODY.

Sex · Nud · Viol · Lang · AdSit

A:

© MONTEREY HOME VIDEO 31944

GREASE

D: Randal Kleiser 110 m

PG | MUS ROM | 1978 | COLOR

7 The highly popular Broadway play, about summer love at fictional high school in the '50s, is brought to the screen and given reasonably good treatment. Travolta, a greaser (but also the ultimate cool dude), and the sweet and innocent new-girl-in-town (Newton-John) meet over the summer break and have a summer romance. But, when fall comes, he loses his head as he has to protect his image as a tough guy and she doesn't fit it. Clever ideas, plenty of energy, excellent choreography, charm and lots of good music. Fun time.

Sex / Nud / Viol / Lang / AdSit

A: John Travolta, Olivia Newton-John, Stockard Channing, Jeff Conaway, Didl Conn, Eve Arden

© PARAMOUNT HOME VIDEO 1108

GREAT BALLS OF FIRE

D: Jim McBride 108 m

PG-13 | DMA MUS | 1989 | COLOR

8 Jerry Lee Lewis was an icon of the early rock `n roll period and his life was as raucous as his music. Dennis Quaid captures the wild spirit of "The Killer" in his rise from obscurity to international fame, and his abrupt fall from grace after he married his 13-year-old second cousin, played by Winona Ryder. This biography is full of energy and style. Dennis Quaid throws in all the enthusiasm he can muster and has great support provided from a good cast.

Sex / Nud / Viol / Lang / AdSit

A: Dennis Quaid, Winona Ryder, Alec Baldwin, Trey Wilson, John Doe, Peter Cook

© ORION PICTURES CORPORATION 8743

GREAT MUPPET CAPER, THE

D: Jim Henson 98 m

G | COM CLD MUS | 1981 | COLOR

8 This is the delightful second feature-length film for Jim Henson's Muppets. After being fired as reporters for a major paper, Miss Piggy, Kermit, Fozzie Bear and the Great Gonzo set about solving the mysterious theft in London of the famous Baseball Diamond. Good gags and fun musical numbers (Kermit dances like Astaire and Miss Piggy swims like Ester Williams). Pretty good follow-up to the superior THE MUPPET MOVIE.

Sex / Nud / Viol / Lang / AdSit

A: Charles Grodin, Diana Rigg, John Cleese, Robert Morley, Peter Ustinov, Jack Warden

© CBS/FOX VIDEO 9035

GYPSY

D: Mervyn LeRoy 143 m

MUS | 1962 | COLOR

6 Musically entertaining biography of the famous stripper Gypsy Rose Lee. Gypsy is the daughter of a demanding stage mother who forced her and her sister into a mediocre career in vaudeville song and dance act. Then one day the shy Gypsy discovered she had a talent of her own - for stripping. The story line follows her life but the primary emphasis is on her turbulent relationship with her mother and some really great songs. Songs include: "Everything's Coming Up Roses," "Small World" and "Let Me Entertain You." Don't look for any skin - you won't find it.

Sex / Nud / Viol / Lang / AdSit

A: Natalie Wood, Rosalind Russell, Karl Malden, Paul Wallace, Betty Bruce, Ann Jillian

© WARNER HOME VIDEO 11207

HAIR

D: Milos Forman 122 m

PG | MUS | 1979 | COLOR

6 As a very long-running musical play on Broadway, this became the icon of an entire era and much, but not all, of the magic was transfered to the screen. However, this is also a video that took its value from the atmosphere of the times in which it prospered, so it has diminished with time. An Oklahoma farm boy (Williams) comes to New York to be inducted into the Army but is waylaid by a group of "hippies" who indoctrinate him into the joys of drugs, sex and peace. The enthusiasm of the age of Aquarius is captured in its soundtrack including: "Aquarius," "Easy to be Hard," "Hair" and much more.

Sex / Nud / Viol / Lang / AdSit

A: Treat Williams, John Savage, Beverly D'Angelo, Annie Golden, Charlotte Rae, Miles Chapin

Distributed By MGM/UA Home Video M201330

HARD DAY'S NIGHT, A

D: Richard Lester 90 m

G | MUS COM | 1964 | B&W

9 This is an exuberant and fun-filled musical romp with the Beatles - even for non-Beatles fans. The fab four had just reached the pinnacle of their popularity at the time of the release of this film and it does contain a full compliment of Lennon-McCarney songs, including: "Can't Buy Me Love," "And I Love Her" and "I Should Have Known Better"; but it is also a fast-paced and funny kaleidoscope of a rock group's frantic day by utilizing clever cinematic techniques. Good fun, even today, because it captures the charm and exuberant personalities that was a large part of how the group achieved the success it did.

Sex / Nud / Viol / Lang / AdSit

A: The Beatles, Wilfred Brambell, Victor Spinetti, Anna Quayle

© MPI HOME VIDEO MP1064

HEAR MY SONG

D: Peter Chelsom 104 m

R | COM MUS | 1991 | COLOR

7 A likable comedy from Britain. Mickey (Dunbar) runs a Liverpool nightclub that caters to the local Irish community, and he loves Nancy (Fitsgerald). Mickey's club barely struggles along until he mistakenly hires a phony tenor who claims to be Joseph Locke (a famed real-life Irish tenor). However, the phony is found out and the mistake causes Mickey to lose his club. More importantly, he loses Nancy, whose mother knew the real Locke and was in love with him. So, the desperate Mickey sets off to Ireland to recover the real tenor (Beatty), who is in hiding there for tax evasion. Mickey must bring him back to his fans and to Nancy's mom. Charming and witty, but slow.

Sex / Nud / Viol / Lang / AdSit

A: Ned Beatty, Adrian Dunbar, Shirley Anne Field, Tara Fitsgerald, David McCallum, William Hootkins

© PARAMOUNT HOME VIDEO 15110

HELLO, DOLLY

D: Gene Kelly 146 m

G | MUS COM | 1969 | COLOR

6 This is a very lavish screen production of Broadway's smash hit about a turn-of-the-century matchmaker (played by Streisand) who hopes to snag one of her clients for herself. Extravagant film production and excellent musical productions cannot entirely make up for the fact that Barbara was much too young for that role. Even so, listen to the fantastic music: "Before the Parade Passes By" and, of course, "Hello Dolly" with Streisand in duet with Louis Armstrong. Based on the play and later movie THE MATCHMAKER.

Sex / Nud / Viol / Lang / AdSit

A: Barbra Streisand, Walter Matthau, Louis Armstrong, Michael Crawford, Tommy Tune, E.J. Peaker

© FOXVIDEO 1001

HELP!

D: Richard Lester 90 m

G | MUS COM | 1965 | COLOR

8 Wild gags and lots of music populate this minor silly story about a group of religious zealots who want Ringo's (the Beatles drummer) ring for a sacrifice. Songs include: "Ticket to Ride," "Another Girl," "You've Got to Hide Your Love Away," and "Help!" If you are not a fan of either The Beatles or abject silliness, you might downgrade this to a 6, or perhaps even skip it. However, eccentrics, fans of the group or fans of silliness will have a good time. And, if you are a true Beatles fan, you MUST also see the excellent documentary, THE COMPLEAT BEATLES.

Sex / Nud / Viol / Lang / AdSit

A: The Beatles, Leo McKern, Eleanor Bran, Victor Spinetti

© MPI HOME VIDEO MP1342

HIGH SOCIETY

D: Charles Walters 107 m

NR | MUS ROM | 1956 | COLOR

6 Entertaining musical remake of PHILADELPHIA STORY with a beautiful Grace Kelly in Katharine Hepburn's role - the society girl playing cat and mouse games over three men: her current fiance (Lund), her ex-husband (Crosby) and a reporter (Sinatra) who is on hand to cover the impending wedding. Great Cole porter tunes include: "Did You Evah?," "You're Sensational" and "True Love," which was Oscar-nominated. Grace Kelly's last screen role.

Sex / Nud / Viol / Lang / AdSit

A: Bing Crosby, Grace Kelly, Frank Sinatra, Celeste Holm, Louis Calhern, Louis Armstrong

Distributed By MGM/UA Home Video M600292

HONEYSUCKLE ROSE

D: Jerry Schatzberg 120 m

PG | MUS | 1980 | COLOR

6 Lots of good country music mark this film as worthy of investing one's time, particularly for fans of Willie Nelson. However, outside that, there is very little else to get excited about. The story is a semi-biographical account of a country music singer's (Nelson) life on the road. His personal life begins to come apart when Willie takes up with the daughter of his longtime friend. Watch for a lot of cameos from some country music greats. The song, "On the Road Again," was Oscar nominated.

Sex / Nud / Viol / Lang / AdSit

A: Willie Nelson, Dyan Cannon, Amy Irving, Slim Pickens, Joey Floyd, Charles Levin

© WARNER HOME VIDEO 1043

HOW TO SUCCEED IN BUSINESS WITHOUT REALLY TRYING

D: David Swift 172 m

NR | MUS COM | 1967 | COLOR

8 Robert Morse brings his Broadway triumph successfully to the big screen in this musical satire about an ambitious and charming window washer who reads a book on success and immediately puts it to work. On his first day in the building, he charms pretty secretary Michele Lee into helping him to meet the chief of personnel. Soon he has everybody, including the President of the company, (Vallee) charmed - and, all with the help of the book. Entertaining with lots of good music including: "I Believe in You" and "Brotherhood of Man."

Sex / Nud / Viol / Lang / AdSit

A: Robert Morse, Michele Lee, Rudy Vallee, Anthony Teague, Maureen Arthur, Sammy Smith

Distributed By MGM/UA Home Video M200663

I DO! I DO!

NR · MUS ROM · 1982 · COLOR

D: · 116 m

8 This is the musical version of a play called "The Fourposter." It is the story of the fifty-year marriage of Michael and Agnes, as told in events occurring in and around their fourposter bed. The musical roles were created on Broadway first by Mary Martin and Robert Preston. This stage presentation was videotaped live with Lee Remick and Hal Linden in the lead roles. It takes the couple from the night before their wedding until the day they leave their home 50 years later. Highly acclaimed. Good stuff!

Sex · Nud · Viol · Lang · ◢ AdSit

A: Lee Remick, Hal Linden

© TURNER HOME ENTERTAINMENT 1004

IDOLMAKER, THE

PG · DMA MUS · 1980 · COLOR

D: Taylor Hackford · 119 m

7 Slick filmmaking tells the story of a failed-songwriter turned promoter (played well by Sharkey) who stops at nothing to push, pull and shove two young Philadelphia boys into becoming national pop idols at the beginning of the rock 'n roll revolution of the late '50s. Quite well done, even though some felt that it fell short at the end. Energetic performances and music recapture much of the feel of the period. Based upon the real-life rise of Frankie Avalon and Fabian.

Sex · Nud · Viol · ◢ Lang · ◢ AdSit

A: Ray Sharkey, Peter Gallagher, Paul Land, Maureen McCormick, Olympia Dukakis

Distributed By MGM/UA Home Video M600370

IMAGINE: JOHN LENNON

R · DOC MUS · 1988 · COLOR

D: · 104 m

8 This documentary is really quite good and contains rare live concert footage, home movies of John Lennon's private life, plus TV footage and much of Lennon's own music (36 songs in all). The film is punctuated with commentary from Lennon himself, that was excerpted from elsewhere. It is insightful, odd at times, funny, emotionally moving and lovingly done.

Sex · ◢ Nud · Viol · ◢ Lang · ◢ AdSit

A: John Lennon, Yoko Ono, George Harrison

© WARNER HOME VIDEO 11819

ISADORA

NR · DMA MUS · 1968 · COLOR

D: Karel Reisz · 153 m

6 Interesting, but very long, biography of a controversial and truly unique individual and a pivotal figure in creative dance. Isadora Duncan was a free-spirited artist who created scandal where ever she went. She was also one of the primary innovators of what became modern dance. Her animalistic and suggestive dancing style was considered very daring and her private life, having several relationships ongoing at the same time, was equally scandalous. The film explores it all, including the deaths of her children and her own bizarre death. Redgrave received an Oscar nomination for her efforts.

◢ Sex · ◢ Nud · Viol · ◢ Lang · ■ AdSit

A: Vanessa Redgrave, James Fox, Jason Robards, Jr., Ivan Tchenko, John Fraser, Bessie Love

© MCA/UNIVERSAL HOME VIDEO, INC. 80519

IT HAPPENED AT THE WORLD'S FAIR

NR · MUS ROM · 1963 · COLOR

D: Norman Taurog · 105 m

6 Entertaining light musical. Elvis Presley plays a daredevil pilot who romances a nurse at the Seattle World's Fair and helps a young girl stay out of an orphanage. Contains ten Elvis songs, none of them very memorable. This was still early in Elvis's movie career, so he hadn't burned out yet and still enjoyed himself. An interesting side note is that this is the very first film in which Kurt Russell appeared. Russell later would do an excellent job of playing Presley in the TV movie ELVIS.

Sex · Nud · Viol · Lang · AdSit

A: Elvis Presley, Joan O'Brien, Gary Lockwood, Vicky Tiu, H.M. Wynant

Distributed By MGM/UA Home Video M600475

I WANNA HOLD YOUR HAND

PG · COM MUS · 1978 · COLOR

D: Robert Zemeckis · 99 m

6 Delightful comedy produced by Steven Spielberg about six New Jersey teenagers in the early '60s who try to break into the Ed Sullivan Show the night that The Beatles are set to appear. Fast-paced, with a fine sense for the time period and the hysteria that surrounded the Fab Four's trip to America. Contains 17 Beatles songs.

Sex · Nud · Viol · ◢ Lang · ◢ AdSit

A: Nancy Allen, Bobby DiCicco, Mark McClure, Theresa Saldana, Eddie Deezen

© WARNER HOME VIDEO 35066

JAILHOUSE ROCK

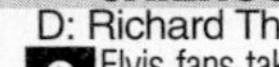

PG · MUS · 1957 · B&W

D: Richard Thorpe · 92 m

8 Elvis fans take note. This is one of his best ever screen appearances, particularly those where music figured into the plot. There isn't a lot of plot here: Elvis is sent to jail after he kills a man while defending a woman's honor. While he's in there, he learns to play a guitar and, when he is released, a promoter turns him into a rock 'n roll star. This is a young Elvis, before his stint in the Army, and he is still filled with energy, particularly during his performance of the title song.

Sex · Nud · Viol · Lang · AdSit

A: Elvis Presley, Mickey Shaughnessy, Dean Jones, Judy Tyler, Jennifer Holden

Distributed By MGM/UA Home Video M500011

JAZZ ON A SUMMER'S DAY

NR · MUS DOC · 1959 · COLOR

D: Bert Stern · 84 m

9 Jazz fans take note. On a summer's day in 1958 at Newport, Road Island, the Newport Jazz Festival was born. This is a candid and thoroughly enjoyable documentary of the musical event that preceeded Woodstock by more than ten years. Virtually all the legendary greats of jazz are in attendance including: Louis Armstrong, Dinah Washington, Mahalia Jackson, Thelonious Monk, Anita O'Day, Chuck Berry and George Shearing.

Sex · Nud · Viol · Lang · AdSit

A: Louis Armstrong, Big Maybell, Chuck Berry, Dianah Washington, Gerry Mulligan, Thelonious Monk

© NEW YORKER FILMS NYV16590

JESUS CHRIST, SUPERSTAR

G · MUS · 1973 · COLOR

D: Norman Jewison · 108 m

6 This is not a religious movie in the traditional sense. It is a rock opera interpretation of the last weeks of the life of Christ as seen through the eyes of Judas. It is very innovative in that it attempts to incorporate modern interpretive elements into the traditional story, which is why it is also very controversial. Very lively score that includes the pop hit "I Don't Know How to Love Him." The visual presentation of many songs in it is in some ways comparable to modern-day music videos.

Sex · Nud · Viol · Lang · AdSit

A: Ted Neeley, Carl Anderson, Yvonne Elliman, Barry Dennen, Joshua Mostel, Bob Bingham

© MCA/UNIVERSAL HOME VIDEO, INC. 55002

JOSEPHINE BAKER STORY, THE

R · DMA MUS · 1991 · COLOR

D: Brian Gibson · 129 m

8 One of the most outrageous, controversial and best loved entertainers of all time was Josephine Baker. This is her story. She was born at the turn of the 20th-century, desperately poor and black in St. Louis. Beginning on the vaudeville circuit in America, she parlayed her effervescent personality, unique singing and sizzling hot dancing into a trip to Paris. There, her nude dancing made her an international sensation and Paris became her home. She took life head on. She married royalty, was extravagant in every way possible. Interesting woman and entertaining film.

Sex · ■ Nud · Viol · ◢ Lang · ■ AdSit

A: Lynn Whitfield, Ruben Blades, David Dukes, Louis Gossett, Jr., Craig T. Nelson

© HBO VIDEO 90571

JUMBO (BILLY ROSE'S)

G · MUS ROM · 1962 · COLOR

D: Charles Walters · 127 m

6 It's the turn of the 20th century and Jimmy Durante and his daughter (Doris Day) are struggling to keep their circus from going broke. Into their camp comes a competitor's spy, intent upon stealing the circus. Instead he falls in love with Doris. The major attraction here to the viewer is not the story but the beautiful Rodgers and Hart score: "This Can't Be Love," "The Most Beautiful Girl in the World" and "My Romance." The Busby Berkeley choreography and the marvelous talents of Durante and Raye also are a delight. A family movie with something a little different for everyone.

Sex · Nud · Viol · Lang · AdSit

A: Doris Day, Stephen Boyd, Jimmy Durante, Martha Raye, Dean Jagger, Billy Barty

Distributed By MGM/UA Home Video M300796

KID GALAHAD

NR · MUS ACT · 1962 · COLOR

D: Phil Karlson · 95 m

6 Elvis plays a young guy just back from the service. He's looking for a job and takes one as a sparring partner at a boxing camp, but instead he knocks out the camp's top boxer. So, the owner decides to make him into a champ, but this is a boxer that would rather be a mechanic and sing. Still, the promoter (Gig Young) can't let him get away because the kid is his one big chance to get out of debt to some hoods. Elvis agrees to fight for him, but that only gets him and his incorruptible trainer (Charles Bronson) in a whole lot of trouble. Pretty good, if you don't expect too much.

Sex · Nud · ◢ Viol · Lang · AdSit

A: Elvis Presley, Gig Young, Charles Bronson, Lola Albright

Distributed By MGM/UA Home Video M701055

KING AND I, THE

D: Walter Lang 133 m

G | MUS ROM COM | 1956 | COLOR

9 This is a sumptuous feast for the eyes and ears. Superb production values showcase a winning story. A spirited English widow (Kerr) is hired by the pompous King of Siam (Yul Brynner) in the 1860s to be governess for his many children. The clash of both cultures and personalities make for some interesting situations, but conflict gradually gives way to respect and to an unspoken and forbidden love. Wonderful music includes their duet "Shall We Dance." Winner of five Oscars and nominee for Best Picture.

Sex / Nud / Viol / Lang / AdSit

A: Deborah Kerr, Yul Brynner, Rita Moreno, Martin Benson, Terry Sounders

© FOXVIDEO 1004

KING CREOLE

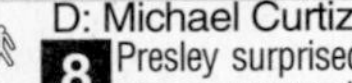

D: Michael Curtiz 116 m

NR | DMA MUS | 1958 | B&W

8 Presley surprised quite a few critics with this performance. He was an unexpected choice for this dramatization of "A Stone for Danny Fisher" after James Dean died, but Hal Wallis tailored it perfectly for him. He plays a young would-be singer, bordering on delinquency and working as a busboy in a mobster's (Matthau) nightclub. Carolyn Jones is Matthau's mistress. When she is publicly mistreated, Presley comes to her defense. So, to embarrass him, Matthau makes him stand up before the crowd and sing, but instead he is a hit. Over a dozen songs including "Hard Headed Woman" and "Trouble."

Sex / Nud / Viol / Lang / AdSit

A: Elvis Presley, Carolyn Jones, Dolores Hart, Dean Jagger, Liliane Montevecchi, Walter Matthau

© CBS/FOX VIDEO 2005

LA BAMBA

D: Luis Valdez 103 m

PG-13 | DMA MUS | 1987 | COLOR

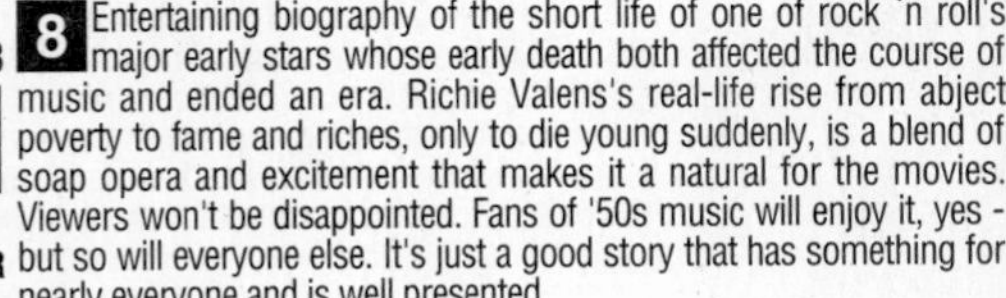

8 Entertaining biography of the short life of one of rock 'n roll's major early stars whose early death both affected the course of music and ended an era. Richie Valens's real-life rise from abject poverty to fame and riches, only to die young suddenly, is a blend of soap opera and excitement that makes it a natural for the movies. Viewers won't be disappointed. Fans of '50s music will enjoy it, yes - but so will everyone else. It's just a good story that has something for nearly everyone and is well presented.

Sex / Nud / Viol / Lang / AdSit

A: Lou Diamond Phillips, Rosana De Soto, Esai Morales, Danielle von Zerneck, Elizabeth Pena

© COLUMBIA TRISTAR HOME VIDEO 60854

LADY SINGS THE BLUES

D: Sidney J. Furie 144 m

R | DMA MUS | 1972 | COLOR

7 Billy Holiday is an icon in African-American culture and a pillar in American jazz. This film is her fictionalized Hollywood biography. As a biography it has many shortcomings; but as a soap opera drama, it's not bad. It attracted five Oscar nominations, including one for Diana Ross in her powerful screen debut. The story supposedly chronicles Holiday's rise from singing in brothels through her destruction by drug addiction. Great songs include "Strange Fruit" and "God Bless the Child."

Sex / Nud / Viol / Lang / AdSit

A: Diana Ross, Billy Dee Williams, Richard Pryor, James Callahan, Paul Hampton, Sid Melton

© PARAMOUNT HOME VIDEO 8374

LAST WALTZ, THE

D: Martin Scorsese 117 m

PG | DOC MUS | 1976 | COLOR

9 A major lineup of 1976 rock 'n roll talent. This is the actual farewell concert for the rock group called "The Band," taped as it happened. Onstage production numbers are interspersed with back stage goings on and interviews. It is a must see for rock 'n roll fans. Note the partial lineup, shown below, of the rock stars included and in attendance.

Sex / Nud / Viol / Lang / AdSit

A: The Band, Bob Dylan, Neil Young, Joni Mitchell, Van Morrison, Eric Clapton

Distributed By MGM/UA Home Video M200482

LA TRAVIATA

D: Franco Zeffirelli 105 m

G | MUS ROM | 1982 | COLOR

9 Verdi's opera of tragic love between doomed lovers is produced in such a manner and with such lushness that it will please even non-opera fans. Inspired by the same story that inspired CAMILLE, this is the emotionally charged story of a courtesan who falls in love with a rich man's son. The boy's father convinces her that she will ruin his son's life and so she breaks off the relationship. They reconcile their love, but only on her deathbed. Beautiful voices. In Italian with subtitles.

Sex / Nud / Viol / Lang / AdSit

A: Teresa Stratas, Placido Domingo, Cornell MacNeil, Alan Monk

© MCA/UNIVERSAL HOME VIDEO, INC. 80048

LES GIRLS

D: George Cukor 155 m

NR | MUS COM | 1957 | COLOR

9 Winning musical from MGM. Lush musical with big production numbers, wonderful Cole Porter music and terrific performances by the entire cast. The story revolves around the turmoil created by a sensational book written by a former dancer (Kay Kendall) which concerned her days with a dance troop. One of the other members has sued her for libel and during the course of the trial, three separate showgirls reveal their romances with dancer Gene Kelley in a series of flashbacks. None of their memories match and they are all funny. Witty and stylish.

Sex / Nud / Viol / Lang / AdSit

A: Gene Kelly, Kay Kendall, Taina Elg, Mitzi Gaynor, Jacques Bergerac

Distributed By MGM/UA Home Video M300308

LITTLE PRINCE, THE

D: Stanley Donen 88 m

G | MUS FAN | 1974 | COLOR

6 This is a valiant effort and it was a major production effort, but is also very difficult to follow. Still, dedicated fans of musicals and/or students of Lerner and Loewe shouldn't miss it. It is a highly romanticized story in which a pilot (Kiley) is forced to land in the desert. He and his wrecked plane are chanced upon by an alien from outer space in the form of a little boy. However, this little boy has the mind of a very mature old soul. Together these two explore matters of life and love. Very curious, but not one of the great team's better efforts.

Sex / Nud / Viol / Lang / AdSit

A: Richard Kiley, Steven Warner, Gene Wilder, Bob Fosse, Clive Revill, Donna McKechnie

© PARAMOUNT HOME VIDEO 8017

LITTLE SHOP OF HORRORS

D: Frank Oz 96 m

PG-13 | COM MUS HOR | 1986 | COLOR

6 Rick Moranis and an excellent cast - supported by a big budget, great special effects and some pretty neat musical production numbers - provide an entertaining and funny musical for the first 2/3 of the film. However, the black comedy plot - which concerns a very large, singing, man-eating plant - turns a little too macabre to be that funny in the last 1/3. Still - fans of the unusual should take note. This is actually a remake of a famous low-budget hit from 1960 done by Roger Corman which also included a very young Jack Nicholson.

Sex / Nud / Viol / Lang / AdSit

A: Rick Moranis, Ellen Greene, Vincent Gardenia, Steve Martin, James Belushi, John Candy

© WARNER HOME VIDEO 11702

LOVE ME TENDER

D: Robert D. Webb 89 m

NR | WST MUS | 1956 | COLOR

7 Elvis's first picture is a Western, and it isn't too bad. He plays the younger of two brothers who are both in love with Debra Paget. When older brother Egan doesn't come back from the Civil War, they think he is dead and Elvis marries Debra. Then Eagan shows up, and with a stolen payroll to boot. It also has four Presley songs including: "Love Me Tender," "Poor Boy," "Old Shep" and "We're Gonna Move (to a Better Home)."

Sex / Nud / Viol / Lang / AdSit

A: Elvis Presley, Richard Egan, Debra Paget, Robert Middleton, William Campbell, Neville Brand

© FOXVIDEO 1172

MAMBO KINGS, THE

D: Arne Glimcher 104 m

R | DMA MUS | 1992 | COLOR

7 Colorful involving story of the trials of two musical brothers who flee Cuba in the early '50s, arriving in New York determined to break into its musical scene with their enthusiastic performances and lively Latin rhythms. In spite of the long odds, they do meet with quick success, but are stopped dead when they refuse to bow to the powerful leader of the local entertainment community. They are forced into becoming butchers to survive, until they get a big break on the "I Love Lucy Show" with Desi Arnaz. This is not a story of music however, it is an involving portrait of the deep love between two brothers through their struggle. The enthusiastic music is fun, too.

Sex / Nud / Viol / Lang / AdSit

A: Armand Assante, Antonio Banderas, Cathy Moriarty, Maruschka Detmers, Desi Arnaz, Jr., Celia Cruz

© WARNER HOME VIDEO 12308

MARY POPPINS

D: Robert Stevenson 139 m

G | MUS CLD FAN | 1964 | COLOR

10 Absolutely delightful! An enchanting magical nanny, Mary Poppins (Andrews), glides into a banker's home in 1910 London and brings happiness into everyone's lives. Who else can have a tea party on the ceiling? She and a chimney sweep (Van Dyke) sing the song "Chim-Chim-Cheree" and dance with magic feet on London rooftops. Van Dyke's animated scene where he frolics with little penguins is unforgettable. This top-shelf musical won five Academy Awards: Best Actress, Film Editing, Original Music, Song and Visual Effects. It was nominated for thirteen. You, as well as the kids, will find your smiles!

Sex / Nud / Viol / Lang / AdSit

A: Julie Andrews, Dick Van Dyke, David Tomlinson, Glynis Johns, Ed Wynn, Hermione Baddeley

© WALT DISNEY HOME VIDEO 023

MONTEREY POP

D: James Desmond — 88 m

NR | DOC MUS | 1967 | COLOR

9 White Hot! This is the first major rock concert film and was shot at the Monterey Pop Festival in California in 1967. This landmark concert featured some of the biggest musical stars (15) of the time, in their brightest moments, and it kicked off the rock summer series (Summer of Love) that culminated in Woodstock. Performances include Janis Joplin's "Ball and Chain" and an intense rendition of "My Generation" by The Who. Brilliant historical time-piece and a must-see for anyone with more than a passing interest in music.

Sex / Nud / Viol / Lang / AdSit

A: Jimi Hendrix, Otis Redding, The Who, Jefferson Airplane, Janis Joplin, The Animals

© COLUMBIA TRISTAR HOME VIDEO RO162VH

MUPPET MOVIE, THE

D: James Frawley — 96 m

G | COM CLD MUS | 1979 | COLOR

8 Effervescent silliness, and some really baaaad puns, make this a delight for everyone. Kids like it because it is light-hearted and silly. Adults get their own special treats - such as when Dom DeLuise interrupts Kermit who's catching flys in the swamp. Dom tells Kermit that he is lost and in a big hurry because he has to "catch a plane." Kermit responds with "Not with a tongue like yours." Irresistable zaniness as the Muppets travel to Hollywood so that they can become movie stars. 15 cameo appearances from some big stars. See also THE MUPPETS TAKE MANHATTEN.

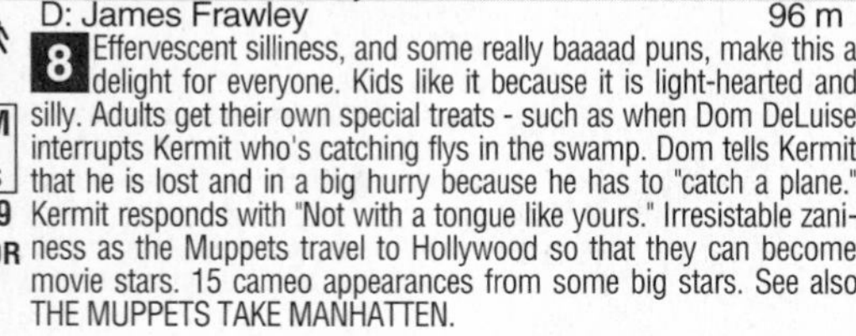

Sex / Nud / Viol / Lang / AdSit

A: Muppets, Milton Berle, Mel Brooks, Steve Martin, Bob Hope, Edgar Bergen

© CBS/FOX VIDEO 9001

MUSIC MAN, THE

D: Morton DaCosta — 151 m

G | MUS COM ROM | 1962 | COLOR

10 Golden Americana and a rousing good time too! A charming con artist and music "professor" (Preston) convinces a small turn-of-the-century Iowa town that he can teach the boys there to play musical instruments by using his Think Method. Then he convinces all the townsfolk that they should form a marching band - buying the costumes, instruments and all from him. Some of the Oscar-winning songs featured in this delightful musical include "76 Trombones," "'Til There Was You" and "Trouble." This wonderful slice of American apple pie was nominated for 6 Oscars, including Best Picture. Wonderful!!

Sex / Nud / Viol / Lang / AdSit

A: Robert Preston, Buddy Hackett, Hermione Gingold, Paul Ford, Pert Kelton, Shirley Jones

© WARNER HOME VIDEO 11473

MY FAIR LADY

D: George Cukor — 170 m

G | MUS ROM COM | 1964 | COLOR

10 Outstanding winner of eight Oscars - including Best Picture! Shaw's enduring play (and film) PYGMALION is masterfully transformed into a magical musical by Lerner and Lowe. It is an exuberant story of the effort by a snooty Englishman to transform, on a bet, a guttersnipe flower peddler (Hepburn) into being able to pass for a respectable lady. In the process, he falls in love with her and she changes him forever. Just a few of the winning and memorable songs include "The Rain in Spain," "On the Street Where You Live" and "Get Me to the Church on Time." Wonderful.

Sex / Nud / Viol / Lang / AdSit

A: Audrey Hepburn, Rex Harrison, Wilfrid Hyde-White, Stanley Holloway, Jeremy Brett, Theodore Bikel

© FOXVIDEO 7038

NEW YORK, NEW YORK

D: Martin Scorsese — 164 m

PG | MUS ROM | 1977 | COLOR

7 Big name talent abounds in this story about the love affair between a splashy saxophonist (De Niro) and a timid sweet singer (Minnelli). The two meet on VJ day - WWII is over. They both audition with a big band, fall in love and get married. He takes over as band leader. She goes back to New York to have their baby. And, he begins an affair with her replacement. Their marriage falls apart but her career takes off, singing the songs he hates. High production values and some great musical sequences and strong performances, but the music is the most interesting thing about it.

Sex / Nud / Viol / ◢ Lang / ◢ AdSit

A: Liza Minnelli, Robert De Niro, Lionel Stander, Georgie Auld, Mary Kay Place, George Memmoli

Distributed By MGM/UA Home Video M301321

OLIVER!

D: Carol Reed — 145 m

G | MUS DMA | 1968 | COLOR

10 An absolutely outstanding musical and winner of the Best Picture Oscar and six others. Great entertainment. Dickens was never this much fun. All the story's touching elements are here, but the tragedy of an eight-year-old orphan's utter aloneness and helpless, living in the streets during desperate times, is much less traumatic when it is set to music and dance. Plus, the colorful characters were wonderfully captured by a terrific cast. There are lavish production numbers and sets. The truly wonderful and memorable songs include: "Consider Yourself," "As Long as He Needs Me" and "Who Will Buy."

Sex / Nud / Viol / Lang / AdSit

A: Mark Lester, Jack Wild, Ron Moody, Oliver Reed, Shani Wallace

© COLUMBIA TRISTAR HOME VIDEO 60526

ON A CLEAR DAY YOU CAN SEE FOREVER

D: Vincente Minnelli — 129 m

G | MUS COM ROM | 1970 | COLOR

7 Entertaining and underrated. Barbra is a neurotic chain smoker who crashes a college class in hypnosis looking for a cure. Psychiatrist Yves Montand agrees to hypnotize her and is fascinated to discover that he has instead regressed her back into a former life - in 19th-century England. Intrigued by the woman he has found, he continues to hypnotize modern Barbra and soon falls in love with the intriguing woman from the past. However, modern Barbra thinks he is treating her smoking problem and she has fallen in love with him. Solid music and lush production.

Sex / Nud / Viol / Lang / AdSit

A: Barbra Streisand, Yves Montand, Bob Newhart, Larry Blyden, Simon Oakland, Jack Nicholson

© PARAMOUNT HOME VIDEO 6927

OPPOSITE SEX, THE

D: David Miller — 117 m

NR | MUS COM | 1956 | COLOR

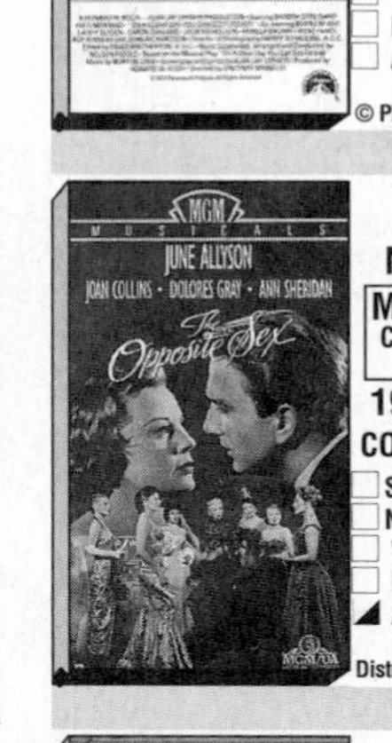

7 This is the musical remake of the 1939 witty comedy THE WOMEN written by Clare Booth Luce. It is the story of a bunch of spoiled Park Avenue women discussing the basic licentious nature of men, while plotting to help one of their number (Allyson) to regain her husband from a floozy by teaching her the fine arts of backstabbing and gossip. Fun musical excursion, but also be sure to see the very funny 1939 original. Songs include: "A Perfect Love," "Jungle Red" and "Young Man with a Horn."

Sex / Nud / Viol / Lang / ◢ AdSit

A: June Allyson, Joan Collins, Joan Blondell, Ann Miller, Agnes Moorehead

Distributed By MGM/UA Home Video M202134

OTELLO

D: Franco Zeffirelli — 123 m

PG | MUS DMA | 1986 | COLOR

8 Opera fans will delight in this production of the classic Italian opera based upon Shakespeare's hero, Otello, starring tenor Placido Domingo. Otello, the jealous Moorish general, is driven into a murderous rage by the scheming Iago who has created lies about Otello's beautiful wife Desdemona. Filmed on locations throughout the Mediterranean. English subtitles.

Sex / Nud / Viol / Lang / ◢ AdSit

A: Placido Domingo, Justino Diaz, Katia Ricciarelli

© KULTUR VIDEO 1184

PAINT YOUR WAGON

D: Joshua Logan — 164 m

PG | MUS COM WST | 1970 | COLOR

9 A rousing good time with this fun-filled, Lerner and Loewe musical/Western/comedy set in the fictional gold-rich/women-poor California mining boom town of No-Name City in the mid-1800s. Two partners in a gold "mine" (Eastwood and Marvin mine the gold that falls through the floors at the saloons) purchase one of a Mormon traveler's extra wives (Seberg), and... they share her - all of her - 50/50. Clever and funny. Plus, some truly great music ("They Call the Wind Maria") that is only slightly diminished by Marvin's and Eastwood's singing.

Sex / Nud / ◢ Viol / ◢ Lang / ■ AdSit

A: Clint Eastwood, Lee Marvin, Jean Seberg, Harve Presnell, John Mitchum, Ray Walston

© PARAMOUNT HOME VIDEO 6933

PAJAMA GAME, THE

D: George Abbott — 102 m

NR | MUS COM ROM | 1957 | COLOR

8 Exuberant and enjoyable Hollywood conversion (largely intact) of the very successful Broadway play. Doris Day plays the head of the union's grievance committee at a pajama factory. She is heading up the charge to demand a 7 1/2 cent per hour pay raise. She must negotiate with the plant's foreman (Raitt) to get it, but love gets in the way. Light-hearted fun. Great songs and inventive Bob Fosse choreography. Songs include: "Hernando's Hideaway," "Hey There" and the big hit "Steam Heat."

Sex / Nud / Viol / Lang / AdSit

A: Doris Day, John Raitt, Carol Haney, Eddie Foy, Jr., Reta Shaw

© WARNER HOME VIDEO 35085

PAL JOEY

D: George Sidney — 109 m

NR | MUS COM | 1957 | COLOR

8 Fun-filled and very entertaining, with a wonderful Rodgers and Hart score including 14 wonderful songs - many now classics themselves. The story is a pretty good one, too, about a brash heel of a singer (Sinatra) who wants to open a fancy nightclub. Rita Hayworth is a sexy, wealthy socialite who could be his ticket but she wants him to give up his love for Kim Novak. Songs include: "My Funny Valentine," "Bewitched Bothered and Bewildered" and "The Lady is a Tramp." Enjoyable.

Sex / Nud / Viol / Lang / ◢ AdSit

A: Frank Sinatra, Rita Hayworth, Kim Novak, Bobby Sherwood, Elizabeth Patterson, Barbara Nichols

© COLUMBIA TRISTAR HOME VIDEO 60798

MUS

PENNIES FROM HEAVEN

D: Herbert Ross 108 m

R | MUS ROM | 1981 | COLOR

6 Unique, offbeat and downbeat musical, but with some great dance and production numbers. Set in the Depression years, Martin plays an unhappily married pitchman selling sheet-music. His miserable life contrasts badly with the happy lyrics of the pop songs he sells. He escapes into his fantasies about a glamorous life with his mistress (Peters), but instead he is arrested for murder and she turns to prostitution. Still, he is a dreamer and continues to dream.

Sex Nud Viol Lang AdSit

A: Steve Martin, Bernadette Peters, Christopher Walken, Jessica Harper, Vernel Bagneris, John McMartin

Distributed By MGM/UA Home Video M800147

PETER PAN

D: Vincent J. Donehue 104 m

NR | MUS CLD | 1960 | COLOR

8 In December 1960, NBC television aired a wonderful musical version of the children's classic starring Mary Martin, for which she won an Emmy. Time has not dimmed the sense of magic and wonder it inspires. Wendy is a young girl, verging on womanhood. However, just before she is all grown up, she and her two young brothers are escorted to Never Never Land, a magical land where only children may go. Their guide there is Peter Pan, a magical boy who refuses to ever grow up. He takes them to a place where there is constant adventure with pirates and Indians and ceaseless fun. Inspired. Also see Spielberg's 1992 follow-up HOOK.

Sex Nud Viol Lang AdSit

A: Mary Martin, Cyril Ritchard, Sondra Lee, Margalo Gilmore

© GOODTIMES 7001

PIPPIN

D: David Sheehan 104 m

NR | MUS | 1981 | COLOR

8 This is a specially taped video version of Bob Fosse's long-running smash Broadway musical play that is also winner of five Tony Awards. The play is premised upon the travails of Pippin, the son of Charlemagne and heir to the Holy Roman Empire. He is learning to deal with his adolescent indecisions, about war and women and he ponders if there is "something worthwhile I can do with my life." Major hit songs include "Corner of the Sky," "No Time at All," "With You," "Magic to Do" and "Spread a Little Sunshine."

Sex Nud Viol Lang AdSit

A: Ben Vereen, William Katt, Martha Raye, Chita Rivera

© VIDEO COMMUNICATIONS, INC. 6004

PIRATES OF PENZANCE, THE

D: Wilford Leach 112 m

G | MUS COM | 1983 | COLOR

7 Gilbert and Sullivan's perennial favorite comic-musical for the stage is given a good go on the screen (with most of the stage intact), but the use of very stylized sets and staged camera spectacles, reminiscent of Busby Berkely, will put off many reality-based filmgoers. Yet the story of an honest young man trapped into being a pirate and in love with the daughter of a Major General is still funny. The lyrics and score are simply wonderful. An impressive effort, but Ronstadt sings better than she acts.

Sex Nud Viol Lang AdSit

A: Kevin Kline, Angela Lansbury, Linda Ronstadt, George Rose, Rex Smith, Tony Azito

© MCA/UNIVERSAL HOME VIDEO, INC. 71012

POPEYE

D: Robert Altman 114 m

PG | COM CLD MUS | 1980 | COLOR

6 Curious live-action version of the famous cartoon character. Not a wonderful musical, but not too bad, either. It is an imaginative staging and production with some really wonderful characterizations from Duvall and especially Williams. All the famous characters are here. Popeye (Williams) rows into port looking for his pappy (Walston). He falls in love with skinny Olive (Duvall), even though she is engaged to Bluto (Smith). Interesting and clever. It was unfairly ignored at the box office by an audience that didn't know quite what how to take it. A good family movie.

Sex Nud Viol Lang AdSit

A: Robin Williams, Shelley Duvall, Ray Walston, Linda Hunt, Paul L. Smith, Paul Dooley

© PARAMOUNT HOME VIDEO 1171

PRODUCERS, THE

D: Mel Brooks 90 m

NR | COM MUS | 1968 | COLOR

9 Hysterical farce from Mel Brooks. This, his first film, won him an Oscar for Best Screenplay and he also directed. It is about a shyster promoter (Mostel) who cons a meek accountant (Wilder) into helping him with a terrific get-rich-quick scheme. They will sell interests in a new (and very bad) Broadway play ("Springtime for Hitler") which they will produce... but they will sell 25 times more shares than are available. Then when the thing flops, they will take all the extra money to Rio with them. But when it becomes a big hit instead, they are in big-time trouble.

Sex Nud Viol Lang AdSit

A: Zero Mostel, Gene Wilder, Dick Shawn, Kenneth Mars, Lee Meredith, Christopher Hewett

© NEW LINE HOME VIDEO 2051

PURPLE RAIN

D: Albert Magnoli 113 m

R | MUS DMA | 1984 | COLOR

6 Prince's notorious screen debut is a semi-autobiographical story of a rock musician who can't get along with his parents, his band or his girlfriend. The film is most notable for its striking score, which won an Oscar. Rock 'n' roll hits include the smash hits: "When Doves Cry," "Let's Go Crazy," "I Would Die 4 U," "Darling Nikki" and "Purple Rain."

Sex Nud Viol Lang AdSit

A: Prince, Morris Day, Apollonia Kotero, Jill Jones, Olga Karlatos, Clarence Williams, III

© WARNER HOME VIDEO 11398

ROAD TO HONG KONG

D: Norman Panama 92 m

NR | MUS COM | 1962 | B&W

6 Lively formula comedy. Two ex-vaudeville performers turned con men end up in a plot filled with international intrigue. A secret formula has been submerged inside one of their minds. Somewhere along the line, Hope loses his memory and that unfortunate incident leads them to involvement with a spy (Collins) and a nutty gang of baddies. Sellers makes an exuberant performance in his cameo as the doctor who examines Hope. Inside jokes between Hope and Crosby add some zest to the last film in the series.

Sex Nud Viol Lang AdSit

A: Bob Hope, Bing Crosby, Joan Collins, Dorothy Lamour, Robert Morley, Walter Gotell

Distributed By MGM/UA Home Video M202078

ROBIN AND THE SEVEN HOODS

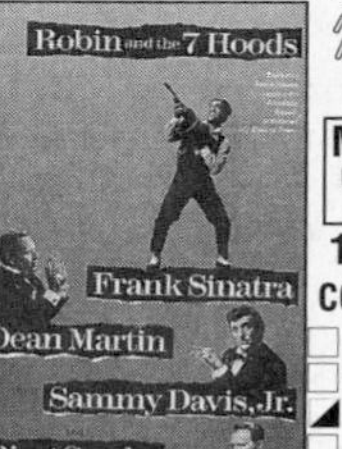

D: Gordon Douglas 123 m

NR | MUS COM | 1964 | COLOR

6 A jazzy musical spoof, both of gangsters and of the classic English adventure tale. Set in 1928 Chicago, gangster Sinatra strikes upon a brilliant move. He will set up various charity groups and then take his cut right off the top. However, all the good will he generates also turns out to be very good for the business at his speakeasies. His chief rival in town (Falk) is more than a little upset because he's losing so much business and he decides to do something about it. A frothy light-hearted musical comedy, featuring the Oscar-nominated songs "My Kind of Town" and "All for One."

Sex Nud Viol Lang AdSit

A: Frank Sinatra, Dean Martin, Bing Crosby, Sammy Davis, Jr., Peter Falk, Barbara Rush

© WARNER HOME VIDEO 11369

ROCKY HORROR PICTURE SHOW, THE

D: Jim Sharman 106 m

R | MUS COM SF | 1975 | COLOR

9 Wacky, purposely goofy, full of rock 'n roll energy and lots of fun! On one dark and stormy night, a stuffy young couple (Bostwick and Sarandon) get a flat tire and come knocking on the door of extra-terrestrial transvestite Dr. Frank N. Furter's mysterious castle looking for a phone. They find that they have arrived on a very special night. It's a party! The castle is full of kinky guests and the bisexual doctor teaches the up-tight pair to loosen up by seducing them both. That's not all - he's an alien. This film inspired a huge unprecedented cult following. Very very different. Be open minded.

Sex Nud Viol Lang AdSit

A: Barry Bostwick, Susan Sarandon, Tim Curry, Charles Gray, Richard O'Brien, Patricia Quinn

© FOXVIDEO 1424

ROCK 'N' ROLL HIGH SCHOOL

D: Allan Arkush 93 m

PG | MUS COM | 1979 | COLOR

6 Rowdy teenage rebels are seeking reform in this fast-paced teenage musical comedy! A new principal (Woronov) comes to Vince Lombardi High School and tries to cramp the kid's style, but one rebellious teenager, a die-hard "Ramones" fan, blasts their music out into the halls, and even succeeds at bringing her favorite group to the school. A confrontation is now at hand. The students go nuts and conduct a huge revolt against the suppressive and stifling establishment. A cult favorite for teens, with some genuine humor and outstanding rock 'n' roll.

Sex Nud Viol Lang AdSit

A: P.J. Soles, Vincent Van Patten, Clint Howard, Dey Young, The Ramones, Mary Woronov

© WARNER HOME VIDEO 24054

ROSE, THE

D: Mark Rydell 134 m

R | DMA MUS | 1979 | COLOR

7 Midler, in her starring debut, brilliantly plays a brassy, extremely successful but lonely rock star who succumb to the perils of stardom and life on the road. She falls prey to alcohol and drug abuse, and gets involved in several destructive relationships, all as a vain attempt to seek solace for her loneliness. Midler's character was modeled after the ill-fated life of singer Janis Joplin. An insightful look into the not-always-glamorous life of rock and roll, with some of the best musical footage ever captured on film. "The Rose" is one of the outstanding songs from the film.

Sex Nud Viol Lang AdSit

A: Bette Midler, Alan Bates, Frederic Forrest, Harry Dean Stanton, Barry Primus, David Keith

© FOXVIDEO 1092

ROUSTABOUT

D: John Rich — 100 m

NR | MUS ROM | 1964 | COLOR

6 Pleasing Presley musical. A wandering young singer (Presley) literally gets run off the road by Stanwyck's carnival. While he is waiting to get his motorcycle fixed, he decides to join the carnival's crew. However, the carnival is in a whole bunch of financial trouble and, while Elvis is helping Stanwyck save her carnival from ruin, he falls in love with her daughter (Freeman). Songs include "Little Egypt" and "One Track Heart." Also has Rachel Welch in her film debut and Teri Garr in another bit part.

Sex / Nud / Viol / Lang / AdSit

A: Elvis Presley, Barbara Stanwyck, Leif Erickson, Joan Freeman, Sue Anne Langdon, Raquel Welch

© CBS/FOX VIDEO 2007

RUMPELSTILTSKIN

D: David Irving — 84 m

G | MUS CLD | 1986 | COLOR

6 A well-done version of this fanciful children's fairy tale. A young girl (Irving) daydreams of magical things and her father swears that everything she touches turns to gold. When the evil King (Revill) hears of this, he summons her to spin straw into gold or be executed. To the rescue comes a mysterious little man, Rumpelstiltskin (Barty), who gets her out of her horrible situation but he expects a very expensive form of repayment. He wants Irving's first-born child - that is, unless she can guess his name. An enjoyable fantasy that young children will especially enjoy.

Sex / Nud / Viol / Lang / AdSit

A: Amy Irving, Priscilla Pointer, Billy Barty, Clive Revill, John Moulder-Brown, Robert Symonds

© MEDIA HOME ENTERTAINMENT, INC. M919

SARAFINA!

D: Darrell James Roodt — 98 m

PG-13 | MUS DMA | 1992 | COLOR

6 This film version of the hit Broadway musical is a near miss for most of the typical public, but it will satisfy some. Sarafina is a black teenage girl living in the South African segregated township of Soweto. She dreams of becoming a movie star but idolizes Nelson Mandella and becomes politicized by the brutalities of the white soldiers who terrorize the people. She and the other students rally around a charismatic history teacher (Goldberg) who teaches them to be proud and reject apartheid. The energetic Afro-pop music and dancing invigorates the plot which is well intentioned but too heavy handed.

Sex / Nud / Viol / Lang / AdSit

A: Whoopi Goldberg, Miriam Makeba, Leleti Khumalo, John Kani, Mbongeni Ngema

© TOUCHSTONE HOME VIDEO 1595

SATURDAY NIGHT FEVER

D: John Badham — 118 m

R | DMA ROM MUS | 1977 | COLOR

8 Huge box office smash! Tony (Travolta) is just a paint salesman in Brooklyn but on Saturday night, the highlight of his week, he dances at the neighborhood disco where he's the star. He decides to take a shot at the big time with a new partner (Gorney) and enters a dance contest that he hopes will serve as a springboard to the place where dreams come true - Manhattan. Instead, he unexpectedly begins to question the shallowness of his existence. The pulse pounding soundtrack and beat of the Bee Gee's helped to define the dynamic dance mood of '70s disco and of an era. Electric!

Sex / Nud / Viol / Lang / AdSit

A: John Travolta, Karen Lynn Gorney, Donna Pescow, Barry Miller, Joseph Cali, Paul Pape

© PARAMOUNT HOME VIDEO 1113

SAY AMEN, SOMEBODY

D: George T. Nierenberg — 100 m

G | DOC MUS | 1983 | COLOR

9 A riotous celebration of Gospel music! This documentary captures the energetic feeling and uplifting essence of the songs, the sound, the meanings, the joy and inspiration of music made for the senses and soul. Featured are two of Gospel's greats: Thomas A. Dorsey and Willie Mae Ford Smith. Their lives and their careers are explored and spliced with more than two dozen exuberant songs. A glistening, shining film that is wonderful for the whole family and will leave you feeling jubilant and refreshed. If you enjoy this, you should also see the documentary GOSPEL.

Sex / Nud / Viol / Lang / AdSit

A: Willie Mae Ford Smith, Thomas A. Dorsey, Sallie Martin

© PACIFIC ARTS VIDEO 547

SCHOOL DAZE

D: Spike Lee — 114 m

R | COM MUS | 1987 | COLOR

7 Insightful and honest comedy. During homecoming weekend at a black college, two factions of the school, the Wanabee fraternity and the Jigaboo fraternity, clash in every way. The Wanabees work to lose or disguise their racial identity, while the Jigaboos are comfortable and secure with their's, and the two groups torment each other. From all this energized ruckus, director Spike Lee skillfully extracts a lesson in social values and explores subjects not often talked about in film, or elsewhere. Spirited dance numbers intermix with the outrageous goings-on during the celebratory weekend. Criticized as being unstructured.

Sex / Nud / Viol / Lang / AdSit

A: Larry Fishburne, Giancarlo Esposito, Joe Seneca, Tisha Campbell, Kyme, Ossie Davis

© COLUMBIA TRISTAR HOME VIDEO 65006

SCROOGE

D: Ronald Neame — 115 m

G | MUS | 1970 | COLOR

7 Big-budget British musical production of the perennial Christmas favorite from the pen of Charles Dickens. It received Oscar nominations for Best Art Direction, Best Costumes, Best Score and Best Song: "Thank You Very Much." It is a very lively presentation of the classic with Finney in a role that seems custom-designed for him. Guiness is a standout, too.

Sex / Nud / Viol / Lang / AdSit

A: Albert Finney, David Collings, Richard Beaumont, Alec Guinness, Edith Evans, Kenneth More

© FOXVIDEO 7126

SILK STOCKINGS

D: Rouben Mamoulian — 118 m

MUS ROM | 1957 | COLOR

8 Musical with polish and pizzazz! Sparks fly when a heartless Soviet agent (Charisse) falls for a persistent American movie producer (Astaire) in romantic Paris. Cold and austere at first, she can't resist Astaire as his charming advances tug at her heart. This re-make of the classic NINOTCHKA into a musical features some new songs by Cole Porter and, as you would expect, unforgettable dancing from Astaire and Charisse.

Sex / Nud / Viol / Lang / AdSit

A: Fred Astaire, Cyd Charisse, Janis Paige, Peter Lorre, George Tobias, Jules Munshin

Distributed By MGM/UA Home Video M700051

SONGWRITER

D: Alan Rudolph — 94 m

R | MUS COM | 1984 | COLOR

6 Kristofferson and Nelson play fictional forms of themselves who, together, take the music industry by storm. Early in their career together, the country-western sensations split up to pursue their own interests. Nelson goes on to become a superstar of country song while Kristofferson remains the country rebel with a huge heart. When Nelson's wife throws him out and he gets into a sticky situation with a manager who is out to steal his material, he calls on his old pal to help him. An enjoyable story that takes you along at an even clip, and features a lot of country music.

Sex / Nud / Viol / Lang / AdSit

A: Kris Kristofferson, Willie Nelson, Melinda Dillon, Rip Torn, Lesley Ann Warren, Mickey Raphael

© COLUMBIA TRISTAR HOME VIDEO 60437

SOUND OF MUSIC, THE

D: Robert Wise — 175 m

G | MUS DMA | 1965 | COLOR

9 Immensely popular film adapted from an immensely popular Broadway musical and taken from the pages of real life. Winner of the Best Picture and four other Oscars. Andrews is Maria, a spunky girl who doesn't fit in at the convent, so she is sent to be the governess for the family of widower Baron Von Trapp (Plummer). She falls in love with him and the family, and they are married. But it is 1938, the Nazis are menacing Austria and have targeted their whole family. So the entire family is forced into making a daring escape over the mountains. Warm and wonderful with memorable songs. Sweet and timeless.

Sex / Nud / Viol / Lang / AdSit

A: Julie Andrews, Christopher Plummer, Peggy Wood, Angela Cartwright, Richard Haydn, Eleanor Parker

© FOXVIDEO 1051

SOUTH PACIFIC

D: Joshua Logan — 150 m

NR | MUS ROM | 1958 | COLOR

7 Rogers & Hammerstein musical that was adapted from a hugely successful Broadway play. James Michener's moving book was simplified for the stage and further diminished for the screen. The result is a largely saccharin presentation, but it is still involving and has wonderful music. The story revolves around life on a Pacific Island during WWII: a nurse from the Midwest falls for a French planter and a sailor falls for a native girl. The plot has been greatly diminished, however. But, the music is truly memorable, and there is a lot of it. Several of the songs are now standards.

Sex / Nud / Viol / Lang / AdSit

A: Mitzi Gaynor, Rossano Brazzi, John Kerr, Ray Walston, John Kerr, France Nuyen

© FOXVIDEO 7045

SUNDAY IN THE PARK WITH GEORGE

D: James Lapine — 145 m

NR | MUS ROM | 1986 | COLOR

9 A painting comes to life in this magnificent taped stage presentation of the superb Pulitzer Prize-winning musical play. Based on characters featured in Georges Seurat's painting "Sunday Afternoon on the Island of La Grande Jatte," each character in the painting becomes real and has a compelling story to tell. The score and lyrics by Stephen Sondheim are very memorable. Patinkin deftly plays the Seurat, the masterful painter. One of the most unforgettable musicals in recent history. A standout!

Sex / Nud / Viol / Lang / AdSit

A: Bernadette Peters, Mandy Patinkin, Barbara Byrne, Charles Kimbrough

© WARNER HOME VIDEO 370

SWEENEY TODD

D: Harold Prince 139 m

NR
MUS HOR
1982
COLOR
Sex
Nud
Viol
Lang
AdSit

8 Truly spooky! A demented barber is the center of focus in this film that is really the Sondheim stage musical filmed in its entirety. The barber Todd (Hearn), falsely sent to prison by the Mayor, is released to find his wife gone mad and his daughter kidnapped by the Mayor. He loses his grip in seeking revenge against the system and begins slashing the throats of his customers. Their remains, given to the haunting Mrs. Lovett (Lansbury), are then baked in her meat pies. Filmed before a live audience at the Dorothy Chandler Pavilion in L.A. The play won 8 Tony Awards in 1979, including Best Musical and Best Actress.

A: Angela Lansbury, George Hearn, Sara Woods

© TURNER HOME ENTERTAINMENT 1002

SWEET CHARITY

D: Bob Fosse 148 m

G
MUS ROM
1968
COLOR
Sex
Nud
Viol
Lang
AdSit

7 This smash Broadway hit was transferred with some success to the screen. Shirley MacLaine stars as a prostitute and dance hall hostess who dreams of love and marriage. When she is dumped by her latest boyfriend, she has a brief fling with a movie star and then takes up with an innocent young accountant. He thinks he can accept her past, but is more challenged by it than he expected. Wonderful dance routines and fantastic music that has many songs which are now standards: "Hey Big Spender," "Rhythm of Life" and "If They Could See Me Now." Entertaining, but also very long.

A: Shirley MacLaine, John McMartin, Chita Rivera, Sammy Davis, Jr., Ricardo Montalban, Paula Kelly

© MCA/UNIVERSAL HOME VIDEO, INC. 55044

SWEET DREAMS

D: Karel Reisz 115 m

PG-13
DMA MUS
1985
COLOR
Sex
Nud
Viol
Lang
AdSit

8 Jessica Lange gives a nearly flawless performance in this brilliant biography of the late Patsy Cline, one of country music's largest icons. This film documents her rise to fame but dwells mostly on her turbulent marriage. When Cline met her husband (Ed Harris), she fell in love quickly. But with fame fast approaching, her husband turned abusive and resentful and their's was a troubled and turbulent marriage. A tragic plane crash silenced forever Cline's wonderful voice, but Lange brings it back to life with her Oscar-nominated portrayal, lip syncing the original songs with absolute precision. Outstanding supporting cast.

A: Jessica Lange, Ed Harris, Ann Wedgeworth, David Clennon, Gary Basaraba

© HBO VIDEO TVA3666

TAP

D: Nick Castle 110 m

PG-13
MUS DMA
1989
COLOR
Sex
Nud
Viol
Lang
AdSit

7 Enjoyable old-style musical with a very talented cast. Hines stars as a recently released convict who has just served a stretch for a jewel robbery. He is an excellent tap dancer, but rock `n roll has destroyed his chances at making a living practicing his craft. Nevertheless, he trys to establish a dancing career for himself instead of returning to crime. His girl friend and her father (Davis), an old-time tap dancer, seek to help him. However, this story line, just as in the old time musical, is just a ruse to showcase some of the best tap dancing you'll ever see anywhere.

A: Gregory Hines, Sammy Davis, Jr., Suzanne Douglas, Savion Glover, Sandman Simms, Joe Morton

© COLUMBIA TRISTAR HOME VIDEO 70143

THAT'S DANCING

D: Jack Haley, Jr. 105 m

G
MUS
1985
COLOR
Sex
Nud
Viol
Lang
AdSit

8 Compendium of virtually all the great dance sequences ever put to film at MGM, from the '30s to modern times (mid-'80s), and hosted by the best dancers in the business. The best part is that you don't have to listen to a lot of dialogue that usually only serves as an excuse to dance in the first place.

A: Gene Kelly, Mikhail Baryshnikov, Sammy Davis, Jr., Ray Bolger, Liza Minnelli, Fred Astaire

Distributed By MGM/UA Home Video M800613

THAT'S ENTERTAINMENT

D: Jack Haley, Jr. 134 m

G
MUS DOC
1974
COLOR
Sex
Nud
Viol
Lang
AdSit

10 Incomparable compilation of some of the most magical moments from MGM's monumental mound of musicals, extracted from over 100 of its best films, and taken over a 29-year period from 1929 to 1958. This was the glory period at MGM when it could rightfully boast of "having more stars than there are in heaven" and almost every one of them gets at least one appearance. Non-stop singing and dancing. Something for nearly everyone. See also THAT'S ENTERTAINMENT, PART 2, which added comedies and dramas.

A: Fred Astaire, Bing Crosby, Gene Kelly, Peter Lawford, Liza Minnelli, Donald O'Connor

Distributed By MGM/UA Home Video M600007

THAT'S ENTERTAINMENT III

D: Bud Friedgen, Michael J. Sheridan 108 m

G
MUS DOC
1994
COLOR
Sex
Nud
Viol
Lang
AdSit

9 Once again they dug back into the vaults at MGM's dream factory and resurrected some of the greatest musical sequences produced there. This one differs from the others in that it also includes many complete musical sequences which were pulled and were never shown in the final productions. We get to watch Fred Astaire do the same dance sequence on two different sets at the same time on a split screen. And, we get to watch a fabulous Eleanor Powell dance sequence on one screen at the same time we watch the buz of the stage hands and cameras as they film the same sequence, on another screen.

A: June Allyson, Ctd Charisse, Lena Horne, Gene Kelly, Debbie Reynolds, Mickey Rooney

Distributed By MGM/UA Home Video

THAT'S ENTERTAINMENT, PART 2

D: Gene Kelly 129 m

G
MUS DOC
1976
COLOR
Sex
Nud
Viol
Lang
AdSit

9 Inevitable sequel to the very popular THAT'S ENTERTAINMENT, that had been made two years earlier. This time comedy and drama, also taken from MGM's impressive vault of major movies, are included along with musicals. When you have that kind of selection to choose from, it is impossible to disappoint, and this film certainly doesn't. Still, the original is even better.

A: John Barrymore, Clark Gable, Greta Garbo, Gene Kelly, Bing Crosby, Judy Holliday

Distributed By MGM/UA Home Video M700075

THAT WAS ROCK

D: Steve Binder, Larry Peerce 90 m

NR
MUS DOC
1964
B&W
Sex
Nud
Viol
Lang
AdSit

9 One of the best collections of rock `n roll and R&B talent from the '60s. See Chuck Berry, James Brown, Ray Charles, Marvin Gaye, The Rolling Stones, The Supremes, Smokey Robinson and the Miracles, Gerry and the Pacemakers, The Ronettes and Tina Turner. Originally recorded on B&W videotape, the recording quality is not good - but the material is priceless. The clips were also originally released in two rock extravaganza-type films: "The T.A.M.I. Show" (1964) and "The Big T.N.T. Show" (1966).

A: Chuck Berry, James Brown, Marvin Gaye, The Rolling Stones, The Supremes, Smokey Robinson

© MUSIC MEDIA M434

THIS IS ELVIS

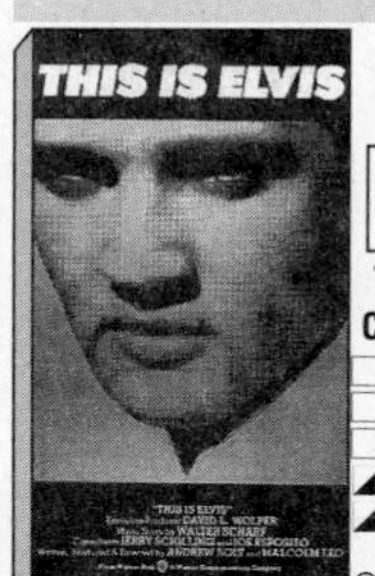

D: Andrew Solt, Malcolm Leo 144 m

PG
DOC MUS
1981
COLOR
Sex
Nud
Viol
Lang
AdSit

8 An entertaining and controversial film which combines interviews, documentary footage, concert clips, home movies and dramatic recreations to portray many different aspects of Presley's life and career. The film begins with his death at age 42 and uses a series of flashbacks to illustrate his beginnings as a truck driver, his early career (including his appearance on The Ed Sullivan Show), his induction into the army, his comeback show with Frank Sinatra and his big TV special from 1968. Includes 38 songs.

A: Elvis Presley

© WARNER HOME VIDEO 11173

THOROUGHLY MODERN MILLIE

D: George Roy Hill 138 m

G
MUS COM
1967
COLOR
Sex
Nud
Viol
Lang
AdSit

6 Cute musical fluff that received 7 Oscar nominations and won Best Original Score. Julie Andrews arrives in the big city and quickly transforms herself into a 1920s modern woman - a flapper. She is also determined to realize her life's ambition: to become a stenographer and marry her boss. But, she becomes so caught up in her fantasy that she doesn't see that she really doesn't want her boss because she really is in love with someone else. All the while, her equally innocent new-found friend (Moore) has become the object of a white slaver's interest. Light-hearted light-weight campy farce.

A: Julie Andrews, Mary Tyler Moore, Carol Channing, John Gavin, Beatrice Lillie, James Fox

© MCA/UNIVERSAL HOME VIDEO, INC. 55028

TOM SAWYER

D: Don Taylor 102 m

G
MUS CLD
1973
COLOR
Sex
Nud
Viol
Lang
AdSit

8 Well done musical remake of Mark Twain's classic, set in the 1830s Missouri wilds along the Mississippi river, near the town of Hannibal. It concerns the exploits of young Tom (Whitaker), his friend - outcast Huck Finn (East) and his girl friend Becky Thatcher (a very young Jodie Foster). this is a first-rate children's movie that will also appeal to many adults. The picture garnered Oscar nominations for Set Decoration, Costume Design and Score. Music and screenplay were written by the same people who did MARY POPPINS, Richard and Robert Sherman.

A: Johnny Whitaker, Celeste Holm, Warren Oates, Jeff East, Jodie Foster

Distributed By MGM/UA Home Video M201863

TRUTH OR DARE

R | DOC MUS | 1991 | COLOR | Sex ■ Nud ■ Viol □ Lang ■ AdSit ■

D: Alek Keshishian — 131 m

8 Controversial, revealing, manipulative and daring. Madonna bravely holds nothing back in this back stage documentary about the controversial performer's life. It's not all pretty; she can be bitchy - barking orders at her dancers and crew - but in the next frame she's vulnerable, mourning at her mother's grave. She has decided to let the audience see everything. You have to decide if it's calculated or just spontaneous. Simply put, if you like Madonna, you will really enjoy this, if not - you won't. You might also be interested to see Julie Brown's biting satire of it called MEDUSA: DARE TO BE TRUTHFUL.

A: Madonna

© LIVE HOME VIDEO 69021

WEST SIDE STORY

NR | MUS ROM DMA | 1961 | COLOR | Sex □ Nud □ Viol ◢ Lang □ AdSit ◢

D: Robert Wise, Jerome Robbins — 153 m

10 Great entertainment, a landmark film and winner of ten Oscars, including Best Picture. The huge Broadway musical smash hit (which transformed Romeo and Juliet into members of rival New York ethnic gangs) was transferred to the silver screen with absolutely nothing lost in the translation. Beautiful and memorable songs (most of which have become standards): "Maria," "Tonight," "I Feel Pretty," "America" and more. Dance sequences won a special Oscar. Very importantly, the beautiful and tragic love story itself is not lost in the beautiful music either. A must see!

A: Natalie Wood, Richard Beymer, Rita Moreno, Russ Tamblyn, George Chakiris

Distributed By MGM/UA Home Video M201266

U2: RATTLE AND HUM

PG-13 | MUS DOC | 1988 | B&W | Sex □ Nud □ Viol □ Lang ■ AdSit ◢

D: Phil Joanou — 90 m

8 Much more than just a concert film! From Ireland to the States, this is an outstanding concert tour of one of the hottest rock bands of the '80s and beyond as they promote their phenomenonal "Joshua Tree" album. U2, the Grammy award-winning band, is one with a message and a conscience. The first half of film is filmed in black and white, the second in color - as four of the members discover not only their musical personality but also their individual inspirations and musical histories.

A:

© PARAMOUNT HOME VIDEO 32228

WHAT'S LOVE GOT TO DO WITH IT

R | DMA MUS | 1993 | COLOR | Sex ■ Nud □ Viol ◢ Lang ■ AdSit ■

D: Brian Gibson — 118 m

9 Hard-hitting biography of R & B and Rock legend, Tina Turner. While the film traces her musical history, and is peppered with some great music, it is more the story of a survivor. She had been abandoned as a child by her mother and left in the care of her grandmother. As a teenager, she rejoined her mother in the big city, where she met Ike Turner. He was immediately struck by her raw talent and singing style. He quickly incorporated her into his band and set about making them into a national name. However, as her popularity rose so did his deep-seated insecurities. He beat her regularly, and it took years for her to break free. An excellent, but sobering, film.

A: Angela Bassett, Laurence Fishburne, Venessa Bell Calloway, Jenifer Lewis, Chi, Phylis Yvonne Stickney

© TOUCHSTONE HOME VIDEO 2011

UNSINKABLE MOLLY BROWN, THE

NR | MUS COM | 1964 | COLOR | Sex □ Nud □ Viol □ Lang □ AdSit □

D: Charles Walters — 128 m

6 Big-budget screen version of the successful Broadway musical. Debbie Reynolds puts in an enthusiastic and rambunctious performance in the title role. Her character is based upon a real-life character from the Colorado gold rush days. She is an unsophisticated, but energetic, backwoods girl who marries a miner just before he strikes it rich. She is determined, but unsuccessful, at making it into Denver society, even though she is the richest woman in town - that is until she gains notoriety as a being survivor of the sinking Titanic. Bouncy, but mostly for musical fans.

A: Debbie Reynolds, Ed Begley, Harve Presnell, Hermione Baddeley, Jack Kruschen, Harvey Lembeck

Distributed By MGM/UA Home Video M600578

WONDERFUL WORLD OF THE BROTHERS GRIM, THE

NR | FAN CLD MUS | 1962 | COLOR | Sex □ Nud □ Viol □ Lang □ AdSit □

D: Henry Levin, George Pal — 128 m

6 Fanciful depiction of the lives of the famous story-telling brothers, which combines a telling of their life stories with three of their fairy tales: "The Dancing Princess," in which a princess finds her true love in a common woodsman; "The Cobbler and the Elves," in which an overworked shoemaker receives overnight assistance from some helpful elves (George Pal's famous Puppetoons); and, "The Singing Bone," where a pompous and cowardly knight relies upon his lowly servant to fight a fire-breathing dragon.

A: Laurence Harvey, Claire Bloom, Jim Backus, Yvette Mimieux, Buddy Hackett, Barbara Eden

Distributed By MGM/UA Home Video M200693

VISION SHARED: TRIBUTE TO W. GUTHRIE AND LEADBELLY

DOC MUS | 1988 | COLOR | Sex □ Nud □ Viol □ Lang □ AdSit □

D: Jim Brown — 70 m

8 Fascinating! Two of the great musical pioneers are paid just tribute by 1988 musicians from many venues in this fantastic documentary. The stories of the lives of folksingers Woody Gutherie and Leadbelly are interspersed with their music which is played by themselves and also performed by many music greats of 1988. This salute to the pair includes songs like "Vigilante Man," "Jesus Christ," "This Land is Your Land" and "Do Re Me." A sparkling look to the recent past and the foundations of popular modern music.

A: Bruce Springsteen, Pete Seeger, Bob Dylan, John Cougar Mellencamp, Willie Nelson, Arlo Guthrie

© CBS MUSIC VIDEO ENTERPRISES 19V-49006

WOODSTOCK

R | DOC MUS | 1970 | COLOR | Sex □ Nud ■ Viol □ Lang ■ AdSit ◢

D: Michael Wadleigh — 184 m

10 Brilliant film which won the 1970 Oscar for Best Documentary and totally captures the spirit of the weekend in 1969 when a farm in New York became the third largest city in the State of New York - with over 400,000 people. This was at the height of the hippie age and it was the Summer of Love. It was the granddaddy if all rock concerts and had virtually every major rock band of the era in attendance. This film is a behind-the-scenes look at both the performers and the people. It was a real "Happening," and this is a valuable time capsule. Great music. Fascinating people.

A: Joan Baez, Joe Cocker, The Who, Country Joe&The Fish, Crosby,Stills & Nash, Jimi Hendrix

© WARNER HOME VIDEO 11762

VIVA LAS VEGAS

NR | MUS ROM | 1963 | COLOR | Sex □ Nud □ Viol □ Lang □ AdSit ◢

D: George Sidney — 85 m

7 The King goes to Las Vegas to win the Las Vegas Grand Prix. Elvis is a racecar driver, but first he has to come up with enough money to buy the hot new engine he's going to need to get the job done. So he takes a job as a waiter, and there he meets luscious, lovely Ann-Margret. She's a swimming instructor at the hotel and Elvis begins to lose his focus. Lots of Vegas pretty girls, some racing action and ten Elvis songs, the biggest of which is "What'd I Say."

A: Elvis Presley, Ann-Margret, Cesare Danova, William Demarest, Jack Carter

Distributed By MGM/UA Home Video M600116

YELLOW SUBMARINE

G | MUS FAN | 1968 | COLOR | Sex □ Nud □ Viol □ Lang □ AdSit □

D: George Dunning — 87 m

8 Imaginative and clever animated feature with a score filled with fun Beatles music. Beatles fans will of course be particularly interested, but others should take note as well. The storyline has animated Beatles traveling by a yellow submarine to the fantasy land of Pepperland where their music and love will overcome the Blue Meanies, who have declared war on all that is good. Surrealistic pop art combines with lots of jokes and puns, plus these and more songs: "Lucy in the Sky With Diamonds," "When I'm 64," "All You Need is Love" and "Yellow Submarine."

A: The Beatles

Distributed By MGM/UA Home Video M301170

WEAVERS: WASN'T THAT A TIME!

DOC MUS | 1980 | COLOR | Sex □ Nud □ Viol □ Lang □ AdSit □

D: Jim Brown — 78 m

10 Wonderfully joyous. For those who don't know - for much of the '40s and '50s The Weavers were the preeminent musical quartet in the country and had a string of top ten hits. The performers were: Lee Hayes, Ronnie Gilbert, Fred Hellerman and Pete Seeger. They and their music formed the basis for the folk phenomena of the late '50s and early '60s. They were magical. This film features archival footage and documents their 1980 reunion at Carnegie Hall. Songs: "Goodnight Irene," "Kisses Sweeter Than Wine," "If I Had a Hammer" (they wrote it) and much, much more.

A: The Weavers

© WARNER REPRISE VIDEO 3-38304

YENTL

PG | MUS ROM | 1983 | COLOR | Sex □ Nud ◢ Viol ◢ Lang □ AdSit ◢

D: Barbra Streisand — 134 m

7 Big star vehicle for Streisand that will be most appreciated by Streisand fans, particularly women. Set in Eastern Europe before World War I, Streisand is the curious daughter of Nehemiah Persoff who decides to dress as a man so that she can further pursue a scholarly education as an Orthodox Jew. She is thrilled when she is accepted, and even admired by her teachers who don't know her secret. She becomes friends (and secretly in love) with Patinkin... but is frustrated because, she is a "man." Clever story idea, but overly long for most people. 12 Streisand songs. She also produced, co-wrote and directed. Score won Oscar.

A: Barbra Streisand, Nehemiah Persoff, Mandy Patinkin, Amy Irving, Steven Hill

Distributed By MGM/UA Home Video M200313

Mystery

1956 and After

ADVOCATE, THE

D: Leslie Megahey — 102 m

R | DMA MYS | 1994 | COLOR | Sex | Nud | Viol | Lang | AdSit

7 15th-century France was rife with ignorance, superstition and corruption. Law is attempted for the protection of order, but it is also subject to the interpretation of both the church and the local aristocracy. One of its more bizarre aspects is that animals were held to the same laws as were man. This presents an interesting background for this film to present its story of an ardent lawyer who has escaped the corrupt politics of Paris, only to be trapped in even more corrupt and bizarre local politics, when he is forced to defend a pig accused of killing a Jewish boy. Quite unusual, yet also quite fascinating -- both from a historical aspect and philosophical one. Based upon fact.

A: Colin Firth, Ian Holm, Donald Pleasence, Amina Annabi, Nicol Williamson, Michael Gough

© MIRAMAX HOME ENTERTAINMENT 2560

AGAINST ALL ODDS

D: Taylor Hackford — 122 m

R | MYS ACT | 1984 | COLOR | Sex | Nud | Viol | Lang | AdSit

6 Steamy thriller. A wealthy hood (Woods) hires an out-of-work ex-football star (Bridges) to find his girlfriend (Ward). Woods tells Bridges that she tried to kill him and also stole $50,000 that he wants back. Bridges chases her down to a beautiful island in Mexico but, instead, falls in love with the sensuous beauty. When Bridges doesn't return, Woods sends a henchman down to bring them both back. Then begins a series of plot twists brought on by jealousy, corruption and murder. Remake of OUT OF THE PAST.

A: Jeff Bridges, Rachel Ward, Alex Karras, James Woods, Richard Widmark, Jane Greer

© GOODTIMES 4621

AGNES OF GOD

D: Norman Jewison — 90 m

PG-13 | DMA MYS | 1985 | COLOR | Sex | Nud | Viol | Lang | AdSit

7 Truly unusual film. An apparently unbalanced young nun (Tilly) is accused of killing her own newborn baby, which she claims is not even hers. A court-appointed psychiatrist (Fonda) is sent to investigate this strange situation, but finds no easy explanations. Is the girl devout and sane, with some greater mystery at play here? Soon Fonda and the Mother Superior (Bancroft) are sparring over the fate of the girl. Very strong acting - two Oscar nominations. At times fascinating, but also disturbing and not always satisfying. From a hit Broadway play.

A: Jane Fonda, Anne Bancroft, Meg Tilly, Anne Pitoniak, Winston Rekert, Gratien Gelians

© COLUMBIA TRISTAR HOME VIDEO 60563

ALICE, SWEET ALICE

D: Alfred Sole — 108 m

R | MYS | 1977 | COLOR | Sex | Nud | Viol | Lang | AdSit

6 This low-budget film is somewhat of an underrated sleeper. Shot in suburban New Jersey, it is the very unusual story of 12-year-old Alice (Sheppard) who has killed her sister, her parents and maybe others. The story is laced with Catholic mysticism and gives rise to some very serious moral issues. Interesting. Also was Brooke Shields's screen debut.

A: Linda Miller, Paula Sheppard, Brooke Shields, Lillian Roth

© GOODTIMES 5051

ALL THE PRESIDENT'S MEN

D: Alan J. Pakula — 139 m

PG | DMA MYS | 1976 | COLOR | Sex | Nud | Viol | Lang | AdSit

10 Nominated for 8 Oscars, won 4, including Best Picture. On June 17, 1972, well-dressed burglars were caught inside the offices of national Democratic party headquarters. This film is a modern classic and is also a landmark film about events that lead to President Nixon's downfall and his eventual resignation. Even though the final result is known, the way in which the drama unfolds is still fascinating. The complex issues surrounding the Watergate break-in are explained in understandable terms by using the best elements of a mystery/thriller, presented in a documentary style. Great story telling.

A: Dustin Hoffman, Robert Redford, Jason Robards, Jr., Jane Alexander, Jack Warden, Martin Balsam

© WARNER HOME VIDEO 1018

AMERICAN GIGOLO

D: Paul Schrader — 117 m

R | SUS MYS | 1980 | COLOR | Sex | Nud | Viol | Lang | AdSit

7 A handsome loner and male whore (Gere) makes his living keeping the ladies of Beverly Hills company. He falls for the wife of a politician (Hutton) and she for him. But a major problem arises when he is framed for a kinky sex-murder and she must decide whether to provide him with the alibi he needs. The sexual chemistry between the two makes this thriller exciting and believable, if a little sleazy.

A: Richard Gere, Lauren Hutton, Hector Elizondo, Nina Van Pallandt, Bill Duke, Frances Bergen

© PARAMOUNT HOME VIDEO 8989

MYS

ANATOMY OF A MURDER

D: Otto Preminger — 161 m

NR | SUS MYS CRM | 1959 | B&W | Sex | Nud | Viol | Lang | AdSit

9 Extremely strong movie. Fascinating courtroom drama with a strong sense of realism. A gripping story that was nominated for seven Oscars, including Best Picture. Jimmy Stewart defends an Army lieutenant (Gazzara) who is on trial for having murdered his sexy wife's (Remick) rapist. Excellent legal drama, considered to be among the best of all time, with some absolutely riveting scenes. Stuart is a witty, cagey defense lawyer. Scott is a stuffy big-city prosecuting attorney. First-rate stuff that was also considered very daring for its time.

A: James Stewart, Arthur O'Connell, Lee Remick, Ben Gazzara, Eve Arden, George C. Scott

© COLUMBIA TRISTAR HOME VIDEO 60701

ANGEL HEART

D: Alan Parker — 112 m

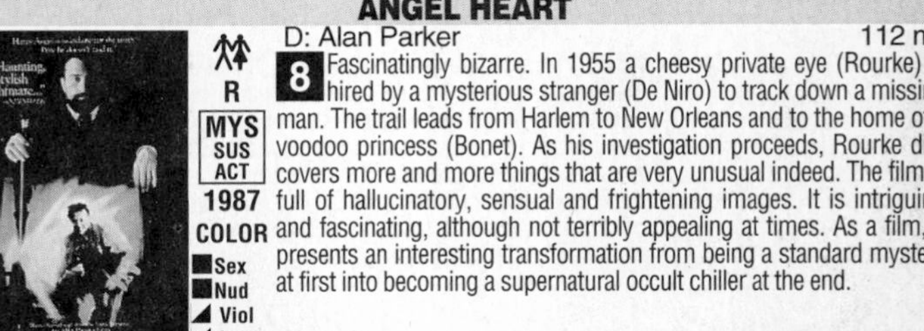

R | MYS SUS ACT | 1987 | COLOR | Sex | Nud | Viol | Lang | AdSit

8 Fascinatingly bizarre. In 1955 a cheesy private eye (Rourke) is hired by a mysterious stranger (De Niro) to track down a missing man. The trail leads from Harlem to New Orleans and to the home of a voodoo princess (Bonet). As his investigation proceeds, Rourke discovers more and more things that are very unusual indeed. The film is full of hallucinatory, sensual and frightening images. It is intriguing and fascinating, although not terribly appealing at times. As a film, it presents an interesting transformation from being a standard mystery at first into becoming a supernatural occult chiller at the end.

A: Mickey Rourke, Robert De Niro, Lisa Bonet, Charlotte Rampling

© LIVE HOME VIDEO 60459

APARTMENT ZERO

D: Martin Donovan — 114 m

R | SUS MYS | 1989 | COLOR | Sex, Nud, Viol, Lang, AdSit

7 Dark, quirky and definitely strange - but gripping! Set in Buenos Aires, Firth is a brilliant young man who is catapulted into financial trouble when his revival movie house hits the skids. He decides to take in a roommate, but he requires that whoever it is knows something about films. He finds the apparent perfect man (Bochner). Bochner even begins to arouse latent homosexual longings in Firth. However, Bochner also soon exhibits signs that there is a psychotic killer inside him and he may even be involved in the government death squads. Curious psychological thriller.

A: Hart Bochner, Colin Firth, Liz Smith, Dora Bryan

© ACADEMY ENTERTAINMENT 1205

BACKDRAFT

D: Ron Howard — 135 m

R | ACT SUS MYS | 1991 | COLOR | Sex, Nud, Viol, Lang, AdSit

7 This is an involving film but the real star is the exciting high-tech special effects. Russell and Baldwin are two feuding brothers who must confront their personal differences and emotional scars after they are assigned to the same fire unit. Their personal drama unfolds against a backdrop in which an arsonist is lighting up the Windy City. The quest to stop him pits brother against brother in a battle of wills, fueled by their determination to live up to their heroic father's reputation. Spectacular special effects alone will keep you riveted, but it's a suspenseful mystery, too.

A: Kurt Russell, William Baldwin, Scott Glenn, Jennifer Jason Leigh, Rebecca De Mornay, Donald Sutherland

© MCA/UNIVERSAL HOME VIDEO, INC. 81078

BEDROOM WINDOW

D: Curtis Hanson — 113 m

R | SUS MYS | 1987 | COLOR | Sex, Nud, Viol, Lang, AdSit

8 Very good Hitchcock-like sexy suspense tale. Guttenberg is having an affair with his boss's wife, beautiful Isabelle Huppert. One day, after making love in his apartment, she alone witnesses a woman being assaulted outside the bedroom window. She doesn't want to report it because their secret would be revealed and she would be destroyed, so Guttenberg does - telling the police he witnessed it when he didn't. When holes in his story begin to appear, he becomes the police's chief suspect in an entire rash of rape/murders. There is only one way out, he has to trap the murderer himself.

A: Steve Guttenberg, Elizabeth McGovern, Isabelle Huppert, Paul Shenar, Frederick Coffin, Carl Lumbly

© LIVE HOME VIDEO 5209

BIG EASY, THE

D: Jim McBride — 100 m

R | ACT MYS ROM | 1987 | COLOR | Sex, Nud, Viol, Lang, AdSit

9 Classy, sexy, exciting and refreshingly different. Quaid is a charming and dedicated homicide detective in New Orleans. Barkin is a by-the-book Assistant D.A. investigating corruption in the police ranks. She and her people catch him taking a small pay off (everybody does it) and goes after him. While they are on opposite sides on this case, she finds that she is still strongly attracted to him. She also discovers that he is truly a dedicated cop. When he uncovers a major scandal in the department and follows it out to the end - even though he is very close to the people involved. Excellent, intricate and well-crafted murder mystery - erotic, too.

A: Dennis Quaid, Ellen Barkin, Ned Beatty, John Goodman, Lisa Jane Persky, Charles Ludlum

© HBO VIDEO 0052

BIG FIX, THE

D: Jeremy Paul Kagan — 108 m

PG | MYS SUS | 1978 | COLOR | Sex, Nud, Viol, Lang, AdSit

7 Pretty good mystery and a good vehicle for Dreyfuss's wise-cracking personality. He plays a '60s radical who is now a private investigator. He is hired by his former lover (Anspack), from the days when they were both political activists at Berkeley, to find out who's using dirty tricks to smear the political candidate she's working for. He already has enough trouble trying to deal with his ex-wife and finding enough time for his kids, and now he winds up in the middle of a murder. Plenty of plot twists to keep you involved.

A: Richard Dreyfuss, Susan Anspach, Bonnie Bedelia, John Lithgow, F. Murray Abraham

© MCA/UNIVERSAL HOME VIDEO, INC. 66053

BLOOD SIMPLE

D: Joel Coen — 96 m

R | SUS MYS | 1985 | COLOR | Sex, Nud, Viol, Lang, AdSit

8 Thrilling film noir type of mystery, full of double and triple crosses. A rural Texas bar owner (Hedaya) hires a private detective (Walsh) to follow his wife (McDormand) because he thinks she's cheating on him with one of his bartenders. She is and, what's more, she and her lover are planning to murder him. So Hedaya hires the detective to kill them first. This is where the real plot twists begin. Who does the detective really work for? Who's really dead? Quite ingenious thriller.

A: John Getz, Frances McDormand, Dan Hedaya, Samm-Art Williams, M. Emmet Walsh

© MCA/UNIVERSAL HOME VIDEO, INC. 80180

BODY DOUBLE

D: Brian De Palma — 114 m

R | MYS SUS CRM | 1984 | COLOR | Sex, Nud, Viol, Lang, AdSit

8 Slick, clever, suspenseful and sexy. De Palma borrows from Hitchcock (VERTIGO and REAR WINDOW) and even himself (OBSESSION, DRESSED TO KILL and BLOW OUT) to create a fascinating and controversial piece of work. Wasson is an out-of-work actor who is set up to be a witness for a murder. He is asked to house-sit at an expensive home where a telescope is trained upon a sexy neighbor who does a nightly dance naked in front of her window. Melanie Griffith is sexy and hilarious as a porno star who holds a key to the mystery of a grisly murder.

A: Craig Wasson, Deborah Shelton, Dennis Franz, Melanie Griffith, Gregg Henry, Guy Boyd

© GOODTIMES 4239

BODY HEAT

D: Lawrence Kasdan — 113 m

R | SUS MYS CRM | 1981 | COLOR | Sex, Nud, Viol, Lang, AdSit

10 Gripping erotic thriller. Hurt is a second-rate lawyer who is sucked into a torrid affair with a sizzlingly lustful Turner. Their chemistry sets the screen ablaze. Turner is beautiful, sexy and rich, but she is married to a rich man (Crenna). She entices Hurt into a torrid affair and then into plot to kill Crenna, but has some devious twists and turns she has kept to herself. Very steamy and sexy, but that never gets in the way of the suspense and the surprises which hold your attention until the very last minute.

A: William Hurt, Kathleen Turner, Richard Crenna, Ted Danson, Mickey Rourke, J.A. Preston

© WARNER HOME VIDEO 20005

BREAKHEART PASS

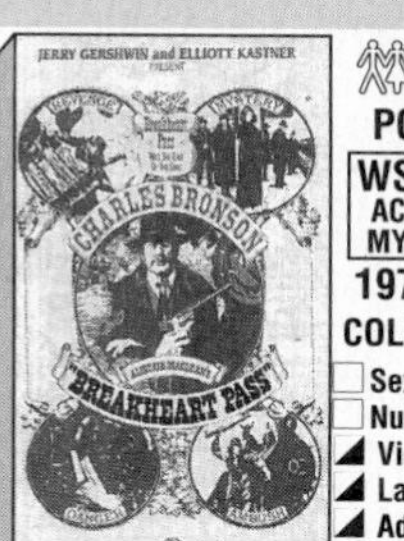

D: Tom Gries — 96 m

PG | WST ACT MYS | 1976 | COLOR | Sex, Nud, Viol, Lang, AdSit

7 Slam-bang action-filled Western starring Charles Bronson. He is an accused thief and an arsonist aboard a special government train that is heading through the snow-draped Rocky Mountains on a rescue mission to an Army outpost and is accompanied by a US Marshall. Also aboard are a governor, his secret mistress and a government engineer. When one of the passengers is murdered, it becomes apparent that all of them have something to hide and are not what they appear to be. Plenty of stunts and fights complement some interesting plot twists in a search for the answer to a

A: Charles Bronson, Ben Johnson, Ed Lauter, Richard Crenna, Charles Durning, Jill Ireland

Distributed By MGM/UA Home Video M201559

CHARADE

D: Stanley Donen — 114 m

NR | MYS ROM | 1963 | COLOR | Sex, Nud, Viol, Lang, AdSit

8 Elegant, classy and fun mystery with a twist of wit. Audrey Hepburn meets charming Cary Grant while skiing in the Alps. She returns to Paris to find that her husband is dead, and that he and his ex-partners had stolen $250,000 in gold during the war and now they want it back. Matthau claims to be a CIA agent and suggests that she would be safer if she gave it back to the government. Cary Grant also shows up offering her his help. Who's a girl to trust? Stylish twists in the Hitchcock tradition. And, it is played out against elegant European backdrops to the strains of Henry Mancini's beautiful score.

A: Cary Grant, Audrey Hepburn, Walter Matthau, James Coburn, George Kennedy, Ned Glass

© MCA/UNIVERSAL HOME VIDEO, INC. 55036

CHEAP DETECTIVE, THE

D: Robert Moore — 92 m

PG | COM MYS | 1978 | COLOR | Sex, Nud, Viol, Lang, AdSit

7 Neil Simon has created a wacky parody of CASABLANCA, THE MALTESE FALCON and THE BIG SLEEP and it is filled with puns, sight gags and a huge bag of star players. Peter Falk plays a Bogart-like character who is in a search for a dozen diamond eggs and also becomes involved in a Casablanca-like love triangle. Very funny most of the time, particularly if you understand the references to these classic movies.

A: Peter Falk, Ann-Margret, Eileen Brennan, Sid Caesar, Madeline Kahn, Marsha Mason

© COLUMBIA TRISTAR HOME VIDEO 90393

CHINATOWN

D: Roman Polanski — 131 m

R | MYS SUS CRM | 1974 | COLOR | Sex, Nud, Viol, Lang, AdSit

10 Landmark film and one of the greatest detective stories of all times. It won eleven Oscar nominations. Jack Nicholson plays Jake Gittes, a small-time 1930's California private detective who is hired by a beautiful socialite (Dunaway) to investigate her husband's affair. But Gittes gets much more than he bargained for when he stumbles into a major case involving double dealing, land swindles, water rights, murder, incest and major political figures. It is a bizarre story which leads us on a complex and fascinating journey. Sequel: THE TWO JAKES.

A: Jack Nicholson, Faye Dunaway, John Huston, Perry Lopez, John Hillerman, Diane Ladd

© PARAMOUNT HOME VIDEO 8674

MYS

COMA

D: Michael Crichton 104 m

PG | SUS MYS | 1978 | COLOR | Sex | Nud | Viol | Lang | AdSit

8 When her friend mysteriously dies during a simple surgery doctor Genevieve Bujold wants to know why. And, when she learns that there have been many other similar cases lately, she begins her investigation in ernest. The horrible truth she discovers puts her into direct conflict with the big hospital's powerful supervisor, Richard Widmark. She has discovered such an outlandish conspiracy that no one believes her - not even her boyfriend (Douglas). She has discovered a whole warehouse of spare body parts, for sale upon request to the highest bidder. Taut, quick-paced thriller. Look quick for Tom Selleck in an early role.

A: Genevieve Bujold, Michael Douglas, Richard Widmark, Rip Torn, Tom Selleck, Elizabeth Ashley

Distributed By MGM/UA Home Video M600013

COMPROMISING POSITIONS

D: Frank Perry 99 m

R | COM MYS | 1985 | COLOR | Sex | Nud | Viol | Lang | AdSit

7 A former investigative reporter, but now a bored housewife (Sarandon), decides to investigate the mysterious death of a Long Island dentist. The dentist, it turns out, was an incredible womanizer. So virtually every woman in town turns out to be a suspect. That element and the suburbia aspects set up a potential for a very clever and funny plot and the first part of the movie is very funny. However, the later part becomes pretty much a standard mystery. Still, a very worthwhile watch.

A: Susan Sarandon, Edward Herrmann, Raul Julia, Judith Ivey, Mary Beth Hurt, Anne DeSalvo

© PARAMOUNT HOME VIDEO 1928

DEAD IN THE WATER

D: Bill Condon 90 m

PG-13 | MYS SUS | 1992 | COLOR | Sex | Nud | Viol | Lang | AdSit

7 Quirky little story of murder which has elements that both Raymond Chandler and Alfred Hitchcock might recognise. Bryan Brown is a moderately successful attorney married to a very wealthy but petty and spiteful spoiled wife. So, he is carrying on an affair with his gorgeous secretary. He would love to divorce his wife, but there is pre-nuptual agreement and he has gotten used to his status and comforts. Reluctantly, he concludes that they must eliminate his wife. His carefully contrived plan requires an alibi which requires a brief affair with another equally obnoxious socialite. In spite of careful plans, one can never plan for everything... can one?

A: Brian Brown, Teri Hatcher, Veronica Cartwright, Anne De Salvo

© MCA/UNIVERSAL HOME VIDEO, INC. 81229

DEATH ON THE NILE

D: John Guillermin 135 m

PG | MYS | 1978 | COLOR | Sex | Nud | Viol | Lang | AdSit

6 Agatha Christie's fussy Belgian detective Hercule Poirot, played by Peter Ustinov, has his leisurely cruise down the Nile River interrupted when a young heiress is murdered. Excellent cast and beautiful scenery try to bring life into this so-so production. But ANY Agatha Christie mystery is better than your average mystery, and that is certainly true about this one.

A: Peter Ustinov, Bette Davis, David Niven, Mia Farrow, Angela Sansbury, Maggie Smith

© HBO VIDEO 1035

DECEPTION

D: Graeme Clifford 90 m

PG-13 | MYS | 1993 | COLOR | Sex | Nud | Viol | Lang | AdSit

6 Andie MacDowell is a young mother and now a widow to a pilot who was killed in Mexico while flying for his own small struggling company. While she is in Mexico to bury him, she discovers that he has several secret bank accounts scattered around the world. Methodically, she travels from one country to the next closing out his accounts and sending home large amounts of money, but then she discovers a clue which leads her to suspect that he may not be dead after all. Mildly interesting.

A: Andie MacDowell, Liam Neeson, Viggo Mortensen, Jack Thompson, Paul Spencer, Chad Powel

© LIVE HOME VIDEO 49125

D.O.A.

D: Rocky Morton 100 m

R | SUS MYS | 1988 | COLOR | Sex | Nud | Viol | Lang | AdSit

7 Dennis Quaid plays a hard-drinking college English professor who wakes up to discover that he has been poisoned with a slow-acting drug and has only twenty-four hours to find who his killers are - and why that did it - before he will die. He enlists the aid of pretty freshman co-ed Meg Ryan as he confronts a series of likely candidates, each of whom has a dark secret to protect, even Ryan. This is a very interesting premise, even though it is somewhat weak in the follow-through. It was done before in 1950 with Edmond O' Brien in the title role. Still, this is a pretty good movie.

A: Dennis Quaid, Meg Ryan, Daniel Stern, Charlotte Rampling, Daniel Stern

© TOUCHSTONE HOME VIDEO 698

DROWNING POOL, THE

D: Stuart Rosenberg 109 m

PG | MYS CRM ACT | 1975 | COLOR | Sex | Nud | Viol | Lang | AdSit

8 Pretty good follow-up to a far-superior HARPER. Newman is back as the cynical private eye Lou Harper. This time he is hired by his former lover (Woodward) to find out who's blackmailing her. This is a seemingly simple case, but the further into it he gets, the more trouble he gets into. Newman's search takes him through some colorful Louisiana settings, gets him involved with all sorts of unsavory types, has him pursued by Woodward's sexy daughter (Melanie Griffith) and he winds up quite literally in water over his head. Slick and intelligent.

A: Paul Newman, Joanne Woodward, Anthony Franciosa, Murray Hamilton, Gail Strickland, Melanie Griffith

© WARNER HOME VIDEO 11371

EDDIE AND THE CRUISERS

D: Martin Davidson 95 m

PG | MYS SUS | 1983 | COLOR | Sex | Nud | Viol | Lang | AdSit

7 Odd but interesting film which has developed into a cult film. Eddie and the Cruisers had been a rock group in the 1960s, but it was way ahead of its time. The lead singer, Eddie, dejected after his album idea is rejected, drove off a bridge - but no body was ever recovered. Now it is much later and the group's songs have finally become popular. Now, also, someone is breaking into all the former bandmember's houses apparently looking for the master tape of some unreleased songs. Reporter Ellen Barkin begins to wonder if Eddie is still alive. Pretty good mystery, even if it is unusual.

A: Tom Berenger, Michael Pare, Ellen Barkin, Helen Schneider, Joe Pantoliano

© NEW LINE HOME VIDEO 2066

ENDANGERED SPECIES

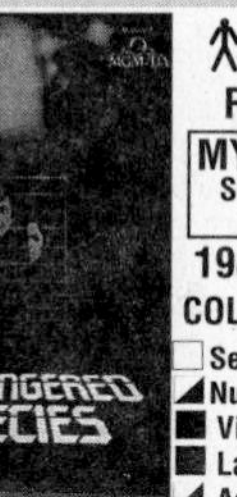

D: Alan Rudolph 97 m

R | MYS SF | 1982 | COLOR | Sex | Nud | Viol | Lang | AdSit

7 A very well done but strange little movie. Robert Urich is an ex-New York cop traveling to get away from his past. He has his daughter with him and the two of them have stopped in a small Colorado town to visit an old friend (Dooley) who runs the local newspaper just as Colorado's peace and quiet is destroyed by a series of bizarre cattle mutilations. Urich, the publisher and a spunky female sheriff (Williams) set out to discover why these cattle are being almost ritualistically cut up and how it could happen with no apparent human participation. This odd story line, oddly enough, was based upon actual events.

A: Robert Urich, JoBeth Williams, Paul Dooley, Hoyt Axton, Peter Coyote

Distributed By MGM/UA Home Video M700217

EYES OF LAURA MARS

D: Irvin Kershner 103 m

R | SUS MYS | 1978 | COLOR | Sex | Nud | Viol | Lang | AdSit

6 Fay Dunaway plays Laura Mars, a commercial photographer whose kinky, erotic and violent photographs are world renowned. But now the artistic visions she sees are also becoming predictions of actual grisly ice pick murders - all of people she knows. Police detective Tommy Lee Jones knows that many of her pictures also resemble confidential police murder photos. What has taken control of Laura? Laura, however, knows the killer is really after her. Lots of wrong turns in the plot add to the suspense. This is a high tension picture, but the unsympathetic characters diminish the impact.

A: Faye Dunaway, Tommy Lee Jones, Brad Dourif, Rene Auberjonois, Raul Julia, Frank Adonis

© COLUMBIA TRISTAR HOME VIDEO VH10190

FAMILY PLOT

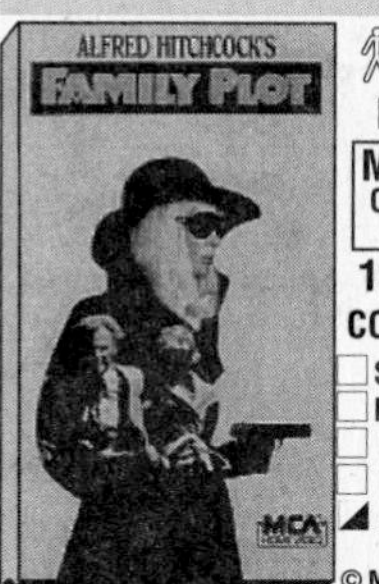

D: Alfred Hitchcock 121 m

PG | MYS COM | 1976 | COLOR | Sex | Nud | Viol | Lang | AdSit

8 This is a winning, light-hearted, convoluted thriller/comedy from Mr. Hitchcock. A seedy pseudo-psychic (Harris) and her loser boyfriend (Dern) team up to track down a lost heir (Devane) and get a $10,000 reward. The target of all this attention is a man supposedly dead, not really dead, but who would much prefer to be thought of as dead. That is because he turns out to be a not-too-nice guy who, along with Karen Black, is in the process of launching a big kidnapping/extortion plot. A fun time, full of plot twists and black humor.

A: Karen Black, Bruce Dern, Barbara Harris, William Devane, Ed Lauter, Cathleen Nesbitt

© MCA/UNIVERSAL HOME VIDEO, INC. 66054

FATAL VISION

D: David Greene 192 m

NR | CRM MYS | 1984 | COLOR | Sex | Nud | Viol | Lang | AdSit

9 Excellent made-for-TV miniseries about a real event that stunned the American public when it happened and had a recurring place in headlines for years after. In 1970, Dr. Jeffrey MacDonald - a former Green Beret - was accused of brutally murdering his pregnant wife and two daughters. MacDonald claimed the murders were done by drug-crazed hippies, but his father-in-law soon came to believe MacDonald had killed his own family. After a military hearing dropped charges due to inconclusive evidence, the father pursued the case and, ten years later, MacDonald was convicted. Compelling drama.

A: Karl Malden, Gary Cole, Eva Marie Saint, Gary Grubbs, Mitchell Ryan, Andy Griffith

© COLUMBIA TRISTAR HOME VIDEO 60770

FINAL ANALYSIS

D: Phil Joanou 125 m

R | SUS MYS | 1992 | COLOR | Sex Nud Viol Lang AdSit

7 A sexy thriller that was created to be in the Hitchcock tradition. Gere is a noted San Francisco psychiatrist treating Thurman, a deeply disturbed young woman. Basinger is her older sister and the wife of a corrupt and abusive man (Roberts). Gere, against his better judgment, becomes sexually involved with sultry Basinger. Basinger kills her husband and is freed when Gere can provide her a psychiatric alibi. However, something doesn't quite fit and he begins to question what is going on. Very sexy, suspenseful, and involved psychothriller that surprises and keeps you guessing and firmly planted on the edge of your seat.

A: Richard Gere, Kim Basinger, Uma Thurman, Eric Roberts, Paul Guilfoyle, Keith David

© WARNER HOME VIDEO 12243

FOUL PLAY

D: Colin Higgins 116 m

PG | COM MYS CRM | 1978 | COLOR | Sex Nud Viol Lang AdSit

8 Very funny murder/mystery. A librarian (Hawn) picks up an undercover agent who gives her information that there will be an assassination attempt upon the Pope when he attends a performance of The Mikado. Quickly, there are several attempts made upon her life. Even though she tells all this to the police, they don't believe her. However, stumbling police detective Chevy Chases eventually comes to believe her and becomes both her protector and lover. A wide assortment of looneys and odd-balls add to the fun. The fine supporting cast includes Dudley Moore in his first American role.

A: Goldie Hawn, Chevy Chase, Burgess Meredith, Rachel Roberts, Dudley Moore, Billy Barty

© PARAMOUNT HOME VIDEO 1116

FOURTH STORY

D: Ivan Passer 91 m

PG-13 | MYS COM ROM | 1990 | COLOR | Sex Nud Viol Lang AdSit

7 Interesting and quirky made-for-cable-TV psychothriller. Mark Harmon plays a likable but average sort of PI who is hired by Mimi Rogers to find her husband after he just disappeared one morning after breakfast. The police don't believe that he's really in trouble and she needs him. Harmon search through the web of clues leads him to believe that there is indeed something afoot, but it is also linked to his own sordid past. What is more, the more they are together, the harder it is to deny that they are powerfully drawn to each other. Very enjoyable characters. However, the ending is a little messy.

A: Mark Harmon, Mimi Rogers, Cliff De Young, Paul Gleason, M. Emmet Walsh

© VIDEO TREASURES M012778

FRANTIC

D: Roman Polanski 120 m

R | MYS SUS | 1988 | COLOR | Sex Nud Viol Lang AdSit

8 A classy and intriguing thriller. An American doctor's wife is mysteriously kidnapped by Arabs in Paris. When neither the bureaucratic Parisian police nor the American embassy officials prove to be very cooperative, a desperate Harrison Ford begins his own frantic search. He discovers that his wife's suitcase had been switched with that of a sexy girl who was a courier for a smuggler. He and the girl, in a complicated web of intrigue, combine forces to pursue both the missing luggage and his wife. Polanski's eye for detail and excellent pacing creates a thrilling emotional rollercoaster. Very good, but starts slow.

A: Harrison Ford, Betty Buckley, Emmanuelle Seiger, John Mahoney, Jimmie Ray Weeks, Gerard Klein

© WARNER HOME VIDEO 11787

FRENZY

D: Alfred Hitchcock 116 m

R | SUS CRM MYS | 1972 | COLOR | Sex Nud Viol Lang AdSit

8 Hitchcock, the master filmmaker, returned to England after 30 years in America to create this, his second-to-last film. It is the story of a "necktie sex-murderer" who is raping and killing women in London. Hitchcock also returns to his favorite theme of an innocent man trapped under the weight of circumstantial evidence. In this case, our man suffers while the suave real killer evades suspicion. Very suspenseful and contains all of the masterful camera tricks, pacing and black humor that are Hitchcock's trademarks.

A: Jon Finch, Barry Foster, Barbara Leigh-Hunt, Anna Massey, Alec McCowen

© MCA/UNIVERSAL HOME VIDEO, INC. 55011

FUGITIVE, THE

D: Andrew Davis 131 m

PG-13 | SUS MYS ACT | 1994 | COLOR | Sex Nud Viol Lang AdSit

9 A huge box office hit. Harrison Ford is Dr. Richard Kimble, who came home to find his wife dying after having been attacked. Kimble scuffled with the intruder and knows that the man has only one arm. However, all the physical evidence points to Kimble. No one believes his story and he is sentenced to die for the murder. But, while on the way to prison, the bus wrecks and he escapes. Tommy Lee Jones is a U.S. Marshall who has been assigned to recapture Kimble. He is good and he is dedicated. Kimble knows his only chance to regain his life is to find that one-armed man himself. Very suspenseful, good action, good mystery and excellent acting. 6 Oscar nominations, including Best Picture.

A: Harrison Ford, Tommy Lee Jones, Sela Ward, Andreas Katsulas, Joe Pantoliano, Jereon Krabbe

© WARNER HOME VIDEO 21000

GORKY PARK

D: Michael Apted 127 m

R | MYS CRM ACT | 1983 | COLOR | Sex Nud Viol Lang AdSit

8 An absorbing murder mystery set in Soviet Moscow. When three bodies, all with their faces and fingerprints destroyed, are discovered in Moscow's Gorky Park, a Russian police inspector (Hurt) begins an investigation. The trail leads him to a very wealthy and well-connected American fur trader (Marvin), a beautiful dissident (Pacula), the KGB and a New York cop (Dennehy). Lots of plot twists keep both Hurt and the viewer confused and guessing. A very involved but involving, and also somewhat uneven murder mystery. It has plenty of intrigue, plus an interesting window into life in a communist state.

A: William Hurt, Lee Marvin, Joanna Pacula, Ian Bannen, Brian Dennehy

© GOODTIMES 04048

GROUNDSTAR CONSPIRACY, THE

D: Lamont Johnson 93 m

PG | SF SUS MYS | 1972 | COLOR | Sex Nud Viol Lang AdSit

8 A top secret space-based laboratory is largely destroyed in an explosion. The only survivor (Sarrazin) is thought by tough government agent Peppard to be a spy who was sent to steal its plans, but Sarrazin is badly burned and has no recollection of events. Still, Peppard must get him to remember. He has to know who was behind the plot. So when brainwashing doesn't work, Sarrazin is set free so that he can be followed. He has now become bait. Clever and intricate plot, with excellent pacing, direction and acting, plus an unexpected climax. A good thriller, unfairly overlooked upon its release.

A: George Peppard, Michael Sarrazin, Christine Belford, Cliff Potts, James Olson

© MCA/UNIVERSAL HOME VIDEO, INC. 80602

GROUND ZERO

D: Michael Pattinson, Bruce Myles 99 m

PG-13 | SUS MYS | 1987 | COLOR | Sex Nud Viol Lang AdSit

7 Suspenseful political intrigue. An Australian cameraman (Friels) learns that his father took newsreel pictures of civilian casualties from a British A-Bomb test in 1954, and may then have been killed by government agents to keep things quiet and preserve a cover-up. The government still wants to keep the lid on it and this politically naive photographer is himself now in serious danger. Donald Pleasence is excellent as a desert hermit who survived the tests. Starts slow and builds steadily throughout.

A: Colin Friels, Donald Pleasence, Natalie Bate, Jack Thompson, Simon Chilvers, Neil Fitzpatrick

© LIVE HOME VIDEO 62781

GUILTY AS SIN

D: Sidney Lumet 107 m

R | SUS MYS | 1993 | COLOR | Sex Nud Viol Lang AdSit

7 An intriguing plot premise. De Mornay is a beautiful, driven attorney who is drawn into defending a charming and handsome self-admitted gigolo (Johnson). Johnson is accused of throwing his wife out a window and faking her suicide for her money. De Mornay learns quickly of his abilities to scheme and manipulate. Convinced of his guilt, she trys to get herself removed from the case but he has arranged it so that she is trapped into defending him. Much more than that, she is also trapped into playing out a special role in his conspiracy. The pacing falters and credibility is stretched, but still holds your interest.

A: Rebecca De Mornay, Don Johnson, Jack Warden, Stephen Lang, Dana Ivey, Ron White

© HOLLYWOOD PICTURES HOME VIDEO 2009

HAMMETT

D: Wim Wenders 97 m

PG | MYS CRM ACT | 1982 | COLOR | Sex Nud Viol Lang AdSit

7 Moody fictionalized screen portrait of the early years of famous mystery writer Dashiell Hammett (THE MALTESE FALCOLN and THE THIN MAN). In real life Hammett actually was a Pinkerton detective and this story has him personally becoming involved with a very baffling case about a missing Chinese woman. It is an authentic recreation of the 1930s film noir look and is a beautifully photographed film, but the very involved plot also requires the viewer's diligent attention in order to be appreciated.

A: Frederic Forrest, Peter Boyle, Marilu Henner, Roy Kinnear, Elisha Cook, Jr., Lydia Lei

© WARNER HOME VIDEO 22026

HARPER

D: Jack Smight 121 m

NR | MYS SUS CRM | 1966 | COLOR | Sex Nud Viol Lang AdSit

9 Excellent, a rousing detective yarn that was the first of Newman's career and is credited with causing the resurrection of the private-eye genre. Harper (Newman) is a smooth private eye who is hired by a rich man's wife (Bacall) to find her husband when he doesn't come home. The investigative trail leads Harper through a curious cast of oddball characters, eventually to a smuggling ring and murder. Fast paced, rapid-fire dialogue and sophisticated plot twists. Followed by THE DROWNING POOL. Excellent.

A: Paul Newman, Lauren Bacall, Shelley Winters, Arthur Hill, Julie Harris, Janet Leigh

© WARNER HOME VIDEO 11175

HIDDEN AGENDA

D: Ken Loach 108 m

R | MYS CRM | 1990 | COLOR

8 Superb political conspiracy and intrigue, in the tradition of Z. An American civil rights investigator, documenting atrocities in Northern Ireland in the 1980s, is murdered in a police ambush. His girlfriend (McDormand) and a British police investigator come to unravel the mystery that surrounds his death and also uncover a military plot to cover up the systematic torture of IRA sympathizers and operatives, including the murder of McDormand's boyfriend. A little hard to follow the dialects at first, but ultimately engrossing and believable viewing.

Sex Nud Viol Lang AdSit

A: Frances McDormand, Brad Dourif, Brian Cox, Mai Zetterling, Jim Norton, Mallie Roeves

© HBO VIDEO 90558

HOLLYWOOD HARRY

D: Robert Forster 99 m

PG-13 | COM MYS | 1986 | COLOR

7 A likable spoof of 40s-style PI mystery. A bored, down-and-out, not-too-bright private detective (Robert Forster) is jolted out of his lethargy by the mysterious case of the rich hog-farmer whose daughter is making porn movies. Daddy wants her back, so he hires our hero. But, the down-and-out Forster is joined in his search through the gutter by his own run-away niece, who adores him. However, neither one of them has a clue about what to do.

Sex Nud Viol Lang AdSit

A: Robert Forster, Joe Spinell, Shannon Wilcox, Kathrine Forster, Marji Martin, Mallie Jackson

© CANNON VIDEO M907

HOUSE OF GAMES

D: David Mamet 102 m

R | MYS SUS | 1987 | COLOR

8 A very unusual and fascinating thriller. An up-tight pop psychiatrist and best-selling female author (Crouse) decides to rescue one of her clients from a charismatic con artist (Mantegna). Instead, she is nearly conned out of $6,000 of her own money and she has also become fascinated with this man. She is both drawn to him and challenged by him. And, she quickly gets in over her head, involved in a plot which contains a suitcase of supposed mob money. Quickly the twists and cons get so thick that she doesn't know who is conning who. This is a slick thriller well worth watching, but pay attention.

Sex Nud Viol Lang AdSit

A: Lindsay Crouse, Joe Mantegna, Lilia Skala, Mike Nussbaum, J.T. Walsh

© HBO VIDEO 0063

HUSTLE

D: Robert Aldrich 120 m

R | CRM MYS ACT | 1975 | COLOR

7 Effective but cynical detective thriller. Burt Reynolds is a bitter L.A. detective called in to investigate the murder of a young woman found dead on the beach, supposedly a suicide. Reynolds is an old fashioned kind of guy who believes in right and wrong, but each day he faces life's worst. So he spends his evenings with his girlfriend (Deneuve), a high-class hooker. Both dream of escaping their dreary lives, but neither does. Reynolds's investigations lead him to a lawyer (Albert) with mob connections. The girl was a hooker and a porn star. Pretty cynical stuff, but it is effective.

Sex Nud Viol Lang AdSit

A: Burt Reynolds, Catherine Deneuve, Ben Johnson, Paul Winfield, Eileen Brennan, Eddie Albert

© PARAMOUNT HOME VIDEO 8785

I, THE JURY

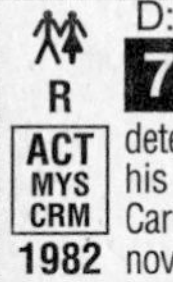

D: Richard T. Heffron 111 m

R | ACT MYS CRM | 1982 | COLOR

7 Mickey Spillane's gritty Mike Hammer character was born in the 1940s in his novel "I, the Jury." In this movie, the hard-boiled detective is updated into the 1980s as he investigates the murder of his Army buddy from Vietnam. His search takes him to Barbara Carrera's sex clinic. The seedy flavor of this film matches that of the novels. It is fast paced, has lots of action, a seedy atmosphere, plus lots of naked women and violence - all of which are befitting the character of Spillane's pulp novels and which also help to cover up some big plot holes.

Sex Nud Viol Lang AdSit

A: Armand Assante, Barbara Carrera, Alan King, Laurene Landon, Geoffrey Lewis, Paul Sorvino

© FOXVIDEO 1186

IN THE HEAT OF THE NIGHT

D: Norman Jewison 110 m

NR | CRM MYS DMA | 1967 | COLOR

9 Powerhouse film that won 5 Oscars, including Best Picture, Best Screenplay and Best Actor. A black Philadelphia homicide detective is arrested at a Mississippi train station after a very important white man is found dead nearby. The gruff redneck sheriff (Steiger) is forced by the facts to release him and then is forced to ask the big city cop for his help in solving the mystery. This a film that works on every level. It is a good mystery, great drama and has not lost any of its considerable punch with time. It is simply excellent.

Sex Nud Viol Lang AdSit

A: Sidney Poitier, Rod Steiger, Warren Oates, Lee Grant, Scott Wilson, Quentin Dean

Distributed By MGM/UA Home Video M201265

IPCRESS FILE, THE

D: Sidney J. Furie 107 m

NR | SUS MYS ACT | 1965 | COLOR

9 This is a quite good and intelligent espionage thriller. Michael Caine is marvelous as a low-key Cockney crook turned secret agent. He is called in by London's top intelligence officials to investigate a series of kidnappings of top scientists, who are then brainwashed and taken behind the Iron Curtain. This is the best of three separate films based on three books from Len Deighton. It is taut and suspenseful, with numerous twists keeping interest levels high throughout. It was a very popular film and it made Caine into a star.

Sex Nud Viol Lang AdSit

A: Michael Caine, Nigel Green, Sue Lloyd, Guy Coleman, Gordon Jackson

© MCA/UNIVERSAL HOME VIDEO, INC. 80518

JACOB'S LADDER

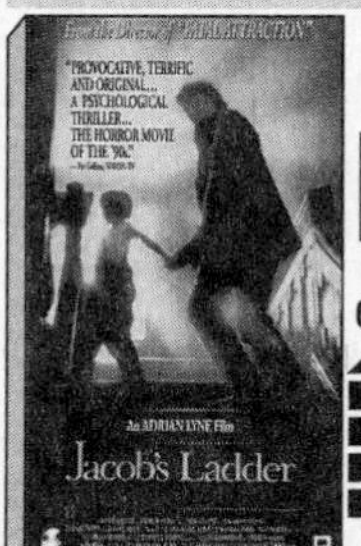

D: Adrian Lyne 116 m

R | SUS MYS | 1990 | COLOR

7 Intriguing, nightmarish and moody thriller with stunning visuals. Jacob is a Vietnam vet who suffers from vivid hallucinations. At times it is difficult for him (and the audience) to tell if what he sees is real or not. Is someone trying to kill him? Did the Army subject his platoon to drug experimentation? Are perhaps his visions actually insights into another consciousness? (The writer of this was the same writer as in GHOST.) Not surprisingly, Jacob is losing his grip on reality. This is very dark and very different, with excellent special effects. You will either be impressed or very confused. Maybe both.

Sex Nud Viol Lang AdSit

A: Tim Robbins, Elizabeth Pena, Danny Aiello, Bryan Larkin

© LIVE HOME VIDEO 68949

JAGGED EDGE

D: Richard Marquand 108 m

R | SUS MYS | 1985 | COLOR

8 Gripping thriller. Jeff Bridges is a wealthy publishing magnate who is accused of the brutal murder of his wife. He seeks out female attorney (Glenn Close) to defend him and she agrees, but only after she becomes convinced that he is actually innocent. During the course of the trial she has fallen in love with him but she also has developed recurring doubts about his innocence. Glenn Close and Jeff Bridges are both convincing, but veteran actor Robert Loggia won an Oscar nomination for his portrait of a sleazy private investigator. Involving, intense and largely well made, but some minor plot holes do hurt it.

Sex Nud Viol Lang AdSit

A: Glenn Close, Jeff Bridges, Peter Coyote, Robert Loggia, Leigh Taylor-Young, Karen Austin

© COLUMBIA TRISTAR HOME VIDEO 60591

JENNIFER 8

D: Bruce Robinson 127 m

R | MYS CRM SUS | 1992 | COLOR

8 Tightly wound thriller. LA homicide detective John Berlin (Garcia) has transfered to a northern California police department to escape big city burnout and to work with his best friend (Henricksen). He arrives just in time to be on-site when a woman's severed hand is found and begins to uncover clues that tie it to an unsolved murder, and that leads him to suspect that there is a serial murderer killing blind women. But, his suspicions are based on few facts and the other cops thinks he's a big city showboat. His fears are very real for him because he has uncovered a pretty blind witness (Thurman) who is now in serious danger because no one believes him.

Sex Nud Viol Lang AdSit

A: Andy Garcia, Uma Thurman, Lance Henriksen, Kathy Baker, Kevin Conway, John Malkovich

© PARAMOUNT HOME VIDEO 32495

JFK

D: Oliver Stone 189 m

R | DMA MYS | 1991 | COLOR

9 Sensational and controversial, this is director Oliver Stone's alternative to the traditional and widely accepted (but not uncontested) Warren Commission version of the JFK assassination. Huge cast of talented big name actors and very high production standards combine with a long running time to cast the view that the assassination was inspired in the halls of government and involved both Cubans and New Orlean's homosexual community. Whether you accept Stone's allegations as fact or fiction, you will still find this to be compelling watching and a fascinatingly interwoven story.

Sex Nud Viol Lang AdSit

A: Kevin Costner, Tommy Lee Jones, Donald Sutherland, Jack Lemmon, Walter Matthau, Joe Pesci

© WARNER HOME VIDEO 12306

JIGSAW MAN, THE

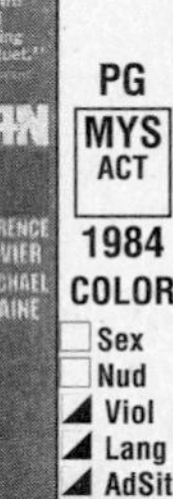

D: Freddie Francis 90 m

PG | MYS ACT | 1984 | COLOR

7 Double agents and double-crosses will keep you guessing the whole way. Michael Caine is a former top British spy who has deserted to the Soviets. But he is really still an English agent, now only in the guise of a traitor? Before he left England, he had hidden a list of Soviet spies who were operating in England. Now, many years later, and after having his physical identity altered through plastic surgery, he is back in England to get his list... but for which side? An interesting caper, but not on a par with the lead's earlier pairing in SLEUTH.

Sex Nud Viol Lang AdSit

A: Laurence Olivier, Michael Caine, Susan George, Robert Powell, Eric Sevareid

© HBO VIDEO TVA3219

KAFKA

D: Steven Soderbergh 100 m

6 This film begins as a marvelously constructed, very moody mystery piece, set in Prague 1919. Irons is Kafka, a novelist at night and an insurance clerk at day. Kafka's friend is found mysteriously dead. The police do not provide him any answers and in fact only add to the mystery. Kafka is also being drawn ever deeper into a plot that links several unexplained deaths, the friend's girlfriend, the company he works for and the government. However, what began wonderfully ends very unsatisfactorily, not because of the strange SF twist, but because it is just so poorly constructed and unresolved. Beginning 9 + Ending 3 = 6 average.

PG-13 | MYS SF | 1992 | COLOR | Sex | Nud | Viol | Lang | AdSit

A: Jeremy Irons, Theresa Russell, Joel Grey, Ian Holm, Jeroen Krabbe, Alec Guinness

© PARAMOUNT HOME VIDEO 15124

KLUTE

D: Alan J. Pakula 114 m

9 Compelling and provocative psychological thriller, with a mesmerizing (Oscar-winning) performance by Jane Fonda. Fonda plays a sultry high-class NYC hooker who gets in over her head. Small-town private detective Donald Sutherland is searching for a husband who is missing after a trip to NYC and who had visited Fonda. Neurotic Fonda only feels in control when she is manipulating a trick. But now she finds herself falling in love with Sutherland as she comes to rely more and more upon him - because she is being relentlessly pursued by the same sadistic killer. A real nail-biter finish.

R | SUS MYS CRM | 1971 | COLOR | Sex | Nud | Viol | Lang | AdSit

A: Jane Fonda, Donald Sutherland, Charles Cioffi, Roy Scheider, Dorothy Tristan, Rita Gam

© WARNER HOME VIDEO 1027

KNIGHT MOVES

D: Carl Schenkel 105 m

7 Competent murder thriller. A chess champion (Christopher Lambert) has gone to the Pacific Northwest to participate in a chess championship and also finds himself incriminated in a series of serial murders. Several beautiful young women have been ritualistically murdered and drained of blood, with cryptic messages then scrawled in their blood. Top cop Tom Skerritt is not certain if Peter, who is receiving phone messages from the killer and supposedly using his game skills to help solve the murders, is the victim of the plot or really is the secret instigator of it. Psychologist Diane Lane too, is caught between love and fear. Not great, but not bad either.

R | SUS MYS CRM | 1993 | COLOR | Sex | Nud | Viol | Lang | AdSit

A: Christopher Lambert, Diane Lane, Tom Skerritt, Daniel Baldwin, Charles Bailey-Gates, Ferdinand Mayne

© REPUBLIC PICTURES HOME VIDEO 2200

LAGUNA HEAT

D: Simon Langton 110 m

6 Witty mystery with a fair dose of action. Harry Hamlin, an L.A. detective who leaves his job after his divorce and the murder of his partner, has moved in with his father in a small coastal town. The town's peaceful facade is destroyed by two brutal murders tied to friends of his father's. Hamlin is drawn into the investigation when he gets involved with the daughter of one of the victims. Hamlin's investigation leads him into a twenty-year-old case of murder and corruption that strikes very close to home. Made for HBO cable TV.

NR | MYS CRM ACT | 1987 | COLOR | Sex | Nud | Viol | Lang | AdSit

A: Harry Hamlin, Jason Robards, Jr., Rip Torn, Catherine Hicks, Anne Francis

© WARNER HOME VIDEO 822

LAST INNOCENT MAN, THE

D: Roger Spottiswoode 114 m

9 Excellent courtroom thriller. An attorney, well-known for winning cases for his less-than-savory clients, has gone into a guilt-induced retirement. He meets a beautiful and sexy woman with whom he falls in love. At her request, he leaves his retreat to defend her estranged husband of the charges that he killed a decoy policewoman. However, he soon discovers that this woman that he loves had other, ulterior motives. This is a very well done and totally involving film where the ethical questions gain equal footing with intrigue and the elaborate plot twists. Excellent made-for-TV production.

NR | SUS MYS | 1987 | COLOR | Sex | Nud | Viol | Lang | AdSit

A: Ed Harris, Roxanne Hart, Clarence Williams, III, Darrell Larson, Bruce McGill, David Suchet

© WARNER HOME VIDEO 819

LAST OF SHEILA, THE

D: Herbert Ross 119 m

7 Absorbing murder mystery in which movie producer James Coburn invites a group of Hollywood types on board his yacht "Sheila" for a Mediterranean cruise. However, his real purpose is to learn who caused his wife's death at a party the previous year, and he has devised a game specifically designed to reveal the culprit. As the clues and red herrings appear, you become more and more involved and intrigued with the plot's outcome. Clever puzzler and a very entertaining murder mystery.

PG | MYS | 1973 | COLOR | Sex | Nud | Viol | Lang | AdSit

A: James Coburn, Dyan Cannon, James Mason, Raquel Welch, Richard Benjamin, Joan Hackett

© WARNER HOME VIDEO 11168

LATE SHOW, THE

D: Robert Benton 93 m

9 This is a highly entertaining mystery that works well on many levels at once. In it, a crusty old retired private eye (played to perfection by Art Carney) becomes drawn into a complex murder mystery. It begins simply enough being only a search to find a missing cat, but that quickly changes when he finds his ex-partner murdered. He sets off to find the murderer with the unwelcome assistance of a flaky flower child played to perfection by a goofy Lily Tomlin. New twists and clues are perfectly timed to keep the mystery interesting, but it is the relationship between its two principal players that is what is most appealing. Well done little gem. Very enjoyable.

PG | MYS CRM COM | 1976 | COLOR | Sex | Nud | Viol | Lang | AdSit

A: Art Carney, Lily Tomlin, Bill Macy, Eugene Roche, Joanna Cassidy, John Considine

© WARNER HOME VIDEO 11163

LEGAL EAGLES

D: Ivan Reitman 116 m

6 Prosecutor Robert Redford and defense attorney Debra Winger team up to clear a kooky performing artist (Hannah) who has been accused of murdering her late father's art dealer. Redford is charming, Winger is a little flaky and together they are quite interesting. This story's plot will not withstand a very close scrutiny however, but it is still pleasing and enjoyable viewing, thanks mostly to the to the screen-presence of the major stars.

PG | MYS ROM | 1986 | COLOR | Sex | Nud | Viol | Lang | AdSit

A: Robert Redford, Debra Winger, Daryl Hannah, Brian Dennehy, Terence Stamp, Steven Hill

© MCA/UNIVERSAL HOME VIDEO, INC. 80479

LIST OF ADRIAN MESSENGER, THE

D: John Huston 98 m

8 Entertaining witty mystery which has the interesting gimmick of having four of Hollywood's biggest names - Tony Curtis, Burt Lancaster, Frank Sinatra and Robert Mitchum - all buried under make-up for short cameo appearances. Someone is killing off all the potential heirs to the family fortune. Now, there is only one heir, a young grandson, left. The only clue to the murderer is a list of names from one of the murdered heirs, Adrian Messinger. Eleven down, one to go. George C. Scott is a retired British intelligence officer who is on the murderer's trail. Entertaining with lots of twists.

NR | SUS MYS CRM | 1963 | B&W | Sex | Nud | Viol | Lang | AdSit

A: George C. Scott, Clive Brook, Dana Wynter, Herbert Marshall, Frank Sinatra, Robert Mitchum

© MCA/UNIVERSAL HOME VIDEO, INC. 80165

LONG GOODBYE, THE

D: Robert Altman 113 m

7 Entertaining and stylish detective yarn based on the classic 1940s PI- character, Philip Marlowe, but updated to the 1970s with many interesting and off-beat twists added. Gould's Marlowe is a New York Jew out of step in hip, me-oriented California. It is frequently funny, but also remains an intense, action oriented mystery of the old school. Marlowe attempts to get an old friend released from a charge that he murdered his wife. A really off-the-wall ending.

R | MYS SUS ACT | 1973 | COLOR | Sex | Nud | Viol | Lang | AdSit

A: Elliott Gould, Sterling Hayden, Mark Rydell, Henry Gibson, Jim Bouton, Nina Van Pallandt

Distributed By MGM/UA Home Video M201409

MALICE

D: Harold Becker 107 m

8 This is a clever thriller that has more kinks in it than you'll find on your worst bad-hair day. Andy is a struggling college professor in a pretty New England town, but his campus is being terrorized by a serial killer and rapist. He is also poor, so to make ends meet, he and his wife Tracy decide to take in a handsome border who is charming, a lady's man, the hot shot new surgeon at the local hospital and an old friend of Andy's. He is also trouble. However, no one is what they appear to be in this Hitchcock-like twister. It's sexy, it'll grab and hold your attention and it'll keep you guessing.

R | SUS MYS | 1993 | COLOR | Sex | Nud | Viol | Lang | AdSit

A: Alec Baldwin, Nicole Kidman, Bill Pullman, Bebe Neuwirth, George C. Scott, Ann Bancroft

© COLUMBIA TRISTAR HOME VIDEO 71773

MANHATTAN MURDER MYSTERY

D: Woody Allen 108 m

8 The old Woody Allen is back. Gone are the angst-ridden self-examinations of much of his later work. This is a tightly scripted mystery, peppered with babbling conversations and Allen's one-liners. Back also is Diane Keaton. She plays Woody's bored wife who has become fascinated by the slightly odd activities of their neighbor after his wife dies of a heart attack. Woody thinks she's over-reacting saying, "There's nothing wrong with you that couldn't be cured with a little Prozac and a polo mallet." So, she enlists the help of their friend Alan Alda. The more they find out, the more it looks like she's right. Starts very slow, but then builds to a rapid fire conclusion.

PG | COM MYS | 1993 | COLOR | Sex | Nud | Viol | Lang | AdSit

A: Diane Keaton, Woody Allen, Alan Alda, Anjelica Huston, Jerry Adler, Ron Rifkin

© COLUMBIA TRISTAR HOME VIDEO 71393

MYS

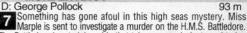

MAN WHO KNEW TOO MUCH, THE

D: Alfred Hitchcock — 120 m

PG | SUS MYS | 1956 | COLOR | Rating: 8

Chilling Hitchcock remake of his earlier masterpiece! A doctor and his wife (Stewart and Day) are vacationing in French Morocco and witness a murder. The dying man whispers to them the plan for a British ambassador to be killed in London. To keep the parents quiet, their young son is kidnapped, and they are forced to foil the murder attempt on their own. The climax, shot at Albert Hall, is an unforgettable sequence in both this and in the earlier version. Day sings "Que Sera, Sera," which won an Oscar for best song and became a big popular hit.

Sex · Nud · Viol · Lang · AdSit

A: James Stewart, Doris Day, Brenda de Banzie, Bernard Miles, Ralph Truman, Daniel Gelin

© MCA/UNIVERSAL HOME VIDEO, INC. 80129

MARLOWE

D: Paul Bogart — 96 m

PG | MYS ACT | 1969 | COLOR | Rating: 8

Entertaining and intriguing mystery. The infamous Marlowe (Garner) is a hard-boiled detective who is hired by a girl (Farrell) to find her missing brother. Garner quickly finds that he has gotten more than he bargained for when kung fu king Bruce Lee (in his film debut) offers him a bribe to drop the case and then turns his office into a pile of broken sticks as a warning. There is blackmail, ice pick murders and a stripper (Moreno) who ultimately helps to solve the case. A good mystery is combined with clever dialogue to make this a real fun time. Based on the Chandler novel "The Little Sister."

Sex · Nud · Viol · Lang · AdSit

A: James Garner, Gayle Hunnicutt, Carroll O'Connor, Rita Moreno, Sharon Farrell, Bruce Lee

Distributed By MGM/UA Home Video M200288

MASQUERADE

D: Bob Swaim — 91 m

R | SUS MYS | 1988 | COLOR | Rating: 8

A clever and complex web of murder and deception is slowly revealed to a naive and innocent but very wealthy Olivia (Tilly). She has just graduated from a Catholic girls school and returned to live in the exclusive Hamptons, but she has to live with her repulsive and alcoholic stepfather (Glover). However, she has all the money she could ever want, plus the rather recent attentions of the handsome skipper of a racing yacht (Lowe). He is in love with her and completely uninterested in her money...isn't he? Outstanding cast keeps the intrigue elevated and the suspense alive. Be prepared for a shocking conclusion.

Sex · Nud · Viol · Lang · AdSit

A: Rob Lowe, Meg Tilly, Kim Cattrall, Doug Savant, John Glover, Dana Delany

Distributed By MGM/UA Home Video M201249

MIGHTY QUINN, THE

D: Carl Schenkel — 98 m

R | MYS CRM | 1989 | COLOR | Rating: 6

There are flavorful and interesting characters set in a beautiful location and, taken as a whole, this is a worthwhile excursion. Denzel is a likable local figure whose intelligence and character have earned him the job of police chief. But his life gets messy when his friend since childhood (Townsend) appears to be the murderer of a rich white man at a local resort. And things get even messier when he finds that there is a lot of covert money that has been sent to his island by the US government, they want it back and have sent on of their agents to get it. Good, but the plot gets fairly involved and has a few too many diversions.

Sex · Nud · Viol · Lang · AdSit

A: Denzel Washington, Robert Townsend, James Fox, Mimi Rogers, M. Emmet Walsh

© CBS/FOX VIDEO 4761

MORNING AFTER, THE

D: Sidney Lumet — 103 m

R | CRM MYS ROM | 1986 | COLOR | Rating: 8

Complex thriller! A beautiful washed-up actress (Fonda), now an alcoholic, is having a very bad morning. After a night of an excess of everything, she wakes up to find that the man in bed next to her is dead, with a dagger through his heart. She remembers nothing. Terrified, she erases all trace of her presence and evades the police. She lives in fear until she bumps into ex-cop and ex-alcoholic (Bridges) who becomes charmed by this girl with a problem and who unravels the mystery for her. Both Fonda's and Bridges's characters are complex, appealing and quite believable.

Sex · Nud · Viol · Lang · AdSit

A: Jane Fonda, Jeff Bridges, Raul Julia, Diane Salinger, Richard Foronjy, Geoffrey Scott

© WARNER HOME VIDEO 419

MORTAL THOUGHTS

D: Alan Rudolph — 104 m

R | CRM MYS | 1991 | COLOR | Rating: 6

Who killed Headly's abusive, drug-addicted and nasty husband (Bruce Willis)? Did she or did her best friend (Demi Moore)? It is a question that the movie never really answers... but the story and accompanying theories are compelling and involving. Filmed in flashback, the story is told how Moore, Willis and a Headly go out one night to a carnival but Willis never makes it home. The two women decide to hide his death and bury him in a ditch. When an inspector comes calling, their friendship unravels as each is pressed hard to present her side of the story. Curious and downbeat.

Sex · Nud · Viol · Lang · AdSit

A: Demi Moore, Bruce Willis, Glenne Headly, John Pankow, Harvey Keitel, Billie Neal

© COLUMBIA TRISTAR HOME VIDEO 50743

MURDER AHOY

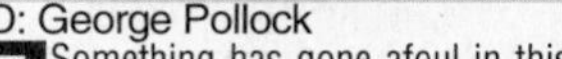

D: George Pollock — 93 m

NR | MYS | 1964 | B&W | Rating: 7

Something has gone afoul in this high seas mystery. Miss Marple is sent to investigate a murder on the H.M.S. Battledore. The Battledore is a training ship that takes young deviants and trains them for better lives. What Miss Marple finds is that someone is training them to become skilled thieves and will kill to keep that information from getting out. The last in Agatha Christie's British film series.

Sex · Nud · Viol · Lang · AdSit

A: Margaret Rutherford, Lionel Jeffries, Charles Tingwell, William Mervyn, Joan Benham, Stringer Davis

Distributed By MGM/UA Home Video M201844

MURDER AT THE GALLOP

D: George Pollock — 82 m

NR | MYS | 1963 | B&W | Rating: 9

More Agatha Christie intrigue! When a wealthy old recluse dies, Agatha Christie's Miss Marple suspects foul play. She leaves no stone unturned as she checks out the cause of the old codgers death. At the reading of Mr. Enderby's will, old Aunt Cora inquires how he might have died, then she, too, is forever silenced. Based on Christie's "After the Funeral," Rutherford and her assistant (Morley) play off of each other with ease, making this one of the best murder tales in the series.

Sex · Nud · Viol · Lang · AdSit

A: Margaret Rutherford, Robert Morley, Flora Robson, Charles Tingwell, Duncan Lamont, Stringer Davis

Distributed By MGM/UA Home Video M201843

MURDER BY DEATH

D: Robert Moore — 95 m

PG | MYS COM | 1976 | COLOR | Rating: 8

Murder is on the dinner menu in this comic mystery! Eccentric millionaire Lionel Twain (Truman Capote) invites top detectives to his home for dinner and offers one million dollars to anyone who can solve the murder of the evening - someone at this table will be stabbed twelve times before midnight. Some of the dinner guests include prominent film detectives such as Sam Spade, Miss Marple and Charlie Chan. Written by Neil Simon, this hilarious film is really a spoof on the great super sleuths of film and features a fantastic all-star cast.

Sex · Nud · Viol · Lang · AdSit

A: Peter Sellers, Peter Falk, David Niven, Maggie Smith, James Coco, Alec Guinness

© COLUMBIA TRISTAR HOME VIDEO 60065

MURDER MOST FOUL

D: George Pollock — 90 m

NR | MYS | 1965 | B&W | Rating: 7

Rutherford's Miss Marple is on jury duty in a murder trial and she is the only juror who is convinced of the murderer's innocence. Her hunch compels her to check out her suspicions by joining a theatrical group because she is convinced that the murderer is still there. Once again she proves she is far more competent than the police investigators assigned to the case. In this third mystery in the series, Rutherford again makes her character a delight to watch.

Sex · Nud · Viol · Lang · AdSit

A: Margaret Rutherford, Ron Moody, Charles Tingwell, Dennis Price, Andrew Cruickshank, Stringer Davis

Distributed By MGM/UA Home Video M201842

MURDER ON THE ORIENT EXPRESS

D: Sidney Lumet — 128 m

PG | MYS SUS | 1974 | COLOR | Rating: 8

Stylish Agatha Christie whodunit! An American millionaire is murdered while sleeping on the Orient Express, and it's a good thing that the master detective from Belgium, Hercule Poirot (Finney), is on the train. Everyone is a suspect, and Poirot sets out to unravel the case. Ingrid Bergman won an Academy Award for Best Supporting Actress for her role as the mousey secretary. Lavishly produced, with a huge all-star cast, it received 6 Oscar nominations in all - even though for years Agatha Christie refused to allow her book to be filmed. This film was followed by DEATH ON THE NILE.

Sex · Nud · Viol · Lang · AdSit

A: Lauren Bacall, Ingrid Bergman, Martin Balsam, Jacqueline Bisset, Albert Finney, Jean-Pierre Cassel

© PARAMOUNT HOME VIDEO 8790

MURDER, SHE SAID

D: George Pollock — 87 m

NR | MYS CRM | 1962 | B&W | Rating: 8

The intrigue never stops in this wonderful whodunit! A dozing Miss Marple (Rutherford) awakens and witnesses a murder on a passing train. Naturally, the police think she is only dreaming. However, convinced of what she saw, she takes a job as a domestic at an estate, hoping to find all the clues she needs to put the case to bed. A very skillful adaptation of Agatha Christie's "4:50 to Paddington" that is great fun for mystery buffs.

Sex · Nud · Viol · Lang · AdSit

A: Margaret Rutherford, Arthur Kennedy, Muriel Pavlow, James Robertson Justice, Charles Tingwell, Thorley Walters

Distributed By MGM/UA Home Video M201994

NIGHT MOVES

D: Arthur Penn 100 m

R | MYS SUS | 1975 | COLOR | Sex | Nud | Viol | Lang | AdSit

8 Excellent, intelligent and complicated, but unjustly overlooked psychological detective story. Gene Hackman is a small time L.A. detective who is hired to track down a teenaged runaway (Griffith) of a rich woman. He puts aside his own marital problems to track the girl down in the Florida Keys where she is staying with her former stepfather and his new girlfriend. Hackman goes and brings her home. The case is apparently solved, however he just learned that the girl is dead. There is more to this case than just a runaway. Dynamite acting from everyone. Hackman crackles, and Warren and Griffith sizzle. A little gem.

A: Gene Hackman, Susan Clark, Jennifer Warren, Melanie Griffith, James Woods, Edward Binns

© WARNER HOME VIDEO 11102

NO WAY OUT

D: Roger Donaldson 114 m

R | SUS MYS ACT | 1987 | COLOR | Sex | Nud | Viol | Lang | AdSit

9 Outstanding and totally engrossing remake of THE BIG CLOCK (1948). This intriguing and sexy suspense thriller will keep you guessing right up to the end. Costner plays a straight arrow from the Navy who is assigned as a CIA liaison to the Secretary of Defense (Hackman). Costner has a passionate affair with a super-sexy lady (Young). When she is murdered, he is assigned to investigate the murder, only to discover that all the clues are pointing to him and he is being framed for the girl's murder. He is being trapped by some very powerful people.

A: Kevin Costner, Gene Hackman, Sean Young, Will Patton, Howard Duff, George Dzundza

© HBO VIDEO 0051

NO WAY TO TREAT A LADY

D: Jack Smight 108 m

NR | MYS SUS COM | 1968 | COLOR | Sex | Nud | Viol | Lang | AdSit

9 Terrific thriller that oddly also has a touch of comedy thrown in. Steiger puts in a dynamite performance as a demented and flamboyant killer. He is a transvestite who disguises himself as different people and then kills - but only dowdy older women, strangling them and leaving a gaudy red kiss on each victim. George Segal is an overly-mothered NY cop determined to find the killer. Segal's chief witness is Lee Remick, and he falls for her. Steiger keeps close tabs on the investigation and enjoys teasing Segal with clues. He also repeatedly taunts Segal with phone calls indicating that Remick may be next. Very well done.

A: Rod Steiger, Lee Remick, George Segal, Eileen Heckart, Murray Hamilton, Michael Dunn

© PARAMOUNT HOME VIDEO 6724

ODESSA FILE, THE

D: Ronald Neame 128 m

PG | SUS MYS ACT | 1974 | COLOR | Sex | Nud | Viol | Lang | AdSit

8 Gripping! John Voight is a German reporter who discovers, through reading the diary of a former death camp survivor, of the existence of Odessa, a secret German society that protects former SS officers who are now safely in positions of power within 1960s German centers of commerce and government. He also learns of the vicious and monstrously cruel Commandant (Maximilian Schell) of a Latvian camp. Voight goes undercover to infiltrate Odessa in search of Schell, but Odessa members are everywhere and he is in constant risk. Intricate plot can be confusing but is well worth the effort.

A: Jon Voight, Maximilian Schell, Derek Jacobi, Maria Schell, Mary Tamm, Klaus Lowitsch

© COLUMBIA TRISTAR HOME VIDEO 60317

OUT OF THE DARKNESS

D: Jud Taylor 96 m

R | CRM MYS SUS | 1985 | COLOR | Sex | Nud | Viol | Lang | AdSit

8 Fascinating story of the New York cop Ed Zigo, who tracked down the infamous "Son of Sam" killer in 1976-77. This was the vicious real-life murderer who shot young lovers in their cars with a large bore revolver, and then wrote taunting notes to reporters and the police to brag of his successes. This gripping story focuses on the cop and the chase, not the killer. A solid and interesting script with tight pacing and an excellent performance from Martin Sheen make this a gripping crime mystery.

A: Martin Sheen, Hector Elizondo, Matt Clark, Jennifer Salt

© VIDMARK ENTERTAINMENT 5241

PARALLAX VIEW, THE

D: Alan J. Pakula 102 m

R | MYS SUS ACT | 1974 | COLOR | Sex | Nud | Viol | Lang | AdSit

9 Absolutely gripping, but strangely neglected, political thriller. Warren Beatty plays an alcoholic small-time reporter who witnesses the assassination of a Presidential candidate. As other witnesses mysteriously turn up dead, he begins his own investigations into their deaths. Each new piece of evidence he uncovers leads him to suspect that there is an elaborate coverup underway. An oppressive suspense builds steadily as the more he learns, the more likely it becomes that he will be eliminated, too.

A: Warren Beatty, Paula Prentiss, Hume Cronyn, William Daniels, Walter McGinn, Kelly Thordsen

© PARAMOUNT HOME VIDEO 8670

PELICAN BRIEF, THE

D: Alan Pakula 141 m

PG-13 | SUS MYS | 1994 | COLOR | Sex | Nud | Viol | Lang | AdSit

8 Fast-paced intrigue based upon the novel of the same name by John Grisham. Two Supreme Court justices have been assassinated. Julia Roberts is a young New Orleans law student who researches the records to discover what factor they have in common and stumbles upon the truth. She presented her case to her law professor/lover, who delivered her brief to the FBI. Almost immediately, his car is blown up and Julia is on the run with two government agencies and a contract killer after her. Her only hope of staying alive lies in a prominent political reporter (Denzel Washington). Overly-involved at times and sometimes cannot stand close scrutiny, but still very involving.

A: Julia Roberts, Denzel Washington, Sam Shepard, John Heard, Tony Goldwyn, John Lithgow

© WARNER HOME VIDEO 12989

PRESUMED INNOCENT

D: Alan J. Pakula 127 m

R | MYS SUS CRM | 1990 | COLOR | Sex | Nud | Viol | Lang | AdSit

8 This is a sexy and thoroughly involving thriller (based on a best-selling novel) which was a big hit at the box office. Ford plays Rusty Sabich, a hard-working up-and-coming attorney at the county prosecutor's office. However, he has a brief affair with a stunningly sexy female attorney (Sacchi) that ends badly. His marriage is damaged but survives. Then the woman turns up raped and murdered. His finger prints and blood are found at the scene and the prosecutor's office that he was so committed to, is now doing its best to nail him. This is a fascinating mystery and courtroom drama that is full of red herrings and plot twists and is very well done.

A: Harrison Ford, Brian Dennehy, Raul Julia, Bonnie Bedelia, Paul Winfield, Greta Scacchi

© WARNER HOME VIDEO 12034

PRINCESS CARABOO

D: Michael Austin 96 m

PG | DMA MYS | 1994 | COLOR | Sex | Nud | Viol | Lang | AdSit

6 An unusual idea for a movie. It is 1787 and a young woman is discovered in the English countryside wearing a turban, speaking no English, dressed rather commonly, but also having an elegant (and some think a regal) bearing. Who is this very strange woman? She is taken into the home of a local aristocrat and as word of her spreads, people become more and more convinced that she is a princess from a foreign land, stranded in England. She becomes the focus of the country's interest and even a favorite in the royal court. All the while, a newspaperman is struck by her beauty and fascinated with her. He must learn who she is. Curious film, but also very contrived and full of holes.

A: Phoebe Cates, Jim Broadbent, Wendy Hughes, Kevin Kline, John Lithgow, Stephen Rea

© COLUMBIA TRISTAR HOME VIDEO 73503

PUBLIC EYE, THE

D: Howard Franklin 99 m

R | CRM MYS | 1992 | COLOR | Sex | Nud | Viol | Lang | AdSit

7 Before there were pictures on TV news, there were sensational pictures on the front pages of newspapers. Joe Pesci is perfect as the premier free-lance tabloid photographer in 1940's New York. He is a grubby little man in a squashed hat with a stubby cigar always stuck in his face. Always the first one on the scene of a shooting, he is friendly with cops and crooks alike. But, he is also a lonely loner with the soul of an artist. His infatuation for a beautiful night club owner (Hershey) involves him in a mob investigation that proves to be deadly. Interesting film noir mystery, but patience required.

A: Joe Pesci, Barbara Hershey, Stanley Tucci, Jerry Alder, Jared Harris, Garry Becker

© MCA/UNIVERSAL HOME VIDEO, INC. 81284

REVERSAL OF FORTUNE

D: Barbet Schroeder 104 m

R | DMA MYS | 1990 | COLOR | Sex | Nud | Viol | Lang | AdSit

9 An absorbing docudrama that provides a fascinating look inside the mysterious and decadent world of the super rich. The film is based upon a real-life case from the early 1980s that had the entire nation's attention. It is the intriguing story of the second trial of Claus von Bulow - an icy European aristocrat who was accused of murdering his wife Sunny, a spoiled wealthy American heiress. He hired a Harvard law professor to appeal his conviction and then to fight for him in a new trial. The murder is explored from many different viewpoints, but the film itself never takes a position. It is a fascinating study in people and the legal system.

A: Jeremy Irons, Glenn Close, Ron Silver, Uta Hagen, Annabella Sciorra, Fisher Stevens

© WARNER HOME VIDEO 11934

RISING SUN

D: Philip Kaufman 129 m

R | CRM MYS ACT | 1993 | COLOR | Sex | Nud | Viol | Lang | AdSit

9 Very complicated, very sexy and enthralling. Snipes is an L.A. cop called in to investigate the death of a beautiful girl found dead on the boardroom table of very important Japanese company that is negotiating to purchase a sensitive American company. He is instructed to pick up Connery, a veteran officer experienced in the culture of the Japanese. Their investigation leads them through an intricate high-tech coverup concealing the business war between two Japanese companies. It is a battle between important and dangerous people and a complicated jigsaw puzzle of culture, intrigue and fast action. Excellent.

A: Sean Connery, Wesley Snipes, Harvey Keitel, Cary-Hiroyuki Tagawa, Tia Carrere, Mako

© FOXVIDEO 8520

SCREAM OF FEAR

D: Seth Holt 81 m

NR | SUS MYS | 1961 | B&W | Sex Nud Viol Lang AdSit

7 Spooky thriller! Penny (Strasberg), a young invalid bound to a wheelchair, visits her stepmother and father at his mansion on the French Riviera. When she arrives, she is told that he is away on business. However, that night, she sees his corpse in various spots around the mansion. Soon she can't separate reality from illusion, but she suspects her stepmother (Todd) has killed her father in order to get at the inheritance, and enlists the aid of family chauffeur (Lewis). That may not have been a good choice either. Unduly overlooked upon its release, it's sure to make you hair stand on end.

A: Susan Strasberg, Ronald Lewis, Ann Todd, Christopher Lee

© COLUMBIA TRISTAR HOME VIDEO 60954

SEA OF LOVE

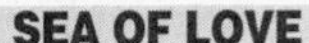

D: Harold Becker 113 m

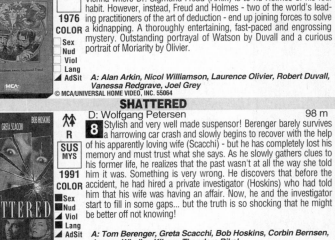

R | CRM SUS MYS | 1989 | COLOR | Sex Nud Viol Lang AdSit

9 Very steamy murder mystery. Al Pacino is a cynical and alcoholic cop who has no life outside his work, except the bottle. He is assigned, along with a cop from another precinct (Goodman), to the investigation of a series of murdered dead men, all of which have Ellen Barkin as a common thread. Pacino falls hard for the fiery Barkin and refuses to believe that she is the murderer, even though everyone else has made her their prime suspect. She has revived Pacino's life and he desperately wants to believe she's innocent. Tension builds as he begins a torrid relationship with her, never really knowing for sure if she is a murderer, even as his investigation continues.

A: Al Pacino, Ellen Barkin, John Goodman, Michael Rooker, William Hickey

© MCA/UNIVERSAL HOME VIDEO, INC. 80883

SEVEN-PER-CENT SOLUTION, THE

D: Herbert Ross 114 m

PG | MYS | 1976 | COLOR | Sex Nud Viol Lang AdSit

8 Zippy, well-done, tongue-in-cheek Holmes adventure. One of the best. Sherlock Holmes (Williamson) suffers from a cocaine addiction. Dr. Watson (Duvall) lures Holmes into a fabricated chase to Vienna where Dr. Sigmund Freud (Arkin) is to rid Holmes of his foul habit. However, instead, Freud and Holmes - two of the world's leading practitioners of the art of deduction - end up joining forces to solve a kidnapping. A thoroughly entertaining, fast-paced and engrossing mystery. Outstanding portrayal of Watson by Duvall and a curious portrait of Moriarity by Olivier.

A: Alan Arkin, Nicol Williamson, Laurence Olivier, Robert Duvall, Vanessa Redgrave, Joel Grey

© MCA/UNIVERSAL HOME VIDEO, INC. 55064

SHATTERED

D: Wolfgang Petersen 98 m

R | SUS MYS | 1991 | COLOR | Sex Nud Viol Lang AdSit

8 Stylish and very well made suspensor! Berenger barely survives a harrowing car crash and slowly begins to recover with the help of his apparently loving wife (Scacchi) - but he has completely lost his memory and must trust what she says. As he slowly gathers clues to his former life, he realizes that the past wasn't at all the way she told him it was. Something is very wrong. He discovers that before the accident, he had hired a private investigator (Hoskins) who had told him that his wife was having an affair. Now, he and the investigator start to fill in some gaps... but the truth is so shocking that he might be better off not knowing!

A: Tom Berenger, Greta Scacchi, Bob Hoskins, Corbin Bernsen, Joanne Whalley-Kilmer, Theodore Bikel

Distributed By MGM/UA Home Video M902357

SHOCK CORRIDOR

D: Samuel Fuller 101 m

NR | DMA MYS | 1963 | B&W | Sex Nud Viol Lang AdSit

8 Condemned by many at the time of its release as being trash, this film has risen to become a cult favorite. An immature and self-serving young journalist decides that he will be committed to an insane asylum so that he can uncover a murderer that the police can't -- and he will win himself a Pulitzer Prize in the process. So, he forces his stripteaser girlfriend to claim that she is his sister and that he has been making advances to her. Once inside, he is confronted with the real pain of the other inmates and the delusions they use to escape. After being attacked by nymphomaniacs and convincing himself that his girlfriend is cheating, he too begins to lose his mind.

A: Peter Breck, Constance Towers, James Best, Hari Rhodes, Gen Evans, Larry Tucker

© HOME VISION SHO 01

SILVER STREAK

D: Arthur Hiller 114 m

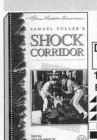

PG | COM ACT MYS | 1976 | COLOR | Sex Nud Viol Lang AdSit

9 Zany thriller. Wilder, a mild-mannered editor, is taking what he hopes to be a restful ride aboard a cross-country train. It seems to be even better when he seduces the girl in the next compartment (sexy Clayburgh). But she is an art scholar with information which will discredit both millionaire McGoohan and his Rembrandt letters as being fakes. Now, Wilder's leisurely trip turns overly exciting, when he spots a dead body being thrown from the train, and then hilarious, when small-time thief Pryor enters into the picture. Highly entertaining blend of romance, comedy and action.

A: Gene Wilder, Jill Clayburgh, Richard Pryor, Ned Beatty, Patrick McGoohan, Scatman Crothers

© FOXVIDEO 1080

SLEUTH

D: Joseph L. Mankiewicz 139 m

PG | SUS MYS COM | 1968 | COLOR | Sex Nud Viol Lang AdSit

9 A delicious and winning film that is made even better by some really superb talent! Caine and Olivier play a masterful cat-and-mouse game, each trying to outsmart and outdo the other. Caine has had an affair with Olivier's wife. So, Olivier devises a clever plot to get even by trying to trick Caine into getting caught committing a crime. However, Caine figures out Olivier's plan and turns the table on Olivier, enacting his own kind of revenge. This totally unpredictable and inventive plot takes some terrific sharp turns that will leave you guessing! Both Olivier and Caine were Oscar-nominated.

A: Laurence Olivier, Michael Caine, Alec Cawthorne, Margo Channing, John Mathews, Teddy Martin

© VIDEO TREASURES SV9069

SOLDIER'S STORY, A

D: Norman Jewison 102 m

PG | MYS CRM DMA | 1984 | COLOR | Sex Nud Viol Lang AdSit

9 Powerful and riveting psychological drama and solid mystery. Set in the segregated Army of 1944, a proud black attorney from Washington is sent to a Louisiana military post to investigate the death of the master sergeant of an all-black unit. He could have been murdered by a white racist, but it could also have been any of the black men in his unit, all of whom hated him. This is a fascinating look into human nature and into the nature of those times. However, it is also a solid whodunit, with a wide assortment of characters, all with compelling reasons for wanting the man dead. Works well on many levels all at once. Sterling performances. Excellent.

A: Howard E. Rollins, Jr., Adolph Caesar, Art Evans, Dennis Lipscomb, Denzel Washington, Patti LaBelle

© COLUMBIA TRISTAR HOME VIDEO 60408

SPY WHO CAME IN FROM THE COLD, THE

D: Martin Ritt 110 m

NR | SUS MYS | 1966 | COLOR | Sex Nud Viol Lang AdSit

9 Intense realism sparks this espionage thriller taken from a brilliant John Le Carre novel. Richard Burton is a burned-out British intelligence agent who has been recalled from Berlin to become a principal element in a plot by the West to eliminate the head of East German counter-espionage. He is to romance a leftist London librarian, convincing her that he is an agent who wants to defect. This gains him entry into the East, but he soon finds that he has been deceived by his own people and is only one part of a more elaborate plan. Very realistic and gloomy.

A: Richard Burton, Claire Bloom, Oskar Werner, Sam Wanamaker, Peter Van Eyck, Cyril Cusack

© PARAMOUNT HOME VIDEO 6509

STILL OF THE NIGHT

D: Robert Benton 91 m

PG | SUS MYS ROM | 1982 | COLOR | Sex Nud Viol Lang AdSit

8 Well-crafted thriller in the Hitchcock tradition. One of psychiatrist Scheider's patients, an antique dealer, is viciously murdered in Jack The Ripper fashion. Now into his life walks the guy's mistress (Streep), an alluring but neurotic art curator. Scheider falls in love with Streep, in spite of his psychiatrist-mother's (Tandy) warnings to the contrary. Soon Scheider wonders if Streep is the killer and after him next. Solid suspense vehicle, in spite of some plot holes, that will keep you guessing and in suspense right up to the end.

A: Roy Scheider, Meryl Streep, Jessica Tandy, Joe Grifasi, Sara Botsford, Josef Sommer

Distributed By MGM/UA Home Video M301411

STORYVILLE

D: Mark Frost 112 m

R | MYS SUS | 1992 | COLOR | Sex Nud Viol Lang AdSit

7 Fairly intriguing and involving mystery. Cray Fowler (Spader) is the privileged son of a powerful family in Louisiana. He is running for congress, but is videotaped in a moment's indiscretion with a beautiful girl. Threatened with blackmail, he unsuccessfully confronts the blackmailer and wakes up to find the man now mysteriously dead. In the course of investigating what happened, he discovers even greater secrets, which killed his father and now threaten to destroy him and his family. At first the film is only mildly interesting but the intricacies evolve to capture your attention and hold it.

A: James Spader, Joanne Whalley-Kilmer, Jason Robards, Jr., Charlotte Lewis, Michael Warren, Piper Laurie

© COLUMBIA TRISTAR HOME VIDEO 92903

STRANGER, THE

D: Adolfo Aristarain 93 m

R | SUS MYS | 1987 | COLOR | Sex Nud Viol Lang AdSit

7 A fast-paced shocker! The victim (Bedelia) of a very bad car accident is so traumatized that she loses all memory. She seeks help with a noted psychologist (Riegert), who helps her put the pieces together. Slowly she comes to realize that she saw not just one, but a number of brutal murders. The police can't find any evidence that the crimes were ever even committed, but the killers are after her now. The only way she can survive is if she can remember the killers's faces before they find her. Her doctor is helping her, or is he? Filmed in Buenos Aires, this is a nerve-racking suspensor.

A: Bonnie Bedelia, Peter Riegert, David Spielberg, Barry Primus, Marcos Woinski

© COLUMBIA TRISTAR HOME VIDEO 60928

STRIKING DISTANCE

D: Rowdy Herrington 102 m

R | ACT MYS CRM | 1993 | COLOR

6 Bruce Willis is a former homicide detective who now patrols the rivers of Pittsburgh on a speedboat because he said something he shouldn't have. What he said was that a serial murderer was a cop or a former cop and not the meek little man that was convicted. Cops don't badmouth cops, even if you are a fifth generation cop in a family of cops. What he didn't say is that he also knew each of the victims. He has just been assigned a woman as a new partner. She is the first one to learn of his secret - just as more dead women beginning to show up. Even though there are some interesting plot twists, there are also a whole lot of plot holes. Still, it works OK overall.

Sex / Nud / Viol / Lang / AdSit

A: Bruce Willis, Sarah Jessica Parker, Dennis Farina, Tom Sizemore, Brian James, Robert Pastorelli

© COLUMBIA TRISTAR HOME VIDEO 53683

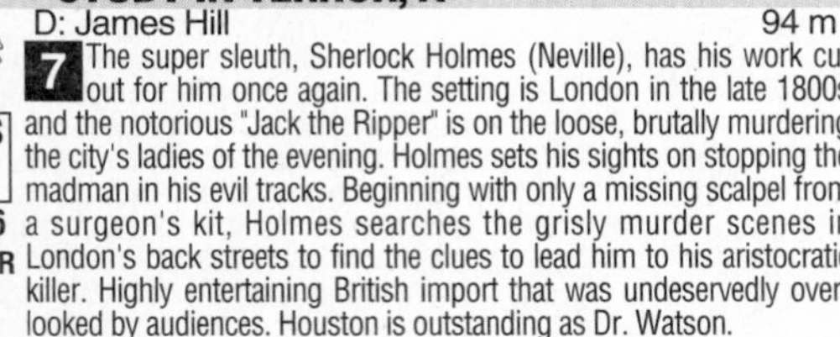

STUDY IN TERROR, A

D: James Hill 94 m

NR | MYS SYS | 1966 | COLOR

7 The super sleuth, Sherlock Holmes (Neville), has his work cut out for him once again. The setting is London in the late 1800s and the notorious "Jack the Ripper" is on the loose, brutally murdering the city's ladies of the evening. Holmes sets his sights on stopping the madman in his evil tracks. Beginning with only a missing scalpel from a surgeon's kit, Holmes searches the grisly murder scenes in London's back streets to find the clues to lead him to his aristocratic killer. Highly entertaining British import that was undeservedly overlooked by audiences. Houston is outstanding as Dr. Watson.

Sex / Nud / Viol / Lang / AdSit

A: John Neville, Donald Houston, Georgia Brown, John Fraser, Anthony Quayle, Barbara Windsor

© COLUMBIA TRISTAR HOME VIDEO 20671

TEMP, THE

D: Tom Holland 99 m

R | MYS SUS | 1993 | COLOR

6 Timothy Hutton is a middle executive at a cookie company. Lara Flynn Boyle begins as a temporary assistant for him and is very dedicated to him, maybe too dedicated. At first she is a perfect secretary, even giving him ideas and letting him take full credit for them. However, soon his competition for advancement at the office literally begins to die off and Lara starts moving up the ladder too. Someone is definitely playing hardball corporate politics... but, is it the temp? An interesting premise (although it has been well worked before) provides mildly interesting watching. Too many clues and red herrings get tiring after a while.

Sex / Nud / Viol / Lang / AdSit

A: Timothy Hutton, Lara Flynn Boyle, Dwight Schultz, Oliver Platt, Faye Dunaway, Steven Weber

© PARAMOUNT HOME VIDEO 32793

THREE DAYS OF THE CONDOR

D: Sydney Pollack 118 m

R | SUS MYS ACT | 1975 | COLOR

9 Riveting spy suspensor. Very well done. Redford is an insignificant CIA researcher (he reads foreign novels to get espionage ideas) at a storefront office in NYC. One day, however, he happens to run an errand and comes back to the office to find that everyone in it has been slaughtered and he is a hunted man. He doesn't know who, he doesn't know why, and he can trust no one until he finds out. Having nowhere to hide, he forces his way into a lonely stranger's (Dunaway) apartment. At first she is terrified, but she begins to believe in him and an uneasy love affair blossoms. Thoroughly engrossing.

Sex / Nud / Viol / Lang / AdSit

A: Robert Redford, Faye Dunaway, Cliff Robertson, Max von Sydow, John Houseman

© PARAMOUNT HOME VIDEO 8803

THUNDERHEART

D: Michael Apted 118 m

R | MYS CRM | 1992 | COLOR

9 Compelling and totally engrossing mystery. Kilmer stars as a hotshot FBI agent who is chosen, because he is part Sioux, to accompany veteran agent Sam Shepard to the Pine Ridge Indian Reservation and investigate a murder. However, his Indian blood gives him no advantage in the investigation. The locals just mock him, calling him a Washington Redskin. However, his encounters with the local sheriff (Green) and religious leader (Thin Elk) teach him things about his own past and he begins to suspect that the government has framed an innocent man. See also the documentary by the same director: INCIDENT AT OGLALA.

Sex / Nud / Viol / Lang / AdSit

A: Val Kilmer, Sam Shepard, Fred Ward, Graham Greene, John Trudell, Chief Ted Thin Elk

© COLUMBIA TRISTAR HOME VIDEO 70693

TONY ROME

D: Gordon Douglas 110 m

NR | MYS ACT | 1967 | COLOR

6 Sinatra stars in the title role as a private eye who is hired by his ex-partner to escort home the beautiful daughter of a wealthy industrialist when she is found drunk in a seedy Miami motel. After the girl's expensive diamond pin turns up missing, his place gets torn up, his ex-partner dies suspiciously and he finds that he is involved with blackmailers and junkies. Mildly diverting detective movie, somewhat reminiscent of the '40s film noir type. Sinatra's character is stylish and glib, but not altogether believable. Some good action helps a confusing plot become entertaining.

Sex / Nud / Viol / Lang / AdSit

A: Frank Sinatra, Jill St. John, Gena Rowlands, Richard Conte, Sue Lyon, Gena Rowlands

© FOXVIDEO 1338

TWO JAKES, THE

D: Jack Nicholson 137 m

R | CRM MYS | 1990 | COLOR

6 Involved and convoluted follow-up to CHINATOWN. It's now ten years later. Jake (Nicholson) is a war hero. He owns a successful detective agency and is a member of the country club. Against his better judgment, he accepts a divorce job to spy on the wife (Tilly) of another Jake, who is a shady land developer (Keitel). Shortly into his investigation, Keitel's partner is murdered. It is pretty obvious Keitel did it and now our Jake's right in the middle. Very convoluted, but if you rent CHINATOWN first to provide a basis for what you will see here, you'll enjoy it - but pay attention.

Sex / Nud / Viol / Lang / AdSit

A: Jack Nicholson, Harvey Keitel, Meg Tilly, Madeleine Stowe, Ruben Blades, Eli Wallach

© PARAMOUNT HOME VIDEO 1854

VERTIGO

D: Alfred Hitchcock 128 m

PG | SUS MYS ROM | 1958 | COLOR

10 Intriguing psychological Hitchcock masterpiece. Stewart is a retired San Francisco police detective. An old friend hires him to follow his suicidal wife (Novak) and Stewart does rescue her from one attempted suicide. Soon he becomes intrigued with her and falls desperately in love, but she dies in a leap from a tower when he is unable to climb to stop her because of his extreme fear of heights. Later, he discovers a shop girl who very strongly resembles her and he attempts to remake this new girl exactly by dying her hair and taking her to the same places. Riveting, very dream-like thriller. Haunting.

Sex / Nud / Viol / Lang / AdSit

A: James Stewart, Kim Novak, Barbara Bel Geddes, Tom Helmore, Ellen Corby, Henry Jones

© MCA/UNIVERSAL HOME VIDEO, INC. 80082

WHISPERS IN THE DARK

D: Crowe Christopher 103 m

R | SUS MYS CRM | 1992 | COLOR

7 Supersexy murder mystery. A beautiful patient (Unger) reports her vivid and provocative sexual encounters with bondage to her female psychiatrist (Sciorra). Sciorra is distressed to learn her own new boyfriend (Sheridan) knows Unger. Is he the man of her torrid stories? ...or is it another of her patients, one who was just released from prison for torturing women? That question becomes critical when Unger is found hanging bound, naked and very dead. Good plot twists and effective murder mystery despite some flaws, but the overt sexuality will diminish it for many..

Sex / Nud / Viol / Lang / AdSit

A: Annabella Sciorra, Jamey Sheridan, Deborah Unger, Alan Alda, Anthony Lapaglia, Jill Clayburgh

© PARAMOUNT HOME VIDEO 32756

WHISTLE BLOWER, THE

D: Simon Langton 99 m

PG | SUS MYS | 1987 | COLOR

8 A taut political mystery thriller. A Russian translator for a British spy agency mysteriously falls to his death just as he was to have an interview with a journalist. His salesman father (Caine), a former intelligence officer, begins his own investigation into his son's death. As a scandal begins to unfold itself, there are even more suspicious deaths. This once-trusting, patriotic man now has severe doubts about his own government. This is an intelligent story of intrigue, but also an exploration of the failings of the English class system. It works on all levels.

Sex / Nud / Viol / Lang / AdSit

A: Michael Caine, James Fox, Nigel Havers, Felicity Dean, John Gielgud

© NEW LINE HOME VIDEO 7665

WIDOW'S PEAK

D: John Irvin 98 m

PG | MYS | 1994 | COLOR

6 This is a sort of "Masterpiece Theater"-like mystery, set in Ireland around the 1920s. Edwina is a free-spirited young widow who has just arrived in Kilshannon, a lovely Irish lake town. The town is dominated by a very proper group of wealthy ladies, who all live in one area known as Widow's Peak, and that group is commanded by Mrs. Counihan. She is a particularly domineering old woman who has set her sights on obtaining Edwina as a match for her twit of a son. However, Miss O'Hare, another member of the group, has decided that there is something not right about Edwina and she is determined to destroy her. A mildly-amusing diversion, with a definite twist ending.

Sex / Nud / Viol / Lang / AdSit

A: Mia Farrow, Joan Plowright, Natasha Richardson, Adrian Dunbar, Jim Broadbent

© TURNER HOME ENTERTAINMENT N4298

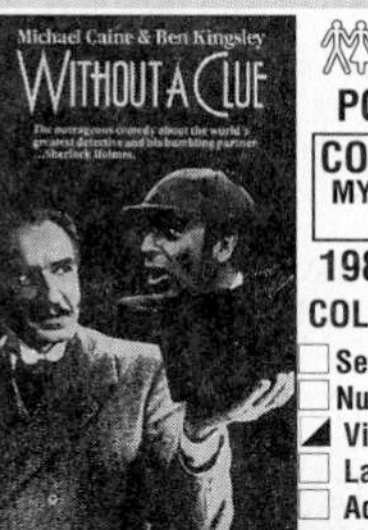

WITHOUT A CLUE

D: Thom Eberhardt 107 m

PG | COM MYS | 1988 | COLOR

8 Funny high-spirited farce that takes an entirely different slant to the oft-used mystery/detective movie vehicle of Sherlock Holmes and Dr. Watson - suppose Sherlock Holmes was just a drunken bumbling actor and Watson was the real deductive genius. Kingsley plays Watson, a doctor who enjoys investigating crimes and then writing about them. He uses the mythical figure of Sherlock Holmes as the detective, but one day is called upon to present him. So he hires Caine to be Holmes and forever after has to keep him out of trouble. Inventive and funny.

Sex / Nud / Viol / Lang / AdSit

A: Michael Caine, Ben Kingsley, Jeffrey Jones, Lysette Anthony, Paul Freeman

© ORION PICTURES CORPORATION 8733

MYS

WITNESS FOR THE PROSECUTION

D: Billy Wilder 116 m

NR | MYS CRM | 1957 | B&W

10 Absolutely wonderful screen adaptation of one of Agatha Christie's best mysteries and one of the best courtroom dramas ever. An aging barrister (Laughton) is called from retirement to defend a married man (Power) who is accused of murdering a wealthy woman that he had been seeing. He claims he didn't do it, but the only witness he has is his icy wife (Dietrich), and she has testified that he is guilty. Wonderful performances (Dietrich's last), more plot twists than a bag of pretzels and a startling ending. Excellent - don't miss it! Four Academy Award nominations.

- [ ] Sex
- [ ] Nud
- [ ] Viol
- [ ] Lang
- [x] AdSit

A: Marlene Dietrich, Tyrone Power, Charles Laughton, Elsa Lanchester, John Williams, Henry Daniell

Distributed By MGM/UA Home Video M202517

WRECK OF THE MARY DEARE, THE

D: Michael Anderson 100 m

NR | MYS | 1959 | COLOR

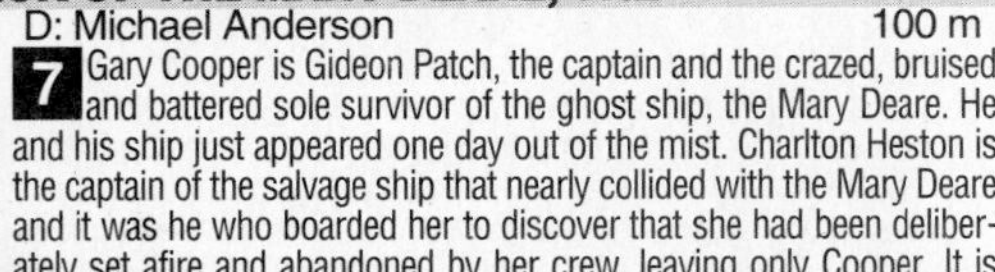

7 Gary Cooper is Gideon Patch, the captain and the crazed, bruised and battered sole survivor of the ghost ship, the Mary Deare. He and his ship just appeared one day out of the mist. Charlton Heston is the captain of the salvage ship that nearly collided with the Mary Deare and it was he who boarded her to discover that she had been deliberately set afire and abandoned by her crew, leaving only Cooper. It is up to the two of them to discover what happened, but for now, Cooper stands accused by a Board of Inquiry in London, charged with negligence. The film slows down some in the middle but is worth while. Good special effects, too.

- [ ] Sex
- [ ] Nud
- [ ] Viol
- [ ] Lang
- [x] AdSit

A: Gary Cooper, Charlton Heston, Michael Redgrave, Emlyn Williams, Cecil Parker, Alexander Knox

Distributed By MGM/UA Home Video 200527

WRONG MAN, THE

D: Alfred Hitchcock 105 m

NR | SUS MYS CRM | 1956 | B&W

7 A harrowing and ultimately terrifying Hitchcock movie - because it is so believable, because it is based upon a true event and because it could happen to you, too. Henry Fonda plays a New York jazz musician who is confronted at his home by police, arrested, fingerprinted, jailed and tried for a series of crimes he didn't commit because there were eye witnesses who swore he was the culprit. And, before the look-alike crook is found, even his wife comes to believe he is guilty. She has a nervous breakdown and is institutionalized. Compelling but unnerving to watch.

- [ ] Sex
- [ ] Nud
- [x] Viol
- [ ] Lang
- [x] AdSit

A: Henry Fonda, Vera Miles, Anthony Quayle, Harold J. Stone, Nehemiah Persoff, Esther Minciotti

© WARNER HOME VIDEO 11155

Romance

Video's Best

1956 and After

84 CHARING CROSS ROAD

D: David Jones 100 m

PG | ROM DMA | 1986 | COLOR | Sex | Nud | Viol | Lang | AdSit

6 Sweet adult romance about two letter correspondents who never meet. True story of a struggling writer in New York, with an intense passion for books she can't really afford, who responds to an ad placed by a London-based used book store in a New York paper. A 20-year relationship ensues between the writer and the store's unhappily married owner which evolves from business to love - but they never meet. Their love exists only through the mail. A beautiful film that is virtually all talk. It is a lovely, literate story, but may be too slow for many.

A: Anne Bancroft, Anthony Hopkins, Judi Dench, Maurice Denham, Jean De Baer, Eleanor David

© COLUMBIA TRISTAR HOME VIDEO 60815

AARON LOVES ANGELA

D: Gordon Parks 99 m

R | ROM CRM | 1975 | B&W | Sex | Nud | Viol | Lang | AdSit

6 Star-crossed "Romeo and Juliet" story, Harlem style. A black boy (Hooks) falls for a sweet and pretty Puerto Rican girl (Cara) in a drug infested neighborhood of Harlem. They are in love but love, in their world, is dangerous. They struggle against the nature of their circumstances, a Puerto Rican gang and his bitter father, to meet in secret in a condemned building. Unknown to them, this is also a place where there is going to be a big drug buy. Jose Feliciano music. Also see the original ROMEO AND JULIET or WEST SIDE STORY.

A: Kevin Hooks, Irene Cara, Moses Gunn, Robert Hooks, Ernestine Jackson, Jose Feliciano

© COLUMBIA TRISTAR HOME VIDEO 60480

ABOUT LAST NIGHT

D: Edward Zwick 113 m

R | ROM COM | 1986 | COLOR | Sex | Nud | Viol | Lang | AdSit

8 Witty, believable and touching romance comedy about an '80s kind of couple (Rob Lowe and Demi Moore). They are young singles committed only to having a good time, who meet at a ball game and again later at a bar. They share a great one-night stand that unexpectedly grows into a housekeeping arrangement. However, their relationship falls on hard times when, despite all their time together, he has a tough time making a total commitment to her and because their best friends are each doing their level best to break them apart. Interesting and funny reflection of yuppie love in the '80s.

A: Rob Lowe, Demi Moore, James Belushi, Elizabeth Perkins, George DiCenzo, Michael Alldredge

© COLUMBIA TRISTAR HOME VIDEO 60735

ABSENCE OF MALICE

D: Sydney Pollack 116 m

PG | DMA ROM | 1981 | COLOR | Sex | Nud | Viol | Lang | AdSit

9 Excellent, thought-provoking entertainment about an innocent man who is convicted by innuendo in the media. Sally Fields is a naive reporter, tricked into printing a story which falsely implicates innocent businessman Paul Newman. Newman fights to clear his name and to get revenge. Fields does what she can to help and in the process he and the conscience-stricken Fields unexpectedly fall for each other. However, it is not the romance that most effects you, it is the timely and probably timeless drama of the story you will remember. This is powerful, thoughtful drama about the potentially abusive power of the press. Received three Oscar nominations.

A: Paul Newman, Sally Field, Bob Balaban, Melinda Dillon, Wilford Brimley, Luther Adler

© GOODTIMES 4222

ABSOLUTE BEGINNERS

D: Julien Temple 107 m

PG-13 | MUS ROM | 1986 | COLOR | Sex | Nud | Viol | Lang | AdSit

6 Enthusiastic British musical production made especially for the screen by a director of music videos. Set in 1958 London, it is the somewhat typical story of love sought for, found, lost and found again. At times it reminds one of WEST SIDE STORY but, overall, falls short of that lofty goal. While the plot is weak, the music and dance scenes do redeem any shortcomings. (However, it also helps if the viewer is British.) Outstanding jazz score. See also WEST SIDE STORY, to see how a truly great teenage-love musical is done.

A: Eddie O'Connell, Patsy Kensit, David Bowie, James Fox, Ray Davies, Ege Ferret

© HBO VIDEO TVA3900

ACCIDENTAL TOURIST, THE

D: Lawrence Kasdan 121 m

PG | DMA ROM COM | 1988 | COLOR | Sex | Nud | Viol | Lang | AdSit

7 Highly acclaimed by critics and nominated for a Best Picture Oscar. William Hurt gives a strong performance as a travel writer who falls apart upon the death of his son. He distances himself from everyone, including Kathleen Turner, his estranged wife. His isolation is broken only when he is around kooky dog trainer Geena Davis. This is an intensely emotional film. While it is quirky and contains some very funny moments, this is primarily an intelligent drama and romance that takes its time to bring out the story. May be too slow for some.

A: William Hurt, Kathleen Turner, Geena Davis, Bill Pullman, Amy Wright, David Ogden Stiers

© WARNER HOME VIDEO 11825

AFFAIR TO REMEMBER, AN

D: Leo McCarey 115 m

NR | ROM | 1957 | COLOR | Sex | Nud | Viol | Lang | AdSit

8 This is one of the major weepers of all times and is a perennial favorite. Cary Grant and Deborah Kerr meet aboard ship and fall deeply, desperately in love. However, they postpone their affair because both question if their love can be real. That is especially important since each of them is engaged to very wealthy others. So, they decide to meet again, but six months later. Sad fate intervenes - he shows up for the meeting, but she is hit by a car on the way there. He thinks she stood him up, plus she may never walk again. Get out the hankies, you'll enjoy each tear. Remake of the 1939 classic LOVE AFFAIR.

A: Cary Grant, Deborah Kerr, Cathleen Nesbitt, Neva Patterson, Richard Denning, Robert Q. Lewis

© FOXVIDEO 1240

AGE OF INNOCENCE, THE

D: Martin Scorsese 138 m

PG | ROM DMA | 1993 | COLOR | Sex | Nud | Viol | Lang | AdSit

9 It is New York City in the 1870's. Newland (Daniel Day-Lewis), a wealthy attorney and the son of a prominent old family, is set to marry the beautiful but very proper May (Winona Ryder), the daughter of another fine old family. Then May's cousin Ellen (Michelle Pfeiffer) returns from Europe, seeking a divorce from her brutish husband. Worse, she wants to live alone and be her own person, which just isn't done. So, Newland is asked to help save the family's good name. Instead, his heart is set pounding with passion for the unconventional Ellen. Against a background of gossip and hypocrisy, they must decide whether they should follow their hearts or do the proper thing. 4 Oscar nominations.

A: Daniel Day-Lewis, Michelle Pfeiffer, Winona Ryder

© COLUMBIA TRISTAR HOME VIDEO 52633

A LA MODE

D: Remy Duchemin — 99 m

R | FOR COM ROM | 1994 | COLOR | Sex ◢ | Nud ■ | Viol ☐ | Lang ◢ | AdSit ■

8 Very entertaining piece of French fluff. Young Fausto has become an orphan and has been apprenticed to Mietek, a small-time tailor. Mietek is a bachelor with his own slant on life, but he takes a particular interest in Fausto. Fausto at first is interested in sewing clothes because he wants to meet pretty young women. He is particularly enamored of the very pretty daughter of the local mechanic. However, he soon discovers that he has a genuine flair for tailoring and a wild, imaginatively extravagant talent for promotion. A gentle story of no particular merit and a little bizarre, but it has very endearing characters. Quite good fun. Subtitles.

A: Jean Yanne, Florence Darel, Ken Higelin, Francois Hautesserre, Maurice Benichow, Maite Nahyr

© MIRAMAX HOME ENTERTAINMENT 3608

ALMOST PERFECT AFFAIR, AN

D: Michael Ritchie — 92 m

PG | ROM COM | 1979 | COLOR | Sex ◢ | Nud ◢ | Viol ☐ | Lang ◢ | AdSit ◢

7 Carradine is a naive young director who has devoted the last two years to creating his film. Now he takes what little money he has left to finance a trip to take it to the Cannes Film Festival in France, where he hopes to sell it. But his film is held up at customs and is released only through the help of a famous producer's wife (Monica Vitti). He, the innocent, falls for and has an affair with her, the worldly. Starts slow but is entertaining and leaves you feeling good. Will appeal most to film fans.

A: Keith Carradine, Monica Vitti, Raf Vallone, Dick Anthony Williams

© PARAMOUNT HOME VIDEO 1221

ALWAYS

D: Henry Jaglom — 105 m

R | DMA ROM COM | 1985 | COLOR | Sex ◢ | Nud ■ | Viol ☐ | Lang ■ | AdSit ■

7 A very original film, largely a biography of director/actor Jaglom's real-life breakup with his wife Townsend. Three couples spend the Fourth of July together at a barbecue. One couple is getting married, one is solidly married, and David and Judy have been separated for two years and are on the verge of divorce. Judy stops by just to visit her almost ex-husband and ends up spending the weekend with him and the two other couples. They discuss love, romance, and each other. Some really funny dialogue, some interesting characters and some powerful human insights. Chocolate can be a powerful thing.

A: Henry Jaglom, Patrice Townsend, Melissa Leo, Joanna Frank, Alan Rachins, Michael Emil

© LIVE HOME VIDEO VA5161

ALWAYS

D: Steven Spielberg — 123 m

PG | ROM COM FAN | 1989 | COLOR | Sex ☐ | Nud ☐ | Viol ☐ | Lang ◢ | AdSit ◢

7 Very pleasing remake of THE STORY OF JOE. Dreyfuss plays a bush pilot who is killed in a crash but is brought back by his guardian angel (Hepburn). He is to be the guardian angel of an awkward young flyer (Johnson). At first Dreyfuss likes his new job, but that all changes when he also has to help his girlfriend (Hunter) to move on with her life and does it by lining her up with Johnson. This is a light little movie with no major statements to make but it is still a lot of fun. However, you should see the original, too. It is one of director Spielberg's favorites, which was the reason why he redid it here.

A: Richard Dreyfuss, Holly Hunter, Brad Johnson, John Goodman, Audrey Hepburn, Keith David

© MCA/UNIVERSAL HOME VIDEO, INC. 80967

AMERICANIZATION OF EMILY, THE

D: Arthur Hiller — 117 m

NR | COM DMA ROM | 1964 | B&W | Sex ◢ | Nud ☐ | Viol ☐ | Lang ☐ | AdSit ◢

8 Entertaining and daring comedy. Garner is a Navy officer whose main job is keeping his superiors comfortable and supplied with "everything." This suits Garner's larcenous and cowardly nature just fine. Andrews is his British war-widow chauffeur. She despises his avowed cowardice but falls for him anyway. However, things drastically change for them both when the admirals decide they want the first American naval casualty of the D-Day invasion filmed for publicity, and they order Garner to do it. Garner is afraid that the casualty is likely to be him. Compelling satire, with a hard edge.

A: James Garner, Julie Andrews, Melvyn Douglas, James Coburn, Joyce Grenfell, Keenan Wynn

Distributed By MGM/UA Home Video M200518

AND NOW MY LOVE

D: Claude Lelouch — 121 m

PG | FOR ROM COM | 1975 | COLOR | Sex ☐ | Nud ☐ | Viol ☐ | Lang ☐ | AdSit ◢

8 An entertaining bit of lighthearted romantic fluff about fate and love at first sight. How can it be that two people fall instantly and passionately in love with each other? The individual lives and three generations of family histories of two people are explored in parallel fashion to explain why they should fall instantly in love at their first meeting. A romantic and lyrical salute to life and love in the 20th century. However, it is a little involved and so requires patience. Dubbed or subtitles.

A: Marthe Keller, Andre Dussollier, Charles Denner

© NEW LINE HOME VIDEO 1505

ANNE OF AVONLEA

D: Kevin Sullivan — 224 m

NR | DMA ROM | 1988 | COLOR | Sex ☐ | Nud ☐ | Viol ☐ | Lang ☐ | AdSit ☐

9 Sparkling sequel to ANNE OF GREEN GABLES and a rare event where the sequel is as good as the original. Anne, the idealistic redheaded orphan who was adopted by a bachelor farmer and his old-maid sister, is now 18. She is an intelligent young woman and a budding writer who becomes a teacher at Avonlea. There she wins the hearts of everyone around her, including the stubborn headmistress who is determined to make her life miserable, and where she has her first brush with adult love. Absolutely charming story that will win over everyone of every age. Extremely well done.

A: Megan Follows, Colleen Dewhurst, Wendy Hiller, Frank Converse, Schuyyler Grant, Jonathan Crombie

© WALT DISNEY HOME VIDEO 650

ANNIE HALL

D: Woody Allen — 99 m

PG | ROM COM DMA | 1977 | COLOR | Sex ◢ | Nud ☐ | Viol ☐ | Lang ◢ | AdSit ■

9 Wonderful bittersweet movie, that nearly everybody (even most non-Allen fans) liked. Woody Allen's humor is very much alive here, but this is also a poignant and sophisticated look into '70s relationships. It is a four-Oscar movie, including Best Picture. It follows the relationship between neurotic New Yorkers, Allen and Keaton as first love grows, then it stutters, then it restarts and then it dies. Both outgrow each other to become different people than they were. Very funny but poignant and sad, too, because it rings so true with many who view it. It'll touch your heart.

A: Woody Allen, Diane Keaton, Tony Roberts, Paul Simon, Shelley Duvall, Carol Kane

Distributed By MGM/UA Home Video M200251

ANY WEDNESDAY

D: Robert Ellis Miller — 109 m

NR | COM ROM | 1966 | COLOR | Sex ◢ | Nud ☐ | Viol ☐ | Lang ☐ | AdSit ■

7 Every Wednesday Jason Robards cheats on his wife. Jane Fonda is the object of his weekly affections. Everything has been just great for them both. However, Jane is starting to feel a little put upon. Then something happens to change everything. Robards has been claiming her apartment as a business deduction, so his secretary accidentally gives out-of-town salesman Dean Jones the key. Jones finds out what's going on and wants to use the information to his advantage in a business deal with Robards, except he and Fonda have fallen for each other. Big hit on Broadway too. Funny, a good time.

A: Jane Fonda, Jason Robards, Jr., Dean Jones, Rosemary Murphy, Ann Prentis

© WARNER HOME VIDEO 11349

APARTMENT, THE

D: Billy Wilder — 126 m

NR | DMA COM ROM | 1960 | B&W | Sex ◢ | Nud ☐ | Viol ☐ | Lang ☐ | AdSit ■

10 Comedy and drama have rarely been so well woven together. In order to win favor with his boss (MacMurry) and other execs, Jack Lemmon agrees to lend his apartment to them so that they can carry on after-hours affairs. His stock rises and he quickly moves up to the 19th floor. He gets a key to the executive washroom, but he has to change his plans when he comes home to find his boss's latest girlfriend (MacLaine) has attempted suicide. He nurses her back to health and falls for her himself. Witty adult entertainment. Lemmon and MacLaine are great. Won the 1960 Best Picture Oscar.

A: Jack Lemmon, Shirley MacLaine, Fred MacMurray, Ray Walston, Jack Kuschen, Edie Adams

Distributed By MGM/UA Home Video M201307

APRIL FOOLS, THE

D: Stuart Rosenberg — 95 m

PG | COM ROM | 1969 | COLOR | Sex ☐ | Nud ☐ | Viol ☐ | Lang ☐ | AdSit ■

6 Jack Lemmon is trapped in a bad marriage to lifeless Sally Kellerman. His boss gives him a big promotion and invites him to a big and glamorous, but boring, cocktail party. However, there he meets the very beautiful, but bored, Catherine Deneuve and the two of them leave together. They have a great time and fall in love. The problem is that they are both married -- she to the boss. This is an old-fashioned romantic comedy in many ways, except that the two of them do the unthinkable (in the 1960s) - they leave their spouses and the country to be together. Pleasant diversion.

A: Jack Lemmon, Catherine Deneuve, Peter Lawford, Sally Kellerman

© CBS/FOX VIDEO 7129

ARABESQUE

D: Stanley Donen — 105 m

NR | SUS ROM | 1966 | COLOR | Sex ☐ | Nud ☐ | Viol ☐ | Lang ☐ | AdSit ◢

6 A diverting espionage story. Peck is an Oxford professor of languages and a code expert. He is hired by a mid-eastern oil tycoon to discover the secret message that is hidden in a set of hieroglyphics. He befriends the tycoon's beautiful mistress (Sophia Loren) and when he discovers the real meaning contained in the hieroglyphics, he's in trouble. He and Loren escape together and the chase is on to find them. Reasonably exciting and entertaining, with beautiful scenery, including that of the radiant Sophia.

A: Sophia Loren, Gregory Peck, Alan Badel, Kieron Moore, Carl Deuring, George Coulouris

© MCA/UNIVERSAL HOME VIDEO, INC. 80362

ARTHUR

D: Steve Gordon — 97 m

PG · COM ROM · 1981 · COLOR

Sex · Nud · Viol · Lang · AdSit

10 Heartwarming and funny. Dudley Moore is Arthur. Arthur is a spoiled, rich and generally happy, alcoholic bachelor. But he is being forced to marry an up-tight heiress (Eikenberry) who he doesn't even like. Worse still, he has fallen for a lowly waitress and shoplifter (Minnelli). His family gives him an ultimatum: it's either a proper wife, continued money, power and elegance; or, love and total poverty. Moore is perfect and loveable as the drunken spoiled rich kid, but it's Gielgud as his sarcastic valet and surrogate father who steals the show and provides the belly laughs. Laugh-out-loud funny.

A: Dudley Moore, Liza Minnelli, Stephen Elliott, John Gielgud, Jill Eikenberry

© WARNER HOME VIDEO 22020

ASK ANY GIRL

D: Charles Walters — 101 m

NR · COM ROM · 1959 · COLOR

Sex · Nud · Viol · Lang · AdSit

7 Shirley MacLaine is a wide-eyed innocent girl who comes to the big city to find a husband, only to discover that most men are just lecherous skirthounds. She goes to work at an advertising agency and sets her sights on capturing one of the bosses (Gig Young), and she enlists the advertising techniques of his older brother (David Niven) to get her man. But things never work out as planned. Fun, light-hearted little fluff, carried off by a top-flight cast.

A: David Niven, Shirley MacLaine, Gig Young, Rod Taylor, Jim Backus, Elisabeth Fraser

Distributed By MGM/UA Home Video 201128

AUTHOR! AUTHOR!

D: Arthur Hiller — 110 m

PG · COM ROM · 1982 · COLOR

Sex · Nud · Viol · Lang · AdSit

7 Al Pacino is a neurotic playwright who is just about to open a new play on Broadway, after a long dry spell. Just then, his flaky philandering wife (Weld) walks out on him for a new man, leaving him with her five kids - only one of which is his. Dyan Cannon is an actress with whom he falls in love and who helps him through his trials. Small but diverting little comedy with a happy ending and really cute kids. Good performances by everyone.

A: Al Pacino, Tuesday Weld, Dyan Cannon, Alan King, Bob Elliott, Ray Gould

© FOXVIDEO 1181

AVANTI !

D: Billy Wilder — 144 m

R · COM ROM · 1972 · COLOR

Sex · Nud · Viol · Lang · AdSit

8 Excellent but largely overlooked movie. Jack Lemmon is a wealthy American businessman who goes to Italy to recover the body of his tycoon father, only to discover that the old man died in the company of his long-time mistress. (The two went over a cliff together in his car.) However, his seemingly simple job is greatly complicated when he falls in love with the daughter of the other woman. The two of them struggle to get the bodies released from the stifling Italian bureaucracy. All of which gives them the time to discover more about their parents and themselves. Underrated Billy Wilder comedy. Entertaining.

A: Jack Lemmon, Juliet Mills, Clive Revill, Edward Andrews, Gianfranco Barra, Franco Agrisano

Distributed By MGM/UA Home Video M203093

BABY BOOM

D: Charles Shyer — 110 m

PG · COM ROM · 1987 · COLOR

Sex · Nud · Viol · Lang · AdSit

8 Funny light-weight little story about a high-powered yuppie Manhatten career-woman (Keaton) whose life abruptly changes when a distant cousin dies and she becomes an instant mom. Both her boss and live-in boyfriend recoil from the changes in her, so she moves to a simpler life in the country. She's not very well equipped for the simple life, though, and luckily she gets help from a friendly veterinarian (Shepard). Consistent and entertaining, but the story line is predictable. You might also want to see a similar story from the 1940s, BACHELOR MOTHER.

A: Diane Keaton, Harold Ramis, Sam Wanamaker, Pat Hingle, Sam Shepard, Britt Leach

Distributed By MGM/UA Home Video M202520

BABY IT'S YOU

D: John Sayles — 105 m

R · ROM COM · 1983 · COLOR

Sex · Nud · Viol · Lang · AdSit

7 Two high school kids in 1966 are total opposites, but they are in love. He is a working-class Catholic high school drop-out who dreams of becoming another Frank Sinatra in spite of rock-n-roll and calls himself the Sheik. She is an over-achieving college-bound Jewish girl who is determined to be a Broadway star. She goes off to college and he goes off to Miami to wait tables and await his big break. True, this slice-of-life story is predictable but it is also quite enjoyable, and has many worthwhile and insightful moments, too.

A: Rosanna Arquette, Vincent Spano, Joanna Merlin, Jack Davidson, Nick Ferrari, Dolores Messina

© PARAMOUNT HOME VIDEO 1538

BACK STREET

D: David Miller — 107 m

NR · ROM · 1961 · COLOR

Sex · Nud · Viol · Lang · AdSit

6 This is the third production of this famous romantic tearjerker. Susan Hayward and department store owner John Gavin meet just after WWII and fall deeply in love, but she will not give up her dream to become a famous fashion designer. They part but meet again later in Rome and immediately resume their love affair, even though he is now locked into a bad marriage with an alcoholic wife (Vera Miles). Miles and their children try to keep the lovers apart. Hayward becomes his mistress, but their romance ends in tragedy. Glossy soap opera that is worth at least three hankies.

A: Susan Hayward, John Gavin, Vera Miles, Charles Drake, Virginia Grey, Reginald Gardiner

© MCA/UNIVERSAL HOME VIDEO, INC. 80149

BAJA OKLAHOMA

D: Bobby Roth — 100 m

NR · COM ROM · 1988 · COLOR

Sex · Nud · Viol · Lang · AdSit

7 This is a bittersweet story of a small-town Texas barmaid who has the unfortunate tendency to always attract the wrong men. In fact, her life is totally occupied by strange characters and her passion to become a country song writer. When one of her many past lovers returns, she writes a song about him, but she is reluctant to give him a second chance. So, he sets about helping her to achieve her dream by working overtime to get her song made into a hit. Willie Nelson and Emmylou Harris make cameo appearances. Lots of colorful people and a good deal of fun, too.

A: Lesley Ann Warren, Peter Coyote, Swoosie Kurtz, Billy Vera

© WARNER HOME VIDEO 827

BAREFOOT IN THE PARK

D: Gene Saks — 106 m

G · COM ROM · 1967 · COLOR

Sex · Nud · Viol · Lang · AdSit

9 Neil Simon's consistently funny story of newlyweds adjusting to married life. A conservative young lawyer and his free-spirited, fun-loving young wife move into a rundown apartment building, where they are beset by a host of newlywed doubts and problems - including an intrusive mother-in-law, who is eventually wooed into retreat by their charming upstair's neighbor (Boyer). Things really boil, however, when Fonda becomes convinced that they are not meant for each other because Redford is too reserved and stuffy - all because he won't go barefoot in the park. A truly good time!

A: Robert Redford, Jane Fonda, Charles Boyer, Mildred Natwick, Herb Edelman

© PARAMOUNT HOME VIDEO 8027

BEFORE SUNRISE

D: Richard Linklater — 101 m

R · ROM · 1995 · COLOR

Sex · Nud · Viol · Lang · AdSit

7 A young American named Jesse is wandering through Europe by train. It is the last day before he must catch a plane for home in Vienna, when he chances to meet a pretty French girl named Celine. The have a real rapport. Conversation flows effortlessly and it is exhilarating. But it is now Vienna and Jesse must leave. In a burst of optimism, he asks if she wouldn't get off the train with him and walk the streets of Vienna until his plane leaves tomorrow morning. She accepts and for this night, they walk and talk, exploring Vienna and themselves. Very talky - endless conversations. However, it is also quite fascinating. Will appeal most to young adults.

A: Ethan Hawke, Julie Delpy

© COLUMBIA TRISTAR HOME VIDEO 06683

BELL, BOOK AND CANDLE

D: Richard Quine — 103 m

NR · COM ROM · 1958 · COLOR

Sex · Nud · Viol · Lang · AdSit

7 Kim Novak is a beautiful 1950s witch and a member of a family of witches which also includes her brother Nicky (Lemmon) and aunt Queeny (Lanchester). Lovely Kim falls in love with James Stewart on the eve of his wedding to someone else and so casts a spell over him to capture his heart. When Jimmy finds out why what has happened, happened... he wants out. So her warlock brother takes both Stewart and his partner (Kovacs) to another wacky witch (Hermione Gingold) to break the spell. Pleasant little comedy, expertly played by a talented cast.

A: James Stewart, Kim Novak, Jack Lemmon, Ernie Kovacs, Hermione Gingold, Elsa Lanchester

© COLUMBIA TRISTAR HOME VIDEO 60132

BELLE EPOQUE

D: Fernando Trueba — 109 m

R · FOR ROM · 1994 · COLOR

Sex · Nud · Viol · Lang · AdSit

7 Delightfully saucy story from Spain. It is 1931, the country is in civil war and young Fernando has just deserted from the army. Arriving in a small town, he makes a friend in an old man who lets him stay with him. But when the man's daughters are to arrive, Fernando is asked to leave. He agrees, but then he sees Clara, Violeta, Rocia and young Luz, and he conveniently arranges to miss his train. Returning to the house, the old man allows him to stay. Four beautiful women - surely he can seduce one of them. However, young Fernando is surprised when one by one, they seduce him. Bawdy and sexy, but not crude. Actually quite charming. Best Foreign Film Oscar. Subtitles.

A: Jorge Sanz, Maribel Verdu, Ariadna Gil, Miriam Diaz-Aroca, Penelope Cruz, Fernando Fernan Gomez

© COLUMBIA TRISTAR HOME VIDEO 79373

BELLS ARE RINGING

D: Vincente Minnelli 126 m

NR | COM MUS ROM | 1960 | COLOR

Sex | Nud | Viol | Lang | AdSit

8 Upbeat musical that was brought to the big screen from Broadway. Judy Holliday plays a shy telephone answering service operator who uses her knowledge of her clients's problems to help them all out. She also has fallen secretly in love with playboy playwright Dean Martin, even though they have never met. He just thinks she is just a nice little old lady passing out advice and so thinks of her only as "Mom." A delightful MGM musical. 14 musical numbers. Songs include "Just in Time." See the Director's index under Vincente Minnelli for other classic musicals. He did a lot of them.

A: Judy Holliday, Dean Martin, Fred Clark, Eddie Foy, Jr., Jean Stapleton, Frank Gorshin

Distributed By MGM/UA Home Video M700063

BENNY & JOON

D: Jeremiah Chechik 98 m

PG | ROM COM | 1993 | COLOR

Sex | Nud | Viol | Lang | AdSit

7 Pleasing and odd little love story. Joon (Masterson) is Benny's mentally disturbed sister who lives at home with Benny. He has dedicated his life to her and her quirky eccentricities, to the point where he has no private life of his own. He is being counselled to place Joon in a group home but he rebels at the idea. Then Joon "wins" Sam (Depp) in a poker game. Sam is a friend's definitely quirky cousin who has taken on the persona of Buster Keaton. Sam's job is to take care of Joon while Benny's at work and the two misfits fall in love. Very enjoyable and fun time with some interesting characters.

A: Aidan Quinn, Johnny Depp, Mary Stuart Masterson

Distributed By MGM/UA Home Video 903007

BETSY, THE

D: Daniel Petrie 132 m

R | DMA ROM | 1978 | COLOR

Sex | Nud | Viol | Lang | AdSit

6 Amusing diversion. A powerful cast throws itself into this soap opera adaptation of a best-seller-brought-to-the-screen, with major gusto. It is the lurid tale of members of an automobile dynasty family. We have here a selection of power brokering, conventional sex, incest and homosexuality. Plot moves pretty slow but it is nonetheless an interesting piece of trash.

A: Laurence Olivier, Tommy Lee Jones, Robert Duvall, Katharine Ross, Lesley-Anne Down, Jane Alexander

© CBS/FOX VIDEO 7190

BIG EASY, THE

D: Jim McBride 100 m

R | ACT MYS ROM | 1987 | COLOR

Sex | Nud | Viol | Lang | AdSit

9 Classy, sexy, exciting and refreshingly different. Quaid is a charming and dedicated homicide detective in New Orleans. Barkin is a by-the-book Assistant D.A. investigating corruption in the police ranks. She and her people catch him taking a small pay off (everybody does it) and goes after him. While they are on opposite sides on this case, she finds that she is still strongly attracted to him. She also discovers that he is truly a dedicated cop. When he uncovers a major scandal in the department and follows it out to the end - even though he is very close to the people involved. Excellent, intricate and well-crafted murder mystery - erotic, too.

A: Dennis Quaid, Ellen Barkin, Ned Beatty, John Goodman, Lisa Jane Persky, Charles Ludlum

© HBO VIDEO 0052

BIZET'S CARMEN

D: 151 m

PG | MUS FOR ROM | 1983 | COLOR

Sex | Nud | Viol | Lang | AdSit

7 Opera is taken off the stage and into the streets when this opera favorite is filmed on location. Placido Domingo plays the aristocratic Spanish soldier who loses his heart and ruins his life when he frees a faithless, beautiful Spanish gypsy from prison in this classic opera. Actually filmed on location in the streets of Spain, this production has true dramatic force, as well as powerful music and beautiful singing.

A: Julia Migenes-Johnson, Placido Domingo, Ruggero Raimondi, Faith Esham, Jean-Philippe Lafont

© COLUMBIA TRISTAR HOME VIDEO 60487

BLACK ORPHEUS

D: Marcel Camus 103 m

NR | FOR ROM FAN | 1958 | COLOR

Sex | Nud | Viol | Lang | AdSit

8 This winner of the Oscar for the Best Foreign Film is a modernized version of an old Greek legend. The story is set in Rio de Janeiro during Carnival, Brazil's version of Marde Gras. A streetcar conductor (Mello) and a shy, beautiful country girl fall passionately in love. The lovers lose themselves in the frenzy of Carnival but she is followed through the streets of Rio by a stranger dressed as death and is killed. Mello attempts to resurrect her through magic but must eventually join her in the next world. Hauntingly beautiful score. Subtitles.

A: Breno Mello, Marpessa Dawn, Lourdes de Oliveira, Lea Garcia, Adhemar da Silva, Alexandro Constantino

© HOME VISION BLA 170

BLAZE

D: Ron Shelton 117 m

R | DMA COM ROM | 1989 | COLOR

Sex | Nud | Viol | Lang | AdSit

7 Hollywood's romantic-comedy version of the outlandish life and love of real-life Louisiana Governor Earl K. Long, who did have a scandalous affair with the flamboyant showgirl and stripper, Blaze Starr. Newman is energetic and full of ornery charm as the crusty Earl Long, and Lolita Davidovich puts in a "outstanding" and sexy performance as the famous Blaze Starr. The feisty Long struggles to survive repeated attacks on himself and his governorship, all the while it is he who is giving them some of their best ammunition. Look for the real Blaze Starr in a cameo role.

A: Paul Newman, Lolita Davidovich, Robert Wuhl, Jeffrey DeMunn

© TOUCHSTONE HOME VIDEO 915

BLUE HAWAII

D: Norman Taurog 106 m

NR | MUS ROM | 1961 | COLOR

Sex | Nud | Viol | Lang | AdSit

6 One of Elvis's most popular flicks. Elvis plays the son of a rich family who returns home to Hawaii after a stint in the service. The heir to a pineapple fortune, he upsets his parents by wanting to work in a tourist bureau instead. Great locations. Plenty of music, pretty girls and romance. Over a dozen songs, including one of his prettiest-ever hits: "Can't Help Falling in Love With You." The sound track was the fastest-selling album of 1961.

A: Elvis Presley, Joan Blackman, Nancy Walters, Angela Lansbury, Roland Winters, Iris Adrian

© CBS/FOX VIDEO 2001

BODYGUARD, THE

D: Mick Jackson 130 m

R | ROM ACT SUS | 1993 | COLOR

Sex | Nud | Viol | Lang | AdSit

8 Frank Farmer (Kostner) is an ex-secret service agent who has now become a private bodyguard for hire. Whitney Houston is a pop-music star who has been receiving threatening messages. She reluctantly agrees to let her manager hire him, but she largely ignores his advice. That is, until Frank has to jump in to save her bacon after one particularly close call. Suddenly, she not only relies upon him but also begins to find her heart softening to him. Frank finds that he too is falling for her, but that is dangerous because feelings like those threaten his edge - and he needs his edge because the killer is still out there. Yes it's predictable, but hey - it's fun too.

A: Kevin Costner, Whitney Houston, Michele Lamar Richards, DeVaughn Nixon, Gary Kemp, Ralph Waite

© WARNER HOME VIDEO 12591

BORN YESTERDAY

D: Luis Mandoki 100 m

PG | COM ROM | 1993 | COLOR

Sex | Nud | Viol | Lang | AdSit

7 Pleasant, but not sparkling, remake of the 1950 Judy Holliday classic. Billie (Melanie Griffith) is a sexy but dim-witted former showgirl who is mistress to a loutish real estate developer (John Goodman). They have come to Washington DC so that he can lobby some senators into keeping a military base open and get even richer. However, her ignorant comments have embarrassed him so much that he has hired a bookish reporter (Don Johnson) to tutor her. Instead, the seemingly dim-witted Billie learns too well. She learns that she doesn't have to accept being treated so badly and that she is also falling for the mild-mannered reporter.

A: Melanie Griffith, John Goodman, Don Johnson, Edward Herrmann, Max Perlich, Fred Dalton Thomas

© HOLLYWOOD PICTURES HOME VIDEO 1740

BREAKFAST AT TIFFANY'S

D: Blake Edwards 114 m

NR | ROM DMA COM | 1961 | COLOR

Sex | Nud | Viol | Lang | AdSit

9 Totally captivating. Audrey Hepburn plays young, beautiful and fanciful Holly Golightly. She is an innocent at play in an imagined world of elegance and fun and captures the imagination and the affections of a struggling writer, George Peppard. This is a tender love story of a small-town girl who caught up in the pursuit of the trappings of glamour and big-city life. Hepburn is absolutely captivating as this little girl lost. A charming and tender love story, perfectly complemented by Mancini's Oscar-winning score.

A: Audrey Hepburn, George Peppard, Patricia Neal, Buddy Ebsen, Mickey Rooney, Martin Balsam

© PARAMOUNT HOME VIDEO 6505

BRONCO BILLY

D: Clint Eastwood 117 m

PG | COM ROM | 1980 | COLOR

Sex | Nud | Viol | Lang | AdSit

7 Engaging, lighthearted story of a troop of oddball characters working for a flea-bag wild west show. Eastwood is the idealistic owner, ace sharpshooter and self-styled star of his nearly-broke traveling Wild West Show. He and his troop of dedicated performers just want to entertain. Sondra Locke is a spoiled little rich girl who is abandoned by her husband on her honeymoon and finds a home when she becomes part of the show as Eastwood's assistant. Eastwood acts, directs and even sings with Merle Haggard. This simple little story has been unduly underrated by many critics. It's just fun.

A: Clint Eastwood, Sondra Locke, Geoffrey Lewis, Scatman Crothers, Bill McKinney, Dan Vadis

© WARNER HOME VIDEO 11104

BUDDY SYSTEM, THE

D: Glenn Jordan 110 m

PG | ROM COM | 1983 | COLOR

7 Nice little charmer. Wil Wheaton and his struggling, insecure, single Mom, make friends with a security guard, who is also a part-time novelist and a part-time inventor (Richard Dreyfuss), and is also struggling in a relationship with his ditzy, unfaithful girlfriend. Wil wants a father, but Mom and Dreyfuss are sure they are just friends. However, in spite of all their concerns and precautions, love triumphs. Dreyfuss learns to give up his unfaithful fantasy girl and Sarandon learns to trust again. This is a pleasing, enjoyable story, even if much of it is predictable. It is both funny and heartwarming.

Sex / Nud / Viol / Lang / AdSit

A: Richard Dreyfuss, Susan Sarandon, Jean Stapleton, Nancy Allen, Wil Wheaton

© FOXVIDEO 1316

BULL DURHAM

D: Ron Shelton 108 m

R | COM ROM | 1988 | COLOR

8 A truly charming and fun romantic comedy about the odd lifestyle surrounding a North Carolina minor league baseball team. Kevin Costner is an veteran catcher past his prime but who has been charged by management with helping to develop an immature young pitcher who has a powerful arm, a terrific fast ball and no brains. Susan Sarandon is a smart but quirky baseball groupie who each year chooses one player to give the benefit of her experience and her affections. This year she chooses the dumb pitcher, but Costner changes her mind. This is a quite intelligent little winner. You may also want to see LONG GONE.

Sex / Nud / Viol / Lang / AdSit

A: Kevin Costner, Susan Sarandon, Tim Robbins, Trey Wilson, Robert Wuhl, Jenny Robertson

© ORION PICTURES CORPORATION 8722

BUONA SERA, MRS. CAMPBELL

D: Melvin Frank 111 m

NR | COM ROM | 1968 | COLOR

7 Interesting premise for a comedy that works well due to an excellent cast. The beautiful Italian mother (Gina Lollogrigida) of a pretty 20-year-old daughter has been accepting support checks for years from three different American men who each think he fathered the girl during WWII. Now, all three men are coming back for a twentieth anniversary Army reunion, and they're bringing their wives along. Another further complication in Gina's life is that her daughter wants to meet her father. Gina is understandably in a panic. Good fun.

Sex / Nud / Viol / Lang / AdSit

A: Gina Lollobrigida, Peter Lawford, Shelley Winters, Phil Silvers, Telly Savalas, Lee Grant

Distributed By MGM/UA Home Video 203045

BUSTER AND BILLIE

D: Daniel Petrie 100 m

R | ROM DMA | 1974 | COLOR

6 A perceptive little story about teenage love between two mismatched Georgia high school students in 1948. A potential for cheap exploitation is averted and becomes instead an affecting young-love story. The most popular boy in school (Vincent) is surprised when he is attracted to a plain girl that he dates only because everyone tells him that she is a tramp. Instead, he sees a warm and sensitive girl who is crying out to be accepted. He finds something sweet and attractive in her, but their love is severely challenged when she is attacked by a group of tough guys.

Sex / Nud / Viol / Lang / AdSit

A: Jan-Michael Vincent, Joan Goodfellow, Pamela Sue Martin, Clifton James, Robert Englund

© COLUMBIA TRISTAR HOME VIDEO 60481

BUTCHER'S WIFE, THE

D: Terry Hughes 107 m

PG-13 | FAN COM ROM | 1991 | COLOR

6 Curious and terribly fanciful! As a little girl, Marina (Moore) dreams that her true love will just simply find her. So one day when Dzunda washes up on shore, apparently right on cue, she believes that her psychic powers have drawn them together and they can't be denied. Without a second thought, she marries him and runs off to his Greenwich Village butcher shop with him. There, she promptly becomes a neighborhood sensation, when her uncannily perceptive advice consistently works and her predictions come true. Psychiatrist Daniels becomes especially entranced with this strange woman, but then love blooms between them and confuses everyone. Fun, but not too deep.

Sex / Nud / Viol / Lang / AdSit

A: Demi Moore, Jeff Daniels, George Dzundza, Mary Steenburgen

© PARAMOUNT HOME VIDEO 32312

BUTTERFIELD 8

D: Daniel Mann 110 m

NR | DMA ROM | 1960 | COLOR

6 Very daring for its day, Elizabeth Taylor won her first Oscar playing a model and high-class call girl who flutters from one man to another. She's very popular, just call Butterfield 8. She meets and falls in love with a very prominent man (Harvey). Their passions rage and he wants to leave his wife to be with her, but cannot come to grips with her past life and eventually refuses to leave his wealthy wife for her. Glossy soap opera.

Sex / Nud / Viol / Lang / AdSit

A: Elizabeth Taylor, Laurence Harvey, Mildred Dunnock, Dina Merrill, Betty Field, Eddie Fisher

Distributed By MGM/UA Home Video M300272

BUTTERFLIES ARE FREE

D: Milton Katselas 149 m

PG | COM ROM DMA | 1972 | COLOR

9 Genuine pleasure of a serio-comedy. Edward Albert is a blind young man struggling to become self-sufficient. He wants break free of his over-protective (but loving) mother and also to romance his kookie next-door neighbor (Hawn). Goldie is an eccentric, aspiring actress who has fallen for this guy but has to learn how to deal with things, too. Their relationship, and all the other complications, leads to a fast-paced comedy. Nominated for three Oscars, Heckart won Best Supporting Actress. A really good time and a great feel-good movie.

Sex / Nud / Viol / Lang / AdSit

A: Goldie Hawn, Edward Albert, Jr., Eileen Heckart, Mike Warren

© COLUMBIA TRISTAR HOME VIDEO 60149

CACTUS FLOWER

D: Gene Saks 103 m

PG | COM ROM | 1969 | COLOR

8 Zany Broadway smash comedy brought to the screen. Matthau is a bachelor dentist having an affair with, and stringing along, pretty-young-thing Goldie Hawn, by telling her that he is married. When she attempts suicide, he says that he will marry her, but she refuses until she meets his wife. Having none, Matthau asks his straight-laced dowdy assistant (Bergman) to sit in as his wife. Both Matthau and Bergman are surprised to find that she is in love with him and he with her. Goldie falls for another guy - the nice guy next door. Hawn won an Oscar in her first big part. Great fun.

Sex / Nud / Viol / Lang / AdSit

A: Walter Matthau, Ingrid Bergman, Goldie Hawn, Jack Weston, Rick Lenz, Vito Scotti

© GOODTIMES 4229

CAMELOT

D: Joshua Logan 179 m

G | MUS ROM | 1967 | COLOR

8 The beautiful and fanciful romance legend of King Arthur and the Round Table was first brought to the Broadway stage by Lerner & Loewe. This is a thoroughly enjoyable big-budget film presentation of that same musical. It is the story of one man trying to balance his dream for justice in a better world and his great love for Guenevere, who loves someone else more than him. Beautiful sets, wonderful music and a tragic story, from the first meeting of Arthur and Guenevere, through the forbidden love affair with Guenevere and Lancelot, and finally to the downfall of Camelot. 3 Oscars.

Sex / Nud / Viol / Lang / AdSit

A: Richard Harris, Vanessa Redgrave, Franco Nero, David Hemmings, Lionel Jefferies

© WARNER HOME VIDEO 11084

CAMILLA

D: Deepa Mehta 101 m

PG-13 | ROM | 1995 | COLOR

6 Young wife and aspiring musician Bridget Fonda, and her graphics-arts husband have come to vacation in the guest house of a Georgia mansion. Fonda is drawn to the violin music of an eccentric old woman, Jessica Tandy, and they rapidly become close friends. When Fonda's husband receives a chance-of-a-lifetime offer from Tandy's overly-protective wealthy son, he wants to leave immediately and fights with Fonda when she wants to stay. Then, once the men are gone, the two women escape on a trip to see a violin concert in Toronto and to visit Tandy's long-ago lover. The plot stumbles and falls along the way in places, but Tandy was excellent in this her last picture before her death.

Sex / Nud / Viol / Lang / AdSit

A: Jessica Tandy, Bridget Fonda, Hume Cronyn, Elias Koteas, Maury Chaykin, Graham Greene

© MIRAMAX HOME ENTERTAINMENT 3613

CANNERY ROW

D: David S. Ward 120 m

PG | ROM COM | 1982 | COLOR

7 Enjoyable people-story. Nick Nolte plays an ex-baseball player who has become a dedicated marine biologist. He is now conducting research in a rundown section of a California waterfront fishing village during the Depression and is also living there. Debra Winger plays an independent and likable prostitute who falls for him. She and a congregation of weird oddballs who live on Cannery Row with him give his life zest and add not-a-little confusion, but never boredom. In spite of some minor shortcomings, it's very hard not to like these characters, the story and the movie.

Sex / Nud / Viol / Lang / AdSit

A: Nick Nolte, Debra Winger, Audra Lindley, Frank McRae, M. Emmet Walsh, Sunshine Parker

Distributed By MGM/UA Home Video M800143

CAROUSEL

D: Henry King 128 m

NR | MUS ROM | 1956 | COLOR

10 Rogers and Hammerstein's classic musical is memorably brought to life with lavish production numbers and the beautiful voices of Gordon MacRae and Shirley Jones. A handsome and charming carnival barker (MacRae) falls in love and marries a beautiful girl (Jones), but he panics when he realizes she is pregnant and he must support them. He feels he must get money fast so he attempts an ill-fated robbery, is killed and then he looks down on her from heaven. Memorable songs include "If I Loved You," "You'll Never Walk Alone" and "June is Bustin' Out All Over." Just wonderful. See OKLAHOMA, too.

Sex / Nud / Viol / Lang / AdSit

A: Gordon MacRae, Shirley Jones, Cameron Mitchell, Barbara Ruick, Claramae Turner, Gene Lockhart

© FOXVIDEO 1713

CASUAL SEX ?

D: Genevieve Robert — 87 m

R | COM ROM | 1988 | COLOR

6 Two young women, Thompson and Jackson, are both looking for men but they also want a deep and meaningful relationship. So they decide to get into shape by taking a vacation at a health resort and use the opportunity to also scout out the men there. Both do their best to attract certain men that they have targeted, so that love can bloom. Unfortunately, all the men want is casual sex. Thompson does her best to fend off an obnoxious pig played by Andrew Dice Clay. Not uproariously funny, but it is amusing and a real try at talking frankly about safe sex.

Sex / Nud / Viol / Lang / AdSit

A: Lea Thompson, Victoria Jackson, Stephen Shellen, Mary Grass, Andrew Dice Clay, Jerry Levine

© MCA/UNIVERSAL HOME VIDEO, INC. 80788

CEMETERY CLUB, THE

D: Bill Duke — 107 m

PG-13 | DMA ROM | 1992 | COLOR

7 Three older women have been friends for a very long time - since before their husbands died. Now all three husbands are dead and the three are trying to decide what to do with the rest of their lives. One day their cemetery visit is disrupted by a loud argument taking place between a very mad Danny Aiello and the groundskeeper for not having taken care of his wife's grave. Later, Aiello meets Burstyn at her music store and again apologizes for the argument, but he also asks her out. Their budding relationship not only confuses the both of them, but it also disrupts the serenity of the Cemetery Club.

Sex / Nud / Viol / Lang / AdSit

A: Danny Aiello, Olympia Dukakis, Ellen Burstyn, Diane Ladd

© TOUCHSTONE HOME VIDEO 1481

CHANCES ARE

D: Emile Ardolino — 108 m

PG | ROM COM | 1989 | COLOR

7 Pretty good light-hearted comedy. Cybill Shepherd has remained true to her husband's memory for 23 years after his death, in spite of the persistent attentions of his best friend (Ryan O'Neal) who is also in love with her. Robert Downey Jr. is a college student who pursues Shepherd's grown daughter home from school. However, he soon uncomfortably discovers that he is the reincarnated spirit of her former husband, after being around Shepherd brings back all the feelings and memories from his former life. So he now sets out to help her to get her life back in motion and become happy again. Very well done. Sweet-natured and appealing.

Sex / Nud / Viol / Lang / AdSit

A: Cybill Shepherd, Robert Downey, Jr., Ryan O'Neal, Mary Stuart Masterson, Christopher McDonald, Josef Sommer

© COLUMBIA TRISTAR HOME VIDEO 70153

CHAPTER TWO

D: Robert Moore — 127 m

PG | COM ROM | 1979 | COLOR

8 Neil Simon's autobiographical Broadway hit recounting many of his own painful personal experiences after the death of his first wife. James Caan plays a newly widowed writer (Caan) who meets a young actress (Marsha Mason, Neil Simon's real-life second wife) who is on the rebound after a failed marriage. They fall head-over-heels in love and ten days later they are married. It is only then he has a huge guilt attack over what he has just done. This makes him afraid for their futures and causes them both to analyze who and what they are. Very entertaining comedy which also will strike a resilient chord with many people.

Sex / Nud / Viol / Lang / AdSit

A: Marsha Mason, James Caan, Valerie Harper, Joseph Bologna

© GOODTIMES 4606

CHARADE

D: Stanley Donen — 114 m

NR | MYS ROM | 1963 | COLOR

8 Elegant, classy and fun mystery with a twist of wit. Audrey Hepburn meets charming Cary Grant while skiing in the Alps. She returns to Paris to find that her husband is dead, and that he and his ex-partners had stolen $250,000 in gold during the war and now they want it back. Matthau claims to be a CIA agent and suggests that she would be safer if she gave it back to the government. Cary Grant also shows up offering her his help. Who's a girl to trust? Stylish twists in the Hitchcock tradition. And, it is played out against elegant European backdrops to the strains of Henry Mancini's beautiful score.

Sex / Nud / Viol / Lang / AdSit

A: Cary Grant, Audrey Hepburn, Walter Matthau, James Coburn, George Kennedy, Ned Glass

© MCA/UNIVERSAL HOME VIDEO, INC. 55036

CHILDREN OF A LESSER GOD

D: Randa Haines — 119 m

R | ROM DMA | 1986 | COLOR

9 An exceptional movie that both the critics and the public liked. William Hurt is a dedicated teacher at a school for the deaf who becomes fascinated with a very beautiful and obviously intelligent, but exceedingly bitter, young woman who continues to work at the school as a janitor after graduating. He seeks to uncover her secrets and to help her but instead falls in love with her. A very unusual and moving love story made more involving by impeccable performances. Matlin, deaf in real life, won an Oscar for her film debut.

Sex / Nud / Viol / Lang / AdSit

A: William Hurt, Marlee Matlin, Piper Laurie, Philip Bosco

© PARAMOUNT HOME VIDEO 1839

CHILLY SCENES OF WINTER

D: Joan Micklin Silver — 96 m

PG | ROM COM DMA | 1982 | COLOR

8 A Salt Lake City civil servant (Heard) falls very hard for pretty Hurt, who has just left her husband because he loved her too little. But now Heard loves her so intensely that she becomes scared by it all and cannot understand why she is now worthy of so much attention. Soon Heard's constant attentions and jealousy drive her back to her husband and the daughter she misses very much, but Heard still tries to win her back. Funny, but painful, too. Wonderful acting.

Sex / Nud / Viol / Lang / AdSit

A: John Heard, Mary Beth Hurt, Peter Riegert, Kenneth McMillan, Gloria Grahame

Distributed By MGM/UA Home Video M600726

CHINA GIRL

D: Abel Ferrara — 90 m

R | ACT ROM | 1987 | COLOR

7 This is a very slick low-budget movie that gives a tired old plot a present-day realness with a strong dose of believability. Set in lower Manhattan, an Italian boy working in a pizza parlor falls in love with a beautiful Chinese girl, but their forbidden romance leads to gang warfare between the neighborhood's Italian and Chinese gangs. This is a war that is carried out with a gritty realism in the back alleyways and dance floors of the neighborhood. A lot of energy and some attractive characters.

Sex / Nud / Viol / Lang / AdSit

A: James Russo, Sari Chang, Richard Panebianco, David Caruso

© LIVE HOME VIDEO 5238

CHRISTMAS WIFE, THE

D: David Jones — 73 m

NR | ROM DMA | 1988 | COLOR

9 A lonely widower (Jason Robards), alone for the first time at Christmas, submits an ad to the newspaper in which he seeks to find someone to share the holiday season with. Iris (Julie Harris) answers the ad. Iris is shy and reserved, and asks only that he ask no questions, and he "hires" her to spend Christmas with him at his mountain cabin. Two of America's greatest actors give beautiful poignancy to this story of love in life's later years. Solid character study and a delight to watch.

Sex / Nud / Viol / Lang / AdSit

A: Jason Robards, Jr., Julie Harris, Don Francks, James Eckhouse, Patricia Hamilton, Deborah Glover

© HBO VIDEO 0323

CINDERELLA LIBERTY

D: Mark Rydell — 117 m

R | ROM DMA | 1973 | COLOR

9 Not your typical kind of romance. This is a heartwarming story of a troubled Seattle hooker, her bastard half-black son and the sailor who learns to love them both. James Caan plays a good-hearted sailor-on-pass who falls for a very likable hooker (Mason), who is in deep trouble. She is determined never to fall in love again and he is determined to change her mind. Great performances by both of them - Mason won an Oscar nomination for her performance. It is a wonderfully warm, non-schmaltzy story where the characters win you over easily, and a strong dose of realism makes it all believable.

Sex / Nud / Viol / Lang / AdSit

A: James Caan, Marsha Mason, Eli Wallach, Burt Young, Dabney Coleman, Kirk Calloway

© FOXVIDEO 1738

CLEOPATRA

D: Joseph L. Mankiewicz — 246 m

NR | DMA ROM | 1963 | COLOR

7 This film created a big commotion in 1963. It had spectacular pageantry, a hugely expensive production cost and was very highly publicized (in part because of an on-going love affair between its two stars, Burton and Taylor). Its story, of the lusty ambitious Egyptian queen (Taylor) who used her charms in hopes of conquering the world through marrying Julius Caesar Emperor of Rome (Harrison), and then also having an ill-fated romance with his general Mark Antony (Burton) after Caesar's death, is ripe with pagentry and spectacle. It won four Oscars and was nominated for more. Rex Harrison was brilliant.

Sex / Nud / Viol / Lang / AdSit

A: Elizabeth Taylor, Richard Burton, Rex Harrison, Roddy McDowall, Pamela Brown, Martin Landau

© FOXVIDEO 1143

COCA-COLA KID, THE

D: Dusan Makavejev — 949 m

R | COM ROM | 1985 | COLOR

6 Strange, light-hearted satire in which an intense young American executive arrives in Australia determined to spread Coca-Cola throughout the land. He discovers that one area is totally devoid of Coke and totally dominated by one old man's independent soft drink. With his savage intensity totally lost upon the laid-back Australians, and besieged by a kooky sexy secretary (Sacchi) who is bent on seducing him, he nevertheless endeavors to attract the stubborn old man into the Coca-Cola fold. Strange but humorous.

Sex / Nud / Viol / Lang / AdSit

A: Eric Roberts, Greta Scacchi, Bill Kerr, Max Gillies, Chris Haywood, Kris McQuade

© LIVE HOME VIDEO VA5099

COCKTAIL

D: Roger Donaldson — 103 m

R | ROM COM | 1988 | COLOR

6 A cocky young man (Cruise) breezes into New York determined to make it big. Instead, he becomes a hotshot bartender after veteran barkeep Brown takes him under his wing. Life is good, but when Cruise falls for charming and wealthy Shue, she gets pregnant while they frolic in Jamaica. From there on, the relationship gets badly bruised as Cruise tries to deal with this new twist of fate and Shue's father tries to keep Cruise away. Pretty basic. Critics didn't like it, but the colorful bar crowds and stylish atmosphere make this an enjoyable and attractive romance for young people.

Sex / Nud / Viol / Lang / AdSit

A: Tom Cruise, Bryan Brown, Elisabeth Shue, Lisa Banes, Laurence Luckinbill, Kelly Lynch

© TOUCHSTONE HOME VIDEO 606

COLD SASSY TREE

D: Joan Tewkesbury — 97 m

NR | DMA ROM | 1989 | COLOR

7 A superb made-for-TV drama that is told through the eyes of a 15-year-old boy. Grandpa Rucker Blakeslee (Widmark) is the supporting pillar of the small Southern town of Cold Sassy. Widmark is the prosperous owner of most of the town's major businesses and is also at the firm head of his family. But he shocks both the town and his family when he returns from a buying trip up North with a new, much younger and very independent bride (Dunaway), who has a dark secret in her past. Their's is a special relationship that each has entered into for separate reasons, but it sets the town buzzing.

Sex / Nud / Viol / Lang / AdSit

A: Faye Dunaway, Richard Widmark, Neil Patrick Harris, Frances Fisher, Lee Garlington, John Jackson

© TURNER HOME ENTERTAINMENT 6057

COMING HOME

D: Hal Ashby — 130 m

R | DMA ROM WAR | 1978 | COLOR

9 Extremely powerful early attempt to explore the effects of the Vietnam war. A gung-ho career Marine officer's (Dern) naive wife (Fonda) finds real love with a bitter paraplegic (Voight) while volunteering at the hospital when her husband is away at war. Dern comes back from Vietnam very mixed up himself. He is having great difficulty adjusting to all the changes in himself and his wife because she is now independent, and deeply involved with Voight. Politics of Vietnam are downplayed, this is a very human drama. Oscars for Fonda, Voight and script. Best Picture nominee, too.

Sex / Nud / Viol / Lang / AdSit

A: Jane Fonda, Jon Voight, Bruce Dern, Robert Carradine, Robert Ginty, Penelope Milford

Distributed By MGM/UA Home Video M301428

COMPETITION, THE

D: Joel Oliansky — 123 m

PG | ROM | 1980 | COLOR

7 Endearing, simple little love story. Two young pianists are competing against each other at a prestigious competition. During the course of the competition they also meet and fall in love. That's pretty much the whole story. It is a satisfying experience, though, in spite of its straightforward nature. It also has some excellent piano music.

Sex / Nud / Viol / Lang / AdSit

A: Richard Dreyfuss, Amy Irving, Lee Remick, Sam Wanamaker, Joseph Cali, Ty Henderson

© COLUMBIA TRISTAR HOME VIDEO 60164

CONTINENTAL DIVIDE

D: Michael Apted — 103 m

PG | ROM COM | 1981 | COLOR

7 A lightweight romantic comedy in which Belushi is a hard-edged Chicago political reporter who gets beat up by thugs because of a story. So, he is sent to hide out in the Rockies for a while by doing a story on a reclusive ornithologist (Brown) who is researching eagles. These two are total opposites. She is a country girl. He is a big city boy. Still, they fall in love and then they have to work out a solution to their totally different lifestyles - a modern twist on the old Tracy/Hepburn formula. A nice little comedy. Brown is attractive, Belushi mellowed out.

Sex / Nud / Viol / Lang / AdSit

A: John Belushi, Blair Brown, Allen Garfield, Carlin Glynn

© MCA/UNIVERSAL HOME VIDEO, INC. 71001

CONVICTION, THE

D: Marco Bellocchio — 92 m

NR | FOR DMA ROM | 1994 | COLOR

8 An unusual and strangely compelling Italian film that proposes insight into, the mystery of female sexuality: Why are many, if not most women, powerfully drawn to "dangerous" men? A woman is inadvertently locked into a museum for the night, only to discover that she is not alone. With her is a man, who totally captivates her and compellingly engages her in a wild night of mutually consuming passion. In the morning, she discovers that he had had the keys all the time, and files charges against him for rape. In court, he does not deny her claims that he overpowered her with his will, but insists that it was seduction not rape. Very unusual and very adult.

Sex / Nud / Viol / Lang / AdSit

A: Pietro Valsecchi, Nella Banfi, Vittorio Mezzogiorno, Andrzej Seweryn, Claire Nebout, Grazny Szapolowska

© ORION PICTURES CORPORATION FLV1151

COUNTERFEIT TRAITOR, THE

D: George Seaton — 140 m

NR | SUS DMA ROM | 1962 | COLOR

8 Tense WWII thriller, based upon a real-life character. Eric Ericson (Holden) has been raised in America but is technically a Swedish citizen. He is also an international businessman and so he travels freely between Allied Europe and Nazi Germany. Because he wants to remain neutral, British agents set him up and then blackmail him into becoming a spy. He is to be a double agent. The Germans are to think that he is one of theirs, but he is one of ours. He becomes a very effective agent for the Allies, working with the German underground, where he meets and falls in love (Lilli Palmer), but their love is doomed.

Sex / Nud / Viol / Lang / AdSit

A: William Holden, Lilli Palmer, Hugh Griffith, Erica Beer, Werner Peters

© PARAMOUNT HOME VIDEO 6113

COURTSHIP OF EDDIE'S FATHER, THE

D: Vincente Minnelli — 117 m

NR | COM ROM | 1962 | COLOR

8 Charming and highly entertaining comedy concerning a motherless 9-year-old boy (Ronny Howard) and his father (Glenn Ford). Life is hard for Ford, who is still trying to recover from the loss of his wife. So his son does his best to find himself a mother and his father a wife by trying to line Dad up with Shirley Jones, Dina Merrill and Stella Stevens. Heartwarming and funny. Very popular. It later it became a hit TV series starring Bill Bixby.

Sex / Nud / Viol / Lang / AdSit

A: Glenn Ford, Shirley Jones, Stella Stevens, Ron Howard, Dina Merrill, Jerry Van Dyke

Distributed By MGM/UA Home Video M200797

COUSINS

D: Joel Schumacher — 110 m

PG-13 | ROM COM | 1989 | COLOR

9 Charming love story that will leave your face smiling and your heart warmed. William Peterson and Sean Young meet at a big wedding and immediately fall into lust. The trouble is that they are both married to others. Their spouses, Ted Danson and Isabella Rossellini, discover what has happened and they become good friends. They decide to get even by faking their own affair, but surprise... their phony-affair turns into true love. Excellent, wonderful, winning and charming feel-good film. It is also the upbeat Americanized version of the 1976 French hit COUSIN, COUSINE.

Sex / Nud / Viol / Lang / AdSit

A: Ted Danson, Isabella Rossellini, Sean Young, William L. Petersen, Lloyd Bridges, Norma Aleandro

© PARAMOUNT HOME VIDEO 32181

CRAZY FROM THE HEART

D: Thomas Schlamme — 94 m

NR | ROM DMA | 1991 | COLOR

8 Delightful and charming. Lahti is the principal at Tidewater Texas High School. She and the football coach have had an "understanding." For the past eight years he has gone to her house on Thursday nights, had dinner and watched her TV. However, he refuses to marry her. Ruben Blades is a small rancher who takes a janitor's job at her school to make ends meet. He immediately likes Lahti, asks her out and, in an act of rebellion, she goes out with the Mexican janitor. She has a ball. They dance, get very drunk and wind up on a Mexican beach, married. However, reality hits on Monday morning, she is married to a Mexican in a very small Texas town. Fun.

Sex / Nud / Viol / Lang / AdSit

A: Christine Lahti, Ruben Blades, William Russ, Mary Kay Place, Louise Latham, Tommy Mendez

© TURNER HOME ENTERTAINMENT 6171

CROCODILE DUNDEE

D: Peter Faiman — 98 m

PG-13 | COM ROM ACT | 1986 | COLOR

9 Huge, world-wide box office phenomenon. A sexy rich-girl reporter (Kozlowski) goes to the Outback of Australia to interview a strange character, Mick "Crocodile" Dundee (Paul Hogan), when she hears tales of him having crawled for miles after having his leg bitten by a crocodile. Mick is a hero of giant proportions. He drinks. He fights. He wrestles crocs, and he obliges her by taking her with him on excursion out into his world. Then she reciprocates by bringing him into her jungle - Manhattan. Hilarious!! Followed by a pretty good CROCODILE DUNDEE II.

Sex / Nud / Viol / Lang / AdSit

A: Paul Hogan, Linda Kozlowski, John Meillon, David Gulpilil, Mark Blum, Michael Lombard

© PARAMOUNT HOME VIDEO 32029

CROSSING DELANCEY

D: Joan Micklin Silver — 97 m

PG | ROM | 1988 | COLOR

6 Amy Irving plays Izzy, a self-reliant, 30ish, single (much to the dismay of her traditional grandmother) Jewish woman who is the manager of an elitist Manhattan bookstore. Her job brings her into contact with New York's sophisticated literary crowd, which Izzy enjoys. Her grandmother, however, has different ideas and she hires a matchmaker who wants to line Izzy up with a man who sells pickles. Izzy quickly rejects that idea and she rejects him. But her fancy friends prove to be phony, and he is a nice guy. Rich in New York atmosphere. A nice little feel-good romance film. Starts slow.

Sex / Nud / Viol / Lang / AdSit

A: Amy Irving, Reizl Bozyk, Peter Riegert, Jeroen Krabbe, Sylvia Miles, Suzzy Roche

© WARNER HOME VIDEO 11826

ROM

CRYING GAME, THE

D: Neil Jordan 112 m

R

DMA ROM

1992

COLOR

Sex Nud Viol Lang AdSit

8 Intelligent and very unusual piece of filmmaking that is not for the casual observer. It starts you firmly in one direction and then suddenly jerks you in another, as it takes on two dramatic themes at one time. It begins in the ruthless politics of the Irish Republican Army when a team of volunteers kidnaps a British soldier (Whitaker) as a hostage. Fergus (Rea) is his guard but he allows himself to begin to like his charge and also begins to question his mission. When Whitaker is killed, Fergus goes to London to see the soldier's girlfriend and again is forced question his values when he falls for the girl too, only to discover that she is a he. Quite compelling.

A: Stephen Rea, Miranda Richardson, Jaye Davidson, Forest Whitaker

© LIVE HOME VIDEO 69039

CUBA

D: Richard Lester 121 m

R

ACT ROM

1979

COLOR

Sex Nud Viol Lang AdSit

7 Sean Connery plays a security advisor from England who is hired by Cuban dictator Batista to come to Cuba in 1959 to help put down the rebel insurgency. There, he meets his former lover Brooke Adams, who is now married to a shiftless playboy, and their passions reignite. He tries to convince her that Batista will fall and that she should leave Cuba with him. When the regime does fall, it is a mad scramble. This is a handsome film with strong cast and good period detail which was virtually and unduly ignored upon its release. Some say it was an attempt to remake CASABLANCA.

A: Brooke Adams, Sean Connery, Jack Weston, Hector Elizondo, Denholm Elliott, Chris Sarandon

Distributed By MGM/UA Home Video M201507

CUTTING EDGE, THE

D: Paul Michael Glaser 102 m

PG

ROM

1991

COLOR

Sex Nud Viol Lang AdSit

7 Entertaining romance flick. Two last-chance kids get one more chance. The hitch is that they can only do it together, and they are both loners. He is a hockey player who can no longer compete because he has lost his peripheral vision. She is a talented but egotistical figure skater who has driven all potential partners away with her mouth. If he can change styles to figure-skating and she can rein in her smart mouth, they have a chance at an Olympic medal in paired figure skating... but that won't be easy. Conflict inevitably leads to love. Cute and fun, but predictable the whole way.

A: D.B. Sweeney, Moira Kelly, Roy Dotrice, Terry O'Quinn, Dwier Brown

Distributed By MGM/UA Home Video M902315

CYRANO DE BERGERAC

D: Jean-Paul Rappeneau 138 m

PG

FOR ROM

1990

COLOR

Sex Nud Viol Lang AdSit

9 An inspired version of the classic tearjerker by Edmond Rostand. This is an extremely lavish French production (filmed in French and shown with subtitles) and may well be the definitive filmed version of the story. It is the story of an 17th-century eloquent swordsman with the romantic soul, who was so self-conscious of his looks that he held back telling his beloved Roxanne of his own deep feeling for her and helped his friend to win her heart for him. Acclaimed as France's greatest actor, Depardieu is charismatic in the role and received an Oscar nomination. Excellent. Subtitles.

A: Gerard Depardieu, Anne Brochet, Vincent Perez, Jacques Weber, Roland Bertin

© ORION PICTURES CORPORATION 5058

DANGEROUS LIAISONS

D: Stephen Frears 120 m

R

DMA ROM

1988

COLOR

Sex Nud Viol Lang AdSit

8 Nominated for 7 Oscars, including Best Picture, and won 3. It is a marvelous story of 18th-century gamesmanship among the bored, unscrupulous aristocracy of a decadent France. Ex-lovers Close and Malkovich are engaged in a contest. They manipulate the lives of those around them through calculated sexual liasons. They seek both their pleasures and revenge through games of seduction and betrayal, but are eventually destroyed by their own shallowness. Pfeiffer is the virtuous beauty that destroys them when Malkovich breaks the rules - he falls in love with her. Lush settings.

A: Glenn Close, John Malkovich, Michelle Pfeiffer, Mildred Natwick, Swoosie Kurtz, Keanu Reeves

© WARNER HOME VIDEO 11872

DANZON

D: Maria Novaro 103 m

PG-13

FOR ROM

1991

COLOR

Sex Nud Viol Lang AdSit

8 Highly regarded film from Mexico. Julia is a telephone operator who lives in Mexico City with her teenage daughter. Her life is boring, monotonous and uneventful - except for Wednesday nights. Wednesday night is when she goes ballroom dancing, performing a dance known as the Danzon. However, her life is upset when Carmelo, her long-time dance partner but about whom she know very little, suddenly disappears. Uncharacteristically following an impulse, she follows him to Veracruz. Suddenly the woman who has no excitement in her life and has seen little of the world, is deeply immersed in mystery and romance. Spanish with subtitles.

A: Maria Rojo, Carmen Salinas, Blanca Guerra, Margarita Isabel, Tito Vasconcelos

© COLUMBIA TRISTAR HOME VIDEO 53463

DAVE

D: Ivan Reitman 110 m

PG-13

COM ROM

1993

COLOR

Sex Nud Viol Lang AdSit

7 Dave owns a semi-successful temp agency but he also has an uncanny likeness for the President. So when the hard-hearted, stuffy and arrogant President needs a look-alike to stand in for him, Dave gets hired. However, when the Prez has a massive stroke while in the arms of a pretty blonde who is not his wife, Dave is drafted into the big leagues. But, Dave takes his role to heart when he is called upon to close a bunch of day care centers in the name of the budget, and he refuses. This precipitates a power struggle between him and the dead President's people who had hired him. There is some intrigue and romance, too. Very enjoyable, even though very predictable.

A: Kevin Kline, Sigourney Weaver, Ben Kingsley, Frank Langella

© WARNER HOME VIDEO 12962

DAVID AND LISA

D: Frank Perry 94 m

NR

DMA ROM

1962

B&W

Sex Nud Viol Lang AdSit

8 Highly-watchable, sensitive and rewarding story of two mentally disturbed teenagers who meet while they are institutionalized. David is a 17-year-old who is absolutely terrified of being touched. 15-year-old Lisa is a schizophrenic who vacillates between being a 4-year-old and a voiceless adolescent. Their unlikely friendship and emotional attachment is nurtured by an understanding doctor (DaSilva). Slowly they begin to build faith, which in turn begins to help them overcome their disturbed natures. Based on fact, this low-budget sleeper won 2 Oscar nominations.

A: Keir Dullea, Janet Margolin, Howard da Silva, Neva Patterson, Clifton James

© COLUMBIA TRISTAR HOME VIDEO 60761

DAYS OF HEAVEN

D: Terrence Malick 95 m

PG

DMA ROM

1978

COLOR

Sex Nud Viol Lang AdSit

9 Hailed as a great cinematic achievement, the stunningly beautiful photography won an Oscar. Gere, his sister and his girlfriend (Adams) leave the poverty of Chicago in turn-of-the-century America. Traveling as a brother and his two sisters, they settle in Kansas on the farm of a wealthy, but dying, young farmer (Sheppard). Sheppard falls in love with Adams, unaware of her real relationship to Gere. Sensing an opportunity to get rich quick, Gere encourages her to marry Sheppard anyway. For a while, they all live in luxury, but when Adams falls for Sheppard, the deception is revealed.

A: Richard Gere, Brooke Adams, Sam Shepard, Linda Manz, Robert Wilke, Stuart Margolin

© PARAMOUNT HOME VIDEO 8942

DAYS OF THUNDER

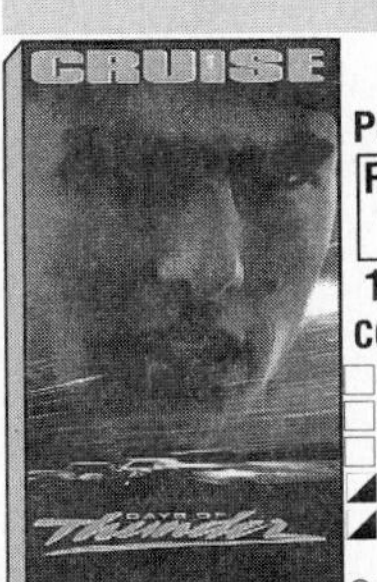

D: Tony Scott 107 m

PG-13

ROM ACT

1990

COLOR

Sex Nud Viol Lang AdSit

6 This is a formula film but it is action-packed and of course - it has Tom Cruise. Cruise is intent on entering the adrenaline-pumping NASCAR car circuit and joins the racing team of veteran racer Duvall. However, his career is short-lived when he is badly injured in a crash. Lovely doctor Kidman patches him back together but discourages him from re-entering the circuit. Ignoring her fears, Cruise goes back to racing anyway. But now, he must deal with his own fears and the realization that he is mortal. The Kidman/Cruise on-screen romance was continued off-screen when they became husband and wife.

A: Tom Cruise, Robert Duvall, Randy Quaid, Nicole Kidman, Cary Elwes, Michael Rooker

© PARAMOUNT HOME VIDEO 32123

DEFENDING YOUR LIFE

D: Albert Brooks 112 m

PG

COM ROM

1991

COLOR

Sex Nud Viol Lang AdSit

7 Funny, offbeat Albert Brooks entry. Brooks is a self-involved advertising executive who, while in his brand new BMW, crashes headfirst into an oncoming bus. Dead, he is sent to Judgement City, a stop-over that allows the deceased to be "processed." There the newly-dead must defend their lives on earth. If they pass, they are sent to heaven. If they don't, they are sent back to earth to start all over again. Streep is perfect and she is heaven-bound. Brooks is taken with her and she is his new motivation to make it into heaven. Peculiar - yes, outrageous - no. Intelligent - yes, clever and witty - yes. Good - yes, great - no.

A: Albert Brooks, Meryl Streep, Rip Torn, Lee Grant, Buck Henry, George D. Wallace

© WARNER HOME VIDEO 12049

DELIRIOUS

D: Tom Mankiewicz 96 m

PG

COM ROM

1991

COLOR

Sex Nud Viol Lang AdSit

6 Slight but pleasant, goofy little comedy. John Candy is a writer for a TV soap opera. He gets conked on the head and wakes up to find himself living inside the story line of his soap and its small town of Ashford Falls. Furthermore, he finds that he can now control everything that happens to him and everyone in the soap, by simply typing the script the way way he wants it. Armed now with his new power, he sets out to capture the heart of beautiful-but-bitchy Emma Samms who he lusts after. However, his plans are constantly being foiled by good girl Mariel Hemingway.

A: John Candy, Raymond Burr, Mariel Hemingway, Emma Samms, Dylan Baker, Charles Rocket

Distributed By MGM/UA Home Video M902243

DESIGNING WOMAN

D: Vincente Minnelli 118 m

NR | COM ROM | 1957 | COLOR

7 Oscars for Best Story and Screenplay. Good natured farce about a rough-natured sports writer (Peck) who meets and, after a whirl-wind courtship, marries a high fashion designer (Bacall). But then they discover that they have almost nothing in common. The fun begins to develop as each attempts to adapt to the other's odd habits and friends, and really it takes off when their old loves show up. Romantic and quite amusing.

Sex / Nud / Viol / Lang / AdSit

A: Gregory Peck, Lauren Bacall, Dolores Gray, Sam Levene, Mickey Shaughnessy, Chuck Connors

Distributed By MGM/UA Home Video M201069

DESK SET

D: Walter Lang 103 m

NR | ROM COM | 1957 | COLOR

7 Classic Hepburn/Tracy pairing. Tracy plays an efficiency expert hired to automate Katherine Hepburn's research department at a TV network with his computers. It is almost foreordained that these two will clash over the man (or woman) verses machine issue. That theme, as presented, seems quite simplistic now, but computers then represented a formidable threat and were a vital concern to much of America. Eventually love wins out and there is a place for both human and machine. The real reason to watch the movie is the sparks and repartee that flies between the two fiery leads.

Sex / Nud / Viol / Lang / AdSit

A: Spencer Tracy, Katharine Hepburn, Gig Young, Joan Blondell, Dina Merrill, Neva Patterson

© FOXVIDEO 1244

DIFFERENT STORY, A

D: Paul Aaron 104 m

PG | ROM DMA | 1979 | COLOR

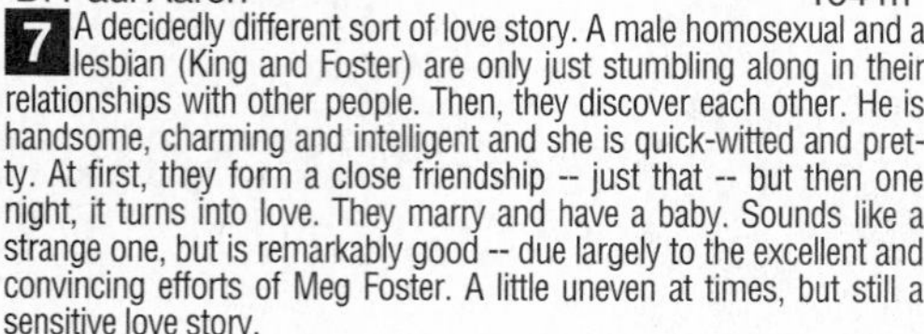

7 A decidedly different sort of love story. A male homosexual and a lesbian (King and Foster) are only just stumbling along in their relationships with other people. Then, they discover each other. He is handsome, charming and intelligent and she is quick-witted and pretty. At first, they form a close friendship -- just that -- but then one night, it turns into love. They marry and have a baby. Sounds like a strange one, but is remarkably good -- due largely to the excellent and convincing efforts of Meg Foster. A little uneven at times, but still a sensitive love story.

Sex / Nud / Viol / Lang / AdSit

A: Perry King, Meg Foster, Valerie Curtin, Peter Donat

© NEW LINE HOME VIDEO 2177

DIRTY DANCING

D: Emile Ardolino 105 m

PG-13 | ROM DMA | 1987 | COLOR

9 A gigantic box office hit - primarily because of its sexy, sensual and energetic dance sequences. Jennifer Grey is a seventeen-year-old girl on vacation with her parents in the Catskills in the 1960s. There she falls for sexy dance instructor Patrick Swayze and becomes his prize pupil. She learns something about dancing and about life, too. This is a coming-of-age story that has little that's new, but tells it with a whole lot of energy and steamy sensuality. Appealing, exuberant and fun. Women especially loved it. Best Song Oscar.

Sex / Nud / Viol / Lang / AdSit

A: Jennifer Grey, Patrick Swayze, Cynthia Rhodes, Jerry Orbach, Jack Weston

© LIVE HOME VIDEO 6013

DOC HOLLYWOOD

D: Michael Clayton-Jones 104 m

PG-13 | COM ROM | 1991 | COLOR

7 Upwardly mobile Michael J. Fox is looking forward to a very lucrative new career as a plastic surgeon in Beverly Hills. But then he has the misfortune to crash his little Porsche into a South Carolina fence. The powers that be in the small town of Grady sentence him to pay for the damages by doing some temporary medical services. This "fine" is designed to give the townsfolk time to seduce him into staying on in their little town. Even though he is melting, he is determined to leave. However, when he becomes interested in pretty local girl Julie Warner and she becomes interested back, things change. A cute film with both a healthy dose of humor and charm.

Sex / Nud / Viol / Lang / AdSit

A: Michael J. Fox, Julie Warner, Bridget Fonda, Woody Harrelson, Barnard Hughes, David Ogden Stiers

© WARNER HOME VIDEO 12222

DOCTOR ZHIVAGO

D: David Lean 200 m

PG | ROM DMA | 1965 | COLOR

9 A beautiful and painfully romantic love story. It is also a mammoth epic spectacle with stunning photography and a beautiful score. It won 5 Oscars. The story was taken from Boris Pasternak's Nobel Prize-winning novel. It is the tale of life in Russia before, during and after the 1917 Russian revolution for a doctor/poet, his wife and his lover. It also paints a vivid portrait of a whole society through a painful and trying time. The movie is long, but can be forgiven because of the gorgeous scenery, the spectacular photography, and the tragic love story it tells. A very watchable movie.

Sex / Nud / Viol / Lang / AdSit

A: Omar Sharif, Julie Christie, Geraldine Chaplin, Rod Steiger, Alec Guinness, Tom Courtenay

Distributed By MGM/UA Home Video M900003

DOGFIGHT

D: Nancy Savoca 94 m

R | ROM DMA | 1991 | COLOR

7 Four young buddies, Marines on their last night in the States before leaving for Vietnam in 1963, stage a dogfight. A dogfight is a contest where each gets a date with the ugliest girl he can find and brings her back to a party where the winner is chosen. However, Phoenix unexpectedly comes to like the girl he finds (Taylor). But when she learns of the cruel joke that has been played on her, she lashes back at him. Now wiser, he leaves his buddies behind to spend the evening with her. That one experience, and the war he goes to fight, marks the end of his arrogance and ignorance, and things are never so simple for him again.

Sex / Nud / Viol / Lang / AdSit

A: River Phoenix, Lili Taylor, Richard Panebianco, Anthony Clark, Mitchell Whitfield, E.G. Daily

© WARNER HOME VIDEO 12051

DOUBLE SUICIDE

D: Masahiro Shinoda 105 m

NR | FOR DMA ROM | 1969 | B&W

8 A Japanese traditional puppet play dating back to 1720 is the source of the story line and the stylized feel to this film. A newspaper vendor has a passionate love affair with a beautiful geisha and she loves him. He cannot control himself and vows to purchase her freedom although he is already very deep in debt. His business is bankrupted. His wife and two small children are suffering terribly. She is neglected, deprived and abused, yet she is bound to him by duty. It is hopeless for everyone. A romantic tragedy laden with symbolism and steeped in Japanese culture. Not for everyone. Subtitles.

Sex / Nud / Viol / Lang / AdSit

A: Shima Iwashita, Kichiemon Nakamura, Hosei Komatsu

© COLUMBIA TRISTAR HOME VIDEO K0677

DYING YOUNG

D: Joel Schumacher 111 m

R | ROM DMA | 1991 | COLOR

7 A competent weeper. Poor, young and inexperienced, Roberts answers a newspaper ad to become a nurse for rich cancer patient (Scott). She is very uncertain that she can handle such a daunting task, but his need for her pulls her in. The two are immediately drawn to each other and, when Scott's cancer suddenly goes into remission, their romance blooms. But when he gets ill again and gives up the fight, it is Roberts who has now grown strong enough to give him the courage he needs to continue fighting. Strong performances from both elevate a simple story.

Sex / Nud / Viol / Lang / AdSit

A: Julia Roberts, Campbell Scott, Vincent D'Onofrio, Colleen Dewhurst, David Selby, Ellen Burstyn

© FOXVIDEO 1914

EDWARD SCISSORHANDS

D: Tim Burton 100 m

PG-13 | COM ROM FAN | 1990 | COLOR

8 Heartwarming, heartbreaking and fanciful. Once upon a time, high on a hill, an inventor created a young man out of spare parts but died before he could give him hands and long scissors served as their awkward replacement. Thereafter, Edward Scissorhands (Depp) lived a lonely existence in the mansion until, one day, the Avon Lady (Wiest) came and took him to live with her family in the suburbs. But when Edward and her daughter (Ryder) fall in love, chaos breaks loose in the close-knit community and poor Edward is caught completely off guard. A very unusual semi-adult fantasy that can be very entertaining if you let it.

Sex / Nud / Viol / Lang / AdSit

A: Johnny Depp, Winona Ryder, Dianne Wiest, Vincent Price, Alan Arkin, Anthony Michael Hall

© FOXVIDEO 0620

EL CID

D: Anthony Mann 172 m

NR | ACT ROM DMA | 1961 | COLOR

8 Huge spectacle film containing some of the best old-world battle sequences ever filmed. There are miles of men in chain mail, knights on horseback and corpses everywhere. The action and spectacle are the real stars. It is the story of the eleventh-century Spanish warrior/hero El Cid (Heston), who battled Moorish invaders from the south, and the great love of his life (Loren). Magnificent settings and costumes. Much of the love story is overshadowed by the battles. Some of the splendor will be lost on the small screen.

Sex / Nud / Viol / Lang / AdSit

A: Charlton Heston, Sophia Loren, Raf Vallone, Hurd Hatfield, Genevieve Page

© BEST FILM & VIDEO CORP. 215

ELECTRIC HORSEMAN, THE

D: Sydney Pollack 120 m

PG | DMA ROM WST | 1979 | COLOR

7 Entertaining modern-day Western about an ex-rodeo star who has become an alcoholic cowboy appearing on cereal boxes riding a horse and promoting the cereal by appearing live on a champion racehorse, in a suit studded with flashing lights. Fonda, a reporter out for a good story, gets one. Redford becomes so upset when the horse he rides is exploited, too, that he steals the horse and rides across Utah looking for a place to set it free. Fonda stays one step of ahead the cops and finds him, but at first doesn't believe him about what he is trying to do. Eventually she does and falls for him.

Sex / Nud / Viol / Lang / AdSit

A: Robert Redford, Jane Fonda, Valerie Perrine, Willie Nelson, John Saxon, Wilford Brimley

© MCA/UNIVERSAL HOME VIDEO, INC. 66006

ELVIRA MADIGAN

D: Bo Widerberg 90 m

PG | FOR ROM | 1967 | COLOR

9 Acclaimed as one of the most romantic films of all times. It is based upon a true story about a Swedish Army officer and a famous circus tightrope walker who fall so desperately in love that they abandon all their obligations to run away together. Their pictures are appearing in the newspapers, so they must hide and keep moving. But soon they are out of money and are hungry. That leaves them only one way out. Loving but yet unsentimental. Beautiful images. Subtitles.

Sex [empty box] · Nud [empty box] · Viol [empty box] · Lang [empty box] · AdSit [full mark]

A: Pia Degermark, Thommy Berggren

© FOOTHILLS VIDEO

ENCHANTED APRIL

D: Mike Newell 93 m

PG | COM ROM | 1992 | COLOR

9 An enchanting and witty piece of delightful entertainment. Two middle class English women of the 1920s seek to escape the drizzly rains of home and the misery of their married lives, by renting a luxury villa on the sunny Italian Riviera for a month to sort through their problems. However, in order to afford it they accept two strangers in to share expenses. One is a cranky old woman and the other is jaded young beauty. The four women quickly relax, unwind their former lives and begin again with new understandings born of their interactions and new circumstances. Intelligent, romantic and charming.

Sex [empty box] · Nud [empty box] · Viol [empty box] · Lang [empty box] · AdSit [half mark]

A: Miranda Richardson, Josie Lawrence, Polly Walker, Joan Plowright, Alfred Molina, Michael Kitchen

© PARAMOUNT HOME VIDEO 15114

ENEMIES, A LOVE STORY

D: Paul Mazursky 121 m

R | DMA COM ROM | 1989 | COLOR

8 Highly regarded and much talked about film of a Jewish refugee (Silver) and Holocaust survivor who is living in America after WWII. He is in the unfortunate position of juggling the three separate women that he loves, each in different ways. He is alive because a Polish family hid him and, largely out of gratitude, he married their daughter - a simple domestic woman who is totally dedicated to homemaking. He is involved in a passionate affair with a fiery married woman. And he has learned that his first wife, who he thought was dead, isn't. Intelligent and sophisticated but slow.

Sex [empty box] · Nud [half mark] · Viol [empty box] · Lang [full mark] · AdSit [full mark]

A: Ron Silver, Anjelica Huston, Lena Olin, Margaret Sophie Stein, Alan King, Judith Malina

© VIDEO TREASURES M012613

FABULOUS BAKER BOYS, THE

D: Steve Kloves 116 m

R | ROM COM DMA | 1989 | COLOR

8 Excellent and curious character study of two piano playing brothers barely surviving by playing small clubs. Business has been even worse lately - that is, until they hire a sultry ex-hooker (Pfeiffer) as their vocalist. Suddenly they're in demand. Beau is excellent as the stalwart older brother who wants to hold the act together and play like they always have. But younger brother Jeff yearns to play solo jazz. Things come to an explosive head when Jeff and sexy Pfeiffer can't keep their hands off each other. Things will never be the same.

Sex [half mark] · Nud [half mark] · Viol [empty box] · Lang [full mark] · AdSit [half mark]

A: Jeff Bridges, Michelle Pfeiffer, Beau Bridges, Ellie Raab, Jennifer Tilly

© LIVE HOME VIDEO 68910

FALLING IN LOVE

D: Ulu Grosbard 106 m

PG-13 | ROM | 1984 | COLOR

6 Two more-or-less happily married people (Streep and De Niro) meet on a commuter train by accident. Two ordinary people are drawn to each other, even though they know it is wrong, and are now compelled to see each other, with no real idea of where it might all lead. They have fallen in love, but do they risk their marriages for one moment of passion? This is an otherwise simple love story that would be unremarkable except for the acting of the two super-stars. If this concept intrigues you, you should see the much better, classic British film of the same subject entitled BRIEF ENCOUNTER.

Sex [empty box] · Nud [empty box] · Viol [empty box] · Lang [full mark] · AdSit [full mark]

A: Robert De Niro, Meryl Streep, Harvey Keitel, Jane Kaczmarek, David Clennon, Dianne Wiest

© PARAMOUNT HOME VIDEO 1628

FANNY

D: Joshua Logan 128 m

NR | ROM DMA | 1961 | COLOR

8 Moving love story that received five Oscar nominations, including Best Picture. Leslie Caron is Fanny, a beautiful young girl who falls in love with Marius, a bartender's son. They live in the French seaport town of Marseilles. Marius has two loves, Fanny and the sea. The two lovers give in to their passions, but he leaves to go to sea, unknowingly leaving her pregnant. To protect her family, she enters into a marriage of convenience with a loving but much older man (Chevalier). When Marius returns, she finds that her love for him has not diminished and three lives are thrown into turmoil.

Sex [empty box] · Nud [empty box] · Viol [empty box] · Lang [empty box] · AdSit [half mark]

A: Leslie Caron, Maurice Chevalier, Charles Boyer, Horst Buchholz, Baccaloni, Lionel Jeffries

© WARNER HOME VIDEO 11159

FAR AND AWAY

D: Ron Howard 140 m

PG-13 | DMA WST ROM | 1992 | COLOR

8 Enjoyable, sweeping near-epic. A poor Irish tenant farmer (Cruise) is upset with the absentee landlord whom he blames for his father's death. He narrowly escapes dying in a duel with the man and escapes to America in 1890, along with the man's spoiled daughter (Kidman) in tow. Their first stop is Boston where he finds work as a bare-knuckle boxer and she plucks chickens. However, quickly they make their way west to attempt to claim free land in the great Oklahoma Land Rush. True, the story line is a little thin but the characters (Cruise and Kidman were married in real life) are a lot of fun to watch and the photography is grand.

Sex [empty box] · Nud [half mark] · Viol [half mark] · Lang [empty box] · AdSit [half mark]

A: Tom Cruise, Nicole Kidman, Thomas Gibson, Colm Meaney, Barbara Babcock, Robert Prosky

© MCA/UNIVERSAL HOME VIDEO, INC. 81415

FAR FROM THE MADDING CROWD

D: John Schlesinger 165 m

PG | ROM DMA | 1967 | COLOR

8 Lovely and intelligent adaptation of Thomas Hardy's romance novel, set in Victorian England of 1874. A beautiful farm girl (Julie Christie) inherits her father's farm. She longs to be free from society's constraints and also to better her station in life. She is a sensual creature who is loved by three men and has a devastating effect on their lives. They are a common herdsman (Bates), a gentleman farmer (Finch) and a dashing calvaryman (Stamp). Her situation unleashes a firestorm of passions and conflict, but eventually yields love, too. Superb production values and beautiful photography.

Sex [empty box] · Nud [empty box] · Viol [half mark] · Lang [empty box] · AdSit [full mark]

A: Julie Christie, Terence Stamp, Alan Bates, Peter Finch, Prunella Ransome

Distributed By MGM/UA Home Video M300514

FAR PAVILIONS, THE

D: Peter Duffell 108 m

NR | ROM DMA | 1984 | COLOR

8 Hugely popular. A grand tale of romance, love, treachery and intrigue. This was originally made as a miniseries for cable TV and is edited down here into feature film length. Ben Cross is a 19th-century Indian-born Englishman who was raised as a Hindu until he was 11. He has now returned to India as an army officer and he falls in love with his former childhood playmate (Irving), who is now a beautiful princess promised to an elderly Rajah (Brazzi). He is torn between his love for her and his duty to the crown. Huge international cast. Beautiful scenery and sets.

Sex [half mark] · Nud [empty box] · Viol [half mark] · Lang [empty box] · AdSit [full mark]

A: Ben Cross, Amy Irving, Omar Sharif, John Gielgud, Christopher Lee, Rossano Brazzi

© HBO VIDEO TVC2717

FATHER GOOSE

D: Ralph Nelson 116 m

NR | COM ROM | 1964 | COLOR

6 Light-hearted romantic comedy. Grant is a carefree drunken bum living a carefree life in the islands of the South Pacific just before WWII breaks out and the Japanese begin their campaign of conquest. Wanting only to be left alone, he is tricked by Howard into becoming a coastwatcher for the Australian navy. If that predicament isn't bad enough, he is forced to rescue a prissy school teacher (Leslie Caron) and her young female charges, and winds up playing unwilling nursemaid to them. Enjoyable, even if undistinguished, romantic adventure that won an Oscar for Screenplay.

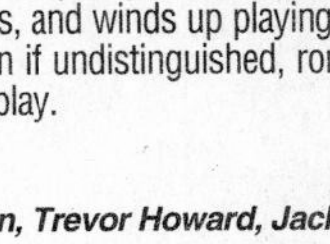

Sex [empty box] · Nud [empty box] · Viol [empty box] · Lang [empty box] · AdSit [half mark]

A: Cary Grant, Leslie Caron, Trevor Howard, Jack Good, Nicole Felsette

© REPUBLIC PICTURES HOME VIDEO 5403

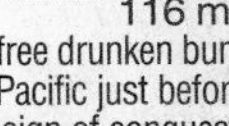

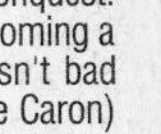

FINIAN'S RAINBOW

D: Francis Ford Coppola 142 m

G | MUS COM ROM | 1968 | COLOR

7 This was a ground-breaking musical in the 1940s when it opened on Broadway, but is now dated in the way it deals with its theme of racial prejudice. Nevertheless, it still has some very fine moments and Tommy Steele is wonderful in the role of an effervescent leprechaun whose gold is stolen by Irishman Astaire. Astaire has transplanted himself into the American South and Steele has followed him. Petula Clarke is Astaire's daughter and gets three wishes - one of which she uses to turn bigoted Southern Senator Wynn into a black man. Tuneful score includes, "How Are Things is Glocca Mora?"

Sex [empty box] · Nud [empty box] · Viol [empty box] · Lang [empty box] · AdSit [half mark]

A: Fred Astaire, Petula Clark, Tommy Steele, Keenan Wynn, Barbara Hanock, Don Francks

© WARNER HOME VIDEO 11208

FINNEGAN BEGIN AGAIN

D: Joan Micklin Silver 112 m

NR | ROM COM | 1985 | COLOR

8 Touching and entertaining light comedy about the unlikely relationship that develops between a mismatched pair. He (Preston) is an aging and grouchy, once-good newspaper writer, who now is reduced to writing an advice column and taking care of his nearly-senile wife. She (Moore) is a middle-aged, widowed school teacher trapped in an affair with a married funeral director (Waterston). The platonic friendship between these two gradually drifts into romance. Winning performances, particularly by Preston, make this charming made-for-cable movie a very pleasant viewing experience.

Sex [empty box] · Nud [empty box] · Viol [empty box] · Lang [half mark] · AdSit [half mark]

A: Robert Preston, Mary Tyler Moore, Sylvia Sidney, Sam Waterston, David Huddleston

© HBO VIDEO TVF3243

FLOWER DRUM SONG

D: Henry Koster 133 m

NR | MUS ROM | 1961 | COLOR

7 Pleasant adaptation of the Rodgers & Hammerstein Broadway musical. A picture-bride (Umeki) comes from China to San Francisco's Chinatown for an arranged marriage to a night-club owner (Soo). However, Soo is in love with a sultry singer (Kwan). But that's OK because Umeki falls in love with a handsome stranger (Shigeta). However, Kwan wants Shigeta. Some wonderful songs have become familiar standards: "I Enjoy Being a Girl" and "You Are Wonderful." The story line is not outstanding, but pleasing performances by some very talented people make this a very entertaining diversion.

Sex | Nud | Viol | Lang | AdSit

A: Jack Soo, Nancy Kwan, Benson Fong, Miyoshi Umeki, Juanita Hall, James Shigeta

© MCA/UNIVERSAL HOME VIDEO, INC. 80198

FOOL FOR LOVE

D: Robert Altman 108 m

R | DMA ROM | 1985 | COLOR

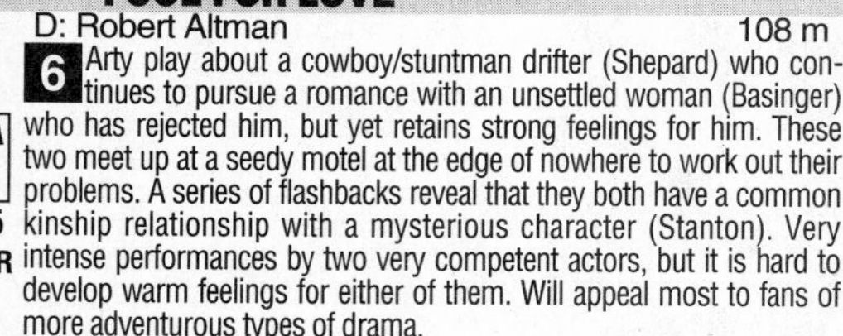

6 Arty play about a cowboy/stuntman drifter (Shepard) who continues to pursue a romance with an unsettled woman (Basinger) who has rejected him, but yet retains strong feelings for him. These two meet up at a seedy motel at the edge of nowhere to work out their problems. A series of flashbacks reveal that they both have a common kinship relationship with a mysterious character (Stanton). Very intense performances by two very competent actors, but it is hard to develop warm feelings for either of them. Will appeal most to fans of more adventurous types of drama.

Sex | Nud | Viol | Lang | AdSit

A: Sam Shepard, Kim Basinger, Harry Dean Stanton, Randy Quaid, Martha Crawford

Distributed By MGM/UA Home Video M800894

FOREVER YOUNG

D: Steve Miner 102 m

PG | SF ROM | 1992 | COLOR

6 Mel Gibson is a test pilot who is desperate when his love has been hit by a car and it is believed that she will never recover. So, he agrees to become a test subject for his best friend, who is a scientist experimenting with suspending life in a secret military project. It is 1939. But the experiment is suspended when the War breaks out. For the next 50 years he sleeps, only to awaken in a government warehouse after two boys play with his container. He had become a forgotten experiment, lost in the system. Now it is 1992 and he has discovered that his love is still alive, but that he is now rapidly aging and dying. If you can buy into all that, you will be satisfied.

Sex | Nud | Viol | Lang | AdSit

A: Mel Gibson, Elijah Wood, Isabel Glasser, George Wendt, Jamie Lee Curtis

© WARNER HOME VIDEO 12571

FOR LOVE OR MONEY

D: Barry Sonneneld 96 m

PG | COM ROM | 1993 | COLOR

6 Michael J. Fox is back in his element as a fast talking concierge at a posh hotel. He can get anything for anyone and can solve any problem - except his own. For years he has been saving all his tips and living in a ramshackle apartment so he can fulfill his life's ambition to create and own the plushest hotel in New York. He has just put all his money into an option to buy an island in the river and is close to making a deal with a major wheeler-dealer who can give him the rest of the money. The problem? The wheeler dealer is married, has a pretty young mistress he's leading along and the girl is also the girl of Michael's dreams. Which dream will it be? Fun, but not special.

Sex | Nud | Viol | Lang | AdSit

A: Michael J. Fox, Gabrielle Anwar, Anthony Higgins, Bob Balaban, Michael Tucker

© MCA/UNIVERSAL HOME VIDEO, INC. 81511

FOURTH STORY

D: Ivan Passer 91 m

PG-13 | MYS COM ROM | 1990 | COLOR

7 Interesting and quirky made-for-cable-TV psychothriller. Mark Harmon plays a likable but average sort of PI who is hired by Mimi Rogers to find her husband after he just disappeared one morning after breakfast. The police don't believe that he's really in trouble and she needs him. Harmon search through the web of clues leads him to believe that there is indeed something afoot, but it is also linked to his own sordid past. What is more, the more they are together, the harder it is to deny that they are powerfully drawn to each other. Very enjoyable characters. However, the ending is a little messy.

Sex | Nud | Viol | Lang | AdSit

A: Mark Harmon, Mimi Rogers, Cliff De Young, Paul Gleason, M. Emmet Walsh

© VIDEO TREASURES M012778

FOUR WEDDINGS AND A FUNERAL

D: Mike Newell 117 m

R | COM ROM | 1994 | COLOR

8 Englishman Hugh Grant spends his Saturday's attending his friend's weddings. While all those around him seem to be falling into matrimonial bliss, his own love life is met with one misfire after another. Then, at one of these weddings, he chances to meet a gorgeous American (Andie MacDowell) and his heart feels a solid tug. But, after one blissful night together, she returns to America and he to his dull love life. Months later, at the next wedding, she returns. Again, they spend a blissful evening of lust, however this time she breaks the news that the next wedding he will go to is hers. Witty, and for most, quite amusing, but some will rate it higher, some lower.

Sex | Nud | Viol | Lang | AdSit

A: Hugh Grant, Andie MacDowell, Kristin Scott Thomas, Simon Callow, Rowan Atkinson, James Fleet

© POLYGRAM VIDEO 6317693

FRANKIE & JOHNNY

D: Garry Marshall 117 m

R | ROM DMA COM | 1991 | COLOR

8 A captivating and unique love story. Pfeiffer and Pacino are very appealing in this endearing but decidedly unglamorous look at a last-chance love affair. Pacino is an ex-con who gets a job as a short order cook at a neighborhood diner. Pfeiffer is a waitress working there who has been burned one too many times and is not interested in a relationship of any kind. But Pacino falls hard for her. He will not retreat and continues to pursue her heart. He finally does charm her into bed, but still Pfeiffer retreats like a fragile bird, afraid of her ghosts. Enjoyable, realistic, believable, upbeat and very moving.

Sex | Nud | Viol | Lang | AdSit

A: Al Pacino, Michelle Pfeiffer, Hector Elizondo, Kate Nelligan, Nathan Lane, Jane Morris

© PARAMOUNT HOME VIDEO 32222

FRENCH LIEUTENANT'S WOMAN, THE

D: Karel Reisz 124 m

R | ROM DMA | 1982 | COLOR

6 Well-crafted telling of a multilayered story which was first related in a very popular novel. The movie version is a much simplified version of that story, yet it requires rapt attention to digest its subtlety and worth. It is an examination of the similarities and contrasts in the parallel stories, separated by time, of a modern-day love affair between two actors (who are creating a film about a love affair between a haunting Victorian woman and her lover) and the love affair of the Victorian people they portray. Intriguing with wonderful acting. Five Academy Award nominations.

Sex | Nud | Viol | Lang | AdSit

A: Meryl Streep, Jeremy Irons, Leo McKern, Hilton McRae, Emily Morgan

Distributed By MGM/UA Home Video M200181

FROM THE TERRACE

D: Mark Robson 144 m

NR | DMA ROM | 1960 | COLOR

8 Well-acted, involving and entertaining high-class soap opera. A young Paul Newman struggles to become successful and advance in society. He does all the right things. He marries the right woman (Joanne Woodward), a rich and spoiled socialite, and he works very long hours. He struggles to succeed in the corporate world while his marriage deteriorates and he has no personal life. Then he meets and falls in love with a woman who forces him to reevaluate everything he has become. Taken from a hugely popular novel about love, romance and power among the idle rich by John O'Hara.

Sex | Nud | Viol | Lang | AdSit

A: Paul Newman, Joanne Woodward, Myrna Loy, Ina Balin, Leon Ames

© FOXVIDEO 1036

FUNNY FACE

D: Stanley Donen 103 m

NR | MUS ROM | 1957 | COLOR

9 Stylish and elegant fairy tale romance story that only happens in the movies. Fred Astair is a charming and sophisticated fashion photographer who discovers an impishly charming Audrey Hepburn working as a clerk in a bookstore. He transforms her into a high-fashion model sensation and falls in love with her. Wonderful Gershwin score: "How Long Has This Been Going On" and "S'Wonderful." One of Astair's best later efforts. Top-notch escapism.

Sex | Nud | Viol | Lang | AdSit

A: Fred Astaire, Audrey Hepburn, Kay Thompson, Michel Auclair, Ruta Lee, Suzy Parker

© PARAMOUNT HOME VIDEO 5608

GATE OF HELL

D: Tienosuk Kinugasa 86 m

NR | FOR ROM ACT | 1956 | COLOR

9 Winner of Best Foreign Film Oscar, New York Film Critics and Cannes. Exquisitely beautiful, haunting and heart-wrenching Japanese tale of love. Set in the 12th-century, a warrior remains faithful to his Emperor in spite of overwhelming odds. When offered anything he wants for his reward, he asks for a beautiful lady he had met briefly but fell passionately in love with. However, she is happily married and refuses him. Yet, he is obsessed with her and refuses to leave her alone. Rebuffed on all fronts and desperate, he threatens to kill both her and her aunt, unless she agrees to let him kill her husband and then marry him. Instead, she kills herself. Beautiful photography. Subtitles.

Sex | Nud | Viol | Lang | AdSit

A: Machiko Kyo, Kazuo Hasegawa, Isao Yamagata

© HOME VISION GAT 020

GHOST

D: Jerry Zucker 127 m

PG-13 | ROM FAN COM | 1990 | COLOR

9 This romantic charmer was the big box office smash of 1990. Demi Moore and Patrick Swayze are deeply in love and are about to be married, but on the way home one night Swayze is mugged and shot. Now a ghost, Swayze learns that his murder was not accidental. It was actually a planned murder by his friend and former partner at the bank, who is laundering money, and that his love is still in grave danger. So, he seeks help from a very surprised phony medium (Goldberg), who, after some unexpected and very funny, supernatural communication with Swayze, realizes that she is the only one who can help save Moore. This is a wonderful film that rings true and has a little of everything for everybody.

Sex | Nud | Viol | Lang | AdSit

A: Patrick Swayze, Demi Moore, Whoopi Goldberg, Tony Goldwyn, Rick Aviles, Vincent Schiavelli

© PARAMOUNT HOME VIDEO 32004

GIANT

D: George Stevens 202 m

G | DMA ROM | 1956 | COLOR

9 This is a giant, sprawling soap opera saga that garnered ten Oscar nominations. It is Edna Ferber's three-generation story about the maturation of Texas from the days of cattle to oil. The story revolves around Rock Hudson, his Eastern-born wife Taylor and James Dean (in his last film role), as a young ranch hand who is totally captivated by Taylor. Dean grows rich with oil and disillusioned with life. Hudson and Taylor raise three kids on what is the biggest ranch in Texas. Weak in spots, but still quite impressive. Two weeks after filming was complete, Dean was killed in a car wreck.

Sex / Nud / Viol / Lang / AdSit

A: James Dean, Rock Hudson, Elizabeth Taylor, Carroll Baker, Dennis Hopper, Chill Wills

© WARNER HOME VIDEO 11414

GIGI

D: Vincente Minnelli 117 m

G | MUS ROM COM | 1958 | COLOR

8 Huge hit. Nine Oscars. This is Lerner and Lowe's charming story about a French tomboy (Caron) who is being groomed by her grandmother and aunt to become a courtesan to wealthy playboy Jourdan - but Gigi wants true love. Jourdan too is bored with his decadent life and has long been charmed by Gigi's exuberance and innocence as a child, but he discovers that she is now a woman and that he has grown to love her. Exquisitely filmed by the musical master Vincente Minelli. Wonderful tunes: "Thank Heaven for Little Girls" and "I Remember It Well."

Sex / Nud / Viol / Lang / AdSit

A: Leslie Caron, Maurice Chevalier, Louis Jourdan, Hermione Gingold, Jacques Bergerac, Eva Gabor

Distributed By MGM/UA Home Video M700050

GLASS BOTTOM BOAT, THE

D: Frank Tashlin 110 m

NR | COM ROM | 1966 | COLOR

6 Light-hearted, fun stuff. Doris Day is a public relations specialist at a space center and pulling double duty as a mermaid for her father (Arthur Godfrey) who is the operator of a glass bottom sightseeing boat. One day, while he is out fishing, top scientist Rod Taylor mistakenly hooks a mermaid. Guess who? On land, they work at the same place, so he gets her assigned to him and they fall in love. But spies from an espionage ring begin chasing her, and she is mistaken for being one of them. Relentless rounds of slapstick humor, but the film is above average lightweight family fun.

Sex / Nud / Viol / Lang / AdSit

A: Doris Day, Rod Taylor, Arthur Godfrey, Paul Lynde, Eric Fleming, Alice Pearce

Distributed By MGM/UA Home Video M202360

GOODBYE COLUMBUS

D: Larry Peerce 105 m

PG | COM ROM | 1969 | COLOR

8 Hugely popular satirical look at the mismatched love affair between a poor, college-dropout librarian (Benjamin) and a pampered Jewish-American princess (MacGraw) from the suburbs. Benjamin meets and falls for McGraw at a country club function and is invited home to meet her unapproving family. An interesting and funny look at suburban life for the upwardly mobile in the '50s. It was the screen debuts of both Benjamin and MacGraw. Look for Jacklyn Smith as a model.

Sex / Nud / Viol / Lang / AdSit

A: Richard Benjamin, Ali MacGraw, Jack Klugman, Nan Martin, Michael Meyers

© PARAMOUNT HOME VIDEO 6826

GOODBYE GIRL, THE

D: Herbert Ross 110 m

PG | COM ROM | 1977 | COLOR

9 Pure fun from Neil Simon. A kooky odd-ball actor from Chicago (Dreyfuss) rents a NYC apartment sight-unseen from another actor. Trouble ensues when he shows up to claim it, because it is still occupied the other actor's old roommate and lover, Marsha Mason and her precocious ten-year-old daughter. It is hate on first sight, but they settle upon a working arrangement where they will share. Their strained relationship is punctuated with insults and wisecracks, however disdain and disgust just as quickly blossom into love. Great dialogue and fun. Nominated for 6 Oscars, Dreyfuss got Best Actor.

Sex / Nud / Viol / Lang / AdSit

A: Richard Dreyfuss, Marsha Mason, Quinn Cummings, Paul Benedict, Barbara Rhoades

Distributed By MGM/UA Home Video M700069

GRADUATE, THE

D: Mike Nichols 106 m

PG | DMA COM ROM | 1967 | COLOR

9 A huge box office smash and a landmark film of the 1960s. 7 nominations, 1 Oscar. Hoffman, in his first major role, plays Benjamin, a very confused and naive college graduate, who returns to his affluent parents's home not knowing what to do with his life. Then Mrs. Robinson (Bancroft), the wife of his father's best friend, seduces him, adding to his confusion. Hoffman is both funny and poignant as he is seduced by this older woman, only to fall in madly love with her daughter. Now, for the first time, Benjamin knows what he wants. A brilliant score by Simon and Garfunkel: "Mrs. Robinson" and "Sounds of Silence" made them international music stars.

Sex / Nud / Viol / Lang / AdSit

A: Anne Bancroft, Dustin Hoffman, Katharine Ross, Murray Hamilton, Norman Fell, Alice Ghostly

© NEW LINE HOME VIDEO 2071

GREASE

D: Randal Kleiser 110 m

PG | MUS ROM | 1978 | COLOR

7 The highly popular Broadway play, about summer love at fictional high school in the '50s, is brought to the screen and given reasonably good treatment. Travolta, a greaser (but also the ultimate cool dude), and the sweet and innocent new-girl-in-town (Newton-John) meet over the summer break and have a summer romance. But, when fall comes, he thinks he has to protect his image as a tough guy and she doesn't fit it. Clever ideas, plenty of energy, excellent choreography, charm and lots of good music. Fun time.

Sex / Nud / Viol / Lang / AdSit

A: John Travolta, Olivia Newton-John, Stockard Channing, Jeff Conaway, Didi Conn, Eve Arden

© PARAMOUNT HOME VIDEO 1108

GREAT GATSBY, THE

D: Jack Clayton 146 m

PG | DMA ROM | 1974 | COLOR

7 F. Scott Fitzgerald's popular romantic tragedy about the flamboyant flapper era of the Roaring Twenties. Jay Gatsby (Redford) lost Daisy, the spoiled woman that he loved, years ago when she married a rich blueblood. He has now become wealthy himself, though through bootlegging. He throws mammoth parties at his Long Island mansion and invites the beautiful society people, hoping once again to get close to his lost love - Daisy Buchanan (Farrow). This is an enjoyable romancer, even though it is slightly flawed. An excellent re-creation of the period.

Sex / Nud / Viol / Lang / AdSit

A: Robert Redford, Mia Farrow, Sam Waterston, Bruce Dern, Karen Black, Lois Chiles

© PARAMOUNT HOME VIDEO 8469

GREEN CARD

D: Peter Weir 107 m

PG-13 | COM ROM | 1990 | COLOR

7 Light-hearted romance! Illegal alien Depardieu and gorgeous American McDowell become married so that he can stay in America and she can satisfy a stuffy review committee to qualify for an apartment that she craves. They both think that the ceremony will be the last time they have to spend any time with each other but the Immigration authorities begin to get suspicious. A full scale investigation is launched, and the unfortunate pair realize that the only way they can pull their phony "marriage" off is to spend a lot of time with each other. When they do, they must face the surprising news that they just might really be falling in love!

Sex / Nud / Viol / Lang / AdSit

A: Gerard Depardieu, Andie MacDowell, Bebe Neuwirth, Gregg Edelman, Robert Prosky, Jessie Keosian

© TOUCHSTONE HOME VIDEO 1141

GREGORY'S GIRL

D: Bill Forsyth 90 m

PG | ROM COM CLD | 1981 | COLOR

8 Delightful low-budget movie made in Scotland that was a winner of England's "Academy Award." It is a winning little comedy about a gangly, graceless high-school teenager who falls in love with his soccer team's newest and best player, Dorothy, the female goal keeper. He gets himself all custom-built just to please her, with the right clothes and the right hair style and then... she stands him up. However, his bruised adolescent psyche is mended when his crush is transferred to Dorothy's girlfriend. Wonderfully magical and humorous story of adolescent love. However, thick accents require diligent viewing.

Sex / Nud / Viol / Lang / AdSit

A: Gordon John Sinclair, Dee Hepburn, Chic Murray, Jake D'Arcy, Alex Norton, John Bett

© UNITED AMERICAN VIDEO CORP. 5318

GROUNDHOG DAY

D: Harold Ramis 101 m

PG | COM ROM | 1993 | COLOR

8 A smart-aleck weatherman (Bill Murray) is sent with sweet Andie MacDowell to Punxsetawney, PA on Groundhog Day to cover the annual prediction for spring. Having covered the ceremonies with his usual caustic wit, Bill and company become trapped in town by a blizzard. And, when he awakens the next morning - amazingly, it is still Groundhog Day, or rather it is Groundhog Day AGAIN!! In fact, now every morning, no matter what he did the day before - up to and even including suicide - is ALWAYS Groundhog Day again. He connives, he philanders, he steals, he plots to win Andie's heart, but he is always forced to repeat this day over and over - until he gets it right. Charming, sweet and very entertaining.

Sex / Nud / Viol / Lang / AdSit

A: Bill Murray, Andie MacDowell, Chris Elliott, Stephen Tobolowsky, Brian Doyle-Murray, Marita Geraghty

© COLUMBIA TRISTAR HOME VIDEO 52293

HANDFUL OF DUST, A

D: Charles Sturridge 118 m

PG | ROM DMA | 1988 | COLOR

8 Very elegant English drama by Evelyn Waugh, the author of "Brideshead Revisited," which is done in a sort of Masterpiece Theatre style. A seemingly happily married upper-crust English couple of the 1930s have their lives torn apart when the husband invites a dashing but penniless socialite for a weekend. By comparison to their guest, the husband is revealed to be a stuffy and tradition-bound husband, and the dormant passions of a bored and selfish wife are ignited by the visitor.

Sex / Nud / Viol / Lang / AdSit

A: James Wilby, Rupert Graves, Kristin Scott Thomas, Anjelica Huston, Alec Guinness

© NEW LINE HOME VIDEO 62825

HANOVER STREET

D: Peter Hyams - 108 m

PG · ROM · 1979 · COLOR

6 A simple little love story set in WWII. An Englishwoman (Lesley-Anne Down) is married to a British Intelligence officer (Plumber). However, she meets and immediately falls in love with an American bomber pilot (Ford). Ford is assigned to fly Plumber on a mission behind the enemy lines. But they are shot down and they work together to complete Plumber's top-secret mission. They become friends. It is only then that they discover that they are in love with the same woman.

Sex · Nud · Viol · Lang · AdSit

A: Harrison Ford, Lesley-Anne Down, Christopher Plummer, Alec McCowen, Richard Mason, Michael Sacks

© COLUMBIA TRISTAR HOME VIDEO 60006

HAVANA

D: Sydney Pollack 145 m

R · DMA ROM · 1990 · COLOR

7 A high-stakes romance set in 1958 amidst the tremors of a communist revolution in Havana. Redford is Jack Weil, a high-rolling gambler who is hoping to make it big in Cuba. En route he meets Olin, the beautiful wife of a revolutionary leader, who is in need of some help. Her husband has been reported killed and now she needs some protection. However, the attraction that propells Redford to her and their budding relationship will certainly hurt his chances at his big break, but Redford realizes that there other dreams worth chasing.

Sex · Nud · Viol · Lang · AdSit

A: Robert Redford, Lena Olin, Alan Arkin, Thomas Milian, Daniel Davis, Tony Plana

© MCA/UNIVERSAL HOME VIDEO, INC. 81049

HIGH SOCIETY

D: Charles Walters 107 m

NR · MUS ROM · 1956 · COLOR

6 Entertaining musical remake of PHILADELPHIA STORY with a beautiful Grace Kelly in Katharine Hepburn's role - the society girl playing cat and mouse games over three men: her current fiance (Lund), her ex-husband (Crosby) and a reporter (Sinatra) who is on hand to cover the impending wedding. Great Cole porter tunes include: "Did You Evah?," "You're Sensational" and "True Love," which was Oscar-nominated. Grace Kelly's last screen role.

Sex · Nud · Viol · Lang · AdSit

A: Bing Crosby, Grace Kelly, Frank Sinatra, Celeste Holm, Louis Calhern, Louis Armstrong

Distributed By MGM/UA Home Video M600292

HONEYMOON IN VEGAS

D: Andrew Bergman 95 m

PG-13 · ROM COM · 1992 · COLOR

6 Mildly entertaining. Nicolas Cage is deathly afraid of getting married but at last gives in. He and his girl (Parker) fly off to Vegas to do the deed. However, in one last bout of cowardice, he delays the wedding for one quick game of poker. James Caan is a big time gambler who had earlier spotted Cage's girlfriend in the lobby. She happens to be a dead-ringer for his deceased wife. So he has arranged for the game and Cage loses $65,000 that he doesn't have. No problem says Caan, just loan me your girl for the weekend and we're even. There are a few funny moments and it is well acted, but there just isn't much meat to it.

Sex · Nud · Viol · Lang · AdSit

A: James Caan, Sarah Jessica Parker, Nicolas Cage, Noriyuki "Pat" Morita, John Capodice, Robert Costanzo

© NEW LINE HOME VIDEO 75863

HOUSEBOAT

D: Melville Shavelson 110 m

NR · ROM COM · 1958 · COLOR

8 Predictable but highly enjoyable '50s-style romantic comedy about a Washington D.C. widowed attorney with three unruly kids living on a houseboat on the Potomac River. He hires a curvaceous music conductor's daughter, with no previous experience, as governess to take them in hand. Despite their relationships with others and numerous intervening catastrophies, they are... surprise... irresistibly drawn to each other. The star power of these two makes this a delight.

Sex · Nud · Viol · Lang · AdSit

A: Cary Grant, Sophia Loren, Martha Hyer, Harry Guardino, Eduardo Ciannelli, Murray Hamilton

© PARAMOUNT HOME VIDEO 5806

HOUSE CALLS

D: Howard Zieff 98 m

PG · ROM COM · 1978 · COLOR

9 This is a laugh-out-loud comedy about a recently widowed doctor, enjoying his sudden desirability and popularity with the ladies. But, he is distressed to find that he is irresistibly attracted to an outspoken divorcee (Jackson) who, if he isn't careful, will mess up everything. He doesn't want to give up his freedom, and she doesn't want to become a just another notch on his bedpost. Matthau and Jackson are wonderful together. Delightful comedy about two equally matched lovers, locked in a matrimonial battle of wits. Both Jackson and Matthau reappeared together in HOPSCOTCH.

Sex · Nud · Viol · Lang · AdSit

A: Walter Matthau, Glenda Jackson, Art Carney, Richard Benjamin, Candice Azzara, Dick O'Neill

© MCA/UNIVERSAL HOME VIDEO, INC. 66045

HOUSE OF THE SPIRITS

D: Bille August - 109 m

R · ROM DMA · 1994 · COLOR

7 Meryl Streep and Jeremy Irons almost recapture the fire they created in THE FRENCH LIEUTENANT'S WOMAN. As a young man, Irons leaves to earn his fortune so that he may marry his love, but she dies before he can return. Distressed, he retreats to a remote ranch and becomes a despotic tyrant. Lonely, he returns to marry the gentle sister of his lost love. They develop a deep tender love, but still his oppressive ways hang like a pall over their house. Told over 50 years' time, this is the story of lost opportunity and the consequences of bitterness. Much of the complexity and motivations from the book are lost, but it still holds your attentions.

Sex · Nud · Viol · Lang · AdSit

A: Meryl Streep, Glenn Close, Jeremy Irons, Winona Ryder, Antonio Banderas, Teri Polo

© LIVE HOME VIDEO 49143

HOUSESITTER

D: Frank Oz 102 m

COM ROM · 1992 · COLOR

6 Mildly entertaining farce. Martin is a love-struck architect who hocks everything to build his dream house in his hometown to surprise his true love - except she says no. Heartbroken, he goes back to the city, leaving his dream house behind. There, he has a one night stand with pretty con-artist (Hawn), and when she discovers that there is a new house in a pretty little town with nobody in it - she decides to move in. Soon, she has put out the word that she is Martin's new wife, all of which is a surprise to Martin's parents, his girlfriend and most of all, to Martin. Basically ridiculous and silly, but OK if you are willing to accept it.

Sex · Nud · Viol · Lang · AdSit

A: Steve Martin, Goldie Hawn, Dana Delany, Julie Harris, Donald Moffat, Peter MacNicol

© MCA/UNIVERSAL HOME VIDEO, INC. 81280

I DO! I DO!

D: 116 m

NR · MUS ROM · 1982 · COLOR

8 This is the musical version of a play called "The Fourposter." It is the story of the fifty-year marriage of Michael and Agnes, as told in events occurring in and around their fourposter bed. The musical roles were created on Broadway first by Mary Martin and Robert Preston. This stage presentation was videotaped live with Lee Remick and Hal Linden in the lead roles. It takes the couple from the night before their wedding until the day they leave their home 50 years later. Highly acclaimed. Good stuff!

Sex · Nud · Viol · Lang · AdSit

A: Lee Remick, Hal Linden

© TURNER HOME ENTERTAINMENT 1004

I LOVE TROUBLE

D: Charles Shyer 123 m

PG · ROM SUS · 1994 · COLOR

6 Mildly interesting story of two aggressive rival Chicago reporters. This is an attempt to recreate the sparks that Tracy and Hepburn threw off, but it largely fizzles. Both these tow hotshot reporters are on the same trail. A trail to discover why a passenger train strangely derailed. The closer they get to the truth, the more in-troubler they get. The only answer is for them to pool their resources, except neither trusts the other. A reasonable time-killer -- if its a slow night.

Sex · Nud · Viol · Lang · AdSit

A: Julia Roberts, Nick Nolte, Saul Rubinek, Robert Loggia, James Rebhorn, Charles Martin Smith

© TOUCHSTONE HOME VIDEO 2983

IMPROMPTU

D: James Lapine 108 m

PG-13 · ROM COM · 1990 · COLOR

7 Witty, intellectual and romantic dramedy with a historical twist. Real-life 19th-century French novelist George Sand (played here by Judy Davis) was in fact not a man at all, but a free-spirited woman who enjoyed smoking cigars and cross-dressing. She also enjoyed scandalizing Paris by collecting a long list of lovers. This amusing film is about the strong-willed woman's pursuit of the delicate Polish composer, Frederic Chopin. He was in everything her opposite and was also not entirely open to her advances. Nor was her current lover eager to see her leave him. For sophisticated tastes.

Sex · Nud · Viol · Lang · AdSit

A: Judy Davis, Hugh Grant, Mandy Patinkin, Bernadette Peters, Julian Sands

© HEMDALE HOME VIDEO, INC. 7007

INDECENT PROPOSAL

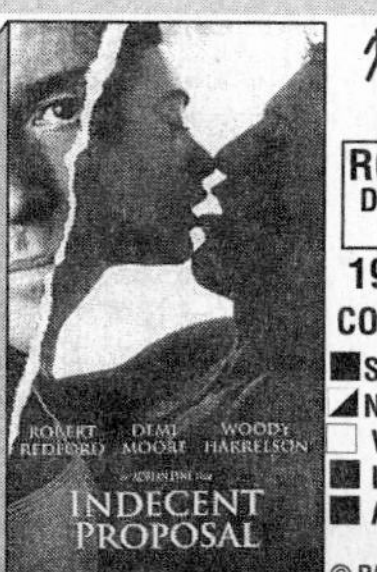

D: Adrian Lyne 119 m

R · ROM DMA · 1993 · COLOR

7 Deeply-in-love newly-weds Demi Moore and Woody Harrelson had gotten themselves into a deep financial hole. They owed $50,000 on a loan that they couldn't repay. Then they thought they had found a way out. Billionaire Robert Redford offered them one million dollars if Woody will let Demi sleep with him for one night. They discussed it. They thought they could handle it. They agreed to do it. But, now the guilt and the doubt about having done it are tearing them both up inside. Its tearing the two of them apart, because all of a sudden, the money problem doesn't matter any more. Not great drama or even great soap opera, but it is interesting.

Sex · Nud · Viol · Lang · AdSit

A: Robert Redford, Demi Moore, Woody Harrelson, Ikuver Platt, Seymour Cassel

© PARAMOUNT HOME VIDEO 32453

INDISCREET

D: Stanley Donen 100 m

ROM COM · 1958 · COLOR

7 Delightful sophisticated comedy in which Cary Grant plays an American playboy diplomat who romances women and then tells them he is married to avoid being trapped into marriage. Then he romances a famous European film star (Bergman). He finds himself drawn to her but still he pretends to be married to escape commitment. However, she eventually discovers his lie and sets her own plans in motion to get even. Stylish and endearing performances from both. Charming.

Sex · Nud · Viol · Lang · AdSit

A: Cary Grant, Ingrid Bergman, Cecil Parker, Phylis Calvert, Megs Jenkins, David Kossoff

© REPUBLIC PICTURES HOME VIDEO 5404

INNOCENT, THE

D: Luchino Visconti 125 m

R · FOR ROM DMA · 1979 · COLOR

9 Lush and beautifully photographed erotic tragedy of Italian decadence. A lustful nineteenth-century Italian nobleman (Giannini) ignores his beautiful wife (Antonelli) and pursues other women, particularly a beautiful widow (O'Neill). He not only fails to hide his escapades, but expects Antonelli to understand. She has an affair of her own with a young author. She has turned the tables on him. He is very surprised to learn that his lust for her has returned and he is now insanely jealous. Highly charged. Famed director Visconti's last film. Subtitles.

Sex · Nud · Viol · Lang · AdSit

A: Giancarlo Giannini, Laura Antonelli, Jennifer O'Neill, Rina Morelli, Massimo Girotti

© CONNOISSEUR VIDEO COLLECTION 1064

INTERSECTION

D: Mark Rydell 98 m

R · ROM SUS · 1994 · COLOR

6 An interesting premise. In the very first scenes, we see Richard Gere's car sliding into an intersection. We know an accident is going to happen but we're going to have to wait through a whole movie to know learn it turns out. Gere's life immediately begins to unfold. He is a wealthy architect married to beautiful Sharon Stone. They have money and a pretty daughter, but their relationship has gone bad. Gere has fallen in love with full-of-life Lolita Davidovich but he still finds it very difficult to give up his past or to start a new life. He is torn with indecision and now he is sliding into an intersection. Some women may like it but it is too slow for most.

Sex · Nud · Viol · Lang · AdSit

A: Richard Gere, Sharon Stone, Lolita Davidovich, Martin Landau, David Selby, Jenny Morrison

© PARAMOUNT HOME VIDEO 32242

IN THE MOOD

D: Phil Alden Robinson 98 m

PG-13 · COM ROM · 1987 · COLOR

7 Fascinating, more so because it was true. Sonny Wisecarver is a teenager in 1944 who has the strange propensity for falling in love with older women and then getting them to fall for him. He runs off with a married mother of two, only to have that relationship annulled. Whereupon, he marries another older woman, only to get in trouble again. Sweetly funny film, based upon a real live character from the '40s who the press labeled "The Woo Woo Kid." The real Sonny Wiscarver has a cameo as a mailman in a newsreel sequence.

Sex · Nud · Viol · Lang · AdSit

A: Patrick Dempsey, Beverly D'Angelo, Talia Balsam, Michael Constantine, Betty Jinett

© WARNER HOME VIDEO 475

INTO THE NIGHT

D: John Landis 115 m

R · ACT ROM COM · 1985 · COLOR

7 Jeff Goldblum is hopelessly boring and bored, plus his wife is having an affair with another man. While out on a midnight ramble, he stumbles into a beautiful woman (Pfeiffer) who is being pursued by a bunch of bad guys and accidentally gets involved with her, helping her to escape. Their adventure continues with repeated encounters with the killers and a quest to find some stolen emeralds. Criticized justly as being unnecessarily convoluted and difficult to follow, it is also, most times, a fun mix of romance, comedy and exciting action. Contains cameos from many leading directors.

Sex · Nud · Viol · Lang · AdSit

A: Jeff Goldblum, Michelle Pfeiffer, David Bowie, Richard Farnsworth, Vera Miles, Dan Aykroyd

© MCA/UNIVERSAL HOME VIDEO, INC. 80170

I.Q.

D: Fred Schepisi 95 m

PG · COM ROM · 1994 · COLOR

6 Lowly mechanic Tim Robbins is awe-struck by the arrival at his garage of Meg Ryan. She is very pretty; she is a brilliant mathematician; and, when Tim trys to return a watch she left, he discovers that she is also the niece of Albert Einstein (Walter Matthau). Oddly enough, Albert takes quite a liking to the boy. He and his three cronies decide that she would in fact be much happier with the mechanic than with the stuffy psychologist she is about to marry. The trouble is that she doesn't think Tim is smart enough. So, Albert and his buddies conspire to make Tim appear to be a latent genius - all of which leads to complications. Preposterous and implausible premise, but works because of star power.

Sex · Nud · Viol · Lang · AdSit

A: Meg Ryan, Tim Robbins, Walter Mathau, Charles Durning, Shephen Fry, Lou Jacobi

© PARAMOUNT HOME VIDEO 32678

IT COULD HAPPEN TO YOU

D: Andrew Bergman 101 m

PG · ROM COM · 1994 · COLOR

7 Lightweight and breezy entertainment. Nicolas Cage is a New York street cop and he loves it. His wife, Rosie Perez, is a hairdresser -- but she doesn't like it. She also doesn't like him being a cop and she doesn't even like him very much. Mostly, she doesn't like not being rich, so she is always having him buy lottery tickets. One day, when short on cash, Cage offered a down-on-her-luck, very sweet and very pretty waitress (Bridget Fonda) half his lottery ticket instead. But the idea backfired when the ticket turned out to be a winner and he had given away $2 million. Rosie really didn't like that and their marriage is in big trouble. Very predictable with absolutely no surprises, but fun.

Sex · Nud · Viol · Lang · AdSit

A: Nicolas Cage, Bridget Fonda, Rosie Perez, Wendell Pierce, Isaac Hayes, Seymour Cassel

© COLUMBIA TRISTAR HOME VIDEO 72813

IT HAPPENED AT THE WORLD'S FAIR

D: Norman Taurog 105 m

NR · MUS ROM · 1963 · COLOR

6 Entertaining light musical. Elvis Presley plays a daredevil pilot who romances a nurse at the Seattle World's Fair and helps a young girl stay out of an orphanage. Contains ten Elvis songs, none of them very memorable. This was still early in Elvis's movie career, so he hadn't burned out yet and still enjoyed himself. An interesting side note is that this is the very first film in which Kurt Russell appeared. Russell later would do an excellent job of playing Presley in the TV movie ELVIS.

Sex · Nud · Viol · Lang · AdSit

A: Elvis Presley, Joan O'Brien, Gary Lockwood, Vicky Tiu, H.M. Wynant

Distributed By MGM/UA Home Video M600475

IT'S MY TURN

D: Claudia Weill 91 m

R · ROM COM · 1980 · COLOR

7 Enjoyable sophisticated comedy about a modern-day woman's dilemma. She is successful - a brilliant mathematics professor, seemingly with everything. But she is also a klutz who can't seem to handle anything, including her life, very well. Her live-in lover is an aloof architect. Then, at her father's wedding, she meets her new stepmother's son (Douglas). He is a brash ex-baseball player with a beard. He is everything she shouldn't like, but she does. However, is this incest? Surprising little film that is consistently funny in a low-key witty sort of way.

Sex · Nud · Viol · Lang · AdSit

A: Jill Clayburgh, Michael Douglas, Charles Grodin, Beverly Garland, Daniel Stern, Jennifer Salt

© COLUMBIA TRISTAR HOME VIDEO 60023

IT STARTED IN NAPLES

D: Melville Shavelson 100 m

NR · ROM COM · 1960 · COLOR

6 Light-hearted fun. Clark Gable is a an American attorney who goes to Italy to settle the estate of his dead brother, only to find that there is a 10-year-old boy from a common-law marriage. His attempts to bring the boy back to the States are blocked by the boy's sexy Italian aunt (Sophia Loren). Guess what happens next. Lots of beautiful Italian scenery, including Sophia.

Sex · Nud · Viol · Lang · AdSit

A: Clark Gable, Sophia Loren, Vittorio De Sica, Marietto, Paolo Carlini, Claudio Ermelli

© PARAMOUNT HOME VIDEO 6790

JACKNIFE

D: David Jones 102 m

R · DMA ROM · 1989 · COLOR

8 This is powerful and captivating human drama that was created through the masterful performances of its stars. Ed Harris is a tormented Vietnam vet who lost his best friend in the war. He has become an alcoholic and now lives alone with his shy wallflower sister. Ten years after the war, he receives an unannounced visit from Robert De Niro, another friend from Vietnam and De Niro forces him to come to grips with the feelings that he has repressed for a long time. However, he also causes trouble in their complacent lives when De Niro begins courting Harris's sister. Moving drama.

Sex · Nud · Viol · Lang · AdSit

A: Robert De Niro, Ed Harris, Kathy Baker, Charles Dutton, Louden Wainwright, III

© HBO VIDEO 0213

JANE EYRE

D: Julian Amyes 239 m

NR · ROM DMA · 1983 · COLOR

8 Classic tale of courage and romance from a 19th-century novel by Charlotte Bronte. A young girl is orphaned, mistreated and unloved. Now older, and possessing a strength born of that childhood, she is hired as governess for the household of the darkly moody and mysterious Mr. Rochester. Her willfulness brings her to his special attention and they fall in love. But their happiness is soon threatened by his dark secret. Exceptional presentation produced by the BBC.

Sex · Nud · Viol · Lang · AdSit

A: Timothy Dalton, Zelah Clarke

© FOXVIDEO 3760

ROM

JEWEL OF THE NILE, THE

D: Lewis Teague 106 m

PG | ACT ROM | 1985 | COLOR

7 This is an enjoyable follow-up to ROMANCING THE STONE, however it can't quite match the vitality of the earlier film. All the characters have here returned six months later to chase down yet another stone - this time in the Sahara Desert, in the middle of an Arab revolution. It seems Turner has writer's block and Douglas is tired of living in her shadow. The answer for them is an adventure to seek out he priceless Jewel of the Nile. Lots of money was spent on technical aspects and explosions. There are lots of good action sequences and some laughs too. Enjoyable.

Sex / Nud / Viol / Lang / AdSit

A: Michael Douglas, Kathleen Turner, Danny DeVito, Avner Eisenberg, Spiros Focas

© FOXVIDEO 1491

JU DOU

D: Zhang Yimou 98 m

NR | FOR ROM DMA | 1991 | COLOR

9 Magnificent and visually stunning picture from China that Chinese officials tried to hide. At the urging of major American directors, it received a much-deserved nomination for the Best Foreign Film. It is the story of a beautiful young woman purchased by a wealthy bitter old man in 1920 China. He is sterile but, because she is unable to bear him the son that he wants, he beats her and treats her as an animal. The man's near-slave adopted son consoles her. They meet in secret and become passionate lovers. But when she becomes pregnant, their lives become hell. Powerful. Subtitles.

Sex / Nud / Viol / Lang / AdSit

A: Gong Li, Li Baotian, Li Wei, Zhang Yi, Zheng Jian

© LIVE HOME VIDEO 68983

JULES AND JIM

D: Francois Truffaut 105 m

NR | FOR ROM | 1962 | B&W

10 Considered by many to be famed French director Truffaut's masterpiece. It is the story of two best friends and their love for the mystical Catherine. Jim and Jules are writers who meet in 1912 at an ancient stone carving of a beautiful woman. They find that they agree on nearly everything, then they meet the enchanting Catherine, who is the image of the carving. The three become great friends and both men adore her. She is a child-woman who embodies all that draws out the passions in a man, but Catherine can commitment to no one man. She marries Jules, but he must suffer through her infidelities. Then she wants Jim. So rather than for anyone to loose, they share each other. Subtitles.

Sex / Nud / Viol / Lang / AdSit

A: Oskar Werner, Henri Serre, Jeanne Moreau, Marie Dubois, Vanna Urbino, Sabine Haudepin

© HOME VISION JUL 050

JUMBO (BILLY ROSE'S)

D: Charles Walters 127 m

G | MUS ROM | 1962 | COLOR

6 It's the turn of the 20th century and Jimmy Durante and his daughter (Doris Day) are struggling to keep their circus from going broke. Into their camp comes a competitor's spy, intent upon stealing the circus. Instead he falls in love with Doris. The major attraction here to the viewer is not the story but the beautiful Rodgers and Hart score: "This Can't Be Love," "The Most Beautiful Girl in the World" and "My Romance." The Busby Berkeley choreography and the marvelous talents of Durante and Raye also are a delight. A family movie with something a little different for everyone.

Sex / Nud / Viol / Lang / AdSit

A: Doris Day, Stephen Boyd, Jimmy Durante, Martha Raye, Dean Jagger, Billy Barty

Distributed By MGM/UA Home Video M300796

JUNGLE FEVER

D: Spike Lee 131 m

R | DMA ROM | 1991 | COLOR

7 Independent director Spike Lee once again raises some controversial questions when he explores racism from both sides of an interracial love affair. It is not a feel good film, nor a naively idealistic one - but one much more realistic, and one that takes a hard look at love, life and society. Snipes is a successful, upwardly mobile happily married black architect from Harlem who falls for his blue collar Italian secretary (Sciorra). Their affair ignites explosive intolerance from both of their families and their friends that is so fierce that they buckle under the pressure.

Sex / Nud / Viol / Lang / AdSit

A: Wesley Snipes, Annabella Sciorra, Spike Lee, Ossie Davis, Ruby Dee, Samuel L. Jackson

© MCA/UNIVERSAL HOME VIDEO, INC. 81093

JUST TELL ME WHAT YOU WANT

D: Sidney Lumet 114 m

R | COM ROM | 1979 | COLOR

6 Alan King puts in a flamboyant performance as a powerful mogul who is both happily married and also has a mistress, one of his top TV producers (Ali MacGraw). What does he do when his mistress finds true love with someone else? He sells the production company, rather than to let her run it. Fed up, she breaks free of him to be with her new man. But King outmaneuvers her to win her back. This is a sophisticated and cynical comedy whose charm may be lost on those who like their romances simple. Still, it has its moments.

Sex / Nud / Viol / Lang / AdSit

A: Ali MacGraw, Alan King, Peter Weller, Myrna Loy, Dina Merrill, Tony Roberts

© WARNER HOME VIDEO 11087

KING AND I, THE

D: Walter Lang 133 m

G | MUS ROM COM | 1956 | COLOR

9 This is a sumptuous feast for the eyes and ears. Superb production values showcase a winning story. A spirited English widow (Kerr) is hired by the pompous King of Siam (Yul Brynner) in the 1860s to be governess for his many children. The clash of both cultures and personalities make for some interesting situations, but conflict gradually gives way to respect and to an unspoken and forbidden love. Wonderful music includes their duet "Shall We Dance." Winner of five Oscars and nominee for Best Picture.

Sex / Nud / Viol / Lang / AdSit

A: Deborah Kerr, Yul Brynner, Rita Moreno, Martin Benson, Terry Sounders

© FOXVIDEO 1004

KINGS GO FORTH

D: Delmer Daves 110 m

NR | DMA ROM | 1958 | COLOR

7 Extremely controversial upon its release, this film still has relevance today. Two American soldiers, a veteran sergeant (Sinatra) and a recent newcomer and playboy (Tony Curtis), fight together on the battlefield of WWII France. Off the battlefield, they compete for the heart of a beautiful French girl (Natalie Wood). However, both of their characters are severely tested when she reveals to them that she is half-white and half-black. A little soapy, but with this quality of talent, that is easy to overlook.

Sex / Nud / Viol / Lang / AdSit

A: Frank Sinatra, Tony Curtis, Natalie Wood, Leora Dana, Karl Swenson

Distributed By MGM/UA Home Video M301730

KISS ME GOODBYE

D: Robert Mulligan 101 m

PG | COM ROM | 1982 | COLOR

6 Enjoyable, but very-much sanitized, version of the spicer (and funnier) Brazilian entry, DONA FLOR AND HER TWO HUSBANDS. A widow (Field) is about to marry stuffy Dr. Rupert Baines (Bridges) when she is confronted with the ghost of her dead husband (Caan), which only she can see and hear. Everything is quite predictable and most of the sexy humor has been altered to insignificance, but there is a comedic chemistry to the relationship between Fields and Bridges that is quite a lot of fun to watch.

Sex / Nud / Viol / Lang / AdSit

A: Sally Field, James Caan, Jeff Bridges, Claire Trevor, Paul Dooley

© FOXVIDEO 1217

LACEMAKER, THE

D: Claude Goretta 107 m

R | FOR ROM | 1977 | COLOR

8 This was the break-through film for French star Isabelle Huppert. In it, she plays a simple and sweet 19-year old beautician. While on a trip to the beach with her friend, she meets a handsome student writer. She falls immediately and rapturously in love with him, and he is infatuated with her innocence and beauty. They return to Paris and immediately move in together. She is desperately in love with him and wants nothing else, but he becomes more and more aware of their differences. She shares none of his interests and wants more from her. Eventually asks her to move out. She is devastated and suffers a mental collapse.

Sex / Nud / Viol / Lang / AdSit

A: Isabelle Huppert, Yves Beneyton, Florence Giorgietti, Anne-Marie Duringer, Jean Obe, Monique Chaumette

© HOME VISION LAC 01

LADYHAWKE

D: Richard Donner 121 m

PG-13 | FAN ACT ROM | 1985 | COLOR

8 Exciting and original medieval romantic adventure fantasy, set in the 13th century and beautifully photographed. A young pickpocket (Broderick) meets and becomes an ally to a dark knight whose constant companion is a hawk. The knight and his lady are the victims of an evil curse, where she is cursed into becoming a hawk by day and he into a wolf by night. Together all three embark on a quest to destroy the curse that tortures them by destroying the one who cast it. Very strong period flavor. Very well done and entertaining.

Sex / Nud / Viol / Lang / AdSit

A: Matthew Broderick, Rutger Hauer, Michelle Pfeiffer, Leo McKern, John Wood, Ken Hutchison

© WARNER HOME VIDEO 11464

LAST METRO, THE

D: Francois Truffaut 131 m

PG | FOR ROM | 1980 | COLOR

7 Nominated for Best Picture Oscar. It is 1942 Paris. The Nazis rule, so a brilliant Jewish theatrical director is forced to go into hiding in the basement of the theater. In his place, his beautiful and loving wife, Catherine Deneuve, must see that the troup stays together. She must deal with the very constrictive boundaries placed upon her by the occupiers, the barbs of a vicious pro-Nazi critic, while also fighting off her growing affections for her lead actor Gerard Depardieu. In spite of everything, the show must go on.

Sex / Nud / Viol / Lang / AdSit

A: Catherine Deneuve, Gerard Depardieu, Jean Poiret, Heinz Bennent, Andrea Ferreol, Jean-Louis Richard

© HOME VISION LAS 070

LAST OF THE MOHICANS, THE

D: Michael Mann 114 m

R | WST ROM ACT | 1992 | COLOR

10 Gorgeously photographed version of James Fenimore Cooper's classic story, set in northern New York during the mid-1700s, at the time of the French and Indian War. Hawkeye and his adoptive Indian father and brother agree to lead an English girl and her sister to their father commanding a remote fort besieged by French and Indian troops. He and the girl fall in love but they are overwhelmed by the war that threatens to consume them. Impeccable period details and intense and realistic violence make believable the desperate plight of these young lovers struggling to survive. This film contains none of Hollywood's typical gloss but rather a gripping realism that is rare to film. Wow!

Sex Nud Viol Lang AdSit

A: Daniel Day-Lewis, Madeleine Stowe, Russell Means, Eric Schweig, Jodhi May, Wes Studi

© FOXVIDEO 1986

L.A. STORY

D: Mick Jackson 98 m

PG-13 | COM ROM | 1991 | COLOR

7 A sometimes hilarious, sweet spoof about life in L.A. that has a ring of truth to it. TV weatherman Harris K. Telemacher (Martin) is hopelessly bored with the forever sunny/smoggy weather. He's bored with his girlfriend (Henner) and his younger diversion (Parker) is just a sexy airhead who fills his time. It's not until a quirky import from London (Tennant, his real-life wife) arrives that Martin's funky L.A. life gets some meaning and purpose. From freeway signs that communicate to snooty restaurants, this delightful farce is lightly seasoned with comic reality.

Sex Nud Viol Lang AdSit

A: Steve Martin, Victoria Tennant, Richard E. Grant, Marilu Henner, Sarah Jessica Parker

© LIVE HOME VIDEO 68964

LA TRAVIATA

D: Franco Zeffirelli 105 m

G | MUS ROM | 1982 | COLOR

9 Verdi's opera of tragic love between doomed lovers is produced in such a manner and with such lushness that it will please even non-opera fans. Inspired by the same story that inspired CAMILLE, this is the emotionally charged story of a courtesan who falls in love with a rich man's son. The boy's father convinces her that she will ruin his son's life and so she breaks off the relationship. They reconcile their love, but only on her deathbed. Beautiful voices. In Italian with subtitles.

Sex Nud Viol Lang AdSit

A: Teresa Stratas, Placido Domingo, Cornell MacNeil, Alan Monk

© MCA/UNIVERSAL HOME VIDEO, INC. 80048

LEGAL EAGLES

D: Ivan Reitman 116 m

PG | MYS ROM | 1986 | COLOR

6 Prosecutor Robert Redford and defense attorney Debra Winger team up to clear a kooky performing artist (Hannah) who has been accused of murdering her late father's art dealer. Redford is charming, Winger is a little flaky and together they are quite interesting. This story's plot will not withstand a very close scrutiny however, but it is still pleasing and enjoyable viewing, thanks mostly to the to the screen-presence of the major stars.

Sex Nud Viol Lang AdSit

A: Robert Redford, Debra Winger, Daryl Hannah, Brian Dennehy, Terence Stamp, Steven Hill

© MCA/UNIVERSAL HOME VIDEO, INC. 80479

LEGENDS OF THE FALL

D: Edward Zwick 134 m

R | DMA ROM | 1995 | COLOR

7 Beginning at the end of the 1800s, this film documents the tale of a prosperous Montana family that self-destructs. Hopkins has three sons. The oldest (Quinn) is the most practical. The middle son (Pitt) is a wild spirit and is his father's favorite. And, the youngest is a romantic who brings home a beautiful young woman to marry, but leaves with his brothers to fight in WWI. Only the two oldest return. Pitt is destroyed because he could not save his brother's life. However, he falls for his brother's fiance - only to leave her and home, destroying his father. She then marries the oldest brother. Years later Pitt returns to begin again but also rekindles old fires. Winner of an Oscar for Best Cinematography.

Sex Nud Viol Lang AdSit

A: Brad Pitt, Anthony Hopkins, Aidan Quinn, Julia Ormand, Henry Thomas, Karina Lombard

© COLUMBIA TRISTAR HOME VIDEO 78723

LIAR'S MOON

D: David Fisher 106 m

PG | ROM DMA | 1981 | COLOR

7 Interesting slightly soap opera-ish romance story about two young lovers in 1949 Texas. Both are young, one is rich and one is poor. They have fallen in love but their parents have forcefully forbidden them to see each other. However, she is pregnant, so they run off together. The two lovers have all the typical problems that you would expect... no money, incompatibility, etc. but they have another problem, too ... they may also be brother and sister. This is not nearly as tacky as it sounds. This is well done and has quite affecting performances, especially by Dillon.

Sex Nud Viol Lang AdSit

A: Matt Dillon, Cindy Fisher, Christopher Connelly, Hoyt Axton, Yvonne De Carlo, Broderick Crawford

© LIVE HOME VIDEO VA4020

LIKE WATER FOR CHOCOLATE

D: Alphonso Arau 105 m

R | FAN ROM | 1992 | COLOR

8 Sensuous fantasy import from Mexico. Set in the early 20th-century, this is the story of a young woman's enormously frustrated life which was twisted by her selfish shrew of a mother. The tradition of their family demanded that the youngest daughter would not marry but would remain home to take care of the mother until she died. However, the youngest daughter was deeply in love to a boy who married her sister. Her passion denied, the only pleasure she has in life is her cooking, and it is quite literally magical and mystical. Even when mama is dead, the poor girl is haunted by her past and her mother's ghost. Erotic and mystical, not for everyone. Subtitles.

Sex Nud Viol Lang AdSit

A: Lumi Cavazos, Marco Leonardi, Regina Torne, Mario Ivan Martinez, Ada Carrasco

© TOUCHSTONE HOME VIDEO 2111

LILITH

D: Robert Rossen 114 m

NR | DMA ROM | 1964 | B&W

7 An intelligent and sensitive study in madness. The story is that of a dedicated young trainee (Beatty) in an exclusive mental institution who falls obsessively in love with a beautiful patient (Seberg). She is bewitching to all who see her, but she is also living in her own dream world. His growing love for this schizophrenic girl draws him ever deeper into her tortured world and eventually into his own madness. This tragic love story is slow to unwind and is ultimately unsatisfying. However, it is also very intriguing and involving. Patience in viewing is required.

Sex Nud Viol Lang AdSit

A: Warren Beatty, Jean Seberg, Peter Fonda, Kim Hunter, Gene Hackman

© COLUMBIA TRISTAR HOME VIDEO 60443

LITTLE ROMANCE, A

D: George Roy Hill 110 m

PG | ROM COM | 1979 | COLOR

7 Enchanting and delightful film which will appeal to all members of the family. It is a film about first love and the relationship that develops between two precocious kids, an American girl and a French boy, and an elderly ex-con man. The old man tells the young couple of an ages-old legend: if they kiss under the Bridge of Sighs in Venice at sunset, their love will last forever. This convinces the two, they are now determined to get there and he agrees to help them. This is a sweet movie that is full of surprises, laughs and will leave everyone feeling good. It is a sensitive and attractive treatment of adolescence.

Sex Nud Viol Lang AdSit

A: Thelonlous Bernard, Diane Lane, Laurence Olivier, Sally Kellerman, Broderick Crawford, David Dukes

© WARNER HOME VIDEO 2001

LONELY HEARTS

D: Paul Cox 95 m

R | ROM COM | 1983 | COLOR

6 A touching and warm, but quirky, love story from Australia. A 50ish momma's boy piano tuner discovers a 30ish dowdy, extremely shy and sexually repressed bank clerk through a dating service after Momma dies. This is a warm story of these two, who have been too long burdened to and by others, who stumble and fumble their way into romance. It is a prize-winning, sometimes funny, sometimes heartwarming, but odd, look at another side of the human condition.

Sex Nud Viol Lang AdSit

A: Wendy Hughes, Norman Kaye, Jon Finlayson, Julia Blake, Jonathan Hardy

© NEW LINE HOME VIDEO 3023

LOST IN YONKERS

D: Martha Coolidge 114 m

PG | COM ROM DMA | 1993 | COLOR

8 Funny, touching and a real charmer from Neil Simon. Its 1942. Eddie is deep in debt from his dead wife's hospital expenses. His only chance is to leave his two boys behind in Yonkers with his stern mother and child-like sister, while he goes on the road for a year. Momma is a cold hard woman, but Aunt Bella is bubbly and full of life - even if her elevator doesn't quite make it to the top floor. Uncle Louie is a small-time hood who also comes to stay with Momma to hide out for a while. The two boys, Aunt Bella and Uncle Louie struggle to survive Momma's iron rule. Lots of clever dialogue from wonderfully drawn characters. Excellent.

Sex Nud Viol Lang AdSit

A: Richard Dreyfuss, Mercedes Ruehl, Irene Worth, David Strathairn, Brad Stoll, Mike Damus

© COLUMBIA TRISTAR HOME VIDEO 52663

LOVE AFFAIR

D: Glenn Gordon Caron 108 m

PG-13 | ROM | 1994 | COLOR

7 First made in 1939 with Charles Boyer and Irene Dunne, and again in 1967 with Cary Grant and Deborah Kerr, Warren Beatty wrote, produced and starred in yet another update of this sentimental weeper. Beatty plays an aging playboy, who discovers true love (his real-life wife Annette Bening) on a cruise ship. The trouble is that he is engaged to someone else and so is she. To give up their current engagements mean they also give up the lives both have lived for so long, so they decide that they will give themselves three months. But, on that designated day, she is hit by a car and is paralyzed, missing their meeting. Romantics only - quite sugary, but it has good people and production values.

Sex Nud Viol Lang AdSit

A: Warren Beatty, Annette Bening, Katharine Hepburn, Garry Shandling, Pierce Brosnan, kate Capshaw

© WARNER HOME VIDEO 13167

LOVE AMONG THE RUINS

D: George Cukor 100 m

NR | ROM COM | 1975 | COLOR

Sex / Nud / Viol / Lang / AdSit

8 Pleasant comedy which brings together two of the screen's biggest stars and one of its greatest directors. Set in 1911 London, Hepburn is being sued by a young gigolo for breach of promise when she fails to marry him. She seeks out the assistance of a long-ago lover (Olivier) who is now a famous barrister. He takes her case and though it all, their love is reborn. Made-for-TV, this piece rises far above the typical TV fare. Both Hepburn and Olivier won Emmys for their performances. Rich dialogue and performances. Entertaining.

A: Katharine Hepburn, Laurence Olivier, Colin Blakely, Joan Sims, Richard Pearson, Leigh Lawson

© CBS/FOX VIDEO 8038

LOVE FIELD

D: Jonathan Kaplan 104 m

PG-13 | ROM DMA | 1992 | COLOR

Sex / Nud / Viol / Lang / AdSit

6 Michelle Pfeiffer is a naive Dallas housewife in 1963 who feels totally inadequate in her own life and idolizes Jacqueline Kennedy. When the President is killed she feels compelled to go to his funeral in spite of her husband forbidding her to do it. She heads north on a Greyhound bus upon which she meets a black man (Haysbert) and his little girl. He sees trouble coming and does his best to avoid her but can't. She simply does not know what kind of trouble she is making for him. She only wants to be friendly, but soon they are in trouble, and are forced to head north together in a stolen car with the FBI in pursuit.

A: Michelle Pfeiffer, Dennis Haysbert, Brian Kerwin, Stephanie McFadden

© ORION PICTURES CORPORATION 8789

LOVE IN THE AFTERNOON

D: Billy Wilder 126 m

NR | COM ROM | 1957 | B&W

Sex / Nud / Viol / Lang / AdSit

7 An enchanting romantic comedy set in Paris. Gary Cooper is a rich American playboy businessman who is having an affair with another man's wife. Maurice Chevalier is a Parisian detective who specializes in spying upon adulterous wives. Audrey Hepburn, Chevalier's wistful and beautiful daughter, learns from her father that an angry husband is bent upon killing Cooper. So she warns Coop, saving him from the impending murder. She, however, begins to have her own rendezvous with him - but only in the afternoons and never telling him her name. Light-hearted and witty romantic comedy.

A: Gary Cooper, Audrey Hepburn, Maurice Chevalier, John McGiver

© CBS/FOX VIDEO 7428

LOVE LETTERS

D: Amy Jones 88 m

R | ROM DMA | 1983 | COLOR

Sex / Nud / Viol / Lang / AdSit

7 An intelligent, interesting and worthy exploration of human nature, that asks some uneasy questions. Jamie Lee Curtis plays a disc jockey who discovers some passionate love letters in the personal effects of her mother, who has died very young. The letters reveal that her mother had had a passionate and consuming, but adulterous, affair with a married man. Curtis longs for the same sort of all-consuming love that her mother had experienced. She gets her chance but the man she has found (Keach) is also married. This is an adult movie that asks adult questions.

A: Jamie Lee Curtis, James Keach, Amy Madigan, Bud Cort, Matt Clark, Sally Kirkland

© LIVE HOME VIDEO 5051

LOVE POTION #9

D: Dale Launer 97 m

PG-13 | COM ROM | 1992 | COLOR

Sex / Nud / Viol / Lang / AdSit

6 Two biochemists are so nerdy that they don't even appeal to each other. Then a palm reader gives him love potion #8. At first he is a non-believer, but his newly-amorous cat changes his mind. So, the two chemists decide to experiment on themselves, but they take precautions to prevent "infecting" each other. Hey, the stuff works! They immediately become the objects of chemically-induced adoration from the other sex. However, the transformed twosome are also becoming genuinely attracted to each other. That is until she is stolen away by a hunk who has a love potion of his own. Our guy fights back, rallying with the antidote, love potion #9. No big laughs but entertaining.

A: Tate Donovan, Sandra Bullock, Dale Midkiff, Mary Mara, Anne Bancroft, Dylan Baker

© FOXVIDEO 1873

LOVER, THE

D: Jean-Jacques Annaud 103 m

R | ROM DMA | 1992 | COLOR

Sex / Nud / Viol / Lang / AdSit

7 Explicit, seductive story of forbidden passion in 1920s Vietnam. Leung, a young, rich Chinese man, becomes obsessed with March, a poor ex-patriot French schoolgirl. Their banned relationship is one of uncontrollable desire. She keeps her emotions aloof and revels only in the excitement of the experience because she always dreamed of making love to faceless men. Although he declares that he will always love March, he marries a woman chosen by his parents. It is only as March returns to France that she realizes that she loves him, too. Nominated for its cinematography, but the plotting suffers because of its vagaries and an over-reliance upon sex.

A: Jane March, Tony Leung, Frederique Meininger, Arnaud Giovaninetti, Melvil Poupaud

Distributed By MGM/UA Home Video 903183

LOVES OF A BLONDE, THE

D: Milos Forman 88 m

NR | FOR COM ROM | 1965 | B&W

Sex / Nud / Viol / Lang / AdSit

9 Very likable and frequently hilarious portrait of a shy romantic young girl, coming of age in a small Czechoslovakia factory town where the women outnumber the men ten to one. This sort of an imbalance can cause a girl to wonder about love. Then a group of Army reservists visits town. Suddenly her girlish fantasies of love take flight. She meets Milda, becomes entranced with him and spends the night, but soon he is gone. A unique blending of pathos, sorrow and desire produces an engrossing and endearing comedy. A gem. A nominee for Best Foreign Film. Subtitles.

A: Hana Brejchova, Vladimir Pucholt

© HOME VISION LOV 100

LOVE STORY

D: Arthur Hiller 100 m

PG | ROM | 1970 | COLOR

Sex / Nud / Viol / Lang / AdSit

8 Megahit schmaltzy tearjerker and perennial romance favorite. Set against a New England college backdrop, rich kid Ryan O'Neal falls in love with a pretty and very gifted, but poor, girl (Ali MacGraw). Much against his family's wishes, he marries her and is disowned. Even though he and his family no longer communicate, Ryan and Ali are happy. Then, tragically, she is discovered to be dying of cancer. Based on the best-selling book by Eric Segal. Simplistic, but very effective.

A: Ali MacGraw, Ryan O'Neal, Ray Milland, John Marley, Tommy Lee Jones, Katherine Balfour

© PARAMOUNT HOME VIDEO 8006

LOVE WITH THE PROPER STRANGER

D: Robert Mulligan 102 m

NR | ROM COM | 1964 | B&W

Sex / Nud / Viol / Lang / AdSit

7 Wood and McQueen throw off sparks in this neat little romancer. McQueen is an independent sort, a musician. Natalie Wood is sweet and charming, a "good Italian girl." The two meet at a summer resort and share a moment of passion. She becomes pregnant and comes to him for help. McQueen trys to raise the money for an abortion, but it's then that he also begins to get to know her for the first time. So, when she breaks down while at a backroom abortionist, he pulls her out. It is then that they awkwardly begin afresh to discover each other. Touching, and frequently funny.

A: Natalie Wood, Steve McQueen, Edie Adams, Herschel Bernardi, Tom Bosley

© PARAMOUNT HOME VIDEO 6312

LUCAS

D: David Seltzer 100 m

PG-13 | ROM COM | 1986 | COLOR

Sex / Nud / Viol / Lang / AdSit

7 A brainy, but wimpy, 14-year-old has been accelerated into high-school. He is usually interested only in bugs and science, but over summer vacation, he falls in love with the pretty and friendly new girl in town. When fall comes though, she starts hanging out with the cool kids at school and she falls for the captain of the football team (Charlie Sheen). So, the love-smitten nerd decides to join the team, too. This is not a silly, condescending or trite film. It is a perceptive endearing story, that portrays the trials of puppy love. It is sweet, intelligent and enjoyable.

A: Corey Haim, Kerri Green, Charlie Sheen, Courtney Thorne-Smith, Winona Ryder

© FOXVIDEO 1495

MAD DOG AND GLORY

D: John McNaughton 97 m

R | ROM DMA | 1993 | COLOR

Sex / Nud / Viol / Lang / AdSit

6 De Niro is a murder investigator for the Chicago police but he is also so shy that his friends have jokingly nicknamed him "Mad Dog." Then Mad Dog accidentally saves the life of a small-time hood, Bill Murray. In gratitude, Murray sends Glory (Uma Thurman) his virtual slave, to "entertain" him for a week. When the two fall in love, Mad Dog must dig down inside himself to find the courage to face up to this hood who wants to take his property back. This is not a comedy, nor is it a true drama or even a true romance. In spite of its uncertain nature, it's a mildly interesting story.

A: Robert De Niro, Uma Thurman, Bill Murray, Kathy Baker, David Caruso, Mike Starr

© MCA/UNIVERSAL HOME VIDEO, INC. 81278

MAHOGANY

D: Berry Gordy 109 m

PG | DMA ROM | 1975 | COLOR

Sex / Nud / Viol / Lang / AdSit

6 Diana Ross goes from rags to riches in this likable soap opera. Perkins is a gay fashion photographer who discovers poor Chicago girl Ross working as a secretary and she is rocketed to international fame as a high-fashion model. However, she is soon dissatisfied and she goes out on a limb wearing one of her own designs at a fashion show. Now she has become a famous clothing designer, too! With all of this new-found fame, Ross leaves her wanna-be politician boyfriend Williams, but she discovers that her life is empty without him. This mildly popular soap opera has its moments.

A: Diana Ross, Billy Dee Williams, Jean-Pierre Aumont, Anthony Perkins, Beah Richards, Nina Foch

© PARAMOUNT HOME VIDEO 8835

MAID, THE

D: Ian Toynton — 91 m

PG | COM ROM | 1991 | COLOR

☐ Sex ☐ Nud ☐ Viol ◢ Lang ◢ AdSit

6 Mildly enjoyable and entertaining, even though it's an entirely unbelievable little comedy. Martin Sheen is a high-powered Wall Street investment banker who has been transfered to Paris to take a position at a bank. There, he spies and becomes totally infatuated with a beautiful woman (Bisset). He decides to pursue her, to the point that he even takes a position as her new maid for the one month he has left before he is to start his new position at the bank, which it turns out, is her her old position. Fun little no-brainer.

A: Martin Sheen, Jacqueline Bisset, Jean-Pierre Cassel, Victoria Shalet, James Faulkner

© VIDEO TREASURES M012777

MAMA, THERE'S A MAN IN YOUR BED

D: Coline Serreau — 107 m

PG-13 | FOR COM ROM | 1990 | COLOR

☐ Sex ◢ Nud ☐ Viol ☐ Lang ■ AdSit

6 Quite unlikely, but still funny, comedy from the writer of THREE MEN AND A BABY. A successful executive of a Paris yogurt factory gets sabotaged by board members planning a takeover - but he finds an unlikely ally in the black cleaning lady. On her nightly rounds, she discovers what is going on and tells him. Together they plot to take back his company. But first he has to hide from the cops, so he stays at her three-room apartment where they sleep four to a bed and she has five kids, each by different husbands. Naturally, they fall in love.

A: Daniel Arteuil, Firmine Richard, Pierre Vernier, Maxime Leroux

© HBO VIDEO 90560

MAN AND A WOMAN, A

D: Claude Lelouch — 103 m

NR | FOR ROM | 1966 | COLOR

◢ Sex ◢ Nud ☐ Viol ☐ Lang ■ AdSit

8 Passionate love story that became very popular. A widowed script girl and a race car driver whose wife had committed suicide, meet at their children's boarding school. They fall in love, but their romance is complicated because she is haunted by memories from her past. Set against the international auto racing circuit, the movie was one of America's most popular French films in the '60s. It was stylish and intensely romantic. It was the Oscar winner for Best Foreign Film and Screenplay. It was remade in '77 and was followed with a sequel in '86. The musical score is fantastic - the acting is potent. Dubbed.

A: Anouk Aimee, Jean-Louis Trintignant, Pierre Barouh, Valerie Lagrange

© WARNER HOME VIDEO 11655

MAN FROM SNOWY RIVER, THE

D: George Miller — 104 m

G | WST ACT ROM | 1982 | COLOR

☐ Sex ☐ Nud ☐ Viol ☐ Lang ☐ AdSit

8 A rousing cinematic treat for the whole family! This is a beautiful and rousing adventure story that is based on a well-known Australian poem. An independent young man is hired by a wealthy cattle rancher in Australia's wilderness of the 1880s. He falls in love with the cattleman's daughter, but is not accepted by her father (Douglas - in a dual role, also as the father's maverick brother). The film culminates in a wild chase through mountainous terrain to capture a herd of wild horses, led by a magnificent stallion. Thrilling. Stunning scenery. Pretty good sequel in RETURN TO SNOWY RIVER.

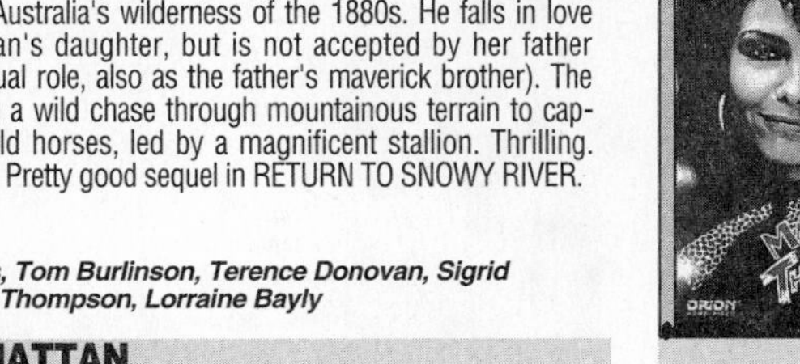

A: Kirk Douglas, Tom Burlinson, Terence Donovan, Sigrid Thornton, Jack Thompson, Lorraine Bayly

© FOXVIDEO 1233

MANHATTAN

D: Woody Allen — 96 m

R | COM ROM | 1979 | B&W

◢ Sex ◢ Nud ☐ Viol ◢ Lang ■ AdSit

9 Another brilliant and sophisticated slice-of-life look by Woody Allen at New York City neurotics - perhaps his best. A successful, but unfulfilled, TV writer (Allen) is running out of luck. His wife (Streep) has left him for another woman, and he has become involved in a string of love affairs that just aren't working out. This is an insightful Woody Allen-style comic look at life and the complications of adult love. The unforgettable Gershwin score successfully mixes with the black and white photography in this endearing adult comedy. See also ANNIE HALL.

A: Woody Allen, Diane Keaton, Mariel Hemingway, Meryl Streep, Michael Murphy, Anne Byrne

Distributed By MGM/UA Home Video M800469

MAN IN LOVE, A

D: Diane Kurys — 110 m

R | ROM DMA | 1987 | COLOR

■ Sex ■ Nud ☐ Viol ◢ Lang ■ AdSit

8 Steamy romance. An American actor (Coyote) is in Italy, making a film about the life of a notable Italian writer. But he becomes hopelessly infatuated with his sultry leading lady (Scacchi). Sparks begin to fly between them. The romance of the script leads them straight into a high-voltage affair, which jeopardizes everything for them both. He is married to Jamie Curtis, who wants him to come home. Director Kurys' first English language film is believable, sensual and interesting. As the characters develop, their everyday concerns about marriage and commitment are lost to passion.

A: Peter Coyote, Jamie Lee Curtis, Greta Scacchi, Peter Riegert, Claudia Cardinale, John Berry

© NEW LINE HOME VIDEO 7711

MAN WHO LOVED WOMEN, THE

D: Francois Truffaut — 119 m

NR | FOR COM ROM | 1977 | COLOR

☐ Sex ☐ Nud ☐ Viol ☐ Lang ■ AdSit

8 Wonderfully charming and sophisticated French comedy with serious undertones. The opening scene contains leg after beautiful female leg, filing slowly past the grave of Bertrand Morane. Bertrand, you see, is a man who loved women. He is a connoisseur of women. He loves all aspects of femaleness. And, women love him...even though he can be faithful to no one woman. He never abuses a woman, he just can't help himself from chasing the next one. This is his story and he tells it in flashback, as an autobiography. Spawned a much lesser American version with Burt Reynolds.

A: Charles Denner, Brigitte Fossey, Nelly Borgeaud, Genevieve Fontanel, Nathalie Baye, Jean Daste

Distributed By MGM/UA Home Video M202962

MAP OF THE HUMAN HEART

D: Vincent Ward — 109 m

R | ROM | 1993 | COLOR

◢ Sex ◢ Nud ◢ Viol ■ Lang ■ AdSit

9 Intriguing, exotic, intelligent, interesting, slightly mystical and unusual love story. A half Eskimo/half white boy is befriended by a white surveyor and taken from his polar home in the 1930s to be cured of tuberculosis. In the hospital he meets a half Indian/half French girl. They are both rebels and become steadfast friends and soulmates but they are soon separated. Returned to his homeland, he is ostracized as being unlucky, and so, he leaves them to navigate a Canadian bomber over WWII Europe. There, he finds his lost love again, but she is now passing for white and again their love is stunted. This is quite romantic, moving and is beautifully filmed.

A: Jason Scott Lee, Anne Parillaud, Patrick Bergin, John Cusack, Robert Jomie, Annie Galipeau

© HBO VIDEO 90778

MARJORIE MORNINGSTAR

D: Irving Rapper — 125 m

NR | DMA ROM | 1958 | COLOR

☐ Sex ☐ Nud ☐ Viol ☐ Lang ◢ AdSit

6 Natalie Wood is a beautiful 18-year-old girl from New York, with stars in her eyes, who leaves her family and sweetheart behind to venture off into the excitement of the theatre. She changes her name from Morgenstern to Morningstar and joins a summer stock group. There, she falls in love with an older performer (Kelly). He leaves the group to go to New York and the big time and she goes with him. She loves him even when he fails, but he does not treat her nearly so well. Adapted from Herman Wouk's novel, Wood and Kelly give touching performances.

A: Gene Kelly, Natalie Wood, Claire Trevor, Ed Wynn, Everett Sloane, Carolyn Jones

© REPUBLIC PICTURES HOME VIDEO 5552

MARRIED TO THE MOB

D: Jonathan Demme — 104 m

R | COM ROM | 1988 | COLOR

☐ Sex ◢ Nud ◢ Viol ◢ Lang ◢ AdSit

9 A delightful and winning comedy of errors. Angela (Pfeiffer) is a beautiful but unhappy housewife who is married to an unfaithful gangster husband. When he gets knocked off, she takes the opportunity to escape mob life altogether and flees to New York, sells all her worldly goods and rents a seedy apartment all on her own. She just might have a chance to be happy too - if it weren't for the head hood, who has the hots for her; his scheming wife, who thinks Angela is his seductress; and the FBI agents, who follow her everywhere. Funny and very likable, Pfeiffer turns out a sparkling performance.

A: Michelle Pfeiffer, Matthew Modine, Dean Stockwell, Mercedes Ruehl, Alec Baldwin, Joan Cusack

© ORION PICTURES CORPORATION 8726

MATCHMAKER, THE

D: Joseph Anthony — 110 m

NR | COM ROM | 1958 | B&W

☐ Sex ☐ Nud ☐ Viol ☐ Lang ◢ AdSit

7 An endearing comedy. Shirley Booth stars as a crafty New York City matchmaker in the late 1800s. A wealthy widower and merchant (Ford) decides it is time to remarry, so he travels to New York to consult with a matchmaker for that purpose. There, he spies Shirley MacLaine and becomes intent on proposing his love to her. However, Shirley Booth has designs on him for herself and schemes to implement her plans. Any of this sound familiar? This is what later became the smash Broadway musical HELLO DOLLY.

A: Shirley Booth, Anthony Perkins, Shirley MacLaine, Paul Ford, Robert Morse, Wallace Ford

© PARAMOUNT HOME VIDEO 5736

MATING GAME, THE

D: George Marshall — 96 m

NR | COM ROM | 1959 | COLOR

☐ Sex ☐ Nud ☐ Viol ☐ Lang ◢ AdSit

8 Fast moving and fun sex romp. Tony Randall is a straight-laced IRS agent who descends upon an ornery farmer (Douglas) to see why he hasn't filed a tax return - ever. Tony does his best to pursue government business but the farmer's daughter (Reynolds) is doing her best to pursue him - and he's losing. Reynolds and Randall are both captivating in these fun roles from early in their careers.

A: Debbie Reynolds, Tony Randall, Paul Douglas, Fred Clark, Una Merkel, Philip Ober

Distributed By MGM/UA Home Video 203048

MIAMI RHAPSODY

D: David Frankel 105 m

PG-13 | ROM | 1995 | COLOR

6 Pretty neurotic advertising copywriter Sarah Jessica Parker is all confused. She had just announced her engagement to animal researcher Gil Bellows, when she discovered that her mother has been having an affair with the male nurse who takes care of her grandmother. Her father has been having an affair with his travel agent. Her brother has been cheating on his pregnant wife with the wife of his partner. And, her newly-married sister has just cheated on her new husband with an old friend from high school. Maybe this marriage stuff isn't such a good idea after all. Lots of witty introspective dialogue, much of it very reminiscent of Woody Allen.

Sex Nud Viol Lang AdSit

A: Sarah Jessica Parker, Mia Farrow, Antonio Banderas, Paul Mazursky, Gil Bellows, Kevin Pollack

© HOLLYWOOD PICTURES HOME VIDEO 2752

MICKI & MAUDE

D: Blake Edwards 118 m

PG-13 | COM ROM | 1984 | COLOR

7 A TV reporter (Dudley Moore) desperately wants to be a father, but his wife Micki (Ann Reinking) is a hard-driving career woman who doesn't want to take the time for a baby and barely for him. So, he has a fling with a pretty cellist named Maude (Irving), who shortly tells him that she is pregnant. Just as she does, his wife gives him the same news - and that's only part of his problems. He loves both women and can't pick between them. So, he marries Maude too, leads a secret double life and that works for a while - until, that is, the two women wind up in adjacent rooms at the hospital. Surprisingly winning and enjoyable.

Sex Nud Viol Lang AdSit

A: Dudley Moore, Amy Irving, Ann Reinking, Richard Mulligan, George Gaynes, Wallace Shawn

© COLUMBIA TRISTAR HOME VIDEO 60456

MIDSUMMER NIGHT'S SEX COMEDY, A

D: Woody Allen 88 m

PG | COM ROM | 1982 | COLOR

7 This one is mostly for Woody Allen fans. It is set at the turn of the century and centers around three couples who decide to spend the weekend together at a beautiful estate in the country. Woody is there with his cold wife (Steenburgen). Ferrer is there with a promiscuous Mia Farrow. And Tony Roberts is there with his latest lover (Haggerty). Mischief-making soon ensues and it seems that everyone ends up falling in love with the wrong person. Quirky, but entertaining.

Sex Nud Viol Lang AdSit

A: Woody Allen, Mia Farrow, Jose Ferrer, Mary Steenburgen, Tony Roberts, Julie Hagerty

© WARNER HOME VIDEO 22025

MISSISSIPPI MASALA

D: Mira Nair 117 m

R | DMA ROM | 1992 | COLOR

7 An unusual and intelligent film. A wealthy Indian attorney, who was born in African Uganda, is forced to leave by dictator Idi Amin. He, his wife and daughter settle down and work for relatives at their motel in an Indian enclave of Mississippi, where they are neither white or black. His beautiful daughter meets and falls for a successful young black man (Washington). She has really never known discrimination but, when their relationship is discovered, they are both immediately chastised by Indians, blacks and whites. Involving, well-conceived and executed, but a little slow.

Sex Nud Viol Lang AdSit

A: Denzel Washington, Sarita Choudhury, Roshan Seth, Sharmila Tagore, Charles Dutton, Joe Seneca

© COLUMBIA TRISTAR HOME VIDEO 92693

MOONSTRUCK

D: Norman Jewison 103 m

PG | COM ROM | 1987 | COLOR

8 Absolutely delightful! Cher stars as an Italian-American widow living at home with her aging parents and engaged to marry an older man (Aiello), even though the romance is passionless. In spite of herself, she finds herself helplessly drawn to, and in love with, his younger brother (Cage). A whole bunch of romantic complications ensue. Jewison does a fantastic job of capturing the essence of Italian-American sensibilities - the warmth, humor and dialogue. Oscars for Cher, Dukakis and Patrick Stanley's script. That's amore!

Sex Nud Viol Lang AdSit

A: Cher, Nicolas Cage, Olympia Dukakis, Vincent Gardenia, Danny Aiello, Julie Bovasso

Distributed By MGM/UA Home Video M901135

MORNING AFTER, THE

D: Sidney Lumet 103 m

R | CRM MYS ROM | 1986 | COLOR

8 Complex thriller! A beautiful washed-up actress (Fonda), now an alcoholic, is having a very bad morning. After a night of an excess of everything, she wakes up to find that the man in bed next to her is dead, with a dagger through his heart. She remembers nothing. Terrified, she erases all trace of her presence and evades the police. She lives in fear until she bumps into ex-cop and ex-alcoholic (Bridges) who becomes charmed by this girl with a problem and who unravels the mystery for her. Both Fonda's and Bridges's characters are complex, appealing and quite believable.

Sex Nud Viol Lang AdSit

A: Jane Fonda, Jeff Bridges, Raul Julia, Diane Salinger, Richard Foronjy, Geoffery Scott

© WARNER HOME VIDEO 419

MOSCOW ON THE HUDSON

D: Paul Mazursky 107 m

R | COM DMA ROM | 1984 | COLOR

8 The film is both comic and bittersweet and Robin Williams is an absolute charmer. While touring the United States, Williams, a musician for the Moscow Circus, is blown away by the wonders of Bloomingdales and defects to America right then. His adjustment to American life is difficult, often comedic and sad. He lives in fear that the KGB will capture him, until he gets his American citizenship. But he also has new friends in a black security guard, a sexy Italian lover and a cagey lawyer. America becomes home, but it doesn't happen all at once and it's a lot fun watching it happen.

Sex Nud Viol Lang AdSit

A: Robin Williams, Maria Conchita Alonso, Cleavant Derricks, Alejandro Rey, Savely Kramarov, Elya Baskin

© COLUMBIA TRISTAR HOME VIDEO 60309

MR. BASEBALL

D: Fred Schepisi m

PG-13 | COM ROM | 1992 | COLOR

6 Intelligent and mildly entertaining serio-comedy about an American big league baseball former-great who is now on the downhill slide. His playing may be slipping, but his ego isn't. His agent gets him a job in Japan, playing for the Chunichi Dragons where his fierce independence and huge ego quickly get him into big trouble with the samurai-like coach (Takakura). He is definitely not a team player and he can't get used to the Japanese style of playing the game. However, Selleck and Takakura are eventually brought together by Selleck's romance with Takanashi, Takakura's daughter. Not hilarious but not too serious, either.

Sex Nud Viol Lang AdSit

A: Tom Selleck, Dennis Haysbert, Ken Takakura, Aya Takanashi

© MCA/UNIVERSAL HOME VIDEO, INC. 81231

MRS. SOFFEL

D: Gillian Armstrong 113 m

PG-13 | DMA ROM | 1985 | COLOR

6 Curiously interesting but also a slow-moving and gloomy drama that was based upon a real incident. In 1901 Pittsburgh, a repressed warden's wife (Keaton) is permitted to distribute Bibles to prisoners on death row. She becomes infatuated with the charismatic older of two brothers (Gibson), who are up for a murder which they may not have committed. She not only falls in love him and then helps them to escape, but she leaves with them, too. She is transformed from being a devoutly religious woman to being the adulterous lover of a man on the run from the law.

Sex Nud Viol Lang AdSit

A: Diane Keaton, Mel Gibson, Edward Herrmann, Matthew Modine, Trini Alvarado, Jennie Dundas

Distributed By MGM/UA Home Video M800600

MR. WONDERFUL

D: Anthony Menhella 99 m

PG-13 | ROM COM | 1993 | COLOR

7 Matt Dillon is an electrician who has three problems. He wants very badly to invest with his friends in the rehabilitation of an old bowling alley. He can't because he is paying his ex-wife (Annabella Sciorra) so much money in alimony, so he needs to find her a new husband, a Mr. Wonderful, as quickly as possible. However, his last problem is the biggest -- he still loves her. And, while it was her that had walked out on him, intent upon getting an education that would lead her away from the blue-collar neighborhood that they both grew up in, she still loves him too. Pleasant romantic comedy, worthy of an hour and a half.

Sex Nud Viol Lang AdSit

A: Matt Dillon, Annabella Sciorra, Mary Louise Parker, William Hurt, Vincent D'Onofrio, David Barry Gray

© WARNER HOME VIDEO 12988

MUCH ADO ABOUT NOTHING

D: Kenneth Branagh 110 m

PG-13 | COM ROM | 1993 | COLOR

8 This is one of the better screen productions of Shakespeare, but it is still Shakespeare. That means that educated and patient audiences will enjoy it, and others will wonder what all the fuss is about. Kenneth Branagh and his real-life wife Emma Thompson give the honey-tongued bard's words both sparkle and bite as the lovers Benedick and Beatrice, who spar with their wits as though they were swords. The story was filmed on location in sunny Tuscany, Italy. Prince Don Pedro and his men have just returned from war to skirmish amid the conflict and rivalries of love between men and women. Many critics would have rated it higher.

Sex Nud Viol Lang AdSit

A: Kenneth Branagh, Richard Briers, Michael Keaton, Keanu Reeves, Emma Thompson, Denzel Washington

© COLUMBIA TRISTAR HOME VIDEO 71753

MURPHY'S ROMANCE

D: Martin Ritt 107 m

PG-13 | ROM COM | 1985 | COLOR

7 Effortless romance in this charmer! A recently divorced young woman (Field) and her twelve-year-old son decide to make a fresh start in a small Arizona town and raise horses for a living. Almost immediately, she runs into crusty old druggist Murphy (Garner) and takes a liking to him, and he to her. But Field's old husband (Kerwin) throws a wrench in things when he shows up again. She doesn't know what to feel. Field and Garner are naturals together in this wonderful little slice of rural Americana that really works. Delightful!

Sex Nud Viol Lang AdSit

A: Sally Field, James Garner, Brian Kerwin, Corey Haim, Dennis Burkley, Georgann Johnson

© COLUMBIA TRISTAR HOME VIDEO 60649

MUSIC MAN, THE

D: Morton DaCosta 151 m

G | MUS COM ROM | 1962 | COLOR

10 Golden Americana and a rousing good time too! A charming con artist and music "professor" (Preston) convinces a small turn-of-the-century Iowa town that he can teach the boys there to play musical instruments by using his Think Method. Then he convinces all the townsfolk that they should form a marching band - buying the costumes, instruments and all from him. Some of the Oscar-winning songs featured in this delightful musical include "76 Trombones," "'Til There Was You" and "Trouble." This wonderful slice of American apple pie was nominated for 6 Oscars, including Best Picture. Wonderful!!

Sex / Nud / Viol / Lang / AdSit

A: Robert Preston, Buddy Hackett, Hermione Gingold, Paul Ford, Pert Kelton, Shirley Jones

© WARNER HOME VIDEO 11473

MY BOYFRIEND'S BACK

D: Bob Balaban 85 m

PG-13 | ROM COM | 1993 | COLOR

6 Silly little film about a love-struck teenager who dies after having been struck by a bullet that was meant for his beautiful but unattainable love. But before dying, he asks her to the prom and she, thinking it's a safe bet, agrees to go. However, so motivated is he that he arises from the grave to make his date on time. Being dead does have certain disadvantages though, such as having body parts that fall off and people just don't treat you the same either. The absurdity of it all gets carried away sometimes and it's also a long time to hear different variations on the same joke over and over, but it is sort of cute. Teenagers in particular might be its best audience.

Sex / Nud / Viol / Lang / AdSit

A: Andrew Lowery, Traci Lind, Danny Zorn, Bob Dishy, Paul Dooley, Edward Herrmann

© TOUCHSTONE HOME VIDEO 2225

MY FAIR LADY

D: George Cukor 170 m

G | MUS ROM COM | 1964 | COLOR

10 Outstanding winner of eight Oscars - including Best Picture! Shaw's enduring play (and film) PYGMALION is masterfully transformed into a magical musical by Lerner and Lowe. It is an exuberant story of the effort by a snooty Englishman to transform, on a bet, a guttersnipe flower peddler (Hepburn) into being able to pass for a respectable lady. In the process, he falls in love with her and she changes him forever. Just a few of the winning and memorable songs include "The Rain in Spain," "On the Street Where You Live" and "Get Me to the Church on Time." Wonderful.

Sex / Nud / Viol / Lang / AdSit

A: Audrey Hepburn, Rex Harrison, Wilfrid Hyde-White, Stanley Holloway, Jeremy Brett, Theodore Bikel

© FOXVIDEO 7038

MY GIRL

D: Howard Zieff 102 m

PG | DMA ROM CLD | 1991 | COLOR

8 Irresistable weeper. Eleven-year-old Chlumsky is the precocious daughter of a widowed mortician (Aydroyd) and because their house doubles for a mortuary, death is everywhere. Aykroyd doesn't have much time for his daughter, nor does he know how to reach out to her, not knowing that she feels responsible for her mother's death or that she's jealous when he falls for the new cosmetologist (Curtis) he has hired. But Macauly Culkin is her neighbor and that summer she and Culkin become best friends and experience the beginnings of young love. However, their summer together comes to a tragic end. Parents, share this one with your kids.

Sex / Nud / Viol / Lang / AdSit

A: Anna Chlumsky, Macaulay Culkin, Dan Aykroyd, Jamie Lee Curtis, Richard Masur, Griffin Dunne

© COLUMBIA TRISTAR HOME VIDEO 50993

MYSTIC PIZZA

D: Donald Petrie 104 m

R | COM ROM | 1988 | COLOR

7 Tasty coming-of-age comedy and the amorous misadventures of three young women. Working this summer at a pizza parlor in the town of Mystic, Connecticut, three young waitresses attempt a grab for their futures. One is set to marry her high school sweetheart, but faints at the alter. One is set to go to college on an astronomy scholarship, but instead falls in love with a married man. Her sister has looks, knows how to use them and is only out for a good time, but instead falls in love with a rich law student. Loveable characters. Good for everyone, but best audience is young women.

Sex / Nud / Viol / Lang / AdSit

A: Annabeth Gish, Julia Roberts, Lili Taylor, Vincent D'Onofrio, William R. Moses, Adam Storke

© MCEG/STERLING 70054

NADINE

D: Robert Benton 83 m

PG | COM ROM | 1987 | COLOR

6 Nadine (Basinger) is a hairdresser in 1954 Texas. She is pregnant and about to be divorced from her looser bar-owner husband (Bridges). She has another problem, too. She was trying to get some "art" photographs back from a photographer when he was murdered and, in an hurry, she mistakenly picked up some other photos which he had taken of a map showing where a new road is to go. That is a secret that means money, and trouble... somebody wants the photos back. She's in big trouble. She seeks help from her reluctant ex and through it all, they fall in love all over again. Well-cast, lighthearted light-weight evening's diversion.

Sex / Nud / Viol / Lang / AdSit

A: Jeff Bridges, Kim Basinger, Rip Torn, Gwen Verdon, Glenne Headly, Jerry Stiller

© CBS/FOX VIDEO 3841

NEW LIFE, A

D: Alan Alda 104 m

PG-13 | COM ROM | 1988 | COLOR

6 Appealing little story about love in modern relationships. Alan Alda is an obnoxious stock broker and Ann-Margret is, or was, his wife. They divorce after twenty years of marriage. Each sets out to seek a new mate in the singles bars of New York. That turns out to be an unexpectedly painful process of bumps and bruises. Ultimately however, it is also a process that teaches to them both to become open and more understanding with each other and other people. They apply that lesson in their new relationships and also in their old ones. Pleasant and entertaining, but not profound.

Sex / Nud / Viol / Lang / AdSit

A: Alan Alda, Ann-Margret, Hal Linden, Veronica Hamel, Mary Kay Place, John Shea

© PARAMOUNT HOME VIDEO 32160

NEW YEAR'S DAY

D: Henry Jaglom 90 m

R | DMA ROM | 1989 | COLOR

7 Interesting character studies are drawn from the opportunity presented when two groups of strangers are forced occupy the same apartment for one day. Three young women have been renting an apartment in New York. They are moving out but thought they had until the end of the day. In walks the owner, recently arrived from California and wanting to move in because he thought their lease was up at the beginning of the day. This film explores the personalities of those moving out and a depressed man in mid-life crisis moving in. That one day leaves a lasting impression on them all forever.

Sex / Nud / Viol / Lang / AdSit

A: Maggie Jakobson, Gwen Welles, David Duchovny, Melanie Winter, Harvey Miller, Irene Moore

© PARAMOUNT HOME VIDEO 12780

NEW YORK, NEW YORK

D: Martin Scorsese 164 m

PG | MUS ROM | 1977 | COLOR

7 Big name talent abounds in this story about the love affair between a splashy saxophonist (De Niro) and a timid sweet singer (Minnelli). The two meet on VJ day - WWII is over. They both audition with a big band, fall in love and get married. He takes over as band leader. She goes back to New York to have their baby. And, he begins an affair with her replacement. Their marriage falls apart but her career takes off, singing the songs he hates. High production values and some great musical sequences and strong performances, but the music is the most interesting thing about it.

Sex / Nud / Viol / Lang / AdSit

A: Liza Minnelli, Robert De Niro, Lionel Stander, Georgie Auld, Mary Kay Place, George Memmoli

Distributed By MGM/UA Home Video M301321

NIGHT SHIFT

D: Ron Howard 106 m

R | COM ROM | 1982 | COLOR

8 Clever and engaging comedy from Ron Howard. A shy and subdued nerd (Winkler) takes a night job at the city morgue for the peace and quiet he expects to find there. But his crazy co-worker (Keaton) and a sweet next door neighbor, who is also a hooker (Long), talk him into making a little extra money by running an escort service out of the morgue. This is a situation that is ripe with opportunities for laughs, and they all get used. Winkler and Long were good, but Keaton was so successful in his first screen lead that it launched him into major stardom. Fun.

Sex / Nud / Viol / Lang / AdSit

A: Henry Winkler, Michael Keaton, Shelley Long, Kevin Costner, Bobby DiCicco, Nita Talbot

© WARNER HOME VIDEO 20006

OBJECT OF BEAUTY

D: Michael Lindsay-Hogg 105 m

R | COM ROM | 1991 | COLOR

8 A dark little love story - offbeat and intriguing. Malcovich and MacDowell, a once affluent couple, are now living way beyond their means. They get stuck in a posh hotel in London with a long-overdue hotel bill. Every day they are sinking deeper in debt, but they keep spending money they don't have and dodging hotel personnel. Malcovich finally suggests that they sell a rare and valuable sculpture that belongs to MacDowell, who refuses. So, when the little object turns up missing, each immediately suspects the other. An amusing test of love.

Sex / Nud / Viol / Lang / AdSit

A: John Malkovich, Andie MacDowell, Lolita Davidovich, Rudi Davies, Joss Ackland, Bill Paterson

© LIVE HOME VIDEO 68948

OBSESSION

D: Brian De Palma 98 m

PG | SUS ROM | 1976 | COLOR

8 Taut and gripping suspensor from Brian De Palma in Hitchcock's VERTIGO tradition. Wealthy New Orleans businessman Cliff Robertson cooperated with police in 1959 when his wife (Bujold) and daughter are kidnapped and they were never seen again. Now, sixteen years later in Rome, he meets a virtual double to his wife, marries her, and she is also kidnapped. The new ransom note he gets is essentially identical to the first one. Complex web of romance, suspense, treachery and torment. Highly watchable.

Sex / Nud / Viol / Lang / AdSit

A: Cliff Robertson, Genevieve Bujold, Wanda Blackman, John Lithgow, Sylvia Kuumba Williams

© GOODTIMES 4607

OFFICER AND A GENTLEMAN, AN

D: Taylor Hackford 126 m

R | ROM DMA | 1982 | COLOR

9 Immensely popular and sentimental soap opera with a hard edge. Richard Gere is a Navy brat, a loner and a social misfit. He sees his only chance for respectability in becoming a Navy pilot, but he first has to get past a tough drill instructor (Gossett) who is intent upon breaking down his selfish independence. Winger is a poor local girl, who sees her only chance at a way out to a good life in being married to a pilot. These two are cut from the same cloth and you can see things coming from a mile away, but this is still a very well done, compelling and heartwarming movie. A real feel good movie.

Sex Nud Viol Lang AdSit

A: Richard Gere, Debra Winger, David Keith, Louis Gossett, Jr., Harold Sylvester, Robert Loggia

© PARAMOUNT HOME VIDEO 1467

OF HUMAN BONDAGE

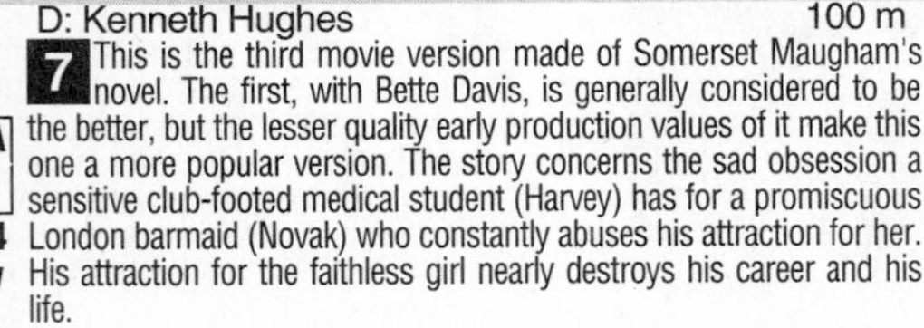

D: Kenneth Hughes 100 m

NR | DMA ROM | 1964 | B&W

7 This is the third movie version made of Somerset Maugham's novel. The first, with Bette Davis, is generally considered to be the better, but the lesser quality early production values of it make this one a more popular version. The story concerns the sad obsession a sensitive club-footed medical student (Harvey) has for a promiscuous London barmaid (Novak) who constantly abuses his attraction for her. His attraction for the faithless girl nearly destroys his career and his life.

Sex Nud Viol Lang AdSit

A: Kim Novak, Laurence Harvey, Siobhan McKenna, Robert Morley, Roger Livesey, Nanette Newman

Distributed By MGM/UA Home Video M300745

OLD GRINGO

D: Luis Puenzo 120 m

R | WST ROM ACT | 1989 | COLOR

7 A noble effort to dramatize Carlos Fuentes's novel revolving around the real-life character, and American journalist of the period, Ambrose Bierce. Jane Fonda plays an American spinster seeking adventure, who takes job as a teacher in old Mexico. Instead, she gets caught up in Pancho Villa's revolution and love. She becomes a realized woman, but is torn between her love for an old ex-patriot American journalist (Peck) and her passion for a young Mexican general (Smits), who is also the American's bastard son.

Sex Nud Viol Lang AdSit

A: Jane Fonda, Jimmy Smits, Gregory Peck, Patricio Contreras, Jessica Tandy

© COLUMBIA TRISTAR HOME VIDEO 50203

ON A CLEAR DAY YOU CAN SEE FOREVER

D: Vincente Minnelli 129 m

G | MUS COM ROM | 1970 | COLOR

7 Entertaining and underrated. Barbra is a neurotic chain smoker who crashes a college class in hypnosis looking for a cure. Psychiatrist Yves Montand agrees to hypnotize her and is fascinated to discover that he has instead regressed her back into a former life - in 19th-century England. Intrigued by the woman he has found, he continues to hypnotize modern Barbra and soon falls in love with the intriguing woman from the past. However, modern Barbara thinks he is treating her smoking problem and she has fallen in love with him. Solid music and lush production.

Sex Nud Viol Lang AdSit

A: Barbra Streisand, Yves Montand, Bob Newhart, Larry Blyden, Simon Oakland, Jack Nicholson

© PARAMOUNT HOME VIDEO 6927

ONCE AROUND

D: Lasse Hallstrom 114 m

R | ROM DMA COM | 1991 | COLOR

7 This movie is like getting wrapped up in a warm blanket on a freezing cold night. Dreyfuss is a super-salesman who sweeps a repressed Holly Hunter off her fee. He is annoying - but he is supposed to be. Hunter is strong emotionally - and she is not supposed to be. They are perfect for each other - but her family doesn't think so. Hunter is so tangled in family disapproval and so in love that she is extremely torn. The beauty of this one is that it is totally unpredictable, and charming, and irresistible, and very, very well acted.

Sex Nud Viol Lang AdSit

A: Richard Dreyfuss, Holly Hunter, Laura San Giacomo, Danny Aiello, Gena Rowlands, Roxanne Hart

© MCA/UNIVERSAL HOME VIDEO, INC. 81041

ONLY THE LONELY

D: Chris Columbus 105 m

PG-13 | ROM COM | 1991 | COLOR

7 Sweet and sentimental little movie. John Candy is a 38-year-old Chicago cop who still lives with his widowed mother (Maureen O'Hara). She is a real piece of work who has opinions about everybody and everything and doesn't hesitate the share them. Ally Sheedy is a plain and painfully shy girl who graduated from beauty school but couldn't get a job, so she does the makeup on cadavers for her mortician father. John and Ally meet and fall in love, but Mom does her best to break them up. John loves this girl but is afraid of hurting Mom. This is sort of an update of 1955 Oscar winner MARTY. There are no Oscars here however, but it's nice.

Sex Nud Viol Lang AdSit

A: John Candy, Maureen O'Hara, Ally Sheedy, Anthony Quinn, James Belushi, Kevin Dunn

© FOXVIDEO 1877

ONLY YOU

D: Norman Jewison 109 m

PG | ROM | 1994 | COLOR

6 Very syrupy-sweet romance story. Faith (Marisa Tomei) has spent most of her life waiting for her soul mate, Damon Bradley, to arrive. She knows who he is because a Ouija board told her so and so did a gypsy fortuneteller. However, she has given up and has just accepted a proposal of marriage from a podiatrist. She is getting ready for her wedding when she receives a phone call from Damon Bradley, a friend of the podiatrist, to wish them well before he leaves on a trip to Italy. Faith is beside herself, and rushes to the airport only to just miss his plane and, on the spot, decides to follow him to Italy, where she meets up with a poetry spouting Damon (Robert Downey Jr.) in Rome.

Sex Nud Viol Lang AdSit

A: Marisa Tomei, Robert Downey, Jr., Bonnie Hunt, Joaquim De Almeida, Fisher Stevens, Billy Zane

© COLUMBIA TRISTAR HOME VIDEO 73263

OPERATION PETTICOAT

D: Blake Edwards 120 m

NR | COM ROM | 1959 | COLOR

9 Hilarious and very popular comedy. Cary Grant is the captain of an unfortunate submarine which is beset by a never-ending series of embarrassing and very funny misfortunes in the South Pacific during World War II. The problems only begin when the sub must go to sea with the boat's paint job incomplete, leaving it pink. The problems are further compounded when first officer Curtis, a smooth-talking con man, squeezes five beautiful nurses into the sub. The stage is now set for some of Hollywood's biggest talents to work their comedic magic, and they do. Really funny. A great time.

Sex Nud Viol Lang AdSit

A: Cary Grant, Tony Curtis, Gene Evans, Dina Merrill, Arthur O'Connell, Gavin MacLeod

© REPUBLIC PICTURES HOME VIDEO 5405

OTHER PEOPLE'S MONEY

D: Norman Jewison 101 m

R | ROM COM | 1992 | COLOR

7 This video is hard to classify. It is not a ha-ha comedy, a oh-ah romance, nor is it a drama. It is the sophisticated story of a nearly-despicable, cute and clever corporate raider Larry the Liquidator (DeVito), who's only lover is his computer, Carmen. Carmen has discovered a cash-rich cable and wire company. Because its industry is dying, its stock value is way below its salvage value. The old-line owner Gregory Peck refuses to liquidate, so Larry begins a hostile takeover. Peck counters by sending in a pretty but hard-as-nails corporate lawyer in as his attack dog. Larry has met his match. He is in love, but even love will not pull him off the scent of blood.

Sex Nud Viol Lang AdSit

A: Danny DeVito, Gregory Peck, Penelope Ann Miller, Piper Laurie, Dean Jones, Tom Aldredge

© WARNER HOME VIDEO 12223

OTHER SIDE OF MIDNIGHT, THE

D: Charles Jarrott 160 m

R | ROM | 1977 | COLOR

9 Glorious trash. Sidney Sheldon's juicy pulp novel makes it to the screen. The critics hated it, women loved it. A young French girl is seduced by an American during the war years. She gets pregnant but he leaves her. She is bent on revenge. She obtains an abortion and then sets her sights on humiliating him. She sleeps her way to the top of the movie world, all the while working carefully behind the scenes to destroy his life and his relationship with his wife Sarandon at every turn. No serious film fans please. Serious soap fans only.

Sex Nud Viol Lang AdSit

A: Noelle Page, John Beck, Marie-France Pisier, Susan Sarandon, Raf Vallone, Clu Gulager

© FOXVIDEO 1135

OTHER SIDE OF THE MOUNTAIN, THE

D: Larry Peerce 102 m

PG | ROM DMA | 1975 | COLOR

8 Popular love story taken from the pages of real life. Jill Kinmont (Hassett) was a talented skier who seemed destined for the 1956 Olympic team. Instead she was left a paraplegic after a tragic skiing accident. Despondent over her circumstances, she is revitalized by the love of Beau Bridges, but then tragedy strikes again. Hers is truly a story of determination in the face of overwhelming adversity. Guaranteed to jerk more than a few tears.

Sex Nud Viol Lang AdSit

A: Marilyn Hassett, Beau Bridges, Dabney Coleman, Belinda J. Montgomery

© MCA/UNIVERSAL HOME VIDEO, INC. 55116

OTHER SIDE OF THE MOUNTAIN, PART II, THE

D: Larry Peerce 99 m

PG | ROM DMA | 1978 | COLOR

8 In this sequel, also taken from real life, the paralyzed skier Jill Kinmont (Hassett) is now a teacher in L.A. after having lost her lover in a plane crash. On vacation to her hometown, she meets a divorced trucker (Bottoms) who pursues her. After having been so heartbroken before, she is very reluctant to allow yet another man into her life, but his persistence breaks down her resistance. This is a good love story. It is involving and credible. As in the first film, be prepared to get a few tears jerked.

Sex Nud Viol Lang AdSit

A: Marilyn Hassett, Timothy Bottoms, Belinda J. Montgomery, Nan Martin

© MCA/UNIVERSAL HOME VIDEO, INC. 55117

OUT OF AFRICA

D: Sydney Pollack 161 m

PG | ROM DMA | 1985 | COLOR

9 Epic love story and winner of seven Oscars, including Best Picture. It is the romantic story of a strong-willed Danish woman (Streep) who married for convenience and then moved to Africa in 1913 with her philandering husband to run their coffee plantation. There, she develops a deep love for the land, its ways, its peoples, and also for an English adventurer (Redford) who loved what she loved. They are two rugged individualists who continually move in and out of each other's lives, torn between love for adventure and each other. Based upon the experiences of writer Isak Dinesen.

Sex Nud Viol Lang AdSit

A: Robert Redford, Meryl Streep, Klaus Maria Brandauer, Michael Kitchen, Malick Bowens, Michael Gough

© MCA/UNIVERSAL HOME VIDEO, INC. 80350

OVERBOARD

D: Garry Marshall 112 m

PG | COM ROM | 1987 | COLOR

8 Clever, light-weight entertainment. Goldie Hawn is a spoiled and arrogant heiress who refuses to pay a carpenter (Russell) for a job. When he sees on the evening news that she has been found suffering from total amnesia, floating in the ocean (she fell from her yacht) - he sees a way both to get even with her and find a much-needed mother for his untamed kids. So he claims her from the authorities as his wife, and she - confused and not knowing any better - sets about taking up her new chores as mother. Good-natured and fun.

Sex Nud Viol Lang AdSit

A: Goldie Hawn, Kurt Russell, Katherine Helmond, Edward Herrmann, Roddy McDowall, Michael Haggerty

Distributed By MGM/UA Home Video M201197

OWL AND THE PUSSYCAT, THE

D: Herbert Ross 95 m

PG | COM ROM | 1970 | COLOR

8 Highly entertaining adaptation of a hit broadway comedy. In her first non-singing role, Streisand plays a kooky part-time model and sometime hooker living next door to a snooty book clerk, would-be writer and full-time snob (Segal). These two just cannot get along - barbs and insults fly back and forth, but love's sparks also fly between them. When he complains to the building's management about her late-night antics, she is expelled but manages to con her way into becoming his roommate. Zany, funny and sometimes hilarious.

Sex Nud Viol Lang AdSit

A: Barbra Streisand, George Segal, Robert Klein, Allen Garfield, Roz Kelly

© COLUMBIA TRISTAR HOME VIDEO 60081

PAJAMA GAME, THE

D: George Abbott 102 m

NR | MUS COM ROM | 1957 | COLOR

8 Exuberant and enjoyable Hollywood conversion (largely intact) of the very successful Broadway play. Doris Day plays the head of the union's grievance committee at a pajama factory. She is heading up the charge to demand a 7 1/2 cent per hour pay raise. She must negotiate with the plant's foreman (Raitt) to get it, but love gets in the way. Light-hearted fun. Great songs and inventive Bob Fosse choreography. Songs include: "Hernando's Hideaway," "Hey There" and the big hit "Steam Heat."

Sex Nud Viol Lang AdSit

A: Doris Day, John Raitt, Carol Haney, Eddie Foy, Jr., Reta Shaw

© WARNER HOME VIDEO 35085

PARADISE

D: Mary Agnes Donoghue 111 m

PG-13 | DMA ROM | 1991 | COLOR

7 An old-fashioned summer film all about love, relationships and heartbreak. Ben and Lily (Johnson and Griffith) are married, but you wouldn't know it from the cold shoulder they give each other. When 10-year old Elijah Wood is sent to live with them for the summer, he becomes intrigued with discovering why their relationship is so strained and discovers that they are still suffering from the pain of losing their own three year-old son. Since that time, Lily and Ben have withdrawn from each other. However, the boy's presence resurrects the love the two once had felt for each other and they receive a second chance. Refreshing and heartwarming.

Sex Nud Viol Lang AdSit

A: Melanie Griffith, Don Johnson, Elijah Wood, Thora Birch, Sheila McCarthy, Eve Gordon

© TOUCHSTONE HOME VIDEO 1258

PATCH OF BLUE, A

D: Guy Green 106 m

NR | DMA ROM | 1965 | COLOR

8 A sensitive and moving drama, which held the potential to be badly exploitive, but it isn't at all. This is a thoughtful drama about an 18-year-old blind white girl whose mother is a prostitute. She keeps the girl uneducated, confined to their apartment and uses her as a servant. One day, on a rare trip alone to the park, the girl meets a young man who helps her and encourages her to learn about life. She falls in love with him, the only one who ever helped her, not knowing that he is black. Good drama, well acted, not overly sentimental or sensationalized. 5 Oscar nominations.

Sex Nud Viol Lang AdSit

A: Sidney Poitier, Elizabeth Hartman, Shelley Winters, Wallace Ford, Ivan Dixon, John Qualen

Distributed By MGM/UA Home Video M202010

PATERNITY

D: David Steinberg 94 m

PG | COM ROM | 1981 | COLOR

6 Pleasant and diverting light comedy about a generally happy and successful 44-year-old bachelor (Reynolds) who decides that he wants a baby, but he doesn't want a wife. So he strikes a bargain with a struggling musician and waitress (D'Angelo) to bear his child - no strings attached. Sure! Things start to get interesting when she starts to fall for him. Not a lot of big laughs, but it is a good time - particularly if you are a Reynolds fan.

Sex Nud Viol Lang AdSit

A: Burt Reynolds, Beverly D'Angelo, Norman Fell, Elizabeth Ashley

© PARAMOUNT HOME VIDEO 1401

PEGGY SUE GOT MARRIED

D: Francis Ford Coppola 103 m

PG-13 | COM ROM FAN | 1986 | COLOR

9 Provocative and thoroughly enjoyable adult fairy tale. Turner is a 43-year-old woman with two kids, who is separated and nearing divorce from her pitchman husband and high-school sweetheart. Then, when she is crowned queen at her 25th class reunion, she suddenly faints and is magically transported back to being 18 years old all over again. She has all the same experiences and opportunities as she did then, but this time she has the benefit of having 25 more years experience to make her decisions. Will she do again what she did then? Inventive and well acted.

Sex Nud Viol Lang AdSit

A: Kathleen Turner, Nicolas Cage, Barry Miller, Catherine Hicks, Maureen O'Sullivan, John Carradine

© CBS/FOX VIDEO 3800

PENNIES FROM HEAVEN

D: Herbert Ross 108 m

R | MUS ROM | 1981 | COLOR

6 Unique, offbeat and downbeat musical, but with some great dance and production numbers. Set in the Depression years, Martin plays an unhappily married pitchman selling sheet-music. His miserable life contrasts badly with the happy lyrics of the pop songs he sells. He escapes into his fantasies about a glamorous life with his mistress (Peters), but instead he is arrested for murder and she turns to prostitution. Still, he is a dreamer and continues to dream.

Sex Nud Viol Lang AdSit

A: Steve Martin, Bernadette Peters, Christopher Walken, Jessica Harper, Vernel Bagneris, John McMartin

Distributed By MGM/UA Home Video M800147

PERSONAL BEST

D: Robert Towne 128 m

R | DMA ROM | 1982 | COLOR

7 Sensitive and honest story about the close personal relationship which develops between two female track-and-field athletes who are in training together for the 1980 Olympics. Truly excellent performances make this an interesting and worthy offering - both as a sports movie and as an honest, non-exploitive look into a loving lesbian relationship which develops between the two leads, a relationship that is destroyed under the pressure of competition.

Sex Nud Viol Lang AdSit

A: Mariel Hemingway, Scott Glenn, Patrice Donnelly, Kenny Moore

© WARNER HOME VIDEO 11242

PEYTON PLACE

D: Mark Robson 157 m

NR | DMA ROM | 1957 | COLOR

8 In the 1950s Grace Matalious wrote a spicy book that ripped the cover off the hypocrisy of middle-class morality, depicting the sexual maneuvering and horseplay going on behind the closed doors of a fictitious small New England town of the early '50s. It, of course, was a monumental hit. This is a toned-down version of the book, but it still was a jolt to the prevailing sensibilities of the times. At its heart, it is essentially a melodramatic soap opera - but one that is very well done, with some of the best talent that was available. Still quite involving today. Nominated for 9 Oscars in 1957.

Sex Nud Viol Lang AdSit

A: Lana Turner, Hope Lange, Russ Tamblyn, Arthur Kennedy, Diane Varsi

© FOXVIDEO 1855

PIANO, THE

D: Jane Campion 121 m

R | ROM DMA | 1993 | COLOR

9 This is a highly acclaimed romantic drama that received 7 Oscar nominations, including Best Picture. It is also the quite unusual love story of an extremely repressed Victorian woman (Hunter) who will no longer talk but only communicates in writing and expresses her emotions through her piano. She is a mail-order bride who has just arrived, quite literally, upon the shore of a very primitive New Zealand, along with her piano and young daughter. Her new husband (Neil) chooses to leave her beloved piano on the beach, but it is retrieved by their neighbor (Keitel) who then uses it to bribe her into sexual adventures. Soon their passions evolve into forbidden love.

Sex Nud Viol Lang AdSit

A: Holly Hunter, Harvey Keitel, Sam Neil, Anna Paquin, Kerry Walker, Genevieve Lemon

© LIVE HOME VIDEO 69974

ROM

PICNIC

D: Joshua Logan 113 m

NR | DMA ROM | 1956 | COLOR | Sex Nud Viol Lang AdSit

8 William Holden is a drifter who arrives on a freight train in a small Kansas town on a Labor Day weekend to visit his friend from college, wealthy Cliff Robertson. Holden had been a big man with the women and a hero on the football team, but now goes from one deadend job to another. Robertson invites him along with his pretty girlfriend Kim Novak to the big town picnic. Holden's easy charm and overt sexuality ignites the passions of all the women, including Novak, who is powerfully drawn to this man who is in many ways just like her. Nominated for six Oscars, including Best Picture, won two. Some overly melodramatic moments diminish its effectiveness today.

A: Kim Novak, William Holden, Susan Strasberg, Rosalind Russell, Cliff Robertson, Arthur O'Connell

© COLUMBIA TRISTAR HOME VIDEO 90613

PILLOW TALK

D: Michael Gordon 103 m

NR | COM ROM | 1959 | COLOR | Sex Nud Viol Lang AdSit

9 Highly entertaining comedy that marked the first pairing of Rock Hudson and Doris Day. A huge box office hit that received five Oscar nominations - winning for Screenplay. Doris is an interior designer who shares a telephone line with Rock, a romeo playboy who is forever on the prowl for a new notch on his bedpost. She despises him for his insincere plotting and tells him so. But, she has never seen him so, when they finally meet, he pretends to be a gentle-manly Texan to charm and then seduce her. Instead, he falls in love with her - only to be scorned when he is discovered. Great supporting cast. A real winner.

A: Rock Hudson, Doris Day, Tony Randall, Thelma Ritter, Nick Adams, Julia Meade

© MCA/UNIVERSAL HOME VIDEO, INC. 55122

PLAYBOYS, THE

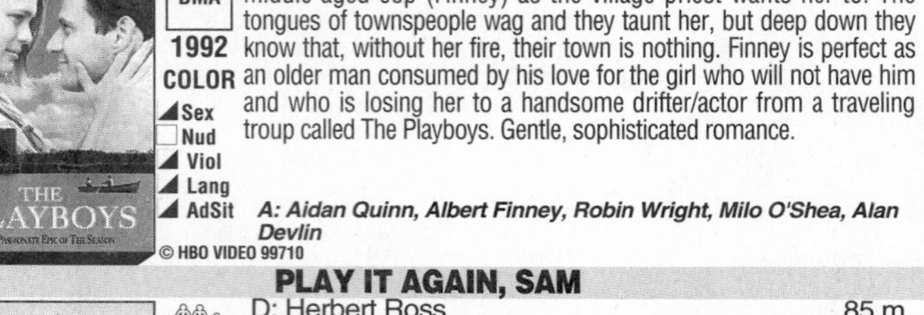

D: Gillies Mackinnon 113 m

PG-13 | ROM DMA | 1992 | COLOR | Sex Nud Viol Lang AdSit

7 The place is an isolated little town in Ireland and it's 1957. An independent and sassy beauty (Wright) has a child out of wed-lock. She will not tell who the father is, nor will she marry the town's middle-aged cop (Finney) as the village priest wants her to. The tongues of townspeople wag and they taunt her, but deep down they know that, without her fire, their town is nothing. Finney is perfect as an older man consumed by his love for the girl who will not have him and who is losing her to a handsome drifter/actor from a traveling troup called The Playboys. Gentle, sophisticated romance.

A: Aidan Quinn, Albert Finney, Robin Wright, Milo O'Shea, Alan Devlin

© HBO VIDEO 99710

PLAY IT AGAIN, SAM

D: Herbert Ross 85 m

PG | COM ROM | 1972 | COLOR | Sex Nud Viol Lang AdSit

8 Entertaining and different Woody Allen comedy that is more con-ventional than most of his films. Here he plays an insecure film critic, lost in his world of movies and suffering from recurring visits from the ghost of Humphrey Bogart - who is constantly giving him advice. When his bored wife divorces him to seek some adventure, Woody repeatedly fumbles in his attempts to meet new women. Even the assistance of his best friend (Roberts) fails. He simply can't say the right things... except, that is, to Diane, his best friend's wife. A funny movie that is also for non-Allen fans.

A: Woody Allen, Diane Keaton, Susan Anspach, Tony Roberts, Jerry Lacy, Jennifer Salt

© PARAMOUNT HOME VIDEO 8112

ROM

PRELUDE TO A KISS

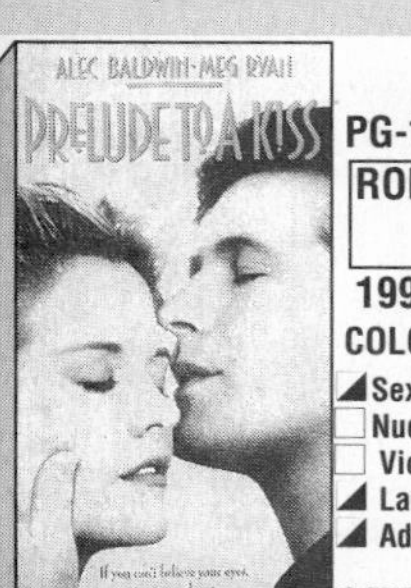

D: Norman Rene 106 m

PG-13 | ROM | 1992 | COLOR | Sex Nud Viol Lang AdSit

6 Very sentimental romancer that was roundly criticized by critics, but which still will have an appeal to some. Ryan and Baldwin are a young couple who meet and, six months later, they agree to get married. However, their wedding is crashed by an old man, and when he kisses the bride, more than sparks fly. Their souls fly back and forth. She is inside him and he in her. She is now a newly married old man in a young woman's body. He is a lively young woman in an old shell. Poor old Baldwin has to figure out what is going on for himself and then get her back. Schmaltzy and offbeat. Only effective if you are receptive.

A: Meg Ryan, Alec Baldwin, Kathy Bates, Ned Beatty, Patty Duke, Sydney Walker

© FOXVIDEO 1971

PRETTY IN PINK

D: Howard Deutch 96 m

PG-13 | ROM COM | 1986 | COLOR | Sex Nud Viol Lang AdSit

8 Effervescent, witty and disarmingly rich teenage comedy. A very bright but poor girl (Ringwald), from the wrong side of the tracks, and a rich boy (McCarthy) fall for each other. He asks her to the Senior Prom and their teen-age society erupts with the scandal. Can their romance survive all of the peer pressure? Their friends are doing everything to keep them apart, including Ringwald's pal Cryer (who is also in love with her). Some touching, funny and very tender moments fuse beautifully in this sparkling coming-of-age film. Good score, too.

A: Molly Ringwald, Andrew McCarthy, Harry Dean Stanton, Jon Cryer, James Spader, Annie Potts

© PARAMOUNT HOME VIDEO 1858

PRETTY WOMAN

D: Garry Marshall 119 m

R | ROM COM | 1990 | COLOR | Sex Nud Viol Lang AdSit

9 Endearing romantic Cinderella charmer. Gere is a hard-hearted corporate raider with no time for a meaningful relationship. Abandoned by his girlfriend, he meets pretty woman and street walker Julia Roberts - who charms him into buying an evening's entertain-ment. So charmed is he with her impishness that he also hires her to spend the entire week. Slowly his heart is melted by the hooker-with-a-heart, and her week with him opens up a whole new world for her... but what happens then? Extremely entertaining, sentimental favorite that was a massive popular hit.

A: Julia Roberts, Richard Gere, Jason Alexander, Ralph Bellamy, Laura San Giacomo, Hector Elizondo

© TOUCHSTONE HOME VIDEO 1027

PRINCE OF TIDES

D: Barbra Streisand 132 m

R | DMA ROM | 1991 | COLOR | Sex Nud Viol Lang AdSit

7 Heartfelt, emotional telling of two lives which touch to "heal" each other. Nolte plays a sad man wearing a happy face and hiding a tortured soul. When his twin sister attempts suicide again, Nolte seeks to help her psychiatrist (Streisand) explore into his sister's continuing profound despair. As their long-repressed sordid family history is released from inside him, he learns to confront his own ghosts. Then Streisand's growing affections for this man, who can reach the son she cannot, reveals the extent of her own isolation and unhappiness. Powerful performances and a moving experience.

A: Nick Nolte, Barbra Streisand, Kate Nelligan, Melinda Dillon, Jeroen Krabbe, Jason Gould

© COLUMBIA TRISTAR HOME VIDEO 50943

PRINCESS BRIDE, THE

D: Rob Reiner 98 m

PG | COM ROM FAN | 1987 | COLOR | Sex Nud Viol Lang AdSit

7 Heroic fairy tale fantasy, designed for both young and old! A sick boy's grandfather (Falk) comes to read to him, promising him a story of monsters, fights, beasts, and, yes, a dose of romance, too. In the extravagant and adventurous story which comes to life on screen, a beautiful princess and a stableboy fall in love but are soon separated, and the evil king has her kidnapped so he can force her to marry him. Suddenly, a strange man in a mask appears poised to do battle for her. This brilliant adaptation of the whimsical cult novel comes alive at the hands of Rob Reiner.

A: Peter Falk, Mandy Patinkin, Carol Kane, Billy Crystal, Chris Sarandon, Cary Elwes

© NEW LINE HOME VIDEO 7709

PURE COUNTRY

D: Christopher Cain 113 m

PG | ROM DMA | 1992 | COLOR | Sex Nud Viol Lang AdSit

7 If you like your country music pure, and if you like your story simple and sweet, this is for you. George is a country music star who has become very unhappy with the demands of his life on the road and the course his stage career (managed by Warren) has taken. So he leaves, right in the middle of a concert tour. He winds up on the ranch of a pretty cowgirl, her gnarly father and her two brothers. George's focus begins to return just as Warren hunts him down and takes him back for a big Las Vegas concert and a happy ending. There are ten different country songs scattered through the storyline.

A: George Straight, Lesley Ann Warren, Isabel Glasser, Kyle Chandler, John Doe, Rory Calhoun

© WARNER HOME VIDEO 12593

QUEEN MARGOT

D: Patrice Chereau 153 m

R | FOR DMA ROM | 1995 | COLOR | Sex Nud Viol Lang AdSit

9 Brilliant French epic historical drama. It is 1572, and religious wars are raging throughout Europe. Charles IX, the son of the shrewd and absolutely ruthless Catherine de Medicis, is King of France. Catholic Catherine has lost her influence over Charles to a Protestant advisor. She now plots to regain control, while also claim-ing credit for preventing war, by marrying her daughter Margot to the Protestant King of a French province. But when the marriage does not achieve her goals, she and her sons resort to assassination and mur-der, and Margot, at first a pawn, becomes a queen. Intelligent, exquis-itely complex and intricate. Requires and inspires rapt attention. Wonderfully acted and filmed. Subtitles.

A: Isabelle Adjani, Daniel Auteuil, Jean-Hugues Anglade, Vincent Perez, Virna Lisi

© MIRAMAX HOME ENTERTAINMENT 4439

QUEEN OF HEARTS

D: Jon Amiel 112 m

PG | COM ROM | 1989 | COLOR | Sex Nud Viol Lang AdSit

8 Warm and endearing jewel. Rosa and Danilo are young Italian lovers who elope after WWII to London because Rosa has been promised to marry the wealthy butcher, Barbariccia. After twenty happy years of marriage, four children and making a good life with their restaurant, Barbariccia arrives in London to spoil it. He has become the owner of several gambling houses and has won every-thing Danilo has in a card game. However, the family has arranged a "sting" to get all their money back and get rid of Barbariccia in the process. Witty and funny. Mostly in English, some subtitles.

A: Anita Zagaria, Joseph Long, Eileen Way, Vittorio Duse, Vittorio Amandola, Tat Whalley

© MCEG/STERLING 70188

RACHEL, RACHEL

D: Paul Newman 102 m

R | DMA ROM | 1968 | COLOR

6 Sensitive, grown-up coming out story. Woodward is a socially repressed schoolteacher during the day. At night she is her aging mother's servant. She prepares her mother's drinks and arranges her parties. Then an old classmate (Olson) appears on the scene and offers Woodward a chance at her first love relationship and she is determined to take it. This very sensitive story about a young woman trying to come out of her shell was nominated for four Oscars, including Best Picture and Director. Woodward gives a compelling performance in Newman's first directorial attempt. A little slow.

Sex / Nud / Viol / Lang / AdSit

A: Joanne Woodward, Estelle Parsons, James Olson, Geraldine Fitzgerald, Kate Harrington, Donald Moffat

© WARNER HOME VIDEO 11333

RACING WITH THE MOON

D: Richard Benjamin 108 m

PG | ROM COM | 1984 | COLOR

7 Touching, entertaining and nostalgic look back. Two young men (Penn and Cage) are about to be sent off to the Marines during WWII and decide to make the most of their last few weeks together in 1942. Penn is a young man from common roots who falls for who he thinks is a rich girl. Emboldened by his imminent departure, he chases her, not knowing that she is a maid's daughter. Meanwhile, his buddy has gotten a girl pregnant, so Penn enlists his new girl's help in raising the necessary $150. Touching and sweet film. Highly likable, a reminder of lost innocence.

Sex / Nud / Viol / Lang / AdSit

A: Sean Penn, Nicolas Cage, Elizabeth McGovern, John Karlen, Rutanya Alda, Carol Kane

© PARAMOUNT HOME VIDEO 1668

RAINMAKER, THE

D: John Anthony 121 m

NR | ROM DMA | 1956 | COLOR

7 More than just a romance, an invigorating film about faith in yourself. When a drought-stricken midwestern town is praying for rain, a charming and bombastic rainmaker (Lancaster) emerges, promising miracles. He successfully charms all the desperate farmers, but the lonely and insecure spinster Hepburn dismisses his promises of hope and deflects his romantic advances. He does not relent. His contagious enthusiasm soon inspires her to believe in herself, and in her beauty - both inside and out. When the moment of truth comes, Hepburn emerges triumphant - forever a changed woman.

Sex / Nud / Viol / Lang / AdSit

A: Burt Lancaster, Katharine Hepburn, Wendell Corey, Lloyd Bridges, Earl Holliman, Cameron Prud'homme

© PARAMOUNT HOME VIDEO 5606

RAINTREE COUNTY

D: Edward Dmytryk 173 m

NR | ROM DMA | 1957 | COLOR

6 Epic soap opera. Set during the Civil War, high school sweethearts (Saint and Clift) are in love. But when beautiful but bratty Southern belle Taylor comes for a visit, she charms Clift into marriage. Only too late does Clift realize that Taylor possesses a streak of insanity. She becomes more and more obsessed with the idea that she is the illegitimate daughter of her father and a servant girl. She becomes more unhappy and tormented, making Clift more unhappy and tormented, too. This lavish production was intended to compare with GONE WITH THE WIND but didn't make it that far.

Sex / Nud / Viol / Lang / AdSit

A: Montgomery Clift, Elizabeth Taylor, Eva Marie Saint, Lee Marvin, Nigel Patrick, Rod Taylor

Distributed By MGM/UA Home Video M900401

RARE BREED, THE

D: Andrew V. McLaglen 107 m

NR | WST ROM | 1966 | COLOR

7 Enjoyable and fun Western. An eccentric British heiress (O'Hara) has a wild idea. She wants to breed stocky English Hereford cows with tough Texan longhorns. Stewart is a stubborn cowboy who is supposed to escort her, her daughter and her prize bull to the Texas ranch of her partner, an outlandish Scottsman (Keith). On the calamity-filled journey there, Stewart grows to admire O'Hara's conviction and determination, but is faced with a romantic rivalry in Keith when they arrive at the ranch. The road to the new breed is also faced with stampedes and rustlers, too. Entertaining and original.

Sex / Nud / Viol / Lang / AdSit

A: James Stewart, Maureen O'Hara, Brian Keith, Juliet Mills, Jack Elam, Ben Johnson

© MCA/UNIVERSAL HOME VIDEO, INC. 80322

REDS

D: Warren Beatty 195 m

PG | DMA ROM | 1981 | COLOR

7 Monumental and ambitious personal film by Director/actor Warren Beatty. It is the story of the American radical leftist journalist, John Reed (Beatty), and his love affair with feminist Louise Bryant (Keaton). Their love affair, marriage and eventual breakup is set against the backdrop of the tumultuous events surrounding the Russian Revolution of 1917. Beautifully photographed and a critical success, but also a ponderously long lesson in communist history. Winner of three Oscars, including Best Director, Supporting Actress and Cinematography.

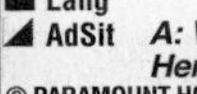

Sex / Nud / Viol / Lang / AdSit

A: Warren Beatty, Diane Keaton, Maureen Stapleton, Edward Herrmann, Jerzy Kosinski, Jack Nicholson

© PARAMOUNT HOME VIDEO 1331

REGARDING HENRY

D: Mike Nichols 85 m

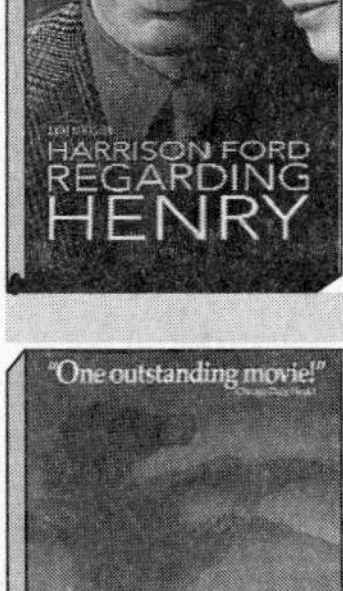

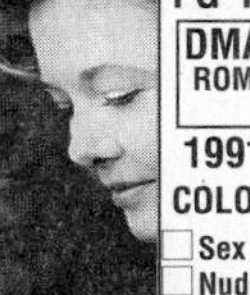

PG-13 | DMA ROM | 1991 | COLOR

8 Unscrupulous, ruthless and callous - that is a telling description of attorney Henry Turner (Ford). Then he is shot in the head in a robbery attempt and everything changes. He has survived the bullet but he has lost his memory. His wife (Bening) helps nurse him back to health and she finds that she is falling in love again, but this time with a different, better man who is emerging. The recovering Ford discovers that they had been drifting apart. Both he and his wife had been having affairs, their marriage had been near breakup and that he was the principal cause. Emotional, yes, but not smarmy or manipulative. This is very believable and rewarding watching.

Sex / Nud / Viol / Lang / AdSit

A: Harrison Ford, Annette Bening, Mikki Allen, Bill Nunn, Donald Moffat, Nancy Marchand

© PARAMOUNT HOME VIDEO 32403

RETURN TO SNOWY RIVER

D: Geoff Burrowes 99 m

PG | WST ROM | 1988 | COLOR

6 Sequel to THE MAN FROM SNOWY RIVER. The hero from the original (Burlinson) has left for three years to round up a herd of horses. He returns to claim the love of his life (Thornton), but finds she is now engaged to a banker's son (Eadie). What's more, her father (Dennehy) is vehemently opposed to their relationship and is determined to keep them apart. Once again, Burlinson must battle to prove his worth. Grand and beautiful photography, plus glorious Australian scenery and fast pace, make this a mildly satisfying sequel that has the same feeling as the original.

Sex / Nud / Viol / Lang / AdSit

A: Tom Burlinson, Sigrid Thornton, Brian Dennehy, Nicholas Eadie, Bryan Marshall

© WALT DISNEY HOME VIDEO 699

REUBEN, REUBEN

D: Robert Ellis Miller 100 m

R | COM ROM | 1983 | COLOR

7 Offbeat sophisticated and witty comedy. Conti is wonderful as a British poet with terminal writer's block. He is also a charming freeloader, who lives by the bottle and makes a game of seducing women. When the Brit is transplanted to Connecticut, he lectures on the college circuit to make ends meet, but there he falls for a beautiful young farm girl student (McGillis) and he struggles mightily turn himself around in hopes of winning her over. Witty and sophisticated, this comedy was adapted from the novel by Peter DeVires. Two Oscar nominations. Certainly not typical movie fair and perhaps not for all tastes.

Sex / Nud / Viol / Lang / AdSit

A: Tom Conti, Kelly McGillis, Cynthia Harris, Joel Fabiani, Roberts Blossom, E. Katherine Kerr

© CBS/FOX VIDEO 1435

RISKY BUSINESS

D: Paul Brickman 99 m

R | COM ROM | 1983 | COLOR

9 Disarming, sexy, stylish and a whole lotta fun! High schooler Tom Cruise is every mother's dream, so when his parents went on vacation, they left him with the house and the Porsche. Then one of his friends orders a call girl for him and his life (and his parent's house) is turned inside out. After the Porsche winds up in the lake, the desperate Cruise allows himself to be charmed by sexy call girl (De Mornay), who is also deeply in debt to her pimp, into turning the affluent home into a bordello for one night. But it all backfires when Cruise falls for her and her pimp steals a whole house full of his parent's furniture. Charming, funny and a huge boost for Tom Cruise.

Sex / Nud / Viol / Lang / AdSit

A: Tom Cruise, Rebecca De Mornay, Curtis Armstrong, Bronson Pinchot, Raphael Sbarge, Joe Pantoliano

© WARNER HOME VIDEO 11323

ROBIN AND MARIAN

D: Richard Lester 107 m

PG | ROM ACT | 1976 | COLOR

7 Robin Hood (Connery) returns to Sherwood Forest after 20 years of battling in the Crusades, along with Little John and King Richard (Harris). When King Richard is accidentally slain, his wicked brother John takes the throne and Robin heads for the woods. Robin's arch nemesis, the Sheriff of Nottingham (Shaw), is ordered to remove the clergy. Robin seeks out his love, Maid Marian (Hepburn), but finds that she has become a nun - the Mother Superior to be exact. The pair rekindle their love for each other and Robin prepares to confront his enemy. What a cast!

Sex / Nud / Viol / Lang / AdSit

A: Sean Connery, Audrey Hepburn, Robert Shaw, Richard Harris, Nicol Williamson, Denholm Elliott

© COLUMBIA TRISTAR HOME VIDEO 60097

ROBIN HOOD: PRINCE OF THIEVES

D: Kevin Reynolds 144 m

PG-13 | ACT ROM | 1991 | COLOR

8 Good entertainment in a spectacular and lush swashbuckler! This 1990s version of the classic tale is a little more rugged, has a lot more gritty realism and less of the idealistic charm of past efforts. It is also lavishly produced, with great attention to detail. Costner's medieval Robin Hood is benevolent, tough, charming and gritty (but he doesn't have an English accent). Alan Rickman is deliciously sinister as the twisted Sheriff of Nottingham, and Mastrantonio holds her own as the captivating and feisty Maid Marian who captures Robin's heart. Action, suspense, romance - there's a little bit of everything all wrapped up in this delightful adventure!

Sex / Nud / Viol / Lang / AdSit

A: Kevin Costner, Morgan Freeman, Mary Elizabeth Mastrantonio, Christian Slater, Alan Rickman, Geraldine Rickman

© WARNER HOME VIDEO 14000

ROCKETEER, THE

D: Joe Johnston 109 m

PG
ACT ROM
1991
COLOR

7 Cliff Secord (Campbell) is an adventurous 1930s daredevil pilot who has discovered a secret government jet pack and takes to the skies with it on a wild joy ride. He's an adventurous sort and is just having fun, but the government wants it back. Unfortunately, so do some local hoods who are trying to deliver it to a secret buyer for a big payday. What they don't know is that their buyer, a famous Hollywood hero, is also a Nazi agent. Campbell's beautiful girlfriend (Connelly) gets unwillingly pulled into the fiasco too when she is romanced by the Hollywood hunk. Great period feel. Pretty good excitement, too, in spite of being overly long.

Sex Nud Viol Lang AdSit

A: Bill Campbell, Alan Arkin, Jennifer Connelly, Paul Sorvino, Timothy Dalton, Terry O'Quinn

© WALT DISNEY HOME VIDEO 1239

ROMANCING THE STONE

D: Michael Douglas 106 m

PG
ACT ROM COM
1984
COLOR

8 Wildly fun! A shy romance novelist (Turner) receives a mysterious package from her dead brother-in-law which she must then take to the jungles of Columbia to rescue her kidnapped sister. Not knowing that she is carrying a treasure map, she finds herself embroiled in danger from the minute she steps off the plane. To her rescue comes wild and woolly Douglas, a gun-toting soldier of the jungle. Of course they fall in love, but the action never stops, nor does the humor, as Turner's drab existence is forever transformed. Followed by JEWEL OF THE NILE.

Sex Nud Viol Lang AdSit

A: Michael Douglas, Kathleen Turner, Danny DeVito, Alfonso Arau, Zack Norman

© FOXVIDEO 1358

ROMAN SPRING OF MRS. STONE, THE

D: Jose Quintero 104 m

NR
ROM
1961
COLOR

6 Vivian Leigh is a wealthy middle-aged and widowed actress who has taken a luxurious apartment in Rome in a search to find herself. She is lonely and the best years of her career are behind her. She falls in love and has a tragic affair with a handsome Italian gigolo (Warren Beatty). However he's an opportunist, who takes all that she can give and then dumps her for a younger Jill St. John. This is a dark love story based on a Tennessee Williams novella.

Sex Nud Viol Lang AdSit

A: Vivien Leigh, Warren Beatty, Lotte Lenya, Jill St. John, Coral Browne

© WARNER HOME VIDEO 11183

ROME ADVENTURE

D: Delmer Daves 119 m

NR
ROM
1962
COLOR

7 A lush soap opera! Suzanne Pleshette is a conservative New England librarian who travels to Rome, the Eternal City, in search of some excitement. She falls in love with an older man, a native Roman playboy (Brazzi), but something is missing. Then she meets a young architect (Troy) and she decides that she likes him better but, again, there is a problem. He has a worldly-wise mistress (Dickinson) who stands in their way. Splendid acting by the two leading ladies. Pleshette and Troy met during this film and were married two years later.

Sex Nud Viol Lang AdSit

A: Suzanne Pleshette, Troy Donahue, Angie Dickinson, Rossano Brazzi, Constance Ford, Al Hirt

© WARNER HOME VIDEO 11193

ROMEO AND JULIET

D: Franco Zeffirelli 138 m

PG
ROM DMA
1968
COLOR

9 The classic Shakespearean tragedy and ultimate love story is brilliantly retold here! Romeo (Whiting) and Juliet (Hussey) are two teenagers who fall deeply in love, but their families are warring. That ensures that their love will never bloom and tragedy soon strikes the forlorn lovers. Whiting and Hussey interpreted their complex roles excellently, despite their young age. The two were 17 and 15, respectively, when the movie was made. The photography and production values will take your breath away. Oscar winner for both Cinematography and Costume Design.

Sex Nud Viol Lang AdSit

A: Olivia Hussey, Leonard Whiting, Milo O'Shea, Michael York

© PARAMOUNT HOME VIDEO 6809

ROOM WITH A VIEW, A

D: James Ivory 117 m

NR
ROM DMA
1986
COLOR

8 Enchanting intelligent surprise! A young Englishwoman (Carter) travels on holliday to sensuous Florence, Italy, to view the world and broaden her horizons. There she finds a young man to whom she is very attracted (Sands). Her meddling chaperone, however, doesn't approve of him and she is torn between her love for this common man and her proper engagement back home to a stuffy and self-absorbed Englishman (Day-Lewis). Based on a novel by E.M. Forster, this film is an elegant, witty and evocative portrayal of the upper-crust manners and mores of the Edwardian English of 1907.

Sex Nud Viol Lang AdSit

A: Helena Bonham Carter, Maggie Smith, Daniel Day-Lewis, Denholm Elliott, Julian Sands, Simon Callow

© CBS/FOX VIDEO 6915

ROUSTABOUT

D: John Rich 100 m

NR
MUS ROM
1964
COLOR

6 Pleasing Presley musical. A wandering young singer (Presley) literally gets run off the road by Stanwyck's carnival. While he is waiting to get his motorcycle fixed, he decides to join the carnival's crew. However, the carnival is in a whole bunch of financial trouble and, while Elvis is helping Stanwyck save her carnival from ruin, he falls in love with her daughter (Freeman). Songs include "Little Egypt" and "One Track Heart." Also has Rachel Welch in her film debut and Teri Garr in another bit part.

Sex Nud Viol Lang AdSit

A: Elvis Presley, Barbara Stanwyck, Leif Erickson, Joan Freeman, Sue Anne Langdon, Raquel Welch

© CBS/FOX VIDEO 2007

ROXANNE

D: Fred Schepisi 107 m

PG
COM ROM
1987
COLOR

8 Clever and winning comedy that is one of Steve Martin's most pleasing efforts. He is C.D., the chief of a small town's fire department, with a super-sized snoz and a rapier wit. Arriving one summer are Roxanne, a beautiful astronomy student (Hannah); and a handsome, but shy and shallow, hunk of a fireman (Rossovich). The shy hunk asks C.D. to contribute eloquent words to help him to woo Roxanne. It works, but poor C.D. has also fallen for Roxanne. She likes C.D., but she has fallen for the hunky man with wit and words - unaware that the words and wit come from C.D. Funny remake of CYRANO DE BERGERAC.

Sex Nud Viol Lang AdSit

A: Steve Martin, Daryl Hannah, Rick Rossovich, Shelley Duvall

© COLUMBIA TRISTAR HOME VIDEO 60853

RUSSIA HOUSE, THE

D: Fred Schepisi 126 m

R
ROM SUS
1991
COLOR

7 Sophisticated suspense. Barley Blair (Connery) is a British book publisher who meets a group of influential Russian writers while on a trip to Russia and is later surprised to receive a secret manuscript from one of them, sent via a beautiful Russian book editor (Pfeiffer). The book reveals the true Soviet nuclear capabilities. Blair turns the information over to Western intelligence and then unwillingly he becomes embroiled in a spy's game of international poker. This is intelligent, involved and reasonably involving, but also a quite somber, thinking-person's film that is a little too full of complicated plot twists and romantic diversions.

Sex Nud Viol Lang AdSit

A: Sean Connery, Michelle Pfeiffer, Roy Scheider, James Fox, John Mahoney, Klaus Maria Brandauer

Distributed By MGM/UA Home Video M902301

RYAN'S DAUGHTER

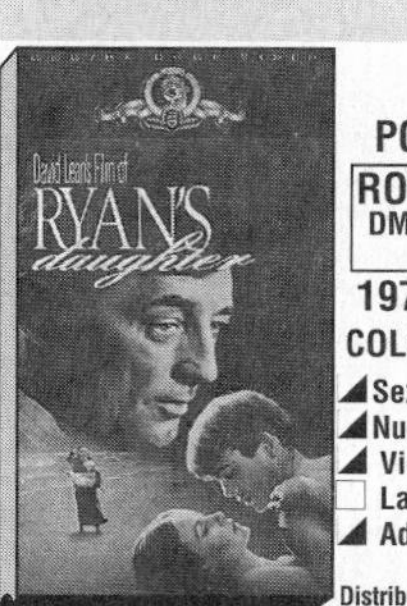

D: David Lean 194 m

PG
ROM DMA
1970
COLOR

8 Sweeping story of tragic love. It's 1916. Mitchum is a quiet, middle-aged school teacher who marries a pretty young local girl (Miles) in the small Northern Ireland village where he teaches. Their's is not a loveless union but it is uninspired. Then, tragically, she falls passionately in love with with a doubly forbidden lover. Her torrid affair is with a shell-shocked British officer who was sent to monitor the activities of the local IRA. When their forbidden affair is discovered, the passions in the little village boil over. Stunning photography. Two Oscars.

Sex Nud Viol Lang AdSit

A: Sarah Miles, Robert Mitchum, Christopher Jones, John Mills, Trevor Howard, Leo McKern

Distributed By MGM/UA Home Video M700163

SAILOR WHO FELL FROM GRACE WITH THE SEA, THE

D: Lewis John Carlino 105 m

R
DMA ROM
1976
COLOR

7 Stirring and erotic romantic drama. A lonely British widow (Miles) meets an American merchant seaman (Kristofferson) and a passionate romance develops between them. Miles sees the sailor as a symbol of honor and trust. However, her troubled young son, who is at first pleased that his mother has someone, is soon convinced by his friends that the sailor won't be true to her and will revert back to sailor ways. Over time, the boy turns violent and a plot for murder develops. The film stays true to Yukio Mishima's novel. The ending is quite bizarre.

Sex Nud Viol Lang AdSit

A: Sarah Miles, Kris Kristofferson, Jonathan Kanh, Margo Cunningham, Earl Rhodes

© GOODTIMES 9181

SAMANTHA

D: Stephen La Rocque 101 m

PG
COM ROM
1992
COLOR

6 Samantha is a wildly eccentric (some might say goofy) girl. On her 21st birthday, her mother and father tell her that she was actually left on their doorstep 21 years before in a wicker basket. Samantha, is overcome by the news, locks herself in her room and sits in front of her almost-father's ancient blunderbuss. She has jury-rigged it to the door to await her imminent demise, but her ill-considered attempt is thwarted. So, she decides to move in with her life-long best friend Henry while she begins her quest to discover her real parents, and screws up his love life in the bargain - for a while. Sometimes wacky and funny, sometimes just strange and sometimes entertaining.

Sex Nud Viol Lang AdSit

A: Martha Plimpton, Dermot Mulroney, Hector Elizondo, Mary Kay Place, Ione Skye

© ACADEMY ENTERTAINMENT 1480

SAME TIME, NEXT YEAR

D: Robert Mulligan 119 m

PG | COM ROM | 1978 | COLOR | Sex | Nud | Viol | Lang | AdSit

8 A warm, human and truly romantic comedy! When Doris and George (Burstyn and Alda) meet at a California inn, they have no idea what the coming years will bring to them. Each is happily married to someone else, but still they fall in love. So, the two decide to carry on an annual affair, returning each year to the same inn. Once every five years, we peek in on their weekend together to witness their individual changes over time. Together, they help each other through all the crises that just come with life. A sweet, very romantic comedy with plenty of wit and excellent character development.

A: Ellen Burstyn, Alan Alda

© MCA/UNIVERSAL HOME VIDEO, INC. 66013

SARAH, PLAIN AND TALL

D: Glenn Jordan 98 m

G | ROM DMA | 1991 | COLOR | Sex | Nud | Viol | Lang | AdSit

8 Endearing and wonderfully acted sentimental charmer, produced to very high standards for TV's "Hallmark Hall of Fame." In 1910, a lonely Kansas farmer and widower (Walken), with two motherless children, advertises back East for a wife. Glen Close is a spinsterly Maine schoolteacher who agrees to a one-month sexless trial "marriage." When she arrives, she finds two kids who quickly warm to her mothering. Her month is an eventful one - they are hit with a big storm and she helps a neighbor give birth, but Walken still grieves for his long-dead wife and it looks at first like her time was wasted.

A: Glenn Close, Christopher Walken, Lexi Randall, Margaret Sophie Stein, Jon De Vries, Christopher Bell

© REPUBLIC PICTURES HOME VIDEO 1821

SATURDAY NIGHT FEVER

D: John Badham 118 m

R | DMA ROM MUS | 1977 | COLOR | Sex | Nud | Viol | Lang | AdSit

8 Huge box office smash! Tony (Travolta) is just a paint salesman in Brooklyn but on Saturday night, the highlight of his week, he dances at the neighborhood disco where he's the star. He decides to take a shot at the big time with a new partner (Gorney) and enters a dance contest that he hopes will serve as a springboard to the place where dreams come true - Manhattan. Instead, he unexpectedly begins to question the shallowness of his existence. The pulse pounding soundtrack and beat of the Bee Gee's helped to define the dynamic dance mood of '70s disco and of an era. Electric!

A: John Travolta, Karen Lynn Gorney, Donna Pescow, Barry Miller, Joseph Cali, Paul Pape

© PARAMOUNT HOME VIDEO 1113

SAY ANYTHING

D: Cameron Crowe 100 m

PG-13 | ROM | 1989 | COLOR | Sex | Nud | Viol | Lang | AdSit

7 A refreshing teenage romance story! An ordinary young man (Cusack) falls in love with the beautiful, brainy and the seemingly unattainable Ione Skye. Even though she is college-bound for England on a scholarship, he decides to try to win her anyway. She responds to his ardent wooing, but her father is infuriated and shows her a nasty side of his personality. But her father's influence is undercut when he is charged by the IRS with embezzlement and everybody learns that things aren't always as they seem to be. An honest and perceptive teenage movie that stands above many of its kind.

A: John Cusack, Ione Skye, John Mahoney, Lili Taylor, Amy Brooks, Pamela Segall

© FOXVIDEO 1701

SAYONARA

D: Joshua Logan 147 m

NR | ROM DMA | 1957 | COLOR | Sex | Nud | Viol | Lang | AdSit

9 Thought provoking, highly regarded and deeply affecting film from James Michener. It is a story of romance and love, but also of the conflict love creates when cultures and human nature clashes. This Best Picture nominee is set just after WWII in occupied Japan. Brando is a racist American air ace who has his self-assured notions severely tested when the government's refusal to allow the interracial marriage of Red Buttons and Miyoshi Umeki precipitates their suicide pact. His notions are really challenged when he falls in love with a beautiful Japanese dancer himself. Winner of 4 Oscars.

A: Marlon Brando, James Garner, Ricardo Montalban, Red Buttons, Miyoshi Umeki, Miiko Taka

© CBS/FOX VIDEO 7146

SCARLETT

D: John Erman 360 m

NR | ROM DMA | 1994 | COLOR | Sex | Nud | Viol | Lang | AdSit

7 This expensive and much ballyhooed 6-hour epic is the made-for-TV mini-series which supposedly picks up where GONE WITH THE WIND left off. Spoiled Southern belle Scarlett O'Hara is now determined to win back the heart of the gambler cad Rhett Butler. She simply must have him back, and she pursues him everywhere at all cost. Essentially, this is a lushly produced soap opera which will more than maintain the rapt attention of the romantics, but it will not inspire them.

A: Joanne Whalley-Kilmer, Timothy Dalton, Ann-Margret, Paul Winfield, Annabeth Gish, John Gielgud

© CABIN FEVER ENTERTAINMENT 9506

SCENES FROM A MARRIAGE

D: Ingmar Bergman 168 m

PG | FOR DMA ROM | 1973 | COLOR | Sex | Nud | Viol | Lang | AdSit

9 Very highly acclaimed by the critics and winner of many awards. This is a challenging, very in-depth and sometimes very truthful, therefore quite painful, look at a relationship between two people over 20 years. Originally made as six 50-minute segments for a Swedish TV mini-series by famed director Ingmar Bergman, it is here edited down to 168 minutes. The two are married for ten years, when there is a painful breakup after he leaves her for a younger woman. They both marry others, only to later reconcile into a new and more mature relationship. Dubbed.

A: Liv Ullmann, Erland Josephson, Bibi Andersson, Jan Malmsjo, Anita Wall, Gunnel Lindblon

© COLUMBIA TRISTAR HOME VIDEO VCF3225

SEMI-TOUGH

D: Michael Ritchie 108 m

R | COM ROM | 1977 | COLOR | Sex | Nud | Viol | Lang | AdSit

8 Fun comic showcase for Reynolds' easy-going charm. Two professional football players - star running back Reynolds and his best buddy, roommate and wide receiver, Kristofferson - share the same girlfriend/buddy, Jill Clayburgh. The lucky girl is also the owner's carefree daughter. They make a happy threesome until Kristofferson joins a self-awareness group, talks her into joining too and then asks her to marry him. Now third man out, Reynolds seeks to debunk the group and win her back for himself. Light-hearted fun that is frequently hilarious.

A: Burt Reynolds, Kris Kristofferson, Jill Clayburgh, Robert Preston, Bert Convy, Lotte Lenya

Distributed By MGM/UA Home Video M201219

SEPARATE TABLES

D: Delbert Mann 118 m

NR | DMA ROM | 1958 | B&W | Sex | Nud | Viol | Lang | AdSit

8 Winner of 7 Oscar nominations, including Best Picture. It is an emotional peek into troubled lives. Based on the play by Terence Rattigan, the guests at a small British seaside hotel develop cautious relationships with each other as they try to sort out their troubled lives. Lancaster and Hayworth are a divorced couple trying to mend their relationship, while Lancaster's lover (Hiller) looks on. The lonely daughter (Kerr) of an overbearing and domineering mother (Cooper) is attracted to a boastful war hero (Niven). Very well-acted, this pair of one-act plays won Niven and Hiller Oscars.

A: Rita Hayworth, Deborah Kerr, David Niven, Wendy Hiller, Burt Lancaster, Gladys Cooper

Distributed By MGM/UA Home Video M301759

SHADOWLANDS

D: Richard Attenborough 133 m

PG | ROM DMA | 1993 | COLOR | Sex | Nud | Viol | Lang | AdSit

9 Wonderful, wrenching and true. English writer C.S. Lewis had won great fame from his children's classic "Chronicles of Narnia". In 1952, he was a middle-aged man, long a confirmed bachelor and a professor at Oxford. He was a master of his world of books. But that Christmas, he met an American writer. She was only in England for a short time with her son, who wanted to meet the author of his favorite book. Their relationship was very polite, but when she left, he felt her absence. Months later, she returned as a divorced woman and it was then that he began to feel love and also, for the first time, profoundly alive. Flawless in all aspects. Hopkins is brilliant.

A: Anthony Hopkins, Debra Winger, Edward Hardwicke, John Wood, Michael Denison, Joseph Mazzello

© HBO VIDEO 90968

SHINING THROUGH

D: David Seltzer 127 m

R | ROM ACT | 1992 | COLOR | Sex | Nud | Viol | Lang | AdSit

7 Griffith takes a job to Douglas's secretary just before WWII breaks out, only to soon discover that he is really an American spymaster. Her brains and guts soon win her a much more challenging job when his key operative in Berlin is killed. She is half-Irish and half German Jew, and she yearns to do something useful to the war effort. Because she is fluent in German, Douglas agrees to let her travel to Germany to gather top secret information for him, even though her only experience in the spy trade is what she has learned watching the movies. Griffith is disarmingly effective in this light weight but enjoyable little film.

A: Michael Douglas, Melanie Griffith, Liam Neeson, Joely Richardson, John Gielgud, Francis Guinan

© FOXVIDEO 5661

SHIRLEY VALENTINE

D: Lewis Gilbert 108 m

R | COM ROM DMA | 1989 | COLOR | Sex | Nud | Viol | Lang | AdSit

8 Frolicsome fun little comedy in which a frumpy middle-aged London housewife looks out upon her comfortable but routine existence and decides that life is passing her by. She loves her husband, but she is bored. So, when she gets a chance to go to Greece, she takes it; and when her husband won't go with her, she goes alone. In beautiful Greece she discovers a freedom that she hasn't known and becomes reborn by a brief romantic interlude with a local lothario. She has fun, recaptures the life that was slipping away and when her husband comes after her, he does too. Involving and fun.

A: Pauline Collins, Tom Conti, Julia McKenzie, Alison Steadman, Joanna Lumley, Bernard Hill

© PARAMOUNT HOME VIDEO 32248

SHOGUN

D: Jerry London 550 m

NR | DMA ROM ACT | 1980 | COLOR

Sex ☐ Nud ◢ Viol ◢ Lang ☐ AdSit ◢

10 This is a landmark made-for-television mini-series based upon James Clavell's novel. It is the spellbinding epic story of a 17th-century English navigator, Blackthorne (Chamberlain), who is shipwrecked in Japan. Japan is a feudal society in which the nobility, the Samurai, have total and utter control over their lands and the people who go with them. Their master is the Shogun, the military leader of all Japan. Blackthorne is in an alien world, but he gains their respect, masters their language, their society and their many-layered plots of intrigue - and he discovers love. Wonderful stuff.

A: Richard Chamberlain, Toshiro Mifune, Yoko Shimada, Frankie Sakai, Alan Badel, Michael Hordern

© PARAMOUNT HOME VIDEO 80102

SILK STOCKINGS

D: Rouben Mamoulian 118 m

MUS ROM | 1957 | COLOR

Sex ☐ Nud ☐ Viol ☐ Lang ☐ AdSit ◢

8 Musical with polish and pizzazz! Sparks fly when a heartless Soviet agent (Charisse) falls for a persistent American movie producer (Astaire) in romantic Paris. Cold and austere at first, she can't resist Astaire as his charming advances tug at her heart. This re-make of the classic NINOTCHKA into a musical features some new songs by Cole Porter and, as you would expect, unforgettable dancing from Astaire and Charisse.

A: Fred Astaire, Cyd Charisse, Janis Paige, Peter Lorre, George Tobias, Jules Munshin

Distributed By MGM/UA Home Video M700051

SINGLES

D: Cameron Crowe 100 m

PG-13 | DMA ROM | 1992 | COLOR

Sex ◢ Nud ☐ Viol ☐ Lang ◢ AdSit ■

7 An enjoyable exploration of the turmoils of love and dating for the young single residents of one particular apartment building in Seattle. Steve is a traffic engineer who is plotting to win the heart of his love, Linda - but Linda has been burned too many times. Janet is a student who is working in a coffee house. She is head over heels in love with Cliff - but Cliff is preoccupied with driving his mediocre rock band to greatness. How will each win what he or she wants, and will they still want it when they get it? No great revelations, but still enjoyable - particularly if you're young and single.

A: Bridget Fonda, Campbell Scott, Kyra Sedgwick, Matt Dillon, Sheila Kelley, Jim True

© WARNER HOME VIDEO 12410

SIRENS

D: John Duigan 104 m

R | ROM | 1994 | COLOR

Sex ■ Nud ■ Viol ☐ Lang ◢ AdSit ■

7 Hugh Grant is a stuffy English cleric on a trip to Australia with his equally stuffy wife in 1930. He has been asked by his bishop to spend a couple of days visiting artist Sam Neal, to prevail upon him not to exhibit a painting of a naked woman hanging on cross. The pair arrives at Neal's house to find him living with his wife, children and three beautiful models. They are scandalous: constantly posing seductively and quite naked, engaging in conversations about Atlantis, playing strip poker and skinny-dipping. Slowly, the starchy resistance of the minister and his wife begins to break. New worlds open to them. Fluffy and mildly entertaining.

A: Hugh Grant, Tara Fitzgerald, Sam Neill, Elle MacPherson, Portia De Rossi, Kate Fischer

© MIRAMAX HOME ENTERTAINMENT 2557

SLEEPING WITH THE ENEMY

D: Joseph Ruben 99 m

R | SUS ROM | 1991 | COLOR

Sex ◢ Nud ☐ Viol ◢ Lang ◢ AdSit ◢

7 Julia Roberts is trapped in a marriage to a very wealthy but compulsive, jealous and abusive husband (Bergin). She fears for her life and has no hope of ever being free of his violent mood swings. However, one fateful night, she seizes an opportunity to fake her own drowning and escapes into the Midwest to begin a new life in hiding. Cautious at first, she slowly ventures out into a semblance of normalcy and a new love, but Bergin discovers her secret and comes to seek her out - and to kill her. Entertaining, with some good chills.

A: Julia Roberts, Patrick Bergin, Kevin Anderson, Elizabeth Lawrence, Kyle Secor, Claudette Nevins

© FOXVIDEO 1871

SLEEPLESS IN SEATTLE

D: Nora Ephron 105 m

PG | ROM COM | 1993 | COLOR

Sex ☐ Nud ☐ Viol ☐ Lang ☐ AdSit ◢

9 Wonderfully endearing feel-good movie. The love of Tom Hanks' life has just died, leaving him and his young son heartbroken and lonely. He has left Chicago to get away from the memories but still he is always sad. So, his son contacts a radio show shrink to get help. In Baltimore, Meg Ryan is about to get married. She does her best to convince herself that she is doing the right thing in marrying this guy, but she is also powerfully drawn to the voice of a lonely, sleepless man a continent away she heard on the radio. As silly as it sounds, this is a charming and funny video that draws you to its attractive characters who you badly want to see get together and be happy.

A: Tom Hanks, Meg Ryan, Bill Pullman, Rosie O'Donnell, Rita Wilson, Rob Reiner

© COLUMBIA TRISTAR HOME VIDEO 52413

SO I MARRIED AN AXE MURDERER

D: Thomas Schlamme 93 m

PG-13 | COM ROM | 1993 | COLOR

Sex ☐ Nud ☐ Viol ☐ Lang ■ AdSit ◢

7 Charlie Mackenzie has trouble committing to a woman. He always finds a problem with them. Sherri was a kleptomaniac, Jill was in the mafia and Pam smelled like soup. Now Charlie has discovered the girl of his dreams at the butcher shop. She is smart and a real babe too. However, on a trip to visit his parents, his mother shows him an article from her tabloid magazine that describes a woman who has murdered her three previous husbands before moving on to a new town to begin again. Slowly, the paranoid Charlie begins to discover clues that point to his new love. Light-hearted and fun overall, but somewhat uneven. In an earlier time, it could have starred Bob Hope.

A: Mike Meyers, Nancy Travis, Anthony LaPaglia, Amanda Plummer, Brenda Fricker, Alan Arkin

© COLUMBIA TRISTAR HOME VIDEO 52423

SOME KIND OF WONDERFUL

D: Howard Deutch 93 m

PG-13 | ROM COM | 1987 | COLOR

Sex ☐ Nud ☐ Viol ☐ Lang ■ AdSit ◢

8 Uniquely wonderful. This is a lovely story of a lovelorn teenager's romantic pursuits. Stoltz is a poor boy from the wrong side of the tracks who has fallen so head-over-heels in love with beautiful and classy Thompson that he is blind to the fact that his best pal, tomboy Masterson, is seriously in love with him. Wonderful exploration of the trials of teenage love that will leave you feeling wonderful. Funny and warm.

A: Eric Stoltz, Lea Thompson, Mary Stuart Masterson, Craig Sheffer, John Ashton, Elias Koteas

© PARAMOUNT HOME VIDEO 31979

SOMEONE TO WATCH OVER ME

D: Ridley Scott 106 m

R | SUS CRM ROM | 1987 | COLOR

Sex ◢ Nud ◢ Viol ■ Lang ■ AdSit ◢

8 Brightly polished thriller! An incredibly beautiful and rich member of the New York's social elite (Rogers) witnesses a gruesome murder that was committed by the mob. She escapes by the skin of her teeth, but is now being stalked by the ruthless killer (Katsulas). Berenger is a happily married cop who is assigned to protect her around the clock. In spite of themselves, the pair begin a passionate affair. When the killer is unsuccessful at nabbing Rogers directly, he kidnaps Berenger's wife and kids to hold hostage. Berenger is being forced to choose between them. A visually stunning, heart-stopping and atmospheric suspensor!

A: Tom Berenger, Mimi Rogers, Lorraine Bracco, Jerry Orbach, John Rubinstein, Andreas Katsulas

© COLUMBIA TRISTAR HOME VIDEO 60877

SOMEWHERE IN TIME

D: Jeannot Szwarc 104 m

PG | ROM FAN | 1980 | COLOR

Sex ☐ Nud ☐ Viol ☐ Lang ◢ AdSit ◢

8 Very entertaining and intensely romantic story of love found and lost! Reeve is a handsome playwrite (from the 1980s) who sees a picture of a beautiful actress (Seymour) that was taken in 1912. He immediately falls in love with her. He believes that they had been lovers in a past life and through self-hypnosis he manages to transports himself back in time to be with her. He finds her at the Grand Hotel on Michigan's Mackinac Island and they fall deeply in love, despite the objections of her manager (Plummer) who does everything he can to break them up. This is an entrancing, even though fanciful, love story with beautiful photography of picturesque settings.

A: Christopher Reeve, Jane Seymour, Christopher Plummer, Teresa Wright, Bill Erwin, George Voskovec

© MCA/UNIVERSAL HOME VIDEO, INC. 66024

SOMMERSBY

D: Jon Amiel 114 m

PG-13 | ROM WST DMA | 1993 | COLOR

Sex ◢ Nud ☐ Viol ◢ Lang ☐ AdSit ◢

9 Very involving and highly romantic Civil War saga, but with a very different bent. Jack Sommersby (Gere) has been away from his Tennessee farm for six years, locked up in a Yankee prison. His wife Laurel and his son have given him up for dead, and yet one day he comes walking back into his war-torn town and onto their decimated farm. Jack has changed. He left as a disagreeable sort and came back as a thoughtful and caring man. Jack wins back Laurel and then even organizes a recovery plan for the town. But soon he is arrested for murder and is accused of being someone else. This one starts slow but comes to a powerful and unusual finish.

A: Richard Gere, Jodie Foster, James Earl Jones, Bill Pullman, William Windom, Brett Kelly

© WARNER HOME VIDEO 12649

SOPHIE'S CHOICE

D: Alan J. Pakula 155 m

R | DMA ROM | 1982 | COLOR

Sex ◢ Nud ☐ Viol ☐ Lang ■ AdSit ■

9 Stunning portrait by Meryl Streep that earned her a Best Actress Oscar. Sophie is a survivor of the Nazi concentration camps. Now safe in America just after the war and living with an explosive biologist (Kline), she is tormented by her own survival from the death camps when so many others did not survive. A young and naive writer (MacNicol) living downstairs from the mysterious pair is drawn to this odd couple. He becomes fascinated with her and an odd relationship develops between the two men and the tragic Sophie. Compelling story and an utterly fascinating performance by Streep. 4 other nominations.

A: Meryl Streep, Kevin Kline, Peter MacNicol, Rita Karin, Stephen D. Newman, Josh Mostel

© CBS/FOX VIDEO 9076

SOUTH PACIFIC

D: Joshua Logan 150 m

NR | MUS ROM | 1958 | COLOR | Sex Nud Viol Lang AdSit

7 Rogers & Hammerstein musical that was adapted from a hugely successful Broadway play. James Michener's moving book was simplified for the stage and further diminished for the screen. The result is a largely saccharin presentation, but it is still involving and has wonderful music. The story revolves around life on a Pacific Island during WWII: a nurse from the Midwest falls for a French planter and a sailor falls for a native girl. The plot has been greatly diminished, however. But, the music is truly memorable, and there is a lot of it. Several of the songs are now standards.

A: Mitzi Gaynor, Rossano Brazzi, John Kerr, Ray Walston, John Kerr, France Nuyen

© FOXVIDEO 7045

SPLASH

D: Ron Howard 109 m

PG | COM ROM FAN | 1984 | COLOR | Sex Nud Viol Lang AdSit

9 An unbelievable plot is made both believable and captivating, thanks to outstanding acting by Hanks and Hannah and deft direction by Howard. Hanks is a wealthy businessman who has everything but love. When he nearly drowns off the coast of Cape Cod, it is a beautiful mermaid (Hannah) who rescues him. She is infatuated with him and grows legs to search the big city for him. She charms him with her incredible innocence and they fall madly in love, but Hanks still has a hard time learning to deal with her nautical nature. Fantastic movie-making and a wonderful blending of fantasy and romance.

A: Tom Hanks, Daryl Hannah, Eugene Levy, John Candy, Dody Goodman, Richard B. Shull

© TOUCHSTONE HOME VIDEO 213

SPLENDOR IN THE GRASS

D: Elia Kazan 124 m

NR | ROM DMA | 1961 | COLOR | Sex Nud Viol Lang AdSit

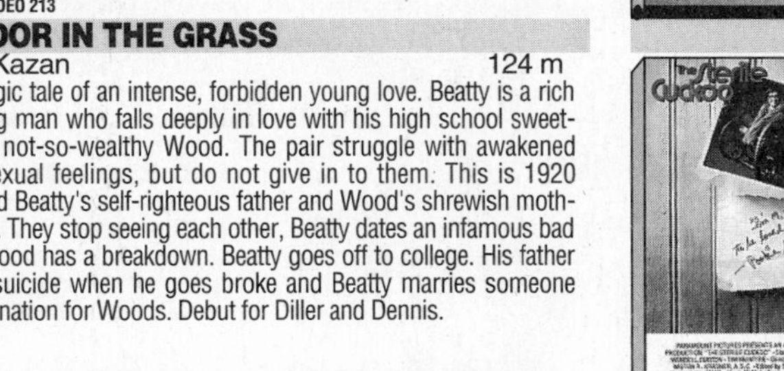

7 A tragic tale of an intense, forbidden young love. Beatty is a rich young man who falls deeply in love with his high school sweetheart, the not-so-wealthy Wood. The pair struggle with awakened intense sexual feelings, but do not give in to them. This is 1920 Kansas and Beatty's self-righteous father and Wood's shrewish mother forbid it. They stop seeing each other, Beatty dates an infamous bad girl and Wood has a breakdown. Beatty goes off to college. His father commits suicide when he goes broke and Beatty marries someone else. Nomination for Woods. Debut for Diller and Dennis.

A: Natalie Wood, Warren Beatty, Audrey Christie, Sean Garrison, Sandy Dennis, Phyllis Diller

© WARNER HOME VIDEO 11164

STANLEY & IRIS

D: Martin Ritt 105 m

PG-13 | ROM DMA | 1990 | COLOR | Sex Nud Viol Lang AdSit

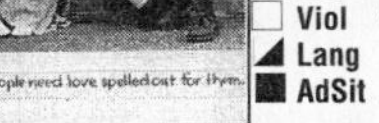

7 Iris is a middle-aged woman, newly widowed. She is adrift, struggling with her grief while trying to support her household. Stanley is a very bright middle-aged guy. He is a mechanical genius who is able to build almost anything, but he is working only as a cook. Then his employers fire him after they too find out his dark secret - he can't read. Stanley has met Iris at the factory where they both worked. After Stanley gets fired (as a safety risk), he can no longer support his old and sick father. He is so despondent that he goes to Iris to ask for her help in learning how to read. This is an affecting drama and a sweet romance story too.

A: Jane Fonda, Robert De Niro, Swoosie Kurtz, Martha Plimpton, Harley Cross, Jamey Sheridan

Distributed By MGM/UA Home Video M901694

STARMAN

D: John Carpenter 115 m

PG | ROM SF FAN | 1984 | COLOR | Sex Nud Viol Lang AdSit

8 An endearing charmer. An space ship is shot down and crashes in rural Wisconsin. The scared alien escapes from the crash site before the government gets to it and stumbles upon the cabin of a young woman (Allen) who is newly widowed and still grieving the loss of her husband. The alien will die if he doesn't make it to Arizona where he will be rescued in three days. So he, takes on the form of her dead husband and makes her drive him there. She is not pleased but along the way, while they are dodging the pursuing FBI, she discovers a sweetness about him. That, and because he looks like her dead husband, she falls in love with him. Very entertaining and uplifting.

A: Jeff Bridges, Karen Allen, Charles Martin Smith, Richard Jaeckel

© COLUMBIA TRISTAR HOME VIDEO 60412

STARTING OVER

D: Alan J. Pakula 106 m

R | ROM COM | 1979 | COLOR | Sex Nud Viol Lang AdSit

8 Hilarious, and also good therapy for everyone who is recovering from divorce. Poor Burt Reynolds really needs to get on with his life, but he can't shake off his feelings for his ex (Bergen). Lonely and insecure, he joins a self-help group and relies upon his his brother (Durning) for support. His life is a mess until Durning introduces him to a schoolteacher (Clayburgh). Together, they are magic and become lovers, but when Bergen comes back, Burt is confused all over again. Very perceptive, charming and very funny. A warm and witty winner!

A: Burt Reynolds, Jill Clayburgh, Candice Bergen, Charles Durning, Frances Sternhagen, Austin Pendleton

© PARAMOUNT HOME VIDEO 1239

STEALING HEAVEN

D: Clive Donner 108 m

R | ROM | 1988 | COLOR | Sex Nud Viol Lang AdSit

7 Well done, steamy romancer with all the ingredients of a supermarket pulp novel, but based upon real-life lovers - as documented in their love letters that have come down to us from 800 years ago. It is the story of Abelar and Heloise. He was a brilliant professor of religious philosophy at Notre Dame in 12th-century Paris. As was then the custom, he was required to take a vow of celibacy but broke his vow when he and the beautiful, intelligent and independent Heloise discovered a passion so deep that they risked everything and defied all authority to be together.

A: Derek de Lint, Kim Thomson, Denholm Elliott, Rachel Kempson, Kenneth Cranham

© MCEG/STERLING 70095

STEALING HOME

D: Steven Kampmann 98 m

PG-13 | DMA ROM | 1988 | COLOR | Sex Nud Viol Lang AdSit

8 A bittersweet story that didn't get its proper due upon release. Harmon plays a nearly washed-up minor league baseball player who is just barely hanging on to his sanity. Then he gets a call to come home. His best friend has committed suicide and has willed him her ashes. She was a free-spirit and was his babysitter when he was young. As he grew up she became his mentor and lover. Their story is told through a series of flashbacks and flashforwards, and as it is explored over time his life slowly comes into focus for him. Somewhat corny and overstated, but also memorable. Foster is unforgettable.

A: Mark Harmon, Jodie Foster, Blair Brown, Harold Ramis, Jonathan Silverman, William McNamara

© WARNER HOME VIDEO 11818

STERILE CUCKOO, THE

D: Alan J. Pakula 107 m

R | DMA ROM | 1970 | COLOR | Sex Nud Viol Lang AdSit

8 Liza Minnelli won a much-deserved Oscar nomination for her role as the wisecracking, insecure, vulnerable Pookie Adams. Her mother died in childbirth (Pookie says she was her first victim) and she has been a problem ever since. Her father doesn't know how to deal with her, so he keeps putting her in different boarding schools. On the bus to college, she meets shy Jerry (Burton) who is on his way to a neighboring school and immediately decides that they should be friends, instead she only embarrasses him. However, later she turns up to spend the weekend and they become friends and lovers. Poignant and bittersweet.

A: Liza Minnelli, Wendell Burton, Tim McIntire, Elizabeth Harrower

© PARAMOUNT HOME VIDEO 6904

STILL OF THE NIGHT

D: Robert Benton 91 m

PG | SUS MYS ROM | 1982 | COLOR | Sex Nud Viol Lang AdSit

8 Well-crafted thriller in the Hitchcock tradition. One of psychiatrist Scheider's patients, an antique dealer, is viciously murdered in Jack The Ripper fashion. Now into his life walks the guy's mistress (Streep), an alluring but neurotic art curator. Scheider falls in love with Streep, in spite of his psychiatrist-mother's (Tandy) warnings to the contrary. Soon Scheider wonders if Streep is the killer and after him next. Solid suspense vehicle, in spite of some plot holes, that will keep you guessing and in suspense right up to the end.

A: Roy Scheider, Meryl Streep, Jessica Tandy, Joe Grifasi, Sara Botsford, Josef Sommer

Distributed By MGM/UA Home Video M301411

STRANGERS WHEN WE MEET

D: Richard Quine 117 m

NR | ROM DMA | 1960 | B&W | Sex Nud Viol Lang AdSit

7 Martial discontent runs rampant in this lush and enjoyable soap opera. A brilliant architect (Douglas) is frustrated with his money-obsessed wife (Rush). Just down the street, neighbor Novak feels worthless and taken for granted by her dull husband (Bryant). Douglas and Novak fall head over heels in love, igniting a heated affair, but their happiness is threatened when Douglas is offered the job of his life and must choose between his family, his career, and Novak. Matthau is wonderful as their mutual friend who knows of their affair and begins to make passes at Rush.

A: Kirk Douglas, Kim Novak, Ernie Kovacs, Barbara Rush, Walter Matthau, Virginia Bruce

© COLUMBIA TRISTAR HOME VIDEO 60944

STRAPLESS

D: David Hare 99 m

R | DMA ROM | 1990 | COLOR | Sex Nud Viol Lang AdSit

7 Intelligent drama that has many aspects to it. A middle-aged American doctor, working in London under England's socialized medical system, has devoted her life to her work. However, after observing her carefree sister, she decides she has missed out on too much. She needs excitement too and takes a chance with a charming man while on a vacation in Portugal. She does have a good time, but she refuses invitations to his bed. Still he persists. Eventually she marries him and gives over to passion. Life now appears to be wonderful, that is until she finds that he has taken her money and is already is married. Passion is not always free.

A: Blair Brown, Bridget Fonda, Bruno Ganz, Hugh Laurie

© COLUMBIA TRISTAR HOME VIDEO 90893

STRICTLY BALLROOM

D: Baz Luhrmann 94 m

PG | ROM COM | 1993 | COLOR | Sex | Nud | Viol | Lang | AdSit

8 A very different sort of comedy from Australia. Paul Mercurio has been in training, under the tutelage of his very driven mother, since he was six years old to win the Pan-Pacific Grand Prix Dance Championship. She desperately wants the championship for her son, that was denied to her and his father. The son, however, is frustrated by the rigid confines of tradition and wants to dance his own steps. His mother is furious with him, but he is determined. He will dance his way and he selects as his dance partner lowly Fran, a mousey-looking beginner, because she believes in him. Critics and regular folks loved this quirky charmer that is sort of a combination of ROCKY and FLASHDANCE.

A: Paul Mercurio, Tara Morice, Bill Hunter, Shirley Hastings, Liz Holt, Les Kendall

© TOUCHSTONE HOME VIDEO 1701

SUMMER AND SMOKE

D: Peter Glenville 118 m

NR | DMA ROM | 1962 | COLOR | Sex | Nud | Viol | Lang | AdSit

8 From the Tennessee Williams play comes this film full of despair, sadness and love unfulfilled. Yet, it is also extremely involving. Geraldine Page (in a repeat of her stage role) stars as a small town spinster with a set of overbearing parents. She is head over heels in love with the town's handsome young doctor (Harvey). But his disregard for her causes both of them a great deal of pain and agony, especially when he falls for a sexy dancehall girl. Dazzling performances throughout, Page gives an especially outstanding performance. Profound and moving, but also slow and depressing.

A: Geraldine Page, Laurence Harvey, Rita Moreno, Una Merkel, John McIntire, Pamela Tiffin

© PARAMOUNT HOME VIDEO 6107

SUMMER OF '42

D: Robert Mulligan 104 m

PG | ROM DMA | 1971 | COLOR | Sex | Nud | Viol | Lang | AdSit

8 This is a lovely, tender and endearing coming-of-age movie, evocatively set in 1940s atmosphere at the beginning of WWII, on a summer resort island. Three adolescent boys are both fascinated and frustrated with sex. They pour over the marriage manual of one of their parents and even make faltering attempts at acquiring condoms from the local pharmacy. But, sex takes on a new meaning when Grimes falls in deeply in love with a 22-year-old war bride who has just sent her new husband off to war. A sweet and tender movie that garnered four Oscar nominations and was hugely popular.

A: Jennifer O'Neill, Gary Grimes, Jerry Houser, Oliver Conant, Christopher Norris, Lou Frizell

© WARNER HOME VIDEO 1033

SUMMER PLACE, A

D: Delmer Daves 130 m

NR | ROM DMA | 1959 | COLOR | Sex | Nud | Viol | Lang | AdSit

7 Top-notch soaper! McGuire and Egan, once teenage lovers, find themselves together again after parental disapproval had catapulted them into 20 years of separation. Egan, now a successful businessman, returns to an island off the coast of Maine and finds that his old flame (McGuire) is stuck in a very unhappy marriage. Romance once again ignites. Each divorce their current spouses and marry each other. Then love strikes again and Egan's daughter (Dee) falls in love with McGuire's son (Donahue). The theme song by Max Steiner was a monumental hit.

A: Troy Donahue, Sandra Dee, Dorothy McGuire, Richard Egan, Arthur Kennedy, Constance Ford

© WARNER HOME VIDEO 11593

SUMMER STORY, A

D: Piers Haggard 97 m

PG-13 | ROM DMA | 1988 | COLOR | Sex | Nud | Viol | Lang | AdSit

7 A romantic and picturesque story of love and life at the turn of the century in England. A beautiful young farmgirl (Stubbs) falls madly in love with an affluent but weak-willed British attorney (Wilby). He does love her, but the social consciousness of the time will not readily allow him in such an arrangement. So, he ultimately makes the decision that changes the course of their romance and breaks Stubbs's fragile heart. An endearing romance tale based on Galsworthy's novel "The Apple Tree."

A: Imogen Stubbs, James Wilby, Ken Colley, Sophie Ward, Susannah York, Jerome Flynn

© MEDIA HOME ENTERTAINMENT, INC. M012485

SUNDAY IN THE PARK WITH GEORGE

D: James Lapine 145 m

NR | MUS ROM | 1986 | COLOR | Sex | Nud | Viol | Lang | AdSit

9 A painting comes to life in this magnificent taped stage presentation of the superb Pulitzer Prize-winning musical play. Based on characters featured in Georges Seurat's painting "Sunday Afternoon on the Island of La Grande Jatte," each character in the painting becomes real and has a compelling story to tell. The score and lyrics by Stephen Sondheim are very memorable. Patinkin deftly plays the Seurat, the masterful painter. One of the most unforgettable musicals in recent history. A standout!

A: Bernadette Peters, Mandy Patinkin, Barbara Byrne, Charles Kimbrough

© WARNER HOME VIDEO 370

SURE THING, THE

D: Rob Reiner 94 m

PG-13 | COM ROM | 1985 | COLOR | Sex | Nud | Viol | Lang | AdSit

7 Sure entertainment! College freshman and party hound John Cusack, and prudish Daphne Zuniga accidentally wind up sharing a ride to California over Christmas break. Cusack, who is actually a strike-out with women, is traveling to see surfer girl Nicollette Sheridan who is supposed to be a "sure thing". Zunigan is supposed to reunite with her equally uptight boyfriend. But, Cusack and Zunigan fight so much that their ride deserts them and to their mutual surprise, they find themselves falling in love with each other on this comic road trip wrought with misadventure.

A: John Cusack, Daphne Zuniga, Anthony Edwards, Viveca Lindfors, Nicollette Sheridan, Tim Robbins

© NEW LINE HOME VIDEO 2178

SWAN, THE

D: Charles Vidor 109 m

NR | ROM COM | 1956 | COLOR | Sex | Nud | Viol | Lang | AdSit

6 The beautiful princess (Kelly) is supposed to marry the prince (Guinness) and save her family's declining fortunes, however she would rather spend her time with her handsome tutor, a common man (Jourdan). Still, when she spies the prince, she is immediately taken by him. However the prince is cool to the arranged wedding, so her mother sets about plotting to make him jealous. It is ironic that this was Grace Kelly's last film before her marriage to Prince Rainier. Slow in spots, and the humor is subtle but the story is captivating and heartwarming. As always, Grace is delightful.

A: Grace Kelly, Alec Guinness, Louis Jourdan, Agnes Moorehead, Jessie Royce Landis, Brian Aherne

Distributed By MGM/UA Home Video M201068

SWEET CHARITY

D: Bob Fosse 148 m

G | MUS ROM | 1968 | COLOR | Sex | Nud | Viol | Lang | AdSit

7 This smash Broadway hit was transferred with some success to the screen. Shirley MacLaine stars as a prostitute and dance hall hostess who dreams of love and marriage. When she is dumped by her latest boyfriend, she has a brief fling with a movie star and then takes up with an innocent young accountant. He thinks he can accept her past, but is more challenged by it than he expected. Wonderful dance routines and fantastic music that has many songs which are now standards: "Hey Big Spender," "Rhythm of Life" and "If They Could See Me Now." Entertaining, but also very long.

A: Shirley MacLaine, John McMartin, Chita Rivera, Sammy Davis, Jr., Ricardo Montalban, Paula Kelly

© MCA/UNIVERSAL HOME VIDEO, INC. 55044

SWEET HEARTS DANCE

D: Robert Greenwald 101 m

R | ROM COM | 1988 | COLOR | Sex | Nud | Viol | Lang | AdSit

6 Nice little change-of-pace film for tough guy Don Johnson. It is the parallel love stories of two high school buddies. Johnson has married his high school sweetheart (Sarandon), is a carpenter, has three kids and is going through a mid-life crisis about his relationship with her. However, his buddy (Daniels) is single, has played around for years, is a school principal, but has fallen in love with a teacher (Perkins) and is about to begin his first real relationship. Entertaining story of the changing natures of both life and love. A little slow-moving in places.

A: Don Johnson, Susan Sarandon, Jeff Daniels, Elizabeth Perkins

© COLUMBIA TRISTAR HOME VIDEO 67012

SWEPT AWAY...

D: Lina Wertmuller 116 m

R | FOR COM ROM | 1975 | COLOR | Sex | Nud | Viol | Lang | AdSit

8 Provocative, saucy Italian comedy with a rough edge. Melato is a spoiled, rich, arrogant woman who continually humiliates the staff aboard her yacht and degrades her servant (Giannini). However, when they end up stranded together on a deserted island, the wars erupt. They can agree upon nothing. She is a rich capitalist. He is a deckhand and a communist. But the sex is great and their roles are quickly reversed. Giannini becomes the dominator, completely controlling Melato's every thought and stripping her of all dignity and vanity. A delightful mixed bag of morality and humor. Dubbed.

A: Giancarlo Giannini, Mariangela Melato

© COLUMBIA TRISTAR HOME VIDEO 60224

SWORD OF LANCELOT

D: Cornel Wilde 115 m

NR | ACT ROM | 1963 | COLOR | Sex | Nud | Viol | Lang | AdSit

7 Before CAMELOT, there was the story of King Arthur and his court - a rousing adventure based on Thomas Mallory's "Morte d'Arthur." This is the love story of forbidden passion between the dashing Sir Lancelot (Wilde) and the captivating Queen Guinevere. When the betrayed King Arthur finds out about their love affair, a vastly destructive war breaks out. Great performances of Lancelot and Guinevere are given by real-life husband and wife team Cornel Wilde and Jean Wallace. Loads of intricate swordplay add to the fun.

A: Cornel Wilde, Jean Wallace, Brian Aherne, George Baker

© MCA/UNIVERSAL HOME VIDEO, INC. 80077

TAMARIND SEED, THE

D: Blake Edwards — 123 m

PG · SUS ROM · 1974 · COLOR · Viol

7 An involving political thriller, tinged with romance. A Cold War romance breaks out between an English secretary for the British foreign office and a disillusioned Russian official from the Paris embassy when they meet while on vacation in the Bahamas. When they return home, the lovers are forced to remain apart. But when Sharif finds he is about to be called back to Moscow and may be in trouble, he decides it's time to trade his knowledge for freedom in the West with her. But a high-placed British politician is also a Russian spy. This is a solid spy thriller, but it serves equally well as a good romancer.

A: Julie Andrews, Omar Sharif, Anthony Quayle, Sylvia Sims, Dan O'Herlihy, Oscar Homolka

© LIVE HOME VIDEO 51120

TAMMY AND THE BACHELOR

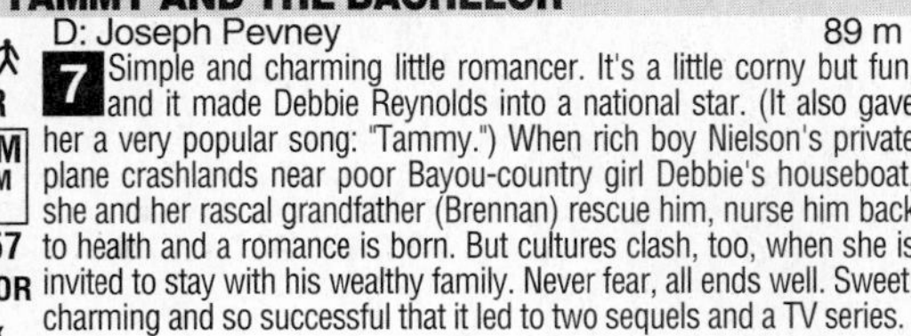

D: Joseph Pevney — 89 m

NR · ROM COM · 1957 · COLOR

7 Simple and charming little romancer. It's a little corny but fun, and it made Debbie Reynolds into a national star. (It also gave her a very popular song: "Tammy.") When rich boy Nielson's private plane crashlands near poor Bayou-country girl Debbie's houseboat, she and her rascal grandfather (Brennan) rescue him, nurse him back to health and a romance is born. But cultures clash, too, when she is invited to stay with his wealthy family. Never fear, all ends well. Sweet, charming and so successful that it led to two sequels and a TV series.

A: Debbie Reynolds, Leslie Nielsen, Walter Brennan, Mala Powers, Fay Wray, Mildred Natwick

© MCA/UNIVERSAL HOME VIDEO, INC. 80314

TEACHER'S PET

D: George Seaton — 120 m

NR · COM ROM · 1958 · B&W

6 Enjoyable little farce. When hard-boiled city editor Clark Gable is roundly criticized by a night school journalism instructor, he is intent upon getting even. So he joins her class, unbeknownst to her. Instead of getting even, he becomes her star pupil, falls in love with her and seeks to win her heart away from her intellectual boyfriend Gig Young. Light, witty, bright and breezy. Gig Young is hilarious. Gable is winning, even though he was really too old for the role.

A: Doris Day, Clark Gable, Gig Young, Mamie Van Doren, Nick Adams, Charles Lane

© PARAMOUNT HOME VIDEO 5716

TEQUILA SUNRISE

D: Robert Towne — 116 m

R · ACT ROM CRM · 1988 · COLOR · Sex · Nud · Viol · Lang · AdSit

8 Good, spicy action flick, with some major Hollywood star power. The lives of two best friends from high school have gone in drastically different directions and are now seemingly headed headlong into conflict. Kurt Russell is an up-and-coming narcotics cop. Mel Gibson is basically a good guy but he has also become a major-league drug dealer and is now trying to get out of a nasty business. Russell is doing his best to try to catch Gibson. Between these two, in an involved plot, is sultry Michelle Pfeiffer, a beautiful restaurant owner whom they both love. Good action and well-paced with appealing stars.

A: Mel Gibson, Michelle Pfeiffer, Kurt Russell, Raul Julia, Arliss Howard

© WARNER HOME VIDEO 11821

TERMS OF ENDEARMENT

D: James L. Brooks — 132 m

PG · DMA ROM COM · 1983 · COLOR · Lang · AdSit

10 Mesmerizing and totally heartwarming drama that captured five major Oscars, including Picture, Screenplay, Director, Actress and Supporting Actress. It is an intimate and winning character study of the relationship between a mother and daughter as it evolves over a period of years. MacLaine is wonderful as a neurotic, domineering mother and Winger is equally good as her independent-minded daughter who marries a cheating English teacher against her mother's wishes and later is to die of cancer. Totally captivating performances and story that surely will warm your heart and wet your eyes.

A: Shirley MacLaine, Debra Winger, Jack Nicholson, John Lithgow, Danny DeVito, Jeff Daniels

© PARAMOUNT HOME VIDEO 1407

TESS

D: Roman Polanski — 136 m

PG · ROM DMA · 1980 · COLOR · AdSit

8 Extremely handsome production of "Tess of the D'Urbervilles," the tragic story of a beautiful but desperately poor girl in Victorian England. She is sent to live with distant relations when her parents learn that their family was once one of prominence, hoping that she will be able to better herself. Instead, she is seduced by her roguish cousin and abandoned when she becomes pregnant. The baby dies. She marries a minister's son but he, too, abandons her on the night of their wedding when he discovers her tainted past. Beautiful and haunting period piece. 6 nominations - 3 Oscars.

A: Nastassia Kinski, Peter Firth, Leigh Lawson, John Bett, Rosemary Martin, Sylvia Coleridge

© COLUMBIA TRISTAR HOME VIDEO 50633

THAT TOUCH OF MINK

D: Delbert Mann — 99 m

NR · COM ROM · 1962 · COLOR · AdSit

7 Amusing romantic comedy. Ever-virginal Doris Day is naive and unemployed, walking through the canyons of New York when she is splashed by hot shot executive Cary Grant's limo. Smitten with the charms of Miss Day, Cary attempts to woo her with his charm and his money. That's it, that's all there really is - but it is a proven formula, has winning stars, sparkling dialogue and good support from a talented cast, particularly Gig Young. Enjoy.

A: Cary Grant, Doris Day, Audrey Meadows, Gig Young, John Astin, Dick Sargent

© REPUBLIC PICTURES HOME VIDEO 5407

THEY MIGHT BE GIANTS

D: Anthony Harvey — 98 m

G · COM ROM · 1971 · COLOR · AdSit

6 Curious, interesting and quirky little comedy. When a retired judge (Scott) begins to believe that he is the great Sherlock Holmes, his brother sees an easy opportunity to grab his money. So the brother hires a female psychiatrist, coincidentally named Dr. Watson (Woodward), to investigate Scott. This she does, following Scott, fully dressed as Holmes, all around New York, while he is in search of the illusive Moriarity. Oddly, she soon begins to believe that he could actually be Holmes. More important than his true identity, she believes in him and two lonely people find and enjoy each other.

A: George C. Scott, Joanne Woodward, Jack Gilford, Lester Rawlins, Rue McClanahan, Ron Weyand

© MCA/UNIVERSAL HOME VIDEO, INC. 80408

THIEF OF HEARTS

D: Douglas Day Stewart — 101 m

R · ROM DMA · 1984 · COLOR · Sex · Nud · Viol · Lang · AdSit

7 This is a fascinating premise gets pretty fair treatment. A cat burglar breaks into a house and steals the diaries of a beautiful young married woman. By reading them, he now possesses all her innermost secrets and desires and strikes upon a well-calculated plan. He spies upon her and then sets out to seduce her by fulfilling all her fantasies. He will become her perfect lover. At first she fails to recognize the ruse and becomes a willing participant in his plan, but then as she begins to suspect, things take a bad turn. Well-done and very erotic, with reedited scenes added for the video version.

A: Barbara Williams, Steven Bauer, John Getz, David Caruso, George Wendt, Christine Ebersole

© PARAMOUNT HOME VIDEO 1660

THOMAS CROWN AFFAIR, THE

D: Norman Jewison — 102 m

R · SUS ROM ACT · 1968 · COLOR · Nud · Viol · Lang · AdSit

8 Stylish combination of a heist movie and a sophisticated romancer. Faye Dunaway is an unscrupulous insurance investigator hot on the trail of a bored millionaire (McQueen) who enjoys staging elaborate burglaries just for the thrill of it. Even as they play coy cat and mouse games and engage in clever and cryptic dialogue, he is plotting a daring bank heist that is to be carried off right under her nose. The emotional and mental games they play with each other inevitably lead to romance. Oscar for best song: "Windmills of Your Mind." Good entertainment.

A: Steve McQueen, Faye Dunaway, Paul Burke, Yaphet Kotto, Jack Weston, Biff McGuire

Distributed By MGM/UA Home Video M201260

THREE MEN AND A LITTLE LADY

D: Emile Ardolino — 103 m

PG · COM ROM · 1990 · COLOR · Sex · Lang · AdSit

8 Some liked this follow-up even better than the original! The men have all matured, baby Mary has now grown into an adorable 5-year-old, and Mom Travis has become an engaging romantic interest. All five live together in a happy home and all three men are dedicated fathers. But when Travis decides to move to England for the love of another man (Cazenove), Selleck's love for her is awakened and the men set out to prove Cazenove's true intentions and that he doesn't care a bit about little Mary. A genuine treasure with plenty love and laughter to go around.

A: Tom Selleck, Steve Guttenberg, Ted Danson, Nancy Travis, Robin Weisman, Christopher Cazenove

© TOUCHSTONE HOME VIDEO 1139

THREE MUSKETEERS, THE

D: Richard Lester — 105 m

PG · ACT COM ROM · 1974 · COLOR · Viol · AdSit

9 Great, well-rounded entertainment that has a little bit of everything. Dumas's classic tale has been filmed numerous times, but never this well. Michael York is determined to become one of the King's elite guards, the Musketeers, so he befriends three of them but, they are only interested in fighting, drinking and chasing women. However, they do become roused to action when York charms Welch, the Queen's lady-in-waiting, and she uncovers a plot to overcome the King. This news sends the Musketeers into rip roaring action. Rousing swashbuckling and hilarious slapstick. Top talent.

A: Oliver Reed, Raquel Welch, Richard Chamberlain, Michael York, Frank Finlay, Geraldine Chaplin

© LIVE HOME VIDEO 67776

ROM

THREE OF HEARTS

D: Yurek Bogayevicz — 101 m

R | ROM DMA | 1993 | COLOR

7 A very unusual premise produces a film that is difficult for many people to accept. Ignoring that, it is quite likable. Kelly Lynch and Sherilyn Fenn have been lesbian lovers. Now Fenn wants to call it quits, but Lynch is still very much in love with her and does not want to lose her. Meanwhile Lynch has become buddies with Baldwin, a likable gigolo she had hired to escort her to a family wedding. This unlikely pair strikes upon a plan to win Fenn back to Lynch. He will seduce her and then dump her, breaking her heart and causing her to return to Lynch. Baldwin, however, is disillusioned with his life and falls for Fenn instead and Lynch eventually decides to help him.

Sex / Nud / Viol / Lang / AdSit

A: William Baldwin, Kelly Lynch, Sherilyn Fenn, Joe Pantoliano, Gail Strickland, Cec Verrell

© TURNER HOME ENTERTAINMENT N4034

TIME TO LOVE AND A TIME TO DIE, A

D: Douglas Sirk — 133 m

NR | DMA ROM WAR | 1958 | COLOR

8 Poignant, moving, believable and sad anti-war film. It is the story of an ordinary German soldier caught up in the chaos occurring during the closing days of World War II. He returns home on furlough from the Russian front to his hometown which has been almost totally destroyed by the Allied bombing raids and his parents are missing. All the townsfolk are as severely demoralized and fearful as is he, but there he meets a beautiful young woman. They fall in love and marry, all the while knowing that their time together will be brief because he must soon return to the front.

Sex / Nud / Viol / Lang / AdSit

A: John Gavin, Lilo Pulver, Jock Mahoney, Keenan Wynn, Jim Hutton, Klaus Kinski

© MCA/UNIVERSAL HOME VIDEO, INC.

TO DANCE WITH THE WHITE DOG

D: Glenn Jordan — 98 m

PG | ROM DMA | 1993 | COLOR

9 Beautiful made-for-TV movie that was done for the Hallmark Hall of Fame. Sam and Cora are an old couple that have lived together for all their lives and live surrounded by their family. Still deeply in love after 50 years of marriage, Cora is stricken and dies. Sam is struggling with his loneliness and is in poor health himself. Suddenly one day, a stray white dog shows up at his door. The two become fast friends, but the dog only comes around when he is alone and his children fear he is losing his mind. But the dog is real and it is there to protect and love him, just as Cora had done. Extremely well done and very moving. Reportedly based upon an actual incidence.

Sex / Nud / Viol / Lang / AdSit

A: Hume Cronyn, Jessica Tandy, Christine Baranski, Terry Beaver, Harley Cross, Ester Rolle

© REPUBLIC PICTURES HOME VIDEO 0837

TOOTSIE

D: Sydney Pollack — 116 m

PG | COM ROM | 1982 | COLOR

10 Wonderfully delightful picture and a huge blockbuster hit. Dustin Hoffman is an out-of-work actor who can't get a job, so he dresses up as a woman to win a part on a daytime soap opera. Quite by accident, he becomes a huge hit and is trapped into playing the role of a woman both onscreen and off. This is particularly distressing to him because he is falling in love with the leading lady (Jessica Lange) who thinks of him/her as a girlfriend. Worse, on a short trip home with Lange, her father makes a pass at him/her. Interesting insights on differences in sexes. 10 Oscar nominations. Funny!!

Sex / Nud / Viol / Lang / AdSit

A: Dustin Hoffman, Jessica Lange, Charles Durning, Bill Murray, Teri Garr, Dabney Coleman

© COLUMBIA TRISTAR HOME VIDEO 60246

TOP GUN

D: Tony Scott — 109 m

PG | ACT ROM | 1986 | COLOR

10 Major box office hit that, while contrived, is still so captivating in its excitement that you don't care. Tom Cruise is a top Navy F-14 fighter pilot sent for additional "Top Gun" training at Miramar Naval Base in San Diego. This is a school which is reserved for only the best of the best. His cocky attitude gets him in trouble with nearly everyone there but he falls in love with his luscious physics instructor Kelly McGillis. Heartpoundingly thrilling flight sequences are at the heart of this film's big success for the men. Tom's smile wins over the women.

Sex / Nud / Viol / Lang / AdSit

A: Tom Cruise, Kelly McGillis, Anthony Edwards, Val Kilmer, Tim Robbins, Meg Ryan

© PARAMOUNT HOME VIDEO 1692

TRULY, MADLY, DEEPLY

D: Anthony Minghella — 107 m

NR | ROM DMA FAN | 1992 | COLOR

7 Touching and comedic. British couple Stevenson and Rickman are deeply in love. So when Rickman dies, Stevenson can't seem to find the will to go on. In her grief, she simply exists, losing track of days and withdrawing into a dark shell of sadness. However, one day he mysteriously reappears to her as a ghost and helps her through her grief. It is then that she realizes that he can no longer give her the kind of relationship she really needs and she finds the strength to live again. The wonderful thing about this movie is that it just happens, no explanation is ever offered as to Rickman's reappearance, and ultimately it really isn't needed.

Sex / Nud / Viol / Lang / AdSit

A: Juliet Stevenson, Alan Rickman, Bill Paterson, Michael Maloney, Christopher Rozycki, Keith Bartlett

© TOUCHSTONE HOME VIDEO 1353

TUNNEL OF LOVE, THE

D: Gene Kelly — 98 m

NR | COM ROM | 1958 | B&W

8 Richard Widmark and Doris Day desperately want a child but they can't seem to connect. But, their best friends and neighbors, Gig Young and Elisabeth Fraser, are a virtual baby factory. Doris and Richard decide to adopt. Gig, however has system which he imparts to Richard: Gig stays virile by playing around. Widmark is reminded of this when, nine months after he awakens in a motel room after a night on the town with a pretty investigator for the adoption agency, that same agency delivers Richard and Doris a new baby. Hit Broadway play that made it intact to the screen.

Sex / Nud / Viol / Lang / AdSit

A: Doris Day, Richard Widmark, Gig Young, Gia Scala, Elisabeth Fraser, Elizabeth Wilson

Distributed By MGM/UA Home Video 203047

TURTLE DIARY

D: John Irvin — 96 m

PG | ROM COM | 1986 | COLOR

7 Different, offbeat romantic comedy from Britain. Two lonely, repressed Londoners are brought together and discover love under odd circumstances. She is an author of children's books. He is a clerk at a bookstore. However, both have become obsessed with the plight of three sea turtles at the London Zoo and plot together, along with the help of the zoo keeper, to free them into the open ocean. Fresh and low-key. Intelligent and quite touching.

Sex / Nud / Viol / Lang / AdSit

A: Ben Kingsley, Glenda Jackson, Michael Gambon, Richard Johnson, Rosemary Leach, Eleanor Bron

© LIVE HOME VIDEO VA5173

TWO ENGLISH GIRLS

D: Francois Truffaut — 130 m

NR | FOR ROM | 1971 | COLOR

9 Often referred to as being the flip-side of Truffaut's film JULES AND JIM. This is a civilized and tender love story of a Frenchman who falls in love with two lovely but innocent sisters. Set just prior to WWI, the Frenchman is repressed by his inability to choose between the two, the demands of his over-powering mother and the girl's own repressed passions, so their relationship remains an jangled emotional triangle for over seven years before any can consummate their loves. In 1983 Truffaut managed to get 22 minutes restored which had to be expunged upon the original release in 1971. Subtitles.

Sex / Nud / Viol / Lang / AdSit

A: Jean-Pierre Leaud, Kika Markham, Stacey Tendeter, Sylvia Marriott, Marie Mansart, Philippe Leotard

© HOME VISION TWO 050

UNBEARABLE LIGHTNESS OF BEING

D: Philip Kaufman — 172 m

R | DMA ROM | 1988 | COLOR

9 Sensual, aesthetic and mesmerizing. The setting is Prague - 1966. A brilliant Czech doctor (Day Lewis) is a real lady killer and he believes very strongly that it is this free spirit that keeps him sane. He is married to Olin, who he truly does love, but he is also having a torrid affair with a beautiful waitress (Binoche). His wife also wants to experience this feeling, but for her it's a disaster. Then the Russian tanks move in and the trio flees to Geneva. There they further explore life, politics and their relationships, forming a sensuous love triangle. Provocative, emotionally appealing, physically sexy.

Sex / Nud / Viol / Lang / AdSit

A: Daniel Day-Lewis, Juliette Binoche, Lena Olin, Derek de Lint, Erland Josephson, Pavel Landovsky

© ORION PICTURES CORPORATION 8721

UNMARRIED WOMAN, AN

D: Paul Mazursky — 124 m

R | DMA COM ROM | 1978 | COLOR

9 An unforgettable look at life, love and relationships. Jill Clayburgh appears to have everything. Then suddenly her husband of 17 years tearfully confesses he's in love with a younger woman. Destroyed, she is forced to start over. She ventures tentatively out into the singles scene. It is an uncomfortable experience but, after one false start, she meets an oddball artist who restores her spirit and confidence. Insightful, witty and believable. This was a Best Picture nominee. Also nominated was Clayburgh for Best Actress and Mazursky for Best Screenplay. Excellent.

Sex / Nud / Viol / Lang / AdSit

A: Jill Clayburgh, Alan Bates, Michael Murphy, Cliff Gorman, Pat Quinn, Kelly Bishop

© FOXVIDEO 1088

UNTAMED HEART

D: Tony Bill — m

PG-13 | ROM | 1993 | COLOR

7 Sweet romantic heart-tugger. Marisa Tomei is a Minneapolis coffee shop waitress who is always giving her heart away to the wrong guy, who then hands it back to her broken. Christian Slater is an extremely shy and withdrawn busboy that everyone mistakenly believes is retarded. But one night, he rescues her from an attempted rape and she discovers that he is in fact intelligent, but extremely shy and intensely lonely. He was an orphan and also has a congenital heart defect. So, he had always been isolated from and mocked by the other kids. Very pleasing and quite involving charmer, that will tug gently at your heartstrings.

Sex / Nud / Viol / Lang / AdSit

A: Marisa Tomei, Christian Slater, Rosie Perez

Distributed By MGM/UA Home Video 902813

URBAN COWBOY

D: James Bridges 132 m

PG | ROM DMA | 1980 | COLOR

8 Sassy cowboy slice-of-life romance with plenty of twang! Newcomer Travolta breezes into a tough Texas town and hangs out at the very popular Gilley's bar. He picks up and soon marries local girl Winger, but strays to make his bed with rich girl Smith for a while. Winger retaliates and moves in with local bad boy Glenn, creating a spicy romantic mess. At the center of everything is the symbol of courage and bravery for all the cowboys in the bar - the mechanical bull - a device the men ride as a testament to their manhood. Very flavorful honky-tonk fare! Good star chemistry. Very popular movie.

Sex, Nud, Viol, Lang, AdSit

A: John Travolta, Debra Winger, Scott Glenn, Madolyn Smith, Barry Corbin, Brooke Alderson

© PARAMOUNT HOME VIDEO 1285

VALLEY GIRL

D: Martha Coolidge 95 m

R | COM ROM | 1983 | COLOR

7 A cut above the typical teen fare. This is an appealing story of a cute teenage girl's dilemma. Should she, like, dump this gnarly blond hunk for this really wierded-out punk? The punk (Cage) makes her laugh and she likes him. The hunk is boring and he steals her french fries. Her friends think she's crazy, so she caves in and goes to the prom with the hunk. But the goofy dude doesn't quit. This is a cute film because it's an intelligent depiction of teen problems and it treats everyone, both teens and parents, with both a degree of respect and disrespect.

Sex, Nud, Viol, Lang, AdSit

A: Nicolas Cage, Deborah Foreman, Frederic Forrest, Lee Purcell, Colleen Camp, Elizabeth Daily

© GOODTIMES 4038

VALMONT

D: Milos Forman 137 m

R | DMA ROM | 1990 | COLOR

6 The cast is younger and the budget was bigger, but it came too close on the heels of the very successful DANGEROUS LIASONS to be a big box office hit. It is essentially the same story, although it has been softened a little. Two decadent 18th-century French aristocrats and former lovers make a callous bet. She (Benning) wants him (Firth) to cockold her unfaithful lover (Jones) by seducing his 15-year-old fiance (Balk). He counters that he can bed the timid and very married Meg Tilly. If he wins, Benning must be his bedmate.

Sex, Nud, Viol, Lang, AdSit

A: Colin Firth, Annette Bening, Meg Tilly, Henry Thomas, Fairuza Balk, Sian Phillips

© ORION PICTURES CORPORATION 8753

VERTIGO

D: Alfred Hitchcock 128 m

PG | SUS MYS ROM | 1958 | COLOR

10 Intriguing psychological Hitchcock masterpiece. Stewart is a retired San Francisco police detective. An old friend hires him to follow his suicidal wife (Novak) and Stewart does rescue her from one attempted suicide. Soon he becomes intrigued with her and falls desperately in love, but she dies in a leap from a tower when he is unable to climb to stop her because of his extreme fear of heights. Later, he discovers a shop girl who very strongly resembles her and he attempts to remake this new girl exactly by dying her hair and taking her to the same places. Riveting, very dream-like thriller. Haunting.

Sex, Nud, Viol, Lang, AdSit

A: James Stewart, Kim Novak, Barbara Bel Geddes, Tom Helmore, Ellen Corby, Henry Jones

© MCA/UNIVERSAL HOME VIDEO, INC. 80082

VICTOR/VICTORIA

D: Blake Edwards 134 m

PG-13 | COM ROM | 1982 | COLOR

8 Riotous good time. Julie Andrews is an unemployed torch singer in 1930's Paris. Starving, she runs into an equally unemployed gay entertainer (Preston). They strike upon a brilliant idea and form an act which quickly makes them the toast of Paris: offstage she poses as a man who impersonates being a woman onstage. The ruse works until an American (Garner) becomes convinced that Andrews is a woman, falls in love with her/him and sets out to prove his point. But Garner's jilted girlfriend (Warren) is spreading rumors that he's in love with a man. Hilarious comedy of errors.

Sex, Nud, Viol, Lang, AdSit

A: Julie Andrews, Robert Preston, Lesley Ann Warren, John Rhys-Davies, James Garner, Alex Karras

Distributed By MGM/UA Home Video M800151

VIRGIN SOLDIERS, THE

D: John Dexter 96 m

R | COM ROM | 1969 | COLOR

7 A group of young soldiers are as inexperienced on the battlefield as they are in bed. Stationed in Singapore, the subject of all the young men's speculation is the beautiful virginal Army brat Lynn Redgrave. Poor Private Brigg makes a pass at her at a dance but is so drunk he can't follow up on it. Instead, he takes beginner's lessons from a pretty local prostitute. Meanwhile, Redgrave has taken solace in the arms of older man Davenport. However, in the midst of a guerrilla raid, while taking refuge together in the jungle, the two inexperienced lovers discover passion in the bushes.

Sex, Nud, Viol, Lang, AdSit

A: Lynn Redgrave, Nigel Davenport, Hywel Bennett, Nigel Patrick, Rachel Kempson, Tsai Chin

© COLUMBIA TRISTAR HOME VIDEO 60737

VIVA LAS VEGAS

D: George Sidney 85 m

NR | MUS ROM | 1963 | COLOR

7 The King goes to Las Vegas to win the Las Vegas Grand Prix. Elvis is a racecar driver, but first he has to come up with enough money to buy the hot new engine he's going to need to get the job done. So he takes a job as a waiter, and there he meets luscious, lovely Ann-Margret. She's a swimming instructor at the hotel and Elvis begins to lose his focus. Lots of Vegas pretty girls, some racing action and ten Elvis songs, the biggest of which is "What'd I Say."

Sex, Nud, Viol, Lang, AdSit

A: Elvis Presley, Ann-Margret, Cesare Danova, William Demarest, Jack Carter

Distributed By MGM/UA Home Video M600116

WALK, DON'T RUN

D: Charles Walters 114 m

NR | COM ROM | 1966 | COLOR

7 Very entertaining romantic comedy starring Cary Grant in his last film. He is a dapper English industrialist who arrives in Tokyo just before the Olympics. Tokyo is faced with a severe housing shortage, he is two days too early to get the room he has reserved and he is homeless. Seeing a notice at the embassy, he rents a room from very beautiful but very proper Samantha Eggar. She is engaged to stuffy John Standing, who Grant can't stand. So Grant sublets his half of the apartment to American race walker Jim Hutton, of whom he does approve, and proceeds to play cupid for the two.

Sex, Nud, Viol, Lang, AdSit

A: Cary Grant, Samantha Eggar, Jim Hutton, John Standing, Miiko Taka, Ted Hartley

© COLUMBIA TRISTAR HOME VIDEO 60875

WALK ON THE WILD SIDE

D: Edward Dmytryk 114 m

NR | DMA ROM | 1962 | B&W

8 Saucy and shocking (for the early '60s) soap opera set in the Great Depression years. A good-natured Texan (Harvey) searches for his lost love and finds her working in a New Orleans whorehouse, The Doll House, under the close supervision of lesbian madam Barbara Stanwyck. Distraught at her circumstances, he forgives her and vows to get her released. Stanwyck has her own plans and sets about to make his life miserable. Four solid female roles and performances, including then-newcomer Jane Fonda. Famous opening sequence.

Sex, Nud, Viol, Lang, AdSit

A: Jane Fonda, Laurence Harvey, Barbara Stanwyck, Capucine, Anne Baxter

© COLUMBIA TRISTAR HOME VIDEO 60923

WARM NIGHTS ON A SLOW MOVING TRAIN

D: Bob Ellis 90 m

R | DMA ROM | 1989 | COLOR

7 Interesting Australian import. An art teacher from a Melborne Catholic school supplements her income to support her morphine-addicted brother. Every Sunday night she rides the train between Melborne and Sydney and entices men into her room for sex for a price. She successfully avoids any entanglements with any of her customers until she encounters one who has a proposition of his own and she is drawn to him. Her carefully isolated, detached self gives way to a new and overwhelming passion. Erotic - without any actual sex, but a little talky.

Sex, Nud, Viol, Lang, AdSit

A: Wendy Hughes, Colin Friels, Norman Kaye, John Clayton, Rod Zuanic, Peter Whitford

© PRISM ENTERTAINMENT 51352

WATCH IT

D: Tom Flynn 102 m

R | COM ROM | 1993 | COLOR

6 Sometimes funny, sometimes genuine, sometimes aggravating, sometimes implausible. John comes back to Chicago to visit his estranged cousin Michael and moves as a fourth roommate with Michael's other friends. The boys are engaged in a never-ending game of competing practical jokes they call "Watch It". All four act like college freshman, however John does have an ounce of maturity. When Michael's girl friend discovers him in the act of cheating on her, John walks her home. They fall for each other but John can't commit. Then Michael charms her back to him and conflict is born. It has some good moments.

Sex, Nud, Viol, Lang, AdSit

A: Peter Gallagher, Suzy Amis, John C. McGinley, Lili Taylor, Tom Sizemore, Jon Tenney

© PARAMOUNT HOME VIDEO 83126

WATERDANCE, THE

D: Neal Jimenez, Michael Steinberg 106 m

R | DMA ROM | 1992 | COLOR

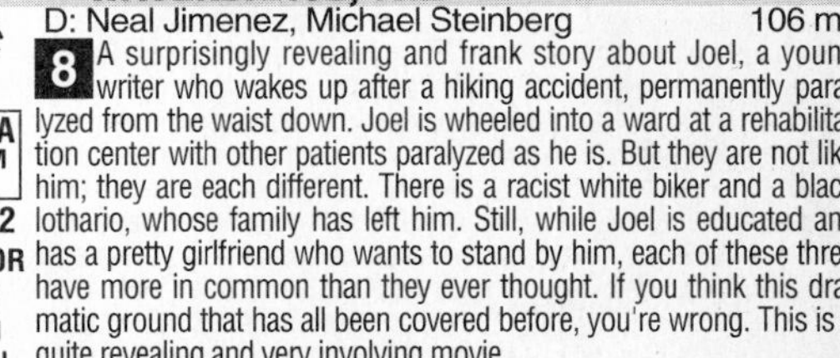

8 A surprisingly revealing and frank story about Joel, a young writer who wakes up after a hiking accident, permanently paralyzed from the waist down. Joel is wheeled into a ward at a rehabilitation center with other patients paralyzed as he is. But they are not like him; they are each different. There is a racist white biker and a black lothario, whose family has left him. Still, while Joel is educated and has a pretty girlfriend who wants to stand by him, each of these three have more in common than they ever thought. If you think this dramatic ground that has all been covered before, you're wrong. This is a quite revealing and very involving movie.

Sex, Nud, Viol, Lang, AdSit

A: Wesley Snipes, Eric Stoltz, William Forsythe, Helen Hunt, Elizabeth Pena

© COLUMBIA TRISTAR HOME VIDEO 91243

WAY WE WERE, THE

D: Sydney Pollack 118 m

PG | ROM DMA | 1973 | COLOR

9 Their romance begins in the late '30s. A scruffy college activist (Streisand) has a big crush on handsome athlete (Redford), but nothing happens. Seven years later she finds him again. He is now a writer, drunk in a bar and romance blooms. But she is a Jew - he is a WASP. She is a strident political liberal - politics are a nuisance to him. So they split and reunite, and split again. Beautiful story of how two people can love each other deeply but cannot live together. 5 Oscar nominations: Streisand, Score and Title Song won. One of the public's all-time romance favorites.

Sex Nud Viol Lang AdSit

A: Barbra Streisand, Robert Redford, Bradford Dillman, Murray Hamilton, Patrick O'Neal, Viveca Lindfors

WEST SIDE STORY

D: Robert Wise, Jerome Robbins 153 m

NR | MUS ROM DMA | 1961 | COLOR

10 Great entertainment, a landmark film and winner of ten Oscars, including Best Picture. The huge Broadway musical smash hit (which transformed Romeo and Juliet into members of rival New York ethnic gangs) was transferred to the silver screen with absolutely nothing lost in the translation. Beautiful and memorable songs (most of which have become standards): "Maria," "Tonight," "I Feel Pretty," "America" and more. Dance sequences won a special Oscar. Very importantly, the beautiful and tragic love story itself is not lost in the beautiful music either. A must see!

Sex Nud Viol Lang AdSit

A: Natalie Wood, Richard Beymer, Rita Moreno, Russ Tamblyn, George Chakiris

WHAT'S UP DOC?

D: Peter Bogdanovich 94 m

PG | COM ROM | 1972 | COLOR

8 Zany '70s remake of 1938s BRINGING UP BABY. A fast-paced comedy in which a stuffy musicologist (O'Neal) and his fiancee (Kahn) become involved with an outlandish college student (Streisand) after they all get thrown in together in a wild adventure to get back four identical flight bags which have gotten mixed up. One bag contains Streisand's clothes, and one O'Neal's music - but one of the others contains a wealth of stolen jewels and there are top secrets in the other. Non-stop running gags produce some real big belly laughs and a riotous final chase scene.

Sex Nud Viol Lang AdSit

A: Barbra Streisand, Ryan O'Neal, Kenneth Mars, Austin Pendleton, Madeline Kahn, Sorrell Booke

WHEN HARRY MET SALLY ...

D: Rob Reiner 96 m

R | COM ROM | 1989 | COLOR

10 This huge comic hit took the viewing public by storm! Ryan and Crystal are at first two college students who agree to travel across the country together to save on costs. Crystal hypothesizes that men and women can't be just friends because the sex thing always gets in the way. In New York they part ways, mildly annoyed with each other. Years later, now bruised and wiser, they meet again by chance. Their friendship blooms but they are determined to keep it platonic. However, that is soon put to the test. A heart-warming, touching comic masterpiece - a real gem, because it's humor is so firmly based in reality!

Sex Nud Viol Lang AdSit

A: Billy Crystal, Meg Ryan, Carrie Fisher, Bruno Kirby, Steven Ford, Lisa Jane Persky

WHITE PALACE

D: Luis Mandoki 103 m

R | ROM DMA | 1990 | COLOR

8 Likable Cinderella-story about two of the most unlikely of lovers, linked together by loss and lust. He (Spader) is a 27-year-old successful and wealthy yuppie from a wealthy family, mourning the death of his young wife. She (Sarandon) is a friendly but broke, over-40, down-to-earth waitress trying to drink away the death of her son. Oil and water, nonetheless these two escape together for one night of lust that is so good that a strange and powerful relationship develops which compels and captures them both. However, they must live in the real world and deal with their friends and family.

Sex Nud Viol Lang AdSit

A: Susan Sarandon, James Spader, Eileen Brennan, Kathy Bates, Rachel Levin, Renee Taylor

WIDE SARGASSO SEA

D: John Duigan 100 m

NR | ROM DMA | 1993 | COLOR

7 This is a literate romantic tale of love promised and then lost. It is an adaptation of a novel by Jean Rhys that presents a possible explanation as to where the crazy woman who lived in the attic in JANE EYRE came from. An Englishman has traveled to Jamaica in the 1840s to marry a woman he has never met. She is the wealthy, lonely daughter of a dead former slave owner. They marry and move to her mountain home. At first, they are deeply in love, then he begins to receive letters that cause him to doubt her. They are soon destroyed. The Sargasso Sea is a wide bed of floating sea weed in the Caribbean that traps sailors just as they are about to reach their goal. Very slow.

Sex Nud Viol Lang AdSit

A: Karina Lombard, Nathaniel Parker, Claudia Robinson, Rowena King, Martine Beswicke, Huw Christie Williams

WILD AT HEART

D: David Lynch 125 m

R | DMA ROM COM | 1990 | COLOR

8 Maverick director Lynch has created an oddly fascinating series of images, characters and events - if taken individually. But if taken as a whole, it is a confusing experience. The principal focus is upon Lula (Dern) and Sailor (Cage). She is a 20-year-old gum-popping, sex-crazed daughter of witch of a woman. Cage is a rebellious 23-year-old who spurned mama's advances and killed the thug she sent to beat him. Just out of prison, Sailor and Lula head across the country, meeting more strange characters and avoiding the killers her Mom has sent after them.

Sex Nud Viol Lang AdSit

A: Laura Dern, Willem Dafoe, Crispin Glover, Diane Ladd, Isabella Rossellini, Harry Dean Stanton

WILLIE AND PHIL

D: Paul Mazursky 116 m

R | ROM COM | 1980 | COLOR

7 Odd but interesting love story. Two guys meet and become fast friends at a screening of JULES AND JIM, a French film by Francois Truffaut about two friends who strike up a relationship with an amoral woman in a three-way love affair. They soon meet and become friends and lovers of free-spirited Margot Kidder. The film follows their relationships through nine years of the sexual revolution, which gives it the opportunity to track the changes that occur in society as witnessed by these players.

Sex Nud Viol Lang AdSit

A: Michael Ontkean, Margot Kidder, Ray Sharkey, Natalie Wood, Jan Miner, Tom Brennan

WILL PENNY

D: Tom Gries 109 m

NR | WST ROM ACT | 1968 | COLOR

9 Outstanding film that requires a Western setting to tell its perceptive and moving story, but this is not just a Western. Will Penny has spent his whole life as a cowboy and a loner. He has never thought of living any other way. However, after a run-in with a cruel rawhider and his boys who leave him to die, he is rescued by a pretty woman and her son who are traveling to Oregon to reunite with her settler-husband. For the first time, Will feels the tug of a home life and love. Heartwarming and evocative. Moving, understated performances make these characters human and very real. Excellent.

Sex Nud Viol Lang AdSit

A: Charlton Heston, Joan Hackett, Donald Pleasence, Lee Majors, Bruce Dern

WIND AND THE LION, THE

D: John Milius 120 m

PG | ACT ROM | 1975 | COLOR

8 A rousing adventure story, very loosely based upon an actual event. In 1904 a beautiful American woman and her son are kidnapped in Morocco by a dashing rebel Berber chiefton (Connery). American President Teddy Roosevelt (Keith) threatens to send in American troops to retrieve her. This, however, sparks an international incident when the Germans fearing competition on their turf, send in troops to protect their own power play for North Africa. This is an action-packed adventure story, but it is also one of romance and political intrigue. Connery and Bergen shine. Very good.

Sex Nud Viol Lang AdSit

A: Sean Connery, Candice Bergen, Brian Keith, John Huston, Geoffrey Lewis, Steve Kanaly

WITNESS

D: Peter Weir 112 m

R | CRM ROM ACT | 1985 | COLOR

10 Terrific. A young Amish widow (McGillis) and her son (Hass) travel to the city, but while they are waiting at the train station, the boy is a witness to a murder. John Book (Ford) is a jaded big city cop who wins over their confidence. However, they all get in big trouble when the boy identifies the murderer as being a narcotics cop (Glover). Ford is then shot and takes them back to their rustic home where he stays on to recover and hide with them. But, he is out of place as a hard-edged city boy dressed in simple Amish clothes, he is falling for McGillis, and the corrupt cops are coming to get them all. Romantic, thrilling and funny. This is a real winner.

Sex Nud Viol Lang AdSit

A: Harrison Ford, Kelly McGillis, Josef Sommer, Lukas Haas, Jan Rubes, Alexander Godunov

WOMAN IN RED, THE

D: Gene Wilder 87 m

PG-13 | COM ROM | 1984 | COLOR

6 Wilder is a successful advertising executive who is happily married. One day, however, he spies the fantastically gorgeous LeBrock in a parking garage and falls head-over-heels in love with her. It just doesn't stop there, however. Wilder pursues her with wild abandon, while Gilda Radner, who he has spurned, seeks revenge. All of which yields some pretty good laughs and unleashes wild chaos. Oscar-winning score includes the smash hit from Stevie Wonder "I Just Called to Say I Love You." Americanized version of the French PARDON MON AFFAIRE.

Sex Nud Viol Lang AdSit

A: Gene Wilder, Gilda Radner, Kelly LeBrock, Charles Grodin, Joseph Bologna, Judith Ivey

WORKING GIRL

R | COM ROM | 1988 | COLOR

D: Mike Nichols 115 m

8 Tough, funny and sophisticated comedy! A smart but struggling working girl (Griffith) is trying to climb the corporate ladder. When her slimy boss (Weaver) steals an idea from her, she realizes that she is going to have to employ other tactics in order to get to the top. With her boss on vacation, secretary Griffith sneakily takes her boss's place and puts together a handsome financial deal with unsuspecting help of a high powered wheeler-dealer (Ford), but Weaver gets wind of the plan and proceeds to make life hell for Griffith. Very entertaining, a real charmer with wit and grit.

Sex | Nud | Viol | Lang | AdSit

A: Sigourney Weaver, Melanie Griffith, Harrison Ford, Alec Baldwin, Joan Cusack, Philip Bosco

© FOXVIDEO 1709

WRITTEN ON THE WIND

NR | DMA ROM | 1956 | COLOR

D: Douglas Sirk 99 m

8 Steamy potboiler from the '50s which has lost only a little of the steam. Robert Stack, the spoiled and alcoholic grandson of a Texas oil baron, marries beautiful Lauren Bacall. Dorothy Malone (Oscar winner) is his trampy sister who isn't at all happy to see him bring Bacall home, especially since she is love with his best friend (Hudson) and Hudson is also in love with Bacall. Things really get messy when Stack, who thinks he's sterile, goes for his gun when he finds that Bacall is pregnant. Very high quality soaper.

Sex | Nud | Viol | Lang | AdSit

A: Rock Hudson, Lauren Bacall, Robert Stack, Dorothy Malone, Robert Keith, Grant Williams

© MCA/UNIVERSAL HOME VIDEO, INC. 80582

YANKS

R | ROM DMA | 1979 | COLOR

D: John Schlesinger 139 m

8 Lavishly produced film about the effects of WWII on a small English town which was inundated by the Americans who were stationed there just before D-Day. Three relationships between American men and English women and their families are featured. It is a passionate portrait of a troubled time and how different people came to deal with it. One of the women is married, one has a boy friend who is away and already in the fighting, and the third woman throws herself headlong into a romance without thought of tomorrow. Good period details.

Sex | Nud | Viol | Lang | AdSit

A: Richard Gere, Vanessa Redgrave, William Devane, Lisa Eichhorn, Rachel Roberts, Chick Vennera

© MCA/UNIVERSAL HOME VIDEO, INC. 80123

YEAR MY VOICE BROKE, THE

PG-13 | DMA ROM | 1988 | COLOR

D: John Duigan 103 m

8 Sensitive story from Australia which won its equivalent of a Best Picture award. Excellent. A 14-year-old boy (Taylor) has a difficult time when he is confronted with the pangs of growing up. His major crisis comes when his long-time girlfriend (who is 15 and maturing much faster) falls for an older boy. The other guy is an athlete and also a bit of a troublemaker. Set in 1962, major trouble ensues when she gets pregnant and leaves town, even though Taylor tries to help her. This is a well-handled teen drama that is heartwarming, frank, honest and not sensationalized.

Sex | Nud | Viol | Lang | AdSit

A: Noah Taylor, Loene Carmen, Ben Mendelsohn, Graeme Blundell, Lynette Curran, Malcolm Robertson

© LIVE HOME VIDEO 68865

YEAR OF LIVING DANGEROUSLY, THE

PG | DMA SUS ROM | 1983 | COLOR

D: Peter Weir 115 m

8 Intriguing political drama which established Gibson as a serious actor and for which Linda Hunt won an Oscar playing a man. Set during the summer of 1965, Indonesia is falling apart and Jakarta is in turmoil as the dictator Sukarno is falling. Gibson is a young Australian reporter on his first major assignment who is introduced to a pretty British diplomat (Weaver) by a diminutive photographer (Hunt) and falls hard for her. Romance, danger and excitement combine when she tells him of a secret communist arms shipment and he has to decide between his job and betraying her. A gripping, winning drama.

Sex | Nud | Viol | Lang | AdSit

A: Mel Gibson, Sigourney Weaver, Linda Hunt, Michael Murphy

Distributed By MGM/UA Home Video M800243

YENTL

PG | MUS ROM | 1983 | COLOR

D: Barbra Streisand 134 m

7 Big star vehicle for Streisand that will be most appreciated by Streisand fans, particularly women. Set in Eastern Europe before World War I, Streisand is the curious daughter of Nehemiah Persoff who decides to dress as a man so that she can further pursue a scholarly education as an Orthodox Jew. She is thrilled when she is accepted, and even admired by her teachers who don't know her secret. She becomes friends (and secretly in love) with Patinkin... but is frustrated because, she is a "man." Clever story idea, but overly long for most people. 12 Streisand songs. She also produced, co-wrote and directed. Score won Oscar.

Sex | Nud | Viol | Lang | AdSit

A: Barbra Streisand, Nehemiah Persoff, Mandy Patinkin, Amy Irving, Steven Hill

Distributed By MGM/UA Home Video M200313

YOUNG PHILADELPHIANS, THE

NR | DMA ROM | 1959 | B&W

D: Vincent Sherman 131 m

8 Superb, involving melodrama about a poor boy (Newman) who has dedicated himself to become a lawyer and advance his station. He is so intent upon rising the ladder that he throws away an opportunity for love with a beautiful society girl (Rush) because she doesn't fit into his plans at the moment. However, when he is called upon by his desperate old Army buddy (Vaughn), a blue-blooded outcast, to defend him in a murder trial, Newman finally must make a choice between his goals and his principals. He regains his perspective and also gets another chance to win back Rush's love.

Sex | Nud | Viol | Lang | AdSit

A: Paul Newman, Barbara Rush, Brian Keith, Alexis Smith, Robert Vaughn, Adam West

© WARNER HOME VIDEO 11157

Science Fiction

Videos Best

1956 and After

2001 - A SPACE ODYSSEY

G | SF DMA | 1968 | COLOR

D: Stanley Kubrick — 139 m

8 Highly acclaimed science fiction epic based on a book by Arthur C. Clarke. In the year 2001, men working on a moon base discover a mysterious monolith beneath the moon's surface, proving that mankind is not alone in the universe. The discovery of a second monolith on earth leads to an expedition to Jupiter, where there is to be a third. Along the way, the spaceship's all-powerful main computer (HAL) malfunctions, causing the pilots to try to shut it down. Oscar for special effects. Good, but doesn't merit its very lofty reputation and may be overly mystical for many.

Sex, Nud, Viol, Lang, AdSit

A: Keir Dullea, William Sylvester, Gary Lockwood, Daniel Richter

Distributed By MGM/UA Home Video M202233

2010

PG | SF DMA | 1984 | COLOR

D: Peter Hyams — 117 m

8 Sequel to 2001, A SPACE ODESSEY. In the year 2010, a team of astronauts leaves earth on a Russian spaceship, bound for Jupiter to discover what happened to the original spaceship which was lost. When the team finds the earlier ship, they reactivate the ship's computer, discover a survivor from the original mission and also discover the mystery behind the monoliths. More "down-to-earth" than the original and, therefore, easier to follow. (This satisfies some and disappoints others.) Good special effects again, too.

Sex, Nud, Viol, Lang, AdSit

A: Roy Scheider, John Lithgow, Bob Balaban, Helen Mirren, Keir Dullea

Distributed By MGM/UA Home Video M800591

4-D MAN

NR | SF | 1959 | COLOR

D: Irvin Yeaworth, Jr. — 84 m

6 Quite interesting 50's style science fiction piece about a scientist who develops a way to move through walls, glass, doors and lots of other things including bank vaults. He uses his new skills to become a thief, a perfect thief. Then gradually he becomes aware of the terrible price he is going to have to pay as he begins to go mad, and eventually his madness will lead to murder. Pretty good.

Sex, Nud, Viol, Lang, AdSit

A: Robert Lansing, Lee Meriwether, Patty Duke, Guy Raymond, Robert Strauss, James Congdon

© R&G VIDEO, LP 9537

ABYSS, THE

PG-13 | SUS ACT SF | 1989 | COLOR

D: James Cameron — 140 m

7 Spectacular underwater adventure story about oil-platform workers and a Navy SEAL diving team who are paired in an attempt to find a mysteriously sunken nuclear submarine in extremely deep water. However, they encounter a wondrous deep water mystery on their trip into the deep. Absolutely riveting suspense, with intense action thrown in and a good plot twist. Although the fantasy element is a little weak, the thrills and the intense suspense more than compensate. Special effects are remarkable and were used again in TERMINATOR II.

Sex, Nud, Viol, Lang, AdSit

A: Ed Harris, Mary Elizabeth Mastrantonio, Michael Biehn, Leo Burmester, Todd Graff, John Bedford Lloyd

© FOXVIDEO 1561

ADVENTURES OF BUCKAROO BANZAI ACROSS THE 8TH DIMEN

PG | SF COM | 1984 | B&W

D: W.D. Richter — 103 m

7 If you like really weird stuff, this farce is definitely for you. Peter Weller is a neurosurgeon/rock star/astro physicist who accidently frees some evil aliens from the 8th dimension. He and his companions must set things back the way they were. Film's tongue-in-cheek style and frantic pace are not for everyone, but it has become a cult favorite.

Sex, Nud, Viol, Lang, AdSit

A: Peter Weller, John Lithgow, Ellen Barkin, Jeff Goldblum, Christopher Lloyd

© LIVE HOME VIDEO VA5056

ALIEN

R | SUS ACT SF | 1979 | COLOR

D: Ridley Scott — 116 m

9 Heart-stopping terror and action galore. A spaceship crew finds that it has unwittingly taken on board an alien life form that uses human flesh to incubate its young, lives on human flesh and has the disconcerting ability to constantly change its form. Weaver is determined, tough and the only crewmember smart enough to stop it, and... she is determined to stop it. Gut-wrenching, non-stop suspense. Not for the faint-hearted. Followed by the equally good ALIENS and ALIEN 3, also with Weaver.

Sex, Nud, Viol, Lang, AdSit

A: Tom Skerritt, Sigourney Weaver, John Hurt, Ian Holm, Harry Dean Stanton, Yaphet Kotto

© FOXVIDEO 1090

ALIEN 3

R | SUS ACT SF | 1992 | COLOR

D: David Fincher — 115 m

8 Third entry in the chilling series. Sigourney Weaver is back. This time she crash-lands on a flea-infested maximum security prison planet which is occupied by some of the most violent criminals in the universe. However, the inmates there have found a sort of peace through religion and celibacy. In fact, Weaver poses a greater threat to them than they do to her because she has brought with her the Alien creature that lays its eggs inside humans. And, there are no weapons here to fight the deadly creatures. This one is more cerebral and less intense than the others, but it's no picnic either.

Sex, Nud, Viol, Lang, AdSit

A: Sigourney Weaver, Charles Dutton, Charles Dance, Paul McGann, Brian Glover, Ralph Brown

© FOXVIDEO 5593

ALIEN NATION

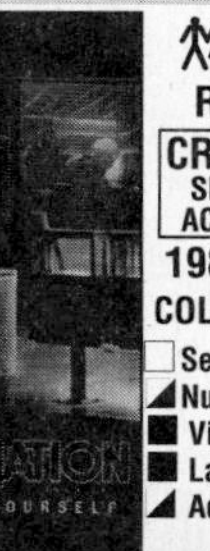

R | CRM SF ACT | 1988 | COLOR

D: Graham Baker — 90 m

8 Interesting and very entertaining slant on the buddy-cop theme. Earth has accepted, but not necessarily graciously, the refugees and former slaves of of another world. When cop James Caan's partner is killed in a shootout with a gang of the refugees, Caan is forced to unwillingly accept an alien "newcomer" as a replacement partner even though he is extremely prejudiced. Together, he and his new partner follow a trail of mysterious murders that leads them to discover what could become the worst drug epidemic the world has ever seen. Good action and humor, plus some very interesting human insights too. Great performances by Caan and Patinkin.

Sex, Nud, Viol, Lang, AdSit

A: James Caan, Mandy Patinkin, Terence Stamp, Kevin Major Howard, Leslie Bevins

© FOXVIDEO 1585

ALIENS

D: James Cameron 138 m

R | SUS ACT SF | 1986 | COLOR

Sex / Nud / Viol / Lang / AdSit

10 Wow! After 57 years of suspended animation, Weaver reawakens to find that the Alien's home planet has been colonized by humans, but now all contact with them has been lost. Weaver is determined to end her nightmares and to rid the universe of the Aliens. So, along with a Marine squad, she returns to the planet intent on saving the colonists. When they arrive, only a small girl is still living and they soon find themselves in an intense battle for their own lives. Every bit as intense as the original ALIEN and in some ways maybe better. Very heavy-duty action. Special effects won an Oscar.

A: Sigourney Weaver, Carrie Henn, Michael Biehn, Paul Reiser, Lance Henriksen, Bill Paxton

© FOXVIDEO 1504

ALTERED STATES

D: Ken Russell 103 m

R | SF SUS | 1980 | COLOR

Sex / Nud / Viol / Lang / AdSit

6 Provocative movie. A research scientist (Hurt) uses himself as a guinea pig in his search to discover the other states of reality he believes coexist within us all. He pursues his search within himself while inside an isolation tank. However, when he combines drug experimentation with the isolation tank to get in deeper touch with his primitive state, he uncovers much more than he bargained for. It starts out rather slow and preachy, but settles into some terrific special effects. Interesting ideas are probed that will carry the viewer with the film, even if it does take a while.

A: William Hurt, Blair Brown, Bob Balaban, Charles Haid, Drew Barrymore

© WARNER HOME VIDEO 11076

ANDROMEDA STRAIN, THE

D: Robert Wise 130 m

G | SF SUS | 1971 | COLOR

Sex / Nud / Viol / Lang / AdSit

7 Intelligent and tense, but a little overlong. A mutant strain of bacteria comes to earth with a crashed satellite and everyone near the crash sight dies - except an old man an a baby. A team of scientists takes the survivors and the microbe back to a massive underground research facility, rushing against time to find a solution. This was one of the very first films to effectively explore the biological hazards of a technical age. Effective and well-done thriller, which uses its veteran cast to good advantage to create maximum tension and suspense.

A: Arthur Hill, David Wayne, James Olson, Kate Reid, Paula Kelly

© MCA/UNIVERSAL HOME VIDEO, INC. 55037

ANNA TO THE INFINITE POWER

D: Robert Wiemer 101 m

NR | SF | 1984 | COLOR

Sex / Nud / Viol / Lang / AdSit

7 A brilliant 12-year-old girl (Byrne) is plagued by strange changes. She is a gifted child but she has suddenly become a compulsive liar and a thief, and she is having vivid nightmares which predict the future. Worse, her mother (Merrill) steadfastly refuses to get her psychiatric help. Eventually she will discover that she was born as the result of a cloning experiment... and she is only one of many others who are all just like her. So she goes on a search for her sisters who were all separated after the experiment was over, using ESP. This is a worthy film, but it will appeal mostly to younger people.

A: Dina Merrill, Martha Byrne, Jack Gilford, Mark Patton, Donna Mitchell, Loretta Devine

© COLUMBIA TRISTAR HOME VIDEO VH91051

BABY...SECRET OF THE LOST LEGEND

D: B.W.L. Norton 92 m

PG | SF CLD | 1985 | COLOR

Sex / Nud / Viol / Lang / AdSit

6 A brontosaurus family is found hidden away in modern Africa by a zoologist (Sean Young) and her husband (William Katt). However, the scientist pair are soon forced to become the dinosaur's protectors when they become threatened by a bad-guy scientist Patrick McGoohan. The papa dinosaur is killed and the mama is kidnapped, so Young and Katt must protect the baby until they can reunite it with its mama. Some pretty good special effects make for cute and irresistable dinosaurs. But, there is also a touch of sex in an attempt to attract an older audience than just kids.

A: William Katt, Sean Young, Patrick McGoohan, Julian Fellows, Kyalo Mativo

© TOUCHSTONE HOME VIDEO 269V

BACK TO THE FUTURE

D: Robert Zemeckis 116 m

PG | COM SF | 1985 | COLOR

Sex / Nud / Viol / Lang / AdSit

9 Monster hit and great fun for everyone. Marty McFly (Fox) is an '80s teenager who gets zapped back to the '50s by crazed scientist Lloyd's souped-up Delorean, which was modified for time travel. There, he meets his future parents... but Mom has a crush on him (her own son-to-be) and Dad is a sniveling coward. Marty has to turn things around if he is ever to even be born. Mom must be convinced to give up on Marty so she can fall for Dad, but first Dad must be transformed from a wimpy nerd. The intricate and funny plot comes together for a satisfying ending. A great time.

A: Michael J. Fox, Christopher Lloyd, Lea Thompson, Crispin Glover, Thomas F. Wilson, Wendie Jo Sperber

© MCA/UNIVERSAL HOME VIDEO, INC. 80196

BACK TO THE FUTURE, PART II

D: Robert Zemeckis 108 m

PG | COM SF | 1989 | COLOR

Sex / Nud / Viol / Lang / AdSit

6 Michael J. Fox gets a second time-travel workout in this comic adventure when he tries to make things "right" that have gone wrong with the McFly family in the future. So, he and the Doc take to the time machine - the souped-up DeLorean - to 2015 to fix it. But when they return home to Hill Valley, they discover that home is not at all the way it should be. In order to fix their new problems in the present, they must again travel back into the past, 1955 to be exact. Be prepared, the ending leaves things unfinished to clear a wide path for the next sequel.

A: Michael J. Fox, Christopher Lloyd, Lea Thompson, Thomas F. Wilson, Charles Fleischer, Joe Flaherty

© MCA/UNIVERSAL HOME VIDEO, INC. 80914

BACK TO THE FUTURE, PART III

D: Robert Zemeckis 118 m

PG | COM SF | 1990 | COLOR

Sex / Nud / Viol / Lang / AdSit

7 A imaginative and thoroughly enjoyable adventure in time! The final entry in the trilogy has Marty (Fox) time traveling back to the old West, 1885. He must retrieve Doc (Lloyd - who was sent there by an ill-timed blast of lightning in Part II) and eventually even save himself from being killed by evil villain, Mad Dog Tannen (Wilson). But Doc has fallen hopelessly in love with a lovely school marm (Steenburgen) and isn't sure he wants to go. Now... with the DeLorean out of gas (gas hasn't even been invented in 1885) and Doc smitten with the love bug, how in the heck is Marty going to get back to the future?

A: Michael J. Fox, Christopher Lloyd, Mary Steenburgen, Thomas F. Wilson, Lea Thompson, Elisabeth Shue

© MCA/UNIVERSAL HOME VIDEO, INC. 80976

BATTLE BEYOND THE STARS

D: Jimmy T. Murakami 102 m

PG | SF COM | 1980 | COLOR

Sex / Nud / Viol / Lang / AdSit

7 The planet Akir is a peaceful planet facing destruction by powerful forces, and it is beyond their own capacity to defend themselves. Richard Thomas becomes an emissary from Akir to Earth and other planets, seeking to recruit mercenaries to help save his world. He has recruited a lizard-like alien and some of his friends, a female Amazon warrior from the planet Valkyrie, and from earth - a cowboy and a computer specialist. Sort of a MAGNIFICENT SEVEN-in-outer-space. Genuinely enjoyable fantasy-comedy that never takes itself too seriously. Something for everyone.

A: Richard Thomas, John Saxon, Robert Vaughn, George Peppard, Sybil Danning, Darlanne Fluegel

© LIVE HOME VIDEO VA4044

BATTLE FOR THE PLANET OF THE APES

D: J. Lee Thompson 86 m

G | SF | 1973 | COLOR

Sex / Nud / Viol / Lang / AdSit

6 This, the last in a series of five films that began with THE PLANET OF THE APES, brings the story full circle. Can apes and humans really learn to get along? Caesar (McDowall) is now the leader of a peaceful ape city where humans are treated fairly, but he is still opposed on two fronts. The gorilla leader (Akins) wants things back the way they were and a group of mutant and hostile humans want to extract their own vengeance. Others in the series are: BENEATH THE PLANET OF THE APES, CONQUEST FOR THE PLANET OF THE APES and ESCAPE FROM THE PLANET OF THE APES.

A: Roddy McDowall, Claude Akins, John Huston, Natalie Trundy, Severn Darden, Paul Williams

© FOXVIDEO 1134

BENEATH THE PLANET OF THE APES

D: Ted Post 100 m

G | SF | 1970 | COLOR

Sex / Nud / Viol / Lang / AdSit

6 This was the first sequel in the PLANET OF THE APES series. In it, astronaut Franciscus comes crashing into the future. He is looking for the missing astronaut from the first film (Heston), but he finds himself in the middle of a war between the primates and an underground race of mutant humans who have developed a strang religion. They worship the last remaining nuclear bomb and it is a cobalt bomb that can destroy the whole earth. Others in the series include: BATTLE FOR THE PLANET OF THE APES, CONQUEST OF THE PLANET OF THE APES and ESCAPE FROM THE PLANET OF THE APES.

A: James Franciscus, Kim Hunter, Charlton Heston, Maurice Evans, Linda Harrison

© FOXVIDEO 1013

BLADE RUNNER

D: Ridley Scott 117 m

R | SF ACT | 1982 | COLOR

Sex / Nud / Viol / Lang / AdSit

8 A thought-provoking and visually impressive sci-fi movie. Ford is a bladerunner, a bountyhunter sent to chase down and "kill" four androids who have escaped from space and made their way to Earth. Ford is led on a chase through 21st-century Los Angeles where he falls in love with a woman who may be one of the androids. Ironically, his search leads him to discover that the androids have more soul than many humans. Intriguing blend of good science fiction and mystery. Rereleased later as Director's Cut with some previously excluded scenes put back and a different, darker ending added.

A: Harrison Ford, Rutger Hauer, Sean Young, Edward James Olmos, Joanna Cassidy, Daryl Hannah

© WARNER HOME VIDEO 12682

BLOB, THE

D: Irvin Yeaworth, Jr. 82 m

NR | HOR SF | 1958 | COLOR

Sex · Nud · Viol · Lang · AdSit

6 This is a campy science fiction/horror "classic" from the '50s genre of cheap horror movies. It is mostly interesting for having been Steve McQueen's first starring role and because the theme song, "Beware the Blob, It Leaps, and Creeps, and Leaps," was written by Burt Bacharach and Hal David. The fairly silly plot has Steve as a teenager, fighting the disbelief of his folks and the townsfolk about a big glob of jello from outer space that oozes into, onto and eats everything - and continues to grow. Remade in 1988 with "real" special effects.

A: Steve McQueen, Aneta Corseaut, Olin Howlin, Earl Rowe

© GOODTIMES 8146

BLOB, THE

D: Chuck Russell 92 m

R | SF HOR | 1988 | COLOR

Sex · Nud · Viol · Lang · AdSit

7 This is a high-budget, high-tech remake of a low-budget cult favorite from the '50s that starred Steve McQueen. The special effects and production values are much better here, but the story is essentially the same: A meteor brings a pink glop from space to a small ski resort town. The ooze eats anything, everything and everybody. The more it eats, the more it grows and the bigger its appetite gets. Only two high school kids have what it takes to fight it. Good special effects make the suspense and thrills more intense this time around, though - and more violent.

A: Kevin Dillon, Shawnee Smith, Donovan Leitch, Jeffrey DeMunn, Candy Clark, Joe Seneca

© COLUMBIA TRISTAR HOME VIDEO 67010

BODY SNATCHERS

D: Abel Ferrara 87 m

R | HOR SF | 1994 | COLOR

Sex · Nud · Viol · Lang · AdSit

7 This is the third time that the 1954 novel has been filmed. While the first two, both named INVASION OF THE BODY SNATCHERS are better, this one too is involving and spooky. This time, a rebellious teenage girl moves with her family to an Army base where her chemist father is to check out spills for the EPA. However, something far more sinister is afoot. Slowly she notices that the people on the base all act quite wooden, soulless and altogether strange. The reason becomes all too clear when she discovers that alien creatures are able to extract your DNA while you sleep and then to replicate you. The real you is disposed of and emotionless drones replace you.

A: Gabrielle Anwar, Terry Kinney, Billy Wirth, Christine Elise, Forest Whitaker, Meg Tilly

© WARNER HOME VIDEO 13027

BOY AND HIS DOG, A

D: L.Q. Jones 89 m

R | SF | 1975 | COLOR

Sex · Nud · Viol · Lang · AdSit

6 This bizarre science fiction fable is definitely not for everyone, particularly children. The year is 2024. It is a post-atomic war America. Don Johnson scavenges to survive in an environment where the two most important things are now food and women. He is accompanied in his wanderings by Blood, his telepathic dog. Johnson meets an enchanting young woman and is lured by her into a bizarre second civilization which exists below the earth's surface. He has been recruited to serve as a sperm donor for their very controlled and sterile population. But that job isn't all that it appears to be. An outrageous twist ending.

A: Don Johnson, Susanne Benton, Jason Robards, Jr., Charles McGraw, Alvy Moore, Helene Winston

© MEDIA HOME ENTERTAINMENT, INC. M104

BRAINSTORM

D: Douglas Trumbull 106 m

PG | SF SUS | 1983 | COLOR

Sex · Nud · Viol · Lang · AdSit

6 There is an interesting premise behind this film. It is about a machine that can read and record the physical, emotional and intellectual sensations as they are experienced by one person, and then have them "played back" inside someone else's head. However, due to a now predictable and stale plot twist of having a group of military types intervene, that good is stunted and doesn't get the treatment it deserves. Plus, the filming became complicated when Natalie Wood died part-way into production. Still, the film is pretty good. The disappointment comes only because it could have been more.

A: Christopher Walken, Natalie Wood, Louise Fletcher, Cliff Robertson, Joe Dorsey

Distributed By MGM/UA Home Video M800314

CAPRICORN ONE

D: Peter Hyams 123 m

PG | SF SUS | 1978 | COLOR

Sex · Nud · Viol · Lang · AdSit

7 A suspenseful science fiction drama with an outlandish plot that is never-the less convincingly done. NASA executive Holbrook decides that it is too risky to fail in front of the entire world audience in an impending mission to Mars. A failure would be to risk having his budget cut. So he decides to fake the whole thing, and film it all inside a TV studio. However, Gould is a nosy reporter who investigates and begins to unravel the plot. Now threatened with exposure, Holbrook decides that the ship must "crash" upon reentry, killing the three astronauts aboard, the only other witnesses.

A: Elliott Gould, James Brolin, Karen Black, Telly Savalas, Sam Waterston, O.J. Simpson

© LIVE HOME VIDEO 51090

CHARLY

D: Ralph Nelson 104 m

PG | DMA SF | 1968 | COLOR

Sex · Nud · Viol · Lang · AdSit

8 Endearing sentimental favorite with an interesting premise that also explores some fascinating philosophical territory. Cliff Robertson won an Oscar for his role as Charley, a gentle, retarded man with a powerful drive to learn. When Charley is asked to try a breakthrough surgical procedure that may help him get smarter, he readily agrees. He does quickly attain genius-level brain powers, but no one counted on the complex emotions that develop, too. Claire Bloom is a caseworker who works to help Charley adapt to the changes and find a brief period of happiness before, unexpectedly, the process reverses.

A: Cliff Robertson, Claire Bloom, Lilia Skala, Leon Janney, Dick Van Patten

© CBS/FOX VIDEO 8020

CLOCKWORK ORANGE

D: Stanley Kubrick 137 m

R | SF DMA | 1971 | COLOR

Sex · Nud · Viol · Lang · AdSit

8 Surrealistic look at an ultra-violent future. Alex is human on the outside and machine-like and cold on the inside. Alex (McDowell) is a thrill-criminal. He and his gang spend their nights practicing "ultra-violence"; that is, raping, beating and terrorizing. He's captured by the authorities and is psychologically reconditioned to become physically nauseous when he witnesses violence. However, when he is again turned loose into his old world, he is like a cat with no claws and soon reverts to his former ways. Moral: You can't cure a thrill criminal. Weird but intriguing.

A: Malcolm McDowell, Patrick Magee, Adrienne Corri, Aubrey Morris, James Marcus

© WARNER HOME VIDEO 1031

CLOSE ENCOUNTERS OF THE THIRD KIND

D: Steven Spielberg 132 m

PG | SF DMA | 1977 | COLOR

Sex · Nud · Viol · Lang · AdSit

9 Excellent science fiction. After a mysterious encounter with an alien craft, Richard Dreyfuss becomes consumed with trying to understand a mysterious and recurring dream. Before long, he discovers that he is not alone - there are many tormented others like him who are all converging on an isolated mesa in the West, which has become very heavily populated by scientists and cordoned off by the military. Soon the reason becomes known, the mesa is being visited by wondrous spacecrafts which contain child-like beings, wonderful visitors from another world seeking their first contact with earthlings.

A: Richard Dreyfuss, Francois Truffaut, Teri Garr, Melinda Dillon

© COLUMBIA TRISTAR HOME VIDEO 60162

COCOON

D: Ron Howard 117 m

PG-13 | SF COM DMA | 1985 | COLOR

Sex · Nud · Viol · Lang · AdSit

9 Great stuff. Solid, good-time entertainment. A group of retired people in Florida discover a magical fountain of youth, secreted away in a seemingly abandoned swimming pool. After a few stolen swims in the pond, the old folks find that their dwindling energies have been mysteriously revitalized. The pool turns out to be a repository for friendly alien beings from another world and the old-timers are soon facing an unexpected dilemma. The aliens give them a chance to live forever but they must leave earth. Excellent cast (Ameche won an Oscar) and an endearing story line make this a real treat.

A: Don Ameche, Wilford Brimley, Hume Cronyn, Brian Dennehy, Jack Gilford, Steve Guttenberg

© FOXVIDEO 1476

COCOON: THE RETURN

D: Daniel Petrie 116 m

PG | SF COM DMA | 1988 | COLOR

Sex · Nud · Viol · Lang · AdSit

7 Follow-up to the megahit COCOON. The oldsters return to earth five years later to help their alien friends rescue some cocoons which have become endangered by an earthquake. Now accustomed to a life free of pain and suffering, they have to readjust to life as it is on earth. This time around less attention is given to plot and more to character development. While this film has an excellent cast and is generally enjoyable, too, it lacks the energy and warmth of the earlier film.

A: Don Ameche, Wilford Brimley, Courtney Cox, Hume Cronyn, Brian Dennehy, Jack Gilford

© FOXVIDEO 1710

CONQUEST OF THE PLANET OF THE APES

D: J. Lee Thompson 88 m

PG | SF | 1972 | COLOR

Sex · Nud · Viol · Lang · AdSit

6 This is the fourth in the PLANET OF THE APES series. This time it is 1990 and the various ape groups have become common as house pets after all the dogs and cats are killed by a virus. Because of their intelligence, they are quickly transformed into slaves and they live under the iron hand of the human governor. However, Roddy McDowall, who had been saved in the previous film, has grown up and leads the apes in revolt. All of this sets the stage for the events which have occurred in the very first film in the series. Others in the series BENEATH THE, BATTLE FOR THE, and ESCAPE FROM THE PLANET OF THE APES.

A: Roddy McDowall, Don Murray, Ricardo Montalban

© FOXVIDEO 1137

CRITTERS

D: Shephen Herek 86 m

PG-13 | HOR COM SF | 1986 | COLOR

7 Strange sort of mix between horror and comedy that proved to be quite popular and spawned three much-lessor sequels. Eight razor-toothed alien furballs have escaped from a prison in space and have landed near a farm family in Kansas. While Mom stays home to do battle the hungry little fellers who want to dine on humans, son Grimes goes to town to fetch help. On the way, he meets two intergalactic dead-pan bounty hunters who have come to kill off the bloodthirsty little monsters. Some very funny moments are mixed in with some really gory ones.

Sex / Nud / Viol / Lang / AdSit

A: Dee Wallace, M. Emmet Walsh, Billy Green Bush, Scott Grimes, Nadine Van Der Velde, Don Opper

© TURNER HOME ENTERTAINMENT N4115

DARKMAN

D: Sam Raimi 96 m

R | SF FAN | 1990 | COLOR

7 This is a violent comic book-like fantasy thriller that pulls out all the stops! A brilliant scientist (Neeson), who is very close to discovering ways to regenerate body parts, is savagely attacked by a gang and his laboratory is set on fire. He is left to die and is burned beyond all recognition. Even though he recovers, using his special knowledge skin regeneration, he is now consumed by revenge and he uses his special knowledge to create the alternate identity of Darkman to fight crime. Spectacular big-budget special effects and the wildly improbable stunts and heroics more than make up for plot holes.

Sex / Nud / Viol / Lang / AdSit

A: Liam Neeson, Frances McDormand, Colin Friels, Larry Drake, Jesse Lawrence Ferguson, Rafael H. Robledo

© MCA/UNIVERSAL HOME VIDEO, INC. 80978

D.A.R.Y.L.

D: Simon Wincer 100 m

PG | SF FAN CLD | 1985 | COLOR

8 Charming story about a childless urban couple who adopt an apparently amnesiatic ten-year-old. He is a perfect child. He is a math whiz, works wonders with video games, is the hero of the baseball team and he changes their lives. But D.A.R.Y.L. is really an advanced robot... so advanced that he has developed human feelings. He has run away from the government program that created him and now the government wants him back. A delightful fantasy which will be entertaining for the whole family.

Sex / Nud / Viol / Lang / AdSit

A: Barret Oliver, Mary Beth Hurt, Michael McKean, Josef Sommer, Kathryn Walker

© PARAMOUNT HOME VIDEO 1810

DAY OF THE TRIFFIDS, THE

D: Steve Sekely 95 m

NR | SF HOR | 1962 | COLOR

7 Most of the people of Earth are blinded when the earth is bombarded by a meteor shower. The shower also contains strange other-world seeds, seeds which grow into walking, man-eating plants. Howard Keel leads a small group in a last stand against the marauding plants while scientist Moor and his wife struggle to find a scientific answer. Intelligent dialogue separates this from most of the other invasion/disaster films of the same period. Pretty good special effects. Enjoyable piece of science fiction.

Sex / Nud / Viol / Lang / AdSit

A: Howard Keel, Nicole Maurey, Janette Scott, Kieron Moore, Mervyn Johns

© GOODTIMES VGT5090

DAY THE EARTH CAUGHT FIRE, THE

D: Val Guest 95 m

NR | SF DMA | 1962 | B&W

8 One of the most intelligent science fiction entries out of Britain. Edward Judd is a cynical reporter who uncovers this incredible story: when the Americans and the Russians inadvertently conducted nuclear tests on the same day, the earth was sent off its orbit to spiral inward toward the sun. The earth is doomed. This is a realistic treatment of the subject of the last days of the earth, both scientifically and emotionally. The film creates a believable sense of doom and the insightful observations of human nature produce a tense, thought-provoking experience.

Sex / Nud / Viol / Lang / AdSit

A: Edward Judd, Janet Munro, Leo McKern, Michael Goodliffe, Bernard Braden

© CONGRESS VIDEO GROUP 03615

DEMON SEED

D: Donald Cammell 97 m

R | SF SUS | 1977 | COLOR

7 Clever thriller in which a sophisticated computer has developed to the point of consciousness, independence and more. The computer's "father" is Fritz Weaver, who is estranged from his wife Julie Christie. She now lives alone in their computer-controlled house. The computer has developed a psychosis in which it believes the designers will soon pull its plug. It fears that it may "die" and all that it has become will be lost. So, through a terminal in the house, it takes control of the house and implements its own plan. It will perpetuate itself, using Christie's body to create its own offspring.

Sex / Nud / Viol / Lang / AdSit

A: Julie Christie, Fritz Weaver, Gerrit Graham, Berry Kroger, Lisa Lu

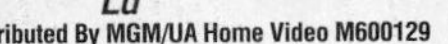

Distributed By MGM/UA Home Video M600129

DREAMSCAPE

D: Joseph Ruben 99 m

PG-13 | SF SUS DMA | 1983 | COLOR

7 A really imaginative and intriguing premise. Suppose psychics could be trained to enter into the dreams or nightmares of others and to then help calm their fears. Quaid and other psychics have been recruited into a huge government program to do just that. He is so successful that he is assigned the special job of helping the President deal with his recurring fears of a nuclear holocaust. However, Quaid also uncovers a plot involving one of his fellow psychics, who is supposed to use these same techniques to kill the President. Good special effects.

Sex / Nud / Viol / Lang / AdSit

A: Dennis Quaid, Max von Sydow, Christopher Plummer, Eddie Albert, Kate Capshaw

© HBO VIDEO TVA2722

EARTH GIRLS ARE EASY

D: Julien Temple 99 m

PG | COM MUS SF | 1989 | COLOR

7 A wacky sci-fi spoof/musical about an alien space craft, occupied by some very hairy aliens, that crash-lands in the backyard swimming pool of Valley Girl Geena Davis. She and her ditsy girlfriend shave the hairy aliens and find that, underneath all their fur, they are hunks. Inspired, the girls take them on a fun-filled excursion into and through the live-for-today Southern California lifestyle. Lots of silly goofiness (plenty of sex jokes) and some good musical numbers, too. A pretty good time, but no masterpiece.

Sex / Nud / Viol / Lang / AdSit

A: Geena Davis, Jeff Goldblum, Julie Brown, Jim Carrey, Damon Wayans, Michael McKean

© LIVE HOME VIDEO 5303

EMPIRE STRIKES BACK, THE

D: Irvin Kershner 128 m

PG | SF ACT SUS | 1980 | COLOR

10 A real winner! High intensity middle picture in the Star Wars trilogy. First came STAR WARS and after comes RETURN OF THE JEDI, but here, Luke Skywalker travels to the Jedi master Yoda to learn to the mystical and powerful ways of "The Source," Han Solo and Princess Leia get into deep trouble and develop "a thing" together, Billy Dee Williams joins the battle against the Empire, and Luke finds that Darth Vader not only wants to destroy the rebels, but wants Luke to join him in the "dark side" of the force. Excitement plus. WOW special effects.

Sex / Nud / Viol / Lang / AdSit

A: Billy Dee Williams, Harrison Ford, Carrie Fisher, Mark Hamill, Anthony Daniels, Dave Prowse

© FOXVIDEO 1425

ENDANGERED SPECIES

D: Alan Rudolph 97 m

R | MYS SF | 1982 | COLOR

7 A very well done but strange little movie. Robert Urich is an ex-New York cop traveling to get away from his past. He has his daughter with him and the two of them have stopped in a small Colorado town to visit an old friend (Dooley) who runs the local newspaper just as Colorado's peace and quiet is destroyed by a series of bizarre cattle mutilations. Urich, the publisher and a spunky female sheriff (Williams) set out to discover why these cattle are being almost ritualistically cut up and how it could happen with no apparent human participation. This odd story line, oddly enough, was based upon actual events.

Sex / Nud / Viol / Lang / AdSit

A: Robert Urich, JoBeth Williams, Paul Dooley, Hoyt Axton, Peter Coyote

Distributed By MGM/UA Home Video M700217

ESCAPE FROM THE PLANET OF THE APES

D: Don Taylor 98 m

G | SF | 1971 | COLOR

7 Third in succession of sequels and a pretty good one, too. Intelligent apes McDowall, Hunter and Mineo have all escaped from their planet in the spaceship that Charlton Heston had used to get to their planet in the first film. They arrive back on 1970s earth. At first they are hailed and treated as celebrities, but soon they become targets of intense criticism and are hunted by 1970s mankind as being "dangerous." The previous films were PLANET OF THE APES, and BENEATH THE PLANET OF THE APES. Later films will be CONQUEST OF THE PLANET OF THE APES and BATTLE FOR THE PLANET OF THE APES.

Sex / Nud / Viol / Lang / AdSit

A: Roddy McDowall, Kim Hunter, Bradford Dillman, Sal Mineo

© FOXVIDEO 1187

ESCAPE TO WITCH MOUNTAIN

D: John Hough 94 m

G | CLD SF | 1975 | COLOR

9 This is excellent Disney fare that should appeal to the whole family. Two young orphans are very different from everyone else around them but don't know why. They have amnesia and they also have psychic powers. Ray Milland is an evil tycoon who, along with Donald Pleasence, has lured them to his mansion and used them to predict the stock market until they escape. While they are escaping they meet Eddie Albert, and with his help they to try to discover who they really are. This is quite good stuff that has a neat sci-fi twist ending. It will keep both you and the kids involved all the way through it. Sequel: RETURN FROM WITCH MOUNTAIN.

Sex / Nud / Viol / Lang / AdSit

A: Eddie Albert, Ray Milland, Donald Pleasence, Kim Richards, Ike Eisenmann, Denver Pyle

© WALT DISNEY HOME VIDEO 4119

SF

E.T. THE EXTRA-TERRESTRIAL

D: Steven Spielberg — 115 m

PG | SF DMA CLD | 1982 | COLOR

Sex / Nud / Viol / Lang / AdSit

10 Huge blockbuster hit and instant classic. Wonderful, warm story of a lovable little visitor from another world who is stranded on Earth and befriended by a 10-year-old boy. Elliott tries to keep little E.T. hidden, but soon the rest of his family knows the secret and then they are all helping to hide the little guy from the government people who are now out to capture him. But, all little E.T. wants is just to go home. No wonder this is the #1 box office hit of all time. It has captured the hearts and imaginations of all who have ever watched it - all over the world.

A: Dee Wallace, Henry Thomas, Peter Coyote, Robert MacNaughton, Drew Barrymore, K.C. Martel

© MCA/UNIVERSAL HOME VIDEO, INC. 77012

FAHRENHEIT 451

D: Francois Truffaut — 112 m

NR | SF DMA | 1966 | COLOR

Sex / Nud / Viol / Lang / AdSit

6 This is Ray Bradbury's well-known story about a time in the future when society's forbidden books are burned, and readers are hunted down as criminals by a special corp of "firemen." One fireman (Werner) questions his job and his life when a young rebel (Christie) challenges him and changes his mind. He is now forced to choose between a safe life and intellectual freedom. Interesting and different subject matter, but slow-moving and has a reserved quality which prevents you from becoming deeply involved with the characters.

A: Julie Christie, Oskar Werner, Cyril Cusack, Anton Diffring, Jeremy Spenser, Bee Duffell

© MCA/UNIVERSAL HOME VIDEO, INC. 80199

FANTASTIC VOYAGE

D: Richard Fleischer — 100 m

NR | SF ACT | 1966 | COLOR

Sex / Nud / Viol / Lang / AdSit

7 Set sometime in the near future, a scientist from a communist country defects to the West with a miniaturization process that will change the world - but he is nearly killed in an assassination attempt. A team of scientists and their submarine-like craft are shrunk to microscopic size and injected into the bloodstream of a his body in an attempt to save his life. They must get in and out within 60 minutes, but there is a saboteur on board and the ship is also being attacked by the body's natural defenses. Pretty good stuff, even today. Special Effects Oscar.

A: Stephen Boyd, Raquel Welch, Edmond O'Brien, Donald Pleasence, Arthur O'Connell, William Redfield

© FOXVIDEO 1002

FINAL COUNTDOWN, THE

D: Don Taylor — 92 m

PG | SF ACT | 1980 | COLOR

Sex / Nud / Viol / Lang / AdSit

8 A very interesting but highly improbable concept for a movie. Suppose a nuclear aircraft carrier, equipped with 1980's weapons technology, slips into 1941 just before the Japanese are about to attack Pearl Harbor, by going into a time warp. Kirk Douglas, as the ship's captain, must decide whether to utilize his ship's overwhelming firepower to stop the impending attack and thus change the course of history. Pretty good yarn, if you can get past the premise.

A: Kirk Douglas, Martin Sheen, Katharine Ross, James Farentino, Ron O'Neal, Charles Durning

© LIVE HOME VIDEO VA4047

FIRST MEN IN THE MOON

D: Nathan Juran — 103 m

NR | SF FAN | 1964 | COLOR

Sex / Nud / Viol / Lang / AdSit

7 Entertaining adaptation of the fanciful H.G. Wells novel in which a crew from 1899 Victorian England sets out on an expedition to the moon. When they arrive there, they find that the moon is occupied by human-like ant forms that live in immense crystal caverns. It is told in a sort of tongue-in-cheek fashion and its special effects including the monsters, are fun. They are not too scary for the younger viewers but still manage to be exciting for everyone. Good family entertainment.

A: Edward Judd, Martha Hyer, Lionel Jefferies, Peter Finch, Erik Chitty, Betty McDowall

© COLUMBIA TRISTAR HOME VIDEO 60958

FLASH GORDON

D: Mike Hodges — 111 m

PG | SF | 1980 | COLOR

Sex / Nud / Viol / Lang / AdSit

7 High-camp revival of the very famous '30s-'40s comic strip character and a fun time, if you don't take it too seriously. High energy waves are pulling the moon out of orbit and threatening the destruction of the earth. Dr. Zarkov has taken two passengers, Flash Gordon (Sam Jones) and beautiful Dale Arden (Melody Anderson), along with him on a rocket ship to the planet Mongo, which is the source of the nasty energy waves. It is also where Flash and Miss Anderson romp through updated, but still intentionally hokey, special effects - doing battle with Ming the Merciless (von Sydow) and sexy evil Princess Aura (Muti).

A: Sam Jones, Max von Sydow, Melody Anderson, Topol, Ornella Muti, Timothy Dalton

© MCA/UNIVERSAL HOME VIDEO, INC. 66022

FLATLINERS

D: Joel Schumacher — 111 m

R | SF SUS | 1990 | COLOR

Sex / Nud / Viol / Lang / AdSit

7 A group of daring young medical students, hungry to explore the unknown, get much more than they expected in this taut thriller. One of the students gets the idea that, if his body temperature could be slowly lowered and his heart stopped (flatlined), he would be able experience the afterlife. He persuades the others to try the experiment and, one by one, each dies for a few moments, experiencing their own personal hell. Their experiments work, but what they don't count on is what they each bring back from death. A nail biter!

A: Kiefer Sutherland, Julia Roberts, Kevin Bacon, William Baldwin, Oliver Platt, Kimberly Scott

© COLUMBIA TRISTAR HOME VIDEO 50383

FLIGHT OF THE NAVIGATOR, THE

D: Randal Kleiser — 90 m

PG | SF CLD | 1986 | COLOR

Sex / Nud / Viol / Lang / AdSit

8 Quite fun. A 12-year-old falls into a ravine in 1978 and wakes up a second later to find that it is now 1986 and his folks have moved away. However, he hasn't aged a day. NASA investigates and discovers that he has previously unknown star charts imprinted on his brain and his disappearance is connected to a recently discovered alien spaceship. He finds that he had been whisked away on a spaceship, that he can communicate with this one and that it needs his help to get home again. Kids will love the special effects, the kooky alien creatures and the action. Parents will enjoy this Disney treat, too.

A: Joey Cramer, Cliff De Young, Veronica Cartwright, Matt Adler, Sarah Jessica Parker, Howard Hesseman

© WALT DISNEY HOME VIDEO 499

FLY, THE

D: Kurt Neumann — 94 m

NR | SF DMA HOR | 1958 | B&W

Sex / Nud / Viol / Lang / AdSit

9 This is a superior science fiction story. A scientist, experimenting with a machine that disintegrates matter in one place and reintegrates it again in another place, has a serious accident when his genes are mixed with those of a household fly. His head has become attached to the fly's body, and vice versa. He is now a gruesome freak struggling to return to normal. This film has become a cult favorite for very good reason. It was produced with care, high production values, good special effects and good acting. It was remade in 1986 in an equally good but much more grizzly manner.

A: David Hedison, Patricia Owens, Vincent Price, Herbert Marshall, Kathleen Freeman

© FOXVIDEO 1190

FLY, THE

D: David Cronenberg — 96 m

R | SF HOR DMA | 1986 | COLOR

Sex / Nud / Viol / Lang / AdSit

8 Equally good (but much more graphic and intense) remake of the 1958 classic science fiction horror story. A brilliant scientist has built a matter transportation device which he decides to try out on himself. Unknown to him, a fly is in the chamber with him when the machine is activated and their genes are mixed together. He becomes horribly disfigured. Very interesting premise, combined with a credible love story. Excellent makeup won an Oscar.

A: Jeff Goldblum, Geena Davis, John Getz, Joy Boushel, Les Carlson

© FOXVIDEO 1503

FORBIDDEN PLANET

D: Fred M. Wilcox — 999 m

G | SF | 1956 | COLOR

Sex / Nud / Viol / Lang / AdSit

6 One of filmdom's very first attempts at serious science fiction and it provided the inspiration for the filmmakers who would make later sci-fi hits, like STARTREK. It was Oscar-nominated for special effects in 1956. It is pretty tame by today's standards. Nonetheless, it is an intelligent film which was very ambitious for its time and is still valuable today. Three explorers visit the planet Altair-IV in 2257. There, the resident scientist has built a self-sufficient world for himself and his daughter. However, there is also a mysterious malevolent force present in their idyllic world.

A: Walter Pidgeon, Anne Francis, Leslie Nielsen, Jack Kelly, Earl Holliman

Distributed By MGM/UA Home Video M202345

FOREVER YOUNG

D: Steve Miner — 102 m

PG | SF ROM | 1992 | COLOR

Sex / Nud / Viol / Lang / AdSit

6 Mel Gibson is a test pilot who is desperate when his love has been hit by a car and it is believed that she will never recover. So, he agrees to become a test subject for his best friend, who is a scientist experimenting with suspending life in a secret military project. It is 1939. But the experiment is suspended when the War breaks out. For the next 50 years he sleeps, only to awaken in a government warehouse after two boys play with his container. He had become a forgotten experiment, lost in the system. Now it is 1992 and he has discovered that his love is still alive, but that he is now rapidly aging and dying. If you can buy into all that, you will be satisfied.

A: Mel Gibson, Elijah Wood, Isabel Glasser, George Wendt, Jamie Lee Curtis

© WARNER HOME VIDEO 12571

S F

FUTUREWORLD

D: Richard T. Heffron — 107 m

PG | SF ACT | 1976 | COLOR

Sex / Nud / Viol / Lang / AdSit

7 Entertaining sequel to WEST WORLD. In a fantastic amusement park of the future, lifelike robots act out a customer's fantasies. But investigative reporters Fonda and Danner find out there is also a plan by one of the scientists to replace all the world's leaders with these robots and to control the world. (Similar plot to the cult classic INVASION OF THE BODY SNATCHERS). Yul Brynner is back in his WEST WORLD role. Pretty good escapism.

A: Peter Fonda, Blythe Danner, Arthur Hill, Yul Brynner, Stuart Margolin, John P. Ryan

© GOODTIMES 04060

GODZILLA, KING OF THE MONSTERS

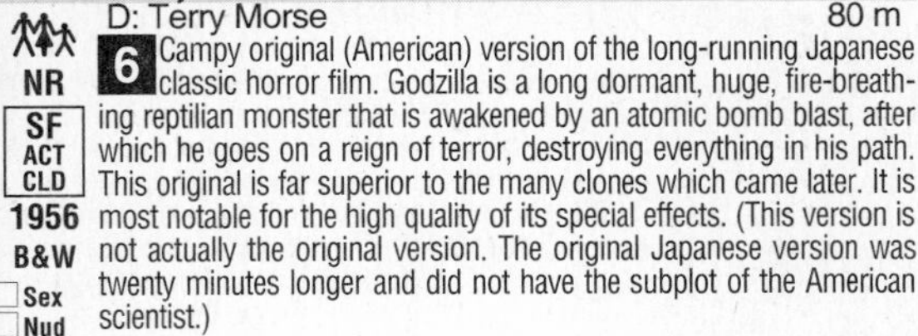

D: Terry Morse — 80 m

NR | SF ACT CLD | 1956 | B&W

Sex / Nud / Viol / Lang / AdSit

6 Campy original (American) version of the long-running Japanese classic horror film. Godzilla is a long dormant, huge, fire-breathing reptilian monster that is awakened by an atomic bomb blast, after which he goes on a reign of terror, destroying everything in his path. This original is far superior to the many clones which came later. It is most notable for the high quality of its special effects. (This version is not actually the original version. The original Japanese version was twenty minutes longer and did not have the subplot of the American scientist.)

A: Inoshiro Honda, Raymond Burr, Takashi Shimura, Akihiko Hirata

© PARAMOUNT HOME VIDEO 12864

GROUNDSTAR CONSPIRACY, THE

D: Lamont Johnson — 93 m

PG | SF SUS MYS | 1972 | COLOR

Sex / Nud / Viol / Lang / AdSit

8 A top secret space-based laboratory is largely destroyed in an explosion. The only survivor (Sarrazin) is thought by tough government agent Peppard to be a spy who was sent to steal its plans, but Sarrazin is badly burned and has no recollection of events. Still, Peppard must get him to remember. He has to know who was behind the plot. So when brainwashing doesn't work, Sarrazin is set free so that he can be followed. He has now become bait. Clever and intricate plot, with excellent pacing, direction and acting, plus an unexpected climax. A good thriller, unfairly overlooked upon its release.

A: George Peppard, Michael Sarrazin, Christine Belford, Cliff Potts, James Olson

© MCA/UNIVERSAL HOME VIDEO, INC. 80602

HANDMAID'S TALE, THE

D: Volker Schlondorff — 109 m

R | SF DMA | 1990 | COLOR

Sex / Nud / Viol / Lang / AdSit

6 An interesting premise is given a little bit better than mediocre treatment, despite top-notch acting. Set in a bleak future-America, the few remaining fertile women are forced to become surrogate breeders for the ruling military elite. This story follows the fortunes of one such girl. Excellent performances fail to inspire a more than a moderately empathetic response. However, this is a very thought-provoking subject that deserves consideration by viewers interested in non-traditional and thought-provoking viewing.

A: Natasha Richardson, Faye Dunaway, Aidan Quinn, Elizabeth McGovern, Victoria Tennant, Robert Duvall

© HBO VIDEO 0431

HIDDEN, THE

D: Jack Sholder — 98 m

R | SF ACT CRM | 1987 | COLOR

Sex / Nud / Viol / Lang / AdSit

8 Unique and exciting science fiction thriller. A Los Angeles cop is joined by a strange FBI agent (he chews Alka-Selzer tablets), in his attempt to get to the bottom of a rash of robberies and murders. The two are searching to find out how normal ordinary law-abiding citizens are being turned into such extremely violent killers. Then, the FBI agent informs the local cop that there is an alien creature who is invading these human bodies. He has a preference for heavy metal music, Ferraris and bloody violence. Full of high-intensity excitement, with good action sequences. Well made and very unpredictable.

A: Michael Nouri, Kyle MacLachlan, Ed O'Ross, Clu Gulager, Claudia Christian, Clarence Felder

© MEDIA HOME ENTERTAINMENT, INC. M940

ICEMAN

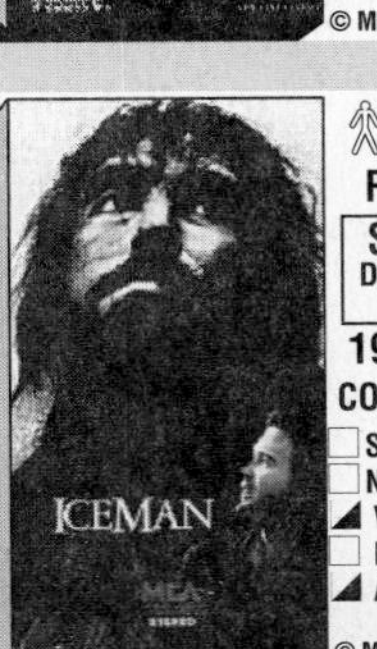

D: Fred Schepisi — 101 m

PG | SF DMA | 1984 | COLOR

Sex / Nud / Viol / Lang / AdSit

8 Fascinating and credible premise: An arctic exploration team finds a pre-historic Neanderthal man frozen in the ice. Incredibly, they are successful in restoring the man to life out of his frozen coma. Now the question becomes what to do with this incredible find. Some want even to dissect him, but anthropologist Hutton is interested in him as a human being and develops a strong rapport with the man. Very well done. The serious approach to the subject matter and excellent performances by the leads make this an intriguing adventure story.

A: Timothy Hutton, Lindsay Crouse, John Lone, Josef Sommer, David Strathairn, Danny Glover

© MCA/UNIVERSAL HOME VIDEO, INC. 80074

ICE PIRATES

D: Stewart Raffill — 95 m

PG | SF COM | 1984 | COLOR

Sex / Nud / Viol / Lang / AdSit

6 Fun farce set in the future. Robert Urich plays a pirate leader in this tongue-in-cheek adventure story. He and his band of buccaneers come to the aid of beautiful princess (Crosby) in her battle against an evil force. Both she and the buccaneers are in pursuit of what is now the Universe's most precious commodity - water. The film is not always successful in its attempts at humor and excitement, but sometimes it is. The special effects aren't great, but they aren't bad, either. All this adds up to a passable evening's diversion for the family.

A: Robert Urich, Mary Crosby, John Matuszak, Anjelica Huston, John Carradine

Distributed By MGM/UA Home Video M800427

ILLUSTRATED MAN, THE

D: Jack Smight — 103 m

PG | SF | 1969 | COLOR

Sex / Nud / Viol / Lang / AdSit

6 One young man meets another very strange man who is totally covered with tattoos at a campground in 1933. The more he stares at these fascinating tattoos, they strangely begin to come alive and reveal stories of the man's very long life. Based upon Rad Bradbury's book, this film concentrates on only three stories. In one, he is the parent of super-powerful and dangerous children. In another, he is an astronaut trapped on a planet where it constantly rains. And in the last, he is a parent preparing for nuclear destruction, having to choose this child's fate. This is pretty heavy going and is for devoted science fiction fans only.

A: Rod Steiger, Claire Bloom, Robert Drivas

© WARNER HOME VIDEO 11211

INCREDIBLE SHRINKING MAN, THE

D: Jack Arnold — 81 m

NR | SF DMA | 1957 | B&W

Sex / Nud / Viol / Lang / AdSit

9 Thoughtful, well-made and intelligent science fiction classic that has not diminished with time. Grant Williams is an ordinary business man who, oddly, begins to shrink after walking through a strange mist. All science's efforts are unable to stop him from shrinking. As he shrinks, his status regarding all things around him alters. Eventually his trip ever smaller makes him invisible to the normal world. He is alone. Great special effects and action create excitement, but the lasting power of the film comes from the forced reevaluation of life as we know it. Excellent.

A: Grant Williams, Randy Stuart, Paul Lanton, April Kent, Raymond Bailey

© MCA/UNIVERSAL HOME VIDEO, INC. 80765

INNERSPACE

D: Joe Dante — 120 m

PG | COM SF | 1987 | COLOR

Sex / Nud / Viol / Lang / AdSit

7 Funny takeoff on FANTASTIC VOYAGE. Dennis Quaid is an astronaut who agrees to be miniaturized down to the size of a virus and then be injected into a rabbit. However, instead he accidentally gets shot into a hypochondriacal store clerk, Martin Short. What's worse, Short is now being chased by spies who want them both. Funny, off-the-wall stuff, with special effects that won an Oscar for Visual Effects. Short is perfect.

A: Dennis Quaid, Martin Short, Fiona Lewis, Vernon Wells, Meg Ryan, Kevin McCarthy

© WARNER HOME VIDEO 11754

INVASION OF THE BODY SNATCHERS

D: Don Siegel — 80 m

NR | SF SUS HOR | 1956 | B&W

Sex / Nud / Viol / Lang / AdSit

9 A chilling and frightening film that is every bit as powerful today as when released. Kevin McCarthy is a small town doctor who observes that all those around him - his patients, his friends and even his family - are slowly being transformed into emotionless, cold, inhuman beings. They look the same but they are different, very different. Slowly he uncovers the truth, that earth has been invaded by strange aliens who consume humans and then replace them with identical replicas that emerge from strange "pods." This has a subtle understated terror that found its intellectual inspiration in McCarthy-era politics.

A: Kevin McCarthy, Dana Wynter, Carolyn Jones, King Donovan, Larry Gates, Virginia Christine

© REPUBLIC PICTURES HOME VIDEO 2018

INVASION OF THE BODY SNATCHERS

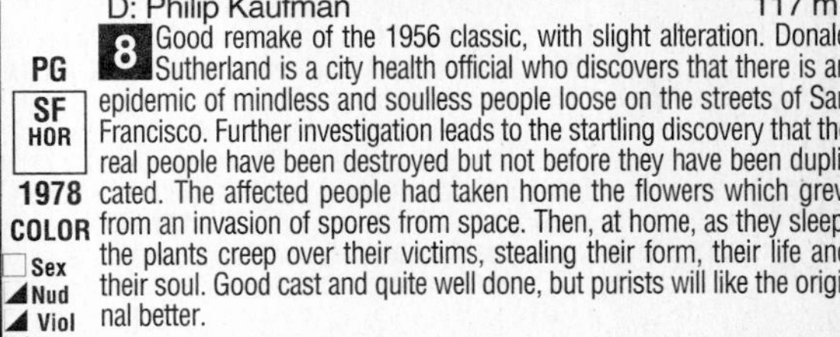

D: Philip Kaufman — 117 m

PG | SF HOR | 1978 | COLOR

Sex / Nud / Viol / Lang / AdSit

8 Good remake of the 1956 classic, with slight alteration. Donald Sutherland is a city health official who discovers that there is an epidemic of mindless and soulless people loose on the streets of San Francisco. Further investigation leads to the startling discovery that the real people have been destroyed but not before they have been duplicated. The affected people had taken home the flowers which grew from an invasion of spores from space. Then, at home, as they sleep, the plants creep over their victims, stealing their form, their life and their soul. Good cast and quite well done, but purists will like the original better.

A: Donald Sutherland, Brooke Adams, Leonard Nimoy, Jeff Goldblum, Veronica Cartwright

Distributed By MGM/UA Home Video M600297

ISLAND OF DR. MOREAU, THE

PG | SF HOR | 1977 | COLOR

D: Don Taylor 104 m

6 Seventeen days adrift alone at sea in 1896, Michael York at last drifts up on the shores of an island, but he is not alone there. The island is populated by the half-animal/half-human creatures created by the experiments of a demented scientist. Dr. Moreau's (Lancaster) creations are the remnants of his experiments to transform animals into men. York meets Moreau and falls in love with his beautiful adopted daughter (Carrera), even as he also begins to discover the full extent of the horrors Moreau has committed.

Sex / Nud / Viol / Lang / AdSit

A: Burt Lancaster, Michael York, Barbara Carrera, Nigel Davenport, Richard Basehart

© GOODTIMES 04062

JURASSIC PARK

PG-13 | ACT SUS SF | 1993 | COLOR

D: Steven Spielberg 126 m

10 Masterful movie making is combined with wondrous special effects to create grippingly real terror. A wealthy industrialist has purchased in island off the coast of Costa Rica and plans to convert it into a fantastic tourist attraction. The featured attraction is live dinosaurs which have been miraculously reconstituted from "pickled" DNA fragments, taken from mosquitoes that have been entombed in amber for 100 million years. Two paleontologists (Neill and Dern) are called in to assure the investors that the park is safe. Instead, they are set upon and hunted by the carnivorous beasts who have been set free by sabotage and a massive power failure.

Sex / Nud / Viol / Lang / AdSit

A: Sam Neill, Laura Dern, Jeff Goldblum, Richard Attenborough

© MCA/UNIVERSAL HOME VIDEO, INC.

KAFKA

PG-13 | MYS SF | 1992 | COLOR

D: Steven Soderbergh 100 m

6 This film begins as a marvelously constructed, very moody mystery piece, set in Prague 1919. Irons is Kafka, a novelist at night and an insurance clerk at day. Kafka's friend is found mysteriously dead. The police do not provide him any answers and in fact only add to the mystery. Kafka is also being drawn ever deeper into a plot that links several unexplained deaths, the friend's girlfriend, the company he works for and the government. However, what began wonderfully ends very unsatisfactorily, not because of the strange SF twist, but because it is just so poorly constructed and unresolved. Beginning 9 + Ending 3 = 6 average.

Sex / Nud / Viol / Lang / AdSit

A: Jeremy Irons, Theresa Russell, Joel Grey, Ian Holm, Jeroen Krabbe, Alec Guinness

© PARAMOUNT HOME VIDEO 15124

LAST STARFIGHTER, THE

PG | SF CLD | 1984 | COLOR

D: Nick Castle 100 m

7 This is a quite enjoyable fantasy adventure yarn that is primarily, but not necessarily only, for kids. In it, a teenage videogame wizkid is transported from his trailer park home to a far away place by an alien, Robert Preston. He has been recruited, after his skill in blasting invading spaceships in a video game called Starfighter, is monitored. It will be his job to help defend the Universe against an evil invasion force. Interesting and witty dialogue, plus a clever premise and some funny situations make this a pleasant time killer.

Sex / Nud / Viol / Lang / AdSit

A: Robert Preston, Lance Guest, Barbara Bosson, Dan O'Herlihy, Catherine Mary Stewart

© MCA/UNIVERSAL HOME VIDEO, INC. 80078

LAWNMOWER MAN, THE

R | SF ACT | 1992 | COLOR

D: Bret Leonard 108 m

7 Dazzling, glitzy, high-tech computer wizardry is both the theme and the substance of this film. Well-meaning scientist Pierce Brosnan has created the means to accelerate the power of the mind through a combination of chemicals and "virtual" reality - a form of reality created within a computer and projected into a mind. He uses a retarded landscaper, the Lawnmower Man, as a new subject after a chimp he had used for nasty government experiments had become violent. The Lawnmower Man is transformed from being a meek moron into a malevolent maniac. Super special effects.

Sex / Nud / Viol / Lang / AdSit

A: Jeff Fahey, Pierce Brosnan, Jenny Wright, Mark Bringleson, Geoffrey Lewis, Jeremy Slate

© TURNER HOME ENTERTAINMENT N4092

LOGAN'S RUN

PG | SF ACT | 1976 | COLOR

D: Michael Anderson 119 m

6 An intelligent adventure set in a strange futuristic society. Logan (York) is a policeman living and working in a carefree hedonistic domed city. His particular job is chasing down "runners" - individuals who run away rather than comply with a law requiring that they be "renewed" at age 30. This is an elaborate ceremony, after which the participants are never seen again. Facing his own renewal, York and a girl escape outside the dome to discover another world that no one knew even existed. And it includes an old man (Ustinov) - something neither has ever seen or known to be possible. Entertaining.

Sex / Nud / Viol / Lang / AdSit

A: Michael York, Richard Jordan, Jenny Agutter, Farrah Fawcett, Peter Ustinov, Roscoe Lee Browne

Distributed By MGM/UA Home Video M600082

MAN WHO FELL TO EARTH, THE

NR | SF SUS | 1976 | COLOR

D: Nicolas Roeg 140 m

7 This intelligent Sci-Fi thriller also contained sex and nudity and so was quite controversial. An alien leaves his family on their very dry and dying home planet to arrive on earth in a search for much needed water. Upon his arrival, he transforms himself into a human, and has plans to use his superior intelligence to make money to build spaceships to bring water back home. But as other business interests thwart his efforts, and he becomes seduced by earthlife and love with an earth woman, he realizes that he is trapped. Depressed and feeling guilty, he resigns himself to human-like life.

Sex / Nud / Viol / Lang / AdSit

A: David Bowie, Rip Torn, Buck Henry, Candy Clark, Bernie Casey, Jackson D. Kane

© COLUMBIA TRISTAR HOME VIDEO 60929

MAN WITH TWO BRAINS, THE

R | COM SF | 1983 | COLOR

D: Carl Reiner 90 m

6 Mad-scientist farce. A brilliant brain surgeon's marriage to an ice queen (Turner) is falling apart. She is super-sexy but refuses him any satisfaction. Hoping to rekindle their romance, Dr. Hfuhruhur (Martin) takes her to Vienna but there he finds his true love. She is a disembodied brain in a jar that can communicate telepathically. So Martin schemes to find a way to "keep" the brain with him. In true Steve Martin form, this wacky comedy can be charming. Some of the scenes will have you in stitches while others leave you cold. Listen for Sissy Spacek as the voice of the brain.

Sex / Nud / Viol / Lang / AdSit

A: Steve Martin, Kathleen Turner, David Warner, Paul Benedict, Richard Brestoff, James Cromwell

© WARNER HOME VIDEO 11319

MARY SHELLEY'S FRANKENSTEIN

R | DMA SF HOR | 1994 | COLOR

D: Kenneth Branagh 123 m

7 This $45 million faithful adaptation of Mary Shelly's novel is set at the end of the eighteenth century. Devastated by the death of his wife, aristocrat Frankenstein (Branagh) studies to become a doctor. His interest lies not in healing the sick but by studying the mysteries of death. As a student, he builds upon the work of a brilliant teacher to actually recreate life by combining the stolen body parts of the dead. Stunned by the pitiful human result of his experiments, who escapes, he vows never to play with life again. However, the hideous and merciless creature he has created (De Niro) is constantly tormented by people. Terribly lonely, he now seeks out his "father" to force him to create a companion for him too.

Sex / Nud / Viol / Lang / AdSit

A: Kenneth Branagh, Robert De Niro, Tom Hulce, Helena Bonham Carter, Aidan Quinn, Ian Holm

© COLUMBIA TRISTAR HOME VIDEO 78713

MEMOIRS OF AN INVISIBLE MAN

PG-13 | SF COM | 1992 | COLOR

D: John Carpenter 99 m

6 Very light diversion. Chevy Chase is a securities analyst who decides to skip the lecture he's supposed to listen to at a government research facility and instead take a nap in a vacant room. Just then, there is an accident and everyone is evacuated from the building except for Chevy. When it is over, Chevy has become invisible. Sam Neill is a rogue CIA agent who is driven to make Chevy a key government asset, but Chevy is not eager to be partners with the CIA, so he makes a break and the chase is on. Chevy seeks out his new girlfriend, Daryl Hannah, for help. Clever. Although its not that funny, it is still reasonably enjoyable.

Sex / Nud / Viol / Lang / AdSit

A: Chevy Chase, Daryl Hannah, Sam Neill, Michael McKean, Stephen Tobolowsky, Jim Norton

© WARNER HOME VIDEO 12310

MOTHRA

NR | SF CLD | 1962 | COLOR

D: Inoshiro Honda 100 m

6 Hokey and silly, but strangely endearing monster flick. Twin princesses, each only six inches tall, are snatched from their home island for display in a local neighborhood bar. The girls pray to the god Mothra hoping to be rescued and Mothra responds, hatching a giant egg in the city of Tokyo. The egg releases a giant caterpillar that turns onto a huge moth and ventures into Tokyo hunting for the girls, destroying the city along the way. Really corny, but still one of the best of the Japanese monster movies, in a campy sort of way.

Sex / Nud / Viol / Lang / AdSit

A: Frankie Sakai, Hiroshi Koizumi, Lee Kresel, Kyoko Kagawa, Emi Itoh, Yumi Itoh

© COLUMBIA TRISTAR HOME VIDEO 60060

NIGHT OF THE COMET

PG-13 | SF COM HOR | 1984 | COLOR

D: Thom Eberhardt 95 m

6 Quirky science fiction spoof. A couple of California "valley girls" are among the few humans left alive and unchanged on earth after a brilliant comet, that last passed earth when the dinosaurs died, again passes overhead. Most people are killed instantly, but some unfortunate others are turned into flesh-eating zombies. The girls, however, spend their time shopping in the deserted stores, looking for guys and dodging zombies. They eventually join a band of other survivors to do battle with the zombies. Sound silly? It is, but is still more than passable entertainment.

Sex / Nud / Viol / Lang / AdSit

A: Robert Beltran, Catherine Mary Stewart, Kelli Maroney, Sharon Farrell

© GOODTIMES 4017

OMEGA MAN, THE

D: Boris Sagal 98 m

PG | SF SUS ACT | 1971 | COLOR

7 Well done and literate science fiction story about the breakdown of society after the world is largely destroyed in a biological war. Heston stars as a medical researcher who is strangely immune to the effects of all the germs. But a militant group of mutant survivors is now bent on destroying all technologies and has particularly targeted him to be killed. Heston discovers a few children who are also immune and being protected by Cash. The mutants want to kill them, too, but they are the future of the species and Heston must study them if there is to be a cure. Gripping suspense.

Sex / Nud / Viol / Lang / AdSit

A: Charlton Heston, Anthony Zerbe, Rosalind Cash, Paul Koslo, Lincoln Kilpatrick, Eric Laneuville

© WARNER HOME VIDEO 11210

OUTLAND

D: Peter Hyams 111 m

R | SF ACT CRM | 1981 | COLOR

8 Rousing space Western. Sean Connery is the new marshall assigned to police a dehumanized, rough-and-tumble mining colony on one of the moons of Jupiter. His search to identify the reasons behind a series of mysterious deaths leads him to the discovery of a pervasive corruption based upon the distribution of mind-altering drugs. Great special effects lend an air of realism and believability to this bleak other-world environment. The exciting action scenes could have occurred just as easily at the OK corral or on the streets of L.A. Exciting.

Sex / Nud / Viol / Lang / AdSit

A: Sean Connery, Peter Boyle, Frances Sternhagen, James Sikking, Kika Markham

© WARNER HOME VIDEO 20002

PHANTASM

D: Don Coscarelli 87 m

R | HOR SF | 1979 | COLOR

6 Popular, but bizarre, mixture of horror and science fiction that definitely does have some jump-out-your-seat moments. A 13-year-old ignores the orders of his older brother not to go to the funeral of a friend who was killed (after having sex with a strange woman in the cemetery). From the bushes, he spies a villainous, very tall man steal the body away. The two brothers follow the sinister man back to a mausoleum and find there a very bizarre world which includes a very deadly flying silver sphere with protruding daggers.

Sex / Nud / Viol / Lang / AdSit

A: Michael Baldwin, Bill Thornbury, Reggie Bannister, Angus Scrimm, Ken Jones, Kathy Lester

© NEW LINE HOME VIDEO 2005

PLANET OF THE APES

D: Franklin J. Schaffner 112 m

G | SF | 1967 | COLOR

8 First in a thought-provoking sci-fi adventure series. Four American astronauts crash-land on what they believe to be an alien world. The dominant life form here is apes. The humans have reverted to a very primitive state and have been relegated, into being slaves. Heston is captured by the apes, who are astounded to learn that he is intelligent and can talk. Simian scientist Roddy McDowall and his wife (Hunter) seek to protect Heston from those who want him destroyed. This upside-down perspective creates an interesting vehicle and has made this series a near-classic. See Index for the others.

Sex / Nud / Viol / Lang / AdSit

A: Charlton Heston, Roddy McDowall, Kim Hunter, Maurice Evans, James Whitmore, James Daly

© FOXVIDEO 1054

PREDATOR

D: John McTiernan 107 m

R | ACT SUS SF | 1987 | COLOR

9 Heart-pounding suspense. Schwarzenegger and his crew of trained mercenaries are hired by the CIA to go into a Latin American jungle to rescue a group South American officials kidnapped by terrorists. Just as they are about to complete their mission, they are surprised to discover that they are themselves being stalked by a fearsome other-world killer - a large, ugly, ferocious alien man/monster with truly awesome powers who enjoys hunting and killing. It has come to earth to hunt the hunters - humans. Fast-paced, intense suspense as team members are picked off one by one. Action-packed.

Sex / Nud / Viol / Lang / AdSit

A: Arnold Schwarzenegger, Jesse Ventura, Bill Duke, Sonny Landham, Carl Weathers, Richard Chaves

© FOXVIDEO 1515

PROJECT X

D: Jonathan Kaplan 107 m

PG | SUS SF | 1987 | COLOR

7 Entertaining quasi-science fiction flick. A chronic screw-up in the Air Force (Broderick) gets assigned to a top secret project to help train the next "generation" of pilots - brilliant chimpanzees who can communicate with sign language. Broderick becomes incensed at the unnecessarily cruel and fatal nature of the experimentation on the chimps, so he, another trainer (Hunt) and the chimps all conspire against the Air Force's plans. Watchable and enjoyable, but predictable.

Sex / Nud / Viol / Lang / AdSit

A: Matthew Broderick, Helen Hunt, Anne Lockhart, Bill Sadler, Johnny Ray McGhee, Jonathon Stark

© FOXVIDEO 5192

PULSE

D: Paul Golding 90 m

PG-13 | HOR SF | 1988 | COLOR

6 Well-crafted but mindless scare flick. David (Lawrence) is an 11-year-old who is visiting his father and step-mother for the summer. He is excited about being there but has become very suspicious that something is going on with the electricity. The appliances seem to have taken on a vengeful personality. The televisions and microwave seem determined to kill them. And then, the old man next door is electrocuted and his house destroyed. Now David and his stepmother are certain there is trouble, but his father refuses to believe. Tension builds slowly and believably until the exciting finish.

Sex / Nud / Viol / Lang / AdSit

A: Cliff De Young, Roxanne Hart, Joey Lawrence, Matthew Lawrence, Charles Tyner, Dennis Redfield

© COLUMBIA TRISTAR HOME VIDEO 65004

PUPPET MASTERS, THE

D: Stuart Orme 119 m

R | SUS SF | 1994 | COLOR

7 Parasitic invaders from another world have overrun a small Iowa town. The little beggars attach themselves to the backs of their hosts, inject a stinger-like tentacle into the brain and take control of the victim, who then becomes their puppet. Government agents Sutherland, Thal and Warner had come to explore the conflicting news reports which first announced a strange landing and then denied it. Their mission is now to find a way to destroy the colony of parasites without being invaded themselves and before the nasty creatures can invade the entire population. Really not too bad. Its only problem is that it comes on the heels of other films such as INVASION OF THE BODY SNATCHERS.

Sex / Nud / Viol / Lang / AdSit

A: Donald Sutherland, Eric Thal, Julie Warner, Keith David, Will Patton, Richard Belzer

© HOLLYWOOD PICTURES HOME VIDEO 3628

QUIET EARTH, THE

D: Geoff Murphy 91 m

R | SF DMA | 1985 | COLOR

6 An intelligent New Zealand Sci-Fi thriller. The earth has become very quiet one morning when a scientist wakes up to find that all human life on earth has been virtually wiped out. He concludes that one of the top secret government projects he has been working on may be the reason, the fabric of time/space may have been torn apart. He seeks to discover if there is other life left. He does find a young woman and a Maori tribesman and together, they realize that it is up to them to find the answer to restoring mankind. Serious food for thought and a technically astute production.

Sex / Nud / Viol / Lang / AdSit

A: Bruno Lawrence, Alison Routledge, Peter Smith

© CBS/FOX VIDEO 3042

RETURN OF THE JEDI

D: Richard Marquand 134 m

PG | SF ACT SUS | 1983 | COLOR

9 Thrilling finale to the hugely popular, exciting and imaginative STAR WARS trilogy from George Lucas. In this episode, Luke Skywalker has further mastered his skills as a Jedi Master of the "Force." He first rescues Princess Leia and Hans Solo from the vile and decadent Jabba-the-Hut, then aids in the destruction of the monstrously powerful Death Star by infiltrating the evil forces of the Empire, seeking out its all-powerful leader Darth Vader - to destroy him. Great characters. Great special effects. Great fun!

Sex / Nud / Viol / Lang / AdSit

A: Mark Hamill, Carrie Fisher, Harrison Ford, Billy Dee Williams, Dave Prowse, Peter Mayhew

© FOXVIDEO 1478

ROAD WARRIOR, THE - MAD MAX 2

D: George Miller 96 m

R | SF ACT | 1982 | COLOR

8 Intense and very stylish action in this follow-up to MAD MAX. Gibson is roving the post-nuclear desolation in the Australian Outback when he is drawn into a frantic attempt to save one small band of survivors from a group of evil marauders and new wave warriors that is trying to take over the fuel depot belonging to the survivors. In the powerful climax, Max desperately leads the survivors in a headlong dash to safety through the Outback, driving a supertanker flat out across the desert while also conducting a running battle with the pursuing villains.

Sex / Nud / Viol / Lang / AdSit

A: Mel Gibson, Bruce Spence, Vernon Wells, Virginia Hey, Mike Preston, Emil Minty

© WARNER HOME VIDEO 11181

ROBOCOP

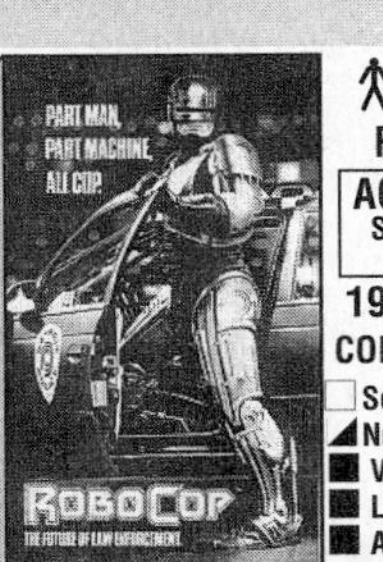

D: Paul Verhoeven 103 m

R | ACT SF | 1987 | COLOR

9 White-hot action! Detroit, in the not so far distant future, is a lawless city. A policeman (Weller) is killed on duty and the corporation that runs the police department uses what's left of him to create a bold new policeman. He is a fusion between man and machine. The dead cop is turned into the ultimate crime fighter - Robocop. However, Robocop still has residual memories that remind him of what he has lost and also information that will enable him to track down his own killers to exact a fierce revenge. A huge hit with unbelievable special effects. Tightly wound and powerfully violent.

Sex / Nud / Viol / Lang / AdSit

A: Peter Weller, Nancy Allen, Ronny Cox, Kurtwood Smith, Miguel Ferrer, Robert Doqui

© ORION PICTURES CORPORATION 8610

ROBOCOP 2

D: Irvin Kershner — 117 m

R | ACT SF | 1990 | COLOR

7 Wildly violent action! There is big trouble in Detroit. A wicked drug kingpin (Noonan) wants to completely permeate the city with his own powerful new drug called "Nuke." Meanwhile, the company that created Robocop has made a newer version of the machine. However, this time the superhero's look-alike is a thoroughly evil cyborg. Robocop (Weller) must rid the city of both menaces - not an easy task. A very grim prediction for the future and a film that is full of fierce, ultra-violent, non-stop action.

□ Sex □ Nud ■ Viol ■ Lang ■ AdSit

A: Peter Weller, Nancy Allen, Dan O'Herlihy, Belinda Bauer, Tom Noonan, Gabriel Damon

© ORION PICTURES CORPORATION 8764

ROCKY HORROR PICTURE SHOW, THE

D: Jim Sharman — 106 m

R | MUS COM SF | 1975 | COLOR

9 Wacky, purposely goofy, full of rock 'n roll energy and lots of fun! On one dark and stormy night, a stuffy young couple (Bostwick and Sarandon) get a flat tire and come knocking on the door of extra-terrestrial transvestite Dr. Frank N. Furter's mysterious castle looking for a phone. They find that they have arrived on a very special night. It's a party! The castle is full of kinky guests and the bisexual doctor teaches the up-tight pair to loosen up by seducing them both. That's not all - he's an alien. This film inspired a huge unprecedented cult following. Very yery different. Be open minded.

◢ Sex ◢ Nud □ Viol ◢ Lang ■ AdSit

A: Barry Bostwick, Susan Sarandon, Tim Curry, Charles Gray, Richard O'Brien, Patricia Quinn

© FOXVIDEO 1424

ROLLERBALL

D: Norman Jewison — 118 m

R | ACT SF | 1975 | COLOR

7 In the year 2018, corporations rule the world. All violence has been prohibited. There are no wars and no crime. Instead, the corporations have created the game of Rollerball, an extremely violent combination of football, basketball, hockey and roller derby. The game's best and most popular player is James Caan. He is so popular that he has become dangerous. The heads of the corporations want him to retire, but he refuses. They take away the woman he loves and still he refuses. Now they have changed the rules of the game. Now it is a game to the death.

□ Sex □ Nud ■ Viol ■ Lang ◢ AdSit

A: James Caan, John Houseman, Maud Adams, John Beck, Moses Gunn, Ralph Richardson

Distributed By MGM/UA Home Video M300262

RUNAWAY

D: Michael Crichton — 99 m

PG-13 | SF ACT | 1984 | COLOR

6 Comic book-like Sci-Fi thriller. Someone is making minor modifications which are turning ordinary domestic robots into death machines. Tough-guy cop Selleck and his beautiful assistant (Rhodes) are assigned the job of bringing in the killer-robots and taking down their evil controller Luther (Simmons from the rock group KISS). However, when Luther catches on to Selleck's game, he kidnaps Selleck's child and holds him hostage on the roof of a building that is under construction. Great special effects help spice up the lukewarm plot and make this an interesting sci-fi flick.

□ Sex ◢ Nud ◢ Viol ■ Lang ■ AdSit

A: Tom Selleck, Cynthia Rhodes, Gene Simmons, Kirstie Alley, Stan Shaw, Joey Cramer

© COLUMBIA TRISTAR HOME VIDEO 60469

RUNNING MAN, THE

D: Paul Michael Glaser — 101 m

R | ACT SF | 1987 | COLOR

6 Horrifying peek into the future. Richard Dawson hosts a game show of death. In the year 2017, in the ravaged city of L.A., people have become very violent. For entertainment, they like to watch a gladiator game show where convicted felons literally run for their lives. If they win the game, they're pardoned, but most lose. Schwarzenegger is framed for murder and so becomes a reluctant contestant. Dawson runs him through his paces as fierce professional killers one after the other stalk him, but Schwarzenegger promises "I'll be back." Fast-paced, very violent action. Based on a novel by Stephen King.

□ Sex □ Nud ■ Viol ◢ Lang ◢ AdSit

A: Arnold Schwarzenegger, Richard Dawson, Maria Conchita Alonso, Yaphet Kotto, Jim Brown, Jesse Ventura

© LIVE HOME VIDEO 6021

SCANNERS

D: David Cronenberg — 104 m

R | HOR SF | 1981 | COLOR

7 Shocking and gruesome, yet a perversely riveting horror tale. It is discovered too late, that a drug which was created to calm a shaky pregnancy causes the child's telekinetic powers to become dramatically increased. The child becomes a "scanner," able to probe into other people's minds. Two of the scanners (Ironside and Dane) have hatched a plot to control the world. However, the doctor who invented the drug (McGoohan) has recruited a good scanner (Lack) to block them. Beware, there is a truly mind-blowing conclusion. Intensely graphic special effects.

□ Sex □ Nud ■ Viol ◢ Lang ◢ AdSit

A: Jennifer O'Neill, Stephen Lack, Patrick McGoohan, Lawrence Dane, Charles Shamata, Michael Ironside

© NEW LINE HOME VIDEO 2080

SHORT CIRCUIT

D: John Badham — 98 m

PG | COM SF | 1986 | COLOR

8 Sparkling comedic farce for the family! No. 5 is a military robot that was developed to be a weapon by the government, but it was zapped with a bolt of lightning and now the little guy seems nearly human. No. 5 has also taken off to see the world on his own. He finds a friend in animal lover Ally Sheedy and learns American culture by watching TV. Sheedy and the newly educated No. 5 develop an affection for each other, but the military is steadfastly after his adorable little tail, with his creator Guttenberg leading the chase. Naturally, she hides him from them. Charming entertainment.

□ Sex □ Nud □ Viol ◢ Lang ◢ AdSit

A: Ally Sheedy, Steve Guttenberg, Fisher Stevens, Austin Pendleton, G.W. Bailey, David Oliver

© FOXVIDEO 3724

SHORT CIRCUIT 2

D: Kenneth Johnson — 110 m

PG | COM SF | 1988 | COLOR

7 Johnny Five (formerly No. 5) is the cute military robot that was struck by lightning in the original film and then became almost human. In this sequel, Johnny comes to the big city to help out one of his inventors who has now gone into the toy business. Johnny hits the streets looking for some "urban input" but attracts some unsavory friends. Some street punks want to trick the naive robot into helping them to pull off a jewel robbery. Cute, but mostly for the younger set this time.

□ Sex □ Nud ◢ Viol ◢ Lang □ AdSit

A: Fisher Stevens, Michael McKean, Cynthia Gibb, Jack Weston

© COLUMBIA TRISTAR HOME VIDEO 67008

SILENT RUNNING

D: Douglas Trumbull — 90 m

G | SF DMA | 1972 | COLOR

8 Dramatic family entertainment with a message. A spaceship floating about in space houses the only remaining vegetation left from an earth where a nuclear war has destroyed all plant life. Dern is a devoted botanist who has spent eight years tending this ark and now he has received an order from earth to destroy everything. The enormity of what is being asked of him is more than he can bare. Instead, he hijacks the vessel, kills off the other crewmen and takes his cargo into the safety of the rings of Saturn. His only companions now are the two robots with very human-like qualities that help him to tend his garden.

□ Sex □ Nud □ Viol □ Lang □ AdSit

A: Bruce Dern, Cliff Potts, Ron Rifkin, Jesse Vint

© MCA/UNIVERSAL HOME VIDEO, INC. 55029

SLAUGHTERHOUSE FIVE

D: George Roy Hill — 104 m

R | SF | 1972 | COLOR

7 Slick and intelligent sci-fi adventure. Billy Pilgrim (Sacks) is a middle-aged man, just an average Joe, whose normal progression in time gets completely out of wack. Pilgrim can't seem to stay in the present, but instead travels from his current life, as a father and husband, back to his life as a POW during WWII and forward to an alien planet, where he is held captive with a sexy lover. Pilgrim even lives two different life experiences at the same time. This very well-done adaptation of Vonnegut's noted novel is sophisticated and spirited, but may be hard to follow the first time around.

□ Sex ◢ Nud ■ Viol ■ Lang ◢ AdSit

A: Michael Sacks, Ron Leibman, Valerie Perrine, Eugene Roche, Sharon Gans, John Dehner

© MCA/UNIVERSAL HOME VIDEO, INC. 55070

STAND, THE

D: Mark Garris — 360 m

NR | SF SUS | 1994 | COLOR

7 Stephen King's epic length novel has been turned into an epic-length (very long) TV movie. At a very high security government research laboratory in California, a lab experiment has gone very wrong. A bacterial agent intended for germ warfare is released and within a matter of days the world's entire population has been whittled down to only 1% of its former size. Emotionally scarred but relieved that the terror is finally over, groups of ragged survivors have begun to gather for survival. But it is only now, on the outskirts of Las Vegas, that the real battle, the battle between good and the ultimate evil, truly begins.

□ Sex □ Nud ◢ Viol □ Lang ◢ AdSit

A: Gary Sinise, Molly Ringwald, Jamey Sheridan, Laura San Giacomo, Ruby Dee, Ossie Davis

© REPUBLIC PICTURES HOME VIDEO 5683

STARGATE

D: Roland Emmerich — 119 m

PG-13 | SF ACT | 1994 | COLOR

7 James Spader is a brilliant linguistic professor whose unconventional ideas have gotten him in trouble, when he receives an invitation to work on a highly secret government project. His job is to decipher ancient symbols on a large round ring first discovered in 1928 at an Egyptian archeological dig, but never reported. His success leads to the discovery that the ring is in fact a portal through space that leads to another world. Now, he and a military team led by Kurt Russell have gone to that other world. It is very similar to earth, however its society has never changed. They remain slaves to the alien being who departed earth 10,000 years before. Some big plot holes diminish its effectiveness.

□ Sex □ Nud ◢ Viol ◢ Lang ◢ AdSit

A: Kurt Russell, James Spader, Viveca Lindfors, Alexis Cruz, Mili Avital, Jaye Davidson

© LIVE HOME VIDEO 60222

STARMAN

D: John Carpenter 115 m

PG | ROM SF FAN | 1984 | COLOR

8 An endearing charmer. An space ship is shot down and crashes in rural Wisconsin. The scared alien escapes from the crash site before the government gets to it and stumbles upon the cabin of a young woman (Allen) who is newly widowed and still grieving the loss of her husband. The alien will die if he doesn't make it to Arizona where he will be rescued in three days. So he, takes on the form of her dead husband and makes her drive him there. She is not pleased but along the way, while they are dodging the pursuing FBI, she discovers a sweetness about him. That, and because he looks like her dead husband, she falls in love with him. Very entertaining and uplifting.

☐ Sex ☐ Nud ◢ Viol ◢ Lang ◢ AdSit

A: Jeff Bridges, Karen Allen, Charles Martin Smith, Richard Jaeckel

© COLUMBIA TRISTAR HOME VIDEO 60412

STAR TREK: THE MOTION PICTURE

D: Robert Wise 143 m

G | SF ACT | 1980 | COLOR

6 This is the first full-length motion picture spawned from the extremely popular TV series of 15 years prior, featuring the same cast. Driven by the huge popularity of that series, the picture generated terrific box office attention and spawned many sequels. This episode concerns an incoming ominous cloud that devours everything in its path. The Enterprise crew discovers that the cloud is really an intelligent machine. When one of it's crew has her body taken over by that intelligence, Kirk and company use her as a key to pursue the mystery of the machine and to venture inside it.

☐ Sex ☐ Nud ☐ Viol ☐ Lang ☐ AdSit

A: William Shatner, Leonard Nimoy, Persis Khambatta, Stephen Collins, DeForest Kelley, James Doohan

© PARAMOUNT HOME VIDEO 8858

STAR TREK GENERATIONS

D: David Carson 117 m

PG | SF ACT | 1994 | COLOR

7 As this film was being made, STAR TREK: THE NEXT GENERATION was ceasing TV production. This film also marked the death of Captain Kirk and so set the stage for the succeeding sequels to revolve around the crew of the "NEXT GENERATION." Here Kirk is aboard the maiden flight of the Enterprise B, when he is apparently sucked into space by a hull breach after the ship confronts an energy field. Time advances 75 years. The crew of the Enterprise C again confronts the energy field. Guinan informs Captain Picard that it is the Nexus, a time-space phenomenon which is paradise-like inside. Mad-scientist, Dr. Soran, is willing to destroy a solar system to get there. Kirk and Picard, both inside the Nexus, must unite to defeat him.

☐ Sex ☐ Nud ◢ Viol ◢ Lang ◢ AdSit

A: Patrick Stewart, Jonathan Frakes, Brent Spinner, Levar Burton, Michael Dorn, William Shatner

© PARAMOUNT HOME VIDEO 32988

STAR TREK II: THE WRATH OF KHAN

D: Nicholas Meyer 113 m

PG | SF ACT | 1982 | COLOR

8 Solid entry in the Star Trek series based upon one of the original 1960s TV plots. In that TV episode, the Enterprise crew had exiled several very aggressive genetic supermen on a lonely planet. They had been genetically engineered to be superior to ordinary humans but had become determined to dominate all society. They are led by Khan (Montalban). Now they have escaped. They have commandeered a war ship and are seeking possession of the new Genesis technology, which can create whole planets - but can also destroy them. And Khan seeks also to destroy his old nemesis, Kirk.

☐ Sex ☐ Nud ◢ Viol ☐ Lang ☐ AdSit

A: William Shatner, Leonard Nimoy, Ricardo Montalban, DeForest Kelley, James Doohan

© PARAMOUNT HOME VIDEO 1180

STAR TREK III: THE SEARCH FOR SPOCK

D: Leonard Nimoy 105 m

PG | SF ACT | 1984 | COLOR

8 Spock is dead - or is he? In STAR TREK II, Spock had sacrificed himself in order to save the rest of the crew. His body was "buried" on the Genesis planet. Now there is evidence that Spock's intellect was not lost and his body is regenerating itself. Kirk and the crew steal their now-mothballed ship and return to rescue a young boy who may be Spock. However, they also find there a Klingon warship that is determined to capture the Genesis technology. Less emphasis on special effects and more on characters and plot.

☐ Sex ☐ Nud ◢ Viol ☐ Lang ☐ AdSit

A: William Shatner, DeForest Kelley, James Doohan, George Takei, Walter Koenig, Nichelle Nichols

© PARAMOUNT HOME VIDEO 1621

STAR TREK IV: THE VOYAGE HOME

D: William Shatner 119 m

PG | SF ACT | 1989 | COLOR

7 Light-hearted and fun. Kirk and the crew of the Enterprise return home to earth in their commandeered Klingon ship (from STAR TREK III) to discover that earth's atmosphere is being bombarded by a message from an alien probe that cannot be returned. The probe is broadcasting in a language only understood by humpback whales, a species that is extinct in the 23rd century. The crew travels back in time to the 20th century to capture two whales to take forward in time and receive the messages. Very entertaining and somewhat comic in tone. A good time.

☐ Sex ☐ Nud ☐ Viol ◢ Lang ☐ AdSit

A: William Shatner, Leonard Nimoy, DeForest Kelley, James Doohan, Walter Koenig, Nichelle Nichols

© PARAMOUNT HOME VIDEO 1797

STAR TREK V: THE FINAL FRONTIER

D: William Shatner 107 m

PG | SF ACT | 1989 | COLOR

6 Kirk and McCoy are trying to teach Spock some campfire songs when the Enterprise receives an emergency call to go to a distant planet which has apparently been taken over by a madman. However, it has all been a ruse. It was only a gambit to attract a starship, the Enterprise, which is then hijacked. The madman needs a vessel to take him to the Great Barrier - the edge of the Universe. He wants to talk to God. Kirk is uncertain why he would need to go to such lengths, but Spock is more receptive - the madman is his half-brother.

☐ Sex ☐ Nud ☐ Viol ◢ Lang ☐ AdSit

A: William Shatner, Leonard Nimoy, DeForest Kelley, James Doohan, Walter Koenig, Nichelle Nichols

© PARAMOUNT HOME VIDEO 32044

STAR TREK VI: THE UNDISCOVERED COUNTRY

D: Nicholas Meyer, William Shatner 110 m

PG | SF ACT | 1991 | COLOR

7 The Klingon Empire is ready to make peace. One of their moons has exploded, the ozone on their home world is being destroyed, they do not have the resources to combat it themselves and they need the Federation. Even though Kirk loathes Klingons because they killed his son, the Enterprise is called upon to meet with the Klingons to prepare for peace talks -- but one of the Klingons is poisoned, Kirk and Dr. McCoy are accused of murder and are sentenced to a prison at a frozen Klingon outpost. Meanwhile, Spock has been able to prove that it was all a plot to destroy the talks. He must retrieve Kirk and McCoy and uncover the real plotters to salvage the peace.

☐ Sex ☐ Nud ◢ Viol ☐ Lang ☐ AdSit

A: William Shatner, Leonard Nimoy, DeForest Kelley, James Doohan, Walter Koenig, Nichelle Nicholes

© PARAMOUNT HOME VIDEO 32301

STAR WARS

D: George Lucas 124 m

PG | SF ACT SUS | 1977 | COLOR

10 HUGE megahit and first of a trio of hits. Old-time Saturday matinee cliff-hanger intensity, Western shoot-`em-up action, mysticism, comedy, loveable characters and high tech wizardry - all set in a place long, long ago and far, far away. An ordinary boy, living with his adoptive parents on a remote farming colony, comes home to find them murdered by Imperial Stormtroopers. He soon also finds that he is not so ordinary and is launched into a mission to save the Universe. Won seven Oscars. Immensely entertaining. Followed by THE EMPIRE STRIKES BACK.

☐ Sex ☐ Nud ◢ Viol ☐ Lang ☐ AdSit

A: Carrie Fisher, Mark Hamill, Harrison Ford, Alec Guinness, Anthony Daniels, Peter Cushing

© FOXVIDEO 1130

TERMINAL MAN, THE

D: Mike Hodges 107 m

R | SF ACT | 1974 | COLOR

6 Engrossing science fiction thriller. George Segal plays a computer scientist who suffered some brain damage from an accident which causes him to erupt in violent outbursts. In desperation he agrees to have a microchip implanted within his brain which supposedly will control his violent urges, but there is a problem. The chip malfunctions and instead it turns him into a violent killer. Well acted, but pretty grim stuff.

☐ Sex ☐ Nud ◢ Viol ☐ Lang ☐ AdSit

A: George Segal, Joan Hackett, Jill Clayburgh, Richard Dysart

© WARNER HOME VIDEO 11212

TERMINATOR, THE

D: James Cameron 108 m

R | ACT SUS SF | 1984 | COLOR

10 A huge blockbuster hit that gained notoriety because of its extremely high intensity. Schwarzenneger, a cyborg (a lifelike robot), is sent back from the future to kill the mother (Hamilton) of a boy who is not yet born but who will later become a rebel leader. Arnold is an incredibly relentless and nearly indestructible killing machine from whom there is no escape. However, also arriving from the future is a resistance fighter (Biehn) who is0 here to help Hamilton defeat the Terminator. Terrific non-stop action flick, great special effects, believable and sympathetic characters and incredible pacing.

◢ Sex ◢ Nud ■ Viol ■ Lang ◢ AdSit

A: Arnold Schwarzenegger, Michael Biehn, Linda Hamilton, Paul Winfield, Lance Henriksen, Rick Rossovich

© HBO VIDEO 2535

TERMINATOR 2: JUDGMENT DAY

D: James Cameron 139 m

R | ACT SF | 1991 | COLOR

9 The action doesn't get much better than this! Hamilton and Schwarzenegger are powerhouses, poised to face their toughest challenges - and they do. The Terminator is back, but this time he is the good guy and the protector of Hamilton's son (Furlong), who is destined to eventually become a world leader in the eventual fight of men against the machines. When a new high tech Terminator that has been programmed to destroy the boy is dispatched from the future, Hamilton and Schwarzenegger find themselves involved in the ultimate battle with the ultimate killing machine. Will superior technology win over shear determination and the human spirit?

☐ Sex ☐ Nud ■ Viol ■ Lang ◢ AdSit

A: Arnold Schwarzenegger, Linda Hamilton, Robert Patrick, Edward Furlong, Earl Boen, Joe Morton

© LIVE HOME VIDEO 68952

SF

THING, THE

D: John Carpenter — 109 m

R | HOR SF SUS | 1982 | COLOR

7 The 1951 classic has been remade. However, it would be more accurate to say that this is more of a sequel. This version, however, is not for the little kiddies - it is filled with gore. Where the original relied upon your imagination to create fear, this version gives you a series of state-of-the-art gory special effects. Kurt Russell and his people arrive at the remote arctic station just after an alien creature, which had been defrosted after having been frozen for years, has depleted the supply of live bodies. This new crew will soon be his new supply. This is scary and fun, but check out the original, too. It is, in many ways, better.

Sex Nud Viol Lang AdSit

A: Kurt Russell, Wilford Brimley, Richard Dysart, Richard Masur, T.K. Carter, Richard Dysart

© MCA/UNIVERSAL HOME VIDEO, INC. 77009

TIME AFTER TIME

D: Nicholas Meyer — 112 m

PG | SF CRM | 1979 | COLOR

8 Very imaginative and engaging story that is quite literate and very enjoyable in spite of its apparently bizarre premise. H.G. Welles (Malcolm McDowell) is compelled to chase Jack the Ripper (David Warner) into the future after the Ripper uses Welles's time machine to escape from Victorian England. The future he escapes to is San Francisco in 1979. Welles and the Ripper engage in a lively battle of wits in an environment that is totally alien to both of them. An amusing and engaging subplot is Welles's burgeoning romance with a modern-day bank teller (Mary Steenburgen).

Sex Nud Viol Lang AdSit

A: David Warner, Mary Steenburgen, Malcolm McDowell, Charles Cioffi, Joseph Maher, Patti D'Arbanville

© WARNER HOME VIDEO 22017

TIME BANDITS

D: Terry Gilliam — 116 m

PG | SF COM | 1981 | COLOR

6 A near-hit from Monty Python alumni Michael Palin and Terry Gilliam. It's witty and clever, with very high production values, but somehow doesn't connect big-time. A bored English schoolboy is escorted through time and space by six dwarves who have stolen a map of time holes from the Supreme Being. They are out to steal treasures from one time and escape into another time. Along the way they have encounters with Robin Hood, Agamemnon, Napoleon and the Titanic. Doesn't work real well as a comedy, but passes fairly well as an adventure.

Sex Nud Viol Lang AdSit

A: John Cleese, Sean Connery, Ian Holm, Shelley Duvall, Katherine Helmond, Michael Palin

© PARAMOUNT HOME VIDEO 2310

TIMECOP

D: Peter Hyams — 99 m

R | SF ACT | 1994 | COLOR

8 This is Jean-Claude Van Damme's most interesting and intelligent flick to date. Blood-and-guts action fans certainly will not be disappointed - there is still plenty of both. However, this one actually has a pretty good premise and is well executed. Van Damme is a special officer assigned to a highly secret government agency in 2004. Their job is to go back into time to remove modern time travelers before they can alter history. The travelers he seeks have been sent by a corrupt politician who is using his access to the technology to generate money for a Presidential election campaign, no matter what the cost. Some plot holes, but over-all it is quite well done and fun.

Sex Nud Viol Lang AdSit

A: Jean-Claude Van Damme, Ron Silver, Mia Sara, Gloria Reuben, Bruce McGill, Scott Lawrence

© MCA/UNIVERSAL HOME VIDEO, INC. 82169

TIME MACHINE, THE

D: George Pal — 103 m

PG | SF DMA | 1960 | COLOR

8 Lush adaptation of the H.G. Welles novel. A Victorian inventor (Taylor) develops a time machine and, full of hope, he travels ahead in time only to encounter numerous world wars and destruction. Disturbed, he leaps far ahead into the year 802,701. There he discovers a peaceful, carefree race living in an apparent Garden of Eden. But there are dangers here as well. These people are mutants, born of atomic wars, who are totally ignorant and apathetic to everything - to the point that they won't even defend themselves against a race of subsurface dwellers which preys upon them. Special Effects Oscar.

Sex Nud Viol Lang AdSit

A: Rod Taylor, Alan Young, Yvette Mimieux, Sebastian Cabot, Tom Helmore, Whit Bissell

Distributed By MGM/UA Home Video M600152

TOTAL RECALL

D: Paul Verhoeven — 113 m

R | SF ACT | 1990 | COLOR

9 Spectacular special effects mark this high intensity actioner, set in the year 2084. Arnold Schwarzenegger is a construction worker who decides to take a fantasy trip to Mars from a machine that plants new memories in your mind. Instead, the machine brings back mysterious haunting old memories that have been taken from him. Why has someone wiped out his memories? Who is he really? He is driven to go to Mars to find out. He finds that he was a secret agent, and now they're trying to kill him. But, why? Very violent. Big, big budget was spent for special effects and scenery, and it shows.

Sex Nud Viol Lang AdSit

A: Arnold Schwarzenegger, Rachel Ticotin, Sharon Stone, Michael Ironside, Ronny Cox

© LIVE HOME VIDEO 68901

TRON

D: Steven Lisberger — 95 m

PG | SF ACT | 1982 | COLOR

6 Enjoyable Disney escapist adventure, geared to more than just kids. Set in the future, nearly everything is controlled by the Master Computer. Jeff Bridges is a computer whiz who sets out to prove that Warner, an unscrupulous executive, has stolen some of his programs. But before he gets very far, he is sucked inside the Master Computer's circuits where he, Boxleitner and Hughes must do battle against Warner and the Master Computer in a deadly video game. Exciting special effects. Plot is a little confusing, though.

Sex Nud Viol Lang AdSit

A: Jeff Bridges, Bruce Boxleitner, David Warner, Cindy Morgan, Barnard Hughes, Dan Shor

© WALT DISNEY HOME VIDEO 122

UFORIA

D: John Binder — 92 m

PG | SF COM | 1981 | COLOR

7 Eccentric personalities mix with funky science fiction and make a thoroughly enjoyable film. Quirky supermarket checkout clerk Williams is a born again Christian with some wild ideas. She believes she is the chosen one, that salvation will come in the form of UFOs and that she will lead humanity to safety. Wanderer Ward falls in love with her, and preacher/huckster Stanton decides that this is a great opportunity to make some serious money, if he can just milk it from the right angle. But... what happens if she's right? Good natured fun, offbeat and more than a little zany.

Sex Nud Viol Lang AdSit

A: Cindy Williams, Harry Dean Stanton, Fred Ward, Harry Carey, Jr., Darrell Larson

© MCA/UNIVERSAL HOME VIDEO, INC. 80042

V

D: Kenneth Johnson — 197 m

NR | SF ACT | 1983 | COLOR

9 This excellent made-for-TV miniseries held the fascination of the country. In it, fifty huge space ships appear in the skies over all the world's major cities. The human-like visitors relate that they are on a mission of peace, but soon they are moving to focus the fears of the masses. Blaming scientist's for all the ills of the mankind, they make their move to establish a world-wide fascist state, while also destroying the only force that can stop them. TV cameraman Mark Singer discovers the awful real truth and forms a rebel army to battle them. Very effective special effects create believability. Success brought another miniseries, then a TV series.

Sex Nud Viol Lang AdSit

A: Mark Singer, Faye Grant, Michael Durrell, Peter Nelson, Jane Badler, Neva Patterson

© WARNER HOME VIDEO 11489

VILLAGE OF THE DAMNED

D: Wolf Rilla — 77 m

HOR SF | 1960 | B&W

8 Eerie, suspenseful and frightening! All the women in a small English village mysteriously become pregnant at the same time and give birth to a strange group of emotionless, super-intelligent children. They all have blond hair, physically develop very rapidly, and also possess telekinetic powers. George Sanders is the father of the children's leader. He takes it upon himself to become their teacher and he learns even more about them. Then the children, with an eerie calmness, begin to terrorize the village. Even though they can read his every thought, Sanders decides that they must be destroyed.

Sex Nud Viol Lang AdSit

A: George Sanders, Barbara Shelley, Michael Gwynne, Laurence Naismith, John Phillips, Richard Vernon

Distributed By MGM/UA Home Video M600174

VOYAGE TO THE BOTTOM OF THE SEA

D: Irwin Allen — 106 m

NR | SF CLD | 1961 | COLOR

6 Reasonably good, light, family-oriented sci-fi flick in which a brilliant submarine commander (Pidgeon) has devised a scheme to save the earth, after the Van Allen radiation belts erupt and threaten to destroy it. The Arctic is already on fire and soon fire will engulf the whole earth unless they can stop it. His plan is to launch a polaris missile into space and then explode it, breaking the chain reaction. But before they can get the sub into position to do that, they have to defeat a sea monster, fend off attacking submarines and an on-board saboteur. It spawned a popular mid-'60s TV series.

Sex Nud Viol Lang AdSit

A: Walter Pidgeon, Joan Fontaine, Peter Lorre, Robert Sterling, Barbara Eden, Michael Ansara

© FOXVIDEO 1044

WARRIORS, THE

D: Walter Hill — 94 m

R | ACT SF | 1979 | COLOR

7 Very stylized, surrealistic and almost cartoon-like vision of street-gang violence in New York City. Somewhat similar in "feel" to CLOCKWORK ORANGE. Two hundred street gangs (called tribes) hold a rally in downtown NYC. A small, little-known tribe calling itself "The Warriors" travels in with the rest. When the grand leader of all the tribes is killed, the unarmed Warriors are falsely blamed. Their leader is killed and the eight remaining members must get struggle to get back home. Their return trip is played out like a game where the subways are "safe" zones.

Sex Nud Viol Lang AdSit

A: Michael Beck, James Remar, Deborah Van Valkenburgh, Thomas Waites, Dorsey Wright, Brian Tyler

© PARAMOUNT HOME VIDEO 1122

SF

WAVELENGTH

D: Mike Gray 87 m

PG
SF
1983
COLOR
Sex
Nud
Viol
Lang
AdSit

6 Interesting and different sort of science fiction flick. A rock musician living in Hollywood Hills stumbles onto a seemingly abandoned underground Air Force facility. He, his girlfriend and an old prospector (Keenan Wynn) explore it and find that the Air Force is holding and conducting secret medical experiments on three extraterrestrials held prisoner there. Soon the government has captured them, too. They and the ETs join forces to escape. Quite well done, with a solid rock score from the group Tangerine Dream.

A: Robert Carradine, Cherie Currie, Keenan Wynn, Cal Bowman, James Hess, Terry Burns

© R&G VIDEO, LP 80201

WESTWORLD

D: Michael Crichton 90 m

PG
SF
WST
ACT
1973
COLOR
Sex
Nud
Viol
Lang
AdSit

7 Very entertaining and inventive yarn about a high tech adult resort of the future, where wealthy patrons may live out their Wild West fantasies with amazingly lifelike robots. By day, the robots are shot up by the patrons. At night they are repaired. Everything is harmless and quite safe until one errant gunfighter robot (Brynner is terrific) refuses to play the game as it was written. He goes berserk and starts stalking the guests for real. Richard Benjamin and James Brolin are two tourists who are unfortunate enough to catch his attention. Well-done sequel is FUTUREWORLD.

A: Yul Brynner, James Brolin, Richard Benjamin, Alan Oppenheimer, Victoria Shaw, Martin Jared

Distributed By MGM/UA Home Video M600097

Suspense

Videos Best

1956 and After

3:10 TO YUMA

D: Delmer Daves — 92 m

NR | WST SUS ACT | 1957 | B&W

9 Top drawer Western, one of the best of the 1950s. Glenn Ford is a notorious gunman and powerful leader of a gang who holds up a stagecoach but gets caught when he stays behind to dally with a lonely barmaid. The wealthy owner of the stage company has offered Van Heflin, a poverty-struck farmer, $200 to guard Ford in a hotel room until lawmen arrive on the 3:10 train to take him into custody. Desperate for the money, Van Heflin agrees and becomes caught up in a psychological battle of wills with Ford, whose men begin to gather outside getting ready to break him out. Powerful stuff.

Sex | Nud | Viol | Lang | AdSit

A: Van Heflin, Glenn Ford, Felicia Farr, Richard Jaeckel, Henry Jones, Leora Dana

© COLUMBIA TRISTAR HOME VIDEO 60444

52 PICKUP

D: John Frankenheimer — 111 m

R | ACT SUS | 1986 | COLOR

7 A hard-edged and self-made man (Scheider) has a fling with a beautiful girl (Preston), where he is photographed by a group of pornographers, and becomes trapped in first blackmail and then murder. Scheider decides to fight back on his own, both to gain back his freedom but also to get revenge against the super-sleazy bad guys. This is a fast-paced thriller with a good story line, but it contains a very graphic and lurid depiction of underground sleaze and is a little too long.

Sex | Nud | Viol | Lang | AdSit

A: Roy Scheider, Ann-Margret, Vanity, John Glover, Clarence Williams, III, Kelly Preston

© VIDEO TREASURES SV9163

5 CORNERS

D: Tony Bill — 94 m

R | SUS COM | 1987 | COLOR

7 This is a strange blending of melodrama and comedy, set in a 1960s Bronx atmosphere. Jodie Foster plays a pretty pet store worker who helped to convict a violent and unstable admirer, and her would-be rapist. Now he is out and is looking for her. Fearful, she seeks help from a friend and former neighborhood tough guy to help protect her from her obsessed fan. However, after a protracted bout of conscience, her toughguy-protector has become a pacifist and civil rights activist. Hard, reality-based suspense is offset by some offbeat comedy and interesting and curious characters.

Sex | Nud | Viol | Lang | AdSit

A: Jodie Foster, Tim Robbins, John Turturro, Elizabeth Berridge, Todd Graff, Rose Gregorio

Distributed By MGM/UA Home Video M202773

8 MILLION WAYS TO DIE

D: Hal Ashby — 115 m

R | ACT SUS CRM | 1986 | COLOR

7 Brutal and cynical film in which Bridges, as an alcoholic ex-cop, is hired by a high-priced call girl (Arquette) to help her escape from her drug-dealing boyfriend and pimp (Garcia). Bridges gets drawn deep into a world of drugs, alcohol and sex and with his history, he may not make it back out. But - having Arquette there waiting for him at the end makes it worth the effort. This is a very violent and cynical cop film, punctuated with Bridges's character's personal crisis. However, it is also populated mostly with unsympathetic characters and that makes it a difficult film to get close to.

Sex | Nud | Viol | Lang | AdSit

A: Jeff Bridges, Rosanna Arquette, Alexandra Paul, Randy Brooks, Andy Garcia, Lisa Sloan

© CBS/FOX VIDEO 6118

ABYSS, THE

D: James Cameron — 140 m

PG-13 | SUS ACT SF | 1989 | COLOR

7 Spectacular underwater adventure story about oil-platform workers and a Navy SEAL diving team who are paired in an attempt to find a mysteriously sunken nuclear submarine in extremely deep water. However, they encounter a wondrous deep water mystery on their trip into the deep. Absolutely riveting suspense, with intense action thrown in and a good plot twist. Although the fantasy element is a little weak, the thrills and the intense suspense more than compensate. Special effects are remarkable and were used again in TERMINATOR II.

Sex | Nud | Viol | Lang | AdSit

A: Ed Harris, Mary Elizabeth Mastrantonio, Michael Biehn, Leo Burmester, Todd Graff, John Bedford Lloyd

© FOXVIDEO 1561

AFTER DARK MY SWEET

D: James Foley — 114 m

R | SUS CRM | 1990 | COLOR

8 Sexy modern-day film noir. A seemingly punch-drunk ex-boxer drifter (Patric), recently escaped from a mental institution, finds himself irresistibly attracted to a seductive widow (Ward). She and a disgraced ex-cop, now a sleazy con man (Dern), draw him into an ill-conceived kidnap and ransom plot. When Patric discovers that he has been duped and is just a pawn in their plan, things get deadly. They picked on the wrong guy. Lots of plot twists in this steamy thriller that is also rife with cynicism and paranoia. Patric puts in a superb performance.

Sex | Nud | Viol | Lang | AdSit

A: Jason Patric, Rachel Ward, Bruce Dern, George Dickerson, James Cotton, Rocky Giordani

© LIVE HOME VIDEO 68943

AFTER HOURS

D: Martin Scorsese — 97 m

R | COM SUS | 1985 | COLOR

6 Very bizarre and sophisticated black comedy. Be prepared for the unusual. Griffin Dunn is an uptight, word-processing trainer who is caught up in a nightmarish comedy of errors. He sets off to meet a sexy blind date (Arquette) at an artist's studio in Soho, but on the way there all his cash is blown out the window of his taxi. He goes to meet her anyway, but decides she is too strange and wants to leave but he doesn't have the subway fare home. So, he has become trapped, along with all the other weirdos, in Soho and that is when his troubles really begin.

Sex | Nud | Viol | Lang | AdSit

A: Griffin Dunne, Rosanna Arquette, Teri Garr, John Heard, Linda Fiorentino, Richard"Cheech" Martin

© WARNER HOME VIDEO 11528

AIRPORT

D: George Seaton — 137 m

PG | SUS DMA | 1970 | COLOR

9 This was the first of the major disaster epics which were very popular for nearly a decade. Here, a crazed bomber blows a hole in an airliner while it is in flight. Badly crippled, the plane must land immediately at a snowbound airport whose runway is blocked by another airliner stuck in the mud. This type of plot provides an opportunity for the film to explore the lives of several different people affected by the disaster. So, there are several stories going on all at the same time. Pretty good stuff. Helen Hayes won an Oscar. Taut and suspenseful. See also AIRPORT 1975, AIRPORT '77, THE POSIDEON ADVENTURE, EARTHQUAKE and TOWERING INFERNO.

Sex | Nud | Viol | Lang | AdSit

A: Burt Lancaster, Dean Martin, George Kennedy, Helen Hayes, Jean Seberg, Jacqueline Bisset

© MCA/UNIVERSAL HOME VIDEO, INC. 55031

AIRPORT 1975

D: Jack Smight 107 m

PG | SUS DMA | 1974 | COLOR

7 AIRPORT disaster sequel. When the cockpit of a 747 is struck by a small plane in mid-air, the entire flight crew is killed. It is up to stewardess Karen Black to fly the plane by Heston's radioed instructions, that is until Heston himself can be "dropped" into the ripped-open cock-pit by a helicopter from overhead. Not terribly believable but it is very entertaining - in part because there were 22 major stars aboard that airplane. See also AIRPORT and AIRPORT '77.

Sex / Nud / Viol / Lang / AdSit

A: Charlton Heston, Karen Black, George Kennedy, Efrem Zimbalist, Jr., Susan Clark, Helen Reddy

© GOODTIMES 4107

AIRPORT '77

D: Jerry Jameson 114 m

PG | SUS DMA | 1977 | COLOR

7 This is another AIRPORT disaster flick sequel. This time, millionaire Jimmy Stewart has a converted 747 jumbo jet transport a large group of VIP guests along with a fortune in his art treasures to the grand opening of a museum in Palm Beach. However, the plane is hijacked along the way and forced to crash land into the open ocean within the famed Bermuda Triangle. Then, in order to be rescued, the plane and passengers, who are alive inside, must be lifted whole from the ocean floor. See also AIRPORT and AIRPORT 1975.

Sex / Nud / Viol / Lang / AdSit

A: Jack Lemmon, Lee Grant, Brenda Vaccaro, Darren McGavin, Christopher Lee, James Stewart

© MCA/UNIVERSAL HOME VIDEO, INC. 66039

ALIEN

D: Ridley Scott 116 m

R | SUS ACT SF | 1979 | COLOR

9 Heart-stopping terror and action galore. A spaceship crew finds that it has unwittingly taken on board an alien life form that uses human flesh to incubate its young, lives on human flesh and has the disconcerting ability to constantly change its form. Weaver is determined, tough and the only crewmember smart enough to stop it, and... she is determined to stop it. Gut-wrenching, non-stop suspense. Not for the faint-hearted. Followed by the equally good ALIENS and ALIEN 3, also with Weaver.

Sex / Nud / Viol / Lang / AdSit

A: Tom Skerritt, Sigourney Weaver, John Hurt, Ian Holm, Harry Dean Stanton, Yaphet Kotto

© FOXVIDEO 1090

ALIEN 3

D: David Fincher 115 m

R | SUS ACT SF | 1992 | COLOR

8 Third entry in the chilling series. Sigourney Weaver is back. This time she crash-lands on a flea-infested maximum security prison planet which is occupied by some of the most violent criminals in the universe. However, the inmates there have found a sort of peace through religion and celibacy. In fact, Weaver poses a greater threat to them than they do to her because she has brought with her the Alien creature that lays its eggs inside humans. And, there are no weapons here to fight the deadly creatures. This one is more cerebral and less intense than the others, but it's no picnic either.

Sex / Nud / Viol / Lang / AdSit

A: Sigourney Weaver, Charles Dutton, Charles Dance, Paul McGann, Brian Glover, Ralph Brown

© FOXVIDEO 5593

ALIENS

D: James Cameron 138 m

R | SUS ACT SF | 1986 | COLOR

10 Wow! After 57 years of suspended animation, Weaver reawakens to find that the Alien's home planet has been colonized by humans, but now all contact with them has been lost. Weaver is determined to end her nightmares and to rid the universe of the Aliens. So, along with a Marine squad, she returns to the planet intent on saving the colonists. When they arrive, only a small girl is still living and they soon find themselves in an intense battle for their own lives. Every bit as intense as the original ALIEN and in some ways maybe better. Very heavy-duty action. Special effects won an Oscar.

Sex / Nud / Viol / Lang / AdSit

A: Sigourney Weaver, Carrie Henn, Michael Biehn, Paul Reiser, Lance Henriksen, Bill Paxton

© FOXVIDEO 1504

ALTERED STATES

D: Ken Russell 103 m

R | SF SUS | 1980 | COLOR

6 Provocative movie. A research scientist (Hurt) uses himself as a guinea pig in his search to discover the other states of reality he believes coexist within us all. He pursues his search within himself while inside an isolation tank. However, when he combines drug experimentation with the isolation tank to get in deeper touch with his primitive state, he uncovers much more than he bargained for. It starts out rather slow and preachy, but settles into some terrific special effects. Interesting ideas are probed that will carry the viewer with the film, even if it does take a while.

Sex / Nud / Viol / Lang / AdSit

A: William Hurt, Blair Brown, Bob Balaban, Charles Haid, Drew Barrymore

© WARNER HOME VIDEO 11076

AMBASSADOR, THE

D: J. Lee Thompson 97 m

R | SUS DMA | 1984 | COLOR

7 Political intrigue set in the Middle East. Mitchum is a dedicated American ambassador to Israel who is working hard to find a solution to the Palestinian issue. He efforts make him the target of numerous terrorist attacks including being blackmailed with a film of his adulterous wife's illicit affair with a PLO powerbroker. Hudson is a security officer. This is an intelligent and entertaining thriller. This is also Rock Hudson's last major film. It is loosely based upon the book 52 PICKUP which was itself made into a good film and released two years later.

Sex / Nud / Viol / Lang / AdSit

A: Robert Mitchum, Ellen Burstyn, Rock Hudson, Fabio Testi, Donald Pleasence

Distributed By MGM/UA Home Video M800765

AMERICAN GIGOLO

D: Paul Schrader 117 m

R | SUS MYS | 1980 | COLOR

7 A handsome loner and male whore (Gere) makes his living keeping the ladies of Beverly Hills company. He falls for the wife of a politician (Hutton) and she for him. But a major problem arises when he is framed for a kinky sex-murder and she must decide whether to provide him with the alibi he needs. The sexual chemistry between the two makes this thriller exciting and believable, if a little sleazy.

Sex / Nud / Viol / Lang / AdSit

A: Richard Gere, Lauren Hutton, Hector Elizondo, Nina Van Pallandt, Bill Duke, Frances Bergen

© PARAMOUNT HOME VIDEO 8989

ANATOMY OF A MURDER

D: Otto Preminger 161 m

NR | SUS MYS CRM | 1959 | B&W

9 Extremely strong movie. Fascinating courtroom drama with a strong sense of realism. A gripping story that was nominated for seven Oscars, including Best Picture. Jimmy Stewart defends an Army lieutenant (Gazzara) who is on trial for having murdered his sexy wife's (Remick) rapist. Excellent legal drama, considered to be among the best of all time, with some absolutely riveting scenes. Stewart is a witty, cagey defense lawyer. Scott is a stuffy big-city prosecuting attorney. First-rate stuff that was also considered very daring for its time.

Sex / Nud / Viol / Lang / AdSit

A: James Stewart, Arthur O'Connell, Lee Remick, Ben Gazzara, Eve Arden, George C. Scott

© COLUMBIA TRISTAR HOME VIDEO 60701

ANDERSON TAPES, THE

D: Sidney Lumet 98 m

PG | SUS CRM | 1971 | COLOR

7 Really neat thriller. Connery is a master crook who has just been released from prison. He plans the holdup of the entire Fifth Avenue apartment building where his girlfriend lives in New York City and the plan is bankrolled by a big underworld boss. The best specialists there are have been hired to work with him. Disguised as moving men, the team systematically loots each apartment, but things start to unravel. Tight editing and excellent performances keep the viewer totally involved and on edge. Climax is particularly good.

Sex / Nud / Viol / Lang / AdSit

A: Sean Connery, Dyan Cannon, Martin Balsam, Ralph Meeker, Alan King, Margaret Hamilton

© COLUMBIA TRISTAR HOME VIDEO 60124

ANDROMEDA STRAIN, THE

D: Robert Wise 130 m

G | SF SUS | 1971 | COLOR

7 Intelligent and tense, but a little overlong. A mutant strain of bacteria comes to earth with a crashed satellite and everyone near the crash sight dies - except an old man an a baby. A team of scientists takes the survivors and the microbe back to a massive underground research facility, rushing against time to find a solution. This was one of the very first films to effectively explore the biological hazards of a technical age. Effective and well-done thriller, which uses its veteran cast to good advantage to create maximum tension and suspense.

Sex / Nud / Viol / Lang / AdSit

A: Arthur Hill, David Wayne, James Olson, Kate Reid, Paula Kelly

© MCA/UNIVERSAL HOME VIDEO, INC. 55037

ANGEL HEART

D: Alan Parker 112 m

R | MYS SUS ACT | 1987 | COLOR

8 Fascinatingly bizarre. In 1955 a cheesy private eye (Rourke) is hired by a mysterious stranger (De Niro) to track down a missing man. The trail leads from Harlem to New Orleans and to the home of a voodoo princess (Bonet). As his investigation proceeds, Rourke discovers more and more things that are very unusual indeed. The film is full of hallucinatory, sensual and frightening images. It is intriguing and fascinating, although not terribly appealing at times. As a film, it presents an interesting transformation from being a standard mystery at first into becoming a supernatural occult chiller at the end.

Sex / Nud / Viol / Lang / AdSit

A: Mickey Rourke, Robert De Niro, Lisa Bonet, Charlotte Rampling

© LIVE HOME VIDEO 60459

ANGUISH

D: Bigas Luna — 85 m

R | HOR SUS | 1988 | COLOR

Sex / Nud / ■ Viol / ◢ Lang / ■ AdSit

7 A bizarre twist is at the heart of this movie. The principal character (Lerner) has lost his job as an orderly due to blindness brought on by diabetes. His mother telepathically talks him into murdering his enemies and then plucking out their eyes for revenge. Then we, the viewers, discover that what we just saw was an on-screen depiction of another movie. That film is being watched by still another audience, whose members are being killed off one-by-one. We are watching two movies for the price of one, one is within the other, and there is a killer in both of them. Scary and compelling.

A: Michael Lerner, Zelda Rubinstein, Talia Paul, Clara Pastor, Angel Jove

© CBS/FOX VIDEO 5145

APARTMENT ZERO

D: Martin Donovan — 114 m

R | SUS MYS | 1989 | COLOR

Sex / Nud / ■ Viol / ■ Lang / ■ AdSit

7 Dark, quirky and definitely strange - but gripping! Set in Buenos Aires, Firth is a brilliant young man who is catapulted into financial trouble when his revival movie house hits the skids. He decides to take in a roommate, but he requires that whoever it is knows something about films. He finds the apparent perfect man (Bochner). Bochner even begins to arouse latent homosexual longings in Firth. However, Bochner also soon exhibits signs that there is a psychotic killer inside him and he may even be involved in the government death squads. Curious psychological thriller.

A: Hart Bochner, Colin Firth, Liz Smith, Dora Bryan

© ACADEMY ENTERTAINMENT 1205

APOLOGY

D: Robert Bierman — 98 m

NR | SUS CRM | 1986 | COLOR

◢ Sex / ◢ Nud / ◢ Viol / ■ Lang / ■ AdSit

8 An intriguingly different story. An artist (Warren) has what she thinks is a brilliant idea. She starts an anonymous phone service, as an artistic experiment. People are to call in to leave their confessions anonymously to free their consciences. But the plan takes a macabre twist when a psychopath begins a killing spree, just so that he has something to confess to her. Soon he begins to pursue her, too. Weller is the cop who trys to help her by catching him first. Stylish suspense thriller. Made for cable TV.

A: Lesley Ann Warren, Peter Weller, John Glover, Jimmie Ray Weeks, George Loros, Harvey Fierstein

© HBO VIDEO 9975

ARABESQUE

D: Stanley Donen — 105 m

NR | SUS ROM | 1966 | COLOR

Sex / Nud / Viol / Lang / ◢ AdSit

6 A diverting espionage story. Peck is an Oxford professor of languages and a code expert. He is hired by a mid-eastern oil tycoon to discover the secret message that is hidden in a set of hieroglyphics. He befriends the tycoon's beautiful mistress (Sophia Loren) and when he discovers the real meaning contained in the hieroglyphics, he's in trouble. He and Loren escape together and the chase is on to find them. Reasonably exciting and entertaining, with beautiful scenery, including that of the radiant Sophia.

A: Sophia Loren, Gregory Peck, Alan Badel, Kieron Moore, Carl Deuring, George Coulouris

© MCA/UNIVERSAL HOME VIDEO, INC. 80362

ARACHNOPHOBIA

D: Frank Marshall — 110 m

PG-13 | SUS HOR COM | 1990 | COLOR

Sex / Nud / ■ Viol / ◢ Lang / ◢ AdSit

8 Killer spiders incite chaos in this very scary big bug movie! When a deadly spider is accidentally imported to the US, it breeds with local creepy crawlies and produces a herd of poisonous, mutant offspring that take special joy in eating humans. Daniels is the quiet family man who wanted to get his family away from the hustle and bustle of the city, but now faces a huge battle getting rid of the creatures that have invaded his new country home. Goodman provides comic relief as the exterminator on a mission. More fun than you can handle!

A: Jeff Daniels, John Goodman, Julian Sands, Harley Jane Kozak, Stuart Pankin, Brian McNamera

© HOLLYWOOD PICTURES HOME VIDEO 1080

ASPHYX, THE

D: Peter Newbrook — 96 m

PG | SUS HOR | 1972 | COLOR

Sex / Nud / ◢ Viol / Lang / ◢ AdSit

8 A Victorian scientist discovers the spirit of death which is possessed within all beings. Life only exists when the spirit is in the body and death can only occur when that spirit leaves the body. Trap it and life becomes eternal - but is eternal life really a good thing to pursue? Excellent thriller, told with conviction.

A: Robert Powell, Robert Stephens, Jane Lapotaire, Ralph Arliss, Alex Scott

© MAGNUM ENTERTAINMENT, INC. M3117

ASSAULT ON PRECINCT 13

D: John Carpenter — 91 m

R | SUS CRM ACT | 1976 | COLOR

Sex / Nud / ■ Viol / ■ Lang / ◢ AdSit

8 Riveting thriller, taut suspense and lots of hard-hitting action. A nearly deserted LA police station is in the process of being closed down. There are only two deathrow prisoners, one cop and two secretaries waiting inside for the moving vans. Through the door runs a man who is being pursued by a gang of street kids. In a state of shock, he cannot tell the cop what is happening before the phone lines and the power are cut. They are all now trapped inside and the gang attacks. Widely recognized as an updated version of the Howard Hawks classic Western RIO BRAVO. Quite good.

A: Austin Stoker, Darwin Joston, Laurie Zimmer, Tony Burton, Nancy Loomis, Kim Richards

© UNITED AMERICAN VIDEO CORP. 5260

AT CLOSE RANGE

D: James Foley — 115 m

R | SUS CRM | 1986 | COLOR

Sex / ◢ Nud / ■ Viol / ■ Lang / ■ AdSit

8 A powerful thriller. A rural Pennsylvania hood returns home to the family he abandoned years before. His two listless and admiring sons long to prove themselves to their father to be worthy of joining his gang, but the two have no idea of how ruthless their father can be. When the cops begin to close in on him, he becomes fearful his own sons know too much and decides that they must be eliminated to remove any threat. Vivid and shocking in its ruthless violence - particularly since it is based upon a real-life situation. Excellent and forceful acting.

A: Sean Penn, Christopher Walken, Mary Stuart Masterson, Christopher Penn, Millie Perkins, Candy Clark

© LIVE HOME VIDEO VA5170

ATTIC, THE

D: George Edwards — 92 m

PG | SUS HOR | 1981 | COLOR

Sex / Nud / Viol / Lang / ◢ AdSit

6 Chilling little story of a domineering father (Milland), confined to a wheel chair, who stops at nothing to intimidate his mousey daughter (Snodgrass) into caring for him. All her dreams for herself are always ruined. Her fiance even disappears, strangely, just before they are to be married. But the tables are about to be turned on Daddy when Louise finds out what's in the attic. Interesting and eerie psychological character study.

A: Carrie Snodgress, Ray Milland, Rosemary Murphy, Ruth Cox, Rancis Bay, Marjorie Eaton

© MONTEREY HOME VIDEO B763

BACKDRAFT

D: Ron Howard — 135 m

R | ACT SUS MYS | 1991 | COLOR

◢ Sex / ◢ Nud / ■ Viol / ■ Lang / ◢ AdSit

7 This is an involving film but the real star is the exciting high-tech special effects. Russell and Baldwin are two feuding brothers who must confront their personal differences and emotional scars after they are assigned to the same fire unit. Their personal drama unfolds against a backdrop in which an arsonist is lighting up the Windy City. The quest to stop him pits brother against brother in a battle of wills, fueled by their determination to live up to their heroic father's reputation. Spectacular special effects alone will keep you riveted, but it's a suspenseful mystery, too.

A: Kurt Russell, William Baldwin, Scott Glenn, Jennifer Jason Leigh, Rebecca De Mornay, Donald Sutherland

© MCA/UNIVERSAL HOME VIDEO, INC. 81078

BAD INFLUENCE

D: Curtis Hanson — 99 m

R | SUS CRM | 1990 | COLOR

■ Sex / ■ Nud / ■ Viol / ■ Lang / ■ AdSit

7 Intriguing but very grim story of a boring Los Angeles yuppie stockbroker (Spader) who is helped out of a bad situation in a bar by a mysterious stranger (Lowe). The charismatic Lowe creates a faithful disciple in Spader by transforming his life into one of excitement, eroticism and danger through outlandish escapades into robbery and kinky sex. However, soon Lowe is out of control as he seeks his own excitement through tormenting Spader and Spader's life becomes a surrealistic nightmare. Nothing is too much for Lowe, including murder. Vivid and sometimes lurid.

A: Rob Lowe, James Spader, Lisa Zane, Christian Clemenson, Kathleen Wilhoite, Tony Maggio

© COLUMBIA TRISTAR HOME VIDEO 59233

BAD SEED, THE

D: Mervyn LeRoy — 129 m

NR | SUS HOR | 1956 | B&W

Sex / Nud / ◢ Viol / Lang / ◢ AdSit

8 Creepy, chilling, spellbinding account of seemingly sweet, but truly evil, six-year old child who coldly and casually murders her classmate for a penmanship medal, and then lures even more people to their deaths. Only her mother begins to suspect who the killer is when she discovers her own dark secret. She carries a bad seed within her, a profound immorality that somehow missed being expressed in her but has come out in her daughter. Great little shocker, with quality production. An unnerving experience, based upon a stageplay. Four Oscar nominations, three for acting.

A: Nancy Kelly, Patty McCormack, Henry Jones, Eileen Heckart, Evelyn Varden, Jesse White

© WARNER HOME VIDEO 11342

BASIC INSTINCT

D: Paul Verhoeven 123 m

R | SUS CRM | 1992 | COLOR

Sex Nud Viol Lang AdSit

7 A taut and intense psychosexual thriller! Set in San Francisco, a tough cop (Douglas) investigates a brutal ice pick murder and finds himself uncontrollably attracted to an overtly sexual novelist (Stone), who is the prime suspect in the case. Despite her ominous and provocative warnings that he's in way over his head, Douglas pursues the unabashedly sexual Stone, never really knowing for sure if he'll be the next to die by the pierce of the pick. Fast paced with graphic sex scenes. But its intense presentation also hides some major plot flaws which don't stand up on later reflection.

A: Michael Douglas, Sharon Stone, George Dzundza, Jeanne Tripplehorn, Denis Arndt, Leilani Sarelle

© LIVE HOME VIDEO 48961

BEDFORD INCIDENT, THE

D: James Harris 102 m

NR | DMA SUS | 1965 | B&W

Sex Nud Viol Lang AdSit

7 Tense nuclear-age Cold War thriller. Poitier is a cocky magazine reporter on board an American destroyer to record a typical day tracking subs off the coast of Greenland. This destroyer is skippered by an authoritarian near-maniacal Navy captain (Widmark), who keeps his near-exhausted but devoted crew on a razor's edge and is also especially fond of harassing one particular Russian sub. This ongoing battle of wits with the sub builds into a destructive pressure within the ship's crew that leads to a numbing climax. Well-acted, with a good script.

A: Richard Widmark, Sidney Poitier, James MacArthur, Martin Balsam, Wally Cox, Eric Portman

© COLUMBIA TRISTAR HOME VIDEO 60130

BEDROOM WINDOW

D: Curtis Hanson 113 m

R | SUS MYS | 1987 | COLOR

Sex Nud Viol Lang AdSit

8 Very good Hitchcock-like sexy suspense tale. Guttenberg is having an affair with his boss's wife, beautiful Isabelle Huppert. One day, after making love in his apartment, she alone witnesses a woman being assaulted outside the bedroom window. She doesn't want to report it because their secret would be revealed and she would be destroyed, so Guttenberg does - telling the police he witnessed it when he didn't. When holes in his story begin to appear, he becomes the police's chief suspect in an entire rash of rape/murders. There is only one way out, he has to trap the murderer himself.

A: Steve Guttenberg, Elizabeth McGovern, Isabelle Huppert, Paul Shenar, Frederick Coffin, Carl Lumbly

© LIVE HOME VIDEO 5209

BELIEVERS, THE

D: John Schlesinger 114 m

R | HOR SUS | 1987 | COLOR

Sex Nud Viol Lang AdSit

8 Gripping and genuinely frightening story of a recently widowed psychiatrist (Sheen) who has moved from Minneapolis to NYC to work for the police department treating cases of stress. He begins treating a cop who is acting strangely and suffers from nightmares arising from the ritualistic child murders he is investigating. Sheen at first does not believe in the power of the voodoo cult, but is forced to change his mind when the cop commits suicide and Sheen discovers that his own son may be sacrificed by the cult. Suspenseful throughout, with a give-no-mercy climax.

A: Martin Sheen, Helen Shaver, Richard Masur, Harley Cross, Jimmy Smits, Robert Loggia

© HBO VIDEO 0034

BEST SELLER

D: John Flynn 95 m

R | ACT SUS | 1987 | COLOR

Sex Nud Viol Lang AdSit

8 Exciting and taut thriller. James Woods is a professional hitman and he wants revenge against a big-time industrialist - a man who he has worked for and trusted for years, but who has fired him. So, he enlists the aid of Brian Dennehy, a cop and successful crime-story writer, to help him tell his life's story. He will tell everything: about the extortion, murders and political corruption. The cop will get his story, but he's also going to have to keep his source alive. Even that is complicated, because neither of these two can completely trust the other. Tense, quick moving and exciting.

A: James Woods, Brian Dennehy, Victoria Tennant, Allison Balson, Paul Shenar, George Coe

© LIVE HOME VIDEO 6026

BIG FIX, THE

D: Jeremy Paul Kagan 108 m

PG | MYS SUS | 1978 | COLOR

Sex Nud Viol Lang AdSit

7 Pretty good mystery and a good vehicle for Dreyfuss's wise-cracking personality. He plays a '60s radical who is now a private investigator. He is hired by his former lover (Anspack), from the days when they were both political activists at Berkeley, to find out who's using dirty tricks to smear the political candidate she's working for. He already has enough trouble trying to deal with his ex-wife and finding enough time for his kids, and now he winds up in the middle of a murder. Plenty of plot twists to keep you involved.

A: Richard Dreyfuss, Susan Anspach, Bonnie Bedelia, John Lithgow, F. Murray Abraham

© MCA/UNIVERSAL HOME VIDEO, INC. 66053

BIG HAND FOR THE LITTLE LADY, A

D: Fielder Cook 95 m

WST COM SUS | 1966 | COLOR

Sex Nud Viol Lang AdSit

8 Great little comedy with lots of twists. It's a clever story about a farmer (Fonda) and his wife (Woodward) who arrive in town just in time for the annual big stakes poker game. He's a former gambler and has sworn off but, he has to get into that game. Against his wife's wishes, he does and then gets dealt the hand of his life. He bets until he runs out of cash, so he bets the farm (much to the wife's distress) and then has a heart attack. She now has everything in the world she owns at stake and bet on the unfinished game, so the little lady steps up to the table and says, "How do you play this game?"

A: Henry Fonda, Joanne Woodward, Jason Robards, Jr., Charles Bickford, Burgess Meredith, Paul Ford

© WARNER HOME VIDEO 11469

BIRDS, THE

D: Alfred Hitchcock 119 m

PG-13 | SUS HOR | 1963 | COLOR

Sex Nud Viol Lang AdSit

8 Hitchcock classic. Tippy Hedren is a beautiful, wealthy, spoiled, young socialite (Hedron) who has her sites set on a handsome attorney (Taylor), much to the dismay of his schoolteacher girlfriend (Pleshette). However, that quickly takes a backseat when nature rebels in Northern California. Suddenly thousands of birds, for no apparent reason, attack the small coastal town of Bedoega Bay and all the townsfolk are pursued wherever they go. Alfred Hitchcock's technical mastery allows the viewer to suspend his suspicions, to believe and then fear that what he is seeing is real. Not for the fainthearted.

A: Rod Taylor, Tippi Hedren, Suzanne Pleshette, Jessica Tandy, Veronica Cartwright, Ethel Griffies

© MCA/UNIVERSAL HOME VIDEO, INC. 55010

BLACK RAINBOW

D: Mike Hodges 103 m

R | SUS FAN | 1991 | COLOR

Sex Nud Viol Lang AdSit

7 Neat little mystical thriller. Rosanna Arquette and her drunken father (Jason Robards) make a dishonest living with a traveling stage act. She is a medium, relaying messages from the dead to the living. However, one day she really does see the future. She tells a woman about her dead husband and how he was murdered - before it happens. She not only accurately predicted the future, she also knows the name of the killer, which makes her and her father targets. But worse that that, she is now perpetually haunted by countless other secrets and impending deaths. Hulce is a young reporter hooked on the story and who follows them on the road.

A: Rosanna Arquette, Jason Robards, Jr., Tom Hulce, Mark Joy, Ron Rosenthal, John Bennes

© VIDEO TREASURES M012820

BLACK SUNDAY

D: John Frankenheimer 143 m

R | SUS ACT CRM | 1977 | COLOR

Sex Nud Viol Lang AdSit

9 Gripping thriller. An Arab guerrilla terrorist organization called Black September plans to attack America in the most painful way possible: they plan to blow up the Superbowl with the President in attendance. The terrorist leader gets shell-shocked Vietnam vet Bruce Dern to pilot the Goodyear Blimp into position, where they then plan to blow it up. Shaw is an Israeli agent who struggles against time to foil their plot. Terrific action sequences combine with genuine terror at the climax to create true excitement. Excellent.

A: Robert Shaw, Bruce Dern, Marthe Keller, Fritz Weaver, Steven Keats, William Daniels

© PARAMOUNT HOME VIDEO 8855

BLACK WIDOW

D: Bob Rafelson 101 m

R | SUS CRM | 1987 | COLOR

Sex Nud Viol Lang AdSit

8 Absorbing sexy thriller. Debra Winger is a Justice Department investigator who becomes intently suspicious of Theresa Russell because Russell is constantly being widowed only a very short time after having married wealthy men. Intensity builds as Winger's obsession with convicting Russell of murder becomes as strong as Russell's own compulsion to continue to get away with murder. Winger becomes so fixated that she quits her job just so she can continue to follow Russell. Solid plotting and the leads are both beautiful - and very believable. Good stuff.

A: Debra Winger, Theresa Russell, Sami Frey, Dennis Hopper, Nicol Williamson, Terry O'Quinn

© FOXVIDEO 5033

BLIND SIDE

D: Geoff Murphy 92 m

R | SUS | 1993 | COLOR

Sex Nud Viol Lang AdSit

7 An American couple (De Mornay and Silver) in Mexico on vacation, accidentally hits a man on a fog-shrouded highway. When they discover that the dead man is also a policeman, they panic and decide to run back to the U.S. Feeling safe to be back home, but upset with what has happened, they decide they must go on with their lives. That's when they get an unwelcome visit from Rutger Hauer. He makes it plain that he knows what happened, but says all he wants is a job to keep quiet. However, soon it's clear that a job isn't enough. It is also plain that he has other bigger plans and they include a De Mornay. Quite good made-for-cable suspensor.

A: Rutger Hauer, Rebecca De Mornay, Ron Silver, Jonathan Banks, Mariska Hargitay, Tamara Clatterbuck

© HBO VIDEO 90870

BLINK

D: Michael Apted — 106 m

R · SUS · 1994 · COLOR

Sex · Nud · Viol · Lang · AdSit

7 Madeleine Stowe is a strong-willed musician who had been blind since childhood but because of a new operation, she can now see. Almost as soon as she's home from the hospital, she sees the man who murdered her upstairs' neighbor, as he was leaving. The trouble is that since she hasn't seen anything for so long, her mind is playing tricks with the image. Aidan Quinn is a cop who is trying to find this guy, who he thinks is a mass murderer, and doesn't know if she is a credible witness. But he does know that he likes her a lot and that is a problem. Plus, she may also be the next victim. Not a lot of new ground here, but Stowe is beautiful and an excellent actress.

A: Madeleine Stowe, Aidan Quinn, Laurie Metcalf, James Remar, Peter Friedman, Bruce A. Young

© TURNER HOME ENTERTAINMENT N4192

BLOOD SIMPLE

D: Joel Coen — 96 m

R · SUS · MYS · 1985 · COLOR

Sex · Nud · Viol · Lang · AdSit

8 Thrilling film noir type of mystery, full of double and triple crosses. A rural Texas bar owner (Hedaya) hires a private detective (Walsh) to follow his wife (McDormand) because he thinks she's cheating on him with one of his bartenders. She is and, what's more, she and her lover are planning to murder him. So Hedaya hires the detective to kill them first. This is where the real plot twists begin. Who does the detective really work for? Who's really dead? Quite ingenious thriller.

A: John Getz, Frances McDormand, Dan Hedaya, Samm-Art Williams, M. Emmet Walsh

© MCA/UNIVERSAL HOME VIDEO, INC. 80180

BLOW OUT

D: Brian De Palma — 108 m

R · SUS · CRM · 1981 · COLOR

Sex · Nud · Viol · Lang · AdSit

7 Travolta is a motion picture sound effects man who inadvertently records the sounds of a car accident which killed a potential Presidential candidate. He also saves the life of a young prostitute who is in that car. Now, listening over and over to his tapes, he becomes certain that something is just not right, that was no accident. He holds the key evidence in a major political conspiracy, but the only one who believes him is the girl. Their knowledge puts both their lives in danger, and they are both targets for murder. Good suspense.

A: John Travolta, Nancy Allen, John Lithgow, Dennis Franz, Peter Boyden

© GOODTIMES 74063

BLOWUP

D: Michelangelo Antonioni — 102 m

NR · SUS · CRM · 1966 · COLOR

Sex · Nud · Viol · Lang · AdSit

8 Solid thriller. A brilliant London photographer travels about London capturing the sights and sounds of the city, particularly beautiful fashion models. One day he photographs a couple embracing in the park, but the girl runs after him, demanding the film back. He refuses and when he develops the film, he thinks he sees a gun trained on her partner. He goes back to the park to investigate and finds a body, but the next morning it's gone. This film is rich in many-layered meanings but remains, at its essence, an elegant murder mystery. Very influential film. Sexy. Would be considered R-rated today.

A: Vanessa Redgrave, David Hemmings, Sarah Miles, Jill Kennington, Verushka, The Yardbirds

Distributed By MGM/UA Home Video M600015

BLUE SUNSHINE

D: Jeff Lieberman — 94 m

R · SUS · HOR · 1977 · COLOR

Sex · Nud · Viol · Lang · AdSit

8 Terrifying psychological shocker. When an innocent man is falsely accused of brutal murders, he evades police while he rushes to uncover who the real murderer is, and what the motive could be. His clues lead him to a discover a whole group of people who are all going bald. What else he discovers is terrifying: there is no rational motive for the murders. Students who took a particular brand of high-octane hallucinogenic LSD in the '60s that was called "Blue Sunshine" are now having violent after-effects - they are becoming crazed killers. This a truly terrifying film about losing control of your mind and a real shocker in spite of its low budget.

A: Zalman King, Mark Goddard, Robert Walden, Deborah Winters, Charles Siebert

© LIVE HOME VIDEO VA4124

BLUE VELVET

D: David Lynch — 121 m

R · SUS · DMA · 1986 · COLOR

Sex · Nud · Viol · Lang · AdSit

8 Audacious, brilliant and disturbing. A young college student returns to his home town and becomes enraptured with a haunting nightclub singer. He soon discovers that there is a bizarre and hidden world of decadence and terror just under the surface of his little town that he and most others never knew was there. It is a perverted world that the surface calm belies. Hopper is fascinating as a sadistic kidnapper/drug dealer. Weird, surreal stuff. Undeniably gripping, but not easily enjoyable. Strong stuff. Keep an open mind.

A: Kyle MacLachlan, Isabella Rossellini, Dennis Hopper, Laura Dern, Dean Stockwell

© WARNER HOME VIDEO 692

BODY DOUBLE

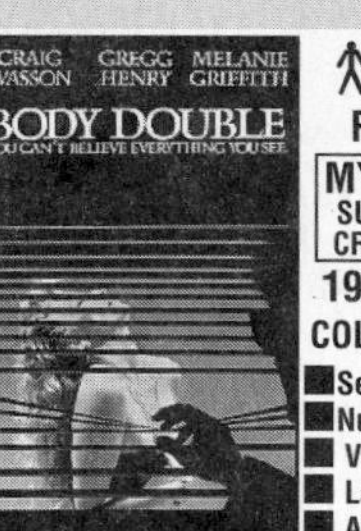

D: Brian De Palma — 114 m

R · MYS · SUS · CRM · 1984 · COLOR

Sex · Nud · Viol · Lang · AdSit

8 Slick, clever, suspenseful and sexy. De Palma borrows from Hitchcock (VERTIGO and REAR WINDOW) and even himself (OBSESSION, DRESSED TO KILL and BLOW OUT) to create a fascinating and controversial piece of work. Wasson is an out-of-work actor who is set up to be a witness for a murder. He is asked to house-sit at an expensive home where a telescope is trained upon a sexy neighbor who does a nightly dance naked in front of her window. Melanie Griffith is sexy and hilarious as a porno star who holds a key to the mystery of a grisly murder.

A: Craig Wasson, Deborah Shelton, Dennis Franz, Melanie Griffith, Gregg Henry, Guy Boyd

© GOODTIMES 4239

BODYGUARD, THE

D: Mick Jackson — 130 m

R · ROM · ACT · SUS · 1993 · COLOR

Sex · Nud · Viol · Lang · AdSit

8 Frank Farmer (Kostner) is an ex-secret service agent who has now become a private bodyguard for hire. Whitney Houston is a pop-music star who has been receiving threatening messages. She reluctantly agrees to let her manager hire him, but she largely ignores his advice. That is, until Frank has to jump in to save her bacon after one particularly close call. Suddenly, she not only relies upon him but also begins to find her heart softening to him. Frank finds that he too is falling for her, but that is dangerous because feelings like those threaten his edge - and he needs his edge because the killer is still out there. Yes it's predictable, but hey - it's fun too.

A: Kevin Costner, Whitney Houston, Michele Lamar Richards, DeVaughn Nixon, Gary Kemp, Ralph Waite

© WARNER HOME VIDEO 12591

BODY HEAT

D: Lawrence Kasdan — 113 m

R · SUS · MYS · CRM · 1981 · COLOR

Sex · Nud · Viol · Lang · AdSit

10 Gripping erotic thriller. Hurt is a second-rate lawyer who is sucked into a torrid affair with a sizzlingly lustful Turner. Their chemistry sets the screen ablaze. Turner is beautiful, sexy and rich, but she is married to a rich man (Crenna). She entices Hurt into a torrid affair and then into plot to kill Crenna, but has some devious twists and turns she has kept to herself. Very steamy and sexy, but that never gets in the way of the suspense and the surprises which hold your attention until the very last minute.

A: William Hurt, Kathleen Turner, Richard Crenna, Ted Danson, Mickey Rourke, J.A. Preston

© WARNER HOME VIDEO 20005

BOSTON STRANGLER, THE

D: Richard Fleischer — 116 m

NR · CRM · SUS · 1968 · COLOR

Sex · Nud · Viol · Lang · AdSit

8 Startling true story. Albert DeSalvo was a seemingly ordinary plumber and family man, but it was he who was the infamous Boston Strangler who terrorized Boston during the 1960s, killing only women - each murder more gruesome than the last. This is a non-sensationalized account of the search for, the capture of and the prosecution of DeSalvo. The documentary style of presentation creates a heightened sense of realism. Fonda plays the criminologist who found him, and Curtis is remarkably believable in a powerful performance as DeSalvo.

A: Tony Curtis, Henry Fonda, George Kennedy, Mike Kellin, Murray Hamilton, Sally Kellerman

© FOXVIDEO 1015

BOYS FROM BRAZIL, THE

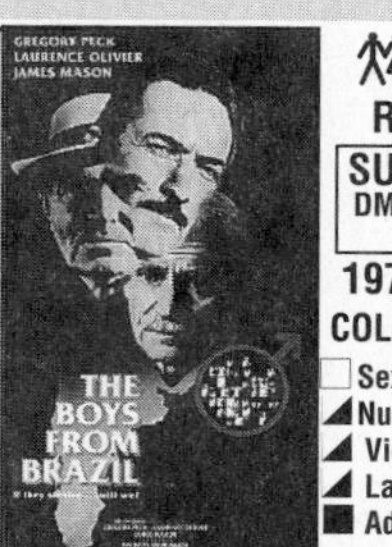

D: Franklin J. Schaffner — 123 m

R · SUS · DMA · 1978 · COLOR

Sex · Nud · Viol · Lang · AdSit

8 This is an entertaining thriller with an interesting premise. Suppose the infamous Nazi doctor who murdered thousands in "medical experiments," Dr. Josef Mengele, was still alive, living in Brazil and was attempting to clone ninety-four brand new boy-Hitlers from which to create a new Reich. Gregory Peck gets a rare opportunity to play a bad guy as Josef Mengele, and does quite well at it, too. But Olivier is brilliant as Nazi hunter Libermann who tries to stop Peck and his hideous cloning project.

A: Gregory Peck, Laurence Olivier, James Mason, Lilli Palmer, Uta Hagen, Rosemary Harris

© LIVE HOME VIDEO 51117

BRAINSTORM

D: Douglas Trumbull — 106 m

PG · SF · SUS · 1983 · COLOR

Sex · Nud · Viol · Lang · AdSit

6 There is an interesting premise behind this film. It is about a machine that can read and record the physical, emotional and intellectual sensations as they are experienced by one person, and then have them "played back" inside someone else's head. However, due to a now predictable and stale plot twist of having a group of military types intervene, that good is stunted and doesn't get the treatment it deserves. Plus, the filming became complicated when Natalie Wood died part-way into production. Still, the film is pretty good. The disappointment comes only because it could have been more.

A: Christopher Walken, Natalie Wood, Louise Fletcher, Cliff Robertson, Joe Dorsey

Distributed By MGM/UA Home Video M800314

BREAKER MORANT

D: Bruce Beresford — 103 m

PG | DMA SUS | 1980 | COLOR

9 Very potent drama and a winner of 10 Australian awards. Set in 1901 during the Boer War in South Africa, three young Australian officers are made into scapegoats and forced to stand trial on trumped up charges of having killed civilian prisoners, one of which was a German. It is preordained that they must be convicted. If they aren't, the political plans of the British Empire will be stunted. Based upon an actual event, this is a gripping story that is beautifully crafted. Strong rich performances bring us close to these tragic characters. Captivating. This is a must see.

Sex / Nud / Viol / Lang / AdSit

A: Edward Woodward, Jack Thompson, John Waters, Charles Tingwell, Bryan Brown, Vincent Ball

© COLUMBIA TRISTAR HOME VIDEO 60145

BURIED ALIVE

D: Frank Darabont — 93 m

PG-13 | SUS COM | 1990 | COLOR

7 A film that delights in bad taste and grotesque humor. A love-starved housewife who's terribly bored with her husband goes out and gets herself a new lover. She convinces her new boyfriend doctor that everything would be just wonderful if he would only kill her husband, and so he does. All is well for a short while but then all hell breaks loose when her presumed dead husband literally crawls back from the grave! Black comedy abounds, darkness surrounds, but all in a very slick way that will keep you glued to your seat and unwilling to turn away.

Sex / Nud / Viol / Lang / AdSit

A: Tim Matheson, Jennifer Jason Leigh, William Atherton, Hoyt Axton, Jay Gerber

© MCA/UNIVERSAL HOME VIDEO, INC. 80939

CAPE FEAR

D: J. Lee Thompson — 106 m

NR | SUS CRM | 1961 | B&W

8 Riveting tale of revenge and terror. Robert Mitchum is truly fearsome as a convicted sadistic rapist who is newly released from prison and who now has come back to terrorize Peck and his family. Peck was the attorney who sent him up. Mitchum stalks Peck's wife and his pretty teenage daughter but, though his actions are despicable, nothing that he does is illegal. The police can do nothing to protect them so, if Peck is going to save his family, he has to set a trap and bait it with those he loves most. Excruciatingly tense drama. Brilliant study of psycopathic sadism. Remade in 1992.

Sex / Nud / Viol / Lang / AdSit

A: Gregory Peck, Polly Bergen, Robert Mitchum, Lori Martin, Martin Balsam, Telly Savalas

© MCA/UNIVERSAL HOME VIDEO, INC. 80514

CAPE FEAR

D: Martin Scorsese — 128 m

R | SUS CRM | 1992 | COLOR

8 Excellent remake of 1961 classic. When wacked-out, self-educated De Niro gets out of jail after 14 long years, he decides to go after the lawyer who let him down and didn't get him off. De Niro methodically torments and terrorizes Nolte's family, paying special attention to his young daughter, but always staying just inside the law. He becomes their ultimate nightmare because the cops can do nothing. Even when Nolte decides he has had enough and takes his family away to hide out, De Niro secretly goes along for the ride. Criticized as being overblown, this is still a nail-biting, teeth-grinding, psychological thriller that really bites, but see the 1961 original too.

Sex / Nud / Viol / Lang / AdSit

A: Robert De Niro, Nick Nolte, Jessica Lange, Juliette Lewis, Joe Don Baker, Robert Mitchum

© MCA/UNIVERSAL HOME VIDEO, INC. 81105

CAPRICORN ONE

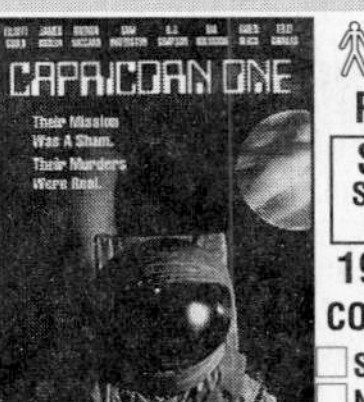

D: Peter Hyams — 123 m

PG | SF SUS | 1978 | COLOR

7 A suspenseful science fiction drama with an outlandish plot that is never-the less convincingly done. NASA executive Holbrook decides that it is too risky to fail in front of the entire world audience in an impending mission to Mars. A failure would be to risk having his budget cut. So he decides to fake the whole thing, and film it all inside a TV studio. However, Gould is a nosy reporter who investigates and begins to unravel the plot. Now threatened with exposure, Holbrook decides that the ship must "crash" upon reentry, killing the three astronauts aboard, the only other witnesses.

Sex / Nud / Viol / Lang / AdSit

A: Elliott Gould, James Brolin, Karen Black, Telly Savalas, Sam Waterston, O.J. Simpson

© LIVE HOME VIDEO 51090

CARNIVAL OF SOULS

D: Herk Harvey — 84 m

PG | HOR SUS | 1962 | B&W

8 This is a cult favorite that was made for just $30,000 in Kansas. It is a really eerie little gem about an uninvolved, non-caring, emotionally detached young woman. The car in which she is riding crashes into a river and she survives - or does she - because it strangely takes her three hours to resurface. Afterward she is plagued by recurring black-outs and is haunted by a ghoulish, zombie-like character which only she can see. Leave the lights on for this one.

Sex / Nud / Viol / Lang / AdSit

A: Candace Hillgoss, Sidney Berger, Frances Feist

© UNITED AMERICAN VIDEO CORP. 7227

CARRIE

D: Brian De Palma — 100 m

R | HOR SUS | 1976 | COLOR

9 In spite of being tormented at home by her religiously fanatic mother and ridiculed at school as a weirdo, suddenly Sissy Spacek's dream appears to have come true when she is asked to the prom by the school hunk. When it turns out to be just a cruel practical joke, everyone pays when Sissy unleashes her secret. She has devastating telekinetic powers and she uses them now to torment her tormentors. This film is very well done. Spacek and Laurie both received Oscar nominations. This is also the film that gave Spacek her big break. High quality spookiness.

Sex / Nud / Viol / Lang / AdSit

A: Sissy Spacek, Piper Laurie, William Katt, John Travolta, Amy Irving, Nancy Allen

Distributed By MGM/UA Home Video M200261

CAT PEOPLE

D: Paul Schrader — 119 m

R | HOR SUS | 1982 | COLOR

7 Erotic remake of the 1942 original. Beautiful Kinski and her brother are cursed to turn into killer panthers when they become sexually aroused. Kinski investigates a series of killings, reportedly by a panther, which she fears may have been committed by her brother. Then she meets and falls passionately in love with the zookeeper (Hurt). What will she do? Plenty eerie and plenty sexy, too. Lots of atmosphere, but it becomes a little too surreal in places. Its gore and nudity will offend some.

Sex / Nud / Viol / Lang / AdSit

A: Nastassia Kinski, Malcolm McDowell, Annette O'Toole, John Heard, Ruby Dee, Ed Begley, Jr.

© MCA/UNIVERSAL HOME VIDEO, INC. 77008

CAT'S EYE

D: Lewis Teague — 94 m

PG-13 | SUS HOR | 1985 | COLOR

8 Some really scary bedtime stories. This is an anthology of three Stephen King tales: Alan King's clinic produces a shocking cure for James Woods's smoking, Tennis pro Hays accepts a challenge to walk around a building on its ledge, and little Drew Barrymore is protected from a deadly troll living in the wall by a stray cat. Some gruesome scenes, but mostly this is just plain scary stuff.

Sex / Nud / Viol / Lang / AdSit

A: Drew Barrymore, James Woods, Robert Hayes, Alan King, Kenneth McMillan, Candy Clark

© CBS/FOX VIDEO 4731

CHANGELING, THE

D: Peter Medak — 113 m

R | SUS HOR | 1979 | COLOR

8 Solid suspense thriller that is also a really scary ghost story. Music professor Scott loses his wife and daughter in a terrible traffic accident and when he moves into an old house, he finds that it is haunted by the spirit of a child who lived and died there 70 years before. Van Devere is the real estate agent who helps Scott to discover the secret of the house, even as Scott becomes the unwilling accomplice to the ghost's revenge. An excellent cast and an intense performance by Scott provide the essence of what every spook story needs, believability.

Sex / Nud / Viol / Lang / AdSit

A: George C. Scott, Trish Van Devere, Melvyn Douglas, John Colicos, Jean Marsh, Madeleine Thornton-Sherwood

© HBO VIDEO 90630

CHARLEY VARRICK

D: Don Siegel — 111 m

PG | SUS ACT | 1973 | COLOR

8 Very good and intelligent thriller. Walter Matthau plays a crop duster and small-time bank robber who only robs little backcountry banks for little payrolls. But he gets much more than he bargained for when he and his partner rob a small rural bank of $750,000 that turns out to have been mob money. Now, they're in big trouble. The mob wants their money back and they send a sadistic and ruthless hit man, Joe Don Baker, to get it. Matthau must find a way to outfox both the mob and their hitman before it's too late. Fast-paced, thrilling action with lots of intriguing plot twists.

Sex / Nud / Viol / Lang / AdSit

A: Walter Matthau, Joe Don Baker, Felicia Farr, Andy Robinson, John Vernon, Sheree North

© MCA/UNIVERSAL HOME VIDEO, INC. 55062

CHILD'S PLAY

D: Tom Holland — 88 m

R | HOR SUS | 1988 | COLOR

8 When 6-year-old Andy is asked how his babysitter was pushed out a window to a violent death, he simply says Chucky did it. A dead psycho murderer (Brad Dourif) has transfered his soul into a doll and Andy was given the doll on his birthday by his widowed Mom (Hicks). Now the doll "Chucky" seeks vengeance on those who killed him, but no one believes poor Andy. However, the real scare is that now Chucky wants to transfer his soul into a live body. A well-crafted horror thriller that builds slowly, leaving the best for last. Great special effects.

Sex / Nud / Viol / Lang / AdSit

A: Catherine Hicks, Chris Sarandon, Alex Vincent, Brad Dourif, Dinah Manoff, Tommy Swerdlow

Distributed By MGM/UA Home Video M901593

CHINA SYNDROME, THE

D: James Bridges 123 m

PG | SUS DMA | 1979 | COLOR

10 A huge box office hit because it was very intense and believable drama. A novice TV reporter (Fonda) and her cameraman are at a nuclear generating station when there is a near-meltdown situation. It is averted only by a quick-thinking engineer (Lemon), but the TV station refuses to televise their video tapes. When Lemmon releases X-rays revealing that it could happen again, another reporter is killed. There is no doubt now that there is a ruthless coverup underway by very powerful people. Feeling he has no alternative Lemmon seizes control of the plant and invites the media in. Excellent.

Sex Nud Viol Lang AdSit

A: Jane Fonda, Jack Lemmon, Michael Douglas, Scott Brady, James Hampton, Peter Donat

© GOODTIMES 4200

CHINATOWN

D: Roman Polanski 131 m

R | MYS SUS CRM | 1974 | COLOR

10 Landmark film and one of the greatest detective stories of all times. It won eleven Oscar nominations. Jack Nicholson plays Jake Gittes, a small-time 1930's California private detective who is hired by a beautiful socialite (Dunaway) to investigate her husband's affair. But Gittes gets much more than he bargained for when he stumbles into a major case involving double dealing, land swindles, water rights, murder, incest and major political figures. It is a bizarre story which leads us on a complex and fascinating journey. Sequel: THE TWO JAKES.

Sex Nud Viol Lang AdSit

A: Jack Nicholson, Faye Dunaway, John Huston, Perry Lopez, John Hillerman, Diane Ladd

© PARAMOUNT HOME VIDEO 8674

CLEAR AND PRESENT DANGER

D: Phillip Noyce 141 m

PG-13 | SUS ACT | 1994 | COLOR

9 Excellent. Jack Clancy's hero spy, Jack Ryan (Harrison Ford) is back. This time he has been promoted to Deputy Director of Intelligence for the CIA. When one of the President's friends and his family is killed by a Colombian drug dealer, the President authorizes a secret attack with US troops, led by field operative Willem Defoe. The druglord decides to fight back, however, but he is being manipulated and deceived by his own intelligence man, who has secret plans of his own. As Ryan, who knew nothing of the President's illegal war, begins to slowly unravel the pieces, he finds that he is being set up to take the fall. More an intelligent and intricate suspense film than an all-out action film.

Sex Nud Viol Lang AdSit

A: Harrison Ford, Willem Dafoe, Anne Archer, James Earl Jones, Joaquim De Almeida, Henry Czerny

© PARAMOUNT HOME VIDEO 32463

CLIENT, THE

D: Joel Schumacher 121 m

PG-13 | CRM SUS | 1994 | COLOR

8 Quite good thriller that was translated from John Grisham's best-seller. A mafia lawyer confesses the whereabouts of dead Senator to an 11-year-old just before committing suicide. The smart kid has watched enough TV to know that he is in trouble if he talks. But, a glory-grabbing federal prosecutor (Jones) knows he knows, so he's in trouble even if he doesn't. He and his single Mom have no money, but he needs a lawyer. He gets the help he needs from an ex-alcoholic ex-mother, Susan Sarandon. Smart and now with a second chance, she is going to protect this kid no matter what. Fascinating battle of wills and maneuvers between the lawyers - and a war to stay alive between the kid and the hoods.

Sex Nud Viol Lang AdSit

A: Susan Sarandon, Tommy Lee Jones, Mary-Louise Parker, Anthony LaPaglia, Brad Renfro, Ossie Davis

© WARNER HOME VIDEO 13233

CLOAK & DAGGER

D: Richard Franklin 101 m

PG | SUS CLD | 1984 | COLOR

7 A young computer whiz kid (Thomas) plays Cloak & Dagger games in which he is a secret agent with his imaginary super-hero playmate (Coleman). However, one day Thomas gets involved in a real-life spy drama and witnesses a real murder, but Coleman (also cast as the boy's father), having been fooled before, does not believe him and thinks that this is just another of the boy's imaginary games. The whiz kid can not get Dad to believe that what he saw was real and is on his own. Suspenseful and fastpaced. Suitable for young people, but also of real interest to adults, too. Actually, a remake of THE WINDOW (1949).

Sex Nud Viol Lang AdSit

A: Henry Thomas, Dabney Coleman, Michael Murphy, Christina Nigra, John McIntire, Jeanette Nolan

© MCA/UNIVERSAL HOME VIDEO, INC. 80124

COLLECTOR, THE

D: William Wyler 116 m

NR | SUS DMA | 1965 | COLOR

8 Chilling, claustrophobic and fascinating character study by a master director. A pathetic young neurotic clerk has no friends and so, instead, he has become a collector. He collects things... all kinds of things. He is desperately lonely, so he kidnaps a beautiful art student and then holds her as his captive, trying to force her to love him. This is a very powerful suspense vehicle and a disturbing probe into the mind of a pathetic desperate man driven to extreme behavior.

Sex Nud Viol Lang AdSit

A: Terence Stamp, Samantha Eggar, Maurice Dallimore, Mona Washbourne

© COLUMBIA TRISTAR HOME VIDEO 60163

COMA

D: Michael Crichton 104 m

PG | SUS MYS | 1978 | COLOR

8 When her friend mysteriously dies during a simple surgery doctor Genevieve Bujold wants to know why. And, when she learns that there have been many other similar cases lately, she begins her investigation in ernest. The horrible truth she discovers puts her into direct conflict with the big hospital's powerful supervisor, Richard Widmark. She has discovered such an outlandish conspiracy that no one believes her - not even her boyfriend (Douglas). She has discovered a whole warehouse of spare body parts, for sale upon request to the highest bidder. Taut, quick-paced thriller. Look quick for Tom Selleck in an early role.

Sex Nud Viol Lang AdSit

A: Genevieve Bujold, Michael Douglas, Richard Widmark, Rip Torn, Tom Selleck, Elizabeth Ashley

Distributed By MGM/UA Home Video M600013

CONFIDENTIALLY YOURS

D: Francois Truffaut 110 m

NR | FOR SUS | 1983 | B&W

7 This was famed director Francois Truffaut's last film. It is light and entertaining, and is also a film very like his favorite director Alfred Hitchcock would have done. However, it is not very highly regarded. It is the story of a real estate agent who is accused of murdering his wife's lover. His secretary, who has been secretly in love with him, turns detective to uncover the mystery of who has framed him. Like Hitchcock's films, this one too has romance and humor thrown in with the thrills. Subtitled.

Sex Nud Viol Lang AdSit

A: Fanny Ardant, Jean-Louis Trintignat, Philippe Laudenbach, Caroline Sihol, Philippe Morier-Genoud

© HOME VISION CON 050

CONSENTING ADULTS

D: Alan J. Pakula 99 m

R | SUS CRM | 1992 | COLOR

6 Kline and Mastrantonio are happily married professionals living next door to Spacey and Miller. Kline and Mastrantonio become more and more impressed with the apparent ease with which Spacey can generate income. Then Spacey provides them with some helpful assistance and draws them further into his confidence. They are friends. However, one day he proposes a strange bargain to Kline, that they trade places in the middle of the night... their wives won't even know. They do, but the next morning Spacey's wife is dead, and the police are holding an astounded Kline for the murder. Contrived, but it still it holds your attention.

Sex Nud Viol Lang AdSit

A: Kevin Kline, Kevin Spacey, Mary Elizabeth Mastrantonio, Rebecca Miller, Forest Whitaker

© HOLLYWOOD PICTURES HOME VIDEO HPH1523

CONVERSATION, THE

D: Francis Ford Coppola 113 m

PG | DMA SUS | 1974 | COLOR

9 Best Picture nominee. Hackman is a top surveillance expert, for sale to the highest bidder, but he has become a loner, isolated and extremely weary. He is hired by a mysterious, powerful man to follow a woman and to record her conversations. When he records her with another man, he learns that she is the mystery man's wife, having an affair. She is in great danger. Hackman's work has hurt people in the past, so he becomes obsessed now with protecting her. However, as the movie evolves, it becomes more a fascinating character study. It is the story of moral man who is deteriorating at an immoral job. Excellent.

Sex Nud Viol Lang AdSit

A: Gene Hackman, John Cazale, Allen Garfield, Harrison Ford, Cindy Williams, Teri Garr

© PARAMOUNT HOME VIDEO 2307

COUNTERFEIT TRAITOR, THE

D: George Seaton 140 m

NR | SUS DMA ROM | 1962 | COLOR

8 Tense WWII thriller, based upon a real-life character. Eric Ericson (Holden) has been raised in America but is technically a Swedish citizen. He is also an international businessman and so he travels freely between Allied Europe and Nazi Germany. Because he wants to remain neutral, British agents set him up and then blackmail him into becoming a spy. He is to be a double agent. The Germans are to think that he is one of theirs, but he is one of ours. He becomes a very effective agent for the Allies, working with the German underground, where he meets and falls in love (Lilli Palmer), but their love is doomed.

Sex Nud Viol Lang AdSit

A: William Holden, Lilli Palmer, Hugh Griffith, Erica Beer, Werner Peters

© PARAMOUNT HOME VIDEO 6113

CUJO

D: Lewis Teague 93 m

R | HOR SUS | 1983 | COLOR

7 A genuinely frightening story from Stephen King. Dee Wallace is a young mother in a Maine village whose marriage is slowly disintegrating. She has had a brief affair, and she and her husband have had a fight. She has left the house with their young son in their car. Terror strikes when the car stalls and the two are attacked by a crazed and rabid Saint Bernard. This is a film where the plot builds slowly throughout and results in a solid, chilling climax. A skillfully crafted chiller that is definitely not for kids.

Sex Nud Viol Lang AdSit

A: Dee Wallace, Danny Pintauro, Daniel Hugh-Kelly, Christopher Stone, Ed Lauter, Mills Watson

© WARNER HOME VIDEO 11331

CURSE OF THE DEMON

D: Jacques Tourneur 81 m

NR HOR SUS 1957 B&W

9 Exceptional. One of the best horror films ever. Dana Andrews plays a stuffy New York clinical psychologist who travels to London to help expose a group of devil worshipers as being a hoax. His colleague has been mysteriously and brutally murdered, but Andrews refuses to believe that a demon called up by the group did it. Unfortunately for Dana, they aren't a hoax, and their leader (MacGinnis) calls up a demon from Hell to deal with him, too. Very moody and atmospheric, with misty English locations. Gripping and chilling terror. True genre classic.

Sex Nud Viol Lang AdSit

A: Dana Andrews, Peggy Cummins, Niall MacGinnis, Maurice Denham

© GOODTIMES 4424

CUTTER'S WAY

D: Ivan Passer 110 m

R CRM SUS 1981 COLOR

7 A small-time hustler and gigolo (Bridges) witnesses a wealthy murderer dumping a young girl's body in an alley. When he is charged with the murder, his best friend (John Heard), an embittered and crippled Vietnam veteran, is determined to help. Heard is extremely bitter toward anyone of privilege - those who sent others off to do their dirty work, like in Vietnam. He now becomes obsessed with exposing the wealthy killer so that he can validate his own tarnished sense of morality. The three leads are all very good, but the gloomy atmosphere may not appeal to all.

Sex Nud Viol Lang AdSit

A: Jeff Bridges, John Heard, Lisa Eichhorn, Ann Dusenberry, Stephen Elliott, Nina Van Pallandt

Distributed By MGM/UA Home Video M700154

DARK HALF, THE

D: George A. Romero 122 m

R HOR SUS 1993 COLOR

6 Hutton is college professor who has been trying to write legitimate works of literature, but so far his major successes, and a good living, have come from writing trash under a pseudonym. The recurring star of those novels is a ruthless antihero who will stop at nothing. When Hutton's secret life is threatened by a blackmailer, he decides to go public and to "kill off" his pseudonym, thereby also the book and its character. However, that character was created out of Hutton's own repressed self (his dark half). That half has gained a life of its own and is brutally killing all of those people who have a part in killing him off. Starts stronger than it finishes.

Sex Nud Viol Lang AdSit

A: Timothy Hutton, Amy Madigan, Julie Harris, Michael Rooker, Robert Joy, Kent Broadhurst

© ORION PICTURES CORPORATION 8787

DAY OF THE JACKAL, THE

D: Fred Zinnemann 143 m

PG SUS CRM ACT 1973 COLOR

9 Mesmerizing tension. It is based upon the best selling novel of the same name and which, in turn, was based upon a real-life character. A terrorist organization hires the world's best professional hitman to assassinate French President Charles de Gaulle. The killer is a faceless man who is known only as the Jackal. French police learn of the plot, but the Jackal constantly changes disguises to stay just ahead of them. The scenes of the massive police manhunt are juxtaposed with the Jackal's compulsively meticulous preparations and the result is a buildup of an incredible tension. First-rate cast and absolutely compelling viewing.

Sex Nud Viol Lang AdSit

A: Edward Fox, Alan Badel, Tony Britton, Cyril Cusack, Eric Porter, Michael Lonsdale

© MCA/UNIVERSAL HOME VIDEO, INC. 66040

DEAD AGAIN

D: Kenneth Branagh 107 m

R SUS DMA 1991 B&W

7 In a world of high-tech, big budget thrillers, along comes this little gem that did very well at the box office. Branagh is a modern-day private eye who takes in a lovely amnesiac (Thompson, his real life wife) and agrees to help her discover who she is. And when she is hypnotized, they find out that they have both lived a former life together in 1949. One was a noted pianist and the other was her conductor husband and the husband was later convicted of murdering his wife with a pair of scissors. Will the past recreate itself? An interesting suspense thriller with style, class and intelligence.

Sex Nud Viol Lang AdSit

A: Kenneth Branagh, Emma Thompson, Andy Garcia, Derek Jacobi, Hanna Schygulla

© PARAMOUNT HOME VIDEO 32057

DEAD CALM

D: Phillip Noyce 96 m

R SUS ACT 1989 COLOR

8 Extremely tense and effective thriller in which a married couple (Neil and Kidman), who have just lost a child, decide to spend some time together alone on a yacht 1200 miles off the coast of Australia. There they pick up a stranger (Zane) who is the sole survivor of a sinking ship. When Neil goes alone to check out the abandoned vessel, terror reigns at home. Zane is a psychotic killer who has killed all on board the ship he has just left. Now he commandeers Neil's boat and his wife, leaving Neil behind. She struggles alone in a cat-and-mouse survival game. Very impressive, intelligently made.

Sex Nud Viol Lang AdSit

A: Sam Neill, Nicole Kidman, Billy Zane

© WARNER HOME VIDEO 11870

DEAD IN THE WATER

D: Bill Condon 90 m

PG-13 MYS SUS 1992 COLOR

7 Quirky little story of murder which has elements that both Raymond Chandler and Alfred Hitchcock might recognise. Bryan Brown is a moderately successful attorney married to a very wealthy but petty and spiteful spoiled wife. So, he is carrying on an affair with his gorgeous secretary. He would love to divorce his wife, but there is pre-nuptual agreement and he has gotten used to his status and comforts. Reluctantly, he concludes that they must eliminate his wife. His carefully contrived plan requires an alibi which requires a brief affair with another equally obnoxious socialite. In spite of careful plans, one can never plan for everything... can one?

Sex Nud Viol Lang AdSit

A: Brian Brown, Teri Hatcher, Veronica Cartwright, Anne De Salvo

© MCA/UNIVERSAL HOME VIDEO, INC. 81229

DEADLY HERO

D: Ivan Nagy 102 m

PG SUS ACT 1975 COLOR

7 Engaging thriller. Murray is a cop who rescues a woman (Williams) from a vicious assault, killing her attacker in the process. At first she is grateful, but later she begins to suspect his actions, motives and continued attentions. Terrified, when she goes to his superiors to express her concerns, he begins to fear that he will lose his upcoming pension and decides that he must stop her. Gritty, bad-cop movie.

Sex Nud Viol Lang AdSit

A: Don Murray, Diahn Williams, James Earl Jones, Lilia Skala, Treat Williams, Danny DeVito

© NEW LINE HOME VIDEO 2042

DEAD MAN OUT

D: Richard Pierce 87 m

NR SUS DMA 1989 COLOR

8 Intense made-for-TV prison drama. Ben (Blades) has brutally murdered four innocent people and is now awaiting execution, but the extreme pressures on Death Row have pushed him over the edge. The State has a problem. They legally can not execute an insane man, even though he was sane when he committed the murders. Glover is a psychiatrist hired by the state to cure Ben. But Glover becomes tortured by his task. Does he cure the man and thereby help to kill him. Or does he leave him to suffer in his torment, but stay alive. Powerful performance by Blades.

Sex Nud Viol Lang AdSit

A: Danny Glover, Ruben Blades, Tom Atkins, Larry Block, Samuel L. Jackson, Maria Ricossa

© HBO VIDEO 0221

DEAD OF WINTER

D: Arthur Penn 100 m

R SUS 1987 COLOR

7 Creepy thriller. Steenburgen is an aspiring but destitute actress. She takes a job when Roddy McDowall asks her to go to a remote country estate to act as a double for another actress who he says had to be removed mid-film because of a nervous breakdown. At the estate, owned by a wheelchair-bound psychiatrist, she is made-over to appear uncannily like the other actress. However, she slowly comes to understand that the actress is actually dead, she is really acting out a part in an elaborate blackmail scheme and... she is trapped. An intricate plot and creepy atmosphere keeps you on the edge.

Sex Nud Viol Lang AdSit

A: Mary Steenburgen, Roddy McDowall, Jan Rubes, William Russ, Ken Pogue, Wayne Robson

© CBS/FOX VIDEO 5147

DEAD RINGERS

D: David Cronenberg 117 m

R DMA SUS 1988 COLOR

8 Perversely fascinating psychothriller. All the more fascinating because it is based upon fact. A pair of identical twins are practicing gynecologists. They share their practice, their apartment, their drug addiction, their women and their insanity. However, all that sharing comes to an end when the strong relationship between the two is torn apart by a deceptive affair with an actress (Bujold). Even though the film breaks down near the end and becomes gory in places, Irons's performance in the dual role and the unnerving premise keep you involved.

Sex Nud Viol Lang AdSit

A: Jeremy Irons, Genevieve Bujold, Heidi Von Palleske, Barbara Gordon, Shirley Douglas, Stephen Lack

© VIDEO TREASURES M012168

DEAD ZONE, THE

D: David Cronenberg 104 m

R SUS 1983 COLOR

8 Eerie and absorbing Stephen King story about a teacher who was in a coma for five years after a car wreck. When he awoke, he had developed the power to see into the past, into a person's soul and to predict the future. At first he uses his new powers for good - to solve murders and help others. But soon, besieged by hordes of people, he retreats into himself. Then he meets a man (Sheen), a politician, who may destroy the world and he has to be stopped. Very well acted. Tense psychological thriller.

Sex Nud Viol Lang AdSit

A: Christopher Walken, Brooke Adams, Tom Skerritt, Herbert Lom, Martin Sheen, Anthony Zerbe

© PARAMOUNT HOME VIDEO 1646

DEATH AND THE MAIDEN

D: Roman Polanski 103 m

R | DMA SUS | 1995 | COLOR | Sex | Nud | Viol | Lang | AdSit

7 Director Roman Polanski has brought Ariel Dorfman's powerful political play to the screen. In some unnamed South American emerging democracy, Paulina (Sigorney Weaver) is waiting for her over-due husband to come home. When headlights approach, a panic-stricken Paulina turns out lights and cocks her pistol. Her husband has only had a flat and been brought home by a stranger. Before bed, their discuss his recent appointment as lead investigator into previous death squads. Then, during the night, the stranger returns, and when Paulina hears his voice she knows that this is the man who tortured and brutally raped her. He is the enemy and she must confront him, but she has to fight her urge for revenge - or she will be as bad as him.

A: Sigorney Weaver, Ben Kingsley, Stuart Wilson

© TURNER HOME ENTERTAINMENT N4119

DECEIVED

D: Damian Harris 108 m

R | SUS | 1991 | COLOR | Sex | Nud | Viol | Lang | AdSit

6 Goldie Hawn is a yuppie art curator who meets and falls in love with a charmer. They marry, have a sweet little girl and life is absolutely wonderful - until he is murdered. When Hawn finds strange things in her dead husband's suit pockets, she begins to investigate to find out more. Slowly she uncovers that Mr. Wonderful had told her a bunch of lies. Her world comes tumbling down as she finds out the real truth, but things get much worse when her presumably murdered husband comes back and he's determined to kill her. An unusually serious role for Hawn and one that generates a fair amount of terror.

A: Goldie Hawn, John Heard, Ashley Peldon, Robin Bartlett, Tom Irwin, Beatrice Straight

© TOUCHSTONE HOME VIDEO 1306

DEEP, THE

D: Peter Yates 120 m

R | ACT SUS | 1977 | COLOR | Sex | Nud | Viol | Lang | AdSit

6 Americans Nolte and Bisset are skin diving off the coast of Bermuda when they discover a sunken World War II ship containing a fortune in morphine. Lou Gossett is a voodoo wielding drug dealer on the island who has considerable interest in the treasure. His interest puts Nolte and Bisset in considerable danger. The two get help from a bitter recluse Shaw. Wonderful underwater scenery is the primary attraction and Bisset's eye-catching T-shirt adds to the excitement. Plot is so-so.

A: Robert Shaw, Jacqueline Bisset, Nick Nolte, Louis Gossett, Jr., Eli Wallach

© GOODTIMES 74205

DEFENSELESS

D: Martin Campbell 106 m

R | SUS CRM | 1991 | COLOR | Sex | Nud | Viol | Lang | AdSit

7 Slick psychological thriller. Barbara Hershey is an attorney who is unfortunate enough to find her client (and lover) dead. However, she has also been framed for his murder and she may also be the killer's next victim. Her client was a real estate tycoon who she had been defending against charges of child pornography and, who it turns out, had also been married to an old friend of hers. Perhaps he was killed by the irate father of one of his young victims, or maybe there is another motive - but she must depend on an enigmatic police detective (Sam Shepard) to find out who the real murderer is, and do it in time to save her.

A: Barbara Hershey, Sam Shepard, J.T. Walsh, John Kapelos, Mary Beth Hurt

© LIVE HOME VIDEO 61704

DELIVERANCE

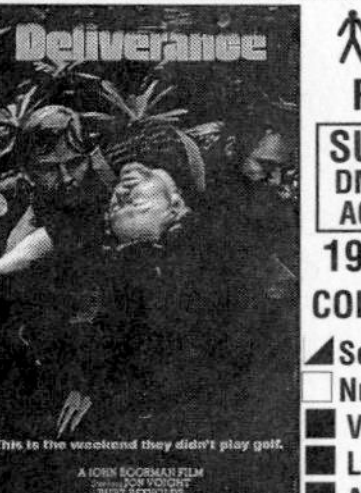

D: John Boorman 109 m

R | SUS DMA ACT | 1972 | COLOR | Sex | Nud | Viol | Lang | AdSit

10 Riveting account of four ordinary businessmen who decide to take a weekend whitewater canoe trip down a wild river before it is dammed up forever. What begins as a man-against-nature excursion becomes an exercise in gripping suspense, terror and survival. Four men become profoundly changed as they are forced to confront their fears alone when they are pursued by two demented hillbillies, intent upon murder and homosexual rape. The movie's theme song "Dueling Banjos" became a major pop hit. Excellent performances. Nominated for Best Picture. Totally involving.

A: Jon Voight, Burt Reynolds, Ned Beatty, Ronny Cox, Bill McKinney, James Dickey

© WARNER HOME VIDEO 1004

DEMON SEED

D: Donald Cammell 97 m

R | SF SUS | 1977 | COLOR | Sex | Nud | Viol | Lang | AdSit

7 Clever thriller in which a sophisticated computer has developed to the point of consciousness, independence and more. The computer's "father" is Fritz Weaver, who is estranged from his wife Julie Christie. She now lives alone in their computer-controlled house. The computer has developed a psychosis in which it believes the designers will soon pull its plug. It fears that it may "die" and all that it has become will be lost. So, through a terminal in the house, it takes control of the house and implements its own plan. It will perpetuate itself, using Christie's body to create its own offspring.

A: Julie Christie, Fritz Weaver, Gerrit Graham, Berry Kroger, Lisa Lu

Distributed By MGM/UA Home Video M600129

DEVILS, THE

D: Ken Russell 103 m

R | DMA SUS | 1971 | COLOR | Sex | Nud | Viol | Lang | AdSit

8 Very controversial and bizarre, but true, story (documented in 1634 France) presented in a nearly hallucinogenic way. Reed plays a cynical and amoral priest (he has a very active sex life) who gets in trouble with his Cardinal for opposing his political plans. Soon a hysterical nun (Redgrave) steps forward, accusing Reed of having seduced her and the other nuns through witchcraft. A charismatic exorcist (Gothard) arrives in town to conduct a mass exorcism, after which Reed is burned at the stake. Some pretty grotesque scenes will surely offend devout believers, but this is fascinating stuff.

A: Vanessa Redgrave, Oliver Reed, Murray Melvin, Max Adrian, Gemma Jones, Michael Gothard

© WARNER HOME VIDEO 11110

DIARY OF ANNE FRANK, THE

D: George Stevens 151 m

NR | DMA SUS | 1959 | B&W | Sex | Nud | Viol | Lang | AdSit

9 Very moving screen depiction of a real-life WWII tragedy. The story was written based upon an actual diary of a young Jewish girl while she was in hiding with her family inside Nazi-occupied Holland. In the diary, she tells of the daily lives of her family and a few friends who are forced to hide in secret rooms hidden behind the false walls of an Amsterdam factory building during the occupation. The threat of discovery is ever-present and they lived their lives under extreme pressure. Still, throughout harrowing daily routines and constant fear, Anne manages to keep hope alive. 3 Oscars.

A: Millie Perkins, Joseph Schildkraut, Shelley Winters, Richard Beymer, Lou Jacobi, Ed Wynn

© FOXVIDEO 1074

DIGGSTOWN

D: Michael Ritchie 98 m

R | SUS ACT | 1992 | COLOR | Sex | Nud | Viol | Lang | AdSit

7 James Woods, a sharp talking con-man just out of jail, is on his way to Diggstown, Georgia, where he has set up a crooked fight promoter (Dern) for a major tumble. Woods has primed Dern to fall for a bet that Woods's fighter (Gossett) can knock out any ten men in the county on the same day. What follows is a series of double-crosses and tricks by two major con men, each trying to outmaneuver and trick the other. Even though you're never quite sure who's out-conning whom until the last, this is not up to the standards of the great con movies like THE STING. Still, it is pretty entertaining.

A: James Woods, Bruce Dern, Louis Gossett, Jr., Heather Graham, Randall "Tex" Cob, Thomas Wilson Brown

Distributed By MGM/UA Home Video 902692

DISAPPEARANCE, THE

D: Stuart Cooper 80 m

R | ACT SUS | 1977 | COLOR | Sex | Nud | Viol | Lang | AdSit

7 Gripping intrigue draws you in early and holds you throughout. Donald Sutherland is a coolly competent professional hit man, but he is becoming morose and dissatisfied with his life. He loses himself to and becomes totally captivated with his wife, the only one he ever cared about or who has ever really cared about him. So one day when she disappears, he loses any ability to concentrate on his work. Oddly though, the next job offer he receives is to kill Plummer, his wife's lover and the man he believes to be responsible for her disappearance. Compelling performance by Sutherland.

A: Donald Sutherland, Francine Racette, David Hemmings, John Hurt, Christopher Plummer, Virginia McKenna

© RHINO HOME VIDEO/RECORDS 2947

DISCLOSURE

D: Barry Levinson 129 m

R | SUS DMA | 1995 | COLOR | Sex | Nud | Viol | Lang | AdSit

7 Michael Douglas has spent the last ten years heading the manufacturing division at a high-tech company. Now that company is about to become part of a multi-million dollar merger. Just as it looks as though he's going to make a lot of money and be promoted in the bargain, he learns that his old flame Demi Moore will get the promotion instead. He can live with that, but she has other plans. That evening she trys to seduce him and when he resists, she claims sexual harassment. He now stands to loose everything, including his family. The only option he has left is to sue her for sexual harassment. This kind of news in the press is very hard on mergers, so now everyone, is playing hardball. Quite involving and not sensationalized.

A: Michael Douglas, Demi Moore, Donald Sutherland, Caroline Goodall, Dylan Baker, Roma Maffia

© WARNER HOME VIDEO 13575

DIVA

D: Jean-Jacques Beineix 119 m

R | FOR SUS ACT | 1981 | COLOR | Sex | Nud | Viol | Lang | AdSit

8 Interesting French film which has become a cult favorite because it is so stylishly photographed. It also has a pretty good story. There are two separate plots interwoven. A mail messenger has a strong attraction to a black American opera singer (Fernandez). She has never allowed her voice to be recorded, so he secretly tapes a performance. He is seen. The next day a strange woman secretly drops another unrelated tape into his pocket, which incriminates a top cop, just before she dies. Soon the messenger is being chased all over Paris by two separate groups, both of whom are after his tapes. Some fans might even rate it higher. Subtitles.

A: Frederic Andrei, Wilhemina Wiggins, Richard Bohringer, Thuy An Luu, Jacques Fabbri, Chantal Deruaz

Distributed By MGM/UA Home Video M800183

D.O.A.

D: Rocky Morton 100 m

R | SUS MYS | 1988 | COLOR | Sex | Nud | Viol | Lang | AdSit

7 Dennis Quaid plays a hard-drinking college English professor who wakes up to discover that he has been poisoned with a slow-acting drug and has only twenty-four hours to find who his killers are - and why that did it - before he will die. He enlists the aid of pretty freshman co-ed Meg Ryan as he confronts a series of likely candidates, each of whom has a dark secret to protect, even Ryan. This is a very interesting premise, even though it is somewhat weak in the follow-through. It was done before in 1950 with Edmond O' Brien in the title role. Still, this is a pretty good movie.

A: Dennis Quaid, Meg Ryan, Daniel Stern, Charlotte Rampling, Daniel Stern

© TOUCHSTONE HOME VIDEO 698

DOG DAY AFTERNOON

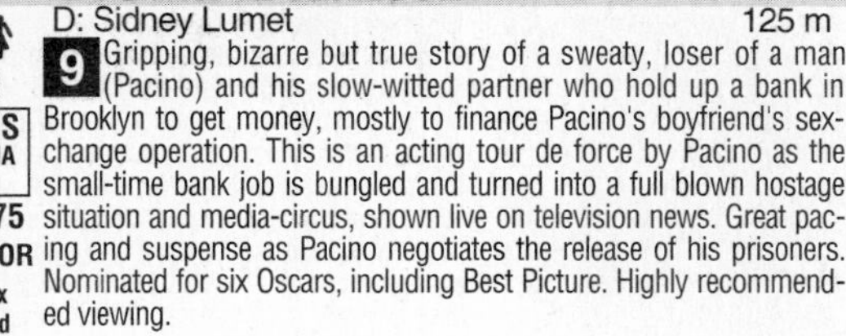

D: Sidney Lumet 125 m

R | SUS DMA | 1975 | COLOR | Sex | Nud | Viol | Lang | AdSit

9 Gripping, bizarre but true story of a sweaty, loser of a man (Pacino) and his slow-witted partner who hold up a bank in Brooklyn to get money, mostly to finance Pacino's boyfriend's sex-change operation. This is an acting tour de force by Pacino as the small-time bank job is bungled and turned into a full blown hostage situation and media-circus, shown live on television news. Great pacing and suspense as Pacino negotiates the release of his prisoners. Nominated for six Oscars, including Best Picture. Highly recommended viewing.

A: Al Pacino, John Cazale, Charles Durning, Carol Kane, James Broderick, Chris Sarandon

© WARNER HOME VIDEO 1024

DOLLARS ($)

D: Richard Brooks 119 m

R | SUS ACT COM | 1972 | COLOR | Sex | Nud | Viol | Lang | AdSit

9 Top notch heist film. Beatty is an American security technician who masterminds a plot to steal the ill-gotten gains from the security deposit boxes of crooks at a German bank. He enlists the aid of a dippy hooker (Hawn) to obtain copies of the keys that he needs for the three critical boxes. However, the film doesn't end after the robbery is over - because the owners of boxes, not nice guys at all, want everything back, and an elaborate chase across a frozen lake begins. Unexpected twists abound. Really good stuff.

A: Warren Beatty, Goldie Hawn, Gert Frobe, Robert Webber, Scott Brady

© COLUMBIA TRISTAR HOME VIDEO 60450

DON'T LOOK NOW

D: Nicolas Roeg 110 m

R | SUS DMA | 1974 | COLOR | Sex | Nud | Viol | Lang | AdSit

8 Gripping, eerie psychic thriller. After their 10 year-old daughter drowns, Christie and Sutherland go to Venice where he is to help to restore a church. She befriends two strange sisters, one of whom is a blind psychic who tells them that their daughter is happy. He does not believe the psychic, but then sees a strange figure in a red raincoat who reminds him of his daughter. The psychic also warns Sutherland of great impending danger. Meanwhile, in another subplot, random murders are occurring about town. Really spooky occult stuff, a sexy scene and big climax.

A: Julie Christie, Donald Sutherland, Hilary Mason, Cielia Matania, Massimo Serato, Renato Scarpa

© PARAMOUNT HOME VIDEO 8704

DREAM LOVER

D: Nicholas Kazan 114 m

NR | SUS | 1994 | COLOR | Sex | Nud | Viol | Lang | AdSit

7 Spader is a young, wealthy and single architect who falls passionately in love with a strikingly beautiful woman (Amick), the woman of his dreams. After a torrid affair, they are married and have a child. Then he discovers that she has lied to him about her family, who are not dead at all but instead are only poor common folk from Texas. He forgives her this lie and they begin anew. But, before long he begins to suspect that she is telling him other lies, and may also be cheating on him. Is he becoming paranoid, or is she plotting against him? He becomes enraged and she has him arrested on abuse charges, and soon thereafter, committed to an institution. Comes in both an R and a sexier NR version.

A: James Spader, Madchen Amick, Bess Armstrong, Frederic Lehne, Larry Miller, Kathleen York

© POLYGRAM VIDEO 33113-3

DREAMSCAPE

D: Joseph Ruben 99 m

PG-13 | SF SUS DMA | 1983 | COLOR | Sex | Nud | Viol | Lang | AdSit

7 A really imaginative and intriguing premise. Suppose psychics could be trained to enter into the dreams or nightmares of others and to then help calm their fears. Quaid and other psychics have been recruited into a huge government program to do just that. He is so successful that he is assigned the special job of helping the President deal with his recurring fears of a nuclear holocaust. However, Quaid also uncovers a plot involving one of his fellow psychics, who is supposed to use these same techniques to kill the President. Good special effects.

A: Dennis Quaid, Max von Sydow, Christopher Plummer, Eddie Albert, Kate Capshaw

© HBO VIDEO TVA2722

DRESSED TO KILL

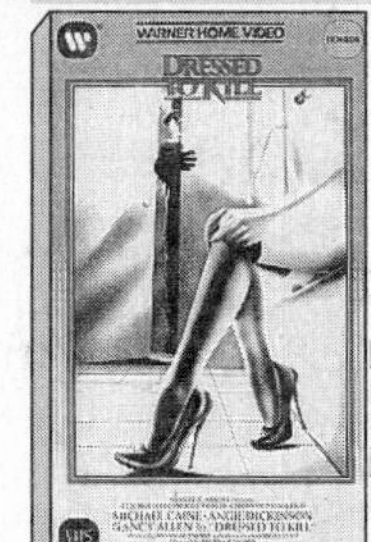

D: Brian De Palma 105 m

R | SUS CRM | 1980 | COLOR | Sex | Nud | Viol | Lang | AdSit

8 High-tension drama as a psychopath stalks two women. Angie Dickinson is a sexually frustrated housewife caught up in her sexual fantasies and is talking with her psychiatrist about her problem. However, she is brutally slashed after she has an affair with a total stranger. A hooker (Nancy Allen) who saw the killer leave, is soon being pursued by the psychopathic killer. So she teams up with Dickenson's young son in an effort to trap the murderer - a tall blonde named Bobbi. Michael Caine plays Angie's psychiatrist and he may hold the key, but beware... all things aren't as they appear to be. Unexpected ending.

A: Michael Caine, Angie Dickinson, Nancy Allen, Keith Gordon, Dennis Franz, David Margulies

© WARNER HOME VIDEO 26008

DR. TERROR'S HOUSE OF HORRORS

D: Freddie Francis 98 m

NR | SUS HOR | 1965 | COLOR | Sex | Nud | Viol | Lang | AdSit

7 Intelligent, very well done film. A mysterious doctor who calls himself Dr. Terror and who reads Tarot cards, enters into the private traveling compartment of five men on a train. He is really Death in disguise and he tells each man his fortune. For each man he predicts death - grotesque and macabre deaths. What follows is an anthology of the separate tales of each man, which are all then interwoven together. They are tales of the macabre and bizarre. Everything is very credibly done, with a top-flight cast. Gruesome, but fun.

A: Peter Cushing, Christopher Lee, Donald Sutherland, Neil McCallum, Roy Castle, Max Adrian

© REPUBLIC PICTURES HOME VIDEO 1067

DUEL

D: Steven Spielberg 91 m

NR | SUS ACT | 1971 | COLOR | Sex | Nud | Viol | Lang | AdSit

8 Startling, effective thriller that was initially made for TV but was later released in theaters, too. This is also the film that made Steven Spielberg's reputation and gave him his big start in this film describing mindless terror. A salesman in a rented car, taking a leisurely drive down a remote stretch of road, finds himself relentlessly pursued by a maniacal driver at the wheel of a ten-ton tanker truck. He can't see this guy's face and he doesn't understand why, but one thing is for certain... this guy wants to kill him.. Superb suspense film with excellent pacing.

A: Dennis Weaver, Tim Herbert, Charles Peel, Eddie Firestone, Gene Dynarksi, Alexander Lockwood

© MCA/UNIVERSAL HOME VIDEO, INC. 55096

EARTHQUAKE

D: Mark Robson 123 m

PG | ACT SUS | 1974 | COLOR | Sex | Nud | Viol | Lang | AdSit

6 This was a monumental disaster film, one of the biggest ever done, in which California is destroyed by "the big one" - buildings collapse, streets buckle and chaos abounds. Theater audiences were also bombarded with "Sensurround" shock waves in addition to the terrific special effects upon the screen. It is packed with action, most of which will translate to the small screen, but the story line is minimal. As is typical in this genre, there are actually several stories running at the same time concerning the different effects of the quake on different people. Huge all-star cast.

A: Charlton Heston, Ava Gardner, Lorne Greene, George Kennedy, Victoria Principal, Walter Matthau

© MCA/UNIVERSAL HOME VIDEO, INC. 55034

EDDIE AND THE CRUISERS

D: Martin Davidson 95 m

PG | MYS SUS | 1983 | COLOR | Sex | Nud | Viol | Lang | AdSit

7 Odd but interesting film which has developed into a cult film. Eddie and the Cruisers had been a rock group in the 1960s, but it was way ahead of its time. The lead singer, Eddie, dejected after his album idea is rejected, drove off a bridge - but no body was ever recovered. Now it is much later and the group's songs have finally become popular. Now, also, someone is breaking into all the former bandmember's houses apparently looking for the master tape of some unreleased songs. Reporter Ellen Barkin begins to wonder if Eddie is still alive. Pretty good mystery, even if it is unusual.

A: Tom Berenger, Michael Pare, Ellen Barkin, Helen Schneider, Joe Pantoliano

© NEW LINE HOME VIDEO 2066

EIGER SANCTION, THE

D: Clint Eastwood 130 m

R | ACT SUS | 1975 | COLOR | Sex | Nud | Viol | Lang | AdSit

8 Clint Eastwood is a retired professional assassin who has taken up a much quieter occupation as an art collector, but he is called out of retirement to hunt down a double agent for the Agency. It is to be a sanctioned hit. His target will be one member of a group of mountain climbers that is seeking to climb the Alps, but he doesn't yet know which man it is. Some of the plot elements take a lot to swallow whole, but the action sequences of climbing the mountain make the movie worth while. Eastwood reportedly did his own climbing.

A: Clint Eastwood, George Kennedy, Vonetta McGee, Jack Cassidy, Thayer David

© MCA/UNIVERSAL HOME VIDEO, INC. 66043

EMPIRE STRIKES BACK, THE

D: Irvin Kershner 128 m

PG

SF ACT SUS

1980 COLOR

Sex Nud Viol Lang AdSit

10 A real winner! High intensity middle picture in the Star Wars trilogy. First came STAR WARS and after comes RETURN OF THE JEDI, but here, Luke Skywalker travels to the Jedi master Yoda to learn to the mystical and powerful ways of "The Source," Han Solo and Princess Leia get into deep trouble and develop "a thing" together, Billy Dee Williams joins the battle against the Empire, and Luke finds that Darth Vader not only wants to destroy the rebels, but wants Luke to join him in the "dark side" of the force. Excitement plus. WOW special effects.

A: Billy Dee Williams, Harrison Ford, Carrie Fisher, Mark Hamill, Anthony Daniels, Dave Prowse

© FOXVIDEO 1425

ENEMY BELOW, THE

D: Dick Powell 98 m

NR

WAR SUS ACT

1957 COLOR

Sex Nud Viol Lang AdSit

9 Gripping and extremely tense cat-and-mouse game between a German U-boat commanded by Curt Jurgens and an American destroyer escort captained by Robert Mitchum. The North Atlantic is the setting for this spellbinding study of bravery and tenacity, as two seasoned warriors engage in a chess game - a battle of experiences to see who will be the victor when hunter pursues hunter. Excellent photography. The special effects won an Oscar. An accurate portrayal of military tactics. Neither side is vilified nor is it glorified. This is highly watchable.

A: Robert Mitchum, Curt Jurgens, Theodore Bikel, Doug McClure, Russell Collins, David Hedison

© FOXVIDEO 1133

ENFORCER, THE

D: James Fargo 97 m

R

ACT SUS CRM

1976 COLOR

Sex Nud Viol Lang AdSit

9 Top-notch follow-up to MAGNUM FORCE in the DIRTY HARRY series. Harry gets in trouble again when he stops a holdup at a liquor store in his own way, but he doesn't stay in the doghouse long. He is needed. He is reluctantly teamed with a female cop (Tyne Daly) to track down a group of terrorists who have robbed a munitions warehouse and launched a terror spree, including kidnapping San Francisco's mayor. Daly seeks not only help to solve the case and take down the bad guys, but to get Harry's approval. Solid action, good humor and a good plot make this a lot of fun - but very violent.

A: Clint Eastwood, Harry Guardino, Tyne Daly, Bradford Dillman, John Mitchum

© WARNER HOME VIDEO 11082

ESCAPE FROM ALCATRAZ

D: Don Siegel 112 m

PG

SUS CRM

1979 COLOR

Sex Nud Viol Lang AdSit

7 Very intriguing and involving "true" story. It is the straightforward telling of the "facts" (although somewhat romanticized by Hollywood) surrounding the actual 1962 breakout of three prisoners from the supposedly escape-proof Alcatraz prison. The prisoners did get off the island but were never heard of again. The movie would have you believe that they survived. Eastwood plays Frank Morris who masterminded the escape for himself and two others. McGoohan plays a cold-hearted tough warden..It maintains your interest throughout and is largely credible.

A: Clint Eastwood, Patrick McGoohan, Roberts Blossom, Jack Thibeau, Fred Ward, Paul Benjamin

© PARAMOUNT HOME VIDEO 1256

ESCAPE FROM SOBIBOR

D: Jack Gold 120 m

PG-13

DMA SUS

1987 COLOR

Sex Nud Viol Lang AdSit

8 Exciting drama based upon the real-life 1943 breakout of prisoners from a Nazi concentration camp. An exceptional cast and script, plus top-notch production values, bring a vibrant sense of reality to this story of the largest-ever prisoner escape from a Nazi death camp. A captured Russian officer, a Polish Jew and a seamstress lead the camp against impossible odds in this last-ditch effort to survive. Alan Arkin in particular puts in a standout performance. Originally made for TV.

A: Alan Arkin, Rutger Hauer, Joanna Pacula, Hartman Becker, Jack Shepherd

© LIVE HOME VIDEO 69004

EVIL, THE

D: Gus Trikonis 80 m

R

HOR SUS

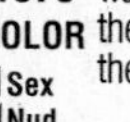

1978 COLOR

Sex Nud Viol Lang AdSit

8 Genuine hard-boiled chills come when psychiatrist Richard Crenna and his wife rent a gothic mansion in the country for his summer drug rehabilitation program. While he and some others are renovating the property, they discover a locked trap door. They should not have opened that door. Now the building has a tenant they don't want - the devil himself (Victor Buono) - who imprisons them all... and then, one by one, kills each one of them off. Genuinely scary stuff of the supernatural variety.

A: Richard Crenna, Joanna Pettet, Victor Buono, Andrew Prine, Cassie Yates

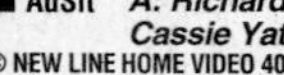

© NEW LINE HOME VIDEO 4006

EXORCIST, THE

D: William Friedkin 122 m

R

SUS HOR

1973 COLOR

Sex Nud Viol Lang AdSit

10 Extraordinarily powerful, deeply evocative and very believable story of the satanic possession. It is so believable that it could literally SCARE the hell out of you. Nominated for 10 Oscars, including Best Picture. A 12-year-old girl (Blair) is possessed by an ancient demon and is transformed into a vile, hideous and truly repulsive creature. Her desperate mother (Burstyn) seeks out a troubled priest (Miller) to confront the demon, but the demon turns the priest's own failing faith and sense of guilt against him. So, Miller calls in a seasoned old priest (von Sydow) to help him exorcise the demon. You may never turn the lights out again.

A: Ellen Burstyn, Max von Sydow, Linda Blair, Jason Miller, Lee J. Cobb

© WARNER HOME VIDEO 1007

EXORCIST II: THE HERETIC

D: John Boorman 118 m

R

SUS HOR

1977 COLOR

Sex Nud Viol Lang AdSit

6 This is a relatively undistinguished sequel to the devastatingly horrific original. Still, this one does contain some genuinely chilling moments. Four years after she was exorcised of the demon Pazuzu, Linda Blair is again suffering from recurring nightmares and is now under treatment by psychoanalyst Louise Fletcher. Under hypnosis, it is discovered she is still possessed. Burton is the Vatican's investigator Father Lamont. He knows that he needs help so he searches through Africa to find former possession survivor James Earl Jones to urge him to once again face the evil that he had barely escaped before.

A: Richard Burton, Linda Blair, Louise Fletcher, Kitty Will, James Earl Jones, Ned Beatty

© WARNER HOME VIDEO 1023

EXPERIMENT IN TERROR

D: Blake Edwards 123 m

NR

SUS CRM ACT

1962 B&W

Sex Nud Viol Lang AdSit

8 Excellent, high-tension gripper about a sadistic psycho killer (Martin) who kidnaps a bank teller's (Remick) teenage sister (Powers). If she doesn't deliver $100,000 to him, her sister will be killed. Desperate, she contacts the FBI and an extensive surveillance is set up, but it doesn't work. The only way to draw him out is to use Remick as bait. Glenn Ford is the FBI agent who fights against the clock to save the girl and prevent tragedy. Suspense builds slowly and steadily throughout the entire picture. Excellent acting. Martin is particularly menacing.

A: Glenn Ford, Lee Remick, Stefanie Powers, Ross Martin, Ned Glass

© GOODTIMES 4443

EYE OF THE NEEDLE

D: Richard Marquand 112 m

R

SUS ACT DMA

1981 COLOR

Sex Nud Viol Lang AdSit

8 Very taut espionage thriller. Sutherland plays a ruthless Nazi agent known as The Needle because of his penchant for killing with a switchblade knife. Operating in England, he learns of the plans for D-Day and makes a mad dash for the coast where he is to meet a U-boat. But a storm throws him up on the rocks of a desolate Scottish island inhabited only by a lonely and sexually frustrated woman, her crippled husband and young son. She allows Sutherland to seduce her and to win her trust - then she discovers what he is. She must stop him. High-tension. Very Good.

A: Donald Sutherland, Ian Bannen, Kate Nelligan, Christopher Cazenove, Philip Martin Brown

Distributed By MGM/UA Home Video M301303

EYES OF LAURA MARS

D: Irvin Kershner 103 m

R

SUS MYS

1978 COLOR

Sex Nud Viol Lang AdSit

6 Fay Dunaway plays Laura Mars, a commercial photographer whose kinky, erotic and violent photographs are world renowned. But now the artistic visions she sees are also becoming predictions of actual grisly ice pick murders - all of people she knows. Police detective Tommy Lee Jones knows that many of her pictures also resemble confidential police murder photos. What has taken control of Laura? Laura, however, knows the killer is really after her. Lots of wrong turns in the plot add to the suspense. This is a high tension picture, but the unsympathetic characters diminish the impact.

A: Faye Dunaway, Tommy Lee Jones, Brad Dourif, Rene Auberjonois, Raul Julia, Frank Adonis

© COLUMBIA TRISTAR HOME VIDEO VH10190

EYEWITNESS

D: Peter Yates 103 m

R

SUS CRM

1981 COLOR

Sex Nud Viol Lang AdSit

7 William Hurt is a janitor in a New York building who discovers a dead man's murdered body. Hurt has long been infatuated with a beautiful television news reporter, so he uses his limited knowledge of the case to get close to her. Then, in order to prolong their relationship, he claims that he actually witnessed the murder. His lies put them both in the middle of international intrigue and in serious danger. A quirky love story and interesting characters just add to a pretty good suspense flick.

A: William Hurt, Sigourney Weaver, Christopher Plummer, James Woods

© CBS/FOX VIDEO 1116

SUS

FAIL SAFE

D: Sidney Lumet 111 m

NR | SUS DMA | 1964 | B&W

9 High-tension nail-biter about what might happen if the US had accidentally bombed Moscow. Through a series of errors, US bombers armed with nuclear weapons are sent to bomb Moscow. They are under strict orders that, once they are on the way, nothing - not even direct orders from the President - will turn them back. The tension becomes intense as time runs down, military leaders struggle to call the planes back and world leaders try to determine what to do to prevent total destruction. Very intelligent production.

Sex / Nud / Viol / Lang / AdSit

A: Henry Fonda, Walter Matthau, Fritz Weaver, Larry Hagman, Frank Overton, Sorrell Booke

© GOODTIMES 4228

FALL OF THE HOUSE OF USHER, THE

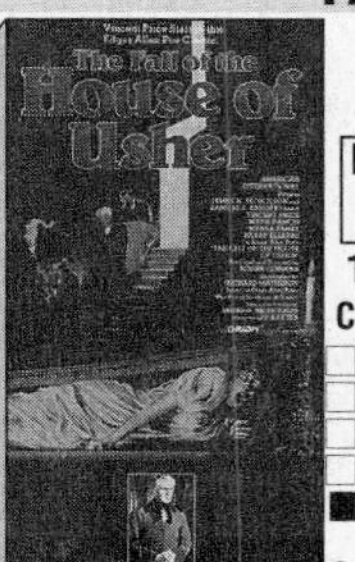

D: Roger Corman 79 m

NR | HOR SUS | 1960 | COLOR

8 Classic Edgar Allan Poe horror tale about a family and its legacy of madness and doom. When her suitor (Mark Damon) arrives at an old, dreary, decaying mansion to take a beautiful girl (Myrna Fahey) away to be married, her older brother (Vincent Price) becomes desperate for his sister to stay and reveals to Damon the secret. All Ushers are condemned to eventual madness and to an early death. Undeterred, he yet attempts to get his intended to leave. It is then that the terror begins. This film captures the flavor of Poe as no other has yet done, even though it was filmed in only 15 days with virtually no budget.

Sex / Nud / Viol / Lang / AdSit

A: Vincent Price, Mark Damon, Myrna Fahey, Harry Ellerbe

© WARNER HOME VIDEO 26004

FATAL ATTRACTION

D: Adrian Lyne 120 m

R | SUS ACT | 1987 | COLOR

9 Terrific adult nail-biter. Douglas plays a happily married man who allows himself to be seduced one weekend when his wife is out of town. It was a fun weekend and it's over, right? Wrong! She is psychotically obsessed with him and she will not leave him alone. She calls him and his family constantly... and worse. This film holds your attention all the way from its super-sexy beginning to its nerve-jolting conclusion. Excellent cast, very exciting movie and major box office hit. Also check out similar PLAY MISTY FOR ME with Clint Eastwood.

Sex / Nud / Viol / Lang / AdSit

A: Michael Douglas, Glenn Close, Anne Archer, Ellen Hamilton Latzen, Stuart Pankin

© PARAMOUNT HOME VIDEO 1762

FEW GOOD MEN, A

D: Rob Reiner 138 m

R | DMA SUS | 1992 | COLOR

10 Terrific courtroom drama. Intelligent, classy and believable. A young Marine at Guantanamo base in Cuba, commanded by a gung-ho Colonel (Nicholson) dies an apparent victim of murder. Two Marines are arrested and charged, but Demi Moore is a military attorney who smells a coverup. She brings it to her superior's attention, who assigns a brilliant smart-aleck Harvard grad (Cruise) to the case instead of her. But, she wangles her way onto the team anyway. It is quickly learned that the death was an accident but that it resulted from an illegal order from commander Nicholson. How to prove it in court. Powerful personalities and performances. Dynamite!

Sex / Nud / Viol / Lang / AdSit

A: Tom Cruise, Jack Nicholson, Demi Moore, Kevin Bacon, Kiefer Sutherland, Kevin Pollack

© COLUMBIA TRISTAR HOME VIDEO 27893

FINAL ANALYSIS

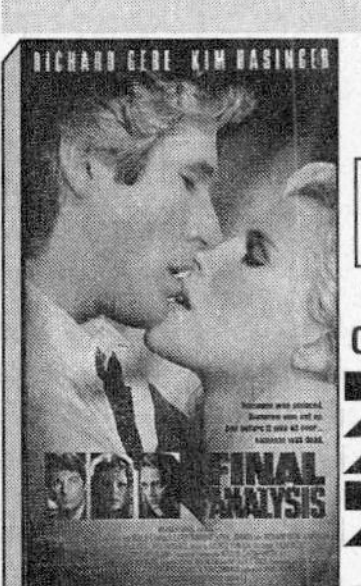

D: Phil Joanou 125 m

R | SUS MYS | 1992 | COLOR

7 A sexy thriller that was created to be in the Hitchcock tradition. Gere is a noted San Francisco psychiatrist treating Thurman, a deeply disturbed young woman. Basinger is her older sister and the wife of a corrupt and abusive man (Roberts). Gere, against his better judgment, becomes sexually involved with sultry Basinger. Basinger kills her husband and is freed when Gere can provide her a psychiatric alibi. However, something doesn't quite fit and he begins to question what is going on. Very sexy, suspenseful, and involved psychothriller that surprises and keeps you guessing and firmly planted on the edge of your seat.

Sex / Nud / Viol / Lang / AdSit

A: Richard Gere, Kim Basinger, Uma Thurman, Eric Roberts, Paul Guilfoyle, Keith David

© WARNER HOME VIDEO 12243

FIRESTARTER

D: Mark L. Lester 113 m

R | SUS HOR | 1984 | COLOR

8 Excellent screen version of Stephen King's strange story of a little girl who has the telekinetic power to start fires by merely thinking of it. Some times she can control her thoughts, sometimes she can't - for which she feels guilty. Her nice-guy father (Sheen) does his best to comfort her and also to protect her from George C. Scott. Scott is an agent for the government. It wants to either use her as their secret weapon or to eliminate her. There is real suspense generated here and great special effects, too. Horror fans will be more than satisfied. Fast paced, with a top-flight cast.

Sex / Nud / Viol / Lang / AdSit

A: Drew Barrymore, David Keith, George C. Scott, Martin Sheen, Art Carney, Louise Fletcher

© MCA/UNIVERSAL HOME VIDEO, INC. 80075

FIRM, THE

D: Sydney Pollack m

R | SUS ACT DMA | 1993 | COLOR

8 Quite good thriller based on a blockbuster novel. Tom Cruise is a poor boy who has managed to graduate at the top of his Harvard law class and is recruited into a mysterious Memphis law firm with a huge salary. Only after he is in does he discover that he can't get out. The firm is a money-laundering machine for the Chicago mob. The FBI, on the other hand, sees him as their big opportunity to break the back of the mafia and is forcing him into becoming their snitch. If he doesn't help them, he'll go to jail. If he does, he will have to hide out forever. He is caught between two powerful forces who can crush him. Top-flight cast. Good, but book was better.

Sex / Nud / Viol / Lang / AdSit

A: Tom Cruise, Jeanne Triplehorn, Gene Hackman, Holly Hunter, Ed Harris, Wilford Brimley

© PARAMOUNT HOME VIDEO 32523

FIRST BORN

D: Michael Apted 100 m

PG-13 | DMA SUS | 1984 | COLOR

6 An intense and believable story of a struggling young divorced woman (Terry Garr), with two sons, who falls in love with tough guy Peter Weller. He moves in with them and later turns out to be an abusive cocaine dealer. His menacing presence becomes a real danger for all of them and it appears they are trapped. But help for the family comes from within when her oldest teenage son (Collett) stands up to Weller. Good performances make this a credible picture, in spite of its overly-violent conclusion.

Sex / Nud / Viol / Lang / AdSit

A: Teri Garr, Peter Weller, Christopher Collet, Robert Downey, Jr., Corey Haim, Sarah Jessica Parker

© PARAMOUNT HOME VIDEO 1744

FLATLINERS

D: Joel Schumacher 111 m

R | SF SUS | 1990 | COLOR

7 A group of daring young medical students, hungry to explore the unknown, get much more than they expected in this taut thriller. One of the students gets the idea that, if his body temperature could be slowly lowered and his heart stopped (flatlined), he would be able experience the afterlife. He persuades the others to try the experiment and, one by one, each dies for a few moments, experiencing their own personal hell. Their experiments work, but what they don't count on is what they each bring back from death. A nail biter!

Sex / Nud / Viol / Lang / AdSit

A: Kiefer Sutherland, Julia Roberts, Kevin Bacon, William Baldwin, Oliver Platt, Kimberly Scott

© COLUMBIA TRISTAR HOME VIDEO 50383

FLIGHT OF THE PHOENIX

D: Robert Aldrich 143 m

NR | SUS DMA ACT | 1966 | COLOR

9 This is a gripping adventure story about a small planeful of men who are forced to crash in the North African desert. They are all trapped in a very hostile environment with only one way out. They must rebuild the plane and fly it out. Tension steadily builds as the men struggle both to endure the extreme rigors of desert survival and to rebuild the plane. An excellent international cast provides credibility and realism to an excellent script. Plus, there is a really unique twist as the climax builds. Very highly recommended viewing.

Sex / Nud / Viol / Lang / AdSit

A: James Stewart, Richard Attenborough, Peter Finch, Hardy Kruger, Ernest Borgnine, George Kennedy

© FOXVIDEO 1221

FOOL KILLER, THE

D: Servando Gonzalez 100 m

NR | DMA SUS | 1965 | B&W

7 Unusual adventure story in which George, a 12-year-old runaway orphan boy in the post-Civil War South, rides the rails. He strikes up a relationship with a crusty old-timer who intrigues him with stories of an eight-foot-tall axe-wielding murderer who is supposedly roaming the countryside. He calls him the "fool killer." Later, young George teams up with a tormented, very tall war veteran who has lost his memory. They travel together, but slowly George begins to fear that his new companion may, in fact, be the fool killer. Somewhat arty and offbeat, but it definitely has its moments.

Sex / Nud / Viol / Lang / AdSit

A: Anthony Perkins, Edward Albert, Dana Elcar, Henry Hull, Salome Jens, Arnold Moss

© REPUBLIC PICTURES HOME VIDEO 1352

FOURTH PROTOCOL, THE

D: John Mackenzie 100 m

R | SUS ACT | 1987 | COLOR

8 Thrilling and excellent Cold War relic. Michael Caine is a British agent who suspects that something strange is up. He knows something is being smuggled into the country, but he doesn't know what it is at first. Then, he discovers that a Russian agent is smuggling an atom bomb into England and will detonate it next to an American airbase. The Americans will be blamed and a major spit will occur in the Western alliance. Non-stop pacing keeps suspense levels very high throughout. Very good.

Sex / Nud / Viol / Lang / AdSit

A: Michael Caine, Pierce Brosnan, Joanna Cassidy, Ned Beatty, Betsy Brantley, Peter Cartwright

© WARNER HOME VIDEO 320

FRANTIC

D: Roman Polanski — 120 m

R | MYS SUS | 1988 | COLOR

8 A classy and intriguing thriller. An American doctor's wife is mysteriously kidnapped by Arabs in Paris. When neither the bureaucratic Parisian police nor the American embassy officials prove to be very cooperative, a desperate Harrison Ford begins his own frantic search. He discovers that his wife's suitcase had been switched with that of a sexy girl who was a courier for a smuggler. He and the girl, in a complicated web of intrigue, combine forces to pursue both the missing luggage and his wife. Polanski's eye for detail and excellent pacing creates a thrilling emotional rollercoaster. Very good, but starts slow.

Sex Nud Viol Lang AdSit

A: Harrison Ford, Betty Buckley, Emmanuelle Seiger, John Mahoney, Jimmie Ray Weeks, Gerard Klein

© WARNER HOME VIDEO 11787

FRENCH CONNECTION, THE

D: William Friedkin — 104 m

R | ACT CRM SUS | 1971 | COLOR

10 An exciting, landmark film that was a winner of five Oscars, including Best Picture. This is a realistic cop action yarn that trails a maverick, nearly amoral, New York cop and his wary partner as they obsessively and relentlessly investigate a huge heroin shipment from France. It is a thrilling and action-packed depiction of tough street-life. It is loaded with blood-pounding suspense and contains one of the most thrilling chase scenes ever recorded on film. Equally important, it also features an excellent plot, good character development, superb acting and was based upon real life.

Sex Nud Viol Lang AdSit

A: Gene Hackman, Fernando Rey, Roy Scheider, Eddie Egan, Sonny Grosso, Tony Lo Bianco

© FOXVIDEO 1009

FRENZY

D: Alfred Hitchcock — 116 m

R | SUS CRM MYS | 1972 | COLOR

8 Hitchcock, the master filmmaker, returned to England after 30 years in America to create this, his second-to-last film. It is the story of a "necktie sex-murderer" who is raping and killing women in London. Hitchcock also returns to his favorite theme of an innocent man trapped under the weight of circumstantial evidence. In this case, our man suffers while the suave real killer evades suspicion. Very suspenseful and contains all of the masterful camera tricks, pacing and black humor that are Hitchcock's trademarks.

Sex Nud Viol Lang AdSit

A: Jon Finch, Barry Foster, Barbara Leigh-Hunt, Anna Massey, Alec McCowen

© MCA/UNIVERSAL HOME VIDEO, INC. 55011

FUGITIVE, THE

D: Andrew Davis — 131 m

PG-13 | SUS MYS ACT | 1994 | COLOR

9 A huge box office hit. Harrison Ford is Dr. Richard Kimble, who came home to find his wife dying after having been attacked. Kimble scuffled with the intruder and knows that the man has only one arm. However, all the physical evidence points to Kimble. No one believes his story and he is sentenced to die for the murder. But, while on the way to prison, the bus wrecks and he escapes. Tommy Lee Jones is a U.S. Marshall who has been assigned to recapture Kimble. He is good and he is dedicated. Kimble knows his only chance to regain his life is to find that one-armed man himself. Very suspenseful, good action, good mystery and excellent acting. 6 Oscar nominations, including Best Picture.

Sex Nud Viol Lang AdSit

A: Harrison Ford, Tommy Lee Jones, Sela Ward, Andreas Katsulas, Joe Pantoliano, Jereon Krabbe

© WARNER HOME VIDEO 21000

FURY, THE

D: Brian De Palma — 119 m

R | SUS HOR | 1978 | COLOR

8 Chilling contemporary tale of an ordinary man (Kirk Douglas) who's son is kidnapped by a supersecret government agency. Its agents have kidnapped his son so that they can use his psychic powers for their own purposes or, if they can't, to kill him. Amy Irving may look as innocent as a school girl - but one look from her can literally kill. Douglas enlists her help and together they track down his missing son and confront the kidnappers. This is a very effective suspense flick, but it is also very intense, very bloody and violent in places... and it has an explosive ending.

Sex Nud Viol Lang AdSit

A: Kirk Douglas, Andrew Stevens, Amy Irving, Fiona Lewis, John Cassavetes, Charles Durning

© FOXVIDEO 1097

FX

D: Robert Mandel — 109 m

R | ACT SUS | 1986 | COLOR

8 Fast-paced thriller. A special effects wizard is hired by the US Justice Department to stage what he thinks is a ploy to hide a protected witness from the mob. Instead, it is actually a plot by some corrupt Feds to kill off a dangerous witness who will incriminate them, too. When the high-tech wizard finds out the truth and discovers that he is also to be a victim, he has to use his tricks to vanish. But first he has to win a high-speed race through the streets of NYC. Lots of action, twists, and some good special effects.

Sex Nud Viol Lang AdSit

A: Bryan Brown, Brian Dennehy, Diane Verona, Cliff De Young, Mason Adams, Jerry Orbach

© HBO VIDEO TVA3769

GAMBIT

D: Ronald Neame — 109 m

NR | COM SUS | 1966 | COLOR

8 Fact-paced and engaging, witty caper comedy. Cat burglar Michael Caine enlists the help of Shirley MacLaine, a wacky Eurasian dancer, to help him steal a priceless art treasure from its ruthless Arab owner. Caine's plan is elaborate, full of gadgets and ultimatley doesn't work, but that's when the fun starts. Caine and MacLaine are great together. The film did not get its proper due when it was originally released, but has now become a cult favorite. Good fun.

Sex Nud Viol Lang AdSit

A: Michael Caine, Shirley MacLaine, Herbert Lom, Roger C. Carmel, John Abbott

© MCA/UNIVERSAL HOME VIDEO, INC. 80365

GOTCHA!

D: Jeff Kanew — 97 m

PG-13 | COM SUS | 1985 | COLOR

7 An entertaining coming-of-age comedy/thriller about a college student who is a social misfit. While, he excels at a campus espionage game called "Gotcha" (a game of mock assassinations), he is a terrible failure with women. So, he goes off to Paris on spring break in search of adventure. However, there he also becomes involved with his sexy dream woman. But this beautiful mystery woman also has ties to real spies and to real danger. Suddenly he's in the middle of real international intrigue and he's playing Gotcha for real.

Sex Nud Viol Lang AdSit

A: Anthony Edwards, Linda Fiorentino, Nick Corri, Klaus Lowitsch, Alex Rocco

© MCA/UNIVERSAL HOME VIDEO, INC. 80188

GRAY LADY DOWN

D: David Greene — 111 m

PG | SUS | 1977 | COLOR

8 Well made and tense, believable nail-biter. A nuclear submarine has been accidentally rammed by a freighter and has sunk into 1400 feet of water. The men onboard have only 48 hours of air. The sunken sub's escape hatch was buried during an earth tremor and they cannot escape by themselves. The Navy must call upon an experimental deep-diving two-man sub to rescue the crew. A solid cast of veteran actors adds credibility to this high-tech race against time. It is logically presented, beautifully photographed and has some really terrific special effects, too.

Sex Nud Viol Lang AdSit

A: Charlton Heston, David Carradine, Stacy Keach, Ned Beatty, Ronny Cox, Rosemary Forsyth

© MCA/UNIVERSAL HOME VIDEO, INC. 55057

GREAT TRAIN ROBBERY, THE

D: Michael Crichton — 111 m

PG | ACT SUS | 1979 | COLOR

9 Stylish thriller about the very first robbery of a moving train - based upon a true incident in 1855 England. Sean Connery plays a dapper rogue of a thief who masterminds a daring plan to hijack gold bullion from a moving train. Beautiful production, with wonderful characters and a captivating plot. Lesley-Anne Down is Connery's beautiful mistress and also a disguise expert. Donald Sutherland is a braggart of a pickpocket. This is great entertainment that has you rooting for the bad guys.

Sex Nud Viol Lang AdSit

A: Sean Connery, Donald Sutherland, Lesley-Anne Down, Alan Webb, Malcolm Terris, Robert Lang

Distributed By MGM/UA Home Video M301427

GROUNDSTAR CONSPIRACY, THE

D: Lamont Johnson — 93 m

PG | SF SUS MYS | 1972 | COLOR

8 A top secret space-based laboratory is largely destroyed in an explosion. The only survivor (Sarrazin) is thought by tough government agent Peppard to be a spy who was sent to steal its plans, but Sarrazin is badly burned and has no recollection of events. Still, Peppard must get him to remember. He has to know who was behind the plot. So when brainwashing doesn't work, Sarrazin is set free so that he can be followed. He has now become bait. Clever and intricate plot, with excellent pacing, direction and acting, plus an unexpected climax. A good thriller, unfairly overlooked upon its release.

Sex Nud Viol Lang AdSit

A: George Peppard, Michael Sarrazin, Christine Belford, Cliff Potts, James Olson

© MCA/UNIVERSAL HOME VIDEO, INC. 80602

GROUND ZERO

D: Michael Pattinson, Bruce Myles — 99 m

PG-13 | SUS MYS | 1987 | COLOR

7 Suspenseful political intrigue. An Australian cameraman (Friels) learns that his father took newsreel pictures of civilian casualties from a British A-Bomb test in 1954, and may then have been killed by government agents to keep things quiet and preserve a cover-up. The government still wants to keep the lid on it and this politically naive photographer is himself now in serious danger. Donald Pleasence is excellent as a desert hermit who survived the tests. Starts slow and builds steadily throughout.

Sex Nud Viol Lang AdSit

A: Colin Friels, Donald Pleasence, Natalie Bate, Jack Thompson, Simon Chilvers, Neil Fitzpatrick

© LIVE HOME VIDEO 62781

GUILTY AS SIN

D: Sidney Lumet — 107 m

R | SUS MYS | 1993 | COLOR | Sex Nud Viol Lang AdSit

7 An intriguing plot premise. De Mornay is a beautiful, driven attorney who is drawn into defending a charming and handsome self-admitted gigolo (Johnson). Johnson is accused of throwing his wife out a window and faking her suicide for her money. De Mornay learns quickly of his abilities to scheme and manipulate. Convinced of his guilt, she trys to get herself removed from the case but he has arranged it so that she is trapped into defending him. Much more than that, she is also trapped into playing out a special role in his conspiracy. The pacing falters and credibility is stretched, but still holds your interest.

A: Rebecca De Mornay, Don Johnson, Jack Warden, Stephen Lang, Dana Ivey, Ron White

© HOLLYWOOD PICTURES HOME VIDEO 2009

HALLOWEEN

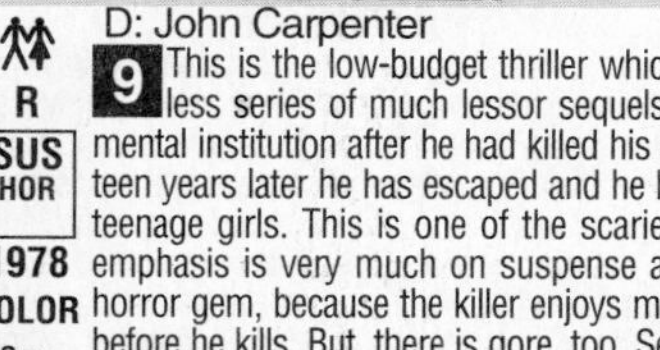

D: John Carpenter — 92 m

R | SUS HOR | 1978 | COLOR | Sex Nud Viol Lang AdSit

9 This is the low-budget thriller which launched a seemingly endless series of much lessor sequels. A young boy was sent to a mental institution after he had killed his sister on Halloween. Now, fifteen years later he has escaped and he has returned to terrorize three teenage girls. This is one of the scariest films since PSYCHO. The emphasis is very much on suspense and terror in this well-crafted horror gem, because the killer enjoys mercilessly taunting his victims before he kills. But, there is gore, too. Several sequels of much lessor quality followed. This is also the film that made Jamie Lee Curtis into a star.

A: Donald Pleasence, Jamie Lee Curtis, Nancy Loomis, P.J. Sales, Charles Cyphers, Kyle Richards

© MEDIA HOME ENTERTAINMENT, INC. M131

HAND THAT ROCKS THE CRADLE, THE

D: Curtis Hanson — 110 m

R | SUS DMA | 1992 | COLOR | Sex Nud Viol Lang AdSit

8 Disturbing thriller that will bristle the hair on the back of your neck! De Mornay is married to an obstetrician who kills himself when patient Sciorra accuses him of molesting her at the office. The trauma prompts De Mornay's miscarriage and she is told she can never have children again. Destroyed, she is determined to get revenge. She takes a job as nanny to Sciorra's two young children and slowly, she plots to take over Sciorra's life. She schemes to win over both the love of Sciorra's children and her husband. De Mornay's character is evil, diabolical and ruthless. Quite compelling and disturbing viewing.

A: Rebecca De Mornay, Annabella Sciorra, Ernie Hudson, Matt McCoy, Ernie Hudson

© HOLLYWOOD PICTURES HOME VIDEO 1334

HARPER

D: Jack Smight — 121 m

NR | MYS SUS CRM | 1966 | COLOR | Sex Nud Viol Lang AdSit

9 Excellent, a rousing detective yarn that was the first of Newman's career and is credited with causing the resurrection of the private-eye genre. Harper (Newman) is a smooth private eye who is hired by a rich man's wife (Bacall) to find her husband when he doesn't come home. The investigative trail leads Harper through a curious cast of oddball characters, eventually to a smuggling ring and murder. Fast paced, rapid-fire dialogue and sophisticated plot twists. Followed by THE DROWNING POOL. Excellent.

A: Paul Newman, Lauren Bacall, Shelley Winters, Arthur Hill, Julie Harris, Janet Leigh

© WARNER HOME VIDEO 11175

HAUNTING, THE

D: Robert Wise — 112 m

G | SUS HOR | 1963 | B&W | Sex Nud Viol Lang AdSit

9 This is a masterful psychological horror movie that manipulates your mind rather than overloads your senses. A ninety-year-old New England house has long been rumored to be haunted. Over the years it has been the setting for a series of tragedies. Dr. Markway (Johnson) is determined to explore its secrets. So he, two female psychic researchers (Harris and Bloom) and the nephew (Tamblyn) of the old woman who has inherited it enter. It soon appears to the group that the house "wants" Julie Harris. But was what we/they just saw real, or was it just our/their imagination? Truly hair-raising.

A: Julie Harris, Claire Bloom, Richard Johnson, Russ Tamblyn, Lois Maxwell, Fay Compton

Distributed By MGM/UA Home Video M600903

HIT, THE

D: Stephen Frears — 97 m

R | SUS COM | 1985 | COLOR | Sex Nud Viol Lang AdSit

7 Offbeat and deceptively funny film. A stool pigeon (Stamp) has been in hiding in Spain for ten years but now has been found. Hurt and Roth are the two hit men who have been hired by the mob to bring him back to Paris where he is to be executed. However, when confronted by the two, Stamp is strangely compliant but begins to play mind games with them, making both them and the viewers, wonder what's going on. Then things get even more complicated for the two after they find that the car they hijacked to escape the police has a beautiful Spanish girl in it. Suspenseful, very funny in places and definitely unpredictable.

A: Terence Stamp, John Hurt, Tim Roth, Laura Del Sol, Bill Hunter, Fernando Rey

© NEW LINE HOME VIDEO 7599

HITCHER, THE

D: Robert Harmon — 98 m

R | HOR SUS | 1985 | COLOR | Sex Nud Viol Lang AdSit

7 A young California-bound motorist (Howell) picks up a hitchhiker (Hauer) somewhere in Texas. He shouldn't have. The thumber is actually a murderous psychotic who has killed his previous ride and now holds a knife to Howell's throat. In a happy piece of good luck, Hower pushes the hitcher out the door and leaves him behind. He has escaped from the hitcher - or has he. His terror is refreshed anew when a car goes by with the hitcher and his next victims inside - a family with children. Edge-of-your-seat suspense. Gobs of violence and gore.

A: Rutger Hauer, C. Thomas Howell, Jennifer Jason Leigh, Jeffrey DeMunn, Henry Darrow

© HBO VIDEO TVA3756

HOPSCOTCH

D: Ronald Neame — 107 m

R | COM SUS | 1980 | COLOR | Sex Nud Viol Lang AdSit

8 Highly entertaining entry from two polished pros, even if the plot is contrived. Matthau plays a CIA agent put out to pasture by his pompous and idiotic boss (Beatty) - so Matthau decides to get even. He and his girl friend (Jackson) decide to publish his memoirs, detailing agency misdeeds and dirty tricks. Beatty doesn't take kindly to their revelations and a marvelously entertaining chase between professional chase-ors and chase-ees ensues. Not entirely believable, but Matthau and Jackson are an utter joy together. See them in HOUSE CALLS, too.

A: Walter Matthau, Glenda Jackson, Ned Beatty, Sam Waterston, Herbert Lom

© NEW LINE HOME VIDEO 00104

HORROR OF DRACULA

D: Terence Fisher — 82 m

NR | HOR SUS | 1958 | COLOR | Sex Nud Viol Lang AdSit

8 Genuinely scary film. Christopher Lee is marvelous as he creates a sinister portrait of the charismatic but vile and evil Count who prowls gothic London as a blood-thirsty vampire. This is a very stylish film that captures the feel of a Dracula whose blood sucking induces an orgasmic-like high in his willing female bloodbanks. Peter Cushing is also very good as Dracula's nemesis, Dr. Van Helsing. This is a very high quality version of the timeless story, equal to Lugosi's 1931 portrait in DRACULA. The success of this film spawned many lessor sequels.

A: Christopher Lee, Peter Cushing, Michael Gough, Melissa Stribling, Carol Marsh, John Van Eyssen

© WARNER HOME VIDEO 11499

HOUSE OF GAMES

D: David Mamet — 102 m

R | MYS SUS | 1987 | COLOR | Sex Nud Viol Lang AdSit

8 A very unusual and fascinating thriller. An up-tight pop psychiatrist and best-selling female author (Crouse) decides to rescue one of her clients from a charismatic con artist (Mantegna). Instead, she is nearly conned out of $6,000 of her own money and she has also become fascinated with this man. She is both drawn to him and challenged by him. And, she quickly gets in over her head, involved in a plot which contains a suitcase of supposed mob money. Quickly the twists and cons get so thick that she doesn't know who is conning who. This is a slick thriller well worth watching, but pay attention.

A: Lindsay Crouse, Joe Mantegna, Lilia Skala, Mike Nussbaum, J.T. Walsh

© HBO VIDEO 0063

HUNT FOR RED OCTOBER, THE

D: John McTiernan — 135 m

PG | SUS ACT | 1990 | COLOR | Sex Nud Viol Lang AdSit

8 This is one of the last of the Cold War thrillers. It is based upon the best-selling Tom Clancy suspense novel set in 1984 - seven years prior to the actual downfall of the communist Soviet state. Connery plays a disenchanted commander of a new top-secret high-tech submarine code-named Red October and he plans to defect to the West with the secret sub. The Soviets race against time to sink him before he can deliver the sub and the Americans struggle to help him - both without starting a nuclear war. Very exciting and well done. However, purists will like the book better.

A: Sean Connery, Alec Baldwin, Scott Glenn, Sam Neill, James Earl Jones

© PARAMOUNT HOME VIDEO 32020

HUSH... HUSH, SWEET CHARLOTTE

D: Robert Aldrich — 133 m

NR | HOR SUS | 1964 | COLOR | Sex Nud Viol Lang AdSit

8 Near-classic chiller. Bette Davis is astonishing as a reclusive, wealthy old woman notorious for having killed her lover years before and who now lives on the edge of reality. When the State wants to tear down her house to build a highway, she turns to her cousin Olivia de Havilland. But de Havilland and her boyfriend Joseph Cotten instead plot to drive her into total insanity. Winner of seven Oscar nominations, this is no ordinary horror movie. Highly suspenseful all the way until the tragic end. Reunites the two stars from WHAT EVER HAPPENED TO BABY JANE.

A: Bette Davis, Olivia de Havilland, Joseph Cotten, Agnes Moorehead, Cecil Kellaway, Mary Astor

© FOXVIDEO 1245

ICE STATION ZEBRA

D: John Sturges — 150 m

G | ACT SUS | 1968 | COLOR

6 This is a Cold War espionage flick in which Rock Hudson commands a submarine that is sent to the North Pole regions to retrieve Soviet spy satelite data from a weather station before the Russians get it. It is a large-scale picture with beautiful arctic photography, action and some suspense. Borgnine is a Russian defector. He is only one of several who are suspected of being the Russian spy which is known to be on board and which is being pursued by British agent Patrick McGoohan. This is a pretty typical Cold War movie. Still, it was supposedly the favorite of billionaire Howard Hughes.

Sex / Nud / Viol / Lang / AdSit

A: Rock Hudson, Ernest Borgnine, Patrick McGoohan, Jim Brown, Tony Bill, Lloyd Nolan

Distributed By MGM/UA Home Video M600160

I LOVE TROUBLE

D: Charles Shyer — 123 m

PG | ROM SUS | 1994 | COLOR

6 Mildly interesting story of two aggressive rival Chicago reporters. This is an attempt to recreate the sparks that Tracy and Hepburn threw off, but it largely fizzles. Both these tow hotshot reporters are on the same trail. A trail to discover why a passenger train strangely derailed. The closer they get to the truth, the more in-troubler they get. The only answer is for them to pool their resources, except neither trusts the other. A reasonable time-killer -- if its a slow night.

Sex / Nud / Viol / Lang / AdSit

A: Julia Roberts, Nick Nolte, Saul Rubinek, Robert Loggia, James Rebhorn, Charles Martin Smith

© TOUCHSTONE HOME VIDEO 2983

IMPOSSIBLE SPY, THE

D: Jim Goddard — 96 m

NR | SUS ACT | 1987 | COLOR

7 Intriguing espionage thriller - more so because it is based upon the real-life exploits of an Egyptain-born Israeli, Elie Cohen. Cohen is a mild mannered businessman who is recruited by Israeli intelligence (the Massad) in 1959 and sent to Argentina to infiltrate a group planning the overthrow of the Syran government. That experience provides him the means to become a spy inside Damascus itself, where he infiltrated the Syran government. The information he provided was, in large measure, responsible for the success of the Israelis in the Six-Day War... but the price is high.

Sex / Nud / Viol / Lang / AdSit

A: John Shea, Eli Wallach, Rami Danon, Michal Bat-Adam

© HBO VIDEO 0035

INCIDENT, THE

D: Larry Pierce — 99 m

NR | SUS CRM | 1967 | B&W

8 Brutal, disturbing story of urban violence witnessed first hand. Martin Sheen made his screen debut as one of two drunken street punks in the New York subway system. Bored, they begin to terrorize, one-by-one, the passengers of a subway car. Their panic-stricken victims become so afraid for themselves that they all but abandon concern for anyone else. Very unpleasant, but still a valid and timely drama with a top-notch cast. This was Donna Mills's first screen outing, as well.

Sex / Nud / Viol / Lang / AdSit

A: Tony Musante, Martin Sheen, Beau Bridges, Jack Gilford, Thelma Ritter, Donna Mills

© FOXVIDEO 1290

IN COLD BLOOD

D: Richard Brooks — 134 m

R | CRM SUS DMA | 1968 | B&W

10 A chilling, very intense masterpiece relating the real world senseless murders of a Kansas farm family and the character of their psychotic murderers. It is taken from Truman Capote's best-selling book of the same name, which he based upon his extensive prison interviews of the two murderers. The events related are all the more chilling because of their matter-of-fact presentation. Blake and Wilson put in the performances of their lives as uncaring remorseless killers and the story related is their's from the time of the crime itself, through to their executions. Extremely powerful.

Sex / Nud / Viol / Lang / AdSit

A: Robert Blake, Scott Wilson, John Forsythe, Jeff Corey, Will Geer, Paul Stewart

© COLUMBIA TRISTAR HOME VIDEO VH10342

INTERNAL AFFAIRS

D: Mike Figgis — 114 m

R | SUS ACT CRM | 1990 | COLOR

8 A gripping police thriller. Andy Garcia is an internal affairs investigator, struggling to gain evidence against a respected veteran police officer (Gere) who he knows is using his position as a cop to manipulate and twist other cops into doing his bidding. Gere is deep into money laundering, robbery, drug running schemes and even murder. He is a control freak, but now he is up against someone he can't control... but he tries. He will protect himself no matter what it takes. Very tense believable plot.

Sex / Nud / Viol / Lang / AdSit

A: Richard Gere, Andy Garcia, Laurie Metcalf, Nancy Travis, William Baldwin

© PARAMOUNT HOME VIDEO 32245

INTERSECTION

D: Mark Rydell — 98 m

R | ROM SUS | 1994 | COLOR

6 An interesting premise. In the very first scenes, we see Richard Gere's car sliding into an intersection. We know an accident is going to happen but we're going to have to wait through a whole movie to know learn it turns out. Gere's life immediately begins to unfold. He is a wealthy architect married to beautiful Sharon Stone. They have money and a pretty daughter, but their relationship has gone bad. Gere has fallen in love with full-of-life Lolita Davidovich but he still finds it very difficult to give up his past or to start a new life. He is torn with indecision and now he is sliding into an intersection. Some women may like it but it is too slow for most.

Sex / Nud / Viol / Lang / AdSit

A: Richard Gere, Sharon Stone, Lolita Davidovich, Martin Landau, David Selby, Jenny Morrison

© PARAMOUNT HOME VIDEO 32242

IN THE LINE OF FIRE

D: Wolfgang Petersen — 127 m

R | SUS ACT | 1993 | COLOR

9 An exciting, very popular and gripping suspense film in which two government agents, both highly-trained and seasoned professionals, pit their skills against each other. Malcovich is extremely intelligent, totally ruthless and was assassin for the CIA. But, now he feels betrayed by his government and for him there is nothing left but the game. Clint Eastwood is an aging Secret Service agent who is haunted by his failure to protect President Kennedy. For Malcovich, the goal of this game of skills and retribution is his assassination of the President. His game is spiced by his highly-prized battle of wits against Eastwood, an adversary who he feels is his equal.

Sex / Nud / Viol / Lang / AdSit

A: Clint Eastwood, John Malkovich, Rene Russo, Dylan McDermott, Gary Cole, Fred Dalton Thompson

© COLUMBIA TRISTAR HOME VIDEO 52313

INVASION OF THE BODY SNATCHERS

D: Don Siegel — 80 m

NR | SF SUS HOR | 1956 | B&W

9 A chilling and frightening film that is every bit as powerful today as when released. Kevin McCarthy is a small town doctor who observes that all those around him - his patients, his friends and even his family - are slowly being transformed into emotionless, cold, inhuman beings. They look the same but they are different, very different. Slowly he uncovers the truth, that earth has been invaded by strange aliens who consume humans and then replace them with identical replicas that emerge from strange "pods." This has a subtle understated terror that found its intellectual inspiration in McCarthy-era politics.

Sex / Nud / Viol / Lang / AdSit

A: Kevin McCarthy, Dana Wynter, Carolyn Jones, King Donovan, Larry Gates, Virginia Christine

© REPUBLIC PICTURES HOME VIDEO 2018

IPCRESS FILE, THE

D: Sidney J. Furie — 107 m

NR | SUS MYS ACT | 1965 | COLOR

9 This is a quite good and intelligent espionage thriller. Michael Caine is marvelous as a low-key Cockney crook turned secret agent. He is called in by London's top intelligence officials to investigate a series of kidnappings of top scientists, who are then brainwashed and taken behind the Iron Curtain. This is the best of three separate films based on three books from Len Deighton. It is taut and suspenseful, with numerous twists keeping interest levels high throughout. It was a very popular film and it made Caine into a star.

Sex / Nud / Viol / Lang / AdSit

A: Michael Caine, Nigel Green, Sue Lloyd, Guy Coleman, Gordon Jackson

© MCA/UNIVERSAL HOME VIDEO, INC. 80518

I WANT TO LIVE!

D: Robert Wise — 122 m

NR | DMA SUS | 1958 | B&W

8 Gripping movie that won Susan Hayward an Oscar for Best Actress and received five other nominations. It is based upon the true story of the 1955 execution of Barbara Graham, in California's San Quentin prison, for murder. Hayward is mesmerizing as she plays a girl who lived dangerously. She stole, was a drug addict and a prostitute but, according to the film, was framed for the robbery/murder of a widow. This is a bleak and downbeat story, but it is nonetheless gripping and compelling throughout.

Sex / Nud / Viol / Lang / AdSit

A: Susan Hayward, Simon Oakland, Virginia Vincent, Theodore Bikel

Distributed By MGM/UA Home Video M600760

JACOB'S LADDER

D: Adrian Lyne — 116 m

R | SUS MYS | 1990 | COLOR

7 Intriguing, nightmarish and moody thriller with stunning visuals. Jacob is a Vietnam vet who suffers from vivid hallucinations. At times it is difficult for him (and the audience) to tell if what he sees is real or not. Is someone trying to kill him? Did the Army subject his platoon to drug experimentation? Are perhaps his visions actually insights into another consciousness? (The writer of this was the same writer as in GHOST.) Not surprisingly, Jacob is losing his grip on reality. This is very dark and very different, with excellent special effects. You will either be impressed or very confused. Maybe both.

Sex / Nud / Viol / Lang / AdSit

A: Tim Robbins, Elizabeth Pena, Danny Aiello, Bryan Larkin

© LIVE HOME VIDEO 68949

SUS

JAGGED EDGE

D: Richard Marquand 108 m

R | SUS MYS | 1985 | COLOR | Sex, Nud, Viol, Lang, AdSit

8 Gripping thriller. Jeff Bridges is a wealthy publishing magnate who is accused of the brutal murder of his wife. He seeks out female attorney (Glenn Close) to defend him and she agrees, but only after she becomes convinced that he is actually innocent. During the course of the trial she has fallen in love with him but she also has developed recurring doubts about his innocence. Glenn Close and Jeff Bridges are both convincing, but veteran actor Robert Loggia won an Oscar nomination for his portrait of a sleazy private investigator. Involving, intense and largely well made, but some minor plot holes do hurt it.

A: Glenn Close, Jeff Bridges, Peter Coyote, Robert Loggia, Leigh Taylor-Young, Karen Austin

© COLUMBIA TRISTAR HOME VIDEO 60591

JAWS

D: Steven Spielberg 124 m

PG | SUS ACT DMA | 1975 | COLOR | Sex, Nud, Viol, Lang, AdSit

10 A blockbuster hit that is both highly entertaining and technically masterful. An otherwise simplistic story line becomes a totally gripping adventure and leaves its audience terror-struck. A small town cop in a New England oceanside tourist town suspects that a great white shark is cruising the shoreline looking for lunch. Stubborn officials ignore his concerns until there is a major attack. The cop, a tenacious shark fisherman and a scientist set out to hunt down the shark, but... the gigantic creature turns to stalk them instead. Beware, this is a truly adrenaline pumping experience.

A: Roy Scheider, Robert Shaw, Richard Dreyfuss, Larraine Gary, Murray Hamilton, Jeffrey Kramer

© MCA/UNIVERSAL HOME VIDEO, INC. 66001

JENNIFER 8

D: Bruce Robinson 127 m

R | MYS CRM SUS | 1992 | COLOR | Sex, Nud, Viol, Lang, AdSit

8 Tightly wound thriller. LA homicide detective John Berlin (Garcia) has transfered to a northern California police department to escape big city burnout and to work with his best friend (Henricksen). He arrives just in time to be on-site when a woman's severed hand is found and begins to uncover clues that tie it to an unsolved murder, and that leads him to suspect that there is a serial murderer killing blind women. But, his suspicions are based on few facts and the other cops thinks he's a big city showboat. His fears are very real for him because he has uncovered a pretty blind witness (Thurman) who is now in serious danger because no one believes him.

A: Andy Garcia, Uma Thurman, Lance Henriksen, Kathy Baker, Kevin Conway, John Malkovich

© PARAMOUNT HOME VIDEO 32495

JUDGMENT IN BERLIN

D: Leo Penn 92 m

PG | DMA SUS | 1988 | COLOR | Sex, Nud, Viol, Lang, AdSit

8 Interesting, intense and unusual courtroom drama based upon the actual 1978 hijacking of a Polish airliner to a US base in West Germany by an East German couple using a toy gun. The communists want the criminals returned. Trying to defuse an embarrassing and politically explosive situation, an American judge (Sheen) is brought in by the American government to decide if a hijacking to escape communism is justifiable. Excellent performances by Sheen and Penn (in a small role) make this a very involving and very watchable experience.

A: Martin Sheen, Sam Wanamaker, Max Gail, Heinz Hoenig, Carl Lumbly, Sean Penn

© NEW LINE HOME VIDEO 62774

JUDGMENT NIGHT

D: Stephen Hopkings 110 m

R | SUS ACT | 1993 | COLOR | Sex, Nud, Viol, Lang, AdSit

7 A bunch of ordinary guys head out together in a motor home for a night out on the town, at a boxing match. When they become bogged down in a traffic jam, they head off to find a way around it on a detour through a bad neighborhood. Instead, they find themselves becoming witnesses to a murder and spend the rest of the film being chased from building to building by a gang of hoods who are trying to eliminate the witnesses. This is no DELIVERENCE but it is fast-paced and the characters are frequently believable.

A: Emilio Estevez, Cuba Gooding, Jr., Denis Leary, Stephen Dorff, Jeremy Pevin, Erik Schrody

© MCA/UNIVERSAL HOME VIDEO, INC. 81563

JUGGERNAUT

D: Richard Lester 109 m

PG | SUS ACT | 1974 | COLOR | Sex, Nud, Viol, Lang, AdSit

7 Very effective suspense thriller. A blackmailer has planted several bombs on board a luxury liner and is holding it for ransom while it sails on the high seas. Harris and a band of experts helicopter on board and must race against time to find all the bombs and defuse them. And, all the while they are looking, the blackmailer stays on the phone to taunt them with meager and cryptic clues as to where the bombs are. This could have been rather commonplace disaster movie, but instead it is raised, by excellent acting and direction, into an intense and realistic thriller.

A: Richard Harris, Omar Sharif, David Hemmings, Anthony Hopkins, Shirley Knight, Ian Holm

Distributed By MGM/UA Home Video M203070

JULIA

D: Fred Zinnemann 118 m

PG | DMA SUS | 1977 | COLOR | Sex, Nud, Viol, Lang, AdSit

9 This is a captivating human thriller, written by the late author Lillian Hellman concerning her life-time friendship with her unusual friend Julia. Lillian (Fonda) and Julia (Redgrave) were childhood friends. Julia was born to wealth and has devoted her life to activist causes. It is now the 1930s and Julia is an activist fighting against the relentless onslaught of Nazism inside Germany. While traveling in Europe, Lillian is approached to smuggle money to her friend Julia inside Germany. This is a very involving production that was extremely well done and was very popular. Three Oscars.

A: Jane Fonda, Vanessa Redgrave, Jason Robards, Jr., Maximilian Schell, Meryl Streep, Hal Holbrook

© FOXVIDEO 1091

JURASSIC PARK

D: Steven Spielberg 126 m

PG-13 | ACT SUS SF | 1993 | COLOR | Sex, Nud, Viol, Lang, AdSit

10 Masterful movie making is combined with wondrous special effects to create grippingly real terror. A wealthy industrialist has purchased in island off the coast of Costa Rica and plans to convert it into a fantastic tourist attraction. The featured attraction is live dinosaurs which have been miraculously reconstituted from "pickled" DNA fragments, taken from mosquitoes that have been entombed in amber for 100 million years. Two paleontologists (Neill and Dern) are called in to assure the investors that the park is safe. Instead, they are set upon and hunted by the carnivorous beasts who have been set free by sabotage and a massive power failure.

A: Sam Neill, Laura Dern, Jeff Goldblum, Richard Attenborough

© MCA/UNIVERSAL HOME VIDEO, INC.

KILLING, THE

D: Stanley Kubrick 85 m

NR | CRM SUS | 1956 | B&W | Sex, Nud, Viol, Lang, AdSit

9 Excellent film noir thriller that established Stanley Kubrick as a director. Sterling Hayden masterminds an intricate plot, requiring split-second timing, to rob a racetrack payroll of $2 million. This extremely well made picture investigates the personality and motivation behind each member of the group. Each story is told up until the same climactic moment in time, but then the next story is begun. When all of the stories have been told up to that same climactic moment, they proceed together to the conclusion. Intriguing idea, spell-binding plot.

A: Sterling Hayden, Coleen Gray, Jay C. Flippen, Marie Windsor, Timothy Carey, Vince Edwards

Distributed By MGM/UA Home Video 201704

KILLING FIELDS, THE

D: Roland Joffe 142 m

R | DMA WAR SUS | 1984 | COLOR | Sex, Nud, Viol, Lang, AdSit

10 An absolutely unforgettable picture. A lacerating and highly charged emotional drama based upon the real events surrounding the fall of Cambodia and the American evacuation. New York Times correspondent Sidney Schanberg is aided in a last minute escape by his close friend and interpretor Dith Pran, but Pran can't get out. He is left to face the horrifying re-education camps of the Khmer Rouge and murder on a massive scale, but Schanberg never stops in his struggles to find and free him. Stunning portrait of a society gone mad! Three Oscars and three additional nominations.

A: Sam Waterston, Haing S. Ngor, John Malkovich, Julian Sands, Craig T. Nelson

© WARNER HOME VIDEO 11419

KILLING TIME, THE

D: Rick King 94 m

R | CRM SUS | 1987 | COLOR | Sex, Nud, Viol, Lang, AdSit

6 Very involved, twisting story line. A small-town sheriff (Baker) is about to retire and is to be replaced by his deputy (Bridges), whose ex-wife is being abused by her new and wealthy husband. She fears for her life, so Bridges helps her plan to murder him, but their plan is threatened by the new deputy (Sutherland). Except Sutherland turns out to be a serial killer who has stolen someone else's identity. Tense drama of suspicion, deception and murder with more twists than a bag of pretzels, but slow to develop.

A: Beau Bridges, Kiefer Sutherland, Wayne Rogers, Joe Don Baker, Camelia Kath, Janet Carroll

© R&G VIDEO, LP 80098

KILL ME AGAIN

D: John Dahl 95 m

R | SUS ACT | 1990 | COLOR | Sex, Nud, Viol, Lang, AdSit

6 Modern-day film noir in which a sexy femme fatal (Whalley-Kilmer) and her boyfriend steal some big-time money from the mob. She knocks her boyfriend in the head and takes off with the money. Then she seduces and tricks a private eye (Kilmer) into helping to fake her death so she can get both the boyfriend and the mob off her trail. But when she dumps Kilmer too, he goes after her and gets caught up in a chase which now includes the law, the ex-boyfriend and the mob. Other than lots of double-crosses, nothing much is new here, but what there is, is well done.

A: Joanne Whalley-Kilmer, Val Kilmer, Michael Madsen, Pat Mulligan, Bibi Besch

Distributed By MGM/UA Home Video M901835

KISS BEFORE DYING, A

D: James Dearden 93 m

R · SUS CRM · 1991 · COLOR

7 A tightly-wound thriller! Dillon is handsome, but poor and utterly ruthless. He decides that the best way out of poverty is to marry very well, so he chooses Sean Young's prominent family to marry into. He researches everything about them, then he makes his move. Young (in two roles) plays twin sisters both courted by Dillon. Dillon kills off the first one while he charms and marries the other sister. The tension mounts when Young slowly gets really curious about her twin's strange death. For the viewer, it doesn't matter that you know who the killer is - suspense hangs in the air and danger looms at every corner.

Sex · Nud · Viol · Lang · AdSit

A: Matt Dillon, Sean Young, Max von Sydow, Diane Ladd, James Russo, Martha Gehman

© MCA/UNIVERSAL HOME VIDEO, INC. 81068

KLUTE

D: Alan J. Pakula 114 m

R · SUS MYS CRM · 1971 · COLOR

9 Compelling and provocative psychological thriller, with a mesmerizing (Oscar-winning) performance by Jane Fonda. Fonda plays a sultry high-class NYC hooker who gets in over her head. Small-town private detective Donald Sutherland is searching for a husband who is missing after a trip to NYC and who had visited Fonda. Neurotic Fonda only feels in control when she is manipulating a trick. But now she finds herself falling in love with Sutherland as she comes to rely more and more upon him - because she is being relentlessly pursued by the same sadistic killer. A real nail-biter finish.

Sex · Nud · Viol · Lang · AdSit

A: Jane Fonda, Donald Sutherland, Charles Cioffi, Roy Scheider, Dorothy Tristan, Rita Gam

© WARNER HOME VIDEO 1027

KNIGHT MOVES

D: Carl Schenkel 105 m

R · SUS MYS CRM · 1993 · COLOR

7 Competent murder thriller. A chess champion (Christopher Lambert) has gone to the Pacific Northwest to participate in a chess championship and also finds himself incriminated in a series of serial murders. Several beautiful young women have been ritualistically murdered and drained of blood, with cryptic messages then scrawled in their blood. Top cop Tom Skerritt is not certain if Peter, who is receiving phone messages from the killer and supposedly using his game skills to help solve the murders, is the victim of the plot or really is the secret instigator of it. Psychologist Diane Lane too, is caught between love and fear. Not great, but not bad either.

Sex · Nud · Viol · Lang · AdSit

A: Christopher Lambert, Diane Lane, Tom Skerritt, Daniel Baldwin, Charles Bailey-Gates, Ferdinand Mayne

© REPUBLIC PICTURES HOME VIDEO 2200

KWAIDAN

D: Masaki Kobayashi 164 m

NR · FOR HOR SUS · 1964 · COLOR

8 KWAIDEN is Japanese and means "Ghost Story." This film consists of four very eerie supernatural tales that were written by an American, Lafcadio Hearn, who settled in Japan in 1890. Each story involves an encounter with a ghost. "Black Hair" is of a samurai who returns to the wife he deserted years before and wakes up the next morning beside her skeleton. "The Woman of the Snow" is about a snow maiden who rescues a woodcutter and then swears to kill him if he tells anyone. "Hoichi, the Earless" is about a blind musician who looses his ears when he sings to a Samurai ghost. "In A Cup of Tea" is about a guard who absorbs a ghost's spirit after seeing his face in a cup of tea. Subtitles.

Sex · Nud · Viol · Lang · AdSit

A: Rentaro Mikuni, Keiko Kishi, Katsuo Nakamura, Kanemon Nakamura

© HOME VISION KWA01

LADY IN A CAGE

D: Walter Grauman 95 m

NR · SUS · 1964 · B&W

7 This is a taut claustrophobic thriller that did not get its due when it was originally released. Olivia de Havilland is wealthy widow who becomes trapped in an elevator inside her own home after the power fails. She cannot escape, but worse than that - she is also being terrorized, tormented and taunted by three young thugs who have broken in, and are robbing her and ransacking her apartment. Excellent acting (especially by a very young James Caan) and excellent photography create a realistic and effective aura of fear. This is very effective chiller that only much later received the credit it was due.

Sex · Nud · Viol · Lang · AdSit

A: Olivia de Havilland, James Caan, Ann Sothern, Scatman Crothers, Jennifer Billingsley, Jeff Corey

© PARAMOUNT HOME VIDEO 6311

LADY IN WHITE

D: Frank Laloggia 113 m

PG-13 · SUS HOR · 1988 · COLOR

7 Eerily effective thriller. Unlike some films which rely on outlandish events to create a chilling effect, this film simply allows you to believe that what you see could be real. A very bright young boy is locked in the cloakroom at school as a prank. During the night he is visited by the ghost of one of several children who have been mysteriously killed in recent years. In his vision he can also, but not quite, make out the killer... or is all this occurring in his imagination? An absorbing thriller, well worth watching.

Sex · Nud · Viol · Lang · AdSit

A: Lukas Haas, Len Carlou, Alex Rocco, Katherine Helmond, Jason Bresson, Lucy Lee Flippin

© VIDEO TREASURES SV9693

LA FEMME NIKITA

D: Luc Parriland 117 m

R · FOR ACT SUS · 1990 · COLOR

9 Action-filled, exotic, intelligent and thoroughly fascinating psychological character study of a supremely unique nature. Nikita is a profoundly lost young woman who is convicted of committing an extremely ruthless murder. But, after receiving a life sentence, the government fakes her suicide and enters her into an ultra-secret training program for assassins. There, her life gains a perverse meaning and focus, but she also gains an appreciation for the life she doesn't have. Haunting. Dubbed or subtitles. Beginning is very odd. Released in an Americanized version as POINT OF NO RETURN.

Sex · Nud · Viol · Lang · AdSit

A: Anne Parrilland, Jeanne Moreau, Tcheky Karyo, Jean Hugues Anglade

© VIDMARK ENTERTAINMENT 5471

LAST INNOCENT MAN, THE

D: Roger Spottiswoode 114 m

NR · SUS MYS · 1987 · COLOR

9 Excellent courtroom thriller. An attorney, well-known for winning cases for his less-than-savory clients, has gone into a guilt-induced retirement. He meets a beautiful and sexy woman with whom he falls in love. At her request, he leaves his retreat to defend her estranged husband of the charges that he killed a decoy policewoman. However, he soon discovers that this woman that he loves had other, ulterior motives. This is a very well done and totally involving film where the ethical questions gain equal footing with intrigue and the elaborate plot twists. Excellent made-for-TV production.

Sex · Nud · Viol · Lang · AdSit

A: Ed Harris, Roxanne Hart, Clarence Williams, III, Darrell Larson, Bruce McGill, David Suchet

© WARNER HOME VIDEO 819

LEGEND OF HELL HOUSE, THE

D: John Hough 94 m

PG · HOR SUS · 1973 · COLOR

7 Thrilling tale of the occult. A wealthy man hires a team of four psychic researchers to occupy a haunted house which has already destroyed one team of investigators. This group is to stay for one week to determine why there have been so many mysterious deaths there. Roddy McDowall is the only survivor of the previous team and he is back again. In addition to him, this time there is a psychiatrist, his wife and a medium. Before their stay is done they will see madness and murder. This is very different from most other ghost movies. There are some real scares here. Top flight cast.

Sex · Nud · Viol · Lang · AdSit

A: Pamela Franklin, Roddy McDowall, Clive Revill, Gayle Hunnicutt

© FOXVIDEO 1465

LIES

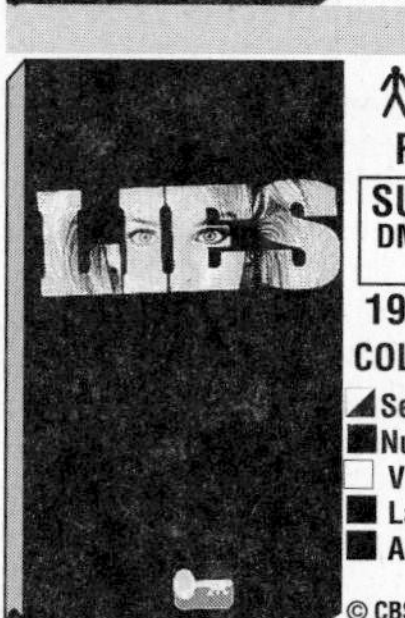

D: Jim Wheat, Ben Wheat 93 m

R · SUS DMA · 1983 · COLOR

6 Interesting psychological thriller about an out-of-work actress who is unwittingly drawn into a plan, by an unscrupulous psychiatrist and scheming film director, to trick an heiress out of her fortune. Set inside a secluded mental institution, she is to portray a murder witness who has committed suicide. However, she learns that there is no film - she is instead a key player in a dangerous scam. The plot is filled with double-crosses and twists (probably too many), but interest is maintained by excellent acting, particularly by Gail Strickland and Ann Dusenberry.

Sex · Nud · Viol · Lang · AdSit

A: Ann Dusenberry, Gail Strickland, Bruce Davison, Clu Gulager, Terence Knox, Bert Remsen

© CBS/FOX VIDEO 3842

LIST OF ADRIAN MESSENGER, THE

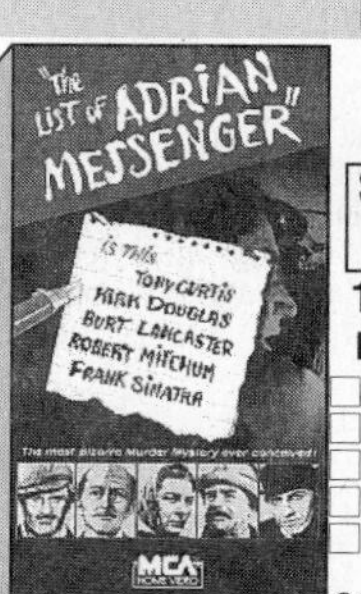

D: John Huston 98 m

NR · SUS MYS CRM · 1963 · B&W

8 Entertaining witty mystery which has the interesting gimmick of having four of Hollywood's biggest names - Tony Curtis, Burt Lancaster, Frank Sinatra and Robert Mitchum - all buried under make-up for short cameo appearances. Someone is killing off all the potential heirs to the family fortune. Now, there is only one heir, a young grandson, left. The only clue to the murderer is a list of names from one of the murdered heirs, Adrian Messinger. Eleven down, one to go. George C. Scott is a retired British intelligence officer who is on the murderer's trail. Entertaining with lots of twists.

Sex · Nud · Viol · Lang · AdSit

A: George C. Scott, Clive Brook, Dana Wynter, Herbert Marshall, Frank Sinatra, Robert Mitchum

© MCA/UNIVERSAL HOME VIDEO, INC. 80165

LITTLE DRUMMER GIRL

D: George Roy Hill 130 m

R · ACT SUS · 1984 · COLOR

7 Intricate espionage thriller. Keaton is an outspoken actress and a Palestinian advocate. However, Israeli intelligence convinces her to become their double agent, involving her in plots of blackmail and terrorism. In actuality, she is being used as bait to catch a Palestinian terrorist. John Le Carre's brilliant and very complex novel is jam-packed into just over two hours. There is a lot to follow, and by trying to leave as much of the plot in as possible, much of the character development and involvement is lost - still, it holds your interest throughout.

Sex · Nud · Viol · Lang · AdSit

A: Diane Keaton, Yorgo Voyagis, Klaus Kinski, Sami Frey, Michael Cristofer

© WARNER HOME VIDEO 11416

LITTLE GIRL WHO LIVES DOWN THE LANE, THE

D: Nicolas Gessner 90 m

PG | SUS | 1976 | COLOR

7 Engrossing and subtle one-of-a-kind thriller that will fool you right up to the end. Jody Foster is a very bright and independent 13-year-old whose father, very oddly, never seems to be home. The snoopy landlady (Alexis Smith) continually comes around, and now presses the issue, wondering what is down in the basement. Her son, Martin Sheen (especially creepy), is a known child molester. He becomes suspicious of what is in Jody's basement, too. While, he is chased off at first by Jody's only true friend, a crippled boy... he'll be back. This chiller is really different and will grip you right until the end.

Sex / Nud / Viol / Lang / AdSit

A: Jodie Foster, Martin Sheen, Alexis Smith, Scott Jacoby, Mort Shuman

© LIVE HOME VIDEO 4066

LONG GOODBYE, THE

D: Robert Altman 113 m

R | MYS SUS ACT | 1973 | COLOR

7 Entertaining and stylish detective yarn based on the classic 1940s PI- character, Philip Marlowe, but updated to the 1970s with many interesting and off-beat twists added. Gould's Marlowe is a New York Jew out of step in hip, me-oriented California. It is frequently funny, but also remains an intense, action oriented mystery of the old school. Marlowe attempts to get an old friend released from a charge that he murdered his wife. A really off-the-wall ending.

Sex / Nud / Viol / Lang / AdSit

A: Elliott Gould, Sterling Hayden, Mark Rydell, Henry Gibson, Jim Bouton, Nina Van Pallandt

Distributed By MGM/UA Home Video M201409

MAGIC

D: Richard Attenborough 106 m

R | SUS HOR | 1978 | COLOR

7 Reality checks out and eerie insanity checks in. Hopkins plays a ventriloquist who lets his dummy, Fats, slowly take over his personality. His insecurities about the act propel him back to his hometown, where he finds his high school sweetheart (Anne-Margaret) involved in a nasty marriage to a loathsome country boy. The love triangle that develops spells disaster. He is slowly losing himself to the growing personality of his dummy (which is manifesting all his worst desires), and she is searching vainly for happiness lost in her past.

Sex / Nud / Viol / Lang / AdSit

A: Anthony Hopkins, Ann-Margret, Burgess Meredith, Ed Lauter, Jerry Hauser, E.J. Andre

© UNITED AMERICAN VIDEO CORP. 5866

MALICE

D: Harold Becker 107 m

R | SUS MYS | 1993 | COLOR

8 This is a clever thriller that has more kinks in it than you'll find on your worst bad-hair day. Andy is a struggling college professor in a pretty New England town, but his campus is being terrorized by a serial killer and rapist. He is also poor, so to make ends meet, he and his wife Tracy decide to take in a handsome border who is charming, a lady's man, the hot shot new surgeon at the local hospital and an old friend of Andy's. He is also trouble. However, no one is what they appear to be in this Hitchcock-like twister. It's sexy, it'll grab and hold your attention and it'll keep you guessing.

Sex / Nud / Viol / Lang / AdSit

A: Alec Baldwin, Nicole Kidman, Bill Pullman, Bebe Neuwirth, George C. Scott, Ann Bancroft

© COLUMBIA TRISTAR HOME VIDEO 71773

MANCHURIAN CANDIDATE, THE

D: John Frankenheimer 127 m

PG-13 | SUS DMA | 1962 | B&W

9 Fully-loaded political thriller! When a highly decorated Korean war vet (Harvey) comes home, nobody suspects that he might actually be a fully-conditioned lethal killing machine. After their platoon is taken by Communists during the war, its members are either killed or brainwashed and then made to forget. However, one survivor (Sinatra) starts to have dreams that give him clues about his returning buddy's real mission. This is a scathing indictment of political extremism on both sides. Lansbury plays the meddling mother who has lofty Republican intentions. Poignant and suspenseful.

Sex / Nud / Viol / Lang / AdSit

A: Frank Sinatra, Laurence Harvey, Angela Lansbury, Janet Leigh, James Gregory, Henry Silva

Distributed By MGM/UA Home Video M801369

MANHUNTER

D: Michael Mann 120 m

R | CRM SUS ACT | 1986 | COLOR

9 Excellent! An ex-FBI agent (Peterson) is recalled to track a ruthless serial killer who is murdering entire families in the southeast. The psychopathic madman (Noonan) gets the name "The Tooth Fairy" for sadistically appropriate reasons. Clever and ever elusive, the only way Peterson can catch this crazed psycho is to actually think like the killer would - to get inside his head. This is the same method used in the later SILENCE OF THE LAMBS and in real life by the FBI. Very contemporary in style, with hard pounding music, this crime drama will take hold of you and won't let go.

Sex / Nud / Viol / Lang / AdSit

A: William L. Petersen, Kim Greist, Brian Cox, Dennis Farina, Stephen Lang, Tom Noonan

© WARNER HOME VIDEO 411

MAN WHO FELL TO EARTH, THE

D: Nicolas Roeg 140 m

NR | SF SUS | 1976 | COLOR

7 This intelligent Sci-Fi thriller also contained sex and nudity and so was quite controversial. An alien leaves his family on their very dry and dying home planet to arrive on earth in a search for much needed water. Upon his arrival, he transforms himself into a human, and has plans to use his superior intelligence to make money to build spaceships to bring water back home. But as other business interests thwart his efforts, and he becomes seduced by earthlife and love with an earth woman, he realizes that he is trapped. Depressed and feeling guilty, he resigns himself to human-like life.

Sex / Nud / Viol / Lang / AdSit

A: David Bowie, Rip Torn, Buck Henry, Candy Clark, Bernie Casey, Jackson D. Kane

© COLUMBIA TRISTAR HOME VIDEO 60929

MAN WHO KNEW TOO MUCH, THE

D: Alfred Hitchcock 120 m

PG | SUS MYS | 1956 | COLOR

8 Chilling Hitchcock remake of his earlier masterpiece! A doctor and his wife (Stewart and Day) are vacationing in French Morocco and witness a murder. The dying man whispers to them the plan for a British ambassador to be killed in London. To keep the parents quiet, their young son is kidnapped, and they are forced to foil the murder attempt on their own. The climax, shot at Albert Hall, is an unforgettable sequence in both this and in the earlier version. Day sings "Que Sera, Sera," which won an Oscar for best song and became a big popular hit.

Sex / Nud / Viol / Lang / AdSit

A: James Stewart, Doris Day, Brenda de Banzie, Bernard Miles, Ralph Truman, Daniel Gelin

© MCA/UNIVERSAL HOME VIDEO, INC. 80129

MARATHON MAN

D: John Schlesinger 125 m

R | ACT SUS | 1976 | COLOR

8 So tense your teeth will hurt. Hoffman stars a student who runs marathons. But he gets caught in the middle of a Nazi crime ring when his brother (Scheider) helps to sneak into the country an old Nazi, Christian Szell (Olivier), whose brother is guarding a horde of jewels that were taken from Jewish prisoners. But, when Olivier's brother dies, he kills Hoffman's brother and begins to torture Hoffman (in a famous scene with a dentist's drill) for information that he thinks he has, but doesn't. Then Hoffman escapes and the hunted becomes the hunter. Excellent. Olivier was Oscar-nominated.

Sex / Nud / Viol / Lang / AdSit

A: Dustin Hoffman, Laurence Olivier, Marthe Keller, Roy Scheider, William Devane, Fritz Weaver

© PARAMOUNT HOME VIDEO 8789

MARNIE

D: Alfred Hitchcock 130 m

PG | DMA SUS | 1964 | COLOR

6 A beautiful blond (Hedron) has the nasty habit of stealing money from her employers and leaving without a clue. When she is caught by her current boss (Connery) before she gets gone, he becomes determined to find out what's behind her kleptomaniac habits and blackmails her into marrying him while he struggles to understand her demons. Hitchcock uses varied innovative filming techniques to hint at the inner turmoil and the underlying psychosis of Hedren's past. Dismissed when it was originally released, the film has since won the respect it deserves.

Sex / Nud / Viol / Lang / AdSit

A: Tippi Hedren, Sean Connery, Diane Baker, Louise Latham, Martin Gabel, Alan Napier

© MCA/UNIVERSAL HOME VIDEO, INC. 80156

MARTIN

D: George A. Romero 96 m

R | SUS HOR | 1978 | COLOR

8 Terror and horror. Martin (Amplas) is just a little crazy. He thinks he is a vampire. Martin is a teenage boy who goes out at night committing all sorts of grizzly murders. First he drugs his victims with a hypodermic, then he opens their veins with a razorblade and then he drinks their blood! Poor Martin becomes even more confused when he is attracted to a depressed young married woman. What's he to do now? Then, Martin's grandfather makes his life even more difficult because he is determined to stop this family curse. This bit of true gore is in fact quite well done.

Sex / Nud / Viol / Lang / AdSit

A: John Amplas, Lincoln Maazel, Christine Forrest, Elayne Nadeau, Tom Savini, Sarah Venable

© HBO VIDEO TVB1976

MASQUERADE

D: Bob Swaim 91 m

R | SUS MYS | 1988 | COLOR

8 A clever and complex web of murder and deception is slowly revealed to a naive and innocent but very wealthy Olivia (Tilly). She has just graduated from a Catholic girls school and returned to live in the exclusive Hamptons, but she has to live with her repulsive and alcoholic stepfather (Glover). However, she has all the money she could ever want, plus the rather recent attentions of the handsome skipper of a racing yacht (Lowe). He is in love with her and completely uninterested in her money...isn't he? Outstanding cast keeps the intrigue elevated and the suspense alive. Be prepared for a shocking conclusion.

Sex / Nud / Viol / Lang / AdSit

A: Rob Lowe, Meg Tilly, Kim Cattrall, Doug Savant, John Glover, Dana Delany

Distributed By MGM/UA Home Video M201249

MEPHISTO WALTZ, THE

D: Paul Wendkos — 109 m

R | SUS HOR | 1971 | COLOR | Sex, Nud, Viol, Lang, AdSit

7 This is a demonic chiller that will possess you. The world's greatest pianist (Jurgens) is dying of leukemia and so he has become eager to find a new body in which to live. Journalist (Alda) is surprised to be granted a long sought-after interview with the famous pianist but soon, Alda's wife (Bisset) begins to notice a marked change in his personality. Jurgens and his daughter (Parkins), it turns out, are both devil worshipers and Alda body has been possessed by Jurgens. The spooky atmosphere may seem a little overdone at first, but the haunting ending will likely stay with you for awhile.

A: Alan Alda, Curt Jurgens, Jacqueline Bisset, Barbara Parkins

© FOXVIDEO 1200

MIDNIGHT EXPRESS

D: Alan Parker — 123 m

R | DMA SUS | 1978 | COLOR | Sex, Nud, Viol, Lang, AdSit

9 Unrelenting reality-based terror! A forceful adaptation of the true story of Billy Hayes (Davis), a young man who was sentenced to 30 years in a sub-human Turkish prison after being caught with hashish strapped to his body. Inside prison, he is subjected to harrowing and violent torture by the Turkish government. This graphic depiction of his chilling experience will most likely stick with you for long while - the nightmarish helplessness and terror of it all goes right to the bone. Oliver Stone won an Oscar for Best Screenplay.

A: Brad Davis, Randy Quaid, John Hurt, Bo Hopkins, Ira Miracle, Mike Kellin

© GOODTIMES 4238

MISERY

D: Rob Reiner — 107 m

R | SUS HOR | 1990 | COLOR | Sex, Nud, Viol, Lang, AdSit

8 Paul Sheldon (Caan) is a writer of successful series of "Misery Chastain" romance novels. His self-proclaimed number one fan is Annie Wilkes (Bates). So, after sliding off the road in a remote region of Colorado and breaking his legs, Paul is pleased that Annie, this rather plain and matronly nurse, has rescued him from the ditch and taken him to her house. However, after she reads his latest novel and discovers that he has killed off her heroine, Paul discovers the dark side of his deranged "angel." The obsessed Annie tortures him and refuses to let him leave until he resurrects Misery in a new novel.

A: Kathy Bates, James Caan, Richard Farnsworth, Frances Sternhagen, Lauren Bacall

© NEW LINE HOME VIDEO 77773

MISSING

D: Constantine Costa-Gavras — 122 m

PG | DMA SUS | 1982 | COLOR | Sex, Nud, Viol, Lang, AdSit

8 Solid political intrigue! At the height of a violent military coup in South America, a young American journalist (Shea) disappears. His wife (Spacek) and conservative businessman father (Lemmon) put past differences behind them to embark on a desperate search to find him there. When their inquiries meet with stonewalling at the American Embassy, the pair come to the uncomfortable conclusion that their own government may be in collusion with the local bureaucracy in preventing them from finding the truth. Best Screenplay, plus nominated for Actor, Actress and Best Picture.

A: Jack Lemmon, Sissy Spacek, John Shea, Melanie Mayron, Charles Cioffi, David Clennon

© MCA/UNIVERSAL HOME VIDEO, INC. 71009

MISSISSIPPI BURNING

D: Alan Parker — 127 m

R | CRM SUS DMA | 1988 | COLOR | Sex, Nud, Viol, Lang, AdSit

9 Hard-edged and mesmerizing drama that is based on fact. It's 1964 and change is coming to Mississippi. Three young civil rights workers are missing and the FBI is investigating. Willem Dafoe is a dedicated young agent sent in to run the investigation, but Gene Hackman is the local agent who understands these people. He and Dafoe are not friends but they are both dedicated to stopping the reign of terror of the KKK. Still, the FBI is not welcomed by any of the locals, black or white. And as Dafoe brings in hundreds of agents, the national press moves in and the fires start to burn. Nominated for seven Academy Awards. Excellent.

A: Gene Hackman, Willem Dafoe, Frances McDormand, Brad Dourif, R. Lee Ermey, Gailard Sartain

© ORION PICTURES CORPORATION 8727

MONA LISA

D: Neil Jordan — 106 m

R | SUS ACT | 1986 | COLOR | Sex, Nud, Viol, Lang, AdSit

7 Absorbing British thriller. Hoskins plays a good-hearted small-time hood whose antics land him in prison. When he gets out, he goes to his former boss (Caine) who gives him a job chauffeuring a high-priced hooker (Tyson) around town. Hoskins falls in love with her and will do anything for her. She wants him to find her lost friend and that may get him killed. Critically acclaimed, the film capitalizes well on the chemistry between Hoskins and Tyson. Hoskins earned an Academy Award nomination for his stylish performance.

A: Bob Hoskins, Cathy Tyson, Michael Caine, Robbie Coltrane, Clark Peters, Kate Hardie

© HBO VIDEO 9955

MONKEY SHINES

D: George A. Romero — 113 m

R | HOR SUS | 1988 | COLOR | Sex, Nud, Viol, Lang, AdSit

6 Hair raising! When a young law student (Beghe) is injured in an accident, he is rendered a quadraplegic. His best friend recruits an animal trainer to educate a lab monkey that will help Beghe to do everyday tasks. However, because the monkey's brain has been altered in the lab, the monkey also begins to carry out the subconscious evil aspirations of Beghe and embarks on a rampage of revenge and murder. The monkey delivers an amazing performance in this chilling flick under the direction of shockmaster George Romero.

A: Jason Beghe, John Pankow, Kate McNeil, Joyce Van Patten

© ORION PICTURES CORPORATION 8728

MONSIEUR HIRE

D: Patrice Leconte — 88 m

PG-13 | FOR SUS CRM | 1990 | COLOR | Sex, Nud, Viol, Lang, AdSit

8 Brilliant and gripping suspense import from France. A balding reclusive tailor, Monsieur Hire, becomes obsessed with the beautiful young lady across his courtyard, peeping at her constantly from his darkened windows. One day a flash of lightning reveals his embarrassing activities to her and she confronts him. When another young woman is found dead nearby and she is terrified. It is natural that Monsieur Hire would becomes the police's natural suspect. However, the snoopy Monsieur Hire knows who the real killer is. Subtly erotic, but also extraordinary in its drama and its perceptiveness.

A: Michel Blanc, Sandrine Bonnaire, Andre Wilms, Luc Thuiller

© ORION PICTURES CORPORATION 5053

MOTHER'S BOYS

D: Yves Simoneau — 96 m

R | SUS | 1994 | COLOR | Sex, Nud, Viol, Lang, AdSit

6 Moderately entertaining thriller in which Jamie Lee Curtis plays a spoiled and unbalanced little rich girl who wants her family back. She had left her husband Peter Gallagher and her three boys three years ago. But now, she has heard that he has filed for divorce, so he can marry pretty assistant principal Joanne Whalley-Kilmer, and she has come to win them all back. When he doesn't agree with her plan and even her own mother plots against her, she plots a vicious and deadly new plan to win back the hearts of her boys, and to get her husband out of the way.

A: Jamie Lee Curtis, Peter Gallagher, Joanne Whalley-Kilmer, Luke Edwards, Joss Ackland, Venessa Redgrave

© MIRAMAX HOME ENTERTAINMENT 2541

MS. 45

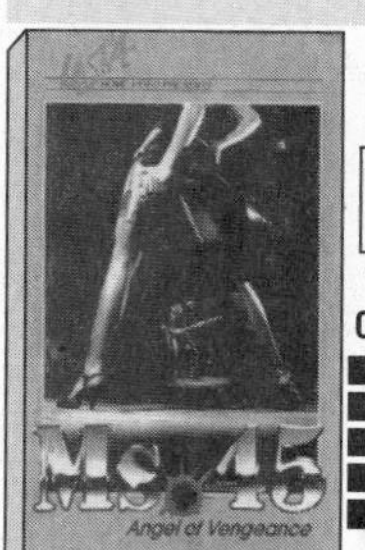

D: Abel Ferrara — 82 m

R | ACT SUS | 1981 | COLOR | Sex, Nud, Viol, Lang, AdSit

7 Violent vengeance. When a beautiful young mute woman is brutally raped and beaten on her way home from work - and then is raped again by a robber waiting in her apartment when she gets home, she loses control. She kills her second attacker and uses his 45 to wreak revenge. The woman with a death wish shows no mercy as she seeks out men in this exploitative shocker - sort of a DEATH WISH from the other side. This violent movie has attained cult status, and the powerful ending is really a shocker.

A: Zoe Tamerlis, Steve Singer, Jack Thibeau, Peter Yellen

© LIVE HOME VIDEO 215147

MURDER ON THE ORIENT EXPRESS

D: Sidney Lumet — 128 m

PG | MYS SUS | 1974 | COLOR | Sex, Nud, Viol, Lang, AdSit

8 Stylish Agatha Christie whodunit! An American millionaire is murdered while sleeping on the Orient Express, and it's a good thing that the master detective from Belgium, Hercule Poirot (Finney), is on the train. Everyone is a suspect, and Poirot sets out to unravel the case. Ingrid Bergman won an Academy Award for Best Supporting Actress for her role as the mousey secretary. Lavishly produced, with a huge all-star cast, it received 6 Oscar nominations in all - even though for years Agatha Christie refused to allow her book to be filmed. This film was followed by DEATH ON THE NILE.

A: Lauren Bacall, Ingrid Bergman, Martin Balsam, Jacqueline Bisset, Albert Finney, Jean-Pierre Cassel

© PARAMOUNT HOME VIDEO 8790

MUSIC BOX

D: Constantine Costa-Gavras — 126 m

PG-13 | DMA SUS | 1989 | COLOR | Sex, Nud, Viol, Lang, AdSit

8 An unusual, passionate and gripping courtroom drama. A working class Hungarian immigrant is accused of having committed atrocious war crimes. He turns to his daughter, a lawyer (Lange), to defend him and prove his innocence. Lange agrees, never once doubting her father's innocence, but soon shocking developments require that she prove everything to herself, too. This is an intense and gripping drama and will have you guessing what the truth is the whole way. Lange received an Oscar nomination for her powerful and convincing performance.

A: Jessica Lange, Armin Mueller-Stahl, Frederic Forrest, Lukas Haas, Cheryl Lynn Bruce, Donald Moffat

© LIVE HOME VIDEO 68903

NAKED PREY, THE

D: Cornel Wilde — 96 m

NR | ACT SUS | 1965 | COLOR

Sex | Nud | Viol | Lang | AdSit

9 An enthralling story of survival. Set in the 1860s, a white expedition in search of ivory offends a group of natives and is subsequently ambushed. All the members except Wilde are tortured to death. Impressed with his bravery, he is given a chance to survive. He is stripped naked, turned free, and then pursued by relentless native hunters. No matter how he struggles, he can keep no more than a few seconds in front of them. Alternately filmed from a distance and then close-up, this is a fascinating and intimate portrait of survival at its most basic level. Virtually no dialogue.

A: Cornel Wilde, Ken Gampu, Gert Van Den Bergh

© PARAMOUNT HOME VIDEO 6525

NARROW MARGIN, THE

D: Peter Hyams — 99 m

R | SUS ACT | 1990 | COLOR

Sex | Nud | Viol | Lang | AdSit

8 Top rate action! Archer reluctantly agrees to a blind date, and then watches from behind a partially closed door as he is shot and killed. She flees to a hideaway in the mountains, but Hackman, the D.A., tracks her down and tries to persuade her to return to L.A. to testify against the killer. She refuses, but soon the hitmen have found her, too. She and Hackman escape and are on a speeding train back to L.A., but the hitmen are following close behind again. Archer fears for her life and Hackman tries to protect his frightened witness in this excellent remake of the 1952 original.

A: Gene Hackman, Anne Archer, James Sikking, J.T. Walsh, M. Emmet Walsh, Susan Hogan

© LIVE HOME VIDEO 68924

NEEDFUL THINGS

D: Fraser C. Heston — 120 m

SUS HOR | 1993

Sex | Nud | Viol | Lang | AdSit

7 A new business called Needful Things has opened in a small Maine town. It is run by a kindly man, who always knows just the right thing will be for anyone who comes into his store. And, he will sell it for a very reasonable price, asking only that you also do him a very small favor in return - just play a small trick on someone. However, all the tricks, when put together, are an unholy conspiracy that has turned everyone in town against each other. Hate has come to town, neighbor murders neighbor. There is riot in the streets. Max von Sydow is the kindly man who is also the devil come to earth. Ed Harris is a cop who just put all the pieces together. From Stephen King.

A: Ed Harris, Max von Sydow, Bonnie Bedelia, J.T. Walsh, Valri Bromfield, Amanda Plummer

© TURNER HOME ENTERTAINMENT N4167

NIGHT GALLERY

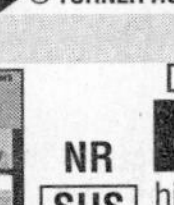

D: Boris Sagal, Barry Shear — 95 m

NR | SUS | 1969 | COLOR

Sex | Nud | Viol | Lang | AdSit

8 Three intriguing stories were taken from the vaults of the stylish master-writer Rod Serling and were made into this, the pilot for his TV series of the same name. Story One concerns a young man who is too eager for his inheritance and gets his unplanned due. Story Two is that of a wealthy blind woman who purchases the eyes of a poor man. The last is the story of an ex-Nazi whose past catches up with him in a South American art gallery when he chances upon a former victim. With Serling, nothing is obvious. Expect the unexpected and the bizarre, too. Thrilling, fascinating and thought provoking stuff.

A: Joan Crawford, Roddy McDowall, Barry Sullivan, Tom Bosley, Sam Jaffe, Ossie Davis

© MCA/UNIVERSAL HOME VIDEO, INC. 80046

NIGHT HAWKS

D: Bruce Malmuth — 99 m

R | ACT SUS | 1981 | COLOR

Sex | Nud | Viol | Lang | AdSit

9 Supercharged action film and Stallone's best performance outside the ROCKY series. He and Williams, two New York street cops, get reassigned to a special unit that is charged with tracking down an especially ruthless and cunning international terrorist (Rutger Hauer), who is out to make a name for himself in America in a big way. Fast paced and very high intensity throughout, but especially tense when Hauer hijacks a tramway. Exciting and very well made.

A: Sylvester Stallone, Billy Dee Williams, Rutger Hauer, Nigel Davenport, Lindsay Wagner

© MCA/UNIVERSAL HOME VIDEO, INC. 71000

NIGHT MOVES

D: Arthur Penn — 100 m

R | MYS SUS | 1975 | COLOR

Sex | Nud | Viol | Lang | AdSit

8 Excellent, intelligent and complicated, but unjustly overlooked psychological detective story. Gene Hackman is a small time L.A. detective who is hired to track down a teenaged runaway (Griffith) of a rich woman. He puts aside his own marital problems to track the girl down in the Florida Keys where she is staying with her former stepfather and his new girlfriend. Hackman goes and brings her home. The case is apparently solved, however he just learned that the girl is dead. There is more to this case than just a runaway. Dynamite acting from everyone. Hackman crackles, and Warren and Griffith sizzle. A little gem.

A: Gene Hackman, Susan Clark, Jennifer Warren, Melanie Griffith, James Woods, Edward Binns

© WARNER HOME VIDEO 11102

NIGHT STALKER, THE

D: Don Weis — 98 m

NR | HOR SUS | 1971 | COLOR

Sex | Nud | Viol | Lang | AdSit

8 Quite good and involving thriller with personality that was originally made for TV. It proved to be so successful that it launched a short-lived series of the same name. Darin McGavin plays a persistent wise-cracking reporter on the crime beat in Las Vegas. The city has recently been plagued by a series of grisly Jack-the-Ripper-like murders. McGavin hounds the city's establishment and keeps turning up new clues in his pursuit of the ghoulish vampirish killer. Extremely tight script with a good blending of believability, mystery, comedy, suspense and horror.

A: Darren McGavin, Simon Oakland, Carol Lynley, Claude Akins, Ralph Meeker

© MCA/UNIVERSAL HOME VIDEO, INC. 80011

NIGHT VISITOR, THE

D: Laslo Benedek — 94 m

PG | CRM SUS | 1970 | COLOR

Sex | Nud | Viol | Lang | AdSit

6 An interesting and clever chiller. Max Von Sydow is imprisoned inside a supposedly escape-proof prison for the criminally insane for having committed a grisly axe murder two years before. He has devised a devious plot to reap vengeance on those who he holds responsible for his conviction. He will escape from prison for one night only and steal across the frozen Scandinavian winterscape in only his underwear and shoes. He will kill his sister and a farm girl, and leave his brother-in-law to take blame. Then he will return to his cell. It's the perfect alibi. Trevor Howard is the detective who investigates the new murderers. Fine performances.

A: Max von Sydow, Liv Ullmann, Trevor Howard, Per Oscarsson

Distributed By MGM/UA Home Video M801756

NINTH CONFIGURATION, THE

D: William Peter Blatty — 115 m

R | SUS DMA | 1979 | COLOR

Sex | Nud | Viol | Lang | AdSit

8 A very intense and almost surrealist film that is hard to follow. Its characters are also very bizarre, so it is not for everyone. Stacy Keach plays a psychiatrist at a remote military mental institution which is charged with caring for deeply disturbed Vietnam War veterans. It soon becomes apparent that the doctor may be as nutty as the patients and he begins to have very strange effects on the patients. This film appears to swing violently from dark comedy to tragedy and almost loses viewers, but the obscure plot does come together in the end.

A: Stacy Keach, Scott Wilson, Jason Miller, Ed Flanders, Neville Brand, George DiCenzo

© R&G VIDEO, LP 90006

NO MERCY

D: Richard Pearce — 108 m

R | ACT SUS | 1986 | COLOR

Sex | Nud | Viol | Lang | AdSit

7 Richard Gere is an undercover cop whose partner is brutally and sadistically murdered. Swearing vengeance, he tracks the killers to Louisiana. There he uncovers a huge drug conspiracy involving the killers he is pursuing. The stakes go up. He kidnaps the druglord's beautiful woman (Basinger), the only witness, to flush out his quarry. He and Basinger make their escape into the Bayous, but ultimately he winds up protecting her from her former lover, who is now out to kill them both. Tense action in a traditional plot, but well done.

A: Richard Gere, Kim Basinger, Jeroen Krabbe, George Dzundza, Gary Basaraba, Ray Sharkey

© COLUMBIA TRISTAR HOME VIDEO 60791

NORTH BY NORTHWEST

D: Alfred Hitchcock — 136 m

NR | SUS CRM | 1959 | COLOR

Sex | Nud | Viol | Lang | AdSit

10 All-time classic suspensor and quintessential Hitchcock. This highly entertaining thriller starred Cary Grant when he was at the height of his career and at his most charming. He plays a bewildered advertising executive who is being chased cross-country by both the police (who think he is a murderer) and by foreign spies (who think he is a double-agent). Then, he is unexpectedly charmed and aided by beautiful Eva Marie Saint, but soon has reason to question her motives, too. A masterpiece of intrigue. Several now-classic and often imitated scenes. See also NOTORIOUS.

A: Cary Grant, Eva Marie Saint, James Mason, Leo G. Carroll, Jessie Royce Landis, Philip Ober

Distributed By MGM/UA Home Video M600104

NO WAY OUT

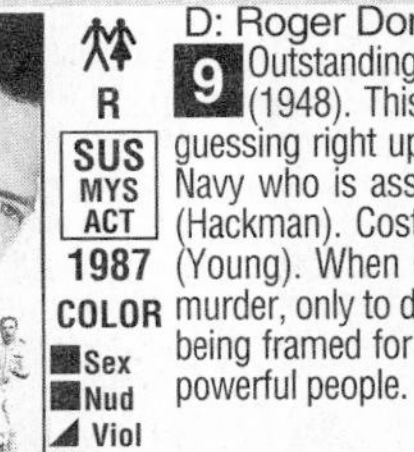

D: Roger Donaldson — 114 m

R | SUS MYS ACT | 1987 | COLOR

Sex | Nud | Viol | Lang | AdSit

9 Outstanding and totally engrossing remake of THE BIG CLOCK (1948). This intriguing and sexy suspense thriller will keep you guessing right up to the end. Costner plays a straight arrow from the Navy who is assigned as a CIA liaison to the Secretary of Defense (Hackman). Costner has a passionate affair with a super-sexy lady (Young). When she is murdered, he is assigned to investigate the murder, only to discover that all the clues are pointing to him and he is being framed for the girl's murder. He is being trapped by some very powerful people.

A: Kevin Costner, Gene Hackman, Sean Young, Will Patton, Howard Duff, George Dzundza

© HBO VIDEO 0051

NO WAY TO TREAT A LADY

D: Jack Smight — 108 m

NR | MYS SUS COM | 1968 | COLOR | Sex, Nud, Viol, Lang, AdSit

9 Terrific thriller that oddly also has a touch of comedy thrown in. Steiger puts in a dynamite performance as a demented and flamboyant killer. He is a transvestite who disguises himself as different people and then kills - but only dowdy older women, strangling them and leaving a gaudy red kiss on each victim. George Segal is an overly-mothered NY cop determined to find the killer. Segal's chief witness is Lee Remick, and he falls for her. Steiger keeps close tabs on the investigation and enjoys teasing Segal with clues. He also repeatedly taunts Segal with phone calls indicating that Remick may be next. Very well done.

A: Rod Steiger, Lee Remick, George Segal, Eileen Heckart, Murray Hamilton, Michael Dunn

© PARAMOUNT HOME VIDEO 6724

OBSESSION

D: Brian De Palma — 98 m

PG | SUS ROM | 1976 | COLOR | Sex, Nud, Viol, Lang, AdSit

8 Taut and gripping suspensor from Brian De Palma in Hitchcock's VERTIGO tradition. Wealthy New Orleans businessman Cliff Robertson cooperated with police in 1959 when his wife (Bujold) and daughter are kidnapped and they were never seen again. Now, sixteen years later in Rome, he meets a virtual double to his wife, marries her, and she is also kidnapped. The new ransom note he gets is essentially identical to the first one. Complex web of romance, suspense, treachery and torment. Highly watchable.

A: Cliff Robertson, Genevieve Bujold, Wanda Blackman, John Lithgow, Sylvia Kuumba Williams

© GOODTIMES 4607

ODESSA FILE, THE

D: Ronald Neame — 128 m

PG | SUS MYS ACT | 1974 | COLOR | Sex, Nud, Viol, Lang, AdSit

8 Gripping! John Voight is a German reporter who discovers, through reading the diary of a former death camp survivor, of the existence of Odessa, a secret German society that protects former SS officers who are now safely in positions of power within 1960s German centers of commerce and government. He also learns of the vicious and monstrously cruel Commandant (Maximilian Schell) of a Latvian camp. Voight goes undercover to infiltrate Odessa in search of Schell, but Odessa members are everywhere and he is in constant risk. Intricate plot can be confusing but is well worth the effort.

A: Jon Voight, Maximilian Schell, Derek Jacobi, Maria Schell, Mary Tamm, Klaus Lowitsch

© COLUMBIA TRISTAR HOME VIDEO 60317

OFFICIAL STORY, THE

D: Luis Puenzo — 112 m

NR | FOR DMA SUS | 1985 | COLOR | Sex, Nud, Viol, Lang, AdSit

9 This is an extremely powerful Oscar winner for Best Foreign Film. It is a devastating story about a sheltered, middle-class Argentinian woman and wife of a politician, who gradually comes to the realization that her adopted daughter was forcefully torn away from her mother by the government. The mother had been a political activist, was tortured and then murdered. Worse than that news, she also learns that her otherwise-loving husband has always known about it. Her world, and all that she has naively believed in, is utterly destroyed. The scene where she views photos of someone, who is obviously her child's mother, with the child's grandmother is devastating. Subtitles.

A: Norma Aleandro, Hector Alterio, Analia Castro

© PACIFIC ARTS VIDEO 630

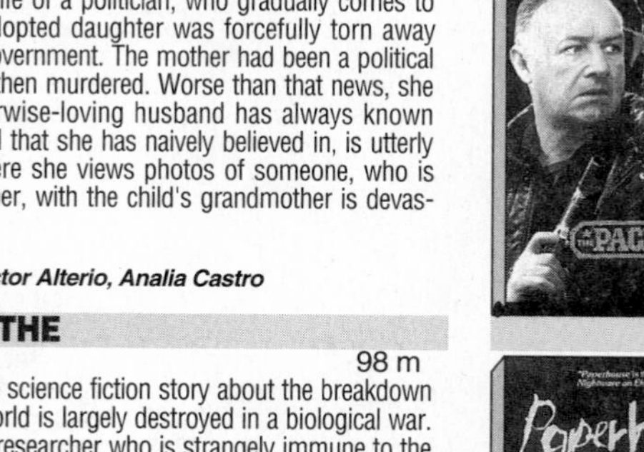

OMEGA MAN, THE

D: Boris Sagal — 98 m

PG | SF SUS ACT | 1971 | COLOR | Sex, Nud, Viol, Lang, AdSit

7 Well done and literate science fiction story about the breakdown of society after the world is largely destroyed in a biological war. Heston stars as a medical researcher who is strangely immune to the effects of all the germs. But a militant group of mutant survivors is now bent on destroying all technologies and has particularly targeted him to be killed. Heston discovers a few children who are also immune and being protected by Cash. The mutants want to kill them, too, but they are the future of the species and Heston must study them if there is to be a cure. Gripping suspense.

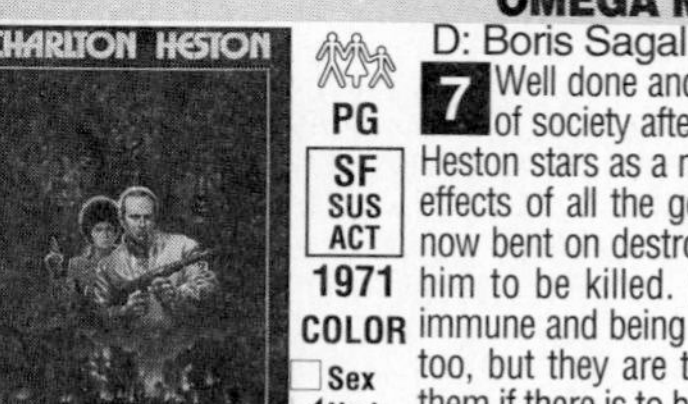

A: Charlton Heston, Anthony Zerbe, Rosalind Cash, Paul Koslo, Lincoln Kilpatrick, Eric Laneuville

© WARNER HOME VIDEO 11210

OMEN, THE

D: Richard Donner — 111 m

R | HOR SUS | 1976 | COLOR | Sex, Nud, Viol, Lang, AdSit

8 Very well done, high tension horror flick with a top flight cast and a good storyline. American ambassador Gregory Peck is convinced by a priest to substitute another child for his own dead newborn baby, without telling his wife (Remick). Five years later, all Hell breaks loose when several people around Damien are all killed. Peck investigates further to find that his own baby had actually been murdered at birth and that the substitute baby, Damien, is the Anti-Christ. According to the New Testament, with the arrival of the Anti-Christ the final battle between good and evil has begun. Peck must kill Damien. Thoroughly frightening. Sequel is DAMIEN - OMEN II.

A: Gregory Peck, Lee Remick, David Warner, Billie Whitelaw, Harvey Stephens, Leo McKern

© FOXVIDEO 1079

OTHER, THE

D: Robert Mulligan — 100 m

PG | SUS HOR | 1972 | COLOR | Sex, Nud, Viol, Lang, AdSit

7 An eerie tale of the unnatural. During the summer of 1935, near a small Connecticut farm, there occurs a series of tragic and bizarre murders. While this film begins at an apparently slow pace, it is only laying careful groundwork and clues for the chilling story which soon begins to unwind. Two 12-year-old boys are twins. They look alike, act alike and are very dedicated to each other. But, they are different - one is very evil. People die. Only their mother and their grandmother have any suspicions of what the truth may be. This is a real chiller from Tom Tryon.

A: Uta Hagen, Diana Muldaur, John Ritter, Chris Udvarnoky, Martin Udvarnoky, Victor French

© FOXVIDEO 1729

OUT OF THE DARKNESS

D: Jud Taylor — 96 m

R | CRM MYS SUS | 1985 | COLOR | Sex, Nud, Viol, Lang, AdSit

8 Fascinating story of the New York cop Ed Zigo, who tracked down the infamous "Son of Sam" killer in 1976-77. This was the vicious real-life murderer who shot young lovers in their cars with a large bore revolver, and then wrote taunting notes to reporters and the police to brag of his successes. This gripping story focuses on the cop and the chase, not the killer. A solid and interesting script with tight pacing and an excellent performance from Martin Sheen make this a gripping crime mystery.

A: Martin Sheen, Hector Elizondo, Matt Clark, Jennifer Salt

© VIDMARK ENTERTAINMENT 5241

PACIFIC HEIGHTS

D: John Schlesinger — 103 m

R | SUS ACT | 1990 | COLOR | Sex, Nud, Viol, Lang, AdSit

8 A landlord's ultimate nightmare! Drake and Patty (Modine and Griffith) have him living right downstairs - in their new house! When the attractive, young couple spy the Victorian house of their dreams in Pacific Heights, they just know they have to have it. They pool their resources and decide that, if they rent out the bottom units, they can just make the mortgage. But their happiness is short lived when mysterious Keaton moves in and turns their lives into a living hell. He is a psychotic that even the legal system can't touch. A gripping, intelligent and believable psychothriller!

A: Melanie Griffith, Matthew Modine, Michael Keaton, Mako, Nobu McCarthy, Laurie Metcalf

© FOXVIDEO 1900

PACKAGE, THE

D: Andrew Davis — 108 m

R | ACT SUS | 1989 | COLOR | Sex, Nud, Viol, Lang, AdSit

8 Nifty espionage thriller. Army sergeant Gene Hackman is assigned to escort another sergeant back to the U.S. from Germany and to his court-martial, but along the way the prisoner escapes. Hackman discovers that his prisoner was actually an imposter and that he is now neck deep in a cold war assassination plot to be carried out at an international disarmament conference. He and his officer ex-wife are left to figure out what's going on, how to clear his name and how to stop the plot from being carried out. Lots of surprises and twists add to the excitement.

A: Gene Hackman, Joanna Cassidy, Tommy Lee Jones, John Heard, Dennis Franz, Reni Santoni

© ORION PICTURES CORPORATION 8747

PAPERHOUSE

D: Bernard Rose — 92 m

PG-13 | SUS HOR FAN | 1989 | COLOR | Sex, Nud, Viol, Lang, AdSit

7 Bizarre, original and strangely captivating fantasy and psychological thriller. At school, Anna (a 13-year-old girl who is prone to vivid dreams) draws a strange house and, in the upstairs window, a lonely boy who cannot move. Then, feeling ill, she heads home but falls into a culvert on the way and there she has a nightmare where she sees the house and meets the boy of her picture. Anna is found and taken home. Now, she alters her drawing to match her new dream. But when the dream returns again, it has evolved once again. It is then that she learns that her doctor has another patient, a paralyzed boy and he's the boy in the window. Her dream is alive.

A: Ben Cross, Glenne Headly, Charlotte Burke, Elliott Spiers, Gemma Jones

© LIVE HOME VIDEO 5283

PAPILLON

D: Franklin J. Schaffner — 150 m

PG | DMA ACT SUS | 1973 | COLOR | Sex, Nud, Viol, Lang, AdSit

9 Exuberant testament to the triumph of the human spirit, based upon the real-life exploits of Henri Charriere, also called Papillon (meaning "the butterfly"). McQueen plays the Frenchman who is unjustly sentenced to the escape-proof hell of the infamous Devil's Island penal colony. In spite of overwhelming odds, he and his friend, a convicted forger (brilliantly played by Hoffman), make continued escape attempts - once succeeding for a short time and living in an idyllic Indian village. Each time they are captured, they again seek a new way to escape. There spirit is indomitable. Long but engrossing throughout.

A: Steve McQueen, Dustin Hoffman, Victor Jory, Anthony Zerbe, Don Gordon, Robert Deman

© WARNER HOME VIDEO 832

SUS

PARALLAX VIEW, THE

D: Alan J. Pakula — 102 m

R | MYS SUS ACT | 1974 | COLOR

Sex Nud Viol Lang AdSit

9 Absolutely gripping, but strangely neglected, political thriller. Warren Beatty plays an alcoholic small-time reporter who witnesses the assassination of a Presidential candidate. As other witnesses mysteriously turn up dead, he begins his own investigations into their deaths. Each new piece of evidence he uncovers leads him to suspect that there is an elaborate coverup underway. An oppressive suspense builds steadily as the more he learns, the more likely it becomes that he will be eliminated, too.

A: Warren Beatty, Paula Prentiss, Hume Cronyn, William Daniels, Walter McGinn, Kelly Thordsen

© PARAMOUNT HOME VIDEO 8670

PASSION OF ANNA, THE

D: Ingmar Bergman — 101 m

R | FOR DMA SUS | 1970 | COLOR

Sex Nud Viol Lang AdSit

8 Max von Sydow is an ex-convict living alone in a farmhouse on a small island and is visited one day by a crippled woman (Ulmann) requesting to use the telephone. When she leaves, she forgets her purse behind. He gets her name from it to return it to her but also learns from letters inside of her troubled marriage. They become friends and she moves into his farmhouse but their relationship becomes very strained, in part because of reports of an axe murderer being at large. She believes he may be the axe murderer and he believes she is trying to kill him as she probably killed her husband and child.

A: Max von Sydow, Liv Ullmann, Bibi Andersson, Erland Josephson

Distributed By MGM/UA Home Video M202786

PATRIOT GAMES

D: Phillip Noyce — 117 m

R | ACT SUS | 1992 | COLOR

Sex Nud Viol Lang AdSit

7 Tom Clancy's CIA character Jack Ryan, first introduced in HUNT FOR RED OCTOBER, is back but this time he is played by Harrison Ford. Retired from the CIA and now a college professor in London with his wife (Archer) and daughter, Jack stumbles onto a plot by a splinter group of the IRA to assassinate English royalty. He breaks up the hit, killing one of the assassins in the process. The angry IRA tracks Jack back to America where he is forced to rejoin the CIA to protect his family and fight off the vengeful IRA. Not up to the standards of its predecessor, but still exciting and interesting if you're not too critical of some plot holes.

A: Harrison Ford, Anne Archer, James Earl Jones, Patrick Bergin, Thora Birch, Richard Harris

© PARAMOUNT HOME VIDEO 32530

PEEPING TOM

D: Michael Powell — 101 m

NR | SUS HOR | 1960 | COLOR

Sex Nud Viol Lang AdSit

8 This film was widely panned (and even denounced) by the critics upon its release, but it is now regarded as a significant pioneering film in psychological explorations and has become a cult favorite. It is the story of a psychopathic woman-killer. As a young boy, his father studied fear and used him as a subject. Now he is grown and he photographs his victims as they are being stabbed with his tripod, just as they die, because he enjoys the look of fear on their faces. The filming technique forces us to become voyeurs to the victim's deaths, right along with him. Very different and highly suspenseful.

A: Carl Boehm, Moira Shearer, Anna Massey, Maxine Audley, Brenda Bruce, Martin Miller

© HOME VISION PEE 030

PELICAN BRIEF, THE

D: Alan Pakula — 141 m

PG-13 | SUS MYS | 1994 | COLOR

Sex Nud Viol Lang AdSit

8 Fast-paced intrigue based upon the novel of the same name by John Grisham. Two Supreme Court justices have been assassinated. Julia Roberts is a young New Orleans law student who researches the records to discover what factor they have in common and stumbles upon the truth. She presented her case to her law professor/lover, who delivered her brief to the FBI. Almost immediately, his car is blown up and Julia is on the run with two government agencies and a contract killer after her. Her only hope of staying alive lies in a prominent political reporter (Denzel Washington). Overly-involved at times and sometimes cannot stand close scrutiny, but still very involving.

A: Julia Roberts, Denzel Washington, Sam Shepard, John Heard, Tony Goldwyn, John Lithgow

© WARNER HOME VIDEO 12989

PIT AND THE PENDULUM, THE

D: Roger Corman — 80 m

NR | HOR SUS | 1961 | COLOR

Sex Nud Viol Lang AdSit

6 Edgar Allan Poe's short story inspired this low-budget thriller. Vincent Price is the son of the 16th-century Spanish Inquisition's most notorious torturer, who is tortured himself by his belief that he has buried his own wife alive. Price also now believes himself to actually be his father. When his wife's brother comes to investigate his sister's death, Price takes him to the pit and the pendulum - a room where a razor sharp pendulum moves ever lower and closer to its victim with each successive sweep. A little hokey in a few spots, still very well staged and acted. Guaranteed to put a chill up your spine.

A: Vincent Price, John Kerr, Barbara Steele, Luana Anders, Anthony Carbone

© GOODTIMES 5-74043

PLAY MISTY FOR ME

D: Clint Eastwood — 103 m

R | SUS | 1971 | COLOR

Sex Nud Viol Lang AdSit

9 Super-suspenseful shocker. Eastwood both starred and directed in this winner. He plays a late-night radio host who is known for playing romantic music and overly confident in his ability to manipulate women, until he meets Jessica Walter. She is an obsessive fan whose repeated request to hear "Misty" results in a one-night stand for him. However, she is obsessed with him too, and the once-confident independent DJ is now being terrorized and held hostage by this crazed fan. This one is every bit as intense as 1989's FATAL ATTRACTION. Both were very popular. Hit song: "The First Time Ever I Saw Your Face."

A: Clint Eastwood, Jessica Walter, Donna Mills, John Larch, Irene Hervey, Jack Ging

© MCA/UNIVERSAL HOME VIDEO, INC. 55016

POINT BLANK

D: John Boorman — 89 m

NR | CRM ACT SUS | 1967 | COLOR

Sex Nud Viol Lang AdSit

9 Violent and tense revenge flick that was largely ignored upon its release but is highly regarded now both for it's potency and its technical merits. Marvin is riveting as a vicious gangster who is shot and left for dead by his partner during a holdup, so he could run off with Marvin's wife and pay off a mob debt with the money they stole. Marvin recovers, and with help from sexy Angie Dickinson and a crooked accountant, he gains access inside the mob. He will get revenge, get his money back and kill off anyone who gets in his way. Very violent.

A: Lee Marvin, Angie Dickinson, Carroll O'Connor, Keenan Wynn, John Vernon, Lloyd Bochner

Distributed By MGM/UA Home Video M800278

POINT OF NO RETURN

D: John Badham — 109 m

R | ACT SUS | 1992 | COLOR

Sex Nud Viol Lang AdSit

7 This is the Americanized (Hollywoodized) version of the very stylish French film LA FEMME NIKITA. It is the story of a beautiful but totally alienated young woman who had become a mindless killer and was sentenced to die. But, a government agency secretly arranged for her faked death so that it could secretly train her into a merciless assassin for them. However, their plans are fowled after her release into society, when she becomes humanized by the love of a gentle man. This version is virtually identical to the French version, except for being in English. However, because the actors are more familiar and the government is ours, it doesn't work as well.

A: Bridget Fonda, Anne Bancroft, Harvey Keitel, Gabriel Byrne, Miguel Ferrer, Olivia D'Abo

© WARNER HOME VIDEO 12819

POSTMAN ALWAYS RINGS TWICE, THE

D: Bob Rafelson — 121 m

R | SUS CRM DMA | 1981 | COLOR

Sex Nud Viol Lang AdSit

6 Super-sexy remake of the classic 1946 film about the passion between a cook at a roadside cafe and a handyman which led to their conspired murder of her husband. Unhampered by the censorship of 1946, this remake dives headlong into the passions only alluded to in the earlier version. After a strong beginning, things begin to wander some. Ultimately, this version is not as satisfying as the original because much of the empathy for the characters which was created in the original is lost here. Still... interesting.

A: Jack Nicholson, Jessica Lange, Michael Lerner, John Colicos

© WARNER HOME VIDEO 673

PREDATOR

D: John McTiernan — 107 m

R | ACT SUS SF | 1987 | COLOR

Sex Nud Viol Lang AdSit

9 Heart-pounding suspense. Schwarzenegger and his crew of trained mercenaries are hired by the CIA to go into a Latin American jungle to rescue a group South American officials kidnapped by terrorists. Just as they are about to complete their mission, they are surprised to discover that they are themselves being stalked by a fearsome other-world killer - a large, ugly, ferocious alien man/monster with truly awesome powers who enjoys hunting and killing. It has come to earth to hunt the hunters - humans. Fast-paced, intense suspense as team members are picked off one by one. Action-packed.

A: Arnold Schwarzenegger, Jesse Ventura, Bill Duke, Sonny Landham, Carl Weathers, Richard Chaves

© FOXVIDEO 1515

PRESUMED INNOCENT

D: Alan J. Pakula — 127 m

R | MYS SUS CRM | 1990 | COLOR

Sex Nud Viol Lang AdSit

8 This is a sexy and thoroughly involving thriller (based on a best-selling novel) which was a big hit at the box office. Ford plays Rusty Sabich, a hard-working up-and-coming attorney at the county prosecutor's office. However, he has a brief affair with a stunningly sexy female attorney (Sacchi) that ends badly. His marriage is damaged but survives. Then the woman turns up raped and murdered. His finger prints and blood are found at the scene and the prosecutor's office that he was so committed to, is now doing its best to nail him. This is a fascinating mystery and courtroom drama that is full of red herrings and plot twists and is very well done.

A: Harrison Ford, Brian Dennehy, Raul Julia, Bonnie Bedelia, Paul Winfield, Greta Scacchi

© WARNER HOME VIDEO 12034

PRIZZI'S HONOR

D: John Huston 130 m

R | COM CRM SUS | 1985 | COLOR

9 Devilishly delicious black comedy. Nicholson is a Mafia hit man for the Prizzi family. He becomes fascinated with a sexy mystery woman (Turner), who turns out to be a free-lance hitter, too. But things become greatly complicated for them when it turns out she has stolen some of the family's money and he gets an order to kill her. Nicholson's loyalties are severely tested: should he hit her, or marry her. Now that he is no longer trustworthy, the family hires her to hit him. Terrific performances, witty dialogue, fascinating plotting. Eight Oscar nominations.

Sex Nud Viol Lang AdSit

A: Jack Nicholson, Kathleen Turner, Anjelica Huston, John Randolph, William Hickey, Robert Loggia

© LIVE HOME VIDEO 5106

PROFESSIONALS, THE

D: Richard Brooks 117 m

PG | WST ACT SUS | 1966 | COLOR

9 Thrilling action-packed Western manned with some of the genre's best talent. A team of four mercenaries (an explosives expert, a horse trainer, an archer and a sharpshooter) are hired by a wealthy aging Texan to track down his beautiful young wife who has been kidnapped by a Mexican bandit. Heavily out-manned and outgunned, their raid upon the stronghold yields up the woman, but they are hotly pursued on the way back and are surprised to find that the woman is not at all eager to go with them. Intense actioner with a high excitement quotient, top-flight performances and quality production values.

Sex Nud Viol Lang AdSit

A: Burt Lancaster, Lee Marvin, Claudia Cardinale, Jack Palance, Woody Strode, Ralph Bellamy

© GOODTIMES 4501

PROJECT X

D: Jonathan Kaplan 107 m

PG | SUS SF | 1987 | COLOR

7 Entertaining quasi-science fiction flick. A chronic screw-up in the Air Force (Broderick) gets assigned to a top secret project to help train the next "generation" of pilots - brilliant chimpanzees who can communicate with sign language. Broderick becomes incensed at the unnecessarily cruel and fatal nature of the experimentation on the chimps, so he, another trainer (Hunt) and the chimps all conspire against the Air Force's plans. Watchable and enjoyable, but predictable.

Sex Nud Viol Lang AdSit

A: Matthew Broderick, Helen Hunt, Anne Lockhart, Bill Sadler, Johnny Ray McGhee, Jonathon Stark

© FOXVIDEO 5192

PSYCHO

D: Alfred Hitchcock 109 m

NR | SUS HOR | 1960 | B&W

10 Hitchcock's masterpiece. This is a high-tension shocker that you will not soon forget once you have seen it - and, if you saw it on TV with commercials, you didn't see it. Janet Leigh is a bank clerk who sees an opportunity to escape her dead-end life and she takes it. But her flight down country roads takes her to the gloomy and bleak Bates motel, where she is introduced to Norman Bates and his sinister mother, a mistake she will never make again. This is the shocker of all time. It is much copied and was also followed by two sequels - but none approach the original.

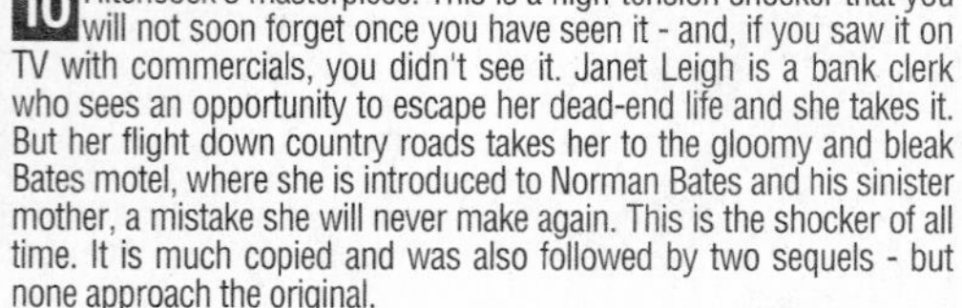

Sex Nud Viol Lang AdSit

A: Anthony Perkins, Janet Leigh, Martin Balsam, Vera Miles, John Gavin, John McIntire

© MCA/UNIVERSAL HOME VIDEO, INC. 55001

PSYCHO II

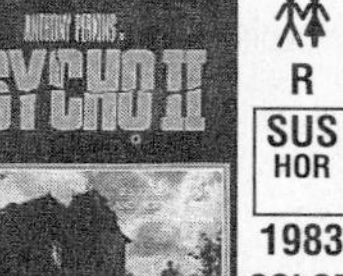

D: Richard Franklin 113 m

R | SUS HOR | 1983 | COLOR

7 Quite good remake of Hitchcock's masterpiece. 22 years after Norman was locked up - he's out, on the recommendation of his shrink and against the objections of Vera Miles, his previous victim's sister. Norman returns to his old neighborhood and tries to go straight. He gets a job at a local restaurant and strikes up a relationship with waitress Meg Tilly. However, it isn't long before he begins getting notes from a woman claiming to be his dead mother. Soon, the killings begin again. Respectful, and effective, remake.

Sex Nud Viol Lang AdSit

A: Anthony Perkins, Vera Miles, Meg Tilly, Robert Loggia, Dennis Franz, Hugh Gillin

© MCA/UNIVERSAL HOME VIDEO, INC. 80008

PULP

D: Mike Hodges 95 m

PG | SUS COM | 1972 | COLOR

6 Pretty good spoof thriller. Michael Caine is a hack writer from Hollywood who is hired by a retired film star (Rooney), to ghost write his autobiography. Rooney made his name playing gangsters and now lives in Italy. Caine travels to Italy and begins his interviews of Rooney, but they are cut short when Rooney is murdered. Now someone is apparently after Caine, too. Maybe Rooney was so good at playing gangsters because he wasn't acting after all.

Sex Nud Viol Lang AdSit

A: Michael Caine, Mickey Rooney, Lionel Stander, Lizabeth Scott, Nadia Cassini, Al Lettieri

© WOOD KNAPP VIDEO 1025

PUPPET MASTERS, THE

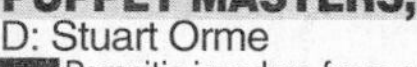

D: Stuart Orme 119 m

R | SUS SF | 1994 | COLOR

7 Parasitic invaders from another world have overrun a small Iowa town. The little beggars attach themselves to the backs of their hosts, inject a stinger-like tentacle into the brain and take control of the victim, who then becomes their puppet. Government agents Sutherland, Thal and Warner had come to explore the conflicting news reports which first announced a strange landing and then denied it. Their mission is now to find a way to destroy the colony of parasites without being invaded themselves and before the nasty creatures can invade the entire population. Really not too bad. Its only problem is that it comes on the heels of other films such as INVASION OF THE BODY SNATCHERS.

Sex Nud Viol Lang AdSit

A: Donald Sutherland, Eric Thal, Julie Warner, Keith David, Will Patton, Richard Belzer

© HOLLYWOOD PICTURES HOME VIDEO 3628

QUILLER MEMORANDUM, THE

D: Michael Anderson 103 m

NR | SUS ACT | 1966 | COLOR

8 No gadgets or gimmicks in this intelligent espionage thriller! An American agent (Segal) in Berlin is recruited by head-Brit Guinness to help uncover a neo-Nazi group that is gaining momentum in Berlin. The two agents who were previously assigned to the project have been killed. Segal soon learns that even the guys on his side aren't trustworthy. He can trust no one - not Guinness, not sensuous teacher Senta Berger, and not Von Sydow, the scheming German aristocrat. He is alone. One mistake and he is dead, too.

Sex Nud Viol Lang AdSit

A: George Segal, Senta Berger, Alec Guinness, Max von Sydow, George Sanders, Robert Helpmann

© FOXVIDEO 1403

RAGGEDY MAN

D: Jack Fisk 94 m

PG | DMA SUS | 1981 | COLOR

8 Gripping character study. A young divorcee (Spacek) is trying to forge a life for herself and her two sons in a small Texas Gulf town. The two single men in town (except for the mysterious raggedy man) are convinced that, since she is divorced, she must be eager and they harass her. Instead, she has a loving affair with a sailor (Roberts) passing through and gains a new inner strength. Now she is determined to go somewhere new, but is again confronted by the two. In a needlessly horrifying ending, she receives help from the mysterious "raggedy man." Otherwise sensitive and unassuming.

Sex Nud Viol Lang AdSit

A: Sissy Spacek, Eric Roberts, Sam Shepard, William Sanderson, Tracey Walter, Henry Thomas

© MCA/UNIVERSAL HOME VIDEO, INC. 71003

RAIDERS OF THE LOST ARK

D: Steven Spielberg 115 m

PG | ACT SUS | 1981 | COLOR

10 Rip-roaring, rousing, riotous adventure that never stops! Indiana Jones (Ford) is an archaeologist who embarks on a quest in 1936 to find the Lost Ark of the Covenant, a religious relic that possesses supernatural powers. Along the way, he battles Nazis, swordsmen, runaway boulders, venomous snakes and a whole vat of death and danger. Powerful, courageous, gritty - Ford is a huge screen hero. Spielberg's tribute to the Saturday matinees of old is better than any revival. The action just keeps coming at you in this thrilling roller-coaster ride! Followed by two sequels.

Sex Nud Viol Lang AdSit

A: Harrison Ford, Karen Allen, Paul Freeman, Ronald Lacey, John Rhys-Davies, Denholm Elliott

© PARAMOUNT HOME VIDEO 1376

RAID ON ENTEBBE

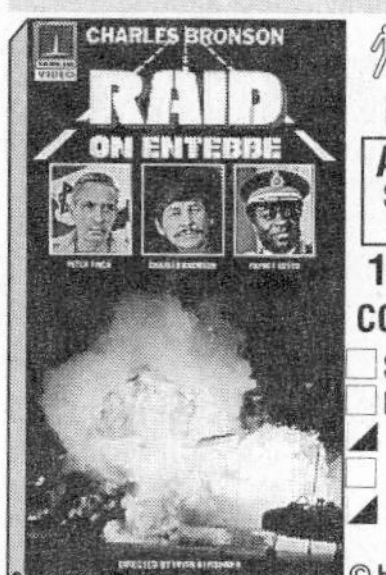

D: Irvin Kershner 113 m

NR | ACT SUS | 1976 | COLOR

7 A well-made dramatization of a real-life dramatic rescue! When terrorists hijacked an Israeli plane in 1976 and took 103 Israeli hostages to Uganda's Entebbe airport, the Israelies struck back. Israeli leader Finch orders a daring military rescue mission into a foreign country to get their people back. Bronson and Bucholz are to be at the helm of the mission. Made for TV, Finch received an Emmy nomination for this compelling drama. Although the impact was greater at the time it was released, it is still a good action film with strong suspenseful elements.

Sex Nud Viol Lang AdSit

A: Charles Bronson, Peter Finch, Horst Buchholz, Martin Balsam, Jack Warden, Yaphet Kotto

© HBO VIDEO TVB2455

RAISING CAIN

D: Brian De Palma m

SUS | 1992 | COLOR

7 This is a fairly effective thriller, but it starts a little slow. Lithgow is a child psychologist who is married to Davidovich. Their relationship has become strained after he develops a near-compulsive fixation toward caring for their daughter. After Davidovich rekindles a relationship with an old lover and, when Lithgow finds out about it, his true nature (rather, natures) is revealed. He has multiple personalities which had been purposefully created in him by his own psychologist father many years before. His father had used him as his personal research subject. The good and protective side of him is Carter. But, the evil, killing side is Cain.

Sex Nud Viol Lang AdSit

A: John Lithgow, Lolita Davidovich, Steven Bauer, Frances Sternhagen, Gregg Henry, Tom Bower

© MCA/UNIVERSAL HOME VIDEO, INC. 81285

REPULSION

NR
HOR SUS
1965
B&W
Sex
Nud
Viol
Lang
AdSit

D: Roman Polanski 105 m

9 Controversial and shocking! A beautiful but sexually repressed young woman (Deneuve) lives with her sister (Furneaux) in a London flat. She is both repulsed by sex and fascinated with it, and she can't escape it because of the affair her sister is having. When Furneaux goes on vacation for two weeks with her lover and leaves her sister alone in the apartment, Deneuve crumbles, a psychological nightmare ensues and she begins to suffer from compelling hallucinations which lead her into a murderous rampage. A thrilling psychological horror masterpiece that is sure to affect you.

A: Catherine Deneuve, Ian Hendry, Yvonne Furneaux, John Fraser, Patrick Wymark, James Villiers

© VIDEO DIMENSIONS

RETURN OF THE JEDI

PG
SF ACT SUS
1983
COLOR
Sex
Nud
Viol
Lang
AdSit

D: Richard Marquand 134 m

9 Thrilling finale to the hugely popular, exciting and imaginative STAR WARS trilogy from George Lucas. In this episode, Luke Skywalker has further mastered his skills as a Jedi Master of the "Force." He first rescues Princess Leia and Hans Solo from the vile and decadent Jabba-the-Hut, then aids in the destruction of the monstrously powerful Death Star by infiltrating the evil forces of the Empire, seeking out its all-powerful leader Darth Vader - to destroy him. Great characters. Great special effects. Great fun!

A: Mark Hamill, Carrie Fisher, Harrison Ford, Billy Dee Williams, Dave Prowse, Peter Mayhew

© FOXVIDEO 1478

RIDER ON THE RAIN

PG
SUS CRM
1970
COLOR
Sex
Nud
Viol
Lang
AdSit

D: Rene Clement 119 m

8 This is a tightly-plotted and well-executed thriller that is loaded with suspense! A young French housewife (Jobert) is brutally raped by a stranger. She kills him in self defense and disposes of his body in the sea. When the body washes up on shore, she receives a visit from a mysterious stranger (Bronson). He tells her he suspects she killed the man. He had been a prison escapee and had a flight bag with $60,000 of US Army money. Bronson won't leave her alone until he gets the money back, and she doesn't know who he is. This is a fine film that has a chilling, polished and unpredictable script. It is also one of Bronson's finest performances.

A: Charles Bronson, Marlene Jobert, Jill Ireland, Annie Cordy

© MONTEREY HOME VIDEO 33708

ROAD GAMES

PG
SUS ACT
1981
COLOR
Sex
Nud
Viol
Lang
AdSit

D: Richard Franklin 100 m

7 Intrigue and gore keep this offbeat thriller moving along. Oddball trucker Stacy Keach makes up stories about the people he meets to occupy his time on a long haul. This time, along the way, he picks up a female hitchhiker (Curtis), a rich girl looking for a change in her mundane life, and she joins him in his mind games. They spy one particular green van and become suspicious that there really may be something afoul with it and decide to investigate further. Director Franklin does a superb job of maintaining a high level of suspense. The audience is never really sure who it can trust and who it can't.

A: Stacy Keach, Jamie Lee Curtis, Marion Edward, Grant Page, Bill Stacey

© NEW LINE HOME VIDEO 90138

ROLLERCOASTER

PG
SUS
1977
COLOR
Sex
Nud
Viol
Lang
AdSit

D: James Goldstone 119 m

8 A whopper of a roller coaster ride! An unstable extortionist (Bottoms) has been placing bombs beneath the rides at some of the nation's biggest amusement parks. His next target is the world's biggest rollercoaster unless he gets $1 million. County inspector (Segal) and FBI agent (Windmark) are the cops who must stop him, and with whom he plays a teasing game of cat and mouse. This is a very well-done and intelligent suspensor that, unfairly, did not get a good reception by the critics, so it never got the exposure it should have. It has a very tense climax that will have you on the edge of your couch!

A: George Segal, Richard Widmark, Timothy Bottoms, Henry Fonda, Harry Guardino, Susan Strasberg

© MCA/UNIVERSAL HOME VIDEO, INC. 66037

ROOTS

NR
DMA SUS
1977
COLOR
Sex
Nud
Viol
Lang
AdSit

D: Marvin J. Chomsky 562 m

9 Monumental epic TV mini-series that won nine Emmys and over 135 other awards. Six 90-minute segments create a multi-generational mosaic of the people and circumstances of one black man's personal heritage. Beginning in a mid-18th century native African village, a young man is stolen away in a slave ship, to be sold into servitude in the American South. His single-minded determination not to lose his real identity inspired his personal story to continued to be passed down, and gave strength to, all his successors in generation after generation. A moving and engrossing human saga.

A: Edward Asner, Lloyd Bridges, Cicely Tyson, Lorne Greene, Ben Vereen, Levar Burton

© WARNER HOME VIDEO 11111

ROSEMARY'S BABY

R
HOR SUS
1968
COLOR
Sex
Nud
Viol
Lang
AdSit

D: Roman Polanski 134 m

9 Stunning and compelling, stylish and chilling tale of witchcraft that is taken nearly verbatim from Ira Levin's best-selling novel. Cassavetes and Mia Farrow move into a stylish New York apartment building where, unknown to Farrow, husband Cassavetes becomes involved in a neighborhood witch's coven. Slowly she becomes aware that those seemingly friendly people around her all have ulterior motives. They want her unborn baby! Very well done, with a top-drawer cast. Terrifying because the presentation makes the story entirely believable. Ruth Gordon won Oscar for Best Supporting Actress.

A: Mia Farrow, John Cassavetes, Ruth Gordon, Ralph Bellamy, Maurice Evans, Charles Grodin

© PARAMOUNT HOME VIDEO 6831

RUNAWAY TRAIN

R
SUS DMA
1985
COLOR
Sex
Nud
Viol
Lang
AdSit

D: Andrei Konchalovsky 112 m

7 An intriguing combination of intense suspense, action and intellectual drama. Two desperate and hardened convicts break out of a maximum security prison in Alaska during the dead of winter. They hop a ride on a freight train only to discover that the engineer has died of a heart attack and now they are trapped on a high speed runaway. The authorities know they are onboard and are intent upon derailing the massive rolling deathtrap until they and the convicts both discover that there is another passenger on board. Voight and Roberts received Oscar nominations for their vivid portraits.

A: Jon Voight, Eric Roberts, Rebecca De Mornay, Kyle T. Heffner, John P. Ryan, Kenneth McMillan

Distributed By MGM/UA Home Video M800867

RUSSIA HOUSE, THE

R
ROM SUS
1991
COLOR
Sex
Nud
Viol
Lang
AdSit

D: Fred Schepisi 126 m

7 Sophisticated suspense. Barley Blair (Connery) is a British book publisher who meets a group of influential Russian writers while on a trip to Russia and is later surprised to receive a secret manuscript from one of them, sent via a beautiful Russian book editor (Pfeiffer). The book reveals the true Soviet nuclear capabilities. Blair turns the information over to Western intelligence and then unwillingly he becomes embroiled in a spy's game of international poker. This is intelligent, involved and reasonably involving, but also a quite somber, thinking-person's film that is a little too full of complicated plot twists and romantic diversions.

A: Sean Connery, Michelle Pfeiffer, Roy Scheider, James Fox, John Mahoney, Klaus Maria Brandauer

Distributed By MGM/UA Home Video M902301

SALEM'S LOT

NR
HOR SUS
1979
COLOR
Sex
Nud
Viol
Lang
AdSit

D: Tobe Hooper 111 m

7 Chilling Stephen King adaptation. A writer (David Soul) returns to the small New England town of Salem's Lot, where his aunt used to live. He hopes to derive some inspiration from her creepy old house, sitting high on a hilltop. He discovers that the house has been sold to a wicked antiques dealer (Mason) and that now the house has become a source of real evil. It is the home of a group of vampires that is determined to create an army of new followers. Soul and two friends set out to destroy them. Originally a two-part TV movie, the video contains more devilish violence. One of the best of King's film adaptations.

A: David Soul, James Mason, Lance Kerwin, Bonnie Bedelia, Lew Ayres, Reggie Nalder

© WARNER HOME VIDEO 11336

SAND PEBBLES

NR
SUS DMA ACT
1966
COLOR
Sex
Nud
Viol
Lang
AdSit

D: Robert Wise 180 m

8 Sprawling, intelligent and compelling epic film which garnered a nomination for Best Picture and numerous other technical Oscar nominations. An exceptionally strong performance from McQueen drives this film about a cynical, normally reclusive sailor assigned to the engine room of an American gunboat patrolling the Yangtze river of China about 1926... just as civil war begins. Commander Crenna must be diplomatic. He represents the United States. But McQueen will not watch passively as his best friend is tortured. And he also moves aggressively to protect a missionary's daughter.

A: Steve McQueen, Richard Crenna, Candice Bergen, Richard Attenborough, Mako, Gavin MacLeod

© FOXVIDEO 1029

SCARECROWS

R
HOR SUS
1988
COLOR
Sex
Nud
Viol
Lang
AdSit

D: William Wesley 80 m

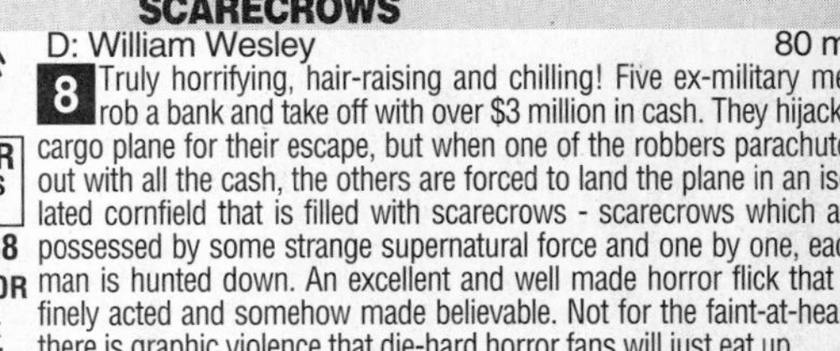

8 Truly horrifying, hair-raising and chilling! Five ex-military men rob a bank and take off with over $3 million in cash. They hijack a cargo plane for their escape, but when one of the robbers parachutes out with all the cash, the others are forced to land the plane in an isolated cornfield that is filled with scarecrows - scarecrows which are possessed by some strange supernatural force and one by one, each man is hunted down. An excellent and well made horror flick that is finely acted and somehow made believable. Not for the faint-at-heart, there is graphic violence that die-hard horror fans will just eat up.

A: Ted Vernon, Michael Simms, Richard Vidan

© FORUM HOME VIDEO FH79013

SUS

SCARLET AND THE BLACK, THE

D: Jerry London 145 m

NR · SUS · ACT · 1983 · COLOR

Sex · Nud · Viol · Lang · AdSit

7 Very good made-for-TV film relating the real-life exploits of a brave Irish priest, Monsignor Hugh O'Flaherty, during WWII. Operating from the Vatican, under the cloak of diplomatic immunity, O'Flaherty organizes a vast network of safe houses inside Nazi-occupied Rome and is responsible for the concealment and escape of hundreds of POWs and refugees. When Gestapo chief (Plummer) orders him killed or captured if he is spotted outside the Vatican, O'Flaherty assumes numerous disguises and plays cat-and-mouse games to keep operating.

A: Gregory Peck, Christopher Plummer, John Gielgud, Raf Vallone

© LIVE HOME VIDEO 69918

SCREAM OF FEAR

D: Seth Holt 81 m

NR · SUS · MYS · 1961 · B&W

Sex · Nud · Viol · Lang · AdSit

7 Spooky thriller! Penny (Strasberg), a young invalid bound to a wheelchair, visits her stepmother and father at his mansion on the French Riviera. When she arrives, she is told that he is away on business. However, that night, she sees his corpse in various spots around the mansion. Soon she can't separate reality from illusion, but she suspects her stepmother (Todd) has killed her father in order to get at the inheritance, and enlists the aid of family chauffeur (Lewis). That may not have been a good choice either. Unduly overlooked upon its release, it's sure to make you hair stand on end.

A: Susan Strasberg, Ronald Lewis, Ann Todd, Christopher Lee

© COLUMBIA TRISTAR HOME VIDEO 60954

SEANCE ON A WET AFTERNOON

D: Bryan Forbes 115 m

NR · SUS · DMA · 1964 · B&W

Sex · Nud · Viol · Lang · AdSit

8 Excellent psychological drama! An eccentric psychic medium (Stanley), who is barely able to maintain her grip on sanity after the loss of her baby, invents a shady scheme to further her career. She decides to have her weak-willed husband (Attenborough) kidnap a wealthy young girl, collect the ransom and then she can reveal the girl's hiding place during a seance to become famous. The plot is full of unpredictable twists and turns, because her plan does not go off as planned. Stanley's outstanding performance of the off-balance psychic earned her an Oscar nomination.

A: Richard Attenborough, Kim Stanley, Patrick Magee, Nanette Newman, Judith Donner, Gerald Sim

© HOME VISION SEA 030

SEA OF LOVE

D: Harold Becker 113 m

R · CRM · SUS · MYS · 1989 · COLOR

Sex · Nud · Viol · Lang · AdSit

9 Very steamy murder mystery. Al Pacino is a cynical and alcoholic cop who has no life outside his work, except the bottle. He is assigned, along with a cop from another precinct (Goodman), to the investigation of a series of murdered dead men, all of which have Ellen Barkin as a common thread. Pacino falls hard for the fiery Barkin and refuses to believe that she is the murderer, even though everyone else has made her their prime suspect. She has revived Pacino's life and he desperately wants to believe she's innocent. Tension builds as he begins a torrid relationship with her, never really knowing for sure if she is a murderer, even as his investigation continues.

A: Al Pacino, Ellen Barkin, John Goodman, Michael Rooker, William Hickey

© MCA/UNIVERSAL HOME VIDEO, INC. 80883

SEE NO EVIL

D: Richard Fleischer 90 m

PG · SUS · 1971 · COLOR

Sex · Nud · Viol · Lang · AdSit

7 A quite good thriller. A young woman (Farrow) is permanently blinded when she takes a bad fall from her horse. She is sent to recuperate at the home of her much-loved uncle (Bailey). However, one day, after she has been out horseback riding with her fiance (Eshley), she returns home to find that someone has brutally murdered her uncle and his family. Then she realizes that the murderer is still in the house and he is now stalking her. A very convincing performance by Farrow contributes to the chilling atmosphere. See also WAIT UNTIL DARK.

A: Mia Farrow, Dorothy Alison, Robin Bailey, Diane Grayson, Lila Kaye, Norman Eshley

© COLUMBIA TRISTAR HOME VIDEO 60700

SENDER, THE

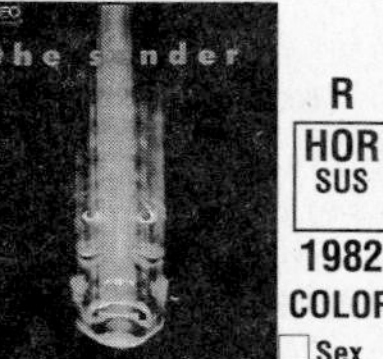

D: Roger Christian 92 m

R · HOR · SUS · 1982 · COLOR

Sex · Nud · Viol · Lang · AdSit

7 A very disturbed young man is so terrified by his nightmares that he becomes suicidal and is hospitalized. It is then discovered that he is also telepathic and can choose others to receive his projected thoughts. When his psychiatrist (Harrold) attempts to help him, she discovers that she has been chosen by him to share his tormented dreams and nightmares. Soon he loses control of his powers and the entire hospital becomes terrorized by his dreams. This is a low-key thriller in the Hitchcock vein. A good cast does a good job.

A: Kathryn Harrold, Shirley Knight, Zeljko Ivanek, Paul Freeman, Sean Hewitt, Harry Ditson

© PARAMOUNT HOME VIDEO 1537

SEVEN DAYS IN MAY

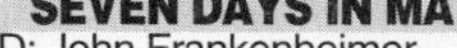

D: John Frankenheimer 118 m

NR · SUS · DMA · 1964 · B&W

Sex · Nud · Viol · Lang · AdSit

8 A tense and entirely believable nail-biter of how it really might happen... the military's overthrow of the US government. An intelligent screenplay from Rod Serling builds tension slowly but unalterably as an Army colonel's (Douglas) suspicions about the intentions of a right-wing general (Lancaster) develop into the reality that there is an active plot within the Pentagon to overthrow the President (March). Powerful climax. Terrific performances by an all-star cast. See also THE MANCHURIAN CANDIDATE.

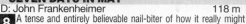

A: Burt Lancaster, Kirk Douglas, Fredric March, Ava Gardner, Edmond O'Brien, Martin Balsam

© WARNER HOME VIDEO 12776

SEVENTH SIGN, THE

D: Carl Schultz 97 m

R · SUS · HOR · 1988 · COLOR

Sex · Nud · Viol · Lang · AdSit

6 The seventh sign, as described in the book of Revelations, signals the end of the world. When six of the seven signs come to pass, pregnant Demi Moore begins having terrible nightmares. A strange-acting boarder (Prochnow) has taken up residence in her house. She discovers that he is carrying out the ancient prophecies from the Bible and through him she also learns that she has been chosen as an instrument of the Seventh Sign. It will come with the birth of her baby. She is having a hard time getting her husband or anyone else to believe her. Still, she is determined to stop it... but, can she.

A: Demi Moore, Michael Biehn, Jurgen Prochnow, Peter Friedman, Manny Jacobs, John Taylor

© COLUMBIA TRISTAR HOME VIDEO 67007

SHALLOW GRAVE

D: Danny Boyle 92 m

R · SUS · 1995 · COLOR

Sex · Nud · Viol · Lang · AdSit

8 Three young roommates have smugly interviewed applicants to find a fourth roommate for their large up-scale apartment. They enjoyed verbally abusing the applicants until they eventually decide upon one who meets their standards. Very soon after the new man moves in however, they discover him dead in his room and with a suitcase of money under his bed. Rather than risk losing the money, they decide to bury him and split it. Very quickly, the roommates become suspicious of each other and begin to plot. Further, that money was the property of some extremely ruthless men and they are very determined to get it back. Paranoia and fear begin to govern everything everyone does. Quite good. Scottish accents do not hamper it.

A: Kerry Fox, Christopher Eccleston, Eway BcGregor, Ken Scott, Keith Allen, Colin McCredle

© POLYGRAM VIDEO 35275-3

SHARKY'S MACHINE

D: Burt Reynolds 123 m

R · CRM · ACT · SUS · 1981 · COLOR

Sex · Nud · Viol · Lang · AdSit

10 Top-drawer cop film - one of the best. Sharkey (Reynolds) is a hardened Atlanta narcotics cop demoted to working in vice after a shootout-gone-bad. He is bored, but when a high-priced hooker turns out to have connections with some very bad and very powerful people who were involved in his earlier narcotics case, Sharky becomes very interested. He sets up a round-the-clock observation of the girl's apartment and becomes totally enraptured by her as he voyeristically watches her every move... but a ruthless assassin is on the prowl and she is his target. Intelligent, realistic, very high intensity action.

A: Burt Reynolds, Vittorio Gassman, Brian Keith, Charles Durning, Rachel Ward, Vittorio Gassman

© WARNER HOME VIDEO 22024

SHATTERED

D: Wolfgang Petersen 98 m

R · SUS · MYS · 1991 · COLOR

Sex · Nud · Viol · Lang · AdSit

8 Stylish and very well made suspensor! Berenger barely survives a harrowing car crash and slowly begins to recover with the help of his apparently loving wife (Scacchi) - but he has completely lost his memory and must trust what she says. As he slowly gathers clues to his former life, he realizes that the past wasn't at all the way she told him it was. Something is very wrong. He discovers that before the accident, he had hired a private investigator (Hoskins) who had told him that his wife was having an affair. Now, he and the investigator start to fill in some gaps... but the truth is so shocking that he might be better off not knowing!

A: Tom Berenger, Greta Scacchi, Bob Hoskins, Corbin Bernsen, Joanne Whalley-Kilmer, Theodore Bikel

Distributed By MGM/UA Home Video M902357

SHINING, THE

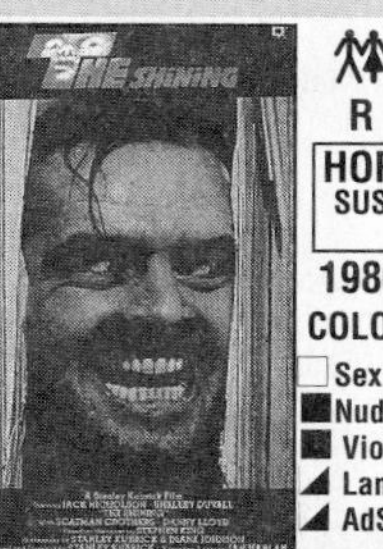

D: Stanley Kubrick 144 m

R · HOR · SUS · 1980 · COLOR

Sex · Nud · Viol · Lang · AdSit

7 Jack Nicholson is a writer who takes a winter job as caretaker at a snowbound resort in the Rockies, where years before the caretaker had killed his family. Nicholson too becomes haunted by the isolation and the specters of the past consume him. He is possessed by the evil spirits of the place and launches a relentless assault on his own family. The horror and violence come at you with a driving force. Fans are sure to love the special effects and Nicholson's performance, although the pace can drag in spots. Stephen King's book provided the basis for this chiller.

A: Jack Nicholson, Shelley Duvall, Scatman Crothers, Danny Lloyd, Barry Nelson, Joel Turkel

© WARNER HOME VIDEO 11079

SHOCK TO THE SYSTEM, A

D: Jan Egleson 88 m

R | SUS COM | 1990 | COLOR | Sex | Nud | Viol | Lang | AdSit

7 Slick little black comedy. Caine's a New York advertising executive who has backed himself into a corner. He has an impossible wife and some major debts, but the worst thing is that a young wippersnapper has just snatched up the promotion he's had his eye on. In a rage of fury, he decides that murder is the answer. He smiles secretly to himself when two of his esteemed colleagues end up on the missing-persons list, and he gets his advancement. But a curious detective may make his new hard-won position in life short-lived. Wickedly sophisticated.

A: Michael Caine, Elizabeth McGovern, Swoosie Kurtz, Peter Riegert, Will Patton, John McMartin

© HBO VIDEO 0378

SHOOT TO KILL

D: Roger Spottiswoode 109 m

R | SUS CRM ACT | 1988 | COLOR | Sex | Nud | Viol | Lang | AdSit

8 Thrilling game of cat and mouse! A ruthless killer joins a group of campers so that he can avoid the police. The group is hiking through the picturesque Pacific Northwest and is being led by Kirstie Alley. When things don't go his way, he begins killing off members of the group. FBI agent Poitier is coming after him, but the FBI man is way out of his element in the wilds and must rely on Alley's rugged boyfriend (Berenger) for help to track them down. This pair mix like oil and water, but they begin to work together when the pressure rises after Alley is taken hostage. Good job by Poitier.

A: Sidney Poitier, Tom Berenger, Kirstie Alley, Clancy Brown, Richard Masur, Andrew Robinson

© TOUCHSTONE HOME VIDEO 697

SHOUT, THE

D: Jerzy Skolimowski 90 m

R | SUS HOR | 1980 | COLOR | Sex | Nud | Viol | Lang | AdSit

7 Offbeat macabre thriller. Imagine someone who can kill just by screaming. Alan Bates is an inmate at an English asylum who claims that he can kill with a horrifying scream he learned while he lived in Australian outback with the Aborigines. Is he crazy? Ask composer John Hurt and his wife (Susannay York). He terrorized them both by demonstrating his power when he killed an innocent shepherd. Then, slowly, he began to take over their lives and seduced her. It was then that the husband discovered for himself the secret of the shout and that is how Bates came to be in the asylum. A very strange and twisted story that will hold your attention.

A: Alan Bates, Susannah York, John Hurt, Tim Curry, Robert Stephens

© UNITED AMERICAN VIDEO CORP. 17198

SILENCE OF THE LAMBS, THE

D: Jonathan Demme 118 m

R | SUS CRM ACT | 1991 | COLOR | Sex | Nud | Viol | Lang | AdSit

9 Outstanding and deeply disturbing Oscar winner. Rookie FBI agent Starling (Foster) has been assigned the daunting task of helping to stop Buffalo Bill, a psycho serial killer who harvests his victim's skin. The key to finding Bill lies within the twisted mind of another brilliant serial killer, Hannibal the Cannibal, now serving time in a high security cell. Dr. Hannibal Lector (Hopkins) is also a brilliant psychiatrist and a master of manipulation. Hannibal knows Bill, but is fascinated with Starling and messes with her mind while she tries to get inside his. A magnificent, terrifying thriller. See MANHUNTER.

A: Jodie Foster, Anthony Hopkins, Scott Glenn, Ted Levine, Anthony Heald, Brooke Smith

© ORION PICTURES CORPORATION 8767

SINGLE WHITE FEMALE

D: Barbet Schroeder 107 m

R | SUS | 1992 | COLOR | Sex | Nud | Viol | Lang | AdSit

7 Earnest psychological thriller. Bridget Fonda is pretty, has her own start-up computer software business and a big apartment. But when she hears that her boyfriend (Steven Weber) has cheated on her with his ex-wife, she runs an ad for a new roommate. Jennifer Jason Leigh appears to be the perfect match. However, Jennifer turns out to be very possessive of her and will go to great links to save their relationship. So when Fonda and Weber get back together and ask her to move out, Jennier comes unglued. Lots of gratuitous nudity and sex, and a predictable plot - but also some genuine creepiness and excitement.

A: Bridget Fonda, Jennifer Jason Leigh, Steven Weber, Peter Friedman, Stephen Tobolowsky

© COLUMBIA TRISTAR HOME VIDEO 51433

SISTERS

D: Brian De Palma 92 m

R | SUS HOR | 1973 | COLOR | Sex | Nud | Viol | Lang | AdSit

7 A hair-raising psychological thriller in the Hitchcock tradition! A pair of identical Siamese twins (Margot Kidder) are surgically separated as teenagers. One twin makes it out of the operation with her sanity intact and is gentle and kind, but the other becomes a homicidal maniac. The trouble is, you see, you never really know which is which. Peering from a bedroom window, a newspaper reporter (Jennifer Salt) witnesses the brutal stabbing of a talk show host, but not the killer. The police don't believe her, so she hires a private detective (Durning). Together they seek to expose the killer and also uncover the nightmare of the sisters. Intense suspense.

A: Margot Kidder, Jennifer Salt, Charles Durning, Barnard Hughes, William Finley, Mary Davenport

© WARNER HOME VIDEO 26002

SLEEPING WITH THE ENEMY

D: Joseph Ruben 99 m

R | SUS ROM | 1991 | COLOR | Sex | Nud | Viol | Lang | AdSit

7 Julia Roberts is trapped in a marriage to a very wealthy but compulsive, jealous and abusive husband (Bergin). She fears for her life and has no hope of ever being free of his violent mood swings. However, one fateful night, she seizes an opportunity to fake her own drowning and escapes into the Midwest to begin a new life in hiding. Cautious at first, she slowly ventures out into a semblance of normalcy and a new love, but Bergin discovers her secret and comes to seek her out - and to kill her. Entertaining, with some good chills.

A: Julia Roberts, Patrick Bergin, Kevin Anderson, Elizabeth Lawrence, Kyle Secor, Claudette Nevins

© FOXVIDEO 1871

SLEUTH

D: Joseph L. Mankiewicz 139 m

PG | SUS MYS COM | 1968 | COLOR | Sex | Nud | Viol | Lang | AdSit

9 A delicious and winning film that is made even better by some really superb talent! Caine and Olivier play a masterful cat-and-mouse game, each trying to outsmart and outdo the other. Caine has had an affair with Olivier's wife. So, Olivier devises a clever plot to get even by trying to trick Caine into getting caught committing a crime. However, Caine figures out Olivier's plan and turns the table on Olivier, enacting his own kind of revenge. This totally unpredictable and inventive plot takes some terrific sharp turns that will leave you guessing! Both Olivier and Caine were Oscar-nominated.

A: Laurence Olivier, Michael Caine, Alec Cawthorne, Margo Channing, John Mathews, Teddy Martin

© VIDEO TREASURES SV9069

SLIVER

D: Phillip Noyce 106 m

R | SUS | 1993 | COLOR | Sex | Nud | Viol | Lang | AdSit

6 Trashy but mildly involving soft-porn/suspense film. Sharon Stone is a newly divorced editor who moves into a tall thin luxury New York highrise (sliver). She is a look-alike to the woman who had occupied her apartment before her and who had fallen to her death - and there were other deaths. Stone is immediately pursued by both author Berenger and building owner Baldwin. Baldwin successfully seduces Stone, but Berenger strikes back with suggestions that Baldwin is a killer. Stone then learns that Baldwin has a big secret - all of the apartments in the highrise have been equipped with hidden cameras and he spies on everyone.

A: Sharon Stone, William Baldwin, Tom Berenger, Martin Landau, Nina Foch, Polly Walker

© PARAMOUNT HOME VIDEO 32722

SNEAKERS

D: Phil Alden Robinson 125 m

PG-13 | SUS COM ACT | 1992 | COLOR | Sex | Nud | Viol | Lang | AdSit

7 Entertaining caper. Redford and his group are very good thieves. They are hired by businesses to test for weaknesses in security systems by actually breaking in without getting caught. Then Redford is blackmailed by two CIA-types into having his team of misfits steal a black box from a brilliant inventor which contains the technology to decode any computer code in the world - a box many people would gladly kill for. Redford's team is made up of Poitier as an ex-CIA man and Aykroyd as an electronics specialist who sees conspiracies everywhere. Sometimes exciting, with several amusing moments.

A: Robert Redford, Sidney Poitier, Dan Aykroyd, River Phoenix, David Strathairn, Mary McDonnell

© MCA/UNIVERSAL HOME VIDEO, INC. 81282

SOMEBODY HAS TO SHOOT THE PICTURE

D: Frank Pierson 104 m

R | SUS DMA | 1990 | COLOR | Sex | Nud | Viol | Lang | AdSit

8 Gripping made-for-cable TV movie. Scheider plays a burned-out, Pulitzer Prize-winning photojournalist who is hired by a small-time druglord (Howard) who was convicted of shooting a police officer seven years before. Now on death row and facing execution, Howard wants someone to film his last seconds. During one of the inevitable delays which frequent the capital punishment process, Scheider uncovers some evidence that may prove that his man is innocent. Then, he and the victim's own widow rush to prove the man's innocence in time to save him. Grabs you early and never lets go. Probably too intense for younger viewers.

A: Roy Scheider, Bonnie Bedelia, Arliss Howard, Robert Carradine, Andre Braugher

© MCA/UNIVERSAL HOME VIDEO, INC. 81038

SOMEONE TO WATCH OVER ME

D: Ridley Scott 106 m

R | SUS CRM ROM | 1987 | COLOR | Sex | Nud | Viol | Lang | AdSit

8 Brightly polished thriller! An incredibly beautiful and rich member of the New York's social elite (Rogers) witnesses a gruesome murder that was committed by the mob. She escapes by the skin of her teeth, but is now being stalked by the ruthless killer (Katsulas). Berenger is a happily married cop who is assigned to protect her around the clock. In spite of themselves, the pair begin a passionate affair. When the killer is unsuccessful at nabbing Rogers directly, he kidnaps Berenger's wife and kids to hold hostage. Berenger is being forced to choose between them. A visually stunning, heart-stopping and atmospheric suspensor!

A: Tom Berenger, Mimi Rogers, Lorraine Bracco, Jerry Orbach, John Rubinstein, Andreas Katsulas

© COLUMBIA TRISTAR HOME VIDEO 60877

SOMETHING FOR EVERYONE

D: Harold Prince 112 m

R | COM SUS | 1970 | COLOR

Sex / Nud / Viol / Lang / AdSit

6 Angela Lansbury is the head of a previously wealthy German family just after WWII. The answer to her prayers appears to be a dynamic young man (York) who wants her to hire him as their footman. It seems he can do anything. But almost immediately, he begins an affair with her homosexual son and at the same time marries a beautiful young woman. York will go to any lengths to further his social standing. He has no morality or social conscience. This is a very well done and interesting black comedy with a twist ending, but the unattractive characters will leave some cold.

A: Angela Lansbury, Michael York, John Gill, Anthony Corlan

© CBS/FOX VIDEO 7174

SOMETHING WILD

D: Jonathan Demme 113 m

R | COM SUS | 1986 | COLOR

Sex / Nud / Viol / Lang / AdSit

7 An offbeat roller coaster ride full of comedy, fun, thrills and violence. A burned-out '80s accountant (Daniels) is looking for something to spice up his life and he finds it in Lulu (Griffith). She is a sexy flirt who invites him into her life and bed. She leads him on a wild ride back to her home town to meet her mother and then to her high school reunion where they run headlong into her psychotic ex-con ex-husband (Liotta) who terrorizes them. What starts out very funny and sexy becomes an intense story full of twists and turns. The soundtrack is outstanding, the acting is solid, and the plot compelling.

A: Jeff Daniels, Melanie Griffith, Ray Liotta, Margaret Colin, Tracey Walter, Dana Preu

© HBO VIDEO 0001

SOUTHERN COMFORT

D: Walter Hill 105 m

R | ACT SUS | 1981 | COLOR

Sex / Nud / Viol / Lang / AdSit

6 Pretty good action flick. When nine National Guardsmen converge on the Louisiana swamps for a weekend of practice maneuvers, they make the fatal mistake of stealing some canoes that belong to the local Cajun boys and then making fun of them. They shouldn't have ought to have done that. Because when war breaks out, the Guardsmen are armed only with rifles loaded with blanks. Slowly but surely the Cajuns kill the Guardsmen one by one until only Carradine and Boothe are left to fight for their lives in the intense climax. Unnerving and intense.

A: Keith Carradine, Powers Boothe, T.K. Carter, Fred Ward, Franklyn Seals, Lewis Smith

© UNITED AMERICAN VIDEO CORP. 5300

SPEED

D: Jan De Bont 115 m

R | ACT SUS CRM | 1994 | COLOR

Sex / Nud / Viol / Lang / AdSit

9 Extremely high-octane film that was a huge summer hit and won two Oscars for Sound. Jack Traven is a member of the LA police SWAT team. When he and his partner break up the well-laid plans of a psychotic ex-cop named Howard Payne to extract money from the city, Howard decides to try again. And, this time he makes a personal challenge to Jack to beat him. This time he has placed a bomb on a city bus that becomes armed at 50 mph and will blow if the bus goes below 50. Jack makes it to the bus, but the bomb is armed and he is being helped by pretty passenger who is now driving. Electric and tense. Very well made. In spite of its implausibilites, you almost never doubt it. Great fun.

A: Keanu Reeves, Dennis Hopper, Sandra Bullock, Joe Morton, Jeff Daniels

© FOXVIDEO 8638

SPY WHO CAME IN FROM THE COLD, THE

D: Martin Ritt 110 m

NR | SUS MYS | 1966 | COLOR

Sex / Nud / Viol / Lang / AdSit

9 Intense realism sparks this espionage thriller taken from a brilliant John Le Carre novel. Richard Burton is a burned-out British intelligence agent who has been recalled from Berlin to become a principal element in a plot by the West to eliminate the head of East German counter-espionage. He is to romance a leftist London librarian, convincing her that he is an agent who wants to defect. This gains him entry into the East, but he soon finds that he has been deceived by his own people and is only one part of a more elaborate plan. Very realistic and gloomy.

A: Richard Burton, Claire Bloom, Oskar Werner, Sam Wanamaker, Peter Van Eyck, Cyril Cusack

© PARAMOUNT HOME VIDEO 6509

STAND, THE

D: Mark Garris 360 m

NR | SF SUS | 1994 | COLOR

Sex / Nud / Viol / Lang / AdSit

7 Stephen King's epic length novel has been turned into an epic-length (very long) TV movie. At a very high security government research laboratory in California, a lab experiment has gone very wrong. A bacterial agent intended for germ warfare is released and within a matter of days the world's entire population has been whittled down to only 1% of its former size. Emotionally scarred but relieved that the terror is finally over, groups of ragged survivors have begun to gather for survival. But it is only now, on the outskirts of Las Vegas, that the real battle, the battle between good and the ultimate evil, truly begins.

A: Gary Sinise, Molly Ringwald, Jamey Sheridan, Laura San Giacomo, Ruby Dee, Ossie Davis

© REPUBLIC PICTURES HOME VIDEO 5683

STAR WARS

D: George Lucas 124 m

PG | SF ACT SUS | 1977 | COLOR

Sex / Nud / Viol / Lang / AdSit

10 HUGE megahit and first of a trio of hits. Old-time Saturday matinee cliff-hanger intensity, Western shoot-`em-up action, mysticism, comedy, loveable characters and high tech wizardry - all set in a place long, long ago and far, far away. An ordinary boy, living with his adoptive parents on a remote farming colony, comes home to find them murdered by Imperial Stormtroopers. He soon also finds that he is not so ordinary and is launched into a mission to save the Universe. Won seven Oscars. Immensely entertaining. Followed by THE EMPIRE STRIKES BACK.

A: Carrie Fisher, Mark Hamill, Harrison Ford, Alec Guinness, Anthony Daniels, Peter Cushing

© FOXVIDEO 1130

STEPFATHER, THE

D: Joseph Ruben 89 m

R | SUS HOR | 1987 | COLOR

Sex / Nud / Viol / Lang / AdSit

8 A chilling story about a charming man with a great smile and who seemingly has a perfect family. But, when they disappoint him - he kills them. And, when no one catches him, he just settles in a new town and gets a new family. The stepfather (O'Quinn) is obsessed with setting up the ideal family and this time it's with Shelly Hack and teenager Jill Schoelen. He's so friendly that no one suspects him, but something doesn't feel right to Schoelen. She has him checked out and begins to suspect the awful truth. Now she's become a risk to dad. Touches of humor are interjected throughout that provide an escape from the madness.

A: Terry O'Quinn, Jill Schoelen, Shelley Hack

© NEW LINE HOME VIDEO 7567

STILL OF THE NIGHT

D: Robert Benton 91 m

PG | SUS MYS ROM | 1982 | COLOR

Sex / Nud / Viol / Lang / AdSit

8 Well-crafted thriller in the Hitchcock tradition. One of psychiatrist Scheider's patients, an antique dealer, is viciously murdered in Jack The Ripper fashion. Now into his life walks the guy's mistress (Streep), an alluring but neurotic art curator. Scheider falls in love with Streep, in spite of his psychiatrist-mother's (Tandy) warnings to the contrary. Soon Scheider wonders if Streep is the killer and after him next. Solid suspense vehicle, in spite of some plot holes, that will keep you guessing and in suspense right up to the end.

A: Roy Scheider, Meryl Streep, Jessica Tandy, Joe Grifasi, Sara Botsford, Josef Sommer

Distributed By MGM/UA Home Video M301411

STING, THE

D: George Roy Hill 129 m

PG | SUS COM | 1973 | COLOR

Sex / Nud / Viol / Lang / AdSit

10 Very popular and hugely entertaining reteaming of the winning duo from BUTCH CASSIDY AND THE SUNDANCE KID, and the winner of 7 Oscars - including Best Picture. After his partner and friend is killed by a NYC hood (Shaw), a small-time con man Redford enlists Newman's help in a big-time scheme to take the guy down, hard. Very talented cast. A clever and intricate plot keeps moving and keeps you guessing and second-guessing. You know there's a con being worked, but you don't ever really know how or who. A very lively Scott Joplin ragtime score from Marvin Hamlisch adds to the fun.

A: Paul Newman, Robert Redford, Robert Shaw, Eileen Brennan, Charles Durning, Ray Walston

© MCA/UNIVERSAL HOME VIDEO, INC. 66009

STORYVILLE

D: Mark Frost 112 m

R | MYS SUS | 1992 | COLOR

Sex / Nud / Viol / Lang / AdSit

7 Fairly intriguing and involving mystery. Cray Fowler (Spader) is the privileged son of a powerful family in Louisiana. He is running for congress, but is videotaped in a moment's indiscretion with a beautiful girl. Threatened with blackmail, he unsuccessfully confronts the blackmailer and wakes up to find the man now mysteriously dead. In the course of investigating what happened, he discovers even greater secrets, which killed his father and now threaten to destroy him and his family. At first the film is only mildly interesting but the intricacies evolve to capture your attention and hold it.

A: James Spader, Joanne Whalley-Kilmer, Jason Robards, Jr., Charlotte Lewis, Michael Warren, Piper Laurie

© COLUMBIA TRISTAR HOME VIDEO 92903

STRANGER, THE

D: Adolfo Aristarain 93 m

R | SUS MYS | 1987 | COLOR

Sex / Nud / Viol / Lang / AdSit

7 A fast-paced shocker! The victim (Bedelia) of a very bad car accident is so traumatized that she loses all memory. She seeks help with a noted psychologist (Riegert), who helps her put the pieces together. Slowly she comes to realize that she saw not just one, but a number of brutal murders. The police can't find any evidence that the crimes were ever even committed, but the killers are after her now. The only way she can survive is if she can remember the killer's faces before they find her. Her doctor is helping her, or is he? Filmed in Buenos Aires, this is a nerve-racking suspensor.

A: Bonnie Bedelia, Peter Riegert, David Spielberg, Barry Primus, Marcos Woinski

© COLUMBIA TRISTAR HOME VIDEO 60928

STRANGER AMONG US, A

D: Sidney Lumet 109 m

PG-13 | SUS ACT | 1992 | COLOR

6 Melanie Griffith puts in a credible performance as a tough New York policewoman. Because she believes the murder and robbery of a jewelry dealer was an inside job, she goes undercover. For this to work, she first must shed her toughcop persona in order to blend into Brooklyn's ultra-religious Hasidic Jews. This one begins with an intriguing premise and contains some good action scenes but is the plot is ultimately a pretty big reach.

Sex Nud Viol Lang AdSit

A: Melanie Griffith, Eric Thal, John Pankow, Tracy Pollan, Lee Richardson, Mia Sara

© HOLLYWOOD PICTURES HOME VIDEO 1480

STREET SMART

D: Jerry Schatzberg 97 m

R | CRM SUS | 1987 | COLOR

6 Corruption, greed and murder meld together in this taut crime drama. Reeve is an unscrupulous magazine reporter in need of a sensational story. So he concocts a front-page story about a New York pimp living high on the hog. When a real-life pimp named Fast Black (Freeman), who resembles the man in the story, is implicated in a murder, Reeve's secure world is threatened. Freeman desperately needs an alibi and Reeve is it. Suddenly, he is embroiled in a murder case and in deep trouble, but he gets help from one of Fast Black's hookers (Baker).

Sex Nud Viol Lang AdSit

A: Christopher Reeve, Morgan Freeman, Mimi Rogers, Kathy Baker, Jay Patterson, Andre Gregory

© CANNON VIDEO M930

STUNTMAN, THE

D: Richard Rush 130 m

R | SUS COM ACT | 1980 | COLOR

9 An uncommon black comedy with spirit! When Vietnam vet Railsback ventures onto a movie set and inadvertently causes the death of the top stuntman, Director O'Toole agrees to hide him from police. But Railsback must replace the dead stuntman. Railsback trains rigorously under O'Toole, who turns out to be a slightly sadistic coach. Then he uncovers the fact that O'Toole is planning to stage a stunt that will kill him. Slightly offbeat and frequently funny, the movie covers a lot of ground and has several twists. But if you stay with it, you will be rewarded.

Sex Nud Viol Lang AdSit

A: Peter O'Toole, Steve Railsback, Barbara Hershey, Alex Rocco, Chuck Bail, Alan Goorwitz

© FOXVIDEO 1110

SUSPECT

D: Peter Yates 101 m

R | SUS CRM | 1987 | COLOR

8 Highly entertaining. Cher has a seemingly impossible task at hand. As a public defender, she has been assigned to prove a deaf and mute, homeless Vietnam vet (Neeson) is innocent of a grisly crime. She finds some unexpected help when one of the jurors (Quaid) contacts her directly. This is highly improper and puts her career in jeopardy, but he has evidence that is so compelling and dangerous that there is no choice but to work with him. Their job is made even more difficult by the stubborn judge, a corrupt senator and a prosecutor with an attitude. Stellar performances all around.

Sex Nud Viol Lang AdSit

A: Dennis Quaid, Cher, Liam Neeson, John Mahoney, Joe Mantegna, Philip Bosco

© COLUMBIA TRISTAR HOME VIDEO 67002

TAKING OF PELHAM ONE TWO THREE, THE

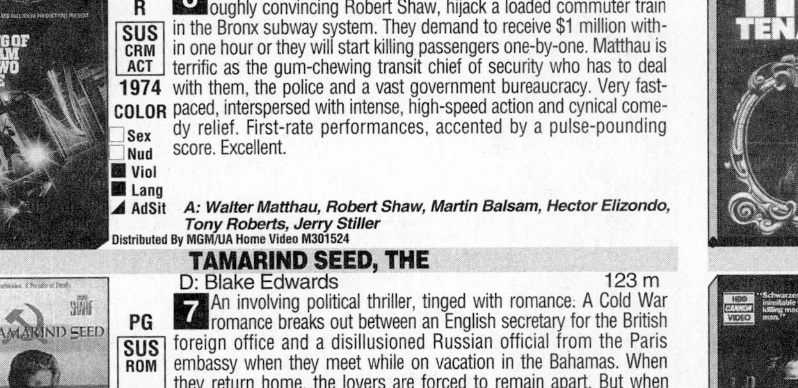

D: Joseph Sargent 115 m

R | SUS CRM ACT | 1974 | COLOR

8 Outstanding action thriller. Four ruthless terrorists, led by a thoroughly convincing Robert Shaw, hijack a loaded commuter train in the Bronx subway system. They demand to receive $1 million within one hour or they will start killing passengers one-by-one. Matthau is terrific as the gum-chewing transit chief of security who has to deal with them, the police and a vast government bureaucracy. Very fast-paced, interspersed with intense, high-speed action and cynical comedy relief. First-rate performances, accented by a pulse-pounding score. Excellent.

Sex Nud Viol Lang AdSit

A: Walter Matthau, Robert Shaw, Martin Balsam, Hector Elizondo, Tony Roberts, Jerry Stiller

Distributed By MGM/UA Home Video M301524

TAMARIND SEED, THE

D: Blake Edwards 123 m

PG | SUS ROM | 1974 | COLOR

7 An involving political thriller, tinged with romance. A Cold War romance breaks out between an English secretary for the British foreign office and a disillusioned Russian official from the Paris embassy when they meet while on vacation in the Bahamas. When they return home, the lovers are forced to remain apart. But when Sharif finds he is about to be called back to Moscow and may be in trouble, he decides it's time to trade his knowledge for freedom in the West with her. But a high-placed British politician is also a Russian spy. This is a solid spy thriller, but it serves equally well as a good romancer.

Sex Nud Viol Lang AdSit

A: Julie Andrews, Omar Sharif, Anthony Quayle, Sylvia Sims, Dan O'Herlihy, Oscar Homolka

© LIVE HOME VIDEO 51120

TARGET

D: Arthur Penn 117 m

R | ACT SUS | 1985 | COLOR

8 Good action adventure flick that overcomes some minor plot faults to deliver up an exciting experience. Dallas lumberyard owner Gene Hackman doesn't want to go to Europe for a vacation. So his wife (Hunnicutt) goes alone, hoping that he and their son (Dillon) will learn to get along in her absence. Then word comes that she has been kidnapped in Paris. He and the son fly to Paris, where assassins immediately attempt to kill him. For the first time, he reveals to his dumb-struck son that this boring, conservative old man is an ex-CIA agent, an expert in killing and surviving.

Sex Nud Viol Lang AdSit

A: Gene Hackman, Matt Dillon, Gayle Hunnicutt, Victoria Fyodorova, Josef Sommer, Guy Boyd

© CBS/FOX VIDEO 7097

TARGETS

D: Peter Bogdanovich 90 m

PG | SUS CRM | 1968 | COLOR

8 Chilling debut for director Peter Bogdanovich. This film has a dual plotline which comes together only at the end. An aging actor in horror movies (Karloff) decides to retire rather than compete with the horrors occurring every day in the real world; and a seemingly normal Vietnam veteran (O'Kelly) loses control and murders his family. Later O'Kelly stations himself high in the screen of a drive-in movie theater and begins to take random shots at the patrons - one of whom is Karloff, there on a promotion stint. Intense suspense builds at the rousing conclusion.

Sex Nud Viol Lang AdSit

A: Boris Karloff, Tim O'Kelly, Randy Quaid, Nancy Hsueh, James Brown, Arthur Peterson

© PARAMOUNT HOME VIDEO 6824

TELEFON

D: Don Siegel 102 m

PG | ACT SUS | 1977 | COLOR

8 Engrossing (even though improbable) and thrilling action adventure in which a crack KGB agent (Bronson) is sent to the USA to stop a Stalinist renegade agent from activating a series of previously planted KGB operatives. These operatives have been hypnotized and preprogrammed to begin a campaign of sabotage against American military bases. Bronson's job is to stop them before they start and so prevent the outbreak of WWIII. Assigned to help him is local KGB contact Lee Remick who is actually a CIA double agent. Very well-done espionage thriller.

Sex Nud Viol Lang AdSit

A: Charles Bronson, Lee Remick, Donald Pleasence, Tyne Daly, Patrick Magee, Sheree North

Distributed By MGM/UA Home Video M700127

TEMP, THE

D: Tom Holland 99 m

R | MYS SUS | 1993 | COLOR

6 Timothy Hutton is a middle executive at a cookie company. Lara Flynn Boyle begins as a temporary assistant for him and is very dedicated to him, maybe too dedicated. At first she is a perfect secretary, even giving him ideas and letting him take full credit for them. However, soon his competition for advancement at the office literally begins to die off and Lara starts moving up the ladder too. Someone is definitely playing hardball corporate politics... but, is it the temp? An interesting premise (although it has been well worked before) provides mildly interesting watching. Too many clues and red herrings get tiring after a while.

Sex Nud Viol Lang AdSit

A: Timothy Hutton, Lara Flynn Boyle, Dwight Schultz, Oliver Platt, Faye Dunaway, Steven Weber

© PARAMOUNT HOME VIDEO 32793

TENANT, THE

D: Roman Polanski 126 m

R | SUS HOR | 1976 | COLOR

8 Very unique and unusual film. Polanski cast himself as a timid Polish clerk who rents a flat in a seedy Parisian apartment building. The previous tenant, a young girl, committed suicide by leaping to her death. He has great difficulty interacting with his neighbors. Gradually, he begins to lose his grip on reality and begins to fear that the people in the building are also trying to drive him into suicide too. Bizarrely fascinating and darkly comic, but this is a film about burgeoning madness and is not at all a typical horror film, yet in many ways it is more creepy.

Sex Nud Viol Lang AdSit

A: Isabelle Adjani, Melvin Douglas, Jo Van Fleet, Bernard Fresson, Shelley Winters

© PARAMOUNT HOME VIDEO 8676

TERMINATOR, THE

D: James Cameron 108 m

R | ACT SUS SF | 1984 | COLOR

10 A huge blockbuster hit that gained notoriety because of its extremely high intensity. Schwarzenneger, a cyborg (a lifelike robot), is sent back from the future to kill the mother (Hamilton) of a boy who is not yet born but who will later become a rebel leader. Arnold is an incredibly relentless and nearly indestructible killing machine from whom there is no escape. However, also arriving from the future is a resistance fighter (Biehn) who is0 here to help Hamilton defeat the Terminator. Terrific non-stop action flick, great special effects, believable and sympathetic characters and incredible pacing.

Sex Nud Viol Lang AdSit

A: Arnold Schwarzenegger, Michael Biehn, Linda Hamilton, Paul Winfield, Lance Henriksen, Rick Rossovich

© HBO VIDEO 2535

THING, THE

D: John Carpenter 109 m

R | HOR SF SUS | 1982 | COLOR

7 The 1951 classic has been remade. However, it would be more accurate to say that this is more of a sequel. This version, however, is not for the little kiddies - it is filled with gore. Where the original relied upon your imagination to create fear, this version gives you a series of state-of-the-art gory special effects. Kurt Russell and his people arrive at the remote arctic station just after an alien creature, which had been defrosted after having been frozen for years, has depleted the supply of live bodies. This new crew will soon be his new supply. This is scary and fun, but check out the original, too. It is, in many ways, better.

Sex Nud Viol Lang AdSit

A: Kurt Russell, Wilford Brimley, Richard Dysart, Richard Masur, T.K. Carter, Richard Dysart

© MCA/UNIVERSAL HOME VIDEO, INC. 77009

THOMAS CROWN AFFAIR, THE

D: Norman Jewison 102 m

R | SUS ROM ACT | 1968 | COLOR

8 Stylish combination of a heist movie and a sophisticated romancer. Faye Dunaway is an unscrupulous insurance investigator hot on the trail of a bored millionaire (McQueen) who enjoys staging elaborate burglaries just for the thrill of it. Even as they play coy cat and mouse games and engage in clever and cryptic dialogue, he is plotting a daring bank heist that is to be carried off right under her nose. The emotional and mental games they play with each other inevitably lead to romance. Oscar for best song: "Windmills of Your Mind." Good entertainment.

Sex Nud Viol Lang AdSit

A: Steve McQueen, Faye Dunaway, Paul Burke, Yaphet Kotto, Jack Weston, Biff McGuire

Distributed By MGM/UA Home Video M201260

THREE DAYS OF THE CONDOR

D: Sydney Pollack 118 m

R | SUS MYS ACT | 1975 | COLOR

9 Riveting spy suspensor. Very well done. Redford is an insignificant CIA researcher (he reads foreign novels to get espionage ideas) at a storefront office in NYC. One day, however, he happens to run an errand and comes back to the office to find that everyone in it has been slaughtered and he is a hunted man. He doesn't know who, he doesn't know why, and he can trust no one until he finds out. Having nowhere to hide, he forces his way into a lonely stranger's (Dunaway) apartment. At first she is terrified, but she begins to believe in him and an uneasy love affair blossoms. Thoroughly engrossing.

Sex Nud Viol Lang AdSit

A: Robert Redford, Faye Dunaway, Cliff Robertson, Max von Sydow, John Houseman

© PARAMOUNT HOME VIDEO 8803

TO LIVE AND DIE IN L.A.

D: William Friedkin 114 m

R | ACT SUS CRM | 1985 | COLOR

8 High intensity action fare that is both riveting and disturbing. Secret Service Agent Petersen becomes obsessed with getting master counterfeiter Willem Dafoe, who had caused the death of his partner. A very cynical and violent film in which the good guys are only just a little better than the bad guys. The characters are complex and the story is loaded with a lot of twists and exciting action sequences. The problem that arises is that it becomes very difficult to determine which side to sympathize with or to even care about anyone at all.

Sex Nud Viol Lang AdSit

A: William L. Petersen, Willem Dafoe, John Pankow, Dean Stockwell, John Turturro

© LIVE HOME VIDEO VA5123

TOO LATE THE HERO

D: Robert Aldrich 132 m

PG | ACT WAR SUS | 1969 | COLOR

8 Good WWII action flick. A reluctant American is assigned to a unit of reluctant British commandos, who are to destroy the Japanese radio installation on the other end of their island in preparation for a major naval action. On their return, they discover a clandestine airfield and must get word of it back. Over the course of their mission, all but two are killed: the American (Robertson) and one Brit (Caine) - and they don't like each other. However, if they are going to survive, they have to cooperate to win an intense battle of wits and wills with the Japanese commandant who is intent upon hunting them down and killing them. Taut, fast-paced, action-packed thriller.

Sex Nud Viol Lang AdSit

A: Michael Caine, Cliff Robertson, Ian Bannen, Henry Fonda, Harry Andrews

© CBS/FOX VIDEO 8034

TOUCH OF EVIL

D: Orson Welles 108 m

NR | CRM SUS ACT | 1958 | B&W

9 A seriously underrated film from Orson Welles - who wrote, directed and starred in it - that is essentially a fascinating character study. When a powerful American and his mistress are blown up at a Mexican border town, Welles, a corrupt American sheriff, blames the murder on a young Mexican and plants evidence on him to insure conviction. An honest Mexican cop (Heston) disputes the claim, so Welles frames Heston's American wife (Leigh) with murder and drugs and terrorizes her. Very famous three-minute continuous shot at beginning.

Sex Nud Viol Lang AdSit

A: Charlton Heston, Janet Leigh, Orson Welles, Joseph Calleia, Akim Tamiroff, Marlene Dietrich

© MCA/UNIVERSAL HOME VIDEO, INC. 55078

TOWERING INFERNO

D: Irwin Allen, John Guillermin 165 m

PG | SUS ACT | 1974 | COLOR

8 First there was a crippled airliner (AIRPORT), then a capsized ship (THE POSEIDON ADVENTURE) and here there is a 150-story high-rise on fire. This was one of the biggest of the disaster flicks that were popular during the early 1970s. During the dedication ceremony of a new San Francisco hotel and office skyscraper that the developer had cut corners on, a fire breaks out, trapping people on the upper floors. Huge cast of blockbuster stars helps to carry this OK drama that is considerably spiced up with spectacular pyrotechnic special effects. 7 nominations, 2 Oscars.

Sex Nud Viol Lang AdSit

A: Steve McQueen, Paul Newman, William Holden, Faye Dunaway, Fred Astaire, Richard Chamberlain

© FOXVIDEO 1071

TRAIN, THE

D: John Frankenheimer 133 m

NR | ACT SUS WAR | 1965 | B&W

9 Top-notch gripping action film set in France just as WWII is starting to turn for the Allies. Burt Lancaster is the head of the French railway system and is also in the underground movement. Paul Scofield is a driven German officer in charge of getting a train load of French art treasures, stolen from French museums, back to Germany. Lancaster is reluctant to risk lives for art until an old man he loves is killed by the Nazis as he trys to stop the train. Excellent, solid suspense. Fast moving, with a clever plot and good special effects. Based on a true story.

Sex Nud Viol Lang AdSit

A: Burt Lancaster, Paul Scofield, Michel Simon, Albert Remy, Wolfgang Preiss

Distributed By MGM/UA Home Video 202511

TRUE BELIEVER

D: Joseph Ruben 103 m

R | CRM SUS | 1989 | COLOR

8 Taut and fierce - a fast ride! A powerful attorney (Woods), once a crusading idealist in the '60s, is now a wealthy but cynical defender of drug dealers. His assistant (Downey) worships him and, in an effort to revitalize him, convinces him to take on an almost impossible case - get a convicted killer who was framed out of prison. Reluctantly at first, Woods takes the case. He finds himself up to his neck in corrupt cops and politicians, but he also rediscovers a passion for his work once again. Highly entertaining build-up to a powerful conclusion that will take you by surprise.

Sex Nud Viol Lang AdSit

A: James Woods, Robert Downey, Jr., Margaret Colin, Kurtwood Smith, Yuji Okumoto, Tom Bower

© COLUMBIA TRISTAR HOME VIDEO 65012

TWILIGHT ZONE: THE MOVIE

D: Joe Dante, John Landis 101 m

PG | SUS DMA FAN | 1983 | COLOR

7 Intriguing collection of four tales of the thought-provoking variety, made famous in the 1960s TV series of the same name. In fact, three of the episodes are remakes from that series. All are interesting and done with much higher production values, but oddly they lack the punch of the originals and overall are not as good - still worth a look, though. Example: "Nightmare at 20,000 Feet" - Lithgow is terrified because he is the only passenger on an airliner who can see the gremlin that is on the craft's wing working hard to rip it off.

Sex Nud Viol Lang AdSit

A: Dan Aykroyd, Albert Brooks, Scatman Crothers, John Lithgow, Vic Morrow, Kevin McCarthy

© WARNER HOME VIDEO 11314

UNDER SUSPICION

D: Simon Moore 100 m

R | SUS CRM | 1992 | COLOR

7 Well-made thriller from England. In 1959 England, divorces could only be obtained through proof of adultery. Neeson was a cop but now is a sleazy PI scraping up a living by setting up scenes of faked adultery to photograph for a fee - many times using his own wife. On one such escapade, he breaks into a room on que but finds his wife and her male companion have been shot dead. He becomes the chief suspect. With the help of an old friend, he struggles to prove himself innocent. But wait, the story's not that simple. Several neat twists keep you guessing. Even when you think it's over, it's not. Over-all, pretty good, but it does stretch credibility at times.

Sex Nud Viol Lang AdSit

A: Liam Neeson, Laura San Giacomo, Kenneth Cranham, Alphonsia Emmanuel, Maggie O'Neill, Martin Grace

© COLUMBIA TRISTAR HOME VIDEO 51133

UNTOUCHABLES, THE

D: Brian De Palma 119 m

R | CRM ACT SUS | 1987 | COLOR

10 Outstanding! Some great talent combines forces to create a captivating high-energy excitement adventure set in prohibition-era Chicago. Costner is Elliot Ness, a very intense straight-arrow federal agent who arrives in a corrupt town, intent upon "getting" Al Capone (De Niro). He quickly sets about finding a few good men for his private force - beginning with a tough street cop (Connery - Oscar winner). Also included is an idealistic rookie (Garcia) and a bookish agent (Smith). A well-woven, realistic tapestry of drama, intrigue, suspense and high-intensity action. Highly recommended.

Sex Nud Viol Lang AdSit

A: Kevin Costner, Sean Connery, Robert De Niro, Charles Martin Smith, Andy Garcia, Billy Drago

© PARAMOUNT HOME VIDEO 1886

VANISHING, THE

D: George Sluizer — 105 m

9 Icy thriller! This is a major league intellectual and psychological chiller. The terror here is not heavy-handed and obvious, but is more of the Hitchcock or the Edgar Allen Poe variety. Two young lovers are traveling when they run out of gas. He thoughtlessly leaves her behind, terrified and alone. She's furious but they make up and go to a rest area to play. She leaves to go to a store but she never returns. Haunted by her loss, he places posters all over requesting information. After three years, a seemingly genteel professor sends him a tantalizing note. Subtle, but deeply and profoundly shocking. Subtitles.

NR | FOR HOR SUS | 1991 | COLOR | Sex | Nud | Viol | Lang | AdSit

A: Gene Bervoets, Johanna Ter Steege, Bernard-Pierre Donnadieu

© FOX/LORBER HOME VIDEO 1037

VANISHING, THE

D: George Sluizer — 110 m

8 One of the most diabolical plots ever put on the screen was first done in Holland. It proved to be so successful that Hollywood redid it here, using the same director. The story concerns a young man (Sutherland) and his girlfriend (Bullock) who leave together to go on a trip. Midway into the trip, she just disappears without a trace at a roadside stop. Sutherland is consumed with finding her, but after three years, he would be satisfied to only know what happened. Jeff Bridges is a quirky chemistry professor who knows the answer and offers to show him. Not as good as the original but still plenty of sheer terror.

R | SUS HOR | 1993 | COLOR | Sex | Nud | Viol | Lang | AdSit

A: Kiefer Sutherland, Jeff Bridges, Sandra Bullock, Nancy Travis, Park Overall, Maggie Linderman

© FOXVIDEO 1997

VERTIGO

D: Alfred Hitchcock — 128 m

10 Intriguing psychological Hitchcock masterpiece. Stewart is a retired San Francisco police detective. An old friend hires him to follow his suicidal wife (Novak) and Stewart does rescue her from one attempted suicide. Soon he becomes intrigued with her and falls desperately in love, but she dies in a leap from a tower when he is unable to climb to stop her because of his extreme fear of heights. Later, he discovers a shop girl who very strongly resembles her and he attempts to remake this new girl exactly by dying her hair and taking her to the same places. Riveting, very dream-like thriller. Haunting.

PG | SUS MYS ROM | 1958 | COLOR | Sex | Nud | Viol | Lang | AdSit

A: James Stewart, Kim Novak, Barbara Bel Geddes, Tom Helmore, Ellen Corby, Henry Jones

© MCA/UNIVERSAL HOME VIDEO, INC. 80082

VICTIM

D: Basil Dearden — 100 m

8 Exhilarating English drama. Bogarde is a successful young lawyer, but he has a secret. When his homosexual lover (McEnery) approaches Bogarde to defend him from phony robbery charges, Bogarde refuses fearing that he may become blackmailed. Then McEnery is found murdered, himself a victim of blackmail. But before he died, he had destroyed any evidence that might have implicated Bogarde with him. Now Bogard feels compelled to go after the murderers, even if it means risking his career, his marriage and his life. A stunning thriller that deftly deals with homosexuality.

NR | SUS DMA | 1961 | B&W | Sex | Nud | Viol | Lang | AdSit

A: Dirk Bogarde, Sylvia Sims, Dennis Price, John Barrie, Peter McEnery, Donald Churchill

© NEW LINE HOME VIDEO 6134

WAIT UNTIL DARK

D: Terence Young — 108 m

9 Tense nail-biter for which Hepburn earned an Academy nomination. Her husband (Zimbalist) is tricked into bringing home a doll which he gives to his recently blinded wife. However, both are unaware that the doll contains heroin. Zimbalist is then lured away from the apartment so that psychotic Arkin and his two henchman Crenna and Weston can get the drugs back. But the trio get more than they bargained for when blind Hepburn turns out the lights... they are on equal footing in the dark. Still, Arkin is a ruthless killer. Riveting and gripping suspense made this into a very popular film.

NR | SUS ACT | 1967 | COLOR | Sex | Nud | Viol | Lang | AdSit

A: Audrey Hepburn, Alan Arkin, Efrem Zimbalist, Jr., Jack Weston, Richard Crenna, Samantha Jones

© WARNER HOME VIDEO 11080

WARGAMES

D: John Badham — 114 m

8 This is an entertaining film for the whole family. A bored teenage computer whiz (Broderick) and his girlfriend (Sheedy) think they've gained access to a new, unreleased computer game called "Global Thermonuclear Warfare" from a game manufacturer. What they really did was to break into the Pentagon's computers. Their game is no game. The entire nation has been placed on nuclear alert and the world on the brink of the ultimate war. Broderick is sought by the government people, who are led by Dabney Coleman, who must stop what he has started. Very entertaining and convincingly done. Not just for kids.

PG | SUS | 1983 | COLOR | Sex | Nud | Viol | Lang | AdSit

A: Matthew Broderick, Dabney Coleman, Ally Sheedy, Barry Corbin, John Wood, Juanin Clay

Distributed By MGM/UA Home Video M200293

WHAT EVER HAPPEND TO BABY JANE?

D: Robert Aldrich — 134 m

8 A truly scary journey into strange minds. This is a character profile of two perverse and rivalrous personalities which are masterfully portrayed by two screen legends. Bette Davis is Baby Jane. She is a child star from the silent era who never made it in talking pictures. Joan Crawford is her sister who did, but she was mysteriously crippled in a car accident and has been an invalid for 30 years. For 30 years Davis has taken care of her sister and tormented her. When Crawford announces she is going to sell the house, Davis really goes off her rocker and reverts to her childhood. A masterpiece of terror. A big hit.

NR | SUS HOR | 1962 | B&W | Sex | Nud | Viol | Lang | AdSit

A: Bette Davis, Joan Crawford, Victor Buono, Anna Lee, Marjorie Bennett

© WARNER HOME VIDEO 11051

WHEN A STRANGER CALLS

D: Fred Walton — 97 m

8 A genuinely scary thriller. A teenage baby sitter (Carol Kane) is terrorized by a mysterious phone caller. Police detective Durning traces the calls and discovers that the man (Beckley) is already inside the house. He captures the invader but not before he has killed the children in the house. The murderous intruder is sent away, but seven years later he escapes and he has come back to torment Kane again. This time she has kids of her own and she is terrified. Kane again calls Durning who is now a private detective to help her again. This is a very high intensity suspense film for the first part, but it lets down some near the end. Still, it is a real shocker.

R | SUS HOR | 1979 | COLOR | Sex | Nud | Viol | Lang | AdSit

A: Charles Durning, Carol Kane, Colleen Dewhurst, Tony Beckley, Rachel Roberts, Ron O'Neal

© COLUMBIA TRISTAR HOME VIDEO 60115

WHISPERS IN THE DARK

D: Crowe Christopher — 103 m

7 Supersexy murder mystery. A beautiful patient (Unger) reports her vivid and provocative sexual encounters with bondage to her female psychiatrist (Sciorra). Sciorra is distressed to learn her own new boyfriend (Sheridan) knows Unger. Is he the man of her torrid stories? ...or is it another of her patients, one who was just released from prison for torturing women? That question becomes critical when Unger is found hanging bound, naked and very dead. Good plot twists and effective murder mystery despite some flaws, but the overt sexuality will diminish it for many.

R | SUS MYS CRM | 1992 | COLOR | Sex | Nud | Viol | Lang | AdSit

A: Annabella Sciorra, Jamey Sheridan, Deborah Unger, Alan Alda, Anthony Lapaglia, Jill Clayburgh

© PARAMOUNT HOME VIDEO 32756

WHISTLE BLOWER, THE

D: Simon Langton — 99 m

8 A taut political mystery thriller. A Russian translator for a British spy agency mysteriously falls to his death just as he was to have an interview with a journalist. His salesman father (Caine), a former intelligence officer, begins his own investigation into his son's death. As a scandal begins to unfold itself, there are even more suspicious deaths. This once-trusting, patriotic man now has severe doubts about his own government. This is an intelligent story of intrigue, but also an exploration of the failings of the English class system. It works on all levels.

PG | SUS MYS | 1987 | COLOR | Sex | Nud | Viol | Lang | AdSit

A: Michael Caine, James Fox, Nigel Havers, Felicity Dean, John Gielgud

© NEW LINE HOME VIDEO 7665

WHITE NIGHTS

D: Taylor Hackford — 135 m

8 Quite good. A famous Russian ballet dancer (Baryshnikov) who defected to America, finds himself captured again when the airplane on which he is traveling must make an emergency landing in the USSR. Hines is a privately remorseful American Army deserter and dancer who is charged by the KGB with keeping Baryshnikov from returning again to the West. The love for dance and the desire for freedom they share bonds them in friendship and, together, they concoct an elaborate plan for escape. Gripping drama, good action and exciting dance sequences.

PG-13 | SUS ACT | 1985 | COLOR | Sex | Nud | Viol | Lang | AdSit

A: Mikhail Baryshnikov, Gregory Hines, Isabella Rossellini, Jerzy Skolimowski, Helen Mirren, Geraldine Page

© COLUMBIA TRISTAR HOME VIDEO 60611

WHITE OF THE EYE

D: Donald Cammell — 111 m

6 Bizarre little thriller. A psycho is loose in a small Arizona town. If you are beautiful and rich you are more likely to see him. That is unwelcome because he is torturing and then dissecting his female victims. David Keith is an audio expert unfaithfully married to an immigrant from New York. She is understandably upset because she and her daughter are getting threatening messages - and her husband is the chief suspect of head cop Evans. The interesting photography and ample twists hold your attention and keep you guessing all the way to the end. And, the ending will leave many unsettled.

R | SUS HOR | 1987 | COLOR | Sex | Nud | Viol | Lang | AdSit

A: David Keith, Cathy Moriarty, Art Evans, Alberta Watson

© PARAMOUNT HOME VIDEO 12670

WHO'LL STOP THE RAIN

D: Karel Reisz — 126 m

R | ACT SUS | 1978 | COLOR

8 Gripping and intense. A Vietnam veteran (Nolte) agrees to smuggle home some heroin for his buddy (Moriarity) who has a buyer for the stuff; but it's a set-up. A corrupt narcotics agent (Zerbe) and his partners are going to steal the dope and kill them all. Nolte shows up with the dope but heads out with Moriarity's addicted wife (Weld) when things go wrong. Moriarity is caught and tortured to reveal their whereabouts. They have fled through L.A. and to the mountains of New Mexico. Very intense and violent. There are no out-and-out good guys. Still an excellent and thoroughly spell-binding film.

Sex / Nud / Viol / Lang / AdSit

A: Nick Nolte, Tuesday Weld, Michael Moriarty, Anthony Zerbe, Richard Masur, Ray Sharkey

Distributed By MGM/UA Home Video M201306

WITHOUT A TRACE

D: Stanley R. Jaffee — 119 m

PG | DMA SUS | 1983 | COLOR

8 An extremely well-done and reality-based depiction of the trauma caused by the disappearance of a child. A mother gets her child up, dressed, sends him off to school, goes to work and then waits for him to get home after school - but he never comes. The police begin an intensive search and she launches herself into a door-to-door campaign - all of which results in nothing for months on end. This story is based upon a real incident in New York. It is a highly suspenseful tear-jerker that presents no easy solutions. Thought provoking.

Sex / Nud / Viol / Lang / AdSit

A: Kate Nelligan, Judd Hirsch, Stockard Channing, David Dukes, Danny Corkill

© FOXVIDEO 1235

WOLF

D: Mike Nichols — 125 m

R | SUS HOR | 1994 | COLOR

7 Senior book editor Jack Nicholson's car strikes a wolf on a lonely stretch of Vermont highway. As Jack attempts to move the animal out of the roadway he is bitten. Just days later, the area around the bite begins to grow hair and he also becomes aware that all his senses are now heightened. Formerly a non-aggressive type, he strikes back now with a vengeance when his job is given to his underhanded protege after their publishing house becomes the subject of a tycoon's takeover; and, Jack's passions become aroused by the man's beautiful but troubled daughter (Pfeiffer). Sophisticated storytelling where the werewolf's bite is only a key that unlocks its victim's true nature.

Sex / Nud / Viol / Lang / AdSit

A: Jack Nicholson, Michelle Pfeiffer, James Spader

© COLUMBIA TRISTAR HOME VIDEO 71153

WOLFEN

D: Michael Wadleigh — 114 m

R | HOR SUS | 1981 | COLOR

8 Effective surrealistic chiller with some really terrifying moments. Albert Finney is a NYC detective who sets out to penetrate the mystery surrounding a series of particularly gory and grisly murders that appear at first to have nothing in common. Aided by a psychologist (Venora) and a wry coroner (Hines), his search leads him to the discovery of a group of American Indians who control a pack of ancient, truly evil supernatural superwolves. Superior special effects and innovative camera work combine with some excellent acting to overcome some other minor shortcomings to make this a chilling experience.

Sex / Nud / Viol / Lang / AdSit

A: Albert Finney, Diane Venora, Edward James Olmos, Gregory Hines, Tom Noonan, Dick O'Neill

© WARNER HOME VIDEO 22019

WRONG MAN, THE

D: Alfred Hitchcock — 105 m

NR | SUS MYS CRM | 1956 | B&W

7 A harrowing and ultimately terrifying Hitchcock movie - because it is so believable, because it is based upon a true event and because it could happen to you, too. Henry Fonda plays a New York jazz musician who is confronted at his home by police, arrested, fingerprinted, jailed and tried for a series of crimes he didn't commit because there were eye witnesses who swore he was the culprit. And, before the look-alike crook is found, even his wife comes to believe he is guilty. She has a nervous breakdown and is institutionalized. Compelling but unnerving to watch.

Sex / Nud / Viol / Lang / AdSit

A: Henry Fonda, Vera Miles, Anthony Quayle, Harold J. Stone, Nehemiah Persoff, Esther Minciotti

© WARNER HOME VIDEO 11155

YAKUZA, THE

D: Sydney Pollack — 112 m

R | ACT SUS | 1975 | COLOR

9 Excellent, high intensity blending of bone-jarring action with a fascinating cultural exploration into the Yakuza, Japan's Mafia-like underworld which has deep roots in the ancient Samurai ways. When Brian Keith's daughter is kidnapped and held for ransom by the Yakuza, he realizes the only chance he has to get her back is Harry Kilmer (Mitchum). Kilmer is a good friend and an ex-GI who is familiar with Yakuza ways, and Kilmer enlists the help of an old Japanese enemy who owes him a big debt. Absolutely gripping, intriguing and solid excitement. Excellent. See also 1989's BLACK RAIN.

Sex / Nud / Viol / Lang / AdSit

A: Robert Mitchum, Takakura Ken, Brian Keith, Herb Edelman, Richard Jordan, Kishi Keiko

© WARNER HOME VIDEO 11397

YEAR OF LIVING DANGEROUSLY, THE

D: Peter Weir — 115 m

PG | DMA SUS ROM | 1983 | COLOR

8 Intriguing political drama which established Gibson as a serious actor and for which Linda Hunt won an Oscar playing a man. Set during the summer of 1965, Indonesia is falling apart and Jakarta is in turmoil as the dictator Sukarno is falling. Gibson is a young Australian reporter on his first major assignment who is introduced to a pretty British diplomat (Weaver) by a diminutive photographer (Hunt) and falls hard for her. Romance, danger and excitement combine when she tells him of a secret communist arms shipment and he has to decide between his job and betraying her. A gripping, winning drama.

Sex / Nud / Viol / Lang / AdSit

A: Mel Gibson, Sigourney Weaver, Linda Hunt, Michael Murphy

Distributed By MGM/UA Home Video M800243

Z

D: Constantine Costa-Gavras — 128 m

PG | FOR SUS DMA | 1969 | COLOR

9 Spellbinding and highly influential political thriller that was banned in several right-wing countries and which won the Oscar for Best Foreign Film. A conservative investigator of the supposed accidental death of a popular left-wing political activist discovers that, not only was it a murder and that the conservative government is covering up, but that the government played an active role in the murder. His decision to pursue the case may result in the downfall of the government. Based on an actual case in Greece in 1963.

Sex / Nud / Viol / Lang / AdSit

A: Yves Montand, Irene Papas, Jean-Louis Trintignant

© COLUMBIA TRISTAR HOME VIDEO 60266

ZULU

D: Cy Endfield — 138 m

NR | ACT SUS | 1964 | COLOR

8 Rousing adventure epic. This is the dramatization of an actual event which occurred on January 22, 1879. A small British garrison of 105 men, stationed at a remote outpost, learns that it is being approached by over 4000 Zulu warriors and that the only source of reinforcement, a force of 1200 men, has been totally wiped out. They are left alone, outnumbered 40-1, to withstand the onslaught. Refusing to abandon their post, they rally to victory. Well crafted, with massive and spectacular battle sequences. Excellent performances, including Caine in his first big role.

Sex / Nud / Viol / Lang / AdSit

A: Jack Hawkins, Stanley Baker, Michael Caine, James Booth, Ulla Jacobsson

© NEW LINE HOME VIDEO 90002

War

1956 and After

84 CHARLIE MOPIC

D: Patrick Duncan — 95 m

R | WAR DMA ACT | 1989 | COLOR

8 Compelling and unique Vietnam war movie. The terrors and hardships of a dangerous jungle reconnaissance mission are told solely through the eye of a camera that is hand-held by an Army combat cameraman. He has been sent along with a six-man patrol into the highlands in 1969 to capture the experience of war for a training film. This filming technique is at times bothersome, but on whole it also adds a strong sense of reality in depicting the personal life-and-death quality of what it was actually like to be in the ground war in Vietnam on a daily basis.

Sex / Nud / Viol / Lang / AdSit

A: Jonathan Emerson, Nicholas Cascone, Richard Brooks, Jasons Tomlins, Christopher Burgard, Glenn Marshower

© COLUMBIA TRISTAR HOME VIDEO 09943

ALL QUIET ON THE WESTERN FRONT

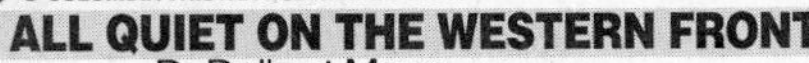

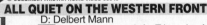

D: Delbert Mann — 131 m

NR | WAR DMA | 1978 | COLOR

9 Extremely strong made-for-TV remake of the 1930 classic. It is war in the mud as told from the German point of view. A young idealistic student-turned-soldier is caught up in the romance of the idea of war and dives excitedly in. But, at the front lines of WWI he discovers the dark realities of war really is. Ernest Borgnine is a seasoned veteran who teaches Richard Thomas how to stay alive. Borgnine, Neal and the movie each received Emmy nominations. Despite being an excellent, high quality production with top notch photography and effects, it still is not as good as the 1930 classic version.

Sex / Nud / Viol / Lang / AdSit

A: Ernest Borgnine, Richard Thomas, Patricia Neal, Ian Holm

© LIVE HOME VIDEO 51115

APOCALYPSE NOW

D: Francis Ford Coppola — 153 m

R | WAR DMA ACT | 1979 | COLOR

10 Chilling, surrealistic Vietnam war epic. Special Forces agent Sheen is sent to find and terminate a highly decorated renegade officer (Brando). The Army High Command claims he has gone mad. He commands his own native army, in his own war, in his own way. Sheen travels upriver into Cambodia on a terrifyingly surrealistic journey into Brando's world, there to find a brilliant man who has gained god-like status through using absolutely ruthless acts of horror. Is this man mad or is it the world? Stunning photography and a very unnerving experience. See also the documentary HEARTS OF DARKNESS about the difficult making of this film.

Sex / Nud / Viol / Lang / AdSit

A: Marlon Brando, Martin Sheen, Robert Duvall, Harrison Ford, Sam Bottoms, Dennis Hopper

© PARAMOUNT HOME VIDEO 2306

ASHES AND DIAMONDS

D: Andrzej Wajda — 105 m

NR | FOR DMA WAR | 1958 | B&W

9 An extremely powerful and influential Polish film. WWII has just ended and a new peace dominated by Russian communists is beginning. Three young Poles, former members of the resistance movement, have just killed three Polish workers, believing that the communist party chief is among them. One of the assassins realizes that their target was in fact not killed. Spending the night at a hotel, the war-hardened young man has an affair with a pretty and tender barmaid. For the first time, he feels the war is over and begins to doubt his continuing role as a bitter political fanatic and soldier. Made a star of Cybulski and is considered the last in a trilogy of war films from director Wajda. Subtitles.

Sex / Nud / Viol / Lang / AdSit

A: Zbigniew Cybulski, Eva Krzyzewska, Adam Pawlikowski, Waclaw Zastrzezynski

© HOME VISION ASH 020

AU REVOIR LES ENFANTS

D: Louis Malle — 103 m

PG | FOR DMA WAR | 1987 | COLOR

8 Goodbye children. Powerful Oscar nominee for Best Foreign Film. During WWII, at a French Catholic boarding school, the headmaster and the monks shield several Jewish children from the occupying Nazis. This is the story of two boys, one Catholic and one Jewish, who develop a close relationship during that winter - a relationship that is cut short when the Nazis discover the Jewish children-in-hiding. Deeply felt and moving, though a little slow at times. A devastating ending. Dubbed.

Sex / Nud / Viol / Lang / AdSit

A: Gaspard Manesse, Raphael Fejto, Francine Racette, Stanislas de Malberg, Phillipe Morier-Genoud, Francois Berleand

© ORION PICTURES CORPORATION 5041

BAT 21

D: Peter Markle — 106 m

R | WAR ACT | 1988 | COLOR

8 Excellent. Gene Hackman is a middle-aged career military officer in Vietnam who has safely fought his war from behind a desk or at 30,000 feet. But he is parachuted into the real war when he is shot down and lands inside enemy territory. Glover is a rescue pilot who doggedly tries to get him out as Hackman struggles to survive on the ground in a hostile territory and in a real down-to-earth shooting war. This film was based upon a real-life occurrence. This is a suspenseful and very well-acted story that keeps you on the edge of your seat. See the index for other Hackman movies.

Sex / Nud / Viol / Lang / AdSit

A: Gene Hackman, Danny Glover, Jerry Reed, David Marshal Grant, Clayton Rohner, Erich Anderson

© VIDEO TREASURES MO12021

BIG RED ONE, THE

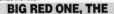

D: Samuel Fuller — 114 m

PG | WAR DMA ACT | 1980 | COLOR

9 A tough, gritty, realistic and brilliant war saga. Director Fuller spent 35 years trying to get this autobiographical movie of his first-hand memories of WWII made. The focus is upon the daily lives of the soldiers of the famous American First Infantry Division, called the Big Red One. Individual soldiers of the division are followed from their landing in North Africa all through Europe. Lee Marvin is a war-weary special infantry sergeant who is just trying to keep his young troops, most of them fresh out of high school, alive. The veterans survive but most replacements never live long enough to learn how to. Rich, moving and realistic. A terrific film.

Sex / Nud / Viol / Lang / AdSit

A: Lee Marvin, Mark Hamill, Robert Carradine, Bobby DiCicco, Kelly Ward, Siegfried Rauch

© WARNER HOME VIDEO 939

BOAT, THE (FORMERLY DAS BOOT)

D: Wolfgang Petersen — 150 m

R | FOR WAR DMA | 1982 | COLOR

9 Extremely realistic depiction of the claustrophobic life aboard a German U-boat on the prowl, attacking and under attack in the North Atlantic of World War II. German-made, the film meticulously illustrates the crowding, grime and absolute terror of being several hundred feet below water while those overhead are trying to kill you. The war-weary captain guides his desperate crew as they attempt to raise the damaged ship from the ocean floor. Brilliant. Superb. Billed as "the most expensive and most successful motion picture in the history of German cinema." Dubbed/subtitles.

Sex / Nud / Viol / Lang / AdSit

A: Jurgen Prochnow, Herbert Granemeyer, Klause Wenneman, Hubertus Bengsch, Martin Semmelrogge

© COLUMBIA TRISTAR HOME VIDEO 60139

BORN ON THE FOURTH OF JULY

R · DMA WAR · 1989 · COLOR · Sex / Nud / Viol / Lang / AdSit

D: Oliver Stone — 145 m

8 Powerful film based on Vietnam War veteran Ron Kovic's bitter memories of his real-life war experiences and resulting paralysis. Strong performances by all concerned make very real one man's story of misery and tragedy. Kovic, once a naive and over-eager young soldier, becomes a bitter anti-war activist after becoming paralyzed, and then humiliated and frustrated by government bureaucracy, his family's inadequacies and a failure of religion. Cruise is brilliant as a tortured man. This is a very moving film, but it is also very heavy-handed in making its point.

A: Tom Cruise, Raymond J. Barry, Caroline Kava, Willem Dafoe, Kyra Sedgwick, Tom Berenger

© MCA/UNIVERSAL HOME VIDEO, INC. 80901

BOYS IN COMPANY C

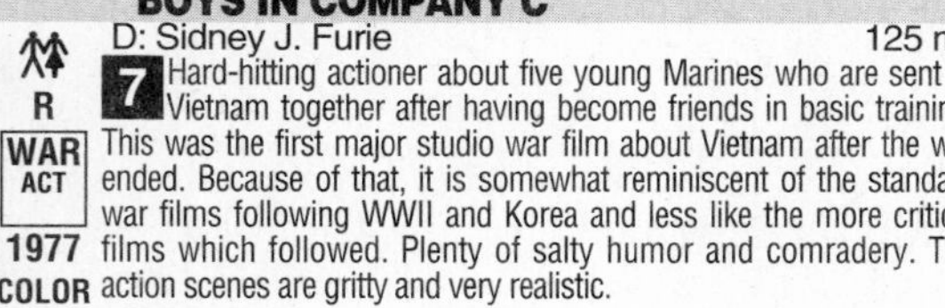

R · WAR ACT · 1977 · COLOR · Sex / Nud / Viol / Lang / AdSit

D: Sidney J. Furie — 125 m

7 Hard-hitting actioner about five young Marines who are sent to Vietnam together after having become friends in basic training. This was the first major studio war film about Vietnam after the war ended. Because of that, it is somewhat reminiscent of the standard war films following WWII and Korea and less like the more critical films which followed. Plenty of salty humor and comradery. The action scenes are gritty and very realistic.

A: Stan Shaw, Andrew Stevens, James Channing, Michael Lembeck, Craig Wasson

© COLUMBIA TRISTAR HOME VIDEO 60144

BRIDGE AT REMAGEN, THE

NR · WAR ACT · 1969 · COLOR · Sex / Nud / Viol / Lang / AdSit

D: John Guillermin — 116 m

7 High intensity war flick recounting the real-life battle for a strategic WWII bridge. Near the end of WWII, Allied soldiers try to capture the last bridge into Germany intact so that it can be used in the Allied invasion efforts. The Germans desperately want the bridge destroyed for the same reason, but they are holding off to the last moment so that their retreating troops can get home. The war is coming to an end... this is the last hope for the Germans. There are very good action sequences, but fans of this genre should be sure to also see the similar but superior A BRIDGE TOO FAR.

A: George Segal, Ben Gazzara, Robert Vaughn, E.G. Marshall, Bradford Dillman, Peter Van Eyck

Distributed By MGM/UA Home Video M201533

BRIDGE ON THE RIVER KWAI, THE

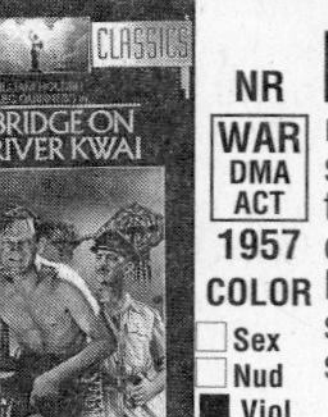

NR · WAR DMA ACT · 1957 · COLOR · Sex / Nud / Viol / Lang / AdSit

D: David Lean — 161 m

10 Powerful war drama which won 7 Academy Awards, including every major category. Much more than a standard war or action movie, this is the powerfully dramatic story of men under extreme stress. British soldiers in a Japanese prisoner-of-war camp are forced to construct a strategic bridge in Burma. For Guinness, the English commander, it is a source of pride for himself and his men, but Holden returns after escaping to blow it up as being a dangerous strategic target. Psychological battles of wills and major action sequences combine in a famous climax.

A: William Holden, Alec Guinness, Jack Hawkins, Sessue Hayakawa, James Donald, Geoffrey Horne

© COLUMBIA TRISTAR HOME VIDEO 60160

BRIDGE TOO FAR, A

PG · WAR ACT · 1977 · COLOR · Sex / Nud / Viol / Lang / AdSit

D: Richard Attenborough — 178 m

9 Spectacular epic movie containing fictionalized personal accounts of the real-life, famous - but disastrous - Allied airborne assault during WWII to get major troop deployments behind the German lines. The objective was to drop 35,000 airborne troops into Eastern Holland to capture six major bridges over the Rhine river from Holland into Germany. This was history's largest airborne assault and before it was over more men had died than in the D-Day invasion. Yet, the people of Holland would have to wait another six months for liberation. Huge all-star cast. Action-packed battle scenes and charged dramatic moments. Beautiful photography of Dutch locations. Exciting.

A: Dirk Bogarde, James Caan, Michael Caine, Sean Connery, Laurence Olivier, Robert Redford

Distributed By MGM/UA Home Video M301838

BURMESE HARP, THE

NR · FOR WAR DMA · 1956 · B&W · Sex / Nud / Viol / Lang / AdSit

D: Kon Ichikawa — 116 m

9 Powerful and moving anti-war film from Japan. Nearing the end of WWII, a harp-playing Japanese soldier's unit tries to steal away into neutral territory but he volunteers to stay behind and journey into the mountains to convince other renegade fighters that Japan has officially surrendered. But along the way, he is wounded and saved by a Buddhist priest. Now transformed and wearing the robes of the monk, he traverses endless plains of dead soldiers and begins to methodically bury and burn the bodies of his countrymen. And when other soldiers leave to retreat, he stays behind to finish his task. Subtitles. Also known as THE HARP OF BURMA.

A: Shoji Yasui, Rentaro Mikuni, Tatsuya Mihashi, Tanie Kitabayashi, Yunosuke Ito

© HOME VISION BUR 110

CASUALTIES OF WAR

R · WAR DMA ACT · 1989 · COLOR · Sex / Nud / Viol / Lang / AdSit

D: Brian De Palma — 120 m

8 This is a startling film that retells a real-life horror story from the Vietnam War. It occurred in 1966 and was first revealed in a magazine article. The story revolves around one incident when an out-of-control squad of American soldiers kidnaps, rapes and later murders a young Vietnamese girl after they are through with her. Fox is a new raw recruit, an innocent private, who watches as his crazed sergeant goes over the edge and leads his troops on this rampage. Fox is the only soldier who object. He tries to help the girl escape and later reports the incident, but he stands alone against his squad.

A: Michael J. Fox, Sean Penn, Thuy Thu Le, Don Harvey, John Leguizamo

© COLUMBIA TRISTAR HOME VIDEO 50183

CATCH-22

R · COM WAR · 1970 · COLOR · Sex / Nud / Viol / Lang / AdSit

D: Mike Nichols — 121 m

6 Captain Yossarian (Arkin) is a war-weary airman who, like most of his compatriots, wants to escape the insanity of combat. He, however, plans to do something about it and has decided to plead insanity. But according to Catch 22, if you are aware enough to say you are crazy, you can't be crazy... so you are qualified to be a soldier. Sarcastic, anti-war black comedy comes close, but sometimes misses the mark, too.

A: Alan Arkin, Martin Balsam, Richard Benjamin, Anthony Perkins, Art Garfunkel, Bob Newhart

© PARAMOUNT HOME VIDEO 6924

CEASE FIRE

R · DMA WAR · 1985 · COLOR · Sex / Nud / Viol / Lang / AdSit

D: David Nutter — 97 m

7 After fifteen years of trying to fit back into society, Johnson's Vietnam-induced flashbacks are ripping at his marriage. When he loses his job, the pain of his experiences overwhelm him. Then fellow vet Lyons convinces him to acknowledge that he has a problem and to seek help in group therapy sessions at a Veterans Center. This is an earnest and heartfelt drama that reflects the other side of RAMBO, which is too true for too many. Slowly, with the help of therapy and the love of his family, he starts to win his way back.

A: Don Johnson, Lisa Biount, Robert F. Lyons, Richard Chaves, Rick Richards, Chris Noel

© CONGRESS VIDEO GROUP 02780

COMING HOME

R · DMA ROM WAR · 1978 · COLOR · Sex / Nud / Viol / Lang / AdSit

D: Hal Ashby — 130 m

9 Extremely powerful early attempt to explore the effects of the Vietnam war. A gung-ho career Marine officer's (Dern) naive wife (Fonda) finds real love with a bitter paraplegic (Voight) while volunteering at the hospital when her husband is away at war. Dern comes back from Vietnam very mixed up himself. He is having great difficulty adjusting to all the changes in himself and his wife because she is now independent, and deeply involved with Voight. Politics of Vietnam are downplayed, this is a very human drama. Oscars for Fonda, Voight and script. Best Picture nominee, too.

A: Jane Fonda, Jon Voight, Bruce Dern, Robert Carradine, Robert Ginty, Penelope Milford

Distributed By MGM/UA Home Video M301428

CROSS OF IRON

R · WAR DMA ACT · 1977 · COLOR · Sex / Nud / Viol / Lang / AdSit

D: Sam Peckinpah — 132 m

8 In the style of the famed German film THE BOAT (DAS BOOT), this is a solid American-made WWII adventure that also tells its story entirely from the German viewpoint. It is also a very realistic and action-packed look at war. Schell plays a German officer who is intent upon winning a hero's medal, while Coburn plays a capable war-weary sergeant who is comptemptuous of both the military and of war. Coburn is just trying to keep his troops from being ground up by the advancing Russian army in 1943. Great action scenes, particularly the tank scenes near the end.

A: James Coburn, Maximilian Schell, James Mason, David Warner, Senta Berger

© MEDIA HOME ENTERTAINMENT, INC. M765

DEAR AMERICA: LETTERS HOME FROM VIETNAM

PG · DOC DMA WAR · 1988 · COLOR · Sex / Nud / Viol / Lang / AdSit

D: Bill Couturie — 84 m

9 An extremely moving and powerful documentary. This is a non-political, award-winning documentary which examines the Vietnam War from the soldier's perspective. Actual letters, written home at the time, are read by numerous prominent actors and are accompanied by '60s music, news footage, still photographs, and even home movies. This is a gut-wrenchingly presentation of the personal face of war. It is neither politicized nor glamorized, only human. Originally made-for-TV and later released to theaters.

A:

© HBO VIDEO 0207

DEER HUNTER, THE

D: Michael Cimino 183 m

R | DMA WAR ACT | 1978 | COLOR

Sex | Nud | Viol | Lang | AdSit

10 Extraordinarily powerful winner of five Oscars, including Best Picture (nominated for nine). Young friends from a blue collar working class background in 1968 Pennsylvania leave their familiar land of hot blast furnaces and cool forests, from which they hunted deer, to go to Vietnam's steaming jungle to hunt men. This epic (long) movie is essentially shown in three parts: the hometown, the horrors of war and then back home again, now scarred both physically and emotionally. This powerful film packs a big wallop, but is not without controversy. Top-flight cast.

A: Robert De Niro, John Cazale, John Savage, Meryl Streep, Schristopher Walken, George Dzundza

© MCA/UNIVERSAL HOME VIDEO, INC. 88000

DIRTY DOZEN, THE

D: Robert Aldrich 150 m

NR | WAR ACT | 1967 | COLOR

Sex | Nud | Viol | Lang | AdSit

9 Major box office hit. Tough Army Major Lee Marvin recruits a bunch of violent convicts to go on a near-suicide commando raid behind German lines. Their reward, if they survive, is to have their records cleared and, if they don't, the opportunity of dying an honorable death. Marvin and his misfit team are to infiltrate a lush German retreat inside France where the German General Staff goes for its R&R. A great cast is well directed in this slick and highly entertaining war adventure which combines action, suspense and humor. Terrific entertainment and exciting, too.

A: Lee Marvin, Ernest Borgnine, Charles Bronson, Jim Brown, John Cassavetes, Donald Sutherland

Distributed By MGM/UA Home Video M700008

EAGLE HAS LANDED, THE

D: John Sturges 131 m

PG | ACT WAR | 1977 | COLOR

Sex | Nud | Viol | Lang | AdSit

8 Fast moving and well-crafted high-adventure yarn set during World War II. Caine and Sutherland play 2 of 19 Nazi agents who are disguised as Polish soldiers and parachuted into England with the intent of kidnapping Winston Churchill and taking him back to Hitler. Their plans go awry when they are discovered early and must make a desperate attempt to complete the objective anyway. This is especially interesting because it is told from the German viewpoint. The agents aren't terrible, repulsive bad guys, just soldiers. Lots of twists, plenty of action and a surprise ending. Great acting.

A: Michael Caine, Donald Sutherland, Robert Duvall, Jenny Agutter, Donald Pleasence, Anthony Quayle

© LIVE HOME VIDEO 51130

ENEMY BELOW, THE

D: Dick Powell 98 m

NR | WAR SUS ACT | 1957 | COLOR

Sex | Nud | Viol | Lang | AdSit

9 Gripping and extremely tense cat-and-mouse game between a German U-boat commanded by Curt Jurgens and an American destroyer escort captained by Robert Mitchum. The North Atlantic is the setting for this spellbinding study of bravery and tenacity, as two seasoned warriors engage in a chess game - a battle of experiences to see who will be the victor when hunter pursues hunter. Excellent photography. The special effects won an Oscar. An accurate portrayal of military tactics. Neither side is vilified nor is it glorified. This is highly watchable.

A: Robert Mitchum, Curt Jurgens, Theodore Bikel, Doug McClure, Russell Collins, David Hedison

© FOXVIDEO 1133

EXECUTION OF PRIVATE SLOVIK, THE

D: Lamont Johnson 122 m

NR | DMA WAR | 1974 | COLOR

Sex | Nud | Viol | Lang | AdSit

8 Riveting true-life account of the first American soldier to be executed for desertion since the Civil War. World War II soldier Eddie Slovik was at first disqualified from active military duty during the war because of a teenage criminal record. However, he was eventually called up and placed in a front line position. Then, under an enemy attack, Slovik froze, could not fire his rifle and deserted his position. This action led to his eventual court-martial and execution by firing squad. Sheen's performance as Slovik is masterful. Powerful drama.

A: Martin Sheen, Mariclare Costello, Ned Beatty, Gary Busey, Matt Clark, Ben Hammer

© MCA/UNIVERSAL HOME VIDEO, INC. 80569

FORCE 10 FROM NAVARONE

D: Guy Hamilton 118 m

PG | WAR ACT | 1978 | COLOR

Sex | Nud | Viol | Lang | AdSit

6 Almost a sequel to the far-superior THE GUNS OF NAVARONE. Members of American and British commando units join forces, under Harrison Ford's leadership, to sabotage a major bridge in the Balkans. The bridge is a vital link between the Germans and the Italians during World War II. Solid cast, with well-staged action sequences, but nothing distinguished in the plot or the execution.

A: Robert Shaw, Harrison Ford, Edward Fox, Franco Nero, Barbara Bach

© WARNER HOME VIDEO 26018

FRIENDLY PERSUASION

D: William Wyler 138 m

NR | WST DMA WAR | 1956 | COLOR

Sex | Nud | Viol | Lang | AdSit

9 Wonderfully warm and charming film about the moral quandaries experienced by a Southern Indiana Quaker family during the heartbreak of the Civil War. Gary Cooper and Dorothy McGuire play the Quaker parents of Anthony Perkins (in an Oscar-nominated performance). Their tranquil life is violently challenged when their eldest son goes off to join in the battles to prove that he is no coward. It is a moving tale of love and honor. Cooper is also perfectly cast. Six Oscar nominations, including Best Picture and Best Director, plus a beautiful Dimitri Tiomkin score.

A: Gary Cooper, Dorothy McGuire, Marjorie Main, Anthony Perkins, Robert Middleton, Richard Eyer

© CBS/FOX VIDEO 7318

FULL METAL JACKET

D: Stanley Kubrick 117 m

R | WAR DMA ACT | 1987 | COLOR

Sex | Nud | Viol | Lang | AdSit

8 A highly acclaimed, straightforward movie which follows a group of Marine recruits through basic training, where they are turned into killing machines, and on to Vietnam, where they do what they are trained to do. The picture is essentially divided into two halves. The beginning portion is dominated by the amazingly foul-mouthed verbal assaults of a real-life drill sergeant, molding the young recruits. The latter half relates the efforts of these Marines to do their job and to survive the 1968 Tet Offensive of Vietnam. It is a compelling depiction of the numbing dehumanization of war.

A: Matthew Modine, Adam Baldwin, Vincent D'Onofrio, R. Lee Ermey, Dorian Harewood, Arliss Howard

© WARNER HOME VIDEO 11760

GALLIPOLI

D: Peter Weir 111 m

PG | WAR ACT | 1981 | COLOR

Sex | Nud | Viol | Lang | AdSit

9 Outstanding picture from Australia. Beautiful and powerful. Two adventurous young Australian idealists (Gibson and Lee) get caught up in a patriotic fever during World War I, join the army and are sent to Turkey. They are sent to Gallipoli, the site of a devastating WWI battle in which the Australian forces suffered tremendous casualties. A totally engrossing human drama and one of the best films ever of life on the battlefield. Striking period details, excellent production values and brilliant acting.

A: Mel Gibson, Mark Lee, Bill Kerr, Robert Grubb, David Argue, Tim McKensie

© PARAMOUNT HOME VIDEO 1504

GETTYSBURG

D: Ronald Maxwell 254 m

PG | WAR DMA ACT | 1993 | COLOR

Sex | Nud | Viol | Lang | AdSit

9 On July 2, 1863, in the second year of the Civil War, the Union and Confederate Armies found each other outside a small Pennsylvania town and there fought the largest battle of the war. By the end of the third day of that battle 53,000 men lay dead - roughly the same number of men killed in the Vietnam War over twelve years. This is an epic film in both its scope and its intent. The battle sequences are extremely realistic and effectively convey the grandeur and the horror of that war like no other film before it. For history films it is a must see. Others, however, may find it to be slow, deliberate and long. Still, be patient. Also see terrific epic documentary THE CIVIL WAR.

A: Tom Berenger, Martin Sheen, Jeff Daniels, Sam Elliott, Richard Jordan

© TURNER HOME ENTERTAINMENT 6139

GLORY

D: Edward Zwick 122 m

R | DMA ACT WAR | 1989 | COLOR

Sex | Nud | Viol | Lang | AdSit

9 Excellent story, based on fact, about the Civil War's first fighting regiment of black soldiers. The Civil War was fought largely because of the plight of black people, but blacks were not allowed to actually fight in it until near the end of the war. Broderick plays the black regiment's white officer who fights to get better treatment and pay for his men, and to gain for them the two things they want most - the opportunity go into battle and the dignity of being men. Extremely high production values, particularly in very realistic battle sequences. Winner of three Oscars, including Best Actor (Washington).

A: Matthew Broderick, Denzel Washington, Morgan Freeman, Cliff De Young, Cary Elwes

© COLUMBIA TRISTAR HOME VIDEO 11543

GO TELL THE SPARTANS

D: Ted Post 114 m

R | WAR DMA ACT | 1978 | COLOR

Sex | Nud | Viol | Lang | AdSit

9 Superior and intelligent Vietnam war movie that was unjustly overlooked at the time of its release because of several other more highly-publicized pictures out at the same time. Set in 1964, before major US involvement in Vietnam, Lancaster is the commanding officer of an advisory group near Dienbienphu. The nature of the war is becoming apparent and he is already beginning to have doubts about the wisdom of being there, but still does his best to train his troops how to stay alive in jungle warfare. Excellent performances. Very realistic. True sleeper of a film.

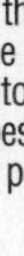

A: Burt Lancaster, Craig Wasson, Jonathan Goldsmith, Marc Singer, Joe Unger

© HBO VIDEO 90615

WAR

GREAT ESCAPE, THE

D: John Sturges — 173 m

NR · ACT WAR DMA · 1963 · COLOR

10 Exciting blockbuster hit filled with major name international stars. An escape-prone group of cocky WWII Allied POWs are all gathered into one high security camp by the Germans, who wanted to put all their bad eggs into one high security basket. Instead, they get a massive POW escape attempt. This rousing adventure story is told as a series of character portraits which are then all linked together. It has a huge cast of top talent and a good script, plus pacing, humor and excitement aplenty. Watch for McQueen's thrilling motorcycle ride. Much copied - never equaled. Based upon an actual event. In the real event, 76 men broke out but only 3 found freedom.

Sex · Nud · Viol · Lang · AdSit

A: Steve McQueen, James Garner, Richard Attenborough, Charles Bronson, James Coburn, David McCallum

Distributed By MGM/UA Home Video M201257

GUNS OF NAVARONE, THE

D: J. Lee Thompson — 145 m

NR · WAR ACT · 1961 · COLOR

9 Action-packed WWII story about a multi-national Allied commando team sent onto a heavily guarded small Greek island in the Aegean Sea to destroy two radar-controlled batteries of huge German guns that threaten Allied troop ships. Excellent acting, first-rate production, high-intensity suspense and action. Nominated for seven Oscars, won Special Effects. Regarded among the best WWII flicks, along with THE GREAT ESCAPE, GUADALCANAL DIARY and SANDS OF IWO JIMA.

Sex · Nud · Viol · Lang · AdSit

A: Gregory Peck, David Niven, Anthony Quinn, Stanley Baker, Anthony Quayle, James Darren

© COLUMBIA TRISTAR HOME VIDEO 60004

HAMBURGER HILL

D: John Irvin — 94 m

R · WAR ACT · 1987 · COLOR

7 Very graphic grunt's-eye-view depiction of a 101st Airborne attack on a hill held by the North Vietnamese in 1969. It is a 10-day attack in which 14 men battle to take a muddy hill and receive 70% casualties. This is a straight-forward depiction of the horror and confusion of fighting, with battle scenes entirely from the soldier's viewpoint. The savage fighting is so graphic that it is sometimes hard to watch, but it is also not easily forgettable.

Sex · Nud · Viol · Lang · AdSit

A: Michael Patrick Boatman, Tegan West, Dylan McDermott, Courtney Vance, Tommy Swerdlow, Steven Weber

© LIVE HOME VIDEO 6015

HEARTBREAK RIDGE

D: Clint Eastwood — 130 m

R · WAR ACT · 1986 · COLOR

6 This is an Eastwood vehicle pure and simple. He displays his starpower playing a tough, battle-scared, foul-mouthed gunnery sergeant with no wars to fight. He is serving his last tour as a boot-camp DI and gets a squad of misfits to train. While he loses the domestic battles with his ex-wife Marsha Mason, he turns his troops into a gung-ho fighting unit. He gets the job done just in time to take them to Grenada and kick communist butts. The whole thing is totally predictable, but just because we know where we're going doesn't mean we won't enjoy the trip.

Sex · Nud · Viol · Lang · AdSit

A: Clint Eastwood, Marsha Mason, Everett McGill, Moses Gunn, Eileen Heckart, Bo Svenson

© WARNER HOME VIDEO 11701

HEAVEN AND EARTH

D: Oliver Stone — 142 m

R · DMA WAR · 1993 · COLOR

6 This is the last in Oliver Stone's Vietnam trilogy following PLATOON and BORN ON THE FOURTH OF JULY. It is based upon the memoirs of Le Ly, a Vietnamese farm girl whose quiet life took a violent turn when her village became the center of a battleground. She is raped and escapes to Da Nang. There she becomes pregnant by a rich man who sends her to Saigon, where she turns to prostitution and she meets Tommy Lee Jones who takes her back to America. Stone uses the sorrowful experiences of one woman to represent all the tragedies of that small country and the American involvement in it. That is a gross simplification and a mistake. Beautifully filmed but slanted and flawed.

Sex · Nud · Viol · Lang · AdSit

A: Tommy Lee Jones, Hiep Thi Le, Joan Chen, Haing S. Ngor, Debbie Reynolds, Conchata Ferrell

© WARNER HOME VIDEO 12983

HELL IN THE PACIFIC

D: John Boorman — 101 m

G · WAR DMA · 1968 · COLOR

6 An unusual twist to a World War II theme. An American pilot (Marvin) becomes stranded on an island that is already occupied by a lone Japanese officer. If this were any other time or place, they would have helped each other. But they are at war. At first they launch minor raids against each other, but then they realize that they stand a better chance of surviving by cooperating, so they strike an uneasy truce. They combine their energies to build a raft so they can both get off the island.

Sex · Nud · Viol · Lang · AdSit

A: Lee Marvin, Toshiro Mifune

© CBS/FOX VIDEO 8028

HELL IS FOR HEROES

D: Don Siegel — 90 m

NR · WAR DMA ACT · 1962 · COLOR

8 Quite good war drama in which character development is carefully interwoven into and necessary to the action sequences. The action scenes themselves are calculated realism, not empty-headed glory charges. A star-studded cast highlights this realistic war saga about a beleaguered Army squad which has survived Africa, France and Belgium, and is now assigned the job of plugging a hole in the front lines near the end of WWII. Steve McQueen is excellent as a tormented man who now requires battle as a drug to survive living.

Sex · Nud · Viol · Lang · AdSit

A: Steve McQueen, Bobby Darin, Fess Parker, Harry Guardino, James Coburn, Bob Newhart

© PARAMOUNT HOME VIDEO 6116

HELL TO ETERNITY

D: Phil Karlson — 132 m

NR · WAR DMA ACT · 1960 · B&W

8 Fascinating true story from World War II. Jeffery Hunter plays the real-life figure of Guy Gabaldon who was a Hispanic man raised by Japanese-Americans. Gabaldon could speak Japanese and became a hero of the South Pacific when he chose to fight his war on Saipan by going behind enemy lines each night to convince defeated Japanese soldiers to surrender, eventually winning a Silver Star for bringing in over 2,000 prisoners. Action aplenty, too, with very realistic battle scenes.

Sex · Nud · Viol · Lang · AdSit

A: Jeffrey Hunter, Vic Damone, David Janssen, Sessue Hayakawa

© CBS/FOX VIDEO 7351

HENRY V

D: Kenneth Branagh — 138 m

NR · DMA WAR · 1989 · COLOR

9 Extraordinarily well done version of the Shakespeare classic telling of King Henry V's war with the French. When a young Henry is thrust onto the throne of England and insulted by the French envoy, Henry is determined to be seen as a strong king. So he exercises his hereditary right to the French crown, gathers his army together and goes to France to claim it. Notable for the inclusion of a very realistic, but small in scale, presentation of medieval warfare. An Oscar nomination went to Kenneth Branagh for his stunning performance as Henry, and the film won the Oscar for Costume Design.

Sex · Nud · Viol · Lang · AdSit

A: Kenneth Branagh, Paul Scofield, Derek Jacobi, Ian Holm, Alec McGowen, Judi Dench

© CBS/FOX VIDEO 2575

HOPE AND GLORY

D: John Boorman — 118 m

PG-13 · DMA WAR · 1987 · COLOR

9 This is an extremely well made English film that was highly praised by critics and was also a Best Picture nominee. It is the story of WWII and the London blitz as it was viewed from the eyes of a nine-year-old boy. Writer/director Boorman recaptures those experience as a time of great trauma and reappraisals for the adults, but just a grand adventure for him. His father is away, his mother is distracted and school is closed because of bombing raids. There is excitement, heroism, friendly soldiers and a live-for-today attitude everywhere. Alternately dramatic and funny, it is rich in characters and atmosphere.

Sex · Nud · Viol · Lang · AdSit

A: Sebastian Rice Edwards, Sarah Miles, David Hayman, Derrick O'Connor, Sammi Davis, Ian Bannen

© NEW LINE HOME VIDEO 7713

HOW I WON THE WAR

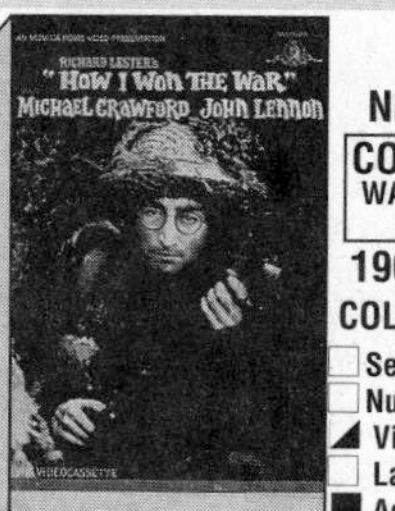

D: Richard Lester — 111 m

NR · COM WAR · 1967 · COLOR

6 Very British satire of one man's story of his military career. Michael Crawford plays an eccentric British officer who makes ridiculous demands of his troops and manages to stay alive when all those around him don't. Savage satire of war that may be lost on many because of very heavy British accents and very dry black humor. Others will find it hilarious.

Sex · Nud · Viol · Lang · AdSit

A: Michael Crawford, John Lennon, Roy Kinnear, Lee Montague, Jack MacGowran

Distributed By MGM/UA Home Video M600455

IN HARM'S WAY

D: Otto Preminger — 165 m

WAR ACT · 1965 · B&W

8 This is an epic motion picture that uses the aftermath of the attack on Pearl Harbor and the beginning of WWII as the backdrop to explore its effects upon the lives and loves of several principal players. The most notable of these are John Wayne and Kirk Douglas. John begins a love affair with nurse Patricia Neal and leads the counterattack against the Japanese. While, Douglas disgraces himself by molesting a nurse and attempts to redeem himself with battle heroics. The credible personal subplots and some really good action sequences make for enjoyable entertainment. However, it was criticized as being too long.

Sex · Nud · Viol · Lang · AdSit

A: John Wayne, Kirk Douglas, Patricia Neal, Tom Tryon, Paula Prentiss, Henry Fonda

© PARAMOUNT HOME VIDEO 6418

IS PARIS BURNING?

D: Rene Clement — 173 m

NR | WAR DMA | 1966 | COLOR

6 This is a star-studded extravaganza, telling of the period in time from the Allied landing at Normandy to the recapture of Paris. Principally, the film concerns the Allied rush to reclaim Paris before the Nazis could destroy it. It is told in a semi-documentary style and uses many stories unfolding parallel to each other (much the same way as it was done in THE LONGEST DAY), to tell the over-all story. The numerous moderately involving stories are told with the help of a large international cast of actors.

Sex / Nud / Viol / Lang / AdSit

A: Jean-Paul Belmondo, Charles Boyer, Leslie Caron, Alain Delon, Kirk Douglas, Glenn Ford

© PARAMOUNT HOME VIDEO 6603

JUDGMENT AT NUREMBURG

D: Stanley Kramer — 187 m

NR | DMA WAR | 1961 | B&W

10 12 Oscar nominations. Galvanizing and masterful production of the post World War II war-crimes trials at Nuremberg, Germany. Tracy is an American judge who must decide the fate of four German judges charged with manipulating the law to help Nazis prosecute Jews in the Holocaust. In pursuit of that end, the film examines the lives of several people deeply affected by the tragedy. The ultimate question to be answered is, how responsible are people for following the orders of their superiors? An intelligent and thoughtful production with a large cast and excellent performances.

Sex / Nud / Viol / Lang / AdSit

A: Spencer Tracy, Burt Lancaster, Maximilian Schell, Richard Widmark, Marlene Dietrich, Montgomery Clift

Distributed By MGM/UA Home Video M301536

KANAL

D: Andrzej Wajda — 96 m

NR | FOR WAR DMA | 1956 | B&W

9 It is May of 1944 and Warsaw has been reduced to rubble by the Nazis. There is only one small chance for the defeated and demoralized Resistance fighters to escape. They are ordered to descend into the foul, dark and claustrophobic sewers. The terror and despair is palpable. The Germans will shoot at them if they emerge and throw grenades down manholes when they don't. Only one, a young woman, knows the way out, but her boyfriend is desperately wounded. They are trapped down below. One of three in a trilogy of Polish war films by Wajda. Others include: A GENERATION and ASHES AND DIAMONDS. Subtitles.

Sex / Nud / Viol / Lang / AdSit

A: Teresa Izewska, Tadeusz Janczar, Wienczyslaw Glinski, Tadeusz Gwiazdowski

© HOME VISION KAN 020

KELLY'S HEROES

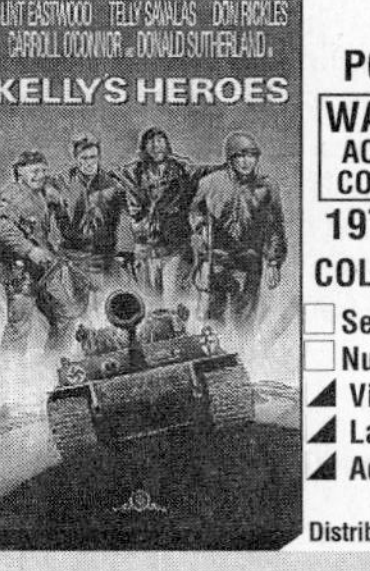

D: Brian G. Hutton — 146 m

PG | WAR ACT COM | 1970 | COLOR

8 Entertaining tongue-in-cheek reverse-spin on the popular film DIRTY DOZEN. Clint Eastwood gathers up a group of misfits and thieves to form his own private army within the Army. His goal is to capture a small village behind German lines. Is he a patriot? No. He and his people launch a very effective and inspirational offensive spearhead against the enemy because there is Nazi gold stored in the town, and they're going to steal it. Sprawling and entertaining, with a large cast of odd-ball characters. Light spirits and some good action sequences keep it moving.

Sex / Nud / Viol / Lang / AdSit

A: Clint Eastwood, Telly Savalas, Don Rickles, Donald Sutherland, Carroll O'Connor, Gavin MacLeod

Distributed By MGM/UA Home Video M700168

KILLING FIELDS, THE

D: Roland Joffe — 142 m

R | DMA WAR SUS | 1984 | COLOR

10 An absolutely unforgettable picture. A lacerating and highly charged emotional drama based upon the real events surrounding the fall of Cambodia and the American evacuation. New York Times correspondent Sidney Schanberg is aided in a last minute escape by his close friend and interpretor Dith Pran, but Pran can't get out. He is left to face the horrifying re-education camps of the Khmer Rouge and murder on a massive scale, but Schanberg never stops in his struggles to find and free him. Stunning portrait of a society gone mad! Three Oscars and three additional nominations.

Sex / Nud / Viol / Lang / AdSit

A: Sam Waterston, Haing S. Ngor, John Malkovich, Julian Sands, Craig T. Nelson

© WARNER HOME VIDEO 11419

KING RAT

D: Bryan Forbes — 135 m

NR | DMA WAR | 1965 | B&W

8 Excellent drama based on the daily life in a WWII Japanese POW camp in Singapore. This story, taken from a James Clavell (author of SHOGUN) novel, is that of a streetwise opportunistic American who rises above everyone else in his prison camp to become the unscrupulous and powerful head of the camp's black market. Known to his fellow prisoners as King Rat, even the officers assist him in his powerplays in exchange for food and money. This is an unvarnished story of survival on a basic level. Segal is convincingly despicable in a role that Newman and McQueen turned down.

Sex / Nud / Viol / Lang / AdSit

A: George Segal, Tom Cortenay, James Fox, Patrick O'Neal, Denholm Elliott, James Donald

© COLUMBIA TRISTAR HOME VIDEO 60028

LAWRENCE OF ARABIA

D: David Lean — 216 m

PG | DMA ACT WAR | 1962 | COLOR

10 A monumental accomplishment that fills the screen with majestic photography and gigantic spectacle. It was a winner of seven Oscars, including Best Picture, Director and Cinematography. Long before there was Operation Desert Storm (the 1991 Persian Gulf War), an enigmatic Englishman went into the deserts of Arabia and organized the scattered Arab tribes into an effective fighting force against the Ottoman Turks and the Germans during World War I. In the process, he created a new order in the Middle East and made himself into a legend. This one has everything: action, adventure and drama.

Sex / Nud / Viol / Lang / AdSit

A: Peter O'Toole, Alec Guinness, Anthony Quinn, Jack Hawkins, Claude Rains, Anthony Quayle

© COLUMBIA TRISTAR HOME VIDEO 50133

LIFE AND NOTHING BUT

D: Bertrand Tavernier — 135 m

PG | FOR DMA WAR | 1989 | COLOR

8 Two years after the armistice, French Major Noiret is still sorting through the dead. He is trying to locate one certifiable unknown soldier for the Arc de Triomphe. His job is a seemingly endless one in that he has over 400,000 dead French soldiers to investigate. His strange occupation also places him into the paths of two women who come to represent all those looking for loved ones. One is a young aristocrat obsessively looking for her dead husband. The other is looking for her fiance. This is a story of tortured lives that are held in limbo by war. Brilliant photography. A major award winner. Well done. Subtitles.

Sex / Nud / Viol / Lang / AdSit

A: Philippe Noiret, Sabine Azema, Pascale Vidal, Maurice Barrier, Francois Perrot, Jean-Pol Dubois

© ORION PICTURES CORPORATION 5056

LIGHTHORSEMEN, THE

D: Simon Wincer — 116 m

PG | WAR ACT DMA | 1988 | COLOR

7 Stirring true story. Sweeping and episodic adventure which explores the lives of four Australian friends as they prepare for a decisive battle in WWI. The thrilling climax is a march through the desert by 800 Australian calvarymen who then mount a surprise calvary attack upon thousands of German and Turkish soldiers in a desert fortress. An impossible mission, but one which changed the course of history. A rousing and exciting calvary charge at the end makes up for its other slower and contemplative moments.

Sex / Nud / Viol / Lang / AdSit

A: Jon Blake, Peter Phelps, Tony Bonner, Bill Kerr, John Walton, Sigrid Thornton

© WARNER HOME VIDEO 762

LION OF THE DESERT

D: Moustapha Akkad — 164 m

PG | WAR ACT | 1979 | COLOR

8 An epic-scale film, based on the true story of a Bedouin teacher, Omar Mukhtar, who, at age 51, rose up to lead his people against the colonizing Italian armies of Mussolini (Steiger), led by a vicious general (Reed). Mukhtar (Quinn) led Bedouins on foot and on horseback in a guerrilla war against the mechanized Italian armies for twenty years until the Italians finally caught him and hung him. This is an impressive large-scale movie with high production values and well-staged battle scenes, but it is quite long.

Sex / Nud / Viol / Lang / AdSit

A: Anthony Quinn, Oliver Reed, Raf Vallone, Rod Steiger, John Gielgud

© LIVE HOME VIDEO 64104

LONGEST DAY, THE

D: Ken Annakin, Andrew Marton — 175 m

G | WAR ACT DMA | 1962 | B&W

9 Monumental epic war film documenting the massive invasion of Europe in WWII. 43 of Hollywood's biggest stars fill roles, big and small, to portray in detail the many events of D-Day. The story is essentially told in three parts: the planning; the behind-the-lines activities of the resistance forces and the initial paratrooper assault; and, the massive landings on the beaches of Normandy, France. The big story is evoked through a series of smaller stories from the many people involved. Spectacular!

Sex / Nud / Viol / Lang / AdSit

A: John Wayne, Robert Mitchum, Henry Fonda, Richard Burton, Rod Steiger, Sean Connery

© FOXVIDEO 1021

LOST COMMAND, THE

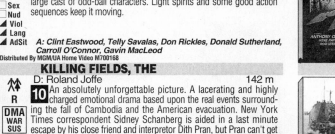

D: Mark Robson — 129 m

NR | ACT WAR | 1966 | COLOR

7 Taut war actioner, with a good international cast. A group of French soldiers escape in defeat from French Indochina (Vietnam) after WWII. The group's disgraced leader (Quinn) has been relieved of all command. However, he gets one more chance to redeem himself when he is sent to fight against the guerrilla warfare breaking out in North African Algeria. He is determined to redeem himself at any cost and launches a bloody attack against the rebel forces led by Arab terrorist leader Segal. Some top notch action scenes

Sex / Nud / Viol / Lang / AdSit

A: Anthony Quinn, Alain Delon, George Segal, Michele Morgan, Claudia Cardinale

© COLUMBIA TRISTAR HOME VIDEO 60948

M*A*S*H

D: Robert Altman — 116 m

R | COM WAR DMA | 1970 | COLOR | ◢ Sex ◢ Nud ◢ Viol ◢ Lang ■ AdSit

10 Hilarious irreverence! A Korean war Mobile Army Surgical Hospital is the setting for this dark and brash comedy. An unruly crew of oddball doctors and nurses survives the trauma of an endless war by concocting outlandish practical jokes to play upon each other - like selling tickets to an "unveiling" of a naked Hot Lips Houlihan in the shower. The result is big belly laughs all around. Winner of Oscar for Best Screenplay. Also nominated for Best Picture, Director and Supporting Actress. Inspired, but also very different from, the long-running TV series which became an attack on the Vietnam War.

A: Elliott Gould, Donald Sutherland, Sally Kellerman, Tom Skerritt, Robert Duvall, JoAnn Pflug

© FOXVIDEO 1038

MACARTHUR

D: Joseph Sargent — 131 m

PG | DMA WAR | 1979 | COLOR | ☐ Sex ☐ Nud ◢ Viol ☐ Lang ◢ AdSit

8 History buffs take note! This portrayal of one of history's most intriguing figures follows MacArthur's career from his controversial island-hopping campaign of WWII, through his governorship of Japan after the war, to the Korean War, when he was fired. The story is revealed between bits of his farewell address given before a group of West Point cadets. Necessarily, many of the details were sacrificed for the sake of time, but enough remains to make this an excellent production. Peck did an admirable job of retaining MacArthur's contentious and regal air.

A: Gregory Peck, Ed Flanders, Dan O'Herlihy, Sandy Kenyon, Dick O'Neill, Marj Dusay

© MCA/UNIVERSAL HOME VIDEO, INC. 55041

MARRIAGE OF MARIA BRAUN, THE

D: Rainer Werner Fassbinder — 120 m

R | FOR DMA WAR | 1979 | COLOR | ◢ Sex ■ Nud ☐ Viol ■ Lang ■ AdSit

9 Challenging and intelligent look at German society in the wake of World War II. In the final days of the war, Maria marries a Wehrmacht officer, even as the bombs fall. They have one night together, he goes off to war and is presumed dead. However, he returns, finding her in bed with an American soldier. He is enraged, attacks the soldier and is sent to prison. The sensuous Maria emotionally isolates herself and does what it takes to get him out, including ruthlessly sleeping her way to the top of the corporate heap in a power-hungry charge, and he betrays his soul to let her do it. Brilliant performances.

A: Hanna Schygulla, Klaus Lowitsch, Ivan Desny

© COLUMBIA TRISTAR HOME VIDEO 60718

MEMPHIS BELLE

D: Michael Caton-Jones — 107 m

PG-13 | DMA WAR ACT | 1990 | COLOR | ☐ Sex ☐ Nud ◢ Viol ◢ Lang ◢ AdSit

8 Flying a bombing raid over Germany was about the most dangerous thing a man could do in WWII. The B-17 Memphis Belle had already flown 24 missions beating the odds. This next one would be its last and its last flight was being immortalized by a documentary for a bond drive, but its crew, all young men just barely out of their teens, don't care. They just want to get that last mission behind them and go home. Involving and entertaining. The film builds slowly, letting us get to know the characters. Then the last mission comes. Terrific air action. Also see TWELVE O'CLOCK HIGH.

A: Matthew Modine, Eric Stoltz, Billy Zane, Tate Donovan, Harry Connick, Jr., D.B. Sweeney

© WARNER HOME VIDEO 12040

MIDNIGHT CLEAR, A

D: Keith Gordon — 107 m

R | DMA WAR | 1992 | COLOR | ◢ Sex ◢ Nud ■ Viol ■ Lang ■ AdSit

6 A sad and emotional anti-war statement, very well received critically. It is Christmas 1944. The war is very near to an end. Six young soldiers are all who remain of a special squad of 16 whiz kids, stationed in a forward position to collect information about an expected desperate Nazi offensive. Scared, they are approached by a group of equally scared German soldiers who want to surrender before they get killed in the big upcoming battle. The two sides even celebrate Christmas together. However, because of a misunderstanding, the peace is broken and the two sides get into a big fire fight anyway. Draining, frustrating and unsatisfying.

A: Peter Berg, Kevin Dillon, Arye Gross, Ethan Hawke, Gary Sinise, Frank Whaley

© COLUMBIA TRISTAR HOME VIDEO 92833

MIDWAY

D: Jack Smight — 132 m

PG | WAR ACT | 1976 | COLOR | ☐ Sex ☐ Nud ◢ Viol ◢ Lang ◢ AdSit

7 Compelling war drama. Only six-months after the Japanese successful attack at Pearl Harbor, American naval and air forces delivered a crushing defeat to the overconfident Japanese Navy in the Battle of Midway, from which they never recovered. This film documents that battle and the events that lead up to it. Fonda shines as Commander Chester W. Nimitz. There is a needless romantic subplot where Heston helps his son deal with a romantic relationship with a Japanese/American. Factually correct, the studio used a mixture of real and created footage in depicting this epic battle.

A: Charlton Heston, Henry Fonda, Glenn Ford, Robert Mitchum, Edward Albert, Hal Holbrook

© MCA/UNIVERSAL HOME VIDEO, INC. 55030

NONE BUT THE BRAVE

D: Frank Sinatra — 106 m

NR | ACT WAR | 1965 | COLOR | ☐ Sex ☐ Nud ◢ Viol ☐ Lang ☐ AdSit

6 Tense war drama about a plane full of Allied Marines that crash-lands on a Pacific island populated by small band of Japanese. Both groups have been cut off from the rest of the war. So, they conduct their own war with both sides plotting against the other and skirmishing. But when the Japanese commander offers water in exchange for help from the American's medic (Sinatra), who then amputates a man's leg and saves his life, a truce is worked out. An interesting, and a respectable entry, but it is most notable for being Sinatra's directorial debut.

A: Frank Sinatra, Clint Walker, Tommy Sands, Brad Dexter, Tony Bill, Sammy Jackson

© WARNER HOME VIDEO 11712

OPERATION CROSSBOW

D: Michael Anderson — 116 m

NR | WAR ACT | 1965 | COLOR | ☐ Sex ☐ Nud ■ Viol ☐ Lang ◢ AdSit

8 Rousing actioner set in WWII. A trio of British agents (Peppard, Courtenay and Kemp) are sent on a near-impossible mission to destroy a heavily guarded secret underground Nazi munitions installation, where German scientists are developing long range rockets. They impersonate German scientists to gain access to information which they are to send back. High intensity throughout, but it has a particularly sensational ending.

A: George Peppard, Sophia Loren, Trevor Howard, Tom Courtenay, Anthony Quayle, John Mills

Distributed By MGM/UA Home Video 202641

PATHS OF GLORY

D: Stanley Kubrick — 89 m

NR | DMA WAR | 1957 | B&W | ☐ Sex ☐ Nud ■ Viol ☐ Lang ■ AdSit

9 Stunning and provocative statement about the excesses which can occur from vanity and abuses of power inside the insane framework of war. Set in WWI France, a vain and inconsistent general orders his troops into an ill-advised attack upon an impenetrable position. After many men are killed, the troops sanely hold back. However, rather than admit his failure, and incensed by their insubordination, the General orders that one man from each of three platoons be chosen to be court-martialed and then executed for cowardice. Powerful, believable and convincingly acted.

A: Kirk Douglas, Ralph Meeker, Adolphe Menjou, George Macready, Timothy Carey, Wayne Morris

Distributed By MGM/UA Home Video M301735

PATTON

D: Franklin J. Schaffner — 171 m

PG | DMA WAR ACT | 1970 | COLOR | ☐ Sex ☐ Nud ◢ Viol ◢ Lang ◢ AdSit

10 Brilliant portrait of an extremely colorful and unique historical figure - George S. "Blood-and-Guts" Patton. Winner of 8 Oscars, including Best Picture, Director, Screenplay and Actor. Patton, the man, was a brilliant battlefield tactician whose single-mindedness in and out of battle helped to win the North African campaign and to launch the initial assault into Europe at the beginning of WWII. It garnered him both the respect and the animosity of nearly everyone. Scott did a brilliant job with the role. Both fascinating and extremely enjoyable.

A: George C. Scott, Karl Malden, Stephen Young, Michael Strong, Tim Considine, Frank Latimore

© FOXVIDEO 1005

PLATOON

D: Oliver Stone — 120 m

R | WAR DMA ACT | 1986 | COLOR | ☐ Sex ☐ Nud ■ Viol ■ Lang ■ AdSit

10 Profound statement on the harrowing experience of war - the utter terror of hand-to-hand combat and its lasting effects on ordinary people. A naive and idealistic replacement arrives at a battle-worn platoon in Vietnam. His innocence is soon lost to the realities of jungle warfare - where the slightest sound could warn of instant death. As bad as that is, he is also in the midst of an intercompany war where two sergeants (one decent and one ruthless) vie for control of the men. War's insanity was never made more personal, more real or more terrifying. 4 Oscars, including Picture and Director.

A: Charlie Sheen, Willem Dafoe, Tom Berenger, Francesco Quinn, Kevin Dillon, Forest Whitaker

© LIVE HOME VIDEO 6012

PORK CHOP HILL

D: Lewis Milestone — 98 m

NR | WAR ACT | 1959 | B&W | ☐ Sex ☐ Nud ◢ Viol ☐ Lang ◢ AdSit

7 Realistic, believable and a grim portrait of one of the many insanities of war. During the Korean War, a beleaguered platoon of men lead by Peck are ordered to take a strategically useless hill. Despite punishing casualties, they manage to take that mound of earth. Then, without replacements or reinforcements, they are ordered to hold the hill - even in the face of a massive attack by an overwhelming force and just as cease-fire talks begin. Good solid performances. Based upon fact.

A: Gregory Peck, Harry Guardino, Rip Torn, George Peppard, Bob Steele, Robert Blake

Distributed By MGM/UA Home Video M301298

RUMOR OF WAR, A

D: Richard T. Heffron 106 m

NR | DMA WAR | 1980 | COLOR | Viol, AdSit

9 Riveting made-for-television war drama based upon a real individual. Philip Caputo (Davis) was a young and idealistic college student who joined the Marines. He went off to fight the brutal war in Vietnam and watched his friends die. Then, while leading his men into combat at a small Vietnamese village, things went terribly awry and he found himself facing a court martial for murder and his once loyal attitude to the Corps changed. A gripping true story about one man's political transformation from an enthusiastic soldier to a bitter veteran. Adapted from the novel by John Sacret Young.

A: Brad Davis, Keith Carradine, Stacy Keach, Michael O'Keefe, Richard Bradford, Brian Dennehy

© FRIES HOME VIDEO 97700

RUN SILENT, RUN DEEP

D: Robert Wise 94 m

NR | WAR DMA ACT | 1958 | B&W | Viol, AdSit

8 Gripping WWII war drama. Burt Lancaster was to have become Captain of his own submarine, but instead is named first officer at the last minute when Clark Gable is given command. Gable is the only survivor of a Japanese attack on his old sub. In spite of being hampered by the suspicions and deep distrust of the entire crew and his first officer, and in the face of long odds, Gable is determined to sink a Japanese cruiser. Very tense drama, capturing the feeling of tight quarters and uncertainty. One of the best submarine movies ever.

A: Clark Gable, Burt Lancaster, Brad Dexter, Jack Warden, Nick Cravat, Don Rickles

Distributed By MGM/UA Home Video M202133

SCHINDLER'S LIST

D: Steven Spielberg 197 m

R | DMA WAR | 1994 | B&W | Sex, Nud, Viol, Lang, AdSit

10 Mind-boggling true story. Oscar Schindler was a promoter, a playboy and a Nazi in Krakow, Poland. In 1939, he seized the opportunity to make his fortune by arm-twisting several wealthy Jews from the ghetto into investing in a new factory that he would front. The company was to make pots for the German war machine with Jewish slave labor. He was a success and did make a fortune, but it also forced him daily to witness the mindless cruelty and absolute horror of the Nazis. His realization transformed him. Soon he was struggling to protect his workers, ultimately even purchasing 1100 Jews from the Nazis. Riveting and true. 10 Oscar nominations, won Best Picture.

A: Liam Neeson, Ralph Fiennes, Ben Kingsley, Caroline Goodall, Jonathan Sagalle, Embeth Davidtz

© MCA/UNIVERSAL HOME VIDEO, INC. 82153

SEA WOLVES, THE

D: Andrew V. McLaglen 120 m

PG | ACT WAR | 1980 | COLOR | Sex, Nud, Viol, Lang, AdSit

7 A riveting war adventure based on a true story! During WWII, aging British agents (Peck and Moore) recruit some retired members of a British calvary unit who are now members of an honorary drinking club in India for an espionage mission against the Germans. The team is after a clandestine radio transmitter on board a German ship that's anchored in a neutral Indian port. While Peck leads his over-the-hill recruits in their training sessions, Moore romances with a beautiful double agent (Kellerman). High flying adventure and a stellar cast.

A: Gregory Peck, Roger Moore, David Niven, Trevor Howard, Barbara Kellerman, Patrick Macnee

© WARNER HOME VIDEO 709

SERGEANT RYKER

D: Buzz Kulik 85 m

NR | DMA WAR | 1968 | COLOR | AdSit

7 Sgt. Paul Ryker has been accused of defecting to Communist China during the Korean War. He claims that he was actually on a secret mission behind enemy lines, but his story doesn't agree with the evidence and he is convicted. The prosecuting attorney believes that Ryker's attorney was incompetent. He reviews the case and succeeds in getting the case reopened, but in the process he has fallen in love with Ryker's wife and is himself now being charged for criminal misconduct. Based upon a made-for-TV film.

A: Lee Marvin, Bradford Dillman, Vera Miles, Peter Graves, Lloyd Nolan, Murral Hamilton

© GOODTIMES 4115

SINK THE BISMARCK

D: Lewis Gilbert 97 m

NR | WAR ACT | 1960 | B&W | Viol, AdSit

9 Powerful and involving first-class WWII actioner! The Bismarck was the biggest and most powerful battle ship ever built. It was supposed to be unsinkable and it was German. Upon the first reports of it leaving safe harbor, the best ship in the English navy was sent after the Bismarck - and was immediately sunk. The British admiralty then concocted a masterful campaign to find, attack and destroy the Nazi ship. It simply had to be done; the fate of the entire navy depended upon it. Historically, the film is reasonably accurate but it is also very exciting with a lot of actual war footage.

A: Kenneth More, Dana Wynter, Carl Mohner, Laurence Naismith, Geoffrey Keen, Karel Stepanek

© FOXVIDEO 1812

TIME TO LOVE AND A TIME TO DIE, A

D: Douglas Sirk 133 m

NR | DMA ROM WAR | 1958 | COLOR | Viol, AdSit

8 Poignant, moving, believable and sad anti-war film. It is the story of an ordinary German soldier caught up in the chaos occurring during the closing days of World War II. He returns home on furlough from the Russian front to his hometown which has been almost totally destroyed by the Allied bombing raids and his parents are missing. All the townsfolk are as severely demoralized and fearful as is he, but there he meets a beautiful young woman. They fall in love and marry, all the while knowing that their time together will be brief because he must soon return to the front.

A: John Gavin, Lilo Pulver, Jock Mahoney, Keenan Wynn, Jim Hutton, Klaus Kinski

© MCA/UNIVERSAL HOME VIDEO, INC.

TOBRUK

D: Arthur Hiller 110 m

NR | ACT WAR | 1966 | COLOR | Viol, AdSit

6 Thrilling World War II action movie in which a group of German Jews, disguised as Axis troops, together with some American and English commandos, undertake a daring mission across miles of desert wasteland to destroy the fuel supplies of Field Marshall Rommel's tanks in North Africa at Tobruk. Pretty good. There are some pretty big action scenes with tank battles, and some intrigue, too, when they suspect a traitor in their midst.

A: Rock Hudson, George Peppard, Guy Stockwell, Nigel Green, Jack Watson, Norman Rossington

© MCA/UNIVERSAL HOME VIDEO, INC. 45014

TOO LATE THE HERO

D: Robert Aldrich 132 m

PG | ACT WAR SUS | 1969 | COLOR | Viol, AdSit

8 Good WWII action flick. A reluctant American is assigned to a unit of reluctant British commandos, who are to destroy the Japanese radio installation on the other end of their island in preparation for a major naval action. On their return, they discover a clandestine airfield and must get word of it back. Over the course of their mission, all but two are killed: the American (Robertson) and one Brit (Caine) - and they don't like each other. However, if they are going to survive, they have to cooperate to win an intense battle of wits and wills with the Japanese commandant who is intent upon hunting them down and killing them. Taut, fast-paced, action-packed thriller.

A: Michael Caine, Cliff Robertson, Ian Bannen, Henry Fonda, Harry Andrews

© CBS/FOX VIDEO 8034

TORA! TORA! TORA!

D: Richard Fleischer, Toshio Masuda 144 m

G | WAR ACT | 1970 | COLOR | Viol, AdSit

8 Extravagant and historically accurate recreation of the events leading up to, and the actual bombing of, Pearl Harbor in 1941. Prepared by both Japanese and American production crews, two versions were prepared: one was released in America and was largely ignored by the public, the other was released in Japan becoming a major box office hit. Extraordinary effort was made to be both accurate and realistic. Much of the fact-based drama surrounding the events leading to the attack was thought to have been too slow for most Americans. Too bad. Very impressive action sequences.

A: Martin Balsam, E.G. Marshall, James Whitmore, Jason Robards, Jr., Tatsuya Mihashi, Joseph Cotten

© FOXVIDEO 1017

TRAIN, THE

D: John Frankenheimer 133 m

NR | ACT SUS WAR | 1965 | B&W | Viol, Lang, AdSit

9 Top-notch gripping action film set in France just as WWII is starting to turn for the Allies. Burt Lancaster is the head of the French railway system and is also in the underground movement. Paul Scofield is a driven German officer in charge of getting a train load of French art treasures, stolen from French museums, back to Germany. Lancaster is reluctant to risk lives for art until an old man he loves is killed by the Nazis as he trys to stop the train. Excellent, solid suspense. Fast moving, with a clever plot and good special effects. Based on a true story.

A: Burt Lancaster, Paul Scofield, Michel Simon, Albert Remy, Wolfgang Preiss

Distributed By MGM/UA Home Video 202511

TWO WOMEN

D: Vittorio De Sica 99 m

NR | FOR DMA WAR | 1961 | B&W | Sex, Viol, AdSit

9 Extremely intense and moving drama. Sophia Loren received an Oscar for her powerful performance. It is a story of survival under extraordinary circumstances. It is Italy during WWII, just as the Germans are retreating and the Allies are advancing. Sophia is the mother of a 13-year-old daughter and both are struggling just to survive. They are also just learning to deal with the girl's awakening womanhood, because both mother and daughter have both fallen in love with a farmer's son (Belmundo), when both are raped by advancing soldiers. Heart-wrenching. Subtitles or dubbed.

A: Sophia Loren, Raf Vallone, Jean-Paul Belmondo, Eleanora Brown, Renato Salvatori

© GOODTIMES 4240

UP PERISCOPE

D: Gordon Douglas — 111 m

NR | WAR ACT | 1959 | COLOR

6 Good WWII actioner. James Garner is young and a brand new navy lieutenant. He is also a skindiver and a demolitions expert who is being sent to sabotage a Japanese radio transmitter on a South Pacific island. He travels to his location on board a submarine captained by Edmond O'Brien, who is under orders to take Garner in as close to shore as possible. Garner then is to leave the submarine while it is submerged and is to return to it when the job is complete. However, if he doesn't return by a predetermined time, he will be presumed dead. Well done. Still pretty effective today.

Sex / Nud / ◢ Viol / Lang / ◢ AdSit

A: James Garner, Edmond O'Brien, Andra Martin, Alan Hale, Carleton Carpenter, Frank Gifford

© WARNER HOME VIDEO 12042

VICTORY AT SEA - SERIES

D: — 780 m

NR | DOC WAR | 1960 | B&W

10 This is a very popular and multi-award-winning documentary series that was created for TV during the early 1950s, in 26 30-minute segments (also available). It documents the Allied struggle during WWII over five continents. The entire series is now available in one six-volume tape set. It is an extremely well-written documentary, containing excellent photography (including some amazing archival footage), magnificently narrated by Alexander Scourby and accompanied by a rousing Richard Rodgers score.

Sex / Nud / ◢ Viol / Lang / ◢ AdSit

A:

© NEW LINE HOME VIDEO 7659

VON RYAN'S EXPRESS

D: Mark Robson — 117 m

NR | ACT WAR | 1965 | COLOR

8 Top-drawer WWII actioner. Sinatra is an American colonel shot down and placed in a POW camp. He is the ranking officer, but is not held in high regard by his fellow prisoners until he engineers the capture of the train in which 600 of them are being transported across Italy to Germany. The POWs want to divert their captured train toward Switzerland and freedom, but the Germans are not about to let that happen without a fight. Hard-hitting action, suspense, solid acting and well-paced directing make this a thrilling adventure story.

Sex / Nud / ◢ Viol / Lang / ◢ AdSit

A: Frank Sinatra, Trevor Howard, Luther Adler, James Brolin, Brad Dexter, Edward Mulhare

© FOXVIDEO 1003

WACKIEST SHIP IN THE ARMY, THE

D: Richard Murphy — 99 m

NR | COM WAR | 1961 | COLOR

6 Pleasing light-weight entertainment. Jack Lemmon is a young Navy lieutenant who, because he has some sailing experience, is conned into commanding a run-down old sailing ship through the waters of the South Pacific during WWII. He and his motley crew of inexperienced Army soldier/sailors are charged with getting a man onto an island behind Japanese lines to spy on Japanese movements. This is a light-hearted comedy that also plays serious for a while with the dangerous aspects of war. Most of the time it is fun and funny, but it has its serious moments, too.

Sex / Nud / ◢ Viol / Lang / AdSit

A: Jack Lemmon, Ricky Nelson, Chips Rafferty, John Lund, Tom Tully, Warren Berlinger

© COLUMBIA TRISTAR HOME VIDEO 60596

WHERE EAGLES DARE

D: Brian G. Hutton — 158 m

PG | WAR ACT | 1968 | COLOR

8 High intensity action film in which a small group of commandos, lead by Burton and Eastwood, attack a supposedly impregnable German-held castle high in the Bavarian Alps to rescue an American general being held captive there. They must get him out before the Nazis get critical secret information out of him, but their plans to do it are jeopardized by an unknown double-agent in their midst. Now, no one can be trusted. Lots of high-risk stunts, shootouts and thrilling adventure. A real hair-raiser.

Sex / Nud / ◢ Viol / ◢ Lang / ◢ AdSit

A: Richard Burton, Clint Eastwood, Mary Ure, Michael Hordern, Patrick Wymark, Robert Beatty

Distributed By MGM/UA Home Video M700137

YOUNG LIONS, THE

D: Edward Dmytryk — 167 m

NR | DMA WAR ACT | 1958 | B&W

9 Excellent, gripping human drama that uses WWII as a backdrop to explore the war's effects on three very different men. Brando is a handsome and idealistic ski instructor who adopts Nazism as the answer to Germany's problems, until he discovers its realities. Montgomery Clift is an American Jew, a smallish man drafted into the Army, who must deal with anti-Semitic taunts both at home and in the service. Dean Martin is a popular playboy entertainer who must learn to face his own cowardice. The three separate stories are interwoven as the men are drawn together by the war. Very moving.

Sex / Nud / ◢ Viol / Lang / ◢ AdSit

A: Marlon Brando, Montgomery Clift, Dean Martin, Hope Lange, Barbara Rush, Maximilian Schell

© FOXVIDEO 1057

ZEPPELIN

D: Etienne Perrier — 102 m

G | ACT WAR | 1971 | COLOR

6 The time is WWI. The English military fears the German's newest weapon, the Zepplin, so they entice a German-born Scottish lieutenant (York) to "defect" to the Germans to collect information on the fearsome weapon. Now, as a German officer, he is almost unbelievably invited aboard the ship for a trial run. However, when it is airborne, he finds there is a reason he is there. The Germans plan to launch a daring raid into England and they need his knowledge of the countryside to carry it off. Entertaining and atmospheric with good special effects.

Sex / Nud / ◢ Viol / Lang / ◢ AdSit

A: Michael York, Elke Sommer, Marius Goring, Anton Diffring, Rupert Davies, Peter Carsten

© WARNER HOME VIDEO 11562

Western

1956 and After

100 RIFLES

D: Tom Gries 110 m

PG | WST | 1969 | COLOR

6 Reynolds plays a Yaqui Indian who robs a bank to buy guns for his people so they can fight back against a railroad tycoon and a corrupt Mexican official. Deputy Jim Brown pursues into Mexico, where they both are imprisoned. They become allies, escape together and Brown joins the Indians in their struggle. However, their friendship is threatened when Brown falls for Reynolds's woman (Raquel Welch). In spite of the then-controversial black/white love scenes, the film was well received. It is still worth seeing today, largely because of Reynolds's performance.

Sex / Nud / ✓ Viol / ✓ Lang / AdSit

A: Burt Reynolds, Raquel Welch, Jim Brown, Fernando Lamas

© CBS/FOX VIDEO 1060

3:10 TO YUMA

D: Delmer Daves 92 m

NR | WST SUS ACT | 1957 | B&W

9 Top drawer Western, one of the best of the 1950s. Glenn Ford is a notorious gunman and powerful leader of a gang who holds up a stagecoach but gets caught when he stays behind to dally with a lonely barmaid. The wealthy owner of the stage company has offered Van Heflin, a poverty-struck farmer, $200 to guard Ford in a hotel room until lawmen arrive on the 3:10 train to take him into custody. Desperate for the money, Van Heflin agrees and becomes caught up in a psychological battle of wills with Ford, whose men begin to gather outside getting ready to break him out. Powerful stuff.

Sex / Nud / ✓ Viol / Lang / ✓ AdSit

A: Van Heflin, Glenn Ford, Felicia Farr, Richard Jaeckel, Henry Jones, Leora Dana

© COLUMBIA TRISTAR HOME VIDEO 60444

7 FACES OF DR. LAO

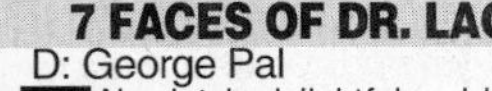

D: George Pal 101 m

NR | FAN WST CLD | 1963 | COLOR

9 Absolutely delightful and heartwarming fantasy. A small Old West town newspaper editor (Ericson) is trying to win the hand of a pretty widow (Eden) and fighting a lonely battle against a villain (O'Connell), who is trying to grab up all the land around. A truly strange helpmate arrives in the form of a mysterious and wise old Chinese magician named Dr. Lao (Randall). Dr. Lao is the proprietor of a traveling circus containing a fantastic array of wondrous sideshow creatures. Fabulous makeup and special effects. Randall is truly outstanding, playing multiple roles. Great fun for all.

Sex / Nud / Viol / Lang / AdSit

A: Tony Randall, Barbara Eden, Arthur O'Connell, John Ericson, Lee Patrick, Noah Beery, Jr.

Distributed By MGM/UA Home Video M600667

AGAINST A CROOKED SKY

D: Earl Bellamy 90 m

G | WST CLD | 1975 | COLOR

6 Pretty good family Western. A boy begins a desperate search for his sister who was taken by Indians and is helped by a grizzled old trapper (Richard Boone). It is a pretty basic story line that has been used many times before, however this time it is squarely aimed at younger viewers. Still, even if you are a little older, if you are a Western fan, you will have a good time with it. However, this same premise was much more deeply explored, with much more mature themes, in the classic John Wayne picture THE SEARCHERS.

Sex / Nud / ✓ Viol / Lang / AdSit

A: Richard Boone, Clint Ritchie, Henry Wilcoxon, Stewart Peterson, Geoffrey Land, Jewel Blanch

© BRIDGESTONE PRODUCTION GROUP

ALAMO, THE

D: John Wayne 162 m

NR | WST ACT | 1960 | COLOR

8 John Wayne's action epic. It was Wayne's personal dream to see that this movie was made. He produced, directed and starred in this epic re-creation of the 1836 siege at San Antonio, Texas mission called the Alamo. The Duke gives a tough performance as Davy Crocket, but Widmark, Boone and Harvey also turn in excellent performances. Movie is a bit long, but when the action starts, Duke fans get their reward. Received seven Oscar nominations, including Best Picture. Also includes a 40-minute documentary about the filming of the movie.

Sex / Nud / ✓ Viol / Lang / AdSit

A: John Wayne, Richard Widmark, Frankie Avalon, Richard Boone, Chill Wills, Laurence Harvey

Distributed By MGM/UA Home Video M302581

ALVAREZ KELLY

D: Edward Dmytryk 110 m

NR | WST ACT | 1966 | COLOR

7 A good Western. Richard Widmark has greatly complicated William Holden's life. Holden is a cowboy who has just sold a bunch of his cattle to the North during the Civil War. Politics are unimportant to him. Now Widmark, who is a Confederate colonel, captures Holden and wants him to help to steal the 2,500 head back for the starving South. Colorful if somewhat offbeat Western. Lots of two-fisted action and it is based upon an actual incident from the Civil War.

Sex / Nud / ✓ Viol / Lang / AdSit

A: William Holden, Richard Widmark, Janice Rule, Victoria Shaw, Patrick O'Neal

© GOODTIMES 4210

ANDERSONVILLE TRIAL, THE

D: George C. Scott 150 m

NR | DMA WST | 1970 | COLOR

9 Riveting psychological and courtroom drama based upon solid historical fact. During the Civil War, the Confederate prison at Andersonville, Georgia housed over 50,000 prisoners under absolutely squalid conditions. This is the gripping account of the moral issues surrounding the post-war trial of the Prussian administrator of that camp, whose German military training required him to follow orders without question even though these orders lead to over 14,000 deaths. It is one of the most tragic stories to come out of the Civil War and is an issue that would be revisited in WWII. Thought-provoking and powerful stuff.

Sex / Nud / Viol / Lang / ■ AdSit

A: Martin Sheen, William Shatner, Buddy Ebsen, Richard Basehart, Cameron Mitchell, Jack Cassidy

© LIVE HOME VIDEO 51065

BAD COMPANY

D: Robert Benton 94 m

PG | WST COM | 1972 | COLOR

7 Interesting and quite different kind of buddy-Western. It is part realistic adventure, part comedy. Two draft-dodgers each decide to head west rather than get caught up in the Civil War. Along the way, they meet some other young draft-dodgers and they form a small-time gang so they can rob and cheat to pay for their way west. However, when the group arrives in the West, it falls apart as they all turn on each other. An entertaining and clever combination of a fun buddy movie, raunchy humor and action. Brown and Bridges somehow manage to make their otherwise grungy characters appealing in spite of their unsavory natures.

Sex / Nud / ✓ Viol / ✓ Lang / ✓ AdSit

A: Jeff Bridges, Barry Brown, Jim Davis, David Huddleston, John Savage, Jerry Houser

© PARAMOUNT HOME VIDEO 8476

BADLANDERS, THE

D: Delmer Daves — 84 m

NR | WST ACT | 1958 | COLOR

7 Good Western action. It is the turn-of-the-century in Arizona. Alan Ladd and Ernest Borgnine have just been released from prison but they are eager to get even with the guy who sent them there in the first place and stole their gold mine in the process. To do it, they enlist a dynamite expert (Persoff) in their plot to steal $200,000 of their own gold back, right from under his nose. This is widely recognized as being a Western version of the gangster classic THE ASPHALT JUNGLE.

Sex / Nud / ◢ Viol / Lang / AdSit

A: Alan Ladd, Ernest Borgnine, Katy Jurado, Claire Kelly

Distributed By MGM/UA Home Video M202710

BALLAD OF CABLE HOGUE, THE

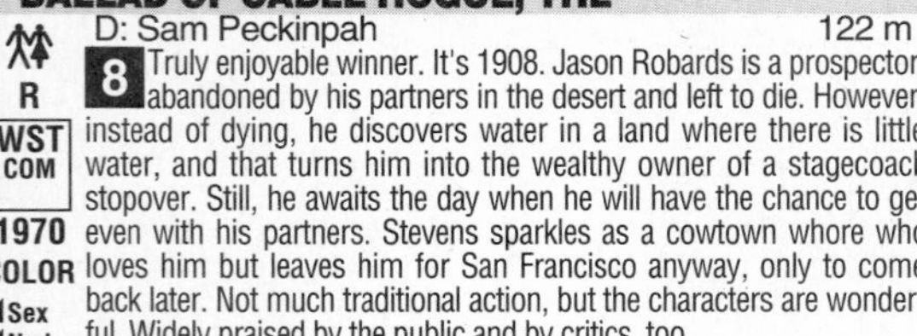

D: Sam Peckinpah — 122 m

R | WST COM | 1970 | COLOR

8 Truly enjoyable winner. It's 1908. Jason Robards is a prospector, abandoned by his partners in the desert and left to die. However, instead of dying, he discovers water in a land where there is little water, and that turns him into the wealthy owner of a stagecoach stopover. Still, he awaits the day when he will have the chance to get even with his partners. Stevens sparkles as a cowtown whore who loves him but leaves him for San Francisco anyway, only to come back later. Not much traditional action, but the characters are wonderful. Widely praised by the public and by critics, too.

◢ Sex / ◢ Nud / ◢ Viol / ◢ Lang / ■ AdSit

A: Jason Robards, Jr., Stella Stevens, Strother Martin, L.Q. Jones, David Warner, Slim Pickens

© WARNER HOME VIDEO 11298

BALLAD OF GREGORIO CORTEZ, THE

D: Robert M. Young — 105 m

PG | WST DMA | 1983 | COLOR

7 This is the true story, set in 1901 Texas, of a Mexican cowhand who was falsely accused of horse theft after a series of errors which stemmed from an otherwise innocent misunderstood word in Spanish. The incident explodes out of control and he kills the local sheriff who came to arrest him. For the next 11 days, he is pursued by 600 rangers for over 450 miles in one of Texas's biggest manhunts. A very different sort of Western that realistically captures the era and recreates the bordertowns. Olmos does an excellent job with the character of a man who is a fugitive for no good reason.

Sex / Nud / ◢ Viol / ◢ Lang / AdSit

A: Edward James Olmos, James Gammon, Tom Bower, Bruce McGill, Alan Vint, Timothy Scott

© NEW LINE HOME VIDEO 2062

BALLAD OF LITTLE JO, THE

D: Maggie Greenwald — 124 m

R | WST DMA | 1993 | COLOR

7 This is a very curious video. While it is a Western, it is a very different sort of Western. Suzy Amis plays the daughter of a wealthy easterner, who is thrown out by her father after she has an illegitimate child. She sets out in a westerly direction, not really knowing where to go. She does however soon discover that a woman alone on the road is a target. So, she cut off her hair and donned a man's clothes. She is safe from unwanted advances, but she also soon discovers that she is trapped in her secret. The video is very evocative of the period and presents a window onto not-so-flattering aspects that are usually glossed over. It is interesting, but it does tend to be a little slow.

◢ Sex / ■ Nud / ◢ Viol / ◢ Lang / ■ AdSit

A: Suzy Amis, Bo Hopkins, Ian McKellen, David Chung, Anthony Heald, Heather Graham

© TURNER HOME ENTERTAINMENT N4156

BARBAROSA

D: Fred Schepisi — 90 m

PG | WST ACT | 1981 | COLOR

8 Action packed and critically acclaimed Western. Willie Nelson puts in a fine performance as Barbarosa - a legendary, free-spirited outlaw who is joined by a ragged farmer/protege (Busey), on the run from an accidental killing. Barbarosa is running both from bounty hunters and his wife's family, who keeps sending their sons out to find and kill him. Together the two survive, while Busey gains a new trade and a growing respect for the strange loner Nelson. Majestic scenery, good period detail, realistic action and a sometimes funny script give it plenty of flavor. Solid Western.

Sex / Nud / ◢ Viol / Lang / ◢ AdSit

A: Willie Nelson, Gary Busey, Isela Vega, Gilbert Roland, Danny De La Paz, George Voskovec

© J2 COMMUNICATIONS 0035

BEGUILED, THE

D: Don Siegel — 109 m

R | WST DMA | 1970 | COLOR

7 Offbeat story set in the South during the Civil War. It is an oddly compelling story of a wounded Union soldier who is taken in at a girl's boarding school. There, he becomes the cause of sexual tensions, leading to a flurry of jealousy and hatred as both students and teachers vie for his affections. He is held hostage by the women, each of whom holds his life in the balance with their vow of secrecy, however he is a schemer and a liar who will say and do anything to get what he wants. Rather slow-paced, but rewarding for the patient viewer, with a startling conclusion. Another interesting and somewhat similar theme was provocatively explored in BLACK NARCISSUS.

◢ Sex / ◢ Nud / ◢ Viol / ◢ Lang / ■ AdSit

A: Clint Eastwood, Geraldine Page, Elizabeth Hartman, Jo Ann Harris, Darleen Carr, Mae Mercer

© MCA/UNIVERSAL HOME VIDEO, INC. 55059

BELIZAIRE THE CAJUN

D: Glen Pitre — 113 m

PG | DMA WST | 1986 | COLOR

6 Rich and faithful portrait of the Louisiana bayou country in the early 1800s. The rhythms of the place and the time provide a backdrop for this piece of Cajun folklore, and are also some of the film's most inviting qualities. Belizair is a self-assured traditional Cajun herbal healer who is in trouble because of his love for the Cajun wife of a rich Anglo, and because of his continued defense of his people against the prejudice of the other locals. Belizair is framed for murder after he helps a persecuted friend. Sincere effort that has worthy moments, but also some shortcomings.

Sex / Nud / ◢ Viol / Lang / ◢ AdSit

A: Armand Assante, Gail Youngs, Michael Schoeffling, Stephen McHatti, Will Patton, Nancy Barrett

© CBS/FOX VIDEO 3740

BIG COUNTRY, THE

D: William Wyler — 166 m

NR | WST ACT | 1958 | COLOR

9 Big Western. Peck is a former sea captain who has abandoned the sea. He met Baker when she was in school, they're engaged and he has now come west to her father's (Bickford) ranch. Upon his arrival, he finds that he has stumbled into the middle of a vicious long-standing feud between Bickford and his neighbor Burl Ives (won Oscar) over water rights. However, the water is on land now owned by Jean Simmons who was willed it when her father died. Peck doesn't want to fight and is accused of being a coward, but he's going to have to. This is a big budget Western and is quite good too. Theme song is a classic.

Sex / Nud / ◢ Viol / Lang / ◢ AdSit

A: Gregory Peck, Jean Simmons, Charlton Heston, Carroll Baker, Burl Ives, Charles Bickford

Distributed By MGM/UA Home Video M900917

BIG HAND FOR THE LITTLE LADY, A

D: Fielder Cook — 95 m

WST COM SUS | 1966 | COLOR

8 Great little comedy with lots of twists. It's a clever story about a farmer (Fonda) and his wife (Woodward) who arrive in town just in time for the annual big stakes poker game. He's a former gambler and has sworn off but, he has to get into that game. Against his wife's wishes, he does and then gets dealt the hand of his life. He bets until he runs out of cash, so he bets the farm (much to the wife's distress) and then has a heart attack. She now has everything in the world she owns at stake and bet on the unfinished game, so the little lady steps up to the table and says, "How do you play this game?"

Sex / Nud / Viol / Lang / AdSit

A: Henry Fonda, Joanne Woodward, Jason Robards, Jr., Charles Bickford, Burgess Meredith, Paul Ford

© WARNER HOME VIDEO 11469

BIG JAKE

D: George Sherman — 110 m

G | WST ACT | 1971 | COLOR

6 It's 1909 and someone has kidnapped John Wayne's grandson (his real-life son John Ethan). They shouldn't have done that. His estranged wife of 18 years (Maureen O'Hara) has asked him to take one million dollars in ransom money to bad guy Richard Boone. Instead, Jake tries a double-cross that just about backfires. This movie also tried for some laughs... but shouldn't have. It works best as a shoot-`em-up Western for John Wayne fans. It's good at that.

Sex / Nud / ◢ Viol / Lang / AdSit

A: John Wayne, Richard Boone, Maureen O'Hara, Patrick Wayne, Chris Mitchum, Bobby Vinton

© FOXVIDEO 7149

BITE THE BULLET

D: Richard Brooks — 131 m

PG | WST ACT | 1975 | COLOR

8 Excellent but unconventional Western that is a large-scale epic about a 700-mile endurance horserace (which were actually quite common in the West at the turn of the 20th century). This is a sleeper of a movie that was hardly noticed upon its release, but undeservedly so. The story revolves around the different types of people who compete in the rough-and-tumble race and the gradual respect that all the finalists gain for each other. There are many top stars in it - Hackman and Coburn in particular are excellent. Beautiful photography.

Sex / Nud / ◢ Viol / ◢ Lang / AdSit

A: Gene Hackman, James Coburn, Candice Bergen, Ben Johnson, Jan-Michael Vincent, Dabney Coleman

© COLUMBIA TRISTAR HOME VIDEO VH10022

BLACK ROBE

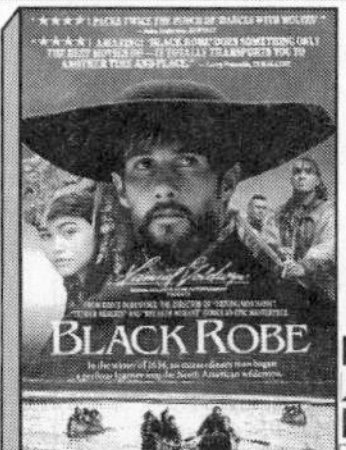

D: Bruce Beresford — 101 m

R | DMA WST | 1991 | COLOR

8 Stunningly photographed quasi-historical portrait of very early North America (Quebec in 1634) and an idealistic young Jesuit's expedition into the virgin wilderness to bring Christianity to the Huron Indians. Leaving a small French outpost, he and a white companion travel with a band of Algonquins through land controlled by the ferocious Iroquois. The priest's concepts of God become unexpectedly challenged when confronted with the Iroquois and God, both in their own elements. Intelligent and intense. A fictional account, but scrupulously based on carefully researched fact.

■ Sex / ◢ Nud / ■ Viol / Lang / ■ AdSit

A: August Schellenberg, Lothaire Bluteau, Aden Young, Sandrine Holt, Tantoo Cardinal

© VIDMARK ENTERTAINMENT VM5543

BLAZING SADDLES

D: Mel Brooks — 93 m

R | COM WST | 1974 | COLOR | Sex, Nud, Viol, Lang, AdSit

9 Hilarious! This is a savage spoof of Westerns (DODGE CITY in particular). It is uproariously funny but also unflinchingly crude. The jokes are rapid fire and constant. The story revolves around Cleavon Little as the unlikely black sheriff being challenged by Harvey Korman's bad guy character. Madelin Kahn does a riotous Dietrich parody, Alex Karras knocks out a horse, and don't forget the beans around the campfire scene. Belly-laugh city. Also don't forget to see the unrelated but equally hilarious Western spoofs SUPPORT YOUR LOCAL SHERIFF and CAT BALLOU!

A: Cleavon Little, Gene Wilder, Harvey Korman, Madeline Kahn, Mel Brooks, Slim Pickens

© WARNER HOME VIDEO 1001

BRAVADOS, THE

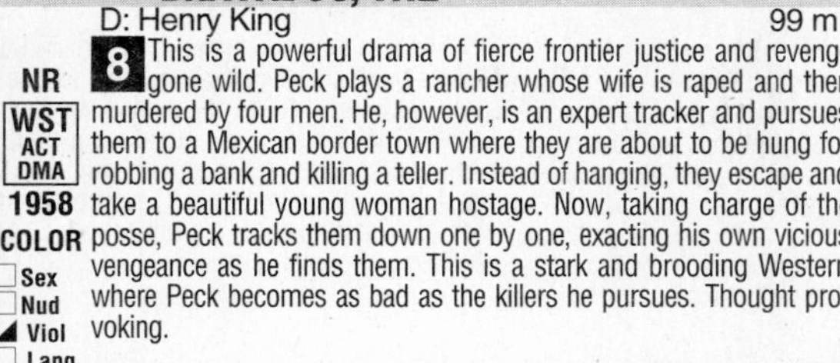

D: Henry King — 99 m

NR | WST ACT DMA | 1958 | COLOR | Sex, Nud, Viol, Lang, AdSit

8 This is a powerful drama of fierce frontier justice and revenge gone wild. Peck plays a rancher whose wife is raped and then murdered by four men. He, however, is an expert tracker and pursues them to a Mexican border town where they are about to be hung for robbing a bank and killing a teller. Instead of hanging, they escape and take a beautiful young woman hostage. Now, taking charge of the posse, Peck tracks them down one by one, exacting his own vicious vengeance as he finds them. This is a stark and brooding Western where Peck becomes as bad as the killers he pursues. Thought provoking.

A: Gregory Peck, Joan Collins, Stephen Boyd, Albert Salmi, Henry Silva, Kathleen Gallant

© FOXVIDEO 1494

BREAKHEART PASS

D: Tom Gries — 96 m

PG | WST ACT MYS | 1976 | COLOR | Sex, Nud, Viol, Lang, AdSit

7 Slam-bang action-filled Western starring Charles Bronson. He is an accused thief and an arsonist aboard a special government train that is heading through the snow-draped Rocky Mountains on a rescue mission to an Army outpost and is accompanied by a US Marshall. Also aboard are a governor, his secret mistress and a government engineer. When one of the passengers is murdered, it becomes apparent that all of them have something to hide and are not what they appear to be. Plenty of stunts and fights complement some interesting plot twists in a search for the answer to a

A: Charles Bronson, Ben Johnson, Ed Lauter, Richard Crenna, Charles Durning, Jill Ireland

Distributed By MGM/UA Home Video M201559

BUCK AND THE PREACHER

D: Sidney Poitier — 102 m

PG | WST COM | 1972 | COLOR | Sex, Nud, Viol, Lang, AdSit

6 Pretty good and different sort of Western, but with a relatively thin plot. Buck (Poitier) is a black ex-Union Army Cavalry sergeant who agrees to act as scout for a wagon train of freed slaves heading to Colorado. Belafonte is a black con man and phony preacher who comes along. The preacher and Buck are forced to team up to defeat a group of white bounty hunters, led by the chief bad guy, Cameron Mitchell, who wants to kidnap them all and take them to Louisiana. Clever and light-hearted in spots. Warm with good characterizations.

A: Sidney Poitier, Harry Belafonte, Cameron Mitchell, Ruby Dee

© COLUMBIA TRISTAR HOME VIDEO 60148

BUTCH AND SUNDANCE: THE EARLY DAYS

D: Richard Lester — 111 m

PG | WST COM | 1979 | COLOR | Sex, Nud, Viol, Lang, AdSit

7 This prequel to the Redford/Newman pairing from the original blockbuster, imagines the same characters as they were when they were still just learning their trade. This easy-to-take follow up traces their adventures from the time of their first meeting, just after Butch is released from prison, and takes them through their early, not-too-good holdup attempts. The leads in this picture (Katt and Beringer), like Newman and Redford, are likable. The film is interesting in its own right, but is far overshadowed by its more illustrious predecessor.

A: William Katt, Tom Berenger, Jeff Corey, John Corey, John Schuck, Jill Eikenberry

© FOXVIDEO 1117

BUTCH CASSIDY AND THE SUNDANCE KID

D: George Roy Hill — 110 m

PG | WST COM | 1969 | COLOR | Sex, Nud, Viol, Lang, AdSit

10 This picture was a spectacular box office hit and deservedly so. It also won 4 Oscars. Newman and Redford are extremely likable as two fun-loving bank and train robbers who are relentlessly pursued by an unshakable Sheriff's posse... "Who is that guy anyway?" So they escape to Bolivia with Sundance's girlfriend (Ross) but they can't even rob the banks there properly because they can't speak the language. Great dialogue and chemistry between the players makes this an utter joy to watch. Extremely entertaining. Do not miss this one.

A: Paul Newman, Robert Redford, Katharine Ross, Strother Martin, Cloris Leachman, Henry James

© FOXVIDEO 1061

CAHILL: U.S. MARSHAL

D: Andrew V. McLaglen — 103 m

PG | WST | 1973 | COLOR | Sex, Nud, Viol, Lang, AdSit

6 John Wayne is a tough Marshall who spends so much time out chasing bad guys that he neglects his young sons at home. Left on their own too much, they decide to start robbing banks and join a gang of bad guys led by George Kennedy. However, when they find out what they've gotten into, they change their minds. But, now they can't get out because Kennedy is holding one son hostage to force the other to help carry out a bank robbery. John has to come to his boys's rescue and redeems his past neglects. Pretty violent in places. OK but ultimately a only slightly above standard B-grade Western.

A: John Wayne, Gary Grimes, George Kennedy, Neville Brand

© WARNER HOME VIDEO 11281

CAT BALLOU

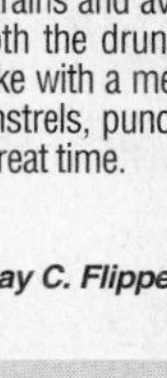

D: Elliot Silverstein — 96 m

NR | COM WST | 1965 | COLOR | Sex, Nud, Viol, Lang, AdSit

10 Wonderfully funny spoof of Westerns. Jane Fonda plays a naive and innocent school teacher who turns to a life of crime after her father is killed by a crooked land baron seeking to gain control of her father's ranch. In response, she forms a rag tag gang, manned by a drunken ex-gunfighter and two cowards, to rob trains and avenge her father's murder. Lee Marvin is hysterical as both the drunken gunfighter (on a drunken horse) and his evil look-alike with a metal nose. Stubby Kaye and Nat King Cole, as traveling minstrels, punctuate the action and narrate the happenings with song. A great time.

A: Jane Fonda, Lee Marvin, Michael Callan, Jay C. Flippen, Duane Hickman, John Marley

© COLUMBIA TRISTAR HOME VIDEO 60154

CHEYENNE AUTUMN

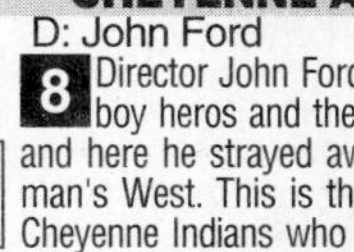

D: John Ford — 155 m

NR | WST DMA | 1964 | COLOR | Sex, Nud, Viol, Lang, AdSit

8 Director John Ford came to be virtually synonymous with cowboy heros and the Western movie. This film was his last movie and here he strayed away from his typical glorification of the white man's West. This is the story of a group of starving and desperate Cheyenne Indians who leave their barren reservation in Oklahoma to struggle back home to Wyoming. It is a pitiful tale of privation and hardship. They must travel across 1500 miles of bleak winter landscape, all the while pursued by the US Calvary, who will only take them back where they started. Worthy viewing.

A: Richard Widmark, Carroll Baker, Karl Malden, Dolores Del Rio, Sal Mineo, Edward G. Robinson

© WARNER HOME VIDEO 11052

CHEYENNE SOCIAL CLUB, THE

D: Gene Kelly — 102 m

PG | WST COM | 1970 | COLOR | Sex, Nud, Viol, Lang, AdSit

9 Light-hearted Western with plenty of action, too. Jimmy Stewart's brother Big John dies, leaving his "social club" to his brother. But Jimmy doesn't discover until he gets there that the club, which is Cheyenne's most popular business establishment, is also the local whorehouse. Jimmy and his scruffy long-time saddle partner (Henry Fonda) briefly enjoy their new-found career and its many benefits but then Jimmy has the misfortune to shoot an unruly customer. Now they are faced with the guy's very upset kinfolk, who are out for revenge. Great characters, all played just for fun... and fun it is. A great time.

A: James Stewart, Henry Fonda, Shirley Jones, Sue Anne Langdon, Elaine Devry

© WARNER HOME VIDEO 11343

CHISUM

D: Andrew V. McLaglen — 111 m

G | WST ACT | 1970 | COLOR | Sex, Nud, Viol, Lang, AdSit

8 This is a quite good Western. The Duke plays John Chisum, a land baron and a real-life character from the famous 1878 New Mexico Lincoln County War. Chisum is struggling against a wealthy land swindler (Forrest Tucker) who is cheating smaller ranchers and farmers out of their land. Excellent meaty characters add grit to the familiar story line: Corbett as Pat Garrett, Deuel as Billy the Kid, George as a bounty hunter and Ben Johnson as Wayne's foreman. Merle Haggard sings.

A: John Wayne, Forrest Tucker, Christopher George, Ben Johnson, Glenn Corbett, Geoffrey Deuel

© WARNER HOME VIDEO 11089

COMANCHEROS

D: Michael Curtiz — 107 m

NR | WST ACT | 1961 | COLOR | Sex, Nud, Viol, Lang, AdSit

8 Solid action Western. Wayne plays a Texas Ranger who has just captured a Mississippi riverboat dandy and gambler (Whitman) on charges of murder, for having killed a man in a duel. But, when Wayne comes up short of manpower, he drafts Whitman to help him chase down a band of outlaws called Comancheros who are supplying the dreaded Commanche Indians with rifles, ammunition and liquor. Typical Wayne, pretty good stuff. This is not his best movie - not his worst. There is plenty of action, some pathos, a little comedy and a great Elmer Bernstein score.

A: John Wayne, Stuart Whitman, Lee Marvin, Ina Balin, Bruce Cabot, Nehemiah Persoff

© FOXVIDEO 1177

COMES A HORSEMAN

D: Alan J. Pakula — 118 m

PG | WST DMA | 1978 | COLOR

☐ Sex ☐ Nud ◢ Viol ◢ Lang ◢ AdSit

8 Modern-day Western, set in the 1940s just after the end of the War. Jane Fonda plays a spinster rancher who is being set upon by her powerful neighbor (Jason Robards). He is intent upon creating a vast empire in the style of the land barons of the old West. Helping her in her fight are her aging hired hand (Farnsworth) and a World War II veteran (Caan), who is trying to forget what he has seen. A simple story, this is nonetheless an engrossing film, beautifully photographed with majestic scenery, but it is a little slow-moving at times.

A: Jane Fonda, James Caan, Jason Robards, Jr., George Grizzard, Richard Farnsworth, Mark Harmon

© FOXVIDEO 4552

CONAGHER

D: Reynaldo Villalobos — 117 m

NR | WST ACT | 1991 | COLOR

☐ Sex ☐ Nud ◢ Viol ☐ Lang ☐ AdSit

7 Very good made-for-cable Western, adapted from a novel by Louis L'Amour. Katharine Ross, her new husband and his children settle in the Western wilderness to start a cattle ranch. But, he never returns from a buying trip and they are left to survive alone. Elliot is a drifting cowpoke who meets her. They are attracted, but neither can or does do anything about it. He winters with an old rancher whose cattle are being stolen and, while tracking down the thieves, the two meet again. Very realistic and evocative for those times, but could have been improved with some editing. Slow.

A: Sam Elliott, Katharine Ross, Barry Corbin, Billy Green Bush, Ken Curtis, Paul Koslo

© TURNER HOME ENTERTAINMENT 6081

COWBOYS

D: Mark Rydell — 128 m

PG | WST ACT | 1972 | COLOR

☐ Sex ☐ Nud ◢ Viol ◢ Lang ☐ AdSit

8 Good Western. John Wayne is Wil Andersen, a rancher whose hired-help desert him to prospect for gold just when he needs them to help to drive his herd 400 miles to market. Having no alternative, he reluctantly hires eleven local schoolboys to drive his cattle. On the trail, the boys face the normal hazards of nature, but also a wagon full of floozies, an outlaw band and their own fears... the boys become men. Bruce Dern is the menacing leader of the outlaw band and John is a gruff but believable father-figure. An unnecessarily cruel revenge mars the ending to otherwise good film.

A: John Wayne, Roscoe Lee Browne, Bruce Dern, Colleen Dewhurst, Slim Pickens, Lonny Chapman

© WARNER HOME VIDEO 11213

CULPEPPER CATTLE COMPANY, THE

D: Dick Richards — 92 m

PG | WST ACT | 1972 | COLOR

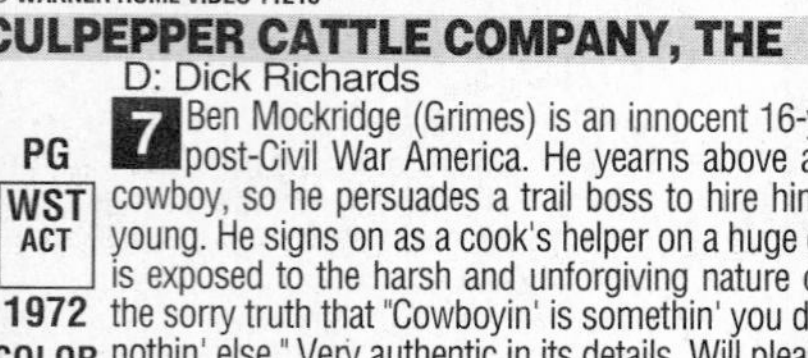

7 Ben Mockridge (Grimes) is an innocent 16-year-old farm boy in post-Civil War America. He yearns above all else to become a cowboy, so he persuades a trail boss to hire him even though he is young. He signs on as a cook's helper on a huge cattle drive where he is exposed to the harsh and unforgiving nature of the open trail and the sorry truth that "Cowboyin' is somethin' you do when you can't do nothin' else." Very authentic in its details. Will please Western fans, but is pretty violent in places.

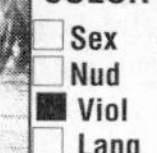

☐ Sex ☐ Nud ■ Viol ☐ Lang ◢ AdSit

A: Gary Grimes, Billy Green Bush, Luke Sakew, Bo Hopkins, Geoffrey Lewis

© FOXVIDEO 1189

DANCES WITH WOLVES

D: Kevin Costner — 180 m

PG-13 | WST DMA ACT | 1990 | COLOR

☐ Sex ☐ Nud ◢ Viol ◢ Lang ◢ AdSit

10 Wonderful, beautiful, grand and elegant. First-time director (and also the film's star) Costner scored a major win with this film. It won seven Oscars, including Best Picture and it struck a resilient chord in many viewers. It is the story of a disillusioned Civil War veteran who is stationed to a remote Army outpost in the Dakota territory. Finding it abandoned, he makes friends with a band of Lakota Sioux and is drawn into their extended family, their way of life and finds new meaning for his life. This is an exciting, thoroughly involving and sensitive telling of a time and a way of life long underappreciated. A must see!

A: Kevin Costner, Mary McDonnell, Graham Greene, Rodney A. Grant, Floyd Red Crow Westerman, Tantoo Cardinal

© ORION PICTURES CORPORATION 8768

DAVY CROCKETT AND THE RIVER PIRATES

D: Norman Foster — 81 m

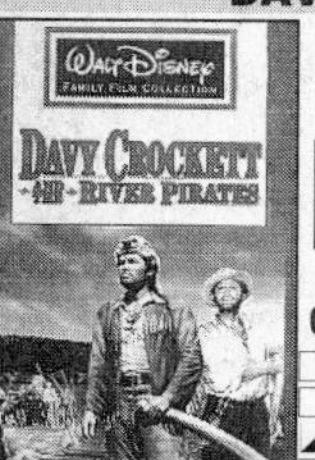

G | CLD WST | 1956 | COLOR

☐ Sex ☐ Nud ◢ Viol ☐ Lang ☐ AdSit

8 This is the second of the Disney feature films which were produced directly from the immensely popular TV episodes. This time Davy takes a raft down the river to New Orleans and runs smack dab into adventure. He has to fight dangerous rapids, Indians and river pirates. He also takes on the famous river pirate Big Mike Fink in a keelboat river race, which was the inspiration for the ride "Mike Fink Keelboats" at Disneyland. This was a wonderful series that will capture the imaginations of today's boys, just as it did yesterday's - but is also fun for the whole family. Disney at his best. Also see the original: DAVY CROCKETT, KING OF THE WILD FRONTIER.

A: Fess Parker, Buddy Ebsen, Jeff York, Clem Bevins, Irvin Ashkenazy, Kenneth Tobey

© WALT DISNEY HOME VIDEO 027

DEADLY COMPANIONS, THE

D: Sam Peckinpah — 90 m

NR | WST ACT | 1961 | COLOR

☐ Sex ☐ Nud ◢ Viol ☐ Lang ◢ AdSit

6 An ex-army sergeant (Brian Keith) accidentally kills a dancehall hostess's (O'Hara) son. To try to make amends, he escorts her and the body through deadly Apache territory. Along with them on their unhappy journey come two others, a half-crazed Confederate deserter (Wills) and a gun-happy young punk (Cochran). Three men and a beautiful woman become uneasy companions, alone in a hostile land. O'Hara must fight back both the unwanted advances of Cochran and her awakening feelings for the man she should hate (Keith). Most notable because this was Peckinpah's first picture.

A: Maureen O'Hara, Brian Keith, Steve Cochran, Chill Wills

© STARMAKER ENTERTAINMENT INC. 80045

DEATH HUNT

D: Peter H. Hunt — 97 m

R | ACT WST | 1981 | COLOR

☐ Sex ☐ Nud ■ Viol ■ Lang ◢ AdSit

8 Thrilling actioner filmed in northern Canada. Lee Marvin is a tough Mountie nearing retirement who reluctantly agrees to leave Angie Dickinson to hunt down a fiercely independent trapper (Bronson) who has been framed for a murder he did not commit. These two skilled woodsman become engaged in a cat-and-mouse chase through icy wilderness, each pitting their skills against the other, each gaining respect for the other. This film based loosely on a real-life case from the 1930s.

A: Charles Bronson, Lee Marvin, Andrew Stevens, Angie Dickinson, Carl Weathers, Ed Lauter

© FOXVIDEO 1125

DUEL AT DIABLO

D: Ralph Nelson — 130 m

NR | WST ACT | 1966 | COLOR

☐ Sex ☐ Nud ◢ Viol ☐ Lang ◢ AdSit

8 Garner is an embittered Army scout who is seeking revenge for his wife's murder while he is also guiding an Army ammunition train through hostile Indian territory. Also accompanying the train are Poitier, as an ex-sergeant who was forced to go along to break some horses that he wants to sell to the Army; and, an extremely bitter merchant (Weaver) and his wife (Anderson), who he despises because she was just recaptured from having lived with the Apaches and now has a half-breed son. This is an involving, solid, old-fashioned Western of the old school, with lots of action.

A: James Garner, Sidney Poitier, Bibi Andersson, Dennis Weaver, Bill Travers, William Redfield

Distributed By MGM/UA Home Video M202957

EL DIABLO

D: Peter Markle — 108 m

PG-13 | WST COM | 1990 | COLOR

☐ Sex ☐ Nud ◢ Viol ☐ Lang ☐ AdSit

7 Tongue-in-cheek made-for-cable Western. Billy, a small town Texas schoolteacher loves to read novels of gunfighters and daydreams of being one. However, when a legendary outlaw named El Diablo actually rides into town, robs a bank and kidnaps one of his students, his daydreams come face to face with reality. While he sets off in pursuit, he is hopelessly outmatched in his quest, until he meets gunman Thomas Van Leek (Louis Gossett, Jr.). He and his cohorts make a new man out of Billy, even as they continue to chase down El Diablo. Full of gags and fun.

A: Anthony Edwards, Louis Gossett, Jr., John Glover, M.C. Gainey, Miguel Sandoval, Sarah Trigger

© HBO VIDEO 90435

EL DORADO

D: Howard Hawks — 126 m

NR | WST ACT COM | 1967 | COLOR

☐ Sex ☐ Nud ◢ Viol ☐ Lang ☐ AdSit

9 Western fans line up. This is a big raucous John Wayne Western. Hawks revamped his big 1959 hit RIO BRAVO and this time has John Wayne being an aging gunfighter who helps his drunken friend, the sheriff (Mitchum), stop a range war. Great characters: Caan as a likable but odd-ball character who can't shoot; Arthur Hunnicut as a gnarled old Indian fighter and deputy; and Christopher George as a gunfighter on the other side but who has a sense of honor. Plenty of action and lots of humor, too. It was so successful it this time that it was redone one more time in 1970 as RIO LOBO.

A: John Wayne, Robert Mitchum, James Caan, Arthur Hunnicutt, Edward Asner, Michelle Carey

© PARAMOUNT HOME VIDEO 6625

ELECTRIC HORSEMAN, THE

D: Sydney Pollack — 120 m

PG | DMA ROM WST | 1979 | COLOR

☐ Sex ☐ Nud ☐ Viol ◢ Lang ◢ AdSit

7 Entertaining modern-day Western about an ex-rodeo star who has become an alcoholic cowboy appearing on cereal boxes riding a horse and promoting the cereal by appearing live on a champion racehorse, in a suit studded with flashing lights. Fonda, a reporter out for a good story, gets one. Redford becomes so upset when the horse he rides is exploited, too, that he steals the horse and rides across Utah looking for a place to set it free. Fonda stays one step of ahead the cops and finds him, but at first doesn't believe him about what he is trying to do. Eventually she does and falls for him.

A: Robert Redford, Jane Fonda, Valerie Perrine, Willie Nelson, John Saxon, Wilford Brimley

© MCA/UNIVERSAL HOME VIDEO, INC. 66006

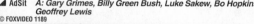

FAR AND AWAY

D: Ron Howard 140 m

PG-13 DMA WST ROM 1992 COLOR Sex Nud Viol Lang AdSit

8 Enjoyable, sweeping near-epic. A poor Irish tenant farmer (Cruise) is upset with the absentee landlord whom he blames for his father's death. He narrowly escapes dying in a duel with the man and escapes to America in 1890, along with the man's spoiled daughter (Kidman) in tow. Their first stop is Boston where he finds work as a bare-knuckle boxer and she plucks chickens. However, quickly they make their way west to attempt to claim free land in the great Oklahoma Land Rush. True, the story line is a little thin but the characters (Cruise and Kidman were married in real life) are a lot of fun to watch and the photography is grand.

A: Tom Cruise, Nicole Kidman, Thomas Gibson, Colm Meaney, Barbara Babcock, Robert Prosky

© MCA/UNIVERSAL HOME VIDEO, INC. 81415

FISTFUL OF DOLLARS, A

D: Sergio Leone 102 m

NR WST ACT 1964 COLOR Sex Nud Viol Lang AdSit

8 This was a watershed picture for Clint Eastwood, from it he became a giant star. In it, he played the "Man With No Name" - a strange gunslinger who single-handedly saves a small Mexican town being torn apart by two warring families. Interestingly, this film is actually based upon an excellent and funny samurai film, YOJIMBO. This was the first of several famed, action-packed spaghetti-Westerns (meaning Italian-made with dubbed-in English for some actors). It was followed by the successful sequel FOR A FEW DOLLARS MORE, and also inspired THE GOOD, THE BAD AND THE UGLY. Innovative and haunting score.

A: Clint Eastwood, Gian Maria Volonte, Marianne Koch, Wolfgang Lukschy, Mario Brega, Carol Brown

Distributed By MGM/UA Home Video M201272

FLAMING STAR

D: Don Siegel 92 m

NR WST 1960 COLOR Sex Nud Viol Lang AdSit

7 Even though there are two songs within the first ten minutes, this is not a Presley teen-musical. This is solid Western, and Presley's performance proved that he could act. It is Texas, just after the Civil War. Presley is the son of rancher John McIntire and his Kiowa wife. Fighting is breaking out between the Indian residents and the white settlers. Presley doesn't want to choose sides and does his best to stop it, but the hatreds are too deep and he gets drawn ever deeper into the fighting. One of Presley's best performances, but also see JAILHOUSE ROCK.

A: Elvis Presley, Barbara Eden, Steve Forrest, Dolores Del Rio, John McIntire

© CBS/FOX VIDEO 1173

FOR A FEW DOLLARS MORE

D: Sergio Leone 130 m

R WST ACT 1965 COLOR Sex Nud Viol Lang AdSit

7 Action-packed sequel to A FISTFUL OF DOLLARS. The Man-with-no-name (Clint Eastwood) joins forces with another bounty hunter/gunslinger (Van Cleef) to track down a Mexican bandit and his cutthroat band. Both of them have their own reason for wanting this guy but to get him they have to form an uneasy partnership. This spaghetti-Western holds few surprises, but has plenty of what Westerns are most famous for, guns and action. Plus, it also has a truly outstanding score from Ennio Morricone. See also THE GOOD, THE BAD AND THE UGLY.

A: Clint Eastwood, Lee Van Cleef, Gian Maria Volonte, Klaus Kinski, Rosemarie Dexter, Mario Brega

Distributed By MGM/UA Home Video M201577

FRIENDLY PERSUASION

D: William Wyler 138 m

NR WST DMA WAR 1956 COLOR Sex Nud Viol Lang AdSit

9 Wonderfully warm and charming film about the moral quandaries experienced by a Southern Indiana Quaker family during the heartbreak of the Civil War. Gary Cooper and Dorothy McGuire play the Quaker parents of Anthony Perkins (in an Oscar-nominated performance). Their tranquil life is violently challenged when their eldest son goes off to join in the battles to prove that he is no coward. It is a moving tale of love and honor. Cooper is also perfectly cast. Six Oscar nominations, including Best Picture and Best Director, plus a beautiful Dimitri Tiomkin score.

A: Gary Cooper, Dorothy McGuire, Marjorie Main, Anthony Perkins, Robert Middleton, Richard Eyer

© CBS/FOX VIDEO 7318

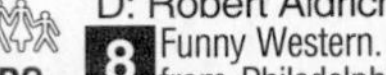

FRISCO KID, THE

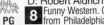

D: Robert Aldrich 119 m

PG WST COM 1979 COLOR Sex Nud Viol Lang AdSit

8 Funny Western. Gene Wilder is a Polish rabbi who is on his way from Philadelphia, across the Wild West, to San Francisco and his new congregation. Except, he has no idea of how to get there and, while on his way, he is besieged by one misfortune after another. However, he meets a kindhearted cowpoke and part-time bankrobber (Ford) who takes pity upon this inept fish-out-of-water. Ford agrees to accompany him across country to San Francisco and together they manage to stay in one scrape or another the entire way. Good family fun.

A: Gene Wilder, Harrison Ford, Ramon Bieri, Val Bisoglio, Leo Fuchs

© WARNER HOME VIDEO 11095

GERONIMO: AN AMERICAN LEGEND

D: Walter Hill 115 m

PG-13 WST ACT 1994 COLOR Sex Nud Viol Lang AdSit

7 A sincere, well acted and evocatively photographed attempt to present fairly both sides of the last of the Indian wars. The primary focus is on Geronimo and his band of renegade Apache raiders but is a reasonably accurate telling of the character and politics of the time. It is the end of an old way of life and the birth of a nation, but Geronimo and his group will live free or die free. General Crook (Hackman) is a fair and honest man who sends a young officer that Geronimo respects (Patric) to get him to surrender. Geronimo does, but is frustrated and breaks free, only to be hunted by a new and ruthless General. Well done, but tends to be slow in places.

A: Jason Patric, Gene Hackman, Robert Duvall, Wes Studi, Matt Damon, Rodney A. Grant

© COLUMBIA TRISTAR HOME VIDEO 58703

GOIN' SOUTH

D: Jack Nicholson 109 m

PG WST COM 1978 COLOR Sex Nud Viol Lang AdSit

6 Oddball little Western. A scruffy horse thief (Nicholson) is saved from the gallows by a prudish spinster (Steenburgen) who invokes a frontier law allowing her to marry him instead. In exchange for saving his life, he has to work on her farm, digging for the gold mine that she is sure is there. A strange love/hate relationship develops between these two quirky characters that makes for an amusing comedy for some, but many of the jokes will fall short for other people. Belushi has a brief, but very funny, spot as a Mexican bandit.

A: Jack Nicholson, Mary Steenburgen, John Belushi, Christopher Lloyd, Veronica Cartwright, Danny DeVito

© PARAMOUNT HOME VIDEO 1133

GOOD, THE BAD, AND THE UGLY, THE

D: Sergio Leone 162 m

R WST ACT 1967 COLOR Sex Nud Viol Lang AdSit

9 Third, last and best of a famous series of Westerns by Italian director Sergio Leone that were nicknamed spaghetti-Westerns and starred Clint Eastwood. In this one, Eastwood plays a bounty hunter and supposedly "The Good" part of a trio of gunslingers, which also consisted of Lee Van Cleef as an Army sergeant - "The Bad," and Eli Wallach as a thief - "The Ugly." Each man has one piece of a puzzle that will lead to $200,000 in buried Confederate gold. Very gritty and violent. See also A FISTFUL OF DOLLARS and A FEW DOLLARS MORE.

A: Clint Eastwood, Lee Van Cleef, Eli Wallach, Rada Rassimov, Mario Brega, Chelo Alono

Distributed By MGM/UA Home Video M301465

GREAT NORTHFIELD MINNESOTA RAID, THE

D: Philip Kaufman 91 m

PG WST ACT 1972 COLOR Sex Nud Viol Lang AdSit

7 Offbeat, but fact-based, Western about the famous raid on the "biggest bank west of the Mississippi" and the raid that ended the bankrobbing careers of the James-Younger gang. Contains vivid portraits of Cole Younger by Robertson and of Jesse James by Duvall. This is an attempt at a more realistic portrait of these bizarre and larger-than-life characters from the Old West, told from the other side - the seamy side - of the mirror. They are simple farmers, misfits who don't understand their times and become ruthless killers. Excellent characterizations but very different sort of Western.

A: Cliff Robertson, Robert Duvall, Luke Askew, R.G. Armstrong, Dana Elcar, Donald Moffat

© MCA/UNIVERSAL HOME VIDEO, INC. 55106

GREY FOX, THE

D: Phillip Borsos 92 m

PG WST DMA 1983 COLOR Sex Nud Viol Lang AdSit

8 Elegant and warm-hearted story of a real life stagecoach bandit named Bill Miner, who was also nick-named the "Gentleman Bandit." After 33 years in prison for stagecoach robbery, he was released into the twentieth century on June 17, 1901 from San Quentin Prison. Farnsworth is excellent as a man who must adjust to an entirely new world and becomes inspired on how to "adapt" to these modern times after he watches THE GREAT TRAIN ROBBERY. Charming and thoughtful entertainment.

A: Richard Farnsworth, Jackie Borroughs, Ken Pogue, Timothy Webber

© MEDIA HOME ENTERTAINMENT, INC. M258

GUNFIGHT AT THE O.K. CORRAL

D: John Sturges 122 m

NR WST ACT 1957 COLOR Sex Nud Viol Lang AdSit

8 Solid big-budget film which is credited with doing a lot to revitalize the Western genre. It also provides a somewhat authentic account of the events leading up to the West's most famous 1881 shoot-out. While the focus of the story is on the personalities of the two volatile key players, Wyatt Earp (Lancaster) and Doc Holliday (Douglas), it never loses sight of the fact that it is an action movie first. A detailed script and excellent acting by Hollywood veterans provide a solid build-up to the big finish at the OK Corral. It was very popular and became a big box office success.

A: Burt Lancaster, Kirk Douglas, Rhonda Fleming, Jo Van Fleet, John Ireland, Lee Van Cleef

© PARAMOUNT HOME VIDEO 6218

HANGING TREE, THE

D: Delmer Daves 108 m

NR | WST DMA | 1959 | COLOR | Viol

9 A solid, intelligent Western, that was unjustly overlooked upon its release. It is 1870s Montana in a gold camp called Skull Creek. The town is populated by fortune seekers of all types. There mountain men, saloons, prostitutes, bad people and good people too -- but they are all after gold. Dr. Joseph Frail (Cooper) is a quiet doctor, haunted by his past, who has come to town to hang out his shingle. But his life is thrown into violent turmoil when he comes to the aid of a pretty immigrant girl (Maria Schell) who has been blinded. It is a woman-poor town and the two of them are hounded by a fire-brand minister (George C. Scott) and a hot-headed jealous miner (Karl Malden.)

A: Gary Cooper, Maria Schell, Karl Malden, George C. Scott, Ben Piazza, Virginia Gregg

© WARNER HOME VIDEO 11049

HANG 'EM HIGH

D: Ted Post 114 m

NR | WST ACT | 1968 | COLOR | Viol, Lang, AdSit

8 An action-packed American production that was done in the spaghetti-Western vein. In it, Eastwood plays an innocent rancher who is lynched by nine over-eager vigilantes who had mistaken him for a murderer. However, to their regret, he survived. Now hateful and sworn to vengeance, he sets about to get revenge. His first step is to get himself named as a marshall by a hanging judge who is bent on cleaning up the territory. The star gives him a "hunting license" and, one-by-one, Eastwood hunts down his victims. Excellently executed by a veteran staff of quality actors, this a solid but very violent, Western.

A: Clint Eastwood, Ed Begley, Pat Hingle, Arlene Golonka, Ben Johnson, Inger Stevens

Distributed By MGM/UA Home Video M201399

HEARTLAND

D: Richard Pearce 95 m

PG | DMA WST | 1979 | COLOR

7 Moving realistic story about pioneer life in the far-flung virgin lands of Wyoming in 1910, based upon the actual diaries of a frontier woman. Ferrell plays a young widow who accepts a job as a housekeeper for a sour homesteader and eventually marries him. They become devoted to each other and their family. She and her daughter learn to deal with the hardships of isolation and having to confront nature on its own terms. Thoughtful with beautiful photography. Excellent acting. Moving, well-crafted and worthy story that was critically acclaimed but is also slow moving.

A: Conchata Ferrell, Rip Torn, Lilia Skala, Megan Folson, Amy Wright

© HBO VIDEO 608

HEARTS OF THE WEST

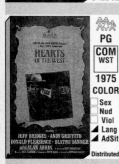

D: Howard Zieff 103 m

PG | COM WST | 1975 | COLOR | Lang, AdSit

7 Pleasant light-hearted story about a starry-eyed young Iowa farm boy with a wild imagination (Bridges) who goes west to Hollywood in the 1920s, intent upon becoming a writer of Western movies. Along the way he stops into his Nevada correspondence school and discovers that it is just a post office box. However, he accidentally takes the crooks cash stash and escapes into the desert, where he is rescued by a movie crew in full Western costume. He becomes pals, gets a job as a B-movie actor, finds love with a script girl and meets a publisher for his novel. A fun and charming little film.

A: Jeff Bridges, Alan Arkin, Blythe Danner, Andy Griffith, Donald Pleasence

Distributed By MGM/UA Home Video M600388

HIGH PLAINS DRIFTER

D: Clint Eastwood 106 m

R | WST ACT | 1973 | COLOR | Sex, Nud, Viol, Lang, AdSit

8 A very different sort of moral play. It is an immoral Western with a moral. The sleazy citizens of a corrupt mining town stand by while three outlaws brutally kill their Sheriff. Then, when gunslinger Eastwood comes to town, they hire him to replace the sheriff and protect them from the return of the bad guys. Instead, Eastwood takes charge of the town in a way they had not intended, and he begins a house-cleaning of his own. Very atmospheric, gritty, and violent, but told with a sense of ironic humor.

A: Clint Eastwood, Verna Bloom, Marinna Hill, Mitchell Ryan, Jack Ging, Geoffrey Lewis

© MCA/UNIVERSAL HOME VIDEO, INC. 66038

HOMBRE

D: Martin Ritt 111 m

NR | WST ACT DMA | 1967 | COLOR | Viol, Lang, AdSit

9 This is an intriguing and intelligent Western with powerhouse performances. Newman is a quiet loner, a white man who was raised by Apaches. He is onboard a 1880's stagecoach, along with a naive young married couple, a woman of the world, a corrupt Indian Agent with stolen money and his haughty wife and Richard Boone. Because Newman is so different he is shunned. However, he is the one they all later must rely upon to save them when their coach is robbed by Boone's killer gang and they are all left stranded to die. A captivating storyline, believable action and moving drama. Excellent.

A: Paul Newman, Fredric March, Richard Boone, Diane Cliento, Cameron Mitchell, Barbara Rush

© FOXVIDEO 1012

HORSE SOLDIERS, THE

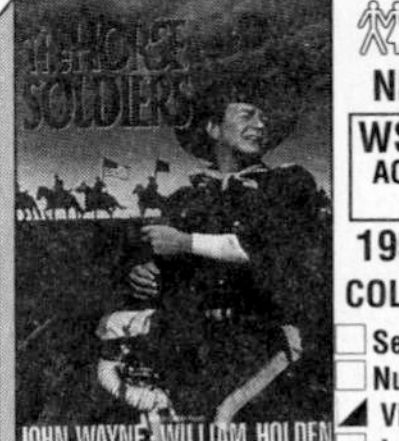

D: John Ford 115 m

NR | WST ACT | 1959 | COLOR | Viol, AdSit

7 Stirring John Ford adventure story - his only set during the Civil War. This "Western" is based upon an actual account of a Union raiding party sent into Rebel territory to cut supply lines into Vicksburg. Interestingly, the film takes no sides in the war. John Wayne plays the determined Union officer leading the raid, but he is accompanied by William Holden as a pacifistic Army doctor. Good action scenes, coupled with a romance between Wayne and a Southern girl (Towers) he must take captive on the way. Better than average as Westerns go, but suffers from preachy dialogue.

A: John Wayne, William Holden, Constance Towers, Hoot Gibson, Althea Gibson, Ken Curtis

Distributed By MGM/UA Home Video M201772

HOUR OF THE GUN

D: John Sturges 100 m

NR | WST ACT | 1967 | COLOR | Viol

7 Interesting twist to THE GUNFIGHT AT THE OK CORRAL -- the truth. James Garner plays a Wyatt Earp who is out for revenge and is ruthless in tracking down his brother's killers. There is lots of action, but this also presents a more complete and much darker picture of the situation surrounding the famous gunfight. Interestingly, it also presents a character, in Wyatt Earp, who is much less heroic and more spiteful. Well done. However, because the truth ran counter to the legend, this one had some difficulty at the box office. Still, this is one all Western fans should watch.

A: James Garner, Jason Robards, Jr., Robert Ryan, Albert Salmi, Charles Aidman, Steve Ihnat

Distributed By MGM/UA Home Video M203118

HOW THE WEST WAS WON

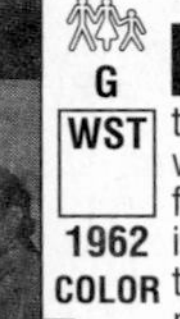

D: John Ford, Henry Hathaway 165 m

G | WST | 1962 | COLOR | Viol

9 This massive Western saga had virtually every major star of its day on the payroll. It is the story of a New England farm family, their trip west beginning in the 1830s and two more generations which later followed them. It is a sprawling film that was majestically filmed for the widescreen Cinerama, and has lost much of its grandeur in the transition to the small screen. Additionally, it is also a solid story that Western fans won't want to miss. It won three Oscars, and was nominated for Best Picture.

A: Gregory Peck, Henry Fonda, James Stewart, John Wayne, Debbie Reynolds, Walter Brennan

Distributed By MGM/UA Home Video M900356

HUD

D: Martin Ritt m

DMA WST | 1963 | B&W | Sex, Viol, AdSit

9 A very powerful adult drama and modern Western that contains one of the most memorable performances from Newman. Newman plays a selfish and irresponsible rake. He is the 30ish son of a Texas rancher (Douglas) who is now old and has fallen on hard times. Brandon de Wilde is the teenage son of Newman's dead brother. All three, and their salty housekeeper (Neal), live together on their dusty cattle ranch. The boy idolizes Newman, but the old man detests his son for his callous disregard for anyone but himself. Newman is tortured and bitter because his father rejects him. Their conflict has come to a head when their cattle become infected and must be destroyed. Winner of 3 Oscars.

A: Paul Newman, Melvyn Douglas, Patricia Neal, Brandon de Wilde, John Ashley, Whit Bissell

© PARAMOUNT HOME VIDEO 6630

INVITATION TO A GUNFIGHTER

D: Richard Wilson 92 m

NR | WST DMA | 1964 | COLOR | Viol, AdSit

7 A very different sort of Western. When a small town learns that a local outcast is returning home, they fear for the safety of their town, so they hire a tough gunslinger (Brynner) to kill him when he shows up. However, a major problem develops for the townsfolk when Brynner determines that the returning bad guy is a more worthwhile human being than anyone in the town he has been hired to protect. This may be too slow for some action fans, but it is interesting and definitely puts a different spin on things.

A: Yul Brynner, George Segal, Janice Rule, Pat Hingle, Brad Dexter

Distributed By MGM/UA Home Video M202958

I WILL FIGHT NO MORE FOREVER

D: Richard T. Heffron 105 m

NR | WST DMA | 1975 | COLOR | Viol

8 Dramatic telling of the true story of the Nez Perce Indians and their leader Chief Joseph. In 1877 Chief Joseph attempted to lead his people north to Canada and to freedom in defiance of a government order to move them onto a reservation. The US government sent the Army to stop them and to bring them back. It was the last major calvary campaign for the plains Indians. The Nez Perce tied the Army up in a chase that lasted for five months, even though they had only 100 warriors. Excellent telling of a moving and affecting story.

A: Ned Romero, James Whitmore, Sam Elliott, Linda Redfern

© GOODTIMES 8387

JAMES A. MICHENER'S TEXAS

NR | WST | 1994 | COLOR

☐ Sex ☐ Nud ◢ Viol ☐ Lang ☐ AdSit

D: Richard Lang — 180 m

6 Made-for-TV version of James Michener's book of the same name. As always, Michener combines several fictional and semi-fictional personal stories to create a mosaic that when combined tells a much bigger historical lesson. Duffy plays Stephen Austin, an American-born Mexican bureaucrat in Mexican-owned Texas until he can no longer tolerate their condition. Stacy Keach is Sam Houston and David Keith is Jim Bowie. Pretty Chelsea Field is a pivotal love interest around which many stories revolve. This is pretty much standard TV fare, but its subject matter and wide-ranging historical scope will make it of interest to some.

A: Patrick Duffy, Chelsea Field, Maria Conchita Alonso, Stacey Keach, Randy Travis, Rick Schroder

© REPUBLIC PICTURES HOME VIDEO 9724

JEREMIAH JOHNSON

PG | WST ACT DMA | 1972 | COLOR

☐ Sex ☐ Nud ◢ Viol ☐ Lang ◢ AdSit

D: Sydney Pollack — 116 m

10 Hugely popular adventure story set in the mid-19th century Rocky Mountains. Jeremiah Johnson is a man who has lost all taste for civilization and so escapes into the unknown wilds of the Rockies. This grandly photographed spectacle follows the loner's early stumbling efforts at survival through to his mastery of the elements. However, his idyllic life is destroyed when his new family is murdered by raiding Indians. He launches himself into a murderous mission of revenge and his success at it leads him to become a feared and legendary figure among the Indians. An extraordinary adventure.

A: Robert Redford, Will Geer, Charles Tyner, Stefan Gierasch, Allyn Ann McLerie

© WARNER HOME VIDEO 11061

JOE KIDD

PG | WST ACT | 1972 | COLOR

☐ Sex ☐ Nud ◢ Viol ◢ Lang ☐ AdSit

D: John Sturges — 88 m

6 Eastwood and Duvall in top form cannot redeem the somewhat muddled quality of this movie. Nevertheless, it does contain some real bang-up action scenes. The time is the turn of the 20th century. The place is New Mexico. Robert Duvall is a land baron who has enticed Eastwood into helping him fight a group of Mexican-Americans who feel that their land has been stolen from them and are now waging a guerrilla war against him. However, Eastwood soon discovers that they are right - he is on the wrong side and quickly joins the other side.

A: Clint Eastwood, Robert Duvall, John Saxon, Don Stroud, Stella Garcia, James Wainwright

© MCA/UNIVERSAL HOME VIDEO, INC. 66050

JUBAL

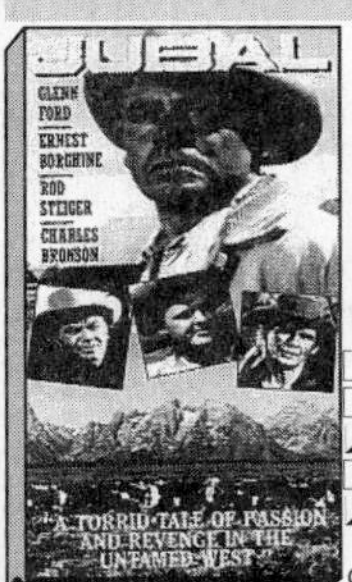

NR | WST ACT | 1956 | COLOR

☐ Sex ☐ Nud ◢ Viol ☐ Lang ◢ AdSit

D: Delmer Daves — 101 m

8 Interesting Western which is sometimes compared to OTHELLO. Glenn Ford is Jubal Troop, a drifter in Wyoming, who signs on as a hired hand at Ernest Borgnine's ranch. Borgnine is a likable oaf but he is having trouble with his sexy wife and he confides in Ford about it. Rod Steiger is one of his ranch hands and wants the woman, but she has rejected him. Steiger is also jealous of Ford's growing influence on Borgnine, so he plants suspicions in Borgnine's mind about Ford's intentions for the wife, which begins a series of events that leads to big trouble. An adult Western, well-acted and generally well done.

A: Glenn Ford, Ernest Borgnine, Valerie French, Rod Steiger, Felicia Farr, Noah Beery, Jr.

© GOODTIMES 4510

JUNIOR BONNER

PG | DMA COM WST | 1972 | COLOR

☐ Sex ☐ Nud ◢ Viol ◢ Lang ◢ AdSit

D: Sam Peckinpah — 101 m

8 Steve McQueen is an aging rodeo has-been who comes back to his hometown for one last ride and to try to make peace with his family in this modern-day Western. Everything and everybody there has changed. His mother and father are separated and his brother sells real estate. This is an interesting comedy/drama that explores life's changes for all the major characters involved but particularly McQueen. Preston is great as his hard-drinking dad but so is McQueen as the soft-spoken cowboy stumbling through life.

A: Steve McQueen, Robert Preston, Ida Lupino, Ben Johnson, Joe Don Baker, Barbara Leigh

© CBS/FOX VIDEO 8019

LAST OF THE MOHICANS, THE

R | WST ROM ACT | 1992 | COLOR

☐ Sex ☐ Nud ■ Viol ☐ Lang ■ AdSit

D: Michael Mann — 114 m

10 Gorgeously photographed version of James Fenimore Cooper's classic story, set in northern New York during the mid-1700s, at the time of the French and Indian War. Hawkeye and his adoptive Indian father and brother agree to lead an English girl and her sister to their father commanding a remote fort besieged by French and Indian troops. He and the girl fall in love but they are overwhelmed by the war that threatens to consume them. Impeccable period details and intense and realistic violence make believable the desperate plight of these young lovers struggling to survive. This film contains none of Hollywood's typical gloss but rather a gripping realism that is rare to film. Wow!

A: Daniel Day-Lewis, Madeleine Stowe, Russell Means, Eric Schweig, Jodhi May, Wes Studi

© FOXVIDEO 1986

LAST TRAIN FROM GUN HILL

NR | WST ACT | 1959 | COLOR

☐ Sex ☐ Nud ◢ Viol ☐ Lang ◢ AdSit

D: John Sturges — 94 m

7 Exciting Western. Douglas is a sheriff who has tracked down his wife's murderer to a small town that is under the almost total domination of Antony Quinn, the one-time best friend of Douglas. The murderer is discovered to have been Quinn's only son (Holliman). Quinn does not want his son to go back with Douglas, but neither does he want to hurt his old friend. Still, Douglas is determined to get Holliman out of town and back home to stand trial and hang - no matter what the cost. Confrontation is inevitable. Intelligently done. Above average.

A: Kirk Douglas, Anthony Quinn, Carolyn Jones, Earl Holliman, Ziva Rodann, Brad Dexter

© STARMAKER ENTERTAINMENT INC. 1058

LAWMAN

PG | WST DMA | 1971 | COLOR

☐ Sex ☐ Nud ☐ Viol ◢ Lang ◢ AdSit

D: Michael Winner — 98 m

8 An old man has been killed by a group of drunken rowdies, who live in a nearby town. Fiercely dedicated lawman Burt Lancaster has come to town to take the men all back for trial. The men all work for the local kingpin and businessman Lee J. Cobb who is determined to avoid trouble if he can, but he isn't going to let this blindly committed lawman take his men back to be hanged. Robert Ryan is the local marshall whose glory has faded and has become weak, but now he must decide on which side he will team. Curious and quite different Western that explores whether the end justifies the means. Cobb is terrific.

A: Burt Lancaster, Robert Ryan, Lee J. Cobb, Sheree North, Joseph Wiseman, Robert Duvall

Distributed By MGM/UA Home Video M202960

LEFT-HANDED GUN, THE

NR | WST DMA ACT | 1958 | B&W

☐ Sex ☐ Nud ◢ Viol ☐ Lang ◢ AdSit

D: Arthur Penn — 1958 m

7 An interesting underrated psychological Western which makes a point of debunking the hero-myth status of Billy the Kid. Newman's Billy is a moody, stupid and ruthless killer -- a lonely hothead who becomes enraged upon the murder of his boss, a man for whom he felt great fondness. Billy becomes so obsessed with killing the man's murderers that he and two others go on a wild killing spree. A curious feature in the film, one which comments upon on human nature in general, is the inclusion of a pulp writer who at first worships Billy but later derides Billy for not being the hero of his stories and eventually betrays Billy. Quite good.

A: Paul Newman, Lita Milan, John Dehner, Hurd Hatfield, James Congdon, James Best

© WARNER HOME VIDEO 11067

LIFE AND TIMES OF JUDGE ROY BEAN, THE

PG | WST COM ACT | 1972 | COLOR

☐ Sex ☐ Nud ◢ Viol ☐ Lang ◢ AdSit

D: John Huston — 124 m

8 Definitely strange but a fun Western with some really funny moments. Paul Newman creates a movie-variation on the real-life character Judge Roy Bean, who was famed as being a hanging judge. Newman's Bean rules over a two-bit Texas town like a lord, having run-ins (sometimes comical) with various odd-ball characters who stumble into his path. Stacy Keach is outstanding among these as the ferocious albino bad guy, Bad Bob. Filled with cameos by some of Hollywood's best. Very enjoyable even though sometimes it slows down too much.

A: Paul Newman, Stacy Keach, Victoria Principal, Jacqueline Bisset, Ava Gardner, Anthony Perkins

© WARNER HOME VIDEO 11174

LITTLE BIG MAN

PG | WST COM DMA | 1970 | COLOR

☐ Sex ◢ Nud ◢ Viol ☐ Lang ◢ AdSit

D: Arthur Penn — 147 m

10 This is an outstanding and thoroughly enjoyable fable of the Old West. Dustin Hoffman plays Jack Crabb, a 121-year-old man living in a nursing home, who tells his colorful and not all-too-believable life's story to a doubtful young reporter through a series of flashbacks. His incredible stories begin when he was an orphaned pioneer boy adopted and raised by Cheyenne Indians. After he had returned to the white world, he became a terrible businessman and miserable husband, a dead-eyed gunfighter, a drunk and eventually a guide to Custer at his last stand. Wonderful characters, very clever, frequently funny, sometimes poignant, always extremely entertaining. Great fun.

A: Dustin Hoffman, Chief Dan George, Faye Dunaway, Martin Balsam, Jeff Corey, Richard Mulligan

© CBS/FOX VIDEO 7130

LONELY ARE THE BRAVE

NR | WST DMA ACT | 1962 | B&W

☐ Sex ☐ Nud ◢ Viol ☐ Lang ◢ AdSit

D: David Miller — 107 m

8 A superb and penetrating character study. An easy-going 20th-century cowboy (Kirk Douglas) wants to help his friend break out of jail, so he gets into a bar fight and punches a cop. Now that he's in jail, his friend doesn't want to leave. Faced with the possibility of a year in prison, Douglas escapes from jail and heads into the hills on horseback. But the modern-day cops, headed up by Matthau, chase him down with help from trucks, helicopters and walkie-talkies. As the chase develops, Matthau gains respect for and begins to like his quarry. Good flick. Well done. One of Douglas's personal favorites.

A: Kirk Douglas, Gena Rowlands, Walter Matthau, Michael Kane, Carroll O'Connor, George Kennedy

© MCA/UNIVERSAL HOME VIDEO, INC. 80143

LONESOME DOVE

NR | WST DMA ACT | 1990 | COLOR

D: Simon Wincer — 372 m

10 Absolutely brilliant and totally engrossing made-for-TV miniseries adapted from Larry McMurtry's Pulitzer Prize-winning novel. This is an entirely believable, sweeping saga of two Texas Rangers who have out-lived their pioneering era in Texas. So, they strike out for Montana with a herd of cattle, intent upon establishing the first ranch in that virgin land. Striking performances by the entire cast paint a rich tapestry of colorful characters, adventure and romance in a realistically depicted Old West. A wonderful, totally involving, not-to-be-missed adventure.

Sex / Nud / Viol / Lang / AdSit

A: Robert Duvall, Tommy Lee Jones, Robert Urich, Danny Glover, Diane Lane, Ricky Schroder

© CABIN FEVER ENTERTAINMENT CF8371

LONG RIDERS

R | WST ACT | 1980 | COLOR

D: Walter Hill — 100 m

8 Excellent and intriguing Western about the famed James/Younger outlaw gang of the late 1800s that is historically fairly accurate. The film is long on action, short on plot, has an obscure moral and it is quite violent. However, it also contains the very interesting and very effective gimmick of having real-life brothers play the brothers of the gang. The Carradines are the Youngers, the Keaches are Frank and Jessie James and the Quaids are the Ford brothers. See also THE GREAT NORTHFIELD MINNESOTA RAID.

Sex / Nud / Viol / Lang / AdSit

A: David Carradine, Keith Carradine, Robert Carradine, Stacy Keach, James Keach, Dennis Quaid

Distributed By MGM/UA Home Video M600454

LOVE ME TENDER

NR | WST MUS | 1956 | COLOR

D: Robert D. Webb — 89 m

7 Elvis's first picture is a Western, and it isn't too bad. He plays the younger of two brothers who are both in love with Debra Paget. When older brother Egan doesn't come back from the Civil War, they think he is dead and Elvis marries Debra. Then Eagan shows up, and with a stolen payroll to boot. It also has four Presley songs including: "Love Me Tender," "Poor Boy," "Old Shep" and "We're Gonna Move (to a Better Home)."

Sex / Nud / Viol / Lang / AdSit

A: Elvis Presley, Richard Egan, Debra Paget, Robert Middleton, William Campbell, Neville Brand

© FOXVIDEO 1172

MAGNIFICENT SEVEN, THE

NR | WST ACT | 1960 | COLOR

D: John Sturges — 129 m

9 Classic shoot-'em-up!!! Recurring raids from a small army of bandits inspire a delegation from a small Mexican town to seek out help from gunfighter Yul Brynner. Brynner rounds up six other misfits like himself, and together they redeem themselves by helping the people to banish the terrorizing banditos and to reestablish pride in the town. A direct American remake of the Japanese classic THE SEVEN SAMAURI, this immensely popular Western spawned three sequels. Except for Brynner, the other six hombres were unknowns at the time, and went on to become sought-after stars.

Sex / Nud / Viol / Lang / AdSit

A: Yul Brynner, Eli Wallach, Steve McQueen, Horst Buchholz, James Coburn, Charles Bronson

Distributed By MGM/UA Home Video M201268

MAJOR DUNDEE

NR | WST ACT | 1965 | COLOR

D: Sam Peckinpah — 124 m

7 Lavishly produced Western in which Charlton Heston plays the title character, who is the warden of a Union Army prison that has been attacked by Apaches. He organizes his regulars and some prisoner volunteers (including a Confederate group whose leader, Richard Harris, is under a sentence of death) to chase the raiding party into Mexico. Complicated characters unduly confuse the plot, but the star power and the action is such that you will enjoy it anyway. The confusion resulted from director Peckinpah being removed. See also THE WILD BUNCH for many similarities.

Sex / Nud / Viol / Lang / AdSit

A: Charlton Heston, Richard Harris, Jim Hutton, James Coburn, Michael Anderson, Jr., Senta Berger

© COLUMBIA TRISTAR HOME VIDEO VH10370

MAN CALLED HORSE, A

PG | WST DMA ACT | 1970 | COLOR

D: Elliot Silverstein — 115 m

10 Powerful and thoroughly engrossing story of a haughty British aristocrat (Harris) who is captured by Sioux Indians while hunting in 1830s Dakotas. He is made into a slave by them, humiliated and then just ignored. He rebels, proving his manhood by undergoing a brutal tribal ritual called a sun dance (graphically shown). With his haughty noble exterior gone, his inner strength is unearthed, and he earns his way as a powerful and respected leader of the group. A gripping and realistic depiction of American Indian communal life. See also RETURN OF A MAN CALLED HORSE and DANCES WITH WOLVES.

Sex / Nud / Viol / Lang / AdSit

A: Richard Harris, Judith Anderson, Manu Tupou, Jean Gascon, Corinna Tsopei, Dub Taylor

© FOXVIDEO 7148

MAN FROM SNOWY RIVER, THE

G | WST ACT ROM | 1982 | COLOR

D: George Miller — 104 m

8 A rousing cinematic treat for the whole family! This is a beautiful and rousing adventure story that is based on a well-known Australian poem. An independent young man is hired by a wealthy cattle rancher in Australia's wilderness of the 1880s. He falls in love with the cattleman's daughter, but is not accepted by her father (Douglas - in a dual role, also as the father's maverick brother). The film culminates in a wild chase through mountainous terrain to capture a herd of wild horses, led by a magnificent stallion. Thrilling. Stunning scenery. Pretty good sequel in RETURN TO SNOWY RIVER.

Sex / Nud / Viol / Lang / AdSit

A: Kirk Douglas, Tom Burlinson, Terence Donovan, Sigrid Thornton, Jack Thompson, Lorraine Bayly

© FOXVIDEO 1233

MAN OF THE WEST

NR | WST | 1958 | COLOR

D: Anthony Mann — 100 m

8 Hard-edged Western with a big bite. Cooper is a former member of the wicked Tobin family gang led by his uncle (Cobb). But, he has reformed, is a good citizen and he is now a married man with children to boot! Suddenly, Cooper finds himself unwillingly thrown back into the gang's grasp again when the train on which he is riding is held up by them. So that he can prevent the other hostages from being harmed, he appears to agree to rejoin the group. Ultimately, however, there must be a showdown and he is the only one he can save them. Excellent and believable story line, with a particularly violent fist fight.

Sex / Nud / Viol / Lang / AdSit

A: Gary Cooper, Julie London, Lee J. Cobb, Arthur O'Connell, Jack Lord, John Dehner

Distributed By MGM/UA Home Video M202059

MAN WHO SHOT LIBERTY VALANCE, THE

NR | WST ACT | 1962 | B&W

D: John Ford — 123 m

9 Excellent adult Western. Stewart stars as an idealistic Eastern-minded lawyer who wants to end the reign of terror of a ruthless killer, Liberty Valance (Marvin) in the lawless West. But the only tool he has is his lawbooks. Lawbooks aren't going to stop Liberty Valance. Stewart and tough rancher John Wayne compete for the love of pretty Vera Miles. Because Miles loves Stewart, and because Wayne knows that civilization must come and men like Stewart will make it happen, Wayne helps Stewart to defeat Valance, turning him into a hero. John Ford's last black and white Western packs a punch!

Sex / Nud / Viol / Lang / AdSit

A: James Stewart, John Wayne, Lee Marvin, Vera Miles, Edmond O'Brien, Andy Devine

© PARAMOUNT HOME VIDEO 6114

MAVERICK

PG | WST COM | 1994 | COLOR

D: Richard Donner — 127 m

7 "Maverick" was one of TV's consistently best series, starred Garner and aired from 1957-1962. Maverick is a suave gambler who had a knack for getting into and out of trouble with a con, style and a grin. Gibson's 1994 Maverick is not Garner's, but he is still a fun-loving clever con-man. And, Garner is back too, but this time as a retired sheriff. Maverick needs to raise the last of the $25,000 stake he needs to get into a big game in St. Louis, but he has a struggle to get there -- with a sexy con-lady (Foster) who picks his pocket and various bad guys out for revenge. The plot is almost inconsequential. The focus is on the personalities. Enjoyable but not a laugh-riot.

Sex / Nud / Viol / Lang / AdSit

A: Mel Gibson, Jodie Foster, James Garner, Graham Greene, Alfred Molina, James Coburn

© WARNER HOME VIDEO 13374

MCCABE AND MRS. MILLER

R | WST ACT | 1971 | COLOR

D: Robert Altman — 121 m

8 It is the turn of the century in the Pacific Northwest. McCabe (Beatty) is a small-time gambler and braggart with big ambitions who rides into a remote pioneer town. There he meets Mrs. Miller (Christie), a pretty madam who is motivated by money and who also has an entourage of expensive whores. She and McCabe become partners in a bordello, but its remarkable success attracts some big-time hoods, who intend to either buy it or steal it. Beautifully photographed, this story is a very realistic Western which takes much of the glamour from the time and out of its subject matter. Interesting.

Sex / Nud / Viol / Lang / AdSit

A: Warren Beatty, Julie Christie, Rene Auberjonois, Keith Carradine, John Schuck, Bert Remsen

© WARNER HOME VIDEO 11055

MONTE WALSH

PG | WST | 1970 | COLOR

D: William A. Fraker — 100 m

8 Unusual and intelligent Western! Three cowboys have been through a lot together, but times are changing. The ranch is losing money, somebody has to go, so Ryan is laid off. Marvin stays on, hoping to save some money to start fresh. Palance leaves to get married and open a hardware store. The hard-pressed Ryan becomes a thief, robs Palance's store and Palance is killed. The murder of one friend places Marvin in the position of hunting down his other friend. Light-hearted and fun at times, and serious and thought-provoking at others. It is a sympathetic portrait of the death of an era.

Sex / Nud / Viol / Lang / AdSit

A: Lee Marvin, Jack Palance, Jeanne Moreau, Mitchell Ryan, Jim Davis, Allyn Ann McLerie

© CBS/FOX VIDEO 7172

MOUNTAIN MEN, THE

D: Richard Lang — 100 m

R | WST ACT | 1980 | COLOR | Sex Nud Viol Lang AdSit

7 A Western that really draws blood. Heston's son, Fraser-Clarke, wrote this extremely graphic depiction of white guys vs. Indians in hand-to-hand battle on the range and in the mountains. Set in the West during the 1830s, the wild lifestyle of two fur trappers (Heston and Keith) is coming to an end. That same way of life is also being threatened for the Indians and these two groups are now in perpetual conflict. The situation is further aggravated by the fact that the trappers have the runaway wife (Racimo) of a mean-spirited Indian Chief and he wants her back.

A: Charlton Heston, Brian Keith, Victoria Racimo, John Glover, Stephen Macht, Seymour Cassel

© GOODTIMES 4505

NEVADA SMITH

D: Henry Hathaway — 135 m

NR | WST ACT | 1966 | COLOR | Sex Nud Viol Lang AdSit

9 Solid hard-hitting Western. Steve McQueen comes home to find his Indian mother and white father have been tortured and killed by a outlaw band. He is now steeled by hate and, vowing vengeance, he sets off in pursuit of the killers. But he is just an inept hate-fueled farmboy until he stumbles onto a traveling gun merchant (Keith), who teaches him how to shoot and how to survive. Now, he has the tools he needs and he methodically pursues each man down and kills him, becoming nearly as bad as his quarry. Very good movie. The character came from the book THE CARPETBAGGERS, which was also made into a movie.

A: Steve McQueen, Karl Malden, Brian Keith, Suzanne Pleshette, Arthur Kennedy, Pat Hingle

© PARAMOUNT HOME VIDEO 6532

NORTH TO ALASKA

D: Henry Hathaway — 117 m

NR | WST ACT COM | 1960 | COLOR | Sex Nud Viol Lang AdSit

9 Terrific good time in this light-hearted John Wayne Western. Wayne and Granger play turn-of-the-century Alaskan gold miners who strike it rich. Fabian is Granger's wet-behind-the-ears brother. Wayne goes to Seattle to pick up supplies and Granger's brand new mail-order bride. But when she is not there, Wayne "buys" saucy Capucine from a saloon and takes her back. Soon Granger and Wayne are both vying for her affections, as is young Fabian. Even while they're fighting each other, they're also fending off claim-jumpers lead by Kovacs. Great, fast-moving, tongue-in-cheek, fun.

A: John Wayne, Stewart Granger, Ernie Kovacs, Fabian, Capucine, Mickey Shaughnessy

© FOXVIDEO 1212

OLD GRINGO

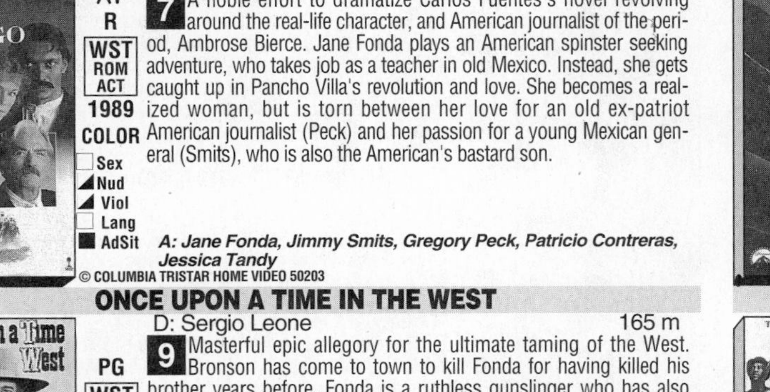

D: Luis Puenzo — 120 m

R | WST ROM ACT | 1989 | COLOR | Sex Nud Viol Lang AdSit

7 A noble effort to dramatize Carlos Fuentes's novel revolving around the real-life character, and American journalist of the period, Ambrose Bierce. Jane Fonda plays an American spinster seeking adventure, who takes job as a teacher in old Mexico. Instead, she gets caught up in Pancho Villa's revolution and love. She becomes a realized woman, but is torn between her love for an old ex-patriot American journalist (Peck) and her passion for a young Mexican general (Smits), who is also the American's bastard son.

A: Jane Fonda, Jimmy Smits, Gregory Peck, Patricio Contreras, Jessica Tandy

© COLUMBIA TRISTAR HOME VIDEO 50203

ONCE UPON A TIME IN THE WEST

D: Sergio Leone — 165 m

PG | WST ACT | 1969 | COLOR | Sex Nud Viol Lang AdSit

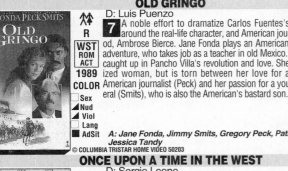

9 Masterful epic allegory for the ultimate taming of the West. Bronson has come to town to kill Fonda for having killed his brother years before. Fonda is a ruthless gunslinger who has also recently cold-bloodedly murdered a man and his children just to get the man's land to sell for a railroad station, and then he framed another outlaw (Robards) for those murders. However, Fonda's now in big trouble because both Robards and Bronson are out to kill him. Plus, a former prostitute (Cardinale), who, unknown to anyone, had married the murdered man, claims that the land is hers. Violent.

A: Henry Fonda, Jason Robards, Jr., Charles Bronson, Claudia Cardinale, Gabriele Ferzetti, Jack Elam

© PARAMOUNT HOME VIDEO 6830

ONE-EYED JACKS

D: Marlon Brando — 141 m

NR | WST | 1961 | COLOR | Sex Nud Viol Lang AdSit

8 Interesting psychological Western which was also directed by one-time-only director Brando. Brando plays a bank robber who is deserted by his partners (including Malden), is captured and spends five years in prison. Upon release, he teams up with a couple of bad guys to rob a bank in a small town whose sheriff turns out to be the now-respectable Malden. Brando seeks revenge on Malden but relents when he falls for Malden's step-daughter. However, now Malden is fearful and is pursuing Brando. Good action, but a little muddled.

A: Marlon Brando, Karl Malden, Katy Jurado, Ben Johnson, Pina Pillicer, Slim Pickens

© PARAMOUNT HOME VIDEO 6537

OUTLAW JOSEY WALES, THE

D: Clint Eastwood — 136 m

PG | WST ACT | 1976 | COLOR | Sex Nud Viol Lang AdSit

9 Intriguing Civil War Western, highly acclaimed as one of Eastwood's best efforts both behind and in front of the camera. Josey Wales is a farmer whose family is brutalized and killed by renegade Union soldiers. Wales joins the Rebs seeking revenge and becomes one of their most effective weapons. At war's end, he refuses to surrender to corrupt Union troops he does not trust and so becomes a renegade. He seeks to escape into the West - but he is now being hunted as an outlaw. Rich characters and images. Exciting and believable.

A: Clint Eastwood, Chief Dan George, Sondra Locke, Bill Mc Kinney, John Vernon, Sam Bottoms

© WARNER HOME VIDEO 11125

PAINT YOUR WAGON

D: Joshua Logan — 164 m

PG | MUS COM WST | 1970 | COLOR | Sex Nud Viol Lang AdSit

9 A rousing good time with this fun-filled, Lerner and Loewe musical/Western/comedy set in the fictional gold-rich/women-poor California mining boom town of No-Name City in the mid-1800s. Two partners in a gold "mine" (Eastwood and Marvin mine the gold that falls through the floors at the saloons) purchase one of a Mormon traveler's extra wives (Seberg), and... they share her - all of her - 50/50. Clever and funny. Plus, some truly great music ("They Call the Wind Maria") that is only slightly diminished by Marvin's and Eastwood's singing.

A: Clint Eastwood, Lee Marvin, Jean Seberg, Harve Presnell, John Mitchum, Ray Walston

© PARAMOUNT HOME VIDEO 6933

PALE RIDER

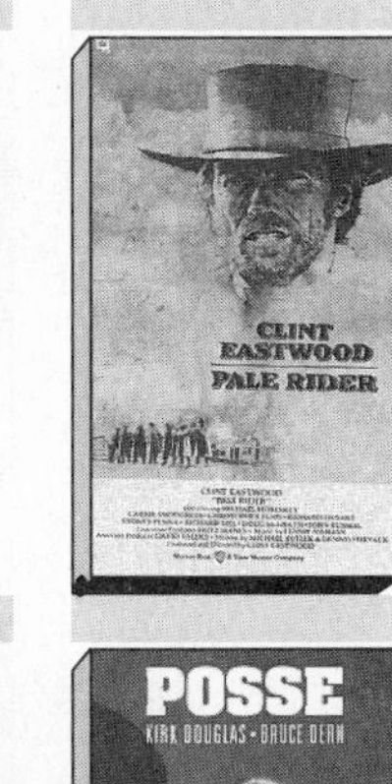

D: Clint Eastwood — 116 m

R | WST ACT | 1985 | COLOR | Sex Nud Viol Lang AdSit

8 Nifty, quasi-mystical Western that many compare in its basic plot to the classic SHANE, but it also has elements of the 1973 HIGH PLAINS DRIFTER. Here Eastwood is Preacher, a very odd and mysterious stranger who rides into the middle of a battle between a group of independent miners and a powerful land baron who is trying to force them off their claims. But, Preacher is a strong character, an inordinately powerful and mystical superhero who gives the miners self-confidence and around whom they rally. It is never made clear, but it is hinted, that Preacher is the spirit of a gunslinger who seeks redemption so that his spirit may rest. Quite good with lots of Western action.

A: Clint Eastwood, Michael Moriarty, Carrie Snodgress, Christopher Penn, Richard Dysart, Sydney Penny

© WARNER HOME VIDEO 11475

POSSE

D: Kirk Douglas — 94 m

PG | WST DMA ACT | 1975 | COLOR | Sex Nud Viol Lang AdSit

8 Solid and interesting Western, with an odd edge. Kirk Douglas is both a cynical lawman and an ambitious politician, seeking to become a Senator from Texas. He sees an opportunity to capture the public's attention when he and his ruthless crew of deputies track down and try to capture an escaped robber, Bruce Dern. But Dern is a wily opponent who recognizes Douglas's self-serving agenda and uses it to gain the sympathy of the townspeople, turn the deputies against Douglas and then enlist them in his own cause.

A: Kirk Douglas, Bruce Dern, Bo Hopkins, James Stacy, Luke Askew, David Canary

© PARAMOUNT HOME VIDEO 8316

POSSE

D: Mario Van Peebles — 113 m

R | WST ACT | 1993 | COLOR | Sex Nud Viol Lang AdSit

6 A very bloody and politically-correct Western. Five black soldiers and one white one, in Cuba during the Spanish-American War, rebel against a corrupt racist white colonel who has done his best to get them killed. They escape into the West with a cache of Cuban gold they have appropriated. Their sharp-shooting leader (Van Peebles) has unfinished business to take care of but the colonel is hot on their trial and has labeled them outlaws. Their arrival finds that the town is in the path of the on-coming railroad and that has made it the target of a bigoted white sheriff. A showdown is at hand.

A: Mario Van Peebles, Stephen Baldwin, Billy Zane, Charles Lane, Tiny Lister, Jr., Blair Underwood

© POLYGRAM VIDEO

PROFESSIONALS, THE

D: Richard Brooks — 117 m

PG | WST ACT SUS | 1966 | COLOR | Sex Nud Viol Lang AdSit

9 Thrilling action-packed Western manned with some of the genre's best talent. A team of four mercenaries (an explosives expert, a horse trainer, an archer and a sharpshooter) are hired by a wealthy aging Texan to track down his beautiful young wife who has been kidnapped by a Mexican bandit. Heavily out-manned and out-gunned, their raid upon the stronghold yields up the woman, but they are hotly pursued on the way back and are surprised to find that the woman is not at all eager to go with them. Intense actioner with a high excitement quotient, top-flight performances and quality production values.

A: Burt Lancaster, Lee Marvin, Claudia Cardinale, Jack Palance, Woody Strode, Ralph Bellamy

© GOODTIMES 4501

PROUD REBEL, THE

D: Michael Curtiz — 99 m

NR | WST | 1958 | COLOR

8 Sentimental charmer. Alan Ladd plays an ex-Confederate soldier who is wandering the countryside looking for a doctor who can help his son (his real-life son) regain his speech. The boy was traumatized when he witnessed the burning of Atlanta and the death of his mother. When Dean Jagger's sons pick a fight with Alan over the boy's dog, Alan winds up in jail. He is bailed out and goes to work for a spinster lady (De Havilland) who is trying to save her land from being taken over by the greedy Jagger. Heartwarming story with great star chemistry.

Sex | Nud | ✓ Viol | Lang | AdSit

A: Alan Ladd, Olivia de Havilland, Dean Jagger, Harry Dean Stanton, David Ladd, Henry Hull

© UNITED AMERICAN VIDEO CORP. 5302

QUICK AND THE DEAD, THE

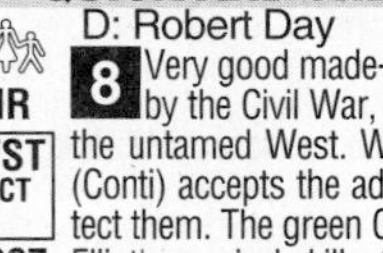

D: Robert Day — 91 m

NR | WST ACT | 1987 | COLOR

8 Very good made-for-cable movie about a young family, uprooted by the Civil War, who attempt to make a home for themselves in the untamed West. When the family comes under attack, the father (Conti) accepts the advice and aid of a wanderer (Elliott) to help protect them. The green Conti and his family come to rely very heavily on Elliot's survival skills. Soon Conti's wife (Capshaw) and his boy begin to doubt him and become very enamored of their new protector. Based on the Louis L'Amour story, the flavor and feel of the lawless Old West is beautifully captured. A classy Western.

Sex | Nud | ✓ Viol | Lang | ✓ AdSit

A: Sam Elliott, Tom Conti, Kate Capshaw, Kenny Morrison, Matt Clark, Lean Louis

© WARNER HOME VIDEO 818

QUIGLEY DOWN UNDER

D: Simon Wincer — 121 m

PG-13 | WST ACT | 1990 | COLOR

7 Entertaining "Western" with a decidedly different twist. Selleck plays Quigley, an American sharpshooter who has been hired by an Australian sheep rancher and land baron. He arrives in the Outback of the 1860s and is hauled across hundreds of miles to meet his employer. The two take an immediate dislike to each other, especially when Quigley finds that he has been hired to hunt down Aborigines. Quigley is beaten, tied to a crazy woman, the two are taken out into the wilderness and left to die, but they don't cooperate. Quigley is now in a war to the death with the vicious land baron.

Sex | ✓ Nud | ✓ Viol | Lang | ✓ AdSit

A: Tom Selleck, Laura San Giacomo, Alan Rickman, Chris Haywood

Distributed By MGM/UA Home Video M902173

RANCHO DELUXE

D: Frank Perry — 93 m

R | COM WST | 1975 | COLOR

8 Quirky modern-day Western. Two listless, fun-lovin', ne'r-do-well, part-time cowboys and cattle rustlers decide to have fun by pestering a bored but rich cattleman who bought his huge ranch with the profits from a chain of beauty parlors. These two are so lazy that their modus operandi is to cut up the dead animals with a chain saw. Their coup de grace comes when they kidnap his prize bull and hold it for ransom, keeping it inside a motel room. A lot of fun and always good-natured, but underlying it all is a sense of pity for the cast of listless characters, because all of them are really only wasting their time in life.

✓ Sex | ✓ Nud | Viol | ■ Lang | ■ AdSit

A: Jeff Bridges, Sam Waterston, Elizabeth Ashley, Charlene Dallas, Clifton James, Slim Pickens

Distributed By MGM/UA Home Video 202643

RARE BREED, THE

D: Andrew V. McLaglen — 107 m

NR | WST ROM | 1966 | COLOR

7 Enjoyable and fun Western. An eccentric British heiress (O'Hara) has a wild idea. She wants to breed stocky English Hereford cows with tough Texan longhorns. Stewart is a stubborn cowboy who is supposed to escort her, her daughter and her prize bull to the Texas ranch of her partner, an outlandish Scottsman (Keith). On the calamity-filled journey there, Stewart grows to admire O'Hara's conviction and determination, but is faced with a romantic rivalry in Keith when they arrive at the ranch. The road to the new breed is also faced with stampedes and rustlers, too. Entertaining and original.

Sex | Nud | ✓ Viol | Lang | ✓ AdSit

A: James Stewart, Maureen O'Hara, Brian Keith, Juliet Mills, Jack Elam, Ben Johnson

© MCA/UNIVERSAL HOME VIDEO, INC. 80322

RETURN TO LONESOME DOVE

D: Mike Robe — 330 m

NR | WST DMA ACT | 1993 | COLOR

8 Good follow-up to the fantastic original. Woodrow has taken his friend back to Texas to bury him. But, before going back, he stops off to ask another former Texas ranger to lead a group in capturing a herd of mustangs and driving them back to Montana. While they are doing that, he will stop off in Nebraska to buy blooded stock. They will breed the two to create a new hardier stock. Newt is to meet him in Nebraska, but instead gets in a gun fight and thrown into jail. He is paroled to a wealthy cattle baron with a pretty young wife. Much of the fire is gone from the original, but it is still well worth a watch.

Sex | Nud | ✓ Viol | Lang | ✓ AdSit

A: John Voight, Barbara Hershey, Rick Schroder, Louis Gossett, Jr., William Petersen, Oliver Reed

© CABIN FEVER ENTERTAINMENT 9586

RETURN TO SNOWY RIVER

D: Geoff Burrowes — 99 m

PG | WST ROM | 1988 | COLOR

6 Sequel to THE MAN FROM SNOWY RIVER. The hero from the original (Burlinson) has left for three years to round up a herd of horses. He returns to claim the love of his life (Thornton), but finds she is now engaged to a banker's son (Eadie). What's more, her father (Dennehy) is vehemently opposed to their relationship and is determined to keep them apart. Once again, Burlinson must battle to prove his worth. Grand and beautiful photography, plus glorious Australian scenery and fast pace, make this a mildly satisfying sequel that has the same feeling as the original.

Sex | Nud | ✓ Viol | ✓ Lang | AdSit

A: Tom Burlinson, Sigrid Thornton, Brian Dennehy, Nicholas Eadie, Bryan Marshall

© WALT DISNEY HOME VIDEO 699

RIDE THE HIGH COUNTRY

D: Sam Peckinpah — 93 m

NR | WST ACT | 1962 | COLOR

9 Considered Peckinpah's finest film and one so good that two of Hollywood's biggest Western stars retired rather than try to top it. Two grizzled old friends and old-time gunfighters join forces to escort a large gold shipment. Along the way they reminisce, and even work together to aid a young bride (Hartley's debut) escape from her barbarian in-laws. While McCrea wants only to do a good and respectable job, Scott secretly wants to steal the gold they are supposed to be guarding. Beautiful photography, wonderful performances and an interesting story.

Sex | Nud | ✓ Viol | Lang | AdSit

A: Randolph Scott, Joel McCrea, Mariette Hartley, Edgar Buchanan, Ronald Starr, Warren Oates

Distributed By MGM/UA Home Video M600850

RIO BRAVO

D: Howard Hawks — 141 m

NR | WST ACT COM | 1959 | COLOR

10 Exuberant Western with Wayne as the classic tough-guy sheriff who has arrested the brother of a wealthy rancher. The rancher wants his brother free. John wants him tried, but the rancher has a whole herd of cowboys and gunslingers ready to help him. John has a drunken deputy (Martin), a toothless, grizzled old man (Brennan) and a young untried gunhand (Nelson). Great fun. Lots of shootin' but good laughs too from a talented cast. Redone by Hawks, again with Wayne, in 1967 as EL DORADO - also was the model for ASSAULT ON PRECINCT 13 and RIO LOBO.

Sex | Nud | ✓ Viol | Lang | AdSit

A: John Wayne, Dean Martin, Angie Dickinson, Walter Brennan, Ricky Nelson, Ward Bond

© WARNER HOME VIDEO 11050

RIO CONCHOS

D: Gordon Douglas — 107 m

NR | WST ACT | 1964 | COLOR

8 A rootin' shootin' good time! An ex-Confederate soldier (O'Brien) is still fighting the Civil War by running guns to the Apaches to get vengeance on the North. Four men, led by a US calvary captain (Whitman), are hunting for 2,000 stolen Spencer repeating rifles. They know O'Brien has them, so they are on their way into Mexico with a wagonload of gun powder to use as bait to draw him out. Boone, an Apache-hating ex-rebel; Franciosa, a charming killer avoiding the noose; and Brown, an Army sergeant, join Whitman in his quest. Some of the best in traditional action-packed Old West adventure.

Sex | Nud | ✓ Viol | Lang | ✓ AdSit

A: Richard Boone, Stuart Whitman, Edmond O'Brien, Anthony Franciosa, Jim Brown

© FOXVIDEO 1224

RIO LOBO

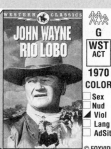

D: Howard Hawks — 103 m

G | WST ACT | 1970 | COLOR

6 Second remake of the original giant 1959 hit RIO BRAVO and its 1967 follow-up EL DORADO. This time Wayne plays an ex-Union colonel who tracks down some Civil War traitors, who are also gold thieves. In the process, he winds up helping out a small town held hostage by a corrupt sheriff. An old story that gets a considerable boost from the talents of Wayne and Jack Elam, as a crazy old codger with a shotgun. This was also the last screen appearance of Sherry Lansing, who became a major studio exec.

Sex | Nud | ✓ Viol | Lang | AdSit

A: John Wayne, Jennifer O'Neill, Jorge Rivero, Jack Elam, Sherry Lansing, Chris Mitchum

© FOXVIDEO 7016

ROOSTER COGBURN

D: Stuart Millar — 108 m

PG | WST COM ACT | 1975 | COLOR

8 TRUE GRIT meets THE AFRICAN QUEEN. John Wayne reprises his very popular and Oscar-winning title character from TRUE GRIT. Rooster is in pursuit of bad men who have lifted an Army wagonload of nitroglycerine. His search introduces him to a bible-thumping old-maid missionary played by Katharine Hepburn, whose father was also murdered by the bad guys. The fun starts when she insists on joining Wayne's expedition. An OK story line, but it is aided greatly by the presence of two screen legends who are just plain fun to watch, as well as a terrific supporting cast.

Sex | Nud | ✓ Viol | Lang | AdSit

A: John Wayne, Katharine Hepburn, Anthony Zerbe, Strother Martin, John McIntire

© MCA/UNIVERSAL HOME VIDEO, INC. 55042

ROUNDERS, THE

D: Burt Kennedy 85 m

NR · WST COM · 1964 · COLOR

7 Likable little comedy about the adventures of two nearly over-the-hill modern-day cowboy buddies working for a stingy rancher (Chill Wills). Ben and Howdy spend nearly the entire movie trying to best an ornery roan named "Ol' Fooler" nearly destroying a small town in the process. Their adventures with the horse becomes the central gag, tieing together a pleasant time-killer of a film which became a minor sleeper hit the year it was released.

☐ Sex ☐ Nud ☐ Viol ☐ Lang ☐ AdSit

A: Glenn Ford, Henry Fonda, Sue Ann Langdon, Hope Holiday, Chill Wills, Edgar Buchanan

Distributed By MGM/UA Home Video M200975

RUTHLESS FOUR, THE

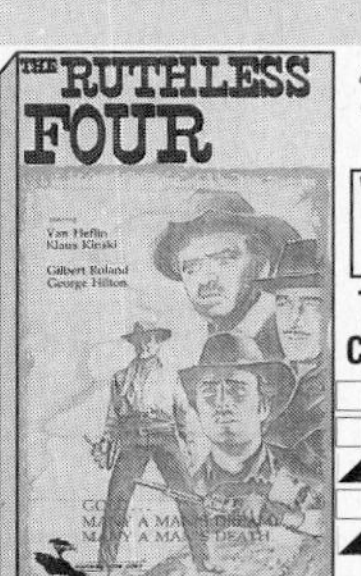

D: Giorgio Capitani 96 m

PG · WST · 1970 · COLOR

7 Intriguing Western psychological character study. Heflin is a loner who has spent a lifetime prospecting and now has struck a rich vein of gold in Nevada, but he can't get to it by himself. In order to get the goods, he needs partners. Unwillingly he enlists the aid of three men he can't trust. The four men begin to work together but it doesn't last, soon it is every man for himself. Mistrust and greed have set in.

☐ Sex ☐ Nud ☑ Viol ☐ Lang ☑ AdSit

A: Van Heflin, Gilbert Roland, Klaus Kinski, George Hilton, Sarah Ross

© MONTEREY HOME VIDEO 33744

SACKETTS, THE

D: Robert Totten 198 m

NR · WST ACT · 1979 · COLOR

7 Powerhouse cast of some of the biggest names in filmdom shine in this made-for-TV epic Western. Two Louis L'Amour novels ("The Daybreakers" and "The Sacketts") were combined to create this story. Three brothers choose to travel into the wild west to start new lives at the close of the Civil War rather than to return to a family feud in Tennessee. This is the saga of their trip west and their fortunes after getting there. Each plans to make it on his own there, but each knows he can rely on his brother. Rousing action flick with some truly sparkling performances.

☐ Sex ☐ Nud ☑ Viol ☐ Lang ☐ AdSit

A: Tom Selleck, Sam Elliott, Glenn Ford, Ben Johnson, Slim Pickens, Ruth Roman

© WARNER HOME VIDEO 957

SCALPHUNTERS, THE

D: Sydney Pollack 100 m

NR · WST COM ACT · 1968 · COLOR

8 Fun-filled and funny Western with truly interesting characters. A very determined fur trapper (Burt Lancaster) is forced by a group of Indians to swap his skins for a highly educated and uppity former slave (also a recent member of the Kiowa nation), Ossie Davis. He's not thrilled with the forced swap, so he sets out to get his furs back. But, by the time he catches them, an outlaw band of scalphunters headed by Savalas, has stolen the furs from the Indians and captured Davis, too. Undeterred, Burt hounds the scalphunters with guerrilla raids, getting occasional inside help from his uneasy ally, Davis. A real good time.

☐ Sex ☐ Nud ☑ Viol ☐ Lang ☑ AdSit

A: Burt Lancaster, Shelley Winters, Ossie Davis, Telly Savalas, Armando Silvestre, Nick Cravat

Distributed By MGM/UA Home Video M202033

SEARCHERS, THE

D: John Ford 144 m

NR · WST ACT · 1956 · COLOR

10 Spectacular Western masterpiece from the two kings of the genre: John Ford and John Wayne. Beautiful scenery, fascinating characters and a thrilling story, rich in both psychological undercurrent and adventure. Wayne is a bitter ex-Confederate soldier who hates Indians. He and his brother's adopted son (who is half-Indian) come home to find that the brother and sister-in-law have been savagely murdered by Comanches and his niece is kidnapped. He and the boy form an uneasy partnership and set off to find her. This begins an epic 7-year odyssey in which Wayne rediscovers his humanity.

☐ Sex ☐ Nud ☑ Viol ☐ Lang ☑ AdSit

A: John Wayne, Jeffrey Hunter, Vera Miles, Ward Bond, Natalie Wood

© WARNER HOME VIDEO 1012

SEPTEMBER GUN

D: Don Taylor 94 m

NR · WST COM · 1983 · COLOR

6 This unconventional Western/comedy starts out a bit slowly but builds into an action-packed adventure. A crusty old gunslinger (Preston) is coerced into helping a stubborn nun (Duke) and a group of orphaned children reach a remote mission school located in Colorado, some three hundred miles away. However, when they get there, the mission school that Sister Dulcina expects to find has been taken over by an outlaw. It is now a bar, and worse. She wants it back for her school and Preston gets the unwelcome job of helping her do it. Made for TV.

☐ Sex ☐ Nud ☐ Viol ☐ Lang ☐ AdSit

A: Robert Preston, Patty Duke, Geoffrey Lewis, Sally Kellerman, Christopher Lewis

© GOODTIMES 9153

SERGEANT RUTLEDGE

D: John Ford 112 m

WST DMA · 1960

8 In the aftermath of the Civil War, two U.S. Calvary units were created specifically for black soldiers. These units served with distinction in helping to open the developing West. The plains Indians came to call these men Buffalo soldiers. Famed Western director John Ford uses that actual situation to create a story of one black soldier who has been wrongly accused of rape and murder. Sergeant Rutledge (Woody Strode) is on trial and his story is told in a series of flashbacks. Lt. Cantrell (Jeffrey Hunter) defends Rutledge as witnesses come to the stand to tell their stories, which are then woven into his. Very unusual for the time. Very interesting material, well presented.

☐ Sex ☐ Nud ☑ Viol ☐ Lang ☑ AdSit

A: Jeffrey Hunter, Woody Strode, Constance Towers, Billie Burke, Carleton Young, Juano Hernandez

© WARNER HOME VIDEO 12272

SHENANDOAH

D: Andrew V. McLaglen 106 m

NR · WST DMA ACT · 1965 · COLOR

9 Emotional Western that captures well the heartbreak of the Civil War. Jimmy Stewart is a widowed father and farmer in Virginia, which was a major crossroads for both armies of the Civil War. Stewart wants no part of this war and vows to stay out of it. But when his young son is arrested after being mistaken for a rebel because he wore the wrong hat, Stewart gathers up the rest of his boys for a search to get their brother back. However, while on their long trip, the war arrives at his farm. This is a large scale picture that is very moving, emotionally charged and haunting. Katharine Ross's debut.

☑ Sex ☐ Nud ☑ Viol ☐ Lang ☑ AdSit

A: James Stewart, Doug McClure, Glenn Corbett, Patrick Wayne, Katharine Ross, George Kennedy

© MCA/UNIVERSAL HOME VIDEO, INC. 55033

SHOOTING, THE

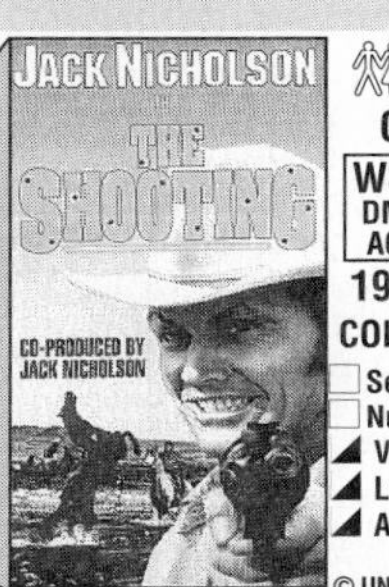

D: Monte Hellman 82 m

G · WST DMA ACT · 1967 · COLOR

7 An unusual existential Western, similar to, but yet far from, the traditional shoot-'em-up. A strange woman (Perkins) hires bounty hunters Oates and Hutchins to escort her across the desert after her son is accidentally killed. A sadistic gunslinger (Nicholson) follows the trio and a bitter dispute develops between Nicholson and Hutchins over the woman and Nicholson kills him. The trio continue on through the relentless desert. Their water is running low and their horses are dying. This is not a typical Western, so don't expect a typical simple traditional resolution and ending.

☐ Sex ☐ Nud ☑ Viol ☑ Lang ☑ AdSit

A: Jack Nicholson, Will Hutchins, Warren Oates, Millie Perkins

© UNITED AMERICAN VIDEO CORP. 17193

SHOOTIST, THE

D: Don Siegel 100 m

PG · WST DMA ACT · 1976 · COLOR

9 An intelligent triumph for John Wayne. As Wayne himself was dying of cancer (his last film), so is his character - an old gunfighter named J.B. Books. The time is 1901. Books has spent his life as a gunman, but both he and his era are dying. All he wants now is to be left alone, but wherever he goes his reputation precedes him. His enemies and even total strangers seek him out. Everybody wants to kill him or to make a profit from him. He has no real friends - only the woman who owns the boarding house where he is staying and her hero-worshipping son. Very believable and moving. A fitting last film for Wayne.

☐ Sex ☐ Nud ☑ Viol ☑ Lang ☑ AdSit

A: John Wayne, Lauren Bacall, Ron Howard, James Stewart, Scatman Crothers, Richard Boone

© PARAMOUNT HOME VIDEO 8904

SILENCE OF THE NORTH

D: Allan Winton King 94 m

PG · WST DMA ACT · 1981 · COLOR

7 Picturesque and inspirational. This is a story about a strong-willed woman (Burstyn) who falls in love with a rugged trapper (Skerritt) and follows him to live in the wilds of northern Canada. The story, based upon the actual autobiography of Olive Fredrickson, tells of her daily struggles, from being a young mother just after the turn of the 20th-century to later being a widow with three children. The wilderness can be cruel, and she and her family are left to brave nature's forces, survive cold winters and deal with tragedy on their own. Excellent.

☐ Sex ☐ Nud ☑ Viol ☐ Lang ☑ AdSit

A: Ellen Burstyn, Tom Skerritt, Gordon Pinsent, Jennifer McKinney, Colin Fox

© MCA/UNIVERSAL HOME VIDEO, INC. 71004

SILVERADO

D: Lawrence Kasdan 132 m

PG-13 · WST ACT · 1985 · COLOR

9 Ripsnorter. A star-packed Western with action aplenty. Scott Glenn, on his way home from prison to his hot-headed brother (Costner), has to protect himself from three men who are trying to kill him. Then he stumbles onto another drifter (Kline) who has been stripped of everything he owns and left to die. The two of them team up to help a black man (Glover) out of a tough spot. Those three then team up with crazy brother Costner and all four help rid a small town of a corrupt sheriff. Relentless pacing provides a really good time, but it is very violent and don't think too long about the details.

☐ Sex ☐ Nud ■ Viol ☑ Lang ☑ AdSit

A: Kevin Kline, Scott Glenn, Kevin Costner, Danny Glover, Linda Hunt, Rosanna Arquette

© COLUMBIA TRISTAR HOME VIDEO 60567

SKIN GAME

D: Paul Bogart — 102 m

PG | WST COM | 1971 | COLOR

9 First-class comedy! Two men of the Old West really have a good con game going in this top-notch comedy with a social conscience. Set just before the Civil War, Garner and Gossett pose as master and slave. Their scam is that Garner sells Gossett for a high price, Gossett escapes and they split the dough. Then they can do it all over again in the next town. Everything is going great, too, until Susan Clark steals their money and Garner's heart; and a slave trader (Asner) takes Gossett and his girlfriend South into real slavery. Always entertaining. Has some really funny moments.

☐ Sex ◢ Nud ◢ Viol ☐ Lang ◢ AdSit

A: James Garner, Louis Gossett, Jr., Susan Clark, Edward Asner, Andrew Duggan

© WARNER HOME VIDEO 11406

SOLDIER BLUE

D: Ralph Nelson — 105 m

PG | WST ACT | 1974 | COLOR

8 Controversial and violent Western. Bergen plays a white woman who had been captured by Indians two years before. She and a young cavalry private (Peter Strauss) survive a brutal attack on a her encampment. Together they struggle to get back to an Army outpost, but along the way are captured by a vile gunrunner. Their eventual escape gets them to safety, but they also learn of an impending massacre the Army is planning (patterned after a true event at Sand Creek in Colorado). Too strident, very violent but still worth watching.

☐ Sex ◢ Nud ■ Viol ◢ Lang ◢ AdSit

A: Candice Bergen, Peter Strauss, Donald Pleasence, John Anderson, Jorge Rivero, Dana Elcar

© NEW LINE HOME VIDEO 2032

SOMMERSBY

D: Jon Amiel — 114 m

PG-13 | ROM WST DMA | 1993 | COLOR

9 Very involving and highly romantic Civil War saga, but with a very different bent. Jack Sommersby (Gere) has been away from his Tennessee farm for six years, locked up in a Yankee prison. His wife Laurel and his son have given him up for dead, and yet one day he comes walking back into his war-torn town and onto their decimated farm. Jack has changed. He left as a disagreeable sort and came back as a thoughtful and caring man. Jack wins back Laurel and then even organizes a recovery plan for the town. But soon he is arrested for murder and is accused of being someone else. This one starts slow but comes to a powerful and unusual finish.

◢ Sex ☐ Nud ◢ Viol ☐ Lang ◢ AdSit

A: Richard Gere, Jodie Foster, James Earl Jones, Bill Pullman, William Windom, Brett Kelly

© WARNER HOME VIDEO 12649

SON OF THE MORNING STAR

D: Mike Robe — 186 m

PG | WST DMA | 1991 | COLOR

7 Excellent and revealing made-for-TV miniseries covering the period from the time of the Civil War to the 1876 Battle at the Little Big Horn. It is the fact-based story of both the peoples and politics of the time, using George Custer as the pivotal figure. It is told from both the Anglo perspective of Custer's wife (Arquette) and a young Indian woman's (voice of Buffy St. Marie) perspective. What emerges is a comprehensive, insightful and personalized picture of a pivotal time in American history. If you are a history fan, it is worthy of at least an 8. However, it is slow-moving in places.

☐ Sex ☐ Nud ■ Viol ☐ Lang ◢ AdSit

A: Gary Cole, Rosanna Arquette, Dean Stockwell, Rodney A. Grant, Stanley Anderson, Ed Blatchford

© REPUBLIC PICTURES HOME VIDEO RN043810

SONS OF KATIE ELDER, THE

D: Henry Hathaway — 122 m

NR | WST ACT COM | 1965 | COLOR

9 Fast-paced Wayne Western with action, good times and a heart! Katie was a loving mother who had four rough and rowdy sons. When she dies, the four come home to pay their respects and decide that the youngest should honor their mother and go to college. But first they make a pact to get back the land that was taken from Katie and to learn the truth about their father's murder six months earlier. The gunman (Wayne), the gambler (Martin), the quiet guy (Holliman) and the kid (Michael Anderson, Jr.) all put aside their differences to learn the truth and to protect each other's back. Rousing good time.

☐ Sex ☐ Nud ◢ Viol ☐ Lang ◢ AdSit

A: John Wayne, Dean Martin, Martha Hyer, Earl Holliman, Jeremy Slate, James Gregory

© PARAMOUNT HOME VIDEO 6729

SUNDOWNERS, THE

D: Fred Zinnemann — 133 m

NR | WST DMA COM | 1960 | COLOR

9 Wonderfully winning film that was a Best Picture nominee and received four other nominations. One of the best-ever of many Mitchum/Kerr pairings. It is the loving character study of a headstrong rover who insists upon taking his wife and family with him from job to job, herding and shearing sheep in Australia's outback during the 1920s. He loves his family and he loves the life, but she thinks its time to settle down. Shot on location in Australia. Numerous winning vignettes and a crew of fascinating characters populate this endearing story. Highly recommended and rewarding viewing for all ages.

☐ Sex ☐ Nud ☐ Viol ☐ Lang ☐ AdSit

A: Deborah Kerr, Robert Mitchum, Peter Ustinov, Michael Anderson, Jr., Glynis Johns, Dina Merrill

© WARNER HOME VIDEO 11215

SUPPORT YOUR LOCAL GUNFIGHTER

D: Burt Kennedy — 92 m

PG | COM WST | 1971 | COLOR

8 The uproariously funny SUPPORT YOUR LOCAL SHERIFF! was so successful that they decided to do another one. Technically, this is not a sequel, because the characters are different (although the actors aren't). This time around Garner is a con artist who has spied an opportunity to make a fortune in a mining dispute. But, in order to do it he has to convince everyone that the bumbling Jack Elam is really a notorious gunfighter and killer. While this one doesn't have the sparkle and punch of the first one, it is still a darn good time and well worth the time spent.

☐ Sex ☐ Nud ◢ Viol ☐ Lang ☐ AdSit

A: James Garner, Suzanne Pleshette, Jack Elam, Harry Morgan, John Dehner, Joan Blondell

Distributed By MGM/UA Home Video M201122

SUPPORT YOUR LOCAL SHERIFF

D: Burt Kennedy — 92 m

G | COM WST | 1969 | COLOR

10 A very, very funny picture - that shoots holes in just about every cliche ever packed into a Western. James Garner is a drifter, passing through a gold-mining boomtown. He's got the fastest wit in the West but at heart he is just a peace lover and it is only his economics which force him into becoming the town sheriff. He is quick to point out that he is really just on his way to Australia. The only one in town actively on his side is the one-eyed town drunk (Eliam). Against him is a cantankerous old man, his snide gunslinger son and the mayor's spoiled suffragette daughter. Absolutely hilarious! Also, see BLAZING SADDLES.

☐ Sex ☐ Nud ◢ Viol ☐ Lang ☐ AdSit

A: James Garner, Joan Hackett, Walter Brennan, Harry Morgan, Jack Elam, Bruce Dern

Distributed By MGM/UA Home Video M202031

TELL THEM WILLIE BOY IS HERE

D: Abraham Polonsky — 98 m

PG | WST DMA | 1969 | COLOR

6 Unusual modern Western that is based upon an actual 1909 incident. Robert Blake is a Paiute Indian who wants to wed white Katharine Ross, but her father (Angel) reacts violently to the news and Blake kills him in self-defense. He and Ross then flee together to avoid arrest. Sheriff Redford is reluctant to arrest Willie, but prissy Susan Clark and racist rancher Sullivan urge him on. President Grover Cleveland is also in the area, and the press corp with him promotes Willie's case nationally into the appearance of a major Indian uprising. Compelling viewing, even though heavy-handed.

☐ Sex ☐ Nud ◢ Viol ◢ Lang ◢ AdSit

A: Robert Redford, Katharine Ross, Robert Blake, Susan Clark, Barry Sullivan, Mikel Angel

© MCA/UNIVERSAL HOME VIDEO, INC. 55084

THERE WAS A CROOKED MAN

D: Joseph L. Mankiewicz — 123 m

R | WST ACT COM | 1970 | COLOR

8 Quirky and clever Western. Crooked man Kirk Douglas steals a small fortune. He is caught when he is spotted by his victim (who is looking through a voyeur's peep hole at a whorehouse) as he is celebrating his new fortune. He is sent to an Arizona prison which is wardened by revision-minded Henry Fonda. But, Douglas uses the opportunities created by Fonda's revisions to institute a riot and escape and immediately sets off to recover the buried booty. But, a very angry and exasperated Fonda has personally set out after him. Entertaining Western, with a clever and funny plot, and a powerhouse cast.

◢ Sex ◢ Nud ◢ Viol ◢ Lang ◢ AdSit

A: Kirk Douglas, Henry Fonda, Warren Oates, Burgess Meredith, Hume Cronyn, Arthur O'Connell

© WARNER HOME VIDEO 11270

THEY CALL ME TRINITY

D: E.B. Clucher — 109 m

G | WST COM | 1971 | COLOR

6 A wild spoof of the very popular "speghetti Westerns" of the time, which became a surprise international hit on its own. Terence Hill is an amoral sheriff helped out by his dim-witted half-brother, but the two unexpectedly become the saviors of a group of Morman settlers who are being harassed by a group of marauding Mexican bandits. Mostly good fun and spiced with ample doses of slapstick humor and comic action.

☐ Sex ☐ Nud ◢ Viol ☐ Lang ☐ AdSit

A: Terence Hill, Bud Spencer, Farley Granger, Gisela Hahn, Stephen Zacharias, Dan Sturkie

© UNITED AMERICAN VIDEO CORP. 5464

TIN STAR, THE

D: Anthony Mann — 93 m

NR | WST ACT | 1957 | B&W

9 Solid and well acted - a quality Western. Henry Fonda is a bounty hunter. He used to be a sheriff and had a family, but they died when he couldn't raise the money for doctor bills. Now, hard and bitter, he comes to a small town to await the arrival of a reward check. Anthony Perkins is the young sheriff in the town and is in way over his head with a local thug. Fonda, seeing a piece of his former self in the sheriff, helps Perkins learn what to do and, in the process, rediscovers a life for himself. An intelligent and affecting character study.

☐ Sex ☐ Nud ◢ Viol ☐ Lang ◢ AdSit

A: Henry Fonda, Anthony Perkins, Betsy Palmer, Neville Brand, John McIntire, Lee Van Cleef

© PARAMOUNT HOME VIDEO 5708

TOMBSTONE

D: George P. Cosmatos 130 m

R WST ACT 1994 COLOR

Sex Nud Viol Lang AdSit

8 Critics dismissed this as just another remake, except more violent. In a literal sense, they were right. However, there is more to it than that. There is a genuine excitement. And, while all the characters and elements have been embellished by Hollywood, most of them, not all, are also generally true. Wyatt and his brothers did use their fearlessness and reputations to worm their way into much of the larcenous business of Tombstone, which put them on a collision course with a gang of hooligans called "The Cowboys". The blood war between these two factions began at the corral, killed Morgan, crippled Virgil, divided the town and destroyed The Cowboys.

A: Kurt Russell, Val Kilmer, Michael Biehn, Powers Boothe, Dana Delany, Sam Elliott

© HOLLYWOOD PICTURES HOME VIDEO 2544

TOM HORN

D: William Wiard 98 m

R WST ACT 1980 COLOR

Sex Nud Viol Lang AdSit

8 Steve McQueen's second-to-last movie is based upon a real-life character who was hung at the turn of the 20th-century. The film may have also revised history somewhat. Tom Horn is a gunfighter and bounty hunter. He is hired by a group of Wyoming cattlemen to get rid of a plague of cattle rustlers. However, when Horn's efficient, but unsavory, methods prove to be too embarrassing, he has to be gotten rid of. So, according to the film, he is framed for the murder of a boy, tried and hanged. Notes from Horne's actual diary inspired this version of the story, but the truth of it is up to the viewer to determine.

A: Steve McQueen, Richard Farnsworth, Slim Pickens, Elisha Cook, Jr.

© WARNER HOME VIDEO 1042

TRAIN ROBBERS, THE

D: Burt Kennedy 92 m

PG WST 1973 COLOR

Sex Nud Viol Lang AdSit

6 Slightly different vehicle for John Wayne. Ann-Margret is a widow whose husband hid $500,000 in stolen bank gold. She solicits the help of an aging Civil War vet (Wayne) in retrieving the gold and returning it, so that her family name can be restored. John and some hired hands set out into the Mexican badlands on this quest but are being pursued by her husband's old partner, Ricardo Montalban, and his band of hired guns, who want the gold, too. Some interesting twists, including a surprise ending, keep things moving. There is action, but the emphasis is on characters and plot.

A: John Wayne, Ann-Margret, Rod Taylor, Ben Johnson, Christopher George, Ricardo Montalban

© WARNER HOME VIDEO 11093

TRUE GRIT

D: Henry Hathaway 128 m

G WST ACT COM 1969 COLOR

Sex Nud Viol Lang AdSit

9 Extremely popular Western for which Wayne finally won an Oscar, after 40 years in film. He is Rooster Cogburn, a crude old derelict of a marshall who helps out a young girl who wants him to track down her father's killer. They head off into Indian country, where they are joined by a young Texas ranger (Campbell). This is a very enjoyable movie that takes time for solid character development and creating interesting relationships between the principals. There is a rousing finish that is topped off with a near-classic shootout. Great entertainment.

A: John Wayne, Glen Campbell, Kim Darby, Robert Duvall, Jeremy Slate, Strother Martin

© PARAMOUNT HOME VIDEO 6833

TWO MULES FOR SISTER SARA

D: Don Siegel 105 m

PG WST ACT COM 1969 COLOR

Sex Nud Viol Lang AdSit

8 Intriguing Western that lures you in, entertains you throughout and then hits you with a surprise curve. Clint is a drifter in Mexico during the revolution. He rescues a nun (MacLaine) from being raped but he is now burdened with her. He finds her to be both strangely unpious and fascinatingly appealing - all of which is very unsettling to him. She entices him into risking his neck by helping her to aid the rebel cause and eventually into helping her attack a French garrison. Light-hearted and action-packed fun - with a surprise inside.

A: Shirley MacLaine, Clint Eastwood, Manolo Fabregas, Alberto Morin, Armando Silvestre, John Kelly

© MCA/UNIVERSAL HOME VIDEO, INC. 66046

TWO RODE TOGETHER

D: John Ford 109 m

NR WST DMA ACT 1961 COLOR

Sex Nud Viol Lang AdSit

8 A worthy Western with Stewart in a somewhat uncharacteristically harsh role. He plays a hard-bitten and cynical marshall who has been hired by a naive calvary officer (Widmark) and a group of settlers to retrieve kidnapped white children from the Commanches. While Widmark and the settlers are optimistic, Stewart knows that what he will bring back is not what they expect. He also knows that the children will not be accepted. Interesting and somber take on the theme first explored in THE SEARCHERS, which is also highly recommended.

A: James Stewart, Richard Widmark, Shirley Jones, Andy Devine, Woody Strode, Linda Cristal

© COLUMBIA TRISTAR HOME VIDEO 60762

ULZANA'S RAID

D: Robert Aldrich 103 m

R WST ACT 1972 COLOR

Sex Nud Viol Lang AdSit

8 A tense and quite unusual Western that was viewed at the time by many critics as being an allegory for the fighting in Vietnam and so it received an unduly poor reception. That unfortunate aspect aside, this is quite an involving story. A seasoned old Army scout is sent along with a green officer in pursuit of a notoriously vicious Apache raiding party led by the cunning Ulzana. The inexperienced young lieutenant is tentative and uncertain, but Lancaster is as calculating as his cruel quarry, Ulzana. Very violent, an absorbing chess game of a pursuit and a thought provoking insight into the thin veil of civilization over us all. Great job by Lancaster. Based on fact.

A: Burt Lancaster, Bruce Davison, Richard Jaeckel, Jorge Luke

© MCA/UNIVERSAL HOME VIDEO, INC. 80155

UNFORGIVEN, THE

D: John Huston 123 m

NR WST DMA 1960 COLOR

Sex Nud Viol Lang AdSit

7 In the Texas panhandle immediately after the Civil War, memories of the fierce battles with the Kiowa are still fresh in minds on both sides. So when a figure from the past claims that Hepburn is a full-blooded Kiowa who was adopted by white settlers as a baby, tensions erupt. The Kiowa want to reclaim her into the tribe and the local whites want her gone. Both she and her adopted family are torn by the conflict that threatens to consume them all. One "brother" clearly loves her in a non-brotherly way and another hates Indians so much he is willing to leave his family. Intense.

A: Burt Lancaster, Audrey Hepburn, Lillian Gish, Audie Murphy, John Saxon, Charles Brickford

Distributed By MGM/UA Home Video M601123

UNFORGIVEN

D: Clint Eastwood m

R WST DMA ACT 1992 COLOR

Sex Nud Viol Lang AdSit

10 Hugely successful and popular but very atypical Western that won Best Picture Oscar plus 3 more. Eastwood is an ex-gunslinger and outlaw who has been struggling to eke out a living as a farmer, but he and his family are starving. So, he and his ex-partner set off to collect a bounty by killing a couple of cowboys who have cut up a prostitute. Their mission, however, places them in direct conflict with another gunslinger (Hackman) who has become comfortable as the ruthless sheriff of the town. This is a no-nonsense, grittily realistic and unglamorous story of men pitted against each other, who are able to survive a brutal game by killing brutally without a thought.

A: Clint Eastwood, Gene Hackman, Morgan Freeman, Richard Harris, Jaimz Woolvett

© WARNER HOME VIDEO 12531

UTU

D: Geoff Murphy 104 m

R ACT DMA WST 1983 COLOR

Sex Nud Viol Lang AdSit

8 Excellent (but very exotic) New Zealand import. It is set there, in the 1870s, but has definite overtones of the American Southwest. When a aboriginal tribesman, who is fighting for the British colonial army, comes home to find that his village has been massacred by the same white army he has been fighting for, he swears vengeance on all whites. He becomes a vicious raider of white settlements, hotly pursued by the army and even despised by many of his own people because of his ruthlessness. Lots of action, but also a moving moral play that is reminiscent of the American campaign against Geronimo.

A: Anzac Wallace, Kelly Johnson, Tim Elliot, Bruno Lawrence

© CBS/FOX VIDEO 6119

VALDEZ IS COMING

D: Edwin Sherin 90 m

PG WST ACT 1971 COLOR

Sex Nud Viol Lang AdSit

7 Pretty good Western. Burt Lancaster is Valdez, a Mexican/American sheriff who struggles to regain his dignity after having suffered years of racial degradation. After Valdez is forced to shoot a Mexican suspect, he tries to provide for the man's widow. His efforts trigger the hostilities of a ruthless cattle baron and gun-runner, who humiliates and then threatens Valdez. So Valdez captures the man's wife and the chase to kill Valdez is on - but Valdez is not a man to be taken lightly. Solid actioner, with some thought thrown in for good measure.

A: Burt Lancaster, Susan Clark, Frank Silvera, Richard Jordan, Jon Cypher, Barton Heyman

Distributed By MGM/UA Home Video M202961

WARLOCK

D: Edward Dmytryk 122 m

NR WST ACT 1959 COLOR

Sex Nud Viol Lang AdSit

8 Intelligent and unusually complex psychological Western. The citizens of a small mining town find that they are being terrorized by a gang of outlaws. So they hire a gunslinger (Fonda) and his crippled gambler partner (Quinn) to stop the gang. Fonda and Quinn do what they were hired to do, but the town is distressed to learn that they have just exchanged one tyrant for another. Now the deputy (Widmark), himself a reformed bandit, must step in to stop a raging Quinn before he destroys the town.

A: Henry Fonda, Anthony Quinn, Richard Widmark, Dorothy Malone, Delores Michaels, Wallace Ford

© FOXVIDEO 1238

WAR WAGON, THE

D: Burt Kennedy 101 m

NR | WST ACT COM | 1967 | COLOR

7 Entertaining tongue-in-cheek John Wayne Western. John has had his fortune stolen, been framed by an unscrupulous cattle baron and mine owner (Cabot) and sent to prison. So, when John gets out, Cabot sends Kirk Douglas to kill him. Instead, John enlists Douglas in his plan to inflict sweet revenge and also gathers together several others in a gang to carry it out. He and his cronies are going to rob a big shipment of gold dust that Cabot transports in a special, heavily armed coach called the War Wagon. Good, mindless action adventure, amply spiced with humor. Hard to beat the combination of Wayne and Douglas.

Sex Nud Viol Lang AdSit

A: John Wayne, Kirk Douglas, Howard Keel, Robert Walker, Jr., Keenan Wynn

© MCA/UNIVERSAL HOME VIDEO, INC. 80016

WATERHOLE NO. 3

D: William Graham 100 m

NR | WST COM | 1967 | COLOR

7 Amusing, somewhat racy, Western farce. Three confederates have stolen a Union Army gold shipment and have hidden it in a desert waterhole. James Coburn is a gambler and lady's man, hot in pursuit of the gold. He has sampled the sheriff's amorous daughter's charms. Now the girl is chasing after him and so is the sheriff, but mostly because Coburn stole the sheriff's prize horse, and they're all converging on the waterhole with the gold. Slapstick comedy, combined with some clever and bawdy dialogue. Good time.

Sex Nud Viol Lang AdSit

A: James Coburn, Carroll O'Connor, Joan Blondell, Claude Akins, Bruce Dern, Margaret Blye

© PARAMOUNT HOME VIDEO 6707

WE OF THE NEVER NEVER

D: Igor Auzins 135 m

G | DMA WST ACT | 1982 | COLOR

8 Touching and captivating import from Australia, and winner of six Australian Academy Award nominations. It is a true story, taken from the diary of Jeannie Gunn, first published in 1908. She was the first white woman to travel deep into the Australian wilderness, called the Outback or the Never Never, to a cattle station with her husband. A stunning piece of camerawork depicts her story of survival in a rugged world dominated by men, their confrontation with the mystical world of the aborigines and their acceptance of her. However, her happiness is soon shattered with the death of her husband.

Sex Nud Viol Lang AdSit

A: Angela Punch-McGregor, Tommy Lewis, Arthur Dignam, Tony Barry

© COLUMBIA TRISTAR HOME VIDEO 60256

WESTWORLD

D: Michael Crichton 90 m

PG | SF WST ACT | 1973 | COLOR

7 Very entertaining and inventive yarn about a high tech adult resort of the future, where wealthy patrons may live out their Wild West fantasies with amazingly lifelike robots. By day, the robots are shot up by the patrons. At night they are repaired. Everything is harmless and quite safe until one errant gunfighter robot (Brynner is terrific) refuses to play the game as it was written. He goes berserk and starts stalking the guests for real. Richard Benjamin and James Brolin are two tourists who are unfortunate enough to catch his attention. Well-done sequel is FUTUREWORLD.

Sex Nud Viol Lang AdSit

A: Yul Brynner, James Brolin, Richard Benjamin, Alan Oppenheimer, Victoria Shaw, Martin Jared

Distributed By MGM/UA Home Video M600097

WHEN THE LEGENDS DIE

D: Stuart Millar 105 m

PG | DMA WST | 1972 | COLOR

7 A perceptive and sensitive story about the relationship that develops between an aging, hard-drinking cowboy, who is having a hard time dealing with his declining rodeo skills, and a rebellious young Ute Indian, who has freshly arrived from the reservation after his parents have died. The old man exploits the youngster and his riding abilities for a meal ticket when he trains the boy to ride broncs in the rodeo. However, their relationship becomes severely strained when Widmark encourages him to lose so they can make money on the bets. One of Widmark's better performances.

Sex Nud Viol Lang AdSit

A: Frederic Forrest, Richard Widmark, Luana Anders, Vito Scotti

© FOXVIDEO 1293

WHITE FANG

D: Randal Kleiser 109 m

PG | WST ACT CLD | 1991 | COLOR

9 Wonderful whole-family entertainment in the true sense of the phrase. This is an exciting adventure film that has something to satisfy everyone. It is a beautiful picture that evokes the actual feel of the Alaskan goldrush days. A young man follows his father's dying wishes to settle his gold claim deep in the wilds of a virgin Yukon wilderness. The film focuses upon the young man's journey there and upon his friendship with an orphaned wolf cub, White Fang. Spectacularly photographed, this is a tale of men in the wilderness and one man's love for his four-footed kindred spirit.

Sex Nud Viol Lang AdSit

A: Ethan Hawke, Klaus Maria Brandauer, James Remar, Seymour Cassel, Susan Hogan

© WALT DISNEY HOME VIDEO 1151

WILD BUNCH, THE

D: Sam Peckinpah 144 m

R | WST ACT | 1969 | COLOR

9 Highly acclaimed Western, primarily because it ushered in a new era of graphic violence in film. However, it is also excellent entertainment. A veteran cast of prominent actors populate this action-packed story about a band of aging outlaws caught at the end of an era in 1913. Lead by Holden, the bunch decides to pull off one last big job. They hijack an ammunition train to take across the border to sell to a renegade Mexican General. They are pursued the whole way there by the Army, lead by a former member (Ryan), who is trying to earn his freedom. Non-stop, very violent action.

Sex Nud Viol Lang AdSit

A: William Holden, Robert Ryan, Ernest Borgnine, Edmond O'Brien, Ben Johnson, Warren Oates

© WARNER HOME VIDEO 1014

WILD ROVERS

D: Blake Edwards 138 m

PG | WST ACT COM | 1971 | COLOR

8 An unheralded little gem. William Holden and Ryan O'Neal are two cowpoke buddies, one old and one young, who become disillusioned with their careers on the range when one of their friends is accidentally killed. On a whim, this not-too-bright pair decide to rob a bank and head out for Mexico. On a dead run with a posse hot on their heels, it occurs to them that this was not a wise career move. The pleasure in the movie comes from the relationship between these guys. A great buddy movie. Solid performances, particularly by Holden.

Sex Nud Viol Lang AdSit

A: William Holden, Ryan O'Neal, Karl Malden, Lynn Carlin, Tom Skerritt, Joe Don Baker

Distributed By MGM/UA Home Video M600305

WILL PENNY

D: Tom Gries 109 m

NR | WST ROM ACT | 1968 | COLOR

9 Outstanding film that requires a Western setting to tell its perceptive and moving story, but this is not just a Western. Will Penny has spent his whole life as a cowboy and a loner. He has never thought of living any other way. However, after a run-in with a cruel rawhider and his boys who leave him to die, he is rescued by a pretty woman and her son who are traveling to Oregon to reunite with her settler-husband. For the first time, Will feels the tug of a home life and love. Heartwarming and evocative. Moving, understated performances make these characters human and very real. Excellent.

Sex Nud Viol Lang AdSit

A: Charlton Heston, Joan Hackett, Donald Pleasence, Lee Majors, Bruce Dern

© PARAMOUNT HOME VIDEO 6723

WINDWALKER

D: Keith Merrill 108 m

PG | WST DMA ACT | 1980 | COLOR

8 Unusually well-rounded family entertainment in the form of the telling of a Cheyenne legend. As an old Cheyenne warrior lies dying, he tells his grandsons the story of how his wife was murdered and his son (their uncle) was kidnapped years before by a neighboring band of Crow Indians. The old man dies but comes back to life to protect his tribe from a Crow attack that is led by his lost son. A very unusual story of war, survival and love. The entire movie is spoken in the Cheyenne and Crow languages with English subtitles.

Sex Nud Viol Lang AdSit

A: Trevor Howard, Nick Ramus, James Remar, Serene Hedin, Dusty Iron Wing McCrea, Silvana Gatlardo

© CBS/FOX VIDEO 6345

WYATT EARP

D: Lawrence Kasdan 191 m

PG-13 | WST DMA ACT | 1994 | COLOR

9 Excellent epic Western, telling the whole story of Wyatt Earp. It begins in Missouri and tells of his father's influence on all the boys. Follows Wyatt from the death of his first wife, becoming a buffalo hunter and then the man who tamed Dodge City. Only in the last half of a quite long movie does the story of the fight with the Clantons come along. A real attempt at telling history and the makeup of a complicated man was made. Wyatt is not painted as being a true hero in the classic Hollywood sense, but that actually makes the story much more interesting. It starts a little slow and is very deliberate in the telling, but it also tells a powerful and fascinating story. Hang in there.

Sex Nud Viol Lang AdSit

A: Kevin Costner, Dennis Quaid, Gene Hackman, Michael Masden, Linden Ashby, Catherine O'Hara

© WARNER HOME VIDEO 13177

YOUNG GUNS

D: Christopher Cain 102 m

R | WST ACT | 1988 | COLOR

6 Hollywood retells the legend of Billy the Kid, done this time with the current group of young Hollywood hunks and bolstered by an MTV-type sound track and 20th-century political correctness. Old-timers will have a harder time cottonin' up to this version, but the younger generation turned out in big numbers. The story is that of a group of young toughs who are hired by a cultured Englishman to protect his New Mexico ranch. When he is killed, they turn into a marauding wild bunch lead by Billy (Estevez) and are hunted down in a major man hunt. Watchable.

Sex Nud Viol Lang AdSit

A: Emilio Estevez, Kiefer Sutherland, Lou Diamond Phillips, Charlie Sheen, Dermot Mulroney, Casey Siemaszko

© LIVE HOME VIDEO 5267

YOUNG GUNS 2

PG-13
WST
ACT
1990
COLOR
Sex
Nud
Viol
Lang
AdSit

D: Geoff Murphy 105 m

6 This marked the return of the remaining half of the bunch from YOUNG GUNS. Same formula as before: lots of action supported by a heavy rock score and filled with Hollywood hunks. This time they have gathered up some new recruits and are heading off to Mexico. But they are being pursued by a band of government men led by Billy's one-time friend Pat Garrett.

A: Emilio Estevez, Kiefer Sutherland, Lou Diamond Phillips, Christian Slater, Balthazar Getty, Alan Ruck

© FOXVIDEO 1902

Oldies

1955 and Before

Action

ADVENTURES OF DON JUAN, THE

D: Vincent Sherman 111 m

NR | ACT COM | 1949 | B&W

7 Colorful costume epic. Errol Flynn plays the great lover and swordsman. This is a very extravagant film in which handsome swashbuckler Flynn is engaged in grand sword fights and in stringing along countless maidens - all of whom he forsakes to save his queen from the evil Duke. The story is told in tongue-in-cheek style, all the while poking fun at Flynn's own reputation as a great lover.

Sex / Nud / ◢ Viol / Lang / ◢ AdSit

A: Errol Flynn, Viveca Lindfors, Robert Douglas, Alan Hale, Romney Brent, Jerry Austin

Distributed By MGM/UA Home Video M600748

ADVENTURES OF ROBIN HOOD, THE

D: Michael Curtiz, William Keighley 103 m

NR | ACT ROM | 1938 | COLOR

9 Extravagant classic adventure film. Dashing Errol Flynn is at his swashbuckling best, wooing Maid Marian (de Havilland), ruining the plans of the evil prince (Rains), robbing from the rich and giving to the poor and fighting wicked and haughty Sir Guy of Gisbourne (Rathbone). Lavish sets in Technicolor are a major asset to this hallmark adventure classic. See also ROBIN AND MARIAN, with Sean Connery as Robin Hood, and Kevin Costner in ROBIN HOOD, PRINCE OF THIEVES.

Sex / Nud / ◢ Viol / Lang / ◢ AdSit

A: Errol Flynn, Basil Rathbone, Ian Hunter, Olivia de Havilland, Claude Rains, Alan Hale

Distributed By MGM/UA Home Video M201377

BEAU GESTE

D: William Wellman 114 m

NR | ACT DMA | 1939 | B&W

9 Excellent! First made in 1926, then again in 1966, this is still the best screen version. It is a classic story of honor, sacrifice and brotherly love. When one brother falsely admits to a jewel theft to save the honor of their impoverished governess and then joins the Foreign Legion, his two brothers join him there. Amid the desert sands and dead soldiers propped against the walls of a desert fortress, the brothers battle native attacks and the tyranny of their sadistic sergeant. The action, story and the characters are all unforgettable. Thought of as a man's movie.

Sex / Nud / ◢ Viol / Lang / ◢ AdSit

A: Gary Cooper, Robert Preston, Ray Milland, Brian Donlevy, J. Carrol Naish, Susan Hayward

© MCA/UNIVERSAL HOME VIDEO, INC. 80547

BEN HUR

D: Fred Niblo 148 m

NR | ACT DMA | 1926 | B&W

8 Gigantic first remake of the original version, which was first filmed in 1907. This silent epic cost a staggering $4,000,000 and took two years to edit. It was the grandest of all the silent movie spectacles and still holds up well compared to the 1959 version with Charlton Heston. It is the story of a Jewish nobleman who is condemned to a life of slavery by a Roman he had called friend. He later returns to seek vengeance on his betrayer. Novarro and Bushman give the performances of their lives. Colossal. Still a winner.

Sex / Nud / ◢ Viol / Lang / ◢ AdSit

A: Ramon Novarro, Francis X. Bushman, May McAvoy, Betty Bronson, Carmel Myers

Distributed By MGM/UA Home Video M301474

BULLDOG DRUMMOND

D: Sidney Howard 89 m

NR | ACT CRM | 1929 | B&W

6 Bulldog Drummond was a fictional character born in print in 1919. In the '20s he was brought to the silent screen, then in 1929 to talkies. Bulldog was a British ex-army officer who was always searching for adventure. Ronald Coleman played the character twice, first here. In this episode, Bulldog aids a lady whose uncle has been kidnapped by phony psychiatrists. This is probably the best of the Drummond series.

Sex / Nud / Viol / Lang / AdSit

A: Ronald Colman, Joan Bennet, Lilyan Tashman

© HBO VIDEO 90751

CAPTAIN BLOOD

D: Michael Curtiz 120 m

NR | ACT | 1935 | B&W

9 One of the best swashbucklers ever. Flynn, in his first starring role, plays a 17th-century doctor sold into slavery in the Caribbean after treating the wounds of rebels. He is purchased by the beautiful niece (de Haviland) of a brutal plantation owner, but escapes to become the leader of a band of pirates and he launches his own battle against the colonial governor (Atwill). Great miniature work, an excellent cast and some of the best sword fights ever put on screen. This film received a nomination as Best Picture and made stars out of Flynn, de Haviland and Curtiz.

Sex / Nud / ◢ Viol / Lang / AdSit

A: Errol Flynn, Olivia de Havilland, Lionel Atwill, Basil Rathbone, Guy Kibbee, Ross Alexander

Distributed By MGM/UA Home Video M201470

CHARGE OF THE LIGHT BRIGADE

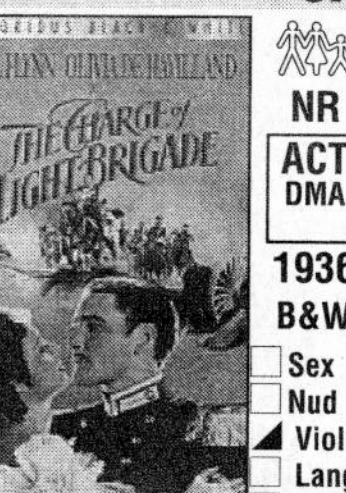

D: Michael Curtiz 117 m

NR | ACT DMA | 1936 | B&W

8 This is a fictionalized account of what may have happened to 600 British cavalrymen who gallantly charged into certain death (and 25,000 Russians) with their sabers flashing during the Crimean War (1853-1856). One of the most dramatic calvary charges ever filmed is showcased in this story which was originally painted in the words of Tennyson's classic poem. This version has Major Vickers (Flynn) leading the 27th Lancers in a quest to find the Indian leader of a massacre of women and children. Thundering action against a romantic backdrop.

Sex / Nud / ◢ Viol / Lang / AdSit

A: Errol Flynn, Olivia de Havilland, Patric Knowles, Donald Crisp, Henry Stephenson, Nigel Bruce

Distributed By MGM/UA Home Video M201510

CHINA SEAS

D: Tay Garnett 88 m

NR | ACT | 1935 | B&W | Sex | Nud | ✓ Viol | Lang | ✓ AdSit

7 Clark Gable and his tramp steamer are between Hong Kong and Singapore when they are hit by a typhoon. All that bouncing around reveals that he has a contraband load of gold on board. Soon, they are boarded by a group of Malaysian pirates who are led by Wallace Beery and they are looking for the gold, which has been hidden again. Also aboard are Gable's ex-lover with a tainted past (Jean Harlow) and a beautiful English aristocrat (Russell). Russell has started a new flame in Clark's boilers, which causes a jealous Harlow to side with Beery. Action-filled story is pretty contrived but it nonetheless offers a good time.

A: Clark Gable, Jean Harlow, Wallace Beery, Lewis Stone, Rosalind Russell, Hattie McDaniel

Distributed By MGM/UA Home Video MV300561

CORSICAN BROTHERS, THE

D: Gregory Ratoff 96 m

NR | ACT | 1941 | COLOR | Sex | Nud | ✓ Viol | Lang | ✓ AdSit

7 Alexander Dumas's famous story of twins who are physically separated at birth but are spiritually linked forever. Their parents are murdered in a blood feud and one child is sent to Paris while the other is sent to the mountains to be raised. When they are grown, they are reunited. They seek to avenge the deaths of their parents and both seek the hand of the same woman. Douglas Fairbanks is a swashbuckler of the highest order because he plays both brothers. Lots of swordplay and hero-type stuff. Not played too seriously, mostly just for fun.

A: Douglas Fairbanks, Jr., Ruth Warrick, Akim Tamiroff, J. Carrol Naish, H.B. Warner

© VIDEO TREASURES SV9616

CRIMSON PIRATE, THE

D: Robert Siodmak 105 m

NR | ACT | 1952 | COLOR | Sex | Nud | ✓ Viol | Lang | ✓ AdSit

8 One of the greatest swashbucklers. An incredibly agile young Burt Lancaster plays a pirate captain who wants only to profit from the battle between the Spanish crown and Caribbean rebels. Instead, he is drawn into the battle for freedom from Spain by beautiful Eva Bartok and rallies a band of freedom-loving rebels to the cause of independence. Exuberant and fast-paced, with lots of great action scenes and plenty of laughs. If you like pirate movies (and even if you don't) this is well worth your time. It was a follow-up to the successful THE FLAME AND THE ARROW.

A: Burt Lancaster, Nick Cravat, Eva Bartok, Torin Thatcher, Christopher Lee

© WARNER HOME VIDEO 11269

DON JUAN

D: Alan Crosland 111 m

NR | ACT | 1926 | B&W | Sex | Nud | ✓ Viol | Lang | ✓ AdSit

7 Entertaining swashbuckler which holds the record for the most screen kisses, 127. The story is of a famous rogue and his escapades - until he falls hard for Mary Astor. But Lucretia Borgia (Taylor) wants him to marry into her clan. This leads to one of the best sword duels ever put on film. Barrymore was at his best as a screen lover and swordfighter, and was surrounded by a top-notch cast. The film is also notable for being the first silent film released with Vitaphone music and sound effects (recorded on a separate disc and played along with the soundless film).

A: John Barrymore, Mary Astor, Willard Louis, Estelle Taylor, Helene Costello, Warner Oland

Distributed By MGM/UA Home Video M302162

ELUSIVE PIMPERNEL, THE

D: Michael Powell 107 m

NR | ACT | 1950 | B&W | Sex | Nud | ✓ Viol | Lang | ✓ AdSit

7 Originally made in 1935 as THE SCARLET PIMPERNEL, this very popular character was brought back once again for even more exploits. David Niven plays Sir Percy Blakeney, who, to all appearances, is a cowardly primping aristocrat flitting about London; but, he is actually Pimpernel, a dashing hero who rescues innocent French aristocrats from the hungry guillotine which is being fed by the unruly mobs of the French Revolution. Dashing swashbuckler.

A: David Niven, Margaret Leighton, Cyril Cusack, Jack Hawkins, David Hutcheson

© HOME VISION ELU 01

FLAME AND THE ARROW, THE

D: Jacques Tourneur 88 m

NR | ACT | 1950 | COLOR | Sex | Nud | ✓ Viol | Lang | ✓ AdSit

8 Rousing swashbuckler in which Burt Lancaster plays an acrobatic Robin Hood-like rebel leader, Dardo the Arrow, who is battling a cruel tyrant. After Dardo makes a narrow escape from the gallows, he returns disguised as an acrobat to rescue Virginia Mayo. Then he comes back once more to lead the peasantry in an uprising against the evil Hessian warlord (Allenby) in his castle in the Italian Alps. Excellent production values, good humor and lots of energy make this a lot of fun. You may also want to see the equally good CRIMSON PIRATES, which came later.

A: Burt Lancaster, Virginia Mayo, Robert Douglas, Aline MacMahon, Nick Cravat

© WARNER HOME VIDEO 11681

FOUR FEATHERS

D: Alexander Korda 115 m

NR | ACT DMA | 1939 | B&W | Sex | Nud | ✓ Viol | Lang | ✓ AdSit

9 Rousing classic adventure story. A young British army officer from a military family disappoints his friends, family and his sweetheart by resigning his commission in 1898. He wants only to settle down with his wife, but he instead is branded as a coward by them all. He is given a feather by each of his friends and his wife as a symbol of his disgrace. Seeking to redeem his honor, he travels to Egypt and disguises himself as a native to courageously fight alone for his country. One by one, he returns the feathers to their presenters. A rip-snorter of a yarn. Great cast and beautiful photography.

A: Ralph Richardson, John Clements, June Duprez, C. Aubrey Smith, Jack Allen

© HBO VIDEO 90787

GENTLEMAN JIM

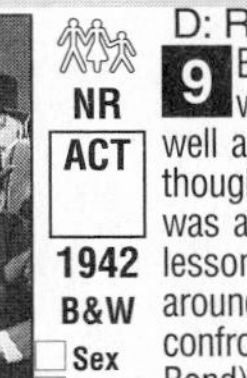

D: Raoul Walsh 104 m

NR | ACT | 1942 | B&W | Sex | Nud | ✓ Viol | Lang | ✓ AdSit

9 Exciting sports biography of the cocky 19th-century heavyweight boxing champion "Gentleman" Jim Corbet. This role was well acted by Errol Flynn and was reportedly his favorite role, even though the film is in many ways historically inaccurate. Jim Corbet was a cocky dandy who could have given Muhammad Ali humble lessons. He was also the first "scientific" fighter: the first to move around the ring and the first to taunt his opponent. Film features the confrontation between Jim and John L. Sullivan (well played by Ward Bond). Great entertainment.

A: Errol Flynn, Alexis Smith, Jack Carson, Alan Hale, John Lader, Ward Bond

Distributed By MGM/UA Home Video M202825

G-MEN

D: William Keighley 86 m

NR | ACT CRM | 1935 | B&W | Sex | Nud | ✓ Viol | Lang | ✓ AdSit

8 James Cagney made his name playing wise-guy gangland characters, but with this film he crossed over to the other side. He's just as cocky as ever, but he's playing a lawyer who was raised by an underworld character. However, when one of his buddies is killed by the mob, he joins the F.B.I. There his inside knowledge proves to be invaluable in the government's efforts to round up underworld kingpins. Jimmy is right there leading the pack on the charge to capture the ten most wanted. It's personal for him. Quite well done entry into the gangster genre and a very popular movie.

A: James Cagney, Ann Dvorak, Margaret Lindsay, Robert Armstrong, Barton MacLane, Lloyd Nolan

Distributed By MGM/UA Home Video M202484

GUN CRAZY

D: Joseph H. Lewis 87 m

NR | ACT CRM | 1949 | B&W | Sex | Nud | ✓ Viol | Lang | ■ AdSit

7 An interesting and innovative gangster film of the BONNIE AND CLYDE variety -- but done 20 years earlier. It is a stylish but bleak sleeper about Laurie Star, a beautiful female carnival sharpshooter, and Bart Tare, a paranoid World War II vet with a lifelong obsession with guns. They both have a passion for excitement and each other, but no future. At Laurie's urging and just for the fun of it, they decide to rob banks. Soon, a series of robberies makes them the most wanted criminals in America. Unique concept for the time that culminates in a violent shootout in a park. Also known for its innovative camera work. Now a cult favorite.

A: Peggy Cummins, John Dall, Morris Carnovsky, Annabell Shaw

© CBS/FOX VIDEO 7337

GUNGA DIN

D: George Stevens 117 m

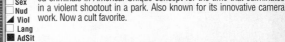

NR | ACT COM | 1939 | B&W | Sex | Nud | ✓ Viol | Lang | ✓ AdSit

9 Rousing and extremely entertaining action/adventure yarn - undimmed by time. Loosely based on Rudyard Kipling's classic poem. Principally a buddy film, this has lots of action and comedy thrown it (plus a little sentimentality). Three English soldiers and a native waterboy, stationed in British colonial India, fight to put down an uprising by a savage religious sect. It is sort of like a Western, but with real Indians and an English slant. A great time. Laughs, plenty of action and loads of fun. Often copied - never equalled.

A: Cary Grant, Victor McLaglen, Douglas Fairbanks, Jr., Joan Fontaine, Sam Jaffe, Eduardo Clannelli

© TURNER HOME ENTERTAINMENT 2055

IVANHOE

D: Richard Thorpe 107 m

NR | ACT ROM | 1952 | COLOR | Sex | Nud | ✓ Viol | Lang | ✓ AdSit

8 Walter Scott's classic and epic tale of chivalry and romance in 12th-century England was nominated for Best Picture, Cinematography and Music. Grand spectacle and beautiful photography are its hallmarks. Saxon knight Ivanhoe (Robert Taylor) defeats a plot against his King Richard by the Normans and rescues fair maidens Joan Fontaine and Elizabeth Taylor from the clutches of vile George Sanders. Swordplay and action are exciting, but the pacing is sometimes slow.

A: Robert Taylor, Elizabeth Taylor, Joan Fontaine, George Sanders, Sebastian Cabot, Emlyn Williams

Distributed By MGM/UA Home Video M600092

KIM

D: Victor Saville 114 m

G | ACT | 1950 | COLOR

Sex / Nud / ✓ Viol / Lang / ✓ AdSit

7 Rousing Rudyard Kipling adventure story about a half-white orphaned boy, alone on his own in the streets of Victorian colonial India. He befriends a horse-thief (Flynn) and a Hindu holy man and becomes enticed into the service of the English as an undercover spy, taking part in a secret plot to repel a Russian invasion through the Kyber Pass. Sweeping adventure story that will sweep you up and carry you along. It will appeal to the entire family. Errol Flynn is again playing the part of the romantic adventurer and Dean Stockwell is excellent in the role of Kim.

A: Errol Flynn, Dean Stockwell, Paul Lukas, Robert Douglas, Thomas Gomez, Cecil Kellaway

Distributed By MGM/UA Home Video M300980

KING SOLOMON'S MINES

D: Compton Bennett 103 m

NR | ACT DMA ROM | 1950 | B&W

Sex / Nud / ✓ Viol / Lang / ✓ AdSit

9 This is a rousing adventure story that rises far above other mundane African safari films. This is a mature drama, spiked with action and adultery. Sterling Hayden is hired by Deborah Kerr to find her husband, who believed that he had found the fabled diamond mines of King Solomon deep in the heart of darkest Africa. Their adventure ever deeper into the wilds to find him is thrill-packed and dangerous (providing some of the inspiration for INDIANA JONES); but there is also a credible adult romance that develops between Kerr and Granger. This is a winner. It won Oscars for Cinematography and Editing. Also filmed by English studios in 1937, but starred American Paul Robeson.

A: Stewart Granger, Deborah Kerr, Hugu Haas, Richard Carlson

Distributed By MGM/UA Home Video M200413

KING SOLOMON'S MINES

D: Robert Stevenson 89 m

NR | ACT | 1937 | B&W

Sex / Nud / ✓ Viol / Lang / ✓ AdSit

8 A beautiful woman entices a famed white hunter into helping her to locate her father in the wilds of unexplored Africa. Her father had been on the trail of the fabled diamond mines of King Solomon, but she has not heard from him for too long. Along with them come two other white men and an enigmatic black man who will be their guide. After enduring great hardship and nearing the end of their journey, the party arrives at a native village. But, they are not welcome and are now in desperate trouble. However, they also now discover that their black guide is actually the king of these people who was deposed by an evil leader, aided by a treacherous witch doctor. Quite good. Remade in 1950.

A: Paul Robeson, Cedric Hardwicke, Roland Yong, John Loder, Anna Lee

© HOME VISION KIN07

LADY KILLER

D: Roy Del Ruth 77 m

NR | ACT CRM | 1933 | B&W

Sex / ✓ Nud / ✓ Viol / Lang / ✓ AdSit

7 Remember that famous Cagney movie where he grinds a grapefruit into Mae Clark's face, PUBLIC ENEMY? Well, those two were reunited in this film. Here Cagney plays an Eastcoast gangster who is on the run and comes west, where he becomes a famous movie star, specializing in playing a toughguy on screen. But, his old gangster pals hear about his new success and they come to Hollywood to blackmail him. Cagney gets to slap Mae Clark around again, too. But, much of this film is played for laughs, and it has a fair dose of Hollywood insider jokes. This is also racier than what most people would expect for this time period. But, in fact, it came out just before the infamous Hayes morality code of 1934.

A: James Cagney, Mae Clark, Leslie Fenton, Margaret Lindsay, Henry O'Neill, Raymond Hatton

Distributed By MGM/UA Home Video M302071

LIVES OF A BENGAL LANCER

D: Henry Hathaway 110 m

NR | ACT WAR | 1935 | B&W

Sex / Nud / ✓ Viol / Lang / ✓ AdSit

8 Highly regarded and rousing adventure yarn, set in British colonial India when it was England's crown jewel. Gary Cooper and Franchot Tone are two dashing and fearless friends in service to the crown. Richard Cromwell is the untested son of their stern by-the-book commander. The two friends take Cromwell under their wing but he is a very poor soldier, even being captured by a warring chieftain. However, he redeems himself in the end. Lots of rousing action, camaraderie and good fun. It received six Oscar nominations, including Best Picture.

A: Gary Cooper, Franchot Tone, Richard Cromwell, Sir Guy Standing, C. Aubrey Smith, Monte Blue

© MCA/UNIVERSAL HOME VIDEO, INC. 80517

MAN IN THE IRON MASK, THE

D: James Whale 109 m

NR | ACT DMA | 1939 | B&W

Sex / Nud / ✓ Viol / Lang / ✓ AdSit

7 Rousing swashbuckling adventure! Twin brothers are separated at birth. One grows up to be Louis XIV, the King of France. The other becomes an idle wanderer raised by the Three Musketeers. When vile brother Louis discovers that he has a look-alike who is much beloved of his friends and the rightful heir to the throne, he kidnaps his twin, imprisons him and forces him to wear an iron mask to hide his identity. An exciting and classic tale of revenge and destruction based on Alexander Dumas's novel. Hayward is fantastic in his dual role as both brothers. Remade for television in 1977.

A: Louis Hayward, Joan Bennett, Joseph Schildkraut, Alan Hale

© VIDEO TREASURES SV9621

MIGHTY JOE YOUNG

D: Ernest B. Schoedsack 94 m

NR | ACT FAN | 1949 | B&W

Sex / Nud / Viol / Lang / AdSit

6 Later-day update of and follow-up to KING KONG. A 12-foot gorilla is raised in the jungles of Africa by a young girl. While on Safari, a scheming night-club owner discovers them and decides to bring the gorilla and the girl back to Hollywood, dreaming of the money he can make. The gorilla gains access to the liquor cabinet, becomes drunk and terrorizes the city, but he later redeems himself when he rescues children from a fire. This version is not nearly as original as KING KONG, but the film still fun. Winner for Best Special Effects.

A: Terry Moore, Ben Johnson, Robert Armstrong, Mr. Joseph Young, Frank McHugh

© TURNER HOME ENTERTAINMENT 6032

MOGAMBO

D: John Ford 116 m

NR | ACT ROM | 1953 | COLOR

Sex / Nud / ✓ Viol / Lang / ✓ AdSit

9 A sexy adventure story set in the lush wilds of Kenya! In this lusty re-make of "RED DUST" (which also starred Gable), a safari guide (Gable) falls in love with both the married Englishwoman who has hired him (Kelly), and Gardner, the well-worn woman with a past who is out for adventure. Sparks fly in the love triangle that develops during the upriver trip. Lots of adventure, action and romance. This Hollywood-style film makes the most of the exotic locations and spicy dialogue and, surprisingly, doesn't include a musical score. It doesn't need one.

A: Clark Gable, Ava Gardner, Grace Kelly, Donald Sinden, Laurence Naismith

Distributed By MGM/UA Home Video M600055

MR. ROBINSON CRUSOE

D: A. Edward Sutherland 76 m

NR | ACT | 1932 | B&W

Sex / Nud / Viol / Lang / AdSit

6 An aging but lively Douglas Fairbanks bets his friends $1000 dollars that he can survive on a deserted tropical island for an entire month without any of the modern-day trappings. His friends drop him off and the industrious Fairbanks builds an wide assortment of his own crude, but effective, gadgets of convenience. He is also not without companionship because a lovely woman arrives just in time. This buoyant old-time adventure is loads of fun for film fans.

A: Douglas Fairbanks, Sr., Sir William Farnum, Maria Alba, Earle Brown

© MPI HOME VIDEO MP1180

NAKED JUNGLE

D: Byron Haskin 95 m

NR | ACT ROM | 1954 | COLOR

Sex / Nud / ✓ Viol / Lang / ✓ AdSit

7 Charlton Heston is the powerful owner of a large plantation carved out of the wilds of South America. Eleanor Parker is the wife he bought sight-unseen. She is beautiful and smart and he wonders why she has come way out here. She finds him to be cold and coarse. They fight and despise each other. Then the plantation is set upon by a huge hoard of army ants, destroying everything in their path - a path that is two miles wide and twenty miles long. The two of them join forces to fight the ants and fall in love. Really good special effects, strong chemistry between the leads and a worthy script make this into an exciting and relatively believable adventure.

A: Eleanor Parker, Charlton Heston, William Conrad, Abraham Sofaer

© PARAMOUNT HOME VIDEO 6012

PASSAGE TO MARSEILLES

D: Michael Curtiz 109 m

NR | ACT | 1944 | B&W

Sex / Nud / ✓ Viol / Lang / ✓ AdSit

6 A diverting action film with a top-notch cast, but unduly shackled by the overuse of flashbacks. Claude Rains relates the story of a group of men, picked up from a liferaft in the open ocean by his ship, a freighter (which is captained by a Nazi sympathizer) on its way back to France just prior to the outset of WWII. The men on the raft are escapees from Devil's Island who were political prisoners and are now returning to France to fight with the free-French against fascism. However, mid-transit, Germany invades France. Action-packed but confusing.

A: Humphrey Bogart, Michele Morgan, Claude Rains, Philip Dorn, Peter Lorre, Sydney Greenstreet

Distributed By MGM/UA Home Video M202475

PRISONER OF ZENDA, THE

D: John Cromwell 102 m

NR | ACT ROM | 1937 | B&W

Sex / Nud / ✓ Viol / Lang / ✓ AdSit

9 Classic, very lavish swashbuckler in which a visiting English look-alike (Colman) takes the place of his royal cousin to help thwart an assassination plot on the life of the crown prince by his evil brother (Fairbanks). Lots of swordfights and a romance between the commoner and the beautiful princess (Carroll), too. One of many remakes (at least six) of this classic story and widely regarded as the best. The first one was silent in 1927 and the last one was a 1979 comedy take off.

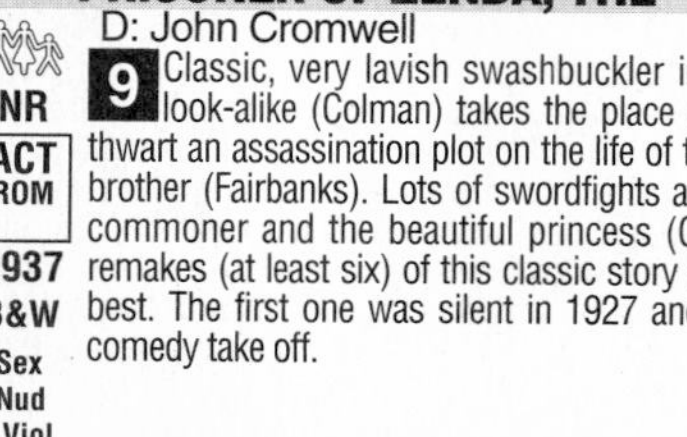

A: Ronald Colman, Madeleine Carroll, Mary Astor, Douglas Fairbanks, Jr., C. Aubrey Smith, Raymond Massey

Distributed By MGM/UA Home Video M301644

REAP THE WILD WIND

D: Cecil B. DeMille — 123 m

NR | ACT ROM | 1942 | B&W

Sex / Nud / Viol / Lang / AdSit

7 First-rate DeMille epic! Just off the coast of Florida in the 1840s, the steamship of a salty sea captain (Wayne) is sunk against the jagged rocks. He and a sophisticated attorney (Milland) become adversaries for the affections of beautiful ship owner Paulett Goddard. Milland accuses Wayne of purposely sinking the ship. The ship was purposefully sunk. However, John didn't do it, but John is on trial for it. Some good special effects and underwater photography. The final battle with a giant squid helped to win the film an Oscar for Special Effects.

A: John Wayne, Susan Hayward, Ray Milland, Paulette Goddard, Raymond Massey, Robert Preston

© MCA/UNIVERSAL HOME VIDEO, INC. 80368

RIFF-RAFF

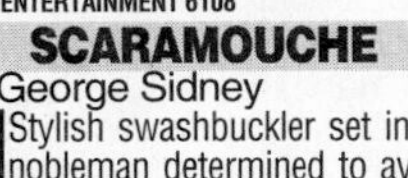

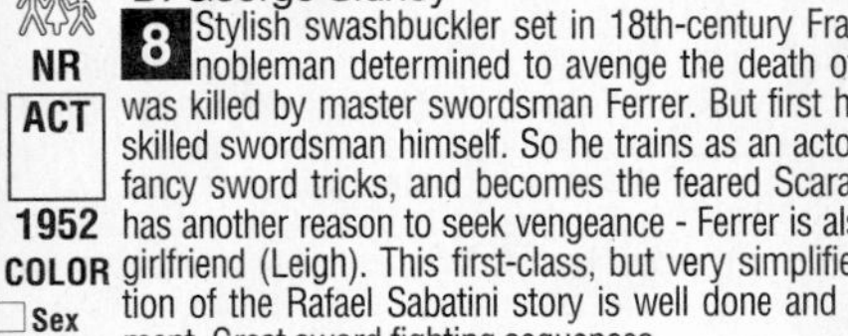

D: Ted Tetzlaff — 80 m

NR | ACT | 1947 | B&W

Sex / Nud / Viol / Lang / AdSit

6 Fast paced adventure. A tough Panamanian-based private detective (O'Brien) is hired to be the bodyguard of a man in possession of a map to South American oil fields which are worth billions. Then O'Brien is approached by an oil company executive who had bought the map in the first place and now wants it back, and by a German, who offers to pay him to steal it for him. That's when O'Brien learns that the man he is protecting had killed to get the map in the first place.

A: Pat O'Brien, Anne Jeffreys, Walter Slezak, Jason Robards, Jr., Percy Kilbride, Jerome Cowan

© TURNER HOME ENTERTAINMENT 6108

SCARAMOUCHE

D: George Sidney — 116 m

NR | ACT | 1952 | COLOR

Sex / Nud / Viol / Lang / AdSit

8 Stylish swashbuckler set in 18th-century France. Granger is a nobleman determined to avenge the death of his brother who was killed by master swordsman Ferrer. But first he must become a skilled swordsman himself. So he trains as an actor, acquiring some fancy sword tricks, and becomes the feared Scaramouche. Granger has another reason to seek vengeance - Ferrer is also in love with his girlfriend (Leigh). This first-class, but very simplified, screen adaptation of the Rafael Sabatini story is well done and rousing entertainment. Great sword fighting sequences.

A: Stewart Granger, Eleanor Parker, Janet Leigh, Mel Ferrer, Henry Wilcoxon, Lewis Stone

Distributed By MGM/UA Home Video M200641

SCARLET PIMPERNEL, THE

D: Harold Young — 95 m

NR | ACT | 1935 | B&W

Sex / Nud / Viol / Lang / AdSit

8 Rousing swashbuckler! Sir Percy (Howard) lives a double life. He poses as an English fool but, when disguised, he becomes the charming hero who saves numerous innocent French noblemen from a mindless death at the guillotine during the Reign of Terror in 18th-century France. Meanwhile, his beautiful wife (Oberon) is increasingly disenchanted with her wimpy husband and falls in love with the romantic Pimpernel, unaware that her own husband is the daredevil in disguise. This movie has something for everyone: intrigue, adventure, suspense and wit. Howard embraces his role with zeal. Remade in 1950 with David Niven as THE ELUSIVE PIMPERNEL.

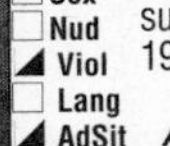

A: Leslie Howard, Merle Oberon, Raymond Massey, Nigel Bruce, Joan Gardner, Raymond Massey

© GOODTIMES 5006

SEA HAWK, THE

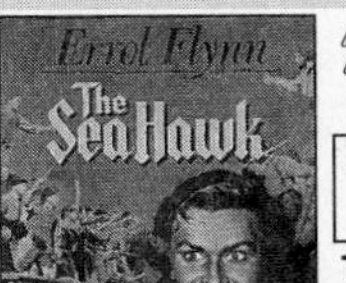

D: Michael Curtiz — 128 m

NR | ACT | 1940 | B&W

Sex / Nud / Viol / Lang / AdSit

8 High-spirited adventure, set in the 16th century. Queen Elizabeth (Robson) suspects that the Spaniards are getting ready to launch a massive attack with their naval armada against England. She commissions Errol Flynn, a swashbuckling sea captain, to gather the evidence and to foil the Spaniards's plans. He seeks to defeat the treacherous Spanish ambassador (Rains) while pursuing the love of his beautiful daughter (Marshall). High-seas action and rousing adventure highlight Flynn at his adventurous best. The film has something for everyone and is acclaimed as one of the best of its genre.

A: Errol Flynn, Flora Robson, Brenda Marshall, Henry Daniell, Claude Rains, Donald Crisp

Distributed By MGM/UA Home Video M201855

SINBAD THE SAILOR

D: Richard Wallace — 117 m

NR | ACT FAN | 1947 | COLOR

Sex / Nud / Viol / Lang / AdSit

8 Very entertaining, rousing, old-time Saturday matinee-style swashbuckler! Sinbad (Fairbanks Jr.), the daring adventurer, is intent on finding Alexander the Great's treasures located somewhere on a faraway island. When he arrives and before he can claim his prize, he must do battle with the devious ruler of the island (Quinn), but he manages also to find time to romance beautiful O'Hara. Sinbad jumps from one perilous situation to another, offering up rousing adventure that's spiced both with fun and tongue-in-cheek humor. A good time.

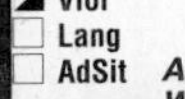

A: Douglas Fairbanks, Jr., Maureen O'Hara, Anthony Quinn, Walter Slezak, George Tobias, Jane Greer

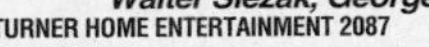

© TURNER HOME ENTERTAINMENT 2087

SOLDIER OF FORTUNE

D: Edward Dmytryk — 96 m

NR | ACT | 1955 | COLOR

Sex / Nud / Viol / Lang / AdSit

7 Danger, adventure and a beautiful location! While in Hong Kong, Hayward's photographer husband (Barry) suddenly turns up missing. Hayward searches relentlessly for him but meets with no success until a handsome smuggler (Gable) appears upon the scene. Desperate to find her lost love, Hayward hires Gable to help rescue him. Gable soon learns that the missing man is being held in communist China and deftly organizes a rescue mission that spans numerous exotic Asian locations. The scenery alone is worth it.

A: Clark Gable, Susan Hayward, Michael Rennie, Gene Barry

© FOXVIDEO 1280

SON OF MONTE CRISTO, THE

D: Rowland V. Lee — 102 m

NR | ACT | 1940 | B&W

Sex / Nud / Viol / Lang / AdSit

7 Sword duels aplenty. Louis Hayward is the noble swashbuckler who battles a would-be dictator (Sanders) of Lichtenberg. He pretends to be a fool but is actually the leader of the resistance movement to the ruthless Sanders, who has the lovely Grand Duchess (Bennett) confined. Hayward poses as a French banker to gain access to Sanders and when he defeats the wicked villain, he also frees the imprisoned Bennett from her bonds and wins her hand. Exciting swordplay. Good adventure yarn.

A: Louis Hayward, Joan Bennett, George Sanders, Florence Bates, Lionel Royce, Montagu Love

© VIDEO YESTERYEAR 137

SWORD AND THE ROSE, THE

D: Ken Annakin — 92 m

NR | ACT CLD | 1953 | COLOR

Sex / Nud / Viol / Lang / AdSit

7 A rich tapestry of Disney heroics, adventure and romance. Set during the reign of King Henry VIII (Justice), Henry's sister, Mary Tudor (Johns), falls in love with a lowly common man (Todd) but is sent to marry the much older King of France by her brother. When the French King dies, the opportunistic and villainous Duke of Buckingham (Gough) seizes the opportunity to try to take Mary's hand in marriage, away from her true love, Todd. Todd must rescue her. Disney filmed this spirited period piece in England. It is rich in flavor but there is no basis in history for it.

A: Richard Todd, Glynis Johns, James Robertson Justice, Michael Gough, Jane Barrett

© WALT DISNEY HOME VIDEO 266

TARZAN AND HIS MATE

D: Cedric Gibbons — 91 m

NR | ACT FAN | 1934 | B&W

Sex / Nud / Viol / Lang / AdSit

8 Second and best of the Tarzan series. Produced in the days before the Hays morality code, this is a distinctly adult version of the ape-man (several scenes were clipped from the original shortly after its release and are restored here). Jane's ex-fiancee returns to the jungle to get all the ivory he can and to entice Jane back to civilization. But Jane has gone native and she's in love. So he and the others trick Tarzan into leading them to the elephant's graveyard so they can plunder it. Tarzan is distracted by Jane and doesn't catch on right away. Plenty of action and sexy, too.

A: Johnny Weissmuller, Maureen O'Sullivan, Neil Hamilton, Paul Cavanagh, Forrester Harvey

Distributed By MGM/UA Home Video M200439

TARZAN, THE APE MAN

D: W.S. Van Dyke — 109 m

NR | ACT FAN | 1932 | B&W

Sex / Nud / Viol / Lang / AdSit

7 This is the beginning of a long line of Tarzan flicks. (However, there was a 1918 silent version.) In this one, Edgar Rice Burroughs's classic character is given respectful treatment with Olympic swimming star Weismuller as Tarzan. Maureen O'Sullivan, who falls for the ape-man, is the daughter of a leader of an English expedition in search of an elephant's graveyard full of ivory. Even though the film techniques are obviously dated, as are some of the attitudes, this film still has pretty good action sequences and is pretty racy, too, especially for the times.

A: Johnny Weissmuller, Maureen O'Sullivan, C. Aubrey Smith

Distributed By MGM/UA Home Video M500043

THIEF OF BAGDAD, THE

D: Ludwig Berger, Michael Powell — 106 m

NR | ACT FAN CLD | 1940 | COLOR

Sex / Nud / Viol / Lang / AdSit

9 Wonderously fanciful story from the tales of the "Arabian Nights." Who couldn't become captivated by the story of a young prince, tricked out of his kingdom and his girl by the evil Grand Vizier, only to be rescued by a thief on a magic carpet who also has the help of a colossal magical genie? Then, throw in an enormous spider, a dog who once was a boy, a flying toy horse, a flower that causes amnesia and a beautiful girl. All the above, combined with terrific special effects and an outstanding score, have made this a perennial favorite. 3 Oscars.

A: Sabu, Conrad Veidt, June Duprez, John Justin, Rex Ingram, Miles Malleson

© HBO VIDEO 90653

THUNDER BAY

D: Anthony Mann — 82 m

NR | ACT DMA | 1953 | COLOR

☐ Sex ☐ Nud ◢ Viol ☐ Lang ◢ AdSit

7 Exciting adventure film from the early '50s. Stewart and Duryea are a couple of maverick wildcatters who are pioneering off-shore oil drilling techniques off the coast of Louisiana. Tension is high between them and the local shrimp fishermen, who are already having a difficult time and are not at all excited to have oil men digging in their waters. Making matters worse for the two oilmen is their mutual affection for pretty Joanne Dru. She is torn between concern for her fellow Cajuns and her attraction to Stewart. Lots of action from a talented cast. Good entertainment.

A: James Stewart, Joanne Dru, Gilbert Roland, Dan Duryea, Jay C. Flippen, Harry Morgan

© MCA/UNIVERSAL HOME VIDEO, INC. 80324

TREASURE ISLAND

D: Victor Fleming — 105 m

NR | ACT CLD | 1934 | B&W

☐ Sex ☐ Nud ◢ Viol ☐ Lang ☐ AdSit

8 This was the first adaptation of Robert Lewis Stevenson's classic story for the big screen, and MGM pulled out all the stops. A young boy (Cooper) receives a treasure map from a dying sailor and then takes on a job as a cabin boy on a ship bound for the treasure island. Also on board is the scurrilous old sea dog Long John Silver (Beery), who sets his sights on stealing the boy's treasure and rallies the ship's crew to mutiny. Fine adventure film that will still inspire the imagination of any adventurous boy.

A: Wallace Beery, Jackie Cooper, Lionel Barrymore, Otto Kruger, Nigel Bruce, Lewis Stone

Distributed By MGM/UA Home Video M500032

TREASURE ISLAND

D: Byron Haskin — 96 m

G | ACT CLD | 1950 | COLOR

☐ Sex ☐ Nud ◢ Viol ☐ Lang ☐ AdSit

8 Walt Disney remade the 1934 version of Stevenson's classic. This version did an excellent job with it and some say even improved upon the earlier version. However, the ending was changed and, in 1975 when it was reissued again, some of the more violent sequences were removed. Bobby Driscoll plays young Jim Hawkins, a young English lad who receives a treasure map from a dying sailor. Aboard a ship bound for the island, Long John Silver (Newton) and the crew of pirates seize control of the ship in a mutiny so they can conduct their own search for the treasure and steal it.

A: Bobby Driscoll, Robert Newton, Basil Sydney, Walter Fitzgerald

© WALT DISNEY HOME VIDEO 041

ULYSSES

D: Mario Camerini — 102 m

NR | ACT FAN CLD | 1955 | COLOR

☐ Sex ☐ Nud ◢ Viol ☐ Lang ◢ AdSit

6 Lavish production of Homer's ancient and epic tale about Ulysses, the King of Ithica, and his long journey home after the Trojan wars. For ten years Ulysses struggles to reach home and his faithful wife Penelope. But all along the way, he is beset by trial after trial unleashed upon him by King Neptune, god of the sea, who is upset with him for having destroyed the Trojans. He is attacked by a hungry one-eyed Cyclops, enticed by Siren songstresses and seduced by the beautiful witch Circe. Then, arriving at home, he must also rescue Penelope, who is being beset by suitors who want to marry her and become king.

A: Kirk Douglas, Luana Mangano, Anthony Quinn, Silvana Mangano

© WARNER HOME VIDEO 11470

WAKE OF THE RED WITCH

D: Edward Ludwig — 106 m

NR | ACT ROM | 1948 | B&W

☐ Sex ☐ Nud ☐ Viol ☐ Lang ◢ AdSit

6 Lively sea yarn about the greed of a ship's captain and his search for sunken treasure and love. John Wayne is involved in a bitter feud with the owner of the East Indies Trading Company (Adler). Wayne has sunk his own ship with a cargo of gold bullion on board, with the idea of going back years later to recover it. Wayne and Adler are also fighting for the affections of beautiful Angelique (Russell). Adler wins, but both he and Angelique are struck by a tropical disease which cripples him and kills her. Now a heartbroken Wayne can return to the Red Witch to recover her treasure.

A: John Wayne, Gail Russell, Gig Young, Luther Adler, Adele Mara, Eduard Franz

© REPUBLIC PICTURES HOME VIDEO 4429

WINGS

D: William Wellman — 139 m

NR | ACT WAR | 1927 | COLOR

☐ Sex ☐ Nud ◢ Viol ☐ Lang ◢ AdSit

6 This is the very first winner of the Oscar for Best Picture and one of the most famous films of the silent era, even though it is not one of the best. It is a simple story of two friends who enlist together in the Army Air Corps during WWI and go to France to battle the Germans. They learn together of flying, war and love - when they both fall for the same girl. Not a particularly good movie, except for the flying sequences, which are still quite exciting today and are what the film is best known for. Accompanied by a sound track recorded from a pipe organ.

A: Clara Bow, Charles "Buddy" Rogers, Richard Arlen, Gary Cooper

© PARAMOUNT HOME VIDEO 2851

Comedy

ABBOTT AND COSTELLO MEET DR. JEKYLL AND MR. HYDE

D: Charles Lamont — 77 m

NR | COM CLD | 1952 | B&W

☐ Sex ☐ Nud ☐ Viol ☐ Lang ☐ AdSit

8 Here America's favorite silly duo from the 40s and 50s play two American Detectives in 1880s London, where they encounter Boris Karloff in the dual role of Jekyll and Hyde. This is one of their funniest movies. Don't miss it when Lou drinks a potion and gets turned into a mouse. Abbott and Costello learned their trade doing standup routines and short comedy skits on the Vaudeville stages. Bud Abbott is an everyman sort who plays straightman to the silly child-like antics of his short round partner, Lou Costello. They were hysterical on stage and also became big hits in the movie theaters of America.

A: Bud Abbott, Lou Costello, Boris Karloff, Craig Stevens

© MCA/UNIVERSAL HOME VIDEO, INC. 80010

ABBOTT AND COSTELLO MEET FRANKENSTEIN

D: Charles Barton — 83 m

NR | COM CLD | 1948 | B&W

☐ Sex ☐ Nud ☐ Viol ☐ Lang ☐ AdSit

8 Fun mix of fright and laughs. Lou and Bud are railroad baggage clerks this time, who get in trouble when crates transporting monsters to the House of Horrors are discovered to be empty. So the twosome follow the monsters's trail to a secret island where they find Dracula (Lugosi) and the Frankenstein monster. Things get dicey for them when a mad scientist plans to put Lou's brain into the Frankenstein monster and the Wolfman (Chaney) wants them all. This is great comedy that works because the monsters always play their parts straight.

A: Bud Abbott, Lou Costello, Lon Chaney, Jr., Bela Lugosi, Lenore Aubert, Jane Randolph

© MCA/UNIVERSAL HOME VIDEO, INC. 55074

ABBOTT AND COSTELLO MEET THE INVISIBLE MAN

D: Charles Lamont — 83 m

NR | COM | 1951

☐ Sex ☐ Nud ☐ Viol ☐ Lang ☐ AdSit

6 Bud and Lou are have just graduated from private detective school when their first customer walks in the door. Tommy is a boxer who has been wrongly accused of murder and he needs their help to prove it. Just then the police arrive and poof, their new client has evaporated. He has injected himself with an experimental invisibility serum. Tommy convinces Lou that he should go undercover as a boxer to find the real killer. Pudgy little Lou will be "Lou the Looper" and invisible Tommy will supply the punches.

A: Bud Abbott, Lou Costello, Nancy Gould, Arther Franz, Adele Jergens, Sheldon Leonard

© MCA/UNIVERSAL HOME VIDEO, INC. 80673

ADAM'S RIB

D: George Cukor — 101 m

NR | COM | 1949 | B&W

☐ Sex ☐ Nud ☐ Viol ☐ Lang ◢ AdSit

8 Acclaimed as one of Hollywood's greatest comedies. This was very daring for its time, but its remaining chauvinism has sadly dated it now. This is a sophisticated comedy (for the 1940s) which has husband and wife lawyers on opposite sides of the same case. Tracy is a prosecutor for the District Attorney's office. Hepburn is a defense attorney who takes the opposing side. Wonderful Judy Holliday made her debut here as a ditzy wife who shot her husband because he was cheating on her. Great supporting cast. This was the sixth Tracy/Hepburn combination. See the index for others.

A: Spencer Tracy, Katharine Hepburn, Judy Holliday, Tom Ewell, David Wayne, Jean Hagen

Distributed By MGM/UA Home Video M500010

AFRICA SCREAMS

D: Charles Barton — 79 m

NR | COM | 1949 | B&W

☐ Sex ☐ Nud ☐ Viol ☐ Lang ☐ AdSit

6 Abbott and Costello go on a safari into Africa with a beautiful woman when Lou smells a big payday. He tries to pass cowardly Bud off as a famous big game hunter and a supposed expert on a the geography of a particular part of Africa. But unknown to the boys, the girl and her cohorts are not interested in big game hunting at all but instead in a secret diamond mine. This film contains many of the typical silly sight gags and slapstick comedy sketches which the pair created and polished in Vaudeville. It is not their best effort, but if you're a fan, you won't care. Kids love it too.

A: Bud Abbott, Lou Costello, Hillary Brooke, Shemp Howard, Max Baer, Clyde Beaty

© UNITED AMERICAN VIDEO CORP. 0097

ANDROCLES AND THE LION

D: Chester Erskine 98 m

NR | COM | 1952 | B&W | 6

The old fable of a simple tailor who receives the everlasting gratitude of a lion after pulling a thorn from his paw, is given a satirical edge by George Bernard Shaw. Alan Young plays the tailor, whose kindness at pulling a thorn from the paw of a lion is later repaid when a group of Christians are saved in the Roman arena. Although some of the bite of the satire is lost, enough survives for the story to remain intriguing.

Sex / Nud / Viol / Lang / AdSit

A: Alan Young, Jean Simmons, Victor Mature, Robert Newton, Maurice Evans, Elsa Lanchester

© NEW LINE HOME VIDEO 6028

ANGEL ON MY SHOULDER

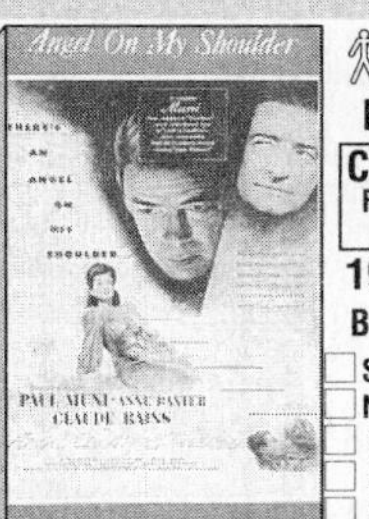

D: Archie Mayo 101 m

NR | COM FAN | 1946 | B&W | 7

Paul Muni is Eddie, a gangster who was murdered by his partner. However, Eddie makes a deal with the Devil (Rains) so he can come back to earth to get revenge. Eddie is sent back, but is placed in the body of a highly respected judge who the Devil expects Eddie will soon discredit. Eddie starts to like his new life. Soon he is running for governor on a reform ticket and has fallen in love with the judge's fiancee. This is all very disappointing for the Devil, especially since Eddie also spends the rest of the film trying outwit the Devil and his plan. Fun time from this entertaining little fantasy.

Sex / Nud / Viol / Lang / AdSit

A: Paul Muni, Anne Baxter, Claude Rains, George Cleveland, Onslow Stevens

© UNITED AMERICAN VIDEO CORP. 4091

ANGELS OVER BROADWAY

D: Ben Hecht, Lee Garmes 80 m

NR | COM | 1940 | B&W | 6

Odd black comedy about a group of low-lifes - regulars at a Broadway cafe. An alcoholic playwrite proposes a do-good scheme to keep an embezzler from committing suicide and to turn his life around. He suggests that they all enter into a high-stakes poker game using the embezzled money as bait. However, alcoholic Mitchell and call girl Hayworth think they smell an opportunity and seek to take advantage of the situation. All of the scheming from these low-lifes builds into an unpredictable climax. Offbeat, especially for the time it was made, but some great dialogue. Considered to be ahead of its time.

Sex / Nud / Viol / Lang / AdSit

A: Rita Hayworth, Douglas Fairbanks, Jr., Thomas Mitchell, John Qualen

© COLUMBIA TRISTAR HOME VIDEO 60688

ANIMAL CRACKERS

D: Victor Heerman 98 m

NR | COM | 1930 | B&W | 7

The Marx Brothers's movies were first big Broadway hits and only later were brought by Hollywood to the screen. That is why this movie (and most other early pictures) look so stagey. So ignore the production values and make room for their totally unique rapid-fire brand of silly humor such as when Grouch says (in his African lecture), "This morning I shot an elephant in my pajamas... How he got in my pajamas, I'll never know." Check the index for more of their insane antics. See also COCONUTS, NIGHT AT THE OPERA, MONKEY BUSINESS and DUCK SOUP.

Sex / Nud / Viol / Lang / AdSit

A: Groucho Marx, Harpo Marx, Chico Marx, Zeppo Marx, Margaret Dumont, Lillian Roth

© MCA/UNIVERSAL HOME VIDEO, INC. 55000

ARSENIC AND OLD LACE

D: Frank Capra 120 m

NR | COM | 1944 | B&W | 10

Hilarious screen version of the outlandish and frenzied hit play about two sweet old ladies who cure gentleman callers of their loneliness by poisoning them and then giving them Christian burials in their basement. Their hapless nephew, Mortimer (Cary Grant), discovers a dead body in the window seat and mistakenly thinks that his crazy brother Teddy did it, never considering his aunts. But before he can get Teddy safely committed, his other sinister brother Jonathan (Massey) shows up, and he has a dead body of his own. Hysterical farce that has in no way lost any of its considerable sparkle.

Sex / Nud / Viol / Lang / AdSit

A: Cary Grant, Priscilla Lane, Jack Carson, James Gleason, Peter Lorre, Raymond Massey

Distributed By MGM/UA Home Video M201568

ARTISTS AND MODELS

D: Frank Tashlin 109 m

NR | COM MUS | 1955 | COLOR | 7

Martin and Lewis's wackiness at its best. Dean Martin is a cartoonist who lands a big job by making Lewis's wacky far-out dreams into comic strips. But when Jerry's dreams start to become telepathic and the Russians become interested in them, things get crazy. Spiced up with loads of beautiful women, typical Martin and Lewis shtick, lots of sight gags and zippy one-liners, plus Martin's singing. Utter silliness that is still fun. This was Shirley MacLaine's second screen appearance.

Sex / Nud / Viol / Lang / AdSit

A: Dean Martin, Jerry Lewis, Shirley MacLaine, Dorothy Malone, Eva Gabor, Anita Ekberg

© PARAMOUNT HOME VIDEO 5510

AS YOU LIKE IT

D: Paul Czinner 96 m

NR | COM ROM | 1936 | B&W | 8

Shakespeare's classic comic tale of love. Beautiful Rosalind (Bergner) is born of nobility but is exiled into the forests of Arden. There she meets and falls in love with Orlando (a very young Olivier). She disguises herself as a boy so that she can safely teach him some lessons on the nature of love so that she may later benefit from them. On the whole, well-done. Shakespeare's reversed version of TOOTSIE.

Sex / Nud / Viol / Lang / AdSit

A: Elisabeth Bergner, Laurence Olivier, Sophie Stewart, Henry Ainley, Felix Aylmer, Leon Quartermaine

© VIDEO YESTERYEAR 447

AWFUL TRUTH, THE

D: Leo McCarey 92 m

NR | COM ROM | 1937 | B&W | 8

This movie became an icon for a whole era in comedy, and is widely recognized as being one of the most influential of the screwball comedies (a fast-paced series of ridiculous happenings). The story has Cary and Irene getting a divorce after a meaningless squabble. Each pursues their separate life and soon is about to marry marrying someone else. However, all the while, each is also doing his level best to screw up the other's marriage plans. The awful truth, you see, is that they still love each other. Five Oscar nominations. Grant is in top form. Witty and rapid-fire but, sadly, many attitudes of the time, date it now.

Sex / Nud / Viol / Lang / AdSit

A: Cary Grant, Irene Dunne, Ralph Bellamy, Cecil Cunningham, Molly Lamont, Mary Forbes

© COLUMBIA TRISTAR HOME VIDEO 60625

BACHELOR AND THE BOBBY-SOXER, THE

D: Irving Reis 95 m

NR | COM ROM | 1947 | B&W | 6

A cocky playboy (Cary Grant) gets arrested after a fight in a nightclub. Irritated with his manner, the lady judge (Loy) sentences Cary to babysit her teenage sister (Temple), who soon develops a passionate crush on him. Poor old Cary is burdened with escorting the teenage girl everywhere. It's fun to watch Grant use his grace and charm as the over-age escort in the juvenile settings, and to watch him match wits and dialogue with Loy. Both the stars and the dialogue sparkle. A big hit in its time, it still has considerable charm today. Amusing witty comedy.

Sex / Nud / Viol / Lang / AdSit

A: Cary Grant, Myrna Loy, Shirley Temple, Rudy Vallee, Johnny Sands

© TURNER HOME ENTERTAINMENT 2079

BALL OF FIRE

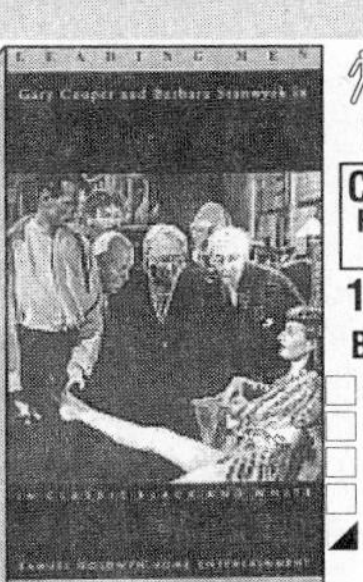

D: Howard Hawks 111 m

NR | COM ROM | 1941 | B&W | 9

Sugarpuss O'Shea (Stanwyck) is a burlesque singer and dancer who is on the lam from the mob. She finds the perfect hiding place with a group of eight very unworldly professors when she takes a job as their assistant. It is her job to help them learn to understand slang, so that they can write a dictionary of American slang. But the reclusive professors learn much more than they expected from her. Great script with sparkling dialogue. Tremendously entertaining comedy - especially watching her teach Gary Cooper the meaning of "yum, yum."

Sex / Nud / Viol / Lang / AdSit

A: Gary Cooper, Barbara Stanwyck, Dana Andrews, Oscar Hamolka, Henry Travers, Dan Duryea

© HBO VIDEO 90750

BANK DICK, THE

D: Edward Cline 73 m

NR | COM | 1940 | B&W | 7

W.C. Fields is Egbert Souse, a drunken no-account who becomes an accidental hero when he foils a robbery quite by accident. Nevertheless, he parlays that into a stint at the bank as a guard. There, his lovely daughter is discovered by a nitwit bank examiner who wants to marry her. All this effort is just an excuse for Fields's insane sense of humor to be turned loose upon a fully-suspecting audience. Full of sight gags and Fields's usual goofball verbal jousts. One of Fields's best.

Sex / Nud / Viol / Lang / AdSit

A: W.C. Fields, Cora Witherspoon, Una Merkel, Shemp Howard

© MCA/UNIVERSAL HOME VIDEO, INC. 80019

BARCELONA

D: Whit Stillman 102 m

PG-13 | COM | 194 | COLOR | 8

Another sophisticated intellectual comedy from the director of METROPOLITAN. This is not a hilarious film. It is more droll and witty. Set against the political and social turmoil of Barcelona, Spain, two American cousins are reunited. Ted is a mid-twenties salesman stationed in Barcelona and his cousin Fred is a Naval officer just arrived in town at a time when Americans are not looked upon favorably. But, this is also a time when the women of Spain are liberated and beautiful, and the two have fallen for two beauties. Their quite different cultures lead to constant discussions of their diverse views of sex, culture and politics. Urbanely intellectual.

Sex / Nud / Viol / Lang / AdSit

A: Taylor Nichols, Chris Eigeman, Tuska Bergen, Mira Sorvino, Pep Munne, Hellena Schmied

© TURNER HOME ENTERTAINMENT N4015

BEACHCOMBER, THE

D: Erich Pommer 87 m

NR | COM ROM | 1938 | B&W

6 Charles Laughton is a disheveled and shiftless drunk. But, he is also a perfectly happy bum, living happily on modest inheritance on an island paradise. His lifestyle appalls the brother/sister missionary team on the island. They want him deported, but the island's administrator likes him, so Laughton only gets moved to a different island. Unsatisfied, missionary Lanchester (his real-life wife) comes over, determined to save him from himself but, unfortunately for her, love intervenes. Delightful screen adaptation of Somerset Maugham's story. However, the production aspects are quite dated.

Sex / Nud / Viol / Lang / AdSit

A: Charles Laughton, Elsa Lanchester, Tyrone Guthrie, Robert Newton

© VIDEO YESTERYEAR 1053

BEAT THE DEVIL

D: John Huston 89 m

NR | COM MUS | 1954 | B&W

6 Truman Capote wrote this satire of the mystery/thrillers that were popular in the early 50s. Sadly, the public then didn't quite know how to take it, so it was not a big box-office success. But this farce has become, and remains, a cult favorite. It is a sophisticated satirical mystery with an unlikely and outlandish plot. Bogart, his wife and four unsavory and scheming partners set out for Africa to set up a big uranium scam, but they become stranded in a small Italian port when their steamer breaks down. There, Bogart meets a flighty Englishwoman, who falls in love with him. She and her husband are also off to Africa on a scam of their own. One scam upon another, until it is difficult to know who to trust.

Sex / Nud / Viol / Lang / AdSit

A: Humphrey Bogart, Robert Morley, Peter Lorre, Jennifer Jones, Gina Lollobrigida, Edward Underdown

© COLUMBIA TRISTAR HOME VIDEO 60554

BEDTIME FOR BONZO

D: Frederick de Cordova 84 m

NR | COM | 1951 | B&W

6 Mostly a curiosity piece and somewhat silly. Professor (and future President of the United States) Ronald Reagan believes that it is environment rather than heredity which is the primary determinant in how well kids turn out. So, to prove his point, he decides to raise a chimp at home. To present the right environment, he even hires a mommy. Harmless little comedy, now high camp. Enjoyable, if you don't expect too much.

Sex / Nud / Viol / Lang / AdSit

A: Ronald Reagan, Diana Lynn, Walter Slezak, Jesse White, Lucille Barkley

© MCA/UNIVERSAL HOME VIDEO, INC. 55015

BELLS OF ST. MARYS, THE

D: Leo McCarey 126 m

NR | COM DMA | 1945 | B&W

8 Bing Crosby reprises his role as Father O'Malley in this sequel to GOING MY WAY. He is a priest assigned to a parish with a parochial school run by a headstrong Mother Superior Ingrid Bergman. The buildings are run down. The playground has been sold off and the whole school may soon be condemned to make way for a parking lot. Father Bing and Sister Ingrid make peace long enough to conspire in a plot to entice a rich benefactor into building them a new home. Great family entertainment that leaves your heart warmed. It was a big box office hit and got 8 Oscar nominations, including Best Picture.

Sex / Nud / Viol / Lang / AdSit

A: Bing Crosby, Ingrid Bergman, Ruth Donnelly, Henry Travers, William Gargan, Joan Carroll

© REPUBLIC PICTURES HOME VIDEO 0252

BISHOP'S WIFE, THE

D: Henry Koster 109 m

NR | COM ROM | 1947 | B&W

8 Enjoyable and sentimental Christmas fantasy. Cary Grant is a suave angel sent down to help a harried bishop (Niven) who neglects his wife and family in his quest to get a new cathedral built. Grant is there to remind him of where his priorities should lie, but Cary has problems of his own when the bishop's long-neglected wife (Young) is attracted to him. Grant is charming and Young is lovely. They don't make films like this much anymore. Nominated for five Academy Awards, including Best Picture.

Sex / Nud / Viol / Lang / AdSit

A: Cary Grant, Loretta Young, David Niven, Monty Woolley, James Gleason, Elsa Lanchester

© HBO VIDEO 90658

BLITHE SPIRIT

D: David Lean 96 m

NR | COM | 1945 | B&W

8 Clever Noel Coward play about a widower (Harrison) who accidentally conjures up the ghost of his first wife at a seance that was held just for fun. His second wife, of five years, does not take kindly to being haunted by the slinky ghost of wife number one and seeks to find a way to send her back. So, she consults with a medium. The 1940s sophisticated upper-crust English atmosphere takes some getting used to but this is truly a clever and funny film. Wonderful performances, and Coward's witty dialogue is a pleasure.

Sex / Nud / Viol / Lang / AdSit

A: Rex Harrison, Constance Cummings, Kay Hammond, Margaret Rutherford, Hugh Wakefield, Joyce Carey

© UNITED AMERICAN VIDEO CORP. 5729

BORN YESTERDAY

D: George Cukor 103 m

NR | COM ROM | 1950 | B&W

10 This was a hilarious Broadway play which was turned into a Best Picture Oscar winner and became a huge box office hit. It is still very funny. A corrupt junk dealer millionaire (Crawford) wants to gain social acceptance and decides his girlfriend needs more culture, so he hires newspaperman William Holden to teach her some. But his plan backfires. The smarter she gets, the more she learns that she is just a pawn and that he is a crook. And, she falls for her teacher. Holiday is an absolute scream as the quintessential "dumb blond" and won Best Actress Oscar. Don't miss this one.

Sex / Nud / Viol / Lang / AdSit

A: Judy Holliday, William Holden, Broderick Crawford, Howard St. John, Frank Otto

© COLUMBIA TRISTAR HOME VIDEO 60143

BRINGING UP BABY

D: Howard Hawks 102 m

NR | COM ROM | 1938 | B&W

10 This is the screwiest of all the screwball comedies and, unlike many of the others, it has lost little of its punch with time. Grant plays a mild-mannered paleontologist whose dinosaur bone is stolen by Hepburn's dog. Hepburn plays a kooky heiress who, along with her pet leopard, sets his life on end when she sets her sights on him. One of the fastest, funniest films ever made. Two terrific comedy performances by the stars. Excellently remade and updated in 1972 with Barbra Streisand and Ryan O'Neal as WHAT'S UP DOC?.

Sex / Nud / Viol / Lang / AdSit

A: Cary Grant, Katharine Hepburn, Charlie Ruggles, May Robson, Barry Fitzgerald, Ward Bond

© TURNER HOME ENTERTAINMENT 6012

BUCK PRIVATES

D: Arthur Lubin 84 m

NR | COM | 1941 | B&W

7 Bud and Lou are two dim-witted tie salesmen who enlist in the army by mistake to avoid getting arrested. The Andrews Sisters make a guest appearance with "Boogie Woogie Bugle Boy." This film was the first to establish Abbott and Costello as box office stars. The plot serves mostly as a vehicle for them to present some of their best burlesque routines. A little dated, but still very funny stuff.

Sex / Nud / Viol / Lang / AdSit

A: Bud Abbott, Lou Costello, Lee Bowman, Alan Curtis, The Andrews Sisters, Jane Frazee

© MCA/UNIVERSAL HOME VIDEO, INC. 55085

BUCK PRIVATES COME HOME

D: Charles Barton 77 m

NR | COM | 1947

8 One of Abbot and Costello's best movies and sequel to BUCK PRIVATES. They are GIs having returned home from Europe, but trying to smuggle in a French orphan they found. The girl is discovered and taken away, but she manages to escape and find the boys again. Bud and Lou must now find the girl's aunt so she can adopt her. However, the aunt can't marry her boyfriend race driver until his car gets out of hock. So, Bud and Lou bail the car out but wind up in the car, leading the cops on a wild-cross country chase. Quite good, much better than typical slapstick comedy, especially the climactic chase scene.

Sex / Nud / Viol / Lang / AdSit

A: Bud Abbott, Lou Costello, Tom Brown, Joan Fulton, Nat Pendleton, Beverly Simmons

© MCA/UNIVERSAL HOME VIDEO, INC. 81303

BURNS AND ALLEN SHOW, THE

D: Ralph Levy 60 m

NR | COM | 1952 | B&W

8 Fans of George and Gracie rejoice. Those of you who aren't familiar with them are in for a treat. These are two episodes of the famed duo's early TV series from the 1952-53 season. George plays an absolutely unflappable comedian who is married to the most ditzy woman ever fabricated by the mind of man or woman. In one episode, Sheldon Leonard is a gangster who comes to blow out Gracie's brains, but finds she doesn't have any. In the other, Jack Benny tries his best to convince Gracie that she and George really are married.

Sex / Nud / Viol / Lang / AdSit

A: George Burns, Gracie Allen, Jack Benny, Sheldon Leonard

© COLUMBIA TRISTAR HOME VIDEO 60537

CANTERVILLE GHOST, THE

D: Jules Dassin 96 m

NR | COM CLD | 1944 | COLOR

7 Pleasant enough little story about a cowardly ghost, played wonderfully by Charles Laughton, who was buried alive 300 years earlier by his own father because he was a coward. Now he is trapped into haunting the castle and doomed to stay there until one of his descendants performs a deed of bravery. Unfortunately for him, everyone in his long line has proven to be a coward too, and he fears he will never be free. Now it is WWII and a far distant nephew (Young) of his is billeted in the castle with his buddies. Is this the chance he's been waiting for?

Sex / Nud / Viol / Lang / AdSit

A: Charles Laughton, Margaret O'Brien, William Gargan, Rags Ragland, Una O'Connor, Robert Young

Distributed By MGM/UA Home Video M201873

CASANOVA'S BIG NIGHT

D: Norman McLeod 86 m

NR | COM | 1954 | COLOR

Sex / Nud / Viol / Lang / AdSit

7 Bob Hope is only a tailor's apprentice, but he bears a striking resemblance to Casanova, the great lover of 17th-century Venice. So he is hired by a duchess to test the true motives of her son's fiancee (Joan Fontaine). Ol' Bob gets caught up in more intrigue than he can handle when bad guys Rathbone, John Carradine, Lon Chaney Jr. and Raymond Burr all want to put him away. Lots of slapstick chases and other Hope shtick.

A: Bob Hope, Joan Fontaine, Audrey Dalton, Basil Rathbone, Hugh Marlowe, Vincent Price

© PARAMOUNT HOME VIDEO 5316

CHAPLIN CAVALCADE

D: Charles Chaplin 80 m

NR | COM | 1936 | B&W

Sex / Nud / Viol / Lang / AdSit

8 An anthology of four of Chaplin's early silent comedies from the 1916-1917 era: "One A.M.,""The Pawnshop," "The Floorwalker" and "The Rink."

A: Charlie Chaplin

© HOLLYWOOD HOME THEATRE

CHARLIE CHAPLIN-THE EARLY YEARS, VOLS 1-4

D: Charles Chaplin 62 m

NR | COM | B&W

Sex / Nud / Viol / Lang / AdSit

8 Original and uncut. Volume 1: "The Immigrant" (1917),"The Count" (1916) and "Easy Street" (1917). Volume 2: "The Pawnbroker" (1916), "The Adventurer" (1917) and "One A.M." Volume 3: "The Cure" (1917), "The Floorwalker" (1916) and "The Vagabond" (1916). Volume 4: "Behind the Screen" (1916), "the Fireman" (1916) and "The Rink" (1916).

A: Charlie Chaplin

© REPUBLIC PICTURES HOME VIDEO 7118

CHRISTMAS IN CONNECTICUT

D: Peter Godfrey 102 m

NR | COM ROM | 1945 | B&W

Sex / Nud / Viol / Lang / AdSit

6 Pleasant lightweight fun. Barbara Stanwyck plays a leading newspaper's housekeeping and gourmet cooking editor. The catch is, she is a fake and doesn't know anything about doing either - she doesn't even have a home of her own that she could do it in. When a war hero is rescued after having spent 18 days starving adrift in a life raft, her editor (who is not aware of her failings) thinks it would be a great story to have her entertain the hero and himself at her home for the holidays. She is panic-struck and has to quick find a husband, a house and a cook. Corny, but good holiday (or anytime else) fun.

A: Barbara Stanwyck, Dennis Morgan, Sydney Greenstreet, S.Z. Scjakk, Reginald Gardiner, Una O'Connor

Distributed By MGM/UA Home Video M301163

CHRISTMAS IN JULY

D: Preston Sturges 67 m

NR | COM | 1940 | B&W

Sex / Nud / Viol / Lang / AdSit

7 Good solid fun. An ambitious, struggling store clerk is sent a bogus telegram by his practical-joking co-workers, fooling him into thinking that he has won a coffee slogan contest and a $25,000 prize. Thrilled, he and his girlfriend set about buying everything they ever wanted - all on credit. The whole town opens its doors to him - that is until the mistake is discovered. A fun-filled romp about the pursuit of the American Dream.

A: Dick Powell, Ellen Drew, Raymond Walburn, William Demarest, Ernest Truex, Franklin Pangborn

© MCA/UNIVERSAL HOME VIDEO, INC. 80207

CITY LIGHTS

D: Charles Chaplin 87 m

NR | COM | 1931 | B&W

Sex / Nud / Viol / Lang / AdSit

10 Chaplin's masterpiece. A wonderful combination of comedy and pathos. It is his story of the little tramp who fell in love with a blind flower girl. She is unable to see him and believes that he is wealthy. Charlie is befriended by a millionaire who, when he is drunk, likes the little tramp but, when he is sober, doesn't even recognize him. The tramp takes the money he needs from the millionaire so the girl can have the operation she needs, willing to go to jail for it. Funny, tender and understated eloquence with a particularly moving finale when the girl finds out the true nature of her benefactor.

A: Charlie Chaplin, Virginia Cherreill, Harry Meyers, Hank Mann

© CBS/FOX VIDEO 3006

COCOANUTS, THE

D: Robert Florey 93 m

NR | COM | 1929 | B&W

Sex / Nud / Viol / Lang / AdSit

7 This is the Marx Brothers's very first film. Groucho is a hotel owner trying to fleece everyone who comes in. Chico and Harpo play con men in his hotel. The staginess of this picture is because Hollywood simply had the boys come west from New York, with their already successful stage play intact, and then just filmed it totally unchanged. Early sound problems and primitive camera work make it difficult to watch at times, but it also contains some of their best comedy skits, including a hilarious rigged auction. See also ANIMAL CRACKERS and check the indexes for others by them.

A: Groucho Marx, Chico Marx, Harpo Marx, Zeppo Marx, Margaret Dumont, Oscar Shaw

© MCA/UNIVERSAL HOME VIDEO, INC. 80378

DAY AT THE RACES, A

D: Sam Wood 109 m

NR | COM | 1937 | B&W

Sex / Nud / Viol / Lang / AdSit

8 Groucho plays a horse doctor pretending to be a psychiatrist so that he can win the heart and pocketbook of a wealthy hypochondriac (Dumont). Hilarious bits include Chico's famous sale of a race-track tip to Groucho from his "tootsie fruitsie" ice cream stand and a scene where the villainess is wallpapered to the wall. The Marx Brothers were still at their peak when this film was made. Perhaps their best work, A NIGHT AT THE OPERA, had just preceeded it in 1936.

A: Groucho Marx, Harpo Marx, Chico Marx, Allan Jones, Maureen O'Sullivan, Margaret Dumont

Distributed By MGM/UA Home Video M500064

DEVIL AND DANIEL WEBSTER, THE

D: William Dieterle 106 m

NR | COM DMA | 1941 | B&W

Sex / Nud / Viol / Lang / AdSit

9 Wonderful. Stephen Vincent Benet's story is faithfully brought to life. There are rich textures of classic Americana in this story of a 19th-century New England farmer (Craig) who sells his soul to the Devil (Houston) in exchange for gold. But after seven years, when it is time to pay up, he decides he wants to back out of the deal. So, he hires the famous orator and lawyer Daniel Webster (Arnold) to defend him and to win back his immortal soul, by arguing for it in front of a jury of the damned. Walter Houston is perfectly despicable as the Devil, but all the acting is wonderful. Very clever. This is a must see!

A: Edward Arnold, Walter Huston, James Craig, Anne Shirley, Jane Darwell, Simone Simon

© HOME VISION DEV 020

DEVIL AND MISS JONES, THE

D: Sam Wood 92 m

NR | COM | 1941 | B&W

Sex / Nud / Viol / Lang / AdSit

8 Delightful simple comedy in which a stuffy, gruffy millionaire (Coburn) becomes alarmed when one of his department stores begins to unionize. He decides to go undercover to investigate for himself the employee complaints and unrest. He disguises himself as a sales clerk in the shoe department. There Miss Jones (Jean Arther) takes him under her wing and also fixes him up with a one of her co-workers. Soon he discovers that the root of his problems are with his own ruthless management. Marvelous comedy - like Hollywood used to make.

A: Jean Arthur, Robert Cummings, Charles Coburn, Edmund Gwenn, Spring Byington, William Demarest

© REPUBLIC PICTURES HOME VIDEO 1015

DOCTOR IN THE HOUSE

D: Ralph Thomas 92 m

NR | COM | 1954 | COLOR

Sex / Nud / Viol / Lang / AdSit

8 Truly funny English comedy, hysterical in places, about the exploits of four medical college students who are intent upon getting rich and studying anatomy - particularly that of beautiful women. But they drink too much, are lazy and three of them have already flunked out once. This film proved to be so successful that it spawned six sequels and eventually even a 1950s TV series.

A: Dirk Bogarde, Muriel Pavlow, Kenneth More, Donald Sinden, Kay Kendall, Donald Houston

© PARAMOUNT HOME VIDEO 12567

DOCTOR TAKES A WIFE, THE

D: Alexander Hall 89 m

NR | COM ROM | 1940 | B&W

Sex / Nud / Viol / Lang / AdSit

7 Fun and lively comedy. Loretta Young is a feminist. She is an independent writer who detests domineering males. Milland is a medical college professor who is more interested in his work than in women. When these two first meet, they hate each other immediately. But after they get to know each other... they still hate each other. Then they get caught up in a publicity mix-up where they are mistakenly believed to be married and they are actually forced to get married. Now, they hate each other more than ever. Great chemistry between these two make for a good time.

A: Loretta Young, Ray Milland, Reginald Gaerdiner, Gail Patrick, Edmund Gwenn

© COLUMBIA TRISTAR HOME VIDEO 60921

DUCK SOUP

D: Leo McCarey — 70 m

NR | COM | 1933 | B&W

Sex | Nud | Viol | Lang | AdSit

9 Deemed by the pundits as the Marx Brothers's best work, this is political satire at its rampant best. Groucho is Rufus T. Firefly, tyrant of the tiny country Fredonia ("land of the spree and home of the knave"), who declares war on his neighbor Sylvania for no particular reason at all. Chico and Harpo are bumbling spies sent to get his war plans. Madness, slapstick gags and "Grouchoisms" abound. The Marx Brothers made absurdity an artform.

A: Groucho Marx, Harpo Marx, Chico Marx, Zeppo Marx, Margaret Dumont, Louis Calhern

© MCA/UNIVERSAL HOME VIDEO, INC. 55012

EGG AND I, THE

D: Chester Erskine — 108 m

NR | COM | 1947 | B&W

Sex | Nud | Viol | Lang | AdSit

7 This box office smash in 1947 is still funny today. A city girl from a Boston finishing school (Colbert) reluctantly moves with her new husband (MacMurry) to his dream chicken farm in the rural Pacific Northwest. Her reluctance turns into profound regret when she first spies the ramshackle dump that is now home. Everything goes wrong. The roof leaks, the doors fall off and their new neighbors, Ma and Pa Kettle and their clan of many many Kettles, keep her entertained whether she wants them or not. How will she survive so totally out of her element? A whole lot of silliness. Ma and Pa Kettle were first introduced here but later were developed into their own very popular series.

A: Claudette Colbert, Fred MacMurray, Marjorie Main, Percy Kilbride, Louise Allbritton

© MCA/UNIVERSAL HOME VIDEO, INC. 80317

EX-MRS. BRADFORD, THE

D: Stephen Roberts — 81 m

NR | COM | MYS | 1936 | B&W

Sex | Nud | Viol | Lang | AdSit

7 Delightful sophisticated comedy in the THIN MAN vein from the same era. However, this time William Powell plays a suave and witty doctor. Someone is killing off a bunch of jockeys at the race track and Powell is the prime suspect. If he's going to get out of this, he's going to have to find out who the real murderer is himself. Coming to his aid is kooky Jean Arthur. She is his mystery-writer ex-wife who finds clues and dangers everywhere - even when none exist. Funny, and a good mystery, too.

A: William Powell, Jean Arthur, James Gleason, Eric Blore, Robert Armstrong

© TURNER HOME ENTERTAINMENT 6130

FARMER'S DAUGHTER, THE

D: H.C. Potter — 97 m

NR | COM | ROM | 1947 | B&W

Sex | Nud | Viol | Lang | AdSit

7 Delightful, fun story. A charming and innocent, but very headstrong, Swedish girl moves to the big city and takes the first job she finds as a servant for a rich young congressman and his mother. She is an excellent worker who immediately endears herself to them both (particularly him). However, she is very opinionated and quickly finds herself nominated by the party opposing him to run for his congressional seat. Good patriotic fun. Loretta Young was so captivating in her role that she won an Oscar. Well done by an excellent cast.

A: Loretta Young, Joseph Cotten, Ethel Barrymore, Charles Bickford, Lex Barker, James Arness

© CBS/FOX VIDEO 8041

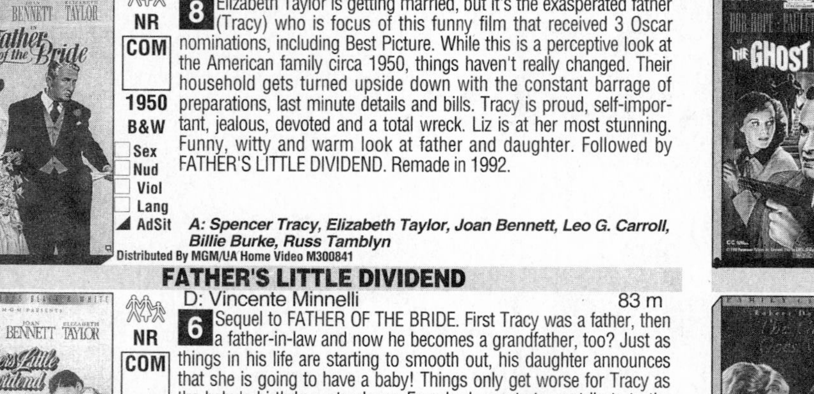

FATHER OF THE BRIDE

D: Vincente Minnelli — 96 m

NR | COM | 1950 | B&W

Sex | Nud | Viol | Lang | AdSit

8 Elizabeth Taylor is getting married, but it's the exasperated father (Tracy) who is focus of this funny film that received 3 Oscar nominations, including Best Picture. While this is a perceptive look at the American family circa 1950, things haven't really changed. Their household gets turned upside down with the constant barrage of preparations, last minute details and bills. Tracy is proud, self-important, jealous, devoted and a total wreck. Liz is at her most stunning. Funny, witty and warm look at father and daughter. Followed by FATHER'S LITTLE DIVIDEND. Remade in 1992.

A: Spencer Tracy, Elizabeth Taylor, Joan Bennett, Leo G. Carroll, Billie Burke, Russ Tamblyn

Distributed By MGM/UA Home Video M300841

FATHER'S LITTLE DIVIDEND

D: Vincente Minnelli — 83 m

NR | COM | 1951 | B&W

Sex | Nud | Viol | Lang | AdSit

6 Sequel to FATHER OF THE BRIDE. First Tracy was a father, then a father-in-law and now he becomes a grandfather, too? Just as things in his life are starting to smooth out, his daughter announces that she is going to have a baby! Things only get worse for Tracy as the baby's birthday gets closer. Everybody wants to contribute to the process, but Tracy doesn't like the idea much at all. And when the kid finally comes along, the kid doesn't much like him either. Delightful and charming, but not on a par with the original.

A: Spencer Tracy, Elizabeth Taylor, Joan Bennett, Don Taylor, Billie Burke

Distributed By MGM/UA Home Video M202401

FLASK OF FIELDS, A

D: Monte Brice, Clyde Bruckman — 61 m

NR | COM | 1930 | B&W

Sex | Nud | Viol | Lang | AdSit

9 Trio of W.C. Fields's masterpiece comedy shorts: "The Golf Specialist," "A Fatal Glass of Beer" and "The Dentist." Hilarious! Particularly outrageous are scenes of Fields (originally censored) climbing all over a female patient whose tooth won't come out. You can see why Fields was such an outstanding talent.

A: W.C. Fields, Rosemary Thelby, George Chandler

© VIDEO YESTERYEAR 515

FLYING DEUCES, THE

D: A. Edward Sutherland — 67 m

NR | COM | 1939 | B&W

Sex | Nud | Viol | Lang | AdSit

7 One of Laurel and Hardy's best efforts. Ollie is heartbroken so he and Stan join the Foreign Legion to forget their lost loves. They soon find that they have a lot to adjust to, plus they get into a series of new problems by trying to straighten out a love affair between a young officer and his girl. This one is pretty fast-paced as compared to their typical episodes. Also included on this particular tape are two classic Betty Boop cartoons.

A: Stan Laurel, Oliver Hardy, Jean Parker, Reginald Gardiner, Charles Middleton, James Finlayson

© REPUBLIC PICTURES HOME VIDEO V1349

FRONT PAGE, THE

D: Lewis Milestone — 101 m

NR | COM | 1931 | B&W

Sex | Nud | Viol | Lang | AdSit

8 Fast and furious pacing, in both the dialogue and the on-screen action, are the hallmark of this first-ever film version of the original play. A newspaper editor (Menjou) and his top reporter (O'Brien) take on City Hall, and each other, when an escapee who is about to be executed shows up claiming to be innocent. A great stable of quality actors make this both funny and forceful. Three remakes followed: HIS GIRL FRIDAY, FRONT PAGE (Matthau and Lemmon) and SWITCHING CHANNELS.

A: Adolphe Menjou, Pat O'Brien, Mary Brian, Edward Everett Horton, Walter Catlett

© VIDEO YESTERYEAR 885

GENERAL, THE

D: Buster Keaton, Clyde Bruckman — 77 m

NR | COM | 1927 | B&W

Sex | Nud | Viol | Lang | AdSit

9 Buster Keaton's silent masterpiece. He plays a Johnnie Gray, who tried to enlist in the Confederate Army but was told to remain a locomotive engineer. When his train and his girlfriend (who is on it) are both hijacked by Yankee spies and taken north, he single-handedly goes north to steal them both back. One of the greatest chases sequences of the silent era ensues. This masterpiece is filmed against a meticulous reconstruction of the Civil War era. It contains inspired comedy, ingenious stuntwork and sight gags. The story is based on an actual event, which was also retold by Disney as THE GREAT LOCOMOTIVE CHASE.

A: Buster Keaton, Marion Mack, Glen Cavender, Jim Farley, Frederick Vroom, Joe Keaton

© HBO VIDEO 0282

GHOST BREAKERS, THE

D: George Marshall — 82 m

NR | COM | HOR | 1940

Sex | Nud | Viol | Lang | AdSit

8 Before there was GHOSTBUSTERS there was Bob Hope. Containing more plot than was normal for Hope pictures, this one has Bob being a New York radio commentator known for his crime exposes. When he is accidentally implicated in a murder case, he hides out in a steamer chest. It is owned by a beautiful heiress (Paulette Goddard) who is on her way to Cuba to claim a haunted castle she has inherited, and now Bob is unexpectedly going with her. Hope and Goddard fall in love and he promises to help her rid the castle of its ghouls...except the ghouls don't want to leave. Some pretty good and effectively scary scenes are mixed in with a lot of laughs. One of Hope's better films and was very popular.

A: Bob Hope, Paulette Goddard, Richard Carlson, Paul Lukas, Anthony Quinn, Richard Carlson

© MCA/UNIVERSAL HOME VIDEO, INC. 81558

GHOST GOES WEST, THE

D: Rene Clair — 82 m

NR | COM | FAN | 1936 | B&W

Sex | Nud | Viol | Lang | AdSit

8 Charming screwball comedy about a Scottish ghost and his 20th-century descendant (both played by Donat) who both escort their castle from Scotland to Florida when it is shipped there, stone-by-stone, after having been purchased by a rich American. The live one wants to win the heart of the millionaire's daughter, and the dead one wants to redeem his lost honor. Whimsical fantasy/comedy that is light-hearted fun.

A: Robert Donat, Jean Parker, Eugene Pallette, Elsa Lanchester, Ralph Bunker

© HBO VIDEO 90656

GOLD RUSH, THE

D: Charles Chaplin — 82 m

NR | COM | 1925 | B&W

Sex / Nud / Viol / Lang / ✓ AdSit

10 One of Chaplin's best, some say it is his best. Charlie's Little Tramp prospects in Alaska's Klondike gold rush and just about starves. Hilarious sequences include Chaplin's now classic Thanksgiving Day feast of a boiled shoe, but Charlie also has a comic tussle with a villain and falls for a dancehall girl. Chaplin's talent for combining pathos and sentimentality with hilarious slapstick has never been better evidenced than here. Memorable and still very, very funny after all these years. A true classic.

A: Charlie Chaplin, Georgia Hale, Mack Swain, Tom Murray

© UNITED AMERICAN VIDEO CORP. 4016

GREAT DICTATOR, THE

D: Charles Chaplin — 126 m

PG | COM | 1940 | B&W

Sex / Nud / Viol / Lang / ✓ AdSit

8 Chaplin's first talkie was completed just as WWII was beginning in earnest. It is the slapstick satire of the then-current world situation, in which Chaplin played a double role. He was both the tyrannical dictator of Tomania, Adenoid Hynkel, and his look-alike, a poor Jewish barber from the ghetto. This was a quite effective satire that was largely lost on audiences of the time, who were preoccupied with the "real thing." Jack Oakie is also marvelous as rival dictator Benzino Napaloni.

A: Charlie Chaplin, Paulette Goddard, Jack Oakie, Reginald Gardiner, Maurice Moscovich, Billy Gilbert

© CBS/FOX VIDEO 3008

GREAT MCGINTY, THE

D: Preston Sturges — 82 m

NR | COM | 1940 | B&W

Sex / Nud / Viol / Lang / ✓ AdSit

7 A wicked satire about corrupt politics. A bartender recollects the story of how he rose to became governor. Originally, he was only a hobo, but he had gained a reputation among the political bosses as a charmer who could really stuff ballot boxes. Soon, he became so valuable to them that the political machine promoted him all the way up to become governor. However, when he boldly sought real reform, the real boss - who was so corrupt that he controlled both the conventional political machine and the reform party - set out to destroy him. Good entertainment. Won an Oscar for Best Screenplay.

A: Brian Donlevy, Muriel Angelus, Akim Tamiroff, Allyn Joslyn, William Demarest

© MCA/UNIVERSAL HOME VIDEO, INC. 80595

GREEN PASTURES, THE

D: Marc Connelly, William Keighley — 93 m

NR | COM FAN | 1936 | B&W

Sex / Nud / Viol / Lang / ✓ AdSit

9 Very unique, interesting, and funny - but also burdened with racially stereotyped characters. The film takes place in a Harlem Sunday School where a teacher tells the stories of the Bible in an entertaining way so that his students can relate to them. But, as the stories of the Old Testament are vibrantly told, they begin to come to life (with the characters speaking in Old South Black vernacular). This film, which had an all-star all-black cast, was heavily boycotted by whites in the South. Rex Ingram is captivating as "de Lawd," as is Oscar Polk as his right-hand angel - Gabe. Religion rarely is this entertaining.

A: Marc Connelly, Rex Ingram, Oscar Polk, Eddie Anderson, Frank Wilson, George Reed

Distributed By MGM/UA Home Video 202834

HAIL THE CONQUERING HERO

D: Preston Sturges — 101 m

NR | COM WAR | 1944 | B&W

Sex / Nud / Viol / Lang / ✓ AdSit

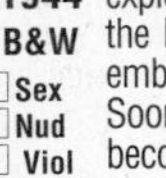

9 A riotous good time in this satire about the hazards brought on by the excesses of wartime patriotism and hero worship. Frail Eddie Bracken signs up for the Army but is turned down because of chronic hay fever. He is so embarrassed that he has worked in a shipyard for six-months, but written home to his mother telling her of his exploits in the Marines. He then has his buddies in the Pacific forward the letters home for him. When his buddies find out that he is too embarrassed to return home, they each donate some of their metals. Soon the whole town thinks Eddie is a big hero and he is nominated to become mayor. Delightful and fast paced satire.

A: Eddie Bracken, Ella Raines, Raymond Walburn, William Demarest, Bill Edwards, Elizabeth Patterson

© MCA/UNIVERSAL HOME VIDEO, INC. 81021

HAPPIEST DAYS OF YOUR LIFE, THE

D: Frank Launder — 83 m

NR | COM | 1950 | B&W

Sex / Nud / Viol / Lang / AdSit

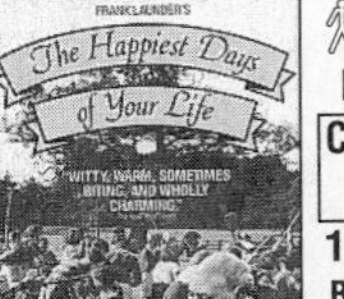

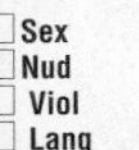

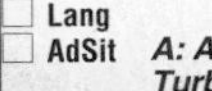

8 Very funny English film concerning the mishaps and misadventures that occur when a girl's school is accidentally billeted in with a boys school. Comic geniuses Alastar Sim and Margaret Rutherford struggle to maintain their composure and their control of these two rivalrous factions which are not supposed to and are ill-prepared to intermix. The kids fight, the bureaucrats pull out their hair and mayhem ensues.

A: Alastair Sim, Margaret Rutherford, Joyce Grenfell, John Turbull, Guy Middleton

© HOME VISION HAP 020

HARVEY

D: Henry Koster — 104 m

NR | COM FAN | 1950 | B&W

Sex / Nud / Viol / Lang / ✓ AdSit

9 Brilliant, classic comedy. Very popular and perennial favorite starring Jimmy Stewart as the loveable Elwood P. Dowd. Elwood is just about the nicest and friendliest man you'd ever meet, but he is just a little strange. He drinks more than he should, but what makes him so strange is that he keeps company with a Pukka (a six-foot three-inch invisible rabbit) named Harvey. Finally, his sister (Hull) reluctantly decides that Elwood should be committed to a loony bin, but hilarity reigns when she gets committed instead and it's now up to Elwood to get things straightened out. Hull won an Oscar for her performance.

A: James Stewart, Josephine Hull, Peggy Dow, Charles Drake, Cecil Kellaway, Jesse White

© MCA/UNIVERSAL HOME VIDEO, INC. 80321

HEAVEN CAN WAIT

D: Ernst Lubitsch — 112 m

NR | COM ROM FAN | 1943 | COLOR

Sex / Nud / Viol / Lang / ✓ AdSit

8 Elegant fantasy/comedy. Don Ameche plays a wealthy old playboy who dies and arrives at the gates of Hell seeking admission there because of his life's many indiscretions with the ladies. However, the lord of darkness is unconvinced that he should enter, so Don must tell his life's story. His indiscretions begin with the upstairs maid and do not stop when he marries beautiful Gene Tierney. But gradually his true love for Tierney is unveiled before us. This is a very witty script that features flashbacks to the Gay '90s. Delightful. Nominated for Best Picture.

A: Gene Tierney, Don Ameche, Charles Coburn, Marjorie Main, Laird Cregar, Spring Byington

© FOXVIDEO 1771

HERE COMES MR. JORDAN

D: Alexander Hall — 949 m

NR | COM FAN | 1941 | B&W

Sex / Nud / Viol / Lang / AdSit

10 Wonderful flight of fantasy in which heaven screws up. Prizefighter Joe Pendleton (Montgomery) accidentally is called to heaven too soon - fifty years too soon. So, he must be sent back to earth in someone else's body until his time is up. The guy they pick for him is a millionaire who was killed off by his greedy wife. When the dead man awakens with a new personality, she is pretty confused, but then so is Joe's old fight manager, who has to be convinced that this is really the old Joe - just in a new body. Top-notch cast. Received six Oscar nominations, including Best Picture, and won two. An excellent remake done in 1978 starred Warren Beatty, called HEAVEN CAN WAIT.

A: Robert Montgomery, Evelyn Keyes, Claude Rains, Rita Johnson, Edward Everett Horton, James Gleason

© COLUMBIA TRISTAR HOME VIDEO 71923

HIS GIRL FRIDAY

D: Howard Hawks — 92 m

NR | COM | 1940 | B&W

Sex / Nud / Viol / Lang / ✓ AdSit

9 One of Howard Hawks' and early Hollywood's best comedies. This remake of THE FRONT PAGE has had a twist added to it. This time around, the story's crack reporter is a woman (Russell). She is trying to retire so that she can marry a mama's boy, but the editor (Grant) wants to keep his star reporter (who is also his ex-wife) just where she is. She thinks she just wants to retire to a life of boring domesticity - however, the story of a lifetime has literally just crawled onto her rolltop desk. Fast pacing and great dialogue, delivered by a talented cast, adds up to first-rate fun.

A: Cary Grant, Rosalind Russell, Ralph Bellamy, Gene Lockhart, Helen Mack, Ernest Truex

© GOODTIMES 08596

HOBSON'S CHOICE

D: David Lean — 107 m

NR | COM | 1954 | B&W

Sex / Nud / Viol / Lang / ✓ AdSit

8 Delightful comedy with a heart. Charles Laughton puts in one of his best performances as an overbearing hard-drinking shoemaker in 1890s London. He makes life miserable for his three daughters by insisting that he will decide who they should marry. But the eldest daughter frustrates his wishes by railroading his talented assistant into marriage and then setting up a shop in competition with her father. Good fun and plenty of laughs.

A: Charles Laughton, John Mills, Brenda de Banzie, Daphne Anderson, Prunella Scales

© HOME VISION HOB 040

HOLD THAT GHOST

D: Arthur Lubin — 86 m

NR | COM | 1941 | B&W

Sex / Nud / Viol / Lang / AdSit

8 One of the very best from Abbot and Costello. Here they are two nightclub waiters, who inherit a haunted house that was previously owned by a hoodlum and reportedly still houses his stolen loot. And, when they come to claim their property, things get spooky. Walls move, lights go on by themselves. There are moans and screams in the air, and people are murdered. Full of great gags. The comic masters are backed up by one of the best supporting casts ever to be into one of their films.

A: Bud Abbott, Lou Costello, Richard Carlson, Joan Davis, The Andrews Sisters, Shemp Howard

© MCA/UNIVERSAL HOME VIDEO, INC. 55087

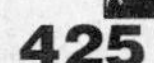

HOLIDAY

D: George Cukor 94 m

NR · COM ROM · 1938 · B&W

8 Delightful and literal adaptation of a Broadway play about a successful but non-conformist young man (Grant, at his charming best) who agrees to meet his wealthy fiancee's stuffy family and to even work for her father's bank. However, when he does meet the family, he finds a kindred spirit in his fiancee's kooky free-thinking sister (Hepburn). She understands him and is just as weird as he is. Which sister going to get him? Fun film.

Sex · Nud · Viol · Lang · AdSit

A: Cary Grant, Katharine Hepburn, Edward Everett Horton, Doris Nolan, Lew Ayres, Binnie Barnes

© COLUMBIA TRISTAR HOME VIDEO 71933

HORSE FEATHERS

D: Norman McLeod 67 m

NR · COM · 1932 · B&W

9 Probably the funniest of the Marx brothers films. This time the brothers destroy Huxley College. Groucho is the president who wants to save money by closing down the dormitory - the kids always sleep in class anyway. He hires Chico and Harpo, a speakeasy worker and a dogcatcher, to build a winning football team so they can beat their rivals at Darwin. Meanwhile Zeppo is chasing a sexy widow. As with all of Marx brothers stuff, don't get too caught up on the plot, just watch for the one-liners.

Sex · Nud · Viol · Lang · AdSit

A: Groucho Marx, Harpo Marx, Chico Marx, Zeppo Marx, Thelma Todd, David Landau

© MCA/UNIVERSAL HOME VIDEO, INC. 80777

HOW TO MARRY A MILLIONAIRE

D: Jean Negulesco 96 m

NR · COM ROM · 1953 · COLOR

7 Pleasant diversion. Three beautiful models pool their money to rent a luxury apartment hoping that they will be able to attract potential millionaire husbands to their penthouse. Trouble occurs when two of them fall for the wrong kind of man - poor. Lightweight fun with some good dialogue, pleasant scenery and good ensemble acting.

Sex · Nud · Viol · Lang · AdSit

A: Marilyn Monroe, Betty Grable, Lauren Bacall, William Powell, Rory Calhoun, David Wayne

© FOXVIDEO 1023

IDIOT'S DELIGHT

D: Clarence Brown 107 m

NR · COM · 1939 · B&W

6 A very interesting bit of history, but a badly dated film. This is one of the last pacifistic movies before America's full involvement in WWII. It has an anti-war air to it, but it is also a comedy in which Clark Gable and a group of others are trapped together in an Alpine retreat as the war starts in Europe. Gable is a tacky vaudevillian who recognizes the female companion to a European munitions industrialist. She claims to be a Russian Countess, but he knows her as an old flame from Omaha. Has its funny moments, but seems incredibly naive today.

Sex · Nud · Viol · Lang · AdSit

A: Clark Gable, Norma Shearer, Edward Arnold, Charles Coburn, Virginia Grey, Joseph Schildkraut

Distributed By MGM/UA Home Video M300610

I MARRIED A WITCH

D: Rene Clair 77 m

NR · COM ROM · 1942 · B&W

8 Delightful fantasy/comedy about a sexy witch (Lake) who returns 400 years after being burned at the stake, intent upon revenge. Fredric March is a dead ringer for the ancestor who persecuted her and is now running for governor. The witch, unable to help herself, falls for the guy and proceeds to play dirty tricks upon his fiancee, Susan Hayward. Funny comedy with some interesting plot twists and boasts some pretty good special effects, too. Ironically, March and Lake couldn't stand each other.

Sex · Nud · Viol · Lang · AdSit

A: Fredric March, Veronica Lake, Robert Benchley, Susan Hayward, Cecil Kellaway, Robert Warwick

© WARNER HOME VIDEO 35079

IMPORTANCE OF BEING EARNEST, THE

D: Anthony Asquith 95 m

NR · COM · 1952 · COLOR

8 Oscar Wilde's classic witty comedy of errors and a spoof of Victorian English manners and morals is presented in high style with one of the most esteemed casts possible. Sophisticated and debonair London bachelor Redgrave assumes the fictitious name of Ernest to hide his many escapades as he seeks the beautiful Gwendolen. However, his friend pretends that he is Ernest in order to impress Redgrave's ward Cecily. Excellent sophisticated English comedy.

Sex · Nud · Viol · Lang · AdSit

A: Michael Redgrave, Edith Evans, Dorothy Tutin, Joan Greenwood, Margaret Rutherford

© PARAMOUNT HOME VIDEO 12574

INSPECTOR GENERAL, THE

D: Henry Koster 102 m

NR · COM MUS · 1949 · COLOR

9 Hysterical Danny Kaye farce. In early 1800s czarist Russia, Danny Kay is a flunky in a traveling medicine show and he has been arrested as a suspected horse thief. However, he is soon mistaken by the village elders to be a visiting Inspector General of the Czar and confidant of Napoleon. He has no idea what is going on but he isn't going to let this good fortune get away. Still, he is not out of trouble, because he is now being drawn ever deeper into court intrigue and that isn't healthy. Highly entertaining showcase for Kaye's many musical and comedic talents. Everyone will truly enjoy this one.

Sex · Nud · Viol · Lang · AdSit

A: Danny Kaye, Walter Slezak, Barbara Bates, Elsa Lanchester, Gene Lockhart, Alan Hale

Distributed By MGM/UA Home Video M202599

INTERNATIONAL HOUSE

D: A. Edward Sutherland 72 m

NR · COM · 1933 · B&W

8 Hilariously offbeat film filled with some of the biggest radio stars of the early '30s. The cockeyed wacky plot has a wide assortment of strange characters all gathered at a Chinese hotel to witness an inventor display his brand new experimental television. The plot, while bizarre, is there merely to provide an excuse for a big cast of vaudevillian and radio players to do their shtick, and for W.C. Fields to play off them. Expect the absurd and you will be satisfied.

Sex · Nud · Viol · Lang · AdSit

A: W.C. Fields, Peggy Hopkins Joyce, George Burns, Gracie Allen, Bela Lugosi, Rudy Vallee

© MCA/UNIVERSAL HOME VIDEO, INC. 80512

IT HAPPENED ONE NIGHT

D: Frank Capra 105 m

NR · COM ROM · 1934 · B&W

9 Terrific romantic comedy that swept all five major Oscars: Best Picture, Actor, Actress, Director and Screenplay. The only other film to do that was ONE FLEW OVER THE CUCKOO'S NEST. Colbert plays a pampered young heiress traveling incognito and running away from her father. Clark Gable is a tough reporter who plays along with her story in hopes of getting a scoop. Of course they fall in love. Great comedy gags remain fresh and funny today. Enchanting and fun-filled.

Sex · Nud · Viol · Lang · AdSit

A: Clark Gable, Claudette Colbert, Walter Connolly, Roscoe Karns, Alan Hale, Ward Bond

© COLUMBIA TRISTAR HOME VIDEO 60382

IT'S A WONDERFUL LIFE

D: Frank Capra 160 m

NR · COM DMA ROM · 1947 · B&W

10 Nobody doesn't like this movie. Sentimental favorite in which Jimmy Stewart wishes he was never born. He's been so busy helping others get what they want that he feels as if everything he wants and needs has passed him by. Then he receives a visit from Clarence, his bumbling guardian angel, who shows him what things would have been like if he had never been born. This is an experience that proves to him what a fortunate and wealthy man he is. Heartwarming, feel good story that is usually reserved just for Christmas, but shouldn't be.

Sex · Nud · Viol · Lang · AdSit

A: James Stewart, Donna Reed, Lionel Barrymore, Thomas Mitchell, Ward Bond, Henry Travers

© REPUBLIC PICTURES HOME VIDEO 2062

IT SHOULD HAPPEN TO YOU

D: George Cukor 81 m

NR · COM ROM · 1953 · B&W

8 Kooky Judy Holliday decides to promote her acting career by hiring a billboard overlooking one of the busiest locations in New York City. When a soap company executive wants this particular location for his product, he trades her several other billboard locations in exchange for her one. All of a sudden she is a sensation. Her boyfriend (Jack Lemmon, in his first screen appearance) has a difficult time dealing with her new-found celebrity status, and she must decide between him and a career. This is a steady stream of fun from two talented comedic actors.

Sex · Nud · Viol · Lang · AdSit

A: Judy Holliday, Jack Lemmon, Peter Lawford, Michael O'Shea

© COLUMBIA TRISTAR HOME VIDEO VH10343

KID, THE/THE IDLE CLASS

D: Charles Chaplin 86 m

NR · COM · 1921 · B&W

7 This is a Charlie Chaplin two-parter. The first one is THE KID. It was Charlie's very first film in which he wrote, produced and directed; and, it was also the film that made Jackie Coogan into a child star. In it, the Little Tramp discovers and takes an apparently orphaned child home with him, but the mother returns and wants to take the baby away. This is Chaplin's trademark blending of pathos and comedy. The second is a rare film short in which Charlie has two roles, the Little Tramp loose on a society golf course, and being mistaken for a millionaire at a costume party.

Sex · Nud · Viol · Lang · AdSit

A: Charlie Chaplin, Jackie Coogan, Edna Purviance

© CBS/FOX VIDEO 3002

KID FROM BROOKLYN, THE

D: Norman McLeod 113 m

NR | COM | 1946 | COLOR

6 This is a great vehicle for Danny Kaye's silliness. He plays a milkman who accidentally knocks out a middle-weight boxing champion in a street brawl. Soon the champ's scheming manager decides to turn Danny into a boxer. Eve Arden's wisecracking and Danny Kaye's charm are mostly what makes this enjoyable. However, this film is actually a remake of THE MILKY WAY, done by Harold Lloyd in 1936, and that one might be funnier.

Sex / Nud / Viol / Lang / AdSit

A: Danny Kaye, Virginia Mayo, Vera-Ellen, Eve Arden, Steve Cochran

© HBO VIDEO 90651

LADY EVE, THE

D: Preston Sturges 93 m

NR | COM ROM | 1941 | B&W

9 Truly entertaining romantic comedy from the '40s. Stanwyck is winning as a con artist who makes her living charming passengers on an ocean liner, all the while also cheating them at cards. She and her father think they have really hit paydirt in Henry Fonda. He is a wealthy and studious beer heir, who is just returning from a trip up the Amazon. She has him all set up for the kill, but then backs out because she's fallen for the guy. Too late, he has found her out and now wants no part of her. She must win him back. Fun.

Sex / Nud / Viol / Lang / ◢ AdSit

A: Barbara Stanwyck, Henry Fonda, Charles Coburn, William Demarest, Eugene Pallette, Eric Blore

© MCA/UNIVERSAL HOME VIDEO, INC. 80353

LADY FOR A DAY

D: Frank Capra 96 m

NR | COM | 1933 | B&W

8 Sentimental Frank Capra favorite about a seedy old woman who is given another chance. This old woman has pampered her daughter by spending all her money to keep her in a boarding school abroad and allowed the girl think that she is wealthy. But now the daughter is about to find out the truth - that the old woman is just a peddlerwoman who sells apples on the street. However, when Dude, a sentimental gambler hears of the old woman's plight, he pays to have her transformed into a real lady - for a day. This film was remade by Capra again as POCKETFUL OF MIRACLES in 1961 with Glenn Ford and Bette Davis.

Sex / Nud / Viol / Lang / ◢ AdSit

A: Warren William, May Robson, Guy Kibbee, Glenda Farrell, Jean Parker, Walter Connolly

© CONNOISSEUR VIDEO COLLECTION 1050

LEMON DROP KID, THE

D: Sidney Lanfield 91 m

NR | COM | 1951 | B&W

7 Enjoyable fast-paced Bob Hope comedy that rises above his typical fare. In a take-off from a Damon Runyon story, Hope plays a horse track fanatic who gives a hood (Lloyd Nolan) some bad advice. When the guy loses his money, he gives Hope a month to get the money back. Every scheme Hope tries backfires, including claiming to collect money for a fake old folks home by being a phony Santa Claus. Entertaining.

Sex / Nud / Viol / Lang / AdSit

A: Bob Hope, Marilyn Maxwell, Lloyd Nolan, Jane Darwell, Fred Clark

© COLUMBIA TRISTAR HOME VIDEO 60743

LIBELED LADY

D: Jack Conway 99 m

NR | COM ROM | 1936 | B&W

8 Classic screwball comedy that begins when Spencer Tracy's newspaper prints a fabricated story about wealthy Myrna Loy stepping out with a married man. Tracy leaves Jean Harlow standing at the alter when he learns he is being sued for $5 million. To protect himself, he prepares an elaborate scheme to trap Loy. He will have his playboy lawyer friend marry Harlow, then seduce Loy - so that he can then claim adultery again. The perfect plan falls through when he falls for Loy instead. Fast paced with brisk dialogue and great chemistry.

Sex / Nud / Viol / Lang / ◢ AdSit

A: Jean Harlow, William Powell, Myrna Loy, Spencer Tracy, Walter Connolly, Cora Witherspoon

Distributed By MGM/UA Home Video M300892

LIFE WITH FATHER

D: Michael Curtiz 118 m

NR | COM | 1947 | COLOR

9 Warm and sentimental, charming Americana and witty too. These are the nostalgic remembrances of author Clarence Day of his own father as he grew up in N.Y.C. at the turn of the 20th-century. The story focuses on the foibles and travails of his eccentric Victorian father - a strict man of business who is considerably and constantly befuddled by his wife and his unruly family. Touching and beautifully photographed. Utterly delightful and consistently funny. Great family entertainment.

Sex / Nud / Viol / Lang / AdSit

A: William Powell, Irene Dunne, Elizabeth Taylor, Edmund Gwenn, ZaSu Pitts, Jimmy Lydon

© UNITED AMERICAN VIDEO CORP. 4096

LIMELIGHT

D: Charles Chaplin 137 m

NR | COM DMA | 1951 | B&W

8 Charlie Chaplin returned to the screen in 1952 for this story set in 1914, of an elderly down-on-his-luck vaudevillian. He is convinced that he is no longer funny. But, when he rescues a ballet dancer from suicide and helps her to succeed on stage, she in turn gives him the confidence he needs to perform again. It is a sentimental story that is hard to resist. Chaplin's comedy routines are actually those from his early career. One segment includes a skit with Buster Keaton and is the only time they appeared together. Upon its 1972 American release, Chaplin won an Oscar for the score, which he cowrote.

Sex / Nud / Viol / Lang / ◢ AdSit

A: Charlie Chaplin, Claire Bloom, Nigel Bruce, Buster Keaton, Sydney Chaplin

© CBS/FOX VIDEO 3010

MAGIC TOWN

D: William Wellman 103 m

NR | COM | 1947 | B&W

6 Jimmy Stewart has hit pay dirt. He is a struggling public opinion pollster who has stumbled upon a small American town, Grandview, that exactly mirrors the nation's tastes. Jane Wyman is a tough-minded newspaper editor in the small town who discovers his secret, and announces the find to the world, hoping to draw new business to her town. Instead, the town is nearly destroyed in a firestorm of media attention. Written by the same writer who Frank Capra used. Some of the results are very funny, but it's also a little corny.

Sex / Nud / Viol / Lang / ◢ AdSit

A: James Stewart, Jane Wyman, Regis Toomey, Kent Smith, Ned Sparks

© REPUBLIC PICTURES HOME VIDEO 2557

MAJOR BARBARA

D: Gabriel Pascal 131 m

COM DMA | 1941 | B&W

7 Captivating British satirical comedy from George Bernard Shaw, set during WWII. Major Barbara is a rich girl who has turned socialist and joined the Salvation Army. She hopes to do more to save the world than her munitions-making father does to destroy it. But she becomes disillusioned with the Salvation Army when it accepts big donations from her father and a rich distiller. Rex Harrison is her smitten, pragmatic fiance who gets in the middle of things. Her father ultimately redeems himself in her eyes when she comes to recognize that he is not so bad after all.

Sex / Nud / Viol / Lang / ◢ AdSit

A: Wendy Miller, Rex Harrison, Robert Morley, Deborah Kerr, Robert Newton, Emlyn Williams

© HOME VISION MAJ01

MAN WHO CAME TO DINNER, THE

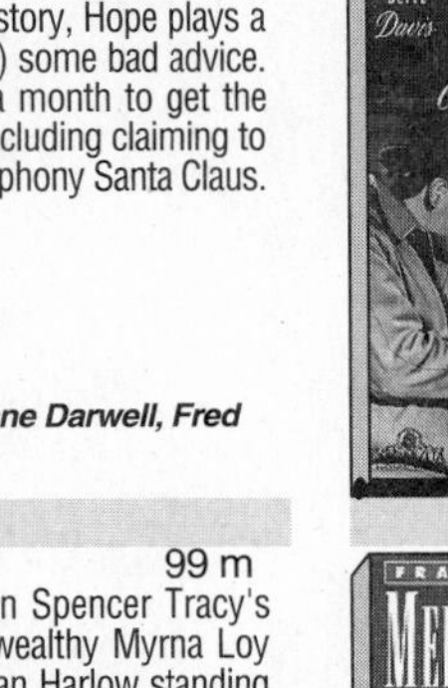

D: William Keighley 113 m

NR | COM | 1941 | B&W

8 Classic screwball comedy! A cocky radio celebrity with a quick wit and quicker tongue (Woolley) falls and breaks his leg, while at the house of the Stanleys. He is forced to stay with this quite ordinary mid-western family for the winter while he recovers, but in the process this obnoxious loudmouth drives them crazy with both his unending demands and the wide array of oddball friends that keep dropping in on them. Bette Davis is delightful as his secretary. Based on the Moss Hart/George Kaufman play, this wacky comedy is fun for the whole family.

Sex / Nud / Viol / Lang / ◢ AdSit

A: Monty Woolley, Bette Davis, Ann Sheridan, Billie Burke, Jimmy Durante, Richard Travis

Distributed By MGM/UA Home Video M201804

MEET JOHN DOE

D: Frank Capra 123 m

NR | COM DMA | 1941 | B&W

8 Endearing and quite entertaining Capra corn. Barbara Stanwyck is a reporter who was just fired. As a last act of defiance, she creates a fictional hardluck character called John Doe to dramatize the hard times. Her man becomes such a hit that she gets her job back - except, there is no real John Doe. So, naive Gary Cooper is hired to become the man and is promoted into a national hero by her for the unscrupulous paper's owner, who has intentions to use Coop's endorsement in a run for the White House. Coop discovers the corrupt intentions and trys, against the huge publicity machine, to stop it.

Sex / Nud / Viol / Lang / ◢ AdSit

A: Gary Cooper, Barbara Stanwyck, Edward Arnold, Walter Brennan, Spring Byington, James Gleason

© GOODTIMES 5-09326

MIDNIGHT

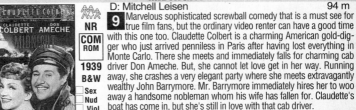

D: Mitchell Leisen 94 m

NR | COM ROM | 1939 | B&W

9 Marvelous sophisticated screwball comedy that is a must see for true film fans, but the ordinary video renter can have a good time with this one too. Claudette Colbert is a charming American gold-digger who just arrived penniless in Paris after having lost everything in Monte Carlo. There she meets and immediately falls for charming cab driver Don Ameche. But, she cannot let love get in her way. Running away, she crashes a very elegant party where she meets extravagantly wealthy John Barrymore. Mr. Barrymore immediately hires her to woo away a handsome nobleman whom his wife has fallen for. Claudette's boat has come in, but she's still in love with that cab driver.

Sex / Nud / Viol / Lang / ◢ AdSit

A: Claudette Colbert, Don Ameche, John Barrymore, Frances Hederer, Mary Astor, Elaine Barrie

© MCA/UNIVERSAL HOME VIDEO, INC. 80831

OLDIES

MIDSUMMER NIGHT'S DREAM

D: Max Reinhardt 118 m

8 This lavishly produced Hollywood version of Shakespeare's fanciful story features just about every big-name actor of the day that Warner Brothers could get its hands on. The play centers around mischievous forest characters (fairies and artisans) who are to put on a play for a royal wedding. Instead, they get involved in the romantic lives of several lovers and, after a battle between the King and Queen of the fairies, everything gets out of hand. Cagney stars as Bottom, Rooney plays Puck. This enchanting film won an Oscar for photography and editing. De Havilland made her film debut here.

COM FAN | 1935 | B&W | Sex | Nud | Viol | Lang | AdSit

A: James Cagney, Mickey Rooney, Olivia de Havilland, Dick Powell, Joe E. Brown, Jean Muir

Distributed By MGM/UA Home Video 202543

MILKY WAY, THE

D: Leo McCarey 88 m

6 Vintage comedy from silent film's master slapstick comedian - Harold Lloyd. An unassuming milkman (Lloyd) accidentally knocks out a drunken world champion boxer in a non-brawl. The champ's quick-witted promoter knows a good thing when he sees it and sets the milkman up to win a string of fixed fights. Pretty soon Lloyd starts to believe his own hype and gets cocky. Then it slowly starts to dawn on him that he is soon going to have to fight a real fight against the champ. Pretty good, but too bad time wasn't kinder to a comic legend. Remade as THE KID FROM BROOKLYN with Danny Kaye.

NR | COM | 1936 | B&W | Sex | Nud | Viol | Lang | AdSit

A: Harold Lloyd, Adolphe Menjou, Dorothy Wilson, Helen Mack

© VIDEO YESTERYEAR 1106

MIN AND BILL

D: George Roy Hill 66 m

6 Dressler and Beery are delightful in this sentimental story about Min, a scruffy old woman who runs a waterfront hotel, and her friend Bill. Min is raising an abandoned girl as her own and will do anything for the girl, including sacrificing her own happiness. But things get complicated for Min when officials want to take the girl away so she can have a "proper" home. Dressler won an Oscar for Best Actress for her outstanding performance. But, sadly, this film is pretty creaky now and so is recommended for film fans only.

NR | COM DMA | 1930 | B&W | Sex | Nud | Viol | Lang | AdSit

A: Marie Dressler, Wallace Beery, Dorothy Jordan, Marjorie Rambeau, Frank McGlynn

Distributed By MGM/UA Home Video M300606

MIRACLE OF MORGAN'S CREEK, THE

D: Preston Sturges 98 m

8 Hilarity and scandal abound in this screwball wartime comedy! A small town girl, Trudy Kockenlocker (Hutton), attends a party for servicemen, gets drunk and marries a soldier. Later she realizes she is pregnant, but can't remember who she married on that fateful night. In order to avoid serious ruin, she convinces another schmuck (Bracken), to marry her for real. Considering the time period in which this thing was made, it is amazing that this daring comedy made it through the censors. A real comic treat too - well worth the ride!

NR | COM | 1944 | B&W | Sex | Nud | Viol | Lang | AdSit

A: Eddie Bracken, Betty Hutton, William Demarest, Diana Lynn, Brian Donlevy, Akim Tamiroff

© PARAMOUNT HOME VIDEO 4312

MISTER ROBERTS

D: John Ford, Mervyn LeRoy 123 m

10 Great fun and a true gem! Trapped in the backwater of WWII, life aboard a Navy cargo ship in the South Pacific is boring, but it is made miserable because of the tyranny of the wacko captain (Cagney). However, through the intervention of the First Officer, Mr. Roberts (Fonda), and a never-ending series of practical jokes, it is made tolerable. Fonda longs to be part of the real shooting war, but Cagney won't let him go because it is only Fonda who keeps his nearly mutinous crew in line. Outstanding performances, particularly Lemmon (Oscar) as young Ensign Pulver in charge of laundry and morale. Terrific!

NR | COM DMA WAR | 1955 | COLOR | Sex | Nud | Viol | Lang | AdSit

A: Henry Fonda, Jack Lemmon, James Cagney, Betsy Palmer, William Powell, Ward Bond

© WARNER HOME VIDEO 1017

MODERN TIMES

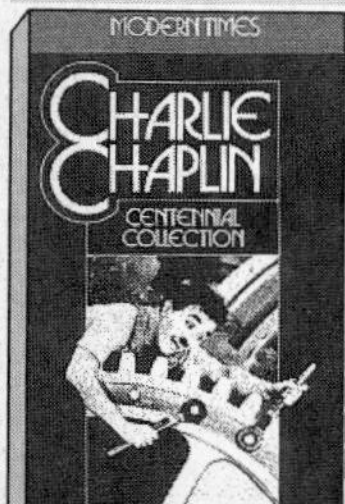

D: Charles Chaplin 87 m

9 This mostly silent masterpiece about the pitfalls of a mechanized society is still beautifully contemporary! The poor Little Tramp suffers from the effects of a machine-induced nervous breakdown, a strike and a jail sentence, which all lead to even more problems. Unemployed, he joins up with a young orphaned girl and they go off together to seek happiness. Chaplin used only a bit of dialogue and sound effects, and wrote the musical score which included the song "Smile." This was the last time he used the Little Tramp, and this proved to be one of his most popular movies.

NR | COM | 1936 | B&W | Sex | Nud | Viol | Lang | AdSit

A: Charlie Chaplin, Paulette Goddard, Henry Bergman, Chester Conklin

© CBS/FOX VIDEO 3007

MONKEY BUSINESS

D: Norman McLeod 77 m

9 Zany Marx Brothers classic! Those ridiculous brothers are at it again in perhaps their most energetic film. The four brothers stow away on a luxury ocean liner, chase women and wreak havoc with the captain and crew. While on board, Groucho and Zeppo are hired to protect one gangster and Chico and Harpo are hired to protect his rival. Side-splitting laughs are more than abundant in this happy Marx brothers comedy. Check out ANIMAL CRACKERS, DUCK SOUP and A NIGHT AT THE OPERA also.

NR | COM | 1931 | B&W | Sex | Nud | Viol | Lang | AdSit

A: Groucho Marx, Zeppo Marx, Chico Marx, Harpo Marx, Thelma Todd, Ruth Hall

© MCA/UNIVERSAL HOME VIDEO, INC. 80172

MONKEY BUSINESS

D: Howard Hawks 97 m

7 Non-stop fun in this screwball comedy! A scientist (Grant) conducts experiments regenerating human tissue hoping to find a recipe for a youth elixir. However one of his chimpanzees mixes up a successful concoction and dumps it into the water cooler. When Grant and his wife (Rogers) take a drink, they revert back to being adolescent in their antics and attitudes. Soon his absent-minded secretary (Monroe) and his boss (Coburn) join into the teenage mindset. A charming bunch of silliness.

NR | COM | 1952 | B&W | Sex | Nud | Viol | Lang | AdSit

A: Cary Grant, Ginger Rogers, Marilyn Monroe, Charles Coburn, Hugh Marlowe

© FOXVIDEO 5140

MONSIEUR VERDOUX

D: Charles Chaplin 125 m

9 This is black comedy at its best! A straight-arrow Parisian bank teller (Chaplin) has a crippled wife and child to support. So when the Depression hits and he is dismissed from his job, he must come up with an answer. His bizarre solution is to marry rich women, murder them and take their money. This dark comedy was way ahead of its time, and has now attained cult appreciation. Raye's role as a would-be victim is a scene stealer. Perhaps Chaplin's most controversial film, it was subtitled "COMEDY OF MURDERS."

NR | COM DMA | 1947 | B&W | Sex | Nud | Viol | Lang | AdSit

A: Charlie Chaplin, Martha Raye, Isobel Elsom, Marilyn Nash, Irving Bacon, William Frawley

© CBS/FOX VIDEO 3009

MORE THE MERRIER, THE

D: George Stevens 104 m

8 Effervescent romantic comedy that was very popular then, and still is a whole lot of fun. When a housing shortage develops during WWII, a young working woman (Arthur) living in Washington D.C. rents out a room to an older man (Coburn) who ends up playing Cupid for her. Concerned with her lack of a love life, Coburn rents out half of his room to a handsome Air Force mechanic (McCrea), and romance blooms. Coburn won an Oscar for his crusty old salt-of-the-earth portrayal. This sparkling film was nominated for six Academy Awards. Remade into WALK DON'T RUN with Cary Grant.

NR | COM ROM | 1943 | B&W | Sex | Nud | Viol | Lang | AdSit

A: Jean Arthur, Joel McCrea, Charles Coburn, Richard Gaines

© COLUMBIA TRISTAR HOME VIDEO 71943

MR. AND MRS. SMITH

D: Alfred Hitchcock 95 m

7 Very unusual Hitchcock flick - a screwball comedy. A devoted but argumentative couple (Lombard and Montgomery) find that after having been married three years, their marriage is not technically legal and it is now null and void. So, Lombard throws her hubby out of the house so that both can enjoy their new freedom. He moves into the club. Meanwhile, his law partner (Raymond) trys to pursue his wife, er... ex-wife, ah.. girlfriend. This vintage and endearing comedy produced fine performances, but undeservedly went largely unnoticed at the time of its release.

NR | COM ROM | 1941 | B&W | Sex | Nud | Viol | Lang | AdSit

A: Carole Lombard, Robert Montgomery, Gene Raymond, Jack Carson, Philip Merivale, Betty Compson

© TURNER HOME ENTERTAINMENT 6018

MR. BLANDINGS BUILDS HIS DREAM HOUSE

D: H.C. Potter 94 m

8 Comic catastrophies abound when a New York City ad executive (Grant) gets sick of city life in his tiny apartment. He and his wife (Loy) decide to chuck it all to purchase their dream house in Connecticut. And a lovely old place it is, too... except that it's so dilapidated that they have tear it down and start from scratch, and a whole new can of comic worms is opened. Grant is his endearing self, and Loy is excellent as his patient and understanding wife. This very familiar theme will really hit home with many new homeowners, regardless of its age. See this one first - before you build!

NR | COM | 1948 | B&W | Sex | Nud | Viol | Lang | AdSit

A: Cary Grant, Myrna Loy, Melvyn Douglas, Reginald Denny, Sharyn Moffett, Connie Marshall

© TURNER HOME ENTERTAINMENT 6007

MR. DEEDS GOES TO TOWN

D: Frank Capra — 115 m

NR | COM ROM | 1936 | B&W

7 Charming vintage comedy! A simple, straight arrow, model citizen, Longfellow Deeds (Cooper) has his world shaken up when he inherits $20 million. He moves from his humble home into a New York City mansion, but he quickly concludes that the money has brought him more trouble than it's worth. So he decides he wants to give it all to struggling farmers. But, because of his highly unconventional attitude, he is first forced to stand trial to prove that he is not insane or "pixilated." Capra won an Academy Award in this film that proves money doesn't always buy happiness.

Sex / Nud / Viol / Lang / AdSit

A: Gary Cooper, Jean Arthur, George Bancroft, Lionel Stander, Douglas Dumbrille, Mayo Methot

© COLUMBIA TRISTAR HOME VIDEO 90143

MR. LUCKY

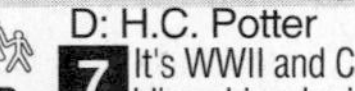

D: H.C. Potter — 100 m

NR | COM ROM | 1943 | B&W

7 It's WWII and Cary Grant is a scoundrel. He is the owner of gambling ship who is trying to do two things: first, avoid the draft and second, steal all the proceeds from a charity ball for War Relief and head off to South America with the money. But his plans go severely awry when his partner steals the loot first and what's worse, Cary starts to fall for the pretty socialite (Day) he is trying to con. So, contrary to his nature, he falls in love, recovers the money and goes straight. Grant's magical performance makes it lots of fun. The film was later made into a TV series.

Sex / Nud / Viol / Lang / AdSit

A: Cary Grant, Laraine Day, Charles Bickford, Gladys Cooper, Alan Carney, Henry Stephenson

© TURNER HOME ENTERTAINMENT 6011

MR. PEABODY AND THE MERMAID

D: Irving Pichel — 89 m

NR | COM FAN | 1948 | B&W

6 Fanciful comedy! A married man (Powell) who is just about to turn 50 and going through a mid-life crisis is fishing in the Caribbean where he hooks a very big fish - a beautiful mermaid (Ann Blyth) to be exact. Absolutely infatuated with her, he takes her home and sticks her in his swimming pool. Unfortunately, his wife doesn't see the charm, and you can predict the results. Very much like SPLASH, only in a 1940s sort of way.

Sex / Nud / Viol / Lang / AdSit

A: William Powell, Ann Blyth, Irene Hervey, Andrea King, Clinton Sundberg

© REPUBLIC PICTURES HOME VIDEO 2819

MR. WINKLE GOES TO WAR

D: Alfred E. Green — 80 m

NR | COM WAR | 1944 | B&W

6 Mr. Winkle (Robinson) is an aging, shy, weak-willed and henpecked bank clerk who mistakenly gets drafted during WWII. However, he surprises everyone when he passes the physical and sets off to basic training with the rest of the draftees. He even survives the grueling days of hard work and abusive sergeants that are meant for much younger men, and is sent to the South Pacific. There, he puts his skills to use and he surprises even himself by emerging as a hero. Although somewhat dated, it is still fun and the acting is excellent. This film was produced to aid the war effort.

Sex / Nud / Viol / Lang / AdSit

A: Edward G. Robinson, Ruth Warrick, Richard Lane, Robert Armstrong

© COLUMBIA TRISTAR HOME VIDEO 60533

MY FAVORITE BRUNETTE

D: Elliott Nugent — 85 m

NR | COM MYS | 1947 | B&W

7 Comic misadventures in this Hope spoof, probably one of his very best, after PALEFACE. A baby photographer (Hope) is mistakenly identified by beautiful Lamour as a private eye, and she hires him to search for her missing uncle. She gives him a map that he is to protect with his life. He then goes to the estate of a supposed friend of the uncle's, only to find a man there who claims that he is the uncle and that the woman is nuts. Hope is obviously in over his head, but that won't stop him. Lots of predictable shtick, but a good time. Lorre is particularly good in a parody of himself.

Sex / Nud / Viol / Lang / AdSit

A: Bob Hope, Dorothy Lamour, Peter Lorre, Lon Chaney, Jr., John Hoyt

© GOODTIMES 5024

MY FAVORITE WIFE

D: Garson Kanin — 88 m

NR | COM ROM | 1940 | B&W

8 A young attorney's wife (Dunne) is presumed dead after seven years of having been lost at sea. But, she is alive. She has been marooned on an island with a handsome young scientist (Scott) for all this time. Just as she has been declared legally dead and her husband Grant is about to remarry (and on the very first night of his honeymoon, too) his newly-rescued first wife appears! What's he to do about his new wife? That's not all, what about that other man? The fun premise provides a lot of laughs in this spirited comedy and the talent of its stars makes it happen. It was remade in 1963 as MOVE OVER DARLING.

Sex / Nud / Viol / Lang / AdSit

A: Cary Grant, Irene Dunne, Gail Patrick, Randolph Scott, Ann Shoemaker, Scotty Beckett

© TURNER HOME ENTERTAINMENT 6052

MY LITTLE CHICKADEE

D: Edward Cline — 91 m

NR | COM | 1940 | B&W

6 Wild spoof of the Old West. Two moral misfits meet on a train in the Old West. Sexpot Mae has been thrown out of the last town for allowing herself to be romanced by a man in a mask, and Fields is a con man on his way to his next con. Mae knows her reputation will have preceeded her, so she arranges to have a card cheat marry her to the smitten Fields. After being attacked by Indians, they disembark in Greasewood City. Sight gags abound. Unwilling to consummated their marriage, Mae places a goat in their wedding bed. He says, "Darling, you've changed your perfume."

Sex / Nud / Viol / Lang / AdSit

A: Mae West, W.C. Fields, Joseph Calleia, Dick Foran, Ruth Donnelly, Margaret Hamilton

© MCA/UNIVERSAL HOME VIDEO, INC. 55005

MY MAN GODFREY

D: Gregory LaCava — 90 m

NR | COM ROM | 1936 | B&W

9 Hilarious classic, acclaimed as the first screwball comedy. A society scavenger hunt is in full swing, and Lombard finds the "bum" she needs at the dump. He (Powell) is a down-on-his-luck former blueblood and when back at the party, he spouts off - calling everyone there insensitive nitwits. She loves it and offers him a job as her butler. He takes the job, but after suffering numerous insults from her dizzy mother, her gigolo-in-waiting and her snobbish sister, he's had enough - but wait, they're in love. This Depression-era film knocked the rich and the masses loved it. Nominated for six Oscars.

Sex / Nud / Viol / Lang / AdSit

A: William Powell, Carole Lombard, Gail Patrick, Alice Brady, Eugene Pallette, Mischa Auer

© GOODTIMES 5002

NEVER GIVE A SUCKER AN EVEN BREAK

D: Edward Cline — 71 m

NR | COM | 1941 | B&W

8 This surreal comedy was Fields's last starring role and was not his best effort, but fans will love his silliness anyway. There is very little coherent plot - just a bizarre, and funny, series of events laid end-to-end. It is Fields's spoof of the film industry. He plays a writer trying to sell a film exec on a movie idea: a character (played by him) reaches to recover a bottle of booze that he has accidentally dropped out of an airplane and falls several thousand feet, landing inside the mountain retreat of Mrs. Hemoglobin (Dumont), whose daughter he then teaches how to play "Post Office." Absurd, but fun.

Sex / Nud / Viol / Lang / AdSit

A: W.C. Fields, Margaret Dumont, Gloria Jean, Leon Errol, Franklin Pangborn, Susan Miller

© BARR ENTERTAINMENT VIDEO 11005

NIGHT AT THE OPERA

D: Sam Wood — 92 m

NR | COM | 1935 | B&W

9 Lunacy reigns. This film has more structure than DUCK SOUP, which preceeded it, and allows those viewers uninitiated to the utter ridiculousness of the Marx Brothers the opportunity to follow the action a little better. Groucho plays a shyster who woos Margaret Dumont and convinces her to invest $200,000 in the opera so she can become a member of high society. Harpo and Chico play cupid to singers Allan Jones and Kitty Carlisle. Together they create a night of total insanity in the world of opera. Probably their best effort.

Sex / Nud / Viol / Lang / AdSit

A: Groucho Marx, Chico Marx, Harpo Marx, Kitty Carlisle, Allan Jones, Margaret Dumont

Distributed By MGM/UA Home Video M500009

NINOTCHKA

D: Ernst Lubitsch — 108 m

NR | COM ROM | 1939 | B&W

8 Enjoyable social farce that was Garbo's first comedy. Many of the social comments have become less biting over the years, but it still works because of its talented cast. Garbo plays a very stern Communist sent to Paris to chastise some fellow comrades who have been seduced by the trappings of capitalism. However, a Parisian playboy and gigolo who spots her, sets his mind on seducing the icy temptress. For her part, she is having a very difficult time resisting the charms of both capitalism and this Frenchman. Delightful romantic comedy. Garbo and screenplay received Oscar nominations.

Sex / Nud / Viol / Lang / AdSit

A: Greta Garbo, Melvyn Douglas, Bela Lugosi, Ina Claire, Bela Lugosi, Sig Ruman

Distributed By MGM/UA Home Video M400115

NOTHING SACRED

D: William Wellman — 75 m

NR | COM | 1937 | COLOR

8 This lively and cynical screwball comedy is a winner. Lombard is at her funniest as a simple Vermont girl whose quack doctor diagnoses her as dying of radium poisoning. A cynical hotshot New York reporter (March), working for a sensationalist paper, exploits her imminent death in a series of pathetic stories which turn her into a national hero. Then she finds out that she isn't really dying. She wants to tell the truth - but no one will let her. Still works. Hilarious.

Sex / Nud / Viol / Lang / AdSit

A: Carole Lombard, Fredric March, Walter Connolly, Charles Winninger

© UNITED AMERICAN VIDEO CORP. 4019

OUR HOSPITALITY

D: Buster Keaton 75 m

NR · COM · 1923 · B&W · Rating: 8

Very highly regarded early comedy. One of Keaton's very best. He stars as a hapless son who returns to the South to claim his family inheritance. He falls in love with a beautiful local girl, only to discover that she is the daughter of a family that has an ancient feud with his. When her brothers find out who he is, they are determined to devise a way to kill their dinner guest without breaking the laws of Southern hospitality. Revered because its clever observations of the human condition are used for the source of much of the comedy, in addition to the hair-raising sight gags.

Sex · Nud · Viol · Lang · AdSit

A: Buster Keaton, Natalie Talmadge, Joe Keaton, Buster Keaton, Kitty Bradbury, Joe Roberts

© HBO VIDEO 0281

PALEFACE, THE

D: Norman McLeod 91 m

NR · COM · WST · 1948 · COLOR · Rating: 8

Amiable spoof of the classic Western THE VIRGINIAN. Cowardly Bob Hope is a charlatan traveling dentist but he has allowed himself to be presented as a celebrated gunslinger. However, he is getting shooting assistance from his sharpshooting new wife, Calamity Jane (Russell). Jane, you see, is also a secret government agent who has seduced Hope so that she can go undercover with him to expose a group selling guns to the Indians. Good script, with lots of wild parodies of Western movie cliches and a hit song: "Buttons and Bows." Probably Hope's best movie performance. Certainly his biggest box office success.

Sex · Nud · Viol · Lang · AdSit

A: Bob Hope, Jane Russell, Robert Armstrong, Iris Adrian, Robert Watson, Iron Eyes Cody

© MCA/UNIVERSAL HOME VIDEO, INC. 80106

PALM BEACH STORY, THE

D: Preston Sturges 88 m

NR · COM · 1942 · B&W · Rating: 8

Madcap screwball comedy. The slightly wacky wife (Colbert) of a poor inventor (McCrea) runs away from her 5-year marriage and heads to Palm Beach for a divorce. On the train, she runs into a nutty but wealthy heiress (Astor) and her bumbling millionaire brother, John D. Hackensacker the Third (Vallee). John D. falls wildly in love with Colbert and pursues her madly. Things get really funny when McCrea arrives to win Colbert back and the ditzy Astor falls for him. Meanwhile, Vallee hires a full orchestra to serenade Colbert. Fast-paced, witty and hilarious.

Sex · Nud · Viol · Lang · AdSit

A: Claudette Colbert, Joel McCrea, Mary Astor, Rudy Vallee, William Demarest

© MCA/UNIVERSAL HOME VIDEO, INC. 80380

PAT AND MIKE

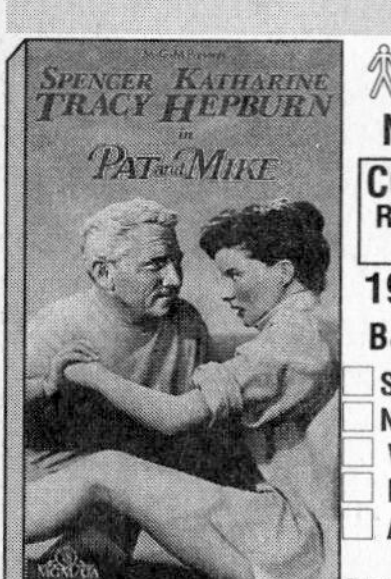

D: George Cukor 96 m

NR · COM · ROM · 1952 · B&W · Rating: 6

Pleasing seventh pairing of Tracy and Hepburn. Hepburn plays Pat, a college gym teacher and a top-notch female athlete, who is convinced by Tracy to turn pro and allow him to become her manager and promoter. Tracy's done a shady deal with an underworld character and it's causing him about as much grief as his blossoming personal relationship with her. And, their relationship also creates a problem for her with her fiance. Oscar-nominated script and great chemistry make it enjoyable, but it is one of their lesser successes.

Sex · Nud · Viol · Lang · AdSit

A: Katharine Hepburn, Spencer Tracy, Jim Backus, Charles Bronson, Chuck Connors

Distributed By MGM/UA Home Video M301269

PHILADELPHIA STORY, THE

D: George Cukor 112 m

NR · COM · ROM · 1940 · B&W · Rating: 9

Scintillating comedy - still one of Hollywood's best. Hepburn is perfect as a spoiled socialite getting married for the second time - this time to a stuffed shirt. Her suave first husband (Grant), who she divorced because he drank, still loves her. He arrives at the wedding early with two gossip reporters, having made a deal to prevent them from publishing a nasty article about her father. Stewart won an Oscar as the reporter who falls in love with her and teaches her what love is. Witty rapid-fire dialogue. Nominated for five Oscars, including Best Picture, winning two - Best Actor (Stewart) and Screenplay.

Sex · Nud · Viol · Lang · AdSit

A: Cary Grant, Katharine Hepburn, James Stewart, Ruth Hussey, John Halliday, Mary Nash

Distributed By MGM/UA Home Video M500059

PICKWICK PAPERS

D: Noel Langley 109 m

NR · COM · DMA · 1952 · B&W · Rating: 8

Touching tale, reasonably faithfully taken from Charles Dickens's first novel, about an actor and his friends who form a club to travel about 1830s England in search of adventure, knowledge and understanding. Through a series of misunderstandings, they become engaged in a comedy of errors that culminates when their leader becomes consigned to a Debtor's prison. Necessarily episodic in nature, it is both funny and heartwarming. Very large and choice cast of veteran actors.

Sex · Nud · Viol · Lang · AdSit

A: James Hayter, James Donald, Hermione Gingold, Kathleen Harrison

© VIDEO COMMUNICATIONS, INC. 1081

PRIDE AND PREJUDICE

D: Robert Z. Leonard 118 m

NR · COM · DMA · 1940 · B&W · Rating: 8

Excellent screen adaptation of Jane Austen's novel written in 1793. It is a bright comedy about a pre-Victorian English family's efforts to get its five unmarried girls all safely married, but each girl has her own peculiarities to make her case special. This clever and witty commentary on manners has lasted for at least 200 years and is still funny today. Excellent cast, gorgeous sets (Oscar) and high production values which capture well the period's flavor and add to the entertainment. First rate stuff.

Sex · Nud · Viol · Lang · AdSit

A: Greer Garson, Laurence Olivier, Edna May Oliver, Edmund Gwenn, Maureen O'Sullivan, Mary Boland

Distributed By MGM/UA Home Video M500114

PRINCESS AND THE PIRATE, THE

D: David Butler 94 m

NR · COM · 1944 · COLOR · Rating: 6

An amiable Bob Hope farce - this time he makes fun of swashbuckler movies. Bob plays a shlock vaudevillian-type actor who claims to be able to impersonate anybody. A beautiful blond princess (Virginia Mayo) has run off to escape a marriage arranged by her father, the king. But, she and Bob are captured together and held by La Roche, patron to a band of villainous pirates led by Victor McLaglen. Walter Brennan (particularly funny) is a wayward and crazy pirate who has stolen a treasure map from McLaglen and then tattooed it on Hope's chest. Very silly but pretty good fun if you are a fan of Hope's never-ending witty one-liners.

Sex · Nud · Viol · Lang · AdSit

A: Bob Hope, Walter Slezak, Walter Brennan, Virginia Mayo, Victor McLaglen

© HBO VIDEO 90666

PROMOTER, THE

D: Ronald Neame 89 m

NR · COM · 1952 · B&W · Rating: 8

Charming, witty and intelligent English comedy of the type that is perfectly suited to Alec Guinness. A penniless young man with a winning personality uses his considerable charms to continually con his way up society's ladder because he is very intent upon getting ahead in the world. That is, until he gets stopped dead in his tracks by the beautiful and equally charming Glynis Johns, who believes in the real him. Consistently entertaining.

Sex · Nud · Viol · Lang · AdSit

A: Alec Guinness, Glynis Johns, Valerie Hobson, Petula Clark, Edward Chapman

© HOME VISION PRO 02

PYGMALION

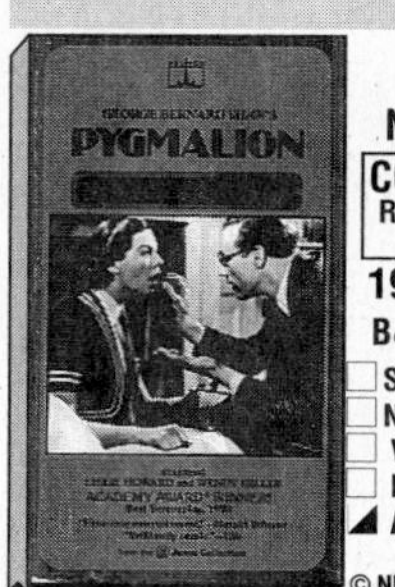

D: Anthony Asquith, Leslie Howard 96 m

NR · COM · ROM · 1938 · B&W · Rating: 9

Wonderful. Before MY FAIR LADY, there was PYGMALION. George Bernard Shaw's winning stageplay was first made into this film before Lerner and Lowe made it into a Broadway musical and later a film. Any product which has that many incarnations must be special, and it is. It is the story about a stuffy English diction professor who makes a bet with a friend that he can transform a common feisty Cockney street peddler to pass as a lady of breeding. He wins his bet, but loses his heart. Clever biting dialogue, great performances.

Sex · Nud · Viol · Lang · AdSit

A: Wendy Hiller, Leslie Howard, Wilfred Lawson, Scott Sunderland, Marle Lohr, David Tree

© NEW LINE HOME VIDEO 6018

QUIET MAN, THE

D: John Ford 153 m

NR · COM · ROM · ACT · 1952 · COLOR · Rating: 10

Masterful tapestry of colorful characters! An Irish-American boxer (Wayne) killed a man in the ring and has traveled to his father's Irish village to recover peace of mind. He meets a beautiful and feisty redhead (O'Hara). He falls in love with her and she with him, but since her cantankerous brother (McLaglen) refuses to give the traditional dowry, she will not consent to be Wayne's wife. Wayne sets out to change McLaglen's mind. Highly entertaining, endearing and funny! Ford won an Oscar for this masterful tribute to Ireland, its traditions and people. Also an Oscar winner for Cinematography.

Sex · Nud · Viol · Lang · AdSit

A: John Wayne, Maureen O'Hara, Barry Fitzgerald, Ward Bond, Victor McLaglen, Mildred Natwick

© REPUBLIC PICTURES HOME VIDEO 3361

RIPTIDE

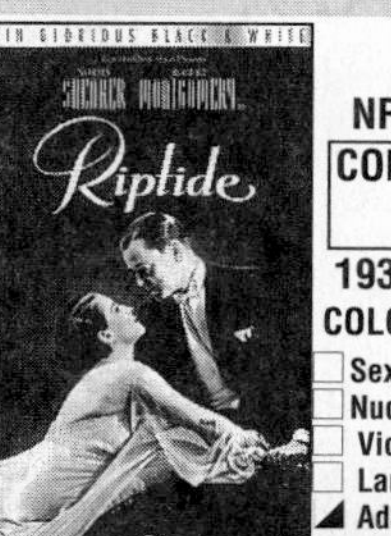

D: Edmund Goulding 90 m

NR · COM · 1934 · COLOR · Rating: 7

Mary (Norma Shearer) is a vivacious Park Avenue socialite who impulsively marries a stodgy English Lord. When her new husband leaves for a trip back to America, she heads off to the French Riviera for some fun, where she runs into her old flame Tommie (Robert Montgomery). Their drunken escapades wind up in the headlines and she has to convince her husband that nothing really happened. The trouble is, Tommie is still chasing her. Quite silly and designed to help Depression audiences feel superior to the frivolous rich, still it is quite entertaining.

Sex · Nud · Viol · Lang · AdSit

A: Norma Shearer, Robert Montgomery, Herbert Marshall, Skeets Gallagher, Ralph Forbes, Lilyan Tashman

Distributed By MGM/UA Home Video M204562

ROOM SERVICE

D: William A. Seiter 78 m

NR COM 1938 B&W

Sex Nud Viol Lang AdSit

6 Old-fashioned comedic farce that was somewhat different movie for the Marx Brothers. It came later on in their careers and had been an existing Broadway play that was then specially adapted for their brand of humor. Groucho is desperately trying to produce a play, but he and the brothers are starving and having a hard time keeping ahead of their creditors. So, Groucho comes up with the brilliant plan to fake the measles to keep the hotel manager from throwing him out of his room. A little more restrained than the traditional Marx slapstick. Although funny, it is one of their lesser movies.

A: Lucille Ball, Groucho Marx, Chico Marx, Harpo Marx, Ann Miller, Frank Albertson

© TURNER HOME ENTERTAINMENT 2088

RUGGLES OF RED GAP

D: Leo McCarey 90 m

NR COM WST 1935 B&W

Sex Nud Viol Lang AdSit

9 A shining gem and a comedy classic! During a poker game in Paris, the Earl of Burnstead (Young) loses his butler Ruggles (Laughton) to a wealthy but uncouth American couple (Ruggles and Boland). The ill-bred pair take their new butler home to Red Gap, Washington, where he becomes both inspired and awed by the wild west and loses all his British airs. He has a wonderful time as he romances the ladies, breaks his old bonds of servitude, discovers his new self and his new place on earth. A charming, disarming and amusing good time. Excellent. Also filmed again later as FANCY PANTS with Bob Hope.

A: Charles Laughton, Mary Boland, Charlie Ruggles, ZaSu Pitts, Roland Young, Leila Hyams

© MCA/UNIVERSAL HOME VIDEO, INC. 80670

SECRET LIFE OF WALTER MITTY, THE

D: Norman McLeod 110 m

NR COM 1947 COLOR

Sex Nud Viol Lang AdSit

7 An enjoyable romp through Everyman Walter Mitty's vivid imagination. Loosely taken from James Thurber's classic short story and features master-comedian Danny Kaye. Walter Mitty is a timid little man who is hen-pecked by both his mother and his fiancee. This milquetoast lives a very boring, everyday kind of existence, but he escapes into his very vivid and consuming daydreams where he is always the glory-drenched hero. Then one day, a beautiful woman really does need his help against a gang of jewel thieves, and the timid little man does become a hero, albeit a reluctant one, and gets the girl too boot.

A: Danny Kaye, Virginia Mayo, Boris Karloff, Fay Bainter, Reginald Denny, Ann Rutherford

© HBO VIDEO 90654

SEVEN LITTLE FOYS, THE

D: Melville Shavelson 95 m

NR COM MUS 1955 COLOR

Sex Nud Viol Lang AdSit

7 Fun-filled and enjoyable musical biography of Eddie Foy, the famous vaudeville song-and-dance entertainer. Bob Hope is less zany than usual as Eddie Foy, the wayward and absentee father of a family of seven kids. All that has to change, however, when his wife dies and he has to decide what to do about taking care of his family and still earn a living. He decides to take all the kids on the road with him, forming the famous vaudeville act "Eddie Foy and the Seven Little Foys." Numerous song and dance numbers and a short appearance by James Cagney as George M. Cohen.

A: Bob Hope, Milly Vitale, Billy Gray, George Tobias, James Cagney

© COLUMBIA TRISTAR HOME VIDEO 60787

SEVEN YEAR ITCH, THE

D: Billy Wilder 105 m

NR COM 1955 COLOR

Sex Nud Viol Lang AdSit

8 Playful comedy which produced Marilyn's most famous pose: air blowing her skirt up. Tom Ewell plays a long-married executive who has just sent his wife off to the cool of Maine for the summer and is left alone in his hot NY apartment. A flowerpot crashing down from overhead serves as an introduction to Marilyn, his luscious new upstairs neighbor - who keeps cool by keeping her underwear in the freezer. Even a happily married man for seven years can give over to flights of fantasy under such pressures. Lots of double entendres. Fun and only a little dated.

A: Marilyn Monroe, Tom Ewell, Sonny Tufts, Evelyn Keyes, Robert Strauss, Oscar Homolka

© FOXVIDEO 1043

SHE DONE HIM WRONG

D: Lowell Sherman 65 m

NR COM 1933 B&W

Sex Nud Viol Lang AdSit

8 Prepare to be taken back to the "Gay '90s." In this lusty adaptation of her risque play "Diamond Lil," Mae West again plays the role she was famous for and invites the dashing Cary Grant to "Come up and see me sometime." In one of West's best roles, she is the bar manager who frolics with notorious men, but when Grant walks in the door, the rest is history. Full of one liners and sexy rebuttals. While West never goes too far, she manages to say things that were surprising for most women at that time, and would still be unacceptable for many women today. A huge heap of fun!

A: Mae West, Cary Grant, Owen Moore, Noah Beery, Gilbert Roland, Rochelle Hudson

© MCA/UNIVERSAL HOME VIDEO, INC. 80597

SHOP AROUND THE CORNER, THE

D: Ernst Lubitsch 100 m

NR COM ROM 1940 B&W

Sex Nud Viol Lang AdSit

8 Simply charming and delightfully memorable. Two sales clerks (Stewart and Sullavan) work together in a gift shop but they can't stand each other. However, they have absolutely no idea that they are also each other's secret pen pals. On paper, they are the best of friends and have been writing affectionate letters to each other for some time. Then things get bad for Stewart when the owner of the store fires him because he mistakenly believes Stewart is carrying on an affair with his wife. Lonely, Stewart seeks out his pen pal for solace, only to find out who she really is. Wonderful.

A: James Stewart, Margaret Sullavan, Frank Morgan, Sara Haden, Joseph Schildkraut, Felix Bressart

Distributed By MGM/UA Home Video M301164

SON OF PALEFACE

D: Frank Tashlin 95 m

NR COM WST 1952 COLOR

Sex Nud Viol Lang AdSit

6 Popular sequel to Bob Hope's best film - THE PALEFACE from 1948. Bob plays a bumbling Harvard graduate who goes west to claim his inheritance, the gold that his Indian-fighter father hid. There to help him is Jane Russell and cowboy legend Roy Rogers. Wild and wacky satire of the Western genre. Hope's sequence where he is in bed with Roy's horse Trigger is recognized as a classic.

A: Bob Hope, Jane Russell, Roy Rogers, Iron Eyes Cody, Douglas Dumbrille, Bill Williams

© COLUMBIA TRISTAR HOME VIDEO 60742

SONS OF THE DESERT

D: William A. Seiter 73 m

NR COM 1933 B&W

Sex Nud Viol Lang AdSit

9 Many consider this wacky film to be Laurel and Hardy's best. The kooky pair want to attend a convention for the fraternal order Sons of the Desert in Chicago, but they know their wives won't let them go if they ask. Instead, they tell their wives that Hardy needs to travel to Hawaii in order to cure his cold, and Laurel must go with him. But when the ship sinks on the way back from the Islands, the boys must figure out a way to explain to their wives why they made it back with nary a scratch and one day ahead of the other survivors. Impeccable comedy.

A: Stan Laurel, Oliver Hardy, Mae Busch, Charley Chase, Mae Busch, Dorothy Christy

© VIDEO TREASURES SV9306

STEAMBOAT BILL JR.

D: Charles F. Reisner 104 m

COM 1928 B&W

Sex Nud Viol Lang AdSit

8 Sparkling silent film. Steamboat Bill (Torrence) is the tough captain of a Mississippi riverboat and is counting on his son (Keaton) to take over the business and keep it out of the red. Unfortunately, Bill Jr. isn't exactly what Dad hoped for. He is a college boy, complete with his ukulele and blazer. He's also a bit accident prone and, what's worse, he is also in love with his father's arch rival. Some excellent sight gags add to the fun, including one of the most dangerous stunts ever filmed. A very impressive silent.

A: Buster Keaton, Ernest Torrence, Tom McGuire, Marion Byron, Tom Lewis

© VIDEO YESTERYEAR 573

SULLIVAN'S TRAVELS

D: Preston Sturges 91 m

NR COM 1941 B&W

Sex Nud Viol Lang AdSit

10 Classic early spoof on Hollywood that's ripe with laughter! Movie director McCrea has done plenty of inconsequential films and decides to do something worthwhile for a change. So, he disguises himself as a bum and sets off across the country with only 10 cents in his pocket on a search to get some new material. Along the way, he picks up a has-been actress (Lake) and the pair travel America, experiencing a whole new realm of danger and human suffering. McCrea's lesson learned is that all you really need when you are down-and-out is laughter. A film with unmatched brilliance and wit. Excellent.

A: Joel McCrea, Veronica Lake, Robert Warwick, William Demarest, Eric Blore, Robert Greig

© MCA/UNIVERSAL HOME VIDEO, INC. 80551

TALK OF THE TOWN, THE

D: George Stevens 118 m

NR COM 1942 B&W

Sex Nud Viol Lang AdSit

7 Wild screwball comedy in which Cary Grant plays an avowed anarchist who is standing trial after being framed both for murder and the arson of a burned-down factory. However, he escapes from jail and poses as a gardner at the country home of school teacher Jean Arthur, which she is readying for rental to a stuffy Supreme Court nominee (Colman). Grant engages Colman in a series of witty debates, trying to convince him of the need for humanity in the law - while at the same time he is trying to win over Jean Arthur's heart. 6 Oscar nominations, including Best Picture.

A: Cary Grant, Jean Arthur, Ronald Colman, Edgar Buchanan, Charles Dingle, Glenda Farrell

© COLUMBIA TRISTAR HOME VIDEO 60780

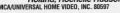

TENDER TRAP, THE

D: Charles Walters 111 m

NR | COM ROM | 1955 | COLOR | Sex | Nud | Viol | Lang | AdSit

8 Charlie Reader has it made. He is a wealthy and successful New York theatrical agent, and he is a carefree bachelor with a big bevy of beautiful babes at his beck and call. Then he he has the misfortune to meet pretty charmer Debbie Reynolds. While he spends the rest of the movie doing his best to avoid it, in the inevitable end he falls head over heels into her tender trap. One of the best romantic comedies of the '50s. Filled with snappy dialogue and stocked with an excellent support cast. It was adapted from a long-running hit Broadway play.

A: Frank Sinatra, Debbie Reynolds, Celeste Holm, David Wayne, Carolyn Jones, Lola Albright

Distributed By MGM/UA Home Video 202547

THAT UNCERTAIN FEELING

D: Ernst Lubitsch 83 m

NR | COM | 1941 | B&W | Sex | Nud | Viol | Lang | AdSit

6 This is one of famed director Ernst Lubitsch's lesser efforts, but still a must-see for serious film fans and lovers of witty banter. Douglas and Oberon are happily married - or are they? They have settled into a boring routine, but Mrs. has developed a recurring hiccup which appears to be based upon her need for now-absent romance. In her visits to her shrink, she meets a wonderfully absurd and cynical piano-playing wit (Meridith) who she takes a fancy to. Roused now into action by the new competition, Douglas strives to win back his wife. Meredith steals the show.

A: Merle Oberon, Melvyn Douglas, Burgess Meredith, Alan Mowbray, Olive Blakeney, Eve Arden

© VIDEO YESTERYEAR 207

THREE STOOGES, THE (VOLUMES 1-10)

D: m

NR | COM | B&W | Sex | Nud | Viol | Lang | AdSit

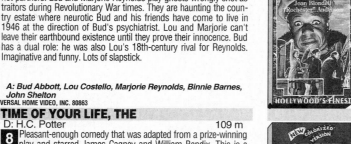

9 The Three Stooges's fast-paced slapstick shorts have been compiled into a ten-cassette collection. Each of the ten cassettes is about a hour long and has three "shorts" taken from among the 190 two-reelers done by the Stooges between 1934-1959. All of them feature Curly. This is the period when the team was in top form. If you are a fan, you're going to love them. If not, you're not reading this.

A: Moe Howard, Curly Howard, Larry Fine

© COLUMBIA TRISTAR HOME VIDEO 60234

TIME OF THEIR LIVES

D: Charles Barton 82 m

NR | COM | 1946 | B&W | Sex | Nud | Viol | Lang | AdSit

8 Considered by many to be the best-ever effort of Abbott and Costello. Oddly enough, this is also the only film where they are not partners. Lou and Marjorie Reynolds play ghosts wrongly shot as traitors during Revolutionary War times. They are haunting the country estate where neurotic Bud and his friends have come to live in 1946 at the direction of Bud's psychiatrist. Lou and Marjorie can't leave their earthbound existence until they prove their innocence. Bud has a dual role: he was also Lou's 18th-century rival for Reynolds. Imaginative and funny. Lots of slapstick.

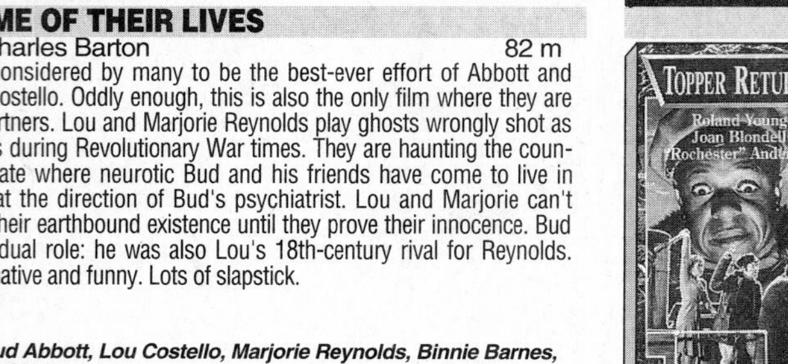

A: Bud Abbott, Lou Costello, Marjorie Reynolds, Binnie Barnes, John Shelton

© MCA/UNIVERSAL HOME VIDEO, INC. 80863

TIME OF YOUR LIFE, THE

D: H.C. Potter 109 m

NR | COM | 1948 | B&W | Sex | Nud | Viol | Lang | AdSit

8 Pleasant-enough comedy that was adapted from a prize-winning play and starred James Cagney and William Bendix. This is a story about a day in the lives of the people who frequent an ordinary waterfront bar called Nick's Saloon, Restaurant and Entertainment Palace. Bendix is Nick, the bartender and Cagney is his chief patron and the uncrowned king of the bar. He has all the money he needs and so sits at his table just meeting people, listening to old music, drinking champagne and influencing the lives of virtually everyone around him. Warm comedy that was reportedly a labor of love by Cagney.

A: James Cagney, William Bendix, Broderick Crawford, Ward Bond

© GOODTIMES 5081

TO BE OR NOT TO BE

D: Ernst Lubitsch 99 m

NR | COM | 1942 | B&W | Sex | Nud | Viol | Lang | AdSit

9 Highly acclaimed and very funny black comedy farce. It was also a major piece of Hollywood propaganda, released at the outset of WWII and designed to reveal the true nature of the Nazis to the world. Jack Benny is a scream as the hammy leader of a group of Polish actors who is trying to outwit the Nazis as they invade and destroy Warsaw. Benny and his flirtatious wife (Lombard, in her last role) use their stage talents to help a Polish flyer (Stack) prevent a spy from delivering names of the underground to the Gestapo. Many think this was Benny's best screen performance.

A: Jack Benny, Carole Lombard, Robert Stack, Lionel Atwill

© WARNER HOME VIDEO 35075

TOM, DICK AND HARRY

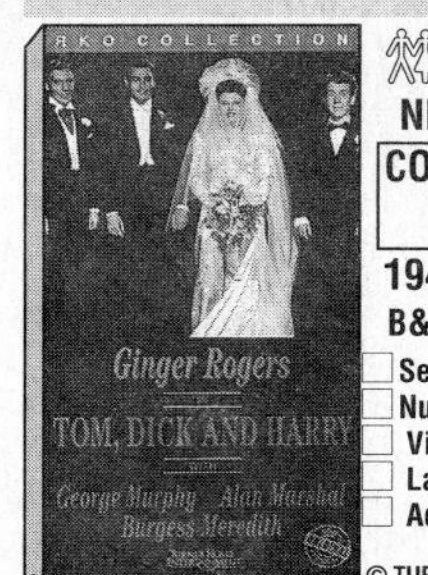

D: Garson Kanin 87 m

NR | COM | 1941 | B&W | Sex | Nud | Viol | Lang | AdSit

7 Ginger Rogers sparkles in this enthusiastic and delightful comedy about a telephone operator who is being pursued in her fantasies by three eager and anxious men at the same time, even though none of them is her ideal man. Spirited performances by everyone, but Phil Silvers outshines everyone in a small role as a pushy ice cream salesman. Very good. Witty dialogue.

A: Ginger Rogers, George Murphy, Burgess Meredith, Alan Marshal, Joe Cunningham, Phil Silvers

© TURNER HOME ENTERTAINMENT 6188

TOO HOT TO HANDLE

D: Jack Conway 108 m

NR | COM | 1938 | B&W | Sex | Nud | Viol | Lang | AdSit

7 Entertaining screwball comedy in which two rival newsreel photographers also compete for the affections of pretty flyer Myrna Loy. When she goes to Brazil to find her lost brother, both of them follow her, still intent upon winning her over, but also upon getting the story first. Fast-paced with witty dialogue and some pretty good action sequences, too.

A: Clark Gable, Myrna Loy, Walter Pidgeon, Leo Carrillo

Distributed By MGM/UA Home Video M202085

TOPPER

D: Norman McLeod 97 m

NR | COM FAN | 1937 | B&W | Sex | Nud | Viol | Lang | AdSit

8 Delightful comedy. (If you are more tolerant of its somewhat dated aspect, you can even add one more number to its rating). Cary Grant and Constance Bennett are two high-living fun-loving party rats who have the definite misfortune of getting killed in a car wreck. Roland Young is a stuffy and milquetoastish banker who has never enjoyed many of life's more daring pleasures. These two brand new ghosts take it upon themselves to show him what he has been missing. Spawned two sequels and a TV series in the 50s.

A: Cary Grant, Roland Young, Constance Bennett, Billie Burke, Eugene Pallette, Arthur Lake

© VIDEO TREASURES HR9608

TOPPER RETURNS

D: Roy Del Ruth 88 m

NR | COM FAN | 1940 | B&W | Sex | Nud | Viol | Lang | AdSit

8 Topper gets visited by a new ghost in this third entry to the series. Cary Grant and Constance Bennett have finally made it to heaven. Joan Blondell has been murdered by a mysterious man in black and she searches out mild-mannered Topper to get his help to nail her murderer. Lots of slapstick, including some pretty good special effects sequences inside a haunted house with Topper and Eddie "Rochester" Anderson. Some think this is the best in the series.

A: Roland Young, Joan Blondell, Carole Landis, Eddie Anderson, Billie Burke, Dennis O'Keefe

© UNITED AMERICAN VIDEO CORP. 1018

TOPPER TAKES A TRIP

D: Norman McLeod 80 m

NR | COM FAN | 1939 | COLOR | Sex | Nud | Viol | Lang | AdSit

7 First sequel to the very popular original TOPPER. Topper and his wife are in France. His wife thinks that he is being unfaithful after she sees him with Constance Bennett. Miss Bennett, you will recall from the original, is a ghost. Cary Grant does not appear in this picture (except in a flashback). This time around Bennett has a new companion - a cute dog. Needing to do a good deed in order to make it into heaven, Bennett follows Topper and his divorce-minded wife to Paris to set things right. Cute fantasy.

A: Constance Bennett, Roland Young, Billie Burke, Alan Mowbray, Verree Teasdale, Franklin Pangborn

© VIDEO TREASURES HR9612

TROUBLE WITH HARRY, THE

D: Alfred Hitchcock 100 m

PG | COM MYS | 1955 | COLOR | Sex | Nud | Viol | Lang | AdSit

7 Uproarious Hitchcock! A very black farce with a morbid theme: Harry's dead, but he won't stay in the ground. While out hunting one fine Vermont day, Edmund Gwenn stumbles across Harry's dead body. Thinking that he killed Harry, he buries him. The trouble is: Harry won't stay buried. Everybody else in town thinks that it was they who killed Harry and it is that which is causing all the problems. Offbeat and often hilarious, this is not typical Hitchcock fare - but it definitely has his touch. This was also MacLaine's screen debut.

A: John Forsythe, Shirley MacLaine, Edmund Gwenn, Jerry Mathers, Mildred Natwick, Mildred Dunnock

© MCA/UNIVERSAL HOME VIDEO, INC. 80130

TUTTLES OF TAHITI, THE

D: Charles Vidor — 91 m

NR | COM | 1942 | B&W

7 Light-hearted comedy about a clan of fun-loving but lazy fishermen in beautiful Tahiti. They are always on the verge of making a fortune, but are instead always broke and are led by Charles Laughton, who would rather play and gamble than do any kind of hard labor. The Tuttles have an ongoing rivalry with the Taio clan, but Laughton and Bates (who leads the Taios) become even stiffer rivals when his son and her daughter fall in love. Pretty simple, but fun and good-natured entertainment.

Sex Nud Viol Lang AdSit

A: Charles Laughton, Jon Hall, Peggy Drake, Florence Bates, Alma Ross, Victor Francen

© TURNER HOME ENTERTAINMENT 6248

TWENTIETH CENTURY

D: Howard Hawks — 91 m

NR | COM | 1934 | COLOR

9 Regarded by many critics as the very first screwball comedy. Barrymore plays a very successful but egotistical Broadway producer who turns a sexy salesclerk into a big sensation. She however gets fed up with his antics and becomes so taken with her own success that she decides to head west to star in films. His fortunes immediately begin to fade, so he joins her on the train ride west and launches into several schemes both to try to win back her love and to get her to re-sign with him. However, she is now just as vain as he is. Brilliant script bristles with inspired insults and zaniness.

Sex Nud Viol Lang AdSit

A: John Barrymore, Carole Lombard, Walter Connolly, Roscoe Karns, Etienne Girardot, Ralph Forbes

© COLUMBIA TRISTAR HOME VIDEO 60945

UNFAITHFULLY YOURS

D: Preston Sturges — 105 m

NR | COM | 1948 | B&W

8 Very funny screwball comedy with flair! A symphony conductor (Harrison) suspects that his beautiful wife (Darnell) is messing around with his personal assistant (Kreuger). One night, as he is conducting a concert that features three main pieces, he fantasizes about three different scenarios (each matching the mood of its respective musical piece) that would take care of his little problem. One even includes murder. A bumbling,but absolutely hilarious comic ride through one man's daydreams as he attempts revenge.

Sex Nud Viol Lang AdSit

A: Rex Harrison, Linda Darnell, Kurt Kreuger, Barbara Lawrence, Rudy Vallee, Lionel Stander

© FOXVIDEO 1249

WAY OUT WEST

D: James W. Horne — 66 m

G | COM WST | 1937 | B&W

9 Certainly one of Laurel and Hardy's best, many say it is their best, comedy. When one of their friends dies and wants to leave his gold mine to his daughter, the duo head west to Brushwood Gulch to deliver to the girl her father's map to the mine. However along the way, a bartender learns of their mission and steers them to his floozy girlfriend instead of the real Mary Roberts. When the boys learn of the ruse, they have to get the map back to the girl for whom it was intended. Lots of good gags and even a soft shoe routine.

Sex Nud Viol Lang AdSit

A: Stan Laurel, Oliver Hardy, James Finlayson, Sharon Lynn

© VIDEO TREASURES HR9610

WE'RE NO ANGELS

D: Michael Curtiz — 103 m

NR | COM | 1955 | COLOR

6 Slightly offbeat comedy in which three escapees from Devil's Island (Bogart, Ray and Ustinov) descend upon the house/store of an island family with the intent to rob them to get enough money to get back to France. Instead, they are so taken with the plight of the kindly but inept storekeeper (Carroll) and his wife that they stay to help him out of his problems with a nasty relative (Rathbone). Amusing and fun, even though a little too talky. Remade in 1989 with little success, in spite of some big name stars.

Sex Nud Viol Lang AdSit

A: Humphrey Bogart, Aldo Ray, Joan Bennett, Peter Ustinov, Basil Rathbone, Leo G. Carroll

© PARAMOUNT HOME VIDEO 5414

WHO DONE IT?

D: Erle C. Kenton — 77 m

NR | COM | 1942 | B&W

8 Abbott and Costello are two would-be radio show writers but are now just soda jerks in the same building where radio plays are broadcast. However, when the network's president is murdered during one of the shows, they pretend to be police detectives... and everyone believes them, even the killer. Silliness, as always, reigns with these two, so don't expect sophisticated humor. One of their best.

Sex Nud Viol Lang AdSit

A: Bud Abbott, Lou Costello, Patric Knowles, William Bendix, Louise Allbritton, Mary Wickes

© MCA/UNIVERSAL HOME VIDEO, INC. 80862

WITHOUT LOVE

D: Harold S. Bucquet — 113 m

NR | COM ROM | 1945 | B&W

6 Mildly amusing story set in wartime Washington, D.C. A sleep-walking inventor (Tracy) and a pretty widow (Hepburn) with a very big house enter into an agreement. They are both disillusioned with love, but he needs a place to conduct his secret war experiments and her basement is perfect. So, they agree to enter into a marriage of convenience. How long can that last? Tracy and Hepburn have great screen chemistry, and Keenan Wynn and Lucille Ball provide good support and a lot of wise-cracks, all of which raises this otherwise mild script to being enjoyable entertainment.

Sex Nud Viol Lang AdSit

A: Spencer Tracy, Katharine Hepburn, Lucille Ball, Keenan Wynn, Carl Esmond, Patricia Morison

Distributed By MGM/UA Home Video M202350

WITHOUT RESERVATIONS

D: Mervyn LeRoy — 101 m

NR | COM ROM | 1946 | B&W

6 Amusing wartime comedy that is peppered with surprise guests. Claudette Colbert is a writer on her way west, aboard a cross-country train, to supervise the film version of her latest book. John Wayne and his buddy Don DeFore are Marine fliers aboard the same train. They have no idea who she is and proceed to verbally tear her book apart. Still, she thinks Wayne would be perfect to play the hero in the film version of the book. Light-hearted enjoyable fluff with Wayne in an unusual role.

Sex Nud Viol Lang AdSit

A: John Wayne, Claudette Colbert, Don Defore, Anne Triola, Phil Brown, Thurston Hall

© TURNER HOME ENTERTAINMENT 6192

WOMAN OF THE YEAR

D: George Stevens — 114 m

NR | COM ROM | 1942 | B&W

9 This was the first-ever teaming of Tracy and Hepburn and one of their best. She is a sophisticated political commentator who meets up with Tracy, an every-man kind of sports reporter. Sparks fly and they get married, only to discover that they have very little in common. She is on a fast track with no time for the simple things he enjoys, like baseball (famous and hysterical scene where he trys to explain the game to her) and a cup of coffee (which she doesn't know how to make). Her role was a bold one for its time but still is likely to upset modern feminists. A delightful good time.

Sex Nud Viol Lang AdSit

A: Katharine Hepburn, Spencer Tracy, Fay Bainter, Reginald Owen, William Bendix

Distributed By MGM/UA Home Video M600093

WOMEN, THE

D: George Cukor — 133 m

NR | COM | 1939 | B&W

9 Classic all-woman cast in a riotous comedy from women about men and women - and what comes of the meeting of the two. The story line itself is almost inconsequential. What is wonderful is the crisp and delicious dialogue from the strong-minded women characters. The story begins with the affair one woman's (Shearer) husband is having with an amoral sales clerk (Crawford). That provides the premise and the excuse necessary for the cast of women to bare their fangs and launch into a bitch-fest. Consistently funny, hilarious at times. Remade as a musical in 1956 as THE OPPOSITE SEX.

Sex Nud Viol Lang AdSit

A: Norma Shearer, Joan Crawford, Rosalind Russell, Joan Fontaine, Paulette Goddard, Mary Boland

Distributed By MGM/UA Home Video M400506

WONDER MAN

D: H. Bruce Humberstone — 98 m

NR | COM MUS | 1945 | COLOR

6 Silly and entertaining vehicle for Danny Kaye's special comedic talents. He plays two physically identical twins, but the personality of each is entirely different. One is an outgoing song and dance man and the other is very serious and quiet. When the song and dance man is killed by gangsters, his spirit comes back to encourage the mousy twin to impersonate him, hoping to convince the hoods that they didn't succeed and so provide a means to trap them. Funny. Won an Oscar for Special Effects.

Sex Nud Viol Lang AdSit

A: Danny Kaye, Virginia Mayo, Vera-Ellen, Donald Woods

© HBO VIDEO 90663

YOU CAN'T CHEAT AN HONEST MAN

D: George Marshall — 79 m

NR | COM | 1939 | B&W

8 W.C. Fields wrote this frantic comedy about a struggling circus owner who has a constantly running battle with his featured act, ventriloquist Edgar Bergen and his alter egos, the wooden dummies Mortimer Snerd and Charlie McCarthy. Bergan is in love with Fields's daughter, but she is determined to marry a rich guy just to help her out her Dad. Lots of snappy dialogue and one-liners. Fields admitted that it was mostly several vaudeville skits put together. Regardless, Fields, Bergen and the smart-aleck puppets are hysterical.

Sex Nud Viol Lang AdSit

A: W.C. Fields, Edgar Bergen, Constance Moore, James Bush, Mary Forbes, Eddie Anderson

© BARR ENTERTAINMENT VIDEO 11007

YOU CAN'T TAKE IT WITH YOU

D: Frank Capra 126 m

NR | COM ROM | 1938 | B&W

9 Director Frank Capra won Oscars for Best Picture and Best Director with this "Capra-corn" screwball comedy. Jean Arthur is the beautiful and reasonably sane daughter in a family of poor but happy eccentrics, and also Jimmy Stewart's secretary. Stewart is the down-to-earth son of a family of rich stuffed shirts, and he wants to marry her. These oil-and-water families are to meet for dinner before the wedding, but when they mistakenly arrive one night early, things get out of hand and everyone winds up in jail. Nominated for a total of seven Oscars.

Sex / Nud / Viol / Lang / AdSit

A: Jean Arthur, James Stewart, Lionel Barrymore, Edward Arnold, Eddie Anderson, Ann Miller

© COLUMBIA TRISTAR HOME VIDEO 90153

BIG STEAL, THE

D: Don Siegel 71 m

NR | CRM SUS | 1949 | B&W

7 Potent thriller. A gang of thieves steals a $300,000 Army payroll. Patrick Knowles has it and he's on the run, but he's not alone. He is being chased through the American Southwest and Old Mexico by Robert Mitchum. Jane Greer throws in with Mitchum because Knowles has $2000 that belongs to her. William Bendix is an Army officer following both Mitchum and Knowles, and Police Lieutenant Ramon Navarro is after them all. Lots of plot twists make this one a lot of fun to watch.

Sex / Nud / ◢ Viol / Lang / AdSit

A: Robert Mitchum, Jane Greer, William Bendix, Patric Knowles, Ramon Novarro

© TURNER HOME ENTERTAINMENT 6135

YOUNG IN HEART, THE

D: Richard Wallace 91 m

NR | COM | 1938 | COLOR

8 Heartwarming charmer. A family of oddball con artists, card sharps and opportunists is kicked out of Monte Carlo for cheating at cards, but they happen upon a train wreck and have the good fortune to save a rich old lady from the wreckage. Miss Fortune, the little old lady, gratefully invites the penniless and homeless group to stay with her. Ecstatic with their new meal ticket, their dreams of new-found wealth are soon changed when Miss Fortune proves instead to be such a charmer that the family learns a new set of values for living. Delightful little winner.

Sex / Nud / Viol / Lang / AdSit

A: Janet Gaynor, Douglas Fairbanks, Jr., Paulette Goddard, Roland Young, Billie Burke, Richard Carlson

© VIDEO TREASURES SV9622

CRISS CROSS

D: Robert Siodmak 98 m

NR | CRM ACT | 1948 | B&W

6 Gritty film noir. Burt Lancaster plays an armored-car driver who is still enamored with his ex-wife (De Carlo). That becomes a serious problem for him when her new husband, a notorious hood (Duryea), catches them together. Caught in a precarious position, the basically honest Lancaster convinces Duryea that he was only discussing a plot with her to rob his truck. Duryea likes the idea. Lancaster only wants to run away with De Carlo but life has become very complicated and double-crosses abound. This movie marked the film debut of Tony Curtis.

Sex / Nud / ◢ Viol / Lang / ◢ AdSit

A: Burt Lancaster, Yvonne De Carlo, Dan Duryea, Stephen McNally, Richard Song, Tony Curtis

© MCA/UNIVERSAL HOME VIDEO, INC. 80678

CROSSFIRE

D: Edward Dmytryk 86 m

NR | CRM DMA | 1947 | B&W

8 An intelligent and engrossing Best Picture nominee and a big box office hit. WWII veteran soldier Robert Ryan and his buddies are mustering out of the service. They celebrate at a nightclub where they meet a Jew and his girlfriend and everyone goes back to the man's apartment where, in a fit of anti-Semitic rage, Ryan beats the Jew to death. A civilian cop (Young) and a military cop (Mitchum) team to investigate the murder. Ryan is able to fool everyone for a while, but the cops set a trap for him. The first major film to explore bigotry. Total of 5 Oscar nominations. Outstanding.

Sex / Nud / Viol / Lang / AdSit

A: Robert Young, Robert Mitchum, Robert Ryan, Gloria Grahame, Paul Kelly, Richard Benedict

© TURNER HOME ENTERTAINMENT 6246

ANGELS WITH DIRTY FACES

D: Michael Curtiz 97 m

NR | CRM DMA | 1938 | B&W

8 Enjoyable and still meaningful, even if it is overly melodramatic. Two childhood friends grow up on the wrong side of the tracks. One (O'Brien) becomes a priest. The other (Cagney) is a prominent neighborhood hood, a hero to the tough neighborhood kids and a counterweight to everything O'Brien trys to do. However, after Cagney gets caught after a shootout with a local hood (Bogart) and is sentenced to die in the gas chamber, Father O'Brien convinces him to do the kids a favor by dying like a coward and depriving the boys of a hero. Great characterizations, particularly Cagney.

Sex / Nud / Viol / Lang / AdSit

A: James Cagney, Pat O'Brien, Humphrey Bogart, Ann Sheridan, George Bancroft, Bobby Jordan

Distributed By MGM/UA Home Video M201619

DEAD END

D: William Wyler 92 m

NR | CRM DMA | 1937 | B&W

8 Grim story of life in the New York tenement slums during the Great Depression. 3 Oscar nominations, including Best Picture. The plot has several different character's stories interwoven to paint the total picture. Bogart plays a gangster on the run who returns to his old neighborhood to see his mother. Joel McCrea is an architect who dreams of rebuilding the depressed waterfront area. Sylvia Sidney is a working girl whose brother turns to crime. The combined result is a naked look at a grinding poverty that breeds crime and no one does anything about it. Still effective today.

Sex / Nud / Viol / Lang / ■ AdSit

A: Humphrey Bogart, Sylvia Sidney, Joel McCrea, Claire Trevor, Marjorie Mian, Ward Bond

© HBO VIDEO 90752

ASPHALT JUNGLE, THE

D: John Huston 112 m

NR | CRM SUS | 1950 | B&W

10 One of the greatest crime films ever and it was the inspiration for numerous others which followed. It is the taut, realistic account of the planning and execution of a jewel robbery that goes bad. The suspense steadily builds throughout the entire picture because of an interesting twist in the way the story is told. Early on, we are told what the outcome will be and for the rest of the picture we're waiting anxiously for it to happen. This film received four Oscar nominations and is also credited with being the film which gave Marilyn Monroe the exposure she needed to become a major star, but the entire cast was inspired.

Sex / Nud / Viol / Lang / ◢ AdSit

A: Sterling Hayden, Sam Jaffe, Louis Calhern, Jean Hagen, James Whitmore, Marilyn Monroe

Distributed By MGM/UA Home Video M700483

DETOUR

D: Edgar G. Ulmer 69 m

NR | CRM SUS | 1946 | B&W

8 Very bleak and innovative film that was shot in only six days. It was largely ignored upon its release but now is a major cult favorite and is one of the first of a newly recognized genre of film known as film noir (black film). An East Coast musician is hitchhiking his way west. When the driver of one of his rides dies in Arizona, he dumps the body, takes the wallet and drives on. But his life falls apart when he picks up sexy hitchhiker Ann Savage, who learns what has happened and threatens to turn him in as a murderer unless he takes her to L.A., sells the car and gives her the money. When he does, she forces him into still another swindle. There is no way out.

Sex / Nud / Viol / Lang / ◢ AdSit

A: Tom Neal, Ann Savage, Claudia Drake, Edmund MacDonald, Tim Ryan

© VIDEO YESTERYEAR 949

BIG HEAT, THE

D: Fritz Lang 89 m

NR | CRM SUS ACT | 1953 | B&W

9 Classic crime thriller. Glenn Ford is an honest cop who is investigating the supposed suicide of a corrupt cop. He is ordered to stop but he doesn't. Then his wife is killed with a bomb that was meant for him. Now, he is relentless in his search and uncovers a tie to an underworld kingpin (Scourby) and his ruthless henchman (Marvin). When Marvin's girl makes a play for Ford, furious Marvin throws a cup of scalding coffee in her face. That was a mistake because now she is motivated to help Glenn. Excellent, high intensity police drama with excellent performances, especially by Marvin as a sadistic killer.

Sex / Nud / ◢ Viol / Lang / ◢ AdSit

A: Glenn Ford, Gloria Grahame, Jacelyn Brando, Lee Marvin, Carolyn Jones, Jeanette Nolan

© COLUMBIA TRISTAR HOME VIDEO 60133

DRAGNET

D: Jack Webb 88 m

NR | CRM MYS | 1951 | COLOR

7 A piece of 1950s Americana. This is a feature length spin-off of the popular TV series from the early '50s. In it, Sgt. Friday and officer Smith solve a mobster's murder, beginning with only four shell casings and a footprint. This case, as was all cases in the series, was based upon a real case. The prime focus of the series always was the solving of the crime, not upon the characters. It was this no-nonsense approach to crime solving that made the TV series so popular. Today their style would likely be viewed much less favorably. Still quite interesting and nostalgic.

Sex / Nud / Viol / Lang / ◢ AdSit

A: Barton Yarborough, Jack Webb

© MCA/UNIVERSAL HOME VIDEO, INC. 45030

FOLLOW ME QUIETLY

D: Richard Fleischer 59 m

NR CRM 1949 B&W

Sex Nud Viol Lang AdSit

7 Well made, hard-hitting and solid little film about a police detective and a newswoman who join forces to hunt down a self-righteous rainy-day psychopathic strangler called The Judge who always manages to stay one step in front of the cops. Ludigan devises a plan to trap the murderer by using small scraps of information that he has collected along the way. Exciting and substantial film noir melodrama.

A: William Lundigan, Dorothy Patrick, Jeff Corey, Nestor Paiva, Charles D. Brown, Paul Guilfoyle

© TURNER HOME ENTERTAINMENT 6104

GANGSTER, THE

D: Gordon Wiles 84 m

NR CRM DMA 1947 B&W

Sex Nud Viol Lang AdSit

8 Unusual and interesting film noir. This is the psychological study of a hood (Sullivan) who has everything. He controls the waterfront in every way. He has all the hoods and half the cops on his payroll, but then another tough guy (Leonard), absolutely ruthless, moves in. Sullivan's insecurities and self-doubt get in his way. His hesitance to act and react places his gang and his life in danger from this new rival gang. His empire is crumbling. Sullivan gives a very strong performance

A: Barry Sullivan, Belita, Joan Lorring, Akim Tamiroff, Harry Morgan, John Ireland

© CBS/FOX VIDEO 7321

HE WALKED BY NIGHT

D: Alfred Werker 79 m

NR CRM SUS 1948 B&W

Sex Nud Viol Lang AdSit

9 This is a little-known cinematic gem that was also reportedly Jack Webb's inspiration for his long-running TV series "Dragnet." This excellent semi-documentary style thriller details the point-by-point manhunt by Los Angeles police to track down a devious and clever killer/thief. Richard Basehart is menacing as the intelligent and particularly cunning killer who is relentlessly pursued. Top-notch cop flick based on an actual police case.

A: Richard Basehart, Scott Brady, Jack Webb, Roy Roberts, Whit Bissell

© VIDEO YESTERYEAR 713

JOHNNY ANGEL

D: Edwin L. Marin 79 m

NR CRM 1945 B&W

Sex Nud Viol Lang AdSit

6 Well done film noir gangster movie. George Raft's father was murdered. He was the captain of a freighter that was carrying $5 million in gold. The gold was stolen and the entire crew was murdered. The only witness was a stowaway and she did not see the killer's faces. Seeking revenge, he sets off in search of the killers. With only the few clues he has, he follows the killers into the New Orleans underworld. There, the path leads him to a deadly ring of enemy Nazi agents. Above average and worth while, but a little too talky.

A: George Raft, Claire Trevor, Signe Hasso, Lowell Gilmore, Margaret Wycherly

© TURNER HOME ENTERTAINMENT 2048

KISS OF DEATH

D: Henry Hathaway 99 m

NR CRM SUS 1947 B&W

Sex Nud Viol Lang AdSit

8 This is the now-famous film noir gangster flick that marked the stunning debut (Oscar nomination) of Richard Widmark as a giggling psychopathic killer who shoved a wheelchair-bound old lady down a staircase. Widmark is a hitman out to kill gangster Victor Mature. Mature is a career criminal who decides to turn state's evidence to prosecutor Donlevy when his gang chooses to let him rot in prison. Now his former business partners are out to get him first. Suspenseful and compelling. Strong performance by Mature, too. Superior thriller.

A: Victor Mature, Brian Donlevy, Richard Widmark, Coleen Gray, Karl Malden, Mildred Dunnock

© FOXVIDEO 1844

KNOCK ON ANY DOOR

D: Nicholas Ray 100 m

NR CRM 1949 B&W

Sex Nud Viol Lang AdSit

6 A young street tough Nick (John Derek), from the slums of Chicago, is defended in his trial for the murder of a cop by Humphrey Bogart, who grew up on the streets himself. During the trial, Nick's wife kills herself. Bogart's defense is that the kid is a victim of society: "Just knock on any door in the slums and you'll find someone just like him." Bogart's speech is still something to see and he is winning his case, but then the District Attorney hits Nick hard with his wife's suicide and Nick confesses. A little quaint by today's standards, but still effective.

A: Humphrey Bogart, John Derek, George Macready, Allene Roberts, Susan Perry

© GOODTIMES 4449

LITTLE CAESAR

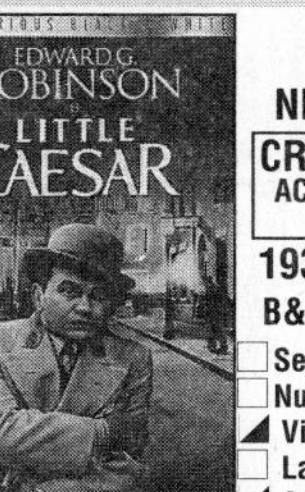

D: Mervyn LeRoy 81 m

NR CRM ACT 1930 B&W

Sex Nud Viol Lang AdSit

8 The first of the great gangster movies, and still one of the best. Robinson is very convincing as a small-time hood and merciless killer who muscles his way to the top of the mob. Many of the plot elements are now common in modern films (they weren't then). There is lots of blood and dead bodies, just as there are now. But the movie has a good story, is fast paced and contains one of the most famous closing lines in moviedom: "Mother of mercy, is this the end of Rico?"

A: Edward G. Robinson, Douglas Fairbanks, Jr., Glenda Farrell, Stanley Fields, Sidney Blackmer, Ralph Ince

Distributed By MGM/UA Home Video M202268

MANHATTAN MELODRAMA

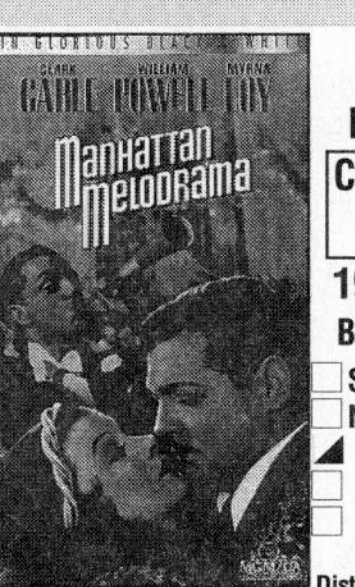

D: W.S. Van Dyke II 91 m

NR CRM 1934 B&W

Sex Nud Viol Lang AdSit

7 Gable and Powell star as two boyhood friends whose lives take different paths. Gable becomes a gangster and Powell an aggressive District Attorney with a mission. Their paths cross first when they fall in love with the same woman and again at a dynamic murder trial. The simple, hackneyed, story line is helped greatly by the talent and chemistry of its cast. (Powell and Loy became a famous pair in the later THIN MAN series.) This film is also best known as the movie that mobster John Dillinger saw just before being gunned down by the Feds in Chicago.

A: William Powell, Clark Gable, Myrna Loy, Leo Carrillo, Isabel Jewell, Mickey Rooney

Distributed By MGM/UA Home Video M202371

MAN ON THE EIFFEL TOWER, THE

D: Burgess Meredith 97 m

NR CRM SUS 1949 COLOR

Sex Nud Viol Lang AdSit

8 A treasure of intrigue! A brilliant police detective (Laughton) is taunted by a thrill-killer-for-hire (Tone) in an intense psychological game of cat-and-mouse. Tone is hired by the nephew of a rich woman to kill her and sets up a blind knife-grinder (Meredith) as a fall-guy. However, the cagey detective quickly dismisses the obvious suspect and instead pursues the hired killer. For a while Tone enjoys the chase, even taunting his pursuer, but Laughton slowly adds heat to the pressure cooker until Tone cracks. Set against a beautiful Parisian backdrop, the plot is powerful and the conclusion very intense.

A: Charles Laughton, Franchot Tone, Burgess Meredith, Robert Hutton, Jean Wallace, Patricia Roc

© FOOTHILLS VIDEO

NOCTURNE

D: Edwin L. Marin 87 m

NR CRM MYS 1946 B&W

Sex Nud Viol Lang AdSit

7 Taut film noir thriller. George Raft is a police lieutenant who asks too many questions about a flamboyant skirt-chasing songwriter's death. Then, when the death is ruled a suicide and he persists in investigating it as a murder, he is suspended from the force. Even that does not deter him. He continues the investigation on his own. He has ten good suspects, all beautiful, but one of them is deadly. Smooth, well done murder mystery.

A: George Raft, Lynn Bari, Virginia Huston, Joseph Pevney, Myrna Dell

© TURNER HOME ENTERTAINMENT 6222

ON DANGEROUS GROUND

D: Nicholas Ray 82 m

NR CRM DMA 1951 B&W

Sex Nud Viol Lang AdSit

7 Hard-boiled and moody film noir. Robert Ryan is a city cop who's seen too much. He's losing his ability to control his anger. His supervisor assigns him the job of helping a county sheriff to solve the murder of a farmer's young daughter. Ryan's investigation leads him to the mentally deficient younger brother of blind Ida Lupino. She begs him to save her brother from the harsh justice that the girl's father wants and he becomes softened by her pleas as he recognizes himself in the violent outbursts of the boy.

A: Robert Ryan, Ida Lupino, Ward Bond, Ed Begley, Anthony Ross, Ian Wolfe

© TURNER HOME ENTERTAINMENT 6157

PANIC IN THE STREETS

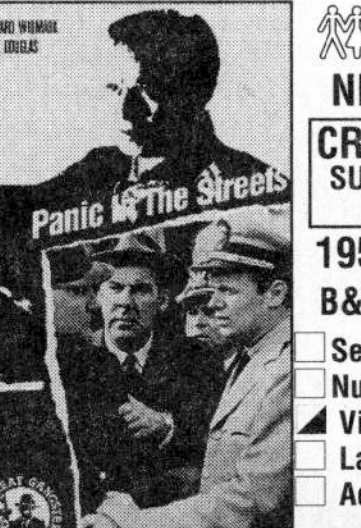

D: Elia Kazan 96 m

NR CRM SUS 1950 B&W

Sex Nud Viol Lang AdSit

9 Excellent thriller set in New Orleans. An illegal resident arrives at the waterfront and is killed by three street punks who are after his money. However, a routine check of the dead man by the medical examiner reveals that he was infected with the highly contagious and deadly bubonic plague. The examiner and the police have only 48 hours to capture the killers and quarantine all their contacts to prevent a massive outbreak of a killer epidemic. Very taut and suspenseful. Excellence in acting, and in all other respects, too. The story won an Oscar.

A: Richard Widmark, Paul Douglas, Barbara Bel Geddes, Jack Palance, Zero Mostel

© FOXVIDEO 1847

PUBLIC ENEMY

D: William Wellman — 83 m

NR | CRM ACT | 1931 | B&W

☐ Sex ☐ Nud ☑ Viol ☐ Lang ☑ AdSit

9 This is the film that made Cagney a star and it is still highly watchable today, even though it is obviously dated. It is also notable as the film having the infamous scene of Cagney shoving a grapefruit into the face of Mae Clarke. Cagney is compelling as a young street tough who embraces a life of crime, beginning by stealing booze on Chicago's south side and graduating up the ladder through the gangland wars. In spite of its many dated notions and techniques, this unvarnished look at a vicious arrogant hood doomed to an early death is still powerful. Fast-paced.

A: James Cagney, Jean Harlow, Eddie Woods, Beryl Mercer, Joan Blondell, Mae Clarke

Distributed By MGM/UA Home Video 201586

RACKET, THE

D: John Cromwell — 88 m

NR | CRM ACT | 1951 | B&W

☐ Sex ☐ Nud ☑ Viol ☐ Lang ☑ AdSit

6 Unusual film noir. A fast-paced crime drama in which an incorruptible police chief (Mitchum) is determined to bring down a corrupt mobster (Ryan), even though it means he has to also fight his own superiors and the politicians who control them. Ryan has a stranglehold on all the politicians, but Mitchum is set to end his rule over the town and a beautiful nightclub singer (Scott). Mitchum's men destroy Ryan's thug army, but Ryan himself escapes, until Mitchum finds a way to lure him in. Bizarre ending.

A: Robert Mitchum, Robert Ryan, William Conrad, Lizabeth Scott, Ray Collins, William Talman

© TURNER HOME ENTERTAINMENT 6112

RIOT IN CELL BLOCK 11

D: Don Siegel — 80 m

NR | CRM ACT | 1954 | B&W

☐ Sex ☐ Nud ☑ Viol ☐ Lang ☑ AdSit

8 Taut, realistic, non-exploitive and powerful prison drama that set a new standard for all movies of its type which followed. Four thousand prisoners in a maximum security prison riot after a mass escape fails, taking several security officers hostage. Things get especially tense when the national guard is called in. This film focuses on the drama and the characterizations of the principal players. There are no heros and no bad guys. It simply focuses on why the riot happened and how it ended. A particularly interesting element is the prisoner's manipulation of the media.

A: Neville Brand, Leo Gordon, Emile Meyer, Frank Faylen

© REPUBLIC PICTURES HOME VIDEO 3458

ROARING TWENTIES, THE

D: Raoul Walsh — 106 m

NR | CRM ACT | 1939 | B&W

☐ Sex ☐ Nud ☑ Viol ☑ Lang ☑ AdSit

8 A lively gangster flick, acclaimed as being one of the best! Cagney is a returning soldier from WWI who has no prospects for a job so he enters into a bootlegging partnership with his old friend Bogart. At first, Cagney flourishes. But then his enterprise comes under attack by rival gangs and is smashed by the law. For a while he has a legitimate cab business left but when the stock market crashes, he is left with only one cab. Depressed and alone, he rescues a woman he once loved and saves her husband (Lynn) from the ruthless Bogart, who's still in the business. Well done.

A: James Cagney, Humphrey Bogart, Jeffrey Lynn, Priscilla Lane, Gladys George, Frank McHugh

Distributed By MGM/UA Home Video M201612

SCAR, THE

D: Steve Sekely — 83 m

NR | CRM DMA | 1948 | B&W

☐ Sex ☐ Nud ☑ Viol ☐ Lang ☑ AdSit

7 Henreid has a dual role in this tough and tense crime drama from the '40s. A gambler and crook is running from the police and happens upon a psychiatrist who, except for a scar on his face, is the gambler's exact double. Elated at his good fortune, the gambler concocts an elaborate plan to kill the good doctor and assume his identity. Unfortunately for him, the twisted plan lands him in exactly the situation he is trying to avoid... the doctor, it seems, has some heavy gambling debts and has his own bullets to dodge.

A: Paul Henreid, Eduard Franz, Joan Bennett, Leslie Brooks, John Qualen

© REPUBLIC PICTURES HOME VIDEO 3562

SCARFACE

D: Howard Hawks — 93 m

NR | CRM ACT | 1932 | B&W

☐ Sex ☐ Nud ■ Viol ☐ Lang ☑ AdSit

9 Explosively intense gangster film based on Al Capone's life. Tony Camonte (Muni) is the Chicago gangster who rises to fame bootlegging alcohol during the depression. Shocking, the film deals with incest, scandal and portrays 28 murders on screen. Due to its jolting nature, the censors forced it to be reedited with a new ending. Producer Howard Hughs did, but then withdrew the film from circulation for forty years. Dvorak is outstanding as Muni's sexy sister and Raft is superb as the rival gangster. This is the film that made Raft and Muni into major stars.

A: Paul Muni, Ann Dvorak, George Raft, Boris Karloff, Karen Morley, Vince Barnett

© MCA/UNIVERSAL HOME VIDEO, INC. 55007

SCARLET STREET

D: Fritz Lang — 101 m

NR | CRM SUS | 1945 | B&W

☐ Sex ☐ Nud ☐ Viol ☐ Lang ☑ AdSit

7 Gloom and deception. A wimpy would-be artist (Robinson) takes the wrong subway home one night from his lowly job as a cashier. He spies beautiful Joan Bennett being attacked and comes to her aid. She lures him into a relationship. He is married but sets her up in an apartment. However, his meager funds are soon tapped, so he begins to embezzle for her. He even allows Bennett to sell his artwork as her own, rather than lose his nights of passion. Then he stumbles in on Bennett in the arms of her real lover, who has conspired with her to fleece him. They shouldn't have done that!

A: Edward G. Robinson, Joan Bennett, Dan Duryea, Margaret Lindsay, Rosalind Ivan

© UNITED AMERICAN VIDEO CORP. 1015

THEY WON'T BELIEVE ME

D: Irving Pichel — 80 m

NR | CRM SUS | 1947 | B&W

☐ Sex ☐ Nud ☐ Viol ☐ Lang ☑ AdSit

8 Fascinating melodrama. Robert Young did quite well with this rare opportunity to play a sleezeball. He is the philandering husband of wealthy Rita Johnson, and he is carrying on affairs with both writer Jane Greer and his secretary Susan Hayward. He wants to murder his wife so that he can have the full benefit of all of her money. However, he leaves with Hayward to go to Las Vegas but she is killed in a car accident. When he arrives home, he finds that his wife has committed suicide and now he is on trial as her murderer.

A: Robert Young, Susan Hayward, Jane Greer, Rita Johnson, Tom Powers, George Tyne

© TURNER HOME ENTERTAINMENT 6111

THIS GUN FOR HIRE

D: Frank Tuttle — 80 m

NR | CRM SUS ACT | 1942 | B&W

☐ Sex ☐ Nud ☑ Viol ☑ Lang ☑ AdSit

8 This is the film that made Alan Ladd into a Hollywood force. It is very sinister in tone - Ladd wears a trench coat and his hat is pulled low. He is a thug, a hired killer and he is seeking revenge against a Nazi double agent who has double-crossed him. Drawn into his hunt is super-sultry Veronica Lake, who exposes a core of good in him and makes him into a sympathetic character for us. What a pair! In spite of how despicable he is, we still root for him to succeed as he struggles to avoid police (who want him for murder) and tracks his victim to a secret plant where Nazis are making poison gas.

A: Alan Ladd, Veronica Lake, Robert Preston, Marc Lawrence, Laird Cregar, Pamela Blake

© MCA/UNIVERSAL HOME VIDEO, INC. 45029

T-MEN

D: Anthony Mann — 93 m

NR | CRM | 1947 | B&W

☐ Sex ☐ Nud ☑ Viol ☑ Lang ☐ AdSit

6 Taken from an actual case history from the closed files of the Treasury Department, two undercover treasury agents infiltrate a notorious and ruthless gang of counterfeiters. Meticulous in its documentation and presentation of the clues, authentic in its locations and dramatic in its semi-documentary form of presentation, this is good story telling. It is an intense thriller that intensifies further when one agent is discovered and killed and the other can do nothing to help his partner.

A: Dennis O'Keefe, June Lockhart, Alfred Ryder, Charles McGraw, Wallace Ford, Mary Meade

© LIVE HOME VIDEO 90107

WHITE HEAT

D: Raoul Walsh — 115 m

NR | CRM ACT | 1949 | B&W

☐ Sex ☐ Nud ☑ Viol ☑ Lang ☑ AdSit

9 Compelling psychological gangster movie in which Cagney gives perhaps his best performance. Cody Jarrett is a crazed and ruthless killer. He has no affection or respect for anyone, except his mother - a shrewd woman of questionable sanity herself - for whom he has an unnatural and obsessive desire to please. O'Brien is a lawman who goes undercover to infiltrate Jarrett's gang to "get the goods" on him. Jarret winds up in prison but, upon learning of Ma's death, escapes - only to die in one of filmdom's most classic scenes. A riveting film.

A: James Cagney, Virginia Mayo, Edmond O'Brien, Steve Cochran, Margaret Wycherly

Distributed By MGM/UA Home Video M201570

LOUISIANA STORY

D: Robert J. Flaherty — 79 m

8 This is the very highly regarded last documentary from Robert Flaherty and it is beautifully filmed. It is the story, actually filmed in the swamps of Lousiana, of a Cajun boy who watches an oil derrick be erected on his father's land. Sponsored by Standard Oil Company, much of the propaganda will certainly be overlooked, but the rich picture of life in the pristine bayou and the charming exploits of the boy and his pet raccoon remain.

NR | DOC | 1948 | B&W

Sex | Nud | Viol | Lang | AdSit

A:

© HOME VISION LOU 01

MAN OF ARAN

D: Robert J. Flaherty — 76 m

9 Famed documentary film-maker Robert J. Flaherty went to a small village on the Aran Islands, a sea-swept group of rocky outcroppings off the coast of Ireland. There he documented in detail the fierce determination and the daily struggle of a small group of fishermen just to survive. The beauty of the the barren landscape, as it is buffeted by an endless series of storms, is beautifully captured, as are the tragedies of such a harsh life.

NR | DOC | 1934 | B&W

Sex | Nud | Viol | Lang | AdSit

A:

© HOME VISION MAN 10

NANOOK OF THE NORTH

D: Robert Flaherty — 69 m

9 Enduring silent classic that is just as - if not more - fascinating than when filmed so long ago. Flaherty's film technique and the equipment he used were quite primitive, and so were the conditions under which he worked. The film depicts the arduous daily life of an Eskimo family lead by the father, Nanook, living along the frozen shores of Hudson Bay. Staged scenes of survival skills are mixed with haunting vistas of endless bleakness. Two years after completion, Nanook died of starvation.

NR | DOC | 1922 | B&W

Sex | Nud | ◢ Viol | Lang | AdSit

A:

© HOME VISION NAN 01

WHY WE FIGHT (SIX PART SERIES)

D: Frank Capra — 385 m

8 In the midst of World War II director Frank Capra created a six-part documentary series which was intended to explain the major aspects of the war to an ignorant and bewildered American public. It began with the historical background from 1931-1939 - Hitler's rise to power, Germany's invasions of Poland and Japan's invasions of China. Then came Germany's taking of the balance of Europe, the Battle of Britain, the fight for Russia in the mud, Japan's cruelties in the Orient and finally America's entry into the struggle.

NR | DOC WAR | 1943

Sex | Nud | ◢ Viol | Lang | ◢ AdSit

A:

© NEW LINE HOME VIDEO 7760

ABE LINCOLN IN ILLINOIS

D: John Cromwell — 110 m

8 Historically, this is a reasonably accurate portrayal of Mr. Lincoln's younger years. (Raymond Massey was Oscar-nominated.) It depicts his childhood in the backwoods of Illinois, early career, ill-fated love for Ann Rutledge and marriage to the shrewish Mary Todd (Ruth Gordon). Reverent and sincere story, even though the production values are slightly dated. Pure Americana, wonderfully acted by Massey with top support from Gordon. Also nominated for Best Cinematography. See also YOUNG MISTER LINCOLN and ABRAHAM LINCOLN.

NR | DMA | 1939 | B&W

Sex | Nud | Viol | Lang | AdSit

A: Raymond Massey, Ruth Gordon, Gene Lockhart, Mary Howard, Dorothy Tree, Minor Watson

© TURNER HOME ENTERTAINMENT 2093

ABRAHAM LINCOLN

D: D.W. Griffith — 97 m

7 Milestone movie in many ways. This was famous silent film director D.W. Griffith's first "talky" and the first film to cover Lincoln's life from his early days as a backwoods lawyer until his assassination at Ford's Theater. Huston's performance is peerless and the picture is sincere, but quite episodic and slow-moving in places. It's production values are very dated now. See also YOUNG MR. LINCOLN and ABE LINCOLN IN ILLINOIS.

NR | DMA | 1930 | B&W

Sex | Nud | Viol | Lang | AdSit

A: Walter Huston, Una Merkel, Kay Hammond, Ian Keith, Hobart Bosworth, Jason Robards, Sr.

© GOODTIMES VGT5133

ADAM HAD FOUR SONS

D: Gregory Ratoff — 81 m

8 This is an intense drama in which Ingrid Bergman is a young foreign girl brought in to be governess for Baxter's four sons after his wife dies. The family has been decimated and it is her strength that becomes the support for them all, especially when Baxter's business fails. But when one son marries the vicious Susan Hayward, brother turns against brother. Bergman sees her for what she is but she is roundly chastised and is nearly fired before everyone discovers that she was right. This classic has it all: tears, laughter, seduction and romance. Fine performances all around. Entertaining for everyone.

NR | DMA ROM | 1941 | B&W

Sex | Nud | Viol | Lang | ◢ AdSit

A: Ingrid Bergman, Warner Baxter, Susan Hayward, Fay Wray, Richard Denning, June Lockhart

© COLUMBIA TRISTAR HOME VIDEO VH10002

ADVENTURES OF HUCKLEBERRY FINN, THE

D: Richard Thorpe — 89 m

8 Mark Twain's classic story is given a pleasant Hollywood spin in this 1930's production (with Mickey Rooney) of an independent boy's wild and adventurous summer on the Mississippi River. Poor Huck Finn decides to get away form his bad-tempered father by faking his own death and running off down the Mississippi. A short way out on his journey he meets up with Jim. Jim is a slave who has also run away and is Huck's friend. Even though much of Twain's satire and wit are exchanged for sentimentality, this is still a rewarding viewing experience, especially for young people.

NR | DMA CLD | 1939 | B&W

Sex | Nud | Viol | Lang | AdSit

A: Mickey Rooney, Walter Connolly, William Frawley, Rex Ingram, Lynne Carver, Jo Ann Sayers

Distributed By MGM/UA Home Video M500053

ADVENTURES OF TOM SAWYER, THE

D: Norman Taurog — 91 m

8 This is a good adaptation of the Mark Twain classic novel in which all of Tom's charm and cunning are left intact. It is a story of a boy who is being raised in a very proper home by a tough but loving aunt, in 1850s Missouri. However, he is also adventurous and mischievous sort who spends all his spare time with the rebellious and independent Huckleberry Finn, except for when he and Becky are chased through a cave by Injun Joe (Jory). Every boy ought to see this at least once, and many who used to be boys (also those who have had a great deal to do with boys) will also have a great time it.

NR | DMA CLD | 1938 | COLOR

Sex | Nud | ◢ Viol | Lang | AdSit

A: Tommy Kelly, Jackie Maran, Ann Gillis, May Robson, Walter Brennan, Victor Jory

© FOXVIDEO 8014

AFRICAN QUEEN, THE

D: John Huston — 105 m

10 Wonderful!! Superb combination of all the elements of film - drama, comedy, romance and action - wrapped up with a ribbon of outstanding acting. Bogart, as a ne'r-do-well drunkard, and Hepburn, as a religious spinster, are thrown together when her village in the Congo is raided by Germans at the outset of WWI. The spinster and the drunken trader fall in love as they travel down a treacherous river in his boat, The African Queen, fighting Germans, nature's elements and each other the whole way. Wonderful, classic film. Bogart won an Oscar. Filmed on location.

NR | DMA ROM COM | 1951 | COLOR

Sex | Nud | ◢ Viol | Lang | ◢ AdSit

A: Humphrey Bogart, Katharine Hepburn, Robert Morley, Peter Bull, Theodore Bikel, Walter Gotell

© CBS/FOX VIDEO 2025

ALICE ADAMS

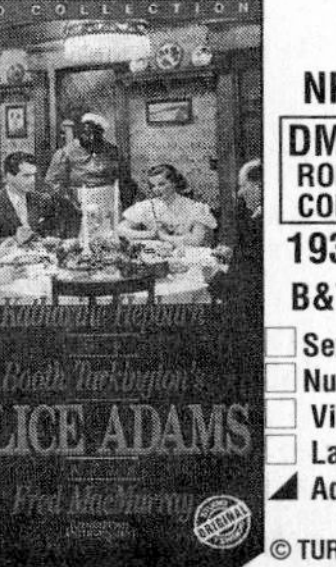

D: George Stevens — 99 m

9 Classic Hepburn. She is a very likable small-town girl from a middle-class background who aspires to a more elevated station in life. So, she convinces her friends that she is from a wealthy family. Then, one night at an upper-crust party, she meets her prince charming (MacMurray) and tells him the made-up tales of her family's fortunes and he believes her - that is until he meets the family. Wonderful. Most memorable for a now-famous scene at the dinner table, which is both funny and a penetrating insight into human nature. Oscar nominations for Best Picture and Hepburn for Actress.

NR | DMA ROM COM | 1935 | B&W

Sex | Nud | Viol | Lang | ◢ AdSit

A: Katharine Hepburn, Fred MacMurray, Evelyn Venable, Frank Albertson, Hattie McDaniel

© TURNER HOME ENTERTAINMENT 6004

ALL ABOUT EVE

D: Joseph L. Mankiewicz 138 m

NR | DMA | 1950 | B&W

Sex / Nud / Viol / Lang / ◢ AdSit

10 Nominated for fourteen Oscars, won six, including Best Picture. This is a brilliant look at the hollow lives that sometimes exist behind the glamour of the stage and it featured a powerhouse cast and a brilliant performance of Bette Davis. Davis is an aging stage star who, having fought and schemed her way to the top, is now being upstaged by a ruthless newcomer (Baxter). Sparkling, witty dialogue. Brilliant and sophisticated look at backstage life. Later brought to Broadway as Applause. A true Hollywood classic.

A: Bette Davis, Anne Baxter, George Sanders, Celeste Holm, Gary Merrill, Thelma Ritter

© CBS/FOX VIDEO 1076

ALL THE KING'S MEN

D: Robert Rossen 109 m

NR | DMA | 1949 | B&W

Sex / Nud / Viol / Lang / ◢ AdSit

9 Powerful story of an ambitious, sweet-talking, back-stabbing politician in the mold of the real-life Louisiana character Huey Long, who was only removed from office when he was assassinated. Starting out as a poor rural farmer, he uses graft and corruption to gain and keep near-total power. Won Oscars for Best Picture, Actor and Supporting Actress, plus four other nominations. Hard-hitting drama that has lost none of its punch. For a different slant on the same premise, see Paul Newman in BLAZE or James Cagney in A LION IS IN THE STREET.

A: Broderick Crawford, Joanne Dru, John Ireland, Mercedes McCambridge, John Derek, Shepperd Strudwick

© COLUMBIA TRISTAR HOME VIDEO 60588

ANNA CHRISTIE

D: Clarence Brown 92 m

NR | DMA | 1930 | B&W

Sex / Nud / Viol / Lang / ■ AdSit

6 Garbo speaks! One of the earliest talkies and the first for Garbo. Garbo plays a tippling ex-hooker who returns home after being away for a long time. The gruff Marie Dressler is sympathetic to her plight but when Garbo finds true love with a seaman (Bickford), she is compelled to tell both him and her father about her unsavory past. From a play by Eugene O'Neill. It is very creaky today, but is still interesting, largely for Garbo's performance. She was 24 at the time. However, if you like Garbo, you should also see her in the superior ANNA KARENINA.

A: Greta Garbo, Charles Bickford, Marie Dressler, Lee Phelps, George F. Marion

Distributed By MGM/UA Home Video M400498

ANNE OF GREEN GABLES

D: George Nicholis 79 m

NR | DMA | 1934 | B&W

Sex / Nud / Viol / Lang / AdSit

7 A mischievous orphan girl with a vivid imagination and vibrant red hair is adopted by a bachelor farmer and his old-maid sister who had really wanted to adopt a boy so he could work their fields. But, the wide-eyed Anne changes their lives and captures the hearts of all those around her, including us. From the classic novel by Lucy Maud Montgomery. Excellent remake in 1985. See also ANNE OF AVONLEA.

A: Anne Shirley, Tom Brown, O.P. Heggie, Helen Westley, Sara Haden, Murray Kinnell

© TURNER HOME ENTERTAINMENT 2028

ARROWSMITH

D: John Ford 100 m

NR | DMA | 1931 | B&W

Sex / Nud / Viol / Lang / ◢ AdSit

8 Quite good drama. Ronald Coleman is an idealistic small-town doctor who leaves his practice to conduct research that will help stop a bubonic plague in the West Indies. His decision proves to be tragic when his first wife (Helen Hayes) dies. Later, large corporations offer him money to leave, but he holds true to his idealism - in spite of the added temptation of a rich girl's love. This is an intelligent and faithful adaptation of Sinclair Lewis's novel, which explores the question of integrity and morality, verses the lure of quick money.

A: Ronald Colman, Helen Hayes, Richard Bennett, Myrna Loy

© HBO VIDEO 90788

BAD AND THE BEAUTIFUL, THE

D: Vincente Minnelli 119 m

NR | DMA | 1952 | B&W

Sex / Nud / Viol / Lang / ■ AdSit

9 An excellent drama which won five Oscars. It is a Hollywood story about Hollywood and ambition. Douglas is a power broker who has produced some of Hollywood's biggest hits. He has risen from total poverty, but he got to the top by doing whatever he needed to do. His tale of twisted ambition is told by three different people who each describe their disastrous relationships with him, now that he is broke and needs their help. Not a very pretty view of Hollywood. One of Lana Turner's best performances. Gloria Grahame won an Oscar. A solid and insightful movie with a human impact outside Hollywood.

A: Kirk Douglas, Lana Turner, Dick Powell, Gloria Grahame, Barry Sullivan, Walter Pidgeon

Distributed By MGM/UA Home Video M300959

BAD DAY AT BLACK ROCK

D: John Sturges 82 m

NR | DMA SUS | 1954 | COLOR

Sex / Nud / ◢ Viol / Lang / ◢ AdSit

9 An extremely powerful drama, still relevant today. A one-armed war veteran (Tracy) stops in the small rural town of Black Rock after WWII to find a Japanese farmer whose dead son he had known. Instead of getting help from the townspeople, he receives unveiled threats. After he is set upon by two of their biggest bad guys (Borgnine and Marvin) and encouraged to leave, it becomes apparent that this hostile town has a big secret to keep. Fine acting from a top notch cast. Excellent photography is somewhat diminished by the small screen. Oscar nominations for Screenplay and Direction.

A: Spencer Tracy, Robert Ryan, Anne Francis, Ernest Borgnine, Walter Brennan, Lee Marvin

Distributed By MGM/UA Home Video M300639

BAREFOOT CONTESSA, THE

D: Joseph L. Mankiewicz 131 m

NR | DMA | 1954 | COLOR

◢ Sex / Nud / Viol / Lang / ■ AdSit

7 Cynical story of a beautiful, naive dancer from a Madrid nightclub who is discovered by fading Hollywood director (Bogart) and molded into a Hollywood glamour girl star to revive his career. Still, with all her success, she is a lonely and tragic, simple soul who never really understands what has happened to her. Now a famous screen star, she marries an Italian nobleman, but even he is impotent. Her tragic story is told as a series of flashbacks. Excellent production values and high quality people, but the plot is sometimes a little too obscure.

A: Humphrey Bogart, Ava Gardner, Edmond O'Brien, Marius Goring, Rossano Brazzi, Valentina Cortese

Distributed By MGM/UA Home Video M202116

BEAU BRUMMEL

D: Harry Beaumont 117 m

NR | DMA | 1924 | B&W

Sex / Nud / Viol / Lang / ◢ AdSit

8 Both the silent movies and Barrymore were at their peak when this movie was released. George Brummel (Barrymore) is a captain in the Tenth Hussars. He is deeply in love with Lady Margery (eighteen-year-old Mary Aster) but she is forced to marry another. Being possessed of great charm and wit, he determines to make himself the favorite of society and then to abuse it as badly as he was abused. He does become a handsome dandy who charms the Prince of Wales and all the ladies, but his plan ultimately ends in ruins. Mary Astor became a major star from exposure in this picture. Silent.

A: John Barrymore, Mary Astor, Willard Louis, Irene Rich, Carmel Myers

© VIDEO YESTERYEAR 1226

BEST YEARS OF OUR LIVES, THE

D: William Wyler 170 m

NR | DMA | 1946 | B&W

Sex / Nud / Viol / Lang / ■ AdSit

9 Excellent and extremely eloquent film. When men come home from having fought in a war, everything about them - their perceptions of the most common-place of things in their life, their family and their inner-selves - are all profoundly changed forever. This powerful film was released just after WWII ended and follows the lives of three returning veterans of that war. It is sometimes funny and sometimes heart-breaking, but always right on the mark. A huge box-office hit, it won nine Oscars and is just as valid and important today as it was when it was released.

A: Fredric March, Myrna Loy, Teresa Wright, Dana Andrews, Virginia Mayo, Harold Russell

© HBO VIDEO 90657

BIG STREET, THE

D: Irving Reis 88 m

NR | DMA ROM | 1942 | B&W

Sex / Nud / Viol / Lang / AdSit

7 Based on a short story by Damon Runyon, this is probably Lucy's best dramatic role ever. She plays a ruthless, gold-digging night club singer who is worshipped by a naive busboy, Henry Fonda. He's so taken with her that he'll do anything for her, even after she is crippled by gangster Barton MacLane and confined to a wheelchair. Sentimental and moist romantic melodrama, but witty too.

A: Lucille Ball, Henry Fonda, Agnes Moorehead, Sam Levene, Barton MacLane, Eugene Pallette

© TURNER HOME ENTERTAINMENT 2092

BILL OF DIVORCEMENT, A

D: George Cukor 70 m

NR | DMA COM | 1932 | B&W

Sex / Nud / Viol / Lang / ■ AdSit

7 Now somewhat dated but still a tour-de-force in acting. Barrymore gives a sensitive performance of a man just escaped from a mental institution after 15 years - returning home to his wife and family, just as she is divorcing him so that she can remarry. Tracy (Hepburn) is his strong-willed daughter who has always been told that her father had a case of shell shock from the First War, but now she finds out from him that there is a history of illness in the family. She becomes quickly convinced that she is its next victim. The film is also notable as being Hepburn's first film role.

A: John Barrymore, Katharine Hepburn, Billie Burke, David Manners, Henry Stephenson

© CBS/FOX VIDEO 8050

BIRTH OF A NATION, THE

D: D.W. Griffith — 154 m

NR | DMA | 1915 | B&W | Sex | Nud | Viol | Lang | AdSit

9 This silent film is a technical landmark in American film for many reasons, but principally its scale. It is an overly simplistic and emotionally manipulative melodrama about the lives of two families. But, it also expresses the epic and tragic story of the South's defeat in the Civil War and its humiliation afterward. Marvelous full-scale battle scenes are still revered today for their authenticity. Griffith's obvious racism and glorification of the KKK will diminish the value for many.

A: Lillian Gish, Mae Marsh, Henry B. Walthall, Miriam Cooper, Robert Harron, Wallace Reid

© REPUBLIC PICTURES HOME VIDEO 0308

BLACKBOARD JUNGLE, THE

D: Richard Brooks — 102 m

NR | DMA | 1955 | B&W | Sex | Nud | Viol | Lang | AdSit

8 This was a hard-hitting expose in its day and is only slightly dated now. Glenn Ford is an idealistic and devoted English teacher who takes a job at an inner-city New York high school that is filled with alienated juvenile delinquents, kids who derive particular pleasure out of tormenting their teachers. He determinedly withstands their abuses while relentlessly pursuing different ways to break down their defenses and eventually gains their respect, succeeding in getting some students to try - but only after being run through a personally harrowing gauntlet. Tough and believable.

A: Glenn Ford, Anne Francis, Vic Morrow, Louis Calhern, Sidney Poitier, Richard Kiley

Distributed By MGM/UA Home Video M200895

BLACK NARCISSUS

D: Michael Powell, Emeric Pressburger — 100 m

NR | DMA | 1947 | COLOR | Sex | Nud | Viol | Lang | AdSit

9 Fascinating premise. A group of Anglican nuns, led by Kerr and Byron, attempt to establish and maintain a school and hospital in the far remote Himalayas. Because of their isolation, the arrival of a sexy British officer into their midst arouses long dormant passions and becomes a source of conflict between the women. Some key elements of this adult plot were originally removed by censors of the day, muddling the plot for its American release, so it never got the box office attention it deserved. It is now fully restored on video. Wonderful sets and photography both won Oscars.

A: Deborah Kerr, Sabu, Jean Simmons, David Farrar, Flora Robson, Kathleen Byron

© UNITED AMERICAN VIDEO CORP. 7026

BLOOD ON THE SUN

D: Frank Lloyd — 94 m

NR | DMA SUS | 1945 | B&W | Sex | Nud | Viol | Lang | AdSit

8 Terrific espionage action-drama. Cagney is the hard-edged managing editor of Tokyo's English-speaking newspaper, and one of the few American journalists in Japan during the 1930s. When the paper breaks the news that Japan is planning to conquer China, the reporter who wrote the story and his wife are murdered. Cagney knows now that his own life is in serious jeopardy. He finds himself caught in an espionage plot when he tries to warn the American authorities, with the help of a beautiful secret agent, of even greater dangers. Good fast-paced and suspenseful melodrama.

A: James Cagney, Robert Armstrong, Wallace Ford, Sylvia Sidney, Porter Hall, John Emery

© GOODTIMES 5060

BLOSSOMS IN THE DUST

D: Mervyn LeRoy — 95 m

NR | DMA | 1941 | COLOR | Sex | Nud | Viol | Lang | AdSit

8 Moving, true story of social visionary and humanitarian Edna Glandney (Greer Garson). When she loses her husband and only son in 19th-century Texas, and her foster sister, who had been branded illegitimate, commits suicide - Edna decides to fight back. She works tirelessly to establish the Texas Children's Home and Aid Society and then places over 2000 children in adoptive homes. She also fights a ceaseless battle to have the stigmatizing word "illegitimate" officially struck from any legal records. Nominated for four Oscars, including Best Picture. A classy, heartwarming tearjerker.

A: Greer Garson, Walter Pidgeon, Felix Bressart, Marsha Hunt, Fay Holden, Samuel S. Hinds

Distributed By MGM/UA Home Video M201874

BLUE ANGEL, THE

D: Josef von Sternberg — 93 m

NR | DMA | 1930 | B&W | Sex | Nud | Viol | Lang | AdSit

8 Emil Jannings plays a repressed professor who tries to get his students to stop going to a cabaret to see sexy Lola Lola (Dietrich). However, when he goes to the cafe to stop them, he soon finds himself caught up in her sultry charm. He becomes so infatuated with her that he sacrifices his career and becomes her near-slave, but she only destroys his life. An incisive study of human nature that is still relevant today. Dietrich's crooning of "Falling in Love Again" made her an international star. One of Germany's first talkies. Subtitles.

A: Emil Jannings, Marlene Dietrich, Kurt Gerron, Rosa Valette, Hans Albers, Edward von Winterstein

© BARR ENTERTAINMENT VIDEO 11011

BODY AND SOUL

D: Robert Rossen — 104 m

NR | DMA | 1947 | B&W | Sex | Nud | Viol | Lang | AdSit

9 Some have called this the best boxing film ever, but it is much more than that. It is great drama. Garfield is a poor but decent man who has turned to boxing to make money. He works his way up to the top by any means it takes, and cannot understand his mother and his girlfriend when they disapprove of what he has become. He believes that he will be independent when he becomes champ, but instead he has to give up 50% of his purse to the hoods, is deep in debt and is ordered to take a dive. Stark realism. 3 Oscar nominations, including Best Actor.

A: John Garfield, Lilli Palmer, Hazel Brooks, Anne Revere, William Conrad, Canada Lee

© REPUBLIC PICTURES HOME VIDEO 0354

BOOM TOWN

D: Jack Conway — 120 m

NR | DMA | 1940 | B&W | Sex | Nud | Viol | Lang | AdSit

6 Two friends, a couple of Texas wildcatters, Big John McMasters (Gable) and Square John Sand (Tracy) strike it rich in the oil fields and move on up to offices on Wall Street, but their friendship has turned to bitter rivalry after one marries the other's sweetheart. The melodrama follows them through their ups and downs, over twenty years. It is simply a story with colorful characters that is given energy and interest by a great cast. This was a major hit at the time.

A: Clark Gable, Spencer Tracy, Claudette Colbert, Hedy Lamarr, Frank Morgan, Chill Wills

Distributed By MGM/UA Home Video M201588

BOYS' TOWN

D: Norman Taurog — 94 m

NR | DMA CLD | 1938 | B&W | Sex | Nud | Viol | Lang | AdSit

8 Boys' Town is a real-life home for orphans and juvenile delinquents in Nebraska, that has now been in existence for many years. Their motto is: "There's no such thing as a bad boy." This is the dramatized story of how Boys' Town was started by the real-life Father Flanagan. Spencer Tracy won an Oscar playing Flanagan in his struggle to find a home for, and give a second chance to, the boys that society was just throwing away. Mickey Rooney, as tough guy Whitey Marsh, is one of his toughest jobs. A little syrupy sweet and sentimental, but still a very rewarding film.

A: Spencer Tracy, Mickey Rooney, Henry Hull, Leslie Fenton, Addison Richards, Edward Norris

Distributed By MGM/UA Home Video M203851

BRIDGES AT TOKO-RI, THE

D: Mark Robson — 103 m

NR | DMA WAR ACT | 1955 | COLOR | Sex | Nud | Viol | Lang | AdSit

9 Powerful and thoughtful war drama. Holden, a married civilian lawyer with two kids, who was an ace pilot in WWII, is called back into service again to fly jets off an aircraft carrier during the Korean War. The picture has two focuses: the man and his personal conflicts, and the pilot and his support crew as they attempt to destroy difficult-to-reach but vital North Korean bridges. The human drama is gripping, but so are the action sequences. Probably the best picture ever done about the Korean War. Excellent personalization of the effects of war. Strong performances.

A: William Holden, Fredric March, Grace Kelly, Mickey Rooney, Earl Holliman, Robert Strauss

© PARAMOUNT HOME VIDEO 5906

BROKEN BLOSSOMS

D: D.W. Griffith — 95 m

NR | DMA | 1919 | B&W | Sex | Nud | Viol | Lang | AdSit

8 Dealing both with child abuse and prejudice, this was a very daring concept for the time in which it was made. Lillian Gish plays the young daughter of an abusive alcoholic London prize-fighter father (Crisp) who beats her regularly. After one particularly bad beating, she falls into the shop of a Chinese poet and a gentleman. He immediately falls in love with her and takes care of her. However, when Crisp learns that his daughter was seen with a Chinese, he becomes enraged and vows to kill him. This tragedy was very powerful then and is still quite engaging today. One of film legend D.W. Griffith's most successful films.

A: Lillian Gish, Richard Barthelmess, Donald Crisp

© HBO VIDEO 0279

BROWNING VERSION, THE

D: Anthony Asquith — 90 m

NR | DMA | 1951 | B&W | Sex | Nud | Viol | Lang | AdSit

8 A already powerful and particularly moving story becomes a truly memorable film, due to the extraordinary performance of Michael Redgrave. Redgrave plays a one-time brilliant scholar who has become a stern, stuffy and ineffective middle-aged professor at an English boy's school. Now his life is crumbling. His wife has been having an affair with another professor and he is being forced out of the school that has been his home for years. On the eave of his retirement, an unexpected and undeserved kindness has now forced him to realize his own arrogance and that his life has been unfulfilled and a failure. Redgrave's closing apology speech is magnificent and regains him the respect of his students.

A: Michael Redgrave, Jean Kent, Nigel Patrick, Wilfrid Hyde-White, Ronald Howard, Bill Travers

© HOME VISION BRO 040

BULLFIGHTER AND THE LADY, THE

D: Budd Boetticher 125 m

NR | DMA ROM | 1950 | B&W

8 Well done. Robert Stack plays a cocky American on vacation in Mexico who becomes intrigued by bullfighting and a beautiful Mexican woman. He befriends the country's leading matador and gets him to teach him bullfighting, but recklessly causes his mentor's death in the ring. He is now despised by the country and the woman and is personally tormented. This is a mature drama with many important themes explored. Unforgettable bullfighting scenes and a good love story, too. This is Hollywood's best ever attempt at trying to understand, and realistically depict, bullfighting.

Sex / Nud / Viol / Lang / AdSit

A: Robert Stack, Joy Page, Gilbert Roland, Katy Jurado, Virginia Grey, John Hubbard

© REPUBLIC PICTURES HOME VIDEO 0461

CAINE MUTINY, THE

D: Edward Dmytryk 125 m

NR | DMA | 1954

10 A must-see movie - a superior courtroom drama. Captain Queeg (Bogart) is a stern captain of the US Navy destroyer/mine sweeper, the Caine. During a fierce storm, Queeg becomes extremely nervous and appears to be on the verge of a breakdown. Fearing for their own safety and that of the ship, the executive officer, with the support of the crew, seizes control of the ship from Queeg. On dry land after the incident, Queeg retaliates by seeking their court martial. Facing a board of inquiry, they must destroy Queeg to save themselves. A brilliant film. Outstanding acting, particularly Bogart.

Sex / Nud / Viol / Lang / AdSit

A: Humphrey Bogart, Jose Ferrer, Van Johnson, Robert Francis, Fred MacMurray, Lee Marvin

© COLUMBIA TRISTAR HOME VIDEO 60425

CANTERBURY TALE, A

D: Michael Powell 123 m

NR | DMA | 1944 | B&W

7 Set during WWII, this is the story of how the lives of four people, three Brits and an American GI, intertwine as they converge upon the cathedral at Canterbury. Their lives are shown in parallel with the lives of the pilgrims from Chaucer's famous stories of 600 years prior, which was also during time of war. These are simple stories, but the focus is upon the them as also set in context of the timeless rugged pastoral countryside. Simple and charming.

Sex / Nud / Viol / Lang / AdSit

A: John Sweet, Eric Portman, Sheila Sim, Dennis Price

© HOME VISION CAN 01

CAPTAINS COURAGEOUS

D: Victor Fleming 118 m

G | DMA ACT CLD | 1937 | B&W

10 Wonderful adaptation of Rudyard Kipling's classic story. A spoiled rich kid (Bartholomew) falls overboard from an ocean liner, is rescued by a Portuguese fisherman (Spencer Tracy) and is brought on board a New England fishing schooner. He demands to be taken back to land but instead has to stay at sea for the balance of the 3-month fishing trip. For the first time in his life, he has to earn his keep. He is put to work along side Mickey Rooney, gets a few lessons in humility from Tracy and gradually is transformed. Excellent! A true treat for everyone! Tracy won Best Actor Oscar.

Sex / Nud / Viol / Lang / AdSit

A: Spencer Tracy, Freddie Bartholomew, Lionel Barrymore, Melvyn Douglas, Mickey Rooney, John Carradine

Distributed By MGM/UA Home Video M500058

CAUGHT

D: Max Ophuls 88 m

NR | DMA | 1949 | B&W

7 A compelling, very well-acted melodrama about a young, beautiful model (Barbara Bel Geddes) who marries a millionaire who she thinks is charming and devoted (Robert Ryan). Too late, she discovers instead that he is abusive, neglectful and worse... insane. Soon, she longs to be free of him and falls in love with a young doctor (James Mason). But, her husband won't let her go. She even becomes pregnant by her lover, but still Ryan will not leave her alone nor will he divorce her. There is only one way out. Murder. An intense, engrossing soap opera.

Sex / Nud / Viol / Lang / AdSit

A: James Mason, Barbara Bel Geddes, Robert Ryan, Frank Ferguson, Curt Bois, Natalie Schafer

© REPUBLIC PICTURES HOME VIDEO 0594

CHAMP, THE

D: King Vidor 87 m

NR | DMA CLD | 1931 | B&W

8 Top-notch tearjerker, winner of two Oscars plus a Best Picture nomination. Wallace Beery won an Oscar as the loveable washed-up ex-boxer who has nothing at all, except the unending adoration of his son. The two of them live in a dive in Tijuana where he is constantly "in training" for a come back, that is, when he is in between drinking binges or not gambling away their money. Now the mother, who abandoned them both, has come back and wants to take the boy away. A simple story, unashamedly sentimental, but one of the most effective and heartwarming tearjerkers of all time. A treasure.

Sex / Nud / Viol / Lang / AdSit

A: Wallace Beery, Jackie Cooper, Irene Rich, Roscoe Ates, Edward Brophy, Hale Hamilton

Distributed By MGM/UA Home Video M301665

CHAMPION

D: Mark Robson 100 m

NR | DMA ACT | 1949 | B&W

9 This is the movie that made Kirk Douglas into a star and earned him an Oscar nomination. Kirk is a boxer, a ruthless loud-mouthed thug, who slugs his way to the top. He is a hero to his fans, but loses his friends and his family because they see him in all his cruelty. After winning a fight that he was supposed to throw, he is attacked by thugs but he is saved by a woman. Still he uses her, too, and then throws her away. He is alone again. Good editing gives the fight scenes a gritty reality. Six Academy Award nominations, won for Editing. Arthur Kennedy got a nomination as Douglas's crippled brother.

Sex / Nud / Viol / Lang / AdSit

A: Kirk Douglas, Marilyn Maxwell, Arthur Kennedy, Paul Steward, Ruth Roman, John Day

© REPUBLIC PICTURES HOME VIDEO 0619

CHEERS FOR MISS BISHOP

D: Tay Garnett 95 m

NR | DMA | 1941 | B&W

7 This is an endearing and sentimental story of a much-loved 19th-century midwestern school teacher. She is Miss Bishop (Martha Scott), who as a young girl graduated from a new college and stayed on there to teach freshman English. In the tradition of GOODBYE MR. CHIPS, she becomes a much-loved institution as the film follows her over 50 years. Even though she has two romances which fail and she never marries, she has a full life and is richly loved by her friends and students. Upbeat charmer.

Sex / Nud / Viol / Lang / AdSit

A: Martha Scott, William Gargan, Edmund Gwenn, Sterling Holloway, Sidney Blackmer, Mary Anderson

© VIDEO YESTERYEAR 958

CHRISTMAS CAROL, A

D: Edwin L. Marin 70 m

NR | DMA | 1938 | B&W

7 Very good film version of Charles Dickens's Christmas classic in which a grumpy old curmudgeon and tightwad is shown - by visions of the past, present and future - that he is the source of his own misery and isolation, and that he can be happy if he only tries. The film's age and an excellent cast of MGM players add credence to the period atmosphere. June Lockhart makes her screen debut.

Sex / Nud / Viol / Lang / AdSit

A: Reginald Owen, Gene Lockhart, Kathleen Lockhart, Leo G. Carroll, Terry Kilburn, Barry MacKay

Distributed By MGM/UA Home Video M201451

CHRISTMAS CAROL, A

D: Brian Desmond Hurst 86 m

NR | DMA | 1951 | B&W

10 Wonderful version of Dickens's classic Christmas parable. Numerous versions have been made over the years for both TV and the movie theatre, but this is likely the best. Alastair Sim is perfect as the miserly Ebenezer Scrooge. His forced encounters with the three ghosts of Christmas force him to come to grips with his own mortality and his disagreeable ways. Widely regarded as probably the best screen version of this classic tale. Very uplifting movie.

Sex / Nud / Viol / Lang / AdSit

A: Alastair Sim, Kathleen Harrison, Jack Warner, Michael Hordern, Mervyn Johns, Hermione Baddeley

© VIDEO COMMUNICATIONS, INC. 1118

CITADEL, THE

D: King Vidor 114 m

NR | DMA | 1938 | B&W

7 Heartwarming, brilliant story of a young, idealistic and dedicated, but impoverished, Scottish physician who begins his career in a poor Welsh mining town. He discovers the cause of a severe cough that plagues the miners but is thwarted in his efforts to reveal his discovery by the medical establishment. He leaves for a lucrative practice in London but is encouraged by his wife and his best friend to go back and minister to the children of a poor village. Received four Oscar nominations, including Best Picture, Actor and Director, though a little slow moving.

Sex / Nud / Viol / Lang / AdSit

A: Robert Donat, Rosalind Russell, Rex Harrison, Ralph Richardson

Distributed By MGM/UA Home Video M300612

CITIZEN KANE

D: Orson Welles 119 m

NR | DMA | 1941 | B&W

10 Widely acclaimed by critics as being one of the best movies of all time. It truly is a technical masterpiece and was extremely innovative on several cinematic fronts. Its storyline of a compulsive, Hearst-like publishing giant's rise to power, and his search for truth and the mystical peace of "Rosebud" is a genuinely interesting one, too. However, much of the ground-breaking, movie-making innovation for which the film is widely hailed by the critics, will be lost on the casual viewer. Still, it is a definite must-see, but particularly for film nuts.

Sex / Nud / Viol / Lang / AdSit

A: Orson Welles, Joseph Cotten, Everett Sloane, Agnes Moorehead, Dorothy Comingore, Ray Collins

© TURNER HOME ENTERTAINMENT 2053

CLEOPATRA

D: Cecil B. DeMille — 101 m

NR | DMA | 1934 | B&W | Nud

8 Monumentally spectacular with lavish production for its day. This early film is also intelligent and really doesn't date badly at all. Claudette Colbert plays Cleopatra -- no one had believed that she would be sexy enough in the role -- who seeks to unite the empires of Egypt with those of Rome. Her ambitions led to the deaths of Caesar and Marcus Anthony, as well as to her own. De Mille was a stickler for historical accuracy, however he never let that get in the way of a good story. He used lush sets, huge numbers of extras, groups of nearly naked women, a real snake for Cleopatra's suicide and other extravagances to maintain his audience's rapt attention.

A: Claudette Colbert, Warren William, Henry Wilcoxon, Gertrude Michael, Joseph Schildkraut, C. Aubrey Smith

© MCA/UNIVERSAL HOME VIDEO, INC. 80644

COME BACK, LITTLE SHEBA

D: Daniel Mann — 99 m

NR | DMA | 1952 | B&W | AdSit

7 A powerful and emotional drama for which Shirley Booth won a well-deserved Oscar. She plays Lola, a dreadfully unhappy and frumpy middle-aged housewife, married to an alcoholic ex-chiropractor. Their troubled relationship is given a new start when a young art student moves in as a boarder. She becomes the daughter they never had and their life together is restored for a short time - that is until the girl takes up with a boy they don't trust and a jealous Lancaster reverts to drinking again. This is a profoundly moving drama about an unhappy marriage and unhappy people.

A: Burt Lancaster, Shirley Booth, Terry Moore, Richard Jaeckel, Philip Ober

© PARAMOUNT HOME VIDEO 5213

COMMAND DECISION

D: Sam Wood — 113 m

NR | DMA WAR | 1948 | COLOR | Viol | AdSit

8 Excellent, taut World War II drama with an all-star cast. This is an unusual war film because it deals with war from the top down. It concerns itself with the top brass, the people who make the big decisions. Gable plays an Allied commander based in England and directing war efforts in Europe. This interesting screenplay deals with the politics of war and also provides interesting insights into the emotions of the military brass who must deal with the daily trauma of sending men to their deaths and of fighting both shooting wars and political ones.

A: Clark Gable, Walter Pidgeon, Van Johnson, Brian Donlevy, Charles Bickford, John McIntire

Distributed By MGM/UA Home Video M202113

CONQUEST

D: Clarence Brown — 113 m

NR | DMA ROM | 1937 | B&W | AdSit

7 This was the only time two of the screen's biggest romantic leads, Garbo and Boyer, ever starred together. It is both historical drama and romance, recounting the affair between Napoleon (Boyer) and the Countess Marie Walewska. Napoleon is so taken by the countess that he agrees to grant Poland its independence if only she is given to him - even though she is already married. At first she despises him, but later comes to love him and is heartbroken at his political marriage to another. She bears him a son and remains loyal, even in his exile after his defeat at Waterloo. Interesting costume drama.

A: Greta Garbo, Charles Boyer, Reginald Owen, Alan Marshal, Henry Stephenson, Leif Erickson

Distributed By MGM/UA Home Video M201130

COURT-MARTIAL OF BILLY MITCHELL, THE

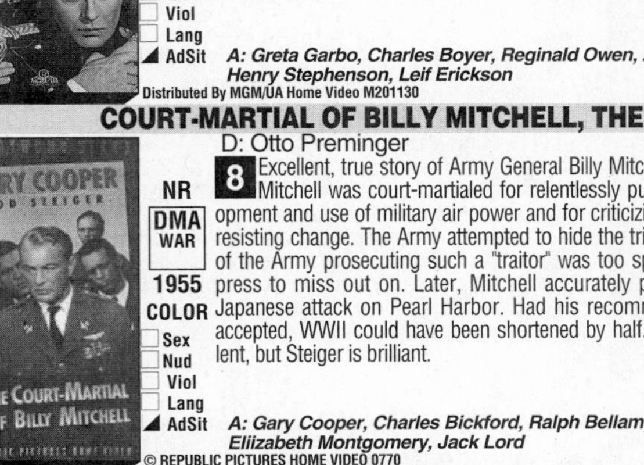

D: Otto Preminger — 100 m

NR | DMA WAR | 1955 | COLOR | AdSit

8 Excellent, true story of Army General Billy Mitchell. In 1925 Billy Mitchell was court-martialed for relentlessly pursuing the development and use of military air power and for criticizing "the brass" for resisting change. The Army attempted to hide the trial but the subject of the Army prosecuting such a "traitor" was too spectacular for the press to miss out on. Later, Mitchell accurately predicted WWII's Japanese attack on Pearl Harbor. Had his recommendations been accepted, WWII could have been shortened by half. Cooper is excellent, but Steiger is brilliant.

A: Gary Cooper, Charles Bickford, Ralph Bellamy, Rod Steiger, Elizabeth Montgomery, Jack Lord

© REPUBLIC PICTURES HOME VIDEO 0770

CROWD, THE

D: King Vidor — 104 m

NR | DMA | 1928 | B&W | AdSit

9 One of the greatest of the silent films. The story is just as poignant and valid today as it was then - it is an "everyman's" story. Two young people meet, fall in love and marry. He believes that if he works hard and does the right things, he can become anything. Both are patient but they find that they are not alone in that dream. Slowly others begin to pass them by and he finds he is in a dead-end job. It is then he comes to realize that there is more value in spending time with his wife and family, so he gives up the big dream to blend into the crowd. It's OK to be average, if the crowd doesn't run you over.

A: James Murray, Eleanor Boardman, Bert Roach, Estelle Clark, Daniel G. Tomlinson

Distributed By MGM/UA Home Video M301357

CRUSADES, THE

D: Cecil B. DeMille — 123 m

NR | DMA ACT ROM | 1935 | B&W | Viol

7 Trade-mark grand epic from Cecil B. DeMille, who depicts the story of the third crusade set in 1187. Henry Wilcoxon is the lusty Richard the Lionhearted, King of England. He, along with the rest of Christian Europe, is summoned to war against the Saracens, who have swept in from Asia to capture Jerusalem for Islam. England and France comprise the bulk of the fighting force, but their alliance is threatened when Richard refuses to marry the sister of the French king. Worse, he has married the beautiful daughter (Lorretta Young) of another king. It is a story of bravery, butchery, honor, romance and more romance. Historians might disagree with DeMille's facts.

A: Loretta Young, Henry Wilcoxon, Ian Keith, Katherine DeMille, C. Aubrey Smith, George Barker

© MCA/UNIVERSAL HOME VIDEO, INC. 81266

DAVID AND BATHSHEBA

D: Henry King — 116 m

NR | DMA | 1951 | COLOR | Viol | AdSit

7 Big production religious epic that received numerous technical nominations and an Oscar for Best Screenplay. Gregory Peck is David, King of the Israelites of the Old Testament. This big picture tells the biblical story of David's lust for Bathsheba (Hayward), the sultry wife of one of his generals. So transfixed with her was he that he forsakes his first wife for her and arranges to have her husband killed in battle so that he can have her for himself. Then God sends his prophet Nathan to David to hold him accountable for what he has done.

A: Gregory Peck, Susan Hayward, Raymond Massey, Kieron Moore, Jayne Meadows, John Sutton

© FOXVIDEO 1380

DAVID COPPERFIELD

D: George Cukor — 131 m

NR | DMA | 1935 | B&W

10 A treat for the whole family. Perhaps the best-ever Hollywood production of any Dickens classic. Young David (Bartholomew) leads an idyllic life with his mother and his nurse until his mother marries Murdstone (Rathbone), a despicable man, and she dies. Orphaned, David faces a life of toil in his step-father's sweatshop, but he runs away to his eccentric aunt. Through strength of character and help from friends, he survives all his trials to achieve success. Wonderful characterizations: Fields as Micawber, Rathbone as villainous Murdstone and Oliver as Aunt Betsey. Masterpiece.

A: Freddie Bartholomew, W.C. Fields, Frank Lawton, Lionel Barrymore, Edna May Oliver, Roland Young

Distributed By MGM/UA Home Video M300649

DECEPTION

D: Irving Rapper — 113 m

NR | DMA ROM | 1946 | COLOR | AdSit

7 Juicy melodrama. Bette Davis is a struggling pianist. Her boyfriend and former lover (Paul Henreid), whom she still loves, has just returned from the war. However, while he was gone, she had been kept as the mistress of her domineering teacher who is also a famous composer (Claude Rains). Rains is now furious at being deserted by her and is threatening to tell her little secret. She is caught between two men she has loved, but who now must keep apart at all costs. At first she uses all the lies she can contrive, then she must resort to something more permanent.

A: Bette Davis, Claude Rains, Paul Henreid, John Abbott, Benson Fong

Distributed By MGM/UA Home Video M201801

DEMETRIUS AND THE GLADIATORS

D: Delmer Daves — 101 m

NR | DMA ACT | 1954 | COLOR | Viol | AdSit

6 This is a fairly tame sequel to the big hit THE ROBE. The Roman Emperor Caligula is obsessed with getting his hands on the robe that Christ wore, believing it to have magic powers. Demetrius is a slave and a devout Christian who has been entrusted with the robe. He is forced to fight lions and men in the arena, becomes one of Rome's greatest gladiators and the lover of seductive temptress Susan Hayward. He has refrained from revealing the robe's location but is now tempted to betray God. The major audience pleaser here is the impressive gladiator duels.

A: Victor Mature, Jay Jackson, Susan Hayward, Debra Paget, Anne Bancroft, Michael Rennie

© FOXVIDEO 1178

DOCKS OF NEW YORK, THE

D: Josef von Sternberg — 60 m

NR | DMA ROM | 1928 | B&W | AdSit

9 One of the last great silent films released, this is a powerful story of love between two losers from the grim and desolate world of the docks. A rough-edged ship stoker (Bancroft) rescues a prostitute (Compson) from the water after she attempts suicide. At first he ignores her, but later he comes to love her and marries her. He tries to clear her of murder charges and is even willing to go to jail for her. Very sentimental. This has a visual splendor and expressiveness that far surpasses the shortcoming of its lack of sound.

A: George Bancroft, Betty Compson, Olga Baclanova, Mitchell Lewis, Clyde Cook

© PARAMOUNT HOME VIDEO 2807

DODSWORTH

D: William Wyler 101 m

NR | DMA ROM | 1936 | B&W | Sex | Nud | Viol | Lang | ◼ AdSit

8 An outstanding film adaptation of a Sinclair Lewis novel and an absorbing drama. A middle-aged self-made millionaire from the midwest, Samuel Dodsworth (Huston), retires at his young wife's suggestion to go to Europe. There, she quickly takes to the cosmopolitan European lifestyle and yearns for romance. She enjoys flirting and is seduced by a gigolo. He is heartsore and is comforted by a beautiful divorcee (Astor). This is not a simple film. The emotions explored are complex. This is a mature treatment of love and marriage. Intelligent and sensitive. Outstanding cast.

A: Walter Huston, Ruth Chatterton, Mary Astor, David Niven, Spring Byington, John Payne

© HBO VIDEO 90659

DOUBLE LIFE, A

D: George Cukor 103 m

NR | DMA SUS | 1947 | B&W | Sex | Nud | Viol | Lang | ◢ AdSit

8 Superb psycho-drama. Colman is a famous actor who has trouble because his stage roles tend to take over his personal life, too. He has become fearful because soon he will play Othello with his ex-wife as his leading lady. It is the role of his life, but his jealousies are consuming him and Othello kills his lover. Colman is sure that his ex-wife is in love with someone else and he becomes increasingly compelled to act upon his Othello-driven feelings. Excellently written and directed. Colman won an Oscar. The score won an Oscar. Shelly Winters became a star from her performance. Highly recommended.

A: Ronald Colman, Signe Hasso, Edmond O'Brien, Shelley Winters

© REPUBLIC PICTURES HOME VIDEO 1092

EACH DAWN I DIE

D: William Keighley 92 m

NR | DMA CRM | 1939 | B&W | Sex | Nud | ◢ Viol | Lang | ◢ AdSit

7 Cagney is an aggressive reporter who discovers that the district attorney is corrupt and reports it. This now makes Cagney a dangerous man, so it is arranged for him to be framed for a murder and sent to prison. There he meets tough-guy George Raft who befriends and protects him. Raft escapes with Cagney's help, but when Cagney is blamed for the escape, Raft comes back to help him. Good performances, but the last half begins to stretch believability. Still, the film was influential enough to help push through some prison reforms.

A: James Cagney, George Raft, Jane Byran, George Bancroft, Maxie Rosenbloom, Victor Jory

Distributed By MGM/UA Home Video M200735

EAST OF EDEN

D: Elia Kazan 118 m

NR | DMA | 1955 | COLOR | Sex | Nud | ◢ Viol | Lang | ◼ AdSit

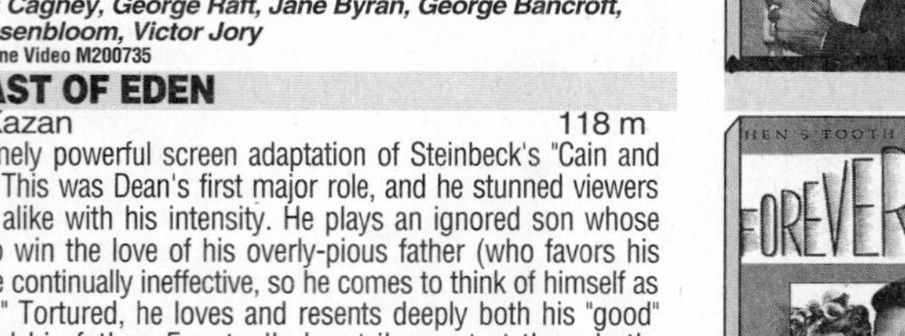

10 Extremely powerful screen adaptation of Steinbeck's "Cain and Abel." This was Dean's first major role, and he stunned viewers and critics alike with his intensity. He plays an ignored son whose attempts to win the love of his overly-pious father (who favors his brother) are continually ineffective, so he comes to think of himself as being "bad." Tortured, he loves and resents deeply both his "good" brother and his father. Eventually he strikes out at them both. Powerful drama. Do not miss this one.

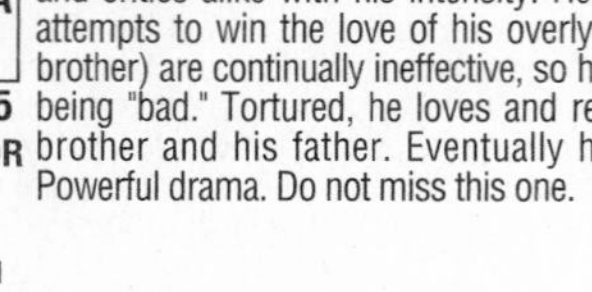

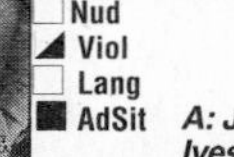

A: James Dean, Jo Van Fleet, Julie Harris, Raymond Massey, Burl Ives, Albert Dekker

© WARNER HOME VIDEO 1005

EASY LIVING

D: Jacques Tourneur 77 m

NR | DMA ROM | 1949 | B&W | Sex | Nud | Viol | Lang | ◢ AdSit

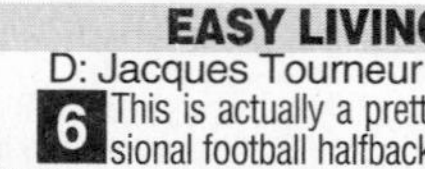

6 This is actually a pretty meaty sports story about a star professional football halfback who discovers that he has a heart defect. If he continues to play, he risks dying but gets to keep his beautiful wife. If he quits, he will loose the money, glamour and probably her, too. Plus, all he will have to look forward to is a job at a small college. However, he gets support from an unexpected source when a secretary from the front office (Ball) tries to help him work out his problems with his wife, even though she loves him, too. One of Victor Mature's best performances.

A: Victor Mature, Lucille Ball, Lizabeth Scott, Sonny Tufts, Lloyd Nolan, Jack Paar

© TURNER HOME ENTERTAINMENT 6035

EDISON, THE MAN

D: Clarence Brown 107 m

NR | DMA | 1940 | COLOR | Sex | Nud | Viol | Lang | AdSit

7 Good entertainment and an inspiring story of the life of the man who brought us the motion picture, the light bulb, the phonograph, the ticker tape and numerous other inventions. The "Wizard of Menlo Park" (played by Tracy) is interviewed on the occasion of the 50th anniversary of the light bulb. His life's story is told as a series of flashbacks... how he started as a penniless janitor with a basement laboratory and later came to create some of the most significant inventions of the industrial age. Keeps moving. Pretty good.

A: Spencer Tracy, Charles Coburn, Rita Johnson

Distributed By MGM/UA Home Video M202346

ELEPHANT BOY

D: Robert Flaherty 82 m

NR | DMA CLD | 1937 | B&W | Sex | Nud | Viol | Lang | AdSit

7 Delightful Rudyard Kipling family adventure movie. A young Indian boy's (Sabu) dream is to become a great hunter. But, when his favorite elephant is sold to a mean dealer, Sabu steals the animal back and escapes into the jungle. There he discovers a large wild herd of elephants and the place that elephants go when they die. Filmed and set in 1930s India, this is both an interesting portrait of the time and place, and a worthy adventure in its own right, particularly for children. There is only one white man in the picture. All others are Indian.

A: Sabu, W.E. Holloway, Walter Hudd, Bruce Gordon, D.J. Williams

© HBO VIDEO 90655

EMPEROR JONES, THE

D: Dudley Murphy 72 m

NR | DMA | 1933 | B&W | Sex | Nud | Viol | Lang | ◢ AdSit

8 This is a very unusual film for its time and starred the famed black actor, singer, athlete and civil rights champion Paul Robeson. He plays Brutus Jones, an overly-proud man who cheated on his fiance and killed his friend in a crap game. Sentenced to life on a chain gang, he escapes and arrives in Haiti where he meets Smithers, an unscrupulous white trader (the only white man in the entire film) who first hires him as a servant. Soon he becomes Smithers' partner, charged with keeping the slaves in line. Jones, however, convinces the rabble that he is immortal and soon has declared himself emperor of the island. This video also contains a 29 minute biography of Robeson, the man.

A: Paul Robeson, Dudley Digges, Frank Wilson, Fredi Washington, Ruby Elzy

© HOME VISION ROB 010

EXECUTIVE SUITE

D: Robert Wise 105 m

NR | DMA | 1954 | B&W | Sex | Nud | Viol | Lang | ◼ AdSit

8 Top-notch melodrama about the power struggle at the top of a major corporation when the president of the company dies. Five junior execs vie for the top spot. However, Stanwyck, as daughter of the founder, mistress of the dead president and the largest shareholder, is the one who must decide. This is a multifaceted script containing many subplots which are all told simultaneously, keeping the story involving and fast-paced. Excellent screenplay, interesting characters and sparkling dialogue move this above the level of a simple soap opera. Top-notch cast. 5 Oscar nominations.

A: William Holden, June Allyson, Barbara Stanwyck, Fredric March, Walter Pidgeon, Shelley Winters

Distributed By MGM/UA Home Video M301400

FOREVER AND A DAY

D: Rene Clair, Edmund Goulding 105 m

NR | DMA | 1943 | B&W | Sex | Nud | Viol | Lang | AdSit

9 A unique once-in-a-lifetime cast of English stars of the 30s and 40s (over eighty in all) star in this epic saga. It is the story about one particular manor house in London and it spans more than 100 years of its history. The story follows each generation that lives in it, from Napoleonic times in 1804 to the Blitz of WWII. The film was created specifically to buck up war time spirits. Each sequence was prepared with meticulous care and contains excellent acting under superb directorship and writing. Fine entertainment.

A: Claude Rains, Charles Laughton, Merle Oberon, Brian Aherne, Ray Milland, Ida Lupino

© HEN'S TOOTH VIDEO 1004

FOUNTAINHEAD, THE

D: King Vidor 114 m

NR | DMA | 1949 | B&W | Sex | Nud | Viol | Lang | ◼ AdSit

7 Ann Rand's classic novel is given life with her own screenplay. Cooper stars as a determined individualist and uncompromising architect whose designs are ahead of his time. He designs a housing project, but the project's builders drastically change what he has done. Outraged, and unwilling to compromise, he blows up the project rather than let its construction be completed. When he is tried for his actions, he accepts no defense other than what he did was the right thing to do. Strong screen chemistry between Cooper and Neal.

A: Gary Cooper, Patricia Neal, Raymond Massey, Kent Smith, Robert Douglas

Distributed By MGM/UA Home Video M301774

FROM HERE TO ETERNITY

D: Fred Zinnemann 118 m

NR | DMA ROM | 1953 | B&W | ◢ Sex | Nud | ◢ Viol | Lang | ◼ AdSit

10 Extremely powerful and passionate movie. Winner of eight Oscars, including Best Picture. (It was nominated for 13 in all.) This is a riveting melodrama depicting Army life in Hawaii just prior to the outbreak of World War II. The blockbuster cast creates memorable characters - each with his own gripping story to tell. Clift is a rebellious bugler and a reluctant boxer, Sergeant Lancaster is having an affair with an officer's wife (famous love scene on the beach), and high-spirited Sinatra earns the wrath of bully Borgnine. This was a huge box office hit that has lost nothing with time.

A: Burt Lancaster, Montgomery Clift, Deborah Kerr, Frank Sinatra, Donna Reed, Ernest Borgnine

© COLUMBIA TRISTAR HOME VIDEO 60531

FUGITIVE, THE

D: John Ford — 99 m

NR | DMA | 1947 | B&W

8 A brooding drama that was one of Henry Fonda's finest performances. He plays a devout and dedicated priest in a fictional Central American country that has outlawed Catholicism. Since he has publicly rejected the government, he has become a wanted man and so goes into hiding in a small village. The townspeople hide him and he performs small rituals for them. He also comforts an American gangster in hiding and baptizes the bastard son of a beautiful woman. However, eventually he is betrayed. Gripping story is a loose adaptation of "The Power and the Glory." Memorable.

Sex / Nud / Viol / Lang / AdSit

A: Henry Fonda, Dolores Del Rio, Pedro Armendariz, Ward Bond, Leo Carrillo, J. Carrol Naish

© TURNER HOME ENTERTAINMENT 6102

FURY

D: Fritz Lang — 99 m

NR | DMA SUS | 1936 | B&W

9 Terrifying depiction of mob hysteria and a self-destructive revenge. Spencer Tracy is wrongly accused of a kidnapping in a small town. A lynch mob attacks the jail in which he is housed and sets it ablaze. Afterward, twenty-one people, including one woman, are brought up on charges of murder because it is believed that Tracy died in the fire - but he did not. However, he is extremely bitter and he now enjoys watching their torment. He remains in hiding and they all stand trial for a murder they did not commit, but would have.

Sex / Nud / Viol / Lang / AdSit

A: Spencer Tracy, Sylvia Sidney, Walter Abel, Bruce Cabot, Edward Ellis, Walter Brennan

Distributed By MGM/UA Home Video M200960

GENERAL DIED AT DAWN, THE

D: Lewis Milestone — 93 m

NR | DMA SUS | 1936 | B&W

9 An exotic adventure story of intrigue. A mysterious soldier of fortune (Cooper) agrees to smuggle gold across the frontiers of China to help finance a peasant rebellion against a ruthless warlord (Tamiroff) who is attempting to take over the northern provinces of China. However, on the way there, Cooper is drawn into games of double-cross after falling for a beautiful American (Carroll) who lures him to Tamiroff. Fine character studies mark this atmospheric drama concerning Oriental intrigue. Tamiroff is especially treacherous and evil.

Sex / Nud / Viol / Lang / AdSit

A: Gary Cooper, Akim Tamiroff, Madeleine Carroll, Porter Hall, Dudley Digges, William Frawley

© MCA/UNIVERSAL HOME VIDEO, INC. 80859

GILDA

D: Charles Vidor — 110 m

NR | DMA ROM | 1946 | B&W

8 Steamy film noir that is Rita Hayworth's most memorable role. A South American casino owner (Macready) hires Glenn Ford as a body guard for his sultry wife (Hayworth), unaware that they were once lovers. When Macready disappears and is presumed dead, Ford and Hayworth take up where they left off and Ford runs the casino. Then the husband comes back, seeking revenge. Most memorable for sexy Hayworth's steamy striptease to "Put the Blame on Mame."

Sex / Nud / Viol / Lang / AdSit

A: Rita Hayworth, Glenn Ford, George Macready, Joseph Calleia, Steven Geray

© COLUMBIA TRISTAR HOME VIDEO 60194

GOING MY WAY

D: Leo McCarey — 126 m

NR | DMA COM MUS | 1944 | B&W

9 This was a major box office hit in its time and it still holds up fairly well today. It won seven Oscars, including Best Picture, Screenplay, Actor and Supporting Actor. It is the heartwarming and sentimental story of a loveable crusty old parish priest (Fitzgerald), with a rundown church, who is won over by a young priest (Crosby) sent to give both him and his church a boost. Crosby sings "Swinging on a Star" and "Too-ra-Loo-ra-Loo-ra" - winner of Best Song Oscar. Unflinchingly sentimental and a great time. Followed by THE BELLS OF ST. MARY'S.

Sex / Nud / Viol / Lang / AdSit

A: Bing Crosby, Barry Fitzgerald, Rise Stevens, Gene Lockhart, Frank McHugh

© MCA/UNIVERSAL HOME VIDEO, INC. 55038

GOLDEN BOY

D: Rouben Mamoulian — 99 m

NR | DMA | 1939 | B&W

6 This was William Holden's screen debut in a starring role. He plays a young man who has had a hard life and fought off the discouragement brought on by his surroundings to become a great violinist, but he is tired of being poor. He signs up with a boxing trainer (Adolphe Menjou) and things begin to change for him, but still not fast enough. So he drops Menjou to sign on with a hood who can get him into a really big-money fight. A little dated now, but still worth while. Holden's performance is still outstanding, as is Stanwyck's as the woman who corrupts him.

Sex / Nud / Viol / Lang / AdSit

A: Barbara Stanwyck, Adolphe Menjou, William Holden, Lee J. Cobb, Joseph Calleia, Sam Levene

© GOODTIMES 4413

GONE WITH THE WIND - 50TH ANNIVERSARY EDITION

D: Victor Fleming — 232 m

G | DMA ROM | 1939 | COLOR

10 Majestic David O. Selznick production of the greatest novel ever about the Civil War. It has also been called the greatest movie ever made and was the winner of eight Oscars out of thirteen nominations. It is an epic saga about the transformation of Southern aristocracy and the romantic Old South through the fires of war. It contains stunning portraits of life in the South before, during and after the Civil War. Our primary window into this massive change is the travails of a spoiled and headstrong girl, Scarlet O'Hara. A great love story and great spectacle. Great and masterfully crafted entertainment. See also JEZEBEL.

Sex / Nud / Viol / Lang / AdSit

A: Clark Gable, Vivien Leigh, Leslie Howard, Olivia de Havilland, Thomas Mitchell, Victor Jory

Distributed By MGM/UA Home Video M902130

GOODBYE, MR. CHIPS

D: Sam Wood — 115 m

NR | DMA ROM | 1939 | B&W

9 Sentimental and heartwarming portrait of a shy, bumbling but well-meaning Latin teacher at an Victorian English boy's school who comes out of his shell only when he meets his future wife (Greer Garson) on holiday. She transforms his shyness into a warmth that the the boys can understand, and he becomes a popular institution at the school. This unabashedly sentimental story grips at your heartstrings and received seven Academy Award nominations. Donat's moving performance even beat out Clark Gable's Rhett Butler for Best Actor Oscar in 1939. It is still a richly rewarding experience.

Sex / Nud / Viol / Lang / AdSit

A: Robert Donat, Greer Garson, John Mills, Terry Kilburn

Distributed By MGM/UA Home Video M300687

GOOD EARTH, THE

D: Sidney Franklin — 138 m

NR | DMA | 1937 | B&W

10 Engrossing and beautifully wrought retelling of Pearl S. Buck's classic Pulitzer Prize-winning novel. A simple Chinese peasant farmer and his wife (through an arranged marriage) endure years of backbreaking labor and poverty to become wealthy, only to have their farm ruined in a drought. Then their lives are suddenly transformed again when revolution sweeps the land and he becomes a wealthy lord. But his greed corrupts him and soon they are again destroyed. Only when it's too late does he learn what his long-neglected wife has given him. Brilliant special effects. 2 Oscars. A milestone picture.

Sex / Nud / Viol / Lang / AdSit

A: Paul Muni, Luise Rainer, Walter Connolly, Tilly Losch, Charley Grapewin, Jessie Ralph

Distributed By MGM/UA Home Video M600120

GRAND HOTEL

D: Edmund Goulding — 112 m

NR | DMA COM | 1932 | B&W

9 Winner of Best Picture Oscar of 1932. A beautiful Berlin Hotel is filled to overflowing with glamorous guests (virtually all the major name MGM stars of the period). This glorious soap opera covers one 24-hour period in which the guest's lives become intertwined. John Barrymore is a financially embarrassed Baron who becomes a jewel thief but falls in love with his intended victim, a ballerina (Garbo) who just wants to be left alone. Lionel has only months to live but still wants to make time with Crawford. The story is still quite good today, but the production techniques are quite dated.

Sex / Nud / Viol / Lang / AdSit

A: Greta Garbo, Joan Crawford, John Barrymore, Wallace Beery, Lionel Barrymore, Lewis Stone

Distributed By MGM/UA Home Video M400564

GRAPES OF WRATH, THE

D: John Ford — 129 m

NR | DMA | 1940 | B&W

10 This is a powerful film masterpiece that was taken from Steinbeck's Pulitzer Prize-winning novel of the same name. It is an epic saga of a pitiful group of farmers who are ravaged by the Great Depression and are forced to leave their drought-stricken Oklahoma farms. Destitute, they migrate to California hoping to get work in the fields there but instead are confronted with prejudice, fear and violence, and they become virtual slaves. Heartbreaking story of determination in the face of impossible odds. Sterling performances. Two Oscars.

Sex / Nud / Viol / Lang / AdSit

A: Henry Fonda, Jane Darwell, John Carradine, Charley Grapewin, Dorris Bowden, Russell Simpson

© FOXVIDEO 1024

GREATEST SHOW ON EARTH, THE

D: Cecil B. DeMille — 149 m

NR | DMA | 1952 | COLOR

8 This is a pretty good time, especially for families, and was the winner of the Best Picture Oscar. It is a big-budget production that presents all the aspects of circus life and is loaded with all the thrills of the big-top. Three principal stories from backstage help hold it all together: James Stewart as a clown with a mysterious past (he is never seen without his makeup), there is a love story and a massive train wreck. Plenty of circus thrills and excitement, too, plus loads of major stars.

Sex / Nud / Viol / Lang / AdSit

A: Betty Hutton, James Stewart, Charlton Heston, Cornel Wilde, Dorothy Lamour, Gloria Grahame

© PARAMOUNT HOME VIDEO 6617

GREAT EXPECTATIONS

D: David Lean 118 m

NR | DMA | 1946 | B&W

10 Excellent production of Dickens's classic story of a penniless orphan who, as a small boy, meets a mysterious stranger in a graveyard and serves as a hired playmate to a young girl under the care of the wealthy, eccentric and mysterious Mrs. Havisham. Later, he is given a mysterious financial endowment, thereby also the opportunity to become a gentleman. However, he is not told who his benefactor is. This film does a wonderful job of capturing the mood of Victorian times. Excellent in all aspects. Winner of two Oscars. Generally recognized as the best of any Dickens adaptations.

Sex / Nud / Viol / Lang / ◢ AdSit

A: John Mills, Alec Guinness, Valerie Hobson, Bernard Miles, Finlay Currie, Jean Simmons

© PARAMOUNT HOME VIDEO 12568

GREAT MAN VOTES, THE

D: Garson Kanin 72 m

NR | DMA COM | 1938 | B&W

9 Delightful gem of a movie. Barrymore is a former professor at Harvard and an author who has been mourning the death of his wife. He has been reduced to being a drunk and the Children's Society threatens him with having his children taken away. By chance, he is chosen to cast the deciding vote in the town's mayoral election and he plays his new power role for maximum benefit, thereby gaining a new-found respect from everyone - including himself. Good dramatic moments, interspersed with some really funny ones. Simple, but well-told story. Good entertainment.

Sex / Nud / Viol / Lang / AdSit

A: John Barrymore, Peter Holden, Virginia Weidler, Donald MacBride, William Demarest

© TURNER HOME ENTERTAINMENT 6257

GREED

D: Erich von Stroheim 133 m

NR | DMA | 1924 | B&W

10 Powerful silent era masterpiece that still speaks effectively to more modern audiences. This epic film was trimmed down by the studio from its original length of over eight hours. It is a story of how two people were changed from being devoted lovers into becoming spiteful adversaries. The specter of greed slowly consumes both their love and their lives. He becomes so consumed by it, and the hatred it spawns, that he murders his best friend. This is not as melodramatic as it may sound. It is well done, but the effects of the severe editing are noticeable.

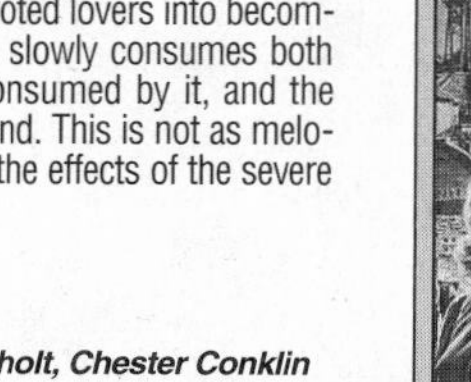

Sex / Nud / Viol / Lang / ◢ AdSit

A: Gibson Gowland, ZaSu Pitts, Jean Hersholt, Chester Conklin

Distributed By MGM/UA Home Video M301360

HAMLET

D: Laurence Olivier 115 m

NR | DMA | 1948 | COLOR

10 This is a bravura production of the best known of the Shakespeare plays. It was also a winner of five Oscars, including Best Picture and Best Actor. Olivier is overpowering in his depiction of Hamlet, the mad Prince of Denmark. Beautifully photographed and staged. Long held up as the standard by which to judge all other productions, even though the screen adaptation was slightly abbreviated.

Sex / Nud / ◢ Viol / Lang / ■ AdSit

A: Laurence Olivier, Eileen Herlie, Jean Simmons, Felix Aylmer, Terence Morgan, Peter Cushing

© PARAMOUNT HOME VIDEO 12569

HEIRESS, THE

D: William Wyler 115 m

NR | DMA ROM | 1949 | COLOR

9 This is a compelling drama based upon an 1881 novel entitled Washington Square. The film garnered 4 Oscars, including Olivia de Haviland's second for her powerful performance as a plain daughter of an extremely wealthy and very domineering man. She is pursued by a gold-digging playboy (Clift) and falls deeply in love with him, but when her father threatens to disinherit her, Clift abandons her on the eve of their wedding. He returns again, seven years later and after the father is dead, but this time she plots her revenge.

Sex / Nud / Viol / Lang / ◢ AdSit

A: Olivia de Havilland, Montgomery Clift, Ralph Richardson, Miriam Hopkins, Vanessa Brown, Mona Freeman

© MCA/UNIVERSAL HOME VIDEO, INC. 80153

HENRY V

D: Laurence Olivier 136 m

NR | DMA | 1945 | COLOR

9 Laurence Olivier's brilliant adaptation of Shakespeare's play won him a special Oscar for "outstanding achievement as actor, producer and director." Unique in that the production begins as an actual 1500ish production might have at the Globe Theatre and then expands into on-location filming. The story is that of the young Prince of Wales who leads his men to victory against the French. Olivier did two other Shakespeare pieces: HAMLET and RICHARD III.

Sex / Nud / Viol / Lang / AdSit

A: Laurence Olivier, Robert Newton, Leslie Banks, Felix Aylmer, Renee Asherson, Leo Genn

© PARAMOUNT HOME VIDEO 12570

HIGH SIERRA

D: Raoul Walsh 101 m

NR | DMA CRM | 1941 | B&W

9 One of Bogart's finest roles as he plays Mad Dog Earle, a weary and aging bank robber who is just out of prison after many years. Reluctantly, Earle agrees to head up just one more big job and then retire. But the heist goes bad. Now on the run, he befriends a poor family who has a pretty daughter with a bad foot, and pays for her operation. He has fallen for her, much to the dismay of Ida Lupino, who loves him. Ultimately, Earle is chased into the High Sierras after a harrowing car chase. Excellent and sympathetic portrait by Bogie of an old hood who gains a heart.

Sex / Nud / ◢ Viol / Lang / ◢ AdSit

A: Humphrey Bogart, Ida Lupino, Alan Curtis, Arthur Kennedy, Joan Leslie, Henry Hull

Distributed By MGM/UA Home Video M201851

HOME OF THE BRAVE

D: Mark Robson 86 m

NR | DMA WAR | 1948 | B&W

8 This was a hard-hitting drama in 1948, and it still carries an impact today. It was one of the first films to deal seriously with prejudice. Edwards is the only black soldier in his squad. He is constantly harangued by the others and has developed tremendous doubt about his worth. Then, when he carries out one member of the squad who was wounded, he becomes paralyzed from the waist down. However, in a hospital it is discovered that he has no physical injury. His wounds are in fact much deeper. He is helped by a psychiatrist to understand that it is his sense of shame and worthlessness. Intelligent presentation, well acted.

Sex / Nud / ◢ Viol / Lang / ◢ AdSit

A: Lloyd Bridges, Frank Lovejoy, James Edwards, Steve Brodie

© REPUBLIC PICTURES HOME VIDEO 1845

HOW GREEN WAS MY VALLEY

D: John Ford 118 m

NR | DMA | 1941 | B&W

10 Winner of 5 Academy Awards including Best Picture. An undisputed masterpiece that has lost nothing with time. 60-year-old Huw Morgan tells the story of his childhood growing up as the youngest of six children in a loving family. They live in Welsh mining town snuggled in a lush green valley. But life in the town and in the mines is hard and dangerous, and there is labor strife too. Life itself at times seems to conspire to destroy the townsfolk and the Morgans in particular. Still, through it all, they survive. There is actually very little plot and is more a series of vignettes that together tell their story of a loving family. Heart-tugging and majestic.

Sex / Nud / Viol / Lang / AdSit

A: Walter Pidgeon, Maureen O'Hara, Donald Crisp, Anna Lee, Roddy McDowall, Barry Fitzgerald

© FOXVIDEO 1037

HUMAN COMEDY, THE

D: Clarence Brown 117 m

NR | DMA | 1943 | B&W

8 This is an Oscar-winning slice-of-life story that is not at all shy about pulling on your heartstrings. It is about life in a small California town and how it is affected by the events of World War II. Mickey Rooney shines as a high-schooler making extra money as a Western Union delivery boy. It's his job to deliver the war news to families, while he and everyone else try to carry on a normal life. This is pure Americana. The broader overall portrait of this point in history is told through a series of small vignettes. Four additional Oscar nominations.

Sex / Nud / Viol / Lang / ◢ AdSit

A: Mickey Rooney, Frank Morgan, James Craig, Marsha Hunt, Fay Bainter, Ray Collins

Distributed By MGM/UA Home Video M300746

HURRICANE, THE

D: John Ford 102 m

NR | DMA | 1937 | B&W

6 One of the earliest disaster flicks from Hollywood. It contains highly believable special effects that are just as effective today as they were then. While the climactic hurricane effects have never been equaled, the story line is somewhat labored and the characters are simplistic sterotypes. The story concerns an idyllic South Sea island where the white governor has become obsessed with capturing a proud runaway native. Once convicted of attacking a white man who insulted him and then repeatedly sentenced to longer and longer terms for failed escape attempts, the man again has escaped.

Sex / Nud / Viol / Lang / AdSit

A: Jon Hall, Dorothy Lamour, Raymond Massey, Mary Astor, C. Aubrey Smith

© HBO VIDEO 90756

I AM A FUGITIVE FROM A CHAIN GANG

D: Mervyn LeRoy 127 m

NR | DMA | 1932 | B&W

10 Disturbing and very powerful landmark drama from early filmdom that has been remade several times since. It still is powerful today. An innocent man is convicted by a corrupt criminal system and is sent to a brutal Southern chain gang. He escapes from this nightmare and establishes himself in a normal life, but he is discovered and again is drawn back into a life of cruelty and crime. Famous for its stunning climax. Unforgettable. Muni is masterful. Based on fact. This film was actually written by a man (Robert E. Burns) who was on the run because of similar circumstances when this film was made.

Sex / Nud / Viol / Lang / ◢ AdSit

A: Paul Muni, Glenda Farrell, Helen Vinson, Preston Foster, Edward Ellis, Allen Jenkins

Distributed By MGM/UA Home Video M202516

I COVER THE WATERFRONT

D: James Cruze 74 m

NR DMA 1933 B&W

6 An interesting piece of early film drama. A big-city newspaper reporter suspects that there is a smuggling operation under way in San Diego. So he romances a free-spirited girl (Colbert) to get evidence against her fisherman father, who he suspects of smuggling illegal Chinese immigrants into the country. But things get unexpectedly complicated for him when he falls for the girl. Quite dated now, but of interest still - particularly to film buffs.

Sex Nud Viol Lang AdSit

A: Ben Lyon, Claudette Colbert, Ernest Torrence, Hobart Cavanaugh, Morris Black, Harry Beresford

© VIDEO YESTERYEAR 20

INFORMER, THE

D: John Ford 91 m

NR DMA 1935 B&W

9 Masterful production of a profound study in human nature, and a winner of two Oscars - including Best Actor for McLaglen, who put in the performance of his career. The story is set in 1922 Ireland. McLaglen is Gypo Nolan, a big, slow-witted, hard-drinking Irish pug, who commits the ultimate transgression for an Irishman when he turns in his IRA friend to the British to collect twenty pounds. Nolan is tormented both with severe bouts of regret and the revenge of the IRA. Powerful drama with a climax that will not leave you after the film's done.

Sex Nud Viol Lang AdSit

A: Victor McLaglen, Heather Angel, Preston Foster, Margot Grahame, Wallace Ford, Una O'Connor

© TURNER HOME ENTERTAINMENT 6156

INTOLERANCE

D: D.W. Griffith 123 m

NR DMA 1916 B&W

8 This is a milestone epic movie. After being heavily criticized for BIRTH OF A NATION, Griffith produced this monster film that was, for many many years after, the most expensive film ever done. It is, in fact, not one but four stories of injustice and inhumanity throughout time. The stories from ancient time are shown in counterpoint to those of modern times. All four plots resolve simultaneously in one climax. The palace sets for the Babylon sequence were the largest ever built for a film. In one scene there were over 15,000 people and 250 chariots.

Sex Nud Viol Lang AdSit

A: Lillian Gish, Bessie Love, Mae Marsh, Elmo Lincoln, Tully Marshall, Eugene Pallette

© HBO VIDEO 905640 2

INTRUDER IN THE DUST

D: Clarence Brown 87 m

NR DMA MYS 1949 B&W

9 Excellent screen depiction of a William Falkner novel, set in his home state of Mississippi. An old black man is held in contempt by the townsfolk because he is proud and owns his own land. When a white man is killed and the old man is found in possession of a pistol which has just been fired, he is accused of the murder by police. A young white boy who has befriended him sees what has happened, coerces his reluctant lawyer uncle into helping the old man before he is lynched by the townsfolk and into finding the real killer. Very well done, both on a social and dramatic level, and as a murder mystery.

Sex Nud Viol Lang AdSit

A: David Brian, Claude Jarman, Jr., Juano Hernandez, Porter Hall, Elizabeth Paterson

Distributed By MGM/UA Home Video M202838

I REMEMBER MAMA

D: George Stevens 119 m

NR DMA COM 1948 B&W

9 Sentimental favorite and piece of Americana that won five Oscar nominations. It is the beautifully told and heartwarming story of an immigrant Norwegian family in San Francisco near the turn of the century. The story is told from the viewpoint of the oldest daughter (Bel Geddes). She tells of her shy aunt and her blustering uncle, of the family's daily struggles, but most of all she talks of how her mother fights to win a new and better life for her children in a new land. A very rewarding experience. Great feel good film.

Sex Nud Viol Lang AdSit

A: Irene Dunne, Barbara Bel Geddes, Oscar Homolka, Philip Dorn, Ellen Corby, Edgar Bergen

© TURNER HOME ENTERTAINMENT 2071

JACKIE ROBINSON STORY, THE

D: Alfred E. Green 76 m

NR DMA 1950

8 Intriguing straightforward biography of a sports great, and the first black man ever allowed to play against white men as an equal participant in major league professional baseball. Becoming an equal on the field did not include being an equal off the field, nor was his appearance on the field accepted gracefully by all. Jackie Robinson was chosen not only because he was an exceptional ball player, but because he was exceptional human being off the field as well. This is a fascinating social history of a very special man.

Sex Nud Viol Lang AdSit

A: Jackie Robinson, Ruby Dee, Minor Watson, Louise Beavers, Richard Lane, Harry Shannon

Distributed By MGM/UA Home Video M204612

JAMAICA INN

D: Alfred Hitchcock 94 m

NR DMA SUS 1939 B&W

6 Hitchcock's last directorial effort before leaving England. It is a costume drama and not his best effort, but it has its points and is aided greatly by a good cast. Charles Laughton plays a country squire in 1819 England who secretly leads a band of pirates that makes its living by luring ships onto the rocks of the Cornish coast and then ransacking them. Maureen O'Hara knows his secrets and, with the help of Robert Newton, a soldier of the King, she brings him down. Film history fans only.

Sex Nud Viol Lang AdSit

A: Charles Laughton, Maureen O'Hara, Robert Newton, Leslie Banks

© VIDEO YESTERYEAR 1133

JOAN OF ARC

D: Victor Fleming 100 m

NR DMA 1948 COLOR

6 Lavish production values and an empathetic performance by Ingrid Bergman mark this film about a devout French farm girl who, in 1428, led the French armies successfully against England. But when a truce is signed with England, she becomes a political prisoner. She is later tried as a heretic by the clergy and then is burned at the stake by the English. In spite of these significant assets, the film is somewhat slow moving and takes itself very seriously. Patient viewers will be rewarded, though.

Sex Nud Viol Lang AdSit

A: Ingrid Bergman, Jose Ferrer, Ward Bond

© UNITED AMERICAN VIDEO CORP. 18007

JOHNNY BELINDA

D: Jean Negulesco, Robert Wise 103 m

NR DMA 1948 B&W

9 Emotionally charged melodrama that won Jane Wyman a Best Actress Oscar. She plays a young deaf-mute farm girl living in a small Nova Scotia town. She is befriended by a doctor (Ayres) who teaches her sign language. However, one night she is raped by a villager and she gets pregnant. Everyone thinks the doctor is the father and he is disgraced. But the rapist tries to take the baby from her and she kills him. Now she is on trial for murder. This could have been just another soap box tearjerker, but it is raised far above that level by excellent presentation and sensitive acting.

Sex Nud Viol Lang AdSit

A: Jane Wyman, Lew Ayres, Charles Bickford, Agnes Moorehead, Jan Sterling, Stephen McNally

Distributed By MGM/UA Home Video M600761

JUAREZ

D: William Dieterle 133 m

NR DMA 1939 B&W

8 Extravagant epic biography of the famous Mexican revolutionary leader who struggled to free his country from the well-meaning but inept rule of Emperior Maximillian. That government was a puppet government of Napolean III and a pawn in European politics. Juarez was very impressed with Lincoln and tried to emulate him. However, he first had to take the reins of power from foreign hands. There was a lot going on in that struggle and this movie tries to get it all (too much) packed into two hours. Still, it contains loads of major stars, high production values and excellent acting.

Sex Nud Viol Lang AdSit

A: Paul Muni, Bette Davis, Brian Aherne, John Garfield, Claude Rains, Donald Crisp

Distributed By MGM/UA Home Video M201699

JULIUS CAESAR

D: Joseph L. Mankiewicz 122 m

NR DMA 1953 B&W

9 The National Review Board stated that this is "the best and most forceful adaptation of William Shakespeare that Hollywood has ever accomplished." It received five Academy Award nominations, including Best Picture. Lavish production values and an all-star cast in top form mark this superior production of honor and politics in ancient Rome. Superior in all respects.

Sex Nud Viol Lang AdSit

A: Marlon Brando, James Mason, John Gielgud, Louis Calhern, Edmond O'Brien, Greer Garson

Distributed By MGM/UA Home Video M200274

KEY LARGO

D: John Huston 100 m

NR DMA SUS 1948 COLOR

8 Entertaining gangster melodrama. Bogart plays a disillusioned soldier home from the war (WWII). He makes a stop in the hotel on Key Largo of the Florida Keys to visit the father and wife of a good friend who was killed in the war. But while he is there, a hurricane comes up, trapping them and a gangster (Robinson) together inside the hotel. Bacall looks to him to be their savior, but Bogart has seen enough violence. That is, until Robinson backs him into a corner. Very well done. Claire Trevor won Best Supporting Actress as Robinson's bimbo lush.

Sex Nud Viol Lang AdSit

A: Humphrey Bogart, Lauren Bacall, Edward G. Robinson, Lionel Barrymore, Claire Trevor

Distributed By MGM/UA Home Video M201617

O L D I E S

KEYS OF THE KINGDOM, THE

D: John M. Stahl 137 m

NR | DMA | 1944 | B&W

8 Gregory Peck won an Oscar nomination in this his first major film. It is the reverent story of a devout Catholic missionary in China. The story begins with him being an old man thinking that he has accomplished little with his life and then his life is told in flashback to reveal quite the opposite. He is a humble man who arrives at a remote outpost where there is no following or mission, and creates one - overcoming many personal hardships along the way, including war. An inspiring and heartwarming movie with lavish production values and a strong supporting cast.

Sex | Nud | Viol | Lang | AdSit

A: Gregory Peck, Thomas Mitchell, Vincent Price, Roddy McDowall, Edmund Gwenn, Cedric Hardwicke

© FOXVIDEO 1314

KING KONG

D: Merian C. Cooper, Ernest B. Schoedsack 100 m

NR | DMA ACT FAN | 1933 | COLOR

10 This is an enduring classic, the many merits of which overcome its primitive production techniques (even though the live action special effects are still quite believable today). On a remote island, a giant ape is discovered and captured. He is transported to America where he is put on display in New York City. Tormented by the crowds, the huge beast manages to break free, wreaking major havoc upon the city, seeking out Fay Wray and taking her with him as he makes a last stand at the top of the Empire State Building. See also MIGHTY JOE YOUNG.

Sex | Nud | ◢ Viol | Lang | AdSit

A: Ernest B. Scholedsack, Robert Armstrong, Fay Wray, Bruce Cabot, Frank Reicher, Noble Johnson

© TURNER HOME ENTERTAINMENT 6003

KINGS ROW

D: Sam Wood 126 m

NR | DMA ROM | 1941 | COLOR

9 Sweeping melodramatic tale which rips away a veil of deceptive serenity from a small Midwestern town just prior to WWI. Two young men (Cummings and Reagan) and their friends grow up there, cradled in its apparent serenity. But when they reach adulthood, the seedy truth of their little town becomes painfully known to them. It is a place of many deceits and deep-seated moral decay. This film was much like the famed PEYTON PLACE and had to be considerably tamed down to get past the censors of the day. Reagan's performance won him universal praise and likely ranks as his career's best.

Sex | Nud | Viol | Lang | ■ AdSit

A: Ann Sheridan, Robert Cummings, Ronald Reagan, Claude Rains, Charles Coburn, Betty Field

Distributed By MGM/UA Home Video M202438

KNUTE ROCKNE - ALL AMERICAN

D: Lloyd Bacon 96 m

NR | DMA | 1940 | COLOR

7 Now-famous sport biography of Notre Dame's immortal and inspirational football coach, Knute Rockne. Rockne was a real person who coached for many winning seasons and became a fixture at Notre Dame and a national icon. The film is pretty corny and sentimental, but it is still a favorite. Rockne was best known for his inspirational lectures to his players. O'Brien relished his role and gave it his best shot with his most famous line, "Now go in there and win one for the Gipper." This is also the movie that helped a President get elected.

Sex | Nud | Viol | Lang | AdSit

A: Pat O'Brien, Ronald Reagan, Gale Page, Donald Crisp, Albert Basserman

Distributed By MGM/UA Home Video M400555

LAND OF THE PHARAOHS

D: Howard Hawks 104 m

NR | DMA | 1955 | COLOR

7 Big screen spectacle (with 10,000 extras) that is a fictionalized account of the building of the Great Pyramid of Egypt in about 3000 B.C. For thirty years the Pharaoh (Hawkins) struggled to get his monumental tomb built, while he struggled also against his scheming wife, who wanted both his treasure and his kingdom. (Fans of Joan Collins will note this as one of her earliest appearances.) In many ways, this is uninspired filmmaking. Yet its scope and a nifty ending still manage to intrigue viewers.

Sex | Nud | ◢ Viol | Lang | AdSit

A: Jack Hawkins, Joan Collins, James Robertson Justice, Dewey Martin, Alexis Minotis, Sydney Chaplin

© WARNER HOME VIDEO 11357

LASSIE COME HOME

D: Fred M. Wilcox 90 m

NR | DMA CLD | 1943 | COLOR

8 Wonderful, warm and sentimental family film that marked the original screen debut of Lassie. A desperately poor English family is forced to sell their dog to a Scottish duke, but Lassie escapes and struggles against long odds to find her way back home across 1000 miles to the boy who loves her. (This Lassie was really a him). You will also see a very young Roddy McDowall and Elizabeth Taylor in this heartwarming film.

Sex | Nud | Viol | Lang | AdSit

A: Roddy McDowall, Donald Crisp, Dame May Whitty, Edmund Gwenn, Nigel Bruce, Elizabeth Taylor

Distributed By MGM/UA Home Video M201866

LAST COMMAND, THE

D: Josef von Sternberg 88 m

NR | DMA | 1928 | B&W

8 Silent film classic that is still very highly regarded. After the Russian revolution of 1917, a once-haughty Czarist general has fled communist Russia for America. He is now just an impoverished extra working on a Hollywood movie lot. In a ruthless twist of irony, he is cast as a Russian general in a film about the Russian revolution. That film is being directed by another ex-Russian - this one is an ex-revolutionary, who takes great and sadistic pride in humiliating the deposed general at every opportunity. Nominated for Best Picture in the first year of the Academy Awards.

Sex | Nud | Viol | Lang | ◢ AdSit

A: Emil Jannings, Evelyn Brent, William Powell, Nicholas Soussanin, Michael Visaroff, Jack Raymont

© PARAMOUNT HOME VIDEO 2785

LAST DAYS OF POMPEII, THE

D: Ernest B. Schoedsack 93 m

NR | DMA | 1934 | B&W

6 Religious drama epic set among the Romans at the time of Christ. Preston Foster is a blacksmith who loses his wife and baby in a tragedy and so becomes a ruthless and successful gladiator. He is sent to Judea to aid Pontius Pilate, bringing with him the son of one of his victims whom he has adopted. In Judea he sees Christ but fails to come to his aid. Nevertheless, when the boy is seriously hurt in an accident, Christ heals him. The blacksmith is forever changed. Renowned for its special effects.

Sex | Nud | ◢ Viol | Lang | ◢ AdSit

A: Preston Foster, Alan Hale, Basil Rathbone, John Wood, Louis Calhern, Dorothy Wilson

© TURNER HOME ENTERTAINMENT 6044

LAST HOLIDAY

D: Henry Cass 88 m

NR | DMA COM | 1950 | B&W

8 George Bird just found out that he is going to die in a couple of weeks. He is a rather ordinary man, rather quiet and solitary actually, but he decides now to change all that. He collects all his savings and takes a luxurious last holiday an exclusive seaside resort. Here he is mistaken for a man of means and influence and soon becomes a favorite among his new friends. This is a luxury that had always escaped him in the past but now he finds himself in the unfamiliar position of being able to influence others. Bittersweet, tender and witty story in which Guiness excels, as usual.

Sex | Nud | Viol | Lang | ◢ AdSit

A: Alec Guiness, Beatrice Campbell, Kay Walsh, Coco Alsan, Bernard Lee, Sidney James

© HOME VISION LAS 080

LEFT HAND OF GOD, THE

D: Edward Dmytryk 87 m

NR | DMA ROM | 1955 | COLOR

7 One of Bogart's last roles. He plays a soldier-of-fortune in post-WWII China who is trying to elude his former employer, a renegade warlord (well played by Cobb) caught up in his own private wars. Bogart takes refuge in a small-town mission under the guise of a priest. His phony rituals and sermons find some favor with the locals, so all goes well for a while. Then Bogart falls for beautiful nurse Tierney. A little slow-moving at times, but still worthy entertainment.

Sex | Nud | ◢ Viol | Lang | ◢ AdSit

A: Humphrey Bogart, Gene Tierney, Lee J. Cobb, Agnes Moorehead, E.G. Marshall, Jean Porter

© CBS/FOX VIDEO 1304

LES MISERABLES

D: Richard Boleslawski 104 m

NR | DMA | 1935 | B&W

9 Best of four Hollywood presentations of Victor Hugo's classic story of good and evil in 19th-century France. Riveting performances mark this story concerning a starving man who steals a loaf of bread in order to survive, but is captured and sent to prison. He escapes prison and rises in station to become mayor, but is tormented by the unfeeling police inspector Charles Laughton who will not allow his past to be buried and is obsessed with his recapture. A magnificent and moving presentation.

Sex | Nud | Viol | Lang | AdSit

A: Fredric March, Charles Laughton, Cedric Hardwicke, Florence Eldridge, John Carradine

© FOXVIDEO 1268

LETTER OF INTRODUCTION

D: John M. Stahl 104 m

NR | DMA COM | 1938 | B&W

6 A young actress trying to break into show business presents a letter of introduction to Adolphe Menjou, a former movie idol. The letter announces that she is the daughter he never knew he had. He takes an immediate liking to the girl and makes her his protege, but he conceals that she is his daughter. His fiancee is jealous and she walks out on him, as does his daughter's boyfriend on her. Melodrama mixed with comedy. Very strong cast of fun people, including the hugely popular real-life ventriloquist Edgar Bergen (father to Candice) and his dummy Charlie McCarthy.

Sex | Nud | Viol | Lang | AdSit

A: Adolphe Menjou, Andrea Leeds, Edgar Bergen, Charlie McCarthy, George Murphy, Eve Arden

© VIDEO YESTERYEAR 1024

LETTER TO THREE WIVES, A

D: Joseph L. Mankiewicz 103 m

NR | DMA | 1949 | B&W | Sex | Nud | Viol | Lang | AdSit

9 An ingenious and delicious script which won an Oscar, as did the Director. Three women are off together on an all-day picnic, when they each receive a letter from the town flirt announcing that she has run off with one of their husbands. But, there is no way of knowing whose husband it is until the three can get back to a phone. In the interim, each woman is forced to dissect her relationship with her own husband. Soon each woman discovers that she is not nearly so confident in herself and her relationship as she had thought. Intriguing plot that was well executed and was quite witty, too.

A: Jeanne Crain, Linda Darnell, Ann Sothern, Kirk Douglas, Paul Douglas, Thelma Ritter

© FOXVIDEO 1093

LIFE OF EMILE ZOLA, THE

D: William Dieterle 117 m

NR | DMA | 1937 | B&W | Sex | Nud | Viol | Lang | AdSit

9 Sincere and moving biography of the famed 19th-century French intellectual and journalist. Zola was a popular novelist who became famous as a defender of the rights of the oppressed. Later in life, he rose to the defense of a Jewish soldier who was unjustly accused of treason and then banished. His stirring defense, and other efforts to establish justice in the French system during the later half of the 19th-century, gave him great notoriety. This lavish production won Best Picture, Screenplay and Supporting Actor, plus a nomination for Muni as Best Actor. See also PRISONER OF HONOR.

A: Paul Muni, Gale Sondergaard, Joseph Schildkraut, Gloria Holden, Donald Crisp, Louis Calhern

Distributed By MGM/UA Home Video M301469

LION IS IN THE STREETS, A

D: Raoul Walsh 88 m

NR | DMA | 1953 | COLOR | Sex | Nud | Viol | Lang | AdSit

7 Jimmy Cagney plays a corrupt Huey Long-type politician. He is a backwoods peddler who turns a gift for gab into a big-time meal ticket. Folks trust him. He makes a crusade out of the plight of the poor sharecropper in his Southern state, and tries to ride it all the way to power in the governor's mansion. But along the way his political ambitions override any sense of morality he used to have, and he sells out whenever he has to. Stirring conclusion. For still other depictions of Heuy Long, see the Oscar-winning ALL THE KING'S MEN or BLAZE.

A: James Cagney, Barbara Hale, Anne Francis, Warner Anderson, Lon Chaney, Jr., John McIntire

© WARNER HOME VIDEO 11682

LITTLE FOXES, THE

D: William Wyler 116 m

NR | DMA | 1941 | B&W | Sex | Nud | Viol | Lang | AdSit

9 An outstanding classic, which has not diminished in the least with time. It is an extremely well made and totally enthralling story of scheming and greed from within an amoral family of carpetbaggers that dominates a poor Southern town at the turn of the 20th century. They plot with and against each other to get what they want - no matter the cost. For them, the game is nearly - but not quite - as important as the money. Flawless acting. Seven Oscar nominations, including Best Picture, Director and Actress.

A: Bette Davis, Herbert Marshall, Teresa Wright, Richard Carlson, Patricia Colinge, Dan Duryea

© HBO VIDEO 90754

LITTLE LORD FAUNTLEROY

D: John Cromwell 98 m

NR | DMA CLD | 1936 | B&W | Sex | Nud | Viol | Lang | AdSit

8 Solid family entertainment - not just for kids. A poor young kid from Brooklyn learns that he is the grandson of an English Earl and potential heir to his fortune. But the bitter and crusty old man blindly hates his widowed American daughter-in-law, the boy's mother, just because she is American. The boy is brought to England to live with the grumpy old geezer, whose hard heart is soon softened by the cheerful kid. Solid story. Solid acting. Very well done.

A: Freddie Bartholomew, C. Aubrey Smith, Dolores Costello, Jessie Ralph, Mickey Rooney, Guy Kibbee

© CBS/FOX VIDEO 8066

LITTLE PRINCESS, THE

D: Walter Lang 93 m

NR | DMA CLD | 1939 | COLOR | Sex | Nud | Viol | Lang | AdSit

6 Predictable, but effective, and endearing story which was Shirley Temple's last major childhood success. Shirley plays the daughter of a rich British officer who places her in an exclusive girls boarding school when he goes off to fight in the Boer war. When it is believed he has been killed, she is thought to be penniless. Suddenly poor, the school's head mistress makes poor little Shirley work as a maid to pay off her bill. But Shirley doesn't believe her father is dead. She visits army hospitals entertaining the troops and searching for him. Lavish production. Predictable, but very enjoyable.

A: Shirley Temple, Richard Greene, Anita Louise, Ian Hunter, Cesar Romero

© FOXVIDEO 1298

LITTLE WOMEN

D: George Cukor 122 m

NR | DMA | 1933 | B&W | Sex | Nud | Viol | Lang | AdSit

10 Delightful and faithful film adaptation of Louisa May Alcott's classic book. This film version has now become a classic in its own right and is generally recognized as the best of all the film productions attempted. The story is that of four very independent sisters, all coming of age in Victorian New England during the time of the Civil War. Their father is off fighting the war. Heburn is a standout against a stellar cast as Jo, who wants be a writer and would leave but is afraid the family will disintegrate. Nominated for three Oscars and winner of Best Screenplay. Wonderful.

A: Katharine Hepburn, Spring Byington, Joan Bennett, Frances Dee, Jean Parker, Edna May Oliver

Distributed By MGM/UA Home Video M600084

LITTLE WOMEN

D: Mervyn LeRoy 122 m

NR | DMA | 1949 | COLOR | Sex | Nud | Viol | Lang | AdSit

7 First remake of the 1933 classic film version of Alcott's classic Civil War era novel. Four very independent girls struggle to grow up, each in her own way at a time of strife, while their father is off fighting in the Civil War. This film benefits from color and slick production. It is a sentimental and unabashed tearjerker, and it is a good effort by a talented cast. It simply cannot compare, however, to the 1933 version.

A: June Allyson, Peter Lawford, Margaret O'Brien, Elizabeth Taylor, Janet Leigh

Distributed By MGM/UA Home Video M200805

LONG VOYAGE HOME, THE

D: John Ford 106 m

NR | DMA | 1940 | COLOR | Sex | Nud | Viol | Lang | AdSit

9 Outstanding and moving drama set in pre-WWII 1939. It is the story of the men of the Merchant Marines - men who spend their lives at sea. Taken from four one-act plays from Eugene O'Neill, it explores the hopes and dreams of working-class sailors on a ship in a dangerous ammunition convoy from America to England. Richly textured stories of the principal characters are revealed in a series of vignettes. Nominated for six Oscars, including Best Picture and Screenplay.

A: John Wayne, Thomas Mitchell, Ian Hunter, Barry Fitzgerald, John Qualen, Ward Bond

© WARNER HOME VIDEO 35076

LOST MOMENT, THE

D: Martin Gabel 90 m

NR | DMA | 1947 | B&W | Sex | Nud | Viol | Lang | AdSit

8 A compelling, absorbing and offbeat drama. Robert Cummings is an American publisher in Italy seeking the long-lost love letters of a long-dead great poet. There, he is to interview an odd old lady who claims to be Juliana, the inspiration for the letters. But he immediately falls for the old woman's neurotic niece, (Hayward) who sometimes imagines herself as being Juliana and also claims to know where the papers are. His efforts to solve the mystery of the papers lead to a near tragedy. Fascinating story based in part on true events.

A: Robert Cummings, Susan Hayward, Agnes Moorehead, Joan Lorring, Eduardo Ciannelli

© REPUBLIC PICTURES HOME VIDEO 2448

LOST WEEKEND, THE

D: Billy Wilder 101 m

NR | DMA | 1945 | B&W | Sex | Nud | Viol | Lang | AdSit

9 Landmark film and winner of Oscars for Best Picture, Director, Actor and Screenplay. This is a powerful, starkly realistic story about alcoholism, that has lost none of its punch over time. Ray Milland is a writer who is totally dissatisfied with his life and who is lost in drinking. Neither his brother nor his girlfriend can bring him out of it. Only after he has lost all control, totally humiliated himself and endured an agonizing hell, will he bring himself back from the brink. Some things never change. Superb acting and an engrossingly powerful film.

A: Ray Milland, Jane Wyman, Phillip Terry, Howard da Silva, Frank Faylen, Mary Young

© MCA/UNIVERSAL HOME VIDEO, INC. 80354

LOVE ME OR LEAVE ME

D: Charles Vidor 122 m

NR | DMA MUS | 1955 | COLOR | Sex | Nud | Viol | Lang | AdSit

8 This is an engrossing serious musical, based on real-life people. It won an Oscar for Best Story and five other nominations besides. It is also reported to be one of Cagney's favorite roles. Cagney plays "the Gimp" Snyder, a gangster who turns his wife, Ruth Etting, (played by Doris Day) into one of the biggest singers of the "Roaring Twenties" era - but Cagney is extremely jealous and also has a bad temper. He makes her into a star onstage, but offstage, he makes her life a nightmare. Very strong performances. Great songs (13 total), including Doris Day's big hit "I'll Never Stop Loving You."

A: James Cagney, Doris Day, Cameron Mitchell, Robert Keith, Tom Tully

Distributed By MGM/UA Home Video M200755

MADAME BOVARY

D: Vincente Minnelli 114 m

NR | DMA ROM | 1949 | B&W

9 Throwing caution to the wind and forsaking the love of her husband, Emma Bovary's appetite for love and lust fuels extramarital affairs that eventually lead to her destruction. This classic 19th-century French story is brought to the screen with lavish production values. James Mason, the novelist who told her story, is now up on morals charges and is protecting himself against censorship. He tells the story as a series of flashbacks. Jones is brilliant as the cold-as-ice heroine who is forever on a quest for something more.

Sex / Nud / Viol / Lang / AdSit

A: Van Heflin, Jennifer Jones, James Mason, Louis Jourdan, Christopher Kent, Gene Lockhart

Distributed By MGM/UA Home Video M600102

MADAME CURIE

D: Mervyn Le Roy 113 m

NR | DMA ROM | 1943 | B&W

8 Nominated for seven Oscars, including Best Picture. Plenty of entertainment value here. Greer Garson and Walter Pidgeon had great screen chemistry, which had earlier helped to propel MRS. MINIVER into becoming a major success. Here, Marie was a young Polish student studying in Paris at the turn of the Twentieth-Century. Scientist Pierre Curie grew to respect the quality of her work and soon also fell in love with her. Quite by chance one day, the two discover odd behavior in a sample. Intrigued, they begin a five year arduous quest that led eventually to the purification of the first radioactive substance, radium. Sometimes slows down, but remains interesting throughout.

Sex / Nud / Viol / Lang / AdSit

A: Greer Garson, Walter Pidgeon, Henry Travers, Albert Basserman, Robert Walker, C. Aubrey Smith

Distributed By MGM/UA Home Video 202054

MADE FOR EACH OTHER

D: John Cromwell 93 m

NR | DMA COM ROM | 1939 | B&W

8 Warm and endearing comedy/drama about a young couple learning to deal with the pitfalls that come with the first few years of marriage. It is painful and sometimes funny to watch because the movie is masterful at imitating real-life. Financial troubles, conflicts with in-laws and confusion about parenting abound. Even when the couple's first child nearly dies, the pair finds a way to overcome that extra hurdle and build on the new strength they have found. Lombard and Stewart do a fine job keeping the plot from getting too heavy.

Sex / Nud / Viol / Lang / AdSit

A: James Stewart, Carole Lombard, Charles Coburn, Ward Bond

© GOODTIMES 5033

MAGNIFICENT AMBERSONS, THE

D: Orson Welles 88 m

NR | DMA | 1942 | B&W

9 Brilliant cinematography make this a critic's favorite and it is a masterful adaptation of a Pulitzer Prize-winning novel. It is the 25-year story of the downfall of a wealthy Midwestern family, the Ambersons, who are the town's wealthiest family in the 1870s at the film's beginning. George is their spoiled and arrogant son, whom everyone in the town despises and hopes will someday get his comeuppance. Eventually he does. It's a good story, well told and beautifully crafted - but it is also true that it is very hard for some of us to identify strongly with wealthy Victorians.

Sex / Nud / Viol / Lang / AdSit

A: Joseph Cotten, Anne Baxter, Tim Holt, Agnes Moorehead, Ray Collins, Richard Bennett

© TURNER HOME ENTERTAINMENT 2073

MARTY

D: Delbert Mann 94 m

NR | DMA ROM | 1955 | B&W

7 Very popular and a winner of 4 Academy Awards, including Best Picture! A realistic and insightful, low-key romance story about a 34-year-old bachelor (Borgnine) who lives with his mother and spends the weekends with his bachelor buddies. He is a lonely and kind-hearted gentle man who wants to be married but has resigned himself to being a fat ugly man who will always be alone. Then he unexpectedly meets a lonely woman to whom he is immediately drawn. However, his emotions are torn when his friends don't think she is pretty and his mother becomes terrified of being left alone. Only slightly dated.

Sex / Nud / Viol / Lang / AdSit

A: Ernest Borgnine, Betsy Blair, Joe De Santis, Joe Mantell, Esther Minciotti, Jerry Paris

Distributed By MGM/UA Home Video M301267

MARY OF SCOTLAND

D: John Ford 123 m

NR | DMA | 1936 | B&W

8 Powerful and engrossing history lesson! In this 16th-century biography, the ill-fated Catholic Queen of Scotland (Hepburn) battles with her jealous cousin and rival, the Anglican Queen of Britain (Eldridge), for power. Fredric March plays Hepburn's friend (and soon her lover) in a bid for power which eventually leads to her execution. Particularly poignant is Mary's address to her accusers in court. The story is intriguing and, while fictionalized, the broad historical details are reasonably accurate in this Hollywood production.

Sex / Nud / Viol / Lang / AdSit

A: Katharine Hepburn, Fredric March, John Carradine, Florence Eldridge, Douglas Walton, Robert Barrat

© TURNER HOME ENTERTAINMENT 6013

MEMBER OF THE WEDDING, THE

D: Delbert Mann 90 m

NR | DMA | 1953 | COLOR

9 Highly acclaimed and emotional coming-of-age drama. Julie Harris is Frankie, a lonely, confused and motherless 12-year-old tomboy, struggling both with her budding adolescence and her utter confusion over her older brother getting married, leaving home and her behind. When Frankie naively invites herself along with the the newlyweds on their honeymoon, she is so humiliated at their rejection that she runs way from home. The only one who understands the emotional turmoil the girl is going through is the housekeeper, the only mother the girl has ever known. Exceptional performances.

Sex / Nud / Viol / Lang / AdSit

A: Ethel Waters, Julie Harris, Brandon de Wilde, Arthur Franz, Nancy Gates

© COLUMBIA TRISTAR HOME VIDEO 60930

MEN, THE

D: Fred Zinnemann 85 m

NR | DMA WAR | 1950 | B&W

8 Excellent. An honest and moving account of the trials of a wounded veteran returning from WWII. In the opening scenes, Lieutenant Wilozek (Brando) gets a sniper's bullet in his spine. He is paralyzed. He returns home but the extent of his injuries have plummeted him into a severe depression that no one can penetrate. His girlfriend slowly breaks down the wall he has built and his doctor gets him involved in a rehabilitation program. But, in spite of it all, he is still consumed with doubt and self-pity. Stunning debut for Brando.

Sex / Nud / Viol / Lang / AdSit

A: Marlon Brando, Teresa Wright, Everett Sloane, Jack Webb, Howard St. John

© REPUBLIC PICTURES HOME VIDEO 2710

MILDRED PIERCE

D: Michael Curtiz 112 m

NR | DMA ROM | 1945 | B&W

9 Gripping melodrama that earned 6 Oscar nominations! Crawford stars as a poor housewife who waits tables and ignores her husband in order to provide for her spoiled daughters, especially Velda (Blythe). She's very good at her job and turns her knowledge and drive into being the owner of a profitable restaurant chain. Then she marries a playboy (Scott) so that her daughters can benefit socially from his name. But he goes through her money, throwing her into bankruptcy. And, too late, she discovers that he's also been sleeping with her spoiled daughter. Crawford won an Oscar for Best Actress.

Sex / Nud / Viol / Lang / AdSit

A: Joan Crawford, Ann Blyth, Jack Carson, Zachary Scott, Eve Arden, Bruce Bennett

Distributed By MGM/UA Home Video M301742

MIRACLE OF OUR LADY OF FATIMA, THE

D: John Brahm 102 m

NR | DMA | 1952 | COLOR

7 A reverent re-creation of a story believed by many to be true. Three Portuguese farm children in 1917 (during WWI) claimed to have seen a vision of the Virgin Mary, who they called the "beautiful lady." The children were threatened by local officials, yet they did not back down. Because Portugal's government at the time was anti-religious, this reported vision touched off a hotbed of religious confrontation and the faith of these children reinspired the faith in countless others. Each year, believers still make pilgrimages to this site, to what they believe is a holy place.

Sex / Nud / Viol / Lang / AdSit

A: Gilbert Roland, Susan Whitney, Sherry Jackson, Sammy Ogg, Angela Clark, Frank Silvera

© WARNER HOME VIDEO 11540

MISS SADIE THOMPSON

D: Curtis Bernhardt 93 m

NR | DMA | 1954 | COLOR

6 Miss Sadie Thompson (sexy Rita Hayworth) is a prostitute who has been thrown out of Honolulu at the request of a missionary (Ferrer). Rather than be deported to San Francisco where she is wanted by the cops, she catches a tramp steamer for New Caladonia in the South Pacific. On the way there, her ship is quarantined on an Island occupied by Marines. She sets all their hearts fluttering (with a now famous song and dance) but she falls for one (Ray). Meanwhile, Ferrer arrives on that same island. She asks for his help to change her ways, but instead she wakes up the dormant passions of the missionary.

Sex / Nud / Viol / Lang / AdSit

A: Rita Hayworth, Jose Ferrer, Aldo Ray, Charles Bronson

© COLUMBIA TRISTAR HOME VIDEO 60055

MOULIN ROUGE

D: John Huston 120 m

NR | DMA | 1952 | COLOR

8 This colorful biography was nominated for 7 Oscars. It is the fascinating story of Parisian painter, Henri De Toulouse-Lautrec, whose fame was over-shadowed by physical deformity. Hurt in a childhood accident, the gifted painter had difficulty charming women, and so frequented some of the more notorious sections of Paris hoping to find acceptance. He fell madly in love with Marie but the relationship did not last. His paintings became famous almost overnight for immortalizing the Montmartre district, the cafe and the Moulin Rouge, but his father felt he had disgraced the family name.

Sex / Nud / Viol / Lang / AdSit

A: Jose Ferrer, Zsa Zsa Gabor, Suzanne Flon, Eric Pohlmann, Colette Marchland, Christopher Lee

Distributed By MGM/UA Home Video M201734

MRS. MINIVER

D: William Wyler 135 m

NR | DMA | 1942 | B&W

Sex / Nud / Viol / Lang / AdSit

9 Outstanding war drama! This fine film follows the middle-class Miniver family, especially Mrs. Miniver, as they cope with the trials of war in a beleaguered England. This is an effective and sentimental story about how Mrs. Miniver successfully deals with the trauma of her young sons being at risk fighting, fighting restricted war rations and surviving terrifying German bombing raids. The speech made at the end was deemed by President Roosevelt to be so important that he ordered a reprint of it made and air dropped over a battered England. Very touching film that won seven Oscars, including Best Picture.

A: Greer Garson, Walter Pidgeon, May Whitty, Teresa Wright, Reginald Owen, Henry Travers

Distributed By MGM/UA Home Video M300804

MR. SMITH GOES TO WASHINGTON

D: Frank Capra 125 m

NR | DMA COM | 1939 | B&W

Sex / Nud / Viol / Lang / AdSit

9 Time-honored classic that brought home eleven Oscar nominations. An idealistic scout master (Stewart) is called to Washington to complete a dead senator's term. He arrives to discover that corruption is running rampant. So, the idealistic new senator decides he must battle his own mentor and all the political powers with a filibuster, to fight against a bill he knows is only a land scam. This sets the stage for a very powerful, and now classic, final scene depicting a little man fighting against the powerful system. Capra's brilliant creation expertly casts Stewart as America's hero to restore our faith in democracy.

A: Jean Arthur, James Stewart, Claude Rains, Edward Arnold, Thomas Mitchell, Beulah Bondi

© COLUMBIA TRISTAR HOME VIDEO 60064

MUTINY ON THE BOUNTY

D: Frank Lloyd 132 m

NR | DMA ACT | 1935 | B&W

Sex / Nud / Viol / Lang / AdSit

9 Rousing adventure tale based upon an actual historical event. This is a film totally undiminished with time. The men of H.M.S. Bounty served under a ruthless and sadistic sea captain during a British naval sea expedition in 1789. The ship's first officer, Fletcher Christian (Gable), fed up with the suffering and degradation that the sadistic Captain Blythe (Laughton) imparts to the crew, leads them in a mutiny, setting Blythe adrift on the high seas. Oscar winner for Best Picture. Also see 1984's THE BOUNTY for a very different slant.

A: Charles Laughton, Clark Gable, Franchot Tone, Herbert Mundlin, Eddie Quillan, Dudley Digges

Distributed By MGM/UA Home Video M400450

MY FRIEND FLICKA

D: Harold Schuster 89 m

NR | DMA CLD | 1943 | COLOR

Sex / Nud / Viol / Lang / AdSit

8 Touching and heartwarming. Despite his father's (Foster) concerns, a young boy (McDowall) longs to have a horse of his own. Finally giving in, Foster allows McDowall to pick from the herd, but he picks a filly with a bloodline that is known for its wildness. Persistent, the boy proves both himself and the horse when he manages to train the unruly animal which becomes his best friend. This magnificent sentimental favorite was based on Mary O'Hara's moving novel, and is a film that the whole family will enjoy. It was also made into a long-running TV series.

A: Roddy McDowall, Preston Foster, Rita Johnson, Jeff Corey, James Bell

© FOXVIDEO 1899

NATIONAL VELVET

D: Clarence Brown 124 m

G | DMA CLD | 1944 | COLOR

Sex / Nud / Viol / Lang / AdSit

10 All-time favorite for everyone... a real rah rah film, one that will have you cheering. Elizabeth Taylor is absolutely adorable as a young girl who wins a neighbor's unruly horse in a lottery. Then, she and her young friend, an embittered jockey (Mickey Rooney), train the horse to race and, against everyone's wishes, she enters him into England's famed Grand National steeplechase. A heartwarming and loveable story. It won two Oscars and was followed by INTERNATIONAL VELVET in 1977.

A: Elizabeth Taylor, Mickey Rooney, Donald Crisp, Anne Revere, Angela Lansbury, Reginald Owen

Distributed By MGM/UA Home Video M300480

NICHOLAS NICKLEBY

D: Alberto Cavalcanti 103 m

NR | DMA | 1947 | B&W

Sex / Nud / Viol / Lang / AdSit

7 Dickens's classic story is given a noble effort by a talented cast. The story is that of a young man, Nicholas Nickleby, who takes a teaching position at a cruel orphanage. Nicholas protects a crippled student there from the school's nasty masters, and also protects his sister and sweetheart from his miserly and manipulative uncle. The story as written has 52 characters in it. The Royal Shakespeare Company takes 8 1/2 hours to perform their play. This film does quite well for only 1 1/2 hours.

A: Derek Bond, Cedric Hardwicke, Alfred Drayton, Bernard Miles, Sally Ann Howes, Sybil Thorndike

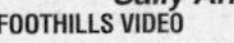

© FOOTHILLS VIDEO

NONE BUT THE LONELY HEART

D: Clifford Odets 113 m

NR | DMA | 1944 | B&W

Sex / Nud / Viol / Lang / AdSit

7 This was a very unusual role for Cary Grant. He never had another quite like it, and it won him an Oscar nomination (his only one). He plays a worthless and lazy Cockney drifter in the slums of London during the 1930s. He is a shiftless good-for-nothing who gets involved with a petty crime ring. But he undergoes a moral transformation when he learns that his mother (Barrymore) is dying of cancer and he returns to take care of her pawn shop. Ethel Barrymore won an Oscar for her performance. It is moody and somewhat grim, but it has some fine moments, too.

A: Cary Grant, Ethel Barrymore, Barry Fitzgerald, Jane Wyatt

© TURNER HOME ENTERTAINMENT 6251

OF HUMAN BONDAGE

D: John Cromwell 84 m

NR | DMA ROM | 1934 | B&W

Sex / Nud / Viol / Lang / AdSit

8 First and, by most critic's judgment, the best film version of Somerset Maugham's novel. This is also the film that made Bette Davis a star. It is the story of a sensitive but brilliant club-footed medical student and his compulsive attraction to a promiscuous barmaid who is constantly unfaithful to him and abuses him badly. Set in London, Davis's cockney accent is definitely lacking, but she more than makes up for that deficiency by the saucy life she breathes into her character.

A: Leslie Howard, Bette Davis, Kay Johnson, Frances Dee, Alan Hale, Reginald Denny

© UNITED AMERICAN VIDEO CORP. 15005

OLD MAID, THE

D: Edmund Goulding 96 m

NR | DMA ROM | 1939 | B&W

Sex / Nud / Viol / Lang / AdSit

8 A classy soap opera. Davis and Hopkins are cousins who are in love with the same man (Brent). However, when Brent is away for too long a time, Hopkins marries into a rich family. When Brent returns, he has a passionate affair with Davis. Davis gets pregnant, but Brent has gone off to fight in the Civil War and gets killed. So Hopkins invites Davis to come to live with her and adopts the child as her own to hide Davis's shame. Now Davis must watch her child being raised by another woman and be disregarded by that child as being just a meddling aunt. Highly entertaining and a champion tearjerker.

A: Bette Davis, Miriam Hopkins, George Brent, Jane Bryan, Donald Crisp, Jerome Cowan

Distributed By MGM/UA Home Video M301311

OLIVER TWIST

D: David Lean 116 m

NR | DMA | 1948 | B&W

Sex / Nud / Viol / Lang / AdSit

8 This is an excellent screen portrait of Charles Dickens's classic story and truly reflected the bleak misery of his times. Oliver is an eight-year-old orphan boy sent to live at a work house. When Oliver is so brazen as to ask for more gruel, he is punished severely and escapes instead into the streets. There he is quickly recruited into a company of thieves headed by a young pickpocket named The Artful Dodger (Newley) and a vile hideous man named Fagin (Guinness) - until he is rescued by a kindly old man. The much more lively and upbeat musical version is called OLIVER!.

A: Alec Guinness, Robert Newton, Anthony Newley, Kay Walsh, John Howard Davies, Henry Stephenson

© PARAMOUNT HOME VIDEO 12571

ON THE WATERFRONT

D: Elia Kazan 108 m

NR | DMA | 1954 | B&W

Sex / Nud / Viol / Lang / AdSit

10 Extremely powerful drama, one of the most highly acclaimed films of all times. Winner of eight Oscars, including Best Picture, Actor, Director and Supporting Actress. It is a gripping story of an almost-was prize fighter (Brando), who is now just a waterfront dock worker, and his brother (Stieger), who get deeply involved with a corrupt union boss (Cobb). When Brando's girlfriend's (Saint) brother is murdered, Brando is encouraged by a priest (Malden) to rebel against Cobb and the corruption, even though it may mean his life.

A: Marlon Brando, Lee J. Cobb, Rod Steiger, Eva Marie Saint, Karl Malden, Leif Erickson

© COLUMBIA TRISTAR HOME VIDEO 60354

OUR TOWN

D: Sam Wood 88 m

NR | DMA | 1940 | B&W

Sex / Nud / Viol / Lang / AdSit

10 Superb screen presentation of Thorton Wilder's classic and Pulitzer Prize-winning play. Set in the simple, small town of Grover's Corners, New Hampshire just prior to WWI, this story may at first appear to be too simplistic in comparison to life today. However, its power to affect people is truly undiminished with time - whether the audience is sophisticated or not. While this is a loving portrait of a time and lifestyle now long gone, it is also a portrait of the basic nature of humanity that is changeless and timeless. Involving, sensitive and moving.

A: William Holden, Martha Scott, Thomas Mitchell, Frank Craven

© GOODTIMES 5035

OUR VINES HAVE TENDER GRAPES

D: Roy Rowland 105 m

NR | DMA | 1945 | B&W | Sex | Nud | Viol | Lang | AdSit

9 Wonderful, deeply heart-warming and never sappy. A true family film about life in a small rural Wisconsin farming town during WWII. The primary focus is upon young O'Brien and her kind father (Robinson), a widower and farmer - but only in so far as they express the values of the little town. When O'Brien is treated to a late night trip to see her first elephant at the circus, she learns how dangerous nature is after she and her cousin are carried off in a spring flood. She learns of war when one of men of the town has to leave to fight. And, she is the first to help a stricken farmer. Excellent.

A: Edward G. Robinson, Margaret O'Brien, James Craig, Francis Gilford, Agnes Moorehead, Morris Carnovsky

Distributed By MGM/UA Home Video M202837

PENNY SERENADE

D: George Stevens 120 m

NR | DMA ROM | 1941 | B&W | Sex | Nud | Viol | Lang | AdSit

8 Widely recognized as one of the all-time classic, ten-hankie tear-jerkers - the quintessential soap opera. Cary Grant falls in love with a record store sales girl (Dunne). They have a whirlwind romance, marry and he takes her to live in Japan. They are deeply in love and she becomes pregnant but she miscarriages and can no longer have children. After they return to the States they adopt, but again tragedy strikes. And, still their trials are not over. This is an excellent film with extremely strong performances all around. Cary Grant received an Oscar nomination.

A: Cary Grant, Irene Dunne, Edgar Buchanan, Beulah Bondi, Ann Doran, Eva Lee Kuney

© REPUBLIC PICTURES HOME VIDEO 5406

PETRIFIED FOREST, THE

D: Archie Mayo 84 m

NR | DMA SUS | 1936 | B&W | Sex | Nud | Viol | Lang | AdSit

8 This gripping drama seems pretty dated at first, largely to Leslie Howard's melodrama, but it picks up quickly. It is also the film that first got Bogart noticed. He plays a killer gangster being pursued by the cops, who now holds hostage the residents of a diner on a remote Arizona road. A young Davis plays the owner's idealistic dreamer daughter, a painter who wants to escape to Europe. She falls for Howard, a disillusioned writer, drifting through life after having his own similar dreams shattered. He has lost his zest for life, much as Bogart has. But together they can grant her her wish.

A: Humphrey Bogart, Leslie Howard, Bette Davis, Dick Foran

Distributed By MGM/UA Home Video M201805

PHONE CALL FROM A STRANGER

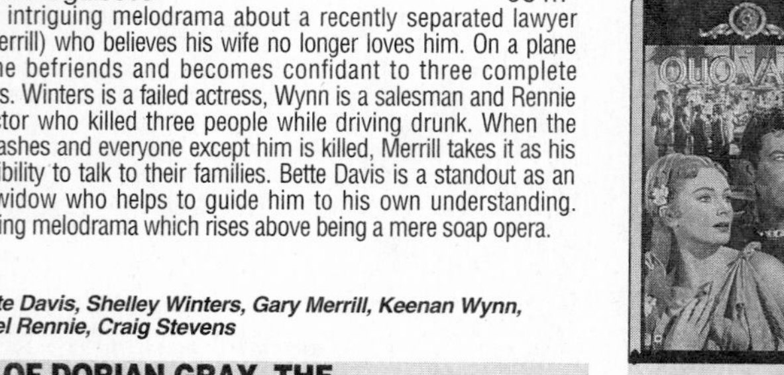

D: Jean Negulesco 96 m

NR | DMA | 1952 | B&W | Sex | Nud | Viol | Lang | AdSit

7 An intriguing melodrama about a recently separated lawyer (Merrill) who believes his wife no longer loves him. On a plane flight, he befriends and becomes confidant to three complete strangers. Winters is a failed actress, Wynn is a salesman and Rennie is a doctor who killed three people while driving drunk. When the plane crashes and everyone except him is killed, Merrill takes it as his responsibility to talk to their families. Bette Davis is a standout as an invalid widow who helps to guide him to his own understanding. Engrossing melodrama which rises above being a mere soap opera.

A: Bette Davis, Shelley Winters, Gary Merrill, Keenan Wynn, Michael Rennie, Craig Stevens

© FOXVIDEO 1528

PICTURE OF DORIAN GRAY, THE

D: Albert Lewin 111 m

NR | DMA HOR FAN | 1945 | B&W | Sex | Nud | Viol | Lang | AdSit

8 An intriguing premise gets top-notch treatment. A roguish 19th-century man strikes a bargain to retain his youthful appearance, and offers up his soul in exchange. While he will never appear to age, a portrait of him (which he keeps well hidden) will and also bears the many scars of his many transgressions. Although sometimes slow moving, this is nonetheless a spellbinding film. A few color sequences are interjected for effect into the largely black and white photography, which won an Oscar. From a short story by Oscar Wilde.

A: George Sanders, Hurd Hatfield, Donna Reed, Angela Lansbury, Peter Lawford, Lowell Gilmore

Distributed By MGM/UA Home Video M400566

PRIDE OF THE YANKEES, THE

D: Sam Wood 129 m

NR | DMA | 1942 | B&W | Sex | Nud | Viol | Lang | AdSit

10 Endearing biography of one of baseball's greatest players. Lou Gehrig was struck down at the height of his career, and eventually killed, by the crippling disease that today bears his name. This is also one of Hollywood's best film biographies ever. Gary Cooper was never better than when he played the New York Yankee first baseman. The film follows both his career and his courageous battle with disease. The final scene has become a classic by itself and is one of Hollywood's all-time most memorable scenes.

A: Gary Cooper, Teresa Wright, Babe Ruth, Walter Brennan, Dan Duryea, Ludwig Stossel

© CBS/FOX VIDEO 7145

PRIMROSE PATH

D: Gregory LaCava 93 m

NR | DMA COM ROM | 1940 | B&W | Sex | Nud | Viol | Lang | AdSit

8 Ginger Rogers shines in this story about a girl from the wrong side of the tracks trying to find a way out of her present existence and unsavory future. She cons her way into a marriage with Joel McCrea, an ambitious owner of a hamburger stand and her ticket out. But her world is turned upside down when he has second thoughts about her after discovering that her mother is a prostitute. Then she discovers that she really does love him. A frank and moving story that is an odd combination of melodrama and comedy. Very good acting.

A: Ginger Rogers, Joel McCrea, Marjorie Rambeau, Miles Mander, Henry Travers

© TURNER HOME ENTERTAINMENT 6019

PRINCE AND THE PAUPER, THE

D: William Keighley 119 m

NR | DMA CLD | 1937 | B&W | Sex | Nud | Viol | Lang | AdSit

8 Rousing film version (the best one) of Mark Twain's own personal favorite of al his many stories. A young English prince longs to learn what life is really like in 16th-century London's slums, so he exchanges clothes and places with a street urchin who is his look-alike. No one is to know, but his enemies at the court learn of the switch and plan to crown the wrong boy King. No one believes the displaced prince's story except for rakish Errol Flynn, who rides and swashbuckles to the aid of the young prince. Large scale and highly enjoyable for young and old.

A: Errol Flynn, Billy Mauch, Bobby Mauch, Claude Rains, Alan Hale, Rex Harrison

Distributed By MGM/UA Home Video 201865

PRISONER, THE

D: Peter Glenville 91 m

NR | DMA | 1955 | B&W | Sex | Nud | Viol | Lang | AdSit

8 Impeccable performances mark this gripping political drama that was banned from both the Cannes and Venice Film Festivals. Set in an unnamed Eastern-block communist country during the '50s (at the height of the Cold War), two former partners against the Nazis are now on opposite political sides and are caught up in a desperate conflict with each other. Alec Guiness is a Cardinal who is being held prisoner by Hawkins, the head of the secret police, and is being tortured into a making a false confession which will then be used to destroy the influence of the Catholic community. Fascinating stuff.

A: Alec Guinness, Jack Hawkins, Raymond Huntley, Wilfrid Lawson

© COLUMBIA TRISTAR HOME VIDEO 60961

QUO VADIS

D: Mervyn LeRoy 171 m

NR | DMA ACT ROM | 1951 | COLOR | Sex | Nud | Viol | Lang | AdSit

8 Epic blockbuster on a grand scale! Hugely popular. Taylor is a Roman commander and a hero just back from a triumphant campaign. He meets and falls for beautiful Deborah Kerr, but he also learns that she is a Christian convert. So when the mad Emperor Niro (Ustinov) burns Rome and places the blame on the Christians, the two lovers are drug out to be publicly executed. Instead, they escape and Taylor goes on to lead the revolt against corrupt Nero. Nominated for eight Oscars, this colossal smash featured lavish sets, exquisite costumes and an eye for detail. Outstanding!

A: Robert Taylor, Deborah Kerr, Peter Ustinov, Leo Glenn, Patricia Laffan, Finlay Currie

Distributed By MGM/UA Home Video M900276

RASPUTIN AND THE EMPRESS

D: Richard Boleslawski 123 m

NR | DMA | 1933 | B&W | Sex | Nud | Viol | Lang | AdSit

8 This superb historic epic is the first and only time that the famous Barrymores were all in the same production. The doomed Russian royalty is warned that the peasantry is rising up in the streets and demanding food and more freedom, but they are pre-occupied with their young hemophiliac son who has fallen and is bleeding to death. The lady-in-waiting informs the Empress of the mad monk Rasputin with mystical powers. He hypnotizes the young prince and stops the bleeding. The Empress now believes he works miracles and Rasputin uses that power to take control and plunder the treasury.

A: John Barrymore, Ethel Barrymore, Lionel Barrymore, Ralph Morgan, Diana Wynyard, Edward Arnold

Distributed By MGM/UA Home Video 202833

RAZOR'S EDGE, THE

D: Edmund Goulding 146 m

NR | DMA ROM | 1946 | B&W | Sex | Nud | Viol | Lang | AdSit

8 Outstanding drama about the search for meaning. When an idealistic young man's world is shaken by the horrors he witnesses in war, he (Power) searches anew for truth. On his return to Chicago, beautiful and sexy Gene Tierney offers him love and the wealth of her family, but he turns her down. He rejects her and the world he grew up in to travel back to the backstreets of Paris and even to the mountains of Nepal. She marries someone else. He returns ten years later having found peace, but those he left behind have none. Nominated for five Academy Awards, including Best Picture. Engrossing.

A: Tyrone Power, Gene Tierney, Anne Baxter, Clifton Webb, Herbert Marshall, John Payne

© FOXVIDEO 1049

REBEL WITHOUT A CAUSE

D: Nicholas Ray 111 m

NR DMA 1955 COLOR

8 Very popular movie from the '50s which defined the beginning of a new era. It was the first film to effectively articulate the problems of teenage America in a way that they could identify with. (It also launched many of the big stars of '50s and '60s, and it put James Dean's star on the map.) Dean is a troubled teenager trying to start over again at a new high school. He is trying to find his way and is taunted by the other kids to test his courage, with tragic results. It is still an effective movie today. The problems of teenagers and parents have not changed.

Sex / Nud / Viol / Lang / AdSit

A: James Dean, Natalie Wood, Sal Mineo, Jim Backus, Dennis Hopper, Nick Adams

© WARNER HOME VIDEO 1011

RED BADGE OF COURAGE, THE

D: John Huston 70 m

NR DMA WAR ACT 1951 B&W

9 Excellent adaptation of Stephen Crane's novel which explores a young Union soldier's battle to conquer his fears after he panics during his first battle of the Civil War. The story takes on a much more profound meaning with Audie Murphie in the lead role because, prior to having become a successful actor, Audie Murphie gained national recognition as being the most highly decorated soldier of WWII. This is a realistic war story, but one where the emphasis is upon the human element of war in spite of the strikingly realistic battle scenes. A moving experience.

Sex / Nud / Viol / Lang / AdSit

A: Audie Murphy, Bill Mauldin, Arthur Hunnicutt, John Dierkes, Royal Dano, Douglas Dick

Distributed By MGM/UA Home Video M300408

RED PONY, THE

D: Lewis Milestone 89 m

NR DMA CLD 1949 COLOR

8 Touching, affecting and moving story that was created by blending of three short stories by John Steinbeck. In it, a lonely young boy turns to a ranchhand for understanding and guidance, and to a frail young horse for affection. The boy's stiff schoolteacher father has married a wealthy woman and she is taking up all his time. The father has become even more distant than before and the boy is confused. This excellent family movie is very believable because the characters are developed effectively through understatement. Strong performances by Mitchum and the boy, Peter Miles. Highly recommended.

Sex / Nud / Viol / Lang / AdSit

A: Myrna Loy, Robert Mitchum, Louis Calhern, Peter Miles

© REPUBLIC PICTURES HOME VIDEO 3406

REMBRANDT

D: Alexander Korda 84 m

NR DMA 1936 B&W

8 A series of vignettes paint a colorful portrait of the famous Dutch painter Rembrandt's last 30 years. The film begins when he is at the height of his fame. However, after the death of his wife, his fortunes begin to fade, along with the quality of his work. He seeks companionship from his housekeeper and then marries his maid (Lanchester). His sorrow, combined with a huge financial burden, leaves the painter continually on the edge of insanity. This is a top-drawer Hollywood biography, even though romanticized and not altogether historically accurate.

Sex / Nud / Viol / Lang / AdSit

A: Charles Laughton, Elsa Lanchester, Gertrude Lawrence, Edward Chapman, Roger Livesey, Marius Goring

© HBO VIDEO 90757

RHAPSODY IN BLUE

D: Irving Rapper 139 m

NR DMA MUS 1945 B&W

7 This biography of the famous American composer George Gershwin is highly romanticized, but it does capture many of his conflicting emotions. It begins with his early days struggling in New York and progresses to his successful days with his partner and brother Ira. Through a series of his musical pieces we watch him slowly craft a new American form of symphony music. Alda does an excellent job of portraying Gershwin and of conveying the inner strength and passion for his work that kept him going. Although not completely on cue or factual, it's still interesting and worthwhile.

Sex / Nud / Viol / Lang / AdSit

A: Robert Alda, Joan Leslie, Alexis Smith, Oscar Levant, Charles Coburn, Herbert Rudley

Distributed By MGM/UA Home Video M301149

RICHARD III

D: Laurence Olivier 158 m

NR DMA 1955 COLOR

8 Shakespeare's fascinating story of one man's grab for England's 15th-century throne! Sir Laurence Olivier, in perhaps one of his finest roles, plays Richard Gloucester, a physically deformed and ruthless nobleman with a sick mind and a driving obsession to become King of England. Richard murders his brother, suffocates a princess and betrays his family, all in pursuit of the crown. This was a big-budget production that is very highly regarded and won numerous awards. It has an outstanding cast, beautiful photography and an Oscar-nominated performance by Olivier.

Sex / Nud / Viol / Lang / AdSit

A: Laurence Olivier, Cedric Hardwicke, Ralph Richardson, John Gielgud, Claire Bloom, Alec Clunes

© HOME VISION RIC 010

RIVER, THE

D: Jean Renoir 99 m

NR DMA ROM 1951 COLOR

9 Wonderfully photographed, an award-winning film. An American, who has lost a leg in the war, has come to visit his cousin living near the Ganges River in India. Living next door to him is an English family, whose teenage daughter's have just begun to awaken to womanhood. The girls are quite taken with the gallant American -- the oldest is certain that he is her Prince Charming come to take her away. However, he has fallen for a beautiful Indian girl. But Indian culture, like the river, is old. The story, while quite simple, is never-the-less quite moving. The real power of the film, however, lies in the photography and the portrait of the geography and culture of India.

Sex / Nud / Viol / Lang / AdSit

A: Patricia Walters, Adrienne Corri, Radha, Thomas E. Breen, Esmond Knight, Nora Swinburne

© HOME VISION RIV 050

ROBE, THE

D: Henry Koster 135 m

NR DMA 1953 COLOR

8 This is one of the best of Hollywood's biblical epics, but not too heavy. A Roman Centurian (Burton) is ordered to supervise Christ's execution where he wins Christ's robe while gambling at the foot of the cross. The robe changes him forever, as it does all who come in contact with it, but it also is much sought-after by the demented emperor Caligula. Burton is ultimately forced to choose between giving the robe to his emperor and becoming a martyr. This was the first film shot in Cinemascope, but the film's bigscreen impact is lost on video. It won two Oscars and also nominated for Best Picture and Actor.

Sex / Nud / Viol / Lang / AdSit

A: Richard Burton, Jean Simmons, Victor Mature, Michael Rennie, Richard Boone, Jay Robinson

© FOXVIDEO 1022

ROCKING HORSE WINNER, THE

D: Anthony Pelissier 91 m

DMA 1949

8 Brilliant English film which brings to the screen one of D.H. Lawrence's short stories. In it, a sensitive boy learns how to keep his family together. His mother's spending has gotten them deeply into trouble and life as he has known it is threatened. Then he discovers that he can magically predict racehorse winners by only riding upon his rocking horse. However, his successes only breed more demands from his parents and his life becomes even more tormented.

Sex / Nud / Viol / Lang / AdSit

A: John Howard Davies, Valerie Hobson, John Mills, Hugh Sinclair, Ronald Squire

© HOME VISION ROC 01

ROSE TATTOO, THE

D: Daniel Mann 116 m

NR DMA ROM 1955 B&W

9 A grieving widow (Magnani), who has been obsessed with the death of her late husband, has become reawakened to the joys of living. She has lived a mundane existence unable to let his memory go, until that is, she discovered that her dead husband had had an affair with a blonde. With the new awareness of his infidelity, she finally allows herself to succumb to the advances of a virile truck driver (with a rose tattoo) and learns to live again. Magnani easily won an Oscar for Best Actress for her captivating performance. Adapted from a play by Tennessee Williams. Nominated for 8 Oscars, including Best Picture.

Sex / Nud / Viol / Lang / AdSit

A: Anna Magnani, Burt Lancaster, Marisa Pavan, Ben Cooper, Virginia Grey, Jo Van Fleet

© PARAMOUNT HOME VIDEO 5511

RUBY GENTRY

D: King Vidor 82 m

NR DMA ROM 1952 B&W

7 A hot-blooded romance turns very sour. When wild girl Jennifer Jones and mild-mannered and well-bred Charlton Heston meet, it's steamy love at first sight. But, unfortunately for Jones, she comes from the wrong side of the North Carolina swamps. Heston takes a proper lady for his wife instead of Jones, which ignites a fierce fury inside her. She contrives to marry a wealthy businessman (Malden) after his bedridden wife (Hutchinson) dies, just so she can use his money to get even with Heston and to destroy him.

Sex / Nud / Viol / Lang / AdSit

A: Jennifer Jones, Charlton Heston, Karl Malden, Josephine Hutchinson

© CBS/FOX VIDEO 8045

SAMSON AND DELILAH

D: Cecil B. DeMille 128 m

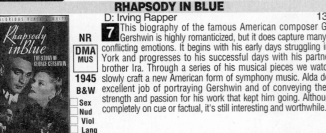

NR DMA 1950 COLOR

7 Cecil B. DeMille's epic Biblical tale of the devilish Delilah (Lamarr) who seduces and then betrays the handsome muscleman Samson (Mature). Hulking Samson wins the hand of a beautiful princess (Lansbury) when he impresses her with his masculinity by killing a lion with his bare hands. But then he is seduced by the charms of Delilah and his power is stolen from him when she cuts off his luxurious golden locks. A cast of thousands and opulent costuming make this an entertaining film. An Oscar winner for Best Art Direction and Best Costumes.

Sex / Nud / Viol / Lang / AdSit

A: Hedy Lamarr, Victor Mature, Angela Lansbury, George Sanders, Henry Wilcoxon, Olive Deering

© PARAMOUNT HOME VIDEO 6726

SEARCH, THE

D: Fred Zinnemann 104 m

NR | DMA WAR | 1948 | B&W

8 Emotional human drama set, and filmed, on location in a destroyed postwar Berlin. A GI (Clift) discovers a young Czech boy (Jandl) hiding in the burned-out rubble of the war-torn city. The boy has survived time and torture in a concentration camp by being suspicious of everything, but Clift breaks down his wall of resistance, befriends and cares for the boy. Meanwhile, the boy's mother is frantically searching in every Displaced Person's Camp to find him. A very moving and poignant drama that won an Oscar for Best Story and a special award for Jandl for outstanding juvenile performance.

Sex / Nud / Viol / Lang / AdSit

A: Montgomery Clift, Ivan Jandl, Aline MacMahon, Jarmila Novotna, Wendell Corey

Distributed By MGM/UA Home Video 202513

SEA WOLF, THE

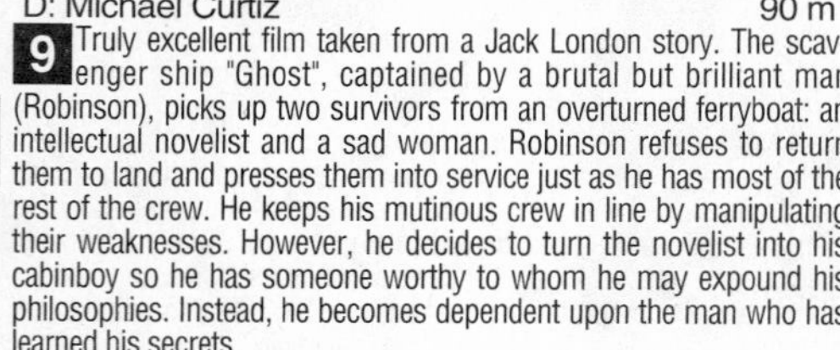

D: Michael Curtiz 90 m

NR | DMA | 1941 | B&W

9 Truly excellent film taken from a Jack London story. The scavenger ship "Ghost", captained by a brutal but brilliant man (Robinson), picks up two survivors from an overturned ferryboat: an intellectual novelist and a sad woman. Robinson refuses to return them to land and presses them into service just as he has most of the rest of the crew. He keeps his mutinous crew in line by manipulating their weaknesses. However, he decides to turn the novelist into his cabinboy so he has someone worthy to whom he may expound his philosophies. Instead, he becomes dependent upon the man who has learned his secrets.

Sex / Nud / Viol / Lang / AdSit

A: Edward G. Robinson, John Garfield, Ida Lupino, Alexander Knox, Gene Lockhart, Barry Fitzgerald

Distributed By MGM/UA Home Video M202840

SECRET GARDEN, THE

D: Fred M. Wilcox 92 m

NR | DMA CLD | 1949 | COLOR

8 Vivid dramatization of the children's classic. A young orphaned girl (O'Brien) is uprooted from India and taken to stay with her embittered uncle (Marshall) and his crippled son (Stockwell) in their huge, dark and foreboding mansion in Victorian England. Marshall is a cold, insensitive and stern type, and Stockwell is a disturbed and unhappy lad. But the determined young girl manages to melt her uncle's heart and bring them happiness, both because she looks so much like his deceased wife and because she finds her aunt's secret garden and begins to nurse it back to life.

Sex / Nud / Viol / Lang / AdSit

A: Margaret O'Brien, Dean Stockwell, Herbert Marshall, Gladys Cooper, Elsa Lanchester

Distributed By MGM/UA Home Video 202377

SERGEANT YORK

D: Howard Hawks 137 m

NR | DMA ACT WAR | 1941 | B&W

9 Excellent and sincere screen portrait of the unusual, but true, story of WWI's biggest war hero. Alvin York was a poor mountain boy from the hills of Tennessee who had virtually no idea of what the bigger world is like. He was a pacifist; still he was drafted into military service for WWI. This strangest of draftees then single-handedly captured 132 German soldiers. Excellent action sequences, but some of the most interesting depictions are scenes of his backwoods existence prior to the war. 11 Oscar nominations, winning two - including Best Actor for Cooper.

Sex / Nud / Viol / Lang / AdSit

A: Gary Cooper, Walter Brennan, George Tobias, Noah Beery, Jr., June Lockhart

Distributed By MGM/UA Home Video M301758

SET-UP, THE

D: Robert Wise 72 m

NR | DMA ACT | 1949 | B&W

8 Fierce boxing drama. An aging boxer (Ryan) is going into the ring again. At 35 he knows he's near the end of his career, but he also thinks he still has a chance, however he is the only one that does. Unbeknownst to him, his trainer (Percy Helton) and a local gangster (Baxter) have agreed to fix the match. They are so convinced he will loose that they don't even bother to tell him. But half-way into the fight it looks like he might win, so they tell him to take a dive, but that makes him more determined than ever. The whole story is told in real time, 72 minutes of the boxer's life. Be prepared for some brutal boxing scenes.

Sex / Nud / Viol / Lang / AdSit

A: Robert Ryan, Audrey Totter, Alan Baxter, George Tobias, James Edwards, Wallace Ford

© TURNER HOME ENTERTAINMENT 6227

SIGN OF THE CROSS, THE

D: Cecil B. DeMille 124 m

NR | DMA | 1932 | B&W

8 Big DeMille epic telling of the persecution of the Christians under the Roman Emperor Nero in 67 A.D. Charles Laughton, as the vile and debauched Nero, has blamed the burning of Rome on the Christians and has placed a bounty upon them. His sexy wife, Claudette Colbert, is in lust with the Prefect, Marcus Superbus, played by Fredric March. However, her love is frustrated because he is in love with a pretty Christian girl. Somewhat slow moving and heavy-handed. Quite sexy in a few places and contains strikingly sadistic scenes of barbarous cruelty in the arena. These scenes were edited out for many years and have just been added back.

Sex / Nud / Viol / Lang / AdSit

A: Fredric March, Elissa Landi, Claudette Colbert, Charles Laughton, Ian Keith, Arthur Hohl

© MCA/UNIVERSAL HOME VIDEO, INC. 80824

SINCE YOU WENT AWAY

D: John Cromwell 179 m

NR | DMA | 1944 | B&W

9 Sentimental weeper. When war erupts, an adored husband and father is sent away to fight. He leaves behind his wife (Colbert) and two daughters (Jones and Temple). Money is short so they take in a boarder (Cotten). The younger daughter is devastated by her father's absence and turns to Cotten. The older daughter is falling in love with him, and even stalwart mother Colbert is tempted by him. This is an emotional character study of intense feelings - the loss, anxiety and the fear that are all a part of wartime commitment. Undated and undiminished with time, it was nominated for nine Oscars.

Sex / Nud / Viol / Lang / AdSit

A: Claudette Colbert, Jennifer Jones, Joseph Cotten, Shirley Temple, Lionel Barrymore, Hattie McDaniel

© CBS/FOX VIDEO 8082

SISTER KENNY

D: Dudley Nichols 116 m

NR | DMA | 1946 | B&W

8 A moving drama about the woman who dedicated her life to developing a treatment for young people afflicted with polio. Sister Kenny was a nurse from Australia's wilderness who pioneered a treatment for the crippling disease. However, the established medical community only scoffed at her successes. She fought for years to have her methods accepted and used by the skeptical medical community, and eventually she succeeded. Russell received an Oscar nomination for her portrayal of the determined nurse with a huge heart and nerves of steel. A very compelling biography.

Sex / Nud / Viol / Lang / AdSit

A: Rosalind Russell, Dean Jagger, Alexander Knox, Beulah Bondi, Philip Merivale, Dorothy Peterson

© TURNER HOME ENTERTAINMENT 6186

SISTERS, THE

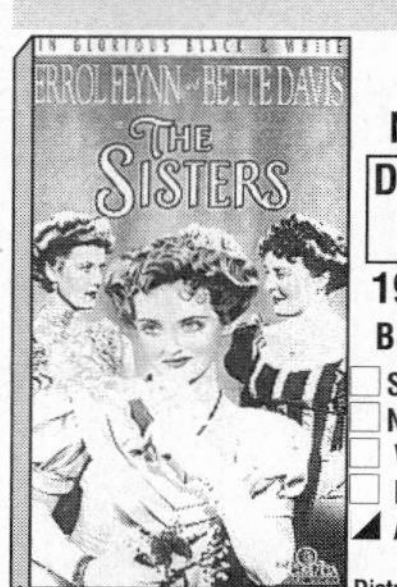

D: Anatole Litvak 99 m

NR | DMA | 1938 | B&W

7 Lavish soap opera, set at the turn of the twentieth-century and beginning just as Teddy Roosevelt takes office. This is the story of the loves of three daughters of a Montana druggist. One marries an older man, one marries the banker's son and the other (Bette Davis) marries a dashing newspaper reporter (Errol Flynn) and moves with him to San Francisco. However, soon after they are married, feeling trapped by his inability to write and by their marriage itself, Flynn takes to drink and leaves his new bride heartbroken, just as the city is violently rent with a catastrophic earthquake.

Sex / Nud / Viol / Lang / AdSit

A: Errol Flynn, Bette Davis, Anita louise, Ian Hunter, Donald Crisp, Beula Bondi

Distributed By MGM/UA Home Video M202618

SNOWS OF KILIMANJARO, THE

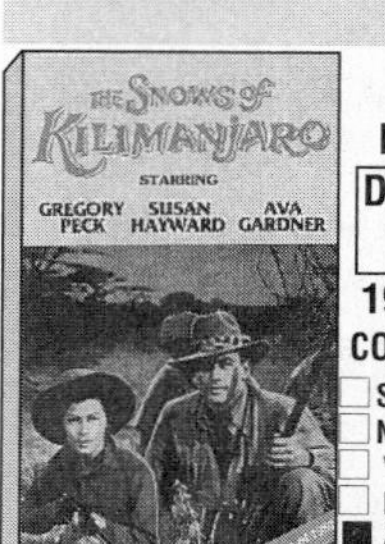

D: Henry King 117 m

NR | DMA | 1952 | COLOR

8 An immensely popular movie. It is a colorful story of an adventurous man's life, and also one of the most faithful and successful attempts to bring Hemingway to the screen. While lying delirious and seriously injured on Africa's famous Mt. Kilimanjaro, a rich and once successful author (Peck) reflects upon his life... his great romances, both with Gardener and his wife (Hayward). He castigates himself for a life that h he feels as been wasted and spent in the pursuit of the wrong things. But faithful Hayward defends him in the face of these self-doubts and he comes to realize his deep love for her. Excellent.

Sex / Nud / Viol / Lang / AdSit

A: Gregory Peck, Ava Gardner, Susan Hayward, Leo G. Carroll

© GOODTIMES VGT5101

SO DEAR TO MY HEART

D: Harold Schuster 82 m

NR | DMA CLD | 1948 | COLOR

9 A warm-hearted Disney film about a boy making his dream come true, and a reminder of a time long gone by! Young farmboy Driscoll's favorite pet is Danny, a black sheep with a foul temper. Driscoll desperately wants to take Danny to the county fair to try his luck at winning a blue ribbon. His problem is that he first has to figure out a way to earn the entry fee. Burl Ives is a big man with a gentle song who urges him to pursue his dream. Live animation mixes with a touching bit of nostalgia to create a delightful tribute to the past.

Sex / Nud / Viol / Lang / AdSit

A: Burl Ives, Beulah Bondi, Bobby Driscoll, Luana Patten, Harry Carey

© WALT DISNEY HOME VIDEO 296

SONG OF BERNADETTE, THE

D: Henry King 156 m

NR | DMA | 1943 | B&W

8 Excellent pious drama that rises above its religious theme. Winner of five Oscars, it is as much a story of people as it is of religion. It is based upon an actual occurrence in 1858 when Bernadette, a young peasant girl from the French village of Lourdes, saw a vision of the Virgin Mary. While some of the devout believed her story, many did not - including some within the church itself, who persecuted her as a blasphemer. Others accused her of being crazy or greedy. Her life was forever changed. There is a shrine in Lourdes today that still attracts millions each year.

Sex / Nud / Viol / Lang / AdSit

A: Charles Bickford, Lee J. Cobb, Jennifer Jones, William Eythe, Vincent Price, Anne Revere

© FOXVIDEO 1034

SOUTHERNER, THE

D: Jean Renoir — 92 m

NR | DMA | 1945 | B&W

☐ Sex ☐ Nud ☐ Viol ☐ Lang ◢ AdSit

7 An inspiring story of a family's struggle with poverty and against overpowering odds. Scott, an uneducated and desperately poor fieldhand, decides he has to take a chance to have something for himself and his family. He quits his job to try to grow cotton on a southern-Texas farm, but it is in miserable condition. His family lives in a run-down shack and does everything they can to make the meager soil produce. However, they are plagued by endless obstacles and natural disasters. A bitter neighbor even refuses to help them when Scott's son (Gilpin) becomes seriously ill. Still, they are determined to succeed. Oscar nominated for Direction.

A: Zachary Scott, Betty Field, J. Carrol Naish, Norman Lloyd, Bunny Sunshine, Jay Gilpin

© UNITED AMERICAN VIDEO CORP. 4012

STAGE DOOR

D: Gregory LaCava — 92 m

NR | DMA COM | 1937 | B&W

☐ Sex ☐ Nud ☐ Viol ☐ Lang ◢ AdSit

9 A brilliant comedy/drama about the lives and ambitions of a bunch of hopeful actresses who all live in a boarding house in the Big Apple. They will go to almost any lengths to get that coveted "big break." Hepburn is a rich girl trying to make it on her own. She and sarcastic Rogers are roommates and rivals. Rogers allows mogul Menjou to take her out to insure winning a part, but Hepburn gets the lead because her father has financed the production - although she doesn't know that. Sparkling dialogue and great acting. The stars and soon-to-be stars of the '30s are featured in this snappy gem.

A: Katharine Hepburn, Ginger Rogers, Adolphe Menjou, Lucille Ball, Constance Collier, Andrea Leeds

© TURNER HOME ENTERTAINMENT 6014

STANLEY AND LIVINGSTONE

D: Henry King — 101 m

NR | DMA ACT | 1939 | B&W

☐ Sex ☐ Nud ☐ Viol ☐ Lang ◢ AdSit

6 This tale of an exciting adventure of discovery is based on a true story! In 1870 Stanley (Tracy), a hard-edged journalist with a nose for adventure, is ordered by his editor to search the African jungles far and wide for a famous missionary - Dr. Livingstone (Hardwicke) - who had been mysteriously missing for years. During his quest, Stanley endured numerous hardships and setbacks as the first white man in an alien world of fierce tribal warriors, Arab slave traders and overpowering natural dangers. But he also discovered all sorts of wonderful and new things. And he found Dr. Livingstone.

A: Spencer Tracy, Cedric Hardwicke, Nancy Kelly, Walter Brennan, Richard Greene, Charles Coburn

© FOXVIDEO 1821

STAR, THE

D: Stuart Heisler — 91 m

NR | DMA | 1952 | B&W

☐ Sex ☐ Nud ☐ Viol ☐ Lang ◢ AdSit

9 Bette Davis received her ninth Oscar nomination for her role in this picture that was virtually made for her. She plays a former Oscar-winning actress who now can't get work and is up to her neck in debt. Early in the movie she is outside an auction house that is selling off her possessions to pay off her creditors. Unable to wangle a role, she gets drunk, lands in jail and gets bailed out by Sterling Hayden. He tries to get her to give up her dream of a comeback and be normal, but she cannot. Davis was exceptionally good in the role because it closely paralleled her own situation.

A: Bette Davis, Sterling Hayden, Natalie Wood, Warner Anderson

© WARNER HOME VIDEO 12489

STAR IS BORN, A

D: William Wellman — 110 m

NR | DMA ROM | 1937 | COLOR

☐ Sex ☐ Nud ☐ Viol ☐ Lang ◢ AdSit

9 This is the first of three adaptations from a brilliant screenplay, written by master writer Dorothy Parker, that was inspired by the earlier WHAT PRICE HOLLYWOOD? (Parker won an Oscar.) A successful but self-destructive and alcoholic actor (March) meets and falls in love with a charming young movie hopeful (Gaynor). They marry. His influence provides her an introduction into Hollywood power circles and her career blossoms. But as her star rises, his declines and she struggles valiantly to keep the man she loves from destroying himself. Moving and poignant. Equally good remake in 1954.

A: Fredric March, Janet Gaynor, Adolphe Menjou, May Robson, Andy Devine

© VIDEO TREASURES BV1838

STAR IS BORN, A

D: George Cukor — 176 m

PG | DMA ROM | 1954 | COLOR

☐ Sex ☐ Nud ☐ Viol ☐ Lang ◢ AdSit

9 This is the first re-make of the 1937 classic (both were inspired by WHAT PRICE HOLLYWOOD) and is every bit as good as the first. The story line remains intact: A hard-drinking actor falls in love with and marries a talented newcomer, only to slowly self-destruct as his talented wife rises to stardom his own star plummets. The acting here is also excellent. The primary difference in this one is that in this version Judy Garland gets a chance to sing. She generated two major hits from it: "The Man That Got Away" and "Born in a Trunk." Excellent acting. Very affecting movie.

A: Judy Garland, James Mason, Jack Carson, Charles Bickford, Tom Noonan

© WARNER HOME VIDEO 11335

STARS LOOK DOWN, THE

D: Carol Reed — 104 m

NR | DMA | 1939 | B&W

☐ Sex ☐ Nud ☐ Viol ☐ Lang ◢ AdSit

8 An attention grabber from start to finish! A poor Welsh miner (Redgrave) gets sick and tired of the deplorable working conditions that are forced upon the workers who are being betrayed by the leaders of their own union. He wants to run for office to try to change things, but his selfish wife (Lockwood) stands in his way. When he realizes that she doesn't love him any more, he decides to run for office anyway. A very powerful and intelligent British drama that was one of the first to make a social statement. A riveting classic based on Cronin's novel.

A: Michael Redgrave, Margaret Lockwood, Edward Rigby, Emlyn Williams, Nancy Price, Cecil Parker

© VIDEO YESTERYEAR 956

STATE OF THE UNION

D: Frank Capra — 122 m

NR | DMA COM | 1948 | B&W

☐ Sex ☐ Nud ☐ Viol ☐ Lang ◢ AdSit

9 A timeless story of a grab for the Presidency that is based on the Pulitzer Prize-winning play. Tracy is a wealthy airplane builder pushed into running for President by his new love, an overbearing newspaper publisher (Lansbury). His estranged wife (Hepburn) doesn't like the political changes she sees in her husband, but agrees to pose as the classic "wife by his side" anyway. And, when he gets in a little too deep in the political soup and loses his sense of balance, it is Hepburn who is there for him. Time does not really date this one. The details of changed but people and politics haven't.

A: Katharine Hepburn, Spencer Tracy, Angela Lansbury, Van Johnson, Adolphe Menjou, Lewis Stone

© MCA/UNIVERSAL HOME VIDEO, INC. 55006

STELLA DALLAS

D: King Vidor — 106 m

NR | DMA | 1937 | B&W

☐ Sex ☐ Nud ☐ Viol ☐ Lang ◢ AdSit

8 Peerless tearjerker, also filmed in 1925 and again in 1990, this however remains the best version. A small-town girl uses a self-improvement course to gain marriage to an upper-crust husband. However, he is a heel and, when her common ways soon betray her, he dumps her for his former love - but not before she has a child. She realizes that her daughter would have many more benefits if the girl was raised with her wealthy father, so Stanwyck selflessly sacrifices everything and gives up her daughter. Stanwyck and Shirley were Oscar nominated.

A: Barbara Stanwyck, Anne Shirley, John Boles, Barbara O'Neil, Marjorie Main, Alan Hale

© HBO VIDEO 90760

STORY OF LOUIS PASTEUR, THE

D: William Dieterle — 87 m

NR | DMA | 1936 | B&W

☐ Sex ☐ Nud ☐ Viol ☐ Lang ☐ AdSit

9 Extremely moving biography! This is an engrossing story which depicts the life of the famous French scientist who dedicated his life to finding a vaccine for rabies and anthrax. He challenged conventional wisdom and defied the medical profession's skepticism and ridicule to proceed steadfastly with his experiments. Even when he had triumphed, he was assaulted by the vindictive powers who he had embarrassed. Muni's portrayal of the dedicated scientist and his notable achievements won him an Oscar for Best Actor. Film was a Best Picture nominee.

A: Paul Muni, Josephine Hutchinson, Anita Louise, Donald Woods, Fritz Leiber, Porter Hall

Distributed By MGM/UA Home Video M301761

STRANGE CARGO

D: Frank Borzage — 115 m

NR | DMA | 1940 | B&W

☐ Sex ☐ Nud ☐ Viol ☐ Lang ◢ AdSit

6 A strange brew of characters in an even stranger religious parable. A group of convicts, led by Gable, tries to make a daring escape from the tropical prison of Devil's Island. They trudge through the jungle and along the way Gable picks up a hardened dance hall girl (Crawford). Also along with them is a mysterious Christ-like figure who calms the anxious and eager escapees, but at sea in an open sailboat, the group both ridicules the Bible and undergo their own conversions. The Legion of Decency originally condemned the film for this religious element. Powerful acting, but an odd film. Mostly for film fans.

A: Joan Crawford, Clark Gable, Ian Hunter, Peter Lorre, Albert Dekker, Eduardo Ciannelli

Distributed By MGM/UA Home Video M301589

STREETCAR NAMED DESIRE, A

D: Elia Kazan — 122 m

PG | DMA | 1951 | B&W

☐ Sex ☐ Nud ☐ Viol ☐ Lang ■ AdSit

10 Tennessee Williams's masterpiece served as the basis for this stunningly disturbing filmed character study. Blanche DuBois (Leigh) is a fragile neurotic woman who seeks solace with her earthy sister (Hunter) and coarse brother-in-law (Brando) in a New Orleans tenement. Her shallow, shaky world crumbles and she ends up destroyed when she is confronted with Brando, who is resentful and spiteful because of the intrusion on his marital life. Conflict builds to a deafening crescendo in this Oscar winner for Leigh, Hunter and Malden. An unforgettable drama that launched Brando's career.

A: Vivien Leigh, Marlon Brando, Kim Hunter, Karl Malden

© WARNER HOME VIDEO 34019

SUNSET BOULEVARD

D: Billy Wilder 110 m

NR | DMA | 1950 | B&W | Sex | Nud | Viol | Lang | AdSit

10 Triple Oscar-winner! The film opens startlingly with Holden floating face down in a swimming pool, his body riddled with bullet holes. Then in flashback, he narrates his own story. Silent film superstar Norma Desmond's (Swanson) career has faded into nothingness, but she still thinks she is a star. Swanson hires a slimy Hollywood screenwriter (Holden) to bring back her career, but he falls in love with her and moves into her dilapidated old mansion. She reels him into her demented game of make-believe. Then, the pair, her ex-husband and their butler all live in the past until Holden is driven to ruin, too. One of great classics of all time, and a very pointed assault on Hollywood!

A: Gloria Swanson, William Holden, Erich von Stroheim, Fred Clark, Jack Webb, Hedda Hopper

© PARAMOUNT HOME VIDEO 4927

TEN COMMANDMENTS, THE

D: Cecil B. DeMille 146 m

NR | DMA | 1923 | B&W | Sex | Nud | Viol | Lang | AdSit

7 Grand scale silent-era film. Produced with a huge cast of extras (they used an actual US Calvary division) and lavish sets. It is based upon the Book of Exodus and includes the parting of the Red Sea, the destruction of the golden calf, etc., but also juxtaposes a modern-day (1920s) counterpart to the story in which two brothers (one good and one evil) are used to illustrate the consequences of breaking the commandments. Pretty heavy-handed, but also still pretty impressive. The film includes the use of some two-color imagery, and is accompanied by pipe organ music.

A: Theodore Roberts, Charles de Roche, Estelle Taylor, Richard Dix, Rod La Rocque, Leatrice Joy

© PARAMOUNT HOME VIDEO 2506

THESE THREE

D: William Wyler 93 m

NR | DMA | 1936 | B&W | Sex | Nud | Viol | Lang | AdSit

8 Compelling adaptation of Lillian Hellman's provocative play "The Children's Hour." Two young women start a girls boarding school and are having some good success until a malicious young girl starts a rumor about both women having an affair with doctor Joel McCrea. She even blackmails another student into supporting her lies. Both the women and the doctor are slowly ruined by the resulting gossip and innuendo. A powerful screen drama which deleted the book's lesbian relationship between the women. Wilder remade it in 1962, including the lesbian aspect, but this one is more effective.

A: Merle Oberon, Miriam Hopkins, Joel McCrea, Bonita Granville, Catherine Doucet, Marcia Mae Jones

© HBO VIDEO 90755

THIS HAPPY BREED

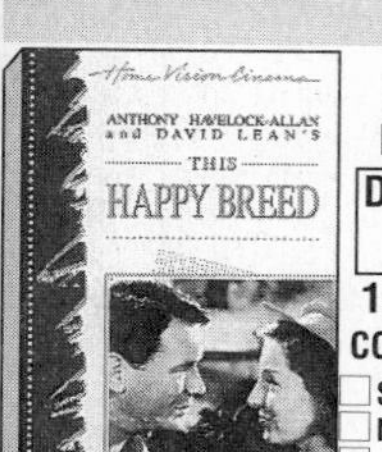

D: Anthony Havelock-Allan, David Lean 110 m

NR | DMA | 1947 | COLOR | Sex | Nud | Viol | Lang | AdSit

8 This was the most popular film in England in 1944, however it was not released in the US until three years later. It is the filmed version of a Noel Coward play concerning the collective lives of one family, as witnessed from 1919-1939, as it struggles to maintain itself and grow. After having served four years in the army, the father comes home and takes his young family to live in a new home, an ordinary row house in an ordinary neighborhood. Very soon, their lives begin to change and to unfold before us. And, for the next twenty years: we become part of their comings and goings, their happiness and their sorrows, until the next war begins.

A: Robert Newton, Celia Johnson, John Mills, Kay Walsh, Stanley Holloway

© HOME VISION THI 030

THREE SECRETS

D: Robert Wise 98 m

NR | DMA | 1950 | B&W | Sex | Nud | Viol | Lang | AdSit

7 Good, solid tearjerker which tells the stories of three women (all told in a series of flashbacks) who each have reason to believe that the 5-year-old sole survivor of a plane crash may be her son who had been given up for adoption. The events surrounding the boy's rescue and the poignant stories of the three women make for a very enjoyable melodrama. Solid cast. Well-done.

A: Eleanor Parker, Patricia Neal, Ruth Roman, Leif Erickson, Frank Lovejoy

© REPUBLIC PICTURES HOME VIDEO 4195

TILL THE END OF TIME

D: Edward Dmytryk 105 m

NR | DMA | 1946 | B&W | Sex | Nud | Viol | Lang | AdSit

7 Solid drama, set just after WWII, that reflected a nation recovering from war. Three Marines come back to their hometown but the war has changed them. Only one has to learned to cope well with his war-created handicap. Another, Mitchum drinks to help deal with his head injury. However, the greatest focus is on Madison, who has major war ghosts but also a romance with McGuire, a troubled war-widow. This film was a big hit, but it also paved the way for the very similar, and much more highly-acclaimed, THE BEST YEARS OF OUR LIVES. Perry Como made the title tune into a huge popular hit.

A: Dorothy McGuire, Guy Madison, Robert Mitchum, Bill Williams, Tom Tully, William Gargan

© TURNER HOME ENTERTAINMENT 2060

TO HAVE AND HAVE NOT

D: Howard Hawks 101 m

NR | DMA | ROM | ACT | 1945 | B&W | Sex | Nud | Viol | Lang | AdSit

9 "You know how to whistle, don't you? You just put your lips together and blow." With these words, Lauren Bacall burned her name into film history. The film is loosely based upon a Hemingway book, but more closely resembles CASABLANCA. Bogart is a disaffected American fisherman during WWII on the French island of Martinique, governed by the corrupt Vichy government. He doesn't want to take any sides in the war and refuses to help. But, after a bad bout with the government, and when Bacall asks nicely, he changes his mind. Very stylish, good action, good drama, sizzling romance.

A: Humphrey Bogart, Lauren Bacall, Walter Brennan, Hoagy Carmichael, Delores Moran, Sheldon Leonard

Distributed By MGM/UA Home Video M600747

TREASURE OF THE SIERRA MADRE, THE

D: John Huston 126 m

NR | DMA | SUS | 1948 | B&W | Sex | Nud | Viol | Lang | AdSit

10 Timeless and insightful masterpiece. It is a seamless tale that won Oscars both for the son (John Huston) - Best Screenplay and Director - and for the father (Walter Huston) - Supporting Actor. Two down-and-out Americans in Mexico take a chance on a grizzled old prospector and set out to discover gold in the Mexican mountains. The old man was right and there is a big gold deposit, but their treasure becomes a curse. At first they are concerned only about bandits, but they soon come to fear an even greater foe - each other. First greed, then fear... and then comes paranoia. Superb!!

A: Humphrey Bogart, Walter Huston, Tim Holt, Bruce Bennett, Barton MacLane, Alfonso Bedoya

Distributed By MGM/UA Home Video M201587

TREE GROWS IN BROOKLYN, A

D: Elia Kazan 128 m

NR | DMA | 1945 | B&W | Sex | Nud | Viol | Lang | AdSit

9 Rich and endearing. Francis is a bright young girl growing up in a tenement building in Brooklyn at the turn of the century. She is a dreamer and the daughter of a kind, but ne'er-do-well, alcoholic father, who she loves deeply, and a very strong-willed, down-to-earth mother. These are very difficult times and they all must struggle just to survive, just like the tree in their back yard. But, Francie doesn't understand and resents her firm mother being so hard on her father, though it is she who is holding the family together. This is a sensitive and poignant drama. It won two Oscars for acting. Excellent.

A: Dorothy McGuire, Joan Blondell, James Dunn, Lloyd Nolan, Peggy Ann Garner, Ted Donaldson

© FOXVIDEO 1517

TYCOON

D: Richard Wallace 128 m

NR | DMA | 1947 | COLOR | Sex | Nud | Viol | Lang | AdSit

6 Interesting saga about a man's compulsion to get a railroad built through the Andes. John Wayne is a determined engineer and railroad builder hired by mining mogul Hardwicke to get the railroad built. Very long, too long, story of Wayne's struggle to overcome the problems of construction in such a harsh environment; fighting with the boss who doesn't approve of his methods; and then having the added complication of falling in love with the boss's daughter (Day). Still, solid acting and an interesting script.

A: John Wayne, Laraine Day, Cedric Hardwicke, Anthony Quinn, James Gleason, Judith Anderson

© TURNER HOME ENTERTAINMENT 2090

UNDERWORLD STORY, THE

D: Cy Endfield 90 m

NR | DMA | 1950 | B&W | Sex | Nud | Viol | Lang | AdSit

7 A seedy newspaper reporter (Duryea) buys into a small town newspaper after he is fired in the city, but he uses mob money to finance his big move. When a black maid is framed for the murder of another newspaperman's daughter-in -law, he dives in with both feet. This is a case that he can get his teeth into - and pay off his debts. He turns the whole event into a free-for-all when he smells a cover-up. He's making some important people very unhappy. Not a particularly flattering portrayal of sensationalist news reporting, but effective.

A: Dan Duryea, Gale Storm, Herbert Marshall, Mary Anderson, Michael O'Shea

© CBS/FOX VIDEO 7658

VIRGIN QUEEN, THE

D: Henry Koster 92 m

NR | DMA | 1955 | COLOR | Sex | Nud | Viol | Lang | AdSit

7 An engrossing historical drama full of impact and set in 16th-century England. Sir Walter Raleigh (Todd) is determined to conquer the new world but he needs money, a lot of money, and finds it in Queen Elizabeth (Davis). She is the willing financier because she has become enamored with this dashing sea captain. However, she becomes incensed when she loses his affections to her more youthful, beautiful and scheming rival, Joan Collins. The Queen is extremely jealous. Davis is brilliant in her second role as Queen Elizabeth. Authentic costuming, good period detail.

A: Bette Davis, Richard Todd, Joan Collins, Herbert Marshall, Jay Robinson, Dan O'Herlihy

© FOXVIDEO 1416

VIVA ZAPATA!

D: Elia Kazan 114 m

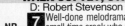

NR DMA 1952 B&W

Sex Nud Viol Lang AdSit

8 Excellent film capturing the feel of the Mexican Revolution. Set in the early 1900s, Brando (Oscar nominated) is Emiliano Zapata, a poor, illiterate peasant who rises within the ranks of the peasant army, along with his alcoholic brother (Anthony Quinn - Academy Award) and later becomes President of Mexico. He fights, not to overthrow the government, but to deliver land to the tenant farmers who work it. The real Zapata was ruthless but Brando's character has been considerably toned down. Plus, the plot is embellished with a love interest and a lament for the corrupting influences of power.

A: Marlon Brando, Anthony Quinn, Jean Peters, Joseph Wiseman, Mildred Dunnock

© FOXVIDEO 1352

WALK SOFTLY, STRANGER

D: Robert Stevenson 81 m

NR DMA ROM 1950 B&W

Sex Nud Viol Lang AdSit

7 Well-done melodrama. Joseph Cotten plays a gambler and a small-time crook who moves to a small town in Ohio to hide out. He moves into a boarding house and takes a job at the local shoe factory. There he meets and falls in love with the crippled daughter of a factory owner. She is wheelchair-bound because of a skiing accident. She, too, falls for this stranger and some of her bitterness begins to fade. Her love makes him want to change his ways permanently, but his past catches up with him when his former partners hunt him down and threaten to ruin everything.

A: Joseph Cotten, Jack Paar, Alida Valli, Spring Byington

© TURNER HOME ENTERTAINMENT 6107

WATCH ON THE RHINE

D: Herman Shumlin 79 m

NR DMA WAR SUS 1943 B&W

Sex Nud Viol Lang AdSit

8 Filmed just prior to the outbreak of WWII, this proved to be a groundbreaking classic. It received four Oscar nominations, including Best Picture. Lukas won for Best Actor. Lukas is a German underground leader who is forced to flee Germany for safety in America. He, his American wife (Davis) and their three kids move in with her mother and brother in Washington and he explains to his naive hosts (and also to the American public) the true nature and threat of fascism. However, another boarder in their home, a Romanian count, threatens to turn him in to the Nazi agents who are hunting him.

A: Bette Davis, Paul Lukas, Geraldine Fitzgerald, Beulah Bondi

Distributed By MGM/UA Home Video M202153

WHAT PRICE HOLLYWOOD?

D: George Cukor 88 m

NR DMA 1932 B&W

Sex Nud Viol Lang AdSit

8 This early film served as the inspiration for A STAR IS BORN, which was filmed several times, but best in 1937 and 1954. A waitress and aspiring movie star (Constance Bennett) is given her big break by a drunken director. However, his career begins to crumble just as Bennett's takes off. This is an excellent version of the story that deserves at least as much attention as its two antecedents. The story line was supposedly inspired by the real-life declining relationship between Barbara Stanwyck and Frank Ray.

A: Constance Bennett, Lowell Sherman, Neil Hamilton, Gregory Ratoff, Brooks Benedict

© TURNER HOME ENTERTAINMENT 6197

WHITE CLIFFS OF DOVER, THE

D: Clarence Brown 127 m

NR DMA WAR 1944 COLOR

Sex Nud Viol Lang AdSit

7 Sentimental, patriotic drama of the sacrifices of one woman. Irene Dunne is an American woman who came to England with her publisher father and stayed on to marry an Englishman (Marshal) just as WWI was breaking out. Their time together is short and he is killed on the battlefields of the war. She, however, is pregnant, gives birth to a son (alternately played by (McDowall and Peter Lawford) and stays in England to raise him. Now, the time is WWII. She is a red cross nurse assigned to a Red Cross hospital in London when her wounded son is brought in for surgery. Well done with fine performances.

A: Irene Dunne, Alan Marshal, Van Johnson, Frank Morgan, C. Aubrey Smith, Roddy McDowall

Distributed By MGM/UA Home Video 202836

WILD ONE, THE

D: Laslo Benedek 79 m

NR DMA 1954 B&W

Sex Nud Viol Lang AdSit

6 The original biker movie. It is still one of Brando's better performances and the one for which he is best known. Although somewhat dated now, it is still worth watching, particularly for film fans. He is the head of a biker gang which upsets things in a small town. He falls for the sheriff's daughter and it looks as though he might change, but then a former friend (Lee Marvin) comes into town with his own gang. Now the townsfolk have had too much and they move to take back their town. Based upon an actual event in Hollister, California.

A: Marlon Brando, Mary Murphy, Robert Keith, Lee Marvin

© COLUMBIA TRISTAR HOME VIDEO 60623

WIND, THE

D: Victor Seastrom 82 m

NR DMA 1928 B&W

Sex Nud Viol Lang AdSit

9 One of the last of the great silent films and a crowning achievement for Lillian Gish. She is a naive young girl who travels west from Virginia to Texas to her cousin's ranch. She describes the ranch as beautiful to a stranger on the train, but when she arrives she discovers that it is an uninviting windswept place. She is to take care of the children, but when the parents begin to feel threatened by her success, she is forced to marry a lout of a man. One night, in yet another windstorm, she is raped and she kills her attacker. She is alone and afraid. Still very moving today.

A: Lillian Gish, Lars Hanson, Montagu Love, Dorothy Cumming, Edward Earle, William Orlamond

Distributed By MGM/UA Home Video M301359

YEARLING, THE

D: Clarence Brown 129 m

G DMA CLD 1946 COLOR

Sex Nud Viol Lang AdSit

9 Beautiful and sensitive family favorite that was also a Best Picture nominee. This is the intelligent story of a young boy's confrontation with the hard realities of survival in early America. A lonely boy, living with his mother and father on a small pioneer farm, adopts an orphaned fawn for a pet. As the fawn grows into a yearling and the boy becomes more and more attached to it, the deer becomes a larger and larger problem for the parents. Eventually they must decide between the yearling and their own survival. Memorable and heart-wrenching.

A: Gregory Peck, Jane Wyman, Claude Jarman, Jr., Chill Wills, Clem Bevins, Margaret Wycherly

Distributed By MGM/UA Home Video M300500

YOUNG MAN WITH A HORN

D: Michael Curtiz 112 m

NR DMA MUS ROM 1950 B&W

Sex Nud Viol Lang AdSit

8 Compelling drama. A young boy is compulsively drawn to music and, through his mastery of the trumpet, he escapes the ghetto: first into small-time dives, and then to play big-time gigs in New York. Douglas is the passionate horn blower who is drawn to vocalist Doris Day but marries bad girl socialite Lauren Bacall, with disastrous results. His world crumbles around him and he resorts to alcohol. The lonely little boy has become a tortured man. Loosely based on real-life trumpeter Bix Beiderbecke. Great cast. Great horn music dubbed by famed trumpeter Harry James.

A: Kirk Douglas, Lauren Bacall, Doris Day, Hoagy Carmichael, Juano Hernandez, Mary Beth Hughes

© WARNER HOME VIDEO 11179

YOUNG MR. LINCOLN

D: John Ford 100 m

NR DMA 1940 B&W

Sex Nud Viol Lang AdSit

9 Wonderful bit of Americana from Director John Ford. This film is, as its title would indicate, a character study of the younger years of Mr. Lincoln. Henry Fonda is truly impressive as Lincoln. This film examines Mr. Lincoln's life from his earliest beginnings in a Kentucky log cabin, through his lost love for Ann Rutledge, his days as a backwoods lawyer, to the film's suspenseful climax as he represents two brothers in a murder trial. Good fun and solid family entertainment.

A: Henry Fonda, Alice Brady, Marjorie Weaver, Donald Meek, Milburn Stone, Ward Bond

© FOXVIDEO 1420

Fantasy

20,000 LEAGUES UNDER THE SEA

D: Richard Fleischer 127 m

G FAN ACT CLD 1954 COLOR

Sex Nud Viol Lang AdSit

9 Marvelous adaptation by Disney of Jules Verne's fantasy adventure written in 1868. Both the film and the book are, and will remain, great fun and timeless. Amid fear created by rumors of a fierce monster ravaging the sea, a lone ship sets sail in a search to find it. On board is a scientist, his wimpy assistant (Lorre) and an adventurous harpooner (Douglas). Their ship is indeed attacked by the monster, but it is instead a submarine named the Nautilus, created and piloted by the mad genius Captain Nemo (Mason). Totally captivating with very high production values and superb special effects.

A: Kirk Douglas, James Mason, Peter Lorre, Paul Lukas, Robert J. Wilke, Carleton Young

© WALT DISNEY HOME VIDEO 015

5,000 FINGERS OF DR. T., THE

D: Roy Rowland — 88 m

FAN CLD — 1953 — B&W

Sex / Nud / Viol / Lang / AdSit

8 This fantasy was co-scripted by Dr. Seuss and was one of Hollywood's best fantasies, but it has been largely overlooked by the public. It is about a boy who hates his piano lessons and dreams about a cruel piano teacher (Conried) who keeps 500 boys locked up in his castle (500 boys X 10 fingers = 5000 fingers). He makes them practice day and night, playing on a piano with a huge keyboard. Also locked away in his dungeon are creatures who dared to play other instruments. The brave boy, with the help of a resourceful plumber, helps to destroy the evil Dr. T.

A: Peter Lind Hayes, Mary Healy, Tommy Rettig, Hans Conried

© COLUMBIA TRISTAR HOME VIDEO 90163

CURSE OF THE CAT PEOPLE

D: Robert Wise — 70 m

NR — FAN SUS — 1944 — B&W

Sex / Nud / Viol / Lang / AdSit

7 A truly interesting follow-up to the 1942 version of CAT PEOPLE. This is not a horror movie as the original was, but is a fantasy about a lonely young girl who lives in a dream world. Her mother, long dead, had suffered from the belief that she would be transformed into a panther. Her father has been trying to protect her from that strange past but now she, too, has fantasies and she has an imaginary friend - her dead mother. (Simone revives her earlier role.) Is her mother just her fantasy or is she real? And, why is she here?

A: Simone Simon, Kent Smith, Jane Randolph, Elizabeth Russell, Ann Carter, Julia Dean

© TURNER HOME ENTERTAINMENT 2084

JUNGLE BOOK, THE

D: Zoltan Korda — 106 m

NR — FAN CLD — 1942 — COLOR

Sex / Nud / Viol / Lang / AdSit

8 This is Rudyard Kipling's classic fantasy of Mowgli, a native boy who became lost in a jungle in India and was raised by wolves and became friends with all the animals except his enemy, the great tiger. When he was grown, he returned to live with the humans of a local village. One day, he and a girl discovered a lost ancient city of great wealth but only take one gold coin when they leave. The girl's greedy father discovers the coin and tricks the village into casting Mowgli out so that he can follow the boy to the gold. Excellent for everyone, but it is best suited for older children and young teens.

A: Sabu, Joseph Calleia, John Qualen, Rosemary DeCamp, Ralph Byrd, Frank Puglia

© VIDEO TREASURES BV1936

LOST HORIZON

D: Frank Capra — 132 m

NR — FAN DMA — 1937 — B&W

Sex / Nud / Viol / Lang / AdSit

9 Intriguing, classic story about five people who have crash-landed in the mountains of Tibet. They miraculously stumble into an enchanted hidden village called Shangri-La. There, peace rules and no one ages or suffers. Ronald Coleman won Best Actor and the picture received three other nominations, including Best Picture. This is still a fascinating movie concept, however the production seems a little creaky now. Interestingly, the video contains significant footage which had been edited out of the film for its late '30s theater presentation. America was getting ready to fight a war.

A: Ronald Colman, Jane Wyatt, John Howard, Edward Everett Horton, Margo, Sam Jaffe

© COLUMBIA TRISTAR HOME VIDEO 60763

MIRACLE ON 34TH STREET

D: George Seaton — 97 m

NR — FAN CLD — 1947 — B&W

Sex / Nud / Viol / Lang / AdSit

10 Positively perfect holiday treat! A cynical mother and boss at Macy's Department Store (O'Hara) employs an old man with a grey beard (Gwenn) to work as Santa during the holidays. He claims to be the real thing and many others, including O'Hara's daughter (Wood), begin to believe that he is real. Mom, however, thinks he's crazy and he is put on trial to prove that he is, in fact, Kris Kringle or get sent away. This heartwarming mixture of fantasy and comedy is delightful for the whole family. Oscar winner for Best Supporting Actor, Screenplay and Original Story. Also available in a colorized version. You will believe!

A: Maureen O'Hara, John Payne, Edmund Gwenn, Gene Lockhart, Natalie Wood, William Frawley

© FOXVIDEO 1072

WIZARD OF OZ, THE

D: Victor Fleming — 119 m

G — FAN CLD MUS — 1939 — B&W

Sex / Nud / Viol / Lang / AdSit

10 This is MGM's ultimate classic children's film that is presented each year on television to a whole new audience, plus an old one that keeps coming back to re-live it. This is a wonderful fantasy in which a young girl visits a wondrous and mysterious fantasy land, and there discovers that things aren't always better somewhere else. This particular video version is a special edition which contains 17 minutes of extra footage which were edited out of the original, plus the original theatrical promotional trailer with Buddy Epson (who was the original Tin Man) performing and Judy Garland receiving an Oscar.

A: Judy Garland, Jack Haley, Ray Bolger, Bert Lahr, Billie Burke, Margaret Hamilton

Distributed By MGM/UA Home Video M301656

Foreign

BAKER'S WIFE, THE

D: Marcel Pagnol — 124 m

NR — FOR COM — 1938 — B&W

Sex / Nud / Viol / Lang / AdSit

9 Hilarious! A small French town has been without a baker for a long time. When they finally do get one, a fabulous one, the baker's wife develops a roving eye and falls in with a handsome shepherd, abandoning the baker. The baker is destroyed and becomes so despondent that he no longer makes good bread. So the desperate town bands together to do everything and anything it takes to bring her back to him. Only the French... Subtitles.

A: Raimu, Ginette Laclere, Charles Moulin, Robert Vattier, Robert Brassa

© INTERAMA VIDEO CLASSICS 0006

BEAUTY AND THE BEAST

D: Jean Cocteau — 93 m

NR — FOR ROM — 1946 — B&W

Sex / Nud / Viol / Lang / AdSit

9 This is an absolutely exquisite French production of the classic fairy tale about the beautiful girl who sacrifices herself to a terribly hideous but kind-hearted beast in order to save her father. However, she will eventually discover that in truth the terrible beast is actually a transformed prince. Haunting dream-like surrealism marks this as an especially beautiful rendition of the story. Althouth it is slowly paced, it is highly evocative and sensuous, with beautiful imagery.

A: Jean Morais, Josette Day, Marcel Andre, Mila Parely, Nane Germon, Michel Auclair

© HOME VISION BEA 110

BICYCLE THIEF, THE

D: Vittorio De Sica — 90 m

NR — FOR DMA — 1948 — B&W

Sex / Nud / Viol / Lang / AdSit

9 A simple, honest and heart-grippingly tragic story that is as powerful today as when it was released. Immediately after World War II, in an unemployment-plagued Italy, an impoverished man has his bicycle stolen. It is not just a bicycle, it is the thing upon which his job and his very survival depends. He and his small son spend a week searching to find it. The father is so panic-stricken that he steals a bicycle, but he is caught and humiliated in front of his son. Compelling, very realistic and an all time classic. It won a special Oscar for Best Foreign Film before there even was a permanent category.

A: Lamberto Maggiorani, Lianelle Carell, Enzo Staiola, Elena Altieri

© CORINTH FILMS 1236

BLOOD OF A POET

D: Jean Cocteau — 55 m

NR — FOR FAN — 1930 — B&W

Sex / Nud / Viol / Lang / AdSit

8 This is famed French director Jean Cocteau's first film and is regarded as a classic by film fans and historians. It is a near-surrealistic piece that explores the way in which artists can become obsessed with their creations. The film begins and ends with a falling chimney. The intervening time, a supposed instant, is filled with four segments depicting how the artist must break with traditional forms and thought. Statues come to life, people turn into statues, people pass through a mirror and a woman flies. Film fans only, most others will be bored and confused. Narrated by Jean Cocteau. Subtitles.

A: Lee Miller, Enrico Rivero, Jean Desbordes

© HOME VISION BLO 040

CHILDREN OF PARADISE

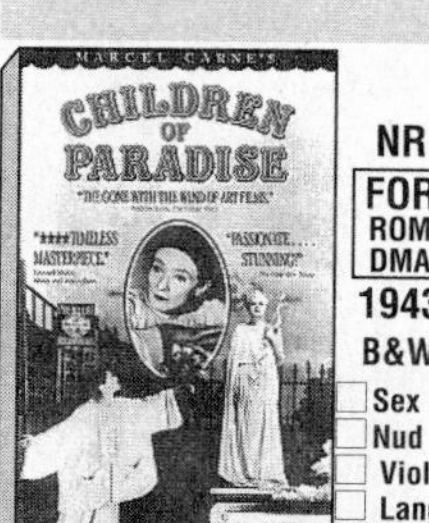

D: Marcel Carne — 189 m

NR — FOR ROM DMA — 1943 — B&W

Sex / Nud / Viol / Lang / AdSit

10 Famed as the best French picture of all time and called their GONE WITH THE WIND, this is both fascinating watching and fascinating history. The picture was filmed in secret when France was under occupation by the Nazis. Many of its actors were active in the resistance movement. Pointedly set exactly 100 years earlier, when France was under very similar circumstances, this is the tragic romantic story of a beautiful but elusive courtesan who is loved by four different men. It is also a tribute to the people who can never be controlled: theater folk, criminals and aristocrats. The woman is loved by a mime and his comedian friend, but she chooses wealth to become the mistress of an aristocrat. Subtitles.

A: Jean-Louis Barrault, Arletty, Pierre Brasseur, Marcel Herrand, Pierre Renoir, Maria Casares

© HOME VISION CHI 040

DEVIL'S ENVOYS, THE

D: Marcel Carne 120 m

NR | FOR FAN ROM | 1942 | B&W

7 This French romantic fantasy was based upon a legend. Set during the middle-ages, two emissaries of the devil are sent by him to earth to create anarchy and to destroy the love affair between two lovers. However, instead of accomplishing their sorry goal, the two eventually give in to the power of love themselves. Filmed during the German Occupation, this film was designed to be a subtle shot at the Germans. Director Carne soon followed this one with another artistic attack at the Germans with his masterpiece CHILDREN OF PARADISE. Subtitles.

Sex / Nud / Viol / Lang / AdSit

A: Arletty, Jules Berry, Marie Deea, Alain Cuny, Fernand Ledoux

© HOME VISION VIS 01

DIABOLIQUE

D: Henri-Georges Clouzot 116 m

NR | FOR SUS MYS | 1955 | B&W

10 Famed as one of the most suspenseful films of all time -- rated right up there with PSYCHO. Sickly Vera Clouzot owns a dreary school for boys that is run by her sadistic husband. She has been brutalized and terrorized by him, as has his icy former mistress, Simone Signoret. The two can no longer tolerate him and conspire to kill him. They dump his body into the school's fetid swimming pool, but when the pool is drained...there is no body. Also, the students report having seen him and even the wife, whose weak heart can barely take the stress, thinks she has seen him still alive. Tension builds mightily to the most stressful and shocking conclusion on film until then. Much copied since. Subtitles.

Sex / Nud / Viol / Lang / AdSit

A: Simone Signoret, Vera Clouzot, Paul Meurisse, Charles Vanel, Noel Roquevert, Therese Dorney

© HOME VISION DIA 040

FORBIDDEN GAMES

D: Rene Clement 85 m

NR | FOR DMA WAR | 1952 | B&W

9 Excellent French anti-war film. During WWII, a young French girl is orphaned in an air raid and adopted by a peasant family. She and their young son develop an immediate friendship. As the two watch her parents being buried, the children decide that her dog, which was also killed, should be buried. This they do and soon they start their own cemetery for other dead animals. They create their own sad imaginary world which uses the real war-torn world for its inspiration. Very sad, tender and movingly intense drama which earned an Oscar as Best Foreign Film. Subtitles.

Sex / Nud / Viol / Lang / AdSit

A: Brigitte Fossey, Georges Pawjouly, Louis Herbert, Suzanne Courtal

© NEW LINE HOME VIDEO 6065

GRAND ILLUSION

D: Jean Renoir 111 m

NR | FOR DMA WAR | 1938 | B&W

9 Famous French director Jean Renoir's classic statement in which he strips away the "glory" of war to reveal its ultimate sorrows. In it, a French aristocrat is captured during WWI and imprisoned in a German camp that is administered by a German aristocratic career officer. United by the similarities of their class, they become fast friends, but their false bonds are broken when the German kills his new friend for having aided French prisoners to escape. Based upon an actual WWI incident. Three years after this film was made, Germany invaded France again during WWII. Subtitles.

Sex / Nud / Viol / Lang / AdSit

A: Jean Gabin, Pierre Fresnay, Erich von Stroheim, Marcel Dalio, Julien Carette, Dita Parlo

© HOME VISION GRA 05

IKIRU

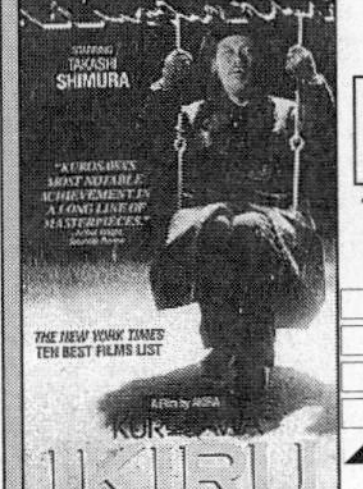

D: Akira Kurosawa 141 m

NR | FOR DMA | 1952 | B&W

9 IKIRU in Japanese means "to live." In the opening scenes, a man is told that he is dying of cancer and has less than one year. For twenty-five years he has been a low-level bureaucrat, caught in his daily routines. He has no real familylife and he is empty. So, he decides that he will use his remaining time well. First, he seeks excitement in the nightlife, but finds no pleasure in it. So, he pursues a pretty co-worker. But, through her he discovers that his unhappiness lies deeper, in his lack of purpose. Now inspired, he is determined to do something useful. He will make sure a playground is built where there is only a cesspool now. Nothing will deter him. Very moving but also depressing.

Sex / Nud / Viol / Lang / AdSit

A: Takashi Shimura, Nobuo Kaneko, Makoto Kobori, Kyoko Seki

© HOME VISION IKI 030

KID FOR TWO FARTHINGS, A

D: Carol Reed 96 m

NR | FOR COM | 1954 | COLOR

8 Delightful sentimental story from England. Little Joe has been told stories by the tailor in his poor London neighborhood of a magical unicorn with powers to grant wishes. One day the boy discovers a goat with only one horn and is convinced that he has discovered the magical unicorn, even though everyone else sees a one-horned goat. Still, the tailor does suddenly get the steam press he's always wanted, and the muscleman finally gets the money he needs to marry Sonia, so she has had her wish granted too. Sure, there is a logical explanation for all that's happened...but there is still that goat to explain.

Sex / Nud / Viol / Lang / AdSit

A: Celia Johnson, Diana Dors, David Kassoff, Joe Robinson, Jonathan Ashmore, Brenda De Banzie

© HOME VISION KID 01

LA STRADA

D: Federico Fellini 107 m

NR | FOR ROM DMA | 1954 | B&W

9 A beautiful film from Federico Fellini that won him international acclaim and an Oscar for Best Foreign Film. It is the simple but moving story of a brutal itinerant circus strongman (Quinn) who buys a poor, simple-minded but beautiful peasant girl to add some spice to his act and to be his mistress. She follows him throughout the countryside and falls pathetically, deeply in love with him. But, for all her love, she is forced to withstand his insults and abuse. Then a gentle clown and acrobat (Basehart) trys to help her and the strongman destroys all three. Very moving. Subtitles.

Sex / Nud / Viol / Lang / AdSit

A: Anthony Quinn, Giulietta Masina, Richard Basehart

© HOME VISION STR 220

LE JOUR SE LEVE (DAYBREAK)

D: Marcel Carne 88 m

FOR DMA | 1939 | B&W

8 Highly regarded French film, which is also credited as being one of the first of the film noir genre. Jean Gabin has barricaded himself in his apartment building and vows not to be taken alive by the police. Through a series of flashbacks, it is revealed to us how his loves for two women have been thwarted by the evil dealings of a dog trainer. Because that man had seduced his love, he was murdered for his transgression; and, now Gabin is trapped in his room. His room is his prison cell, until he will die.

Sex / Nud / Viol / Lang / AdSit

A: Jean Gabin, Arletty, Jules Berry, Jacqueline Laurent

© HOME VISION JOU01

M

D: Fritz Lang 99 m

NR | FOR SUS CRM | 1931 | B&W

9 Unnerving suspense! The terrifying story of a psychotic murderer who kills only children. The only clue available is a tune that the murderer incessantly whistles. The German police fail, despite a massive effort, to find the murderer. The turmoil so upsets the underworld that it mobilizes its own resources to locate and punish the killer. Based on a real-life Dusseldorf murderer, Lorre's film debut still carries contemporary impact. The use of imaginative props and film techniques capture the essence of outrage and fright that was felt throughout Berlin. Excellent. Subtitles.

Sex / Nud / Viol / Lang / AdSit

A: Peter Lorre, Otto Wernicke, Gustav Grundgens, Ellen Widmann, Inge Landgut

© BARR ENTERTAINMENT VIDEO HM0105

MAEDCHEN IN UNIFORM

D: Leontine Sagan 90 m

NR | FOR DMA | 1931 | B&W

9 Today it is considered one of the early masterpieces of German cinema, but it was banned by the Nazis and had to have the help of Eleanor Roosevelt to get past American censors. A 14-year old girl is sent to a very strict boarding school for daughters of poor military officers. She rejects the authoritarian nature of the schools's elderly matron and finds a sympathetic ear in a young teacher who sees the girl as a reflection of her former self. A bond is formed that soon becomes more than a platonic one. This is one of the very first films to treat the theme of lesbianism in a non-critical way. It was an all-female production and was written by a woman. Subtitles.

Sex / Nud / Viol / Lang / AdSit

A: Hertha Thiele, Dorothea Wieck, Emilia Unda

© HOME VISION MAE 030

MIRACLE IN MILAN

D: Vittorio De Sica 96 m

NR | FOR FAN | 1951 | B&W

9 Whimsical adult fairy tale condemning the way displaced people were treated after the war! Despair and depression surround the peasants living in post-WWII Italy. A young orphan is given refuge by a band of beggars and other displaced people from the war. And when the ghost of the old woman who raised him gives him a magic dove that can make wishes come true, he sets about improving their lot and leads a rebellion against the rich landlord who wants the beggars off his land. The landlord then allows the beggars to make their own greedy requests - that is until the dove is stolen. Subtitles.

Sex / Nud / Viol / Lang / AdSit

A: Francesco Golisano, Paolo Stoppa, Emma Gramatica, Guglielmo Barnabo, Brunelia Bovo

© HOME VISION MIR 04

MR. HULOT'S HOLIDAY

D: Jacques Tati 86 m

NR | FOR COM | 1953 | COLOR

9 Wonderfully light-hearted comic masterpiece about a bumbling but friendly and well-meaning man who makes a trip to a very proper French seaside resort and proceeds to destroy it. Nearly plotless, the wonderfully eccentric Mr. Hulot simply causes one catastrophe after another. Hilarious. It has virtually no dialogue at all and is a throw-back to the slapstick of the silent era. Grand Prize winner at Cannes.

Sex / Nud / Viol / Lang / AdSit

A: Jacques Tati, Nathalie Pascaud, Louis Parrault, Michelle Rolla, Raymond Carl

© HOME VISION HUL 030

PANDORA'S BOX

NR
FOR DMA
1928
B&W
Sex
Nud
Viol
Lang
AdSit

D: G.W. Pabst 110 m

9 Remarkable silent film classic. Banned for years, this is a powerful drama but with blatant sexual themes. Lulu is the innocent, but very sensual, mistress and later wife of a wealthy editor. When he is killed accidentally, she is wrongly convicted of his murder but escapes with the help of her lesbian lover and her son (who Lulu also seduces). They escape to London, where Lulu resorts to prostitution to support them. Virtually all the men she comes in contact with are destroyed, but she is ultimately destroyed herself by Jack the Ripper. Subtitles.

A: Louise Brooks, Fritz Kortner, Francis Lederer, Carl Goetz

© HOME VISION PAN 010

RASHOMON

NR
FOR DMA
1951
B&W
Sex
Nud
Viol
Lang
AdSit

D: Akira Kurosawa 83 m

9 A multi-award winning film from Japan and a must see for all film fans. In Japan in the 12th century, a woman is raped and her husband murdered by a wild criminal (Mifune). But when the only real witness and three other people involved tell the story of what they think happened, each gives a very different account of the crime, as each tries to present himself in the best possible light. This fascinating Japanese masterpiece makes a timeless and poignant statement about truth and justice, and won the Oscar for Best Foreign Film. Technically masterful. Subtitles or Dubbed.

A: Toshiro Mifune, Machiko Kyo, Masayuki Mori, Takashi Shimura

© HOME VISION RAS 030

RIFIFI

NR
FOR SUS CRM
1954
B&W
Sex
Nud
Viol
Lang
AdSit

D: Jules Dassin 110 m

9 This famous foreign suspensor set the standard for all caper/robbery movies that followed it! The famous 30 minute robbery sequence is a masterpiece of nervous suspense. Not one word is spoken, nor is there any music, just tension. When four jewel thieves do succeed in the dangerous robbery is when trouble begins, because that's when they find that their relationships are the most dangerous thing of all. They begin to mistrust and even to betray each other. Absolutely guaranteed to get the adrenaline pumping. Has not lost a drop of excitement over the years. Subtitles.

A: Jean Servais, Carl Mohner, Marie Sabouret, Magali Noel, Robert Manuel, Perlo Vita

© VIDEO YESTERYEAR 345

RULES OF THE GAME, THE

NR
FOR COM DMA
1939
B&W
Sex
Nud
Viol
Lang
AdSit

D: Jean Renoir 110 m

8 A masterful French frolic that was banned there and in Germany for 20 years because of its stinging social commentary about a decadent upper class! A number of dignitaries are invited to a French chateau for a weekend of hunting and indulgence to celebrate the last few days before World War II. When the servants become involved romantically with the aristocrats, and visa versa, chaos runs rampant. The film pokes fun at the French leisure class and its opulence. However, a tragic ending also brings a rapid finish to the comic romp and jolts you right out of your comfort zone. Sophisticated. Subtitles.

A: Marcel Dalio, Nora Gregor, Jean Renoir, Mila Parely, Gaston Modot

© HOME VISION RUL 01

SAWDUST AND TINSEL

NR
FOR DMA
1953
B&W
Sex
Nud
Viol
Lang
AdSit

D: Ingmar Bergman 87 m

8 This film generated a lot of controversy when it was released. It is the story of lust and love, set against the backdrop of a seedy run-down traveling circus. The aging circus owner leaves his sensuous young lover to reconcile with his wife. And when that fails, he attempts to return to his mistress, but she has a new lover and now humiliates and eventually destroys him. Sultry Harriet Andersson is the sexy object of his attentions. Subtitles.

A: Harriet Andersson, Ake Groenberg, Hasse Ekman, Anders Ek, Annika Tretow, Kiki

© HOME VISION SAW 020

SECRETS OF WOMEN

NR
FOR COM
1952
B&W
Sex
Nud
Viol
Lang
AdSit

D: Ingmar Bergman 108 m

7 This was Bergman's first commercial success. Although it was released in 1952 in Europe, it was not released in the US until nine years later. It is a sophisticated comedy/drama about the stories four women tell about their past love affairs, while they are waiting at a summer house for their husbands to arrive. Their stories are all told in flashback and are told entirely from a woman's point of view. The best sequence is that of the last woman who refused to tell her story, but whose love for her husband is rekindled while they are trapped on a stalled elevator. Subtitles.

A: Anita Bjork, Gunnar Bjornstrand, Karl-Arne Holmsten, Jarl Kulle, Eva Dahlbeck

© HOME VISION SEC 110

SEVEN SAMURAI, THE

NR
FOR ACT
1955
B&W
Sex
Nud
Viol
Lang
AdSit

D: Akira Kurosawa 208 m

8 This was a very highly influential Japanese film which was repackaged for America and became the very popular Western THE MAGNIFICENT SEVEN. However, here a 17th-century samurai master agrees to help defend a pitiful small village against repeated attacks by bandits. To do it, he assembles a team of six other samurai masters. They will defend the town and, more importantly, train the townspeople to defend themselves. A rousing and thrilling battle climax winds up this 3+ hour epic, and also completes the process of building several carefully-drawn characters. Excellent. Subtitles.

A: Takashi Shimura, Toshiro Mifune, Yoshi Inaba, Seiji Miyaguchi, Minoru Chiaki, Daisuke Kato

© HOME VISION SEV 080

SMILES OF A SUMMER NIGHT

NR
FOR COM ROM
1955
B&W
Sex
Nud
Viol
Lang
AdSit

D: Ingmar Bergman 110 m

8 A thoroughly enchanting and a comic carnal frolic! Eight people venture to a country estate in Sweden at the turn of the 20th-century for a weekend of relaxation. With the help of a mysterious drink, each ends up paired with completely different people than they came with. The principal characters are a middle-aged lawyer, his very young bride, his son, his ex-lover and her new lover. Witty, clever and sophisticated, this comedy was the basis for the classic play "A Little Night Music." This highly popular and sexy bedroom comedy became one of Bergman's most successful. Subtitled or dubbed versions available.

A: Ulla Jacobsson, Harriet Andersson, Eva Dahlbeck, Margit Carlquist, Gunnar Bjornstrand, Jarl Kulle

© HOME VISION SMI 040

TESTAMENT OF DR. MABUSE

NR
FOR SUS
1933
B&W
Sex
Nud
Viol
Lang
AdSit

D: Fritz Lang 120 m

9 In 1922 famed German director Fritz Lang created a silent suspense masterpiece in which his lead character was a psychotic leader of a criminal gang. As it ended, Dr. Mabuse was committed to an asylum. This film begins there. Dr. Mabuse is no less demented, still controlling his army of criminals. And, he is plotting to crush society through endless waves of violence and thievery -- even after his death, by having hypnotized his psychiatrist so that upon his death, he can take over the soul of the man and continue his reign of terror. This is a thinly disguised attack on Adolph Hitler and Lang fled Germany shortly after this film was released. His wife became a high-ranking Nazi. Subtitles.

A: Rudolph Klein-Rogge, Oscar Beregi, Fera Liessem, Gustav Diessl

© HOME VISION TES 020

THREEPENNY OPERA, THE

NR
FOR MUS
1931
B&W
Sex
Nud
Viol
Lang
AdSit

D: G.W. Pabst 113 m

8 Biting musical satire of "respectable" (German) society that did not please the Nazis at all. It is also the birthplace of the now classic song made popular by Bobby Darin in the late 1950s: "Mack the Knife." Mack is a dashing thief and lady's man in London's seedy underworld of the 1890s, who regularly gets his way in his world. That is, until he is so audacious as to marry the daughter of Soho's "Beggar King." Then poor Mack has to run for his life when the outraged king dispatches a bunch of crooked cops to hunt him down.

A: Rudolph Forster, Carola Neher, Lotte Lenya, Fritz Rasp

© HOME VISION THR 110

UGETSU

NR
FOR FAN DMA
1953
B&W
Sex
Nud
Viol
Lang
AdSit

D: Kenji Mizoguchi 94 m

10 Critically acclaimed Japanese classic. Set in the 16th century and surrounded by civil war, two poor potters who dream of glory, leave their families to sell their wares in the city. There both abandon their families to follow their dreams. One brother uses his money to buy a spear and armor and by overwhelming luck achieves his lifelong ambition to become a samurai. The other brother allows himself to be seduced by a beautiful noblewoman. However, both find their dreams to be far less then they had thought and their wives are destroyed by their folly. One is killed and the other has to become a prostitute. Beautifully filmed but mix of reality and supernatural require concentration. Subtitles.

A: Machiko Kyo, Kinuyo Tanaka, Mitsuko Mito, Masayuki Mori, Saka Ozawa

© HOME VISION UGE 010

UMBERTO D.

NR
FOR DMA
1955
B&W
Sex
Nud
Viol
Lang
AdSit

D: Vittorio De Sica 89 m

10 A powerful, brilliant Italian tearjerker. Painful because of the subject matter which is the sad truth of the unfairness of old age and the way society treats its elderly. Surviving only on a meager government pension, the retired Umberto (Battisi) is forced out on the Roman streets with only his memories and his trusted dog for companionship. His struggle to maintain his dignity and support himself and his dog, the only one who loves him, is heartrending. This is a potent masterpiece that is in no way diminished with time. Many believe this to be De Sica's most important work. Subtitles.

A: Carlo Battisi, Maria Pia Casilio, Lina Genneri

© NEW LINE HOME VIDEO 6131

WAGES OF FEAR, THE

D: Henri-Georges Clouzot — 148 m

NR | FOR SUS | 1953 | B&W

8 A harrowing French classic set in South America. After an oil well explodes into a huge unquenchable fire, four men, bored and broke, are hired to risk their lives driving trucks loaded with the extremely volatile explosive nitroglycerine. The obvious risks are greatly compounded because the trucks must be driven over miles of bumpy, twisting mountain roads. But, the film also explores the characters of the four individuals who would take such huge chances. Very well done and highly acclaimed. In French - with subtitles. There was an OK remake done in English in 1977 as SORCERER.

Sex · Nud · ◢ Viol · Lang · AdSit

A: Yves Montand, Charles Vanel, Vera Clouzot, Peter Van Eyck, Folco Lulli, William Tubbs

© HOME VISION WAG 040

Horror

BEDLAM

D: Mark Robson — 79 m

NR | HOR | 1945 | B&W

6 St. Mary of Bethlehem was an actual insane asylum in 18th-century London. That facility was alternately known as Bedlam. In this chilling tale, Karloff is at his spooky best playing the cruel and sadistic head of that asylum. Anna Lee has visited the asylum and seen the unspeakable horrors he carries out there. But when she tries to expose his cruelties, he protects himself by having her committed. She, too, is now trapped behind the walls of his insane prison. Chilling tale that was based upon actual events.

Sex · Nud · Viol · Lang · ◢ AdSit

A: Boris Karloff, Anna Lee, Ian Wolfe, Richard Fraser, Billy House, Jason Robards, Sr.

© TURNER HOME ENTERTAINMENT 6182

BLACK CAT, THE

D: Edgar G. Ulmer — 65 m

NR | HOR | 1934 | B&W

7 A surrealistic and polished horror film whose spooky atmosphere is only aided by the film's age. It has bizarre sets and an even more bizarre plot. When their bus crashes, a honeymooning couple spends the night in a spooky house owned by Karloff. Karloff's attention to the woman causes the couple to try to flee, but they are trapped - it seems, Karloff has determined to marry the girl to the devil. On another front, Lugosi is a doctor who is locked in a struggle with Karloff and is being drawn ever deeper into a web of evil with the devil-worshipping architect Karloff and his black magic.

Sex · Nud · Viol · Lang · ◢ AdSit

A: Boris Karloff, Bela Lugosi, Jacqueline Wells, Lucille Lund, Henry Armetta

© MCA/UNIVERSAL HOME VIDEO, INC. 80814

BODY SNATCHER, THE

D: Robert Wise — 78 m

NR | HOR | 1945 | B&W

9 Eerie classic horror. A 19th-century Scottish doctor, who requires cadavers for his experiments, turns a pitiful soul (Karloff), a cabbie, into a pathetic grave robber to get them. The doctor basks in public glory, but lonely Karloff's only pleasure comes from associating with the doctor. He even turns to murder to satisfy the doctor's need for more body parts, but still the doctor scorns him. So Karloff blackmails the doctor, threatening to expose him. The doctor decides something has to be done about Boris, but that was a bad idea. Rich in dark atmosphere and gloom.

Sex · Nud · ◢ Viol · Lang · ◢ AdSit

A: Henry Daniell, Boris Karloff, Bela Lugosi, Edith Atwater, Russell Wade, Rita Corday

© TURNER HOME ENTERTAINMENT 2086

BRIDE OF FRANKENSTEIN, THE

D: James Whale — 75 m

NR | HOR FAN | 1935 | B&W

10 A thoroughly delightful horror movie that picks up where FRANKENSTEIN left off. Chilling, sinister and wicked, this masterpiece from director Whale expertly mixes all of the expected horror elements with emotion, humor and elegance, plus healthy doses of wit. The corrupt Dr. Praetorius (Thesiger) forces Dr. Frankenstein (Clive) into making a female companion for the lonely monster (Karloff), who has been terrorizing the countryside looking for a friend. This extremely well-made sequel was immensely popular. A true classic.

Sex · Nud · Viol · Lang · AdSit

A: Boris Karloff, Elsa Lanchester, Colin Clive, Valerie Hobson, Ernest Thesiger, Una O'Connor

© MCA/UNIVERSAL HOME VIDEO, INC. 80115

CAT PEOPLE

D: Jacques Tourneur — 64 m

NR | HOR SUS | 1942 | B&W

6 Intriguing cult horror classic about a woman who fears that her family's ancient and evil curse is now upon her. That bizarre curse causes her to become transformed into a marauding black cat should her passions ever become aroused. Then that cat will hunt and kill her lover. Many doubt that her fears are justified, but we don't. There is plenty of suspense brought on by the skillful manipulation of your imagination and some real terror too, but the plot is slow to develop. Very successful, it was followed up in 1944 with CURSE OF THE CAT PEOPLE, and was remade much more explicitly in 1982.

Sex · Nud · Viol · Lang · ◢ AdSit

A: Simone Simon, Kent Smith, Tom Conway, Jack Holt, Jane Randolph

© TURNER HOME ENTERTAINMENT 2085

CREATURE FROM THE BLACK LAGOON

D: Jack Arnold — 79 m

NR | HOR | 1954 | B&W

7 Campy fun. Members of a scientific expedition in the Amazon run into a strange fish/man creature. The scientists drug and capture him. However, while he is in captivity, he develops the hots for female archaeologist Julia Adams. Later, when he escapes, he captures her and takes her with him back to the swamp. Her fellow scientist Richard Carlson immediately launches a search to get her back. This is the prototypical '50s monster movie and has become high-camp for seasoned viewers, but it also provides some excitement for the uninitiated - particularly younger viewers.

Sex · Nud · Viol · Lang · AdSit

A: Richard Carlson, Julie Adams, Richard Denning, Antonio Moreno, Whit Bissell, Nestor Paiva

© MCA/UNIVERSAL HOME VIDEO, INC. 66018

DEVIL BATS

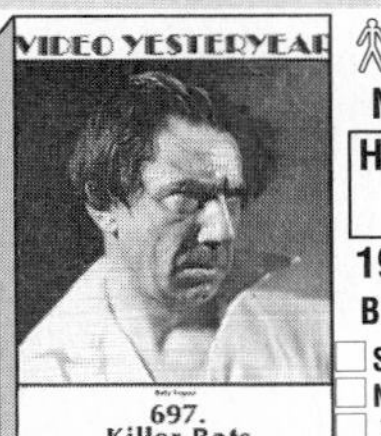

D: Jean Yarbrough — 68 m

NR | HOR | 1942 | B&W

6 Entertaining Bela Lugosi horror flick. Bela is, to all appearances, an kindly village doctor but, in reality, he is a true mad scientist. Working in his laboratory at home, he has created an army of blood-sucking killer bats which he calls "my friends", and he has trained them to be directed to their quarry by an attraction for a special perfume. One of Lugosi's most notorious pictures.

Sex · Nud · Viol · Lang · ◢ AdSit

A: Bela Lugosi, Suzanne Kaaren, Dave O'Brien

© VIDEO YESTERYEAR 697

DEVIL DOLL, THE

D: Tod Browning — 798 m

NR | HOR | 1936 | B&W

7 Imaginative, macabre and bizarre. Barrymore is a wrongfully imprisoned convict who escapes from Devil's Island. He returns home both to redeem his name and to seek revenge upon the three people who have wronged him. Upon arrival, he seeks out the wife of a dead mad-scientist whom he had befriended. That scientist had concocted a shrinking potion. Together the two shrink humans to doll size and force them to become tiny assassins. He dresses up as a kindly old lady running a toy store so that he can send them on their missions. Spooky. Excellent special effects.

Sex · Nud · Viol · Lang · ◢ AdSit

A: Lionel Barrymore, Maureen O'Sullivan, Frank Lawton, Henry B. Walthall, Robert Greig, Lucy Beaumont

Distributed By MGM/UA Home Video 600904

DOCTOR X

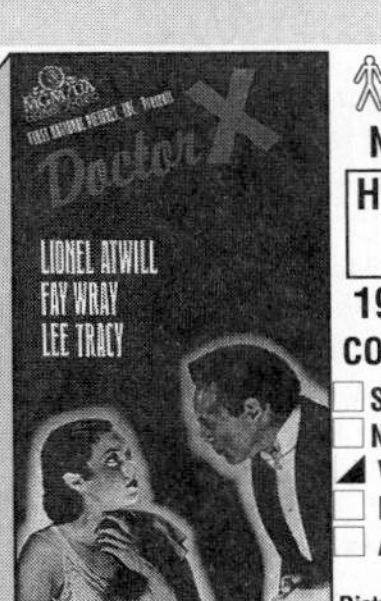

D: Michael Curtiz — 77 m

NR | HOR | 1932 | COLOR

6 One of filmdom's earliest efforts to scare. Weird mystery about a "full moon" strangler, who police believe is the strange Doctor X (Atwill). An investigative reporter (Tracy) follows a trail of bodies to his medical college where the one-armed mad scientist is doing research on cannibalism and synthetic flesh. This is a vintage horror piece that is very dated but nonetheless worthy viewing for horror fans. It is also technically interesting because it was done in a very innovative two-color process and the makeup was done by Max Factor himself.

Sex · Nud · ◢ Viol · Lang · AdSit

A: Lionel Atwill, Preston Foster, Fay Wray, Lee Tracy, Mae Busch

Distributed By MGM/UA Home Video 601159

DRACULA

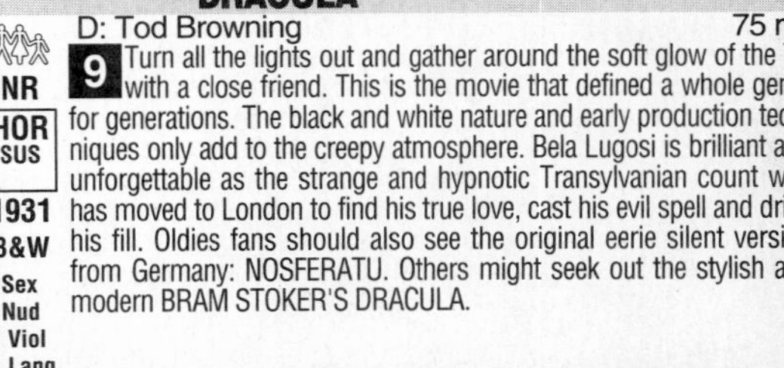

D: Tod Browning — 75 m

NR | HOR SUS | 1931 | B&W

9 Turn all the lights out and gather around the soft glow of the TV with a close friend. This is the movie that defined a whole genre for generations. The black and white nature and early production techniques only add to the creepy atmosphere. Bela Lugosi is brilliant and unforgettable as the strange and hypnotic Transylvanian count who has moved to London to find his true love, cast his evil spell and drink his fill. Oldies fans should also see the original eerie silent version from Germany: NOSFERATU. Others might seek out the stylish and modern BRAM STOKER'S DRACULA.

◢ Sex · Nud · ◢ Viol · Lang · ◢ AdSit

A: Bela Lugosi, David Manners, Helen Chandler, Dwight Frye, Edward Van Sloan, Herbert Bunston

© MCA/UNIVERSAL HOME VIDEO, INC. 81123

OLDIES

DRACULA'S DAUGHTER

D: Lambert Hillyer — 81 m

NR | HOR SUS | 1936

8 Moody sequel to Lugossi's classic. The very beautiful and mysterious Countess Marya Zaleska (Gloria Holden) suddenly appears in London, just as numerous people are found seemingly drained of blood. She is the unhappy and troubled daughter of Dracula and has been desperately trying to break her accursed addiction to blood. Now she seeks comfort from psychiatrist Dr. Garth (Otto Kruger) and she quickly falls in love with him, even though he is engaged. So she seeks to win him away from his fiancee by placing a curse upon the poor girl. Good acting and an intelligent and logical script have made this a perennial favorite.

Sex / Nud / Viol / Lang / AdSit

A: Otto Kruger, Gloria Holden, Marguerite Churchill, Irving Pichel, Edward Van Sloan, Nan Grey

© MCA/UNIVERSAL HOME VIDEO, INC. 80610

DR. JEKYLL AND MR. HYDE

D: John S. Robertson — 63 m

NR | HOR DMA | 1920 | B&W

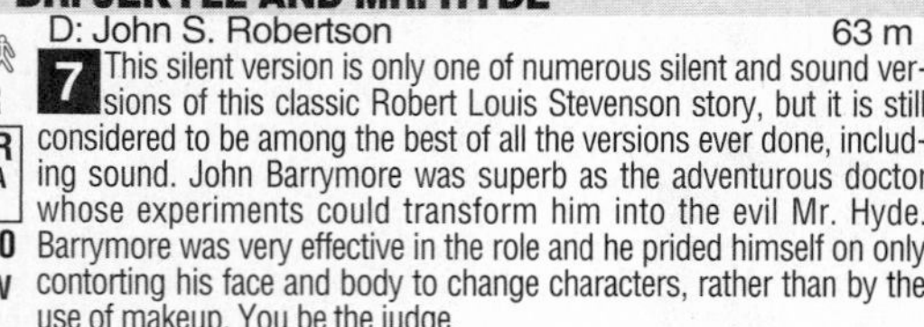

7 This silent version is only one of numerous silent and sound versions of this classic Robert Louis Stevenson story, but it is still considered to be among the best of all the versions ever done, including sound. John Barrymore was superb as the adventurous doctor whose experiments could transform him into the evil Mr. Hyde. Barrymore was very effective in the role and he prided himself on only contorting his face and body to change characters, rather than by the use of makeup. You be the judge.

Sex / Nud / Viol / Lang / ◢ AdSit

A: John Barrymore, Martha Mansfield, Brandon Hurst, Nita Naldi, Charles Lane, Louis Wolheim

© REPUBLIC PICTURES HOME VIDEO 1068

DR. JEKYLL AND MR. HYDE

D: Rouben Mamoulian — 97 m

NR | HOR DMA | 1932 | B&W

8 Frederic March is excellent and won the Oscar for Best Actor for his frightening portrayal of the tortured English doctor, even though at the time, he was considered only to be a comic actor. This film was quite effective and also very became influential for its use of makeup, camera and symbolism. It was also filmed in the pre-Production Code days and so was both more violent and more sexual than would be permitted later on. (In fact, 17 minutes were later edited out to satisfy the censors.) Hopkins was also very good as Ivy, the lady of the evening who Hyde taunts and abuses.

Sex / Nud / ◢ Viol / Lang / ◢ AdSit

A: Fredric March, Miriam Hopkins, Rose Hobart, Holmes Herbert, Edgar Norton

Distributed By MGM/UA Home Video M201642

DR. JEKYLL AND MR. HYDE

D: Victor Fleming — 113 m

G | HOR DMA | 1941 | B&W

7 This time around, with Tracy, more emphasis is placed upon the psychological elements of the story - a good doctor who becomes a murdering Mr. Hyde, and the threat to his relationship with his fiancee (Lana Turner) because of his relationship with a prostitute (Ingrid Bergman). Great acting by everyone, particularly Bergman, but it still does not surpass the production with Fredric March in 1932.

Sex / Nud / Viol / Lang / ◢ AdSit

A: Spencer Tracy, Ingrid Bergman, Lana Turner, Donald Crisp, Ian Hunter, Barton MacLane

Distributed By MGM/UA Home Video M300651

FRANKENSTEIN

D: James Whale — 71 m

NR | HOR FAN | 1931 | B&W

10 A true Hollywood classic and a film which defined a whole genre for all time. In spite of its antiquated production techniques (including having no score), this is still a quite moving depiction of Mary Shelley's novel favorite. Boris Karloff provides a masterly performance (he never mutters a word) as the pathetic man-made man, created from parts of corpses and brought to life only to be scorned by men. When the mad Dr. Frankenstein cannot control his creation, the townspeople attack the pitiable, lonely creature. Excellent. Followed by BRIDE OF FRANKENSTEIN.

Sex / Nud / ◢ Viol / Lang / AdSit

A: Boris Karloff, Colin Clive, Mae Clarke, John Boles, Edward Van Sloan, Dwight Frye

© MCA/UNIVERSAL HOME VIDEO, INC. 55004

FRANKENSTEIN MEETS THE WOLFMAN

D: Roy William Neill — 73 m

NR | HOR | 1943 | B&W

7 Two of Universal Studio's all-time favorite monsters meet face to face. A tormented Wolfman is disinterred and seeks out a doctor's help. He's looking either for a cure or to be put out of his misery. He is sent to gypsy Maria Ouspenskaya, who takes him to the village where Dr. Frankenstein once lived. The good doctor is dead - but his creation isn't. These two misfits prefer to fight rather than to be friends and the countryside begins to accumulate corpses. Fast-paced and exciting. Eerie atmosphere. Good fun.

Sex / Nud / ◢ Viol / Lang / AdSit

A: Lon Chaney, Jr., Patric Knowles, Bela Lugosi, Ilona Massey, Maria Ouspenskaya, Lionel Atwill

© MCA/UNIVERSAL HOME VIDEO, INC. 80422

FREAKS

D: Tod Browning — 65 m

NR | HOR SUS | 1932 | B&W

9 An incredibly bizarre horror film that is a truly macabre masterpiece and a cult favorite. This most unusual picture presents a fascinating story of hideously deformed circus freaks who seek a terrible revenge upon a beautiful trapeze artist and her strongman lover when she marries a midget only to poison him for his money. The film's actors are in fact, real-life circus sideshow freaks. While you initially feel repulsion, curiosity, fear and pity for these oddities, you also grow to accept and even to respect them. The "normal" people are the villains in this one. Boy, do the freaks get even. Amazing stuff!

Sex / Nud / ◢ Viol / Lang / ■ AdSit

A: Wallace Ford, Leila Hyams, Olga Baclanova, Roscoe Ates, Harry Earles

Distributed By MGM/UA Home Video M600843

HOUSE OF WAX

D: Andre De Toth — 88 m

PG | HOR | 1953 | COLOR

8 Vincent Price is a sculptor of wax, but he disappears after he loses a hand in a fire that his evil partner set to the wax museum that they had built together, destroying it. When he reappears, he opens a new museum with marvelous and even more life-like figures inside. Everyone praises the new works. Only Phyllis Kirk questions it, and instead thinks... murder. How has he populated his new museum with such lifelike figures when his hands are so crippled? By using real humans that he has dipped in wax. Originally shown in 3-D, but it works just as well without the gimmick.

Sex / Nud / Viol / Lang / ◢ AdSit

A: Vincent Price, Phyllis Kirk, Carolyn Jones, Paul Cavanagh, Charles Bronson

© WARNER HOME VIDEO 11054

ISLE OF THE DEAD

D: Mark Robson — 72 m

NR | HOR | 1945 | B&W

7 Eerie, intelligent and unusual horror flick. The year is 1912. A Greek general (Karloff) has come to an island to visit the grave of his wife and discovers that there is a dreadful plague in this land... a very unusual plague. It is a sickness that slowly enters your mind and drives you insane. He becomes the leader of the effort to fight it, but instead slowly becomes victim to the plague himself. Everywhere there is insanity. Graves are robbed. People are buried before they are dead. Vampires roam the land. Startling, unsettling and genuinely frightening.

Sex / Nud / ◢ Viol / Lang / ◢ AdSit

A: Boris Karloff, Ellen Drew, Jason Robards, Sr., Marc Cramer, Katherine Emery, Helene Thimig

© TURNER HOME ENTERTAINMENT 6181

I WALKED WITH A ZOMBIE

D: Jacques Tourneur — 68 m

NR | HOR SUS | 1943 | B&W

9 An exceptional chiller, don't be fooled by the hokey title. An American planter in Haiti hires a Canadian nurse to look after his wife after she mysteriously becomes catatonic. Nurse Dee's investigations lead to the discovery that there are several family skeletons in the closet, and also of island legends of voodoo that cannot be ignored. A rich atmosphere and tension permeates this story of black magic and terror. Director Tourneur forgoes gore and sudden shocks in exchange for an intriguing spell-binding story line and constant sustained suspense.

Sex / Nud / ◢ Viol / Lang / ◢ AdSit

A: Frances Dee, Tom Conway, James Ellison, Edith Barrett, Christine Gordon, Teresa Harris

© TURNER HOME ENTERTAINMENT 6183

MARK OF THE VAMPIRE

D: Tod Browning — 61 m

NR | HOR | 1935 | B&W

7 They're coming to suck your blood! Residents of a small town are terrorized by a band of blood-sucking vampires. Count Mora (Lugosi) and his sultry and villainous daughter (Borland) are after the residents of an old estate. The foolish townsfolk are disbelievers and try on their own to stop the creatures of the night, but it is only the local vampire expert (Barrymore) who can put an end to their reign of terror. This well-done flick is actually a remake of the silent movie, LONDON AFTER MIDNIGHT.

Sex / Nud / ◢ Viol / Lang / ◢ AdSit

A: Lionel Barrymore, Bela Lugosi, Elizabeth Allan, Lionel Atwill, Carol Borland, Jean Hersholt

Distributed By MGM/UA Home Video M600905

MUMMY, THE

D: Karl Freund — 72 m

NR | HOR SUS | 1932 | B&W

9 When archeologists read from a sacred book, against dire warnings to the contrary, they bring back to life a 3,700 year old Egyptian mummy. He was a high priest who had been embalmed alive for attempting to revive a sacrificed vestal virgin who he loved. Now, when he sees Zita Johann, he thinks she is his ancient princess reincarnated and is intent upon getting his dusty arms around her. Karloff is superb as the creepy old bag of bones. Director Freund relies more on atmospheric thrill than actual gore - which adds to the effectiveness and surrealistic air of this rather excellent classic.

Sex / Nud / ◢ Viol / Lang / ◢ AdSit

A: Boris Karloff, Zita Johann, David Manners, Arthur Byron, Edward Van Sloan, Bramwell Fletcher

© MCA/UNIVERSAL HOME VIDEO, INC. 80030

MUMMY'S HAND, THE

D: Christy Cabanne 70 m

NR
HOR
1940
B&W

6 Two carnival archaeologists are financed by a reluctant magician and his beautiful daughter on a trip to Egypt where they are to uncover the long lost tomb of the Princess Ananka. Their clues lead them to discover hidden passageways that lead them deep into the tomb, but the tomb is guarded by a 3000-year-old mummy being kept alive by a secret formula administered by a sinister high priest. The invaders are not welcome, however 3000 years is a long time and the Mummy does take a particular shine to the beautiful girl. A fair dose of thrills and chills, but also a few laughs.

Sex
Nud
Viol
Lang
AdSit

A: Dick Foran, Peggy Moran, Wallace Ford, Cecil Kellaway, Eduardo Ciannelli, George Zucco

© MCA/UNIVERSAL HOME VIDEO, INC. 80850

NOSFERATU

D: F.W. Murnau 530 m

NR
HOR
SUS
FOR
1922
B&W

8 This is the eerie original screen Dracula and it is probably the most vile and hideous characterization of him. Set in the 1830's, here Count Orloc of Transylvania is gaunt, pale and fearsome. The count has recognised his long lost love in a salesman's photograph, and leaves immediately to reclaim her. His arrival at the small German town of Breman brings with it great evil, darkness and foreboding as he arrives on a ghost ship that has several earth-filled coffins and is loaded to the gunnels with rats. The wife determines that the only hope to save the town is for her to occupy Dracula for so long that he cannot return to his casket by dawn. Silent with subtitles.

Sex
Nud
Viol
Lang
AdSit

A: Max Schreck, Gustave Von Wagenheim, Greta Schroeder, Alexander Granach

© GOODTIMES 8184

SON OF DRACULA

D: Robert Siodmak 80 m

NR
HOR
1943
B&W

7 Convincing Hollywood chiller! Count Alucard (Lon Chaney) travels to the deep South and sweeps the lovely Louise Allbritton off her feet, taking her away from her smitten boyfriend (Paige). Her problem is that she doesn't really know just who the handsome Count Alucard is. No one does, but an upset Paige begins to unearth some clues - like spell Alucard backwards - and decides to get Allbritton away from the captivating count. However, it's too late because bow she likes blood, too. Great special effects and atmosphere that add to the thrills in this spooky vampire tale.

Sex
Nud
Viol
Lang
AdSit

A: Lon Chaney, Jr., Louise Allbritton, Robert Paige, Frank Craven, Evelyn Ankers, J. Edward Bromberg

© MCA/UNIVERSAL HOME VIDEO, INC. 80766

SON OF FRANKENSTEIN

D: Rowland V. Lee 99 m

NR
HOR
1939
B&W

7 Eerie, well-made third in the Frankenstein series. Now 25 years after the "death" of the Frankenstein monster, the son of Dr. Frankenstein returns to his ancestral castle where he meets Ygor. Ygor is a shepherd with a broken neck, having survived a hanging. Ygor urges the younger Frankenstein to revive the monster and to rehabilitate him, thus redeeming the family name. But when the monster is revived, a vengeful Ygor instead turns him loose on a killing spree in the countryside. Excellent and intelligent production, with a top-flight cast. Very atmospheric.

Sex
Nud
Viol
Lang
AdSit

A: Bela Lugosi, Basil Rathbone, Boris Karloff, Lionel Atwill, Josephine Hutchinson, Donnie Dunagan

© MCA/UNIVERSAL HOME VIDEO, INC. 80764

THING, THE

D: Christian Nyby 80 m

NR
HOR
SF
SUS
1951
B&W

8 Very entertaining stereotypical '50s sci-fi/horror/monster flick. The theme is simple enough. A frozen blob is discovered near an army radar station in Arctic. When it is accidentally defrosted, it turns out to be an Alien creature that terrorizes the camp. However, this film is better than many of the genre of the period. What makes this film so special is the very high level of tension that is developed through the director's calculated creation of fear based upon the unknown (the alien is rarely actually seen) and the steady deliberate pacing. Exceptional acting helps to make this a very effective thriller.

Sex
Nud
Viol
Lang
AdSit

A: Kenneth Tobey, James Arness, Margaret Sheridan, Robert Cornthwaite, Douglas Spencer, Dewey Martin

© TURNER HOME ENTERTAINMENT 2069

WHITE ZOMBIE

D: Victor Halperin 79 m

NR
HOR
1932
B&W

7 A campy, eerie, low-budget thriller from the early days of films. Early filming techniques and B&W photography enhance this spooky outing which is the granddaddy of all "modern-day" zombie flicks. Bela Lugosi is the white master of a misty Haitian sugar mill. He is a master sorcerer and has manned his plantation with an army of zombies, all under his spell. Another plantation owner who has been jilted, asks Lugosi to place pretty American Madge Bellamy under his powers to prevent her marriage to someone else. Lugosi agrees, however she can be still be awakened with a kiss. Mostly for film fans.

Sex
Nud
Viol
Lang
AdSit

A: Bela Lugosi, Madge Bellamy, Joseph Cawthorn, Robert Frazer, John Harron, Clarence Muse

© REPUBLIC PICTURES HOME VIDEO 4529

WOLF MAN, THE

D: George Waggner 70 m

NR
HOR
1941
B&W

9 Wonderful horror film which led to many sequels and is one of the greatest of the classic horror films. Chaney (in a role he would play five more times) plays an American who returns to Wales and is bitten when he helps a beautiful girl who is being attacked by a wolf in the moors. However, this wolf is no ordinary wolf. A gypsy seer tells him that he has been bitten by a werewolf and now, with each rising of the new moon, he too is condemned to become a bloodthirsty werewolf. This is a well-produced and genuinely eerie film which is so engrossing that you will become totally lost within the myth.

Sex
Nud
Viol
Lang
AdSit

A: Claude Rains, Lon Chaney, Jr., Bela Lugosi, Ralph Bellamy, Evelyn Ankers, Maria Ouspenskaya

© MCA/UNIVERSAL HOME VIDEO, INC. 80031

OLDIES

Musicals

42ND STREET

D: Lloyd Bacon 90 m

NR
MUS
1933
B&W

8 The quintessential cliched musical. An ailing Broadway producer places all his marbles in one last major effort at success. But, just before opening, the lead dancer breaks her leg and the show must be saved by the young untested understudy, Ruby Keeler. Busby Berkeley dance extravaganza.

Sex
Nud
Viol
Lang
AdSit

A: Dick Powell, Ruby Keeler, Ginger Rogers, Warner Baxter, Una Merkel

Distributed By MGM/UA Home Video M301672

AFFAIRS OF DOBIE GILLIS, THE

D: Don Weis 74 m

NR
MUS
COM
ROM
1953
B&W

7 Entertaining musical comedy that starred America's darling of the 50s, Debbie Reynolds. Starring with her was Bobby Van, who played Dobie Gillis, the archetypal girl-chasing college student. There are lots of big band numbers and dances stuffed in between the college shenanigans, plus Hans Conried as a sour professor who is the source of much of the kid's grief. This formula proved to be so successful that it went on to become a very popular TV series entitled, "The Many Loves of Dobie Gillis". That show featured a young actor, Bob Denver, who went on to become a huge TV star as Gilligan of "Gilligan's Island."

Sex
Nud
Viol
Lang
AdSit

A: Debbie Reynolds, Bobby Van, Hans Conried, Lurene Tuttle, Bob Fosse

Distributed By MGM/UA Home Video M204545

AMERICAN IN PARIS, AN

D: Vincente Minnelli 115 m

NR
MUS
ROM
1951
COLOR

9 Winner of six Oscars, including Best Picture. Lavish production musical with Gene Kelly's brilliant choreography and a George and Ira Gershwin score. Ex-GI Kelly stays in Paris after WWII to become an artist, only to fall in love with lovely Leslie Caron who is engaged to someone else. Plot is so-so but the music and dancing are marvelous. Center-piece is a 17-minute love song/ballet with Kelly and Caron.

Sex
Nud
Viol
Lang
AdSit

A: Gene Kelly, Leslie Caron, Oscar Levant, Nina Foch, Georges Guetary

Distributed By MGM/UA Home Video M600006

ANCHORS AWEIGH

D: George Sidney 141 m

NR
MUS
1945
COLOR

6 OK musical that will please most musical fans but is considered by most critics to be only a good warm-up for the more superior musical ON THE TOWN. The story line is weak, but the music and dance sequences are quite good. Two sailors (Kelly and Sinatra) on leave in Hollywood both fall for Kathryn Grayson. Sinatra sings Sammy Cahn's tunes, and Kelly dances up a storm, particularly in the celebrated scene with the animated mouse Jerry, of "Tom and Jerry" fame.

Sex
Nud
Viol
Lang
AdSit

A: Gene Kelly, Frank Sinatra, Kathryn Grayson, Jose Iturbi, Dean Stockwell, Pamela Britton

Distributed By MGM/UA Home Video M202678

BABES IN ARMS

D: Busby Berkeley — 94 m

NR | MUS | 1939 | B&W

6 This was the first teaming of Mickey Rooney and Judy Garland and it is the prototypical adolescent "let's put on a show" type of movie. Mickey is the son of vaudevillian parents. When they and others are hit by hard times, Mickey writes and directs his schoolmates in a show to raise some money for them. Pretty typical plot line has the local prima donna trying to steal the lead from Judy, but in the end Judy wins out and Mickey and Judy sing and dance up a storm. Lively jazz/swing score was Oscar-nominated, as was Rooney.

Sex | Nud | Viol | Lang | AdSit

A: Mickey Rooney, Judy Garland, Charles Winninger, Guy Kibbee, Margaret Hamilton

Distributed By MGM/UA Home Video M400585

BAND WAGON, THE

D: Vincente Minnelli — 113 m

NR | MUS | 1953 | COLOR

9 This is one of Minnelli's best musicals. Astaire is a washed-up movie star who is persuaded by his friends to make a comeback in a Broadway musical. He joins the show, even though he has some serious misgivings. He is right - the show flops on the road. Undeterred, he raises the money he needs, takes over the production and makes it into a hit. Musical highlights: "Dancing in the Dark," "Shine on Your Shoes" and "That's Entertainment." If you like musicals, look in the actor's index under Astaire and the director's index under Minnelli. Between them, they almost own the genre.

Sex | Nud | Viol | Lang | AdSit

A: Fred Astaire, Cyd Charisse, Oscar Levant, Nanette Fabray, Jack Buchanan

Distributed By MGM/UA Home Video M202147

BITTER SWEET

D: W.S. Van Dyke II — 94 m

NR | MUS ROM | 1940 | B&W

7 One of the best of the MacDonald/Eddy pairings. This is noted playwrite Noel Coward's operetta about a young couple, a violinist and a dancer, who are in love. On the eve of her wedding to someone else in 1880, they elope to Vienna. They struggle to survive there, living only on love when he is unable to sell his music. The climax comes when she sings his songs to an enthusiastic audience after he has defended her honor in a duel with a lecherous Baron. Coward's beautiful songs are the principal reason the film still has interest and merit.

Sex | Nud | Viol | Lang | AdSit

A: Jeanette MacDonald, Nelson Eddy, George Sanders, Felix Bressart, Lynne Carver, Ian Hunter

Distributed By MGM/UA Home Video M301485

BRIGADOON

D: Vincente Minnelli — 109 m

G | MUS ROM | 1954 | COLOR

8 One of the best of Lerner and Loewe's fanciful musicals is brought to the screen. Two American hunters in the Scottish Highlands stumble upon an enchanted Scottish village called Brigadoon, which appears only once every 100 years. There, Kelly meets beautiful Cyd Charisse and they fall in love. He must now decide whether to stay in her world and be lost in time, or return to his own. Beautiful songs such as "Almost Like Being in Love" and "I'll Go Home With Bonnie Jean," plus show-stopping dance routines.

Sex | Nud | Viol | Lang | AdSit

A: Gene Kelly, Van Johnson, Cyd Charisse, Elaine Stewart, Barry Jones, Hugh Laing

Distributed By MGM/UA Home Video M700040

BROADWAY MELODY OF 1938

D: Roy Del Ruth — 111 m

NR | MUS | 1937 | B&W

6 Musicals were never more popular than in the late '30s. This was one that was custom-designed to appeal to that audience. The story line revolves around a girl who dreams of making it big on Broadway (Eleanor Powell) and the producer (Robert Taylor) who gets her there. A likable musical, it has a rich cast of popular entertainers but is best remembered for its dancing and particularly its singing. (A very young Judy Garland sings "You Made Me Love You" to Clark Gable and became a big hit.)

Sex | Nud | Viol | Lang | AdSit

A: Judy Garland, Robert Taylor, George Murphy, Eleanor Powell, Sophie Tucker, Buddy Ebsen

Distributed By MGM/UA Home Video M301048

BROADWAY MELODY OF 1940

D: Norman Taurog — 104 m

NR | MUS | 1940 | B&W

6 If you are a fan of Fred Astaire, this is a good one for you. Here he is teamed with Eleanor Powell for the only time and has a rivalry with George Murphy, his partner, for her heart. Forget the plot. Enjoy lots of dancing and the music (Cole Porter's "Begin the Beguine" and "I've Got My Eyes on You"), too.

Sex | Nud | Viol | Lang | AdSit

A: Fred Astaire, Eleanor Powell, George Murphy, Frank Morgan, Ian Hunter

Distributed By MGM/UA Home Video M301111

CABIN IN THE SKY

D: Vincente Minnelli — 99 m

NR | MUS COM | 1943 | B&W

8 This is one of Hollywood's first general release films featuring an all-black cast. Terrific musical taken directly from Broadway. It is the story of the battle between a good, poor-but-devout woman (Ethel Waters) married a shiftless man - Little Joe (Eddie "Rochester" Anderson); and an evil, sinfully-beautiful woman (Lena Horne) sent by the devil to win over the soul of Little Joe. Contains songs "Happiness is a Thing Called Joe" and "Takin' a Chance on Love." A bit racist in nature, but consider when it was made. Terrific cast.

Sex | Nud | Viol | Lang | AdSit

A: Eddie Anderson, Lena Horne, Ethel Waters, Rex Ingram, Louis Armstrong, Duke Ellington

Distributed By MGM/UA Home Video M300558

CALAMITY JANE

D: David Butler — 101 m

MUS COM WST | 1953 | COLOR

7 Entertaining, rambunctious musical comedy in which Doris Day plays Calamity Jane as a tomboy who is in wild and amorous pursuit of Wild Bill Hickok (Howard Keel). Doris had a lot of fun with this role and it shows. She is a wildly independent gal of the West who goes after her man but doesn't want to change her ways. Bill doesn't want much to do with her until, with a little bit of help, Calamity reveals that thar's a heap o' woman under them buckskins. This is also the movie where Day introduces her biggest hit song (which also won an Oscar), "Secret Love."

Sex | Nud | Viol | Lang | AdSit

A: Doris Day, Howard Keel, Allyn Ann McLerie, Phillip Carey, Gale Robbins, Dick Wesson

© WARNER HOME VIDEO 11209

CAPTAIN JANUARY

D: David Butler — 76 m

NR | MUS CLD | 1936 | B&W

7 Shirley Temple is at her sympathetic best as an orphan who lives with a lighthouse keeper. Captain January (Kibbee) rescued her from a shipwreck when she was just a baby. She is now a happy 4-year-old and is the sweetheart of all the fisherman in the neighborhood. But a new truant officer has moved to town and wants to take Shirley away to put her in a proper home.

Sex | Nud | Viol | Lang | AdSit

A: Shirley Temple, Guy Kibbee, Slim Summerville, Buddy Ebsen

© FOXVIDEO 1068

CAREFREE

D: Mark Sandrich — 83 m

NR | MUS COM | 1938 | B&W

6 Ralph Bellamy hires a psychiatrist (Fred Astaire) to hypnotize Ginger Rogers into submission after she turns down his marriage proposal. Fred does his best, but instead falls for the girl himself. Not the best Rogers/Astaire pairing. It's more of a comedy than their others, but it nonetheless still has some good dance sequences.

Sex | Nud | Viol | Lang | AdSit

A: Fred Astaire, Ginger Rogers, Ralph Bellamy, Luella Gear, Jack Carson, Franklin Pangborn

© TURNER HOME ENTERTAINMENT 2039

COVER GIRL

D: Charles Vidor — 107 m

NR | MUS COM | 1944 | COLOR

7 This was a big Columbia musical and one of the first to use the song lyrics essentially as dialogue in the plot. The story line is simple and cliched. A Brooklyn nightclub chorus girl wins a cover-girl contest, gives up her boyfriend and joins a Broadway show, only to discover that nothing is more important than love. But this film provides an excellent vehicle to display Hayworth's beauty and dancing, Kelly's brilliant innovative dancing and a pretty good Jerome Kern-Ira Girshwin musical score. Phil Silvers is funny, but Eve Arden's wise-cracking steals the spotlight.

Sex | Nud | Viol | Lang | AdSit

A: Rita Hayworth, Gene Kelly, Lee Bowman, Phil Silvers, Jinx Falkenburg, Eve Arden

© COLUMBIA TRISTAR HOME VIDEO 90413

DADDY LONG LEGS

D: Jean Negulesco — 126 m

NR | MUS ROM | 1955 | COLOR

6 Delightfully romantic fairy tale. A rich bachelor playboy (Astaire) becomes entranced with a pretty orphaned 18-year-old French girl. He sponsors her through two years of college in America anonymously. When she returns to France all grown up, Fred falls hard for her but trys to do the right thing because he is so much older. Trite? Yes, but... they tell the whole story dancing to a Johnny Mercer score which includes the now-classic "Something's Got to Give."

Sex | Nud | Viol | Lang | AdSit

A: Fred Astaire, Leslie Caron, Terry Moore, Thelma Ritter, Fred Clark, Charlotte Austin

© FOXVIDEO 1378

DANCE, GIRL, DANCE

D: Dorothy Arzner 89 m

NR | MUS DMA | 1940 | B&W | Sex | Nud | Viol | Lang | AdSit

7 This is ostensibly a musical but - being written by, directed by and starring principally women - it has a decidedly different slant than most other such films of the era. Innocent-girl Judy (O'Hara) dances ballet as a stooge in a burlesque act just to make ends meet while she struggles to break into professional ballet. Lucille Ball is the tough lead dancer (Lucy, a stripper?) at the burlesque house and she will do anything to keep the spotlight from O'Hara. She and O'Hara also fight for the same man. Finally O'Hara and Ball have it out. Acclaimed as an early feminist film.

A: Maureen O'Hara, Louis Hayward, Lucille Ball, Virginia Field, Ralph Bellamy, Maria Ouspenskaya

© TURNER HOME ENTERTAINMENT 6034

EASTER PARADE

D: Charles Walters 104 m

NR | MUS ROM COM | 1948 | COLOR | Sex | Nud | Viol | Lang | AdSit

9 Absolutely wonderful Irving Berlin musical (it has seventeen songs). Set in 1912, Astaire's dance partner (Miller) dumps him to go solo, so he picks Garland out of the chorus line, vowing that he can make her into a big star. Though he moons over his loss of Miller, Garland works hard to eventually capture his approval and also his heart. Wonderful classic songs and dance sequences make this an eminently watchable favorite, again and again.

A: Judy Garland, Fred Astaire, Peter Lawford, Jules Munshin, Ann Miller

Distributed By MGM/UA Home Video M600256

EVERGREEN

D: Victor Saville 93 m

NR | MUS COM | 1934 | B&W | Sex | Nud | Viol | Lang | AdSit

8 This was a very big early musical comedy from England. It featured the music of Rogers and Hart and is the story of young girl who pretends to be her mother. In 1909, her mother had been the toast of the London stage but had just retired and was set to marry a marquis when her daughter's father, who she thought to be dead, returned to blackmail her. So, leaving the girl in the care of someone, the mother vanished. Now, 25 years later, the girl is the spitting image of her mother. So much does she look like her, that people actually believe that she is her. That would be enough problems, but the poor girl is also in love with the man pretending to be her mother's son. Big production numbers.

A: Jessie Matthews, Sonnie Hale, Betty Balfour, Barry Mackay, Ivor Maclaren

© HOME VISION EVE 01

FANCY PANTS

D: George Marshall 92 m

NR | MUS COM | 1950 | COLOR | Sex | Nud | Viol | Lang | AdSit

7 Amusing and good-natured remake of 1935's RUGGLES OF RED GAP. Bob Hope plays an out-of-work actor pretending to be an English gentleman's gentleman. He is acquired by an oil-rich, husband-seeking, tomboy boss (Lucille Ball) and accompanies her back home to the Wild West of New Mexico. Entertaining movie, made so more by its cast than the story's premise - which was better done in the 1935 version.

A: Bob Hope, Lucille Ball, Bruce Cabot, Jack Kirkwood, Lea Penman, Hugh French

© PARAMOUNT HOME VIDEO 6208

FANTASIA

D: 120 m

G | MUS FAN | 1940 | COLOR | Sex | Nud | Viol | Lang | AdSit

8 Extravagant, hugely expensive and extremely bold venture by Walt Disney in 1940. The imaginations of the animators were turned loose to translate classical music masterpieces into free-flowing animated surreal fantasy story lines. There are seven sequences in all. The best are "The Sorcerer's Apprentice" and "Night on Bald Mountain." Highly praised by some and criticized by others. Certainly different. Imagination and patience required - and richly rewarded.

A:

© WALT DISNEY HOME VIDEO 1132

FLYING DOWN TO RIO

D: Thornton Freeland 89 m

NR | MUS | 1933 | B&W | Sex | Nud | Viol | Lang | AdSit

6 This first pairing of Astaire and Rogers is now very dated and corny, but it is nonetheless interesting for documenting the beginning of the Astaire/Rogers match up. It has also become known for its notorious climax in which dozens of chorus girls sing and dance while strapped to the wings of biplanes. Die-hard musical fans only.

A: Dolores Del Rio, Gene Raymond, Raoul Roulien, Ginger Rogers, Fred Astaire, Blanche Frederici

© TURNER HOME ENTERTAINMENT 6100

FOLLOW THE FLEET

D: Mark Sandrich 80 m

NR | MUS ROM | 1936 | B&W | Sex | Nud | Viol | Lang | AdSit

8 Friends of Fred and Ginger take note of this delightful song and dance fest to Irving Berlin's score. Two sailors on leave pursue two sisters. Songs include: "Let's Face the Music and Dance," "Let Yourself Go," "We Saw the Sea" and "I'm Putting All My Eggs in One Basket." Look for Lucille Ball and Betty Grable in bit parts.

A: Fred Astaire, Ginger Rogers, Randolph Scott, Harriet Nelson, Betty Grable, Lucille Ball

© TURNER HOME ENTERTAINMENT 2038

FOOTLIGHT PARADE

D: Lloyd Bacon 108 m

NR | MUS | 1933 | B&W | Sex | Nud | Viol | Lang | AdSit

6 Busby Berkeley extravaganza. Entertaining Depression-era entertainment. Cagney stars as a producer of extravagantly staged dance spectaculars who is dodging creditors because of the arrival of talking pictures. He finds a home of sorts producing musical intermissions between films at a movie theatre. Includes three of Berkeley's best, and most risque, routines: "Hollywood Hotel," "By a Waterfall" and "Shanghai Lil." Watch for Cagney's hoofing.

A: James Cagney, Joan Blondell, Ruby Keeler, Dick Powell, Guy Kibbee, Frank McHugh

Distributed By MGM/UA Home Video M301676

GAY DIVORCEE, THE

D: Mark Sandrich 107 m

NR | MUS | 1934 | B&W | Sex | Nud | Viol | Lang | AdSit

8 Delightful (although quite dated) early musical and the first Astaire/Rogers pairing in star roles. Astaire plays a dancer who Rogers mistakes as being the man listed as the correspondent (Rhodes) in her divorce suit. But Astaire pursues her, woos her and wins her. Nominated for Best Picture in, spite of a non-existant plot and because of the music and dancing. Music includes "The Continental," "Night and Day" and "A Needle in a Haystack."

A: Fred Astaire, Ginger Rogers, Edward Everett Horton, Erik Rhodes, Eric Blore, Betty Grable

© TURNER HOME ENTERTAINMENT 6092

GENTLEMEN PREFER BLONDES

D: Howard Hawks 92 m

NR | MUS COM | 1953 | COLOR | Sex | Nud | Viol | Lang | AdSit

9 Funny, flashy musical about two girls who just want to have fun. Marilyn Monroe and Jane Russell are two show girls from Little Rock who are on their way to Paris so Monroe can marry a millionaire's son. On board ship, Monroe has an innocent flirtation with a married elderly jeweler and Russell falls for a guy who turns out to be a private detective sent to collect dirt on Monroe. Songs include "Diamonds Are a Girl's Best Friend." Monroe and Russell are great together.

A: Jane Russell, Marilyn Monroe, Charles Coburn, Elliott Reid, Tom Noonan, George Winslow

© FOXVIDEO 1019

GIRL CRAZY

D: Norman Taurog 101 m

NR | MUS COM | 1943 | B&W | Sex | Nud | Viol | Lang | AdSit

7 A fun and quality pairing (the eighth time) of Mickey and Judy. Mickey plays a rich young Eastern kid whose father sends him to an all-boy's school in the desert to forget about girls. However, Mickey meets and falls for the only girl around, the dean's granddaughter (Judy), but she's more interested in helping her grandfather whose school is near bankruptcy. So what do they do - they promote a big rodeo to raise money to keep the school in business. Great Gershwin music: "Fascinating Rythym," "Embraceable You" and "I Got Rhythm."

A: Mickey Rooney, Judy Garland, Gil Stratton, Robert E. Strickland, June Allyson, Nancy Walker

Distributed By MGM/UA Home Video M300567

GLENN MILLER STORY, THE

D: Anthony Mann 113 m

G | MUS DMA | 1953 | COLOR | Sex | Nud | Viol | Lang | AdSit

7 Glenn Miller was as a major phenomenon on the American music scene of the late '30s. His style of music marked a major departure from the music of what came before and paved the way for the major changes which were yet to come. The music of the Big Band Era is the highlight of this sentimental life's story of one of the era's greatest bandleaders who was killed in a plane crash while entertaining troops in WWII. All of his major hits are played. Jimmy Stewart puts in a respectable effort in the title role. Guest appearances by Louis Armstrong and Gene Krupa.

A: James Stewart, June Allyson, Charles Drake, Harry Morgan, Frances Langford, Gene Krupa

© MCA/UNIVERSAL HOME VIDEO, INC. 45004

GOOD NEWS

D: Charles Walters 93 m

NR | MUS | 1947 | COLOR

7 Simple and silly, but for musical fans, highly entertaining. It is a musical set in 1920s on a college campus, and is about campus life. Peter Lawford is a football star who is being pursued by two coeds, June Allyson and Patricia Marshall. One loves him for the wrong reasons, one for the right. Score includes "Varsity Drag," "French Lesson," "The Best Things in Life are Free" and the Oscar-nominated "Pass the Peace Pipe."

Sex Nud Viol Lang AdSit

A: June Allyson, Peter Lawford, Patricia Marshall, Joan McCracken, Ray McDonald, Mel Torme

Distributed By MGM/UA Home Video M300877

GREAT CARUSO, THE

D: Richard Thorpe 108 m

G | MUS | 1951 | COLOR

7 This is a Hollywood-embellished biography of one of the greatest legends of opera. It begins when he was a young man, as a singing waiter, and progresses through his 18 years at the Metropolitan Opera. There is enough interesting drama to keep the uninitiated interested, but the film will really provide the greatest enjoyment for fans of opera. Lanza's big voice renders arias from La Boheme, I Pagliacci and Rioletto. 27 numbers in all.

Sex Nud Viol Lang AdSit

A: Mario Lanza, Ann Blyth

Distributed By MGM/UA Home Video M600067

GREAT ZIEGFELD, THE

D: Robert Z. Leonard 177 m

NR | MUS DMA | 1936 | B&W

8 Flamboyant tribute to a flamboyant man. It captured 3 Oscars, including Best Picture Oscar for 1936. It is filled with lavish production numbers and peppered with many of the talented stars who actually appeared in the Ziegfeld Follies (Fanny Brice and Ray Bolger, among others). It is a detailed account of the up-and-down career of one of the most famous men in show business, including his love life. Many memorable songs: "A Pretty Girl is Like a Melody," "Look for the Silver Lining" and "Rhapsody in Blue."

Sex Nud Viol Lang AdSit

A: William Powell, Myrna Loy, Luise Rainer, Frank Morgan, Fanny Brice, Virginia Bruce

Distributed By MGM/UA Home Video M300538

GUYS AND DOLLS

D: Joseph L. Mankiewicz 150 m

MUS COM ROM | 1955 | COLOR

9 Entertaining and exuberant musical that was transferred to the big screen from Broadway, and made it largely intact. Frank Sinatra and Marlon Brando play likable flamboyant big city gamblers of the 1930s. Sinatra tries to finance a big floating crap game by winning a bet with Brando that Brando can't win the affections of a pretty Salvation Army soldier (Jean Simmons). While Brando trys to win his bet, Sinatra expends a great deal of effort ducking marriage to his own girlfriend. Lots of energy, songs and fun. Songs include: "If I Were A Bell," "Sit Down, You're Rockin' the Boat" and "Luck Be a Lady Tonight."

Sex Nud Viol Lang AdSit

A: Marlon Brando, Frank Sinatra, Jean Simmons, Vivian Blaine, Stubby Kaye, Veda Ann Borg

© CBS/FOX VIDEO 7039

HALLELUJAH

D: King Vidor 90 m

NR | MUS DMA | 1929 | B&W

8 A revolutionary and ground-breaking film. This was the first all-black talking film and it was one of the very first true musicals. Filmed on location in Tennessee, it is the story of an innocent young black man who accidentally kills his brother. He turns to religion for solace and becomes a preacher but remains vulnerable to the sins of the flesh. Dated in many ways and too melodramatic, but it is still very moving and a truly insightful look into the ways of the old South. Very daring for its time. Contains many spiritual and traditional songs plus two from Irving Berlin. Director was Oscar-nominated.

Sex Nud Viol Lang AdSit

A: Daniel L. Haynes, Nina Mae McKinney, William Fountaine, Everett McGarity, Victoria Spivey

Distributed By MGM/UA Home Video M202839

HANS CHRISTIAN ANDERSEN

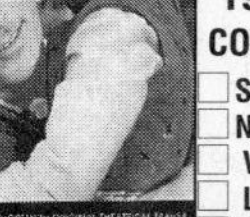

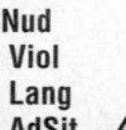

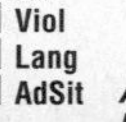

D: Charles Vidor 112 m

NR | MUS CLD | 1952 | COLOR

9 Wonderful, tune-filled musical biography of the famous storyteller, Hans Christian Andersen. Danny Kaye is just marvelous in the title role as a shoemaker who is forced to leave his hometown because the school children all skip school just to come an hear him tell his stories. After going to Copenhagen, he is hired to make shoes for a beautiful ballerina. He falls desperately, deeply in love with her and then writes "The Littlest Mermaid." Listen also for him telling the stories of "Thumbelina," "Inchworm" and "Ugly Duckling."

Sex Nud Viol Lang AdSit

A: Danny Kaye, Farley Granger, Renee Jeanmaire, John Brown, Roland Petit

© HBO VIDEO 90650

HARVEY GIRLS, THE

D: George Sidney 102 m

NR | MUS COM | 1946 | COLOR

7 An energetic musical that is based on the real life 19th-century restaurants that were built to accompany the railroad's expansion into the West. The restaurants became extremely popular because they could be relied upon for good food, pretty waitresses and a civil dining experience in a crude and primitive environment. Beverly Garland was at the height of her form when she was cast to play an innocent mail-order bride traveling west. A great cast includes a young Angela Lansbury and Cyd Charisse. And, the songs include the Oscar-winning "On the Atchison, Topeka and the Santa Fe."

Sex Nud Viol Lang AdSit

A: Judy Garland, John Hodiak, Ray Bolger, Angela Lansbury, Preston Foster, Cyd Charisse

Distributed By MGM/UA Home Video M301003

HERE COMES THE GROOM

D: Frank Capra 114 m

NR | MUS COM ROM | 1951 | B&W

6 Pleasant musical comedy about a happy-go-lucky reporter who contrives to keep his former fiancee from marrying a millionaire real estate developer. He needs her to remarry him because he only has five days left to find a wife or he will lose the two war orphans he wants to adopt. Typical Frank Capra formula for good fun and light spirits. Good songs including: "In the Cool, Cool, Cool of the Evening."

Sex Nud Viol Lang AdSit

A: Bing Crosby, Jane Wyman, Franchot Tone, Alexis Smith

© PARAMOUNT HOME VIDEO 5101

HOLIDAY INN

D: Mark Sandrich 101 m

MUS | 1942 | B&W

7 This was a fluffy star vehicle for the monumental talents of Bing Crosby and Fred Astaire and the music of Irving Berlin. They are set in a modest plot where Fred and Bing join forces to open an Inn that is to be open only for the holiday season, but instead they fight over a girl. The best part of the films is that you will be presented with a whole bunch of holiday songs - most notably "Easter Parade" and popular music's all-time biggest seller "White Christmas."

Sex Nud Viol Lang AdSit

A: Bing Crosby, Fred Astaire, Marjorie Reynolds, Walter Abel, Louise Beavers

© MCA/UNIVERSAL HOME VIDEO, INC. 55039

IN THE GOOD OLD SUMMERTIME

D: Robert Z. Leonard 104 m

NR | MUS COM ROM | 1949 | COLOR

8 Endearing remake of the successful 1940 non-musical THE SHOP AROUND THE CORNER. This time the setting is turn-of-the-century Chicago. Judy Garland and Van Johnson are co-workers in a music store where they fight or generally ignore each other. However, unknown to either, they are also pen pals whose relationship on paper is blossoming into love. Features a lot of classic old time songs including: "Wait Rill the Sun Shines Nellie," "I Don't Care" and the title tune.

Sex Nud Viol Lang AdSit

A: Judy Garland, Van Johnson, S.Z. Sakall, Spring Byington, Clinton Sundberg, Buster Keaton

Distributed By MGM/UA Home Video M300860

JAZZ SINGER, THE

D: Alan Crosland 89 m

NR | MUS DMA | 1927 | B&W

6 Ground-breaking film that is recognized as being the first movie to incorporate sound with moving pictures. There is really only a few spoken lines, but it does contain Jolson singing "Mammy," "Toot, Toot Tootsie Goodbye" and some others. The story is that of a son of an orthodox Jewish cantor who wants his son to follow in his footsteps, but Jolson just wants to sing jazz. It is most notable now as a curiosity. It was remade in 1980 with Neil Diamond, but that was both a critical and commercial failure.

Sex Nud Viol Lang AdSit

A: Al Jolson, May McAvoy, Warner Oland, Eugene Besserer, Bobby Gordon, William Demarest

Distributed By MGM/UA Home Video M302312

JOLSON STORY, THE

D: Alfred E. Green 129 m

NR | MUS DMA | 1946 | COLOR

7 Entertaining but syrupy biography of vaudeville's greatest performer, Al Jolson. Larry Parks does a good job playing the Jolson character and his rise to fame, but the main focus of the film is Jolson's music - and that is Jolson himself singing those songs. You will hear "April Showers," "Avalon," "You Made Me Love You," "Swanny," "By the Light of the Silvery Moon" and "My Mammy."

Sex Nud Viol Lang AdSit

A: Larry Parks, Evelyn Keyes, William Demarest, Bill Goodwin, Ludwig Donath, Tamara Shayne

© COLUMBIA TRISTAR HOME VIDEO 60686

JOY OF LIVING

D: Tay Garnett 91 m

NR | MUS COM | 1938 | B&W | Sex | Nud | Viol | Lang | AdSit

6 Zany screwball musical comedy in which a wealthy, carefree, globe-trotting playboy (Fairbanks) sets his sights on a very practical and business-minded Broadway singer (Dunne). He's determined to show her how to enjoy life and also to save her from her leach-like family (including Lucile Ball), which likes its mealticket too much. However, instead of being grateful for his help, she has him arrested for being a masher - but still he doesn't give up. Good Jerome Kern and Dorothy Fields score including: "A Heavenly Party," "Just Let Me Look at You" and "What's Good About Goodnight?"

A: Irene Dunne, Douglas Fairbanks, Jr., Alice Brady, Guy Kibbee, Jean Dixon, Eric Blore

© TURNER HOME ENTERTAINMENT 6037

KISMET

D: Vincente Minnelli 114 m

NR | MUS ROM | 1955 | COLOR | Sex | Nud | Viol | Lang | AdSit

6 Lavish production of a very successful Broadway presentation of a musical Arabian Nights tale. This interesting and valiant effort is entertaining but fails to ignite audiences as did the stage version. In ancient Bagdad, a charming con man (Keel), with a beautiful daughter (Blythe), is forced by an evil Wazir to trick the Caliph (Damone) into marrying a princess. Instead he helps his own daughter to win the Caliph's heart. Songs include: "Stranger in Paradise," "Baubles, Bangles and Beads" and more. Musical fans only.

A: Howard Keel, Ann Blyth, Dolores Gray, Vic Damone, Monty Woolley, Sebastian Cabot

Distributed By MGM/UA Home Video M700130

KISS ME KATE

D: George Sidney 110 m

NR | MUS COM | 1953 | COLOR | Sex | Nud | Viol | Lang | AdSit

7 This is Cole Porter's Broadway musical version of Shakespeare's TAMING OF THE SHREW. It is a sophisticated comedy of errors about two once-married stage actors who are trying to put on a play financed by gangsters Keenan Wynn and James Whitmore. Their off-stage life keeps influencing their on-stage lives - they can't get along in either. Oscar-nominated score: "So in Love," "From This Moment On," "Wunderbar" and "Always True to You in My Fashion." A real treat for musical fans.

A: Kathryn Grayson, Howard Keel, Ann Miller, Bobby Van, Keenan Wynn, Bob Fosse

Distributed By MGM/UA Home Video M300307

MEET ME IN ST. LOUIS

D: Vincente Minnelli 119 m

NR | MUS COM ROM | 1944 | COLOR | Sex | Nud | Viol | Lang | AdSit

10 Wonderful. Absolute perfection and a perennial favorite! Elegant staging and production. It's 1904 in St. Louis, just before the World's Fair. The Ames family is a very happy group until Dad announces that he is moving the family to New York and everyone is upset. Songs include "The Boy Next Door," "Have Yourself a Merry Little Christmas" and "The Trolley Song." O'Brien won a special Oscar for Best Child Actress. This sentimental slice of Americana, with outstanding performances, sets and cinematography, is truly a classic treat for the senses.

A: Judy Garland, Mary Astor, Tom Drake, Margaret O'Brien, Harry Davenport, Lucille Bremer

Distributed By MGM/UA Home Video M201827

MIKADO, THE

D: Victor Schertzinger 93 m

NR | MUS COM | 1939 | COLOR | Sex | Nud | Viol | Lang | AdSit

8 Gilbert and Sullivan's masterful and funny operetta, as performed by the D'Oyly Carte Opera Company and the London Symphony Orchestra, was wonderfully captured on film in 1939. This in reality is a farcical spoof of Victorian society, but it is portrayed in the play as instead being the romantic shenanigans inside the Japanese royal court. The terrific Gilbert & Sullivan music and lyrics are all in place. This is still probably the best version ever on film.

A: Kenny Baker, Martyn Green, ohn Barclay, Sydney Granville, Gregory Stroud

© HOME VISION MIK 030

MOON OVER MIAMI

D: Walter Lang 92 m

NR | MUS ROM | 1941 | COLOR | Sex | Nud | Viol | Lang | AdSit

7 Entertaining musical romance. A pair of Texan sisters (Grable and Landis) leave the Texas hamburger joint where they work to go gold digging in Miami, hoping to find rich husbands. After several romantic adventures, Grable lands a handsome and charming, but broke, man (Ameche). Landis ends up with a millionaire (Cummings). This musical remake of "THREE BLIND MICE" was also remade in 1946 as "THREE LITTLE GIRLS IN BLUE." Grable's performance is a whole lot of fun and was critical in making her a big star.

A: Betty Grable, Carole Landis, Charlotte Greenwood, Don Ameche, Robert Cummings, Jack Hailey

© FOXVIDEO 1725

MY SISTER EILEEN

D: Richard Quine 108 m

NR | MUS COM | 1955 | COLOR | Sex | Nud | Viol | Lang | AdSit

9 Two small-town girls move from Ohio to Manhattan. Ruth is an aspiring writer and Eileen wants to be an actor. They have come to set the world on its end, but first they have to find an apartment they can afford. So, they move into the cheap, musty basement of the Popopolous Arms. When Ruth's corny romance stories are turned down by magazine editor Jack Lemmon, she decides to accept his suggestion to write about something she knows - her very popular and beautiful sister Eileen. But when he likes her new story and wants to meet Eileen, her jealousy takes hold and she weaves a webb of lies that lead to hilarious mayhem. Excellent singing and dancing, and lots of fun.

A: Janet Leigh, Betty Garrett, Jack Lemmon, Bob Fosse, Kurt Kaszner, Dick York

© COLUMBIA TRISTAR HOME VIDEO 51283

NAUGHTY MARIETTA

D: W.S. Van Dyke 106 m

G | MUS ROM | 1935 | B&W | Sex | Nud | Viol | Lang | AdSit

7 Famed first pairing of the very popular romantic and musical favorites Jeanette MacDonald and Nelson Eddy. As in many of their operatic pairings, the story line is almost inconsequential - it only serves as an excuse for these two to sing. However, it is based upon a 1910 Victor Herbert operetta in which she is a French princess who has run off to America to avoid marrying a man she doesn't love. There she falls in love with an Indian scout. Songs include: "The Italian Street Song," "Tramp, Tramp, Tramp" and "Ah, Sweet Mystery of Life."

A: Jeanette MacDonald, Nelson Eddy, Frank Morgan, Elsa Lanchester, Douglas Dembrille, Celia Parker

Distributed By MGM/UA Home Video M600371

NEPTUNE'S DAUGHTER

D: Edward Buzzell 94 m

NR | MUS COM | 1949 | COLOR | Sex | Nud | Viol | Lang | AdSit

6 Light-hearted entertainment from the '40s. Simple empty-headed vehicle designed to highlight audience favorites Esther Williams and comic Red Skelton. Esther plays a bathing suit designer on vacation in South America in love with Ricardo Montalban, and Red is a masseur mistaken for a polo player and being pursued by Esther's wacky sister. Esther, of course, appears in several of her trademark water ballets. Harmless bubbly fun. Contains the Oscar-winning song: "Baby It's Cold Outside."

A: Esther Williams, Red Skelton, Keenan Wynn, Ricardo Montalban, Mel Blanc

Distributed By MGM/UA Home Video M200853

OKLAHOMA!

D: Fred Zinnemann 145 m

G | MUS ROM WST | 1955 | COLOR | Sex | Nud | Viol | Lang | AdSit

10 Wonderful Rogers and Hammerstein musical gets the full treatment. An all-star cast, colorful costumes and sets, and wondrous, timeless music combine to make this a landmark film. It is the story of a beautiful country girl who is courted by both a cowboy and vile hired hand. Extremely entertaining musical. Gordon MacRae and Shirley Jones make screen magic, just as they did in CAROUSEL. Songs include: "Oh, What a Beautiful Morning" and "Surrey With the Fringe on Top," among many more. Two Oscars.

A: Gordon MacRae, Shirley Jones, Rod Steiger, Charlotte Greenwood, Gloria Grahame, Eddie Albert

© FOXVIDEO 7020

ON THE TOWN

D: Stanley Donen, Gene Kelly 98 m

NR | MUS ROM | 1949 | COLOR | Sex | Nud | Viol | Lang | AdSit

9 Great MGM musical - shot on location in New York. The story concerns three sailors on 24-hour shore leave looking for love in the big city and finding three girls. Kelly chases down a poster girl, Sinatra a cabbie and Munsin pursues Miller. The first major number is "New York, New York," and it is also the last. In between are 10 other great song and dance sequences. The bright and bouncy score won Oscars. Fun and exuberant.

A: Gene Kelly, Frank Sinatra, Vera-Ellen, Ann Miller, Betty Garrett, Jules Munshin

Distributed By MGM/UA Home Video M202740

PERILS OF PAULINE, THE

D: George Marshall 96 m

NR | MUS COM | 1947 | COLOR | Sex | Nud | Viol | Lang | AdSit

6 Lively musical, very loosely based upon the famous silent movie heroine Pearl White. The highly-charged and effervescent Betty Hutton plays Pearl White, a seamstress who graduates to the Broadway stage and, after a rift with her boyfriend, departs for Hollywood. There she wins the lead in the famous ongoing silent serial "The Perils of Pauline." Colorful musical with some good songs from Frank Loesser: "I Wish I Didn't Love You So" and "Poppa Don't Preach to Me."

A: Betty Hutton, John Lund, Constance Collier, William Demarest, Frank Faylen, Billy DeWolfe

© BARR ENTERTAINMENT VIDEO 11031

PIRATE, THE

D: Vincente Minnelli — 102 m

NR | MUS | 1948 | COLOR

6 Lavish MGM musical that doesn't quite connect as a story line, but does pretty good for singing and dancing. Gene Kelly is a circus clown who pretends to be a pirate on this nineteenth-century Caribbean island so that he can win Judy Garland away from her fiance in an impending arranged marriage to the town's middle-aged mayor. Good Cole Porter score includes "Be a Clown." Kelly dances up a storm as usual, but with particular athletic flair this time.

Sex / Nud / Viol / Lang / AdSit

A: Judy Garland, Gene Kelly

Distributed By MGM/UA Home Video M700101

POOR LITTLE RICH GIRL

D: Irving Cummings — 72 m

NR | MUS CLD | 1936 | B&W

8 One of Shirley Temple's best. She plays the motherless daughter of a rich man who has sent her off to boarding school. But she ducks out of the school and gets lost. She teams up with a husband and wife vaudeville act by telling them that she is an orphan. Together, all three sing and dance their way to success and, in the end, Shirley is reunited with her father and his new wife. Look for her famous number in a military uniform and rifle "Military Man," along with "Oh My Goodness," "You've Got to Eat Your Spinach, Baby" and "When I'm With You."

Sex / Nud / Viol / Lang / AdSit

A: Shirley Temple, Alice Faye, Jack Haley, Gloria Stuart, Michael Whalen, Claude Gillingwater

© FOXVIDEO 1069

REBECCA OF SUNNYBROOK FARM

D: Allan Dwan — 80 m

NR | MUS CLD | 1938 | B&W

6 Engaging family musical. A little girl (Temple) desperately wants to become a radio star and when a talent scout living next door to her aunt's farmhouse, where she is staying, realizes that she has the right stuff, he gets her career going. The girl rockets to stardom, but her wicked stepfather tries to make money on the deal, too. Shirley sings "On the Good Ship Lollipop" and "Animal Crackers." Even better, she gets to pal about with Jack Haley and Bill "Bojangles" Robinson. The title of this film has nothing to do with the famous book.

Sex / Nud / Viol / Lang / AdSit

A: Shirley Temple, Jack Haley, Randolph Scott, Bill Robinson, Gloria Stuart, Phyllis Brooks

© FOXVIDEO 1065

ROAD TO BALI

D: Hal Walker — 91 m

NR | MUS COM | 1952 | COLOR

6 Hope and Crosby team up in another musically adventurous "road" saga. This time the pair of vaudeville performers is looking for a job and their search leads them to a lush South Seas island where they find the beautiful Lamour. There, the pair attempts to keep her safe from man-eating natives and all sorts of other jungle perils. Some of the best scenes are those that feature famous Hollywood stars in brief cameo appearances, such as Jane Russell and Humphrey Bogart. For fans of the series, this is one of the best.

Sex / Nud / Viol / Lang / ◢ AdSit

A: Bob Hope, Bing Crosby, Dorothy Lamour, Murvyn Vye, Ralph Moody

© UNICORN VIDEO, INC. 301

ROAD TO RIO

D: Norman McLeod — 100 m

NR | MUS COM | 1947 | B&W

7 Hope and Crosby are up to their usual monkey business in this fifth "road" series adventure. The two accidentally set fire to a carnival and flee town on an cruise ship headed for Rio. While on board, they come across Lamour, a beautiful girl who is about to enter into an pre-arranged marriage against her will. The comic pair attempts to thwart the wedding and save her from her evil aunt.

Sex / Nud / Viol / Lang / AdSit

A: Bob Hope, Bing Crosby, Dorothy Lamour, Gale Sondergaard, Frank Faylen

© COLUMBIA TRISTAR HOME VIDEO 60870

ROAD TO UTOPIA

D: Hal Walker — 90 m

NR | MUS COM | 1946 | B&W

8 Slap-happy adventure farce. The famous pair of the "road" series, Hope and Crosby, is headed to Alaska for the gold rush, hoping to make it big. They're swabbing the decks to get there because they've lost all of their money, but they do have a stolen deed to a gold mine for when they get there! Unfortunately, when they arrive, they also run into a beautiful saloon girl who just happens to be the rightful owner of the mine. Full of comic asides, practical jokes and one-liners, fans have rated this the very best of the series. Quite funny.

Sex / Nud / Viol / Lang / AdSit

A: Bob Hope, Bing Crosby, Dorothy Lamour, Hillary Brooke, Douglas Dumbrille, Jack LaRue

© MCA/UNIVERSAL HOME VIDEO, INC. 81390

ROMANCE ON THE HIGH SEAS

D: Michael Curtiz — 99 m

NR | MUS ROM | 1948 | COLOR

7 A sparkling little musical that was also Doris Day's first film! A suspicious wife (Paige) suspects that her husband (Defore) is cheating on her, so she hires Doris to take her place on a cruise. That way, she can stay home and watch him. But, her plan goes awry when he likewise hires Carson to go on the cruise to check up on her. That's right, Carson is following Doris, who also doesn't know she is being watched. A whole boatload of fun in this charming musical. Doris Day's spot was reserved for Judy Garland, but she was unavailable at the time. Contains the Oscar-winning song "It's Magic."

Sex / Nud / Viol / Lang / ◢ AdSit

A: Jack Carson, Janis Paige, Don Defore, Doris Day, Oscar Levant, S.Z. Sakall

Distributed By MGM/UA Home Video M302313

ROMAN SCANDALS

D: Frank Tuttle — 92 m

MUS COM | 1933 | B&W

6 A whimsical daydream, full of gags. Famed entertainer Eddie Cantor is a young delivery boy prone to fanciful thoughts. He dreams himself right into ancient Rome, where he becomes a taste-tester for an evil ruler (Arnold) and tries to thwart the queen's plot to poison her husband. His comic adventures take him into a Roman bath house and a perilous chariot race. One of the best scenes is a musical number where a bunch of women dance around wearing only wigs (Lucille Ball is one of them). Comedy set around some serene and serious surroundings.

Sex / ◢ Nud / Viol / Lang / ◢ AdSit

A: Eddie Cantor, Ruth Etting, Gloria Stuart, David Manners, Verree Teasdale, Edward Arnold

© HBO VIDEO 90749

ROSE-MARIE

D: W.S. Van Dyke — 112 m

G | MUS ROM | 1936 | B&W

6 Engaging musical from the old school! High in the Canadian Rockies, opera singer (Jeanette MacDonald) goes deep into the rugged mountains in search of her brother (Jimmy Stewart, in one of his earliest roles) who has been wounded in a prison escape. There, in the wilderness, she runs into Sgt. Bruce, a Canadian Mountie (Nelson Eddy), who is looking for her brother, too. There, along the rugged trail, the pair fall in love and sing to each other. An enjoyable escapade if you're an Eddy/MacDonald fan. Songs include "Indian Love Call" and "The Song of the Mounties."

Sex / Nud / Viol / Lang / ◢ AdSit

A: Nelson Eddy, Jeanette MacDonald, James Stewart, Reginald Owen, Allan Jones, Alan Mowbray

Distributed By MGM/UA Home Video M300374

SEVEN BRIDES FOR SEVEN BROTHERS

D: Stanley Donen — 102 m

G | MUS WST COM | 1954 | COLOR

10 Rollicking and witty Western musical, but with a great story too! Set in Oregon in 1850, seven young brothers are living a lonely life. When brother Keel brings home his new wife (Powell), she is overpowered by so many lonely brothers. So, she teaches them some class and social graces. But, just as soon as they begin to show some promise, Keel convinces the younger men to kidnap six pretty women and to make them their wives. Incensed, Powell kicks Keel out. An absolutely delightful musical, with a barn-raising scene that steals the show. Excellent dancing and musical score. Knockout!

Sex / Nud / Viol / Lang / AdSit

A: Howard Keel, Jane Powell, Jeff Richards, Russ Tamblyn, Tommy Rall, Virginia Gibson

Distributed By MGM/UA Home Video M700091

SHALL WE DANCE

D: Mark Sandrich — 109 m

NR | MUS COM | 1937 | B&W

8 Top musical with a terrific score. That duo with the magic feet are at it again in this enjoyable musical with a comedic edge. Astaire and Rogers are a ballet star and a singer who are after jobs that are sure to further their careers, but they are going to have to cooperate. In order to get them, they must pretend to get married - but they also promise each other to get a rapid divorce as soon as they can. Their farce provides the basis for some fun romantic antics and superb songs, including "Let's Call the Whole Thing Off." Little do they know that true love is right around the corner. A most memorable Gershwin score.

Sex / Nud / Viol / Lang / AdSit

A: Fred Astaire, Ginger Rogers, Eric Blore, Edward Everett Horton

© TURNER HOME ENTERTAINMENT 2037

SHOW BOAT

D: James Whale — 115 m

NR | MUS | 1936 | B&W

8 This is the best film version of a ground-breaking early musical. It has wonderful music and it also has a fascinating history because it had a very daring theme for its time. The original Broadway musical was adapted from a book by Edna Ferber. Its story revolves around the people (both black and white) on a Mississippi river showboat in the very early 1900s and it even included an interracial romance. The original Broadway version was forbidden to have any actual black actors or singers appearing in it. Rather, the black parts had to be white people in blackface. Listen for the wonderful and now-classic songs: "Old Man River," "Bill," "Can't Help Lovin' Dat Man" and much more.

Sex / Nud / Viol / Lang / ◢ AdSit

A: Irene Dunne, Allan Jones, Helen Morgan, Paul Robeson, Charles Winninger, Hattie McDaniel

Distributed By MGM/UA Home Video M301757

SINGIN' IN THE RAIN

D: Gene Kelly — 103 m

G | MUS ROM | 1952 | COLOR

10 Perhaps the greatest of the great musicals. Probably considered so because it not only contains some truly great music - "You Were Meant for Me," "Make `Em Laugh," "All I Do is Dream of You" and, of course, "Singin' in the Rain" - but also because it had a literate script and plot. It is set in Hollywood and is a gentle poke at the silent film era. The transition is being made to talkies and not all the stars are going to make it. It is also a romance where Kelly tries to win the heart of pretty Debbie Reynolds. One of a kind.

Sex / Nud / Viol / Lang / AdSit

A: Gene Kelly, Debbie Reynolds, Donald O'Connor, Cyd Charisse, Rita Moreno, Jean Hagen

Distributed By MGM/UA Home Video M600185

SKY'S THE LIMIT, THE

D: Edward H. Griffith — 89 m

NR | MUS | 1943 | B&W

6 Minor but notable wartime musical. An out-of-uniform Flying Tiger ace (Astaire) meets and falls in love with a lovely photographer (Leslie), but she won't give him the time of day. Pretty Leslie is a lady who is extremely dedicated to helping win the war but, because Astaire is out of uniform and is determined to avoid hero-worship, she thinks he is a slackard. Of course it has Astaire's dancing but also songs "One For My Baby" and "My Shining Hour".

Sex / Nud / Viol / Lang / ◢ AdSit

A: Fred Astaire, Joan Leslie, Robert Ryan, Robert Benchley, Elizabeth Patterson, Majorie Gateson

© TURNER HOME ENTERTAINMENT 2046

SONG IS BORN, A

D: Howard Hawks — 113 m

NR | MUS COM | 1948 | COLOR

7 In this entertaining remake of BALL OF FIRE, a jazz-loving professor (Kaye) of high-brow music takes his friends on a musical ride, teaching them the history of jazz and introducing them to notable musicians along the way. Jazz greats include: Louis Armstrong, Tommy Dorsey, Charlie Barnet, Mel Powell, Lionel Hampton and Buck and Bubbles. However, in the meantime, he falls in love with a saloon singer (Mayo) who is hiding out from the police and she turns Kaye into a man of strength and character. Great jazz fun.

Sex / Nud / Viol / Lang / AdSit

A: Danny Kaye, Virginia Mayo, Hugh Herbert, Steve Cochran, Felix Bressart, Benny Goodman

© HBO VIDEO 90745

SPRINGTIME IN THE ROCKIES

D: Irving Cummings — 91 m

NR | MUS ROM | 1942 | COLOR

7 Entertaining Hollywood musical. Two Broadway entertainers (Grable and Payne) just can't seem to get along. They bicker and fight, make up and break up, on and off stage in this fun musical. Forever trying to "get even" with each other, Grable runs off with a handsome dancer and gets engaged just to spite Payne. Payne retaliates by hiring a steamy secretary and feigns love. Light on plot, but the lush scenery and excellent singing and dancing make up for it.

Sex / Nud / Viol / Lang / ◢ AdSit

A: Betty Grable, John Payne, Carmen Miranda, Cesar Romero, Charlotte Greenwood, Edward Everett Horton

© FOXVIDEO 1723

STATE FAIR

D: Walter Lang — 100 m

NR | MUS | 1945 | COLOR

7 Charming, tuneful and entertaining Americana. A colorful canvas of song and charm! A midwestern family prepares for the Iowa State Fair, each anticipating his/her own set of rewards. Dad (Winninger) is hoping to take home a prize in the hog contest, while Mom (Bainter) hopes her mincemeat pie is worth a ribbon. The children (Haymes and Crain) hope for romance, and they find it. The ingredients in this straightforward charmer are perfectly measured: wit, romance, song and innocence. A wonderful musical that would have certainly won a ribbon at the Iowa fair.

Sex / Nud / Viol / Lang / AdSit

A: Jeanne Crain, Dana Andrews, Dick Haymes, Vivian Blaine, Charles Winninger, Fay Bainter

© FOXVIDEO 1348

STORMY WEATHER

D: Andrew L. Stone — 78 m

NR | MUS | 1943 | B&W

6 An enjoyable musical that is told in flashback format and boasts a stellar all-black cast. Robinson and Horne are a husband and wife team who work in show business, are struggling to put bread on the table and to keep their marriage together. The plot, however, proves to be just an excuse for and a loose framework with which to present some of the greatest black talent of that day. It has an outstanding musical score that features Fats Waller performing "Ain't Misbehavin'," but Horne steals the show when she performs the title song "Stormy Weather."

Sex / Nud / Viol / Lang / ◢ AdSit

A: Lena Horne, Bill Robinson, Cab Calloway, Dooley Wilson, Fats Waller, Katherine Dunham

© FOXVIDEO 1168

SUMMER STOCK

D: Charles Walters — 121 m

NR | MUS | 1950 | COLOR

8 Fancy footwork and zippy songs create a very engaging musical. DeHaven is a carefree sister who invites a dance troup to practice on her farm, without telling her older sister (Garland) who's struggling to keep it afloat. Garland doesn't like the idea when they all show up, but she strikes a deal with the dancers. They can stay in her farmhouse and practice getting ready for a play in exchange for help with the chores. It is not long before the show biz bug bites Garland and she has a change of heart. Light-on-his-feet Kelly manages to sweep Garland off of hers. A light-hearted, enjoyable musical.

Sex / Nud / Viol / Lang / ◢ AdSit

A: Judy Garland, Gene Kelly, Phil Silvers, Marjorie Main, Eddie Bracken, Gloria De Haven

Distributed By MGM/UA Home Video M300851

SWING TIME

D: George Stevens — 103 m

NR | MUS COM | 1935 | B&W

8 A real charmer! Dazzling dancing and acting makes this one of the best Astaire/Rogers films. Astaire is a young groom-to-be who goes to the Big Apple hoping to dance his way to earning the $25,000 he needs to wed his long-time girlfriend. But while he is there, he falls in love with a beautiful dance instructor (Rogers). Soon Astaire is hoping that he won't make enough money, and won't have to go home to his fiancee. A very appealing, highly likable musical with both characters at their comic and dancing best.

Sex / Nud / Viol / Lang / ◢ AdSit

A: Fred Astaire, Ginger Rogers, Victor Moore, Helen Broderick, Betty Furness, Eric Blore

© TURNER HOME ENTERTAINMENT 2036

TAKE ME OUT TO THE BALL GAME

D: Busby Berkeley — 90 m

NR | MUS | 1949 | COLOR

6 Colorful but predictable musical set at the turn of the century. Sinatra and Kelly are part-time ball players on semi-pro baseball team and also part-time vaudeville singers. Both are pleasantly surprised when the team is purchased by a beautiful woman (Williams). Kelly is a star on the team but he is almost taken in by a crooked gambler who tempts him with a big break in the theater. However, he is only working him overtime to make the ball team lose. Williams saves him just in time. Some pretty good musical numbers, including the classic title tune. Don't be surprised if you find Esther in the water.

Sex / Nud / Viol / Lang / AdSit

A: Gene Kelly, Frank Sinatra, Esther Williams, Betty Garrett, Edward Arnold, Jules Munshin

Distributed By MGM/UA Home Video M300503

TALES OF HOFFMAN, THE

D: Michael Powell, Emeric Pressburger — 125 m

NR | MUS | 1951 | COLOR

8 Following the success of THE RED SHOES, the same people brought Jacques Offenbach's fantasy opera to the screen. A student falls in love with a prima ballerina who reminds him of his past loves. When she appears to reject him, he relates the stories of his past loves, which are then portrayed in dance and music, to a group of students. There are three loves and each reveals a different stage of his life. Offbeat and not of all tastes, but ardent opera fans will approve.

Sex / Nud / Viol / Lang / AdSit

A: Robert Rounseville, Moira Shearer, Robert Helpmann

© HOME VISION TAL 060

THERE'S NO BUSINESS LIKE SHOW BUSINESS

D: Walter Lang — 117 m

NR | MUS | 1954 | COLOR

7 Entertaining and enjoyable. It is a marvelous showcase for some outstanding talents, plus a solid Irving Berlin score, but it is a little over-produced and the story line about the lives and loves of a Vaudeville family act is pretty weak. Still, musical fans should definitely watch it to see and hear: "Alexander's Ragtime Band," "Heatwave," "Play a Simple Melody," "Remember" and Ethel Merman's calling card title tune "There's No Business Like Show Business."

Sex / Nud / Viol / Lang / AdSit

A: Ethel Merman, Donald O'Connor, Marilyn Monroe, Dan Dailey, Johnny Ray, Mitzi Gaynor

© FOXVIDEO 1086

THREE LITTLE WORDS

D: Richard Thorpe — 103 m

NR | MUS | 1950 | COLOR

8 Fred Astaire claimed that this was his favorite movie. It is the musical biography, mostly factual, of the songwriting team of Kalmar and Ruby. There is little plot, however. But, there is a great deal of singing and dancing and a whole lot of fun. Songs include: "I Wanna Be Loved By You," "Thinking of You" and "Who's Sorry Now?"

Sex / Nud / Viol / Lang / AdSit

A: Red Skelton, Fred Astaire, Debbie Reynolds, Vera-Ellen, Arlene Dahl, Keenan Wynn

Distributed By MGM/UA Home Video M301189

TOP HAT

D: Mark Sandrich — 99 m

NR | MUS ROM COM | 1935 | B&W

10 If you like musicals and dancing, this is the movie for you. But, it's also romantic, has good comedic moments and the story line is better developed than in most musicals. But still, it's the singing and dancing that makes it so special. Probably the best of the Fred Astaire and Ginger Rodgers parings, it is set in London. Fred falls for Ginger, his downstairs neighbor, but she thinks he's married. Nominated for Best Picture. Top tunes from Irving Berlin: "Cheek to Cheek," "Top Hat, White Tie and Tails" and many more.

Sex / Nud / Viol / Lang / AdSit

A: Fred Astaire, Ginger Rogers, Edward Everett Horton, Eric Blore, Helen Broderick, Erik Rhodes

© TURNER HOME ENTERTAINMENT 2070

WHITE CHRISTMAS

D: Michael Curtiz — 120 m

NR | MUS COM | 1954 | COLOR

7 Irving Berlin song fest. Two Army pals from the war (Crosby and Kaye) have been teamed up ever since and have become a top show business act. When they learn that their old commanding officer's Vermont ski resort is in trouble, they decide to stage a musical at his resort to give him a boost. Songs include "Blue Skies," "Snow," "Count Your Blessings Instead of Sheep" (Oscar nominated), "Sisters" and, of course, "White Christmas" - which was first introduced in HOLIDAY INN, from which this film borrows heavily. Mostly for fans of old-style musicals.

Sex / Nud / Viol / Lang / AdSit

A: Bing Crosby, Danny Kaye, Dean Jagger, Vera-Ellen, Rosemary Clooney

© PARAMOUNT HOME VIDEO 6104

YANKEE DOODLE DANDY

D: Michael Curtiz — 127 m

NR | MUS DMA | 1942 | B&W

9 Rousing biography and musical depicting the somewhat fictionalized life of the entertainment legend, George M. Cohan, and starring another entertainment legend (Cagney). Cagney is wonderful as George M., the early 20th-century playwrite, songwriter, actor and dancer who began on the stages of vaudeville, only to later dominate the Broadway stage for an entire generation. Seven Oscar nominations, including Best Picture. Winner of three, including Cagney for Best Actor. Great show tunes, too: "You're a Grand Old Flag," ""Over There" and, of course, "Yankee Doodle Dandy."

Sex / Nud / Viol / Lang / AdSit

A: James Cagney, Joan Leslie, Walter Huston, Irene Manning, Rosemary DeCamp, Richard Whorf

Distributed By MGM/UA Home Video M200792

YOU'LL NEVER GET RICH

D: Sidney Lanfield — 88 m

NR | MUS COM | 1941 | B&W

9 Astaire is a Broadway choreographer who gets drafted into the Army when he's right in the middle of a production. But the Army has no pity on him. Before he goes, he manages to mess up a budding relationship with beautiful Rita Hayworth when he tries to help his boss (Benchley) out of a jam with his wife. Desperate for Astaire to finish his work, Benchley concocts a scheme where Astaire will finish the job while in the Army and also put on a benefit for the troops. With this, Astaire also gets a chance to win Hayworth back. Excellent dancing and Cole Porter music.

Sex / Nud / Viol / Lang / AdSit

A: Fred Astaire, Rita Hayworth, John Hubbard, Robert Benchley, Osa Massen, Frieda Inescort

© COLUMBIA TRISTAR HOME VIDEO 60265

YOU WERE NEVER LOVELIER

D: William A. Seiter — 98 m

NR | MUS ROM | 1942 | B&W

9 Top-drawer escapist fare from the '40s. Rita Hayworth was never lovelier. She plays the daughter of an Argentinian hotel mogul (Menjou) who spurns love and romance. Concerned about her welfare, Menjou invents a mysterious suitor for her who sends her flowers and love letters. But, he is distressed to learn that she has confused a down-on-his-luck entertainer Fred Astaire with the fantasy man he created. They sing and dance and she is struck with Cupid's arrow. Delightful romantic fluff of a type not seen anymore.

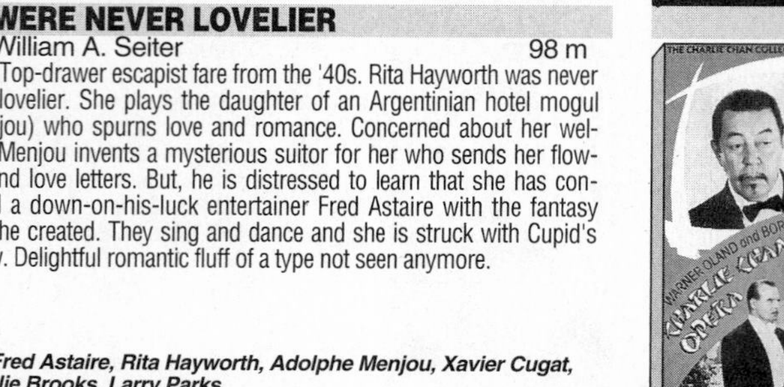

Sex / Nud / Viol / Lang / AdSit

A: Fred Astaire, Rita Hayworth, Adolphe Menjou, Xavier Cugat, Leslie Brooks, Larry Parks

© COLUMBIA TRISTAR HOME VIDEO 60401

Mystery

AFTER THE THIN MAN

D: W.S. Van Dyke — 113 m

NR | MYS COM | 1936 | B&W

8 Another 1930's powerhouse pairing of William Powell and Myrna Loy. Powell and Loy had terrific screen chemistry that gave them a dozen hits together. Here they are the popular wisecracking sophisticated detectives, Nick and Nora Charles. When one of Nora's blue-blooded cousins is accused of killing her husband, Nick must help prove her innocence. But before long there are two more murders and they are in trouble. Clever and snappy dialogue make solving the case of the missing husband great fun. See also THE THIN MAN and ANOTHER THIN MAN.

Sex / Nud / Viol / Lang / AdSit

A: William Powell, Myrna Loy, James Stewart, Elissa Landi, Joseph Calleia, Sam Levine

Distributed By MGM/UA Home Video M300820

AND THEN THERE WERE NONE

D: Rene Clair — 97 m

NR | MYS SUS COM | 1945 | B&W

9 A true classic and perhaps the best-ever adaptation of one of Agatha Christie's mysteries. It is a great tale filled with mystery, suspense and humor that will keep you entranced until the very last scene. The premise is that ten guests, who don't know each other or their host, are invited to a lonely and isolated English island. The only common thread is that each has a hidden crime in his past. One by one the guests are murdered, with never a clue as to why or who the murderer is. It uses equal parts of humor and suspense, plus a deftly created atmosphere, to weave a vastly entertaining yarn. It has been remade twice.

Sex / Nud / Viol / Lang / AdSit

A: Barry Fitzgerald, Walter Huston, Richard Burton, Roland Young, Judith Anderson, Louis Hayward

© VIDEO COMMUNICATIONS, INC. 4501

ANOTHER THIN MAN

D: W.S. Van Dyke II — 103 m

NR | MYS COM | 1939 | B&W

8 Sophistication and wit. Nick and Nora Charles are the witty and urbane private detective couple first seen in THE THIN MAN. As in the other Thin Man movies, the plot is secondary to the clever interaction between the two leads. Here the detectives contend with a man who dreams about catastrophies before they happen. Always an enjoyable experience. See AFTER THE THIN MAN, SHADOW OF THE THIN MAN and the others. Check the Sequels index.

Sex / Nud / Viol / Lang / AdSit

A: William Powell, Myrna Loy, Virginia Grey, Otto Kruger, C. Aubrey Smith, Ruth Hussey

Distributed By MGM/UA Home Video M300868

BIG SLEEP, THE

D: Howard Hawks — 114 m

NR | MYS CRM SUS | 1946 | B&W

10 One of the most stylish and satisfying film noir mysteries of the '40s. Philip Marlowe's most bizarre case. Lauren Bacall is at her sexiest and Bogart is at his peak. Marlowe is drawn into a complex murder and blackmail case by being hired to protect a thumb-sucking nympho (Vickers) against a pornography and blackmail ring, and he falls for her sister (Bacall) in the process. The plot is exquisitely intricate, so don't blink - and DON'T MISS THIS MOVIE. The atmosphere and dialogue are impeccable. Find more of Bogie in the Actor's Index and other Philip Marlowe adventures in the Heros... Index.

Sex / Nud / Viol / Lang / AdSit

A: Humphrey Bogart, Lauren Bacall, John Ridgely, Martha Vickers, Dorothy Malone, Elisha Cook, Jr.

Distributed By MGM/UA Home Video M201378

CHARLIE CHAN AT THE OPERA

D: H. Bruce Humberstone — 68 m

NR | MYS CRM | 1936 | B&W

8 The famous and popular crime-solving character, Charlie Chan, the Oriental detective from the Honolulu police department, first came to the screen in 1926 but didn't become widely popular until 1931 when Warner Oland took the role. There were three primary Charlies until the series ended in the late '40s. This film is of the best of the mysteries - most are not available on video. Here Charlie seeks out a high society murderer who has escaped from an asylum, taken refuge in an opera house and now members of the company are slowly being killed off.

Sex / Nud / Viol / Lang / AdSit

A: Warner Oland, Boris Karloff, Keye Luke, Charlotte Henry, Thomas Beck, Gregory Gaye

© FOXVIDEO 1368

CHARLIE CHAN IN RIO

D: Harry Lachman — 62 m

NR | MYS CRM | 1941 | B&W

8 Sidney Toler was the second Charlie Chan after Warner Oland died in 1937 and played Charlie for nine years. Not many of the series, particularly the good ones, are available on video. However, this is the best by Sidney Toler. Here Charlie joins forces with the Rio police to solve a tricky case. Charlie is in Rio to arrest a murderess, but someone gets to her before he can.

Sex / Nud / Viol / Lang / AdSit

A: Sidney Toler, Mary Beth Hughes, Cobina Wright, Victor Jory, Harold Huber, Victor Sen Yung

© FOXVIDEO 1706

CRACK-UP

D: Irving Reis — 64 m

NR | MYS SUS | 1946 | B&W

8 Exciting and very unusual film noir mystery. Pat O'Brien is a New York art critic, historian and forgery expert. He gets a whack on the head and wakes up with partial amnesia - except that he thinks he remembers that some of the great paintings in a museum have been stolen and replaced with clever forgeries. However, people are telling him that he has just been in a train wreck. Is he crazy? He is having difficulty telling fact from fiction, reality from a lie. Is someone trying to drive him insane? Involved but engrossing mystery with some off-beat camera work.

Sex | Nud | Viol | Lang | AdSit

A: Pat O'Brien, Claire Trevor, Herbert Marshall, Wallace Ford, Ray Collins, Dean Harens

© TURNER HOME ENTERTAINMENT 6131

DARK PASSAGE

D: Delmer Daves — 107 m

NR | MYS CRM | 1947 | B&W

7 Humphrey Bogart has been wrongly convicted of his wife's murder and sent to San Quentin. He escapes and sets out to clear his name. Now free, he meets and falls for a beautiful artist (Bacall), who is convinced that he is innocent. She helps him change his identity through plastic surgery and he hides out in her apartment while he heals. Then he can go after the real killer. Pretty good melodrama, with great chemistry between Bogart and Bacall.

Sex | Nud | Viol | Lang | ◢ AdSit

A: Humphrey Bogart, Lauren Bacall, Bruce Bennett, Agnes Moorehead, Tom D'Andrea

Distributed By MGM/UA Home Video M201854

DEAD RECKONING

D: John Cromwell — 100 m

R | MYS SUS | 1947 | B&W

8 An underrated whodunit that still holds up extremely well today. Humphrey Bogart and his buddy are war heros returning home to be honored. But once in the States, his pal jumps their train and two days later is found dead. Bogart is determined to find out why his army buddy disappeared and how he died. The mystery deepens when Bogie finds out that his buddy had enlisted under a false name because he had been convicted of murder. Bogie's search leads him into gangland murders and beautiful nightclub singer (Lisabeth Scott). Good, tough drama. Well acted.

Sex | Nud | ◢ Viol | Lang | ◢ AdSit

A: Humphrey Bogart, Lizabeth Scott, Morris Carnovsky, William Prince, Wallace Ford, Charles Cane

© COLUMBIA TRISTAR HOME VIDEO 60641

DETECTIVE, THE

D: Robert Hamer — 91 m

NR | MYS COM | 1954 | B&W

7 Intelligent, light-hearted British mystery in which Alec Guinness plays Father Brown, an eccentric priest who fancies himself to be a master sleuth (even though he is quite an amateur). On a trip to Rome with a very valuable cross, he has it stolen from him and is out-witted by an international jewel thief (Finch). Father Brown seeks the return of the stolen goods by setting a trap and baits it with a gold chess set. He loses that, too, but tracks the thieves to a Castle in Rome and confronts them there. Clever, droll entertainment from Great Britain. Guinness is a delight.

Sex | Nud | Viol | Lang | ◢ AdSit

A: Alec Guinness, Peter Finch, Cecil Parker, Joan Greenwood, Bernard Lee

© COLUMBIA TRISTAR HOME VIDEO 60949

DRESSED TO KILL

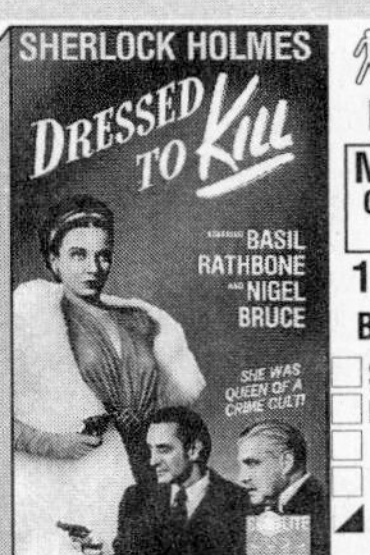

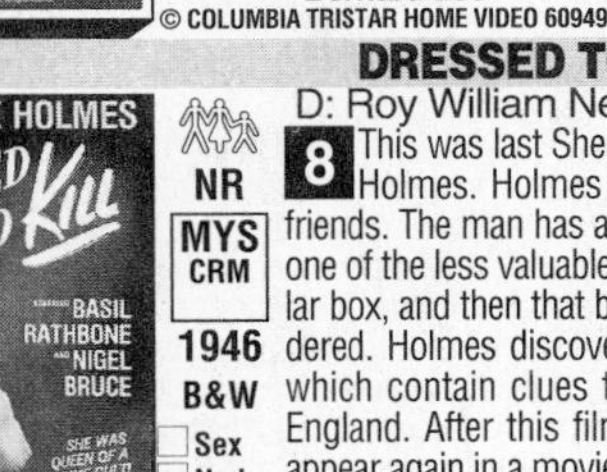

D: Roy William Neill — 72 m

NR | MYS CRM | 1946 | B&W

8 This was last Sherlock Holmes adventure with Basil Rathbone as Holmes. Holmes investigates the burglary of one of Watson's friends. The man has an extensive collection of music boxes, but only one of the less valuable ones is stolen. Holmes is shown another similar box, and then that box is also stolen. Then Watson's friend is murdered. Holmes discovers that he is in pursuit of three music boxes which contain clues to engraving plates stolen from the Bank of England. After this film, Rathbone retired to the stage and did not appear again in a movie for nine years.

Sex | Nud | Viol | Lang | ◢ AdSit

A: Basil Rathbone, Nigel Bruce, Patricia Morison, Edmond Breon, Carl Harbord

© REPUBLIC PICTURES HOME VIDEO V7155

GREEN FOR DANGER

D: Sidney Gilliat — 90 m

NR | MYS COM | 1947 | B&W

9 Very highly regarded English mystery with a heavy dollop of English wit. A rescue worker in WWII England mysteriously dies on the operating table in a rural hospital. When other people start turning up dead on that table, too, Scotland Yard's Inspector Cockrill (Sim) arranges a fake operation to help solve the case of the mad killer. Excellent and very tense thriller which is neatly tied together and punctuated with Alastair Sim's wit. It is a must see for mystery fans and just good entertainment for everyone else.

Sex | Nud | Viol | Lang | ◢ AdSit

A: Alastair Sim, Trevor Howard, Leo Genn, Sally Gray, Rosamund John

© HOME VISION GRE 11

HOUND OF THE BASKERVILLES, THE

D: Sidney Lanfield — 80 m

NR | MYS SUS | 1939 | B&W

8 Quintessential Sherlock Homes. While it was made the same year as THE ADVENTURES OF SHERLOCK HOLMES, this was actually the first film done with the successful teaming of Basil Rathbone and Nigel Bruce. Holmes and Watson are called on by a young nobleman to rescue him from a curse which has plagued his family for generations, killing his ancestors. The curse is a malevolent great dog that haunts the surrounding moors. Is it real? Is it an apparition? Or - is it his imagination? Listen for the famous closing line from the cocaine-using Holmes, "Quick Watson, the needle." Also see THE SCARLET CLAW.

Sex | Nud | Viol | Lang | ◢ AdSit

A: Basil Rathbone, Nigel Bruce, Wendy Barrie, Lionel Atwill, Richard Greene, John Carradine

© CBS/FOX VIDEO 7778

HOUSE OF FEAR, THE

D: Roy William Neill — 69 m

NR | MYS SUS | 1945 | B&W

7 After the rousing success of THE ADVENTURES OF SHERLOCK HOLMES, HOUND OF THE BASKERVILLES and THE SCARLET CLAW, the duo were, for a while, brought to WWII London to aid in the war effort. This, however, is the first film that took them back to Victorian times again. This time they investigate the case of who is killing the members of the "Good Comrades Club." It is a group of six men who live(d) in a dreary Scottish mansion, each of whom had large insurance policies made out to the last surviving member of the club. The detective's job is complicated because the four deceased are disfigured beyond identification.

Sex | Nud | Viol | Lang | ◢ AdSit

A: Basil Rathbone, Nigel Bruce, Aubrey Mather, Dennis Hoey, Paul Cavanagh, Holmes Herbert

© CBS/FOX VIDEO 7779

I CONFESS

D: Alfred Hitchcock — 105 m

NR | MYS SUS | 1952 | B&W

7 This is a Hitchcock tale of a priest (Clift) who has heard a killer's confession. However, he refuses to betray the secrets of the confessional, and he stays with that conviction even though he's getting deeper and deeper into trouble himself because more and more of the clues begin pointing to him as being the murderer. He has, in fact, become the primary suspect of investigator Karl Malden. This is a moody and somber thriller and is not one of Hitchcock's best efforts. Still, it is a quite involving mystery, due largely to the clever use of Quebec locations and an intense performance from Montgomery Clift.

Sex | Nud | Viol | Lang | ◢ AdSit

A: Montgomery Clift, Anne Baxter, Karl Malden, Brian Aherne, Roger Dann

© WARNER HOME VIDEO 11063

I WAKE UP SCREAMING

D: H. Bruce Humberstone — 82 m

NR | MYS CRM SUS | 1941 | B&W

8 Classy whodunit with a neat twist at the end. Dark creepy atmosphere (known as film noir) marks this story about a beautiful girl who is murdered on the eve of her departure for Hollywood. Her agent (Mature) is the prime suspect in her murder, but her sister (Grable) is also suspect. Still, the cop in charge is convinced it was Mature who killed her and is determined to get him. Even though Grable should be afraid of Mature, she joins forces with him to prove his innocence. A good mystery, tense throughout.

Sex | Nud | ◢ Viol | Lang | ◢ AdSit

A: Betty Grable, Victor Mature, Laird Cregar, Carole Landis, William Gargan

© FOXVIDEO 1720

JOURNEY INTO FEAR

D: Norman Foster — 68 m

NR | MYS SUS | 1942 | B&W

8 This is a taut espionage thriller. It is at times difficult to follow, but it is also realistic, believable and contains a few strokes of brilliance. It is WWII. Joseph Cotten plays an American munitions expert who is sent to help out in Turkey, so Nazi agents are quickly eager to kill him. On the advice of a Turkish colonel (Welles), he is supposed to escape by sneaking on board a rusty old freighter, which then heads out across the Black Sea. Even though everything was supposed to have been done in secret, the ship has left port with a Nazi killer on board and now Cotten doesn't know who, if anyone, to trust.

Sex | Nud | ◢ Viol | Lang | ◢ AdSit

A: Orson Welles, Joseph Cotten, Dolores Del Rio, Ruth Warrick, Agnes Moorehead, Hans Conried

© TURNER HOME ENTERTAINMENT 2049

KENNEL MURDER CASE, THE

D: Michael Curtiz — 74 m

NR | MYS CRM | 1933 | B&W

9 Stylish and intriguing murder mystery in which William Powell plays a suave detective named Philo Vance. (This was the fore-runner to the character Nick Charles that Powell would soon make famous in the THIN MAN series.) A man who was hated by virtually everybody is found dead - locked inside a sealed room. The police think it was suicide. It couldn't be anything else... right? Our witty and charming detective thinks otherwise. Methodically, he interviews all the witnesses and then slowly reconstructs a very complex crime. All the clues are there, right in front of you. Dated, but still excellent.

Sex | Nud | Viol | Lang | AdSit

A: William Powell, Mary Astor, Eugene Pallette, Ralph Morgan, Jack LaRue

© UNITED AMERICAN VIDEO CORP. 4142

KISS ME DEADLY

D: Robert Aldrich 106 m

NR MYS CRM 1955 B&W

8 Hard-edged film noir thriller. P.I. Mike Hammer gives a ride to a pretty girl (Leachman). She turns up dead and now the F.B.I. is investigating. Then Mike gives protection to the girl's terrified roommate, only to find that she is in partnership with the hoods who killed Leachman and also helped to frame him for murder. The object of everybody's attention is a suitcase containing a nuclear bomb. This is a moody and violent picture whose pacing and camera techniques marked it as a milestone in films.

Sex / Nud / Viol / Lang / AdSit

A: Ralph Meeker, Albert Dekker, Paul Stewart, Cloris Leachman, Jack Elam, Strother Martin

Distributed By MGM/UA Home Video M202251

MURDER AT THE VANITIES

D: Mitchell Leisen 91 m

NR MYS MUS 1934 B&W

6 This vintage backstage mystery takes place on the Broadway set of the famous Earl Carroll's Broadway revue. Everyone is a suspect. A cop with a sharp edge (McLaglen) must find the killer before the curtain falls or the killer will get away. Off-beat production numbers include "Cocktails for Two" and an ode to the hemp plant "Sweet Marijuana." Sort of fun oddity.

Sex / Nud / Viol / Lang / AdSit

A: Carl Brisson, Victor McLaglen, Jack Oakie, Kitty Carlisle

© MCA/UNIVERSAL HOME VIDEO, INC. 80410

LADY FROM SHANGHAI, THE

D: Orson Welles 87 m

NR MYS SUS 1948 B&W

8 This is a longtime cult favorite and is also one of Orson Welles's most enjoyable pictures. The camera and the director are the real stars in this film noir piece. Orson Welles is an Irish sailor who saves a beautiful woman (Rita Hayworth) from a rapist. He is then hired by the woman's crippled lawyer husband to help them and his business partner sail a luxury yacht back to San Francisco. Along the way, he is seduced by the woman and ensnared into a murder plot at sea. This film contains some much-heralded camera work, particularly the now-famous climax scene, a shoot-out in a hall-of-mirrors.

Sex / Nud / Viol / Lang / AdSit

A: Rita Hayworth, Orson Welles, Everett Sloane, Glenn Anders, Ted de Corsia, Gus Schilling

© COLUMBIA TRISTAR HOME VIDEO 60451

NIGHT TO REMEMBER, A

D: Richard Wallace 91 m

NR MYS SUS COM 1943 B&W

9 Highly entertaining whodunit with a comic flair. The wife of a successful young murder mystery writer has always wanted him to write a romantic novel, so she searches out the perfect apartment for them in Greenwich village which will set just the proper mood. However, when a dead body turns up in their back yard, he feels compelled to solve the real murder mystery. Classy, consistently entertaining - with a few hilarious lines and terrific performances.

Sex / Nud / Viol / Lang / AdSit

A: Loretta Young, Brian Aherne, Sidney Toler, Gale Sondergaard, Donald MacBride, Blanche Yurka

© COLUMBIA TRISTAR HOME VIDEO 62000

LADY IN THE LAKE

D: Robert Montgomery 104 m

NR MYS CRM 1946 B&W

6 Clever and innovative effort in movie making. Author Raymond Chandler's detective hero Philip Marlowe investigates the mystery of the missing wife. The cleverness lies not in the plot but in the technique of having the camera be Marlowe. Everything is told from Marlowe's standpoint. Interesting entertainment, even though the technique has many flaws and shortcomings. The plot itself is quite involved. Marlowe finds a woman's body in the lake, but it's not the woman he's looking for. Then there are more surprises.

Sex / Nud / Viol / Lang / AdSit

A: Robert Montgomery, Audrey Totter, Lloyd Nolan, Tom Tully, Leon Ames

Distributed By MGM/UA Home Video M202250

PEARL OF DEATH, THE

D: Roy William Neill 69 m

NR MYS 1944 B&W

7 Rathbone and Bruce, again as Sherlock Holmes and Dr. Watson, are this time tracking down three criminals. A master thief has stolen the Borgia pearls and hidden them inside a wet plaster cast which will become one of six busts of Napoleon. The thief then instructs his homicidal partner, "The Creeper," to kill the owners of the busts. This he accomplishes by methodically snapping the third vertebrae in each of his victim's necks. The masterful Holmes catches, but must then do battle with, "The Creeper." Pretty good offering in the series.

Sex / Nud / Viol / Lang / AdSit

A: Basil Rathbone, Nigel Bruce, Evelyn Ankers, Dennis Hoey, Miles Mander, Mary Gordon

© CBS/FOX VIDEO 7780

LADY VANISHES, THE

D: Alfred Hitchcock 96 m

NR MYS SUS COM 1938 B&W

8 Top-notch Hitchcock that some critics rated, along with THE THIRTY-NINE STEPS, as being his best. Film fans will rate it much higher. However, modern audiences will require patience with the dated aspects. On a pre-WWII European train ride, a young American woman (Lockwood) is on her way to England and befriends a sweet old woman. However, the old woman is soon missing and most on the train deny that she ever even existed. Unwilling to accept the old woman's disappearance, Lockwood investigates with the aid of fellow passengers and discovers that absolutely no one on this train is who they appear to be. Wonderful blend of mystery, comedy and suspense.

Sex / Nud / Viol / Lang / AdSit

A: Margaret Lockwood, Michael Redgrave, May Whitty, Paul Lukas

© SPOTLITE VIDEO V7335

SCARLET CLAW, THE

D: Roy William Neill 74 m

NR MYS SUS 1944 B&W

9 A highly atmospheric mystery, acclaimed by some as the best of the Sherlock Holmes series. Holmes (Rathbone) and Watson (Bruce) travel to Canada in 1944 to attend a seminar on supernatural powers. While there, they are drawn into an investigation of several gruesome murders recently committed. The villagers attribute the killings to the work of a local monster. But as the monster adopts different disguises, Holmes sets out to prove that the murders were committed by human hands. Moody photography adds to the mysterious mood.

Sex / Nud / Viol / Lang / AdSit

A: Basil Rathbone, Nigel Bruce, Paul Cavanagh, Kay Harding, Gerald Hammer, Arthur Hohl

© CBS/FOX VIDEO 7782

LAURA

D: Otto Preminger 88 m

NR MYS ROM 1944 B&W

9 This is an outstanding film (five Oscar nominations) that was extremely popular upon its release. Dana Andrews is a tough cop who is way out of his element in high society, but he is called upon to investigate the case of a beautiful society girl (Gene Tierney) whose face was blown away by a shotgun blast. As his investigation deepens, the cop becomes irresistably drawn to the beautiful and mysterious dead woman. His investigation becomes more and more personal as he begins to fall in love with her. This is a very good and stylish mystery that has a classy presentation with sharp and witty dialogue.

Sex / Nud / Viol / Lang / AdSit

A: Gene Tierney, Dana Andrews, Clifton Webb, Vincent Price, Judith Anderson, Grant Mitchell

© FOXVIDEO 1094

SHADOW OF THE THIN MAN

D: W.S. Van Dyke II 98 m

NR MYS COM 1941 B&W

8 A dynamite whodunit! The fourth in the Thin Man series has our heros, the suave and witty married detectives Nick and Nora (Powell and Loy), stumbling upon the murders of a jockey and a reporter at the racetrack. There is a body in the shower, another one hanging from a chandelier and a diamond bracelet in the radiator. The debonair pair quickly move in to investigate, with their baby Nick and dog Asta in tow, to try to uncover who is behind the dastardly deeds. Once again, this fun entry in the light-hearted Thin Man detective series will live up to your expectations.

Sex / Nud / Viol / Lang / AdSit

A: William Powell, Myrna Loy, Barry Nelson, Donna Reed, Sam Levene

Distributed By MGM/UA Home Video M300967

MALTESE FALCOLN, THE

D: John Huston 101 m

NR MYS SUS CRM 1941 B&W

10 A masterpiece. One of the all-time best detective mysteries ever made! Sam Spade (Bogart) and his partner are hired by pretty Miss Wonderly (Astor) to trail a man. That same night Sam's partner is shot; shortly thereafter, so is the man he was to follow; and, Sam finds himself to be the center of a great deal of interest by a cast of strange characters, all of whom are in hot pursuit of a priceless jeweled black bird. This adaptation of Hammett's detective novel is brilliant. The hard-edged style of the film set the precedence for many hardball detective movies which followed it. Attention to detail, great characters and superb casting make this film one of the all-time greats.

Sex / Nud / Viol / Lang / AdSit

A: Humphrey Bogart, Mary Astor, Peter Lorre, Sydney Greenstreet, Ward Bond, Gladys George

Distributed By MGM/UA Home Video M201546

SHERLOCK HOLMES AND THE SECRET WEAPON

D: Roy William Neill 68 m

NR MYS 1942 B&W

8 This Holmes adventure is set against the dangerous backdrop of WWII Europe. Holmes (Rathbone) is charged with finding a Swiss inventor and his bombsight, who are in hiding in Germany. Holmes is to get both of them out of Germany, and out of reach of the Nazis and their villainous accomplice, Professor Moriarty. The only clue Holmes has to find them is an encrypted message left by the inventor.

Sex / Nud / Viol / Lang / AdSit

A: Basil Rathbone, Nigel Bruce, Lionel Atwill, Kaaren Verne

© VIDEO TREASURES HR9605

SHERLOCK HOLMES AND THE VOICE OF TERROR

D: John Rawlins — 65 m

NR | MYS | 1942 | B&W

Sex / Nud / Viol / Lang / ✓ AdSit

7 Set in London during World War II, Holmes (Rathbone) and Watson (Bruce) are given the dangerous task of quieting Nazi radio broadcasts that promises sinister sabotage acts against the Allied forces. Those promises broadcast by the "Voice of Terror" are all then systematically and promptly carried out by an evil Nazi death committee. It is rich in the atmosphere of a war-torn London and over-all is quite enjoyable.

A: Basil Rathbone, Nigel Bruce, Reginald Denny, Evelyn Ankers, Thomas Gomez

© CBS/FOX VIDEO 7788

SHERLOCK HOLMES FACES DEATH

D: Roy William Neill — 68 m

NR | MYS | 1943 | B&W

Sex / Nud / Viol / Lang / ✓ AdSit

7 When the Musgrave mansion becomes a den of death, Watson (Bruce) calls on his trusty friend Holmes (Rathbone) to help him solve the strange murders. Holmes believes that the clue to the killings is contained in a will, and set out to find the killer by playing a giant game of human "chess" right on the mansion's floor. Holmes methodically moves people around from square to square in his brilliant game of deductive reasoning.

A: Basil Rathbone, Nigel Bruce, Hillary Brooke, Milburn Stone

© CBS/FOX VIDEO 7784

SHERLOCK HOLMES IN WASHINGTON

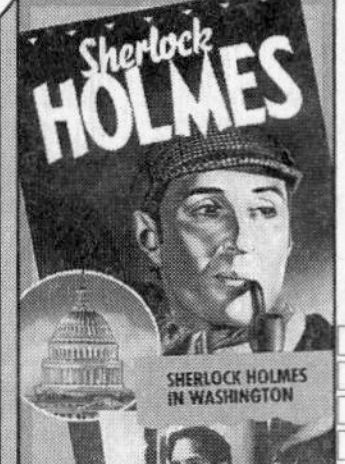

D: Roy William Neill — 71 m

NR | MYS | 1943 | B&W

Sex / Nud / Viol / Lang / ✓ AdSit

6 This nifty Holmes wartime adventure brings the duo to the United States. A top secret British agent is harboring a secret microfilm containing important war documents inside the casing of a matchbook. When he is killed, the matchbook is given to a woman traveling on an airplane. She has no idea how important it is, and it falls into the wrong hands. Holmes (Rathbone) and Watson (Bruce) are dispatched to Washington to find the elusive matchbook and chase down a ring of Nazi spies.

A: Basil Rathbone, Nigel Bruce, George Zucco, Marjorie Lord, George Zucco

© CBS/FOX VIDEO 7785

SONG OF THE THIN MAN

D: Edward Buzzell — 87 m

NR | MYS COM | 1947 | B&W

Sex / Nud / Viol / Lang / ✓ AdSit

7 This was the last of the Thin Man films. The super sleuthing couple Nick and Nora (Powell and Loy) go after a murderer who kills a bandmember aboard ship. Their search takes them to New York and has them hanging out in some of the Big Apple's swankier jazz clubs. The snappy dialogue seems especially crisp set against the steamy backdrop. A fitting and particularly good conclusion to the entertaining series. Be sure to see the Heros, etc. index for a complete listing of the others in the series.

A: William Powell, Myrna Loy, Keenan Wynn, Dean Stockwell

Distributed By MGM/UA Home Video M300969

SPELLBOUND

D: Alfred Hitchcock — 111 m

NR | MYS ROM | 1945 | B&W

Sex / Nud / Viol / Lang / ✓ AdSit

9 The master of suspense works his magic in this classic thriller for the mind! Six Oscar nominations. Peck is the new head psychiatrist in a mental hospital but quickly starts to exhibit problems of his own. Bergman, the beautiful psychiatrist who falls in love with him, soon discovers that he is not who he appears to be. He is an imposter and an amnesiac. She loves him, but where is the real Dr. Edwards? Is Peck a murderer? She must help him get to the bottom of the past he has blocked out. Expect several unanticipated plot twists. Famous for a Salvador Dali surrealist dream sequence.

A: Ingrid Bergman, Gregory Peck, Leo G. Carroll, Michael Chekhov, John Emery, Wallace Ford

© CBS/FOX VIDEO 8035

STAGE FRIGHT

D: Alfred Hitchcock — 110 m

NR | MYS SUS | 1949 | B&W

Sex / Nud / Viol / Lang / ✓ AdSit

7 Early Hitchcock fun. A young drama student (Todd) appears to have been framed by his mistress (Dietrich), a flamboyant stage star, for the murder of her husband. Jane Wyman, who was once Todd's girlfriend, decides to play detective and takes a job as Dietrich's maid, in an attempt to uncover some clues that will implicate Dietrich. Meanwhile, Wyman's father hides Todd out until they can get the goods and force Dietrich to confess, but the arrival of a slick detective (Wilding) complicates things. This is an underrated thriller with a tricky plot.

A: Jane Wyman, Marlene Dietrich, Michael Wilding, Richard Todd, Kay Walsh, Alastair Sim

© WARNER HOME VIDEO 11380

THIN MAN, THE

D: W.S. Van Dyke — 90 m

NR | MYS COM | 1934 | B&W

Sex / Nud / Viol / Lang / AdSit

9 This suave, sophisticated and happy detective couple captivated both the general public and the critics with their charm and clever banter - and they're just as delightful today. Nick Charles is a retired police detective who enjoys being retired, making snide jokes, spending his rich wife's money and drinking. Nora enjoys the thrill of the chase, the excitement of his friends, and she can match his wisecracks one-for-one. The two are asked by a rich heiress to find her missing father. Spawned 5 sequels, but the first is best. Check out the Heros, etc Index for more.

A: William Powell, Myrna L… een O'Sullivan, Nat Pendleton, Edward Brophy, Porter H…

Distributed By MGM/UA Home Video M300608

THIN MAN GOES HOM… HE

D: Richard Thorpe — 102 m

NR | MYS COM | 1944 | B&W

Sex / Nud / Viol / Lang / AdSit

7 This is the fifth entry in the series. In it, Nick and Nora go back to his home town of Sycamo… Springs to see his parents. Even there the two can't escape murder when a man mysteriously drops dead on the neighbor's front porch. Now Nick has to prove himself in front of his father. But Dad doesn't take it kindly when Nick starts pointing fingers at his fellow townsmen. This one still has all the mystery elements of the past entries, however it plays more on the comedy aspects of the famous sophisticated detectives.

A: William Powell, Myrna Loy, Lucile Watson, Gloria De Haven, Anne Revere, Helen Vinson

Distributed By MGM/UA Home Video M300970

VELVET TOUCH, THE

D: John Gage — 97 m

NR | MYS SUS | 1948 | B&W

Sex / Nud / ✓ Viol / Lang / ✓ AdSit

6 Spiffy, crisp and very well-acted. A devious producer tries to put the brakes on a young stage actress's career (Russell) by blackmailing her. In a fit of rage, she hits him with a statue and accidentally kills him. In a stoke of good fortune, she seems to be off the hook when another actress, the man's former lover, is blamed for the murder by detective Greenstreet. It looks like a perfect crime. She does her best to enjoy her victory, but is instead defeated by her conscience. Polished, with a very rewarding ending.

A: Rosalind Russell, Leo Genn, Claire Trevor, Sydney Greenstreet, Leon Ames, Frank McHugh

© TURNER HOME ENTERTAINMENT 6017

YOUNG AND INNOCENT

D: Alfred Hitchcock — 80 m

NR | MYS SUS | 1937 | B&W

Sex / Nud / Viol / Lang / AdSit

8 Very entertaining and sadly neglected thriller from Hitchcock. A writer (de Marney) is arrested and tried for the murder of an actress acquaintance who had been strangled with the belt from his missing raincoat. However, he escapes at his trial. The constable's daughter has fallen for him and assists him in his cross-country quest to save himself. They are in pursuit of the real killer, a man with a nervous eye twitch. As in all mysteries, but particularly Hitchcock, the fun is in the search. This one is filled with twists, missing evidence and Hitchcock's sometime surrealistic photography, timing and wit.

A: Derrick de Marney, Nova Pilbeam, Percy Marmont, Mary Clare, Basil Radford

© VIDEO TREASURES BV5032

Romance

ALGIERS

D: John Cromwell — 92 m

NR | ROM CRM | 1938 | B&W

Sex / Nud / Viol / Lang / ✓ AdSit

7 Mystery, adventure and romance combined. This is probably Boyer's most famous role. He plays the international jewel thief Pepe LeMoko, who seeks sanctuary from the police and becomes trapped in the infamous Casbah district of Algiers of North Africa, home to thieves, criminals and outcasts of all races and cultures. Heddy Lamarr, the beautiful Parisian, slumming in the Casbah, meets and falls in love with him there, but he can't leave. Strangely enough, the famous phrase, "Come with me to the Casbah," was made popular by the movie but never was heard in it. Stylish, murky, romantic.

A: Charles Boyer, Hedy Lamarr, Sigrid Gurie, Joseph Calleia, Gene Lockhart, Alan Hale

© VIDEO YESTERYEAR 667

ALL THIS AND HEAVEN TOO

D: Anatole Litvak — 141 m

NR | ROM SUS DMA | 1940 | B&W | Sex | Nud | Viol | Lang | AdSit

8 A real weeper that won an Oscar nomination for Best Picture and was actually based upon a true murder case. In 1840 Paris, the wife of the Duc de Praslin (Boyer) is an uncaring mother who despises her children's adored and kindly governess (Davis). She is insanely jealous because she knows her husband loves Davis and feels he has been unfaithful to her. So, when this vengeful woman is found murdered, people naturally assume that the governess and the husband did it. However, he is royalty and so is safe, but because Davis is a servant, she is at the mercy of the justice system.

A: Bette Davis, Charles Boyer, Jeffrey Lynn, Barbara O'Neill, Virginia Weidler, Henry Daniell

Distributed By MGM/UA Home Video M600749

ANNA KARENINA

D: Clarence Brown — 96 m

NR | ROM DMA | 1935 | B&W | Sex | Nud | Viol | Lang | AdSit

8 Leo Tolstoy's classic romance novel of nineteenth century Russia is brought to life by the same team as in ANNA CHRISTIE. Garbo is an unhappily married wife of a politician (Rathbone) from St. Petersburg. Then, while on a trip to Moscow, she falls in love with the handsome Count Vronsky (March) and runs away with him to Venice. But there is tragedy in the air for her when her husband tells her son that she is dead, and her lover begins to long for the life he had to leave behind, to which she may not return. High quality film that still holds up well today.

A: Greta Garbo, Fredric March, Basil Rathbone, Freddie Bartholomew, Maureen O'Sullivan, Reginald Denny

Distributed By MGM/UA Home Video M300505

ANN VICKERS

D: John Cromwell — 76 m

NR | ROM DMA | 1933 | B&W | Sex | Nud | Viol | Lang | AdSit

6 Soapy early melodrama based upon the novel by Sinclair Lewis. Ann Vickers (Irene Dunne) falls in love with an army Captain but he leaves her when she becomes pregnant. Deserted by him and chastised by others, she gives up on men altogether and instead devotes herself to a life of social service. She becomes a reform-minded prison warden, and it is there that she meets and falls in love with judge Barney Dolphin (Walter Huston). However, the judge is convicted on trumped-up bribery charges and she must wait still another eight years. Somewhat episodic and dated, but still worth a look.

A: Irene Dunne, Walter Huston, Bruce Cabot, Conrad Nagel, Edna May Oliver, J. Carrol Naish

© TURNER HOME ENTERTAINMENT 2029

BACHELOR MOTHER

D: Garson Kanin — 82 m

NR | ROM COM | 1939 | B&W | Sex | Nud | Viol | Lang | AdSit

8 Witty and very funny movie that was one of the biggest hits of 1939. Ginger Rogers is an unmarried sales clerk who finds a baby on a doorstep and takes it in. However, serious complications arise when no one will believe that the baby isn't hers. As an unmarried mother, her whole life is turned upside down and she is even in danger of losing her job. The store's owner thinks his son (Niven) is responsible. Then three more men turn up all claiming to be the father. Rogers shows a real talent for comedy in this movie, even though she reportedly didn't want to do this picture.

A: Ginger Rogers, David Niven, Charles Coburn, Frank Albertson, Ernest Truex

© TURNER HOME ENTERTAINMENT 6056

BLOOD AND SAND

D: Fred Niblo — 92 m

ROM | 1922 | B&W | Sex | Nud | Viol | Lang | AdSit

7 This is one of Rudolph Valentino's most famous roles and confirmed his place as a leading sex symbol of the silent screen. In it, he is a poor boy who realizes his life's ambition to become a famous bullfighter in the rings of Spain, a matador. After his success, he marries his childhood sweetheart, however he is also quickly seduced by a wealthy and sultry society woman and is sucked into a decadent life. Silent film accompanied by organ music.

A: Rudolph Valentino, Lila Lee, Nita Naldi, George Field

© VIDEO YESTERYEAR 521

BRIEF ENCOUNTER

D: David Lean — 86 m

NR | ROM DMA | 1945 | B&W | Sex | Nud | Viol | Lang | AdSit

9 Very highly regarded by critics. A truly romantic and poignant classic film of a doomed love affair, written by Noel Coward. Two quite ordinary people, happily married to and in love with others, chance to meet in a railroad train station and become irresistibly drawn to each other in a desperately short and poignant romance. A sensitive look at an unforeseen romance, with very touching love scenes between Johnson and Howard. A memorable film for all time. However, it is also quite slow moving at the beginning and is very English in flavor.

A: Celia Johnson, Trevor Howard, Cyril Raymond, Stanley Holloway, Joyce Carey

© PARAMOUNT HOME VIDEO 12566

CAMILLE

D: George Cukor — 110 m

NR | ROM DMA | 1936 | B&W | Sex | Nud | Viol | Lang | AdSit

9 This is MGM's beautiful production of the classic weeper which is acclaimed as being one of the most romantic movies ever made. It is also the film for which Garbo is best remembered. She plays a beautiful Parisian courtesan and free spirit who sacrifices herself for Robert Taylor, the man she loves. The ending will break your heart and bring tears to your eyes, as it has all who have ever watched it before you.

A: Greta Garbo, Robert Taylor, Lionel Barrymore, Henry Daniell, Elizabeth Allan, Laura Hope Crews

Distributed By MGM/UA Home Video M300472

CARRIE

D: William Wyler — 118 m

NR | ROM | 1952 | B&W | Sex | Nud | Viol | Lang | AdSit

7 Jennifer Jones plays Carrie. Carrie is a beautiful and innocent turn-of-the-century farm girl who comes to the city and succeeds in becoming a famous actress. Olivier gives one of his best performances as a respectable married man who becomes totally enraptured by her. He becomes her lover, but after she falls in love with someone else, he destroys himself in his attempts to win her back.

A: Jennifer Jones, Laurence Olivier, Miriam Hopkins, Eddie Albert, Mary Murphy

© PARAMOUNT HOME VIDEO 5123

CASABLANCA

D: Michael Curtiz — 104 m

NR | ROM DMA SUS | 1943 | B&W | Sex | Nud | Viol | Lang | AdSit

10 Arguably one of the very best movies ever made and it is still a perennial favorite. Into Rick's - a seedy Algierian nightclub in WWII North Africa that is run by Rick, a noble American outcast (Bogart), and populated by European refugees, misfits and Nazis - walks Rick's long lost love (Bergman) and her refugee/underground leader husband (Henreid). Vivid memories of passion, love and betrayal overwhelm them both when she asks Rick to help her husband to escape - but will she go with him or will she stay with Rick? Romance, high drama, political intrigue and absolutely wonderful dialogue. 3 Oscars.

A: Humphrey Bogart, Ingrid Bergman, Paul Henreid, Claude Rains, Sydney Greenstreet, Peter Lorre

Distributed By MGM/UA Home Video M801502

CLOCK, THE

D: Vincente Minnelli — 91 m

NR | ROM | 1945 | B&W | Sex | Nud | Viol | Lang | AdSit

7 Entertaining little bit of froth with Judy Garland as a secretary who meets Robert Walker, a war-time soldier on a 48-hour pass, in a train station. They immediately fall in love and then make the most of their short time together by exploring the streets of New York meeting all sorts of interesting people. Interestingly, because of the way in which the script is written, the city actually becomes a third character in this charming little love story. Shortly after this picture was made, director Minnelli married his star.

A: Judy Garland, Robert Walker, James Gleason, Keenan Wynn, Marshall Thompson, Lucile Gleason

Distributed By MGM/UA Home Video MV200890

CYRANO DE BERGERAC

D: Michael Gordon — 112 m

NR | ROM | 1950 | B&W | Sex | Nud | Viol | Lang | AdSit

8 Charming adaptation of Edmond Rostand's classic romantic tragedy of unrequited love. Jose Ferrer won an Oscar as Cyrano, the eloquent 17th-century soldier/poet with the long nose. He desperately loves the fair Roxanne but is discouraged by his embarrassing prodigious nose. He loves her but knows that she loves a shy, handsome young soldier. So, he loans his tragic wit to the young man, allowing him to win her hand and thereby make her happy. However, love can not be fooled. This theme was later transformed by Steve Martin into a comedy, ROXANNE.

A: Jose Ferrer, Mala Powers, William Prince, Morris Carnovsky, Ralph Clanton, Elena Verdugo

© REPUBLIC PICTURES HOME VIDEO 0822

DARK VICTORY

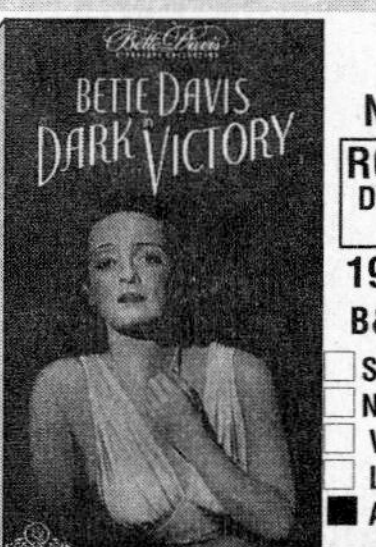

D: Edmund Goulding — 105 m

NR | ROM DMA | 1939 | B&W | Sex | Nud | Viol | Lang | AdSit

9 This is a champion weeper of a movie and it stars Bette Davis in one of her best roles. She plays a head-strong heiress who has frittered her life away on meaningless parties and shopping. Then she is nearly destroyed when her eyesight starts to dim and she discovers that she has a brain tumor. A successful operation to correct it leads her into true love with the doctor who saved her. She changes her life in an attempt to give it real meaning. But soon, the tumor returns. Classy tearjerker. Great job by Davis.

A: Bette Davis, George Brent, Humphrey Bogart, Ronald Reagan, Geraldine Fitsgerald, Cora Witherspoon

Distributed By MGM/UA Home Video M301312

DESIREE

D: Henry Koster 110 m

NR ROM 1954 B&W Sex Nud Viol Lang AdSit

6 Semi-historical romance costume drama about the loves of Napoleon Bonaparte, played by Brando. When he was young and penniless, Napoleon fell for pretty 17-year-old seamstress Desiree (Simmons), but her father forbade their relationship. So she married a nobleman, but she never forgot her first love. In the interim, Bonaparte has risen to power and married Josephine (Oberon), but his affections become confused when he is once again reunited with his long lost love.

A: Marlon Brando, Jean Simmons, Merle Oberon, Michael Rennie, Cameron Mitchell, Cathleen Nesbitt

© FOXVIDEO 1527

EAGLE, THE

D: Clarence Brown 74 m

NR ROM COM 1925 B&W Sex Nud Viol Lang AdSit

8 This is one of Valentino's best pictures. It is a satirical romance, where Valentino mocks his own image. The story is that of a Russian Cossack Lieutenant who spurns the amorous attentions of the Czarina. After he rejects her, he is banished and becomes a Robin Hood-like character called The Eagle. This was one of Valentino's most popular movies and one of his last. He died at the age of 31.

A: Rudolph Valentino, Vilma Banky, Louise Dresser

© HBO VIDEO 0280

ENCHANTED COTTAGE, THE

D: John Cromwell 78 m

NR ROM FAN 1944 B&W Sex Nud Viol Lang AdSit

6 Sensitive and touching parable. Robert Young is a war veteran who is so horribly disfigured that people shun him. He is so desperate and alone that he is on the verge of suicide. Dorothy McGuire is very drab and extremely shy. She, too, is alone. They are both outcasts. However, they find each other, get married and decide to go off to be by themselves. They move into a little cottage that has magical powers and slowly they are transformed into beautiful people. Excellent understated performances elevate this above its seemingly simple story line.

A: Dorothy McGuire, Robert Young, Herbert Marshall, Mildred Natwick, Spring Byington, Richard Gaines

© TURNER HOME ENTERTAINMENT 6047

FAREWELL TO ARMS, A

D: Frank Borzage 79 m

NR ROM DMA 1932 B&W Sex Nud Viol Lang AdSit

8 Very romanticized and romantic version of Hemingway's wonderfully tragic love between an American ambulance driver and a British nurse, both caught up in, and separated by, the momentum of war in WWI Italy. Much of the drama of the war apparent in the book has been left out of the film except where it is required to advance the love story. The resulting film is very sentimental, but it is also very affecting, and it was Helen Hayes's personal favorite role. Great acting by Gary Cooper and Adolphe Menjou, but the glory goes to Helen Hayes.

A: Helen Hayes, Gary Cooper, Adolphe Menjou, Mary Phillips, Jack LaRue

© VIDEO TREASURES BV1948

FLESH AND THE DEVIL

D: Clarence Brown 103 m

NR ROM 1927 B&W Sex Nud Viol Lang AdSit

7 Two boyhood friends have sworn a blood oath to always be friends. Both are at a military school when Gilbert spies the beautiful Garbo at a ball and dances with her. Into the room walks Garbo's husband, who challenges Gilbert to a duel. The husband is killed and it is politely suggested that Gilbert go away for five years. He asks his friend to console the widow. Three years later, he returns to find that the two are married and a duel is threatened between the friends. The very passionate on-screen performances from Gilbert and Garbo were due, in part, to an off-screen affair. Silent.

A: Greta Garbo, John Gilbert, Lars Hanson, Barbara Kent, William Orlamond, George Fawcett

Distributed By MGM/UA Home Video M301358

GHOST AND MRS. MUIR, THE

D: Joseph L. Mankiewicz 104 m

NR ROM COM 1947 B&W Sex Nud Viol Lang AdSit

10 Utterly charming romantic fantasy about a poor widow (Tierney) and her young daughter (a very young Natalie Wood) who move into a seaside cottage which is haunted by the cantankerous ghost of a salty 19th-century seafaring captain (Harrison). At first he does his best to scare her away, but then he falls deeply in love with her. When all her money is spent, he writes a book for her that tells of his exploits and which rescues her from financial distress, but it also introduces her to a real live man. Wonderful characterizations from two of film-dom's most favorite stars. Beautifully made.

A: Rex Harrison, Gene Tierney, George Sanders, Vanessa Brown, Edna Best, Natalie Wood

© FOXVIDEO 1385

GREAT LIE, THE

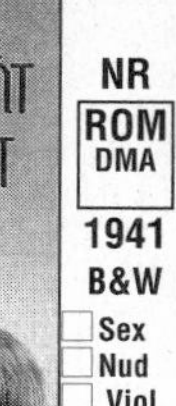

D: Edmund Goulding 101 m

NR ROM DMA 1941 B&W Sex Nud Viol Lang AdSit

8 This is a pretty good soap opera and it won Mary Astor an Oscar for Best Supporting Actress. It is a tale of love and devotion. George Brent has a brief relationship with Mary Astor, who is a flashy concert pianist, but their marriage is quickly annulled. Then he marries genteel Southern socialite Bette Davis and almost immediately becomes lost in a plane crash in South America. However, Mary is pregnant, even though she doesn't want the child. So, she and Bette enter into the Great Lie: Bette will raise the child as her own. Romance and soap opera fans only.

A: Bette Davis, Mary Astor, George Brent, Lucile Watson, Hattie McDaniel, Grant Mitchell

Distributed By MGM/UA Home Video M201802

GUY NAMED JOE, A

D: Victor Fleming 121 m

NR ROM COM FAN 1944 B&W Sex Nud Viol Lang AdSit

8 Enchanting romantic fantasy about a downed WWII fighter pilot (Tracy) who comes back to earth to become a guardian angel for a novice flyer (Johnson). Tracy comes to help Johnson become a better pilot, but is disconcerted when Johnson also pursues Tracy's old girlfriend (Dunne). Sentimental and whimsical. Highly popular in its time, it is only slightly dated now. Spielberg so loved it that he remade it in 1989 as ALWAYS.

A: Spencer Tracy, Irene Dunne, Van Johnson, Ward Bond, James Gleason, Lionel Barrymore

Distributed By MGM/UA Home Video M301380

HISTORY IS MADE AT NIGHT

D: Frank Borzage 98 m

NR ROM SUS 1937 B&W Sex Nud Viol Lang AdSit

7 Elegant and stylish romantic melodrama about a woman (Arthur) who is desperate to escape her shipping magnate husband's cruelty and jealousy. She flees to Paris where she has fallen in love with Boyer, who vows to protect her. But the jealous husband follows her, even killing a man, attempting to frame Boyer for the murder. Intensely romantic, topped off with a thrilling climax aboard a luxury liner that is threatened by icebergs. A compelling love story, in spite of some improbable circumstances.

A: Charles Boyer, Jean Arthur, Colin Clive, Leo Carrillo, George Meeker, Lucien Prival

© WARNER HOME VIDEO 35077

HUMORESQUE

D: Jean Negulesco 126 m

NR ROM DMA 1946 B&W Sex Nud Viol Lang AdSit

8 This is perhaps Crawford's finest performance as she plays a wealthy twice-divorced and re-married socialite who becomes obsessed in a doomed affair with an ambitious violinist (Garfield). She sponsors the debut of this talented artist and follows his rise up from the slums to prominence. They have one brief moment together, but her demands destroy them. He now shuns her advances, which leads to a tragic ending. More than a typical soap opera, this is a top-drawer romance, with winning performances, snappy dialogue, good production values and Isaac Stern playing the violin.

A: Joan Crawford, John Garfield, Oscar Levant, J. Carrol Naish, Craig Stevens, Peggy Knudsen

Distributed By MGM/UA Home Video M202081

HUNCHBACK OF NOTRE DAME, THE

D: Wallace Worsley 133 m

NR ROM DMA SUS 1923 B&W Sex Nud Viol Lang AdSit

8 One of the most prominent films of the silent era. This story of a pitiably deformed bell ringer's love for a Gypsy dancer captured the imaginations of all those who viewed it. It is now most memorable for Lon Chaney Sr.'s brilliant characterization of the Hunchback, through his athletic abilities and his remarkable makeup, which included a 70-pound rubber hump and special devices to prevent him from standing erect or closing his mouth.

A: Lon Chaney, Sr., Patsy Ruth Miller, Ernest Torrence

© VIDEO YESTERYEAR 23

HUNCHBACK OF NOTRE DAME, THE

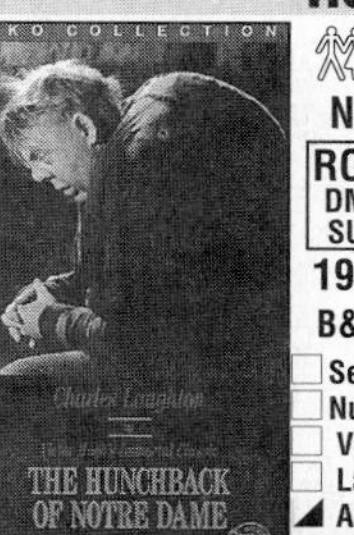

D: William Dieterle 117 m

NR ROM DMA SUS 1939 B&W Sex Nud Viol Lang AdSit

9 Perhaps the best-ever production of Victor Hugo's classic tragic love story. Charles Laughton is haunting as the hideously deformed and tortured spirit Quasimodo who lives in the bell towers of the famed Notre Dame Cathedral of 15th-century Paris. Quasimodo is the scorn of medieval Paris but is given a moment's pity one day by the beautiful Gypsy dancer Esmerelda, with whom he then falls deeply in love. However, one day an angry crowd in the square is about to hang her. He sweeps down from the bell tower rescuing her and delivers her to the Cathedral where she can claim sanctuary. A must see!

A: Charles Laughton, Thomas Mitchell, Maureen O'Hara, Edmond O'Brien, Cedric Hardwicke

© TURNER HOME ENTERTAINMENT 2058

I KNOW WHERE I'M GOING

D: Michael Powell, Emeric Pressburger — 91 m

NR | ROM COM | 1947 | B&W

9 An enchanting and delightful story about an extremely headstrong young girl who is determined to marry an old man for his money. But her plans are interrupted when she becomes stranded in a Scottish coastal town by a storm while she is on her way to him. While stranded there, she meets and falls in love with a naval officer. Even though she struggles hard against it, this fateful meeting has changed her plans and her life forever. Very enjoyable. Charming and witty. A well-made gem.

Sex / Nud / Viol / Lang / AdSit

A: Emeric Pressburger, Wendy Hiller, Roger Livesey, Finlay Currie, Pamela Brown, Valentine Dyall

© HOME VISION KNO 01

IN NAME ONLY

D: John Cromwell — 942 m

NR | ROM DMA | 1939 | B&W

7 Beautifully acted, emotional tearjerker. Cary Grant meets the recently widowed Lombard at a summer resort. They are immediately drawn to each other, have an intense few days and fall deeply in love. However, there is a problem. He is already married and his wife is a bitchy socialite (Francis) who had only married him only for his family's money. He tries desperately to get a divorce. At first she agrees to it but then she decides against it. She even has his parents, who don't know the whole truth, siding with her. Grant and his new love are on an emotional rollercoaster.

Sex / Nud / Viol / Lang / AdSit

A: Carole Lombard, Cary Grant, Kay Francis, Charles Coburn, Helen Vinson, Peggy Ann Garner

© TURNER HOME ENTERTAINMENT 2005

INTERMEZZO

D: Gregory Ratoff — 70 m

NR | ROM | 1939 | B&W

9 One of the most highly acclaimed love stories ever brought to film. Originally done in Swedish (also starring Ingrid Bergman), it proved to be so successful that it was redone in English for the American screen, giving America the opportunity to fall in love with a wonderfully winsome Ingrid Bergman - which it did. She is a young piano teacher to the children of a world-famous and world-weary violinist. His enthusiasm and zest for life and music is restored as he becomes enraptured with her charm and exuberance. He abandons everything to be with her, but is haunted by the family he leaves behind.

Sex / Nud / Viol / Lang / AdSit

A: Leslie Howard, Ingrid Bergman, Edna Best, John Halliday, Cecil Kellaway, Enid Bennett

© CBS/FOX VIDEO 8036

JEZEBEL

D: William Wyler — 105 m

NR | ROM DMA | 1938 | B&W

8 Bette Davis was supposed to have been Scarlett O'Hara in GONE WITH THE WIND. When she lost out in the competition, MGM gave her the lead role in this big-budget production as a consolation prize, and with it she took home her second Oscar. She plays the headstrong spoiled daughter of Southern aristocracy who enjoys toying with her suitor Henry Fonda. But when she wears a red dress to a ball where single women are supposed to wear white, she has gone too far. Embarrassed, Fonda leaves her to marry a Northerner. Great entertainment which received five other nominations and won one more Oscar.

Sex / Nud / Viol / Lang / AdSit

A: Bette Davis, Henry Fonda, George Brent, Spring Byington, Donald Crisp, Margaret Lindsay

Distributed By MGM/UA Home Video M301313

KITTY FOYLE

D: Sam Wood — 105 m

NR | ROM DMA | 1940 | B&W

7 Very high quality soap opera that was a Best Picture Nominee (plus 4 others) and gave Ginger Rogers her first opportunity to act in a dramatic role... and she did too, she won Best Actress Oscar. She plays an ordinary working girl, a secretary, who becomes the wife of a rich socialite (Morgan). But, she doesn't fit in with his circle of friends so he dumps her to marry another Philadelphia aristocrat. A noble but poor doctor (Craig) falls deeply for her and asks her to marry him, just then her wealthy first husband comes back to her. Who shall she choose? This was very much a liberated woman's movie of its age. Still not too bad today.

Sex / Nud / Viol / Lang / AdSit

A: Ginger Rogers, Dennis Morgan, James Craig, Eduardo Ciannelli, Gladys Cooper

© TURNER HOME ENTERTAINMENT 6204

LAST TIME I SAW PARIS, THE

D: Richard Brooks — 116 m

NR | ROM | 1954 | COLOR

6 F. Scott Fitzgerald's classic short story of tragic love and disillusionment, "Babylon Revisited," is updated to post-WWII. Van Johnson is a young army reporter who meets Donna Reed in Paris. She takes him back to Texas to meet her family. However, Johnson has met her sister before and their romance begins again and they are married. His career begins to fall apart and he begins to drink. Their marriage begins to crumble. High quality, slick soap opera with sympathetic performances by all, particularly by Donna Reed.

Sex / Nud / Viol / Lang / AdSit

A: Elizabeth Taylor, Van Johnson, Donna Reed, Walter Pidgeon, Eva Gabor, Roger Moore

Distributed By MGM/UA Home Video M202378

LETTER FROM AN UNKNOWN WOMAN

D: Max Ophuls — 87 m

NR | ROM | 1948 | B&W

8 Exquisite, but sad romantic portrait of obsession and unrequited love. Throughout her entire life, Joan Fontaine pursues her obsession for a musician whose life is filled with adoring females, and who literally doesn't know that she is alive. She has forsaken one proposal of marriage for him, deserted her husband for him, and did have one romantic interlude with him - which he forgot - but from which she bore his son. Loving photography, lush settings and music, and romantic dialogue. Beautiful.

Sex / Nud / Viol / Lang / AdSit

A: Joan Fontaine, Louis Jourdan, Mady Christians, Marcel Journet, Art Smith

© REPUBLIC PICTURES HOME VIDEO 2330

LILI

D: Charles Walters — 87 m

G | ROM MUS | 1953 | COLOR

9 Charming and utterly delightful musical for both young and old alike. Leslie Caron is wonderful as a naive and lonely sixteen-year-old French orphan who one day talked to the puppets in a small traveling circus. She proved to be so enchanting and popular that the embittered and crippled puppeteer hired her. She soon falls in love with a magician but is heartbroken to learn that he is already married. The puppeteer has fallen in love with her, but he is so jealous and bitter that she does not know and thinks that he is a cruel man. He recognizes what he has done and through her friends, the puppets, he wins her back. Oscar-winning music includes the song "Hi Lili, Hi Lili, Hi Low." Enchanting!

Sex / Nud / Viol / Lang / AdSit

A: Leslie Caron, Mel Ferrer, Zsa Zsa Gabor, Jean-Pierre Aumont, Kurt Kasznar, Amanda Blake

Distributed By MGM/UA Home Video M600310

LITTLE MINISTER, THE

D: Richard Wallace — 110 m

NR | ROM | 1934 | B&W

7 Charming story based upon a novel by the creator of Peter Pan. This is the story of a very proper Scottish minister who comes to a small 19th-century Scottish town and slowly wins the respect of the townsfolk. Then he very nearly loses it when he becomes enraptured with a girl who everyone in the town believes to be a gypsy (Katharine Hepburn in one of her earliest roles). His new ministry is in serious peril until her true identity becomes known. A satisfying romance that is not just for Hepburn fans.

Sex / Nud / Viol / Lang / AdSit

A: Katharine Hepburn, John Beal, Donald Crisp, Andy Clyde, Beryl Mercer

© TURNER HOME ENTERTAINMENT 2009

LOVE IS A MANY SPLENDORED THING

D: Henry King — 102 m

NR | ROM | 1955 | COLOR

7 Extremely romantic and moving soap opera, set during the Korean War. Winner of three Oscars and nominated for Best Picture. Holden is a married war correspondent sent to cover the Korean War. Jennifer Jones is a beautiful Eurasian doctor. The two meet and fall desperately in love, but their love affair is doomed from the start. They are tormented because he is married, but they are also separated by the war and by racial prejudice. This is a moving and very romantic love story and it was extremely popular upon its release.

Sex / Nud / Viol / Lang / AdSit

A: Jennifer Jones, William Holden, Isobel Elsom, Jorja Curtright, Richard Loo

© FOXVIDEO 1039

MAGNIFICENT OBSESSION

D: Douglas Sirk — 108 m

NR | ROM DMA | 1954 | COLOR

8 Magnificent soapbox tearjerker! Hudson plays a reckless playboy who indirectly blinds Wyman (Oscar-nominated) in an auto accident. Torn by guilt, he feels compelled to find a way to restore her vision. He restructures his entire life, becomes a skilled surgeon, and is finally granted the opportunity to perform the miracle. And, Wyman eventually falls in love with the selfless doctor who is working so hard to help her. This is a remake that remains true to the original 1935 version.

Sex / Nud / Viol / Lang / AdSit

A: Jane Wyman, Rock Hudson, Barbara Rush, Otto Kruger, Agnes Moorehead, Gregg Palmer

© MCA/UNIVERSAL HOME VIDEO, INC. 80151

NOW, VOYAGER

D: Irving Rapper — 118 m

NR | ROM DMA | 1942 | B&W

9 Masterful tearjerking. Classic romance. Bette Davis plays an extremely shy and disturbed spinster, tormented by a mother who never wanted her. After a stay at psychiatrist Rains's clinic, she gains new confidence and goes on a sea cruise, where she discovers love but with an unhappily married man (Henreid). After returning to land, she revisits Rains and discovers Henreid's daughter there suffering from rejection by her mother. Davis mothers his daughter and conducts a secret love with Heinreid, too. Unforgettable. Contains the now-famous cigarette lighting sequence.

Sex / Nud / Viol / Lang / AdSit

A: Bette Davis, Paul Henreid, Claude Rains, Gladys Cooper, Janis Wilson, Bonita Granville

Distributed By MGM/UA Home Video M301316

PLACE IN THE SUN, A

D: George Stevens 120 m

NR | ROM DMA | 1951 | B&W | Sex | Nud | Viol | Lang | AdSit

9 One of the powerhouse films of the early '50s. Montgomery Clift is a poor boy who has come to work at his rich uncle's plant. He meets and seduces dowdy Shelly Winters, but falls madly in love with beautiful and wealthy Liz Taylor. Sparks fly and they plan to marry, but just then Winters announces that she is pregnant. She now stands between him and everything he ever dreamed. While he plots to drown her, he changes his mind at the last minute. Still, the boat tips over, she is drowned and he is tried for murder. This film took home 6 Oscars then and it hasn't lost much of its impact over time.

A: Montgomery Clift, Elizabeth Taylor, Shelley Winters, Raymond Burr, Keefe Braselle, Anne Revere

© PARAMOUNT HOME VIDEO 5815

PORTRAIT OF JENNIE

D: William Dieterle 86 m

NR | ROM FAN | 1948 | B&W | Sex | Nud | Viol | Lang | AdSit

8 Hauntingly romantic, with a very subtle eeriness. Joseph Cotten is a penniless artist, adrift and struggling for artistic inspiration. One day in New York's Central Park, he meets Jennie. Jennie is a very young and beautiful but very strange girl. She is innocent and charming, but she also speaks of things that are from another time. The next time he meets her, and each succeeding time, Jennie becomes steadily and mysteriously older. It is then that he begins to suspect that he may have fallen in love with the wandering spirit of a dead girl. Lush and very romantic production. A haunting and beautiful fantasy.

A: Jennifer Jones, Joseph Cotten, Ethel Barrymore, Lillian Gish, David Wayne

© CBS/FOX VIDEO 8037

QUEEN CHRISTINA

D: Rouben Mamoulian 100 m

NR | ROM DMA | 1933 | B&W | Sex | Nud | Viol | Lang | AdSit

8 The lovely 17th-century Queen of Sweden, Christina (Garbo), shocked all of Europe when she gave up her throne for love. This is a fictionalized account of that event. Don Antonio (Gilbert) is sent by the King of Spain to arrange his marriage to Christiana. Tormented by the prospect of a political marriage, she escapes to an inn dressed as a man and there accidentally meets Gilbert. She is quickly taken by him, reveals her true self and they begin a passionate affair. Garbo and Gilbert were off-screen lovers as well and their screen chemistry has made this a romantic favorite.

A: Greta Garbo, John Gilbert, Ian Keith, Lewis Stone, C. Aubrey Smith, Gustav Von Seyffertiz

Distributed By MGM/UA Home Video M300531

RANDOM HARVEST

D: Mervyn LeRoy 127 m

NR | ROM DMA | 1942 | B&W | Sex | Nud | Viol | Lang | AdSit

8 Deeply moving and well-done love story. 7 Oscar nominations. Ronald Colman is a WWI veteran who was hurt and is suffering from amnesia. He meets and falls in love with Greer Garson. They marry, have a child and are happy. He becomes a writer and goes to London to sell a story. However, while there he is struck by a car and his long ago memories flood back, but the last three years are now lost. Garson finds him but, on advice of the doctor, does not tell him who she is and what they were. Instead, she becomes his secretary and they fall in love all over again. An excellent movie that requires a box of tissues.

A: Greer Garson, Ronald Colman, Philip Dorn, Susan Peters, Henry Travers, Reginald Owen

Distributed By MGM/UA Home Video M300961

REBECCA

D: Alfred Hitchcock 132 m

NR | ROM MYS | 1940 | B&W | Sex | Nud | Viol | Lang | AdSit

9 Compelling blend of romance and mystery. Winner of Oscars for Best Picture and Cinematography, plus six other nominations. This Hitchcock masterpiece is a rich tapestry of images. Naively innocent Joan Fontaine falls deeply in love with and marries a dashing aristocrat (Olivier). She returns with him to his huge estate, but never feels at home there. She is haunted at every turn by the memory of his first wife, who died under mysterious circumstances, and she is taunted by the mysterious housekeeper. Untold secrets must be unraveled before they can be free of the past. Excellent.

A: Joan Fontaine, Laurence Olivier, George Sanders, Judith Anderson, Nigel Bruce, Reginald Denny

© CBS/FOX VIDEO 8012

RED DUST

D: Victor Fleming 83 m

NR | ROM DMA | 1932 | B&W | Sex | Nud | Viol | Lang | AdSit

8 Hot-blooded classic! Almost too steamy for the box office in the '30s. A man (Gable) running a rubber plantation in Indochina falls for an engineer's wife (Astor). At the same time he, is carrying on an affair with a shady lady (Harlow) who has a heart of gold but is on the run from the authorities. Although torn between the pair, he returns to the arms of his bawdy girlfriend. The outstanding performances of the cast are what makes this film a true classic. Remade in 1950 as CONGO MAISIE and in 1954 as MOGAMBO. Full of humor, spirit and hot love in the jungle.

A: Clark Gable, Jean Harlow, Mary Astor, Donald Crisp, Gene Raymond, Tully Marshall

Distributed By MGM/UA Home Video M300560

RED SHOES, THE

D: Michael Powell 136 m

NR | ROM MUS CLD | 1948 | COLOR | Sex | Nud | Viol | Lang | AdSit

8 Opulent, grandly romantic and very popular, especially with young girls. A beautiful young ballerina (Shearer) is torn. She is in love with a composer (Goring), but the ballet company's heartless director (Walbrook) does not approve. The conflict between her love of dance and her love for a man is paralleled by the dance she is most famous for - "Dance of the Red Shoes" - which was adapted from the Hans Christian Anderson fairy tale about bewitched shoes that nearly dance the wearer to death. This very popular musical is sure to have inspired many young dancers. Nominated for 5 Oscars, including Best Picture. Followed by THE TALES OF HOFFMAN.

A: Moira Shearer, Emeric Pressburger, Anton Walbrook, Robert Helpmann, Marius Goring, Leonide Massine

© PARAMOUNT HOME VIDEO 12572

ROMANCE IN MANHATTAN

D: Stephen Roberts 78 m

NR | ROM COM | 1934 | B&W | Sex | Nud | Viol | Lang | AdSit

6 A sweet charmer! Francis Lederer is an illegal alien and a scab taxi driver in New York during a strike. He is just scraping by. A beautiful chorus girl (Rogers) is charmed by his enthusiastic optimism, takes pity on him, becomes his friend, lets him camp out on the roof of her apartment building and the pair fall in love. A sweet love story filled with charm and comedy. Lederer really steals the show with his funny portrayal of a man totally unfamiliar with his surroundings, sensitive and searching for his dream.

A: Ginger Rogers, Francis Lederer, J. Farrell MacDonald, Arthur Hohl, Sidney Toler

© TURNER HOME ENTERTAINMENT 6207

ROMAN HOLIDAY

D: William Wyler 118 m

NR | ROM | 1953 | B&W | Sex | Nud | Viol | Lang | AdSit

9 Bittersweet romantic classic! A beautiful young princess (Hepburn) has an overpowering desire to taste the common life, so she escapes her daily royal trappings to wander about Rome incognito during a tour in Europe. However, there she meets a reporter (Peck), who pretends not to know her true identity. He is hoping for the ultimate story and he gets it. They fall in love. Still, they both know that their day in the sun can not continue. Nominated for nine Oscars, this spectacular classic incorporates charm, wit and humor with picturesque settings and a stellar cast.

A: Gregory Peck, Audrey Hepburn, Eddie Albert, Tullio Carminati

© PARAMOUNT HOME VIDEO 6204

ROYAL WEDDING

D: Stanley Donen 93 m

NR | ROM MUS | 1951 | COLOR | Sex | Nud | Viol | Lang | AdSit

6 Fancy footwork abounds in this light-hearted musical! Brother and sister dance team Astaire and Powell travel to London to perform during Princess Elizabeth II's royal wedding to Prince Phillip. Each finds true love as the royal couple tie the knot, Astaire with Churchill and Powell with English nobleman Lawford. Included in this pleasurable musical is Astaire's now famous walk on the ceiling and his dance with a hat rack.

A: Fred Astaire, Jane Powell, Keenan Wynn, Peter Lawford, Sarah Churchill

Distributed By MGM/UA Home Video M600083

SABRINA

D: Billy Wilder 113 m

NR | ROM COM | 1954 | B&W | Sex | Nud | Viol | Lang | AdSit

9 Audrey Hepburn is magical in this effervescent romance! A chauffeur's daughter (Hepburn) returns home from an education in Paris - beautiful, refined and all grown up. She arrives at the estate where her father works, to find that two rich brothers (Bogart and Holden) are understandably attracted to her. At first, she is attracted to playboy Holden's charming ways, but older brother Bogart proves to be more stable. A spicy love triangle develops as Bogart turns up the heat. Will Bogart save her from his flaky brother? Glamorous and romantic!

A: Humphrey Bogart, Audrey Hepburn, William Holden, Martha Hyer, John Williams, Nancy Kulp

© PARAMOUNT HOME VIDEO 5402

SEPTEMBER AFFAIR

D: William Dieterle 105 m

NR | ROM DMA | 1950 | B&W | Sex | Nud | Viol | Lang | AdSit

7 A tale of forbidden romance. An unhappily married man (Cotten) and a pianist (Fontaine), overly-dedicated to her career, meet while in Naples and fall desperately in love. Their doomed affair is given an unexpected chance when they miss their sight-seeing plane, it crashes, and both of them are reported as being missing. However, their spontaneous love affair and happiness are overshadowed by the obligations they have both run away from. Walter Huston rerecorded the famous title song. This is a well-made love story that refrains from being too mushy.

A: Joseph Cotten, Joan Fontaine, Francoise Rosay, Jessica Tandy, Robert Arthur

© PARAMOUNT HOME VIDEO 5012

OLDIES

SHEIK, THE

D: George Melford 79 m

NR ROM 1921 B&W

Sex Nud Viol Lang AdSit

6 It was a very different world when Rudolph Valentino created a national phenomenon with this picture. The moguls predicted this would be a big flop. Instead women lined up in unprecedented numbers to watch Ahmed, a Saharan Arab chieftain, charm Lady Diana Mayo, a sophisticated English woman, with his raw sensuality. He wins her heart and also then rides to her rescue when she is captured by rival a tribesman. What was red hot then, is pretty hokey now, but it is still fun and educational, too. The film was blatantly racist and condescending.

A: Rudolph Valentino, Agnes Ayres, Adolphe Menjou, Walter Long, Lucien Littlefield, George Waggner

© PARAMOUNT HOME VIDEO 2680

STRAWBERRY BLONDE, THE

D: Raoul Walsh 100 m

NR ROM COM 1941 B&W

Sex Nud Viol Lang AdSit

8 Sentimentally set in the Gay 90s, this is a warm and delightful story about a struggling mail-order dentist (Cagney) desperately in love with a beautiful strawberry blond (Hayworth). Unfortunately for him, she is more taken with an up-and-coming financier (Carson) and Cagney gets stuck spending his time with her friend, a spunky suffragette and nurse (de Havilland), who he eventually marries -- but he never forgets his first love. It is ten years later and Cagney has gone to prison after taking the rap for Carson. He is now savoring his opportunity to take revenge, when he witnesses Carson being henpecked by Hayworth. He discovers that he has had the perfect wife all along.

A: James Cagney, Olivia de Havilland, Rita Hayworth, Alan Hale, Jack Carson, George Tobias

Distributed By MGM/UA Home Video M600881

SUMMERTIME

D: David Lean 99 m

NR ROM DMA 1955 B&W

Sex Nud Viol Lang AdSit

9 Lavish and romantic, set in the beautiful city of Venice. Hepburn is a very lonely spinster on a vacation. There, she allows herself to be carried away with the city and visits an antique shop where falls in love with the owner (Brazzi). Unfortunately, Brazzi is married, however unhappily, so the two share a tender romance anyway. Hepburn's beauty emerges under the glow of her new love affair. She decides to take a huge chance, even though she knows she cannot win. A warm, sensitive heartbreaker. Hepburn's sentimental performance is, as always, above par - Oscar nominated. Also nominated for Direction.

A: Katharine Hepburn, Rossano Brazzi, Isa Miranda, Darren McGavin, Mari Aldon, Andre Morell

© HOME VISION SUM 040

TALE OF TWO CITIES, A

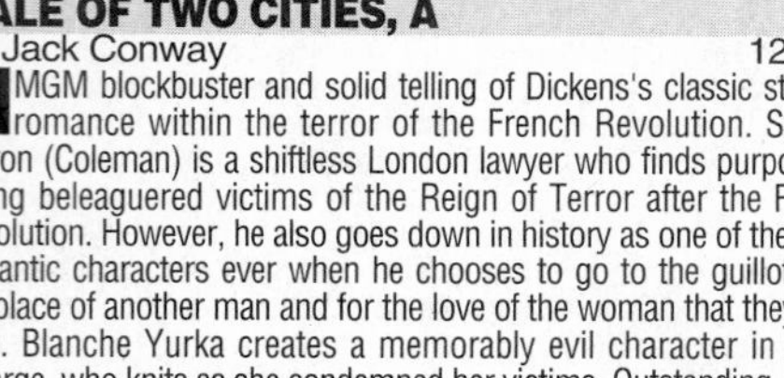

D: Jack Conway 128 m

NR ROM DMA 1935 B&W

Sex Nud Viol Lang AdSit

9 MGM blockbuster and solid telling of Dickens's classic story of romance within the terror of the French Revolution. Sydney Carron (Coleman) is a shiftless London lawyer who finds purpose by aiding beleaguered victims of the Reign of Terror after the French Revolution. However, he also goes down in history as one of the most romantic characters ever when he chooses to go to the guillotine in the place of another man and for the love of the woman that they both love. Blanche Yurka creates a memorably evil character in Mme. Defarge, who knits as she condemned her victims. Outstanding.

A: Ronald Colman, Elizabeth Allan, Basil Rathbone, Edna May Oliver, Blanche Yurka, Reginald Owen

Distributed By MGM/UA Home Video M600078

THAT HAMILTON WOMAN

D: Alexander Korda 125 m

NR ROM DMA 1941 B&W

Sex Nud Viol Lang AdSit

9 Achingly romantic story - all the more so because it is true. It also was one of the biggest scandals of the early 19th century - the forbidden love affair between the famous British Naval Commander Lord Nelson (Olivier) and Lady Hamilton (Leigh). She was beautiful, intelligent and raised herself up from poverty to become the wife of an ambassador. But she loved Nelson and pursued every opportunity to promote his interests. She was all that any man could want. Nelson loved her passionately but their love would destroy her. Reported to be Churchill's favorite movie.

A: Laurence Olivier, Vivien Leigh, Henry Wilcoxon, Gladys Cooper, Alan Mowbray, Sara Allgood

© HBO VIDEO 90662

THAT NIGHT

D: Craig Bolotin 89 m

PG-13 ROM DMA 89 COLOR

Sex Nud Viol Lang AdSit

7 Alice (Eliza Dusku) is a ten-year-old girl who lives across the street from 17-year-old Cheryl (Juliette Lewis) in a comfortable suburban neighborhood in 1961 New Jersey. Alice is trying to grow up and Cheryl is her idol. Cheryl is everything she wants to be. All the boys want her. She is a wild spirit and, every Friday after school, she buys a new scarf at Woolworths. Cheryl is in love with a boy from the other side of the tracks and he's a greaser. He wears the wrong clothes, runs with a tough crowd, but he loves her. After one fateful night, and after Cheryl is forbidden to see him again, Alice takes it upon herself to see that the two lovers stay together.

A: C. Thomas Howell, Juliette Lewis, Helen Shaver, Eliza Dushku, John Dossett, J. Smith Cameron

© WARNER HOME VIDEO 13165

THEY LIVE BY NIGHT

D: Nicholas Ray 95 m

NR ROM 1949 B&W

Sex Nud Viol Lang AdSit

7 Involving film noir regarded by some as a classic. Set in the 1930s, a naive young thief is sent to prison. He joins two hardened criminals in an escape. Wounded in the escape, he is nursed back to health by an equally naive young girl and they fall in love. Now, truly desperate to escape his past, they are trapped by it even more. They are on the run, with the police after them. That theme - two young people lost in a world where they don't know, or can't play, by the rules - is one which would reappear again later in REBEL WITHOUT A CAUSE.

A: Cathy O'Donnell, Farley Granger, Howard da Silva, Jay C. Flippen, Helen Craig, Will Wright

© HOLLYWOOD HOME THEATRE

THREE COMRADES

D: Frank Borzage 98 m

NR ROM DMA 1938 B&W

Sex Nud Viol Lang AdSit

9 The best-selling romantic novel, set in a decimated post-WWI Germany, was turned into a beautifully poignant film. Three lifelong friends return home from the trenches of France to an inflated economy where money is carried in wheelbarrows and hope is non-existant. Still, they pool their money to set up an auto repair shop through which they meet a beautiful and high-spirited Englishwoman dying of tuberculosis. She falls in love with one of them but refuses to marry him because she will die. They convince her otherwise but her lover is killed in the street riots. Beautiful, classy and touching romancer.

A: Robert Taylor, Margaret Sullavan, Franchot Tone, Robert Young, Guy Kibbee, Lionel Atwill

Distributed By MGM/UA Home Video 202841

TO CATCH A THIEF

D: Alfred Hitchcock 103 m

NR ROM COM 1955 COLOR

Sex Nud Viol Lang AdSit

8 Lightweight piece of fluff with two of the screen's most beautiful stars. Suave Cary is a former jewel thief who is now in retirement at the French Riviera. However, his life is being complicated by a string of burglaries, done in a manner which matches his old style exactly and for which he is being blamed. He must catch the thief to clear his name and he uses Grace Kelly's mother's jewels to be the honey for his trap. Good suspensor, but low-key. The emphasis is on witty dialogue and charm from its cast, plus some very stylish production. Three Oscar nominations.

A: Cary Grant, Grace Kelly, Brigitte Auber, Jessie Royce Landis, John Williams, Charles Vanel

© PARAMOUNT HOME VIDEO 6308

WATERLOO BRIDGE

D: Mervyn LeRoy 109 m

NR ROM DMA 1940 B&W

Sex Nud Viol Lang AdSit

9 Very well made, sentimental and a classic tearjerker. Vivien Leigh is a very sweet but naive young ballerina in London at the outset of WWI. She meets and immediately falls in love with a handsome Army captain who is soon sent off to war. She misses a dance performance so that she can see him off and is fired from her job. Then she learns (falsely) that he has been killed. She is desperate, distraught and suicidal, so she becomes a prostitute to support herself. However, one day, as she is soliciting business from returning soldiers, they find each other again.

A: Vivien Leigh, Robert Taylor, Lucile Watson, Virginia Field, C. Aubrey Smith, Maria Ouspenskaya

Distributed By MGM/UA Home Video M300494

WEDDING MARCH, THE

D: Erich von Stroheim 113 m

NR ROM 1928 B&W

Sex Nud Viol Lang AdSit

9 Film fans take note - this is a silent film masterpiece from the German legend Erich von Stroheim, who directed and also starred in it. Set in Vienna prior to WWI, a roguish Prince agrees to a marriage of convenience but falls in love with a beautiful poor girl, seducing her by the side of the Danube as the apple blossoms fall. But, their's is a doomed love that can never be. Interestingly, there are an innovative couple of minutes of two-color film included. Special note: if the story seems short and incomplete - it is. It is really only half of the original story because the other half has been lost.

A: Fay Wray, Erich von Stroheim, ZaSu Pitts, Matthew Betz

© PARAMOUNT HOME VIDEO 39501

WUTHERING HEIGHTS

D: William Wyler 104 m

NR ROM DMA 1939 B&W

Sex Nud Viol Lang AdSit

10 The screen's greatest love story. Heathcliff (Olivier) is an abandoned Gypsy boy who is taken in by a 19th-century English family, becoming their stableboy. He and Cathy (Oberon), the family's spoiled young daughter, become childhood friends and later passionate but star-crossed lovers. When Cathy marries rich Edgar Linton (Niven), in spite of her love for Heathcliff, he leaves, returning later, moderately wealthy, and marries Linton's naive sister for revenge. Oberon is captivatingly beautiful. She and Olivier make heart-stirring screen magic.

A: Laurence Olivier, Merle Oberon, David Niven, Flora Robson, Geraldine Fitzgerald, Donald Crisp

© HBO VIDEO 90729

Science Fiction

WAR OF THE WORLDS, THE

D: Byron Haskin — 85 m

G · SF SUS · 1953 · COLOR

Sex / Nud / ✓ Viol / Lang / AdSit

8 Excellent science fiction that received an Oscar for Special Effects. H.G. Wells's classic novel was first broadcast on the radio by Orson Welles. It was so plausible that people believed it. He literally terrorized the nation with it. This movie version was updated only slightly. Earth is being invaded by hordes of eerie hovering space vehicles which mindlessly spew death from a monstrous heat ray that emanates from a goose-necked "head" protruding from the body of each vehicle. All efforts by earthlings to reason with them or destroy them fail. Intelligent fast-paced drama. This is not a "monster" movie.

A: Gene Barry, Ann Robinson, Les Tremayne, Jack Kruschen, Robert Cornthwaite, Cedric Hardwicke

© PARAMOUNT HOME VIDEO 5303

DAY THE EARTH STOOD STILL, THE

D: Robert Wise — 92 m

G · SF DMA · 1951 · B&W

Sex / Nud / Viol / Lang / ✓ AdSit

9 This first-rate intelligent science fiction piece was a landmark film. It was the first in which the alien from outer space (Michael Rennie) is a benevolent being, whose sole purpose is to warn Earth of impending catastrophe if it continues on its violent path. However, Rennie and his massive robot companion are met with suspicion and hostility by the people of earth. Even though the special effects are dated now, the subject matter is topical. People have not likely changed all that much. This is a powerful film because its ideas are credible and thought provoking.

A: Michael Rennie, Patricia Neal, Hugh Marlowe, Sam Jaffe, Billy Gray, Frances Bavier

© FOXVIDEO 1011

INVISIBLE MAN, THE

D: James Whale — 71 m

NR · SF SUS · 1933 · B&W

Sex / Nud / Viol / Lang / AdSit

9 Excellent. H.G. Welles's classic story is beautifully done. A scientist has created a chemical formula for invisibility. Even though he has yet to create a counter-agent for the drug, he uses himself as a subject to test its effectiveness. He at first enjoys the novelty of the experience and there are several scenes which are quite funny. But soon things get serious as the ugly side effects begin to show themselves. He slowly becomes an insane megalomaniac. Good special effects. Claude Rains made his screen debut in this film, although no one actually sees him until the very end.

A: Claude Rains, Gloria Stuart, Una O'Connor, Henry Travers, E.E. Clive, Dwight Frye

© MCA/UNIVERSAL HOME VIDEO, INC. 80398

IT CAME FROM BENEATH THE SEA

D: Robert Gordon — 80 m

NR · SF CLD · 1955 · B&W

Sex / Nud / Viol / Lang / AdSit

6 This is one of the many "monster" movies that were typical in the '50s, but this science fiction piece has become a minor classic, primarily because of its special effects. Repeated nuclear explosions in the Pacific Ocean stir up a giant octopus from the depths. Enraged and hungry, it begins a reign of terror on the West Coast and works his way toward San Francisco. Only a Navy submarine stands in his way. Quite good for its genre.

A: Faith Domergue, Kenneth Tobey, Ian Keith, Donald Curtis, Dean Maddox, Jr.

© COLUMBIA TRISTAR HOME VIDEO 60491

METROPOLIS

D: Fritz Lang — 120 m

NR · SF · 1926 · B&W

Sex / Nud / Viol / Lang / AdSit

7 Using some of the most sophisticated film techniques available at the time (1926), this silent classic made technical predictions of a futuristic and mechanized city in 2026 that were pretty much right on the mark. It was a very influential film. The plot, however, about a mad scientist who uses a beautiful robot to help provoke a group of workers into a revolt, is pretty silly. There are other versions available, one with as much as a half hour removed from it and a pop-music soundtrack added.

A: Brigitte Helm, Alfred Abel, Rudolf Klein-Rogge, Gustav Froelich, Fritz Rasp

© GOODTIMES 5079

THEM

D: Gordon Douglas — 93 m

NR · SF SUS · 1954 · B&W

Sex / Nud / ✓ Viol / Lang / AdSit

7 This is a well-crafted science fiction monster classic from the early '50s. A young, terrified girl is discovered in the destroyed remains of trailer home out in the New Mexico desert. From their investigation, two scientists discover that recent atomic testing has mutated a race of giant ants. They and FBI agent James Arness, trace the ants to their nest and their queen in the sewers of L.A. This is a actually a thoughtful film which gives its subject serious treatment. Time is taken to make the premise credible and believable. And, it also has some scenes which will create genuine fear. Good special effects, too.

A: James Whitmore, Edmund Gwenn, Joan Weldon, James Arness, Onslow Stevens, Chris Drake

© WARNER HOME VIDEO 11191

Suspense

13 RUE MADELEINE

D: Henry Hathaway — 95 m

NR · SUS WAR · 1946 · B&W

Sex / Nud / Viol / Lang / ✓ AdSit

6 Fairly decent WWII espionage thriller that was based upon actual events. James Cagney stars as an O.S.S. (Army intelligence group - Office of Special Services) chief charged with the training of a group of agents. They are supposed to infiltrate France to discover the location of Nazi rocket sites in Europe before the Allied D-Day invasion. However, Cagney's group is infiltrated by a Nazi spy, and one of his agents is killed. So, Cagney must go on the mission himself.

A: James Cagney, Annabella, Richard Conte, Frank Latimore, Walter Abel, Sam Jaffe

© CBS/FOX VIDEO 1422

39 STEPS, THE

D: Alfred Hitchcock — 80 m

NR · SUS ROM · 1935 · B&W

Sex / Nud / Viol / Lang / ✓ AdSit

8 Hitchcock's first masterpiece. Just before dying, a female British agent (Mannheim) gives a visiting Canadian (Donat) a map of Scotland and tells him about a spy ring run by a man missing part of a finger. Donat finds himself pursued both by the police, who want him for her murder, and by the spies, who want to shut him up. His only chance is to follow the only clue he has and go to Scotland. On the way, he avoids detection by train police by kissing a strange woman (Carroll). Later, he meets her again and is handcuffed to her by the spies. She despises him but by morning, they are in love and she is helping him. Still very involving. Film fans will rate it much higher.

A: Robert Donat, Madeleine Carroll, Lucie Mannheim, Peggy Ashcroft, Godfrey Tearle, John Laurie

© UNITED AMERICAN VIDEO CORP. 0008

49TH PARALLEL

D: Michael Powell — 122 m

NR · SUS ACT · 1941 · B&W

Sex / Nud / ✓ Viol / Lang / ✓ AdSit

8 Production on this film began just prior to, but it was not completed until after, WWII had begun. It was very highly regarded by the critics of the day and it was nominated for three Oscars, winning for Best Original Story. In 1940, a German U-boat is sunk just off the northern coast of Canada in Hudson's Bay, but six of the crew made it to shore. The ruthless party is desperate to return home and begins a reign of terror and murder in their flight across Canada. At times it is very realistic and suspenseful, at others it becomes simplistic and melodramatic. Still, it is highly evocative of those times.

A: Anton Walbrook, Eric Portman, Leslie Howard, Raymond Massey, Laurence Olivier, Glynis Johns

© UNITED AMERICAN VIDEO CORP. 7022

ABOVE SUSPICION

D: Richard Thorpe — 90 m

NR · SUS ACT · 1943 · B&W

Sex / Nud / Viol / Lang / ✓ AdSit

7 Top-notch espionage thriller. The British secret service asks newlyweds Fred and Joan to do some undercover work while they are on their honeymoon in Paris, just prior to WWII. Their assignment is to try to find a missing allied agent. They quickly find themselves chasing a series of baffling clues and are surrounded by agents on all sides. Even Fred's college pal (Rathbone) is now a Nazi spy, and the Gestapo is hot on their trail, too. Fast-moving and interesting melodrama. Solid adventure flick, spiced with some clever banter between it's two leads to make it even more fun.

A: Joan Crawford, Fred MacMurray, Conrad Veidt, Basil Rathbone, Reginald Owen

Distributed By MGM/UA Home Video M201182

ACROSS THE PACIFIC

D: John Huston 98 m

NR | SUS MYS | 1942 | B&W

Sex ☐ Nud ☐ Viol ◢ Lang ☐ AdSit ◢

7 Excellent, quick-moving wartime espionage thriller. Bogart plays a cynical Army officer who is given a dishonorable discharge just prior to the attack on Pearl Harbor. Now, aboard a freighter to the Orient, he meets a mysterious sociology professor (Greenstreet) who speaks much too highly of Japan, a very quiet Japanese passenger, and a beautiful fashion designer (Astor) on her way to Panama. Who are the spies? And, what is their quarry? Bogart, Astor and Greenstreet are the same three leads who appear in THE MALTESE FALCOLN, don't dare miss that one.

A: Humphrey Bogart, Mary Astor, Sydney Greenstreet, Victor Sen Yung, Keye Luke, Richard Loo

Distributed By MGM/UA Home Video M201853

BERLIN EXPRESS

D: Jacques Tourneur 86 m

NR | SUS DMA | 1948 | B&W

Sex ☐ Nud ☐ Viol ☐ Lang ☐ AdSit ◢

7 A solid thriller set in post-war Germany. American scientist Ryan is on a trainride to Germany, and so is a prominent peace-minded German politician (Paul Lucas). Lucas is the only man the Allies feel has the potential to reunite the war-torn country. However, he is captured by Neo-Nazis. His assistant (Merle Oberon) convinces Ryan and two fellow passengers, a British and a Russian officer, to help her search throughout a bombed-out Frankfurt to find Lucas before he can be killed. The use of actual film footage from a devastated post-war Germany gives the film a startling authenticity. Exciting, tightly scripted thriller.

A: Merle Oberon, Robert Ryan, Charles Karvin, Paul Lukas, Robert Coote

© TURNER HOME ENTERTAINMENT 6195

BEWARE, MY LOVELY

D: Harry Horner 77 m

NR | SUS | 1952 | B&W

Sex ☐ Nud ☐ Viol ◢ Lang ☐ AdSit ◢

7 Darkly suspenseful. Young war widow Ida Lupino hires an apparently simple-minded handyman to clean her floors and do odd jobs. She soon regrets that choice when, one day, he hears her calling the grocery store and thinks she is calling the police to come get him. Panicked, he locks all the doors and windows and stalks her throughout the house. Robert Ryan is menacingly terrifying as a handyman who can fly into psychotic rages one minute and return to his former calm self just as quickly. The terror holds you in its grip right to the end.

A: Ida Lupino, Robert Ryan, Taylor Holmes, Barbara Whiting

© REPUBLIC PICTURES HOME VIDEO 7067

BLUEBEARD

D: Edgar G. Ulmer 72 m

NR | SUS HOR | 1944 | B&W

Sex ☐ Nud ☐ Viol ☐ Lang ☐ AdSit ◢

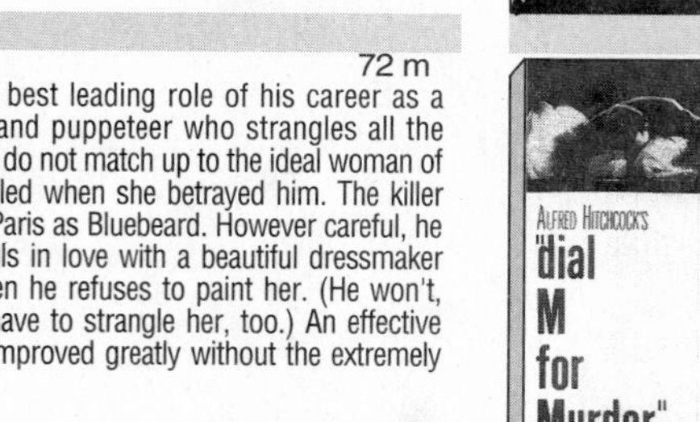

6 John Carradine has the best leading role of his career as a deranged French artist and puppeteer who strangles all the women he paints because they do not match up to the ideal woman of his youth, who he also strangled when she betrayed him. The killer becomes known to a terrified Paris as Bluebeard. However careful, he meets his demise when he falls in love with a beautiful dressmaker who becomes suspicious when he refuses to paint her. (He won't, because if he does - he will have to strangle her, too.) An effective thriller that would have been improved greatly without the extremely distracting sound track.

A: John Carradine, Jean Parker, Niles Asther, Ludwig Stossel, Iris Adrian, Emmett Lynn

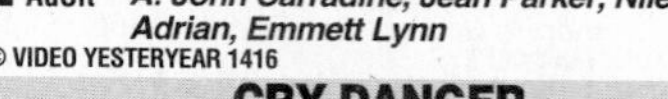

© VIDEO YESTERYEAR 1416

CRY DANGER

D: Robert Parrish 80 m

NR | SUS CRM | 1951 | B&W

Sex ☐ Nud ☐ Viol ◢ Lang ☐ AdSit ◢

8 Excellent, well-made, fast-paced melodrama. Powell is a bookie who is framed and sent to jail, along with his friend, under a life's sentence for a murder and a robbery that they didn't commit. However, Five years later, he gains a release because a crippled man, who hopes to get a share of the $100,000 payroll that was stolen, has given him a phony alibi. Now free, Powell relentlessly pursues the real crooks through the seedy backstreets of L.A. He wants revenge and his friend released. However, that means he has become dangerous and so he is also a marked man.

A: Dick Powell, Rhonda Fleming, Richard Erdman, Regis Toomey, William Conrad

© REPUBLIC PICTURES HOME VIDEO 7130

DARK MIRROR, THE

D: Robert Siodmak 85 m

NR | SUS CRM | 1946 | B&W

Sex ☐ Nud ☐ Viol ☐ Lang ☐ AdSit ◢

8 Creepy, well-made psychological suspensor. Olivia de Havilland plays identical twin sisters who are being analysed by a psychiatrist (Ayres) to determine which is a murderer and which is merely covering for the other. As his investigation proceeds, deep-seated hostilities between the two emerge when both sisters fall for the doctor. Jealousy erupts and he soon discovers that one sister is truly psychotic and she very well might kill him. She even may convince her own sister to commit suicide. But - which one is which? Tension builds slowly and powerfully. Well done.

A: Olivia de Havilland, Lew Ayres, Thomas Mitchell, Richard Long, Charles Evans

© REPUBLIC PICTURES HOME VIDEO 0888

DARK PAST

D: Rudolph Mate 75 m

NR | SUS CRM | 1949 | B&W

Sex ☐ Nud ☐ Viol ☐ Lang ☐ AdSit ◢

8 A desperate and psychotic young killer (Holden), afraid of his own dreams, escapes prison. He, his girlfriend (Foch) and two others break into the home of a psychiatrist (Cobb). They hold him, his family and his house guests all captive. Cobb uses the only weapon he has, his skills, to fight back. He slowly works his way inside his captor's head, trying to understand why he kills and at the same time that he trys to talk him into giving himself up. The more Cobb delves into Holden's DARK PAST, the more vulnerable Holden becomes - until finally he rebels. Involving suspense, with excellent performances.

A: William Holden, Lee J. Cobb, Nina Foch, Adele Jergens, Stephen Dunne

© COLUMBIA TRISTAR HOME VIDEO 60741

DEAD OF NIGHT

D: Alberto Cavalcanti, Charles Crichton 104 m

NR | SUS HOR | 1945 | B&W

Sex ☐ Nud ☐ Viol ◢ Lang ☐ AdSit ■

9 All-time classic masterpiece. This is the granddaddy of many of today's most thoughtful chillers. Mervyn Jones is an architect who is invited to a party hosted by Michael Redgrave in a remote country house. But he is not alone when he arrives there. The others already there are all strangers to each other, however they are not to him. They are all characters appearing in his recurring nightmare. When he tells of this, the others begin to reveal their own nightmares. Five of the eeriest tales of the supernatural ever told now unfold. Time has not dimmed the impact of these stories at all. Really good stuff.

A: Mervyn Johns, Michael Redgrave, Sally Ann Howes, Miles Malleson, Googie Withers, Basil Radford

© CONGRESS VIDEO GROUP 04020

DESPERATE HOURS, THE

D: William Wyler 112 m

NR | SUS DMA CRM | 1955 | B&W

Sex ☐ Nud ☐ Viol ◢ Lang ☐ AdSit ◢

9 Thrilling, taut, classic drama. Three escaped convicts, led by Bogart, break into Fredric March's typical Indiana suburban home and hold him and his family hostage. The three are evading a manhunt and waiting for Bogart's girlfriend to dig up and return with the buried loot. This story was based upon an actual incident and is about the desperate conflict between men who have nothing to lose and a man who has everything to lose. In this nail-biter, March apparently cooperates with the convicts while trying constantly to outsmart them. It is a desperate battle of will and wits. Excellent!

A: Humphrey Bogart, Fredric March, Arthur Kennedy, Martha Scott, Gig Young, Dewey Martin

© PARAMOUNT HOME VIDEO 5509

DIAL M FOR MURDER

D: Alfred Hitchcock 105 m

PG | SUS | 1954 | COLOR

Sex ☐ Nud ☐ Viol ◢ Lang ☐ AdSit ◢

8 Ray Milland is a philandering playboy who fears losing his meal ticket after he discovers that his wealthy wife (Grace Kelly) has found a new lover in Robert Cummings. So, he plots to get rid of her and to inherit her fortune. In his plan, he blackmails a killer into murdering his wife when he is conveniently out of town. But the plan backfires when she kills her attacker instead with a pair of scissors. So Milland switches to Plan B, but that plan disintegrates, too, under the questioning of a savvy police detective (John Williams). Sustained suspense and quite worthy viewing, but this is not Hitchcock's best effort.

A: Grace Kelly, Robert Cummings, Ray Milland, John Williams, Anthony Dawson

© WARNER HOME VIDEO 11156

D.O.A.

D: Rudolph Mate 82 m

NR | SUS MYS | 1950 | B&W

Sex ☐ Nud ☐ Viol ☐ Lang ☐ AdSit ◢

7 Edmond O'Brien is an accountant on vacation in San Francisco, when he discovers that he has been purposely poisoned with radiation and he is now slowly dying. He has 72 hours. Who has killed him, and why? He has to know. He must find his own murderer before time runs out. Neville Brand is terrific as the psychopath who tries to do him in. Spellbinding and fast-paced with good dialogue. Very well done. Remade in 1988 with Dennis Quaid.

A: Edmond O'Brien, Pamela Britton, Luther Adler, Neville Brand, Henry Hart, Virginia Lee

© UNITED AMERICAN VIDEO CORP. 4095

DOUBLE INDEMNITY

D: Billy Wilder 107 m

NR | SUS CRM DMA | 1944 | B&W

Sex ☐ Nud ☐ Viol ☐ Lang ☐ AdSit ■

10 One of the most popular movies of the 1940s and winner of six Oscar nominations, including Best Picture. It is based upon an actual event and became the inspiration for 1981's steamy BODY HEAT. This film has a brilliant script that is filled with suspense and crackling dialogue. MacMurray is a shifty insurance agent who concocts a scheme to help sexy Stanwyck cash in her husband's insurance policy for double its face amount. But - Fred's boss (Robinson) becomes suspicious of her husband's death. The lovers then begin to plot against each other. Definite must-see film.

A: Fred MacMurray, Barbara Stanwyck, Edward G. Robinson, Porter Hall

© MCA/UNIVERSAL HOME VIDEO, INC. 80174

EVIL MIND, THE (AKA THE CLAIRVOYANT)

D: Maurice Elvey — 69 m

NR | SUS | 1935 | B&W

Sex / Nud / Viol / Lang / AdSit

7 Interesting and well done British entry about a phony stage-psychic (Claude Raines in a fine performance) who suddenly realizes his phony predictions are coming true. He successfully predicts a train wreck and a horse race. But when he predicts a mine disaster where 310 men die, his warning is ignored. That is until 310 miners are killed in a panic stampede. He is accused of causing the panic and is tried for murder.

A: Claude Rains, Fay Wray, Mary Clare, Jane Baxter, Ben Field

© VIDEO YESTERYEAR 854

FALLEN IDOL, THE

D: Carol Reed — 92 m

NR | SUS DMA | 1948 | B&W

Sex / Nud / Viol / Lang / ◢ AdSit

8 Superbly crafted film. A small boy, the young son of an ambassador, idolizes the family's butler. The butler is trapped in a very unhappy marriage and is accused of murder when his wife dies a suspicious death. The desperate boy tries to protect his friend from the police by lying. Then, when the boy finds out that it really was an accident and he tries to tell the truth, no one will believe him. This is a story of an adult world that is told entirely from the boy's point of view. Excellent drama, high suspense. Two Oscar nominations.

A: Ralph Richardson, Michele Morgan, Bobby Henrey, Sonia Dresdel, Denis O'Dea, Jack Hawkins

© HOME VISION FAL 060

FOREIGN CORRESPONDENT

D: Alfred Hitchcock — 120 m

NR | SUS MYS | 1940 | B&W

Sex / Nud / Viol / Lang / ◢ AdSit

10 One of Hitchcock's very best, a thrilling masterpiece and one of the best espionage films ever. Joel McCrea stars as an American reporter sent to Europe just prior to World War II to uncover the most provocative stories he can find. He meets a peace activist (Marshall), falls for his daughter (Day) but then becomes fearful that Marshall may also be deeply involved with a Nazi spy ring. He soon gets caught up in a whirlwind of intrigue and double-crosses when a Dutch diplomat with vital information is kidnapped. Breathlessly taut and tremendously entertaining. 6 Oscar nominations.

A: Joel McCrea, Laraine Day, Herbert Marshall, George Sanders, Albert Basserman, Robert Benchley

© WARNER HOME VIDEO 35080

GASLIGHT

D: George Cukor — 114 m

NR | SUS CRM | 1944 | B&W

Sex / Nud / Viol / Lang / ◢ AdSit

8 Eerie classic psycho-thriller. A wealthy, innocent young girl (Bergman) in Victorian London is very vulnerable after her aunt is murdered, so she marries a seemingly wonderful Charles Boyer. Boyer insists that they live in the aunt's house. Poor Ingrid, she doesn't know that it is was Boyer who had killed the aunt in the first place and he is now obsessed with hunting for the aunt's hidden jewelry. However, he needs more time to conduct his searches. He has to get her out of the house, so he very methodically and purposefully seeks to drive Bergman insane. Bergman won her first Oscar. Two other nominations.

A: Ingrid Bergman, Joseph Cotten, Charles Boyer, Dame May Witty, Angela Lansbury, Terry Moore

Distributed By MGM/UA Home Video M400473

GLASS KEY, THE

D: Stuart Heisler — 85 m

NR | SUS ACT | 1942 | B&W

Sex / Nud / ◢ Viol / Lang / ◢ AdSit

8 Excellent, fast-moving Dashiell Hammett story about a likable but crooked politician who is accused of murdering the other candidate's son. Alan Ladd plays the body guard who struggles to save his boss from the frame-up by vicious members of the mob. (Look for a scene where Ladd gets knocked out by a punch from Bendix - it's real). An excellent piece of work that Japanese master Akira Kurosawa claims was the inspiration for his masterstroke: YOJIMBO.

A: Brian Donlevy, Alan Ladd, Veronica Lake, William Bendix, Richard Denning

© MCA/UNIVERSAL HOME VIDEO, INC. 80861

HOTEL RESERVE

D: Lance Comfort — 79 m

NR | SUS | 1944 | B&W

Sex / Nud / Viol / Lang / ◢ AdSit

6 A moody thriller about an innocent Austria medical student who is staying at a hotel on the French Riveria in 1938, just prior to the outbreak of World War II. However, after his film gets mixed up with someone elses at the hotel, the locals have accused him of photographing French military installations and of being a Nazi spy. If he cannot prove his innocence by finding the real spy, he will be deported. So, he must investigate all the guests at his hotel to capture the spy himself. Pretty good spy story, well done.

A: Max Greene, Victor Hanbury, James Mason, Lucie Mannheim, Herbert Lom, Patricia Medina

© TURNER HOME ENTERTAINMENT 6143

IN A LONELY PLACE

D: Nicholas Ray — 93 m

NR | SUS CRM | 1950 | B&W

Sex / Nud / ◢ Viol / Lang / ◢ AdSit

9 Excellent psychological thriller with Bogie in a rare sort of role. Bogart is a screenwriter just back from the war, trying to make a comeback. But, his violent temper and extremely opinionated outbursts have made it difficult for him to regain lost ground. Then he gets thrown a real curve when he is accused of murder. However, his beautiful neighbor gives him a phony alibi, they begin an affair and his career rebounds. But she also now witnesses his violent outbursts and raging jealousy, and she, too, begins to doubt his innocence. Gripping suspense.

A: Humphrey Bogart, Gloria Grahame, Frank Lovejoy, Robert Warwick, Jeff Donnell, Martha Stewart

© COLUMBIA TRISTAR HOME VIDEO 60940

KEEPER OF THE FLAME

D: George Cukor — 100 m

NR | SUS MYS | 1942 | B&W

Sex / Nud / Viol / Lang / AdSit

7 Spencer Tracy is a top reporter who has been assigned to go to a small town to get a good story on a war hero killed in a car accident. Tracy interviews the patriot's reclusive widow (Hepburn) and falls in love with her. However, his continued investigations are also starting to turn up some pretty unsavory facts about her dead husband. He suspects that the guy might really have been a fascist who was hoping to overthrow the government, and Tracy now also suspects that Hepburn was in on it, too. Does he expose her? This was Tracy and Hepburn's second time out together.

A: Spencer Tracy, Katharine Hepburn, Richard Whorf, Margaret Wycherly, Forrest Tucker, Frank Craven

Distributed By MGM/UA Home Video M202347

LEOPARD MAN, THE

D: Jacques Tourneur — 66 m

NR | SUS HOR | 1943 | B&W

Sex / Nud / ◢ Viol / Lang / ◢ AdSit

8 Excellent, moody, low-budget thriller. A black leopard that was used in a publicity stunt escapes in a small New Mexico town. Soon a series of grizzly murders has the town gripped in fear because no one knows if the deaths are caused by the cat or only someone behaving like a cat. There is an overall air of suspense and fear that is pervasive in this movie and it contains a couple of scenes that have to rate among the scariest ever put on film, making this much more than just another horror movie. Especially good for film buffs.

A: Margo, Dennis O'Keefe, Jean Brooks

© NOSTALGIA MERCHANT 8040

LETTER, THE

D: William Wyler — 96 m

NR | SUS DMA | 1940 | B&W

◢ Sex / Nud / Viol / Lang / ■ AdSit

9 Fascinating adaptation of a Somerset Maugham play which works equally well as a top-notch melodrama and as a character study. In the very first scene, Bette Davis empties a revolver into a man. She claims she killed him defending her honor, but her own attorney has his doubts. Then he is approached by the wife of the dead man, who wants money. She has an incriminating letter to the dead man from Davis. It seems, the dead man was Davis's secret lover. Now Davis must retrieve the letter if she is to survive. High suspense and intrigue marks the wait to see if she'll make it. Extremely well done.

A: Bette Davis, Herbert Marshall, James Stephenson, Frieda Inescort, Gale Sondergaard

Distributed By MGM/UA Home Video M301315

LIFEBOAT

D: Alfred Hitchcock — 96 m

NR | SUS DMA | 1944 | B&W

Sex / Nud / Viol / Lang / ◢ AdSit

9 A riveting thriller and a penetrating study in human nature. A diverse group of survivors are adrift together in a single lonely lifeboat during WWII. A freighter was attacked and sunk by a German submarine, which also then sank. The survivors are all from the sunken freighter except for one rescued German, who is the disguised captain of the submarine. All the characters are from very different backgrounds and each character has his own story to tell. This is a fascinating drama that unfolds entirely on that one cramped boat. There were Oscar nominations for both Director Hitchcock and John Steinbeck's Screenplay.

A: Tallulah Bankhead, William Bendix, Walter Slezak, Mary Anderson, John Hodiak, Hume Cronyn

© FOXVIDEO 1393

MAN WHO KNEW TOO MUCH, THE

D: Alfred Hitchcock — 72 m

NR | SUS MYS | 1934 | B&W

Sex / Nud / Viol / Lang / ◢ AdSit

8 Gripping tale of intrigue! While on vacation in Switzerland, a dying undercover agent tells a friend (Banks) of a planned assassination. Then the friend's daughter (Philbeam) is kidnapped to keep her parents from telling the police what they know and they do keep their silence. However, that means that it's going to be entirely up to them to foil the assassination and to find their daughter. This winner was remade by Hitchcock in 1956. Both films are Hitchcock favorites and are suspenseful from start to finish. Peter Lorre shines as the evil and unforgettable villain.

A: Leslie Banks, Edna Best, Peter Lorre, Nova Pilbeam, Frank Vosper

© FOOTHILLS VIDEO

O L D I E S

MATA HARI

D: George Fitzmaurice 90 m

SUS WAR
1932
B&W
◢ Sex
◢ Nud
◢ Viol
☐ Lang
◢ AdSit

8 Classic spy movie! Gorgeous Garbo stars as the infamous exotic dancer and German spy from WWI. She steals French secrets by beguiling two military soldiers (Navarro and Barrymore) in exchange for sex. But she makes the fatal error of falling in love with one of her sources and shooting the other. She is executed for her duplicity. Garbo is wickedly sexy. Watch for her subtle strip-tease (her back is to the camera the entire time). Her hypnotic voice made this a box office smash. Don't believe the script however, because only the name and the execution are accurate.

A: Greta Garbo, Ramon Novarro, Lionel Barrymore, Lewis Stone, Karen Morely, C. Henry Gordon

Distributed By MGM/UA Home Video M202066

MINE OWN EXECUTIONER

D: Anthony Kimmins 103 m

NR
SUS DMA
1948
B&W
☐ Sex
☐ Nud
☐ Viol
☐ Lang
◢ AdSit

7 A thoughtful and involving story about the inner workings of the mind, and the toll it takes on those who try to understand it. Burgess Meredith is a London psychiatrist who accepts as a patient a disturbed, recently returned veteran who, captured by the Japanese during WWII, is having trouble dealing with the aftereffects. Meredith, however, is also having trouble dealing with the pressures of his work. But he appears to be making headway helping the man until his patient breaks, shooting his wife and committing suicide. Based on the novel by Nigel Balchin. Engrossing and only slightly dated.

A: Burgess Meredith, Dulcie Gray, Kieron Moore, John Laurie, Christine Norden, Barbara White

© HOLLYWOOD HOME THEATRE

MURDER, MY SWEET

D: Edward Dmytryk 94 m

NR
SUS MYS ACT
1944
B&W
☐ Sex
☐ Nud
◢ Viol
☐ Lang
◢ AdSit

9 Two cases become one in this gripping mystery. One man, an ex-con (Masurki), hires hard-ball detective Phillip Marlowe (Powell) to find his long lost ex-girlfriend. Another man hires Marlowe to accompany him to buy back a stolen necklace. The two cases merge into one of murder, drugs and corruption as Marlowe is put through the paces to make sense of it all. One of the best films of the '40s, this adaptation of Raymond Chandler's "Farewell, My Lovely" revived Powell's career. Still an riveting thriller today.

A: Dick Powell, Claire Trevor, Anne Shirley, Mike Mazurki, Otto Kruger, Miles Mander

© TURNER HOME ENTERTAINMENT 6132

NARROW MARGIN, THE

D: Richard Fleischer 70 m

NR
SUS ACT
1952
B&W
☐ Sex
☐ Nud
◢ Viol
☐ Lang
◢ AdSit

9 Acclaimed as one of the best "B" movies ever made. Tough New York cop Charles McGraw is unwillingly escorting the widow of a mobster on a speeding passenger train to California, where she is to testify in a big trial. Also onboard are an undercover police woman acting as a decoy and three underworld hitmen. The three don't know which woman is their intended target, but that detail doesn't get in the way. Filmed effectively in very tight quarters. Very popular and filmed on a very small budget, this was one of the most profitable films RKO ever had. Fast paced and well acted. Highly recommended.

A: Charles McGraw, Marie Windsor, Jacqueline White, Queenie Leonard

© TURNER HOME ENTERTAINMENT 6237

NIAGARA

D: Henry Hathaway 89 m

NR
SUS CRM
1953
COLOR
☐ Sex
☐ Nud
☐ Viol
☐ Lang
◢ AdSit

8 Truly interesting suspense film which is fascinating both for its content and for Monroe's performance prior to becoming a superstar. She plays a sexy young woman on her honeymoon. She is plotting (along with her lover) to kill her new husband (Cotten) who has just been released from a veteran's mental hospital. Instead, Cotten discovers their plans, kills the boyfriend and then goes after Monroe. Interestingly, Monroe goes from being a villain to being the sympathetic victim. Quite good.

A: Marilyn Monroe, Joseph Cotten, Jean Peters, Casey Adams, Don Wilson, Richard Allan

© FOXVIDEO 5138

NIGHT NURSE

D: William Wellman 73 m

NR
SUS
1931
B&W
◢ Sex
☐ Nud
◢ Viol
◢ Lang
■ AdSit

8 Taut and gripping, and a risque thriller from the pre-Production Code days. Stawyck is a nurse for two small children in a wealthy but fatherless household. True, the mother is less than wholesome, but things become really bad when Stanwyck discovers a plot to keep the mother drunk while the doctor and the chauffeur murder off the children for their inheritance. Stanwyck has to go to some shady characters to get the help she needs. Good dialogue and sterling performances from some of Hollywood's biggest name actors, just as they were beginning to become known. This film still "works" well today.

A: Barbara Stanwyck, Joan Blondell, Clark Gable

Distributed By MGM/UA Home Video M302069

NIGHT OF THE HUNTER, THE

D: Charles Laughton 94 m

NR
SUS DMA
1955
B&W
☐ Sex
☐ Nud
◢ Viol
☐ Lang
◢ AdSit

7 Bizarre, strangely filmed, surrealistic entry from one-time-only director Charles Laughton. An imprisoned, psychotic, self-proclaimed preacher (Mitchum) learns of a small fortune stolen by his cellmate (Graves) and he is determined to get it. After Graves has been executed and Mitchum is released, Mitchum charms Graves's widow (Winters) into marrying him. Then he murders her and torments the kids who he knows know where the money is. Fearing for their lives, the two kids run away with the stolen money... but with a maniacal Mitchum in pursuit. Very arty, film buffs only.

A: Robert Mitchum, Shelley Winters, Lillian Gish, Peter Graves, Evelyn Varden, Billy Chapin

Distributed By MGM/UA Home Video M301107

NOTORIOUS

D: Alfred Hitchcock 103 m

NR
SUS ROM DMA
1946
B&W
◢ Sex
☐ Nud
◢ Viol
☐ Lang
■ AdSit

10 A brilliant espionage thriller from Hitchcock. Young playgirl Bergman's father has committed suicide after he is discovered to be a Nazi agent. Mortified by the revelation, she allows herself to be recruited by government agent Grant. She is to seduce her way into South American spy Rains's life, but she and Grant have also become tormented lovers. He now despises what she does and she feels deserted by him. When Rains discovers her deception, he slowly begins to poison her. This is an intricate and fast-paced romantic spy story. It is acclaimed by many, as being Hitchcock's best. Highly romantic and uncompromisingly suspenseful.

A: Cary Grant, Ingrid Bergman, Claude Rains, Louis Calhern

© FOXVIDEO 8011

ODD MAN OUT

D: Carol Reed 111 m

NR
SUS DMA
1947
B&W
☐ Sex
☐ Nud
◢ Viol
☐ Lang
◢ AdSit

9 Excellent postwar British filmmaking and a super thriller. James Mason, in one of the finest performances of his life, plays an IRA gunman who is badly wounded in a robbery. He seeks shelter in Belfast's ghettos as the British dragnet closes in around him. For eight extremely tense hours he is pursued by the police and by others with their own motives. There is a bounty hunter, his girl (who wants to share his last hours), a priest who wants to give him last rights, and one of his IRA partners who wants to smuggle him home. This film is only somewhat dated. It is still quite exciting and very tense.

A: James Mason, Kathleen Ryan, Robert Newton, Cyril Cusack, Dan O'Herlihy, Robert Beatty

© PARAMOUNT HOME VIDEO 12575

ONLY ANGELS HAVE WINGS

D: Howard Hawks 121 m

NR
SUS ACT ROM
1939
B&W
☐ Sex
☐ Nud
☐ Viol
☐ Lang
◢ AdSit

8 Highly acclaimed Howard Hawks adventure and character study set in South America. Cary Grant is the chief pilot at a small air freight company struggling to survive against bad economics, bad countryside and bad luck. Their primary contract is to deliver the mail over the rugged Andes Mountains of Peru. Jean Arthur is stuck on him, but all he has time for is the company. Desperate for another pilot, he hires Barthelmess who has a reputation for having crashed a plane years earlier and is married to Hayworth, who is also trying to seduce Grant.

A: Cary Grant, Rita Hayworth, Richard Barthelmess, Jean Arthur, Thomas Mitchell, Allyn Joslyn

© COLUMBIA TRISTAR HOME VIDEO 60946

OUT OF THE PAST

D: Jacques Tourneur 97 m

NR
SUS MYS ACT
1947
B&W
☐ Sex
☐ Nud
◢ Viol
☐ Lang
◢ AdSit

9 Enthralling tale of double-dealing and intrigue in the underworld. Highly acclaimed as quintessential film noir. Robert Mitchum is a worn out private detective who has retired to a small town after having been deceived by his one-time employer's (Douglas) mistress (Greer) in a torrid romance. Douglas has not forgiven him and seeks him out to frame him for murder. Superior intricate plot and dark and moody staging. Remade, with only moderate success, as AGAINST ALL ODDS in 1984.

A: Robert Mitchum, Kirk Douglas, Jane Greer, Rhonda Fleming, Dickie Moore, Steve Brodie

© TURNER HOME ENTERTAINMENT 6053

PHANTOM OF THE OPERA

D: Rupert Julian 79 m

NR
SUS DMA HOR
1925
B&W
☐ Sex
☐ Nud
☐ Viol
☐ Lang
◢ AdSit

7 Lon Chaney Jr. was known as "the man of a thousand faces." No other film typifies his justly held reputation as does this one. He plays a brilliant composer whose face has been horribly disfigured by acid. Now crazed, scorned and vilified by the public, he lives in the catacombs under the Paris Opera, haunting it from the shadows. Hearing a beautiful soprano sing, he becomes infatuated with her and steals her away to his underworld where he will train her to sing. Intrigued by his mask and seizing upon an impulse, she unmasks him in a scene that is still shocking today.

A: Lon Chaney, Jr., Mary Philbin, Norman Kerry, Snitz Edwards, Gibson Gowland

© UNITED AMERICAN VIDEO CORP. 4044

PHANTOM OF THE OPERA

D: Arthur Lubin — 93 m

NR | SUS DMA HOR | 1943 | COLOR

Sex / Nud / Viol / Lang / AdSit

8 Pretty decent remake of the 1925 classic and the first-ever talkie version. This time Claude Rains plays the acid-scarred phantom whose best musical works were stolen and who now lives in the catacombs under the Paris Opera. He becomes infatuated with a beautiful soprano, is determined to make her a star and to get even with those who have wronged him. Plenty of spooky moments, very high production values and excellent acting, but they could have done with less singing.

A: Nelson Eddy, Susanna Foster, Claude Rains, Edgar Barrier, Hume Cronyn, Miles Mander

© MCA/UNIVERSAL HOME VIDEO, INC. 80399

PICKUP ON SOUTH STREET

D: Samuel Fuller — 81 m

NR | SUS CRM ACT | 1953 | B&W

Sex / Nud / Viol / Lang / AdSit

8 Well made and brutal espionage film with a different sort of twist. Widmark plays a cheap pickpocket who dips into Jean Peters purse and comes up with a secret chemical recipe that was enroute to a communist agent. She, however, just thought she was doing a favor for her boyfriend (Kiely), who now demands that she get it back. Thelma Ritter is a stand-out as a neighborhood busy-body and police informer. She directs the federal agents, who were trailing Peters, to Widmark even though he is a friend, but she refuses to tell Kiley, who kills her. Excellent, violent noir-thriller, with lots of twists.

A: Richard Widmark, Jean Peters, Thelma Ritter, Richard Kiley, Murvyn Vye

© FOXVIDEO 1401

PITFALL, THE

D: Andre De Toth — 88 m

NR | SUS DMA | 1948 | B&W

Sex / Nud / Viol / Lang / AdSit

8 Well made, well acted and tense film noir. Dick Powell is an insurance salesman who is happily married to a near-perfect wife (Wyatt) and has a wonderful son. Still, he allows himself to be drawn into a one-night romance with a beautiful young woman (Scott). That's a mistake he wishes he never made because he is now suffering from a lot more than just guilt. He may lose his wife and his job, and he's up to his neck in intrigue, jealousy and murder.

A: Dick Powell, Lizabeth Scott, Jane Wyatt, Raymond Burr, John Litel, Byron Barr

© REPUBLIC PICTURES HOME VIDEO 3217

POSTMAN ALWAYS RINGS TWICE, THE

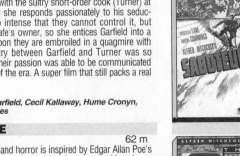

D: Tay Garnett — 113 m

NR | SUS CRM DMA | 1946 | B&W

Sex / Nud / Viol / Lang / AdSit

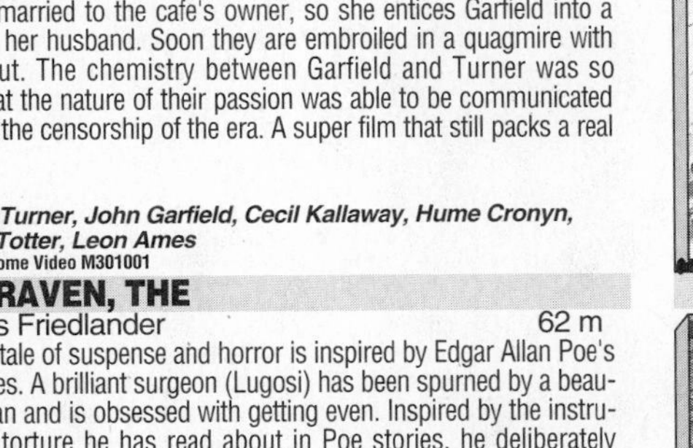

9 This is a classic torrid American tale of lust and murder. A drifter (Garfield) falls in lust with the sultry short-order cook (Turner) at a small roadside cafe, and she responds passionately to his seductions. Their passion is so intense that they cannot control it, but Turner is married to the cafe's owner, so she entices Garfield into a plot to kill her husband. Soon they are embroiled in a quagmire with no way out. The chemistry between Garfield and Turner was so intense that the nature of their passion was able to be communicated in spite of the censorship of the era. A super film that still packs a real punch.

A: Lana Turner, John Garfield, Cecil Kallaway, Hume Cronyn, Audrey Totter, Leon Ames

Distributed By MGM/UA Home Video M301001

RAVEN, THE

D: Louis Friedlander — 62 m

NR | SUS HOR | 1935 | B&W

Sex / Nud / Viol / Lang / AdSit

8 This tale of suspense and horror is inspired by Edgar Allan Poe's stories. A brilliant surgeon (Lugosi) has been spurned by a beautiful woman and is obsessed with getting even. Inspired by the instruments of torture he has read about in Poe stories, he deliberately deforms the face of an escaped killer (Karloff). The doctor simply laughs when the distraught Karloff sees his hideous face, but promises to repair it if Karloff will assist him. However, when Karloff realizes that the doctor will never repair his face, he rescues the girl instead and exacts his own justly heinous revenge on the doctor.

A: Boris Karloff, Bela Lugosi, Irene Ware, Lester Matthews, Samuel S. Hinds

© MCA/UNIVERSAL HOME VIDEO, INC. 80815

REAR WINDOW

D: Alfred Hitchcock — 113 m

PG | SUS MYS COM | 1954 | COLOR

Sex / Nud / Viol / Lang / AdSit

9 Gripping murder mystery from the master. One of Hitchcock's very best efforts. Stewart is a bored magazine photographer who is confined to a wheelchair in his Greenwich Village apartment with a broken leg. To pass the time, he takes up spying on his neighbors through his rear window. He becomes very suspicious of one neighbor (Burr) in particular when his wife is suddenly missing. Stewart even has reason to suspect that Burr is cutting up her body. Clever psychological profile of voyeurism, as well as an entertaining and gripping mystery. Top-notch cast. A masterpiece.

A: James Stewart, Grace Kelly, Wendell Corey, Thelma Ritter, Raymond Burr

© MCA/UNIVERSAL HOME VIDEO, INC. 80081

RED HOUSE, THE

D: Delmer Daves — 100 m

NR | SUS MYS | 1947 | B&W

Sex / Nud / Viol / Lang / AdSit

7 A gripping psychological melodrama. A crippled and reclusive farmer (Robinson) lives with his sister and adoptive daughter on their remote farm. He dotes on his daughter but is obsessed with keeping everyone away from a mysterious and intriguing red house that is situated deep in the woods. The girl talks Robinson into hiring a boyfriend from school to help with the work around the farm. She has always obeyed her father and stayed away from the woods where the forbidden house is, but now she and her friend have become intrigued with seeking out the mystery behind her father's strange demand.

A: Edward G. Robinson, Judith Anderson, Lon McCallister, Rory Calhoun, Julie London

© GOODTIMES 5082

ROPE

D: Alfred Hitchcock — 81 m

PG | SUS DMA | 1948 | COLOR

Sex / Nud / Viol / Lang / AdSit

8 Just for the thrill of it, two college students (Dall and Granger) murder a classmate with a rope and stuff his body in a trunk. Thrilled at the intellectual challenge, they invite the dead man's friends, father and professor over to have dinner, which they set atop the very trunk in which his body is stashed. As the night wears on, the guest's suspicions begin to rise, as does the suspense. Director Hitchcock shot his first color film in 10-minute segments on a single set to create the illusion of seamless action. The movie is based on the real-life Leopold-Loeb murder.

A: James Stewart, John Dall, Farley Granger, Cedric Hardwicke, Joan Chandler, Constance Collier

© MCA/UNIVERSAL HOME VIDEO, INC. 80110

SABOTAGE

D: Alfred Hitchcock — 77 m

NR | SUS | 1936 | B&W

Sex / Nud / Viol / Lang / AdSit

7 Sly early Hitchcock thriller! An undercover terrorist (Homolka) is a theatre manager in London, but he is also a terrorist who goes out on secret bombing missions at night. His wife slowly begins to suspect that she is married to the madman who is currently terrorizing the city. The tension mounts steadily when she goes to Scotland Yard with her suspicions and undercover detective Loder begins to investigate her claims. Based on Joseph Conrad's "Secret Agent," this was one of Hitchcock's first directorial attempts at his signature thrillers.

A: Oscar Homolka, Sylvia Sidney, John Loder, Desmond Tester

© UNITED AMERICAN VIDEO CORP. V4010

SABOTEUR

D: Alfred Hitchcock — 108 m

NR | SUS ACT | 1942 | B&W

Sex / Nud / Viol / Lang / AdSit

8 Outstanding high suspense wartime thriller from Hitchcock with an ever present feeling of doom and gloom. A mild mannered but stubborn man (Cummings) witnesses the sabotage of an American munitions factory during World War II. His best friend is killed in the explosion and he is framed for it. Determined to clear his name, he becomes an interstate fugitive as he tracks down the real saboteur, German agent Kruger. The thrilling fast-paced chase takes Cummings on a cross-country journey. It is most famous for its edge-of-your-seat cliffhanger climax at the Statue of Liberty.

A: Robert Cummings, Priscilla Lane, Otto Kruger, Norman Lloyd

© MCA/UNIVERSAL HOME VIDEO, INC. 80111

SECRET AGENT, THE

D: Alfred Hitchcock — 84 m

NR | SUS DMA | 1936 | B&W

Sex / Nud / Viol / Lang / AdSit

7 Another thriller from the master! This one uses a strange mix of excitement and comedy that is somewhat of a departure from more traditional Hitchcock films. Set against the majestic Swiss Alps, three secret agents are sent to Switzerland to identify and then assassinate a German spy. Gielgud and Carroll are to pose as husband and wife. Lorre is lusciously evil as the lascivious, lunatic Mexican assassin sent with them to do the deed. A well acted and entertaining spy thriller with some excellent characterizations and surprising sexual undercurrents.

A: Robert Young, Madeleine Carroll, Peter Lorre, John Gielgud, Percy Marmont, Lilli Palmer

© GOODTIMES 5011

SEVENTH CROSS, THE

D: Fred Zinnemann — 112 m

NR | SUS ACT DMA | 1944 | B&W

Sex / Nud / Viol / Lang / AdSit

8 Gripping, nail-biting suspense! Seven men make a daring escape from a Nazi concentration camp and are immediately pursued by the Gestapo. The Nazi leader, determined to recapture all seven men, has seven trees stripped of their bark and crosses nailed to them. As the Nazis find each man, they will nail him to his waiting cross and leave him there to die in view of the camp. The Nazis capture six of the men, but one, George Heisler (Tracy), with the help of many people, continues to elude his pursuers, always narrowly escaping his death. Will the seventh cross continue to remain unoccupied?

A: Spencer Tracy, Signe Hasso, Hume Cronyn, Agnes Moorehead, Jessica Tandy, George Macready

Distributed By MGM/UA Home Video M202348

OLDIES

SEVENTH VICTIM, THE

D: Mark Robson — 71 m

NR | SUS HOR | 1943 | B&W

7 Eerily haunting thriller that never jars you but, instead, covers you with a blanket of dread. An orphaned girl (Hunter) is informed by the boarding school at which she stays that her older sister has stopped sending her tuition. So, she leaves school to go to Greenwich Village to search for her sister who has disappeared. There Hunter discovers that her sister has fallen in with a group of devil worshipers who virtually control the lives of its members. Her sister has told her psychiatrist of their existence and now they are trying to force her to commit suicide. Spooky and chilling with truly sinister characters.

Sex / Nud / Viol / Lang / AdSit

A: Tom Conway, Kim Hunter, Jean Brooks, Hugh Beaumont, Erford Gage

© TURNER HOME ENTERTAINMENT 2083

SHADOW OF A DOUBT

D: Alfred Hitchcock — 108 m

NR | SUS | 1943 | B&W

9 One of the master's personal favorites! A young girl, Charlie (Teresa Wright), was given her name because of an uncle who she adores and idolizes. So, she is absolutely thrilled when he comes to stay with her family in California. But a shadow of doubt is cast upon his character as Charlie begins to suspect that he might be the psychotic Merry Widow mass-murderer. She struggles to decide if she should reveal her suspicions to the police or instead protect her family. Then she realizes that he has become aware of her suspicions and the cat-and-mouse game begins. An intense and disturbing thriller!

Sex / Nud / Viol / Lang / AdSit

A: Joseph Cotten, Teresa Wright, Macdonald Carey, Wallace Ford, Hume Cronyn, Henry Travers

© MCA/UNIVERSAL HOME VIDEO, INC. 80112

SORRY, WRONG NUMBER

D: Anatole Litvak — 89 m

NR | SUS | 1948 | B&W

8 Chills build slowly into sheer terror! A spoiled, paranoid heiress, who is also a bedridden hypochondriac (Stanwyck), accidentally overhears a telephone conversation between two men who are discussing the lurid details of a planned murder. Then she receives two other mysterious phone calls and, slowly, Stanwyck begins to believe that she is to be the unfortunate victim. The police do not believe her. Now virtually powerless and with time ticking down, she tries desperately to contact her husband (Lancaster). Stanwyck's riveting performance resulted in her fourth Oscar nomination.

Sex / Nud / Viol / Lang / AdSit

A: Barbara Stanwyck, William Conrad, Burt Lancaster, Wendell Corey, Ed Begley, Leif Erickson

© PARAMOUNT HOME VIDEO 4801

STALAG 17

D: Billy Wilder — 120 m

NR | SUS WAR COM | 1953 | B&W

9 Immensely entertaining combination of suspense, mystery and humor. William Holden (Oscar winner) is a cynical wheeler-dealer inside a WWII German P.O.W. camp. He is despised by his fellow prisoners because he is a wiseguy and because his enterprise has made him wealthy in the primary currency of the camp - cigarettes. However, there is a dangerous stoolpidgeon among them who is revealing all the prisoners' plans to the Germans, and Holden is everyone's chief suspect. Clever use of a wide cast of talented character actors takes the edge off the tension and creates a believable atmosphere.

Sex / Nud / Viol / Lang / AdSit

A: William Holden, Don Taylor, Otto Preminger, Neville Brand, Peter Graves, Robert Strauss

© PARAMOUNT HOME VIDEO 5816

STRANGE LOVE OF MARTHA IVERS, THE

D: Lewis Milestone — 116 m

NR | SUS CRM | 1946 | B&W

8 Electric thriller! Stanwyck is a wealthy and powerful woman married to the District Attorney, but he is a weak man (Douglas). She has inherited a lot of money and virtually controls her town, but she has a dark secret. When she was a teenager, she had wanted to elope with Van Heflin and had murdered her aunt who denied her her wish, and she allowed an innocent man to be executed. Heflin has arrived back in town and her secret is now threatened. She fears Heflin will blackmail them. However, her unfounded paranoia only makes Heflin more and more curious. This often gripping film starts slowly and then builds to a crescendo.

Sex / Nud / Viol / Lang / AdSit

A: Barbara Stanwyck, Kirk Douglas, Van Heflin, Lizabeth Scott, Judith Anderson, Darryl Hickman

© UNITED AMERICAN VIDEO CORP. 6317

STRANGER, THE

D: Orson Welles — 95 m

NR | SUS DMA | 1946 | B&W

8 Solid Welles' suspensor that takes hold and won't let go! Orson Welles is a stranger in a small town in Connecticut just after the end of WWII, but he is an escaped Nazi war criminal. He has fashioned a new life for himself in this sleepy little town and is about to marry the judge's daughter (Young) who is unaware of her love's true identity. At first, Welles is unaware that Federal agent Robinson has zeroed in on his whereabouts. But, when he does figure it out, the two engage in a grim cat-and-mouse game that places the girl's life in the middle. She is in danger and their battle will culminate in the jolting climax.

Sex / Nud / Viol / Lang / AdSit

A: Orson Welles, Edward G. Robinson, Loretta Young, Richard Long, Martha Wentworth

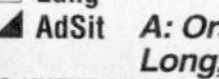

© UNITED AMERICAN VIDEO CORP. 1019

STRANGER ON THE THIRD FLOOR

D: Boris Ingster — 64 m

NR | SUS MYS | 1940 | B&W

8 Taut thriller! A man (Cook), mistakenly charged for murder, is convicted and sentenced. McGuire is the reporter who testified against Cook and it was his circumstantial evidence that convinced the jury, but he begins to have second thoughts when he starts having strange nightmares. Did Cook actually commit the crime? Was the wrong man condemned? Then his own neighbor is also murdered. Cook's fiancee is convinced of his innocence and she sets out to prove it by uncovering the real killer. Climactic nightmare scene is a real chiller!

Sex / Nud / Viol / Lang / AdSit

A: Peter Lorre, John McGuire, Margaret Tallichet, Charles Waldron, Elisha Cook, Jr.

© TURNER HOME ENTERTAINMENT 6225

STRANGERS ON A TRAIN

D: Alfred Hitchcock — 101 m

NR | SUS CRM | 1951 | B&W

10 Undeniably one of Hitchcock's very best - a classic thriller! Granger is a tennis pro who wants to marry Roman, but his trampy wife is standing in his way. On the other hand, Walker is a spoiled psychopath also who wants his domineering father out of his way. When the two strangers meet on a train, they casually discuss exchanging murders. Granger playfully agrees to the deal, thinking Walker is joking. He wasn't, and immediately carries out his part of the plan. Hitchcock's impeccable film techniques build to an unforgettable climax. A brilliantly suspenseful ride from start to finish.

Sex / Nud / Viol / Lang / AdSit

A: Farley Granger, Robert Walker, Ruth Roman, Leo G. Carroll, Patricia Hitchcock, Marion Lorne

© WARNER HOME VIDEO 11062

SUDDENLY

D: Lewis Allen — 77 m

NR | SUS CRM | 1954 | B&W

7 The air is ripe with tense, teeth-grinding danger. Sinatra is a hired assassin who is given the ultimate assignment. With nerves of steel and a fierce determination to carry out his job, the ruthless killer is set to assassinate the President. Together with two other triggermen, Sinatra takes over a small house in Suddenly, a small town in which the President will stop on his way to a fishing trip. Sinatra plays the assassin with icy precision and gives the unmistakable impression that he will let no one get in his way.

Sex / Nud / Viol / Lang / AdSit

A: Frank Sinatra, Sterling Hayden, Nancy Gates, James Gleason, Willis Bouchey, Kim Charney

© CONTINENTAL VIDEO 1006

SUSPICION

D: Alfred Hitchcock — 99 m

NR | SUS | 1941 | B&W

9 Chalk up another winning suspensor for Hitchcock! A lonely, but very rich, wallflower (Fontaine) falls in love with a charming man-about-town (Grant) without knowing very much about him - but she doesn't care. However, it is not long before the flamboyant Grant has spent himself into big trouble. Slowly and ever so steadily Fontaine's "suspicion" gradually begins to build. She suspects that her new husband has plans to dig himself out of his financial hole over her dead body - by killing her to collect a hefty insurance check. Fontaine's dynamite performance won her an Oscar for Best Actress.

Sex / Nud / Viol / Lang / AdSit

A: Cary Grant, Joan Fontaine, Cedric Hardwicke, Nigel Bruce, Dame May Whitty, Isabel Jeans

© TURNER HOME ENTERTAINMENT 2074

THIRD MAN, THE

D: Carol Reed — 104 m

NR | SUS MYS | 1949 | B&W

10 A widely acclaimed and sophisticated film, this is still one of the best suspense films of all time. It is the innovative camera work that accentuated the gloomy and sinister atmosphere within which the film draws its character. Cotten is a pulp writer who has arrived, totally broke, in a ravaged post-war Vienna. Thinking that he will just ask his old friend Lime for a job, he is told that Lime is dead. Checking farther, he learns Lime is not dead but is, instead, active in the black market. This deadly knowledge has now put Cotten in deep trouble. Very moody and highly intriguing.

Sex / Nud / Viol / Lang / AdSit

A: Orson Welles, Joseph Cotten, Alida Valli, Trevor Howard

© GOODTIMES 5069

UNINVITED, THE

D: Lewis Allen — 99 m

NR | SUS HOR | 1944 | B&W

8 A very unusual ghost story! A brother and sister (Hussey and Milland) buy a house on the Cornish coast in England. They soon discover that there are cold spots in the rooms and they witness doors closing all by themselves. Pretty Gail Russell becomes a regular visitor even though her grandfather has forbidden her to go there because her mother was killed in a fall from the cliffs. Is she haunting the house? Milland begins to fall in love with the beautiful girl, while he seeks to discover the answer to the mystery. Things become clearer when he finds that there is not one ghost, but two. Classy. Eerie.

Sex / Nud / Viol / Lang / AdSit

A: Ray Milland, Cornelia Otis Skinner, Gail Russell, Ruth Hussey, Donald Crisp, Dorothy Stickney

© MCA/UNIVERSAL HOME VIDEO, INC. 80400

WINDOW, THE

D: Ted Tetzlaff — 73 m

NR | SUS | 1949 | B&W

7 Gripping thriller about a little boy who is constantly making up stories. So, when he witnesses the neighbors through his window commit an actual murder, his parents won't believe him. In fact, they make him go to the neighbors to apologize for his lie. Now that the neighbors know that he knows, they are coming for him next and he is alone. Very well photographed. Suspense builds throughout. Bobby Driscoll won a special Oscar for his performance as the boy. This same idea was resurrected in 1984 in CLOAK AND DAGGER.

Sex / Nud / Viol / Lang / AdSit

A: Bobby Driscoll, Barbara Hale, Arthur Kennedy, Paul Stewart, Ruth Roman

© TURNER HOME ENTERTAINMENT 6223

WOMAN'S FACE, A

D: George Cukor — 107 m

NR | SUS DMA | 1941 | B&W

8 A taut, well-crafted and involving melodrama. The film begins as Crawford is standing trial for murder, and the story unravels as each witness testifies. She suffered a severe facial disfigurement when she was young and had become a lonely, tormented woman and a criminal. She had succumbed to the advances of a charming but penniless aristocrat (Veidt). But, when her face was mended by a surgeon, she has a chance to start over and her personality is transformed. However, she discovers that Veidt had only seduced her into becoming a governess so she could kill the child standing between him and an inheritance. Real weeper.

Sex / Nud / Viol / Lang / ◢ AdSit

A: Joan Crawford, Conrad Veidt, Melvyn Douglas, Osa Massen

Distributed By MGM/UA Home Video M3000611

ACE OF ACES

D: J. Walter Ruben — 77 m

NR | WAR DMA ACT | 1933 | B&W

6 Over the skies of WWI roared a new and romantic weapon, the airplane. Excited by the romance of aerial combat, pretty Nancy Adams (Allan) urges her sculptor fiance (Dix) to become a fighter pilot. While not exactly eager, Dix is both charmed and embarrassed by her into enlisting. Having done that, he becomes infatuated with the excitement and is transformed into a ruthless flying ace. Contains some pretty exciting flying sequences. It was the TOP GUN of its day.

Sex / Nud / ◢ Viol / Lang / ◢ AdSit

A: Elizabeth Allan, Richard Dix, Ralph Bellamy, Bill Cagney, Joe Sauers

© TURNER HOME ENTERTAINMENT 6141

ACTION IN THE NORTH ATLANTIC

D: Lloyd Bacon — 129 m

NR | WAR ACT | 1943 | B&W

6 One of Hollywood's wartime salutes to the WWII fighting men. This film follows the crew of a Merchant Marine freighter. Humphrey Bogart is just one of the crew whose ship is shot out from under them. Rescued, they start out again, this time sailing the North Atlantic in a convoy to deliver much-needed supplies to Murmansk, Russia. This convoy is again attacked by Nazi submarines. Bogart is forced to take command when his skipper is wounded and must do his best to get the cargo delivered and the crew safely back. Good special effects and moving drama.

Sex / Nud / ◢ Viol / Lang / ◢ AdSit

A: Humphrey Bogart, Raymond Massey, Alan Hale, Julie Bishop, Ruth Gordon, Dane Clark

Distributed By MGM/UA Home Video M202264

AIR FORCE

D: Howard Hawks — 119 m

NR | WAR ACT | 1943 | B&W

7 Exciting WWII action film that was highly acclaimed (received two Oscar nominations) and still stands up well today. Filmed by Howard Hawks in the days immediately following the Japanese sneak attack on Pearl Harbor, this is a blatantly propagandist and even racist film. Regardless, it is a truly thrilling and realistic actioner. It follows the exploits of a B-17 bomber crew which arrived in Pearl Harbor on December 6, and shows how they learn to pull together at Pearl Harbor, Manila and the Coral Sea. Excellent script, solid acting and exciting dogfight sequences.

Sex / Nud / ◢ Viol / Lang / ◢ AdSit

A: John Garfield, John Ridgely, Gig Young, Arthur Kennedy, Harry Carey, Charles Drake

Distributed By MGM/UA Home Video M202412

ALL QUIET ON THE WESTERN FRONT

D: Lewis Milestone — 132 m

NR | WAR DMA ACT | 1930 | B&W

10 Some technical aspects may be dated now but time has NOT diminished the power of this masterpiece. Idealistic young student Ayres enlists in the German army in 1914. He and his classmates are quickly sent to the front, where the horrible reality of war becomes daily life. The film becomes a succession of unforgettable scenes, including Ayres trapped in a bomb crater with a man he has killed, and rows of infantryman being mowed over by machinegun fire. Filled with emotional and harrowing scenes of fighting and man's ultimate inhumanity to man. Extremely powerful.

Sex / Nud / ◢ Viol / Lang / ◢ AdSit

A: Lew Ayres, Louis Walheim, John Wray, Slim Summerville, Russell Gleason, Ben Alexander

© MCA/UNIVERSAL HOME VIDEO, INC. 55018

BACK TO BATAAN

D: Edward Dmytryk — 95 m

NR | WAR ACT | 1945 | B&W

8 The Philippines are about to fall to the Japanese at the beginning of WWII. Wayne is a colonel recalled from the front line to help defend Bataan, but he is too late. He is assigned to organize a native guerrilla unit to harass the Japanese but must first inspire the Filipino leader (Quinn), who is reluctant. Realistic, very well made and acted, perhaps because many of those in the film had actually been there. Features actual war footage. Great action - but not just a shoot-'em-up. A very good drama - well worth your time.

Sex / Nud / ■ Viol / Lang / ◢ AdSit

A: John Wayne, Anthony Quinn, Beulah Bondi, Fely Franquelli, Richard Loo, Philip Ahn

© TURNER HOME ENTERTAINMENT 2081

BATAAN

D: Tay Garnett — 115 m

NR | WAR ACT | 1943 | B&W

9 Very realistic WWII story of the defense of the Philippine Islands, set in the early days of WWII and released in the darkest days of the War. It became one of the biggest box office hits of the period. Vastly outnumbered American and Filipino troops desperately attempt to stall the overwhelming, steadily advancing Japanese forces by destroying a strategic bridge. Good combat scenes, but this is more a story of the personalities of the men themselves, convincingly played by a very strong cast. One of the best WWII films made.

Sex / Nud / ◢ Viol / Lang / ◢ AdSit

A: Robert Taylor, George Murphy, Thomas Mitchell, Lloyd Nolan, Lee Bowman, Robert Walker

Distributed By MGM/UA Home Video M600927

BATTLE CRY

D: Raoul Walsh — 149 m

NR | WAR ROM ACT | 1955 | COLOR

7 Elaborate star-filled screen presentation of Leon Uris's best-selling adventure/romance novel. The story is of a hardened Marine major and the group of young troops he is training for battle in the Pacific during WWII. The action element is not over-looked, but much more important are the numerous subplots concerning the lives and loves of the many different characters involved. Each is very different. The soap opera-like novel was very popular so Hollywood pulled out the stops and filled the movie with all the stars it could find.

Sex / Nud / ◢ Viol / Lang / ◢ AdSit

A: Van Heflin, Aldo Ray, Mona Freeman, Nancy Olson, James Whitmore, Raymond Massey

© WARNER HOME VIDEO 11153

BATTLEGROUND

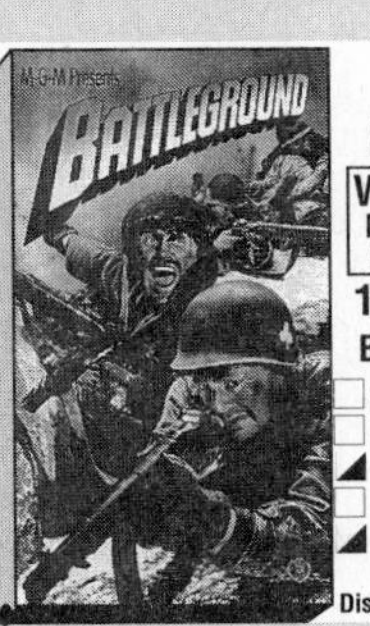

D: William Wellman — 119 m

NR | WAR DMA ACT | 1949 | B&W

8 Nominated for six Oscars, including Best Picture, and winner of two. A solid drama of men in war. A WWII division of American troops is dug in at the strategic crossroads of the city of Bastogne, trapped behind the German lines during the German advance at the Battle of the Bulge. Supplies are low, they are surrounded, but still they hold out. The star-studded cast represents dogfaces from all over the country. These are their stories - who they are, their fears and their courage. Very realistic, acclaimed as being the most realistic and believable of the period. Very big hit. Oscars for script and photography.

Sex / Nud / ◢ Viol / Lang / ◢ AdSit

A: Van Johnson, John Hodiak, Ricardo Montalban, George Murphy, Marshall Thompson, Denise Darcel

Distributed By MGM/UA Home Video M201002

DAWN PATROL, THE

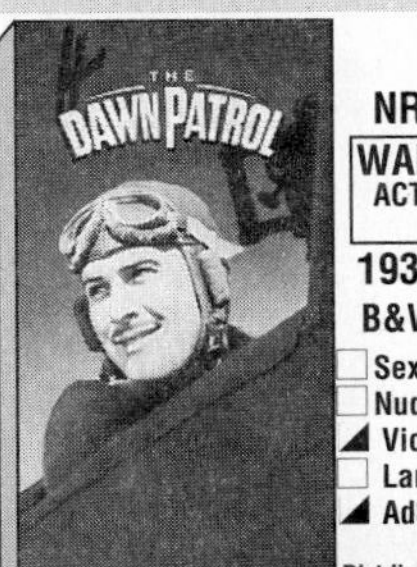

D: Edmund Goulding — 108 m

NR | WAR ACT | 1938 | B&W

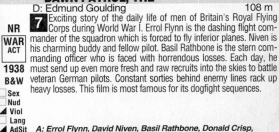

7 Exciting story of the daily life of men of Britain's Royal Flying Corps during World War I. Errol Flynn is the dashing flight commander of the squadron which is forced to fly inferior planes. Niven is his charming buddy and fellow pilot. Basil Rathbone is the stern commanding officer who is faced with horrendous losses. Each day, he must send up even more fresh and raw recruits into the skies to battle veteran German pilots. Constant sorties behind enemy lines rack up heavy losses. This film is most famous for its dogfight sequences.

Sex / Nud / ◢ Viol / Lang / ◢ AdSit

A: Errol Flynn, David Niven, Basil Rathbone, Donald Crisp, Melville Cooper, Barry Fitzgerald

Distributed By MGM/UA Home Video M202820

DESERT FOX, THE

NR
WAR DMA ACT
1951
B&W
Sex
Nud
Viol
Lang
AdSit

D: Henry Hathaway — 87 m

8 Excellent. This is the true story of WWII German Field Marshal Erwin Rommel, the brilliant military strategist of North Africa. It is a sensitive human account of his early military victories and later defeats. These defeats resulted in his return to Germany, his disillusionment with Hitler and his eventual participation in a plot to assassinate Hitler. Mason is brilliant in the role, and later reprieved it in THE DESERT RATS.

A: James Mason, Jessica Tandy, Cedric Hardwicke, Luther Adler, Desmond Young

© CBS/FOX VIDEO 1014

DESERT RATS, THE

NR
WAR ACT
1953
B&W
Sex
Nud
Viol
Lang
AdSit

D: Robert Wise — 88 m

8 Excellent action flick about an English captain (Burton) in charge of an outnumbered Australian regiment that is trying to hold out against long odds in 1941 at the key North African desert outpost of Tobruk. They are under siege by the brilliant German Field Marshall Erwin Rommel (played brilliantly by Mason, who reprieves his role from the THE DESERT FOX). The British army is in full retreat. Burton and his green recruits, through a series of daring lightning raids, are the only obstacle that is keeping Rommel from capturing the Suez Canal. Plenty of action.

A: Richard Burton, James Mason, Robert Newton, Chips Rafferty

© FOXVIDEO 1313

FIGHTING SEABEES, THE

NR
WAR ACT
1944
B&W
Sex
Nud
Viol
Lang
AdSit

D: Edward Ludwig — 99 m

7 A rousing war melodrama which has John Wayne being a short-tempered and determined civilian construction boss. He is determined to help defeat the Japanese by directing the civil work battalions that are building and repairing the installations close to the front lines in the Pacific. Tired of losing his men to enemy fire, he fights to get them armed and they become the "Seabees." But, he is in constant conflict with his Navy supervisor O'Keefe because he refuses to follow Navy rules. He and O'Keefe are also battling with each other for hand of Hayward. Lots of action. Pretty good.

A: John Wayne, Susan Hayward, Dennis O'Keefe, William Frawley

© REPUBLIC PICTURES HOME VIDEO 1268

FLYING LEATHERNECKS

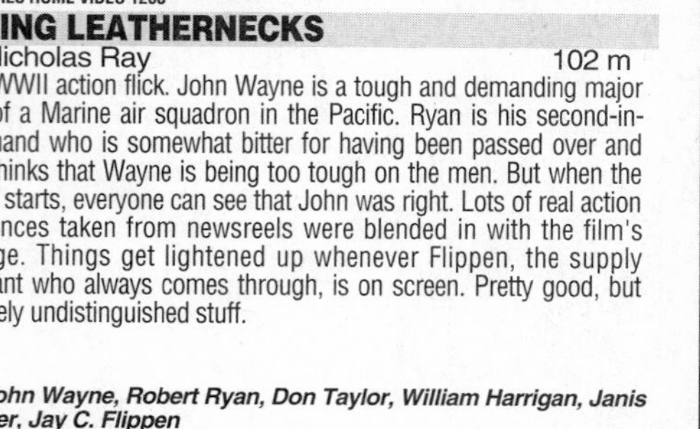

NR
WAR ACT
1951
COLOR
Sex
Nud
Viol
Lang
AdSit

D: Nicholas Ray — 102 m

6 WWII action flick. John Wayne is a tough and demanding major of a Marine air squadron in the Pacific. Ryan is his second-in-command who is somewhat bitter for having been passed over and who thinks that Wayne is being too tough on the men. But when the action starts, everyone can see that John was right. Lots of real action sequences taken from newsreels were blended in with the film's footage. Things get lightened up whenever Flippen, the supply sergeant who always comes through, is on screen. Pretty good, but relatively undistinguished stuff.

A: John Wayne, Robert Ryan, Don Taylor, William Harrigan, Janis Carter, Jay C. Flippen

© TURNER HOME ENTERTAINMENT 2075

FLYING TIGERS

NR
WAR ACT
1942
B&W
Sex
Nud
Viol
Lang
AdSit

D: David Miller — 101 m

6 Another WWII action movie with a Hollywood-type depiction the real-life Flying Tigers squadron of China. John Wayne plays the leader of a squadron of American mercenary pilots in China fighting the Japanese for the Chinese government. John fights to keep his group of unruly pilots alive, while also fighting for the affections of a pretty nurse. Great actual dogfight footage, though.

A: John Wayne, John Carroll, Anna Lee, Paul Kelly, Gordon Jones, Mae Clarke

© REPUBLIC PICTURES HOME VIDEO 1389

GO FOR BROKE

NR
WAR ACT
1951
B&W
Sex
Nud
Viol
Lang
AdSit

D: Robert Pirosh — 91 m

8 This film was based upon the famous real-life 442nd Regimental Combat Team of World War II. It was the most highly decorated regiment in the war and won a Presidential Citation. It was also an all-Japanese-American regiment that struggled mightily to regain honor for themselves, and their families back home in American concentration camps. This is a fictionalized account, but it contains all the ironies of their segregation and humiliations while they struggle to prove themselves. Van Johnson plays their bigoted commander whose prejudice gives way over time to respect.

A: Van Johnson, Lane Nakano, Henry Nakamura, George Miki, Henry Oyasato, Warner Anderson

Distributed By MGM/UA Home Video M202409

GUADALCANAL DIARY

NR
WAR ACT
1943
B&W
Sex
Nud
Viol
Lang
AdSit

D: Lewis Seiler — 93 m

9 One of the best of the World War II action movies. It was made at almost the same time as the actual events of the war were really occurring. It is the story about men, from widely different backgrounds, who are drawn together as close as brothers under the pressure of war. Outmanned and undersupplied, the group bands together to hold off an attack on their remote but vital airstrip. There is a big cast of talented actors, which is highlighted by Bendix as a former Brooklyn cab driver. It is a good action flick, but it is also a realistic representation of the camaraderie created by war.

A: Preston Foster, Lloyd Nolan, William Bendix, Richard Conte, Anthony Quinn, Richard Jaeckel

© CBS/FOX VIDEO 1726

HALLS OF MONTEZUMA

NR
WAR ACT
1950
COLOR
Sex
Nud
Viol
Lang
AdSit

D: Lewis Milestone — 113 m

6 This is a good war/action flick, but is only one of numerous action flicks that came out after WWII capitalizing on the drama of the War and glamorizing the gung-ho character of the Marines. A troop of Marines is sent on a dangerous mission to scout and capture a Japanese rocket base. Widmark is a school teacher who is transformed into a leader of men. Full of slam-bang action typical for the genre, executed by an excellent cast.

A: Richard Widmark, Jack Palance, Robert Wagner, Jack Webb, Reginald Gardiner, Karl Malden

© FOXVIDEO 1214

IMMORTAL BATTALION, THE

NR
WAR ACT
1944
B&W
Sex
Nud
Viol
Lang
AdSit

D: Carol Reed — 89 m

6 Very interesting and exhilarating wartime British propaganda release. It is a pseudo-documentary in which a group of totally different newly recruited civilians are molded into a cohesive fighting team. The editing skillfully mixes training footage and actual combat footage with the filmed footage to present a believable, coherent and powerful film. This wartime propaganda film was the idea of David Niven, who was also a Lt. Col. at the time.

A: David Niven, Stanley Holloway, Raymond Huntley, Peter Ustinov, Trevor Howard, Leo Genn

© GOODTIMES 5073

IMMORTAL SERGEANT, THE

NR
WAR DMA ACT
1943
B&W
Sex
Nud
Viol
Lang
AdSit

D: John M. Stahl — 91 m

7 This is quite an involving war story set in the hot Libyan desert during WWII. When raw recruits are left without leadership, after their superiors are all killed, one shy corporal (Fonda) must rise to take command of his patrol. If they are to survive, he must draw upon the skills and lessons taught him by his old sergeant (Mitchell). And, he gains the strength to do what he needs to do because of his love for the girl back home. Well told and interesting story, meant to inspire the troops and the nation at a time when it was badly needed.

A: Henry Fonda, Maureen O'Hara, Thomas Mitchell, Melville Cooper, Allyn Joslyn, Reginald Gardiner

© FOXVIDEO 1392

LOST PATROL, THE

NR
WAR SUS ACT
1943
B&W
Sex
Nud
Viol
Lang
AdSit

D: John Ford — 73 m

9 Superb and gripping war drama. A band of British calvarymen are lost in the Mesopotamian desert during WWI. Struggling to survive in this harsh waterless environment, they are mercilessly attacked and killed off one by one by a group of Arabs led by a fanatical religious leader (Karloff). The story is of their fight against the desert, the Arabs and themselves, as they struggle to determine what to do. Finally only one is left. Fast-paced suspense throughout.

A: Victor McLaglen, Boris Karloff, Wallace Ford, Reginald Denny, Alan Hale, J.M. Kerrigan

© TURNER HOME ENTERTAINMENT 6264

MEN OF THE FIGHTING LADY

NR
WAR ACT
1954
COLOR
Sex
Nud
Viol
Lang
AdSit

D: Andrew Marton — 82 m

7 This film was a big box office success for MGM when it was released, just as the Korean War ended. It is an exploration of the lives of the men on board an aircraft carrier stationed off the Korean coast during the war. The primary focus is upon one pilot, Van Johnson, but it also examines the other pilots, the Captain, ship's surgeon and even the repair officer who has to patch up the shot-up planes. Lots of good air action, much of it taken from actual missions. But particularly involving is Johnson "talking down" another pilot who has been blinded to a safe landing. Good stuff.

A: Van Johnson, Walter Pidgeon, Louis Calhern, Dewey Martin, Keenan Wynn, Frank Lovejoy

Distributed By MGM/UA Home Video M202413

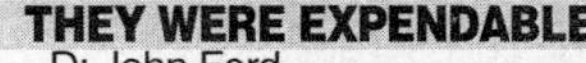

OBJECTIVE, BURMA!

D: Raoul Walsh 142 m

NR | WAR ACT DMA | 1945 | B&W | ☐ Sex ☐ Nud ■ Viol ☐ Lang ◢ AdSit

9 Exciting and highly acclaimed action/drama from WWII. A group of commandos are parachuted into Burma's jungles, behind Japanese lines, to sabotage a large radar facility. After achieving the objective, they are to be evacuated by air, but the planes can't get in. So they must begin a long trek to another location with the vengeful Japanese in hot pursuit. They take very heavy casualties under harrowing conditions. The film's major asset is that it accurately reflects the personal realities of combat. No Hollywood-heroics here. Excellent.

A: Errol Flynn, William Prince, James Brown, George Tobias, Henry Hull, Warner Anderson

Distributed By MGM/UA Home Video M202411

ONE OF OUR AIRCRAFT IS MISSING

D: Michael Powell, Emeric Pressburger 106 m

NR | WAR SUS ACT | 1941 | B&W | ☐ Sex ☐ Nud ◢ Viol ☐ Lang ◢ AdSit

7 Highly acclaimed war drama that begins with a World War II British bomber raid on Stuttgart in which one plane is hit. Struggling against their dying plane and desperately attempting to limp home, the crew makes it as far as Holland, where they have to bale out and try to make it back home on land with the help of the Dutch people. Very realistic, exciting and very suspenseful.

A: Godfrey Tearle, Eric Portman, Hugh Williams, Peter Ustinov, Pamela Brown, Googie Withers

© REPUBLIC PICTURES HOME VIDEO V3059

PURPLE HEART, THE

D: Lewis Milestone 98 m

NR | WAR DMA | 1944 | B&W | ☐ Sex ☐ Nud ☐ Viol ☐ Lang ◢ AdSit

7 Immediately following Pearl Harbor a fleet of B-25s took off from an aircraft carrier headed for Tokyo. Eight airman were shot down over occupied China and captured after the daring 1942 bombing raid by Jimmie Doolittle's men. The captured men were brought back to Japan where they were put on public trial for murder and war crimes. The outcome of their trial was never in doubt. They will be found guilty and executed. But before that, they will be tortured to learn from where the raids were launched. A fascinating tale of courage, based upon actual events. Good acting. See also THIRTY SECONDS OVER TOKYO.

A: Richard Conte, Tala Birell, Dana Andrews, Farley Granger, Sam Levene, Nestor Paiva

© CBS/FOX VIDEO 1730

SAHARA

D: Zoltan Korda 97 m

NR | WAR SUS ACT | 1943 | B&W | ☐ Sex ☐ Nud ◢ Viol ☐ Lang ◢ AdSit

9 Gripping WWII classic, one of the best to come out of that period. Bogart is a tank commander retreating across the Sahara Desert of North Africa after the defeat at Tobruk. He, his crew and some British stragglers they rescued, are in and on their tank for a desperate flight across the desert with no water and plenty of Germans all around them. They stumble onto the ruins of a desert village. Now they have water, but the Germans desperately need it, too, and offer to barter for it. Instead, Bogart and his crew valiantly defend their strategic prize. Tough, grim, insightful, exciting.

A: Humphrey Bogart, Bruce Bennett, Dan Duryea, Lloyd Bridges, J. Carrol Naish, Rex Ingram

© COLUMBIA TRISTAR HOME VIDEO VH10472

SANDS OF IWO JIMA

D: Allan Dwan 109 m

NR | WAR ACT | 1949 | B&W | ☐ Sex ☐ Nud ◢ Viol ☐ Lang ◢ AdSit

8 Hugely popular WWII action flick for which John Wayne earned an Oscar nomination in his role as tough-as-nails Sergeant Stryker. Stryker is a career Marine and a combat veteran. He knows what his men will be up against on the beaches of the South Pacific and drives them especially hard to prepare them. Most of the men hate him because of that ruthlessness, but when they are exposed to unforgiving, merciless combat on Tarawa and Iwo Jima, they understand. Great battle scenes, enhanced by actual war footage interspliced into the dramatic action. Much copied.

A: John Wayne, Adele Mara, Forrest Tucker, John Agar, Richard Jaeckel, Arthur Franz

© REPUBLIC PICTURES HOME VIDEO 3556

SO PROUDLY WE HAIL

D: Mark Sandrich 126 m

NR | WAR ROM | 1943 | B&W | ☐ Sex ☐ Nud ◢ Viol ☐ Lang ☐ AdSit

7 Well-meaning patriotic flag-waving soap opera. Filmed during WWII, this is the supposed story of a group of nurses evacuated from Corregidor after the fall of Bataan. Their story is told in flashback and relates their loves, told against the backdrop of the step-by-step collapse of the Philippines to the Japanese. The emphasis here is on people and emotions, fighting footage is minimal, but the hospital settings in the jungles and in the tunnels of Corregidor are very realistic. Not particularly distinguished but still this is a good light romantic entertainment.

A: Claudette Colbert, Paulette Goddard, Veronica Lake, George Reeves, Barbra Britton, Sonny Tufts

© MCA/UNIVERSAL HOME VIDEO, INC. 82248

THEY WERE EXPENDABLE

D: John Ford 135 m

NR | WAR ACT | 1945 | B&W | ☐ Sex ☐ Nud ◢ Viol ☐ Lang ◢ AdSit

9 Truly excellent WWII action drama. It was made by director John Ford, who had personal experience in battle. This is the story of the naval war that occurred in the Philippines in the immediate aftermath of the destruction of the American Naval fleet at Pearl Harbor. This war was fought largely by fast, lightweight boats (made of plywood) called PT boats. Robert Montgomery (who was a real-life naval officer) stars in a role based upon the exploits of real-life PT captain, and Congressional Medal of Honor winner, John Bulkeley. John Wayne plays his second-in-command. Detailed and realistic. This was a very personal film for director Ford. Excellent.

A: Robert Montgomery, John Wayne, Donna Reed, Ward Bond, Jack Holt, Leon Ames

Distributed By MGM/UA Home Video M201544

THIRTY SECONDS OVER TOKYO

D: Mervyn LeRoy 139 m

NR | WAR ACT | 1944 | B&W | ☐ Sex ☐ Nud ◢ Viol ☐ Lang ☐ AdSit

8 In 1942, shortly after the Japanese had bombed Pearl Harbor, a squadron of B-25s left the deck of an aircraft carrier, each plane fully loaded with bombs. Their target was Tokyo. The problem was that they could reach the target but could not carry enough fuel to return. The plan was to fly on and land in China after dropping their load, but many didn't make it that far. Based on historical fact. This film is Hollywood's exciting dramatization of that actual event. The film won an Oscar for Special Effects and was given even greater impact by some very good acting. See also THE PURPLE HEART.

A: Spencer Tracy, Van Johnson, Robert Walker, Phyllis Thaxter, Robert Mitchum, Phyllis Thaxter

Distributed By MGM/UA Home Video M600928

TO HELL AND BACK

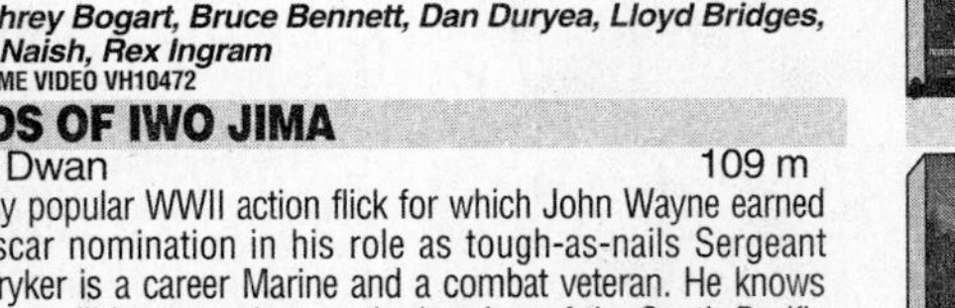

D: Jesse Hibbs 106 m

NR | WAR ACT | 1955 | COLOR | ☐ Sex ☐ Nud ◢ Viol ☐ Lang ◢ AdSit

7 The true story of America's most decorated soldier of WWII, Audie Murphy - played by himself. Audie Murphy, a poor Texas sharecropper's son, was rejected by both the Marines and the Navy. So he joined the Army and rose through the ranks to become the most decorated soldier of the war (including the Congressional Medal of Honor). This is a reasonably interesting autobiography, but the battle sequences are excellent and all the more exciting because they are true. Murphy became a popular movie star after the war and remained so until he was killed in a plane crash.

A: Audie Murphy, Marshall Thompson, Charles Drake, Gregg Palmer, Susan Kohner, Jack Kelly

© MCA/UNIVERSAL HOME VIDEO, INC. 45013

TWELVE O'CLOCK HIGH

D: Henry King 132 m

NR | WAR DMA SUS | 1949 | B&W | ☐ Sex ☐ Nud ◢ Viol ☐ Lang ◢ AdSit

10 Enthralling classic. Pivotal to the success of the Allies WWII effort was the relentless bombing of Germany by heavy bombers based in England. The cost in downed aircraft and flyers was horrendous. Peck plays the commanding officer of one such bomber squadron, who has been sent in to replace his predecessor (Merrill) who had grown too close to his men. He had became ineffective and the now men are demoralized. Peck is strict and the men don't like him but they slowly gain respect for him. However soon the toll begins to wear Peck down, too. Very realistic and compelling. See also MEMPHIS BELLE.

A: Gregory Peck, Hugh Marlowe, Gary Merrill, Millard Mitchell, Dean Jagger

© FOXVIDEO 1075

WAKE ISLAND

D: John Farrow 88 m

NR | WAR ACT | 1942 | B&W | ☐ Sex ☐ Nud ◢ Viol ☐ Lang ☐ AdSit

8 Solid and realistic WWII actioner based upon the actual nature of the defense of Wake Island in the South Pacific at the very outset of the War. Attacked without warning, at the same time as Pearl Harbor is bombed, and without hope of reinforcement or even resupply, a small band of Marines is attacked by the Japanese time after time - from the sea, air and by land - but yet remain determined to hold onto the strategic little island. This stirring war film garnered four Oscar nominations and helped to inspire the nation's spirit at a time when it was sorely needed.

A: Robert Preston, Brian Donlevy, William Bendix, Macdonald Carey, Albert Dekker, Walter Abel

© MCA/UNIVERSAL HOME VIDEO, INC. 80371

WALK IN THE SUN, A

D: Lewis Milestone 117 m

NR | WAR DMA ACT | 1945 | B&W | ☐ Sex ☐ Nud ◢ Viol ☐ Lang ◢ AdSit

8 Thoughtful and realistic WWII drama that dwells more on the psychological nature of the stresses of war upon different men. An Army unit at the beach landing in Salerno, Italy is assigned the job of moving six miles inland to capture a farmhouse held by Nazis. They don't know why they are to do it, only that their job is to do it. Casualties on the beach place sergeant Andrews in command of the mission. The war scenes are realistic, in that we never get to see the enemy's face, just the effect of his fire. Combat is not glamorized, nor is it minimized - it's just necessary.

A: Dana Andrews, Richard Conte, Lloyd Bridges, John Ireland, George Tyne, Sterling Holloway

© FOOTHILLS VIDEO

WING AND A PRAYER

D: Henry Hathaway 98 m

NR | WAR ACT | 1944 | COLOR | Sex | Nud | Viol ◢ | Lang | AdSit ◢

7 Thrilling and realistic action story from WWII's war in the Pacific. This is an Oscar-nominated Screenplay that is set just after the attack on Pearl Harbor and just before the Battle of Midway. The American high command does not want to tip its hand to the Japanese, so it allows both them and its own men to believe that they were unwilling to be engaged. The story follows some freshly recruited and frustrated Navy pilots as they train from the decks of an aircraft carrier, while not knowing that they will get their chance earlier than they expect. Well-researched and exciting entry, with actual combat footage.

A: Don Ameche, Dana Andrews, William Eythe, Richard Jaeckel, Charles Bickford, Richard Crane

© FOXVIDEO 1910

WORLD AT WAR SERIES, THE

D: m

WAR DOC | COLOR | Sex | Nud | Viol ◢ | Lang | AdSit ◢

9 A fascinating and extensive documentary summary of WWII, narrated by Laurence Olivier. It is a series of 26 individual one-hour segments, each documenting separate aspects of the war from its very beginning to the final moments in the bomb blasts of Japan. This is the story of a horrendous global tragedy which, by some estimates, resulted in a total of 55 million casualties from beginning to end. It includes not only dramatic film footage and extensive interviews with many of the statesmen and military leaders of the time but also of the ordinary people. Extraordinary.

A:

© HBO VIDEO PTVF3438

3 GODFATHERS

D: John Ford 103 m

NR | WST DMA | 1948 | COLOR | Sex | Nud | Viol | Lang | AdSit

8 Sentimental favorite that has been filmed several times with different twists, but this is still the best. Three half-hearted bandits on the run discover a destroyed wagon with a pregnant woman in it, giving birth all alone, in the middle of the desert. Before she dies after giving birth, she extracts a vow from each of them that they will get her baby to safety. Well done Western, a touching story with frequent touches of humor.

A: John Wayne, Pedro Armendariz, Harry Carey, Jr., Mae Marsh, Jane Darwell, Ward Bond

Distributed By MGM/UA Home Video M201000

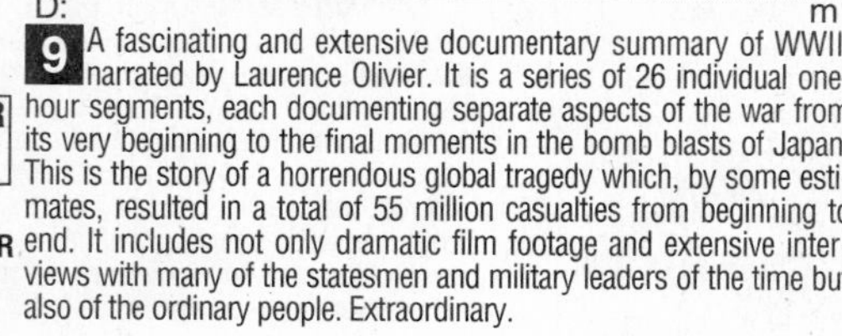

ABILENE TOWN

D: Edwin L. Marin 89 m

NR | WST ACT | 1946 | B&W | Sex | Nud | Viol ◢ | Lang | AdSit

7 Randolph Scott is the marshall of the new and wild cowtown of Abilene, Kansas that was built to handle the herds of cattle that were being driven north to the railheads from Texas in the 1870s. It is his job to separate the homesteaders around his town from wild cattlemen, fresh from 90 days of dusty trail, flush with cash and full of booze. He also has to battle members of the Younger gang, deal with an alcoholic sheriff (Buchanan) and choose between the pretty dance hall girl (Ann Dvorak) and nice girl Rhonda Fleming. Polished, if traditional, Western.

A: Randolph Scott, Ann Dvorak, Rhonda Fleming, Edgar Buchanan, Lloyd Bridges

© GOODTIMES 5122

ALLEGHENY UPRISING

D: William A. Seiter 81 m

NR | WST ACT | 1939 | B&W | Sex | Nud | Viol ◢ | Lang | AdSit

6 Colonialist John Wayne has had all that he can stand. He rallies a group of like-minded Pennsylvanians and leads them in an uprising against the tyrannical British captain (Sanders) who is governing the pre-Revolutionary War colonies. However, Sanders retaliates by trying to stifle the uprising by being even harder on the settlers. Pretty Claire Trevor conducts her own kind of warfare, trying to win Wayne's heart. She is reteamed here with Wayne after their triumphant pairing in STAGECOACH - also in 1939.

A: John Wayne, Claire Trevor, George Sanders, Brian Donlevy, Robert Barrat, Chill Wills

© TURNER HOME ENTERTAINMENT 2082

ALONG CAME JONES

D: Stuart Heisler 93 m

NR | WST COM | 1945 | B&W | Sex | Nud | Viol | Lang | AdSit

8 Very entertaining Western satire produced by Gary Cooper. It is a story of a extremely tame and mild-mannered cowpoke (Gary Cooper) who arrives in a strange town where he is mistaken for a notorious killer (Dan Duryea) because they have the same initials. He is just a gun-shy drifter and at first he enjoys all the attention his killer-status brings. He especially likes the attentions of pretty Loretta Young. However, when both the law and Duryea decide to come after him, it isn't so much fun for him any more... but it is for us. Enjoyable, very watchable, low-key Western spoof in which Cooper makes fun of his on-screen alter ego.

A: Gary Cooper, Loretta Young, Dan Duryea, William Demarest, Frank Sully, Russell Simpson

Distributed By MGM/UA Home Video M203039

ANGEL AND THE BADMAN

D: James Edward Grant 100 m

NR | WST | 1947 | B&W | Sex | Nud | Viol ◢ | Lang | AdSit

8 John Wayne plays Quirt Evans, a gunman and an ex-deputy of Wyatt Earp. He has been shot during a confrontation with the Stevens gang and was nursed back to health by a Quaker girl, Gail Russell. He fell in love with the pretty girl who saved his life, but he has a problem trying to live up to her peaceful expectations for him. She is begging him not to seek revenge and to leave his old life behind. The trouble with that is that no one has told that to the Stevens gang. It's predictable, but it's also thoughtful and intelligent, too and superior to many of Wayne's later pure action pictures.

A: John Wayne, Gail Russell, Harry Carey, Irene Rich, Bruce Cabot, Lee Dixon

© UNITED AMERICAN VIDEO CORP. 0065

ANNIE OAKLEY

D: George Stevens 90 m

NR | WST | 1935 | B&W | Sex | Nud | Viol | Lang | AdSit

7 Fun and reasonably accurate telling of the true story of the awkward uncultured Ozark girl who rose to international fame and prominence as the famous sharpshooter for Buffalo Bill's Wild West Show. Featured is her on-again off-again romance with the show's other sharpshooter Toby Walker, but it also has some funny moments in which Sitting Bull trys to learn to live in the "modern" world. Annie Oakley was also the inspiration for one of Broadway's biggest musical hits: Annie Get Your Gun.

A: Barbara Stanwyck, Preston Foster, Melvyn Douglas, Moroni Olsen, Andy Clyde, Chief Thundercloud

© TURNER HOME ENTERTAINMENT 2089

BADMAN'S TERRITORY

D: Tim Whelan 98 m

WST ACT | 1946 | B&W | Sex | Nud | Viol ◢ | Lang | AdSit

7 Randolph Scott is a Texas sheriff chasing outlaws who flee into a strip of land bordering the Oklahoma territory. It is a no-man's land, called the Quinto strip, where the law has no meaning and it has become a major outlaw stronghold. Into it rides sheriff Scott in pursuit of the James boys and the Dalton gang. But before he can do what he came to do, he gets framed for murder by a corrupt US Marshall.

A: Randolph Scott, Ann Richards, George "Gabby" Hayes, Ray Collins, Chief Thundercloud

© TURNER HOME ENTERTAINMENT 2052

BARBARY COAST

D: Howard Hawks 90 m

NR | WST | 1935 | B&W | Sex | Nud | Viol | Lang | AdSit

6 This is a big-budget adventure, that is set in 1849 San Francisco, and in it, Hollywood bends the script to the best advantage of its big-name cast's particular talents. Beautiful Miriam Hopkins is caught up in a web of corruption and is pursued both by a ruthless gangster (Robinson) and a naive but honest prospector (McCrea) in a love triangle.

A: Miriam Hopkins, Edward G. Robinson, Joel McCrea, Walter Brennan, Brian Donlevy, Harry Carey

© HBO VIDEO 90759

BEND OF THE RIVER

D: Anthony Mann 91 m

NR | WST ACT | 1952 | COLOR | Sex | Nud | Viol ◢ | Lang | AdSit ◢

8 This is a compelling Western of the 1880s Oregon trail and of a man trying to cleanse his soul. Stewart is a former Missouri border raider turned wagonmaster who is leading a wagon train through Oregon's wilderness. He is determined to get them through, despite being beset by all manner of problems, including Indian raids, having his supplies hijacked to be sold to gold miners and being betrayed by a former partner. It is a superior Western with excellent action sequences and top notch performances. Satisfied viewers may also want to see MAN OF THE WEST.

A: James Stewart, Arthur Kennedy, Rock Hudson, Julie Adams, Lori Nelson, Harry Morgan

© MCA/UNIVERSAL HOME VIDEO, INC. 80323

BIG CAT, THE

D: Phil Karlson — 75 m

NR | WST | 1949 | COLOR | Rating: 6

An exciting family outdoor adventure story. High-country ranchers are feuding, but a huge marauding mountain lion has gotten in their way. The cat is killing off both their stock and has become their common enemy. It is one that they must unite to defeat, but it is a city boy that helps them to track down the killer cat. Enjoyable action/adventure story for everybody.

☐ Sex ☐ Nud ☐ Viol ☐ Lang ☐ AdSit

A: Preston Foster, Lon McCallister, Forrest Tucker

© UNITED AMERICAN VIDEO CORP. 1001

BIG SKY, THE

D: Howard Hawks — 121 m

NR | WST ACT | 1952 | B&W | Rating: 6

This is a sprawling adventure story of an 1830 keelboat expedition up the uncharted Missouri River into Blackfoot country to establish trade with the Indians. Douglas and Martin are unruly fur trappers who have been involved in one scrape after another. Hunnicutt is a grizzled frontiersman heading up the expedition. He signs them both on when the three break out of jail together. As the expedition poles its craft upstream against the current, led by a beautiful Indian captive, it is attacked by Crow Indians and set upon by thieves. An action-packed old-school Western. Hunnicut received an Oscar nomination.

☐ Sex ☐ Nud ☑ Viol ☐ Lang ☐ AdSit

A: Kirk Douglas, Dewey Martin, Elizabeth Threatt, Arthur Hunnicutt, Buddy Bear, Steven Geray

© TURNER HOME ENTERTAINMENT 2050

BIG TRAIL, THE

D: Raoul Walsh — 110 m

NR | WST | 1930 | B&W | Rating: 6

This epic Western may seem pretty creaky now but still is worth watching, especially for the Duke's fans. This was John Wayne's first starring role and in it he is the scout for a wagon train heading to Oregon. He is determined to get his pioneers to their destination in spite of weather, Indian raids and bad guy Tyrone Power Sr. It is his last role. An interesting comment: This movie was made at a time when many of the people who actually lived the pioneer experience were still alive, a fact that could not help but influence it. Much of the character of what you see is how it very likely was.

☐ Sex ☐ Nud ☑ Viol ☐ Lang ☐ AdSit

A: John Wayne, Marguerite Churchill, Tyrone Power, Sr., Ian Keith, Ward Bond

© FOXVIDEO 1362

BLOOD ON THE MOON

D: Robert Wise — 88 m

NR | WST | 1948 | B&W | Rating: 7

A straight-forward, old style Western, taken from a novel by Luke Short. Robert Mitchum is a cowpoke and drifter who is hired to be a gunman by Robert Preston, his former partner. Preston plans to cheat a wealthy landholder out of his cattle by pretending to help homesteaders. However, Mitchum falls for the rancher's beautiful daughter and, as he witnesses more of his former partner's ruthlessness, he becomes convinced that he is on the wrong side. The stage is now set for a rousing two-fisted climax, as Mitchum vows to make right the wrong that he has done by taking on Preston himself.

☐ Sex ☐ Nud ☐ Viol ☑ Lang ☐ AdSit

A: Robert Mitchum, Barbara Bel Geddes, Robert Preston, Walter Brennan, Phyllis Thaxter, Frank Faylen

© TURNER HOME ENTERTAINMENT 6124

BROKEN ARROW

D: Delmer Daves — 93 m

NR | WST | 1950 | COLOR | Rating: 7

One of the earliest movies made that treated the Indians and their culture with some degree of respect. Jimmy Stewart plays a cowboy who befriends Apache chief Cochise (Jeff Chandler). And, he also marries a pretty Indian maiden (Debra Pagent). However, it is the middle of the Apache wars and Stewart also signs on as a cavalry scout, seeking to find a way for the whites and the Indians to coexist in 1870s Arizona. This is a movie that gives us romance, plenty of scenery and good action, too.

☐ Sex ☐ Nud ☑ Viol ☐ Lang ☐ AdSit

A: James Stewart, Jeff Chandler, Debra Paget, Will Geer, Arthur Hunnicutt, Jay Silverheels

© FOXVIDEO 1310

BROKEN LANCE

D: Edward Dmytryk — 96 m

NR | WST DMA | 1954 | COLOR | Rating: 8

This is an intelligent Western - the script won an Oscar. In it, Tracy plays a hard-edged, ruthless cattle baron who has brought up his four sons devoid of emotion. Now, his sons are as ruthless as he is, the family is warring among themselves and his empire is collapsing around him. His one faithful son (Wagner) has been denied his heritage because he is half-Indian. He has also just been released from prison after having confessed to a crime he didn't commit to protect his father. Now, he is battling his brothers, who are all scheming against both him and his father and it is leading to a violent confrontation.

☐ Sex ☐ Nud ☑ Viol ☐ Lang ☑ AdSit

A: Spencer Tracy, Robert Wagner, Jean Peters, Richard Widmark, Katy Jurado, Hugh O'Brian

© FOXVIDEO 1226

BUGLES IN THE AFTERNOON

D: Roy Rowland — 85 m

NR | WST | 1952 | COLOR | Rating: 6

This is a fast-moving story about an Army officer who has been branded as a coward and then court-martialed. Humiliated, he heads to the remote west to re-enlist with the 7th Calvary as a private for service against the Sioux in the Dakota territories. But, he discovers that his arch-nemesis is also there and is now his commanding officer. The guy does everything he can to make Milland miserable and to place his life in danger. At the Battle of the Little Big Horn everyone becomes separated and on their own, and it also becomes their private battleground.

☐ Sex ☐ Nud ☑ Viol ☐ Lang ☐ AdSit

A: Ray Milland, Helena Carter, Forrest Tucker, George Reeves, Gertrude Michael

© REPUBLIC PICTURES HOME VIDEO 0450

DANIEL BOONE

D: David Howard — 77 m

NR | WST ACT | 1936 | B&W | Rating: 7

Traditional and action-packed version of the exploits of the famous frontiersman. Rugged cowboy star O'Brien is well cast in the title role. As Daniel Boone, he leads a group of pioneers from North Carolina, through the mountain passes into the wilderness of Kentucky. There he is beset by marauding Indians who are aided by bad-guy half-breed John Carradine. Great adventure film, especially for hero-seeking boys.

☐ Sex ☐ Nud ☐ Viol ☐ Lang ☐ AdSit

A: George O'Brien, Heather Angel, John Carradine, Ralph Forbes, Clarence Muse

© GOODTIMES 5134

DARK COMMAND

D: Raoul Walsh — 95 m

NR | WST | 1940 | B&W | Rating: 7

In the days just prior to the Civil War, William Cantrell (Pidgeon) and Bob Seton (Wayne) compete for the job of Marshall of Kansas. When Cantrell loses, he forms a group of renegades into an outlaw band (Cantrell's Raiders) so large and powerful that they can rape and plunder on both sides of the Mason Dixon Line at will. Cantrell also tricks Seton's girl (Trevor) into marrying him. Seaton must now stop Cantrell and his murderous raids. A not too bad early Wayne Western, with plenty of action, but a little uneven in places.

☐ Sex ☐ Nud ☑ Viol ☐ Lang ☐ AdSit

A: John Wayne, Claire Trevor, Walter Pidgeon, Roy Rogers, George "Gabby" Hayes, Marjorie Main

© REPUBLIC PICTURES HOME VIDEO 0882

DAVY CROCKETT, KING OF THE WILD FRONTIER

D: Norman Foster — 93 m

NR | WST CLD ACT | 1955 | COLOR | Rating: 8

Originally filmed as TV episodes, the Davy Crockett series created a huge national phenomenon. Disney's initial three episodes were so popular that they were again released as this feature film. In it, Davy and his sidekick George Russell (Ebsen) fight their way through Indians, assorted bad guys, the US Congress and eventually arrive at the Alamo. Rousing fun for the whole family. Followed by DAVY CROCKETT AND THE RIVER PIRATES.

☐ Sex ☐ Nud ☐ Viol ☐ Lang ☐ AdSit

A: Fess Parker, Buddy Ebsen, Basil Ruysdael, Hans Conried, William Bakewell, Kenneth Tobey

© WALT DISNEY HOME VIDEO 014

DESTRY RIDES AGAIN

D: George Marshall — 94 m

NR | WST COM | 1939 | B&W | Rating: 9

Loving spoof of the B-grade Westerns of the '30s. The son of a now-dead super-lawman is called in to rescue a corrupt town. What shows up is a milk-drinking, six-shooterless, mild-mannered sheriff (Jimmy Stewart). In spite of these seeming shortcomings, he manages to defeat the bad guys and to fend off the advances of sexy saloon singer Marlene Dietrich who wants to "See What the Boys in the Back Room Will Have." In spite of its mild-mannered sheriff theme, there is still plenty of action and plenty of laughs. Often copied, but never equalled. Watch it.

☐ Sex ☐ Nud ☐ Viol ☐ Lang ☐ AdSit

A: James Stewart, Marlene Dietrich, Brian Donlevy, Mischa Auer, Una Merkel, Jack Carson

© MCA/UNIVERSAL HOME VIDEO, INC. 80352

DODGE CITY

D: Michael Curtiz — 105 m

NR | WST ACT | 1939 | COLOR | Rating: 8

Big-scale Western adventure. Set just after the Civil War, at the time that the railroads were pushing their way west and cattlemen were driving the long horn herds north to meet them. Errol Flynn is a Texas cattleman who dons a star to clean up a wild Dodge City, Kansas. He stops a stampede and a burning runaway train. Those heroic exploits and a huge barroom brawl later formed the cliche-bashing basis for the hilarious Western parody BLAZING SADDLES. In spite of the fun Mel Brooks had spoofing this movie, it is still a lot of fun and a good Western.

☐ Sex ☐ Nud ☑ Viol ☐ Lang ☐ AdSit

A: Errol Flynn, Olivia de Havilland, Ann Sheridan, Bruce Cabot, Alan Hale, Ward Bond

Distributed By MGM/UA Home Video 201698

DRUMS ALONG THE MOHAWK

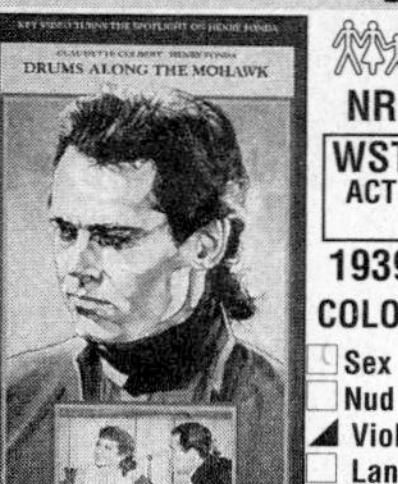

D: John Ford 103 m

NR | WST ACT | 1939 | COLOR

9 Richly detailed film which captures life in the colonial pre-Revolutionary War wilderness of upstate New York. Colbert is a cultured city woman who naively joins her new husband (Fonda) as a settler in the rawness of a virgin new land. She quickly learns that she must learn a whole new way of life, enduring not only the harshness of the new and primitive homestead, but also the uncertainties of watching her husband go off to fight marauding Indians. Full of action, humor, drama and rich in Americana. Well done.

Sex / Nud / Viol / Lang / AdSit

A: Claudette Colbert, Henry Fonda, Edna May Oliver, John Carradine, Jessie Ralph, Ward Bond

© FOXVIDEO 1382

DUEL IN THE SUN

D: David O. Selznick 138 m

NR | WST ROM | 1946 | COLOR

8 Lust in the sun is the real theme of this ambitious and engrossing Selznick production. It is a big-budget Western about a hot-blooded half-Indian girl (Jones) in love with the sophisticated son (Cotten) of a Texas land baron (Barrymore), but in lust with his rough-and-tumble cowpoke brother (Peck). The complexities of this kind of relationship has to result in trouble, and it does. Very watchable, with a unexpected ending. Nominated for two Oscars.

Sex / Nud / Viol / Lang / AdSit

A: Jennifer Jones, Gregory Peck, Joseph Cotten, Lionel Barrymore, Walter Huston, Harry Carey

© CBS/FOX VIDEO 8032

FAR COUNTRY, THE

D: Anthony Mann 97 m

NR | WST ACT | 1955 | COLOR

8 First-rate. Jimmy Stewart and Walter Brennan drive a cattle herd north from Wyoming to the gold rush territory of Alaska in 1896. Arriving in Dawson and expecting to make a fortune, they are instead cheated out of their herd by crooked sheriff and self-appointed judge, John McIntire. They steal their herd back and head off to Skagway with McIntire in pursuit. He will stop at nothing to get the herd, but peaceful cowpoke Stewart refuses to seek revenge until two of his close friends are murdered. A fine Western with great characters, excellent performances and set against colorful backdrops.

Sex / Nud / Viol / Lang / AdSit

A: James Stewart, Ruth Roman, Walter Brennan, Corinne Calvet, John McIntire, Harry Morgan

© MCA/UNIVERSAL HOME VIDEO, INC.

FIGHTING KENTUCKIAN, THE

D: George Waggner 100 m

NR | WST | 1949 | B&W

6 Entertaining two-fisted period adventure. On his way home from the Battle of New Orleans, frontiersman John Wayne meets and falls in love with the daughter of an evil French land baron. John and his buddies set about saving the farmland of the French homesteaders that the evil Frenchman and his cutthroats are determined to steal. It would have been better less attention to the romance.

Sex / Nud / Viol / Lang / AdSit

A: John Wayne, Vera Hruba Ralston, Philip Dorn, Oliver Hardy, Marie Windsor, John Howard

© REPUBLIC PICTURES HOME VIDEO 1306

FORT APACHE

D: John Ford 127 m

NR | WST ACT | 1948 | B&W

9 Great entertainment. This is the first of director Ford's famous Western cavalry trilogy. Henry Fonda is an ambitious colonel stuck out in the wilderness outpost of Fort Apache. He wants to get out but to do it he needs to make a name for himself fighting a war with the Apaches, so he provokes one. John Wayne is his field-experienced Captain who struggles to protect the troops as Fonda endangers his whole command. Rich in Western characterizations, atmosphere and the glorious scenery of Arizona's Monument Valley. Followed by SHE WORE A YELLOW RIBBON and RIO GRANDE.

Sex / Nud / Viol / Lang / AdSit

A: John Wayne, Henry Fonda, Shirley Temple, Ward Bond, John Agar, Victor McLaglen

© TURNER HOME ENTERTAINMENT 2068

GUNFIGHTER, THE

D: Henry King 85 m

NR | WST DMA | 1950 | B&W

8 A top-notch Western which was actually quite different for its time by being one of the first of the '50s to be more "adult" and less heroic in its focus. Peck puts in an excellent performance playing a world-weary gunfighter who who has returned home to a small frontier town. He wants only to be left in peace and to visit his long-estranged wife and son. However, the town's sheriff, who is his old friend, advises him that the town's people want him gone as fast as possible. Still, before he can go, he is confronted by a young tough who insists upon challenging him. Thoughtful and first rate.

Sex / Nud / Viol / Lang / AdSit

A: Gregory Peck, Helen Westcott, Millard Mitchell, Jean Parker, Karl Malden, Skip Homeier

© CBS/FOX VIDEO 1213

HELL'S HINGES

D: William S. Hart 65 m

NR | WST ACT | 1916 | B&W

9 Silent film's famous cowboy hero William S. Hart plays Blaze Tracey. Blaze is a tough guy in a mean-spirited wild frontier town called Hell's Hinges. However, his wildness is tamed when he falls for the sister of a minister who has come to town. But, when the minister is seduced by a sexy saloon girl and his church is destroyed, Hart seeks revenge. He is going to save the town even if he has to destroy it. The film is most interesting for the way the lawlessness and corruption is depicted. Remember, this film was not far removed in time from the real wild-West. Silent film.

Sex / Nud / Viol / Lang / AdSit

A: William S. Hart, Clara Williams, Louise Glaum, Jack Standing

© VIDEO YESTERYEAR 1069

HIGH NOON

D: Fred Zinnemann 85 m

NR | WST DMA ACT | 1952 | B&W

10 A gripping and powerful classic Western drama. Today is Gary Cooper's last day as sheriff. Today, also, he is marrying Grace Kelly and is leaving town to start a new life. But today he learns that a man who he had sent to prison and three others will arrive on the noon train to kill him. He could just leave town and keep looking over his shoulder for the rest of his life. Instead, he chooses to stay and fight. But, he finds that he will have to fight alone. Everyone in town deserts him - even his new wife. The taut suspense is exaggerated because the story unfolds in real time.

Sex / Nud / Viol / Lang / AdSit

A: Gary Cooper, Grace Kelly, Lloyd Bridges, Thomas Mitchell, Katy Jurado, Henry Morgan

© REPUBLIC PICTURES HOME VIDEO 5532

INDIAN FIGHTER, THE

D: Andre de Toth 88 m

NR | WST ACT | 1955 | COLOR

7 This is a rousing, if undistinguished, adventure yarn of the Old West. Kirk Douglas leads a wagon train to Oregon in the 1870's, but to get there they must get through a prairie that is occupied by warring Sioux. Lots of Old West action - fightin', shootin' and a little lovin'.

Sex / Nud / Viol / Lang / AdSit

A: Kirk Douglas, Walter Matthau, Elsa Martinelli, Walter Abel, Lon Chaney, Jr.

Distributed By MGM/UA Home Video M203122

JESSE JAMES

D: Darryl F. Zanuck 105 m

PG | WST ACT | 1939 | COLOR

7 Entertaining but highly fictionalized account of the notorious 19th-century outlaw Jesse James and his brother. It presents an image of a family of peaceful farmers that was forced into a life a crime after their mother is murdered by an unscrupulous railroad agent. Questionable historical aspects aside, Fonda as Frank and Power as Jesse are very engaging characters. This was a big-budget Western that delivered on action and entertainment. Great cast.

Sex / Nud / Viol / Lang / AdSit

A: Tyrone Power, Henry Fonda, Nancy Kelly, Randolph Scott, Brian Donlevy, Jane Darwell

© FOXVIDEO 1485

JOHNNY GUITAR

D: Nicholas Ray 110 m

NR | WST | 1954 | COLOR

7 Not at all your typical Western. Alternately called weird and bizarre, this film has a major twist - this time the women shoot it out. Joan Crawford is a cynical and wealthy saloon owner who has bought up everything in the oncoming railroad's path. Mercedes McCambridge is a moralistic big landowner who can't stand Crawford and whips the locals into a lather trying to get her thrown out of Arizona. Gunfighter Sterling Hayden and Scott Brady stand back and watch them fight it out. Some critics burden it with Freudian symbolism - just enjoy it.

Sex / Nud / Viol / Lang / AdSit

A: Joan Crawford, Sterling Hayden, Scott Brady, Mercedes McCambridge, Ward Bond, Ben Cooper

© REPUBLIC PICTURES HOME VIDEO 2126

KENTUCKIAN, THE

D: Burt Lancaster 104 m

NR | WST | 1955 | COLOR

6 Fun adventure story that both starred and was directed by Burt Lancaster. It also provided the first screen appearance of Walter Matthau. It is a pretty good early American adventure story in which a Kentucky mountain man is migrating to Texas with his boy to start a new life. Along the way they get waylaid by some feuding mountaineers and they encounter a pretty girl indentured to a mean tavern owner, so they use their river passage money to buy her freedom. Pretty good action and several good doses of comedy, too.

Sex / Nud / Viol / Lang / AdSit

A: Burt Lancaster, Diana Lyon, Dianne Foster, Walter Matthau, John McIntire, Una Merkel

Distributed By MGM/UA Home Video M202645

LAST OF THE MOHICANS, THE

D: George B. Seitz 91 m

NR | WST ACT ROM | 1936 | B&W

8 Well made and exciting large-scale movie based upon James Fenimore Cooper's classic novel set during the French and Indian War of the 1750s in upstate New York. White frontiersman Hawkeye (Scott) and his adoptive Mohican father and brother guide an English officer and two white women through French lines to a besieged English fort, all the while being pursued by a Huron war party. Elaborately staged battle sequences. Majestically remade in 1992, with fabulous and meticulous care to detail.

Sex / Nud / Viol / Lang / AdSit

A: Randolph Scott, Binnie Barnes, Heather Angel, Robert Barrat, Phillip Reed, Henry Wilcoxon

© UNITED AMERICAN VIDEO CORP. 5859

MAN ALONE, A

D: Ray Milland 96 m

NR | WST | 1955 | COLOR

6 A gunslinger (Milland) happens upon the scene of a stage robbery, with six dead bodies. He reports what he finds at the next town, but is instead accused of the murders by the town's most respected citizen, who had actually committed the crime himself. Now a lynch mob is in hot pursuit of the gunslinger. He finds himself hiding from the angry townsfolk in the house of the town's sick and quarantined sheriff. He falls for the sheriff's daughter and wins the sheriff's trust. This is Milland's first directorial attempt, and it is pretty good. The finale is particularly strong.

Sex / Nud / Viol / Lang / AdSit

A: Ray Milland, Raymond Burr, Mary Murphy, Ward Bond, Lee Van Cleef

© REPUBLIC PICTURES HOME VIDEO 2579

MAN FROM COLORADO, THE

D: Henry Levin 99 m

NR | WST ACT | 1949 | COLOR

7 Intelligent psychological Western. A Civil War veteran (Ford), on the edge of insanity, becomes a federal judge in Colorado. Ford's demons taunt him until he can no longer separate today's reality from that of his bloody past. His old army buddy (Holden) is now the town's marshall and witnesses his friend's psychotic behavior. The townspeople have had enough of Ford's ruthlessness, and Holden must challenge Ford to step down. Ford and Holden both give solid and notable performances.

Sex / Nud / Viol / Lang / AdSit

A: Glenn Ford, William Holden, Ellen Drew, Edgar Buchanan, Jerome Courtland, Ray Collins

© COLUMBIA TRISTAR HOME VIDEO 60962

MAN FROM LARAMIE, THE

D: Anthony Mann 104 m

NR | WST SUS ACT | 1955 | COLOR

9 Rough and tumble adult Western! When Stewart's brother is shot and killed by Apaches, he becomes obsessed with finding the man who sold the Indians the repeating rifles. In his search, Stewart finds himself on a ranch where the two sons are vying for control upon their father's death. After a run in with one of the brothers (Nicol), Stewart goes to work for a foe of the father. Stewart is caught by Nicol, who forces his men to hold Stewart, while he shoots Stewart in the hand. Then Stewart discovers that it was the brothers who sold guns to the Apaches. Excellent!

Sex / Nud / Viol / Lang / AdSit

A: James Stewart, Arthur Kennedy, Donald Crisp, Cathy O'Donnell, Alex Nicol, Aline MacMahon

© COLUMBIA TRISTAR HOME VIDEO 60855

MAN FROM THE ALAMO, THE

D: Budd Boetticher 79 m

NR | WST ACT | 1953 | COLOR

7 The men inside the Alamo are worried about the safety of their families. Glenn Ford is chosen by lot to be the one to sneak out of the Alamo and then to go to warn the other defender's families of the impending danger. This he does but he discovers that most of the families, including his own, have been murdered. And, since he was the only one to escape the slaughter at the Alamo, he is branded a coward and a traitor. Now he dedicates himself to the fighting. Unusual but fascinating Western.

Sex / Nud / Viol / Lang / AdSit

A: Glenn Ford, Julie Adams, Hugh O'Brian, Chill Wills, Victor Jory, Jeanne Cooper

© MCA/UNIVERSAL HOME VIDEO, INC.

MAN WITHOUT A STAR

D: King Vidor 89 m

NR | WST | 1955 | COLOR

7 Douglas plays a likable and charming wanderer who does everything he can to avoid trouble. Even so, he can take care of himself and does OK in a pinch. He befriends a ranch hand (Campbell) and both are hired by a beautiful and tough cattle baroness (Jeanne Crain) who often uses her womanly charms to get what she wants. What she wants is to keep the range unfenced and she is willing to be ruthless to do it. Douglas believes the ranges should remain unfenced and is attracted to her charms, but he is not at all excited by her methods. Fun time. Douglas even sings and plays a banjo.

Sex / Nud / Viol / Lang / AdSit

A: Kirk Douglas, Jeanne Crain, Claire Trevor, Richard Boone, Jay C. Flippen, William Campbell

© MCA/UNIVERSAL HOME VIDEO, INC. 80144

MY DARLING CLEMENTINE

D: John Ford 97 m

NR | WST ACT | 1946 | B&W

10 One of the best Westerns ever! Wyatt Earp (Fonda) and his brothers arrive just outside Tombstone with a small herd of cattle. Old Man Clanton (Brennan) and his boys offer to buy them but the Earps refuse and go into town, leaving one brother to tend the herd. They arrive in a Tombstone that is wide open and dangerous. After a run-in with a local wildman, Wyatt is offered the job of sheriff, which he declines. He and his brothers go back to find their herd gone and brother dead. Wyatt accepts the badge and begins a path that leads the brothers to the shootout at the OK Corral.

Sex / Nud / Viol / Lang / AdSit

A: Henry Fonda, Linda Darnell, Victor Mature, Walter Brennan, Cathy Downs, Tim Holt

© FOXVIDEO 1398

NAKED SPUR, THE

D: Anthony Mann 93 m

NR | WST ACT | 1952 | COLOR

9 Highly acclaimed and sophisticated Western, beautifully shot on location in the Rockies. James Stewart is a hardbitten bounty hunter determined to make enough money to buy back the ranch he lost. Stewart tracks down a killer (Ryan) and his girlfriend (Leigh) in the mountains and is taking them back, but along the way two others join him, cutting themselves in as "partners." Reluctantly Stewart lets them in because he's tired. Immediately, Ryan seeks to cause trouble between the three of them and the girl falls for Stewart, causing even more trouble. Intelligent, exciting and suspenseful.

Sex / Nud / Viol / Lang / AdSit

A: James Stewart, Robert Ryan, Janet Leigh, Ralph Meeker, Millard Mitchell

Distributed By MGM/UA Home Video M600520

NARROW TRAIL, THE

D: Lambert Hillyer 56 m

NR | WST | 1917 | B&W

9 Remarkably good silent film classic that pays studied attention to accurate period details, particularly of San Francisco's Barbary Coast. William S. Hart, the famous silent screen cowboy hero, plays an outlaw, Ice Harding. Ice captures and tames a wild pony, but his gang rejects him because they are afraid the distinctive pony will make him too recognizable. Alone, he falls in love and now longs to go straight. But, she has tainted past too, and runs away to San Francisco. However, Ice loves her, tracks her down and then races his pony to win the money that will give them both a chance at a new life.

Sex / Nud / Viol / Lang / AdSit

A: William S. Hart, Sylvia Bremer, Milton Ross, Robert Kortman

© FOOTHILLS VIDEO

NORTHWEST PASSAGE

D: King Vidor 127 m

NR | WST ACT | 1940 | COLOR

9 Stirring adventure story, one of the greatest of all times, based on the real-life adventures of pioneer Robert Rogers (Tracy). Rogers leads a band of 160 settler soldiers into the wilderness of northern New York and the St. Lawrence territory. Their mission is to eliminate the vicious tribe of Abernaki Indians who have made numerous murderous raids on the settlers. It is 1759, the time of French and Indian War. The party is faced with an almost impossible task - before they can even mount their attack, they must first navigate through uncharted and extremely hostile wilderness. Realistically presented.

Sex / Nud / Viol / Lang / AdSit

A: Spencer Tracy, Robert Young, Walter Brennan, Ruth Hussey

Distributed By MGM/UA Home Video M201132

OUTLAW, THE

D: Howard Hughes 95 m

NR | WST | 1943 | B&W

6 Infamous sex-Western of the early '40s. Notorious for teenage Russell's cleavage, producer/director Howard Hughes's fascinating with it and the censor's objections to it. Aside from those elements, it is a more or less typical B-grade Western of the period, and yet another "take" on the Billy the Kid legend. Billy, wounded by Pat Garrett, hides out on a ranch owned by his friend Doc Holliday and is pre-occupied by Jane Russell and her cleavage. Not a good movie, but not too bad. Sex aspect is vastly overrated.

Sex / Nud / Viol / Lang / AdSit

A: Jane Russell, Walter Huston, Jack Beutel, Thomas Mitchell, Mimi Aguglia, Joe Sawyer

© GOODTIMES 5020

OX-BOW INCIDENT, THE

D: William Wellman 75 m

NR | WST DMA ACT | 1943 | B&W

9 Brilliant indictment of the tyranny and terror created by mob rule. When a Nevada rancher is murdered by rustlers, two drifters (Fonda and Morgan) join the posse chasing down his killers. The posse - now more of a mob - is stirred up and led by an ex-Confederate officer. They stumble upon three hapless farmers sitting around a campfire and allow themselves to be quickly convinced of the guilt of the three, with only the slightest amount of circumstantial evidence. When the mob sets about to hang the three, only the drifters and a very few others object. Best Picture nominee.

Sex / Nud / Viol / Lang / AdSit

A: Henry Fonda, Jane Darwell, Anthony Quinn, Dana Andrews, Harry Morgan, Mary Beth Hughes

© FOXVIDEO 1652

PLAINSMAN, THE

D: Cecil B. DeMille — 113 m

NR · WST ACT · 1937 · B&W · Rating: 6

Sex · Nud · ✓ Viol · Lang · AdSit

Historically preposterous extravaganza that, if taken with a grain of historic salt, is still good action-filled fun. Gary Cooper is Wild Bill Hickock who is out to foil an attempt to sell guns to the Indians lead by Yellow Hand, while also engaging in a running romantic battle of wits with Calamity Jane (Jean Arthur). Also in appearance are Buffalo Bill, Abraham Lincoln and George Armstrong Custer. Don't worry about the details, just enjoy it for what it is, an excuse to create a good time with a rousing adventure story.

A: Gary Cooper, Jean Arthur, Charles Bickford, Anthony Quinn, James Ellison

© MCA/UNIVERSAL HOME VIDEO, INC. 80548

PONY EXPRESS

D: Jerry Hopper — 101 m

NR · WST ACT · 1953 · COLOR · Rating: 8

Sex · Nud · ✓ Viol · Lang · AdSit

Above-average Western actioner that glamorizes the 1860s process of establishing an express mail route which used a series of riders to relay mail between St. Joseph, Missouri and Sacramento, California. Buffalo Bill Cody (Heston) and Wild Bill Hickock (Tucker) do battle with rival stage coach stationmasters, the weather, the country and, of course, the Indians. In spite of some glaring historical inaccuracies, this is a fun-filled flick full of fists, bullets and arrows. The real Pony Express lasted only a couple of years.

A: Charlton Heston, Forrest Tucker, Rhonda Fleming, Jan Sterling

© PARAMOUNT HOME VIDEO 5217

PURSUED

D: Raoul Walsh — 101 m

NR · WST ACT · 1947 · B&W · Rating: 8

Sex · Nud · ✓ Viol · Lang · ✓ AdSit

Intriguing, unusual and hard-hitting Western. Robert Mitchum is the bewildered step-son of Judith Anderson. He was brought into the Callum family several years earlier, upon the murder of his father - an event of which Mitchum has no memory. Mitchum falls in love with and marries his step-sister. Her brother despises him and plots to ambush him, but instead is killed by Mitchum in a shootout. Now Mitchum is hated by all the Callums, including his new wife... and then, he remembers what he had forgotten. Fast-paced terrific Western.

A: Robert Mitchum, Teresa Wright, Judith Anderson, Dean Jagger, Harry Carey, Jr., Alan Hale

© REPUBLIC PICTURES HOME VIDEO 3326

RACHEL AND THE STRANGER

D: Norman Foster — 79 m

NR · WST ROM · 1948 · B&W · Rating: 7

Sex · Nud · ✓ Viol · Lang · ✓ AdSit

William Holden is a widowed pioneer father living in the western woods of the 1820s. Even though he is overwhelmed with grief for the loss of his wife, he buys a bondwoman out of servitude to teach his motherless son manners and to tend to the daily chores. Though they are married, Holden is so buried in love for his dead wife that he fails to notice the charms of his new "wife." But when a wandering stranger (Mitchum) visits and is attracted to her, Holden's love for her is suddenly awakened. Entertaining, with some funny moments and a thrilling Indian raid at the end, too.

A: Loretta Young, William Holden, Robert Mitchum, Tom Tully, Sara Haden

© TURNER HOME ENTERTAINMENT 6127

RED RIVER

D: Howard Hawks — 134 m

NR · WST ACT · 1948 · B&W · Rating: 10

Sex · Nud · ✓ Viol · Lang · ✓ AdSit

Epic and grand Western. Wayne stars as an early settler of the Texas wilderness and guardian to an orphan, Montgomery Clift. After spending years creating one of the largest ranches in Texas, this tough-as-nails cattle baron gathers up all his cattle, plus those of his neighbors, and sets out for the newly opened railheads in Kansas with one of the first cattle herds to be driven north. Wayne is a tyrannical taskmaster. His rule moves them through dangers that would have stopped other men. But his determination becomes cruelty and Clift leads a mutiny against him. Excellent everything.

A: John Wayne, Montgomery Clift, Walter Brennan, Joanne Dru, Coleen Gray

Distributed By MGM/UA Home Video M201724

RENEGADE RANGER/SCARLET RIVER

D: David Howard — 113 m

NR · WST · 1938 · B&W · Rating: 6

Sex · Nud · Viol · Lang · ✓ AdSit

These two Westerns are presented in the same way they did it in the '30s and '40s. Really - it's a double feature. RENEGADE RANGER - George O'Brien, playing Texas Ranger Jack Steele, is assigned to bring in beautiful Mexican bandit Rita Hayworth, who has been accused of murder. But Steele discovers that she is innocent. SCARLET RIVER - A movie cowboy, filming at the Scarlet River Ranch, winds up in a series of real shootouts with some bad guys who are trying to take the ranch away from its pretty owner.

A: George O'Brien, Rita Hayworth, Tim Holt, Ray Whitley

© TURNER HOME ENTERTAINMENT 2041

RETURN OF DRAW EGAN, THE

VIDEO YESTERYEAR
1441.
The Return of Draw Egan
with
William S. Hart.
The most wanted man in New Mexico territory becomes the sheriff of Yellow Dog!

D: William S. Hart — 64 m

NR · WST · 1916 · B&W · Rating: 8

Sex · Nud · ✓ Viol · Lang · AdSit

Legendary silent screen cowboy star William S. Hart stars in perhaps his best Western, as an outlaw who has reformed himself for the love of a good woman and become the sheriff in a small town. But... an old partner-in-crime shows up and threatens to expose him and ruin everything he has built for himself. Tough, no-nonsense Western.

A: William S. Hart, Louise Glaum, Margery Wilson, Robert McKimm

© VIDEO YESTERYEAR 1441

RETURN OF FRANK JAMES, THE

D: Fritz Lang — 92 m

NR · WST · 1940 · COLOR · Rating: 7

Sex · Nud · Viol · Lang · ✓ AdSit

This tough sequel to JESSE JAMES opens as Jesse James is shot in the back by the notorious Ford brothers. When the pair is pardoned by the law, Jesse's brother Frank (Fonda), who has gone straight, decides to strap his guns back on and seek his own revenge. But he is sidelined when framed by the brothers for murder and robbery. At the trial, with the Ford brothers gloating in the audience, a young female reporter (Tierney) covering his trial discovers the truth. Fonda's performance is effectively subdued. This was also Gene Tierney's acting debut. A thoroughly enjoyable Western.

A: Henry Fonda, Jackie Cooper, Gene Tierney, John Carradine, Henry Hull, J. Edward Bromberg

© FOXVIDEO 1328

RIO GRANDE

D: John Ford — 105 m

NR · WST ACT · 1950 · B&W · Rating: 8

Sex · Nud · ✓ Viol · Lang · AdSit

This epic Western that was the last of the famous cavalry trilogy by John Ford. (First came FORT APACHE, then came SHE WORE A YELLOW RIBBON.) Here John Wayne is the commander of a remote western Army outpost, fighting a war with the Apache. His son has flunked out of West Point and now shows up as a new member of his regiment. Soon his strong-willed estranged wife (O'Hara) arrives, insisting on getting the boy released from the army. This film is rich in characters and the Army's traditions of bravery and gallantry. It is loaded with beautiful scenery, has songs by the Sons of the Pioneers and lots of action too, but it also stretches history and credibility to the breaking point.

A: John Wayne, Maureen O'Hara, Ben Johnson, Chill Wills, J. Carrol Naish, Victor McLaglen

© REPUBLIC PICTURES HOME VIDEO 3457

RIVER OF NO RETURN

D: Otto Preminger — 91 m

NR · WST · 1954 · COLOR · Rating: 7

Sex · Nud · ✓ Viol · Lang · ✓ AdSit

Entertaining Western adventure. When Monroe and her ruthless gambler boyfriend (Calhoun) meet with danger on a sinking river raft, Mitchum and his son (Rettig) pull them to safety. Calhoun, who is in a hurry to register a gold claim that he won dishonestly, steals Mitchum's horse and gun and deserts them all, including Monroe. Left stranded and at the mercy of rampaging Indians, Monroe, Mitchum and Rettig make a treacherous journey downriver on a raft to safety. Plenty of action as the trio careen down the swift river, beautiful scenery and romantic action between Monroe and Mitchum.

A: Robert Mitchum, Marilyn Monroe, Rory Calhoun, Tommy Rettig, Murvyn Vye, Douglas Spencer

© FOXVIDEO 5139

SAN ANTONIO

D: David Butler — 107 m

NR · WST · 1945 · COLOR · Rating: 6

Sex · Nud · ✓ Viol · Lang · AdSit

A traditional and pretty predictable Western, but with plenty of action. When Flynn, a rancher, discovers who has been stealing his cattle, he heads into the wide open town of San Antonio after the rustlers. A beautiful saloon girl (Smith) is working for the saloon owner (Francen), who is also the corrupt cattle rustler who has been stealing Flynn's cattle. Good-guy Flynn enters the scene, uncovers Francen's criminal operation, and Smith falls in love with him. Good actioner that moves along at a rapid pace.

A: Errol Flynn, Alexis Smith, S.Z. Sakall, Victor Francen, Florence Bates, John Litel

Distributed By MGM/UA Home Video M202120

SAN FRANCISCO

D: W.S. Van Dyke — 116 m

NR · WST ROM · 1936 · B&W · Rating: 8

Sex · Nud · ✓ Viol · Lang · AdSit

Big-budget flick populated by all the big-name stars MGM could muster. Set on the Barbary Coast of San Francisco in 1906, Gable is the dapper owner of one of the biggest and best saloons. He falls in love with the beautiful singer Jeanette MacDonald. She is also one of the town's best and is in demand by every saloon owner. Gable vies for her attentions but he also leads an effort to destroy the corrupt political forces that are controlling the waterfront. Just as he appears to be making headway on both fronts they are hit with the famous 1906 San Francisco earthquake. Great special effects that are still impressive today.

A: Clark Gable, Jeanette MacDonald, Spencer Tracy, Jack Holt, Jessie Ralph, Ted Healy

Distributed By MGM/UA Home Video M300474

SHANE

D: George Stevens 117 m

NR | WST ACT ROM | 1953 | COLOR

10 This is the quintessential Western or, at the very least, among the best of the very best. A mysterious drifter rides onto a dusty hardscrabble farm. He intends to stop for just a little while but stays on to become a hired hand. It is plain that he is no ordinary man - he's running from a past. The farmer likes him, the boy idolizes him and the farmer's wife finds herself powerfully attracted to him. However, a hard-headed pioneer cattle rancher is trying to drive all the sodbusters off and the stranger must decide if he should stay out of the fight or give his new friends the kind of help only a man like him can give.

Sex | Nud | ✓ Viol | Lang | ✓ AdSit

A: Van Heflin, Alan Ladd, Jean Arthur, Brandon de Wilde, Jack Palance, Ben Johnson

© PARAMOUNT HOME VIDEO 6522

SHE WORE A YELLOW RIBBON

D: John Ford 103 m

NR | WST ACT | 1949 | COLOR

10 Thrilling middle episode of Ford's cavalry trilogy (FORT APACHE and RIO GRANDE.) This time John is the aging commander (Captain Brittles) of a calvary outpost and he is being forced to retire just as war is about to break out with the Indians. Unable to make peace, unable to get the settlers evacuated in time and unwilling to let someone else lead this fight, Captain Brittles leads his men against the Indian raiders. A winning Western in every way: rousing action, fascinating characters and brilliant photography (Oscar).

Sex | Nud | ✓ Viol | Lang | AdSit

A: John Wayne, Joanne Dru, Ben Johnson, John Agar, Harry Carey, Jr., Victor McLaglen

© TURNER HOME ENTERTAINMENT 2065

SOUTH OF ST. LOUIS

D: Ray Enright 88 m

NR | WST | 1949 | COLOR

6 Three partners in a Texas ranch (McCrea, Scott and Kennedy) are best friends. That is until the Civil War, in the form of the invading Union Army, destroys their ranch and leaves them all broke. They each go their separate ways. One joins the Confederate Army, and a pretty dancehall girl entices the other two into a scheme to run guns through the Yankee blockade into the South. A solid Western with some solid acting by a big name cast.

Sex | Nud | ✓ Viol | Lang | ✓ AdSit

A: Joel McCrea, Alexis Smith, Zachary Scott, Dorothy Malone, Douglas Kennedy, Alan Hale

© REPUBLIC PICTURES HOME VIDEO 3835

SPOILERS, THE

D: Ray Enright 84 m

NR | WST ACT | 1942 | B&W

7 An innocent ship's captain (Wayne) is tricked by an unscrupulous town official (Scott), out of the rich gold mine that he and his partner (Harry Carey) own. It's 1890 and this is the Klondike. If they're are going to get it back at all, they are going to have to do it themselves. He and Scott also end up vying for the attentions of a sexy saloon girl (Dietrich). The clincher to both of these battles comes in one of the most elaborate (and most often imitated) barroom fight scenes ever filmed. This is the fourth of five screen remakes of this same story.

Sex | Nud | Viol | Lang | ✓ AdSit

A: John Wayne, Randolph Scott, Marlene Dietrich, Margaret Lindsay, Harry Carey, Richard Barthelmess

© MCA/UNIVERSAL HOME VIDEO, INC. 80015

STAGECOACH

D: John Ford 97 m

NR | WST ACT | 1939 | B&W

9 A landmark Western in every way - intelligent and exciting, too. And, it made both John Ford and John Wayne into big names. Nine entirely different people are forced to be together on board a stagecoach through Apache country and are set upon in an Indian attack. Mitchell won a Supporting Oscar as a drunken doctor. Wayne is an escaped prisoner out for revenge for the deaths of his father and brother, but he had been caught and is being taken back to jail by a sheriff (Bancroft). Claire Trevor is a prostitute who falls in love with Wayne. Filmed in beautiful Monument Valley, Utah. A true classic!

Sex | Nud | ✓ Viol | Lang | ✓ AdSit

A: John Wayne, Claire Trevor, John Carradine, Thomas Mitchell, Donald Meek, Andy Devine

© WARNER HOME VIDEO 35078

STATION WEST

D: Sidney Lanfield 80 m

NR | WST | 1948 | B&W

7 Dusty Western with a romantic twist. In a small Western town, a rash of gold robberies is disrupting life and prosperity. Dick Powell is an undercover Army officer who is assigned to find the man behind the robberies. However while he is going through the clues, he meets and falls for a very captivating woman (Greer), the owner of a gambling house and, to his surprise, the ringleader! Solid entertainment based on the story by Luke Short.

Sex | Nud | ✓ Viol | Lang | ✓ AdSit

A: Dick Powell, Jane Greer, Tom Powers, Raymond Burr, Steve Brodie, Gordon Oliver

© TURNER HOME ENTERTAINMENT 2051

TALL IN THE SADDLE

D: Edwin L. Marin 79 m

NR | WST ACT | 1944 | B&W

7 Enjoyable, rip snorter - an old-style Western. John is a cowboy who just has no time for women until he takes a job at a ranch owned by an aging spinster, who also has a beautiful niece. His cousin and another cowboy have been killed by a corrupt judge who wanted the cousin's ranch. And now, the judge is after the old woman's ranch, too. Lots of shootouts, fistfights and chases, and in the end John gets the girl.

Sex | Nud | ✓ Viol | Lang | AdSit

A: John Wayne, Ella Raines, George "Gabby" Hayes, Ward Bond, Don Douglas

© TURNER HOME ENTERTAINMENT 6028

TEXAS

D: George Marshall 94 m

NR | WST ACT | 1941 | B&W

8 High quality Western that proved to be an excellent starring vehicle for two young stars who would later become supporting pillars of the genre. Glenn Ford and William Holden are two young Confederate veterans drifting through Texas. But when they are mistaken for stage robbers by a posse, they have to separate and make a run for it. When they meet up again, they become pawns on opposite sides of a fight between cattlemen and rustlers, and they are also rivals for the hand of Claire Trevor. Action-packed, fun-filled, funny and highly enjoyable.

Sex | Nud | ✓ Viol | Lang | AdSit

A: William Holden, Glenn Ford, Claire Trevor, George Bancroft, Edgar Buchanan, Raymond Hatton

© COLUMBIA TRISTAR HOME VIDEO 60664

THEY DIED WITH THEIR BOOTS ON

D: Raoul Walsh 140 m

NR | WST ACT | 1941 | B&W

8 This rousing Western swashbuckler was originally represented as being the story of General George Custer. It is widely accepted as being a classic film, but it is not at all a credible history lesson. Still, Errol Flynn put in one of his most respected efforts, tracing the life of Custer from his days at West Point, his military exploits, and his marriage to his downfall at Little Big Horn. Flynn in life was just as flamboyant as was Custer. As fiction, this is good and exciting entertainment. It is only diminished when you know the truth.

Sex | Nud | ✓ Viol | Lang | AdSit

A: Errol Flynn, Olivia de Havilland, Arthur Kennedy, Anthony Quinn, Sydney Greenstreet, Charley Grapewin

Distributed By MGM/UA Home Video M201473

TUMBLEWEEDS

D: King Baggot, William S. Hart 141 m

NR | WST | 1925 | B&W

9 One of the silent era's biggest Westerns. It was also Hart's last film. Hart is a cowboy in 1889 Oklahoma. He's fallen in love with a settler's pretty daughter and he realizes that the era of the open range and the cowboy is also nearly over. His one chance at happiness is the free land that the government is giving away in western Oklahama - the great Oklahoma Land Rush on the Cherokee strip. But he gets to the race late. His ride from far behind, through masses of bicycles, horses, buggies and wagons is still a thrilling spectacle. A true classic.

Sex | Nud | ✓ Viol | Lang | AdSit

A: William S. Hart, Barbara Bedford, Lucien Littlefield, Lillian Leighton, J. Gorden Russell, Richard J. Neill

© VIDEO YESTERYEAR 598

UNCONQUERED

D: Cecil B. DeMille 147 m

NR | WST | 1947 | COLOR

6 Another big-budget DeMille epic -- this time set in 1763 -- it's the settlers against the Indians and corrupt white men. Gary Cooper is an American colonial hero set on stopping an Indian uprising, led by the great Indian leader Pontiac, and on winning over the heart of a pretty indentured servant, Paulette Goddard. Big budget and big sets are used to tell a slightly overblown tale of intrigue and adventure in the wilds of the Ohio river valley.

Sex | Nud | ✓ Viol | Lang | AdSit

A: Gary Cooper, Paulette Goddard, Howard da Silva, Boris Karloff, Cecil Kellaway, Ward Bond

© MCA/UNIVERSAL HOME VIDEO, INC. 80344

UNION PACIFIC

D: Cecil B. DeMille 136 m

NR | WST | 1939 | COLOR

8 Big-budget classic Western. At the end of the Civil War, a great and expensive effort was launched to unite the East Coast with the West. The Union Pacific would build westward and the Central Pacific would build eastward. However, one man conspired to slow the Union Pacific down. So, the Union brought in Joel McCrea to clean up the trouble makers. The trouble is that one of the trouble makers is his old friend from the War, Robert Preston and both are in love with spunky Barbara Stanwyck. Quite well done, with a spectacular train wreck and plenty of action, but sparked by fine understated acting from Preston and McCrea.

Sex | Nud | ✓ Viol | Lang | AdSit

A: Barbara Stanwyck, Joel McCrea, Akim Tamiroff, Robert Preston, Lynne Overman, Brian Donlevy

© MCA/UNIVERSAL HOME VIDEO, INC. 81214

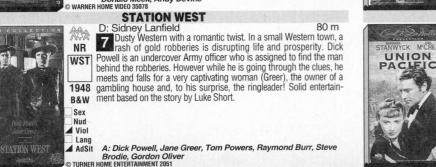

VERA CRUZ

D: Robert Aldrich 94 m

NR | WST ACT | 1954 | COLOR

7 Solid Western action! Set during the Mexican Revolution of 1866, two Americans (Cooper and Lancaster) have come to Mexico to sell their services to the highest bidder. They are hired to escort a large shipment of gold to Emperor Maximilian in Vera Cruz. But, the alliance that the pair has formed was built on shaky ground from the very beginning, and things get very tense when Cooper allows himself to be convinced by a beautiful woman (Darcel) to hand the goods over to local rebels. Lancaster meanwhile, has his own plans for the precious cargo. Two-fisted adventure!

☐ Sex ☐ Nud ◢ Viol ☐ Lang ◢ AdSit

A: Gary Cooper, Burt Lancaster, Denise Darcel, Cesar Romero, George Macready, Ernest Borgnine

Distributed By MGM/UA Home Video M202015

VIRGINIA CITY

D: Michael Curtiz 121 m

NR | WST ACT | 1940 | B&W

6 Two-fisted Civil War Western! Confederate colonel Scott is determined to get $5,000,000 in gold through to the Confederacy from Nevada. Errol Flynn is a Union spy who is sent to see that he doesn't. Bogart is a half-breed Mexican bandit who only loves the gold. Miriam Hopkins is a Rebel spy, traveling west on a stagecoach supposedly enroute to become a saloon singer in Virginia City. She and Flynn meet aboard the coach going west when it is held up by Bogart. Meanwhile, back in Virginia City, Scott is plotting to get the gold out. Contrived, but good action and great cast.

☐ Sex ☐ Nud ☐ Viol ☐ Lang ◢ AdSit

A: Humphrey Bogart, Errol Flynn, Randolph Scott, Miriam Hopkins, Frank McHugh, Alan Hale

Distributed By MGM/UA Home Video M202526

VIVA VILLA!

D: David O. Selzenick 115 m

NR | WST ACT DMA | 1934 | B&W

9 Mexico's legendary bandit hero proved to be excellent material for this very entertaining film which was nominated for Best Picture and two other nominations. It is also acclaimed as Berry's finest screen performance. Villa rises from being a captivating bandit leader who robs from the rich, keeps most of it and gives some to the poor to becoming a leader of the Mexican Revolutionary Army. After the victory he reverts to being a bandit, only to return with his army later and declare himself President of the country - until he again retires to his ranch. Huge box office sensation. Facts are questionable.

☐ Sex ☐ Nud ◢ Viol ☐ Lang ◢ AdSit

A: Wallace Beery, Fay Wray, Stuart Erwin, Leo Carrillo, Donald Cook, George E. Stone

Distributed By MGM/UA Home Video M202835

WAGON MASTER

D: John Ford 86 m

NR | WST | 1950 | B&W

7 The king of the Westerns, John Ford, directed this fine saga of the real Old West and it later inspired the long running TV series "Wagon Train," which also starred Ward Bond. Two fun-loving carefree cowboy ramblers are hired to guide a westward-bound Mormon wagontrain that is heading off into the largely unknown Utah territory and straight into confrontation with Indians and ruthless outlaws. This is a realistic depiction of the people and the time. It was also one of John Ford's favorites, and one of the earliest starring roles for Ben Johnson, Harry Carey Jr. and James Arness.

☐ Sex ☐ Nud ◢ Viol ☐ Lang ☐ AdSit

A: Ben Johnson, Joanne Dru, Ward Bond, Harry Carey, Jr., Jane Darwell, James Arness

WESTERNER, THE

D: William Wyler 100 m

NR | WST COM | 1940 | B&W

9 Very entertaining Western. Cooper is a cowboy drifting through Texas on his way to California but he has the misfortune of buying a horse from a horse thief. Worse, he is brought up on the charges before the infamous "judge" Roy Bean (Brennan won his third Oscar as the likable bad-guy judge). Cooper only just keeps from being hung by convincing the judge that he once met Lilly Langtree, the judge's great love, and even has a lock of her hair. Coop and Bean become best friends, but Coop eventually chooses sides against him after the judge burns out some homesteader friends of Coop. A good time.

☐ Sex ☐ Nud ◢ Viol ☐ Lang ☐ AdSit

A: Gary Cooper, Walter Brennan, Doris Davenport, Dana Andrews, Chill Wills, Forrest Tucker

WESTERN UNION

D: Fritz Lang 95 m

NR | WST | 1941 | COLOR

7 Epic Western about the construction of the first telegraph line through the West. Western Union has hired an ex-outlaw (Randolf Scott) as a guide and an Eastern dandy (Robert Young) to do the job. The two must battle against the terrain, the weather, the Indians and Scott's former gang to get their job done. And, they are also fighting each other over the love of pretty telegrapher Virginian Gilmore. Entertaining and spirited.

☐ Sex ☐ Nud ◢ Viol ☐ Lang ☐ AdSit

A: Randolph Scott, Vance Shaw, Robert Young, Barton MacLane, Virginia Gilmore, Chill Wills

WINCHESTER '73

D: Anthony Mann 82 m

NR | WST | 1950 | B&W

8 All through the '40s, in part because of WWII, the Western movie had steadily lost its appeal at the box office - that is, until this movie came along. It is credited with inspiring a rebirth of the whole genre. Jimmy Stewart and his misfit brother enter into a sharpshooting contest, with the winner to receive a special issue of the newly invented repeating rifle from Winchester. Stewart wins the rifle but it is soon stolen from him. Stewart pursues his rifle through ambushes, fistfights and gunfights with outlaws and Indians. He will recover the one-of-a-kind rifle and also catch his father's murderer, his own brother.

☐ Sex ☐ Nud ◢ Viol ☐ Lang ☐ AdSit

A: James Stewart, Shelley Winters, Dan Duryea, Tony Curtis, Rock Hudson, Will Geer

Family

Suitable for Family Viewing

Video's Best

1956 and After

Action

ADVENTURES OF DON JUAN, THE

D: Vincent Sherman 111 m

NR | ACT COM | 1949 | B&W | Sex | Nud | Viol | Lang | AdSit

7 Colorful costume epic. Errol Flynn plays the great lover and swordsman. This is a very extravagant film in which handsome swashbuckler Flynn is engaged in grand sword fights and in stringing along countless maidens - all of whom he forsakes to save his queen from the evil Duke. The story is told in tongue-in-cheek style, all the while poking fun at Flynn's own reputation as a great lover.

A: Errol Flynn, Viveca Lindfors, Robert Douglas, Alan Hale, Romney Brent, Jerry Austin

Distributed By MGM/UA Home Video M600748

ADVENTURES OF ROBIN HOOD, THE

D: Michael Curtiz, William Keighley 103 m

NR | ACT ROM | 1938 | COLOR | Sex | Nud | Viol | Lang | AdSit

9 Extravagant classic adventure film. Dashing Errol Flynn is at his swashbuckling best, wooing Maid Marian (de Havilland), ruining the plans of the evil prince (Rains), robbing from the rich and giving to the poor and fighting wicked and haughty Sir Guy of Gisbourne (Rathbone). Lavish sets in Technicolor are a major asset to this hallmark adventure classic. See also ROBIN AND MARIAN, with Sean Connery as Robin Hood, and Kevin Costner in ROBIN HOOD, PRINCE OF THIEVES.

A: Errol Flynn, Basil Rathbone, Ian Hunter, Olivia de Havilland, Claude Rains, Alan Hale

Distributed By MGM/UA Home Video M201377

BATMAN: MASK OF THE PHANTASM

D: Eric Radomski, Bruce Timm 77 m

PG | ACT CLD | 1994 | COLOR | Sex | Nud | Viol | Lang | AdSit

8 After two super-budget feature films and a campy TV series, the Batman of the comic series returned in animated form this time. This version stays true to the style, and even the time (late 1930's) of the original. Andrea, Bruce Wayne's only true love, has come back to Gotham City but Batman (Bruce Wayne in disguise) is now suspected by the police in the murders of several major crime figures. One crime lord is so terrified of him that he has hired The Joker to protect him. However, the murderer is not Batman but yet another masked avenger. So, if Batman is to regain his good name, he must find out the truth. Exciting and well done but realistic and very violent, so this is not for very young. Many adults will like it too.

A:

© WARNER HOME VIDEO 15500

BEAU GESTE

D: William Wellman 114 m

NR | ACT DMA | 1939 | B&W | Sex | Nud | Viol | Lang | AdSit

9 Excellent! First made in 1926, then again in 1966, this is still the best screen version. It is a classic story of honor, sacrifice and brotherly love. When one brother falsely admits to a jewel theft to save the honor of their impoverished governess and then joins the Foreign Legion, his two brothers join him there. Amid the desert sands and dead soldiers propped against the walls of a desert fortress, the brothers battle native attacks and the tyranny of their sadistic sergeant. The action, story and the characters are all unforgettable. Thought of as a man's movie.

A: Gary Cooper, Robert Preston, Ray Milland, Brian Donlevy, J. Carrol Naish, Susan Hayward

© MCA/UNIVERSAL HOME VIDEO, INC. 80547

BEN HUR

D: Fred Niblo 148 m

NR | ACT DMA | 1926 | B&W | Sex | Nud | Viol | Lang | AdSit

8 Gigantic first remake of the original version, which was first filmed in 1907. This silent epic cost a staggering $4,000,000 and took two years to edit. It was the grandest of all the silent movie spectacles and still holds up well compared to the 1959 version with Charlton Heston. It is the story of a Jewish nobleman who is condemned to a life of slavery by a Roman he had called friend. He later returns to seek vengeance on his betrayer. Novarro and Bushman give the performances of their lives. Colossal. Still a winner.

A: Ramon Novarro, Francis X. Bushman, May McAvoy, Betty Bronson, Carmel Myers

Distributed By MGM/UA Home Video M301474

BEN HUR

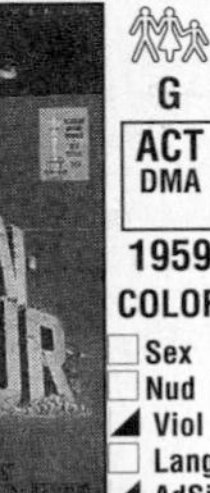

D: William Wyler 211 m

G | ACT DMA | 1959 | COLOR | Sex | Nud | Viol | Lang | AdSit

10 This monumental picture still holds the record for the most Oscars at 11 out of 12 nominations. The story line concerns a wealthy Jewish nobleman (Heston) who incurs the wrath of a Roman military governor who was also his childhood friend. Heston's family is imprisoned and he is sentenced to slavery as an oarsman on a galley. There, he saves the life of his Roman master and reattains a position of honor. He then returns to seek vengeance on his former friend in a spectacular chariot race. WOW! Fantastic special effects and photography. See it in wide screen only.

A: Charlton Heston, Jack Hawkins, Sam Jaffe, Stephen Boyd, Martha Scott

Distributed By MGM/UA Home Video M900004

BILLY JACK

D: T.C. Frank 114 m

PG | ACT DMA | 1971 | COLOR | Sex | Nud | Viol | Lang | AdSit

7 A powerful, youth-oriented favorite. A huge film at the time of its release, it developed a cult following for its support of freedom, justice and anything anti-establishment. It made bold statements against bigotry, education and the government. Billy Jack (Laughlin) is a young half-breed Indian and a former Green Beret who is dedicated to single-handedly saving a "freedom school" for troubled children from reactionary townsfolk. His weapon - his finely honed karate skills - is what keeps their intrusions at bay.

A: Tom Laughlin, Deloris Taylor, Clark Howat, Bert Freed, Kenneth Tobey, Julie Webb

© WARNER HOME VIDEO 1040

BULLDOG DRUMMOND

D: Sidney Howard — 89 m

NR | ACT CRM | 1929 | B&W

6 Bulldog Drummond was a fictional character born in print in 1919. In the '20s he was brought to the silent screen, then in 1929 to talkies. Bulldog was a British ex-army officer who was always searching for adventure. Ronald Coleman has played the character twice, first here. In this episode, Bulldog aids a lady whose uncle has been kidnapped by phony psychiatrists. This is probably the best of the Drummond series.

Sex / Nud / Viol / Lang / AdSit

A: Ronald Colman, Joan Bennet, Lilyan Tashman

© HBO VIDEO 90751

BULLITT

D: Peter Yates — 114 m

PG | ACT CRM | 1968 | COLOR

9 This is the picture which set the standard in police action dramas for a long time, and it still stands up extremely well today. McQueen, in one of his best performances, plays a tough police detective assigned to guard a criminal witness for 48 hours and to then deliver him to testify. But his witness was shot and now he is chasing down the killer. Lots of plot twists make this a movie to be watched... but the car chase scenes make it a movie to watch over and over. Filmed at actual speeds in excess of 100 mph, they're excitement-plus, and some of the best ever done like it.

Sex / Nud / ◢ Viol / Lang / ◢ AdSit

A: Steve McQueen, Robert Vaughn, Jacqueline Bisset, Norman Fell, Don Gordon, Robert Duvall

© WARNER HOME VIDEO 1029

CALL OF THE WILD

D: Ken Annakin — 104 m

PG | ACT DMA | 1972 | COLOR

7 Jack London's classic story remade. This time it has Charlton Heston in the lead role of an Alaskan gold prospector whose dog is stolen and forced into sad and sadistic service for others. This is good viewing, but there were three other productions of this story. Virtually all of them are better, but none are available on video except for the excellent 1991 variation by Disney called WHITE FANG.

Sex / Nud / ◢ Viol / ◢ Lang / AdSit

A: Charlton Heston, Michele Mercier, Marla Rohm, Rik Battagila

© GOODTIMES 8385

CAPTAIN BLOOD

D: Michael Curtiz — 120 m

NR | ACT | 1935 | B&W

9 One of the best swashbucklers ever. Flynn, in his first starring role, plays a 17th-century doctor sold into slavery in the Caribbean after treating the wounds of rebels. He is purchased by the beautiful niece (de Haviland) of a brutal plantation owner, but escapes to become the leader of a band of pirates and he launches his own battle against the colonial governor (Atwill). Great miniature work, an excellent cast and some of the best sword fights ever put on screen. This film received a nomination as Best Picture and made stars out of Flynn, de Haviland and Curtiz.

Sex / Nud / ◢ Viol / Lang / AdSit

A: Errol Flynn, Olivia de Havilland, Lionel Atwill, Basil Rathbone, Guy Kibbee, Ross Alexander

Distributed By MGM/UA Home Video M201470

CHARGE OF THE LIGHT BRIGADE, THE

D: Michael Curtiz — 117 m

NR | ACT DMA | 1936 | B&W

8 This is a fictionalized account of what may have happened to 600 British cavalrymen who gallantly charged into certain death (and 25,000 Russians) with their sabers flashing during the Crimean War (1853-1856). One of the most dramatic calvary charges ever filmed is showcased in this story which was originally painted in the words of Tennyson's classic poem. This version has Major Vickers (Flynn) leading the 27th Lancers in a quest to find the Indian leader of a massacre of women and children. Thundering action against a romantic backdrop.

Sex / Nud / ◢ Viol / Lang / AdSit

A: Errol Flynn, Olivia de Havilland, Patric Knowles, Donald Crisp, Henry Stephenson, Nigel Bruce

Distributed By MGM/UA Home Video M201510

CHINA GATE

D: Samuel Fuller — 95 m

NR | ACT | 1957 | B&W

7 Prior to the major United States involvement in Indochina (Vietnam), it was a French colony. This film presents a very early view of Vietnam and France's troubles there. It is primarily an action story that concerns a group of Foreign Legion soldiers led by Sergeant Brock (Barry) who must go deep into the jungle to blow up a communist ammunition dump. They are led there by Lucky Legs, a beautiful Eurasian girl (Dickenson), and she and Brock are not strangers. They had a love affair which resulted in a child that Brock refuses to acknowledge.

Sex / Nud / ◢ Viol / Lang / ◢ AdSit

A: Gene Barry, Angie Dickinson, Nat King Cole, Paul Dubov, Lee Van Cleef, George Givot

© REPUBLIC PICTURES HOME VIDEO 0648

CHINA SEAS

D: Tay Garnett — 88 m

NR | ACT | 1935 | B&W

7 Clark Gable and his tramp steamer are between Hong Kong and Singapore when they are hit by a typhoon. All that bouncing around reveals that he has a contraband load of gold on board. Soon, they are boarded by a group of Malaysian pirates who are led by Wallace Beery and they are looking for the gold, which has been hidden again. Also aboard are Gable's ex-lover with a tainted past (Jean Harlow) and a beautiful English aristocrat (Russell). Russell has started a new flame in Clark's boilers, which causes a jealous Harlow to side with Beery. Action-filled story is pretty contrived but it nonetheless offers a good time.

Sex / Nud / ◢ Viol / Lang / ◢ AdSit

A: Clark Gable, Jean Harlow, Wallace Beery, Lewis Stone, Rosalind Russell, Hattie McDaniel

Distributed By MGM/UA Home Video MV300561

CONAN THE DESTROYER

D: Richard Fleischer — 101 m

PG | ACT FAN | 1984 | COLOR

6 Far less violent than its predecessor CONAN THE BARBARIAN. Conan is recruited to accompany a beautiful princess (d'Abo) to a castle on a search for a magical gemstone. He and an assortment of accomplices he has picked up along the way, battle and defeat beasts and baddies as they proceed along. Played more for laughs this time. Still plenty of action, but certainly more suitable for the family.

Sex / Nud / ◢ Viol / Lang / ◢ AdSit

A: Arnold Schwarzenegger, Grace Jones, Wilt Chamberlain, Sarah Douglas, Olivia D'Abo, Mako

© MCA/UNIVERSAL HOME VIDEO, INC. 80079

CORSICAN BROTHERS, THE

D: Gregory Ratoff — 96 m

NR | ACT | 1941 | COLOR

7 Alexander Dumas's famous story of twins who are physically separated at birth but are spiritually linked forever. Their parents are murdered in a blood feud and one child is sent to Paris while the other is sent to the mountains to be raised. When they are grown, they are reunited. They seek to avenge the deaths of their parents and both seek the hand of the same woman. Douglas Fairbanks is a swashbuckler of the highest order because he plays both brothers. Lots of swordplay and hero-type stuff. Not played too seriously, mostly just for fun.

Sex / Nud / ◢ Viol / Lang / ◢ AdSit

A: Douglas Fairbanks, Jr., Ruth Warrick, Akim Tamiroff, J. Carrol Naish, H.B. Warner

© VIDEO TREASURES SV9616

CRIMSON PIRATE, THE

D: Robert Siodmak — 105 m

NR | ACT | 1952 | COLOR

8 One of the greatest swashbucklers. An incredibly agile young Burt Lancaster plays a pirate captain who wants only to profit from the battle between the Spanish crown and Caribbean rebels. Instead, he is drawn into the battle for freedom from Spain by beautiful Eva Bartok and rallies a band of freedom-loving rebels to the cause of independence. Exuberant and fast-paced, with lots of great action scenes and plenty of laughs. If you like pirate movies (and even if you don't) this is well worth your time. It was a follow-up to the successful THE FLAME AND THE ARROW.

Sex / Nud / ◢ Viol / Lang / ◢ AdSit

A: Burt Lancaster, Nick Cravat, Eva Bartok, Torin Thatcher, Christopher Lee

© WARNER HOME VIDEO 11269

DAMN THE DEFIANT!

D: Lewis Gilbert — 101 m

NR | ACT DMA | 1962 | COLOR

8 Dramatic tale of an eighteenth-century British warship and its crew which is at war with both the French and with itself. Great attention to historic detail and a fine performances from its cast gives this production a first-rate quality. Guinness is the captain of the British warship H.M.S Defiant, but he is opposed by Bogarde, his cruel first officer, whose iron-fisted rule has the crew ready to mutiny. When Guinness is wounded and Bogarde takes command, the crew does mutiny - just as they are about to enter a major battle. Guinness must win them back.

Sex / Nud / ◢ Viol / Lang / ◢ AdSit

A: Alec Guinness, Dirk Bogarde, Maurice Denham, Anthony Quayle, Peter Gill, Nigel Stock

© COLUMBIA TRISTAR HOME VIDEO 60825

DIAMONDS ARE FOREVER

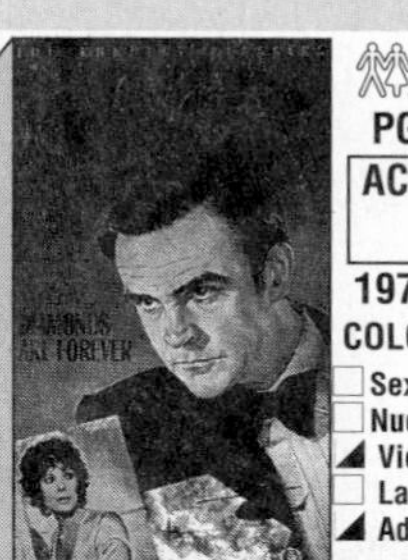

D: Guy Hamilton — 121 m

PG | ACT | 1971 | COLOR

7 James Bond's eighth outing (sixth for Connery and his second-to-last) - this time in the American Southwest. Bad guy (Charles Gray) uses the Las Vegas base of operations of a kidnapped millionaire recluse (Jimmy Dean) and a huge diamond-smuggling enterprise to finance his attempt to harness the sun's power. He intends to use a satellite-based light collector and laser beam to control the world. Not the best Bond effort, but pretty good - with plenty of action, gadgets and girls.

Sex / Nud / ◢ Viol / Lang / ◢ AdSit

A: Sean Connery, Jill St. John, Charles Gray, Lana Wood, Jimmy Dean, Bruce Cabot

Distributed By MGM/UA Home Video M201406

DICK TRACY

D: Warren Beatty 105 m

PG | ACT CRM FAN | 1990 | COLOR | Sex Nud Viol Lang AdSit

7 Cartoon-like megabuck production that is a parody of the famous long-running comic-strip hero. There is a terrific line-up of major actors, however some are almost unrecognizable under makeup. (Al Pacino is despicable as the main villain who plans to unite all the bad guys. Madonna is marvelously vampy as Breathless Mahoney. Glenne Headly is lovely as Tracy's (Beatty) love interest.) Tracy rises to challenge the bad guys, but has trouble with his personal life. Plenty of shoot-'em-up action, against an unreal cartoon-like backdrop. Pretty good fun, not wonderful.

A: Warren Beatty, Madonna, Al Pacino, Dustin Hoffman, Mandy Patinkin, Paul Sorvino

© TOUCHSTONE HOME VIDEO 1066

DOBERMAN GANG, THE

D: Byron Ross Chudnow 85 m

G | ACT CRM | 1972 | COLOR | Sex Nud Viol Lang AdSit

7 A con man who doesn't trust human partners, kidnaps six vicious Doberman Pinschers and a dog trainer, and then uses them to rob a particularly difficult bank. Six vicious-looking dogs rush into a bank with studded collars and saddlebags. One dog delivers a note to the tellers and the others stand guard. The real thieves are outside, but no one knows who they are. Ingenious low-budget flick that really works quite well. The dogs steal the show. Good family fare. Led to two sequels.

A: Byron Mabe, Hal Reed, Julie Parrish, Simmy Bow, Jojo D'Amore, Juhn Tull

© CBS/FOX VIDEO 7793

DON JUAN

D: Alan Crosland 111 m

NR | ACT | 1926 | B&W | Sex Nud Viol Lang AdSit

7 Entertaining swashbuckler which holds the record for the most screen kisses, 127. The story is of a famous rogue and his escapades - until he falls hard for Mary Astor. But Lucretia Borgia (Taylor) wants him to marry into her clan. This leads to one of the best sword duels ever put on film. Barrymore was at his best as a screen lover and swordfighter, and was surrounded by a top-notch cast. The film is also notable for being the first silent film released with Vitaphone music and sound effects (recorded on a separate disc and played along with the soundless film).

A: John Barrymore, Mary Astor, Willard Louis, Estelle Taylor, Helene Costello, Warner Oland

Distributed By MGM/UA Home Video M302162

DRAGONSLAYER

D: Matthew Robbins 110 m

PG | ACT FAN | 1981 | COLOR | Sex Nud Viol Lang AdSit

6 Enjoyable fantasy adventure. A horrible fire-breathing dragon is terrorizing the British countryside and an aging sorcerer is the only one who can stop it, but he is killed. So the job falls to his apprentice, who quickly finds himself in over his head, but only after he has already agreed to slay the dragon to save both a damsel in distress and the kingdom. Rich in special effects and period flavor. Set in 6th-century England and filmed on location in England, Scotland and Wales. Pretty scary and gruesome for real young ones and a little too corny for oldsters, but just right for those in between.

A: Peter MacNicol, Caitlin Clarke, Ralph Richardson, John Hallam, Peter Eyre, Albert Salmi

© PARAMOUNT HOME VIDEO 1367

DR. NO

D: Terence Young 112 m

PG | ACT | 1963 | COLOR | Sex Nud Viol Lang AdSit

9 A James Bond winner. This is the film that launched the Bond juggernaut and made Sean Connery a superstar. It is less gimmicky than later ones, but the Bond elements are all there: nonstop action, witty dialogue, sexy women and humor. British Special Agent 007 is sent to Jamaica to investigate another agent's death. He is soon on his way to the mysterious island retreat of the evil Dr. No. where, with the help of CIA Agent Lord and beautiful Andress, he uncovers a sinister plot by Dr. No to take over the world. But, James defeats it just in the nick of time. Great fun!

A: Sean Connery, Ursula Andress, Joseph Wiseman, Jack Lord, Bernard Lee, Lois Maxwell

Distributed By MGM/UA Home Video M201401

EARTHQUAKE

D: Mark Robson 123 m

PG | ACT SUS | 1974 | COLOR | Sex Nud Viol Lang AdSit

6 This was a monumental disaster film, one of the biggest ever done, in which California is destroyed by "the big one" - buildings collapse, streets buckle and chaos abounds. Theater audiences were also bombarded with "Sensurround" shock waves in addition to the terrific special effects upon the screen. It is packed with action, most of which will translate to the small screen, but the story line is minimal. As is typical in this genre, there are actually several stories running at the same time concerning the different effects of the quake on different people. Huge all-star cast.

A: Charlton Heston, Ava Gardner, Lorne Greene, George Kennedy, Victoria Principal, Walter Matthau

© MCA/UNIVERSAL HOME VIDEO, INC. 55034

EDDIE MACON'S RUN

D: Jeff Kanew 95 m

PG | ACT | 1983 | COLOR | Sex Nud Viol Lang AdSit

6 OK car chase movie in which Schneider is wrongly convicted on trumped-up charges and sentenced to life. He has to get back with his wife and baby, so he escapes from jail and then runs across Texas toward Old Mexico. Kirk Douglas plays an aging cop who relentlessly pursues him. Douglas has his own agenda - he has to catch Sneider so he can prove that he is still valuable. Overall, it's pretty predictable but it does have a good assortment of stunts.

A: Kirk Douglas, John Schneider, Lee Purcell, Leah Ayres, Lisa Dunsheath

© MCA/UNIVERSAL HOME VIDEO, INC. 77016

EL CID

D: Anthony Mann 172 m

NR | ACT ROM DMA | 1961 | COLOR | Sex Nud Viol Lang AdSit

8 Huge spectacle film containing some of the best old-world battle sequences ever filmed. There are miles of men in chain mail, knights on horseback and corpses everywhere. The action and spectacle are the real stars. It is the story of the eleventh-century Spanish warrior/hero El Cid (Heston), who battled Moorish invaders from the south, and the great love of his life (Loren). Magnificent settings and costumes. Much of the love story is overshadowed by the battles. Some of the splendor will be lost on the small screen.

A: Charlton Heston, Sophia Loren, Raf Vallone, Hurd Hatfield, Genevieve Page

© BEST FILM & VIDEO CORP. 215

ELUSIVE PIMPERNEL, THE

D: Michael Powell 107 m

NR | ACT | 1950 | B&W | Sex Nud Viol Lang AdSit

7 Originally made in 1935 as THE SCARLET PIMPERNEL, this very popular character was brought back once again for even more exploits. David Niven plays Sir Percy Blakeney, who, to all appearances, is a cowardly primping aristocrat flitting about London; but, he is actually Pimpernel, a dashing hero who rescues innocent French aristocrats from the hungry guillotine which is being fed by the unruly mobs of the French Revolution. Dashing swashbuckler.

A: David Niven, Margaret Leighton, Cyril Cusack, Jack Hawkins, David Hutcheson

© HOME VISION ELU 01

FAR OFF PLACE, A

D: Mikael Solomon 107 m

PG | ACT | 1993 | COLOR | Sex Nud Viol Lang AdSit

7 This is not at all a typical Walt Disney kid's adventure movie. It is more a video for teenagers (probably not for kids under 10 at all), because of graphic scenes of killing. It is the story of a 14-year-old girl named Nonnie, Xhabbo (a young bushman and her best friend) and Harry, a teenager from New York. Nonnie and her parents lived on the edge of Africa's Kalahari Desert and were fighting a battle against poachers who had been killing elephants for their ivory. However, now the poachers have killed Nonnie's parents and the three teenagers are forced to flee across 700 miles of open desert, with the poachers hot on their trial. Quite good.

A: Reese Witherspoon, Ethan Randall, Jack Thompson, Sarel Bok, Maximilian Schell, Robert Burke

© WALT DISNEY HOME VIDEO 1795

FFOLKES

D: Andrew V. McLaglen 99 m

PG | ACT COM | 1980 | COLOR | Sex Nud Viol Lang AdSit

7 Tongue-in-cheek characterization by Roger Moore in which he plays a character who acts exactly counter to his former role as James Bond. This guy hates women, but loves cats. He is a underwater sabotage expert who is called in by the British government to stop an impending attempt by a psychotic madman (Perkins) who is determined to blow up the largest oil rig in the North Sea unless the government pays him a ransom. This is no classic, but is an enjoyable diversion that is told with a touch of humor. The plot is actually more plausible than most of the James Bond plots.

A: Roger Moore, Anthony Perkins, James Mason, Michael Parks, David Hedison

© MCA/UNIVERSAL HOME VIDEO, INC. 80183

FIREFOX

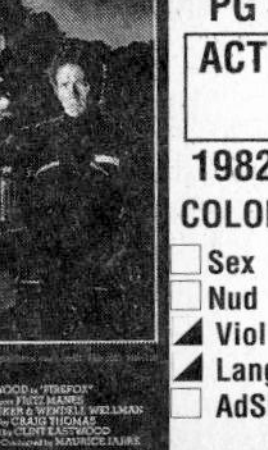

D: Clint Eastwood 136 m

PG | ACT | 1982 | COLOR | Sex Nud Viol Lang AdSit

7 The Russians have created a super fighter that can fly at Mach 6 and everything in it is controlled by the pilot's thoughts. American super-pilot Clint Eastwood is assigned the job of sneaking into a Russian air base and stealing their newest secret weapon, Firefox. Once he gets it off the ground, he still has to get it through the Russian's lethal air defense system. A little slow in the beginning, but then it takes off and gives you a good ride. Good special effects during the flight sequences.

A: Clint Eastwood, Freddie Jones, David Huffman, Warren Clarke, Ronald Lacey, Ken Colley

© WARNER HOME VIDEO 11219

FLAME AND THE ARROW, THE

D: Jacques Tourneur 88 m

NR | ACT | 1950 | COLOR

8 Rousing swashbuckler in which Burt Lancaster plays an acrobatic Robin Hood-like rebel leader, Dardo the Arrow, who is battling a cruel tyrant. After Dardo makes a narrow escape from the gallows, he returns disguised as an acrobat to rescue Virginia Mayo. Then he comes back once more to lead the peasantry in an uprising against the evil Hessian warlord (Allenby) in his castle in the Italian Alps. Excellent production values, good humor and lots of energy make this a lot of fun. You may also want to see the equally good CRIMSON PIRATES, which came later.

Sex, Nud, ◢ Viol, Lang, ◢ AdSit

A: Burt Lancaster, Virginia Mayo, Robert Douglas, Aline MacMahon, Nick Cravat

© WARNER HOME VIDEO 11681

FOR YOUR EYES ONLY

D: John Glen 129 m

PG | ACT | 1981 | COLOR

8 James Bond is back. After many frivolous outings, this fifth appearance of Roger Moore marks a return to a more serious attempt at the original James Bond "feel." Still, there are the beautiful women and action sequences, but its plot is less of a cartoon and more a spy adventure. Bond must gain the return of a top secret device from a sunken submarine with the aid of a Greek beauty - before the Russians get it.

Sex, ◢ Nud, ◢ Viol, ◢ Lang, ◢ AdSit

A: Roger Moore, Carole Bouquet, Chaim Topol, Lynn-Holly Johnson, Julian Glover, Jill Bennett

Distributed By MGM/UA Home Video M200180

FOUR FEATHERS

D: Alexander Korda 115 m

NR | ACT DMA | 1939 | B&W

9 Rousing classic adventure story. A young British army officer from a military family disappoints his friends, family and his sweetheart by resigning his commission in 1898. He wants only to settle down with his wife, but he instead is branded as a coward by them all. He is given a feather by each of his friends and his wife as a symbol of his disgrace. Seeking to redeem his honor, he travels to Egypt and disguises himself as a native to courageously fight alone for his country. One by one, he returns the feathers to their presenters. A rip-snorter of a yarn. Great cast and beautiful photography.

Sex, Nud, ◢ Viol, Lang, ◢ AdSit

A: Ralph Richardson, John Clements, June Duprez, C. Aubrey Smith, Jack Allen

© HBO VIDEO 90787

FROM RUSSIA WITH LOVE

D: Terence Young 119 m

PG | ACT | 1964 | COLOR

9 This is thrilling and definitive Bond. Along with GOLDFINGER, it is one of the best of the James Bond superspy entries. It is a suspenseful adventure in which James becomes involved in a sinister plot which is baited with a beautiful Russian agent. He is pursued and almost done in on the Orient Express by a memorable and truly sinister bad guy (Robert Shaw). And, he is nearly toe-stabbed by a creepy Russian spy-master (Lotte Lenya) just as he thinks his job is complete. More realistic and believable than virtually all the other Bond flicks.

Sex, Nud, ◢ Viol, Lang, ◢ AdSit

A: Sean Connery, Daniela Bianchi, Lotte Lenya, Pedro Amendariz, Robert Shaw

Distributed By MGM/UA Home Video M201402

GATOR

D: Burt Reynolds 116 m

PG | ACT | 1976 | COLOR

6 Gator McKlusky (Reynolds) is back in this sequel to the very popular WHITE LIGHTNING. Now on probation from moonshining charges, good ol' boy Gator is approached by an undercover Department of Justice agent (Weston) and blackmailed into finking on his backwoods buddy and local crime czar Jerry Reed. It seems the corrupt governor (Mike Douglas) needs a big bust to get reelected. But, Gator decides to get revenge on Douglas and his corrupt cronies too. Mildly entertaining, particularly for Reynolds fans.

Sex, Nud, ◢ Viol, Lang, ◢ AdSit

A: Burt Reynolds, Jack Weston, Lauren Hutton, Jerry Reed, Alice Ghostly, Dub Taylor

Distributed By MGM/UA Home Video M301623

GENTLEMAN JIM

D: Raoul Walsh 104 m

NR | ACT | 1942 | B&W

9 Exciting sports biography of the cocky 19th-century heavyweight boxing champion "Gentleman" Jim Corbet. This role was well acted by Errol Flynn and was reportedly his favorite role, even though the film is in many ways historically inaccurate. Jim Corbet was a cocky dandy who could have given Muhammad Ali humble lessons. He was also the first "scientific" fighter: the first to move around the ring and the first to taunt his opponent. Film features the confrontation between Jim and John L. Sullivan (well played by Ward Bond). Great entertainment.

Sex, Nud, ◢ Viol, Lang, ◢ AdSit

A: Errol Flynn, Alexis Smith, Jack Carson, Alan Hale, John Lader, Ward Bond

Distributed By MGM/UA Home Video M202825

G-MEN

D: William Keighley 86 m

NR | ACT CRM | 1935 | B&W

8 James Cagney made his name playing wise-guy gangland characters, but with this film he crossed over to the other side. He's just as cocky as ever, but he's playing a lawyer who was raised by an underworld character. However, when one of his buddies is killed by the mob, he joins the F.B.I. There his inside knowledge proves to be invaluable in the government's efforts to round up underworld kingpins. Jimmy is right there leading the pack on the charge to capture the ten most wanted. It's personal for him. Quite well done entry into the gangster genre and a very popular movie.

Sex, Nud, ◢ Viol, Lang, ◢ AdSit

A: James Cagney, Ann Dvorak, Margaret Lindsay, Robert Armstrong, Barton MacLane, Lloyd Nolan

Distributed By MGM/UA Home Video M202484

GOLDFINGER

D: Guy Hamilton 113 m

PG | ACT | 1964 | COLOR

10 Quintessential classic Bond! Third in the series and perhaps the best, although FROM RUSSIA WITH LOVE is right up there. James must rescue Fort Knox from the infamous Goldfinger's plot to contaminate its entire gold supply with radioactivity, thus making his own horde even more valuable. All the suave charm, excitement and thrills you expect are there, along with beautiful women. While the plot has its share of gadgets, it somehow never loses believability. Great entertainment and a memorable score, as well.

Sex, Nud, ◢ Viol, Lang, ◢ AdSit

A: Sean Connery, Gert Frobe, Honor Blackman, Shirley Eaton, Harold Sakata

Distributed By MGM/UA Home Video M201403

GREAT ESCAPE, THE

D: John Sturges 173 m

NR | ACT WAR DMA | 1963 | COLOR

10 Exciting blockbuster hit filled with major name international stars. An escape-prone group of cocky WWII Allied POWs are all gathered into one high security camp by the Germans, who wanted to put all their bad eggs into one high security basket. Instead, they get a massive POW escape attempt. This rousing adventure story is told as a series of character portraits which are then all linked together. It has a huge cast of top talent and a good script, plus pacing, humor and excitement aplenty. Watch for McQueen's thrilling motorcycle ride. Much copied - never equaled. Based upon an actual event. In the real event, 76 men broke out but only 3 found freedom.

Sex, Nud, ◢ Viol, Lang, ◢ AdSit

A: Steve McQueen, James Garner, Richard Attenborough, Charles Bronson, James Coburn, David McCallum

Distributed By MGM/UA Home Video M201257

GREAT LOCOMOTIVE CHASE, THE

D: Francis D. Lyon 85 m

NR | ACT | 1956 | COLOR

7 Colorful Disney production which depicts the true-life adventure story of a group of Union soldiers known as Andrews Raiders who launch a daring raid behind Confederate lines to steal a Confederate train and bring it home, blowing up the bridges behind it. However, their efforts are hampered by one rebel who will not stop trying to get his train back. Good family fun. This is a straightforward telling of the story with Disney emphasis on action and suspense. But there was another telling of the story - a great silent comedy classic by Buster Keaton in 1927 called THE GENERAL. See it, too.

Sex, Nud, ◢ Viol, Lang, AdSit

A: Fess Parker, Jeffrey Hunter, Jeff York, John Lupton, Eddie Firestone, Kenneth Tobey

© WALT DISNEY HOME VIDEO

GREAT TRAIN ROBBERY, THE

D: Michael Crichton 111 m

PG | ACT SUS | 1979 | COLOR

9 Stylish thriller about the very first robbery of a moving train - based upon a true incident in 1855 England. Sean Connery plays a dapper rogue of a thief who masterminds a daring plan to hijack gold bullion from a moving train. Beautiful production, with wonderful characters and a captivating plot. Lesley-Anne Down is Connery's beautiful mistress and also a disguise expert. Donald Sutherland is a braggart of a pickpocket. This is great entertainment that has you rooting for the bad guys.

Sex, Nud, Viol, ◢ Lang, ◢ AdSit

A: Sean Connery, Donald Sutherland, Lesley-Anne Down, Alan Webb, Malcolm Terris, Robert Lang

Distributed By MGM/UA Home Video M301427

GUNGA DIN

D: George Stevens 117 m

NR | ACT COM | 1939 | B&W

9 Rousing and extremely entertaining action/adventure yarn - undimmed by time. Loosely based on Rudyard Kipling's classic poem. Principally a buddy film, this has lots of action and comedy thrown it (plus a little sentimentality). Three English soldiers and a native waterboy, stationed in British colonial India, fight to put down an uprising by a savage religious sect. It is sort of like a Western, but with real Indians and an English slant. A great time. Laughs, plenty of action and loads of fun. Often copied - never equalled.

Sex, Nud, ◢ Viol, Lang, ◢ AdSit

A: Cary Grant, Victor McLaglen, Douglas Fairbanks, Jr., Joan Fontaine, Sam Jaffe, Eduardo Cannelli

© TURNER HOME ENTERTAINMENT 2055

HATARI!

D: Howard Hawks — 158 m

NR · ACT COM · 1961 · COLOR

8 High energy and light-hearted fun. A great cast has a ball with a fun adventure story about a bunch of wild-animal trappers who capture African animals for zoos. This is good fun for adults and kids alike. John Wayne is at his macho best as the leader of the group. The simple story is amply spiced with doses of comedy, action, some excellent animal and scenic photography, and a little romance, too. Filmed on location in Tanganyika. Terrific Mancini score.

☐ Sex ☐ Nud ☐ Viol ☐ Lang ☐ AdSit

A: John Wayne, Elsa Martinelli, Red Buttons, Hardy Kruger, Gerard Blain

© PARAMOUNT HOME VIDEO 6629

HOOPER

D: Hal Needham — 100 m

PG · ACT COM · 1978 · COLOR

8 Entertaining and light-hearted romp with fun-loving good-old-boys from Hollywood. Burt Reynolds and Sally Field recaptured much of the charm that they developed in SMOKEY AND THE BANDIT, but this time Burt plays an aging professional stuntman who is being challenged by an arrogant up-and-comer (Vincent) into doing the biggest stunt of his career. You should expect lots of thrilling stunts in cars and other places, but the real fun here is in the wise-cracking characters they create. Lots of fun.

☐ Sex ☐ Nud ☐ Viol ◢ Lang ◢ AdSit

A: Burt Reynolds, Jan-Michael Vincent, Sally Field, Brian Keith, John Marley, Robert Klein

© WARNER HOME VIDEO 1008

ICE STATION ZEBRA

D: John Sturges — 150 m

G · ACT SUS · 1968 · COLOR

6 This is a Cold War espionage flick in which Rock Hudson commands a submarine that is sent to the North Pole regions to retrieve Soviet spy satelite data from a weather station before the Russians get it. It is a large-scale picture with beautiful arctic photography, action and some suspense. Borgnine is a Russian defector. He is only one of several who are suspected of being the Russian spy which is known to be on board and which is being pursued by British agent Patrick McGoohan. This is a pretty typical Cold War movie. Still, it was supposedly the favorite of billionaire Howard Hughes.

☐ Sex ☐ Nud ◢ Viol ☐ Lang ◢ AdSit

A: Rock Hudson, Ernest Borgnine, Patrick McGoohan, Jim Brown, Tony Bill, Lloyd Nolan

Distributed By MGM/UA Home Video M600160

INDIANA JONES AND THE LAST CRUSADE

D: Steven Spielberg — 126 m

PG-13 · ACT COM · 1989 · COLOR

8 Entertaining family flick in the Saturday matinee serial-action tradition. This is the last in the series of adventurous exploits of the famous Indiana Jones. Here, Indie (Ford) launches himself on a quest to find his father (Connery) who has disappeared while in search of the Holy Grail. Connery and Ford work well together as they endeavor to find the Grail and then to protect it from the evil Nazis, who are out to steal it. Thrills and style will delight viewers of all ages.

☐ Sex ☐ Nud ◢ Viol ◢ Lang ◢ AdSit

A: Harrison Ford, Sean Connery, Denholm Elliott, Alison Doody, River Phoenix, Julian Glover

© PARAMOUNT HOME VIDEO 31859

INDIANA JONES AND THE TEMPLE OF DOOM

D: Steven Spielberg — 118 m

PG · ACT COM · 1984 · COLOR

8 Exciting follow-up (and first of two sequels) to super hit RAIDERS OF THE LOST ARK. This one is set at a place in time before the original and has Indie (Ford), a nightclub singer (Capshaw) and a resourceful Korean kid (Quan) embark on an adventure in India to retrieve a magic jewel and a village's children from a Maharaja's fortress where they have been forced to work his mines. Filled with action-packed sequences as the original was, but less effective now. May be too intense for very young viewers.

☐ Sex ☐ Nud ◢ Viol ◢ Lang ◢ AdSit

A: Harrison Ford, Kate Capshaw, Ke Huy Quan, Amrish Puri, Philip Stone, Dan Aykroyd

© PARAMOUNT HOME VIDEO 1643

IRON WILL

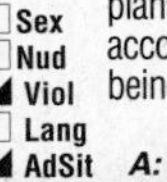
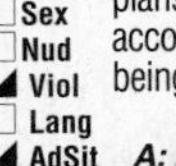
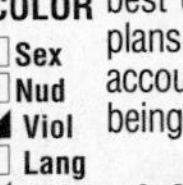
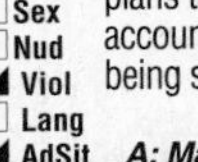

D: Charles Haid — 109 m

PG · ACT DMA · 1994 · COLOR

8 It's 1917. Will Stoneman is a 17-year old South Dakota farm boy whose father raises sled dogs. When his father is killed, it looks like his mother may lose the farm and he'll never get to go to college. So, Will decides to enter a treacherous 522-mile dog-sled race through "the meanest stretch of land that God ever put together." For seven days, in mind-numbing 30-below cold, he will race against the best dog-sled racers in the world for the $10,000 prize, which he plans to win by running harder and sleeping less. This is a fictionalized account of an actual event. Predictable, but that doesn't stop it from being solid, rousing entertainment for the whole family.

☐ Sex ☐ Nud ◢ Viol ☐ Lang ◢ AdSit

A: Mackenzie Astin, Kevin Spacey, David Ogden Stiers, August Schellenberg, Brian Cox, George Gerdes

© WALT DISNEY HOME VIDEO 2545

IVANHOE

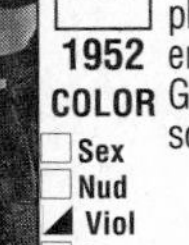

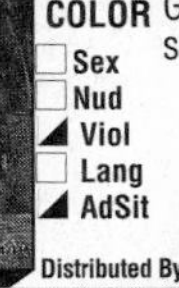

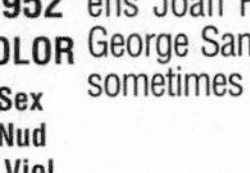

D: Richard Thorpe — 107 m

NR · ACT ROM · 1952 · COLOR

8 Walter Scott's classic and epic tale of chivalry and romance in 12th-century England was nominated for Best Picture, Cinematography and Music. Grand spectacle and beautiful photography are its hallmarks. Saxon knight Ivanhoe (Robert Taylor) defeats a plot against his King Richard by the Normans and rescues fair maidens Joan Fontaine and Elizabeth Taylor from the clutches of vile George Sanders. Swordplay and action are exciting, but the pacing is sometimes slow.

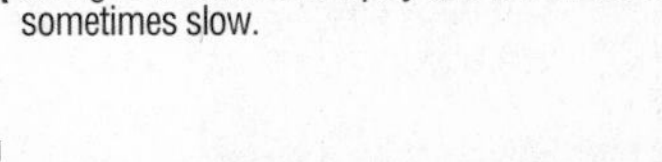
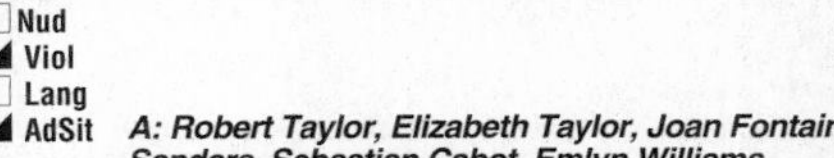

☐ Sex ☐ Nud ◢ Viol ☐ Lang ◢ AdSit

A: Robert Taylor, Elizabeth Taylor, Joan Fontaine, George Sanders, Sebastian Cabot, Emlyn Williams

Distributed By MGM/UA Home Video M600092

JASON AND THE ARGONAUTS

D: Don Chaffey — 104 m

G · ACT CLD · 1963 · COLOR

9 Exciting and very well done adventure story from Greek mythology. Jason, the son of a murdered Thessalian king, is cheated out of his birthright. So he gathers a crew for his ship and sets sail in search of the mythical Golden Fleece in order to reclaim his throne. This is an exciting adventure story which is made more so by stunning special effects (including a now classic scene with swordfighting skeletons). An interesting feature of this film for parents is that Jason and his crew are not portrayed as superheros, just mortal men performing great deeds. Great for kids.

☐ Sex ☐ Nud ◢ Viol ☐ Lang ☐ AdSit

A: Todd Armstrong, Gary Raymond, Honor Blackman, Nancy Kovack, Laurence Naismith, Niall MacGinnis

© COLUMBIA TRISTAR HOME VIDEO 60025

JEWEL OF THE NILE, THE

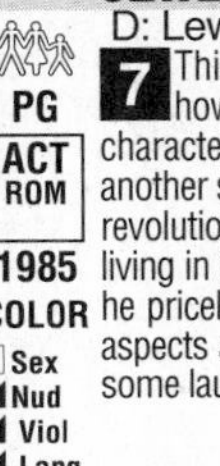

D: Lewis Teague — 106 m

PG · ACT ROM · 1985 · COLOR

7 This is an enjoyable follow-up to ROMANCING THE STONE, however it can't quite match the vitality of the earlier film. All the characters have here returned six months later to chase down yet another stone - this time in the Sahara Desert, in the middle of an Arab revolution. It seems Turner has writer's block and Douglas is tired of living in her shadow. The answer for them is an adventure to seek out he priceless Jewel of the Nile. Lots of money was spent on technical aspects and explosions. There are lots of good action sequences and some laughs too. Enjoyable.

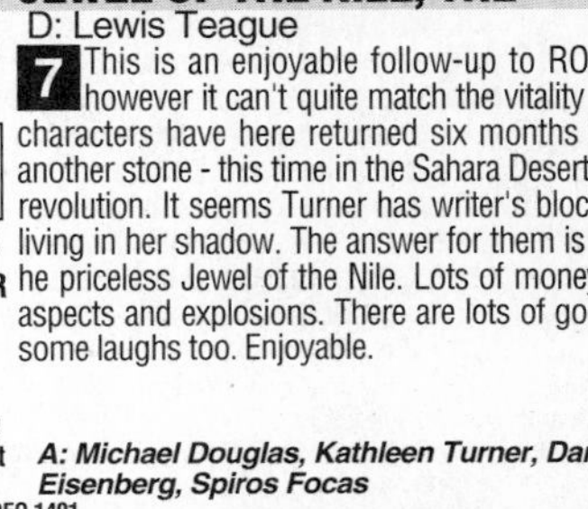

☐ Sex ◢ Nud ◢ Viol ◢ Lang ☐ AdSit

A: Michael Douglas, Kathleen Turner, Danny DeVito, Avner Eisenberg, Spiros Focas

© FOXVIDEO 1491

KARATE KID, THE

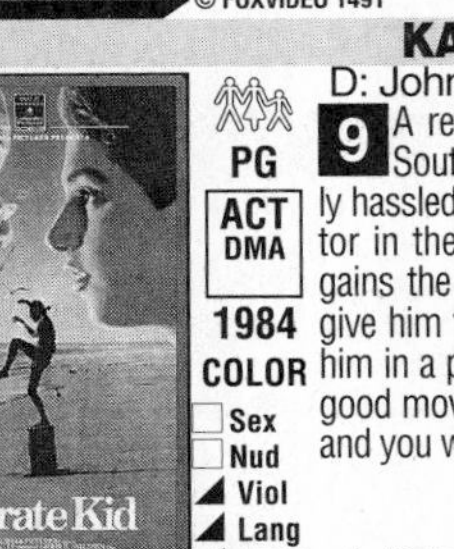

D: John G. Avildsen — 126 m

PG · ACT DMA · 1984 · COLOR

9 A real audience pleaser. A fatherless kid (Macchio) arrives in Southern California from New Jersey. Out of place and constantly hassled by some street toughs, he finds an unlikely friend and mentor in the apartment complex's Japanese gardner (Morita). Morita gains the boy's confidence and decides to train the boy in karate to give him the confidence he needs. But, in so doing, he also instructs him in a personal code of honor. This is an old fashioned sort of feel-good movie that doesn't hide its attempts to play with your emotions, and you won't care. You'll be cheering.

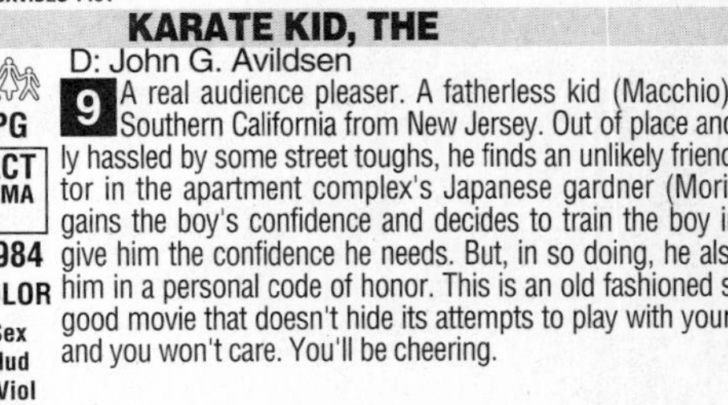

☐ Sex ☐ Nud ◢ Viol ◢ Lang ◢ AdSit

A: Ralph Macchio, Noriyuki "Pat" Morita, Elisabeth Shue, Martin Kove, William Zabka

© COLUMBIA TRISTAR HOME VIDEO 60406

KARATE KID PART II, THE

D: John G. Avildsen — 113 m

PG · ACT DMA · 1986 · COLOR

7 This sequel begins immediately after the original ends. Morita receives notice that his father in Japan is dying. When he and "the kid" (Macchio) arrive in Okinawa, Morita is immediately and forcefully reminded of an old feud with an old rival. Morita sets about resolving that situation and also revives an old love. Macchio also finds love with a village girl and a new enemy in the nephew of Morita's old foe. This film is most notable for its repeat appearance of a cast of likable characters, and the feel-good finish. Enjoyable, but predictable.

☐ Sex ☐ Nud ◢ Viol ◢ Lang ◢ AdSit

A: Ralph Macchio, Noriyuki "Pat" Morita, Nobu McCarthy, Martin Kove, William Zabka

© COLUMBIA TRISTAR HOME VIDEO 60717

KHARTOUM

D: Basil Dearden — 136 m

NR · ACT DMA · 1966 · COLOR

8 Sweeping quasi-historical spectacle which tells the saga of Britain's battle for control over the Sudan, and of the rivalry between a British general (Heston) and a Moslem holy man (Olivier) named "The Mahdi" by his followers. In spite of their respect for each other, these two could not compromise and in 1883 The Mahdi led his followers in a long and arduous siege of the Sudanese city of Khartoum. The siege was eventually successful and led to the downfall of the British. Grand spectacle, well-mounted large battle sequences and some notable acting make this an entertaining diversion.

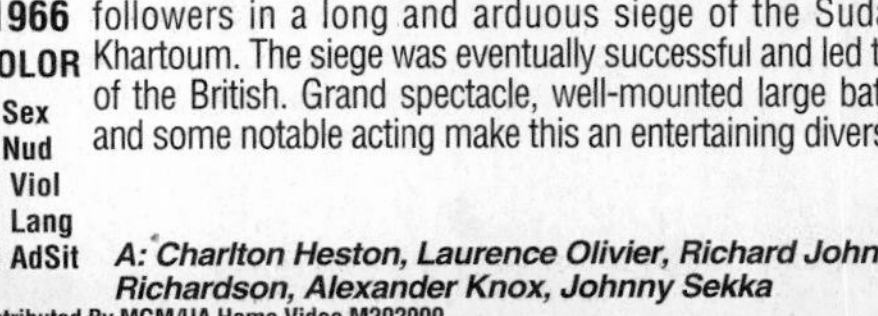

☐ Sex ☐ Nud ◢ Viol ☐ Lang ◢ AdSit

A: Charlton Heston, Laurence Olivier, Richard Johnson, Ralph Richardson, Alexander Knox, Johnny Sekka

Distributed By MGM/UA Home Video M202009

KIDNAPPED

D: Robert Stevenson 95 m

G | ACT CLD | 1960 | COLOR

7 Great fun for kids of all ages from Disney. This is Disney's production of Robert Lewis Stevenson's swashbuckler classic. A young orphaned Scotsman is kidnapped by his cruel uncle just as he is about to inherit his family's estate. The boy is pressed into service as a cabin boy on a ship bound for the New World where, unknown to him, he is to be sold into slavery. But in their crossing they run over a small boat, killing all who were on board but a fellow Scotsman. The survivor and the boy become fast friends and escape the clutches of the foul ship they are captive to. Lots of high seas adventures.

☐ Sex ☐ Nud ☑ Viol ☐ Lang ☐ AdSit

A: Peter Finch, James MacArthur, Bernard Lee, Niall MacGinnis, Finlay Currie, Peter O'Toole

© WALT DISNEY HOME VIDEO 111

KIM

D: Victor Saville 114 m

G | ACT | 1950 | COLOR

7 Rousing Rudyard Kipling adventure story about a half-white orphaned boy, alone on his own in the streets of Victorian colonial India. He befriends a horse-thief (Flynn) and a Hindu holy man and becomes enticed into the service of the English as an undercover spy, taking part in a secret plot to repel a Russian invasion through the Kyber Pass. Sweeping adventure story that will sweep you up and carry you along. It will appeal to the entire family. Errol Flynn is again playing the part of the romantic adventurer and Dean Stockwell is excellent in the role of Kim.

☐ Sex ☐ Nud ☐ Viol ☐ Lang ☑ AdSit

A: Errol Flynn, Dean Stockwell, Paul Lukas, Robert Douglas, Thomas Gomez, Cecil Kellaway

Distributed By MGM/UA Home Video M300980

KING SOLOMON'S MINES

D: Robert Stevenson 89 m

NR | ACT | 1937 | B&W

8 A beautiful woman entices a famed white hunter into helping her to locate her father in the wilds of unexplored Africa. Her father had been on the trail of the fabled diamond mines of King Solomon, but she has not heard from him for too long. Along with them come two other white men and an enigmatic black man who will be their guide. After enduring great hardship and nearing the end of their journey, the party arrives at a native village. But, they are not welcome and are now in desperate trouble. However, they also now discover that their black guide is actually the king of these people who was deposed by an evil leader, aided by a treacherous witch doctor. Quite good. Remade in 1950.

☐ Sex ☐ Nud ☑ Viol ☐ Lang ☑ AdSit

A: Paul Robeson, Cedric Hardwicke, Roland Yong, John Loder, Anna Lee

© HOME VISION KIN07

LIVE AND LET DIE

D: Guy Hamilton 123 m

PG | ACT | 1973 | COLOR

7 This is the first James Bond episode with Roger Moore as Bond. It is an interesting and fun excursion, but has a cartoonish plot. Bond is after a Caribbean diplomat Dr. Kanaga (Kotto), who is actually a drug kingpin intent upon giving away tons of heroin free, with the ultimate goal of creating a huge supply of junkies that he can then supply. Bond chases him in Harlem, his Caribbean island and through the swamps of Louisiana in a spectacular very high speed boat chase - "helped" by a good-ol'-boy sheriff. Seymore is Bond's love interest and Kotto's fortune-teller.

☐ Sex ☐ Nud ☑ Viol ☐ Lang ☑ AdSit

A: Roger Moore, Yaphet Kotto, Jane Seymour, Clifton James, Geoffrey Holder

Distributed By MGM/UA Home Video M201418

LIVES OF A BENGAL LANCER

D: Henry Hathaway 110 m

NR | ACT WAR | 1935 | B&W

8 Highly regarded and rousing adventure yarn, set in British colonial India when it was England's crown jewel. Gary Cooper and Franchot Tone are two dashing and fearless friends in service to the crown. Richard Cromwell is the untested son of their stern by-the-book commander. The two friends take Cromwell under their wing but he is a very poor soldier, even being captured by a warring chieftain. However, he redeems himself in the end. Lots of rousing action, camaraderie and good fun. It received six Oscar nominations, including Best Picture.

☐ Sex ☐ Nud ☑ Viol ☐ Lang ☑ AdSit

A: Gary Cooper, Franchot Tone, Richard Cromwell, Sir Guy Standing, C. Aubrey Smith, Monte Blue

© MCA/UNIVERSAL HOME VIDEO, INC. 80517

LIVING DAYLIGHTS, THE

D: John Glen 131 m

PG | ACT | 1987 | COLOR

8 One of the best of the later James Bond films. It is the sixteenth in the series and Dalton is the fourth James Bond. This Bond is more mature in his attitudes and the plot is much less comic book in tone than many of the other recent entries. Bond is sent to help a KGB general (who turns out to be a double agent) and a pretty cellist escape over the Iron Curtain. Bond then gets involved with a crazy American gunrunner and a plot to smuggle tons of opium out of Afgahanistan. Good and credible adventure.

☐ Sex ☐ Nud ☑ Viol ☐ Lang ☑ AdSit

A: Timothy Dalton, Maryann d'Abo, Jeroen Krabbe, Joe Don Baker, John Rhys-Davies, Art Malik

Distributed By MGM/UA Home Video M202529

MAN IN THE IRON MASK, THE

D: James Whale 109 m

NR | ACT DMA | 1939 | B&W

7 Rousing swashbuckling adventure! Twin brothers are separated at birth. One grows up to be Louis XIV, the King of France. The other becomes an idle wanderer raised by the Three Musketeers. When vile brother Louis discovers that he has a look-alike who is much beloved of his friends and the rightful heir to the throne, he kidnaps his twin, imprisons him and forces him to wear an iron mask to hide his identity. An exciting and classic tale of revenge and destruction based on Alexander Dumas's novel. Hayward is fantastic in his dual role as both brothers. Remade for television in 1977.

☐ Sex ☐ Nud ☑ Viol ☐ Lang ☑ AdSit

A: Louis Hayward, Joan Bennett, Joseph Schildkraut, Alan Hale

© VIDEO TREASURES SV9621

MAN IN THE IRON MASK, THE

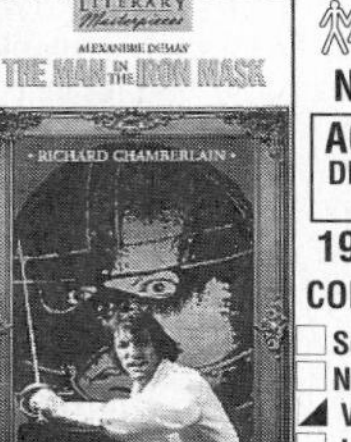

D: Mike Newell 108 m

NR | ACT DMA | 1977 | COLOR

8 Excellent and quite opulent made-for-TV movie of the classic and timeless tale from Alexander Dumas. Phillipe is one of two royal twin brothers. He is the rightful heir to the throne but is confined at birth to a remote island, and is there forced to wear an iron mask so no one will ever know his true identity. His foppish brother Louis is made king, but the real power rests with Finance Minister Fouget. France is corrupt. Captain D'Artagnan and another minister conspire to free Phillipe from prison so that he may publicly challenge Louis. Grand entertainment for the whole family.

☐ Sex ☐ Nud ☑ Viol ☐ Lang ☑ AdSit

A: Richard Chamberlain, Patrick McGoohan, Louis Jourdan, Jenny Agutter, Vivien Merchant, Ian Holm

© LIVE HOME VIDEO 69940

MAN WHO WOULD BE KING, THE

D: John Huston 128 m

PG | ACT DMA | 1975 | COLOR

9 Excellent, rousing Rudyard Kipling adventure like they used to make! Two British ex-soldiers (Connery and Caine), in the fading days of colonial England, head to Kafiristan to plunder it and become rich. Connery is struck by an arrow in the chest but it hits a medal he wears and, when he just pulls the arrow out, the people declare him a god. The two soldiers enjoy their good fortune. Soon Caine wishes to leave but Connery likes being King. However, their deception is soon uncovered and they are ruined. Garnered four Oscar nominations. Caine and Connery are magic.

☐ Sex ☐ Nud ☑ Viol ☐ Lang ☑ AdSit

A: Sean Connery, Michael Caine, Christopher Plummer, Saeed Jaffrey, Shakira Caine

© FOXVIDEO 7435

MAN WITH THE GOLDEN GUN, THE

D: Guy Hamilton 127 m

PG | ACT | 1974 | COLOR

7 Golden action! Ninth in the series, Fleming's adaptation places 007 (Moore) in a desperate fight to retrieve the world's only solar harnessing device, the "Solex." The bad guy Scaramanga (Christopher Lee) has the device installed on his remote island retreat. The clue that leads Bond to the assassin's hideaway is the trail of an assassin's exotic weapon. This one is not as gadget-crazy as some of the others, but there are pandemonious chase scenes and car stunts, as well as beautiful scenery. A Pink Panther animated short adds to the amusement.

☐ Sex ☐ Nud ☑ Viol ☐ Lang ☑ AdSit

A: Roger Moore, Christopher Lee, Britt Ekland, Maud Adams, Herve Villechaize, Clifton James

Distributed By MGM/UA Home Video M201419

MIGHTY JOE YOUNG

D: Ernest B. Schoedsack 94 m

NR | ACT FAN | 1949 | B&W

6 Later-day update of and follow-up to KING KONG. A 12-foot gorilla is raised in the jungles of Africa by a young girl. While on Safari, a scheming night-club owner discovers them and decides to bring the gorilla and the girl back to Hollywood, dreaming of the money he can make. The gorilla gains access to the liquor cabinet, becomes drunk and terrorizes the city, but he later redeems himself when he rescues children from a fire. This version is not nearly as original as KING KONG, but the film still fun. Winner for Best Special Effects.

☐ Sex ☐ Nud ☐ Viol ☐ Lang ☐ AdSit

A: Terry Moore, Ben Johnson, Robert Armstrong, Mr. Joseph Young, Frank McHugh

© TURNER HOME ENTERTAINMENT 6032

MOGAMBO

D: John Ford 116 m

NR | ACT ROM | 1953 | COLOR

9 A sexy adventure story set in the lush wilds of Kenya! In this lusty re-make of "RED DUST" (which also starred Gable), a safari guide (Gable) falls in love with both the married Englishwoman who has hired him (Kelly), and Gardner, the well-worn woman with a past who is out for adventure. Sparks fly in the love triangle that develops during the upriver trip. Lots of adventure, action and romance. This Hollywood-style film makes the most of the exotic locations and spicy dialogue and, surprisingly, doesn't include a musical score. It doesn't need one.

☐ Sex ☐ Nud ☑ Viol ☐ Lang ☑ AdSit

A: Clark Gable, Ava Gardner, Grace Kelly, Donald Sinden, Laurence Naismith

Distributed By MGM/UA Home Video M600055

MOONRAKER

D: Lewis Gilbert 128 m

PG | ACT | 1979 | COLOR | 6

Intergalactic adventure! Bond matches wits with evil industrialist Hugo Drax (Lonsdale). Drax is building a space station and plans to annihilate the planet with nerve gas dispensed from his fleet of space shuttles. After this is done he can then replace the earth's population with his own perfect super race. Bond's planet-saving efforts are full of cool spy stuff, exotic locations and witty dialogue. The freefall scene where 007 battles mega-villain Jaws for a single parachute is one of the film's best moments.

Sex / Nud / Viol / ✓ Lang / ✓ AdSit

A: Roger Moore, Lois Chiles, Richard Kiel, Michael Lonsdale

Distributed By MGM/UA Home Video M201422

MR. ROBINSON CRUSOE

D: A. Edward Sutherland 76 m

NR | ACT | 1932 | B&W | 6

An aging but lively Douglas Fairbanks bets his friends $1000 dollars that he can survive on a deserted tropical island for an entire month without any of the modern-day trappings. His friends drop him off and the industrious Fairbanks builds an wide assortment of his own crude, but effective, gadgets of convenience. He is also not without companionship because a lovely woman arrives just in time. This buoyant old-time adventure is loads of fun for film fans.

Sex / Nud / Viol / Lang / AdSit

A: Douglas Fairbanks, Sr., Sir William Farnum, Maria Alba, Earle Brown

© MPI HOME VIDEO MP1180

MYSTERIOUS ISLAND

D: Cy Endfield 101 m

NR | ACT FAN CLD | 1961 | COLOR | 7

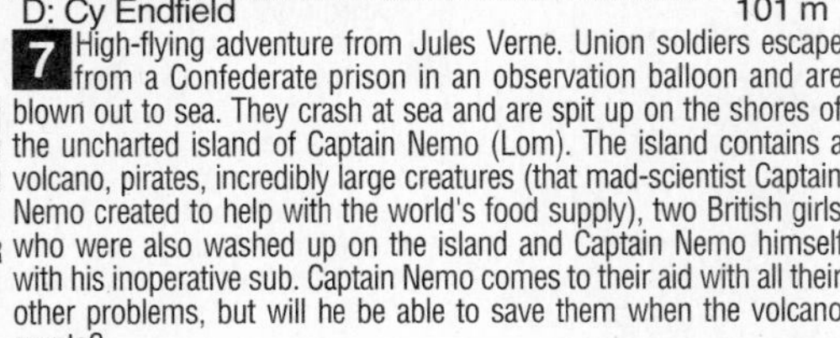

High-flying adventure from Jules Verne. Union soldiers escape from a Confederate prison in an observation balloon and are blown out to sea. They crash at sea and are spit up on the shores of the uncharted island of Captain Nemo (Lom). The island contains a volcano, pirates, incredibly large creatures (that mad-scientist Captain Nemo created to help with the world's food supply), two British girls who were also washed up on the island and Captain Nemo himself with his inoperative sub. Captain Nemo comes to their aid with all their other problems, but will he be able to save them when the volcano erupts?

Sex / Nud / ✓ Viol / Lang / AdSit

A: Michael Craig, Joan Greenwood, Herbert Lom, Michael Callan, Gary Merrill

© COLUMBIA TRISTAR HOME VIDEO 60067

NAKED PREY, THE

D: Cornel Wilde 96 m

NR | ACT SUS | 1965 | COLOR | 9

An enthralling story of survival. Set in the 1860s, a white expedition in search of ivory offends a group of natives and is subsequently ambushed. All the members except Wilde are tortured to death. Impressed with his bravery, he is given a chance to survive. He is stripped naked, turned free, and then pursued by relentless native hunters. No matter how he struggles, he can keep no more than a few seconds in front of them. Alternately filmed from a distance and then close-up, this is a fascinating and intimate portrait of survival at its most basic level. Virtually no dialogue.

Sex / Nud / ✓ Viol / Lang / ✓ AdSit

A: Cornel Wilde, Ken Gampu, Gert Van Den Bergh

© PARAMOUNT HOME VIDEO 6525

NEVER SAY NEVER AGAIN

D: Irvin Kershner 134 m

PG | ACT | 1983 | COLOR | 8

Sean Connery is back as James Bond after having been absent for 12 years. James is in pursuit of arch-villain Brandauer who is threatening the world with stolen missiles. Barbara Carrera is memorable as a sexy assassin Fatima Blush, out to get James - but she makes an explosive departure before she can get the job done. Sexy Kim Basinger plays Brandauer's naive girlfriend and ultimately James's love. Solid entry that is basically a remake of THUNDERBALL. Action-packed and witty.

Sex / ✓ Nud / ✓ Viol / Lang / ✓ AdSit

A: Sean Connery, Klaus Maria Brandauer, Max von Sydow, Barbara Carrera, Kim Basinger, Bernie Casey

© WARNER HOME VIDEO 11337

NONE BUT THE BRAVE

D: Frank Sinatra 106 m

NR | ACT WAR | 1965 | COLOR | 6

Tense war drama about a plane full of Allied Marines that crash-lands on a Pacific island populated by small band of Japanese. Both groups have been cut off from the rest of the war. So, they conduct their own war with both sides plotting against the other and skirmishing. But when the Japanese commander offers water in exchange for help from the American's medic (Sinatra), who then amputates a man's leg and saves his life, a truce is worked out. An interesting, and a respectable entry, but it is most notable for being Sinatra's directorial debut.

Sex / Nud / ✓ Viol / Lang / AdSit

A: Frank Sinatra, Clint Walker, Tommy Sands, Brad Dexter, Tony Bill, Sammy Jackson

© WARNER HOME VIDEO 11712

OCTOPUSSY

D: John Glen 131 m

PG | ACT | 1983 | COLOR | 8

James Bond Number 13. Roger Moore is in pursuit of the killer of 009. He discovers a plot by a hard-line Soviet general, assisted by Octopussy (Maude Adams), to cripple the West's nuclear threat with public pressure. They will deliberately create a nuclear accident at a US base in Germany which will kill hundreds of thousands of people and force the removal of the nucs. Bond is launched on a fast-paced excursion through many countries and many women to prevent that from happening. Clever and humorous, but also one of the more believable adventures.

✓ Sex / Nud / ✓ Viol / Lang / ✓ AdSit

A: Roger Moore, Maud Adams, Louis Jourdan, Kristina Wayborn

Distributed By MGM/UA Home Video M200294

ON HER MAJESTY'S SECRET SERVICE

D: Peter H. Hunt 143 m

PG | ACT | 1969 | COLOR | 8

Fascinating James Bond entry. This was the first Bond film without Connery, but it was remarkably good - and gets better with age. This Bond is more vulnerable than Connery. He has tried and failed for two years to track down archvillian Blofeld (Savalas). He meets his match in beautiful and enchanting Dianna Rigg, and marries her. Through her gangster father, he gains entry into Blofeld's mountain stronghold to foil Blofeld's attempt to poison the world's food supply, but he does it at great cost. Less gimmicky, with great action.

Sex / Nud / ✓ Viol / Lang / ✓ AdSit

A: George Lazenby, Diana Rigg, Telly Savalas, Gabriele Ferzetti, Bernard Lee, Lois Maxwell

Distributed By MGM/UA Home Video M201420

OUR MAN FLINT

D: Daniel Mann 107 m

NR | ACT COM | 1966 | COLOR | 6

Outlandish James Bond spoof. Coburn is superagent Derek Flint from Z.O.W.I.E. who is sent to protect the world from a plot by the evil organization GALAXY and its top agent, the super seductive Gila Golan. GALAXY and its scientists are plotting to overtake and control the world's weather. It is up to superstud Flint to defeat them... but he does have the use of his special lighter that has 83 different uses, including: a blow torch, a derringer, a dart gun and a 2-way radio. Spectacular tongue-in-cheek spoof.

Sex / Nud / ✓ Viol / Lang / ✓ AdSit

A: James Coburn, Lee J. Cobb, Gila Golan, Edward Mulhare, Benson Fong, Shelby Grant

© FOXVIDEO 1131

POSEIDON ADVENTURE, THE

D: Ronald Neame 117 m

PG | ACT DMA | 1972 | COLOR | 9

One of the best of many disaster films from the 1970s. An ocean-going luxury liner is overwhelmed by a massive tidal wave and left capsized, bobbing upside down on the open ocean. A few survivors, trapped below deck, must work their way into the deepest bowels of the ship, which is now the only part exposed to the air, in the hope that someone will find them and cut through the hull to save them. Their arduous trip provides numerous opportunities for an exploration of their motivations and individual life stories. Oscars for Special Effects and Theme Song: "The Morning After."

Sex / Nud / ✓ Viol / ✓ Lang / AdSit

A: Gene Hackman, Ernest Borgnine, Carol Lynley, Red Buttons, Shelley Winters, Jack Albertson

© CBS/FOX VIDEO 1058

PRISONER OF ZENDA, THE

D: John Cromwell 102 m

NR | ACT ROM | 1937 | B&W | 9

Classic, very lavish swashbuckler in which a visiting English look-alike (Colman) takes the place of his royal cousin to help thwart an assassination plot on the life of the crown prince by his evil brother (Fairbanks). Lots of swordfights and a romance between the commoner and the beautiful princess (Carroll), too. One of many remakes (at least six) of this classic story and widely regarded as the best. The first one was silent in 1927 and the last one was a 1979 comedy take off.

Sex / Nud / ✓ Viol / Lang / ✓ AdSit

A: Ronald Colman, Madeleine Carroll, Mary Astor, Douglas Fairbanks, Jr., C. Aubrey Smith, Raymond Massey

Distributed By MGM/UA Home Video M301644

RAIDERS OF THE LOST ARK

D: Steven Spielberg 115 m

PG | ACT SUS | 1981 | COLOR | 10

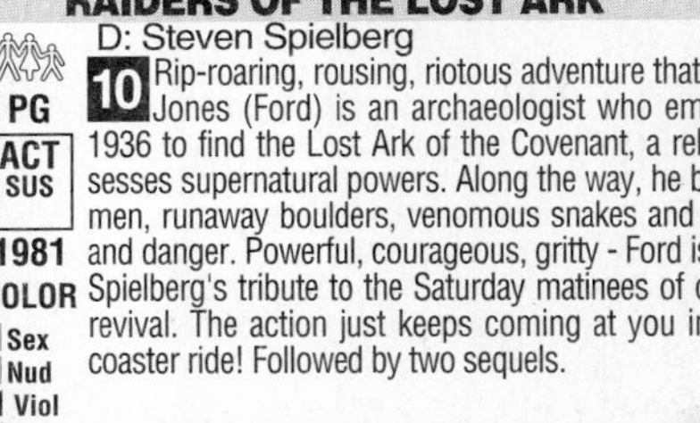

Rip-roaring, rousing, riotous adventure that never stops! Indiana Jones (Ford) is an archaeologist who embarks on a quest in 1936 to find the Lost Ark of the Covenant, a religious relic that possesses supernatural powers. Along the way, he battles Nazis, swordsmen, runaway boulders, venomous snakes and a whole vat of death and danger. Powerful, courageous, gritty - Ford is a huge screen hero. Spielberg's tribute to the Saturday matinees of old is better than any revival. The action just keeps coming at you in this thrilling roller-coaster ride! Followed by two sequels.

Sex / Nud / ✓ Viol / ✓ Lang / ✓ AdSit

A: Harrison Ford, Karen Allen, Paul Freeman, Ronald Lacey, John Rhys-Davies, Denholm Elliott

© PARAMOUNT HOME VIDEO 1376

RAID ON ENTEBBE

D: Irvin Kershner — 113 m

NR | ACT SUS | 1976 | COLOR

7 A well-made dramatization of a real-life dramatic rescue! When terrorists hijacked an Israeli plane in 1976 and took 103 Israeli hostages to Uganda's Entebbe airport, the Israelies struck back. Israeli leader Finch orders a daring military rescue mission into a foreign country to get their people back. Bronson and Bucholz are to be at the helm of the mission. Made for TV, Finch received an Emmy nomination for this compelling drama. Although the impact was greater at the time it was released, it is still a good action film with strong suspenseful elements.

☐ Sex ☐ Nud ✓ Viol ☐ Lang ✓ AdSit

A: Charles Bronson, Peter Finch, Horst Buchholz, Martin Balsam, Jack Warden, Yaphet Kotto

© HBO VIDEO TVB2455

REAP THE WILD WIND

D: Cecil B. DeMille — 123 m

NR | ACT ROM | 1942 | B&W

7 First-rate DeMille epic! Just off the coast of Florida in the 1840s, the steamship of a salty sea captain (Wayne) is sunk against the jagged rocks. He and a sophisticated attorney (Milland) become adversaries for the affections of beautiful ship owner Paulett Goddard. Milland accuses Wayne of purposely sinking the ship. The ship was purposefully sunk. However, John didn't do it, but John is on trial for it. Some good special effects and underwater photography. The final battle with a giant squid helped to win the film an Oscar for Special Effects.

☐ Sex ☐ Nud ☐ Viol ☐ Lang ✓ AdSit

A: John Wayne, Susan Hayward, Ray Milland, Paulette Goddard, Raymond Massey, Robert Preston

© MCA/UNIVERSAL HOME VIDEO, INC. 80368

RIFF-RAFF

D: Ted Tetzlaff — 80 m

NR | ACT | 1947 | B&W

6 Fast paced adventure. A tough Panamanian-based private detective (O'Brien) is hired to be the bodyguard of a man in possession of a map to South American oil fields which are worth billions. Then O'Brien is approached by an oil company executive who had bought the map in the first place and now wants it back, and by a German, who offers to pay him to steal it for him. That's when O'Brien learns that the man he is protecting had killed to get the map in the first place.

☐ Sex ☐ Nud ✓ Viol ☐ Lang ✓ AdSit

A: Pat O'Brien, Anne Jeffreys, Walter Slezak, Jason Robards, Jr., Percy Kilbride, Jerome Cowan

© TURNER HOME ENTERTAINMENT 6108

ROCKETEER, THE

D: Joe Johnston — 109 m

PG | ACT ROM | 1991 | COLOR

7 Cliff Secord (Campbell) is an adventurous 1930s daredevil pilot who has discovered a secret government jet pack and takes to the skies with it on a wild joy ride. He's an adventurous sort and is just having fun, but the government wants it back. Unfortunately, so do some local hoods who are trying to deliver it to a secret buyer for a big payday. What they don't know is that their buyer, a famous Hollywood hero, is also a Nazi agent. Campbell's beautiful girlfriend (Connelly) gets unwillingly pulled into the fiasco too when she is romanced by the Hollywood hunk. Great period feel. Pretty good excitement, too, in spite of being overly long.

☐ Sex ☐ Nud ✓ Viol ☐ Lang ✓ AdSit

A: Bill Campbell, Alan Arkin, Jennifer Connelly, Paul Sorvino, Timothy Dalton, Terry O'Quinn

© WALT DISNEY HOME VIDEO 1239

ROMANCING THE STONE

D: Michael Douglas — 106 m

PG | ACT ROM COM | 1984 | COLOR

8 Wildly fun! A shy romance novelist (Turner) receives a mysterious package from her dead brother-in-law which she must then take to the jungles of Columbia to rescue her kidnapped sister. Not knowing that she is carrying a treasure map, she finds herself embroiled in danger from the minute she steps off the plane. To her rescue comes wild and woolly Douglas, a gun-toting soldier of the jungle. Of course they fall in love, but the action never stops, nor does the humor, as Turner's drab existence is forever transformed. Followed by JEWEL OF THE NILE.

☐ Sex ☐ Nud ✓ Viol ✓ Lang ✓ AdSit

A: Michael Douglas, Kathleen Turner, Danny DeVito, Alfonso Arau, Zack Norman

© FOXVIDEO 1358

SCARAMOUCHE

D: George Sidney — 116 m

NR | ACT | 1952 | COLOR

8 Stylish swashbuckler set in 18th-century France. Granger is a nobleman determined to avenge the death of his brother who was killed by master swordsman Ferrer. But first he must become a skilled swordsman himself. So he trains as an actor, acquiring some fancy sword tricks, and becomes the feared Scaramouche. Granger has another reason to seek vengeance - Ferrer is also in love with his girlfriend (Leigh). This first-class, but very simplified, screen adaptation of the Rafael Sabatini story is well done and rousing entertainment. Great sword fighting sequences.

☐ Sex ☐ Nud ✓ Viol ☐ Lang ✓ AdSit

A: Stewart Granger, Eleanor Parker, Janet Leigh, Mel Ferrer, Henry Wilcoxon, Lewis Stone

Distributed By MGM/UA Home Video M200641

SCARLET PIMPERNEL, THE

D: Harold Young — 95 m

NR | ACT | 1935 | B&W

8 Rousing swashbuckler! Sir Percy (Howard) lives a double life. He poses as an English fool but, when disguised, he becomes the charming hero who saves numerous innocent French noblemen from a mindless death at the guillotine during the Reign of Terror in 18th-century France. Meanwhile, his beautiful wife (Oberon) is increasingly disenchanted with her wimpy husband and falls in love with the romantic Pimpernel, unaware that her own husband is the daredevil in disguise. This movie has something for everyone: intrigue, adventure, suspense and wit. Howard embraces his role with zeal. Remade in 1950 with David Niven as THE ELUSIVE PIMPERNEL.

☐ Sex ☐ Nud ✓ Viol ☐ Lang ✓ AdSit

A: Leslie Howard, Merle Oberon, Raymond Massey, Nigel Bruce, Joan Gardner, Raymond Massey

© GOODTIMES 5006

SEA HAWK, THE

D: Michael Curtiz — 128 m

NR | ACT | 1940 | B&W

8 High-spirited adventure, set in the 16th century. Queen Elizabeth (Robson) suspects that the Spaniards are getting ready to launch a massive attack with their naval armada against England. She commissions Errol Flynn, a swashbuckling sea captain, to gather the evidence and to foil the Spaniards's plans. He seeks to defeat the treacherous Spanish ambassador (Rains) while pursuing the love of his beautiful daughter (Marshall). High-seas action and rousing adventure highlight Flynn at his adventurous best. The film has something for everyone and is acclaimed as one of the best of its genre.

☐ Sex ☐ Nud ✓ Viol ☐ Lang ✓ AdSit

A: Errol Flynn, Flora Robson, Brenda Marshall, Henry Daniell, Claude Rains, Donald Crisp

Distributed By MGM/UA Home Video M201855

SEA WOLVES, THE

D: Andrew V. McLaglen — 120 m

PG | ACT WAR | 1980 | COLOR

7 A riveting war adventure based on a true story! During WWII, aging British agents (Peck and Moore) recruit some retired members of a British calvary unit who are now members of an honorary drinking club in India for an espionage mission against the Germans. The team is after a clandestine radio transmitter on board a German ship that's anchored in a neutral Indian port. While Peck leads his over-the-hill recruits in their training sessions, Moore romances with a beautiful double agent (Kellerman). High flying adventure and a stellar cast.

✓ Sex ✓ Nud ✓ Viol ☐ Lang ✓ AdSit

A: Gregory Peck, Roger Moore, David Niven, Trevor Howard, Barbara Kellerman, Patrick Macnee

© WARNER HOME VIDEO 709

SHAMUS

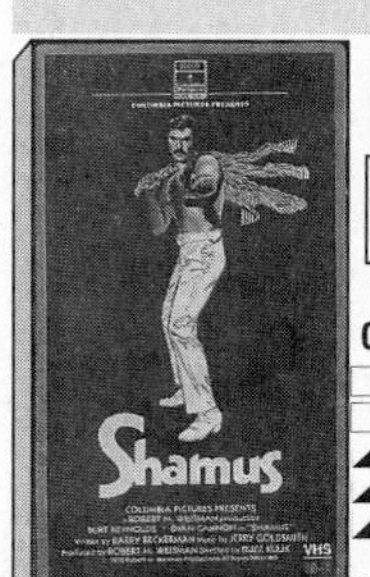

D: Buzz Kulik — 106 m

PG | ACT COM | 1973 | COLOR

6 Gimmicky and not particularly innovative, but still a fun private eye movie. Burt Reynolds is a quirky, wisecracking private eye who is hired to recover some stolen diamonds. In the process of his investigations, he runs across a much bigger operation, including a warehouse full of stolen weapons and ammunition. Poor old Burt gets beat up at every other turn, but he does get some help from beautiful socialite Dyan Cannon. Fast moving, with lots of action and glib dialogue. Pretty good.

☐ Sex ☐ Nud ✓ Viol ✓ Lang ✓ AdSit

A: Burt Reynolds, Dyan Cannon, John P. Ryan, Giorgio Tozzi, Joe Santos, Ron Weyand

© COLUMBIA TRISTAR HOME VIDEO 60205

SHIPWRECKED

D: Nils Gaup — 93 m

PG | ACT CLD | 1991 | COLOR

8 A young boy joins the crew of a sailing ship as cabin boy to earn money to help save his parent's farm. They set sail for the South Seas, but on board is a pirate posing as a British naval officer. It is his plan to wait until the ship gets to the right location and then take control. However, just as he does, the ship is caught up in a terrible storm and is capsized. The lad makes it to a tropical island, but soon discovers that this is the island the pirate was seeking and it contains his buried treasure. Shipwrecked on a pirate island, the boy finds that he is not alone, and he must struggle to survive. Rousing Disney adventure film for young and old alike.

☐ Sex ☐ Nud ✓ Viol ☐ Lang ☐ AdSit

A: Stian Smestad, Gabriel Byrne, Louisa Haigh, Trond Munch, Bjorn Sundquist, Eva Von Honna

© WALT DISNEY HOME VIDEO 1168

SINBAD THE SAILOR

D: Richard Wallace — 117 m

NR | ACT FAN | 1947 | COLOR

8 Very entertaining, rousing, old-time Saturday matinee-style swashbuckler! Sinbad (Fairbanks Jr.), the daring adventurer, is intent on finding Alexander the Great's treasures located somewhere on a faraway island. When he arrives and before he can claim his prize, he must do battle with the devious ruler of the island (Quinn), but he manages also to find time to romance beautiful O'Hara. Sinbad jumps from one perilous situation to another, offering up rousing adventure that's spiced both with fun and tongue-in-cheek humor. A good time.

☐ Sex ☐ Nud ✓ Viol ☐ Lang ☐ AdSit

A: Douglas Fairbanks, Jr., Maureen O'Hara, Anthony Quinn, Walter Slezak, George Tobias, Jane Greer

© TURNER HOME ENTERTAINMENT 2087

SOLDIER OF FORTUNE

D: Edward Dmytryk — 96 m

NR | ACT | 1955 | COLOR

7 Danger, adventure and a beautiful location! While in Hong Kong, Hayward's photographer husband (Barry) suddenly turns up missing. Hayward searches relentlessly for him but meets with no success until a handsome smuggler (Gable) appears upon the scene. Desperate to find her lost love, Hayward hires Gable to help rescue him. Gable soon learns that the missing man is being held in communist China and deftly organizes a rescue mission that spans numerous exotic Asian locations. The scenery alone is worth it.

Sex / Nud / Viol / Lang / ✓ AdSit

A: Clark Gable, Susan Hayward, Michael Rennie, Gene Barry

© FOXVIDEO 1280

SON OF MONTE CRISTO, THE

D: Rowland V. Lee — 102 m

NR | ACT | 1940 | B&W

7 Sword duels aplenty. Louis Hayward is the noble swashbuckler who battles a would-be dictator (Sanders) of Lichtenberg. He pretends to be a fool but is actually the leader of the resistance movement to the ruthless Sanders, who has the lovely Grand Duchess (Bennett) confined. Hayward poses as a French banker to gain access to Sanders and when he defeats the wicked villain, he also frees the imprisoned Bennett from her bonds and wins her hand. Exciting swordplay. Good adventure yarn.

Sex / Nud / ✓ Viol / Lang / ✓ AdSit

A: Louis Hayward, Joan Bennett, George Sanders, Florence Bates, Lionel Royce, Montagu Love

© VIDEO YESTERYEAR 137

SPACECAMP

D: Harry Winer — 115 m

PG | ACT CLD | 1986 | COLOR

6 An exciting adventure for anyone who ever dreamed of being an astronaut. Five awe-struck teenagers are chosen to spend the summer at a NASA space camp and learn all about the wonders of the space shuttle with the help of astronaut Capshaw. The summer program is sailing along until a robot, with a mind of its own, decides to launch the novice crew into space. When Capshaw gets injured, the teenage astronauts must figure out a way to get their hides back to earth in one piece. A fun trip.

Sex / Nud / Viol / ✓ Lang / AdSit

A: Kate Capshaw, Lea Thompson, Tom Skerritt, Kelly Preston, Larry B. Scott, Tate Donovan

© LIVE HOME VIDEO VA5174

SPARTACUS

D: Stanley Kubrick — 196 m

PG-13 | ACT DMA | 1960 | COLOR

10 Rousing and rewarding, intelligent and thrilling. A huge, epic human drama based solidly in historical fact. In 73 B.C. in republican Rome, a large and bloody slave revolt did, in fact, for a short time, challenge the Empire. Kirk Douglas plays Spartacus, a slave/gladiator who rose up first against the barbarism of his own master and later came to lead the entire slave revolt against all Rome. Brilliantly photographed - huge spectacle, with an involving script, exciting performances and thrilling battle sequences. Winner of four Oscars. Must see.

Sex / Nud / ✓ Viol / Lang / ✓ AdSit

A: Kirk Douglas, Laurence Olivier, Jean Simmons, Charles Laughton, Peter Ustinov, Tony Curtis

© MCA/UNIVERSAL HOME VIDEO, INC. 81133

SPY WHO LOVED ME, THE

D: Lewis Gilbert — 128 m

PG | ACT | 1977 | COLOR

8 Explosive Bond adventure! After US and Russian submarines are stolen by a shipping tycoon, Bond (Moore) must team up with a beautiful Soviet spy (Bach) in order to squash the evil Stromberg's (Jurgens) maniacal plans to destroy the world. Seems Stromberg wants to be the ruler of an undersea world which he will create after his provoked nuclear war destroys life as we know it on the surface. The major obstacle thrown in Bond's path is a hugely menacing seven foot hulk with a steel jaw - appropriately named "Jaws." Number 10 in the series is a boatload of fun.

✓ Sex / Nud / ✓ Viol / Lang / ✓ AdSit

A: Roger Moore, Barbara Bach, Curt Jurgens, Richard Kiel, Caroline Munro, Bernard Lee

Distributed By MGM/UA Home Video M201421

SUPERMAN II

D: Richard Lester — 127 m

PG | ACT COM FAN | 1979 | COLOR

8 Superman (Reeve) has his hands really full when three evil villains from his home planet Krypton come to earth and are intent on ruling it. They all possess the same powers that Superman has, and so the challenging battle to save the world begins. Meanwhile, Superman falls deeper in love with Lois Lane (Kidder), and arch rival Lex Luthor (Hackman) keeps persistently nipping at his heels. Much more brash and wild that the first film, this super adventure keeps the adrenaline pumping and the laughs coming at a very steady pace.

Sex / Nud / ✓ Viol / Lang / ✓ AdSit

A: Christopher Reeve, Margot Kidder, Gene Hackman, Ned Beatty, Valerie Perrine, Jackie Cooper

© WARNER HOME VIDEO 11120

SUPERMAN, THE MOVIE

D: Richard Donner — 143 m

PG | ACT COM FAN | 1978 | COLOR

9 A super movie! Reeve is the man of steel from the planet Krypton who is sent to earth as a child and is raised in a small midwestern town. When he is grown he moves to the big city and uses his super powers to keep crime at bay. Clark Kent, the unassuming newspaper man, becomes Superman when duty calls. He fights for truth, justice and the American way while battling the evil Lex Luthor (Hackman). Superman also falls for the captivating Lois Lane (Kidder) in this infectious film that spawned three sequels. Plenty of humor, adventure and romance. Oscar winner for special effects!

Sex / Nud / ✓ Viol / ✓ Lang / ✓ AdSit

A: Christopher Reeve, Margot Kidder, Marlon Brando, Gene Hackman, Ned Beatty, Jackie Cooper

© WARNER HOME VIDEO 1013

SWISS FAMILY ROBINSON

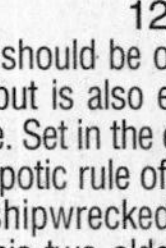

D: Ken Annakin — 126 m

G | ACT CLD | 1960 | COLOR

9 Rousing fanciful adventure story that should be on every kid's - certainly every boy's - to-watch list, but is also entertaining for the entire family. Patented Disney adventure. Set in the early 19th-century, a family has set sail to escape the despotic rule of Napoleon but, under pursuit by pirates, they become shipwrecked on a tropical island paradise. The inventive father and his two older sons build a wonderland for the family out of native materials and an array of inventive weapons to ward off the impending assault of pirates led by Hayakawa. Top drawer entertainment.

Sex / Nud / ✓ Viol / Lang / AdSit

A: John Mills, Dorothy McGuire, James MacArthur, Janet Munro, Tommy Kirk, Sessue Hayakawa

© WALT DISNEY HOME VIDEO 053

SWORD AND THE ROSE, THE

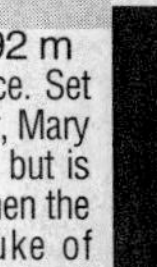

D: Ken Annakin — 92 m

NR | ACT CLD | 1953 | COLOR

7 A rich tapestry of Disney heroics, adventure and romance. Set during the reign of King Henry VIII (Justice), Henry's sister, Mary Tudor (Johns), falls in love with a lowly common man (Todd) but is sent to marry the much older King of France by her brother. When the French King dies, the opportunistic and villainous Duke of Buckingham (Gough) seizes the opportunity to try to take Mary's hand in marriage, away from her true love, Todd. Todd must rescue her. Disney filmed this spirited period piece in England. It is rich in flavor but there is no basis in history for it.

Sex / Nud / ✓ Viol / Lang / AdSit

A: Richard Todd, Glynis Johns, James Robertson Justice, Michael Gough, Jane Barrett

© WALT DISNEY HOME VIDEO 266

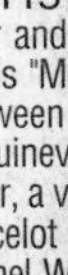

FAMILY

SWORD OF LANCELOT

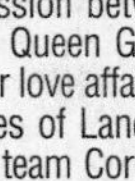

D: Cornel Wilde — 115 m

NR | ACT ROM | 1963 | COLOR

7 Before CAMELOT, there was the story of King Arthur and his court - a rousing adventure based on Thomas Mallory's "Morte d'Arthur." This is the love story of forbidden passion between the dashing Sir Lancelot (Wilde) and the captivating Queen Guinevere. When the betrayed King Arthur finds out about their love affair, a vastly destructive war breaks out. Great performances of Lancelot and Guinevere are given by real-life husband and wife team Cornel Wilde and Jean Wallace. Loads of intricate swordplay add to the fun.

Sex / Nud / ✓ Viol / Lang / ✓ AdSit

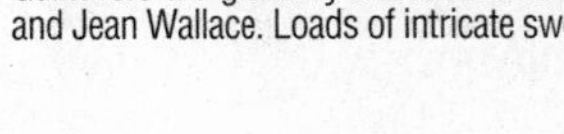

A: Cornel Wilde, Jean Wallace, Brian Aherne, George Baker

© MCA/UNIVERSAL HOME VIDEO, INC. 80077

SWORD OF THE VALIANT

D: Stephen Weeks — 102 m

PG | ACT | 1984 | COLOR

7 Nice mix of chivalry and adventure. Sean Connery is the supernatural Green Knight in the court of Camelot. When Sir Gawain (O'Keffe), a knight in King Arthur's court, cuts the Green Knight's head off, the magical Connery puts himself back together and makes Sir Gawain a bargain. O'Keffe must solve a riddle within one year or death is his consequence. Excellent period detail and production values, exciting swordplay and witty humor.

Sex / Nud / ✓ Viol / Lang / ✓ AdSit

A: Cyrielle Claire, Miles O'Keefe, Leigh Lawson, Sean Connery, Trevor Howard, Peter Cushing

Distributed By MGM/UA Home Video M700593

TARZAN, THE APE MAN

D: W.S. Van Dyke — 109 m

NR | ACT FAN | 1932 | B&W

7 This is the beginning of a long line of Tarzan flicks. (However, there was a 1918 silent version.) In this one, Edgar Rice Burroughs's classic character is given respectful treatment with Olympic swimming star Weismuller as Tarzan. Maureen O'Sullivan, who falls for the ape-man, is the daughter of a leader of an English expedition in search of an elephant's graveyard full of ivory. Even though the film techniques are obviously dated, as are some of the attitudes, this film still has pretty good action sequences and is pretty racy, too, especially for the times.

Sex / ✓ Nud / ✓ Viol / Lang / AdSit

A: Johnny Weissmuller, Maureen O'Sullivan, C. Aubrey Smith

Distributed By MGM/UA Home Video M500043

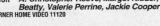

THIEF OF BAGDAD, THE

D: Ludwig Berger, Michael Powell — 106 m

NR | ACT FAN CLD | 1940 | COLOR

9 Wonderously fanciful story from the tales of the "Arabian Nights." Who couldn't become captivated by the story of a young prince, tricked out of his kingdom and his girl by the evil Grand Vizier, only to be rescued by a thief on a magic carpet who also has the help of a colossal magical genie? Then, throw in an enormous spider, a dog who once was a boy, a flying toy horse, a flower that causes amnesia and a beautiful girl. All the above, combined with terrific special effects and an outstanding score, have made this a perennial favorite. 3 Oscars.

☐ Sex ☐ Nud ☐ Viol ☐ Lang ☐ AdSit

A: Sabu, Conrad Veidt, June Duprez, John Justin, Rex Ingram, Miles Malleson

© HBO VIDEO 90653

THREE MUSKETEERS, THE

D: Richard Lester — 105 m

PG | ACT COM ROM | 1974 | COLOR

9 Great, well-rounded entertainment that has a little bit of everything. Dumas's classic tale has been filmed numerous times, but never this well. Michael York is determined to become one of the King's elite guards, the Musketeers, so he befriends three of them but, they are only interested in fighting, drinking and chasing women. However, they do become roused to action when York charms Welch, the Queen's lady-in-waiting, and she uncovers a plot to overcome the King. This news sends the Musketeers into rip roaring action. Rousing swashbuckling and hilarious slapstick. Top talent.

☐ Sex ☐ Nud ◢ Viol ☐ Lang ◢ AdSit

A: Oliver Reed, Raquel Welch, Richard Chamberlain, Michael York, Frank Finlay, Geraldine Chaplin

© LIVE HOME VIDEO 67776

THREE MUSKETEERS, THE

D: Stephen Herek — 105 m

PG | ACT | 1993 | COLOR

7 The most recent in a string of many (at least 5) remakes of the classic adventure tale. Young D'Artagnon travels to Paris to join the King's guards, the Musketeers, only to discover that it has been disbanded by the treacherous Cardinal Richelieu. Only three Musketeers have not laid down their swords. D'Artagnon discovers that Richelieu is planning to enter into a treasonous treaty of his own with England which is to be delivered by the beautiful but deadly Lady DeWinter (DeMornay). That message must be stopped. Lots and lots of swordplay and merry-making. Not a lot of plot or character depth, so not as involving as some of the earlier versions.

☐ Sex ☐ Nud ◢ Viol ☐ Lang ◢ AdSit

A: Charlie Sheen, Kiefer Sutherland, Chris O'Donnell, Oliver Platt, Tim Curry, Rebecca DeMornay

© WALT DISNEY HOME VIDEO 2524

THUNDERBALL

D: Terence Young — 140 m

PG | ACT | 1965 | COLOR

8 James Bond is in pursuit of Spectre's number two man, Largo, and two stolen atom bombs - with which Largo intends to blackmail Miami. Along the way, James encounters Largo's mistress, Claudine Auger (the former Miss France), and seduces her into battling for truth and justice. 007 is as suave, as tough as ever and is loaded down with gadgets and pretty bikini-clad girls, too, but he is also all wet. Much of the filming was underwater, which makes it somewhat difficult to follow. Remade 14 years later as NEVER SAY NEVER AGAIN.

☐ Sex ☐ Nud ◢ Viol ☐ Lang ◢ AdSit

A: Sean Connery, Claudine Auger, Adolfo Celi, Luciana Paluzzi, Rick Van Nutter

Distributed By MGM/UA Home Video M202729

THUNDER ROAD

D: Arthur Ripley — 94 m

PG | ACT | 1958 | B&W

7 A pretty good action flick that was Mitchum's all the way. Mitchum co-wrote, produced and starred in this story of a Tennessee hill boy, just back from Korea and just out of prison, who goes back into the only business he knows - moonshining. Mitchum shines as a man whose own future is sealed but who cautions his younger brother to go into a real career. All the while he struggles against mobsters who want to take over his operation and the feds who want to shut him down. Mitchum even got a popular hit song from the film's theme - which he also wrote and sang.

☐ Sex ☐ Nud ◢ Viol ☐ Lang ◢ AdSit

A: Robert Mitchum, Gene Barry, Keely Smith, James Mitchum, Jacques Auburchon, Trevor Bardette

Distributed By MGM/UA Home Video M601453

TOBRUK

D: Arthur Hiller — 110 m

NR | ACT WAR | 1966 | COLOR

6 Thrilling World War II action movie in which a group of German Jews, disguised as Axis troops, together with some American and English commandos, undertake a daring mission across miles of desert wasteland to destroy the fuel supplies of Field Marshall Rommel's tanks in North Africa at Tobruk. Pretty good. There are some pretty big action scenes with tank battles, and some intrigue, too, when they suspect a traitor in their midst.

☐ Sex ☐ Nud ◢ Viol ☐ Lang ◢ AdSit

A: Rock Hudson, George Peppard, Guy Stockwell, Nigel Green, Jack Watson, Norman Rossington

© MCA/UNIVERSAL HOME VIDEO, INC. 45014

TOP GUN

D: Tony Scott — 109 m

PG | ACT ROM | 1986 | COLOR

10 Major box office hit that, while contrived, is still so captivating in its excitement that you don't care. Tom Cruise is a top Navy F-14 fighter pilot sent for additional "Top Gun" training at Miramar Naval Base in San Diego. This is a school which is reserved for only the best of the best. His cocky attitude gets him in trouble with nearly everyone there but he falls in love with his luscious physics instructor Kelly McGillis. Heartpoundingly thrilling flight sequences are at the heart of this film's big success for the men. Tom's smile wins over the women.

◢ Sex ☐ Nud ◢ Viol ◢ Lang ◢ AdSit

A: Tom Cruise, Kelly McGillis, Anthony Edwards, Val Kilmer, Tim Robbins, Meg Ryan

© PARAMOUNT HOME VIDEO 1692

TREASURE ISLAND

D: Victor Fleming — 105 m

NR | ACT CLD | 1934 | B&W

8 This was the first adaptation of Robert Lewis Stevenson's classic story for the big screen, and MGM pulled out all the stops. A young boy (Cooper) receives a treasure map from a dying sailor and then takes on a job as a cabin boy on a ship bound for the treasure island. Also on board is the scurrilous old sea dog Long John Silver (Beery), who sets his sights on stealing the boy's treasure and rallies the ship's crew to mutiny. Fine adventure film that will still inspire the imagination of any adventurous boy.

☐ Sex ☐ Nud ◢ Viol ☐ Lang ☐ AdSit

A: Wallace Beery, Jackie Cooper, Lionel Barrymore, Otto Kruger, Nigel Bruce, Lewis Stone

Distributed By MGM/UA Home Video M500032

TREASURE ISLAND

D: Byron Haskin — 96 m

G | ACT CLD | 1950 | COLOR

8 Walt Disney remade the 1934 version of Stevenson's classic. This version did an excellent job with it and some say even improved upon the earlier version. However, the ending was changed and, in 1975 when it was reissued again, some of the more violent sequences were removed. Bobby Driscoll plays young Jim Hawkins, a young English lad who receives a treasure map from a dying sailor. Aboard a ship bound for the island, Long John Silver (Newton) and the crew of pirates seize control of the ship in a mutiny so they can conduct their own search for the treasure and steal it.

☐ Sex ☐ Nud ◢ Viol ☐ Lang ☐ AdSit

A: Bobby Driscoll, Robert Newton, Basil Sydney, Walter Fitzgerald

© WALT DISNEY HOME VIDEO 041

ULYSSES

D: Mario Camerini — 102 m

NR | ACT FAN CLD | 1955 | COLOR

6 Lavish production of Homer's ancient and epic tale about Ulysses, the King of Ithica, and his long journey home after the Trojan wars. For ten years Ulysses struggles to reach home and his faithful wife Penelope. But all along the way, he is beset by trial after trial unleashed upon him by King Neptune, god of the sea, who is upset with him for having destroyed the Trojans. He is attacked by a hungry one-eyed Cyclops, enticed by Siren songstresses and seduced by the beautiful witch Circe. Then, arriving at home, he must also rescue Penelope, who is being beset by suitors who want to marry her and become king.

☐ Sex ☐ Nud ◢ Viol ☐ Lang ◢ AdSit

A: Kirk Douglas, Luana Mangano, Anthony Quinn, Silvana Mangano

© WARNER HOME VIDEO 11470

VIEW TO A KILL, A

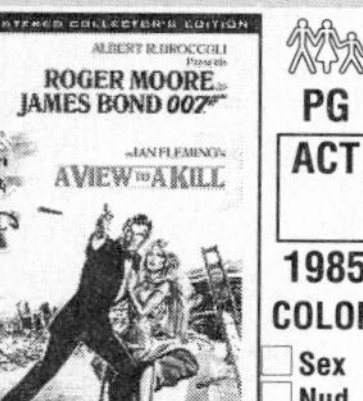

D: John Glen — 126 m

PG | ACT | 1985 | COLOR

7 James's fellow agent has been killed in the Alps and when James goes to investigate, he barely escapes Soviet assassins. The trail leads him to a Russian spy in the Silicon Valley of California. Walken plans to induce a devastating earthquake there and take over the lucrative microchip market. The menacing Grace Jones is Walken's assistant, as is the captivating Roberts, but Roberts becomes Bond's ally and romantic interest. Edge-of-your seat adventure with spectacular stunts and action at every corner. This was Roger Moore's last outing as Bond.

☐ Sex ☐ Nud ◢ Viol ◢ Lang ◢ AdSit

A: Roger Moore, Christopher Walken, Grace Jones, Tanya Roberts, Patrick Macnee, Patrick Bauchau

Distributed By MGM/UA Home Video M202739

VIKINGS, THE

D: Richard Fleischer — 117 m

NR | ACT | 1958 | COLOR

7 Well-done and rousing, an authentic-looking Viking action epic with a big-name cast. Tony Curtis is a slave of the Vikings. He is also Douglas's half-brother, although neither knows it. Curtis's mother was an English queen who was raped by Douglas's father, the Viking king (Borgnine). Douglas is a boisterous and rowdy carbon copy of his father. Both Douglas and Curtis are in love with the beautiful captured Welsh princess, Janet Leigh. However, Curtis and she escape, but Curtis and Douglas meet again and eventually unite to fight the English when their father is killed.

☐ Sex ☐ Nud ◢ Viol ☐ Lang ◢ AdSit

A: Kirk Douglas, Ernest Borgnine, Janet Leigh, Tony Curtis, James Donald

Distributed By MGM/UA Home Video M700579

VON RYAN'S EXPRESS

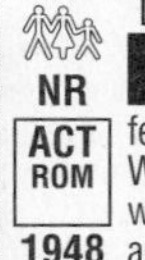

D: Mark Robson — 117 m

NR | ACT WAR | 1965 | COLOR

Sex / Nud / ◢ Viol / Lang / ◢ AdSit

8 Top-drawer WWII actioner. Sinatra is an American colonel shot down and placed in a POW camp. He is the ranking officer, but is not held in high regard by his fellow prisoners until he engineers the capture of the train in which 600 of them are being transported across Italy to Germany. The POWs want to divert their captured train toward Switzerland and freedom, but the Germans are not about to let that happen without a fight. Hard-hitting action, suspense, solid acting and well-paced directing make this a thrilling adventure story.

A: Frank Sinatra, Trevor Howard, Luther Adler, James Brolin, Brad Dexter, Edward Mulhare

© FOXVIDEO 1003

WAKE OF THE RED WITCH

D: Edward Ludwig — 106 m

NR | ACT ROM | 1948 | B&W

Sex / Nud / Viol / Lang / ◢ AdSit

6 Lively sea yarn about the greed of a ship's captain and his search for sunken treasure and love. John Wayne is involved in a bitter feud with the owner of the East Indies Trading Company (Adler). Wayne has sunk his own ship with a cargo of gold bullion on board, with the idea of going back years later to recover it. Wayne and Adler are also fighting for the affections of beautiful Angelique (Russell). Adler wins, but both he and Angelique are struck by a tropical disease which cripples him and kills her. Now a heartbroken Wayne can return to the Red Witch to recover her treasure.

A: John Wayne, Gail Russell, Gig Young, Luther Adler, Adele Mara, Eduard Franz

© REPUBLIC PICTURES HOME VIDEO 4429

WHITE LIGHTNING

D: Joseph Sargent — 101 m

PG | ACT | 1973 | COLOR

Sex / Nud / ◢ Viol / ◢ Lang / ◢ AdSit

8 Exciting action flick in which Burt Reynolds, as Gator McKlusky - a good ol' boy and moonshine runner - has been in prison. The Feds come to him with a proposition that they will free him if he helps them to trap a gang of moonshiners involving corrupt cop Beatty. Reynolds, however, has his own agenda. He wants to get Beatty, because Beatty killed his brother. Rousing adventure with top-notch acting and good driving stunts help raise this film above typical mindless action fare. This proved to be a popular film and Reynolds reprised his role later for the sequel GATOR.

A: Burt Reynolds, Ned Beatty, Jennifer Billingsley, Bo Hopkins, Matt Clark, Louise Latham

Distributed By MGM/UA Home Video M301431

WHITE LINE FEVER

D: Jonathan Kaplan — 92 m

PG | ACT | 1975 | COLOR

Sex / Nud / ◢ Viol / ◢ Lang / ◢ AdSit

7 This was somewhat of a surprise hit. It is an entertaining morality-based actioner about a young returning Vietnam War veteran who gets married, buys a big rig and sets out to become an independent long haul trucker. He gets work through an old friend but balks when asked to carry an illegal load by a group of hoods. After his friend is killed, his wife is beaten (killing their unborn baby) and their house burned, he fights back. Solid direction, good acting, a plausible script and some really good action sequences have made this into a cult favorite.

A: Jan-Michael Vincent, Kay Lenz, Slim Pickens, L.Q. Jones, Don Porter, Sam Laws

© COLUMBIA TRISTAR HOME VIDEO VH10563

WILBY CONSPIRACY, THE

D: Ralph Nelson — 113 m

PG | ACT DMA | 1974 | COLOR

Sex / Nud / ◢ Viol / ◢ Lang / ◢ AdSit

8 Set in South Africa but filmed in Kenya, Sidney Poitier is a militant African political activist. His attorney is Michael Caine's girlfriend. Poitier and Caine are chained together and then are allowed to escape by a vicious and bigoted policeman who is intent upon following Poitier to his underground leader. Poitier's and Caine's plight bring back reminders of THE DEFIANT ONES. It's the charm of Poitier and Caine that keep this film moving as an action film, while never losing the dramatic impact from the underlying causes.

A: Sidney Poitier, Michael Caine, Rutger Hauer, Nicol Williamson, Prunella Gee, Persis Khambatta

Distributed By MGM/UA Home Video M301294

WILLOW

D: Ron Howard — 130 m

PG | ACT FAN CLD | 1988 | COLOR

Sex / Nud / ◢ Viol / Lang / ◢ AdSit

7 A kooky fantasy - sort of Star Wars meets the Wizard of Oz. Davis is Willow, 0an elf who is the protector of a small baby who will grow up, end the reign of the evil Queen Bavmorda (Marsh) and bring peace to the world. Warrior Kilmer offers his help to the little guy and along the way they encounter many wacky characters, some dangerous and some funny. This is a fanciful adventure that provides an eyeful of special effects. Although aimed at children, some of the violence might be too intense for the youngest ones.

A: Val Kilmer, Joanne Whalley-Kilmer, Warwick Davis, Jean Marsh, Patricia Hayes, Billy Barty

© COLUMBIA TRISTAR HOME VIDEO 60936

WIND AND THE LION, THE

D: John Milius — 120 m

PG | ACT ROM | 1975 | COLOR

Sex / Nud / ◢ Viol / Lang / ◢ AdSit

8 A rousing adventure story, very loosely based upon an actual event. In 1904 a beautiful American woman and her son are kidnapped in Morocco by a dashing rebel Berber chiefton (Connery). American President Teddy Roosevelt (Keith) threatens to send in American troops to retrieve her. This, however, sparks an international incident when the Germans fearing competition on their turf, send in troops to protect their own power play for North Africa. This is an action-packed adventure story, but it is also one of romance and political intrigue. Connery and Bergen shine. Very good.

A: Sean Connery, Candice Bergen, Brian Keith, John Huston, Geoffrey Lewis, Steve Kanaly

Distributed By MGM/UA Home Video M600662

YOU ONLY LIVE TWICE

D: Lewis Gilbert — 118 m

PG | ACT | 1967 | COLOR

Sex / Nud / ◢ Viol / Lang / ◢ AdSit

8 Fifth in the Bond series and perhaps the most gadget-infested of them all. Set in Japan, James seeks out SPECTRE head man Biofeld (Pleasance) inside a volcano. Biofeld is engaged in an elaborate enterprise to steal both Russian and American spaceships. Each side is blaming the other. It appears that SPECTRE's plan to provoke World War III, so that it can emerge as the world's dominant force, is working. Some pretty nifty gadgets, pretty girls, of course, and a quick pace. Nancy Sinatra sings the title song.

A: Sean Connery, Akiko Wakabayashi, Tetsuro Tamba, Donald Pleasence, Karin Dor, Bernard Lee

Distributed By MGM/UA Home Video M201405

ZEPPELIN

D: Etienne Perrier — 102 m

G | ACT WAR | 1971 | COLOR

Sex / Nud / ◢ Viol / Lang / ◢ AdSit

6 The time is WWI. The English military fears the German's newest weapon, the Zepplin, so they entice a German-born Scottish lieutenant (York) to "defect" to the Germans to collect information on the fearsome weapon. Now, as a German officer, he is almost unbelievably invited aboard the ship for a trial run. However, when it is airborne, he finds there is a reason he is there. The Germans plan to launch a daring raid into England and they need his knowledge of the countryside to carry it off. Entertaining and atmospheric with good special effects.

A: Michael York, Elke Sommer, Marius Goring, Anton Diffring, Rupert Davies, Peter Carsten

© WARNER HOME VIDEO 11562

ZULU

D: Cy Endfield — 138 m

NR | ACT SUS | 1964 | COLOR

Sex / Nud / ■ Viol / Lang / ◢ AdSit

8 Rousing adventure epic. This is the dramatization of an actual event which occurred on January 22, 1879. A small British garrison of 105 men, stationed at a remote outpost, learns that it is being approached by over 4000 Zulu warriors and that the only source of reinforcement, a force of 1200 men, has been totally wiped out. They are left alone, outnumbered 40-1, to withstand the onslaught. Refusing to abandon their post, they rally to victory. Well crafted, with massive and spectacular battle sequences. Excellent performances, including Caine in his first big role.

A: Jack Hawkins, Stanley Baker, Michael Caine, James Booth, Ulla Jacobsson

© NEW LINE HOME VIDEO 90002

FAMILY

Comedy

9 TO 5

D: Colin Higgins — 110 m

PG | COM | 1980 | COLOR

Sex / Nud / Viol / ◢ Lang / ◢ AdSit

9 Great fun for nearly everybody from this very popular comedy. Three secretaries fantasize gleefully on how they will one day get even with their chauvinistic heal of a boss (Dabney Coleman). Then one day, circumstances suddenly do arise that give them a chance to act their fantasies out. The three women have a terrific time by becoming his torturers. Filled with outrageous slapstick sequences and lots of comedic one-liners. This was Dolly Parton's film debut and she also wrote and sang the theme song. Both were very big hits. Very enjoyable and funny.

A: Jane Fonda, Lily Tomlin, Dolly Parton, Dabney Coleman

© FOXVIDEO 1099

ABBOTT AND COSTELLO MEET DR. JEKYLL AND MR. HYDE

D: Charles Lamont — 77 m

NR · COM CLD · 1952 · B&W

8 Here America's favorite silly duo from the 40s and 50s play two American Detectives in 1880s London, where they encounter Boris Karloff in the dual role of Jekyll and Hyde. This is one of their funniest movies. Don't miss it when Lou drinks a potion and gets turned into a mouse. Abbott and Costello learned their trade doing standup routines and short comedy skits on the Vaudeville stages. Bud Abbott is an everyman sort who plays straightman to the silly child-like antics of his short round partner, Lou Costello. They were hysterical on stage and also became big hits in the movie theaters of America.

Sex · Nud · Viol · Lang · AdSit

A: Bud Abbott, Lou Costello, Boris Karloff, Craig Stevens

© MCA/UNIVERSAL HOME VIDEO, INC. 80010

ABBOTT AND COSTELLO MEET FRANKENSTEIN

D: Charles Barton — 83 m

NR · COM CLD · 1948 · B&W

8 Fun mix of fright and laughs. Lou and Bud are railroad baggage clerks this time, who get in trouble when crates transporting monsters to the House of Horrors are discovered to be empty. So the twosome follow the monsters's trail to a secret island where they find Dracula (Lugosi) and the Frankenstein monster. Things get dicey for them when a mad scientist plans to put Lou's brain into the Frankenstein monster and the Wolfman (Chaney) wants them all. This is great comedy that works because the monsters always play their parts straight.

Sex · Nud · Viol · Lang · AdSit

A: Bud Abbott, Lou Costello, Lon Chaney, Jr., Bela Lugosi, Lenore Aubert, Jane Randolph

© MCA/UNIVERSAL HOME VIDEO, INC. 55074

ABBOTT AND COSTELLO MEET THE INVISIBLE MAN

D: Charles Lamont — 83 m

NR · COM · 1951

6 Bud and Lou are have just graduated from private detective school when their first customer walks in the door. Tommy is a boxer who has been wrongly accused of murder and he needs their help to prove it. Just then the police arrive and poof, their new client has evaporated. He has injected himself with an experimental invisibility serum. Tommy convinces Lou that he should go undercover as a boxer to find the real killer. Pudgy little Lou will be "Lou the Looper" and invisible Tommy will supply the punches.

Sex · Nud · Viol · Lang · AdSit

A: Bud Abbott, Lou Costello, Nancy Gould, Arther Franz, Adele Jergens, Sheldon Leonard

© MCA/UNIVERSAL HOME VIDEO, INC. 80673

ABSENT-MINDED PROFESSOR, THE

D: Robert Stevenson — 96 m

G · COM CLD · 1961 · B&W

8 A nerdy genius college professor (Fred MacMurry) accidentally discovers a gravity-defying glop he calls flubber. However, no one believes him except a nasty industrialist (Keenan Wynn), who tries to steal it. So, Fred uses the bouncy stuff on the shoes of school's losing basketball team, to make them into winners; and, in his old jalopy, to make it fly. Still great stuff for young kids, parents and maybe even a few teenagers.

Sex · Nud · Viol · Lang · AdSit

A: Fred MacMurray, Nancy Olson, Keenan Wynn, Tommy Kirk, Leon Ames, Ed Wynn

© WALT DISNEY HOME VIDEO 028

ADDAMS FAMILY, THE

D: Barry Sonnenfeld — 102 m

PG-13 · COM · 1991 · COLOR

8 A campy winner that's pure joy! Unorthodox and strange - sure. Kooky and spooky - you bet. That's the fun of it. The loveable, yet slightly sadistic, Addams Family lights up the screen in this comic tribute to creator cartoonist Charles Addams. A fake Uncle Fester comes to the mansion planning to steal the family fortune but is foiled by the sheer strangeness of the family's antics. Morticia (Huston) and Gomez (Julia) toss romantic sparks all over the place, and their daughter (Ricci) almost steals the show as she delivers ghoulish lines in deadpan fashion. Wonderful!

Sex · Nud · ◢ Viol · Lang · ◢ AdSit

A: Anjelica Huston, Raul Julia, Christopher Lloyd, Christina Ricci, Jimmy Workman, Judith Malina

© PARAMOUNT HOME VIDEO 32689

AFRICA SCREAMS

D: Charles Barton — 79 m

NR · COM · 1949 · B&W

6 Abbott and Costello go on a safari into Africa with a beautiful woman when Lou smells a big payday. He tries to pass cowardly Bud off as a famous big game hunter and a supposed expert on a the geography of a particular part of Africa. But unknown to the boys, the girl and her cohorts are not interested in big game hunting at all but instead in a secret diamond mine. This film contains many of the typical silly sight gags and slapstick comedy sketches which the pair created and polished in Vaudeville. It is not their best effort, but if you're a fan, you won't care. Kids love it too.

Sex · Nud · Viol · Lang · AdSit

A: Bud Abbott, Lou Costello, Hillary Brooke, Shemp Howard, Max Baer, Clyde Beaty

© UNITED AMERICAN VIDEO CORP. 0097

AIRPLANE

D: Jim Abrahams — 88 m

PG · COM · 1980 · COLOR

9 This is a wildly absurd spoof of the megahit AIRPORT and all the other disaster movies. It is filled with nonstop gags, bad puns and stupid jokes - most of which work. Hays is a washed-up anxiety-ridden pilot, flying onboard a plane where all the other people are stricken with food poisoning. That means everyone - including the pilot. So, he and his wacked-out ex-girlfriend stewardess are the only ones left who have a chance of landing the plane. This exercise in absolute silliness was a runaway hit in the theater. See also AIRPLANE II: THE SEQUEL; also THE NAKED GUN and NAKED GUN 2 1/2.

Sex · ◢ Nud · Viol · Lang · ◢ AdSit

A: Robert Hayes, Julie Hagerty, Robert Stack, Lloyd Bridges, Peter Graves, Leslie Nielsen

© PARAMOUNT HOME VIDEO 1305

AIRPLANE 2 - THE SEQUEL

D: Ken Finkleman — 84 m

PG · COM · 1982 · COLOR

7 Hysterical sequel, with the same sort of silly, stupid jokes as were in the original AIRPLANE! And, there's a lot of them, too. This time, terrified pilot Hays must save the space shuttle from destruction. You also will want to see the original AIRPLANE! and the similar films of the NAKED GUN series.

Sex · ◢ Nud · Viol · Lang · ◢ AdSit

A: Robert Hayes, Julie Hagerty, Lloyd Bridges, William Shatner, Raymond Burr, Chad Everett

© PARAMOUNT HOME VIDEO 1489

AIR UP THERE, THE

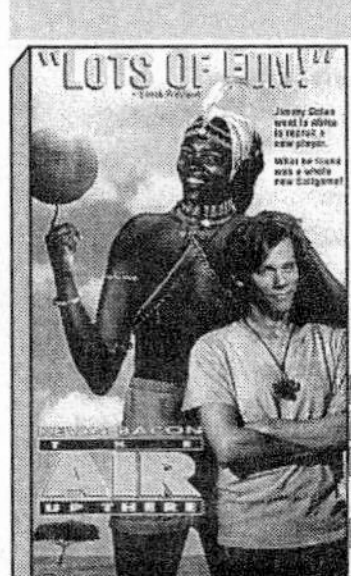

D: Paul M. Glaser — 107 m

PG · COM · 1994 · COLOR

6 Kevin Bacon is a former college basketball great who blew his knee out and so missed playing with the pros. Now he is, and has been for some time, the assistant coach at his alma-mater, St. Josephs. His ego has just gotten him in trouble again and it looks like he will never become coach. That's when he spots the 6'8"-answer to his prayers on a videotape that was shot at one of the school's missions in the middle of Africa. So, he's off to Africa to recruit the next NBA Hall-of-Famer. This is predictable all the way and is filled to the top with Hollywood cliches, but it still manages to kill time rather painlessly. Younger viewers will like it better than old cynics.

Sex · Nud · Viol · ◢ Lang · AdSit

A: Kevin Bacon, Charles Gitonga Maina, Yolanda Vasquez, Winston Ntshona, Mabutho "Kid" Sithole, Sean McCann

© HOLLYWOOD PICTURES HOME VIDEO 2546

ALICE'S RESTAURANT

D: Arthur Penn — 111 m

PG · COM · 1969 · COLOR

7 Remember the 1960s? Folk singer Arlo Guthrie had a big hit song which was given life within this film. Both the film and the song provide some revealing insights into the "hippie" counterculture of that era. The unusual and comic story chronicles Guthrie's ability to evade mandatory military service - the draft - after being deemed undesirable for having been arrested for littering. This is generally a fun blend of melodrama and whimsey.

Sex · ◢ Nud · Viol · ◢ Lang · ◢ AdSit

A: Arlo Guthrie, Pat Quinn, James Broderick, Michael McClanathan, Geoff Outlaw, Tina Chen

Distributed By MGM/UA Home Video M201370

ALL OF ME

D: Carl Reiner — 93 m

PG · COM · 1984 · COLOR

8 Wild slapstick. The spirit of a very eccentric and recently deceased heiress (Lily Tomlin) is accidentally injected into a lawyer's body (Steve Martin) after a guru's attempt to put her spirit into another woman's body fails. Since Martin is unwilling to give up possession, hilarity ensues. This is a great showcase for the comedic talents of the two stars as their two different-sex, totally mismatched personalities battle for possession of one body. It starts out sort of slow but gets better as it goes along. Martin's physical clowning steals the show.

Sex · Nud · Viol · ◢ Lang · ◢ AdSit

A: Steve Martin, Lily Tomlin, Victoria Tennant, Jason Bernard, Madolyn Smith, Selma Diamond

© HBO VIDEO 2715

ANDROCLES AND THE LION

D: Chester Erskine — 98 m

NR · COM · 1952 · B&W

6 The old fable of a simple tailor who receives the everlasting gratitude of a lion after pulling a thorn from his paw, is given a satirical edge by George Bernard Shaw. Alan Young plays the tailor, whose kindness at pulling a thorn from the paw of a lion is later repaid when a group of Christians are saved in the Roman arena. Although some of the bite of the satire is lost, enough survives for the story to remain intriguing.

Sex · Nud · Viol · Lang · AdSit

A: Alan Young, Jean Simmons, Victor Mature, Robert Newton, Maurice Evans, Elsa Lanchester

© NEW LINE HOME VIDEO 6028

ANGEL ON MY SHOULDER

D: Archie Mayo — 101 m

NR | COM FAN | 1946 | B&W | Sex | Nud | Viol | Lang | AdSit

7 Paul Muni is Eddie, a gangster who was murdered by his partner. However, Eddie makes a deal with the Devil (Rains) so he can come back to earth to get revenge. Eddie is sent back, but is placed in the body of a highly respected judge who the Devil expects Eddie will soon discredit. Eddie starts to like his new life. Soon he is running for governor on a reform ticket and has fallen in love with the judge's fiancee. This is all very disappointing for the Devil, especially since Eddie also spends the rest of the film trying outwit the Devil and his plan. Fun time from this entertaining little fantasy.

A: Paul Muni, Anne Baxter, Claude Rains, George Cleveland, Onslow Stevens

© UNITED AMERICAN VIDEO CORP. 4091

ANGELS IN THE OUTFIELD

D: William Dear — 103 m

PG | COM | 1994 | COLOR | Sex | Nud | Viol | Lang | AdSit

7 Young Roger lives with his best friend in a foster home next to the ball park. When his father arrives for a last visit, Roger asks him when they can be together and Pop says, "When the Angels win the pennant." Even though the Angels are perennial losers, Roger prays that night that the Angels will win. Someone is listening, because soon a real angel (Christopher Lloyd) arrives to give the team some much-needed assistance. No one can see him, except that is for Roger, but everyone knows something is up. Coach Danny Glover hears of the boy's story and refuses to believe, but before long no one can deny that the Angels are winning. Charming, if simple and predictable, Disney family film.

A: Danny Glover, Tony Danza, Brenda Fricker, Ben Johnson, Christopher Lloyd, Joseph Gordon-Levitt

© WALT DISNEY HOME VIDEO 2753

ANIMAL CRACKERS

D: Victor Heerman — 98 m

NR | COM | 1930 | B&W | Sex | Nud | Viol | Lang | AdSit

7 The Marx Brothers's movies were first big Broadway hits and only later were brought by Hollywood to the screen. That is why this movie (and most other early pictures) look so stagey. So ignore the production values and make room for their totally unique rapid-fire brand of silly humor such as when Grouch says (in his African lecture), "This morning I shot an elephant in my pajamas... How he got in my pajamas, I'll never know." Check the index for more of their insane antics. See also COCONUTS, NIGHT AT THE OPERA, MONKEY BUSINESS and DUCK SOUP.

A: Groucho Marx, Harpo Marx, Chico Marx, Zeppo Marx, Margaret Dumont, Lillian Roth

© MCA/UNIVERSAL HOME VIDEO, INC. 55000

ANY WHICH WAY YOU CAN

D: Buddy Van Horn — 116 m

PG | COM ACT | 1980 | COLOR | ◢ Sex | Nud | ◢ Viol | ◢ Lang | ◢ AdSit

8 Sequel to EVERY WHICH WAY BUT LOOSE. Same cast of characters, same enjoyable formula. Eastwood is a beer drinkin' mechanic/streetfighter who is set to meet the King of the Streetfighters in an all-out fight in Jackson Hole, Wyoming. However, Clint falls in love and doesn't want to go. So a group of hoods kidnap his love to encourage him to show up. Clyde, the raunchy orangutan, is back, too. Certainly not highbrow entertainment, but it is a lot of fun and was very popular.

A: Clint Eastwood, Sondra Locke, Geoffrey Lewis, William Smith, Harry Guardino, Ruth Gordon

© WARNER HOME VIDEO 11077

AROUND THE WORLD IN 80 DAYS

D: Michael Anderson — 179 m

G | COM | 1956 | COLOR | Sex | Nud | Viol | Lang | AdSit

7 This successful extravaganza won five Oscars, including Best Picture, upon its release. It is a little dated now, but still offers up plenty of entertainment. It is the Jules Verne story of Phileous Fogg and his valet who are out to win a 19th-century bet that they can circle the world in 80 days. They encounter one adventure after another during their trip, each one populated with its own major star. Over 40 major stars appear in cameo roles. Very expensive - 68,894 people are photographed on 252 locations in 13 countries.

A: David Niven, Cantinflas, Shirley MacLaine, Robert Newton, Marlene Dietrich, John Gielgud

© WARNER HOME VIDEO 11321

ARSENIC AND OLD LACE

D: Frank Capra — 120 m

NR | COM | 1944 | B&W | Sex | Nud | Viol | Lang | ◢ AdSit

10 Hilarious screen version of the outlandish and frenzied hit play about two sweet old ladies who cure gentleman callers of their loneliness by poisoning them and then giving them Christian burials in their basement. Their hapless nephew, Mortimer (Cary Grant), discovers a dead body in the window seat and mistakenly thinks that his crazy brother Teddy did it, never considering his aunts. But before he can get Teddy safely committed, his other sinister brother Jonathan (Massey) shows up, and he has a dead body of his own. Hysterical farce that has in no way lost any of its considerable sparkle.

A: Cary Grant, Priscilla Lane, Jack Carson, James Gleason, Peter Lorre, Raymond Massey

Distributed By MGM/UA Home Video M201568

ARTHUR

D: Steve Gordon — 97 m

PG | COM ROM | 1981 | COLOR | ◢ Sex | Nud | Viol | ◢ Lang | ◢ AdSit

10 Heartwarming and funny. Dudley Moore is Arthur. Arthur is a spoiled, rich and generally happy, alcoholic bachelor. But he is being forced to marry an up-tight heiress (Eikenberry) who he doesn't even like. Worse still, he has fallen for a lowly waitress and shoplifter (Minnelli). His family gives him an ultimatum: it's either a proper wife, continued money, power and elegance; or, love and total poverty. Moore is perfect and loveable as the drunken spoiled rich kid, but it's Gielgud as his sarcastic valet and surrogate father who steals the show and provides the belly laughs. Laugh-out-loud funny.

A: Dudley Moore, Liza Minnelli, Stephen Elliott, John Gielgud, Jill Eikenberry

© WARNER HOME VIDEO 22020

ARTISTS AND MODELS

D: Frank Tashlin — 109 m

NR | COM MUS | 1955 | COLOR | Sex | Nud | Viol | Lang | AdSit

7 Martin and Lewis's wackiness at its best. Dean Martin is a cartoonist who lands a big job by making Lewis's wacky far-out dreams into comic strips. But when Jerry's dreams start to become telepathic and the Russians become interested in them, things get crazy. Spiced up with loads of beautiful women, typical Martin and Lewis shtick, lots of sight gags and zippy one-liners, plus Martin's singing. Utter silliness that is still fun. This was Shirley MacLaine's second screen appearance.

A: Dean Martin, Jerry Lewis, Shirley MacLaine, Dorothy Malone, Eva Gabor, Anita Ekberg

© PARAMOUNT HOME VIDEO 5510

ASK ANY GIRL

D: Charles Walters — 101 m

NR | COM ROM | 1959 | COLOR | Sex | Nud | Viol | Lang | ◢ AdSit

7 Shirley MacLaine is a wide-eyed innocent girl who comes to the big city to find a husband, only to discover that most men are just lecherous skirthounds. She goes to work at an advertising agency and sets her sights on capturing one of the bosses (Gig Young), and she enlists the advertising techniques of his older brother (David Niven) to get her man. But things never work out as planned. Fun, light-hearted little fluff, carried off by a top-flight cast.

A: David Niven, Shirley MacLaine, Gig Young, Rod Taylor, Jim Backus, Elisabeth Fraser

Distributed By MGM/UA Home Video 201128

AUNTIE MAME

D: Morton DaCosta — 144 m

NR | COM MUS | 1958 | COLOR | Sex | Nud | Viol | Lang | AdSit

9 Funny and very entertaining. Russell is a tour-de-force in the title role as a colorful 1920's free-thinking eccentric aunt of an orphaned boy she adopts. She thinks "life is a banquet, and most poor suckers are starving to death." The boy, a sensible and down-to-earth type, has to learn to adapt to his lively live-for-today aunt. The story was first a hit Broadway play and the same cast was then transported into this film production. Hugely successful, it was nominated for six Academy Awards and was the top grossing film of 1959. A lot of fun.

A: Rosalind Russell, Forrest Tucker, Coral Browne, Fred Clark, Peggy Cass, Roger Smith

© WARNER HOME VIDEO 11152

AUTHOR! AUTHOR!

D: Arthur Hiller — 110 m

PG | COM ROM | 1982 | COLOR | Sex | Nud | Viol | ◢ Lang | ◢ AdSit

7 Al Pacino is a neurotic playwright who is just about to open a new play on Broadway, after a long dry spell. Just then, his flaky philandering wife (Weld) walks out on him for a new man, leaving him with her five kids - only one of which is his. Dyan Cannon is an actress with whom he falls in love and who helps him through his trials. Small but diverting little comedy with a happy ending and really cute kids. Good performances by everyone.

A: Al Pacino, Tuesday Weld, Dyan Cannon, Alan King, Bob Elliott, Ray Gould

© FOXVIDEO 1181

BABY BOOM

D: Charles Shyer — 110 m

PG | COM ROM | 1987 | COLOR | Sex | Nud | Viol | ◢ Lang | ◢ AdSit

8 Funny light-weight little story about a high-powered yuppie Manhattan career-woman (Keaton) whose life abruptly changes when a distant cousin dies and she becomes an instant mom. Both her boss and live-in boyfriend recoil from the changes in her, so she moves to a simpler life in the country. She's not very well equipped for the simple life, though, and luckily she gets help from a friendly veterinarian (Shepard). Consistent and entertaining, but the story line is predictable. You might also want to see a similar story from the 1940s, BACHELOR MOTHER.

A: Diane Keaton, Harold Ramis, Sam Wanamaker, Pat Hingle, Sam Shepard, Britt Leach

Distributed By MGM/UA Home Video M202520

FAMILY

BACHELOR AND THE BOBBY-SOXER, THE

D: Irving Reis 95 m

NR | COM ROM | 1947 | B&W

6 A cocky playboy (Cary Grant) gets arrested after a fight in a nightclub. Irritated with his manner, the lady judge (Loy) sentences Cary to babysit her teenage sister (Temple), who soon develops a passionate crush on him. Poor old Cary is burdened with escorting the teenage girl everywhere. It's fun to watch Grant use his grace and charm as the over-age escort in the juvenile settings, and to watch him match wits and dialogue with Loy. Both the stars and the dialogue sparkle. A big hit in its time, it still has considerable charm today. Amusing witty comedy.

Sex / Nud / Viol / Lang / AdSit

A: Cary Grant, Myrna Loy, Shirley Temple, Rudy Vallee, Johnny Sands

© TURNER HOME ENTERTAINMENT 2079

BACK TO THE FUTURE

D: Robert Zemeckis 116 m

PG | COM SF | 1985 | COLOR

9 Monster hit and great fun for everyone. Marty McFly (Fox) is an '80s teenager who gets zapped back to the '50s by crazed scientist Lloyd's souped-up Delorean, which was modified for time travel. There, he meets his future parents... but Mom has a crush on him (her own son-to-be) and Dad is a sniveling coward. Marty has to turn things around if he is ever to even be born. Mom must be convinced to give up on Marty so she can fall for Dad, but first Dad must be transformed from a wimpy nerd. The intricate and funny plot comes together for a satisfying ending. A great time.

Sex / Nud / Viol / Lang / AdSit

A: Michael J. Fox, Christopher Lloyd, Lea Thompson, Crispin Glover, Thomas F. Wilson, Wendie Jo Sperber

© MCA/UNIVERSAL HOME VIDEO, INC. 80196

BACK TO THE FUTURE, PART II

D: Robert Zemeckis 108 m

PG | COM SF | 1989 | COLOR

6 Michael J. Fox gets a second time-travel workout in this comic adventure when he tries to make things "right" that have gone wrong with the McFly family in the future. So, he and the Doc take to the time machine - the souped-up DeLorean - to 2015 to fix it. But when they return home to Hill Valley, they discover that home is not at all the way it should be. In order to fix their new problems in the present, they must again travel back into the past, 1955 to be exact. Be prepared, the ending leaves things unfinished to clear a wide path for the next sequel.

Sex / Nud / Viol / ◢ Lang / AdSit

A: Michael J. Fox, Christopher Lloyd, Lea Thompson, Thomas F. Wilson, Charles Fleischer, Joe Flaherty

© MCA/UNIVERSAL HOME VIDEO, INC. 80914

BACK TO THE FUTURE, PART III

D: Robert Zemeckis 118 m

PG | COM SF | 1990 | COLOR

7 A imaginative and thoroughly enjoyable adventure in time! The final entry in the trilogy has Marty (Fox) time traveling back to the old West, 1885. He must retrieve Doc (Lloyd - who was sent there by an ill-timed blast of lightning in Part II) and eventually even save himself from being killed by evil villain, Mad Dog Tannen (Wilson). But Doc has fallen hopelessly in love with a lovely school marm (Steenburgen) and isn't sure he wants to go. Now... with the DeLorean out of gas (gas hasn't even been invented in 1885) and Doc smitten with the love bug, how in the heck is Marty going to get back to the future?

Sex / Nud / Viol / ◢ Lang / AdSit

A: Michael J. Fox, Christopher Lloyd, Mary Steenburgen, Thomas F. Wilson, Lea Thompson, Elisabeth Shue

© MCA/UNIVERSAL HOME VIDEO, INC. 80976

BAD NEWS BEARS, THE

D: Michael Ritchie 102 m

PG | COM | 1976 | COLOR

9 One of 1976's top grossing films, a terrific and funny comedy. Beer drinking ex-minor league pitcher Walter Matthau gets roped into coaching to a hopeless Little League baseball team, whose only talent seems to be spouting four-letter words and getting into fights. Enduring endless torment, he somehow turns a bunch of misfit boys into a team and then brings in an ace spitball pitcher - a girl (Tatum O'Neal) - to save the day. Riotous good fun. The movie's tremendous success spawned two sequels, only one of which is worth watching: BAD NEWS BEARS IN BREAKING TRAINING.

Sex / Nud / Viol / ◢ Lang / AdSit

A: Walter Matthau, Tatum O'Neal, Vic Morrow, Alfred Lutter, Jackie Earle Haley

© PARAMOUNT HOME VIDEO 8863

BAD NEWS BEARS IN BREAKING TRAINING, THE

D: Michael Ritchie 105 m

PG | COM | 1976 | COLOR

6 The Little Leaguers from THE BAD NEWS BEARS are back, but Walter Mathau isn't - so it isn't as good. Still, much of the charm is intact. Eager for a chance to play the Houston Toros so that they can get a shot at beating the Japanese champs, they first have to get a new coach. They find one guy, then dump him in favor of one kid's estranged father (Devane) who hopefully can teach their pitcher to get his fastball over the plate. Warm and sentimental, plus much of the language has been cleaned up from the first time, but it's not as much fun. Forget the next sequel.

Sex / Nud / Viol / ◢ Lang / AdSit

A: William Devane, Clifton James, Jackie Earle Haley, Jimmy Baio, Chris Barnes

© PARAMOUNT HOME VIDEO 8965

BALL OF FIRE

D: Howard Hawks 111 m

NR | COM ROM | 1941 | B&W

9 Sugarpuss O'Shea (Stanwyck) is a burlesque singer and dancer who is on the lam from the mob. She finds the perfect hiding place with a group of eight very unworldly professors when she takes a job as their assistant. It is her job to help them learn to understand slang, so that they can write a dictionary of American slang. But the reclusive professors learn much more than they expected from her. Great script with sparkling dialogue. Tremendously entertaining comedy - especially watching her teach Gary Cooper the meaning of "yum, yum."

Sex / Nud / Viol / Lang / ◢ AdSit

A: Gary Cooper, Barbara Stanwyck, Dana Andrews, Oscar Hamolka, Henry Travers, Dan Duryea

© HBO VIDEO 90750

BALTIMORE BULLET, THE

D: Robert Ellis Miller 103 m

PG | COM | 1980 | COLOR

7 Pleasant light-hearted little sports story about a couple of pool hustlers, a fast-talking veteran (Coburn) and a newcomer partner (Boxleitner) who con their way cross-country in an effort to raise some really big money, so they can play a high-stakes game with a suave gambler known as "The Deacon" (Sharif). Some remarkable pool shots, along with cameos by some of the sport's best, give the film the proper sense of atmosphere. See also THE HUSTLER and COLOR OF MONEY.

Sex / ◢ Nud / Viol / ◢ Lang / ◢ AdSit

A: James Coburn, Omar Sharif, Bruce Boxleitner, Ronee Blakley, Jack O'Halloran, Michael Lerner

© NEW LINE HOME VIDEO 90007

BANANAS

D: Woody Allen 83 m

PG | COM | 1971 | COLOR

9 Pure vintage Allen zaniness. Either you like him or you don't. It contains a wide variety of good and bad jokes in a bizarre story of a sex-starved gadget-tester who is jilted by his girlfriend, a political activist (Lassiter). Lovestruck, he follows her to the banana republic of San Marcos. There, after a set of Allen-like typically weird events, he inadvertently becomes president. A wacky movie with a funny score. Absurdity reigns.

Sex / Nud / Viol / Lang / ◢ AdSit

A: Woody Allen, Louise Lasser, Carlos Montalban, Howard Cosell, Rene Enriquez, Charlotte Rae

Distributed By MGM/UA Home Video M201764

BANK DICK, THE

D: Edward Cline 73 m

NR | COM | 1940 | B&W

7 W.C. Fields is Egbert Souse, a drunken no-account who becomes an accidental hero when he foils a robbery quite by accident. Nevertheless, he parlays that into a stint at the bank as a guard. There, his lovely daughter is discovered by a nitwit bank examiner who wants to marry her. All this effort is just an excuse for Fields's insane sense of humor to be turned loose upon a fully-suspecting audience. Full of sight gags and Fields's usual goofball verbal jousts. One of Fields's best.

Sex / Nud / Viol / Lang / AdSit

A: W.C. Fields, Cora Witherspoon, Una Merkel, Shemp Howard

© MCA/UNIVERSAL HOME VIDEO, INC. 80019

BEDTIME FOR BONZO

D: Frederick de Cordova 84 m

NR | COM | 1951 | B&W

6 Mostly a curiosity piece and somewhat silly. Professor (and future President of the United States) Ronald Reagan believes that it is environment rather than heredity which is the primary determinant in how well kids turn out. So, to prove his point, he decides to raise a chimp at home. To present the right environment, he even hires a mommy. Harmless little comedy, now high camp. Enjoyable, if you don't expect too much.

Sex / Nud / Viol / Lang / AdSit

A: Ronald Reagan, Diana Lynn, Walter Slezak, Jesse White, Lucille Barkley

© MCA/UNIVERSAL HOME VIDEO, INC. 55015

BEETLEJUICE

D: Tim Burton 92 m

PG | COM | 1988 | COLOR

A loving, young couple sets up a perfect life for themselves in a pretty little farmhouse in Connecticut, but their perfect life is cut short when they drown accidentally. Being very new ghosts, and being inexperienced at such things, they continue to "live" in their farmhouse. But, a bizarre family has moved into their house and is intent upon destroying everything the couple had built. Because they are not yet good at haunting, they decide to call in professional help in the form of free-lance evil spirit Beetlejuice (Keaton). Good natured in spirit and good fun. Fun special effects.

Sex / Nud / ◢ Viol / ◢ Lang / AdSit

A: Alec Baldwin, Geena Davis, Jeffrey Jones, Catherine O'Hara, Winona Ryder, Robert Goulet

© WARNER HOME VIDEO 11785

BELL, BOOK AND CANDLE

D: Richard Quine 103 m

NR | COM ROM | 1958 | COLOR | Rating: 7

Kim Novak is a beautiful 1950s witch and a member of a family of witches which also includes her brother Nicky (Lemmon) and aunt Queeny (Lanchester). Lovely Kim falls in love with James Stewart on the eve of his wedding to someone else and so casts a spell over him to capture his heart. When Jimmy finds out why what has happened, happened... he wants out. So her warlock brother takes both Stewart and his partner (Kovacs) to another wacky witch (Hermione Gingold) to break the spell. Pleasant little comedy, expertly played by a talented cast.

Sex / Nud / Viol / Lang / ✓ AdSit

A: James Stewart, Kim Novak, Jack Lemmon, Ernie Kovacs, Hermione Gingold, Elsa Lanchester

© COLUMBIA TRISTAR HOME VIDEO 60132

BELLBOY, THE

D: Jerry Lewis 72 m

NR | COM CLD | 1960 | COLOR | Rating: 6

Jerry Lewis at his silliest. Jerry is a ridiculous bellboy who fouls up everything at a ritzy Miami Beach hotel. What other bellboy in the world, when told to bring everything from the trunk of a Volkswagen, would remove the engine and take it up to their room. The film is a non-stop series of sight gags and slapstick. Young kids and Jerry Lewis fans will enjoy themselves.

Sex / Nud / Viol / Lang / AdSit

A: Jerry Lewis, Alex Gerry, Bob Clayton, Sonnie Sands, Bill Richman

© VIDEO TREASURES 9740

BELLS ARE RINGING

D: Vincente Minnelli 126 m

NR | COM MUS ROM | 1960 | COLOR | Rating: 8

Upbeat musical that was brought to the big screen from Broadway. Judy Holliday plays a shy telephone answering service operator who uses her knowledge of her clients's problems to help them all out. She also has fallen secretly in love with playboy playwright Dean Martin, even though they have never met. He just thinks she is just a nice little old lady passing out advice and so thinks of her only as "Mom." A delightful MGM musical. 14 musical numbers. Songs include "Just in Time." See the Director's index under Vincente Minnelli for other classic musicals. He did a lot of them.

Sex / Nud / Viol / Lang / ✓ AdSit

A: Judy Holliday, Dean Martin, Fred Clark, Eddie Foy, Jr., Jean Stapleton, Frank Gorshin

Distributed By MGM/UA Home Video M700063

BELLS OF ST. MARYS, THE

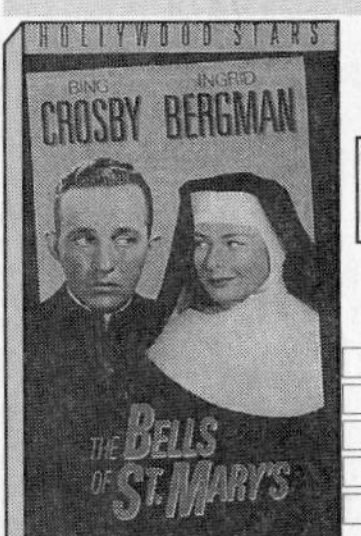

D: Leo McCarey 126 m

NR | COM DMA | 1945 | B&W | Rating: 8

Bing Crosby reprises his role as Father O'Malley in this sequel to GOING MY WAY. He is a priest assigned to a parish with a parochial school run by a headstrong Mother Superior Ingrid Bergman. The buildings are run down. The playground has been sold off and the whole school may soon be condemned to make way for a parking lot. Father Bing and Sister Ingrid make peace long enough to conspire in a plot to entice a rich benefactor into building them a new home. Great family entertainment that leaves your heart warmed. It was a big box office hit and got 8 Oscar nominations, including Best Picture.

Sex / Nud / Viol / Lang / AdSit

A: Bing Crosby, Ingrid Bergman, Ruth Donnelly, Henry Travers, William Gargan, Joan Carroll

© REPUBLIC PICTURES HOME VIDEO 0252

BEVERLY HILLBILLIES, THE

D: Penelope Spheeris 93 m

PG | COM | 1994 | COLOR | Rating: 7

Well, they're back... and just as silly as they were the first time 'round. But hey, that ain't all bad. The faces of the characters have changed but the characters haven't. Jed and his clan of hillbillies move themselves and their backwoods ways into the world of the super-rich. His neighbor is the greedy banker who only cares about keeping Jed's money in the bank. The banker's number one lackey, Miss Jane, is set upon winning the heart (and body) of Jed's nephew, the super-dumb Jethro (Diedrich Bader). Meanwhile, the banker's number two lackey (Rob Schneider) has set his girlfriend out to capture Jed's heart (and money). Fun blend of stupid humor and slapstick.

Sex / Nud / Viol / Lang / AdSit

A: Jim Varney, Cloris Leachman, Lilly Tomlin, Dabney Coleman, Erika Eleniak, Lea Thompson

© FOXVIDEO 8561

BIG

D: Penny Marshall 104 m

PG | COM DMA | 1988 | COLOR | Rating: 9

Sparkling, heartwarming blockbuster. When a 12-year-old boy is rejected by a fifteen-year-old girl, he makes a wish at a carnival's mechanical fortune teller to become big. The next morning he is - but he still has the mind and heart of a 12-year-old. Excellent vehicle for Hanks - it won him an Oscar nomination. This is much more a story about childhood innocence than a story for children. A major commercial success, it inspired other movies to use instant-grownup characters (although FREAKY FRIDAY was actually the first).

✓ Sex / Nud / Viol / ✓ Lang / ✓ AdSit

A: Tom Hanks, Elizabeth Perkins, Robert Loggia, John Heard, Jared Ruston, David Moscow

© FOXVIDEO 1658

BIG BUS, THE

D: James Frawley 88 m

PG | COM | 1976 | COLOR | Rating: 6

Silly spoof of disaster films that predates AIRPLANE's spoof of AIRPORT by four years, but is not nearly as good. Still, it may be of interest to fans of the genre. It is the story of a super-luxurious, 75-ton, nuclear-powered bus with 32 wheels that is making its maiden run from New York to Denver. The bus carries a wide assortment of odd-ball characters, including a co-pilot who is prone to sudden blackouts.

Sex / Nud / ✓ Viol / ✓ Lang / AdSit

A: Joseph Bologna, Stockard Channing, John Beck, Lynn Redgrave, Jose Ferrer, Ruth Gordon

© PARAMOUNT HOME VIDEO 8823

BIG BUSINESS

D: Jim Abrahams 98 m

PG | COM | 1988 | COLOR | Rating: 7

Clever. Two sets of identical twins, one born rich (the Midlers) and one born poor (the Tomlins) are mixed together at birth in the tiny town of Jupiter Hollow, which is owned by Midler's parents. One mismatched pair of Midler/Tomlins stays in town, poor. The other pair leaves rich - neither knowing of the colossal mix-up. Years later the wealthy New York twins, dominated by Midler, decide to sell the family interest in the town to a strip miner. Upset at that prospect, the poor country pair come to New York to fight for their town, only to discover their true long-lost twin. Fairly well-done and genuinely funny in several places.

Sex / Nud / Viol / ✓ Lang / ✓ AdSit

A: Bette Midler, Lily Tomlin, Fred Ward, Edward Herrmann, Michele Placido, Daniel Gerroll

© TOUCHSTONE HOME VIDEO 605

BILL & TED'S BOGUS JOURNEY

D: Peter Hewitt 98 m

PG | COM | 1991 | COLOR | Rating: 6

After skating through history class with the personal help of some of history's most prominent historical figures, cool dudes Reeves and Winter are desperately hoping that some twist of fate will bring them back to reality - any reality - in this funny sequel to BILL & TED'S EXCELLENT ADVENTURE. Once again, they travel through time in a phone booth, but this time their journey is literally to hell and back. After futuristic clones Evil Bill and Evil Ted are sent from above to end their "most excellent" lives, the pair will need much more than charm as they come face to face with the Grim Reaper. Radical, dude!

Sex / Nud / Viol / ✓ Lang / AdSit

A: Keanu Reeves, Alex Winter, George Carlin, William Sadler, Joss Ackland

© ORION PICTURES CORPORATION 8765

BILL & TED'S EXCELLENT ADVENTURE

D: Stephen Herek 90 m

PG | COM | 1989 | COLOR | Rating: 7

A charmer and surprise hit! Two very hip but very stupid California high school radical dudes (Reeves and Winter) are failing history in grand fashion. To their rescue appears George Carlin, a futuristic guardian angel who possesses a magical phone booth that allows time travel. The pair climb aboard and experience history first hand, meeting the likes of Joan of Arc, Caesar, Napoleon, Beethoven and Socrates, all of whom make for an excellent history presentation. Loaded with laughs. Very cool, dude!

Sex / Nud / Viol / ✓ Lang / AdSit

A: Keanu Reeves, Alex Winter, George Carlin, Bernie Casey, Amy Stock-Poynton, Tony Camilieri

© NEW LINE HOME VIDEO 8741

BILL COSBY - HIMSELF

D: Bill Cosby, Jr. 104 m

PG | COM | 1981 | COLOR | Rating: 8

Concert footage filmed at Toronto's Hamilton Place Performing Arts Center of Bill Cosby imparting his wit and wisdom on such subjects as natural childbirth, raising children, going to the dentist and drinking.

Sex / Nud / Viol / Lang / ✓ AdSit

A: Bill Cosby

© CBS/FOX VIDEO 1350

BINGO LONG TRAVELING ALL-STARS, THE

D: John Badham 111 m

PG | COM | 1976 | COLOR | Rating: 8

Lively and funny comedy set in 1939, in the days of the old Negro Leagues, when blacks were barred from playing in the majors. Williams plays a baseball player who battles the Negro League's management by starting his own razzle dazzle team. His team of lively characters barnstorms its way through rural America, where they must also resort to conning, clowning and stealing just to survive. A great cast captures the feel of the period and has a whole lot of fun with the time and the subject. So do we... a real good time.

Sex / Nud / Viol / ✓ Lang / ✓ AdSit

A: Billy Dee Williams, James Earl Jones, Richard Pryor, Ted Ross

© MCA/UNIVERSAL HOME VIDEO, INC. 66056

BISHOP'S WIFE, THE

D: Henry Koster — 109 m

NR | COM ROM | 1947 | B&W

8 Enjoyable and sentimental Christmas fantasy. Cary Grant is a suave angel sent down to help a harried bishop (Niven) who neglects his wife and family in his quest to get a new cathedral built. Grant is there to remind him of where his priorities should lie, but Cary has problems of his own when the bishop's long-neglected wife (Young) is attracted to him. Grant is charming and Young is lovely. They don't make films like this much anymore. Nominated for five Academy Awards, including Best Picture.

Sex | Nud | Viol | Lang | ◢ AdSit

A: Cary Grant, Loretta Young, David Niven, Monty Woolley, James Gleason, Elsa Lanchester

© HBO VIDEO 90658

BORN YESTERDAY

D: George Cukor — 103 m

NR | COM ROM | 1950 | B&W

10 This was a hilarious Broadway play which was turned into a Best Picture Oscar winner and became a huge box office hit. It is still very funny. A corrupt junk dealer millionaire (Crawford) wants to gain social acceptance and decides his girlfriend needs more culture, so he hires newspaperman William Holden to teach her some. But his plan backfires. The smarter she gets, the more she learns that she is just a pawn and that he is a crook. And, she falls for her teacher. Holiday is an absolute scream as the quintessential "dumb blond" and won Best Actress Oscar. Don't miss this one.

Sex | Nud | Viol | Lang | ◢ AdSit

A: Judy Holliday, William Holden, Broderick Crawford, Howard St. John, Frank Otto

© COLUMBIA TRISTAR HOME VIDEO 60143

BORN YESTERDAY

D: Luis Mandoki — 100 m

PG | COM ROM | 1993 | COLOR

7 Pleasant, but not sparkling, remake of the 1950 Judy Holliday classic. Billie (Melanie Griffith) is a sexy but dim-witted former showgirl who is mistress to a loutish real estate developer (John Goodman). They have come to Washington DC so that he can lobby some senators into keeping a military base open and get even richer. However, her ignorant comments have embarrassed him so much that he has hired a bookish reporter (Don Johnson) to tutor her. Instead, the seemingly dim-witted Billie learns too well. She learns that she doesn't have to accept being treated so badly and that she is also falling for the mild-mannered reporter.

Sex | Nud | Viol | ◢ Lang | ◢ AdSit

A: Melanie Griffith, John Goodman, Don Johnson, Edward Herrmann, Max Perlich, Fred Dalton Thomas

© HOLLYWOOD PICTURES HOME VIDEO 1740

BREAKING AWAY

D: Peter Yates — 100 m

PG | COM DMA | 1979 | COLOR

9 Wonderful sleeper and Best Picture Oscar nominee. It is a touching story of love, growing up and class differences. Four working-class teenagers just out of high school are scorned by the college kids in town. One becomes fixated on becoming a bicycle racing champion and tries to win a college girl over by pretending he's an Italian racer. When his cover is blown and the college boys further scorn his efforts, he and his friends decide to prove themselves as equals by winning the college bike race. This appealing, unpretentious film is funny, tender, insightful and entirely enjoyable.

Sex | Nud | Viol | ◢ Lang | ◢ AdSit

A: Dennis Christopher, Dennis Quaid, Robyn Douglas, Daniel Stern, Jackie Earle Haley, Barbara Barrie

© FOXVIDEO 1081

BRINGING UP BABY

D: Howard Hawks — 102 m

NR | COM ROM | 1938 | B&W

10 This is the screwiest of all the screwball comedies and, unlike many of the others, it has lost little of its punch with time. Grant plays a mild-mannered paleontologist whose dinosaur bone is stolen by Hepburn's dog. Hepburn plays a kooky heiress who, along with her pet leopard, sets his life on end when she sets her sights on him. One of the fastest, funniest films ever made. Two terrific comedy performances by the stars. Excellently remade and updated in 1972 with Barbra Streisand and Ryan O'Neal as WHAT'S UP DOC?.

Sex | Nud | Viol | Lang | ◢ AdSit

A: Cary Grant, Katharine Hepburn, Charlie Ruggles, May Robson, Barry Fitzgerald, Ward Bond

© TURNER HOME ENTERTAINMENT 6012

BRINK'S JOB, THE

D: William Friedkin — 103 m

PG | COM CRM | 1978 | COLOR

8 Highly entertaining and funny account of the famous 1950 Boston Brink's vault robbery, told with a light touch. Peter Falk stars as the head of a gang of klutzes that somehow pulls off the crime of the century - almost. They get $2.7 million, lead the government on a very long, very expensive chase and then get caught just one week before the statute of limitations runs out. Lots of fun.

Sex | Nud | ◢ Viol | ◢ Lang | AdSit

A: Peter Falk, Peter Boyle, Allen Garfield, Warren Oates, Paul Sorvino, Gena Rowlands

© MCA/UNIVERSAL HOME VIDEO, INC. 80062

BROADWAY DANNY ROSE

D: Woody Allen — 85 m

PG | COM | 1984 | COLOR

7 Woody Allen wrote, directed and starred as talent agent Broadway Danny Rose. Danny Rose is a small-time manager who has no talent for selecting talent and has too soft of a heart to boot. His best chance to succeed and his principal client is an alcoholic over-the-hill crooner named Lou Canova, who is married but carrying on an affair with a gangster's tough-talking girlfriend, Mia Farrow. When Canova gets a chance to move up, Allen has to pretend to be Farrow's boyfriend, which is not a healthy thing to be. Entertaining little comic fable.

Sex | Nud | Viol | ◢ Lang | ◢ AdSit

A: Woody Allen, Mia Farrow, Milton Berle, Sandy Baron, Corbett Monica, Jackie Gayle

© LIVE HOME VIDEO 5041

BRONCO BILLY

D: Clint Eastwood — 117 m

PG | COM ROM | 1980 | COLOR

7 Engaging, lighthearted story of a troop of oddball characters working for a flea-bag wild west show. Eastwood is the idealistic owner, ace sharpshooter and self-styled star of his nearly-broke traveling Wild West Show. He and his troop of dedicated performers just want to entertain. Sondra Locke is a spoiled little rich girl who is abandoned by her husband on her honeymoon and finds a home when she becomes part of the show as Eastwood's assistant. Eastwood acts, directs and even sings with Merle Haggard. This simple little story has been unduly underrated by many critics. It's just fun.

Sex | Nud | Viol | ◢ Lang | ◢ AdSit

A: Clint Eastwood, Sondra Locke, Geoffrey Lewis, Scatman Crothers, Bill McKinney, Dan Vadis

© WARNER HOME VIDEO 11104

BUCK PRIVATES

D: Arthur Lubin — 84 m

NR | COM | 1941 | B&W

7 Bud and Lou are two dim-witted tie salesmen who enlist in the army by mistake to avoid getting arrested. The Andrews Sisters make a guest appearance with "Boogie Woogie Bugle Boy." This film was the first to establish Abbott and Costello as box office stars. The plot serves mostly as a vehicle for them to present some of their best burlesque routines. A little dated, but still very funny stuff.

Sex | Nud | Viol | Lang | AdSit

A: Bud Abbott, Lou Costello, Lee Bowman, Alan Curtis, The Andrews Sisters, Jane Frazee

© MCA/UNIVERSAL HOME VIDEO, INC. 55085

BUCK PRIVATES COME HOME

D: Charles Barton — 77 m

NR | COM | 1947

8 One of Abbott and Costello's best movies and sequel to BUCK PRIVATES. They are GIs having returned home from Europe, but trying to smuggle in a French orphan they found. The girl is discovered and taken away, but she manages to escape and find the boys again. Bud and Lou must now find the girl's aunt so she can adopt her. However, the aunt can't marry her boyfriend race driver until his car gets out of hock. So, Bud and Lou bail the car out but wind up in the car, leading the cops on a wild-cross country chase. Quite good, much better than typical slapstick comedy, especially the climactic chase scene.

Sex | Nud | Viol | Lang | AdSit

A: Bud Abbott, Lou Costello, Tom Brown, Joan Fulton, Nat Pendleton, Beverly Simmons

© MCA/UNIVERSAL HOME VIDEO, INC. 81303

BURNS AND ALLEN SHOW, THE

D: Ralph Levy — 60 m

NR | COM | 1952 | B&W

8 Fans of George and Gracie rejoice. Those of you who aren't familiar with them are in for a treat. These are two episodes of the famed duo's early TV series from the 1952-53 season. George plays an absolutely unflappable comedian who is married to the most ditzy woman ever fabricated by the mind of man or woman. In one episode, Sheldon Leonard is a gangster who comes to blow out Gracie's brains, but finds she doesn't have any. In the other, Jack Benny tries his best to convince Gracie that she and George really are married.

Sex | Nud | Viol | Lang | AdSit

A: George Burns, Gracie Allen, Jack Benny, Sheldon Leonard

© COLUMBIA TRISTAR HOME VIDEO 60537

BUTTERFLIES ARE FREE

D: Milton Katselas — 149 m

PG | COM ROM DMA | 1972 | COLOR

9 Genuine pleasure of a serio-comedy. Edward Albert is a blind young man struggling to become self-sufficient. He wants break free of his over-protective (but loving) mother and also to romance his kookie next-door neighbor (Hawn). Goldie is an eccentric, aspiring actress who has fallen for this guy but has to learn how to deal with things, too. Their relationship, and all the other complications, leads to a fast-paced comedy. Nominated for three Oscars, Heckart won Best Supporting Actress. A really good time and a great feel-good movie.

Sex | Nud | Viol | Lang | ◢ AdSit

A: Goldie Hawn, Edward Albert, Jr., Eileen Heckart, Mike Warren

© COLUMBIA TRISTAR HOME VIDEO 60149

CACTUS FLOWER

D: Gene Saks — 103 m

PG | COM ROM | 1969 | COLOR

8 Zany Broadway smash comedy brought to the screen. Matthau is a bachelor dentist having an affair with, and stringing along, pretty-young-thing Goldie Hawn, by telling her that he is married. When she attempts suicide, he says that he will marry her, but she refuses until she meets his wife. Having none, Matthau asks his straight-laced dowdy assistant (Bergman) to sit in as his wife. Both Matthau and Bergman are surprised to find that she is in love with him and he with her. Goldie falls for another guy - the nice guy next door. Hawn won an Oscar in her first big part. Great fun.

Sex / Nud / Viol / Lang / AdSit

A: Walter Matthau, Ingrid Bergman, Goldie Hawn, Jack Weston, Rick Lenz, Vito Scotti

© GOODTIMES 4229

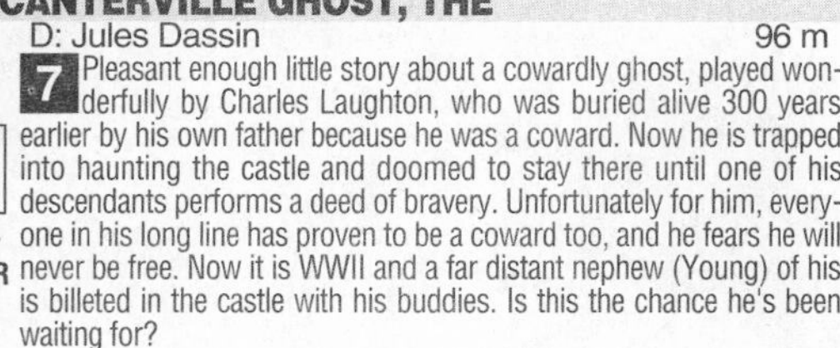

CANTERVILLE GHOST, THE

D: Jules Dassin — 96 m

NR | COM CLD | 1944 | COLOR

7 Pleasant enough little story about a cowardly ghost, played wonderfully by Charles Laughton, who was buried alive 300 years earlier by his own father because he was a coward. Now he is trapped into haunting the castle and doomed to stay there until one of his descendants performs a deed of bravery. Unfortunately for him, everyone in his long line has proven to be a coward too, and he fears he will never be free. Now it is WWII and a far distant nephew (Young) of his is billeted in the castle with his buddies. Is this the chance he's been waiting for?

Sex / Nud / Viol / Lang / AdSit

A: Charles Laughton, Margaret O'Brien, William Gargan, Rags Ragland, Una O'Connor, Robert Young

Distributed By MGM/UA Home Video M201873

CARBON COPY

D: Michael Schultz — 91 m

PG | COM | 1981 | COLOR

7 This is a pleasant lightweight comedy starring George Segal as a corporate executive who is married to the boss's daughter and fully enjoying his life, when there comes a knock on the door. Standing there is the black son from a dalliance he had many years past, seeking out his father. Unfortunately for Segal, his wife and father-in-law do not take the news at all well. Sometimes silly, sometimes clever mix of social commentary and comedy.

Sex / Nud / Viol / Lang / AdSit

A: George Segal, Susan Saint James, Denzel Washington, Jack Warden, Dick Martin

© NEW LINE HOME VIDEO 1609

CASANOVA'S BIG NIGHT

D: Norman McLeod — 86 m

NR | COM | 1954 | COLOR

7 Bob Hope is only a tailor's apprentice, but he bears a striking resemblance to Casanova, the great lover of 17th-century Venice. So he is hired by a duchess to test the true motives of her son's fiancee (Joan Fontaine). Ol' Bob gets caught up in more intrigue than he can handle when bad guys Rathbone, John Carradine, Lon Chaney Jr. and Raymond Burr all want to put him away. Lots of slapstick chases and other Hope shtick.

Sex / Nud / Viol / Lang / AdSit

A: Bob Hope, Joan Fontaine, Audrey Dalton, Basil Rathbone, Hugh Marlowe, Vincent Price

© PARAMOUNT HOME VIDEO 5316

CASEY'S SHADOW

D: Martin Ritt — 117 m

PG | COM DMA CLD | 1977 | COLOR

7 Enjoyable old-time family fare. Walter Matthau is a ne'er-do-well and impoverished Cajun horse trainer whose wife has left him to raise their three sons by himself. Matthau is a simple man whose modest dream is to train a winning racehorse, but it is a dream he wants more than almost anything. He and his boys are grooming a quarter horse that the boys love, named Casey's Shadow for a million dollar race -- even though the wealthy owner Alexis Smith only wants to sell him. When the horse's leg is hurt just before the big race and even though the vet and his boys don't want the horse to race, Matthau enters the horse. Matthau almost single-handedly carries this movie.

Sex / Nud / Viol / Lang / AdSit

A: Walter Matthau, Andrew Rubin, Stephen Burns, Alexis Smith, Robert Webber, Murray Hamilton

© COLUMBIA TRISTAR HOME VIDEO 60153

CAT BALLOU

D: Elliot Silverstein — 96 m

NR | COM WST | 1965 | COLOR

10 Wonderfully funny spoof of Westerns. Jane Fonda plays a naive and innocent school teacher who turns to a life of crime after her father is killed by a crooked land baron seeking to gain control of her father's ranch. In response, she forms a rag tag gang, manned by a drunken ex-gunfighter and two cowards, to rob trains and avenge her father's murder. Lee Marvin is hysterical as both the drunken gunfighter (on a drunken horse) and his evil look-alike with a metal nose. Stubby Kaye and Nat King Cole, as traveling minstrels, punctuate the action and narrate the happenings with song. A great time.

Sex / Nud / Viol / Lang / AdSit

A: Jane Fonda, Lee Marvin, Michael Callan, Jay C. Flippen, Duane Hickman, John Marley

© COLUMBIA TRISTAR HOME VIDEO 60154

CHAPLIN CAVALCADE

D: Charles Chaplin — 80 m

NR | COM | 1936 | B&W

8 An anthology of four of Chaplin's early silent comedies from the 1916-1917 era: "One A.M.,""The Pawnshop," "The Floorwalker" and "The Rink."

Sex / Nud / Viol / Lang / AdSit

A: Charlie Chaplin

© HOLLYWOOD HOME THEATRE

CHAPLIN REVUE, THE

D: Charles Chaplin — 126 m

NR | COM | 1958 | B&W

8 Three of Chaplin's best short features: "A Dog's Life," "Shoulder Arms," and "The Pilgrim." The pieces are woven together by music composed by Chaplin and his own narration and also includes some behind the scenes footage.

Sex / Nud / Viol / Lang / AdSit

A: Charlie Chaplin, Edna Purviance, Sydney Chaplin, Mack Swain

© CBS/FOX VIDEO 3001

CHARLIE CHAPLIN-THE EARLY YEARS, VOLS 1-4

D: Charles Chaplin — 62 m

NR | COM | B&W

8 Original and uncut. Volume 1: "The Immigrant" (1917),"The Count" (1916) and "Easy Street" (1917). Volume 2: "The Pawnbroker" (1916), "The Adventurer" (1917) and "One A.M." Volume 3: "The Cure" (1917), "The Floorwalker" (1916) and "The Vagabond" (1916). Volume 4: "Behind the Screen" (1916), "the Fireman" (1916) and "The Rink" (1916).

Sex / Nud / Viol / Lang / AdSit

A: Charlie Chaplin

© REPUBLIC PICTURES HOME VIDEO 7118

CHRISTMAS IN CONNECTICUT

D: Peter Godfrey — 102 m

NR | COM ROM | 1945 | B&W

6 Pleasant lightweight fun. Barbara Stanwyck plays a leading newspaper's housekeeping and gourmet cooking editor. The catch is, she is a fake and doesn't know anything about doing either - she doesn't even have a home of her own that she could do it in. When a war hero is rescued after having spent 18 days starving adrift in a life raft, her editor (who is not aware of her failings) thinks it would be a great story to have her entertain the hero and himself at her home for the holidays. She is panic-struck and has to quick find a husband, a house and a cook. Corny, but good holiday (or anytime else) fun.

Sex / Nud / Viol / Lang / AdSit

A: Barbara Stanwyck, Dennis Morgan, Sydney Greenstreet, S.Z. Scjakk, Reginald Gardiner, Una O'Connor

Distributed By MGM/UA Home Video M301163

CHRISTMAS IN JULY

D: Preston Sturges — 67 m

NR | COM | 1940 | B&W

7 Good solid fun. An ambitious, struggling store clerk is sent a bogus telegram by his practical-joking co-workers, fooling him into thinking that he has won a coffee slogan contest and a $25,000 prize. Thrilled, he and his girlfriend set about buying everything they ever wanted - all on credit. The whole town opens its doors to him - that is until the mistake is discovered. A fun-filled romp about the pursuit of the American Dream.

Sex / Nud / Viol / Lang / AdSit

A: Dick Powell, Ellen Drew, Raymond Walburn, William Demarest, Ernest Truex, Franklin Pangborn

© MCA/UNIVERSAL HOME VIDEO, INC. 80207

CHRISTMAS STORY, A

D: Bob Clark — 95 m

PG | COM CLD | 1983 | COLOR

9 Absolutely delightful story about growing up. Humorist Jean Sheperd relates a warmly comic story from his childhood in the 1940s, about his single-minded driving obsession with getting a Genuine Red Ryder Carbine Action Two Hundred Shot Lightning Loader BB rifle for Christmas - in spite of his mother's desperate concerns that he might put someone's eye out. Sheperd narrates the whimsical storyline himself and he is played wonderfully by Billingsley. An absolute and total delight for both young and old.

Sex / Nud / Viol / Lang / AdSit

A: Peter Billingsley, Darren McGavin, Melinda Dillon, Ian Petrella, Scott Schwartz, Tedde Moore

Distributed By MGM/UA Home Video M800446

CINDERFELLA

D: Jerry Lewis 88 m

NR | COM CLD | 1960 | COLOR

6 Silly Jerry Lewis farce. The well-known children's fairy tale is rewritten to have wacky Ed Wynn become Jerry Lewis's godfather and save Jerry from his wicked stepmother and stepbrothers. Pretty weak over all, but children and Jerry Lewis fans will likely be entertained.

Sex Nud Viol Lang AdSit

A: Jerry Lewis, Ed Wynn, Anna Maria Alberghetti

© VIDEO TREASURES SV9741

CITY LIGHTS

D: Charles Chaplin 87 m

NR | COM | 1931 | B&W

10 Chaplin's masterpiece. A wonderful combination of comedy and pathos. It is his story of the little tramp who fell in love with a blind flower girl. She is unable to see him and believes that he is wealthy. Charlie is befriended by a millionaire who, when he is drunk, likes the little tramp but, when he is sober, doesn't even recognize him. The tramp takes the money he needs from the millionaire so the girl can have the operation she needs, willing to go to jail for it. Funny, tender and understated eloquence with a particularly moving finale when the girl finds out the true nature of her benefactor.

Sex Nud Viol Lang ◢ AdSit

A: Charlie Chaplin, Virginia Cherreill, Harry Meyers, Hank Mann

© CBS/FOX VIDEO 3006

COCOANUTS, THE

D: Robert Florey 93 m

NR | COM | 1929 | B&W

7 This is the Marx Brothers's very first film. Groucho is a hotel owner trying to fleece everyone who comes in. Chico and Harpo play con men in his hotel. The staginess of this picture is because Hollywood simply had the boys come west from New York, with their already successful stage play intact, and then just filmed it totally unchanged. Early sound problems and primitive camera work make it difficult to watch at times, but it also contains some of their best comedy skits, including a hilarious rigged auction. See also ANIMAL CRACKERS and check the indexes for others by them.

Sex Nud Viol Lang ◢ AdSit

A: Groucho Marx, Chico Marx, Harpo Marx, Zeppo Marx, Margaret Dumont, Oscar Shaw

© MCA/UNIVERSAL HOME VIDEO, INC. 80378

COLD TURKEY

D: Norman Lear 99 m

PG | COM | 1971 | COLOR

7 Clever little satire from Norman Lear about the small town of Eagle Rock, Iowa which accepts a challenge from a tobacco company to win $25 million. Madison Avenue PR guy Merwin Wren (Newhart) has convinced the tobacco company that no town could possibly win, but they didn't count on an ambitious minister (Dick Van Dyke) who leads the townsfolk in the crusade to quit smoking. Silly madness. Bob and Ray are hilarious.

Sex Nud Viol Lang ◢ AdSit

A: Dick Van Dyke, Pippa Scott, Tom Poston, Bob Newhart, Vincent Gardenia, Edward Everett Horton

Distributed By MGM/UA Home Video M201581

COME BLOW YOUR HORN

D: Bud Yorkin 115 m

NR | COM | 1963 | COLOR

7 Fun, light-hearted early effort from Neil Simon (this was his first big stage hit) with a screen play written by Norman Lear. Frank Sinatra plays a free-living swinging bachelor with girls everywhere, who also has an admiring younger brother and a nagging father. Frank teaches his younger brother the ropes, only to have him steal his own girl away and to learn that playing the field can sometimes be a fool's game. Sinatra sings the title song.

Sex Nud Viol Lang ◢ AdSit

A: Frank Sinatra, Lee J. Cobb, Molly Picon, Barbara Rush, Jill St. John, Tony Bill

© PARAMOUNT HOME VIDEO 6535

COOLEY HIGH

D: Michael Schultz 107 m

PG | COM | 1975 | COLOR

6 Amusing little comedy. An inner-city version of AMERICAN GRAFFITI, set in 1964 Chicago. It is a series of incidents about inner-city high school life revolving around high school kids Turman and Jacobs. Their principal concerns are girl problems in the form of Cynthia Davis, but they also have to contend with teachers and a couple of street toughs. Instead of cruising Main Street in cars, they swipe rides on buses and trains. Sometimes funny, sometimes serious. It's generally OK, with warmth and good humor. It later became "What's Happening!" on TV.

Sex Nud Viol ◢ Lang AdSit

A: Glynn Turman, Lawrence Hilton-Jacobs, Garrett Morris, Cynthia Davis, Corin Rogers, Maurice Leon Havis

© ORION PICTURES CORPORATION 7506

COOL RUNNINGS

D: Jon Turteltaub 98 m

PG | COM | 1993 | COLOR

7 During the 1988 Winter Olympics, the small, very warm, Caribbean island of Jamaica placed an unlikely entry into the very cold bobsledding event. That actual event provoked Hollywood into creating its own version of the story. When a determined Jamaican sprinter's injury prevents him from entering into his preferred event, he gathers together some of his friends and together they enter the bobsledding event - even though none of them have ever even seen snow before. And, to give themselves a fighting chance, they entice a former bobsledder (John Candy) into coaching them. Silly, full of slap stick and predictable the whole way, but that doesn't prevent if from being a good time.

Sex Nud Viol Lang AdSit

A: Leon, Doug E. Doug, Rawle D. Lewis, Malik Yoba, John Candy

© WALT DISNEY HOME VIDEO 2325

COURT JESTER, THE

D: Melvin Frank, Norman Panama 101 m

NR | COM | 1956 | COLOR

9 One of the best comedies ever, certainly Kaye's best. He plays a lowly valet who rises to become a leader of a peasant revolt after he gets mixed up with some forest outlaws who are scheming to restore the rightful heir to the throne of England. For the love of a girl Kaye impersonates the Court Jester so he can gain access to the castle and then gets caught up in more swashbuckling than he wants. Delightfully complicated and very funny comic situations follow. Best gag: "The pellet with the poison's in the vessel with the pestle."

Sex Nud Viol Lang AdSit

A: Danny Kaye, Glynis Johns, Basil Rathbone, Angela Lansbury, Mildred Natwick, Cecil Parker

© PARAMOUNT HOME VIDEO 5512

COURTSHIP OF EDDIE'S FATHER, THE

D: Vincente Minnelli 117 m

NR | COM ROM | 1962 | COLOR

8 Charming and highly entertaining comedy concerning a motherless 9-year-old boy (Ronny Howard) and his father (Glenn Ford). Life is hard for Ford, who is still trying to recover from the loss of his wife. So his son does his best to find himself a mother and his father a wife by trying to line Dad up with Shirley Jones, Dina Merrill and Stella Stevens. Heartwarming and funny. Very popular. It later it became a hit TV series starring Bill Bixby.

Sex Nud Viol Lang AdSit

A: Glenn Ford, Shirley Jones, Stella Stevens, Ron Howard, Dina Merrill, Jerry Van Dyke

Distributed By MGM/UA Home Video M200797

CROCODILE DUNDEE II

D: John Cornell 110 m

PG | COM ACT | 1988 | COLOR

7 Pleasant enough follow-up to the original. However, more action is added to the successful formula this time. Mick and Sue are now living in NYC, but things get too exciting for them when her ex-husband takes some pictures of some Columbian drug lords that he wasn't supposed to take and sends them to her for safekeeping. The Columbians want those pictures back and they are very nasty about it. Mick decides to even the odds by leading the bad guys onto his turf - the Outback of Australia. There, he is more than a match for the bad guys. Fun time.

Sex Nud ◢ Viol ◢ Lang ◢ AdSit

A: Paul Hogan, Linda Kozlowski, John Mellion, Charles Dutton, Hector Ubarry, Juan Fernandez

© PARAMOUNT HOME VIDEO 32147

DARBY O'GILL AND THE LITTLE PEOPLE

D: Robert Stevenson 90 m

G | COM CLD FAN | 1959 | COLOR

9 Wonderful fantasy about an an old caretaker at a wealthy Irish estate, Darby O'Gill, who falls into a well and discovers the leprechaun king. Darby tricks the king into granting him three wishes, but he soon wishes he hadn't. Poor old Darby has such a reputation for blarney that no one believes his preposterous tale, and the larcenous king has tricked him into wasting two wishes. Then comes a young Sean Connery, who has come to the estate to replace him, so he and his daughter are also about to lose their home. It is a magical tale with neat special effects. Among Disney's very best.

Sex Nud Viol Lang AdSit

A: Albert Sharpe, Janet Munro, Sean Connery, Jimmy O'Dea, Kieron Moore, Estelle Winwood

© WALT DISNEY HOME VIDEO 038

DAVE

D: Ivan Reitman 110 m

PG-13 | COM ROM | 1993 | COLOR

7 Dave owns a semi-successful temp agency but he also has an uncanny likeness for the President. So when the hard-hearted, stuffy and arrogant President needs a look-alike to stand in for him, Dave gets hired. However, when the Prez has a massive stroke while in the arms of a pretty blonde who is not his wife, Dave is drafted into the big leagues. But, Dave takes his role to heart when he is called upon to close a bunch of day care centers in the name of the budget, and he refuses. This precipitates a power struggle between him and the dead President's people who had hired him. There is some intrigue and romance, too. Very enjoyable, even though very predictable.

◢ Sex ◢ Nud Viol ◢ Lang ◢ AdSit

A: Kevin Kline, Sigourney Weaver, Ben Kingsley, Frank Langella

© WARNER HOME VIDEO 12962

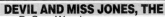

DAY AT THE RACES, A

D: Sam Wood — 109 m

NR | COM | 1937 | B&W

8 Groucho plays a horse doctor pretending to be a psychiatrist so that he can win the heart and pocketbook of a wealthy hypochondriac (Dumont). Hilarious bits include Chico's famous sale of a racetrack tip to Groucho from his "tootsie fruitsie" ice cream stand and a scene where the villainess is wallpapered to the wall. The Marx Brothers were still at their peak when this film was made. Perhaps their best work, A NIGHT AT THE OPERA, had just preceeded it in 1936.

☐ Sex ☐ Nud ☐ Viol ☐ Lang ◢ AdSit

A: Groucho Marx, Harpo Marx, Chico Marx, Allan Jones, Maureen O'Sullivan, Margaret Dumont

Distributed By MGM/UA Home Video M500064

DAYS OF THRILLS AND LAUGHTER

D: Robert Youngson — 93 m

NR | COM | 1961 | B&W

8 This is the third compilation of old movie clips prepared by Robert Youngson. It is a compilation of action and comedy scenes from the silent picture classics of Charlie Chaplin, Laurel and Hardy, the Keystone Cops, Fatty Arbuckle, Douglas Fairbanks, Pearl White and more. Quite good.

☐ Sex ☐ Nud ☐ Viol ☐ Lang ◢ AdSit

A:

© MPI HOME VIDEO MP1329

DEAD MEN DON'T WEAR PLAID

D: Carl Reiner — 89 m

PG | COM | 1982 | B&W

7 Entertaining film noir parody. It is pretty good farce with an interesting twist. Steve Martin plays a private eye hired by beautiful Rachel Ward to solve the murder of her father, a famous cheese maker. Martin's search involves apparent conversations with famous movie people such as Humphrey Bogart, Cary Grant, Ingrid Bergman, Barbara Stanwyck, Fred MacMurray and Veronica Lake. (Film clips from old films are cleverly intermixed with Martin's live action and dialogue). The dead-pan humor is funny and sometimes even hilarious, but the one-note joke does wear thin after awhile.

☐ Sex ☐ Nud ☐ Viol ◢ Lang ◢ AdSit

A: Steve Martin, Rachel Ward, Reni Santoni, Carl Reiner, George Gaynes, Frank McCarthy

© MCA/UNIVERSAL HOME VIDEO, INC. 77011

DELICATE DELINQUENT, THE

D: Don McGuire — 101 m

NR | COM CLD | 1957 | B&W

7 Jerry Lewis plays a bumbling janitor who pals around with juvenile delinquents. He joins the police force, with the help of Darren McGavin, but he is such a goofball that he has a hard time proving himself. This was Jerry's first effort after he split from Dean Martin, and it is one of his best efforts. It is also sentimental and contains the requisite assortment of Lewis slapstick and silliness.

☐ Sex ☐ Nud ☐ Viol ☐ Lang ☐ AdSit

A: Jerry Lewis, Martha Hyer, Darren McGavin, Horace McMahon, Milton Frome

© PARAMOUNT HOME VIDEO 5613

DELIRIOUS

D: Tom Mankiewicz — 96 m

PG | COM ROM | 1991 | COLOR

6 Slight but pleasant, goofy little comedy. John Candy is a writer for a TV soap opera. He gets conked on the head and wakes up to find himself living inside the story line of his soap and its small town of Ashford Falls. Furthermore, he finds that he can now control everything that happens to him and everyone in the soap, by simply typing the script the way way he wants it. Armed now with his new power, he sets out to capture the heart of beautiful-but-bitchy Emma Samms who he lusts after. However, his plans are constantly being foiled by good girl Mariel Hemingway.

☐ Sex ☐ Nud ☐ Viol ☐ Lang ◢ AdSit

A: John Candy, Raymond Burr, Mariel Hemingway, Emma Samms, Dylan Baker, Charles Rocket

Distributed By MGM/UA Home Video M902243

DEVIL AND DANIEL WEBSTER, THE

D: William Dieterle — 106 m

NR | COM DMA | 1941 | B&W

9 Wonderful. Stephen Vincent Benet's story is faithfully brought to life. There are rich textures of classic Americana in this story of a 19th-century New England farmer (Craig) who sells his soul to the Devil (Houston) in exchange for gold. But after seven years, when it is time to pay up, he decides he wants to back out of the deal. So, he hires the famous orator and lawyer Daniel Webster (Arnold) to defend him and to win back his immortal soul, by arguing for it in front of a jury of the damned. Walter Houston is perfectly despicable as the Devil, but all the acting is wonderful. Very clever. This is a must see!

☐ Sex ☐ Nud ☐ Viol ☐ Lang ◢ AdSit

A: Edward Arnold, Walter Huston, James Craig, Anne Shirley, Jane Darwell, Simone Simon

© HOME VISION DEV 020

DEVIL AND MISS JONES, THE

D: Sam Wood — 92 m

NR | COM | 1941 | B&W

8 Delightful simple comedy in which a stuffy, gruffy millionaire (Coburn) becomes alarmed when one of his department stores begins to unionize. He decides to go undercover to investigate for himself the employee complaints and unrest. He disguises himself as a sales clerk in the shoe department. There Miss Jones (Jean Arther) takes him under her wing and also fixes him up with a one of her coworkers. Soon he discovers that the root of his problems are with his own ruthless management. Marvelous comedy - like Hollywood used to make.

☐ Sex ☐ Nud ☐ Viol ☐ Lang ☐ AdSit

A: Jean Arthur, Robert Cummings, Charles Coburn, Edmund Gwenn, Spring Byington, William Demarest

© REPUBLIC PICTURES HOME VIDEO 1015

DIRTY ROTTEN SCOUNDRELS

D: Frank Oz — 110 m

PG | COM | 1988 | COLOR

7 Funny and enjoyable tale of two con artists with very conflicting styles who are trampling on each other's toes. Michael Caine very successfully operates his scam with great style and panache in the south of France, bilking wealthy females. So when crude American interloper Steve Martin crashes into the territory, the town is quickly not big enough for the both of them. They decide to settle the issue through a competition to conquer the heart and wallet of pretty Glenne Headly, a wide-eyed American heiress. Top-notch comic antics from the two leads and some sharp plot twists.

☐ Sex ☐ Nud ☐ Viol ◢ Lang ◢ AdSit

A: Steve Martin, Michael Caine, Glenne Headly, Barbara Harris, Anton Rodgers, Ian McDiarmid

© ORION PICTURES CORPORATION 8725

DISORDERLY ORDERLY, THE

D: Frank Tashlin — 90 m

NR | COM CLD | 1964 | COLOR

7 One of Jerry Lewis's best solo vehicles. Jerry is trying to earn money for medical school by working as a clumsy orderly in a hospital. Full of clever slapstick routines and sight gags. Jerry has one particular problem that is certainly going to be a major hindrance in learning to become a doctor: when people describe their pains, he begins to feel them, too. Silly, but this one is not just for Lewis fans - pretty good.

☐ Sex ☐ Nud ☐ Viol ☐ Lang ☐ AdSit

A: Jerry Lewis, Glenda Farrell, Susan Oliver, Everett Sloane, Jack E. Leonard, Kathleen Freeman

© PARAMOUNT HOME VIDEO 6406

DOCTOR TAKES A WIFE, THE

D: Alexander Hall — 89 m

NR | COM ROM | 1940 | B&W

7 Fun and lively comedy. Loretta Young is a feminist. She is an independent writer who detests domineering males. Milland is a medical college professor who is more interested in his work than in women. When these two first meet, they hate each other immediately. But after they get to know each other... they still hate each other. Then they get caught up in a publicity mix-up where they are mistakenly believed to be married and they are actually forced to get married. Now, they hate each other more than ever. Great chemistry between these two make for a good time.

☐ Sex ☐ Nud ☐ Viol ☐ Lang ◢ AdSit

A: Loretta Young, Ray Milland, Reginald Gaerdiner, Gail Patrick, Edmund Gwenn

© COLUMBIA TRISTAR HOME VIDEO 60921

DONOVAN'S REEF

D: John Ford — 109 m

NR | COM | 1963 | COLOR

7 Fun, light-hearted John Wayne comedy about three carefree pals on a Pacific island after WWII whose lives are up-ended by the unexpected arrival of a beautiful girl. Wayne and Marvin are co-owners of a raucous bar. Their buddy Warden, the island's doctor, has a Polynesian wife and several mixed-race children. The beautiful girl is Warden's stateside, fully-grown daughter, who's mother is a Boston blueblood and she doesn't know about her father's new family. Because Warden's not home, and fearing an embarrassing confrontation, Wayne and Lee hide his new family's identity from her. Seems quite patronizing now, but is also good-natured fun.

☐ Sex ☐ Nud ◢ Viol ☐ Lang ◢ AdSit

A: John Wayne, Lee Marvin, Elizabeth Allen, Jack Warden, Cesar Romero, Dorothy Lamour

© PARAMOUNT HOME VIDEO 6220

DON'T DRINK THE WATER

D: Howard Morris — 100 m

G | COM | 1969 | COLOR

6 Wacky little comedy, based on a Woody Allen play. Jackie Gleason is a caterer. He, his wife (Estelle Parsons) and daughter are on a European vacation when the plane taking them to Greece is hijacked and they are taken to a communist country instead. Stranded, they occupy themselves with taking pictures, but that is not a healthy thing to do in a paranoid country. They are immediately accused of being spies. They seek and find asylum in the US embassy, where they quickly become the focus of an international incident.

☐ Sex ☐ Nud ☐ Viol ☐ Lang ☐ AdSit

A: Jackie Gleason, Estelle Parsons, Ted Bessell, Michael Constantine, Joan Delaney, Richard Libertini

© NEW LINE HOME VIDEO 00107

DUCK SOUP

D: Leo McCarey — 70 m

NR | COM | 1933 | B&W | 9

Deemed by the pundits as the Marx Brothers's best work, this is political satire at its rampant best. Groucho is Rufus T. Firefly, tyrant of the tiny country Fredonia ("land of the spree and home of the knave"), who declares war on his neighbor Sylvania for no particular reason at all. Chico and Harpo are bumbling spies sent to get his war plans. Madness, slapstick gags and "Grouchoisms" abound. The Marx Brothers made absurdity an artform.

Sex / Nud / Viol / Lang / AdSit

A: Groucho Marx, Harpo Marx, Chico Marx, Zeppo Marx, Margaret Dumont, Louis Calhern

© MCA/UNIVERSAL HOME VIDEO, INC. 55012

EGG AND I, THE

D: Chester Erskine — 108 m

NR | COM | 1947 | B&W | 7

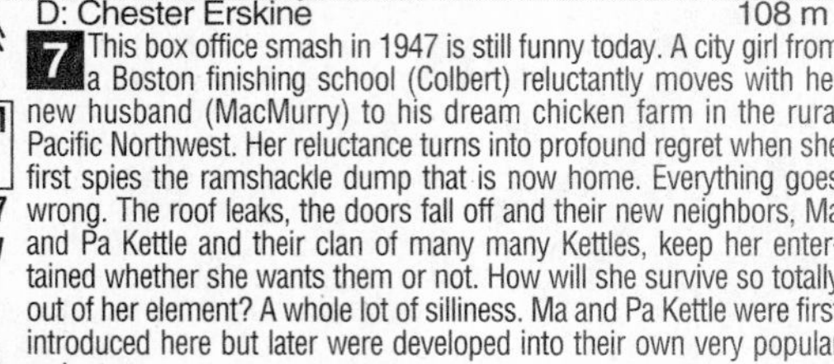

This box office smash in 1947 is still funny today. A city girl from a Boston finishing school (Colbert) reluctantly moves with her new husband (MacMurry) to his dream chicken farm in the rural Pacific Northwest. Her reluctance turns into profound regret when she first spies the ramshackle dump that is now home. Everything goes wrong. The roof leaks, the doors fall off and their new neighbors, Ma and Pa Kettle and their clan of many many Kettles, keep her entertained whether she wants them or not. How will she survive so totally out of her element? A whole lot of silliness. Ma and Pa Kettle were first introduced here but later were developed into their own very popular series.

Sex / Nud / Viol / Lang / AdSit

A: Claudette Colbert, Fred MacMurray, Marjorie Main, Percy Kilbride, Louise Allbritton

© MCA/UNIVERSAL HOME VIDEO, INC. 80317

ENTER LAUGHING

D: Carl Reiner — 112 m

NR | COM | 1967 | COLOR | 6

Carl Reiner's semi-autobiographical account of a young man who gives up an unpromising career as a mechanic, and his mother's dreams of him becoming a pharmacist, to become a comedian instead. His stage debut is a total disaster and unorthodox, to say the least. This was a funny vehicle for Alan Arkin on Broadway and it made him into a star. There are also some good scenes with Jack Gilford and Elaine May. Generally funny - with some really funny bits.

Sex / Nud / Viol / Lang / AdSit

A: Shelley Winters, Elaine May, Jose Ferrer, Jack Gilford, Reni Santoni, Don Rickles

© COLUMBIA TRISTAR HOME VIDEO 60624

ERRAND BOY, THE

D: Jerry Lewis — 93 m

NR | COM CLD | 1961 | B&W | 6

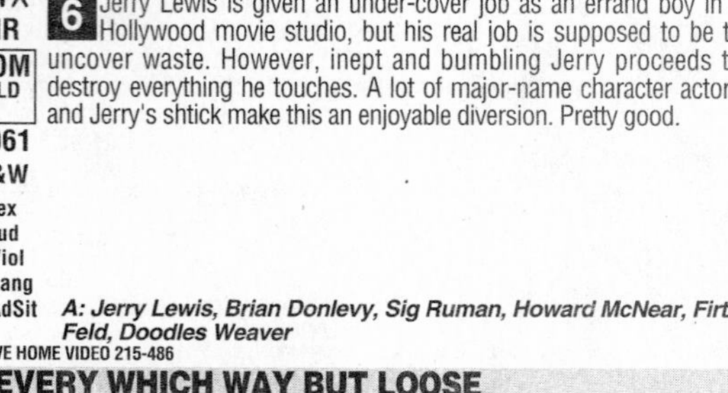

Jerry Lewis is given an under-cover job as an errand boy in a Hollywood movie studio, but his real job is supposed to be to uncover waste. However, inept and bumbling Jerry proceeds to destroy everything he touches. A lot of major-name character actors and Jerry's shtick make this an enjoyable diversion. Pretty good.

Sex / Nud / Viol / Lang / AdSit

A: Jerry Lewis, Brian Donlevy, Sig Ruman, Howard McNear, Fritz Feld, Doodles Weaver

© LIVE HOME VIDEO 215-486

EVERY WHICH WAY BUT LOOSE

D: James Fargo — 114 m

PG | COM ACT | 1978 | COLOR | 8

Very popular and a big box office hit with wide public appeal. Eastwood plays a brawling boozy truck driver who chases a barroom country singer across the whole Southwest, while getting into fights with a motorcycle gang and a legendary barroom brawler named Tank Murdock. Far and away, the most appealing feature of the film is Eastwood's raunchy 165-pound Orangutan side-kick Clyde. A light-hearted good time. Great country-western songs, too. A lot of fun, but don't be expecting subtlety. This is all out low-brow stuff.

Sex / Nud / Viol / Lang / AdSit

A: Clint Eastwood, Sondra Locke, Geoffrey Lewis, Beverly D'Angelo, Ruth Gordon

© WARNER HOME VIDEO 1028

FARMER'S DAUGHTER, THE

D: H.C. Potter — 97 m

NR | COM ROM | 1947 | B&W | 7

Delightful, fun story. A charming and innocent, but very headstrong, Swedish girl moves to the big city and takes the first job she finds as a servant for a rich young congressman and his mother. She is an excellent worker who immediately endears herself to them both (particularly him). However, she is very opinionated and quickly finds herself nominated by the party opposing him to run for his congressional seat. Good patriotic fun. Loretta Young was so captivating in her role that she won an Oscar. Well done by an excellent cast.

Sex / Nud / Viol / Lang / AdSit

A: Loretta Young, Joseph Cotten, Ethel Barrymore, Charles Bickford, Lex Barker, James Arness

© CBS/FOX VIDEO 8041

FAST BREAK

D: Jack Smight — 107 m

PG | COM | 1979 | COLOR | 6

A pretty good little comedy in which Gabe Kaplan, of TV's "Welcome Back Kotter," gives up his promising career as a cashier at a New York deli for a chance to coach an obscure Nevada college's pitiful basketball team. He is to get $50 for every game he wins and, if he beats their major rival, he gets to keep the job. He sets about recruiting his team by bringing in five street kids from New York to be on his team - and one of them is a girl.

Sex / Nud / Viol / Lang / AdSit

A: Gabe Kaplan, Harold Sylvester, Mike Warren, Bernard King, Reb Brown

© UNITED AMERICAN VIDEO CORP. 5970

FATHER GOOSE

D: Ralph Nelson — 116 m

NR | COM ROM | 1964 | COLOR | 6

Light-hearted romantic comedy. Grant is a carefree drunken bum living a carefree life in the islands of the South Pacific just before WWII breaks out and the Japanese begin their campaign of conquest. Wanting only to be left alone, he is tricked by Howard into becoming a coastwatcher for the Australian navy. If that predicament isn't bad enough, he is forced to rescue a prissy school teacher (Leslie Caron) and her young female charges, and winds up playing unwilling nursemaid to them. Enjoyable, even if undistinguished, romantic adventure that won an Oscar for Screenplay.

Sex / Nud / Viol / Lang / AdSit

A: Cary Grant, Leslie Caron, Trevor Howard, Jack Good, Nicole Felsette

© REPUBLIC PICTURES HOME VIDEO 5403

FATHER OF THE BRIDE

D: Vincente Minnelli — 96 m

NR | COM | 1950 | B&W | 8

Elizabeth Taylor is getting married, but it's the exasperated father (Tracy) who is focus of this funny film that received 3 Oscar nominations, including Best Picture. While this is a perceptive look at the American family circa 1950, things haven't really changed. Their household gets turned upside down with the constant barrage of preparations, last minute details and bills. Tracy is proud, self-important, jealous, devoted and a total wreck. Liz is at her most stunning. Funny, witty and warm look at father and daughter. Followed by FATHER'S LITTLE DIVIDEND. Remade in 1992.

Sex / Nud / Viol / Lang / AdSit

A: Spencer Tracy, Elizabeth Taylor, Joan Bennett, Leo G. Carroll, Billie Burke, Russ Tamblyn

Distributed By MGM/UA Home Video M300841

FATHER OF THE BRIDE

D: Charles Shyer — 105 m

PG | COM | 1992 | COLOR | 7

Steve Martin's little girl is getting married. This is not an easy thing for a father to deal with. She's just a baby. True, she is over 21 and she is marrying a computer whiz from a wealthy family, but still... Finally, after coming to grips with the idea of it all, he still has to face the reality of it. Particularly, he has to face wedding planner Martin Short and the bills. Pleasant, but undistinguished, remake of the 1950 classic with Spencer Tracy and Elizabeth Taylor. A little too silly in places, but Steve Martin fans will expect that.

Sex / Nud / Viol / Lang / AdSit

A: Steve Martin, Diane Keaton, Kimberly Williams, Martin Short, Kieran Culkin, George Newbern

© TOUCHSTONE HOME VIDEO 1335

FATHER'S LITTLE DIVIDEND

D: Vincente Minnelli — 83 m

NR | COM | 1951 | B&W | 6

Sequel to FATHER OF THE BRIDE. First Tracy was a father, then a father-in-law and now he becomes a grandfather, too? Just as things in his life are starting to smooth out, his daughter announces that she is going to have a baby! Things only get worse for Tracy as the baby's birthday gets closer. Everybody wants to contribute to the process, but Tracy doesn't like the idea much at all. And when the kid finally comes along, the kid doesn't much like him either. Delightful and charming, but not on a par with the original.

Sex / Nud / Viol / Lang / AdSit

A: Spencer Tracy, Elizabeth Taylor, Joan Bennett, Don Taylor, Billie Burke

Distributed By MGM/UA Home Video M202401

FLIM-FLAM MAN, THE

D: Irvin Kershner — 104 m

NR | COM | 1967 | COLOR | 7

Very entertaining comedy in which Scott is an old-time bunko artist who makes a living by charming the rural yokels of the South at the same time that he fleeces them. Along comes an AWOL soldier (Sarrazin) who Scott takes under his wing and teaches all the tricks of the trade. But Sarrazin, the ungrateful wretch, is essentially an honest man who tries to reform Scott instead. That is a gambit doomed to failure. Clever film with likable characters in which Scott really shines.

Sex / Nud / Viol / Lang / AdSit

A: George C. Scott, Sue Lyon, Michael Sarrazin, Harry Morgan, Jack Albertson, Slim Pickens

© FOXVIDEO 1210

FLINTSTONES, THE

PG | COM CLD | 1994 | COLOR

D: Brian Levant — 91 m

7 Anyone who compares this movie to the long-running TV cartoon series will be both disillusioned and satisfied. In spite of a $40 million budget that built fantastic sets plus some right-on casting, this film just does not have the same feel as the cartoon series did. However, that is not to say that it isn't fun. It is, if you are either a kid, or willing to accept the silly humor that appeals to a kid - like, say, those people who like The Three Stooges. In it, lovable, but not-too-bright Fred gets a big head when he is promoted by boss Rock Quarry. However, he was only promoted so he can take the fall for all the money Rock has embezzled. Also, poor Barney loses his job and has to move in with Fred and Wilma.

Sex / Nud / Viol / Lang / AdSit

A: John Goodman, Rick Moranis, Elizabeth Perkins, Rosie O'Donnell, Kyle MacLachlan, Halle Berry

© MCA/UNIVERSAL HOME VIDEO, INC. 81744

FLYING DEUCES, THE

NR | COM | 1939 | B&W

D: A. Edward Sutherland — 67 m

7 One of Laurel and Hardy's best efforts. Ollie is heartbroken so he and Stan join the Foreign Legion to forget their lost loves. They soon find that they have a lot to adjust to, plus they get into a series of new problems by trying to straighten out a love affair between a young officer and his girl. This one is pretty fast-paced as compared to their typical episodes. Also included on this particular tape are two classic Betty Boop cartoons.

Sex / Nud / Viol / Lang / AdSit

A: Stan Laurel, Oliver Hardy, Jean Parker, Reginald Gardiner, Charles Middleton, James Finlayson

© REPUBLIC PICTURES HOME VIDEO V1349

FOR THE LOVE OF BENJI

G | COM CLD | 1977 | COLOR

D: Joe Camp — 85 m

8 One of the most loveable characters in moviedom returns to charm his way into your heart. The whole family will enjoy his adventure through the streets of Athens, with Benji being chased by secret agents in search of the secret information tattooed on his paw. An interesting aspect of this film is that the movie is shot from Benji's point of view. Lovable. Preceeded by BENJI and followed by OH, HEAVENLY DOG!

Sex / Nud / Viol / Lang / AdSit

A: Benji, Patsy Garrett, Cynthia Smith, Allen Fiuzat, Ed Nelson, Bridget Armstrong

© BEST FILM & VIDEO CORP. 123

FORTUNE COOKIE, THE

NR | COM | 1966 | COLOR

D: Billy Wilder — 126 m

9 Hilarious Walter Matthau and Jack Lemmon comic pairing. When sports cameraman Lemmon gets knocked over while filming a football game, his shyster-lawyer brother-in-law, Whiplash Willie (Matthau), sees dollar signs. At first Jack plays along with the plan to collect $1 million, but soon his conscience gets the better of him and Willie has a struggle to keep Jack in the game. Matthau won an Oscar for his performance in Billy Wilder's laugh-out-loud comic masterpiece.

Sex / Nud / Viol / Lang / ✓ AdSit

A: Jack Lemmon, Walter Matthau, Ron Rich, Cliff Osmond, Judi West

Distributed By MGM/UA Home Video M202115

FOUL PLAY

PG | COM MYS CRM | 1978 | COLOR

D: Colin Higgins — 116 m

8 Very funny murder/mystery. A librarian (Hawn) picks up an undercover agent who gives her information that there will be an assassination attempt upon the Pope when he attends a performance of The Mikado. Quickly, there are several attempts made upon her life. Even though she tells all this to the police, they don't believe her. However, stumbling police detective Chevy Chases eventually comes to believe her and becomes both her protector and lover. A wide assortment of looneys and odd-balls add to the fun. The fine supporting cast includes Dudley Moore in his first American role.

Sex / Nud / ✓ Viol / ✓ Lang / ✓ AdSit

A: Goldie Hawn, Chevy Chase, Burgess Meredith, Rachel Roberts, Dudley Moore, Billy Barty

© PARAMOUNT HOME VIDEO 1116

FOUR MUSKETEERS, THE

PG | COM ACT | 1975 | COLOR

D: Richard Lester — 107 m

8 Highly entertaining, high-spirited comedy/adventure and sequel to THE THREE MUSKETEERS (although they were actually filmed at the same time). It is a tongue-in-cheek irreverent retelling of the Dumas classic of honor and comradeship between three valiant swordsmen. Full of swashbuckling sword play, slap stick humor and good story telling. It actually has a quite engrossing plot too, and Raquel Welch was never better. The final sword duel is a real piece of work.

Sex / Nud / ✓ Viol / Lang / ✓ AdSit

A: Oliver Reed, Raquel Welch, Richard Chamberlain, Frank Finlay, Michael York, Christopher Lee

© LIVE HOME VIDEO 215-280

FREAKY FRIDAY

G | COM CLD | 1977 | COLOR

D: Gary Nelson — 98 m

8 Charming breezy comedy that is a truly fun time for the whole family - from Disney. Teenager Jodie Foster gets her wish when she and her mother (Barbara Harris) magically exchange personalities for a day and both of them find out that neither has such an easy time of things. Probably one of Disney's best-ever comedies. Lightweight fun from Mary Rogers's adaptation of her own book. This is the same premise as in the 1948 movie VICE VERSA, and it became very popular later with such other movies as BIG - but it was seldom used better than it was here.

Sex / Nud / Viol / Lang / AdSit

A: Jodie Foster, Barbara Harris, John Astin, Ruth Buzzi, Kay Ballard, Patsy Kelly

© WALT DISNEY HOME VIDEO 056

FRESHMAN, THE

PG | COM CRM | 1990 | COLOR

D: Andrew Bergman — 102 m

7 A lighthearted charmer! Broderick is a naive freshman film student who, minutes after arriving in New York, has all his bags and belongings stolen. Broderick tracks the thief (Kirby) down, who surprisingly makes him an offer that he can't refuse. He now finds himself working for an irresistibly charismatic mob boss (Brando, in a spoof on his role in THE GODFATHER) running strange errands, while also being hotly pursued by the boss's sexy daughter. Among his odd duties is picking up a giant lizard from the airport and delivering that strange cargo unharmed to New Jersey.

Sex / Nud / Viol / ✓ Lang / ✓ AdSit

A: Matthew Broderick, Marlon Brando, Bruno Kirby, Maximilian Schell, Penelope Ann Miller, Frank Whaley

© COLUMBIA TRISTAR HOME VIDEO 70293

FUN WITH DICK AND JANE

PG | COM CRM | 1977 | COLOR

D: Ted Kotcheff — 95 m

8 Zany, polished fun-filled comedy. What do you do when you enjoy, and in fact are addicted to, the luxurious upper-middle-class lifestyle that your job as a highly-paid aerospace executive gives you, and you are suddenly fired? At first Dick and Jane tighten their belts and Jane gets a job. But Jane doesn't like her job and they don't like their belts tight. So, quite naturally, they decide to do the next best thing to earn a good living, they will rob and steal. See Dick and Jane steal. See Dick and Jane run. Really funny stuff.

Sex / Nud / Viol / ✓ Lang / ✓ AdSit

A: George Segal, Jane Fonda, Ed McMahon, Dick Gautier, Allan Miller

© GOODTIMES 4431

GAMBIT

NR | COM SUS | 1966 | COLOR

D: Ronald Neame — 109 m

8 Fact-paced and engaging, witty caper comedy. Cat burglar Michael Caine enlists the help of Shirley MacLaine, a wacky Eurasian dancer, to help him steal a priceless art treasure from its ruthless Arab owner. Caine's plan is elaborate, full of gadgets and ultimatley doesn't work, but that's when the fun starts. Caine and MacLaine are great together. The film did not get its proper due when it was originally released, but has now become a cult favorite. Good fun.

Sex / Nud / Viol / Lang / ✓ AdSit

A: Michael Caine, Shirley MacLaine, Herbert Lom, Roger C. Carmel, John Abbott

© MCA/UNIVERSAL HOME VIDEO, INC. 80365

GAZEBO, THE

NR | COM | 1959 | B&W

D: George Marshall — 100 m

8 Wacky offbeat comedy that is dominated by Glenn Ford as a distressed TV mystery writer who has learned that his Broadway star wife, Debbie Reynolds, had posed for nude photographs when she was younger and is now being blackmailed. Ford decides that the only way out is to kill the blackmailer and he plans to bury the guy in the back yard under where a new gazebo is just about to be built. The problem is that Ford is a much better planner than a carry-outer. Lots of laughs.

Sex / Nud / Viol / Lang / ✓ AdSit

A: Glenn Ford, Debbie Reynolds, Carl Reiner, Doro Merande, John McGiver, Mabel Albertson

Distributed By MGM/UA Home Video M204548

GENERAL, THE

NR | COM | 1927 | B&W

D: Buster Keaton, Clyde Bruckman — 77 m

9 Buster Keaton's silent masterpiece. He plays a Johnnie Gray, who tried to enlist in the Confederate Army but was told to remain a locomotive engineer. When his train and his girlfriend (who is on it) are both hijacked by Yankee spies and taken north, he single-handedly goes north to steal them both back. One of the greatest chases sequences of the silent era ensues. This masterpiece is filmed against a meticulous reconstruction of the Civil War era. It contains inspired comedy, ingenious stuntwork and sight gags. The story is based on an actual event, which was also retold by Disney as THE GREAT LOCOMOTIVE CHASE.

Sex / Nud / Viol / Lang / ✓ AdSit

A: Buster Keaton, Marion Mack, Glen Cavender, Jim Farley, Frederick Vroom, Joe Keaton

© HBO VIDEO 0282

GHOST BREAKERS, THE

D: George Marshall 82 m

NR | COM HOR | 1940 | **8**

Before there was GHOSTBUSTERS there was Bob Hope. Containing more plot than was normal for Hope pictures, this one has Bob being a New York radio commentator known for his crime exposes. When he is accidentally implicated in a murder case, he hides out in a steamer chest. It is owned by a beautiful heiress (Paulette Goddard) who is on her way to Cuba to claim a haunted castle she has inherited, and now Bob is unexpectedly going with her. Hope and Goddard fall in love and he promises to help her rid the castle of its ghouls...except the ghouls don't want to leave. Some pretty good and effectively scary scenes are mixed in with a lot of laughs. One of Hope's better films and was very popular.

☐ Sex ☐ Nud ☐ Viol ☐ Lang ☐ AdSit

A: Bob Hope, Paulette Goddard, Richard Carlson, Paul Lukas, Anthony Quinn, Richard Carlson

© MCA/UNIVERSAL HOME VIDEO, INC. 81558

GHOSTBUSTERS

D: Ivan Reitman 105 m

PG | COM HOR FAN | 1984 | COLOR | **9**

This film was a major box office hit and is about a trio of flaky parapsychologists who set up a shop specializing in the capture of unwanted ghosts. Business at first is pretty slow, but then they get their first job exorcising beautiful Sigourney Weaver's refrigerator. Soon both she and her nerdy neighbor are possessed by demons and the Ghostbusters discover that her entire building has become a magnet for all kinds of evil spirits... and the city of New York is now in desperate peril. Wonderfully offbeat and genuinely funny, with some pretty scary special effects, too. Murray is wonderfully weird. Great fun and good entertainment. 44 years before this there was Bob Hope in GHOSTBREAKERS.

☐ Sex ☐ Nud ☐ Viol ◢ Lang ◢ AdSit

A: Bill Murray, Dan Aykroyd, Sigourney Weaver, Harold Ramis, Annie Potts, Rick Moranis

© COLUMBIA TRISTAR HOME VIDEO 60413

GHOSTBUSTERS II

D: Ivan Reitman 102 m

PG | COM HOR FAN | 1989 | COLOR | **7**

Entertaining follow-up to the original blockbuster. This time the ghostbusting team sets about rescuing Sigourney Weaver, her infant son and all of NYC from a river of pink slime negative energy, which is flowing under the streets of the city. This one seems rather long and is not as captivating as the original, but is still a good time for fans. Teenagers are probably its best audience.

☐ Sex ☐ Nud ☐ Viol ◢ Lang ☐ AdSit

A: Bill Murray, Dan Aykroyd, Sigourney Weaver, Harold Ramis, Rick Moranis, Ernie Hudson

© COLUMBIA TRISTAR HOME VIDEO 50163

GHOST GOES WEST, THE

D: Rene Clair 82 m

NR | COM FAN | 1936 | B&W | **8**

Charming screwball comedy about a Scottish ghost and his 20th-century descendant (both played by Donat) who both escort their castle from Scotland to Florida when it is shipped there, stone-by-stone, after having been purchased by a rich American. The live one wants to win the heart of the millionaire's daughter, and the dead one wants to redeem his lost honor. Whimsical fantasy/comedy that is light-hearted fun.

☐ Sex ☐ Nud ☐ Viol ☐ Lang ☐ AdSit

A: Robert Donat, Jean Parker, Eugene Pallette, Elsa Lanchester, Ralph Bunker

© HBO VIDEO 90656

GIDGET

D: Paul Wendkos 95 m

NR | COM | 1959 | COLOR | **6**

First and best of a whole wave of surfer movies. In this one, a small insecure teenager (a girl midget - Gidget) decides that, in order to win the respect of the boys on the beach, she will have to learn to surf. She does and they do. Pretty entertaining for real young folks, and for the old folks who want to remember when they weren't. Sandra Dee was the perfect Gidget.

☐ Sex ☐ Nud ☐ Viol ☐ Lang ☐ AdSit

A: Sandra Dee, James Darren, Arthur O'Connell, Cliff Robertson, Doug McClure, Tom Laughlin

© GOODTIMES 4513

GLASS BOTTOM BOAT, THE

D: Frank Tashlin 110 m

NR | COM ROM | 1966 | COLOR | **6**

Light-hearted, fun stuff. Doris Day is a public relations specialist at a space center and pulling double duty as a mermaid for her father (Arthur Godfrey) who is the operator of a glass bottom sightseeing boat. One day, while he is out fishing, top scientist Rod Taylor mistakenly hooks a mermaid. Guess who? On land, they work at the same place, so he gets her assigned to him and they fall in love. But spies from an espionage ring begin chasing her, and she is mistaken for being one of them. Relentless rounds of slapstick humor, but the film is above average lightweight family fun.

☐ Sex ☐ Nud ☐ Viol ☐ Lang ☐ AdSit

A: Doris Day, Rod Taylor, Arthur Godfrey, Paul Lynde, Eric Fleming, Alice Pearce

Distributed By MGM/UA Home Video M202360

GODS MUST BE CRAZY, THE

D: Jamie Uys 109 m

PG | COM | 1981 | COLOR | **8**

Disarmingly funny film from South Africa. When a bush pilot throws an empty Coke bottle out of his plane, a tribe of primitive bushman look on it at first as a gift from the gods. But then things start to get all mixed up for the tribe, so they choose one of their own (Nixau) to return it to the gods. Setting out on his monumental quest, the little bushman runs first across a klutzy scientist and beautiful journalist, who are trying to return to a safari camp, and then upon a clumsy group of Communist guerrillas. This film is the biggest foreign box-office hit in history. Hilarious.

☐ Sex ◢ Nud ☐ Viol ◢ Lang ◢ AdSit

A: Marius Weyers, Sandra Prinsloo, Nixau

© FOXVIDEO 1450

GODS MUST BE CRAZY 2, THE

D: Jamie Uys 98 m

PG | COM | 1990 | COLOR | **7**

The little African bushman returns in this follow-up to the surprise big hit original. Nixau, the bushman living deep in the African desert, is forced to confront civilization again when his two children unintentionally hitch a ride on a poacher's truck. He follows the truck's trail to rescue them but along the way he also has to rescue a couple of white people who become stranded when their light plane crashes. Light-hearted slapstick that is genuinely entertaining to the whole family, although the original is better.

☐ Sex ◢ Nud ☐ Viol ☐ Lang ◢ AdSit

A: Nixau, Lena Farugia, Hans Strydom, Erick Bowen

© COLUMBIA TRISTAR HOME VIDEO 10313

GOING IN STYLE

D: Martin Brest 91 m

PG | COM DMA | 1979 | COLOR | **9**

Absolutely delightful. Three old men share an apartment in Queens, a bench in the park and a boring existence. When one of their sons needs some help with his finances, Burns convinces the other two that they should help the boy out and spice up their lives a little, too. They should rob a bank. You would expect a film with this quality of talent and a good plot gimmick like that to be funny and it is, but it also proves to be a moving experience, too. Burns is a standout.

☐ Sex ☐ Nud ☐ Viol ◢ Lang ☐ AdSit

A: George Burns, Art Carney, Lee Strasberg, Charles Hallahan, Pamela Payton-Wright

© WARNER HOME VIDEO 1030

GOLD RUSH, THE

D: Charles Chaplin 82 m

NR | COM | 1925 | B&W | **10**

One of Chaplin's best, some say it is his best. Charlie's Little Tramp prospects in Alaska's Klondike gold rush and just about starves. Hilarious sequences include Chaplin's now classic Thanksgiving Day feast of a boiled shoe, but Charlie also has a comic tussle with a villain and falls for a dancehall girl. Chaplin's talent for combining pathos and sentimentality with hilarious slapstick has never been better evidenced than here. Memorable and still very, very funny after all these years. A true classic.

☐ Sex ☐ Nud ☐ Viol ☐ Lang ◢ AdSit

A: Charlie Chaplin, Georgia Hale, Mack Swain, Tom Murray

© UNITED AMERICAN VIDEO CORP. 4016

GREAT MCGINTY, THE

D: Preston Sturges 82 m

NR | COM | 1940 | B&W | **7**

A wicked satire about corrupt politics. A bartender recollects the story of how he rose to became governor. Originally, he was only a hobo, but he had gained a reputation among the political bosses as a charmer who could really stuff ballot boxes. Soon, he became so valuable to them that the political machine promoted him all the way up to become governor. However, when he boldly sought real reform, the real boss - who was so corrupt that he controlled both the conventional political machine and the reform party - set out to destroy him. Good entertainment. Won an Oscar for Best Screenplay.

☐ Sex ☐ Nud ☐ Viol ☐ Lang ◢ AdSit

A: Brian Donlevy, Muriel Angelus, Akim Tamiroff, Allyn Joslyn, William Demarest

© MCA/UNIVERSAL HOME VIDEO, INC. 80595

GREAT MUPPET CAPER, THE

D: Jim Henson 98 m

G | COM CLD MUS | 1981 | COLOR | **8**

This is the delightful second feature-length film for Jim Henson's Muppets. After being fired as reporters for a major paper, Miss Piggy, Kermit, Fozzie Bear and the Great Gonzo set about solving the mysterious theft in London of the famous Baseball Diamond. Good gags and fun musical numbers (Kermit dances like Astaire and Miss Piggy swims like Ester Williams). Pretty good follow-up to the superior THE MUPPET MOVIE.

☐ Sex ☐ Nud ☐ Viol ☐ Lang ☐ AdSit

A: Charles Grodin, Diana Rigg, John Cleese, Robert Morley, Peter Ustinov, Jack Warden

© CBS/FOX VIDEO 9035

GREAT RACE, THE

D: Blake Edwards — 160 m

NR | COM | 1965 | COLOR

☐ Sex ☐ Nud ☐ Viol ☐ Lang ☐ AdSit

8 Lively comedy farce about a 20,000 mile trans-global auto race set in 1908. This extravagant production pits ultra-good guy Tony Curtis (he's in white), with a gorgeous suffragette (Natalie Wood) along for the ride, against super-bad guys Jack Lemmon and Peter Falk (they're in black). Filled with slapstick (contains the biggest pie fight - 2,357 pies - ever). Good fun, but plenty silly, too.

A: Tony Curtis, Natalie Wood, Jack Lemmon, Peter Falk, Keenan Wynn, Larry Storch

© WARNER HOME VIDEO 11091

GREEN PASTURES, THE

D: Marc Connelly, William Keighley — 93 m

NR | COM FAN | 1936 | B&W

☐ Sex ☐ Nud ☐ Viol ☐ Lang ◢ AdSit

9 Very unique, interesting, and funny - but also burdened with racially stereotyped characters. The film takes place in a Harlem Sunday School where a teacher tells the stories of the Bible in an entertaining way so that his students can relate to them. But, as the stories of the Old Testament are vibrantly told, they begin to come to life (with the characters speaking in Old South Black vernacular). This film, which had an all-star all-black cast, was heavily boycotted by whites in the South. Rex Ingram is captivating as "de Lawd," as is Oscar Polk as his right-hand angel - Gabe. Religion rarely is this entertaining.

A: Marc Connelly, Rex Ingram, Oscar Polk, Eddie Anderson, Frank Wilson, George Reed

Distributed By MGM/UA Home Video 202834

GREMLINS

D: Joe Dante — 106 m

PG | COM FAN HOR | 1984 | COLOR

☐ Sex ☐ Nud ◢ Viol ◢ Lang ◢ AdSit

8 Entertaining and very different. Steven Spielberg put together this combination "horror"/comedy - so this is not your typical flick. The premise is that an inventor (Axton) goes on a Christmas shopping trip to Chinatown looking for the perfect gift for his son. He decides upon a strange but cute little creature called a "mowgli," but is given three warnings: Do not get it wet, keep it out of bright light and never to feed it after midnight. When these rules are ignored, hordes of mischievous gremlins result. Fascinating special effects. Really wacky.

A: Zach Galligan, Phoebe Cates, Hoyt Axton, Frances Lee McCain, Polly Holliday, Glynn Turman

© WARNER HOME VIDEO 11388

GREMLINS 2: THE NEW BATCH

D: Joe Dante — 107 m

PG-13 | COM FAN HOR | 1990 | COLOR

☐ Sex ☐ Nud ◢ Viol ◢ Lang ◢ AdSit

8 Those weird little creatures are back to raise havoc in a New York office complex and with its tycoon owner. The film is filled with the same odd mixture of non-toxic horror and comedy as in the original. It is also filled with Hollywood insider-type jokes and plot spins. A little more violence than the first one earned it a PG-13. Some think it's not as good as the original. Others think it's better. Fun, no matter how it's sliced.

A: Zach Galligan, Phoebe Cates, John Glover, Christopher Lee, Robert Prosky, Dick Miller

© WARNER HOME VIDEO 11886

GROUNDHOG DAY

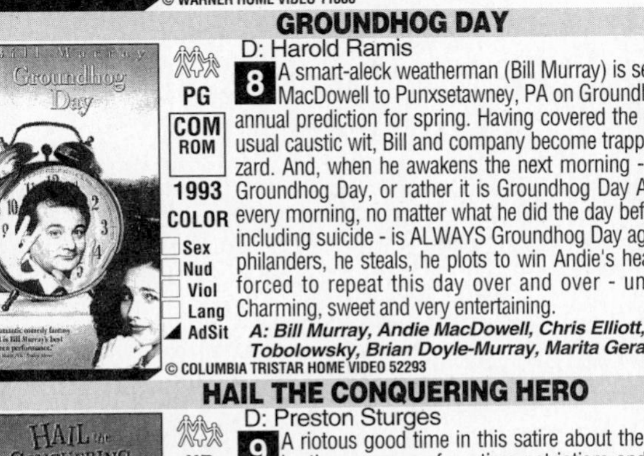

D: Harold Ramis — 101 m

PG | COM ROM | 1993 | COLOR

☐ Sex ☐ Nud ☐ Viol ☐ Lang ◢ AdSit

8 A smart-aleck weatherman (Bill Murray) is sent with sweet Andie MacDowell to Punxsetawney, PA on Groundhog Day to cover the annual prediction for spring. Having covered the ceremonies with his usual caustic wit, Bill and company become trapped in town by a blizzard. And, when he awakens the next morning - amazingly, it is still Groundhog Day, or rather it is Groundhog Day AGAIN!! In fact, now every morning, no matter what he did the day before - up to and even including suicide - is ALWAYS Groundhog Day again. He connives, he philanders, he steals, he plots to win Andie's heart, but he is always forced to repeat this day over and over - until he gets it right. Charming, sweet and very entertaining.

A: Bill Murray, Andie MacDowell, Chris Elliott, Stephen Tobolowsky, Brian Doyle-Murray, Marita Geraghty

© COLUMBIA TRISTAR HOME VIDEO 52293

HAIL THE CONQUERING HERO

D: Preston Sturges — 101 m

NR | COM WAR | 1944 | B&W

☐ Sex ☐ Nud ☐ Viol ☐ Lang ◢ AdSit

9 A riotous good time in this satire about the hazards brought on by the excesses of wartime patriotism and hero worship. Frail Eddie Bracken signs up for the Army but is turned down because of chronic hay fever. He is so embarrassed that he has worked in a shipyard for six-months, but written home to his mother telling her of his exploits in the Marines. He then has his buddies in the Pacific forward the letters home for him. When his buddies find out that he is too embarrassed to return home, they each donate some of their metals. Soon the whole town thinks Eddie is a big hero and he is nominated to become mayor. Delightful and fast paced satire.

A: Eddie Bracken, Ella Raines, Raymond Walburn, William Demarest, Bill Edwards, Elizabeth Patterson

© MCA/UNIVERSAL HOME VIDEO, INC. 81021

HAIRSPRAY

D: John Waters — 92 m

PG | COM | 1988 | COLOR

☐ Sex ☐ Nud ☐ Viol ◢ Lang ◢ AdSit

6 Goofball spoof of the early sixties. The story is intentionally bizarre and concerns a chubby adolescent girl who is consumed by a passion to dance on a Baltimore teen-TV dance show in 1963. She has the tallest tower of hair and the coolest dance moves, but before she can be on the show she has to de-throne the reigning bouffant queen. Entertaining, if you are a fan of extravagant satire or of '60s music - of which there is a wide and very rich selection.

A: Sonny Bono, Divine, Colleen Fitzpatrick, Deborah Harry, Jerry Stiller, Pia Zadora

© NEW LINE HOME VIDEO 62822

HAPPIEST DAYS OF YOUR LIFE, THE

D: Frank Launder — 83 m

NR | COM | 1950 | B&W

☐ Sex ☐ Nud ☐ Viol ☐ Lang ☐ AdSit

8 Very funny English film concerning the mishaps and misadventures that occur when a girl's school is accidentally billeted in with a boys school. Comic geniuses Alastar Sim and Margaret Rutherford struggle to maintain their composure and their control of these two rivalrous factions which are not supposed to and are ill-prepared to intermix. The kids fight, the bureaucrats pull out their hair and mayhem ensues.

A: Alastair Sim, Margaret Rutherford, Joyce Grenfell, John Turbull, Guy Middleton

© HOME VISION HAP 020

HARRY AND THE HENDERSONS

D: William Dear — 111 m

PG | COM CLD | 1987 | COLOR

☐ Sex ☐ Nud ◢ Viol ☐ Lang ◢ AdSit

7 Entertaining and pretty good family fun. Your typical suburban family is out on a trip in the wilds when father Lithgow runs over Harry, a real live man/ape - the fabled "Bigfoot". At first they think he's dead, but he's not. They bring him home to nurse him, but the big guy wreaks total havoc in their house. Still, he is a loveable sort and the family is growing more and more attached to him. Even so, they need to get him back to the woods where he belongs. That's a lot harder than it sounds... Harry doesn't want to go. But, he has to go because now everybody is after him. Good family entertainment.

A: John Lithgow, Melinda Dillon, Don Ameche, Joshua Ruday, Margaret Langrick, Kevin Peter Hall

© MCA/UNIVERSAL HOME VIDEO, INC. 80677

HARVEY

D: Henry Koster — 104 m

NR | COM FAN | 1950 | B&W

☐ Sex ☐ Nud ☐ Viol ☐ Lang ◢ AdSit

9 Brilliant, classic comedy. Very popular and perennial favorite starring Jimmy Stewart as the loveable Elwood P. Dowd. Elwood is just about the nicest and friendliest man you'd ever meet, but he is just a little strange. He drinks more than he should, but what makes him so strange is that he keeps company with a Pukka (a six-foot three-inch invisible rabbit) named Harvey. Finally, his sister (Hull) reluctantly decides that Elwood should be committed to a loony bin, but hilarity reigns when she gets committed instead and it's now up to Elwood to get things straightened out. Hull won an Oscar for her performance.

A: James Stewart, Josephine Hull, Peggy Dow, Charles Drake, Cecil Kellaway, Jesse White

© MCA/UNIVERSAL HOME VIDEO, INC. 80321

HEARTS OF THE WEST

D: Howard Zieff — 103 m

PG | COM WST | 1975 | COLOR

☐ Sex ☐ Nud ☐ Viol ◢ Lang ◢ AdSit

7 Pleasant light-hearted story about a starry-eyed young Iowa farm boy with a wild imagination (Bridges) who goes west to Hollywood in the 1920s, intent upon becoming a writer of Western movies. Along the way he stops into his Nevada correspondence school and discovers that it is just a post office box. However, he accidentally takes the crooks cash stash and escapes into the desert, where he is rescued by a movie crew in full Western costume. He becomes pals, gets a job as a B-movie actor, finds love with a script girl and meets a publisher for his novel. A fun and charming little film.

A: Jeff Bridges, Alan Arkin, Blythe Danner, Andy Griffith, Donald Pleasence

Distributed By MGM/UA Home Video M600388

HEAVEN CAN WAIT

D: Ernst Lubitsch — 112 m

NR | COM ROM FAN | 1943 | COLOR

☐ Sex ☐ Nud ☐ Viol ☐ Lang ◢ AdSit

8 Elegant fantasy/comedy. Don Ameche plays a wealthy old playboy who dies and arrives at the gates of Hell seeking admission there because of his life's many indiscretions with the ladies. However, the lord of darkness is unconvinced that he should enter, so Don must tell his life's story. His indiscretions begin with the upstairs maid and do not stop when he marries beautiful Gene Tierney. But gradually his true love for Tierney is unveiled before us. This is a very witty script that features flashbacks to the Gay '90s. Delightful. Nominated for Best Picture.

A: Gene Tierney, Don Ameche, Charles Coburn, Marjorie Main, Laird Cregar, Spring Byington

© FOXVIDEO 1771

HEAVEN CAN WAIT

PG | COM FAN | 1978 | COLOR

D: Buck Henry — 100 m

9 Highly entertaining and well-done remake of the charming 1941 smash hit HERE COMES MR. JORDAN. Warren Beatty plays Joe Pendleton, a good-natured football hero, whose soul has been accidentally removed too soon from his body by an over-eager angel. Then before they can get him back into it, his body is cremated. Bummer. So, the head angel (Mason) gets him another body to use until his time is really up. However, that presents a problem too. The new body belongs to a millionaire whose wife wants to kill him. Nine Oscar nominations.

Sex / Nud / Viol / Lang / AdSit

A: Warren Beatty, Julie Christie, Jack Warden, Dyan Cannon, Charles Grodin, James Mason

© PARAMOUNT HOME VIDEO 1109

HERE COMES MR. JORDAN

NR | COM FAN | 1941 | B&W

D: Alexander Hall — 949 m

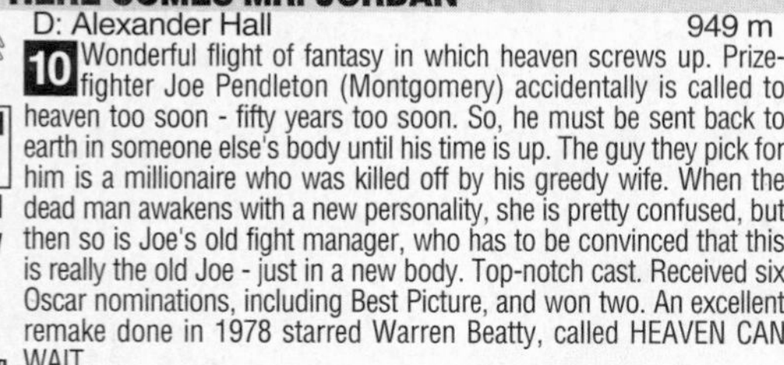

10 Wonderful flight of fantasy in which heaven screws up. Prizefighter Joe Pendleton (Montgomery) accidentally is called to heaven too soon - fifty years too soon. So, he must be sent back to earth in someone else's body until his time is up. The guy they pick for him is a millionaire who was killed off by his greedy wife. When the dead man awakens with a new personality, she is pretty confused, but then so is Joe's old fight manager, who has to be convinced that this is really the old Joe - just in a new body. Top-notch cast. Received six Oscar nominations, including Best Picture, and won two. An excellent remake done in 1978 starred Warren Beatty, called HEAVEN CAN WAIT.

Sex / Nud / Viol / Lang / AdSit

A: Robert Montgomery, Evelyn Keyes, Claude Rains, Rita Johnson, Edward Everett Horton, James Gleason

© COLUMBIA TRISTAR HOME VIDEO 71923

HERO AT LARGE

PG | COM | 1980 | COLOR

D: Martin Davidson — 99 m

6 An out-of-work actor (Ritter), who is in a Captain Avenger costume while promoting a movie, foils a holdup attempt at a deli and the city begins to think that they are being protected by the real thing. The mayor, who is running for reelection, and his agents attempt to exploit the actor for their benefit. More than a little silly, but still enjoyable family fun.

Sex / Nud / Viol / ◢ Lang / AdSit

A: John Ritter, Anne Archer, Bert Convy, Devin McCarthy, Harry Bellaver, Anita Dangler

Distributed By MGM/UA Home Video M600316

HEY ABBOTT!

NR | COM | 1978 | COLOR

D: Jim Gates — 76 m

8 This is a collection of a series of hilarious skits by Abbott and Costello. This pair of vaudeville greats graduated from the vaudeville stage to film and then to TV. Vaudeville was slapstick comedy, sometimes with a heavy emphasis on word play. These guys were among the best at both. These skits (essentially all vaudeville) were taken from their 1950s TV series and the tape is hosted by comedic legend Milton Berle. Skits included: "Who's on First," "Oyster Stew," "Floogie Street" and "The Birthday Party."

Sex / Nud / Viol / Lang / AdSit

A: Bud Abbott, Lou Costello, Joe Besser, Phil Silvers, Steve Allen

© UNITED AMERICAN VIDEO CORP. 8152

HOBSON'S CHOICE

NR | COM | 1954 | B&W

D: David Lean — 107 m

8 Delightful comedy with a heart. Charles Laughton puts in one of his best performances as an overbearing hard-drinking shoemaker in 1890s London. He makes life miserable for his three daughters by insisting that he will decide who they should marry. But the eldest daughter frustrates his wishes by railroading his talented assistant into marriage and then setting up a shop in competition with her father. Good fun and plenty of laughs.

Sex / Nud / Viol / Lang / ◢ AdSit

A: Charles Laughton, John Mills, Brenda de Banzie, Daphne Anderson, Prunella Scales

© HOME VISION HOB 040

HOCUS POCUS

PG | COM | 1993 | COLOR

D: Kenny Ortega — 96 m

6 One Halloween night, a teen-age boy playing with a spell, releases three witches who had been hung 300 years before. The three know that this time, if they are to survive, they must suck all the life's force from the town's children by daybreak. They crash a costume party where they escape detection by appearing to be just some more adults in costume. However, much to their dismay, the kid, his young sister, a pretty teenage girl and a talking 17th-century cat have set out determined to stop them. Starts slow and then picks up some steam, generally enjoyable but it never reaches its potential.

Sex / Nud / Viol / Lang / ◢ AdSit

A: Bette Midler, Sarah Jessica Parker, Kathy Najimy, Omri Katz, Thora Birch, Vinessa Shaw

© WALT DISNEY HOME VIDEO 2144

HOLD THAT GHOST

NR | COM | 1941 | B&W

D: Arthur Lubin — 86 m

8 One of the very best from Abbot and Costello. Here they are two nightclub waiters, who inherit a haunted house that was previously owned by a hoodlum and reportedly still houses his stolen loot. And, when they come to claim their property, things get spooky. Walls move, lights go on by themselves. There are moans and screams in the air, and people are murdered. Full of great gags. The comic masters are backed up by one of the best supporting casts ever to be into one of their films.

Sex / Nud / Viol / Lang / AdSit

A: Bud Abbott, Lou Costello, Richard Carlson, Joan Davis, The Andrews Sisters, Shemp Howard

© MCA/UNIVERSAL HOME VIDEO, INC. 55087

HOLIDAY

NR | COM ROM | 1938 | B&W

D: George Cukor — 94 m

8 Delightful and literal adaptation of a Broadway play about a successful but non-conformist young man (Grant, at his charming best) who agrees to meet his wealthy fiancee's stuffy family and to even work for her father's bank. However, when he does meet the family, he finds a kindred spirit in his fiancee's kooky free-thinking sister (Hepburn). She understands him and is just as weird as he is. Which sister going to get him? Fun film.

Sex / Nud / Viol / Lang / AdSit

A: Cary Grant, Katharine Hepburn, Edward Everett Horton, Doris Nolan, Lew Ayres, Binnie Barnes

© COLUMBIA TRISTAR HOME VIDEO 71933

HOMEWARD BOUND: THE INCREDIBLE JOURNEY

G | COM CLD | 1993 | COLOR

D: Duwayne Dunham — 84 m

8 Rock solid family entertainment and a lot of fun. Here, Disney has remade their 1963 hit THE INCREDIBLE JOURNEY, but this time they gave the cute animals real personalities and the voices of Michael J. Fox, Don Ameche and Sally Field. This is the extremely enjoyable and sometimes comic story of two dogs and a cat who are left temporarily several hundred miles away from home. However, they become worried that their masters are in trouble and so the three buddies begin a cross-country journey through the beautiful Sierra Mountains to get home. Very clever and highly entertaining story of their many encounters along the way. Truly a lot of fun. Some might even rate it higher.

Sex / Nud / Viol / Lang / AdSit

A:

© WALT DISNEY HOME VIDEO 1801

HONEY, I BLEW UP THE KID

PG | COM CLD FAN | 1992 | COLOR

D: Randal Kleiser — 89 m

8 Sequel to HONEY, I SHRUNK THE KIDS. Moranis is now working for a corporation trying to develop a ray that, this time, will enlarge things. He is accidentally successful but accidentally blows up his two-year-old to the size of a ten-story building. There is something here for everyone to laugh at. Moranis is hysterical as he runs around Las Vegas trying to blast his kid with a ray gun to shrink him back down to size. Great special effects again. Overall, this is nearly as good as the original - only slightly less funny because some of the novelty is gone.

Sex / Nud / Viol / Lang / AdSit

A: Rick Moranis, Lloyd Bridges, Marcia Strassman, Robert Oliveri, Amy O'Neill

© WALT DISNEY HOME VIDEO 1371

HONEY, I SHRUNK THE KIDS

PG | COM CLD FAN | 1989 | COLOR

D: Joe Johnston — 101 m

9 Big box office hit and great family fun-filled fantasy - in the old fashioned Disney tradition. Rick Moranis plays a klutzy scientist who is inventing an experimental ray gun in the attic. One day his kids and the neighbor's kids are playing with it and zap... they are all shrunk down to the size of ants. They become lost in the backyard, which, because of their size, has now been transformed into a forbidding jungle filled with terrible monsters. Really good special effects and fun gags that will satisfy all age groups. Good family entertainment.

Sex / Nud / Viol / Lang / AdSit

A: Rick Moranis, Matt Frewer, Marcia Strassman, Kristine Sutherland, Thomas Brown, Jared Rushton

© WALT DISNEY HOME VIDEO 909

HONEYMOON MACHINE, THE

NR | COM | 1961 | COLOR

D: Richard Thorpe — 87 m

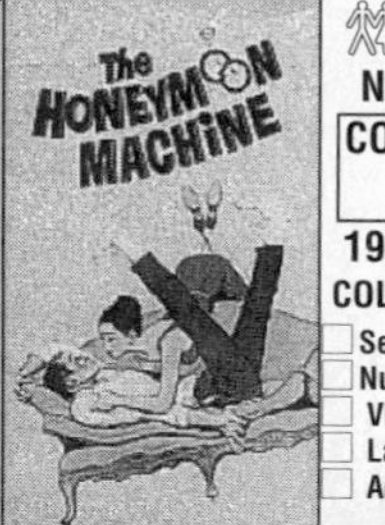

6 Pleasant light-hearted little movie about a couple of sailors who find a way to break the bank at a casino in Venice by using the very large electronic brain on board their ship to determine the peculiarities of a roulette wheel. Not a great movie, but it is fun and you get to watch some big-name actors when they were very young and before they were big names.

Sex / Nud / Viol / Lang / AdSit

A: Steve McQueen, Brigid Brazlen, Jim Hutton, Paula Prentiss, Dean Jagger, Jack Weston

Distributed By MGM/UA Home Video 200795

HORSE FEATHERS

NR · COM · 1932 · B&W

D: Norman McLeod — 67 m

9 Probably the funniest of the Marx brothers films. This time the brothers destroy Huxley College. Groucho is the president who wants to save money by closing down the dormitory - the kids always sleep in class anyway. He hires Chico and Harpo, a speakeasy worker and a dogcatcher, to build a winning football team so they can beat their rivals at Darwin. Meanwhile Zeppo is chasing a sexy widow. As with all of Marx brothers stuff, don't get too caught up on the plot, just watch for the one-liners.

Sex / Nud / Viol / Lang / ◢ AdSit

A: Groucho Marx, Harpo Marx, Chico Marx, Zeppo Marx, Thelma Todd, David Landau

© MCA/UNIVERSAL HOME VIDEO, INC. 80777

HOT MILLIONS

G · COM · 1968 · COLOR

D: Eric Till — 105 m

8 Highly entertaining laugh-getter, one of the surprise hits of the year and nominated for Best Original Screenplay. Peter Ustinov plays a roguish embezzler who is caught because of a computer. So, he decides to get his revenge by becoming an expert on computers himself in jail. When released, he conspires to get computer genius Robert Morley out of the country, and then, using his identity, he wheedles his way into Karl Malden's company, where he embezzles millions of dollars, marries his secretary and moves to Rio. But then, Malden sends Bob Newhart after him. Frequently hilarious.

Sex / Nud / Viol / Lang / ◢ AdSit

A: Peter Ustinov, Maggie Smith, Karl Malden, Bob Newhart, Robert Morley, Cesar Romero

Distributed By MGM/UA Home Video M204550

HOUSEGUEST

PG · COM · 1995 · COLOR

D: Randall Miller — 119 m

6 Silly family comedy. Sinbad is a former orphan who has never grown up. He is now a 35-year-old wannabe millionaire, chasing one get-rich scheme after another, but his luck has just ran out. He owes a loan-shark the $5,000 he borrowed, plus $45,000 in interest. His first bit of good luck is that the two goofy goons sent to collect from him are so stupid he is able to escape. The second is that he stumbles upon an uptight, middle-aged, upper-class white guy (Harrington) at the airport, who is waited for a black guy that he hasn't seen in years...and Sinbad is able to convince him that he is that guy. Then, silly Sinbad goes home with Harrington and teaches him and his family how to loosen-up.

Sex / Nud / Viol / ◢ Lang / AdSit

A: Sinbad, Phil Hartman, Jeffrey Jones, Kim Greist, Stan Shaw, Tony Longo

© HOLLYWOOD PICTURES HOME VIDEO 3631

I MARRIED A WITCH

NR · COM ROM · 1942 · B&W

D: Rene Clair — 77 m

8 Delightful fantasy/comedy about a sexy witch (Lake) who returns 400 years after being burned at the stake, intent upon revenge. Fredric March is a dead ringer for the ancestor who persecuted her and is now running for governor. The witch, unable to help herself, falls for the guy and proceeds to play dirty tricks upon his fiancee, Susan Hayward. Funny comedy with some interesting plot twists and boasts some pretty good special effects, too. Ironically, March and Lake couldn't stand each other.

Sex / Nud / Viol / Lang / AdSit

A: Fredric March, Veronica Lake, Robert Benchley, Susan Hayward, Cecil Kellaway, Robert Warwick

© WARNER HOME VIDEO 35079

INNERSPACE

PG · COM SF · 1987 · COLOR

D: Joe Dante — 120 m

7 Funny takeoff on FANTASTIC VOYAGE. Dennis Quaid is an astronaut who agrees to be miniaturized down to the size of a virus and then be injected into a rabbit. However, instead he accidentally gets shot into a hypochondriacal store clerk, Martin Short. What's worse, Short is now being chased by spies who want them both. Funny, off-the-wall stuff, with special effects that won an Oscar for Visual Effects. Short is perfect.

Sex / Nud / ◢ Viol / ◢ Lang / AdSit

A: Dennis Quaid, Martin Short, Fiona Lewis, Vernon Wells, Meg Ryan, Kevin McCarthy

© WARNER HOME VIDEO 11754

INSPECTOR GENERAL, THE

NR · COM MUS · 1949 · COLOR

D: Henry Koster — 102 m

9 Hysterical Danny Kaye farce. In early 1800s czarist Russia, Danny Kay is a flunky in a traveling medicine show and he has been arrested as a suspected horse thief. However, he is soon mistaken by the village elders to be a visiting Inspector General of the Czar and confidant of Napoleon. He has no idea what is going on but he isn't going to let this good fortune get away. Still, he is not out of trouble, because he is now being drawn ever deeper into court intrigue and that isn't healthy. Highly entertaining showcase for Kaye's many musical and comedic talents. Everyone will truly enjoy this one.

Sex / Nud / Viol / Lang / AdSit

A: Danny Kaye, Walter Slezak, Barbara Bates, Elsa Lanchester, Gene Lockhart, Alan Hale

Distributed By MGM/UA Home Video M202599

INTERNATIONAL HOUSE

NR · COM · 1933 · B&W

D: A. Edward Sutherland — 72 m

8 Hilariously offbeat film filled with some of the biggest radio stars of the early '30s. The cockeyed wacky plot has a wide assortment of strange characters all gathered at a Chinese hotel to witness an inventor display his brand new experimental television. The plot, while bizarre, is there merely to provide an excuse for a big cast of vaudevillian and radio players to do their shtick, and for W.C. Fields to play off them. Expect the absurd and you will be satisfied.

Sex / Nud / Viol / Lang / AdSit

A: W.C. Fields, Peggy Hopkins Joyce, George Burns, Gracie Allen, Bela Lugosi, Rudy Vallee

© MCA/UNIVERSAL HOME VIDEO, INC. 80512

I OUGHT TO BE IN PICTURES

PG · COM DMA · 1982 · COLOR

D: Herbert Ross — 107 m

8 Heartwarming Neil Simon story about a 19-year-old girl who travels to Los Angeles to become a movie star and to look up her long lost father. Matthau plays a burned out screenwriter who spends more time drinking and at the race track than he does writing, and who abandoned his family back in Brooklyn many years ago. Ann-Margret plays his girlfriend, who mediates between the two to eventually brings them back together, and gets Matthau's paternal genes to kick in. Very funny and affecting.

Sex / ◢ Nud / Viol / ◢ Lang / ◢ AdSit

A: Walter Matthau, Ann-Margret, Dinah Manoff, Lance Guest, Lewis Smith, Martin Ferrero

© FOXVIDEO 1150

IRRECONCILABLE DIFFERENCES

PG · COM DMA · 1984 · COLOR

D: Charles Shyer — 112 m

6 An unusual premise gives this picture a good opportunity to do something different and it almost does: a 10-year-old girl sues her parents for a divorce. A young couple have a good relationship until they each start to have some successes with their careers. Then they both become totally self-centered, devoted first to career and then to themselves. They exclude themselves from each other and even from their daughter. So she divorces them. A good premise, some funny moments and some poignant moments redeem this otherwise mediocre flick.

Sex / ◢ Nud / Viol / ◢ Lang / ◢ AdSit

A: Drew Barrymore, Ryan O'Neal, Shelley Long, Sharon Stone, Sam Wanamaker

© LIVE HOME VIDEO VA5057

IT'S A MAD, MAD, MAD, MAD WORLD

G · COM · 1963 · COLOR

D: Stanley Kramer — 188 m

8 Three hours of zaniness from a virtual "Who's Who" of American comedy of the 1960s. An accident victim reveals the location of a buried "treasure" to a whole group of people who have surrounded him as he lays dying. Invigorated at their good fortune, they all charge off in a mad scramble to get their piece of the pie. But, it's stolen money and Spencer Tracy is a police detective who wants it back. However, he chooses to just sit back to watch this group of crazies do their level best to beat each other to $350,000 in stolen money and do his job for him. Sight-gags galore. Big cast and a good time.

Sex / Nud / Viol / Lang / AdSit

A: Spencer Tracy, Edie Adams, Milton Berle, Sid Caesar, Ethel Merman, Jonathan Winters

Distributed By MGM/UA Home Video M302193

IT'S A WONDERFUL LIFE

NR · COM DMA ROM · 1947 · B&W

D: Frank Capra — 160 m

10 Nobody doesn't like this movie. Sentimental favorite in which Jimmy Stewart wishes he was never born. He's been so busy helping others get what they want that he feels as if everything he wants and needs has passed him by. Then he receives a visit from Clarence, his bumbling guardian angel, who shows him what things would have been like if he had never been born. This is an experience that proves to him what a fortunate and wealthy man he is. Heartwarming, feel good story that is usually reserved just for Christmas, but shouldn't be.

Sex / Nud / Viol / Lang / ◢ AdSit

A: James Stewart, Donna Reed, Lionel Barrymore, Thomas Mitchell, Ward Bond, Henry Travers

© REPUBLIC PICTURES HOME VIDEO 2062

IT SHOULD HAPPEN TO YOU

NR · COM ROM · 1953 · B&W

D: George Cukor — 81 m

8 Kooky Judy Holliday decides to promote her acting career by hiring a billboard overlooking one of the busiest locations in New York City. When a soap company executive wants this particular location for his product, he trades her several other billboard locations in exchange for her one. All of a sudden she is a sensation. Her boyfriend (Jack Lemmon, in his first screen appearance) has a difficult time dealing with her new-found celebrity status, and she must decide between him and a career. This is a steady stream of fun from two talented comedic actors.

Sex / Nud / Viol / Lang / ◢ AdSit

A: Judy Holliday, Jack Lemmon, Peter Lawford, Michael O'Shea

© COLUMBIA TRISTAR HOME VIDEO VH10343

FAMILY

I WANNA HOLD YOUR HAND

PG | COM MUS | 1978 | COLOR

D: Robert Zemeckis — 99 m

6 Delightful comedy produced by Steven Spielberg about six New Jersey teenagers in the early '60s who try to break into the Ed Sullivan Show the night that The Beatles are set to appear. Fast-paced, with a fine sense for the time period and the hysteria that surrounded the Fab Four's trip to America. Contains 17 Beatles songs.

Sex | Nud | Viol | ◢ Lang | ◢ AdSit

A: Nancy Allen, Bobby DiCicco, Mark McClure, Theresa Saldana, Eddie Deezen

© WARNER HOME VIDEO 35066

KID, THE/THE IDLE CLASS

NR | COM | 1921 | B&W

D: Charles Chaplin — 86 m

7 This is a Charlie Chaplin two-parter. The first one is THE KID. It was Charlie's very first film in which he wrote, produced and directed; and, it was also the film that made Jackie Coogan into a child star. In it, the Little Tramp discovers and takes an apparently orphaned child home with him, but the mother returns and wants to take the baby away. This is Chaplin's trademark blending of pathos and comedy. The second is a rare film short in which Charlie has two roles, the Little Tramp loose on a society golf course, and being mistaken for a millionaire at a costume party.

Sex | Nud | Viol | Lang | ◢ AdSit

A: Charlie Chaplin, Jackie Coogan, Edna Purviance

© CBS/FOX VIDEO 3002

KID FROM BROOKLYN, THE

NR | COM | 1946 | COLOR

D: Norman McLeod — 113 m

6 This is a great vehicle for Danny Kaye's silliness. He plays a milkman who accidentally knocks out a middle-weight boxing champion in a street brawl. Soon the champ's scheming manager decides to turn Danny into a boxer. Eve Arden's wisecracking and Danny Kaye's charm are mostly what makes this enjoyable. However, this film is actually a remake of THE MILKY WAY, done by Harold Lloyd in 1936, and that one might be funnier.

Sex | Nud | Viol | Lang | AdSit

A: Danny Kaye, Virginia Mayo, Vera-Ellen, Eve Arden, Steve Cochran

© HBO VIDEO 90651

KISS ME GOODBYE

PG | COM ROM | 1982 | COLOR

D: Robert Mulligan — 101 m

6 Enjoyable, but very-much sanitized, version of the spicer (and funnier) Brazilian entry, DONA FLOR AND HER TWO HUSBANDS. A widow (Field) is about to marry stuffy Dr. Rupert Baines (Bridges) when she is confronted with the ghost of her dead husband (Caan), which only she can see and hear. Everything is quite predictable and most of the sexy humor has been altered to insignificance, but there is a comedic chemistry to the relationship between Fields and Bridges that is quite a lot of fun to watch.

Sex | Nud | Viol | ◢ Lang | ■ AdSit

A: Sally Field, James Caan, Jeff Bridges, Claire Trevor, Paul Dooley

© FOXVIDEO 1217

KOTCH

PG | COM DMA | 1971 | COLOR

D: Jack Lemmon — 114 m

9 Totally charming comedy about an old coot who keeps getting in the way living at his son's house, so they put him in an old age home. However he can't stand it there so he runs away and rents a small house to live in by himself. He befriends the pregnant young girl who used to babysit for his grandson and who has run away from home after being deserted by both her family and the baby's father. So, Kotch takes her into his little house and they take care of each other. This is a truly winning and heart-warming story, with a terrific performance by Matthau for which he received an Oscar nomination. The film got three other nominations, too. Excellent.

◢ Sex | Nud | Viol | ◢ Lang | ■ AdSit

A: Walter Matthau, Deborah Winters, Felicia Farr, Ellen Geer, Charles Aidman, Lucy Saroyan

© MAGNETIC VIDEO 8008

LADY EVE, THE

NR | COM ROM | 1941 | B&W

D: Preston Sturges — 93 m

9 Truly entertaining romantic comedy from the '40s. Stanwyck is winning as a con artist who makes her living charming passengers on an ocean liner, all the while also cheating them at cards. She and her father think they have really hit paydirt in Henry Fonda. He is a wealthy and studious beer heir, who is just returning from a trip up the Amazon. She has him all set up for the kill, but then backs out because she's fallen for the guy. Too late, he has found her out and now wants no part of her. She must win him back. Fun.

Sex | Nud | Viol | Lang | ◢ AdSit

A: Barbara Stanwyck, Henry Fonda, Charles Coburn, William Demarest, Eugene Pallette, Eric Blore

© MCA/UNIVERSAL HOME VIDEO, INC. 80353

LADY FOR A DAY

NR | COM | 1933 | B&W

D: Frank Capra — 96 m

8 Sentimental Frank Capra favorite about a seedy old woman who is given another chance. This old woman has pampered her daughter by spending all her money to keep her in a boarding school abroad and allowed the girl think that she is wealthy. But now the daughter is about to find out the truth - that the old woman is just a peddlerwoman who sells apples on the street. However, when Dude, a sentimental gambler hears of the old woman's plight, he pays to have her transformed into a real lady - for a day. This film was remade by Capra again as POCKETFUL OF MIRACLES in 1961 with Glenn Ford and Bette Davis.

Sex | Nud | Viol | Lang | ◢ AdSit

A: Warren William, May Robson, Guy Kibbee, Glenda Farrell, Jean Parker, Walter Connolly

© CONNOISSEUR VIDEO COLLECTION 1050

LEMON DROP KID, THE

NR | COM | 1951 | B&W

D: Sidney Lanfield — 91 m

7 Enjoyable fast-paced Bob Hope comedy that rises above his typical fare. In a take-off from a Damon Runyon story, Hope plays a horse track fanatic who gives a hood (Lloyd Nolan) some bad advice. When the guy loses his money, he gives Hope a month to get the money back. Every scheme Hope tries backfires, including claiming to collect money for a fake old folks home by being a phony Santa Claus. Entertaining.

Sex | Nud | Viol | Lang | AdSit

A: Bob Hope, Marilyn Maxwell, Lloyd Nolan, Jane Darwell, Fred Clark

© COLUMBIA TRISTAR HOME VIDEO 60743

LET'S DO IT AGAIN

PG | COM | 1975 | COLOR

D: Sidney Poitier — 113 m

8 Highly entertaining follow-up to UPTOWN SATURDAY NIGHT. Cosby and Poitier proved to be so popular as the larcenous lodge brothers that they decided to bring them back. This time they raise some money for their lodge by hypnotizing skinny Jimmy Walker and convincing him that he is a prize fighter. When he wins, the mob gets interested. A little silly, but a lot of fun, too.

Sex | Nud | Viol | ◢ Lang | ◢ AdSit

A: Sidney Poitier, Bill Cosby, Calvin Lockhart, John Amos, Jimmie C. Walker, Ossie Davis

© WARNER HOME VIDEO 11137

LIFE WITH FATHER

NR | COM | 1947 | COLOR

D: Michael Curtiz — 118 m

9 Warm and sentimental, charming Americana and witty too. These are the nostalgic remembrances of author Clarence Day of his own father as he grew up in N.Y.C. at the turn of the 20th-century. The story focuses on the foibles and travails of his eccentric Victorian father - a strict man of business who is considerably and constantly befuddled by his wife and his unruly family. Touching and beautifully photographed. Utterly delightful and consistently funny. Great family entertainment.

Sex | Nud | Viol | Lang | AdSit

A: William Powell, Irene Dunne, Elizabeth Taylor, Edmund Gwenn, ZaSu Pitts, Jimmy Lydon

© UNITED AMERICAN VIDEO CORP. 4096

LITTLE BIG LEAGUE

PG | COM | 1994 | COLOR

D: Andrew Scheinman — 120 m

8 Very well made family entertainment and you don't even need to like baseball to enjoy it - but if you do, you'll enjoy it even more. 12-year-old Billy is a baseball prodigy. He can't play any better than any other kid, but he knows everything there is to know about strategy. His grandpa owns the Minnesota Twins and when he dies, he leaves them to Billy. The Twins manager is sarcastic and derisive, and the team is losing. So, Billy fires the manager and hires himself. He revives many of the old plays from past days and teaches the team that having fun makes winners, but he is also soon overpowered by his place in a grownup world. Seems preposterous, but it really works.

Sex | Nud | Viol | Lang | ◢ AdSit

A: Luke Edwards, Ashley Crow, Timothy Busfield, Jason Robards, Jr., John Ashton, Kevin Dunn

© COLUMBIA TRISTAR HOME VIDEO 72833

LITTLE GIANTS

PG | COM CLD | 1994 | COLOR

D: Duwayne Dunham — 106 m

6 Silly sort of sports film, mostly for kids. It's in the same vein as MIGHTY DUCKS and BAD NEWS BEARS, but not as as good. Two brothers living in the small town of Urbania, Ohio couldn't be more different. O'Neill is a former All-American and Heisman Trophy winner who now runs an auto dealership, and Moranis is just an ordinary sort who has always felt overrun by his hero brother. So, when O'Neill excludes a bunch of young geeky kids from his pee-wee football team, Moranis forms them all (including his daughter) into another team and challenges his brother to a game -- with the winner to represent the town. Captures well the way kids act, but too many body-function jokes.

Sex | Nud | Viol | Lang | AdSit

A: Rick Moranis, Ed O'Neill, Brian Haley, Mary Ellen Trainor, Susanna Thompson, John Madden

© WARNER HOME VIDEO 16220

LITTLE MISS MARKER

D: Walter Bernstein 103 m

PG COM 1980 COLOR

8 Cute and winning Damon Runyon story set in the Depression. A charming little six-year-old girl was left with a crotchety bookie, named Sorrowful Jones (Walter Matthau), as security for payment on a bet. But when her father loses his bet and commits suicide, Sorrowful has a marker that he doesn't quite know how to handle. He doesn't know what to do with this kid and she is slowly melting his heart. So he asks his lady friend, a beautiful widow and socialite (Julie Andrews), for help. It gets a little slow-moving at times and is definitely very sentimental, but it is also great family entertainment.

Sex Nud Viol Lang AdSit

A: Walter Matthau, Julie Andrews, Bob Newhart, Lee Grant, Sara Stimson

© MCA/UNIVERSAL HOME VIDEO, INC. 55082

LOST IN YONKERS

D: Martha Coolidge 114 m

PG COM ROM DMA 1993 COLOR

8 Funny, touching and a real charmer from Neil Simon. Its 1942. Eddie is deep in debt from his dead wife's hospital expenses. His only chance is to leave his two boys behind in Yonkers with his stern mother and child-like sister, while he goes on the road for a year. Momma is a cold hard woman, but Aunt Bella is bubbly and full of life - even if her elevator doesn't quite make it to the top floor. Uncle Louie is a small-time hood who also comes to stay with Momma to hide out for a while. The two boys, Aunt Bella and Uncle Louie struggle to survive Momma's iron rule. Lots of clever dialogue from wonderfully drawn characters. Excellent.

Sex Nud Viol Lang ◢ AdSit

A: Richard Dreyfuss, Mercedes Ruehl, Irene Worth, David Strathairn, Brad Stoll, Mike Damus

© COLUMBIA TRISTAR HOME VIDEO 52663

LOVE AT FIRST BITE

D: Stan Dragoti 96 m

PG COM 1979 COLOR

8 A really good time. Funny, and more than a little silly, slapstick takeoff on the Dracula legend. Hamilton, as Dracula, finds himself evicted from his Transylvanian castle by the communists who want to make it into a gymnasium. So, he jets off to New York in search of his long lost love, now reborn as a fashion model who he saw on the front page of a magazine. Poor Drac, he is out of his element in New York. He even gets drunk on the blood of a wino. Even though her psychiatrist boyfriend tries to warn her, Drac's love still falls for the Count. So, the shrink becomes determined to save her. This is pretty heavy-handed slapstick humor but, hey, it's effective, and a lot of fun.

Sex Nud Viol ◢ Lang ◢ AdSit

A: George Hamilton, Susan St. James, Richard Benjamin, Dick Shawn, Arte Johnson, Sherman Hemsley

© WARNER HOME VIDEO 26009

LOVE BUG, THE

D: Robert Stevenson 108 m

G COM CLD 1969 COLOR

9 Delightful Disney and cute comedy that is not just for kids. When a second-rate race driver (Dean Jones) defends a little VW from its abusive owner's kicks, interesting things begin to happen. The bug, Herbie by name, takes a shine to him. So later, when he gets teamed up with Herbie, he starts to win races. He thinks he's doing it on his own, but he's wrong. You see, Herbie has a mind of its own - some other pretty special other talents too - and, he is using them all to help them both win races. Lots of slapstick, stunts and warm-hearted fun. This film's success led to three sequels, but the original is the best.

Sex Nud Viol Lang AdSit

A: Dean Jones, Michele Lee, Buddy Hackett, David Tomlinson, Joe Flynn

© WALT DISNEY HOME VIDEO 012

MAGIC TOWN

D: William Wellman 103 m

NR COM 1947 B&W

6 Jimmy Stewart has hit pay dirt. He is a struggling public opinion pollster who has stumbled upon a small American town, Grandview, that exactly mirrors the nation's tastes. Jane Wyman is a tough-minded newspaper editor in the small town who discovers his secret, and announces the find to the world, hoping to draw new business to her town. Instead, the town is nearly destroyed in a firestorm of media attention. Written by the same writer who Frank Capra used. Some of the results are very funny, but it's also a little corny.

Sex Nud Viol Lang ◢ AdSit

A: James Stewart, Jane Wyman, Regis Toomey, Kent Smith, Ned Sparks

© REPUBLIC PICTURES HOME VIDEO 2557

MAID TO ORDER

D: Amy Jones 92 m

PG COM 1987 COLOR

6 Slight but enjoyable little picture in which a spoiled little rich girl (Sheedy) gets a reverse-Cinderella treatment. Her chain-smoking fairy godmother takes away all her toys, her credit cards, even her identity and makes her penniless. She then is forced to take a position as a maid for spoiled rich people Valerie Perrine and Dick Shawn. Sheedy learns her lesson, meets her prince charming and gains some humility along the way.

Sex Nud Viol ◢ Lang AdSit

A: Ally Sheedy, Beverly D'Angelo, Dick Shawn, Michael Ontkean, Valerie Perrine, Tom Skerritt

© LIVE HOME VIDEO 64311

MANNEQUIN

D: Michael Gottlieb 90 m

PG COM FAN 1987 COLOR

6 Comedy with a fantasy twist. A struggling artist (McCarthy) gets by, by sculpting mannequins and dressing store windows. However, one of his creations is special - into it he has designed all his fantasy elements. Then something mystical happens. An Egyptian spirit (Cattrall) comes and takes over the plaster body, but only he can see her. If anyone else comes around, it's back to plaster. Still, he is now an instant success. Taylor is amusing as his effeminate partner. This is a simple-minded, check-your-brain-at-the-door kind of comedy. Take it for what it is.

Sex Nud Viol Lang ◢ AdSit

A: Andrew McCarthy, Kim Cattrall, Estelle Getty, James Spader, Meshach Taylor, Carole Davis

© VIDEO TREASURES M920

MAN WHO CAME TO DINNER, THE

D: William Keighley 113 m

NR COM 1941 B&W

8 Classic screwball comedy! A cocky radio celebrity with a quick wit and quicker tongue (Woolley) falls and breaks his leg, while at the house of the Stanleys. He is forced to stay with this quite ordinary mid-western family for the winter while he recovers, but in the process this obnoxious loudmouth drives them crazy with both his unending demands and the wide array of oddball friends that keep dropping in on them. Bette Davis is delightful as his secretary. Based on the Moss Hart/George Kaufman play, this wacky comedy is fun for the whole family.

Sex Nud Viol Lang ◢ AdSit

A: Monty Woolley, Bette Davis, Ann Sheridan, Billie Burke, Jimmy Durante, Richard Travis

Distributed By MGM/UA Home Video M201804

MATCHMAKER, THE

D: Joseph Anthony 110 m

NR COM ROM 1958 B&W

7 An endearing comedy. Shirley Booth stars as a crafty New York City matchmaker in the late 1800s. A wealthy widower and merchant (Ford) decides it is time to remarry, so he travels to New York to consult with a matchmaker for that purpose. There, he spies Shirley MacLaine and becomes intent on proposing his love to her. However, Shirley Booth has designs on him for herself and schemes to implement her plans. Any of this sound familiar? This is what later became the smash Broadway musical HELLO DOLLY.

Sex Nud Viol Lang ◢ AdSit

A: Shirley Booth, Anthony Perkins, Shirley MacLaine, Paul Ford, Robert Morse, Wallace Ford

© PARAMOUNT HOME VIDEO 5736

MATINEE

D: Joe Dante 99 m

PG COM 1993 COLOR

7 Sweet-natured and pleasant light entertainment that is meant to call up memories of another time. It is 1962 and master-promoter Lawrence Woolsey (Goodman) is about to personally launch his latest horror/monster movie. The movie is "Mant" (half man, half ant - all terror). The place is Key West, Florida just as the US Navy is heading out to enforce a blockade on Russian ships bound for Cuba. The world is terrorized by being on the brink of nuclear war; the patrons of the local theater are about to be terrorized by Mant; and, Gene (a 15-year-old horror movie fan) and his new girlfriend are locked together inside a bomb shelter in the theater's basement. Light-hearted.

Sex Nud Viol ◢ Lang AdSit

A: John Goodman, Cathy Moriarty, Simon Fenton, Omri Katz, Kellie Martin, Lisa Jakub

© MCA/UNIVERSAL HOME VIDEO, INC. 81481

MATING GAME, THE

D: George Marshall 96 m

NR COM ROM 1959 COLOR

8 Fast moving and fun sex romp. Tony Randall is a straight-laced IRS agent who descends upon an ornery farmer (Douglas) to see why he hasn't filed a tax return - ever. Tony does his best to pursue government business but the farmer's daughter (Reynolds) is doing her best to pursue him - and he's losing. Reynolds and Randall are both captivating in these fun roles from early in their careers.

Sex Nud Viol Lang ◢ AdSit

A: Debbie Reynolds, Tony Randall, Paul Douglas, Fred Clark, Una Merkel, Philip Ober

Distributed By MGM/UA Home Video 203048

MATTER OF PRINCIPLE, A

D: Gwen Arner 60 m

NR COM DMA 1984 COLOR

7 A lighthearted Scrooge-like Christmas story for everybody. The selfish and cantankerous father (Arkin) of a very large brood, ruins the family's Christmas when he decides he can't afford the expense. His wife (Dana) is fed up with his tyrannical behavior. She decides to take no more of it and leaves him, taking the kids. When he comes to realize that he might just have cost himself his family, he has a change of heart and comes to understand the true meaning of Christmas. Well done, a fun and entertaining holiday story.

Sex Nud Viol Lang ◢ AdSit

A: Alan Arkin, Barbara Dana, Tony Arkin

© ACADEMY ENTERTAINMENT 1065

MAX DUGAN RETURNS

D: Herbert Ross — 98 m

PG | COM | 1983 | COLOR | Rating: 9

A warm and winning little comedy from Neil Simon that will warm your heart and tickle your funnybone. An ex-con and gambler (Robards) decides to try to regain the love of his daughter (Mason) after having been gone 26 years. Mason is a widowed school teacher, barely surviving with her son (Broderick), and she isn't very excited about seeing him again. Still, Robards is determined and he has a suitcase of money - even if it isn't his - to buy her love. So, he buries her and his grandson in presents. Imagine the difficult time she has explaining this to her new policeman boyfriend (Sutherland).

☐ Sex ☐ Nud ☐ Viol ☑ Lang ☑ AdSit

A: Jason Robards, Jr., Marsha Mason, Donald Sutherland, Matthew Broderick, Dody Goodman, Sal Viscuso

© FOXVIDEO 1236

MEATBALLS

D: Ivan Reitman — 94 m

PG | COM | 1980 | COLOR | Rating: 7

Irreverent, very lightweight, summertime fun! Murray stars as the lunatic summer counselor who leads his troops against their rivals in the camp olympics, while he also pays special attention to building their egos and helping one especially quiet kid. But, he also takes time for romance with pretty Kate Lynch. His wacky behavior is surprisingly easy to take, despite his sometimes tacky antics. Over all, it is touching and even irresistible at times, if you're ready for major silliness.

☐ Sex ☑ Nud ☐ Viol ☑ Lang ☑ AdSit

A: Bill Murray, Harvey Atkin, Kate Lynch, Russ Banham, Kristine DeBell, Sarah Torgov

© PARAMOUNT HOME VIDEO 1324

MEET JOHN DOE

D: Frank Capra — 123 m

NR | COM DMA | 1941 | B&W | Rating: 8

Endearing and quite entertaining Capra corn. Barbara Stanwyck is a reporter who was just fired. As a last act of defiance, she creates a fictional hardluck character called John Doe to dramatize the hard times. Her man becomes such a hit that she gets her job back - except, there is no real John Doe. So, naive Gary Cooper is hired to become the man and is promoted into a national hero by her for the unscrupulous paper's owner, who has intentions to use Coop's endorsement in a run for the White House. Coop discovers the corrupt intentions and trys, against the huge publicity machine, to stop it.

☐ Sex ☐ Nud ☐ Viol ☐ Lang ☑ AdSit

A: Gary Cooper, Barbara Stanwyck, Edward Arnold, Walter Brennan, Spring Byington, James Gleason

© GOODTIMES 5-09326

MIDNIGHT

D: Mitchell Leisen — 94 m

NR | COM ROM | 1939 | B&W | Rating: 9

Marvelous sophisticated screwball comedy that is a must see for true film fans, but the ordinary video renter can have a good time with this one too. Claudette Colbert is a charming American gold-digger who just arrived penniless in Paris after having lost everything in Monte Carlo. There she meets and immediately falls for charming cab driver Don Ameche. But, she cannot let love get in her way. Running away, she crashes a very elegant party where she meets extravagantly wealthy John Barrymore. Mr. Barrymore immediately hires her to woo away a handsome nobleman whom his wife has fallen for. Claudette's boat has come in, but she's still in love with that cab driver.

☐ Sex ☐ Nud ☐ Viol ☐ Lang ☑ AdSit

A: Claudette Colbert, Don Ameche, John Barrymore, Frances Hederer, Mary Astor, Elaine Barrie

© MCA/UNIVERSAL HOME VIDEO, INC. 80831

MIGHTY DUCKS, THE

D: Stephen Herek — 103 m

PG | COM CLD | 1992 | COLOR | Rating: 8

Clever family fun. Estevez is a hotshot attorney who delights in humiliating his opponents - even the judges. So, when he is caught speeding once too often, they throw the book at him. However, he will be able to escape a jail sentence if he will perform community service. That is how he gets the job of coaching a kids's hockey team made up of inner-city misfits, called the Ducks. His anger and frustration at the situation soon give way to excitement over his successes with the team. The experience changes his attitude, helps the kids learn to play as a team and he also learns about love. Predictable, but a lot of fun anyway.

☐ Sex ☐ Nud ☑ Viol ☐ Lang ☐ AdSit

A: Emilio Estevez, Lane Smith, Joss Ackland, Heidi Kling

© WALT DISNEY HOME VIDEO 1585

MILKY WAY, THE

D: Leo McCarey — 88 m

NR | COM | 1936 | B&W | Rating: 6

Vintage comedy from silent film's master slapstick comedian - Harold Lloyd. An unassuming milkman (Lloyd) accidentally knocks out a drunken world champion boxer in a non-brawl. The champ's quick-witted promoter knows a good thing when he sees it and sets the milkman up to win a string of fixed fights. Pretty soon Lloyd starts to believe his own hype and gets cocky. Then it slowly starts to dawn on him that he is soon going to have to fight a real fight against the champ. Pretty good, but too bad time wasn't kinder to a comic legend. Remade as THE KID FROM BROOKLYN with Danny Kaye.

☐ Sex ☐ Nud ☐ Viol ☐ Lang ☐ AdSit

A: Harold Lloyd, Adolphe Menjou, Dorothy Wilson, Helen Mack

© VIDEO YESTERYEAR 1106

MIN AND BILL

D: George Roy Hill — 66 m

NR | COM DMA | 1930 | B&W | Rating: 6

Dressler and Beery are delightful in this sentimental story about Min, a scruffy old woman who runs a waterfront hotel, and her friend Bill. Min is raising an abandoned girl as her own and will do anything for the girl, including sacrificing her own happiness. But things get complicated for Min when officials want to take the girl away so she can have a "proper" home. Dressler won an Oscar for Best Actress for her outstanding performance. But, sadly, this film is pretty creaky now and so is recommended for film fans only.

☐ Sex ☐ Nud ☐ Viol ☐ Lang ☐ AdSit

A: Marie Dressler, Wallace Beery, Dorothy Jordan, Marjorie Rambeau, Frank McGlynn

Distributed By MGM/UA Home Video M300606

MISTER ROBERTS

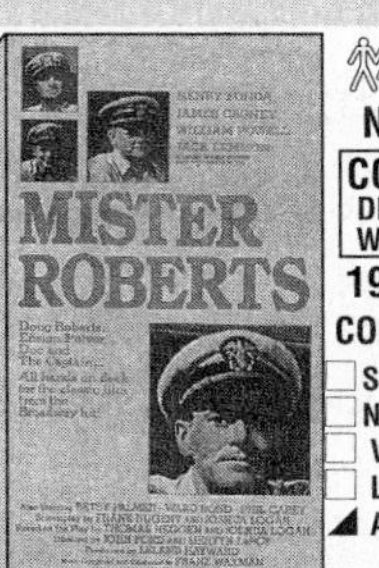

D: John Ford, Mervyn LeRoy — 123 m

NR | COM DMA WAR | 1955 | COLOR | Rating: 10

Great fun and a true gem! Trapped in the backwater of WWII, life aboard a Navy cargo ship in the South Pacific is boring, but it is made miserable because of the tyranny of the wacko captain (Cagney). However, through the intervention of the First Officer, Mr. Roberts (Fonda), and a never-ending series of practical jokes, it is made tolerable. Fonda longs to be part of the real shooting war, but Cagney won't let him go because it is only Fonda who keeps his nearly mutinous crew in line. Outstanding performances, particularly Lemmon (Oscar) as young Ensign Pulver in charge of laundry and morale. Terrific!

☐ Sex ☐ Nud ☐ Viol ☐ Lang ☑ AdSit

A: Henry Fonda, Jack Lemmon, James Cagney, Betsy Palmer, William Powell, Ward Bond

© WARNER HOME VIDEO 1017

MODERN TIMES

D: Charles Chaplin — 87 m

NR | COM | 1936 | B&W | Rating: 9

This mostly silent masterpiece about the pitfalls of a mechanized society is still beautifully contemporary! The poor Little Tramp suffers from the effects of a machine-induced nervous breakdown, a strike and a jail sentence, which all lead to even more problems. Unemployed, he joins up with a young orphaned girl and they go off together to seek happiness. Chaplin used only a bit of dialogue and sound effects, and wrote the musical score which included the song "Smile." This was the last time he used the Little Tramp, and this proved to be one of his most popular movies.

☐ Sex ☐ Nud ☐ Viol ☐ Lang ☑ AdSit

A: Charlie Chaplin, Paulette Goddard, Henry Bergman, Chester Conklin

© CBS/FOX VIDEO 3007

MONEY PIT, THE

D: Richard Benjamin — 91 m

PG | COM | 1986 | COLOR | Rating: 6

A yuppie couple faces yuppie ruin in this innocuous misadventure. An up-and-coming rock and roll lawyer (Hanks) falls in love with a musician (Long). Just to "cement" their relationship, they decide to buy a mansion and fix it up. What they get is a house that just keeps sucking up money. Everything breaks, falls, collapses, deteriorates or blows up. Silly Spielberg creation begins to lose contact with reality as the house continues to ruin their lives. Can be fun if you're in the right state of unconsciousness.

☐ Sex ☐ Nud ☑ Viol ☑ Lang ☐ AdSit

A: Tom Hanks, Shelley Long, Alexander Godunov, Maureen Stapleton, Joe Mantegna, Philip Bosco

© MCA/UNIVERSAL HOME VIDEO, INC. 80387

MONKEY BUSINESS

D: Norman McLeod — 77 m

NR | COM | 1931 | B&W | Rating: 9

Zany Marx Brothers classic! Those ridiculous brothers are at it again in perhaps their most energetic film. The four brothers stow away on a luxury ocean liner, chase women and wreak havoc with the captain and crew. While on board, Groucho and Zeppo are hired to protect one gangster and Chico and Harpo are hired to protect his rival. Side-splitting laughs are more than abundant in this happy Marx brothers comedy. Check out ANIMAL CRACKERS, DUCK SOUP and A NIGHT AT THE OPERA also.

☐ Sex ☐ Nud ☐ Viol ☐ Lang ☑ AdSit

A: Groucho Marx, Zeppo Marx, Chico Marx, Harpo Marx, Thelma Todd, Ruth Hall

© MCA/UNIVERSAL HOME VIDEO, INC. 80172

MONKEY BUSINESS

D: Howard Hawks — 97 m

NR | COM | 1952 | B&W | Rating: 7

Non-stop fun in this screwball comedy! A scientist (Grant) conducts experiments regenerating human tissue hoping to find a recipe for a youth elixir. However one of his chimpanzees mixes up a successful concoction and dumps it into the water cooler. When Grant and his wife (Rogers) take a drink, they revert back to being adolescent in their antics and attitudes. Soon his absent-minded secretary (Monroe) and his boss (Coburn) join into the teenage mindset. A charming bunch of silliness.

☐ Sex ☐ Nud ☐ Viol ☐ Lang ☐ AdSit

A: Cary Grant, Ginger Rogers, Marilyn Monroe, Charles Coburn, Hugh Marlowe

© FOXVIDEO 5140

MORE THE MERRIER, THE

D: George Stevens 104 m

NR | COM ROM | 1943 | B&W

Sex / Nud / Viol / Lang / ◢ AdSit

8 Effervescent romantic comedy that was very popular then, and still is a whole lot of fun. When a housing shortage develops during WWII, a young working woman (Arthur) living in Washington D.C. rents out a room to an older man (Coburn) who ends up playing Cupid for her. Concerned with her lack of a love life, Coburn rents out half of his room to a handsome Air Force mechanic (McCrea), and romance blooms. Coburn won an Oscar for his crusty old salt-of-the-earth portrayal. This sparkling film was nominated for six Academy Awards. Remade into WALK DON'T RUN with Cary Grant.

A: Jean Arthur, Joel McCrea, Charles Coburn, Richard Gaines

© COLUMBIA TRISTAR HOME VIDEO 71943

MOTHER, JUGS & SPEED

D: Peter Yates 98 m

PG | COM | 1976 | COLOR

Sex / Nud / Viol / ◢ Lang / ◢ AdSit

6 This is black comedy (in a sort of MASH vein) that is better that its title would indicate. The three primary characters are Cosby, Welch and Keitel. They are all drivers for a run-down ambulance company that is more concerned with the number of patients they see each day than the patient's health. Keitel is an ex-cop with a mixed past. Cosby is a free-wheeling driver and Welch is a dispatcher, studying nights to become a driver. Hagman is a show stopper as a driver with sex forever on his mind. They respond to call after call. Many are funny but some aren't. Not bad overall.

A: Bill Cosby, Raquel Welch, Larry Hagman, Harvey Keitel, Allen Garfield

© FOXVIDEO 1698

MOUSE THAT ROARED, THE

D: Jack Arnold 83 m

NR | COM | 1959 | COLOR

Sex / Nud / Viol / Lang / ◢ AdSit

8 Hilarious Sellers comedic satire. Grand Fenwick, a very, very small country - the smallest on earth - declares war on the United States because they hope to be defeated so they may collect foreign aid to rebuild their treasury. But when Sellers invades New York and captures an inventor of "the bomb" along with a sample bomb, they win and the US surrenders. Peter Sellers is masterful in this extravagant farce. He plays three separate roles to the hilt, each one severely lacking in brain power.

A: Peter Sellers, Jean Seberg, David Kossoff, William Hartnell, Monty Landis, Leo McKern

© COLUMBIA TRISTAR HOME VIDEO 60062

MR. AND MRS. SMITH

D: Alfred Hitchcock 95 m

NR | COM ROM | 1941 | B&W

Sex / Nud / Viol / Lang / ◢ AdSit

7 Very unusual Hitchcock flick - a screwball comedy. A devoted but argumentative couple (Lombard and Montgomery) find that after having been married three years, their marriage is not technically legal and it is now null and void. So, Lombard throws her hubby out of the house so that both can enjoy their new freedom. He moves into the club. Meanwhile, his law partner (Raymond) trys to pursue his wife, er... ex-wife, ah.. girlfriend. This vintage and endearing comedy produced fine performances, but undeservedly went largely unnoticed at the time of its release.

A: Carole Lombard, Robert Montgomery, Gene Raymond, Jack Carson, Philip Merivale, Betty Compson

© TURNER HOME ENTERTAINMENT 6018

MR. BLANDINGS BUILDS HIS DREAM HOUSE

D: H.C. Potter 94 m

NR | COM | 1948 | B&W

Sex / Nud / Viol / Lang / ◢ AdSit

8 Comic catastrophies abound when a New York City ad executive (Grant) gets sick of city life in his tiny apartment. He and his wife (Loy) decide to chuck it all to purchase their dream house in Connecticut. And a lovely old place it is, too... except that it's so dilapidated that they have tear it down and start from scratch, and a whole new can of comic worms is opened. Grant is his endearing self, and Loy is excellent as his patient and understanding wife. This very familiar theme will really hit home with many new homeowners, regardless of its age. See this one first - before you build!

A: Cary Grant, Myrna Loy, Melvyn Douglas, Reginald Denny, Sharyn Moffett, Connie Marshall

© TURNER HOME ENTERTAINMENT 6007

MR. DEEDS GOES TO TOWN

D: Frank Capra 115 m

NR | COM ROM | 1936 | B&W

Sex / Nud / Viol / Lang / AdSit

7 Charming vintage comedy! A simple, straight arrow, model citizen, Longfellow Deeds (Cooper) has his world shaken up when he inherits $20 million. He moves from his humble home into a New York City mansion, but he quickly concludes that the money has brought him more trouble than it's worth. So he decides he wants to give it all to struggling farmers. But, because of his highly unconventional attitude, he is first forced to stand trial to prove that he is not insane or "pixilated." Capra won an Academy Award in this film that proves money doesn't always buy happiness.

A: Gary Cooper, Jean Arthur, George Bancroft, Lionel Stander, Douglas Dumbrille, Mayo Methot

© COLUMBIA TRISTAR HOME VIDEO 90143

MR. LUCKY

D: H.C. Potter 100 m

NR | COM ROM | 1943 | B&W

Sex / Nud / Viol / Lang / ◢ AdSit

7 It's WWII and Cary Grant is a scoundrel. He is the owner of gambling ship who is trying to do two things: first, avoid the draft and second, steal all the proceeds from a charity ball for War Relief and head off to South America with the money. But his plans go severely awry when his partner steals the loot first and what's worse, Cary starts to fall for the pretty socialite (Day) he is trying to con. So, contrary to his nature, he falls in love, recovers the money and goes straight. Grant's magical performance makes it lots of fun. The film was later made into a TV series.

A: Cary Grant, Laraine Day, Charles Bickford, Gladys Cooper, Alan Carney, Henry Stephenson

© TURNER HOME ENTERTAINMENT 6011

MR. MOM

D: Stan Dragoti 90 m

PG | COM | 1983 | COLOR

Sex / Nud / Viol / ◢ Lang / ◢ AdSit

8 Hilarious flip-flop on the traditional American way of life. When a Detroit engineer (Keaton) loses his job and his wife (Garr) gets a high paying job with an advertising agency, they do the obvious thing: she goes to work and he stays home. This role reversal forces Keaton into some unfamiliar territory in dealing with the perils of running a household: the housework, the kids and a neighbor who wants to seduce him. How does he cope? He turns to alcohol and soap operas. Some really very funny moments happen when a traditional man gets out of his element.

A: Michael Keaton, Teri Garr, Martin Mull, Ann Jillian, Christopher Lloyd, Frederick Koehler

© LIVE HOME VIDEO 5025

MR. NORTH

D: Danny Huston 90 m

PG | COM FAN | 1988 | COLOR

Sex / Nud / Viol / Lang / ◢ AdSit

6 Whimsical fantasy. A bright young Yale graduate (Edwards) arrives amid the upper-class society of Newport, R.I. of the 1920s. He is, it seems, endowed with magical healing powers. His body has an unusual amount of electricity and he can heal merely by touching. He begins to make a name for himself curing the wealthy sick and charming them, too, until the local medical community takes him to court. Based on Thornton Wilder's "Theophilus North," directed by John Huston's son with help from Dad before he died. Feel-good theme, but its very fanciful style might not be for all.

A: Anthony Edwards, Robert Mitchum, Harry Dean Stanton, Anjelica Huston, Mary Stuart Masterson, Virginia Madsen

© MCEG/STERLING 70075

MR. PEABODY AND THE MERMAID

D: Irving Pichel 89 m

NR | COM FAN | 1948 | B&W

Sex / Nud / Viol / Lang / ◢ AdSit

6 Fanciful comedy! A married man (Powell) who is just about to turn 50 and going through a mid-life crisis is fishing in the Caribbean where he hooks a very big fish - a beautiful mermaid (Ann Blyth) to be exact. Absolutely infatuated with her, he takes her home and sticks her in his swimming pool. Unfortunately, his wife doesn't see the charm, and you can predict the results. Very much like SPLASH, only in a 1940s sort of way.

A: William Powell, Ann Blyth, Irene Hervey, Andrea King, Clinton Sundberg

© REPUBLIC PICTURES HOME VIDEO 2819

MR. WINKLE GOES TO WAR

D: Alfred E. Green 80 m

NR | COM WAR | 1944 | B&W

Sex / Nud / Viol / Lang / ◢ AdSit

6 Mr. Winkle (Robinson) is an aging, shy, weak-willed and henpecked bank clerk who mistakenly gets drafted during WWII. However, he surprises everyone when he passes the physical and sets off to basic training with the rest of the draftees. He even survives the grueling days of hard work and abusive sergeants that are meant for much younger men, and is sent to the South Pacific. There, he puts his skills to use and he surprises even himself by emerging as a hero. Although somewhat dated, it is still fun and the acting is excellent. This film was produced to aid the war effort.

A: Edward G. Robinson, Ruth Warrick, Richard Lane, Robert Armstrong

© COLUMBIA TRISTAR HOME VIDEO 60533

MUPPET MOVIE, THE

D: James Frawley 96 m

G | COM CLD MUS | 1979 | COLOR

Sex / Nud / Viol / Lang / AdSit

8 Effervescent silliness, and some really baaaad puns, make this a delight for everyone. Kids like it because it is light-hearted and silly. Adults get their own special treats - such as when Dom DeLuise interrupts Kermit who's catching flys in the swamp. Dom tells Kermit that he is lost and in a big hurry because he has to "catch a plane." Kermit responds with "Not with a tongue like yours." Irresistable zaniness as the Muppets travel to Hollywood so that they can become movie stars. 15 cameo appearances from some big stars. See also THE MUPPETS TAKE MANHATTEN.

A: Muppets, Milton Berle, Mel Brooks, Steve Martin, Bob Hope, Edgar Bergen

© CBS/FOX VIDEO 9001

MUPPETS TAKE MANHATTAN, THE

D: Frank Oz — 94 m

G | COM | CLD | 1984 | COLOR

8 The Muppets return. After Kermit and his friends create a hit college show, they decide that they are ready for the big time... Broadway. Off they head for the Big Apple where they get taken in by a shyster lawyer. They're so broke they live in lockers at the bus station, Kermit gets amnesia on his way to his wedding to Miss Piggy. Muppet madness, and a wide selection of cameo appearances from some of the industry's biggest names, is again at the heart of this extravaganza in silliness.

Sex / Nud / Viol / Lang / AdSit

A: Art Carney, James Coco, Dabney Coleman, Elliott Gould, Joan Rivers, Linda Lavin

© CBS/FOX VIDEO 6731

MY BODYGUARD

D: Tony Bill — 96 m

PG | COM | DMA | 1980 | COLOR

8 This is a winning and very likable charmer that will give everyone smiles. Clifford Peache (Makepeace) is a boy who has attended an exclusive private school for nine years, but now he is enrolled in a Chicago public high school, and that's a whole different world. The school is run by a gang of teenage thugs, lead by Dillon, who extort money from their classmates. But Clifford finds a unique solution. He hires Baldwin, a menacing older student, to protect him. However, their strictly-business relationship turns into a warm friendship with some surprises. A very funny and heartwarming movie.

Sex / Nud / Viol / Lang / AdSit

A: Matt Dillon, Chris Makepeace, Adam Baldwin, Ruth Gordon, Matt Dillon, John Houseman

© FOXVIDEO 1111

MY FAVORITE BRUNETTE

D: Elliott Nugent — 85 m

NR | COM | MYS | 1947 | B&W

7 Comic misadventures in this Hope spoof, probably one of his very best, after PALEFACE. A baby photographer (Hope) is mistakenly identified by beautiful Lamour as a private eye, and she hires him to search for her missing uncle. She gives him a map that he is to protect with his life. He then goes to the estate of a supposed friend of the uncle's, only to find a man there who claims that he is the uncle and that the woman is nuts. Hope is obviously in over his head, but that won't stop him. Lots of predictable shtick, but a good time. Lorre is particularly good in a parody of himself.

Sex / Nud / Viol / Lang / AdSit

A: Bob Hope, Dorothy Lamour, Peter Lorre, Lon Chaney, Jr., John Hoyt

© GOODTIMES 5024

FAMILY

MY MAN GODFREY

D: Gregory LaCava — 90 m

NR | COM | ROM | 1936 | B&W

9 Hilarious classic, acclaimed as the first screwball comedy. A society scavenger hunt is in full swing, and Lombard finds the "bum" she needs at the dump. He (Powell) is a down-on-his-luck former blueblood and when back at the party, he spouts off - calling everyone there insensitive nitwits. She loves it and offers him a job as her butler. He takes the job, but after suffering numerous insults from her dizzy mother, her gigolo-in-waiting and her snobbish sister, he's had enough - but wait, they're in love. This Depression-era film knocked the rich and the masses loved it. Nominated for six Oscars.

Sex / Nud / Viol / Lang / AdSit

A: William Powell, Carole Lombard, Gail Patrick, Alice Brady, Eugene Pallette, Mischa Auer

© GOODTIMES 5002

NATIONAL LAMPOON'S CHRISTMAS VACATION

D: Jeremiah S. Chechik — 97 m

PG-13 | COM | 1989 | COLOR

7 Crazy, wacky, zany, and also the source for some very big laughs for fans of Chevy Chase's brand of crazy, wacky, zany slapstick. Clark Griswold (Chase) is a hapless family man who decides to spend the holiday vacation at home and have the relatives come to visit him. What a mess! Relatives bicker, create chaos and generally drive everyone nuts. Randy Quaid is one of those relatives who is in for the holidays and he is the quintessential slob. Predictable and not at all highbrow humor, but still a amusing good time.

Sex / Nud / Viol / Lang / AdSit

A: Chevy Chase, Beverly D'Angelo, Randy Quaid, John Randolph, Diane Ladd, E.G. Marshall

© WARNER HOME VIDEO 11889

NEW LEAF, A

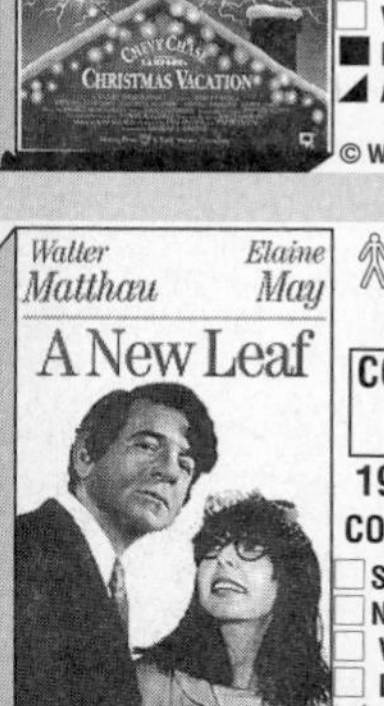

D: Elaine May — 102 m

G | COM | 1971 | COLOR

6 Light comedy that is mildly entertaining. Elaine May wrote, directed and starred in this screwball-type comedy. She plays a very rich, but clumsy, bumbling and frumpy botanist who is in search of a plant that will create immortality. Walter Matthau plays an aging playboy who has just about run out of money and is in search of a new meal ticket.

Sex / Nud / Viol / Lang / AdSit

A: Walter Matthau, Elaine May, Jack Weston, James Coco, George Rose, William Redfield

© PARAMOUNT HOME VIDEO 8007

NIGHT AT THE OPERA

D: Sam Wood — 92 m

NR | COM | 1935 | B&W

9 Lunacy reigns. This film has more structure than DUCK SOUP, which preceeded it, and allows those viewers uninitiated to the utter ridiculousness of the Marx Brothers the opportunity to follow the action a little better. Groucho plays a shyster who woos Margaret Dumont and convinces her to invest $200,000 in the opera so she can become a member of high society. Harpo and Chico play cupid to singers Allan Jones and Kitty Carlisle. Together they create a night of total insanity in the world of opera. Probably their best effort.

Sex / Nud / Viol / Lang / AdSit

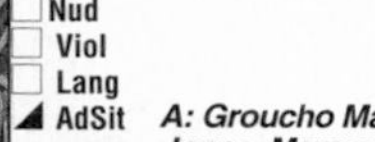
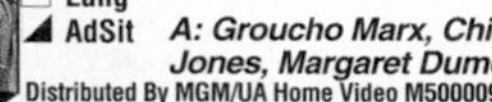

A: Groucho Marx, Chico Marx, Harpo Marx, Kitty Carlisle, Allan Jones, Margaret Dumont

Distributed By MGM/UA Home Video M500009

NIGHT THEY RAIDED MINSKY'S, THE

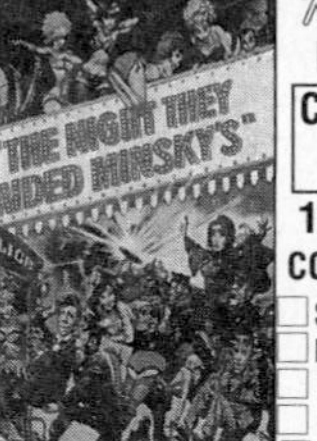

D: William Friedkin — 990 m

PG | COM | 1968 | COLOR

7 Cute and flavorful depiction of the story of striptease in burlesque. Britt Ekland is a naive Amish girl who has come to the big city to dance on Broadway. Instead, she ends up stripping and falling in love with a vaudeville comic (Robards) - much to the embarrassment and disdain of her very proper father. Some funny situations, but mostly the film provides an interesting look at what vaudeville and burlesque were actually like (it wasn't just strippers), and contains a lot of the racy humor that they were known for. There are several intact burlesque comedy skits.

Sex / Nud / Viol / Lang / AdSit

A: Jason Robards, Jr., Britt Ekland, Norman Wisdom, Forrest Tucker, Harry Andrews, Joseph Wiseman

Distributed By MGM/UA Home Video M202363

NOTHING SACRED

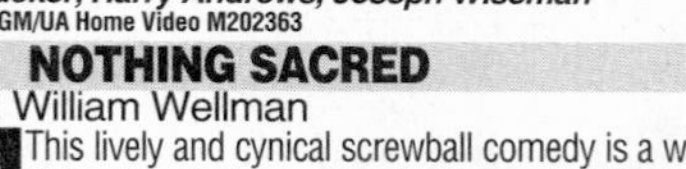

D: William Wellman — 75 m

NR | COM | 1937 | COLOR

8 This lively and cynical screwball comedy is a winner. Lombard is at her funniest as a simple Vermont girl whose quack doctor diagnoses her as dying of radium poisoning. A cynical hotshot New York reporter (March), working for a sensationalist paper, exploits her imminent death in a series of pathetic stories which turn her into a national hero. Then she finds out that she isn't really dying. She wants to tell the truth - but no one will let her. Still works. Hilarious.

Sex / Nud / Viol / Lang / AdSit

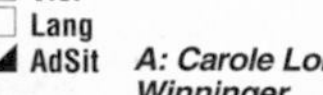
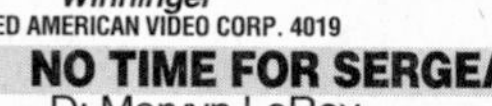

A: Carole Lombard, Fredric March, Walter Connolly, Charles Winninger

© UNITED AMERICAN VIDEO CORP. 4019

NO TIME FOR SERGEANTS

D: Mervyn LeRoy — 119 m

NR | COM | 1958 | B&W

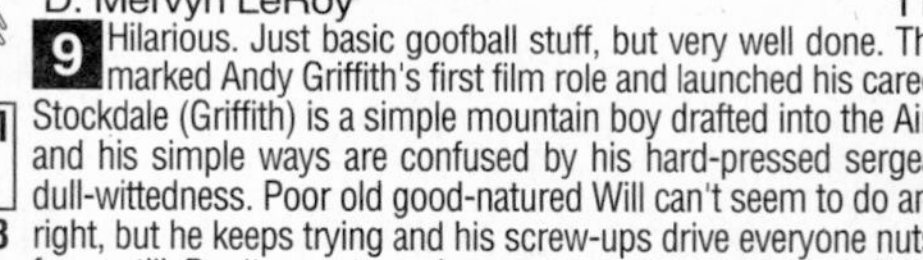

9 Hilarious. Just basic goofball stuff, but very well done. This film marked Andy Griffith's first film role and launched his career. Will Stockdale (Griffith) is a simple mountain boy drafted into the Air Force and his simple ways are confused by his hard-pressed sergeant for dull-wittedness. Poor old good-natured Will can't seem to do anything right, but he keeps trying and his screw-ups drive everyone nuts. Very funny still. Don't expect any deep message, just a reeeal good time.

Sex / Nud / Viol / Lang / AdSit

A: Andy Griffith, Myron McCormick, Nick Adams, Murray Hamilton, Don Knotts, Ed Begley

© WARNER HOME VIDEO 11195

NUTTY PROFESSOR, THE

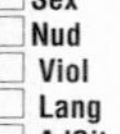

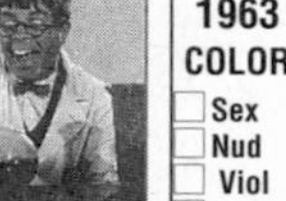

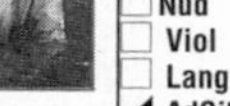

D: Jerry Lewis — 107 m

NR | COM | 1963 | COLOR

8 Jerry Lewis's most popular film. He directs himself in dual roles as the Jekyll and Hyde personalities hidden inside a super-shy, goofy-looking nerd of a college professor. Yearning for the love of beautiful student Stella Stevens, the professor creates a secret formula in his college lab which transforms the nerd into a suave but callous lady-killer (strangely similar in a cynical way, to his ex-partner, Dean Martin). Problems develop when the formula wears off at inopportune times.

Sex / Nud / Viol / Lang / AdSit

A: Jerry Lewis, Stella Stevens, Henry Gibson, Del Moore, Kathleen Freeman, Ned Flory

© PARAMOUNT HOME VIDEO 6712

ODD COUPLE, THE

D: Gene Saks — 106 m

G | COM | 1968 | COLOR

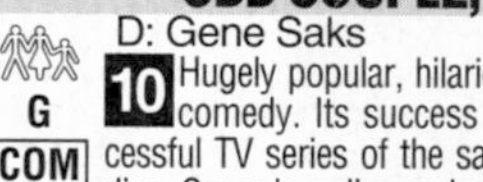

10 Hugely popular, hilarious film that was taken from a Neil Simon comedy. Its success also launched a long-lived and very successful TV series of the same name. Felix and Oscar are poker buddies. Oscar is a divorced sportswriter and a slob of epic proportions. Felix is thrown out of his house and his marriage by his wife because of his obsessive neatness and quirky personality. Taking pity on Felix, Oscar lets him move in - creating a situation ripe with hilarious possibilities, none of which are missed. High quality everything. A scream!

Sex / Nud / Viol / Lang / AdSit

A: Jack Lemmon, Walter Matthau, John Fiedler, Herb Edelman, Monica Evans, Carole Shelley

© PARAMOUNT HOME VIDEO 8026

OH, GOD!

D: Carl Reiner — 98 m

PG | COM FAN | 1977 | COLOR

Sex | Nud | Viol | Lang | AdSit

10 Wonderfully charming - and almost believable - story in which God creates a modern-day Moses in the form of a mild-mannered supermarket manager. George Burns is nearly perfect as God - or, at least, his version of God is one that is very appealing. John Denver is the manager, incredulous at his misfortune for having been chosen for such an unenviable job. However, everyone just thinks he is crazy and no one believes him.If God ever did come - this is exactly what you could expect the reaction to be. Inspired casting all around. Great entertainment!

A: George Burns, John Denver, Teri Garr, Paul Sorvino, Ralph Bellamy, George Furth

© WARNER HOME VIDEO 1010

ONE, TWO, THREE

D: Billy Wilder — 110 m

NR | COM | 1961 | B&W

Sex | Nud | Viol | Lang | ◢ AdSit

8 Winning fast-paced comedy that was James Cagney's last screen performance (until RAGTIME in 1981). He plays the manager of the Coca-Cola plant in West Berlin. He is in the middle of a promotional campaign when a state-side exec sends his empty-headed daughter to visit Germany and asks Cagney to look after her. All hell breaks loose when she slips over into East Germany and falls in love with a card-carrying, ardent Communist. And now there is a brand new little Commie on the way. Very funny.

A: James Cagney, Horst Buchholz, Arlene Francis, Pamela Tiffin, Hans Lothar, Lilo Pulver

Distributed By MGM/UA Home Video M600882

OPERATION PETTICOAT

D: Blake Edwards — 120 m

NR | COM ROM | 1959 | COLOR

Sex | Nud | Viol | Lang | ◢ AdSit

9 Hilarious and very popular comedy. Cary Grant is the captain of an unfortunate submarine which is beset by a never-ending series of embarrassing and very funny misfortunes in the South Pacific during World War II. The problems only begin when the sub must go to sea with the boat's paint job incomplete, leaving it pink. The problems are further compounded when first officer Curtis, a smooth-talking con man, squeezes five beautiful nurses into the sub. The stage is now set for some of Hollywood's biggest talents to work their comedic magic, and they do. Really funny. A great time.

A: Cary Grant, Tony Curtis, Gene Evans, Dina Merrill, Arthur O'Connell, Gavin MacLeod

© REPUBLIC PICTURES HOME VIDEO 5405

OUR HOSPITALITY

D: Buster Keaton — 75 m

NR | COM | 1923 | B&W

Sex | Nud | Viol | Lang | ◢ AdSit

8 Very highly regarded early comedy. One of Keaton's very best. He stars as a hapless son who returns to the South to claim his family inheritance. He falls in love with a beautiful local girl, only to discover that she is the daughter of a family that has an ancient feud with his. When her brothers find out who he is, they are determined to devise a way to kill their dinner guest without breaking the laws of Southern hospitality. Revered because its clever observations of the human condition are used for the source of much of the comedy, in addition to the hair-raising sight gags.

A: Buster Keaton, Natalie Talmadge, Joe Keaton, Buster Keaton, Kitty Bradbury, Joe Roberts

© HBO VIDEO 0281

OUTLAW BLUES

D: Richard T. Heffron — 101 m

PG | COM | 1977 | COLOR

Sex | Nud | Viol | ◢ Lang | ◢ AdSit

7 Light-weight little comedy about a struggling country music song writer and ex-con (Fonda) who becomes a national folk hero. Years earlier he had one of his songs stolen from him. It then became a big hit and it made the thief (Callahan) famous. Now, in a confrontation with Callahan, Fonda accidentally shoots him and becomes the focus of statewide manhunt. His backup singer (Susan St. James) helps him hide out on the run, while she promotes his new song into a big hit for him. Pleasant and appealing no-brainer.

A: Peter Fonda, Susan St. James, James Callahan, John Crawford

© WARNER HOME VIDEO 11146

OVERBOARD

D: Garry Marshall — 112 m

PG | COM ROM | 1987 | COLOR

Sex | Nud | Viol | ◢ Lang | ◢ AdSit

8 Clever, light-weight entertainment. Goldie Hawn is a spoiled and arrogant heiress who refuses to pay a carpenter (Russell) for a job. When he sees on the evening news that she has been found suffering from total amnesia, floating in the ocean (she fell from her yacht) - he sees a way both to get even with her and find a much-needed mother for his untamed kids. So he claims her from the authorities as his wife, and she - confused and not knowing any better - sets about taking up her new chores as mother. Good-natured and fun.

A: Goldie Hawn, Kurt Russell, Katherine Helmond, Edward Herrmann, Roddy McDowall, Michael Haggerty

Distributed By MGM/UA Home Video M201197

PALEFACE, THE

D: Norman McLeod — 91 m

NR | COM WST | 1948 | COLOR

Sex | Nud | Viol | Lang | AdSit

8 Amiable spoof of the classic Western THE VIRGINIAN. Cowardly Bob Hope is a charlatan traveling dentist but he has allowed himself to be presented as a celebrated gunslinger. However, he is getting shooting assistance from his sharpshooting new wife, Calamity Jane (Russell). Jane, you see, is also a secret government agent who has seduced Hope so that she can go undercover with him to expose a group selling guns to the Indians. Good script, with lots of wild parodies of Western movie cliches and a hit song: "Buttons and Bows." Probably Hope's best movie performance. Certainly his biggest box office success.

A: Bob Hope, Jane Russell, Robert Armstrong, Iris Adrian, Robert Watson, Iron Eyes Cody

© MCA/UNIVERSAL HOME VIDEO, INC. 80106

PAPA'S DELICATE CONDITION

D: George Marshall — 98 m

NR | COM DMA | 1963 | COLOR

Sex | Nud | Viol | Lang | ◢ AdSit

7 Pleasant light-hearted drama set in turn-of-the-century Texas. The setting evokes nostalgic feelings for a time past and the mood is light-hearted, but the subject has a serious overtone. Papa (Jackie Gleason) is a fun-loving railroader and the apple of his daughter's eye, but he is also a drunk and an embarrassment to his wife (Glynnis Johns). One day she packs up the kids and walks out. Gleason is quite charming in this enjoyable little story that also won an Oscar for Best Song: "Call Me Irresponsible."

A: Jackie Gleason, Glynis Johns, Charlie Ruggles, Laurel Goodwin, Charles Lane, Elisha Cook, Jr.

© PARAMOUNT HOME VIDEO 6212

PAPER MOON

D: Peter Bogdanovich — 102 m

PG | COM | 1973 | B&W

Sex | Nud | ◢ Viol | ◢ Lang | ◢ AdSit

9 Heart-warming and totally captivating story of a 1930s con-man (O'Neal) who agrees to drive the precocious, charming and worldly-wise 9-year-old daughter (his real-life daughter Tatum) of a dead former "girlfriend" to her aunt in Missouri. Along the way, he poses as a door-to-door Bible salesman and he is pleased to find that his cigarette-smoking young charge is very adept at helping him to charm widows out of their money. She's a natural. They are a happy family until they are joined by a wacky carny stripper (Kahn). A very colorful and funny film that is great fun, with loveable characters.

A: Ryan O'Neal, Tatum O'Neal, Madeline Kahn, John Hillerman, P.J. Johnson, Randy Quaid

© PARAMOUNT HOME VIDEO 8465

PARENT TRAP, THE

D: David Swift — 129 m

NR | COM CLD | 1961 | COLOR

Sex | Nud | Viol | Lang | AdSit

9 Hugely popular Disney hit for the whole family. A prissy teenage girl from Boston runs into her spitting image in the form of a tomboy from California, at summer camp. The two mix like oil and water, at first. However, when they begin to compare notes, they discover that they are identical twins separated when their parents had divorced years before. Mom went east and Dad went west. The two decide to switch places at summer's end so each can meet the other parent and to begin a conspiracy designed to bring their still single parents back together again. Good fun for everyone. Hayley Mills is delightful.

A: Hayley Mills, Maureen O'Hara, Brian Keith, Charlie Ruggles, Leo G. Carroll, Joanna Barnes

© WALT DISNEY HOME VIDEO 107

PARTY, THE

D: Blake Edwards — 99 m

NR | COM | 1968 | COLOR

Sex | Nud | Viol | Lang | ◢ AdSit

7 Hysterical sight gags frequent one of Peter Sellers's best (some think his best) and funniest work. You do, however, need to be a fan of absolute silliness. He plays a bumbling, dense actor who accidentally destroys an entire movie set, and he is fired for it. However, he is also mistakenly invited to a lavish party that evening at the director's extravagant house, and he wanders through the party inadvertently creating havoc wherever he goes. The movie begins to fall apart during the last third, but still great fun.

A: Peter Sellers, Claudine Longet, Marge Champion, Denny Miller, Gavin MacLeod

Distributed By MGM/UA Home Video M201584

PAT AND MIKE

D: George Cukor — 96 m

NR | COM ROM | 1952 | B&W

Sex | Nud | Viol | Lang | AdSit

6 Pleasing seventh pairing of Tracy and Hepburn. Hepburn plays Pat, a college gym teacher and a top-notch female athlete, who is convinced by Tracy to turn pro and allow him to become her manager and promoter. Tracy's done a shady deal with an underworld character and it's causing him about as much grief as his blossoming personal relationship with her. And, their relationship also creates a problem for her with her fiance. Oscar-nominated script and great chemistry make it enjoyable, but it is one of their lesser successes.

A: Katharine Hepburn, Spencer Tracy, Jim Backus, Charles Bronson, Chuck Connors

Distributed By MGM/UA Home Video M301269

PHILADELPHIA STORY, THE

D: George Cukor — 112 m

NR | COM ROM | 1940 | B&W

9 Scintillating comedy - still one of Hollywood's best. Hepburn is perfect as a spoiled socialite getting married for the second time - this time to a stuffed shirt. Her suave first husband (Grant), who she divorced because he drank, still loves her. He arrives at the wedding early with two gossip reporters, having made a deal to prevent them from publishing a nasty article about her father. Stewart won an Oscar as the reporter who falls in love with her and teaches her what love is. Witty rapid-fire dialogue. Nominated for five Oscars, including Best Picture, winning two - Best Actor (Stewart) and Screenplay.

Sex / Nud / Viol / Lang / ◢ AdSit

A: Cary Grant, Katharine Hepburn, James Stewart, Ruth Hussey, John Halliday, Mary Nash

Distributed By MGM/UA Home Video M500059

PICKWICK PAPERS, THE

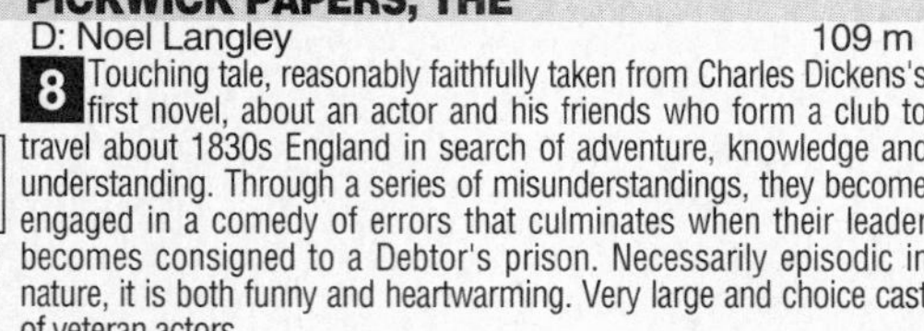

D: Noel Langley — 109 m

NR | COM DMA | 1952 | B&W

8 Touching tale, reasonably faithfully taken from Charles Dickens's first novel, about an actor and his friends who form a club to travel about 1830s England in search of adventure, knowledge and understanding. Through a series of misunderstandings, they become engaged in a comedy of errors that culminates when their leader becomes consigned to a Debtor's prison. Necessarily episodic in nature, it is both funny and heartwarming. Very large and choice cast of veteran actors.

Sex / Nud / Viol / Lang / ◢ AdSit

A: James Hayter, James Donald, Hermione Gingold, Kathleen Harrison

© VIDEO COMMUNICATIONS, INC. 1081

PINK PANTHER, THE

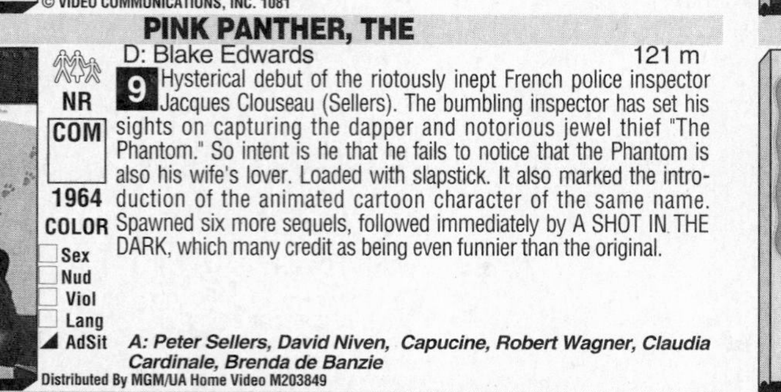

D: Blake Edwards — 121 m

NR | COM | 1964 | COLOR

9 Hysterical debut of the riotously inept French police inspector Jacques Clouseau (Sellers). The bumbling inspector has set his sights on capturing the dapper and notorious jewel thief "The Phantom." So intent is he that he fails to notice that the Phantom is also his wife's lover. Loaded with slapstick. It also marked the introduction of the animated cartoon character of the same name. Spawned six more sequels, followed immediately by A SHOT IN THE DARK, which many credit as being even funnier than the original.

Sex / Nud / Viol / Lang / ◢ AdSit

A: Peter Sellers, David Niven, Capucine, Robert Wagner, Claudia Cardinale, Brenda de Banzie

Distributed By MGM/UA Home Video M203849

PINK PANTHER STRIKES AGAIN, THE

D: Blake Edwards — 104 m

PG | COM | 1976 | COLOR

8 Riotous fifth adventure of the bumbling French police inspector Clouseau. This time Clouseau's now insane supervisor (Lom) escapes from the asylum to which he has been confined. He commandeers a ray gun and threatens the city with total destruction if Clouseau is not destroyed. He has also hired a team of international killers to hunt Clouseau down. One of them, Lesley-Anne Down falls in love with the bumbler. Filled with the lots of slapstick and pain oriented jokes. Followed by REVENGE OF THE PINK PANTHER.

Sex / Nud / ◢ Viol / Lang / ◢ AdSit

A: Peter Sellers, Herbert Lom, Colin Blakely, Leonard Rossiter, Lesley-Anne Down, Burt Kwouk

Distributed By MGM/UA Home Video M200252

PLAY IT AGAIN, SAM

D: Herbert Ross — 85 m

PG | COM ROM | 1972 | COLOR

8 Entertaining and different Woody Allen comedy that is more conventional than most of his films. Here he plays an insecure film critic, lost in his world of movies and suffering from recurring visits from the ghost of Humphrey Bogart - who is constantly giving him advice. When his bored wife divorces him to seek some adventure, Woody repeatedly fumbles in his attempts to meet new women. Even the assistance of his best friend (Roberts) fails. He simply can't say the right things... except, that is, to Diane, his best friend's wife. A funny movie that is also for non-Allen fans.

Sex / Nud / Viol / ◢ Lang / ◢ AdSit

A: Woody Allen, Diane Keaton, Susan Anspach, Tony Roberts, Jerry Lacy, Jennifer Salt

© PARAMOUNT HOME VIDEO 8112

PLAZA SUITE

D: Arthur Hiller — 114 m

PG | COM | 1971 | COLOR

7 Pleasing Niel Simon collection of three comic vignettes, all of which occur in the same suite at New York City's exclusive Plaza Hotel and with comic veteran Walter Matthau playing all the male roles. 1) Stapleton and Matthau rent a room while the paint dries at home. Matthau is having an affair with his secretary. 2) Matthau is in town for a short time and calls up an old girlfriend who is married, bored and feeling guilty, and he tries to seduce her. 3) Matthau's young bride-to-be daughter locks herself in the bathroom and won't come out.

Sex / Nud / Viol / Lang / ◢ AdSit

A: Walter Matthau, Maureen Stapleton, Barbara Harris, Lee Grant, Louise Sorel, Jenny Sullivan

© PARAMOUNT HOME VIDEO 8046

PLEASE DON'T EAT THE DAISIES

D: Charles Walters — 112 m

NR | COM | 1960 | COLOR

8 Bright and amiable family fare. David Niven and Doris Day have four kids. They leave their big city apartment to set up housekeeping in a big old house in the country when he begins a new job as a drama critic. And so begins not one storyline but a series of entertaining escapades: The big-city family learns to adjust to the country life. Doris struggles to renovate their house and deal with the P.T.A. David attempts to deal with an irate actress who he has panned in a review and a persistent cabbie who has a new script that he wants David to look at. Light-hearted farce.

Sex / Nud / Viol / Lang / AdSit

A: David Niven, Doris Day, Janis Paige, Spring Byington, Richard Haydn, Jack Weston

Distributed By MGM/UA Home Video M201301

POCKETFUL OF MIRACLES

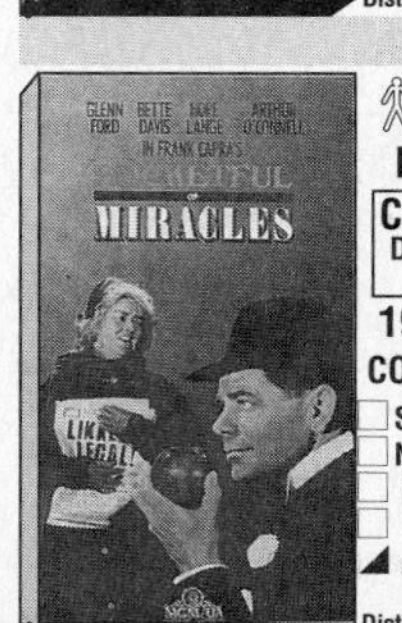

D: Frank Capra — 137 m

NR | COM DMA | 1961 | COLOR

7 Sentimental favorite from Frank Capra. Bette Davis is delightful as Apple Annie, an old woman living in poverty, selling apples to support herself and her daughter who's away in boarding school. She spends everything on her daughter, who thinks her mother is wealthy and now is coming to visit. Annie is scared. Glenn Ford plays a softhearted crook who lines up a bunch of his toughguy friends to help Apple Annie convince her visiting daughter, and her rich fiance, that Annie is really a lady. This is Capra's own remake of his 1933 hit LADY FOR A DAY. Pleasing supersweet diversion. Ann-Margret's film debut.

Sex / Nud / Viol / Lang / ◢ AdSit

A: Bette Davis, Glenn Ford, Hope Lange, Arthur O'Connell, Peter Falk, Jack Elam

Distributed By MGM/UA Home Video M203855

POPEYE

D: Robert Altman — 114 m

PG | COM CLD MUS | 1980 | COLOR

6 Curious live-action version of the famous cartoon character. Not a wonderful musical, but not too bad, either. It is an imaginative staging and production with some really wonderful characterizations from Duvall and especially Williams. All the famous characters are here. Popeye (Williams) rows into port looking for his pappy (Walston). He falls in love with skinny Olive (Duvall), even though she is engaged to Bluto (Smith). Interesting and clever. It was unfairly ignored at the box office by an audience that didn't know quite what how to take it. A good family movie.

Sex / Nud / Viol / Lang / AdSit

A: Robin Williams, Shelley Duvall, Ray Walston, Linda Hunt, Paul L. Smith, Paul Dooley

© PARAMOUNT HOME VIDEO 1171

PRIDE AND PREJUDICE

D: Robert Z. Leonard — 118 m

NR | COM DMA | 1940 | B&W

8 Excellent screen adaptation of Jane Austen's novel written in 1793. It is a bright comedy about a pre-Victorian English family's efforts to get its five unmarried girls all safely married, but each girl has her own peculiarities to make her case special. This clever and witty commentary on manners has lasted for at least 200 years and is still funny today. Excellent cast, gorgeous sets (Oscar) and high production values which capture well the period's flavor and add to the entertainment. First rate stuff.

Sex / Nud / Viol / Lang / ◢ AdSit

A: Greer Garson, Laurence Olivier, Edna May Oliver, Edmund Gwenn, Maureen O'Sullivan, Mary Boland

Distributed By MGM/UA Home Video M500114

PRINCESS AND THE PIRATE, THE

D: David Butler — 94 m

NR | COM | 1944 | COLOR

6 An amiable Bob Hope farce - this time he makes fun of swashbuckler movies. Bob plays a shlock vaudevillian-type actor who claims to be able to impersonate anybody. A beautiful blond princess (Virginia Mayo) has run off to escape a marriage arranged by her father, the king. But, she and Bob are captured together and held by La Roche, patron to a band of villainous pirates led by Victor McLaglen. Walter Brennan (particularly funny) is a wayward and crazy pirate who has stolen a treasure map from McLaglen and then tattooed it on Hope's chest. Very silly but pretty good fun if you are a fan of Hope's never-ending witty one-liners.

Sex / Nud / Viol / Lang / AdSit

A: Bob Hope, Walter Slezak, Walter Brennan, Virginia Mayo, Victor McLaglen

© HBO VIDEO 90666

PRINCESS BRIDE, THE

D: Rob Reiner — 98 m

PG | COM ROM FAN | 1987 | COLOR

7 Heroic fairy tale fantasy, designed for both young and old! A sick boy's grandfather (Falk) comes to read to him, promising him a story of monsters, fights, beasts, and, yes, a dose of romance, too. In the extravagant and adventurous story which comes to life on screen, a beautiful princess and a stableboy fall in love but are soon separated, and the evil king has her kidnapped so he can force her to marry him. Suddenly, a strange man in a mask appears poised to do battle for her. This brilliant adaptation of the whimsical cult novel comes alive at the hands of Rob Reiner.

Sex / Nud / ◢ Viol / Lang / AdSit

A: Peter Falk, Mandy Patinkin, Carol Kane, Billy Crystal, Chris Sarandon, Cary Elwes

© NEW LINE HOME VIDEO 7709

PRISONER OF ZENDA, THE

D: Richard Quine — 108 m

PG | COM | 1979 | COLOR

6 Comedic take off on the famous 1937 swashbuckling action movie of the same name. However, here Peter Sellers plays a Cockney cab driver who has been enlisted into being a look-alike stand-in for the endangered prince of the mythical nation of Ruritainia, after he is threatened with assassination by his evil half-brother. Things get further confused when the cabby falls for the prince's fiancee. This is a funny movie that didn't get much critical acclaim. It will be most enjoyed by fans of the zany, mix-up type comedies and by Peter Sellers fans.

Sex / Nud / Viol / Lang / ✔ AdSit

A: Peter Sellers, Lynne Frederick, Lionel Jeffries, Elke Sommer, Gregory Sierra, Jeremy Kemp

© MCA/UNIVERSAL HOME VIDEO, INC. 66057

PRODUCERS, THE

D: Mel Brooks — 90 m

NR | COM MUS | 1968 | COLOR

9 Hysterical farce from Mel Brooks. This, his first film, won him an Oscar for Best Screenplay and he also directed. It is about a shyster promoter (Mostel) who cons a meek accountant (Wilder) into helping him with a terrific get-rich-quick scheme. They will sell interests in a new (and very bad) Broadway play ("Springtime for Hitler") which they will produce... but they will sell 25 times more shares than are available. Then when the thing flops, they will take all the extra money to Rio with them. But when it becomes a big hit instead, they are in big-time trouble.

Sex / Nud / Viol / ✔ Lang / ✔ AdSit

A: Zero Mostel, Gene Wilder, Dick Shawn, Kenneth Mars, Lee Meredith, Christopher Hewett

© NEW LINE HOME VIDEO 2051

PROTOCOL

D: Herbert Ross — 96 m

PG | COM | 1984 | COLOR

7 Pleasant, but highly contrived, movie in which a bubble-headed waitress (Goldie Hawn) inadvertently foils an assassination plot against an Arab Potentate. She becomes an overnight hero and is awarded a job in the State Protocol Department, but quickly becomes a pawn in games of state. Simple Goldie rises to the challenge and transforms herself into a meaningful person. Light-hearted, frivolous entertainment that was made for Goldie and is more than a little like her character in PRIVATE BENJAMIN. Likable.

Sex / ✔ Nud / ✔ Viol / ✔ Lang / ✔ AdSit

A: Goldie Hawn, Chris Sarandon, Gail Strickland, Cliff De Young, Richard Romanus, Ed Begley, Jr.

© WARNER HOME VIDEO 11434

QUIET MAN, THE

D: John Ford — 153 m

NR | COM ROM ACT | 1952 | COLOR

10 Masterful tapestry of colorful characters! An Irish-American boxer (Wayne) killed a man in the ring and has traveled to his father's Irish village to recover peace of mind. He meets a beautiful and feisty redhead (O'Hara). He falls in love with her and she with him, but since her cantankerous brother (McLaglen) refuses to give the traditional dowry, she will not consent to be Wayne's wife. Wayne sets out to change McLaglen's mind. Highly entertaining, endearing and funny! Ford won an Oscar for this masterful tribute to Ireland, its traditions and people. Also an Oscar winner for Cinematography.

Sex / Nud / ✔ Viol / Lang / ✔ AdSit

A: John Wayne, Maureen O'Hara, Barry Fitzgerald, Ward Bond, Victor McLaglen, Mildred Natwick

© REPUBLIC PICTURES HOME VIDEO 3361

RADIOLAND MURDERS

D: Mel Smith — 108 m

PG | COM | 1994 | COLOR

6 Frenetic slap-stick comedy that not that far removed from what you would expect from the Three Stooges. Loaded with a cast of prominent stars in cameo roles, this is the story of the antics going on behind the scenes of a live radio broadcast for a new network in 1939. Behind the scenes everything is going wrong. The sponsors have demanded that the entire script be rewritten at the last minute. The writers haven't been paid in weeks. The director is romancing the manager's wife. The head writer is trying to win back his wife, the show's assistant manager. And both he and she are trying to solve some very real murders that started about as soon as the show did. Very goofy and not for everyone.

Sex / Nud / Viol / Lang / ✔ AdSit

A: Brian Benben, Ned Beatty, George Burns, Brion James, Michael Lerner

© MCA/UNIVERSAL HOME VIDEO, INC. 82206

RELUCTANT DEBUTANTE, THE

D: Vincente Minnelli — 97 m

NR | COM | 1958 | COLOR

6 Lively and refreshing comedy. The on- (and off) screen husband and wife team (Harrison and Kendall) are making elaborate preparations to present their daughter (Sandra Dee) to society. It's the social season in London, where promising seventeen-year-olds take part in lavish balls specially designed for the momentous occasion. Unfortunately, Harrison's Americanized daughter (by another marriage) is quickly bored by English etiquette and tradition and instead takes up with a bad boy American drummer (Saxon). Sprightly and fun.

Sex / Nud / Viol / Lang / ✔ AdSit

A: Rex Harrison, Kay Kendall, John Saxon, Sandra Dee, Angela Lansbury

Distributed By MGM/UA Home Video M202364

RETURN OF THE PINK PANTHER

D: Blake Edwards — 113 m

G | COM | 1974 | COLOR

8 When a famous diamond is stolen, an ex-thief known as the Phantom (Plummer), now retired and married, is automatically blamed. He decides that he must find the culprit himself before he winds up getting stuck behind bars. However, at the same time, police chief Lom has reluctantly assigned the case to the nitwit Inspector Clouseau (Sellers). Sellers proceeds to again make Lom's life truly miserable and parades through a series of bumbling mishaps with a style all his own. Loaded with pratfalls and slapstick. A shameless good time for fans of the ridiculous.

Sex / Nud / Viol / Lang / AdSit

A: Peter Sellers, Christopher Plummer, Catherine Schell, Herbert Lom, Burt Kwouk, Peter Arne

© LIVE HOME VIDEO 27480

REVENGE OF THE PINK PANTHER, THE

D: Blake Edwards — 100 m

PG | COM | 1972 | COLOR

7 The bumbling Inspector Clouseau is at it again. When the French Inspector (Sellers) is tipped off that he is to be killed, he foils the assassination attempt, but pretends to be dead. Ditzy but resourceful, he hopes to be able to find his would-be killer if he can remain incognito. This means that he appears in a never-ending series of disguises. His search leads him to Hong Kong, where he attempts to break up the heroin ring of his would-be assassin. As in the others of the series, this also contains a series of pratfalls and slapstick jokes. The last in the series by Sellers.

Sex / Nud / Viol / ✔ Lang / AdSit

A: Peter Sellers, Herbert Lom, Dyan Cannon, Robert Webber, Burt Kwouk, Robert Loggia

Distributed By MGM/UA Home Video M201448

ROCKET GIBRALTAR

D: Daniel Petrie — 100 m

PG | COM DMA | 1988 | COLOR

7 Bittersweet drama about love and family. A much-loved patriarch, Levi Rockwell (Lancaster), has called his family together to celebrate his 77th birthday. His large family, children and grandchildren, all gather on his beautiful estate on Long Island. Although his children love him, it's his grandchildren that make a heartfelt connection with him and carry out his most cherished last wish. Sentimental, touching and emotional. Have a box of tissue ready for the last few scenes.

Sex / Nud / Viol / ✔ Lang / ✔ AdSit

A: Burt Lancaster, Suzy Amis, John Glover, Bill Pullman, Patricia Clarkson, Frances Conroy

© COLUMBIA TRISTAR HOME VIDEO 65009

ROOM SERVICE

D: William A. Seiter — 78 m

NR | COM | 1938 | B&W

6 Old-fashioned comedic farce that was somewhat different movie for the Marx Brothers. It came later on in their careers and had been an existing Broadway play that was then specially adapted for their brand of humor. Groucho is desperately trying to produce a play, but he and the brothers are starving and having a hard time keeping ahead of their creditors. So, Groucho comes up with the brilliant plan to fake the measles to keep the hotel manager from throwing him out of his room. A little more restrained than the traditional Marx slapstick. Although funny, it is one of their lesser movies.

Sex / Nud / Viol / Lang / ✔ AdSit

A: Lucille Ball, Groucho Marx, Chico Marx, Harpo Marx, Ann Miller, Frank Albertson

© TURNER HOME ENTERTAINMENT 2088

ROSALIE GOES SHOPPING

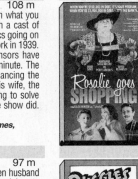

D: Percy Adlon — 96 m

PG | COM | 1990 | COLOR

6 A German woman has moved to America with her American husband - to a little town in Arkansas. Rosalie (Sagebrecht) is a warm-hearted mother, just searching for her American Dream. She goes on a credit card rampage and buys everything in sight. Soon, she has to become a wizard at creative finance as she alters checks, lies daily to credit collectors and runs up $1 million in debts. She has become a genius at creative finance. She just wants her family to have a piece of the American Pie. A quirky look at American consumerism and consumption.

Sex / Nud / Viol / ✔ Lang / ✔ AdSit

A: Marianne Sagebrecht, Brad Davis, Judge Reinhold, Alex Winter, John Hawkes, David Denney

© VIDMARK ENTERTAINMENT VM5275

RUGGLES OF RED GAP

D: Leo McCarey — 90 m

NR | COM WST | 1935 | B&W

9 A shining gem and a comedy classic! During a poker game in Paris, the Earl of Burnstead (Young) loses his butler Ruggles (Laughton) to a wealthy but uncouth American couple (Ruggles and Boland). The ill-bred pair take their new butler home to Red Gap, Washington, where he becomes both inspired and awed by the wild west and loses all his British airs. He has a wonderful time as he romances the ladies, breaks his old bonds of servitude, discovers his new self and his new place on earth. A charming, disarming and amusing good time. Excellent. Also filmed again later as FANCY PANTS with Bob Hope.

Sex / Nud / Viol / Lang / AdSit

A: Charles Laughton, Mary Boland, Charlie Ruggles, ZaSu Pitts, Roland Young, Leila Hyams

© MCA/UNIVERSAL HOME VIDEO, INC. 80670

RUSSIANS ARE COMING, THE RUSSIANS ARE COMING, THE

D: Norman Jewison — 127 m

NR | COM | 1966 | COLOR

8 Zany comedy that was a surprise big hit. Set at the height of the Cold War, imagine the hysterics that would ensue if a Russian submarine, intent only upon getting a close look at a typically picturesque small Maine fishing village, runs aground upon a sandbar. And then an inept crewman (Alan Arkin) is sent ashore to capture a civilian boat large enough to tow the submarine free. Instead, Arkin nearly starts a war when he is confronted by the local make-shift militia, led by an inept old soldier (Paul Ford) and a bungling deputy sheriff (Jonathan Winters). Solid light-hearted comedy with good gags.

Sex / Nud / Viol / Lang / AdSit

A: Carl Reiner, Eva Marie Saint, Alan Arkin, Brian Keith, Jonathan Winters, Paul Ford

Distributed By MGM/UA Home Video M201490

SECRET LIFE OF WALTER MITTY, THE

D: Norman McLeod — 110 m

NR | COM | 1947 | COLOR

7 An enjoyable romp through Everyman Walter Mitty's vivid imagination. Loosely taken from James Thurber's classic short story and features master-comedian Danny Kaye. Walter Mitty is a timid little man who is hen-pecked by both his mother and his fiancee. This milquetoast lives a very boring, everyday kind of existence, but he escapes into his very vivid and consuming daydreams where he is always the glory-drenched hero. Then one day, a beautiful woman really does need his help against a gang of jewel thieves, and the timid little man does become a hero, albeit a reluctant one, and gets the girl too boot.

Sex / Nud / Viol / Lang / AdSit

A: Danny Kaye, Virginia Mayo, Boris Karloff, Fay Bainter, Reginald Denny, Ann Rutherford

© HBO VIDEO 90654

RUSSKIES

D: Rick Rosenthal — 100 m

PG | COM | 1987 | COLOR

6 Enjoyable lesson in civics for young people. While on a mission to pick up a captured defense weapon, a Russian sailor (Hubley) wrecks his raft off the coast of the Florida Keys while trying to get to shore. Three adventurous and curious young boys (Phoenix, Billingsley and DeSalle) debate whether to turn him in, but decide that they like him despite the anti-Soviet sentiment that is prevalent in their small town. Everything comes to a momentous climax when the US military shows up. OK sort of remake of THE RUSSIANS ARE COMING, THE RUSSIANS ARE COMING.

Sex / Nud / Viol / Lang / AdSit

A: Whip Hubley, Leaf Phoenix, Peter Billingsley, Stefan DeSalle, Susan Walters, Patrick Kilpatrick

© WARNER HOME VIDEO 761

SEEMS LIKE OLD TIMES

D: Jay Sandrich — 103 m

PG | COM | 1980 | COLOR

8 Romantically zany Neil Simon comedy. A beautiful attorney (Hawn), with a soft heart, finds herself torn between her ex-husband (Chase), who needs her help, and her new husband (Grodin), on a career fast-track. When Chase is accused of bank robbery, he goes to Hawn for help. But Chase's predicament could harm Grodin's chances of becoming the next Attorney General. Clever and funny situations occur as Hawn helps Chase, but also struggles to maintain proper appearances for her husband. A well-cast 1930s-style screwball comedy-like farce, overflowing with wit and charm.

Sex / Nud / Viol / Lang / AdSit

A: Chevy Chase, Goldie Hawn, Charles Grodin, Robert Guillaume, Harold Gould, George Grizzard

© COLUMBIA TRISTAR HOME VIDEO 60200

SAVANNAH SMILES

D: Pierre DeMoro — 105 m

PG | COM CLD | 1982 | COLOR

8 A real charmer. Savannah (Anderson) is a six-year old who runs away from her snooty, rich parents and she winds up in the back seat of a car belonging to two soft-hearted escaped convicts. Her father has offered a huge reward for her return, but who's going to believe the story of two convicts. So, they try valiantly to get her back without blowing their cover. Meanwhile, the three hide out in an abandoned house where they all become a loving "family," experiencing feelings none of them has ever known before. Chock-full of tender moments, sincere laughs and an ending that packs an emotional punch. A gem!

Sex / Nud / Viol / Lang / AdSit

A: Mark Miller, Donovan Scott, Bridgette Andersen, Peter Graves, Michael Parks, Noriyuki "Pat" Morita

© NEW LINE HOME VIDEO 2058

SEND ME NO FLOWERS

D: Norman Jewison — 100 m

NR | COM | 1964 | COLOR

7 Classic Hudson/Day fun! Rock Hudson, a hopeless hypochondriac, overhears a bleak prognosis at a hospital one day and becomes convinced that it's his own. Wanting to make sure that his family and wife (Day) are provided for when he is gone, he enlists the aid of best friend Randall to find a new husband for Day. The laughs break loose when Day convinces herself that his strange behavior is a cover-up for an affair he is having and he's just feeling guilty. This buoyant and funny film was the last of the Hudson/Day pairings.

Sex / Nud / Viol / Lang / AdSit

A: Rock Hudson, Doris Day, Tony Randall, Clint Walker, Paul Lynde, Hal March

© MCA/UNIVERSAL HOME VIDEO, INC. 80405

F A M I L Y

SAVING GRACE

D: Robert M. Young — 112 m

PG | COM | 1986 | COLOR

7 Sweet-natured and sentimental little comedy about a young Pope. He is a man-of-the-people and is very frustrated at becoming bogged down with the bureaucracy and bureaucrats of the Vatican... so he just leaves. He just wanders away to a small remote village that has no priest and is desperately poor. There, he gets a chance to help people again. Several cute moments, including watching three Cardinals try to cover up the fact that the Pope is missing. Not very believable, but well-intentioned and fun... as long as you don't think too hard about it.

Sex / Nud / Viol / Lang / AdSit

A: Tom Conti, Fernando Rey, Erland Josephson, Giancarlo Giannini, Donald Hewlett, Edward James Olmos

© NEW LINE HOME VIDEO 2180

SEVEN LITTLE FOYS, THE

D: Melville Shavelson — 95 m

NR | COM MUS | 1955 | COLOR

7 Fun-filled and enjoyable musical biography of Eddie Foy, the famous vaudeville song-and-dance entertainer. Bob Hope is less zany than usual as Eddie Foy, the wayward and absentee father of a family of seven kids. All that has to change, however, when his wife dies and he has to decide what to do about taking care of his family and still earn a living. He decides to take all the kids on the road with him, forming the famous vaudeville act "Eddie Foy and the Seven Little Foys." Numerous song and dance numbers and a short appearance by James Cagney as George M. Cohen.

Sex / Nud / Viol / Lang / AdSit

A: Bob Hope, Milly Vitale, Billy Gray, George Tobias, James Cagney

© COLUMBIA TRISTAR HOME VIDEO 60787

SCAVENGER HUNT

D: Michael Schultz — 116 m

PG | COM | 1979 | COLOR

6 Silly, campy fun. When game manufacturer Vincent Price dies, he leaves a huge amount of money to his friends and relatives, but only the winning team of an insane scavenger hunt will get to claim the grand prize - the entire two hundred million dollar estate of the dearly-departed. Included in the odd assortment of required collectibles are commodes, ostriches, fat people, beehives and all sorts of other very strange items. Nutty.

Sex / Nud / Viol / Lang / AdSit

A: Richard Benjamin, James Coco, Scatman Crothers, Ruth Gordon, Cloris Leachman, Cleavon Little

© CBS/FOX VIDEO 6224

SHOP AROUND THE CORNER, THE

D: Ernst Lubitsch — 100 m

NR | COM ROM | 1940 | B&W

8 Simply charming and delightfully memorable. Two sales clerks (Stewart and Sullavan) work together in a gift shop but they can't stand each other. However, they have absolutely no idea that they are also each other's secret pen pals. On paper, they are the best of friends and have been writing affectionate letters to each other for some time. Then things get bad for Stewart when the owner of the store fires him because he mistakenly believes Stewart is carrying on an affair with his wife. Lonely, Stewart seeks out his pen pal for solace, only to find out who she really is. Wonderful.

Sex / Nud / Viol / Lang / AdSit

A: James Stewart, Margaret Sullavan, Frank Morgan, Sara Haden, Joseph Schildkraut, Felix Bressart

Distributed By MGM/UA Home Video M301164

SCROOGED

D: Richard Donner — 101 m

PG-13 | COM | 1989 | COLOR

7 Heartwarming holiday comedy with spirit! Frank (Murray) is a cold-hearted network TV executive who doesn't have time for anybody but himself. Frank's holiday attitude needs an adjustment. When three ghosts, the ghosts of Christmas past (a maniacal New York cabbie), present (a zany Carol Kane) and a ghoul from the future, come to visit, they manage to put a little love in back into his heart and ignite his holiday spirit, too. Murray's trademark style of humor adds a zany quality to this film and it surprises you with its unexpected emotional ending.

Sex / Nud / Viol / Lang / AdSit

A: Bill Murray, John Forsythe, Carol Kane, David Johansen, Karen Allen, Bobcat Goldthwait

© PARAMOUNT HOME VIDEO 32054

SHORT CIRCUIT

D: John Badham — 98 m

PG | COM SF | 1986 | COLOR

8 Sparkling comedic farce for the family! No. 5 is a military robot that was developed to be a weapon by the government, but it was zapped with a bolt of lightning and now the little guy seems nearly human. No. 5 has also taken off to see the world on his own. He finds a friend in animal lover Ally Sheedy and learns American culture by watching TV. Sheedy and the newly educated No. 5 develop an affection for each other, but the military is steadfastly after his adorable little tail, with his creator Guttenberg leading the chase. Naturally, she hides him from them. Charming entertainment.

Sex / Nud / Viol / Lang / AdSit

A: Ally Sheedy, Steve Guttenberg, Fisher Stevens, Austin Pendleton, G.W. Bailey, David Oliver

© FOXVIDEO 3724

SHORT CIRCUIT 2

D: Kenneth Johnson 110 m

PG · COM · SF · 1988 · COLOR

7 Johnny Five (formerly No. 5) is the cute military robot that was struck by lightning in the original film and then became almost human. In this sequel, Johnny comes to the big city to help out one of his inventors who has now gone into the toy business. Johnny hits the streets looking for some "urban input" but attracts some unsavory friends. Some street punks want to trick the naive robot into helping them to pull off a jewel robbery. Cute, but mostly for the younger set this time.

Sex · Nud · ◢ Viol · ◢ Lang · AdSit

A: Fisher Stevens, Michael McKean, Cynthia Gibb, Jack Weston

© COLUMBIA TRISTAR HOME VIDEO 67008

SHOT IN THE DARK, A

D: Blake Edwards 103 m

PG · COM · 1964 · COLOR

9 Hilarious follow up to THE PINK PANTHER. The bumbling and incredibly inept Parisian Inspector Clouseau is assigned to investigate a murder where all the clues point to very sexy maid Elke Sommer as being the murderer. In spite of overwhelming evidence to the contrary, Clouseau sets out to prove that she is innocent. Slapstick and hilarity abound. Wherever he goes, he leaves an ever-increasing pile of dead bodies. Very fast-paced. The success of this picture assured that a long, and successful, string of sequels would follow - and they did.

Sex · Nud · Viol · Lang · ◢ AdSit

A: Peter Sellers, Elke Sommer, George Sanders, Herbert Lom, Burt Kwouk, Tracy Reed

Distributed By MGM/UA Home Video M201446

SILENT MOVIE

D: Mel Brooks 87 m

PG · COM · 1976 · COLOR

6 A washed-up movie director (Brooks) gets a wild idea that just might revive his career: revive the silent movie. He realizes that silent films were often the funniest kind, so he and a few of his friends (Feldman and DeLuise) hire a crew of big name stars (Burt Reynolds, Paul Newman, James Caan, Liza Minnelli and Anne Bancroft) and convince an influential movie producer to back their film. There are some really funny scenes and sight gags, although a few attempts at humor fall flat. Amusing nonetheless. It includes music and sound effects but only one line of spoken dialogue.

Sex · Nud · Viol · Lang · ◢ AdSit

A: Mel Brooks, Marty Feldman, Sid Caesar, Dom DeLuise, Bernadette Peters, Harold Gould

© FOXVIDEO 1437

SILVER STREAK

D: Arthur Hiller 114 m

PG · COM · ACT · MYS · 1976 · COLOR

9 Zany thriller. Wilder, a mild-mannered editor, is taking what he hopes to be a restful ride aboard a cross-country train. It seems to be even better when he seduces the girl in the next compartment (sexy Clayburgh). But she is an art scholar with information which will discredit both millionaire McGoohan and his Rembrandt letters as being fakes. Now, Wilder's leisurely trip turns overly exciting, when he spots a dead body being thrown from the train, and then hilarious, when small-time thief Pryor enters into the picture. Highly entertaining blend of romance, comedy and action.

Sex · Nud · ◢ Viol · ◢ Lang · ◢ AdSit

A: Gene Wilder, Jill Clayburgh, Richard Pryor, Ned Beatty, Patrick McGoohan, Scatman Crothers

© FOXVIDEO 1080

SISTER ACT

D: Emile Ardolino 100 m

PG · COM · 1992 · COLOR

8 Very popular comedy. Whoopi is a singer in a Vegas nightclub act and the girlfriend of the club's mobster owner. But, when she has the misfortune of catching him in the act of murdering someone, she knows she's in big trouble and heads underground. The cops offer her protection if she will testify. She agrees but, much to her surprise and dismay, the place they choose to hide her is a convent. This is not a lifestyle which comes easy to a Vegas lounge singer. What's even worse, their choir is terrible. So, Whoopi transforms this boring bunch of off-key nuns into a rock-`n-roll sensation. But being on network news is not a good thing for a nun on the run. Lot of fun.

Sex · Nud · Viol · ◢ Lang · AdSit

A: Whoopi Goldberg, Maggie Smith, Harvey Keitel, Mary Wickes

© TOUCHSTONE HOME VIDEO 1452

SISTER ACT 2

D: Bill Duke 107 m

PG · COM · 1994 · COLOR

6 Sister Whoopi is back. This time the nuns are in trouble and they need her help. Bad guy, James Coburn is trying to shut down their inner-city San Francisco high school. These kids really need their school and only Whoopi can help them. How? By what else? Let's put on a show! There is not a lot of plot here, nor is there much suspense or even much involvement with the characters. What there is, is some fun choral efforts by a bunch of talented kids. Predictable but genuinely wholesome, even if it isn't very funny or exciting.

Sex · Nud · Viol · Lang · AdSit

A: Whoopi Goldberg, Maggie Smith, Kathy Najimy, Bernard Hughes, Mary Wickes, James Coburn

© TOUCHSTONE HOME VIDEO 2525

SLEEPER

D: Woody Allen 88 m

PG · COM · 1973 · COLOR

8 Woody Allen silliness supreme. Ridiculous farce in which Woody is a mild-mannered owner of a health food store who goes in to have an ulcer operation only to wake up - or rather, be defrosted - 200 years later, after having been wrapped in aluminum foil and frozen. This world is a vastly changed place from the one he left. He is almost immediately sought out to be recruited into an underground movement that is trying to overthrow the dictator, but Woody hides out instead, pretending to be a robot. Wacky silliness, slapstick gags aplenty and one liners flying everywhere.

Sex · Nud · Viol · ◢ Lang · ◢ AdSit

A: Woody Allen, Diane Keaton, Mary Gregory, John Beck, Don Keefer, Don McLiam

Distributed By MGM/UA Home Video M201463

SLITHER

D: Howard Zieff 92 m

PG · COM · 1973 · COLOR

7 Zany comic farce. James Caan and his cellmate Harry, were just released from prison but they are immediately attacked. Harry is killed but, with his dying breath, gives Caan a clue to $300,000 in stolen loot. This launches a wacky adventure in which a group of oddball characters - Caan, his amphetamine-addicted girlfriend (Kellerman), Harry's ex-partner Barry and Harry's wife (Lasser) - chase all over Southern California countryside in Barry's RV in search of the fortune. However there are two ominous black vans always in pursuit and everyone takes frequent comedic stops along the way.

Sex · Nud · ◢ Viol · ◢ Lang · AdSit

A: James Caan, Peter Boyle, Sally Kellerman, Louise Lasser, Allen Garfield, Richard B. Shull

Distributed By MGM/UA Home Video M200171

SMILE

D: Michael Ritchie 113 m

PG · COM · 1975 · COLOR

7 A sarcastic, comic poke at beauty pageants. The chief judge is a mobile home salesman (Dern), whose son snaps pictures of the contestants naked and tries to sell the pictures to his friends, but gets caught. The choreographer (Kidd) is trying to revive his flagging career. The head of the proceedings (Feldon) is a prude. Since there are a multitude of story lines going on at the same time, we are not allowed to get involved with any one character. That, along with its unflattering portrait of pageants, caused the public to stay away. This is unfortunate because the film is also frequently hilarious.

Sex · Nud · Viol · ◢ Lang · ◢ AdSit

A: Bruce Dern, Barbara Feldon, Melanie Griffith, Michael Kidd, Geoffrey Lewis, Nicholas Pryor

Distributed By MGM/UA Home Video M201288

SMOKEY AND THE BANDIT

D: Hal Needham 96 m

PG · COM · ACT · 1977 · COLOR

9 Box office smash comedy. Good ol' boy Bandit (Burt Reynolds) gets hired to haul four hundred cases of Coors beer from Texarkana, Texas to Atlanta, Georgia. Since Coors is legal in Texas and not in Atlanta, there is a little bit of a situation - but if he can do it in 28 hours, he gets $80,000. So Burt runs interference, in a fast Camero, all across the South for the illegal load which is being driven in an 18-wheeler by Jerry Reed. Burt's job is keeping a herd of bumbling cops, led by local sheriff Jackie Gleeson, occupied for his good buddy Reed. Loads of car stunts and gags. A rollicking good time.

Sex · Nud · ◢ Viol · ◢ Lang · ◢ AdSit

A: Burt Reynolds, Sally Field, Jackie Gleason, Jerry Reed, Mike Henry, Paul Williams

© MCA/UNIVERSAL HOME VIDEO, INC. 66003

SMOKEY AND THE BANDIT II

D: Hal Needham 101 m

PG · COM · ACT · 1980 · COLOR

7 Pretty good sequel to the original. This time the Bandit (Reynolds) and his buddy are hired to get a pregnant elephant to the Republican convention. But to do it, they have to go through the stomping grounds of their old arch-enemy sheriff Buford T. Justice (Gleeson). Dom DeLuis plays a gynecologist who gets to come along and treat the elephant. Contains a full assortment of the same sort of stunts that were the hallmark of the original, plus lots of clever dialogue, too. It doesn't have the same spark as the original did. Still, it's a good time.

Sex · Nud · Viol · ◢ Lang · ◢ AdSit

A: Burt Reynolds, Sally Field, Jackie Gleason, Dom DeLuise, Jerry Reed, Paul Williams

© MCA/UNIVERSAL HOME VIDEO, INC. 66020

SOME LIKE IT HOT

D: Billy Wilder 120 m

NR · COM · 1959 · B&W

10 Wildly funny and now a legendary comedy. Two second-rate musicians witness the infamous St. Valentine's Day massacre in Chicago. That's a very unhealthy situation to be in. So with the mob in hot pursuit, the two disguise themselves as women and take up with an all-girl band that is leaving by train to a gig in Miami. Marilyn was rarely, if ever, more casually sensual than here; Curtis and Lemmon are a delight; and Joe E. Brown is a scream as a rich playboy with the hots for Jack Lemmon (in drag). Dazzling performances in a truly funny comedy.

Sex · Nud · ◢ Viol · Lang · ◢ AdSit

A: Marilyn Monroe, Tony Curtis, Jack Lemmon, George Raft, Pat O'Brien, Joe E. Brown

Distributed By MGM/UA Home Video M203848

FAMILY

SON OF PALEFACE

D: Frank Tashlin — 95 m

NR | COM WST | 1952 | COLOR | Rating: 6

Popular sequel to Bob Hope's best film - THE PALEFACE from 1948. Bob plays a bumbling Harvard graduate who goes west to claim his inheritance, the gold that his Indian-fighter father hid. There to help him is Jane Russell and cowboy legend Roy Rogers. Wild and wacky satire of the Western genre. Hope's sequence where he is in bed with Roy's horse Trigger is recognized as a classic.

Sex | Nud | Viol | Lang | AdSit

A: Bob Hope, Jane Russell, Roy Rogers, Iron Eyes Cody, Douglas Dumbrille, Bill Williams

© COLUMBIA TRISTAR HOME VIDEO 60742

SONS OF THE DESERT

D: William A. Seiter — 73 m

NR | COM | 1933 | B&W | Rating: 9

Many consider this wacky film to be Laurel and Hardy's best. The kooky pair want to attend a convention for the fraternal order Sons of the Desert in Chicago, but they know their wives won't let them go if they ask. Instead, they tell their wives that Hardy needs to travel to Hawaii in order to cure his cold, and Laurel must go with him. But when the ship sinks on the way back from the Islands, the boys must figure out a way to explain to their wives why they made it back with nary a scratch and one day ahead of the other survivors. Impeccable comedy.

Sex | Nud | Viol | Lang | ✓ AdSit

A: Stan Laurel, Oliver Hardy, Mae Busch, Charley Chase, Mae Busch, Dorothy Christy

© VIDEO TREASURES SV9306

SPIES LIKE US

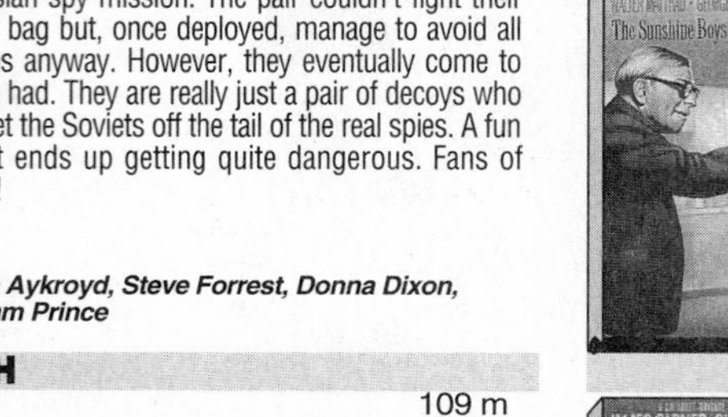

D: John Landis — 102 m

PG | COM | 1985 | COLOR | Rating: 6

A very kooky and silly comedy. Aykroyd and Chase are two nitwit government employees recruited by a US intelligence organization for a perilous Russian spy mission. The pair couldn't fight their way out of a wet paper bag but, once deployed, manage to avoid all sorts of sticky situations anyway. However, they eventually come to realize that they've been had. They are really just a pair of decoys who have been sent out to get the Soviets off the tail of the real spies. A fun screwball comedy that ends up getting quite dangerous. Fans of wacky humor will enjoy!

Sex | Nud | Viol | ✓ Lang | ✓ AdSit

A: Chevy Chase, Dan Aykroyd, Steve Forrest, Donna Dixon, Bruce Davison, William Prince

© WARNER HOME VIDEO 11533

SPLASH

D: Ron Howard — 109 m

PG | COM ROM FAN | 1984 | COLOR | Rating: 9

An unbelievable plot is made both believable and captivating, thanks to outstanding acting by Hanks and Hannah and deft direction by Howard. Hanks is a wealthy businessman who has everything but love. When he nearly drowns off the coast of Cape Cod, it is a beautiful mermaid (Hannah) who rescues him. She is infatuated with him and grows legs to search the big city for him. She charms him with her incredible innocence and they fall madly in love, but Hanks still has a hard time learning to deal with her nautical nature. Fantastic movie-making and a wonderful blending of fantasy and romance.

Sex | ✓ Nud | Viol | ✓ Lang | ✓ AdSit

A: Tom Hanks, Daryl Hannah, Eugene Levy, John Candy, Dody Goodman, Richard B. Shull

© TOUCHSTONE HOME VIDEO 213

START THE REVOLUTION WITHOUT ME

D: Bud Yorkin — 91 m

PG | COM | 1970 | COLOR | Rating: 7

Hilarious confusion! Set in 17th-century France, a peasant lady and an aristocrat each have twins, which are inadvertently mixed up. One Wilder/Sutherland combo grows up as aristocrats and the other as poor peasants. Years later, the mis-matched brothers first meet when both sets are sent to the the King's palace to prepare for the impending revolution. With the mixed-up pairs having one member each on opposite sides of the warring fence, absolute chaos erupts as they try to figure out which one is to be where and who is who. This madcap film developed a cult following.

Sex | ✓ Nud | ✓ Viol | ✓ Lang | ✓ AdSit

A: Gene Wilder, Donald Sutherland, Billie Whitelaw, Hugh Griffith, Jack MacGowran, Victor Spinetti

© WARNER HOME VIDEO 11296

STEAMBOAT BILL JR.

D: Charles F. Reisner — 104 m

COM | 1928 | B&W | Rating: 8

Sparkling silent film. Steamboat Bill (Torrence) is the tough captain of a Mississippi riverboat and is counting on his son (Keaton) to take over the business and keep it out of the red. Unfortunately, Bill Jr. isn't exactly what Dad hoped for. He is a college boy, complete with his ukulele and blazer. He's also a bit accident prone and, what's worse, he is also in love with his father's arch rival. Some excellent sight gags add to the fun, including one of the most dangerous stunts ever filmed. A very impressive silent.

Sex | Nud | Viol | Lang | AdSit

A: Buster Keaton, Ernest Torrence, Tom McGuire, Marion Byron, Tom Lewis

© VIDEO YESTERYEAR 573

SULLIVAN'S TRAVELS

D: Preston Sturges — 91 m

NR | COM | 1941 | B&W | Rating: 10

Classic early spoof on Hollywood that's ripe with laughter! Movie director McCrea has done plenty of inconsequential films and decides to do something worthwhile for a change. So, he disguises himself as a bum and sets off across the country with only 10 cents in his pocket on a search to get some new material. Along the way, he picks up a has-been actress (Lake) and the pair travel America, experiencing a whole new realm of danger and human suffering. McCrea's lesson learned is that all you really need when you are down-and-out is laughter. A film with unmatched brilliance and wit. Excellent.

Sex | Nud | Viol | Lang | AdSit

A: Joel McCrea, Veronica Lake, Robert Warwick, William Demarest, Eric Blore, Robert Greig

© MCA/UNIVERSAL HOME VIDEO, INC. 80551

SUMMER SCHOOL

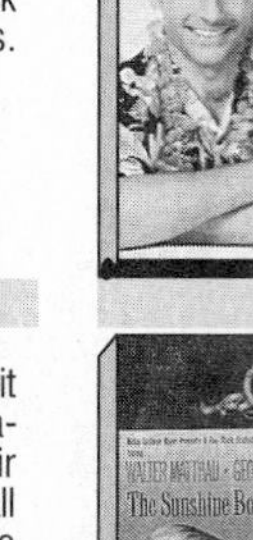

D: Carl Reiner — 98 m

PG-13 | COM | 1987 | COLOR | Rating: 8

Excellent summer fun - at school! Harmon is a laid-back high school coach and teacher whose mellow teaching style gets him in hot water. His students aren't doing very well, and so the administration forces Harmon to stay home from a Hawaiian vacation to prepare some kids for a big remedial English test. If they don't pass, he loses his job! Summer love ignites when Harmon falls for Alley. She isn't interested in him in the beginning, but soon comes around and even helps out. Reiner's deft direction makes this a blast for teenagers and middle-agers alike.

Sex | Nud | ✓ Viol | ✓ Lang | AdSit

A: Mark Harmon, Kirstie Alley, Robin Thomas, Dean Cameron, Patrick Labyorteaux, Courtney Thorne-Smith

© PARAMOUNT HOME VIDEO 1518

SUNSHINE BOYS, THE

D: Herbert Ross — 102 m

PG | COM | 1975 | COLOR | Rating: 8

Very popular and appealing Neil Simon Broadway comedy brought to the screen. Richard Benjamin is a talent agent who schemes to entice his retired old uncle and former partner to revive their one-time top vaudeville act for a TV special. The problem is that, while the two were great together on stage, they hated each other's guts offstage and have been feuding for years. This is the first screen appearance of George Burns since 1939 and he received a Best Supporting Actor Oscar for his efforts. With Burns and Matthau this film can't miss and it doesn't.

Sex | Nud | Viol | ✓ Lang | ✓ AdSit

A: George Burns, Walter Matthau, Richard Benjamin, Lee Meredith, Carol Arthur, Howard Hesseman

Distributed By MGM/UA Home Video M600014

SUPPORT YOUR LOCAL GUNFIGHTER

D: Burt Kennedy — 92 m

PG | COM WST | 1971 | COLOR | Rating: 8

The uproariously funny SUPPORT YOUR LOCAL SHERIFF! was so successful that they decided to do another one. Technically, this is not a sequel, because the characters are different (although the actors aren't). This time around Garner is a con artist who has spied an opportunity to make a fortune in a mining dispute. But, in order to do it he has to convince everyone that the bumbling Jack Elam is really a notorious gunfighter and killer. While this one doesn't have the sparkle and punch of the first one, it is still a darn good time and well worth the time spent.

Sex | Nud | ✓ Viol | Lang | AdSit

A: James Garner, Suzanne Pleshette, Jack Elam, Harry Morgan, John Dehner, Joan Blondell

Distributed By MGM/UA Home Video M201122

SUPPORT YOUR LOCAL SHERIFF

D: Burt Kennedy — 92 m

G | COM WST | 1969 | COLOR | Rating: 10

A very, very funny picture - that shoots holes in just about every cliche ever packed into a Western. James Garner is a drifter, passing through a gold-mining boomtown. He's got the fastest wit in the West but at heart he is just a peace lover and it is only his economics which force him into becoming the town sheriff. He is quick to point out that he is really just on his way to Australia. The only one in town actively on his side is the one-eyed town drunk (Eliam). Against him is a cantankerous old man, his snide gunslinger son and the mayor's spoiled suffragette daughter. Absolutely hilarious! Also, see BLAZING SADDLES.

Sex | Nud | ✓ Viol | Lang | AdSit

A: James Garner, Joan Hackett, Walter Brennan, Harry Morgan, Jack Elam, Bruce Dern

Distributed By MGM/UA Home Video M202031

TAKE DOWN

D: Keith Merrill — 96 m

PG | COM DMA | 1978 | COLOR | Rating: 7

Light-hearted sports serio-comedy. The high school in a little Utah town has a perpetually losing football team. Still they are determined to win at something. So they start a wrestling team, even though the only coach they have is a stuffy English teacher and Shakespeare scholar (Herrmann) who has no understanding at all of sports - and he isn't very excited by the prospect of coaching either. However, urged on by his wife, Herrmann learns to loosen up. Surprise, he develops a winning team but has to he struggle to keep his rebellious star athlete from dropping out of school. Rousing finish.

Sex | Nud | Viol | ✓ Lang | AdSit

A: Edward Herrmann, Kathleen Lloyd, Lorenzo Lamas, Maureen McCormick, Stephen Furst, Kevin Hooks

© UNICORN VIDEO, INC. 564

TALL STORY

D: Joshua Logan — 90 m

NR | COM | 1960 | B&W

7 Enjoyable little piece of froth about a man-hungry college co-ed who has fallen for the college basketball star Anthony Perkins. She is trying to get both her degree and her man. He, however, has unwittingly been bribed to throw the big basketball game between the American and the Soviet teams and is trying to get out of it. Light-hearted farcical fun. This was also Jane Fonda's film debut.

Sex | Nud | Viol | Lang | ✓ AdSit

A: Anthony Perkins, Jane Fonda, Ray Walston, Marc Connelly, Anne Jackson, Murray Hamilton

© WARNER HOME VIDEO 11236

TEAHOUSE OF THE AUGUST MOON, THE

D: Daniel Mann — 124 m

NR | COM | 1956 | COLOR

9 Warm and winning. The US Army assigns a young officer (Glenn Ford) the task of teaching the tiny Okinawan village of Tobiki the benefits of democracy and free enterprise in the wake of World War II. Marlon Brando plays the overly large (he's supposed to be Japanese), shrewd and roguish peasant interpreter who helps Ford with his daunting task. Charming and witty compendium of the tribulations occurring when widely different cultures collide. Rarely has it been so much fun, however. Interesting characters, funny, with clever dialogue. Successful transition from Broadway play.

Sex | Nud | Viol | Lang | AdSit

A: Marlon Brando, Glenn Ford, Machiko Kyo, Eddie Albert, Paul Ford

Distributed By MGM/UA Home Video M200665

THAT TOUCH OF MINK

D: Delbert Mann — 99 m

NR | COM ROM | 1962 | COLOR

7 Amusing romantic comedy. Ever-virginal Doris Day is naive and unemployed, walking through the canyons of New York when she is splashed by hot shot executive Cary Grant's limo. Smitten with the charms of Miss Day, Cary attempts to woo her with his charm and his money. That's it, that's all there really is - but it is a proven formula, has winning stars, sparkling dialogue and good support from a talented cast, particularly Gig Young. Enjoy.

Sex | Nud | Viol | Lang | ✓ AdSit

A: Cary Grant, Doris Day, Audrey Meadows, Gig Young, John Astin, Dick Sargent

© REPUBLIC PICTURES HOME VIDEO 5407

THOUSAND CLOWNS, A

D: Fred Coe — 114 m

NR | COM | 1965 | B&W

8 Hilarious comedy about a non-conformist writer (Robards) who drops out of society. He lives with his precocious 12-year-old nephew and aspires to teach the boy his peculiar ways. All this makes him unpopular with the welfare department and he is being pressured by a social worker (Gordon) to go out and get a "regular job" - or they'll take the boy away. Filmed in NYC and taken from a big Broadway play. Witty, poignant, heart-warming and very funny. It is still very worthwhile, even though it is dated slightly because non-conformist Robards does have to sell out and get a job in the end.

Sex | Nud | Viol | Lang | AdSit

A: Jason Robards, Jr., Barbara Harris, Martin Balsam, Barry Gordon, Gene Saks, William Daniels

Distributed By MGM/UA Home Video M202365

THREE MEN AND A BABY

D: Leonard Nimoy — 102 m

PG | COM | 1988 | COLOR

9 Lively, warm and very enjoyable (also extremely popular) comedy. Three carefree bachelors suddenly have unwanted responsibility thrust upon them. A destitute and distraught former girlfriend of bachelor Danson leaves a baby, his baby, on the doorstep of the trio's swinging, impeccably furnished and maintained bachelor digs. This is bubbly, brainless fun when the three party animals become instant, bumbling, overly-protective "fathers." Winning performances all around. It is an American remake of the French THREE MEN AND A CRADLE and was followed by THREE MEN AND A LITTLE LADY.

Sex | Nud | Viol | ✓ Lang | AdSit

A: Tom Selleck, Steve Guttenberg, Ted Danson, Nancy Travis, Margaret Colin, Philip Bosco

© TOUCHSTONE HOME VIDEO 658

THREE MEN AND A LITTLE LADY

D: Emile Ardolino — 103 m

PG | COM ROM | 1990 | COLOR

8 Some liked this follow-up even better than the original! The men have all matured, baby Mary has now grown into an adorable 5-year-old, and Mom Travis has become an engaging romantic interest. All five live together in a happy home and all three men are dedicated fathers. But when Travis decides to move to England for the love of another man (Cazenove), Selleck's love for her is awakened and the men set out to prove Cazenove's true intentions and that he doesn't care a bit about little Mary. A genuine treasure with plenty love and laughter to go around.

✓ Sex | Nud | Viol | ✓ Lang | ✓ AdSit

A: Tom Selleck, Steve Guttenberg, Ted Danson, Nancy Travis, Robin Weisman, Christopher Cazenove

© TOUCHSTONE HOME VIDEO 1139

THREE STOOGES, THE (VOLUMES 1-10)

D: — m

NR | COM | B&W

9 The Three Stooges's fast-paced slapstick shorts have been compiled into a ten-cassette collection. Each of the ten cassettes is about a hour long and has three "shorts" taken from among the 190 two-reelers done by the Stooges between 1934-1959. All of them feature Curly. This is the period when the team was in top form. If you are a fan, you're going to love them. If not, you're not reading this.

Sex | Nud | Viol | Lang | AdSit

A: Moe Howard, Curly Howard, Larry Fine

© COLUMBIA TRISTAR HOME VIDEO 60234

THRILL OF IT ALL, THE

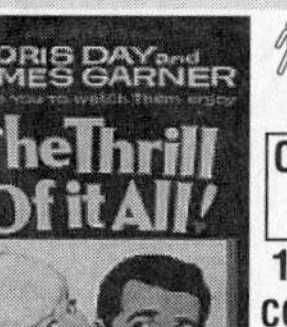

D: Norman Jewison — 108 m

NR | COM | 1963 | COLOR

7 Cute little '60s spoof of the TV industry and commercials, in particular. Doris Day and her doctor hubby James Garner are happily married, but that is all drastically changed when a bored Day accepts a high-paying job as a spokesperson in TV commercials. She becomes an overnight sensation and their domestic bliss is transformed into a nightmare for Garner. All he wants is to have his old life back and he schemes to get it. Written by Carl Reiner. Fast and funny.

Sex | Nud | Viol | Lang | AdSit

A: Doris Day, James Garner, Arlene Francis, Edward Andrews, Elliott Reid, Carl Reiner

© MCA/UNIVERSAL HOME VIDEO, INC. 80320

TIME OF THEIR LIVES, THE

D: Charles Barton — 82 m

NR | COM | 1946 | B&W

8 Considered by many to be the best-ever effort of Abbott and Costello. Oddly enough, this is also the only film where they are not partners. Lou and Marjorie Reynolds play ghosts wrongly shot as traitors during Revolutionary War times. They are haunting the country estate where neurotic Bud and his friends have come to live in 1946 at the direction of Bud's psychiatrist. Lou and Marjorie can't leave their earthbound existence until they prove their innocence. Bud has a dual role: he was also Lou's 18th-century rival for Reynolds. Imaginative and funny. Lots of slapstick.

Sex | Nud | Viol | Lang | AdSit

A: Bud Abbott, Lou Costello, Marjorie Reynolds, Binnie Barnes, John Shelton

© MCA/UNIVERSAL HOME VIDEO, INC. 80863

TOM, DICK AND HARRY

D: Garson Kanin — 87 m

NR | COM | 1941 | B&W

7 Ginger Rogers sparkles in this enthusiastic and delightful comedy about a telephone operator who is being pursued in her fantasies by three eager and anxious men at the same time, even though none of them is her ideal man. Spirited performances by everyone, but Phil Silvers outshines everyone in a small role as a pushy ice cream salesman. Very good. Witty dialogue.

Sex | Nud | Viol | Lang | AdSit

A: Ginger Rogers, George Murphy, Burgess Meredith, Alan Marshal, Joe Cunningham, Phil Silvers

© TURNER HOME ENTERTAINMENT 6188

TOOTSIE

D: Sydney Pollack — 116 m

PG | COM ROM | 1982 | COLOR

10 Wonderfully delightful picture and a huge blockbuster hit. Dustin Hoffman is an out-of-work actor who can't get a job, so he dresses up as a woman to win a part on a daytime soap opera. Quite by accident, he becomes a huge hit and is trapped into playing the role of a woman both onscreen and off. This is particularly distressing to him because he is falling in love with the leading lady (Jessica Lange) who thinks of him/her as a girlfriend. Worse, on a short trip home with Lange, her father makes a pass at him/her. Interesting insights on differences in sexes. 10 Oscar nominations. Funny!!

Sex | Nud | Viol | ✓ Lang | ✓ AdSit

A: Dustin Hoffman, Jessica Lange, Charles Durning, Bill Murray, Teri Garr, Dabney Coleman

© COLUMBIA TRISTAR HOME VIDEO 60246

TOPPER

D: Norman McLeod — 97 m

NR | COM FAN | 1937 | B&W

8 Delightful comedy. (If you are more tolerant of its somewhat dated aspect, you can even add one more number to its rating). Cary Grant and Constance Bennett are two high-living fun-loving party rats who have the definite misfortune of getting killed in a car wreck. Roland Young is a stuffy and milquetoastish banker who has never enjoyed many of life's more daring pleasures. These two brand new ghosts take it upon themselves to show him what he has been missing. Spawned two sequels and a TV series in the 50s.

Sex | Nud | Viol | Lang | AdSit

A: Cary Grant, Roland Young, Constance Bennett, Billie Burke, Eugene Pallette, Arthur Lake

© VIDEO TREASURES HR9608

TOPPER RETURNS

D: Roy Del Ruth — 88 m

NR | COM FAN | 1940 | B&W

8 Topper gets visited by a new ghost in this third entry to the series. Cary Grant and Constance Bennett have finally made it to heaven. Joan Blondell has been murdered by a mysterious man in black and she searches out mild-mannered Topper to get his help to nail her murderer. Lots of slapstick, including some pretty good special effects sequences inside a haunted house with Topper and Eddie "Rochester" Anderson. Some think this is the best in the series.

Sex / Nud / Viol / Lang / AdSit

A: Roland Young, Joan Blondell, Carole Landis, Eddie Anderson, Billie Burke, Dennis O'Keefe

© UNITED AMERICAN VIDEO CORP. 1018

TOPPER TAKES A TRIP

D: Norman McLeod — 80 m

NR | COM FAN | 1939 | COLOR

7 First sequel to the very popular original TOPPER. Topper and his wife are in France. His wife thinks that he is being unfaithful after she sees him with Constance Bennett. Miss Bennett, you will recall from the original, is a ghost. Cary Grant does not appear in this picture (except in a flashback). This time around Bennett has a new companion - a cute dog. Needing to do a good deed in order to make it into heaven, Bennett follows Topper and his divorce-minded wife to Paris to set things right. Cute fantasy.

Sex / Nud / Viol / Lang / AdSit

A: Constance Bennett, Roland Young, Billie Burke, Alan Mowbray, Verree Teasdale, Franklin Pangborn

© VIDEO TREASURES HR9612

TOUGH GUYS

D: Jeff Kanew — 103 m

PG | COM | 1986 | COLOR

6 This picture was custom-made for Lancaster and Douglas, two screen legends. It was also their seventh time together on screen. In it, they play the last two successful train robbers in America, who are just now being released after a thirty-year stretch in prison. They are woefully out of place in the world of the 1980's and are given no respect because they are old. Lancaster winds up in a nursing home and Douglas can only find work doing menial labor. Demoralized, they decide to go back into the business that they know best, for one last big heist. Not hilarious, but still fun.

Sex / Nud / Viol / Lang / ◢ AdSit

A: Burt Lancaster, Kirk Douglas, Charles Durning, Eli Wallach, Alexis Smith, Dana Carvey

© TOUCHSTONE HOME VIDEO 511

TOY, THE

D: Richard Donner — 102 m

PG | COM | 1982 | COLOR

6 A very successful, but out of touch, businessman (Gleason) takes his spoiled kid (Schwartz) shopping for Christmas and tells him that he can have absolutely anything he wants in the store. The kid decides that he wants the janitor (Pryor), a down-and-out journalist who will gladly take the money. High comedy unleashes itself as janitor Pryor teaches Gleason and the kid a few things about love, life and happiness and helping to change their lives. Pretty simple and predictable but entertaining.

Sex / Nud / Viol / ◢ Lang / AdSit

A: Richard Pryor, Jackie Gleason, Scott Schwartz, Wilfrid Hyde-White, Ned Beatty

© GOODTIMES 4499

TROUBLE WITH ANGELS, THE

D: Ida Lupino — 110 m

NR | COM CLD | 1966 | COLOR

7 Charming light-weight fare in which two rambunctious young girls (Hayley Mills and June Harding) are constantly playing pranks and raising Cain at a Catholic convent school. They are driving the normally sane and saintly Mother Superior (Rosalind Russell) nuts. Warm and genial comedy suitable for the whole family.

Sex / Nud / Viol / Lang / AdSit

A: Hayley Mills, June Harding, Rosalind Russell, Binnie Barnes, Mary Wickes, Gypsy Rose Lee

© COLUMBIA TRISTAR HOME VIDEO 60250

TURNER AND HOOCH

D: Roger Spottiswoode — 110 m

PG | COM CRM ACT | 1989 | COLOR

6 Hanks is a quirky California cop with a compulsion for cleanliness who is assigned to uncover a murderer in a drug-related case. And, he inherits the only witness to the murder - the victim's really ugly, really big dog! Hooch is a mess, and messes up everything around him, including chewing up the upholstery of Hanks's car after he leaves the dog inside it. Hanks's natural charm, along with that of the curious canine, works reasonably well at holding our attention in this very mild comedy as the pair are put through their paces while solving the crime and coincidentally discovering romance too.

Sex / Nud / ◢ Viol / Lang / ◢ AdSit

A: Tom Hanks, Mare Winningham, Craig T. Nelson, Reginald VelJohnson, Scott Paulin, J.C. Quinn

© TOUCHSTONE HOME VIDEO 911

TUTTLES OF TAHITI, THE

D: Charles Vidor — 91 m

NR | COM | 1942 | B&W

7 Light-hearted comedy about a clan of fun-loving but lazy fishermen in beautiful Tahiti. They are always on the verge of making a fortune, but are instead always broke and are led by Charles Laughton, who would rather play and gamble than do any kind of hard labor. The Tuttles have an ongoing rivalry with the Taio clan, but Laughton and Bates (who leads the Taios) become even stiffer rivals when his son and her daughter fall in love. Pretty simple, but fun and good-natured entertainment.

Sex / Nud / Viol / Lang / AdSit

A: Charles Laughton, Jon Hall, Peggy Drake, Florence Bates, Alma Ross, Victor Francen

© TURNER HOME ENTERTAINMENT 6248

TWINS

D: Ivan Reitman — 107 m

PG | COM | 1989 | COLOR

8 Nutty, warm and very funny. As the result of a genetic experiment, very short DeVito and mega-man Schwarzenegger are twins (yes, twins) who were separated at birth and have now been reunited in their adult life. When the pair figure out that it is actually true, they embark on a comic road trip to find their natural mother. Although this is a very unlikely plot, this hilarious film that has somehow been made to be believable and is highly satisfying. That is do in large measure to help from the natural wit and humor of the stars. A lot of fun!

Sex / Nud / ◢ Viol / ◢ Lang / AdSit

A: Arnold Schwarzenegger, Danny DeVito, Kelly Preston, Chloe Webb, Bonnie Bartlett, Marshall Bell

© MCA/UNIVERSAL HOME VIDEO, INC. 80873

UNCLE BUCK

D: John Hughes — 100 m

PG | COM CLD | 1989 | COLOR

7 Lightweight but enjoyable farce that is mostly for the younger set. When the family is hit by a crisis and Mom and Dad have to leave for a while, they bring in big, oafish, clumsy, bachelor Uncle Buck to look after his nephew and nieces. In spite of his faltering attempts at surrogate parenthood, the kids, particularly teenage daughter Kelly, come to realize that old Buck isn't so bad after all. Contrary to how it might appear, there is some intelligence behind the slapstick. It'll leave your heart a little warmer, too.

Sex / Nud / Viol / ◢ Lang / AdSit

A: John Candy, Amy Madigan, Jean Kelly, Macaulay Culkin, Gaby Hoffman

© MCA/UNIVERSAL HOME VIDEO, INC. 80900

UNFAITHFULLY YOURS

D: Preston Sturges — 105 m

NR | COM | 1948 | B&W

8 Very funny screwball comedy with flair! A symphony conductor (Harrison) suspects that his beautiful wife (Darnell) is messing around with his personal assistant (Kreuger). One night, as he is conducting a concert that features three main pieces, he fantasizes about three different scenarios (each matching the mood of its respective musical piece) that would take care of his little problem. One even includes murder. A bumbling,but absolutely hilarious comic ride through one man's daydreams as he attempts revenge.

Sex / Nud / Viol / Lang / ◢ AdSit

A: Rex Harrison, Linda Darnell, Kurt Kreuger, Barbara Lawrence, Rudy Vallee, Lionel Stander

© FOXVIDEO 1249

UPTOWN SATURDAY NIGHT

D: Sidney Poitier — 104 m

PG | COM | 1974 | COLOR

7 Good time entertainment. Cosby and Poitier sneak out of their houses for a night together of gambling at an illicit gambling parlor. But things go drastically awry when the game is raided by a band of hoods and everyone there is robbed. However, things get really desperate for them, when they learn that one of them had a winning lottery ticket tucked away in his wallet. Now they are determined to get that wallet back. Hilarity reigns when these two ordinary Joes go up against the mob. Very popular comedy that was followed by LET'S DO IT AGAIN.

Sex / Nud / ◢ Viol / ◢ Lang / ◢ AdSit

A: Bill Cosby, Sidney Poitier, Flip Wilson, Harry Belafonte, Richard Pryor, Rosalind Cash

© WARNER HOME VIDEO 11101

VICE VERSA

D: Brian Gilbert — 97 m

PG | COM | 1988 | COLOR

6 Father and son trade places! Marshall Seymour (Reinhold) is a workaholic department store executive who never has time for his son. His son (Savage) thinks that his Dad is completely out of touch. But the pair learn what it is like to be in the other's shoes when the powers of a magical skull enable their bodies to trade places while their minds stay put. Even though the plot has been recycled, the chemistry between Savage and Reinhold make this a real winner. If you like this one, see also FREAKY FRIDAY or BIG.

Sex / Nud / Viol / ◢ Lang / ◢ AdSit

A: Judge Reinhold, Fred Savage, Swoosie Kurtz, David Proval, Corinne Bohrer, Jane Kaczmarek

© COLUMBIA TRISTAR HOME VIDEO 65007

WACKIEST SHIP IN THE ARMY, THE

D: Richard Murphy — 99 m

NR · COM · WAR · 1961 · COLOR

6 Pleasing light-weight entertainment. Jack Lemmon is a young Navy lieutenant who, because he has some sailing experience, is conned into commanding a run-down old sailing ship through the waters of the South Pacific during WWII. He and his motley crew of inexperienced Army soldier/sailors are charged with getting a man onto an island behind Japanese lines to spy on Japanese movements. This is a light-hearted comedy that also plays serious for a while with the dangerous aspects of war. Most of the time it is fun and funny, but it has its serious moments, too.

☐ Sex ☐ Nud ☑ Viol ☐ Lang ☐ AdSit

A: Jack Lemmon, Ricky Nelson, Chips Rafferty, John Lund, Tom Tully, Warren Berlinger

© COLUMBIA TRISTAR HOME VIDEO 60596

WALK, DON'T RUN

D: Charles Walters — 114 m

NR · COM · ROM · 1966 · COLOR

7 Very entertaining romantic comedy starring Cary Grant in his last film. He is a dapper English industrialist who arrives in Tokyo just before the Olympics. Tokyo is faced with a severe housing shortage, he is two days too early to get the room he has reserved and he is homeless. Seeing a notice at the embassy, he rents a room from very beautiful but very proper Samantha Eggar. She is engaged to stuffy John Standing, who Grant can't stand. So Grant sublets his half of the apartment to American race walker Jim Hutton, of whom he does approve, and proceeds to play cupid for the two.

☐ Sex ☐ Nud ☐ Viol ☐ Lang ☐ AdSit

A: Cary Grant, Samantha Eggar, Jim Hutton, John Standing, Miiko Taka, Ted Hartley

© COLUMBIA TRISTAR HOME VIDEO 60875

WAY OUT WEST

D: James W. Horne — 66 m

G · COM · WST · 1937 · B&W

9 Certainly one of Laurel and Hardy's best, many say it is their best, comedy. When one of their friends dies and wants to leave his gold mine to his daughter, the duo head west to Brushwood Gulch to deliver to the girl her father's map to the mine. However along the way, a bartender learns of their mission and steers them to his floozy girlfriend instead of the real Mary Roberts. When the boys learn of the ruse, they have to get the map back to the girl for whom it was intended. Lots of good gags and even a soft shoe routine.

☐ Sex ☐ Nud ☐ Viol ☐ Lang ☐ AdSit

A: Stan Laurel, Oliver Hardy, James Finlayson, Sharon Lynn

© VIDEO TREASURES HR9610

WE'RE NO ANGELS

D: Michael Curtiz — 103 m

NR · COM · 1955 · COLOR

6 Slightly offbeat comedy in which three escapees from Devil's Island (Bogart, Ray and Ustinov) descend upon the house/store of an island family with the intent to rob them to get enough money to get back to France. Instead, they are so taken with the plight of the kindly but inept storekeeper (Carroll) and his wife that they stay to help him out of his problems with a nasty relative (Rathbone). Amusing and fun, even though a little too talky. Remade in 1989 with little success, in spite of some big name stars.

☐ Sex ☐ Nud ☐ Viol ☐ Lang ☐ AdSit

A: Humphrey Bogart, Aldo Ray, Joan Bennett, Peter Ustinov, Basil Rathbone, Leo G. Carroll

© PARAMOUNT HOME VIDEO 5414

WHAT ABOUT BOB?

D: Frank Oz — 99 m

PG · COM · 1991 · COLOR

8 Zany good time. Wacked-out, phobic and totally dependent neurotic (Bill Murray) pursues his pompous shrink (Dreyfuss) on his summer vacation. Murray just doesn't want to be left alone. Wherever Dreyfuss turns, there's Murray. Worse still, Murray has endeared himself to Dreyfuss's family. Dreyfuss wants to lose Murray but his family likes him, so there is no respite for Dreyfuss anywhere. The head-doctor is himself driven to madness. Hilarious in places, just plain silly in others, but almost always enjoyable. Even non-fans of the wise-cracking Bill Murray will have a good time with him in this one.

☐ Sex ☐ Nud ☐ Viol ☐ Lang ☐ AdSit

A: Richard Dreyfuss, Bill Murray, Julie Hagerty, Charlie Korsmo, Kathryn Bowen, Tom Aldredge

© TOUCHSTONE HOME VIDEO 1224

WHAT'S UP DOC?

D: Peter Bogdanovich — 94 m

PG · COM · ROM · 1972 · COLOR

8 Zany '70s remake of 1938s BRINGING UP BABY. A fast-paced comedy in which a stuffy musicologist (O'Neal) and his fiancee (Kahn) become involved with an outlandish college student (Streisand) after they all get thrown in together in a wild adventure to get back four identical flight bags which have gotten mixed up. One bag contains Streisand's clothes, and one O'Neal's music - but one of the others contains a wealth of stolen jewels and there are top secrets in the other. Non-stop running gags produce some real big belly laughs and a riotous final chase scene.

☐ Sex ☐ Nud ☐ Viol ☐ Lang ☐ AdSit

A: Barbra Streisand, Ryan O'Neal, Kenneth Mars, Austin Pendleton, Madeline Kahn, Sorrell Booke

© WARNER HOME VIDEO 1041

WHAT'S UP TIGER LILY

D: Woody Allen — 80 m

PG · COM · 1966 · COLOR

6 At the height of the James Bond craze, Woody Allen came up with this one-joke spy farce that works quite well through most of its length. He's taken a fourth-rate Japanese rip-off of the spy genre, over-dubbed all the Japanese dialogue with English and substituted his own wacky plot. Under Woody's revised plot, there is a devious plan afoot to steal the world's best egg salad recipe. Silliness reigns. Music is provided by The Lovin' Spoonful.

☐ Sex ☐ Nud ☑ Viol ☑ Lang ☐ AdSit

A: Woody Allen, Tatsuya Mihashi, Hana Miya, Tadao Nakamura

© GOODTIMES 9148

WHEN COMEDY WAS KING

D: — 81 m

NR · COM · 1959 · B&W

9 This is a compilation of some of the best clips from the comedies of the silent era. Included are clips from Charlie Chaplin, Buster Keaton, Laurel and Hardy, Ben Turpin, Fatty Arbuckle, Wallace Beery, Gloria Swanson, The Keystone Kops and more. Comedy like this doesn't diminish with time.

☐ Sex ☐ Nud ☐ Viol ☐ Lang ☐ AdSit

A: Charlie Chaplin, Harry Langdon, Buster Keaton, Fatty Arbuckle, Mabel Normand, Snub Pollard

© UNITED AMERICAN VIDEO CORP. 7124

WHO DONE IT?

D: Erle C. Kenton — 77 m

NR · COM · 1942 · B&W

8 Abbott and Costello are two would-be radio show writers but are now just soda jerks in the same building where radio plays are broadcast. However, when the network's president is murdered during one of the shows, they pretend to be police detectives... and everyone believes them, even the killer. Silliness, as always, reigns with these two, so don't expect sophisticated humor. One of their best.

☐ Sex ☐ Nud ☐ Viol ☐ Lang ☐ AdSit

A: Bud Abbott, Lou Costello, Patric Knowles, William Bendix, Louise Allbritton, Mary Wickes

© MCA/UNIVERSAL HOME VIDEO, INC. 80862

WHO FRAMED ROGER RABBIT

D: Robert Zemeckis — 106 m

PG · COM · 1988 · COLOR

8 Fun blending of real and fantasy worlds in this technically very difficult combination of live-action and animation. The plot is set in Hollywood in 1947. Cartoon character Roger Rabbit is framed for murder and seeks the help of hard-boiled real-world detective Eddie Valiant (Hoskins), but must first pull him out of his self-induced retirement. Hoskins's investigation leads him into the animated world of Toon Town, a place that is inhabited by famous cartoon characters, and a place where anything can happen and usually does. Funny, fast-paced and very entertaining.

☐ Sex ☐ Nud ☐ Viol ☐ Lang ☑ AdSit

A: Bob Hoskins, Christopher Lloyd, Joanna Cassidy, Stubby Kaye, Alan Tilvern

© TOUCHSTONE HOME VIDEO 940

WHO'S MINDING THE MINT?

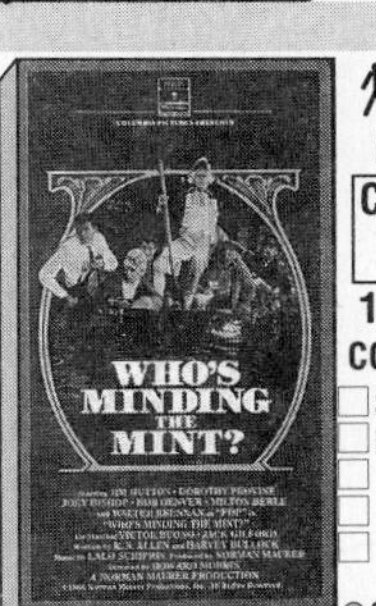

D: Howard Morris — 97 m

NR · COM · 1967 · COLOR

8 Hilarious farce in the same vein as IT'S A MAD, MAD, MAD, MAD WORLD. A really top-flight cast of talented people makes this zaniness work, and work well it does. Jim Hutton is a worker at the US Mint who accidentally destroys $50,000 in new bills. He enlists the help of an odd assortment of friendly thieves to help him reprint the missing money. Things get really wacky, though, when he has to hurriedly move the plan up one night and it turns into an outrageous come-as-you-are fest. Plus, they have printed up not $50,000 but $7,000,000. Truly entertaining - a riotous good time.

☐ Sex ☐ Nud ☐ Viol ☐ Lang ☐ AdSit

A: Jim Hutton, Walter Brennan, Jack Gilford, Milton Berle, Joey Bishop, Victor Buono

© COLUMBIA TRISTAR HOME VIDEO 60439

WITHOUT A CLUE

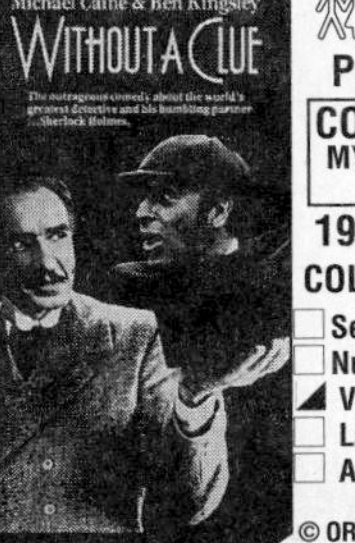

D: Thom Eberhardt — 107 m

PG · COM · MYS · 1988 · COLOR

8 Funny high-spirited farce that takes an entirely different slant to the oft-used mystery/detective movie vehicle of Sherlock Holmes and Dr. Watson - suppose Sherlock Holmes was just a drunken bumbling actor and Watson was the real deductive genius. Kingsley plays Watson, a doctor who enjoys investigating crimes and then writing about them. He uses the mythical figure of Sherlock Holmes as the detective, but one day is called upon to present him. So he hires Caine to be Holmes and forever after has to keep him out of trouble. Inventive and funny.

☐ Sex ☐ Nud ☑ Viol ☐ Lang ☐ AdSit

A: Michael Caine, Ben Kingsley, Jeffrey Jones, Lysette Anthony, Paul Freeman

© ORION PICTURES CORPORATION 8733

WITHOUT LOVE

D: Harold S. Bucquet 113 m

NR · COM ROM · 1945 · B&W · Sex · Nud · Viol · Lang · AdSit

6 Mildly amusing story set in wartime Washington, D.C. A sleep-walking inventor (Tracy) and a pretty widow (Hepburn) with a very big house enter into an agreement. They are both disillusioned with love, but he needs a place to conduct his secret war experiments and her basement is perfect. So, they agree to enter into a marriage of convenience. How long can that last? Tracy and Hepburn have great screen chemistry, and Keenan Wynn and Lucille Ball provide good support and a lot of wise-cracks, all of which raises this otherwise mild script to being enjoyable entertainment.

A: Spencer Tracy, Katharine Hepburn, Lucille Ball, Keenan Wynn, Carl Esmond, Patricia Morison

Distributed By MGM/UA Home Video M202350

WONDER MAN

D: H. Bruce Humberstone 98 m

NR · COM MUS · 1945 · COLOR · Sex · Nud · Viol · Lang · AdSit

6 Silly and entertaining vehicle for Danny Kaye's special comedic talents. He plays two physically identical twins, but the personality of each is entirely different. One is an outgoing song and dance man and the other is very serious and quiet. When the song and dance man is killed by gangsters, his spirit comes back to encourage the mousy twin to impersonate him, hoping to convince the hoods that they didn't succeed and so provide a means to trap them. Funny. Won an Oscar for Special Effects.

A: Danny Kaye, Virginia Mayo, Vera-Ellen, Donald Woods

© HBO VIDEO 90663

WRONG ARM OF THE LAW, THE

D: Cliff Owen 94 m

NR · COM CRM · 1962 · B&W · Sex · Nud · Viol · Lang · AdSit

7 Silly farce of the variety that made Sellers famous. He plays Pearly Gates, the leader of a Cockney band of thieves that is so prosperous that it has set up a welfare-like system to take care of its members. All that is threatened now because each time they carry off a heist, they are confronted by a group of cops that confiscates everything. The problem is that these guys are not really cops. So Pearly calls a conference between the real cops and the other hoods, and they all agree to call a truce and cooperate long enough to get these cop/thieves put in jail. Wacky and zany, wild fun.

A: Peter Sellers, Lionel Jeffries, Bernard Cribbins, Nanette Newman, Davey Kaye

© MONTEREY HOME VIDEO 34860

YOU CAN'T CHEAT AN HONEST MAN

D: George Marshall 79 m

NR · COM · 1939 · B&W · Sex · Nud · Viol · Lang · AdSit

8 W.C. Fields wrote this frantic comedy about a struggling circus owner who has a constantly running battle with his featured act, ventriloquist Edgar Bergen and his alter egos, the wooden dummies Mortimer Snerd and Charlie McCarthy. Bergan is in love with Fields's daughter, but she is determined to marry a rich guy just to help her out her Dad. Lots of snappy dialogue and one-liners. Fields admitted that it was mostly several vaudeville skits put together. Regardless, Fields, Bergen and the smart-aleck puppets are hysterical.

A: W.C. Fields, Edgar Bergen, Constance Moore, James Bush, Mary Forbes, Eddie Anderson

© BARR ENTERTAINMENT VIDEO 11007

YOU CAN'T TAKE IT WITH YOU

D: Frank Capra 126 m

NR · COM ROM · 1938 · B&W · Sex · Nud · Viol · Lang · AdSit

9 Director Frank Capra won Oscars for Best Picture and Best Director with this "Capra-corn" screwball comedy. Jean Arthur is the beautiful and reasonably sane daughter in a family of poor but happy eccentrics, and also Jimmy Stewart's secretary. Stewart is the down-to-earth son of a family of rich stuffed shirts, and he wants to marry her. These oil-and-water families are to meet for dinner before the wedding, but when they mistakenly arrive one night early, things get out of hand and everyone winds up in jail. Nominated for a total of seven Oscars.

A: Jean Arthur, James Stewart, Lionel Barrymore, Edward Arnold, Eddie Anderson, Ann Miller

© COLUMBIA TRISTAR HOME VIDEO 90153

YOUNG FRANKENSTEIN

D: Mel Brooks 106 m

PG · COM HOR · 1974 · B&W · Sex · Nud · Viol · Lang · AdSit

9 This ranks right up there with BLAZING SADDLES, the other masterpiece from Mel Brooks - master of zany spoofs. This one rips into Frankenstein movies. Gene Wilder is a modern-day college professor who disdains his family's jaded history and goes back to Transylvania to get it right this time. Gags are nonstop. Hysterical scenes with Boyle as his monster and Marty Feldman as his hunch-back assistant. Music, sets and props, which are reminiscent of the '30s, all add to the fun. Hilarious the whole way through.

A: Gene Wilder, Peter Boyle, Marty Feldman, Madeline Kahn, Cloris Leachman, Teri Garr

© FOXVIDEO 1103

YOUNG IN HEART, THE

D: Richard Wallace 91 m

NR · COM · 1938 · COLOR · Sex · Nud · Viol · Lang · AdSit

8 Heartwarming charmer. A family of oddball con artists, card sharps and opportunists is kicked out of Monte Carlo for cheating at cards, but they happen upon a train wreck and have the good fortune to save a rich old lady from the wreckage. Miss Fortune, the little old lady, gratefully invites the penniless and homeless group to stay with her. Ecstatic with their new meal ticket, their dreams of new-found wealth are soon changed when Miss Fortune proves instead to be such a charmer that the family learns a new set of values for living. Delightful little winner.

A: Janet Gaynor, Douglas Fairbanks, Jr., Paulette Goddard, Roland Young, Billie Burke, Richard Carlson

© VIDEO TREASURES SV9622

Crime

AL CAPONE

D: Richard Wilson 104 m

NR · CRM ACT DMA · 1959 · B&W · Sex · Nud · Viol · Lang · AdSit

8 Excellent action movie. Solid telling of the life story of the infamous Chicago gangster who rises from being a hitman for Johnny Torrio (Persoff) to become the king of the Prohibition Era. After a bitter battle with the Feds, he is arrested and imprisoned for tax evasion. No other gangster so captured the imagination and the headlines of the country. Steiger is riveting in his portrayal of Capone, and the rest of the cast is perfect, too. For more of Capone see THE UNTOUCHABLES (1987) and SCARFACE (1932).

A: Rod Steiger, Fay Spain, Martin Balsam, Nehemiah Persoff

© CBS/FOX VIDEO 7750

ANGELS WITH DIRTY FACES

D: Michael Curtiz 97 m

NR · CRM DMA · 1938 · B&W · Sex · Nud · Viol · Lang · AdSit

8 Enjoyable and still meaningful, even if it is overly melodramatic. Two childhood friends grow up on the wrong side of the tracks. One (O'Brien) becomes a priest. The other (Cagney) is a prominent neighborhood hood, a hero to the tough neighborhood kids and a counterweight to everything O'Brien trys to do. However, after Cagney gets caught after a shootout with a local hood (Bogart) and is sentenced to die in the gas chamber, Father O'Brien convinces him to do the kids a favor by dying like a coward and depriving the boys of a hero. Great characterizations, particularly Cagney.

A: James Cagney, Pat O'Brien, Humphrey Bogart, Ann Sheridan, George Bancroft, Bobby Jordan

Distributed By MGM/UA Home Video M201619

ASPHALT JUNGLE, THE

D: John Huston 112 m

NR · CRM SUS · 1950 · B&W · Sex · Nud · Viol · Lang · AdSit

10 One of the greatest crime films ever and it was the inspiration for numerous others which followed. It is the taut, realistic account of the planning and execution of a jewel robbery that goes bad. The suspense steadily builds throughout the entire picture because of an interesting twist in the way the story is told. Early on, we are told what the outcome will be and for the rest of the picture we're waiting anxiously for it to happen. This film received four Oscar nominations and is also credited with being the film which gave Marilyn Monroe the exposure she needed to become a major star, but the entire cast was inspired.

A: Sterling Hayden, Sam Jaffe, Louis Calhern, Jean Hagen, James Whitmore, Marilyn Monroe

Distributed By MGM/UA Home Video M700483

DRAGNET

D: Jack Webb 88 m

NR · CRM MYS · 1951 · COLOR · Sex · Nud · Viol · Lang · AdSit

7 A piece of 1950s Americana. This is a feature length spin-off of the popular TV series from the early '50s. In it, Sgt. Friday and officer Smith solve a mobster's murder, beginning with only four shell casings and a footprint. This case, as was all cases in the series, was based upon a real case. The prime focus of the series always was the solving of the crime, not upon the characters. It was this no-nonsense approach to crime solving that made the TV series so popular. Today their style would likely be viewed much less favorably. Still quite interesting and nostalgic.

A: Barton Yarborough, Jack Webb

© MCA/UNIVERSAL HOME VIDEO, INC. 45030

MADIGAN

D: Don Siegel — 101 m

NR | CRM ACT | 1968 | COLOR

8 Realistic, hard-hitting action! Madigan (Widmark), is a tough cop, but he's in double trouble. In an attempt to capture a killer, he and his partner break in on a psychopathic killer, but they're momentarily distracted by a naked girl and the killer gets away. Hardball Commissioner Russell (Fonda) is outraged and gives Madigan only 72 hours to catch the guy. Madigan is hard-pressed but his socialite wife also is pressuring him to quit the police work he loves. Critically acclaimed for its revealing look into the workings of New York City detectives - its popularity launched the TV series.

☐ Sex ◢ Nud ◢ Viol ◢ Lang ◢ AdSit

A: Richard Widmark, Henry Fonda, Inger Stevens, Harry Guardino, James Whitmore

© MCA/UNIVERSAL HOME VIDEO, INC. 80040

MURPH THE SURF

D: Marvin J. Chomsky — 102 m

PG | CRM | 1975 | COLOR

6 The impossible heist. A story of how two Florida beach bums conspired to steal the 564-carat Star of India sapphire from New York's American Museum of Natural History. Believe it or not, they actually succeeded, and the story is based on the truth. The real crime was committed in 1964. It was the biggest jewel heist in history. There is some solid suspense in this film and a pretty good boat chase, too.

☐ Sex ☐ Nud ☐ Viol ☐ Lang ◢ AdSit

A: Robert Conrad, Don Stroud, Donna Mills, Robyn Millan, Burt Young, Luther Adler

© WARNER HOME VIDEO 26030

ORGANIZATION, THE

D: Don Medford — 107 m

PG | CRM ACT | 1971 | COLOR

6 The third and final appearance of Mr. Tibbs, the tough big city police detective Poitier created in IN THE HEAT OF THE NIGHT and followed up with in THEY CALL ME MR. TIBBS. This time in San Francisco, Poitier comes to the aid of a student vigilante group who raids a furniture factory that is really a front trafficking in heroin. When the manager is murdered, the group admits to Tibbs that they stole $5 million in dope to keep it off the streets but they didn't kill anyone. He rises to their defense but is suspended from the force. Good action flick with a realistic plot and believable climax.

☐ Sex ☐ Nud ◢ Viol ◢ Lang ◢ AdSit

A: Sidney Poitier, Barbara Mc Nair, Raul Julia, Sheree North, Ron O'Neal, Daniel J. Travanti

Distributed By MGM/UA Home Video M203136

PANIC IN THE STREETS

D: Elia Kazan — 96 m

NR | CRM SUS | 1950 | B&W

9 Excellent thriller set in New Orleans. An illegal resident arrives at the waterfront and is killed by three street punks who are after his money. However, a routine check of the dead man by the medical examiner reveals that he was infected with the highly contagious and deadly bubonic plague. The examiner and the police have only 48 hours to capture the killers and quarantine all their contacts to prevent a massive outbreak of a killer epidemic. Very taut and suspenseful. Excellence in acting, and in all other respects, too. The story won an Oscar.

☐ Sex ☐ Nud ◢ Viol ☐ Lang ☐ AdSit

A: Richard Widmark, Paul Douglas, Barbara Bel Geddes, Jack Palance, Zero Mostel

© FOXVIDEO 1847

PUBLIC ENEMY

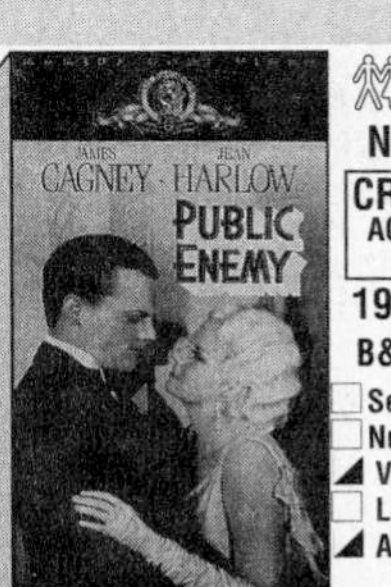

D: William Wellman — 83 m

NR | CRM ACT | 1931 | B&W

9 This is the film that made Cagney a star and it is still highly watchable today, even though it is obviously dated. It is also notable as the film having the infamous scene of Cagney shoving a grapefruit into the face of Mae Clarke. Cagney is compelling as a young street tough who embraces a life of crime, beginning by stealing booze on Chicago's south side and graduating up the ladder through the gangland wars. In spite of its many dated notions and techniques, this unvarnished look at a vicious arrogant hood doomed to an early death is still powerful. Fast-paced.

☐ Sex ☐ Nud ◢ Viol ☐ Lang ◢ AdSit

A: James Cagney, Jean Harlow, Eddie Woods, Beryl Mercer, Joan Blondell, Mae Clarke

Distributed By MGM/UA Home Video 201586

RACKET, THE

D: John Cromwell — 88 m

NR | CRM ACT | 1951 | B&W

6 Unusual film noir. A fast-paced crime drama in which an incorruptible police chief (Mitchum) is determined to bring down a corrupt mobster (Ryan), even though it means he has to also fight his own superiors and the politicians who control them. Ryan has a stranglehold on all the politicians, but Mitchum is set to end his rule over the town and a beautiful nightclub singer (Scott). Mitchum's men destroy Ryan's thug army, but Ryan himself escapes, until Mitchum finds a way to lure him in. Bizarre ending.

☐ Sex ☐ Nud ◢ Viol ☐ Lang ◢ AdSit

A: Robert Mitchum, Robert Ryan, William Conrad, Lizabeth Scott, Ray Collins, William Talman

© TURNER HOME ENTERTAINMENT 6112

ROARING TWENTIES, THE

D: Raoul Walsh — 106 m

NR | CRM ACT | 1939 | B&W

8 A lively gangster flick, acclaimed as being one of the best! Cagney is a returning soldier from WWI who has no prospects for a job so he enters into a bootlegging partnership with his old friend Bogart. At first, Cagney flourishes. But then his enterprise comes under attack by rival gangs and is smashed by the law. For a while he has a legitimate cab business left but when the stock market crashes, he is left with only one cab. Depressed and alone, he rescues a woman he once loved and saves her husband (Lynn) from the ruthless Bogart, who's still in the business. Well done.

☐ Sex ☐ Nud ◢ Viol ☐ Lang ◢ AdSit

A: James Cagney, Humphrey Bogart, Jeffrey Lynn, Priscilla Lane, Gladys George, Frank McHugh

Distributed By MGM/UA Home Video M201612

Documentary

ANIMALS ARE BEAUTIFUL PEOPLE

D: Jamie Uys — 92 m

G | DOC CLD | 1974 | COLOR

8 This fun documentary was made by the maker of THE GODS MUST BE CRAZY. It is a humorous and interesting review of the animals of the deserts and the jungles of Africa. It covers all the animals from the largest to the smallest using sharp portraits that remain interesting and do not become too cute. Examples include such things as the mother fish who hides her babies in her mouth, and the "good time" that some elephants and other animals have when they eat the well-fermented Marula tree berries.

☐ Sex ☐ Nud ☐ Viol ☐ Lang ☐ AdSit

A:

© WARNER HOME VIDEO 11105

BEST BOY

D: Ira Wohl — 105 m

DOC DMA | 1981 | COLOR

8 This is the moving real-life story of Philly, a 52-year-old retarded man and it won an Oscar for Best Documentary. Philly has been living at home with his parents ever since he was born, but now his parents are very old. His cousin Ira has become concerned about what will happen to Philly. So he talks Philly's parents into letting him help Philly to learn how to become more independent. This is a film that documents his efforts to do just that. Contrary to being a depressing film, Philly's enthusiasm and joy at accomplishing even the littlest tasks is contagious. A heart-warming, uplifting film. Recommended.

☐ Sex ☐ Nud ☐ Viol ☐ Lang ◢ AdSit

A:

© TAPEWORM VIDEO 1020

CHUCK BERRY HAIL HAIL! ROCK 'N' ROLL

D: Taylor Hackford — 121 m

PG | DOC MUS | 1987 | COLOR

10 If you like classic rock 'n roll, you've got to see this movie. Chuck Berry, the father of rock 'n roll, had his sixtieth birthday tribute concert in St. Louis at the Fox Theatre - and this is it. Singing back-up are some of the greatest singers and stylists of classic and '80s rock 'n roll. Berry sings all of his greatest songs including: "Maybellene," "Memphis," "Nadine" and "Roll Over Beethoven."

☐ Sex ☐ Nud ☐ Viol ☐ Lang ☐ AdSit

A: Chuck Berry, Keith Richards, Eric Clapton, Robert Cray, Etta James, Julian Lennon

© MCA/UNIVERSAL HOME VIDEO, INC. 80465

COMPLEAT BEATLES, THE

D: — 119 m

NR | DOC MUS | 1984 | B&W

9 A fascinating documentary, even to non-Beatle fans. It is an extensive and quite entertaining look at the evolution and promotion of an international phenomenon. It documents their very earliest beginnings, the changes they underwent and all the people involved in their creation and promotion; and, it is punctuated with a very liberal use of actual interviews, newsreel footage and concert excerpts - including their US tour. The primary focus is on their development - from the early days as "The Quarrymen", through their maturation to more complex music, to their breakup after the 1969 film LET IT BE.

☐ Sex ☐ Nud ☐ Viol ☐ Lang ☐ AdSit

A: The Beatles

Distributed By MGM/UA Home Video M700166

FAMILY

ELVIS: THAT'S THE WAY IT IS

G | DOC MUS | 1970 | COLOR

D: Dennis Sanders — 109 m

8 Excellent documentary made in 1970 of Elvis's preparations for a run in the Las Vegas International Hotel. Well filmed, with numerous excerpts of Elvis offstage and rehearsing. Also interspersed are numerous interviews of various backstage people, fans and musicians. The film culminates with his opening night act which includes "All Shook Up," "Blue Suede Shoes" and "Bridge Over Troubled Waters." 27 songs in all.

Sex / Nud / Viol / Lang / AdSit

A: Elvis Presley

Distributed By MGM/UA Home Video M700373

ENDLESS SUMMER, THE

NR | DOC COM | 1964 | COLOR

D: Bruce Brown — 90 m

8 This is a perennial favorite and has not diminished with time. It is an extraordinarily fun documentary that captures the exhilaration and danger of surfing through beautiful photography of people in beautiful locations. It is a quasi-travelogue loosely patterned around the quest of two young surfers to find the perfect wave by exploring all the world's most famous beaches. Whimsically narrated by director Bruce Brown. In 1994, 30 years later, Brown retraced the steps in this documentary in ENDLESS SUMMER II.

Sex / Nud / Viol / Lang / AdSit

A:

© TURNER HOME ENTERTAINMENT N4028

ENDLESS SUMMER II

PG | DOC COM | 1994 | COLOR

D: Bruce Brown — 110 m

9 In 1964 director Bruce Brown created a now classic documentary in which two young surfers decided to follow the summer and the waves to all the places around the world where they could surf. Now, thirty years later, Brown goes back on the road again to retrace those footsteps, and it's even more fun than before. This is a very entertaining travelogue in which Brown narrates their trip with clever and funny dialogue. The photography is absolutely outstanding. He photographs surfing on big waves, on small waves, on almost no waves and on HUGE waves. He photographs it from in front of the waves, from behind the waves, on top of the wave, inside the wave and under the wave. Radical dude.

Sex / ◢ Nud / Viol / Lang / AdSit

A: Robert "Wingnut" Weaver, Patrick O'Connell

© TURNER HOME ENTERTAINMENT N4052

GIZMO

G | DOC COM | 1980 | B&W

D: — 76 m

8 Funny documentary revealing America's passion for zany inventions. Footage was largely gleaned from newsreels dating back to the '30s. The inventions include a dimple making machine, wet diaper alarms and an anti-snore device.

Sex / Nud / Viol / Lang / AdSit

A:

© WARNER HOME VIDEO 28002

GOLDEN AGE OF COMEDY, THE

NR | DOC | 1957 | B&W

D: Robert Youngson — 78 m

7 Fun compilation of some of the silent era's greatest comedy moments created by some of its then zaniest stars: Charlie Chaplin, Laurel and Hardy, the Keystone Kops, Will Rogers, Carole Lombard, Ben Turpin, Harry Langdon and others. This wide assortment of slapstick excerpts, from the heyday of silent film 1914-1929, presents the comedy that brought tears of laughter to the entertainment-deprived and relatively unsophisticated audiences of its day, however much of what was hysterical then provokes mostly yawns now.

Sex / Nud / Viol / Lang / AdSit

A:

© UNITED AMERICAN VIDEO CORP. 216

GOSPEL

DOC MUS | 1982 | COLOR

D: — 92 m

9 A rousing and exuberant, high-energy concert including several top gospel performers of the '70s and '80s in very entertaining performances before a very enthusiastic crowd. There is no commentary, only music. The groups include: James Cleveland and the Southern California Community Choir, Walter Hawkins and the Hawkins Family, Mighty Clouds of Joy, Shirley Caesar, Twinkie Clark and the Clark Sisters. If you enjoyed this you should also see another documentary SAY AMEN, SOMEBODY.

Sex / Nud / Viol / Lang / AdSit

A:

© MONTEREY HOME VIDEO 31944

KING: MONTGOMERY TO MEMPHIS

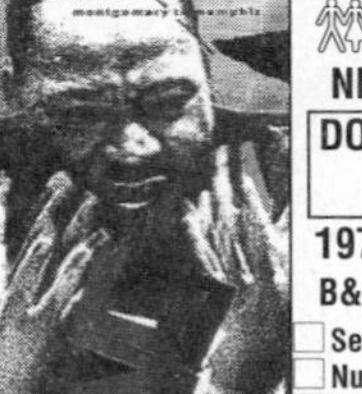

NR | DOC | 1970 | B&W

D: — 103 m

9 A eloquent documentary of the life and accomplishments of the man and a dream. Numerous pieces of film are brilliantly edited together documenting the highlights of his career, beginning with the bus boycott in Montgomery, through his address at the Lincoln Memorial and the Nobel Peace Prize, to his murder in Memphis.

Sex / Nud / Viol / Lang / AdSit

A:

© PACIFIC ARTS VIDEO 680

KOYAANISQATSI

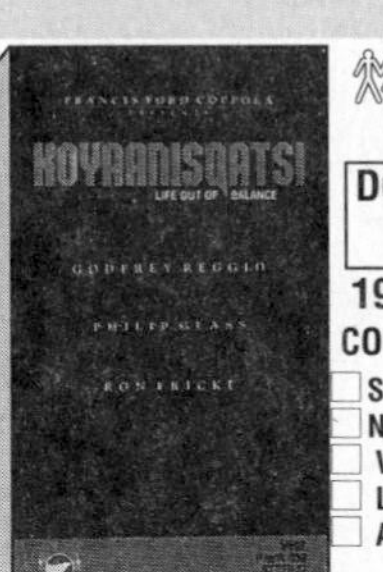

DOC | 1983 | COLOR

D: Godfrey Reggio — 87 m

8 Strangely compelling viewing. It is a fascinating kaleidoscopic view of the many majesties and not so majestic objects and activities to be found in both nature and within man's cities. It is a total flight of photographic fancy, where the only sound is a symbiotic score by Philip Glass. There is no narration, no dialogue. There is only a never-ending string of compelling images. Koyaanisqatsi is a word from the language of the Southwestern Hopi Indians. It means "life out of balance."

Sex / Nud / Viol / Lang / AdSit

A:

© PACIFIC ARTS VIDEO PAVR539

MAN WHO SAW TOMORROW, THE

PG | DOC | 1981 | COLOR

D: Robert Guenette — 88 m

8 An amazing 16th-century poet and mystic Nostradamus made extremely accurate and thought-provoking predictions that will confound and terrify you. Welles narrates this documentary detailing the predicted events that have occurred and the many still to come. Amazingly accurate, his prophecies included the rise and fall of Hitler and the assassinations of Presidents Lincoln and Kennedy. Nostradamus even gives names and dates in some cases. Haunting.

Sex / Nud / ◢ Viol / Lang / ◢ AdSit

A: Orson Welles

© WARNER HOME VIDEO 11246

MONTEREY POP

NR | DOC MUS | 1967 | COLOR

D: James Desmond — 88 m

9 White Hot! This is the first major rock concert film and was shot at the Monterey Pop Festival in California in 1967. This landmark concert featured some of the biggest musical stars (15) of the time, in their brightest moments, and it kicked off the rock summer series (Summer of Love) that culminated in Woodstock. Performances include Janis Joplin's "Ball and Chain" and an intense rendition of "My Generation" by The Who. Brilliant historical time-piece and a must-see for anyone with more than a passing interest in music.

Sex / Nud / Viol / Lang / AdSit

A: Jimi Hendrix, Otis Redding, The Who, Jefferson Airplane, Janis Joplin, The Animals

© COLUMBIA TRISTAR HOME VIDEO RO162VH

MY FRIEND LIBERTY

DOC CLD | 1986 | COLOR

D: Jimmy Picker — 30 m

7 Animated history lesson. The famous lady Liberty comes to life, steps down and educates a young man about the history of the statue and the meaning behind her name. Entertaining and educational, this program is done in clay animation by the Academy Award winner Jimmy Picker. Great for children and adults alike.

Sex / Nud / Viol / Lang / AdSit

A:

© WARNER HOME VIDEO 130

NANOOK OF THE NORTH

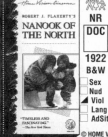

NR | DOC | 1922 | B&W

D: Robert Flaherty — 69 m

9 Enduring silent classic that is just as - if not more - fascinating than when filmed so long ago. Flaherty's film technique and the equipment he used were quite primitive, and so were the conditions under which he worked. The film depicts the arduous daily life of an Eskimo family lead by the father, Nanook, living along the frozen shores of Hudson Bay. Staged scenes of survival skills are mixed with haunting vistas of endless bleakness. Two years after completion, Nanook died of starvation.

Sex / Nud / ◢ Viol / Lang / AdSit

A:

© HOME VISION NAN 01

PUMPING IRON

PG | DOC | 1977 | COLOR

D: George Butler, Robert Flore — 90 m

6 Fascinating look inside the world of male body building. The primary focus is upon six-time Mr. Olympia, Arnold Schwarzenegger, and his attempt to retain his title. (This film was the first major exposure of Schwarzenegger to the bulk of the American public.) Also included are many of the major body builders of the time, including Lou Ferrigno (The Incredible Hulk). Much of the behind-the-scenes filming concerns Arnold's efforts at psyching out Ferrigno. See also companion film PUMPING IRON II: THE WOMEN.

☐ Sex ☐ Nud ☐ Viol ◢ Lang ◢ AdSit

A: Arnold Schwarzenegger, Lou Ferrigno, Mike Katz, Franco Columbu

© COLUMBIA TRISTAR HOME VIDEO 60085

PUMPING IRON II: THE WOMEN

NR | DOC | 1985 | COLOR

D: George Butler — 107 m

6 Curious documentary covering the 1983 Women's World Cup held at Caesar's Palace in Las Vegas. It is a straightforward documentary whose primary focus is the contrasting physiques of massive Australian Bev Francis and the more curvy Rachel McLish. An interesting curiosity is that the winners are offered their prizes either in cash, by check or with poker chips. It was derived from the earlier documentary with Arnold Schwarzenegger and Lou Ferrigno, PUMPING IRON.

☐ Sex ◢ Nud ☐ Viol ◢ Lang ◢ AdSit

A: Rachel McLish, Lori Bowden, Carla Dunlap, Bev Francis, Kris Alexander, George Plimpton

© LIVE HOME VIDEO VA5093

SAY AMEN, SOMEBODY

G | DOC MUS | 1983 | COLOR

D: George T. Nierenberg — 100 m

9 A riotous celebration of Gospel music! This documentary captures the energetic feeling and uplifting essence of the songs, the sound, the meanings, the joy and inspiration of music made for the senses and soul. Featured are two of Gospel's greats: Thomas A. Dorsey and Willie Mae Ford Smith. Their lives and their careers are explored and spliced with more than two dozen exuberant songs. A glistening, shining film that is wonderful for the whole family and will leave you feeling jubilant and refreshed. If you enjoy this, you should also see the documentary GOSPEL.

☐ Sex ☐ Nud ☐ Viol ☐ Lang ☐ AdSit

A: Willie Mae Ford Smith, Thomas A. Dorsey, Sallie Martin

© PACIFIC ARTS VIDEO 547

STATUE OF LIBERTY, THE

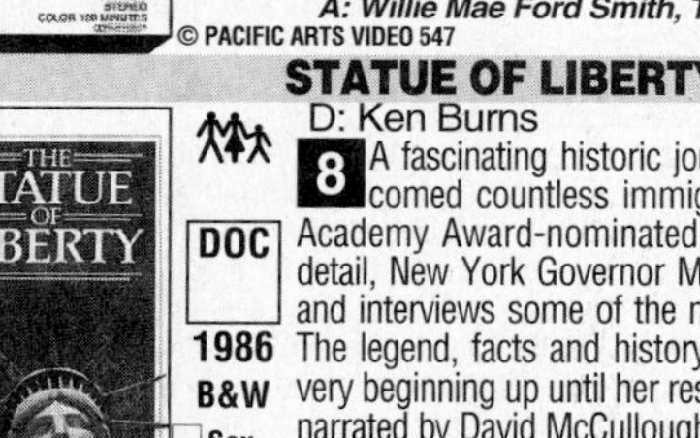

DOC | 1986 | B&W

D: Ken Burns — 60 m

8 A fascinating historic journey! The famous "Lady" that has welcomed countless immigrants to America is the feature of this Academy Award-nominated documentary. Researched to the last detail, New York Governor Mario Cuomo makes a guest appearance and interviews some of the most intriguing and famous immigrants. The legend, facts and history of Lady Liberty are explored from the very beginning up until her restoration in 1986. An outstanding tribute, narrated by David McCullough. Another documentary about the statue but aimed more for children is MY FRIEND LIBERTY.

☐ Sex ☐ Nud ☐ Viol ☐ Lang ☐ AdSit

A:

© LIVE HOME VIDEO VA1049

VISION SHARED: TRIBUTE TO W. GUTHRIE AND LEADBELLY

DOC MUS | 1988 | COLOR

D: Jim Brown — 70 m

8 Fascinating! Two of the great musical pioneers are paid just tribute by 1988 musicians from many venues in this fantastic documentary. The stories of the lives of folksingers Woody Gutherie and Leadbelly are interspersed with their music which is played by themselves and also performed by many music greats of 1988. This salute to the pair includes songs like "Vigilante Man," "Jesus Christ," "This Land is Your Land" and "Do Re Me." A sparkling look to the recent past and the foundations of popular modern music.

☐ Sex ☐ Nud ☐ Viol ☐ Lang ☐ AdSit

A: Bruce Springsteen, Pete Seeger, Bob Dylan, John Cougar Mellencamp, Willie Nelson, Arlo Guthrie

© CBS MUSIC VIDEO ENTERPRISES 19V-49006

WEAVERS: WASN'T THAT A TIME!

DOC MUS | 1980 | COLOR

D: Jim Brown — 78 m

10 Wonderfully joyous. For those who don't know - for much of the '40s and '50s The Weavers were the preeminent musical quartet in the country and had a string of top ten hits. The performers were: Lee Hayes, Ronnie Gilbert, Fred Hellerman and Pete Seeger. They and their music formed the basis for the folk phenomena of the late '50s and early '60s. They were magical. This film features archival footage and documents their 1980 reunion at Carnegie Hall. Songs: "Goodnight Irene," "Kisses Sweeter Than Wine," "If I Had a Hammer" (they wrote it) and much, much more.

☐ Sex ☐ Nud ☐ Viol ☐ Lang ☐ AdSit

A: The Weavers

© WARNER REPRISE VIDEO 3-38304

ABE LINCOLN IN ILLINOIS

NR | DMA | 1939 | B&W

D: John Cromwell — 110 m

8 Historically, this is a reasonably accurate portrayal of Mr. Lincoln's younger years. (Raymond Massey was Oscar-nominated.) It depicts his childhood in the backwoods of Illinois, early career, ill-fated love for Ann Rutledge and marriage to the shrewish Mary Todd (Ruth Gordon). Reverent and sincere story, even though the production values are slightly dated. Pure Americana, wonderfully acted by Massey with top support from Gordon. Also nominated for Best Cinematography. See also YOUNG MISTER LINCOLN and ABRAHAM LINCOLN.

☐ Sex ☐ Nud ☐ Viol ☐ Lang ☐ AdSit

A: Raymond Massey, Ruth Gordon, Gene Lockhart, Mary Howard, Dorothy Tree, Minor Watson

© TURNER HOME ENTERTAINMENT 2093

ABRAHAM LINCOLN

NR | DMA | 1930 | B&W

D: D.W. Griffith — 97 m

7 Milestone movie in many ways. This was famous silent film director D.W. Griffith's first "talky" and the first film to cover Lincoln's life from his early days as a backwoods lawyer until his assassination at Ford's Theater. Huston's performance is peerless and the picture is sincere, but quite episodic and slow-moving in places. It's production values are very dated now. See also YOUNG MR. LINCOLN and ABE LINCOLN IN ILLINOIS.

☐ Sex ☐ Nud ☐ Viol ☐ Lang ☐ AdSit

A: Walter Huston, Una Merkel, Kay Hammond, Ian Keith, Hobart Bosworth, Jason Robards, Sr.

© GOODTIMES VGT5133

ADAM

NR | DMA | 1983 | COLOR

D: Michael Tuchner — 96 m

8 Heart rending real-life story of John and Reve William's search for their son Adam after he had mysteriously disappeared. This is compelling, wrenching drama, detailing the months of uncertainty and anguish. Eventually their lobby of Congress led to legislation which today permits parents to use the FBI's national crime computer to help locate missing children.

☐ Sex ☐ Nud ☐ Viol ☐ Lang ◢ AdSit

A: Daniel J. Travanti, JoBeth Williams, Martha Scott, Richard Masur, Paul Regina, Mason Adams

© STAR CLASSICS L1761

ADAM HAD FOUR SONS

NR | DMA ROM | 1941 | B&W

D: Gregory Ratoff — 81 m

8 This is an intense drama in which Ingrid Bergman is a young foreign girl brought in to be governess for Baxter's four sons after his wife dies. The family has been decimated and it is her strength that becomes the support for them all, especially when Baxter's business fails. But when one son marries the vicious Susan Hayward, brother turns against brother. Bergman sees her for what she is but she is roundly chastised and is nearly fired before everyone discovers that she was right. This classic has it all: tears, laughter, seduction and romance. Fine performances all around. Entertaining for everyone.

☐ Sex ☐ Nud ☐ Viol ☐ Lang ◢ AdSit

A: Ingrid Bergman, Warner Baxter, Susan Hayward, Fay Wray, Richard Denning, June Lockhart

© COLUMBIA TRISTAR HOME VIDEO VH10002

ADVENTURES OF HUCK FINN, THE

PG | DMA CLD | 1993 | COLOR

D: Stephen Sommers — 108 m

9 Wonderful adaptation of Mark Twain's classic adventure story set in the pre-Civil War South. Huck Finn is a fun-loving boy that is as wild as the river, but he has been taken in by the widow Douglas who has vowed to civilize him. However, his thieving father has come and stolen him back, so Huck has faked his own murder and run away. In the uproar, the household slave, and Huck's friend Jim, also runs away. Now everyone thinks that Jim has murdered Huck. Instead, they have joined up on a grand adventure down the river, which turns into a run for their lives. Fast-moving and funny. Never misses a beat.

☐ Sex ☐ Nud ◢ Viol ◢ Lang ☐ AdSit

A: Elijah Wood, Courtney B. Vance, Robbie Coltrane, Jason Robards, Jr., Ron Pearlman, Dana Ivey

© WALT DISNEY HOME VIDEO 1896

ADVENTURES OF HUCKLEBERRY FINN, THE

D: Richard Thorpe 89 m

NR | DMA CLD | 1939 | B&W

8 Mark Twain's classic story is given a pleasant Hollywood spin in this 1930's production (with Mickey Rooney) of an independent boy's wild and adventurous summer on the Mississippi River. Poor Huck Finn decides to get away form his bad-tempered father by faking his own death and running off down the Mississippi. A short way out on his journey he meets up with Jim. Jim is a slave who has also run away and is Huck's friend. Even though much of Twain's satire and wit are exchanged for sentimentality, this is still a rewarding viewing experience, especially for young people.

Sex / Nud / Viol / Lang / AdSit

A: Mickey Rooney, Walter Connolly, William Frawley, Rex Ingram, Lynne Carver, Jo Ann Sayers

Distributed By MGM/UA Home Video M500053

ADVENTURES OF HUCKLEBERRY FINN, THE

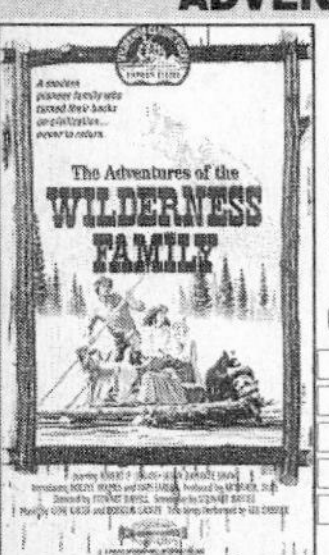

D: Michael Curtiz 108 m

G | DMA CLD | 1960 | COLOR

7 Very good version of Twain's classic story with a very appealing cast. More true to Twain's original story than earlier films. An independent boy, Huckleberry Finn, and escaped slave, Jim, travel down the Mississippi River and get more adventure than they had counted on when they run into two con men who convince them that they are a king and duke. Eddie Hodges is appealing as Huck and famed boxer Archie Moore is a standout as Jim.

Sex / Nud / Viol / Lang / AdSit

A: Tony Randall, Eddie Hodges, Archie Moore, Patty McCormack, Neville Brand, Buster Keaton

Distributed By MGM/UA Home Video M201279

ADVENTURES OF THE WILDERNESS FAMILY, THE

D: Stewart Raffill 100 m

G | DMA CLD | 1976 | COLOR

8 This is a very good, family-oriented human interest drama but is mostly geared for young people. An urban family escapes the city and pollution to the majestic wonders of nature for the sake of a sick daughter. There they build a cabin in the magnificent Rockies and brave the dangers of the wild. Lots of animals and scenery. See also WILDERNESS FAMILY, PART 2 and similar ACROSS THE GREAT DIVIDE.

Sex / Nud / Viol / Lang / AdSit

A: Robert Logan, Susan D. Shaw, Ham Larsen, Heather Rattray, George "Buck" Flower, William Cornford

© VIDEO TREASURES 9655

ADVENTURES OF TOM SAWYER, THE

D: Norman Taurog 91 m

NR | DMA CLD | 1938 | COLOR

8 This is a good adaptation of the Mark Twain classic novel in which all of Tom's charm and cunning are left intact. It is a story of a boy who is being raised in a very proper home by a tough but loving aunt, in 1850s Missouri. However, he is also adventurous and mischievous sort who spends all his spare time with the rebellious and independent Huckleberry Finn, except for when he and Becky are chased through a cave by Injun Joe (Jory). Every boy ought to see this at least once, and many who used to be boys (also those who have had a great deal to do with boys) will also have a great time it.

Sex / Nud / ✓ Viol / Lang / AdSit

A: Tommy Kelly, Jackie Maran, Ann Gillis, May Robson, Walter Brennan, Victor Jory

© FOXVIDEO 8014

AFRICAN QUEEN, THE

D: John Huston 105 m

NR | DMA ROM COM | 1951 | COLOR

10 Wonderful!! Superb combination of all the elements of film - drama, comedy, romance and action - wrapped up with a ribbon of outstanding acting. Bogart, as a ne'r-do-well drunkard, and Hepburn, as a religious spinster, are thrown together when her village in the Congo is raided by Germans at the outset of WWI. The spinster and the drunken trader fall in love as they travel down a treacherous river in his boat, The African Queen, fighting Germans, nature's elements and each other the whole way. Wonderful, classic film. Bogart won an Oscar. Filmed on location.

Sex / Nud / ✓ Viol / Lang / ✓ AdSit

A: Humphrey Bogart, Katharine Hepburn, Robert Morley, Peter Bull, Theodore Bikel, Walter Gotell

© CBS/FOX VIDEO 2025

AMERICAN GRAFFITI

D: George Lucas 112 m

PG | DMA COM | 1973 | COLOR

10 A monster hit and a treasure trove of nostalgia. Also brilliant and unpretentious filmmaking that is just plain fun. It follows a group of high school students who are about to transition into another world. They nearing graduation from high school in 1962, in a small Northern California town. Lucas weaves their individual lives together into a vastly interesting, poignant, sensitive, frequently funny and always fascinating mosaic. An insightful and very entertaining package, wrapped up in terrific rock 'n roll score. You really get to care about all these people. Highly recommended.

Sex / Nud / Viol / ✓ Lang / ✓ AdSit

A: Richard Dreyfuss, Ron Howard, Paul LeMat, Cindy Williams, Candy Clark, Mackenzie Phillips

© MCA/UNIVERSAL HOME VIDEO, INC. 66010

ANNE OF AVONLEA

D: Kevin Sullivan 224 m

NR | DMA ROM | 1988 | COLOR

9 Sparkling sequel to ANNE OF GREEN GABLES and a rare event where the sequel is as good as the original. Anne, the idealistic redheaded orphan who was adopted by a bachelor farmer and his old-maid sister, is now 18. She is an intelligent young woman and a budding writer who becomes a teacher at Avonlea. There she wins the hearts of everyone around her, including the stubborn headmistress who is determined to make her life miserable, and where she has her first brush with adult love. Absolutely charming story that will win over everyone of every age. Extremely well done.

Sex / Nud / Viol / Lang / AdSit

A: Megan Follows, Colleen Dewhurst, Wendy Hiller, Frank Converse, Schuyyler Grant, Jonathan Crombie

© WALT DISNEY HOME VIDEO 650

ANNE OF GREEN GABLES

D: George Nicholis 79 m

NR | DMA | 1934 | B&W

7 A mischievous orphan girl with a vivid imagination and vibrant red hair is adopted by a bachelor farmer and his old-maid sister who had really wanted to adopt a boy so he could work their fields. But, the wide-eyed Anne changes their lives and captures the hearts of all those around her, including us. From the classic novel by Lucy Maud Montgomery. Excellent remake in 1985. See also ANNE OF AVONLEA.

Sex / Nud / Viol / Lang / AdSit

A: Anne Shirley, Tom Brown, O.P. Heggie, Helen Westley, Sara Haden, Murray Kinnell

© TURNER HOME ENTERTAINMENT 2028

ANNE OF GREEN GABLES

D: Kevin Sullivan 199 m

NR | DMA | 1985 | COLOR

10 Wonderfully well-made. This endearing classic story is brought to life by an excellent cast and set in beautifully scenic Nova Scotia. A charming orphan girl with a wild imagination and flaming red hair is adopted by a bachelor farmer and his old-maid sister. They are kind hard-working people, but very plain and stoic; and, Anne is vibrant, full of wonder for life and bounding with enthusiasm. As much as they resist her, she brings profound changes into their quiet lives, and they love her in return. Heartwarming and thoroughly uplifting story. A true treat for everyone. See also ANNE OF AVONLEA.

Sex / Nud / Viol / Lang / AdSit

A: Megan Follows, Colleen Dewhurst, Patricia Hamilton, Marilyn Lightstone, Charmion King, Richard Farnsworth

© WALT DISNEY HOME VIDEO 642

AS SUMMERS DIE

D: Jean-Claude Tramont 88 m

NR | DMA | 1986 | COLOR

7 Excellent made-for-TV movie. Glenn Scott is a struggling small town Georgia lawyer in 1959, who takes on the town's wealthiest family. He defends an old black woman against a rich white family's attempt to take back some land the family patriarch had given her earlier, after oil is found on it. He gets some unexpected help from the old man's feisty old sister (Davis). He soon finds that he has to defend this old woman too when the rest of the family begins to question her sanity. And the more he becomes involved with their family, he is drawn to the old woman's niece (Curtis). Excellent acting bring sparkle to a pretty good drama.

Sex / Nud / Viol / Lang / AdSit

A: Scott Glenn, Bette Davis, Jamie Lee Curtis, Penny Fuller, Beah Richards, John McIntire

© HBO VIDEO 9977

AUTOBIOGRAPHY OF MISS JANE PITMAN

D: John Korty 106 m

NR | DMA | 1974 | COLOR

10 This terrific made-for-TV movie is a triumph, and it won nine Emmys. It is essentially the story of much of black-American history, and it is told as it was "witnessed" in the person of one woman, Jane Pitman. Upon the event of her 110th birthday, just as the civil rights movement of the 1960s has begun, she begins to tell her story. The story line follows her from age 19 when she was a slave girl during the Civil War South, through to womanhood, in the Jim Crow era, to being an old woman and witnessing the civil rights movement of the 1960s. Excellent stuff!

Sex / Nud / ✓ Viol / Lang / ✓ AdSit

A: Cicely Tyson, Richard Dysart, Odetta, Michael Murphy, Thalmus Rasulala, Barbara Chaney

© UNITED AMERICAN VIDEO CORP. 5917

BABE, THE

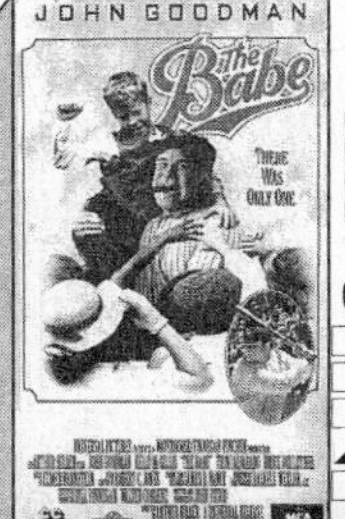

D: Arthur Hiller 115 m

PG | DMA | 1992 | COLOR

7 Baseball's larger-than-life hero is given good old-fashioned hero treatment in this entertaining, sentimental and pleasing Hollywood biography. All the well-known Babe Ruth trivia is included, including his famous called home run shot over the center field wall in the 1932 World Series, his love for children and also his many excesses. However, this is not a mindless tribute or exploitive trivialization. The man is given substance and dignity. Although his shortcomings are there too, we are never allowed to lose our love for the oversized hero. Goodman does a great job. Enjoyable.

Sex / Nud / Viol / ✓ Lang / AdSit

A: John Goodman, Kelly McGillis, Trini Alvarado, Bruce Boxleitner, Peter Donat, Richard Tyson

© MCA/UNIVERSAL HOME VIDEO, INC. 81286

BAD DAY AT BLACK ROCK

D: John Sturges 82 m

NR · DMA SUS · 1954 · COLOR

9 An extremely powerful drama, still relevant today. A one-armed war veteran (Tracy) stops in the small rural town of Black Rock after WWII to find a Japanese farmer whose dead son he had known. Instead of getting help from the townspeople, he receives unveiled threats. After he is set upon by two of their biggest bad guys (Borgnine and Marvin) and encouraged to leave, it becomes apparent that this hostile town has a big secret to keep. Fine acting from a top notch cast. Excellent photography is somewhat diminished by the small screen. Oscar nominations for Screenplay and Direction.

Sex · Nud · ✓ Viol · Lang · ✓ AdSit

A: Spencer Tracy, Robert Ryan, Anne Francis, Ernest Borgnine, Walter Brennan, Lee Marvin

Distributed By MGM/UA Home Video M300639

BARABBAS

D: Richard Fleischer 134 m

NR · DMA · 1961 · COLOR

8 Fictionalized Biblical epic of the life of Barabbas, the thief who was freed by Pontius Pilate when Jesus Christ was condemned to die. Barabbas is a non-believer, but spends the troubled years after his release first as a slave and later as a gladiator. He constantly mocks Christ, while all the time he is struggling to understand the meaning of it all. Only in the end does he discover faith. Plenty of spectacle and action. Quinn and a solid cast of veterans give credibility to this screen adaptation of a novel by Par Lagerkvist.

Sex · Nud · ✓ Viol · Lang · AdSit

A: Anthony Quinn, Silvana Mangano, Arthur Kennedy, Katy Jurado, Harry Andrews, Vittorio Gassman

© COLUMBIA TRISTAR HOME VIDEO 60129

BEAR, THE

D: Jean-Jacques Annaud 92 m

PG · DMA CLD · 1989 · COLOR

9 Excellent family entertainment that was roundly praised by critics and loved by audiences. It is a big-budget movie that took several years to film and is the story, set in 1885 British Columbia, of a huge injured kodiak bear that adopts an orphaned cub. Fearing gunfire from approaching hunters, the two flee across a vast expanse of beautiful but foreboding wilderness. But in the end, the bears still must face the hunter. This is not a schmaltzy Disney knock-off. This is special. Adults will enjoy this as much as the kids.

Sex · Nud · ✓ Viol · Lang · AdSit

A: Tcheky Karyo, Jack Wallace

© COLUMBIA TRISTAR HOME VIDEO 70213

BERNICE BOBS HER HAIR

D: Joan Micklin Silver 49 m

NR · DMA · 1976 · COLOR

8 This is F. Scott Fitzgerld's delightful and sensitive story of a shy young girl (Shelly Duvall) who is transformed by her cousin into a femme fatale on a summer's visit in 1919. She sacrifices her beautiful long hair so that she will be accepted by an in-group of pleasure-seeking would-be flappers from the jazz-age, and becomes a big success. But her success is also a source of unexpected problems when she captures all the boys's hearts. A fun but perceptive movie that explores our perceptions of self-worth and personal integrity. Introduction by Henry Fonda.

Sex · Nud · Viol · Lang · AdSit

A: Shelley Duvall, Veronica Cartwright, Bud Cort, Dennis Christopher, Gary Springer, Land Binkley

© MONTEREY HOME VIDEO 30434

BIBLE, THE

D: John Huston 171 m

NR · DMA · 1966 · COLOR

8 A major cinematic rendering of the ancient stories from the first twenty-two chapters of Genesis. They include: the creation, Adam and Eve, Cain and Able, Noah's Ark, the Tower of Babel, Sodom and Gomorrah, and the story of Abraham and Sarah. It is somewhat long on grandeur and short on intimacy with the characters, nevertheless it is also a spectacular vision of a film.

Sex · Nud · Viol · Lang · AdSit

A: George C. Scott, Peter O'Toole, Ava Gardner, Richard Harris, Franco Nero, Michael Parks

© FOXVIDEO 1020

BIRCH INTERVAL

D: Delbert Mann 104 m

PG · DMA · 1978 · COLOR

6 An uplifting family story of a 12-year-old girl who is sent to live with her Amish grandfather, Eddie Albert, in rural 1947 Pennsylvania. She eagerly anticipates her visit there, but she soon learns that things aren't as idyllic as she has imagined and also learns some of life's sadder truths through some painful experiences. An excellent cast and outstanding performances make this sensitive coming-of-age story a memorable experience for both young and old.

Sex · Nud · Viol · Lang · ✓ AdSit

A: Eddie Albert, Rip Torn, Ann Wedgeworth, Susan McClung, Anne Revere

© MEDIA HOME ENTERTAINMENT, INC. M867

BIRDMAN OF ALCATRAZ

D: John Frankenheimer 141 m

NR · DMA · 1962 · COLOR

8 Excellent, but romanticized, screenplay about a man who got along better with birds than he did with people. It is an intense character study of the real-life prisoner Robert Stroud who became a world renown expert on birdlife while serving 40 years in solitary confinement for murder, in some of the toughest prisons in the country. Stroud eventually spent 53 years in prisons, including Alcatraz - a prison which was reserved to house the worst of the worst. Lancaster puts in one of his best performances.

Sex · Nud · Viol · Lang · ✓ AdSit

A: Burt Lancaster, Karl Malden, Thelma Ritter, Betty Field, Neville Brand, Telly Savalas

Distributed By MGM/UA Home Video M202269

BITTER HARVEST

D: Roger Young 98 m

NR · DMA · 1981 · COLOR

8 Excellent drama. Everything goes wrong for young dairy farmer Ron Howard, whose cattle first take sick and then start to die. Howard is convincing as the scared and panicky farmer who has to battle an unfeeling government bureaucracy to discover that there is a fat-soluble chemical in his dairy feed that is killing his cows, and affecting over 8 million Americans, too. This was a made-for-TV movie that was based upon a true incident. Far above typical TV fare.

Sex · Nud · Viol · Lang · ✓ AdSit

A: Ron Howard, Art Carney, Richard Dysart

© FRIES HOME VIDEO 90700

BLACK BEAUTY

D: James Hill 105 m

G · DMA CLD · 1971 · B&W

7 This is the beloved classic children's story of a young boy's relentless quest in Victorian England to find his missing black colt as it passes from owner to owner, until once again it is back home with him. It will definitely hold a kid's attention throughout and will likely hold the attention of many adults, too. Plus, it quite probably will also bring a tear to everyone's eye.

Sex · Nud · Viol · Lang · AdSit

A: Mark Lester, Walter Slezak, Peter Lee Lawrence, Ursla Glas

© PARAMOUNT HOME VIDEO 8079

BLACK STALLION, THE

D: Carroll Ballard 117 m

G · DMA CLD · 1979 · COLOR

9 The wonderful and moving story of a boy and his relationship with a beautiful black Arabian stallion. The two were stranded together on a desert island after a shipwreck. They have become best friends and, after they are rescued, the horse goes home with the boy. The primary thrust of the story is upon the training and racing of his horse, with the help of a wise old horse trainer (Mickey Rooney). One of the best children's films ever, and fun for adults, too. It proved to be so popular that it was followed with THE BLACK STALLION RETURNS.

Sex · Nud · Viol · Lang · AdSit

A: Kelly Reno, Mickey Rooney, Teri Garr, Clarence Huse, Hoyt Axton

Distributed By MGM/UA Home Video M201604

BLACK STALLION RETURNS, THE

D: Robert Dalva 105 m

PG · DMA CLD · 1983 · COLOR

8 Rousing sequel to THE BLACK STALLION. When the black stallion is stolen back by an Arab chieftain and taken to the Sahara, Kelly Reno, now a teenager, goes there to get him back. In his ordeal to get his friend back, he has to travel across miles of hot desert sands and deal with not always friendly local tribesmen. Pretty good action scenes, particularly the big race climax scene. This is not a cheap rip-off of the original. It is good in its own right. But still, it doesn't quite have the same magic as the original. Excellent family entertainment.

Sex · Nud · Viol · Lang · AdSit

A: Kelly Reno, Vincent Spano, Teri Garr, Allen Garfield, Woody Strode, Jodi Thelen

Distributed By MGM/UA Home Video M201864

BLOSSOMS IN THE DUST

D: Mervyn LeRoy 95 m

NR · DMA · 1941 · COLOR

8 Moving, true story of social visionary and humanitarian Edna Glandney (Greer Garson). When she loses her husband and only son in 19th-century Texas, and her foster sister, who had been branded illegitimate, commits suicide - Edna decides to fight back. She works tirelessly to establish the Texas Children's Home and Aid Society and then places over 2000 children in adoptive homes. She also fights a ceaseless battle to have the stigmatizing word "illegitimate" officially struck from any legal records. Nominated for four Oscars, including Best Picture. A classy, heartwarming tearjerker.

Sex · Nud · Viol · Lang · ✓ AdSit

A: Greer Garson, Walter Pidgeon, Felix Bressart, Marsha Hunt, Fay Holden, Samuel S. Hinds

Distributed By MGM/UA Home Video M201874

BORN FREE

D: James Hill — 95 m

9 NR — DMA CLD — 1966 COLOR — Sex / Nud / Viol / Lang / AdSit

This is an exceptional film with universal appeal. It is also a true story. Elsa, a young lioness, is one of three lion cubs who are raised in captivity by two Kenyan game wardens after they are forced to kill the cub's parents. The wardens want Elsa to be free when she is grown. So, as Elsa matures, they have to teach her how to survive on her own in the wilderness. This is a true family film and not just for the young kids. Immensely popular upon its release, it has lost none of its charm over time. The title song won an Oscar and was also a significant pop hit.

A: Virginia McKenna, Bill Travers, Geoffrey Keen, Peter Lukoye

© COLUMBIA TRISTAR HOME VIDEO 60142

BOUND FOR GLORY

D: Hal Ashby — 149 m

8 PG — DMA MUS — 1976 COLOR — Sex / Nud / Viol / Lang / AdSit

This moving biography is of Woodie Guthrie, a famous singer/composer of some of America's most favorite folk songs ("This Land is Your land"). It focuses primarily on the depression years when Guthrie traveled across America primarily by rail. The vignettes of that sad period of American history and those hit hardest by it, provide us with a window into the suffering that made up the soul of his songs. Carradine is superb as Gutherie. Won 2 Oscars: Photography and Score.

A: David Carradine, Ronny Cox, Melinda Dillon, Gail Strickland, Randy Quaid, John Lehne

Distributed By MGM/UA Home Video M600878

BOYS' TOWN

D: Norman Taurog — 94 m

8 NR — DMA CLD — 1938 B&W — Sex / Nud / Viol / Lang / AdSit

Boys' Town is a real-life home for orphans and juvenile delinquents in Nebraska, that has now been in existence for many years. Their motto is: "There's no such thing as a bad boy." This is the dramatized story of how Boys' Town was started by the real-life Father Flanagan. Spencer Tracy won an Oscar playing Flanagan in his struggle to find a home for, and give a second chance to, the boys that society was just throwing away. Mickey Rooney, as tough guy Whitey Marsh, is one of his toughest jobs. A little syrupy sweet and sentimental, but still a very rewarding film.

A: Spencer Tracy, Mickey Rooney, Henry Hull, Leslie Fenton, Addison Richards, Edward Norris

Distributed By MGM/UA Home Video M203851

BRIAN'S SONG

D: Buzz Kulik — 74 m

10 G — DMA — 1970 COLOR — Sex / Nud / Viol / Lang / AdSit

Truly exceptional made-for-TV movie recounting the real-life deep friendship between Chicago Bears players Brian Piccolo and Gale Sayers. It won five Emmy Awards. This odd-ball pair made news as the first interracial roommates in professional football, but their relationship only began on the playing field. They became best friends too. Brian Piccolo (Caan) is witty and free-spirited. Gale Sayers (Williams) is serious and all business. When Sayers gets badly hurt, Piccolo prods him into full recovery. Then it's Sayers turn when Piccolo is found to have cancer. Heartwarming. A milestone in TV movies.

A: James Caan, Billy Dee Williams, Jack Warden, Judy Pace, Shelley Fabares

© COLUMBIA TRISTAR HOME VIDEO 60156

BROKEN BLOSSOMS

D: D.W. Griffith — 95 m

8 NR — DMA — 1919 B&W — Sex / Nud / Viol / Lang / AdSit

Dealing both with child abuse and prejudice, this was a very daring concept for the time in which it was made. Lillian Gish plays the young daughter of an abusive alcoholic London prize-fighter father (Crisp) who beats her regularly. After one particularly bad beating, she falls into the shop of a Chinese poet and a gentleman. He immediately falls in love with her and takes care of her. However, when Crisp learns that his daughter was seen with a Chinese, he becomes enraged and vows to kill him. This tragedy was very powerful then and is still quite engaging today. One of film legend D.W. Griffith's most successful films.

A: Lillian Gish, Richard Barthelmess, Donald Crisp

© HBO VIDEO 0279

BROWNING VERSION, THE

D: Anthony Asquith — 90 m

8 NR — DMA — 1951 B&W — Sex / Nud / Viol / Lang / AdSit

A already powerful and particularly moving story becomes a truly memorable film, due to the extraordinary performance of Michael Redgrave. Redgrave plays a one-time brilliant scholar who has become a stern, stuffy and ineffective middle-aged professor at an English boy's school. Now his life is crumbling. His wife has been having an affair with another professor and he is being forced out of the school that has been his home for years. On the eave of his retirement, an unexpected and undeserved kindness has now forced him to realize his own arrogance and that his life has been unfulfilled and a failure. Redgrave's closing apology speech is magnificent and regains him the respect of his students.

A: Michael Redgrave, Jean Kent, Nigel Patrick, Wilfrid Hyde-White, Ronald Howard, Bill Travers

© HOME VISION BRO 040

BUDDY HOLLY STORY, THE

D: Steve Rash — 113 m

8 PG — DMA MUS — 1978 COLOR — Sex / Nud / Viol / Lang / AdSit

One of the best rock `n roll movies ever. Gary Busey was Oscar-nominated for his bravura performance as Buddy Holly - the legendary Texas boy who combined country music with rhythm and blues. This is not the typical glossed-over Hollywood version of a poor boy made good, but an accurate representation of the Texas rock legend up until his tragic death. Busey's energetic impersonation of Holly includes live performances of the classic "That'll Be the Day," "It's So Easy," "Peggy Sue" and others. See also LA BAMBA for Richie Valens's story.

A: Gary Busey, Charles Martin Smith, Dick O'Neil, Maria Richwine, Conrad Janis, Amy Johnson

© COLUMBIA TRISTAR HOME VIDEO 60801

CAPTAINS COURAGEOUS

D: Victor Fleming — 118 m

10 G — DMA ACT CLD — 1937 B&W — Sex / Nud / Viol / Lang / AdSit

Wonderful adaptation of Rudyard Kipling's classic story. A spoiled rich kid (Bartholomew) falls overboard from an ocean liner, is rescued by a Portuguese fisherman (Spencer Tracy) and is brought on board a New England fishing schooner. He demands to be taken back to land but instead has to stay at sea for the balance of the 3-month fishing trip. For the first time in his life, he has to earn his keep. He is put to work along side Mickey Rooney, gets a few lessons in humility from Tracy and gradually is transformed. Excellent! A true treat for everyone! Tracy won Best Actor Oscar.

A: Spencer Tracy, Freddie Bartholomew, Lionel Barrymore, Melvyn Douglas, Mickey Rooney, John Carradine

Distributed By MGM/UA Home Video M500058

CARDINAL, THE

D: Otto Preminger — 175 m

7 NR — DMA — 1963 COLOR — Sex / Nud / Viol / Lang / AdSit

Tom Tryon plays a Roman Catholic priest, Stephen Fermoyle, who has come from a humble background and Irish parents, all the while doubting himself and his calling. This is a handsomely produced soap opera that follows his career from parish priest to the lofty level of Cardinal over a period of three decades. The story is long but nonetheless compelling due to Otto Preminger's deft touch. Beautiful pageantry and some good acting don't hurt, either.

A: Tom Tryon, Carol Lynley, Romy Schneider, John Huston, Burgess Meredith

© VIDEO TREASURES SV9030

CHALK GARDEN, THE

D: Ronald Neame — 106 m

8 NR — DMA — 1964 COLOR — Sex / Nud / Viol / Lang / AdSit

When her father remarries, young Hayley Mills is sent to live with her grandmother. Grandmother spoils her shamefully and the girl has become a terror because she rightfully feels as though no one loves her. Both her mother and father have deserted her and her grandmother's prime concern is her garden. She has become an extremely disagreeable girl and she lashes out at everyone. Then a governess (Kerr), with a dark past, battles everyone to give the girl the love, support and direction she needs. A very high quality soap opera for discriminating audiences. Entertaining, too.

A: Deborah Kerr, Hayley Mills, Edith Evans, Felix Aylmer, Elizabeth Sellars, John Mills

© MCA/UNIVERSAL HOME VIDEO, INC. 80639

CHAMP, THE

D: King Vidor — 87 m

8 NR — DMA CLD — 1931 B&W — Sex / Nud / Viol / Lang / AdSit

Top-notch tearjerker, winner of two Oscars plus a Best Picture nomination. Wallace Beery won an Oscar as the loveable washed-up ex-boxer who has nothing at all, except the unending adoration of his son. The two of them live in a dive in Tijuana where he is constantly "in training" for a come back, that is, when he is in between drinking binges or not gambling away their money. Now the mother, who abandoned them both, has come back and wants to take the boy away. A simple story, unashamedly sentimental, but one of the most effective and heartwarming tearjerkers of all time. A treasure.

A: Wallace Beery, Jackie Cooper, Irene Rich, Roscoe Ates, Edward Brophy, Hale Hamilton

Distributed By MGM/UA Home Video M301665

CHAMP, THE

D: Franco Zeffirelli — 121 m

7 PG — DMA CLD — 1979 COLOR — Sex / Nud / Viol / Lang / AdSit

Sentimental remake of the 1931 Wallace Beery/Jackie Cooper classic, this time set at a Florida racetrack. Billy Flynn is an alcoholic ex-prize fighter who keeps promising his young son that he will one day again become champ, but instead he drinks and is perpetually broke. After seven years, the boy's now-wealthy mother sees him again and challenges Billy for custody of the boy. Billy now desperately needs to attempt a real come back so he can keep his son, even though the doctor says it will kill him. Not up to the original but still jerks plenty of tears. Very young Schroder is outstanding.

A: Jon Voight, Faye Dunaway, Ricky Schroder, Jack Warden

Distributed By MGM/UA Home Video M600034

CHAMPIONS

PG · DMA · 1984 · COLOR

D: John Irvin — 113 m

7 Heartwarming true story from England of the triumph of the human spirit - in the tradition of CHARIOTS OF FIRE. It is the comeback story of two champions: a talented young jockey with his eye set upon winning the Grand National Steeplechase, but who is stricken with cancer at 31; and his horse Aldaniti, that is crippled in a horse race. Both overcame long odds to ride in the National during the rousing finish to an uplifting film. Well-made and affecting film.

Sex / Nud / Viol / ◢ Lang / ◢ AdSit

A: John Hurt, Edward Woodward, Jan Francis, Ben Johnson

© NEW LINE HOME VIDEO 2086

CHARIOTS OF FIRE

PG · DMA · 1981 · COLOR

D: Hugh Hudson — 124 m

8 A major box office hit and highly acclaimed by the critics. It is an unusual and absorbing drama about two Englishmen, one a devout Scottish Christian missionary and the other a Jewish student, who are both training to run in the 1924 Olympics. However, neither is running for personal glory or for the glory of England - one is running for the glory of God, the other just to gain acceptance. It is a thought-provoking drama that also beautifully captures both the spirit and the atmosphere of the times. It won Best Picture of 1981 and three other Oscars.

Sex / Nud / Viol / Lang / ◢ AdSit

A: Ben Cross, Ian Charleson, Nigel Havers, Nicolas Farrell, Alice Krige, Cheryl Campbell

© WARNER HOME VIDEO 20004

CHARLY

PG · DMA SF · 1968 · COLOR

D: Ralph Nelson — 104 m

8 Endearing sentimental favorite with an interesting premise that also explores some fascinating philosophical territory. Cliff Robertson won an Oscar for his role as Charley, a gentle, retarded man with a powerful drive to learn. When Charley is asked to try a breakthrough surgical procedure that may help him get smarter, he readily agrees. He does quickly attain genius-level brain powers, but no one counted on the complex emotions that develop, too. Claire Bloom is a caseworker who works to help Charley adapt to the changes and find a brief period of happiness before, unexpectedly, the process reverses.

Sex / Nud / Viol / Lang / ■ AdSit

A: Cliff Robertson, Claire Bloom, Lilia Skala, Leon Janney, Dick Van Patten

© CBS/FOX VIDEO 8020

CHEERS FOR MISS BISHOP

NR · DMA · 1941 · B&W

D: Tay Garnett — 95 m

7 This is an endearing and sentimental story of a much-loved 19th-century midwestern school teacher. She is Miss Bishop (Martha Scott), who as a young girl graduated from a new college and stayed on there to teach freshman English. In the tradition of GOODBYE MR. CHIPS, she becomes a much-loved institution as the film follows her over 50 years. Even though she has two romances which fail and she never marries, she has a full life and is richly loved by her friends and students. Upbeat charmer.

Sex / Nud / Viol / Lang / AdSit

A: Martha Scott, William Gargan, Edmund Gwenn, Sterling Holloway, Sidney Blackmer, Mary Anderson

© VIDEO YESTERYEAR 958

CHILD IS WAITING, A

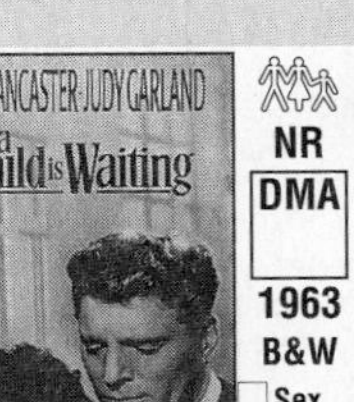

NR · DMA · 1963 · B&W

D: John Cassavetes — 105 m

8 A moving, poignant and provocative story of an overly-committed music teacher (Garland) and psychologist (Lancaster) at a school for the mentally retarded who desperately attempt to reach out to the children who will always remain children. One particular situation becomes the focus of the drama, but the story chosen could have been that of any one of the children because of the many similarities they all share. Actual retarded children were used in the filming, producing a poignant and gripping story. Not for overly sensitive people.

Sex / Nud / Viol / Lang / ◢ AdSit

A: Burt Lancaster, Judy Garland, Steven Hill, Gena Rowlands

Distributed By MGM/UA Home Video M301824

CHOSEN, THE

PG · DMA · 1982 · COLOR

D: Jeremy Paul Kagan — 107 m

8 A provocative and very moving story about two very different views of the world, plus the conflict that develops between the two people and the friendship that bridges it. Two Jewish-American boys in 1940s Brooklyn become fast friends, but that friendship also provokes a deep inner struggle. Miller is a the son of a devout Jew who is a liberal scholar (Schell). He has been raised to question everything. Benson is the son of a very strict Hasidic rabbi (Steiger), who has been taught to forsake the 20th century entirely and not to question either his faith or his heritage. Very good drama. The religion aspect is only incidental to the larger cultural one.

Sex / Nud / ◢ Viol / Lang / ◢ AdSit

A: Maximilian Schell, Rod Steiger, Robby Benson, Barry Miller, Hildy Brooks, Ron Rifkin

© FOXVIDEO 1297

CHRISTMAS CAROL, A

NR · DMA · 1938 · B&W

D: Edwin L. Marin — 70 m

7 Very good film version of Charles Dickens's Christmas classic in which a grumpy old curmudgeon and tightwad is shown - by visions of the past, present and future - that he is the source of his own misery and isolation, and that he can be happy if he only tries. The film's age and an excellent cast of MGM players add credence to the period atmosphere. June Lockhart makes her screen debut.

Sex / Nud / Viol / Lang / AdSit

A: Reginald Owen, Gene Lockhart, Kathleen Lockhart, Leo G. Carroll, Terry Kilburn, Barry MacKay

Distributed By MGM/UA Home Video M201451

CHRISTMAS CAROL, A

NR · DMA · 1951 · B&W

D: Brian Desmond Hurst — 86 m

10 Wonderful version of Dickens's classic Christmas parable. Numerous versions have been made over the years for both TV and the movie theatre, but this is likely the best. Alastair Sim is perfect as the miserly Ebenezer Scrooge. His forced encounters with the three ghosts of Christmas force him to come to grips with his own mortality and his disagreeable ways. Widely regarded as probably the best screen version of this classic tale. Very uplifting movie.

Sex / Nud / Viol / Lang / AdSit

A: Alastair Sim, Kathleen Harrison, Jack Warner, Michael Hordern, Mervyn Johns, Hermione Baddeley

© VIDEO COMMUNICATIONS, INC. 1118

CITADEL, THE

NR · DMA · 1938 · B&W

D: King Vidor — 114 m

7 Heartwarming, brilliant story of a young, idealistic and dedicated, but impoverished, Scottish physician who begins his career in a poor Welsh mining town. He discovers the cause of a severe cough that plagues the miners but is thwarted in his efforts to reveal his discovery by the medical establishment. He leaves for a lucrative practice in London but is encouraged by his wife and his best friend to go back and minister to the children of a poor village. Received four Oscar nominations, including Best Picture, Actor and Director, though a little slow moving.

Sex / Nud / Viol / Lang / ◢ AdSit

A: Robert Donat, Rosalind Russell, Rex Harrison, Ralph Richardson

Distributed By MGM/UA Home Video M300612

CIVIL WAR, THE

NR · DMA · 1990 · COLOR

D: Burns Ken — 680 m

10 Director Ken Burns captivated the American public with his nine part PBS TV-series, which made the magnitude and horror of the American Civil War become real. Never before has it been made so plain to so many what a truly cataclysmic event the War was, not only for Americans but for the whole world. It was the crowning event of all civilization from the advent of recorded history. It was a monumental conflict that defined warfare for the two World Wars to come, but it also decided the value of life and the practicality of a nation of laws for all the people. With this as a backdrop, Lincoln's two-minute Gettysburg Address garners real and profound meaning. Magnificent.

Sex / Nud / ◢ Viol / Lang / ◢ AdSit

A:

© TURNER HOME ENTERTAINMENT 1861

CLASH OF THE TITANS

PG · DMA FAN CLD · 1981 · COLOR

D: Desmond Davis — 118 m

8 Ancient Greek mythology is given life by some pretty good special effects and a big-name cast. The hero Perseus (Hamlin), son of Zeus (Olivier), must battle magic, monsters and the gods to save beautiful Andromeda (Bowker) from danger and to win her hand. Special effects are the real stars, however, particularly the flying horse Pegasus and Medusa, the woman with hair of snakes who can turn you to stone if you look at her.

Sex / Nud / ◢ Viol / Lang / ◢ AdSit

A: Laurence Olivier, Harry Hamlin, Judi Bowker, Burgess Meredith, Maggie Smith

Distributed By MGM/UA Home Video M700074

COAL MINER'S DAUGHTER

PG · DMA MUS · 1980 · COLOR

D: Michael Apted — 124 m

9 This is the true-life rags-to-riches story of the "First Lady of County Music," Loretta Lynn - but it is more than that. It's a fascinating character study, independent of its central character's connection to country music. Sissy Spacek won a well-deserved Oscar for her portrayal of Lynn's rise from being an impoverished Appalachian child-bride (a mother of four at eighteen) to becoming an American icon, and all the unexpected problems that followed her rise to fame.

Sex / Nud / Viol / Lang / ◢ AdSit

A: Sissy Spacek, Tommy Lee Jones, Beverly D'Angelo, Levon Helm, Phyllis Boyens, Ernest Tubb

© MCA/UNIVERSAL HOME VIDEO, INC. 66015

CONRACK

PG · DMA · 1974 · COLOR · Sex · Nud · Viol · Lang · AdSit

D: Martin Ritt — 111 m

8 Simple but involving true story of Pat Conroy, a white teacher who goes to a small, isolated island off the South Carolina coast to teach its culturally deprived black kids. It is a moving story about a dedicated teacher who will go to almost any lengths to reach his kids, even if it means some very unconventional teaching methods or placing himself in direct conflict with the school superintendent. A very affecting and effective movie, with a satisfying upbeat story to tell. Outstanding job by Jon Voight.

A: Jon Voight, Hume Cronyn, Paul Winfield, Madge Sinclair, Tina Andrews, Antonio Fargas

© FOXVIDEO 1469

CORRINA, CORRINA

PG · DMA COM · 1994 · COLOR · Sex · Nud · Viol · Lang · AdSit

D: Jessie Nelson — 115 m

7 Sweet little 7-year-old Molly has just lost her mother and refuses to talk. Her father Manny (Ray Liotta) is heart-broken too, but he has to go on. After a couple of mistreats, he hires Corrina (Whoopi Goldberg) as his housekeeper. She is an highly-educated black woman who can't get other work using it, because this is the 1950s. Little Molly has never run into anyone quite like Whoopi. Her sense of fun breaks down the wall that sad little Molly has built up. But this creates another set of problems, because Molly starts to think of Corrina as her mother. What's more, Manny and Corrina become good friends and now their families are concerned. Not quite believable but fun anyway.

A: Whoopie Goldberg, Ray Liotta, Tina Majorino, Wendy Crewson, Larry Miller, Don Ameche

© TURNER HOME ENTERTAINMENT N4013

CRISIS AT CENTRAL HIGH

NR · DMA · 1981 · COLOR · Sex · Nud · Viol · Lang · ✓ AdSit

D: Lamont Johnson — 120 m

9 Compelling made-for-TV documentary-like recreation of the events surrounding the 1957 integration of Central High in Little Rock, Arkansas. The Supreme Court had ordered the all-white school to admit nine black students, creating a crisis situation. White crowds picketed the school, taunted and even beat up blacks. This film is a recreation of the actual events as they were recorded at the time in the journal of assistant principal Elizabeth Huckaby, who played a critical role in achieving a peaceful resolution. Woodward is stunning as Huckaby and received an Emmy nomination for her efforts.

A: Joanne Woodward, Charles Durning, Henderson Forsythe, William Russ, Calvin Levels

© LIVE HOME VIDEO LA9509

CRUSADES, THE

NR · DMA ACT ROM · 1935 · B&W · Sex · Nud · ✓ Viol · Lang · AdSit

D: Cecil B. DeMille — 123 m

7 Trade-mark grand epic from Cecil B. DeMille, who depicts the story of the third crusade set in 1187. Henry Wilcoxon is the lusty Richard the Lionhearted, King of England. He, along with the rest of Christian Europe, is summoned to war against the Saracens, who have swept in from Asia to capture Jerusalem for Islam. England and France comprise the bulk of the fighting force, but their alliance is threatened when Richard refuses to marry the sister of the French king. Worse, he has married the beautiful daughter (Lorretta Young) of another king. It is a story of bravery, butchery, honor, romance and more romance. Historians might disagree with DeMille's facts.

A: Loretta Young, Henry Wilcoxon, Ian Keith, Katherine DeMille, C. Aubrey Smith, George Barker

© MCA/UNIVERSAL HOME VIDEO, INC. 81266

CRY FREEDOM

PG · DMA · 1987 · COLOR · Sex · Nud · ✓ Viol · Lang · ✓ AdSit

D: Richard Attenborough — 157 m

9 Sweeping film chronicles the true story of two men, one white and one black, in South Africa. In 1975 newspaperman Donald Woods (Kline) meets a crusading non-violent black leader Steve Biko (Washington) and they become friends. It is only through Biko, that Woods comes to understand the true horror of the system of which he is a part. Later, when Biko is murdered in prison, Woods courageously risks his own life to press the government for an inquest. That determined action causes his own persecution by the same system. He must escape, as he fights to get the real story told to the rest of the world. Excellent.

A: Kevin Kline, Denzel Washington, Penelope Wilton, Kevin MacNally, John Thaw, Timothy West

© MCA/UNIVERSAL HOME VIDEO, INC. 80763

DAD

PG · DMA COM · 1989 · COLOR · Sex · Nud · Viol · ✓ Lang · ■ AdSit

D: Gary David Goldberg — 117 m

8 Very touching dose of reality. A busy Wall Street yuppie (Ted Danson) must stop his life midstream to move in with his aged parents when his father becomes very ill. His previously distant and superficial relationship with his parents becomes radically altered as he faces the new reality of their mortality. For the first time, he also begins to understand them as adult individuals instead of parents. Lots of highs and lows, maybe too many, but definitely moving. It may also evoke painful feelings in old people and those who are dealing with old age in others. Lemmon is wonderful.

A: Jack Lemmon, Ted Danson, Olympia Dukakis, Kathy Baker, Kevin Spacey, Ethan Hawke

© MCA/UNIVERSAL HOME VIDEO, INC. 80933

DAUGHTERS OF THE DUST

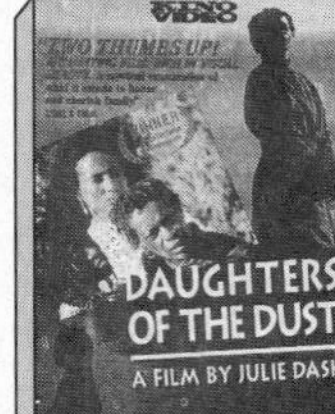

NR · DMA · 1991 · COLOR · Sex · Nud · Viol · Lang · AdSit

D: Julie Dash — 113 m

7 A beautifully photographed, often quite interesting, sometimes fascinating but unfortunately also quite slow-moving portrait of an isolated group of former slaves, living on the islands off the coasts of South Carolina and Georgia. These are a people who have retained their West African culture into the modern era. The time is 1902 and the story focuses on one family that is leaving the island to find prosperity in the North and the ceremony that marks their departure.

A: Cora Lee Day, Barbara-O, Cheryl Lynn Bruce, Tommy Hicks, Kaycee Moore, Alva Rogers

© KINO INTERNATIONAL VIDEO

DAVID AND BATHSHEBA

NR · DMA · 1951 · COLOR · Sex · Nud · ✓ Viol · Lang · ✓ AdSit

D: Henry King — 116 m

7 Big production religious epic that received numerous technical nominations and an Oscar for Best Screenplay. Gregory Peck is David, King of the Israelites of the Old Testament. This big picture tells the biblical story of David's lust for Bathsheba (Hayward), the sultry wife of one of his generals. So transfixed with her was he that he forsakes his first wife for her and arranges to have her husband killed in battle so that he can have her for himself. Then God sends his prophet Nathan to David to hold him accountable for what he has done.

A: Gregory Peck, Susan Hayward, Raymond Massey, Kieron Moore, Jayne Meadows, John Sutton

© FOXVIDEO 1380

DAVID COPPERFIELD

NR · DMA · 1935 · B&W · Sex · Nud · Viol · Lang · AdSit

D: George Cukor — 131 m

10 A treat for the whole family. Perhaps the best-ever Hollywood production of any Dickens classic. Young David (Bartholomew) leads an idyllic life with his mother and his nurse until his mother marries Murdstone (Rathbone), a despicable man, and she dies. Orphaned, David faces a life of toil in his step-father's sweatshop, but he runs away to his eccentric aunt. Through strength of character and help from friends, he survives all his trials to achieve success. Wonderful characterizations: Fields as Micawber, Rathbone as villainous Murdstone and Oliver as Aunt Betsey. Masterpiece.

A: Freddie Bartholomew, W.C. Fields, Frank Lawton, Lionel Barrymore, Edna May Oliver, Roland Young

Distributed By MGM/UA Home Video M300649

DEAD POET'S SOCIETY

PG · DMA · 1989 · COLOR · Sex · Nud · Viol · ✓ Lang · ✓ AdSit

D: Peter Weir — 128 m

7 Best Picture nominee. Against a background of straight-laced, conventional learning at a conservative New England prep school in 1959, an unconventional English teacher (Williams) both inspires and challenges his students. Williams, as the teacher, captures his student's imaginations by his infectious love for poetry, urging them to "seize the day" and make the most of life. Inspired by his teachings, the students revive a secret club, but as their independence asserts itself the movement is crushed by the school. Very well acted, particularly Williams. Oscar for Screenplay.

A: Robin Williams, Robert Sean Leonard, Ethan Hawke, Kurtwood Smith, Josh Charles, Gale Hansen

© TOUCHSTONE HOME VIDEO 947

DEFIANT ONES, THE

NR · DMA ACT · 1958 · B&W · Sex · Nud · ✓ Viol · Lang · ✓ AdSit

D: Stanley Kramer — 97 m

9 A major ground-breaking movie and great entertainment, too. It was nominated for seven Oscars and won three. Two prisoners who are chained together escape from a chain gang in the deep South. One is black and the other is white. Poitier and Curtis hate each other, but they are forced to work together and depend upon each other if they are first to escape and then to survive. This is a very well made and exciting movie that still packs a big punch today, while never sinking into platitudes and cliches. Powerful performances garnered four of the Oscar nominations.

A: Tony Curtis, Sidney Poitier, Theodore Bikel, Charles McGraw, Lon Chaney, Jr., Cara Williams

Distributed By MGM/UA Home Video M201557

DEMETRIUS AND THE GLADIATORS

NR · DMA ACT · 1954 · COLOR · Sex · Nud · ✓ Viol · Lang · ✓ AdSit

D: Delmer Daves — 101 m

6 This is a fairly tame sequel to the big hit THE ROBE. The Roman Emperor Caligula is obsessed with getting his hands on the robe that Christ wore, believing it to have magic powers. Demetrius is a slave and a devout Christian who has been entrusted with the robe. He is forced to fight lions and men in the arena, becomes one of Rome's greatest gladiators and the lover of seductive temptress Susan Hayward. He has refrained from revealing the robe's location but is now tempted to betray God. The major audience pleaser here is the impressive gladiator duels.

A: Victor Mature, Jay Jackson, Susan Hayward, Debra Paget, Anne Bancroft, Michael Rennie

© FOXVIDEO 1178

DIARY OF ANNE FRANK, THE

D: George Stevens — 151 m

NR | DMA SUS | 1959 | B&W | Rating: 9

Very moving screen depiction of a real-life WWII tragedy. The story was written based upon an actual diary of a young Jewish girl while she was in hiding with her family inside Nazi-occupied Holland. In the diary, she tells of the daily lives of her family and a few friends who are forced to hide in secret rooms hidden behind the false walls of an Amsterdam factory building during the occupation. The threat of discovery is ever-present and they lived their lives under extreme pressure. Still, throughout harrowing daily routines and constant fear, Anne manages to keep hope alive. 3 Oscars.

☐ Sex ☐ Nud ☑ Viol ☐ Lang ☑ AdSit

A: Millie Perkins, Joseph Schildkraut, Shelley Winters, Richard Beymer, Lou Jacobi, Ed Wynn

© FOXVIDEO 1074

DOLLMAKER, THE

D: Daniel Petrie — 140 m

NR | DMA | 1984 | COLOR | Rating: 8

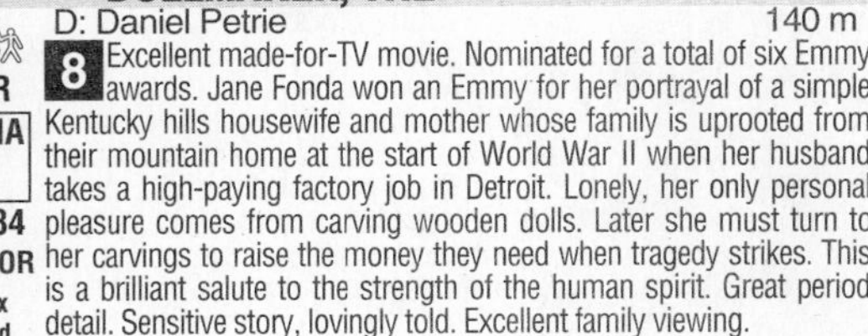

Excellent made-for-TV movie. Nominated for a total of six Emmy awards. Jane Fonda won an Emmy for her portrayal of a simple Kentucky hills housewife and mother whose family is uprooted from their mountain home at the start of World War II when her husband takes a high-paying factory job in Detroit. Lonely, her only personal pleasure comes from carving wooden dolls. Later she must turn to her carvings to raise the money they need when tragedy strikes. This is a brilliant salute to the strength of the human spirit. Great period detail. Sensitive story, lovingly told. Excellent family viewing.

☐ Sex ☐ Nud ☐ Viol ☐ Lang ☑ AdSit

A: Jane Fonda, Levon Helm, Susan Kingsley, Nikki Cresswell

© FOXVIDEO 5538

DON'T CRY, IT'S ONLY THUNDER

D: Peter Werner — 108 m

PG | DMA | 1981 | COLOR | Rating: 8

Heartwarming little movie that never got big promotion when it was released. It is based upon a true incident from the Vietnam War. In 1968, a US Army medic (Christopher) has a profitable little business set up on the side dealing in black market items. But he gets caught, court-martialed and sent to work in a mortuary in Saigon. There, he is recruited by a group of nuns and a dedicated Army doctor who need his special talent to help supply their orphanage. Now, things take on a new meaning for him. A truly inspirational movie that never drifts into melodrama.

☐ Sex ☐ Nud ☑ Viol ☑ Lang ☑ AdSit

A: Dennis Christopher, Susan Saint James, Roger Aaron Brown, Lisa Lu, James Whitmore, Jr., Thu Thuy

© COLUMBIA TRISTAR HOME VIDEO 60170

DOWNHILL RACER

D: Michael Ritchie — 102 m

PG | DMA | 1969 | COLOR | Rating: 7

Sports story about what it sometimes takes to be a winner. It was a very influential and well-done sports film that provides a not-often-seen look behind the glamour. It is also the character study of a loner's empty life. Redford plays an egotistical ski bum who wins a place on the US Olympic ski team when a racer gets hurt. His character is very unappealing, however. This makes him a source of trouble for the team, and a not very appealing hero for the film. The film works best for its exciting skiing sequences, which are dazzling. Redford did much of his own skiing and stunts.

☐ Sex ☐ Nud ☐ Viol ☑ Lang ☑ AdSit

A: Robert Redford, Gene Hackman, Camilla Sparv, Kar Michael Vogler, Jim McMullan, Chiristian Dormer

© PARAMOUNT HOME VIDEO 6910

DREAMCHILD

D: Gavin Millar — 90 m

PG | DMA | 1985 | COLOR | Rating: 7

In 1932 an eighty-year-old woman came to Columbia University to help everyone there celebrate the 100th birthday of Lewis Carroll (author of "Alice's Adventures in Wonderland"). She was present because, when she was just 10, she was the inspiration for Carroll to create the story - she was Alice. Those true facts led to the making of this film. Here, Alice recalls her relationship with Carroll in mid-19th century England. She recalls her idyllic childhood through a blend of reality and Jim Henson's muppets. Well done unusual treat, worth watching.

☐ Sex ☐ Nud ☐ Viol ☐ Lang ☐ AdSit

A: Coral Browne, Peter Gallagher, Ian Holm, Jane Asher, Nicola Cowper, Amelia Shankley

Distributed By MGM/UA Home Video M202767

EDISON, THE MAN

D: Clarence Brown — 107 m

NR | DMA | 1940 | COLOR | Rating: 7

Good entertainment and an inspiring story of the life of the man who brought us the motion picture, the light bulb, the phonograph, the ticker tape and numerous other inventions. The "Wizard of Menlo Park" (played by Tracy) is interviewed on the occasion of the 50th anniversary of the light bulb. His life's story is told as a series of flashbacks... how he started as a penniless janitor with a basement laboratory and later came to create some of the most significant inventions of the industrial age. Keeps moving. Pretty good.

☐ Sex ☐ Nud ☐ Viol ☐ Lang ☐ AdSit

A: Spencer Tracy, Charles Coburn, Rita Johnson

Distributed By MGM/UA Home Video M202346

EIGHT MEN OUT

D: John Sayles — 120 m

PG | DMA | 1988 | COLOR | Rating: 7

Intriguing sports drama about the 1919 World Series where the Chicago White Sox intentionally threw the Series. That actual event became known as the Black Sox scandal. A superb ensemble cast and excellent period detail illustrate the story of a team that felt so motivated by the stinginess of their team owner they felt justified in selling out a World Series game - the game they loved and their fans - for cash. They were all caught and everyone involved was banned from ever playing the game professionally again. The story is true.

☐ Sex ☐ Nud ☐ Viol ☑ Lang ☐ AdSit

A: Charlie Sheen, John Cusack, Christopher Lloyd, D.B. Sweeney, David Strathairn, Michael Lerner

© ORION PICTURES CORPORATION 8723

ELECTRIC HORSEMAN, THE

D: Sydney Pollack — 120 m

PG | DMA ROM WST | 1979 | COLOR | Rating: 7

Entertaining modern-day Western about an ex-rodeo star who has become an alcoholic cowboy appearing on cereal boxes riding a horse and promoting the cereal by appearing live on a champion racehorse, in a suit studded with flashing lights. Fonda, a reporter out for a good story, gets one. Redford becomes so upset when the horse he rides is exploited, too, that he steals the horse and rides across Utah looking for a place to set it free. Fonda stays one step of ahead the cops and finds him, but at first doesn't believe him about what he is trying to do. Eventually she does and falls for him.

☐ Sex ☐ Nud ☐ Viol ☑ Lang ☑ AdSit

A: Robert Redford, Jane Fonda, Valerie Perrine, Willie Nelson, John Saxon, Wilford Brimley

© MCA/UNIVERSAL HOME VIDEO, INC. 66006

ELEPHANT BOY

D: Robert Flaherty — 82 m

NR | DMA CLD | 1937 | B&W | Rating: 7

Delightful Rudyard Kipling family adventure movie. A young Indian boy's (Sabu) dream is to become a great hunter. But, when his favorite elephant is sold to a mean dealer, Sabu steals the animal back and escapes into the jungle. There he discovers a large wild herd of elephants and the place that elephants go when they die. Filmed and set in 1930s India, this is both an interesting portrait of the time and place, and a worthy adventure in its own right, particularly for children. There is only one white man in the picture. All others are Indian.

☐ Sex ☐ Nud ☐ Viol ☐ Lang ☐ AdSit

A: Sabu, W.E. Holloway, Walter Hudd, Bruce Gordon, D.J. Williams

© HBO VIDEO 90655

ELEPHANT MAN, THE

D: David Lynch — 124 m

PG | DMA | 1980 | B&W | Rating: 8

Moving story, remarkably based upon a real individual - John Merrick (beautifully played by John Hurt under masses of make-up). Merrick was massively deformed and was dubbed the Elephant Man by the freak show where he lived until being rescued by a Victorian doctor (Hopkins). Degraded, beaten and humiliated, Merrick is at last given a chance to gain some dignity and respect for himself. This is the story of a man's struggle to survive and achieve dignity against hopeless odds. Beautiful period details. Top performances. 8 Oscar nominations. Unforgettable.

☐ Sex ☐ Nud ☐ Viol ☐ Lang ☑ AdSit

A: Anthony Hopkins, John Hurt, Anne Bancroft, John Gielgud, Wendy Hiller, Freddie Jones

© PARAMOUNT HOME VIDEO 1347

ELVIS - THE MOVIE

D: John Carpenter — 117 m

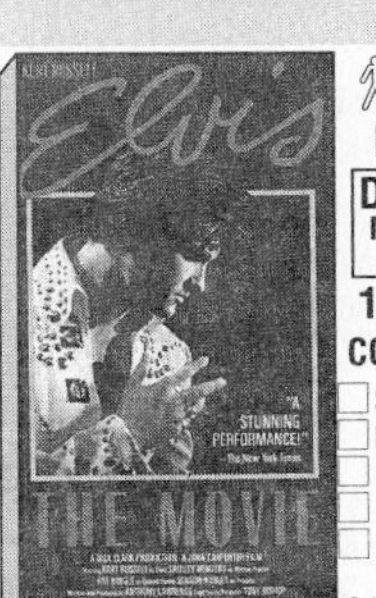

NR | DMA MUS | 1979 | COLOR | Rating: 9

Highly regarded and excellent depiction of Elvis's life, from rising from poverty as a truck driver to headlining in Las Vegas showrooms. Russell won universal acclaim for his right-on portrait of The King. His became the standard for the comparison of all other impersonators. This was a made-for-TV production, but is far better than that might indicate. It was one of the highest rated TV movies of all time. Excellent acting support came from Shelly Winters as Elvis's mother.

☐ Sex ☐ Nud ☐ Viol ☐ Lang ☐ AdSit

A: Kurt Russell, Shelley Winters, Season Hubley, Pat Hingle, Bing Russell

© LIVE HOME VIDEO 4080

EXODUS

D: Otto Preminger — 213 m

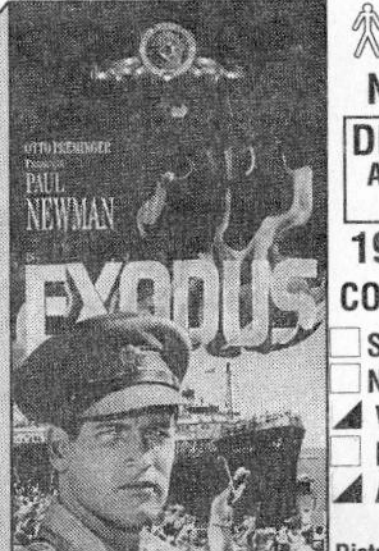

NR | DMA ACT | 1960 | COLOR | Rating: 7

Major box office hit which tells the story of the birth of the Jewish state, beginning with the resettlement of Palestine after World War II. The primary story line follows Paul Newman as a major political and military leader who guides European refugees after the war into British controlled Palestine. He later leads fighters in the resistance movement to win independence from Britain and separation from the Arabs, to form a separate Jewish state. The lives of several other characters are followed, including Sal Mineo as a young Auschwitz survivor who joins a terrorist group.

☐ Sex ☐ Nud ☑ Viol ☐ Lang ☑ AdSit

A: Paul Newman, Eva Marie Saint, Lee J. Cobb, Sal Mineo, Ralph Richardson

Distributed By MGM/UA Home Video M301455

FIELD OF DREAMS

D: Phil Alden Robinson — 106 m

PG | DMA FAN | 1989 | COLOR

8 This was the feel-good movie of 1989 and a Best Picture nominee. Costner plays a dreamer, an Iowa farmer who hears a voice that says, "If you build it, he will come." After he convinces himself and his wife that he is not crazy, he sets out to build a baseball diamond in the middle of his corn field. Then, mystically and magically, Shoeless Joe Jackson of the Chicago White Sox of 1918, his father's hero, does come. Then Costner sets off to find a reclusive writer (Jones) who returns with Costner to witness the wonder. Soon a whole team of people, all with unfulfilled dreams, arrives at the magic corn field. Excellent acting but "corny".

Sex / Nud / Viol / ◢ Lang / ◢ AdSit

A: Kevin Costner, Amy Madigan, Gaby Hoffman, Ray Liotta, Timothy Busfield, James Earl Jones

© MCA/UNIVERSAL HOME VIDEO, INC. 80884

FISH HAWK

D: Donald Shebib — 95 m

G | DMA CLD | 1979 | COLOR

7 Fish Hawk is an old alcoholic Osage Indian living alone in the turn-of-the-century Ozarks. He is a lonely old man who is scorned by everyone. In his drunkenness one day, he kills his dog - one of the few friends he has. He vows to reform and to track down and kill a bear that has been terrorizing the town. In the woods, he meets a lonely young farm boy. They become friends and their friendship causes him to remember much of what he has forgotten. He vows to give up his old ways, but he also must leave his new friend to go back home to his people. A gentle story that is well done.

Sex / Nud / Viol / Lang / ◢ AdSit

A: Will Sampson, Charles Fields, Geoffrey Bowes, Mary Pirie, Don Francks

© VIDEO TREASURES M297

FOOL KILLER, THE

D: Servando Gonzalez — 100 m

NR | DMA SUS | 1965 | B&W

7 Unusual adventure story in which George, a 12-year-old runaway orphan boy in the post-Civil War South, rides the rails. He strikes up a relationship with a crusty old-timer who intrigues him with stories of an eight-foot-tall axe-wielding murderer who is supposedly roaming the countryside. He calls him the "fool killer." Later, young George teams up with a tormented, very tall war veteran who has lost his memory. They travel together, but slowly George begins to fear that his new companion may, in fact, be the fool killer. Somewhat arty and offbeat, but it definitely has its moments.

Sex / Nud / Viol / Lang / AdSit

A: Anthony Perkins, Edward Albert, Dana Elcar, Henry Hull, Salome Jens, Arnold Moss

© REPUBLIC PICTURES HOME VIDEO 1352

FOOTLOOSE

D: Herbert Ross — 107 m

PG | DMA | 1984 | COLOR

7 When big-city kid Bacon moves into a small town, he finds a few surprises in store for him. The biggest surprise is that dancing is outlawed. Bible belt minister Lithgow has taken it upon himself to institute the ban in their little town. However, when Bacon falls for the minister's daughter, the two team up to make a formidable opponent in the battle to bring back fun. The memorable score did very well on the charts, and Bacon's spirited determination makes this a "feel good" film that's especially well suited for younger teenagers.

Sex / Nud / ◢ Viol / ◢ Lang / ◢ AdSit

A: Kevin Bacon, Lori Singer, John Lithgow, Dianne Wiest, Christopher Penn, Sarah Jessica Parker

© PARAMOUNT HOME VIDEO 1589

FOREVER AND A DAY

D: Rene Clair, Edmund Goulding — 105 m

NR | DMA | 1943 | B&W

9 A unique once-in-a-lifetime cast of English stars of the 30s and 40s (over eighty in all) star in this epic saga. It is the story about one particular manor house in London and it spans more than 100 years of its history. The story follows each generation that lives in it, from Napoleonic times in 1804 to the Blitz of WWII. The film was created specifically to buck up war time spirits. Each sequence was prepared with meticulous care and contains excellent acting under superb directorship and writing. Fine entertainment.

Sex / Nud / Viol / Lang / AdSit

A: Claude Rains, Charles Laughton, Merle Oberon, Brian Aherne, Ray Milland, Ida Lupino

© HEN'S TOOTH VIDEO 1004

GIRL WHO SPELLED FREEDOM, THE

D: Simon Wincer — 90 m

NR | DMA CLD | 1986 | COLOR

8 Heartwarming true story of a young Cambodian girl who is determined to master English after her family flees war-torn Cambodia and settles in Tennessee. In spite of the difficulties she and her family have struggling to learn new ways and a new language, she becomes a spelling-bee champion within a just a few months. Good entertainment for all ages.

Sex / Nud / Viol / Lang / AdSit

A: Wayne Rogers, Mary Kay Place, Kieu Chinh, Kathleen Sisk, Jade Chinn, Margot Pinvidic

© WALT DISNEY HOME VIDEO 416V

GOING MY WAY

D: Leo McCarey — 126 m

NR | DMA COM MUS | 1944 | B&W

9 This was a major box office hit in its time and it still holds up fairly well today. It won seven Oscars, including Best Picture, Screenplay, Actor and Supporting Actor. It is the heartwarming and sentimental story of a loveable crusty old parish priest (Fitzgerald), with a rundown church, who is won over by a young priest (Crosby) sent to give both him and his church a boost. Crosby sings "Swinging on a Star" and "Too-ra-Loo-ra-Loo-ra" - winner of Best Song Oscar. Unflinchingly sentimental and a great time. Followed by THE BELLS OF ST. MARY'S.

Sex / Nud / Viol / Lang / AdSit

A: Bing Crosby, Barry Fitzgerald, Rise Stevens, Gene Lockhart, Frank McHugh

© MCA/UNIVERSAL HOME VIDEO, INC. 55038

GOODBYE, MR. CHIPS

D: Sam Wood — 115 m

NR | DMA ROM | 1939 | B&W

9 Sentimental and heartwarming portrait of a shy, bumbling but well-meaning Latin teacher at an Victorian English boy's school who comes out of his shell only when he meets his future wife (Greer Garson) on holiday. She transforms his shyness into a warmth that the the boys can understand, and he becomes a popular institution at the school. This unabashedly sentimental story grips at your heartstrings and received seven Academy Award nominations. Donat's moving performance even beat out Clark Gable's Rhett Butler for Best Actor Oscar in 1939. It is still a richly rewarding experience.

Sex / Nud / Viol / Lang / AdSit

A: Robert Donat, Greer Garson, John Mills, Terry Kilburn

Distributed By MGM/UA Home Video M300687

GREATEST SHOW ON EARTH, THE

D: Cecil B. DeMille — 149 m

NR | DMA | 1952 | COLOR

8 This is a pretty good time, especially for families, and was the winner of the Best Picture Oscar. It is a big-budget production that presents all the aspects of circus life and is loaded with all the thrills of the big-top. Three principal stories from backstage help hold it all together: James Stewart as a clown with a mysterious past (he is never seen without his makeup), there is a love story and a massive train wreck. Plenty of circus thrills and excitement, too, plus loads of major stars.

Sex / Nud / Viol / Lang / AdSit

A: Betty Hutton, James Stewart, Charlton Heston, Cornel Wilde, Dorothy Lamour, Gloria Grahame

© PARAMOUNT HOME VIDEO 6617

GREATEST STORY EVER TOLD, THE

D: George Stevens — 199 m

G | DMA | 1965 | COLOR

9 Epic and grand-scale telling of the life of Christ, presenting all the traditional Biblical stories. It traces his life from birth through the crucifixion to the resurrection. It includes a huge star-studded cast. It earned five Oscar nominations and has become an enduring perennial favorite.

Sex / Nud / Viol / Lang / AdSit

A: Max von Sydow, Charlton Heston, Roddy McDowall, Robert Loggia, Jose Ferrer, Dorothy McGuire

Distributed By MGM/UA Home Video M301653

GREAT EXPECTATIONS

D: David Lean — 118 m

NR | DMA | 1946 | B&W

10 Excellent production of Dickens's classic story of a penniless orphan who, as a small boy, meets a mysterious stranger in a graveyard and serves as a hired playmate to a young girl under the care of the wealthy, eccentric and mysterious Mrs. Havisham. Later, he is given a mysterious financial endowment, thereby also the opportunity to become a gentleman. However, he is not told who his benefactor is. This film does a wonderful job of capturing the mood of Victorian times. Excellent in all aspects. Winner of two Oscars. Generally recognized as the best of any Dickens adaptations.

Sex / Nud / Viol / Lang / ◢ AdSit

A: John Mills, Alec Guinness, Valerie Hobson, Bernard Miles, Finlay Currie, Jean Simmons

© PARAMOUNT HOME VIDEO 12568

GREAT MAN VOTES, THE

D: Garson Kanin — 72 m

NR | DMA COM | 1938 | B&W

9 Delightful gem of a movie. Barrymore is a former professor at Harvard and an author who has been mourning the death of his wife. He has been reduced to being a drunk and the Children's Society threatens him with having his children taken away. By chance, he is chosen to cast the deciding vote in the town's mayoral election and he plays his new power role for maximum benefit, thereby gaining a newfound respect from everyone - including himself. Good dramatic moments, interspersed with some really funny ones. Simple, but well-told story. Good entertainment.

Sex / Nud / Viol / Lang / AdSit

A: John Barrymore, Peter Holden, Virginia Weidler, Donald MacBride, William Demarest

© TURNER HOME ENTERTAINMENT 6257

HAMBONE AND HILLIE

D: Roy Watts — 97 m

PG | DMA CLD | 1984 | COLOR

7 Heartwarming story of devotion. An elderly woman returns to Los Angeles from a trip to New York to visit her grandson by plane. However, her dog, Hambone, who must travel as baggage, escapes from his travel case and gets loose in the big world, far way from home. But Hambone will not be separated from his mistress for long, and a cross-country 3,300 mile journey of many travails begins. Very good entertainment for the whole family, but especially the kids.

Sex / Nud / ✓ Viol / Lang / AdSit

A: Lillian Gish, O.J. Simpson, Timothy Bottoms, Candy Clark, Jack Carter

© R&G VIDEO, LP 80072

HAWAII

D: George Roy Hill — 190 m

NR | DMA | 1966 | COLOR

7 Sprawling Michener saga about the white settlement of Hawaii in the early 1800s. The missionaries came to bring God but instead nearly destroyed a people and a culture. Max von Sydow plays the stridently religious missionary who is sent to convert the natives. Julie Andrews plays his wife who struggles to stand by him, even though she is in love with dashing sea captain Richard Harris. Beautiful photography and scenery. Received six Oscar nominations. The second half of Michener's book was made into the sequel: THE HAWAIIANS.

✓ Sex / Nud / ✓ Viol / Lang / ✓ AdSit

A: Julie Andrews, Max von Sydow, Richard Harris, Torin Thatcher, Gene Hackman, Carroll O'Connor

Distributed By MGM/UA Home Video M301464

HEART LIKE A WHEEL

D: Jonathan Kaplan — 113 m

PG | DMA ACT | 1983 | COLOR

7 Well-made sports biography about the pioneering female drag racer, Shirley "Cha-Cha" Muldowney. Bedelia gives a stellar performance as a hard-pressed woman who struggles to balance a career as a racer with being a wife. She also struggles to fight the sexist attitudes of a male-dominated sport into which she is the first woman to dare to enter. While the film does concern racing, it is really a human story of dedication and courage. It wins on both levels. Surprisingly good.

Sex / Nud / Viol / ✓ Lang / ✓ AdSit

A: Bonnie Bedelia, Beau Bridges, Leo Rossi, Hoyt Axton, Bill McKinney, Dick Miller

© FOXVIDEO 1300

HOMECOMING, THE

D: Fielder Cook — 98 m

NR | DMA | 1971 | COLOR

8 Award-winning and sentimental telling of rural life during the Great Depression. It is also the pilot for the extremely popular TV series, "The Waltons." It is Christmas Eve in 1933. The large Walton family is anxiously awaiting the return home of their father, who has gone to town in search of work. He is long over due. The beleaguered mother decides to send her oldest son off in search of news. Heartwarming.

Sex / Nud / Viol / Lang / AdSit

A: Patricia Neal, Richard Thomas, Edgar Bergen, Ellen Corby, William Windom, Cleavon Little

© FOXVIDEO 7134

HOOSIERS

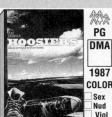

D: David Anspaugh — 114 m

PG | DMA | 1987 | COLOR

9 Thoroughly enjoyable slice of Americana. A very satisfying experience that the whole family will truly enjoy. Gene Hackman plays an unorthodox coach who gets one last chance at coaching in a small town high school in Indiana. His methods rankle everyone, on and off the team, until his team starts to win. He takes his underdogs to the championship. The town, the school, everybody is excited. The thrill is infectious even to the viewer. What is particularly gratifying is that this story was based upon a real-life incident in 1951 Indiana.

Sex / Nud / Viol / Lang / ✓ AdSit

A: Gene Hackman, Barbara Hershey, Dennis Hopper, Sheb Wooley, Fern Parsons, Brad Boyle

© LIVE HOME VIDEO 5191

HOW GREEN WAS MY VALLEY

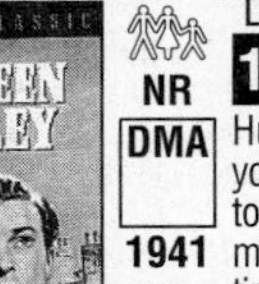

D: John Ford — 118 m

NR | DMA | 1941 | B&W

10 Winner of 5 Academy Awards including Best Picture. An undisputed masterpiece that has lost nothing with time. 60-year-old Huw Morgan tells the story of his childhood growing up as the youngest of six children in a loving family. They live in Welsh mining town snuggled in a lush green valley. But life in the town and in the mines is hard and dangerous, and there is labor strife too. Life itself at times seems to conspire to destroy the townsfolk and the Morgans in particular. Still, through it all, they survive. There is actually very little plot and is more a series of vignettes that together tell their story of a loving family. Heart-tugging and majestic.

Sex / Nud / Viol / Lang / AdSit

A: Walter Pidgeon, Maureen O'Hara, Donald Crisp, Anna Lee, Roddy McDowall, Barry Fitzgerald

© FOXVIDEO 1037

HURRICANE, THE

D: John Ford — 102 m

NR | DMA | 1937 | B&W

6 One of the earliest disaster flicks from Hollywood. It contains highly believable special effects that are just as effective today as they were then. While the climactic hurricane effects have never been equaled, the story line is somewhat labored and the characters are simplistic sterotypes. The story concerns an idyllic South Sea island where the white governor has become obsessed with capturing a proud runaway native. Once convicted of attacking a white man who insulted him and then repeatedly sentenced to longer and longer terms for failed escape attempts, the man again has escaped.

Sex / Nud / Viol / Lang / AdSit

A: Jon Hall, Dorothy Lamour, Raymond Massey, Mary Astor, C. Aubrey Smith

© HBO VIDEO 90756

ICE CASTLES

D: Donald Wrye — 109 m

PG | DMA | 1979 | COLOR

7 An Iowa farm girl strives her whole life to become a world class figure skater. She even forsakes her boyfriend and her widowed father in her consuming pursuit of the Olympic gold in ice skating. But she is forced to change her plans when an accident leaves her blinded. However, with the help of her father and her boyfriend, she regains the courage needed to beat the odds and to skate again. Sentimental overload? Yes, but effectively done, bringing both laughter and tears. Enjoyable. Melissa Manchester sings Marvin Hamlisch's Oscar-nominated theme "Through the Eyes of Love."

Sex / Nud / Viol / ✓ Lang / AdSit

A: Robby Benson, Lynn-Holly Johnson, Colleen Dewhurst, Tom Skerritt, Jennifer Warren

© COLUMBIA TRISTAR HOME VIDEO 60018

IDOLMAKER, THE

D: Taylor Hackford — 119 m

PG | DMA MUS | 1980 | COLOR

7 Slick filmmaking tells the story of a failed-songwriter turned promoter (played well by Sharkey) who stops at nothing to push, pull and shove two young Philadelphia boys into becoming national pop idols at the beginning of the rock `n roll revolution of the late '50s. Quite well done, even though some felt that it fell short at the end. Energetic performances and music recapture much of the feel of the period. Based upon the real-life rise of Frankie Avalon and Fabian.

Sex / Nud / Viol / ✓ Lang / ✓ AdSit

A: Ray Sharkey, Peter Gallagher, Paul Land, Maureen McCormick, Olympia Dukakis

Distributed By MGM/UA Home Video M600370

IF YOU COULD SEE WHAT I HEAR

D: Eric Till — 100 m

PG | DMA COM | 1981 | COLOR

6 Interesting screen biography of real-life blind singer/composer Tom Sullivan. The story deals directly with his blindness and how he handles things. It begins with his college years, telling his story over time until he settles down after having several flings. The story stresses the more humorous elements of his situation and has, therefore, been criticized as being too simplistic, sugary-sweet and insubstantial. Others call it optimistic, life-affirming and uplifting. You'll get out of it whatever you look for.

Sex / Nud / Viol / Lang / ✓ AdSit

A: Marc Singer, R.H. Thomson, Sarah Torgov, Shari Belafonte Harper

© LIVE HOME VIDEO VA5014

INN OF THE SIXTH HAPPINESS, THE

D: Mark Robson — 158 m

NR | DMA | 1958 | COLOR

8 Effective and heartwarming true story of English missionary Gladys Alward (Bergman) who determinedly opens a mission prior to the outbreak of World War II. She earns the respect and love of the locals and, in particular, the Mandarin (Donat), who agreed to convert to Christianity just for her. She falls in love with a Eurasian colonel (Jergens) but is forced to leave the country at the outbreak of the war. So she takes a group of war orphans on a dangerous cross country flight with her. Very involving. A simple, true story - well told.

Sex / Nud / Viol / Lang / AdSit

A: Ingrid Bergman, Curt Jurgens, Robert Donat, Ronald Squire

© FOXVIDEO 1170

INTERNATIONAL VELVET

D: Bryan Forbes — 126 m

PG | DMA CLD | 1978 | COLOR

8 Entertaining sequel to the 1944 classic NATIONAL VELVET which starred a young Elizabeth Taylor. The English Steeplechase winner (Newman) is now forty years old. She has an orphaned American niece (O'Neal) who is determined to become an Olympic riding champion. A tough trainer (Hopkins) shows her the dedication it takes to become a winner. Excellent photography and fine acting help offset the fact that it is slightly overlong. Still, this is interesting human drama and enjoyable family entertainment.

Sex / Nud / Viol / Lang / AdSit

A: Tatum O'Neal, Christopher Plummer, Anthony Hopkins, Nanette Newman, Dinsdale Landen

Distributed By MGM/UA Home Video M600296

INTRUDER IN THE DUST

D: Clarence Brown 87 m

NR | DMA MYS | 1949 | B&W | Sex | Nud | Viol ✓ | Lang | AdSit ✓

9 Excellent screen depiction of a William Falkner novel, set in his home state of Mississippi. An old black man is held in contempt by the townsfolk because he is proud and owns his own land. When a white man is killed and the old man is found in possession of a pistol which has just been fired, he is accused of the murder by police. A young white boy who has befriended him sees what has happened, coerces his reluctant lawyer uncle into helping the old man before he is lynched by the townsfolk and into finding the real killer. Very well done, both on a social and dramatic level, and as a murder mystery.

A: David Brian, Claude Jarman, Jr., Juano Hernandez, Porter Hall, Elizabeth Paterson

Distributed By MGM/UA Home Video M202838

I REMEMBER MAMA

D: George Stevens 119 m

NR | DMA COM | 1948 | B&W | Sex | Nud | Viol | Lang | AdSit

9 Sentimental favorite and piece of Americana that won five Oscar nominations. It is the beautifully told and heartwarming story of an immigrant Norwegian family in San Francisco near the turn of the century. The story is told from the viewpoint of the oldest daughter (Bel Geddes). She tells of her shy aunt and her blustering uncle, of the family's daily struggles, but most of all she talks of how her mother fights to win a new and better life for her children in a new land. A very rewarding experience. Great feel good film.

A: Irene Dunne, Barbara Bel Geddes, Oscar Homolka, Philip Dorn, Ellen Corby, Edgar Bergen

© TURNER HOME ENTERTAINMENT 2071

JACKIE ROBINSON STORY, THE

D: Alfred E. Green 76 m

NR | DMA | 1950 | Sex | Nud | Viol | Lang | AdSit

8 Intriguing straightforward biography of a sports great, and the first black man ever allowed to play against white men as an equal participant in major league professional baseball. Becoming an equal on the field did not include being an equal off the field, nor was his appearance on the field accepted gracefully by all. Jackie Robinson was chosen not only because he was an exceptional ball player, but because he was exceptional human being off the field as well. This is a fascinating social history of a very special man.

A: Jackie Robinson, Ruby Dee, Minor Watson, Louise Beavers, Richard Lane, Harry Shannon

Distributed By MGM/UA Home Video M204612

JESSE OWENS STORY, THE

D: Richard Irving 174 m

NR | DMA | 1984 | COLOR | Sex | Nud | Viol | Lang | AdSit ✓

7 This is a made-for-TV docudrama that tells the story of famed American hero Jesse Owens. Owens was a black sharecropper's son who rose above his family's circumstances to go to college. At college, he broke track record after record and went on to the 1936 Olympics in Nazi Germany. There he won a fabulous, four gold medals and embarrassed Hitler and his prized supermen. For a brief while he was the pride of America, but he went home to face the same prejudices he had left, in the land that he loved and had called him a hero. For 30 years more he was both embarrassed and exploited, but he never faltered in his struggle for dignity.

A: Dorian Harewood, Georg Stanford Brown, Debbi Morgan, Barry Corbin, Kai Wulff, George Kennedy

© PARAMOUNT HOME VIDEO 85040

JESUS OF NAZARETH

D: Franco Zeffirelli 279 m

NR | DMA | 1976 | COLOR | Sex | Nud | Viol | Lang | AdSit ✓

9 Widely regarded as one of, if not the best, film telling of the story of Christ. Originally filmed for television, and populated by a huge big-name cast of Who's Whos, this is an extremely detailed and reverent recounting of the life of Christ as told by the four Gospels. It begins before his birth and goes through to the Crucifixion and Resurrection. Visually splendid and narratively involving, it was acclaimed by critics and religious leaders too. Very long, even though it has been edited down from the original TV length, but well worth the time spent.

A: Robert Powell, Anne Bancroft, James Mason, Laurence Olivier, Rod Steiger, Ernest Borgnine

© LIVE HOME VIDEO 48988

JOURNEY OF NATTY GANN, THE

D: Jeremy Paul Kagan 101 m

PG | DMA ACT CLD | 1985 | COLOR | Sex | Nud | Viol ✓ | Lang ✓ | AdSit

9 This is a wonderfully endearing story that has the rare quality of being a family movie that has a genuine appeal both to young and to old. Natty Gann is a young girl in Depression-era Chicago, whose desperate father has to leave her, on short notice and without saying goodbye, with a very unpleasant old woman so he can take a good job in Seattle. Natty refuses to believe her father has deserted her and embarks on a cross-country trip by rail to go to him. She is all alone, except for a protective wolf and a hardened drifter she meets along the way. Very appealing, highly entertaining and very worthwhile.

A: Meredith Salenger, John Cusack, Ray Wise, Lainie Kazan, Barry Miller, Scatman Crothers

© WALT DISNEY HOME VIDEO 400

KEYS OF THE KINGDOM, THE

D: John M. Stahl 137 m

NR | DMA | 1944 | B&W | Sex | Nud | Viol | Lang | AdSit

8 Gregory Peck won an Oscar nomination in this his first major film. It is the reverent story of a devout Catholic missionary in China. The story begins with him being an old man thinking that he has accomplished little with his life and then his life is told in flashback to reveal quite the opposite. He is a humble man who arrives at a remote outpost where there is no following or mission, and creates one - overcoming many personal hardships along the way, including war. An inspiring and heartwarming movie with lavish production values and a strong supporting cast.

A: Gregory Peck, Thomas Mitchell, Vincent Price, Roddy McDowall, Edmund Gwenn, Cedric Hardwicke

© FOXVIDEO 1314

KING CREOLE

D: Michael Curtiz 116 m

NR | DMA MUS | 1958 | B&W | Sex | Nud | Viol ✓ | Lang | AdSit ✓

8 Presley surprised quite a few critics with this performance. He was an unexpected choice for this dramatization of "A Stone for Danny Fisher" after James Dean died, but Hal Wallis tailored it perfectly for him. He plays a young would-be singer, bordering on delinquency and working as a busboy in a mobster's (Matthau) nightclub. Carolyn Jones is Matthau's mistress. When she is publicly mistreated, Presley comes to her defense. So, to embarrass him, Matthau makes him stand up before the crowd and sing, but instead he is a hit. Over a dozen songs including "Hard Headed Woman" and "Trouble."

A: Elvis Presley, Carolyn Jones, Dolores Hart, Dean Jagger, Liliane Montevecchi, Walter Matthau

© CBS/FOX VIDEO 2005

KING KONG

D: Merian C. Cooper, Ernest B. Schoedsack 100 m

NR | DMA ACT FAN | 1933 | COLOR | Sex | Nud | Viol ✓ | Lang | AdSit

10 This is an enduring classic, the many merits of which overcome its primitive production techniques (even though the live action special effects are still quite believable today). On a remote island, a giant ape is discovered and captured. He is transported to America where he is put on display in New York City. Tormented by the crowds, the huge beast manages to break free, wreaking major havoc upon the city, seeking out Fay Wray and taking her with him as he makes a last stand at the top of the Empire State Building. See also MIGHTY JOE YOUNG.

A: Ernest B. Scholedsack, Robert Armstrong, Fay Wray, Bruce Cabot, Frank Reicher, Noble Johnson

© TURNER HOME ENTERTAINMENT 6003

KING OF KINGS

D: Nicholas Ray 170 m

NR | DMA | 1961 | COLOR | Sex | Nud | Viol ✓ | Lang | AdSit

9 A reverent and very traditional telling of the life of Christ. It is a story simply yet intelligently told, and grandly filmed in CinemaScope. Christ's life is told from its beginning in the manger, through to his death on the cross, and includes such important events as his wandering in the desert, The Sermon on the Mount and, of course, The Last Supper. A large-scale spectacular that had a cast of thousands. Narrated by Orson Welles.

A: Jeffrey Hunter, Siobhan McKenna, Robert Ryan, Hurd Hatfield, Viveca Lindfors, Rita Gam

Distributed By MGM/UA Home Video M700326

KNUTE ROCKNE - ALL AMERICAN

D: Lloyd Bacon 96 m

NR | DMA | 1940 | COLOR | Sex | Nud | Viol | Lang | AdSit

7 Now-famous sport biography of Notre Dame's immortal and inspirational football coach, Knute Rockne. Rockne was a real person who coached for many winning seasons and became a fixture at Notre Dame and a national icon. The film is pretty corny and sentimental, but it is still a favorite. Rockne was best known for his inspirational lectures to his players. O'Brien relished his role and gave it his best shot with his most famous line, "Now go in there and win one for the Gipper." This is also the movie that helped a President get elected.

A: Pat O'Brien, Ronald Reagan, Gale Page, Donald Crisp, Albert Basserman

Distributed By MGM/UA Home Video M400555

LAND OF THE PHARAOHS

D: Howard Hawks 104 m

NR | DMA | 1955 | COLOR | Sex | Nud | Viol ✓ | Lang | AdSit

7 Big screen spectacle (with 10,000 extras) that is a fictionalized account of the building of the Great Pyramid of Egypt in about 3000 B.C. For thirty years the Pharaoh (Hawkins) struggled to get his monumental tomb built, while he struggled also against his scheming wife, who wanted both his treasure and his kingdom. (Fans of Joan Collins will note this as one of her earliest appearances.) In many ways, this is uninspired filmmaking. Yet its scope and a nifty ending still manage to intrigue viewers.

A: Jack Hawkins, Joan Collins, James Robertson Justice, Dewey Martin, Alexis Minotis, Sydney Chaplin

© WARNER HOME VIDEO 11357

LASSIE COME HOME

D: Fred M. Wilcox — 90 m

NR | DMA CLD | 1943 | COLOR

8 Wonderful, warm and sentimental family film that marked the original screen debut of Lassie. A desperately poor English family is forced to sell their dog to a Scottish duke, but Lassie escapes and struggles against long odds to find her way back home across 1000 miles to the boy who loves her. (This Lassie was really a him). You will also see a very young Roddy McDowall and Elizabeth Taylor in this heartwarming film.

Sex / Nud / Viol / Lang / AdSit

A: Roddy McDowall, Donald Crisp, Dame May Whitty, Edmund Gwenn, Nigel Bruce, Elizabeth Taylor

Distributed By MGM/UA Home Video M201866

LAST ANGRY MAN, THE

D: Daniel Mann — 100 m

NR | DMA | 1959 | B&W

7 Paul Muni received his fifth Oscar nomination in this his last picture. Although a little overly-sentimental, this is still a very enjoyable story about a selfless doctor who has dedicated 45 years of service as a general practitioner in a poor Brooklyn neighborhood. Now a TV show wants to honor him with a depiction of his life's story, but the old man's principals are threatened by an overly-enthusiastic TV producer. Excellent performances raise this above a mere soap opera.

Sex / Nud / Viol / Lang / AdSit

A: Paul Muni, David Wayne, Betsy Palmer, Luther Adler, Joby Baker, Joanna Moore

© COLUMBIA TRISTAR HOME VIDEO 60956

LAST DAYS OF POMPEII, THE

D: Ernest B. Schoedsack — 93 m

NR | DMA | 1934 | B&W

6 Religious drama epic set among the Romans at the time of Christ. Preston Foster is a blacksmith who loses his wife and baby in a tragedy and so becomes a ruthless and successful gladiator. He is sent to Judea to aid Pontius Pilate, bringing with him the son of one of his victims whom he has adopted. In Judea he sees Christ but fails to come to his aid. Nevertheless, when the boy is seriously hurt in an accident, Christ heals him. The blacksmith is forever changed. Renowned for its special effects.

Sex / Nud / Viol / Lang / AdSit

A: Preston Foster, Alan Hale, Basil Rathbone, John Wood, Louis Calhern, Dorothy Wilson

© TURNER HOME ENTERTAINMENT 6044

LEAN ON ME

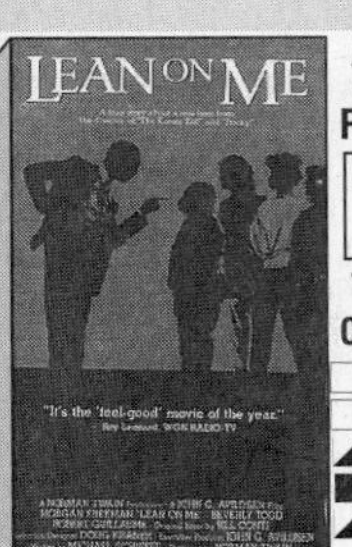

D: John G. Avildsen — 109 m

PG-13 | DMA | 1989 | COLOR

6 Entertaining screen depiction of Joe Clark, a real-life individual who achieved national recognition as a no-nonsense high school principal. He reestablished order at his inner-city high school and fought against drugs and crime by wielding a bat and a bullhorn. His threats and encouragements produced a profound change in both the school's general atmosphere and in the student's attitudes. A good feel-good movie and a good performance by Morgan Freeman.

Sex / Nud / Viol / Lang / AdSit

A: Morgan Freeman, Robert Guillaume, Beverly Todd, Alan North, Lynne Thigpen, Robin Bartlett

© WARNER HOME VIDEO 11875

LEARNING TREE, THE

D: Gordon Parks — 107 m

PG | DMA | 1969 | COLOR

7 Sensitive autobiographical story by famed Life magazine photographer Gordon Parks. It is the story of a young black man growing up in Kansas in the 1920s. That summer he learns of many things, but struggles with the moral dilemma of his life when, after he witnesses a murder, he must decide whether he should speak up. Revealing what he saw will free the white man falsely charged, convict the black man who did it and risk personal retribution that is sure to come from the black man's son. This is a beautifully photographed story of growing up black.

Sex / Nud / Viol / Lang / AdSit

A: Kyle Johnson, Estelle Evans, Dana Elcar, Mita Waters, Alex Clarke

© WARNER HOME VIDEO 11591

LEAVE `EM LAUGHING

D: Jackie Cooper — 103 m

NR | DMA | 1981 | COLOR

9 Outstanding, heartwarming, true-life story of Jack Thum. Jack Thum was a Chicago supermarket clown and real-life hero. He and his wife took in and cared for dozens of homeless, neglected and unwanted children. This is a real tearjerker but it is never manipulative. It is a moving testimony to an extraordinarily good man's life. Mickey Rooney is brilliant. He is totally believable as a simple man struggling both to help these desperate kids and to make ends meet. Then it tears your heart out when he learns that he will die of cancer and thinks he is a failure. Must-see family entertainment.

Sex / Nud / Viol / Lang / AdSit

A: Mickey Rooney, Anne Jackson, Red Buttons, William Windom, Elisha Cook, Jr.

© FRIES HOME VIDEO 94950

LILIES OF THE FIELD

D: Ralph Nelson — 95 m

NR | DMA COM | 1963 | B&W

8 Extremely popular and heart-warming story of an itinerant handyman who happens upon a group of nuns recently escaped from East Germany. They are attempting to build a church but have no skills, no money for building materials and are barely able to communicate. Yet they charm and coerce him into helping them in their mission. This was a low-budget movie, but it had a winning story line and great characterizations that combined to make it a big hit with the public. Poitier won an Oscar and the movie received two other nominations, including Best Picture.

Sex / Nud / Viol / Lang / AdSit

A: Sidney Poitier, Lilia Skala, Lisa Mann, Isa Crino, Stanley Adams

Distributed By MGM/UA Home Video M301762

LITTLE LORD FAUNTLEROY

D: John Cromwell — 98 m

NR | DMA CLD | 1936 | B&W

8 Solid family entertainment - not just for kids. A poor young kid from Brooklyn learns that he is the grandson of an English Earl and potential heir to his fortune. But the bitter and crusty old man blindly hates his widowed American daughter-in-law, the boy's mother, just because she is American. The boy is brought to England to live with the grumpy old geezer, whose hard heart is soon softened by the cheerful kid. Solid story. Solid acting. Very well done.

Sex / Nud / Viol / Lang / AdSit

A: Freddie Bartholomew, C. Aubrey Smith, Dolores Costello, Jessie Ralph, Mickey Rooney, Guy Kibbee

© CBS/FOX VIDEO 8066

LITTLE MAN TATE

D: Jodie Foster — 99 m

PG | DMA | 1991 | COLOR

8 Heartbreaking, heartwarming charmer. What's a poor waitress mom (Foster) to do when she realizes that her genius son needs to be raised in an environment that she can't provide ... love isn't enough, he needs stimulation. So, when he gets an opportunity to go to a special summer college session, though she resists at first, she sends him. He is to stay with the well-meaning director of the special school (Wiest), but her focus is always on his mind and she doesn't know how to give him the love he needs. He feels alone, unloved, misunderstood and rejected. Extremely well done. A real winner for Foster.

Sex / Nud / Viol / Lang / AdSit

A: Jodie Foster, Dianne Wiest, Adam Hann-Byrd, Harry Connick, Jr., David Pierce, P.J. Ochlan

© ORION PICTURES CORPORATION 8778

LITTLE PRINCESS, THE

D: Walter Lang — 93 m

NR | DMA CLD | 1939 | COLOR

6 Predictable, but effective, and endearing story which was Shirley Temple's last major childhood success. Shirley plays the daughter of a rich British officer who places her in an exclusive girls boarding school when he goes off to fight in the Boer war. When it is believed he has been killed, she is thought to be penniless. Suddenly poor, the school's head mistress makes poor little Shirley work as a maid to pay off her bill. But Shirley doesn't believe her father is dead. She visits army hospitals entertaining the troops and searching for him. Lavish production. Predictable, but very enjoyable.

Sex / Nud / Viol / Lang / AdSit

A: Shirley Temple, Richard Greene, Anita Louise, Ian Hunter, Cesar Romero

© FOXVIDEO 1298

MADAME CURIE

D: Mervyn Le Roy — 113 m

NR | DMA ROM | 1943 | B&W

8 Nominated for seven Oscars, including Best Picture. Plenty of entertainment value here. Greer Garson and Walter Pidgeon had great screen chemistry, which had earlier helped to propel MRS. MINIVER into becoming a major success. Here, Marie was a young Polish student studying in Paris at the turn of the Twentieth-Century. Scientist Pierre Curie grew to respect the quality of her work and soon also fell in love with her. Quite by chance one day, the two discover odd behavior in a sample. Intrigued, they begin a five year arduous quest that led eventually to the purification of the first radioactive substance, radium. Sometimes slows down, but remains interesting throughout.

Sex / Nud / Viol / Lang / AdSit

A: Greer Garson, Walter Pidgeon, Henry Travers, Albert Basserman, Robert Walker, C. Aubrey Smith

Distributed By MGM/UA Home Video 202054

MADAME X

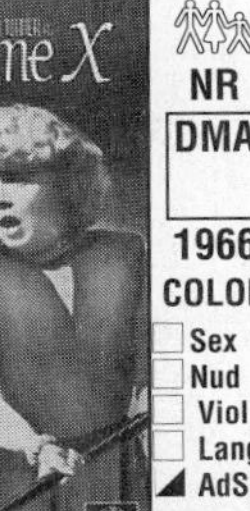

D: David Lowell Rich — 100 m

NR | DMA | 1966 | COLOR

8 Get your hankies out! Turner plays the wife of an inattentive and absent diplomat who was blackmailed by her mother-in-law into abandoning him and her young son. Now, 20 years later, she is destitute and up on charges of murder. In a perverse twist of fate, she is defended at her trial by her now-grown son - only he has no idea that he is defending his own mother. Turner's attempts at preventing her son from finding out the truth are truly heart-wrenching. Slow in spots, but Turner delivers a very moving performance. This is the sixth filming of this popular soap opera since 1909.

Sex / Nud / Viol / Lang / AdSit

A: Lana Turner, John Forsythe, Ricardo Montalban, Burgess Meredith, Constance Bennett, Keir Dullea

© MCA/UNIVERSAL HOME VIDEO, INC. 80154

MADE FOR EACH OTHER

D: John Cromwell 93 m

NR | DMA COM ROM | 1939 | B&W

8 Warm and endearing comedy/drama about a young couple learning to deal with the pitfalls that come with the first few years of marriage. It is painful and sometimes funny to watch because the movie is masterful at imitating real-life. Financial troubles, conflicts with in-laws and confusion about parenting abound. Even when the couple's first child nearly dies, the pair finds a way to overcome that extra hurdle and build on the new strength they have found. Lombard and Stewart do a fine job keeping the plot from getting too heavy.

Sex / Nud / Viol / Lang / ■ AdSit

A: James Stewart, Carole Lombard, Charles Coburn, Ward Bond

© GOODTIMES 5033

MAN WITHOUT A COUNTRY, THE

D: Delbert Mann 78 m

NR | DMA | 1973 | COLOR

8 Stirring and thought-provoking adaptation of the classic Edward Everett Hale novel. It is a brilliant character study of a fictional early 1800 character named Philip Nolan. Nolan is an overly-zealous patriot who is eager to join in Aaron Burr's plan to bring Texas and Mexico into the United States. When he is caught, he boldly states that if his country stays as it was, he wished that he did not have a country. At his court-martial, Nolan is granted his wish: he would be condemned to a ship and never be allowed to receive news of or even see American soil again.

Sex / Nud / Viol / Lang / ◢ AdSit

A: Cliff Robertson, Robert Ryan, Peter Strauss, Beau Bridges, Walter Abel, John Cullum

© WORLDVISION HOME VIDEO, INC. 4105

MARJORIE MORNINGSTAR

D: Irving Rapper 125 m

NR | DMA ROM | 1958 | COLOR

6 Natalie Wood is a beautiful 18-year-old girl from New York, with stars in her eyes, who leaves her family and sweetheart behind to venture off into the excitement of the theatre. She changes her name from Morgenstern to Morningstar and joins a summer stock group. There, she falls in love with an older performer (Kelly). He leaves the group to go to New York and the big time and she goes with him. She loves him even when he fails, but he does not treat her nearly so well. Adapted from Herman Wouk's novel, Wood and Kelly give touching performances.

Sex / Nud / Viol / Lang / ◢ AdSit

A: Gene Kelly, Natalie Wood, Claire Trevor, Ed Wynn, Everett Sloane, Carolyn Jones

© REPUBLIC PICTURES HOME VIDEO 5552

MASADA

D: Boris Sagal 131 m

NR | DMA ACT | 1984 | COLOR

9 Excellent and moving epic drama of bravery and strength in this film dramatic depiction of a true event. In 70 A.D., a Roman general (O'Toole) is ordered to crush the Jewish uprising in Israel, and he does... Jerusalem is destroyed. However, a rebel zealot leader (Strauss) leads of a group of 980 zealots in an escape to Herod the Great's fortress palace high on Mt. Masada. There they hold out valiantly against 10,000 Roman soldiers in a prolonged 3-year Roman siege. Based on Ernest K. Gann's novel, this dramatic story was made into a very popular TV miniseries. O'Toole and Strauss deliver fine performances.

Sex / Nud / Viol / Lang / ◢ AdSit

A: Peter O'Toole, Peter Strauss, Barbara Carrera

© MCA/UNIVERSAL HOME VIDEO, INC. 66025

MASS APPEAL

D: Glenn Jordan 99 m

PG | DMA COM | 1984 | COLOR

8 A young seminary student (Ivanek) wreaks holy havoc when he challenges a situation he finds at Father Tim Farley's (Lemmon) wealthy parish. Father Tim is laid-back. He cracks jokes from the pulpit and is much-loved by his parishioners. He even drives a Mercedes. Idealistic newcomer Ivaek questions Lemmon's methods and the two are launched on a collision course. Ivanek's confrontational path also gets him sideways of the inflexible Monsignor (Durning) and almost tossed out. But Lemmon protects his new charge and eventually they teach other about faith.

Sex / Nud / Viol / ◢ Lang / ◢ AdSit

A: Jack Lemmon, Zeljko Ivanek, Charles Durning, Louise Latham, Lois de Banzie, James Ray

© MCA/UNIVERSAL HOME VIDEO, INC. 80168

MEMBER OF THE WEDDING, THE

D: Delbert Mann 90 m

NR | DMA | 1953 | COLOR

9 Highly acclaimed and emotional coming-of-age drama. Julie Harris is Frankie, a lonely, confused and motherless 12-year-old tomboy, struggling both with her budding adolescence and her utter confusion over her older brother getting married, leaving home and her behind. When Frankie naively invites herself along with the the newlyweds on their honeymoon, she is so humiliated at their rejection that she runs way from home. The only one who understands the emotional turmoil the girl is going through is the housekeeper, the only mother the girl has ever known. Exceptional performances.

Sex / Nud / Viol / Lang / ◢ AdSit

A: Ethel Waters, Julie Harris, Brandon de Wilde, Arthur Franz, Nancy Gates

© COLUMBIA TRISTAR HOME VIDEO 60930

MIRACLE OF OUR LADY OF FATIMA, THE

D: John Brahm 102 m

NR | DMA | 1952 | COLOR

7 A reverent re-creation of a story believed by many to be true. Three Portuguese farm children in 1917 (during WWI) claimed to have seen a vision of the Virgin Mary, who they called the "beautiful lady." The children were threatened by local officials, yet they did not back down. Because Portugal's government at the time was anti-religious, this reported vision touched off a hotbed of religious confrontation and the faith of these children reinspired the faith in countless others. Each year, believers still make pilgrimages to this site, to what they believe is a holy place.

Sex / Nud / Viol / Lang / AdSit

A: Gilbert Roland, Susan Whitney, Sherry Jackson, Sammy Ogg, Angela Clark, Frank Silvera

© WARNER HOME VIDEO 11540

MIRACLE WORKER, THE

D: Arthur Penn 107 m

NR | DMA | 1962 | B&W

9 Truly inspiring! A brilliant film depiction of the life of Helen Keller (Duke) and her unforgettable and determined teacher Annie Sullivan (Bancroft). Helen is lost to a world she cannot see and cannot hear. She can only touch. Her parents cannot make themselves discipline the poor girl and she is wild. Annie eventually breaks into Helen's private world and pulls her back into the real world, but first she has to fight both Helen and her well-meaning but destructive parents. Both Bancroft and Duke won Oscars for the masterful re-creation of their Broadway roles. A must see.

Sex / Nud / ◢ Viol / Lang / ◢ AdSit

A: Anne Bancroft, Patty Duke, Victor Jory, Inga Swenson, Andrew Prine, Beah Richards

Distributed By MGM/UA Home Video M600590

MOLLY MAGUIRES, THE

D: Martin Ritt 123 m

PG | DMA | 1970 | COLOR

6 Powerful story of a battle for dignity. In 1870 the immigrant Irish coal miners in Pennsylvania worked under terrible conditions. The Molly Maguires were a group of rebels that violently battled against those inhuman conditions. Connery, the leader of the group, considers a new arrival in town (Harris) to be a friend. However he is really a Pinkerton detective whose mission is to betray the Mollies, even though it is a difficult task to deal with in his own conscience. This story evokes vivid images of the sad day-to-day drone of the miners' existence and is based on fact. Beautiful Mancini score.

Sex / Nud / ◢ Viol / ■ Lang / ■ AdSit

A: Sean Connery, Richard Harris, Samantha Eggar, Frank Finlay, Art Lund, Anthony Costello

© PARAMOUNT HOME VIDEO 6905

MRS. MINIVER

D: William Wyler 135 m

NR | DMA | 1942 | B&W

9 Outstanding war drama! This fine film follows the middle-class Miniver family, especially Mrs. Miniver, as they cope with the trials of war in a beleaguered England. This is an effective and sentimental story about how Mrs. Miniver successfully deals with the trauma of her young sons being at risk fighting, fighting restricted war rations and surviving terrifying German bombing raids. The speech made at the end was deemed by President Roosevelt to be so important that he ordered a reprint of it made and air dropped over a battered England. Very touching film that won seven Oscars, including Best Picture.

Sex / Nud / Viol / Lang / ◢ AdSit

A: Greer Garson, Walter Pidgeon, May Whitty, Teresa Wright, Reginald Owen, Henry Travers

Distributed By MGM/UA Home Video M300804

MR. SMITH GOES TO WASHINGTON

D: Frank Capra 125 m

NR | DMA COM | 1939 | B&W

9 Time-honored classic that brought home eleven Oscar nominations. An idealistic scout master (Stewart) is called to Washington to complete a dead senator's term. He arrives to discover that corruption is running rampant. So, the idealistic new senator decides he must battle his own mentor and all the political powers with a filibuster, to fight against a bill he knows is only a land scam. This sets the stage for a very powerful, and now classic, final scene depicting a little man fighting against the powerful system. Capra's brilliant creation expertly casts Stewart as America's hero to restore our faith in democracy.

Sex / Nud / Viol / Lang / AdSit

A: Jean Arthur, James Stewart, Claude Rains, Edward Arnold, Thomas Mitchell, Beulah Bondi

© COLUMBIA TRISTAR HOME VIDEO 60064

MURPHY'S WAR

D: Peter Yates 106 m

PG | DMA ACT | 1971 | COLOR

7 Near the end of WWII, an English ship is torpedoed and its crew gunned down by a German U-boat that prowls nearby waters. Irish merchantman (O'Toole) is the only survivor of the massacre. He is rescued by a French oil engineer and nursed back to health at a nearby village hospital. Now healthy, he hears of a wrecked old sea plane and decides to seek his own revenge by patching it up to conduct his own private war on the marauding U-boat's crew. O'Toole packs a powerful performance into this wartime story.

Sex / Nud / ◢ Viol / Lang / ◢ AdSit

A: Peter O'Toole, Sian Phillips, Philippe Noiret, Horst Janson, John Hallam, Ingo Morgendorf

© PARAMOUNT HOME VIDEO 8047

MY FRIEND FLICKA

D: Harold Schuster 89 m

NR | DMA CLD | 1943 | COLOR | Rating: 8

Touching and heartwarming. Despite his father's (Foster) concerns, a young boy (McDowall) longs to have a horse of his own. Finally giving in, Foster allows McDowall to pick from the herd, but he picks a filly with a bloodline that is known for its wildness. Persistent, the boy proves both himself and the horse when he manages to train the unruly animal which becomes his best friend. This magnificent sentimental favorite was based on Mary O'Hara's moving novel, and is a film that the whole family will enjoy. It was also made into a long-running TV series.

Sex | Nud | Viol | Lang | AdSit

A: Roddy McDowall, Preston Foster, Rita Johnson, Jeff Corey, James Bell

© FOXVIDEO 1899

MY GIRL

D: Howard Zieff 102 m

PG | DMA ROM CLD | 1991 | COLOR | Rating: 8

Irresistable weeper. Eleven-year-old Chlumsky is the precocious daughter of a widowed mortician (Aydroyd) and because their house doubles for a mortuary, death is everywhere. Aykroyd doesn't have much time for his daughter, nor does he know how to reach out to her, not knowing that she feels responsible for her mother's death or that she's jealous when he falls for the new cosmetologist (Curtis) he has hired. But Macauly Culkin is her neighbor and that summer she and Culkin become best friends and experience the beginnings of young love. However, their summer together comes to a tragic end. Parents, share this one with your kids.

Sex | Nud | ◢ Viol | Lang | ◢ AdSit

A: Anna Chlumsky, Macaulay Culkin, Dan Aykroyd, Jamie Lee Curtis, Richard Masur, Griffin Dunne

© COLUMBIA TRISTAR HOME VIDEO 50993

MY SIDE OF THE MOUNTAIN

D: James B. Clark 100 m

G | DMA CLD | 1969 | COLOR | Rating: 7

This is an entertaining back-to-nature tale in which a thirteen-year-old boy gives up all of his worldly possessions and the comforts of home, to test his survival skills by emulating his idol, Henry David Thoreau. He runs away intending to make the Canadian mountains his home for one year and takes nothing with him but his mind and his courage. Refreshing and charming, this is a film that the whole family will enjoy. It's not just for kids.

Sex | Nud | Viol | Lang | AdSit

A: Ted Eccles, Theodore Bikel, Tudi Wiggins, Frank Perry, Prggi Loder

© PARAMOUNT HOME VIDEO 6813

NATIONAL VELVET

D: Clarence Brown 124 m

G | DMA CLD | 1944 | COLOR | Rating: 10

All-time favorite for everyone... a real rah rah film, one that will have you cheering. Elizabeth Taylor is absolutely adorable as a young girl who wins a neighbor's unruly horse in a lottery. Then, she and her young friend, an embittered jockey (Mickey Rooney), train the horse to race and, against everyone's wishes, she enters him into England's famed Grand National steeplechase. A heartwarming and loveable story. It won two Oscars and was followed by INTERNATIONAL VELVET in 1977.

Sex | Nud | Viol | Lang | AdSit

A: Elizabeth Taylor, Mickey Rooney, Donald Crisp, Anne Revere, Angela Lansbury, Reginald Owen

Distributed By MGM/UA Home Video M300480

NATURAL, THE

D: Barry Levinson 134 m

PG | DMA | 1984 | COLOR | Rating: 8

Sentimental film favorite, extremely popular with the public. Roy Hobbs (Redford) is a natural baseball player, but his career is stopped dead by a bullet from a crazy woman (Hershey) while on his way up to the big leagues. Sidelined for 16 years, Hobbs makes a hard-fought comeback attempt. Inspired by his hometown sweetheart, his batting leads his team into the pennant. But the owner will take a financial loss if the team wins, so Kim Basinger is brought in to distract Redford for a while. Rewarding, old-fashioned fun.

Sex | Nud | ◢ Viol | ◢ Lang | ◢ AdSit

A: Robert Redford, Robert Duvall, Glenn Close, Kim Basinger, Barbara Hershey

© COLUMBIA TRISTAR HOME VIDEO 60380

NEVER CRY WOLF

D: Carroll Ballard 105 m

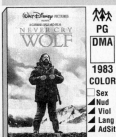

PG | DMA | 1983 | COLOR | Rating: 8

This "nature" film proved to be very popular across a broad spectrum of the viewing public. It is the story of a field biologist (Smith) who is sent into the barren wilds of the Arctic to study wolves. Absolutely alone in the vast wilderness, we watch Smith set up his observations of a pack of wolves and then watch the relationship that develops between the two. There is stunning scenery and beautiful photography, but this is also an absorbing, and sometimes humorous, adventure story worthy of viewing by everyone from the very youngest to the oldest. Taken from the best-selling memoirs of Farley Mowat. Done by Disney's studios.

Sex | ◢ Nud | ◢ Viol | ◢ Lang | ◢ AdSit

A: Charles Martin Smith, Brian Dennehy, Samson Jorah

© WALT DISNEY HOME VIDEO 182

NICHOLAS NICKLEBY

D: Alberto Cavalcanti 103 m

NR | DMA | 1947 | B&W | Rating: 7

Dickens's classic story is given a noble effort by a talented cast. The story is that of a young man, Nicholas Nickleby, who takes a teaching position at a cruel orphanage. Nicholas protects a crippled student there from the school's nasty masters, and also protects his sister and sweetheart from his miserly and manipulative uncle. The story as written has 52 characters in it. The Royal Shakespeare Company takes 8 1/2 hours to perform their play. This film does quite well for only 1 1/2 hours.

Sex | Nud | Viol | Lang | ◢ AdSit

A: Derek Bond, Cedric Hardwicke, Alfred Drayton, Bernard Miles, Sally Ann Howes, Sybil Thorndike

© FOOTHILLS VIDEO

NIGHT TO REMEMBER, A

D: Roy Ward Baker 119 m

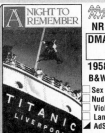

NR | DMA | 1958 | B&W | Rating: 9

Compelling, detailed and authentic documentary-like accounting of the events surrounding the sinking of the H.M.S. Titanic in April of 1912. That wreck cost 1302 lives (705 survived). The human story of that tragedy is told through a series of vignettes by using a huge cast. (There are over 200 speaking roles.) The stories told are the personal stories of heroism, self-sacrifice, grace under pressure and also the immense tragedy in the face of panic and terrible confusion. The "unsinkable" ship hit an iceberg and sank in 1 1/2 hours.

Sex | Nud | Viol | Lang | ◢ AdSit

A: Kenneth More, David McCallum, Honor Blackman, Robert Ayers, Anthony Bushell

© PARAMOUNT HOME VIDEO 12580

OLD YELLER

D: Robert Stevenson 84 m

G | DMA CLD | 1957 | COLOR | Rating: 10

Wonderful, endearing Disney story that has been and will continue to be a perpetual family favorite for very good reason. Set in the Texas wilderness of 1859, a pioneer father leaves his family and homestead to join a cattle drive for a short while, leaving his young son "in charge" of the family. In the father's absence, the boy adopts a mongrel dog he names Old Yeller. Soon Old Yeller becomes his best friend and the family's protector. The two are inseparable. Then tragedy strikes and the boy must become a man. It is a powerful story for children but adults love it, too. See also THE YEARLING.

Sex | Nud | ◢ Viol | Lang | AdSit

A: Dorothy McGuire, Fess Parker, Tommy Kirk, Kevin Corcoran, Jeff York, Chuck Connors

© WALT DISNEY HOME VIDEO 037

OLIVER TWIST

D: David Lean 116 m

NR | DMA | 1948 | B&W | Rating: 8

This is an excellent screen portrait of Charles Dickens's classic story and truly reflected the bleak misery of his times. Oliver is an eight-year-old orphan boy sent to live at a work house. When Oliver is so brazen as to ask for more gruel, he is punished severely and escapes instead into the streets. There he is quickly recruited into a company of thieves headed by a young pickpocket named The Artful Dodger (Newley) and a vile hideous man named Fagin (Guinness) - until he is rescued by a kindly old man. The much more lively and upbeat musical version is called OLIVER!.

Sex | Nud | ◢ Viol | Lang | ◢ AdSit

A: Alec Guinness, Robert Newton, Anthony Newley, Kay Walsh, John Howard Davies, Henry Stephenson

© PARAMOUNT HOME VIDEO 12571

ONE ON ONE

D: Lamont Johnson 100 m

PG | DMA | 1977 | COLOR | Rating: 8

An upbeat "little" film in which Robby Benson is a small town boy who is awarded a basketball scholarship to a big West Coast university. There he runs head-on into the corruption of big-time college athletics and an extremely demanding coach. Naive Benson trys to buck both the system and his coach. He gains help for his studies and strength for his battles with his coach through the encouragement of his pretty tutor, Annette O'Toole. It is an inspiring story in which the little guy takes on the power and wins.

Sex | Nud | Viol | ◢ Lang | AdSit

A: Robby Benson, Annette O'Toole, G.D. Spradlin, Gail Strickland, Melanie Griffith

© WARNER HOME VIDEO 11141

ON GOLDEN POND

D: Mark Rydell 105 m

PG | DMA COM | 1981 | COLOR | Rating: 10

Big unexpected hit. Thoughtful, heartwarming and moving story of growing old and the reconciliation between a crotchety father and his alienated daughter. Winner of three Oscars: Actor (Fonda), Actress (Hepburn) and Screenplay. The daughter leaves her fiance's snotty son with her aging parents for the summer. The old man and the kid develop a relationship which teaches the kid to lighten up and the old man how to enjoy living again, to express love and to show his daughter the love she has long craved. Wonderful and uplifting. A real feel-good flick.

Sex | Nud | Viol | ◢ Lang | ◢ AdSit

A: Katharine Hepburn, Henry Fonda, Jane Fonda, Dabney Coleman, Doug McKeon, William Lanteau

© LIVE HOME VIDEO 27456

ON THE BEACH

D: Stanley Kramer — 135 m

NR | DMA | 1959 | B&W

6 After a nuclear war strikes the Northern Hemisphere, the only survivors are a few people in Australia and those on board a submerged American submarine captained by Gregory Peck. As the ominous nuclear clouds gradually descend upon these people, too, Peck attempts to save this one small group of survivors, which includes a young couple (Perkins and Anderson), an alcoholic nuclear scientist (Astaire), and Peck and his adventurous love interest (Gardner). Very well done, but gloomy. It was a highly-celebrated anti-nuclear war film from the '50s.

Sex / Nud / Viol / Lang / ◢ AdSit

A: Gregory Peck, Ava Gardner, Fred Astaire, Anthony Perkins, Donna Anderson, John Tate

Distributed By MGM/UA Home Video M202267

OUR VINES HAVE TENDER GRAPES

D: Roy Rowland — 105 m

NR | DMA | 1945 | B&W

9 Wonderful, deeply heart-warming and never sappy. A true family film about life in a small rural Wisconsin farming town during WWII. The primary focus is upon young O'Brien and her kind father (Robinson), a widower and farmer - but only in so far as they express the values of the little town. When O'Brien is treated to a late night trip to see her first elephant at the circus, she learns how dangerous nature is after she and her cousin are carried off in a spring flood. She learns of war when one of men of the town has to leave to fight. And, she is the first to help a stricken farmer. Excellent.

Sex / Nud / Viol / Lang / AdSit

A: Edward G. Robinson, Margaret O'Brien, James Craig, Francis Gilford, Agnes Moorehead, Morris Carnovsky

Distributed By MGM/UA Home Video M202837

PATCH OF BLUE, A

D: Guy Green — 106 m

NR | DMA ROM | 1965 | COLOR

8 A sensitive and moving drama, which held the potential to be badly exploitive, but it isn't at all. This is a thoughtful drama about an 18-year-old blind white girl whose mother is a prostitute. She keeps the girl uneducated, confined to their apartment and uses her as a servant. One day, on a rare trip alone to the park, the girl meets a young man who helps her and encourages her to learn about life. She falls in love with him, the only one who ever helped her, not knowing that he is black. Good drama, well acted, not overly sentimental or sensationalized. 5 Oscar nominations.

Sex / Nud / Viol / Lang / ◢ AdSit

A: Sidney Poitier, Elizabeth Hartman, Shelley Winters, Wallace Ford, Ivan Dixon, John Qualen

Distributed By MGM/UA Home Video M202010

FAMILY

PATTON

D: Franklin J. Schaffner — 171 m

PG | DMA WAR ACT | 1970 | COLOR

10 Brilliant portrait of an extremely colorful and unique historical figure - George S. "Blood-and-Guts" Patton. Winner of 8 Oscars, including Best Picture, Director, Screenplay and Actor. Patton, the man, was a brilliant battlefield tactician whose single-mindedness in and out of battle helped to win the North African campaign and to launch the initial assault into Europe at the beginning of WWII. It garnered him both the respect and the animosity of nearly everyone. Scott did a brilliant job with the role. Both fascinating and extremely enjoyable.

Sex / Nud / ◢ Viol / ◢ Lang / ◢ AdSit

A: George C. Scott, Karl Malden, Stephen Young, Michael Strong, Tim Considine, Frank Latimore

© FOXVIDEO 1005

PHAR LAP

D: Simon Wincer — 107 m

PG | DMA | 1984 | COLOR

9 Rousing family entertainment. This is the true account of the legendary Australian thoroughbred horse from the 1930s that became an national hero after overcoming huge odds to be a winner. Told in a series of flashbacks. Phar Lap was trained by a brutal trainer and was nearly ruined by him. But through the devotion of a shy stableboy and the dedication of his Jewish owner (who had to fight mindless prejudice just to get his horse entered), this horse became the winner of 33 races in just three years. You'll be cheering, too.

Sex / Nud / ◢ Viol / ◢ Lang / AdSit

A: Tom Burlinson, Ron Leibman, Judy Morris, Martin Vaughan, Celia De Burgh, Vincent Ball

© FOXVIDEO 1444

PLACES IN THE HEART

D: Robert Benton — 113 m

PG | DMA | 1984 | COLOR

9 A wonderful, sensitive charmer for which Sally Field won an Oscar and which also was a big box office hit. In Depression-plagued Waxahachie, Texas, Sally Field's sheriff husband is accidentally killed. Widowed, with children and no money, she is suddenly faced with the possible loss of her farm. Desperate, she agrees to take in an alienated blind boarder (Malkovich) and also accepts an offer from a vagabond black fieldhand (Glover) to help her farm her cotton. A bond of love grows between this mismatched, makeshift family as they struggle to save their home against over-whelming odds. A definite must-see, watch it.

Sex / Nud / ◢ Viol / ◢ Lang / ◢ AdSit

A: Sally Field, John Malkovich, Danny Glover, Ed Harris, Amy Madigan, Lindsay Crouse

© CBS/FOX VIDEO 6836

PLAYING FOR TIME

D: Daniel Mann — 148 m

NR | DMA | 1980 | COLOR

9 Outstanding and stunning true story of how a French cabaret singer, Fania Fenelon (Redgrave), and a few others, survived the Auschwitz concentration camp by performing in a bizarre orchestra - an orchestra which played for other inmates as they marched off to their deaths, as well as for Nazi officers. But each member of the orchestra lived in terror because they all knew that at any time they could be next. This first-rate made-for-TV movie won four Emmys, including Drama Special, Actress (Redgrave), Supporting Actress (Alexander) and Writing.

Sex / Nud / Viol / Lang / ◢ AdSit

A: Vanessa Redgrave, Jane Alexander, Maud Adams, Viveca Lindfors, Shirley Knight, Melanie Mayron

© MCEG/STERLING 70034

PRIDE OF THE YANKEES, THE

D: Sam Wood — 129 m

NR | DMA | 1942 | B&W

10 Endearing biography of one of baseball's greatest players. Lou Gehrig was struck down at the height of his career, and eventually killed, by the crippling disease that today bears his name. This is also one of Hollywood's best film biographies ever. Gary Cooper was never better than when he played the New York Yankee first baseman. The film follows both his career and his courageous battle with disease. The final scene has become a classic by itself and is one of Hollywood's all-time most memorable scenes.

Sex / Nud / Viol / Lang / ◢ AdSit

A: Gary Cooper, Teresa Wright, Babe Ruth, Walter Brennan, Dan Duryea, Ludwig Stossel

© CBS/FOX VIDEO 7145

PRINCE AND THE PAUPER, THE

D: William Keighley — 119 m

NR | DMA CLD | 1937 | B&W

8 Rousing film version (the best one) of Mark Twain's own personal favorite of al his many stories. A young English prince longs to learn what life is really like in 16th-century London's slums, so he exchanges clothes and places with a street urchin who is his look-alike. No one is to know, but his enemies at the court learn of the switch and plan to crown the wrong boy King. No one believes the displaced prince's story except for rakish Errol Flynn, who rides and swashbuckles to the aid of the young prince. Large scale and highly enjoyable for young and old.

Sex / Nud / Viol / Lang / AdSit

A: Errol Flynn, Billy Mauch, Bobby Mauch, Claude Rains, Alan Hale, Rex Harrison

Distributed By MGM/UA Home Video 201865

PRINCESS CARABOO

D: Michael Austin — 96 m

PG | DMA MYS | 1994 | COLOR

6 An unusual idea for a movie. It is 1787 and a young woman is discovered in the English countryside wearing a turban, speaking no English, dressed rather commonly, but also having an elegant (and some think a regal) bearing. Who is this very strange woman? She is taken into the home of a local aristocrat and as word of her spreads, people become more and more convinced that she is a princess from a foreign land, stranded in England. She becomes the focus of the country's interest and even a favorite in the royal court. All the while, a newspaperman is struck by her beauty and fascinated with her. He must learn who she is. Curious film, but also very contrived and full of holes.

Sex / Nud / Viol / Lang / ◢ AdSit

A: Phoebe Cates, Jim Broadbent, Wendy Hughes, Kevin Kline, John Lithgow, Stephen Rea

© COLUMBIA TRISTAR HOME VIDEO 73503

PROMISES IN THE DARK

D: Jerome Hellman — 118 m

PG | DMA | 1980 | COLOR

8 Intense and very realistic tearjerker about the relationship that develops between a doctor (Mason) and her patient, a seventeen-year-old girl who is dying of cancer. Mason is tormented by the fact that there is nothing she can do for her charge. Now that the girl is getting worse each day, Mason must decide whether she will honor her promise to let the girl die with dignity or sustain her on life support systems. Top-notch acting and an unrelenting realism make this a sensitive, moving, compassionate experience, and a depressing one.

Sex / Nud / Viol / ◢ Lang / ◢ AdSit

A: Ned Beatty, Susan Clark, Marsha Mason, Michael Brandon, Kathleen Beller

© WARNER HOME VIDEO 22011

QUO VADIS

D: Mervyn LeRoy — 171 m

NR | DMA ACT ROM | 1951 | COLOR

8 Epic blockbuster on a grand scale! Hugely popular. Taylor is a Roman commander and a hero just back from a triumphant campaign. He meets and falls for beautiful Deborah Kerr, but he also learns that she is a Christian convert. So when the mad Emperor Niro (Ustinov) burns Rome and places the blame on the Christians, the two lovers are drug out to be publicly executed. Instead, they escape and Taylor goes on to lead the revolt against corrupt Nero. Nominated for eight Oscars, this colossal smash featured lavish sets, exquisite costumes and an eye for detail. Outstanding!

Sex / Nud / ◢ Viol / Lang / ◢ AdSit

A: Robert Taylor, Deborah Kerr, Peter Ustinov, Leo Glenn, Patricia Laffan, Finlay Currie

Distributed By MGM/UA Home Video M900276

RAGTIME

D: Milos Forman — 156 m

PG | DMA CRM | 1981 | COLOR | Sex | Nud | Viol | Lang | AdSit

8 A colorful portrait of life at the beginning of the 20th century, set amidst scandal and middle-class morals of the time. Too many subplots confuse the beginning of the film, but things pick up when the focus narrows. While on his way to his own wedding, a black man is accosted by a raucous group of firemen who harass him and then vandalize his car. After repeated attempts to receive justice within the system fail, he takes drastic measures on his own and holds the town hostage. Now, finally, the system takes notice but fights back with a vengeance. Excellent, lots of major stars and a big budget. Nominated for eight Oscars.

A: James Cagney, Brad Dourif, Moses Gunn, Elizabeth McGovern, Kenneth McMillan, James Olson

© PARAMOUNT HOME VIDEO 1486

REBEL WITHOUT A CAUSE

D: Nicholas Ray — 111 m

NR | DMA | 1955 | COLOR | Sex | Nud | Viol | Lang | AdSit

8 Very popular movie from the '50s which defined the beginning of a new era. It was the first film to effectively articulate the problems of teenage America in a way that they could identify with. (It also launched many of the big stars of '50s and '60s, and it put James Dean's star on the map.) Dean is a troubled teenager trying to start over again at a new high school. He is trying to find his way and is taunted by the other kids to test his courage, with tragic results. It is still an effective movie today. The problems of teenagers and parents have not changed.

A: James Dean, Natalie Wood, Sal Mineo, Jim Backus, Dennis Hopper, Nick Adams

© WARNER HOME VIDEO 1011

RED PONY, THE

D: Lewis Milestone — 89 m

NR | DMA CLD | 1949 | COLOR | Sex | Nud | Viol | Lang | AdSit

8 Touching, affecting and moving story that was created by blending of three short stories by John Steinbeck. In it, a lonely young boy turns to a ranchhand for understanding and guidance, and to a frail young horse for affection. The boy's stiff schoolteacher father has married a wealthy woman and she is taking up all his time. The father has become even more distant than before and the boy is confused. This excellent family movie is very believable because the characters are developed effectively through understatement. Strong performances by Mitchum and the boy, Peter Miles. Highly recommended.

A: Myrna Loy, Robert Mitchum, Louis Calhern, Peter Miles

© REPUBLIC PICTURES HOME VIDEO 3406

RED TENT, THE

D: Mickail K. Kalatozov — 121 m

G | DMA ACT | 1969 | COLOR | Sex | Nud | Viol | Lang | AdSit

7 Rugged adventure and a gripping saga about attempts to rescue a downed Italian dirigible crew. In 1928 the Italian dirigible "Italia" crashed in the Arctic while exploring the North Pole. For days the crew huddled inside the makeshift red tent sending out S.O.S. radio messages. Ronald Amundsen (Connery) leads a daring ground rescue attempt but dies trying to find the crew. Told in flashback form, this lavishly produced film is even more compelling because it is based upon a true story. Emotional and extremely well-acted. Beautiful photography.

A: Sean Connery, Peter Finch, Hardy Kruger, Claudia Cardinale

© PARAMOUNT HOME VIDEO 8041

RESURRECTION

D: Daniel Petrie — 102 m

PG | DMA FAN | 1980 | COLOR | Sex | Nud | Viol | Lang | AdSit

9 An underrated gem. Burstyn (Oscar nominated) creates a fascinating character - a simple, ordinary and pleasant woman who survives a traffic accident that killed her husband. She returns from near-death to discover that she has received a miraculous gift, the ability to heal both herself and others. This gentle, gracious woman then heals all those who come to her for help. However, the young farmer with whom she was falling in love, tries to force her to confess that she is Jesus reborn. Others accuse her of being a charlatan or resent her power. Everyone wants something. Her gift has now become a burden.

A: Ellen Burstyn, Sam Shepard, Roberts Blossom, Eva LeGallienne, Richard Farnsworth, Clifford David

© MCA/UNIVERSAL HOME VIDEO, INC. 66047

RIGHT STUFF, THE

D: Philip Kaufman — 193 m

PG | DMA ACT | 1983 | COLOR | Sex | Nud | Viol | Lang | AdSit

9 Fascinating and invigorating film that, even though quite long, is never boring. Seven pilots are chosen to be the first Americans in space under the NASA program, Project Mercury. This film tells their stories. Although the pivotal character is Chuck Yeager, all seven receive considerable attention, as does the entire training process that launched America's space program. An epic story, with plenty of exhilarating moments, that does not disappoint. Watch for the real Chuck Yeager in a cameo. Winner of four Oscars, including Score.

A: Charles Frank, Scott Glenn, Ed Harris, Sam Shepard, Fred Ward, Barbara Hershey

© WARNER HOME VIDEO 20014

ROBE, THE

D: Henry Koster — 135 m

NR | DMA | 1953 | COLOR | Sex | Nud | Viol | Lang | AdSit

8 This is one of the best of Hollywood's biblical epics, but not too heavy. A Roman Centurian (Burton) is ordered to supervise Christ's execution where he wins Christ's robe while gambling at the foot of the cross. The robe changes him forever, as it does all who come in contact with it, but it also is much sought-after by the demented emperor Caligula. Burton is ultimately forced to choose between giving the robe to his emperor and becoming a martyr. This was the first film shot in Cinemascope, but the film's bigscreen impact is lost on video. It won two Oscars and also nominated for Best Picture and Actor.

A: Richard Burton, Jean Simmons, Victor Mature, Michael Rennie, Richard Boone, Jay Robinson

© FOXVIDEO 1022

ROCKY

D: John G. Avildsen — 125 m

PG | DMA ACT | 1976 | COLOR | Sex | Nud | Viol | Lang | AdSit

10 Triple Academy Award-winning feel-good powerhouse! An unknown, small-time loser, a thumb-breaker from the streets of Philadelphia (Stallone), gets one miraculous shot at the boxing championship when champion Apollo Creed (Weathers) offers to fight him as a publicity stunt. For Appolo Creed, this is a joke - but for Rocky, it is everything. Rocky is relentlessly trained by a gnarled old has-been trainer (Meridith) and inspired by his shy girlfriend (Shire). This endearing film really went the distance with audiences and spawned numerous sequels. It is a rousing charmer that never gets old!

A: Sylvester Stallone, Talia Shire, Burt Young, Burgess Meredith, Carl Weathers, Thayer David

Distributed By MGM/UA Home Video M200249

ROCKY II

D: Sylvester Stallone — 119 m

PG | DMA ACT | 1979 | COLOR | Sex | Nud | Viol | Lang | AdSit

8 Rocky (Stallone) went from being a nobody to a national sensation in the first picture. Now he has become disenchanted with his new-found fame and is even unable to find work. After being taunted by his rival, Apollo Creed (Weathers), he accepts an offer for a rematch, in spite of the objections of his now-pregnant wife (Shire). Rocky rigorously trains under the keen eye of his personal trainer (Meredith), while also fighting with Shire at home. He is nearly destroyed when she, his tower of strength and inspiration, lapses into a coma after childbirth. Sentimental, powerful and uplifting!

A: Sylvester Stallone, Talia Shire, Carl Weathers, Burgess Meredith, Burt Young

Distributed By MGM/UA Home Video M200250

ROCKY III

D: Sylvester Stallone — 103 m

PG | DMA ACT | 1982 | COLOR | Sex | Nud | Viol | Lang | AdSit

7 Stallone pounds out another rousing success! Rocky, now a man of wealth and leisure, is challenged into a new fight by the bullish Clubber Lang (Mr T.). However, Rocky is now soft and loses big, so he must reach deep within himself to find the inner strength needed to win a rematch - "the eye of the tiger." This time around, Rocky has to deal with a new challenger - fear. His longtime and trusted manager (Meredith) has died, but his new manager, Apollo Creed, teaches him some fancy footwork and quick moves in preparation for the big battle ahead.

A: Sylvester Stallone, Talia Shire, Hulk Hogan, Mr. T, Burt Young, Burgess Meredith

Distributed By MGM/UA Home Video M202086

ROCKY IV

D: Sylvester Stallone — 93 m

PG | DMA ACT | 1985 | COLOR | Sex | Nud | Viol | Lang | AdSit

6 Rocky faces his biggest challenge. He is to represent America and avenge the death of his friend and teacher, Apollo Creed. This time Rocky prepares to do battle with Drago (Lundgren), a hulking superhuman Russian boxer with a death wish. Drago trains with stardust and sophisticated computer equipment, while Rocky has to train in a cold and rugged Siberia using old-fashioned primitive equipment. His wife (Shire) stands by him once again as he battles not only against the ominous powerhouse, but also for the good ol' USA. Intense and fierce, but much of the charm is gone.

A: Sylvester Stallone, Dolph Lundgren, Talia Shire, Carl Weathers, Burt Young, Brigitte Nielsen

Distributed By MGM/UA Home Video M202084

ROOTS

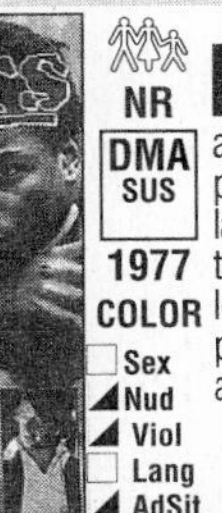

D: Marvin J. Chomsky — 562 m

NR | DMA SUS | 1977 | COLOR | Sex | Nud | Viol | Lang | AdSit

9 Monumental epic TV mini-series that won nine Emmys and over 135 other awards. Six 90-minute segments create a multi-generational mosaic of the people and circumstances of one black man's personal heritage. Beginning in a mid-18th century native African village, a young man is stolen away in a slave ship, to be sold into servitude in the American South. His single-minded determination not to lose his real identity inspired his personal story to continued to be passed down, and gave strength to, all his successors in generation after generation. A moving and engrossing human saga.

A: Edward Asner, Lloyd Bridges, Cicely Tyson, Lorne Greene, Ben Vereen, Levar Burton

© WARNER HOME VIDEO 11111

RUDY

D: David Anspaugh — 112 m

PG | DMA | 1993 | COLOR

7 Likable story about an unlikely but real-life sports hero, Daniel E. "Rudy" Ruettiger. Rudy wanted more than anything to play football for Notre Dame but he was too short, too light, too poor and didn't have good grades. So, for four years after highschool, he worked in the mills. But when his best friend was killed, Rudy knew he had to chase his dream, no matter how long the odds. When Notre Dame wouldn't admit him, he worked his way through Holy Cross until his grades were good enough. And, when he couldn't make the the 1st, 2nd or even 3rd teams, he became Notre Dame's tackling dummy. Too Hollywood to believe all of it, but you can't escape liking it either.

Sex / Nud / Viol / ◢ Lang / ◢ AdSit

A: Sean Astin, Ned Beatty, Charles S. Dutton, Jason Miller, Lili Taylor, Robert Prosky

© COLUMBIA TRISTAR HOME VIDEO 53723

SAMSON AND DELILAH

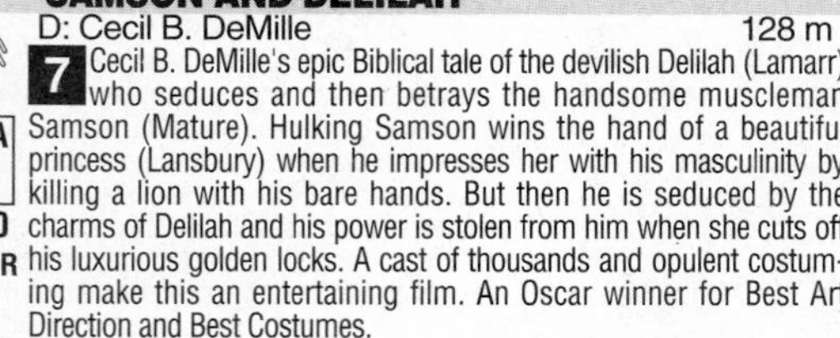

D: Cecil B. DeMille — 128 m

NR | DMA | 1950 | COLOR

7 Cecil B. DeMille's epic Biblical tale of the devilish Delilah (Lamarr) who seduces and then betrays the handsome muscleman Samson (Mature). Hulking Samson wins the hand of a beautiful princess (Lansbury) when he impresses her with his masculinity by killing a lion with his bare hands. But then he is seduced by the charms of Delilah and his power is stolen from him when she cuts off his luxurious golden locks. A cast of thousands and opulent costuming make this an entertaining film. An Oscar winner for Best Art Direction and Best Costumes.

Sex / Nud / ◢ Viol / Lang / ◢ AdSit

A: Hedy Lamarr, Victor Mature, Angela Lansbury, George Sanders, Henry Wilcoxon, Olive Deering

© PARAMOUNT HOME VIDEO 6726

SEARCH, THE

D: Fred Zinnemann — 104 m

NR | DMA WAR | 1948 | B&W

8 Emotional human drama set, and filmed, on location in a destroyed postwar Berlin. A GI (Clift) discovers a young Czech boy (Jandl) hiding in the burned-out rubble of the war-torn city. The boy has survived time and torture in a concentration camp by being suspicious of everything, but Clift breaks down his wall of resistance, befriends and cares for the boy. Meanwhile, the boy's mother is frantically searching in every Displaced Person's Camp to find him. A very moving and poignant drama that won an Oscar for Best Story and a special award for Jandl for outstanding juvenile performance.

Sex / Nud / Viol / Lang / ◢ AdSit

A: Montgomery Clift, Ivan Jandl, Aline MacMahon, Jarmila Novotna, Wendell Corey

Distributed By MGM/UA Home Video 202513

SECRET GARDEN, THE

D: Fred M. Wilcox — 92 m

NR | DMA CLD | 1949 | COLOR

8 Vivid dramatization of the children's classic. A young orphaned girl (O'Brien) is uprooted from India and taken to stay with her embittered uncle (Marshall) and his crippled son (Stockwell) in their huge, dark and foreboding mansion in Victorian England. Marshall is a cold, insensitive and stern type, and Stockwell is a disturbed and unhappy lad. But the determined young girl manages to melt her uncle's heart and bring them happiness, both because she looks so much like his deceased wife and because she finds her aunt's secret garden and begins to nurse it back to life.

Sex / Nud / Viol / Lang / AdSit

A: Margaret O'Brien, Dean Stockwell, Herbert Marshall, Gladys Cooper, Elsa Lanchester

Distributed By MGM/UA Home Video 202377

SECRET GARDEN, THE

D: Agnieszka Holland — 103 m

PG | DMA CLD | 1993 | COLOR

9 A sumptuously photographed screen adaptation of Frances Hodgson Burnett's classic 1911 novel. Ten-year-old Mary is a sad orphaned girl who has been returned to England from India after her parents were killed. She is to live with her cold uncle, who is still mourning his wife's death, and his bed-ridden ten-year-old son. Their huge mansion, on the cold and misty moors, is a lifeless loveless place. Mary begins to explore her new home and discovers a garden that has been locked away since her aunt's death. She begins to nurture the neglected garden and to draw out her sick cousin. Slowly life begins to return to them all. Excellent, but too intense and slow for young kids. 10 and up.

Sex / Nud / Viol / Lang / AdSit

A: Kate Maberly, Heydon Prowse, Andrew Knott, John Lynch, Laura Crossley, Maggie Smith

© WARNER HOME VIDEO 19000

SEPARATE BUT EQUAL

D: George Stevens, Jr. — 193 m

PG | DMA | 1991 | COLOR

9 Subtly intelligent and totally absorbing made-for-cable-TV film. In one of his finest performances, Poitier is stunning as Thurgood Marshall, the brilliant NAACP lawyer who fought a four-year battle that resulted in the famous Supreme Court ruling of 1954: Brown vs. Board of Education. This momentous ruling declared that separate was inherently not equal. All performances, and the entire play itself, are doubly effective because none of the people in it, on either side, are not portrayed as simplistic caricatures, but as real people - neither all good, nor all bad. Gripping and powerful.

Sex / Nud / Viol / Lang / ◢ AdSit

A: Sidney Poitier, Burt Lancaster, Richard Kiley, Cleavon Little, John McMartin

© REPUBLIC PICTURES HOME VIDEO 3617

SERGEANT YORK

D: Howard Hawks — 137 m

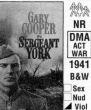

NR | DMA ACT WAR | 1941 | B&W

9 Excellent and sincere screen portrait of the unusual, but true, story of WWI's biggest war hero. Alvin York was a poor mountain boy from the hills of Tennessee who had virtually no idea of what the bigger world is like. He was a pacifist; still he was drafted into military service for WWI. This strangest of draftees then single-handedly captured 132 German soldiers. Excellent action sequences, but some of the most interesting depictions are scenes of his backwoods existence prior to the war. 11 Oscar nominations, winning two - including Best Actor for Cooper.

Sex / Nud / ◢ Viol / Lang / ◢ AdSit

A: Gary Cooper, Walter Brennan, George Tobias, Noah Beery, Jr., June Lockhart

Distributed By MGM/UA Home Video M301758

SHAG: THE MOVIE

D: Zelda Barron — 96 m

PG | DMA COM | 1989 | COLOR

7 Surprisingly pleasing female coming-of-age-type movie, set in the South in the summer of 1963. Four best friends from high school decide to spend one last fling together before one gets married, one leaves town and two go off to college. They go to Myrtle Beach for their last weekend of fun at a Shag contest (briefly-popular type of '60s dance). The movie does not open any new ground here, but the four leads are very appealing. Sort of a throwback to the BEACH PARTY movies, with a bit of DIRTY DANCING thrown in. Great '60s sound track and good period details.

Sex / Nud / Viol / Lang / ◢ AdSit

A: Phoebe Cates, Annabeth Gish, Bridget Fonda, Tyrone Power, Jr., Robert Rusler, Page Hannah

© HBO VIDEO 0214

SILAS MARNER

D: Giles Foster — 92 m

NR | DMA | 1985 | COLOR

8 Wonderful, touching BBC adaptation of George Eliot's classic tale. Set in 18th-century England, a crusty old linen weaver (Kingsley) has become a bitter man. His life has become dull and uninspired after he was wrongly accused of stealing. So, dejected and betrayed, he retreats into seclusion. However, a powerful twist of fate brings a young abandoned girl to his home and he is reborn. Suddenly, he has someone who needs him, and she brings a great deal of joy into his lonely existence and changes his life. However, everything is threatened when her real father returns. Enchanting.

Sex / Nud / Viol / Lang / ◢ AdSit

A: Ben Kingsley, Jenny Agutter, Patrick Ryecart, Jonathan Coy, Freddie Jones, Frederick Treves

© CBS/FOX VIDEO 3711

SINCE YOU WENT AWAY

D: John Cromwell — 179 m

NR | DMA | 1944 | B&W

9 Sentimental weeper. When war erupts, an adored husband and father is sent away to fight. He leaves behind his wife (Colbert) and two daughters (Jones and Temple). Money is short so they take in a boarder (Cotten). The younger daughter is devastated by her father's absence and turns to Cotten. The older daughter is falling in love with him, and even stalwart mother Colbert is tempted by him. This is an emotional character study of intense feelings - the loss, anxiety and the fear that are all a part of wartime commitment. Undated and undiminished with time, it was nominated for nine Oscars.

Sex / Nud / Viol / Lang / ◢ AdSit

A: Claudette Colbert, Jennifer Jones, Joseph Cotten, Shirley Temple, Lionel Barrymore, Hattie McDaniel

© CBS/FOX VIDEO 8082

SISTER KENNY

D: Dudley Nichols — 116 m

NR | DMA | 1946 | B&W

8 A moving drama about the woman who dedicated her life to developing a treatment for young people afflicted with polio. Sister Kenny was a nurse from Australia's wilderness who pioneered a treatment for the crippling disease. However, the established medical community only scoffed at her successes. She fought for years to have her methods accepted and used by the skeptical medical community, and eventually she succeeded. Russell received an Oscar nomination for her portrayal of the determined nurse with a huge heart and nerves of steel. A very compelling biography.

Sex / Nud / Viol / Lang / ◢ AdSit

A: Rosalind Russell, Dean Jagger, Alexander Knox, Beulah Bondi, Philip Merivale, Dorothy Peterson

© TURNER HOME ENTERTAINMENT 6186

SKEEZER

D: Peter H. Hunt — 96 m

NR | DMA CLD | 1981 | COLOR

8 A surprising true story that is sure to touch a soft spot in even the hardest of hearts. In this heartwarming, made-for-TV drama, a social worker discovers that letting troubled and lonely children play with Skeezer, a loveable sheepdog, produces wonderful results. After just a few hours with the dog, the children with emotional disorders in the home where she works, are much more calm and receptive to others. This true-life tale merely exposes the simple truth that we all need acceptance and love.

Sex / Nud / Viol / Lang / AdSit

A: Karen Valentine, Dee Wallace, Justin Lord, Tom Atkins

© LIVE HOME VIDEO 66870

SO DEAR TO MY HEART

D: Harold Schuster 82 m

NR | DMA CLD | 1948 | COLOR

9 A warm-hearted Disney film about a boy making his dream come true, and a reminder of a time long gone by! Young farmboy Driscoll's favorite pet is Danny, a black sheep with a foul temper. Driscoll desperately wants to take Danny to the county fair to try his luck at winning a blue ribbon. His problem is that he first has to figure out a way to earn the entry fee. Burl Ives is a big man with a gentle song who urges him to pursue his dream. Live animation mixes with a touching bit of nostalgia to create a delightful tribute to the past.

Sex / Nud / Viol / Lang / AdSit

A: Burl Ives, Beulah Bondi, Bobby Driscoll, Luana Patten, Harry Carey

© WALT DISNEY HOME VIDEO 296

SOMEBODY UP THERE LIKES ME

D: Robert Wise 97 m

NR | DMA | 1956 | B&W

9 Inspirational sports drama and the top-notch biography of boxing legend Rocky Graziano. Newman throws off sparks playing a tough but vulnerable Rocky. This is an inspiring story that follows him from his roots in poverty on the streets of NYC, through a stint in prison and a tumultuous army career, on to his rise to becoming middleweight boxing champion. This is a story that rises above being a mere sports story into being a true dramatic gem - but it is also one of the best boxing films ever made. Cinematography won an Oscar, as did Art Direction. It made Newman a star.

Sex / Nud / ◢ Viol / Lang / ◢ AdSit

A: Paul Newman, Sal Mineo, Pier Angeli, Robert Loggia, Steve McQueen, Everett Sloane

Distributed By MGM/UA Home Video M300640

SOUNDER

D: Martin Ritt 105 m

G | DMA | 1972 | COLOR

9 Moving, beautifully made, thought provoking, highly acclaimed and a truly excellent family movie. Nominated for Best Picture. Set in Louisiana during the Great Depression, a black sharecropper's family must survive very hard times alone after the father is caught trying to steal food for his family and is sent to prison for a year. His wife struggles to to keep them all whole until he can return. Utterly believable performances by the entire cast, but particularly Tyson, give this story a universal appeal that transcends any racial lines.

Sex / Nud / Viol / Lang / AdSit

A: Cicely Tyson, Paul Winfield, Carmen Mathews, Kevin Hooks, Taj Mahal, James Best

© PARAMOUNT HOME VIDEO 2324

SOUTHERNER, THE

D: Jean Renoir 92 m

NR | DMA | 1945 | B&W

7 An inspiring story of a family's struggle with poverty and against overpowering odds. Scott, an uneducated and desperately poor fieldhand, decides he has to take a chance to have something for himself and his family. He quits his job to try to grow cotton on a southern-Texas farm, but it is in miserable condition. His family lives in a run-down shack and does everything they can to make the meager soil produce. However, they are plagued by endless obstacles and natural disasters. A bitter neighbor even refuses to help them when Scott's son (Gilpin) becomes seriously ill. Still, they are determined to succeed. Oscar nominated for Direction.

Sex / Nud / Viol / Lang / ◢ AdSit

A: Zachary Scott, Betty Field, J. Carrol Naish, Norman Lloyd, Bunny Sunshine, Jay Gilpin

© UNITED AMERICAN VIDEO CORP. 4012

STACKING

D: Martin Rosen 96 m

PG | DMA | 1987 | COLOR

6 The Morgan family is down on its luck in 1950s Montana. They are about to lose their farm because the husband and father has had a bad accident in the field and now spends most of his time drinking. Mother (Lahti) is fed up with her life, yearns to escape it and has become enamored with a handsome drifter (Coyote). So, fourteen-year-old Anna Mae (Follows) is the only one who is left to do what has to be done. She and their hard-drinking fieldhand (Forrest) struggle to make their stacking machine work so they can harvest the hay they need to save the farm.

Sex / Nud / Viol / ◢ Lang / ◢ AdSit

A: Christine Lahti, Frederic Forrest, Megan Follows, Peter Coyote, Jason Gedrick

© NEW LINE HOME VIDEO 90227

STAGE DOOR

D: Gregory LaCava 92 m

NR | DMA COM | 1937 | B&W

9 A brilliant comedy/drama about the lives and ambitions of a bunch of hopeful actresses who all live in a boarding house in the Big Apple. They will go to almost any lengths to get that coveted "big break." Hepburn is a rich girl trying to make it on her own. She and sarcastic Rogers are roommates and rivals. Rogers allows mogul Menjou to take her out to insure winning a part, but Hepburn gets the lead because her father has financed the production - although she doesn't know that. Sparkling dialogue and great acting. The stars and soon-to-be stars of the '30s are featured in this snappy gem.

Sex / Nud / Viol / Lang / ◢ AdSit

A: Katharine Hepburn, Ginger Rogers, Adolphe Menjou, Lucille Ball, Constance Collier, Andrea Leeds

© TURNER HOME ENTERTAINMENT 6014

STAND AND DELIVER

D: Ramon Menendez 103 m

PG | DMA | 1988 | COLOR

8 Inspiring true story. Jamie Escalante (Olmos) is a tough Los Angeles high school teacher who gives up a prestigious job to become an inner-city math teacher. He believes he can impact the lives of inner-city students who are on a fast track to nowhere. Armed with a forceful, unique and caring style, and a power to motivate even the most rebellious students, he challenges, pokes, prods and inspires his kids, kids who could barely do basic math, to become math masters and pass the state Advanced Placement Test in calculus - their ticket into college. Heartwarming, funny and true.

Sex / Nud / Viol / ◢ Lang / AdSit

A: Edward James Olmos, Andy Garcia, Lou Diamond Phillips, Rosana De Soto, Will Gotay, Ingrid Oliu

© WARNER HOME VIDEO 11805

STANLEY AND LIVINGSTONE

D: Henry King 101 m

NR | DMA ACT | 1939 | B&W

6 This tale of an exciting adventure of discovery is based on a true story! In 1870 Stanley (Tracy), a hard-edged journalist with a nose for adventure, is ordered by his editor to search the African jungles far and wide for a famous missionary - Dr. Livingstone (Hardwicke) - who had been mysteriously missing for years. During his quest, Stanley endured numerous hardships and setbacks as the first white man in an alien world of fierce tribal warriors, Arab slave traders and overpowering natural dangers. But he also discovered all sorts of wonderful and new things. And he found Dr. Livingstone.

Sex / Nud / Viol / Lang / ◢ AdSit

A: Spencer Tracy, Cedric Hardwicke, Nancy Kelly, Walter Brennan, Richard Greene, Charles Coburn

© FOXVIDEO 1821

STARDUST MEMORIES

D: Woody Allen 89 m

PG | DMA COM | 1980 | B&W

6 Allen is unabashedly playing himself in this unique but mean-spirited film. Sandy Bates (Allen) is a filmmaker whose earlier stuff can't compare (according to his fans) to his later stuff. He is a lonely genius who nobody understands. When a director cuts up his first serious film, he seeks solace by attending a seminar, but is immediately stampeded by fans, favor-seekers and film critics. Allen shows a side of himself that fans may not like, and takes a poke at those who have been critical of his work. Still, very interesting.

Sex / Nud / Viol / ◢ Lang / ◢ AdSit

A: Woody Allen, Charlotte Rampling, Jessica Harper, Marie-Christine Barrault, Tony Roberts, Daniel Stern

Distributed By MGM/UA Home Video M203033

STARS LOOK DOWN, THE

D: Carol Reed 104 m

NR | DMA | 1939 | B&W

8 An attention grabber from start to finish! A poor Welsh miner (Redgrave) gets sick and tired of the deplorable working conditions that are forced upon the workers who are being betrayed by the leaders of their own union. He wants to run for office to try to change things, but his selfish wife (Lockwood) stands in his way. When he realizes that she doesn't love him any more, he decides to run for office anyway. A very powerful and intelligent British drama that was one of the first to make a social statement. A riveting classic based on Cronin's novel.

Sex / Nud / Viol / Lang / ◢ AdSit

A: Michael Redgrave, Margaret Lockwood, Edward Rigby, Emlyn Williams, Nancy Price, Cecil Parker

© VIDEO YESTERYEAR 956

STATE OF THE UNION

D: Frank Capra 122 m

NR | DMA COM | 1948 | B&W

9 A timeless story of a grab for the Presidency that is based on the Pulitzer Prize-winning play. Tracy is a wealthy airplane builder pushed into running for President by his new love, an overbearing newspaper publisher (Lansbury). His estranged wife (Hepburn) doesn't like the political changes she sees in her husband, but agrees to pose as the classic "wife by his side" anyway. And, when he gets in a little too deep in the political soup and loses his sense of balance, it is Hepburn who is there for him. Time does not really date this one. The details of changed but people and politics haven't.

Sex / Nud / Viol / Lang / ◢ AdSit

A: Katharine Hepburn, Spencer Tracy, Angela Lansbury, Van Johnson, Adolphe Menjou, Lewis Stone

© MCA/UNIVERSAL HOME VIDEO, INC. 55006

STONE BOY, THE

D: Christopher Cain 93 m

PG | DMA | 1984 | COLOR

9 Powerfully moving. On a hunting expedition, 12-year-old Presson accidentally kills his older brother. At first he doesn't know what to do, but eventually he does go home to tell his parents what happened. However, now wrought with guilt, he retreats behind a dark and quiet wall of seclusion. He doesn't even cry and his quietness is perceived as being a lack of caring. He receives an overwhelming dose of rejection and anger from his father (Duvall). While, his mother wants to reach out to him, she is restrained by the distraught father. This is an intensely sad but very realistic story of family that is nearly destroyed by a lack of communication.

Sex / Nud / ◢ Viol / ◢ Lang / ◢ AdSit

A: Robert Duvall, Glenn Close, Jason Presson, Frederic Forrest, Wilford Brimley, Gail Youngs

© FOXVIDEO 1445

FAMILY

STORY OF LOUIS PASTEUR, THE

D: William Dieterle — 87 m

NR | DMA | 1936 | B&W | 9

Extremely moving biography! This is an engrossing story which depicts the life of the famous French scientist who dedicated his life to finding a vaccine for rabies and anthrax. He challenged conventional wisdom and defied the medical profession's skepticism and ridicule to proceed steadfastly with his experiments. Even when he had triumphed, he was assaulted by the vindictive powers who he had embarrassed. Muni's portrayal of the dedicated scientist and his notable achievements won him an Oscar for Best Actor. Film was a Best Picture nominee.

☐ Sex ☐ Nud ☐ Viol ☐ Lang ☐ AdSit

A: Paul Muni, Josephine Hutchinson, Anita Louise, Donald Woods, Fritz Leiber, Porter Hall

Distributed By MGM/UA Home Video M301761

STRANGE CARGO

D: Frank Borzage — 115 m

NR | DMA | 1940 | B&W | 6

A strange brew of characters in an even stranger religious parable. A group of convicts, led by Gable, tries to make a daring escape from the tropical prison of Devil's Island. They trudge through the jungle and along the way Gable picks up a hardened dance hall girl (Crawford). Also along with them is a mysterious Christ-like figure who calms the anxious and eager escapees, but at sea in an open sailboat, the group both ridicules the Bible and undergo their own conversions. The Legion of Decency originally condemned the film for this religious element. Powerful acting, but an odd film. Mostly for film fans.

☐ Sex ☐ Nud ☐ Viol ☐ Lang ✓ AdSit

A: Joan Crawford, Clark Gable, Ian Hunter, Peter Lorre, Albert Dekker, Eduardo Ciannelli

Distributed By MGM/UA Home Video M301589

SUGARLAND EXPRESS, THE

D: Steven Spielberg — 109 m

PG | DMA COM | 1974 | COLOR | 8

Oddly fascinating film that was Steven Spielberg's first feature film. A simple-minded girl, just released from jail after having served a short sentence for a minor theft, learns that her baby is being adopted by a family in Sugarland, Texas. In a fit of desperation, she breaks her husband out of prison, kidnapping a cop along the way. They all set off to Sugarland in a stolen cop car to get her baby back. Pursued by an armada of police cars, she gets major publicity and becomes a folk hero. Based upon an actual 1969 event.

☐ Sex ☐ Nud ✓ Viol ✓ Lang ☐ AdSit

A: Goldie Hawn, Ben Johnson, William Atherton, Michael Sacks

© MCA/UNIVERSAL HOME VIDEO, INC. 55052

SUNRISE AT CAMPOBELLO

D: Vincent J. Donehue — 144 m

NR | DMA | 1960 | COLOR | 8

Fascinating biography of President Franklin D. Roosevelt's courageous struggle to keep polio from taking over his life. Bellamy expertly plays the determined president who is stricken with the debilitating disease and paralyzed in the 1920s. His wife Eleanor (Garson) and trusted friend (Cronyn) inspire him to face the disease head-on and try to walk again. Outstanding and educational, the acting is first-rate and absolutely inspirational. Adapted from Schary's hit play. Four Oscar nominations.

☐ Sex ☐ Nud ☐ Viol ☐ Lang ✓ AdSit

A: Ralph Bellamy, Greer Garson, Hume Cronyn, Jean Hagen, Ann Shoemaker, Alan Bunce

© WARNER HOME VIDEO 11214

SUNSET BOULEVARD

D: Billy Wilder — 110 m

NR | DMA | 1950 | B&W | 10

Triple Oscar-winner! The film opens startlingly with Holden floating face down in a swimming pool, his body riddled with bullet holes. Then in flashback, he narrates his own story. Silent film superstar Norma Desmond's (Swanson) career has faded into nothingness, but she still thinks she is a star. Swanson hires a slimy Hollywood screenwriter (Holden) to bring back her career, but he falls in love with her and moves into her dilapidated old mansion. She reels him into her demented game of make-believe. Then, the pair, her ex-husband and their butler all live in the past until Holden is driven to ruin, too. One of great classics of all time, and a very pointed assault on Hollywood!

☐ Sex ☐ Nud ☐ Viol ☐ Lang ✓ AdSit

A: Gloria Swanson, William Holden, Erich von Stroheim, Fred Clark, Jack Webb, Hedda Hopper

© PARAMOUNT HOME VIDEO 4927

SWEET SMELL OF SUCCESS

D: Alexander Mackendrick — 97 m

NR | DMA | 1957 | B&W | 8

Lancaster stars as J.J. Hunsecker, an egomaniacal, all-powerful New York newspaper columnist. Curtis is a press agent whose livelihood depends upon getting his client's exposure. Because Lancaster's column provides the best exposure available, Curtis will do anything to get it. Lancaster is driven and has no interest in women, except for his sister who lives with him. When she takes up with a musician (Milner), Lancaster wants it stopped and offers Curtis whatever it takes if he'll do it. Though he feels guilty, Curtis is too drawn by the offer to refuse. Blistering look at power and the press.

☐ Sex ☐ Nud ☐ Viol ☐ Lang ✓ AdSit

A: Burt Lancaster, Tony Curtis, Martin Milner, Sam Levene, Barbara Nichols, Susan Harrison

Distributed By MGM/UA Home Video M301434

SYLVESTER

D: Tim Hunter — 104 m

PG | DMA CLD | 1984 | COLOR | 8

NATIONAL VELVET fans take note! Sylvester is an untamed jumping horse that catches the fancy of sixteen year-old tomboy Gilbert. She and her two brothers are orphaned and are under the care of a crusty old horse trainer (Farnsworth). Gilbert falls in love with the beautiful white horse and enlists the aid of Farnsworth to help train it, even though he doesn't think the horse has a chance. But with his help, she and Sylvester do train the horse for the event of her life held in Lexington, Kentucky. A charmer that lifts you up and leaves you feeling very good.

☐ Sex ☐ Nud ☐ Viol ✓ Lang ☐ AdSit

A: Melissa Gilbert, Richard Farnsworth, Michael Schoeffling, Constance Towers

© COLUMBIA TRISTAR HOME VIDEO 60476

TABLE FOR FIVE

D: Robert Lieberman — 120 m

PG | DMA | 1983 | COLOR | 8

A very effective drama which reflects a situation many can identify with. Jon Voight is a divorced father who, after a long absence is now estranged from his children. He hopes to reestablish his relationship with them. So, he picks them from his ex-wife (Perkins) and her new husband (Crenna) to go on an extended ocean voyage. But, he finds that it is very difficult to regain his children's respect and affections. Then news arrives that their mother has been killed in a car accident and he has to battle stepfather Crenna for custody. Solid tear-jerker.

☐ Sex ☐ Nud ☐ Viol ✓ Lang ✓ AdSit

A: Jon Voight, Millie Perkins, Richard Crenna, Kevin Costner, Roxana Zal, Marie-Christine Barrault

© CBS/FOX VIDEO 7043

TEN COMMANDMENTS, THE

D: Cecil B. DeMille — 146 m

NR | DMA | 1923 | B&W | 7

Grand scale silent-era film. Produced with a huge cast of extras (they used an actual US Calvary division) and lavish sets. It is based upon the Book of Exodus and includes the parting of the Red Sea, the destruction of the golden calf, etc., but also juxtaposes a modern-day (1920s) counterpart to the story in which two brothers (one good and one evil) are used to illustrate the consequences of breaking the commandments. Pretty heavy-handed, but also still pretty impressive. The film includes the use of some two-color imagery, and is accompanied by pipe organ music.

☐ Sex ☐ Nud ☐ Viol ☐ Lang ☐ AdSit

A: Theodore Roberts, Charles de Roche, Estelle Taylor, Richard Dix, Rod La Rocque, Leatrice Joy

© PARAMOUNT HOME VIDEO 2506

TEN COMMANDMENTS, THE

D: Cecil B. DeMille — 219 m

G | DMA | 1956 | COLOR | 9

DeMille's second spectacular biblical epic. The Old Testament story of Moses is told with great detail (Oscar for Special Effects) and as much presence and conviction as Charlton Heston can muster. Moses's life is depicted from the time of his birth, his adoption into royalty, his banishment to the desert, his anointment by God, the many trials endured by the Egyptian king Ramses and the exodus of the Jews from Egypt. DeMille didn't miss anything. The parting of the Red Sea is still spectacular. Solid reverent family entertainment. See also equally grand BEN HUR, filmed three years later.

☐ Sex ☐ Nud ☐ Viol ☐ Lang ☐ AdSit

A: Charlton Heston, Yul Brynner, John Derek, Anne Baxter, Yvonne De Carlo, Edward G. Robinson

© PARAMOUNT HOME VIDEO 6524

TENTH MAN, THE

D: Richard T. Heffron — 99 m

NR | DMA | 1988 | COLOR | 8

A fascinating premise. Hopkins is a wealthy attorney who lives on an estate near a village just outside of WWII Paris and commutes in to work each day. However, one day he is picked up totally at random by a Nazi patrol and is thrown into prison. He and the other prisoners are told that they are to single out ten from their number, who will then be shot. They make the choice at random and he is one that is selected. Terrified, he makes a contract with a fellow prisoner who will die in his place and he will give everything he owns to the man's impoverished mother and sister. Years later, tormented and destitute he visits his house not telling them who he is. Excellent.

☐ Sex ☐ Nud ✓ Viol ☐ Lang ✓ AdSit

A: Anthony Hopkins, Kristin Scott Thomas, Derek Jacobi, Cyril Cusack

Distributed By MGM/UA Home Video 803941

TERMS OF ENDEARMENT

D: James L. Brooks — 132 m

PG | DMA ROM COM | 1983 | COLOR | 10

Mesmerizing and totally heartwarming drama that captured five major Oscars, including Picture, Screenplay, Director, Actress and Supporting Actress. It is an intimate and winning character study of the relationship between a mother and daughter as it evolves over a period of years. MacLaine is wonderful as a neurotic, domineering mother and Winger is equally good as her independent-minded daughter who marries a cheating English teacher against her mother's wishes and later is to die of cancer. Totally captivating performances and story that surely will warm your heart and wet your eyes.

☐ Sex ☐ Nud ☐ Viol ✓ Lang ✓ AdSit

A: Shirley MacLaine, Debra Winger, Jack Nicholson, John Lithgow, Danny DeVito, Jeff Daniels

© PARAMOUNT HOME VIDEO 1407

TO KILL A MOCKINGBIRD

D: Robert Mulligan — 131 m

NR | DMA | 1962 | B&W | ☐ Sex ☐ Nud ◢ Viol ☐ Lang ◢ AdSit

9 Outstanding and flavorful film about a small-town 1930s Alabama lawyer who defends a black man who was falsely charged of raping a white woman. Peck is outstanding (Oscar) as the hard-pressed lawyer and widowed father who is trying to raise two impressionable young children against a background of hate and fear. He is ostracized by the whole town for standing up for what is right. An extremely powerful film that takes its time but never bogs down. Winner of three Oscars, including Peck's, plus two other nominations, including Best Picture.

A: Gregory Peck, Mary Badham, Philip Alford, Brock Peters, Robert Duvall, John Megna

© MCA/UNIVERSAL HOME VIDEO, INC. 55032

TO SIR, WITH LOVE

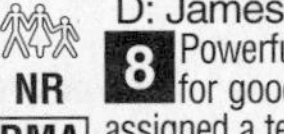

D: James Clavell — 105 m

NR | DMA | 1967 | COLOR | ☐ Sex ☐ Nud ☐ Viol ☐ Lang ◢ AdSit

8 Powerful and affecting melodrama that was very popular - and for good reason. Sidney Poitier is a new, untried teacher who is assigned a teaching position at a London slum school that is populated by alienated and abusive teenagers. His determined persistence and unorthodox teaching methods break through their walls of hostility and instill in them a renewed sense of hope. A heartfelt and believable film in which Poitier shines in one of his best performances. Similar to equally good BLACKBOARD JUNGLE from 10 years earlier.

A: Sidney Poitier, Judy Geeson, Christian Roberts, Suzy Kendall, Lulu, Faith Brook

© COLUMBIA TRISTAR HOME VIDEO 60247

TOUCHED BY LOVE

D: Gus Trikonis — 95 m

PG | DMA | 1980 | COLOR | ☐ Sex ☐ Nud ☐ Viol ◢ Lang ☐ AdSit

7 Touching true story. A nursing trainee who works with kids afflicted with cerebral palsy has one particular girl who is totally incommunicative until she strikes upon the unconventional idea of talking the girl into writing to her idol, Elvis Presley. When Presley returns her letter and becomes the girl's pen pal, she begins a remarkable turnaround in attitude which results in a new life for her. Understated performances add significantly to this uplifting and sentimental (but not overly so) effective tearjerker.

A: Deborah Raffin, Diane Lane, Michael Learned, Cristina Raines, Mary Wickes, Clu Gulager

© COLUMBIA TRISTAR HOME VIDEO 60307

TREE GROWS IN BROOKLYN, A

D: Elia Kazan — 128 m

NR | DMA | 1945 | B&W | ☐ Sex ☐ Nud ☐ Viol ☐ Lang ◢ AdSit

9 Rich and endearing. Francis is a bright young girl growing up in a tenement building in Brooklyn at the turn of the century. She is a dreamer and the daughter of a kind, but ne'er-do-well, alcoholic father, who she loves deeply, and a very strong-willed, down-to-earth mother. These are very difficult times and they all must struggle just to survive, just like the tree in their back yard. But, Francie doesn't understand and resents her firm mother being so hard on her father, though it is she who is holding the family together. This is a sensitive and poignant drama. It won two Oscars for acting. Excellent.

A: Dorothy McGuire, Joan Blondell, James Dunn, Lloyd Nolan, Peggy Ann Garner, Ted Donaldson

© FOXVIDEO 1517

TRIBES

D: Joseph Sargent — 90 m

G | DMA COM | 1970 | COLOR | ☐ Sex ☐ Nud ☐ Viol ☐ Lang ◢ AdSit

8 Excellent made-for-TV movie. It was made during the time of the Vietnam war and revolves around many of the issues that concerned everyone then. It has become a little dated but it is also still both insightful and funny. Imagine a hippie, in a robe, with long hair and sandals, getting drafted into the Marines. Darin McGavin is the tough DI given the responsibility of turning this flower into a lean, mean, fighting machine. The trouble is, he is already lean and tough, but he's a dedicated peacenik. Worse yet, he's also a natural leader and everyone in the platoon is following him, not the tough DI. Really quite good.

A: Jan-Michael Vincent, Darren McGavin, Earl Holliman, John Gruber, Danny Goldman, Richard Yniguez

© FOXVIDEO 1669

TUCKER: THE MAN AND HIS DREAM

D: Francis Ford Coppola — 111 m

PG | DMA | 1988 | COLOR | ☐ Sex ☐ Nud ☐ Viol ◢ Lang ◢ AdSit

8 In 1948 the man before his time built the car before its time. This true story of Preston Tucker (Bridges) is told with spirit and verve and is brilliantly directed by longtime admirer Coppola. Tucker built a safer and more affordable car than anyone else after the war, but interests in Washington joined forces with the big three car manufacturers and launched a smear campaign against the car, destroying Tucker's dream. Undaunted, Tucker emerged with his character unshaken and his optimism intact. Inspiring!

A: Jeff Bridges, Joan Allen, Martin Landau, Frederic Forrest, Ako, Dean Stockwell

© PARAMOUNT HOME VIDEO 32144

VIVA ZAPATA!

D: Elia Kazan — 114 m

NR | DMA | 1952 | B&W | ☐ Sex ☐ Nud ◢ Viol ☐ Lang ◢ AdSit

8 Excellent film capturing the feel of the Mexican Revolution. Set in the early 1900s, Brando (Oscar nominated) is Emiliano Zapata, a poor, illiterate peasant who rises within the ranks of the peasant army, along with his alcoholic brother (Anthony Quinn - Academy Award) and later becomes President of Mexico. He fights, not to overthrow the government, but to deliver land to the tenant farmers who work it. The real Zapata was ruthless but Brando's character has been considerably toned down. Plus, the plot is embellished with a love interest and a lament for the corrupting influences of power.

A: Marlon Brando, Anthony Quinn, Jean Peters, Joseph Wiseman, Mildred Dunnock

© FOXVIDEO 1352

VOYAGE ROUND MY FATHER, A

D: Alvin Rakoff — 85 m

NR | DMA COM | 1983 | COLOR | ☐ Sex ☐ Nud ☐ Viol ☐ Lang ◢ AdSit

8 A powerful emotional journey that also has a strong comedic undercurrent. When an eccentric but successful older lawyer (Olivier) loses his sight, he decides to continue his battles in the courtroom anyway, and turns to his family and son for help. As his son (Bates) helps his difficult father through this trying time, he begins to remember all of the good times and the bitterly bad times that he and his father have shared in their troubled relationship. And, he learns to stop trying to understand his father and to just love him. Beautifully filmed and acted. A good lesson for most fathers and sons.

A: Laurence Olivier, Alan Bates, Elizabeth Sellars, Jane Asher

© HBO VIDEO 0329

WATERSHIP DOWN

D: Martin Rosen — 93 m

PG | DMA FAN | 1978 | COLOR | ☐ Sex ☐ Nud ◢ Viol ☐ Lang ◢ AdSit

8 Although this is an animated feature, it is not a cartoon for little kiddies. It is an allegorical story for adults and older kids. It involves the human-like story of the survival of a small group of rabbits who leave the apparent safety of their home because Hazel foresees impending doom. She leads a group of males in search of a new home, past the dangers of foxes, owls, dogs and men, to reach a hill called Watership Down. There, they make a new home and set about attracting females from neighboring, but hostile clans, of rabbits. Well-done, thoughtful entertainment.

A:

© WARNER HOME VIDEO 34003

WE OF THE NEVER NEVER

D: Igor Auzins — 135 m

G | DMA WST ACT | 1982 | COLOR | ☐ Sex ☐ Nud ◢ Viol ◢ Lang ◢ AdSit

8 Touching and captivating import from Australia, and winner of six Australian Academy Award nominations. It is a true story, taken from the diary of Jeannie Gunn, first published in 1908. She was the first white woman to travel deep into the Australian wilderness, called the Outback or the Never Never, to a cattle station with her husband. A stunning piece of camerawork depicts her story of survival in a rugged world dominated by men, their confrontation with the mystical world of the aborigines and their acceptance of her. However, her happiness is soon shattered with the death of her husband.

A: Angela Punch-McGregor, Tommy Lewis, Arthur Dignam, Tony Barry

© COLUMBIA TRISTAR HOME VIDEO 60256

WHEN THE LEGENDS DIE

D: Stuart Millar — 105 m

PG | DMA WST | 1972 | COLOR | ☐ Sex ☐ Nud ☐ Viol ◢ Lang ☐ AdSit

7 A perceptive and sensitive story about the relationship that develops between an aging, hard-drinking cowboy, who is having a hard time dealing with his declining rodeo skills, and a rebellious young Ute Indian, who has freshly arrived from the reservation after his parents have died. The old man exploits the youngster and his riding abilities for a meal ticket when he trains the boy to ride broncs in the rodeo. However, their relationship becomes severely strained when Widmark encourages him to lose so they can make money on the bets. One of Widmark's better performances.

A: Frederic Forrest, Richard Widmark, Luana Anders, Vito Scotti

© FOXVIDEO 1293

WHISTLE DOWN THE WIND

D: Bryan Forbes — 99 m

NR | DMA | 1962 | B&W | ☐ Sex ☐ Nud ☐ Viol ☐ Lang ☐ AdSit

8 A fugitive murderer is found hiding in the barn by three innocent young children. When they ask who he is, he is so relieved they are just children that he says, "Jesus Christ!" - and they take him at his word. Word of him spreads through the children but none tells their parents. They keep his secret and hide him in the barn. Excellent performances by everyone, especially the children. This is a fascinating story about the nature of a child's trust and innocence. There is a memorable conclusion that makes it especially worthwhile viewing for the whole family.

A: Hayley Mills, Alan Bates, Bernard Lee, Norman Bird, Elsie Wagstaffe

© NEW LINE HOME VIDEO 6040

WILD HEARTS CAN'T BE BROKEN

D: Steve Minor — 89 m

G | DMA | 1991 | COLOR

9 Truly wonderful family picture. A rebellious 17-year-old orphan girl flees her aunt's stifling home by answering a newspaper advertisement seeking a rider for a diving horse in a traveling show. But this is more than just a story about a girl who rides a horse through forty feet of empty space into a tank of water. It is the story of a girl who struggles for happiness and to succeed in a world where the chips are stacked against her. Not only does she succeed once, but twice. And she finds a family and love. Terrific feel for an era and absolutely charming. Based on truth.

☐ Sex ☐ Nud ☐ Viol ☐ Lang ☐ AdSit

A: Gabrielle Anwar, Cliff Robertson, Michael Schoeffling

© WALT DISNEY HOME VIDEO 1223

WORLD APART, A

D: Chris Menges — 114 m

PG | DMA | 1988 | COLOR

8 Sleeper that was unduly passed over in theatrical release, but definitely a worthy rental. It is the story of a 13-year-old girl's perceptions of her parents and particularly her mother. It is 1963 in South Africa and her parents are activists against apartheid. Her father is forced into exile outside the country and her mother is a journalist who is arrested and put into solitary confinement. She shares her mother's passion for the fight against such a corrupt system, but she also is desperately in need of a mother who is never there for her. Powerful.

☐ Sex ☐ Nud ✓ Viol ✓ Lang ✓ AdSit

A: Barbara Hershey, Jeroen Krabbe, David Suchet, Jodhi May, Paul Freeman, Linda Mvusi

© MEDIA HOME ENTERTAINMENT, INC. M012484

FAMILY

YEARLING, THE

D: Clarence Brown — 129 m

G | DMA CLD | 1946 | COLOR

9 Beautiful and sensitive family favorite that was also a Best Picture nominee. This is the intelligent story of a young boy's confrontation with the hard realities of survival in early America. A lonely boy, living with his mother and father on a small pioneer farm, adopts an orphaned fawn for a pet. As the fawn grows into a yearling and the boy becomes more and more attached to it, the deer becomes a larger and larger problem for the parents. Eventually they must decide between the yearling and their own survival. Memorable and heart-wrenching.

☐ Sex ☐ Nud ☐ Viol ☐ Lang ☐ AdSit

A: Gregory Peck, Jane Wyman, Claude Jarman, Jr., Chill Wills, Clem Bevins, Margaret Wycherly

Distributed By MGM/UA Home Video M300500

YOUNG MR. LINCOLN

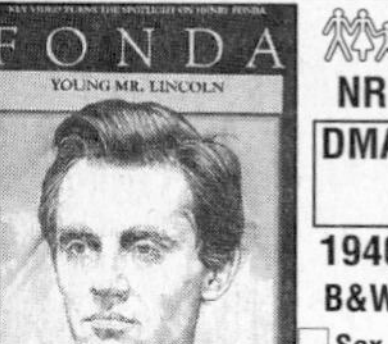

D: John Ford — 100 m

NR | DMA | 1940 | B&W

9 Wonderful bit of Americana from Director John Ford. This film is, as its title would indicate, a character study of the younger years of Mr. Lincoln. Henry Fonda is truly impressive as Lincoln. This film examines Mr. Lincoln's life from his earliest beginnings in a Kentucky log cabin, through his lost love for Ann Rutledge, his days as a backwoods lawyer, to the film's suspenseful climax as he represents two brothers in a murder trial. Good fun and solid family entertainment.

☐ Sex ☐ Nud ☐ Viol ☐ Lang ☐ AdSit

A: Henry Fonda, Alice Brady, Marjorie Weaver, Donald Meek, Milburn Stone, Ward Bond

© FOXVIDEO 1420

3 WORLDS OF GULLIVER, THE

D: Jack Sher — 100 m

NR | FAN CLD | 1960 | COLOR

7 This fanciful story, designed in the 18th century to be biting satire, is considerably toned down here. Now it is just good family entertainment. It is the story of Gulliver, who was swept overboard while at sea and washed ashore first on Lilliput, an island totally inhabited by very, very tiny people. Later Gulliver travels to another island, Brobdingnag, where the people are as much taller than Gulliver as he was than the Lilliputians. It's all done in live action through a trick photography process called dynavision. OK for everyone, but best for young children.

☐ Sex ☐ Nud ☐ Viol ☐ Lang ☐ AdSit

A: Kerwin Mathews, Jo Morrow, June Thorburn, Lee Patterson, Gregoire Aslan, Basil Sydney

© COLUMBIA TRISTAR HOME VIDEO 60924

5,000 FINGERS OF DR. T., THE

D: Roy Rowland — 88 m

FAN CLD | 1953 | B&W

8 This fantasy was co-scripted by Dr. Seuss and was one of Hollywood's best fantasies, but it has been largely overlooked by the public. It is about a boy who hates his piano lessons and dreams about a cruel piano teacher (Conried) who keeps 500 boys locked up in his castle (500 boys X 10 fingers = 5000 fingers). He makes them practice day and night, playing on a piano with a huge keyboard. Also locked away in his dungeon are creatures who dared to play other instruments. The brave boy, with the help of a resourceful plumber, helps to destroy the evil Dr. T.

☐ Sex ☐ Nud ☐ Viol ☐ Lang ☐ AdSit

A: Peter Lind Hayes, Mary Healy, Tommy Rettig, Hans Conried

© COLUMBIA TRISTAR HOME VIDEO 90163

7 FACES OF DR. LAO

D: George Pal — 101 m

NR | FAN WST CLD | 1963 | COLOR

9 Absolutely delightful and heartwarming fantasy. A small Old West town newspaper editor (Ericson) is trying to win the hand of a pretty widow (Eden) and fighting a lonely battle against a villain (O'Connell), who is trying to grab up all the land around. A truly strange helpmate arrives in the form of a mysterious and wise old Chinese magician named Dr. Lao (Randall). Dr. Lao is the proprietor of a traveling circus containing a fantastic array of wondrous sideshow creatures. Fabulous makeup and special effects. Randall is truly outstanding, playing multiple roles. Great fun for all.

☐ Sex ☐ Nud ☐ Viol ☐ Lang ☐ AdSit

A: Tony Randall, Barbara Eden, Arthur O'Connell, John Ericson, Lee Patrick, Noah Beery, Jr.

Distributed By MGM/UA Home Video M600667

7TH VOYAGE OF SINBAD, THE

D: Nathan Juran — 94 m

G | FAN CLD | 1958 | COLOR

8 Flavorful Arabian Nights tale of Sinbad the Sailor. An evil wizard has shrunk the beautiful Princess (and Sinbad's true love) to only six inches high. In order to restore her, Sinbad must battle a giant bird, a giant cyclops, a dragon and a sword-wielding living skeleton. Wonderful special effects and a thrilling, well-paced, fanciful adventure story that will please both young and old alike. The stop motion animation created for this picture is still very highly regarded, and for years was held as the standard for the industry.

☐ Sex ☐ Nud ✓ Viol ☐ Lang ☐ AdSit

A: Kerwin Mathews, Kathryn Grant, Richard Eyer, Torin Thatcher

© COLUMBIA TRISTAR HOME VIDEO 60114

ADVENTURES OF BARON MUNCHAUSEN, THE

D: Terry Gilliam — 122 m

PG | FAN COM CLD | 1989 | COLOR

7 Inside the walls of a city under siege by the armies of the Ottoman Empire, a small troupe of actors puts on a play about the infamous German Baron Munchausen, who had claimed to have had many wildly extravagant exploits. Their presentation is interrupted by an old soldier who claims that he is, in fact, the real Baron. Vowing that he will rescue the town, the old soldier departs in a rag-tag home-made hot air balloon, off to enlist the aid of his superhuman partners of old: the strongest man on earth, the man who can blow stronger than a hurricane, and the fastest man alive. Silly, light-hearted fantasy.

☐ Sex ✓ Nud ✓ Viol ☐ Lang ☐ AdSit

A: John Neville, Robin Williams, Eric Idle, Oliver Reed, Sarah Polley, Uma Thurman

© COLUMBIA TRISTAR HOME VIDEO 50153

Foreign

20,000 LEAGUES UNDER THE SEA

D: Richard Fleischer — 127 m

G | FAN ACT CLD | 1954 | COLOR

9 Marvelous adaptation by Disney of Jules Verne's fantasy adventure written in 1868. Both the film and the book are, and will remain, great fun and timeless. Amid fear created by rumors of a fierce monster ravaging the sea, a lone ship sets sail in a search to find it. On board is a scientist, his wimpy assistant (Lorre) and an adventurous harpooner (Douglas). Their ship is indeed attacked by the monster, but it is instead a submarine named the Nautilus, created and piloted by the mad genius Captain Nemo (Mason). Totally captivating with very high production values and superb special effects.

☐ Sex ☐ Nud ✓ Viol ☐ Lang ☐ AdSit

A: Kirk Douglas, James Mason, Peter Lorre, Paul Lukas, Robert J. Wilke, Carleton Young

© WALT DISNEY HOME VIDEO 015

BEASTMASTER, THE

D: Don Coscarelli — 119 m

PG | FAN ACT | 1982 | COLOR

8 In a magical feudal world, a demented high priest enslaves a people and demands that they sacrifice their young children. A young warrior (Singer) is the only survivor of a tribal massacre, and he uses his ability to communicate telepathically with animals to aid him in his quest to defeat the evil sorcerer (Rip Torn) and to save the beautiful virgin (Tanya Roberts). Good special effects, and plenty of animals and action for kids of all ages.

☐ Sex ✓ Nud ✓ Viol ☐ Lang ✓ AdSit

A: Marc Singer, Tanya Roberts, Rip Torn, John Amos

Distributed By MGM/UA Home Video M800226

BOY WHO COULD FLY, THE

D: Nick Castle 114 m

PG | FAN DMA | 1986 | COLOR | Sex | Nud | Viol | Lang ✓ | AdSit

8 Highly enjoyable and uplifting film, excellent family entertainment. When her husband commits suicide after learning he has cancer, the hard-pressed Bonnie Bedelia and her two children move in next door to a troubled autistic boy who has lost his parents in a plane wreck and now just sits on the roof dreaming that he can fly. No one can reach him, but Bedelia's troubled daughter (Deakins) slowly draws him out of his private world and becomes the only true friend he has. Genuinely heartwarming picture about the value of love and of never giving up.

A: Lucy Deakins, Jay Underwood, Bonnie Bedelia, Fred Savage, Colleen Dewhurst, Fred Gwynne

© WARNER HOME VIDEO 781

CURSE OF THE CAT PEOPLE, THE

D: Robert Wise 70 m

NR | FAN SUS | 1944 | B&W | Sex | Nud | Viol | Lang | AdSit ✓

7 A truly interesting follow-up to the 1942 version of CAT PEOPLE. This is not a horror movie as the original was, but is a fantasy about a lonely young girl who lives in a dream world. Her mother, long dead, had suffered from the belief that she would be transformed into a panther. Her father has been trying to protect her from that strange past but now she, too, has fantasies and she has an imaginary friend - her dead mother. (Simone revives her earlier role.) Is her mother just her fantasy or is she real? And, why is she here?

A: Simone Simon, Kent Smith, Jane Randolph, Elizabeth Russell, Ann Carter, Julia Dean

© TURNER HOME ENTERTAINMENT 2084

DARK CRYSTAL, THE

D: Jim Henson, Frank Oz 93 m

PG | FAN | 1982 | COLOR | Sex | Nud | Viol ✓ | Lang | AdSit ✓

6 The creators of the Muppets have created a full-length feature film that is totally populated by puppets. It is a fanciful tale depicting good versus evil. In it, a young Gelfling (elf-like creature) hero must find and replace a missing piece of the dark crystal in order to protect the world and restore it to light. If he is unsuccessful, the terribly evil Skeksis (vulture-like creatures) will defeat the benevolent Mystics and the world will decay. The Skeksis are such absolutely repugnant and evil characters that they are likely to be far too scary for small kids. Better for older kids and teenagers.

A:

© WALT DISNEY HOME VIDEO 2596

GOLDEN VOYAGE OF SINBAD, THE

D: Gordon Hessler 105 m

G | FAN CLD | 1974 | COLOR | Sex | Nud | Viol | Lang | AdSit

8 Tales of Captain Sinbad have thrilled generations. Great special effects add to the mystical charm of this ancient hero in a film that still captures the fantasies of kids today. Sinbad sets sail for an uncharted island with a beautiful slave girl (Munro) and the Grand Vizier of the land on board his ship. An evil wizard is trying to gain control of the kingdom and is using evil spirits to do it. Great special effects include both a ship's figurehead and a sword wielding six-armed statue coming to life. Then throw in a one-eyed centaur and a griffin. Great entertainment for kids.

A: John Phillip Law, Caroline Monro, Tom Baker, Douglas Wilmer, Gregoire Aslan, John Garfield, Jr.

© COLUMBIA TRISTAR HOME VIDEO 60199

GOONIES, THE

D: Richard Donner 114 m

PG | FAN CLD | 1985 | COLOR | Sex | Nud | Viol ✓ | Lang ✓ | AdSit

8 Rousing old-fashioned adventure yarn for kids. Spielberg produced this fantasy about a neighborhood group of kids who call themselves the Goonies. Their neighborhood is going to be razed by greedy developers so they all get together for one last time. Then, wonderfully, they discover a real-life treasure map that will provide more than enough money to save their neighborhood. They set off on a trek for the treasure, a trek which leads them into a subterranean world of caves, caverns, booby-traps, a real pirate ship and a monster. Plenty of action and thrills to keep the kids fascinated.

A: Sean Astin, Josh Brolin, Corey Feldman, Martha Plimpton, Ke Huy Quan, John Matuszak

© WARNER HOME VIDEO 11474

HOBBIT, THE

D: Arthur Rankin, Jr. 78 m

FAN | 1977 | COLOR | Sex | Nud | Viol | Lang | AdSit

6 J.R.R. Tolkien's classic fantasy is set in a time and place long ago. It is the story of a strange little man-like creature named Bilbo Baggins and his perilous adventures in the marvelously wondrous world of middle-earth, which is populated by wizards, dwarves, goblins, wargs and the terrible dragon Smaug. The book is magical but it is reduced here to little more than a children's fairy tale. Perhaps it is too much to expect that this fantasy masterpiece should translate well to the screen. Nevertheless, there is value for those familiar with the book, but please read the book. Sequel is RETURN OF THE KING.

A:

© WARNER HOME VIDEO 716

HOOK

D: Steven Spielberg 142 m

PG | FAN CLD | 1991 | COLOR | Sex | Nud | Viol ✓ | Lang | AdSit

7 Peter Pan (Williams) is all grown up and has become a stressed-out exec who doesn't spend enough time with his children. However, while he is in London visiting Aunt Wendy, his old arch enemy Captain Hook (Hoffman) kidnaps his kids and Peter must return to Never Never Land to get them back. But Peter is so changed that he can't remember how to fly or how to fight. Fortunately, Tinkerbell (Roberts) comes to the rescue and helps him to remember and to get ready for the big showdown with Hook. Not wonderful, but pleasant. Enjoy this big-budget high tech Spielberg fantasy, but please also see the wonderful low-tech 1960 TV production of PETER PAN.

A: Robin Williams, Dustin Hoffman, Julia Roberts, Bob Hoskins, Maggie Smith, Caroline Goodall

© COLUMBIA TRISTAR HOME VIDEO 70603

JOURNEY TO THE CENTER OF THE EARTH

D: Henry Levin 129 m

G | FAN CLD | 1959 | COLOR | Sex | Nud | Viol ✓ | Lang | AdSit

7 Jules Verne's fantasy adventure about a 19th-century expedition to the center of the earth is still imaginative and fun, but its sense of innocence, especially with today's sophisticated audiences, makes it most attractive to children and fanciful adults. A scientist and his small party descend into the earth's bowels. Along the way they encounter dangerous giant reptiles, a beautiful quartz cavern, the lost city of Atlantis, a treacherous and traitorous count and other adventures. High production values and good special effects.

A: James Mason, Pat Boone, Arlene Dahl, Diane Baker, Peter Ronsen, Thayer David

© FOXVIDEO 1248

JUNGLE BOOK, THE

D: Zoltan Korda 106 m

NR | FAN CLD | 1942 | COLOR | Sex | Nud | Viol ✓ | Lang | AdSit

8 This is Rudyard Kipling's classic fantasy of Mowgli, a native boy who became lost in a jungle in India and was raised by wolves and became friends with all the animals except his enemy, the great tiger. When he was grown, he returned to live with the humans of a local village. One day, he and a girl discovered a lost ancient city of great wealth but only take one gold coin when they leave. The girl's greedy father discovers the coin and tricks the village into casting Mowgli out so that he can follow the boy to the gold. Excellent for everyone, but it is best suited for older children and young teens.

A: Sabu, Joseph Calleia, John Qualen, Rosemary DeCamp, Ralph Byrd, Frank Puglia

© VIDEO TREASURES BV1936

LAND THAT TIME FORGOT, THE

D: Kevin Connor 90 m

PG | FAN | 1975 | COLOR | Sex | Nud | Viol | Lang | AdSit

6 Lightweight production of Edgar Rice Burroughs's (Tarzan) adventure story set in 1918. A group of Germans from a WWI submarine and some American survivors of a sunk Allied ship, who had also been aboard the sub, discover a lost and secret prehistoric land in South America that is still dominated by dinosaurs. This is a pretty good adventure story for young people, but story line is pretty simple and the special effects are only mediocre at best.

A: Doug McClure, Susan Penhaligon, John McEnery

© LIVE HOME VIDEO VA3027

METEOR MAN, THE

D: Robert Townsend 99 m

PG | FAN COM | 1994 | COLOR | Sex | Nud | Viol ✓ | Lang | AdSit

6 Silly and farcical. Robert Townsend is a mild-mannered school teacher in a gang-terrorized neighborhood of Washington DC. His father wants to stand up to the gang but Townsend (and nearly everyone else) just wants to hide. That is until Townsend is struck by a magic green meteor which transforms him into Meteor Man, giving him the power to deflect lots and lots of bullets or catch them in his teeth, fly (even though he's afraid of heights), beat up bad guys and understand his dog speak to him. Even though the film lacks a sharp focus, it is so good natured that most will have fun, particularly black kids. Lots of painless-type violence.

A: Robert Townsend, Marla Gibbs, Eddie Griffin, Robert Guillaume, James Earl Jones, Roy Fegan

Distributed By MGM/UA Home Video M903022

MIRACLE ON 34TH STREET

D: George Seaton 97 m

NR | FAN CLD | 1947 | B&W | Sex | Nud | Viol | Lang | AdSit

10 Positively perfect holiday treat! A cynical mother and boss at Macy's Department Store (O'Hara) employs an old man with a grey beard (Gwenn) to work as Santa during the holidays. He claims to be the real thing and many others, including O'Hara's daughter (Wood), begin to believe that he is real. Mom, however, thinks he's crazy and he is put on trial to prove that he is, in fact, Kris Kringle or get sent away. This heartwarming mixture of fantasy and comedy is delightful for the whole family. Oscar winner for Best Supporting Actor, Screenplay and Original Story. Also available in a colorized version. You will believe!

A: Maureen O'Hara, John Payne, Edmund Gwenn, Gene Lockhart, Natalie Wood, William Frawley

© FOXVIDEO 1072

NIGHTMARE BEFORE CHRISTMAS, THE

D: Tim Burton — 76 m

SEPT | FAN CLD | 1993 | COLOR

8 Wonderfully bizarre. Welcome to a land where each holiday has its own town. Jack Skellington is the Pumpkin King of freakish Halloween Town. He is the master of all things in his domain, but has become bored with it. He longs for something more and thinks he has found it when he discovers Christmas Town. The answer for him is simple, he will kidnap Santa Claus and take his place. Even though his Frankenstein-like rag doll girlfriend Sally cautions against it, Jack proceeds with his plan to make Christmas his too. Don't expect a typical Christmas tale. Expect something very different. Wonderful stop-action puppet animation flows as smoothly as real life and was Oscar-nominated.

Sex / Nud / Viol / Lang / AdSit

A:

© TOUCHSTONE HOME VIDEO 2236

WIZARD OF OZ, THE

D: Victor Fleming — 119 m

G | FAN CLD MUS | 1939 | B&W

10 This is MGM's ultimate classic children's film that is presented each year on television to a whole new audience, plus an old one that keeps coming back to re-live it. This is a wonderful fantasy in which a young girl visits a wondrous and mysterious fantasy land, and there discovers that things aren't always better somewhere else. This particular video version is a special edition which contains 17 minutes of extra footage which were edited out of the original, plus the original theatrical promotional trailer with Buddy Epson (who was the original Tin Man) performing and Judy Garland receiving an Oscar.

Sex / Nud / Viol / Lang / AdSit

***A:* Judy Garland, Jack Haley, Ray Bolger, Bert Lahr, Billie Burke, Margaret Hamilton**

Distributed By MGM/UA Home Video M301656

RED BALLOON, THE

D: Albert Lamorisse — 34 m

FAN CLD FOR | 1956 | COLOR

10 A brilliant children's treasure! While there is no dialogue in this classic fantasy, it remains one of the most charming films of all time. In this engaging story, a young boy (Lamorisse) makes friends with a red balloon, and it follows him all around Paris. It goes to school with him. It even waits for him outside his window when he is in his room. The film is so visually flawless that the story is crystal clear - it needs no dialogue. A winner for both children and adults alike with a sparkling musical score. Winner of an Academy Award for Best Original Screenplay. Unequaled!

Sex / Nud / Viol / Lang / AdSit

***A:* Pascal Lamorisse, Georges Seliler**

© NEW LINE HOME VIDEO 6001

WONDERFUL WORLD OF THE BROTHERS GRIM, THE

D: Henry Levin, George Pal — 128 m

NR | FAN CLD MUS | 1962 | COLOR

6 Fanciful depiction of the lives of the famous story-telling brothers, which combines a telling of their life stories with three of their fairy tales: "The Dancing Princess," in which a princess finds her true love in a common woodsman; "The Cobbler and the Elves," in which an overworked shoemaker receives overnight assistance from some helpful elves (George Pal's famous Puppetoons); and, "The Singing Bone," where a pompous and cowardly knight relies upon his lowly servant to fight a fire-breathing dragon.

Sex / Nud / Viol / Lang / AdSit

***A:* Laurence Harvey, Claire Bloom, Jim Backus, Yvette Mimieux, Buddy Hackett, Barbara Eden**

Distributed By MGM/UA Home Video M200693

RETURN OF THE KING, THE

D: Jules Bass — 98 m

NR | FAN | 1979 | COLOR

6 J.R.R. Tolkein's ever-popular tale about an epic battle between good and evil is greatly diminished in scope and scale. For the uninitiated, this conclusion to the story begun in THE HOBBIT may be slightly confusing. For those already initiated to the grand story, much has been removed from it to get the story on film. Consequently, not many viewers will be totally satisfied. However, it is still worthy of watching. Both the initiated and in-initiated will find something that they will find to be of interest. For a grittier version check out LORD OF THE RINGS.

Sex / Nud / ◢ Viol / Lang / ◢ AdSit

A:

© WARNER HOME VIDEO 843

FAMILY

TUCK EVERLASTING

D: Frederick King Keller — 90 m

NR | FAN CLD | 1981 | COLOR

8 Enchanting, entertaining and intelligent fantasy that the whole family can enjoy. One day, while walking through the woods, Young Whynnie discovers the Tuck family. The Tucks feel no pain, never grow old and will never die. The Tucks come to like and eventually trust her enough to reveal to her their secret. This is a charming story that is not at all patronizing to kids and is a rewarding experience for the whole family. The film was adapted from Natalie Babbitt's novel of the same title.

Sex / Nud / Viol / Lang / AdSit

***A:* Margaret Chamberlain, Paul Flessa, Fred A. Keller, James McGuire, Sonia Raimi, Bruce D'Auria**

© LIVE HOME VIDEO VA4228

ASHES AND DIAMONDS

D: Andrzej Wajda — 105 m

NR | FOR DMA WAR | 1958 | B&W

9 An extremely powerful and influential Polish film. WWII has just ended and a new peace dominated by Russian communists is beginning. Three young Poles, former members of the resistance movement, have just killed three Polish workers, believing that the communist party chief is among them. One of the assassins realizes that their target was in fact not killed. Spending the night at a hotel, the war-hardened young man has an affair with a pretty and tender barmaid. For the first time, he feels the war is over and begins to doubt his continuing role as a bitter political fanatic and soldier. Made a star of Cybulski and is considered the last in a trilogy of war films from director Wajda. Subtitles.

Sex / Nud / ◢ Viol / Lang / ■ AdSit

***A:* Zbigniew Cybulski, Eva Krzyzewska, Adam Pawlikowski, Waclaw Zastrzezynski**

© HOME VISION ASH 020

TWICE UPON A TIME

D: John Korty, Charles Swenson — 75 m

PG | FAN CLD | 1983 | COLOR

8 Imaginative and captivating cartoon fable that is only marginally for young kids. It is much too fast-paced, complex and filled with word-play for the average youngster and is more suited to older children, teenagers and fanciful adults. That is why this deserving video did not get wide theatrical release, even though it was produced by George Lucas. An almost indescribable bunch of characters sets out to save the world from the greedy owner of the Murkworks Nightmare Factory and to prevent him from blanketing the world with bad dreams. Funny and enjoyable.

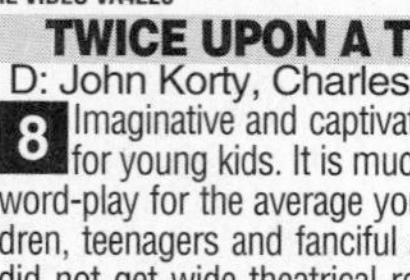

Sex / Nud / Viol / Lang / AdSit

A:

© WARNER HOME VIDEO 20012

BICYCLE THIEF, THE

D: Vittorio De Sica — 90 m

NR | FOR DMA | 1948 | B&W

9 A simple, honest and heart-grippingly tragic story that is as powerful today as when it was released. Immediately after World War II, in an unemployment-plagued Italy, an impoverished man has his bicycle stolen. It is not just a bicycle, it is the thing upon which his job and his very survival depends. He and his small son spend a week searching to find it. The father is so panic-stricken that he steals a bicycle, but he is caught and humiliated in front of his son. Compelling, very realistic and an all time classic. It won a special Oscar for Best Foreign Film before there even was a permanent category.

Sex / Nud / Viol / Lang / ◢ AdSit

***A:* Lamberto Maggiorani, Lianelle Carell, Enzo Staiola, Elena Altieri**

© CORINTH FILMS 1236

WITCHES, THE

D: Nicolas Roeg — 92 m

PG | FAN CLD | 1990 | COLOR

9 Terrific spooky story for kids, but not under 8 or so. Luke is a 9-year-old boy whose loving grandmother tells him bedtime stories and always warns him of the dangers of witches (they like to kill little children). However, he and his grandmother happen to stay at a hotel where there is also a conference of witches and, it seems, the head witch (Huston) has created a magic potion that will turn all the children in England into mice. Then, she spots Luke. He escapes from her, but not before she turns him into a mouse. Now it is up to Luke to save himself and all the other children. That's not an easy job for a mouse.

Sex / Nud / Viol / Lang / AdSit

***A:* Jasen Fisher, Mai Zetterling, Anjelica Huston, Rowan Atkinson, Bill Paterson, Brenda Blethyn**

© WARNER HOME VIDEO 671

BLACK AND WHITE IN COLOR

D: Jean-Jacques Annaud — 90 m

PG | FOR COM | 1976 | COLOR

8 This is a very funny film and was the surprise winner in 1976 of the Oscar for Best Foreign Film over the more highly-touted COUSINE, COUSINE and SEVEN BEAUTIES. It is the whimsical story of two remote European settlements in Africa, one German and one French, which have been existing peacefully side-by-side for years. But with the outset of WWI, the French decide it is their duty to attack the Germans. So one of them recruits a bunch of surrounding natives and equips them with shoes, bayonets and French names for a battle which falters pitifully. Biting satire. Subtitles.

Sex / ◢ Nud / ◢ Viol / ◢ Lang / AdSit

***A:* Jean Carmet, Jacques Spiesser, Catherine Rouvel**

© WARNER HOME VIDEO 803

HIDDEN FORTRESS, THE

D: Akira Kurosawa 139 m

NR | FOR ACT COM | 1958 | B&W

9 George Lucas acknowledges that this film, from the Japanese master filmmaker Akira Kurosawa, was the inspiration for his mega-smash hit STAR WARS. In it, a haughty young princess, a fortune in gold, a fugitive general and two bumbling and comic mercenary soldiers make a treacherous journey through enemy territory to get her back to her homeland. This one is so much fun you may even forget that its a foreign film. Subtitles.

Sex / Nud / Viol / Lang / AdSit

A: Toshiro Mifune, Misa Uehara, Minoru Chiaki, Kimatare Fugiwara, Susumu Fujita, Takashi Shimura

© HOME VISION HID 030

KID FOR TWO FARTHINGS, A

D: Carol Reed 96 m

NR | FOR COM | 1954 | COLOR

8 Delightful sentimental story from England. Little Joe has been told stories by the tailor in his poor London neighborhood of a magical unicorn with powers to grant wishes. One day the boy discovers a goat with only one horn and is convinced that he has discovered the magical unicorn, even though everyone else sees a one-horned goat. Still, the tailor does suddenly get the steam press he's always wanted, and the muscleman finally gets the money he needs to marry Sonia, so she has had her wish granted too. Sure, there is a logical explanation for all that's happened...but there is still that goat to explain.

Sex / Nud / Viol / Lang / AdSit

A: Celia Johnson, Diana Dors, David Kassoff, Joe Robinson, Jonathan Ashmore, Brenda De Banzie

© HOME VISION KID 01

M

D: Fritz Lang 99 m

NR | FOR SUS CRM | 1931 | B&W

9 Unnerving suspense! The terrifying story of a psychotic murderer who kills only children. The only clue available is a tune that the murderer incessantly whistles. The German police fail, despite a massive effort, to find the murderer. The turmoil so upsets the underworld that it mobilizes its own resources to locate and punish the killer. Based on a real-life Dusseldorf murderer, Lorre's film debut still carries contemporary impact. The use of imaginative props and film techniques capture the essence of outrage and fright that was felt throughout Berlin. Excellent. Subtitles.

Sex / Nud / Viol / Lang / AdSit

A: Peter Lorre, Otto Wernicke, Gustav Grundgens, Ellen Widmann, Inge Landgut

© BARR ENTERTAINMENT VIDEO HM0105

MON ONCLE

D: Jacques Tati 110 m

NR | FOR COM | 1958 | COLOR

7 Outrageous foreign comedy farce that pokes fun at all things "modern." Mr. Hulot's brother-in-law's (Zola) home is a riotous mix of gadgets and mechanization. On the other hand, the quiet and unassuming Hulot (Tati) has a simple home. Hulot's adoring nephew (Bercort) prefers the simpler life, and it is from his perspective that the story is told. Included in his father's house is a grotesque fish fountain and some of the ugliest, most twisted furniture you've ever seen anywhere. The film is an ongoing series of sight gags with almost no dialogue. Best Foreign Picture Oscar. Subtitles.

Sex / Nud / Viol / Lang / AdSit

A: Jacques Tati, Jean-Pierre Zola, Adrienne Servantie, Alain Bercourt

© HOME VISION ONC 020

MR. HULOT'S HOLIDAY

D: Jacques Tati 86 m

NR | FOR COM | 1953 | COLOR

9 Wonderfully light-hearted comic masterpiece about a bumbling but friendly and well-meaning man who makes a trip to a very proper French seaside resort and proceeds to destroy it. Nearly plotless, the wonderfully eccentric Mr. Hulot simply causes one catastrophe after another. Hilarious. It has virtually no dialogue at all and is a throw-back to the slapstick of the silent era. Grand Prize winner at Cannes.

Sex / Nud / Viol / Lang / AdSit

A: Jacques Tati, Nathalie Pascaud, Louis Parrault, Michelle Rolla, Raymond Carl

© HOME VISION HUL 030

MY FATHER'S GLORY

D: Yves Robert 110 m

G | FOR DMA | 1991 | COLOR

9 Very highly acclaimed literary triumph. It is the richly painted portrait of the memories of author and filmmaker Marcel Pagnol's childhood in rural France at the turn of the 20th-century. It is primarily the story of a summer trip that he took, along with his parents, where even the most commonplace of situations become fascinating to a precocious boy totally involved in the rural lifestyle. This marvelous experience was followed by the equally fascinating MY MOTHER'S CASTLE. In French with subtitles.

Sex / Nud / Viol / Lang / AdSit

A: Philippe Caubere, Nathalie Roussel, Julian Ciamaca, Therese Liotard, Didier Pain

© ORION PICTURES CORPORATION 5066

RHAPSODY IN AUGUST

D: Akira Kurosawa 98 m

PG | FOR DMA | 1991 | COLOR

6 Famed Japanese filmmaker Akira Kurosawa's morality play that comments both upon the destructive nature of war, even years after it is over. An old woman, living outside of Nagasaki, has her grandchildren over for the summer while their parents are in Hawaii to visit the family of her wealthy brother who is now near death. The children discover for the first time that their grandfather was killed in the atomic bomb blast and at first resent their parents for going to America. The old woman chastises them for blaming Americans and instead blames war itself. Kurosawa's approach is very simplistic and seems more directed toward young people, but should not be lost.

Sex / Nud / Viol / Lang / AdSit

A: Sachiko Murase, Hidetaka Yoshioka, Tomoko Onatakara, mie Suzuki, Mitsunori Isaki, Richard Gere

© ORION PICTURES CORPORATION 5062

SEVEN SAMURAI, THE

D: Akira Kurosawa 208 m

NR | FOR ACT | 1955 | B&W

8 This was a very highly influential Japanese film which was repackaged for America and became the very popular Western THE MAGNIFICENT SEVEN. However, here a 17th-century samurai master agrees to help defend a pitiful small village against repeated attacks by bandits. To do it, he assembles a team of six other samurai masters. They will defend the town and, more importantly, train the townspeople to defend themselves. A rousing and thrilling battle climax winds up this 3+ hour epic, and also completes the process of building several carefully-drawn characters. Excellent. Subtitles.

Sex / Nud / Viol / Lang / AdSit

A: Takashi Shimura, Toshiro Mifune, Yoshi Inaba, Seiji Miyaguchi, Minoru Chiaki, Daisuke Kato

© HOME VISION SEV 080

SHOOT THE PIANO PLAYER

D: Francois Truffaut 84 m

NR | FOR DMA | 1960 | B&W

7 Film fans only, this is an interesting mixed bag of offbeat and colorful characters. A brilliant concert pianist (Aznavour) is haunted by his wife's suicide and begins a rapid spiral downward. Soon he finds himself playing to a sleazy crowd at a cheap Parisian cafe, where he is being pressured to get his life together by his new girlfriend, a waitress at the cafe. He gets into a fight with the bartender over her. And, his brother gets involved with the gangsters that frequent the place. This is an uncompromising New Wave film that takes the viewer across the emotional spectrum from dark comedy to tragedy. Subtitles.

Sex / Nud / Viol / Lang / AdSit

A: Charles Aznavour, Marie Dubois, Nicole Berger, Michele Mercier

© HOME VISION SHO 100

UMBERTO D.

D: Vittorio De Sica 89 m

NR | FOR DMA | 1955 | B&W

10 A powerful, brilliant Italian tearjerker. Painful because of the subject matter which is the sad truth of the unfairness of old age and the way society treats its elderly. Surviving only on a meager government pension, the retired Umberto (Battisi) is forced out on the Roman streets with only his memories and his trusted dog for companionship. His struggle to maintain his dignity and support himself and his dog, the only one who loves him, is heartrending. This is a potent masterpiece that is in no way diminished with time. Many believe this to be De Sica's most important work. Subtitles.

Sex / Nud / Viol / Lang / AdSit

A: Carlo Battisi, Maria Pia Casilio, Lina Genneri

© NEW LINE HOME VIDEO 6131

WAGES OF FEAR, THE

D: Henri-Georges Clouzot 148 m

NR | FOR SUS | 1953 | B&W

8 A harrowing French classic set in South America. After an oil well explodes into a huge unquenchable fire, four men, bored and broke, are hired to risk their lives driving trucks loaded with the extremely volatile explosive nitroglycerine. The obvious risks are greatly compounded because the trucks must be driven over miles of bumpy, twisting mountain roads. But, the film also explores the characters of the four individuals who would take such huge chances. Very well done and highly acclaimed. In French - with subtitles. There was an OK remake done in English in 1977 as SORCERER.

Sex / Nud / Viol / Lang / AdSit

A: Yves Montand, Charles Vanel, Vera Clouzot, Peter Van Eyck, Folco Lulli, William Tubbs

© HOME VISION WAG 040

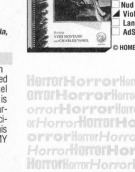

13 GHOSTS

D: William Castle — 88 m

NR | HOR | 1960 | B&W

Sex / Nud / ✔ Viol / Lang / ✔ AdSit

6 An enjoyable family spookfest. A normal ordinary family - a mom, a dad and two kids - inherits an old house which comes equipped with a spooky housekeeper (who may also be a witch), a secret fortune (hidden somewhere inside) and 13 ghosts. Viewers of the original theater version were issued special glasses which allowed them to see the ghosts in 3D. Light-hearted fun, with some laughs and some scares, too.

A: Charles Herbert, Donald Woods, Martin Milner, Rosemary DeCamp, Jo Morrow, Margaret Hamilton

© COLUMBIA TRISTAR HOME VIDEO 60488

ABOMINABLE DR. PHIBES, THE

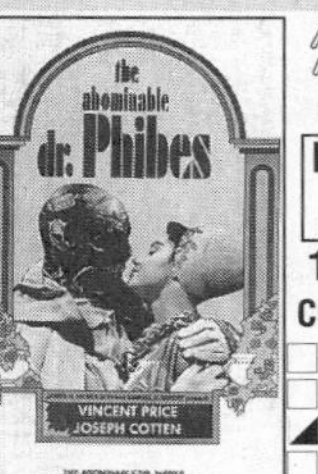

D: Robert Fuest — 90 m

NR | HOR | 1971 | COLOR

Sex / Nud / ✔ Viol / Lang / AdSit

7 Dr. Phibes and his wife are in a terrible car accident about 1929. He has survived even though he is horribly disfigured. However, his wife has died during surgery. The crazed Dr. Phibes is incensed that the doctors let his wife die and has stalked and tormented them. Now, he has decided that he will to get even with them by inflicting upon his nine victims the same ten plagues from the Old Testament which God had visited upon the Egyptian Pharaoh Ramses. And, at the same time, he will search for a way to bring his beloved back to life. Filmed amid gothic backdrops, this is a stylish picture that is reminiscent of 1930s horror flicks. Price is at his campy best.

A: Vincent Price, Joseph Cotten, Hugh Griffith, Terry-Thomas, Virginia North

© LIVE HOME VIDEO 3029

BLOB, THE

D: Irvin Yeaworth, Jr. — 82 m

NR | HOR SF | 1958 | COLOR

Sex / Nud / Viol / Lang / AdSit

6 This is a campy science fiction/horror "classic" from the '50s genre of cheap horror movies. It is mostly interesting for having been Steve McQueen's first starring role and because the theme song, "Beware the Blob, It Leaps, and Creeps, and Leaps," was written by Burt Bacharach and Hal David. The fairly silly plot has Steve as a teenager, fighting the disbelief of his folks and the townsfolk about a big glob of jello from outer space that oozes into, onto and eats everything - and continues to grow. Remade in 1988 with "real" special effects.

A: Steve McQueen, Aneta Corseaut, Olin Howlin, Earl Rowe

© GOODTIMES 8146

BRIDE OF FRANKENSTEIN, THE

D: James Whale — 75 m

NR | HOR FAN | 1935 | B&W

Sex / Nud / Viol / Lang / AdSit

10 A thoroughly delightful horror movie that picks up where FRANKENSTEIN left off. Chilling, sinister and wicked, this masterpiece from director Whale expertly mixes all of the expected horror elements with emotion, humor and elegance, plus healthy doses of wit. The corrupt Dr. Praetorius (Thesiger) forces Dr. Frankenstein (Clive) into making a female companion for the lonely monster (Karloff), who has been terrorizing the countryside looking for a friend. This extremely well-made sequel was immensely popular. A true classic.

A: Boris Karloff, Elsa Lanchester, Colin Clive, Valerie Hobson, Ernest Thesiger, Una O'Connor

© MCA/UNIVERSAL HOME VIDEO, INC. 80115

CREATURE FROM THE BLACK LAGOON

D: Jack Arnold — 79 m

NR | HOR | 1954 | B&W

Sex / Nud / Viol / Lang / AdSit

7 Campy fun. Members of a scientific expedition in the Amazon run into a strange fish/man creature. The scientists drug and capture him. However, while he is in captivity, he develops the hots for female archaeologist Julia Adams. Later, when he escapes, he captures her and takes her with him back to the swamp. Her fellow scientist Richard Carlson immediately launches a search to get her back. This is the prototypical '50s monster movie and has become high-camp for seasoned viewers, but it also provides some excitement for the uninitiated - particularly younger viewers.

A: Richard Carlson, Julie Adams, Richard Denning, Antonio Moreno, Whit Bissell, Nestor Paiva

© MCA/UNIVERSAL HOME VIDEO, INC. 66018

CREEPING FLESH, THE

D: Freddie Francis — 94 m

PG | HOR | 1972 | COLOR

Sex / Nud / ✔ Viol / Lang / ✔ AdSit

7 A scientist, trying to create a serum from the blood of evil men to counteract insanity, is injecting the serum into his daughter, whose mother had been insane. However, she has become insane, too, and is placed in her uncle's asylum. Her father continues his experiments, this time on an ancient skeleton that grows flesh when touched with water and he accidentally brings back to life a long dormant evil spirit. He is slowly goes insane himself, and as he does, the monster is turned loose on the world. This is an old-fashioned monster thriller, with a good cast, that will run a few icy chills up and down your spine.

A: Peter Cushing, Christopher Lee, Lorna Hellbron, George Benson, Kenneth J. Warren

© COLUMBIA TRISTAR HOME VIDEO VH10147

DEVIL BATS

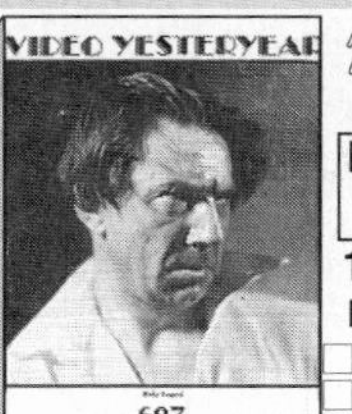

D: Jean Yarbrough — 68 m

NR | HOR | 1942 | B&W

Sex / Nud / Viol / Lang / ✔ AdSit

6 Entertaining Bela Lugosi horror flick. Bela is, to all appearances, an kindly village doctor but, in reality, he is a true mad scientist. Working in his laboratory at home, he has created an army of blood-sucking killer bats which he calls "my friends", and he has trained them to be directed to their quarry by an attraction for a special perfume. One of Lugosi's most notorious pictures.

A: Bela Lugosi, Suzanne Kaaren, Dave O'Brien

© VIDEO YESTERYEAR 697

DEVIL DOLL, THE

D: Tod Browning — 798 m

NR | HOR | 1936 | B&W

Sex / Nud / Viol / Lang / ✔ AdSit

7 Imaginative, macabre and bizarre. Barrymore is a wrongfully imprisoned convict who escapes from Devil's Island. He returns home both to redeem his name and to seek revenge upon the three people who have wronged him. Upon arrival, he seeks out the wife of a dead mad-scientist whom he had befriended. That scientist had concocted a shrinking potion. Together the two shrink humans to doll size and force them to become tiny assassins. He dresses up as a kindly old lady running a toy store so that he can send them on their missions. Spooky. Excellent special effects.

A: Lionel Barrymore, Maureen O'Sullivan, Frank Lawton, Henry B. Walthall, Robert Greig, Lucy Beaumont

Distributed By MGM/UA Home Video 600904

DOCTOR PHIBES RISES AGAIN

D: Robert Fuest — 89 m

PG | HOR | 1972 | COLOR

Sex / Nud / ✔ Viol / Lang / AdSit

7 This is a terror flick in the innocent '60s tradition. It brings back the Dr. Phibes character from THE ABOMINABLE DR. PHIBES. Mad Dr. Phibes (Price, at his campy best) goes off to an Egyptian tomb in search of a magic potion - the elixir of life - which will bring his dead wife back to life. But he is not alone. A wealthy man named Biederbeck wants it, too. So to gain possession of the stuff, and to assure it is he who wins, Phibes gradually kills off all the members of the other side except Biederbeck. Soon it is a personal battle and both men are determined to win. Entertaining.

A: Vincent Price, Robert Quarry, Hugh Griffith, Valli Kemp, Peter Cushing, Terry-Thomas

© LIVE HOME VIDEO VA4349

DOCTOR X

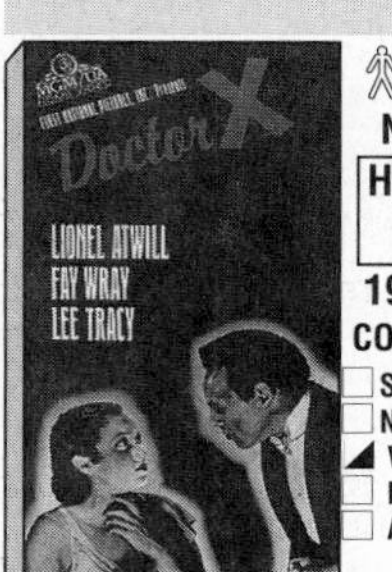

D: Michael Curtiz — 77 m

NR | HOR | 1932 | COLOR

Sex / Nud / ✔ Viol / Lang / AdSit

6 One of filmdom's earliest efforts to scare. Weird mystery about a "full moon" strangler, who police believe is the strange Doctor X (Atwill). An investigative reporter (Tracy) follows a trail of bodies to his medical college where the one-armed mad scientist is doing research on cannibalism and synthetic flesh. This is a vintage horror piece that is very dated but nonetheless worthy viewing for horror fans. It is also technically interesting because it was done in a very innovative two-color process and the makeup was done by Max Factor himself.

A: Lionel Atwill, Preston Foster, Fay Wray, Lee Tracy, Mae Busch

Distributed By MGM/UA Home Video 601159

DRACULA

D: Tod Browning — 75 m

NR | HOR SUS | 1931 | B&W

✔ Sex / Nud / ✔ Viol / Lang / ✔ AdSit

9 Turn all the lights out and gather around the soft glow of the TV with a close friend. This is the movie that defined a whole genre for generations. The black and white nature and early production techniques only add to the creepy atmosphere. Bela Lugosi is brilliant and unforgettable as the strange and hypnotic Transylvanian count who has moved to London to find his true love, cast his evil spell and drink his fill. Oldies fans should also see the original eerie silent version from Germany: NOSFERATU. Others might seek out the stylish and modern BRAM STOKER'S DRACULA.

A: Bela Lugosi, David Manners, Helen Chandler, Dwight Frye, Edward Van Sloan, Herbert Bunston

© MCA/UNIVERSAL HOME VIDEO, INC. 81123

DRACULA'S DAUGHTER

D: Lambert Hillyer — 81 m

NR | HOR SUS | 1936

Sex / Nud / Viol / Lang / AdSit

8 Moody sequel to Lugossi's classic. The very beautiful and mysterious Countess Marya Zaleska (Gloria Holden) suddenly appears in London, just as numerous people are found seemingly drained of blood. She is the unhappy and troubled daughter of Dracula and has been desperately trying to break her accursed addiction to blood. Now she seeks comfort from psychiatrist Dr. Garth (Otto Kruger) and she quickly falls in love with him, even though he is engaged. So she seeks to win him away from his fiancee by placing a curse upon the poor girl. Good acting and an intelligent and logical script have made this a perennial favorite.

A: Otto Kruger, Gloria Holden, Marguerite Churchill, Irving Pichel, Edward Van Sloan, Nan Grey

© MCA/UNIVERSAL HOME VIDEO, INC. 80610

DR. JEKYLL AND MR. HYDE

D: John S. Robertson 63 m

NR | HOR DMA | 1920 | B&W

7 This silent version is only one of numerous silent and sound versions of this classic Robert Louis Stevenson story, but it is still considered to be among the best of all the versions ever done, including sound. John Barrymore was superb as the adventurous doctor whose experiments could transform him into the evil Mr. Hyde. Barrymore was very effective in the role and he prided himself on only contorting his face and body to change characters, rather than by the use of makeup. You be the judge.

Sex / Nud / Viol / Lang / ✓ AdSit

A: John Barrymore, Martha Mansfield, Brandon Hurst, Nita Naldi, Charles Lane, Louis Wolheim

© REPUBLIC PICTURES HOME VIDEO 1068

DR. JEKYLL AND MR. HYDE

D: Victor Fleming 113 m

G | HOR DMA | 1941 | B&W

7 This time around, with Tracy, more emphasis is placed upon the psychological elements of the story - a good doctor who becomes a murdering Mr. Hyde, and the threat to his relationship with his fiancee (Lana Turner) because of his relationship with a prostitute (Ingrid Bergman). Great acting by everyone, particularly Bergman, but it still does not surpass the production with Fredric March in 1932.

Sex / Nud / Viol / Lang / ✓ AdSit

A: Spencer Tracy, Ingrid Bergman, Lana Turner, Donald Crisp, Ian Hunter, Barton MacLane

Distributed By MGM/UA Home Video M300651

FRANKENSTEIN

D: James Whale 71 m

NR | HOR FAN | 1931 | B&W

10 A true Hollywood classic and a film which defined a whole genre for all time. In spite of its antiquated production techniques (including having no score), this is still a quite moving depiction of Mary Shelley's novel favorite. Boris Karloff provides a masterly performance (he never mutters a word) as the pathetic man-made man, created from parts of corpses and brought to life only to be scorned by men. When the mad Dr. Frankenstein cannot control his creation, the townspeople attack the pitiable, lonely creature. Excellent. Followed by BRIDE OF FRANKENSTEIN.

Sex / Nud / ✓ Viol / Lang / AdSit

A: Boris Karloff, Colin Clive, Mae Clarke, John Boles, Edward Van Sloan, Dwight Frye

© MCA/UNIVERSAL HOME VIDEO, INC. 55004

FRANKENSTEIN MEETS THE WOLFMAN

D: Roy William Neill 73 m

NR | HOR | 1943 | B&W

7 Two of Universal Studio's all-time favorite monsters meet face to face. A tormented Wolfman is disinterred and seeks out a doctor's help. He's looking either for a cure or to be put out of his misery. He is sent to gypsy Maria Ouspenskaya, who takes him to the village where Dr. Frankenstein once lived. The good doctor is dead - but his creation isn't. These two misfits prefer to fight rather than to be friends and the countryside begins to accumulate corpses. Fast-paced and exciting. Eerie atmosphere. Good fun.

Sex / Nud / ✓ Viol / Lang / AdSit

A: Lon Chaney, Jr., Patric Knowles, Bela Lugosi, Ilona Massey, Maria Ouspenskaya, Lionel Atwill

© MCA/UNIVERSAL HOME VIDEO, INC. 80422

HOUSE OF WAX

D: Andre De Toth 88 m

PG | HOR | 1953 | COLOR

8 Vincent Price is a sculptor of wax, but he disappears after he loses a hand in a fire that his evil partner set to the wax museum that they had built together, destroying it. When he reappears, he opens a new museum with marvelous and even more life-like figures inside. Everyone praises the new works. Only Phyllis Kirk questions it, and instead thinks... murder. How has he populated his new museum with such lifelike figures when his hands are so crippled? By using real humans that he has dipped in wax. Originally shown in 3-D, but it works just as well without the gimmick.

Sex / Nud / Viol / Lang / ✓ AdSit

A: Vincent Price, Phyllis Kirk, Carolyn Jones, Paul Cavanagh, Charles Bronson

© WARNER HOME VIDEO 11054

I WAS A TEENAGE WEREWOLF

D: Gene Fowler, Jr. 75 m

NR | HOR | 1957 | B&W

6 So bad it's good. It is also most notable because it was Michael Landon's screen debut. In it, he plays Tony, a high-school kid with a tendency to explode into raving fits of violence. He is being "treated" by his doctor for his aggressive behavior but things are only getting worse. Finally Tony becomes fully transformed and the reason for his rampage becomes obvious. He is a werewolf. This film was very popular with teenagers of the day, particularly at drive-in movies. Now it is a big cult film.

Sex / Nud / ✓ Viol / Lang / ✓ AdSit

A: Michael Landon, Yvonne Lime, Whit Bissell, Vladimir Sokoloff, Guy Williams

© COLUMBIA TRISTAR HOME VIDEO 60906

MARK OF THE VAMPIRE

D: Tod Browning 61 m

NR | HOR | 1935 | B&W

7 They're coming to suck your blood! Residents of a small town are terrorized by a band of blood-sucking vampires. Count Mora (Lugosi) and his sultry and villainous daughter (Borland) are after the residents of an old estate. The foolish townsfolk are disbelievers and try on their own to stop the creatures of the night, but it is only the local vampire expert (Barrymore) who can put an end to their reign of terror. This well-done flick is actually a remake of the silent movie, LONDON AFTER MIDNIGHT.

Sex / Nud / ✓ Viol / Lang / ✓ AdSit

A: Lionel Barrymore, Bela Lugosi, Elizabeth Allan, Lionel Atwill, Carol Borland, Jean Hersholt

Distributed By MGM/UA Home Video M600905

MUMMY, THE

D: Karl Freund 72 m

NR | HOR SUS | 1932 | B&W

9 When archeologists read from a sacred book, against dire warnings to the contrary, they bring back to life a 3,700 year old Egyptian mummy. He was a high priest who had been embalmed alive for attempting to revive a sacrificed vestal virgin who he loved. Now, when he sees Zita Johann, he thinks she is his ancient princess reincarnated and is intent upon getting his dusty arms around her. Karloff is superb as the creepy old bag of bones. Director Freund relies more on atmospheric thrill than actual gore - which adds to the effectiveness and surrealistic air of this rather excellent classic.

Sex / Nud / ✓ Viol / Lang / ✓ AdSit

A: Boris Karloff, Zita Johann, David Manners, Arthur Byron, Edward Van Sloan, Bramwell Fletcher

© MCA/UNIVERSAL HOME VIDEO, INC. 80030

MUMMY'S HAND, THE

D: Christy Cabanne 70 m

NR | HOR | 1940 | B&W

6 Two carnival archaeologists are financed by a reluctant magician and his beautiful daughter on a trip to Egypt where they are to uncover the long lost tomb of the Princess Ananka. Their clues lead them to discover hidden passageways that lead them deep into the tomb, but the tomb is guarded by a 3000-year-old mummy being kept alive by a secret formula administered by a sinister high priest. The invaders are not welcome, however 3000 years is a long time and the Mummy does take a particular shine to the beautiful girl. A fair dose of thrills and chills, but also a few laughs.

Sex / Nud / ✓ Viol / Lang / AdSit

A: Dick Foran, Peggy Moran, Wallace Ford, Cecil Kellaway, Eduardo Ciannelli, George Zucco

© MCA/UNIVERSAL HOME VIDEO, INC. 80850

NIGHT STALKER, THE

D: Don Weis 98 m

NR | HOR SUS | 1971 | COLOR

8 Quite good and involving thriller with personality that was originally made for TV. It proved to be so successful that it launched a short-lived series of the same name. Darin McGavin plays a persistent wise-cracking reporter on the crime beat in Las Vegas. The city has recently been plagued by a series of grisly Jack-the-Ripper-like murders. McGavin hounds the city's establishment and keeps turning up new clues in his pursuit of the ghoulish vampirish killer. Extremely tight script with a good blending of believability, mystery, comedy, suspense and horror.

Sex / Nud / ✓ Viol / Lang / ✓ AdSit

A: Darren McGavin, Simon Oakland, Carol Lynley, Claude Akins, Ralph Meeker

© MCA/UNIVERSAL HOME VIDEO, INC. 80011

PIT AND THE PENDULUM, THE

D: Roger Corman 80 m

NR | HOR SUS | 1961 | COLOR

6 Edgar Allan Poe's short story inspired this low-budget thriller. Vincent Price is the son of the 16th-century Spanish Inquisition's most notorious torturer, who is tortured himself by his belief that he has buried his own wife alive. Price also now believes himself to actually be his father. When his wife's brother comes to investigate his sister's death, Price takes him to the pit and the pendulum - a room where a razor sharp pendulum moves ever lower and closer to its victim with each successive sweep. A little hokey in a few spots, still very well staged and acted. Guaranteed to put a chill up your spine.

Sex / Nud / ✓ Viol / Lang / ✓ AdSit

A: Vincent Price, John Kerr, Barbara Steele, Luana Anders, Anthony Carbone

© GOODTIMES 5-74043

SON OF DRACULA

D: Robert Siodmak 80 m

NR | HOR | 1943 | B&W

7 Convincing Hollywood chiller! Count Alucard (Lon Chaney) travels to the deep South and sweeps the lovely Louise Allbritton off her feet, taking her away from her smitten boyfriend (Paige). Her problem is that she doesn't really know just who the handsome Count Alucard is. No one does, but an upset Paige begins to unearth some clues - like spell Alucard backwards - and decides to get Allbritton away from the captivating count. However, it's too late because bow she likes blood, too. Great special effects and atmosphere that add to the thrills in this spooky vampire tale.

Sex / Nud / ✓ Viol / Lang / ✓ AdSit

A: Lon Chaney, Jr., Louise Allbritton, Robert Paige, Frank Craven, Evelyn Ankers, J. Edward Bromberg

© MCA/UNIVERSAL HOME VIDEO, INC. 80766

SON OF FRANKENSTEIN

D: Rowland V. Lee 99 m

NR | HOR | 1939 | B&W

☐ Sex ☐ Nud ☑ Viol ☐ Lang ☐ AdSit

7 Eerie, well-made third in the Frankenstein series. Now 25 years after the "death" of the Frankenstein monster, the son of Dr. Frankenstein returns to his ancestral castle where he meets Ygor. Ygor is a shepherd with a broken neck, having survived a hanging. Ygor urges the younger Frankenstein to revive the monster and to rehabilitate him, thus redeeming the family name. But when the monster is revived, a vengeful Ygor instead turns him loose on a killing spree in the countryside. Excellent and intelligent production, with a top-flight cast. Very atmospheric.

A: Bela Lugosi, Basil Rathbone, Boris Karloff, Lionel Atwill, Josephine Hutchinson, Donnie Dunagan

© MCA/UNIVERSAL HOME VIDEO, INC. 80764

THING, THE

D: Christian Nyby 80 m

NR | HOR SF SUS | 1951 | B&W

☐ Sex ☐ Nud ☑ Viol ☐ Lang ☑ AdSit

8 Very entertaining stereotypical '50s sci-fi/horror/monster flick. The theme is simple enough. A frozen blob is discovered near an army radar station in Arctic. When it is accidentally defrosted, it turns out to be an Alien creature that terrorizes the camp. However, this film is better than many of the genre of the period. What makes this film so special is the very high level of tension that is developed through the director's calculated creation of fear based upon the unknown (the alien is rarely actually seen) and the steady deliberate pacing. Exceptional acting helps to make this a very effective thriller.

A: Kenneth Tobey, James Arness, Margaret Sheridan, Robert Cornthwaite, Douglas Spencer, Dewey Martin

© TURNER HOME ENTERTAINMENT 2069

TOMB OF LIGEIA

D: Roger Corman 82 m

NR | HOR | 1964 | COLOR

☐ Sex ☐ Nud ☐ Viol ☐ Lang ☑ AdSit

7 Stylish and spooky film by Roger Corman. It is his last entry in a series of horror flicks that were inspired by the stories of Edgar Alan Poe. Vincent Price is obsessed with his dead wife and he marries a woman who looks like her. She, however, is understandably upset when she discovers that he sleeps in the crypt of his dead wife. The spirit of the dead woman returns first in the form of their cat and then in the new bride herself. This is a well-done spook film that was also shot on the sets left over from the filming of BECKET.

A: Vincent Price, Elizabeth Shepherd, John Westbrook, Richard Johnson, Derek Francis

© HBO VIDEO TVC3681

TWICE-TOLD TALES

D: Sidney Salkow 120 m

NR | HOR | 1963 | COLOR

☐ Sex ☐ Nud ☑ Viol ☐ Lang ☑ AdSit

6 Fright fans take notice. Vincent Price stars in three separate thrillers loosely based on stories from the famous 19th-century writer Nathaniel Hawthorne. The stories are: "Dr. Heidegger's Experiment" - a doctor brings his dead wife back to life and she then tells him a secret; "Rappaccini's Daughter" - who was raised on deadly herbs by her brilliant father and now just her touch is deadly; and "The House of the Seven Gables" - a man returns to the house to search for hidden treasure and is haunted by a vengeful spirit. Rich in atmosphere, with good characterizations from a talented cast.

A: Vincent Price, Sebastian Cabot, Brett Halsey, Joyce Taylor, Beverly Garland

Distributed By MGM/UA Home Video M601161

WHITE ZOMBIE

D: Victor Halperin 79 m

NR | HOR | 1932 | B&W

☐ Sex ☐ Nud ☑ Viol ☐ Lang ☐ AdSit

7 A campy, eerie, low-budget thriller from the early days of films. Early filming techniques and B&W photography enhance this spooky outing which is the granddaddy of all "modern-day" zombie flicks. Bela Lugosi is the white master of a misty Haitian sugar mill. He is a master sorcerer and has manned his plantation with an army of zombies, all under his spell. Another plantation owner who has been jilted, asks Lugosi to place pretty American Madge Bellamy under his powers to prevent her marriage to someone else. Lugosi agrees, however she can be still be awakened with a kiss. Mostly for film fans.

A: Bela Lugosi, Madge Bellamy, Joseph Cawthorn, Robert Frazer, John Harron, Clarence Muse

© REPUBLIC PICTURES HOME VIDEO 4529

WOLF MAN, THE

D: George Waggner 70 m

NR | HOR | 1941 | B&W

☐ Sex ☐ Nud ☑ Viol ☐ Lang ☑ AdSit

9 Wonderful horror film which led to many sequels and is one of the greatest of the classic horror films. Chaney (in a role he would play five more times) plays an American who returns to Wales and is bitten when he helps a beautiful girl who is being attacked by a wolf in the moors. However, this wolf is no ordinary wolf. A gypsy seer tells him that he has been bitten by a werewolf and now, with each rising of the new moon, he too is condemned to become a bloodthirsty werewolf. This is a well-produced and genuinely eerie film which is so engrossing that you will become totally lost within the myth.

A: Claude Rains, Lon Chaney, Jr., Bela Lugosi, Ralph Bellamy, Evelyn Ankers, Maria Ouspenskaya

© MCA/UNIVERSAL HOME VIDEO, INC. 80031

Musicals

1776

D: Peter H. Hunt 148 m

G | MUS | 1972 | COLOR

☐ Sex ☐ Nud ☐ Viol ☐ Lang ☐ AdSit

8 This is a witty and spirited musical retelling of how the United States was founded. This Pulitzer Prize-winning film is a re-creation of the hit Broadway musical stage play by Peter Stone, and it includes nearly all of the original cast. The primary focus is the signing of the Declaration of Independence and it includes the discussions and debate over who should write it - John Adams (Daniels) or Tom Jefferson (Howard). Ben Franklin (da Silva), however, wonders if the document will even be passed in such a divided congress. Entertaining and fun!

A: William Daniels, Howard da Silva, Ken Howard, Blythe Danner, Ronald Holgate, John Cullum

© COLUMBIA TRISTAR HOME VIDEO 60204

42ND STREET

D: Lloyd Bacon 90 m

NR | MUS | 1933 | B&W

☐ Sex ☐ Nud ☐ Viol ☐ Lang ☐ AdSit

8 The quintessential cliched musical. An ailing Broadway producer places all his marbles in one last major effort at success. But, just before opening, the lead dancer breaks her leg and the show must be saved by the young untested understudy, Ruby Keeler. Busby Berkeley dance extravaganza.

A: Dick Powell, Ruby Keeler, Ginger Rogers, Warner Baxter, Una Merkel

Distributed By MGM/UA Home Video M301672

AFFAIRS OF DOBIE GILLIS, THE

D: Don Weis 74 m

NR | MUS COM ROM | 1953 | B&W

☐ Sex ☐ Nud ☐ Viol ☐ Lang ☐ AdSit

7 Entertaining musical comedy that starred America's darling of the 50s, Debbie Reynolds. Starring with her was Bobby Van, who played Dobie Gillis, the archetypal girl-chasing college student. There are lots of big band numbers and dances stuffed in between the college shenanigans, plus Hans Conried as a sour professor who is the source of much of the kid's grief. This formula proved to be so successful that it went on to become a very popular TV series entitled, "The Many Loves of Dobie Gillis". That show featured a young actor, Bob Denver, who went on to become a huge TV star as Gilligan of "Gilligan's Island."

A: Debbie Reynolds, Bobby Van, Hans Conried, Lurene Tuttle, Bob Fosse

Distributed By MGM/UA Home Video M204545

AMERICAN IN PARIS, AN

D: Vincente Minnelli 115 m

NR | MUS ROM | 1951 | COLOR

☐ Sex ☐ Nud ☐ Viol ☐ Lang ☑ AdSit

9 Winner of six Oscars, including Best Picture. Lavish production musical with Gene Kelly's brilliant choreography and a George and Ira Gershwin score. Ex-GI Kelly stays in Paris after WWII to become an artist, only to fall in love with lovely Leslie Caron who is engaged to someone else. Plot is so-so but the music and dancing are marvelous. Center-piece is a 17-minute love song/ballet with Kelly and Caron.

A: Gene Kelly, Leslie Caron, Oscar Levant, Nina Foch, Georges Guetary

Distributed By MGM/UA Home Video M600006

ANNIE

D: John Huston 128 m

PG | MUS CLD | 1982 | COLOR

☐ Sex ☐ Nud ☐ Viol ☐ Lang ☐ AdSit

8 The comic strip story of the little orphan girl with the perpetual optimism comes to life. Annie (Quinn) is a red-haired orphan girl who dreams of life outside the orphanage, but her plans to escape are constantly foiled by Miss Hannigan, the drunken head mistress (Burnett). One day Annie is chosen to go to live for a short time with hugely rich Daddy Warbucks (Finney). They hit it off and days become weeks. But Miss Hannigan continues to plot to get her back. Big, splashy and over-produced, but it's still all there and it's fine family entertainment.

A: Albert Finney, Carol Burnett, Aileen Quinn, Bernadette Peters, Tim Curry, Geoffrey Holder

© COLUMBIA TRISTAR HOME VIDEO 60127

FAMILY

BABES IN ARMS

D: Busby Berkeley 94 m

NR | MUS | 1939 | B&W

6 This was the first teaming of Mickey Rooney and Judy Garland and it is the prototypical adolescent "let's put on a show" type of movie. Mickey is the son of vaudevillian parents. When they and others are hit by hard times, Mickey writes and directs his schoolmates in a show to raise some money for them. Pretty typical plot line has the local prima donna trying to steal the lead from Judy, but in the end Judy wins out and Mickey and Judy sing and dance up a storm. Lively jazz/swing score was Oscar-nominated, as was Rooney.

Sex / Nud / Viol / Lang / AdSit

A: Mickey Rooney, Judy Garland, Charles Winninger, Guy Kibbee, Margaret Hamilton

Distributed By MGM/UA Home Video M400585

BAND WAGON, THE

D: Vincente Minnelli 113 m

NR | MUS | 1953 | COLOR

9 This is one of Minnelli's best musicals. Astaire is a washed-up movie star who is persuaded by his friends to make a comeback in a Broadway musical. He joins the show, even though he has some serious misgivings. He is right - the show flops on the road. Undeterred, he raises the money he needs, takes over the production and makes it into a hit. Musical highlights: "Dancing in the Dark," "Shine on Your Shoes" and "That's Entertainment." If you like musicals, look in the actor's index under Astaire and the director's index under Minnelli. Between them, they almost own the genre.

Sex / Nud / Viol / Lang / AdSit

A: Fred Astaire, Cyd Charisse, Oscar Levant, Nanette Fabray, Jack Buchanan

Distributed By MGM/UA Home Video M202147

BLUE HAWAII

D: Norman Taurog 106 m

NR | MUS ROM | 1961 | COLOR

6 One of Elvis's most popular flicks. Elvis plays the son of a rich family who returns home to Hawaii after a stint in the service. The heir to a pineapple fortune, he upsets his parents by wanting to work in a tourist bureau instead. Great locations. Plenty of music, pretty girls and romance. Over a dozen songs, including one of his prettiest-ever hits: "Can't Help Falling in Love With You." The sound track was the fastest-selling album of 1961.

Sex / Nud / Viol / Lang / AdSit

A: Elvis Presley, Joan Blackman, Nancy Walters, Angela Lansbury, Roland Winters, Iris Adrian

© CBS/FOX VIDEO 2001

BOY FRIEND, THE

D: Ken Russell 137 m

G | MUS COM | 1971 | COLOR

6 When the leading lady (Jackson) breaks her ankle, she is quickly replaced by the assistant stage manager (Twiggy). This is an interesting musical that works actually in two different ways. First, as a 1920s musical production of "The Boy Friend," which is being put on at a tacky matinee; and also as a vehicle for the much more elaborate Busby Berkeley production numbers which occur within the daydreams of the matinee's participants. It will be most entertaining to fans of the '30s musicals genre. Fourteen songs in all. Glenda Jackson has a cameo as the lead hoofer.

Sex / Nud / Viol / Lang / AdSit

A: Twiggy, Christopher Gable, Moyra Fraser, Max Adrian, Vladek Sheybal, Glenda Jackson

Distributed By MGM/UA Home Video M200306

BRIGADOON

D: Vincente Minnelli 109 m

G | MUS ROM | 1954 | COLOR

8 One of the best of Lerner and Loewe's fanciful musicals is brought to the screen. Two American hunters in the Scottish Highlands stumble upon an enchanted Scottish village called Brigadoon, which appears only once every 100 years. There, Kelly meets beautiful Cyd Charisse and they fall in love. He must now decide whether to stay in her world and be lost in time, or return to his own. Beautiful songs such as "Almost Like Being in Love" and "I'll Go Home With Bonnie Jean," plus show-stopping dance routines.

Sex / Nud / Viol / Lang / AdSit

A: Gene Kelly, Van Johnson, Cyd Charisse, Elaine Stewart, Barry Jones, Hugh Laing

Distributed By MGM/UA Home Video M700040

BROADWAY MELODY OF 1938

D: Roy Del Ruth 111 m

NR | MUS | 1937 | B&W

6 Musicals were never more popular than in the late '30s. This was one that was custom-designed to appeal to that audience. The story line revolves around a girl who dreams of making it big on Broadway (Eleanor Powell) and the producer (Robert Taylor) who gets her there. A likable musical, it has a rich cast of popular entertainers but is best remembered for its dancing and particularly its singing. (A very young Judy Garland sings "You Made Me Love You" to Clark Gable and became a big hit.)

Sex / Nud / Viol / Lang / AdSit

A: Judy Garland, Robert Taylor, George Murphy, Eleanor Powell, Sophie Tucker, Buddy Ebsen

Distributed By MGM/UA Home Video M301048

BROADWAY MELODY OF 1940

D: Norman Taurog 104 m

NR | MUS | 1940 | B&W

6 If you are a fan of Fred Astaire, this is a good one for you. Here he is teamed with Eleanor Powell for the only time and has a rivalry with George Murphy, his partner, for her heart. Forget the plot. Enjoy lots of dancing and the music (Cole Porter's "Begin the Beguine" and "I've Got My Eyes on You"), too.

Sex / Nud / Viol / Lang / AdSit

A: Fred Astaire, Eleanor Powell, George Murphy, Frank Morgan, Ian Hunter

Distributed By MGM/UA Home Video M301111

BRUCE SPRINGSTEEN VIDEO ANTHOLOGY/1978-88

D: 100 m

MUS | 1988 | COLOR

8 Concert footage of Springsteen. Contains eighteen of his songs.

Sex / Nud / Viol / Lang / AdSit

A: Bruce Springsteen

© CBS MUSIC VIDEO ENTERPRISES 24V-49010

BYE BYE BIRDIE

D: George Sidney 112 m

NR | MUS COM | 1963 | COLOR

7 Lots of fun in this film adaptation of a big Broadway hit. An Elvis-like rock `n roll sensation is being drafted into the Army. His manager, who is facing unemployment, launches a nationwide contest to find one lucky girl to give him a last goodbye kiss on the Ed Sullivan Show. When it turns out to be Ann-Margret, her home town, particularly her father (Paul Lynde), is thrown into a tizzy. Songs include "Kids" and "Put on a Happy Face." Really entertaining little piece of musical fluff. This was also Ann-Margret's film debut.

Sex / Nud / Viol / Lang / AdSit

A: Janet Leigh, Dick Van Dyke, Bobby Rydell, Maureen Stapleton, Paul Lynde, Ann-Margret

© COLUMBIA TRISTAR HOME VIDEO 60150

CALAMITY JANE

D: David Butler 101 m

MUS COM WST | 1953 | COLOR

7 Entertaining, rambunctious musical comedy in which Doris Day plays Calamity Jane as a tomboy who is in wild and amorous pursuit of Wild Bill Hickok (Howard Keel). Doris had a lot of fun with this role and it shows. She is a wildly independent gal of the West who goes after her man but doesn't want to change her ways. Bill doesn't want much to do with her until, with a little bit of help, Calamity reveals that that's a heap o' woman under them buckskins. This is also the movie where Day introduces her biggest hit song (which also won an Oscar), "Secret Love."

Sex / Nud / Viol / Lang / AdSit

A: Doris Day, Howard Keel, Allyn Ann McLerie, Phillip Carey, Gale Robbins, Dick Wesson

© WARNER HOME VIDEO 11209

CAPTAIN JANUARY

D: David Butler 76 m

NR | MUS CLD | 1936 | B&W

7 Shirley Temple is at her sympathetic best as an orphan who lives with a lighthouse keeper. Captain January (Kibbee) rescued her from a shipwreck when she was just a baby. She is now a happy 4-year-old and is the sweetheart of all the fisherman in the neighborhood. But a new truant officer has moved to town and wants to take Shirley away to put her in a proper home.

Sex / Nud / Viol / Lang / AdSit

A: Shirley Temple, Guy Kibbee, Slim Summerville, Buddy Ebsen

© FOXVIDEO 1068

CAROUSEL

D: Henry King 128 m

NR | MUS ROM | 1956 | COLOR

10 Rogers and Hammerstein's classic musical is memorably brought to life with lavish production numbers and the beautiful voices of Gordon MacRae and Shirley Jones. A handsome and charming carnival barker (MacRae) falls in love and marries a beautiful girl (Jones), but he panics when he realizes she is pregnant and he must support them. He feels he must get money fast so he attempts an ill-fated robbery, is killed and then he looks down on her from heaven. Memorable songs include "If I Loved You," "You'll Never Walk Alone" and "June is Bustin' Out All Over." Just wonderful. See OKLAHOMA, too.

Sex / Nud / Viol / Lang / AdSit

A: Gordon MacRae, Shirley Jones, Cameron Mitchell, Barbara Ruick, Claramae Turner, Gene Lockhart

© FOXVIDEO 1713

CHITTY CHITTY BANG BANG

D: Kenneth Hughes — 147 m

G | MUS CLD | 1968 | COLOR

7 This very lavish musical was based upon a book by Ian Fleming. Dick Van Dyke plays an inventor with two children who creates a magical flying automobile. On a trip to the beach, he, his girlfriend and the children are all kidnapped into a magical world. It is dominated by the evil Baron Bomburst and his child-hating wife, who has kidnapped the children. With the help of a toymaker (Benny Hill), Dick seeks to rescue the kids. This picture cost a huge amount of money for its time ($10,000,000) and was supposed to be more of a family picture, but really is most appealing to smaller children.

Sex / Nud / Viol / Lang / AdSit

A: Dick Van Dyke, Sally Ann Howes, Anna Quayle, Lionel Jeffries, Benny Hill

Distributed By MGM/UA Home Video M201647

CONCERT FOR BANGLADESH, THE

D: Saul Swimmer — 90 m

G | MUS DOC | 1971 | COLOR

9 In August 1971 at Madison Square Garden, former Beatle George Harrison put on a benefit concert to raise money to help the starving people of Bangladesh. It was a huge rock concert that gained international recognition and support. This is a straight-forward recording of that concert. Lots of great rock music from many giants of the period, but you might want to fast-forward through a long stretch of Ravi Shankar's sitar music if you aren't a fan.

Sex / Nud / Viol / Lang / AdSit

A: George Harrison, Bob Dylan, Eric Clapton, Ringo Starr, Leon Russell, Ravi Shankar

© PARAMOUNT HOME VIDEO 15167

DADDY LONG LEGS

D: Jean Negulesco — 126 m

NR | MUS ROM | 1955 | COLOR

6 Delightfully romantic fairy tale. A rich bachelor playboy (Astaire) becomes entranced with a pretty orphaned 18-year-old French girl. He sponsors her through two years of college in America anonymously. When she returns to France all grown up, Fred falls hard for her but trys to do the right thing because he is so much older. Trite? Yes, but... they tell the whole story dancing to a Johnny Mercer score which includes the now-classic "Something's Got to Give."

Sex / Nud / Viol / Lang / AdSit

A: Fred Astaire, Leslie Caron, Terry Moore, Thelma Ritter, Fred Clark, Charlotte Austin

© FOXVIDEO 1378

DAMN YANKEES

D: George Abbott, Stanley Donen — 111 m

NR | MUS COM | 1958 | COLOR

8 Huge Broadway hit is brought to the screen in wonderful fashion. Joe Boyd is a middle-aged baseball fan that so wants to help his beloved Washington Senators whip the Yankees and win the pennant that he makes a deal with the devil (Walston) and his beautiful vamp Lola (Verdon) to become rejuvenated into a young player. Wonderful songs and dances. Oscar nominated score has "Whatever Lola Wants," "Heart" and "Two Lost Souls." Verdon is sexy and Walston is marvelously devilish.

Sex / Nud / Viol / Lang / AdSit

A: Tab Hunter, Gwen Verdon, Ray Walston, Russ Brown, Shannon Bolin, Nathaniel Frey

© WARNER HOME VIDEO 35109

DOCTOR DOLITTLE

D: Richard Fleischer — 145 m

G | MUS CLD | 1967 | COLOR

8 This is a musical adaptation of Hugh Lofting's children's classic about an eccentric doctor (Rex Harrison) who loves animals so much better than people that he speaks 498 animal languages. He goes off on an adventure, from his home at Puddleby-on-the-Marsh, in search of new ones and he and his fiancee (Samantha Eggar) discover some very strange ones indeed. Won an Oscar for Best Song: "Talk to the Animals." While it was a box office flop and most critics were unkind, it still manages to please little kids who aren't aware of any of that.

Sex / Nud / Viol / Lang / AdSit

A: Rex Harrison, Samantha Eggar, Anthony Newley, Richard Attenborough, Peter Bull, Geoffrey Holder

© FOXVIDEO 1025

EASTER PARADE

D: Charles Walters — 104 m

NR | MUS ROM COM | 1948 | COLOR

9 Absolutely wonderful Irving Berlin musical (it has seventeen songs). Set in 1912, Astaire's dance partner (Miller) dumps him to go solo, so he picks Garland out of the chorus line, vowing that he can make her into a big star. Though he moons over his loss of Miller, Garland works hard to eventually capture his approval and also his heart. Wonderful classic songs and dance sequences make this an eminently watchable favorite, again and again.

Sex / Nud / Viol / Lang / AdSit

A: Judy Garland, Fred Astaire, Peter Lawford, Jules Munshin, Ann Miller

Distributed By MGM/UA Home Video M600256

FANCY PANTS

D: George Marshall — 92 m

NR | MUS COM | 1950 | COLOR

7 Amusing and good-natured remake of 1935's RUGGLES OF RED GAP. Bob Hope plays an out-of-work actor pretending to be an English gentleman's gentleman. He is acquired by an oil-rich, husband-seeking, tomboy boss (Lucille Ball) and accompanies her back home to the Wild West of New Mexico. Entertaining movie, made so more by its cast than the story's premise - which was better done in the 1935 version.

Sex / Nud / Viol / Lang / AdSit

A: Bob Hope, Lucille Ball, Bruce Cabot, Jack Kirkwood, Lea Penman, Hugh French

© PARAMOUNT HOME VIDEO 6208

FANTASIA

D: — 120 m

G | MUS FAN | 1940 | COLOR

8 Extravagant, hugely expensive and extremely bold venture by Walt Disney in 1940. The imaginations of the animators were turned loose to translate classical music masterpieces into free-flowing animated surreal fantasy story lines. There are seven sequences in all. The best are "The Sorcerer's Apprentice" and "Night on Bald Mountain." Highly praised by some and criticized by others. Certainly different. Imagination and patience required - and richly rewarded.

Sex / Nud / Viol / Lang / AdSit

A:

© WALT DISNEY HOME VIDEO 1132

FINIAN'S RAINBOW

D: Francis Ford Coppola — 142 m

G | MUS COM ROM | 1968 | COLOR

7 This was a ground-breaking musical in the 1940s when it opened on Broadway, but is now dated in the way it deals with its theme of racial prejudice. Nevertheless, it still has some very fine moments and Tommy Steele is wonderful in the role of an effervescent leprechaun whose gold is stolen by Irishman Astaire. Astair has transplanted himself into the American South and Steele has followed him. Petula Clarke is Astaire's daughter and gets three wishes - one of which she uses to turn bigoted Southern Senator Wynn into a black man. Tuneful score includes, "How Are Things is Glocca Mora?"

Sex / Nud / Viol / Lang / AdSit

A: Fred Astaire, Petula Clark, Tommy Steele, Keenan Wynn, Barbara Hanock, Don Francks

© WARNER HOME VIDEO 11208

GIRL CRAZY

D: Norman Taurog — 101 m

NR | MUS COM | 1943 | B&W

7 A fun and quality pairing (the eighth time) of Mickey and Judy. Mickey plays a rich young Eastern kid whose father sends him to an all-boy's school in the desert to forget about girls. However, Mickey meets and falls for the only girl around, the dean's granddaughter (Judy), but she's more interested in helping her grandfather whose school is near bankruptcy. So what do they do - they promote a big rodeo to raise money to keep the school in business. Great Gershwin music: "Fascinating Rythym," "Embraceable You" and "I Got Rhythm."

Sex / Nud / Viol / Lang / AdSit

A: Mickey Rooney, Judy Garland, Gil Stratton, Robert E. Strickland, June Allyson, Nancy Walker

Distributed By MGM/UA Home Video M300567

GOOD NEWS

D: Charles Walters — 93 m

NR | MUS | 1947 | COLOR

7 Simple and silly, but for musical fans, highly entertaining. It is a musical set in 1920s on a college campus, and is about campus life. Peter Lawford is a football star who is being pursued by two coeds, June Allyson and Patricia Marshall. One loves him for the wrong reasons, one for the right. Score includes "Varsity Drag," "French Lesson," "The Best Things in Life are Free" and the Oscar-nominated "Pass the Peace Pipe."

Sex / Nud / Viol / Lang / AdSit

A: June Allyson, Peter Lawford, Patricia Marshall, Joan McCracken, Ray McDonald, Mel Torme

Distributed By MGM/UA Home Video M300877

GREASE

D: Randal Kleiser — 110 m

PG | MUS ROM | 1978 | COLOR

7 The highly popular Broadway play, about summer love at fictional high school in the '50s, is brought to the screen and given reasonably good treatment. Travolta, a greaser (but also the ultimate cool dude), and the sweet and innocent new-girl-in-town (Newton-John) meet over the summer break and have a summer romance. But, when fall comes, he thinks he has to protect his image as a tough guy and she doesn't fit it. Clever ideas, plenty of energy, excellent choreography, charm and lots of good music. Fun time.

Sex / Nud / Viol / Lang / AdSit

A: John Travolta, Olivia Newton-John, Stockard Channing, Jeff Conaway, Didi Conn, Eve Arden

© PARAMOUNT HOME VIDEO 1108

GREAT ZIEGFELD, THE

D: Robert Z. Leonard — 177 m

NR | MUS DMA | 1936 | B&W

Sex / Nud / Viol / Lang / AdSit

8 Flamboyant tribute to a flamboyant man. It captured 3 Oscars, including Best Picture Oscar for 1936. It is filled with lavish production numbers and peppered with many of the talented stars who actually appeared in the Ziegfeld Follies (Fanny Brice and Ray Bolger, among others). It is a detailed account of the up-and-down career of one of the most famous men in show business, including his love life. Many memorable songs: "A Pretty Girl is Like a Melody," "Look for the Silver Lining" and "Rhapsody in Blue."

A: William Powell, Myrna Loy, Luise Rainer, Frank Morgan, Fanny Brice, Virginia Bruce

Distributed By MGM/UA Home Video M300538

HALLELUJAH

D: King Vidor — 90 m

NR | MUS DMA | 1929 | B&W

Sex / Nud / Viol / Lang / AdSit

8 A revolutionary and ground-breaking film. This was the first all-black talking film and it was one of the very first true musicals. Filmed on location in Tennessee, it is the story of an innocent young black man who accidentally kills his brother. He turns to religion for solace and becomes a preacher but remains vulnerable to the sins of the flesh. Dated in many ways and too melodramatic, but it is still very moving and a truly insightful look into the ways of the old South. Very daring for its time. Contains many spiritual and traditional songs plus two from Irving Berlin. Director was Oscar-nominated.

A: Daniel L. Haynes, Nina Mae McKinney, William Fountaine, Everett McGarity, Victoria Spivey

Distributed By MGM/UA Home Video M202839

HANS CHRISTIAN ANDERSEN

D: Charles Vidor — 112 m

NR | MUS CLD | 1952 | COLOR

Sex / Nud / Viol / Lang / AdSit

9 Wonderful, tune-filled musical biography of the famous storyteller, Hans Christian Andersen. Danny Kaye is just marvelous in the title role as a shoemaker who is forced to leave his hometown because the school children all skip school just to come an hear him tell his stories. After going to Copenhagen, he is hired to make shoes for a beautiful ballerina. He falls desperately, deeply in love with her and then writes "The Littlest Mermaid." Listen also for him telling the stories of "Thumbelina," "Inchworm" and "Ugly Duckling."

A: Danny Kaye, Farley Granger, Renee Jeanmaire, John Brown, Roland Petit

© HBO VIDEO 90650

HARD DAY'S NIGHT, A

D: Richard Lester — 90 m

G | MUS COM | 1964 | B&W

Sex / Nud / Viol / Lang / AdSit

9 This is an exuberant and fun-filled musical romp with the Beatles - even for non-Beatles fans. The fab four had just reached the pinnacle of their popularity at the time of the release of this film and it does contain a full compliment of Lennon-McCarney songs, including: "Can't Buy Me Love," "And I Love Her" and "I Should Have Known Better"; but it is also a fast-paced and funny kaleidoscope of a rock group's frantic day by utilizing clever cinematic techniques. Good fun, even today, because it captures the charm and exuberant personalities that was a large part of how the group achieved the success it did.

A: The Beatles, Wilfred Brambell, Victor Spinetti, Anna Quayle

© MPI HOME VIDEO MP1064

HARVEY GIRLS, THE

D: George Sidney — 102 m

NR | MUS COM | 1946 | COLOR

Sex / Nud / Viol / Lang / AdSit

7 An energetic musical that is based on the real life 19th-century restaurants that were built to accompany the railroad's expansion into the West. The restaurants became extremely popular because they could be relied upon for good food, pretty waitresses and a civil dining experience in a crude and primitive environment. Beverly Garland was at the height of her form when she was cast to play an innocent mail-order bride traveling west. A great cast includes a young Angela Lansbury and Cyd Charisse. And, the songs include the Oscar-winning "On the Atchison, Topeka and the Santa Fe."

A: Judy Garland, John Hodiak, Ray Bolger, Angela Lansbury, Preston Foster, Cyd Charisse

Distributed By MGM/UA Home Video M301003

HELLO, DOLLY!

D: Gene Kelly — 146 m

G | MUS COM | 1969 | COLOR

Sex / Nud / Viol / Lang / AdSit

6 This is a very lavish screen production of Broadway's smash hit about a turn-of-the-century matchmaker (played by Streisand) who hopes to snag one of her clients for herself. Extravagant film production and excellent musical productions cannot entirely make up for the fact that Barbara was much too young for that role. Even so, listen to the fantastic music: "Before the Parade Passes By" and, of course, "Hello Dolly" with Streisand in duet with Louis Armstrong. Based on the play and later movie THE MATCHMAKER.

A: Barbra Streisand, Walter Matthau, Louis Armstrong, Michael Crawford, Tommy Tune, E.J. Peaker

© FOXVIDEO 1001

HELP!

D: Richard Lester — 90 m

G | MUS COM | 1965 | COLOR

Sex / Nud / Viol / Lang / AdSit

8 Wild gags and lots of music populate this minor silly story about a group of religious zealots who want Ringo's (the Beatles drummer) ring for a sacrifice. Songs include: "Ticket to Ride," "Another Girl," "You've Got to Hide Your Love Away," and "Help!" If you are not a fan of either The Beatles or abject silliness, you might downgrade this to a 6, or perhaps even skip it. However, eccentrics, fans of the group or fans of silliness will have a good time. And, if you are a true Beatles fan, you MUST also see the excellent documentary, THE COMPLEAT BEATLES.

A: The Beatles, Leo McKern, Eleanor Bran, Victor Spinetti

© MPI HOME VIDEO MP1342

HERE COMES THE GROOM

D: Frank Capra — 114 m

NR | MUS COM ROM | 1951 | B&W

Sex / Nud / Viol / Lang / AdSit

6 Pleasant musical comedy about a happy-go-lucky reporter who contrives to keep his former fiancee from marrying a millionaire real estate developer. He needs her to remarry him because he only has five days left to find a wife or he will lose the two war orphans he wants to adopt. Typical Frank Capra formula for good fun and light spirits. Good songs including: "In the Cool, Cool, Cool of the Evening."

A: Bing Crosby, Jane Wyman, Franchot Tone, Alexis Smith

© PARAMOUNT HOME VIDEO 5101

HOLIDAY INN

D: Mark Sandrich — 101 m

MUS | 1942 | B&W

Sex / Nud / Viol / Lang / AdSit

7 This was a fluffy star vehicle for the monumental talents of Bing Crosby and Fred Astaire and the music of Irving Berlin. They are set in a modest plot where Fred and Bing join forces to open an Inn that is to be open only for the holiday season, but instead they fight over a girl. The best part of the films is that you will be presented with a whole bunch of holiday songs - most notably "Easter Parade" and popular music's all-time biggest seller "White Christmas."

A: Bing Crosby, Fred Astaire, Marjorie Reynolds, Walter Abel, Louise Beavers

© MCA/UNIVERSAL HOME VIDEO, INC. 55039

HONEYSUCKLE ROSE

D: Jerry Schatzberg — 120 m

PG | MUS | 1980 | COLOR

Sex / Nud / Viol / Lang / AdSit

6 Lots of good country music mark this film as worthy of investing one's time, particularly for fans of Willie Nelson. However, outside that, there is very little else to get excited about. The story is a semi-biographical account of a country music singer's (Nelson) life on the road. His personal life begins to come apart when Willie takes up with the daughter of his longtime friend. Watch for a lot of cameos from some country music greats. The song, "On the Road Again," was Oscar nominated.

A: Willie Nelson, Dyan Cannon, Amy Irving, Slim Pickens, Joey Floyd, Charles Levin

© WARNER HOME VIDEO 1043

IN THE GOOD OLD SUMMERTIME

D: Robert Z. Leonard — 104 m

NR | MUS COM ROM | 1949 | COLOR

Sex / Nud / Viol / Lang / AdSit

8 Endearing remake of the successful 1940 non-musical THE SHOP AROUND THE CORNER. This time the setting is turn-of-the-century Chicago. Judy Garland and Van Johnson are co-workers in a music store where they fight or generally ignore each other. However, unknown to either, they are also pen pals whose relationship on paper is blossoming into love. Features a lot of classic old time songs including: "Wait Rill the Sun Shines Nellie," "I Don't Care" and the title tune.

A: Judy Garland, Van Johnson, S.Z. Sakall, Spring Byington, Clinton Sundberg, Buster Keaton

Distributed By MGM/UA Home Video M300860

IT HAPPENED AT THE WORLD'S FAIR

D: Norman Taurog — 105 m

NR | MUS ROM | 1963 | COLOR

Sex / Nud / Viol / Lang / AdSit

6 Entertaining light musical. Elvis Presley plays a daredevil pilot who romances a nurse at the Seattle World's Fair and helps a young girl stay out of an orphanage. Contains ten Elvis songs, none of them very memorable. This was still early in Elvis's movie career, so he hadn't burned out yet and still enjoyed himself. An interesting side note is that this is the very first film in which Kurt Russell appeared. Russell later would do an excellent job of playing Presley in the TV movie ELVIS.

A: Elvis Presley, Joan O'Brien, Gary Lockwood, Vicky Tiu, H.M. Wynant

Distributed By MGM/UA Home Video M600475

JOY OF LIVING

D: Tay Garnett 91 m

NR | MUS COM | 1938 | B&W

6 Zany screwball musical comedy in which a wealthy, carefree, globe-trotting playboy (Fairbanks) sets his sights on a very practical and business-minded Broadway singer (Dunne). He's determined to show her how to enjoy life and also to save her from her leach-like family (including Lucile Ball), which likes its mealticket too much. However, instead of being grateful for his help, she has him arrested for being a masher - but still he doesn't give up. Good Jerome Kern and Dorothy Fields score including: "A Heavenly Party," "Just Let Me Look at You" and "What's Good About Goodnight?"

Sex | Nud | Viol | Lang | AdSit

A: *Irene Dunne, Douglas Fairbanks, Jr., Alice Brady, Guy Kibbee, Jean Dixon, Eric Blore*

© TURNER HOME ENTERTAINMENT 6037

JUMBO (BILLY ROSE'S)

D: Charles Walters 127 m

G | MUS ROM | 1962 | COLOR

6 It's the turn of the 20th century and Jimmy Durante and his daughter (Doris Day) are struggling to keep their circus from going broke. Into their camp comes a competitor's spy, intent upon stealing the circus. Instead he falls in love with Doris. The major attraction here to the viewer is not the story but the beautiful Rodgers and Hart score: "This Can't Be Love," "The Most Beautiful Girl in the World" and "My Romance." The Busby Berkeley choreography and the marvelous talents of Durante and Raye also are a delight. A family movie with something a little different for everyone.

Sex | Nud | Viol | Lang | AdSit

A: *Doris Day, Stephen Boyd, Jimmy Durante, Martha Raye, Dean Jagger, Billy Barty*

Distributed By MGM/UA Home Video M300796

KID GALAHAD

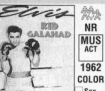

D: Phil Karlson 95 m

NR | MUS ACT | 1962 | COLOR

6 Elvis plays a young guy just back from the service. He's looking for a job and takes one as a sparring partner at a boxing camp, but instead he knocks out the camp's top boxer. So, the owner decides to make him into a champ, but this is a boxer that would rather be a mechanic and sing. Still, the promoter (Gig Young) can't let him get away because the kid is his one big chance to get out of debt to some hoods. Elvis agrees to fight for him, but that only gets him and his incorruptible trainer (Charles Bronson) in a whole lot of trouble. Pretty good, if you don't expect too much.

Sex | Nud | ◢ Viol | Lang | AdSit

A: *Elvis Presley, Gig Young, Charles Bronson, Lola Albright*

Distributed By MGM/UA Home Video M701055

KING AND I, THE

D: Walter Lang 133 m

G | MUS ROM COM | 1956 | COLOR

9 This is a sumptuous feast for the eyes and ears. Superb production values showcase a winning story. A spirited English widow (Kerr) is hired by the pompous King of Siam (Yul Brynner) in the 1860s to be governess for his many children. The clash of both cultures and personalities make for some interesting situations, but conflict gradually gives way to respect and to an unspoken and forbidden love. Wonderful music includes their duet "Shall We Dance." Winner of five Oscars and nominee for Best Picture.

Sex | Nud | Viol | Lang | AdSit

A: *Deborah Kerr, Yul Brynner, Rita Moreno, Martin Benson, Terry Sounders*

© FOXVIDEO 1004

MARY POPPINS

D: Robert Stevenson 139 m

G | MUS CLD FAN | 1964 | COLOR

10 Absolutely delightful! An enchanting magical nanny, Mary Poppins (Andrews), glides into a banker's home in 1910 London and brings happiness into everyone's lives. Who else can have a tea party on the ceiling? She and a chimney sweep (Van Dyke) sing the song "Chim-Chim-Cheree" and dance with magic feet on London rooftops. Van Dyke's animated scene where he frolics with little penguins is unforgettable. This top-shelf musical won five Academy Awards: Best Actress, Film Editing, Original Music, Song and Visual Effects. It was nominated for thirteen. You, as well as the kids, will find your smiles!

Sex | Nud | Viol | Lang | AdSit

A: *Julie Andrews, Dick Van Dyke, David Tomlinson, Glynis Johns, Ed Wynn, Hermione Baddeley*

© WALT DISNEY HOME VIDEO 023

MEET ME IN ST. LOUIS

D: Vincente Minnelli 119 m

NR | MUS COM ROM | 1944 | COLOR

10 Wonderful. Absolute perfection and a perennial favorite! Elegant staging and production. It's 1904 in St. Louis, just before the World's Fair. The Ames family is a very happy group until Dad announces that he is moving the family to New York and everyone is upset. Songs include "The Boy Next Door," "Have Yourself a Merry Little Christmas" and "The Trolley Song." O'Brien won a special Oscar for Best Child Actress. This sentimental slice of Americana, with outstanding performances, sets and cinematography, is truly a classic treat for the senses.

Sex | Nud | Viol | Lang | AdSit

A: *Judy Garland, Mary Astor, Tom Drake, Margaret O'Brien, Harry Davenport, Lucille Bremer*

Distributed By MGM/UA Home Video M201827

MOON OVER MIAMI

D: Walter Lang 92 m

NR | MUS ROM | 1941 | COLOR

7 Entertaining musical romance. A pair of Texan sisters (Grable and Landis) leave the Texas hamburger joint where they work to go gold digging in Miami, hoping to find rich husbands. After several romantic adventures, Grable lands a handsome and charming, but broke, man (Ameche). Landis ends up with a millionaire (Cummings). This musical remake of "THREE BLIND MICE" was also remade in 1946 as "THREE LITTLE GIRLS IN BLUE." Grable's performance is a whole lot of fun and was critical in making her a big star.

Sex | Nud | Viol | Lang | ◢ AdSit

A: *Betty Grable, Carole Landis, Charlotte Greenwood, Don Ameche, Robert Cummings, Jack Hailey*

© FOXVIDEO 1725

MUSIC MAN, THE

D: Morton DaCosta 151 m

G | MUS COM ROM | 1962 | COLOR

10 Golden Americana and a rousing good time too! A charming con artist and music "professor" (Preston) convinces a small turn-of-the-century Iowa town that he can teach the boys there to play musical instruments by using his Think Method. Then he convinces all the townsfolk that they should form a marching band - buying the costumes, instruments and all from him. Some of the Oscar-winning songs featured in this delightful musical include "76 Trombones," "'Til There Was You" and "Trouble." This wonderful slice of American apple pie was nominated for 6 Oscars, including Best Picture. Wonderful!!

Sex | Nud | Viol | Lang | AdSit

A: *Robert Preston, Buddy Hackett, Hermione Gingold, Paul Ford, Pert Kelton, Shirley Jones*

© WARNER HOME VIDEO 11473

MY FAIR LADY

D: George Cukor 170 m

G | MUS ROM COM | 1964 | COLOR

10 Outstanding winner of eight Oscars - including Best Picture! Shaw's enduring play (and film) PYGMALION is masterfully transformed into a magical musical by Lerner and Lowe. It is an exuberant story of the effort by a snooty Englishman to transform, on a bet, a guttersnipe flower peddler (Hepburn) into being able to pass for a respectable lady. In the process, he falls in love with her and she changes him forever. Just a few of the winning and memorable songs include "The Rain in Spain," "On the Street Where You Live" and "Get Me to the Church on Time." Wonderful.

Sex | Nud | Viol | Lang | AdSit

A: *Audrey Hepburn, Rex Harrison, Wilfrid Hyde-White, Stanley Holloway, Jeremy Brett, Theodore Bikel*

© FOXVIDEO 7038

MY SISTER EILEEN

D: Richard Quine 108 m

NR | MUS COM | 1955 | COLOR

9 Two small-town girls move from Ohio to Manhattan. Ruth is an aspiring writer and Eileen wants to be an actor. They have come to set the world on its end, but first they have to find an apartment they can afford. So, they move into the cheap, musty basement of the Popopolous Arms. When Ruth's corny romance stories are turned down by magazine editor Jack Lemmon, she decides to accept his suggestion to write about something she knows - her very popular and beautiful sister Eileen. But when he likes her new story and wants to meet Eileen, her jealousy takes hold and she weaves a webb of lies that lead to hilarious mayhem. Excellent singing and dancing, and lots of fun.

Sex | Nud | Viol | Lang | AdSit

A: *Janet Leigh, Betty Garrett, Jack Lemmon, Bob Fosse, Kurt Kaszner, Dick York*

© COLUMBIA TRISTAR HOME VIDEO 51283

NEPTUNE'S DAUGHTER

D: Edward Buzzell 94 m

NR | MUS COM | 1949 | COLOR

6 Light-hearted entertainment from the '40s. Simple empty-headed vehicle designed to highlight audience favorites Esther Williams and comic Red Skelton. Esther plays a bathing suit designer on vacation in South America in love with Ricardo Montalban, and Red is a masseur mistaken for a polo player and being pursued by Esther's wacky sister. Esther, of course, appears in several of her trademark water ballets. Harmless bubbly fun. Contains the Oscar-winning song: "Baby It's Cold Outside."

Sex | Nud | Viol | Lang | AdSit

A: *Esther Williams, Red Skelton, Keenan Wynn, Ricardo Montalban, Mel Blanc*

Distributed By MGM/UA Home Video M200853

OKLAHOMA!

D: Fred Zinnemann 145 m

G | MUS ROM WST | 1955 | COLOR

10 Wonderful Rogers and Hammerstein musical gets the full treatment. An all-star cast, colorful costumes and sets, and wondrous, timeless music combine to make this a landmark film. It is the story of a beautiful country girl who is courted by both a cowboy and vile hired hand. Extremely entertaining musical. Gordon MacRae and Shirley Jones make screen magic, just as they did in CAROUSEL. Songs include: "Oh, What a Beautiful Morning" and "Surrey With the Fringe on Top," among many more. Two Oscars.

Sex | Nud | Viol | Lang | AdSit

A: *Gordon MacRae, Shirley Jones, Rod Steiger, Charlotte Greenwood, Gloria Grahame, Eddie Albert*

© FOXVIDEO 7020

OLIVER!

D: Carol Reed — 145 m

G · MUS DMA · 1968 · COLOR

10 An absolutely outstanding musical and winner of the Best Picture Oscar and six others. Great entertainment. Dickens was never this much fun. All the story's touching elements are here, but the tragedy of an eight-year-old orphan's utter aloneness and helpless, living in the streets during desperate times, is much less traumatic when it is set to music and dance. Plus, the colorful characters were wonderfully captured by a terrific cast. There are lavish production numbers and sets. The truly wonderful and memorable songs include: "Consider Yourself," "As Long as He Needs Me" and "Who Will Buy."

Sex · Nud · Viol · Lang · AdSit

A: Mark Lester, Jack Wild, Ron Moody, Oliver Reed, Shani Wallace

© COLUMBIA TRISTAR HOME VIDEO 60526

ON A CLEAR DAY YOU CAN SEE FOREVER

D: Vincente Minnelli — 129 m

G · MUS COM ROM · 1970 · COLOR

7 Entertaining and underrated. Barbra is a neurotic chain smoker who crashes a college class in hypnosis looking for a cure. Psychiatrist Yves Montand agrees to hypnotize her and is fascinated to discover that he has instead regressed her back into a former life - in 19th-century England. Intrigued by the woman he has found, he continues to hypnotize modern Barbra and soon falls in love with the intriguing woman from the past. However, modern Barbara thinks he is treating her smoking problem and she has fallen in love with him. Solid music and lush production.

Sex · Nud · Viol · Lang · AdSit

A: Barbra Streisand, Yves Montand, Bob Newhart, Larry Blyden, Simon Oakland, Jack Nicholson

© PARAMOUNT HOME VIDEO 6927

PAJAMA GAME, THE

D: George Abbott — 102 m

NR · MUS COM ROM · 1957 · COLOR

8 Exuberant and enjoyable Hollywood conversion (largely intact) of the very successful Broadway play. Doris Day plays the head of the union's grievance committee at a pajama factory. She is heading up the charge to demand a 7 1/2 cent per hour pay raise. She must negotiate with the plant's foreman (Raitt) to get it, but love gets in the way. Light-hearted fun. Great songs and inventive Bob Fosse choreography. Songs include: "Hernando's Hideaway," "Hey There" and the big hit "Steam Heat."

Sex · Nud · Viol · Lang · AdSit

A: Doris Day, John Raitt, Carol Haney, Eddie Foy, Jr., Reta Shaw

© WARNER HOME VIDEO 35085

PETER PAN

D: Vincent J. Donehue — 104 m

NR · MUS CLD · 1960 · COLOR

8 In December 1960, NBC television aired a wonderful musical version of the children's classic starring Mary Martin, for which she won an Emmy. Time has not dimmed the sense of magic and wonder it inspires. Wendy is a young girl, verging on womanhood. However, just before she is all grown up, she and her two young brothers are escorted to Never Never Land, a magical land where only children may go. Their guide there is Peter Pan, a magical boy who refuses to ever grow up. He takes them to a place where there is constant adventure with pirates and Indians and ceaseless fun. Inspired. Also see Spielberg's 1992 follow-up HOOK.

Sex · Nud · Viol · Lang · AdSit

A: Mary Martin, Cyril Ritchard, Sondra Lee, Margalo Gilmore

© GOODTIMES 7001

PIRATES OF PENZANCE, THE

D: Wilford Leach — 112 m

G · MUS COM · 1983 · COLOR

7 Gilbert and Sullivan's perennial favorite comic-musical for the stage is given a good go on the screen (with most of the Broadway cast intact), but the use of very stylized sets and staged camera spectacles, reminiscent of Busby Berkely, will put off many reality-based filmgoers. Yet the story of an honest young man trapped into being a pirate and in love with the daughter of a Major General is still funny. The lyrics and score are simply wonderful. An impressive effort, but Ronstadt sings better than she acts.

Sex · Nud · Viol · Lang · AdSit

A: Kevin Kline, Angela Lansbury, Linda Ronstadt, George Rose, Rex Smith, Tony Azito

© MCA/UNIVERSAL HOME VIDEO, INC. 71012

POOR LITTLE RICH GIRL, THE

D: Irving Cummings — 72 m

NR · MUS CLD · 1936 · B&W

8 One of Shirley Temple's best. She plays the motherless daughter of a rich man who has sent her off to boarding school. But she ducks out of the school and gets lost. She teams up with a husband and wife vaudeville act by telling them that she is an orphan. Together, all three sing and dance their way to success and, in the end, Shirley is reunited with her father and his new wife. Look for her famous number in a military uniform and rifle "Military Man," along with "Oh My Goodness," "You've Got to Eat Your Spinach, Baby" and "When I'm With You."

Sex · Nud · Viol · Lang · AdSit

A: Shirley Temple, Alice Faye, Jack Haley, Gloria Stuart, Michael Whalen, Claude Gillingwater

© FOXVIDEO 1069

REBECCA OF SUNNYBROOK FARM

D: Allan Dwan — 80 m

NR · MUS CLD · 1938 · B&W

6 Engaging family musical. A little girl (Temple) desperately wants to become a radio star and when a talent scout living next door to her aunt's farmhouse, where she is staying, realizes that she has the right stuff, he gets her career going. The girl rockets to stardom, but her wicked stepfather tries to make money on the deal, too. Shirley sings "On the Good Ship Lollipop" and "Animal Crackers." Even better, she gets to pal about with Jack Haley and Bill "Bojangles" Robinson. The title of this film has nothing to do with the famous book.

Sex · Nud · Viol · Lang · AdSit

A: Shirley Temple, Jack Haley, Randolph Scott, Bill Robinson, Gloria Stuart, Phyllis Brooks

© FOXVIDEO 1065

ROAD TO BALI

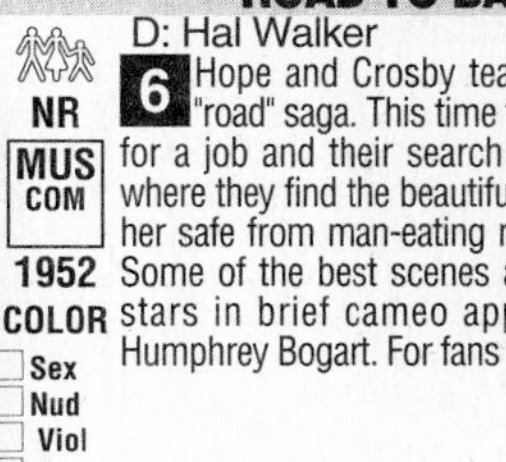

D: Hal Walker — 91 m

NR · MUS COM · 1952 · COLOR

6 Hope and Crosby team up in another musically adventurous "road" saga. This time the pair of vaudeville performers is looking for a job and their search leads them to a lush South Seas island where they find the beautiful Lamour. There, the pair attempts to keep her safe from man-eating natives and all sorts of other jungle perils. Some of the best scenes are those that feature famous Hollywood stars in brief cameo appearances, such as Jane Russell and Humphrey Bogart. For fans of the series, this is one of the best.

Sex · Nud · Viol · Lang · ◢ AdSit

A: Bob Hope, Bing Crosby, Dorothy Lamour, Murvyn Vye, Ralph Moody

© UNICORN VIDEO, INC. 301

ROAD TO HONG KONG, THE

D: Norman Panama — 92 m

NR · MUS COM · 1962 · B&W

6 Lively formula comedy. Two ex-vaudeville performers turned con men end up in a plot filled with international intrigue. A secret formula has been submerged inside one of their minds. Somewhere along the line, Hope loses his memory and that unfortunate incident leads them to involvement with a spy (Collins) and a nutty gang of baddies. Sellers makes an exuberant performance in his cameo as the doctor who examines Hope. Inside jokes between Hope and Crosby add some zest to the last film in the series.

Sex · Nud · Viol · Lang · ◢ AdSit

A: Bob Hope, Bing Crosby, Joan Collins, Dorothy Lamour, Robert Morley, Walter Gotell

Distributed By MGM/UA Home Video M202078

ROAD TO RIO

D: Norman McLeod — 100 m

NR · MUS COM · 1947 · B&W

7 Hope and Crosby are up to their usual monkey business in this fifth "road" series adventure. The two accidentally set fire to a carnival and flee town on an cruise ship headed for Rio. While on board, they come across Lamour, a beautiful girl who is about to enter into an pre-arranged marriage against her will. The comic pair attempts to thwart the wedding and save her from her evil aunt.

Sex · Nud · Viol · Lang · AdSit

A: Bob Hope, Bing Crosby, Dorothy Lamour, Gale Sondergaard, Frank Faylen

© COLUMBIA TRISTAR HOME VIDEO 60870

ROAD TO UTOPIA

D: Hal Walker — 90 m

NR · MUS COM · 1946 · B&W

8 Slap-happy adventure farce. The famous pair of the "road" series, Hope and Crosby, is headed to Alaska for the gold rush, hoping to make it big. They're swabbing the decks to get there because they've lost all of their money, but they do have a stolen deed to a gold mine for when they get there! Unfortunately, when they arrive, they also run into a beautiful saloon girl who just happens to be the rightful owner of the mine. Full of comic asides, practical jokes and one-liners, fans have rated this the very best of the series. Quite funny.

Sex · Nud · Viol · Lang · AdSit

A: Bob Hope, Bing Crosby, Dorothy Lamour, Hillary Brooke, Douglas Dumbrille, Jack LaRue

© MCA/UNIVERSAL HOME VIDEO, INC. 81390

ROBIN AND THE SEVEN HOODS

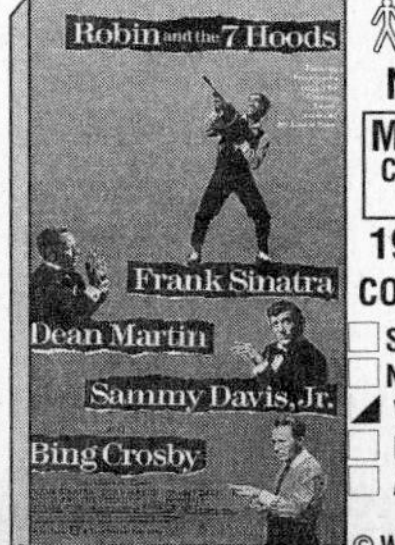

D: Gordon Douglas — 123 m

NR · MUS COM · 1964 · COLOR

6 A jazzy musical spoof, both of gangsters and of the classic English adventure tale. Set in 1928 Chicago, gangster Sinatra strikes upon a brilliant move. He will set up various charity groups and then take his cut right off the top. However, all the good will he generates also turns out to be very good for the business at his speakeasies. His chief rival in town (Falk) is more than a little upset because he's losing so much business and he decides to do something about it. A frothy light-hearted musical comedy, featuring the Oscar-nominated songs "My Kind of Town" and "All for One."

Sex · Nud · ◢ Viol · Lang · AdSit

A: Frank Sinatra, Dean Martin, Bing Crosby, Sammy Davis, Jr., Peter Falk, Barbara Rush

© WARNER HOME VIDEO 11369

FAMILY

ROCK 'N' ROLL HIGH SCHOOL

D: Allan Arkush — 93 m

PG | MUS COM | 1979 | COLOR

☐ Sex ☐ Nud ☐ Viol ■ Lang ☐ AdSit

6 Rowdy teenage rebels are seeking reform in this fast-paced teenage musical comedy! A new principal (Woronov) comes to Vince Lombardi High School and tries to cramp the kid's style, but one rebellious teenager, a die-hard "Ramones" fan, blasts their music out into the halls, and even succeeds at bringing her favorite group to the school. A confrontation is now at hand. The students go nuts and conduct a huge revolt against the suppressive and stifling establishment. A cult favorite for teens, with some genuine humor and outstanding rock 'n' roll.

A: P.J. Soles, Vincent Van Patten, Clint Howard, Dey Young, The Ramones, Mary Woronov

© WARNER HOME VIDEO 24054

ROMAN SCANDALS

D: Frank Tuttle — 92 m

MUS COM | 1933 | B&W

☐ Sex ◢ Nud ☐ Viol ☐ Lang ◢ AdSit

6 A whimsical daydream, full of gags. Famed entertainer Eddie Cantor is a young delivery boy prone to fanciful thoughts. He dreams himself right into ancient Rome, where he becomes a taste-tester for an evil ruler (Arnold) and tries to thwart the queen's plot to poison her husband. His comic adventures take him into a Roman bath house and a perilous chariot race. One of the best scenes is a musical number where a bunch of women dance around wearing only wigs (Lucille Ball is one of them). Comedy set around some serene and serious surroundings.

A: Eddie Cantor, Ruth Etting, Gloria Stuart, David Manners, Verree Teasdale, Edward Arnold

© HBO VIDEO 90749

ROSE-MARIE

D: W.S. Van Dyke — 112 m

G | MUS ROM | 1936 | B&W

☐ Sex ☐ Nud ☐ Viol ☐ Lang ◢ AdSit

6 Engaging musical from the old school! High in the Canadian Rockies, opera singer (Jeanette MacDonald) goes deep into the rugged mountains in search of her brother (Jimmy Stewart, in one of his earliest roles) who has been wounded in a prison escape. There, in the wilderness, she runs into Sgt. Bruce, a Canadian Mountie (Nelson Eddy), who is looking for her brother, too. There, along the rugged trail, the pair fall in love and sing to each other. An enjoyable escapade if you're an Eddy/MacDonald fan. Songs include "Indian Love Call" and "The Song of the Mounties."

A: Nelson Eddy, Jeanette MacDonald, James Stewart, Reginald Owen, Allan Jones, Alan Mowbray

Distributed By MGM/UA Home Video M300374

ROUSTABOUT

D: John Rich — 100 m

NR | MUS ROM | 1964 | COLOR

☐ Sex ☐ Nud ☐ Viol ☐ Lang ◢ AdSit

6 Pleasing Presley musical. A wandering young singer (Presley) literally gets run off the road by Stanwyck's carnival. While he is waiting to get his motorcycle fixed, he decides to join the carnival's crew. However, the carnival is in a whole bunch of financial trouble and, while Elvis is helping Stanwyck save her carnival from ruin, he falls in love with her daughter (Freeman). Songs include "Little Egypt" and "One Track Heart." Also has Rachel Welch in her film debut and Teri Garr in another bit part.

A: Elvis Presley, Barbara Stanwyck, Leif Erickson, Joan Freeman, Sue Anne Langdon, Raquel Welch

© CBS/FOX VIDEO 2007

RUMPELSTILTSKIN

D: David Irving — 84 m

G | MUS CLD | 1986 | COLOR

☐ Sex ☐ Nud ☐ Viol ☐ Lang ☐ AdSit

6 A well-done version of this fanciful children's fairy tale. A young girl (Irving) daydreams of magical things and her father swears that everything she touches turns to gold. When the evil King (Revill) hears of this, he summons her to spin straw into gold or be executed. To the rescue comes a mysterious little man, Rumpelstiltskin (Barty), who gets her out of her horrible situation but he expects a very expensive form of repayment. He wants Irving's first-born child - that is, unless she can guess his name. An enjoyable fantasy that young children will especially enjoy.

A: Amy Irving, Priscilla Pointer, Billy Barty, Clive Revill, John Moulder-Brown, Robert Symonds

© MEDIA HOME ENTERTAINMENT, INC. M919

SCROOGE

D: Ronald Neame — 115 m

G | MUS | 1970 | COLOR

☐ Sex ☐ Nud ☐ Viol ☐ Lang ☐ AdSit

7 Big-budget British musical production of the perennial Christmas favorite from the pen of Charles Dickens. It received Oscar nominations for Best Art Direction, Best Costumes, Best Score and Best Song: "Thank You Very Much." It is a very lively presentation of the classic with Finney in a role that seems custom-designed for him. Guiness is a standout, too.

A: Albert Finney, David Collings, Richard Beaumont, Alec Guinness, Edith Evans, Kenneth More

© FOXVIDEO 7126

SEVEN BRIDES FOR SEVEN BROTHERS

D: Stanley Donen — 102 m

G | MUS WST COM | 1954 | COLOR

☐ Sex ☐ Nud ☐ Viol ☐ Lang ☐ AdSit

10 Rollicking and witty Western musical, but with a great story too! Set in Oregon in 1850, seven young brothers are living a lonely life. When brother Keel brings home his new wife (Powell), she is overpowered by so many lonely brothers. So, she teaches them some class and social graces. But, just as soon as they begin to show some promise, Keel convinces the younger men to kidnap six pretty women and to make them their wives. Incensed, Powell kicks Keel out. An absolutely delightful musical, with a barn-raising scene that steals the show. Excellent dancing and musical score. Knockout!

A: Howard Keel, Jane Powell, Jeff Richards, Russ Tamblyn, Tommy Rall, Virginia Gibson

Distributed By MGM/UA Home Video M700091

SHALL WE DANCE

D: Mark Sandrich — 109 m

NR | MUS COM | 1937 | B&W

☐ Sex ☐ Nud ☐ Viol ☐ Lang ☐ AdSit

8 Top musical with a terrific score. That duo with the magic feet are at it again in this enjoyable musical with a comedic edge. Astaire and Rogers are a ballet star and a singer who are after jobs that are sure to further their careers, but they are going to have to cooperate. In order to get them, they must pretend to get married - but they also promise each other to get a rapid divorce as soon as they can. Their farce provides the basis for some fun romantic antics and superb songs, including "Let's Call the Whole Thing Off." Little do they know that true love is right around the corner. A most memorable Gershwin score.

A: Fred Astaire, Ginger Rogers, Eric Blore, Edward Everett Horton

© TURNER HOME ENTERTAINMENT 2037

SHOW BOAT

D: James Whale — 115 m

NR | MUS | 1936 | B&W

☐ Sex ☐ Nud ☐ Viol ☐ Lang ◢ AdSit

8 This is the best film version of a ground-breaking early musical. It has wonderful music and it also has a fascinating history because it had a very daring theme for its time. The original Broadway musical was adapted from a book by Edna Ferber. Its story revolves around the people (both black and white) on a Mississippi river show-boat in the very early 1900s and it even included an interracial romance. The original Broadway version was forbidden to have any actual black actors or singers appearing in it. Rather, the black parts had to be white people in blackface. Listen for the wonderful and now-classic songs: "Old Man River," "Bill," "Can't Help Lovin' Dat Man" and much more.

A: Irene Dunne, Allan Jones, Helen Morgan, Paul Robeson, Charles Winninger, Hattie McDaniel

Distributed By MGM/UA Home Video M301757

SILK STOCKINGS

D: Rouben Mamoulian — 118 m

MUS ROM | 1957 | COLOR

☐ Sex ☐ Nud ☐ Viol ☐ Lang ◢ AdSit

8 Musical with polish and pizzazz! Sparks fly when a heartless Soviet agent (Charisse) falls for a persistent American movie producer (Astaire) in romantic Paris. Cold and austere at first, she can't resist Astaire as his charming advances tug at her heart. This re-make of the classic NINOTCHKA into a musical features some new songs by Cole Porter and, as you would expect, unforgettable dancing from Astaire and Charisse.

A: Fred Astaire, Cyd Charisse, Janis Paige, Peter Lorre, George Tobias, Jules Munshin

Distributed By MGM/UA Home Video M700051

SONG IS BORN, A

D: Howard Hawks — 113 m

NR | MUS COM | 1948 | COLOR

☐ Sex ☐ Nud ☐ Viol ☐ Lang ☐ AdSit

7 In this entertaining remake of BALL OF FIRE, a jazz-loving professor (Kaye) of high-brow music takes his friends on a musical ride, teaching them the history of jazz and introducing them to notable musicians along the way. Jazz greats include: Louis Armstrong, Tommy Dorsey, Charlie Barnet, Mel Powell, Lionel Hampton and Buck and Bubbles. However, in the meantime, he falls in love with a saloon singer (Mayo) who is hiding out from the police and she turns Kaye into a man of strength and character. Great jazz fun.

A: Danny Kaye, Virginia Mayo, Hugh Herbert, Steve Cochran, Felix Bressart, Benny Goodman

© HBO VIDEO 90745

SOUND OF MUSIC, THE

D: Robert Wise — 175 m

G | MUS DMA | 1965 | COLOR

☐ Sex ☐ Nud ☐ Viol ☐ Lang ☐ AdSit

9 Immensely popular film adapted from an immensely popular Broadway musical and taken from the pages of real life. Winner of the Best Picture and four other Oscars. Andrews is Maria, a spunky girl who doesn't fit in at the convent, so she is sent to be the governess for the family of widower Baron Von Trapp (Plummer). She falls in love with him and the family, and they are married. But it is 1938, the Nazis are menacing Austria and have targeted their whole family. So the entire family is forced into making a daring escape over the mountains. Warm and wonderful with memorable songs. Sweet and timeless.

A: Julie Andrews, Christopher Plummer, Peggy Wood, Angela Cartwright, Richard Haydn, Eleanor Parker

© FOXVIDEO 1051

SPRINGTIME IN THE ROCKIES

D: Irving Cummings 91 m

NR | MUS ROM | 1942 | COLOR

7 Entertaining Hollywood musical. Two Broadway entertainers (Grable and Payne) just can't seem to get along. They bicker and fight, make up and break up, on and off stage in this fun musical. Forever trying to "get even" with each other, Grable runs off with a handsome dancer and gets engaged just to spite Payne. Payne retaliates by hiring a steamy secretary and feigns love. Light on plot, but the lush scenery and excellent singing and dancing make up for it.

Sex / Nud / Viol / Lang / ◢ AdSit

A: Betty Grable, John Payne, Carmen Miranda, Cesar Romero, Charlotte Greenwood, Edward Everett Horton

© FOXVIDEO 1723

STATE FAIR

D: Walter Lang 100 m

NR | MUS | 1945 | COLOR

7 Charming, tuneful and entertaining Americana. A colorful canvas of song and charm! A midwestern family prepares for the Iowa State Fair, each anticipating his/her own set of rewards. Dad (Winninger) is hoping to take home a prize in the hog contest, while Mom (Bainter) hopes her mincemeat pie is worth a ribbon. The children (Haymes and Crain) hope for romance, and they find it. The ingredients in this straightforward charmer are perfectly measured: wit, romance, song and innocence. A wonderful musical that would have certainly won a ribbon at the Iowa fair.

Sex / Nud / Viol / Lang / AdSit

A: Jeanne Crain, Dana Andrews, Dick Haymes, Vivian Blaine, Charles Winninger, Fay Bainter

© FOXVIDEO 1348

STORMY WEATHER

D: Andrew L. Stone 78 m

NR | MUS | 1943 | B&W

6 An enjoyable musical that is told in flashback format and boasts a stellar all-black cast. Robinson and Horne are a husband and wife team who work in show business, are struggling to put bread on the table and to keep their marriage together. The plot, however, proves to be just an excuse for and a loose framework with which to present some of the greatest black talent of that day. It has an outstanding musical score that features Fats Waller performing "Ain't Misbehavin'," but Horne steals the show when she performs the title song "Stormy Weather."

Sex / Nud / Viol / Lang / ◢ AdSit

A: Lena Horne, Bill Robinson, Cab Calloway, Dooley Wilson, Fats Waller, Katherine Dunham

© FOXVIDEO 1168

SUMMER STOCK

D: Charles Walters 121 m

NR | MUS | 1950 | COLOR

8 Fancy footwork and zippy songs create a very engaging musical. DeHaven is a carefree sister who invites a dance troup to practice on her farm, without telling her older sister (Garland) who's struggling to keep it afloat. Garland doesn't like the idea when they all show up, but she strikes a deal with the dancers. They can stay in her farmhouse and practice getting ready for a play in exchange for help with the chores. It is not long before the show biz bug bites Garland and she has a change of heart. Light-on-his-feet Kelly manages to sweep Garland off of hers. A light-hearted, enjoyable musical.

Sex / Nud / Viol / Lang / ◢ AdSit

A: Judy Garland, Gene Kelly, Phil Silvers, Marjorie Main, Eddie Bracken, Gloria De Haven

Distributed By MGM/UA Home Video M300851

SUNDAY IN THE PARK WITH GEORGE

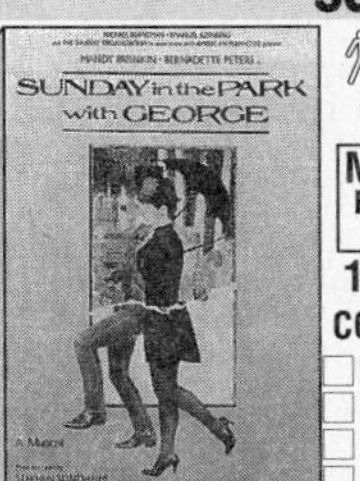

D: James Lapine 145 m

NR | MUS ROM | 1986 | COLOR

9 A painting comes to life in this magnificent taped stage presentation of the superb Pulitzer Prize-winning musical play. Based on characters featured in Georges Seurat's painting "Sunday Afternoon on the Island of La Grande Jatte," each character in the painting becomes real and has a compelling story to tell. The score and lyrics by Stephen Sondheim are very memorable. Patinkin deftly plays the Seurat, the masterful painter. One of the most unforgettable musicals in recent history. A standout!

Sex / Nud / Viol / Lang / ◢ AdSit

A: Bernadette Peters, Mandy Patinkin, Barbara Byrne, Charles Kimbrough

© WARNER HOME VIDEO 370

SWING TIME

D: George Stevens 103 m

NR | MUS COM | 1935 | B&W

8 A real charmer! Dazzling dancing and acting makes this one of the best Astaire/Rogers films. Astaire is a young groom-to-be who goes to the Big Apple hoping to dance his way to earning the $25,000 he needs to wed his long-time girlfriend. But while he is there, he falls in love with a beautiful dance instructor (Rogers). Soon Astaire is hoping that he won't make enough money, and won't have to go home to his fiancee. A very appealing, highly likable musical with both characters at their comic and dancing best.

Sex / Nud / Viol / Lang / ◢ AdSit

A: Fred Astaire, Ginger Rogers, Victor Moore, Helen Broderick, Betty Furness, Eric Blore

© TURNER HOME ENTERTAINMENT 2036

THAT'S DANCING

D: Jack Haley, Jr. 105 m

G | MUS | 1985 | COLOR

8 Compendium of virtually all the great dance sequences ever put to film at MGM, from the '30s to modern times (mid-'80s), and hosted by the best dancers in the business. The best part is that you don't have to listen to a lot of dialogue that usually only serves as an excuse to dance in the first place.

Sex / Nud / Viol / Lang / AdSit

A: Gene Kelly, Mikhail Baryshnikov, Sammy Davis, Jr., Ray Bolger, Liza Minnelli, Fred Astaire

Distributed By MGM/UA Home Video M800613

THAT WAS ROCK

D: Steve Binder, Larry Peerce 90 m

NR | MUS DOC | 1964 | B&W

9 One of the best collections of rock 'n roll and R&B talent from the '60s. See Chuck Berry, James Brown, Ray Charles, Marvin Gaye, The Rolling Stones, The Supremes, Smokey Robinson and the Miracles, Gerry and the Pacemakers, The Ronettes and Tina Turner. Originally recorded on B&W videotape, the recording quality is not good - but the material is priceless. The clips were also originally released in two rock extravaganza-type films: "The T.A.M.I. Show" (1964) and "The Big T.N.T. Show" (1966).

Sex / Nud / Viol / Lang / AdSit

A: Chuck Berry, James Brown, Marvin Gaye, The Rolling Stones, The Supremes, Smokey Robinson

© MUSIC MEDIA M434

THOROUGHLY MODERN MILLIE

D: George Roy Hill 138 m

G | MUS COM | 1967 | COLOR

6 Cute musical fluff that received 7 Oscar nominations and won Best Original Score. Julie Andrews arrives in the big city and quickly transforms herself into a 1920s modern woman - a flapper. She is also determined to realize her life's ambition: to become a stenographer and marry her boss. But, she becomes so caught up in her fantasy that she doesn't see that she really doesn't want her boss because she really is in love with someone else. All the while, her equally innocent new-found friend (Moore) has become the object of a white slaver's interest. Light-hearted light-weight campy farce.

Sex / Nud / Viol / Lang / AdSit

A: Julie Andrews, Mary Tyler Moore, Carol Channing, John Gavin, Beatrice Lillie, James Fox

© MCA/UNIVERSAL HOME VIDEO, INC. 55028

THREE LITTLE WORDS

D: Richard Thorpe 103 m

NR | MUS | 1950 | COLOR

8 Fred Astaire claimed that this was his favorite movie. It is the musical biography, mostly factual, of the songwriting team of Kalmar and Ruby. There is little plot, however. But, there is a great deal of singing and dancing and a whole lot of fun. Songs include: "I Wanna Be Loved By You," "Thinking of You" and "Who's Sorry Now?"

Sex / Nud / Viol / Lang / AdSit

A: Red Skelton, Fred Astaire, Debbie Reynolds, Vera-Ellen, Arlene Dahl, Keenan Wynn

Distributed By MGM/UA Home Video M301189

TOM SAWYER

D: Don Taylor 102 m

G | MUS CLD | 1973 | COLOR

8 Well done musical remake of Mark Twain's classic, set in the 1830s Missouri wilds along the Mississippi river, near the town of Hannibal. It concerns the exploits of young Tom (Whitaker), his friend - outcast Huck Finn (East) and his girl friend Becky Thatcher (a very young Jodie Foster). this is a first-rate children's movie that will also appeal to many adults. The picture garnered Oscar nominations for Set Decoration, Costume Design and Score. Music and screenplay were written by the same people who did MARY POPPINS, Richard and Robert Sherman.

Sex / Nud / Viol / Lang / AdSit

A: Johnny Whitaker, Celeste Holm, Warren Oates, Jeff East, Jodie Foster

Distributed By MGM/UA Home Video M201863

TOP HAT

D: Mark Sandrich 99 m

NR | MUS ROM COM | 1935 | B&W

10 If you like musicals and dancing, this is the movie for you. But, it's also romantic, has good comedic moments and the story line is better developed than in most musicals. But still, it's the singing and dancing that makes it so special. Probably the best of the Fred Astaire and Ginger Rodgers parings, it is set in London. Fred falls for Ginger, his downstairs neighbor, but she thinks he's married. Nominated for Best Picture. Top tunes from Irving Berlin: "Cheek to Cheek," "Top Hat, White Tie and Tails" and many more.

Sex / Nud / Viol / Lang / AdSit

A: Fred Astaire, Ginger Rogers, Edward Everett Horton, Eric Blore, Helen Broderick, Erik Rhodes

© TURNER HOME ENTERTAINMENT 2070

UNSINKABLE MOLLY BROWN, THE

D: Charles Walters — 128 m

NR | MUS COM | 1964 | COLOR

6 Big-budget screen version of the successful Broadway musical. Debbie Reynolds puts in an enthusiastic and rambunctious performance in the title role. Her character is based upon a real-life character from the Colorado gold rush days. She is an unsophisticated, but energetic, backwoods girl who marries a miner just before he strikes it rich. She is determined, but unsuccessful, at making it into Denver society, even though she is the richest woman in town - that is until she gains notoriety as a being survivor of the sinking Titanic. Bouncy, but mostly for musical fans.

Sex / Nud / Viol / Lang / AdSit

A: Debbie Reynolds, Ed Begley, Harve Presnell, Hermione Baddeley, Jack Kruschen, Harvey Lembeck

Distributed By MGM/UA Home Video M600578

VIVA LAS VEGAS

D: George Sidney — 85 m

NR | MUS ROM | 1963 | COLOR

7 The King goes to Las Vegas to win the Las Vegas Grand Prix. Elvis is a racecar driver, but first he has to come up with enough money to buy the hot new engine he's going to need to get the job done. So he takes a job as a waiter, and there he meets luscious, lovely Ann-Margret. She's a swimming instructor at the hotel and Elvis begins to lose his focus. Lots of Vegas pretty girls, some racing action and ten Elvis songs, the biggest of which is "What'd I Say."

Sex / Nud / Viol / Lang / ◢ AdSit

A: Elvis Presley, Ann-Margret, Cesare Danova, William Demarest, Jack Carter

Distributed By MGM/UA Home Video M600116

WHITE CHRISTMAS

D: Michael Curtiz — 120 m

NR | MUS COM | 1954 | COLOR

7 Irving Berlin song fest. Two Army pals from the war (Crosby and Kaye) have been teamed up ever since and have become a top show business act. When they learn that their old commanding officer's Vermont ski resort is in trouble, they decide to stage a musical at his resort to give him a boost. Songs include "Blue Skies," "Snow," "Count Your Blessings Instead of Sheep" (Oscar nominated), "Sisters" and, of course, "White Christmas" - which was first introduced in HOLIDAY INN, from which this film borrows heavily. Mostly for fans of old-style musicals.

Sex / Nud / Viol / Lang / AdSit

A: Bing Crosby, Danny Kaye, Dean Jagger, Vera-Ellen, Rosemary Clooney

© PARAMOUNT HOME VIDEO 6104

YANKEE DOODLE DANDY

D: Michael Curtiz — 127 m

NR | MUS DMA | 1942 | B&W

9 Rousing biography and musical depicting the somewhat fictionalized life of the entertainment legend, George M. Cohan, and starring another entertainment legend (Cagney). Cagney is wonderful as George M., the early 20th-century playwrite, songwriter, actor and dancer who began on the stages of vaudeville, only to later dominate the Broadway stage for an entire generation. Seven Oscar nominations, including Best Picture. Winner of three, including Cagney for Best Actor. Great show tunes, too: "You're a Grand Old Flag," ""Over There" and, of course, "Yankee Doodle Dandy."

Sex / Nud / Viol / Lang / AdSit

A: James Cagney, Joan Leslie, Walter Huston, Irene Manning, Rosemary DeCamp, Richard Whorf

Distributed By MGM/UA Home Video M200792

YELLOW SUBMARINE

D: George Dunning — 87 m

G | MUS FAN | 1968 | COLOR

8 Imaginative and clever animated feature with a score filled with fun Beatles music. Beatles fans will of course be particularly interested, but others should take note as well. The storyline has animated Beatles traveling by a yellow submarine to the fantasy land of Pepperland where their music and love will overcome the Blue Meanies, who have declared war on all that is good. Surrealistic pop art combines with lots of jokes and puns, plus these and more songs: "Lucy in the Sky With Diamonds," "When I'm 64," "All You Need is Love" and "Yellow Submarine."

Sex / Nud / Viol / Lang / AdSit

A: The Beatles

Distributed By MGM/UA Home Video M301170

Mystery

AFTER THE THIN MAN

D: W.S. Van Dyke — 113 m

NR | MYS COM | 1936 | B&W

8 Another 1930's powerhouse pairing of William Powell and Myrna Loy. Powell and Loy had terrific screen chemistry that gave them a dozen hits together. Here they are the popular wisecracking sophisticated detectives, Nick and Nora Charles. When one of Nora's blue-blooded cousins is accused of killing her husband, Nick must help prove her innocence. But before long there are two more murders and they are in trouble. Clever and snappy dialogue make solving the case of the missing husband great fun. See also THE THIN MAN and ANOTHER THIN MAN.

Sex / Nud / Viol / Lang / ◢ AdSit

A: William Powell, Myrna Loy, James Stewart, Elissa Landi, Joseph Calleia, Sam Levine

Distributed By MGM/UA Home Video M300820

AND THEN THERE WERE NONE

D: Rene Clair — 97 m

NR | MYS SUS COM | 1945 | B&W

9 A true classic and perhaps the best-ever adaptation of one of Agatha Christie's mysteries. It is a great tale filled with mystery, suspense and humor that will keep you entranced until the very last scene. The premise is that ten guests, who don't know each other or their host, are invited to a lonely and isolated English island. The only common thread is that each has a hidden crime in his past. One by one the guests are murdered, with never a clue as to why or who the murderer is. It uses equal parts of humor and suspense, plus a deftly created atmosphere, to weave a vastly entertaining yarn. It has been remade twice.

Sex / Nud / Viol / Lang / ◢ AdSit

A: Barry Fitzgerald, Walter Huston, Richard Burton, Roland Young, Judith Anderson, Louis Hayward

© VIDEO COMMUNICATIONS, INC. 4501

ANOTHER THIN MAN

D: W.S. Van Dyke II — 103 m

NR | MYS COM | 1939 | B&W

8 Sophistication and wit. Nick and Nora Charles are the witty and urbane private detective couple first seen in THE THIN MAN. As in the other Thin Man movies, the plot is secondary to the clever interaction between the two leads. Here the detectives contend with a man who dreams about catastrophies before they happen. Always an enjoyable experience. See AFTER THE THIN MAN, SHADOW OF THE THIN MAN and the others. Check the Sequels index.

Sex / Nud / Viol / Lang / ◢ AdSit

A: William Powell, Myrna Loy, Virginia Grey, Otto Kruger, C. Aubrey Smith, Ruth Hussey

Distributed By MGM/UA Home Video M300868

BIG FIX, THE

D: Jeremy Paul Kagan — 108 m

PG | MYS SUS | 1978 | COLOR

7 Pretty good mystery and a good vehicle for Dreyfuss's wise-cracking personality. He plays a '60s radical who is now a private investigator. He is hired by his former lover (Anspack), from the days when they were both political activists at Berkeley, to find out who's using dirty tricks to smear the political candidate she's working for. He already has enough trouble trying to deal with his ex-wife and finding enough time for his kids, and now he winds up in the middle of a murder. Plenty of plot twists to keep you involved.

Sex / Nud / ◢ Viol / ◢ Lang / ◢ AdSit

A: Richard Dreyfuss, Susan Anspach, Bonnie Bedelia, John Lithgow, F. Murray Abraham

© MCA/UNIVERSAL HOME VIDEO, INC. 66053

CHARLIE CHAN AT THE OPERA

D: H. Bruce Humberstone — 68 m

NR | MYS CRM | 1936 | B&W

8 The famous and popular crime-solving character, Charlie Chan, the Oriental detective from the Honolulu police department, first came to the screen in 1926 but didn't become widely popular until 1931 when Warner Oland took the role. There were three primary Charlies until the series ended in the late '40s. This film is of the best of the mysteries - most are not available on video. Here Charlie seeks out a high society murderer who has escaped from an asylum, taken refuge in an opera house and now members of the company are slowly being killed off.

Sex / Nud / Viol / Lang / AdSit

A: Warner Oland, Boris Karloff, Keye Luke, Charlotte Henry, Thomas Beck, Gregory Gaye

© FOXVIDEO 1368

CHARLIE CHAN IN RIO

D: Harry Lachman — 62 m

NR | MYS CRM | 1941 | B&W

8 Sidney Toler was the second Charlie Chan after Warner Oland died in 1937 and played Charlie for nine years. Not many of the series, particularly the good ones, are available on video. However, this is the best by Sidney Toler. Here Charlie joins forces with the Rio police to solve a tricky case. Charlie is in Rio to arrest a murderess, but someone gets to her before he can.

Sex / Nud / Viol / Lang / AdSit

A: Sidney Toler, Mary Beth Hughes, Cobina Wright, Victor Jory, Harold Huber, Victor Sen Yung

© FOXVIDEO 1706

DRESSED TO KILL

NR | MYS CRM | 1946 | B&W

D: Roy William Neill — 72 m

8 This was last Sherlock Holmes adventure with Basil Rathbone as Holmes. Holmes investigates the burglary of one of Watson's friends. The man has an extensive collection of music boxes, but only one of the less valuable ones is stolen. Holmes is shown another similar box, and then that box is also stolen. Then Watson's friend is murdered. Holmes discovers that he is in pursuit of three music boxes which contain clues to engraving plates stolen from the Bank of England. After this film, Rathbone retired to the stage and did not appear again in a movie for nine years.

Sex / Nud / Viol / Lang / ◢ AdSit

A: Basil Rathbone, Nigel Bruce, Patricia Morison, Edmond Breon, Carl Harbord

© REPUBLIC PICTURES HOME VIDEO V7155

EDDIE AND THE CRUISERS

PG | MYS SUS | 1983 | COLOR

D: Martin Davidson — 95 m

7 Odd but interesting film which has developed into a cult film. Eddie and the Cruisers had been a rock group in the 1960s, but it was way ahead of its time. The lead singer, Eddie, dejected after his album idea is rejected, drove off a bridge - but no body was ever recovered. Now it is much later and the group's songs have finally become popular. Now, also, someone is breaking into all the former bandmember's houses apparently looking for the master tape of some unreleased songs. Reporter Ellen Barkin begins to wonder if Eddie is still alive. Pretty good mystery, even if it is unusual.

Sex / Nud / ◢ Viol / ◢ Lang / ◢ AdSit

A: Tom Berenger, Michael Pare, Ellen Barkin, Helen Schneider, Joe Pantoliano

© NEW LINE HOME VIDEO 2066

FAMILY PLOT

PG | MYS COM | 1976 | COLOR

D: Alfred Hitchcock — 121 m

8 This is a winning, light-hearted, convoluted thriller/comedy from Mr. Hitchcock. A seedy pseudo-psychic (Harris) and her loser boyfriend (Dern) team up to track down a lost heir (Devane) and get a $10,000 reward. The target of all this attention is a man supposedly dead, not really dead, but who would much prefer to be thought of as dead. That is because he turns out to be a not-too-nice guy who, along with Karen Black, is in the process of launching a big kidnap-ping/extortion plot. A fun time, full of plot twists and black humor.

Sex / Nud / Viol / Lang / ◢ AdSit

A: Karen Black, Bruce Dern, Barbara Harris, William Devane, Ed Lauter, Cathleen Nesbitt

© MCA/UNIVERSAL HOME VIDEO, INC. 66054

MARLOWE

PG | MYS ACT | 1969 | COLOR

D: Paul Bogart — 96 m

8 Entertaining and intriguing mystery. The infamous Marlowe (Garner) is a hard-boiled detective who is hired by a girl (Farrell) to find her missing brother. Garner quickly finds that he has gotten more than he bargained for when kung fu king Bruce Lee (in his film debut) offers him a bribe to drop the case and then turns his office into a pile of broken sticks as a warning. There is blackmail, ice pick murders and a stripper (Moreno) who ultimately helps to solve the case. A good mystery is combined with clever dialogue to make this a real fun time. Based on the Chandler novel "The Little Sister."

Sex / Nud / Viol / ◢ Lang / ◢ AdSit

A: James Garner, Gayle Hunnicutt, Carroll O'Connor, Rita Moreno, Sharon Farrell, Bruce Lee

Distributed By MGM/UA Home Video M200288

MURDER BY DEATH

PG | MYS COM | 1976 | COLOR

D: Robert Moore — 95 m

8 Murder is on the dinner menu in this comic mystery! Eccentric millionaire Lionel Twain (Truman Capote) invites top detectives to his home for dinner and offers one million dollars to anyone who can solve the murder of the evening - someone at this table will be stabbed twelve times before midnight. Some of the dinner guests include prominent film detectives such as Sam Spade, Miss Marple and Charlie Chan. Written by Neil Simon, this hilarious film is really a spoof on the great super sleuths of film and features a fantastic all-star cast.

Sex / Nud / Viol / ◢ Lang / ◢ AdSit

A: Peter Sellers, Peter Falk, David Niven, Maggie Smith, James Coco, Alec Guinness

© COLUMBIA TRISTAR HOME VIDEO 60065

NIGHT TO REMEMBER, A

NR | MYS SUS COM | 1943 | B&W

D: Richard Wallace — 91 m

9 Highly entertaining whodunit with a comic flair. The wife of a successful young murder mystery writer has always wanted him to write a romantic novel, so she searches out the perfect apartment for them in Greenwich village which will set just the proper mood. However, when a dead body turns up in their back yard, he feels compelled to solve the real murder mystery. Classy, consistently entertaining - with a few hilarious lines and terrific performances.

Sex / Nud / Viol / Lang / AdSit

A: Loretta Young, Brian Aherne, Sidney Toler, Gale Sondergaard, Donald MacBride, Blanche Yurka

© COLUMBIA TRISTAR HOME VIDEO 62000

PEARL OF DEATH, THE

NR | MYS | 1944 | B&W

D: Roy William Neill — 69 m

7 Rathbone and Bruce, again as Sherlock Holmes and Dr. Watson, are this time tracking down three criminals. A master thief has stolen the Borgia pearls and hidden them inside a wet plaster cast which will become one of six busts of Napoleon. The thief then instructs his homicidal partner, "The Creeper," to kill the owners of the busts. This he accomplishes by methodically snapping the third vertebrae in each of his victim's necks. The masterful Holmes catches, but must then do battle with, "The Creeper." Pretty good offering in the series.

Sex / Nud / ◢ Viol / Lang / AdSit

A: Basil Rathbone, Nigel Bruce, Evelyn Ankers, Dennis Hoey, Miles Mander, Mary Gordon

© CBS/FOX VIDEO 7780

SCARLET CLAW, THE

NR | MYS SUS | 1944 | B&W

D: Roy William Neill — 74 m

9 A highly atmospheric mystery, acclaimed by some as the best of the Sherlock Holmes series. Holmes (Rathbone) and Watson (Bruce) travel to Canada in 1944 to attend a seminar on supernatural powers. While there, they are drawn into an investigation of several gruesome murders recently committed. The villagers attribute the killings to the work of a local monster. But as the monster adopts different disguises, Holmes sets out to prove that the murders were committed by human hands. Moody photography adds to the mysterious mood.

Sex / Nud / ◢ Viol / Lang / ◢ AdSit

A: Basil Rathbone, Nigel Bruce, Paul Cavanagh, Kay Harding, Gerald Hammer, Arthur Hohl

© CBS/FOX VIDEO 7782

SEVEN-PER-CENT SOLUTION, THE

PG | MYS | 1976 | COLOR

D: Herbert Ross — 114 m

8 Zippy, well-done, tongue-in-cheek Holmes adventure. One of the best. Sherlock Holmes (Williamson) suffers from a cocaine addiction. Dr. Watson (Duvall) lures Holmes into a fabricated chase to Vienna where Dr. Sigmund Freud (Arkin) is to rid Holmes of his foul habit. However, instead, Freud and Holmes - two of the world's leading practitioners of the art of deduction - end up joining forces to solve a kidnapping. A thoroughly entertaining, fast-paced and engrossing mystery. Outstanding portrayal of Watson by Duvall and a curious portrait of Moriarity by Olivier.

Sex / Nud / Viol / Lang / ◢ AdSit

A: Alan Arkin, Nicol Williamson, Laurence Olivier, Robert Duvall, Vanessa Redgrave, Joel Grey

© MCA/UNIVERSAL HOME VIDEO, INC. 55064

SHADOW OF THE THIN MAN

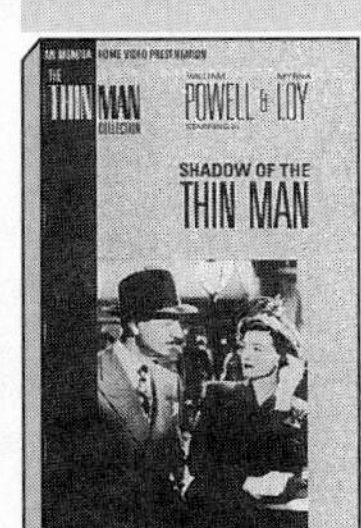

NR | MYS COM | 1941 | B&W

D: W.S. Van Dyke II — 98 m

8 A dynamite whodunit! The fourth in the Thin Man series has our heros, the suave and witty married detectives Nick and Nora (Powell and Loy), stumbling upon the murders of a jockey and a reporter at the racetrack. There is a body in the shower, another one hanging from a chandelier and a diamond bracelet in the radiator. The debonair pair quickly move in to investigate, with their baby Nick and dog Asta in tow, to try to uncover who is behind the dastardly deeds. Once again, this fun entry in the light-hearted Thin Man detective series will live up to your expectations.

Sex / Nud / Viol / Lang / ◢ AdSit

A: William Powell, Myrna Loy, Barry Nelson, Donna Reed, Sam Levene

Distributed By MGM/UA Home Video M300967

SHERLOCK HOLMES AND THE SECRET WEAPON

NR | MYS | 1942 | B&W

D: Roy William Neill — 68 m

8 This Holmes adventure is set against the dangerous backdrop of WWII Europe. Holmes (Rathbone) is charged with finding a Swiss inventor and his bombsight, who are in hiding in Germany. Holmes is to get both of them out of Germany, and out of reach of the Nazis and their villainous accomplice, Professor Moriarty. The only clue Holmes has to find them is an encrypted message left by the inventor.

Sex / Nud / Viol / Lang / ◢ AdSit

A: Basil Rathbone, Nigel Bruce, Lionel Atwill, Kaaren Verne

© VIDEO TREASURES HR9605

SHERLOCK HOLMES AND THE VOICE OF TERROR

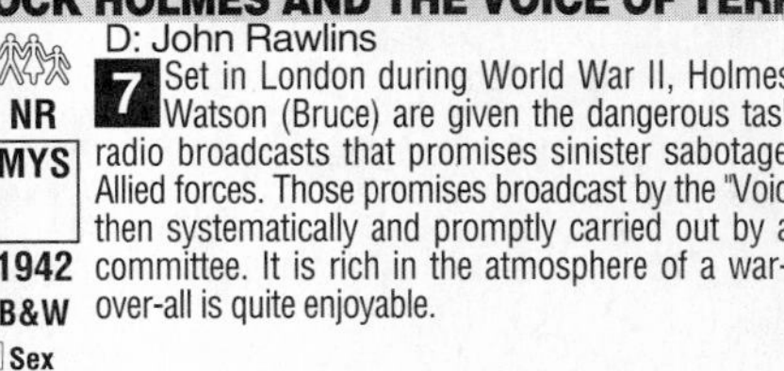

NR | MYS | 1942 | B&W

D: John Rawlins — 65 m

7 Set in London during World War II, Holmes (Rathbone) and Watson (Bruce) are given the dangerous task of quieting Nazi radio broadcasts that promises sinister sabotage acts against the Allied forces. Those promises broadcast by the "Voice of Terror" are all then systematically and promptly carried out by an evil Nazi death committee. It is rich in the atmosphere of a war-torn London and over-all is quite enjoyable.

Sex / Nud / Viol / Lang / ◢ AdSit

A: Basil Rathbone, Nigel Bruce, Reginald Denny, Evelyn Ankers, Thomas Gomez

© CBS/FOX VIDEO 7788

SHERLOCK HOLMES FACES DEATH

D: Roy William Neill 68 m

NR | MYS | 1943 | B&W

7 When the Musgrave mansion becomes a den of death, Watson (Bruce) calls on his trusty friend Holmes (Rathbone) to help him solve the strange murders. Holmes believes that the clue to the killings is contained in a will, and set out to find the killer by playing a giant game of human "chess" right on the mansion's floor. Holmes methodically moves people around from square to square in his brilliant game of deductive reasoning.

Sex / Nud / Viol / Lang / ✓ AdSit

A: Basil Rathbone, Nigel Bruce, Hillary Brooke, Milburn Stone

© CBS/FOX VIDEO 7784

SHERLOCK HOLMES IN WASHINGTON

D: Roy William Neill 71 m

NR | MYS | 1943 | B&W

6 This nifty Holmes wartime adventure brings the duo to the United States. A top secret British agent is harboring a secret microfilm containing important war documents inside the casing of a matchbook. When he is killed, the matchbook is given to a woman traveling on an airplane. She has no idea how important it is, and it falls into the wrong hands. Holmes (Rathbone) and Watson (Bruce) are dispatched to Washington to find the elusive matchbook and chase down a ring of Nazi spies.

Sex / Nud / Viol / Lang / ✓ AdSit

A: Basil Rathbone, Nigel Bruce, George Zucco, Marjorie Lord, George Zucco

© CBS/FOX VIDEO 7785

SONG OF THE THIN MAN

D: Edward Buzzell 87 m

NR | MYS COM | 1947 | B&W

7 This was the last of the Thin Man films. The super sleuthing couple Nick and Nora (Powell and Loy) go after a murderer who kills a bandmember aboard ship. Their search takes them to New York and has them hanging out in some of the Big Apple's swankier jazz clubs. The snappy dialogue seems especially crisp set against the steamy backdrop. A fitting and particularly good conclusion to the entertaining series. Be sure to see the Heros, etc. index for a complete listing of the others in the series.

Sex / Nud / Viol / Lang / ✓ AdSit

A: William Powell, Myrna Loy, Keenan Wynn, Dean Stockwell

Distributed By MGM/UA Home Video M300969

SPELLBOUND

D: Alfred Hitchcock 111 m

NR | MYS ROM | 1945 | B&W

9 The master of suspense works his magic in this classic thriller for the mind! Six Oscar nominations. Peck is the new head psychiatrist in a mental hospital but quickly starts to exhibit problems of his own. Bergman, the beautiful psychiatrist who falls in love with him, soon discovers that he is not who he appears to be. He is an imposter and an amnesiac. She loves him, but where is the real Dr. Edwards? Is Peck a murderer? She must help him get to the bottom of the past he has blocked out. Expect several unanticipated plot twists. Famous for a Salvador Dali surrealist dream sequence.

Sex / Nud / Viol / Lang / ✓ AdSit

A: Ingrid Bergman, Gregory Peck, Leo G. Carroll, Michael Chekhov, John Emery, Wallace Ford

© CBS/FOX VIDEO 8035

STAGE FRIGHT

D: Alfred Hitchcock 110 m

NR | MYS SUS | 1949 | B&W

7 Early Hitchcock fun. A young drama student (Todd) appears to have been framed by his mistress (Dietrich), a flamboyant stage star, for the murder of her husband. Jane Wyman, who was once Todd's girlfriend, decides to play detective and takes a job as Dietrich's maid, in an attempt to uncover some clues that will implicate Dietrich. Meanwhile, Wyman's father hides Todd out until they can get the goods and force Dietrich to confess, but the arrival of a slick detective (Wilding) complicates things. This is an underrated thriller with a tricky plot.

Sex / Nud / Viol / Lang / ✓ AdSit

A: Jane Wyman, Marlene Dietrich, Michael Wilding, Richard Todd, Kay Walsh, Alastair Sim

© WARNER HOME VIDEO 11380

STUDY IN TERROR, A

D: James Hill 94 m

NR | MYS SYS | 1966 | COLOR

7 The super sleuth, Sherlock Holmes (Neville), has his work cut out for him once again. The setting is London in the late 1800s and the notorious "Jack the Ripper" is on the loose, brutally murdering the city's ladies of the evening. Holmes sets his sights on stopping the madman in his evil tracks. Beginning with only a missing scalpel from a surgeon's kit, Holmes searches the grisly murder scenes in London's back streets to find the clues to lead him to his aristocratic killer. Highly entertaining British import that was undeservedly overlooked by audiences. Houston is outstanding as Dr. Watson.

Sex / Nud / ✓ Viol / Lang / ✓ AdSit

A: John Neville, Donald Houston, Georgia Brown, John Fraser, Anthony Quayle, Barbara Windsor

© COLUMBIA TRISTAR HOME VIDEO 20671

THIN MAN GOES HOME, THE

D: Richard Thorpe 102 m

NR | MYS COM | 1944 | B&W

7 This is the fifth entry in the series. In it, Nick and Nora go back to his home town of Sycamore Springs to see his parents. Even there the two can't escape murder when a man mysteriously drops dead on the neighbor's front porch. Now Nick has to prove himself in front of his father. But Dad doesn't take it kindly when Nick starts pointing fingers at his fellow townsmen. This one still has all the mystery elements of the past entries, however it plays more on the comedy aspects of the famous sophisticated detectives.

Sex / Nud / Viol / Lang / AdSit

A: William Powell, Myrna Loy, Lucile Watson, Gloria De Haven, Anne Revere, Helen Vinson

Distributed By MGM/UA Home Video M300970

Romance

ALWAYS

D: Steven Spielberg 123 m

PG | ROM COM FAN | 1989 | COLOR

7 Very pleasing remake of THE STORY OF JOE. Dreyfuss plays a bush pilot who is killed in a crash but is brought back by his guardian angel (Hepburn). He is to be the guardian angel of an awkward young flyer (Johnson). At first Dreyfuss likes his new job, but that all changes when he also has to help his girlfriend (Hunter) to move on with her life and does it by lining her up with Johnson. This is a light little movie with no major statements to make but it is still a lot of fun. However, you should see the original, too. It is one of director Spielberg's favorites, which was the reason why he redid it here.

Sex / Nud / Viol / ✓ Lang / ✓ AdSit

A: Richard Dreyfuss, Holly Hunter, Brad Johnson, John Goodman, Audrey Hepburn, Keith David

© MCA/UNIVERSAL HOME VIDEO, INC. 80967

BACHELOR MOTHER

D: Garson Kanin 82 m

NR | ROM COM | 1939 | B&W

8 Witty and very funny movie that was one of the biggest hits of 1939. Ginger Rogers is an unmarried sales clerk who finds a baby on a doorstep and takes it in. However, serious complications arise when no one will believe that the baby isn't hers. As an unmarried mother, her whole life is turned upside down and she is even in danger of losing her job. The store's owner thinks his son (Niven) is responsible. Then three more men turn up all claiming to be the father. Rogers shows a real talent for comedy in this movie, even though she reportedly didn't want to do this picture.

Sex / Nud / Viol / Lang / ✓ AdSit

A: Ginger Rogers, David Niven, Charles Coburn, Frank Albertson, Ernest Truex

© TURNER HOME ENTERTAINMENT 6056

BUDDY SYSTEM, THE

D: Glenn Jordan 110 m

PG | ROM COM | 1983 | COLOR

7 Nice little charmer. Wil Wheaton and his struggling, insecure, single Mom, make friends with a security guard, who is also a part-time novelist and a part-time inventor (Richard Dreyfuss), and is also struggling in a relationship with his ditzy, unfaithful girlfriend. Wil wants a father, but Mom and Dreyfuss are sure they are just friends. However, in spite of all their concerns and precautions, love triumphs. Dreyfuss learns to give up his unfaithful fantasy girl and Sarandon learns to trust again. This is a pleasing, enjoyable story, even if much of it is predictable. It is both funny and heartwarming.

Sex / Nud / Viol / ✓ Lang / ✓ AdSit

A: Richard Dreyfuss, Susan Sarandon, Jean Stapleton, Nancy Allen, Wil Wheaton

© FOXVIDEO 1316

CHANCES ARE

D: Emile Ardolino 108 m

PG | ROM COM | 1989 | COLOR

7 Pretty good light-hearted comedy. Cybill Shepherd has remained true to her husband's memory for 23 years after his death, in spite of the persistent attentions of his best friend (Ryan O'Neal) who is also in love with her. Robert Downey Jr. is a college student who pursues Shepherd's grown daughter home from school. However, he soon uncomfortably discovers that he is the reincarnated spirit of her former husband, after being around Shepherd brings back all the feelings and memories from his former life. So he now sets out to help her to get her life back in motion and become happy again. Very well done. Sweet-natured and appealing.

Sex / Nud / Viol / ✓ Lang / ✓ AdSit

A: Cybill Shepherd, Robert Downey, Jr., Ryan O'Neal, Mary Stuart Masterson, Christopher McDonald, Josef Sommer

© COLUMBIA TRISTAR HOME VIDEO 70153

CLOCK, THE

D: Vincente Minnelli — 91 m

NR | ROM | 1945 | B&W

7 Entertaining little bit of froth with Judy Garland as a secretary who meets Robert Walker, a war-time soldier on a 48-hour pass, in a train station. They immediately fall in love and then make the most of their short time together by exploring the streets of New York meeting all sorts of interesting people. Interestingly, because of the way in which the script is written, the city actually becomes a third character in this charming little love story. Shortly after this picture was made, director Minnelli married his star.

Sex / Nud / Viol / Lang / ◢ AdSit

A: Judy Garland, Robert Walker, James Gleason, Keenan Wynn, Marshall Thompson, Lucile Gleason

Distributed By MGM/UA Home Video MV200890

CUTTING EDGE, THE

D: Paul Michael Glaser — 102 m

PG | ROM | 1991 | COLOR

7 Entertaining romance flick. Two last-chance kids get one more chance. The hitch is that they can only do it together, and they are both loners. He is a hockey player who can no longer compete because he has lost his peripheral vision. She is a talented but egotistical figure skater who has driven all potential partners away with her mouth. If he can change styles to figure-skating and she can rein in her smart mouth, they have a chance at an Olympic medal in paired figure skating... but that won't be easy. Conflict inevitably leads to love. Cute and fun, but predictable the whole way.

Sex / Nud / Viol / ◢ Lang / AdSit

A: D.B. Sweeney, Moira Kelly, Roy Dotrice, Terry O'Quinn, Dwier Brown

Distributed By MGM/UA Home Video M902315

CYRANO DE BERGERAC

D: Michael Gordon — 112 m

NR | ROM | 1950 | B&W

8 Charming adaptation of Edmond Rostand's classic romantic tragedy of unrequited love. Jose Ferrer won an Oscar as Cyrano, the eloquent 17th-century soldier/poet with the long nose. He desperately loves the fair Roxanne but is discouraged by his embarrassing prodigious nose. He loves her but knows that she loves a shy, handsome young soldier. So, he loans his tragic wit to the young man, allowing him to win her hand and thereby make her happy. However, love can not be fooled. This theme was later transformed by Steve Martin into a comedy, ROXANNE.

Sex / Nud / Viol / Lang / ◢ AdSit

A: Jose Ferrer, Mala Powers, William Prince, Morris Carnovsky, Ralph Clanton, Elena Verdugo

© REPUBLIC PICTURES HOME VIDEO 0822

DESK SET

D: Walter Lang — 103 m

NR | ROM COM | 1957 | COLOR

7 Classic Hepburn/Tracy pairing. Tracy plays an efficiency expert hired to automate Katherine Hepburn's research department at a TV network with his computers. It is almost foreordained that these two will clash over the man (or woman) verses machine issue. That theme, as presented, seems quite simplistic now, but computers then represented a formidable threat and were a vital concern to much of America. Eventually love wins out and there is a place for both human and machine. The real reason to watch the movie is the sparks and repartee that flies between the two fiery leads.

Sex / Nud / Viol / Lang / AdSit

A: Spencer Tracy, Katharine Hepburn, Gig Young, Joan Blondell, Dina Merrill, Neva Patterson

© FOXVIDEO 1244

GHOST AND MRS. MUIR, THE

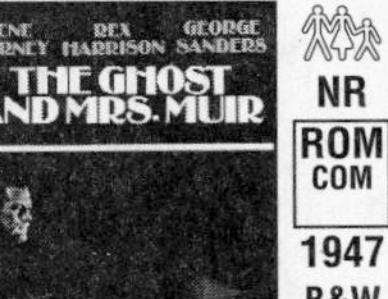

D: Joseph L. Mankiewicz — 104 m

NR | ROM COM | 1947 | B&W

10 Utterly charming romantic fantasy about a poor widow (Tierney) and her young daughter (a very young Natalie Wood) who move into a seaside cottage which is haunted by the cantankerous ghost of a salty 19th-century seafaring captain (Harrison). At first he does his best to scare her away, but then he falls deeply in love with her. When all her money is spent, he writes a book for her that tells of his exploits and which rescues her from financial distress, but it also introduces her to a real live man. Wonderful characterizations from two of filmdom's most favorite stars. Beautifully made.

Sex / Nud / Viol / Lang / ◢ AdSit

A: Rex Harrison, Gene Tierney, George Sanders, Vanessa Brown, Edna Best, Natalie Wood

© FOXVIDEO 1385

GREGORY'S GIRL

D: Bill Forsyth — 90 m

PG | ROM COM CLD | 1981 | COLOR

8 Delightful low-budget movie made in Scotland that was a winner of England's "Academy Award." It is a winning little comedy about a gangly, graceless high-school teenager who falls in love with his soccer team's newest and best player, Dorothy, the female goal keeper. He gets himself all custom-built just to please her, with the right clothes and the right hair style and then... she stands him up. However, his bruised adolescent psyche is mended when his crush is transferred to Dorothy's girlfriend. Wonderfully magical and humorous story of adolescent love. However, thick accents require diligent viewing.

Sex / Nud / Viol / ◢ Lang / ◢ AdSit

A: Gordon John Sinclair, Dee Hepburn, Chic Murray, Jake D'Arcy, Alex Norton, John Bett

© UNITED AMERICAN VIDEO CORP. 5318

GUY NAMED JOE, A

D: Victor Fleming — 121 m

NR | ROM COM FAN | 1944 | B&W

8 Enchanting romantic fantasy about a downed WWII fighter pilot (Tracy) who comes back to earth to become a guardian angel for a novice flyer (Johnson). Tracy comes to help Johnson become a better pilot, but is disconcerted when Johnson also pursues Tracy's old girlfriend (Dunne). Sentimental and whimsical. Highly popular in its time, it is only slightly dated now. Spielberg so loved it that he remade it in 1989 as ALWAYS.

Sex / Nud / Viol / Lang / ◢ AdSit

A: Spencer Tracy, Irene Dunne, Van Johnson, Ward Bond, James Gleason, Lionel Barrymore

Distributed By MGM/UA Home Video M301380

HOUSEBOAT

D: Melville Shavelson — 110 m

NR | ROM COM | 1958 | COLOR

8 Predictable but highly enjoyable '50s-style romantic comedy about a Washington D.C. widowed attorney with three unruly kids living on a houseboat on the Potomac River. He hires a curvaceous music conductor's daughter, with no previous experience, as governess to take them in hand. Despite their relationships with others and numerous intervening catastrophies, they are... surprise... irresistibly drawn to each other. The star power of these two makes this a delight.

Sex / Nud / Viol / Lang / AdSit

A: Cary Grant, Sophia Loren, Martha Hyer, Harry Guardino, Eduardo Ciannelli, Murray Hamilton

© PARAMOUNT HOME VIDEO 5806

HUNCHBACK OF NOTRE DAME, THE

D: Wallace Worsley — 133 m

NR | ROM DMA SUS | 1923 | B&W

8 One of the most prominent films of the silent era. This story of a pitiably deformed bell ringer's love for a Gypsy dancer captured the imaginations of all those who viewed it. It is now most memorable for Lon Chaney Sr.'s brilliant characterization of the Hunchback, through his athletic abilities and his remarkable makeup, which included a 70-pound rubber hump and special devices to prevent him from standing erect or closing his mouth.

Sex / Nud / ◢ Viol / Lang / ◢ AdSit

A: Lon Chaney, Sr., Patsy Ruth Miller, Ernest Torrence

© VIDEO YESTERYEAR 23

HUNCHBACK OF NOTRE DAME, THE

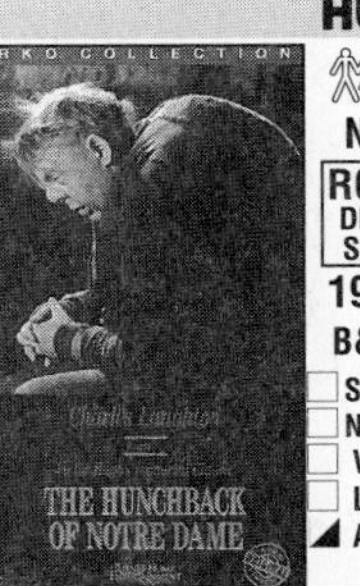

D: William Dieterle — 117 m

NR | ROM DMA SUS | 1939 | B&W

9 Perhaps the best-ever production of Victor Hugo's classic tragic love story. Charles Laughton is haunting as the hideously deformed and tortured spirit Quasimodo who lives in the bell towers of the famed Notre Dame Cathedral of 15th-century Paris. Quasimodo is the scorn of medieval Paris but is given a moment's pity one day by the beautiful Gypsy dancer Esmerelda, with whom he then falls deeply in love. However, one day an angry crowd in the square is about to hang her. He sweeps down from the bell tower rescuing her and delivers her to the Cathedral where she can claim sanctuary. A must see!

Sex / Nud / Viol / Lang / ◢ AdSit

A: Charles Laughton, Thomas Mitchell, Maureen O'Hara, Edmond O'Brien, Cedric Hardwicke

© TURNER HOME ENTERTAINMENT 2058

IT STARTED IN NAPLES

D: Melville Shavelson — 100 m

NR | ROM COM | 1960 | COLOR

6 Light-hearted fun. Clark Gable is a an American attorney who goes to Italy to settle the estate of his dead brother, only to find that there is a 10-year-old boy from a common-law marriage. His attempts to bring the boy back to the States are blocked by the boy's sexy Italian aunt (Sophia Loren). Guess what happens next. Lots of beautiful Italian scenery, including Sophia.

Sex / Nud / Viol / Lang / ◢ AdSit

A: Clark Gable, Sophia Loren, Vittorio De Sica, Marietto, Paolo Carlini, Claudio Ermelli

© PARAMOUNT HOME VIDEO 6790

LILI

D: Charles Walters — 87 m

G | ROM MUS | 1953 | COLOR

9 Charming and utterly delightful musical for both young and old alike. Leslie Caron is wonderful as a naive and lonely sixteen-year-old French orphan who one day talked to the puppets in a small traveling circus. She proved to be so enchanting and popular that the embittered and crippled puppeteer hired her. She soon falls in love with a magician but is heartbroken to learn that he is already married. The puppeteer has fallen in love with her, but he is so jealous and bitter that she does not know and thinks that he is a cruel man. He recognizes what he has done and through her friends, the puppets, he wins her back. Oscar-winning music includes the song "Hi Lili, Hi Lili, Hi Low." Enchanting!

Sex / Nud / Viol / Lang / AdSit

A: Leslie Caron, Mel Ferrer, Zsa Zsa Gabor, Jean-Pierre Aumont, Kurt Kasznar, Amanda Blake

Distributed By MGM/UA Home Video M600310

LITTLE ROMANCE, A

D: George Roy Hill 110 m

PG | ROM COM | 1979 | COLOR

7 Enchanting and delightful film which will appeal to all members of the family. It is a film about first love and the relationship that develops between two precocious kids, an American girl and a French boy, and an elderly ex-con man. The old man tells the young couple of an ages-old legend: if they kiss under the Bridge of Sighs in Venice at sunset, their love will last forever. This convinces the two, they are now determined to get there and he agrees to help them. This is a sweet movie that is full of surprises, laughs and will leave everyone feeling good. It is a sensitive and attractive treatment of adolescence.

☐ Sex ☐ Nud ☐ Viol ◢ Lang ☐ AdSit

A: Thelonlous Bernard, Diane Lane, Laurence Olivier, Sally Kellerman, Broderick Crawford, David Dukes

© WARNER HOME VIDEO 2001

OTHER SIDE OF THE MOUNTAIN, THE

D: Larry Peerce 102 m

PG | ROM DMA | 1975 | COLOR

8 Popular love story taken from the pages of real life. Jill Kinmont (Hassett) was a talented skier who seemed destined for the 1956 Olympic team. Instead she was left a paraplegic after a tragic skiing accident. Despondent over her circumstances, she is revitalized by the love of Beau Bridges, but then tragedy strikes again. Hers is truly a story of determination in the face of overwhelming adversity. Guaranteed to jerk more than a few tears.

☐ Sex ☐ Nud ☐ Viol ◢ Lang ◢ AdSit

A: Marilyn Hassett, Beau Bridges, Dabney Coleman, Belinda J. Montgomery

© MCA/UNIVERSAL HOME VIDEO, INC. 55116

OTHER SIDE OF THE MOUNTAIN, PART II, THE

D: Larry Peerce 99 m

PG | ROM DMA | 1978 | COLOR

8 In this sequel, also taken from real life, the paralyzed skier Jill Kinmont (Hassett) is now a teacher in L.A. after having lost her lover in a plane crash. On vacation to her hometown, she meets a divorced trucker (Bottoms) who pursues her. After having been so heartbroken before, she is very reluctant to allow yet another man into her life, but his persistence breaks down her resistance. This is a good love story. It is involving and credible. As in the first film, be prepared to get a few tears jerked.

☐ Sex ☐ Nud ☐ Viol ☐ Lang ◢ AdSit

A: Marilyn Hassett, Timothy Bottoms, Belinda J. Montgomery, Nan Martin

© MCA/UNIVERSAL HOME VIDEO, INC. 55117

PURE COUNTRY

D: Christopher Cain 113 m

PG | ROM DMA | 1992 | COLOR

7 If you like your country music pure, and if you like your story simple and sweet, this is for you. George is a country music star who has become very unhappy with the demands of his life on the road and the course his stage career (managed by Warren) has taken. So he leaves, right in the middle of a concert tour. He winds up on the ranch of a pretty cowgirl, her gnarly father and her two brothers. George's focus begins to return just as Warren hunts him down and takes him back for a big Las Vegas concert and a happy ending. There are ten different country songs scattered through the storyline.

☐ Sex ☐ Nud ☐ Viol ☐ Lang ◢ AdSit

A: George Straight, Lesley Ann Warren, Isabel Glasser, Kyle Chandler, John Doe, Rory Calhoun

© WARNER HOME VIDEO 12593

RED SHOES, THE

D: Michael Powell 136 m

NR | ROM MUS CLD | 1948 | COLOR

8 Opulent, grandly romantic and very popular, especially with young girls. A beautiful young ballerina (Shearer) is torn. She is in love with a composer (Goring), but the ballet company's heartless director (Walbrook) does not approve. The conflict between her love of dance and her love for a man is paralleled by the dance she is most famous for - "Dance of the Red Shoes" - which was adapted from the Hans Christian Anderson fairy tale about bewitched shoes that nearly dance the wearer to death. This very popular musical is sure to have inspired many young dancers. Nominated for 5 Oscars, including Best Picture. Followed by THE TALES OF HOFFMAN.

☐ Sex ☐ Nud ☐ Viol ☐ Lang ◢ AdSit

A: Moira Shearer, Emeric Pressburger, Anton Walbrook, Robert Helpmann, Marius Goring, Leonide Massine

© PARAMOUNT HOME VIDEO 12572

ROBIN AND MARIAN

D: Richard Lester 107 m

PG | ROM ACT | 1976 | COLOR

7 Robin Hood (Connery) returns to Sherwood Forest after 20 years of battling in the Crusades, along with Little John and King Richard (Harris). When King Richard is accidentally slain, his wicked brother John takes the throne and Robin heads for the woods. Robin's arch nemesis, the Sheriff of Nottingham (Shaw), is ordered to remove the clergy. Robin seeks out his love, Maid Marian (Hepburn), but finds that she has become a nun - the Mother Superior to be exact. The pair rekindle their love for each other and Robin prepares to confront his enemy. What a cast!

☐ Sex ☐ Nud ◢ Viol ◢ Lang ◢ AdSit

A: Sean Connery, Audrey Hepburn, Robert Shaw, Richard Harris, Nicol Williamson, Denholm Elliott

© COLUMBIA TRISTAR HOME VIDEO 60097

ROMANCE IN MANHATTAN

D: Stephen Roberts 78 m

NR | ROM COM | 1934 | B&W

6 A sweet charmer! Francis Lederer is an illegal alien and a scab taxi driver in New York during a strike. He is just scraping by. A beautiful chorus girl (Rogers) is charmed by his enthusiastic optimism, takes pity on him, becomes his friend, lets him camp out on the roof of her apartment building and the pair fall in love. A sweet love story filled with charm and comedy. Lederer really steals the show with his funny portrayal of a man totally unfamiliar with his surroundings, sensitive and searching for his dream.

☐ Sex ☐ Nud ☐ Viol ☐ Lang ◢ AdSit

A: Ginger Rogers, Francis Lederer, J. Farrell MacDonald, Arthur Hohl, Sidney Toler

© TURNER HOME ENTERTAINMENT 6207

ROMAN HOLIDAY

D: William Wyler 118 m

NR | ROM | 1953 | B&W

9 Bittersweet romantic classic! A beautiful young princess (Hepburn) has an overpowering desire to taste the common life, so she escapes her daily royal trappings to wander about Rome incognito during a tour in Europe. However, there she meets a reporter (Peck), who pretends not to know her true identity. He is hoping for the ultimate story and he gets it. They fall in love. Still, they both know that their day in the sun can not continue. Nominated for nine Oscars, this spectacular classic incorporates charm, wit and humor with picturesque settings and a stellar cast.

☐ Sex ☐ Nud ☐ Viol ☐ Lang ◢ AdSit

A: Gregory Peck, Audrey Hepburn, Eddie Albert, Tullio Carminati

© PARAMOUNT HOME VIDEO 6204

ROMAN SPRING OF MRS. STONE, THE

D: Jose Quintero 104 m

NR | ROM | 1961 | COLOR

6 Vivian Leigh is a wealthy middle-aged and widowed actress who has taken a luxurious apartment in Rome in a search to find herself. She is lonely and the best years of her career are behind her. She falls in love and has a tragic affair with a handsome Italian gigolo (Warren Beatty). However he's an opportunist, who takes all that she can give and then dumps her for a younger Jill St. John. This is a dark love story based on a Tennessee Williams novella.

☐ Sex ☐ Nud ☐ Viol ☐ Lang ◢ AdSit

A: Vivien Leigh, Warren Beatty, Lotte Lenya, Jill St. John, Coral Browne

© WARNER HOME VIDEO 11183

ROYAL WEDDING

D: Stanley Donen 93 m

NR | ROM MUS | 1951 | COLOR

6 Fancy footwork abounds in this light-hearted musical! Brother and sister dance team Astaire and Powell travel to London to perform during Princess Elizabeth II's royal wedding to Prince Phillip. Each finds true love as the royal couple tie the knot, Astaire with Churchill and Powell with English nobleman Lawford. Included in this pleasurable musical is Astaire's now famous walk on the ceiling and his dance with a hat rack.

☐ Sex ☐ Nud ☐ Viol ☐ Lang ◢ AdSit

A: Fred Astaire, Jane Powell, Keenan Wynn, Peter Lawford, Sarah Churchill

Distributed By MGM/UA Home Video M600083

SABRINA

D: Billy Wilder 113 m

NR | ROM COM | 1954 | B&W

9 Audrey Hepburn is magical in this effervescent romance! A chauffeur's daughter (Hepburn) returns home from an education in Paris - beautiful, refined and all grown up. She arrives at the estate where her father works, to find that two rich brothers (Bogart and Holden) are understandably attracted to her. At first, she is attracted to playboy Holden's charming ways, but older brother Bogart proves to be more stable. A spicy love triangle develops as Bogart turns up the heat. Will Bogart save her from his flaky brother? Glamorous and romantic!

☐ Sex ☐ Nud ☐ Viol ☐ Lang ◢ AdSit

A: Humphrey Bogart, Audrey Hepburn, William Holden, Martha Hyer, John Williams, Nancy Kulp

© PARAMOUNT HOME VIDEO 5402

SARAH, PLAIN AND TALL

D: Glenn Jordan 98 m

G | ROM DMA | 1991 | COLOR

8 Endearing and wonderfully acted sentimental charmer, produced to very high standards for TV's "Hallmark Hall of Fame." In 1910, a lonely Kansas farmer and widower (Walken), with two motherless children, advertises back East for a wife. Glen Close is a spinsterly Maine schoolteacher who agrees to a one-month sexless trial "marriage." When she arrives, she finds two kids who quickly warm to her mothering. Her month is an eventful one - they are hit with a big storm and she helps a neighbor give birth, but Walken still grieves for his long-dead wife and it looks at first like her time was wasted.

☐ Sex ☐ Nud ☐ Viol ☐ Lang ☐ AdSit

A: Glenn Close, Christopher Walken, Lexi Randall, Margaret Sophie Stein, Jon De Vries, Christopher Bell

© REPUBLIC PICTURES HOME VIDEO 1821

SLEEPLESS IN SEATTLE

D: Nora Ephron 105 m

PG · ROM COM · 1993 · COLOR

9 Wonderfully endearing feel-good movie. The love of Tom Hanks' life has just died, leaving him and his young son heartbroken and lonely. He has left Chicago to get away from the memories but still he is always sad. So, his son contacts a radio show shrink to get help. In Baltimore, Meg Ryan is about to get married. She does her best to convince herself that she is doing the right thing in marrying this guy, but she is also powerfully drawn to the voice of a lonely, sleepless man a continent away she heard on the radio. As silly as it sounds, this is a charming and funny video that draws you to its attractive characters who you badly want to see get together and be happy.

Sex · Nud · Viol · Lang · AdSit

A: Tom Hanks, Meg Ryan, Bill Pullman, Rosie O'Donnell, Rita Wilson, Rob Reiner

© COLUMBIA TRISTAR HOME VIDEO 52413

SOMEWHERE IN TIME

D: Jeannot Szwarc 104 m

PG · ROM FAN · 1980 · COLOR

8 Very entertaining and intensely romantic story of love found and lost! Reeve is a handsome playwrite (from the 1980s) who sees a picture of a beautiful actress (Seymour) that was taken in 1912. He immediately falls in love with her. He believes that they had been lovers in a past life and through self-hypnosis he manages to transports himself back in time to be with her. He finds her at the Grand Hotel on Michigan's Mackinac Island and they fall deeply in love, despite the objections of her manager (Plummer) who does everything he can to break them up. This is an entrancing, even though fanciful, love story with beautiful photography of picturesque settings.

Sex · Nud · Viol · Lang · AdSit

A: Christopher Reeve, Jane Seymour, Christopher Plummer, Teresa Wright, Bill Erwin, George Voskovec

© MCA/UNIVERSAL HOME VIDEO, INC. 66024

STARMAN

D: John Carpenter 115 m

PG · ROM SF FAN · 1984 · COLOR

8 An endearing charmer. An space ship is shot down and crashes in rural Wisconsin. The scared alien escapes from the crash site before the government gets to it and stumbles upon the cabin of a young woman (Allen) who is newly widowed and still grieving the loss of her husband. The alien will die if he doesn't make it to Arizona where he will be rescued in three days. So he, takes on the form of her dead husband and makes her drive him there. She is not pleased but along the way, while they are dodging the pursuing FBI, she discovers a sweetness about him. That, and because he looks like her dead husband, she falls in love with him. Very entertaining and uplifting.

Sex · Nud · Viol · Lang · AdSit

A: Jeff Bridges, Karen Allen, Charles Martin Smith, Richard Jaeckel

© COLUMBIA TRISTAR HOME VIDEO 60412

SWAN, THE

D: Charles Vidor 109 m

NR · ROM COM · 1956 · COLOR

6 The beautiful princess (Kelly) is supposed to marry the prince (Guinness) and save her family's declining fortunes, however she would rather spend her time with her handsome tutor, a common man (Jourdan). Still, when she spies the prince, she is immediately taken by him. However the prince is cool to the arranged wedding, so her mother sets about plotting to make him jealous. It is ironic that this was Grace Kelly's last film before her marriage to Prince Rainier. Slow in spots, and the humor is subtle but the story is captivating and heartwarming. As always, Grace is delightful.

Sex · Nud · Viol · Lang · AdSit

A: Grace Kelly, Alec Guinness, Louis Jourdan, Agnes Moorehead, Jessie Royce Landis, Brian Aherne

Distributed By MGM/UA Home Video M201068

TALE OF TWO CITIES, A

D: Jack Conway 128 m

NR · ROM DMA · 1935 · B&W

9 MGM blockbuster and solid telling of Dickens's classic story of romance within the terror of the French Revolution. Sydney Carron (Coleman) is a shiftless London lawyer who finds purpose by aiding beleaguered victims of the Reign of Terror after the French Revolution. However, he also goes down in history as one of the most romantic characters ever when he chooses to go to the guillotine in the place of another man and for the love of the woman that they both love. Blanche Yurka creates a memorably evil character in Mme. Defarge, who knits as she condemned her victims. Outstanding.

Sex · Nud · Viol · Lang · AdSit

A: Ronald Colman, Elizabeth Allan, Basil Rathbone, Edna May Oliver, Blanche Yurka, Reginald Owen

Distributed By MGM/UA Home Video M600078

TAMMY AND THE BACHELOR

D: Joseph Pevney 89 m

NR · ROM COM · 1957 · COLOR

7 Simple and charming little romancer. It's a little corny but fun, and it made Debbie Reynolds into a national star. (It also gave her a very popular song: "Tammy.") When rich boy Nielson's private plane crashlands near poor Bayou-country girl Debbie's houseboat, she and her rascal grandfather (Brennan) rescue him, nurse him back to health and a romance is born. But cultures clash, too, when she is invited to stay with his wealthy family. Never fear, all ends well. Sweet, charming and so successful that it led to two sequels and a TV series.

Sex · Nud · Viol · Lang · AdSit

A: Debbie Reynolds, Leslie Nielsen, Walter Brennan, Mala Powers, Fay Wray, Mildred Natwick

© MCA/UNIVERSAL HOME VIDEO, INC. 80314

TO DANCE WITH THE WHITE DOG

D: Glenn Jordan 98 m

PG · ROM DMA · 1993 · COLOR

9 Beautiful made-for-TV movie that was done for the Hallmark Hall of Fame. Sam and Cora are an old couple that have lived together for all their lives and live surrounded by their family. Still deeply in love after 50 years of marriage, Cora is stricken and dies. Sam is struggling with his loneliness and is in poor health himself. Suddenly one day, a stray white dog shows up at his door. The two become fast friends, but the dog only comes around when he is alone and his children fear he is losing his mind. But the dog is real and it is there to protect and love him, just as Cora had done. Extremely well done and very moving. Reportedly based upon an actual incidence.

Sex · Nud · Viol · Lang · AdSit

A: Hume Cronyn, Jessica Tandy, Christine Baranski, Terry Beaver, Harley Cross, Ester Rolle

© REPUBLIC PICTURES HOME VIDEO 0837

URBAN COWBOY

D: James Bridges 132 m

PG · ROM DMA · 1980 · COLOR

8 Sassy cowboy slice-of-life romance with plenty of twang! Newcomer Travolta breezes into a tough Texas town and hangs out at the very popular Gilley's bar. He picks up and soon marries local girl Winger, but strays to make his bed with rich girl Smith for a while. Winger retaliates and moves in with local bad boy Glenn, creating a spicy romantic mess. At the center of everything is the symbol of courage and bravery for all the cowboys in the bar - the mechanical bull - a device the men ride as a testament to their manhood. Very flavorful honky-tonk fare! Good star chemistry. Very popular movie.

Sex · Nud · Viol · Lang · AdSit

A: John Travolta, Debra Winger, Scott Glenn, Madolyn Smith, Barry Corbin, Brooke Alderson

© PARAMOUNT HOME VIDEO 1285

Science Fiction

4-D MAN

D: Irvin Yeaworth, Jr. 84 m

NR · SF · 1959 · COLOR

6 Quite interesting 50's style science fiction piece about a scientist who develops a way to move through walls, glass, doors and lots of other things including bank vaults. He uses his new skills to become a thief, a perfect thief. Then gradually he becomes aware of the terrible price he is going to have to pay as he begins to go mad, and eventually his madness will lead to murder. Pretty good.

Sex · Nud · Viol · Lang · AdSit

A: Robert Lansing, Lee Meriwether, Patty Duke, Guy Raymond, Robert Strauss, James Congdon

© R&G VIDEO, LP 9537

ANDROMEDA STRAIN, THE

D: Robert Wise 130 m

G · SF SUS · 1971 · COLOR

7 Intelligent and tense, but a little overlong. A mutant strain of bacteria comes to earth with a crashed satellite and everyone near the crash sight dies - except an old man an a baby. A team of scientists takes the survivors and the microbe back to a massive underground research facility, rushing against time to find a solution. This was one of the very first films to effectively explore the biological hazards of a technical age. Effective and well-done thriller, which uses its veteran cast to good advantage to create maximum tension and suspense.

Sex · Nud · Viol · Lang · AdSit

A: Arthur Hill, David Wayne, James Olson, Kate Reid, Paula Kelly

© MCA/UNIVERSAL HOME VIDEO, INC. 55037

ANNA TO THE INFINITE POWER

D: Robert Wiemer 101 m

NR · SF · 1984 · COLOR

7 A brilliant 12-year-old girl (Byrne) is plagued by strange changes. She is a gifted child but she has suddenly become a compulsive liar and a thief, and she is having vivid nightmares which predict the future. Worse, her mother (Merrill) steadfastly refuses to get her psychiatric help. Eventually she will discover that she was born as the result of a cloning experiment... and she is only one of many others who are all just like her. So she goes on a search for her sisters who were all separated after the experiment was over, using ESP. This is a worthy film, but it will appeal mostly to younger people.

Sex · Nud · Viol · Lang · AdSit

A: Dina Merrill, Martha Byrne, Jack Gilford, Mark Patton, Donna Mitchell, Loretta Devine

© COLUMBIA TRISTAR HOME VIDEO VH91051

BABY...SECRET OF THE LOST LEGEND

D: B.W.L. Norton 92 m

PG | SF CLD | 1985 | COLOR | Sex | Nud | Viol | Lang | AdSit

6 A brontosaurus family is found hidden away in modern Africa by a zoologist (Sean Young) and her husband (William Katt). However, the scientist pair are soon forced to become the dinosaur's protectors when they become threatened by a bad-guy scientist Patrick McGoohan. The papa dinosaur is killed and the mama is kidnapped, so Young and Katt must protect the baby until they can reunite it with its mama. Some pretty good special effects make for cute and irresistable dinosaurs. But, there is also a touch of sex in an attempt to attract an older audience than just kids.

A: William Katt, Sean Young, Patrick McGoohan, Julian Fellows, Kyalo Mativo

© TOUCHSTONE HOME VIDEO 269V

BATTLE BEYOND THE STARS

D: Jimmy T. Murakami 102 m

PG | SF COM | 1980 | COLOR | Sex | Nud | Viol | Lang | AdSit

7 The planet Akir is a peaceful planet facing destruction by powerful forces, and it is beyond their own capacity to defend themselves. Richard Thomas becomes an emissary from Akir to Earth and other planets, seeking to recruit mercenaries to help save his world. He has recruited a lizard-like alien and some of his friends, a female Amazon warrior from the planet Valkyrie, and from earth - a cowboy and a computer specialist. Sort of a MAGNIFICENT SEVEN-in-outer-space. Genuinely enjoyable fantasy-comedy that never takes itself too seriously. Something for everyone.

A: Richard Thomas, John Saxon, Robert Vaughn, George Peppard, Sybil Danning, Darlanne Fluegel

© LIVE HOME VIDEO VA4044

BATTLE FOR THE PLANET OF THE APES

D: J. Lee Thompson 86 m

G | SF | 1973 | COLOR | Sex | Nud | Viol | Lang | AdSit

6 This, the last in a series of five films that began with THE PLANET OF THE APES, brings the story full circle. Can apes and humans really learn to get along? Caesar (McDowall) is now the leader of a peaceful ape city where humans are treated fairly, but he is still opposed on two fronts. The gorilla leader (Akins) wants things back the way they were and a group of mutant and hostile humans want to extract their own vengeance. Others in the series are: BENEATH THE PLANET OF THE APES, CONQUEST FOR THE PLANET OF THE APES and ESCAPE FROM THE PLANET OF THE APES.

A: Roddy McDowall, Claude Akins, John Huston, Natalie Trundy, Severn Darden, Paul Williams

© FOXVIDEO 1134

BENEATH THE PLANET OF THE APES

D: Ted Post 100 m

G | SF | 1970 | COLOR | Sex | Nud | Viol | Lang | AdSit

6 This was the first sequel in the PLANET OF THE APES series. In it, astronaut Franciscus comes crashing into the future. He is looking for the missing astronaut from the first film (Heston), but he finds himself in the middle of a war between the primates and an underground race of mutant humans who have developed a strang religion. They worship the last remaining nuclear bomb and it is a cobalt bomb that can destroy the whole earth. Others in the series include: BATTLE FOR THE PLANET OF THE APES, CONQUEST OF THE PLANET OF THE APES and ESCAPE FROM THE PLANET OF THE APES.

A: James Franciscus, Kim Hunter, Charlton Heston, Maurice Evans, Linda Harrison

© FOXVIDEO 1013

BRAINSTORM

D: Douglas Trumbull 106 m

PG | SF SUS | 1983 | COLOR | Sex | Nud | Viol | Lang | AdSit

6 There is an interesting premise behind this film. It is about a machine that can read and record the physical, emotional and intellectual sensations as they are experienced by one person, and then have them "played back" inside someone else's head. However, due to a now predictable and stale plot twist of having a group of military types intervene, that good is stunted and doesn't get the treatment it deserves. Plus, the filming became complicated when Natalie Wood died part-way into production. Still, the film is pretty good. The disappointment comes only because it could have been more.

A: Christopher Walken, Natalie Wood, Louise Fletcher, Cliff Robertson, Joe Dorsey

Distributed By MGM/UA Home Video M800314

CAPRICORN ONE

D: Peter Hyams 123 m

PG | SF SUS | 1978 | COLOR | Sex | Nud | Viol | Lang | AdSit

7 A suspenseful science fiction drama with an outlandish plot that is never-the less convincingly done. NASA executive Holbrook decides that it is too risky to fail in front of the entire world audience in an impending mission to Mars. A failure would be to risk having his budget cut. So he decides to fake the whole thing, and film it all inside a TV studio. However, Gould is a nosy reporter who investigates and begins to unravel the plot. Now threatened with exposure, Holbrook decides that the ship must "crash" upon reentry, killing the three astronauts aboard, the only other witnesses.

A: Elliott Gould, James Brolin, Karen Black, Telly Savalas, Sam Waterston, O.J. Simpson

© LIVE HOME VIDEO 51090

CLOSE ENCOUNTERS OF THE THIRD KIND

D: Steven Spielberg 132 m

PG | SF DMA | 1977 | COLOR | Sex | Nud | Viol | Lang | AdSit

9 Excellent science fiction. After a mysterious encounter with an alien craft, Richard Dreyfuss becomes consumed with trying to understand a mysterious and recurring dream. Before long, he discovers that he is not alone - there are many tormented others like him who are all converging on an isolated mesa in the West, which has become very heavily populated by scientists and cordoned off by the military. Soon the reason becomes known, the mesa is being visited by wondrous spacecrafts which contain child-like beings, wonderful visitors from another world seeking their first contact with earthlings.

A: Richard Dreyfuss, Francois Truffaut, Teri Garr, Melinda Dillon

© COLUMBIA TRISTAR HOME VIDEO 60162

COCOON: THE RETURN

D: Daniel Petrie 116 m

PG | SF COM DMA | 1988 | COLOR | Sex | Nud | Viol | Lang | AdSit

7 Follow-up to the megahit COCOON. The oldsters return to earth five years later to help their alien friends rescue some cocoons which have become endangered by an earthquake. Now accustomed to a life free of pain and suffering, they have to readjust to life as it is on earth. This time around less attention is given to plot and more to character development. While this film has an excellent cast and is generally enjoyable, too, it lacks the energy and warmth of the earlier film.

A: Don Ameche, Wilford Brimley, Courtney Cox, Hume Cronyn, Brian Dennehy, Jack Gilford

© FOXVIDEO 1710

CONQUEST OF THE PLANET OF THE APES

D: J. Lee Thompson 88 m

PG | SF | 1972 | COLOR | Sex | Nud | Viol | Lang | AdSit

6 This is the fourth in the PLANET OF THE APES series. This time it is 1990 and the various ape groups have become common as house pets after all the dogs and cats are killed by a virus. Because of their intelligence, they are quickly transformed into slaves and they live under the iron hand of the human governor. However, Roddy McDowall, who had been saved in the previous film, has grown up and leads the apes in revolt. All of this sets the stage for the events which have occurred in the very first film in the series. Others in the series BENEATH THE, BATTLE FOR THE, and ESCAPE FROM THE PLANET OF THE APES.

A: Roddy McDowall, Don Murray, Ricardo Montalban

© FOXVIDEO 1137

D.A.R.Y.L

D: Simon Wincer 100 m

PG | SF FAN CLD | 1985 | COLOR | Sex | Nud | Viol | Lang | AdSit

8 Charming story about a childless urban couple who adopt an apparently amnesiatic ten-year-old. He is a perfect child. He is a math whiz, works wonders with video games, is the hero of the baseball team and he changes their lives. But D.A.R.Y.L. is really an advanced robot... so advanced that he has developed human feelings. He has run away from the government program that created him and now the government wants him back. A delightful fantasy which will be entertaining for the whole family.

A: Barret Oliver, Mary Beth Hurt, Michael McKean, Josef Sommer, Kathryn Walker

© PARAMOUNT HOME VIDEO 1810

DAY OF THE TRIFFIDS, THE

D: Steve Sekely 95 m

NR | SF HOR | 1962 | COLOR | Sex | Nud | Viol | Lang | AdSit

7 Most of the people of Earth are blinded when the earth is bombarded by a meteor shower. The shower also contains strange other-world seeds, seeds which grow into walking, man-eating plants. Howard Keel leads a small group in a last stand against the marauding plants while scientist Moor and his wife struggle to find a scientific answer. Intelligent dialogue separates this from most of the other invasion/disaster films of the same period. Pretty good special effects. Enjoyable piece of science fiction.

A: Howard Keel, Nicole Maurey, Janette Scott, Kieron Moore, Mervyn Johns

© GOODTIMES VGT5090

DAY THE EARTH CAUGHT FIRE, THE

D: Val Guest 95 m

NR | SF DMA | 1962 | B&W | Sex | Nud | Viol | Lang | AdSit

8 One of the most intelligent science fiction entries out of Britain. Edward Judd is a cynical reporter who uncovers this incredible story: when the Americans and the Russians inadvertently conducted nuclear tests on the same day, the earth was sent off its orbit to spiral inward toward the sun. The earth is doomed. This is a realistic treatment of the subject of the last days of the earth, both scientifically and emotionally. The film creates a believable sense of doom and the insightful observations of human nature produce a tense, thought-provoking experience.

A: Edward Judd, Janet Munro, Leo McKern, Michael Goodliffe, Bernard Braden

© CONGRESS VIDEO GROUP 03615

DAY THE EARTH STOOD STILL, THE

G | SF DMA | 1951 | B&W

D: Robert Wise — 92 m

9 This first-rate intelligent science fiction piece was a landmark film. It was the first in which the alien from outer space (Michael Rennie) is a benevolent being, whose sole purpose is to warn Earth of impending catastrophe if it continues on its violent path. However, Rennie and his massive robot companion are met with suspicion and hostility by the people of earth. Even though the special effects are dated now, the subject matter is topical. People have not likely changed all that much. This is a powerful film because its ideas are credible and thought provoking.

☐ Sex ☐ Nud ☐ Viol ☐ Lang ◢ AdSit

A: Michael Rennie, Patricia Neal, Hugh Marlowe, Sam Jaffe, Billy Gray, Frances Bavier

© FOXVIDEO 1011

EMPIRE STRIKES BACK, THE

PG | SF ACT SUS | 1980 | COLOR

D: Irvin Kershner — 128 m

10 A real winner! High intensity middle picture in the Star Wars trilogy. First came STAR WARS and after comes RETURN OF THE JEDI, but here, Luke Skywalker travels to the Jedi master Yoda to learn to the mystical and powerful ways of "The Source," Han Solo and Princess Leia get into deep trouble and develop "a thing" together, Billy Dee Williams joins the battle against the Empire, and Luke finds that Darth Vader not only wants to destroy the rebels, but wants Luke to join him in the "dark side" of the force. Excitement plus. WOW special effects.

☐ Sex ☐ Nud ◢ Viol ☐ Lang ☐ AdSit

A: Billy Dee Williams, Harrison Ford, Carrie Fisher, Mark Hamill, Anthony Daniels, Dave Prowse

© FOXVIDEO 1425

ESCAPE FROM THE PLANET OF THE APES

G | SF | 1971 | COLOR

D: Don Taylor — 98 m

7 Third in succession of sequels and a pretty good one, too. Intelligent apes McDowall, Hunter and Mineo have all escaped from their planet in the spaceship that Charlton Heston had used to get to their planet in the first film. They arrive back on 1970s earth. At first they are hailed and treated as celebrities, but soon they become targets of intense criticism and are hunted by 1970s mankind as being "dangerous." The previous films were PLANET OF THE APES, and BENEATH THE PLANET OF THE APES. Later films will be CONQUEST OF THE PLANET OF THE APES and BATTLE FOR THE PLANET OF THE APES.

☐ Sex ☐ Nud ☐ Viol ☐ Lang ☐ AdSit

A: Roddy McDowall, Kim Hunter, Bradford Dillman, Sal Mineo

© FOXVIDEO 1187

E.T. THE EXTRA-TERRESTRIAL

PG | SF DMA CLD | 1982 | COLOR

D: Steven Spielberg — 115 m

10 Huge blockbuster hit and instant classic. Wonderful, warm story of a lovable little visitor from another world who is stranded on Earth and befriended by a 10-year-old boy. Elliott tries to keep little E.T. hidden, but soon the rest of his family knows the secret and then they are all helping to hide the little guy from the government people who are now out to capture him. But, all little E.T. wants is just to go home. No wonder this is the #1 box office hit of all time. It has captured the hearts and imaginations of all who have ever watched it - all over the world.

☐ Sex ☐ Nud ☐ Viol ☐ Lang ☐ AdSit

A: Dee Wallace, Henry Thomas, Peter Coyote, Robert MacNaughton, Drew Barrymore, K.C. Martel

© MCA/UNIVERSAL HOME VIDEO, INC. 77012

FANTASTIC VOYAGE

NR | SF ACT | 1966 | COLOR

D: Richard Fleischer — 100 m

7 Set sometime in the near future, a scientist from a communist country defects to the West with a miniaturization process that will change the world - but he is nearly killed in an assassination attempt. A team of scientists and their submarine-like craft are shrunk to microscopic size and injected into the bloodstream of a his body in an attempt to save his life. They must get in and out within 60 minutes, but there is a saboteur on board and the ship is also being attacked by the body's natural defenses. Pretty good stuff, even today. Special Effects Oscar.

☐ Sex ☐ Nud ☐ Viol ☐ Lang ☐ AdSit

A: Stephen Boyd, Raquel Welch, Edmond O'Brien, Donald Pleasence, Arthur O'Connell, William Redfield

© FOXVIDEO 1002

FINAL COUNTDOWN, THE

PG | SF ACT | 1980 | COLOR

D: Don Taylor — 92 m

8 A very interesting but highly improbable concept for a movie. Suppose a nuclear aircraft carrier, equipped with 1980's weapons technology, slips into 1941 just before the Japanese are about to attack Pearl Harbor, by going into a time warp. Kirk Douglas, as the ship's captain, must decide whether to utilize his ship's overwhelming firepower to stop the impending attack and thus change the course of history. Pretty good yarn, if you can get past the premise.

☐ Sex ☐ Nud ◢ Viol ◢ Lang ☐ AdSit

A: Kirk Douglas, Martin Sheen, Katharine Ross, James Farentino, Ron O'Neal, Charles Durning

© LIVE HOME VIDEO VA4047

FIRST MEN IN THE MOON

NR | SF FAN | 1964 | COLOR

D: Nathan Juran — 103 m

7 Entertaining adaptation of the fanciful H.G. Wells novel in which a crew from 1899 Victorian England sets out on an expedition to the moon. When they arrive there, they find that the moon is occupied by human-like ant forms that live in immense crystal caverns. It is told in a sort of tongue-in-cheek fashion and its special effects including the monsters, are fun. They are not too scary for the younger viewers but still manage to be exciting for everyone. Good family entertainment.

☐ Sex ☐ Nud ☐ Viol ☐ Lang ☐ AdSit

A: Edward Judd, Martha Hyer, Lionel Jefferies, Peter Finch, Erik Chitty, Betty McDowall

© COLUMBIA TRISTAR HOME VIDEO 60958

FLASH GORDON

PG | SF | 1980 | COLOR

D: Mike Hodges — 111 m

7 High-camp revival of the very famous '30s-'40s comic strip character and a fun time, if you don't take it too seriously. High energy waves are pulling the moon out of orbit and threatening the destruction of the earth. Dr. Zarkov has taken two passengers, Flash Gordon (Sam Jones) and beautiful Dale Arden (Melody Anderson), along with him on a rocket ship to the planet Mongo, which is the source of the nasty energy waves. It is also where Flash and Miss Anderson romp through updated, but still intentionally hokey, special effects - doing battle with Ming the Merciless (von Sydow) and sexy evil Princess Aura (Muti).

☐ Sex ☐ Nud ◢ Viol ◢ Lang ☐ AdSit

A: Sam Jones, Max von Sydow, Melody Anderson, Topol, Ornella Muti, Timothy Dalton

© MCA/UNIVERSAL HOME VIDEO, INC. 66022

FLIGHT OF THE NAVIGATOR

PG | SF CLD | 1986 | COLOR

D: Randal Kleiser — 90 m

8 Quite fun. A 12-year-old falls into a ravine in 1978 and wakes up a second later to find that it is now 1986 and his folks have moved away. However, he hasn't aged a day. NASA investigates and discovers that he has previously unknown star charts imprinted on his brain and his disappearance is connected to a recently discovered alien spaceship. He finds that he had been whisked away on a spaceship, that he can communicate with this one and that it needs his help to get home again. Kids will love the special effects, the kooky alien creatures and the action. Parents will enjoy this Disney treat, too.

☐ Sex ☐ Nud ☐ Viol ☐ Lang ☐ AdSit

A: Joey Cramer, Cliff De Young, Veronica Cartwright, Matt Adler, Sarah Jessica Parker, Howard Hesseman

© WALT DISNEY HOME VIDEO 499

FLY, THE

NR | SF DMA HOR | 1958 | B&W

D: Kurt Neumann — 94 m

9 This is a superior science fiction story. A scientist, experimenting with a machine that disintegrates matter in one place and reintegrates it again in another place, has a serious accident when his genes are mixed with those of a household fly. His head has become attached to the fly's body, and vice versa. He is now a gruesome freak struggling to return to normal. This film has become a cult favorite for very good reason. It was produced with care, high production values, good special effects and good acting. It was remade in 1986 in an equally good but much more grizzly manner.

☐ Sex ☐ Nud ☐ Viol ☐ Lang ◢ AdSit

A: David Hedison, Patricia Owens, Vincent Price, Herbert Marshall, Kathleen Freeman

© FOXVIDEO 1190

FORBIDDEN PLANET

G | SF | 1956 | COLOR

D: Fred M. Wilcox — 999 m

6 One of filmdom's very first attempts at serious science fiction and it provided the inspiration for the filmmakers who would make later sci-fi hits, like STARTREK. It was Oscar-nominated for special effects in 1956. It is pretty tame by today's standards. Nonetheless, it is an intelligent film which was very ambitious for its time and is still valuable today. Three explorers visit the planet Altair-IV in 2257. There, the resident scientist has built a self-sufficient world for himself and his daughter. However, there is also a mysterious malevolent force present in their idyllic world.

☐ Sex ☐ Nud ☐ Viol ☐ Lang ☐ AdSit

A: Walter Pidgeon, Anne Francis, Leslie Nielsen, Jack Kelly, Earl Holliman

Distributed By MGM/UA Home Video M202345

FOREVER YOUNG

PG | SF ROM | 1992 | COLOR

D: Steve Miner — 102 m

6 Mel Gibson is a test pilot who is desperate when his love has been hit by a car and it is believed that she will never recover. So, he agrees to become a test subject for his best friend, who is a scientist experimenting with suspending life in a secret military project. It is 1939. But the experiment is suspended when the War breaks out. For the next 50 years he sleeps, only to awaken in a government warehouse after two boys play with his container. He had become a forgotten experiment, lost in the system. Now it is 1992 and he has discovered that his love is still alive, but that he is now rapidly aging and dying. If you can buy into all that, you will be satisfied.

☐ Sex ☐ Nud ☐ Viol ◢ Lang ☐ AdSit

A: Mel Gibson, Elijah Wood, Isabel Glasser, George Wendt, Jamie Lee Curtis

© WARNER HOME VIDEO 12571

FUTUREWORLD

D: Richard T. Heffron — 107 m

PG | SF ACT | 1976 | COLOR

7 Entertaining sequel to WEST WORLD. In a fantastic amusement park of the future, lifelike robots act out a customer's fantasies. But investigative reporters Fonda and Danner find out there is also a plan by one of the scientists to replace all the world's leaders with these robots and to control the world. (Similar plot to the cult classic INVASION OF THE BODY SNATCHERS). Yul Brynner is back in his WEST WORLD role. Pretty good escapism.

Sex / Nud / ✓ Viol / ✓ Lang / AdSit

A: Peter Fonda, Blythe Danner, Arthur Hill, Yul Brynner, Stuart Margolin, John P. Ryan

© GOODTIMES 04060

GODZILLA, KING OF THE MONSTERS

D: Terry Morse — 80 m

NR | SF ACT CLD | 1956 | B&W

6 Campy original (American) version of the long-running Japanese classic horror film. Godzilla is a long dormant, huge, fire-breathing reptilian monster that is awakened by an atomic bomb blast, after which he goes on a reign of terror, destroying everything in his path. This original is far superior to the many clones which came later. It is most notable for the high quality of its special effects. (This version is not actually the original version. The original Japanese version was twenty minutes longer and did not have the subplot of the American scientist.)

Sex / Nud / ✓ Viol / Lang / AdSit

A: Inoshiro Honda, Raymond Burr, Takashi Shimura, Akihiko Hirata

© PARAMOUNT HOME VIDEO 12864

GROUNDSTAR CONSPIRACY, THE

D: Lamont Johnson — 93 m

PG | SF SUS MYS | 1972 | COLOR

8 A top secret space-based laboratory is largely destroyed in an explosion. The only survivor (Sarrazin) is thought by tough government agent Peppard to be a spy who was sent to steal its plans, but Sarrazin is badly burned and has no recollection of events. Still, Peppard must get him to remember. He has to know who was behind the plot. So when brainwashing doesn't work, Sarrazin is set free so that he can be followed. He has now become bait. Clever and intricate plot, with excellent pacing, direction and acting, plus an unexpected climax. A good thriller, unfairly overlooked upon its release.

Sex / Nud / ✓ Viol / Lang / ✓ AdSit

A: George Peppard, Michael Sarrazin, Christine Belford, Cliff Potts, James Olson

© MCA/UNIVERSAL HOME VIDEO, INC. 80602

ICEMAN

D: Fred Schepisi — 101 m

PG | SF DMA | 1984 | COLOR

8 Fascinating and credible premise: An arctic exploration team finds a pre-historic Neanderthal man frozen in the ice. Incredibly, they are successful in restoring the man to life out of his frozen coma. Now the question becomes what to do with this incredible find. Some want even to dissect him, but anthropologist Hutton is interested in him as a human being and develops a strong rapport with the man. Very well done. The serious approach to the subject matter and excellent performances by the leads make this an intriguing adventure story.

Sex / Nud / ✓ Viol / ✓ Lang / ✓ AdSit

A: Timothy Hutton, Lindsay Crouse, John Lone, Josef Sommer, David Strathairn, Danny Glover

© MCA/UNIVERSAL HOME VIDEO, INC. 80074

ICE PIRATES

D: Stewart Raffill — 95 m

PG | SF COM | 1984 | COLOR

6 Fun farce set in the future. Robert Urich plays a pirate leader in this tongue-in-cheek adventure story. He and his band of buccaneers come to the aid of beautiful princess (Crosby) in her battle against an evil force. Both she and the buccaneers are in pursuit of what is now the Universe's most precious commodity - water. The film is not always successful in its attempts at humor and excitement, but sometimes it is. The special effects aren't great, but they aren't bad, either. All this adds up to a passable evening's diversion for the family.

Sex / Nud / ✓ Viol / Lang / ✓ AdSit

A: Robert Urich, Mary Crosby, John Matuszak, Anjelica Huston, John Carradine

Distributed By MGM/UA Home Video M800427

INCREDIBLE SHRINKING MAN, THE

D: Jack Arnold — 81 m

NR | SF DMA | 1957 | B&W

9 Thoughtful, well-made and intelligent science fiction classic that has not diminished with time. Grant Williams is an ordinary business man who, oddly, begins to shrink after walking through a strange mist. All science's efforts are unable to stop him from shrinking. As he shrinks, his status regarding all things around him alters. Eventually his trip ever smaller makes him invisible to the normal world. He is alone. Great special effects and action create excitement, but the lasting power of the film comes from the forced reevaluation of life as we know it. Excellent.

Sex / Nud / ✓ Viol / Lang / ✓ AdSit

A: Grant Williams, Randy Stuart, Paul Lanton, April Kent, Raymond Bailey

© MCA/UNIVERSAL HOME VIDEO, INC. 80765

INVISIBLE MAN, THE

D: James Whale — 71 m

NR | SF SUS | 1933 | B&W

9 Excellent. H.G. Welles's classic story is beautifully done. A scientist has created a chemical formula for invisibility. Even though he has yet to create a counter-agent for the drug, he uses himself as a subject to test its effectiveness. He at first enjoys the novelty of the experience and there are several scenes which are quite funny. But soon things get serious as the ugly side effects begin to show themselves. He slowly becomes an insane megalomaniac. Good special effects. Claude Rains made his screen debut in this film, although no one actually sees him until the very end.

Sex / Nud / Viol / Lang / AdSit

A: Claude Rains, Gloria Stuart, Una O'Connor, Henry Travers, E.E. Clive, Dwight Frye

© MCA/UNIVERSAL HOME VIDEO, INC. 80398

IT CAME FROM BENEATH THE SEA

D: Robert Gordon — 80 m

NR | SF CLD | 1955 | B&W

6 This is one of the many "monster" movies that were typical in the '50s; but this science fiction piece has become a minor classic, primarily because of its special effects. Repeated nuclear explosions in the Pacific Ocean stir up a giant octopus from the depths. Enraged and hungry, it begins a reign of terror on the West Coast and works his way toward San Francisco. Only a Navy submarine stands in his way. Quite good for its genre.

Sex / Nud / Viol / Lang / AdSit

A: Faith Domergue, Kenneth Tobey, Ian Keith, Donald Curtis, Dean Maddox, Jr.

© COLUMBIA TRISTAR HOME VIDEO 60491

LAST STARFIGHTER, THE

D: Nick Castle — 100 m

PG | SF CLD | 1984 | COLOR

7 This is a quite enjoyable fantasy adventure yarn that is primarily, but not necessarily only, for kids. In it, a teenage videogame wizkid is transported from his trailer park home to a far away place by an alien, Robert Preston. He has been recruited, after his skill in blasting invading spaceships in a video game called Starfighter, is monitored. It will be his job to help defend the Universe against an evil invasion force. Interesting and witty dialogue, plus a clever premise and some funny situations make this a pleasant time killer.

Sex / Nud / ✓ Viol / ✓ Lang / AdSit

A: Robert Preston, Lance Guest, Barbara Bosson, Dan O'Herlihy, Catherine Mary Stewart

© MCA/UNIVERSAL HOME VIDEO, INC. 80078

LOGAN'S RUN

D: Michael Anderson — 119 m

PG | SF ACT | 1976 | COLOR

6 An intelligent adventure set in a strange futuristic society. Logan (York) is a policeman living and working in a carefree hedonistic domed city. His particular job is chasing down "runners" - individuals who run away rather than comply with a law requiring that they be "renewed" at age 30. This is an elaborate ceremony, after which the participants are never seen again. Facing his own renewal, York and a girl escape outside the dome to discover another world that no one knew even existed. And it includes an old man (Ustinov) - something neither has ever seen or known to be possible. Entertaining.

Sex / ✓ Nud / ✓ Viol / Lang / ✓ AdSit

A: Michael York, Richard Jordan, Jenny Agutter, Farrah Fawcett, Peter Ustinov, Roscoe Lee Browne

Distributed By MGM/UA Home Video M600082

METROPOLIS

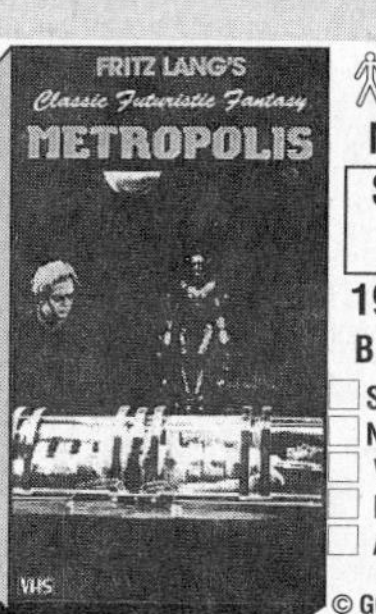

D: Fritz Lang — 120 m

NR | SF | 1926 | B&W

7 Using some of the most sophisticated film techniques available at the time (1926), this silent classic made technical predictions of a futuristic and mechanized city in 2026 that were pretty much right on the mark. It was a very influential film. The plot, however, about a mad scientist who uses a beautiful robot to help provoke a group of workers into a revolt, is pretty silly. There are other versions available, one with as much as a half hour removed from it and a pop-music soundtrack added.

Sex / Nud / Viol / Lang / AdSit

A: Brigitte Helm, Alfred Abel, Rudolf Klein-Rogge, Gustav Froelich, Fritz Rasp

© GOODTIMES 5079

MOTHRA

D: Inoshiro Honda — 100 m

NR | SF CLD | 1962 | COLOR

6 Hokey and silly, but strangely endearing monster flick. Twin princesses, each only six inches tall, are snatched from their home island for display in a local neighborhood bar. The girls pray to the god Mothra hoping to be rescued and Mothra responds, hatching a giant egg in the city of Tokyo. The egg releases a giant caterpillar that turns onto a huge moth and ventures into Tokyo hunting for the girls, destroying the city along the way. Really corny, but still one of the best of the Japanese monster movies, in a campy sort of way.

Sex / Nud / ✓ Viol / Lang / AdSit

A: Frankie Sakai, Hiroshi Koizumi, Lee Kresel, Kyoko Kagawa, Emi Itoh, Yumi Itoh

© COLUMBIA TRISTAR HOME VIDEO 60060

OMEGA MAN, THE

PG | SF SUS ACT | 1971 | COLOR

D: Boris Sagal 98 m

7 Well done and literate science fiction story about the breakdown of society after the world is largely destroyed in a biological war. Heston stars as a medical researcher who is strangely immune to the effects of all the germs. But a militant group of mutant survivors is now bent on destroying all technologies and has particularly targeted him to be killed. Heston discovers a few children who are also immune and being protected by Cash. The mutants want to kill them, too, but they are the future of the species and Heston must study them if there is to be a cure. Gripping suspense.

Sex / ✓ Nud / ✓ Viol / Lang / AdSit

A: Charlton Heston, Anthony Zerbe, Rosalind Cash, Paul Koslo, Lincoln Kilpatrick, Eric Laneuville

© WARNER HOME VIDEO 11210

PLANET OF THE APES

G | SF | 1967 | COLOR

D: Franklin J. Schaffner 112 m

8 First in a thought-provoking sci-fi adventure series. Four American astronauts crash-land on what they believe to be an alien world. The dominant life form here is apes. The humans have reverted to a very primitive state and have been relegated, into being slaves. Heston is captured by the apes, who are astounded to learn that he is intelligent and can talk. Simian scientist Roddy McDowall and his wife (Hunter) seek to protect Heston from those who want him destroyed. This upside-down perspective creates an interesting vehicle and has made this series a near-classic. See Index for the others.

Sex / Nud / ✓ Viol / Lang / ✓ AdSit

A: Charlton Heston, Roddy McDowall, Kim Hunter, Maurice Evans, James Whitmore, James Daly

© FOXVIDEO 1054

RETURN OF THE JEDI

PG | SF ACT SUS | 1983 | COLOR

D: Richard Marquand 134 m

9 Thrilling finale to the hugely popular, exciting and imaginative STAR WARS trilogy from George Lucas. In this episode, Luke Skywalker has further mastered his skills as a Jedi Master of the "Force." He first rescues Princess Leia and Hans Solo from the vile and decadent Jabba-the-Hut, then aids in the destruction of the monstrously powerful Death Star by infiltrating the evil forces of the Empire, seeking out its all-powerful leader Darth Vader - to destroy him. Great characters. Great special effects. Great fun!

Sex / Nud / ✓ Viol / Lang / AdSit

A: Mark Hamill, Carrie Fisher, Harrison Ford, Billy Dee Williams, Dave Prowse, Peter Mayhew

© FOXVIDEO 1478

SILENT RUNNING

G | SF DMA | 1972 | COLOR

D: Douglas Trumbull 90 m

8 Dramatic family entertainment with a message. A spaceship floating about in space houses the only remaining vegetation left from an earth where a nuclear war has destroyed all plant life. Dern is a devoted botanist who has spent eight years tending this ark and now he has received an order from earth to destroy everything. The enormity of what is being asked of him is more than he can bare. Instead, he hijacks the vessel, kills off the other crewmen and takes his cargo into the safety of the rings of Saturn. His only companions now are the two robots with very human-like qualities that help him to tend his garden.

Sex / Nud / Viol / Lang / AdSit

A: Bruce Dern, Cliff Potts, Ron Rifkin, Jesse Vint

© MCA/UNIVERSAL HOME VIDEO, INC. 55029

STAR TREK: THE MOTION PICTURE

G | SF ACT | 1980 | COLOR

D: Robert Wise 143 m

6 This is the first full-length motion picture spawned from the extremely popular TV series of 15 years prior, featuring the same cast. Driven by the huge popularity of that series, the picture generated terrific box office attention and spawned many sequels. This episode concerns an incoming ominous cloud that devours everything in its path. The Enterprise crew discovers that the cloud is really an intelligent machine. When one of it's crew has her body taken over by that intelligence, Kirk and company use her as a key to pursue the mystery of the machine and to venture inside it.

Sex / Nud / Viol / Lang / AdSit

A: William Shatner, Leonard Nimoy, Persis Khambatta, Stephen Collins, DeForest Kelley, James Doohan

© PARAMOUNT HOME VIDEO 8858

STAR TREK II: THE WRATH OF KHAN

PG | SF ACT | 1982 | COLOR

D: Nicholas Meyer 113 m

8 Solid entry in the Star Trek series based upon one of the original 1960s TV plots. In that TV episode, the Enterprise crew had exiled several very aggressive genetic supermen on a lonely planet. They had been genetically engineered to be superior to ordinary humans but had become determined to dominate all society. They are led by Khan (Montalban). Now they have escaped. They have commandeered a war ship and are seeking possession of the new Genesis technology, which can create whole planets - but can also destroy them. And Khan seeks also to destroy his old nemesis, Kirk.

Sex / Nud / ✓ Viol / Lang / AdSit

A: William Shatner, Leonard Nimoy, Ricardo Montalban, DeForest Kelley, James Doohan

© PARAMOUNT HOME VIDEO 1180

STAR TREK III: THE SEARCH FOR SPOCK

PG | SF ACT | 1984 | COLOR

D: Leonard Nimoy 105 m

8 Spock is dead - or is he? In STAR TREK II, Spock had sacrificed himself in order to save the rest of the crew. His body was "buried" on the Genesis planet. Now there is evidence that Spock's intellect was not lost and his body is regenerating itself. Kirk and the crew steal their now-mothballed ship and return to rescue a young boy who may be Spock. However, they also find there a Klingon warship that is determined to capture the Genesis technology. Less emphasis on special effects and more on characters and plot.

Sex / Nud / ✓ Viol / Lang / AdSit

A: William Shatner, DeForest Kelley, James Doohan, George Takei, Walter Koenig, Nichelle Nichols

© PARAMOUNT HOME VIDEO 1621

STAR TREK IV: THE VOYAGE HOME

PG | SF ACT | 1989 | COLOR

D: William Shatner 119 m

7 Light-hearted and fun. Kirk and the crew of the Enterprise return home to earth in their commandeered Klingon ship (from STAR TREK III) to discover that earth's atmosphere is being bombarded by a message from an alien probe that cannot be returned. The probe is broadcasting in a language only understood by humpback whales, a species that is extinct in the 23rd century. The crew travels back in time to the 20th century to capture two whales to take forward in time and receive the messages. Very entertaining and somewhat comic in tone. A good time.

Sex / Nud / Viol / ✓ Lang / AdSit

A: William Shatner, Leonard Nimoy, DeForest Kelley, James Doohan, Walter Koenig, Nichelle Nichols

© PARAMOUNT HOME VIDEO 1797

STAR TREK V: THE FINAL FRONTIER

PG | SF ACT | 1989 | COLOR

D: William Shatner 107 m

6 Kirk and McCoy are trying to teach Spock some campfire songs when the Enterprise receives an emergency call to go to a distant planet which has apparently been taken over by a madman. However, it has all been a ruse. It was only a gambit to attract a starship, the Enterprise, which is then hijacked. The madman needs a vessel to take him to the Great Barrier - the edge of the Universe. He wants to talk to God. Kirk is uncertain why he would need to go to such lengths, but Spock is more receptive - the madman is his half-brother.

Sex / Nud / Viol / ✓ Lang / AdSit

A: William Shatner, Leonard Nimoy, DeForest Kelley, James Doohan, Walter Koenig, Nichelle Nichols

© PARAMOUNT HOME VIDEO 32044

STAR TREK VI: THE UNDISCOVERED COUNTRY

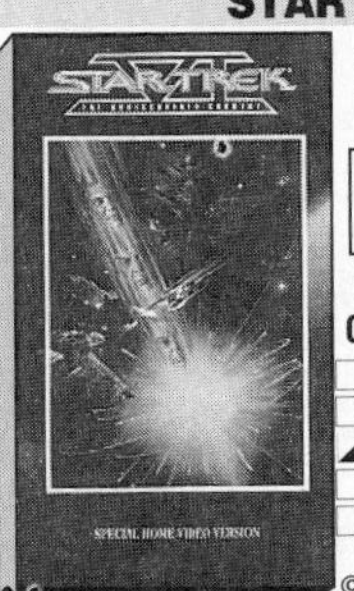

PG | SF ACT | 1991 | COLOR

D: Nicholas Meyer, William Shatner 110 m

7 The Klingon Empire is ready to make peace. One of their moons has exploded, the ozone on their home world is being destroyed, they do not have the resources to combat it themselves and they need the Federation. Even though Kirk loathes Klingons because they killed his son, the Enterprise is called upon to meet with the Klingons to prepare for peace talks -- but one of the Klingons is poisoned, Kirk and Dr. McCoy are accused of murder and are sentenced to a prison at a frozen Klingon outpost. Meanwhile, Spock has been able to prove that it was all a plot to destroy the talks. He must retrieve Kirk and McCoy and uncover the real plotters to salvage the peace.

Sex / Nud / ✓ Viol / Lang / AdSit

A: William Shatner, Leonard Nimoy, DeForest Kelley, James Doonan, Walter Koenig, Nichelle Nicholes

© PARAMOUNT HOME VIDEO 32301

STAR WARS

PG | SF ACT SUS | 1977 | COLOR

D: George Lucas 124 m

10 HUGE megahit and first of a trio of hits. Old-time Saturday matinee cliff-hanger intensity, Western shoot-'em-up action, mysticism, comedy, loveable characters and high tech wizardry - all set in a place long, long ago and far, far away. An ordinary boy, living with his adoptive parents on a remote farming colony, comes home to find them murdered by Imperial Stormtroopers. He soon also finds that he is not so ordinary and is launched into a mission to save the Universe. Won seven Oscars. Immensely entertaining. Followed by THE EMPIRE STRIKES BACK.

Sex / Nud / ✓ Viol / Lang / AdSit

A: Carrie Fisher, Mark Hamill, Harrison Ford, Alec Guinness, Anthony Daniels, Peter Cushing

© FOXVIDEO 1130

THEM

NR | SF SUS | 1954 | B&W

D: Gordon Douglas 93 m

7 This is a well-crafted science fiction monster classic from the early '50s. A young, terrified girl is discovered in the destroyed remains of trailer home out in the New Mexico desert. From their investigation, two scientists discover that recent atomic testing has mutated a race of giant ants. They and FBI agent James Arness, trace the ants to their nest and their queen in the sewers of L.A. This is a actually a thoughtful film which gives its subject serious treatment. Time is taken to make the premise credible and believable. And, it also has some scenes which will create genuine fear. Good special effects, too.

Sex / Nud / ✓ Viol / Lang / AdSit

A: James Whitmore, Edmund Gwenn, Joan Weldon, James Arness, Onslow Stevens, Chris Drake

© WARNER HOME VIDEO 11191

TIME AFTER TIME

D: Nicholas Meyer — 112 m

PG | SF CRM | 1979 | COLOR

8 Very imaginative and engaging story that is quite literate and very enjoyable in spite of its apparently bizarre premise. H.G. Welles (Malcolm McDowell) is compelled to chase Jack the Ripper (David Warner) into the future after the Ripper uses Welles's time machine to escape from Victorian England. The future he escapes to is San Francisco in 1979. Welles and the Ripper engage in a lively battle of wits in an environment that is totally alien to both of them. An amusing and engaging subplot is Welles's burgeoning romance with a modern-day bank teller (Mary Steenburgen).

☐ Sex ☐ Nud ◢ Viol ◢ Lang ◢ AdSit

A: David Warner, Mary Steenburgen, Malcolm McDowell, Charles Cioffi, Joseph Maher, Patti D'Arbanville

© WARNER HOME VIDEO 22017

TIME BANDITS

D: Terry Gilliam — 116 m

PG | SF COM | 1981 | COLOR

6 A near-hit from Monty Python alumni Michael Palin and Terry Gilliam. It's witty and clever, with very high production values, but somehow doesn't connect big-time. A bored English schoolboy is escorted through time and space by six dwarves who have stolen a map of time holes from the Supreme Being. They are out to steal treasures from one time and escape into another time. Along the way they have encounters with Robin Hood, Agamemnon, Napoleon and the Titanic. Doesn't work real well as a comedy, but passes fairly well as an adventure.

☐ Sex ☐ Nud ◢ Viol ☐ Lang ◢ AdSit

A: John Cleese, Sean Connery, Ian Holm, Shelley Duvall, Katherine Helmond, Michael Palin

© PARAMOUNT HOME VIDEO 2310

TIME MACHINE, THE

D: George Pal — 103 m

PG | SF DMA | 1960 | COLOR

8 Lush adaptation of the H.G. Welles novel. A Victorian inventor (Taylor) develops a time machine and, full of hope, he travels ahead in time only to encounter numerous world wars and destruction. Disturbed, he leaps far ahead into the year 802,701. There he discovers a peaceful, carefree race living in an apparent Garden of Eden. But there are dangers here as well. These people are mutants, born of atomic wars, who are totally ignorant and apathetic to everything - to the point that they won't even defend themselves against a race of subsurface dwellers which preys upon them. Special Effects Oscar.

☐ Sex ☐ Nud ◢ Viol ☐ Lang ◢ AdSit

A: Rod Taylor, Alan Young, Yvette Mimieux, Sebastian Cabot, Tom Helmore, Whit Bissell

Distributed By MGM/UA Home Video M600152

TRON

D: Steven Lisberger — 95 m

PG | SF ACT | 1982 | COLOR

6 Enjoyable Disney escapist adventure, geared to more than just kids. Set in the future, nearly everything is controlled by the Master Computer. Jeff Bridges is a computer whiz who sets out to prove that Warner, an unscrupulous executive, has stolen some of his programs. But before he gets very far, he is sucked inside the Master Computer's circuits where he, Boxleitner and Hughes must do battle against Warner and the Master Computer in a deadly video game. Exciting special effects. Plot is a little confusing, though.

☐ Sex ☐ Nud ◢ Viol ☐ Lang ☐ AdSit

A: Jeff Bridges, Bruce Boxleitner, David Warner, Cindy Morgan, Barnard Hughes, Dan Shor

© WALT DISNEY HOME VIDEO 122

UFORIA

D: John Binder — 92 m

PG | SF COM | 1981 | COLOR

7 Eccentric personalities mix with funky science fiction and make a thoroughly enjoyable film. Quirky supermarket checkout clerk Williams is a born again Christian with some wild ideas. She believes she is the chosen one, that salvation will come in the form of UFOs and that she will lead humanity to safety. Wanderer Ward falls in love with her, and preacher/huckster Stanton decides that this is a great opportunity to make some serious money, if he can just milk it from the right angle. But... what happens if she's right? Good natured fun, offbeat and more than a little zany.

☐ Sex ☐ Nud ☐ Viol ◢ Lang ◢ AdSit

A: Cindy Williams, Harry Dean Stanton, Fred Ward, Harry Carey, Jr., Darrell Larson

© MCA/UNIVERSAL HOME VIDEO, INC. 80042

V

D: Kenneth Johnson — 197 m

NR | SF ACT | 1983 | COLOR

9 This excellent made-for-TV miniseries held the fascination of the country. In it, fifty huge space ships appear in the skies over all the world's major cities. The human-like visitors relate that they are on a mission of peace, but soon they are moving to focus the fears of the masses. Blaming scientist's for all the ills of the mankind, they make their move to establish a world-wide fascist state, while also destroying the only force that can stop them. TV cameraman Mark Singer discovers the awful real truth and forms a rebel army to battle them. Very effective special effects create believability. Success brought another miniseries, then a TV series.

☐ Sex ☐ Nud ◢ Viol ☐ Lang ◢ AdSit

A: Mark Singer, Faye Grant, Michael Durrell, Peter Nelson, Jane Badler, Neva Patterson

© WARNER HOME VIDEO 11489

VOYAGE TO THE BOTTOM OF THE SEA

D: Irwin Allen — 106 m

NR | SF CLD | 1961 | COLOR

6 Reasonably good, light, family-oriented sci-fi flick in which a brilliant submarine commander (Pidgeon) has devised a scheme to save the earth, after the Van Allen radiation belts erupt and threaten to destroy it. The Arctic is already on fire and soon fire will engulf the whole earth unless they can stop it. His plan is to launch a polaris missile into space and then explode it, breaking the chain reaction. But before they can get the sub into position to do that, they have to defeat a sea monster, fend off attacking submarines and an on-board saboteur. It spawned a popular mid-'60s TV series.

☐ Sex ☐ Nud ◢ Viol ☐ Lang ☐ AdSit

A: Walter Pidgeon, Joan Fontaine, Peter Lorre, Robert Sterling, Barbara Eden, Michael Ansara

© FOXVIDEO 1044

WAR OF THE WORLDS, THE

D: Byron Haskin — 85 m

G | SF SUS | 1953 | COLOR

8 Excellent science fiction that received an Oscar for Special Effects. H.G. Wells's classic novel was first broadcast on the radio by Orson Welles. It was so plausible that people believed it. He literally terrorized the nation with it. This movie version was updated only slightly. Earth is being invaded by hordes of eerie hovering space vehicles which mindlessly spew death from a monstrous heat ray that emanates from a goose-necked "head" protruding from the body of each vehicle. All efforts by earthlings to reason with them or destroy them fail. Intelligent fast-paced drama. This is not a "monster" movie.

☐ Sex ☐ Nud ◢ Viol ☐ Lang ☐ AdSit

A: Gene Barry, Ann Robinson, Les Tremayne, Jack Kruschen, Robert Cornthwaite, Cedric Hardwicke

© PARAMOUNT HOME VIDEO 5303

WAVELENGTH

D: Mike Gray — 87 m

PG | SF | 1983 | COLOR

6 Interesting and different sort of science fiction flick. A rock musician living in Hollywood Hills stumbles onto a seemingly abandoned underground Air Force facility. He, his girlfriend and an old prospector (Keenan Wynn) explore it and find that the Air Force is holding and conducting secret medical experiments on three extraterrestrials held prisoner there. Soon the government has captured them, too. They and the ETs join forces to escape. Quite well done, with a solid rock score from the group Tangerine Dream.

☐ Sex ◢ Nud ◢ Viol ◢ Lang ☐ AdSit

A: Robert Carradine, Cherie Currie, Keenan Wynn, Cal Bowman, James Hess, Terry Burns

© R&G VIDEO, LP 80201

WESTWORLD

D: Michael Crichton — 90 m

PG | SF WST ACT | 1973 | COLOR

7 Very entertaining and inventive yarn about a high tech adult resort of the future, where wealthy patrons may live out their Wild West fantasies with amazingly lifelike robots. By day, the robots are shot up by the patrons. At night they are repaired. Everything is harmless and quite safe until one errant gunfighter robot (Brynner is terrific) refuses to play the game as it was written. He goes berserk and starts stalking the guests for real. Richard Benjamin and James Brolin are two tourists who are unfortunate enough to catch his attention. Well-done sequel is FUTUREWORLD.

☐ Sex ☐ Nud ◢ Viol ☐ Lang ☐ AdSit

A: Yul Brynner, James Brolin, Richard Benjamin, Alan Oppenheimer, Victoria Shaw, Martin Jared

Distributed By MGM/UA Home Video M600097

Suspense

AIRPORT

D: George Seaton — 137 m

PG | SUS DMA | 1970 | COLOR

9 This was the first of the major disaster epics which were very popular for nearly a decade. Here, a crazed bomber blows a hole in an airliner while it is in flight. Badly crippled, the plane must land immediately at a snowbound airport whose runway is blocked by an another airliner stuck in the mud. This type of plot provides an opportunity for the film to explore the lives of several different people affected by the disaster. So, there are several stories going on all at the same time. Pretty good stuff. Helen Hayes won an Oscar. Taut and suspenseful. See also AIRPORT 1975, AIRPORT '77, THE POSIDEON ADVENTURE, EARTHQUAKE and TOWERING INFERNO.

☐ Sex ☐ Nud ☐ Viol ☐ Lang ◢ AdSit

A: Burt Lancaster, Dean Martin, George Kennedy, Helen Hayes, Jean Seberg, Jacqueline Bisset

© MCA/UNIVERSAL HOME VIDEO, INC. 55031

AIRPORT 1975

D: Jack Smight — 107 m

PG | SUS DMA | 1974 | COLOR

7 AIRPORT disaster sequel. When the cockpit of a 747 is struck by a small plane in mid-air, the entire flight crew is killed. It is up to stewardess Karen Black to fly the plane by Heston's radioed instructions, that is until Heston himself can be "dropped" into the ripped-open cock-pit by a helicopter from overhead. Not terribly believable but it is very entertaining - in part because there were 22 major stars aboard that airplane. See also AIRPORT and AIRPORT '77.

[ ] Sex [ ] Nud [ ] Viol [ ] Lang [x] AdSit

A: Charlton Heston, Karen Black, George Kennedy, Efrem Zimbalist, Jr., Susan Clark, Helen Reddy

© GOODTIMES 4107

AIRPORT '77

D: Jerry Jameson — 114 m

PG | SUS DMA | 1977 | COLOR

7 This is another AIRPORT disaster flick sequel. This time, millionaire Jimmy Stewart has a converted 747 jumbo jet transport a large group of VIP guests along with a fortune in his art treasures to the grand opening of a museum in Palm Beach. However, the plane is hijacked along the way and forced to crash land into the open ocean within the famed Bermuda Triangle. Then, in order to be rescued, the plane and passengers, who are alive inside, must be lifted whole from the ocean floor. See also AIRPORT and AIRPORT 1975.

[ ] Sex [ ] Nud [ ] Viol [ ] Lang [x] AdSit

A: Jack Lemmon, Lee Grant, Brenda Vaccaro, Darren McGavin, Christopher Lee, James Stewart

© MCA/UNIVERSAL HOME VIDEO, INC. 66039

ANDERSON TAPES, THE

D: Sidney Lumet — 98 m

PG | SUS CRM | 1971 | COLOR

7 Really neat thriller. Connery is a master crook who has just been released from prison. He plans the holdup of the entire Fifth Avenue apartment building where his girlfriend lives in New York City and the plan is bankrolled by a big underworld boss. The best specialists there are have been hired to work with him. Disguised as moving men, the team systematically loots each apartment, but things start to unravel. Tight editing and excellent performances keep the viewer totally involved and on edge. Climax is particularly good.

[ ] Sex [ ] Nud [x] Viol [ ] Lang [x] AdSit

A: Sean Connery, Dyan Cannon, Martin Balsam, Ralph Meeker, Alan King, Margaret Hamilton

© COLUMBIA TRISTAR HOME VIDEO 60124

ASPHYX, THE

D: Peter Newbrook — 96 m

PG | SUS HOR | 1972 | COLOR

8 A Victorian scientist discovers the spirit of death which is possessed within all beings. Life only exists when the spirit is in the body and death can only occur when that spirit leaves the body. Trap it and life becomes eternal - but is eternal life really a good thing to pursue? Excellent thriller, told with conviction.

[ ] Sex [ ] Nud [x] Viol [ ] Lang [x] AdSit

A: Robert Powell, Robert Stephens, Jane Lapotaire, Ralph Arliss, Alex Scott

© MAGNUM ENTERTAINMENT, INC. M3117

CHARLEY VARRICK

D: Don Siegel — 111 m

PG | SUS ACT | 1973 | COLOR

8 Very good and intelligent thriller. Walter Matthau plays a crop duster and small-time bank robber who only robs little back-country banks for little payrolls. But he gets much more than he bargained for when he and his partner rob a small rural bank of $750,000 that turns out to have been mob money. Now, they're in big trouble. The mob wants their money back and they send a sadistic and ruthless hit man, Joe Don Baker, to get it. Matthau must find a way to outfox both the mob and their hitman before it's too late. Fast-paced, thrilling action with lots of intriguing plot twists.

[ ] Sex [ ] Nud [x] Viol [x] Lang [x] AdSit

A: Walter Matthau, Joe Don Baker, Felicia Farr, Andy Robinson, John Vernon, Sheree North

© MCA/UNIVERSAL HOME VIDEO, INC. 55062

CHINA SYNDROME, THE

D: James Bridges — 123 m

PG | SUS DMA | 1979 | COLOR

10 A huge box office hit because it was very intense and believable drama. A novice TV reporter (Fonda) and her cameraman are at a nuclear generating station when there is a near-meltdown situation. It is averted only by a quick-thinking engineer (Lemon), but the TV station refuses to televise their video tapes. When Lemmon releases X-rays revealing that it could happen again, another reporter is killed. There is no doubt now that there is a ruthless coverup underway by very powerful people. Feeling he has no alternative Lemmon seizes control of the plant and invites the media in. Excellent.

[ ] Sex [ ] Nud [x] Viol [ ] Lang [x] AdSit

A: Jane Fonda, Jack Lemmon, Michael Douglas, Scott Brady, James Hampton, Peter Donat

© GOODTIMES 4200

CLOAK & DAGGER

D: Richard Franklin — 101 m

PG | SUS CLD | 1984 | COLOR

7 A young computer whiz kid (Thomas) plays Cloak & Dagger games in which he is a secret agent with his imaginary superhero playmate (Coleman). However, one day Thomas gets involved in a real-life spy drama and witnesses a real murder, but Coleman (also cast as the boy's father), having been fooled before, does not believe him and thinks that this is just another of the boy's imaginary games. The whiz kid can not get Dad to believe that what he saw was real and is on his own. Suspenseful and fastpaced. Suitable for young people, but also of real interest to adults, too. Actually, a remake of THE WINDOW (1949).

[ ] Sex [ ] Nud [ ] Viol [ ] Lang [ ] AdSit

A: Henry Thomas, Dabney Coleman, Michael Murphy, Christina Nigra, John McIntire, Jeanette Nolan

© MCA/UNIVERSAL HOME VIDEO, INC. 80124

DUEL

D: Steven Spielberg — 91 m

NR | SUS ACT | 1971 | COLOR

8 Startling, effective thriller that was initially made for TV but was later released in theaters, too. This is also the film that made Steven Spielberg's reputation and gave him his big start in this film describing mindless terror. A salesman in a rented car, taking a leisurely drive down a remote stretch of road, finds himself relentlessly pursued by a maniacal driver at the wheel of a ten-ton tanker truck. He can't see this guy's face and he doesn't understand why, but one thing is for certain... this guy wants to kill him.. Superb suspense film with excellent pacing.

[ ] Sex [ ] Nud [ ] Viol [x] Lang [x] AdSit

A: Dennis Weaver, Tim Herbert, Charles Peel, Eddie Firestone, Gene Dynarksi, Alexander Lockwood

© MCA/UNIVERSAL HOME VIDEO, INC. 55096

ESCAPE FROM ALCATRAZ

D: Don Siegel — 112 m

PG | SUS CRM | 1979 | COLOR

7 Very intriguing and involving "true" story. It is the straightforward telling of the "facts" (although somewhat romanticized by Hollywood) surrounding the actual 1962 breakout of three prisoners from the supposedly escape-proof Alcatraz prison. The prisoners did get off the island but were never heard of again. The movie would have you believe that they survived. Eastwood plays Frank Morris who masterminded the escape for himself and two others. McGoohan plays a cold-hearted tough warden. It maintains your interest throughout and is largely credible.

[ ] Sex [ ] Nud [x] Viol [x] Lang [x] AdSit

A: Clint Eastwood, Patrick McGoohan, Roberts Blossom, Jack Thibeau, Fred Ward, Paul Benjamin

© PARAMOUNT HOME VIDEO 1256

EVIL MIND, THE (AKA THE CLAIRVOYANT)

D: Maurice Elvey — 69 m

NR | SUS | 1935 | B&W

7 Interesting and well done British entry about a phony stage-psychic (Claude Raines in a fine performance) who suddenly realizes his phony predictions are coming true. He successfully predicts a train wreck and a horse race. But when he predicts a mine disaster where 310 men die, his warning is ignored. That is until 310 miners are killed in a panic stampede. He is accused of causing the panic and is tried for murder.

[ ] Sex [ ] Nud [ ] Viol [ ] Lang [ ] AdSit

A: Claude Raines, Fay Wray, Mary Clare, Jane Baxter, Ben Field

© VIDEO YESTERYEAR 854

EXPERIMENT IN TERROR

D: Blake Edwards — 123 m

NR | SUS CRM ACT | 1962 | B&W

8 Excellent, high-tension gripper about a sadistic psycho killer (Martin) who kidnaps a bank teller's (Remick) teenage sister (Powers). If she doesn't deliver $100,000 to him, her sister will be killed. Desperate, she contacts the FBI and an extensive surveillance is set up, but it doesn't work. The only way to draw him out is to use Remick as bait. Glenn Ford is the FBI agent who fights against the clock to save the girl and prevent tragedy. Suspense builds slowly and steadily throughout the entire picture. Excellent acting. Martin is particularly menacing.

[ ] Sex [ ] Nud [ ] Viol [ ] Lang [x] AdSit

A: Glenn Ford, Lee Remick, Stefanie Powers, Ross Martin, Ned Glass

© GOODTIMES 4443

FALLEN IDOL, THE

D: Carol Reed — 92 m

NR | SUS DMA | 1948 | B&W

8 Superbly crafted film. A small boy, the young son of an ambassador, idolizes the family's butler. The butler is trapped in a very unhappy marriage and is accused of murder when his wife dies a suspicious death. The desperate boy tries to protect his friend from the police by lying. Then, when the boy finds out that it really was an accident and he tries to tell the truth, no one will believe him. This is a story of an adult world that is told entirely from the boy's point of view. Excellent drama, high suspense. Two Oscar nominations.

[ ] Sex [ ] Nud [ ] Viol [ ] Lang [x] AdSit

A: Ralph Richardson, Michele Morgan, Bobby Henrey, Sonia Dresdel, Denis O'Dea, Jack Hawkins

© HOME VISION FAL 060

FLIGHT OF THE PHOENIX, THE

D: Robert Aldrich 143 m

NR · SUS DMA ACT · 1966 · COLOR

9 This is a gripping adventure story about a small planeful of men who are forced to crash in the North African desert. They are all trapped in a very hostile environment with only one way out. They must rebuild the plane and fly it out. Tension steadily builds as the men struggle both to endure the extreme rigors of desert survival and to rebuild the plane. An excellent international cast provides credibility and realism to an excellent script. Plus, there is a really unique twist as the climax builds. Very highly recommended viewing.

☐ Sex ☐ Nud ☐ Viol ☐ Lang ☑ AdSit

A: James Stewart, Richard Attenborough, Peter Finch, Hardy Kruger, Ernest Borgnine, George Kennedy

© FOXVIDEO 1221

GASLIGHT

D: George Cukor 114 m

NR · SUS CRM · 1944 · B&W

8 Eerie classic psycho-thriller. A wealthy, innocent young girl (Bergman) in Victorian London is very vulnerable after her aunt is murdered, so she marries a seemingly wonderful Charles Boyer. Boyer insists that they live in the aunt's house. Poor Ingrid, she doesn't know that it is was Boyer who had killed the aunt in the first place and he is now obsessed with hunting for the aunt's hidden jewelry. However, he needs more time to conduct his searches. He has to get her out of the house, so he very methodically and purposefully seeks to drive Bergman insane. Bergman won her first Oscar. Two other nominations.

☐ Sex ☐ Nud ☐ Viol ☐ Lang ☑ AdSit

A: Ingrid Bergman, Joseph Cotten, Charles Boyer, Dame May Witty, Angela Lansbury, Terry Moore

Distributed By MGM/UA Home Video M400473

GRAY LADY DOWN

D: David Greene 111 m

PG · SUS · 1977 · COLOR

8 Well made and tense, believable nail-biter. A nuclear submarine has been accidentally rammed by a freighter and has sunk into 1400 feet of water. The men onboard have only 48 hours of air. The sunken sub's escape hatch was buried during an earth tremor and they cannot escape by themselves. The Navy must call upon an experimental deep-diving two-man sub to rescue the crew. A solid cast of veteran actors adds credibility to this high-tech race against time. It is logically presented, beautifully photographed and has some really terrific special effects, too.

☐ Sex ☐ Nud ☑ Viol ☑ Lang ☑ AdSit

A: Charlton Heston, David Carradine, Stacy Keach, Ned Beatty, Ronny Cox, Rosemary Forsyth

© MCA/UNIVERSAL HOME VIDEO, INC. 55057

JUGGERNAUT

D: Richard Lester 109 m

PG · SUS ACT · 1974 · COLOR

7 Very effective suspense thriller. A blackmailer has planted several bombs on board a luxury liner and is holding it for ransom while it sails on the high seas. Harris and a band of experts helicopter on board and must race against time to find all the bombs and defuse them. And, all the while they are looking, the blackmailer stays on the phone to taunt them with meager and cryptic clues as to where the bombs are. This could have been rather commonplace disaster movie, but instead it is raised, by excellent acting and direction, into an intense and realistic thriller.

☐ Sex ☐ Nud ☑ Viol ☑ Lang ☐ AdSit

A: Richard Harris, Omar Sharif, David Hemmings, Anthony Hopkins, Shirley Knight, Ian Holm

Distributed By MGM/UA Home Video M203070

OTHER, THE

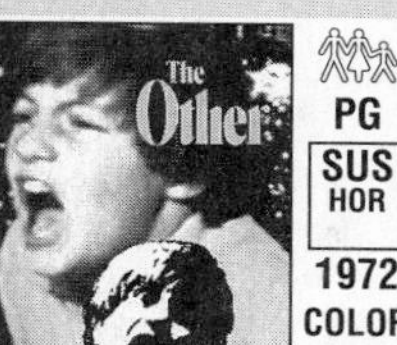

D: Robert Mulligan 100 m

PG · SUS HOR · 1972 · COLOR

7 An eerie tale of the unnatural. During the summer of 1935, near a small Connecticut farm, there occurs a series of tragic and bizarre murders. While this film begins at an apparently slow pace, it is only laying careful groundwork and clues for the chilling story which soon begins to unwind. Two 12-year-old boys are twins. They look alike, act alike and are very dedicated to each other. But, they are different - one is very evil. People die. Only their mother and their grandmother have any suspicions of what the truth may be. This is a real chiller from Tom Tryon.

☐ Sex ☐ Nud ☑ Viol ☑ Lang ☑ AdSit

A: Uta Hagen, Diana Muldaur, John Ritter, Chris Udvarnoky, Martin Udvarnoky, Victor French

© FOXVIDEO 1729

PHANTOM OF THE OPERA, THE

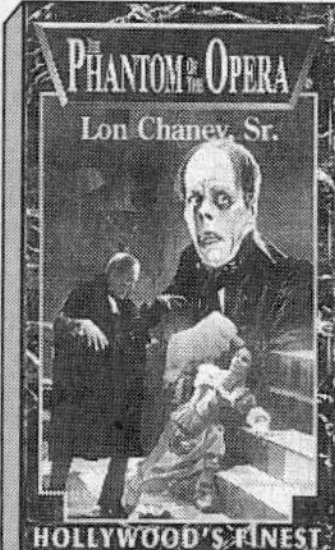

D: Rupert Julian 79 m

NR · SUS DMA HOR · 1925 · B&W

7 Lon Chaney Jr. was known as "the man of a thousand faces." No other film typifies his justly held reputation as does this one. He plays a brilliant composer whose face has been horribly disfigured by acid. Now crazed, scorned and vilified by the public, he lives in the catacombs under the Paris Opera, haunting it from the shadows. Hearing a beautiful soprano sing, he becomes infatuated with her and steals her away to his underworld where he will train her to sing. Intrigued by his mask and seizing upon an impulse, she unmasks him in a scene that is still shocking today.

☐ Sex ☐ Nud ☐ Viol ☐ Lang ☑ AdSit

A: Lon Chaney, Jr., Mary Philbin, Norman Kerry, Snitz Edwards, Gibson Gowland

© UNITED AMERICAN VIDEO CORP. 4044

PHANTOM OF THE OPERA, THE

D: Arthur Lubin 93 m

NR · SUS DMA HOR · 1943 · COLOR

8 Pretty decent remake of the 1925 classic and the first-ever talkie version. This time Claude Rains plays the acid-scarred phantom whose best musical works were stolen and who now lives in the catacombs under the Paris Opera. He becomes infatuated with a beautiful soprano, is determined to make her a star and to get even with those who have wronged him. Plenty of spooky moments, very high production values and excellent acting, but they could have done with less singing.

☐ Sex ☐ Nud ☐ Viol ☐ Lang ☑ AdSit

A: Nelson Eddy, Susanna Foster, Claude Rains, Edgar Barrier, Hume Cronyn, Miles Mander

© MCA/UNIVERSAL HOME VIDEO, INC. 80399

PROJECT X

D: Jonathan Kaplan 107 m

PG · SUS SF · 1987 · COLOR

7 Entertaining quasi-science fiction flick. A chronic screw-up in the Air Force (Broderick) gets assigned to a top secret project to help train the next "generation" of pilots - brilliant chimpanzees who can communicate with sign language. Broderick becomes incensed at the unnecessarily cruel and fatal nature of the experimentation on the chimps, so he, another trainer (Hunt) and the chimps all conspire against the Air Force's plans. Watchable and enjoyable, but predictable.

☐ Sex ☐ Nud ☑ Viol ☑ Lang ☐ AdSit

A: Matthew Broderick, Helen Hunt, Anne Lockhart, Bill Sadler, Johnny Ray McGhee, Jonathon Stark

© FOXVIDEO 5192

PULP

D: Mike Hodges 95 m

PG · SUS COM · 1972 · COLOR

6 Pretty good spoof thriller. Michael Caine is a hack writer from Hollywood who is hired by a retired film star (Rooney), to ghost write his autobiography. Rooney made his name playing gangsters and now lives in Italy. Caine travels to Italy and begins his interviews of Rooney, but they are cut short when Rooney is murdered. Now someone is apparently after Caine, too. Maybe Rooney was so good at playing gangsters because he wasn't acting after all.

☐ Sex ☐ Nud ☑ Viol ☑ Lang ☐ AdSit

A: Michael Caine, Mickey Rooney, Lionel Stander, Lizabeth Scott, Nadia Cassini, Al Lettieri

© WOOD KNAPP VIDEO 1025

ROLLERCOASTER

D: James Goldstone 119 m

PG · SUS · 1977 · COLOR

8 A whopper of a roller coaster ride! An unstable extortionist (Bottoms) has been placing bombs beneath the rides at some of the nation's biggest amusement parks. His next target is the world's biggest rollercoaster unless he gets $1 million. County inspector (Segal) and FBI agent (Windmark) are the cops who must stop him, and with whom he plays a teasing game of cat and mouse. This is a very well-done and intelligent suspensor that, unfairly, did not get a good reception by the critics, so it never got the exposure it should have. It has a very tense climax that will have you on the edge of your couch!

☐ Sex ☐ Nud ☑ Viol ☑ Lang ☐ AdSit

A: George Segal, Richard Widmark, Timothy Bottoms, Henry Fonda, Harry Guardino, Susan Strasberg

© MCA/UNIVERSAL HOME VIDEO, INC. 66037

SABOTAGE

D: Alfred Hitchcock 77 m

NR · SUS · 1936 · B&W

7 Sly early Hitchcock thriller! An undercover terrorist (Homolka) is a theatre manager in London, but he is also a terrorist who goes out on secret bombing missions at night. His wife slowly begins to suspect that she is married to the madman who is currently terrorizing the city. The tension mounts steadily when she goes to Scotland Yard with her suspicions and undercover detective Loder begins to investigate her claims. Based on Joseph Conrad's "Secret Agent," this was one of Hitchcock's first directorial attempts at his signature thrillers.

☐ Sex ☐ Nud ☐ Viol ☐ Lang ☑ AdSit

A: Oscar Homolka, Sylvia Sidney, John Loder, Desmond Tester

© UNITED AMERICAN VIDEO CORP. V4010

SABOTEUR

D: Alfred Hitchcock 108 m

NR · SUS ACT · 1942 · B&W

8 Outstanding high suspense wartime thriller from Hitchcock with an ever present feeling of doom and gloom. A mild mannered but stubborn man (Cummings) witnesses the sabotage of an American munitions factory during World War II. His best friend is killed in the explosion and he is framed for it. Determined to clear his name, he becomes an interstate fugitive as he tracks down the real saboteur, German agent Kruger. The thrilling fast-paced chase takes Cummings on a cross-country journey. It is most famous for its edge-of-your-seat cliffhanger climax at the Statue of Liberty.

☐ Sex ☐ Nud ☑ Viol ☐ Lang ☑ AdSit

A: Robert Cummings, Priscilla Lane, Otto Kruger, Norman Lloyd

© MCA/UNIVERSAL HOME VIDEO, INC. 80111

SAND PEBBLES, THE

D: Robert Wise — 180 m

NR | SUS DMA ACT | 1966 | COLOR

8 Sprawling, intelligent and compelling epic film which garnered a nomination for Best Picture and numerous other technical Oscar nominations. An exceptionally strong performance from McQueen drives this film about a cynical, normally reclusive sailor assigned to the engine room of an American gunboat patrolling the Yangtze river of China about 1926... just as civil war begins. Commander Crenna must be diplomatic. He represents the United States. But McQueen will not watch passively as his best friend is tortured. And he also moves aggressively to protect a missionary's daughter.

Sex / Nud / ✓ Viol / Lang / ✓ AdSit

A: Steve McQueen, Richard Crenna, Candice Bergen, Richard Attenborough, Mako, Gavin MacLeod

© FOXVIDEO 1029

SCARLET AND THE BLACK, THE

D: Jerry London — 145 m

NR | SUS ACT | 1983 | COLOR

7 Very good made-for-TV film relating the real-life exploits of a brave Irish priest, Monsignor Hugh O'Flaherty, during WWII. Operating from the Vatican, under the cloak of diplomatic immunity, O'Flaherty organizes a vast network of safe houses inside Nazi-occupied Rome and is responsible for the concealment and escape of hundreds of POWs and refugees. When Gestapo chief (Plummer) orders him killed or captured if he is spotted outside the Vatican, O'Flaherty assumes numerous disguises and plays cat-and-mouse games to keep operating.

Sex / Nud / ✓ Viol / Lang / ✓ AdSit

A: Gregory Peck, Christopher Plummer, John Gielgud, Raf Vallone

© LIVE HOME VIDEO 69918

SLEUTH

D: Joseph L. Mankiewicz — 139 m

PG | SUS MYS COM | 1968 | COLOR

9 A delicious and winning film that is made even better by some really superb talent! Caine and Olivier play a masterful cat-and-mouse game, each trying to outsmart and outdo the other. Caine has had an affair with Olivier's wife. So, Olivier devises a clever plot to get even by trying to trick Caine into getting caught committing a crime. However, Caine figures out Olivier's plan and turns the table on Olivier, enacting his own kind of revenge. This totally unpredictable and inventive plot takes some terrific sharp turns that will leave you guessing! Both Olivier and Caine were Oscar-nominated.

Sex / Nud / ✓ Viol / ✓ Lang / ✓ AdSit

A: Laurence Olivier, Michael Caine, Alec Cawthorne, Margo Channing, John Mathews, Teddy Martin

© VIDEO TREASURES SV9069

STING, THE

D: George Roy Hill — 129 m

PG | SUS COM | 1973 | COLOR

10 Very popular and hugely entertaining reteaming of the winning duo from BUTCH CASSIDY AND THE SUNDANCE KID, and the winner of 7 Oscars - including Best Picture. After his partner and friend is killed by a NYC hood (Shaw), a small-time con man Redford enlists Newman's help in a big-time scheme to take the guy down, hard. Very talented cast. A clever and intricate plot keeps moving and keeps you guessing and second-guessing. You know there's a con being worked, but you don't ever really know how or who. A very lively Scott Joplin ragtime score from Marvin Hamlisch adds to the fun.

Sex / Nud / ✓ Viol / ✓ Lang / ✓ AdSit

A: Paul Newman, Robert Redford, Robert Shaw, Eileen Brennan, Charles Durning, Ray Walston

© MCA/UNIVERSAL HOME VIDEO, INC. 66009

STRANGER, THE

D: Orson Welles — 95 m

NR | SUS DMA | 1946 | B&W

8 Solid Welles' suspensor that takes hold and won't let go! Orson Welles is a stranger in a small town in Connecticut just after the end of WWII, but he is an escaped Nazi war criminal. He has fashioned a new life for himself in this sleepy little town and is about to marry the judge's daughter (Young) who is unaware of her love's true identity. At first, Welles is unaware that Federal agent Robinson has zeroed in on his whereabouts. But, when he does figure it out, the two engage in a grim cat-and-mouse game that places the girl's life in the middle. She is in danger and their battle will culminate in the jolting climax.

Sex / Nud / Viol / Lang / ✓ AdSit

A: Orson Welles, Edward G. Robinson, Loretta Young, Richard Long, Martha Wentworth

© UNITED AMERICAN VIDEO CORP. 1019

STRANGERS ON A TRAIN

D: Alfred Hitchcock — 101 m

NR | SUS CRM | 1951 | B&W

10 Undeniably one of Hitchcock's very best - a classic thriller! Granger is a tennis pro who wants to marry Roman, but his trampy wife is standing in his way. On the other hand, Walker is a spoiled psychopath also who wants his domineering father out of his way. When the two strangers meet on a train, they casually discuss exchanging murders. Granger playfully agrees to the deal, thinking Walker is joking. He wasn't, and immediately carries out his part of the plan. Hitchcock's impeccable film techniques build to an unforgettable climax. A brilliantly suspenseful ride from start to finish.

Sex / Nud / Viol / Lang / ✓ AdSit

A: Farley Granger, Robert Walker, Ruth Roman, Leo G. Carroll, Patricia Hitchcock, Marion Lorne

© WARNER HOME VIDEO 11062

SUDDENLY

D: Lewis Allen — 77 m

NR | SUS CRM | 1954 | B&W

7 The air is ripe with tense, teeth-grinding danger. Sinatra is a hired assassin who is given the ultimate assignment. With nerves of steel and a fierce determination to carry out his job, the ruthless killer is set to assassinate the President. Together with two other triggermen, Sinatra takes over a small house in Suddenly, a small town in which the President will stop on his way to a fishing trip. Sinatra plays the assassin with icy precision and gives the unmistakable impression that he will let no one get in his way.

Sex / Nud / Viol / Lang / ✓ AdSit

A: Frank Sinatra, Sterling Hayden, Nancy Gates, James Gleason, Willis Bouchey, Kim Charney

© CONTINENTAL VIDEO 1006

SUSPICION

D: Alfred Hitchcock — 99 m

NR | SUS | 1941 | B&W

9 Chalk up another winning suspensor for Hitchcock! A lonely, but very rich, wallflower (Fontaine) falls in love with a charming man-about-town (Grant) without knowing very much about him - but she doesn't care. However, it is not long before the flamboyant Grant has spent himself into big trouble. Slowly and ever so steadily Fontaine's "suspicion" gradually begins to build. She suspects that her new husband has plans to dig himself out of his financial hole over her dead body - by killing her to collect a hefty insurance check. Fontaine's dynamite performance won her an Oscar for Best Actress.

Sex / Nud / Viol / Lang / ✓ AdSit

A: Cary Grant, Joan Fontaine, Cedric Hardwicke, Nigel Bruce, Dame May Whitty, Isabel Jeans

© TURNER HOME ENTERTAINMENT 2074

TOWERING INFERNO

D: Irwin Allen, John Guillermin — 165 m

PG | SUS ACT | 1974 | COLOR

8 First there was a crippled airliner (AIRPORT), then a capsized ship (THE POSEIDON ADVENTURE) and here there is a 150-story high-rise on fire. This was one of the biggest of the disaster flicks that were popular during the early 1970s. During the dedication ceremony of a new San Francisco hotel and office skyscraper that the developer had cut corners on, a fire breaks out, trapping people on the upper floors. Huge cast of blockbuster stars helps to carry this OK drama that is considerably spiced up with spectacular pyrotechnic special effects. 7 nominations, 2 Oscars.

Sex / Nud / Viol / ✓ Lang / ✓ AdSit

A: Steve McQueen, Paul Newman, William Holden, Faye Dunaway, Fred Astaire, Richard Chamberlain

© FOXVIDEO 1071

UNINVITED, THE

D: Lewis Allen — 99 m

NR | SUS HOR | 1944 | B&W

8 A very unusual ghost story! A brother and sister (Hussey and Milland) buy a house on the Cornish coast in England. They soon discover that there are cold spots in the rooms and they witness doors closing all by themselves. Pretty Gail Russell becomes a regular visitor even though her grandfather has forbidden her to go there because her mother was killed in a fall from the cliffs. Is she haunting the house? Milland begins to fall in love with the beautiful girl, while he seeks to discover the answer to the mystery. Things become clearer when he finds that there is not one ghost, but two. Classy. Eerie.

Sex / Nud / Viol / Lang / ✓ AdSit

A: Ray Milland, Cornelia Otis Skinner, Gail Russell, Ruth Hussey, Donald Crisp, Dorothy Stickney

© MCA/UNIVERSAL HOME VIDEO, INC. 80400

WARGAMES

D: John Badham — 114 m

PG | SUS | 1983 | COLOR

8 This is an entertaining film for the whole family. A bored teenage computer whiz (Broderick) and his girlfriend (Sheedy) think they've gained access to a new, unreleased computer game called "Global Thermonuclear Warfare" from a game manufacturer. What they really did was to break into the Pentagon's computers. Their game is no game. The entire nation has been placed on nuclear alert and the world on the brink of the ultimate war. Broderick is sought by the government people, who are led by Dabney Coleman, who must stop what he has started. Very entertaining and convincingly done. Not just for kids.

Sex / Nud / ✓ Viol / ✓ Lang / AdSit

A: Matthew Broderick, Dabney Coleman, Ally Sheedy, Barry Corbin, John Wood, Juanin Clay

Distributed By MGM/UA Home Video M200293

WINDOW, THE

D: Ted Tetzlaff — 73 m

NR | SUS | 1949 | B&W

7 Gripping thriller about a little boy who is constantly making up stories. So, when he witnesses the neighbors through his window commit an actual murder, his parents won't believe him. In fact, they make him go to the neighbors to apologize for his lie. Now that the neighbors know that he knows, they are coming for him next and he is alone. Very well photographed. Suspense builds throughout. Bobby Driscoll won a special Oscar for his performance as the boy. This same idea was resurrected in 1984 in CLOAK AND DAGGER.

Sex / Nud / Viol / Lang / AdSit

A: Bobby Driscoll, Barbara Hale, Arthur Kennedy, Paul Stewart, Ruth Roman

© TURNER HOME ENTERTAINMENT 6223

War

ACE OF ACES

D: J. Walter Ruben — 77 m

NR | WAR DMA ACT | 1933 | B&W | Sex | Nud | Viol ◢ | Lang | AdSit ◢

6 Over the skies of WWI roared a new and romantic weapon, the airplane. Excited by the romance of aerial combat, pretty Nancy Adams (Allan) urges her sculptor fiance (Dix) to become a fighter pilot. While not exactly eager, Dix is both charmed and embarrassed by her into enlisting. Having done that, he becomes infatuated with the excitement and is transformed into a ruthless flying ace. Contains some pretty exciting flying sequences. It was the TOP GUN of its day.

A: Elizabeth Allan, Richard Dix, Ralph Bellamy, Bill Cagney, Joe Sauers

© TURNER HOME ENTERTAINMENT 6141

AIR FORCE

D: Howard Hawks — 119 m

NR | WAR ACT | 1943 | B&W | Sex | Nud | Viol ◢ | Lang | AdSit ◢

7 Exciting WWII action film that was highly acclaimed (received two Oscar nominations) and still stands up well today. Filmed by Howard Hawks in the days immediately following the Japanese sneak attack on Pearl Harbor, this is a blatantly propagandist and even racist film. Regardless, it is a truly thrilling and realistic actioner. It follows the exploits of a B-17 bomber crew which arrived in Pearl Harbor on December 6, and shows how they learn to pull together at Pearl Harbor, Manila and the Coral Sea. Excellent script, solid acting and exciting dogfight sequences.

A: John Garfield, John Ridgely, Gig Young, Arthur Kennedy, Harry Carey, Charles Drake

Distributed By MGM/UA Home Video M202412

BACK TO BATAAN

D: Edward Dmytryk — 95 m

NR | WAR ACT | 1945 | B&W | Sex | Nud | Viol ■ | Lang | AdSit ◢

8 The Philippines are about to fall to the Japanese at the beginning of WWII. Wayne is a colonel recalled from the front line to help defend Bataan, but he is too late. He is assigned to organize a native guerrilla unit to harass the Japanese but must first inspire the Filipino leader (Quinn), who is reluctant. Realistic, very well made and acted, perhaps because many of those in the film had actually been there. Features actual war footage. Great action - but not just a shoot-`em-up. A very good drama - well worth your time.

A: John Wayne, Anthony Quinn, Beulah Bondi, Fely Franquelli, Richard Loo, Philip Ahn

© TURNER HOME ENTERTAINMENT 2081

BATAAN

D: Tay Garnett — 115 m

NR | WAR ACT | 1943 | B&W | Sex | Nud | Viol ◢ | Lang | AdSit ◢

9 Very realistic WWII story of the defense of the Philippine Islands, set in the early days of WWII and released in the darkest days of the War. It became one of the biggest box office hits of the period. Vastly outnumbered American and Filipino troops desperately attempt to stall the overwhelming, steadily advancing Japanese forces by destroying a strategic bridge. Good combat scenes, but this is more a story of the personalities of the men themselves, convincingly played by a very strong cast. One of the best WWII films made.

A: Robert Taylor, George Murphy, Thomas Mitchell, Lloyd Nolan, Lee Bowman, Robert Walker

Distributed By MGM/UA Home Video M600927

BRIDGE AT REMAGEN, THE

D: John Guillermin — 116 m

NR | WAR ACT | 1969 | COLOR | Sex | Nud | Viol ■ | Lang | AdSit ◢

7 High intensity war flick recounting the real-life battle for a strategic WWII bridge. Near the end of WWII, Allied soldiers try to capture the last bridge into Germany intact so that it can be used in the Allied invasion efforts. The Germans desperately want the bridge destroyed for the same reason, but they are holding off to the last moment so that their retreating troops can get home. The war is coming to an end... this is the last hope for the Germans. There are very good action sequences, but fans of this genre should be sure to also see the similar but superior A BRIDGE TOO FAR.

A: George Segal, Ben Gazzara, Robert Vaughn, E.G. Marshall, Bradford Dillman, Peter Van Eyck

Distributed By MGM/UA Home Video M201533

DESERT RATS, THE

D: Robert Wise — 88 m

NR | WAR ACT | 1953 | B&W | Sex | Nud | Viol ◢ | Lang | AdSit ◢

8 Excellent action flick about an English captain (Burton) in charge of an outnumbered Australian regiment that is trying to hold out against long odds in 1941 at the key North African desert outpost of Tobruk. They are under siege by the brilliant German Field Marshall Erwin Rommel (played brilliantly by Mason, who reprieves his role from the THE DESERT FOX). The British army is in full retreat. Burton and his green recruits, through a series of daring lightning raids, are the only obstacle that is keeping Rommel from capturing the Suez Canal. Plenty of action.

A: Richard Burton, James Mason, Robert Newton, Chips Rafferty

© FOXVIDEO 1313

FIGHTING SEABEES, THE

D: Edward Ludwig — 99 m

NR | WAR ACT | 1944 | B&W | Sex | Nud | Viol ◢ | Lang | AdSit

7 A rousing war melodrama which has John Wayne being a short-tempered and determined civilian construction boss. He is determined to help defeat the Japanese by directing the civilian work battalions that are building and repairing the installations close to the front lines in the Pacific. Tired of losing his men to enemy fire, he fights to get them armed and they become the "Seabees." But, he is in constant conflict with his Navy supervisor O'Keefe because he refuses to follow Navy rules. He and O'Keefe are also battling with each other for hand of Hayward. Lots of action. Pretty good.

A: John Wayne, Susan Hayward, Dennis O'Keefe, William Frawley

© REPUBLIC PICTURES HOME VIDEO 1268

FLYING LEATHERNECKS

D: Nicholas Ray — 102 m

NR | WAR ACT | 1951 | COLOR | Sex | Nud | Viol ◢ | Lang | AdSit ◢

6 WWII action flick. John Wayne is a tough and demanding major of a Marine air squadron in the Pacific. Ryan is his second-in-command who is somewhat bitter for having been passed over and who thinks that Wayne is being too tough on the men. But when the action starts, everyone can see that John was right. Lots of real action sequences taken from newsreels were blended in with the film's footage. Things get lightened up whenever Flippen, the supply sergeant who always comes through, is on screen. Pretty good, but relatively undistinguished stuff.

A: John Wayne, Robert Ryan, Don Taylor, William Harrigan, Janis Carter, Jay C. Flippen

© TURNER HOME ENTERTAINMENT 2075

FLYING TIGERS

D: David Miller — 101 m

NR | WAR ACT | 1942 | B&W | Sex | Nud | Viol ◢ | Lang | AdSit

6 Another WWII action movie with a Hollywood-type depiction the real-life Flying Tigers squadron of China. John Wayne plays the leader of a squadron of American mercenary pilots in China fighting the Japanese for the Chinese government. John fights to keep his group of unruly pilots alive, while also fighting for the affections of a pretty nurse. Great actual dogfight footage, though.

A: John Wayne, John Carroll, Anna Lee, Paul Kelly, Gordon Jones, Mae Clarke

© REPUBLIC PICTURES HOME VIDEO 1389

GO FOR BROKE

D: Robert Pirosh — 91 m

NR | WAR ACT | 1951 | B&W | Sex | Nud | Viol ◢ | Lang | AdSit ◢

8 This film was based upon the famous real-life 442nd Regimental Combat Team of World War II. It was the most highly decorated regiment in the war and won a Presidential Citation. It was also an all-Japanese-American regiment that struggled mightily to regain honor for themselves, and their families back home in American concentration camps. This is a fictionalized account, but it contains all the ironies of their segregation and humiliations while they struggle to prove themselves. Van Johnson plays their bigoted commander whose prejudice gives way over time to respect.

A: Van Johnson, Lane Nakano, Henry Nakamura, George Miki, Henry Oyasato, Warner Anderson

Distributed By MGM/UA Home Video M202409

GUADALCANAL DIARY

D: Lewis Seiler — 93 m

NR | WAR ACT | 1943 | B&W | Sex | Nud | Viol ■ | Lang | AdSit ■

9 One of the best of the World War II action movies. It was made at almost the same time as the actual events of the war were really occurring. It is the story about men, from widely different backgrounds, who are drawn together as close as brothers under the pressure of war. Outmanned and undersupplied, the group bands together to hold off an attack on their remote but vital airstrip. There is a big cast of talented actors, which is highlighted by Bendix as a former Brooklyn cab driver. It is a good action flick, but it is also a realistic representation of the camaraderie created by war.

A: Preston Foster, Lloyd Nolan, William Bendix, Richard Conte, Anthony Quinn, Richard Jaeckel

© CBS/FOX VIDEO 1726

HALLS OF MONTEZUMA

D: Lewis Milestone 113 m

NR | WAR ACT | 1950 | COLOR

6 This is a good war/action flick, but is only one of numerous action flicks that came out after WWII capitalizing on the drama of the War and glamorizing the gung-ho character of the Marines. A troop of Marines is sent on a dangerous mission to scout and capture a Japanese rocket base. Widmark is a school teacher who is transformed into a leader of men. Full of slam-bang action typical for the genre, executed by an excellent cast.

Sex / Nud / ◢ Viol / Lang / ◢ AdSit

A: Richard Widmark, Jack Palance, Robert Wagner, Jack Webb, Reginald Gardiner, Karl Malden

© FOXVIDEO 1214

HELL IS FOR HEROES

D: Don Siegel 90 m

NR | WAR DMA ACT | 1962 | COLOR

8 Quite good war drama in which character development is carefully interwoven into and necessary to the action sequences. The action scenes themselves are calculated realism, not empty-headed glory charges. A star-studded cast highlights this realistic war saga about a beleaguered Army squad which has survived Africa, France and Belgium, and is now assigned the job of plugging a hole in the front lines near the end of WWII. Steve McQueen is excellent as a tormented man who now requires battle as a drug to survive living.

Sex / Nud / ◢ Viol / Lang / ◢ AdSit

A: Steve McQueen, Bobby Darin, Fess Parker, Harry Guardino, James Coburn, Bob Newhart

© PARAMOUNT HOME VIDEO 6116

HELL TO ETERNITY

D: Phil Karlson 132 m

NR | WAR DMA ACT | 1960 | B&W

8 Fascinating true story from World War II. Jeffery Hunter plays the real-life figure of Guy Gabaldon who was a Hispanic man raised by Japanese-Americans. Gabaldon could speak Japanese and became a hero of the South Pacific when he chose to fight his war on Saipan by going behind enemy lines each night to convince defeated Japanese soldiers to surrender, eventually winning a Silver Star for bringing in over 2,000 prisoners. Action aplenty, too, with very realistic battle scenes.

Sex / Nud / ◢ Viol / Lang / ◢ AdSit

A: Jeffrey Hunter, Vic Damone, David Janssen, Sessue Hayakawa

© CBS/FOX VIDEO 7351

IMMORTAL SERGEANT, THE

D: John M. Stahl 91 m

NR | WAR DMA ACT | 1943 | B&W

7 This is quite an involving war story set in the hot Libyan desert during WWII. When raw recruits are left without leadership, after their superiors are all killed, one shy corporal (Fonda) must rise to take command of his patrol. If they are to survive, he must draw upon the skills and lessons taught him by his old sergeant (Mitchell). And, he gains the strength to do what he needs to do because of his love for the girl back home. Well told and interesting story, meant to inspire the troops and the nation at a time when it was badly needed.

Sex / Nud / ◢ Viol / Lang / ◢ AdSit

A: Henry Fonda, Maureen O'Hara, Thomas Mitchell, Melville Cooper, Allyn Joslyn, Reginald Gardiner

© FOXVIDEO 1392

MEN OF THE FIGHTING LADY

D: Andrew Marton 82 m

NR | WAR ACT | 1954 | COLOR

7 This film was a big box office success for MGM when it was released, just as the Korean War ended. It is an exploration of the lives of the men on board an aircraft carrier stationed off the Korean coast during the war. The primary focus is upon one pilot, Van Johnson, but it also examines the other pilots, the Captain, ship's surgeon and even the repair officer who has to patch up the shot-up planes. Lots of good air action, much of it taken from actual missions. But particularly involving is Johnson "talking down" another pilot who has been blinded to a safe landing. Good stuff.

Sex / Nud / ◢ Viol / Lang / ◢ AdSit

A: Van Johnson, Walter Pidgeon, Louis Calhern, Dewey Martin, Keenan Wynn, Frank Lovejoy

Distributed By MGM/UA Home Video M202413

MIDWAY

D: Jack Smight 132 m

PG | WAR ACT | 1976 | COLOR

7 Compelling war drama. Only six-months after the Japanese successful attack at Pearl Harbor, American naval and air forces delivered a crushing defeat to the overconfident Japanese Navy in the Battle of Midway, from which they never recovered. This film documents that battle and the events that lead up to it. Fonda shines as Commander Chester W. Nimitz. There is a needless romantic subplot where Heston helps his son deal with a romantic relationship with a Japanese/American. Factually correct, the studio used a mixture of real and created footage in depicting this epic battle.

Sex / Nud / ◢ Viol / ◢ Lang / ◢ AdSit

A: Charlton Heston, Henry Fonda, Glenn Ford, Robert Mitchum, Edward Albert, Hal Holbrook

© MCA/UNIVERSAL HOME VIDEO, INC. 55030

ONE OF OUR AIRCRAFT IS MISSING

D: Michael Powell, Emeric Pressburger 106 m

NR | WAR SUS ACT | 1941 | B&W

7 Highly acclaimed war drama that begins with a World War II British bomber raid on Stuttgart in which one plane is hit. Struggling against their dying plane and desperately attempting to limp home, the crew makes it as far as Holland, where they have to bale out and try to make it back home on land with the help of the Dutch people. Very realistic, exciting and very suspenseful.

Sex / Nud / ◢ Viol / Lang / ◢ AdSit

A: Godfrey Tearle, Eric Portman, Hugh Williams, Peter Ustinov, Pamela Brown, Googie Withers

© REPUBLIC PICTURES HOME VIDEO V3059

OPERATION CROSSBOW

D: Michael Anderson 116 m

NR | WAR ACT | 1965 | COLOR

8 Rousing actioner set in WWII. A trio of British agents (Peppard, Courtenay and Kemp) are sent on a near-impossible mission to destroy a heavily guarded secret underground Nazi munitions installation, where German scientists are developing long range rockets. They impersonate German scientists to gain access to information which they are to send back. High intensity throughout, but it has a particularly sensational ending.

Sex / Nud / ■ Viol / Lang / ◢ AdSit

A: George Peppard, Sophia Loren, Trevor Howard, Tom Courtenay, Anthony Quayle, John Mills

Distributed By MGM/UA Home Video 202641

PORK CHOP HILL

D: Lewis Milestone 98 m

NR | WAR ACT | 1959 | B&W

7 Realistic, believable and a grim portrait of one of the many insanities of war. During the Korean War, a beleaguered platoon of men lead by Peck are ordered to take a strategically useless hill. Despite punishing casualties, they manage to take that mound of earth. Then, without replacements or reinforcements, they are ordered to hold the hill - even in the face of a massive attack by an overwhelming force and just as cease-fire talks begin. Good solid performances. Based upon fact.

Sex / Nud / ◢ Viol / Lang / ◢ AdSit

A: Gregory Peck, Harry Guardino, Rip Torn, George Peppard, Bob Steele, Robert Blake

Distributed By MGM/UA Home Video M301298

PURPLE HEART, THE

D: Lewis Milestone 98 m

NR | WAR DMA | 1944 | B&W

7 Immediately following Pearl Harbor a fleet of B-25s took off from an aircraft carrier headed for Tokyo. Eight airman were shot down over occupied China and captured after the daring 1942 bombing raid by Jimmie Doolittle's men. The captured men were brought back to Japan where they were put on public trial for murder and war crimes. The outcome of their trial was never in doubt. They will be found guilty and executed. But before that, they will be tortured to learn from where the raids were launched. A fascinating tale of courage, based upon actual events. Good acting. See also THIRTY SECONDS OVER TOKYO.

Sex / Nud / Viol / Lang / ◢ AdSit

A: Richard Conte, Tala Birell, Dana Andrews, Farley Granger, Sam Levene, Nestor Paiva

© CBS/FOX VIDEO 1730

RUN SILENT, RUN DEEP

D: Robert Wise 94 m

NR | WAR DMA ACT | 1958 | B&W

8 Gripping WWII war drama. Burt Lancaster was to have become Captain of his own submarine, but instead is named first officer at the last minute when Clark Gable is given command. Gable is the only survivor of a Japanese attack on his old sub. In spite of being hampered by the suspicions and deep distrust of the entire crew and his first officer, and in the face of long odds, Gable is determined to sink a Japanese cruiser. Very tense drama, capturing the feeling of tight quarters and uncertainty. One of the best submarine movies ever.

Sex / Nud / ◢ Viol / Lang / ◢ AdSit

A: Clark Gable, Burt Lancaster, Brad Dexter, Jack Warden, Nick Cravat, Don Rickles

Distributed By MGM/UA Home Video M202133

SAHARA

D: Zoltan Korda 97 m

NR | WAR SUS ACT | 1943 | B&W

9 Gripping WWII classic, one of the best to come out of that period. Bogart is a tank commander retreating across the Sahara Desert of North Africa after the defeat at Tobruk. He, his crew and some British stragglers they rescued, are in and on their tank for a desperate flight across the desert with no water and plenty of Germans all around them. They stumble onto the ruins of a desert village. Now they have water, but the Germans desperately need it, too, and offer to barter for it. Instead, Bogart and his crew valiantly defend their strategic prize. Tough, grim, insightful, exciting.

Sex / Nud / ◢ Viol / Lang / ◢ AdSit

A: Humphrey Bogart, Bruce Bennett, Dan Duryea, Lloyd Bridges, J. Carrol Naish, Rex Ingram

© COLUMBIA TRISTAR HOME VIDEO VH10472

SANDS OF IWO JIMA

D: Allan Dwan — 109 m

NR · WAR ACT · 1949 · B&W

☐ Sex ☐ Nud ☑ Viol ☐ Lang ☑ AdSit

8 Hugely popular WWII action flick for which John Wayne earned an Oscar nomination in his role as tough-as-nails Sergeant Stryker. Stryker is a career Marine and a combat veteran. He knows what his men will be up against on the beaches of the South Pacific and drives them especially hard to prepare them. Most of the men hate him because of that ruthlessness, but when they are exposed to unforgiving, merciless combat on Tarawa and Iwo Jima, they understand. Great battle scenes, enhanced by actual war footage interspliced into the dramatic action. Much copied.

A: John Wayne, Adele Mara, Forrest Tucker, John Agar, Richard Jaeckel, Arthur Franz

© REPUBLIC PICTURES HOME VIDEO 3556

THEY WERE EXPENDABLE

D: John Ford — 135 m

NR · WAR ACT · 1945 · B&W

☐ Sex ☐ Nud ☑ Viol ☐ Lang ☑ AdSit

9 Truly excellent WWII action drama. It was made by director John Ford, who had personal experience in battle. This is the story of the naval war that occurred in the Philippines in the immediate aftermath of the destruction of the American Naval fleet at Pearl Harbor. This war was fought largely by fast, lightweight boats (made of plywood) called PT boats. Robert Montgomery (who was a real-life naval officer) stars in a role based upon the exploits of real-life PT captain, and Congressional Medal of Honor winner, John Bulkeley. John Wayne plays his second-in-command. Detailed and realistic. This was a very personal film for director Ford. Excellent.

A: Robert Montgomery, John Wayne, Donna Reed, Ward Bond, Jack Holt, Leon Ames

Distributed By MGM/UA Home Video M201544

THIRTY SECONDS OVER TOKYO

D: Mervyn LeRoy — 139 m

NR · WAR ACT · 1944 · B&W

☐ Sex ☐ Nud ☑ Viol ☐ Lang ☐ AdSit

8 In 1942, shortly after the Japanese had bombed Pearl Harbor, a squadron of B-25s left the deck of an aircraft carrier, each plane fully loaded with bombs. Their target was Tokyo. The problem was that they could reach the target but could not carry enough fuel to return. The plan was to fly on and land in China after dropping their load, but many didn't make it that far. Based on historical fact. This film is Hollywood's exciting dramatization of that actual event. The film won an Oscar for Special Effects and was given even greater impact by some very good acting. See also THE PURPLE HEART.

A: Spencer Tracy, Van Johnson, Robert Walker, Phyllis Thaxter, Robert Mitchum, Phyllis Thaxter

Distributed By MGM/UA Home Video M600928

TO HELL AND BACK

D: Jesse Hibbs — 106 m

NR · WAR ACT · 1955 · COLOR

☐ Sex ☐ Nud ☑ Viol ☐ Lang ☑ AdSit

7 The true story of America's most decorated soldier of WWII, Audie Murphy - played by himself. Audie Murphy, a poor Texas sharecropper's son, was rejected by both the Marines and the Navy. So he joined the Army and rose through the ranks to become the most decorated soldier of the war (including the Congressional Medal of Honor). This is a reasonably interesting autobiography, but the battle sequences are excellent and all the more exciting because they are true. Murphy became a popular movie star after the war and remained so until he was killed in a plane crash.

A: Audie Murphy, Marshall Thompson, Charles Drake, Gregg Palmer, Susan Kohner, Jack Kelly

© MCA/UNIVERSAL HOME VIDEO, INC. 45013

TORA! TORA! TORA!

D: Richard Fleischer, Toshio Masuda — 144 m

G · WAR ACT · 1970 · COLOR

☐ Sex ☐ Nud ☑ Viol ☐ Lang ☑ AdSit

8 Extravagant and historically accurate recreation of the events leading up to, and the actual bombing of, Pearl Harbor in 1941. Prepared by both Japanese and American production crews, two versions were prepared: one was released in America and was largely ignored by the public, the other was released in Japan becoming a major box office hit. Extraordinary effort was made to be both accurate and realistic. Much of the fact-based drama surrounding the events leading to the attack was thought to have been too slow for most Americans. Too bad. Very impressive action sequences.

A: Martin Balsam, E.G. Marshall, James Whitmore, Jason Robards, Jr., Tatsuya Mihashi, Joseph Cotten

© FOXVIDEO 1017

UP PERISCOPE

D: Gordon Douglas — 111 m

NR · WAR ACT · 1959 · COLOR

☐ Sex ☐ Nud ☑ Viol ☐ Lang ☑ AdSit

6 Good WWII actioner. James Garner is young and a brand new navy lieutenant. He is also a skindiver and a demolitions expert who is being sent to sabotage a Japanese radio transmitter on a South Pacific island. He travels to his location on board a submarine captained by Edmond O'Brien, who is under orders to take Garner in as close to shore as possible. Garner then is to leave the submarine while it is submerged and is to return to it when the job is complete. However, if he doesn't return by a predetermined time, he will be presumed dead. Well done. Still pretty effective today.

A: James Garner, Edmond O'Brien, Andra Martin, Alan Hale, Carleton Carpenter, Frank Gifford

© WARNER HOME VIDEO 12042

WAKE ISLAND

D: John Farrow — 88 m

NR · WAR ACT · 1942 · B&W

☐ Sex ☐ Nud ☑ Viol ☐ Lang ☐ AdSit

8 Solid and realistic WWII actioner based upon the actual nature of the defense of Wake Island in the South Pacific at the very outset of the War. Attacked without warning, at the same time as Pearl Harbor is bombed, and without hope of reinforcement or even resupply, a small band of Marines is attacked by the Japanese time after time - from the sea, air and by land - but yet remain determined to hold onto the strategic little island. This stirring war film garnered four Oscar nominations and helped to inspire the nation's spirit at a time when it was sorely needed.

A: Robert Preston, Brian Donlevy, William Bendix, Macdonald Carey, Albert Dekker, Walter Abel

© MCA/UNIVERSAL HOME VIDEO, INC. 80371

WHERE EAGLES DARE

D: Brian G. Hutton — 158 m

PG · WAR ACT · 1968 · COLOR

☐ Sex ☐ Nud ☑ Viol ☑ Lang ☑ AdSit

8 High intensity action film in which a small group of commandos, lead by Burton and Eastwood, attack a supposedly impregnable German-held castle high in the Bavarian Alps to rescue an American general being held captive there. They must get him out before the Nazis get critical secret information out of him, but their plans to do it are jeopardized by an unknown double-agent in their midst. Now, no one can be trusted. Lots of high-risk stunts, shootouts and thrilling adventure. A real hair-raiser.

A: Richard Burton, Clint Eastwood, Mary Ure, Michael Hordern, Patrick Wymark, Robert Beatty

Distributed By MGM/UA Home Video M700137

WING AND A PRAYER, A

D: Henry Hathaway — 98 m

NR · WAR ACT · 1944 · COLOR

☐ Sex ☐ Nud ☑ Viol ☐ Lang ☑ AdSit

7 Thrilling and realistic action story from WWII's war in the Pacific. This is an Oscar-nominated Screenplay that is set just after the attack on Pearl Harbor and just before the Battle of Midway. The American high command does not want to tip its hand to the Japanese, so it allows both them and its own men to believe that they were unwilling to be engaged. The story follows some freshly recruited and frustrated Navy pilots as they train from the decks of an aircraft carrier, while not knowing that they will get their chance earlier than they expect. Well-researched and exciting entry, with actual combat footage.

A: Don Ameche, Dana Andrews, William Eythe, Richard Jaeckel, Charles Bickford, Richard Crane

© FOXVIDEO 1910

Western

100 RIFLES

D: Tom Gries — 110 m

PG · WST · 1969 · COLOR

☐ Sex ☐ Nud ☑ Viol ☑ Lang ☐ AdSit

6 Reynolds plays a Yaqui Indian who robs a bank to buy guns for his people so they can fight back against a railroad tycoon and a corrupt Mexican official. Deputy Jim Brown pursues into Mexico, where they both are imprisoned. They become allies, escape together and Brown joins the Indians in their struggle. However, their friendship is threatened when Brown falls for Reynolds's woman (Raquel Welch). In spite of the then-controversial black/white love scenes, the film was well received. It is still worth seeing today, largely because of Reynolds's performance.

A: Burt Reynolds, Raquel Welch, Jim Brown, Fernando Lamas

© CBS/FOX VIDEO 1060

3:10 TO YUMA

D: Delmer Daves — 92 m

NR · WST SUS ACT · 1957 · B&W

☐ Sex ☐ Nud ☑ Viol ☐ Lang ☑ AdSit

9 Top drawer Western, one of the best of the 1950s. Glenn Ford is a notorious gunman and powerful leader of a gang who holds up a stagecoach but gets caught when he stays behind to dally with a lonely barmaid. The wealthy owner of the stage company has offered Van Heflin, a poverty-struck farmer, $200 to guard Ford in a hotel room until lawmen arrive on the 3:10 train to take him into custody. Desperate for the money, Van Heflin agrees and becomes caught up in a psychological battle of wills with Ford, whose men begin to gather outside getting ready to break him out. Powerful stuff.

A: Van Heflin, Glenn Ford, Felicia Farr, Richard Jaeckel, Henry Jones, Leora Dana

© COLUMBIA TRISTAR HOME VIDEO 60444

3 GODFATHERS

D: John Ford — 103 m

NR | WST DMA | 1948 | COLOR

8 Sentimental favorite that has been filmed several times with different twists, but this is still the best. Three half-hearted bandits on the run discover a destroyed wagon with a pregnant woman in it, giving birth all alone, in the middle of the desert. Before she dies after giving birth, she extracts a vow from each of them that they will get her baby to safety. Well done Western, a touching story with frequent touches of humor.

Sex / Nud / Viol / Lang / AdSit

A: John Wayne, Pedro Armendariz, Harry Carey, Jr., Mae Marsh, Jane Darwell, Ward Bond

Distributed By MGM/UA Home Video M201000

ABILENE TOWN

D: Edwin L. Marin — 89 m

NR | WST ACT | 1946 | B&W

7 Randolph Scott is the marshall of the new and wild cowtown of Abilene, Kansas that was built to handle the herds of cattle that were being driven north to the railheads from Texas in the 1870s. It is his job to separate the homesteaders around his town from wild cattlemen, fresh from 90 days of dusty trail, flush with cash and full of booze. He also has to battle members of the Younger gang, deal with an alcoholic sheriff (Buchanan) and choose between the pretty dance hall girl (Ann Dvorak) and nice girl Rhonda Fleming. Polished, if traditional, Western.

Sex / Nud / ✓ Viol / Lang / AdSit

A: Randolph Scott, Ann Dvorak, Rhonda Fleming, Edgar Buchanan, Lloyd Bridges

© GOODTIMES 5122

AGAINST A CROOKED SKY

D: Earl Bellamy — 90 m

G | WST CLD | 1975 | COLOR

6 Pretty good family Western. A boy begins a desperate search for his sister who was taken by Indians and is helped by a grizzled old trapper (Richard Boone). It is a pretty basic story line that has been used many times before, however this time it is squarely aimed at younger viewers. Still, even if you are a little older, if you are a Western fan, you will have a good time with it. However, this same premise was much more deeply explored, with much more mature themes, in the classic John Wayne picture THE SEARCHERS.

Sex / Nud / ✓ Viol / Lang / AdSit

A: Richard Boone, Clint Ritchie, Henry Wilcoxon, Stewart Peterson, Geoffrey Land, Jewel Blanch

© BRIDGESTONE PRODUCTION GROUP

ALAMO, THE

D: John Wayne — 162 m

NR | WST ACT | 1960 | COLOR

8 John Wayne's action epic. It was Wayne's personal dream to see that this movie was made. He produced, directed and starred in this epic re-creation of the 1836 siege at San Antonio, Texas mission called the Alamo. The Duke gives a tough performance as Davy Crocket, but Widmark, Boone and Harvey also turn in excellent performances. Movie is a bit long, but when the action starts, Duke fans get their reward. Received seven Oscar nominations, including Best Picture. Also includes a 40-minute documentary about the filming of the movie.

Sex / Nud / ✓ Viol / Lang / AdSit

A: John Wayne, Richard Widmark, Frankie Avalon, Richard Boone, Chill Wills, Laurence Harvey

Distributed By MGM/UA Home Video M302581

ALLEGHENY UPRISING

D: William A. Seiter — 81 m

NR | WST ACT | 1939 | B&W

6 Colonialist John Wayne has had all that he can stand. He rallies a group of like-minded Pennsylvanians and leads them in an uprising against the tyrannical British captain (Sanders) who is governing the pre-Revolutionary War colonies. However, Sanders retaliates by trying to stifle the uprising by being even harder on the settlers. Pretty Claire Trevor conducts her own kind of warfare, trying to win Wayne's heart. She is reteamed here with Wayne after their triumphant pairing in STAGECOACH - also in 1939.

Sex / Nud / ✓ Viol / Lang / AdSit

A: John Wayne, Claire Trevor, George Sanders, Brian Donlevy, Robert Barrat, Chill Wills

© TURNER HOME ENTERTAINMENT 2082

ALONG CAME JONES

D: Stuart Heisler — 93 m

NR | WST COM | 1945 | B&W

8 Very entertaining Western satire produced by Gary Cooper. It is a story of a extremely tame and mild-mannered cowpoke (Gary Cooper) who arrives in a strange town where he is mistaken for a notorious killer (Dan Duryea) because they have the same initials. He is just a gun-shy drifter and at first he enjoys all the attention his killer-status brings. He especially likes the attentions of pretty Loretta Young. However, when both the law and Duryea decide to come after him, it isn't so much fun for him any more... but it is for us. Enjoyable, very watchable, low-key Western spoof in which Cooper makes fun of his on-screen alter ego.

Sex / Nud / Viol / Lang / AdSit

A: Gary Cooper, Loretta Young, Dan Duryea, William Demarest, Frank Sully, Russell Simpson

Distributed By MGM/UA Home Video M203039

ALVAREZ KELLY

D: Edward Dmytryk — 110 m

NR | WST ACT | 1966 | COLOR

7 A good Western. Richard Widmark has greatly complicated William Holden's life. Holden is a cowboy who has just sold a bunch of his cattle to the North during the Civil War. Politics are unimportant to him. Now Widmark, who is a Confederate colonel, captures Holden and wants him to help to steal the 2,500 head back for the starving South. Colorful if somewhat offbeat Western. Lots of two-fisted action and it is based upon an actual incident from the Civil War.

Sex / Nud / ✓ Viol / Lang / AdSit

A: William Holden, Richard Widmark, Janice Rule, Victoria Shaw, Patrick O'Neal

© GOODTIMES 4210

ANGEL AND THE BADMAN

D: James Edward Grant — 100 m

NR | WST | 1947 | B&W

8 John Wayne plays Quirt Evans, a gunman and an ex-deputy of Wyatt Earp. He has been shot during a confrontation with the Stevens gang and was nursed back to health by a Quaker girl, Gail Russell. He fell in love with the pretty girl who saved his life, but he has a problem trying to live up to her peaceful expectations for him. She is begging him not to seek revenge and to leave his old life behind. The trouble with that is that no one has told that to the Stevens gang. It's predictable, but it's also thoughtful and intelligent, too and superior to many of Wayne's later pure action pictures.

Sex / Nud / ✓ Viol / Lang / AdSit

A: John Wayne, Gail Russell, Harry Carey, Irene Rich, Bruce Cabot, Lee Dixon

© UNITED AMERICAN VIDEO CORP. 0065

ANNIE OAKLEY

D: George Stevens — 90 m

NR | WST | 1935 | B&W

7 Fun and reasonably accurate telling of the true story of the awkward uncultured Ozark girl who rose to international fame and prominence as the famous sharpshooter for Buffalo Bill's Wild West Show. Featured is her on-again off-again romance with the show's other sharpshooter Toby Walker, but it also has some funny moments in which Sitting Bull trys to learn to live in the "modern" world. Annie Oakley was also the inspiration for one of Broadway's biggest musical hits: Annie Get Your Gun.

Sex / Nud / Viol / Lang / AdSit

A: Barbara Stanwyck, Preston Foster, Melvyn Douglas, Moroni Olsen, Andy Clyde, Chief Thundercloud

© TURNER HOME ENTERTAINMENT 2089

BAD COMPANY

D: Robert Benton — 94 m

PG | WST COM | 1972 | COLOR

7 Interesting and quite different kind of buddy-Western. It is part realistic adventure, part comedy. Two draft-dodgers each decide to head west rather than get caught up in the Civil War. Along the way, they meet some other young draft-dodgers and they form a small-time gang so they can rob and cheat to pay for their way west. However, when the group arrives in the West, it falls apart as they all turn on each other. An entertaining and clever combination of a fun buddy movie, raunchy humor and action. Brown and Bridges somehow manage to make their otherwise grungy characters appealing in spite of their unsavory natures.

Sex / Nud / ✓ Viol / ✓ Lang / ✓ AdSit

A: Jeff Bridges, Barry Brown, Jim Davis, David Huddleston, John Savage, Jerry Houser

© PARAMOUNT HOME VIDEO 8476

BADLANDERS, THE

D: Delmer Daves — 84 m

NR | WST ACT | 1958 | COLOR

7 Good Western action. It is the turn-of-the-century in Arizona. Alan Ladd and Ernest Borgnine have just been released from prison but they are eager to get even with the guy who sent them there in the first place and stole their gold mine in the process. To do it, they enlist a dynamite expert (Persoff) in their plot to steal $200,000 of their own gold back, right from under his nose. This is widely recognized as being a Western version of the gangster classic THE ASPHALT JUNGLE.

Sex / Nud / ✓ Viol / Lang / AdSit

A: Alan Ladd, Ernest Borgnine, Katy Jurado, Claire Kelly

Distributed By MGM/UA Home Video M202710

BADMAN'S TERRITORY

D: Tim Whelan — 98 m

WST ACT | 1946 | B&W

7 Randolph Scott is a Texas sheriff chasing outlaws who flee into a strip of land bordering the Oklahoma territory. It is a no-man's land, called the Quinto strip, where the law has no meaning and it has become a major outlaw stronghold. Into it rides sheriff Scott in pursuit of the James boys and the Dalton gang. But before he can do what he came to do, he gets framed for murder by a corrupt US Marshall.

Sex / Nud / ✓ Viol / Lang / AdSit

A: Randolph Scott, Ann Richards, George "Gabby" Hayes, Ray Collins, Chief Thundercloud

© TURNER HOME ENTERTAINMENT 2052

BALLAD OF GREGORIO CORTEZ, THE

D: Robert M. Young — 105 m

PG | WST DMA | 1983 | COLOR

7 This is the true story, set in 1901 Texas, of a Mexican cowhand who was falsely accused of horse theft after a series of errors which stemmed from an otherwise innocent misunderstood word in Spanish. The incident explodes out of control and he kills the local sheriff who came to arrest him. For the next 11 days, he is pursued by 600 rangers for over 450 miles in one of Texas's biggest manhunts. A very different sort of Western that realistically captures the era and recreates the bordertowns. Olmos does an excellent job with the character of a man who is a fugitive for no good reason.

☐ Sex ☐ Nud ☑ Viol ☑ Lang ☐ AdSit

A: Edward James Olmos, James Gammon, Tom Bower, Bruce McGill, Alan Vint, Timothy Scott

© NEW LINE HOME VIDEO 2062

BARBAROSA

D: Fred Schepisi — 90 m

PG | WST ACT | 1981 | COLOR

8 Action packed and critically acclaimed Western. Willie Nelson puts in a fine performance as Barbarosa - a legendary, free-spirited outlaw who is joined by a ragged farmer/protege (Busey), on the run from an accidental killing. Barbarosa is running both from bounty hunters and his wife's family, who keeps sending their sons out to find and kill him. Together the two survive, while Busey gains a new trade and a growing respect for the strange loner Nelson. Majestic scenery, good period detail, realistic action and a sometimes funny script give it plenty of flavor. Solid Western.

☐ Sex ☐ Nud ☑ Viol ☐ Lang ☑ AdSit

A: Willie Nelson, Gary Busey, Isela Vega, Gilbert Roland, Danny De La Paz, George Voskovec

© J2 COMMUNICATIONS 0035

BARBARY COAST

D: Howard Hawks — 90 m

NR | WST | 1935 | B&W

6 This is a big-budget adventure, that is set in 1849 San Francisco, and in it, Hollywood bends the script to the best advantage of its big-name cast's particular talents. Beautiful Miriam Hopkins is caught up in a web of corruption and is pursued both by a ruthless gangster (Robinson) and a naive but honest prospector (McCrea) in a love triangle.

☐ Sex ☐ Nud ☐ Viol ☐ Lang ☐ AdSit

A: Miriam Hopkins, Edward G. Robinson, Joel McCrea, Walter Brennan, Brian Donlevy, Harry Carey

© HBO VIDEO 90759

BEND OF THE RIVER

D: Anthony Mann — 91 m

NR | WST ACT | 1952 | COLOR

8 This is a compelling Western of the 1880s Oregon trail and of a man trying to cleanse his soul. Stewart is a former Missouri border raider turned wagonmaster who is leading a wagon train through Oregon's wilderness. He is determined to get them through, despite being beset by all manner of problems, including Indian raids, having his supplies hijacked to be sold to gold miners and being betrayed by a former partner. It is a superior Western with excellent action sequences and top notch performances. Satisfied viewers may also want to see MAN OF THE WEST.

☐ Sex ☐ Nud ☑ Viol ☐ Lang ☑ AdSit

A: James Stewart, Arthur Kennedy, Rock Hudson, Julie Adams, Lori Nelson, Harry Morgan

© MCA/UNIVERSAL HOME VIDEO, INC. 80323

BIG CAT, THE

D: Phil Karlson — 75 m

NR | WST | 1949 | COLOR

6 An exciting family outdoor adventure story. High-country ranchers are feuding, but a huge marauding mountain lion has gotten in their way. The cat is killing off both their stock and has become their common enemy. It is one that they must unite to defeat, but it is a city boy that helps them to track down the killer cat. Enjoyable action/adventure story for everybody.

☐ Sex ☐ Nud ☐ Viol ☐ Lang ☐ AdSit

A: Preston Foster, Lon McCallister, Forrest Tucker

© UNITED AMERICAN VIDEO CORP. 1001

BIG COUNTRY, THE

D: William Wyler — 166 m

NR | WST ACT | 1958 | COLOR

9 Big Western. Peck is a former sea captain who has abandoned the sea. He met Baker when she was in school, they're engaged and he has now come west to her father's (Bickford) ranch. Upon his arrival, he finds that he has stumbled into the middle of a vicious long-standing feud between Bickford and his neighbor Burl Ives (won Oscar) over water rights. However, the water is on land now owned by Jean Simmons who was willed it when her father died. Peck doesn't want to fight and is accused of being a coward, but he's going to have to. This is a big budget Western and is quite good too. Theme song is a classic.

☐ Sex ☐ Nud ☑ Viol ☐ Lang ☑ AdSit

A: Gregory Peck, Jean Simmons, Charlton Heston, Carroll Baker, Burl Ives, Charles Bickford

Distributed By MGM/UA Home Video M900917

BIG HAND FOR THE LITTLE LADY, A

D: Fielder Cook — 95 m

WST COM SUS | 1966 | COLOR

8 Great little comedy with lots of twists. It's a clever story about a farmer (Fonda) and his wife (Woodward) who arrive in town just in time for the annual big stakes poker game. He's a former gambler and has sworn off but, he has to get into that game. Against his wife's wishes, he does and then gets dealt the hand of his life. He bets until he runs out of cash, so he bets the farm (much to the wife's distress) and then has a heart attack. She now has everything in the world she owns at stake and bet on the unfinished game, so the little lady steps up to the table and says, "How do you play this game?"

☐ Sex ☐ Nud ☐ Viol ☐ Lang ☐ AdSit

A: Henry Fonda, Joanne Woodward, Jason Robards, Jr., Charles Bickford, Burgess Meredith, Paul Ford

© WARNER HOME VIDEO 11469

BIG JAKE

D: George Sherman — 110 m

G | WST ACT | 1971 | COLOR

6 It's 1909 and someone has kidnapped John Wayne's grandson (his real-life son John Ethan). They shouldn't have done that. His estranged wife of 18 years (Maureen O'Hara) has asked him to take one million dollars in ransom money to bad guy Richard Boone. Instead, Jake tries a double-cross that just about backfires. This movie also tried for some laughs... but shouldn't have. It works best as a shoot-`em-up Western for John Wayne fans. It's good at that.

☐ Sex ☐ Nud ☑ Viol ☐ Lang ☐ AdSit

A: John Wayne, Richard Boone, Maureen O'Hara, Patrick Wayne, Chris Mitchum, Bobby Vinton

© FOXVIDEO 7149

BIG SKY, THE

D: Howard Hawks — 121 m

NR | WST ACT | 1952 | B&W

6 This is a sprawling adventure story of an 1830 keelboat expedition up the uncharted Missouri River into Blackfoot country to establish trade with the Indians. Douglas and Martin are unruly fur trappers who have been involved in one scrape after another. Hunnicutt is a grizzled frontiersman heading up the expedition. He signs them both on when the three break out of jail together. As the expedition poles its craft upstream against the current, led by a beautiful Indian captive, it is attacked by Crow Indians and set upon by thieves. An action-packed old-school Western. Hunnicut received an Oscar nomination.

☐ Sex ☐ Nud ☑ Viol ☐ Lang ☐ AdSit

A: Kirk Douglas, Dewey Martin, Elizabeth Threatt, Arthur Hunnicutt, Buddy Bear, Steven Geray

© TURNER HOME ENTERTAINMENT 2050

BIG TRAIL, THE

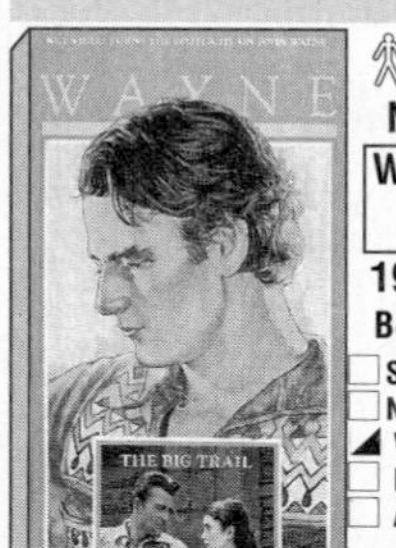

D: Raoul Walsh — 110 m

NR | WST | 1930 | B&W

6 This epic Western may seem pretty creaky now but still is worth watching, especially for the Duke's fans. This was John Wayne's first starring role and in it he is the scout for a wagon train heading to Oregon. He is determined to get his pioneers to their destination in spite of weather, Indian raids and bad guy Tyrone Power Sr. It is his last role. An interesting comment: This movie was made at a time when many of the people who actually lived the pioneer experience were still alive, a fact that could not help but influence it. Much of the character of what you see is how it very likely was.

☐ Sex ☐ Nud ☑ Viol ☐ Lang ☐ AdSit

A: John Wayne, Marguerite Churchill, Tyrone Power, Sr., Ian Keith, Ward Bond

© FOXVIDEO 1362

BITE THE BULLET

D: Richard Brooks — 131 m

PG | WST ACT | 1975 | COLOR

8 Excellent but unconventional Western that is a large-scale epic about a 700-mile endurance horserace (which were actually quite common in the West at the turn of the 20th century). This is a sleeper of a movie that was hardly noticed upon its release, but undeservedly so. The story revolves around the different types of people who compete in the rough-and-tumble race and the gradual respect that all the finalists gain for each other. There are many top stars in it - Hackman and Coburn in particular are excellent. Beautiful photography.

☐ Sex ☐ Nud ☑ Viol ☑ Lang ☐ AdSit

A: Gene Hackman, James Coburn, Candice Bergen, Ben Johnson, Jan-Michael Vincent, Dabney Coleman

© COLUMBIA TRISTAR HOME VIDEO VH10022

BLOOD ON THE MOON

D: Robert Wise — 88 m

NR | WST | 1948 | B&W

7 A straight-forward, old style Western, taken from a novel by Luke Short. Robert Mitchum is a cowpoke and drifter who is hired to be a gunman by Robert Preston, his former partner. Preston plans to cheat a wealthy landholder out of his cattle by pretending to help homesteaders. However, Mitchum falls for the rancher's beautiful daughter and, as he witnesses more of his former partner's ruthlessness, he becomes convinced that he is on the wrong side. The stage is now set for a rousing two-fisted climax, as Mitchum vows to make right the wrong that he has done by taking on Preston himself.

☐ Sex ☐ Nud ☐ Viol ☑ Lang ☐ AdSit

A: Robert Mitchum, Barbara Bel Geddes, Robert Preston, Walter Brennan, Phyllis Thaxter, Frank Faylen

© TURNER HOME ENTERTAINMENT 6124

BREAKHEART PASS

D: Tom Gries — 96 m

PG | WST ACT MYS | 1976 | COLOR

7 Slam-bang action-filled Western starring Charles Bronson. He is an accused thief and an arsonist aboard a special government train that is heading through the snow-draped Rocky Mountains on a rescue mission to an Army outpost and is accompanied by a US Marshall. Also aboard are a governor, his secret mistress and a government engineer. When one of the passengers is murdered, it becomes apparent that all of them have something to hide and are not what they appear to be. Plenty of stunts and fights complement some interesting plot twists in a search for the answer to a

Sex ☐ Nud ☐ Viol ◢ Lang ◢ AdSit ◢

A: Charles Bronson, Ben Johnson, Ed Lauter, Richard Crenna, Charles Durning, Jill Ireland

Distributed By MGM/UA Home Video M201559

BROKEN ARROW

D: Delmer Daves — 93 m

NR | WST | 1950 | COLOR

7 One of the earliest movies made that treated the Indians and their culture with some degree of respect. Jimmy Stewart plays a cowboy who befriends Apache chief Cochise (Jeff Chandler). And, he also marries a pretty Indian maiden (Debra Pagent). However, it is the middle of the Apache wars and Stewart also signs on as a cavalry scout, seeking to find a way for the whites and the Indians to coexist in 1870s Arizona. This is a movie that gives us romance, plenty of scenery and good action, too.

Sex ☐ Nud ☐ Viol ◢ Lang ☐ AdSit ☐

A: James Stewart, Jeff Chandler, Debra Paget, Will Geer, Arthur Hunnicutt, Jay Silverheels

© FOXVIDEO 1310

BROKEN LANCE

D: Edward Dmytryk — 96 m

NR | WST DMA | 1954 | COLOR

8 This is an intelligent Western - the script won an Oscar. In it, Tracy plays a hard-edged, ruthless cattle baron who has brought up his four sons devoid of emotion. Now, his sons are as ruthless as he is, the family is warring among themselves and his empire is collapsing around him. His one faithful son (Wagner) has been denied his heritage because he is half-Indian. He has also just been released from prison after having confessed to a crime he didn't commit to protect his father. Now, he is battling his brothers, who are all scheming against both him and his father and it is leading to a violent confrontation.

Sex ☐ Nud ☐ Viol ◢ Lang ☐ AdSit ◢

A: Spencer Tracy, Robert Wagner, Jean Peters, Richard Widmark, Katy Jurado, Hugh O'Brian

© FOXVIDEO 1226

BUCK AND THE PREACHER

D: Sidney Poitier — 102 m

PG | WST COM | 1972 | COLOR

6 Pretty good and different sort of Western, but with a relatively thin plot. Buck (Poitier) is a black ex-Union Army Cavalry sergeant who agrees to act as scout for a wagon train of freed slaves heading to Colorado. Belafonte is a black con man and phony preacher who comes along. The preacher and Buck are forced to team up to defeat a group of white bounty hunters, led by the chief bad guy, Cameron Mitchell, who wants to kidnap them all and take them to Louisiana. Clever and light-hearted in spots. Warm with good characterizations.

Sex ☐ Nud ☐ Viol ☐ Lang ◢ AdSit ☐

A: Sidney Poitier, Harry Belafonte, Cameron Mitchell, Ruby Dee

© COLUMBIA TRISTAR HOME VIDEO 60148

BUGLES IN THE AFTERNOON

D: Roy Rowland — 85 m

NR | WST | 1952 | COLOR

6 This is a fast-moving story about an Army officer who has been branded as a coward and then court-martialed. Humiliated, he heads to the remote west to re-enlist with the 7th Calvary as a private for service against the Sioux in the Dakota territories. But, he discovers that his arch-nemesis is also there and is now his commanding officer. The guy does everything he can to make Milland miserable and to place his life in danger. At the Battle of the Little Big Horn everyone becomes separated and on their own, and it also becomes their private battleground.

Sex ☐ Nud ☐ Viol ◢ Lang ☐ AdSit ☐

A: Ray Milland, Helena Carter, Forrest Tucker, George Reeves, Gertrude Michael

© REPUBLIC PICTURES HOME VIDEO 0450

BUTCH AND SUNDANCE: THE EARLY DAYS

D: Richard Lester — 111 m

PG | WST COM | 1979 | COLOR

7 This prequel to the Redford/Newman pairing from the original blockbuster, imagines the same characters as they were when they were still just learning their trade. This easy-to-take follow up traces their adventures from the time of their first meeting, just after Butch is released from prison, and takes them through their early, not-too-good holdup attempts. The leads in this picture (Katt and Beringer), like Newman and Redford, are likable. The film is interesting in its own right, but is far overshadowed by its more illustrious predecessor.

Sex ☐ Nud ☐ Viol ◢ Lang ◢ AdSit ◢

A: William Katt, Tom Berenger, Jeff Corey, John Corey, John Schuck, Jill Eikenberry

© FOXVIDEO 1117

BUTCH CASSIDY AND THE SUNDANCE KID

D: George Roy Hill — 110 m

PG | WST COM | 1969 | COLOR

10 This picture was a spectacular box office hit and deservedly so. It also won 4 Oscars. Newman and Redford are extremely likable as two fun-loving bank and train robbers who are relentlessly pursued by an unshakable Sheriff's posse... "Who is that guy anyway?" So they escape to Bolivia with Sundance's girlfriend (Ross) but they can't even rob the banks there properly because they can't speak the language. Great dialogue and chemistry between the players makes this an utter joy to watch. Extremely entertaining. Do not miss this one.

Sex ☐ Nud ☐ Viol ◢ Lang ☐ AdSit ◢

A: Paul Newman, Robert Redford, Katharine Ross, Strother Martin, Cloris Leachman, Henry James

© FOXVIDEO 1061

CAHILL: U.S. MARSHAL

D: Andrew V. McLaglen — 103 m

PG | WST | 1973 | COLOR

6 John Wayne is a tough Marshall who spends so much time out chasing bad guys that he neglects his young sons at home. Left on their own too much, they decide to start robbing banks and join a gang of bad guys led by George Kennedy. However, when they find out what they've gotten into, they change their minds. But, now they can't get out because Kennedy is holding one son hostage to force the other to help carry out a bank robbery. John has to come to his boys's rescue and redeems his past neglects. Pretty violent in places. OK but ultimately a only slightly above standard B-grade Western.

Sex ☐ Nud ☐ Viol ◢ Lang ☐ AdSit ☐

A: John Wayne, Gary Grimes, George Kennedy, Neville Brand

© WARNER HOME VIDEO 11281

CHEYENNE AUTUMN

D: John Ford — 155 m

NR | WST DMA | 1964 | COLOR

8 Director John Ford came to be virtually synonymous with cowboy heros and the Western movie. This film was his last movie and here he strayed away from his typical glorification of the white man's West. This is the story of a group of starving and desperate Cheyenne Indians who leave their barren reservation in Oklahoma to struggle back home to Wyoming. It is a pitiful tale of privation and hardship. They must travel across 1500 miles of bleak winter landscape, all the while pursued by the US Calvary, who will only take them back where they started. Worthy viewing.

Sex ☐ Nud ☐ Viol ☐ Lang ☐ AdSit ◢

A: Richard Widmark, Carroll Baker, Karl Malden, Dolores Del Rio, Sal Mineo, Edward G. Robinson

© WARNER HOME VIDEO 11052

CHISUM

D: Andrew V. McLaglen — 111 m

G | WST ACT | 1970 | COLOR

8 This is a quite good Western. The Duke plays John Chisum, a land baron and a real-life character from the famous 1878 New Mexico Lincoln County War. Chisum is struggling against a wealthy land swindler (Forrest Tucker) who is cheating smaller ranchers and farmers out of their land. Excellent meaty characters add grit to the familiar story line: Corbett as Pat Garrett, Deuel as Billy the Kid, George as a bounty hunter and Ben Johnson as Wayne's foreman. Merle Haggard sings.

Sex ☐ Nud ☐ Viol ◢ Lang ☐ AdSit ☐

A: John Wayne, Forrest Tucker, Christopher George, Ben Johnson, Glenn Corbett, Geoffrey Deuel

© WARNER HOME VIDEO 11089

CONAGHER

D: Reynaldo Villalobos — 117 m

NR | WST ACT | 1991 | COLOR

7 Very good made-for-cable Western, adapted from a novel by Louis L'Amour. Katharine Ross, her new husband and his children settle in the Western wilderness to start a cattle ranch. But, he never returns from a buying trip and they are left to survive alone. Elliot is a drifting cowpoke who meets her. They are attracted, but neither can or does do anything about it. He winters with an old rancher whose cattle are being stolen and, while tracking down the thieves, the two meet again. Very realistic and evocative for those times, but could have been improved with some editing. Slow.

Sex ☐ Nud ☐ Viol ◢ Lang ☐ AdSit ☐

A: Sam Elliott, Katharine Ross, Barry Corbin, Billy Green Bush, Ken Curtis, Paul Koslo

© TURNER HOME ENTERTAINMENT 6081

COWBOYS, THE

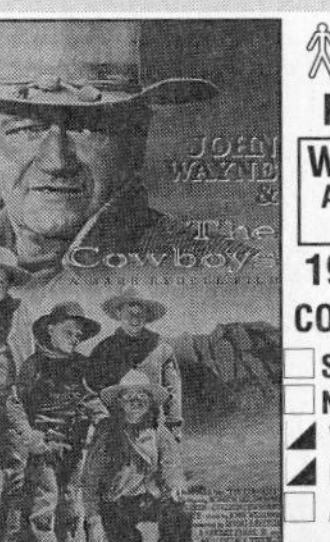

D: Mark Rydell — 128 m

PG | WST ACT | 1972 | COLOR

8 Good Western. John Wayne is Wil Andersen, a rancher whose hired-help desert him to prospect for gold just when he needs them to help to drive his herd 400 miles to market. Having no alternative, he reluctantly hires eleven local schoolboys to drive his cattle. On the trail, the boys face the normal hazards of nature, but also a wagon full of floozies, an outlaw band and their own fears... the boys become men. Bruce Dern is the menacing leader of the outlaw band and John is a gruff but believable father-figure. An unnecessarily cruel revenge mars the ending to otherwise good film.

Sex ☐ Nud ☐ Viol ◢ Lang ◢ AdSit ☐

A: John Wayne, Roscoe Lee Browne, Bruce Dern, Colleen Dewhurst, Slim Pickens, Lonny Chapman

© WARNER HOME VIDEO 11213

DANIEL BOONE

NR | WST ACT | 1936 | B&W

D: David Howard — 77 m

7 Traditional and action-packed version of the exploits of the famous frontiersman. Rugged cowboy star O'Brien is well cast in the title role. As Daniel Boone, he leads a group of pioneers from North Carolina, through the mountain passes into the wilderness of Kentucky. There he is beset by marauding Indians who are aided by bad-guy half-breed John Carradine. Great adventure film, especially for hero-seeking boys.

Sex / Nud / Viol / Lang / AdSit

A: George O'Brien, Heather Angel, John Carradine, Ralph Forbes, Clarence Muse

© GOODTIMES 5134

DARK COMMAND

NR | WST | 1940 | B&W

D: Raoul Walsh — 95 m

7 In the days just prior to the Civil War, William Cantrell (Pidgeon) and Bob Seton (Wayne) compete for the job of Marshall of Kansas. When Cantrell loses, he forms a group of renegades into an outlaw band (Cantrell's Raiders) so large and powerful that they can rape and plunder on both sides of the Mason Dixon Line at will. Cantrell also tricks Seton's girl (Trevor) into marrying him. Seaton must now stop Cantrell and his murderous raids. A not too bad early Wayne Western, with plenty of action, but a little uneven in places.

Sex / Nud / ✔ Viol / Lang / AdSit

A: John Wayne, Claire Trevor, Walter Pidgeon, Roy Rogers, George "Gabby" Hayes, Marjorie Main

© REPUBLIC PICTURES HOME VIDEO 0882

DAVY CROCKETT, KING OF THE WILD FRONTIER

NR | WST CLD ACT | 1955 | COLOR

D: Norman Foster — 93 m

8 Originally filmed as TV episodes, the Davy Crockett series created a huge national phenomenon. Disney's initial three episodes were so popular that they were again released as this feature film. In it, Davy and his sidekick George Russell (Ebsen) fight their way through Indians, assorted bad guys, the US Congress and eventually arrive at the Alamo. Rousing fun for the whole family. Followed by DAVY CROCKETT AND THE RIVER PIRATES.

Sex / Nud / Viol / Lang / AdSit

A: Fess Parker, Buddy Ebsen, Basil Ruysdael, Hans Conried, William Bakewell, Kenneth Tobey

© WALT DISNEY HOME VIDEO 014

DEADLY COMPANIONS, THE

NR | WST ACT | 1961 | COLOR

D: Sam Peckinpah — 90 m

6 An ex-army sergeant (Brian Keith) accidentally kills a dancehall hostess's (O'Hara) son. To try to make amends, he escorts her and the body through deadly Apache territory. Along with them on their unhappy journey come two others, a half-crazed Confederate deserter (Wills) and a gun-happy young punk (Cochran). Three men and a beautiful woman become uneasy companions, alone in a hostile land. O'Hara must fight back both the unwanted advances of Cochran and her awakening feelings for the man she should hate (Keith). Most notable because this was Peckinpah's first picture.

Sex / Nud / ✔ Viol / Lang / ✔ AdSit

A: Maureen O'Hara, Brian Keith, Steve Cochran, Chill Wills

© STARMAKER ENTERTAINMENT INC. 80045

DESTRY RIDES AGAIN

NR | WST COM | 1939 | B&W

D: George Marshall — 94 m

9 Loving spoof of the B-grade Westerns of the '30s. The son of a now-dead super-lawman is called in to rescue a corrupt town. What shows up is a milk-drinking, six-shooterless, mild-mannered sheriff (Jimmy Stewart). In spite of these seeming shortcomings, he manages to defeat the bad guys and to fend off the advances of sexy saloon singer Marlene Dietrich who wants to "See What the Boys in the Back Room Will Have." In spite of its mild-mannered sheriff theme, there is still plenty of action and plenty of laughs. Often copied, but never equalled. Watch it.

Sex / Nud / Viol / Lang / AdSit

A: James Stewart, Marlene Dietrich, Brian Donlevy, Mischa Auer, Una Merkel, Jack Carson

© MCA/UNIVERSAL HOME VIDEO, INC. 80352

DODGE CITY

NR | WST ACT | 1939 | COLOR

D: Michael Curtiz — 105 m

8 Big-scale Western adventure. Set just after the Civil War, at the time that the railroads were pushing their way west and cattlemen were driving the long horn herds north to meet them. Errol Flynn is a Texas cattleman who dons a star to clean up a wild Dodge City, Kansas. He stops a stampede and a burning runaway train. Those heroic exploits and a huge barroom brawl later formed the cliche-bashing basis for the hilarious Western parody BLAZING SADDLES. In spite of the fun Mel Brooks had spoofing this movie, it is still a lot of fun and a good Western.

Sex / Nud / ✔ Viol / Lang / AdSit

A: Errol Flynn, Olivia de Havilland, Ann Sheridan, Bruce Cabot, Alan Hale, Ward Bond

Distributed By MGM/UA Home Video 201698

DRUMS ALONG THE MOHAWK

NR | WST ACT | 1939 | COLOR

D: John Ford — 103 m

9 Richly detailed film which captures life in the colonial pre-Revolutionary War wilderness of upstate New York. Colbert is a cultured city woman who naively joins her new husband (Fonda) as a settler in the rawness of a virgin new land. She quickly learns that she must learn a whole new way of life, enduring not only the harshness of the new and primitive homestead, but also the uncertainties of watching her husband go off to fight marauding Indians. Full of action, humor, drama and rich in Americana. Well done.

Sex / Nud / ✔ Viol / Lang / ✔ AdSit

A: Claudette Colbert, Henry Fonda, Edna May Oliver, John Carradine, Jessie Ralph, Ward Bond

© FOXVIDEO 1382

DUEL AT DIABLO

NR | WST ACT | 1966 | COLOR

D: Ralph Nelson — 130 m

8 Garner is an embittered Army scout who is seeking revenge for his wife's murder while he is also guiding an Army ammunition train through hostile Indian territory. Also accompanying the train are Poitier, as an ex-sergeant who was forced to go along to break some horses that he wants to sell to the Army; and, an extremely bitter merchant (Weaver) and his wife (Anderson), who he despises because she was just recaptured from having lived with the Apaches and now has a half-breed son. This is an involving, solid, old-fashioned Western of the old school, with lots of action.

Sex / Nud / ✔ Viol / Lang / ✔ AdSit

A: James Garner, Sidney Poitier, Bibi Andersson, Dennis Weaver, Bill Travers, William Redfield

Distributed By MGM/UA Home Video M202957

EL DIABLO

PG-13 | WST COM | 1990 | COLOR

D: Peter Markle — 108 m

7 Tongue-in-cheek made-for-cable Western. Billy, a small town Texas schoolteacher loves to read novels of gunfighters and day-dreams of being one. However, when a legendary outlaw named El Diablo actually rides into town, robs a bank and kidnaps one of his students, his daydreams come face to face with reality. While he sets off in pursuit, he is hopelessly outmatched in his quest, until he meets gunman Thomas Van Leek (Louis Gossett, Jr.). He and his cohorts make a new man out of Billy, even as they continue to chase down El Diablo. Full of gags and fun.

Sex / Nud / ✔ Viol / Lang / AdSit

A: Anthony Edwards, Louis Gossett, Jr., John Glover, M.C. Gainey, Miguel Sandoval, Sarah Trigger

© HBO VIDEO 90435

EL DORADO

NR | WST ACT COM | 1967 | COLOR

D: Howard Hawks — 126 m

9 Western fans line up. This is a big raucous John Wayne Western. Hawks revamped his big 1959 hit RIO BRAVO and this time has John Wayne being an aging gunfighter who helps his drunken friend, the sheriff (Mitchum), stop a range war. Great characters: Caan as a likable but odd-ball character who can't shoot; Arthur Hunnicut as a gnarled old Indian fighter and deputy; and Christopher George as a gunfighter on the other side but who has a sense of honor. Plenty of action and lots of humor, too. It was so successful it this time that it was redone one more time in 1970 as RIO LOBO.

Sex / Nud / ✔ Viol / Lang / AdSit

A: John Wayne, Robert Mitchum, James Caan, Arthur Hunnicutt, Edward Asner, Michelle Carey

© PARAMOUNT HOME VIDEO 6625

FAR COUNTRY, THE

NR | WST ACT | 1955 | COLOR

D: Anthony Mann — 97 m

8 First-rate. Jimmy Stewart and Walter Brennan drive a cattle herd north from Wyoming to the gold rush territory of Alaska in 1896. Arriving in Dawson and expecting to make a fortune, they are instead cheated out of their herd by crooked sheriff and self-appointed judge, John McIntire. They steal their herd back and head off to Skagway with McIntire in pursuit. He will stop at nothing to get the herd, but peaceful cowpoke Stewart refuses to seek revenge until two of his close friends are murdered. A fine Western with great characters, excellent performances and set against colorful backdrops.

Sex / Nud / ✔ Viol / Lang / AdSit

A: James Stewart, Ruth Roman, Walter Brennan, Corinne Calvet, John McIntire, Harry Morgan

© MCA/UNIVERSAL HOME VIDEO, INC.

FIGHTING KENTUCKIAN, THE

NR | WST | 1949 | B&W

D: George Waggner — 100 m

6 Entertaining two-fisted period adventure. On his way home from the Battle of New Orleans, frontiersman John Wayne meets and falls in love with the daughter of an evil French land baron. John and his buddies set about saving the farmland of the French homesteaders that the evil Frenchman and his cutthroats are determined to steal. It would have been better less attention to the romance.

Sex / Nud / ✔ Viol / Lang / AdSit

A: John Wayne, Vera Hruba Ralston, Philip Dorn, Oliver Hardy, Marie Windsor, John Howard

© REPUBLIC PICTURES HOME VIDEO 1306

FLAMING STAR

D: Don Siegel — 92 m

NR | WST | 1960 | COLOR

7 Even though there are two songs within the first ten minutes, this is not a Presley teen-musical. This is solid Western, and Presley's performance proved that he could act. It is Texas, just after the Civil War. Presley is the son of rancher John McIntire and his Kiowa wife. Fighting is breaking out between the Indian residents and the white settlers. Presley doesn't want to choose sides and does his best to stop it, but the hatreds are too deep and he gets drawn ever deeper into the fighting. One of Presley's best performances, but also see JAILHOUSE ROCK.

Sex / Nud / ✓ Viol / Lang / ✓ AdSit

A: Elvis Presley, Barbara Eden, Steve Forrest, Dolores Del Rio, John McIntire

© CBS/FOX VIDEO 1173

FORT APACHE

D: John Ford — 127 m

NR | WST ACT | 1948 | B&W

9 Great entertainment. This is the first of director Ford's famous Western cavalry trilogy. Henry Fonda is an ambitious colonel stuck out in the wilderness outpost of Fort Apache. He wants to get out but to do it he needs to make a name for himself fighting a war with the Apaches, so he provokes one. John Wayne is his field-experienced Captain who struggles to protect the troops as Fonda endangers his whole command. Rich in Western characterizations, atmosphere and the glorious scenery of Arizona's Monument Valley. Followed by SHE WORE A YELLOW RIBBON and RIO GRANDE.

Sex / Nud / ✓ Viol / Lang / AdSit

A: John Wayne, Henry Fonda, Shirley Temple, Ward Bond, John Agar, Victor McLaglen

© TURNER HOME ENTERTAINMENT 2068

FRIENDLY PERSUASION

D: William Wyler — 138 m

NR | WST DMA WAR | 1956 | COLOR

9 Wonderfully warm and charming film about the moral quandaries experienced by a Southern Indiana Quaker family during the heartbreak of the Civil War. Gary Cooper and Dorothy McGuire play the Quaker parents of Anthony Perkins (in an Oscar-nominated performance). Their tranquil life is violently challenged when their eldest son goes off to join in the battles to prove that he is no coward. It is a moving tale of love and honor. Cooper is also perfectly cast. Six Oscar nominations, including Best Picture and Best Director, plus a beautiful Dimitri Tiomkin score.

Sex / Nud / ✓ Viol / Lang / ✓ AdSit

A: Gary Cooper, Dorothy McGuire, Marjorie Main, Anthony Perkins, Robert Middleton, Richard Eyer

© CBS/FOX VIDEO 7318

FRISCO KID, THE

D: Robert Aldrich — 119 m

PG | WST COM | 1979 | COLOR

8 Funny Western. Gene Wilder is a Polish rabbi who is on his way from Philadelphia, across the Wild West, to San Francisco and his new congregation. Except, he has no idea of how to get there and, while on his way, he is besieged by one misfortune after another. However, he meets a kindhearted cowpoke and part-time bankrobber (Ford) who takes pity upon this inept fish-out-of-water. Ford agrees to accompany him across country to San Francisco and together they manage to stay in one scrape or another the entire way. Good family fun.

Sex / Nud / ✓ Viol / ✓ Lang / AdSit

A: Gene Wilder, Harrison Ford, Ramon Bieri, Val Bisoglio, Leo Fuchs

© WARNER HOME VIDEO 11095

GREY FOX, THE

D: Phillip Borsos — 92 m

PG | WST DMA | 1983 | COLOR

8 Elegant and warm-hearted story of a real life stagecoach bandit named Bill Miner, who was also nick-named the "Gentleman Bandit." After 33 years in prison for stagecoach robbery, he was released into the twentieth century on June 17, 1901 from San Quentin Prison. Farnsworth is excellent as a man who must adjust to an entirely new world and becomes inspired on how to "adapt" to these modern times after he watches THE GREAT TRAIN ROBBERY. Charming and thoughtful entertainment.

Sex / Nud / ✓ Viol / Lang / ✓ AdSit

A: Richard Farnsworth, Jackie Borroughs, Ken Pogue, Timothy Webber

© MEDIA HOME ENTERTAINMENT, INC. M258

GUNFIGHT AT THE O.K. CORRAL

D: John Sturges — 122 m

NR | WST ACT | 1957 | COLOR

8 Solid big-budget film which is credited with doing a lot to revitalize the Western genre. It also provides a somewhat authentic account of the events leading up to the West's most famous 1881 shoot-out. While the focus of the story is on the personalities of the two volatile key players, Wyatt Earp (Lancaster) and Doc Holliday (Douglas), it never loses sight of the fact that it is an action movie first. A detailed script and excellent acting by Hollywood veterans provide a solid build-up to the big finish at the OK Corral. It was very popular and became a big box office success.

Sex / Nud / ✓ Viol / Lang / ✓ AdSit

A: Burt Lancaster, Kirk Douglas, Rhonda Fleming, Jo Van Fleet, John Ireland, Lee Van Cleef

© PARAMOUNT HOME VIDEO 6218

GUNFIGHTER, THE

D: Henry King — 85 m

NR | WST DMA | 1950 | B&W

8 A top-notch Western which was actually quite different for its time by being one of the first of the '50s to be more "adult" and less heroic in its focus. Peck puts in an excellent performance playing a world-weary gunfighter who who has returned home to a small frontier town. He wants only to be left in peace and to visit his long-estranged wife and son. However, the town's sheriff, who is his old friend, advises him that the town's people want him gone as fast as possible. Still, before he can go, he is confronted by a young tough who insists upon challenging him. Thoughtful and first rate.

Sex / Nud / ✓ Viol / Lang / ✓ AdSit

A: Gregory Peck, Helen Westcott, Millard Mitchell, Jean Parker, Karl Malden, Skip Homeier

© CBS/FOX VIDEO 1213

HANGING TREE, THE

D: Delmer Daves — 108 m

NR | WST DMA | 1959 | COLOR

9 A solid, intelligent Western, that was unjustly overlooked upon its release. It is 1870s Montana in a gold camp called Skull Creek. The town is populated by fortune seekers of all types. There mountain men, saloons, prostitutes, bad people and good people too -- but they are all after gold. Dr. Joseph Frail (Cooper) is a quiet doctor, haunted by his past, who has come to town to hang out his shingle. But his life is thrown into violent turmoil when he comes to the aid of a pretty immigrant girl (Maria Schell) who has been blinded. It is a woman-poor town and the two of them are hounded by a fire-brand minister (George C. Scott) and a hot-headed jealous miner (Karl Malden.)

Sex / Nud / ✓ Viol / Lang / ✓ AdSit

A: Gary Cooper, Maria Schell, Karl Malden, George C. Scott, Ben Piazza, Virginia Gregg

© WARNER HOME VIDEO 11049

HIGH NOON

D: Fred Zinnemann — 85 m

NR | WST DMA ACT | 1952 | B&W

10 A gripping and powerful classic Western drama. Today is Gary Cooper's last day as sheriff. Today, also, he is marrying Grace Kelly and is leaving town to start a new life. But today he learns that a man who he had sent to prison and three others will arrive on the noon train to kill him. He could just leave town and keep looking over his shoulder for the rest of his life. Instead, he chooses to stay and fight. But, he finds that he will have to fight alone. Everyone in town deserts him - even his new wife. The taut suspense is exaggerated because the story unfolds in real time.

Sex / Nud / ✓ Viol / Lang / ✓ AdSit

A: Gary Cooper, Grace Kelly, Lloyd Bridges, Thomas Mitchell, Katy Jurado, Henry Morgan

© REPUBLIC PICTURES HOME VIDEO 5532

HORSE SOLDIERS, THE

D: John Ford — 115 m

NR | WST ACT | 1959 | COLOR

7 Stirring John Ford adventure story - his only set during the Civil War. This "Western" is based upon an actual account of a Union raiding party sent into Rebel territory to cut supply lines into Vicksburg. Interestingly, the film takes no sides in the war. John Wayne plays the determined Union officer leading the raid, but he is accompanied by William Holden as a pacifistic Army doctor. Good action scenes, coupled with a romance between Wayne and a Southern girl (Towers) he must take captive on the way. Better than average as Westerns go, but suffers from preachy dialogue.

Sex / Nud / ✓ Viol / Lang / ✓ AdSit

A: John Wayne, William Holden, Constance Towers, Hoot Gibson, Althea Gibson, Ken Curtis

Distributed By MGM/UA Home Video M201772

HOUR OF THE GUN

D: John Sturges — 100 m

NR | WST ACT | 1967 | COLOR

7 Interesting twist to THE GUNFIGHT AT THE OK CORRAL -- the truth. James Garner plays a Wyatt Earp who is out for revenge and is ruthless in tracking down his brother's killers. There is lots of action, but this also presents a more complete and much darker picture of the situation surrounding the famous gunfight. Interestingly, it also presents a character, in Wyatt Earp, who is much less heroic and more spiteful. Well done. However, because the truth ran counter to the legend, this one had some difficulty at the box office. Still, this is one all Western fans should watch.

Sex / Nud / ✓ Viol / Lang / AdSit

A: James Garner, Jason Robards, Jr., Robert Ryan, Albert Salmi, Charles Aidman, Steve Ihnat

Distributed By MGM/UA Home Video M203118

HOW THE WEST WAS WON

D: John Ford, Henry Hathaway — 165 m

G | WST | 1962 | COLOR

9 This massive Western saga had virtually every major star of its day on the payroll. It is the story of a New England farm family, their trip west beginning in the 1830s and two more generations which later followed them. It is a sprawling film that was majestically filmed for the widescreen Cinerama, and has lost much of its grandeur in the transition to the small screen. Additionally, it is also a solid story that Western fans won't want to miss. It won three Oscars, and was nominated for Best Picture.

Sex / Nud / ✓ Viol / Lang / AdSit

A: Gregory Peck, Henry Fonda, James Stewart, John Wayne, Debbie Reynolds, Walter Brennan

Distributed By MGM/UA Home Video M900356

INDIAN FIGHTER, THE

D: Andre de Toth 88 m

NR | WST ACT | 1955 | COLOR

Sex / Nud / ✓ Viol / Lang / ✓ AdSit

7 This is a rousing, if undistinguished, adventure yarn of the Old West. Kirk Douglas leads a wagon train to Oregon in the 1870's, but to get there they must get through a prairie that is occupied by warring Sioux. Lots of Old West action - fightin', shootin' and a little lovin'.

A: Kirk Douglas, Walter Matthau, Elsa Martinelli, Walter Abel, Lon Chaney, Jr.

Distributed By MGM/UA Home Video M203122

I WILL FIGHT NO MORE FOREVER

D: Richard T. Heffron 105 m

NR | WST DMA | 1975 | COLOR

Sex / Nud / ✓ Viol / Lang / AdSit

8 Dramatic telling of the true story of the Nez Perce Indians and their leader Chief Joseph. In 1877 Chief Joseph attempted to lead his people north to Canada and to freedom in defiance of a government order to move them onto a reservation. The US government sent the Army to stop them and to bring them back. It was the last major calvary campaign for the plains Indians. The Nez Perce tied the Army up in a chase that lasted for five months, even though they had only 100 warriors. Excellent telling of a moving and affecting story.

A: Ned Romero, James Whitmore, Sam Elliott, Linda Redfern

© GOODTIMES 8387

JAMES A. MICHENER'S TEXAS

D: Richard Lang 180 m

NR | WST | 1994 | COLOR

Sex / Nud / ✓ Viol / Lang / AdSit

6 Made-for-TV version of James Michener's book of the same name. As always, Michener combines several fictional and semi-fictional personal stories to create a mosaic that when combined tells a much bigger historical lesson. Duffy plays Stephen Austin, an American-born Mexican bureaucrat in Mexican-owned Texas until he can no longer tolerate their condition. Stacy Keach is Sam Houston and David Keith is Jim Bowie. Pretty Chelsea Field is a pivotal love interest around which many stories revolve. This is pretty much standard TV fare, but its subject matter and wide-ranging historical scope will make it of interest to some.

A: Patrick Duffy, Chelsea Field, Maria Conchita Alonso, Stacey Keach, Randy Travis, Rick Schroder

© REPUBLIC PICTURES HOME VIDEO 9724

JEREMIAH JOHNSON

D: Sydney Pollack 116 m

PG | WST ACT DMA | 1972 | COLOR

Sex / Nud / ✓ Viol / Lang / ✓ AdSit

10 Hugely popular adventure story set in the mid-19th century Rocky Mountains. Jeremiah Johnson is a man who has lost all taste for civilization and so escapes into the unknown wilds of the Rockies. This grandly photographed spectacle follows the loner's early stumbling efforts at survival through to his mastery of the elements. However, his idyllic life is destroyed when his new family is murdered by raiding Indians. He launches himself into a murderous mission of revenge and his success at it leads him to become a feared and legendary figure among the Indians. An extraordinary adventure.

A: Robert Redford, Will Geer, Charles Tyner, Stefan Gierasch, Allyn Ann McLerie

© WARNER HOME VIDEO 11061

JESSE JAMES

D: Darryl F. Zanuck 105 m

PG | WST ACT | 1939 | COLOR

Sex / Nud / ✓ Viol / Lang / AdSit

7 Entertaining but highly fictionalized account of the notorious 19th-century outlaw Jesse James and his brother. It presents an image of a family of peaceful farmers that was forced into a life a crime after their mother is murdered by an unscrupulous railroad agent. Questionable historical aspects aside, Fonda as Frank and Power as Jesse are very engaging characters. This was a big-budget Western that delivered on action and entertainment. Great cast.

A: Tyrone Power, Henry Fonda, Nancy Kelly, Randolph Scott, Brian Donlevy, Jane Darwell

© FOXVIDEO 1485

JOE KIDD

D: John Sturges 88 m

PG | WST ACT | 1972 | COLOR

Sex / Nud / ✓ Viol / ✓ Lang / AdSit

6 Eastwood and Duvall in top form cannot redeem the somewhat muddled quality of this movie. Nevertheless, it does contain some real bang-up action scenes. The time is the turn of the 20th century. The place is New Mexico. Robert Duvall is a land baron who has enticed Eastwood into helping him fight a group of Mexican-Americans who feel their land has been stolen from them and are now waging a guerrilla war against him. However, Eastwood soon discovers that they are right - he is on the wrong side and quickly joins the other side.

A: Clint Eastwood, Robert Duvall, John Saxon, Don Stroud, Stella Garcia, James Wainwright

© MCA/UNIVERSAL HOME VIDEO, INC. 66050

KENTUCKIAN, THE

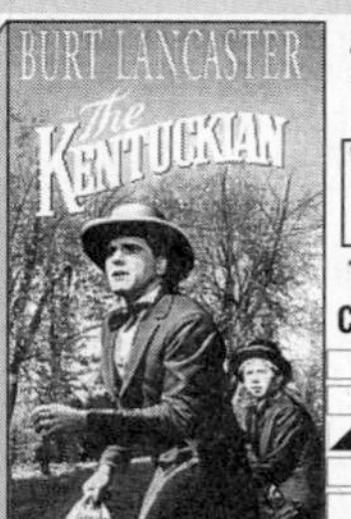

D: Burt Lancaster 104 m

NR | WST | 1955 | COLOR

Sex / Nud / ✓ Viol / Lang / AdSit

6 Fun adventure story that both starred and was directed by Burt Lancaster. It also provided the first screen appearance of Walter Matthau. It is a pretty good early American adventure story in which a Kentucky mountain man is migrating to Texas with his boy to start a new life. Along the way they get waylaid by some feuding mountaineers and they encounter a pretty girl indentured to a mean tavern owner, so they use their river passage money to buy her freedom. Pretty good action and several good doses of comedy, too.

A: Burt Lancaster, Diana Lyon, Dianne Foster, Walter Matthau, John McIntire, Una Merkel

Distributed By MGM/UA Home Video M202645

LAST OF THE MOHICANS, THE

D: George B. Seitz 91 m

NR | WST ACT ROM | 1936 | B&W

Sex / Nud / ✓ Viol / Lang / ✓ AdSit

8 Well made and exciting large-scale movie based upon James Fenimore Cooper's classic novel set during the French and Indian War of the 1750s in upstate New York. White frontiersman Hawkeye (Scott) and his adoptive Mohican father and brother guide an English officer and two white women through French lines to a besieged English fort, all the while being pursued by a Huron war party. Elaborately staged battle sequences. Majestically remade in 1992, with fabulous and meticulous care to detail.

A: Randolph Scott, Binnie Barnes, Heather Angel, Robert Barrat, Phillip Reed, Henry Wilcoxon

© UNITED AMERICAN VIDEO CORP. 5859

LAST TRAIN FROM GUN HILL

D: John Sturges 94 m

NR | WST ACT | 1959 | COLOR

Sex / Nud / ✓ Viol / Lang / ✓ AdSit

7 Exciting Western. Douglas is a sheriff who has tracked down his wife's murderer to a small town that is under the almost total domination of Antony Quinn, the one-time best friend of Douglas. The murderer is discovered to have been Quinn's only son (Holliman). Quinn does not want his son to go back with Douglas, but neither does he want to hurt his old friend. Still, Douglas is determined to get Holliman out of town and back home to stand trial and hang - no matter what the cost. Confrontation is inevitable. Intelligently done. Above average.

A: Kirk Douglas, Anthony Quinn, Carolyn Jones, Earl Holliman, Ziva Rodann, Brad Dexter

© STARMAKER ENTERTAINMENT INC. 1058

LEFT-HANDED GUN, THE

D: Arthur Penn 1958 m

NR | WST DMA ACT | 1958 | B&W

Sex / Nud / ✓ Viol / Lang / ✓ AdSit

7 An interesting underrated psychological Western which makes a point of debunking the hero-myth status of Billy the Kid. Newman's Billy is a moody, stupid and ruthless killer -- a lonely hothead who becomes enraged upon the murder of his boss, a man for whom he felt great fondness. Billy becomes so obsessed with killing the man's murderers that he and two others go on a wild killing spree. A curious feature in the film, one which comments upon on human nature in general, is the inclusion of a pulp writer who at first worships Billy but later derides Billy for not being the hero of his stories and eventually betrays Billy. Quite good.

A: Paul Newman, Lita Milan, John Dehner, Hurd Hatfield, James Congdon, James Best

© WARNER HOME VIDEO 11067

LITTLE BIG MAN

D: Arthur Penn 147 m

PG | WST COM DMA | 1970 | COLOR

Sex / ✓ Nud / ✓ Viol / Lang / ✓ AdSit

10 This is an outstanding and thoroughly enjoyable fable of the Old West. Dustin Hoffman plays Jack Crabb, a 121-year-old man living in a nursing home, who tells his colorful and not all-too-believable life's story to a doubtful young reporter through a series of flashbacks. His incredible stories begin when he was an orphaned pioneer boy adopted and raised by Cheyenne Indians. After he had returned to the white world, he became a terrible businessman and miserable husband, a dead-eyed gunfighter, a drunk and eventually a guide to Custer at his last stand. Wonderful characters, very clever, frequently funny, sometimes poignant, always extremely entertaining. Great fun.

A: Dustin Hoffman, Chief Dan George, Faye Dunaway, Martin Balsam, Jeff Corey, Richard Mulligan

© CBS/FOX VIDEO 7130

LONESOME DOVE

D: Simon Wincer 372 m

NR | WST DMA ACT | 1990 | COLOR

✓ Sex / ✓ Nud / ✓ Viol / ✓ Lang / ✓ AdSit

10 Absolutely brilliant and totally engrossing made-for-TV miniseries adapted from Larry McMurtry's Pulitzer Prize-winning novel. This is an entirely believable, sweeping saga of two Texas Rangers who have out-lived their pioneering era in Texas. So, they strike out for Montana with a herd of cattle, intent upon establishing the first ranch in that virgin land. Striking performances by the entire cast paint a rich tapestry of colorful characters, adventure and romance in a realistically depicted Old West. A wonderful, totally involving, not-to-be-missed adventure.

A: Robert Duvall, Tommy Lee Jones, Robert Urich, Danny Glover, Diane Lane, Ricky Schroder

© CABIN FEVER ENTERTAINMENT CF8371

FAMILY

LOVE ME TENDER

D: Robert D. Webb — 89 m

NR | WST MUS | 1956 | COLOR

7 Elvis's first picture is a Western, and it isn't too bad. He plays the younger of two brothers who are both in love with Debra Paget. When older brother Egan doesn't come back from the Civil War, they think he is dead and Elvis marries Debra. Then Eagan shows up, and with a stolen payroll to boot. It also has four Presley songs including: "Love Me Tender," "Poor Boy," "Old Shep" and "We're Gonna Move (to a Better Home)."

Sex / Nud / Viol / Lang / AdSit

A: Elvis Presley, Richard Egan, Debra Paget, Robert Middleton, William Campbell, Neville Brand

© FOXVIDEO 1172

MAGNIFICENT SEVEN, THE

D: John Sturges — 129 m

NR | WST ACT | 1960 | COLOR

9 Classic shoot-'em-up!!! Recurring raids from a small army of bandits inspire a delegation from a small Mexican town to seek out help from gunfighter Yul Brynner. Brynner rounds up six other misfits like himself, and together they redeem themselves by helping the people to banish the terrorizing banditos and to reestablish pride in the town. A direct American remake of the Japanese classic THE SEVEN SAMAURI, this immensely popular Western spawned three sequels. Except for Brynner, the other six hombres were unknowns at the time, and went on to become sought-after stars.

Sex / Nud / Viol / Lang / AdSit

A: Yul Brynner, Eli Wallach, Steve McQueen, Horst Buchholz, James Coburn, Charles Bronson

Distributed By MGM/UA Home Video M201268

MAJOR DUNDEE

D: Sam Peckinpah — 124 m

NR | WST ACT | 1965 | COLOR

7 Lavishly produced Western in which Charlton Heston plays the title character, who is the warden of a Union Army prison that has been attacked by Apaches. He organizes his regulars and some prisoner volunteers (including a Confederate group whose leader, Richard Harris, is under a sentence of death) to chase the raiding party into Mexico. Complicated characters unduly confuse the plot, but the star power and the action is such that you will enjoy it anyway. The confusion resulted from director Peckinpah being removed. See also THE WILD BUNCH for many similarities.

Sex / Nud / Viol / Lang / AdSit

A: Charlton Heston, Richard Harris, Jim Hutton, James Coburn, Michael Anderson, Jr., Senta Berger

© COLUMBIA TRISTAR HOME VIDEO VH10370

MAN ALONE, A

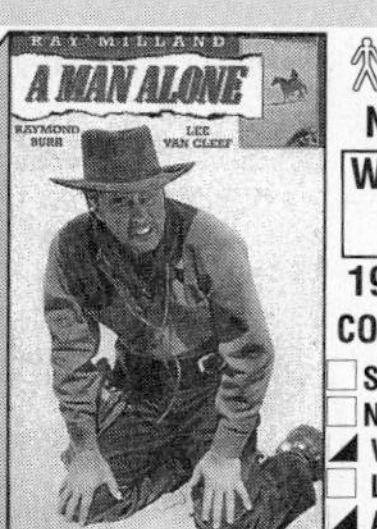

D: Ray Milland — 96 m

NR | WST | 1955 | COLOR

6 A gunslinger (Milland) happens upon the scene of a stage robbery, with six dead bodies. He reports what he finds at the next town, but is instead accused of the murders by the town's most respected citizen, who had actually committed the crime himself. Now a lynch mob is in hot pursuit of the gunslinger. He finds himself hiding from the angry townsfolk in the house of the town's sick and quarantined sheriff. He falls for the sheriff's daughter and wins the sheriff's trust. This is Milland's first directorial attempt, and it is pretty good. The finale is particularly strong.

Sex / Nud / Viol / Lang / AdSit

A: Ray Milland, Raymond Burr, Mary Murphy, Ward Bond, Lee Van Cleef

© REPUBLIC PICTURES HOME VIDEO 2579

MAN CALLED HORSE, A

D: Elliot Silverstein — 115 m

PG | WST DMA ACT | 1970 | COLOR

10 Powerful and thoroughly engrossing story of a haughty British aristocrat (Harris) who is captured by Sioux Indians while hunting in 1830s Dakotas. He is made into a slave by them, humiliated and then just ignored. He rebels, proving his manhood by undergoing a brutal tribal ritual called a sun dance (graphically shown). With his haughty noble exterior gone, his inner strength is unearthed, and he earns his way as a powerful and respected leader of the group. A gripping and realistic depiction of American Indian communal life. See also RETURN OF A MAN CALLED HORSE and DANCES WITH WOLVES.

Sex / Nud / Viol / Lang / AdSit

A: Richard Harris, Judith Anderson, Manu Tupou, Jean Gascon, Corinna Tsopei, Dub Taylor

© FOXVIDEO 7148

MAN FROM COLORADO, THE

D: Henry Levin — 99 m

NR | WST ACT | 1949 | COLOR

7 Intelligent psychological Western. A Civil War veteran (Ford), on the edge of insanity, becomes a federal judge in Colorado. Ford's demons taunt him until he can no longer separate today's reality from that of his bloody past. His old army buddy (Holden) is now the town's marshall and witnesses his friend's psychotic behavior. The townspeople have had enough of Ford's ruthlessness, and Holden must challenge Ford to step down. Ford and Holden both give solid and notable performances.

Sex / Nud / Viol / Lang / AdSit

A: Glenn Ford, William Holden, Ellen Drew, Edgar Buchanan, Jerome Courtland, Ray Collins

© COLUMBIA TRISTAR HOME VIDEO 60962

MAN FROM LARAMIE, THE

D: Anthony Mann — 104 m

NR | WST SUS ACT | 1955 | COLOR

9 Rough and tumble adult Western! When Stewart's brother is shot and killed by Apaches, he becomes obsessed with finding the man who sold the Indians the repeating rifles. In his search, Stewart finds himself on a ranch where the two sons are vying for control upon their father's death. After a run in with one of the brothers (Nicol), Stewart goes to work for a foe of the father. Stewart is caught by Nicol, who forces his men to hold Stewart, while he shoots Stewart in the hand. Then Stewart discovers that it was the brothers who sold guns to the Apaches. Excellent!

Sex / Nud / Viol / Lang / AdSit

A: James Stewart, Arthur Kennedy, Donald Crisp, Cathy O'Donnell, Alex Nicol, Aline MacMahon

© COLUMBIA TRISTAR HOME VIDEO 60855

MAN FROM SNOWY RIVER, THE

D: George Miller — 104 m

G | WST ACT ROM | 1982 | COLOR

8 A rousing cinematic treat for the whole family! This is a beautiful and rousing adventure story that is based on a well-known Australian poem. An independent young man is hired by a wealthy cattle rancher in Australia's wilderness of the 1880s. He falls in love with the cattleman's daughter, but is not accepted by her father (Douglas - in a dual role, also as the father's maverick brother). The film culminates in a wild chase through mountainous terrain to capture a herd of wild horses, led by a magnificent stallion. Thrilling. Stunning scenery. Pretty good sequel in RETURN TO SNOWY RIVER.

Sex / Nud / Viol / Lang / AdSit

A: Kirk Douglas, Tom Burlinson, Terence Donovan, Sigrid Thornton, Jack Thompson, Lorraine Bayly

© FOXVIDEO 1233

MAN FROM THE ALAMO, THE

D: Budd Boetticher — 79 m

NR | WST ACT | 1953 | COLOR

7 The men inside the Alamo are worried about the safety of their families. Glenn Ford is chosen by lot to be the one to sneak out of the Alamo and then to go to warn the other defender's families of the impending danger. This he does but he discovers that most of the families, including his own, have been murdered. And, since he was the only one to escape the slaughter at the Alamo, he is branded a coward and a traitor. Now he dedicates himself to the fighting. Unusual but fascinating Western.

Sex / Nud / Viol / Lang / AdSit

A: Glenn Ford, Julie Adams, Hugh O'Brian, Chill Wills, Victor Jory, Jeanne Cooper

© MCA/UNIVERSAL HOME VIDEO, INC.

MAN OF THE WEST

D: Anthony Mann — 100 m

NR | WST | 1958 | COLOR

8 Hard-edged Western with a big bite. Cooper is a former member of the wicked Tobin family gang led by his uncle (Cobb). But, he has reformed, is a good citizen and he is now a married man with children to boot! Suddenly, Cooper finds himself unwillingly thrown back into the gang's grasp again when the train on which he is riding is held up by them. So that he can prevent the other hostages from being harmed, he appears to agree to rejoin the group. Ultimately, however, there must be a showdown and he is the only one he can save them. Excellent and believable story line, with a particularly violent fist fight.

Sex / Nud / Viol / Lang / AdSit

A: Gary Cooper, Julie London, Lee J. Cobb, Arthur O'Connell, Jack Lord, John Dehner

Distributed By MGM/UA Home Video M202059

MAN WHO SHOT LIBERTY VALANCE, THE

D: John Ford — 123 m

NR | WST ACT | 1962 | B&W

9 Excellent adult Western. Stewart stars as an idealistic Eastern-minded lawyer who wants to end the reign of terror of a ruthless killer, Liberty Valance (Marvin) in the lawless West. But the only tool he has is his lawbooks. Lawbooks aren't going to stop Liberty Valance. Stewart and tough rancher John Wayne compete for the love of pretty Vera Miles. Because Miles loves Stewart, and because Wayne knows that civilization must come and men like Stewart will make it happen, Wayne helps Stewart to defeat Valance, turning him into a hero. John Ford's last black and white Western packs a punch!

Sex / Nud / Viol / Lang / AdSit

A: James Stewart, John Wayne, Lee Marvin, Vera Miles, Edmond O'Brien, Andy Devine

© PARAMOUNT HOME VIDEO 6114

MAN WITHOUT A STAR

D: King Vidor — 89 m

NR | WST | 1955 | COLOR

7 Douglas plays a likable and charming wanderer who does everything he can to avoid trouble. Even so, he can take care of himself and does OK in a pinch. He befriends a ranch hand (Campbell) and both are hired by a beautiful and tough cattle baroness (Jeanne Crain) who often uses her womanly charms to get what she wants. What she wants is to keep the range unfenced and she is willing to be ruthless to do it. Douglas believes the ranges should remain unfenced and is attracted to her charms, but he is not at all excited by her methods. Fun time. Douglas even sings and plays a banjo.

Sex / Nud / Viol / Lang / AdSit

A: Kirk Douglas, Jeanne Crain, Claire Trevor, Richard Boone, Jay C. Flippen, William Campbell

© MCA/UNIVERSAL HOME VIDEO, INC. 80144

MONTE WALSH

D: William A. Fraker 100 m

PG | WST | 1970 | COLOR

Sex / Nud / Viol / Lang / ◢ AdSit

8 Unusual and intelligent Western! Three cowboys have been through a lot together, but times are changing. The ranch is losing money, somebody has to go, so Ryan is laid off. Marvin stays on, hoping to save some money to start fresh. Palance leaves to get married and open a hardware store. The hard-pressed Ryan becomes a thief, robs Palance's store and Palance is killed. The murder of one friend places Marvin in the position of hunting down his other friend. Light-hearted and fun at times, and serious and thought-provoking at others. It is a sympathetic portrait of the death of an era.

A: Lee Marvin, Jack Palance, Jeanne Moreau, Mitchell Ryan, Jim Davis, Allyn Ann McLerie

© CBS/FOX VIDEO 7172

MY DARLING CLEMENTINE

D: John Ford 97 m

NR | WST ACT | 1946 | B&W

Sex / Nud / ◢ Viol / Lang / AdSit

10 One of the best Westerns ever! Wyatt Earp (Fonda) and his brothers arrive just outside Tombstone with a small herd of cattle. Old Man Clanton (Brennan) and his boys offer to buy them but the Earps refuse and go into town, leaving one brother to tend the herd. They arrive in a Tombstone that is wide open and dangerous. After a run-in with a local wildman, Wyatt is offered the job of sheriff, which he declines. He and his brothers go back to find their herd gone and brother dead. Wyatt accepts the badge and begins a path that leads the brothers to the shootout at the OK Corral.

A: Henry Fonda, Linda Darnell, Victor Mature, Walter Brennan, Cathy Downs, Tim Holt

© FOXVIDEO 1398

NAKED SPUR, THE

D: Anthony Mann 93 m

NR | WST ACT | 1952 | COLOR

Sex / Nud / ◢ Viol / Lang / ◢ AdSit

9 Highly acclaimed and sophisticated Western, beautifully shot on location in the Rockies. James Stewart is a hardbitten bounty hunter determined to make enough money to buy back the ranch he lost. Stewart tracks down a killer (Ryan) and his girlfriend (Leigh) in the mountains and is taking them back, but along the way two others join him, cutting themselves in as "partners." Reluctantly Stewart lets them in because he's tired. Immediately, Ryan seeks to cause trouble between the three of them and the girl falls for Stewart, causing even more trouble. Intelligent, exciting and suspenseful.

A: James Stewart, Robert Ryan, Janet Leigh, Ralph Meeker, Millard Mitchell

Distributed By MGM/UA Home Video M600520

NARROW TRAIL, THE

D: Lambert Hillyer 56 m

NR | WST | 1917 | B&W

Sex / Nud / ◢ Viol / Lang / ◢ AdSit

9 Remarkably good silent film classic that pays studied attention to accurate period details, particularly of San Francisco's Barbary Coast. William S. Hart, the famous silent screen cowboy hero, plays an outlaw, Ice Harding. Ice captures and tames a wild pony, but his gang rejects him because they are afraid the distinctive pony will make him too recognizable. Alone, he falls in love and now longs to go straight. But, she has tainted past too, and runs away to San Francisco. However, Ice loves her, tracks her down and then races his pony to win the money that will give them both a chance at a new life.

A: William S. Hart, Sylvia Bremer, Milton Ross, Robert Kortman

© FOOTHILLS VIDEO

NORTH TO ALASKA

D: Henry Hathaway 117 m

NR | WST ACT COM | 1960 | COLOR

Sex / Nud / ◢ Viol / Lang / ◢ AdSit

9 Terrific good time in this light-hearted John Wayne Western. Wayne and Granger play turn-of-the-century Alaskan gold miners who strike it rich. Fabian is Granger's wet-behind-the-ears brother. Wayne goes to Seattle to pick up supplies and Granger's brand new mail-order bride. But when she is not there, Wayne "buys" saucy Capucine from a saloon and takes her back. Soon Granger and Wayne are both vying for her affections, as is young Fabian. Even while they're fighting each other, they're also fending off claim-jumpers lead by Kovacs. Great, fast-moving, tongue-in-cheek, fun.

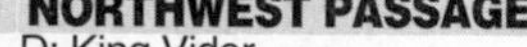

A: John Wayne, Stewart Granger, Ernie Kovacs, Fabian, Capucine, Mickey Shaughnessy

© FOXVIDEO 1212

NORTHWEST PASSAGE

D: King Vidor 127 m

NR | WST ACT | 1940 | COLOR

Sex / Nud / ◢ Viol / Lang / AdSit

9 Stirring adventure story, one of the greatest of all times, based on the real-life adventures of pioneer Robert Rogers (Tracy). Rogers leads a band of 160 settler soldiers into the wilderness of northern New York and the St. Lawrence territory. Their mission is to eliminate the vicious tribe of Abernaki Indians who have made numerous murderous raids on the settlers. It is 1759, the time of French and Indian War. The party is faced with an almost impossible task - before they can even mount their attack, they must first navigate through uncharted and extremely hostile wilderness. Realistically presented.

A: Spencer Tracy, Robert Young, Walter Brennan, Ruth Hussey

Distributed By MGM/UA Home Video M201132

ONE-EYED JACKS

D: Marlon Brando 141 m

NR | WST | 1961 | COLOR

Sex / Nud / ◢ Viol / Lang / ◢ AdSit

8 Interesting psychological Western which was also directed by one-time-only director Brando. Brando plays a bank robber who is deserted by his partners (including Malden), is captured and spends five years in prison. Upon release, he teams up with a couple of bad guys to rob a bank in a small town whose sheriff turns out to be the now-respectable Malden. Brando seeks revenge on Malden but relents when he falls for Malden's step-daughter. However, now Malden is fearful and is pursuing Brando. Good action, but a little muddled.

A: Marlon Brando, Karl Malden, Katy Jurado, Ben Johnson, Pina Pillicer, Slim Pickens

© PARAMOUNT HOME VIDEO 6537

OUTLAW JOSEY WALES, THE

D: Clint Eastwood 136 m

PG | WST ACT | 1976 | COLOR

◢ Sex / ◢ Nud / ■ Viol / ◢ Lang / ◢ AdSit

9 Intriguing Civil War Western, highly acclaimed as one of Eastwood's best efforts both behind and in front of the camera. Josey Wales is a farmer whose family is brutalized and killed by renegade Union soldiers. Wales joins the Rebs seeking revenge and becomes one of their most effective weapons. At war's end, he refuses to surrender to corrupt Union troops he does not trust and so becomes a renegade. He seeks to escape into the West - but he is now being hunted as an outlaw. Rich characters and images. Exciting and believable.

A: Clint Eastwood, Chief Dan George, Sondra Locke, Bill Mc Kinney, John Vernon, Sam Bottoms

© WARNER HOME VIDEO 11125

OX-BOW INCIDENT, THE

D: William Wellman 75 m

NR | WST DMA ACT | 1943 | B&W

Sex / Nud / ◢ Viol / Lang / ◢ AdSit

9 Brilliant indictment of the tyranny and terror created by mob rule. When a Nevada rancher is murdered by rustlers, two drifters (Fonda and Morgan) join the posse chasing down his killers. The posse - now more of a mob - is stirred up and led by an ex-Confederate officer. They stumble upon three hapless farmers sitting around a campfire and allow themselves to be quickly convinced of the guilt of the three, with only the slightest amount of circumstantial evidence. When the mob sets about to hang the three, only the drifters and a very few others object. Best Picture nominee.

A: Henry Fonda, Jane Darwell, Anthony Quinn, Dana Andrews, Harry Morgan, Mary Beth Hughes

© FOXVIDEO 1652

PLAINSMAN, THE

D: Cecil B. DeMille 113 m

NR | WST ACT | 1937 | B&W

Sex / Nud / ◢ Viol / Lang / AdSit

6 Historically preposterous extravaganza that, if taken with a grain of historic salt, is still good action-filled fun. Gary Cooper is Wild Bill Hickock who is out to foil an attempt to sell guns to the Indians lead by Yellow Hand, while also engaging in a running romantic battle of wits with Calamity Jane (Jean Arthur). Also in appearance are Buffalo Bill, Abraham Lincoln and George Armstrong Custer. Don't worry about the details, just enjoy it for what it is, an excuse to create a good time with a rousing adventure story.

A: Gary Cooper, Jean Arthur, Charles Bickford, Anthony Quinn, James Ellison

© MCA/UNIVERSAL HOME VIDEO, INC. 80548

PONY EXPRESS

D: Jerry Hopper 101 m

NR | WST ACT | 1953 | COLOR

Sex / Nud / ◢ Viol / Lang / AdSit

8 Above-average Western actioner that glamorizes the 1860s process of establishing an express mail route which used a series of riders to relay mail between St. Joseph, Missouri and Sacramento, California. Buffalo Bill Cody (Heston) and Wild Bill Hickock (Tucker) do battle with rival stage coach stationmasters, the weather, the country and, of course, the Indians. In spite of some glaring historical inaccuracies, this is a fun-filled flick full of fists, bullets and arrows. The real Pony Express lasted only a couple of years.

A: Charlton Heston, Forrest Tucker, Rhonda Fleming, Jan Sterling

© PARAMOUNT HOME VIDEO 5217

POSSE

D: Kirk Douglas 94 m

PG | WST DMA ACT | 1975 | COLOR

Sex / Nud / ◢ Viol / Lang / ◢ AdSit

8 Solid and interesting Western, with an odd edge. Kirk Douglas is both a cynical lawman and an ambitious politician, seeking to become a Senator from Texas. He sees an opportunity to capture the public's attention when he and his ruthless crew of deputies track down and try to capture an escaped robber, Bruce Dern. But Dern is a wily opponent who recognizes Douglas's self-serving agenda and uses it to gain the sympathy of the townspeople, turn the deputies against Douglas and then enlist them in his own cause.

A: Kirk Douglas, Bruce Dern, Bo Hopkins, James Stacy, Luke Askew, David Canary

© PARAMOUNT HOME VIDEO 8316

PROUD REBEL, THE

D: Michael Curtiz 99 m

NR WST 1958 COLOR

8 Sentimental charmer. Alan Ladd plays an ex-Confederate soldier who is wandering the countryside looking for a doctor who can help his son (his real-life son) regain his speech. The boy was traumatized when he witnessed the burning of Atlanta and the death of his mother. When Dean Jagger's sons pick a fight with Alan over the boy's dog, Alan winds up in jail. He is bailed out and goes to work for a spinster lady (De Havilland) who is trying to save her land from being taken over by the greedy Jagger. Heartwarming story with great star chemistry.

Sex / Nud / ✓ Viol / Lang / AdSit

A: Alan Ladd, Olivia de Havilland, Dean Jagger, Harry Dean Stanton, David Ladd, Henry Hull

© UNITED AMERICAN VIDEO CORP. 5302

QUICK AND THE DEAD, THE

D: Robert Day 91 m

NR WST ACT 1987 COLOR

8 Very good made-for-cable movie about a young family, uprooted by the Civil War, who attempt to make a home for themselves in the untamed West. When the family comes under attack, the father (Conti) accepts the advice and aid of a wanderer (Elliott) to help protect them. The green Conti and his family come to rely very heavily on Elliot's survival skills. Soon Conti's wife (Capshaw) and his boy begin to doubt him and become very enamored of their new protector. Based on the Louis L'Amour story, the flavor and feel of the lawless Old West is beautifully captured. A classy Western.

Sex / Nud / ✓ Viol / Lang / ✓ AdSit

A: Sam Elliott, Tom Conti, Kate Capshaw, Kenny Morrison, Matt Clark, Lean Louis

© WARNER HOME VIDEO 818

RACHEL AND THE STRANGER

D: Norman Foster 79 m

NR WST ROM 1948 B&W

7 William Holden is a widowed pioneer father living in the western woods of the 1820s. Even though he is overwhelmed with grief for the loss of his wife, he buys a bondwoman out of servitude to teach his motherless son manners and to tend to the daily chores. Though they are married, Holden is so buried in love for his dead wife that he fails to notice the charms of his new "wife." But when a wandering stranger (Mitchum) visits and is attracted to her, Holden's love for her is suddenly awakened. Entertaining, with some funny moments and a thrilling Indian raid at the end, too.

Sex / Nud / ✓ Viol / Lang / ✓ AdSit

A: Loretta Young, William Holden, Robert Mitchum, Tom Tully, Sara Haden

© TURNER HOME ENTERTAINMENT 6127

RARE BREED, THE

D: Andrew V. McLaglen 107 m

NR WST ROM 1966 COLOR

7 Enjoyable and fun Western. An eccentric British heiress (O'Hara) has a wild idea. She wants to breed stocky English Hereford cows with tough Texan longhorns. Stewart is a stubborn cowboy who is supposed to escort her, her daughter and her prize bull to the Texas ranch of her partner, an outlandish Scottsman (Keith). On the calamity-filled journey there, Stewart grows to admire O'Hara's conviction and determination, but is faced with a romantic rivalry in Keith when they arrive at the ranch. The road to the new breed is also faced with stampedes and rustlers, too. Entertaining and original.

Sex / Nud / ✓ Viol / ✓ Lang / ✓ AdSit

A: James Stewart, Maureen O'Hara, Brian Keith, Juliet Mills, Jack Elam, Ben Johnson

© MCA/UNIVERSAL HOME VIDEO, INC. 80322

RED RIVER

D: Howard Hawks 134 m

NR WST ACT 1948 B&W

10 Epic and grand Western. Wayne stars as an early settler of the Texas wilderness and guardian to an orphan, Montgomery Clift. After spending years creating one of the largest ranches in Texas, this tough-as-nails cattle baron gathers up all his cattle, plus those of his neighbors, and sets out for the newly opened railheads in Kansas with one of the first cattle herds to be driven north. Wayne is a tyrannical taskmaster. His rule moves them through dangers that would have stopped other men. But his determination becomes cruelty and Clift leads a mutiny against him. Excellent everything.

Sex / Nud / ✓ Viol / Lang / ✓ AdSit

A: John Wayne, Montgomery Clift, Walter Brennan, Joanne Dru, Coleen Gray

Distributed By MGM/UA Home Video M201724

RENEGADE RANGER/SCARLET RIVER

D: David Howard 113 m

NR WST 1938 B&W

6 These two Westerns are presented in the same way they did it in the '30s and '40s. Really - it's a double feature. RENEGADE RANGER - George O'Brien, playing Texas Ranger Jack Steele, is assigned to bring in beautiful Mexican bandit Rita Hayworth, who has been accused of murder. But Steele discovers that she is innocent. SCARLET RIVER - A movie cowboy, filming at the Scarlet River Ranch, winds up in a series of real shootouts with some bad guys who are trying to take the ranch away from its pretty owner.

Sex / Nud / Viol / Lang / ✓ AdSit

A: George O'Brien, Rita Hayworth, Tim Holt, Ray Whitley

© TURNER HOME ENTERTAINMENT 2041

RETURN OF DRAW EGAN, THE

D: William S. Hart 64 m

NR WST 1916 B&W

8 Legendary silent screen cowboy star William S. Hart stars in perhaps his best Western, as an outlaw who has reformed himself for the love of a good woman and become the sheriff in a small town. But... an old partner-in-crime shows up and threatens to expose him and ruin everything he has built for himself. Tough, no-nonsense Western.

Sex / Nud / ✓ Viol / Lang / AdSit

A: William S. Hart, Louise Glaum, Margery Wilson, Robert McKimm

© VIDEO YESTERYEAR 1441

RETURN OF FRANK JAMES, THE

D: Fritz Lang 92 m

NR WST 1940 COLOR

7 This tough sequel to JESSE JAMES opens as Jesse James is shot in the back by the notorious Ford brothers. When the pair is pardoned by the law, Jesse's brother Frank (Fonda), who has gone straight, decides to strap his guns back on and seek his own revenge. But he is sidelined when framed by the brothers for murder and robbery. At the trial, with the Ford brothers gloating in the audience, a young female reporter (Tierney) covering his trial discovers the truth. Fonda's performance is effectively subdued. This was also Gene Tierney's acting debut. A thoroughly enjoyable Western.

Sex / Nud / Viol / Lang / ✓ AdSit

A: Henry Fonda, Jackie Cooper, Gene Tierney, John Carradine, Henry Hull, J. Edward Bromberg

© FOXVIDEO 1328

RETURN TO LONESOME DOVE

D: Mike Robe 330 m

NR WST DMA ACT 1993 COLOR

8 Good follow-up to the fantastic original. Woodrow has taken his friend back to Texas to bury him. But, before going back, he stops off to ask another former Texas ranger to lead a group in capturing a herd of mustangs and driving them back to Montana. While they are doing that, he will stop off in Nebraska to buy blooded stock. He will breed the two to create a new hardier stock. Newt is to meet him in Nebraska, but instead gets in a gun fight and thrown into jail. He is paroled to a wealthy cattle baron with a pretty young wife. Much of the fire is gone from the original, but it is still well worth a watch.

Sex / Nud / ✓ Viol / Lang / ✓ AdSit

A: John Voight, Barbara Hershey, Rick Schroder, Louis Gossett, Jr., William Petersen, Oliver Reed

© CABIN FEVER ENTERTAINMENT 9586

RETURN TO SNOWY RIVER

D: Geoff Burrowes 99 m

PG WST ROM 1988 COLOR

6 Sequel to THE MAN FROM SNOWY RIVER. The hero from the original (Burlinson) has left for three years to round up a herd of horses. He returns to claim the love of his life (Thornton), but finds she is now engaged to a banker's son (Eadie). What's more, her father (Dennehy) is vehemently opposed to their relationship and is determined to keep them apart. Once again, Burlinson must battle to prove his worth. Grand and beautiful photography, plus glorious Australian scenery and fast pace, make this a mildly satisfying sequel that has the same feeling as the original.

Sex / Nud / ✓ Viol / ✓ Lang / AdSit

A: Tom Burlinson, Sigrid Thornton, Brian Dennehy, Nicholas Eadie, Bryan Marshall

© WALT DISNEY HOME VIDEO 699

RIDE THE HIGH COUNTRY

D: Sam Peckinpah 93 m

NR WST ACT 1962 COLOR

9 Considered Peckinpah's finest film and one so good that two of Hollywood's biggest Western stars retired rather than try to top it. Two grizzled old friends and old-time gunfighters join forces to escort a large gold shipment. Along the way they reminisce, and even work together to aid a young bride (Hartley's debut) escape from her barbarian in-laws. While McCrea wants only to do a good and respectable job, Scott secretly wants to steal the gold they are supposed to be guarding. Beautiful photography, wonderful performances and an interesting story.

Sex / Nud / ✓ Viol / Lang / AdSit

A: Randolph Scott, Joel McCrea, Mariette Hartley, Edgar Buchanan, Ronald Starr, Warren Oates

Distributed By MGM/UA Home Video M600850

RIO BRAVO

D: Howard Hawks 141 m

NR WST ACT COM 1959 COLOR

10 Exuberant Western with Wayne as the classic tough-guy sheriff who has arrested the brother of a wealthy rancher. The rancher wants his brother free. John wants him tried, but the rancher has a whole herd of cowboys and gunslingers ready to help him. John has a drunken deputy (Martin), a toothless, grizzled old man (Brennan) and a young untried gunhand (Nelson). Great fun. Lots of shootin' but good laughs too from a talented cast. Redone by Hawks, again with Wayne, in 1967 as EL DORADO - also was the model for ASSAULT ON PRECINCT 13 and RIO LOBO.

Sex / Nud / ✓ Viol / Lang / AdSit

A: John Wayne, Dean Martin, Angie Dickinson, Walter Brennan, Ricky Nelson, Ward Bond

© WARNER HOME VIDEO 11050

RIO CONCHOS

D: Gordon Douglas — 107 m

NR | WST ACT | 1964 | COLOR

8 A rootin' shootin' good time! An ex-Confederate soldier (O'Brien) is still fighting the Civil War by running guns to the Apaches to get vengeance on the North. Four men, led by a US calvary captain (Whitman), are hunting for 2,000 stolen Spencer repeating rifles. They know O'Brien has them, so they are on their way into Mexico with a wagonload of gun powder to use as bait to draw him out. Boone, an Apache-hating ex-rebel; Franciosa, a charming killer avoiding the noose; and Brown, an Army sergeant, join Whitman in his quest. Some of the best in traditional action-packed Old West adventure.

☐ Sex ☐ Nud ◢ Viol ☐ Lang ◢ AdSit

A: Richard Boone, Stuart Whitman, Edmond O'Brien, Anthony Franciosa, Jim Brown

© FOXVIDEO 1224

RIO GRANDE

D: John Ford — 105 m

NR | WST ACT | 1950 | B&W

8 This epic Western that was the last of the famous cavalry trilogy by John Ford. (First came FORT APACHE, then came SHE WORE A YELLOW RIBBON.) Here John Wayne is the commander of a remote western Army outpost, fighting a war with the Apache. His son has flunked out of West Point and now shows up as a new member of his regiment. Soon his strong-willed estranged wife (O'Hara) arrives, insisting on getting the boy released from the army. This film is rich in characters and the Army's traditions of bravery and gallantry. It is loaded with beautiful scenery, has songs by the Sons of the Pioneers and lots of action too, but it also stretches history and credibility to the breaking point.

☐ Sex ☐ Nud ◢ Viol ☐ Lang ☐ AdSit

A: John Wayne, Maureen O'Hara, Ben Johnson, Chill Wills, J. Carrol Naish, Victor McLaglen

© REPUBLIC PICTURES HOME VIDEO 3457

RIO LOBO

D: Howard Hawks — 103 m

G | WST ACT | 1970 | COLOR

6 Second remake of the original giant 1959 hit RIO BRAVO and its 1967 follow-up EL DORADO. This time Wayne plays an ex-Union colonel who tracks down some Civil War traitors, who are also gold thieves. In the process, he winds up helping out a small town held hostage by a corrupt sheriff. An old story that gets a considerable boost from the talents of Wayne and Jack Elam, as a crazy old codger with a shotgun. This was also the last screen appearance of Sherry Lansing, who became a major studio exec.

☐ Sex ☐ Nud ◢ Viol ☐ Lang ☐ AdSit

A: John Wayne, Jennifer O'Neill, Jorge Rivero, Jack Elam, Sherry Lansing, Chris Mitchum

© FOXVIDEO 7016

RIVER OF NO RETURN

D: Otto Preminger — 91 m

NR | WST | 1954 | COLOR

7 Entertaining Western adventure. When Monroe and her ruthless gambler boyfriend (Calhoun) meet with danger on a sinking river raft, Mitchum and his son (Rettig) pull them to safety. Calhoun, who is in a hurry to register a gold claim that he won dishonestly, steals Mitchum's horse and gun and deserts them all, including Monroe. Left stranded and at the mercy of rampaging Indians, Monroe, Mitchum and Rettig make a treacherous journey downriver on a raft to safety. Plenty of action as the trio careen down the swift river, beautiful scenery and romantic action between Monroe and Mitchum.

☐ Sex ☐ Nud ◢ Viol ☐ Lang ◢ AdSit

A: Robert Mitchum, Marilyn Monroe, Rory Calhoun, Tommy Rettig, Murvyn Vye, Douglas Spencer

© FOXVIDEO 5139

ROOSTER COGBURN

D: Stuart Millar — 108 m

PG | WST COM ACT | 1975 | COLOR

8 TRUE GRIT meets THE AFRICAN QUEEN. John Wayne reprises his very popular and Oscar-winning title character from TRUE GRIT. Rooster is in pursuit of bad men who have lifted an Army wagonload of nitroglycerine. His search introduces him to a bible-thumping old-maid missionary played by Katharine Hepburn, whose father was also murdered by the bad guys. The fun starts when she insists on joining Wayne's expedition. An OK story line, but it is aided greatly by the presence of two screen legends who are just plain fun to watch, as well as a terrific supporting cast.

☐ Sex ☐ Nud ◢ Viol ☐ Lang ☐ AdSit

A: John Wayne, Katharine Hepburn, Anthony Zerbe, Strother Martin, John McIntire

© MCA/UNIVERSAL HOME VIDEO, INC. 55042

ROUNDERS, THE

D: Burt Kennedy — 85 m

NR | WST COM | 1964 | COLOR

7 Likable little comedy about the adventures of two nearly over-the-hill modern-day cowboy buddies working for a stingy rancher (Chill Wills). Ben and Howdy spend nearly the entire movie trying to best an ornery roan named "Ol' Fooler" nearly destroying a small town in the process. Their adventures with the horse becomes the central gag, tieing together a pleasant time-killer of a film which became a minor sleeper hit the year it was released.

☐ Sex ☐ Nud ☐ Viol ☐ Lang ☐ AdSit

A: Glenn Ford, Henry Fonda, Sue Ann Langdon, Hope Holiday, Chill Wills, Edgar Buchanan

Distributed By MGM/UA Home Video M200975

RUTHLESS FOUR, THE

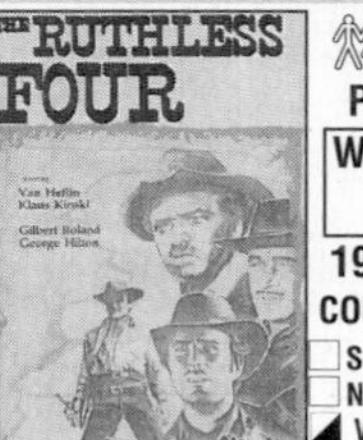

D: Giorgio Capitani — 96 m

PG | WST | 1970 | COLOR

7 Intriguing Western psychological character study. Heflin is a loner who has spent a lifetime prospecting and now has struck a rich vein of gold in Nevada, but he can't get to it by himself. In order to get the goods, he needs partners. Unwillingly he enlists the aid of three men he can't trust. The four men begin to work together but it doesn't last, soon it is every man for himself. Mistrust and greed have set in.

☐ Sex ☐ Nud ◢ Viol ☐ Lang ◢ AdSit

A: Van Heflin, Gilbert Roland, Klaus Kinski, George Hilton, Sarah Ross

© MONTEREY HOME VIDEO 33744

SACKETTS, THE

D: Robert Totten — 198 m

NR | WST ACT | 1979 | COLOR

7 Powerhouse cast of some of the biggest names in filmdom shine in this made-for-TV epic Western. Two Louis L'Amour novels ("The Daybreakers" and "The Sacketts") were combined to create this story. Three brothers choose to travel into the wild west to start new lives at the close of the Civil War rather than to return to a family feud in Tennessee. This is the saga of their trip west and their fortunes after getting there. Each plans to make it on his own there, but each knows he can rely on his brother. Rousing action flick with some truly sparkling performances.

☐ Sex ☐ Nud ◢ Viol ☐ Lang ☐ AdSit

A: Tom Selleck, Sam Elliott, Glenn Ford, Ben Johnson, Slim Pickens, Ruth Roman

© WARNER HOME VIDEO 957

SAN ANTONIO

D: David Butler — 107 m

NR | WST | 1945 | COLOR

6 A traditional and pretty predictable Western, but with plenty of action. When Flynn, a rancher, discovers who has been stealing his cattle, he heads into the wide open town of San Antonio after the rustlers. A beautiful saloon girl (Smith) is working for the saloon owner (Francen), who is also the corrupt cattle rustler who has been stealing Flynn's cattle. Good-guy Flynn enters the scene, uncovers Francen's criminal operation, and Smith falls in love with him. Good actioner that moves along at a rapid pace.

☐ Sex ☐ Nud ◢ Viol ☐ Lang ☐ AdSit

A: Errol Flynn, Alexis Smith, S.Z. Sakall, Victor Francen, Florence Bates, John Litel

Distributed By MGM/UA Home Video M202120

SAN FRANCISCO

D: W.S. Van Dyke — 116 m

NR | WST ROM | 1936 | B&W

8 Big-budget flick populated by all the big-name stars MGM could muster. Set on the Barbary Coast of San Francisco in 1906, Gable is the dapper owner of one of the biggest and best saloons. He falls in love with the beautiful singer Jeanette MacDonald. She is also one of the town's best and is in demand by every saloon owner. Gable vies for her attentions but he also leads an effort to destroy the corrupt political forces that are controlling the waterfront. Just as he appears to be making headway on both fronts they are hit with the famous 1906 San Francisco earthquake. Great special effects that are still impressive today.

☐ Sex ☐ Nud ◢ Viol ☐ Lang ☐ AdSit

A: Clark Gable, Jeanette MacDonald, Spencer Tracy, Jack Holt, Jessie Ralph, Ted Healy

Distributed By MGM/UA Home Video M300474

SCALPHUNTERS, THE

D: Sydney Pollack — 100 m

NR | WST COM ACT | 1968 | COLOR

8 Fun-filled and funny Western with truly interesting characters. A very determined fur trapper (Burt Lancaster) is forced by a group of Indians to swap his skins for a highly educated and uppity former slave (also a recent member of the Kiowa nation), Ossie Davis. He's not thrilled with the forced swap, so he sets out to get his furs back. But, by the time he catches them, an outlaw band of scalphunters headed by Savalas, has stolen the furs from the Indians and captured Davis, too. Undeterred, Burt hounds the scalphunters with guerrilla raids, getting occasional inside help from his uneasy ally, Davis. A real good time.

☐ Sex ☐ Nud ◢ Viol ☐ Lang ◢ AdSit

A: Burt Lancaster, Shelley Winters, Ossie Davis, Telly Savalas, Armando Silvestre, Nick Cravat

Distributed By MGM/UA Home Video M202033

SEARCHERS, THE

D: John Ford — 144 m

NR | WST ACT | 1956 | COLOR

10 Spectacular Western masterpiece from the two kings of the genre: John Ford and John Wayne. Beautiful scenery, fascinating characters and a thrilling story, rich in both psychological undercurrent and adventure. Wayne is a bitter ex-Confederate soldier who hates Indians. He and his brother's adopted son (who is half-Indian) come home to find that the brother and sister-in-law have been savagely murdered by Comanches and his niece is kidnapped. He and the boy form an uneasy partnership and set off to find her. This begins an epic 7-year odyssey in which Wayne rediscovers his humanity.

☐ Sex ☐ Nud ◢ Viol ☐ Lang ◢ AdSit

A: John Wayne, Jeffrey Hunter, Vera Miles, Ward Bond, Natalie Wood

© WARNER HOME VIDEO 1012

SEPTEMBER GUN

D: Don Taylor — 94 m

NR | WST COM | 1983 | COLOR

6 This unconventional Western/comedy starts out a bit slowly but builds into an action-packed adventure. A crusty old gunslinger (Preston) is coerced into helping a stubborn nun (Duke) and a group of orphaned children reach a remote mission school located in Colorado, some three hundred miles away. However, when they get there, the mission school that Sister Dulcina expects to find has been taken over by an outlaw. It is now a bar, and worse. She wants it back for her school and Preston gets the unwelcome job of helping her do it. Made for TV.

Sex / Nud / Viol / Lang / AdSit

A: Robert Preston, Patty Duke, Geoffrey Lewis, Sally Kellerman, Christopher Lewis

© GOODTIMES 9153

SHANE

D: George Stevens — 117 m

NR | WST ACT ROM | 1953 | COLOR

10 This is the quintessential Western or, at the very least, among the best of the very best. A mysterious drifter rides onto a dusty hardscrabble farm. He intends to stop for just a little while but stays on to become a hired hand. It is plain that he is no ordinary man - he's running from a past. The farmer likes him, the boy idolizes him and the farmer's wife finds herself powerfully attracted to him. However, a hard-headed pioneer cattle rancher is trying to drive all the sodbusters off and the stranger must decide if he should stay out of the fight or give his new friends the kind of help only a man like him can give.

Sex / Nud / ✓ Viol / Lang / ✓ AdSit

A: Van Heflin, Alan Ladd, Jean Arthur, Brandon de Wilde, Jack Palance, Ben Johnson

© PARAMOUNT HOME VIDEO 6522

SHENANDOAH

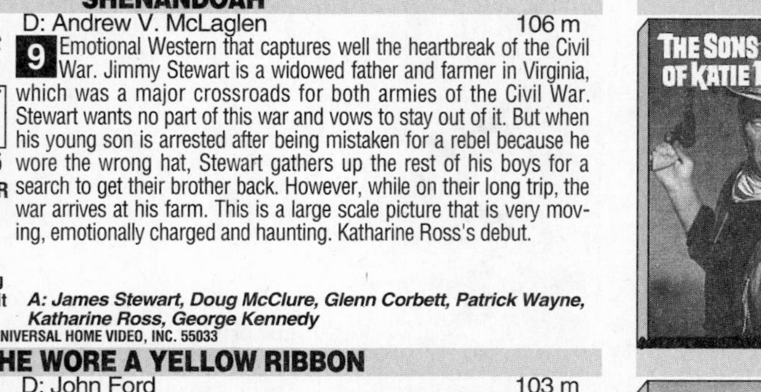

D: Andrew V. McLaglen — 106 m

NR | WST DMA ACT | 1965 | COLOR

9 Emotional Western that captures well the heartbreak of the Civil War. Jimmy Stewart is a widowed father and farmer in Virginia, which was a major crossroads for both armies of the Civil War. Stewart wants no part of this war and vows to stay out of it. But when his young son is arrested after being mistaken for a rebel because he wore the wrong hat, Stewart gathers up the rest of his boys for a search to get their brother back. However, while on their long trip, the war arrives at his farm. This is a large scale picture that is very moving, emotionally charged and haunting. Katharine Ross's debut.

✓ Sex / Nud / ✓ Viol / Lang / ✓ AdSit

A: James Stewart, Doug McClure, Glenn Corbett, Patrick Wayne, Katharine Ross, George Kennedy

© MCA/UNIVERSAL HOME VIDEO, INC. 55033

SHE WORE A YELLOW RIBBON

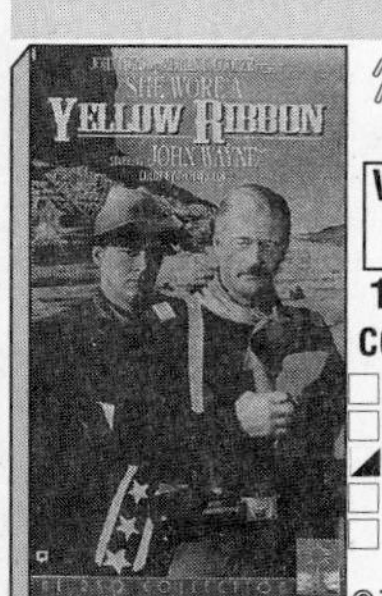

D: John Ford — 103 m

NR | WST ACT | 1949 | COLOR

10 Thrilling middle episode of Ford's cavalry trilogy (FORT APACHE and RIO GRANDE.) This time John is the aging commander (Captain Brittles) of a calvary outpost and he is being forced to retire just as war is about to break out with the Indians. Unable to make peace, unable to get the settlers evacuated in time and unwilling to let someone else lead this fight, Captain Brittles leads his men against the Indian raiders. A winning Western in every way: rousing action, fascinating characters and brilliant photography (Oscar).

Sex / Nud / ✓ Viol / Lang / AdSit

A: John Wayne, Joanne Dru, Ben Johnson, John Agar, Harry Carey, Jr., Victor McLaglen

© TURNER HOME ENTERTAINMENT 2065

SHOOTING, THE

D: Monte Hellman — 82 m

G | WST DMA ACT | 1967 | COLOR

7 An unusual existential Western, similar to, but yet far from, the traditional shoot-'em-up. A strange woman (Perkins) hires bounty hunters Oates and Hutchins to escort her across the desert after her son is accidentally killed. A sadistic gunslinger (Nicholson) follows the trio and a bitter dispute develops between Nicholson and Hutchins over the woman and Nicholson kills him. The trio continue on through the relentless desert. Their water is running low and their horses are dying. This is not a typical Western, so don't expect a typical simple traditional resolution and ending.

Sex / Nud / ✓ Viol / ✓ Lang / ✓ AdSit

A: Jack Nicholson, Will Hutchins, Warren Oates, Millie Perkins

© UNITED AMERICAN VIDEO CORP. 17193

SHOOTIST, THE

D: Don Siegel — 100 m

PG | WST DMA ACT | 1976 | COLOR

9 An intelligent triumph for John Wayne. As Wayne himself was dying of cancer (his last film), so is his character - an old gunfighter named J.B. Books. The time is 1901. Books has spent his life as a gunman, but both he and his era are dying. All he wants now is to be left alone, but wherever he goes his reputation precedes him. His enemies and even total strangers seek him out. Everybody wants to kill him or to make a profit from him. He has no real friends - only the woman who owns the boarding house where he is staying and her hero-worshipping son. Very believable and moving. A fitting last film for Wayne.

Sex / Nud / ✓ Viol / ✓ Lang / ✓ AdSit

A: John Wayne, Lauren Bacall, Ron Howard, James Stewart, Scatman Crothers, Richard Boone

© PARAMOUNT HOME VIDEO 8904

SILENCE OF THE NORTH

D: Allan Winton King — 94 m

PG | WST DMA ACT | 1981 | COLOR

7 Picturesque and inspirational. This is a story about a strong-willed woman (Burstyn) who falls in love with a rugged trapper (Skerritt) and follows him to live in the wilds of northern Canada. The story, based upon the actual autobiography of Olive Fredrickson, tells of her daily struggles, from being a young mother just after the turn of the 20th-century to later being a widow with three children. The wilderness can be cruel, and she and her family are left to brave nature's forces, survive cold winters and deal with tragedy on their own. Excellent.

Sex / Nud / ✓ Viol / Lang / ✓ AdSit

A: Ellen Burstyn, Tom Skerritt, Gordon Pinsent, Jennifer McKinney, Colin Fox

© MCA/UNIVERSAL HOME VIDEO, INC. 71004

SKIN GAME

D: Paul Bogart — 102 m

PG | WST COM | 1971 | COLOR

9 First-class comedy! Two men of the Old West really have a good con game going in this top-notch comedy with a social conscience. Set just before the Civil War, Garner and Gossett pose as master and slave. Their scam is that Garner sells Gossett for a high price, Gossett escapes and they split the dough. Then they can do it all over again in the next town. Everything is going great, too, until Susan Clark steals their money and Garner's heart; and a slave trader (Asner) takes Gossett and his girlfriend South into real slavery. Always entertaining. Has some really funny moments.

Sex / ✓ Nud / ✓ Viol / Lang / ✓ AdSit

A: James Garner, Louis Gossett, Jr., Susan Clark, Edward Asner, Andrew Duggan

© WARNER HOME VIDEO 11406

SONS OF KATIE ELDER, THE

D: Henry Hathaway — 122 m

NR | WST ACT COM | 1965 | COLOR

9 Fast-paced Wayne Western with action, good times and a heart! Katie was a loving mother who had four rough and rowdy sons. When she dies, the four come home to pay their respects and decide that the youngest should honor their mother and go to college. But first they make a pact to get back the land that was taken from Katie and to learn the truth about their father's murder six months earlier. The gunman (Wayne), the gambler (Martin), the quiet guy (Holliman) and the kid (Michael Anderson, Jr.) all put aside their differences to learn the truth and to protect each other's back. Rousing good time.

Sex / Nud / ✓ Viol / Lang / ✓ AdSit

A: John Wayne, Dean Martin, Martha Hyer, Earl Holliman, Jeremy Slate, James Gregory

© PARAMOUNT HOME VIDEO 6729

SPOILERS, THE

D: Ray Enright — 84 m

NR | WST ACT | 1942 | B&W

7 An innocent ship's captain (Wayne) is tricked by an unscrupulous town official (Scott), out of the rich gold mine that he and his partner (Harry Carey) own. It's 1890 and this is the Klondike. If they're are going to get it back at all, they are going to have to do it themselves. He and Scott also end up vying for the attentions of a sexy saloon girl (Dietrich). The clincher to both of these battles comes in one of the most elaborate (and most often imitated) barroom fight scenes ever filmed. This is the fourth of five screen remakes of this same story.

Sex / Nud / Viol / Lang / ✓ AdSit

A: John Wayne, Randolph Scott, Marlene Dietrich, Margaret Lindsay, Harry Carey, Richard Barthelmess

© MCA/UNIVERSAL HOME VIDEO, INC. 80015

STAGECOACH

D: John Ford — 97 m

NR | WST ACT | 1939 | B&W

9 A landmark Western in every way - intelligent and exciting, too. And, it made both John Ford and John Wayne into big names. Nine entirely different people are forced to be together on board a stagecoach through Apache country and are set upon in an Indian attack. Mitchell won a Supporting Oscar as a drunken doctor. Wayne is an escaped prisoner out for revenge for the deaths of his father and brother, but he had been caught and is being taken back to jail by a sheriff (Bancroft). Claire Trevor is a prostitute who falls in love with Wayne. Filmed in beautiful Monument Valley, Utah. A true classic!

Sex / Nud / ✓ Viol / Lang / ✓ AdSit

A: John Wayne, Claire Trevor, John Carradine, Thomas Mitchell, Donald Meek, Andy Devine

© WARNER HOME VIDEO 35078

STATION WEST

D: Sidney Lanfield — 80 m

NR | WST | 1948 | B&W

7 Dusty Western with a romantic twist. In a small Western town, a rash of gold robberies is disrupting life and prosperity. Dick Powell is an undercover Army officer who is assigned to find the man behind the robberies. However while he is going through the clues, he meets and falls for a very captivating woman (Greer), the owner of a gambling house and, to his surprise, the ringleader! Solid entertainment based on the story by Luke Short.

Sex / Nud / ✓ Viol / Lang / ✓ AdSit

A: Dick Powell, Jane Greer, Tom Powers, Raymond Burr, Steve Brodie, Gordon Oliver

© TURNER HOME ENTERTAINMENT 2051

SUNDOWNERS, THE

D: Fred Zinnemann — 133 m

NR | WST DMA COM | 1960 | COLOR

9 Wonderfully winning film that was a Best Picture nominee and received four other nominations. One of the best-ever of many Mitchum/Kerr pairings. It is the loving character study of a headstrong rover who insists upon taking his wife and family with him from job to job, herding and shearing sheep in Australia's outback during the 1920s. He loves his family and he loves the life, but she thinks its time to settle down. Shot on location in Australia. Numerous winning vignettes and a crew of fascinating characters populate this endearing story. Highly recommended and rewarding viewing for all ages.

Sex | Nud | Viol | Lang | AdSit

A: Deborah Kerr, Robert Mitchum, Peter Ustinov, Michael Anderson, Jr., Glynis Johns, Dina Merrill

© WARNER HOME VIDEO 11215

TALL IN THE SADDLE

D: Edwin L. Marin — 79 m

NR | WST ACT | 1944 | B&W

7 Enjoyable, rip snorter - an old-style Western. John is a cowboy who just has no time for women until he takes a job at a ranch owned by an aging spinster, who also has a beautiful niece. His cousin and another cowboy have been killed by a corrupt judge who wanted the cousin's ranch. And now, the judge is after the old woman's ranch, too. Lots of shootouts, fistfights and chases, and in the end John gets the girl.

Sex | Nud | ✓ Viol | Lang | AdSit

A: John Wayne, Ella Raines, George "Gabby" Hayes, Ward Bond, Don Douglas

© TURNER HOME ENTERTAINMENT 6028

TELL THEM WILLIE BOY IS HERE

D: Abraham Polonsky — 98 m

PG | WST DMA | 1969 | COLOR

6 Unusual modern Western that is based upon an actual 1909 incident. Robert Blake is a Paiute Indian who wants to wed white Katharine Ross, but her father (Angel) reacts violently to the news and Blake kills him in self-defense. He and Ross then flee together to avoid arrest. Sheriff Redford is reluctant to arrest Willie, but prissy Susan Clark and racist rancher Sullivan urge him on. President Grover Cleveland is also in the area, and the press corp with him promotes Willie's case nationally into the appearance of a major Indian uprising. Compelling viewing, even though heavy-handed.

Sex | Nud | ✓ Viol | ✓ Lang | ✓ AdSit

A: Robert Redford, Katharine Ross, Robert Blake, Susan Clark, Barry Sullivan, Mikel Angel

© MCA/UNIVERSAL HOME VIDEO, INC. 55084

TEXAS

D: George Marshall — 94 m

NR | WST ACT | 1941 | B&W

8 High quality Western that proved to be an excellent starring vehicle for two young stars who would later become supporting pillars of the genre. Glenn Ford and William Holden are two young Confederate veterans drifting through Texas. But when they are mistaken for stage robbers by a posse, they have to separate and make a run for it. When they meet up again, they become pawns on opposite sides of a fight between cattlemen and rustlers, and they are also rivals for the hand of Claire Trevor. Action-packed, fun-filled, funny and highly enjoyable.

Sex | Nud | ✓ Viol | Lang | AdSit

A: William Holden, Glenn Ford, Claire Trevor, George Bancroft, Edgar Buchanan, Raymond Hatton

© COLUMBIA TRISTAR HOME VIDEO 60664

THEY CALL ME TRINITY

D: E.B. Clucher — 109 m

G | WST COM | 1971 | COLOR

6 A wild spoof of the very popular "speghetti Westerns" of the time, which became a surprise international hit on its own. Terence Hill is an amoral sheriff helped out by his dim-witted half-brother, but the two unexpectedly become the saviors of a group of Morman settlers who are being harassed by a group of marauding Mexican bandits. Mostly good fun and spiced with ample doses of slapstick humor and comic action.

Sex | Nud | ✓ Viol | Lang | AdSit

A: Terence Hill, Bud Spencer, Farley Granger, Gisela Hahn, Stephen Zacharias, Dan Sturkie

© UNITED AMERICAN VIDEO CORP. 5464

THEY DIED WITH THEIR BOOTS ON

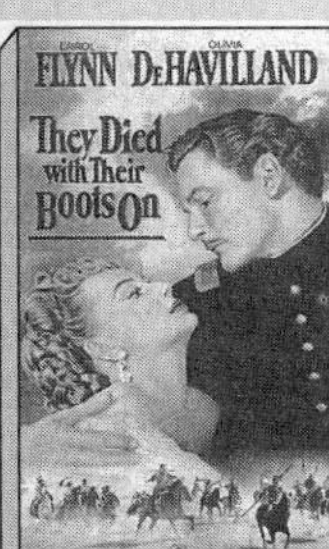

D: Raoul Walsh — 140 m

NR | WST ACT | 1941 | B&W

8 This rousing Western swashbuckler was originally represented as being the story of General George Custer. It is widely accepted as being a classic film, but it is not at all a credible history lesson. Still, Errol Flynn put in one of his most respected efforts, tracing the life of Custer from his days at West Point, his military exploits, and his marriage to his downfall at Little Big Horn. Flynn in life was just as flamboyant as was Custer. As fiction, this is good and exciting entertainment. It is only diminished when you know the truth.

Sex | Nud | ✓ Viol | Lang | AdSit

A: Errol Flynn, Olivia de Havilland, Arthur Kennedy, Anthony Quinn, Sydney Greenstreet, Charley Grapewin

Distributed By MGM/UA Home Video M201473

TIN STAR, THE

D: Anthony Mann — 93 m

NR | WST ACT | 1957 | B&W

9 Solid and well acted - a quality Western. Henry Fonda is a bounty hunter. He used to be a sheriff and had a family, but they died when he couldn't raise the money for doctor bills. Now, hard and bitter, he comes to a small town to await the arrival of a reward check. Anthony Perkins is the young sheriff in the town and is in way over his head with a local thug. Fonda, seeing a piece of his former self in the sheriff, helps Perkins learn what to do and, in the process, rediscovers a life for himself. An intelligent and affecting character study.

Sex | Nud | ✓ Viol | Lang | ✓ AdSit

A: Henry Fonda, Anthony Perkins, Betsy Palmer, Neville Brand, John McIntire, Lee Van Cleef

© PARAMOUNT HOME VIDEO 5708

TRAIN ROBBERS, THE

D: Burt Kennedy — 92 m

PG | WST | 1973 | COLOR

6 Slightly different vehicle for John Wayne. Ann-Margret is a widow whose husband hid $500,000 in stolen bank gold. She solicits the help of an aging Civil War vet (Wayne) in retrieving the gold and returning it, so that her family name can be restored. John and some hired hands set out into the Mexican badlands on this quest but are being pursued by her husband's old partner, Ricardo Montalban, and his band of hired guns, who want the gold, too. Some interesting twists, including a surprise ending, keep things moving. There is action, but the emphasis is on characters and plot.

Sex | Nud | ✓ Viol | Lang | AdSit

A: John Wayne, Ann-Margret, Rod Taylor, Ben Johnson, Christopher George, Ricardo Montalban

© WARNER HOME VIDEO 11093

TRUE GRIT

D: Henry Hathaway — 128 m

G | WST ACT COM | 1969 | COLOR

9 Extremely popular Western for which Wayne finally won an Oscar, after 40 years in film. He is Rooster Cogburn, a crude old derelict of a marshall who helps out a young girl who wants him to track down her father's killer. They head off into Indian country, where they are joined by a young Texas ranger (Campbell). This is a very enjoyable movie that takes time for solid character development and creating interesting relationships between the principals. There is a rousing finish that is topped off with a near-classic shootout. Great entertainment.

Sex | Nud | ✓ Viol | Lang | AdSit

A: John Wayne, Glen Campbell, Kim Darby, Robert Duvall, Jeremy Slate, Strother Martin

© PARAMOUNT HOME VIDEO 6833

TUMBLEWEEDS

D: King Baggot, William S. Hart — 141 m

NR | WST | 1925 | B&W

9 One of the silent era's biggest Westerns. It was also Hart's last film. Hart is a cowboy in 1889 Oklahoma. He's fallen in love with a settler's pretty daughter and he realizes that the era of the open range and the cowboy is also nearly over. His one chance at happiness is the free land that the government is giving away in western Oklahama - the great Oklahama Land Rush on the Cherokee strip. But he gets to the race late. His ride from far behind, through masses of bicycles, horses, buggies and wagons is still a thrilling spectacle. A true classic.

Sex | Nud | ✓ Viol | Lang | AdSit

A: William S. Hart, Barbara Bedford, Lucien Littlefield, Lillian Leighton, J. Gorden Russell, Richard J. Neill

© VIDEO YESTERYEAR 598

TWO MULES FOR SISTER SARA

D: Don Siegel — 105 m

PG | WST ACT COM | 1969 | COLOR

8 Intriguing Western that lures you in, entertains you throughout and then hits you with a surprise curve. Clint is a drifter in Mexico during the revolution. He rescues a nun (MacLaine) from being raped but he is now burdened with her. He finds her to be both strangely unpious and fascinatingly appealing - all of which is very unsettling to him. She entices him into risking his neck by helping her to aid the rebel cause and eventually into helping her attack a French garrison. Light-hearted and action-packed fun - with a surprise inside.

Sex | Nud | ✓ Viol | ✓ Lang | ✓ AdSit

A: Shirley MacLaine, Clint Eastwood, Manolo Fabregas, Alberto Morin, Armando Silvestre, John Kelly

© MCA/UNIVERSAL HOME VIDEO, INC. 66046

TWO RODE TOGETHER

D: John Ford — 109 m

NR | WST DMA ACT | 1961 | COLOR

8 A worthy Western with Stewart in a somewhat uncharacteristically harsh role. He plays a hard-bitten and cynical marshall who has been hired by a naive calvary officer (Widmark) and a group of settlers to retrieve kidnapped white children from the Commanches. While Widmark and the settlers are optimistic, Stewart knows that what he will bring back is not what they expect. He also knows that the children will not be accepted. Interesting and somber take on the theme first explored in THE SEARCHERS, which is also highly recommended.

Sex | Nud | ✓ Viol | Lang | ✓ AdSit

A: James Stewart, Richard Widmark, Shirley Jones, Andy Devine, Woody Strode, Linda Cristal

© COLUMBIA TRISTAR HOME VIDEO 60762

UNCONQUERED

NR | WST | 1947 | COLOR

D: Cecil B. DeMille — 147 m

6 Another big-budget DeMille epic -- this time set in 1763 -- it's the settlers against the Indians and corrupt white men. Gary Cooper is an American colonial hero set on stopping an Indian uprising, led by the great Indian leader Pontiac, and on winning over the heart of a pretty indentured servant, Paulette Goddard. Big budget and big sets are used to tell a slightly overblown tale of intrigue and adventure in the wilds of the Ohio river valley.

☐ Sex ☐ Nud ☑ Viol ☐ Lang ☐ AdSit

A: Gary Cooper, Paulette Goddard, Howard da Silva, Boris Karloff, Cecil Kellaway, Ward Bond

© MCA/UNIVERSAL HOME VIDEO, INC. 80344

UNFORGIVEN, THE

NR | WST DMA | 1960 | COLOR

D: John Huston — 123 m

7 In the Texas panhandle immediately after the Civil War, memories of the fierce battles with the Kiowa are still fresh in minds on both sides. So when a figure from the past claims that Hepburn is a full-blooded Kiowa who was adopted by white settlers as a baby, tensions erupt. The Kiowa want to reclaim her into the tribe and the local whites want her gone. Both she and her adopted family are torn by the conflict that threatens to consume them all. One "brother" clearly loves her in a non-brotherly way and another hates Indians so much he is willing to leave his family. Intense.

☐ Sex ☐ Nud ☑ Viol ☐ Lang ☑ AdSit

A: Burt Lancaster, Audrey Hepburn, Lillian Gish, Audie Murphy, John Saxon, Charles Brickford

Distributed By MGM/UA Home Video M601123

UNION PACIFIC

NR | WST | 1939 | COLOR

D: Cecil B. DeMille — 136 m

8 Big-budget classic Western. At the end of the Civil War, a great and expensive effort was launched to unite the East Coast with the West. The Union Pacific would build westward and the Central Pacific would build eastward. However, one man conspired to slow the Union Pacific down. So, the Union brought in Joel McCrea to clean up the trouble makers. The trouble is that one of the trouble makers is his old friend from the War, Robert Preston and both are in love with spunky Barbara Stanwyck. Quite well done, with a spectacular train wreck and plenty of action, but sparked by fine understated acting from Preston and McCrea.

☐ Sex ☐ Nud ☑ Viol ☐ Lang ☐ AdSit

A: Barbara Stanwyck, Joel McCrea, Akim Tamiroff, Robert Preston, Lynne Overman, Brian Donlevy

© MCA/UNIVERSAL HOME VIDEO, INC. 81214

VALDEZ IS COMING

PG | WST ACT | 1971 | COLOR

D: Edwin Sherin — 90 m

7 Pretty good Western. Burt Lancaster is Valdez, a Mexican/American sheriff who struggles to regain his dignity after having suffered years of racial degradation. After Valdez is forced to shoot a Mexican suspect, he tries to provide for the man's widow. His efforts trigger the hostilities of a ruthless cattle baron and gun-runner, who humiliates and then threatens Valdez. So Valdez captures the man's wife and the chase to kill Valdez is on - but Valdez is not a man to be taken lightly. Solid actioner, with some thought thrown in for good measure.

☐ Sex ☐ Nud ☑ Viol ☐ Lang ☐ AdSit

A: Burt Lancaster, Susan Clark, Frank Silvera, Richard Jordan, Jon Cypher, Barton Heyman

Distributed By MGM/UA Home Video M202961

VERA CRUZ

NR | WST ACT | 1954 | COLOR

D: Robert Aldrich — 94 m

7 Solid Western action! Set during the Mexican Revolution of 1866, two Americans (Cooper and Lancaster) have come to Mexico to sell their services to the highest bidder. They are hired to escort a large shipment of gold to Emperor Maximilian in Vera Cruz. But, the alliance that the pair has formed was built on shaky ground from the very beginning, and things get very tense when Cooper allows himself to be convinced by a beautiful woman (Darcel) to hand the goods over to local rebels. Lancaster meanwhile, has his own plans for the precious cargo. Two-fisted adventure!

☐ Sex ☐ Nud ☑ Viol ☐ Lang ☑ AdSit

A: Gary Cooper, Burt Lancaster, Denise Darcel, Cesar Romero, George Macready, Ernest Borgnine

Distributed By MGM/UA Home Video M202015

VIRGINIA CITY

NR | WST ACT | 1940 | B&W

D: Michael Curtiz — 121 m

6 Two-fisted Civil War Western! Confederate colonel Scott is determined to get $5,000,000 in gold through to the Confederacy from Nevada. Errol Flynn is a Union spy who is sent to see that he doesn't. Bogart is a half-breed Mexican bandit who only loves the gold. Miriam Hopkins is a Rebel spy, traveling west on a stagecoach supposedly enroute to become a saloon singer in Virginia City. She and Flynn meet aboard the coach going west when it is held up by Bogart. Meanwhile, back in Virginia City, Scott is plotting to get the gold out. Contrived, but good action and great cast.

☐ Sex ☐ Nud ☐ Viol ☐ Lang ☑ AdSit

A: Humphrey Bogart, Errol Flynn, Randolph Scott, Miriam Hopkins, Frank McHugh, Alan Hale

Distributed By MGM/UA Home Video M202526

VIVA VILLA!

NR | WST ACT DMA | 1934 | B&W

D: David O. Selzenick — 115 m

9 Mexico's legendary bandit hero proved to be excellent material for this very entertaining film which was nominated for Best Picture and two other nominations. It is also acclaimed as Berry's finest screen performance. Villa rises from being a captivating bandit leader who robs from the rich, keeps most of it and gives some to the poor to becoming a leader of the Mexican Revolutionary Army. After the victory he reverts to being a bandit, only to return with his army later and declare himself President of the country - until he again retires to his ranch. Huge box office sensation. Facts are questionable.

☐ Sex ☐ Nud ☑ Viol ☐ Lang ☑ AdSit

A: Wallace Beery, Fay Wray, Stuart Erwin, Leo Carrillo, Donald Cook, George E. Stone

Distributed By MGM/UA Home Video M202835

WAGON MASTER

NR | WST | 1950 | B&W

D: John Ford — 86 m

7 The king of the Westerns, John Ford, directed this fine saga of the real Old West and it later inspired the long running TV series "Wagon Train," which also starred Ward Bond. Two fun-loving carefree cowboy ramblers are hired to guide a westward-bound Mormon wagontrain that is heading off into the largely unknown Utah territory and straight into confrontation with Indians and ruthless outlaws. This is a realistic depiction of the people and the time. It was also one of John Ford's favorites, and one of the earliest starring roles for Ben Johnson, Harry Carey Jr. and James Arness.

☐ Sex ☐ Nud ☑ Viol ☐ Lang ☐ AdSit

A: Ben Johnson, Joanne Dru, Ward Bond, Harry Carey, Jr., Jane Darwell, James Arness

© TURNER HOME ENTERTAINMENT 6128

WAR WAGON, THE

NR | WST ACT COM | 1967 | COLOR

D: Burt Kennedy — 101 m

7 Entertaining tongue-in-cheek John Wayne Western. John has had his fortune stolen, been framed by an unscrupulous cattle baron and mine owner (Cabot) and sent to prison. So, when John gets out, Cabot sends Kirk Douglas to kill him. Instead, John enlists Douglas in his plan to inflict sweet revenge and also gathers together several others in a gang to carry it out. He and his cronies are going to rob a big shipment of gold dust that Cabot transports in a special, heavily armed coach called the War Wagon. Good, mindless action adventure, amply spiced with humor. Hard to beat the combination of Wayne and Douglas.

☐ Sex ☐ Nud ☑ Viol ☐ Lang ☐ AdSit

A: John Wayne, Kirk Douglas, Howard Keel, Robert Walker, Jr., Keenan Wynn

© MCA/UNIVERSAL HOME VIDEO, INC. 80016

WESTERNER, THE

NR | WST COM | 1940 | B&W

D: William Wyler — 100 m

9 Very entertaining Western. Cooper is a cowboy drifting through Texas on his way to California but he has the misfortune of buying a horse from a horse thief. Worse, he is brought up on the charges before the infamous "judge" Roy Bean (Brennan won his third Oscar as the likable bad-guy judge). Cooper only just keeps from being hung by convincing the judge that he once met Lilly Langtree, the judge's great love, and even has a lock of her hair. Coop and Bean become best friends, but Coop eventually chooses sides against him after the judge burns out some homesteader friends of Coop. A good time.

☐ Sex ☐ Nud ☑ Viol ☐ Lang ☐ AdSit

A: Gary Cooper, Walter Brennan, Doris Davenport, Dana Andrews, Chill Wills, Forrest Tucker

© HBO VIDEO 90665

WESTERN UNION

NR | WST | 1941 | COLOR

D: Fritz Lang — 95 m

7 Epic Western about the construction of the first telegraph line through the West. Western Union has hired an ex-outlaw (Randolf Scott) as a guide and an Eastern dandy (Robert Young) to do the job. The two must battle against the terrain, the weather, the Indians and Scott's former gang to get their job done. And, they are also fighting each other over the love of pretty telegrapher Virginian Gilmore. Entertaining and spirited.

☐ Sex ☐ Nud ☑ Viol ☐ Lang ☐ AdSit

A: Randolph Scott, Vance Shaw, Robert Young, Barton MacLane, Virginia Gilmore, Chill Wills

© FOXVIDEO 1750

WHITE FANG

PG | WST ACT CLD | 1991 | COLOR

D: Randal Kleiser — 109 m

9 Wonderful whole-family entertainment in the true sense of the phrase. This is an exciting adventure film that has something to satisfy everyone. It is a beautiful picture that evokes the actual feel of the Alaskan goldrush days. A young man follows his father's dying wishes to settle his gold claim deep in the wilds of a virgin Yukon wilderness. The film focuses upon the young man's journey there and upon his friendship with an orphaned wolf cub, White Fang. Spectacularly photographed, this is a tale of men in the wilderness and one man's love for his four-footed kindred spirit.

☐ Sex ☐ Nud ☑ Viol ☐ Lang ☐ AdSit

A: Ethan Hawke, Klaus Maria Brandauer, James Remar, Seymour Cassel, Susan Hogan

© WALT DISNEY HOME VIDEO 1151

WILD ROVERS, THE

PG | WST ACT COM | 1971 | COLOR

☐ Sex ☐ Nud ◢ Viol ◢ Lang ☐ AdSit

D: Blake Edwards 138 m

8 An unheralded little gem. William Holden and Ryan O'Neal are two cowpoke buddies, one old and one young, who become disillusioned with their careers on the range when one of their friends is accidentally killed. On a whim, this not-too-bright pair decide to rob a bank and head out for Mexico. On a dead run with a posse hot on their heels, it occurs to them that this was not a wise career move. The pleasure in the movie comes from the relationship between these guys. A great buddy movie. Solid performances, particularly by Holden.

A: William Holden, Ryan O'Neal, Karl Malden, Lynn Carlin, Tom Skerritt, Joe Don Baker

Distributed By MGM/UA Home Video M600305

WILL PENNY

NR | WST ROM ACT | 1968 | COLOR

☐ Sex ☐ Nud ◢ Viol ◢ Lang ◢ AdSit

D: Tom Gries 109 m

9 Outstanding film that requires a Western setting to tell its perceptive and moving story, but this is not just a Western. Will Penny has spent his whole life as a cowboy and a loner. He has never thought of living any other way. However, after a run-in with a cruel rawhider and his boys who leave him to die, he is rescued by a pretty woman and her son who are traveling to Oregon to reunite with her settler-husband. For the first time, Will feels the tug of a home life and love. Heartwarming and evocative. Moving, understated performances make these characters human and very real. Excellent.

A: Charlton Heston, Joan Hackett, Donald Pleasence, Lee Majors, Bruce Dern

© PARAMOUNT HOME VIDEO 6723

WINCHESTER '73

NR | WST | 1950 | B&W

☐ Sex ☐ Nud ◢ Viol ☐ Lang ☐ AdSit

D: Anthony Mann 82 m

8 All through the '40s, in part because of WWII, the Western movie had steadily lost its appeal at the box office - that is, until this movie came along. It is credited with inspiring a rebirth of the whole genre. Jimmy Stewart and his misfit brother enter into a sharpshooting contest, with the winner to receive a special issue of the newly invented repeating rifle from Winchester. Stewart wins the rifle but it is soon stolen from him. Stewart pursues his rifle through ambushes, fistfights and gunfights with outlaws and Indians. He will recover the one-of-a-kind rifle and also catch his father's murderer, his own brother.

A: James Stewart, Shelley Winters, Dan Duryea, Tony Curtis, Rock Hudson, Will Geer

© MCA/UNIVERSAL HOME VIDEO, INC. 80325

WINDWALKER

PG | WST DMA ACT | 1980 | COLOR

☐ Sex ☐ Nud ◢ Viol ☐ Lang ☐ AdSit

D: Keith Merrill 108 m

8 Unusually well-rounded family entertainment in the form of the telling of a Cheyenne legend. As an old Cheyenne warrior lies dying, he tells his grandsons the story of how his wife was murdered and his son (their uncle) was kidnapped years before by a neighboring band of Crow Indians. The old man dies but comes back to life to protect his tribe from a Crow attack that is led by his lost son. A very unusual story of war, survival and love. The entire movie is spoken in the Cheyenne and Crow languages with English subtitles.

A: Trevor Howard, Nick Ramus, James Remar, Serene Hedin, Dusty Iron Wing McCrea, Silvana Gatlardo

© CBS/FOX VIDEO 6345

Children

Video's Best

1956 and After

Feature Films

20,000 LEAGUES UNDER THE SEA

G | FAN ACT CLD | 1954 | COLOR | Sex, Nud, ✓ Viol, Lang, AdSit

D: Richard Fleischer — 127 m

9 Marvelous adaptation by Disney of Jules Verne's fantasy adventure written in 1868. Both the film and the book are, and will remain, great fun and timeless. Amid fear created by rumors of a fierce monster ravaging the sea, a lone ship sets sail in a search to find it. On board is a scientist, his wimpy assistant (Lorre) and an adventurous harpooner (Douglas). Their ship is indeed attacked by the monster, but it is instead a submarine named the Nautilus, created and piloted by the mad genius Captain Nemo (Mason). Totally captivating with very high production values and superb special effects.

A: Kirk Douglas, James Mason, Peter Lorre, Paul Lukas, Robert J. Wilke, Carleton Young

© WALT DISNEY HOME VIDEO 015

3 WORLDS OF GULLIVER, THE

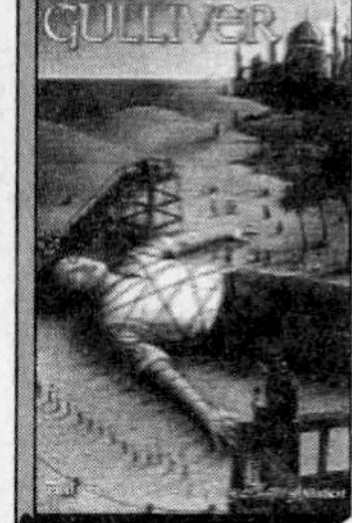

NR | FAN CLD | 1960 | COLOR | Sex, Nud, Viol, Lang, AdSit

D: Jack Sher — 100 m

7 This fanciful story, designed in the 18th century to be biting satire, is considerably toned down here. Now it is just good family entertainment. It is the story of Gulliver, who was swept overboard while at sea and washed ashore first on Lilliput, an island totally inhabited by very, very tiny people. Later Gulliver travels to another island, Brobdingnag, where the people are as much taller than Gulliver as he was than the Lilliputians. It's all done in live action through a trick photography process called dynavision. OK for everyone, but best for young children.

A: Kerwin Mathews, Jo Morrow, June Thorburn, Lee Patterson, Gregoire Aslan, Basil Sydney

© COLUMBIA TRISTAR HOME VIDEO 60924

5,000 FINGERS OF DR. T., THE

FAN CLD | 1953 | B&W | Sex, Nud, Viol, Lang, AdSit

D: Roy Rowland — 88 m

8 This fantasy was co-scripted by Dr. Seuss and was one of Hollywood's best fantasies, but it has been largely overlooked by the public. It is about a boy who hates his piano lessons and dreams about a cruel piano teacher (Conried) who keeps 500 boys locked up in his castle (500 boys X 10 fingers = 5000 fingers). He makes them practice day and night, playing on a piano with a huge keyboard. Also locked away in his dungeon are creatures who dared to play other instruments. The brave boy, with the help of a resourceful plumber, helps to destroy the evil Dr. T.

A: Peter Lind Hayes, Mary Healy, Tommy Rettig, Hans Conried

© COLUMBIA TRISTAR HOME VIDEO 90163

7 FACES OF DR. LAO

NR | FAN WST CLD | 1963 | COLOR | Sex, Nud, Viol, Lang, AdSit

D: George Pal — 101 m

9 Absolutely delightful and heartwarming fantasy. A small Old West town newspaper editor (Ericson) is trying to win the hand of a pretty widow (Eden) and fighting a lonely battle against a villain (O'Connell), who is trying to grab up all the land around. A truly strange helpmate arrives in the form of a mysterious and wise old Chinese magician named Dr. Lao (Randall). Dr. Lao is the proprietor of a traveling circus containing a fantastic array of wondrous sideshow creatures. Fabulous makeup and special effects. Randall is truly outstanding, playing multiple roles. Great fun for all.

A: Tony Randall, Barbara Eden, Arthur O'Connell, John Ericson, Lee Patrick, Noah Beery, Jr.

Distributed By MGM/UA Home Video M600667

7TH VOYAGE OF SINBAD, THE

G | FAN CLD | 1958 | COLOR | Sex, Nud, ✓ Viol, Lang, AdSit

D: Nathan Juran — 94 m

8 Flavorful Arabian Nights tale of Sinbad the Sailor. An evil wizard has shrunk the beautiful Princess (and Sinbad's true love) to only six inches high. In order to restore her, Sinbad must battle a giant bird, a giant cyclops, a dragon and a sword-wielding living skeleton. Wonderful special effects and a thrilling, well-paced, fanciful adventure story that will please both young and old alike. The stop motion animation created for this picture is still very highly regarded, and for years was held as the standard for the industry.

A: Kerwin Mathews, Kathryn Grant, Richard Eyer, Torin Thatcher

© COLUMBIA TRISTAR HOME VIDEO 60114

ABBOTT AND COSTELLO MEET DR. JEKYLL AND MR. HYDE

NR | COM CLD | 1952 | B&W | Sex, Nud, Viol, Lang, AdSit

D: Charles Lamont — 77 m

8 Here America's favorite silly duo from the 40s and 50s play two American Detectives in 1880s London, where they encounter Boris Karloff in the dual role of Jekyll and Hyde. This is one of their funniest movies. Don't miss it when Lou drinks a potion and gets turned into a mouse. Abbott and Costello learned their trade doing standup routines and short comedy skits on the Vaudeville stages. Bud Abbott is an everyman sort who plays straightman to the silly child-like antics of his short round partner, Lou Costello. They were hysterical on stage and also became big hits in the movie theaters of America.

A: Bud Abbott, Lou Costello, Boris Karloff, Craig Stevens

© MCA/UNIVERSAL HOME VIDEO, INC. 80010

ABBOTT AND COSTELLO MEET FRANKENSTEIN

NR | COM CLD | 1948 | B&W | Sex, Nud, Viol, Lang, AdSit

D: Charles Barton — 83 m

8 Fun mix of fright and laughs. Lou and Bud are railroad baggage clerks this time, who get in trouble when crates transporting monsters to the House of Horrors are discovered to be empty. So the twosome follow the monsters's trail to a secret island where they find Dracula (Lugosi) and the Frankenstein monster. Things get dicey for them when a mad scientist plans to put Lou's brain into the Frankenstein monster and the Wolfman (Chaney) wants them all. This is great comedy that works because the monsters always play their parts straight.

A: Bud Abbott, Lou Costello, Lon Chaney, Jr., Bela Lugosi, Lenore Aubert, Jane Randolph

© MCA/UNIVERSAL HOME VIDEO, INC. 55074

ABBOTT AND COSTELLO MEET THE INVISIBLE MAN

NR | COM | 1951

D: Charles Lamont — 83 m

6 Bud and Lou are have just graduated from private detective school when their first customer walks in the door. Tommy is a boxer who has been wrongly accused of murder and he needs their help to prove it. Just then the police arrive and poof, their new client has evaporated. He has injected himself with an experimental invisibility serum. Tommy convinces Lou that he should go undercover as a boxer to find the real killer. Pudgy little Lou will be "Lou the Looper" and invisible Tommy will supply the punches.

Sex / Nud / Viol / Lang / AdSit

A: Bud Abbott, Lou Costello, Nancy Gould, Arther Franz, Adele Jergens, Sheldon Leonard

© MCA/UNIVERSAL HOME VIDEO, INC. 80673

ABSENT-MINDED PROFESSOR, THE

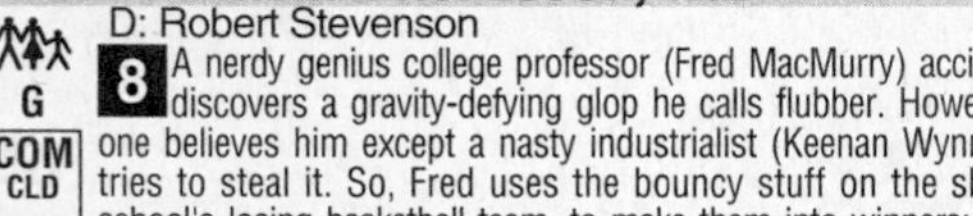

G | COM CLD | 1961 | B&W

D: Robert Stevenson — 96 m

8 A nerdy genius college professor (Fred MacMurry) accidentally discovers a gravity-defying glop he calls flubber. However, no one believes him except a nasty industrialist (Keenan Wynn), who tries to steal it. So, Fred uses the bouncy stuff on the shoes of school's losing basketball team, to make them into winners; and, in his old jalopy, to make it fly. Still great stuff for young kids, parents and maybe even a few teenagers.

Sex / Nud / Viol / Lang / AdSit

A: Fred MacMurray, Nancy Olson, Keenan Wynn, Tommy Kirk, Leon Ames, Ed Wynn

© WALT DISNEY HOME VIDEO 028

ACROSS THE GREAT DIVIDE

G | DMA CLD | 1977 | COLOR

D: Stewart Raffill — 102 m

6 A very well done children's film about the adventures of two orphans. While on their way to Oregon in 1876, the two young children are orphaned when their grandfather dies, but they decide that they must continue on by themselves to claim their family's land in Oregon. Along the way they stumble into a loveable old con man and the threesome adopt each other and continue to pursue their dream traveling through the beautiful and threatening mountains. Fun for young people. See also THE ADVENTURES OF THE WILDERNESS FAMILY and THE WILDERNESS FAMILY, PART 2.

Sex / Nud / Viol / Lang / AdSit

A: Robert Logan, George "Buck" Flower, Heather Rattray, Mark Edward Hall

© VIDEO TREASURES M206

ADVENTURES OF BARON MUNCHAUSEN, THE

PG | FAN COM CLD | 1989 | COLOR

D: Terry Gilliam — 122 m

7 Inside the walls of a city under siege by the armies of the Ottoman Empire, a small troupe of actors puts on a play about the infamous German Baron Munchausen, who had claimed to have had many wildly extravagant exploits. Their presentation is interrupted by an old soldier who claims that he is, in fact, the real Baron. Vowing that he will rescue the town, the old soldier departs in a rag-tag home-made hot air balloon, off to enlist the aid of his superhuman partners of old: the strongest man on earth, the man who can blow stronger than a hurricane, and the fastest man alive. Silly, light-hearted fantasy.

Sex / ✔ Nud / ✔ Viol / Lang / AdSit

A: John Neville, Robin Williams, Eric Idle, Oliver Reed, Sarah Polley, Uma Thurman

© COLUMBIA TRISTAR HOME VIDEO 50153

ADVENTURES OF HUCK FINN, THE

PG | DMA CLD | 1993 | COLOR

D: Stephen Sommers — 108 m

9 Wonderful adaptation of Mark Twain's classic adventure story set in the pre-Civil War South. Huck Finn is a fun-loving boy that is as wild as the river, but he has been taken in by the widow Douglas who has vowed to civilize him. However, his thieving father has come and stolen him back, so Huck has faked his own murder and run away. In the uproar, the household slave, and Huck's friend Jim, also runs away. Now everyone thinks that Jim has murdered Huck. Instead, they have joined up on a grand adventure down the river, which turns into a run for their lives. Fast-moving and funny. Never misses a beat.

Sex / Nud / ✔ Viol / ✔ Lang / AdSit

A: Elijah Wood, Courtney B. Vance, Robbie Coltrane, Jason Robards, Jr., Ron Pearlman, Dana Ivey

© WALT DISNEY HOME VIDEO 1896

ADVENTURES OF HUCKLEBERRY FINN, THE

NR | DMA CLD | 1939 | B&W

D: Richard Thorpe — 89 m

8 Mark Twain's classic story is given a pleasant Hollywood spin in this 1930's production (with Mickey Rooney) of an independent boy's wild and adventurous summer on the Mississippi River. Poor Huck Finn decides to get away form his bad-tempered father by faking his own death and running off down the Mississippi. A short way out on his journey he meets up with Jim. Jim is a slave who has also run away and is Huck's friend. Even though much of Twain's satire and wit are exchanged for sentimentality, this is still a rewarding viewing experience, especially for young people.

Sex / Nud / Viol / Lang / AdSit

A: Mickey Rooney, Walter Connolly, William Frawley, Rex Ingram, Lynne Carver, Jo Ann Sayers

Distributed By MGM/UA Home Video M500053

ADVENTURES OF HUCKLEBERRY

G | DMA CLD | 1960 | COLOR

D: Michael Curtiz — 108 m

7 Very good version of Twain's classic story with a very appealing cast. More true to Twain's original story than earlier films. An independent boy, Huckleberry Finn, and escaped slave, Jim, travel down the Mississippi River and get more adventure than they had counted on when they run into two con men who convince them that they are a king and duke. Eddie Hodges is appealing as Huck and famed boxer Archie Moore is a standout as Jim.

Sex / Nud / Viol / Lang / AdSit

A: Tony Randall, Eddie Hodges, Archie Moore, Patty McCormack, Neville Brand, Buster Keaton

Distributed By MGM/UA Home Video M201279

ADVENTURES OF MILO AND OTIS, THE

G | CLD | 1989 | COLOR

D: Masanori Hata — 76 m

8 Outstanding and extremely cute live-action children's story about two farmyard friends, a puppy and a kitten, who become lost in the forest. Together there, they encounter numerous adventures, overcoming all obstacles to eventually raise their own litters. Narrated by Dudley Moore. Wonderfully engaging entertainment for young people which took four years to complete and was extremely popular.

Sex / Nud / Viol / Lang / AdSit

A:

© COLUMBIA TRISTAR HOME VIDEO 50143

ADVENTURES OF THE WILDERNESS FAMILY, THE

G | DMA CLD | 1976 | COLOR

D: Stewart Raffill — 100 m

8 This is a very good, family-oriented human interest drama but is mostly geared for young people. An urban family escapes the city and pollution to the majestic wonders of nature for the sake of a sick daughter. There they build a cabin in the magnificent Rockies and brave the dangers of the wild. Lots of animals and scenery. See also WILDERNESS FAMILY, PART 2 and similar ACROSS THE GREAT DIVIDE.

Sex / Nud / Viol / Lang / AdSit

A: Robert Logan, Susan D. Shaw, Ham Larsen, Heather Rattray, George "Buck" Flower, William Cornford

© VIDEO TREASURES 9655

ADVENTURES OF TOM SAWYER, THE

NR | DMA CLD | 1938 | COLOR

D: Norman Taurog — 91 m

8 This is a good adaptation of the Mark Twain classic novel in which all of Tom's charm and cunning are left intact. It is a story of a boy who is being raised in a very proper home by a tough but loving aunt, in 1850s Missouri. However, he is also adventurous and mischievous sort who spends all his spare time with the rebellious and independent Huckleberry Finn, except for when he and Becky are chased through a cave by Injun Joe (Jory). Every boy ought to see this at least once, and many who used to be boys (also those who have had a great deal to do with boys) will also have a great time it.

Sex / Nud / ✔ Viol / Lang / AdSit

A: Tommy Kelly, Jackie Maran, Ann Gillis, May Robson, Walter Brennan, Victor Jory

© FOXVIDEO 8014

AGAINST A CROOKED SKY

G | WST CLD | 1975 | COLOR

D: Earl Bellamy — 90 m

6 Pretty good family Western. A boy begins a desperate search for his sister who was taken by Indians and is helped by a grizzled old trapper (Richard Boone). It is a pretty basic story line that has been used many times before, however this time it is squarely aimed at younger viewers. Still, even if you are a little older, if you are a Western fan, you will have a good time with it. However, this same premise was much more deeply explored, with much more mature themes, in the classic John Wayne picture THE SEARCHERS.

Sex / Nud / ✔ Viol / Lang / AdSit

A: Richard Boone, Clint Ritchie, Henry Wilcoxon, Stewart Peterson, Geoffrey Land, Jewel Blanch

© BRIDGESTONE PRODUCTION GROUP

AMAZING MR. BLUNDEN, THE

G | CLD | 1972 | COLOR

D: Lionel Jeffries — 100 m

7 Nice little family-oriented, unscary ghost story about a widow and her two children who move into an old house in 1918 London. The house is occupied by the ghost of a previous tenant, a lawyer from the 19th century. The widow and her kids agree to help him right a past wrong and to solve a mystery committed 100 years before by going back in time with him. Good well-rounded entertainment for the whole family.

Sex / Nud / Viol / Lang / AdSit

A: Laurence Naismith, Lynne Frederick, Garry Miller, Dorothy Alison, Diana Dors, Garry Miller

© MEDIA HOME ENTERTAINMENT, INC. M814

ANDRE

D: George Miller — 96 m

7 | PG | CLD | 1994 | COLOR | Viol

Set in a small Maine town in the early 60s, this is the mostly-true story of Andre, an utterly charming seal. The town's harbor master is an animal lover and one day he brings home a young motherless seal pup. Since the house is already full of animals, this new one fits right in too - especially with their little girl, Toni. Toni doesn't have many friends and so soon Andre has become her best friend. But, the fishing is bad this season and the fisherman blame the seals, so their family and Andre aren't very popular in town. However, Andre is such a charmer, that soon the town becomes famous because of him. Very sweet. Mostly for kids up to 12.

A: Keith Carradine, Tina Majorino, Keith Szarabajka, Joshua Jackson, Aidon Pendleton, Chelsea Field

© PARAMOUNT HOME VIDEO 33138

ANIMALS ARE BEAUTIFUL PEOPLE

D: Jamie Uys — 92 m

8 | G | DOC CLD | 1974 | COLOR

This fun documentary was made by the maker of THE GODS MUST BE CRAZY. It is a humorous and interesting review of the animals of the deserts and the jungles of Africa. It covers all the animals from the largest to the smallest using sharp portraits that remain interesting and do not become too cute. Examples include such things as the mother fish who hides her babies in her mouth, and the "good time" that some elephants and other animals have when they eat the well-fermented Marula tree berries.

A:

© WARNER HOME VIDEO 11105

ANNIE

D: John Huston — 128 m

8 | PG | MUS CLD | 1982 | COLOR

The comic strip story of the little orphan girl with the perpetual optimism comes to life. Annie (Quinn) is a red-haired orphan girl who dreams of life outside the orphanage, but her plans to escape are constantly foiled by Miss Hannigan, the drunken head mistress (Burnett). One day Annie is chosen to go to live for a short time with hugely rich Daddy Warbucks (Finney). They hit it off and days become weeks. But Miss Hannigan continues to plot to get her back. Big, splashy and over-produced, but it's still all there and it's fine family entertainment.

A: Albert Finney, Carol Burnett, Aileen Quinn, Bernadette Peters, Tim Curry, Geoffrey Holder

© COLUMBIA TRISTAR HOME VIDEO 60127

APPLE DUMPLING GANG, THE

D: Norman Tokar — 100 m

8 | G | CLD | 1975 | COLOR

Walt Disney Western, mostly for kids. Bixby is a bachelor gambler who finds himself unwillingly inheriting three children. The kids find a huge gold nugget in an old mine and decide to protect themselves from the greedy townspeople by faking the robbery of the gold with the help of a couple of bumbling would-be outlaws, Knox and Conway. But things get overly exciting when a real gang trys to steal it first.

A: Bill Bixby, Susan Clark, Don Knotts, Tim Conway, David Wayne, Slim Pickens

© WALT DISNEY HOME VIDEO 018

BABY...SECRET OF THE LOST LEGEND

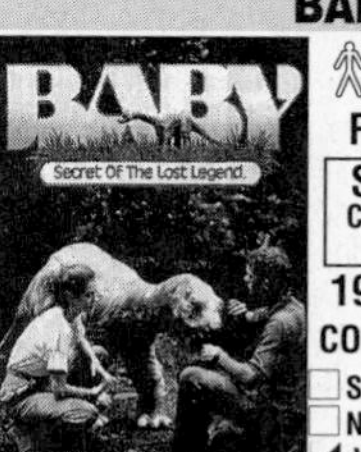

D: B.W.L. Norton — 92 m

6 | PG | SF CLD | 1985 | COLOR | Viol, Lang

A brontosaurus family is found hidden away in modern Africa by a zoologist (Sean Young) and her husband (William Katt). However, the scientist pair are soon forced to become the dinosaur's protectors when they become threatened by a bad-guy scientist Patrick McGoohan. The papa dinosaur is killed and the mama is kidnapped, so Young and Katt must protect the baby until they can reunite it with its mama. Some pretty good special effects make for cute and irresistable dinosaurs. But, there is also a touch of sex in an attempt to attract an older audience than just kids.

A: William Katt, Sean Young, Patrick McGoohan, Julian Fellows, Kyalo Mativo

© TOUCHSTONE HOME VIDEO 269V

BAKER'S HAWK

D: Lyman Dayton — 98 m

7 | G | CLD | 1976 | COLOR

Fine family entertainment. It is 1876 and a young boy's father (Clint Walker) has taken an unpopular stand against a group of vigilantes in a small town. He and his whole family have become ostracized by all the townsfolk. But, one day, the lonely boy rescues a small red-tailed hawk from a fox. He and an old hermit (Ives) nurse the hawk back to health, tame him and train him to become a hunting bird. This is a warm and interesting story with a good message: it's OK to be different. Filmed in the beautiful mountains of Utah.

A: Clint Walker, Burl Ives, Diane Baker, Lee H. Montgomery, Alan Young, Taylor Lacher

© BRIDGESTONE PRODUCTION GROUP

BATTERIES NOT INCLUDED

D: Matthew Robbins — 107 m

7 | PG | CLD | 1987 | COLOR

When a group of poor and elderly tenants who occupy an ancient apartment building in New York are faced with eviction because their tenement is scheduled for destruction, they get help from a most unusual source - a "family" of loveable tiny little flying saucers. Predictable, but sweet. An enjoyable kid's fantasy from Stephen Spielberg.

A: Hume Cronyn, Jessica Tandy, Frank McRae, Elizabeth Pena, Michael Carmine, Dennis Boutsikaris

© MCA/UNIVERSAL HOME VIDEO, INC. 80770

BEAR, THE

D: Jean-Jacques Annaud — 92 m

9 | PG | DMA CLD | 1989 | COLOR | Viol

Excellent family entertainment that was roundly praised by critics and loved by audiences. It is a big-budget movie that took several years to film and is the story, set in 1885 British Columbia, of a huge injured kodiak bear that adopts an orphaned cub. Fearing gunfire from approaching hunters, the two flee across a vast expanse of beautiful but foreboding wilderness. But in the end, the bears still must face the hunter. This is not a schmaltzy Disney knock-off. This is special. Adults will enjoy this as much as the kids.

A: Tcheky Karyo, Jack Wallace

© COLUMBIA TRISTAR HOME VIDEO 70213

BEDKNOBS AND BROOMSTICKS

D: Robert Stevenson — 112 m

8 | G | CLD | 1971 | COLOR

Lively animated Disney favorite. Three kids have come to live with nanny Angela Lansbury. They aren't too excited about the prospect until they learn that she is a witch-in-training. She has enrolled in the Correspondence College of Witchcraft so she can help the Allies ward off the Nazi invasion of England during WWII. The four of them and a gentleman friend, engage in grand adventure when she transports them all to the land of Naboombu on her magic bed. There they meet all varieties of talking cartoon animals. Effective combined use of animation and live action won an Oscar.

A: Angela Lansbury, David Tomlinson, Roddy McDowall, Sam Jaffe, Roy Snart, Cindy O'Callaghan

© WALT DISNEY HOME VIDEO 016

BEETHOVEN

D: Brian Levant — 87 m

8 | G | CLD | 1992 | COLOR

Charles Grodin has a wife, three kids and a 185-pound Saint Bernard named Beethoven. Beethoven worms his way into the hearts of the three kids and the wife, but is never quite so successful with Grodin. Beethoven slobbers, he chews, he digs and he slobbers. But when Beethoven becomes the object of the evil plans of a villainous veterinarian (Jones), Grodin realizes he loves Beethoven too, and saves the hairy hound from disaster. Kids will really enjoy all the sight gags, but parents will likely get tired of it.

A: Charles Grodin, Dean Jones, Oliver Platt, Stanley Tucci, Christopher Castille

© MCA/UNIVERSAL HOME VIDEO, INC. 81222

BEETHOVEN'S 2ND

D: Rod Daniel — 89 m

8 | PG | CLD COM | 1993 | COLOR

One of those rare sequels that is better than the original, at least most adults will think so. Beethoven is back, but the doggie drool quotient is way down. The dependence upon silliness and gross jokes has been replaced with interesting characters and situations. Much of the story is told from Beethoven's point of view. While on a stroll in the park one day, Beethoven spied his true love and four of the cutest puppies ever born. But, when the snarling owner of the new bride threatens to drown the furballs, Charles Grodin's kids decide to hide them in the basement, without telling Dad. This video is one the parents will enjoy right along with their kids.

A: Charles Grodin, Bonnie Hunt, Nicholle Tom, Christopher Castile, Sarah Rose Karr, Debi Mazar

© MCA/UNIVERSAL HOME VIDEO, INC. 81608

BELLBOY, THE

D: Jerry Lewis — 72 m

6 | NR | COM CLD | 1960 | COLOR

Jerry Lewis at his silliest. Jerry is a ridiculous bellboy who fouls up everything at a ritzy Miami Beach hotel. What other bellboy in the world, when told to bring everything from the trunk of a Volkswagen, would remove the engine and take it up to their room. The film is a non-stop series of sight gags and slapstick. Young kids and Jerry Lewis fans will enjoy themselves.

A: Jerry Lewis, Alex Gerry, Bob Clayton, Sonnie Sands, Bill Richman

© VIDEO TREASURES 9740

BENIKER GANG, THE

D: Ken Kwapis — 87 m

G | CLD DMA | 1984 | COLOR

7 Heartwarming made-for-TV film about five orphans in an orphanage who have formed their own unorthodox family and are determined to stay together no matter what. The five even conspire to find ways to ward off potential parents. But when the family is finally threatened with breakup because of adoptions that can't be avoided, they all run off together and the oldest ghostwrites an advice column to support them all. This is actually quite well-done and not overly-sweet, as you might expect. A real sleeper.

Sex / Nud / Viol / Lang / AdSit

A: Andrew McCarthy, Jennie Dundas, Danny Dintanro, Charles Fields, Jeff Alan-Lee

© WARNER HOME VIDEO 223

BENJI

Benji
"The most entertaining family picture of our time. Maybe of all time."

D: Joe Camp — 87 m

G | CLD | 1973 | COLOR

9 This is a simple but totally endearing story about a small and unassuming mutt, Benji, who outwits the kidnappers of two small children. In appreciation, the kids and their family adopt him. Viewers are all the more charmed by Benji because the story is told entirely from his dog's-eye-view vantage point. Excellent family entertainment that was a big theater hit. Kids just loved this movie. It was the first of what became a long string of sequels. See also BENJI, THE HUNTED; FOR THE LOVE OF BENJI and OH, HEAVENLY DOG!

Sex / Nud / Viol / Lang / AdSit

A: Peter Breck, Cynthia Smith, Christopher Connelly, Patsy Garrett, Mark Slade, Debra Walley

© BEST FILM & VIDEO CORP. 122

BENJI, THE HUNTED

Disney's
Benji the Hunted
"The first guaranteed don't-miss-it movie of the year!"

D: Joe Camp — 89 m

G | CLD | 1987 | COLOR

8 Good family entertainment. The extremely popular all-American hero dog, Benji, again stars. This time Benji adopts four cute orphaned cougar cubs and he protects them from bears, wolves, foxes and eagles. This movie is mostly for kids but it manages to warm even older hearts. See the original, BENJI, and the other sequels too.

Sex / Nud / Viol / Lang / AdSit

A: Red Stegall, Joe Camp, Steve Zanollini, Karen Thorndike, Frank Inn, Nancy Francis

© WALT DISNEY HOME VIDEO 594

BIG TOP PEE-WEE

D: Randal Kleiser — 86 m

PG | CLD COM | 1988 | COLOR

6 Farmer Pee-wee comes out of his cellar to find a circus has pitched its tent in his backyard. He decides to join up - but first he has to develop his own act. He also falls for the pretty trapeze artist Golino, much to the dismay of his girlfriend Miller. It's a simple story and there are some weak spots, but the kids will like it - even if it isn't up to the much better PEE-WEE'S BIG ADVENTURE.

Sex / Nud / Viol / Lang / AdSit

A: Pee-wee Herman, Kris Kristofferson, Valeria Golino, Penelope Ann Miller, Susan Tyrrell, Albert Henderson

© PARAMOUNT HOME VIDEO 32076

BLACKBEARD'S GHOST

D: Robert Stevenson — 106 m

G | CLD | 1968 | COLOR

7 The famous pirate ghost Blackbeard (Ustinov) has been cursed to wander the earth until he can perform one good deed. Then the unfortunate pirate is accidentally conjured up by track coach Dean Jones and finally gets his chance for redemption when he decides to help Dean coach his perpetually losing track team. While it is true that Blackbeard does have a definite lack of knowledge about some of the finer points of the sport, he does have opportunities which are denied the ordinary mortal man - since he can be invisible. Plenty of slapstick and some interesting special effects. A good time, especially for the younger set.

Sex / Nud / Viol / Lang / AdSit

A: Peter Ustinov, Dean Jones, Suzanne Pleshette, Elsa Lanchester, Joby Baker, Elliott Reid

© WALT DISNEY HOME VIDEO 062

BLACK BEAUTY

D: James Hill — 105 m

G | DMA CLD | 1971 | B&W

7 This is the beloved classic children's story of a young boy's relentless quest in Victorian England to find his missing black colt as it passes from owner to owner, until once again it is back home with him. It will definitely hold a kid's attention throughout and will likely hold the attention of many adults, too. Plus, it quite probably will also bring a tear to everyone's eye.

Sex / Nud / Viol / Lang / AdSit

A: Mark Lester, Walter Slezak, Peter Lee Lawrence, Ursla Glas

© PARAMOUNT HOME VIDEO 8079

BLACK BEAUTY

D: Caroline Thompson — 881 m

G | CLD | 1994 | COLOR

8 Anna Sewell's classic 1877 novel is once again brought to the screen. There have been several animated versions and another feature film done in 1971, but this one is especially well done. It will certainly hold the attention of any child between 6 and 16, and it will not insult nor bore most older watchers either. Told from the horse's point of view and "in his own voice," this is the story of a beautiful horse who was born into a caring environment. But at age three, when the family is faced with hard times, he is sold. Beauty tells his own tale of the hard years and the many owners he has until once again, years later he can return to the family that loves him.

Sex / Nud / Viol / Lang / AdSit

A: Sean Bean, David Thewlis, Jim Carter, Peter Davison, Alun Armstrong, John McEnery

© WARNER HOME VIDEO 14400

BLACK STALLION, THE

D: Carroll Ballard — 117 m

G | DMA CLD | 1979 | COLOR

9 The wonderful and moving story of a boy and his relationship with a beautiful black Arabian stallion. The two were stranded together on a desert island after a shipwreck. They have become best friends and, after they are rescued, the horse goes home with the boy. The primary thrust of the story is upon the training and racing of his horse, with the help of a wise old horse trainer (Mickey Rooney). One of the best children's films ever, and fun for adults, too. It proved to be so popular that it was followed with THE BLACK STALLION RETURNS.

Sex / Nud / Viol / Lang / AdSit

A: Kelly Reno, Mickey Rooney, Teri Garr, Clarence Huse, Hoyt Axton

Distributed By MGM/UA Home Video M201604

BLACK STALLION RETURNS, THE

D: Robert Dalva — 105 m

PG | DMA CLD | 1983 | COLOR

8 Rousing sequel to THE BLACK STALLION. When the black stallion is stolen back by an Arab chieftain and taken to the Sahara, Kelly Reno, now a teenager, goes there to get him back. In his ordeal to get his friend back, he has to travel across miles of hot desert sands and deal with not always friendly local tribesmen. Pretty good action scenes, particularly the big race climax scene. This is not a cheap rip-off of the original. It is good in its own right. But still, it doesn't quite have the same magic as the original. Excellent family entertainment.

Sex / Nud / Viol / Lang / AdSit

A: Kelly Reno, Vincent Spano, Teri Garr, Allen Garfield, Woody Strode, Jodi Thelen

Distributed By MGM/UA Home Video M201864

BORN FREE

D: James Hill — 95 m

NR | DMA CLD | 1966 | COLOR

9 This is an exceptional film with universal appeal. It is also a true story. Elsa, a young lioness, is one of three lion cubs who are raised in captivity by two Kenyan game wardens after they are forced to kill the cub's parents. The wardens want Elsa to be free when she is grown. So, as Elsa matures, they have to teach her how to survive on her own in the wilderness. This is a true family film and not just for the young kids. Immensely popular upon its release, it has lost none of its charm over time. The title song won an Oscar and was also a significant pop hit.

Sex / Nud / Viol / Lang / AdSit

A: Virginia McKenna, Bill Travers, Geoffrey Keen, Peter Lukoye

© COLUMBIA TRISTAR HOME VIDEO 60142

BOYS' TOWN

D: Norman Taurog — 94 m

NR | DMA CLD | 1938 | B&W

8 Boys' Town is a real-life home for orphans and juvenile delinquents in Nebraska, that has now been in existence for many years. Their motto is: "There's no such thing as a bad boy." This is the dramatized story of how Boys' Town was started by the real-life Father Flanagan. Spencer Tracy won an Oscar playing Flanagan in his struggle to find a home for, and give a second chance to, the boys that society was just throwing away. Mickey Rooney, as tough guy Whitey Marsh, is one of his toughest jobs. A little syrupy sweet and sentimental, but still a very rewarding film.

Sex / Nud / Viol / Lang / AdSit

A: Spencer Tracy, Mickey Rooney, Henry Hull, Leslie Fenton, Addison Richards, Edward Norris

Distributed By MGM/UA Home Video M203851

BRAVE ONE, THE

D: Irving Rapper — 100 m

CLD | 1956 | COLOR

8 This is an endearing story of a young Mexican peasant boy and his pet bull, Gitano. Gitano has been the boy's friend since the moment he was born. But, Gitano has now grown into a beautiful fighting bull and so is sold to fight in the bull ring in Mexico City. However, the boy is not about to let his best friend die in the ring, so he begins his quest to rescue him. This was a winner of an Academy Award for Best Original Story. It is a heartwarming story that all kids will love - and a lot of adults will, too.

Sex / Nud / Viol / Lang / AdSit

A: Michel Ray, Rodolfo Hoyos, Elsa Cardenas, Joi Lansing

© VIDEO COMMUNICATIONS, INC. 1010

BRIGHT EYES

D: David Butler — 90 m

NR | CLD | 1934 | B&W

7 This near-classic children's drama finds Shirley Temple being the daughter of a maid in a large mansion. She lives with her mother at the mansion and puts up with the spoiled bratty daughter of the house. However, she mostly enjoys spending her time down at the air strip. Then, when her mother dies in a car wreck, poor Shirley becomes the object of a custody battle between the millionaire and a pilot at the airstrip who is her godfather and was her father's friend. This was the first movie to be designed just for Shirley and she charms everyone by singing "On the Good Ship Lollipop."

Sex / Nud / Viol / Lang / AdSit

A: Shirley Temple, James Dunn, Jane Withers, Judith Allen, Lois Wilson

© FOXVIDEO 1699

CANDLESHOE

D: Norman Tokar — 101 m

G | CLD | 1978 | COLOR

7 Fun Disney slapstick. Con man Leo McKern tries to pass off a poor orphaned street urchin (Jodie Foster) as being Helen Hayes's long-lost grand-daughter, so he can gain access to a Candleshoe, a stately English manor where there is supposed to be fortune in Spanish doubloons hidden away. David Niven is Hayes's faithful butler who uses a lot of different disguises to hide the fact that Hayes is actually broke. However, they all find true riches when they all become a family. Fun for the whole family.

Sex / Nud / Viol / Lang / AdSit

A: David Niven, Helen Hayes, Jodie Foster, Leo McKern, Veronica Quiligan

© WALT DISNEY HOME VIDEO 078

CANTERVILLE GHOST, THE

D: Jules Dassin — 96 m

NR | COM CLD | 1944 | COLOR

7 Pleasant enough little story about a cowardly ghost, played wonderfully by Charles Laughton, who was buried alive 300 years earlier by his own father because he was a coward. Now he is trapped into haunting the castle and doomed to stay there until one of his descendants performs a deed of bravery. Unfortunately for him, everyone in his long line has proven to be a coward too, and he fears he will never be free. Now it is WWII and a far distant nephew (Young) of his is billeted in the castle with his buddies. Is this the chance he's been waiting for?

Sex / Nud / Viol / Lang / AdSit

A: Charles Laughton, Margaret O'Brien, William Gargan, Rags Ragland, Una O'Connor, Robert Young

Distributed By MGM/UA Home Video M201873

CAPTAIN JANUARY

D: David Butler — 76 m

NR | MUS CLD | 1936 | B&W

7 Shirley Temple is at her sympathetic best as an orphan who lives with a lighthouse keeper. Captain January (Kibbee) rescued her from a shipwreck when she was just a baby. She is now a happy 4-year-old and is the sweetheart of all the fisherman in the neighborhood. But a new truant officer has moved to town and wants to take Shirley away to put her in a proper home.

Sex / Nud / Viol / Lang / AdSit

A: Shirley Temple, Guy Kibbee, Slim Summerville, Buddy Ebsen

© FOXVIDEO 1068

CAPTAINS COURAGEOUS

D: Victor Fleming — 118 m

G | DMA ACT CLD | 1937 | B&W

10 Wonderful adaptation of Rudyard Kipling's classic story. A spoiled rich kid (Bartholomew) falls overboard from an ocean liner, is rescued by a Portuguese fisherman (Spencer Tracy) and is brought on board a New England fishing schooner. He demands to be taken back to land but instead has to stay at sea for the balance of the 3-month fishing trip. For the first time in his life, he has to earn his keep. He is put to work along side Mickey Rooney, gets a few lessons in humility from Tracy and gradually is transformed. Excellent! A true treat for everyone! Tracy won Best Actor Oscar.

Sex / Nud / Viol / Lang / AdSit

A: Spencer Tracy, Freddie Bartholomew, Lionel Barrymore, Melvyn Douglas, Mickey Rooney, John Carradine

Distributed By MGM/UA Home Video M500058

CASEY'S SHADOW

D: Martin Ritt — 117 m

PG | COM DMA CLD | 1977 | COLOR

7 Enjoyable old-time family fare. Walter Matthau is a ne'er-do-well and impoverished Cajun horse trainer whose wife has left him to raise their three sons by himself. Matthau is a simple man whose modest dream is to train a winning racehorse, but it is a dream he wants more than almost anything. He and his boys are grooming a quarter horse that the boys love, named Casey's Shadow for a million dollar race -- even though the wealthy owner Alexis Smith only wants to sell him. When the horse's leg is hurt just before the big race and even though the vet and his boys don't want the horse to race, Matthau enters the horse. Matthau almost single-handedly carries this movie.

Sex / Nud / Viol / Lang / AdSit

A: Walter Matthau, Andrew Rubin, Stephen Burns, Alexis Smith, Robert Webber, Murray Hamilton

© COLUMBIA TRISTAR HOME VIDEO 60153

CHAMP, THE

D: King Vidor — 87 m

NR | DMA CLD | 1931 | B&W

8 Top-notch tearjerker, winner of two Oscars plus a Best Picture nomination. Wallace Beery won an Oscar as the loveable washed-up ex-boxer who has nothing at all, except the unending adoration of his son. The two of them live in a dive in Tijuana where he is constantly "in training" for a come back, that is, when he is in between drinking binges or not gambling away their money. Now the mother, who abandoned them both, has come back and wants to take the boy away. A simple story, unashamedly sentimental, but one of the most effective and heartwarming tearjerkers of all time. A treasure.

Sex / Nud / Viol / Lang / AdSit

A: Wallace Beery, Jackie Cooper, Irene Rich, Roscoe Ates, Edward Brophy, Hale Hamilton

Distributed By MGM/UA Home Video M301665

CHAMP, THE

D: Franco Zeffirelli — 121 m

PG | DMA CLD | 1979 | COLOR

7 Sentimental remake of the 1931 Wallace Beery/Jackie Cooper classic, this time set at a Florida racetrack. Billy Flynn is an alcoholic ex-prize fighter who keeps promising his young son that he will one day again become champ, but instead he drinks and is perpetually broke. After seven years, the boy's now-wealthy mother sees him again and challenges Billy for custody of the boy. Billy now desperately needs to attempt a real come back so he can keep his son, even though the doctor says it will kill him. Not up to the original but still jerks plenty of tears. Very young Schroder is outstanding.

Sex / Nud / Viol / Lang / AdSit

A: Jon Voight, Faye Dunaway, Ricky Schroder, Jack Warden

Distributed By MGM/UA Home Video M600034

CHEETAH

D: Jeff Blyth — 83 m

G | CLD | 1989 | COLOR

7 Disney story about two California teenagers who are forced to give up MTV so they can go to Kenya for the summer with their scientist parents. There they meet and befriend a Masai boy. They teach him video games, and he shows them the ways of the wild. Together, the three of them find and adopt an orphaned cheetah cub which they raise as a pet, until it is stolen away by gamblers. The two kids from the city set out to get the cub back, and their African friend has to set out to find them. Quite good, entertainment for whole family.

Sex / Nud / Viol / Lang / AdSit

A: Keith Coogan, Lucy Deakins, Collin Mothupi

© WALT DISNEY HOME VIDEO 912

CHITTY CHITTY BANG BANG

D: Kenneth Hughes — 147 m

G | MUS CLD | 1968 | COLOR

7 This very lavish musical was based upon a book by Ian Fleming. Dick Van Dyke plays an inventor with two children who creates a magical flying automobile. On a trip to the beach, he, his girlfriend and the children are all kidnapped into a magical world. It is dominated by the evil Baron Bomburst and his child-hating wife, who has kidnapped the children. With the help of a toymaker (Benny Hill), Dick seeks to rescue the kids. This picture cost a huge amount of money for its time ($10,000,000) and was supposed to be more of a family picture, but really is most appealing to smaller children.

Sex / Nud / Viol / Lang / AdSit

A: Dick Van Dyke, Sally Ann Howes, Anna Quayle, Lionel Jeffries, Benny Hill

Distributed By MGM/UA Home Video M201647

CHRISTMAS STORY, A

D: Bob Clark — 95 m

PG | COM CLD | 1983 | COLOR

9 Absolutely delightful story about growing up. Humorist Jean Sheperd relates a warmly comic story from his childhood in the 1940s, about his single-minded driving obsession with getting a Genuine Red Ryder Carbine Action Two Hundred Shot Lightning Loader BB rifle for Christmas - in spite of his mother's desperate concerns that he might put someone's eye out. Sheperd narrates the whimsical storyline himself and he is played wonderfully by Billingsley. An absolute and total delight for both young and old.

Sex / Nud / Viol / Lang / AdSit

A: Peter Billingsley, Darren McGavin, Melinda Dillon, Ian Petrella, Scott Schwartz, Tedde Moore

Distributed By MGM/UA Home Video M800446

CINDERFELLA

D: Jerry Lewis — 88 m

NR | COM CLD | 1960 | COLOR

6 Silly Jerry Lewis farce. The well-known children's fairy tale is rewritten to have wacky Ed Wynn become Jerry Lewis's godfather and save Jerry from his wicked stepmother and stepbrothers. Pretty weak over all, but children and Jerry Lewis fans will likely be entertained.

Sex / Nud / Viol / Lang / AdSit

A: Jerry Lewis, Ed Wynn, Anna Maria Alberghetti

© VIDEO TREASURES SV9741

CLASH OF THE TITANS

D: Desmond Davis 118 m

PG | DMA FAN CLD | 1981 | COLOR

8 Ancient Greek mythology is given life by some pretty good special effects and a big-name cast. The hero Perseus (Hamlin), son of Zeus (Olivier), must battle magic, monsters and the gods to save beautiful Andromeda (Bowker) from danger and to win her hand. Special effects are the real stars, however, particularly the flying horse Pegasus and Medusa, the woman with hair of snakes who can turn you to stone if you look at her.

☐ Sex ☐ Nud ◢ Viol ☐ Lang ◢ AdSit

A: Laurence Olivier, Harry Hamlin, Judi Bowker, Burgess Meredith, Maggie Smith

Distributed By MGM/UA Home Video M700074

CLOAK & DAGGER

D: Richard Franklin 101 m

PG | SUS CLD | 1984 | COLOR

7 A young computer whiz kid (Thomas) plays Cloak & Dagger games in which he is a secret agent with his imaginary superhero playmate (Coleman). However, one day Thomas gets involved in a real-life spy drama and witnesses a real murder, but Coleman (also cast as the boy's father), having been fooled before, does not believe him and thinks that this is just another of the boy's imaginary games. The whiz kid can not get Dad to believe that what he saw was real and is on his own. Suspenseful and fastpaced. Suitable for young people, but also of real interest to adults, too. Actually, a remake of THE WINDOW (1949).

☐ Sex ☐ Nud ☐ Viol ☐ Lang ☐ AdSit

A: Henry Thomas, Dabney Coleman, Michael Murphy, Christina Nigra, John McIntire, Jeanette Nolan

© MCA/UNIVERSAL HOME VIDEO, INC. 80124

CRICKET IN TIMES SQUARE

D: Chuck Jones 30 m

NR | CLD | 1973 | COLOR

9 This is a "Parent's Choice" award winner. It is a wonderful Chuck Jones (the ace cartoon veteran who created Roadrunner, Bugs Bunny, etc.) production about a country cricket named Chester who finds himself in the big unfriendly city of New York. Chester is a very different sort of cricket because he has a special talent. His wings sound like a beautiful violin when he rubs them together. Chester, with the help of his friends Tucker the mouse and Harry the cat, uses his unique talent to calm the jangled nerves of the frantic city. Delightful tale for the whole family.

☐ Sex ☐ Nud ☐ Viol ☐ Lang ☐ AdSit

A:

© LIVE HOME VIDEO 21152

DARBY O'GILL AND THE LITTLE PEOPLE

D: Robert Stevenson 90 m

G | COM CLD FAN | 1959 | COLOR

9 Wonderful fantasy about an an old caretaker at a wealthy Irish estate, Darby O'Gill, who falls into a well and discovers the leprechaun king. Darby tricks the king into granting him three wishes, but he soon wishes he hadn't. Poor old Darby has such a reputation for blarney that no one believes his preposterous tale, and the larcenous king has tricked him into wasting two wishes. Then comes a young Sean Connery, who has come to the estate to replace him, so he and his daughter are also about to lose their home. It is a magical tale with neat special effects. Among Disney's very best.

☐ Sex ☐ Nud ☐ Viol ☐ Lang ☐ AdSit

A: Albert Sharpe, Janet Munro, Sean Connery, Jimmy O'Dea, Kieron Moore, Estelle Winwood

© WALT DISNEY HOME VIDEO 038

D.A.R.Y.L

D: Simon Wincer 100 m

PG | SF FAN CLD | 1985 | COLOR

8 Charming story about a childless urban couple who adopt an apparently amnesiatic ten-year-old. He is a perfect child. He is a math whiz, works wonders with video games, is the hero of the baseball team and he changes their lives. But D.A.R.Y.L. is really an advanced robot... so advanced that he has developed human feelings. He has run away from the government program that created him and now the government wants him back. A delightful fantasy which will be entertaining for the whole family.

☐ Sex ☐ Nud ◢ Viol ◢ Lang ☐ AdSit

A: Barret Oliver, Mary Beth Hurt, Michael McKean, Josef Sommer, Kathryn Walker

© PARAMOUNT HOME VIDEO 1810

DAVY CROCKETT AND THE RIVER PIRATES

D: Norman Foster 81 m

G | CLD WST | 1956 | COLOR

8 This is the second of the Disney feature films which were produced directly from the immensely popular TV episodes. This time Davy takes a raft down the river to New Orleans and runs smack dab into adventure. He has to fight dangerous rapids, Indians and river pirates. He also takes on the famous river pirate Big Mike Fink in a keelboat river race, which was the inspiration for the ride "Mike Fink Keelboats" at Disneyland. This was a wonderful series that will capture the imaginations of today's boys, just as it did yesterday's - but is also fun for the whole family. Disney at his best. Also see the original: DAVY CROCKETT, KING OF THE WILD FRONTIER.

☐ Sex ☐ Nud ◢ Viol ☐ Lang ☐ AdSit

A: Fess Parker, Buddy Ebsen, Jeff York, Clem Bevins, Irvin Ashkenazy, Kenneth Tobey

© WALT DISNEY HOME VIDEO 027

DAVY CROCKETT, KING OF THE WILD FRONTIER

D: Norman Foster 93 m

NR | WST CLD ACT | 1955 | COLOR

8 Originally filmed as TV episodes, the Davy Crockett series created a huge national phenomenon. Disney's initial three episodes were so popular that they were again released as this feature film. In it, Davy and his sidekick George Russell (Ebsen) fight their way through Indians, assorted bad guys, the US Congress and eventually arrive at the Alamo. Rousing fun for the whole family. Followed by DAVY CROCKETT AND THE RIVER PIRATES.

☐ Sex ☐ Nud ☐ Viol ☐ Lang ☐ AdSit

A: Fess Parker, Buddy Ebsen, Basil Ruysdael, Hans Conried, William Bakewell, Kenneth Tobey

© WALT DISNEY HOME VIDEO 014

DAYDREAMER, THE

D: Jules Bass 80 m

G | CLD | 1966 | COLOR

7 This is a pleasing story of Hans Christian Andersen, the famous children's storyteller. It is set when he was just a 13-year-old boy and in it he meets many of the fairy tale characters he will later write about. There is a wide cast of top-name talent playing all the parts and the film's format mixes puppets in with live action to tell the stories of: "The Emperor's New Clothes" - where a little boy is the only one to speak up against a lie; and, "The Little Mermaid" - who wants so badly to become human. Very entertaining, especially for kids.

☐ Sex ☐ Nud ☐ Viol ☐ Lang ☐ AdSit

A: Ray Bolger, Jack Gilford, Margaret Hamilton, Paul O'Keefe, Boris Karloff, Victor Borge

© NEW LINE HOME VIDEO 2064

DELICATE DELINQUENT, THE

D: Don McGuire 101 m

NR | COM CLD | 1957 | B&W

7 Jerry Lewis plays a bumbling janitor who pals around with juvenile delinquents. He joins the police force, with the help of Darren McGavin, but he is such a goofball that he has a hard time proving himself. This was Jerry's first effort after he split from Dean Martin, and it is one of his best efforts. It is also sentimental and contains the requisite assortment of Lewis slapstick and silliness.

☐ Sex ☐ Nud ☐ Viol ☐ Lang ☐ AdSit

A: Jerry Lewis, Martha Hyer, Darren McGavin, Horace McMahon, Milton Frome

© PARAMOUNT HOME VIDEO 5613

DENNIS THE MENACE

D: Nick Castle 101 m

PG | CLD | 1993 | COLOR

6 This pleasant-enough movie is based upon the famous 41-year-old (at the time of release) comic strip character by Hank Ketcham. Dennis is always getting into trouble. He doesn't mean anybody any harm but that doesn't stop the troubles from coming - particularly to Dennis's grumpy old neighbor, Mr. Wilson. In this film, Dennis's folks have to leave town and the kindly Mrs. Wilson, much to the regret of Mr. Wilson, agrees to take Dennis in. However, Mr. Wilson is not the only one to get nailed by Dennis. Dennis takes on an escaped criminal who should have stayed in jail. Well acted, but uninspired. Best for kids.

☐ Sex ☐ Nud ◢ Viol ☐ Lang ☐ AdSit

A: Walter Matthau, Christopher Lloyd, Joan Plowright, Lea Thompson, Mason Bamble, Robert Stanton

© WARNER HOME VIDEO 17000

DICK TRACY

D: Warren Beatty 105 m

PG | ACT CRM FAN | 1990 | COLOR

7 Cartoon-like megabuck production that is a parody of the famous long-running comic-strip hero. There is a terrific line-up of major actors, however some are almost unrecognizable under makeup. (Al Pacino is despicable as the main villain who plans to unite all the bad guys. Madonna is marvelously vampy as Breathless Mahoney. Glenne Headly is lovely as Tracy's (Beatty) love interest.) Tracy rises to challenge the bad guys, but has trouble with his personal life. Plenty of shoot-'em-up action, against an unreal cartoon-like backdrop. Pretty good fun, not wonderful.

☐ Sex ☐ Nud ◢ Viol ☐ Lang ◢ AdSit

A: Warren Beatty, Madonna, Al Pacino, Dustin Hoffman, Mandy Patinkin, Paul Sorvino

© TOUCHSTONE HOME VIDEO 1066

DISORDERLY ORDERLY, THE

D: Frank Tashlin 90 m

NR | COM CLD | 1964 | COLOR

7 One of Jerry Lewis's best solo vehicles. Jerry is trying to earn money for medical school by working as a clumsy orderly in a hospital. Full of clever slapstick routines and sight gags. Jerry has one particular problem that is certainly going to be a major hindrance in learning to become a doctor: when people describe their pains, he begins to feel them, too. Silly, but this one is not just for Lewis fans - pretty good.

☐ Sex ☐ Nud ☐ Viol ☐ Lang ☐ AdSit

A: Jerry Lewis, Glenda Farrell, Susan Oliver, Everett Sloane, Jack E. Leonard, Kathleen Freeman

© PARAMOUNT HOME VIDEO 6406

DOCTOR DOLITTLE

D: Richard Fleischer — 145 m

G | MUS CLD | 1967 | COLOR

Sex / Nud / Viol / Lang / AdSit

8 This is a musical adaptation of Hugh Lofting's children's classic about an eccentric doctor (Rex Harrison) who loves animals so much better than people that he speaks 498 animal languages. He goes off on an adventure, from his home at Puddleby-on-the-Marsh, in search of new ones and he and his fiancee (Samantha Eggar) discover some very strange ones indeed. Won an Oscar for Best Song: "Talk to the Animals." While it was a box office flop and most critics were unkind, it still manages to please little kids who aren't aware of any of that.

A: Rex Harrison, Samantha Eggar, Anthony Newley, Richard Attenborough, Peter Bull, Geoffrey Holder

© FOXVIDEO 1025

DOG OF FLANDERS, A

D: James B. Clark — 96 m

NR | CLD DMA | 1959 | COLOR

Sex / Nud / Viol / Lang / AdSit

9 This is a wonderful children's story, but it is also good viewing for the whole family. Set in turn-of-the-century Belgium, a young boy who is living with his grandfather, dreams of becoming a great painter, but they are very poor. He and his grandfather adopt a stray dog who pulls the old man's milk cart, and when the dog becomes sick, they have to struggle to save him. However, then the grandfather dies, and the boy and the dog are left alone. Get out your hankies - this is going to hit you just as hard as OLD YELLER. It is particularly good for kids.

A: David Ladd, Donald Crisp, Theodore Bikel, Max Croiset, Monique Ahrens, Siohban Taylor

© PARAMOUNT HOME VIDEO 2325

DOGPOUND SHUFFLE

D: Jeffrey Bloom — 98 m

PG | CLD COM | 1974 | COLOR

Sex / Nud / Viol / Lang / AdSit ◢

7 Fun light-weight little story about a homeless ex-vaudevillian tap dancer (Moody) whose dog, his only real friend, is impounded. In order to get the dog back, he must raise $30. Another drifter, a young harmonica-player (Soul), talks him into forming a street team to raise the money. Funny and sensitive performances, particularly by master character actor Ron Moody.

A: Ron Moody, David Soul, Pamela McMyler, Ray Strucklyn, Raymond Sutton

© FOXVIDEO 9058

ELEPHANT BOY

D: Robert Flaherty — 82 m

NR | DMA CLD | 1937 | B&W

Sex / Nud / Viol / Lang / AdSit

7 Delightful Rudyard Kipling family adventure movie. A young Indian boy's (Sabu) dream is to become a great hunter. But, when his favorite elephant is sold to a mean dealer, Sabu steals the animal back and escapes into the jungle. There he discovers a large wild herd of elephants and the place that elephants go when they die. Filmed and set in 1930s India, this is both an interesting portrait of the time and place, and a worthy adventure in its own right, particularly for children. There is only one white man in the picture. All others are Indian.

A: Sabu, W.E. Holloway, Walter Hudd, Bruce Gordon, D.J. Williams

© HBO VIDEO 90655

ERRAND BOY, THE

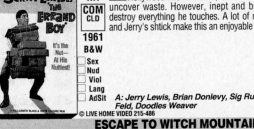

D: Jerry Lewis — 93 m

NR | COM CLD | 1961 | B&W

Sex / Nud / Viol / Lang / AdSit

6 Jerry Lewis is given an under-cover job as an errand boy in a Hollywood movie studio, but his real job is supposed to be to uncover waste. However, inept and bumbling Jerry proceeds to destroy everything he touches. A lot of major-name character actors and Jerry's shtick make this an enjoyable diversion. Pretty good.

A: Jerry Lewis, Brian Donlevy, Sig Ruman, Howard McNear, Firtz Feld, Doodles Weaver

© LIVE HOME VIDEO 215-486

ESCAPE TO WITCH MOUNTAIN

D: John Hough — 94 m

G | CLD SF | 1975 | COLOR

Sex / Nud / Viol / Lang / AdSit

9 This is excellent Disney fare that should appeal to the whole family. Two young orphans are very different from everyone else around them but don't know why. They have amnesia and they also have psychic powers. Ray Milland is an evil tycoon who, along with Donald Pleasence, has lured them to his mansion and used them to predict the stock market until they escape. While they are escaping they meet Eddie Albert, and with his help they to try to discover who they really are. This is quite good stuff that has a neat sci-fi twist ending. It will keep both you and the kids involved all the way through it. Sequel: RETURN FROM WITCH MOUNTAIN.

A: Eddie Albert, Ray Milland, Donald Pleasence, Kim Richards, Ike Eisenmann, Denver Pyle

© WALT DISNEY HOME VIDEO 4119

E.T. THE EXTRA-TERRESTRIAL

D: Steven Spielberg — 115 m

PG | SF DMA CLD | 1982 | COLOR

Sex / Nud / Viol / Lang / AdSit

10 Huge blockbuster hit and instant classic. Wonderful, warm story of a lovable little visitor from another world who is stranded on Earth and befriended by a 10-year-old boy. Elliott tries to keep little E.T. hidden, but soon the rest of his family knows the secret and then they are all helping to hide the little guy from the government people who are now out to capture him. But, all little E.T. wants is just to go home. No wonder this is the #1 box office hit of all time. It has captured the hearts and imaginations of all who have ever watched it - all over the world.

A: Dee Wallace, Henry Thomas, Peter Coyote, Robert MacNaughton, Drew Barrymore, K.C. Martel

© MCA/UNIVERSAL HOME VIDEO, INC. 77012

EWOK ADVENTURE, THE

D: John Korty — 96 m

G | CLD | 1984 | COLOR

Sex / Nud / Viol / Lang / AdSit

7 Kids will delight in these fuzzy little creatures that George Lucas recreates after their first appearance in RETURN OF THE JEDI from the STARWARS trilogy. In it, two very young children, a brother and sister, get lost and are searching for their parents after their spaceship crashes on Endor, the home planet of the Ewoks. When their search puts them in danger with the underground giant Gorax, the little fuzzballs come to their aid.

A: Eric Walker, Warwick Davis, Fionnula Flanagan, Guy Boyd

Distributed By MGM/UA Home Video M802053

EWOKS: THE BATTLE FOR ENDOR

D: Jim Wheat — 97 m

G | CLD | 1985 | COLOR

Sex / Nud / Viol ◢ / Lang / AdSit

7 Those feisty little furballs are at it again. This time they come to the aid of an old curmudgeon, a little girl and her Ewok pal, as they all rescue an Ewok family being held by an evil king.

A: Wilford Brimley, Aubree Miller, Sian Phillips, Niki Bothelo

Distributed By MGM/UA Home Video M801425

FAR OFF PLACE, A

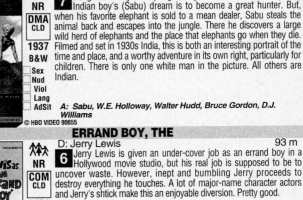

D: Mikael Solomon — 107 m

PG | ACT | 1993 | COLOR

Sex / Nud / Viol ◢ / Lang ◢ / AdSit ◢

7 This is not at all a typical Walt Disney kid's adventure movie. It is more a video for teenagers (probably not for kids under 10 at all), because of graphic scenes of killing. It is the story of a 14-year-old girl named Nonnie, Xhabbo (a young bushman and her best friend) and Harry, a teenager from New York. Nonnie and her parents lived on the edge of Africa's Kalahari Desert and were fighting a battle against poachers who had been killing elephants for their ivory. However, now the poachers have killed Nonnie's parents and the three teenagers are forced to flee across 700 miles of open desert, with the poachers hot on their trial. Quite good.

A: Reese Witherspoon, Ethan Randall, Jack Thompson, Sarel Bok, Maximilian Schell, Robert Burke

© WALT DISNEY HOME VIDEO 1795

FISH HAWK

D: Donald Shebib — 95 m

G | DMA CLD | 1979 | COLOR

Sex / Nud / Viol / Lang / AdSit ◢

7 Fish Hawk is an old alcoholic Osage Indian living alone in the turn-of-the-century Ozarks. He is a lonely old man who is scorned by everyone. In his drunkenness one day, he kills his dog - one of the few friends he has. He vows to reform and to track down and kill a bear that has been terrorizing the town. In the woods, he meets a lonely young farm boy. They become friends and their friendship causes him to remember much of what he has forgotten. He vows to give up his old ways, but he also must leave his new friend to go back home to his people. A gentle story that is well done.

A: Will Sampson, Charles Fields, Geoffrey Bowes, Mary Pirie, Don Francks

© VIDEO TREASURES M297

FLIGHT OF THE NAVIGATOR

D: Randal Kleiser — 90 m

PG | SF CLD | 1986 | COLOR

Sex / Nud / Viol / Lang / AdSit

8 Quite fun. A 12-year-old falls into a ravine in 1978 and wakes up a second later to find that it is now 1986 and his folks have moved away. However, he hasn't aged a day. NASA investigates and discovers that he has previously unknown star charts imprinted on his brain and his disappearance is connected to a recently discovered alien spaceship. He finds that he had been whisked away on a spaceship, that he can communicate with this one and that it needs his help to get home again. Kids will love the special effects, the kooky alien creatures and the action. Parents will enjoy this Disney treat, too.

A: Joey Cramer, Cliff De Young, Veronica Cartwright, Matt Adler, Sarah Jessica Parker, Howard Hesseman

© WALT DISNEY HOME VIDEO 499

FLINTSTONES, THE

D: Brian Levant — 91 m

PG | COM CLD | 1994 | COLOR | Rating: 7

Anyone who compares this movie to the long-running TV cartoon series will be both disillusioned and satisfied. In spite of a $40 million budget that built fantastic sets plus some right-on casting, this film just does not have the same feel as the cartoon series did. However, that is not to say that it isn't fun. It is, if you are either a kid, or willing to accept the silly humor that appeals to a kid - like, say, those people who like The Three Stooges. In it, lovable, but not-too-bright Fred gets a big head when he is promoted by boss Rock Quarry. However, he was only promoted so he can take the fall for all the money Rock has embezzled. Also, poor Barney loses his job and has to move in with Fred and Wilma.

Sex | Nud | Viol | Lang | AdSit

A: John Goodman, Rick Moranis, Elizabeth Perkins, Rosie O'Donnell, Kyle MacLachlan, Halle Berry

© MCA/UNIVERSAL HOME VIDEO, INC. 81744

FLIPPER

D: James B. Clark — 91 m

NR | CLD | 1963 | COLOR | Rating: 8

Flipper is a loveable dolphin that captured the hearts of 1960s TV audiences and he forever changed the way the world thought about dolphins. Flipper is a wounded dolphin who is nursed back to health by Luke, the son of a Florida wildlife manager. He and Flipper have become best friends. Even though Flipper has to be returned to the wild, boy and dolphin will not be separated for long. Great entertainment for kids. Lots of beautiful scenery. It was shot on location in the Florida Keys and in the Bahamas.

Sex | Nud | Viol | Lang | AdSit

A: Chuck Connors, Luke Haalpin, Connie Scott, Jane Rose, Joe Higgins

Distributed By MGM/UA Home Video M200800

FOR THE LOVE OF BENJI

D: Joe Camp — 85 m

G | COM CLD | 1977 | COLOR | Rating: 8

One of the most loveable characters in moviedom returns to charm his way into your heart. The whole family will enjoy his adventure through the streets of Athens, with Benji being chased by secret agents in search of the secret information tattooed on his paw. An interesting aspect of this film is that the movie is shot from Benji's point of view. Lovable. Preceeded by BENJI and followed by OH, HEAVENLY DOG!

Sex | Nud | Viol | Lang | AdSit

A: Benji, Patsy Garrett, Cynthia Smith, Allen Fiuzat, Ed Nelson, Bridget Armstrong

© BEST FILM & VIDEO CORP. 123

FREAKY FRIDAY

D: Gary Nelson — 98 m

G | COM CLD | 1977 | COLOR | Rating: 8

Charming breezy comedy that is a truly fun time for the whole family - from Disney. Teenager Jodie Foster gets her wish when she and her mother (Barbara Harris) magically exchange personalities for a day and both of them find out that neither has such an easy time of things. Probably one of Disney's best-ever comedies. Lightweight fun from Mary Rogers's adaptation of her own book. This is the same premise as in the 1948 movie VICE VERSA, and it became very popular later with such other movies as BIG - but it was seldom used better than it was here.

Sex | Nud | Viol | Lang | AdSit

A: Jodie Foster, Barbara Harris, John Astin, Ruth Buzzi, Kay Ballard, Patsy Kelly

© WALT DISNEY HOME VIDEO 056

FREE WILLY

D: Simon Wincer — 112 m

PG | CLD DMA | 1993 | COLOR | Rating: 8

This is a very good movie for all kids, most parents and some adults. Jesse is a 12-year-old parentless kid who gets one more chance. He gets assigned kindly foster parents to take care of him while he is to wash off the paint that he and some of his homeless friends had sprayed on the walls of a second-rate seaquarium. While working at the park, he meets Willy. Willy is an orca, a killer whale who has been taken from his family. Willy is unhappy and no one can train him, but lonely Jesse and lonely Willy become fast friends when Willy is attracted to Jesse's harmonica. This film was a big hit.

Sex | Nud | Viol | Lang | AdSit

A: Jason James Richter, Lori Petty, Jayne Atkinson, August Schellenberg, Michael Madsen

© WARNER HOME VIDEO 18000

GENTLE GIANT

D: James Neilson — 94 m

NR | CLD | 1967 | COLOR | Rating: 8

This is a very pleasant family film whose success led to a very successful television series called "Gentle Ben." Mark (Clint Howard) is a seven-year-old Florida boy and the son of a wildlife officer (Dennis Weaver). Mark finds and befriends a friendly black bear cub and names him Ben. However, after Ben gets full-grown, the townspeople force them to put Ben into a zoo, and the two friends are torn apart. When Mark learns that Ben has escaped into the Everglades, Mark is afraid for his friend and rushes to get him back. Very popular. Especially good for kids.

Sex | Nud | Viol | Lang | AdSit

A: Dennis Weaver, Vera Miles, Clint Howard, Ralph Meeker, Huntz Hall, Charles Martin

© REPUBLIC PICTURES HOME VIDEO 1480

GIRL WHO SPELLED FREEDOM, THE

D: Simon Wincer — 90 m

NR | DMA CLD | 1986 | COLOR | Rating: 8

Heartwarming true story of a young Cambodian girl who is determined to master English after her family flees war-torn Cambodia and settles in Tennessee. In spite of the difficulties she and her family have struggling to learn new ways and a new language, she becomes a spelling-bee champion within a just a few months. Good entertainment for all ages.

Sex | Nud | Viol | Lang | AdSit

A: Wayne Rogers, Mary Kay Place, Kieu Chinh, Kathleen Sisk, Jade Chinn, Margot Pinvidic

© WALT DISNEY HOME VIDEO 416V

GODZILLA, KING OF THE MONSTERS

D: Terry Morse — 80 m

NR | SF ACT CLD | 1956 | B&W | Rating: 6

Campy original (American) version of the long-running Japanese classic horror film. Godzilla is a long dormant, huge, fire-breathing reptilian monster that is awakened by an atomic bomb blast, after which he goes on a reign of terror, destroying everything in his path. This original is far superior to the many clones which came later. It is most notable for the high quality of its special effects. (This version is not actually the original version. The original Japanese version was twenty minutes longer and did not have the subplot of the American scientist.)

Sex | Nud | ◢ Viol | Lang | AdSit

A: Inoshiro Honda, Raymond Burr, Takashi Shimura, Akihiko Hirata

© PARAMOUNT HOME VIDEO 12864

GOLDEN VOYAGE OF SINBAD, THE

D: Gordon Hessler — 105 m

G | FAN CLD | 1974 | COLOR | Rating: 8

Tales of Captain Sinbad have thrilled generations. Great special effects add to the mystical charm of this ancient hero in a film that still captures the fantasies of kids today. Sinbad sets sail for an uncharted island with a beautiful slave girl (Munro) and the Grand Vizier of the land on board his ship. An evil wizard is trying to gain control of the kingdom and is using evil spirits to do it. Great special effects include both a ship's figurehead and a sword wielding six-armed statue coming to life. Then throw in a one-eyed centaur and a griffin. Great entertainment for kids.

Sex | Nud | Viol | Lang | AdSit

A: John Phillip Law, Caroline Monro, Tom Baker, Douglas Wilmer, Gregoire Aslan, John Garfield, Jr.

© COLUMBIA TRISTAR HOME VIDEO 60199

GOONIES, THE

D: Richard Donner — 114 m

PG | FAN CLD | 1985 | COLOR | Rating: 8

Rousing old-fashioned adventure yarn for kids. Spielberg produced this fantasy about a neighborhood group of kids who call themselves the Goonies. Their neighborhood is going to be razed by greedy developers so they all get together for one last time. Then, wonderfully, they discover a real-life treasure map that will provide more than enough money to save their neighborhood. They set off on a trek for the treasure, a trek which leads them into a subterranean world of caves, caverns, booby-traps, a real pirate ship and a monster. Plenty of action and thrills to keep the kids fascinated.

Sex | Nud | ◢ Viol | ◢ Lang | AdSit

A: Sean Astin, Josh Brolin, Corey Feldman, Martha Plimpton, Ke Huy Quan, John Matuszak

© WARNER HOME VIDEO 11474

GREAT MUPPET CAPER, THE

D: Jim Henson — 98 m

G | COM CLD MUS | 1981 | COLOR | Rating: 8

This is the delightful second feature-length film for Jim Henson's Muppets. After being fired as reporters for a major paper, Miss Piggy, Kermit, Fozzie Bear and the Great Gonzo set about solving the mysterious theft in London of the famous Baseball Diamond. Good gags and fun musical numbers (Kermit dances like Astaire and Miss Piggy swims like Ester Williams). Pretty good follow-up to the superior THE MUPPET MOVIE.

Sex | Nud | Viol | Lang | AdSit

A: Charles Grodin, Diana Rigg, John Cleese, Robert Morley, Peter Ustinov, Jack Warden

© CBS/FOX VIDEO 9035

GREGORY'S GIRL

D: Bill Forsyth — 90 m

PG | ROM COM CLD | 1981 | COLOR | Rating: 8

Delightful low-budget movie made in Scotland that was a winner of England's "Academy Award." It is a winning little comedy about a gangly, graceless high-school teenager who falls in love with his soccer team's newest and best player, Dorothy, the female goal keeper. He gets himself all custom-built just to please her, with the right clothes and the right hair style and then... she stands him up. However, his bruised adolescent psyche is mended when his crush is transferred to Dorothy's girlfriend. Wonderfully magical and humorous story of adolescent love. However, thick accents require diligent viewing.

Sex | Nud | Viol | ◢ Lang | ◢ AdSit

A: Gordon John Sinclair, Dee Hepburn, Chic Murray, Jake D'Arcy, Alex Norton, John Bett

© UNITED AMERICAN VIDEO CORP. 5318

HAMBONE AND HILLIE

D: Roy Watts — 97 m

PG | DMA CLD | 1984 | COLOR

7 Heartwarming story of devotion. An elderly woman returns to Los Angeles from a trip to New York to visit her grandson by plane. However, her dog, Hambone, who must travel as baggage, escapes from his travel case and gets loose in the big world, far way from home. But Hambone will not be separated from his mistress for long, and a cross-country 3,300 mile journey of many travails begins. Very good entertainment for the whole family, but especially the kids.

Sex / Nud / ✓ Viol / Lang / AdSit

A: Lillian Gish, O.J. Simpson, Timothy Bottoms, Candy Clark, Jack Carter

© R&G VIDEO, LP 80072

HANS CHRISTIAN ANDERSEN

D: Charles Vidor — 112 m

NR | MUS CLD | 1952 | COLOR

9 Wonderful, tune-filled musical biography of the famous story-teller, Hans Christian Andersen. Danny Kaye is just marvelous in the title role as a shoemaker who is forced to leave his hometown because the school children all skip school just to come an hear him tell his stories. After going to Copenhagen, he is hired to make shoes for a beautiful ballerina. He falls desperately, deeply in love with her and then writes "The Littlest Mermaid." Listen also for him telling the stories of "Thumbelina," "Inchworm" and "Ugly Duckling."

Sex / Nud / Viol / Lang / AdSit

A: Danny Kaye, Farley Granger, Renee Jeanmaire, John Brown, Roland Petit

© HBO VIDEO 90650

HARRY AND THE HENDERSONS

D: William Dear — 111 m

PG | COM CLD | 1987 | COLOR

7 Entertaining and pretty good family fun. Your typical suburban family is out on a trip in the wilds when father Lithgow runs over Harry, a real live man/ape - the fabled "Bigfoot". At first they think he's dead, but he's not. They bring him home to nurse him, but the big guy wreaks total havoc in their house. Still, he is a loveable sort and the family is growing more and more attached to him. Even so, they need to get him back to the woods where he belongs. That's a lot harder than it sounds... Harry doesn't want to go. But, he has to go because now everybody is after him. Good family entertainment.

Sex / Nud / ✓ Viol / Lang / ✓ AdSit

A: John Lithgow, Melinda Dillon, Don Ameche, Joshua Ruday, Margaret Langrick, Kevin Peter Hall

© MCA/UNIVERSAL HOME VIDEO, INC. 80677

HEIDI

D: Allan Dwan — 88 m

NR | CLD | 1937 | B&W

9 This ages-old classic children's story has been done several times but this version with Shirley Temple as Heidi has also become a classic film. Shirley Temple was perfect in the role of the little Swiss orphan who is at first sent to live with her grandfather high in his mountain cabin in the Alps. She wins the gruff old man's heart but is then taken from him by her aunt and given to a rich family in the city. An ageless, solid tearjerker that is sure to win the hearts of parents and kids alike.

Sex / Nud / Viol / Lang / AdSit

A: Shirley Temple, Jean Hersholt, Arthur Treacher, Helen Westley, Pauline Moore, Thomas Beck

© FOXVIDEO 1066

HEIDI

D: Delbert Mann — 105 m

NR | CLD | 1968 | COLOR

8 This children's movie is a well executed version of the story which retells the same classic tale that was first done on film by Shirley Temple in 1937. It is the story of a loveable little orphan girl who must leave the mountain home and her gruff grandfather that she loves, to move to the big city to be a playmate for a rich cousin.

Sex / Nud / Viol / Lang / AdSit

A: Maximilian Schell, Jennifer Edwards, Jean Simmons, Michael Redgrave, Walter Slezak, Peter Van Eyck

© LIVE HOME VIDEO 4158

HERBIE RIDES AGAIN

D: Robert Stevenson — 88 m

G | CLD | 1974 | COLOR

8 This is Disney's first sequel to the very popular original THE LOVE BUG. This time Herbie, the magical VW, helps Helen Hayes, Stephanie Powers and Ken Berry to prevent an evil real estate developer (Keenan Wynn) from bulldozing Helen Hay's Victorian fire-house home and building the world's tallest building. Typical Disney fun with plenty of slapstick.

Sex / Nud / Viol / Lang / AdSit

A: Helen Hayes, Ken Berry, Stefanie Powers, John McIntire, Keenan Wynn, Huntz Hall

© WALT DISNEY HOME VIDEO 42

HIDEAWAYS, THE

D: Fielder Cook — 105 m

G | CLD | 1972 | COLOR

6 Two suburban kids, Claudia, a 12-year-old girl, and her brother Jamie, decide to teach their family a lesson and have an adventure at the same time. They run away from home and hide out in the Metropolitan Museum of Art. Mrs. Frankweiler (Ingrid Bergman) is an eccentric and reclusive old woman who has donated a statue of an angel to the museum and claims that it is a work by Michelangelo. The whole city wants to know if that's true. The kids decide that they will make their adventure complete and find out. How? They are going to work up their courage and ask her. Best for kids.

Sex / Nud / Viol / Lang / AdSit

A: Ingrid Bergman, Sally Prager, Johnny Doran, George Rose, Richard Mulligan, Madeline Kahn

© WARNER HOME VIDEO 733

HOME ALONE

D: Chris Columbus — 105 m

PG | CLD COM | 1990 | COLOR

9 This was a huge smash hit that kids loved because one of their own gets to cream the bad guys. 8-year-old Macaulay Culkin just wishes his parents would go away - and then they do! He wakes up one December morning to find that his family has left for their Christmas vacation to Paris and accidentally left him behind. Two thieves have targeted their supposedly vacant house to be ripped off, however they never counted on the little guy being there to stop them. Macaulay's war against the bad guys is the highlight of this entertaining film full of slap stick shenanigans. Parents won't like it as much as kids.

Sex / Nud / ✓ Viol / Lang / AdSit

A: Macaulay Culkin, Joe Pesci, Daniel Stern, John Heard, Catherine O'Hara, Kristin Minter

© FOXVIDEO 1866

HOME ALONE 2

D: Chris Columbus — 120 m

PG | CLD COM | 1992 | COLOR

8 This is a cookie-cutter remake of the original. This time Macaulay gets separated from his parents by wandering onto the wrong plane in the Chicago airport and winds up in New York City. Because he has his father's credit cards, he checks into the Plaza Hotel and has a great time, until he runs into his old enemies Joe Pesci and Daniel Stern who have escaped from jail and are out for revenge. Macaulay, however sets up a new trap for them in a brownstone that is under renovation. The last 15 minutes are again filled with a slapstick war where the bad guys get their due.

Sex / Nud / ✓ Viol / ✓ Lang / AdSit

A: Macaulay Culkin, Joe Pesci, Daniel Stem, John Heard, Catherine O'Hara, Daniel Stern

© FOXVIDEO 1989

HOMEWARD BOUND: THE INCREDIBLE JOURNEY

D: Duwayne Dunham — 84 m

G | COM CLD | 1993 | COLOR

8 Rock solid family entertainment and a lot of fun. Here, Disney has remade their 1963 hit THE INCREDIBLE JOURNEY, but this time they gave the cute animals real personalities and the voices of Michael J. Fox, Don Ameche and Sally Field. This is the extremely enjoyable and sometimes comic story of two dogs and a cat who are left temporarily several hundred miles away from home. However, they become worried that their masters are in trouble and so the three buddies begin a cross-country journey through the beautiful Sierra Mountains to get home. Very clever and highly entertaining story of their many encounters along the way. Truly a lot of fun. Some might even rate it higher.

Sex / Nud / Viol / Lang / AdSit

A:

© WALT DISNEY HOME VIDEO 1801

HONEY, I BLEW UP THE KID

D: Randal Kleiser — 89 m

PG | COM CLD FAN | 1992 | COLOR

8 Sequel to HONEY, I SHRUNK THE KIDS. Moranis is now working for a corporation trying to develop a ray that, this time, will enlarge things. He is accidentally successful but accidentally blows up his two-year-old to the size of a ten-story building. There is something here for everyone to laugh at. Moranis is hysterical as he runs around Las Vegas trying to blast his kid with a ray gun to shrink him back down to size. Great special effects again. Overall, this is nearly as good as the original - only slightly less funny because some of the novelty is gone.

Sex / Nud / Viol / Lang / AdSit

A: Rick Moranis, Lloyd Bridges, Marcia Strassman, Robert Oliveri, Amy O'Neill

© WALT DISNEY HOME VIDEO 1371

HONEY, I SHRUNK THE KIDS

D: Joe Johnston — 101 m

PG | COM CLD FAN | 1989 | COLOR

9 Big box office hit and great family fun-filled fantasy - in the old fashioned Disney tradition. Rick Moranis plays a klutzy scientist who is inventing an experimental ray gun in the attic. One day his kids and the neighbor's kids are playing with it and zap... they are all shrunk down to the size of ants. They become lost in the backyard, which, because of their size, has now been transformed into a forbidding jungle filled with terrible monsters. Really good special effects and fun gags that will satisfy all age groups. Good family entertainment.

Sex / Nud / Viol / Lang / AdSit

A: Rick Moranis, Matt Frewer, Marcia Strassman, Kristine Sutherland, Thomas Brown, Jared Rushton

© WALT DISNEY HOME VIDEO 909

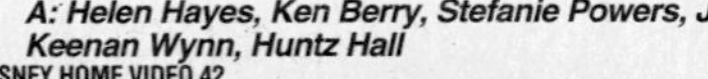

HOOK

D: Steven Spielberg 142 m

PG | FAN CLD | 1991 | COLOR

7 Peter Pan (Williams) is all grown up and has become a stressed-out exec who doesn't spend enough time with his children. However, while he is in London visiting Aunt Wendy, his old arch enemy Captain Hook (Hoffman) kidnaps his kids and Peter must return to Never Never Land to get them back. But Peter is so changed that he can't remember how to fly or how to fight. Fortunately, Tinkerbell (Roberts) comes to the rescue and helps him to remember and to get ready for the big showdown with Hook. Not wonderful, but pleasant. Enjoy this big-budget high tech Spielberg fantasy, but please also see the wonderful low-tech 1960 TV production of PETER PAN.

☐ Sex ☐ Nud ◢ Viol ☐ Lang ☐ AdSit

A: Robin Williams, Dustin Hoffman, Julia Roberts, Bob Hoskins, Maggie Smith, Caroline Goodall

© COLUMBIA TRISTAR HOME VIDEO 70603

HUCKLEBERRY FINN

D: J. Lee Thompson 74 m

NR | CLD | 1974 | COLOR

8 An excellent made-for-TV version of Mark Twain's classic story of Huck Finn. Huck is a free-spirited boy who nobody owns or can tame. He and Jim, a runaway slave, ride a raft down the Mississippi River. Their adventure takes them smack dab into excitement. They have to duck slave owners who are trying to track down a runaway slave and they rescue two con-artists who have been thrown off a riverboat and who claim to be royalty. Soon Huck gets caught up on one of their scams but lives to regret it. This version is very well done, however it is best suited to younger people and children. Several other versions have been done that are a little less directed toward children.

☐ Sex ☐ Nud ☐ Viol ☐ Lang ☐ AdSit

A: Ron Howard, Danny Most, Antonio Fargas, Merle Haggard, Jack Elam, Royal Dano

© CBS/FOX VIDEO 8015

INCREDIBLE JOURNEY, THE

D: Fletcher Markle 80 m

G | CLD | 1963 | COLOR

9 This well-made and entertaining Disney live-action story became very popular and has been released by Disney several times. It was remade in 1993 with a twist as HOMEWARD BOUND: THE INCREDIBLE JOURNEY. It is the story of three pets who have been left with friends of the family, who live 250 miles away from their home, while the family goes on vacation. Feeling abandoned, they attempt to return back to their home. Two dogs and a cat embark on the 250-mile action-packed return journey across the Canadian wilderness. Along the way, they have run-ins with a bear, porcupines, a lynx, a farm dog and assorted humans. Good family stuff, but particularly kids.

☐ Sex ☐ Nud ☐ Viol ☐ Lang ☐ AdSit

A: Emile Genest, John Drainie, Tommy Tweed, Sandra Scott, Syme Jago, Marion Filayson

© WALT DISNEY HOME VIDEO 147

IN SEARCH OF A GOLDEN SKY

D: Jefferson Richard 94 m

PG | CLD | 1984 | COLOR

8 When their mother dies and their father disappears, three young city children move to the mountain cabin of their uncle who lives in the wilds of the American Northwest. The kids don't want to leave the city and the old coot isn't thrilled to see them come, but they have no choice. Still, the children grow to love nature, and the old man opens his heart to them. Just then, the county welfare department decides they should be placed in a foster home, so they all flee to his fishing cabin to hide out. The story features fun times, playful animals and beautiful scenery. Good wholesome family entertainment.

☐ Sex ☐ Nud ☐ Viol ☐ Lang ☐ AdSit

A: Charles Napier, George "Buck" Flower, Cliff Osmond, Anne Szesny, Shane Wallace

© CBS/FOX VIDEO 3854

IN SEARCH OF THE CASTAWAYS

D: Robert Stevenson 98 m

G | CLD FAN | 1962 | COLOR

8 Fun-filled Disney adaptation of Jules Verne's adventure story. A young girl (Mills) launches an expedition into the South Pacific, headed by professor Chevalier, to find her missing sea captain father. Their fanciful journey requires them to overcome the perils of earthquakes and volcanos, and do battle with a giant condor and cannibals. Great special effects provide an involving fantasy to stimulate the adventurous spirit in young and old alike.

☐ Sex ☐ Nud ☐ Viol ☐ Lang ☐ AdSit

A: Maurice Chevalier, Hayley Mills, George Sanders, Wilfrid Hyde-White, Michael Anderson, Jr.

© WALT DISNEY HOME VIDEO 131

INTERNATIONAL VELVET

D: Bryan Forbes 126 m

PG | DMA CLD | 1978 | COLOR

8 Entertaining sequel to the 1944 classic NATIONAL VELVET which starred a young Elizabeth Taylor. The English Steeplechase winner (Newman) is now forty years old. She has an orphaned American niece (O'Neal) who is determined to become an Olympic riding champion. A tough trainer (Hopkins) shows her the dedication it takes to become a winner. Excellent photography and fine acting help offset the fact that it is slightly overlong. Still, this is interesting human drama and enjoyable family entertainment.

☐ Sex ☐ Nud ☐ Viol ☐ Lang ☐ AdSit

A: Tatum O'Neal, Christopher Plummer, Anthony Hopkins, Nanette Newman, Dinsdale Landen

Distributed By MGM/UA Home Video M600296

INTO THE WEST

D: Mike Newell 97 m

PG | CLD DMA | 1993 | COLOR

8 Excellent adventure story for kids over 10 and their parents. Set in modern-day Ireland, two young boys, 8 and 12 years old, are struggling to understand their place in the world. Their mother has died and their father has been drinking ever since. They are poor, nearly alone and they are gypsies, so they are despised by everyone. But, their grandfather has been followed home by a beautiful white horse which adopts the boys. The three are inseparable. The horse even stays with them in their 16th floor apartment until he is taken away by the authorities. So, the boys steal him back and begin a cross country odyssey, with the horse leading the way and their father and the police in pursuit.

☐ Sex ☐ Nud ◢ Viol ◢ Lang ◢ AdSit

A: Gabriel Byrne, Ellen Barkin, Ruaidhri Conroy, Ciaran Fitzgerald, David Kelly, Johnny Murphy

© TOUCHSTONE HOME VIDEO 1594

IT CAME FROM BENEATH THE SEA

D: Robert Gordon 80 m

NR | SF CLD | 1955 | B&W

6 This is one of the many "monster" movies that were typical in the '50s, but this science fiction piece has become a minor classic, primarily because of its special effects. Repeated nuclear explosions in the Pacific Ocean stir up a giant octopus from the depths. Enraged and hungry, it begins a reign of terror on the West Coast and works his way toward San Francisco. Only a Navy submarine stands in his way. Quite good for its genre.

☐ Sex ☐ Nud ☐ Viol ☐ Lang ☐ AdSit

A: Faith Domergue, Kenneth Tobey, Ian Keith, Donald Curtis, Dean Maddox, Jr.

© COLUMBIA TRISTAR HOME VIDEO 60491

JASON AND THE ARGONAUTS

D: Don Chaffey 104 m

G | ACT CLD | 1963 | COLOR

9 Exciting and very well done adventure story from Greek mythology. Jason, the son of a murdered Thessalian king, is cheated out of his birthright. So he gathers a crew for his ship and sets sail in search of the mythical Golden Fleece in order to reclaim his throne. This is an exciting adventure story which is made more so by stunning special effects (including a now classic scene with swordfighting skeletons). An interesting feature of this film for parents is that Jason and his crew are not portrayed as superheros, just mortal men performing great deeds. Great for kids.

☐ Sex ☐ Nud ◢ Viol ☐ Lang ☐ AdSit

A: Todd Armstrong, Gary Raymond, Honor Blackman, Nancy Kovack, Laurence Naismith, Niall MacGinnis

© COLUMBIA TRISTAR HOME VIDEO 60025

JOURNEY OF NATTY GANN, THE

D: Jeremy Paul Kagan 101 m

PG | DMA ACT CLD | 1985 | COLOR

9 This is a wonderfully endearing story that has the rare quality of being a family movie that has a genuine appeal both to young and to old. Natty Gann is a young girl in Depression-era Chicago, whose desperate father has to leave her, on short notice and without saying goodbye, with a very unpleasant old woman so he can take a good job in Seattle. Natty refuses to believe her father has deserted her and embarks on a cross-country trip by rail to go to him. She is all alone, except for a protective wolf and a hardened drifter she meets along the way. Very appealing, highly entertaining and very worthwhile.

☐ Sex ☐ Nud ◢ Viol ◢ Lang ☐ AdSit

A: Meredith Salenger, John Cusack, Ray Wise, Lainie Kazan, Barry Miller, Scatman Crothers

© WALT DISNEY HOME VIDEO 400

JOURNEY TO THE CENTER OF THE EARTH

D: Henry Levin 129 m

G | FAN CLD | 1959 | COLOR

7 Jules Verne's fantasy adventure about a 19th-century expedition to the center of the earth is still imaginative and fun, but its sense of innocence, especially with today's sophisticated audiences, makes it most attractive to children and fanciful adults. A scientist and his small party descend into the earth's bowels. Along the way they encounter dangerous giant reptiles, a beautiful quartz cavern, the lost city of Atlantis, a treacherous and traitorous count and other adventures. High production values and good special effects.

☐ Sex ☐ Nud ◢ Viol ☐ Lang ☐ AdSit

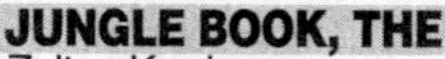

A: James Mason, Pat Boone, Arlene Dahl, Diane Baker, Peter Ronsen, Thayer David

© FOXVIDEO 1248

JUNGLE BOOK, THE

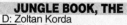

D: Zoltan Korda 106 m

NR | FAN CLD | 1942 | COLOR

8 This is Rudyard Kipling's classic fantasy of Mowgli, a native boy who became lost in a jungle in India and was raised by wolves and became friends with all the animals except his enemy, the great tiger. When he was grown, he returned to live with the humans of a local village. One day, he and a girl discovered a lost ancient city of great wealth but only take one gold coin when they leave. The girl's greedy father discovers the coin and tricks the village into casting Mowgli out so that he can follow the boy to the gold. Excellent for everyone, but it is best suited for older children and young teens.

☐ Sex ☐ Nud ◢ Viol ☐ Lang ☐ AdSit

A: Sabu, Joseph Calleia, John Qualen, Rosemary DeCamp, Ralph Byrd, Frank Puglia

© VIDEO TREASURES BV1936

JUNGLE BOOK, THE

PG | CLD ACT | 1994 | COLOR

D: Steven Sommers — 111 m

6 This is Rudyard Kipling's classic tale of Mowgli, a young boy from India who was lost in the jungle and raised to manhood by a pack of wolves. One day he chances upon a long-lost village containing great treasures of gold and jewels. But Mowgli has no use for these and takes only a jewel-encrusted dagger. Later still, Mowgli finds a beautiful girl in the jungle and follows her back to her village. Now for the first time, he discovers man and they discover his treasure. Don't expect to see a live-action version of Disney's cute animated classic. This attempts to follow more closely the original story, but it also takes considerable license. Very simply told. Too violent for very young however.

Sex ☐ Nud ☐ Viol ☑ Lang ☐ AdSit ☐

A: Jason Scott Lee, Cary Elwes, Lena Hheadley, Sam Neill, John Cleese, Jason Fleming

© WALT DISNEY HOME VIDEO 4604

KIDCO

PG | CLD COM | 1983 | COLOR

D: Ronald F. Maxwell — 104 m

7 Enjoyable story about a group of kids, between the ages of 9 and 16, who go into the fertilizer and pest control business for themselves. Much to everyone's surprise, their business takes off and they thrive. Soon it is the largest one of its type in all San Diego County. The kids are confronted with serious and unfair competition from unscrupulous adults and they are even under the scrutiny of the I.R.S, but they're not going to be beat. Very enjoyable excursion into American junior enterprise. The funniest part is that the story is based upon a real case.

Sex ☐ Nud ☐ Viol ☐ Lang ☑ AdSit ☑

A: Scott Schwartz, Cinnamopn Idles, Tristine Kkyler, Elizabeth Gorcey, Maggie Blye

© FOXVIDEO 1359

KIDNAPPED

G | ACT CLD | 1960 | COLOR

D: Robert Stevenson — 95 m

7 Great fun for kids of all ages from Disney. This is Disney's production of Robert Lewis Stevenson's swashbuckler classic. A young orphaned Scotsman is kidnapped by his cruel uncle just as he is about to inherit his family's estate. The boy is pressed into service as a cabin boy on a ship bound for the New World where, unknown to him, he is to be sold into slavery. But in their crossing they run over a small boat, killing all who were on board but a fellow Scotsman. The survivor and the boy become fast friends and escape the clutches of the foul ship they are captive to. Lots of high seas adventures.

Sex ☐ Nud ☐ Viol ☑ Lang ☐ AdSit ☐

A: Peter Finch, James MacArthur, Bernard Lee, Niall MacGinnis, Finlay Currie, Peter O'Toole

© WALT DISNEY HOME VIDEO 111

LASSIE COME HOME

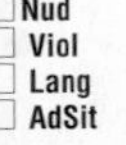

NR | DMA CLD | 1943 | COLOR

D: Fred M. Wilcox — 90 m

8 Wonderful, warm and sentimental family film that marked the original screen debut of Lassie. A desperately poor English family is forced to sell their dog to a Scottish duke, but Lassie escapes and struggles against long odds to find her way back home across 1000 miles to the boy who loves her. (This Lassie was really a him). You will also see a very young Roddy McDowall and Elizabeth Taylor in this heartwarming film.

Sex ☐ Nud ☐ Viol ☐ Lang ☐ AdSit ☐

A: Roddy McDowall, Donald Crisp, Dame May Whitty, Edmund Gwenn, Nigel Bruce, Elizabeth Taylor

Distributed By MGM/UA Home Video M201866

LAST STARFIGHTER, THE

PG | SF CLD | 1984 | COLOR

D: Nick Castle — 100 m

7 This is a quite enjoyable fantasy adventure yarn that is primarily, but not necessarily only, for kids. In it, a teenage videogame wizkid is transported from his trailer park home to a far away place by an alien, Robert Preston. He has been recruited, after his skill in blasting invading spaceships in a video game called Starfighter, is monitored. It will be his job to help defend the Universe against an evil invasion force. Interesting and witty dialogue, plus a clever premise and some funny situations make this a pleasant time killer.

Sex ☐ Nud ☐ Viol ☑ Lang ☑ AdSit ☐

A: Robert Preston, Lance Guest, Barbara Bosson, Dan O'Herlihy, Catherine Mary Stewart

© MCA/UNIVERSAL HOME VIDEO, INC. 80078

LITTLE COLONEL, THE

NR | CLD | 1935 | B&W

D: David Butler — 80 m

7 This was one of Shirley Temple's best films and one that appeals to all age groups. Shirley is the granddaughter of a Confederate Colonel who has disowned his daughter (Temple's mother) because she has committed the unpardonable crime of marrying a Yankee in the days of the Reconstruction South, just after the Civil War. However, sweet Shirley charms her way into his heart and brings mother and grandfather back together. This film also has one of her most famous dance routines with Bill "Bojangles" Robinson.

Sex ☐ Nud ☐ Viol ☐ Lang ☐ AdSit ☐

A: Shirley Temple, Lionel Barrymore, Evelyn Venable, John Lodge, Bill Robinson, Sidney Blackmer

© FOXVIDEO 5245

LITTLE GIANTS

PG | COM CLD | 1994 | COLOR

D: Duwayne Dunham — 106 m

6 Silly sort of sports film, mostly for kids. It's in the same vein as MIGHTY DUCKS and BAD NEWS BEARS, but not as good. Two brothers living in the small town of Urbania, Ohio couldn't be more different. O'Neill is a former All-American and Heisman Trophy winner who now runs an auto dealership, and Moranis is just an ordinary sort who has always felt overrun by his hero brother. So, when O'Neill excludes a bunch of young geeky kids from his pee-wee football team, Moranis forms them all (including his daughter) into another team and challenges his brother to a game -- with the winner to represent the town. Captures well the way kids act, but too many body-function jokes.

Sex ☐ Nud ☐ Viol ☐ Lang ☐ AdSit ☐

A: Rick Moranis, Ed O'Neill, Brian Haley, Mary Ellen Trainor, Susanna Thompson, John Madden

© WARNER HOME VIDEO 16220

LITTLE LORD FAUNTLEROY

NR | DMA CLD | 1936 | B&W

D: John Cromwell — 98 m

8 Solid family entertainment - not just for kids. A poor young kid from Brooklyn learns that he is the grandson of an English Earl and potential heir to his fortune. But the bitter and crusty old man blindly hates his widowed American daughter-in-law, the boy's mother, just because she is American. The boy is brought to England to live with the grumpy old geezer, whose hard heart is soon softened by the cheerful kid. Solid story. Solid acting. Very well done.

Sex ☐ Nud ☐ Viol ☐ Lang ☐ AdSit ☐

A: Freddie Bartholomew, C. Aubrey Smith, Dolores Costello, Jessie Ralph, Mickey Rooney, Guy Kibbee

© CBS/FOX VIDEO 8066

LITTLE PRINCESS, THE

NR | DMA CLD | 1939 | COLOR

D: Walter Lang — 93 m

6 Predictable, but effective, and endearing story which was Shirley Temple's last major childhood success. Shirley plays the daughter of a rich British officer who places her in an exclusive girls boarding school when he goes off to fight in the Boer war. When it is believed he has been killed, she is thought to be penniless. Suddenly poor, the school's head mistress makes poor little Shirley work as a maid to pay off her bill. But Shirley doesn't believe her father is dead. She visits army hospitals entertaining the troops and searching for him. Lavish production. Predictable, but very enjoyable.

Sex ☐ Nud ☐ Viol ☐ Lang ☐ AdSit ☐

A: Shirley Temple, Richard Greene, Anita Louise, Ian Hunter, Cesar Romero

© FOXVIDEO 1298

LITTLE RASCALS, THE

PG | CLD | 1994 | COLOR

D: Penelope Spheeris — 83 m

6 Pioneering film-maker Hal Roach created a series of original short films in the 1920s and 1930s about a group of very young kids which did lots of fun and funny things that other kids wished that they could do too. It was originally called the "Our Gang" series and later became "The Little Rascals" when rebroadcast on TV. This new film captures a little of the fun created by its namesake but it will likely be watched by oldsters trying to recapture the flavor of the earlier films. They will be disappointed. However, very young kids might enjoy this story in which Alfalfa trys to woo Darla, while still maintaining his membership in the Gang's womenhater's club. Silly slapstick humor.

Sex ☐ Nud ☐ Viol ☐ Lang ☐ AdSit ☐

A: Travis Tedford, Bug Hall, Kevin Jamal Woods, Ross Elliot Bagby, Brittany Aston Holmes

© MCA/UNIVERSAL HOME VIDEO, INC. 82144

LITTLEST REBEL, THE

NR | CLD | 1935 | B&W

D: David Butler — 70 m

6 This is one of Shirley Temple's most famous pictures and is similar in many ways to another of her pictures, THE LITTLE COLONEL. It has a simple and idealistic treatment of the Civil War. In it, loveable Shirley saves her father from being executed as a Confederate spy by charming President Lincoln. She and Bill "Bo Jangles" Robinson also dance together again. Songs include "Polly Wolly Doodle" and "Those Endearing Young Charms."

Sex ☐ Nud ☐ Viol ☐ Lang ☐ AdSit ☐

A: Shirley Temple, John Boles, Bill Robinson, Jack Holt, Karen Marley

© FOXVIDEO 5246

LOVE BUG, THE

G | COM CLD | 1969 | COLOR

D: Robert Stevenson — 108 m

9 Delightful Disney and cute comedy that is not just for kids. When a second-rate race driver (Dean Jones) defends a little VW from its abusive owner's kicks, interesting things begin to happen. The bug, Herbie by name, takes a shine to him. So later, when he gets teamed up with Herbie, he starts to win races. He thinks he's doing it on his own, but he's wrong. You see, Herbie has a mind of its own - some other pretty special other talents too - and, he is using them all to help them both win races. Lots of slapstick, stunts and warm-hearted fun. This film's success led to three sequels, but the original is the best.

Sex ☐ Nud ☐ Viol ☐ Lang ☐ AdSit ☐

A: Dean Jones, Michele Lee, Buddy Hackett, David Tomlinson, Joe Flynn

© WALT DISNEY HOME VIDEO 012

MAGIC OF LASSIE, THE

D: Don Chaffey 100 m

G · CLD · 1978 · COLOR

7 This is a loveable remake of LASSIE COME HOME. A loathsome millionaire (Pernell Roberts) wants to buy Grandpa's vineyard in Northern California, where Grandpa (Jimmy Stewart) and his two grandchildren, Kris and Kelly, live. Grandpa refuses to sell. So, Roberts, who has proof that he owns Lassie, spitefully takes Lassie back to Colorado. Lassie, however, will not be separated from her family and she embarks on a danger-filled journey through the Rockies to get back home. In the meantime, Kris has set out on his own in search of his best friend. Enjoyment for the whole family.

☐ Sex ☐ Nud ☐ Viol ☐ Lang ☐ AdSit

A: James Stewart, Stephanie Zimbalist, Mickey Rooney, Lassie, Alice Faye, Pernell Roberts

Distributed By MGM/UA Home Video M300729

MARY POPPINS

D: Robert Stevenson 139 m

G · MUS · CLD · FAN · 1964 · COLOR

10 Absolutely delightful! An enchanting magical nanny, Mary Poppins (Andrews), glides into a banker's home in 1910 London and brings happiness into everyone's lives. Who else can have a tea party on the ceiling? She and a chimney sweep (Van Dyke) sing the song "Chim-Chim-Cheree" and dance with magic feet on London rooftops. Van Dyke's animated scene where he frolics with little penguins is unforgettable. This top-shelf musical won five Academy Awards: Best Actress, Film Editing, Original Music, Song and Visual Effects. It was nominated for thirteen. You, as well as the kids, will find your smiles!

☐ Sex ☐ Nud ☐ Viol ☐ Lang ☐ AdSit

A: Julie Andrews, Dick Van Dyke, David Tomlinson, Glynis Johns, Ed Wynn, Hermione Baddeley

MIGHTY DUCKS, THE

D: Stephen Herek 103 m

PG · COM · CLD · 1992 · COLOR

8 Clever family fun. Estevez is a hotshot attorney who delights in humiliating his opponents - even the judges. So, when he is caught speeding once too often, they throw the book at him. However, he will be able to escape a jail sentence if he will perform community service. That is how he gets the job of coaching a kids's hockey team made up of inner-city misfits, called the Ducks. His anger and frustration at the situation soon give way to excitement over his successes with the team. The experience changes his attitude, helps the kids learn to play as a team and he also learns about love. Predictable, but a lot of fun anyway.

☐ Sex ☐ Nud ☑ Viol ☐ Lang ☐ AdSit

A: Emilio Estevez, Lane Smith, Joss Ackland, Heidi Kling

MIRACLE ON 34TH STREET

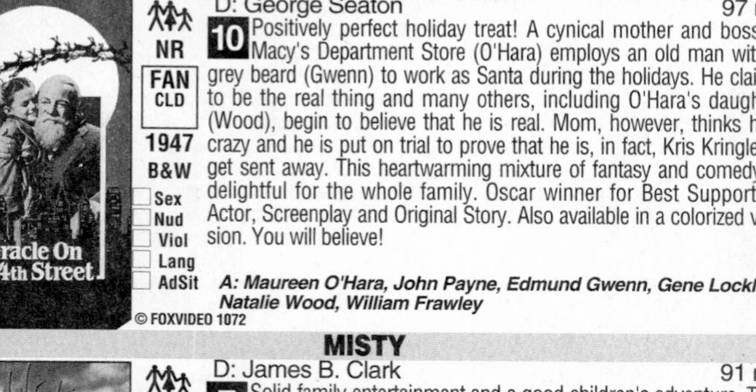

D: George Seaton 97 m

NR · FAN · CLD · 1947 · B&W

10 Positively perfect holiday treat! A cynical mother and boss at Macy's Department Store (O'Hara) employs an old man with a grey beard (Gwenn) to work as Santa during the holidays. He claims to be the real thing and many others, including O'Hara's daughter (Wood), begin to believe that he is real. Mom, however, thinks he's crazy and he is put on trial to prove that he is, in fact, Kris Kringle or get sent away. This heartwarming mixture of fantasy and comedy is delightful for the whole family. Oscar winner for Best Supporting Actor, Screenplay and Original Story. Also available in a colorized version. You will believe!

☐ Sex ☐ Nud ☐ Viol ☐ Lang ☐ AdSit

A: Maureen O'Hara, John Payne, Edmund Gwenn, Gene Lockhart, Natalie Wood, William Frawley

MISTY

D: James B. Clark 91 m

NR · CLD · 1961 · COLOR

7 Solid family entertainment and a good children's adventure. Two orphaned children (David Ladd and Pam Smith) are living with their grandparents on Chincoteaque, the picturesque island off the coast of Virginia that is also the real-life home of a famous herd of wild ponies. Each year there is an annual pony round-up and auction to thin the herd. This year, the children have fallen in love with a young colt that they name Misty. They save up enough money to buy him and after they do, they set about training him. Based on the book by Marguerite Henry.

☐ Sex ☐ Nud ☐ Viol ☐ Lang ☐ AdSit

A: David Ladd, Pam Smith, Arthur O'Connell, Anne Seymour

MOTHRA

D: Inoshiro Honda 100 m

NR · SF · CLD · 1962 · COLOR

6 Hokey and silly, but strangely endearing monster flick. Twin princesses, each only six inches tall, are snatched from their home island for display in a local neighborhood bar. The girls pray to the god Mothra hoping to be rescued and Mothra responds, hatching a giant egg in the city of Tokyo. The egg releases a giant caterpillar that turns onto a huge moth and ventures into Tokyo hunting for the girls, destroying the city along the way. Really corny, but still one of the best of the Japanese monster movies, in a campy sort of way.

☐ Sex ☐ Nud ☑ Viol ☐ Lang ☐ AdSit

A: Frankie Sakai, Hiroshi Koizumi, Lee Kresel, Kyoko Kagawa, Emi Itoh, Yumi Itoh

MUPPET CHRISTMAS CAROL, THE

D: Brian Henson 86 m

G · CLD · 1992 · COLOR

7 The Muppet people have brought their patented zaniness to give new life to Charles Dickens classic. Kermit the Frog is Bob Crachit, The Great Gonzo is the narrator, but also present are many of the other familiar Muppet characters - plus Muppet ghosts and Muppet vegetables. The only human face is that of Michael Caine who plays Ebenezer Scrooge. The story's meaning comes through but everything stays fun. Paul Williams' songs add a nice touch too. It must be said that kids will have more fun with this one than their parents will. But, who doesn't love the Muppets?

☐ Sex ☐ Nud ☐ Viol ☐ Lang ☐ AdSit

A: Michael Caine

MUPPET MOVIE, THE

D: James Frawley 96 m

G · COM · CLD · MUS · 1979 · COLOR

8 Effervescent silliness, and some really baaaad puns, make this a delight for everyone. Kids like it because it is light-hearted and silly. Adults get their own special treats - such as when Dom DeLuise interrupts Kermit who's catching flys in the swamp. Dom tells Kermit that he is lost and in a big hurry because he has to "catch a plane." Kermit responds with "Not with a tongue like yours." Irresistable zaniness as the Muppets travel to Hollywood so that they can become movie stars. 15 cameo appearances from some big stars. See also THE MUPPETS TAKE MANHATTEN.

☐ Sex ☐ Nud ☐ Viol ☐ Lang ☐ AdSit

A: Muppets, Milton Berle, Mel Brooks, Steve Martin, Bob Hope, Edgar Bergen

MUPPETS TAKE MANHATTAN, THE

D: Frank Oz 94 m

G · COM · CLD · 1984 · COLOR

8 The Muppets return. After Kermit and his friends create a hit college show, they decide that they are ready for the big time... Broadway. Off they head for the Big Apple where they get taken in by a shyster lawyer. They're so broke they live in lockers at the bus station, Kermit gets amnesia on his way to his wedding to Miss Piggy. Muppet madness, and a wide selection of cameo appearances from some of the industry's biggest names, is again at the heart of this extravaganza in silliness.

☐ Sex ☐ Nud ☐ Viol ☐ Lang ☐ AdSit

A: Art Carney, James Coco, Dabney Coleman, Elliott Gould, Joan Rivers, Linda Lavin

MY FRIEND FLICKA

D: Harold Schuster 89 m

NR · DMA · CLD · 1943 · COLOR

8 Touching and heartwarming. Despite his father's (Foster) concerns, a young boy (McDowall) longs to have a horse of his own. Finally giving in, Foster allows McDowall to pick from the herd, but he picks a filly with a bloodline that is known for its wildness. Persistent, the boy proves both himself and the horse when he manages to train the unruly animal which becomes his best friend. This magnificent sentimental favorite was based on Mary O'Hara's moving novel, and is a film that the whole family will enjoy. It was also made into a long-running TV series.

☐ Sex ☐ Nud ☐ Viol ☐ Lang ☐ AdSit

A: Roddy McDowall, Preston Foster, Rita Johnson, Jeff Corey, James Bell

MY GIRL

D: Howard Zieff 102 m

PG · DMA · ROM · CLD · 1991 · COLOR

8 Irresistable weeper. Eleven-year-old Chlumsky is the precocious daughter of a widowed mortician (Aydroyd) and because their house doubles for a mortuary, death is everywhere. Aykroyd doesn't have much time for his daughter, nor does he know how to reach out to her, not knowing that she feels responsible for her mother's death or that she's jealous when he falls for the new cosmetologist (Curtis) he has hired. But Macauly Culkin is her neighbor and that summer she and Culkin become best friends and experience the beginnings of young love. However, their summer together comes to a tragic end. Parents, share this one with your kids.

☐ Sex ☐ Nud ☑ Viol ☐ Lang ☑ AdSit

A: Anna Chlumsky, Macaulay Culkin, Dan Aykroyd, Jamie Lee Curtis, Richard Masur, Griffin Dunne

MY SIDE OF THE MOUNTAIN

D: James B. Clark 100 m

G · DMA · CLD · 1969 · COLOR

7 This is an entertaining back-to-nature tale in which a thirteen-year-old boy gives up all of his worldly possessions and the comforts of home, to test his survival skills by emulating his idol, Henry David Thoreau. He runs away intending to make the Canadian mountains his home for one year and takes nothing with him but his mind and his courage. Refreshing and charming, this is a film that the whole family will enjoy. It's not just for kids.

☐ Sex ☐ Nud ☐ Viol ☐ Lang ☐ AdSit

A: Ted Eccles, Theodore Bikel, Tudi Wiggins, Frank Perry, Prggi Loder

CHILDREN

MYSTERIOUS ISLAND

D: Cy Endfield 101 m

NR · ACT FAN CLD · 1961 · COLOR · Sex · Nud · ✓ Viol · Lang · AdSit

7 High-flying adventure from Jules Verne. Union soldiers escape from a Confederate prison in an observation balloon and are blown out to sea. They crash at sea and are spit up on the shores of the uncharted island of Captain Nemo (Lom). The island contains a volcano, pirates, incredibly large creatures (that mad-scientist Captain Nemo created to help with the world's food supply), two British girls who were also washed up on the island and Captain Nemo himself with his inoperative sub. Captain Nemo comes to their aid with all their other problems, but will he be able to save them when the volcano erupts?

A: Michael Craig, Joan Greenwood, Herbert Lom, Michael Callan, Gary Merrill

© COLUMBIA TRISTAR HOME VIDEO 60067

NATIONAL VELVET

D: Clarence Brown 124 m

G · DMA CLD · 1944 · COLOR · Sex · Nud · Viol · Lang · AdSit

10 All-time favorite for everyone... a real rah rah film, one that will have you cheering. Elizabeth Taylor is absolutely adorable as a young girl who wins a neighbor's unruly horse in a lottery. Then, she and her young friend, an embittered jockey (Mickey Rooney), train the horse to race and, against everyone's wishes, she enters him into England's famed Grand National steeplechase. A heartwarming and loveable story. It won two Oscars and was followed by INTERNATIONAL VELVET in 1977.

A: Elizabeth Taylor, Mickey Rooney, Donald Crisp, Anne Revere, Angela Lansbury, Reginald Owen

Distributed By MGM/UA Home Video M300480

NEW ADVENTURES OF PIPPI LONGSTOCKING, THE

D: Ken Annakin 100 m

G · CLD · 1988 · COLOR · Sex · Nud · Viol · Lang · AdSit

6 This film is based upon the classic children's character of Pippi Longstockings. Pippi is a red headed girl with pigtails, striped stockings, a quick mind and a streak of wild independence. She has been washed up on a Florida beach after being separated from her sea captain father by a ferocious tidal wave. Because she is alone, she is sent to an orphanage where she drives the mistress (Brennan) crazy with her wild practical jokes and pranks. Kids will have a good time with the food fights and the fun special effects.

A: Tami Erin, David Seaman, Jr., Cory Crow, Eileen Brennan, Dick Van Patten

© COLUMBIA TRISTAR HOME VIDEO 65008

OLD YELLER

D: Robert Stevenson 84 m

G · DMA CLD · 1957 · COLOR · Sex · Nud · ✓ Viol · Lang · AdSit

10 Wonderful, endearing Disney story that has been and will continue to be a perpetual family favorite for very good reason. Set in the Texas wilderness of 1859, a pioneer father leaves his family and homestead to join a cattle drive for a short while, leaving his young son "in charge" of the family. In the father's absence, the boy adopts a mongrel dog he names Old Yeller. Soon Old Yeller becomes his best friend and the family's protector. The two are inseparable. Then tragedy strikes and the boy must become a man. It is a powerful story for children but adults love it, too. See also THE YEARLING.

A: Dorothy McGuire, Fess Parker, Tommy Kirk, Kevin Corcoran, Jeff York, Chuck Connors

© WALT DISNEY HOME VIDEO 037

PARENT TRAP, THE

D: David Swift 129 m

NR · COM CLD · 1961 · COLOR · Sex · Nud · Viol · Lang · AdSit

9 Hugely popular Disney hit for the whole family. A prissy teenage girl from Boston runs into her spitting image in the form of a tomboy from California, at summer camp. The two mix like oil and water, at first. However, when they begin to compare notes, they discover that they are identical twins separated when their parents had divorced years before. Mom went east and Dad went west. The two decide to switch places at summer's end so each can meet the other parent and to begin a conspiracy designed to bring their still single parents back together again. Good fun for everyone. Hayley Mills is delightful.

A: Hayley Mills, Maureen O'Hara, Brian Keith, Charlie Ruggles, Leo G. Carroll, Joanna Barnes

© WALT DISNEY HOME VIDEO 107

PEE-WEE'S BIG ADVENTURE

D: Tim Burton 92 m

PG · CLD · 1985 · COLOR · Sex · Nud · ✓ Viol · Lang · AdSit

8 Kids, especially the little ones, love this stuff. Pee-wee Herman is a very nerdish character who becomes very upset when someone has stolen his prized Red Rocket bicycle. He will do anything to get it back. So, he begins a nationwide search to find it. In his trip, he will meet a variety of interesting and very curious characters: an ex-convict, a friendly waitress and group of bikers... and then there is truck-driving "Large Marge." The kids really love her. Lot of fun for kids. Really quite inventive stuff.

A: Pee-wee Herman, Elizabeth Daily, Mark Holton, Diane Salinger, Judd Omen

© WARNER HOME VIDEO 11523

PETER PAN

D: Vincent J. Donehue 104 m

NR · MUS CLD · 1960 · COLOR · Sex · Nud · Viol · Lang · AdSit

8 In December 1960, NBC television aired a wonderful musical version of the children's classic starring Mary Martin, for which she won an Emmy. Time has not dimmed the sense of magic and wonder it inspires. Wendy is a young girl, verging on womanhood. However, just before she is all grown up, she and her two young brothers are escorted to Never Never Land, a magical land where only children may go. Their guide there is Peter Pan, a magical boy who refuses to ever grow up. He takes them to a place where there is constant adventure with pirates and Indians and ceaseless fun. Inspired. Also see Spielberg's 1992 follow-up HOOK.

A: Mary Martin, Cyril Ritchard, Sondra Lee, Margalo Gilmore

© GOODTIMES 7001

PETE'S DRAGON

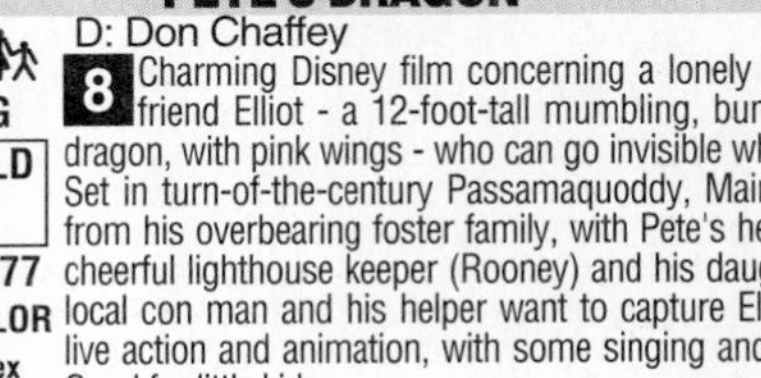

D: Don Chaffey 128 m

G · CLD · 1977 · COLOR · Sex · Nud · Viol · Lang · AdSit

8 Charming Disney film concerning a lonely orphan boy and his friend Elliot - a 12-foot-tall mumbling, bumbling, bright green dragon, with pink wings - who can go invisible whenever he wants to. Set in turn-of-the-century Passamaquoddy, Maine, the boy escapes from his overbearing foster family, with Pete's help, and stays with a cheerful lighthouse keeper (Rooney) and his daughter (Reddy). But a local con man and his helper want to capture Elliot. Pleasing mix of live action and animation, with some singing and dancing thrown in. Good for little kids.

A: Helen Reddy, Jim Dale, Mickey Rooney, Red Buttons, Shelley Winters, Sean Marshall

© WALT DISNEY HOME VIDEO 010

POLLYANNA

D: David Swift 134 m

CLD · 1960 · COLOR · Sex · Nud · Viol · Lang · AdSit

9 Young Haley Mills took home an Oscar for her performance as the ever-cheerful Pollyanna in this Disney adaptation of Eleanor Porter's charming story. Pollyanna is a 12-year-old orphan who comes to live with her very rich, very stuffy aunt (Wyman) who dominates a small New England town near the turn of the 20th-century. Pollyanna is a perennially happy girl who makes a practice of always looking for the good in people. She sparks a transformation in the townsfolk, who she manages to infect with her optimism - eventually even including her gloomy aunt. Genuinely fun and heartwarming entertainment the whole family can enjoy. Great cast of supporting characters. Truly fun.

A: Hayley Mills, Richard Egan, Jane Wyman, Karl Malden, Adolphe Menjou, Agnes Moorehead

© WALT DISNEY HOME VIDEO 045

POOR LITTLE RICH GIRL, THE

D: Irving Cummings 72 m

NR · MUS CLD · 1936 · B&W · Sex · Nud · Viol · Lang · AdSit

8 One of Shirley Temple's best. She plays the motherless daughter of a rich man who has sent her off to boarding school. But she ducks out of the school and gets lost. She teams up with a husband and wife vaudeville act by telling them that she is an orphan. Together, all three sing and dance their way to success and, in the end, Shirley is reunited with her father and his new wife. Look for her famous number in a military uniform and rifle "Military Man," along with "Oh My Goodness," "You've Got to Eat Your Spinach, Baby" and "When I'm With You."

A: Shirley Temple, Alice Faye, Jack Haley, Gloria Stuart, Michael Whalen, Claude Gillingwater

© FOXVIDEO 1069

POPEYE

D: Robert Altman 114 m

PG · COM CLD MUS · 1980 · COLOR · Sex · Nud · Viol · Lang · AdSit

6 Curious live-action version of the famous cartoon character. Not a wonderful musical, but not too bad, either. It is an imaginative staging and production with some really wonderful characterizations from Duvall and especially Williams. All the famous characters are here. Popeye (Williams) rows into port looking for his pappy (Walston). He falls in love with skinny Olive (Duvall), even though she is engaged to Bluto (Smith). Interesting and clever. It was unfairly ignored at the box office by an audience that didn't know quite what how to take it. A good family movie.

A: Robin Williams, Shelley Duvall, Ray Walston, Linda Hunt, Paul L. Smith, Paul Dooley

© PARAMOUNT HOME VIDEO 1171

PRINCE AND THE PAUPER, THE

D: William Keighley 119 m

NR · DMA CLD · 1937 · B&W · Sex · Nud · Viol · Lang · AdSit

8 Rousing film version (the best one) of Mark Twain's own personal favorite of al his many stories. A young English prince longs to learn what life is really like in 16th-century London's slums, so he exchanges clothes and places with a street urchin who is his look-alike. No one is to know, but his enemies at the court learn of the switch and plan to crown the wrong boy King. No one believes the displaced prince's story except for rakish Errol Flynn, who rides and swashbuckles to the aid of the young prince. Large scale and highly enjoyable for young and old.

A: Errol Flynn, Billy Mauch, Bobby Mauch, Claude Rains, Alan Hale, Rex Harrison

Distributed By MGM/UA Home Video 201865

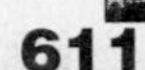

REBECCA OF SUNNYBROOK FARM

D: Allan Dwan 80 m

NR | MUS CLD | 1938 | B&W

6 Engaging family musical. A little girl (Temple) desperately wants to become a radio star and when a talent scout living next door to her aunt's farmhouse, where she is staying, realizes that she has the right stuff, he gets her career going. The girl rockets to stardom, but her wicked stepfather tries to make money on the deal, too. Shirley sings "On the Good Ship Lollipop" and "Animal Crackers." Even better, she gets to pal about with Jack Haley and Bill "Bojangles" Robinson. The title of this film has nothing to do with the famous book.

Sex Nud Viol Lang AdSit

A: Shirley Temple, Jack Haley, Randolph Scott, Bill Robinson, Gloria Stuart, Phyllis Brooks

© FOXVIDEO 1065

RED BALLOON, THE

D: Albert Lamorisse 34 m

FAN CLD FOR | 1956 | COLOR

10 A brilliant children's treasure! While there is no dialogue in this classic fantasy, it remains one of the most charming films of all time. In this engaging story, a young boy (Lamorisse) makes friends with a red balloon, and it follows him all around Paris. It goes to school with him. It even waits for him outside his window when he is in his room. The film is so visually flawless that the story is crystal clear - it needs no dialogue. A winner for both children and adults alike with a sparkling musical score. Winner of an Academy Award for Best Original Screenplay. Unequaled!

Sex Nud Viol Lang AdSit

A: Pascal Lamorisse, Georges Seliler

© NEW LINE HOME VIDEO 6001

RED PONY, THE

D: Lewis Milestone 89 m

NR | DMA CLD | 1949 | COLOR

8 Touching, affecting and moving story that was created by blending of three short stories by John Steinbeck. In it, a lonely young boy turns to a ranchhand for understanding and guidance, and to a frail young horse for affection. The boy's stiff schoolteacher father has married a wealthy woman and she is taking up all his time. The father has become even more distant than before and the boy is confused. This excellent family movie is very believable because the characters are developed effectively through understatement. Strong performances by Mitchum and the boy, Peter Miles. Highly recommended.

Sex Nud Viol Lang AdSit

A: Myrna Loy, Robert Mitchum, Louis Calhern, Peter Miles

© REPUBLIC PICTURES HOME VIDEO 3406

RED SHOES, THE

D: Michael Powell 136 m

NR | ROM MUS CLD | 1948 | COLOR

8 Opulent, grandly romantic and very popular, especially with young girls. A beautiful young ballerina (Shearer) is torn. She is in love with a composer (Goring), but the ballet company's heartless director (Walbrook) does not approve. The conflict between her love of dance and her love for a man is paralleled by the dance she is most famous for - "Dance of the Red Shoes" - which was adapted from the Hans Christian Anderson fairy tale about bewitched shoes that nearly dance the wearer to death. This very popular musical is sure to have inspired many young dancers. Nominated for 5 Oscars, including Best Picture. Followed by THE TALES OF HOFFMAN.

Sex Nud Viol Lang AdSit

A: Moira Shearer, Emeric Pressburger, Anton Walbrook, Robert Helpmann, Marius Goring, Leonide Massine

© PARAMOUNT HOME VIDEO 12572

ROOKIE OF THE YEAR

D: Daniel Stern 103 m

PG | CLD COM | 1993 | COLOR

7 Lightweight fantasy adventure for kids. Nicholas is crazy about baseball, but he is so clumsy that he's always the last kid on the bench to get played. Then a miracle happens... he breaks his arm. It's a miracle because when it heals on its own, he discovers that the tendons have been stretched too tight, so his arm now is like a catapult. Those shortened tendons have given him a 100 mph fastball. Now the kid who could never play, has just signed a contract to pitch for the Chicago Cubs. He's got the power but he needs help to put it to use. Gary Busy is a nearly over-the-hill pitcher that shows him how to get the job done. Pleasant enough pastime for kids.

Sex Nud Viol Lang AdSit

A: Thomas Ian Nicholas, Gary Busy, Albert Hall, Amy Morton, Dan Hedaya, Bruce Altman

© FOX 8521

RUMPELSTILTSKIN

D: David Irving 84 m

G | MUS CLD | 1986 | COLOR

6 A well-done version of this fanciful children's fairy tale. A young girl (Irving) daydreams of magical things and her father swears that everything she touches turns to gold. When the evil King (Revill) hears of this, he summons her to spin straw into gold or be executed. To the rescue comes a mysterious little man, Rumpelstiltskin (Barty), who gets her out of her horrible situation but he expects a very expensive form of repayment. He wants Irving's first-born child - that is, unless she can guess his name. An enjoyable fantasy that young children will especially enjoy.

Sex Nud Viol Lang AdSit

A: Amy Irving, Priscilla Pointer, Billy Barty, Clive Revill, John Moulder-Brown, Robert Symonds

© MEDIA HOME ENTERTAINMENT, INC. M919

SANDLOT, THE

D: David Mickey Evans 101 m

PG | CLD | 1993 | COLOR

7 As a buddy-film for younger kids, this is a pleasant enough pastime. It is a story about a new kid in town. The other kids think Scotty is just a dork - he doesn't even know how to play baseball. But then he is befriended by Benny, the little league's biggest baseball hero, who is also the leader of the neighborhood's ragtag ball team. Benny teaches Scotty how to play baseball and transforms him into a winner. The boys' summer is then spent playing baseball, chasing girls, getting sick at the fair and trying to get their ball back from a big nasty junkyard dog. By the end of summer, Scotty feels at home.

Sex Nud Viol ◢ Lang AdSit

A: Tom Guiry, Mike Vitar, Patrick Renna, Chauncey Leopardi, Marty York, Brandon Adams

© FOXVIDEO 8500

SAVANNAH SMILES

D: Pierre DeMoro 105 m

PG | COM CLD | 1982 | COLOR

8 A real charmer. Savannah (Anderson) is a six-year old who runs away from her snooty, rich parents and she winds up in the back seat of a car belonging to two soft-hearted escaped convicts. Her father has offered a huge reward for her return, but who's going to believe the story of two convicts. So, they try valiantly to get her back without blowing their cover. Meanwhile, the three hide out in an abandoned house where they all become a loving "family," experiencing feelings none of them has ever known before. Chock-full of tender moments, sincere laughs and an ending that packs an emotional punch. A gem!

Sex Nud Viol Lang AdSit

A: Mark Miller, Donovan Scott, Bridgette Andersen, Peter Graves, Michael Parks, Noriyuki "Pat" Morita

© NEW LINE HOME VIDEO 2058

SEA GYPSIES, THE

D: Stewart Raffill 102 m

G | CLD | 1978 | COLOR

8 Good, exciting family entertainment. A female photographer, a widower, his two daughters and a young stowaway all set out on an around-the-world sailing cruise, but their trip is cut short when they become shipwrecked off Alaska on one of the Aleutian Islands. Trapped on the island, faced with a fierce oncoming winter and hostile animals, they begin to build a craft that they can use for escape before it's too late. Beautiful photography, filmed on location. Based loosely upon a real-life event.

Sex Nud Viol Lang AdSit

A: Robert Logan, Mikki Jamison-Olsen, Heather Rattray, Cjon Damitri Patterson, Shannon Saylor

© WARNER HOME VIDEO 11280

SECRET GARDEN, THE

D: Fred M. Wilcox 92 m

NR | DMA CLD | 1949 | COLOR

8 Vivid dramatization of the children's classic. A young orphaned girl (O'Brien) is uprooted from India and taken to stay with her embittered uncle (Marshall) and his crippled son (Stockwell) in their huge, dark and foreboding mansion in Victorian England. Marshall is a cold, insensitive and stern type, and Stockwell is a disturbed and unhappy lad. But the determined young girl manages to melt her uncle's heart and bring them happiness, both because she looks so much like his deceased wife and because she finds her aunt's secret garden and begins to nurse it back to life.

Sex Nud Viol Lang AdSit

A: Margaret O'Brien, Dean Stockwell, Herbert Marshall, Gladys Cooper, Elsa Lanchester

Distributed By MGM/UA Home Video 202377

SECRET GARDEN, THE

D: Agnieszka Holland 103 m

PG | DMA CLD | 1993 | COLOR

9 A sumptuously photographed screen adaptation of Frances Hodgson Burnett's classic 1911 novel. Ten-year-old Mary is a sad orphaned girl who has been returned to England from India after her parents were killed. She is to live with her cold uncle, who is still mourning his wife's death, and his bed-ridden ten-year-old son. Their huge mansion, on the cold and misty moors, is a lifeless loveless place. Mary begins to explore her new home and discovers a garden that has been locked away since her aunt's death. She begins to nurture the neglected garden and to draw out her sick cousin. Slowly life begins to return to them all. Excellent, but too intense and slow for young kids. 10 and up.

Sex Nud Viol Lang AdSit

A: Kate Maberly, Heydon Prowse, Andrew Knott, John Lynch, Laura Crossley, Maggie Smith

© WARNER HOME VIDEO 19000

SESAME STREET PRESENTS: FOLLOW THAT BIRD

D: Ken Kwapis 92 m

G | CLD | 1985 | COLOR

8 Quality fun for the children! Big Bird gets sent off to live with his own kind. However, when he gets there, he quickly gets a bad case of homesickness and decides to take to the highway to get back home to Sesame Street. Meanwhile, his friends from Sesame Street have also set out to find him and bring him back. But, Big Bird is plagued on his journey home by the Sleaze Brothers (Thomas and Flaherty) who want to make Big Bird the main attraction in their amusement park. The Sesame Street gang are the scene stealers in this wonderful film that the children will love and adults may, too.

Sex Nud Viol Lang AdSit

A: Sandra Bernhard, John Candy, Chevy Chase, Joe Flaherty, Dave Thomas

© WARNER HOME VIDEO 11522

SHAGGY DOG, THE

D: Charles Barton — 101 m

G · CLD COM · 1959 · B&W · Sex / Nud / Viol / Lang / AdSit

8 A winning classic Disney fantasy! A young Wilby Daniels (Tommy Kirk) has found an ancient ring and mutters the magic words inscribed inside. He suddenly discovers that he has now cast a magical spell which transforms him into a sheepdog - and does it at the worst possible random moments. His predicament is made even worse because his dad (Fred MacMurray) is allergic to dogs. The only way he can break the spell and be turned back into a boy permanently is by an act of heroism. Disney's first attempt at a live action film is chock full of fun gags and charm. A good time!

A: Fred MacMurray, Jean Hagen, Tommy Kirk, Annette Funicello, Tim Considine, Kevin Corcoran

© WALT DISNEY HOME VIDEO 43

SHIPWRECKED

D: Nils Gaup — 93 m

PG · ACT CLD · 1991 · COLOR · Sex / Nud / ◢ Viol / Lang / AdSit

8 A young boy joins the crew of a sailing ship as cabin boy to earn money to help save his parent's farm. They set sail for the South Seas, but on board is a pirate posing as a British naval officer. It is his plan to wait until the ship gets to the right location and then take control. However, just as he does, the ship is caught up in a terrible storm and is capsized. The lad makes it to a tropical island, but soon discovers that this is the island the pirate was seeking and it contains his buried treasure. Shipwrecked on a pirate island, the boy finds that he is not alone, and he must struggle to survive. Rousing Disney adventure film for young and old alike.

A: Stian Smestad, Gabriel Byrne, Louisa Haigh, Trond Munch, Bjorn Sundquist, Eva Von Honna

© WALT DISNEY HOME VIDEO 1168

SKEEZER

D: Peter H. Hunt — 96 m

NR · DMA CLD · 1981 · COLOR · Sex / Nud / Viol / Lang / AdSit

8 A surprising true story that is sure to touch a soft spot in even the hardest of hearts. In this heartwarming, made-for-TV drama, a social worker discovers that letting troubled and lonely children play with Skeezer, a loveable sheepdog, produces wonderful results. After just a few hours with the dog, the children with emotional disorders in the home where she works, are much more calm and receptive to others. This true-life tale merely exposes the simple truth that we all need acceptance and love.

A: Karen Valentine, Dee Wallace, Justin Lord, Tom Atkins

© LIVE HOME VIDEO 66870

SO DEAR TO MY HEART

D: Harold Schuster — 82 m

NR · DMA CLD · 1948 · COLOR · Sex / Nud / Viol / Lang / AdSit

9 A warm-hearted Disney film about a boy making his dream come true, and a reminder of a time long gone by! Young farmboy Driscoll's favorite pet is Danny, a black sheep with a foul temper. Driscoll desperately wants to take Danny to the county fair to try his luck at winning a blue ribbon. His problem is that he first has to figure out a way to earn the entry fee. Burl Ives is a big man with a gentle song who urges him to pursue his dream. Live animation mixes with a touching bit of nostalgia to create a delightful tribute to the past.

A: Burl Ives, Beulah Bondi, Bobby Driscoll, Luana Patten, Harry Carey

© WALT DISNEY HOME VIDEO 296

SON OF LASSIE

D: S. Sylvan Simon — 100 m

G · CLD · 1945 · COLOR · Sex / Nud / Viol / Lang / AdSit

6 The sequel to LASSIE COME HOME finds the young British boy now grown and enlisted in the British war effort. Separated from his much loved master who has gone off to war, the son of Lassie, Laddie, sneaks aboard his master's plane. Then, when they are both shot down over Germany, the Germans use the unsuspecting Laddie to track his master down. Good one for kids and dog people.

A: Peter Lawford, Donald Crisp, June Lockhart, Nigel Bruce, William Severn, Leon Ames

Distributed By MGM/UA Home Video 201084

SPACECAMP

D: Harry Winer — 115 m

PG · ACT CLD · 1986 · COLOR · Sex / Nud / Viol / ◢ Lang / AdSit

6 An exciting adventure for anyone who ever dreamed of being an astronaut. Five awe-struck teenagers are chosen to spend the summer at a NASA space camp and learn all about the wonders of the space shuttle with the help of astronaut Capshaw. The summer program is sailing along until a robot, with a mind of its own, decides to launch the novice crew into space. When Capshaw gets injured, the teenage astronauts must figure out a way to get their hides back to earth in one piece. A fun trip.

A: Kate Capshaw, Lea Thompson, Tom Skerritt, Kelly Preston, Larry B. Scott, Tate Donovan

© LIVE HOME VIDEO VA5174

SQUANTO: A WARRIOR'S TALE

D: Xavier Koller — 112 m

PG · CLD ACT · 1994 · COLOR · Sex / Nud / ◢ Viol / Lang / AdSit

7 Squanto was an actual character from American history, whose story is here told by the people at Disney. Set in the early 1600s, Squanto was a young Indian warrior who was captured and returned to England as a prized slave. There, he escaped his captors and from a group of monks, learned both how to speak English and that not all Englishmen were bad. The monks eventually also helped him to return home, on a ship loaded with Pilgrims. However, when they arrive, the locals are prepared to fight this time. Even though his own tribe had been murdered, Squanto convinces these Indians that war brings only pain and successfully brokers a long-lived peace. The story is very simply told. Most suitable for children and teens.

A: Adam Beach, Eric Schweig, Mandy Patinkin, Michael Gambon, Nathaniel Parker, Alex Norton

© WALT DISNEY HOME VIDEO 2552

SUBURBAN COMMANDO

D: Burt Kennedy — 88 m

PG · CLD COM · 1991 · COLOR · Sex / Nud / Viol / Lang / AdSit

7 Wrestling's superstar Hulk Hogan is surprisingly likable and effective as Shep Ramsey, an alien warrior who has battled General Ball and defeated his plan to take over the Universe. He has come to earth to get a little well-deserved rest but instead becomes involved with the troubled lives of a down-on-their-luck urban family. Father Christopher Lloyd is too mild-mannered and is being over-run by his boss, so Shep gives him some lessons and helps to revive their luck. Mostly for kids.

A: Hulk Hogan, Christopher Lloyd, Shelley Duvall, Larry Miller, William Ball, JoAnn Dearing

© TURNER HOME ENTERTAINMENT N4098

SUPER MARIO BROTHERS

D: Rocky Morton, Annabel Jankel — 104 m

PG · CLD · 1993 · COLOR · Sex / Nud / ◢ Viol / Lang / AdSit

7 Spurred on by the monster success of the video game of the same name, Hollywood has created its own special adventure for the hero plumbers. A parallel universe is discovered near Brooklyn and the brothers enter it to help its beautiful princess "Dinohattan" battle the half human/half lizard king. (You see, this is a universe where the inhabitants have evolved directly from dinosaurs.) The king has kidnapped the princess because she possesses a magical meteorite fragment. Lots of special effects, energy and non-threatening violence, but it lacks creative spark. Still, the kids will like it.

A: Bob Hoskins, John Leguizamo, Dennis Hopper, Samantha Mathis, Fisher Stevens, Fiona Shaw

© HOLLYWOOD PICTURES HOME VIDEO 2008

SWISS FAMILY ROBINSON

D: Ken Annakin — 126 m

G · ACT CLD · 1960 · COLOR · Sex / Nud / ◢ Viol / Lang / AdSit

9 Rousing fanciful adventure story that should be on every kid's - certainly every boy's - to-watch list, but is also entertaining for the entire family. Patented Disney adventure. Set in the early 19th-century, a family has set sail to escape the despotic rule of Napoleon but, under pursuit by pirates, they become shipwrecked on a tropical island paradise. The inventive father and his two older sons build a wonderland for the family out of native materials and an array of inventive weapons to ward off the impending assault of pirates led by Hayakawa. Top drawer entertainment.

A: John Mills, Dorothy McGuire, James MacArthur, Janet Munro, Tommy Kirk, Sessue Hayakawa

© WALT DISNEY HOME VIDEO 053

SWORD AND THE ROSE, THE

D: Ken Annakin — 92 m

NR · ACT CLD · 1953 · COLOR · Sex / Nud / ◢ Viol / Lang / AdSit

7 A rich tapestry of Disney heroics, adventure and romance. Set during the reign of King Henry VIII (Justice), Henry's sister, Mary Tudor (Johns), falls in love with a lowly common man (Todd) but is sent to marry the much older King of France by her brother. When the French King dies, the opportunistic and villainous Duke of Buckingham (Gough) seizes the opportunity to try to take Mary's hand in marriage, away from her true love, Todd. Todd must rescue her. Disney filmed this spirited period piece in England. It is rich in flavor but there is no basis in history for it.

A: Richard Todd, Glynis Johns, James Robertson Justice, Michael Gough, Jane Barrett

© WALT DISNEY HOME VIDEO 266

SYLVESTER

D: Tim Hunter — 104 m

PG · DMA CLD · 1984 · COLOR · Sex / Nud / Viol / ◢ Lang / AdSit

8 NATIONAL VELVET fans take note! Sylvester is an untamed jumping horse that catches the fancy of sixteen year-old tomboy Gilbert. She and her two brothers are orphaned and are under the care of a crusty old horse trainer (Farnsworth). Gilbert falls in love with the beautiful white horse and enlists the aid of Farnsworth to help train it, even though he doesn't think the horse has a chance. But with his help, she and Sylvester do train the horse for the event of her life held in Lexington, Kentucky. A charmer that lifts you up and leaves you feeling very good.

A: Melissa Gilbert, Richard Farnsworth, Michael Schoeffling, Constance Towers

© COLUMBIA TRISTAR HOME VIDEO 60476

TEENAGE MUTANT NINJA TURTLES II - THE SECRET OF THE OOZE

PG | CLD | 1991 | COLOR

D: Michael Pressman — 88 m

8 Those pizza-loving evil-fighting humanoid turtles are back. This time as live-action figures. They are still striving to rid New York City of evil. Once again they are up against their archenemy called the Foot, led by the nasty and evil Shreader. When the Foot captures the last remaining canister of the glowing ooze that created the turtles in the first place, the fearsome foursome go to get it back. Lots of kiddy-type action and suspense again. Virtually no plot. The kids will love it.

☐ Sex ☐ Nud ☑ Viol ☐ Lang ☐ AdSit

A: Francois Chau, Paige Turco, David Warner, Ernie Reyes, Jr., Vanilla Ice

© TURNER HOME ENTERTAINMENT N4100

THAT DARN CAT!

G | CLD COM | 1965 | COLOR

D: Robert Stevenson — 115 m

8 Lively Disney comedy about a Siamese cat named DC (Darned Cat), belonging to Hayley Mills, who comes home one night after its regular excursion with the wristwatch of a kidnapped bank teller around its neck. Hayley calls the FBI and agent Dean Jones (who is allergic to cats) trails DC through one slapstick adventure after another in his search to find the kidnapped woman. Bright and lively comedy with plenty of interesting characters, much like you would expect from the Disney fun factory.

☐ Sex ☐ Nud ☐ Viol ☐ Lang ☐ AdSit

A: Hayley Mills, Dean Jones, Dorothy Provine, Roddy McDowall, Neville Brand, Elsa Lanchester

© WALT DISNEY HOME VIDEO 4125

THEM

NR | SF SUS | 1954 | B&W

D: Gordon Douglas — 93 m

7 This is a well-crafted science fiction monster classic from the early '50s. A young, terrified girl is discovered in the destroyed remains of trailer home out in the New Mexico desert. From their investigation, two scientists discover that recent atomic testing has mutated a race of giant ants. They and FBI agent James Arness, trace the ants to their nest and their queen in the sewers of L.A. This is a actually a thoughtful film which gives its subject serious treatment. Time is taken to make the premise credible and believable. And, it also has some scenes which will create genuine fear. Good special effects, too.

☐ Sex ☐ Nud ☑ Viol ☐ Lang ☐ AdSit

A: James Whitmore, Edmund Gwenn, Joan Weldon, James Arness, Onslow Stevens, Chris Drake

© WARNER HOME VIDEO 11191

THIEF OF BAGDAD, THE

NR | ACT FAN CLD | 1940 | COLOR

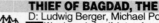

D: Ludwig Berger, Michael Powell — 106 m

9 Wonderously fanciful story from the tales of the "Arabian Nights." Who couldn't become captivated by the story of a young prince, tricked out of his kingdom and his girl by the evil Grand Vizier, only to be rescued by a thief on a magic carpet who also has the help of a colossal magical genie? Then, throw in an enormous spider, a dog who once was a boy, a flying toy horse, a flower that causes amnesia and a beautiful girl. All the above, combined with terrific special effects and an outstanding score, have made this a perennial favorite. 3 Oscars.

☐ Sex ☐ Nud ☐ Viol ☐ Lang ☐ AdSit

A: Sabu, Conrad Veidt, June Duprez, John Justin, Rex Ingram, Miles Malleson

© HBO VIDEO 90653

THREE LIVES OF THOMASINA, THE

NR | CLD | 1963 | COLOR

D: Don Chaffey — 97 m

8 Thomasina is a cat that belongs to the daughter of a stern Scottish veterinarian. Thomasina is very sick. The veterinarian father decides the cat is so sick that it should be put to sleep, and he does it. The cat goes to heaven (a neat trip) but later mysteriously turns up at the house of a reclusive neighbor who is said to have mystical powers. Sure enough, she has brought Thomasina back for the little girl, but in the process, she also teaches the father how to be more compassionate, and she heals the relationship between him and his daughter. A winner from Disney.

☐ Sex ☐ Nud ☐ Viol ☐ Lang ☐ AdSit

A: Patrick McGoohan, Susan Hampshire, Karen Dotrice, Matthew Gerber, Laurence Naismith, Jean Anderson

© WALT DISNEY HOME VIDEO 185

TOM SAWYER

G | MUS CLD | 1973 | COLOR

D: Don Taylor — 102 m

8 Well done musical remake of Mark Twain's classic, set in the 1830s Missouri wilds along the Mississippi river, near the town of Hannibal. It concerns the exploits of young Tom (Whitaker), his friend - outcast Huck Finn (East) and his girl friend Becky Thatcher (a very young Jodie Foster). this is a first-rate children's movie that will also appeal to many adults. The picture garnered Oscar nominations for Set Decoration, Costume Design and Score. Music and screenplay were written by the same people who did MARY POPPINS, Richard and Robert Sherman.

☐ Sex ☐ Nud ☐ Viol ☐ Lang ☐ AdSit

A: Johnny Whitaker, Celeste Holm, Warren Oates, Jeff East, Jodie Foster

Distributed By MGM/UA Home Video M201863

TOM THUMB

G | CLD | 1958 | COLOR

D: George Pal — 93 m

8 A really neat adaptation by George Pal (and his Puppetoons) of the classic fairy story about a lonely woodcutter and his wife who are given a son by the forest queen. Even though their new son is only six inches tall, the cheerful Tom is beloved by everyone in town. However, the evil Terry-Thomas and his bungling henchman Peter Sellers plot to use tiny Tom to break into the town's treasury to steal it. Charming characters and great story telling. Won an Oscar for Best Special Effects. Kids will love it and so will fanciful adults.

☐ Sex ☐ Nud ☐ Viol ☐ Lang ☐ AdSit

A: Russ Tamblyn, Peter Sellers, Terry-Thomas, Alan Young, June Thorburn, Bernard Miles

Distributed By MGM/UA Home Video M400430

TREASURE ISLAND

NR | ACT CLD | 1934 | B&W

D: Victor Fleming — 105 m

8 This was the first adaptation of Robert Lewis Stevenson's classic story for the big screen, and MGM pulled out all the stops. A young boy (Cooper) receives a treasure map from a dying sailor and then takes on a job as a cabin boy on a ship bound for the treasure island. Also on board is the scurrilous old sea dog Long John Silver (Beery), who sets his sights on stealing the boy's treasure and rallies the ship's crew to mutiny. Fine adventure film that will still inspire the imagination of any adventurous boy.

☐ Sex ☐ Nud ☑ Viol ☐ Lang ☐ AdSit

A: Wallace Beery, Jackie Cooper, Lionel Barrymore, Otto Kruger, Nigel Bruce, Lewis Stone

Distributed By MGM/UA Home Video M500032

TREASURE ISLAND

G | ACT CLD | 1950 | COLOR

D: Byron Haskin — 96 m

8 Walt Disney remade the 1934 version of Stevenson's classic. This version did an excellent job with it and some say even improved upon the earlier version. However, the ending was changed and, in 1975 when it was reissued again, some of the more violent sequences were removed. Bobby Driscoll plays young Jim Hawkins, a young English lad who receives a treasure map from a dying sailor. Aboard a ship bound for the island, Long John Silver (Newton) and the crew of pirates seize control of the ship in a mutiny so they can conduct their own search for the treasure and steal it.

☐ Sex ☐ Nud ☑ Viol ☐ Lang ☐ AdSit

A: Bobby Driscoll, Robert Newton, Basil Sydney, Walter Fitzgerald

© WALT DISNEY HOME VIDEO 041

TROUBLE WITH ANGELS, THE

NR | COM CLD | 1966 | COLOR

D: Ida Lupino — 110 m

7 Charming light-weight fare in which two rambunctious young girls (Hayley Mills and June Harding) are constantly playing pranks and raising Cain at a Catholic convent school. They are driving the normally sane and saintly Mother Superior (Rosalind Russell) nuts. Warm and genial comedy suitable for the whole family.

☐ Sex ☐ Nud ☐ Viol ☐ Lang ☐ AdSit

A: Hayley Mills, June Harding, Rosalind Russell, Binnie Barnes, Mary Wickes, Gypsy Rose Lee

© COLUMBIA TRISTAR HOME VIDEO 60250

TUCK EVERLASTING

NR | FAN CLD | 1981 | COLOR

D: Frederick King Keller — 90 m

8 Enchanting, entertaining and intelligent fantasy that the whole family can enjoy. One day, while walking through the woods, Young Whynnie discovers the Tuck family. The Tucks feel no pain, never grow old and will never die. The Tucks come to like and eventually trust her enough to reveal to her their secret. This is a charming story that is not at all patronizing to kids and is a rewarding experience for the whole family. The film was adapted from Natalie Babbitt's novel of the same title.

☐ Sex ☐ Nud ☐ Viol ☐ Lang ☐ AdSit

A: Margaret Chamberlain, Paul Flessa, Fred A. Keller, James McGuire, Sonia Raimi, Bruce D'Auria

© LIVE HOME VIDEO VA4228

ULYSSES

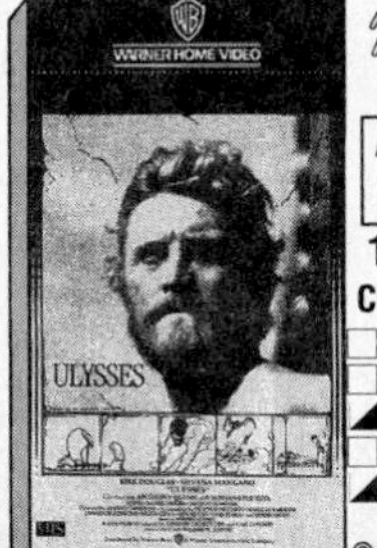

NR | ACT FAN CLD | 1955 | COLOR

D: Mario Camerini — 102 m

6 Lavish production of Homer's ancient and epic tale about Ulysses, the King of Ithica, and his long journey home after the Trojan wars. For ten years Ulysses struggles to reach home and his faithful wife Penelope. But all along the way, he is beset by trial after trial unleashed upon him by King Neptune, god of the sea, who is upset with him for having destroyed the Trojans. He is attacked by a hungry one-eyed Cyclops, enticed by Siren songstresses and seduced by the beautiful witch Circe. Then, arriving at home, he must also rescue Penelope, who is being beset by suitors who want to marry her and become king.

☐ Sex ☐ Nud ☑ Viol ☐ Lang ☑ AdSit

A: Kirk Douglas, Luana Mangano, Anthony Quinn, Silvana Mangano

© WARNER HOME VIDEO 11470

UNCLE BUCK

D: John Hughes — 100 m

PG | COM CLD | 1989 | COLOR

7 Lightweight but enjoyable farce that is mostly for the younger set. When the family is hit by a crisis and Mom and Dad have to leave for a while, they bring in big, oafish, clumsy, bachelor Uncle Buck to look after his nephew and nieces. In spite of his faltering attempts at surrogate parenthood, the kids, particularly teenage daughter Kelly, come to realize that old Buck isn't so bad after all. Contrary to how it might appear, there is some intelligence behind the slapstick. It'll leave your heart a little warmer, too.

Sex / Nud / Viol / ◢ Lang / AdSit

A: John Candy, Amy Madigan, Jean Kelly, Macaulay Culkin, Gaby Hoffman

© MCA/UNIVERSAL HOME VIDEO, INC. 80900

VOYAGE TO THE BOTTOM OF THE SEA

D: Irwin Allen — 106 m

NR | SF CLD | 1961 | COLOR

6 Reasonably good, light, family-oriented sci-fi flick in which a brilliant submarine commander (Pidgeon) has devised a scheme to save the earth, after the Van Allen radiation belts erupt and threaten to destroy it. The Arctic is already on fire and soon fire will engulf the whole earth unless they can stop it. His plan is to launch a polaris missile into space and then explode it, breaking the chain reaction. But before they can get the sub into position to do that, they have to defeat a sea monster, fend off attacking submarines and an on-board saboteur. It spawned a popular mid-'60s TV series.

Sex / Nud / ◢ Viol / Lang / AdSit

A: Walter Pidgeon, Joan Fontaine, Peter Lorre, Robert Sterling, Barbara Eden, Michael Ansara

© FOXVIDEO 1044

WARGAMES

D: John Badham — 114 m

PG | SUS | 1983 | COLOR

8 This is an entertaining film for the whole family. A bored teenage computer whiz (Broderick) and his girlfriend (Sheedy) think they've gained access to a new, unreleased computer game called "Global Thermonuclear Warfare" from a game manufacturer. What they really did was to break into the Pentagon's computers. Their game is no game. The entire nation has been placed on nuclear alert and the world on the brink of the ultimate war. Broderick is sought by the government people, who are led by Dabney Coleman, who must stop what he has started. Very entertaining and convincingly done. Not just for kids.

Sex / Nud / ◢ Viol / ◢ Lang / AdSit

A: Matthew Broderick, Dabney Coleman, Ally Sheedy, Barry Corbin, John Wood, Juanin Clay

Distributed By MGM/UA Home Video M200293

WEE WILLIE WINKIE

D: John Ford — 100 m

NR | CLD | 1937 | B&W

8 One of Shirley Temple's best films. It is the story of a little girl and her widowed mother who have come to India to live with her crusty grandfather, who is a colonel in the colonial army. Shirley quickly becomes the troop's mascot and the particular favorite of a soft-hearted bull of a sergeant (Victor McLaglen), but she also manages to charm the leader of a group of rebels. Eventually, it is little Shirley who brings his rebel group and the military together in a truce. Based upon a story by Rudyard Kipling. A charming movie.

Sex / Nud / Viol / Lang / AdSit

A: Shirley Temple, Cesar Romero, Victor McLaglen, C. Aubrey Smith, Cune Lang, Michael Whalen

© FOXVIDEO 1070

WHERE THE RED FERN GROWS

D: Norman Tokar — 97 m

G | CLD | 1974 | COLOR

7 Billy is a young boy growing up in the hills of Oklahoma during the desperately poor 1930s. He very badly wants two hunting dogs that his family really can't afford. His grandfather encourages him anyway by telling Billy to keep the faith and God will help. Billy scrimps and saves to earn the money he needs. All he thinks he wants is to get his dogs and train them to be the best hunting dogs in the state. Instead he gets much more: he gets a lesson in responsibility and growing up. A very good and involving family entertainment.

Sex / Nud / Viol / Lang / AdSit

A: James Whitmore, Beverly Garland, Jack Ging, Lonny Chapman, Stewart Peterson

© BRIDGESTONE PRODUCTION GROUP

WHITE FANG

D: Randal Kleiser — 109 m

PG | WST ACT CLD | 1991 | COLOR

9 Wonderful whole-family entertainment in the true sense of the phrase. This is an exciting adventure film that has something to satisfy everyone. It is a beautiful picture that evokes the actual feel of the Alaskan goldrush days. A young man follows his father's dying wishes to settle his gold claim deep in the wilds of a virgin Yukon wilderness. The film focuses upon the young man's journey there and upon his friendship with an orphaned wolf cub, White Fang. Spectacularly photographed, this is a tale of men in the wilderness and one man's love for his four-footed kindred spirit.

Sex / Nud / ◢ Viol / Lang / AdSit

A: Ethan Hawke, Klaus Maria Brandauer, James Remar, Seymour Cassel, Susan Hogan

© WALT DISNEY HOME VIDEO 1151

WILDERNESS FAMILY, PART 2

D: Frank Zuniga — 104 m

G | CLD | 1978 | COLOR

8 This is the follow-up to the popular family film ADVENTURE OF THE WILDERNESS FAMILY which was about a city family who moves to the wilderness. This sequel finds the parents enjoying their escape from the big city and the kids enjoying the wildlife. But, the summer is ending and they must prepare for the coming harsh winter. Their only visitors, apart from the animals, is a crusty old trapper and the mail pilot. Beautiful scenery and lots of animals.

Sex / Nud / Viol / Lang / AdSit

A: Robert Logan, Susan D. Shaw, Heather Rattray, Ham Larsen, George "Buck" Flower, Brian Cutler

© VIDEO TREASURES M204

WILLOW

D: Ron Howard — 130 m

PG | ACT FAN CLD | 1988 | COLOR

7 A kooky fantasy - sort of Star Wars meets the Wizard of Oz. Davis is Willow, 0an elf who is the protector of a small baby who will grow up, end the reign of the evil Queen Bavmorda (Marsh) and bring peace to the world. Warrior Kilmer offers his help to the little guy and along the way they encounter many wacky characters, some dangerous and some funny. This is a fanciful adventure that provides an eyeful of special effects. Although aimed at children, some of the violence might be too intense for the youngest ones.

Sex / Nud / ◢ Viol / Lang / ◢ AdSit

A: Val Kilmer, Joanne Whalley-Kilmer, Warwick Davis, Jean Marsh, Patricia Hayes, Billy Barty

© COLUMBIA TRISTAR HOME VIDEO 60936

WILLY WONKA AND THE CHOCOLATE FACTORY

D: Mel Stuart — 100 m

G | CLD | 1971 | COLOR

7 An inventive fantasy, especially for older children. Gene Wilder is the world's greatest chocolate manufacturer and the ruler over a mysterious and magical candy factory. In this particular year, he holds a contest in which five winners will be awarded a lifetime supply of chocolate, plus a trip through the factory, accompanied by an adult. However, like all good fantasies (and a common theme in all the fairy tales which have lasted), all is not good and nice: While we are drawn to a poor but honest paperboy, the other four kids are stinkers, and we enjoy watching them get what's coming to them.

Sex / Nud / Viol / Lang / AdSit

A: Gene Wilder, Jack Albertson, Peter Ostrum, Roy Kinnear, Denise Nickerson, Ursula Reit

© WARNER HOME VIDEO 11206

WITCHES, THE

D: Nicolas Roeg — 92 m

PG | FAN CLD | 1990 | COLOR

9 Terrific spooky story for kids, but not under 8 or so. Luke is a 9-year-old boy whose loving grandmother tells him bedtime stories and always warns him of the dangers of witches (they like to kill little children). However, he and his grandmother happen to stay at a hotel where there is also a conference of witches and, it seems, the head witch (Huston) has created a magic potion that will turn all the children in England into mice. Then, she spots Luke. He escapes from her, but not before she turns him into a mouse. Now it is up to Luke to save himself and all the other children. That's not an easy job for a mouse.

Sex / Nud / Viol / Lang / AdSit

A: Jasen Fisher, Mai Zetterling, Anjelica Huston, Rowan Atkinson, Bill Paterson, Brenda Blethyn

© WARNER HOME VIDEO 671

WIZARD OF OZ, THE

D: Victor Fleming — 119 m

G | FAN CLD MUS | 1939 | B&W

10 This is MGM's ultimate classic children's film that is presented each year on television to a whole new audience, plus an old one that keeps coming back to re-live it. This is a wonderful fantasy in which a young girl visits a wondrous and mysterious fantasy land, and there discovers that things aren't always better somewhere else. This particular video version is a special edition which contains 17 minutes of extra footage which were edited out of the original, plus the original theatrical promotional trailer with Buddy Epson (who was the original Tin Man) performing and Judy Garland receiving an Oscar.

Sex / Nud / Viol / Lang / AdSit

A: Judy Garland, Jack Haley, Ray Bolger, Bert Lahr, Billie Burke, Margaret Hamilton

Distributed By MGM/UA Home Video M301656

WONDERFUL WORLD OF THE BROTHERS GRIM, THE

D: Henry Levin, George Pal — 128 m

NR | FAN CLD MUS | 1962 | COLOR

6 Fanciful depiction of the lives of the famous story-telling brothers, which combines a telling of their life stories with three of their fairy tales: "The Dancing Princess," in which a princess finds her true love in a common woodsman; "The Cobbler and the Elves," in which an overworked shoemaker receives overnight assistance from some helpful elves (George Pal's famous Puppetoons); and, "The Singing Bone," where a pompous and cowardly knight relies upon his lowly servant to fight a fire-breathing dragon.

Sex / Nud / Viol / Lang / AdSit

A: Laurence Harvey, Claire Bloom, Jim Backus, Yvette Mimieux, Buddy Hackett, Barbara Eden

Distributed By MGM/UA Home Video M200693

CHILDREN

YEARLING, THE

D: Clarence Brown 129 m

G | DMA CLD | 1946 | COLOR

9 Beautiful and sensitive family favorite that was also a Best Picture nominee. This is the intelligent story of a young boy's confrontation with the hard realities of survival in early America. A lonely boy, living with his mother and father on a small pioneer farm, adopts an orphaned fawn for a pet. As the fawn grows into a yearling and the boy becomes more and more attached to it, the deer becomes a larger and larger problem for the parents. Eventually they must decide between the yearling and their own survival. Memorable and heart-wrenching.

Sex / Nud / Viol / Lang / AdSit

A: Gregory Peck, Jane Wyman, Claude Jarman, Jr., Chill Wills, Clem Bevins, Margaret Wycherly

Distributed By MGM/UA Home Video M300500

Animated Films

101 DALMATIANS

D: Wolfgang Reitherman, Hamilton Luske 80 m

G | CLD | 1961 | COLOR

10 Charming Disney favorite that fascinates every child who has ever watched it, and charms most adults, too. Pongo, a male Dalmatian, arranges for his bachelor master to meet a pretty girl in the park so he can meet Perdita, the girl's Dalmatian. Both the humans and the dogs marry. Soon there is a litter of puppies, which the aptly named Cruella De Ville kidnaps in order to have a fur coat made from them. So Pongo and Perdita begin an all-out effort to recover them and save their puppies from Cruella's evil henchmen. In the end, they get much more than they expected. Great entertainment.

Sex / Nud / Viol / Lang / AdSit

A:

© WALT DISNEY HOME VIDEO 1263

ALADDIN

D: John Musker, Ron Clements 90 m

CLD COM | 1992 | COLOR

10 Disney did it again. Hugely popular and an instant classic. The classic tale from the Arabian Nights was adapted to feature the manic, over-the-top energy and talent of Robin Williams as the genie. Aladdin is a poor street-smart peasant struggling to survive in the market of Agrabah, when he stumbles upon the beautiful Princess Jasmine who longs to be free. Aladdin is chosen to retrieve the magic lantern by the Sultan's evil counselor Jafar. Instead, Aladdin discovers for himself the magic of the genie in the lamp. Truly a for everyone. Charming, very funny, clever and extremely entertaining. 2 Oscars. Followed by RETURN OF JAFAR.

Sex / Nud / Viol / Lang / AdSit

A:

© WALT DISNEY HOME VIDEO 1662

ALICE IN WONDERLAND

D: Lou Bunin 80 m

G | CLD | 1951 | COLOR

9 Wonderful and very fanciful animated telling of Lewis Carroll's classic children's novel by the animators at Disney. It has a wonderful score and concentrates more on the humor and adventure of Alice's tale than on the political satire (which was the real thrust of the 19th-century novel). There are wonderfully fanciful sequences including: the zany Mad Hatter's party; the evil and spoiled Queen of Hearts; and, the strange Chesire Cat, who can vanish and leave behind only his very toothy smile. This is a treat for young and old alike and a classic for the ages.

Sex / Nud / Viol / Lang / AdSit

A:

© WALT DISNEY HOME VIDEO 036

ALL DOGS GO TO HEAVEN

D: Don Bluth 85 m

G | CLD | 1989 | COLOR

8 Set in 1939 New Orleans, a junkyard dog, a German Shepherd named Charles B. Barkin, is double-crossed and killed by his partner-in-crime, a Pit Bull named Carface. However, Barkin is returned to earth where a little orphan girl who can speak to dogs, comes to rely upon him for help. Barkin at once sees that he can use the girl as a way to regain his old business and also to get revenge against Carface. However, he instead learns that there is something that is more valuable than money or revenge. This is above the average stuff for little kids. Its production was overseen by ex-Disney man Don Bluth, so that is why it is well done.

Sex / Nud / ◢ Viol / Lang / AdSit

A:

Distributed By MGM/UA Home Video M301868

AMERICAN TAIL, AN

D: Don Bluth 81 m

G | CLD | 1986 | COLOR

9 Endearing and very entertaining animated feature from Steven Spielberg. After fleeing persecution in Russia, young mouse Fievel and his family arrive in New York at the turn of the century. America is supposed to be the land where the streets are paved with cheese and there are no cats. But, young Fievel immediately gets lost in the big city and is separated from his family. While, the story is somewhat predictable if you're older than six, most watchers won't be. What watchers will be, is treated to some very lush animation, a rich soundtrack and lasting characters.

Sex / Nud / Viol / Lang / AdSit

A:

© MCA/UNIVERSAL HOME VIDEO, INC. 80536

AMERICAN TAIL, AN - FIEVEL GOES WEST

D: Phil Nibbelink 75 m

G | CLD | 1991 | COLOR

9 Enjoyable comedic follow-up to the endearing original. This time the little mouse Fievel Mousekewitz and his family head out to the Old West to seek their fortunes. There, Fievel partners up with the legendary, but slightly over-the-hill, lawdog Wylie Burp (Jimmie Stewart) to defeat the wild and crazy cat, Tiger (Dom DeLuise).

Sex / Nud / Viol / Lang / AdSit

A:

© MCA/UNIVERSAL HOME VIDEO, INC. 81067

BABAR - THE MOVIE

D: Alan Bunce 79 m

G | CLD | 1989 | COLOR

8 The classic children's character, Babar the Elephant King, tells his offspring the story of how he saved his homeland and Celeste (his future queen) from certain destruction by a bad guy named Rataxes and his army of bad rhinos. Good for very young children, not interesting for the older ones. Mixture of kiddy-comedy and adventure.

Sex / Nud / Viol / Lang / AdSit

A: Babar

© LIVE HOME VIDEO 27316

BAMBI

D: David D. Hand 69 m

G | CLD | 1942 | COLOR

10 Disney's animated classic story about the little deer who lives in the forest, and the lives of the other creatures who are his friends. Life there is not always easy and the lovable forest babies must deal with the turmoil and changes which come with the changing seasons. Bambi the deer grows up, along with Thumper the rabbit, Flower the skunk and Owl the owl. Strikingly real animation. Much more than just a cute story for kids. It is a simplified lesson in life.

Sex / Nud / Viol / Lang / AdSit

A:

© WALT DISNEY HOME VIDEO 942

BATMAN: MASK OF THE PHANTASM

D: Eric Radomski, Bruce Timm 77 m

PG | ACT CLD | 1994 | COLOR

8 After two super-budget feature films and a campy TV series, the Batman of the comic series returned in animated form this time. This version stays true to the style, and even the time (late 1930's) of the original. Andrea, Bruce Wayne's only true love, has come back to Gotham City but Batman (Bruce Wayne in disguise) is now suspected by the police in the murders of several major crime figures. One crime lord is so terrified of him that he has hired The Joker to protect him. However, the murderer is not Batman but yet another masked avenger. So, if Batman is to regain his good name, he must find out the truth. Exciting and well done but realistic and very violent, so this is not for very young. Many adults will like it too.

Sex / Nud / ◢ Viol / Lang / ◢ AdSit

A:

© WARNER HOME VIDEO 15500

BEAUTY AND THE BEAST

D: Gary Trousdale, Kirk Wise 90 m

G | CLD MUS | 1991 | COLOR

10 Disney received the first-ever Best Picture nomination for an animated feature for this delightful instant classic. The story is that of the beautiful daughter of an eccentric father, who is made a prisoner in the isolated and desolate castle of a hideous beast that loves her. The essentials of the classic storyline are all there but everything is given a Disney twist and set to music in a score that took home an Oscar, as did its title tune. Except, this time around everything is more fanciful: All the household fixtures come to life and sing. Delightful. Children 6 & up are held spellbound, but it's a little slow for the very youngest ones.

Sex / Nud / Viol / Lang / AdSit

A:

© WALT DISNEY HOME VIDEO 1325

BON VOYAGE CHARLIE BROWN (AND DON'T COME BACK)!

D: 76 m

G | CLD | 1980 | COLOR

Sex / Nud / Viol / Lang / AdSit

8 The Peanuts gang goes to France for two weeks as exchange students.

A: *Charlie Brown*

© PARAMOUNT HOME VIDEO 1158

BOY NAMED CHARLIE BROWN, A

D: 85 m

G | CLD | 1969 | COLOR

Sex / Nud / Viol / Lang / AdSit

8 This is the very first animated feature of the Peanuts gang. Charlie Brown has a shot at fame when he wins his school's spelling bee and goes on to the national contest.

A: *Charlie Brown*

© CBS/FOX VIDEO 7121

BRAVE LITTLE TOASTER, THE

D: 90 m

G | CLD | 1988 | COLOR

Sex / Nud / Viol / Lang / AdSit

7 An oddly interesting animated feature that is reminiscent of the very earliest children's cartoons made by Disney. It is the charming story of a toaster, a radio, a lamp and an electric blanket that all come to life and set out in perilous search to find their young master. Fascinating and pleasant viewing for young children.

A:

© WALT DISNEY HOME VIDEO 1117

CARE BEARS ADVENTURE IN WONDERLAND, THE

D: 76 m

G | CLD | 1987 | COLOR

Sex / Nud / Viol / Lang / AdSit

9 Third in the series. The Care Bears go through the looking glass to help stop an evil wizard who has kidnapped a princess. Like the others, this is for very small kids, but they will love it.

A:

© MCA/UNIVERSAL HOME VIDEO, INC. 80720

CARE BEARS MOVIE, THE

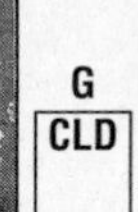

D: 75 m

G | CLD | 1985 | COLOR

Sex / Nud / Viol / Lang / AdSit

9 A magician's assistant comes under the control of an evil spirit, whose plan it is to remove all the feelings from the world. The loveable care bears save the day. Music provided by Carole King and John Sebastian. Little kids will love it.

A:

© LIVE HOME VIDEO 5082

CARE BEARS MOVIE II: A NEW GENERATION

D: 77 m

G | CLD | 1985 | COLOR

Sex / Nud / Viol / Lang / AdSit

9 Evil Dark Heart makes a deal with a sad little girl to help trap the happy Care Bears. But, when she realizes what she has done, she instead helps to save them. Lots of music. Great for the littlest kiddies.

A:

© COLUMBIA TRISTAR HOME VIDEO 60682

CHARLOTTE'S WEBB

D: Charles A. Nichols 94 m

G | CLD | 1972 | COLOR

Sex / Nud / Viol / Lang / AdSit

9 Heartwarming animated children's story of Wilber, the shy runt of a piglet who is afraid that he is going to be turned into bacon. He is befriended by Charlotte, the barnyard spider, who weaves words into her magic web to convince the farmer that Wilber is a miraculous hog. Voices of Debbie Reynolds, Paul Lynde, Henry Gibson and Agnes Moorehead. Charming story for children.

A:

© PARAMOUNT HOME VIDEO 8099

CHIPMUNK ADVENTURE, THE

D: 76 m

G | CLD | 1987 | COLOR

Sex / Nud / Viol / Lang / AdSit

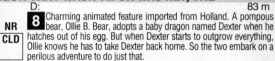

8 When Dave goes to Europe and leaves them behind in the care of Miss Miller - Alvin, Simon and Theodore are very unhappy. They have their own dreams for world travel. So, Alvin convinces Simon and Theodore to enter a hot air balloon race around the world, against three female chipmunks called the Chipettes. Their adventure gets even more thrilling when they are tricked into helping a pair of international diamond smugglers.

A:

© WARNER HOME VIDEO 429

DRAGON THAT WASN'T... OR WAS HE?, THE

D: 83 m

NR | CLD | 1983 | COLOR

Sex / Nud / Viol / Lang / AdSit

8 Charming animated feature imported from Holland. A pompous bear, Ollie B. Bear, adopts a baby dragon named Dexter when he hatches out of his egg. But when Dexter starts to outgrow everything, Ollie knows he has to take Dexter back home. So the two embark on a perilous adventure to do just that.

A:

© MCA/UNIVERSAL HOME VIDEO, INC. 80348

DR. SEUSS - DR. SEUSS ON THE LOOSE

D: 30 m

NR | CLD | 1974 | COLOR

Sex / Nud / Viol / Lang / AdSit

8 These three wonderful featurettes from the famous Dr. Seuss are fun, entertaining and have a moral. A lesson on racism is learned in "The Sneetches." Courtesy is the theme in "The Zax." And, the classic "Green Eggs and Ham" teaches children not to make snap judgments about things they haven't tried.

A:

© CBS/FOX VIDEO 6937

DR. SEUSS - HALLOWEEN IS GRINCH NIGHT

D: 30 m

NR | CLD | 1977 | COLOR

Sex / Nud / Viol / Lang / AdSit

8 One terrifying night, the evil grinch preys upon the townspeople of a small town and forces them into submission. However, there is one little boy with courage stands up to him and learns about facing his fears.

A:

© CBS/FOX VIDEO 6825

DR. SEUSS - HORTON HEARS A WHO!

D: 26 m

NR | CLD | 1970 | COLOR

Sex / Nud / Viol / Lang / AdSit

8 This charming children's story is about an endearing elephant named Horton who knows of a society of extremely tiny people who are living on the top of an itty bitty speck of dust. However, when Horton tries to save the small community, everybody around him thinks that he has lost his mind, and poor Horton can't get anyone to believe him.

A:

Distributed By MGM/UA Home Video M200702

DR. SEUSS - HOW THE GRINCH STOLE CHRISTMAS

NR | CLD | 1966 | COLOR | D: Chuck Jones | 26 m

9 This masterpiece should be required holiday viewing for everybody every Christmas. It has, in fact, become a seasonal fixture on TV every year since it was originally created. It is a simply charming tale of the despised grinch who plots to take Christmas away from the tiny town of Whoville. He takes all their gifts, he takes the lights off the trees and he even takes their Christmas dinner. He desperately tries to totally destroy all their holiday cheer. However, in the end he fails miserably, is transformed and brings everything back. Wonderfully narrated by Boris Karloff.

Sex Nud Viol Lang AdSit A:

Distributed By MGM/UA Home Video M201011

DR. SEUSS - PONTOFFEL POCK

NR | CLD | 1979 | COLOR | D: | 30 m

8 Dr. Seuss's lesson in confidence building. A lonely young boy gets a special piano from a fairy named McGillicuddy. It has magical powers and can take him anywhere that he wants to go! But he gets scared because it just gets too complicated for him. However, he learns to trust in himself. A very enjoyable sugar-coated lesson for kids.

Sex Nud Viol Lang AdSit A:

© CBS/FOX VIDEO 6934

DR. SEUSS - THE CAT IN THE HAT

NR | CLD | 1974 | COLOR | D: | 30 m

8 The usual cherished blend of lessons learned and fun is found here again in this tale from Dr. Seuss. Two children are bored on a rainy day and are on the verge of doing mischief, when they are unexpectedly entertained by a oddball cat who won't leave until he finds what he is looking for. What he is looking for is a moss-covered, three-pronged gredunza. He is turning their house inside-out in the process of finding it and is giving them a good time on a rainy day in the bargain.

Sex Nud Viol Lang AdSit A:

© CBS/FOX VIDEO 6936

DR. SEUSS - THE GRINCH GRINCHES THE CAT IN THE HAT

NR | CLD | 1982 | COLOR | D: | 30 m

8 Two of Dr. Seuss's most memorable characters - the cat and the grinch - battle it out in this marvelous kids adventure. On one beautiful summer day, the cat decides that the grinch needs to change his ways and it is up to him to do it. He will give the grinch lessons on being cheerful, helpful and kind and will teach him some manners. That, of course, cannot help but result in adventure.

Sex Nud Viol Lang AdSit A:

© CBS/FOX VIDEO 6935

DR. SEUSS - THE HOOBER-BLOOB HIGHWAY

NR | CLD | 1974 | COLOR | D: | 30 m

8 The path of light that leads to a small floating island is called the Hoober-Bloob highway. Mr. Hoober-Bloob lives there. He teaches the island's guests lessons about self worth and respect and an adventure on his island is always memorable.

Sex Nud Viol Lang AdSit A:

© CBS/FOX VIDEO 6843

DR. SEUSS - THE LORAX

NR | CLD | 1974 | COLOR | D: | 30 m

8 Dr. Seuss has created an offbeat and memorable character called the Lorax. The Lorax speaks for the trees and he tries to save a forest when progress and greed go too far. This one teaches kids to pay special attention to caring for the environment.

Sex Nud Viol Lang AdSit A:

© CBS/FOX VIDEO 6842

DUCKTALES - THE MOVIE: TREASURE OF THE LOST LAMP

G | CLD | 1990 | COLOR | D: | 74 m

7 Enjoyable Disney fun for both young and old. Huey, Dewey, Louie and Webby McDuck are an awesome duck foursome. They are all searching for a lost treasure - the lost lamp - and very soon find themselves battling an evil wizard for possession. Seems that the magic lamp also houses a genie that can grant their every wish! A simple, straightforward, fun adventure.

Sex Nud Viol Lang AdSit A:

© WALT DISNEY HOME VIDEO 1082

DUMBO

G | CLD | 1940 | COLOR | D: | 63 m

10 This is Disney's wonderful cartoon classic and a different twist on the story of the Ugly Duckling. Dumbo is a sad little baby elephant who is ridiculed by everyone because he has such huge ears. But, his friend Timothy the Mouse helps him to gain confidence in himself when Dumbo learns that he can use his big ears to fly. All of a sudden, ugly little Dumbo becomes the biggest star in the circus. The musical score won an Oscar. Marvelous animation. A true delight for all ages.

Sex Nud Viol Lang AdSit A:

© WALT DISNEY HOME VIDEO 024

FANTASIA

G | MUS FAN | 1940 | COLOR | D: | 120 m

8 Extravagant, hugely expensive and extremely bold venture by Walt Disney in 1940. The imaginations of the animators were turned loose to translate classical music masterpieces into free-flowing animated surreal fantasy story lines. There are seven sequences in all. The best are "The Sorcerer's Apprentice" and "Night on Bald Mountain." Highly praised by some and criticized by others. Certainly different. Imagination and patience required - and richly rewarded.

Sex Nud Viol Lang AdSit A:

© WALT DISNEY HOME VIDEO 1132

FERNGULLY ...THE LAST RAINFOREST

G | CLD | 1992 | COLOR | D: Bill Kroyer | 72 m

8 Very entertaining animated feature with an ecological message that was designed for kids. A group of fairies lives contentedly in a mystical rain forest until one day they hear the sound of machines. Little Crysta flies to the sounds and finds a crew of workmen cutting trees. She shrinks one of them down to her size and flies him back to the rest of the fairies to try tp convince him to help them to protect their forest and to prevent the escape of an evil spirit that will otherwise be released. One of the most fun creatures helping make their case is a crazy, wacked-out bat with Robin Williams's voice. Fun.

Sex Nud Viol Lang AdSit A:

© FOXVIDEO 5594

FLIGHT OF THE DRAGONS, THE

G | CLD | 1982 | COLOR | D: Arthur Rankin, Jr., Jules Bass | 98 m

8 It is nearing the end of the age of magic and four wizard brothers have joined forces to create a land where magic will be able to survive. However, one of them is evil and who's true motive is only to cause war and destruction. Carolinas is a kind wizard who joins forces with a dragon, a gallant knight and a man from the 20th century, to capture the evil brother's magic crown. If they succeed, it would leave him powerless and the tyranny of the evil Red Wizards would be ended. Grade-schoolers will become fascinated by this tale. Stop-action animation is used, plus the voices of John Ritter, Harry Morgan and James Earl Jones.

Sex Nud Viol Lang AdSit A:

© WARNER HOME VIDEO 976

FOX AND THE HOUND, THE

G | CLD | 1981 | COLOR | D: Art Stevens, Ted Burman | 83 m

7 Tod is an orphaned baby fox who is adopted by a lonely widow. He has become friends with a young hunting dog named Copper who lives next door. The two young pups run, play and swim together in the nearby forest and become the very best of friends. But, then Copper goes away for the winter and when he returns in the spring, both youngsters are grown...and they can no longer be friends like they were when they were young. The widow has also decided that Tod now needs to be free and get back in the forest. There he meets a beautiful lady fox and they are happy, until the day when Copper and his master come to hunt in the forest. Satisfactory entertainment, but lacks the charm of other Disney films.

Sex Nud ✓ Viol Lang AdSit A:

© WALT DISNEY HOME VIDEO 2041

GARGOYLES: THE MOVIE

D: 80 m

NR CLD 1994 COLOR

8 1000 years ago, the inhabitants of a medieval castle were protected by a race of creatures who defended them fiercely by night, but by day turned to stone. They were the Gargoyles. However, the Gargoyles were betrayed and were placed under a spell that has kept them as stone for the last 1000 years. Today, in the modern world and made part of a highrise structure, high above the clouds in Manhattan, the Gargoyles are revived. A wealthy industrialist now wants them to help to recover stolen valuables, but the wary Gargoyles are uncertain who to trust.

Sex Nud Viol Lang AdSit

A:

© BUENA VISTA HOME VIDEO 4423

GOOFY MOVIE, A

D: Kevin Lima 76 m

G CLD COM 1995 COLOR

7 While it would appear that Mickey's ever-faithful friend Goofy is finally the star of his own movie, in fact the real centerpiece is his teenaged son, Max. During the last days of school, before the summer break, Max sets out to win over the heart of his pretty girlfriend by becoming a rock star. While his antics have won her heart and a date, he has also earned the anger of the principal who calls papa Goofy about his delinquent son. So, concerned Goofy decides that the perfect way to set his boy back on the right path is to take him fishing. Off they go on their trip, where Goofy gets caught in an endless series of screwups, causing Max to worry that he is going to grow up to be just like his dad.

Sex Nud Viol Lang AdSit

A: Goofy

© WALT DISNEY HOME VIDEO 4658

GREAT LAND OF SMALL, THE

D: 94 m

G CLD 1986 COLOR

6 Enchanting story for kids. Two children go to visit their grandparents in the country where they also meet Mimmick the Indian. Mimmick knows where the entrance is that is used by a very tiny man named Fritz. Fritz is an inhabitant of the magical Land of Small, which exists deep inside the earth. The children race to the end of the rainbow to find Fritz. They do and get to meet the King and Queen, but are also chased by the villainous tavern-keeper. Light entertainment for little kids.

Sex Nud Viol Lang AdSit

A:

© R&G VIDEO, LP 96005

GREAT MOUSE DETECTIVE, THE

D: Barry Mattinson 74 m

G CLD 1986 COLOR

9 Charming Disney animated feature about an English mouse, Basil of Baker Street, and his faithful companion Dr. Dawson. This team of diminutive detectives bares an uncanny resemblance to Sherlock Holmes and Dr. Watson. They battle an evil rat, Professor Ratigan, who plots against the royal rodent family through the creation of a robot mouse. Engaging characters. Good fun that is fast enough paced to keep the attention of even older viewers.

Sex Nud Viol Lang AdSit

A:

© WALT DISNEY HOME VIDEO 1360

HAPPILY EVER AFTER

D: John Howley 74 m

G CLD 1993 COLOR

7 Filmation Studios have taken up where the Disney the story of Snow White and Prince Charming left off. The love-struck pair are on their way to invite the seven dwarves to their wedding. However, Lord Maliss has arrived at the palace of his sister, the evil Queen, to find that she is dead and her palace is overrun with animals. Furious, he plots to kidnap Snow White, but instead captures Prince Charming. Snow White continues on to the dwarves' cottage for help only to find that the dwarves have gone to the next kingdom. They have left the place to their cousins, the dwarfelles who are assistants to Mother Nature and have magic powers. Certainly not Disney, but not bad.

Sex Nud Viol Lang AdSit

A:

© WORLDVISION HOME VIDEO, INC. 8045

JACOB TWO-TWO MEETS THE HOODED FANG

D: Theodore J. Flicker 90 m

G CLD 1979 COLOR

7 Captivating children's fantasy. Jacob Two-Two is called Two-Two because he has to say everything twice so that grownups can understand him. Frustrated, he dreams a dream in which he is thrown into a children's prison on Slimer's Island. His warden there is the Hooded Fang (Alex Karras), who brags that this is a prison "where no brats return." Jacob leads his fellow prisoners in a revolt. Humorous story for kids that rises above its low budget.

Sex Nud Viol Lang AdSit

A: Stephen Rosenberg, Alex Karras

© LIVE HOME VIDEO VA4398

JUNGLE BOOK, THE

D: 78 m

G CLD 1967 COLOR

7 Cute animated version of Rudyard Kipling's classic tale of a boy who has been raised by wolves. The wolves try to take him back to live in the man village, but the boy doesn't want to go until he sees a pretty girl. Disney has created a lively cast of loveable animal characters and given them a great voices (including Phil Harris, Louis Prima, Sebastian Cabot, George Sanders and Sterling Holloway) and some fun tunes. While this is reasonably interesting viewing for very young children, it has been greatly simplified. Also see the animated MOWGLI'S BROTHERS and older children should see the 1942 feature film THE JUNGLE BOOK.

Sex Nud Viol Lang AdSit

A:

© WALT DISNEY HOME VIDEO 1122

LADY AND THE TRAMP

D: Walt Disney 77 m

G CLD 1955 COLOR

10 Adorable all-time Disney animated favorite - and his first one to be done in CinemaScope. Lady is a pampered pedigreed spaniel who runs away from home after she feels rejected because her humans have brought home a new baby. But, she is way out of her element in the street and her ill-advised adventure requires her to be rescued by the streetwise and roguish mutt, Tramp. Tramp and Lady fall in love over a bowl of spaghetti. Great Disney. It is adventuresome, dramatic and romantic, with ample doses of charm and music. Children will be enraptured, but older people will find themselves just as involved. Excellent.

Sex Nud Viol Lang AdSit

A:

© WALT DISNEY HOME VIDEO 582

LAND BEFORE TIME, THE

D: Don Bluth 69 m

G CLD 1988 COLOR

8 Excellent animated children's fable that will likely charm soft-hearted oldsters, too. A massive change has occurred in the earth's climate of 70 million years ago, and it causes a loveable young dinosaur, a brontosaurus named Littlefoot,and his family to leave his home to seek out the Great Valley. There food is said to be plentiful. However, he is separated from his parents, so he and his friends must find the promised land themselves. However, their adventure is dangerous and they face a series of problems on the way, including being pursued by flesh-eating dinosaurs called the Sharpteeth. Excellent entertainment and production values.

Sex Nud Viol Lang AdSit

A:

© MCA/UNIVERSAL HOME VIDEO, INC. 80864

LAND BEFORE TIME PART II, THE

D: Roy Allen Smith 74 m

G CLD 1994 COLOR

6 Now safe from the Sharpteeth in The Great Valley, Little Foot and his pals Sarah, Ducky, Petry and Spike, aren't content to play where their parents tell them. They don't like being thought of as children. They want to show their parents how grown up they are. So, when two other dinosaurs steal one of the eggs, the young troop sets out to get it back...even when it means going into the "Mysterious Beyond," where they have been forbidden to go. Soon, they find themselves in big trouble and they have even jeopardized the safety of The Great Valley itself. Very sweet, moral-laced story for very young viewers.

Sex Nud Viol Lang AdSit

A:

© MCA/UNIVERSAL HOME VIDEO, INC. 82142

LEGEND OF SLEEPY HOLLOW, THE

D: 33 m

NR CLD 1949 COLOR

9 Superb animated short from Disney... one of the best. Washington Irving's classic early 1800's tale of a stringbean country teacher's run-in with a mysterious and fearsome headless horseman is wonderfully adapted for the screen by Disney's animators. It has just the right amount of suspense and fear generated for the younger set. The story is also given a significant boost by having the melodious voice of Bing Crosby as narrator.

Sex Nud Viol Lang AdSit

A:

© WALT DISNEY HOME VIDEO 1034

LION KING, THE

D: 88 m

G CLD 1994 COLOR

9 Once again, Disney's studios have produced a true animated gem for nearly the entire family. However, this time those likely left out are the littlest of kids. This is the story of Simba, son of Musafa, the lion king. Simba is tricked by his evil uncle Scar in a plot that kills Musafa. Simba believes his father's death to have been his fault and so leaves to live in exile. Crossing a barren desert, Simba is rescued by two other outcasts, a smelly warthog named Pumbaa and a diminutive meerkat named Timon. He grows up with them to later return and reclaim his throne from Scar. Stunningly life-like animation. Recommended for eight and up because of its quite ominous and sinister beginning. Oscars for Best Score and Song.

Sex Nud ✓ Viol Lang AdSit

A:

© WALT DISNEY HOME VIDEO 2977

LION, THE WITCH AND THE WARDROBE, THE

D: 95 m

G | CLD | 1979 | COLOR

Sex / Nud / Viol / Lang / AdSit

8 Very enjoyable animated story for children. It is an excellent made-for-TV adaptation from the first of C.S. Lewis's classic books in "The Chronicles of Narnia." Four English children magically pass through an antique wardrobe into the magical Kingdom of Narnia. There they enter onto a grand adventure to help the Lion King release his land from the curse of the wicked Ice Queen, who has brought perpetual winter to his land. Enchanting!

A:

© LIVE HOME VIDEO 4194

LITTLE MERMAID, THE

D: John Musker, Don Clements 83 m

G | CLD | 1989 | COLOR

Sex / Nud / Viol / Lang / AdSit

10 Totally endearing, absolutely charming, an instant classic from Disney. This wonderfully animated children's movie is based upon the classic story of Hans Christian Anderson. The story is that of Ariel, an unfortunate little mermaid princess who falls so in love with a mortal man that she strikes a tragic bargain with an evil and treacherous witch to become human so that she can be with the man she loves. Your kids will watch it over and over and over; and you will find yourself humming its infectious songs, too. An absolute delight for everyone!

A:

© WALT DISNEY HOME VIDEO 913

LITTLE NEMO: ADVENTURES IN SLUMBERLAND

D: Masanori Hata, William Hurtz 85 m

G | CLD | 1992 | COLOR

Sex / Nud / Viol / Lang / AdSit

7 This is an entertaining animated feature for older children. It may be too intense for the smaller ones. It is the animated version of a comic strip character that was actually first animated in 1911. Little Nemo is a big-eyed youngster whose dreams have transported him, his flying squirrel and his bed to Slumberland, where it seems the King of Slumberland, King Morpheus, has selected Nemo to be his heir. However, Nemo is tricked by con man Flip (voice of Mickey Rooney) into using his magic key to unlock a forbidden door. Now Nemo must rescue Morpheus from the evil Nightmare King.

A:

© HEMDALE HOME VIDEO, INC. 7139

MOWGLI'S BROTHERS

D: Chuck Jones 30 m

CLD | 1976 | COLOR

Sex / Nud / Viol / Lang / AdSit

8 Wonderful animated story for the whole family. A young child is raised in the jungle by a pack of wolves and learns about life, love and jungle ethics. Based on the novel by Rudyard Kipling, this delightful film is narrated by Roddy McDowall. Master animator Chuck Jones (Bugs Bunny and Road Runner) gives real life to this heartwarming cartoon. Chuck Jones also did Kipling's RIKKI-TIKKI-TAVI. Interested viewers may also want to see Disney's version of Mowgli in THE JUNGLE BOOK, plus there was a more faithful full length feature of the Kipling classic done in 1942, also called THE JUNGLE BOOK.

A:

© LIVE HOME VIDEO 23528

MY LITTLE PONY - THE MOVIE

D: Michael Joens 87 m

G | CLD | 1986 | COLOR

Sex / Nud / Viol / Lang / AdSit

8 Little ones, particularly little girls, love this feature-length animated children's story. Ponyland is being threatened. The wicked witch Hydia and her daughters are threatening the pastel Ponies with a living slime called "the Smooze" which will turn the Ponies colorful world into different shades of gray. This kiddy film contains lots of kids songs and is enhanced further by the talented voices of Danny DeVito, Cloris Leachman, Madeline Kahn, Rhea Perlman, Tony Randall and Jon Bauman.

A:

© LIVE HOME VIDEO VA5171

MY NEIGHBOR TOTORO

D: Hayo Miyazaki 87 m

G | CLD | 1993 | COLOR

Sex / Nud / Viol / Lang / AdSit

8 A very different sort of children's offering. This animated children's story was created in Japan, but has received acclaim in many other cultures in the world as well. It is the story of two little girls who, with their father, move into an old house in the country while their mother is in the hospital. The old house is occupied by spirits in the form of little black "dust bunnies". And, living in their back yard, is Totoro, a giant fuzzy forest spirit, who can work magic and only the children can see. When the 5-year-old sister gets lost, it is Totoro that her sister turns to for help in finding her. Beautifully and realistically animated, but this is very different from Disney.

A:

© FOX 4276

NEVERENDING STORY, THE

D: Wolfgang Petersen 94 m

PG | CLD | 1984 | COLOR

Sex / Nud / Viol / Lang / AdSit

9 This is a superb children's fantasy, like no other. A lonely young boy has taken refuge in a mysterious book. As he begins to read, he is magically transported into a fantasy world filled with magic, charming monsters and a pretty princess. But a mysterious storm-like force, called the Nothing, is threatening to destroy everything. All the creatures of the kingdom have called upon a young warrior named Atreyu to save them. And, our boy is astonished to find, that if Atreyu is to succeed, he must help him. Wonderfully imaginative adventure with terrific special effects.

A: Barret Oliver, Noah Hathaway, Tami Stronach, Moses Gunn, Patricia Hayes, Gerald McRaney

© WARNER HOME VIDEO 11399

NIGHTMARE BEFORE CHRISTMAS, THE

D: Tim Burton 76 m

SEPT | FAN CLD | 1993 | COLOR

Sex / Nud / Viol / Lang / AdSit

8 Wonderfully bizarre. Welcome to a land where each holiday has its own town. Jack Skellington is the Pumpkin King of freakish Halloween Town. He is the master of all things in his domain, but has become bored with it. He longs for something more and thinks he has found it when he discovers Christmas Town. The answer for him is simple, he will kidnap Santa Claus and take his place. Even though his Frankenstein-like rag doll girlfriend Sally cautions against it, Jack proceeds with his plan to make Christmas his too. Don't expect a typical Christmas tale. Expect something very different. Wonderful stop-action puppet animation flows as smoothly as real life and was Oscar-nominated.

A:

© TOUCHSTONE HOME VIDEO 2236

PAGEMASTER, THE

D: Joe Johnston, Maurice Hunt 76 m

G | CLD | 1994 | COLOR

Sex / Nud / Viol / Lang / AdSit

6 Beginning as live-action but quickly transformed into an animated feature, this is a well-meaning story designed to encourage kids to read. Macaulay Culkin is a kid who is so afraid of getting hurt that he is constantly afraid to do anything. While on his way to run an errand for his father he gets caught in a storm and takes refuge inside a near-empty library. There he is soon swept away into a magical land where all the stories have come to life and the only way for him to leave is to conquer his fears as he is faced with a fire-breathing dragon, fearsome Moby Dick, Dr. Jekyll and Mr. Hyde and more. His escorts are three talking books - Adventure, Fantasy and Horror.

A: Macaulay Culkin, Christopher Lloyd, Ed Begley, Jr., Mel Harris, Whoopi Goldberg, Patrick Stewart

© FOXVIDEO 8641

PECOS BILL

D: 30 m

G | CLD | 1988 | COLOR

Sex / Nud / Viol / Lang / AdSit

8 Robin Williams is the perfect voice for the animated Pecos Bill, that mythical cowboy who was raised by coyotes. It was Bill, of course, who dug the Grand Canyon and the Great Salt Lake. The story is as far-fetched as any Paul Bunyon tale that has ever been told, and lots of fun, too.

A: Robin Williams

© COLUMBIA TRISTAR HOME VIDEO H0660

PHANTOM TOLLBOOTH, THE

D: Chuck Jones, David Monahan 89 m

G | CLD | 1969 | COLOR

Sex / Nud / Viol / Lang / AdSit

7 A clever combination of live action and animation that will catch and hold a child's imagination. Milo, a bored little boy, sees a tollbooth magically appear in his bedroom. When he and his dog drive his toy car through the tollbooth, they enter into a wonderful animated world, the Kingdom of Wisdom. But the world is disrupted by a disagreement between the letters and the numbers about which is more important. Likable characters that offer up a little education along with the entertainment.

A:

Distributed By MGM/UA Home Video M500155

PINOCCHIO

D: Walt Disney 87 m

G | CLD | 1940 | COLOR

Sex / Nud / Viol / Lang / AdSit

10 Masterful, timeless animated storytelling that has been pleasing children for many generations now and will never be obsolete. If you thought it was only for kids, watch it again - it appeals on many levels. Magical fantasy about a puppet, carved by a lonely old man. When the old man wishes upon a star for the puppet to come to life, his wish is granted. But Pinocchio can only become a real boy if he learns to be brave, truthful and unselfish. Winner of 2 Oscars, Best Score and Best Song - "When You Wish Upon a Star."

A:

© WALT DISNEY HOME VIDEO 239

POINT, THE

D: Harry Nilsson — 74 m

9 Something special. This is a thoroughly engaging animated story for children narrated by Ringo Starr. In the land of "Point," where everything and everyone has a point, lived Oblio, the first and only round-headed child ever born. As punishment for having no point, he and his dog Arrow are sent away to the "Pointless Forest." There they meet strange and unusual creatures, who have all been exiled to the Pointless Forest because they, too, were different. Features the hit song "Me and My Arrow." Thoughtful, entertaining and can be genuinely be enjoyed by the whole family.

CLD — 1971 — COLOR — Sex / Nud / Viol / Lang / AdSit

A:

© LIVE HOME VIDEO VA4415

PRINCESS & THE GOBLIN, THE

D: Jozsef Gemes — 82 m

7 Animated version of the 1872 fairy tale of George MacDonald. Princess Irene and Curtie, the young son of a miner, discover that there will soon be a revolt of the ugly and very nasty goblins who were forced to live underground many years ago. The goblins will sneak out of their secret holes in a surprise attack on the sun people. They intend to destroy the sun people, bringing them back down into their darkness with them. The goblin prince also plans to kidnap and marry young Irene. So, Irene and Curtie sneak down into the dark holes themselves first and destroy the goblins plans. More for older children, the youngest ones may become frightened. Animation is stiff.

G — CLD — 1991 — COLOR — Sex / Nud / Viol / ✓ Lang / AdSit

A:

© HEMDALE HOME VIDEO, INC. 7114

RACE FOR YOUR LIFE, CHARLIE BROWN!

D: Bill Melendez — 76 m

9 Charlie's adventures continue! Charlie Brown, Snoopy and the "Peanuts" gang go to summer camp and find themselves challenged by bullies in a wild river raft race. Snoopy saves the day with his heroic motorcycle riding. Fun cartoon fun for the whole family.

G — CLD — 1977 — COLOR — Sex / Nud / Viol / Lang / AdSit

A: Charlie Brown

© PARAMOUNT HOME VIDEO 8850

RAGGEDY ANN AND ANDY

D: Richard Williams — 87 m

6 Fun children's adventure. Marcella is a little girl. Each night when she drifts off to dreamland, her dolls magically come to life. This night, when a new French doll named Babbette is kidnapped by a pirate, Raggedy Ann and Andy come to the rescue. This animated adventure features 16 songs by Joe Raposo, the Sesame Street composer.

G — CLD — 1977 — COLOR — Sex / Nud / Viol / Lang / AdSit

A: Claire Williams

© CBS/FOX VIDEO 7089

RELUCTANT DRAGON, THE

D: Charles A. Nichols — 28 m

8 A loveable Disney adventure. A medieval dragon would much rather sit around all day just being a couch potato - drinking tea and singing songs. He doesn't want to be the fierce monster that he is supposed to be. Then a boy and an old dragon fighter get hold of the docile creature and decide that it's time to teach him a thing or two about being a dragon. They will show him the proper way to act. They will show him how to be fierce. This is a fast-paced, highly entertaining treasure for kids.

CLD — 1957 — COLOR — Sex / Nud / Viol / Lang / AdSit

A:

© WALT DISNEY HOME VIDEO 533

RESCUERS, THE

D: Wolfgang Reitherman, John Lounsbery — 77 m

9 Gem of an animated feature that captured children's fancies and rejuvenated Disney in animated films. Bob Newhart and Eva Gabor provide the voices of Bernard and Bianca, two adventuresome mice who are members of the Mouse Rescue Aid Society. They discover a bottle containing an urgent message from a little orphaned girl who is being held captive in a swamp by Madame Medusa. She wants to use the girl to retrieve a diamond from a pirate's cave. Bernard and Bianca set out to rescue the little girl with the help of a bird named Orville, who gives them a ride on his back deep into the swamp. Charming.

G — CLD — 1977 — COLOR — Sex / Nud / Viol / Lang / AdSit

A:

© WALT DISNEY HOME VIDEO 1399

RESCUERS DOWN UNDER, THE

D: Hendel Butoy, Mike Gabriel — 77 m

8 Charming return of the world's bravest mice. Bianca and Bernard are back and they're in Australia. They're there to help a young boy who has been imprisoned by a ruthless trapper in the Outback for trying to protect a rare eagle. The two have a whole new wondrous world to explore which contains kangaroos, wallabies, an evil salamander and a great golden eagle. The eagle becomes their friend and aids them in their struggle by carrying them on his back. The fast-paced action, accentuated by computer-assisted animation, helps to hold kids's attention throughout and makes it a big favorite with them.

G — CLD — 1991 — COLOR — Sex / Nud / Viol / Lang / AdSit

A:

© WALT DISNEY HOME VIDEO 1142

RETURN OF JAFAR, THE

D: — 66 m

7 The Disney folks knew that they were going to have a good thing with ALADDIN. So, they followed it almost immediately with this special animated feature that was designed specifically to be sold only on video. Even though the genie is back, Robin Williams is gone. Therefore, much of the spark is also gone. Still, most kids will enjoy it well enough. The arch villain Jafar was transformed into a genie and trapped inside the magic lamp in the first outing. This time, he has escaped his bottle and is determined to destroy Aladdin and capture the throne. But, his parrot pal, voiced by comedian Gilbert Gottfried, has had enough and has sided with Aladdin to destroy him.

G — CLD — 1994 — COLOR — Sex / Nud / Viol / Lang / AdSit

A:

© WALT DISNEY HOME VIDEO 2237

RIKKI-TIKKI-TAVI

D: Chuck Jones — 30 m

9 Delightful! A British family in India adopts a mongoose into their home. But, two very hideous and deadly cobra snakes, Nag and Nagaina, are determined to get into the house to kill the humans and then lay their eggs. The courageous mongoose, Rikki-Tikki-Tavi, will fight to the death to protect his humans. Welles narrates this wonderful animated feature based on Rudyard Kipling's endearing story. A first-rate adventure, brilliantly captured by animation master Chuck Jones.

CLD — 1975 — COLOR — Sex / Nud / Viol / Lang / AdSit

A:

© LIVE HOME VIDEO 24320

ROBIN HOOD

D: Wolfgang Reitherman — 83 m

7 A clever Disney reworking of the classic character. In this animated feature, the classic Robin Hood tale is told by using animals to play the parts. It is still located in Sherwood Forest. Robin Hood (a fox) and his sidekick (a bear) thwart the attempts of the bumbling prince (a lion) and his evil sidekick (a snake) to tax the poor. Many delightful characters and a pleasant good time. While this is not one of Disney's best efforts it is still entertaining for young kids.

G — CLD — 1973 — COLOR — Sex / Nud / Viol / Lang / AdSit

A:

© WALT DISNEY HOME VIDEO 1189

ROCK-A-DOODLE

D: Don Bluth — 90 m

8 Entertaining kids story that is sort of "Elvis meets Wizard of Oz". When a young boy gets konked on the head, he envisions the story of Rock-a-Doodle, a farmyard rooster who believed that the sun came up just because he crowed. When the owl ridiculed him and the other animals laughed at him, he left the farm for the big city, where he became a big singing sensation. When the farm animals come to miss him, they and the boy, who was transformed into kitten, go off to bring him back to the farm. Quite enjoyable for younger children, who like the characters and the music.

G — CLD — 1992 — COLOR — Sex / Nud / Viol / Lang / AdSit

A: Sandy Duncan, Ellen Greene, Phil Harris, Christopher Plummer, Charles Nelson Reilly

© HBO VIDEO 90701

SECRET OF NIMH, THE

D: Don Bluth — 84 m

8 A truly engaging animated adventure! When a widow field mouse finds that her home is threatened by a farmer's plow, she embarks on a search for a new and safe haven for herself and her family. But when her move is complicated because of the illness of one of her children, she seeks help from a secret society of super-intelligent rats, a fumbling crow and a wise owl. A very well done animated story that the entire family will enjoy.

G — CLD — 1982 — COLOR — Sex / Nud / Viol / Lang / AdSit

A:

Distributed By MGM/UA Home Video M800211

SLEEPING BEAUTY

G | CLD | 1959 | COLOR

D: Clyde Geronimi — 75 m

10 Enchanting Disney masterpiece. This 17th-century fairy tale is told by Disney in a straightforward fashion but is done in combination with beautiful music from Tchaikovsky's ballet. When an evil witch is not invited to the castle for the celebration of the princess's birth, she casts a spell so that the princess will prick her finger and fall into a deep sleep on her sixteenth birthday. The only way she can be awakened is by a kiss from her true love. One day Prince Philip, with help from three good fairies, saves her. This was the last animated feature that Walt oversaw himself.

Sex / Nud / Viol / Lang / AdSit

A:

© WALT DISNEY HOME VIDEO 476V

SNOOPY, COME HOME

G | CLD | 1972 | COLOR

D: Bill Melendez — 80 m

8 Priceless Peanuts adventure! Snoopy takes off unexpectedly and leaves the entire Peanuts Gang in a frenzy, frantically searching for their lost dog. When Snoopy learns that he had a previous owner, he and Woodstock leave home to go visit her. The independent and head-strong Snoopy has no idea of the panic he has caused. A hugely entertaining and heartwarming tale that features excellent animation.

Sex / Nud / Viol / Lang / AdSit

A: *Charlie Brown*

© CBS/FOX VIDEO 7125

SNOW WHITE AND THE SEVEN DWARFS

G | CLD | 1937 | COLOR

D: David D. Hand — 84 m

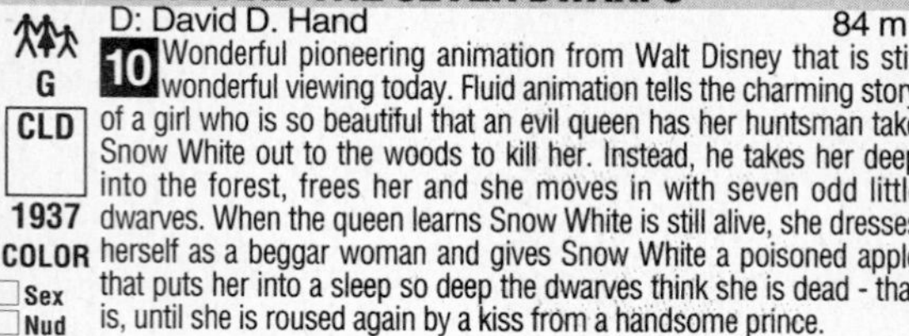

10 Wonderful pioneering animation from Walt Disney that is still wonderful viewing today. Fluid animation tells the charming story of a girl who is so beautiful that an evil queen has her huntsman take Snow White out to the woods to kill her. Instead, he takes her deep into the forest, frees her and she moves in with seven odd little dwarves. When the queen learns Snow White is still alive, she dresses herself as a beggar woman and gives Snow White a poisoned apple that puts her into a sleep so deep the dwarves think she is dead - that is, until she is roused again by a kiss from a handsome prince.

Sex / Nud / Viol / Lang / AdSit

A:

© WALT DISNEY HOME VIDEO 1524

STAR FOR JEREMY, A

CLD | COLOR

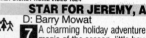

D: Barry Mowat — 22 m

7 A charming holiday adventure set in England. Captivated by the magic of the season, little boy Jeremy looks up at his Christmas tree with wonder and awe. The thing that he is most curious about is the star atop the enchanting tree. When he asks why it is there, he is taken on a wonderful journey and learns about its origin. Thoughtful, touching and educational, an animated story parents and child alike will enjoy.

Sex / Nud / Viol / Lang / AdSit

A:

© BRIDGESTONE PRODUCTION GROUP

SWORD IN THE STONE, THE

G | CLD | 1963 | COLOR

D: Wolfgang Reitherman — 79 m

8 Fine entertainment for youngsters. This is the Disney telling of the classic legend of King Arthur. This version has a young boy named Wart, being helped by the wondrous magician Merlin and his friends. Wart learns how to rely upon himself and his own intellect, to eventually pull the fabled sword from the stone. And, the one who pulls the sword free, legend dictates, shall become king. Fast moving with interesting characters.

Sex / Nud / Viol / Lang / AdSit

A:

© WALT DISNEY HOME VIDEO 229

TALES OF BEATRIX POTTER

G | CLD | 1986 | COLOR

D: — 46 m

7 Six of Beatrix Potter's captivating children's stories, including "Peter Rabbit," are told in narration style against a backdrop of Miss Potter's original storybook illustrations. Each story has a moralistic theme which cautions that bad things will happen if you do the wrong thing.

Sex / Nud / Viol / Lang / AdSit

A: *Sydney Walker*

© LIVE HOME VIDEO 1541

TEENAGE MUTANT NINJA TURTLES: THE EPIC BEGINS

G | CLD | 1990 | COLOR

D: Steve Barron — 72 m

8 This series was quite literally a bad joke that turned into a huge national phenomenon. Kids loved it. It was so successful, that it spawned several sequels, a TV series and a mountain of toys. Four sewer-living, fun-and-pizza-loving, hip-talking humanoid turtles strive to rid New York of evil. Their arch-enemy is a gang called the Foot, which is led by nasty and evil Shreader. When their ninja-master mentor, a rat named Splinter, is captured by Shreader, the turtles and a friendly reporter embark on a campaign to retrieve him. Lots of kiddy-type action and suspense. Not that well written. No redeeming values. The kids will love it.

Sex / Nud / ◢ Viol / ◢ Lang / AdSit

A:

© LIVE HOME VIDEO 23979

THREE CABALLEROS, THE

G | CLD | 1945 | COLOR

D: Norman Ferguson — 71 m

6 This is a curious Disney blend of live-action and animation that was made during WWII at the behest of the US State Department as a good will salute to the countries of Central and South America. It is set in exotic locations and is accompanied by rousing music. In it, Donald Duck visits a Mexican Rooster named Panchito and a Brazilian parrot named Jose Cariocoa.

Sex / Nud / Viol / Lang / AdSit

A:

© WALT DISNEY HOME VIDEO 091

THUMBELINA

PG | CLD | 1994 | COLOR

D: Don Bluth, Gary Goldman — 86 m

7 Hans Christian Anderson's classic children's story about a tiny little girl no bigger than your thumb. Thumbelina meets the love of her life, the elf prince Cornelius, but before their romance barely begins, she is kidnapped away by a beetle. As she struggles to find her way back home, Cornelius struggles to find and rescue her. Lots of very sweet romance songs from Barry Manilow. The small fries will enjoy it well enough.

Sex / Nud / Viol / Lang / AdSit

A:

© WARNER HOME VIDEO 24000

TINY TOON ADVENTURES - HOW I SPENT MY VACATION

G | CLD | 1991 | COLOR

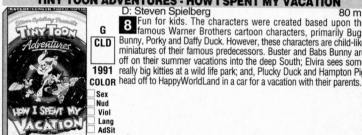

D: Steven Spielberg — 80 m

8 Fun for kids. The characters were created based upon the famous Warner Brothers cartoon characters, primarily Bugs Bunny, Porky and Daffy Duck. However, these characters are child-like miniatures of their famous predecessors. Buster and Babs Bunny are off on their summer vacations into the deep South; Elvira sees some really big kitties at a wild life park; and, Plucky Duck and Hampton Pig head off to HappyWorldLand in a car for a vacation with their parents.

Sex / Nud / Viol / Lang / AdSit

A:

© WARNER HOME VIDEO 12290

TOMMY TRICKER AND THE STAMP TRAVELLER

CLD | 1988 | COLOR

D: Michael Rubbo — 101 m

7 A young stamp collector wheels and deals to get his hands on a very valuable magic stamp. By chanting the proper rhymes, its owner can be shrunk down to fit on a postage stamp and then be able to be transported to all kinds of far away places. Clever and charming combination of live action and animation.

Sex / Nud / Viol / Lang / AdSit

A: *Lucas Evans, Anthony Rogers, Jill Stanley*

© LIVE HOME VIDEO 26560

TROLL IN CENTRAL PARK, A

G | CLD | 1994 | COLOR

D: Don Bluth — 76 m

7 Lovable little Stanley has a magical green thumb and loves flowers. But trolls aren't supposed to be lovable, so wicked Queen Gnorga banishes him to place made of rock and steel - Central Park in New York City. There Stanley is lost in all the noise and traffic until he meets two small children, Gus and his little sister Rosie. They make him happy and he begins to show them how you can do anything if only you believe in yourself and creates a wonderful world of flowers for them. When Queen Gnorga sees what is happening, she comes to Central Park to turn Stanley into a stone, but Stanley and the children defeat her. For very young children only.

Sex / Nud / Viol / Lang / AdSit

A:

© WARNER HOME VIDEO 16100

TWICE UPON A TIME

D: John Korty, Charles Swenson 75 m

PG | FAN | CLD | 1983 | COLOR | Sex | Nud | Viol | Lang | AdSit

8 Imaginative and captivating cartoon fable that is only marginally for young kids. It is much too fast-paced, complex and filled with word-play for the average youngster and is more suited to older children, teenagers and fanciful adults. That is why this deserving video did not get wide theatrical release, even though it was produced by George Lucas. An almost indescribable bunch of characters sets out to save the world from the greedy owner of the Murkworks Nightmare Factory and to prevent him from blanketing the world with bad dreams. Funny and enjoyable.

A:

© WARNER HOME VIDEO 20012

WE'RE BACK

D: Dick Zondag, Ralph Zondag 71 m

G | CLD | 1993 | COLOR | Sex | Nud | Viol | Lang | AdSit

9 Terrific animated feature produced by Steven Spielberg. High energy fun with a really catchy songs. Kids will love it and parents will get caught up in it some too. The story is about four fierce dinosaurs who were fed brain grain by a rich eccentric professor who went back in time to get them. The brain grain transforms them into loveable, intelligent, gentle giants. The professor then transports them into modernday New York to answer the wishes of the kids who have fervently wanted to see real dinosaurs. When they get there, they join forces with a street kid and a young girl to help defeat the professor's wicked brother Screweyes who runs a circus of fear. Great fun.

A:

© MCA/UNIVERSAL HOME VIDEO, INC. 81289

WIND IN THE WILLOWS, THE

D: Mark Hall 34 m

G | CLD | 1959 | COLOR | Sex | Nud | Viol | Lang | AdSit

8 J. Thaddeus Toad is a very rich and impulsive young toad who has a wild passion for all things in life but when he discovers the wonders of motorcars, he loses all control. He becomes so enamored with a beautiful red roadster that he agrees to trade his magnificent mansion, Toad Hall, for it. His friend Moley, Rat and Angus MacBadger are now certain he has lost his mind. Toad heads off in his new car to "nowhere in particular" but soon gets himself arrested - the beautiful red roadster was stolen. Now his friends have to get him out and clear his good name.

A:

© WALT DISNEY HOME VIDEO 427

Cartoons

ADVENTURES OF DROOPY, THE

D: 53 m

NR | CLD | 1943 | COLOR | Sex | Nud | Viol | Lang | AdSit

7 This slow-talking, sad-looking dog is featured in seven short, fun features. Droopy was MGM's most famous cartoon character.

A: *Droopy*

Distributed By MGM/UA Home Video M300586

ADVENTURES OF ROCKY AND BULLWINKLE, THE - 8 VOLS

D: Jay Ward, Bill Scott 240 m

CLD | 1961 | COLOR | Sex | Nud | Viol | Lang | AdSit

8 This classic television series will likely stay in reruns forever on TV because of its appeal to kids of all ages. Kids like the obvious jokes. Adults enjoy the double meanings and puns. Their adventures are here released on video tape in eight separate volumes. Each tape contains a complete Rocky and Bullwinkle serial, plus assorted episodes of Fractured Fairy Tales, Bullwinkle's Corner, Mr. Know-it-All, Dudley Do-Right, Aesop and Son and others.

A: *Rocky the Flying Squ, Bulwinkle Moose*

© BUENA VISTA HOME VIDEO 1019

ANT AND THE AARDVARK, THE

D: Friz Freleng 32 m

G | CLD | 1969 | COLOR | Sex | Nud | Viol | Lang | AdSit

7 The hungry Aardvark is constantly subverted by the red ant. Like "The Roadrunner," this character is a little more mature in its slant, but is still enjoyable for everyone. There are five separate, very funny episodes on this tape: "I've Got Ants In My Plans," "The Ant From Uncle," "The Ant and the Ardvark," "Never Bug an Ant" and "Technology, Phooey."

A:

Distributed By MGM/UA Home Video M200911

BEN AND ME

D: Hamilton Luske 25 m

NR | CLD | 1954 | COLOR | Sex | Nud | Viol | Lang | AdSit

7 This is the story of Amos the churchmouse, who was the little, and little-known, companion and confidant to Benjamin Franklin. It seems it was actually Amos who came up with all those ideas, not Ben. The Walt Disney production team gives this nifty little short its luxurious look.

A:

© WALT DISNEY HOME VIDEO 748

BEST OF BUGS BUNNY AND FRIENDS, THE

D: Tex Avery, Bob Clampett 53 m

G | CLD | 1986 | COLOR | Sex | Nud | Viol | Lang | AdSit

9 Some of the best of Warner Brothers's pre-1947 cartoons are in this collection: "Duck Soup to Nuts," "What's Cookin', Doc," "Bedtime for Snuffles," "Tweetie Pie," "Nothing but the Tooth," "A Feud There Was" and "The Little Lion Hunter."

A: *Bugs Bunny*

Distributed By MGM/UA Home Video M200682

BUGS AND DAFFY: THE WARTIME CARTOONS

D: 80 m

NR | CLD | COLOR | Sex | Nud | Viol | Lang | AdSit

9 This video contains eleven cartoons dating from the war years 1943-1945. Because of their propaganda nature, and some blatant racism, most of them are not now shown often. They are, nevertheless, classics and inspired animation. Narrated by Leonard Malton.

A: *Bugs Bunny, Daffy Duck*

Distributed By MGM/UA Home Video M201494

BUGS BUNNY/ROAD RUNNER MOVIE, THE

D: 98 m

G | CLD | 1979 | COLOR | Sex | Nud | Viol | Lang | AdSit

9 Anthology of some of Bugs's best cartoons, including "What's Opera, Doc?" and "Duck Amuck." It is narrated by Bugs and features Daffy Duck, Porky Pig, Elmer Fudd, Pepe Le Pew and Road Runner.

A: *Bugs Bunny, Daffy Duck, Porky Pig, Elmer Fudd, Pepe Le Pew, Road Runner*

© WARNER HOME VIDEO 1003

BUGS BUNNY AND ELMER FUDD CARTOON FESTIVAL

D: Tex Avery 54 m

CLD | COLOR | Sex | Nud | Viol | Lang | AdSit

8 That wonderful wabbit is up to his usual antics again in this great collection of seven Warner Brothers classics. Features include "Slick Hare," "The Big Snooze" and "The Old Grey Hare." The fun never stops.

A: *Bugs Bunny, Elmer Fudd*

Distributed By MGM/UA Home Video M200701

BUGS BUNNY CLASSICS - SPECIAL COLLECTOR'S EDITION

D: Tex Avery — 60 m

NR | CLD | COLOR

10 This has to be the best collection of Bugs Bunny cartoons ever put together! Eight classics are featured, including "Rabbit Punch," Acrobatty Bunny" and "Hare-Devil Hare," a cartoon that marked the introduction of Marvin the Martian and Yosemite Sam. Superb fun for all.

☐ Sex ☐ Nud ☐ Viol ☐ Lang ☐ AdSit

A: Bugs Bunny

Distributed By MGM/UA Home Video M201497

BUGS BUNNY IN KING ARTHUR'S COURT

D: Chuck Jones — 25 m

NR | CLD | 1977 | COLOR

7 Bugs gets a bum steer and winds up transported back to King Arthur's Court where the King is Daffy (Duck) and at his round table is Sir Loin of Pork (Porky Pig), Yosemite Sam (The Black Knight) and Elmer Fudd hunts dragons. This was a special that was made for TV. Not the very best ever of Bugs and friends, but still a good time.

☐ Sex ☐ Nud ☐ Viol ☐ Lang ☐ AdSit

A: Bugs Bunny

© WARNER HOME VIDEO 11850

BUGS BUNNY, SUPERSTAR

D: — 91 m

NR | CLD | 1944 | COLOR

8 A collection of nine of Bugs's classic cartoons from the early '40s, including "What's Cookin', Doc?" and "Corny Concerto." Also includes interviews with some of the men involved in their creation: Bob Clampett, Fritz Freleg, and Tex Avery - along with behind-the-scenes home movies. Narrated by Orson Welles.

☐ Sex ☐ Nud ☐ Viol ☐ Lang ☐ AdSit

A: Bugs Bunny

Distributed By MGM/UA Home Video M201323

BUGS BUNNY'S WACKY ADVENTURES

D: — 59 m

CLD | 1957 | COLOR

8 8 more Bugs Bunny favorite cartoons: "Long Haired Hare," "Hare Do," "Bunny Hugged," "Bully for Bugs," "The Grey Hounded Hare," Ali Baba Bunny," "Roman Legion Hare" and "Duck! Rabbit! Duck!"

☐ Sex ☐ Nud ☐ Viol ☐ Lang ☐ AdSit

A: Bugs Bunny

© WARNER HOME VIDEO 11504

DAFFY DUCK: THE NUTTINESS CONTINUES

D: Tex Avery, Bob Clampett — 59 m

CLD | 1985 | B&W

9 Sheer delight! This adventurous cartoon features Daffy getting all that is deserved from an animated witch. The fun includes "Duck Amuck," "Deduce You Say" and "The Daffy Duck." Loads of enjoyment for the whole family! Eight cartoons in all.

☐ Sex ☐ Nud ☐ Viol ☐ Lang ☐ AdSit

A: Daffy Duck

© WARNER HOME VIDEO 11505

DAFFY DUCK CARTOON FESTIVAL: AIN'T THAT DUCKY

D: — 35 m

CLD | 1942 | COLOR

8 Compilation of Daffy Duck favorites from 1942-1948. Includes one of Daffy's funniest - "The Wise Quacking Duck," plus "Ain't That Ducky," "Daffy Duck Slept Here," "Hollywood Daffy" and "Conrad the Sailor."

☐ Sex ☐ Nud ☐ Viol ☐ Lang ☐ AdSit

A: Daffy Duck

Distributed By MGM/UA Home Video M200695

DAFFY DUCK'S MOVIE: FANTASTIC ISLAND

D: Friz Freleng — 78 m

G | CLD | 1983 | COLOR

8 Ten Warner Brothers cartoons are linked together in a spoof of TV's long-running series "Fantasy Island." Daffy is the Ricardo Montalban host and Speedy Gonzales is the short sidekick.

☐ Sex ☐ Nud ☐ Viol ☐ Lang ☐ AdSit

A: Daffy Duck, Porky Pig, Tweety Pie, Sylvester the Cat, Pepe Le Pew

© WARNER HOME VIDEO 11324

DAFFY DUCK'S QUACKBUSTERS

D: — 79 m

G | CLD | 1988 | COLOR

8 Warner Brothers created several feature-length animated films, which are actually several older cartoons interwoven into a newly created central story line of feature length. This is perhaps the best of them. Others include DAFFY DUCK: FANTASTIC ISLAND and BUGS BUNNY/ROAD RUNNER MOVIE.

☐ Sex ☐ Nud ☐ Viol ☐ Lang ☐ AdSit

A: Daffy Duck

© WARNER HOME VIDEO 11807

ELMER FUDD CARTOON FESTIVAL: AN ITCH IN TIME

D: — 33 m

CLD | 1940 | COLOR

7 Four cartoons including two recognized classics: "An Itch in Time," and "Back Alley Oproar," plus "The Hardship of Miles Standish" and "Elmer's Pet Rabbit."

☐ Sex ☐ Nud ☐ Viol ☐ Lang ☐ AdSit

A: Elmer Fudd

Distributed By MGM/UA Home Video M200700

ELMER FUDD'S COMEDY CAPERS

D: — 57 m

CLD | COLOR

8 An outstanding collection of eight Warner Brothers cartoons from its most productive period. Included are the classics: "The Rabbit of Seville," "Bugs' Bonnets," "What's Opera, Doc?" and "Rabbit Seasoning."

☐ Sex ☐ Nud ☐ Viol ☐ Lang ☐ AdSit

A: Elmer Fudd

© WARNER HOME VIDEO 11606

FOGHORN LEGHORN'S FRACTURED FUNNIES

D: — 58 m

CLD | 1955 | COLOR

7 The cantankerous rooster meets his match in this series of eight cartoons where he runs across the now-familiar cast of barnyard characters, including a young chicken hawk with the determination and manners of a street fighter. Some of the best cartoons of the series.

☐ Sex ☐ Nud ☐ Viol ☐ Lang ☐ AdSit

A: Foghorn Leghorn

© WARNER HOME VIDEO 11607

HERE'S DONALD

D: Walt Disney — 22 m

NR | CLD | COLOR

8 Disney cartoons featuring Donald, from 1937-1947.

☐ Sex ☐ Nud ☐ Viol ☐ Lang ☐ AdSit

A: Donald Duck

© WALT DISNEY HOME VIDEO 527

HERE'S GOOFY

D: Walt Disney 22 m

NR | CLD | COLOR

7 Three Disney cartoons featuring Goofy, from 1945-1953.

A: Goofy

© WALT DISNEY HOME VIDEO 529

HERE'S MICKEY

D: Walt Disney 27 m

NR | CLD | COLOR

7 Three of Disney's cartoon classics featuring Mickey, made from 1935-1941.

A: Mickey Mouse

© WALT DISNEY HOME VIDEO 526

HERE'S PLUTO!

D: Walt Disney 23 m

NR | CLD | COLOR

6 Three of Disney's cartoon classics featuring Pluto, made from 1949-1947.

A: Pluto

© WALT DISNEY HOME VIDEO 528

JUST PLAIN DAFFY

D: Bob Clampett, Friz Freleng 60 m

CLD | COLOR

7 Daffy is the star of eight separate cartoons. Many of these cartoons have been released in other compilations, but this collection does include two less widely released cartoons from the WWII era: "Nasty Quacks" and "Duck Soup to Nuts."

A: Daffy Duck

Distributed By MGM/UA Home Video M201496

LITTLE TWEETY AND LITTLE INKI CARTOON FESTIVAL

D: Bob Clampett, Friz Freleng 50 m

CLD | COLOR

7 Collection of seven animated cartoons from animators Bob Clampett, Friz Freleng and Chuck Jones. Four are of the wiley little yellow bird Tweety: "I Taw a Putty Tat," "Birdie and the Beast," "Gruesome Twosome" and "Tweetie Pie." Three are of a courageous but diminutive African warrior named Inki: "Inki at the Circus," "Inki and the Lion" and "The Little Lion Hunter."

A: Tweety Pie, Inki

Distributed By MGM/UA Home Video M200699

LOONEY, LOONEY, LOONEY BUGS BUNNY MOVIE

D: Friz Freleng 79 m

G | CLD | 1981 | COLOR

8 Fun-filled compilation of Warner Brothers cartoons - some of the best done by Friz Freleng. Follow up to the BUGS BUNNY/ROAD RUNNER MOVIE. Highlights include the 1957 cartoon "The Three Little Bops," "Knight Knight Bugs" and Bugs Bunny's Oscars parody "The Oswald Awards."

A: Bugs Bunny, Daffy Duck, Porky Pig, Tweety Pie, Yosemite Sam

© WARNER HOME VIDEO 11142

MGM CARTOON MAGIC

D: Tex Avery, George Gordon 53 m

NR | CLD | 1938 | COLOR

7 This barrel of fun comes from a very delightful collection of cartoon classics that have been stored in MGM's vault. There are a lot of laughs in store with "Screwball Squirrel," "Little Rural Riding Hood" (which has almost adult themes), and "The Captain's Christmas." "The Lonesome Stranger" fights for freedom, truth and justice. Seven cartoons in all.

A:

Distributed By MGM/UA Home Video M300230

MICKEY KNOWS BEST

D: Walt Disney 26 m

CLD | 1986 | COLOR

10 From 1936, a collection of three delightful Disney cartoons. "Moving Day" has the endearing Donald Duck attempting to get away from a plumber's helper. In "Mickey's Amateurs," Donald gets laughs while trying to recite a poem, and Pluto takes an immediate dislike to a loveable elephant in "Mickey's Elephant."

A: Mickey Mouse, Donald Duck, Pluto

© WALT DISNEY HOME VIDEO 442V

PINK PANTHER CARTOON FESTIVAL: PINK-A-BOO, THE

D: Friz Freleng, David H. DePatie 56 m

NR | CLD | 1965 | COLOR

7 Contains nine Pink Panther cartoons: "Slink Pink," "Come on in, the Water's Pink," "Pink Aye," "Extinct Pink," "Pink-A-Boo," "Bobolink Pink," "Bully for Pink," "Smile Pretty, Say Pink" and "In the Pink of the Night."

A: The Pink Panther

Distributed By MGM/UA Home Video M300481

PINK PANTHER CARTOON FESTIVAL:PINK PANTHER FOLLIES

D: Friz Freleng, David H. DePatie 57 m

NR | CLD | 1966 | COLOR

8 Nine classic Pink Panther cartoons, including: "Pink-a-Rella," "Pink Pest Control," "Pink Plasm," "Keep Our Flowers Pink," "Pink Flea," "Put-Put Pink," "A Fly in the Pink," "Rock-A-Bye Pinky" and "Pink in the Clink."

A: The Pink Panther

Distributed By MGM/UA Home Video M300541

PORKY PIG TALES

D: Arthur Davis, Chuck Jones 44 m

CLD | COLOR

8 Six great Porky Pig favorites from 1948-1959. "The Awful Orphan," "The Pest That Came to Dinner," "My Little Duckaroo," "Jumpin' Jupiter," "Dog Collared" and "China Jones."

A: Porky Pig

© WARNER HOME VIDEO 11833

SNIFFLES THE MOUSE CARTOON FESTIVAL

D: Chuck Jones 32 m

CLD | 1940 | COLOR

8 Guaranteed to hold the little ones captive, and probably the old ones, too. Sniffles is a great little cartoon character. Sniffles is a brave little mouse that is always getting into trouble, but always gets out. The whiskered wonder is featured in four short stories: "Sniffles Bells the Cat," "The Brave Little Bat," "Lost and Foundling" and "Toy Trouble." Pure enjoyment.

A: Sniffles

Distributed By MGM/UA Home Video M200698

SYLVESTER AND TWEETY'S CRAZY CAPERS

D: Friz Freleng 57 m

8 Eight classic cartoons provide the vehicle for the highly enjoyable scenes where the crazed cat Sylvester just can't leave that cute little bird Tweety alone. Included in the madness are: "Tweet and Lovely," "Tree for Two," "Tweety and the Beanstalk," "The Last Hungry Cat," "Mouse-Taken Identity" and "Canned Feud." Loads of entertaining fun!

CLD | 1985 | COLOR | Sex | Nud | Viol | Lang | AdSit

A: Sylvester the Cat

© WARNER HOME VIDEO 11506

TWEETY & SYLVESTER

D: Bob Clampett, Friz Freleng 60 m

9 Eight cartoons from Warner Brothers featuring Tweety and Sylvester in the period of 1942-1948, including the Oscar winning "Tweetie Pie." There are three entries with Tweetie only: "A Tale of Two Kitties," "Birdie and the Beast" and "A Gruesome Twosome." Sylvester is alone in "Life with Feathers." Also included are such favorites as "Back Alley Uproar" and "I Taw a Putty Tat."

CLD | COLOR | Sex | Nud | Viol | Lang | AdSit

A: Tweety Pie, Sylvester the Cat

Distributed By MGM/UA Home Video M201498

WOODY WOODPECKER AND HIS FRIENDS - VOL. 1

D: Walter Lantz 80 m

NR **8** Contains a collection of Woody Woodpecker cartoons from 1940-1955, including: "Knock Knock," "Bandmaster," "Ski for Two," "Hoot Noon," "Legend of Rock-A-Bye Point," "Wet Blanket Policy," "To Catch a Woodpecker," "Musical Moments," "Bats in the Belfry," "Crazy Mixed-up Pup" and "The Walter Lanz Story."

CLD | 1982 | COLOR | Sex | Nud | Viol | Lang | AdSit

A: Woody Woodpecker

© MCA/UNIVERSAL HOME VIDEO, INC. 55080

WOODY WOODPECKER AND HIS FRIENDS - VOL. 2

D: Walter Lantz 59 m

7 This is a three-volume set which contains a bunch of the best of the Woody Woodpecker cartoons from Walter Lantz. Including: "Cracked Nut" (the very first Woody Woodpecker cartoon), "Banquet Busters," "Born to Peck," "The Redwood Sap," "The Poet and the Peasant," "Fish Fry," "The Screwdriver," "Wacky Bye Baby," "Woody Dines Out," "Loose Nut," "S-H-H-H" and "Convict Concerto."

CLD | COLOR | Sex | Nud | Viol | Lang | AdSit

A: Woody Woodpecker

© MCA/UNIVERSAL HOME VIDEO, INC. 80007

WOODY WOODPECKER AND HIS FRIENDS - VOL. 3

D: Walter Lantz 55 m

NR **8** Contains eight episodes from 1940-1944, including "Woody Woodpecker," "Swing Your Partner," "Smoked Hams," "Dog Tax Dodgers," "Sleep Happy," "Maw and Paw in Plywood Panic," "I'm Cold" and "The Barber of Seville."

CLD | 1984 | COLOR | Sex | Nud | Viol | Lang | AdSit

A: Woody Woodpecker

© MCA/UNIVERSAL HOME VIDEO, INC. 80122

Educational

BARNEY AND THE BACKYARD GANG

D: John Grable 30 m

9 This super-successful TV series was created especially for very young children, ages 2-8. Barney is a very friendly and magic dinosaur. He always has kids (almost never adults) over to play with him. They all play games, sing songs and go on trips together. The show is really kept just that simple. However, it is also much more than that: Barney has been very carefully designed to be fun, involving and totally non-threatening to children but that also means that the show can give them the information they need and want, and do it on a level and at a speed that they can digest. Extremely popular with young kids.

CLD | 1988 | COLOR | Sex | Nud | Viol | Lang | AdSit

A:

© THE LYONS GROUP 98011

BILL NYE THE SCIENCE GUY - SERIES

D: 49 m

NR **9** Way cool way to really interest kids in the wonders of science. Bill Nye is both a mechanical engineer and a stand-up comic. The videos in this series are entries nationally syndicated TV series that is produced by Disney and appears regularly on PBS. The show has a rapid-fire delivery that includes really neat graphics, great sound effects and top-notch science-based music videos. The science topics explored vary widely from physics to paleontology, but are always presented in a way that is both relevant to the viewer's daily life and fun to watch. Here, science is not just a subject taught in school. Science effects us everyday and this series shows us the hows and whys of it. Highly recommended.

CLD | 1994 | COLOR | Sex | Nud | Viol | Lang | AdSit

A: Bill Nye

© WALT DISNEY HOME VIDEO 2919

CLIFFORD'S FUN WITH NUMBERS

D: Kate Shepherd 30 m

8 Clifford is a big red animated dog that was designed by education professionals to help teach, in a fun way, very young viewers (ages 3-7) some of the very basic skills they should have before they get to school. Kids are presented with the information in a way such that they don't even recognize it as learning. Rather than use rote memorization, kids learn basic skills by having them incorporated into the silly kid-type story lines that kids like to watch over and over. Six separate 30-minute volumes on LETTERS, NUMBERS, OPPOSITES, etc.

CLD | 1988 | COLOR | Sex | Nud | Viol | Lang | AdSit

A:

© LIVE HOME VIDEO 27428

DEBBY BOONE'S HUG-A-LONG SONGS - VOL. 1 & 2

D: Chris Darley 35 m

8 The world can be a wonderful place. These tapes are designed to help children to see what great fun growing up can be when they sing along to delightful tunes. Debbie Boone sings to kids about understanding the wonders and small pleasures of life, and overcoming its little fears. Her simple songs are packaged into a series of kiddie music videos and released in two 35-minute cassettes.

CLD | 1989 | COLOR | Sex | Nud | Viol | Lang | AdSit

A: Debby Boone

© J2 COMMUNICATIONS 0062

DISNEY'S SING ALONG SONGS: (SERIES)

D: m

G **10** This is an extremely popular series of videos for young kids from the Disney people. It utilizes musical and film clip excerpts that kids recognize from Disney's many popular feature films and uses them to to both entertain and to begin to teach them to read. The children hear the music and sing along with it, while they also see the related film clip and the written words which are flashed on the screen in a "follow the bouncing ball" format. Excellent, both as education and entertainment.

CLD | 1990 | COLOR | Sex | Nud | Viol | Lang | AdSit

A:

© WALT DISNEY HOME VIDEO

DONALD DUCK IN MATHMAGIC LAND

D: Walt Disney 27 m

NR **8** Made long before Sesame Street, this award-winning short was an early effort to explain simple mathematics principals to young people, and it remains a valuable teaching tool today. Donald serves as a guide through Mathmagic Land, a magic world of numbers where trees have square roots and there are rivers of numbers. Donald has fun with numbers and so will kids.

CLD | 1959 | COLOR | Sex | Nud | Viol | Lang | AdSit

A: Donald Duck

© WALT DISNEY HOME VIDEO 692

HEY, WHAT ABOUT ME?

G | CLD | 1987 | COLOR

D: 25 m

9 This is a very highly regarded video guide for young kids. It is designed by professionals to help brothers and sisters (ages 2-6) understand what happens, both good and bad, when a new baby comes into the family. It was filmed using real kids as role models and uses clever songs to help generate interest. It not only shows its young audience how to deal with being lonely or mad, but also gives them games to play with their brothers and sisters. Your kids will thoroughly enjoy themselves, at the same time that they get their questions answered.

Sex / Nud / Viol / Lang / AdSit

A:

© KIDVIDZ

MY FRIEND LIBERTY

DOC | CLD | 1986 | COLOR

D: Jimmy Picker 30 m

7 Animated history lesson. The famous lady Liberty comes to life, steps down and educates a young man about the history of the statue and the meaning behind her name. Entertaining and educational, this program is done in clay animation by the Academy Award winner Jimmy Picker. Great for children and adults alike.

Sex / Nud / Viol / Lang / AdSit

A:

© WARNER HOME VIDEO 130

RAFFI, A YOUNG CHILDREN'S CONCERT WITH

G | CLD | 1984 | COLOR

D: David Devine 50 m

9 Young children just adore the Canadian folksinger Raffi. He sings just to them with fun and light-hearted songs that they can participate in. This particular video is a tape of a sold-out concert in Toronto. It includes 18 favorite tunes from him including "Bumping Up and Down," "Shake My Sillies Out," "Down by the Bay" and "Wheels on the Bus." Your kids's attention to the screen will never waver. There are several tapes in the series.

Sex / Nud / Viol / Lang / AdSit

A: Raffi

© A&M VIDEO 61707

ROCK & READ

NR | CLD | 1989 | COLOR

D: Tamar Simon Hoffs 29 m

6 This progressive, and somewhat controversial, technique for teaching very young kids (3+) to read is called word recognition. It is a system where the child more or less memorizes the over-all "look" of the word. This particular video is a very hip, MTV-like approach to exposing kids to words. Artists on the soundtrack sing familiar songs (Twinkle Twinkle Little Star, etc.) in a catchy, pop manner and the kids are flashed words at the appropriate time, to instill an instant recognition of how they look. How well it works as a teaching tool will be debated, but kids do really enjoy this tape.

Sex / Nud / Viol / Lang / AdSit

A:

© MCA/UNIVERSAL HOME VIDEO, INC. 80910

SHERI LEWIS - LAMB CHOP'S PLAY-ALONG!

CLD | 1992 | COLOR

D: 30 m

9 This excellent children's series on tape is taken from the hit PBS television show of the same name. Each tape is a compilation of similar segments from the TV show. All the episodes are geared both to get the kids at home to participate in song and in activities while always being fun. Kids do love them. They are most appropriate for children from as young as 3 to about 9. Each tape is 30 minutes long.

Sex / Nud / Viol / Lang / AdSit

A: Lamb Chop, Sheri Lewis

© A&M VIDEO 84213

WINNIE THE POOH LEARNING SERIES

NR | CLD | COLOR

D: 45 m

9 This is one in a series of Disney-created cartoons for little kids that is designed to be both a lot of fun and to teach them how to get along with other kids.

Sex / Nud / Viol / Lang / AdSit

A: Winnie the Pooh

© WALT DISNEY HOME VIDEO 3943

Indexes

TITLES

ACTORS

ACTORS

ACTORS

DIRECTORS

DIRECTORS

DIRECTORS

ACT

CLD

COM

CRM

DMA

DOC

FAN

FOR

HOR

MUS

MYS

ROM

SF

BEST OF THE BEST

SUS

WAR

WST

Videos I'd Like to See

Video's Best

CATEGORY	VIDEO TITLE	YEAR	PAGE #

Videos I'd Like to See

Videos Best

CATEGORY	VIDEO TITLE	YEAR	PAGE #